D0688023

HiSET® Exam Prep

Third Edition

Our 80 years' expertise = Your competitive advantage

Practice Tests + Proven Strategies + Online

ACKNOWLEDGMENTS

Special thanks to the team that made this book possible:
Laura Aitcheson, Arthur Ahn, Mikhail Alexeeff, Gina Allison, Alexis Ferreri Beardsley, Kim Bowers, Erik Bowman, Julie Choi, Margaret Crane, Alisha Crowley, Lola Disparte, Boris Dvorkin, Paula Fleming, Tom Flesher, Joanna Graham, Allison Harm, Jack Hayes, Gar Hong, Kevin Jacobson, Stephanie Jolly, Wyatt Kent, Rebecca Knauer, Jennifer Land, Heather Maigur, Terrence McGovern, Terrence McMullen, Eli Meyer, Kathy Osmus, Anthony Parr, Rachel Pearsall, Neha Rao, Rachel Reina, Teresa Rupp, Scott Safir, Glen Stohr, Kathryn Sollenberger, Alexandra Strelka, Caren Van Slyke, Lee Weiss, and many others who have shaped this book over the years.

Published by Kaplan Publishing, a division of Kaplan, Inc.
750 Third Avenue
New York, NY 10017

10 9 8 7 6 5 4 3 2 1

ISBN: 978-1-5062-4897-4

Kaplan Publishing books are available at special quantity discounts to use for sales promotions, employee premiums, or educational purposes. For more information or to purchase books, please call the Simon & Schuster special sales department at 866-506-1949.

CONTENTS

The material in this book is based on the best information available from the testmaker at the time of writing. However, Educational Testing Service (ETS)® may have instituted changes or refinements to the HiSET exam since this book was published. Visit http://hiset.ets.org/ for the most up-to-date information about the HiSET contents and registration process.

KAPLAN'S HiSET® BOOK AND ONLINE CENTER

WELCOME

Congratulations on your decision to pursue high school equivalency, and thank you for choosing Kaplan for your HiSET exam preparation! This book and the included online resources will be all you need to prepare for the HiSET exam. To help you create a study plan, let's start by walking you through everything you need to know to take advantage of your book and your Online Center.

YOUR BOOK AND ONLINE CENTER

This book and online center combination contains a complete study program, including:

- Detailed instruction covering the essential concepts of Reading, Writing, Mathematics, Social Studies, and Science
- Effective methods and strategies for every question type
- A pretest featuring questions from all sections of the HiSET exam, designed to help you diagnose your strengths and weaknesses
- Over a thousand practice questions, plus answer explanations for each
- A full-length practice test

GETTING STARTED

How to Study

Step 1: Register your Online Center.

Step 2: Take the pretests.

Step 3: Fill out the study planners.

Step 4: Create a study plan.

Step 5: Learn and review, practice and review, assess and review.

Step 6: Take the practice tests.

Step 7: Confirm your readiness to take the HiSET exam.

Step 1: Register your Online Center.

To take full advantage of your Kaplan study resources, visit kaptest.com/moreonline. Click on the word "HiSET" and answer the questions that appear.

After creating your username and password, log in to your syllabus at kaptest.com. There you will be able to access additional chapters that introduce concepts not covered in this book.

Step 2: Take the pretests.

Begin by learning what strengths you're already bringing to the HiSET exam and what subject areas you need to work on most. To do so, take the diagnostic pretests beginning on page 1. These pretests are not designed to simulate the HiSET exam, but rather to assess the essential skills you'll need to master.

When you've completed the pretests, check your responses against the answers and explanations that begin on page 52. Be sure to review the explanations for each question: By doing so, you'll learn a great deal about why the right answer was right and you'll start building your HiSET skills.

Step 3: Fill out the study planners.

Once you've compared your answers to the correct answers, use that information to fill out the study planners on pages 64–68. These study planners will give you a rough estimate of which subjects are your strongest and which need the most work.

If you can, it is wisest to study and review *all* of the topics tested by the HiSET exam. However, if you are pressed for time, the study planners will help you prioritize those topics that present you with the greatest challenges.

Step 4: Create a study plan.

Before you begin your studies, make a plan—and then stick to it.

To begin with, **make a study schedule**. Make a list of all your commitments: jobs, family, sports, holidays, trips, and anything else that takes chunks of your time. Figure out how you can fit a few hours of HiSET study into that schedule each week. The amount of time you have to spend might vary, but try to spend at least six hours a week studying. The amount of time you study in one session can also vary. In the beginning, study for as long as you can hold your focus; if that is only 15 minutes, that's fine. Continue to add time onto each study session until you have built up the stamina to study for two hours straight. You might want to do three study sessions, of two hours each, every week. If you want to take the HiSET exam soon, you might need more time each week.

Be realistic in your planning; if you are overly ambitious in creating your study schedule, you may find it difficult to follow through. Also be sure to take at least one day off from studying each week so that you don't exhaust yourself. Most importantly, once you've made your study schedule, **stick to it.** Treat it like a job and discipline yourself accordingly. Imagine yourself "clocking in" at the beginning of a study session and "clocking out" at the end of it.

Think about how you'll cover all five tests between now and the time you would like to take the HiSET exam. If your state allows you to take the HiSET subject tests on different days, you may choose to study (for example) Reading and Writing first, and then take the Reading test and the Writing test, before you move on to Mathematics or another subject. If you plan to—or if your state requires you to—take the five subject tests all at once, you will have to **allot the months you have to study** among the five subjects.

It's normal to be stressed about taking the HiSET exam. Throughout your studies, **manage your stress** so that it doesn't get in the way of your learning. To do so, keep yourself on a regular sleep schedule, eat right, exercise, and continue to spend time with friends and/or family. If you're studying and find yourself becoming very stressed and anxious, step away for a moment. Take a walk, work out, cook a meal, work on your car, play sports, do breathing exercises, meditate—do something healthy to release your stress and then return to your studies. Don't fuel your studies by loading up on caffeine or sugar: you won't be able to focus well.

Step 5: Learn and review, practice and review, assess and review.

Once you have your study schedule in place, begin work on the concepts presented in this book. You'll do this in three stages:

Learn and Review: Each lesson presents you with information you need to learn to master the HiSET exam. Carefully read and absorb each lesson, paying particular attention to the bolded words and to the "Key Ideas" presented in the left margin of the lesson page. When you are finished, review any concepts that gave you trouble before moving on to the practice questions.

Practice and Review: Each lesson ends with practice questions that will ask you to apply the concepts you just learned. Do the practice questions without worrying about how much time you're taking, but don't stop there! After you do a practice set, review each question's explanation (found in the back of the book). Ask yourself what you did right on that question and what you could have done better. This review will help you learn more about what you need to work on.

Assess and Review: At the end of each chapter, there will be another set of practice problems that test you on all of the concepts presented throughout the chapter. Reviewing your answers and studying the explanations will provide you with a good assessment of which topics you are comfortable with and which topics you should spend more time on.

Another key component of review is periodically revisiting concepts you haven't studied in a while. For example, you might begin by studying reading and then move on to math. If you do, pause every week or so while studying math to review what you learned about reading so your reading skills don't get rusty.

Step 6: Take the practice tests.

Once you have studied all the concepts the HiSET exam assesses, take the practice tests that begin on page 663. These tests are designed to mimic the HiSET exam as much as possible. Time yourself, just as you will be timed on Test Day.

Score your practice tests using the practice test answers and explanations in the back of the book, and fill out the practice test scoring charts that follow those explanations.

Step 7: Confirm your readiness to take the HiSET exam.

You may decide that you need to study some subjects more before taking the real HiSET exam. If you are ready to test, contact your state's department of education, or visit that agency's website, to learn how to register for the exam.

In the week or two before Test Day, do a review of all the concepts in this book. Then, the day before the test, don't study. You need to be rested to do well.

Good Luck!

We wish you the very best of luck on the HiSET exam. If you absorb the concepts presented in this book and do well in your practice, walk into the test feeling confident. As you take the test, be sure to keep breathing deeply and don't let stress get in the way. You can do it!

HiSET® EXAM OVERVIEW

HiSET stands for "High School Equivalency Test." The HiSET exam measures whether you have achieved a level of academic accomplishment equivalent to having graduated from high school. Visit the HiSET website (http://hiset.ets.org) to be sure the HiSET exam is offered in your state or jurisdiction. You should also review the eligibility requirements for your state or jurisdiction.

You may have heard people refer to getting a high school equivalency degree as "getting a GED." However, this way of referring to the degree is inaccurate. The GED® is an exam that has long been used in most states to determine whether a person should be granted a high school equivalency degree by the state. The degree itself is not "a GED." Recently, some states have decided to stop using the GED test or to offer another testing option in addition to the GED test for people who are seeking a high school equivalency degree. The HiSET exam is one such alternative to the GED test. Since 2013, the HiSET exam from Educational Testing Service (ETS) and the TASC Test Assessing Secondary Completion from McGraw-Hill Education CTB have been adopted by numerous states because they are more affordable and more widely accessible than the GED test. What's important to remember is that all three tests allow someone to earn a high school equivalency credential. Contact your state's department of education to find out which exam you should study for.

There are two ways to take the HiSET exam: using paper and pencil or on a computer. Which format you will take may depend on your state. Contact your state's department of education to find out whether you will test on paper or on a computer. It may be that you have a choice, or your state may require you to test in a specific format.

The HiSET exam is also available in Spanish. If you would like to take the Spanish version of the test, contact your state's department of education to find out if and where you can test in Spanish.

The HiSET exam is composed of five subtests in the following subjects:*

Language Arts—Reading: The Reading Test assesses your ability to understand, comprehend, interpret, and analyze a variety of reading material. As defined by CCSS, 60 percent will involve literary content and 40 percent will involve informational content. You will have 65 minutes to answer 40 multiple-choice items.

Language Arts—Writing: The Writing Test assesses your language skills and has two parts. A multiple-choice component assesses your ability to use correct grammar and to edit text for clarity. On that portion of the Writing Test, you will have 75 minutes to answer 51 multiple-choice questions. On the second part of the Writing Test, you will have 45 minutes to create written responses that are evaluated for development of ideas, organization of ideas, language facility, and conventions. These two parts will be separated by a break.

Mathematics: The Mathematics Test assesses your ability to solve quantitative problems using fundamental concepts and reasoning skills. You will have 90 minutes to answer 50 multiple-choice questions. The Mathematics Test is calculator neutral. This means that a calculator is not required; however, if you request a calculator, the test center is required to provide either a four-function or scientific calculator (the type of calculator provided is at the testing center's discretion.) Please refer to the state policies for the state in which you are testing. It is important to note that a test taker may NOT bring his or her own calculator to the testing center for use on the HiSET exam.

Science: The Science Test assesses your ability to use science content knowledge, apply principles of scientific inquiry, and interpret and evaluate scientific information in the content areas of life science, physical science, and earth science. Most Science Test questions will be based on a short passage or graphic, but some may require you to remember a basic science concept. You will have 80 minutes to answer 50 multiple-choice items on the Science Test.

Social Studies: The Social Studies Test assesses your ability to analyze and evaluate various kinds of social studies information and uses material from a variety of content areas including history, political science, psychology, sociology, anthropology, geography, and economics. Most Social Studies Test questions will be based on primary documents or graphics, but some may require you to remember a concept from social studies. You will have 70 minutes to answer 50 multiple-choice items on the Social Studies Test.

***Note:** The information given here was the latest information available as of December 2018. For updates or additional information, visit http://hiset.ets.org.

When to Take the HiSET Exam

When should you plan to take the HiSET exam? The best answer is: When you're ready. You may have to do a significant amount of studying before being ready to test, especially if you have been away from school for some years. That said, it can be helpful for you to set a goal—a date by which you would like to have the HiSET completed. Having a date in mind can motivate you to stick to your study schedule and manage your studies. It can also help you stay focused on your ultimate goal of earning your high school equivalency degree.

Registering for the Exam

How you will register for the exam depends partly on your state. Contact your state's department of education or visit http://hiset.ets.org to learn more.

The HiSET exam provides services and accommodations for those who have a disability or health-related need. If you have a disability that would require an approved accommodation, you can learn more at http://hiset.ets.org/take/disabilities—and plan ahead: Allow at least 6 weeks for your request to be processed.

If you do not meet the minimum HiSET score requirements, you can take it again up to two additional times within a calendar year. For additional information regarding retake policies, visit http://hiset.ets.org/take/schedule/retake.

Scoring Information

Each of the 5 subtests is scored on a scale of 1–20. In order to pass the HiSET exam, you must meet all of the following criteria:

- Achieve a score of at least 8 on each of the 5 subtests
- Score at least 2 out of 6 on the essay portion of the Writing Test
- Achieve a total scaled score on all 5 HiSET subtests of at least 45

It's also important to note that you must score at least an 8 for the subtests and a 2 for the essay on the same test date. You cannot combine scores from multiple tests.

You will receive two types of score reports:

Comprehensive Score Report: This report is a cumulative record of all of your highest subtest scores (including the essay) indicating whether or not you passed the HiSET exam.

Individual Test Report: This report includes your score for an individual subtest and an explanation of what your score means. It also indicates whether or not you demonstrate college and career readiness (at least 15 out of 20 on any of the subtests).

To learn more about these reports, visit http://hiset.ets.org/scores/understand.

Taking the Paper-Based HiSET Exam

You can take the HiSET exam in a paper-based format. You will be given an answer sheet to fill in; this will be a page with circles, or bubbles, for the answer choices for each question. You will fill in the bubble corresponding to the answer choice you think is correct, using a no. 2 or HB pencil. (Remember to take pencils with you!) In the second half of the Writing Test, you will write your essay by hand. You will be allowed to use scratch paper for calculations and to organize your thoughts for the essay. You will also be permitted to use a calculator provided by the test center. You may NOT bring your own calculator on Test Day.

Taking the Computer-Based HiSET exam

Depending on where you live and/or the test center you choose, you may take the HiSET exam on a computer. This means that to succeed on the test, you will need to familiarize yourself with basic computer skills. If you do not have a computer at home and are not familiar with computers, try to find a computer you can use to practice using a mouse, typing on a keyboard, and navigating through items on a computer screen. Many public libraries or community centers have computers you can use. Your state department of education may know of other resources.

If you are taking the computer-based version of the HiSET exam, you must still test at a testing center established by your state. You *cannot* test at home. Unfortunately, there may be unscrupulous people who will try to sell you an "online" version of the HiSET exam for you to take at home over the Internet. *This is not a real HiSET exam, so don't be taken in.*

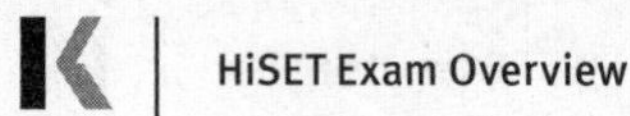

Navigating through questions

You will use the mouse to choose answers to questions, and also to move from one question to the next. The upper right corner of your screen will look something like this:

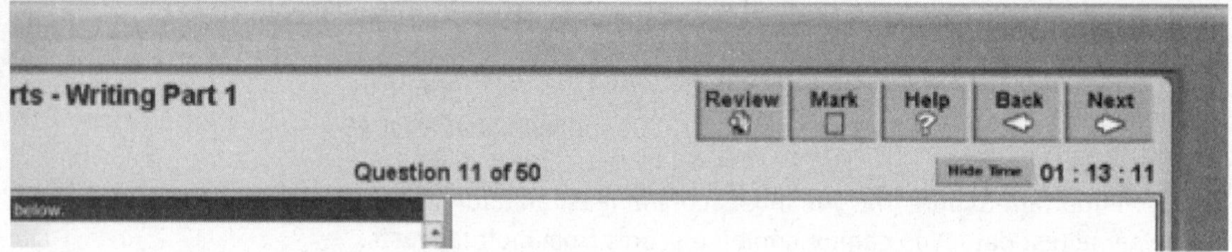

Click "Back" to return to a previous question. Click "Next" to move to the next question.

Tools to use as you are answering questions

If you get stuck on a question or are unsure of your answer, you can check the box labeled "Mark" and return to it later.

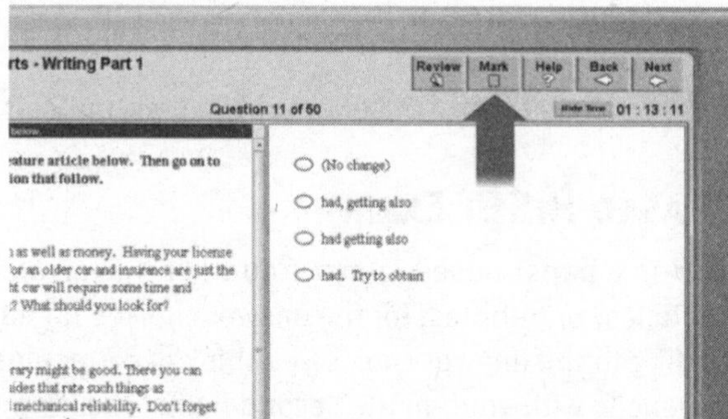

One extremely useful button is labeled "Review."

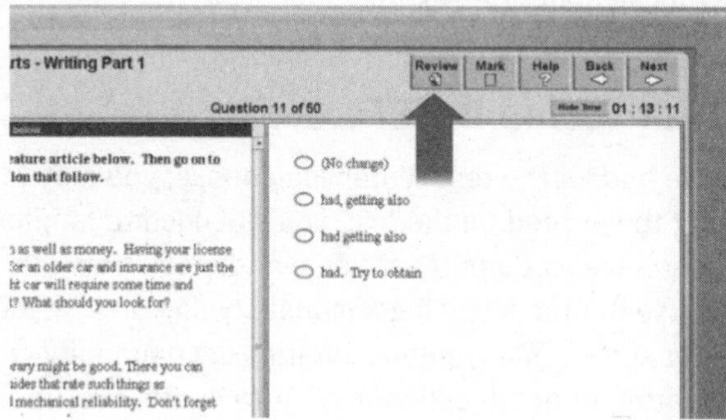

Clicking this will give you an overview of all of the questions in that section: those you've answered, those you haven't answered, those you've marked for review, and those you haven't looked at yet. Using this will allow you to keep track of the status of each question.

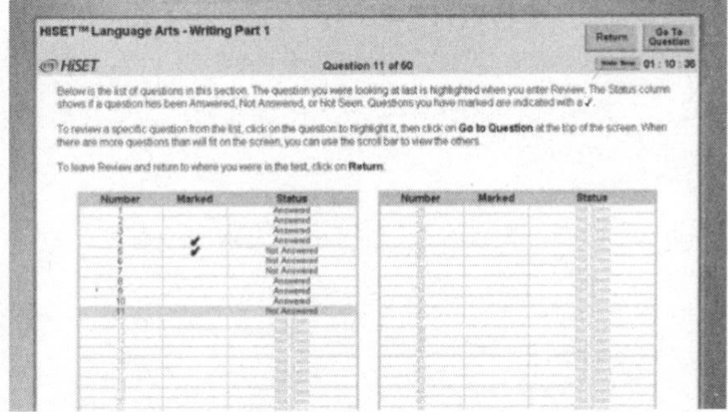

If you are taking the computer version of the HiSET exam, you will be able to use an on-screen calculator that has the basic functions needed for the kinds of questions you'll encounter on the exam. You can access the online calculator at any time during the test by clicking on the word "Calc."

On the Writing Test, you will use the keyboard to type your essay into a text box. You will have some basic word-processing tools such as insert text, delete, cut-and-paste, and undo. You will not have any spelling- or grammar-checking functions. If you are taking the test in Spanish, there will be a toolbar available in the Essay subtest so that you can insert special characters as needed.

Managing your time

At the top-right corner of the screen, you will see a timer telling you how much time remains in that section. You may want to leave the timer up for the entire test or only check it periodically if you find it distracting. When the timer is showing, the button below it will say "Hide Time." Click it to remove the timer from the screen.

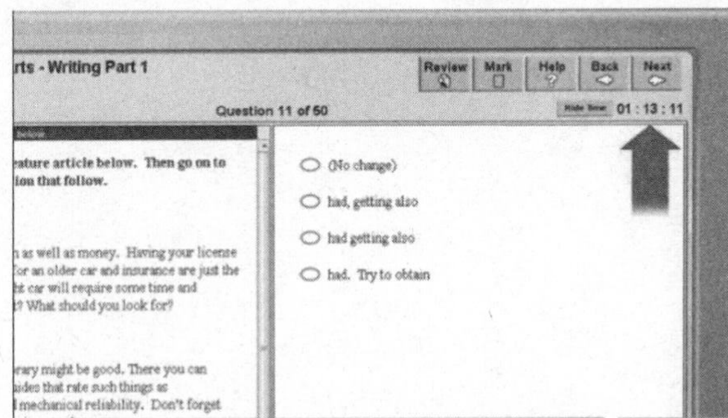

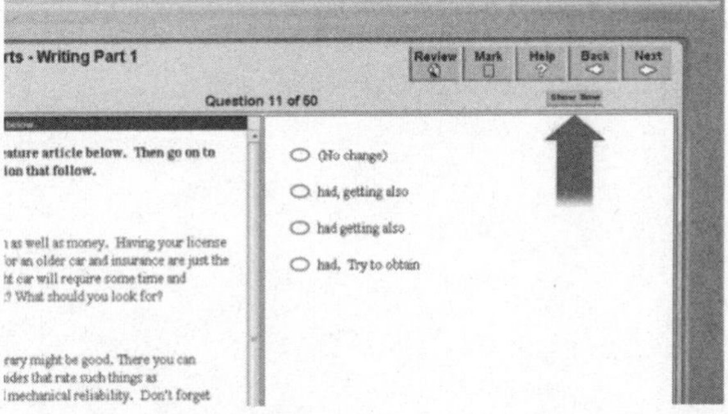

PRETESTS

The pretests are intended to help you decide what you need to study in order to pass the actual HiSET exam. After you take the pretests, you will check your answers and then use the Pretest Study Planners to determine your course of study.

The pretests are designed to assess your skills in an efficient manner. Thus, they are shorter than the actual HiSET exam. To see what the actual HiSET exam will be like, flip through the practice tests beginning on page 663.

STEP 1: Take the following pretests that correspond to the five HiSET test areas.

Language Arts: Reading, pages 2–9

20 Questions

Language Arts: Writing, pages 10–17

Part I: Language Skills—18 Questions

Part II: Essay

Mathematics, pages 18–27

Part I: Quantitative Reasoning—18 Questions

Part II: Algebraic Reasoning and Geometry—22 Questions

Social Studies, pages 28–39

Part I: Social Studies Skills—10 Questions

Part II: Social Studies Content—26 Questions

Science, pages 40–51

Part I: Science Skills—10 Questions

Part II: Science Content—25 Questions

All of the questions are in multiple-choice format, except for the essay, which requires writing an extended response. For the multiple-choice questions, you may fill in the circles next to the correct answers in this book, or you can write your answers on a separate piece of paper.

STEP 2: Check your answers with the Pretest Answers and Explanations that begin on page 52.

STEP 3: Fill in the Pretest Study Planners, starting on page 64. These charts will allow you to target your problem areas so that you can study in the most efficient manner.

STEP 4: Use the study planners on pages 64–68 to map out your work.

Language Arts: Reading Pretest—20 Questions

Directions: You may fill in the circles next to the correct answers or write your answers on a separate piece of paper.

Questions 1 through 5 refer to the following passage about introverts.

Excerpted from "Don't Call Introverted Children 'Shy'"

1 Imagine a 2-year-old who greets you with a huge smile, offering a toy. Now here's another child who regards you gravely and hides behind his parent's leg. How do you feel about these two children? If you're like most people, you think of the first child as social and the second as reserved or . . . "shy." . . . But this misses what's really going on with standoffish kids. Many were born with a careful, sensitive temperament that predisposes them to look before they leap. And this can pay off handsomely as they grow, in the form of strong academics, enhanced creativity, and even a unique brand of leadership and empathy.

2 One way to see this temperament more clearly is to consider how these children react to stimuli. When these children are at 4 months, if you pop a balloon over their heads, they holler and pump their arms more than other babies do. At age 2, they proceed carefully when they see a . . . toy robot for the first time. When they're school age, they play matching games with more deliberation than their peers. . . . Notice that none of these things—popping balloons, toy robots, matching games—has anything to do with people. In other words, these kids are not antisocial. They're simply sensitive to their environments.

3 But if they're not antisocial, these kids are differently social. [Children with this type of temperament are highly likely to grow up to be introverted, but s]hyness and introversion are not the same thing. Shy people fear negative judgment, while introverts simply prefer less stimulation. . . .

4 Children with an alert, sensitive temperament also pay close attention to social cues and moral principles. By age 6, they cheat and break rules less than other kids do—even when they believe they won't be caught. At 7, they're more likely than their peers to be described by parents and caregivers as empathetic or conscientious. As adults, introverted leaders have even been found to deliver better outcomes than extroverts when managing employees, according to a recent study by management professor Adam Grant of the Wharton School of the University of Pennsylvania, because they encourage others' ideas instead of trying to put their own stamp on things. And they're less likely to take dangerous risks. . . .

5 But we wouldn't want to live in a world composed entirely of cautious introverts. . . . The two types [introverts and extroverts] need each other. Many successful ventures are the result of effective partnerships between introverts and extroverts. The famously charismatic Steve Jobs teamed up with powerhouse introverts at crucial points in his career at Apple, cofounding the company with the shy Steve Wozniak and bequeathing it to its current CEO, the quiet Tim Cook. . . .

6 The ideal scenario is when those two toddlers—the one who hands you the toy with the smile and the other who checks you out so carefully—grow up to run the world together.

1. Which one of the following best expresses the main idea of the passage?

   - A. Companies should include both introverted and extroverted workers on teams.
   - B. There are advantages to being sensitive and introverted.
   - C. Children who are sensitive are more deliberate when playing a game.
   - D. Introverts simply prefer less stimulation than others do.

2. According to the passage, children with sensitive temperaments are more likely to be which of the following?

   - A. empathetic
   - B. risk-taking
   - C. antisocial
   - D. noisy

3. According to the passage, the partnership between Steve Jobs and Steve Wozniak is an example of which of the following?

   - A. the negative consequences of a mixture of different personality types in the workplace
   - B. a successful collaboration between two introverts
   - C. a successful collaboration between an introvert and an extrovert
   - D. a combination of people who should "run the world"

4. Which one of the following is the best summary of the second paragraph?

   - A. Some children respond more dramatically than others to unfamiliar or startling events.
   - B. Observing how children respond to stimuli is the best way to study different kinds of social behavior.
   - C. Children who are perceived as "shy" are actually more sensitive than other children to stimuli in their environments.
   - D. If sensitivity in a child is not corrected by around age 2, that child will grow up to be an oversensitive adult.

5. Based on the passage, which one of the following activities would an introvert most likely prefer?

   - A. enjoying a quiet dinner with a handful of friends
   - B. going alone to a club to enjoy loud dance music
   - C. accompanying one friend to a crowded street festival
   - D. participating solo in a sport called "extreme ice-slope surfing"

Questions 6 through 10 refer to the following information about forklifts and the related diagram.

Excerpt from "Forklift Safety Guide"

1 Driving a forklift differs from driving a car. In a car or truck, the front wheels steer the vehicle. A forklift has the steering wheels in the rear. The rear end of the forklift swings in a circle around the front wheels, which support most of the load. The operator must check that there is room for the rear end to swing when making turns. This clearance can be maintained in your workplace by permanently marking aisles with painted lines or arranging storage racks in a way that creates obvious aisles for travel. However, these marked aisles will only be effective if you keep them clear of stored materials.

2 A forklift is not as responsive as a car when the steering wheel is turned. Rear-wheel steering makes it difficult to stop a forklift quickly or swerve and still maintain control. It is important, then, not to drive a forklift fast or around corners quickly.

3 Driving with the load downhill can result in loss of the load and control of the forklift. If you drive a forklift on an incline, you must keep the load on the uphill side. Otherwise, you may have no weight on the wheels that steer, and you can lose control! The load could also fall off or cause the forklift to tip.

4 Often a large forklift load obstructs the driver's view in one direction. It may be necessary to travel long distances with the load to the rear (in reverse for most forklifts). Use extra caution when traveling in reverse.

Adapted with permission from the State of Washington, Department of Labor and Industries.

6. According to the passage, which one of the following is an effect of rear-wheel steering on a forklift?
   - A. The front wheels carry most of the load.
   - B. The driver may have some difficulty in controlling the forklift.
   - C. There is a danger that the forklift will tip over.
   - D. The forklift driver may have little visibility.

7. Which one of the following identifies a pair of things or ideas between which the author draws a contrast?
   - A. driving a forklift and driving a car
   - B. the turning radius of a forklift and the turning radius of a car
   - C. a warehouse with clearly marked aisles and a highway with clearly marked lanes
   - D. driving a forklift in reverse and walking backward

8. Together, the passage and the graphic support which one of the following conclusions?
   - A. A forklift should never carry a load taller than the forklift itself.
   - B. A forklift should travel backward only when traveling downhill.
   - C. A forklift cannot drive uphill unless it is carrying a load.
   - D. A forklift that is traveling downhill with a heavy load should travel backward.

9. Which of the following best describes the author's purpose?
   - A. to inform drivers of cars about the differences between driving a car and driving a forklift
   - B. to warn the general public about the dangers of forklifts
   - C. to explain safe practices to forklift drivers
   - D. to describe the difference between skilled and unskilled forklift drivers

10. Which of the following best describes the organization of the passage?
    - A. The author lists potential dangers inherent in forklift driving and explains how to avoid them.
    - B. The author states that forklift driving is dangerous and gives examples of forklift accidents to support that idea.
    - C. The author lists the features of forklifts and describes their benefits.
    - D. The author explains the pros and cons of forklift driving to present a balanced picture of the value of forklifts.

Questions 11 through 15 refer to the following selections about genetically modified organism (GMO) foods.

World Food Prize Goes to Three Biotech Scientists

1 The World Food Prize Foundation took the bold step of awarding this year's prize to three pioneers of plant biotechnology whose work brought the world genetically modified crops.

2 Van Montagu and Chilton independently developed the technology in the 1980s to stably transfer foreign genes into plants, a discovery that set up a race to develop tools to genetically engineer plants. It allowed other scientists to incorporate genetic traits that allow plants to better withstand drought and extreme heat and to fight off pests and disease. Fraley was the first to successfully transfer immunity to specific bacteria into a plant. Fraley genetically engineered the first herbicide-resistant soybean in 1996.

3 Genetically enhanced crops are grown on more than 420 million acres in nearly 30 countries by over 17 million farmers worldwide, the foundation said. More than 90 percent of the users are small, resource-poor farmers in developing countries.

4 Many U.S. farmers credited genetic modifications in corn with saving last year's crop from all but total devastation, as half of the nation endured the worst drought in 60 years. Modern corn plants are more stable and can withstand a wider variety of climate conditions because of genetically improved leaves, roots, and reproductive capability.

5 Fraley said biotechnology will enable the farming industry to meet the needs of a growing global population. "We know we need from a demand perspective to double food production around the world in the next 30 years," he said.

Adapted from David Pitt, "World Food Prize goes to 3 biotech scientists," Associated Press, June 19, 2013

Dangers of GMO Foods

1 The rise in autoimmune diseases, infertility, gastrointestinal problems, and chronic diseases may be associated with the introduction of GMO (genetically modified organism) foods. In a position paper by the American Academy of Environmental Medicine, the authors ask all physicians to consider the role of GMO foods in the nation's health crisis and advise their patients to avoid all GMO foods whenever possible. The Academy also recommends a moratorium on GMO seeds and calls for immediate independent safety testing and the labeling of all food items containing genetically modified products.

2 As the reliance on GMO seeds expands worldwide, concerns about food supply and safety continue to escalate. Genetically engineered seeds are identical in structure, and if a problem affects one particular crop, a major crop failure can result. For example, following the recent failure of three GMO corn crops in three South African provinces, the Africa Centre for Biosecurity has called for an investigation and immediate ban of all GMO food. Corn is a primary source of food for southern African nations.

3 Most GMO seeds are genetically engineered to be herbicide tolerant and resistant to insect infestation and disease. Environmentalists worry that the characteristics of GMO crops may encourage farmers to increase their use of herbicides and pesticides, which will raise human consumption of dangerous toxins. GMO crops also manufacture their own pesticides, which puts further poisons into humans and soil and may cause unforeseen changes in the environment.

Adapted from Susan Brassard, "Dangers of GMO Foods," Livestrong.com, September 2, 2010

11. The author of Passage 1 most likely notes that the majority of GMO crops are cultivated by “small, resource-poor farmers in developing countries” in order to

- A. highlight how GMO foods can be harmful to struggling farmers.
- B. suggest that GMO foods can be beneficial to struggling farmers.
- C. illustrate how GMO foods can be more expensive for consumers.
- D. explain why GMO crops often fail.

12. Passage 2 is primarily concerned with

- A. the uses and misuses of GMO foods.
- B. the origin and development of GMO foods.
- C. the unexpected benefits of GMO foods.
- D. the safety and reliability of GMO foods.

13. What can be inferred from the first paragraph of Passage 2?

- A. American physicians, as a group, are completely unaware of the potential dangers of GMOs.
- B. The labels of some foods containing GMO ingredients do not indicate that the products contain genetically modified components.
- C. GMO foods have been proven to cause certain chronic conditions.
- D. Independent safety testing has been completed for most GMO foods.

14. The two passages primarily disagree about whether or not

- A. GMO foods can help support a growing world population.
- B. GMO foods are better able to withstand drought and insect infestation than natural foods.
- C. GMO foods are largely a positive development for global food production.
- D. scientists who study GMO foods are worthy of recognition.

15. Passage 2 cites the example of a major crop failure in South Africa to illustrate the dangers of planting with GMO seeds. Which paragraph in Passage 1 offers a counterexample that weakens this position?

- A. Paragraph 1
- B. Paragraph 2
- C. Paragraph 4
- D. Paragraph 5

Questions 16 through 20 refer to the following.

Excerpted from *Black Beauty*

1 The first place that I can well remember was a large, pleasant meadow with a pond of clear water in it. Some shady trees leaned over it, and rushes and water lilies grew at the deep end. Over the hedge on one side we looked into a plowed field, and on the other we looked over a gate at our master's house, which stood by the roadside. . . .

2 One day, when there was a good deal of kicking, my mother whinnied to me to come to her, and then she said:

3 "I wish you to pay attention to what I am going to say to you. The colts who live here are very good colts, but they are cart-horse colts, and of course they have not learned manners. You have been well-bred and well-born; your father has a great name in these parts, and your grandfather won the cup two years at the Newmarket races; your grandmother had the sweetest temper of any horse I ever knew, and I think you have never seen me kick or bite. I hope you will grow up gentle and good, and never learn bad ways; do your work with a good will, lift your feet up well when you trot, and never bite or kick even in play."

4 I have never forgotten my mother's advice; I knew she was a wise old horse, and our master thought a great deal of her. Her name was Duchess, but he often called her Pet.

5 Our master was a good, kind man. He gave us good food, good lodging, and kind words; he spoke as kindly to us as he did to his little children. We were all fond of him, and my mother loved him very much. When she saw him at the gate she would neigh with joy, and trot up to him. . . . All the horses would come to him, but I think we were his favorites. My mother always took him to the town on a market day in a light gig.

6 There was a plowboy, Dick, who sometimes came into our field to pluck blackberries from the hedge. When he had eaten all he wanted, he would have what he called fun with the colts, throwing stones and sticks at them to make them gallop. We did not much mind him, for we could gallop off, but sometimes a stone would hit and hurt us.

7 One day he was at this game, and did not know that the master was in the next field, but he was there, watching what was going on; over the hedge he jumped in a snap, and catching Dick by the arm, he gave him such a box on the ear as made him roar with the pain and surprise. As soon as we saw the master, we trotted up nearer to see what went on.

16. Who is the narrator in this passage?

- A. a servant
- B. a hired plowboy
- C. a young horse
- D. a child

17. What is the setting of the story?

- A. a town
- B. a racetrack
- C. a forest
- D. a farm

18. The narrator's account of his youth can best be described as

- A. melancholy.
- B. contented.
- C. regretful.
- D. humorous.

19. The narrator would most likely describe the master in the story as

- A. affectionate and protective.
- B. arrogant and abusive.
- C. playful and light-hearted.
- D. bold and aggressive.

20. The mother's speech in paragraph three most likely serves to

- A. correct the narrator for playing too roughly.
- B. assure the narrator he will grow up to win races like his grandfather.
- C. reprimand the narrator for insulting the master.
- D. accuse the narrator of stealing blackberries.

LANGUAGE ARTS: WRITING PRETEST

PART I: LANGUAGE SKILLS—18 QUESTIONS

Directions: You may fill in the circles next to the correct answers or write your answers on a separate piece of paper.

Questions 1 through 6 refer to the following paragraphs.

To: Parents and Guardians
From: Sonia Vasquez, School Nurse

(A)

(1) A student in your child's class have been diagnosed with strep throat. (2) Strep throat is a highly contagious disease and a common illness in children. (3) Unlike most sore throats, which are caused by viruses, strep throat is caused by bacteria and is treatable with antibiotics. (4) The time between exposure to the disease and the appearance of symptoms is usually one to three days. (5) To safeguard your child's health, please take the following precautions. (6) Watch your child for strep symptoms. (7) Such as sore throat, fever, swollen glands, and headache. (8) If your child developed any of these symptoms, take him or her to the doctor. (9) If a throat culture is positive, treatment can be started. (10) It is extremely important to take all the prescribed medicine until it is gone.

(B)

(11) Children should get immediate treatment for several reasons. (12) For one, treatment reduces spread of the disease. (13) In addition antibiotics may prevent rheumatic fever. (14) Treatment also prevents other rare but possibly dangerous complications.

(C)

(15) Your child may return to school after taking medicine for 24 hours and the fever must be gone. (16) Please call us with any questions or concerns you have.

1. Sentence 1: **A student in your child's class have been diagnosed with strep throat.**

   Which correction should be made to sentence 1?

   - A. replace your with you're
   - B. change child's to children
   - C. insert a comma after class
   - D. change have to has

2. Sentences 6 and 7: **Watch your child for strep symptoms. Such as** sore throat, fever, swollen glands, and headache.

   Which is the best way to write the underlined portion of these sentences?

   - A. symptoms. Such as
   - B. symptoms, the best known are
   - C. symptoms, such as
   - D. symptoms examples are

3. Sentence 8: **If your child developed any of these symptoms, take him or her to the doctor.**

   Which correction should be made to sentence 8?

   - A. replace your with you're
   - B. change developed to develops
   - C. remove the comma
   - D. replace him or her with them

4. Which revision would improve the effectiveness of the passage?

   Begin a new paragraph with

   - A. sentence 3
   - B. sentence 4
   - C. sentence 5
   - D. sentence 6

5. Sentence 13: **In addition antibiotics may prevent rheumatic fever.**

   Which correction should be made to sentence 13?

   - A. insert a comma after addition
   - B. insert a comma after antibiotics
   - C. change may prevent to are preventing
   - D. change rheumatic fever to Rheumatic Fever

6. Sentence 15: **Your child may return to school after taking medicine for 24 hours and the fever must be gone.**

   The most effective revision of sentence 15 would begin with which group of words?

   - A. After the fever is gone and your child has taken
   - B. Having taken medicine for 24 hours and the fever
   - C. Your child, once having taken medicine for 24 hours, may
   - D. The fever being gone and the medicine being finished,

Questions 7 through 12 refer to the following paragraphs.

Compulsive Gambling

(A)

(1) Most of us can bet on a football game, or buy a lottery ticket with little damage to our finances. (2) In contrast, compulsive gamblers cannot stop even when their behavior had threatened to ruin their lives.

(B)

(3) Gambling frequently occupies the thoughts of compulsive gamblers. (4) For instance, they may be reliving past gambling experiences or coming up with schemes to get more money for gambling. (5) Although they may have tried several times to stop gambling, their efforts met with failure. (6) When trying to stop gambling, they feel irritable and restless. (7) They need to gamble with more and more money in order to enjoy it, losing money increases their desire to gamble. (8) They may even commit fraud forgery, or theft to get the funds to continue their habit. (9) Many of them have lost jobs, important relationships, or career opportunities because of their involvement with gambling.

(C)

(10) Compulsive gambling is like any other addiction. (11) As gamblers lose control over gambling, they lose control over their lives as well. (12) They may become anxious and depressed or they may fail to live up to their obligations, causing others to stop trusting them.

7. Sentence 1: **Most of us can bet on a football game, or buy a lottery ticket with little damage to our finances.**

   Which correction should be made to sentence 1?

   - A. insert a comma after us
   - B. change bet to be betting
   - C. remove the comma
   - D. insert a comma after ticket

8. Sentence 2: **In contrast, compulsive gamblers cannot stop even when their behavior had threatened to ruin their lives.**

   Which is the best way to write the underlined portion of this sentence?

   - A. had threatened
   - B. will threaten
   - C. threatens
   - D. having threatened

9. Which sentence would be most effective if inserted at the beginning of paragraph B?
   - A. Compulsive gamblers have a lot of problems.
   - B. Some people engage in compulsive gambling.
   - C. Gamblers escape from negative emotions.
   - D. Compulsive gamblers display a number of consistent traits.

10. Sentence 7: **They need to gamble with more and more money in order to enjoy it, losing money increases their desire to gamble.**

    Which is the best way to write the underlined portion of this sentence?
    - A. it. Losing
    - B. it but losing
    - C. it, now that losing
    - D. it and losing

11. Sentence 8: **They may even commit fraud forgery, or theft to get the funds to continue their habit.**

    Which correction should be made to sentence 8?
    - A. insert a comma after fraud
    - B. insert a comma after theft
    - C. replace their with there
    - D. replace their with they're

12. Sentence 12: **They may become anxious and depressed or they may fail to live up to their obligations, causing others to stop trusting them.**

    Which is the best way to write the underlined portion of this sentence?
    - A. depressed, or they
    - B. depressed, they
    - C. depressed. And they
    - D. depressed and they

Questions 13 through 18 refer to the following paragraphs.

Choosing a Pet

(A)

(1) People often make impulse buys at Pet Stores just because they see an adorable puppy or kitten. (2) Unhappily, these poor creatures are likely to end up at animal shelters when the owners find he can't care for them. (3) To avoid this outcome, choose your pet wisely. (4) Remember that your pet will become a member of your family and a daily responsibility.

(B)

(5) There's several factors to consider when selecting a pet. (6) First of all, do you have the time to care for a pet? (7) While some pets require little care, puppies and kittens need to be housebroken and to train them. (8) If the animal needs exercise, is your home large enough? (9) Would you enjoy taking your pet outdoors for exercise? (10) Do you think people should get a lot of exercise? (11) Can you afford the costs of food, vaccinations, and health check-ups? (12) Does your building allow pets? (13) Finally, if you must leave home for a few days, can you find someone to care for your pet?

(C)

(14) Once you choose a pet that is appropriate for your lifestyle, bring the animal to a veterinarian for examination. (15) You should be able to return the pet if the animal was unhealthy.

13. Sentence 1: **People often make impulse buys at Pet Stores just because they see an adorable puppy or kitten.**

    Which correction should be made to sentence 1?

    - A. change buys to bys
    - B. change Pet Stores to pet stores
    - C. insert a comma before because
    - D. insert a comma before or

14. Sentence 2: **Unhappily, these poor creatures are likely to end up at animal shelters when the owners find he can't care for them.**

    Which correction should be made to sentence 2?

    - A. remove the comma
    - B. change animal shelters to Animal Shelters
    - C. insert a comma after shelters
    - D. replace he with they

15. Sentence 5: **There's several factors to consider when selecting a pet.**

Which correction should be made to sentence 5?

- A. change There's to There are
- B. insert a comma after factors
- C. replace to with too
- D. insert a comma after consider

16. Sentence 7: **While some pets require little care, puppies and kittens need to be housebroken and to train them.**

Which is the best way to write the underlined portion of the sentence?

- A. be housebroken and to train them
- B. housebreaking and training
- C. be housebroken and trained
- D. be housebroken and training

17. Which revision should be made to the placement of sentence 10?

- A. move sentence 10 to the beginning of paragraph B
- B. move sentence 10 to follow sentence 6
- C. move sentence 10 to the beginning of paragraph C
- D. remove sentence 10

18. Sentence 15: **You should be able to return the pet if the animal was unhealthy.**

Which correction should be made to sentence 15?

- A. change You to One
- B. insert a comma after pet
- C. replace if with and
- D. change was to is

Language Arts: Writing Pretest

Part II: Essay

Directions: Read both the pair of passages and the writing prompt and answer the questions that follow.

Questions 1–9 are based on the process of writing a response to a pair of passages.
Note: Do not start writing your response until you are asked to do so at question 8.

Essay Prompt

The following articles present different views on how best to educate children with disabilities. They were written by educational psychologists and appeared side by side in a recent issue of a magazine for parents. Read both passages carefully, noting the strengths and weaknesses of each discussion.

Then, write an essay in which you explain your own opinion on the issue. Be sure to use evidence from the text passages provided as well as specific reasons and examples from your own experience and knowledge to support your position. Your essay should acknowledge alternate and/or opposing ideas. When you have finished your essay, check your writing for correct spelling, punctuation, and grammar.

Mainstreaming: Beneficial for Everyone

The practice of "mainstreaming" students with developmental disabilities, or including them in the regular classroom and having them participate in as many activities there as possible, is helpful for both those students and their nondisabled classmates.

A key consideration in educational placement is the fact that young children's language ability is significantly influenced by that of their classmates. This has been shown to be particularly true for students who have difficulty speaking or understanding speech. It is believed that children spend much more time one-on-one with one another than with a teacher or other adult, and they imitate one another's behavior. Thus, placing a child with a disability that affects language ability with peers who are less challenged is advantageous to that child's development. In contrast, educating students with language challenges separately, without interaction with more skilled classmates, is detrimental to their social and academic growth.

Furthermore, when these children grow up, they will need to function in a diverse society, not the tailored environment of the special education classroom. Integrating them from a young age into environments where social norms are similar to those they will need to navigate as adults prepares them for success in the future. Likewise, their nondisabled classmates will be better positioned for lifetime success if they develop the ability to interact constructively with people who are different from them in a variety of ways. For this reason, isolating children with developmental disabilities does nondisabled children a disservice by not teaching them the flexibility and empathy necessary to have productive relationships with a wide range of people.

Some argue that students with disabilities are ill-served in the mainstream classroom. However, with appropriate educational and social supports, they will achieve better academic and social outcomes there than if their education is designed entirely around their limitations.

"Equal" Treatment Is Unfair

Imagine a second-grade classroom in which the teacher is asking students to read a paragraph out loud as a group. Some students are shy about reading aloud, but they are carried along by the class and are gaining confidence. However, one student isn't reading at all. Instead, she is banging her fists on her desk. Then she stands up, screams, and jerks the book out of the hands of the student next to her and throws it across the room. Some students are frightened; others see this as an opportunity to engage in some disruptive behavior of their own. Certainly, the reading lesson is completely derailed.

Placing children with developmental disabilities in regular classrooms is unfair to other students, to teachers, and—most of all—to the very children that "mainstreaming" is intended to help. Teachers in the regular classroom often lack specialized training to meet the needs of children with developmental disabilities. These students deserve special education programs that address their academic level and learning style. Being forced to participate in classroom activities they cannot perform batters their self-esteem and does nothing to advance their skills.

Besides finding academic assignments a source of severe frustration, such children often find the regular classroom environment itself very unpleasant. They may experience sensory overload, and instead of making friends, they may find themselves surrounded by classmates whose speech and nonverbal cues are incomprehensible.

Therefore, no one should be surprised when the mainstreamed child acts out in class. When this occurs, other students may feel unsafe and they certainly stop learning. Teachers, already in a stressful and undervalued job, have a classroom management problem and no tools to deal with it. Proponents of mainstreaming argue that it provides students with disabilities that same opportunities that are available to other children. However, even when well-intentioned, mainstreaming is not the right choice for many students.

Unpack the Writing Prompt

1. What is the topic of the writing prompt?

   ____

2. What does the prompt ask you to do?

   ____

3. What does the prompt tell you that you need to include in the response?

   ____

Develop Your Topic Sentence and Supporting Details

4. Write a sentence that introduces the topic of your essay and another sentence stating your position on the topic. These will be the first paragraph of your essay.

   ____

5. What are three details from the passage you will use to develop your argument?

   ____

   ____

   ____

6. Write a concluding sentence that summarizes your argument.

   ____

Plan, Draft, Revise, and Edit Your Response

7. On a piece of paper, make a plan for your response.
8. On a computer or on a piece of paper, write a response to the prompt that includes an introduction, a body, and a conclusion.
9. Make revisions to improve your response and correct any errors in grammar, usage, spelling, capitalization, and punctuation.

Mathematics Pretest

Part I: Quantitative Reasoning—18 Questions

Directions: You may fill in the circles next to the correct answers or write your answers on a separate piece of paper. You MAY use a calculator.

Questions 1–2 refer to the following information and graph.

Video Warehouse has divided the surrounding community into four advertising zones. The graph shows the total number of customers from each zone for a three-week period.

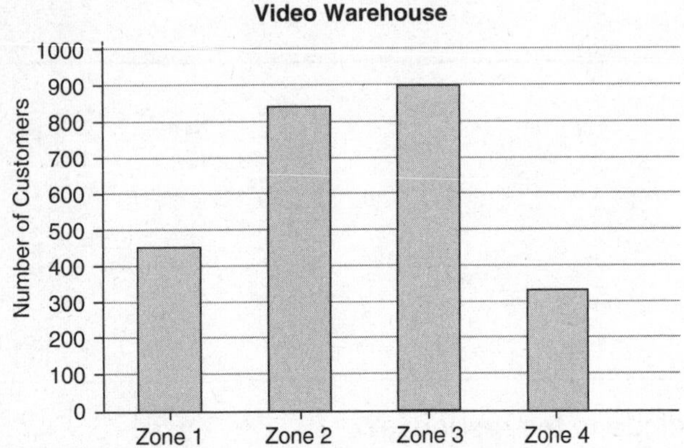

1. During the three weeks, how many customers came from Zones 3 and 4?
   - A. between 900 and 1,000
   - B. between 1,000 and 1,100
   - C. between 1,100 and 1,200
   - D. between 1,200 and 1,300
   - E. between 1,300 and 1,400

2. What is the approximate ratio of customers from Zone 1 to customers from Zone 3?
   - A. 3:5
   - B. 3:2
   - C. 2:1
   - D. 1:3
   - E. 1:2

3. A potter uses $\frac{3}{5}$ of a pound of clay to make a bowl. How many bowls could the potter make from 10 pounds of clay?
   - A. 6
   - B. 8
   - C. 16
   - D. 17
   - E. 19

4. Janelle has recently been hired for the job of library assistant. The following graph shows what percent of her time will be spent on each of five tasks each day.

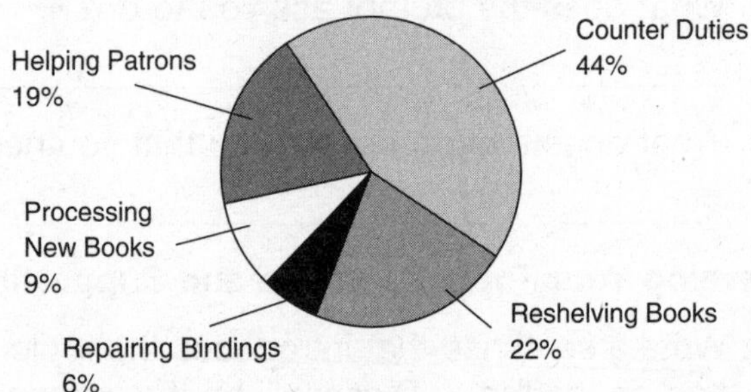

   The number of hours that Janelle will spend working at the counter is about how many times the number of hours that she will spend processing new books and repairing bindings?
   - A. 2
   - B. 3
   - C. 4
   - D. 5
   - E. 6

5. Fifteen percent of the workers at Nationwide Industries earn minimum wage. If 24 workers earn minimum wage, how many total workers are there at Nationwide Industries?

- A. 4
- B. 36
- C. 160
- D. 240
- E. 360

6. An accountant is going to pay the following four bills:

Bill	Amount
W	$27.10
X	$261.00
Y	$2.80
Z	$27.20

The accountant will pay the bills in order from smallest to largest. In what order will he pay them?

- A. W, X, Z, Y
- B. X, W, Z, Y
- C. Y, X, W, Z
- D. X, Z, W, Y
- E. Y, W, Z, X

7. A jar holds 16 ounces of honey. A cook is going to make two recipes. One of the recipes calls for 2.5 ounces of honey, and the other calls for 4.25 ounces of honey. After the cook has made those two recipes, how many ounces of honey will be left in the jar?

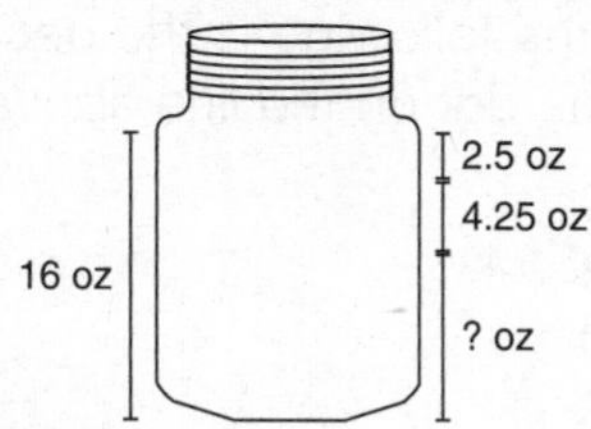

- A. 6.75
- B. 9.25
- C. 10.00
- D. 11.25
- E. 11.75

8. All numbers that are evenly divisible by both 6 and 14 are also divisible by which of the following numbers?

- A. 8
- B. 12
- C. 21
- D. 28
- E. 32

9. Alice, Kathy, and Sheila work as medical assistants at Valley Clinic. Alice has worked 8 years longer than Kathy. Kathy has worked half as long as Sheila. If Sheila has worked at the company for 10 years, how many years has Alice worked there?

- A. 5
- B. 8
- C. 10
- D. 12
- E. 13

Question 10 is based on the spinner below.

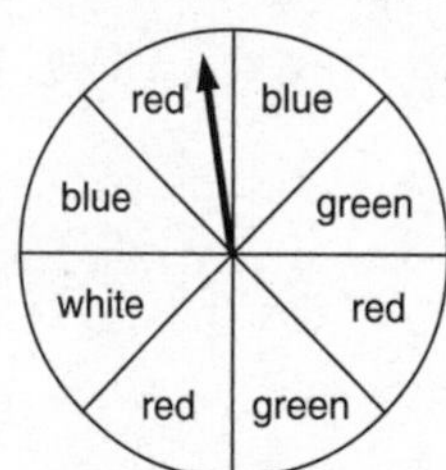

10. The spinner shown in the drawing is divided into eight equal sections. If you spin the spinner one time, what is the probability of not getting blue?

- A. $\frac{1}{8}$
- B. $\frac{1}{4}$
- C. $\frac{1}{2}$
- D. $\frac{3}{4}$
- E. $\frac{7}{8}$

11. A computer monitor is regularly priced at \$320. During a two-day sale, the price was decreased to \$240. Which of the following is the percentage decrease of the monitor's price during the sale?

- A. 25%
- B. 33%
- C. 45%
- D. 75%
- E. 80%

12. For a 10-day period, a bank kept track of the number of new accounts opened each day. The results are shown in the table below. What is the median number of accounts opened per day during this 10-day period?

Day	Accounts	Day	Accounts
May 7	6	May 14	4
May 8	2	May 15	8
May 9	7	May 16	6
May 10	5	May 17	4
May 11	4	May 18	7

- A. 5
- B. 5.3
- C. 5.5
- D. 6
- E. 6.7

13. Jim is a salesperson, and his employers expect him to sell at least \$12,000 in merchandise per month. In April, Jim sold \$2,500 in the first week of the month and twice that much in the second week. How much must he sell in the rest of April combined in order to sell the minimum expected of him?

- A. \$4,500
- B. \$5,500
- C. \$7,500
- D. \$9,500
- E. \$12,000

14. Angela likes to use two walking sticks when she goes hiking, but the two walking sticks she has been given recently are different lengths. One is $3\frac{4}{5}$ feet long, and the other is $3\frac{1}{2}$ feet long.

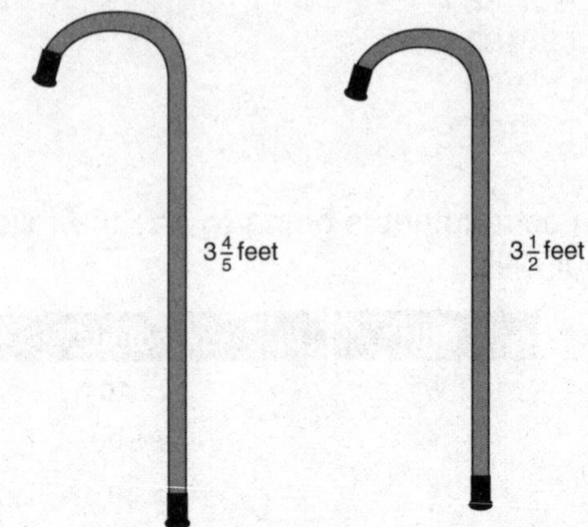

Angela wants to cut the longer stick to match the shorter one. How much should she cut from the longer stick so that the two walking sticks will be the same length?

- A. $\frac{3}{4}$ feet
- B. $\frac{3}{5}$ feet
- C. $\frac{3}{10}$ feet
- D. $\frac{1}{4}$ feet
- E. $\frac{1}{3}$ feet

Question 15 is based on the following number line.

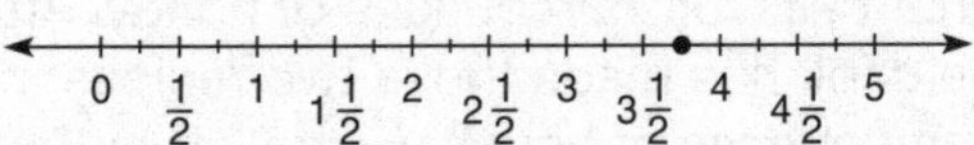

15. Which of the following is the decimal point value of the dot on the line above?

- A. 3.25
- B. 3.33
- C. 3.50
- D. 3.75
- E. 4.00

Question 16 is based on the following information and graph.

Marjorie has a class of 35 students, and she tracked their performance on a recent math exam. The graph below represents how their scores were distributed along the range of possible scores, from F to A.

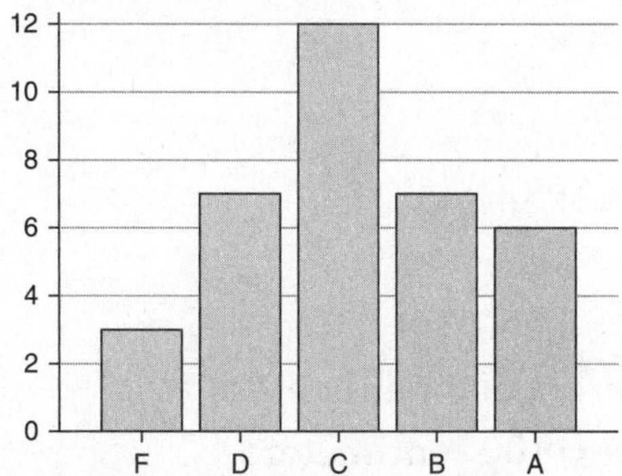

16. Based on the graph, which of the following is a true statement?

- A. None of Marjorie's students received an F on the exam.
- B. Most of Marjorie's students received either an A or a B on the exam.
- C. If Marjorie gave the same exam again to another group of students, most of those students would receive a C.
- D. If Marjorie gave the same exam again to another group of students, more of those students than these students would receive an F.
- E. More students received either an A or a B than received either a D or an F.

---

17. Jason deposits $5,000 in a bank account that will pay him 4% simple interest annually. If Jason deposits no more than the initial $5,000, how much money will be in the account at the end of five years? (The formula for simple interest is $I = prt$ or *interest* = *principal* × *rate* × *time.* Use a decimal to express the interest when using that formula.)

- A. $200
- B. $1,000
- C. $5,000
- D. $6,000
- E. $7,200

18. A local library shows movies on Thursday evenings. The library administrator has chosen the next six movies he will show, but he has not decided in which order to show them. How many possible orderings of the six movies are there?

- A. 21
- B. 36
- C. 720
- D. 1,012
- E. 1,024

MATHEMATICS PRETEST

PART II: ALGEBRAIC REASONING AND GEOMETRY—22 QUESTIONS

This page displays formulas that you will be given when you take the HiSET exam. You can refer to this page on Part II of this pretest.

Perimeter / Circumference

Rectangle

Perimeter = 2(*length*) + 2(*width*)

Circle

Circumference = 2π(*radius*)

Area

Circle

Area = $\pi(radius)^2$

Triangle

Area = $\frac{1}{2}(base)(height)$

Parallelogram

Area = (*base*)(*height*)

Trapezoid

Area = $\frac{1}{2}(base_1 + base_2)(height)$

Volume

Prism/Cylinder

Volume = (*area of the base*)(*height*)

Pyramid/Cone

Volume = $\frac{1}{3}$(*area of the base*)(*height*)

Sphere

Volume = $\frac{4}{3}\pi(radius)^3$

Length

1 foot = 12 inches

1 yard = 3 feet

1 mile = 5,280 feet

1 meter = 1,000 millimeters

1 meter = 100 centimeters

1 kilometer = 1,000 meters

1 mile ≈ 1.6 kilometers

1 inch = 2.54 centimeters

1 foot ≈ 0.3 meter

Capacity / Volume

1 cup = 8 fluid ounces

1 pint = 2 cups

1 quart = 2 pints

1 gallon = 4 quarts

1 gallon = 231 cubic inches

1 liter = 1,000 milliliters

1 liter ≈ 0.264 gallon

Weight

1 pound = 16 ounces

1 ton = 2,000 pounds

1 gram = 1,000 milligrams

1 kilogram = 1,000 grams

1 kilogram ≈ 2.2 pounds

1 ounce ≈ 28.3 grams

Directions: You may fill in the circles next to the correct answers or write your answers on a separate piece of paper. Refer to the formula sheet on page 22 as needed. You MAY use your calculator.

1. Which point on the number line below represents the value $-\frac{16}{6}$?

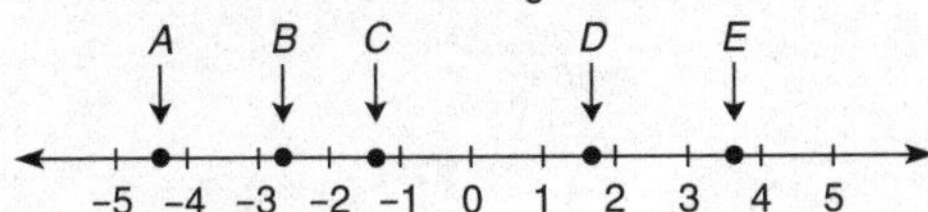

- A. Point *A*
- B. Point *B*
- C. Point *C*
- D. Point *D*
- E. Point *E*

2. Evaluate the expression $2x - (4y - 3) + 5xz$, when $x = -3$, $y = 2$, and $z = -1$.

- A. 45
- B. 16
- C. 4
- D. −10
- E. −16

3. On April 1 of this year, the high temperature in Northville was 46 degrees Fahrenheit. Then a sudden snowstorm arose, and the temperature dropped sharply to a low of −8 degrees Fahrenheit. What was the magnitude of the change in temperature on that day?

- A. 54
- B. 46
- C. 36
- D. −36
- E. −46

Question 4 refers to the following drawing.

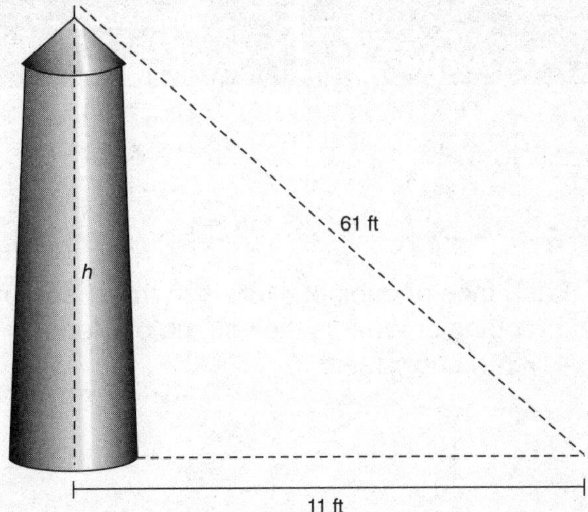

4. A tower casts a shadow 11 feet long. The distance from the top of the tower to the end of the shadow is 61 feet. How many feet tall is the tower?

- A. 50
- B. 60
- C. 61
- D. 72
- E. 81

Question 5 is based on the following information.

Designer Furnishings sells premade cabinets and cupboards, as shown below.

Model	Dimensions (in inches)
411R	32 by 22 by 10
412R	28 by 36 by 15
413S	24 by 72 by 18
414S	25 by 24 by 6

5. Each face of cabinet 413S is in the shape of a rectangle. What is the volume of Model 413S in cubic feet?

- A. 18
- B. 31
- C. 36
- D. 48
- E. 108

6. Together, Levy and Matthew earn $4,680 per month. Levy earns $520 more per month than Matthew earns. How much does Levy earn per month?

- A. $2,080
- B. $2,340
- C. $2,600
- D. $3,260
- E. $4,160

7. The design for a new cone-shaped closed container is shown below. What is the surface area of this container, in square inches? You can select the correct formula from the formula sheet on page 22.

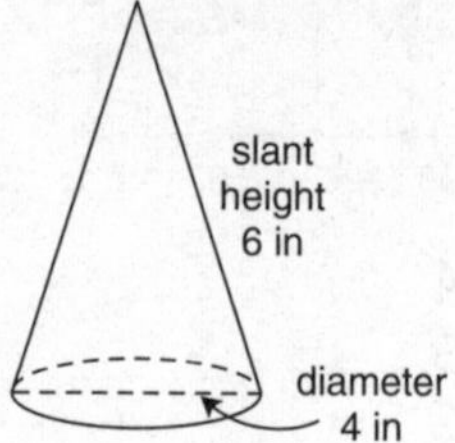

- A. 4π
- B. 12π
- C. 16π
- D. 28π
- E. 32π

8. Simplify this polynomial:
$3x^3 + x + 2x^3 - 4x^2 + 14y - 2(y + x)$.

- A. $3x^3 - 3x^2 + 14(-2y + 2x)$
- B. $5x^3 - 3x^2 + 14y - 2y - 2x$
- C. $3x^3 - x + 4x^2 + 12y$
- D. $5x^3 - 4x^2 - x + 12y$
- E. $5x^3 + 4x^2 + x + 12y$

9. A rectangle is drawn on a coordinate grid. Three of its four vertices are located at points (–1, – 2), (–1, 4), and (2, – 2). What is the location of the fourth vertex?

- A. (–2, –4)
- B. (–1, –4)
- C. (1, 4)
- D. (2, 4)
- E. (4, 2)

10. Which of the following expressions is equal to the expression $4x - 2(3x - 9)$?

- A. $18 - 2x$
- B. $-10x - 18$
- C. $-2x - 18$
- D. $2x + 18$
- E. $10x - 18$

11. In the equation $3x^2 - 10x = 8$, which of the following values for x will make the equation true?

- A. –4
- B. –3
- C. 0
- D. 3
- E. 4

12. Solve for x: $12(x - 2) < 24$

- A. $x < 0$
- B. $x > 0$
- C. $x < 12$
- D. $x > 4$
- E. $x < 4$

13. Scientists estimate that Earth is 4,540,000,000 years old. What is that number expressed in scientific notation?

- A. 4.54×10^7
- B. 4.54×10^9
- C. 454×10^{10}
- D. $2(127 \times 10^7)$
- E. $4(127 \times 10^7)$

14. Joe just purchased an oddly shaped piece of property, depicted in the figure below.

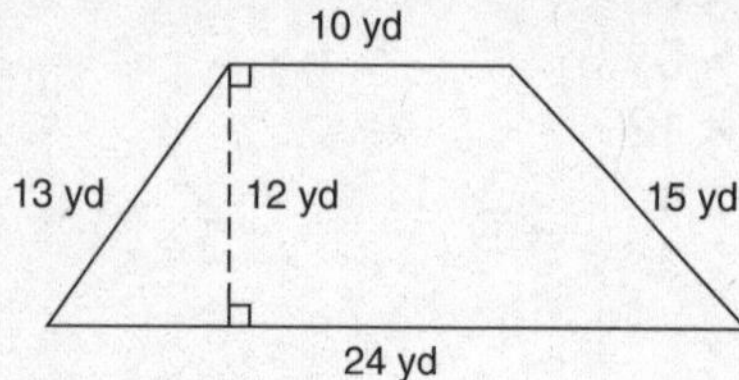

What is the area, in square yards, of Joe's new property?

- A. 120
- B. 134
- C. 140
- D. 156
- E. 204

15. The XYZ Company sells hats and will monogram them if customers choose. The price for each monogram varies depending on how many hats a customer would like to have monogrammed. The monogram prices for several order sizes are shown below:

Number of hats to be monogrammed (n)	Price per monogram (p)
1	\$5.00
2	\$4.50
3	\$4.00
4	\$3.50
5	\$3.00
6	\$2.50

Which of the following best expresses the relationship of price per monogram (for all nonnegative values of p) to number of hats monogrammed shown in the table above?

- A. $p = \$5.00 - (n - 1)\$0.50$
- B. $p = \$5.00 - n(\$0.50)$
- C. $p = (n - 1)\$5.00$
- D. $p = \$0.50(10n)$
- E. $p = \$5.00(10n)$

16. A parallelogram has two obtuse angles and two acute angles. If the measure of one of the obtuse angles is 110°, what is the measure, in degrees, of one of the acute angles?

- A. 10°
- B. 70°
- C. 110°
- D. 240°
- E. 270°

Question 17 refers to the following graph.

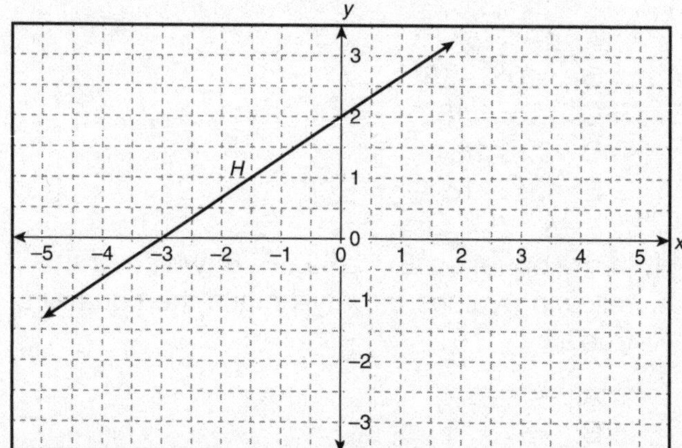

17. Line H is the graph of which of the following equations?

- A. $y = \frac{1}{3}x + 2$
- B. $y + 2 = \frac{2}{3}x$
- C. $y = \frac{2}{3}x + 2$
- D. $y = 3(x - 2) + 2$
- E. $y = 3x - 2$

18. A fountain's pool is enclosed by a circular plastic tank. The distance from the center of the pool to the wall of the tank is 10 feet. How long is the wall of the tank in feet?

- A. 20π
- B. $\frac{20}{\pi}$
- C. 25π
- D. 100π
- E. 200π

19. Line W passes through the following points on the coordinate grid: $(0, -9)$ and $(4, -1)$. What is the slope of line W?

- A. -2
- B. $-\frac{1}{2}$
- C. $\frac{1}{2}$
- D. 2
- E. 4

20. Beansey's Baked Beans, Inc., has developed a new can for its baked beans, shown below:

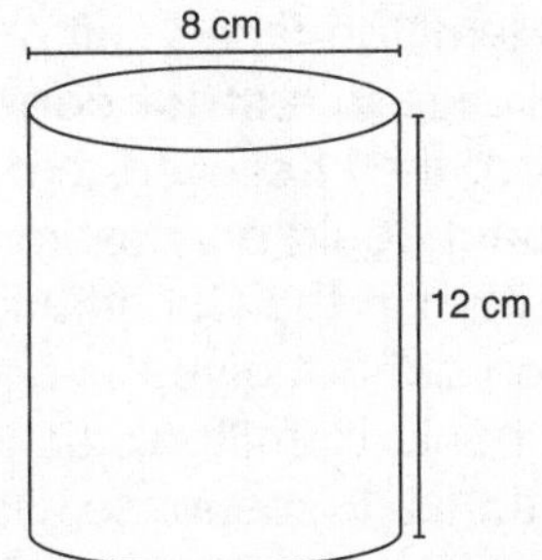

What is the volume of the new can, in cubic centimeters?

- A. 48π
- B. 96π
- C. 192π
- D. 768π
- E. $1{,}024\pi$

21. Tina is considering renting a commercial space for her business. The space is shown below.

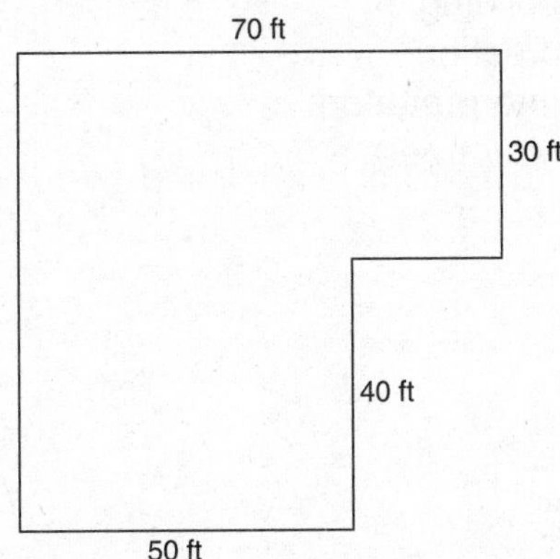

What is the area of the commercial space, in square feet?

- A. 290
- B. 2,100
- C. 2,800
- D. 3,600
- E. 4,100

22. In the system of equations $3x - 3y = -9$ and $2x + y = 9$, solve for both x and y. You may use the coordinate grid below to help your work.

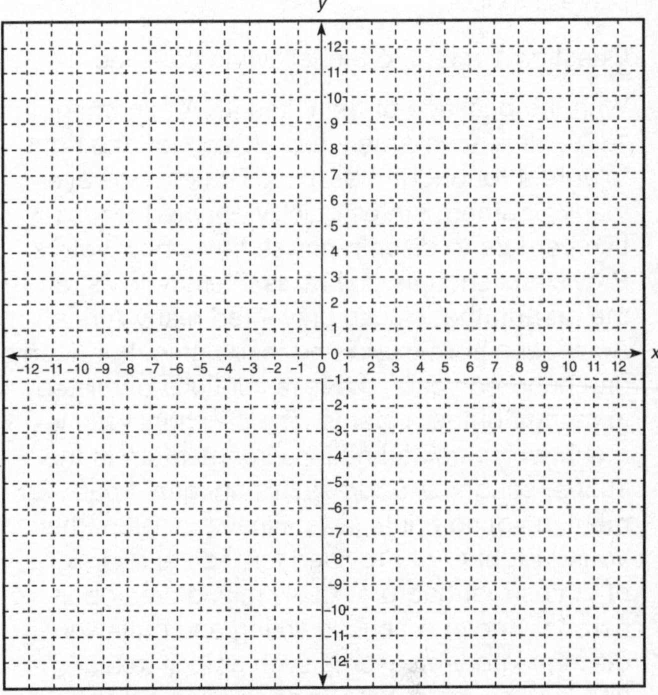

What is the solution set for x and y?

- A. $(2, -5)$
- B. $(0, 3)$
- C. $(0, 9)$
- D. $(2, 5)$
- E. $(5, 2)$

Social Studies Pretest

Part I: Social Studies Skills—10 Questions

Directions: You may fill in the circles next to the correct answers or write your answers on a separate piece of paper.

Question 1 refers to the following passage.

With the passage of the Fifteenth Amendment in 1870, all African Americans were given the right to vote throughout the United States. However, many Southern states quickly enacted legislative barriers to disenfranchise these new voters. Provisions such as poll taxes, literacy tests, and the grandfather clause prevented many African Americans from exercising their rights. For nearly one hundred years, these restrictions persisted in many Southern states. The civil rights movement, which gained national momentum in the 1950s, sought to address this unequal treatment in voting rights laws. Finally, in 1965, the Voting Rights Act provided for federal oversight of states that had previously raised unfair barriers to African American voting and outlawed discriminatory measures such as poll taxes and literacy tests. Voter participation among African Americans dramatically increased in the following years.

1. Which of the following describes the author's main idea?

   - A. The Voting Rights Act of 1965 ended discrimination in all areas of American society.
   - B. The main effect of the Voting Rights Act of 1965 was to empower individual states to end discriminatory measures against African American voting.
   - C. The Voting Rights Act of 1965 gave the federal government oversight of state elections to end barriers against African American voting.
   - D. The Fifteenth Amendment did not end racism in Southern states.

Question 2 refers to the following passage.

To address the nation's financial insolvency after the Revolutionary War, George Washington turned to his Secretary of the Treasury, Alexander Hamilton. Hamilton proposed creating a national bank, which would help to pay back the nation's debt and stabilize the nation's currency. Immediately, Hamilton faced stiff opposition from those who believed in a **strict construction** of the Constitution; they believed that Congress and the president could only exercise powers specifically written in the Constitution. Because the Constitution did not give the power to create a national bank, Hamilton's actions would be unconstitutional. In response, Hamilton offered a justification for the constitutionality of his bank based on a **loose construction** of the Constitution, meaning that Congress could use the Necessary and Proper Clause of the Constitution to stretch its power beyond what was specified in the words of the document. In Washington's first great test of presidential leadership, he sided with Hamilton and the idea of a national bank.

2. What is meant by the term "construction" in the passage?

   - A. building
   - B. creation
   - C. interpretation
   - D. structure

Questions 3 and 4 refer to the following passage.

In an attempt to make consumers more aware of the nutritional value of the foods they purchase, the Food and Drug Administration (FDA) is attempting to impose strict new regulations on all food retailers. These regulations would require that the caloric information of each food product be clearly posted on the premises, typically through signs that would be expensive to create and maintain. While these regulations would place a financial burden on all food retailers—an expense that would necessarily be passed on to consumers—the regulations would be particularly devastating to smaller restaurants, grocery stores, and convenience stores that offer fresh food items. To relieve this burden on smaller businesses, Congress has proposed the Common Sense Nutritional Disclosure Act, which would exempt smaller food establishments that primarily sell prepackaged foods from having to post on-site information. Also, under this legislation, restaurants that take most of their orders remotely can post caloric information online.

3. What is the author's point of view regarding the FDA's new food regulations?

   - A. The FDA's new regulations would place a financial hardship on small food retailers.
   - B. The FDA's new regulations would help consumers choose foods of a higher nutritional value.
   - C. The FDA's new regulations would have a more severe financial impact on chain restaurants than on smaller food retailers.
   - D. The FDA's new regulations would give food retailers more diverse options for displaying caloric information.

4. Which one of the following words points to the author's viewpoint regarding the FDA's strict new regulations?

   - A. "aware"
   - B. "strict"
   - C. "devastating"
   - D. "remotely"

Questions 5 and 6 refer to the following paragraph.

It is known that a significant quantity of oil exists within the Arctic National Wildlife Refuge (ANWR) of Alaska. Shockingly, there are many who would have us ignore this incredible resource housed right within our national borders. One commonly cited reason against drilling for oil in the ANWR is that the drilling process would endanger the existence of the porcupine caribou, whose calving grounds encompass much of the region. But science has shown us that as many as 99 percent of all the species that once existed on Earth are now extinct, and the vast majority of these extinctions were not caused by humans. Clearly, then, extinctions are a sad but natural aspect of life on Earth, and we have no reason not to drill in the ANWR.

5. Which of the following statements is a correct evaluation of the argument?

   - A. The argument is valid, because it relies on scientific evidence that has been shown to be true.
   - B. The argument is valid, because extracting oil would bolster the national economy.
   - C. The argument is invalid, because it confuses correlation with causation.
   - D. The argument is invalid, because it attempts to refute one reason against doing something while ignoring other possible reasons.

6. Which of the following considerations, if true, best illustrates why the author's evidence is inadequate?

   - A. Some people depend on the porcupine caribou for food.
   - B. People who call themselves "scientists" often make claims that are very persuasive.
   - C. There is not enough oil in the ANWR to have a measurable impact on global oil prices.
   - D. Extracting oil from the ANWR would reduce the foreign trade deficit.

Questions 7 and 8 are based on the following information and map.

After World War II, Germany was split into two nations: democratic West Germany and communist East Germany. West Germany was under the control of the victorious Allies, who formed an alliance called the North Atlantic Treaty Organization (NATO). In 1955, NATO decided to allow West Germany to join NATO and to rearm. In response, the U.S.S.R. (that is, the Soviet Union) and a number of communist Eastern European countries formed what they called a "Treaty of Friendship, Co-operation, and Mutual Assistance," commonly referred to as the Warsaw Pact. In the Warsaw Pact, the communist countries agreed to band together if one of them was attacked, and the smaller communist countries agreed to put their military forces under the command of the Soviet Union.

Source: Central Intelligence Agency

7. Some historians believe that, in forming the Warsaw Pact, the Soviet Union wanted to create a buffer between itself and NATO countries. How does the map support that view?
   - A. The map indicates that many of the World War II Allies joined the Warsaw Pact, but not until the 1960s.
   - B. The map shows that most of the Warsaw Pact countries lay between the Soviet Union and Western countries, including France, West Germany, and Great Britain.
   - C. The map shows that the Warsaw Pact involved the building of a wall between the Soviet Union and Western Europe.
   - D. The map indicates that the Soviet Union was made up of smaller republics on its western border.

8. The map could be used to dispute which one of the following claims?
   - A. In forming the Warsaw Pact, the Soviet Union greatly increased its access to oceanic coastline.
   - B. In forming the Warsaw Pact, the Soviet Union wished to increase its trade with Africa.
   - C. The Warsaw Pact benefitted Bulgaria and Romania no less than the Soviet Union.
   - D. The Warsaw Pact initially included Albania.

Question 9 refers to the following table and map.

Average Yearly Rainfall in New England	
State	**Avg. Rainfall/Year**
Connecticut	47 inches
Maine	41 inches
Massachusetts	45 inches
New Hampshire	42 inches
Rhode Island	44 inches
Vermont	39 inches

Source: netstate.com

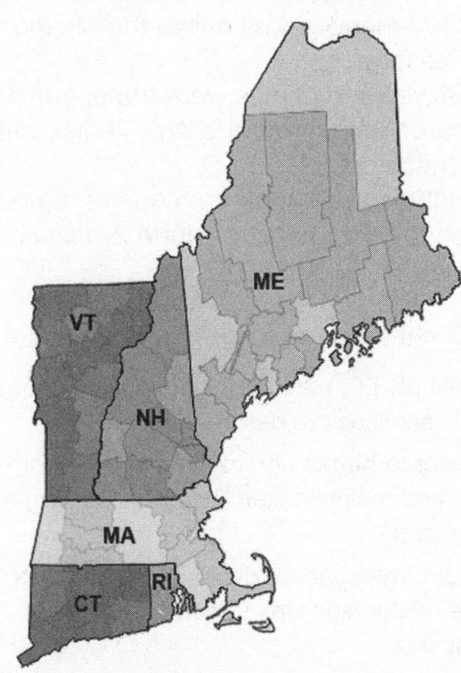

9. What is the average (arithmetic mean) yearly rainfall, in inches, of the three northernmost states in New England?
   - A. $40\frac{2}{3}$
   - B. 41
   - C. 42
   - D. $43\frac{1}{3}$

Question 10 refers to the following graph.

The graph below shows the percentage of people who voted in presidential elections from 1996 to 2012.

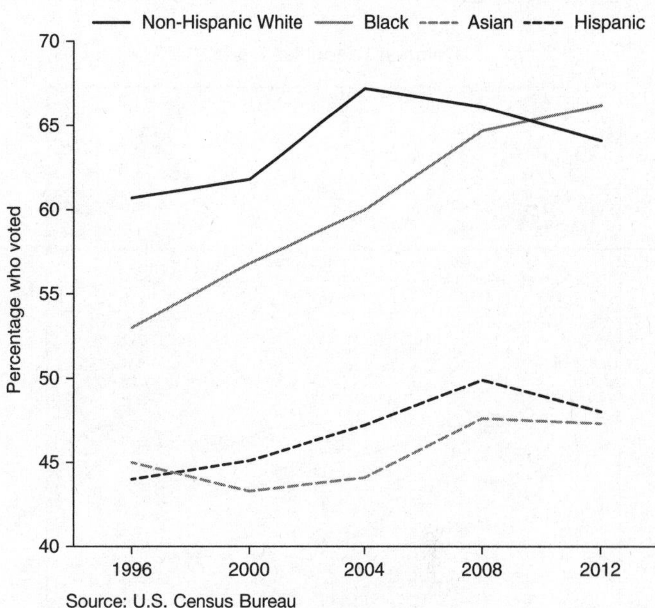

10. Over the period illustrated by the line graph, the rate at which eligible black voters participated in presidential elections
    - A. fluctuated up and down, but ended higher than it began.
    - B. steadily increased, surpassing that of white voters in the 2012 elections.
    - C. increased sharply in the middle of the time period shown on the graph before dropping back closer to its original level.
    - D. was consistently lower than the rates of most other races and ethnic groups.

Social Studies Pretest

Part II: Social Studies Content—26 Questions

Directions: You may fill in the circles next to the correct answers or write your answers on a separate piece of paper.

Question 1 and 2 refer to the following map.

Colonial Triangular Trade

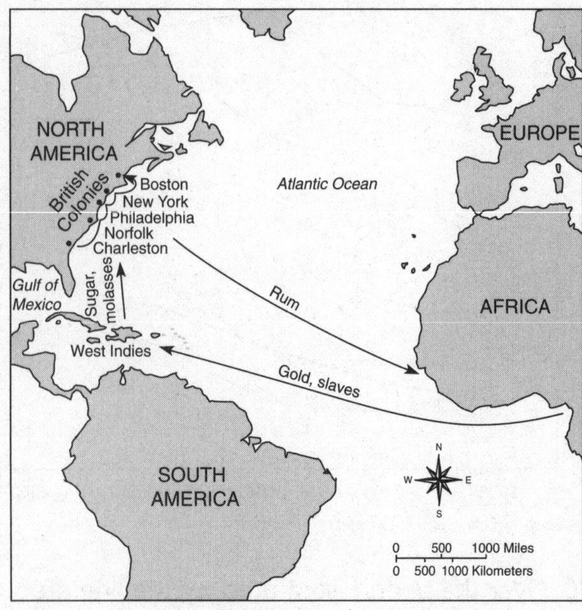

1. Based on this map, what were the three sides of the triangle in the triangular trade?
   - A. Europe to the West Indies; the West Indies to Africa; Africa to the British colonies
   - B. the West Indies to the British colonies; the British colonies to Africa; Africa to the West Indies
   - C. the West Indies to England; England to the British colonies; the British colonies to Africa
   - D. South America to Africa; Africa to the West Indies; the West Indies to the British colonies

2. Which statement is a conclusion based on the map rather than a supporting detail from the map?
   - A. Cargo ships never had to sail empty on any leg of a profitable triangular journey.
   - B. The journey of Africans from Africa to the Americas was called the Middle Passage.
   - C. Slaves sometimes were transported on cargo ships from the West Indies to the British colonies.
   - D. Rum was shipped from one of the ports on the east coast of North America.

Question 3 refers to the following information.

Several types of U.S. banking institutions and some of their main services are described below.

Federal Reserve banks control the nation's monetary policy and maintain stability of the banking and financial systems.

Commercial banks accept deposits, make loans, and provide related services to corporations and other businesses.

Retail banks provide savings and checking accounts, mortgages, personal loans, and debit and credit cards to consumers.

Community development banks serve residents and spur economic development in low- to moderate-income areas.

Credit unions provide their members with checking and savings accounts, mortgages, and other services at a lower interest rate than other financial institutions.

3. At which type of financial institution would the ABC Printing Company be most likely to take out a loan to finance the purchase of a new printing press?
   - A. Federal Reserve bank
   - B. commercial bank
   - C. retail bank
   - D. community development bank

Questions 4 and 5 refer to the following passage.

Somerville has had a long history of corruption. From the 1960s to the 1980s, its mayors, councilors, and tax assessors were involved in a complex network of bribery and favors. The "strong-mayor" system of government is responsible for this corruption; in the history of Massachusetts, all but a single instance of municipal corruption occurred under a strong-mayor government. Because that tainted system is still in place to this day in Somerville, the current mayor must be viewed with strong suspicion.

4. Which of the following words or phrases is based on the author's opinion, not fact?

   - A. "long history"
   - B. "tainted system"
   - C. "bribery"
   - D. "mayors, councilors, and tax assessors"

5. Is the author's conclusion properly supported by evidence?

   - A. Yes, because the corruption in Somerville spreads beyond the office of the mayor.
   - B. Yes, because 20 years of corruption can accurately be called a "long history."
   - C. No, because there is no mention of criminal investigation or charges.
   - D. No, because no indication is given that the current mayor will behave as past mayors did.

6. Most Americans believe it is their duty as citizens to take part in our system of government.

   Which of the following actions represents participation in government?

   - A. pursuing higher education
   - B. displaying the American flag
   - C. volunteering at a hospital
   - D. serving on a jury

7. In many Latin American countries, control passes back and forth between military and civilian rule. Generally, when a civilian government rules, it tries to improve conditions for the nation's citizens, but these attempts lead to turmoil and civil unrest. In response, the military takes power and imposes strict controls on the populace. Such shifts have taken place in Argentina, Peru, and Chile in recent decades.

   Which of the following is highly valued by those who favor military rule?

   - A. social welfare
   - B. freedom
   - C. democracy
   - D. law and order

Questions 8 and 9 refer to the following chart.

Presidential Powers in Several Nations

Constitutional Power	U.S.A.	South Africa	France	Mexico
Control armed forces	✔	✔	✔	✔
Approve legislation	✔	✔	✔	✔
Appoint executive branch officials	✔	✔	✔	✔
Appoint judges	✔	✔	✔	✔
Appoint prime minister			✔	
Dissolve legislature			✔	

8. Which of the following is a difference between the powers of the U.S. and French presidents?
   - A. The U.S. president controls the armed forces, and the French president does not.
   - B. The U.S. president approves legislation, and the French president does not.
   - C. The French president has the power to dissolve the legislature, while the U.S. president does not.
   - D. The French president has the power to appoint judges, while the U.S. president does not.

9. Which of the following statements is a conclusion based on the chart rather than a detail?
   - A. The president of South Africa cannot dissolve the legislature.
   - B. Of all the presidents shown, the French president has the greatest variety of powers.
   - C. The president of Mexico has the power to appoint judges.
   - D. The U.S. president has the power to approve legislation.

Question 10 refers to the following paragraph.

After the Civil War, southern states passed Jim Crow laws, which kept whites and blacks apart in public places like restaurants, buses, and restrooms. In an 1896 case, *Plessy v. Ferguson*, the U.S. Supreme Court upheld a Louisiana law requiring separate railroad cars for white and black passengers. The Court ruled that it was constitutional to have "separate but equal" facilities for whites and blacks and other minorities. The Court reasoned that "legislation is powerless to eradicate racial instincts or to abolish distinctions." One justice dissented, saying that the decision was "inconsistent with the personal liberty of citizens, white and black."

10. Which of the following statements is an opinion rather than a fact?
   - A. In the late 1800s, many southern states passed Jim Crow laws to keep whites and blacks separate in public places.
   - B. In Louisiana, a law required separate railroad cars for white and black passengers.
   - C. *Plessy v. Ferguson* was an 1896 Supreme Court case that challenged the Louisiana law related to segregated railroad cars.
   - D. The U.S. Supreme Court ruling in *Plessy v. Ferguson* was wrong because it infringed on freedoms guaranteed in the Constitution.

Questions 11 and 12 refer to the following paragraph and chart.

When the U.S. government cannot cover its expenses, it borrows money by selling bonds. It pays back the principal and interest on the bonds over a period of many years. The national debt is the total amount the U.S. government owes at any particular point in time. In 2010, this was about $13.2 trillion.

One way of measuring the national debt is by computing the per capita national debt. The per capita national debt is the total national debt divided by the population of the United States. The graph below shows the per capita national debt every five years from 1990 to 2010.

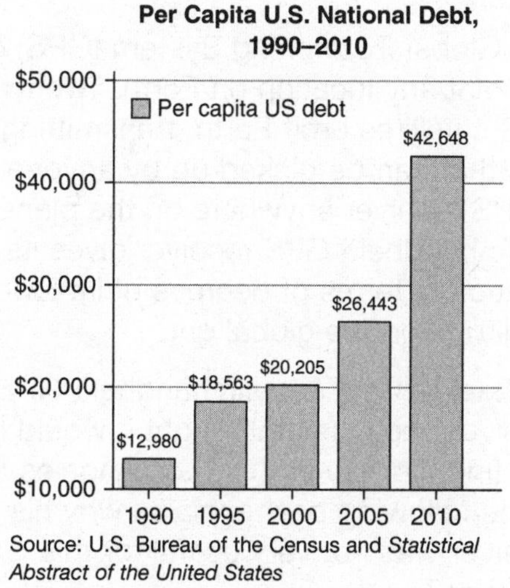

Source: U.S. Bureau of the Census and *Statistical Abstract of the United States*

11. Which of the following conclusions is supported by the data in the paragraph and the graph?
   - A. The nation's debt increased at a faster rate than did the U.S. population during the period shown on the graph.
   - B. Every person in the United States owed an average of $20,000 to the government in the year 2000.
   - C. In 1990, the U.S. government owed every American about $13,000.
   - D. The U.S. government sold about $5.7 trillion worth of bonds in 2000.

12. Which action would enable the U.S. government to reduce its debt?
   - A. Postpone payment of that debt.
   - B. Pay interest to foreign investors.
   - C. Pay interest to U.S. investors.
   - D. Raise taxes and cut spending.

Question 13 refers to the following paragraph.

The ninth-century BCE collapse of the Mayan empire is often attributed to a massive drought. But new geological and archaeological evidence from the Yucatán Peninsula in Mexico shows that the Mayans engaged in massive deforestation, clearing land for crops and burning the wood to bake bricks for their cities and temples. Modern weather models show that the destruction of native vegetation could have contributed to as much as 60 percent of the dry weather that is believed to have ended this civilization.

13. According to the theory presented in the paragraph, what was the effect of Mayan deforestation of the Yucatán Peninsula?
   - A. The Mayans needed more land to grow crops.
   - B. Scientists discovered new evidence in the geological record.
   - C. A drought was significantly worsened due to lack of native vegetation.
   - D. Baking bricks required an enormous amount of wood.

Question 14 refers to the following map.

Great Britain during the Industrial Revolution, 1830

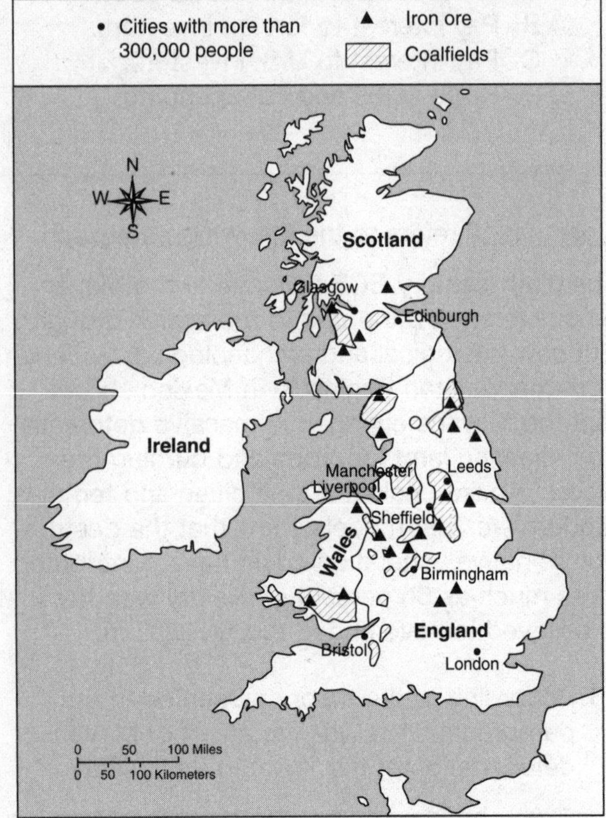

14. Which of the following is a conclusion based on the map rather than a supporting detail from the map?
   - A. The Industrial Revolution took place in Great Britain around the year 1830.
   - B. More than 300,000 people lived in Sheffield around 1830.
   - C. Many cities had large populations because nearby coal and iron ore deposits meant jobs.
   - D. There was a large area with coal deposits in southern Wales around 1830.

15. When a nation follows a policy of appeasement, it makes concessions to an aggressor in order to preserve the peace.

   Which of the following is an example of appeasement?
   - A. Italy's support of Spanish Nationalists in the Spanish Civil War in the late 1930s
   - B. Great Britain's acceptance of Germany's takeover of Austria and Czechoslovakia in the late 1930s
   - C. Germany's 1939 invasion of Poland, which started World War II
   - D. Japan's alliance with Germany and Italy in 1940, which created the Rome-Berlin-Tokyo Axis

16. The Global Positioning System (GPS) can pinpoint any location on Earth. Twenty-four GPS satellites orbit Earth, transmitting signals that can be picked up by anyone with a GPS receiver anywhere on the planet. A basic handheld GPS receiver gives its location in terms of degrees of latitude and longitude on the global grid.

   Michael bought a basic handheld GPS receiver because he thought it would help him find his way around Los Angeles. Which of the following best explains why his GPS receiver was not very useful for this purpose?
   - A. GPS satellites do not orbit over Los Angeles.
   - B. The latitude and longitude grid does not extend over urban areas.
   - C. Knowing only latitude and longitude does not help a person get around a city.
   - D. Not all of the streets in Los Angeles run in a straight line.

Questions 17 through 19 refer to the following poster.

Source: Library of Congress. World War I Posters Collection. Artist Dan Sayre Groesbeck.

17. The person who designed this poster used irony to make a point. Behind this irony was an assumption with which the designer expected viewers to agree.

    Which of the following statements summarizes this assumption?

    - A. People will give to the war effort because they are doing well economically.
    - B. Financing the war requires selling bonds and raising taxes.
    - C. During wartime, people have little money to spend on their sons.
    - D. People value the lives of their children more than they value money.

18. During which war was this poster part of a government advertising campaign?

    - A. the Civil War
    - B. World War I
    - C. World War II
    - D. the Vietnam War

19. If the government were running a similar advertising campaign today, which medium would probably reach the most people?

    - A. posters
    - B. leaflets and brochures
    - C. print ads in financial newspapers
    - D. television ads on primetime

Question 20 refers to the following table.

The Five Most Populous American Colonies, 1750

Colony	Population (estimate)
Massachusetts	188,000
Pennsylvania	119,700
Connecticut	111,300
Maryland	141,000
Virginia	231,000

Source: U.S. Bureau of the Census

20. Which of the following statements is supported by the data in the chart?

    - A. The population of all of the American colonies was less than 700,000.
    - B. Virginia had more than twice as many people as Maryland.
    - C. Most of the population of Massachusetts was of English origin.
    - D. The population of the colony of New York was smaller than that of Connecticut.

Questions 21 through 23 refer to the following paragraph and flowchart.

The U.S. Civil Service system is designed to ensure that people are appointed to government positions because of their skills and abilities rather than because of their political affiliation. Over 90 percent of federal jobs are covered by civil service rules. The typical steps in applying for a civil service job are shown below.

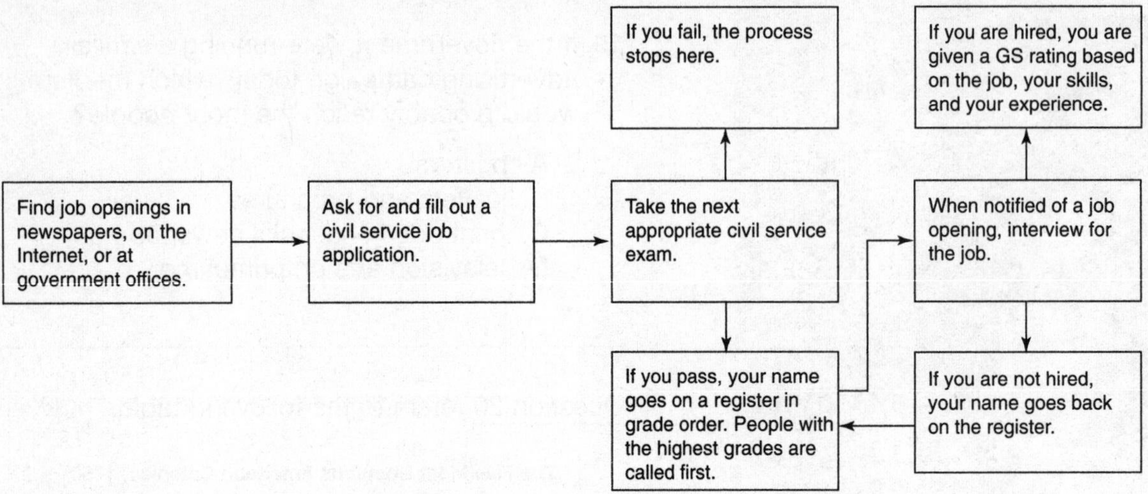

21. Which of the following is the best title for the flowchart?
   - A. A History of the Civil Service
   - B. The Qualifications of Civil Service Workers
   - C. Applying for Civil Service Jobs
   - D. Interviewing for a Civil Service Job

22. What does a civil servant's GS rating probably affect most?
   - A. salary
   - B. length of service
   - C. job security
   - D. education level

23. On which of the following values does the structure of the Civil Service system primarily rest?
   - A. patriotism
   - B. equal opportunity
   - C. freedom of speech
   - D. respect for seniority

Questions 24 and 25 refer to the following graphs.

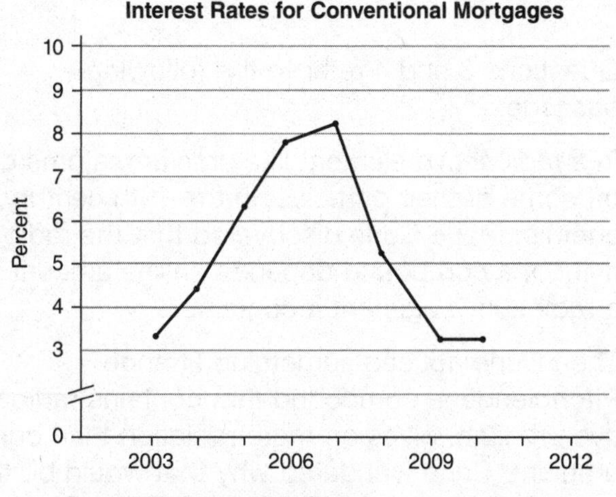

Source: U.S. Bureau of the Census

U.S. Mortgage Debt Outstanding

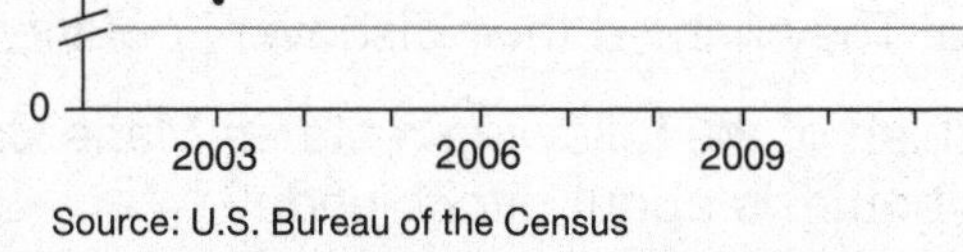

Source: U.S. Bureau of the Census

24. In 2005, what were the approximate interest rate and approximate total mortgage debt outstanding for a conventional mortgage?

- A. 8 percent and $13,000 billion
- B. 4 percent and $11,000 billion
- C. 6 percent and $12,000 billion
- D. 6 percent and $9,000 billion

25. Based on the graphs, how do mortgage interest rates and total mortgage debt outstanding compare?

- A. Interest rates rise in direct proportion to decreases in total mortgage debt outstanding.
- B. The higher the interest rate, the lower the total mortgage debt outstanding.
- C. The lower the interest rate, the higher the total mortgage debt outstanding.
- D. As interest rates rise and then fall, the total mortgage debt will move similarly but not at the same rate.

---

26. A culture hearth refers to the center of a culture—the source of its ideas, values, customs, fashions, and practices. An example of an ancient culture hearth was the area along the Nile River in Egypt. The agricultural, economic, social, artistic, and religious ideas and practices that grew up there spread through trade to other areas of the ancient world.

Which of the following is an example of a modern culture hearth with worldwide influence?

- A. Pyongyang, capital of North Korea, which has a 95 percent literacy rate
- B. Ottawa, capital of Canada, with a population of about one million
- C. New Zealand, which exports wool and textiles
- D. Hollywood, California, which produces movies and television shows enjoyed around the world

SCIENCE PRETEST

PART I: SCIENCE SKILLS—10 QUESTIONS

Directions: You may fill in the circles next to the correct answers or write your answers on a separate piece of paper.

Questions 1 and 2 refer to the following passage.

For many years, scientists believed that all living things depended on sunlight for their energy. For example, human beings derive energy from food. Our food comes either from plants that require sunlight or from animals, which eat plants that require sunlight.

However, in the 1970s scientists discovered hot springs, called *hydrothermal vents*, in the ocean floor. These vents are miles below the surface of the ocean, far beyond the reach of sunlight. Yet these vents are surrounded by fascinating life forms, including giant red tube worms, eyeless shrimp, hairy-looking crabs, and communities of bacteria that grow like carpets on the ocean floor.

Those bacteria feed on minerals, like sulfur, that flow upward through the vents. The bacteria use a process called *chemosynthesis* to turn the minerals into nutrition. The bacteria, in turn, are eaten by many of the animals that live near the vents. Thus, those animals take in a source of energy that does not derive from sunlight.

1. Which of the following would be a good title for this passage?
   - A. "The Advantages and Disadvantages of Life Near Hydrothermal Vents"
   - B. "Hydrothermal Vents: A Potential Fuel Source for Our Energy-Hungry Economy"
   - C. "Hydrothermal Vents Suggest That Not All Life Is Solar Powered"
   - D. "Major 20th-Century Advances in Oceanography"

2. Which of the following is a detail that supports the main idea of the passage?
   - A. Many scientists believe that all living creatures depend on sunlight for their energy.
   - B. Hydrothermal vents were not discovered until the 1970s.
   - C. The hairy-looking crabs are covered in structures that enable them to catch tiny particles of food.
   - D. No sunlight penetrates to the world of hydrothermal ocean vents.

Questions 3 and 4 refer to the following passage.

In a *radioactive* element like uranium, atoms give off some of their particles. In the 19th century, chemist Marie Curie discovered that the radioactivity of a compound depends on the amount of a radioactive element it contains.

Then Curie noticed something strange. Pitchblende, a compound that contains radioactive uranium, gives off more radiation than pure uranium. Curie wondered why that would be the case. She guessed that pitchblende might contain another element that was even more radioactive than uranium.

To find out, Curie and her husband isolated the elements that make up pitchblende. After isolating each element, they measured its radioactivity. As a result of this process, the Curies discovered that pitchblende contains a highly radioactive element, which no one had identified before. They named their discovery *polonium*.

3. Which of the following restates Marie Curie's hypothesis about pitchblende?
   - A. Pitchblende contains uranium.
   - B. Uranium interacts with the nonradioactive elements in pitchblende to increase its radioactivity.
   - C. Polonium was discovered by the Curies as a result of their experiment.
   - D. Pitchblende contains an element that is more radioactive than uranium.

4. Which of the following is a reasonable conclusion based on Curie's experiment?
   - A. Pitchblende is more radioactive than pure uranium because it contains polonium.
   - B. Polonium is only one of many reasons why pitchblende is more radioactive than pure uranium.
   - C. Marie Curie would become famous.
   - D. The Curies were not the first physicists to isolate polonium.

Questions 5 and 6 refer to the following passage.

The **ozone layer** is a part of the upper atmosphere with high concentrations of ozone, a form of oxygen. The ozone layer absorbs between 97 percent and 99 percent of the sun's medium-frequency **ultraviolet light**, which can cause skin damage and even skin cancers. For this reason, depletion of the ozone layer is potentially a global health risk. The ozone layer has been decreasing in thickness for decades due to atmospheric pollution. In particular, **chlorofluorocarbons** (CFCs), used in aerosol sprays and refrigerators, were so harmful to the ozone layer that a global ban was implemented in 1994, and production had almost entirely ceased by 2004. However, this ban was not effective; the hole in the ozone layer that appeared over Antarctica reached its largest recorded size in 2006.

5. Which evidence from the passage supports the conclusion that CFCs remain in the atmosphere for some time after their use?
   - A. The ozone layer started thinning decades ago.
   - B. The hole in the ozone layer reached its largest size after CFCs were banned from production and use.
   - C. CFCs are used both in aerosols and as refrigerants.
   - D. CFCs absorb medium-frequency ultraviolet light.

6. Which of the following additional pieces of evidence would best counter the author's opinion that the ban on CFCs was not effective?
   - A. The ozone hole is not literally a hole but rather an area in which the ozone layer is depleted by more than 50 percent.
   - B. While the ozone layer continues to thin, it is thinning at a rate much lower than it has in the past.
   - C. Skin cancer rates near the equator, far from Antarctica, have not changed significantly since 1994.
   - D. The CFC ban contains a few extremely narrow exceptions for uses where no suitable replacement exists, such as in fire-suppression systems on airplanes.

Questions 7 and 8 refer to the following text.

Adenosine triphosphate (ATP) is one of the most important chemicals for the function of the cells of all known living organisms. It stores and transports energy within and between cells. When a cell needs to use this energy, a chemical reaction releases it. Adenosine triphosphate and water can combine to remove either a **phosphate** (P_i) or **pyrophosphate** (PP_i) from the ATP, leaving **adenosine diphosphate** (ADP) or **adenosine monophosphate** (AMP) respectively.

Equation	Energy released (in kilocalories per mole)
$ATP + H_2O \rightarrow ADP + P_i$	7.3
$ATP + H_2O \rightarrow AMP + PP_i$	10.9

7. Which answer choice describes the process in the equation $ATP + H_2O \rightarrow AMP + PP_i$?
   - A. Adenosine triphosphate is transported from one part of a cell to another.
   - B. Adenosine triphosphate is broken down into adenosine monophosphate and a pyrophosphate, releasing energy.
   - C. Adenosine monophosphate is broken down into water and a pyrophosphate, releasing energy.
   - D. Adenosine monophosphate stores energy, which is transported to another cell.

8. Which of the following chemicals plays a role most similar to that of ATP?
   - A. Lactase, which breaks down the lactose sugar found in milk for easier digestion
   - B. DNA, which is found in the nucleus of every cell and contains instructions for the cell to manufacture proteins
   - C. Hemoglobin, which allows red blood cells to carry oxygen
   - D. Glycogen, which stores sugars that can be broken off in differing amounts when the body needs energy

Question 9 refers to the following information and table.

	P	P
w	Pw	Pw
w	Pw	Pw

	P	w
P	PP	Pw
w	Pw	ww

9. An equal number of seeds are produced from each of two pairs of flowers. One pair is a purebred pink plant with dominant pink genes (P) and a purebred white plant with recessive white genes (w). The other pair is made up of two hybrid plants, which are pink. The Punnett squares above show all possible combinations of alleles for the two pairs. If a seed is selected at random from the offspring of those two pairs, what is the probability that the selected seed will grow to be white?

   A. $\frac{1}{8}$

   B. $\frac{1}{4}$

   C. $\frac{3}{4}$

   D. $\frac{7}{8}$

Question 10 refers to the following graph.

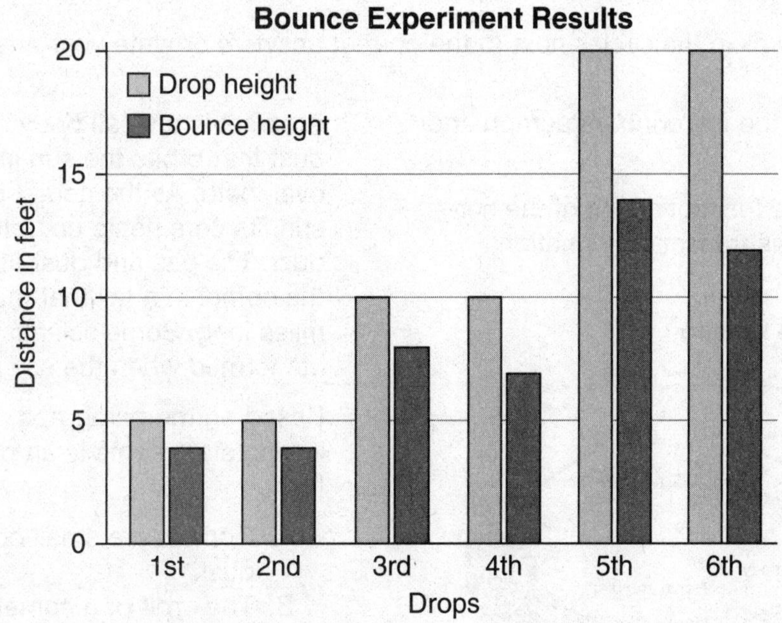

10. A ball was dropped onto a surface from different heights, and the height of the first bounce of each drop was recorded. The graph above illustrates the initial heights and bounce heights of the six trials in the experiment. What was the average (arithmetic mean) difference between the drop height and the first bounce height, in feet?

 A. $2\frac{1}{2}$
 B. $3\frac{1}{2}$
 C. 8
 D. 21

Science Pretest

Part II: Science Content—25 Questions

Directions: You may fill in the circles next to the correct answers or write your answers on a separate piece of paper.

Question 1 refers to the following paragraph and diagram.

A neuron is the basic functional unit of the nervous system. Neurons transmit information throughout the body.

A Neuron

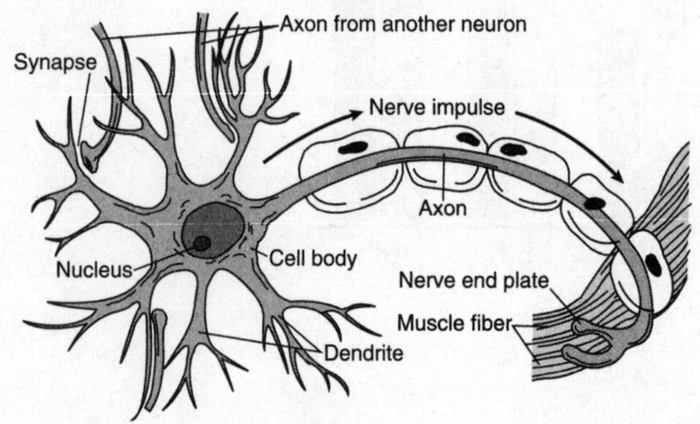

1. Which of the following is implied by the paragraph and the diagram?

 - A. Neurons are part of the endocrine system.
 - B. Oxygen is carried throughout the body by neurons.
 - C. Neurons transmit instructions regarding movement to muscles.
 - D. Nerve impulses travel from the axon to the cell body.

2. A comet is a small body made of ice and dust that orbits the sun in an elliptical, or oval, path. As the comet approaches the sun, its core heats up, releasing gas and dust. The gas and dust stream away from the comet in a tail that may be millions of miles long. Some scientists believe that comets formed when the solar system was born.

 Based on the paragraph, which of the following statements is an opinion rather than a fact?

 - A. Comets are small bodies of ice and dust.
 - B. The orbit of a comet has an elliptical shape.
 - C. Comets release gas and dust as they approach the sun.
 - D. Comets formed when the solar system was born.

3. In a photochemical reaction, light starts the reaction. Light can start a chemical reaction by exciting atoms and molecules, making them unstable and more likely to react with other atoms and molecules.

 Which of the following is an example of a photochemical reaction?

 - A. polymerization, in which long-chain organic compounds are formed from repeating units called monomers
 - B. fractional distillation, in which various petroleum products are separated out of crude oil
 - C. neutralization, in which an acid and a base react to form a salt and water
 - D. photosynthesis, in which green plants use the energy from sunlight to make carbohydrates from water and carbon dioxide

Questions 4 through 6 refer to the following chart.

Some Glands of the Endocrine System

Endocrine Gland	Hormone	Function
Pituitary gland	Growth hormone	Promotes bone and muscle growth
Ovary	Estrogen	Stimulates development of female secondary sexual characteristics
Testis	Testosterone	Stimulates development of male secondary sexual characteristics
Adrenal gland	Adrenaline	Increases heart activity, breathing rate, and blood flow to muscles for "fight or flight"
Thyroid	Thyroxine	Regulates metabolism and growth
Pancreas	Insulin	Regulates blood sugar levels

4. What is the function of the hormone thyroxine?

   - A. It controls female secondary sexual characteristics.
   - B. It controls male secondary sexual characteristics.
   - C. It speeds up the pulse and breathing rate for "fight or flight."
   - D. It helps control metabolism and growth.

5. People who have one form of the disease diabetes mellitus do not produce enough insulin. Based on the chart, what is the general effect of this disease?

   - A. stunted growth
   - B. excess growth
   - C. overproduction of estrogen
   - D. uncontrolled blood sugar levels

6. Paul, a child who was not growing as rapidly as he should, was given growth hormone to stimulate his growth. Paul anticipated that the hormone would enable him to reach an adult height of over six feet, even though his parents are both below average height. In fact, Paul's adult height was 5 feet 7 inches.

   What was wrong with Paul's thinking?

   - A. Growth hormone is only one of several factors that determine a person's adult height.
   - B. Growth hormone, when administered as a drug, does not affect a person's height.
   - C. In order to grow to over six feet tall, Paul would have had to take insulin, too.
   - D. In order to grow to over six feet tall, Paul would have had to take testosterone, too.

---

7. An emulsion is a mixture of two liquids whose particles are evenly scattered in one another without dissolving. Emulsions are unstable. After a time, the liquids separate.

   Which of the following is an emulsion?

   - A. tea with sugar
   - B. salt water
   - C. oil and vinegar salad dressing
   - D. food coloring and water

8. Earth science includes the study of Earth's atmosphere—the layer of gases that surrounds Earth—and Earth's hydrosphere—the oceans, rivers, lakes, and groundwater.

Which of the following scientists would be most likely to apply knowledge from a study of both the atmosphere and hydrosphere to his or her work?

- A. a geologist who studies volcanoes and mountain formation
- B. an astronomer who studies the planets of the solar system
- C. a meteorologist who studies weather patterns and predicts weather
- D. an ecologist who studies the distribution of populations of organisms

Question 9 refers to the following chart.

Organisms in a Food Chain

Role	Description
Producer	A green plant, which produces its own food using energy from sunlight
Herbivore	An animal that gets nutrients by eating plants
Carnivore	An animal that gets nutrients by eating other animals
Omnivore	An animal that gets nutrients by eating both plants and animals
Decomposer	An organism that gets nutrients from feeding on dead organisms and returns nutrients to the soil in the process

9. Earthworms break down large pieces of dead organic material in the soil. What role do earthworms play in the food chain?

- A. They are producers.
- B. They are herbivores.
- C. They are carnivores.
- D. They are decomposers.

Question 10 refers to the following graph.

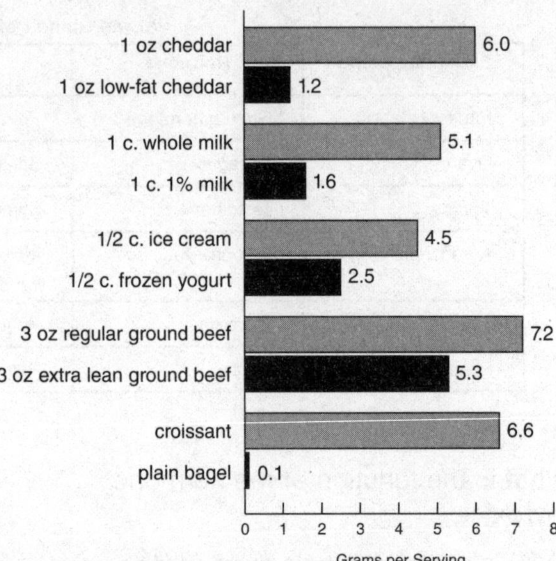

10. Suppose a child's diet usually includes two servings of cheese, four servings of milk, one serving of ice cream or frozen yogurt, one serving of ground beef, and a croissant or bagel every day.

If the child's parent wanted to decrease the amount of saturated fat in the child's daily diet, which of the following actions would be most effective?

- A. switch from regular to low-fat cheddar
- B. switch from whole milk to 1 percent milk
- C. switch from frozen yogurt to ice cream
- D. switch from regular to extra lean ground beef

11. Torque is the ability of a force to produce rotation. The torque of any force is equal to the amount of the force multiplied by the distance from the pivot point to the point where the force is applied. For example, when you go through a revolving door, you are applying force as you push. The torque of your force is equal to the force you apply times the distance between your hand and the axis of the revolving door.

    Which of the following actions would decrease torque as you go through a revolving door?

    - A. moving your hand closer to the center of the revolving door
    - B. moving your hand closer to the outer edge of the revolving door
    - C. pushing with two hands rather than one hand
    - D. leaning toward the door as you push to increase your force

Question 12 refers to the following graph.

U.S. Consumption of Energy by Source, 1997 (in common unit of metric tons oil equivalent [TOE])

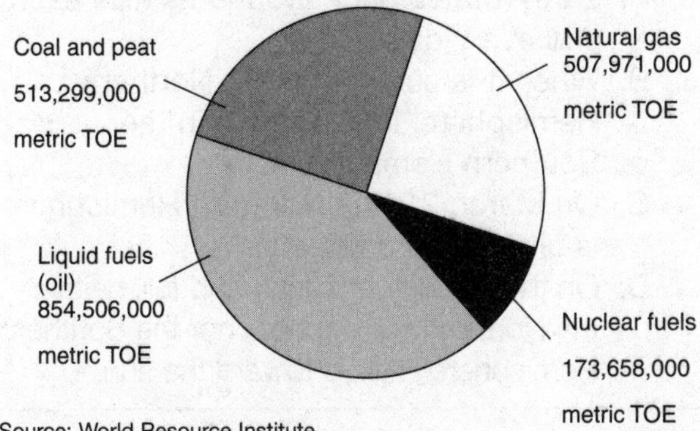

Source: World Resource Institute

12. Of the four energy sources shown, which two are the most similar in the proportion of energy they supply in the United States?

    - A. coal/peat and natural gas
    - B. natural gas and nuclear fuels
    - C. nuclear fuels and liquid fuels
    - D. liquid fuels and natural gas

Question 13 refers to the following paragraph and map.

In 1620, the eastern half of the United States was covered by virgin forest—forest that had never been cut down. Many parts of this region today are covered by second-growth forest—the ecosystem that eventually grows back after farmland is abandoned.

Virgin Forest of the United States 1620–1990

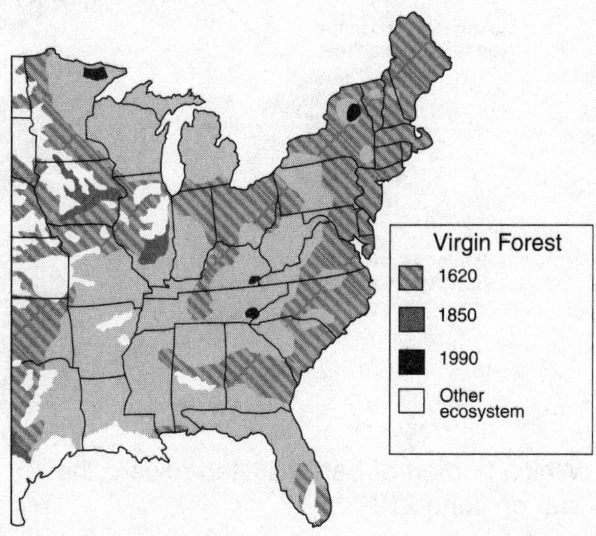

Source: *National Geographic*

13. Which of the following conclusions is supported by the paragraph and the map?

    - A. The western half of the United States had far less forest cover in 1620 than did the eastern half.
    - B. As European Americans moved from the East Coast westward between 1620 and 1850, they cut down forests to build farms.
    - C. A number of relatively large areas of virgin forest remain in the eastern half of the United States today.
    - D. Today's second-growth forests in the eastern United States have fewer species of plants and animals than the virgin forest did.

Questions 14 and 15 refer to the following information and diagram.

The seasons occur because the axis of Earth is tilted. At different times of year, different parts of Earth get more hours of higher-intensity sunlight. As the diagram shows, summer begins in the Southern Hemisphere on December 21, when that hemisphere is tilted toward the sun.

Why Earth Has Seasons

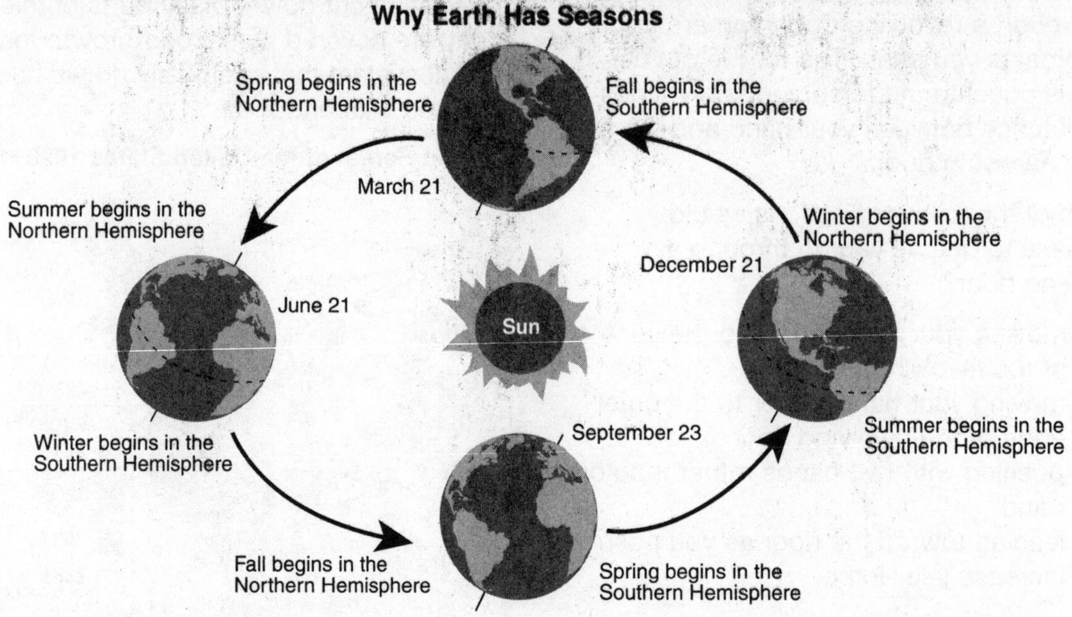

14. Which portion of Earth is tilted toward the sun on June 21?

- A. the Southern Hemisphere
- B. the Northern Hemisphere
- C. the axis
- D. the equator

15. Which of the following statements is supported by the information in the diagram?

- A. Earth rotates once around its axis each and every day.
- B. When it is summer in the Northern Hemisphere, it is summer in the Southern Hemisphere.
- C. On March 21, the Northern Hemisphere is tilted toward the sun.
- D. On the first day of spring and fall, neither the Northern Hemisphere nor the Southern Hemisphere is tilted toward the sun.

16. Ecologists use a tool called a quadrat when doing field studies of plant distribution. A quadrat is an open, four-sided structure about a meter square. It is placed on the ground, whether in a meadow, on a hillside, or at the beach. The ecologist then counts the plants of different species inside the quadrat. By using a quadrat, an ecologist can get a more accurate understanding of species distribution than by doing a random count.

Which of the following statements can be inferred from the given facts?

- A. A quadrat is a tool used by ecologists.
- B. A quadrat is a frame about a meter square.
- C. To use a quadrat, the ecologist places it on the ground.
- D. A quadrat makes plant distribution estimates more reliable.

17. According to Charles's Law, when the pressure of a gas remains constant, the volume of a quantity of gas varies directly with the temperature. In other words, as the temperature of a gas rises, the volume of the gas increases.

Which of the following graphs illustrates Charles's Law?

A.

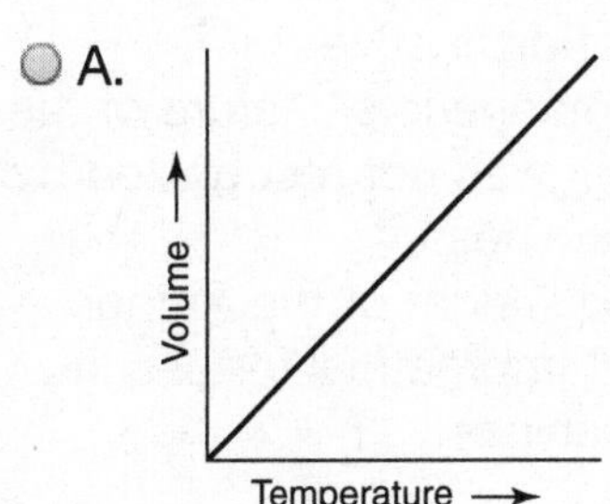

B.

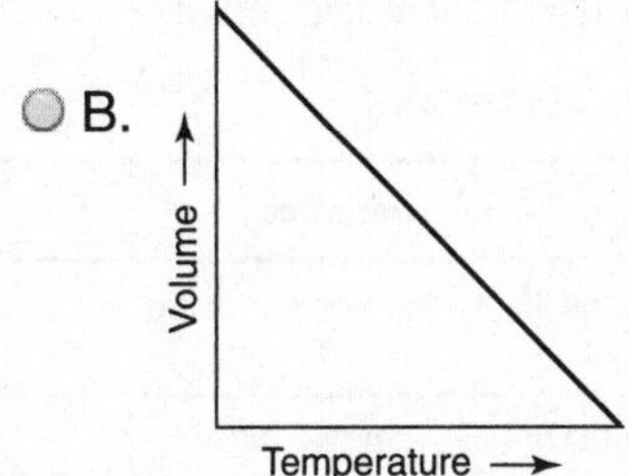

C.

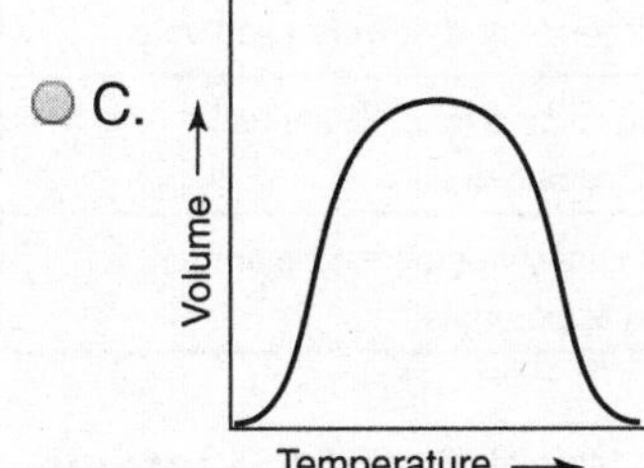

D.

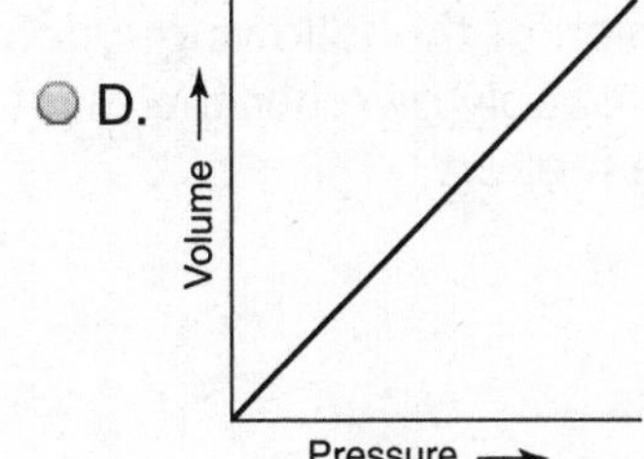

18. At the beginning of the twentieth century, only three subatomic particles were known: protons, neutrons, and electrons. In the last half of the century, dozens of new particles were discovered using new technology. Machines called particle accelerators push particles to tremendous speeds. When two particles collide at high speed, they annihilate each other and new particles are formed.

Which of the following is not stated in the passage?

- A. Protons, neutrons, and electrons are subatomic particles.
- B. Atoms are composed of subatomic particles.
- C. In particle accelerators, particles are pushed to very high speeds.
- D. Particles that collide at high speed annihilate each other, forming new particles.

19. Density is the amount of matter, or mass, in a given volume of a substance. To find the density of an object, you divide its mass by its volume. A student wanted to find the density of a 3-cm cube of lead. First, she used a scale to find the mass of the cube. Next, she calculated the volume by multiplying 3 cm × 3 cm × 3 cm. Finally, she divided the volume by the mass to find the density of the lead cube.

Why was the density the student calculated inaccurate?

- A. A scale cannot be used for finding mass.
- B. Multiplying three sides of the cube will not give the cube's volume.
- C. The student should have found the volume first.
- D. The student should have divided the mass by the volume.

Questions 20 and 21 refer to the following information.

When the U.S. Mint had to design a new dollar coin to replace the old Susan B. Anthony dollar, it faced a problem. It wanted to design an appealing, distinctive golden-color coin that vending machines would recognize as an Anthony dollar, which looks like a quarter. Vending machines identify coins by their weight, size, and electromagnetic signature. They test a coin by passing an electric current through it and measuring the resulting magnetic field. Thus, the new Sacagawea dollar coin had to be similar to the Anthony dollar in size, weight, and electromagnetic signature.

Size and weight were easy to imitate, but the electromagnetic signature was not. The Anthony dollar had a copper core covered by a silver-colored copper-nickel alloy. All the golden alloy sample coins had three times as much electrical conductivity as the Anthony dollar. Vending machines did not recognize them. Finally, metallurgists came up with the idea of adding manganese, which has low conductivity, to zinc and copper. The result was a coin consisting of 77 percent copper, 12 percent zinc, 7 percent manganese, and 4 percent nickel. The pure copper core was covered with a golden alloy of manganese, zinc, copper, and nickel. This golden coin has electromagnetic properties similar to those of the Anthony dollar, so it is recognized by U.S. vending machines.

20. It can be inferred from the passage above that an alloy is

- A. a magnetic material.
- B. a material that stops electricity.
- C. a mixture of metals.
- D. the core of a coin.

21. The U.S. Mint could have solved its technical problems with the Sacagawea dollar by making it out of the same metals as the Anthony dollar. Why did the people at the Mint decide against this?

- A. The metals in the Anthony alloy were too rare and expensive to use in the new coin.
- B. Like nickels, dimes, and quarters, the Anthony dollar was silver-colored and therefore not distinctive.
- C. The electromagnetic signature of the Anthony coin was not recognized by vending machines.
- D. The size and weight of the Anthony coin made it impractical for use in vending machines.

Question 22 refers to the following chart.

Types of Plants

Type	Characteristics
Annual	Completes life cycle in one growing season
Biennial	Completes life cycle in two growing seasons; flowers during second year
Perennial	Lives for years and flowers each year
Tender	Sensitive to cold (can be annual, biennial, or perennial)
Hardy	Can withstand frosts (can be annual, biennial, or perennial)

22. Marion has little interest in or time for gardening, yet she would like to have flowers in her front yard. Which of the following types of plants would probably give her the most flowers for the least effort?

- A. annuals
- B. biennials
- C. tender plants
- D. hardy perennials

Question 23 refers to the following information and diagram.

How a Reflecting Telescope Works

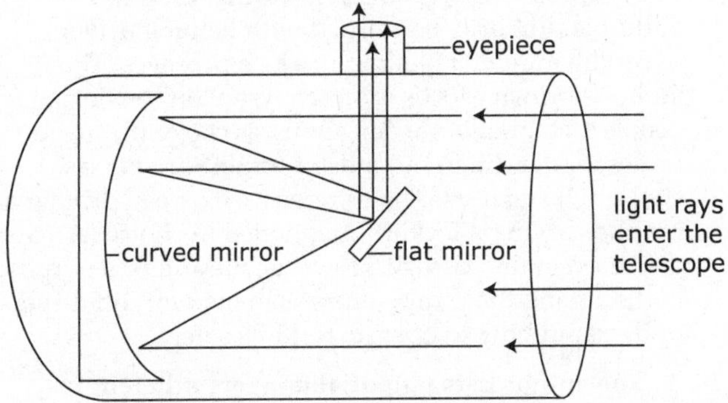

23. If the flat mirror were removed from this telescope, what would happen as a result?
    - A. Light rays would not enter the telescope.
    - B. Light rays would not reflect off the curved mirror.
    - C. A viewer could not see anything through the telescope.
    - D. A viewer could see only objects that were in focus.

24. The discovery of a new drug was once largely the result of trial and error, laboratory experiments, and clinical trials. Although these methods are still used, computer science is being applied to the drug discovery process to refine it and speed it up. For example, computers can analyze genetic material to locate genes that may hold promise in the development of new drugs. Computers can analyze data generated by lab experiments. Computer simulations can even help predict how a particular drug will work under specific circumstances.

    What is the main reason that computers are now being used in the drug discovery process?
    - A. They enable scientists to abandon trial-and-error methods.
    - B. They help scientists analyze large amounts of data in a systematic way.
    - C. They have made laboratory experiments unnecessary.
    - D. They have made clinical trials unnecessary.

25. People planning to visit tropical countries may need to be vaccinated against disease. For example, two to four weeks before a trip, travelers should be vaccinated against typhoid fever. The vaccine is 50 to 80 percent effective. Additional precautions against typhoid fever include avoiding food and water that may be dirty.

    If a traveler is vaccinated against typhoid fever two to four weeks before a brief trip to the tropics, which of the following best explains why he or she should take extra precautions against contracting the disease?
    - A. The typhoid fever vaccination is effective for only a few months.
    - B. The typhoid fever vaccination is only 50 to 80 percent effective.
    - C. The typhoid fever vaccination can cause soreness, fever, and headache.
    - D. Typhoid fever spreads only through air and water.

STOP

Congratulations! You have completed the pretests. Your next step is to check your answers with the Pretest Answers and Explanations that begin on the next page and fill in the study planners that appear on pages 64–68.

Pretest Answers and Explanations

Reading

1. **B. There are advantages to being sensitive and introverted.** The main idea of a passage is the idea that is most important to the author. The author wrote this passage to convey the idea that being introverted can be beneficial. Choices (C) and (D) both contain ideas the author expresses, but neither of those are the main idea of the entire passage. Choice (A) might be a reasonable inference based on the fifth paragraph but is not the author's main point.

2. **A. empathetic** The fourth paragraph states that children with sensitive temperaments "are more likely than their peers to be described by parents and caregivers as empathetic or conscientious." Choice (B) is contradicted by the author's statements that sensitive children tend to grow up to be introverts, and that introverts are less likely than others "to take dangerous risks." The author says explicitly that sensitive children "are not antisocial," so choice (C) is incorrect. Choice (D) is not supported by the passage.

3. **C. a successful collaboration between an introvert and an extrovert** The author mentions the partnership between Jobs and Wozniak in order to support her point that "[m]any successful ventures are the result of effective partnerships between introverts and extroverts."

4. **C. Children who are perceived as "shy" are actually more sensitive than other children to stimuli in their environments.** The author's purpose in the second paragraph is to help her readers understand the temperaments of the so-called "shy" children introduced in the first paragraph.

5. **A. enjoying a quiet dinner with a handful of friends** The author explains that introverts are not antisocial, so an introvert will not necessarily prefer to be alone. However, introverts are more sensitive to stimuli in their environment, so an introvert would not be likely to prefer (B) loud dance music or (C) a crowded street festival. Moreover, the author says that introverts are "less likely to take dangerous risks," and you can infer that (D) "ice slope surfing" is a dangerous sport.

6. **B. The driver may have some difficulty in controlling the forklift.** Paragraphs one and two discuss rear-wheel steering in forklifts. According to the second paragraph, rear-wheel steering is the reason why forklifts are not as responsive as cars and can be difficult to control.

7. **A. driving a forklift and driving a car** The first and second paragraphs discuss the differences between driving a car and driving a forklift.

8. **D. A forklift that is traveling downhill with a heavy load should travel backward.** The third paragraph explains that, when driving a forklift with a load on an incline, "you must keep the load on the uphill side." The graphic reinforces this by showing a forklift with the load on the uphill side. The arrow above the graphic points in two directions, and this suggests that the forklift should keep its load on the uphill side and travel backwards even when going downhill.

9. **C. to explain safe practices to forklift drivers** The author is primarily concerned with helping drivers of forklifts understand and use safe practices. The author's primary focus is on safety, not on convincing people that forklifts are dangerous, as choice (B) suggests, or describing different kinds of forklift drivers, as choice (D) suggests. The differences between driving a car and driving a forklift (mentioned in choice (A)) are discussed in the passage. However, the author's purpose in discussing those differences is to help forklift drivers understand how to operate forklifts safely.

10. **A. The author lists potential dangers inherent in forklift driving and explains how to avoid them.** Each paragraph discusses a different potential danger of forklift driving. 1st paragraph: the forklift's wide swing when turning; 2nd paragraph: the difficulty of controlling a forklift; 3rd paragraph: the dangers of driving on an incline with the load facing downhill; 4th paragraph: large loads that obstruct the driver's view. Each paragraph also discusses how best to deal with those dangers.

11. **B. suggest that GMO foods can be beneficial to struggling farmers.** This detail supports the overall purpose of the passage—to highlight the benefits of GMO foods for world food production. The fact that "small, resource-poor farmers" would choose to produce GMO crops implies that these are more reliable and potentially more lucrative than natural crops.

12. **D. the safety and reliability of GMO foods.** Passage 2 primarily discusses how GMO foods can pose a threat to human health and how GMO crops can be especially susceptible to massive failures.

13. **B. The labels of some foods containing GMO ingredients do not indicate that the products contain genetically modified components.** The last sentence of the first paragraph states that the American Academy of Environmental Medicine called for "the labeling of all food items containing genetically modified products." Therefore, at least some GMO foods do not yet have this labeling.

14. **C. GMO foods are largely a positive development for global food production.** The authors of the two passages disagree primarily about whether GMO foods are beneficial or dangerous.

15. **C. Paragraph 4** In Passage 1, Paragraph 4 details how GMO corn crops survived a devastating drought that natural corn crops would not have been able to withstand. This addresses the issue of reliability raised by the example of the South African corn in Passage 2.

16. **C. a young horse** The context clues in the passage indicate that the speaker is actually a horse. In paragraph 2, we learn that the speaker's mother

"whinnied," and in paragraph 4, she is specifically referred to as a horse. In paragraph 5, the speaker mentions that he and his mother are the master's favorites among all of the horses.

17. **D. a farm** The description of the setting in paragraph 1 indicates that the story takes place in a rural location. In paragraph 6, the speaker's reference to an event that occurred in his "field" also supports this setting.

18. **B. contented.** The overall tone of the speaker's account is positive. The passage describes the pleasant setting of his childhood, the respect he had for his mother, and the kind treatment he received from his master. Even the one negative memory, the occasional teasing by the plowboy, serves to show how the speaker was cared for by his master.

19. **A. affectionate and protective.** Paragraph 5 describes the master's gentle way of treating his horses. Paragraph 7 recounts how the master punished the young boy who was harming the horses.

20. **A. correct the speaker for playing too roughly.** The mother's speech is introduced in paragraph 2 after the phrase "when there was a good deal of kicking." Toward the end of the speech in paragraph 3, the mother implores the speaker to "grow up gentle and good" and "never to bite or kick even in play."

Writing

PART I: LANGUAGE SKILLS

1. **D. change have to has** The third-person singular subject student requires the verb form has.
2. **C. symptoms, such as** This links a fragment to an independent clause to form a complete sentence.
3. **B. change developed to develops** The verb should be in the present tense because the action is occurring in the present. Moreover, the present tense is consistent with the majority of verbs in the passage.
4. **C. sentence 5.** Sentences 1–4 explain basic facts about strep throat. Sentences 5–10 explain what parents should do if their child has strep throat.
5. **A. insert a comma after addition** Generally, an introductory phrase is followed by a comma.
6. **A. After the fever is gone and your child has taken** Combining the detail about taking medicine and the second independent clause about the fever into an introductory subordinate clause results in a smooth, effective sentence.
7. **C. remove the comma** No comma is needed between two verbs in a compound predicate (*bet on a football game or buy a lottery ticket*).
8. **C. threatens** The action is always true, so the present tense is correct. Moreover, the present tense is consistent with the majority of verbs in the passage.
9. **D. Compulsive gamblers display a number of consistent traits.** This is the only topic sentence that sums up the main point and is neither too specific nor too general.
10. **A. it. Losing** Choice (A), which forms two complete sentences, is the only choice given that properly corrects the comma splice here. Choice (D) is incorrect because a comma must precede *and* in a compound sentence.
11. **A. insert a comma after fraud** Commas are required between items in a series.
12. **A. depressed, or they** A comma should precede a coordinating conjunction that joins independent clauses.
13. **B. change Pet Stores to pet stores** This term is not capitalized because it is not the name of a store; it is just a type of a store.
14. **D. replace he with they** The antecedent *owners* is plural, so *they* is the correct pronoun to use.
15. **A. change There's to There are** The verb agrees with the subject, *several factors*, which is plural.
16. **C. be housebroken and trained** Only option (C) has both verbs in parallel structure and creates a correct sentence.
17. **D. remove sentence 10** The sentence about exercise and people is not relevant to pets, the topic of the article.
18. **D. change was to is** The statement is always true, so the present tense is correct. Moreover, the present tense is consistent with the majority of verbs in the passage.

PART II, ESSAY

Unpacking the Writing Prompt Checklist Your responses to items 1 through 3 may vary but should be similar to the following. Give yourself a check mark for each of your responses that reflects the same idea as the one here. Each check mark is worth 1 point, for a score of 0–3.

1. _______ Whether it is better to educate children with disabilities in a regular classroom or separately
2. _______ Take a position—either "mainstreaming" is better or separate instruction is better.
3. _______ Details from the passages indicating strengths or weaknesses of the two arguments given, as well as evidence from my personal experience

Thesis and Evidence Checklist Your responses to items 4 through 6 may vary. Remember that there is no right or wrong position to take on the issue. A strong essay can be written on either side. The following are sample responses reflecting one position on the issue. Give yourself a check mark if your response resembles the example in content and style.

4. _______ All students are entitled to a good education, and educating children with disabilities is important to their success in life and to society. Students with disabilities should be educated alongside students without disabilities as much as possible.
5. _______ Some mainstreamed students make more academic progress than students who are taught separately. Students who are segregated may not make as many friends. Students who do not have disabilities learn important skills by learning side by side with children who are different from them.
6. _______ Even though teaching students with disabilities separately may be easier in some ways, mainstreaming these children is a better option.
7. Responses to item 7 will vary quite a bit. You may have written a rough outline or a map of ideas you wished to include in your essay. Compare your outline or idea map to the generic examples on 213–215 of this book. Give yourself a score of 3 if your essay planning was as comprehensive and thorough as the examples, a score of 2 if you outlined or mapped some of your ideas, and a score of 1 if your outline/map did not assist you much in writing. Give yourself a score of 0 if you did not plan your essay before writing.
8. **Drafting Checklist** Check off each task that you performed. Give yourself a score of 0–6 based on how many checks you made.

   _______ I wrote a first paragraph that clearly introduced the topic and my position on it.

   _______ I developed several paragraphs responding to the prompt.

   _______ In my response, I cited specific details from the text to support my central idea.

   _______ In my response, I provided additional relevant information based on my own knowledge and perspectives.

   _______ In my response, I acknowledged at least one argument for the other side of the issue and discussed its strengths and weaknesses.

   _______ I wrote a conclusion that summarized my argument.
9. **Revising and Editing Checklist** Give yourself a score of 0–6 based on how many checks you made.

   _______ My essay was well organized, with a clear introduction, body, and conclusion.

   _______ I grouped related ideas and their supporting details into paragraphs and put different ideas in different paragraphs.

   _______ I made sure that my sentences were complete, clear, and correct with some variation in sentence length and structure.

   _______ I used words correctly to convey my ideas in a formal academic style.

   _______ I knew how to check for subject-verb agreement, pronoun agreement, and verb tense errors and fixed any I found.

   _______ I knew how to correct punctuation, capitalization, and spelling errors and fixed any I found.

Mathematics

PART I: QUANTITATIVE REASONING

1. **D. between 1,200 and 1,300** The graph shows that roughly 900 customers came from Zone 3 during this period and that somewhere between 300 and 400 customers came from Zone 4 during the same period. Thus, adding them together will result in a number between 1,200 and 1,300.
2. **E. 1:2** The bar for Zone 1 is a little less than halfway between 400 and 500; round to 450. The best estimate for the bar for Zone 3 is 900. Make sure you write the ratio in the order stated in the problem. Zone 1: Zone 3 = 450:900, which simplifies to 1:2.
3. **C. 16** Divide 10 by $\frac{3}{5}$. The answer is 16 with a remainder. Since the question asks for how many bowls the potter can complete, ignore the remainder.
4. **B. 3** The graph doesn't give the actual number of hours Janelle will work, but it does show how her time spent at one activity compares to another. If she works 100 hours, she will spend 44 hours working at the counter, 9 hours processing new books, and 6 hours repairing bindings. Compare 44 to 15. The number 44 is about 3 times as great as 15.
5. **C. 160** To solve, set up a ratio. 15 percent = $\frac{15}{100}$. Set that equal to the ratio of employees who make minimum wage to the total number of employees, and use a variable to represent the total number of employees. $\frac{15}{100} = \frac{24}{x}$. Cross multiply: $24 \times 100 = 2400$. Divide: $2400 \div 15 = 160$.
6. **E. Y, W, Z, X** Compare the numbers and list in order from smallest to largest: \$2.80, \$27.10, \$27.20, \$261.00.
7. **B. 9.25** Add together the amounts of honey the cook will use in the two recipes: $2.5 + 4.25 = 6.75$. Subtract that amount from the total amount of honey in the jar. $16 - 6.75 = 9.25$.
8. **C. 21** One way to solve the problem is to find a number that is evenly divisible by 6 and 14, and then try dividing that number by each of the answer choices. Go through the multiples of 14 until you find one that is divisible by 6: 14, 28, 42. The number 42 is divisible by both 14 and 6. Then review the answer choices: 42 cannot be evenly divided by 8, 12, 28, or 35. It can be evenly divided by 21.
9. **E. 13** Work backward through the facts. Sheila has worked 10 years. Kathy has worked half as long as Sheila, which equals 5 years. Alice has worked 8 years longer than Kathy. $5 + 8 = 13$ years.
10. **D. $\frac{3}{4}$** Two sections, which equal $\frac{2}{8}$ or $\frac{1}{4}$, are marked "blue." Thus, the chance of not getting blue is $1 - \frac{1}{4} = \frac{3}{4}$.
11. **A. 25%** To find percent of change, divide the amount of change by the original price. Then multiply by 100 to change the result from a decimal to a percent: $\frac{\$320 - \$240}{\$320} \times 100 = \frac{\$80}{\$320} \times 100 = 0.25 \times 100 = 25\%$.
12. **C. 5.5** The median is the middle number of a group of numbers. Arrange the numbers of accounts in order: 2, 4, 4, 4, 5, 6, 6, 7, 7, 8. The middle numbers are 5 and 6. When there are two numbers in the middle, find the mean of those two numbers: $\frac{5+6}{2} = 5.5$.
13. **A. \$4,500** Add together the amounts that Jim has sold so far in April: \$2,500 + \$5,000 = \$7,500. Then subtract that amount from the minimum his employers expect him to sell: \$12,000 – \$7,500 = \$4,500.
14. **C. $\frac{3}{10}$ feet** Subtract the length of the shorter stick from the length of the longer one: $3\frac{4}{5} - 3\frac{1}{2}$. To solve, find a common denominator: $3\frac{8}{10} - 3\frac{5}{10} = \frac{3}{10}$.
15. **D. 3.75** The number line is divided into increments, each of which equals one-fourth, or .25. The dot is three increments to the right of the number 3, so its value is 3.75.
16. **E. More students received either an A or a B than received either a D or an F.** Based on the graph, 6 students received an A and 7 students a B. $7 + 6 = 13$. Also, 7 students received a D and 3 received an F. $7 + 3 = 10$. Since 13 is greater than 10, the A-and-B group is larger than the D-and-F group. Choice (A) is not supported because some students did fail the exam. Choice (B) suggests that most—more than half—of Marjorie's students received an A or B. However, the A-and-B group (13 students) is smaller than the total number of students who got a C (12 students), a D (7 students), or an F (3 students). Choice (C) is unsupported because the graph has no information about how any other group of students would perform.
17. **D. \$6,000** Use the formula provided to find the interest Jason's deposit would earn over the five years. As directed, express the percent interest as a decimal, 0.04. \$5000 × 5 (years) × 0.04 = \$1000. Then, to find out how much is in the account at the end of the five years, add that interest to Jason's original deposit: \$5,000 + \$1,000 = \$6,000.
18. **C. 720** To find out how many possible orderings, or sequences, of six items are possible, multiply. There are six possibilities for the first movie. Then after the first movie has been chosen, there are five possibilities for the second movie, then four for the third movie, and so on: $6 \times 5 \times 4 \times 3 \times 2 \times 1 = 720$.

PART II: ALGEBRAIC REASONING AND GEOMETRY

1. **B. Point *B*** Convert the improper fraction to a mixed fraction:

   $-\frac{16}{6} = -2\frac{4}{6} = -2\frac{2}{3}$, which is the value of Point *B*.
2. **C. 4** Substitute and simplify:

   $= 2x - (4y - 3) + 5xz$

   $= 2(-3) - [4(2) - 3] + 5(-3)(-1)$

   $= -6 - (8 - 3) + 15$

   $= -6 - 5 + 15$

   $= -11 + 15$

   $= 4$

3. **A. 54** To find the magnitude of the change in temperature, subtract the lowest temperature from the highest temperature: $46 - (-8) = 46 + 8 = 54$.

4. **B. 60** The tower, its shadow, and the distance between them form a right triangle. Use the Pythagorean relationship to find the missing distance:

$$61^2 = 11^2 + h^2$$
$$3721 = 121 + h^2$$
$$3600 = h^2$$
$$60 = h$$

5. **A. 18** To find the volume of a rectangular prism, multiply *length* × *width* × *height*. Here, however, the question asks for the volume in feet, while the measurements are given in inches. Therefore, start by converting the inches of model 413S to feet: 24 in × 72 in × 18 in = 2 ft × 6 ft × 1.5 ft = 18 ft^3.

6. **C. $2,600** The question stem gives us two equations. First, we know that $M + L = 4{,}680$. Also, since Levy earns $520 more than Matthew earns, that can be expressed as $L = M + 520$, or, put another way, $M = L - 520$. Since the question asks for a solution for Levy, substitute the value of M from the second equation in the first equation:

$$(L - 520) + L = 4{,}680$$
$$2L - 520 = 4{,}680$$
$$2L = 5{,}200$$
$$L = 2{,}600$$

7. **C. 16π** The formula for the surface area of a cone is: $SA = \pi rs + \pi r^2$. In that formula, SA means *surface area*, r represents the *radius*, and s is the *slant height*, or the distance from the bottom of one side of the cone to the point. The diagram indicates that the diameter of the base is 4, so its radius is 2. The slant height is 6. Substitute and simplify:

$$SA = \pi(2)(6) + \pi(2)^2$$
$$SA = 12\pi + 4\pi = 16\pi$$

8. **D. $5x^3 - 4x^2 - x + 12y$** Start by removing the parentheses:
$3x^3 + x + 2x^2 - 4x^2 + 14y - 2(y + x) =$
$3x^3 + x + 2x^3 - 4x^2 + 14y - 2y - 2x$. Then, identify like terms that can be combined:
$3x^3$ and $2x^3$, which add to $5x^3$.
$-4x^2$ cannot be combined with any other term.
x and $-2x$ add to $-x$.
$14y$ and $-2y$ add to $12y$.
Combine into a new expression: $5x^3 - 4x^2 - x + 12y$.

9. **D. (2, 4)** On scratch paper, draw the three points given in the question stem:

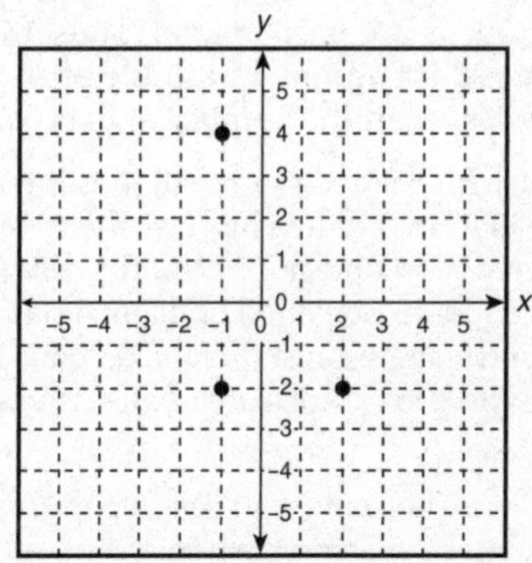

The fourth corner of the rectangle will be at (2, 4).

10. **A. 18 – 2x** Simplify: $4x - 2(3x - 9) = 4x - 6x + 18 = -2x + 18$. That can also be expressed as $18 - 2x$.

11. **E. 4** The simplest way to solve this problem is to try the values of x given in the answer choices in the equation. Starting with (A), where x equals –4: $3(4)^2 - 10(-4) = 3(16) + 40 = 88$. That's a great deal more than 8. That result suggests that (B), where x equals –3, would also be likely to yield a result that's far too large. Try (C) or (D) to see what result a positive number yields. In (C), x equals 3: $3(3)^2 - 10(3) = 3(9) - 30 = -3$. That's a little too small, so the answer must be (E), x equals 4. Try it to confirm: $3(4)^2 - 10(4) = 3(16) - 40 = 8$. (E) is correct.

12. **E. $x < 4$** Simplify the expression:

$$12(x - 2) < 24$$
$$12x - 24 < 24$$
$$12x < 48$$
$$x < 4$$

13. **B. 4.54×10^9** Writing a number in scientific notation involves expressing it as the product of two terms: one term is a number and the other is 10 raised to some power. To find how large the power of ten should be, imagine counting spaces to the left of the decimal point. Choice (B) reflects the correct number and the correct power of 10, or places to the left of the decimal point.

14. **E. 204** The shape of Joe's new property is a trapezoid, and the formula for the area of a trapezoid is $A = \frac{1}{2}h(b_1 + b_2)$. In that formula, A is area and h means the height, which is 12 yards here. The variables b_1 and b_2 are the two bases, which here are 10 yards and 24 yards. Plug those values into the formula: $A = \frac{1}{2}(12)(10 + 24) = (6)(34) = 204$. (You can tell that Joe's property is a trapezoid because the two bases are parallel; the right angles indicated at the two ends of the *height* line indicate this.)

15. **A. $p = \$5.00 - (n - 1)\ \$0.50$** If a customer requests only one monogram, the fee is $5.00. However, if a customer

requests 2, the price per monogram drops by \$0.50 (which you can think of as 1 × \$0.50). If a customer requests 3 monograms, the price per monogram drops another \$0.50, or 2 × \$0.50 in total. Thus, the price per monogram is \$5.00 minus a multiple of \$0.50. The multiple is one less than the number of hats ordered.

16. **B. 70°** In any four-sided figure, all four interior angles add up to 360°. In a parallelogram, the two obtuse angles are equal to one another, and the two acute angles are equal to one another. Here, you know that the two obtuse angles add up to 220°. 360° – 220° = 140°. Since there are two acute angles, divide that number by two.

17. **C.** $y = \frac{2}{3}x + 2$ The answer choices are in slope-intercept form, so begin by finding the *y*-intercept, which is 2. Then find the slope, which represents $\frac{rise}{run}$. Find two points on line H, and count the difference between the *y*-coordinates for those two points in order to find the *rise*. Then count the difference between the *x*-coordinates for those two points to find the *run*. For each vertical increase of two (*rise*), the line moves three numbers on the horizontal axis (*run*). Thus, the slope is $\frac{2}{3}$, and the equation is $y = \frac{2}{3}x + 2$.

18. **A. 20π** The question asks for the circumference of the pool. The question stem gives the distance from the middle of the pool to the edge—that's the radius of the circle, which is half the diameter. Thus, the diameter of the circle is 20 ft. Plug that into the formula for the circumference of a circle: $C = d\pi$. $C = 20\pi$.

19. **D. 2** The slope of a line can be expressed as $\frac{rise}{run}$. To find the slope using two points, subtract one *y*-coordinate from another to find the *rise*, and subtract one *x*-coordinate from another to find the *run*. It does not matter which point you subtract from the other, as long as you are consistent about which point you are subtracting when finding both rise and run.

$\frac{-1-(-9)}{4-0} = \frac{8}{4} = 2.$

20. **C. 192π** The formula for the volume of a cylinder is $V = \pi r^2 h$. In that formula, *V* is volume, *r* is the radius of the base, and *h* is height. In this case, you know that the diameter of the base of the can is 8, so the radius is 4. Plug in the values: $V = \pi \times (4\text{ cm})^2 \times (12\text{ cm}) = \pi \times 16\text{ cm}^2 \times 12\text{ cm} = 192\pi\text{ cm}^3$.

21. **E. 4,100** To find the area of a compound figure like this one, split it up into simpler shapes. Here, the space can be split into two rectangles:

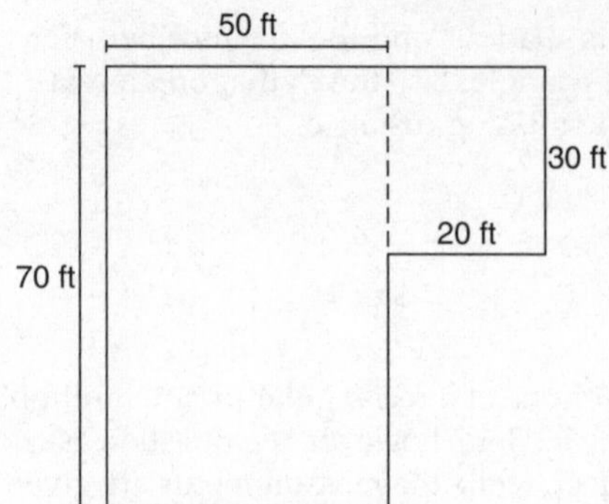

Find the area of the two rectangles and add those two areas together: (70 × 50) + (30 × 20) = 3,500 + 600 = 4,100.

22. **D. (2, 5)** There are two ways to solve this problem. First, you could graph both lines. If you did so, your scratchwork should look like this:

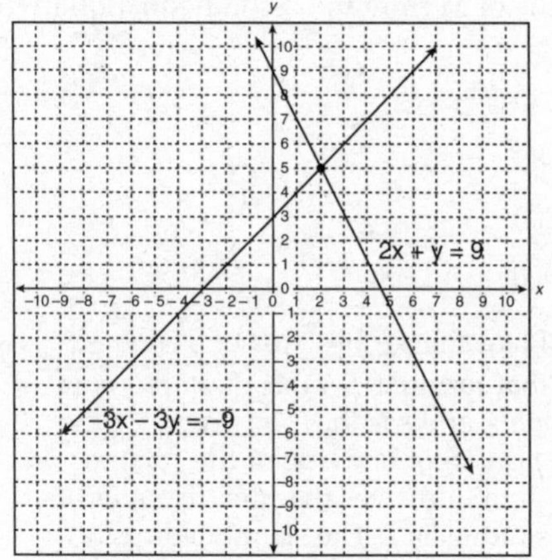

Based on that sketch, the two lines intersect at (2, 5), which means that those coordinates are the solution to the system of equations.

Alternatively, you could also have plugged each answer choice into both equations in order to find the answer choice that works in both equations. For example, to test choice (A) in this way:

Plug (2, –5) into the first equation: $-3x - 3y = -9$.
$-3(2) - 3(-5) \stackrel{?}{=} -9$

$-6 + 15 = -9$. So choice (A) works fine in the first equation. Now try the second: $2x + y = 9$

$2(2) + (-5) \stackrel{?}{=} 9$

$4 - 5 \neq 9$. Answer choice (A) does *not* work in the second equation. Therefore, it is incorrect. Try the other answer choices in a similar way. Only (D) will work in both equations.

Social Studies

Part I: Social Studies Skills

1. **C. The Voting Rights Act of 1965 gave the federal government oversight of state elections to end barriers against African American voting.** The passage described the historical events that led to the Voting Rights Act and how this legislation ended the voting discrimination that certain states enacted after the passage of the Fifteenth Amendment.

2. **C. interpretation** According to the passage, the terms "strict construction" and "loose construction" refer to different ways in which people interpret the range of powers that the Constitution grants to the federal government.

3. **A. The FDA's new regulations would place a financial hardship on small food retailers.** According to the passage, smaller food retailers would feel more of the burden than larger establishments, and the Common Sense Nutritional Disclosure Act seeks to relieve this burden.

4. **C. "devastating"** This word highlights the author's point of view that the FDA's new regulations would be especially harmful to smaller food retailers.

5. **D. The argument is invalid, because it attempts to refute one reason against doing something while ignoring all the others.** The paragraph states that possible danger to the porcupine caribou is "one commonly cited" reason against drilling in the Arctic National Wildlife Refuge. This implies that there are other reasons as well. Thus, the author's conclusion that "we have no reason not to drill in the ANWR" is unsupported, since the author has attempted to refute only one of the possibly many reasons against drilling in the refuge.

6. **A. Some people depend on the porcupine caribou for food.** The primary evidence in this argument is that almost all of the species that have ever lived on Earth have gone extinct, and the vast majority of these extinctions happened naturally. The author uses this evidence to argue that the human threat to the porcupine caribou isn't a big deal. However, the author fails to consider the possibility that human-caused extinctions are worse than naturally occurring ones. Choice (A) shows that the loss of the caribou by human hands would cause a severe problem: the loss of a major food source for some people.

7. **B. The map shows that most of the Warsaw Pact countries lay between the Soviet Union and Western countries, including France, West Germany, and Great Britain.** The passage states that the World War II Allies, which included France and Great Britain, formed NATO. It also states that West Germany was allowed to join NATO. And the map makes clear that the smaller Warsaw Pact countries lay geographically between those nations and the Soviet Union.

8. **A. In forming the Warsaw Pact, the Soviet Union greatly increased its access to oceanic coastlines.** Although most of the Warsaw Pact countries touched the ocean, most of their borders were land borders, and two of the Warsaw Pact countries were completely landlocked.

9. **A. $40\frac{2}{3}$** The three northernmost states are Maine (ME), New Hampshire (NH), and Vermont (VT). To find the average, sum the rainfall of each state and divide by 3. $\frac{41+42+39}{3} = 40\frac{2}{3}$.

10. **B. steadily increased, surpassing that of white voters in the 2012 elections.** The solid gray line corresponds to the rate at which black voters participated in presidential elections. It increases consistently from year to year, and shows the highest rate of all groups in the 2012 election.

Part II: Social Studies Content

1. **B. the West Indies to the British colonies; the British colonies to Africa; Africa to the West Indies** According to the map, the West Indies exported sugar and molasses to the British colonies in North America. The British colonies exported rum to Africa. Finally, Africa exported slaves and gold to the West Indies. The trade routes formed a triangle.

2. **A. Cargo ships never had to sail empty on any leg of a profitable triangular journey.** This is a general conclusion that is supported by the details of the map, which show goods traveling along each leg of the triangular trade route. Therefore, a very profitable journey must have meant a ship carried cargo on each leg of the route. The remaining options state details that may or may not be confirmed by the map.

3. **B. commercial bank** According to the descriptions, commercial banks provide services to businesses and other corporations. None of the other descriptions describe financial institutions making loans to companies. They focus either on national financial systems or on individual borrowers.

4. **B. tainted system** "Tainted" is a loaded word that indicates the author's belief that a "strong-mayor" system is inherently corrupt.

5. **D. No, because no indication is given that the current mayor will behave as past mayors did.** A strong-mayor system may enable—but does not guarantee—corruption. Past corruption is not by itself enough reason to have a strong suspicion toward the current government.

6. **D. serving on a jury** Serving on a jury, like voting, is a civic duty of each citizen. It is a way to participate in the judicial branch of government. Note that although choice (B), displaying the American flag, is a patriotic act, it does not involve participating in government in any way and so is not a way of participating in the political system.

7. **D. law and order** The hallmark of military rule is strict control over the citizenry; in other words, law and order.

8. **C. The French president has the power to dissolve the legislature, while the U.S. president does not.** The checkmark in the last row under "France" indicates that the French president can dissolve the legislature. The U.S. president does not have this power.

9. **B. Of all the presidents shown, the French president has the greatest variety of powers.** This statement is a conclusion, a generalization based on the details in the chart. Choices (A), (C), and (D) are specific details from the chart.

10. **D. The U.S. Supreme Court ruling in *Plessy v. Ferguson* was wrong because it infringed on freedoms guaranteed in the Constitution.** This statement is a rephrasing of the dissenting justice's opinion, or belief, about the case. The other statements are all facts from the paragraph.

11. **A. The nation's debt increased at a faster rate than did the U.S. population during the period shown on the graph.** You can tell this is true because the per capita debt figure increased steadily from 1990 to 2010. This would happen only if the debt increased faster than the population of the United States.

12. **D. Raise taxes and cut spending.** You can conclude from the text that to cut the national debt, the U.S. government would have to increase income (raise taxes) and lower costs (cut spending).

13. **C. A drought was significantly worsened due to lack of native vegetation.** According to the passage, the deforestation caused a significant portion of the drought that led to the Mayan collapse. Choices (A) and (D) are both causes, not effects, of the deforestation.

14. **C. Many cities had large populations because nearby coal and iron ore deposits meant jobs.** Coal and iron ore were among the most important raw materials of the Industrial Revolution. By examining the relationship of the location of the cities to that of the coalfields and iron ore deposits, you can conclude that Great Britain's most populous cities (with the exception of London) were large partly because of their proximity to the important raw materials of the Industrial Revolution. The remaining statements are details from the map.

15. **B. Great Britain's acceptance of Germany's takeover of Austria and Czechoslovakia in the late 1930s** Of all the options, this is the only one that has the element of concession without opposition that is the hallmark of appeasement.

16. **C. Knowing only latitude and longitude does not help a person get around a city.** Being able to pinpoint precise location in terms of latitude and longitude is not of much value in a city unless this information is translated into streets and highways. A basic receiver such as the one described in the paragraph does not do that; however, other more sophisticated models, such as those built into vehicle dashboards or cellular phones, do just that.

17. **D. People value the lives of their children more than they value money.** This is the underlying assumption of the poster: that Americans have been willing to send their sons into battle where they risk their lives, but haven't been donating money to the war cause with equal willingness. The poster thus plays upon their sense of guilt.

18. **B. World War I** The poster is dated 1917, so the war is World War I.

19. **D. television ads on prime time** Today the government could probably reach the most people with TV ads rather than print ads, because so many people watch TV.

20. **D. The population of the colony of New York was smaller than that of Connecticut.** Since the chart shows the five colonies with the largest populations in 1750, it follows that any colony not listed has a population smaller than that of Connecticut, which ranked fifth. The other options are not supported by the data in the table.

21. **C. Applying for Civil Service Jobs.** This title best describes what the flowchart shows—the steps in applying for a civil service job.

22. **A. salary** The GS rating of a job, based on the job description and the candidate's skills and experience, is directly related to the salary level of the position. The other options would not be affected by the GS rating.

23. **B. equal opportunity** Since civil service jobs are open to all who apply and are awarded on merit, they are designed to provide equal opportunity for employment, regardless of gender, race, ethnicity, party affiliation, or other factors.

24. **C. 6 percent and $12,000 billion** Locate 2005 on each graph. (Note that each tick mark on the horizontal axis indicates a year, even if it is not labeled.) The first graph shows the mortgage interest rate was about 6 percent in 2005. The second graph shows the total outstanding mortgage debt was about $12,000 billion in 2005.

25. **D. As interest rates rise and then fall, the total mortgage debt will move similarly but not at the same rate.** Look at the general trend shown by each graph. Note that as interest rates rise and fall, the mortgage debts rise similarly but fall at a different rate.

26. **D. Hollywood, California, which produces movies and television shows enjoyed around the world** The movies and TV shows that originate in Hollywood are distributed worldwide, helping to spread American popular culture to other nations.

Science

Part I: Science Skills

1. **C. "Hydrothermal Vents Suggest That Not All Life Is Solar Powered"** The author's main point is that some of the life forms around hydrothermal vents derive energy from a source other than the sun. Choice (C) captures that idea. Choices (A) and (B) mischaracterize the subject matter of the passage, and choice (D) is far too broad.

2. **D. No sunlight penetrates to the world of hydrothermal ocean vents.** Only choice (D) supports the idea that some life forms derive energy from a source other than the sun. Choice (A) distorts the meaning of the first line of the passage. Choice (B) is true but does not serve to support this idea. Choice (C) is not stated in the passage.

3. **D. Pitchblende contains an element that is more radioactive than uranium.** A hypothesis is a guess made by a scientist before the scientist conducts an experiment. Before Marie Curie and her husband conducted their experiment with pitchblende, she guessed that pitchblende was more radioactive than pure uranium because pitchblende contained a radioactive element other than uranium. Curie already knew choice (A) to be true, so it was not a hypothesis she intended to test. Choice (B) is not stated in the passage. Choice (C) describes the outcome of the Curies' experiment—not their initial hypothesis.

4. **A. Pitchblende is more radioactive than pure uranium because it contains polonium.** As a result of their experiment, the Curies discovered that pitchblende contained polonium, a highly radioactive element. This suggests that Marie Curie's initial hypothesis was correct. Choice (B) is not supported by the passage. Choice (C) is unsupported by the passage.

5. **B. The hole in the ozone reached its largest size after CFCs were banned from production and use.** According to the passage, the hole in the ozone layer reached its largest size after CFCs were discontinued. The presence of CFCs that stayed in the atmosphere for years after use is a likely explanation for this phenomenon.

6. **B. While the ozone layer continues to thin, it is thinning at a rate much lower than it has in the past.** If the rate of ozone depletion has slowed significantly, it is likely that the CFC ban was at least partially effective.

7. **B. Adenosine triphosphate is broken down into adenosine monophosphate and a pyrophosphate, releasing energy.** The text describes this relation between ATP (adenosine triphosphate), AMP (adenosine monophosphate), and PP_i (pyrophosphate).

8. **D. Glycogen, which stores sugars that can be broken off in differing amounts when the body needs energy** Both glycogen and ATP store energy, and both can release different amounts of energy depending on the needs of the cell or organism.

9. **A. $\frac{1}{8}$** Because white is a recessive trait, a plant must have two white genes (ww) in order to be white. Of the 8 possible outcomes illustrated in the Punnett squares, only one has this pair of genes.

10. **B. $3\frac{1}{2}$** The difference between the drop height and the first bounce height for the first drop was 1 foot. For the second, it was also 1 foot, and for the third, 2 feet. Find these differences for all the drops. The average of a set of items is the sum of the items divided by the number of items in the set. Thus, to find the average here, add all the differences and divide by the number of drops:

$$\frac{1+1+2+3+6+8}{6} = \frac{21}{6} = 3\frac{1}{2}$$

Part II: Science Content

1. **C. Neurons transmit instructions regarding movement to muscles.** Since neurons transmit information and the function of muscles is to move, it follows that neurons transmit instructions regarding movement to muscles. The paragraph and the diagrams show that all the other options contain incorrect information.

2. **D. Comets formed when the solar system was born.** Opinions are usually signaled by words like "believe," "think," or "feel." In this case, the last sentence of the paragraph states that scientists believe that comets formed when the solar system was born, showing that this is an opinion.

3. **D. photosynthesis, in which green plants use the energy from sunlight to make carbohydrates from water and carbon dioxide** The key element in a photochemical reaction is light. Of the options listed, only photosynthesis involves light.

4. **D. It helps control metabolism and growth.** First locate thyroxine in the "Hormone" column, then move along the row to the "Function" column to find the answer.

5. **D. uncontrolled blood sugar levels** The chart shows that insulin regulates blood sugar levels, so problems with insulin production will cause problems with blood sugar levels.

6. **A. Growth hormone is only one of several factors that determine a person's adult height.** Growth hormone alone does not determine height. A person's genetic make up—the height of his parents and other family members—contributes, as do nutrition and the action of other hormones. Paul's expectations were therefore unrealistic.

7. **C. oil and vinegar salad dressing** This is an example of an emulsion—two liquids mixed together but not dissolving. If you let oil and vinegar dressing stand, the oil will rise to the top. The other options are all solutions, which do not separate over time.

8. **C. a meteorologist who studies weather patterns and predicts weather** Knowledge gained from a study of the atmosphere and hydrosphere is closely related to the study of weather, which is influenced by both.

9. **D. They are decomposers.** Since earthworms are feeding on dead organic matter, which comes from dead organisms, they must be decomposers.

10. **B. switch from whole milk to 1 percent milk** The switch from whole milk to low-fat milk reduces fat intake by 3.5 grams/serving. While the difference in saturated fat per serving is greater in cheddar cheese than in milk, since the child drinks 4 servings of milk daily, this would be a reduction of 14 grams per day. The reduction from switching cheeses comes to 9.6 grams, since the child eats two servings of cheese per day.

11. **A. moving your hand closer to the center of the revolving door** Moving your hand closer to the center of the door decreases distance to the pivot point. Since the force remains the same in this case, when you multiply distance times force you will come up with a lower number, which indicates decreased torque.

12. **A. coal/peat and natural gas** Look on the circle graph for energy sources occupying wedges of approximately the same size. The only two that are about the same size are coal/peat and natural gas, indicating they provide about the same proportion of energy consumed in the United States.

13. **B. As European Americans moved from the East Coast westward between 1620 and 1850, they cut down forests to build farms.** The map shows and the paragraph implies that the virgin forests of the eastern United States were almost all cut down between 1620 and 1850. The paragraph further implies that the forests were cut down for farmland, which has since been abandoned. Based on this information, choice (B) is the only conclusion that is supported by the map and the paragraph. The map and the paragraph either lack support for or contradict the other options.

14. **B. the Northern Hemisphere** First locate June 21 on the diagram and then examine the tilt of Earth. Note that at that time of year, the Northern Hemisphere tilts toward the sun, and it is summer there.

15. **D. On the first day of spring and fall, neither the Northern Hemisphere nor the Southern Hemisphere is tilted toward the sun.** According to the diagram, on March 21 and September 23 Earth's axis is tilted neither toward nor away from the sun, so neither hemisphere is tilted toward the sun. The remaining choices are not supported by the diagram.

16. **D. A quadrat makes plant distribution estimates more reliable.** This option is a conclusion, or a general statement, that is supported by all the details in the paragraph. The other options are specific details paraphrased from the paragraph.

17. **A.**

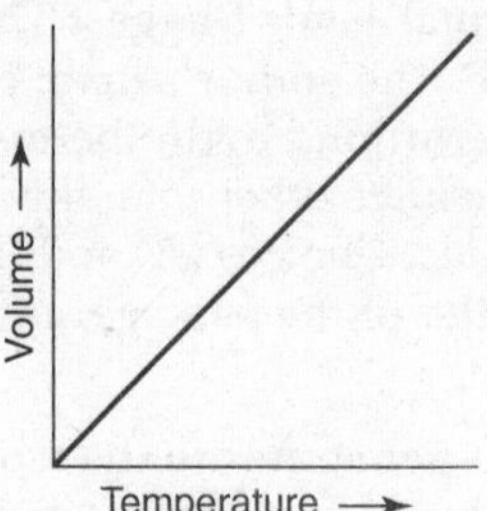

Charles's Law involves the relationship of a gas's volume and temperature. Since volume increases with increases in temperature, the first graph must be correct. Note that you can eliminate choice (D) immediately because it involves changes in pressure, and Charles's Law assumes that pressure remains constant.

18. **B. Atoms are composed of subatomic particles.** This is an assumption made by the writer of the paragraph. He or she does not explain this but assumes it is common knowledge. All the other options are statements made or strongly implied in the passage.

19. **D. The student should have divided the mass by the volume.** The paragraph states that density is calculated by dividing mass by volume. The student did the reverse, which is incorrect. All of the other steps the student followed were correct.

20. **C. a mixture of metals.** According to the passage, the Anthony dollar was made of a copper-nickel alloy, and the final Sacagawea dollar, of a manganese, zinc, copper, and nickel alloy. From these examples, you can infer that an alloy is a mixture of metals.

21. **B. Like nickels, dimes, and quarters, the Anthony dollar was silver-colored and therefore not distinctive.** The Mint wanted to replace the Anthony dollar with a distinctive coin—a coin that looked different from the coins already in circulation. Making the new coin out of the same metals as the silver-colored Anthony dollar would not accomplish this.

22. **D. hardy perennials** Hardy plants withstand frost, so they are more likely to survive than tender plants. Perennials come up and flower for many years. Therefore, hardy perennials are likely to provide the most flowers with the least effort on the gardener's part.

23. **C. A viewer could not see anything through the telescope.** The function of the flat mirror is to redirect the light rays toward the eyepiece so the viewer can see the object in the telescope's sights. If the flat mirror were removed, the reflection of the object would no longer be visible through the eyepiece.

24. **B. They help scientists analyze large amounts of data in a systematic way.** The ability of a computer to process lots of data, far more systematically and quickly than a human being can, has helped speed up and refine the drug discovery process although the older methods of running laboratory experiments and clinical trials are still also important.

25. **B. The typhoid fever vaccine is only 50 to 80 percent effective.** Because getting vaccinated against typhoid fever does not completely eliminate the traveler's chance of getting the disease, it makes sense that he or she should take extra precautions against contracting this food- and water-borne disease.

PRETEST STUDY PLANNERS

If you have not already done so, take the pretests starting on page 1. Then check your answers against the Pretest Answers and Explanations starting on page 52. Use your results to fill in the charts that follow so that you can target the areas that need the most work.

LANGUAGE ARTS: READING, 20 QUESTIONS

Circle the question numbers that you answered correctly in the second column. Write the number correct in the third column. If you do not have time to review all of the Reading sections, target your study to the content areas in which you missed several questions.

Content Area	Question Numbers	Number Correct/Total
Interpreting Informational Text Pages 70–95	1, 2, 3, 4, 5, 6, 7, 12, 13	____/9
Analyzing Informational Text Pages 96–111	8, 9, 10, 11, 14, 15	____/6
Reading Literature Pages 112–127	16, 17, 18, 19, 20	____/5

Language Arts: Writing

Part I: Language Skills, 18 Questions

Circle the question numbers that you answered correctly in the second column. Write the number correct in the third column. If you do not have time to review all of the Writing sections, target your study to the content areas in which you missed several questions.

Content Area	Question Numbers	Number Correct/Total
Writing Effective Sentences and **Connecting Ideas** Pages 136–157 and 158–169	2, 6, 9, 10, 12, 17	_____/6
Using Grammar Correctly Pages 170–187	1, 3, 8, 14, 15, 18	_____/6
Using Writing Mechanics Pages 188–203	5, 7, 11, 13	_____/4
Polishing Your Writing Pages 230–243	4, 16	_____/2

Part II: Essay

Circle the question numbers that you answered correctly in the second column. Write the number correct in the third column. If you do not have time to review all of the Writing sections, target your study to the content areas in which you missed several questions.

Content Area	Question Numbers	Number Correct/Total
Unpack the Writing Prompt Pages 204–205	1, 2, 3	My score is _____/3 based on the Unpacking the Writing Prompt Checklist, page 55.
Read the Passages with the Prompt in Mind, Develop a Thesis Statement, and **Collect Supporting Evidence** Pages 206–211	4, 5, 6	My score is _____/3 based on the Thesis and Evidence Checklist, page 215.
Plan Your Response Pages 212–215	7	My score is _____/3 based on a comparison to the examples on page 55.
Draft Your Response Pages 216–221	8	My score is _____/6 based on the Drafting Checklist, page 55.
Revise and Edit Your Response Pages 222–225	9	My score is _____/6 based on the Revising and Editing Checklist, page 55.

MATHEMATICS

Part I: Quantitative Reasoning, 18 Questions

Circle the question numbers that you answered correctly in the second column. Write the number correct in the third column. If you do not have time to review all of the Mathematics sections, target your study to the content areas in which you missed several questions.

Content Area	Question Numbers	Number Correct/Total
Number and Quantity I: Problem Solving Pages 260–285	6, 8, 9, 13	____/4
Number and Quantity II: Decimals and Fractions Pages 286–309	3, 7, 14, 15	____/4
Number and Quantity III: Ratio, Proportion, and Percent Pages 310–329	2, 5, 11, 17	____/4
Statistics and Probability Pages 330–367	1, 4, 10, 12, 16, 18	____/6

Part II: Algebraic Reasoning and Geometry, 22 Questions

Circle the question numbers that you answered correctly in the second column. Write the number correct in the third column. If you do not have time to review all of the Mathematics sections, target your study to the content areas in which you missed several questions.

Content Area	Question Numbers	Number Correct/Total
Algebraic Expressions Pages 368–401	1, 2, 3, 8, 10, 13	____/6
Functions Pages 402–441	6, 9, 11, 12, 15, 17, 19, 22	____/8
Geometry Pages 442–481	4, 5, 7, 14, 16, 18, 20, 21	____/8

Social Studies

Part I: Social Studies Skills, 10 Questions

Circle the question numbers that you answered correctly in the second column. Write the number correct in the third column. If you do not have time to review all of the Social Studies sections, target your study to the content areas in which you missed several questions.

Content Area	Question Numbers	Number Correct/Total
Determine Central Idea and Draw Conclusions; Interpret Words and Ideas; Make Inferences; Form and Apply Valid Conclusions Pages 518–525	1, 2	_____/2
Analyze and Evaluate Author's Purpose, Reasoning, and Evidence Pages 526–529	3, 4, 5, 6	_____/4
Analyze Relationships Between Materials; Interpret Data and Statistics Pages 532–537	7, 8, 9, 10	_____/4

Part II: Social Studies Content, 26 Questions

Circle the question numbers that you answered correctly in the second column. Write the number correct in the third column. If you do not have time to review all of the Social Studies sections, target your study to the content areas in which you missed several questions.

Content Area	Question Numbers	Number Correct/Total
U.S. History Pages 542–555	1, 2, 10, 17, 18, 19, 20	_____/7
Civics and Government Pages 556–569	4 ,5, 6, 21, 22, 23	_____/6
World History Pages 570–583	7, 8, 9, 14, 15	_____/5
Economics Online chapter	3, 11, 12, 24, 25	_____/5
Geography Online chapter	13, 16, 26	_____/3

Science

Part I: Science Skills, 10 Questions

Circle the question numbers that you answered correctly in the second column. Write the number correct in the third column. If you do not have time to review all of the Science sections, target your study to the content areas in which you missed several questions.

Content Area	Question Numbers	Number Correct/Total
Comprehend Scientific Presentations Pages 596–597	1, 2	____ /2
Use the Scientific Method; Evaluate Experimental Design Pages 598–601	3, 4	____ /2
Reason with, Express, and Apply Scientific Information; Synthesize Relevant Information; Assess the Credibility of Sources Pages 602–609	5, 6, 7, 8	____ /4
Use Statistics and Probability Pages 610–611	9, 10	____ /2

Part II: Science Content, 25 Questions

Circle the question numbers that you answered correctly in the second column. Write the number correct in the third column. If you do not have time to review all of the Science sections, target your study to the content areas in which you missed several questions.

Content Area	Question Numbers	Number Correct/Total
Life Science Pages 616–635	1, 4, 5, 6, 9, 10, 16, 22, 24, 25	____ /10
Physical Science Pages 636–661	3, 7, 11, 17, 18, 19, 20, 21, 23	____ /9
Earth and Space Science Online chapter	2, 8, 12, 13, 14, 15	____ /6

ABOUT THE TEST

Language Arts: Reading

UNIT 1

The HiSET® Reading Test assesses your ability to understand and analyze written passages. You will read a passage and then answer several questions about it. You will have 65 minutes to answer approximately 40 questions. All Reading questions will be multiple choice.

Forty percent of the Reading Test will cover informational content. Questions in this portion target skills such as:

- Identifying an author's main point
- Describing the structure of a passage
- Analyzing an author's argument
- Restating or applying ideas from the passage
- Understanding words in the context of an informational passage

Pages 70–111 of this unit cover these skills.

Sixty percent of the Reading Test will cover literary content. Questions in this portion target skills such as:

- Understanding plot, character, and theme
- Describing the structure of a story and how it is used to develop a theme
- Making inferences about characters and the author's attitude toward them
- Understanding words and figurative language in the context of a fictional passage

Pages 112–127 of this unit cover these skills.

* Note: The information given here was the latest information available as of December 2018. It is possible that some of this information may change between this printing and your test date. For updates, visit http://hiset.ets.org.

LESSON 1

Main Ideas and Details

The Main Idea

A writer has a message, or **main idea**, to get across. Sometimes the main idea is stated directly; often you have to figure it out yourself. You can find the main idea by asking, "What is the *most important* point the writer is making?" Most of the information in a passage will point to and explain the main idea.

As you read this passage, ask yourself what *main* point the writer is making. The answer will be the main idea.

> When I am reading a poem, I rarely feel alone in the room. The poet and I are together. It's as if the poet wrote a secret diary years ago. I am unlocking it as I sit alone and read.
>
> At times I don't understand what a poem means. I just like the way it sounds or the strange images that it provokes. The world is so peculiar in a poem. At the same time, it is so enticing. Sometimes I understand exactly, as if the poet is whispering to me, as if we shared the same experience.
>
> I must be fully concentrated on reading, or I cannot enter the world of a poem. There are too many daily tasks to attend to—tasks that are very far removed from the magic and imagination involved in a poem.
>
> On a cold, snowy day, I cuddle up inside my apartment and read and read. Then, I'm free to ride through the imagination of all those who came before me.

► Which of the following statements expresses the main idea?

(1) The writer has a love of poetry.
(2) The writer cuddles up on cold days to read.

You are correct if you chose **(1)**. While the passage mentions that the writer reads on cold days, the main point of all the information is how much the writer enjoys reading poetry.

Each paragraph has a main idea. To find the main idea of a passage with more than one paragraph, put together the ideas from all the paragraphs.

Supporting Details

A writer explains the main idea of a passage with supporting details. **Supporting details** include facts, examples, descriptions, and specific pieces of information. When you read, you need to identify details that support the main idea.

► Which detail helps you understand the writer's main point?

(1) At times, the writer does not understand a poem.
(2) The writer feels poetry is filled with magic and imagination.

You are correct if you chose **(2)**. That detail helps you see that the main idea is the writer's love of poetry. The fact that the writer doesn't always understand a poem is true, but it alone does not support the main idea.

KEY IDEAS

- The most important point of a passage is called the main idea.
- Sometimes a main idea is stated, but often you must figure it out.
- Supporting details point to and explain the main idea.

HiSET EXAM TIP

Be sure you don't confuse a supporting detail of a passage with the main idea. If you are asked for the main idea, choose the most important, general point.

PRACTICE 1

Questions 1 through 5 refer to the following passage from a diary.

EXCERPTED FROM *ARIADNE'S THREAD*

1 I feel I have never had a home. All my life moving from place to place. The only thing that remained the same, that was stable, was Oklahoma. Even the landscape never changed. The towns there never grew up into cities. The people were the same each year, wearing the same clothing, saying the same things.

2 The search for a homeland is part of the Chickasaw migration legend. It was ordained by the deities and began in the past when the people lived in the land of the "setting sun." During the days they would walk over the land, searching for their home. The priests carried a pole. They carried it in their hands by day and planted it each night. During the night it moved about and by morning it would be pointing the direction they were to travel. For a while it commanded the people to journey east, toward the morning sun. They crossed the Mississippi River eventually, and on the other side, the pole finally ceased to move during the night. The land was settled, crops were planted. It became known as the Old Fields. But one morning the pole leaned westward. The people gathered together and began the long journey back. They abandoned their village but did not feel sorrow because the pole had commanded it.

3 And I am still moving, looking for a home. I don't know if I will ever escape my tradition, my past. It goes with me everywhere, like a shadow.

By Linda Hogan from *Ariadne's Thread,* edited by Lyn Lifshin, New York: Harper & Row, 1982.

1. How does the author describe herself?

She feels as if she is

A. searching for a place to call home
B. doomed to stay in Oklahoma
C. tired of the sameness in her life
D. being shadowed by failure

2. Who do the Chickasaw believe are responsible for making them move?

A. the priests
B. white people
C. themselves
D. the gods

3. Why did the Chickasaw not feel sad when they left their homes in the east?

A. They knew they were headed to a better place to live.
B. They had been forced to move east to begin with.
C. They were returning to their ancient homeland.
D. It was simply part of their beliefs to follow the pole.

4. Which of the following best summarizes the main idea?

The writer

A. has always lived in Oklahoma and plans to stay there
B. feels trapped by tradition and wants to move far away
C. understands that her tendency to search is part of her Chickasaw heritage
D. believes that people in Oklahoma are all the same

5. How does the statement "I don't know if I will ever escape my tradition" (paragraph 3) support the main idea?

It shows that the writer

A. is trying to escape by moving around
B. lives in a more modern time
C. believes in the power of Indian legends
D. accepts that she is Chickasaw

STUDY ADVICE

Remember that practice has three levels: Learn and Review, Practice and Review, Assess and Review. For each lesson, absorb the concepts on the left page. Then practice using the page on the right, and carefully review the explanations in the back of the book. Finally, use the question sets at the end of each chapter to assess your progress. Don't forget to review the explanations for those question sets, too.

LESSON 2

Rephrasing and Summary

Rephrasing Ideas

Rephrasing an idea means putting it into your own words. For example, a friend may tell you that a movie wasn't worth the eight dollars she spent to see it. You might then tell a coworker that your friend said the movie was no good.

KEY IDEAS

- To rephrase an idea, put it in your own words.
- To summarize, choose the most important details that explain the main idea of a piece.

As you read the passage below, rephrase in your mind what you are reading.

> In Canton, Ohio, we take our desserts seriously. There are two local candy stores that receive over 90 percent of the city's candy business: Heggy's and Baldwin's. Those who prefer Heggy's won't befriend anyone who buys their sweets at Baldwin's.
>
> My family has always patronized Heggy's. At the Heggy's factory, Gerty wraps by hand each large chocolate candy in clear cellophane wrap. She's in the back of the store with her hairnet, seated at a table filled with hundreds of chocolates. My favorite chocolates at Heggy's are the dark chocolate creams, peanut clusters, and caramels.
>
> Heggy's aficionados point out that their candy of choice is a larger size and therefore superior. The rivalry runs deep . . . at Easter, Hanukkah, Christmas, Thanksgiving, and all occasions. Baldwin's loyal followers claim its sweets are sweeter. It's a feud over the best chocolate in town.

► How do the people of Canton feel about chocolate candy?
(1) They consider it a serious health issue.
(2) They feel it's important enough to take a stand on.

HiSET EXAM TIP

As you read a HiSET passage, check your understanding by pausing occasionally to see if you can rephrase and summarize what you are reading.

You are correct if you chose **(2)**. The phrase "take our desserts seriously" means that the candy is important to people.

On the Reading Test, the correct answer will not always use the exact words from the passage. You will have to recognize that an idea has been rephrased.

Summarizing

If you want to tell a friend about a movie you liked, you might **summarize** what happens in the movie. You certainly will not give all the details—that would take too long. A summary includes only the most important facts and ideas.

► Which of the following statements best summarizes the difference in opinion over the candy?
(1) Some people prefer Heggy's candy because it's bigger, while others prefer Baldwin's because it's sweeter.
(2) People argue whether to buy Heggy's or Baldwin's candy for different holidays.

You are correct if you chose **(1)**. The last paragraph sums up the difference in people's opinions. Statement (2) merely states a detail in the last paragraph.

PRACTICE 2

<u>Questions 1 through 3</u> refer to the following business letter.

EXCERPTED FROM *THE ENCYCLOPEDIA OF BUSINESS LETTERS*

Dear Richard,

1 Attached is a copy of my June 8th letter to Customer Service. After having my car serviced on June 30th, the list of problems has grown. These matters need your immediate attention.

2 Although I did finally receive my copy of the warranty after waiting two months, it is not bumper-to-bumper as Mr. Schecht promised. It also requires service at your facility unless the warranty administrator waives that requirement. I purchased the car from you at a premium price with the expectation that I would have a bumper-to-bumper warranty that I could use at any dealer. I never would have bought this car from you if I knew about these limitations. I expect two things: A written waiver from the warranty administrator that allows me to have warranty service performed at any dealer, and a wrap-around warranty, provided at your cost, that turns this limited warranty into the promised "bumper-to-bumper" warranty.

3 I expect an itemized list of registration costs, and the exact amount of credit I received from the Department of Motor Vehicles for the canceled plates voucher I gave to Mr. Schecht. If there is a refund due, I expect it within 15 days.

4 I expect a proper bill of sale that itemizes and describes the payments for the alarm system and the extended warranty, and includes all the items on the original bill of sale.

5 Your mechanic was unable to locate a cause for the burning smell. The smell persists. I expect your written assurance that if and when the cause for this smell becomes known, you will repair the problem at your cost.

6 The mechanic did *not* repair the left front marker light, although he promised he would. Enclosed is a copy of your invoice for this repair, which wasn't made, as well as an invoice from another dealer who actually made the repair. I expect reimbursement for $22.90.

cc: Joe Smith, Department of Consumer Affairs

1. The problems that the writer mentions in the first paragraph and outlines in his letter include which of the following?

A. receiving repairs the writer did not ask for
B. rude treatment
C. lack of proper paperwork
D. the premium price paid for the car

2. What does the customer want done about the burning smell?

A. the mechanic to find the cause of the smell
B. the car to be repaired free of charge if the cause of the problem is discovered
C. a refund of the money that was paid to have the problem fixed
D. reimbursement for having the problem fixed by another dealer

3. Which of the following statements best summarizes this letter?

A. A letter to customer service was never responded to and is being attached.
B. Mechanics have been unable to fix one problem and did not fix a second.
C. The service and warranty on the customer's car have been unacceptable.
D. Some dealers and garages are better than others.

LESSON 3

Application of Ideas

When you **apply ideas**, you use information you already know in a new but similar situation. For example, suppose you know that a friend loves country music. When you need to buy a gift for that friend, you walk past the jazz and rock sections in the music store and head straight for the country. You're applying what you've learned about your friend to help you choose a gift.

To apply ideas when reading, look for elements in the new situation that are similar to elements in the passage you have read. Read this selection and then see if you can apply some of the ideas in it.

> When the delivery truck pulled up to my house the day before my mother's birthday, I knew her gift had finally arrived. I was excited. Not only had I ordered a beautiful art book for her, but I'd also ordered a mystery novel for myself and a book each for my nephew and niece. I couldn't resist buying them while I was choosing my mother's gift from an online bookstore. The carton looked bigger than I expected, but perhaps it had a lot of filler to keep the books from becoming damaged.
>
> I lugged the huge box into the kitchen so I could open it and begin wrapping my mother's gift. I tugged at the industrial staples and then tore open the carton. To my surprise, it was filled with many copies of the same book. To make matters worse, it was a book I had not ordered. *Who Moved My Cheese?* What kind of book was that? And who would order *one* copy of that book, let alone 11? I certainly didn't want these books. I knew my family wouldn't want them either. They wanted *The Art of Diego Rivera, Harry Potter,* and Dr. Seuss. So much for buying online. I'm sticking to in-store buying.

▶ Which of the following situations is most like the situation that happened to the writer?
(1) buying groceries only to discover you brought someone else's bag home
(2) buying 11 boxes of the same pasta at the store

Option **(1)** is correct. It shares the elements of intending to buy something and getting the wrong thing by mistake. The second option is wrong because the writer did not intentionally buy 11 copies of the book. Now try this question.

▶ If the writer attended an auction, she would be most likely to
(1) decide which item to bid on and how much she would bid
(2) get involved in the excitement and bid on many things

You are correct if you chose **(2)**. The writer states that she couldn't resist buying additional items when she was shopping online. Therefore, she seems the type to get caught up in buying things. If she had carefully chosen which book to buy her mother and had ordered only that one, then option (1) would be correct.

KEY IDEAS

- Applying ideas means using information in a new but similar situation.
- To apply ideas, ask yourself, "How is this new situation just like the situation in the passage?"

HiSET EXAM TIP

As you work through questions on the HiSET Reading Test, refer back to the passage to confirm whether your answers make sense.

PRACTICE 3

Questions 1 through 4 refer to the following excerpt.

EXCERPTED FROM *MAKING THE MOST OF YOUR MONEY*

1 Once you stop using credit cards, three things will happen.

2 You will buy less—and whatever you do buy will probably be a less expensive model or make. Studies have found that people spend more when they pay with plastic, because it doesn't feel like real money. When it is real money, you're more sensible.

3 Your total debt will shrink rapidly. You are paying *off* back bills, you are not adding new ones, and you have extra money because you're buying less. That surplus cash will reduce your debt faster than you could imagine.

4 You will grow incredibly smug. You're the first on your block to get out of debt. Others will follow, but you'll be the first.

5 I'm not against credit cards. They're easy to use. They're handy. If your card has a low annual fee and a 25-day, interest-free grace period for paying your bills, you're getting monthly loans for practically nothing. What I'm against is buying more on your credit cards than you can pay for at the end of the month.

6 Once you've fought your way out of debt you can start using credit cards again—but only for the convenience of not carrying cash. Your days of debt are done. A big expense may sometimes drive you over the limit. A stereo. A llama. A hot-air balloon. Whenever you limp home, back in debt, recite your mantra: "From now on, I'm not going to put down a charge card for anything." Stick with it until you're free again.

From *Making the Most of Your Money* by Jane Bryant Quinn, New York: Simon & Schuster, 1991

1. According to the writer, becoming debt-free is a behavior most similar to

A. overcoming a bad habit
B. learning a new trick
C. forgetting a friend's birthday
D. setting a good example

2. If you have five credit cards with high interest rates and no grace periods, how can you become debt free?

A. pay your debt off slowly so that you have extra cash for necessities
B. never use the credit cards
C. use them only when it is not convenient to carry cash
D. cut up four of the credit cards right away

3. Which of the following situations is most like the process of becoming debt free?

A. driving a car
B. wearing a patch to give up smoking
C. losing weight by avoiding all-you-can-eat buffets
D. running a marathon race

4. Earlier in the book, the author made the statement "It's so simple that I'm almost embarrassed to mention it. Don't borrow any more."

Based on this information and the information in this passage, with which of the following statements would the author most likely agree?

A. "Money is the root of all evil."
B. "You can never have enough money."
C. "Live within your means."
D. "You deserve only the best."

STUDY ADVICE

Mastering new skills, such as applying ideas from a Reading passage, takes practice. The more you work on these skills, the stronger they will become.

Interpreting Informational Text

LESSON 4

Cause and Effect

When one event or idea influences another, there is a cause-and-effect relationship. For example, if you forget to fill your car with gas, the car will stall. The lack of gas is the **cause,** or the reason. The stalled car is the **effect**.

As you read this passage, look for cause-and-effect relationships.

> He is deceptively sweet upon waking up, and lets out a large yawn, showing his thin pink puppy tongue, and simultaneously letting out a high-pitched squeaking sound. Not two minutes later, he's eaten my favorite magazine and stuffed his entire head in the kitchen wastebasket to find a leftover turkey bone. The pup searches under the bed, on top of the dresser, and beside the nightstand for anything to chew. He's on a rampage in the morning—it's just his puppy nature.
>
> To calm him down, we head to the park for one hour of exercise with the other neighborhood dogs. Afterwards, he plays with his stuffed animal squeaky toy, sleeps for an hour, then finds his favorite bone. He lies down like an angel, chewing with contentment.

KEY IDEAS

- To determine the cause of an event, answer the question "Why did this happen?"
- To determine an effect, ask yourself, "What was the result?"

► What causes the puppy's owners to take him to the park?

(1) They like to see the other neighborhood dogs.
(2) The puppy is acting too wild and energetic.

You are correct if you chose **(2)**. The first paragraph describes wild behavior, and the second paragraph says, "To calm him down, we head to the park . . ."

HiSET EXAM TIP

In a Reading Test passage, a writer might discuss one cause and all its effects, one effect and all its causes, or a chain of events in which each effect becomes the cause of another event.

► Why is the puppy so wild and energetic?

(1) It is just the way a puppy is.
(2) He has a behavioral problem.

You are correct if you chose **(1)**. The writer doesn't indicate that the puppy's behavior is a problem. In fact, she clearly states that it's just the puppy's nature.

► What effect does the activity in the park have on the puppy?

(1) It calms him and tires him out.
(2) It teaches him to obey his owner.

You are correct if you chose **(1)**. When they get back from the park, the puppy plays quietly, sleeps for an hour, and then lies down to chew.

► Why does a walk in the park have a calming effect on the puppy?

(1) because the puppy enjoys seeing the other dogs
(2) because the puppy gets plenty of exercise

You are correct if you chose **(2)**. The exercise brings on the effect—calm behavior. This cause is not directly stated. You have to apply what you know about exercise and its effects in order to understand the relationship.

Questions 1 through 5 refer to the following excerpt from an essay.

EXCERPTED FROM "THE DEPRESSION"

Some events are so important that their influence cuts across class lines, affects all races and ethnic groups, and leaves no region untouched. The depression of the 1930s was such an event. No one who lived through those years in the United States could ever completely forget the bread lines, the millions of unemployed, or the forlorn and discouraged men and women who saw their mortgages foreclosed, their dreams shattered, their children hungry and afraid.

The depression was precipitated by the stock market crash in October 1929, but the actual cause of the collapse was an unhealthy economy. While the ability of the manufacturing industry to produce consumer goods had increased rapidly, mass purchasing power had remained relatively static. Most laborers, farmers, and white-collar workers, therefore, could not afford to buy the automobiles and refrigerators turned out by factories in the 1920s, because their incomes were too low. At the same time, the federal government increased the problem through economic policies that tended to encourage the very rich to over-save.

Herbert Hoover, a sensitive and humane engineer, had the misfortune of being President when the depression began. Even though he broke with the past and used the power of the federal government to stem the tide of depression, especially through loans to businesses and banks, his efforts proved to be too little and too late.

From "The Depression" from *Generations: Your Family in Modern American History*, 2nd ed., edited by James Watts and Allen F. Davis, New York: Alfred A. Knopf, 1974, 1978.

1. According to the authors, why was the depression of the 1930s so important?

A. It could have been prevented.
B. It was a time of economic hardship.
C. It affected nearly everyone.
D. It was unforgettable.

2. According to the passage, which of the following was an effect of the depression?

A. Many people lost the mortgages on their homes.
B. The stock market collapsed in October 1929.
C. Herbert Hoover was elected president.
D. The rich began to save too much of their money.

3. According to the passage, which of the following was one cause of the depression?

A. a static stock market
B. low worker incomes
C. not enough productivity
D. laborers refusing to buy products

4. In the early part of the depression, what effect did government policies have on the economy?

A. Banks and businesses began to need loans.
B. They had little effect.
C. Some of the poorer people were helped.
D. The very rich were helped.

5. One person who lived during the depression stated, "I can remember one time, the only thing in the house to eat was mustard. . . . And we can't stand mustard till today."

This account supports which of the following ideas from the passage?

A. Workers should have been paid more.
B. The depression touched everyone.
C. Herbert Hoover could have done more to help the economy.
D. The depression left people emotionally scarred.

LESSON 5

Comparison and Contrast

You are probably familiar with comparing and contrasting whenever you go shopping. If you are looking at two cars or even two bottles of aspirin, you want to know if the price of the two is the same or different.

Writers **compare** to point out what is similar and **contrast** to point out what is different about ideas or things.

As you read this passage, look for things being compared and contrasted.

> In December, it seems everyone is hurrying to bake holiday treats, decorate, and buy gifts. Some holiday shoppers trek through store after store, while others prefer catalog or online shopping. Just two of the holidays that keep everyone so busy this time of year are Christmas and Hanukkah.
>
> These holidays are, of course, times of celebration. People plan parties and family get-togethers. Both involve gift giving. Both also coincide with the winter solstice in the Northern Hemisphere, a time when many ancient cultures rejoiced.
>
> Christmas is a celebration of the birth of Jesus, though celebrating Christmas on December 25 did not become common until the fourth century.
>
> Hanukkah, the Jewish Festival of Lights, celebrates the belief that a flask of oil sufficient for only one day miraculously burned for eight days in a temple in the second century B.C.E. That's why on Hanukkah an additional candle is lit each evening until, on the eighth night of the holiday, eight candles are burning.

▶ What is the writer comparing and contrasting?
(1) methods of shopping
(2) Christmas and Hanukkah

You are correct if you chose **(2)**. The similarities and differences between the two holidays are the focus of the discussion. Two methods of shopping are merely mentioned.

▶ What is one basis on which the writer compares the two?
(1) time of year celebrated
(2) kinds of meals served

You are correct if you chose **(1)**. The similarities discussed in this passage include the time of the winter solstice in the Northern Hemisphere, close to when each holiday is celebrated.

▶ What is one basis on which the writer contrasts the two?
(1) gift giving
(2) their histories

The correct answer is **(2)**. The two holidays have very different histories. Both holidays involve gift giving, so that is not a point of contrast.

KEY IDEAS

- To compare ideas or things, find out how they are alike.
- To contrast ideas or things, find out how they differ.
- A writer might compare two things, contrast two things, or compare and contrast in one passage.

HiSET EXAM TIP

In a Reading Test passage, a writer may (1) compare in one paragraph and contrast in the next or (2) go back and forth, discussing similarities and differences on different points.

PRACTICE 5

Questions 1 through 5 refer to the following excerpt from a diary.

EXCERPTED FROM *DIARIES OF THE WESTWARD JOURNEY*

1 Mr. West from Peoria, Ill. had another man, his wife, a son Clay about 20 years of age and his daughter, America, eighteen. Unfortunately Mr. West had gone to the extreme of providing himself with such a heavy wagon and load that they were deemed objectionable as fellow argonauts. After disposing of some of their supplies they were allowed to join us. They had four fine oxen. This wagon often got stalled in bad roads much to the annoyance of all, but as he was a wagon maker and his companion a blacksmith by trade and both were accommodating there were always ready hands to "pry the wheel out of mire."

2 A mule team from Washington, D.C. was very insufficiently provisioned . . . [by] Southern gentlemen "unused to work. . . ." They deserted the train at Salt Lake as they could not proceed with their equipment and it was easier to embrace Mormonism than to brave the "American Desert."

3 Much in contrast to these men were four batchelors Messers Wilson, Goodall, Fifield and Martin, who had a wagon drawn by four oxen and two milch cows following behind. The latter gave milk all the way to the sink of the Humboldt where they died, having acted as draught animals for several weeks after the oxen had perished. Many a cup of milk was given to the children of the train and the mothers tried in every way possible to express their gratitude.

By Catherine Haun from *Women's Diaries of the Westward Journey,* edited by Lillian Schlissel, New York: Schocken Books, 1982.

1. What did Mr. West do that allowed his group to join the wagon train?

A. make wagons for the others
B. bring four fine oxen
C. offer milk to the children
D. leave some of his possessions behind

2. What purpose did the cows serve?

A. They led the oxen through rough terrain.
B. They carried children when wagons were full.
C. They provided milk and pulled wagons.
D. They provided food and replaced the mules.

3. Which of the following is contrasted in this excerpt?

A. the provisions of each group of travelers
B. the stability of each of the wagons
C. the number of people in each group
D. the ability of each group to feed the children

4. Suppose the writer were comparing a woman with five children who could sew and cook to one man with an old ox. Which of the following would be her most likely response?

The writer would

A. be happy to have people who could cook and sew
B. prefer to add fewer people to the group of travelers
C. feel sorry for the man and welcome him
D. offer the man one of her own animals

5. Based on the information in this excerpt, how is this trip similar for all the travelers?

A. They must cooperate and work together.
B. They will be rewarded for their efforts.
C. They have similar backgrounds and relate to each other.
D. They have all been forced to go on the journey.

STUDY ADVICE

Practice looking for examples of these concepts in daily life. You can pick out cause/effect and comparison/contrast relationships in TV news stories, articles, and magazines. That will help you to become a stronger reader for your HiSET exam.

LESSON 6

Conclusions and Generalizations

Conclusions

A detective draws a **conclusion** when he looks at different pieces of evidence and figures out who committed a crime. A doctor draws a conclusion when she looks at different symptoms and figures out what illness a patient has. You, as a reader, can draw a conclusion when you take pieces of information and put them together to figure out something that the writer has not directly stated.

KEY IDEAS

- A conclusion is an idea figured out from different pieces of information.
- You can use your knowledge of the real world to help you draw conclusions when you read.

See what conclusions you can draw from this notice sent by an employer.

> Thank you for sending your resume in response to our newspaper advertisement. We consider our company—and especially our employees—to be the best. And we want to keep it that way. For that reason, we carefully review each resume that is sent to us. We want to ensure that our company and the new employee we hire are a perfect match.
>
> This process, of course, takes some time. We want to assure you that your resume is part of this process and will be reviewed. If we feel we have an opening that matches your qualifications, we will contact you. If you have not heard from us within ten business days of the postmark of this notice, be assured that we will keep your resume on file for one year and review it when future openings arise.

► If a job applicant has not heard from this company three weeks after reading this notice, what can she conclude?

(1) The review process is taking longer than expected.
(2) She did not get the job that she applied for.

HiSET EXAM TIP

Be sure to read an entire passage before answering the questions about it. That way, you'll take all the information into account and won't jump to conclusions.

Option **(2)** is correct. The notice says that the review process takes some time. It also says that the company will contact the applicant if it feels she matches the opening. Finally, if she doesn't hear from the company within ten business days, her resume will go on file. You can conclude that the review process takes about ten business days, and if she hasn't been contacted in that time, she didn't get the job.

► What kind of notice can you conclude this is?

(1) a personal note sent to this individual applicant
(2) a form notice sent to all applicants

Again, you're correct if you chose **(2)**. The way the notice is worded, with no personal details, lets you conclude this. You can also use your knowledge of the real world and business form letters to conclude that this, too, is a form letter.

► What conclusion can you draw about the company's attitude?

(1) It cares about its employees and their job satisfaction.
(2) It cares only about profits and employee productivity.

You are correct if you chose **(1)**. The fact that the company states not only that it considers its employees to be the best but also that it takes the time to communicate sincerely with potential employees lets you conclude that.

PRACTICE 6.1

Questions 1 through 5 refer to the following excerpt from an autobiography.

EXCERPTED FROM *THE STORY OF MY LIFE*

1 Once there were eleven tadpoles in a glass globe set in a window full of plants. I remember the eagerness with which I made discoveries about them. It was great fun to plunge my hand into the bowl and feel the tadpoles frisk about, and to let them slip and slide between my fingers. One day a more ambitious fellow leaped beyond the edge of the bowl and fell on the floor, where I found him to all appearance more dead than alive. The only sign of life was a slight wriggling of his tail. But no sooner had he returned to his element than he darted to the bottom, swimming round and round in joyous activity. He had made his leap, he had seen the great world, and was content to stay in his pretty glass house under the big fuchsia tree until he attained the dignity of froghood. Then he went to live in the leafy pool at the end of the garden, where he made the summer nights musical with his quaint love-song.

2 Thus I learned from life itself. At the beginning I was only a little mass of possibilities. It was my teacher who unfolded and developed them. When she came, everything about me breathed of love and joy and was full of meaning. She has never since let pass an opportunity to point out the beauty that is in everything, nor has she ceased trying in thought and action and example to make my life sweet and useful.

3 It was my teacher's genius, her quick sympathy, her loving tact which made the first years of my education so beautiful.

From *The Story of My Life* by Helen Keller.

1. What can you conclude about the writer's view of learning?

A. It is rewarding and one of life's joys.
B. It is better with a strict teacher.
C. It happens very slowly, if at all.
D. It happens most often when you are alone.

2. What conclusion can you draw about the writer's character?

The writer is

A. self-centered and demanding
B. confused and searching
C. fearful and shy
D. insightful and grateful

3. If Helen's teacher was trying to teach her addition, what method would the teacher most likely use?

A. make Helen stand and recite addition facts for one hour every day
B. assign an abundance of addition homework
C. show Helen how addition is used in everyday life
D. ask a well-known mathematician to teach the subject

4. How are the thoughts in this personal account organized?

A. as a comparison with a frog followed by a contrast
B. as a problem followed by its solution
C. in chronological order, or time sequence
D. as an anecdote followed by a generalization based on the anecdote

5. Later in her story, Helen compares a child's mind to a shallow brook "which ripples and dances merrily over the stony course of its education. . . ." Based on this information and the excerpt above, what is similar about the tadpole and a child?

A. They learn from others.
B. They are eager to grow into adulthood.
C. Youth can make them do dangerous things.
D. Their development is not entirely smooth.

Generalizations

A **generalization** is a broad statement about a group of people, objects, or things, or about a type of event. Usually, it takes something that is true in one specific case and extends it to every possible case. For example, "My hometown celebrated Independence Day with fireworks last summer" is a fact about a specific Fourth of July in a specific town; a generalization could be "Every Independence Day, my hometown celebrates with fireworks."

► Identify one statement with *F* for a fact and the other with *G* for generalization.

(1) Every clerk in the store focuses on customer service more than any other aspect of the job.

(2) Tina, the manager of the women's shoe department, helps customers select just the right pair of shoes.

If you identified option **(2)** as being a fact and option **(1)** as being a generalization, you were correct. One hint that **(1)** is the generalization is the word "Every." Words like *all, never,* and *always* show up in sentences that make broad, sweeping statements. The sentence about Tina, on the other hand, gives specific information about a specific person and so is not a generalization.

Generalizations can be valid and true when properly made. A writer can support a generalization with an example (like Tina, above) and information that shows why the example represents the whole group. Often, a generalization is too broad to apply to every member of a group, and a good writer will acknowledge that there are exceptions.

"Dogs are typically more attached to their owners than cats are, due in part to their evolution as pack animals. My dog will jump up to meet me as soon as I get home from work, while my cat will continue napping serenely until hunger motivates him to do otherwise."

► What example is given to support the generalization that "Dogs are typically more attached to their owners than cats"?

(1) Dogs evolved as pack animals.

(2) The author's dog jumps up to meet her, while her cat ignores her.

The example of the author's dog's attachment to her, **(2)**, illustrates and supports the generalization that most dogs show greater attachment to their owners. The specific example helps to show that the statement is based on experience.

Writers sometimes make the mistake of drawing **faulty generalizations** based on too little information. Imagine a person who bites into an apple, finds a worm, and concludes that all apples have worms in them. Since a generalization is a broad statement, a **valid generalization** requires broad knowledge to justify it. A generalization about American cities is more likely to be faulty if the writer bases on it only one city but more likely to be valid if the writer supports it with knowledge of 20 cities. With a larger sample, the writer is also better able to know whether to qualify a generalization as something that is true in most, but not all, cases.

► Identify one statement with *FG* for a faulty generalization and the other with *VG* for a valid generalization.

(1) Every breed of dog has four legs, so almost all dogs have four legs.

(2) Some dogs bark at kids, so all dogs must dislike or fear children.

You are correct if you chose **(1)** as the valid generalization: the writer shows awareness of many different types of dogs. Option **(2)** is a faulty generalization; dogs may bark at children for reasons other than fear or dislike.

KEY IDEAS

- A generalization is a broad statement about a group or class.
- When assessing a generalization, evaluate the writer's evidence.
- An important factor in thoughtful reading is distinguishing between faulty and valid generalizations.

HiSET EXAM TIP

If you see a generalization, look for supporting evidence that may be introduced by phrases such as "for example," "such as," or "for instance."

PRACTICE 6.2

Questions 1 through 3 are based on the following newspaper editorial.

OPINION: DOUBTS ABOUT GLOBAL WARMING

1 Shady Hollow was hit yesterday with record cold temperatures. And yet, despite this deep freeze, we'll continue to be subjected to the doctrine of global warming.

2 There is plenty to be said for fuel economy—anyone who lived through the energy crisis of the 1970s learned that lesson the hard way—but it's time we dispense with the terror campaign of doomsday climatology and recognize it for the pseudoscience that it is. Whenever Shady Hollow gets a big hit of winter weather, common sense tells us that the idea of "warming" seems fishy, yet climatologists insist on playing the same tune. More and more, this tune is taken up by policy-makers and government bodies, who steer our administrations accordingly. It must be the case that ivory towers have good weather stripping and excellent heating systems; as for the man on the street, he's finding his street a chilly one these days.

3 The simple fact is that it is logically impossible to reconcile a record cold temperature with the idea that it's getting warmer. A record cold temperature, and this may be worth spelling out, means exactly this: it has never been colder on this date in recorded history. If "warming" means what it sounds like it means—that temperatures are rising, not falling—then there is a real problem here, because that is quite simply not what is happening.

4 It may take years to get out from under the orthodoxy of the accepted opinion on climate change, but the facts themselves will not go away. Sooner or later, we'll be forced to acknowledge that we're still bundling up, and when that happens, we can stop building policy discussions around fictions.

1. What is a generalization that is made in paragraph 3?

A. Shady Hollow has the coldest temperatures in the region.
B. Global warming can only be valid if it predicts high temperatures.
C. On the whole, temperatures are not rising.
D. If children are taught a simpler theory, then a more complex theory should be set aside.

2. What evidence does the author give to support his generalization about global warming?

A. Shady Hollow was hit with a record cold temperature yesterday.
B. Ivory towers have good weather stripping.
C. It may take years to change opinions on climate change.
D. There is plenty to be said for fuel economy.

3. Which of the following pieces of information would put the author in a better position to make a generalization about climate change?

A. an account of the energy crisis of the 1970s
B. minutes of policy discussions from the 1970s through today
C. interviews with the "man on the street" from the 1990s through today
D. worldwide data tables of temperatures from the 1980s through today

LESSON 7

Word Choice

Writers make careful decisions to select words that will impact their audience. One choice that writers make is to select words that have a **connotation** associated with a particular image or feeling. Think of the different connotations of *dog, mutt,* and *man's best friend*. The word *dog* has a neutral connotation; it just describes the animal. To some, the word *mutt* would have a negative connotation, while the phrase *man's best friend* would have a positive connotation.

KEY IDEAS

- Writers choose words carefully to make an impact on the reader.
- They deliberately choose words with positive, negative, or neutral connotations.
- Writers also use figurative language such as similes, metaphors, and personification to enhance descriptions.

► Assign a *P* (positive) or an *N* (negative) to the following words to indicate the connotation that might be associated with them:
(1) shack
(2) villa

You are correct if you assigned an *N* to (1) and a *P* to (2). The word *shack* probably brings to mind a small, poorly built or run-down building. On the other hand, the word *villa* might be associated with a house in the countryside or a vacation destination.

Writers use **figurative language** to make their descriptions clearer and more vivid. They use **similes**, which use the words *like* or *as* to compare two things; for example, "Her new coat fit like a glove." This indicates that the coat fit perfectly. Another type of figurative language is a **metaphor**, which implies a comparison between two things. One familiar metaphor is "Life is a journey"; this compares two dissimilar things in order to describe life. A third figure of speech is **personification**, by which a writer assigns human characteristics to something that is not human. For example, a writer may describe a storm as "slashing at the windows and knocking on the door."

HiSET EXAM TIP

Read closely to see how a writer's word choice affects how you picture something or feel about it. You may have to answer questions that require an awareness of the impact of both words' connotations and figurative language.

If you look very carefully, you can find the island of Ascension on a map about midway between Angola, in Africa, and Brazil, in South America. This South Atlantic island has a population of about 1,000 people and is home to an important GPS ground antenna and a British air force base. Its volcanic terrain greets visitors with a forbidding aspect; place names like "Comfortless Cove" indicate how rocky and uninviting Ascension Island may appear. Even so, with its dry subtropical weather, excellent sport fishing, and unique wildlife, this barren outpost attracts about 1,000 tourists each year.

► What does the personification in the third sentence suggest about Ascension Island?
(1) Tourists are forbidden to visit the island.
(2) The island doesn't look like a good place to visit.

You are correct if you chose **(2)**. The writer refers to the island as if it were a person with an unfriendly appearance. Since the last sentence states that tourists do visit the island, you know that they are not forbidden to do so.

PRACTICE 7

Questions 1 through 5 refer to the following product description.

A COOL NEW BLANKET

1 Many people rely on electric blankets to keep warm on winter nights without turning on expensive central heating. In summer, though, there's no alternative to noisy fans and energy-hogging air conditioners if you want to stay cool . . . until now. The Starlight company recently introduced its newest product: an electric blanket that keeps you cool even on sweltering summer nights.

2 The CoolForter blanket works like an electric blanket, but it feels like a dream. The blanket contains a full tenth of a mile of flexible hose, fully insulated between layers of soft cotton. A small, quiet compressor refrigerates the safely enclosed cooling chemical and circulates it continuously through the coils. The CoolForter coddles you in refreshing comfort, and you never have to worry about waking up shivering. That's because your sleeping temperature is precisely controlled by the built-in thermostat, which can be adjusted to your exact temperature preference.

3 Your CoolForter blanket also matches your decorating preferences: the replaceable cover comes in a wide variety of bland colors to suit any décor. If you decide to redecorate, choose from a selection of fun and gaudy prints to liven up your room.

4 Best of all, the CoolForter saves you money every time you use it. Consuming an average of just 80 watts, the twin-size blanket is like a regular household light bulb, costing just pennies per day to run. It's an investment in comfort that will pay for itself many times over the lifetime of its generous ten-year warranty and beyond.

STUDY ADVICE

To practice spotting figurative language, similes, metaphors, and personification, pay particular attention to advertisements. Think about how an ad's wording conveys a strong positive connotation about the product being advertised (or a negative connotation about the competitor's product).

1. In paragraph 2, what is compared to a dream?
   A. an electric blanket
   B. the flexible hose used in the CoolForter blanket
   C. the cotton insulating layers
   D. the CoolForter blanket

2. What could be a reason that the writer used the word "coddles" in paragraph 2?
   A. to show that the blanket keeps its user warm
   B. to show that the blanket is a pleasant indulgence
   C. to show that the blanket keeps its user cool
   D. to show that the user can wrap herself up in the blanket

3. What word could the writer have used instead of "chemical" in paragraph 2 that would have a less negative connotation?
   A. fluid
   B. antifreeze
   C. contaminant
   D. water

4. Which word in paragraph 3 means "neutral" but has a negative connotation?
   A. decorating
   B. replaceable
   C. bland
   D. gaudy

5. Why is "like a regular household light bulb" from paragraph 4 an effective use of a comparison using figurative language?
   A. It reminds the consumer that, while a light bulb generates heat, the CoolForter blanket keeps its user cool.
   B. It makes the CoolForter blanket seem ordinary.
   C. It emphasizes the difference in cost between running a regular light bulb and operating a compact fluorescent light bulb.
   D. It allows the consumer to compare the CoolForter's energy usage to that of a familiar item.

LESSON 8

Writer's Tone and Point of View

Tone

A writer usually has a certain attitude toward the subject he or she is writing about. This attitude is the **tone** of the piece. The tone is not directly stated. You have to sense it by the writer's choice of words and manner of expression.

As you read this drama review, ask yourself, "What tone of voice would the author have if she were reading this aloud to me?"

> Watching actor Brian Dennehy as Willy Loman in the stage production of *Death of a Salesman* was transforming. I know intellectually that live theater is better than movies. Movie actors reshoot scenes until they are perfect. An actor on stage has one chance to get it right. It is immediate. The actors are breathing human beings in the same room with you. Theater provides the opportunity for strong emotions to surface, right there, in the moment. Seeing a play often envelops me in energy.
>
> But I've never gone so far as to cry at a theater performance until now. I cried because Dennehy's Loman reminded me of my father, of the brevity of our lives, of how easy it is to waste our lives. This was not an intellectual response. I suddenly heard what this man on stage was saying—his life wasn't worth living, though he had tried hard, had a devoted wife and two sons. It didn't matter that this play was written in the 1940s. Mr. Dennehy stood on stage and roared at us about our lives now. It was hard-hitting, emotional drama.

► Which of the following best describes the tone of this piece?
(1) positive and somewhat awed
(2) cool and objective

The correct response is **(1)**. The writer states positive opinions. She also chooses short, clipped expressions—"It is immediate" and "right there, in the moment"—that by themselves create a sense of drama and awe. If the tone were cool and objective, you would not sense the writer's emotional attitude toward the play.

Point of View

The **point of view** of a piece is "where the author is coming from"—that is, the writer's background and experiences that may affect her opinions. For example, when you read an editorial in a newspaper, you can usually tell whether the writer has a liberal or a conservative point of view.

► What point of view does the writer of the review above have?
(1) that of a person who prefers sitting at home watching TV
(2) that of an enthusiastic theatergoer

You are correct if you chose **(2)**. You can conclude that the writer goes to the theater ("Seeing a play often envelops me") and enjoys it ("theater is better than movies"). Knowing this helps you evaluate the merits of the review.

KEY IDEAS

- The writer's attitude toward a subject is conveyed by the tone of the writing.
- To determine tone, look at word choice and manner of expression. How would the writer sound reading the piece?
- The writer's point of view is the position he or she is writing from.

HiSET EXAM TIP

Some kinds of tone you might see in Reading Test passages are formal or informal, positive or negative, objective, sarcastic, arrogant, concerned, affectionate, or nostalgic.

PRACTICE 8

Questions 1 through 5 refer to the following review.

EXCERPTED FROM "TALKING BACK TO THE TUBE"

1 CBS delivered a television low mark called *Big Brother.* Focusing on ten fame-seeking, people-pleasing, hair-teasing losers willing to submit to surveillance by a nation of snoops for three months, it was so bad that it wasn't even good. Forget about camp reversals that transform trash into the perversely fascinating, forget about the Cheese Factor, which allows a pop-cultural product to be moldy and musty and stinky and still taste good. *Big Brother* was so bad that even Jean-Paul Sartre would have yawned, and the dude wrote hundreds of pages about useless passion in *Being and Nothingness.*

2 But something good did come of *Big Brother,* something wicked and warped and witty, something created by people with way too much time on their hands and way too much venom in their bite. While the reality series was channeling banality through the cable cords and over the airwaves six nights a week, a small crew of writers were deconstructing and eviscerating the tedium on the Internet. They were taking hours and hours of prime-time dross and turning it into decadent, amoral, sharp, electronic gold.

3 Internet sass.

4 You gotta love it, if only because it keeps razor-tongued fanatics and uncensored savants off the streets and out of trouble.

5 Not only was there a site devoted entirely to the ridiculing of CBS, *Big Brother,* its ten cast members, their families, host Julie Chen, and the gaseous *Big Brother* house pug, but a number of other general interest sites, notably Salon.com, spent the summer providing wry daily updates on the non-goings-on of the non-people in the non-house. They, too, took the non-pulse of a DOA television series and gave it a semblance of life on the Internet.

Excerpt from "Talking Back to the Tube," by Matthew Gilbert. Reprinted courtesy of the *Boston Globe.*

1. Who are referred to as "razor-tongued fanatics and uncensored savants" (paragraph 4)?

A. the television writers
B. the television cast of *Big Brother*
C. the Internet writers
D. the Internet audience

2. Which of the following best summarizes the reviewer's point about *Big Brother*?

A. The Internet reviews were much more interesting than the TV show.
B. The TV show was so bad that it was funny.
C. Internet writers are better than TV writers.
D. The main problem was with the ten people on the TV show.

3. What opinion is supported by the statement "even Jean-Paul Sartre would have yawned, and the dude wrote hundreds of pages about useless passion" (paragraph 1)?

A. The show was boring.
B. The show should have been longer.
C. The show needed more passion.
D. The show was incomprehensible.

4. Which of the following best describes the tone of this review?

A. apologetic
B. nostalgic for earlier shows
C. informal and hip
D. objective

5. From whose point of view is this piece likely written?

A. a television script writer
B. a person who hates watching TV
C. someone knowledgeable about the media
D. a disgruntled fan

LESSON 9

Text Structure

Writers make choices about how to organize informational and nonfiction materials based on their purpose. You have already seen two text structures: cause and effect, which shows how one thing made another happen, and comparison and contrast, which illustrates similarities and differences.

There are other **text structures** often used for informational text:

- **Example**—introduces an unfamiliar topic and then follows with common examples to aid understanding.
- **Pros and Cons**—explains a situation by first presenting its benefits and then portraying its deficiencies in order to present both sides.
- **Chronological Order** or **Process**—presents details in the order in which they occur; also referred to as a **sequence** of events.
- **Elaboration**—makes a statement and indicates that additional information or an explanation will follow.

These text structures use different types of **transitions** to guide the reader from one idea to the next. Many of these are familiar to you.

KEY IDEAS

- Writers may use different text structures depending on what they are writing about.
- One of the main tools writers use to create different text structures is transition words, which create relationships between ideas.

Text Structure	Purpose	Sample Transitions
Example	Organizes illustrations that support a concept	for example, for instance, such as, to illustrate
Pros and Cons	Shows benefits and drawbacks	on the one hand, on the other hand
Chronological Order or Process	Describes events and procedures	before, after, next, following, meanwhile, until
Elaboration	Expands with additional details	additionally, furthermore, moreover

HiSET EXAM TIP

You will need to be aware of different types of text structure to answer questions, but you will not need to identify any structures by their names.

Practice using an understanding of text structure by reading the paragraph and answering the question below.

> Today, there are millions of workers who are not employees in the traditional sense; they are called "contract workers." These are self-employed individuals who have contracts with different businesses. For example, a graphic artist may have several different clients and design a newsletter for one and a website for another. Contract workers pay for their own equipment, supplies, and benefits—such as health insurance.

► What is a detail from the passage that explains the concept of "contract workers"?

(1) They are not employees in the traditional sense.
(2) They may have contracts with several businesses.

Choice **(2)** illustrates the concept of contract workers by explaining that they have several different clients rather than one employer. Choice (1) does not help to explain contract work; it just explains what contract workers are not.

PRACTICE 9

Questions 1 and 2 refer to this scientific experiment.

COWPOX, SMALLPOX, AND IMMUNITY

1 In 1796, British physician Edward Jenner conducted an experiment intended to help develop a viable treatment for the deadly smallpox disease. Some time before, he had noticed that dairymaids in his village commonly became infected with cowpox. Cowpox is an illness that is very similar to smallpox, but it is not deadly. The dairymaids who caught cowpox later turned out to be immune to smallpox. This led Jenner to experiment with whether he could make a test subject immune to smallpox by first infecting that person with cowpox. His test subject was a young boy named James. First, Jenner made small cuts on James's skin and inserted liquid from the cowpox sores of a local dairymaid. After being exposed to the disease, James caught cowpox and later recovered. After the boy's recovery from cowpox, Jenner exposed James to smallpox and found that the boy was immune. Today, scientists and medical professionals know that the cowpox and smallpox viruses are so similar that the body's immune system cannot tell them apart.

1. What step in the process came before James's recovery from cowpox?

A. his immunity to smallpox
B. exposure to the cowpox disease
C. scientists' discovery that cowpox and smallpox are similar
D. Jenner exposing James to smallpox

2. Which of the following phrases from the passage provides information about the order of the steps in the process?

A. "cannot tell them apart"
B. "Jenner made small cuts"
C. "After being exposed to the disease"
D. "make a test subject immune"

Question 3 refers to this discussion of gardening.

THE UPS AND DOWNS OF GARDENING

1 Planting and maintaining a backyard garden can have many benefits, but it also brings challenges. On the one hand, successful gardeners often express deep feelings of accomplishment and satisfaction in their gardens. Gardening can involve good exercise and fresh air, and spending time outdoors can be a healthy escape from everyday responsibilities and concerns. A flower garden provides a beautiful view that often attracts delightful visitors, including butterflies and hummingbirds. A vegetable garden provides nutritious food and can add up to significant savings on your grocery bill. An herb garden can supply alternatives to unhealthy ingredients such as salt and oil.

2 On the other hand, planting and maintaining a garden can be very expensive and time-consuming, and a garden may fail despite your best efforts. Proper soil and fertilizers must be bought, and plants or seeds must be chosen. It is also important to consider the watering and feeding of the garden to ensure proper growth. A number of factors beyond your immediate control may affect the success of your garden. If the season's weather is extreme in any way—too dry, too rainy, too hot, or too cold—it can damage tender plants and undo your hard work, wasting your investment of time and money. Similarly, invasive pests and diseases can be devastating to your home garden and can be difficult and expensive to control.

3. Which of the following is one of the writer's arguments against planting and maintaining a backyard garden?

A. Time outdoors often alleviates stress.
B. A number of factors can damage a garden.
C. Having too many daily chores is stressful.
D. Rain is bad for a garden.

LESSON 10

Reading Predictively

Active reading means asking questions of the text as you read. By asking your own questions, you will focus on and understand the most important aspects of the passage, and you will be prepared to answer the test's questions. One of the most important questions to ask is "What will the rest of this paragraph or passage be about?" Use your understanding of the author's main idea and purpose in writing, as well as clues about the structure of the passage, to anticipate what it will say.

KEY IDEAS

- Use clues to the author's purpose in writing to predict the content and structure of the rest of the passage.
- Transition words help you to anticipate the direction the passage is taking.
- Understanding the author's point of view on a topic may allow you to infer what the author would think about another topic or situation.

Practice by reading the first paragraph of a passage and asking yourself what the rest of the passage will be about. Then answer the question below.

> Many bird species migrate, or travel long distances, every spring and fall even though migration requires a great expenditure of energy as well as exposure to dangers such as storms. Some birds do not survive the journey. Scientists have put forward several ideas to explain why birds migrate despite the risks.

► Which of the following statements could be the main idea of the second paragraph?

(1) Birds may migrate to find a better supply of food.
(2) Birds face a number of dangers when they migrate.

The first paragraph ends by saying that scientists have several ideas about migration, so you can predict that the following paragraphs will discuss these possible reasons. Therefore, choice **(1)** states a possible main idea of the next paragraph. According to the paragraph, migration is dangerous, as choice (2) says, but the author has said all he is going to say about this.

HiSET EXAM TIP

Asking questions such as "What is the author likely to say next?" will help you understand the main idea and structure of a passage.

You might also see a question about how the author would approach a different topic from the one in the passage. When the author expresses an opinion, ask, "What criteria did the author use to reach that conclusion?" Predict that the author would apply the same reasoning to another situation.

The author of the passage about bird migration ends with this paragraph.

> As scientists continue to investigate why birds migrate, it will be important to collect data on different bird species. After all, one bird's reason for migrating may not be the same as another's, and a one-size-fits-all theory of bird migration may well fail to explain important distinctions.

► If the author of this passage were asked to express an opinion about a theory of plant seed dispersion, which theory would the author likely prefer?

(1) Plants make seeds in a variety of shapes to take advantage of different methods of dispersion, depending on their particular environment.
(2) All plants seek to maximize how far they can spread their seeds, and plants that make wind-borne seeds are the most successful.

Note that this question is *not* testing your knowledge of plant seed dispersion. That wouldn't be fair because the passage was not about plants. The question is asking about the author's likely opinion of a theory, and the passage tells you the author values theories that take into account differences between species. Therefore, choice **(1)** is correct because it expresses the idea that different plants may achieve seed dispersal in different ways. Choice (2) applies one standard to all plants.

PRACTICE 10

Questions 1 and 2 refer to the following discussion of chemicals used in farming.

CONSEQUENCES OF THE GREEN REVOLUTION

1 The "Green Revolution" took place primarily in the 1960s, when the introduction of a number of technologies made farming much more productive. The effect was most dramatic in the developing world.

The Green Revolution is credited with saving a billion people from starvation. It permanently changed the world's economic and social dynamic, giving people in poor countries the opportunity to grow enough food to feed themselves. However, this dramatic improvement in living conditions has come at a substantial cost, especially to the environment.

2 Many technological improvements led to the Green Revolution. One such improvement was the development of chemicals that killed insects (pesticides) and weeds (herbicides). These pesticides and herbicides increased crop yields. However, their toxic effects spread beyond their target species, affecting helpful animals and plants and even humans themselves. For example, the pesticide DDT caused serious harm to birds and has been banned for routine agricultural use in many countries. In addition, a number of studies have linked long-term exposure to agricultural chemicals to increased risk of cancer in humans.

3 Thus, one cannot pronounce the Green Revolution an unqualified success. Furthermore, when evaluating the impact of new technologies, it is important to identify and assess their unintended effects as well as their intended ones.

1. If the author were to add a new paragraph to this passage, just before the last paragraph, how would that paragraph most logically begin?

A. "However, there is no definitive evidence that agricultural chemicals are causing the collapse of bee colonies, a phenomenon that remains a mystery."

B. "On the other hand, climate change is a far more serious environmental problem and deserves greater attention."

C. "Moreover, harmful insects and weeds develop resistance to agricultural chemicals over time, forcing farmers to purchase more expensive, and more toxic, treatments."

D. "The human population growth fostered in part by the Green Revolution has resulted in some societies having a large proportion of children and young adults."

2. If asked to evaluate the use of genetically modified organisms in agriculture, with which statement would the author be most likely to agree?

A. History shows that new technologies have negative consequences, so genetically modified organisms should not be used in farming.

B. Like other new technologies, genetically modified organisms may have negative consequences as well as positive ones, and it is important to take all effects into account.

C. If genetically modified organisms will help farmers feed more people, thereby preventing starvation, then they should be used.

D. If genetically modified organisms are likely to harm the environment but help people, then farmers should use the technology.

STUDY ADVICE

Congratulations—you're almost done with the first chapter of this book! The last few pages of each chapter will give you additional practice items to reinforce what you've learned in that chapter. Before you begin the first of these on the next page, you may want to review anything that seemed challenging in the lessons so far.

Interpreting Informational Text Practice Questions

Questions 1 through 4 refer to the following excerpt from an autobiography.

EXCERPTED FROM *THE LIARS' CLUB*

1 That fall my school career didn't go much better. I got suspended from my second-grade class twice, first for biting a kid named Phyllis who wasn't, to my mind, getting her scissors out fast enough to comply with the teacher, then again for breaking my plastic ruler over the head of a boy named Sammy Joe Tyler, whom I adored. A pale blue knot rose through the blond stubble of his crew cut. Both times I got sent to the principal, a handsome ex–football coach named Frank Doleman who let Lecia and me call him Uncle Frank. (Lecia and I had impressed Uncle Frank by both learning to read pretty much without instruction before we were three. Mother took us each down to his office in turn, and we each dutifully read the front page of the day's paper out loud to him, so he could be sure it wasn't just some story we'd memorized.)

2 He let me stay in his office playing chess all afternoon with whoever wandered in. He loved pitting me against particularly lunkheaded fifth- and sixth-grade boys who'd been sent down for paddlings they never got. He'd try to use my whipping them at chess to make them nervous about how dumb they were. "Now this little bitty old second-grader here took you clean in six plays. Don't you reckon you need to be listening to Miss Vilimez instead of cutting up?" When Mrs. Hess led me solemnly down the hall to Frank Doleman's office, I would pretend to cry, but thought instead about Brer Rabbit as he was being thrown into the briar patch where he'd been born and raised, and screaming *Please don't throw me in that briar patch!*

From *The Liars' Club* by Mary Karr, New York: Penguin Books, 1995.

1. If the writer had attended an elementary school dance, which of the following might she have done?

   A. made fun of everyone as they danced
   B. sat and played chess with the boys
   C. been too shy to dance with anyone
   D. hit a boy in the arm to get his attention

2. What is meant by the statement "I . . . thought instead about Brer Rabbit as he was being thrown into the briar patch where he'd been born and raised and screaming *Please don't throw me in that briar patch!*" (paragraph 2)?

   A. She was so upset that she wanted to scream.
   B. She was just pretending she didn't want to go to the principal's office.
   C. She hoped the teacher would let her back in class if she pleaded with her.
   D. She was afraid of what would happen in the principal's office.

3. What type of principal was Frank Doleman?

   A. strict
   B. ineffective
   C. unusual
   D. mean

4. Later in the autobiography, the narrator describes herself as "small-boned and skinny, but more than able to make up for that."

   Based on this description and the excerpt, which of the following best describes the narrator?

   A. confident
   B. serious
   C. friendly
   D. hopeful

Questions 5 through 9 refer to this article about soda.

TURNING BACK A SUGARY TIDE

1 The popular soft drinks known as soda, pop, or both trace their origins all the way back to 1767, when English chemist Joseph Priestley invented a method for carbonating water. Over the last two and a half centuries, soda has risen to prominence primarily as a sweet beverage for social occasions. By the mid-1990s, soda had become the beverage of choice for adolescents. This increase in consumption has not been without negative consequences. Since the early 1980s, obesity rates for young Americans have risen steadily, as has the incidence of juvenile diabetes, heart disease, and myriad other ailments related to poor diet.

2 To counteract the harmful effects of overindulging in soda, federal, state, and local governments have taken steps in recent years. Former First Lady Michelle Obama promotes healthier diet choices and campaigns against childhood obesity. Several states now require that restaurants post calorie information next to all menu items, including beverages. In a controversial move, former New York City mayor Michael Bloomberg proposed banning the sale of sodas over 16 ounces in city eateries. Additionally, many school districts around the country have banned the sale of soda in school vending machines.

3 These efforts appear to be paying off: latest statistics indicate that the percentage of teens who consume soda daily has fallen from 75 percent in the 1990s to 62 percent in 2009. However, most teens who abandon soda as a daily beverage replace it with other high-sugar choices, such as juice or energy and sport drinks. While many of these products have slightly less sugar than soda, the net impact of regular consumption is likely to be just as damaging in the long term. Regulating the sale of soda is a step in the right direction, but more can be done to educate young people about the dangers of a diet overflowing with sugary beverages.

5. Which of the following best describes the tone of this article?

   A. playful but informative
   B. pessimistic and sarcastic
   C. concerned but hopeful
   D. neutral and inquisitive

6. Which of the following best describes the author's point of view on reducing soda consumption?

   A. The sale of soda should be outlawed due to the beverage's negative impact on health.
   B. Consuming diet soda is healthier than consuming regular soda.
   C. A young person's decision to consume soda is a personal choice that must be respected.
   D. Young people will choose healthier beverages if they are better educated about the dangers of consumption of sugared beverages.

7. According to paragraph 3, what will likely be the "net impact" of regularly consuming juice, energy, and sport drinks instead of soda?

   A. Teenagers who consume these beverages instead of soda will avoid the health hazards associated with soda.
   B. Soda manufacturers will likely go out of business since fewer consumers will be purchasing their products.
   C. Young people who drink these beverages regularly will eventually suffer from the same ailments as those who drink soda regularly.
   D. Many of the teenagers who drink juice, energy, and sport drinks will choose healthier food options to supplement their diets.

8. According to the passage, the author most likely regards the steps to curb soda consumption described in paragraph 2 as

   A. disruptive but essential
   B. effective to some extent
   C. invasive and extreme
   D. well-intentioned but unenforceable

9. In the beginning of paragraph 3, the words "These efforts" refer to which of the following?

   A. Creating soda from carbonated water
   B. Recommending energy and sport drinks instead of soda
   C. Reducing excessive consumption of soda
   D. Increasing educational programs about the effects of soda

<u>Questions 10 through 12</u> refer to the following business document.

EXCERPTED FROM *INDEPENDENT CONSULTANT'S BROCHURE AND LETTER HANDBOOK* BY HERMAN HOLTZ

1 The National Association of Temporary Services (NATS), which represents the nation's temporary help employers, testified today before the House Ways and Means Committee on the employer mandate and related provisions of the President's Health Security Act (H.R. 3600).

2 Edward A. Lenz, NATS senior vice president, legal and government affairs, said that the temporary help industry supports the principle of universal coverage, but has serious concerns that the cost of mandates could weaken the ability of the temporary help industry to act as a "jobs bridge" to regular, full-time employment.

3 According to Lenz, the temporary help industry has recently "assumed a new and vital role—by helping to ease the burden on individuals during the current restructuring of the American work force. Temporary work offers displaced workers a critical safety net of income, benefits, and skills training and often provides a bridge back to regular, full-time employment."

4 In addition, the Association is concerned that the mandates, as currently structured, would "also impose enormous administrative burdens" due to annual temporary employee turnover in the range of 400 to 600 percent. If employer mandates are adopted, Lenz urged Congress to create a mechanism that relates premium payments to hours worked, such as a simple payroll tax.

10. Which of the following states one of the main concerns of NATS?

A. NATS won't be able to offer skills training to temporary employees if the government mandates coverage.
B. There will be an increase in turnover of temporary employees if the government mandates coverage.
C. The cost of mandated coverage will lessen the ability of NATS to hire and supply temporary workers.
D. Restructuring the work force is a burden to all Americans.

11. According to the press release, why have businesses supplying temporary help become even more necessary?

A. Many workers are losing their jobs and need temporary jobs until they find permanent work again.
B. There is not enough work for everyone to have a full-time permanent job.
C. The job turnover rate has gone as high as 400 to 600 percent.
D. More and more workers do not want permanent full-time work.

12. What is the overall purpose of this piece?

A. to stimulate debate over universal health insurance coverage
B. to impress both the Congress and the president
C. to describe various alternatives to mandated coverage
D. to raise awareness of an issue

Questions 13 through 16 refer to the following excerpt from a historical feminist speech.

EXCERPTED FROM *A TREASURY OF THE WORLD'S GREAT SPEECHES*

1 We have met here today to discuss our rights and wrongs, civil and political, and not, as some have supposed, to go into the detail of social life alone. We do not propose to petition the legislature to make our husbands just, generous, and courteous, to seat every man at the head of a cradle, and to clothe every woman in male attire. None of these points, however important they may be considered by leading men, will be touched in this convention. As to their costume, the gentlemen need feel no fear of our imitating that, for we think it in violation of every principle of taste, beauty, and dignity; notwithstanding all the contempt cast upon our loose, flowing garments, we still admire the graceful folds, and consider our costume far more artistic than theirs. Many of the nobler sex seem to agree with us in this opinion, for the bishops, priests, judges, barristers, and lord mayors of the first nation on the globe, and the Pope of Rome, with his cardinals, too, all wear the loose flowing robes, thus tacitly acknowledging that the male attire is neither dignified nor imposing. No, we shall not molest you in your philosophical experiments with stocks, pants, high-heeled boots, and Russian belts. Yours be the glory to discover, by personal experience, how long the kneepan can resist the terrible strapping down which you impose, in how short time the well-developed muscles of the throat can be reduced to mere threads by the constant pressure of the stock, how high the heel of a boot must be to make a short man tall, and how tight the Russian belt may be drawn and yet have wind enough left to sustain life.

2 But we are assembled to protest against a form of government existing without the consent of the governed—to declare our right to be free. . . .

From a speech at a women's rights convention by Elizabeth Cady Stanton, as reprinted in *A Treasury of the World's Great Speeches,* edited by Houston Peterson, New York: Simon & Schuster, 1954, 1965.

13. Which of the following best rephrases the lines "Yours be the glory to discover . . . how long the kneepad can resist the terrible strapping down which you impose" (paragraph 1)?

    A. Men do not understand how uncomfortable women's clothes are.
    B. Women will not resort to wearing pants or other restrictive men's clothing.
    C. Men will only understand women when women dress like them.
    D. Men and women will be equal only when they both wear belts and collars.

14. What is a "stock" (paragraph 1)?

    A. a man's jacket
    B. a wooden frame holding a prisoner
    C. a loose shirt
    D. a cloth worn around the neck

15. If the speaker attended a fancy tea party, which of the following would she be most likely to do?

    A. be on her best behavior
    B. speak up about current events
    C. treat the hostess like royalty
    D. comment on everyone's clothing

16. Later in the speech, Stanton states that "over the horns of bigotry and prejudice will be our way." Based on this and the excerpt, you can conclude that Stanton is giving this speech for what reason?

    A. Women are fighting for the right to vote.
    B. Women are tired of being made to wear dresses.
    C. Husbands need to be made just and generous.
    D. Many people mistakenly judge others by their appearance.

STUDY ADVICE

Don't forget to review the answers and explanations, and compare them to your own work. Doing so will give you valuable information about what kinds of mistakes you're prone to. Then you can practice to avoid those mistakes!

Analyzing Informational Text

LESSON 1

Purpose of Text

When you read HiSET Reading Test passages, it is important that you comprehend not only what the author is writing about but also the **purpose**—the reason *why* he or she is writing this passage. Authors of nonfiction passages have one or more of the following purposes:

- **Narrate**—Narrative passages typically recount events chronologically, that is, in the order in which they happened. Examples include a person's life story and hour-by-hour developments in a news story.
- **Inform**—The author seeks to present facts and data to explain a subject, situation, or idea. Examples include news articles, financial summaries, and scientific findings.
- **Persuade**—The author seeks to change readers' minds, and the passage includes the author's opinions, recommendations, or conclusions. Examples are political speeches, newspaper editorials, and entertainment reviews.
- **Entertain**—Authors writing to entertain are trying to amuse or interest their readers. Examples include a humorous memoir or articles about celebrities.

KEY IDEAS

- Writers have different reasons, or purposes, for writing.
- The main purposes for writing are to narrate a story, to inform, to persuade, and to entertain.

Read the paragraph and answer questions about the writer's purpose.

According to market research, video games sales—including digital downloads and apps—in the United States topped $15 billion in 2010. The most popular game genres were Action (21.7% of sales), Sports Games (16.3%), and Shooter (15.9%). Family Entertainment games accounted for only 9.1 percent of sales.

► What is the writer's purpose for this paragraph?
(1) to present facts about video game sales
(2) to convince readers that Family Entertainment games' sales should be increased

► Imagine there is an additional sentence at the end of the paragraph. "Because popular games in the Action and Shooter genres may contain extremely graphic violence, parents must be educated about how to monitor their children's purchases and game play." What would be the purpose of the revised paragraph about video games?
(1) to entertain readers with an amusing fact about video games
(2) to persuade parents to become more involved in their children's use of video games

HiSET EXAM TIP

As you are reading passages on the test, ask yourself, "Why did the author write this story, article, or speech?" That will help you to understand the purpose.

In the first question, choice **(1)** is correct because the writer gives facts and not persuasive information. In the second question, once the information about violence has been added, choice **(2)** is correct because the statement offers a recommendation to persuade, not entertain, parents.

After an explosion damaged critical systems on the spacecraft of the Apollo 13 mission, the three astronauts aboard were forced to make the journey back to Earth inside the Lunar Module (LM), the small vessel originally designed to land on the Moon's surface. Using the LM as a "lifeboat" provided the astronauts with enough oxygen and water for the return trip, but it also introduced a new problem: there was no way to recycle used air. To solve the problem, engineers back on Earth cataloged all of the spare parts and detachable pieces inside the Apollo modules. From these, they prototyped various devices the astronauts might use to make filters to use inside the LM. The Earth-based engineers talked the astronauts through the process of constructing and installing the make-shift filters. The engineers' quick thinking and creativity provided the astronauts with a way to maintain breathable air throughout their journey back to Earth.

1. The purpose of the paragraph above is to

A. explain how the Lunar Module worked
B. tell how creative engineers saved astronauts
C. inform about the space program's value
D. convince that engineers are essential workers

Our state should cut all sales taxes on the purchase of new automobiles to encourage buying new cars. Older cars do not run as cleanly as new vehicles and, thus, contribute to air pollution. Additionally, older cars are less safe to operate. One study estimates that last year, as many as 500 deaths or serious injuries from accidents in our state could have been prevented by the sorts of safety features that are standard on newer-model cars.

2. The writer most likely includes the fact about preventable deaths or serious injuries in automobile accidents because it

A. is the conclusion the writer is trying to prove
B. supports the writer's main recommendation
C. may shock readers into becoming safer drivers
D. will encourage legislators to cut sales taxes

<u>Questions 3 and 4</u> are based on this passage.

SILK: NOW AND THEN

Modern consumers do not appreciate the historical importance of the fabric silk. Silk fabric is valued for its smooth texture and shimmering appearance. It is also highly absorbent, making silk clothing comfortable in both high and low temperatures. Today, silk fabrics remain somewhat more expensive than cotton cloth and synthetic textiles, but many would be surprised to learn that silk was arguably the most important product in Asia and Europe for nearly 1,000 years.

Originally, sericulture—the technology of making silk cloth from silkworm cocoons—was known only in China. Around 2,000 years ago, nomads from Central Asia would travel to China to trade horses and other goods for silk cloth. As these nomads ventured West, silk became known to people in the Middle East and Europe. Over time, traders established routes over 4,000 miles long from China to Europe that became known as the Silk Road. Throughout the ancient and medieval world, silk was the preferred fabric for the robes of royalty and the very wealthy.

3. This purpose of this passage is to

A. criticize ancient peoples for overvaluing silk
B. explain how silk fabrics are made
C. entertain readers who enjoy historical travel
D. inform about the historical importance of silk

4. How does the information in the second paragraph support the purpose of the passage?

A. It illustrates why silk remains an expensive product today.
B. It refutes the notion that silk is a valuable product in the modern world.
C. It provides examples of silk's historical importance in trade and culture.
D. It compares the value of silk to that of other products from Asia.

LESSON 2

Effectiveness of Argument

KEY IDEAS

- An argument is a statement that takes a position.
- An argument consists of a conclusion about the issue and supporting evidence.
- Critically reading an argument involves understanding the stated or implied assumptions behind the claim.

HiSET EXAM TIP

On some passages, writers may use terms such as "for these reasons," "it follows that," or "therefore" to indicate their conclusion. In other cases, you may have to carefully analyze the passage to find the argument.

You may think of an argument as being a quarrel between people. However, in reading and writing, an **argument** consists of the following:

- A **conclusion** (that is, main point) about something
- The **evidence**, which is support that is given for the conclusion
- The author's **assumptions**, or ideas the author takes for granted, behind the argument

Writers should provide supporting evidence for their argument; otherwise, they are just making an unsupported claim. You may need to read carefully to **infer** their assumptions.

Read the argument below and answer the questions that follow.

In the past few years, the majority of state governments have passed laws making it illegal to send text messages while driving. These laws are clearly a good decision for which legislators should be praised. Drivers are 23 times more likely to have accidents while texting than they are while driving undistracted. It is common sense that the government has a responsibility to protect its citizens from the recklessness of a careless few.

1. What is the writer's argument about anti-texting laws?
   (1) Such laws are a good idea because drivers are prone to accidents while texting.
   (2) The majority of state governments have passed laws making it illegal to text while driving.

2. What evidence is given in support of the author's argument?
   (1) Drivers are 23 times more prone to accidents while texting.
   (2) Members of state legislatures should be praised.

3. Which of the following is likely one of the author's unstated assumptions?
   (1) Drivers must police themselves to avoid dangerous situations.
   (2) A state government should pass laws to ensure citizens' safety.

The answer to Question 1 is **(1)**. The author's opinion is that anti-texting laws are "good" and "should be praised." The rest of the argument supports that opinion. The answer to Question 2 is **(1)**. A statistic such as "23 times more likely" is typical of the factual evidence you can expect to see on the HiSET. The answer to Question 3 is **(2)**. We know that the assumption that governments should protect citizens is a premise of the author because he praises legislators for passing these laws to make roads and highways safer.

PRACTICE 2

Questions 1 through 4 refer to this passage about the minimum wage.

MAKING MINIMUM WAGE WORK FOR WORKERS

1 The minimum wage is the lowest salary that a company can legally pay its employees. The federal minimum wage is the lowest allowed in the nation, but many states have set minimum wages higher than the national number.

2 Several states have taken the sensible step of automatically raising their minimum wage to adjust for inflation and consumer price increases. This policy ensures that low-paid workers are paid a stable, livable income over the long term. Raising the federal minimum wage, however, requires direct action by lawmakers. As a result, over the past 40 years, the federal minimum wage has not kept pace with the rate of inflation. Nowadays, full-time minimum-wage workers earn so little money that many have fallen below the poverty line. In the case of the minimum wage, the federal government should follow the lead of the states. Congress needs to establish automatic wage increases triggered by increases in inflation and changes to the consumer price index. That is the only way to ensure sustainable earnings for hardworking citizens.

1. Which of the following is the main point of the passage?

A. States' minimum wages differ from the federal minimum wage.
B. The federal government should automatically raise the minimum wage to match price increases.
C. The federal minimum wage ensures a comfortable living for people earning it.
D. State minimum wages are the result of political games played with people's livelihoods.

2. What is the writer's argument about states that automatically raise their minimum wages?

A. Those states' wages have not kept pace with the rate of inflation.
B. People earning more than minimum wage in those states are wealthy.
C. Those states have many workers in poverty.
D. Those states have systems superior to the federal system of manual increases.

3. What evidence is given to support the author's argument?

A. Some states have minimum wages lower than the federal minimum wage.
B. The federal government should adjust its minimum wage automatically.
C. Over the past 40 years, the federal minimum wage has not kept pace with inflation.
D. As a result of inflation, $1 in 1972 was worth more than $5 is worth today.

4. Which of the following is most likely to be one of the author's assumptions?

A. Employees under the age of 18 might be paid less than the minimum wage.
B. Ensuring sustainable incomes for hardworking citizens is a responsibility of lawmakers.
C. Employees earning the federal minimum wage cannot support themselves and their families.
D. The past 40 years have experienced significantly higher inflation than was expected.

STUDY ADVICE

On page 96, you learned to ask yourself *why* an author wrote a passage, and you learned that sometimes authors want to persuade their readers about something. The questions on this page are about *how* an author goes about persuading her readers.

LESSON 3

Validity of Arguments

Just because a writer makes an argument does not mean you have to accept it as **valid**, or convincing. You need to analyze the supporting evidence. Below are some types of **support for arguments** and ways that you can question their legitimacy.

KEY IDEAS

- An argument may or may not be valid.
- For the argument to be valid, it needs to be supported by relevant and provable evidence.
- Critical thinking requires questioning both the method of argument and the source of supporting evidence.

Type of Support	Description	Questions to Ask
Facts	Objective facts that can be tested or measured	Is the information complete, or is it partial or selectively chosen?
Data or Statistics	Numerical data that have been gathered or sampled	Do the numbers accurately represent the subject? How were they gathered?
Examples or Anecdotes	Stories to demonstrate the "truth"	Are the stories true? Are they relevant?
Authority	Testimonials from a recognized authority	Does the person really know the issue, or is he or she a spokesperson or celebrity?
Causality	Assertions that one thing caused another	Is this really a cause, or is it just a related factor?

In addition to analyzing the evidence, you need to be aware that sometimes writers use **emotional appeals** based on fear, pity, or getting you to "jump on the bandwagon" of the argument's popularity.

HiSET EXAM TIP

When you are reading a writer's argument, don't evaluate it based on what you already believe. Think critically about whether or not the writer adequately and validly supports the argument.

Gasoline prices spiked suddenly in the Weston metropolitan area last week when the local oil refinery went offline due to a facility-wide computer malfunction. Shortly thereafter, the average number of miles driven daily by Weston residents fell by a whopping 55 percent. Clearly, the higher gas prices were responsible for the decline in miles driven.

► What is the argument in the paragraph?
(1) Higher gas prices were responsible for the decline in miles driven.
(2) The spike in gas prices was due to a computer malfunction at the local refinery.

► Which of the following undermines the writer's argument?
(1) Oil refineries have stopped production in the past.
(2) Last week, a blizzard struck the Weston area, causing a state of emergency that required all nonemergency vehicles to stay off the roads.

For the first question, choice **(1)** is correct. The writer concludes that high gas prices caused the decline in driving and uses the background about the refinery shutdown as support. For the second question, choice **(2)** is correct. The writer's argument is faulty because she assumes that the high price of gasoline was the only cause of the reduction in driving. Choice **(2)** supplies another reasonable explanation for the reduced driving, thereby weakening the argument.

Questions 1 through 4 refer to this passage about voting technology.

VOTING SYSTEMS IN THE U.S.

1 The large-scale adoption in 1996 of direct-recording electronic (DRE) voting was proclaimed as the beginning of an era of superior voting technology. For as long as elections have been held, voting systems have been flawed in various ways. In mid-18th-century America, voters called out their selections publicly. This assured an accurate count but meant voting could not be private. Paper ballots, on the other hand, were anonymous but could be easily forged or miscounted.

2 The next innovation was the mechanical-lever voting machine, introduced in the late 19th century. The use of this voting system peaked in the 1960s. Over the next several decades, the mechanical-lever machines were replaced by two early electronic voting systems: bubble sheets recorded by optical scanner and punch cards processed electronically. All of these systems were prone to glitches, such as the notorious "hanging chads" and unreadable ballots in Florida after the 2000 U.S. presidential election.

3 Now, many jurisdictions use all-electronic DRE systems. Every step of the voting process is electronic: the ballot appears on a screen, the voter indicates his or her selection via buttons or touch-screen technology, and results are stored on a memory card. In DRE voting, there is always a record of a voter's choices, and there is no chance of voters filling in the wrong bubble or of poorly punched cards that cause votes to go uncounted. For all of these reasons, DRE is clearly the most secure and accurate voting system available.

1. The main point of the passage is that

A. unlike optical-scanning and punch-card voting systems, DRE voting is completely electronic
B. punch-card voting systems caused a problem in the 2000 presidential election
C. voting systems have been developed over time to address previous systems' flaws
D. elections in America have changed greatly over the years

2. Which of the following statements, if true, is evidence to support the writer's argument?

A. When technology changes, voting systems change along with it.
B. DRE voting avoids some problems associated with other voting systems.
C. Several voting systems have become obsolete because they violated voters' privacy
D. No modern-day election would ever be conducted using a public voice vote.

3. What evidence is given to support the writer's argument?

A. DRE systems immediately record voters' choice, while other electronic systems have voters initially use a paper ballot.
B. Mechanical-lever voting machines were replaced by other mechanical voting devices.
C. Punch-card voting involves electronic processing.
D. In the mid-18th century, public votes were popular.

4. Which of the following is an example that strengthens the argument?

A. A local businessowner reported no issues using a DRE system.
B. DRE voting became popular as a result of the 2000 election glitches.
C. In 2018, some DRE voters reported difficulty marking their votes accurately due to the DRE interface or hardware.
D. Audits of elections that use DRE demonstrate this system is more accurate than paper ballots.

LESSON 4

Text Related by Theme or Topic

On the HiSET Reading Test, you may need to read related **paired passages** and answer questions based on your understanding of both of them. The two texts will be related by **topic** (what the passages address) or **theme** (the writer's message about a topic). You will need to understand each passage on its own and be able to **synthesize** (blend) information to draw a conclusion.

Below are two paragraphs about the same topic. One is a news story, and the other is an opinion piece. Read both selections and answer the questions based on your understanding and analysis of both texts.

KEY IDEAS

- The HiSET Reading Test may present two selections on a related topic or theme.
- Some questions will require comprehension and analysis of each piece on its own.
- Other questions will require a synthesis of information from the two sources.

News Story

Candy, greasy meals, and high-calorie sodas may be banned in U.S. elementary and high schools. According to news reports, new standards proposed by the Department of Agriculture would replace such items as fried potato chips with baked chips and sugary sodas with lower-calories sport drinks. These regulations are a result of a child nutrition law, passed by the U.S. Congress to combat childhood obesity.

Response Letter

The paper announced that the government will be mandating "healthier food" in school cafeterias. Doesn't the government have anything better to do than to "babysit" our schools? Shouldn't the schools be focused on improving education, not monitoring behavior? Where is the research to show that school meals account for childhood obesity? This is just one more government intrusion into our personal lives.

HiSET EXAM TIP

When you are presented with two selections, identify the main point of both passages. Doing so will help you to spot what the authors agree or disagree about.

► What is the topic of both of these selections?
  (1) greasy food in school cafeterias
  (2) new guidelines for healthy school meals

► What information is given in the news story?
  (1) The government is "babysitting" our schools.
  (2) Certain unhealthy foods may be banned from public schools.

► Which relevant argument is made in the response letter?
  (1) The new regulations are a good way to help combat childhood obesity.
  (2) The new regulations are a poor idea because monitoring student behavior is not a school's responsibility.

The correct choice in the first question is **(2)** because the news story reports on the regulations while the response letter criticizes them. In the second question, choice **(2)** is correct because it summarizes the factual information in the news story. The correct choice in the third question is **(2)** because the writer of the response letter clearly states her opposition to the new regulations.

Questions 1 through 4 refer to the paired passages below.

Passage 1

The online piracy of digital files is a major problem for the music industry. From 2004 to 2009, 30 billion songs were downloaded illegally, representing a loss of billions of dollars of revenue. Recent legislation, along with the shutdown of certain major file-sharing websites, has begun to stem the tide of piracy. The organization representing the music and recording industry, however, reports that the annual harm to the economy from piracy may be as high as $12.5 billion dollars a year. More must be done.

Passage 2

Online piracy is harmful to the music industry, but not only for the reasons the industry claims. The financial harm caused by piracy is often exaggerated. The recording industry's estimates are based on the prices of songs and the number of songs downloaded; in reality, a person who illegally downloaded 10,000 songs would download only a fraction of that number if forced to pay for each file. As a result, the actual loss of revenue caused by piracy is certainly much lower than the industry estimates. However, a fear of piracy has made investors cautious about signing new, experimental artists. That in itself is a cause for concern and a reason more needs to be done to halt illegal downloading.

---

1. The topic of both passages is

A. ways in which industries can exaggerate financial harm
B. examples of recent legislation to protect an industry
C. online piracy of music files
D. the signing of new, experimental musicians

2. The main argument of Passage 1 is that

A. new, experimental artists are necessary for the music industry to succeed
B. additional action to combat online piracy is warranted because piracy causes financial losses to the music industry
C. the shutdown of major file-sharing websites was a positive development because they contributed to $12.5 billion per year in damages
D. from 2004 to 2009, 30 billion songs were downloaded illegally

3. Which claim in Passage 2 supports the conclusion drawn in Passage 1?

A. Fear of piracy makes it difficult for new, experimental acts to get signed.
B. Recent legislation has begun to reduce the amount of online music piracy.
C. A person who downloads music illegally would likely download fewer songs if he or she had to pay for them.
D. Financial harm from illegal music downloads is often exaggerated.

4. With which of the following statements would the writers of both passages agree?

A. Online piracy of digital files has a harmful effect on the music industry.
B. Online piracy of digital files causes serious damage to the economy.
C. The main reason to combat online piracy is to ensure that new, experimental artists can find investors.
D. Music is important for a healthy society to function properly.

Analyzing Informational Text

LESSON 5

Texts with Opposing Arguments

You have learned about writers' arguments and have seen how the Reading Test may require you to work with two related texts. In some cases, you may read two selections that have **opposing arguments** about the same topic. Read the selections below and think about the authors' claims, the **assumptions** or the thinking behind their positions, and the supporting evidence for each.

KEY IDEAS

- The HiSET Reading Test may present opposing arguments on the same topic.
- Some arguments will reach different conclusions because they use different types of evidence.
- Other opposing pairs of arguments may use the same evidence but have different underlying assumptions.

Argument

Coal, the source of half the energy in the United States, has been the dirtiest of all fossil fuels because it creates harmful emissions when burned. Help is on the way with the development of new "clean coal" technologies that reduce coal's environmental impact. These new technologies purify exhaust gases as coal burns (wet scrubbers) and prevent the formation of harmful emissions in the first place (low-NO*x* burners). There is even gasification, which avoids burning coal altogether.

Opposing Argument

"Clean coal" amounts to just an advertising slogan. Don't be fooled by claims about new technologies making coal a clean-burning fuel. The hazards to our environment start well before that. Coal mining wastes huge amounts of water—70 to 260 million gallons daily. Today's mining companies now use mountaintop removal, instead of traditional mining, to extract coal. Forty-nine states have issued fish intake advisories due to high mercury concentration in water, much of it due to runoff from coal mining.

HiSET EXAM TIP

When you read two selections with opposing viewpoints, carefully analyze each writer's arguments. Don't let your opinions on the topic influence how you answer the questions.

► What is the topic of both of these selections?
(1) preventing air pollution from coal
(2) the usefulness of "clean coal" technologies

You were right to pick choice **(2)**. The Argument suggests that "clean coal" will reduce coal's environmental impact, while the Opposing Argument contends that coal will continue to harm the environment.

► What type of evidence is provided in the Argument?
(1) statistics demonstrating the effectiveness of "clean coal" technologies
(2) facts about new "clean coal" technologies

Here, choice **(2)** is correct. The Argument lists and briefly describes the new technologies.

► How does the Opposing Argument confront the underlying assumption of the Argument?
(1) It points out environmental damage caused by coal before it is burned, when "clean coal" technologies are not used.
(2) It cites studies showing that "clean coal" technologies are less effective than their advocates claim they are.

Choice **(1)** is correct. Impacts from mining, water waste, and mercury runoff are among the other harms cited in the Opposing Argument.

PRACTICE 5

Questions 1 through 4 refer to the Argument and Opposing Argument below.

ARGUMENT: Rating Systems for Movies Are Beneficial

In 1968, the Motion Picture Association of America (MPAA) replaced the complicated, morals-based Hays Code with the current, user-friendly MPAA rating system. This system is designed specifically to help parents decide whether a movie is appropriate for their child. Every parent in America knows what G, PG, PG-13, and R mean and can use these ratings to quickly judge suitability. Moreover, ratings now include descriptions that give even more information that parents can use to assess content and make wise movie-viewing decisions for their children. MPAA ratings take the guesswork out of at least one aspect of parenting!

OPPOSING ARGUMENT: Movie Rating Systems Are a Joke

A movie's MPAA rating—G, PG, PG-13, or R—is a familiar tag that parents, in particular, use to make fundamental decisions about family entertainment. Sadly, the rating system is more a marketing tool for the industry than a useful guide for parents. Consider that, in the early 1980s, unknowing parents exposed their children to alarming gore and violence under the PG rating, prompting the creation of the PG-13 rating. The result is that now, a movie that includes violence, drug use, gore, and sexual content can be marketed as a family-friendly PG-13 experience. Parents are better off finding an unbiased source of realistic reviews than trusting the MPAA rating system.

---

1. The topic of both passages is

A. violence in movies
B. good and bad parenting decisions
C. the MPAA movie rating system
D. motion picture marketing strategies

2. Which of the following is the main point of the Argument?

A. The MPAA rating system replaced the Hays Code.
B. The MPAA rating system is a useful tool for parents.
C. Parents should consult a variety of sources before deciding which movies to allow their children to watch.
D. The G, PG, PG-13, and R ratings are familiar and easy to understand.

3. The writer of the Opposing Argument would agree with which of the following statements?

A. Parents overreacted to movie content in the 1980s.
B. The PG-13 rating introduced a helpful distinction to the system.
C. Violence and drug use are examples of family-friendly movie content.
D. The MPAA rating system should not be trusted.

4. Which of the following conclusions could be drawn about the writer of the Argument?

A. She largely approves of the MPAA rating system as a guideline for parents.
B. She allows her children to watch movies rated PG but not those rated PG-13.
C. She is wary of how the MPAA rating system judges violent content in movies.
D. She believes that the Hays Code was detrimental to the movie industry.

STUDY ADVICE

How long are your study sessions? Start by studying for as long as you can easily focus on the material—which might be 15 minutes or an hour. Gradually train yourself to focus on the material for longer stretches, until your study sessions are two to three hours each. After all, you will need to maintain your focus on Test Day.

LESSON 6

Texts with Related Graphic Information

When you read nonfiction and informational text in a textbook, magazine, or website, it is often accompanied by a **graphic**—an illustration, photograph, or diagram—that helps you to understand the information. On the HiSET Reading Test, you may need to combine information from text and graphics to draw conclusions and to make observations about how the graphic supports the information in the text. Practice with the text and graphic below.

KEY IDEAS

- The HiSET Reading Test may present some selections with accompanying graphics.
- Read the passage carefully and analyze the graphic.
- Evaluate whether each question is based on the text, the graphic, or a combination of the two.

"Mayfield" No More? The Changing American Household

Although *Leave It to Beaver* was a fictional television show, many advertisements, politicians, and movies still echo its portrayal of the typical American household of the 1950s: a married couple with children. A closer look at government statistics shows that it might be time to retool that image; today, fewer than half of American households are husband-wife households. In fact, more than a quarter of American households are now occupied by one person living alone—a significant group for marketers to target, as those who live alone are entirely responsible for all household purchases.

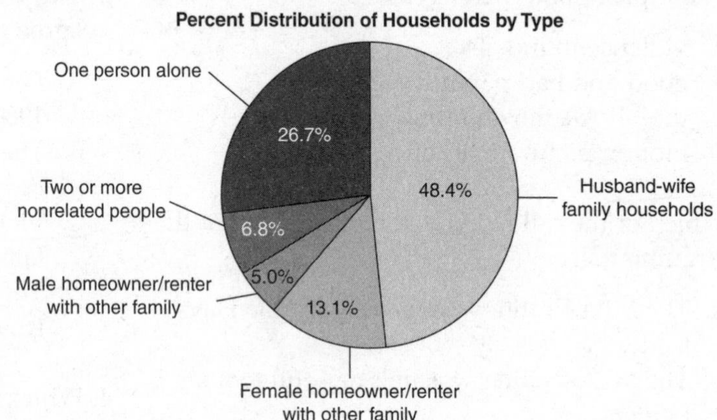

Source: U.S. Census Bureau

HiSET EXAM TIP

When you see that a graphic accompanies a selection, ask yourself, "Is this graphic providing supporting material, or is it providing additional information?" If you understand that, you will be better able to answer the test questions.

▶ What is the topic of the story and the graphic?

(1) the composition of American households
(2) advertising on *Leave It to Beaver*

If you answered **(1)**, you were correct. The story outlines the current make-up of American households, and the graphic supplies factual detail.

▶ How does the pie chart support the information in the story?

(1) It provides statistics comparing American households in the 1950s with American households today.
(2) It confirms the story's point about current household composition and provides additional details not discussed in the story.

Choice **(2)** is correct. The pie chart supplies statistics about husband-wife households (48.4%) and single-resident households (26.7%) that match the article's assertions and show the proportion of Americans living with other family and with roommates to whom they are not related.

<u>**Questions 1 through 3**</u> **refer to the following passage and the two figures below.**

Gerrymandering: An Electoral Advantage

1 The term *gerrymander* is used to describe the process by which electoral districts are given curious shapes in order to favor the interests of the party in power of a state legislature. Through this process, the governing political party tailors the electoral map to group unfavorable neighborhoods into a few districts likely to vote for the opposition while configuring the majority of districts to favor the party in power.

2 Figures 2(a) and 2(b) show how a governing political party can benefit from gerrymandering. In both figures, there are 40 gray squares and 60 white squares, and the area is divided into four equal-sized districts. In Figure 2(a), the white-square party will win only two seats out of four, but in Figure 2(b), the white-square party will take three of the four districts, as most of the gray votes are consolidated into one oddly shaped and geographically separated district. In fact, Illinois's 4th Congressional District is similar in shape to the gray district in Figure 2(b).

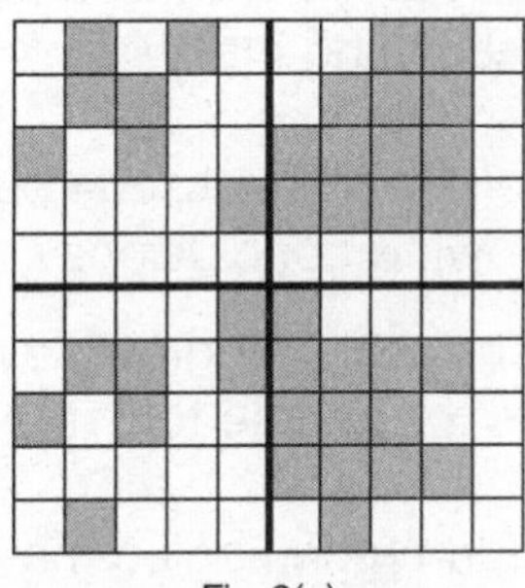

Fig. 2(a)

Geographically Uniform Districts

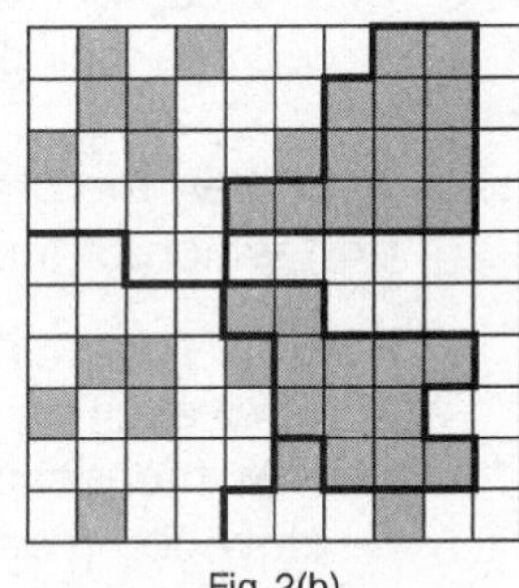

Fig. 2(b)

Gerrymandered Districts

1. Which of the following is the main point of the passage and figures?
   A. Illinois's 4th Congressional District has now been in existence for over 200 years.
   B. Curiosity is the most important ingredient in the democratic process.
   C. Gerrymandered congressional districts are a major threat to the democratic system.
   D. Governing parties can use their power to shape electoral districts to their advantage.

2. Which of the following conclusions can be drawn from the passage and the figures?
   A. Gerrymandering is more common in Illinois than in other American states.
   B. Through gerrymandering, a governing party can be elected to a greater number of seats than its voter support might otherwise allow.
   C. Through gerrymandering, impartial committees draw boundaries to keep elections fair.
   D. Gerrymandering convinces citizens who would ordinarily be unfavorable to a party to change their votes.

3. In what way do the figures support the passage?
   A. They illustrate the advantages a party can obtain through gerrymandering.
   B. They predict victory for the gray party in the upcoming election.
   C. They are more relevant to Chicago than to rural Illinois.
   D. They show that voter turnout will continue to decline if governing parties continue to gerrymander districts.

STUDY ADVICE

On the next few pages, you'll do some Analyzing Text practice questions. If you get most of them correct, pat yourself on the back! If you get several wrong, work through the lessons and practice problems again.

ANALYZING INFORMATIONAL TEXT PRACTICE QUESTIONS

Questions 1 through 4 refer to the following passage about communication technology and the accompanying cartoon.

SOCIAL NETWORKING AT WHAT COST?

1 Sit in any restaurant or coffee shop long enough, and you're bound to witness a familiar scene: a couple, a family, or a group of friends gathered to enjoy a meal, but instead of conversing, each person at the table sits staring at his or her cell phone. In this age of social media, the question arises: does technology enhance or limit our ability to make strong emotional connections with other people?

2 Social networks have broadened with the expansion of communication technology. We connect easily with new acquaintances, old friends, potential clients, and complete strangers. For loved ones who are separated by distance, technology provides an important lifeline. Soldiers, deployed for long tours of duty, meet their newborn children over video chat. Grandparents, limited by ill health, watch their grandchildren grow through pictures and videos posted to social media sites.

3 With all the benefits of social media, however, come considerable costs. Each new connection we make (and old acquaintance we maintain) demands time, energy, and emotional investment. This often comes at the expense of time we could give to the most important people in our lives. Moreover, much of what we share through social media is superficial or entertaining. Only when technology is used to enhance our deepest, most valuable connections can it be considered real progress for humankind.

"A bunch of friends are coming over to stare at their phones."

1. What is the purpose of the passage and the graphic?
   A. to discuss different forms of social media
   B. to suggest a new form of communication technology
   C. to examine ways in which modern families use technology to communicate
   D. to discuss whether communication technology helps or hurts relationships

2. What is the topic of the passage and the graphic?
   A. maintaining long-distance relationships
   B. how technology affects interpersonal connections
   C. the limits of social media
   D. the expense of new technologies

3. Which of the following details in the graphic supports the author's point of view in the passage?
   A. The caption reveals that the woman is expecting friends to visit.
   B. The woman in the cartoon is speaking on the phone with a computer nearby.
   C. The woman in the cartoon is alone.
   D. The caption reveals that the woman's friends will use their phones during their visit.

4. Together, the graphic and the passage support which of the following conclusions?
   A. New communication technologies may offer exciting ways for people to establish new friendships.
   B. New communication technologies may adversely impact important human relationships.
   C. New communication technologies may offer positive solutions for friends who are separated by distance.
   D. New communication technologies may help people to complete several tasks at once.

<u>Questions 5 through 8</u> refer to this passage about the giant squid.

THE GIANT SQUID: MORE THAN COLOSSAL?

1 The giant squid is the world's longest cephalopod. Based on measurements of over 100 full specimens (including adult and adolescent individuals) recovered from the stomachs of sperm whales and other predators, scientists have determined that the giant squid can reach a length of 13 meters.

2 Some have argued that the honor of longest cephalopod should instead go to the colossal squid, a distant relative of the giant squid, but this belief is incorrect. It is true that the colossal squid may outweigh its giant cousin. However, of the few specimens of the colossal squid (all of them juveniles) described in the scientific literature, the longest measured ten meters. Therefore, the giant squid wins the length contest.

3 No other cephalopod is even close in length to either of these animals. For example, the giant Pacific octopus, the world's longest octopus species, has a maximum arm span of only about six meters. The giant squid's status as the world's longest cephalopod remains uncontested.

5. The main point of the passage is that

   A. the colossal squid weighs more than the giant squid
   B. the giant squid is the world's longest cephalopod
   C. the giant Pacific octopus is the world's longest octopus species
   D. the giant squid can reach a length of 13 meters

6. Which of the following best summarizes the writer's argument in paragraph 2?

   A. The colossal squid is the world's longest cephalopod.
   B. The colossal squid is a distant relative of the giant squid.
   C. The giant Pacific octopus is not as long as the giant squid.
   D. The giant squid is longer than the colossal squid.

7. What evidence is given to support the writer's argument in paragraph 2?

   A. The colossal squid can weigh more than the giant squid.
   B. The giant squid is the world's longest cephalopod.
   C. The length of the longest known colossal squid specimen is ten meters.
   D. The giant Pacific octopus has a maximum arm span of only about six meters.

8. Which of the following is an example of faulty reasoning that weakens the writer's argument?

   A. The longest known colossal squid is ten meters long, so there is no colossal squid longer than the longest giant squid.
   B. The giant Pacific octopus is the world's longest species of octopus, but it is not as long as the giant squid.
   C. Many specimens of the giant squid have been measured.
   D. Because sperm whales prey on giant squid, they must also prey on colossal squid.

<u>Questions 9 through 15</u> **refer to these two passages about mercury.**

Passage 1

1 The use of mercury amalgam for dental fillings has already been banned in several European nations, and it should also be banned in the United States. The mercury contained in amalgam fillings slowly leaches into the mouth and is swallowed. It is then absorbed by the small intestine and accumulates in various body tissues, including the brain, kidney, and liver. In 2001, a study reported that patients with a higher number of amalgam fillings also had higher occurrences of cancer, respiratory disease, and diseases of the nervous system. Therefore, it is clear that this accumulated mercury causes a variety of health problems.

2 In addition to its health impact, the mercury released from dental amalgam has a number of damaging environmental consequences. Mercury waste produced by dental offices is sometimes directly disposed of into sewage water or landfills. Mercury can leach from landfills into groundwater and get into rivers and lakes. It has been estimated, for example, that dental amalgam is the source of 4 percent of the mercury found in the water of Lake Superior.

3 Due to the alarming health and environmental consequences of mercury amalgam, dental fillings should be made from resin composites instead. These composites are already becoming popular due to their cosmetic appeal, so banning mercury amalgam will create no consumer backlash. There are demonstrable advantages (and no disadvantages) to banning mercury dental amalgam in the United States.

Passage 2

1 In recent years, uneducated consumers have expressed a growing fear of the mercury commonly found in dental fillings. The environmental impact of mercury is serious, and the release of mercury into the environment must be better controlled. However, the health risks associated with mercury amalgam fillings are minimal.

2 It is well-known that people who have mercury amalgam fillings absorb small amounts of mercury. However, most of this mercury is excreted in the urine. To date, no convincing scientific study has demonstrated that mercury absorbed from dental fillings causes any serious health problems. Because mercury amalgam fillings tend to last longer than resin composite fillings, amalgam is preferable for use whenever there is no cosmetic need for a tooth-colored filling.

3 However, the disposal of mercury amalgam in dental offices absolutely must be regulated. The Environmental Protection Agency estimates that 40 to 50 percent of the mercury in the wastewater processed at public treatment plants comes from dental amalgam. This is inexcusable, especially because devices that remove mercury from wastewater are inexpensive and easy for dental offices to use. While mercury amalgam should remain available because it is more durable than composites, every dental office must have a device to remove mercury from wastewater.

9. The topic of both passages is

   A. groundwater contamination
   B. mercury dental amalgam
   C. resin composite fillings
   D. dental health risks

10. What is the main argument of Passage 1?

   A. Mercury amalgam fillings are not unhealthy, but their disposal should be regulated for environmental reasons.
   B. Resin composite should replace mercury amalgam for dental fillings because it tends to last longer.
   C. Mercury amalgam fillings should be banned because they are unhealthy and bad for the environment.
   D. Mercury dental amalgam leaches mercury into a patient's mouth and can damage the liver.

11. Which statement best describes the supporting evidence in paragraph 3 of Passage 2?

   A. It appears convincing at first glance, but no source is cited.
   B. It is a seemingly convincing statistic, but the source is untrustworthy.
   C. It is an unconvincing statistic from an untrustworthy source.
   D. It is a convincing statistic from a reliable source.

12. In paragraph 3, the author of Passage 1 states that "These composites are already becoming popular due to their cosmetic appeal, so banning mercury amalgam will create no consumer backlash." Which of the following is an assumption the author of Passage 1 makes about consumers?

   A. Consumers have no other reason, such as cost or durability, to prefer mercury amalgam to composite fillings.
   B. Consumers will be happy with whatever material they are offered for dental fillings.
   C. Consumers are not generally vocal about their preferences.
   D. Consumers never discuss the choice of filling material with their dentists.

13. The writer of Passage 2 would be most likely to agree with which of the following statements?

   A. Mercury amalgam fillings should be banned because they are unhealthy.
   B. Resin composite fillings look better than mercury amalgam fillings when each is used on visible tooth surfaces.
   C. Mercury contamination of public wastewater is an unimportant issue.
   D. Resin composite fillings are preferable to mercury amalgam in all cases.

14. Which of the passages has weaker supporting evidence and why?

   A. Passage 1, because it cites no sources for the study or the statistic it cites
   B. Passage 1, because it argues that mercury should be banned in dental fillings
   C. Passage 2, because it cites the Environmental Protection Agency as the source of a statistic it cites
   D. Passage 2, because it argues that mercury used by dental offices should be better regulated

15. The information presented in Passage 2 suggests that Passage 1 includes which of the following examples of faulty reasoning?

   A. Resin composites are already gaining in popularity.
   B. The use of mercury dental amalgam has already been banned in several European nations.
   C. The mercury released from dental amalgam has damaging environmental consequences.
   D. Mercury that accumulates in body tissues causes a variety of health problems.

LESSON 1

Plot Elements

Plot refers to the events in a story. Generally, the events are told in order—what happened first, next, and so on. Understanding the order of events, the sequence, can help you see which events caused or affected others.

A story usually contains at least one **conflict**, or problem. The conflict may be between characters, within a character, or between a character and nature. Conflict creates tension. When it is resolved, the tension ends.

The following excerpt is about a brother and sister whose mother has a tumor. As you read it, look for the order of events and the conflict.

Robert didn't phone until evening. His voice was fatigued and thin. "I've moved her to the university hospital," he said. "They can't deal with it at home."

Kate waited, saying nothing. She concentrated on the toes of her shoes. They needed shining. *You never take care of anything,* her mother would say.

"She has a tumor in her head." He said it firmly, as though Kate might challenge him.

"I'll take a plane tomorrow morning," Kate answered, "I'll be there by noon."

Robert exhaled. "Look," he said, "don't even come back here unless you can keep your mouth shut and do it my way."

"Get to the point."

"The point is they believe she has a malignancy and we're not going to tell her. I almost didn't tell you." His voice faltered. "They're going to operate but if they find what they're expecting, they don't think they can stop it."

For a moment there was no sound except an oceanic vibration of distance on the wire. Even that sound grew still. Robert breathed. Kate could almost see him, in a booth at the hospital, staring straight ahead at the plastic instructions screwed to the narrow rectangular body of the telephone. It seemed to her that she was hurtling toward him.

From "Souvenir" by Jayne Anne Phillips, from *Black Tickets,* NY: Delacorte Press, 1979. Reprinted with permission of Jayne Anne Phillips.

► When did Robert decide not to tell his mother about the tumor?
(1) before talking to Kate
(2) after discussing the issue with Kate

(1) is correct. Robert has already decided what to do when he calls Kate.

► Which of the following identifies a conflict in this excerpt?
(1) Kate tells Robert she will fly there tomorrow.
(2) Robert tells Kate that she must do as he says.

(2) is correct. Robert challenges Kate. That creates tension.

KEY IDEAS

- The plot is the series of events in a story. Understanding the order of the events helps you see how they are related.
- The conflict is a problem between characters, between a character and nature, or within a character.

HiSET EXAM TIP

To understand the events and conflict in a story, pay attention to the dialogue. Remember that every time the speaker changes, a new paragraph begins.

PRACTICE 1

Questions 1 through 4 refer to the following excerpt from a short story.

EXCERPTED FROM "THE PIECE OF STRING"

1 The countryman looked at the Mayor in astonishment, already terrified by this suspicion resting on him without his knowing why.

2 "Me? Me? I picked up the pocket-book?"

3 "Yes, you, yourself."

4 "On my word of honor, I never heard of it."

5 "But you were seen."

6 "I was seen, me? Who says he saw me?"

7 "Monsieur Malandain, the harness-maker."

8 The old man remembered, understood, and flushed with anger.

9 "Ah, he saw me, the clodhopper, he saw me pick up this string, here, Mayor." And rummaging in his pocket he drew out the little piece of string.

10 But the Mayor, incredulous, shook his head.

11 "You will not make me believe, Maître Hauchecorne, that Monsieur Malandain, who is a man we can believe, mistook this cord for a pocket-book."

12 The peasant, furious, lifted his hand, spat at one side to attest his honor, repeating:

13 "It is nevertheless God's own truth, the sacred truth. I repeat it on my soul and my salvation."

14 The Mayor resumed:

15 "After picking up the object, you stood like a stilt, looking a long while in the mud to see if any piece of money had fallen out."

16 The old fellow choked with indignation and fear. . . .

17 He was confronted with Monsieur Malandain, who repeated and maintained his affirmation. They abused each other for an hour. At his own request, Maître Hauchecorne was searched. Nothing was found on him.

18 Finally the Mayor, very much perplexed, discharged him with the warning that he would consult the Public Prosecutor and ask for further orders.

1. What was the peasant doing when he "lifted his hand, spat at one side to attest his honor" (paragraph 12)?

A. thinking of striking the Mayor
B. swearing that he was telling the truth
C. pleading to the Mayor for mercy
D. performing a peasant ritual

2. How did the peasant react when confronted with Malandain, the harness-maker?

He

A. became choked with fear and indignation
B. tried to explain what had actually happened
C. became respectful and subdued
D. confronted him and then asked to be searched

3. Which of the following statements best describes the conflict in this excerpt?

A. A town mayor is abusing his authority.
B. A peasant leads a harsh life and is often at odds with others.
C. A peasant is accused of taking a pocketbook.
D. Someone has lost a pocketbook with a great deal of money in it.

4. What is the most likely reason the harnessmaker is believed?

A. A string can't be mistaken for a pocketbook.
B. The peasant was looking in the mud for money.
C. The harness-maker is higher in social status than the peasant.
D. Other people saw the peasant pick up a pocketbook.

LESSON 2

Inferences

To understand a story, you can't just rely on what is directly stated. You also need to "read between the lines," or make **inferences**. An inference is based on information you are given *plus* what you have learned about the real world—the way things happen and the way people act.

KEY IDEAS

- To understand a story, you must make inferences.
- Making inferences means that you look closely at the details in the story, think about your knowledge of the real world, and then ask yourself, "What does this information point to?"

As you read this excerpt from a story, look for suggested meanings behind people's actions and words.

> "Last night?" The old blue eyes looked blank, then brightened. "Ah no, I must have taken one of my Seconals. Otherwise I'd have heard it surely. 'Auntie,' my niece always says—'what if there should be a fire, and you there sleeping away?' Do what she says, I do sometimes, only to hear every pin drop till morning." She shook her head, entering the elevator. "Going up?"
>
> "N-no," said Mrs. Hazlitt. "I—have to wait here for a minute." She sat down on the bench, the token bench that she had never seen anybody sitting on, and watched the car door close on the little figure still shaking its head, borne upward like a fairy godmother, willing but unable to oblige. The car's hum stopped, then its light glowed on again. Someone else was coming down. . . .
>
> The car door opened. "Wssht!" said Miss Finan, scuttling out again. "I've just remembered. Not last night, but two weeks ago. And once before that. A scream, you said?"
>
> Mrs. Hazlitt stood up. Almost unable to speak, for the tears that suddenly wrenched her throat, she described it.

From "The Scream on Fifty-Seventh Street" by Hortense Calisher, from *Tales for the Mirror,* reprinted in *Women and Fiction,* edited by Susan Cahill, New York: New American Library, 1975.

HiSET EXAM TIP

Do not leave a question unanswered. If you read a tough question, do your best to think about it, look back at the passage for information you may need, and then choose the best answer.

▶ What happened before the beginning of this excerpt?

(1) Mrs. Hazlitt heard a scream the night before and asked Miss Finan if she heard it, too.

(2) Mrs. Hazlitt asked Miss Finan about her health and whether she is sleeping well.

The correct answer is **(1).** You can infer it from details such as "Last night?" and "Not last night, but two weeks ago. And once before that. A scream, you said?"

▶ What is the most likely reason that "tears suddenly wrenched" Mrs. Hazlitt's throat?

(1) She was upset at Miss Finan's inability to remember.

(2) She was relieved that Miss Finan had heard a scream, too.

You are correct if you chose **(2).** Mrs. Hazlitt is so relieved that someone else heard the scream that she has to fight back tears.

PRACTICE 2

Questions 1 through 4 refer to the following excerpt from a short story.

EXCERPTED FROM "THE STORY OF AN HOUR"

1 [Louise] knew that she would weep again when she saw [her husband's] kind, tender hands folded in death; the face that had never looked save with love upon her, fixed and gray and dead. But she saw beyond that bitter moment a long procession of years to come that would belong to her absolutely. And she opened and spread her arms out to them in welcome.

2 There would be no one to live for during those coming years; she would live for herself. There would be no powerful will bending her in that blind persistence with which men and women believe they have a right to impose a private will upon a fellow creature. A kind intention or a cruel intention made the act seem no less a crime as she looked upon it in that brief moment of illumination.

3 And yet she had loved him—sometimes. Often she had not. What did it matter! What could love, the unsolved mystery, count for in face of this possession of self-assertion, which she suddenly recognized as the strongest impulse of her being!

4 "Free! Body and soul free!" she kept whispering. . . .

5 Some one was opening the front door with a latchkey. It was [her husband] Brently Mallard who entered, a little travel-stained, composedly carrying his grip-sack and umbrella. He had been far from the scene of accident, and did not even know there had been one. He stood amazed at [her sister] Josephine's piercing cry; at Richards' quick motion to screen him from the view of his wife.

6 But Richards was too late.

7 When the doctors came they said she had died of heart disease—of joy that kills.

From "The Story of an Hour" by Kate Chopin.

1. How did Brently Mallard generally feel toward his wife?

He

A. had always loved her
B. kept her at arm's length
C. liked to play practical jokes on her
D. had cruel intentions toward her

2. Which detail best expresses Louise's vision of her future?

A. that bitter moment
B. she'd weep again
C. spread her arms out in welcome
D. blind persistence

3. What was the doctors' meaning when they said that Louise died of "joy that kills" (paragraph 7)?

They thought that

A. she was overcome and thrilled to see her husband
B. she was excited about her upcoming life of freedom
C. her heart was worn out from giving so much love
D. her heart was weakened from the strain of living

4. Why did Louise die?

A. She was overcome with relief.
B. She was shocked that she would not be free.
C. She was confused by feelings of love and hate.
D. She thought there would be no one to live for.

STUDY ADVICE

As you're getting settled into your study schedule, remember to build in rewards and breaks. Celebrate a job well done with a fun outing. Commemorate your successes in practice with a study partner or with your cheering section (family or friends). You need these moments to build confidence, which is a necessary component of success.

LESSON 3

Character

Characters are the people who inhabit a story. The personalities and motivations of characters are often stated directly by the **narrator**—the person telling the story. Sometimes you can also infer characters' personalities or motivations by what they do, what they think, and what they say.

As you read this excerpt, look for details that describe each character.

> Axel Olsen was going to paint Helga Crane. Not only was he going to paint her, but he was to accompany her and her aunt on their shopping expedition. Aunt Katrina was frankly elated. Uncle Poul was also visibly pleased. Evidently they were not above kow-towing to a lion. Helga's own feelings were mixed; she was amused, grateful, and vexed. It had all been decided and arranged without her, and, also, she was a little afraid of Olsen. His stupendous arrogance awed her.
>
> The day was an exciting, not easily to be forgotten one. Definitely, too, it conveyed to Helga her exact status in her new environment. A decoration. A curio. A peacock. Their progress through the shops was an event; an event for Copenhagen as well as for Helga Crane. Her dark, alien appearance was to most people an astonishment. Some stared surreptitiously, some openly, and some stopped dead in front of her in order more fully to profit by their stares. "*Den Sorte*" dropped freely, audibly, from many lips.
>
> The time came when she grew used to the stares of the population. And the time came when the population of Copenhagen grew used to her outlandish presence and ceased to stare. But at the end of that first day it was with thankfulness that she returned to the sheltering walls of the house on Maria Kirkplads.

From "Quicksand" by Nella Larsen, in *The Norton Anthology of African American Literature,* edited by Henry Louis Gates, Jr., and Nellie Y. McKay, New York: W.W. Norton, 1997.

▶ Which of the following describes Helga?

(1) attractive, down-to-earth, embarking on a new life
(2) self-centered, smug, enjoys being watched

Choice **(1)** is correct. An artist is painting her, suggesting she is attractive. Yet she prefers not to be the center of attention (see the end of the last paragraph).

▶ Which of the following would Olsen most likely do at a party?

(1) snub the hostess if the wine was below his expectations
(2) offer to drive anyone home who needed a ride

Choice **(1)** is correct. Apply what you know about people with "stupendous arrogance" (see the end of the first paragraph) to answer this question.

KEY IDEAS

- Characters are the people in the story.
- You can understand a character by noting what the narrator tells you directly as well as by inferring from the character's appearance, actions, words, and thoughts.

HiSET EXAM TIP

A common kind of question asks you to choose how a character would act in a different situation, based on what you know about the character's personality.

PRACTICE 3

Questions 1 through 3 refer to the following excerpt from a story.

EXCERPTED FROM "HIZAKURIGE"

1 "I shall never forget it," the witch went on. "When you were ill you gave your sickness to me. Our only child, who had to carry on our name, grew weak and thin because there was no rice to fill his empty stomach. Every day the bill collectors were knocking at the door and the rent remained unpaid. Yet I did not complain—not even when I slipped in the dogs' dirt in the lane."

2 "Don't talk of it," said Yaji. "You'll break my heart."

3 "And then, when through my labors I had saved enough money to buy a kimono, I had to pawn it for your sake and never saw it again. Never again did it come back to me from the pawnbroker's."

4 "At the same time you must remember what a pleasant place you are in now," said Yaji, "while I have to worry along down here."

5 "What? What is there pleasant about it? It is true that by the help of your friends you erected a stone over my grave, but you never go near it, and you never contribute to the temple to get the priests to say prayers for my soul. I am nothing to you. The stone over my grave has been taken away and put into the wall, where all the dogs come and make water against it. Not a drop of water is ever placed on my grave. Truly in death we suffer all sorts of troubles."

6 "True, true," said Yaji.

7 "But while you thus treat me with neglect," the witch went on, "lying in my grave I think of nobody but you and long for the time when you will join me in the underworld. Shall I come to meet you?"

8 "No, no, don't do that," said Yaji. "It's really too far for you."

9 "Well then, I have one request to make."

10 "Yes, yes. What is it?"

11 "Give this witch plenty of money."

12 "Of course, of course."

13 "How sad the parting!" cried the witch. "I have yet much to tell you, countless questions to ask you, but the messenger of Hell recalls me!"

14 Then, recovering from her trance, the witch twanged her bow.

From "Hizakurige" by Jippensha Ikku in *The Longwood Introduction to Fiction*, Boston: Allyn and Bacon, 1992.

1. Why does Yaji say, "No, no, don't do that . . . It's really too far for you" (paragraph 8)?

A. He is trying to be more considerate than he had been in the past.
B. He is reluctant to see the ghost of his wife.
C. He has no real interest in seeing his wife again.
D. His wife can't really travel to him anyway.

2. Which of the following is the best description of the witch?

A. caring
B. unconvincing
C. untrustworthy
D. thoughtful

3. Earlier in the story, the witch, speaking as Yaji's wife, says, "Ah, what agony I went through when I was married to you—time and again suffering the pangs of hunger and shivering with cold in the winter."

Based on this information and the excerpt, what kind of husband did Yaji seem to be?

A. angry
B. kind-hearted
C. responsible
D. neglectful

LESSON 4

Theme

Every story has a subject. The subject might be about fighting a war or growing up in poverty. But there is more to a story than its subject. As a reader, look for what the author is trying to say about the subject. That is the **theme**—the message the author wants the reader to understand. In fiction, the theme is often a statement about life. For example, the theme might be that fighting in a war changes a person's life forever.

The theme may be directly stated. If it is not, you can infer the theme from the characters' thoughts and actions and from the things that happen in the story.

As you read the following excerpt, ask yourself what message about the people and their lives the author is trying to tell you.

> While the boys were getting the Doctor's horse, he went to the window to examine the house plants. "What do you do to your geraniums to keep them blooming all winter, Mary? I never pass this house that from the road I don't see your windows full of flowers."
>
> She snapped off a dark red one, and a ruffled new green leaf, and put them in his buttonhole. "There, that looks better. You look too solemn for a young man, Ed. Why don't you git married? I'm worried about you. . . ."
>
> Sometimes the Doctor heard the gossipers in the drugstore wondering why Rosicky didn't get on faster. He was industrious, and so were his boys, but they were rather free and easy, weren't pushers, and they didn't always show good judgment. They were comfortable, they were out of debt, but they didn't get much ahead. Maybe, Doctor Burleigh reflected, people as generous and warmhearted and affectionate as the Rosickys never got ahead much; maybe you couldn't enjoy your life and put it into the bank, too.

From "Neighbor Rosicky" by Willa Cather, from *Obscure Destinies*.

▶ Which of the following statements is the theme of the story?
(1) A good life is measured in terms of love, not money.
(2) People should not gossip about others.

You are correct if you chose **(1).** Doctor Burleigh's thoughts at the end of the excerpt help you understand that this is the author's main message.

▶ Which of the following details supports the theme?
(1) Mary Rosicky lovingly "worries" about the doctor.
(2) The Rosickys keep out of debt.

Again, you are correct if you chose **(1).** The flowers Mary grows, the fact that she snaps off one to give the doctor, and her expressed concern for him all show her warmth and happiness. They help support the theme that the doctor reflects on.

KEY IDEAS

- The subject of a story is what the story is about.
- The theme of a story is different from the subject. The theme goes beyond the subject and expresses a point of view about life.

HiSET EXAM TIP

Read the whole passage carefully but not too slowly before you begin to answer the questions. If you read a question that really stumps you, skip it and go on. You can come back to it.

PRACTICE 4

Questions 1 through 5 refer to the following excerpt from a short story.

EXCERPTED FROM *GONE FISHIN'*

1 Early morning is the best time. You're fully rested but not awake enough to remember how hard it all is. Morning is like being a child again, and morning before the sun is out is like those magic times that you hid under the bed and in between the clothes hanging in your mother's closet. Times when any kind of miracle could come about just as normal as a spider making her web.

2 I remember waking up in the dark once when I was very small. I jumped right out of bed and went up next to the screen door on the back porch to see what kind of fantastic thing was going on outside. At first I couldn't see anything but there was a clopping sound, nickering, and a deep voice that made me feel calm and wondering. Slowly, coming out from the darkness, I saw a gray shimmering next to a tall black pillar. The shimmer turned into a big horse and the pillar became my father holding out an apple and cooing in his bass voice, "Ho! Yeah, boy," even though the horse was tame and eating from his hand.

3 I drifted into sleep thinking that we were poor and didn't own a horse. When I woke up it was light and there was no horse to be seen. I asked my father about it but he told me that I was dreaming—where were poor people like us going to find big gray stallions?

4 But there were horse chips behind the barn and hoofprints too.

5 I decided that it was a magic horse and man that I'd seen. From that day on I believed that magic hides in the early morning. If you get up early enough you might find something so beautiful that it would be all right if you just died right then because nothing else in life could ever be better.

From *Gone Fishin'* by Walter Mosley, Baltimore: Black Classic Press, 1997.

1. In the story, the boy __________ after hearing his father's explanation.

   A. feels confused
   B. finds a new explanation
   C. no longer trusts his father
   D. tries to convince his father

2. Which of the following is the best description of the boy?

   A. hard-hearted
   B. imaginative
   C. skeptical
   D. chatty

3. What is the most likely reason the boy decides he saw a magic horse and man?

   A. He wants to reconcile what he saw with what his father told him.
   B. He enjoys magic and likes to make up stories.
   C. He wants to prove his father was mistaken.
   D. This kind of miracle can happen.

4. Which of the following would the father probably enjoy most?

   A. daydreaming about the future
   B. having enough money to pay some bills
   C. keeping his son's hopes up about getting a new bicycle for his birthday
   D. sharing ghost stories around a campfire

5. Which of the following statements fits the theme of this story?

   A. False hopes will not get you anywhere.
   B. Dreams really can come true.
   C. Adults cannot see what children see.
   D. Morning and youth are full of possibility.

STUDY ADVICE

Remember, you'll be able to work on more questions at the end of this chapter. So, if you are struggling with a topic and don't feel you have more time to spend on it right now, flag it for later! Keeping a good list of what you should come back to is important in organizing your study plan.

LESSON 5

Style and Point of View

Style

A writer has many choices when deciding how to write a story. A writer may use long, complex sentences; short, clipped sentences; or anything in between. A writer may use flowery or formal language, slang, or spoken dialect. One writer may use vivid images or symbols, while another writes a plain, spare story. The individual characteristics that a writer chooses—sentence structure, choice of words, use of images, and other devices—are all part of the writer's **style.**

KEY IDEAS

- The style of a piece of writing is determined by the choices a writer makes in words, sentence structure, images, and other devices.
- A story is written from a narrator's point of view. The narrator may be an "outsider" or a character who can reveal only what he or she sees and thinks.

As you read this excerpt, look for the characteristics that this particular author chose. Ask yourself what effect they have on your understanding of the writing.

> The only part of the night I recall without feeling anger or sadness is loading the horses. Andy and I hardly had the fencing up before Brett came along with the first ten or twelve. . . . A couple of roans and an Appaloosa stood out in that first bunch in the starlight, and a bay with a roached mane. Then Ed brought up a second bunch, about fifteen mostly dark but a palomino and two paints in there, I remember. Andy and I shooed them up the ramp, which clattered and thundered under their hooves. It was a cool night, still. I could feel the horses on my skin, their body heat swirling around us. I could . . . hear their nostrils fluttering. I felt hard muscle ripple under my hand when I clapped a hip to steer them around. I felt their tails slap my back, and caught a glint in their bared eyes.

From "Stolen Horses" by Barry Lopez, from *Writers Harvest 3,* edited by Tobias Wolff, copyright © 2000 by Share Our Strength. Used by permission of Dell Publishing, a division of Random House, Inc.

HiSET EXAM TIP

You will not have to identify and use terms such as third person *and* first person, *but you should be able to understand and appreciate the effect of the writers' choices.*

► What is the effect of the author's description of the horses?
  (1) It creates a depth of feeling for the horses' vitality.
  (2) It provides insight into what the characters are doing.

You are correct if you chose **(1).** The vivid, descriptive details allow you to imagine the horses and sense their vitality and strength.

Point of View

Another choice a writer makes is which **point of view** to write from. Will the narrator be outside the story, watching and revealing the characters' actions and perhaps even their thoughts and feelings? If so, the writer will use *third person* point of view. Or will the narrator be a character in the story, able to report only what he or she thinks? In that case, the writer will use *first person* point of view.

► Which of the following indicates that the narrator is a character and so we can know only his thoughts?
  (1) "The only part of the night I recall . . ."
  (2) "Then Ed brought up a second bunch . . ."

(1) is correct. The narrator tells his own thoughts. A clue is the word *I.*

PRACTICE 5

Questions 1 through 4 refer to the following excerpt from a short story called "Coach."

EXCERPTED FROM *AN AMATEUR'S GUIDE TO THE NIGHT*

1 "This apartment your mom found is like an office or something. A studio for her to go to and get away every now and then. . . ."

2 "She wants to get away from us," Daphne said.

3 "Definitely not. She gave me a list, is how this whole thing started. She's got stuff she wants to do, and you with your school problems and me with the team—we're too much for her, see? She could spend her entire day on us, if you think about it, and never have one second for herself. If you think about it fairly, Daphne, you'll agree." . . .

4 She made a sigh and marched over to a trash can to deposit her slumping cone. Then she washed up at the children's drinking fountain and rejoined Coach, who had finished his Brown Cow but had kept the plastic spoon in the mouth.

5 "What was on this list of Mom's?" Daphne asked.

6 "Adult stuff," Coach said.

7 "Just give me an example."

8 Coach removed the plastic spoon and cracked it in half.

9 "Your mother's list is for five years. In that time, she wants to be speaking French regularly. She wants to follow up on her printmaking."

10 "This is adult stuff?" Daphne said.

11 Coach raised a hand to Bobby Stark. Stark had three malt cups in a cardboard carrier and he was moving toward the parking lot.

12 "Hey, those all for you?" Coach called out.

13 "I got a month to get fat, Coach. You'll have five months to beat it off me," the boy called back.

14 The people at some of the tables around Coach's lit up with grins. Bobby Stark's parents were grinning.

15 "Every hit of that junk takes a second off your time in the forty—just remember that!" Coach shouted.

16 Stark wagged his head ruefully, his cheeks blushing. He pretended to hide the malts behind his arm.

1. What is Bobby Stark's attitude?

A. He worries about his weight problem.
B. He takes things in stride.
C. He is looking forward to the sports season.
D. He feels unfairly criticized by the coach.

2. Because of the narrator's point of view, what does the reader know?

A. only Bobby Stark's actions
B. thoughts and feelings of the characters
C. the actions and speech of the characters
D. only Daphne's thoughts and feelings

3. Through their dialogue, what kind of relationship can you conclude the characters have with each other?

A. informal
B. tense
C. suspicious
D. deteriorating

4. Later in the story, Coach has this discussion with his wife, Sherry: "'It's like my apartment,' Sherry said. 'A place apart.' Coach cut her off. 'Don't go on about how much you love your apartment.'"

Based on this information and the excerpt, which of the following best describes Coach in his discussion with Daphne?

A. brutally frank
B. angry and hostile
C. loving and warm
D. not entirely honest about his feelings

LESSON 6

Figurative Language

Figurative language refers to words that are being used to mean something other than their actual, literal meaning. Writers and poets use figurative language to help paint a mental picture in the reader's mind. Instead of saying, "His voice was soothing and pleasing," for example, a writer might say, "His voice was like velvet."

Figurative language often compares two different things. Sometimes the comparison is signaled by the words *like* or *as,* but not always. A writer might also say, "His voice was velvet." Another favorite technique of writers and poets is to give a human characteristic to something nonhuman, such as, "The wind sighed."

As you read this poem, look for figurative language and what it might mean.

The School Children

The children go forward with their little satchels.
And all morning the mothers have labored
to gather the late apples, red and gold,
like words of another language.

And on the other shore
are those who wait behind great desks
to receive these offerings.

How orderly they are—the nails
on which the children hang
their overcoats of blue or yellow wool.

And the teachers shall instruct them in silence
and the mothers shall scour the orchards for a way out,
drawing to themselves the gray limbs of the fruit trees
bearing so little ammunition.

From "The House on Marshland" from *The First Four Books* by Louise Gluck. Copyright 1968, 1971, 1972, 1973, 1974, 1975, 1976, 1977, 1978, 1980, 1985, 1995.

► What is suggested by comparing apples to "words of another language" in the fourth line?

(1) a sense of strangeness, not a part of one's world
(2) useless things that have no meaning

You are correct if you chose **(1).** A language different from your own can seem strange and removed. The mothers feel removed from the world of teachers and schoolchildren.

► What does the word "shore" in the fifth line refer to?

(1) the other side of an ocean
(2) the world of the classroom

You are correct if you chose **(2).** The mothers in the poem think of school as far away from them.

KEY IDEAS

- Fiction writers and poets use figurative language—words that do not have their literal meaning—to compare different things.
- Some comparisons are introduced by *like* or *as*; others are not. Some comparisons give human characteristics to nonhuman things.

HiSET EXAM TIP

You are not penalized for wrong answers on the HiSET exam, so do not leave any answers blank. If you return to a skipped multiple-choice question and still cannot determine the answer, narrow the choices to the two most reasonable and then select the one that makes the most sense.

PRACTICE 6

Questions 1 through 5 refer to the following poem.

EXCERPTED FROM "DÉJEUNER SUR L'HERBE" ("LUNCH ON THE GRASS")

1 It's pleasant to board the ferry in the sunscape
As the late light slants into afternoon;
The faint wind ruffles the river, rimmed with foam.
We move through the aisles of bamboo
Towards the cool water-lilies.

2 The young dandies drop ice into the drinks,
While the girls slice the succulent lotus root.
Above us, a patch of cloud spreads, darkening
Like a water-stain on silk.

3 *Write this down quickly, before the rain!*

4 Don't sit there! The cushions were soaked by the shower.
Already the girls have drenched their crimson skirts.
Beauties, their powder streaked with mascara, lament their ruined faces.

5 The wind batters our boat, the mooring-line
Has rubbed a wound in the willow bark.
The edges of the curtains are embroidered by the river foam.

6 Like a knife in a melon, Autumn slices Summer.

7 *It will be cold, going back.*

1. What is compared to "a water-stain on silk" (Stanza 2)?

A. foam on the edge of the river
B. rain clouds approaching
C. lotus root juice on a tablecloth
D. ice cubes dropping into cold drinks

2. What is meant by the statement "lament their ruined faces" (Stanza 4)?

A. They could no longer smile.
B. They were growing old.
C. The rain caused their makeup to run.
D. The wind was chapping their faces.

3. Why is "The edges of the curtains are embroidered by the river foam" (Stanza 5) an effective use of figurative language?

It helps the reader see that

A. the people forgot to close the windows and curtains
B. the wind is so strong that it is blowing spray from the river into the boat
C. the curtains are beautifully edged with lace
D. the river is rising quickly

4. According to the speaker, how was the change from summer to autumn (Stanza 6)?

A. quick and easy
B. halting and uncertain
C. slow and predictable
D. pleasant and smooth

5. Which of the following words best describe the tone of this poem?

A. gentle and calm
B. humorous and playful
C. wry and observant
D. dry and formal

STUDY ADVICE

The Reading Test will include some passages from plays or poems. Use the same skills you've been learning to understand plays and poems: Look for the author's point of view, tone, and use of figurative language.

Reading Literature Practice Questions

Questions 1 through 3 refer to the following excerpt from a story.

EXCERPTED FROM *SHILOH & OTHER STORIES*

1 Leroy Moffitt's wife, Norma Jean, is working on her pectorals. She lifts three-pound dumbbells to warm up, then progresses to a twenty-pound barbell. Standing with her legs apart, she reminds Leroy of Wonder Woman.

2 "I'd give anything if I could just get these muscles to where they're real hard," says Norma Jean. "Feel this arm. It's not as hard as the other one."

3 "That's cause you're right-handed," says Leroy, dodging as she swings the barbell in an arc.

4 "Do you think so?"

5 "Sure."

6 Leroy is a truckdriver. He injured his leg in a highway accident four months ago, and his physical therapy, which involves weights and a pulley, prompted Norma Jean to try building herself up. Now she is attending a body-building class. Leroy has been collecting temporary disability since his tractor-trailer jackknifed in Missouri, badly twisting his left leg in its socket. He has a steel pin in his hip. He will probably not be able to drive his rig again. It sits in the backyard, like a gigantic bird that has flown home to roost. Leroy has been home in Kentucky for three months, and his leg is almost healed, but the accident frightened him and he does not want to drive any more long hauls. He is not sure what to do next. In the meantime, he makes things from craft kits. He started by building a miniature log cabin from notched Popsicle sticks. He varnished it and placed it on the TV set, where it remains. It reminds him of a rustic Nativity scene. Then he tried string art (sailing ships on black velvet), a macramé owl kit, a snap-together B-17 Flying Fortress, and a lamp made out of a model truck, with a light fixture screwed in the top of the cab. At first the kits were diversions, something to kill time, but now he is thinking about building a full-scale log house from a kit. It would be considerably cheaper than building a regular house, and besides, Leroy has grown to appreciate how things are put together. He has begun to realize that in all the years he was on the road he never took time to examine anything. He was always flying past scenery.

1. Which of the following best describes Leroy's wife, Norma Jean?

   A. shy
   B. loving
   C. self-concerned
   D. grumpy

2. By comparing Leroy's truck to a bird that has flown home to roost, the author suggests that Leroy __________.

   A. comes and goes as he pleases
   B. always preferred to be at home "nesting"
   C. won't be driving his truck for a while
   D. is a bit "flighty" and unpredictable

3. Why might Leroy be continually making things from craft kits?

   Because he

   A. is impatient with his leg healing
   B. has always enjoyed working with his hands
   C. grew tired of bodybuilding
   D. doesn't want to consider what to do next

Questions 4 through 7 refer to this excerpt from a story.

EXCERPTED FROM *WINTER'S TALES*

1 A small sailor-boy, named Simon, stood on the wet, swinging deck, held on to a shroud, and looked up towards the drifting clouds, and to the upper top-gallant yard of the main-mast.

2 A bird, that had sought refuge upon the mast, had got her feet entangled in some loose tackle-yarn of the halliard, and, high up there, struggled to get free. The boy on the deck could see her wings flapping and her head turning from side to side.

3 Through his own experience of life he had come to the conviction that in this world everyone must look after himself, and expect no help from others. But the mute, deadly fight kept him fascinated for more than an hour. He wondered what kind of bird it would be. These last days a number of birds had come to settle in the barque's rigging: swallows, quails, and a pair of peregrine falcons; he believed that this bird was a peregrine falcon. He remembered how, many years ago, in his own country and near his home, he had once seen a peregrine falcon quite close, sitting on a stone and flying straight up from it. Perhaps this was the same bird. He thought: "That bird is like me. Then she was there, and now she is here."

4 At that a fellow-feeling rose in him, a sense of common tragedy; he stood looking at the bird with his heart in his mouth. There were none of the sailors about to make fun of him; he began to think out how he might go up by the shrouds to help the falcon out. He brushed his hair back and pulled up his sleeves, gave the deck round him a great glance, and climbed up. He had to stop a couple of times in the swaying rigging.

5 It was indeed, he found when he got to the top of the mast, a peregrine falcon. As his head was on a level with hers, she gave up her struggle, and looked at him with a pair of angry, desperate yellow eyes.

6 He had to take hold of her with one hand while he got his knife out, and cut off the tackle-yarn. He was scared as he looked down, but at the same time he felt that he had been ordered up by nobody, but that this was his own venture, and this gave him a proud, steadying sensation, as if the sea and the sky, the ship, the bird and himself were all one.

From *Winter's Tales* by Isak Dinesen, Random House, Inc. ©1942.

4. What can you infer about the boy's decision to climb the rig?

   A. It took some courage.
   B. It was a familiar task.
   C. It felt like a chore.
   D. He was ordered to do it.

5. Which of the following best describes both the boy and the bird at the beginning of the excerpt?

   A. confident
   B. alone
   C. scared
   D. wary

6. Which ideas are most clearly contrasted in this excerpt?

   A. love and hate
   B. youth and experience
   C. fear and fearlessness
   D. loneliness and sense of belonging

7. The word ____________ best describes the mood created by the author in this excerpt.

   A. mournful
   B. nostalgic
   C. peaceful
   D. triumphant

Questions 8 through 11 refer to this excerpt from a story.

EXCERPTED FROM "THE LEGEND OF SLEEPY HOLLOW"

1 "Who are you?" He received no reply. He repeated his demand in a still more agitated voice. Still there was no answer. Once more he cudgelled the sides of the inflexible Gunpowder, and, shutting his eyes, broke forth with involuntary fervor into a psalm-tune. Just then the shadowy object of alarm put itself in motion, and, with a scramble and a bound, stood at once in the middle of the road. Though the night was dark and dismal, yet the form of the unknown might now in some degree be ascertained. He appeared to be a horseman of large dimensions, and mounted on a black horse of powerful frame. He made no offer of molestation or sociability, but kept aloof on one side of the road, jogging along on the blind side of old Gunpowder, who had now got over his fright and waywardness.

2 Ichabod, who had no relish for this strange midnight companion, and bethought himself of the adventure of Brom Bones with the Galloping Hessian, now quickened his steed, in hopes of leaving him behind. The stranger, however, quickened his horse to an equal pace. Ichabod pulled up, and fell into a walk, thinking to lag behind—the other did the same. His heart began to sink within him; he endeavored to resume his psalm-tune, but his parched tongue clove to the roof of his mouth, and he could not utter a stave. There was something in the moody and dogged silence of this pertinacious companion, that was mysterious and appalling. It was soon fearfully accounted for. On mounting a rising ground, which brought the figure of his fellow-traveller in relief against the sky, gigantic in height, and muffled in a cloak, Ichabod was horror-struck, on perceiving that he was headless!—but his horror was still more increased, on observing that the head, which should have rested on his shoulders, was carried before him on the pommel of the saddle: his terror rose to desperation; he rained a shower of kicks and blows upon Gunpowder, hoping, by a sudden movement, to give his companion the slip—but the spectre started full jump with him.

3 Away then they dashed, through thick and thin; stones flying, and sparks flashing at every bound. Ichabod's flimsy garments fluttered in the air, as he stretched his long lank body away over his horse's head, in the eagerness of his flight.

From "The Legend of Sleepy Hollow" by Washington Irving.

8. What is meant by "he endeavored to resume his psalm-tune" (paragraph 2)?

   Ichabod Crane tried to

   A. recite religious doctrine
   B. ride more steadily
   C. start singing again
   D. think of a realistic solution

9. What is the effect of the author's use of words such as "dashed," "stones flying," and "sparks flashing" (paragraph 3)?

   The words create a feeling of

   A. panic
   B. clumsiness
   C. playfulness
   D. magic

10. Which of the following best describes the mood of this excerpt?

   A. angry
   B. sorrowful
   C. suspenseful
   D. sentimental

11. Later in the story, the narrator implies that the horseman had a pumpkin on the pommel of his saddle. Given this additional information, Ichabod can best be described as ____________ given his actions in the excerpt.

   A. brave in the face of great danger
   B. too scared to think rationally
   C. moving too quickly
   D. quick thinking in his escape

Questions 12 through 14 refer to this excerpt from a play.

A man named John Wright has been murdered, and the County Attorney and Sheriff are trying to determine whether Wright's wife might have had a motive.

EXCERPTED FROM *TRIFLES*

COUNTY ATTORNEY: Well, that's interesting, I'm sure. [*Seeing the birdcage.*] Has the bird flown?

MRS. HALE: [*Putting more quilt pieces over the box.*] We think the—cat got it.

COUNTY ATTORNEY: [*Preoccupied.*] Is there a cat?

[*MRS. HALE glances in a quick covert way at MRS. PETERS.*]

MRS. PETERS: Well, not now. They're superstitious, you know. They leave.

COUNTY ATTORNEY: [*To SHERIFF PETERS, continuing an interrupted conversation.*] No sign at all of anyone having come from the outside. Their own rope. Now let's go up again and go over it piece by piece. [*They start upstairs.*] It would have to have been someone who knew just the—

[*MRS. PETERS sits down. The two women sit there not looking at one another, but as if peering into something and at the same time holding back. When they talk now it is in the manner of feeling their way over strange ground, as if afraid of what they are saying, but as if they cannot help saying it.*]

MRS. HALE: She liked the bird. She was going to bury it in that pretty box.

MRS. PETERS: [*In a whisper.*] When I was a girl—my kitten—there was a boy took a hatchet, and before my eyes—and before I could get there—. [*Covers her face an instant.*] If they hadn't held me back I would have— [*Catches herself, looks upstairs where steps are heard, falters weakly.*]—hurt him.

MRS. HALE: [*With a slow look around her.*] I wonder how it would seem never to have had any children around. [*Pause.*] No, Wright wouldn't like the bird—a thing that sang. She used to sing. He killed that, too.

MRS. PETERS: [*Moving uneasily.*] We don't know who killed the bird.

MRS. HALE: I knew John Wright.

MRS. PETERS: It was an awful thing was done in this house that night, Mrs. Hale. Killing a man while he slept, slipping a rope around his neck that choked the life out of him.

MRS. HALE: His neck. Choked the life out of him. [*Her hand goes out and rests on the birdcage.*]

MRS. PETERS: [*With rising voice.*] We don't know who killed him. We don't know.

MRS. HALE: [*Her own feeling not interrupted.*] If there'd been years and years of nothing, then a bird to sing to you, it would be awful—still, after the bird was still.

Excerpted from *Trifles*, by Susan Glaspell, published by Penguin Putnam, Inc.

12. Who does Mrs. Hale think killed the bird?
    A. John Wright
    B. Mrs. Peters
    C. the cat
    D. Mrs. Wright

13. Based on the excerpt, which of the following best describes John Wright?
    A. a person who is loving and attentive
    B. someone who smothers all the joy in another person
    C. a person capable of murder
    D. someone devoted to law and order

14. Which of the following conclusions can you draw about Mrs. Peters and Mrs. Hale?
    A. Together they committed murder.
    B. Each one thinks the other one is the murderer.
    C. They are eager to tell the police all they know.
    D. They understand how someone could be driven to murder.

LANGUAGE ARTS: READING ANSWERS AND EXPLANATIONS

Interpreting Informational Text

Lesson 1: Main Ideas and Details

Practice 1

1. **A. searching for a place to call home** The author states this feeling directly in the first two lines and in the last paragraph.
2. **D. the gods** The second sentence in the second paragraph says, "It was ordained by the deities."
3. **D. It was simply part of their beliefs to follow the pole.** The meaning of the pole is explained beginning with the fourth sentence of the second paragraph. The last sentence explains that the Chickasaws lacked sorrow because they trusted the pole's command.
4. **C. understands that her tendency to search is part of her Chickasaw heritage** The details about the author's search for a home, combined with the information that "the search for a homeland is part of the Chickasaw migration legend," helps you understand this main idea.
5. **D. accepts that she is Chickasaw** You can see that the writer is saying that her Chickasaw heritage is an inescapable part of who she is.

Lesson 2: Rephrasing and Summary

Practice 2

1. **C. lack of proper paperwork** As the writer discusses the problems, he states that he wants an "itemized list" and "a proper bill of sale." He does mention the premium price, choice (D), but that price is the reason he expects proper paperwork and is not a complaint in and of itself.
2. **B. the car to be repaired free of charge if the cause of the problem is discovered** This expectation is stated in the fifth paragraph of the letter.
3. **C. The service and warranty on the customer's car have been unacceptable.** The letter is a detailed list of the customer's complaints. They can be summed up by saying that both the service and the warranty have not been as promised.

Lesson 3: Application of Ideas

Practice 3

1. **A. overcoming a bad habit** The writer advises those trying to break free of credit card debt: "Stick with it until you're free again."
2. **B. never use the credit cards** The last paragraph implies that the author approves of using credit cards only once you have already gotten out of debt, and then only for convenience. Thus, if you are in debt, you should stop using your credit cards.
3. **C. losing weight by avoiding all-you-can-eat buffets** Basically, the advice is that you gradually lose your debt by not adding anything to it. This is similar to helping yourself lose weight by not adding to it with portions of food you don't need.
4. **C. "Live within your means."** This statement can be inferred from the advice "Don't borrow any more," and "What I'm against is buying more on your credit cards than you can pay for at the end of the month."

Lesson 4: Cause and Effect

Practice 4

1. **C. It affected nearly everyone.** This answer summarizes the meaning of the first two sentences of the passage.
2. **A. Many people lost the mortgages on their homes.** This answer is stated in the first paragraph: "men and women who saw their mortgages foreclosed." Choices (B) and (D) are both mentioned as causes, not effects, of the depression.
3. **B. low worker incomes** The second paragraph states, "but the actual cause of the collapse was an unhealthy economy. . . . Most laborers . . . could not afford to buy the automobiles . . . because their incomes were too low."
4. **B. They had little effect.** The writer tells what Herbert Hoover did as president to curb the depression ("loans to businesses and banks") but then states that "his efforts proved to be too little and too late."
5. **D. The depression left people emotionally scarred.** The first paragraph states, "No one who lived through those years . . . could ever completely forget." The statement about eating mustard that is provided in the question addresses this emotional effect rather than issues related to farmers, workers, the economy, or the number of individuals affected.

Lesson 5: Comparison and Contrast

Practice 5

1. **D. leave some of his possessions behind** This answer is found in the seventh and eighth lines of paragraph 1.
2. **C. They provided milk and pulled wagons.** The selection states that "cows . . . gave milk all the way to the sink of the Humboldt where they died, having acted as draught animals for several weeks after the oxen had perished."
3. **A. the provisions of each group of travelers** Each paragraph talks about a different group and what it had to offer the wagon train. For example, "Much in contrast to these men were four batchelors . . . , who had a wagon drawn by four oxen . . . cows following behind."
4. **A. be happy to have people who could cook and sew** The writer was interested in assessing how self-sufficient the group could be and what each group could offer the entire wagon train. For example, she writes, "but as he was a wagon maker and his companion a blacksmith by trade and both were accommodating there were always ready hands to 'pry the wheel out of mire.'"

5. **A. They must cooperate and work together.** Throughout the excerpt, there is evidence that all the travelers depended on each other for animals, food, and physical help, such as pulling wagons out of the mud.

Lesson 6: Conclusions and Generalizations

Practice 6.1

1. **A. It is rewarding and one of life's joys.** The passage states that "my teacher's genius, . . . made the first years of my education so beautiful." She also delights in observing and learning from the tadpole.
2. **D. insightful and grateful** The writer has insight about the connection between herself and the tadpole: "Thus I learned from life itself. At the beginning I was only a little mass of possibilities." The writer is also grateful to her teacher: "nor has she ceased trying . . . to make my life sweet and useful."
3. **C. show Helen how addition is used in everyday life** You can apply what you learn in the diary entry: "Thus I learned from life itself. . . . She has never since let pass an opportunity to point out the beauty that is in everything. . . ." The teacher would therefore probably use everyday life situations to teach.
4. **D. as an anecdote followed by a generalization based on the anecdote** The writer tells the story of the tadpoles (an anecdote) and relates it to her attitude toward life and learning.
5. **D. Their development is not entirely smooth.** The writer describes the tadpole having difficulty after leaping out of the bowl. This is similar to the quotation about "the stony course" of a child's education.

Practice 6.2

1. **C. On the whole, temperatures are not rising.** The writer states that rising temperatures are "quite simply not what is happening," based on the cold temperatures of the day before.
2. **A. Shady Hollow was hit with a record cold temperature yesterday.** This one piece of information is the example the author uses to support the generalization that temperatures, generally speaking, are not rising.
3. **D. worldwide data tables of temperatures from the 1980s through today** The author's generalization suffers from being based on one temperature reading. His generalization would be more likely to be valid if informed by many temperature readings over time.

Lesson 7: Word Choice

Practice 7

1. **D. the CoolForter blanket** The first sentence of paragraph 2 tells you two things about the CoolForter blanket: that "it works like an electric blanket" and that "it feels like a dream."
2. **B. to show that the blanket is a pleasant indulgence** To "coddle" is to treat gently or take care of a person. Choice (B) describes this idea.
3. **A. fluid** Many people associate the word *chemical* with toxicity or harm. A more neutral word to describe the cooling substance without inaccurate specificity is *fluid*.
4. **C. bland** The word *bland* indicates a lack of interesting features. Unlike the word *neutral*, which also indicates a lack of characteristic features, the word *bland* can carry a negative connotation.
5. **D. It allows the consumer to compare the CoolForter's energy usage to that of a familiar item.** The author's choice of a light bulb, an item with which most readers are probably familiar, emphasizes that the CoolForter blanket will not use excessive amounts of energy.

Lesson 8: Writer's Tone and Point of View

Practice 8

1. **C. the Internet writers** The writer mentions "Internet sass" and then goes on to say that "you gotta love it" because it keeps writers "off the street and out of trouble."
2. **A. The Internet reviews were much more interesting than the TV show.** The review states, "They [Internet writers] were taking hours and hours of primetime dross and turning it into decadent, amoral, sharp, electronic gold."
3. **A. The show was boring.** The reviewer's main opinion of the show is that it was bad and boring ("non-goings-on of the non-people in the non-house"). Someone yawning supports the idea of boredom.
4. **C. informal and hip** Phrases such as "the dude" and "you gotta love it" contribute to an informal and modern, or hip, tone.
5. **C. someone knowledgeable about the media** The reviewer talks knowledgeably about both television and the Internet.

Lesson 9: Text Structure

Practice 9

1. **B. exposure to the cowpox disease** As seen in the text, James's recovery from cowpox followed his exposure to it. Note that choice (D) refers to Jenner exposing James to smallpox, not cowpox.
2. **C. "After being exposed to the disease"** The transition word *After* tells the reader that James's exposure came before his catching cowpox and recovery from it. Thus, it gives the reader explicit information about the order of the steps in the process.
3. **B. A number of factors can damage a garden.** As discussed in the passage, factors such as weather, pests, and diseases can affect plants and cause damage, undoing the time and work that have been invested.

Lesson 10: Reading Predictively

Practice 10

1. **C. "Moreover, harmful insects and weeds develop resistance to agricultural chemicals over time, forcing farmers to purchase more expensive, and more toxic, treatments."** At the end of the first paragraph, the author indicates her main idea will be the negative effects the Green Revolution has had on the environment. The second paragraph says that agricultural chemicals have had adverse environmental effects. Logically, a new third paragraph would discuss either another negative effect of these chemicals (choice (C)) or another Green Revolution technology that has hurt the environment. A statement that chemicals have not been shown to harm bees (A) is the opposite of the author's point. Climate change (B) and the impact of population growth on human societies (D) are outside the scope of the passage.

2. **B. Like other new technologies, genetically modified organisms may have negative consequences as well as positive ones, and it is important to take all effects into account.** At the end of the passage, the author states the opinion that both intended and unintended consequences should be taken into account when evaluating a technology. Choice (B) expresses how the author would apply this view to a technology not discussed in the passage.

Interpreting Informational Text Practice Questions

1. **D. hit a boy in the arm to get his attention** The writer talks about breaking a ruler over the head of a boy she likes; you can therefore conclude that she would hit a boy in the arm to get his attention. She responds physically and without much thought to consequences.
2. **B. She was just pretending she didn't want to go to the principal's office.** The circumstances of Brer Rabbit pretending he was afraid to go into the briar patch where he was born and raised are similar to the speaker pretending to be afraid to go to the principal's office.
3. **C. unusual** From the different examples of how Frank Doleman behaved (allowing a young girl to play chess in his office and not punishing boys sent to his office), you can conclude that he was an unusual principal.
4. **A. confident** The additional information you get from the new quotation and the examples of her behavior, plus the overall tone of the excerpt, suggest a confident young girl.
5. **C. concerned but hopeful.** The author is worried about the health impact of soda consumption on teenagers. But she is also hopeful; in the last sentence, she states that more "can" be done to reduce the consumption of sugary beverages.
6. **D. Young people will choose healthier beverages if they are better educated about the dangers of regular soda consumption.** The last paragraph supports this choice. Choice (A) is unsupported by the passage: even though the author does not condemn the legal measures mentioned in paragraph 2, you do not know whether she would support an overall ban. Choice (B) is unsupported also; the author never mentions diet soda.
7. **C. Young people who drink these beverages regularly will eventually suffer from the same ailments as those who drink soda regularly.** The author points out that, even though juice and energy drinks have somewhat less sugar than soda, regular consumption of those products "is likely to be just as damaging in the long term."
8. **B. effective to some extent.** After describing the measures, the author begins paragraph 3 by stating, "These efforts appear to be paying off" but goes on to explain why they may not fully solve the problem of sugar consumption among teenagers.
9. **C. Reducing excessive consumption of soda.** The author is referring to the efforts described in paragraph 2, all of which attempted to reduce soda consumption.
10. **C. The cost of mandated coverage will lessen the ability of NATS to hire and supply temporary workers.** This question is basically answered in paragraph 2: "the cost of mandates could weaken the ability of the temporary help industry to act as a 'jobs bridge.'"
11. **A. Many workers are losing their jobs and need temporary jobs until they find permanent work again.** The third paragraph explains this reason.
12. **D. to raise awareness of one side of an issue** The whole passage—plus knowledge of who Edward A. Lenz is—helps you see that its purpose is to explain the position of the NATS.
13. **B. Women will not resort to wearing pants or other restrictive men's clothing.** This statement and the lines that follow it help you see that Stanton is saying men can wear their restrictive clothing; women want no part of it.
14. **D. a cloth worn around the neck** By looking at the context clues—or words around the word *stock*—you can see that it is something worn around the neck.
15. **B. speak up about current events** This very direct speech of Stanton's indicates her straight-to-the-point personality. She is not interested in criticism for its own sake but rather speaks up about issues she strongly believes in.
16. **A. Women are fighting for the right to vote.** The phrase "over the horns of bigotry" helps you see that women are fighting for something. The last paragraph of the excerpt helps you see that they are fighting for the right to vote.

Analyzing Informational Text

Lesson 1: Purpose of Text

Practice 1

1. **B. tell how creative engineers saved astronauts** This passage is a narrative about the process of saving the lives of the Apollo 13 astronauts, including in particular the role of engineers. Choices (A), (C), and (D) are all far too broad.
2. **B. supports the writer's main recommendation** The writer recommends that the state cut sales taxes on new vehicles. Preventing deaths with the modern safety features on new cars is one of the reasons for this recommendation.
3. **D. inform about the historical importance of silk** The passage begins by discussing the "historical importance" of silk, and continues throughout to introduce new points about this topic.
4. **C. It provides examples of silk's historical importance in trade and culture.** Nomads traveling to China for silk and the creation of the "Silk Road" are examples of silk's importance.

Lesson 2: Effectiveness of Argument

Practice 2

1. **B. The federal government should automatically raise the minimum wage to match price increases.** The author states that "[s]everal states have taken the sensible step of automatically raising their minimum wage to adjust for inflation and consumer price increases." Later she also states that "the federal government should follow the lead of the states." Thus, the author is recommending that the federal government should adjust the minimum wage for price increases. The rest of the passage serves to support this recommendation.
2. **D. Those states have systems superior to the federal system of manual increases.** The author's main point is that the federal government should adopt automatic minimum wage increases, as some states currently have done. Thus, she believes that the states' systems are better than the current federal system.
3. **C. Over the past 40 years, the federal minimum wage has not kept pace with inflation.** Choice (C) is a historical fact provided in the second paragraph as evidence to support the writer's argument.
4. **B. Ensuring sustainable incomes for hardworking citizens is a responsibility of lawmakers.** The author states that lawmakers must ensure stability for workers but does not justify why they must do so. She assumes that this is part of the job lawmakers should do.

Lesson 3: Validity of Arguments

Practice 3

1. **C. voting systems have been developed over time to address previous systems' flaws** The writer introduces DRE voting, describes several voting systems, and concludes by suggesting that DRE continues the trend of new voting systems correcting some flaws while introducing others.
2. **B. DRE voting avoids problems associated with other voting systems.** The writer supports the assertion that DRE voting has addressed some flaws of older DRE systems voting system by listing problems that might be encountered with other voting systems and then stating that DRE voting avoids such problems.
3. **A. DRE systems immediately record voters' choice, while other electronic systems have voters initially use a paper ballot.** This is one of the facts that the writer cites in support of the assertion that DRE voting addressed some flaws. The other three answer choices cite facts that are included in the passage, but those facts are all background information and do not give direct support to the writer's main point.
4. **D. Audits of elections that use DRE demonstrate this system is more accurate than paper ballots.** The author asserts that DRE systems are the safest and most accurate option available. If these systems have been proven more accurate than paper ballots (one of the alternatives), then this would strengthen the argument, so (D) is correct.

Lesson 4: Text Related by Theme or Topic

Practice 4

1. **C. online piracy of music files** Both passages are focused on reasons why online piracy is harmful and the need to take further action.
2. **B. additional action to combat online piracy is warranted because piracy causes financial loses to the music industry.** The first passage concludes that more must be done to prevent online piracy. The main factual information the writer uses to support this thesis is information about the financial damage that piracy causes.
3. **A. Fear of piracy makes it difficult for new, experimental acts to get signed.** Both passages reach the same conclusion: more must be done to prevent piracy of music files. Choice (A) is the only answer choice that provides direct support for the conclusion of Passage 2, and, therefore, also for that of Passage 1.
4. **A. Online piracy of digital files has a harmful effect on the music industry.** Both authors provide different reasons as to why piracy is potentially harmful, but both agree that it has a negative effect on the industry.

Lesson 5: Texts with Opposing Arguments

Practice 5

1. **C. the MPAA movie rating system** Each writer is making an argument about the relevance and trustworthiness of the MPAA rating system.
2. **B. The MPAA rating system is a useful tool for parents.** The writer of the Argument (Passage 1) uses information about the MPAA rating system to support her argument that the system helps parents to make sound decisions.
3. **D. The MPAA rating system should not be trusted.** In the second sentence, the writer indicates that the MPAA rating system is not a useful guide and concludes by recommending that parents use a different source of advice.
4. **A. She largely approves of the MPAA rating system as a guideline for parents.** The passage provides no information about the writer's own child-rearing decisions, choice (B), or about her opinion of the effect of the Hays Code on the movie industry, choice (D). Also, her statements about the rating system are uniformly positive, making choice (C) incorrect.

Lesson 6: Texts with Related Graphic Information

Practice 6

1. **D. Governing parties can use their power to shape electoral districts to their advantage.** The passage and the figures focus on demonstrating how gerrymandering works. Choices (A) and (B) are not supported at all by the passage, and choice (C) is far too extreme.
2. **B. Through gerrymandering, a governing party can be elected to a greater number of seats than its voter support might otherwise allow.** The second paragraph describes how the second grid figure shows one party winning 75 percent of the seats from 60 percent of the vote, rather than the 50 percent of seats shown in the first grid figure.
3. **A. They illustrate the advantages a party can obtain through gerrymandering.** As discussed in the passage's second paragraph, the figures show how a party can benefit from the process. While choices (C) and (D) may or may not be true statements, they do not describe how the figures support the passage.

Analyzing Informational Text Practice Questions

1. **D. to discuss whether communication technology helps or hurts relationships** This answer choice reflects the scope of the article introduced at the end of the first paragraph.
2. **B. how technology affects interpersonal connections** The question at the end of paragraph 1 introduces this topic. Paragraph 2 discusses positive effects of communication technology while paragraph 3 discusses a negative effect.
3. **D. The caption reveals that the woman's friends will use their phones during their visit.** The caption is similar to a scenario described in the first paragraph of the passage. In both cases, people are choosing to use technology rather than to enjoy the company of those with whom they have an established relationship.
4. **B. New communication technologies may adversely impact important human relationships.** The author's concluding paragraph discusses how communication technology can connect us with so many people that we have less time and energy to spend on relationships with friends and family, and the caption of the image reveals that the visiting friends plan to spend time on their phones rather than in conversing with one another.
5. **B. the giant squid is the world's longest cephalopod** The author's introduction and conclusion both raise this point, and the evidence in the paragraph supports this thesis.
6. **D. The giant squid is longer than the colossal squid.** The author provides scientific evidence about the colossal squid to support the passage's main idea about the giant squid.
7. **C. The length of the longest known colossal squid specimen is ten meters.** This factual evidence supports the author's main idea.
8. **A. The longest known colossal squid is ten meters long, so there is no colossal squid longer than the longest giant squid.** According to paragraph 2, there are very few samples of colossal squid, and all of them have been juveniles. It is improper to draw a conclusion about the entire colossal squid species on the basis of such limited evidence.
9. **B. mercury dental amalgam** Though the authors have somewhat different opinions on the subject, both passages are centrally about mercury dental amalgam.
10. **C. Mercury amalgam fillings should be banned because they are unhealthy and bad for the environment.** The first sentence of Passage 1 states that mercury amalgam should be banned for use in dental fillings. The first paragraph cites health reasons for this opinion. The second paragraph cites environmental reasons. Choice (D) is mentioned in Passage 1, but it serves as support for the author's main point.
11. **D. It is a convincing statistic from a reliable source.** The statement that 40–50 percent of mercury in wastewater is from an easily preventable source is a convincing statistic. The EPA is a large nonpolitical government agency and so is likely to provide reliable information.
12. **A. Consumers have no other reason, such as cost or durability, to prefer mercury amalgam to composite fillings.** The author of Passage 1 states that "banning mercury amalgam would draw no consumer backlash" because resin composite fillings are better for cosmetic reasons. The author assumes that there is no other reason to prefer mercury amalgam.
13. **B. Resin composite fillings look better than mercury amalgam fillings when each is used on visible tooth surfaces.** The author of Passage 2 states that amalgam is preferable to resin composite whenever there is no

cosmetic need for a tooth-colored filling. Thus, you can infer that he believes that resin composite fillings look more like natural teeth than mercury amalgam.

14. **A. Passage 1, because it cites no sources for the study or the statistic it cites** The author of passage 1 says that "it has been estimated" that 4 percent of the mercury in Lake Superior comes from dental amalgam, but the author cites no source. The author also gives no source for the 2001 study that is cited in the first paragraph.
15. **D. Mercury that accumulates in body tissues causes a variety of health problems.** The study cited in the first paragraph of passage 1 found a correlation between mercury amalgam fillings and a number of health conditions. A correlation does not prove causation, but the author of passage 1 states that "this accumulated mercury causes a variety of health problems."

Reading Literature

Lesson 1: Plot Elements

Practice 1

1. **B. swearing that he was telling the truth** The following statement in the excerpt gives the context and meaning: "It is nevertheless God's own truth, the sacred truth. I repeat it on my soul and my salvation."
2. **D. confronted him and then asked to be searched** According to the excerpt, when the harness-maker comes in and repeats his story, the two "abused each other for an hour. At his own request, Maître Hauchecorne was searched."
3. **C. A peasant is accused of taking a pocket-book.** As you read the excerpt, you understand that a harness-maker has accused a peasant of taking a pocket-book, and the mayor of the town believes the harness-maker.
4. **C. The harness-maker is higher in social status than the peasant.** The harness-maker is characterized as "a man we can believe." The countryman is referred to as a "peasant." You can infer that the difference in the two men's social status affects the way their statements are viewed.

Lesson 2: Inferences

Practice 2

1. **A. had always loved her** In the first paragraph, Louise recalls her husband's face: "the face that had never looked save with love upon her." The term *save* means "except."
2. **C. spread her arms out in welcome** The first paragraph explains that although Louise knew she would cry at the sight of her dead husband, "that bitter moment" would soon give way to years of freedom, which she welcomed.
3. **A. she was overcome and thrilled to see her husband** The doctors assumed that Louise was so glad to learn her husband had not died in an accident that she was shocked and overjoyed to see him walk in the door.
4. **B. She was shocked that she would not be free.** Much of the excerpt is about Louise looking forward to the freedom of being without her husband. When she learns that her husband is alive, she also learns that she will not be free.

Lesson 3: Character

Practice 3

1. **B. He is reluctant to see the ghost of his wife.** The witch, supposedly speaking as Yaji's wife, says that she lies in her grave longing for Yaji to die and join her. She then asks, "Shall I come to meet you?" Throughout the passage, Yaji seems uncomfortable. At this moment you can infer that he is reluctant.
2. **C. untrustworthy** The witch is tricking Yaji. The witch has her own interests at heart when she pretends it is the wife requesting, "Give this witch plenty of money."
3. **D. neglectful** The information we are given about Yaji suggests that he treated his wife poorly when she was alive and now does not tend her grave.

Lesson 4: Theme

Practice 4

1. **B. finds a new explanation** After his father tells the boy he is dreaming, the boy states, "I decided that it was a magic horse and man that I'd seen."
2. **B. imaginative** The detailed description of the dream and the boy's insistence on believing in it are signs of his imaginative powers.
3. **A. He wants to reconcile what he saw with what his father told him.** Initially the boy seems to think that he saw a real, ordinary horse, but his father explains why this is unlikely. However, the boy does not accept the explanation that he was merely dreaming. Thus, he thinks of a new explanation.
4. **B. having enough money to pay some bills** The father is a practical man, a realist—"where were poor people like us going to find big gray stallions?" Because of the family's poverty, the father would probably enjoy having money to pay bills.
5. **D. Morning and youth are full of possibility.** The end of the excerpt states, "I believed that magic hides in the early morning. . . . you might find something so beautiful . . . nothing else in life could ever be better."

Lesson 5: Style and Point of View

Practice 5

1. **B. He takes things in stride.** When Coach chides Bobby for having three malts, Bobby jokes with him and then pretends to hide them. Bobby is not angry or defensive in a way that could justify choice (D).

2. **C. the actions and speech of the characters** The narrator reports only what can be seen or heard by any observer. As a reader, you don't learn anyone's thoughts or feelings. You must infer them from their actions and speech.
3. **A. informal** Throughout the excerpt, people speak and act quite informally: Daphne washes up in a drinking fountain, Coach speaks with a spoon in his mouth, Bobby jokes with Coach, and so on.
4. **D. not entirely honest about his feelings** In his discussion with Daphne, Coach tries to explain his wife's need for an apartment of her own. Yet he sounds hostile and cuts his wife off when she speaks of her apartment. You can conclude he was hiding his real feelings from Daphne.

Lesson 6: Figurative Language

Practice 6

1. **B. rain clouds approaching** Lines 8–9 state,"patch of cloud spreads, darkening/Like a water-stain on silk." The following line mentions the coming rain: "*. . . quickly, before the rain!*"
2. **C. The rain caused their makeup to run.** The previous two lines mention "soaked by the shower" and "drenched." Immediately preceding the mention of "ruined faced" is a description of "streaked mascara." The girls' makeup is streaked because of the rain.
3. **B. the wind is so strong that it is blowing spray from the river into the boat** The figurative language helps you "see" the effects of the strong wind by painting a picture of curtains embroidered with white foamy water blown from the river.
4. **A. quick and easy** A knife cuts through a melon quickly and easily, and that is how cold, wet autumn weather has cut through the warm summer day.
5. **C. wry and observant** Throughout the poem the speaker observes and comments on what is going on around him with a dryly humorous, or wry, attitude.

Reading Literature Practice Questions

1. **C. self-concerned** Leroy's condition inspires Norma Jean to care for herself. She discusses herself and her body, and the passage gives no indication that any of the other answers fit her character.
2. **C. won't be driving his truck for a while** The passage tells us Leroy is injured and probably won't drive, so describing the truck as roosting, or sleeping, implies it will not be used.
3. **D. doesn't want to consider what to do next** The passage says that Leroy is "not sure what to do next" and is making his crafts "in the meantime."
4. **A. It took some courage.** The fourth paragraph says the boy's "heart was in his mouth" and the sixth paragraph explains the boy was "scared as he looked down."
5. **B. alone** The boy has come to believe that you cannot rely on anyone but yourself. He is alone on the deck and sees the bird alone atop the mast. Even though it needs help, he is not going to help it at first.
6. **D. loneliness and sense of belonging** The sailor-boy begins the excerpt believing that everyone must look after himself. The final sentence of the excerpt states that his adventure leaves him with the belief that "the sky, the ship, the bird and himself were all one."
7. **D. triumphant** The mood of the piece rises as the boy climbs the mast to save the bird. At the top, he feels proud of what he has chosen to do and succeeded at doing and feels at one with everything.
8. **C. start singing again** A clue is given in the phrase "but his parched tongue clove to the roof of his mouth, he could not utter a stave." His mouth, dry from fear, could not utter a note of the song.
9. **A. panic** Reading those words both alone and in context gives you a sense of Ichabod's panic-stricken haste to get away.
10. **C. suspenseful** There is mystery and tension over whether the headless horseman will catch up with Ichabod and, if so, what he will do. The events that are happening and the way they are told create suspense.
11. **B. too scared to think rationally** When you realize that Ichabod mistakenly thought he saw a head when it was in reality a pumpkin, you can see that he was letting his fear get the better of his judgment.
12. **A. John Wright** Although Mrs. Peters insists they don't know who killed the bird, Mrs. Hale states, "Wright wouldn't like the bird—a thing that sang. She used to sing. He killed that, too. . . . I knew John Wright."
13. **B. someone who smothers all the joy in another person** Mrs. Hale says: "No, Wright wouldn't like the bird—a thing that sang. She used to sing. He killed that, too." From these comments, you can conclude that John Wright was capable of discouraging a person from singing, something that would have made that person happy.
14. **D. They understand how someone could be driven to murder.** The two women seem nervous and are evasive about the bird's death. But they are not protecting themselves. You can tell they suspect who might have murdered Wright and what might have driven the person to murder. References to "she," someone who liked to sing but stopped because of Wright ("He killed that, too"), someone who lived in loneliness and had only the bird as pleasure until the bird was killed, indicate that the women suspect that Mrs. Wright killed her husband.

Language Arts: Writing

UNIT 2

The HiSET Writing Test assesses your language skills in two different ways. You will have 120 minutes to complete the Writing Test.*

1. Expect to spend around 75 minutes answering approximately 51 multiple-choice items that assess language skills. These questions will target skills such as:
   - Constructing sentences
   - Using grammar correctly
   - Using words correctly
   - Organizing ideas into paragraphs
   - Connecting ideas
2. You will have around 45 minutes to write one essay in response to a pair of passages. You will read the passages and then write an essay that argues for a position on the issue discussed. Your essay will be scored on how well it:
   - Supports its conclusion with valid reasoning and relevant evidence
   - Develops ideas in a clear and logical manner
   - Demonstrates control over writing mechanics and expression

If you are taking the paper version of the HiSET exam, you will write your essay on paper. If you are testing on a computer, you will type your essay into a box on the screen.

This unit is organized into skills needed to write effective sentences and paragraphs, skills required to write the essay, and skills needed to edit writing and correct mistakes in grammar and usage. Be aware that the skills you will practice in this unit to answer multiple-choice questions will also be useful to you as you write and revise your essay for the Writing Test.

* Note: The information given here was the latest information available as of December 2018. It is possible that some of this information may change between this printing and your test date. For updates, visit http://hiset.ets.org.

LESSON 1

Simple Sentences

A complete simple sentence has at least one subject and one verb. The **subject** is the person, place, or thing that the sentence is talking about. The subject performs an action or is described. The **verb** is the word that tells what action the subject is doing or links the subject to a modifier.

Action verb: Elaine (subject) took (verb) notes on the meeting.

Linking verb: They (subject) were (verb) long (modifier).

If a sentence is missing either the subject or the verb, it is incomplete. An incomplete sentence is called a **fragment.**

EXAMPLES
No subject: Typed up her notes.
Complete sentence: Elaine typed up her notes.

No verb: The computer in the main office.
Complete sentence: The computer in the main office crashed several times.

A complete sentence must also express a complete thought. The reader should not be left asking questions.

Incomplete thought: When she lost her work. (What happened when she lost her work?)
Complete thought: Elaine was very frustrated when she lost her work.

Incomplete thought: The person in charge of computer support. (What about that person?)
Complete thought: Elaine called the person in charge of computer support.

Incomplete thought: By replacing the hard drive.
Complete thought: Elaine can fix the computer by replacing the hard drive.

Finally, a complete sentence should have correct end punctuation. A statement should end with a period, and so should a command. A question should end with a question mark. An exclamation should end with an exclamation point.

Statement: Elaine has lost several files this way.
Command: Turn off the computer.
Question: Will the computer ever be fixed?
Exclamation: What a mess we're in!

If you find a fragment in your writing, rewrite it to make it a complete sentence.

- If the sentence does not have a subject, add a subject.
- If the sentence does not have a verb, add a verb.
- If the thought is incomplete, add words or combine the incomplete thought with a complete sentence.

KEY IDEAS

- Make sure each sentence has a subject and verb and expresses a complete thought.
- If a sentence doesn't express a complete thought, you may need to add a subject, verb, or other words.
- Use correct end punctuation.

HiSET EXAM TIP

Read each sentence in the passage to yourself and pause at its end. That may help you "hear" whether the sentence is actually an incomplete thought or a sentence fragment.

PRACTICE 1

A. Directions: Write *C* if the sentence is complete or *F* if the sentence is a fragment. Rewrite any fragments to make them complete.

EXAMPLE

Talks all the time on the telephone. *F Dave talks all the time on the telephone.*

1. Drives his girlfriend crazy. ____________________

2. As soon as he comes home from work. ____________________

3. He calls everyone he knows. ____________________

4. Dave's sister and his best friend. ____________________

B. Questions 5 through 7 refer to the following advertisement.

What Is Three-Way Calling?

(A)

(1) Three-way calling is a unique service that enables you to conduct a conference call. (2) From the privacy of your own home. (3) You can talk to your sister in Florida and your mother in Nebraska at the same time. (4) It's even possible to seek a third person's advice when you're in the middle of a regular call. (5) For instance, if you're closing a deal, can bring your lawyer into the conversation.

(B)

(6) Why wait? (7) This useful and convenient service. (8) Can be yours for only pennies a month.

5. Sentences 1 and 2: Three-way calling is a unique service that enables you to conduct a conference call. From the privacy of your own home.

Which is the best way to write the underlined portion of these sentences?

A. call. And from
B. call. It from
C. call from
D. calling from

6. Sentence 5: For instance, if you're closing a deal, can bring your lawyer into the conversation.

Which correction should be made to sentence 5?

A. remove the comma after instance
B. change closing to close
C. insert you before can
D. replace lawyer with closing

7. Sentences 7 and 8: This useful and convenient service. Can be yours for only pennies a month.

Which is the best way to write the underlined portion of these sentences?

A. service is
B. service it can
C. service can
D. service. That can

STUDY ADVICE

Remember that you will use grammar skills in two ways on the Writing Test. You will answer multiple-choice questions about grammar, and you will also be expected to use correct grammar in your essay. Learn to recognize grammatical mistakes not only in others' writing but also in your own.

LESSON 2

Compound and Complex Sentences

Compound Sentences

The simple sentences described in Lesson 1 are also called **independent clauses.** An independent clause has a subject and a verb and expresses a complete thought. You can join two or more independent clauses in one **compound sentence.** To make a compound sentence, you should:

- Choose a logical **coordinating conjunction** to join the independent clauses. The most common coordinating conjunctions are *and, but, or, nor, for, so,* and *yet*.
- Insert a comma before the coordinating conjunction.

KEY IDEAS

- You can join two independent clauses into one compound sentence.
- Use a coordinating conjunction preceded by a comma.
- Choose a conjunction that correctly relates the two ideas.

EXAMPLES

Two independent clauses: Sam saw a design flaw. He wrote a memo.
Joined correctly: Sam saw a design flaw, so he wrote a memo.

No coordinating conjunction: Sam asked his boss, she told him to send it.
Correct: Sam asked his boss, and she told him to send it.

No comma: Sam's boss was busy so she asked Sam to write the memo.
Correct: Sam's boss was busy, so she asked Sam to write the memo.

Be sure the coordinating conjunction expresses the correct relationship between the ideas in the two independent clauses.

Relationship between Ideas	Coordinating Conjunction
join two equally important ideas	and
contrast two ideas	but, yet
show a cause	for
show an effect	so
give a choice	or
give no choice	nor

Incorrect conjunction: Sam showed initiative, **yet** his boss praised him.
Correct conjunction: Sam showed initiative, **so** his boss praised him.

HiSET EXAM TIP

Be sure that a coordinating conjunction separates two independent clauses before you choose the option that inserts a comma before the conjunction.

Be sure that you are actually joining two independent clauses and not just two subjects or two verbs.

Incorrect: The designers, and the builders got the memo.
Correct (no comma): The designers and the builders got the memo.

Incorrect: The designers needed the information, and appreciated the memo.
Correct (two independent clauses): The designers needed the information. They appreciated the memo.
Correct (no comma): The designers needed the information and appreciated the memo.

PRACTICE 2.1

A. Directions: Using the list on page 138, choose a coordinating conjunction for each sentence. On a separate sheet of paper, rewrite the sentence using the conjunction preceded by a comma.

EXAMPLE

I didn't want to seem timid, ____*so*____ I didn't tell anyone about my experience.

1. It was late ______________________________ I was walking home from work.

2. My coworker, Judy, had offered to drive me ____________________ I had refused.

3. It was a warm night ________________________ I decided to get some fresh air.

4. It was really my choice. I could have taken a cab ____________________ I could have walked.

5. I heard a loud noise ________________ I ran the last block to my house. Later, I learned that it was only a car backfiring.

B. Questions 6 through 8 refer to the following paragraph.

Air Couriers

(1) If you want to travel abroad but don't have a lot of money, one option is to be an air courier. (2) An air courier carries shipping documents on an international flight, and gets a cheap ticket in return. (3) Companies use couriers because it often costs less to check freight as baggage than to ship it as cargo. (4) Air couriers fly on the major airlines, so sometimes they can't check any baggage of their own. (5) Couriers usually book their trips in advance but they get their tickets on the day of the flight.

6. Sentence 2: An air courier carries shipping documents on an international flight, and gets a cheap ticket in return.

Which correction should be made to sentence 2?

A. change carries to carry
B. remove the comma
C. replace and with but
D. insert so after and

7. Sentence 4: Air couriers fly on the major airlines, so sometimes they can't check any baggage of their own.

Which is the best way to write the underlined portion of this sentence?

A. airlines, but
B. airlines but
C. airlines nor
D. airlines, or

8. Sentence 5: Couriers usually book their trips in advance but they get their tickets on the day of the flight.

Which correction should be made to sentence 5?

A. replace usually with never
B. insert a comma after advance
C. insert a comma after but
D. replace they with she

Complex Sentences

A **complex sentence** is made up of an independent clause and a **subordinate clause.** A subordinate clause has a subject and verb, but it does not express a complete thought.

KEY IDEAS

- Join a subordinate and an independent clause to form a complex sentence.
- Use a subordinating conjunction that shows the correct relationship between ideas.
- Put a comma after the subordinate clause when it comes at the beginning of a sentence.

EXAMPLES

Subordinate clause: Because their pay was too low.
Complex sentence: Teachers went on strike because their pay was too low.
(independent clause: Teachers went on strike; subordinate clause: because their pay was too low.)

Every subordinate clause begins with a **subordinating conjunction** that shows the relationship between the subordinate clause and the independent clause. Below is a list of common subordinating conjunctions.

Relationship between Clauses	Subordinating Conjunction
cause/reason	because
effect/result	in order that, so that
time	after, as, before, once, since, until, when, whenever, while
place	where, wherever
choice	if, whether
contradiction	although, even though, though

Choose the subordinating conjunction that conveys the meaning you are trying to express.

HiSET EXAM TIP

You may need to select the correct subordinating conjunction to link two clauses. Choose the word or phrase that correctly conveys the relationship between the ideas.

Incorrect meaning: The strike continued for more than a month once it finally ended.
Correct meaning: The strike continued for more than a month before it finally ended.

When a subordinate clause comes at the beginning of a sentence, put a comma after it. If the subordinate clause comes at the end of a sentence, you generally don't need a comma before it.

At beginning of sentence: While teachers were on the picket line, kids stayed home.
At end of sentence: Kids stayed home while teachers were on the picket line.

However, when a subordinate clause at the end of a sentence begins with *although, though,* or *even though,* put a comma before the clause.

At beginning of sentence: Even though the public supported the teachers, the school board did not concede to the teachers' demands.
At end of sentence: The school board did not concede to teachers' demands, even though the public supported the teachers.

A subordinate clause cannot stand independently. By itself, a subordinate clause is a sentence fragment. Make sure that every subordinate clause is joined to an independent clause.

Incorrect: After the strike finished. The school year began.
Corrected by joining independent and subordinate clauses: After the strike finished, the school year began.

PRACTICE 2.2

A. Directions: Join the clauses to form complex sentences. Use the subordinating conjunctions in parentheses.

EXAMPLE

(if) You buy a smoke detector. You can protect your family.

If you buy a smoke detector, you can protect your family. ______________________________

1. Most fatal fires occur. (when) A family is asleep.

____

2. (because) A smoke alarm wakes you up. It can allow you to escape.

____

3. Try to replace the smoke detector's battery. (before) It goes dead.

____

4. (although) Smoke detectors cost money. The expense is worth it.

____

B. Questions 5 through 7 refer to the following paragraph.

Phone Etiquette

(1) When you are making business call, it's wise to keep a few key rules in mind. (2) First of all, be prepared. (3) Have paper and pencil ready so that you won't have to fumble for them. (4) Whenever you identify yourself, ask the person whether this is a good time to talk. (5) Get to the point quickly. (6) Before you hang up. (7) Thank the person for his or her time. (8) Finally, put the phone down gently. (9) Slamming down the receiver makes a poor impression.

5. Sentence 1: When you are making business call, it's wise to keep a few key rules in mind.

Which correction should be made to sentence 1?

A. change are making to is making
B. insert a after making
C. remove the comma
D. change it's to its

6. Sentence 4: Whenever you identify yourself, ask the person whether this is a good time to talk.

Which correction should be made to sentence 4?

A. replace Whenever with After
B. remove the comma
C. insert a comma after person
D. replace the person with them

7. Sentences 6 and 7: Before you hang _______ the person for his or her time.

Choose the option that correctly completes the sentence.

A. up and then Thank
B. up and thank
C. up thank
D. up, thank

STUDY ADVICE

Don't underestimate the value of grammar: Good grammar helps others understand your writing. Being able to write clearly will help you on the Writing Test, on job applications, in advancing your career, in school (if you plan to pursue postsecondary studies), and in your life as a citizen. Therefore, if anything so far is unclear, spend more time on it before moving on.

LESSON 3

Run-Ons and Comma Splices

Run-Ons

There are two errors people commonly make when they join independent clauses to form a sentence. The first type of error is called a **run-on.** In a run-on, two independent clauses are combined without proper punctuation.

Run-On: Banks offer many helpful services you should check them out.

You can correct a run-on in one of several ways:

- Break the run-on into two separate sentences.

  Correct: Banks offer many services. You should check them out.
- Make a compound sentence (add a coordinating conjunction and a comma).

  Correct: Banks offer many services, so you should check them out.
- Make a complex sentence (add a subordinating conjunction and, if necessary, a comma).

  Correct: Because banks offer many services, you should check them out.

A run-on can also consist of independent clauses strung together with *and.* Correct this kind of run-on by dividing it into one or more compound sentences or by combining ideas into one sentence.

Run-On: Banking is getting more and more convenient and you can check on your account using bank-by-phone services and it's possible to do your banking on the Internet.
Correct: Banking is getting more and more convenient. You can check on your account using bank-by-phone services, and it's possible to do your banking on the Internet.

Run-On: Friday I got paid and I went to the bank and I cashed my check.
Correct: Friday I got paid, went to the bank, and cashed my check.

Comma Splices

The second type of error people sometimes make when joining independent clauses is called a **comma splice.** A comma splice occurs when two sentences are joined with just a comma. To correct a comma splice, add a coordinating conjunction after the comma:

Comma splice: You can check on your account using bank-by-phone services, it's possible to do your banking on the Internet.
Correct: You can check on your account using bank-by-phone services, and it's possible to do your banking on the Internet.

You can also correct a comma splice using the methods described above for correcting a run-on. You can also join two related ideas with a semicolon.

Comma splice: There are fewer bank tellers today, banks do offer other services.
Corrected by creating a complex sentence: Although there are fewer bank tellers today, banks do offer other services.

KEY IDEAS

- A run-on sentence is two or more sentences that are connected without correct punctuation.
- In a comma splice, two sentences are joined with only a comma.
- To correct a run-on or comma splice, make a compound or complex sentence or separate the sentences.

HiSET EXAM TIP

When you read a run-on sentence or a comma splice, look for the place where you would pause if you read the sentence aloud. That is where you should make the correction.

PRACTICE 3

A. Directions: Correct the following run-ons and comma splices using the methods explained on page 142.

1. Jeff just got his driver's license, he's very excited.

____

2. He bought a car that has a lot of miles on it it wasn't very expensive.

____

3. He doesn't have a lot of free time, he'd like to take a car trip.

____

4. He needs to find out about car insurance and he needs to get a good map and he needs to join an auto club.

____

B. Questions 5 through 7 refer to the following paragraph.

Photography Tips

(A)

(1) It's not hard to take great pictures just keep these tips in mind. (2) For one thing, you need to get close to your subject, or you won't get a good shot. (3) Be patient, wait for the right moment to shoot. (4) Make sure the lighting is sufficient. (5) Even outdoors, you can use a flash to fill in shadows.

(B)

(6) Think about what you want to emphasize in your picture. (7) You don't have to use the autofocus option, most cameras allow you to select the focus point you prefer. (8) For example, many photographs of people focus on the eyes.

5. **Sentence 1:** It's not hard to take great pictures just keep these tips in mind.

   Which is the best way to write the underlined portion of the sentence?

   A. pictures if you just
   B. pictures if you just that
   C. pictures, if you just
   D. pictures that just

6. **Sentence 3:** Be patient, wait for the right moment to shoot.

   Which correction should be made to sentence 3?

   A. remove the comma
   B. insert and after the comma
   C. insert but then after the comma
   D. insert a comma after moment

7. **Sentence 7:** You don't have to use the autofocus option, most cameras allow you to select the focus point you prefer.

   Which correction should be made to sentence 7?

   A. delete the comma after option
   B. insert and after option
   C. insert because in place of the comma
   D. delete you after allow

LESSON 4

Subordinate Ideas

Writing is more effective when it flows smoothly. Therefore, try to eliminate short, choppy sentences whenever possible. You can do this by using **subordination** in a variety of ways.

You already know how to form a complex sentence with a subordinating clause. You also know how to create compound sentences. Either of these methods can be used to combine short sentences.

EXAMPLES
Short and choppy: Carla ran for the bus. She missed it.
Complex sentence: Although Carla ran for the bus, she missed it.
Compound sentence: Carla ran for the bus, but she missed it.

If two sentences have the same subject, you can combine them to form one sentence with a compound predicate. The **predicate** includes the verb plus anything else that is not part of the subject:

Short and choppy: Carla sat on the bench. She looked at her watch.
With compound predicate: Carla sat on the bench and looked at her watch.

Likewise, when two sentences have the same predicate, you can combine them to form one sentence with a compound subject. The resulting sentence will be less repetitive and wordy:

Short, choppy, and repetitive: Carla missed the bus. Dave missed the bus, too.
With compound subject: Carla and Dave missed the bus.

Finally, several short sentences that are related can be combined into one longer and more detailed sentence:

Short and choppy: Carla missed the bus. It was the 7:45 bus. She was on her way to work.
More detailed sentence: Carla missed the 7:45 bus on her way to work.

Sometimes, you can use two methods at the same time. For instance, in the sentence below, you can make a complex sentence with combined details:

Short and choppy: Carla found a pay phone near the bus stop. She called her boss. Then she called one of her coworkers.
Complex sentence with combined details: After Carla found a pay phone near the bus stop, she called her boss and one of her coworkers.

Repetitive: Her boss thanked her for calling. Her coworker thanked her for calling, and they both offered to pass along any messages.
With compound subject and compound predicate: Both her boss and her coworker thanked her for calling and offered to pass along any messages.

KEY IDEAS

- Use smooth, flowing sentences rather than short, choppy sentences.
- Form compound or complex sentences from short sentences.
- Combine two predicates to make a compound predicate or combine two subjects to make a compound subject.

HiSET EXAM TIP

Read the passages on the test to yourself as if you could hear them in your mind. That "silent hearing" will help you notice sentences that are choppy or repetitive.

PRACTICE 4

A. Directions: Write each set of short, choppy sentences as one longer, smooth sentence.

EXAMPLE

If you are in a tornado, keep the windows closed. You should go to a safe place.

If you are in a tornado, keep the windows closed and go to a safe place.

1. Tornadoes can cause a lot of damage. Earthquakes are also capable of causing a lot of damage.

____

2. Earthquakes are somewhat common in California. Many Californians do not seem to mind.

____

3. On May 20, 2013, there was a tornado. It happened in Oklahoma. Twenty-four people were killed. Almost 400 people were injured.

____

4. Tornadoes can occur anywhere in the United States. They can happen any time of year.

____

B. Questions 5 through 7 refer to the following warranty.

Limited Warranty

(1) If there is any defect, Pantronics will repair this unit free of charge. (2) Audio components will be repaired. (3) Repairs will take place up to one year after the date of purchase. (4) The unit may be brought to the service center. (5) It can also be mailed. (6) A proof of purchase, such as a receipt, must be presented in order to receive service. (7) This warranty does not cover damage due to accidents. (8) It does not cover damage due to mishandling or faulty installation.

5. **Sentences 2 and 3:** Audio components will be ____________ to one year after date of purchase.

   Which is the best way to fill in the blank?

   A. repaired. Repairs will then take up
   B. repaired and repairs will take place up
   C. repaired, the repairs will take place up
   D. repaired up

6. **Sentences 4 and 5:** The unit may be brought to the service center. It can also be mailed.

   The most effective combination of sentences 4 and 5 would include which group of words?

   A. brought or mailed to
   B. once brought to the service center,
   C. units that are mailed to the service center
   D. bringing it to the service center, or mailing

7. **Sentences 7 and 8:** This warranty does not cover damage due to accidents. It does not cover damage due to mishandling or faulty installation.

   The most effective combination of sentences 7 and 8 would include which group of words?

   A. accidents, and it
   B. accidents, and this warranty
   C. accidents, and, in addition, it
   D. accidents, mishandling, or faulty installation

LESSON 5

Modify Ideas

Modifiers are words and phrases used to add descriptive details. A modifier might be a word like *sweaty*, a verb phrase like *dragging the heavy box*, a prepositional phrase like *from the storage room*, or a clause like *that we packed this morning*. Modifiers make writing clearer, more specific, and more interesting.

KEY IDEAS

- Modifiers make writing clearer and more interesting.
- Correct a dangling modifier by turning it into a subordinate clause or by making the word that is modified the subject of the sentence.
- Place a modifier as near as possible to the word or phrase it describes.

EXAMPLES

Without modifiers: Our friends Jack and Tina helped us while we were moving.
With modifiers: Our good friends Jack and Tina helped us while we were moving, watching our baby in their home.

Without modifiers: We realized the weather would not cooperate.
With modifiers: Sweating profusely at 9 A.M., we realized the weather would be uncooperatively hot.

Use modifiers carefully, or your meaning will be unclear. A **dangling modifier** is a word or phrase at the beginning of the sentence that has no clear subject to describe. To correct a dangling modifier, turn it into a subordinate clause, or make the word that the modifier describes into the subject of the sentence.

Dangling modifier: Driving the truck, one of the boxes fell out. (Who was driving the truck—one of the boxes?)
Correct: As we were driving the truck, one of the boxes fell out.
Correct: Driving the truck, we heard one of the boxes fall out.

Dangling modifier: Parking in a tow zone, a police officer gave us a ticket. (It sounds as if the police officer were parking in the tow zone.)
Correct: Because we parked in a tow zone, a police officer gave us a ticket.

Dangling modifier: Never having planned a move before, the real estate agent gave us some tips. (It sounds as if the real estate agent is the one who had never planned a move.)
Correct: Never having planned a move before, we asked the real estate agent for some tips.

HiSET EXAM TIP

When a modifying phrase is at the beginning of a sentence, use a comma to separate it from the rest of the sentence.

A misplaced modifier is poorly placed in the sentence. It is not clear which word it modifies, or it modifies the wrong word in the sentence. To correct a misplaced modifier, put the modifier next to the word it describes.

Misplaced modifier: The moving van was just large enough that we rented.
Correct: The moving van that we rented was just large enough.

Misplaced modifier: We hoisted and lugged all our furniture up two flights of stairs panting heavily. (What was panting heavily—*we* or *the stairs*?)
Correct: Panting heavily, we hoisted and lugged all our furniture up two flights of stairs.

PRACTICE 5

A. Directions: Revise each sentence, correcting the misplaced or dangling modifier.

1. Trent's sister encouraged him to become a nurse, who is a health professional.

____

2. Waking up the patients to take their blood pressure, they get rather annoyed.

____

3. He writes their temperature and blood pressure on their charts carefully.

____

4. Talking with the patients, it is hard to make visitors leave at 9 P.M.

____

B. Questions 5 through 7 refer to the following passage about adoption.

Adoption

(A)

(1) Adoption is a legal procedure that gives a person the rights of a son or daughter who is not the birth child of the adopter. (2) This practice dates back to ancient Greece. (3) People without heirs used it to perpetuate their estates.

(B)

(4) Adoptions may be handled through an agency or by independent placement. (5) Going through an agency, a "home study" to decide whether prospective parents will be fit is required. (6) In an independent placement, there is no study. (7) Lawyers handle these adoptions when parents ask them to frequently.

5. **Sentence 1:** Adoption is a legal procedure that gives a person the rights of a son or daughter who is not the birth child of the adopter.

   The most effective revision of sentence 1 would include which group of words?

   A. a legal procedure, adoption that gives
   B. a person who is not the birth child
   C. the son or daughter of the adopter
   D. the birth child, who is a son or daughter

6. **Sentence 5:** Going through an agency, a "home study" to decide whether prospective parents will be fit is required.

   The most effective revision of sentence 5 would begin with which group of words?

   A. For parents, going through an agency
   B. Requiring a "home study"
   C. An agency requires a "home study"
   D. Deciding whether a parent is fit

7. **Sentence 7:** Lawyers handle these adoptions when parents ask them to frequently.

   Which correction should be made to sentence 7?

   A. insert a comma after adoptions
   B. replace to with too
   C. insert a comma after to
   D. move frequently to follow Lawyers

STUDY ADVICE

Keep in mind that people often do not correctly use modifiers when speaking. Learn the rules in this lesson and don't rely on your ear for modifiers.

LESSON 6

Parallel Structure

When you write a sentence that lists two or more words, phrases, or clauses, the elements in the list must be in the same grammatical form. In other words, the sentence must have **parallel structure.** Writing that has parallel structure is clearer and easier to follow.

KEY IDEAS

- Listed items should be parallel in form and structure.
- Each phrase should have the same elements as other phrases in the series.
- Don't put words and clauses together in the same series.

Examples

Not parallel: Jim wants to eat less, exercise more, and be getting more sleep.
Parallel: Jim wants to eat less, exercise more, and get more sleep.

Not parallel: Walking and to swim are good aerobic exercises.
Parallel: Walking and swimming are good aerobic exercises.

Not parallel: Try to lose weight slowly, sensibly, and be careful.
Parallel: Try to lose weight slowly, sensibly, and carefully.

To be sure that your sentences have parallel structure, follow the guidelines below.

Make sure that verbs in a list are in the same form and tense:

Not parallel: Jim went to the store, bought an exercise mat, and is doing exercises.
Parallel: Jim went to the store, bought an exercise mat, and did exercises.

Be sure that phrases in a list are parallel in form and wording. For example, if one phrase in a list begins with a preposition, the others should, too. If one phrase begins with the word *the*, the others should, too.

Not parallel: Avoid exercising on busy streets, near traffic jams, and polluted areas.
Parallel: Avoid exercising on busy streets, near traffic jams, and in polluted areas.

Not parallel: He left the gym shoes, sweatpants, and the shirt in the gym.
Parallel: He left the gym shoes, the sweatpants, and the shirt in the gym.

Each list must have single words, short phrases, or clauses. Don't put single words and clauses together in the same series:

HiSET EXAM TIP

When you revise a sentence to use parallel structure, use the comma to separate each element as shown in these examples.

Not parallel: The most effective fitness programs are low impact, informal, and you can do them at home.
Parallel: The most effective fitness programs are low impact, informal, and home based.

Finally, notice that a comma separates each item within a list of three or more: *low impact, informal, and home based.*

PRACTICE 6

A. Directions: Rewrite each sentence to make the structure parallel.

EXAMPLE

Jenna works quickly, carefully, and is thorough.

Jenna works quickly, carefully, and thoroughly.

1. Jenna has worked in a factory, a store, and has a waitressed.

2. She would like putting her kids in a better school and to get a better job.

3. She thinks the kids' father is irresponsible, lazy, and doesn't care about them.

4. He doesn't have the time, the energy, or money to give them what they deserve.

B. Questions 5 through 7 refer to the following memo.

TO: All Employees

(A)

(1) A new alarm system has been installed. (2) It is designed to make our workplace safer, more comfortable, and pleasant. (3) However, we need everyone's cooperation.

(B)

(4) If you are the last one to leave, turn off all lights, computers, and check the coffee makers. (5) Then go to the alarm system located by the door. (6) Punch in the secret code, press ON, and be leaving immediately. (7) Lock the door behind you.

5. **Sentence 2:** It is designed to make our workplace safer, more comfortable, and pleasant.

   Which correction should be made to sentence 2?

   A. replace our with are
   B. remove the comma after safer
   C. insert more before pleasant
   D. no correction is necessary

6. **Sentence 4:** If you are the last one to leave, turn off all lights, ________________ coffee makers.

   Choose the option that correctly completes the sentence.

   A. and computers, and the
   B. computers, and check the
   C. computers, and checking the
   D. computers, and

7. **Sentence 6:** Punch in the secret code, press ON, and be leaving immediately.

   Which correction should be made to sentence 6?

   A. change punch to punching
   B. remove the comma after ON
   C. change be leaving to leave
   D. insert a comma after leaving

STUDY ADVICE

Love reading novels or comic books? That's fantastic, because you're building your language skills every time you read. However, sometimes authors deliberately break the rules of grammar to create an artistic effect. That said, don't mimic your favorite writer; rather, use the rules in this chapter when you write your essay.

LESSON 7

Writing Style

Formal and Less Formal Style

Writing style should be more or less formal depending on the purpose of the writing and who will be reading it. Published academic writing is very formal. Because the purpose is to express ideas precisely to other people who study the topic, sentences may be relatively complex and vocabulary advanced. The emotional tone is neutral, as in the example below.

> Although the dynamics of federalism vary, particularly with regard to exchanges of power and influence between the central authority and substate entities (such as municipalities), federalist nations generally tend to exhibit a tendency toward race-to-the-top business-related legislation.

Writing for business, journalism, or school assignments is businesslike. A workplace memo, news article, or paper for class follows the rules of grammar and punctuation and expresses ideas clearly and concisely. Passive voice and wordy constructions, while not exactly wrong, should usually be avoided. The purpose is to be understood by a general audience, so sentences are less complex, and the writer uses familiar words. The tone may be neutral, or the writer may express moderate enthusiasm or dismay, as in the example below.

> A recent government report estimates that 15 percent of American households experienced food insecurity last year. (Food insecurity is defined as the state of being without reliable means of acquiring food.) Food insecurity affected almost 9 million children last year.

An email to a friend, a post on Facebook, or a line of dialogue in a novel will all be casual in tone. Because the primary purpose is to sound like speech, the conventions of written grammar and spelling may not be followed. In fiction, dialogue or interior monologue (the character's unspoken thoughts) must reflect the speaker's personality, level of education or sophistication, and mood. The example below is from a work of fiction.

> "Well, matters ain't gone any too well with him," Harmon said. "When a man's been setting round like a hulk for twenty years or more, seeing things that want doing, it eats inter him, and he loses his grit."

Excerpted from *Ethan Frome*, Edith Wharton, 1911.

Communication via Twitter or text message is not bound by conventional rules of grammar, spelling, and punctuation because the goal is to communicate with a minimum of words.

KEY IDEAS

- Depending on the author's purpose and audience, writing should be formal, businesslike, or casual.
- Departures from the rules of grammar are sometimes acceptable in fiction or informal communications like texts.
- When unsure how to express an idea correctly or appropriately, the writer should consult an authoritative guide to style.

HiSET EXAM TIP

When you evaluate someone else's writing or practice your own writing, try reading it aloud. You will hear whether the language is formal, businesslike, or casual.

PRACTICE 7.1

A. Identify the answer choice that best matches the style required to complete each sentence.

1. The following sentence appears in a paper written for a history class.

____ an underlying cause was the very different economic and social systems that had developed in the industrializing North and the agrarian South.

A. With different attitudes toward slavery being an obvious cause of the American Civil War,
B. While different attitudes toward slavery were an obvious cause of the American Civil War,
C. Despite the obvious cause of the American Civil War being different attitudes toward slavery,
D. It is clear as day that different attitudes toward slavery were a cause of the American Civil War, but

2. The following sentence appears in a letter to the editor of a newspaper.

The city council should consider without delay the proposed lifting of the ban on owning pit bulls within a mile of a school, ____.

A. because this law unfairly restricts the property rights of some citizens
B. due to the fact that some citizens' property rights are being unfairly restricted by the law
C. on account of the law's unfair restriction of some citizens' rights
D. given the unfair restriction of the property rights of some citizens that the law imposes

3. The following sentences are spoken by a character in a novel.

"I'm just saying, it goes to show that not everyone is telling the truth all the time. You need to ____."

A. exercise vigilance against prevarication when you converse with individuals who make inflated claims
B. be careful now, having been burned by this person, not to get hurt again in the same way by someone else another time
C. be aware of the potential for falsehood when someone's stories seem exaggerated
D. watch out when someone makes promises that seem too good to be true

4. The following sentences appear in an email from an office manager to the employees in that office:

Our company vacation policy has changed. From now on, ____ must use at least one week of vacation in October, November, or December.

A. if having more than three weeks of vacation saved up as of the end of September, employees
B. employees with more than three weeks of vacation saved up at the end of September
C. employees swimming in vacation days at the end of September—that is, those with three weeks or more—
D. employees who have accrued in excess of three weeks of vacation as of September's month end

Using Style Guides

What is correct spelling, punctuation, and grammar has varied over time and, at any given time, varies according to the type of publication. Publishers of different types of material use different style guides to determine what is correct. Consider the example below.

> "You are over scrupulous surely. I dare say Mr. Bingley will be very glad to see you; and I will send a few lines by you to assure him of my hearty consent to his marrying which ever he chuses of the girls; though I must throw in a good word for my little Lizzy."

Excerpted from *Pride and Prejudice*, Jane Austen, 1813.

- Today, *overscrupulous* and *whichever* would be spelled as one word, and "chuses" would be spelled *chooses*. However, these spellings were correct when *Pride and Prejudice* was published in Britain in 1813.
- Today one would use commas where semicolons are used here. Again, this punctuation was correct in early 19th-century Britain.
- The quoted dialogue is spoken by a husband having an ordinary conversation with his wife. In the mouth of a modern character, these words would sound extremely stilted, but they conformed to the literary conventions of the time.

There are many style guides. Different style guides may have different guidance about spelling, punctuation, sentence structure, idioms, and other aspects of writing. Consider the differences listed in the two tables below:

Table 4.1: Spelling differences

Style Guide A	***Style Guide B***
e-mail	email
push-up	pushup
Web site	website
whistle-blower	whistleblower

Table 4.2: Various differences in guidance

***Chicago Manual of Style*, 16th edition (used by book publishers)**	***A news website's style guidelines***	***A style guide used by scholarly journals***
In a list of three or more items, use of serial comma (before *and*) is highly recommended.	Do not use serial comma.	Always use serial comma.
When a complete sentence follows a colon, do not capitalize the first word after the colon.	When a complete sentence follows a colon, capitalize the first word after the colon.	When a complete sentence follows a colon, capitalize the first word after the colon.
Usually write out numbers up to one hundred; use numerals for 101 and up.	Usually write out numbers up to nine; use numerals for 10 and up. Use numerals for ages.	Usually write out numbers up to nine; use numerals for 10 and up. Use numerals for quantities of time.
Spell out *United States* when used as a noun; abbreviate *US* when used as an adjective, as in "the US economy."	Abbreviate *United States* as *U.S.* in text, as *US* in headlines.	Spell out *United States* when used as a noun; abbreviate *U.S.* when used as an adjective, as in "the U.S. economy."

Whenever you write, think about what style is appropriate and ask a teacher or supervisor what style guide is recommended.

PRACTICE 7.2

A. Match the sentence to the style guide rule with which it complies.

1. Each of the sentences below conforms to a rule listed in the *Chicago Manual of Style*. Match the rule (in the second table) to the sentence in the first table.

The letters *z* and *q* are the most infrequently used in the English language.	
When viewing a solar eclipse, it is important not to look at the sun directly.	
Many early civilizations arose in the Fertile Crescent, an area that today includes the nations of Egypt and Iraq.	
He was not sure whether he should apply to college or not, but if he did, he would ask Mr. Robson for a letter of recommendation.	

a. 8.140 The words *sun* and *moon* are usually lowercased in nontechnical contexts and always lowercased in the plural.
b. 5.220 While *if* is conditional, *whether* introduces an alternative.
c. 7.59 Individual letters and combinations of letters of the Latin alphabet are usually italicized.
d. 8.47 Popular names of places, or epithets, are usually capitalized [in contexts where they will be readily understood].

2. Use the appropriate rule from a style guide used by students. The rules are in the second table; match them to the examples in the first table.

They asked an impartial mediator to help them resolve their dispute, but the mediator was uninterested in the case.	
The smokejumpers who fight fires in national forests undergo extensive training.	
Before she signed up for Psychology 101, she read that it must be taken prior to Psychology 102.	
The president is the commander in chief of the armed forces.	

a. The job titles *firefighter, smokejumper,* and *bookbinder* are written as one word and are not capitalized.
b. Use *disinterested* to mean impartial. Use *uninterested* to mean that someone lacks interest.
c. In general, only capitalize titles when they are used directly before an individual's name.
d. In general, *before* is preferable to *prior to. Prior to* is appropriate, however, when something is required for something else to happen.

B. Use the material from the given style guide to complete the sentence.

3. A style guide used by scientists advises writers to avoid language that labels a person by his or her condition (such as "she is a neurotic"). The guide instructs writers to use language that puts the person before the condition.

In his study, he will analyze data from surveys of ____________.

A. veterans with disabilities

B. disabled veterans

C. veterans who are experiencing disabilities

D. handicapped veterans

4. *Chicago Manual of Style*: "Chicago prefers the lowercase form [of abbreviations for time of day], with periods. . . . Time zones, where needed, are usually given in parentheses—for example, 4:45 p.m. (CST)."

The tournament will begin at ____________, so it will be on television in the morning in the United States.

A. 1 in the afternoon (Greenwich Mean Time)

B. one o'clock in the afternoon (GMT)

C. 1:00 p.m. (GMT)

D. 1 P.M. GMT

WRITING EFFECTIVE SENTENCES PRACTICE QUESTIONS

Questions 1 through 5 refer to the following paragraphs.

Conserving Household Energy

(A)

(1) According to the Department of Energy, many families spend an average of 14 percent of their yearly income on heating and cooling costs. (2) Although you can't do much about high fuel prices, you can try some energy-saving measures.

(B)

(3) To reduce wintertime energy costs, keep the shades drawn at night. (4) Seal your windows, so that cold air can't get through the cracks. (5) You can use sealing material available at any hardware store. (6) If you have an air conditioner, cover it with thick plastic. (7) Keep your thermostat at 68°F during the day. (8) Keep it at 62°F at night.

(C)

(9) In the summer, use fans and natural breezes rather than air-conditioning whenever possible. (10) If you have windows that get direct sunlight. (11) Keep the shades down during the day. (12) Don't leave your air conditioner running when you're not at home, change the filter every summer. (13) With a clogged filter, the air conditioner's energy use can go up as much as 5 percent. (14) Put your air conditioner on a low setting. (15) Your home will not cool down when your air conditioner is on full blast any faster.

1. Sentence 4: **Seal your windows, so that cold air can't get through the cracks.**

   Which correction should be made to sentence 4?

   A. change seal to sealing
   B. remove the comma
   C. change can't to couldn't
   D. change through to out

2. Sentences 7 and 8: **Keep your thermostat at 68°F during the day. Keep it at 62°F at night.**

   The most effective combination of sentences 7 and 8 would include which group of words?

   A. keeping your thermostat at
   B. during the day and 62°F
   C. the day, keeping it at
   D. at night, it should be kept

3. Sentences 10 and 11: **If you have windows that get direct sunlight. Keep the shades down during the day.**

   Which is the best way to write the underlined portion of these sentences?

   A. sunlight and
   B. sunlight and to keep
   C. sunlight keep
   D. sunlight, keep

4. Sentence 12: **Don't leave your air conditioner running when you're not at home, change the filter every summer.**

   Which is the best way to write the underlined portion of the sentence?

   A. home and change
   B. home change
   C. home, so change
   D. home. Do change

5. Sentence 15: **Your home will not cool down when your air conditioner is on full blast any faster.**

   The most effective revision of sentence 15 would begin with which group of words?

   A. Your home will not cool down any faster
   B. Having the air conditioner on full blast, it
   C. When your home will not cool down,
   D. Air-conditioning your home on full blast,

Questions 6 through 10 refer to the following letter of complaint.

Cole Electronics
2514 Broadway
New York, NY 10057

Dear Manager:

(A)

(1) On August 2, I purchased a television at your store. (2) When I got the television home I discovered that the picture was fuzzy. (3) Returning to the store to see if the problem could be fixed easily. (4) I assumed that there would be no problem because I had just purchased the set.

(B)

(5) The customer service personnel said they had no time to handle my complaint. (6) They were extremely rude and unprofessional. (7) Finally, a salesman told me that I would have to send the TV to a service center in Detroit. (8) At that point, I demanded a refund. (9) Claiming that the TV had been used, it could not be returned.

(C)

(10) I am angry about the treatment I received and I am also very frustrated. (11) I would now like to receive a full refund or getting the TV repaired locally. (12) Please contact me to let me know what action will be taken. (13) My phone number is (212) 555-2719.

Sincerely,
Jeffrey Barnes

6. Sentence 2: **When I got the television home I discovered that the picture was fuzzy.**

   Which correction should be made to sentence 2?

   A. replace When with Since
   B. insert a comma after home
   C. insert a comma after discovered
   D. change was to be

7. Sentence 3: **Returning to the store to see if the problem could be fixed easily.**

   Which correction should be made to sentence 3?

   A. replace Returning with I returned
   B. add a comma after store
   C. change could to can
   D. change easily to easy

8. Sentence 9: **Claiming that the TV had been used, it could not be returned.**

   The most effective revision of sentence 9 would begin with which group of words?

   A. He claimed that because
   B. The TV was claimed to
   C. Returning the TV,
   D. Making a claim about the TV

9. Sentence 10: **I am angry about the treatment I received and I am also very frustrated.**

   The most effective revision of sentence 10 would include which group of words?

   A. angry and frustrated about the
   B. feeling angry about the treatment
   C. being the recipient of such treatment
   D. the manner in which I was treated

10. Sentence 11: **I would now like to receive a full ____________ the TV repaired locally.**

    Choose the option that correctly completes the sentence.

    A. refund, getting
    B. refund, or getting
    C. refund or get
    D. refund to getting

Questions 11 though 15 refer to the following paragraphs.

Workplace Friendships

(A)

(1) Should you make friends at work or keep your distance? (2) Most experts agree that it's not wise to get too chummy with your boss. Relationships with coworkers, however, are a more complex matter. (3) Although workplace friendships between peers can be beneficial, they can also cause problems.

(B)

(4) Workplace friendships have many positive aspects. (5) It's hard to work if you feel alone and in a productive way. (6) Having friends at work can make your day more pleasant, and give you energy. (7) Friends can serve as a sounding board for problems and help you succeed.

(C)

(8) However, like any other friendship, workplace friendships can turn sour. (9) Things get messy, when the friendship unravels in plain view of your boss and coworkers. (10) Discrimination and harassment suits have even been brought in some cases.

(D)

(11) Experts recommend keeping your social life with work friends out of the workplace. (12) For instance, don't exchange presents at work or talking about your evening out. (13) Avoid praising a friend publicly if it could make someone else resentful. (14) Keeping your work life separate from your social life may be hard but it's worth the effort.

11. Sentence 5: **It's hard to work if you feel alone and in a productive way.**

    The most effective revision of sentence 5 would include which group of words?

    A. work productively if you
    B. to work, it isn't easy if
    C. if you feel alone and productive
    D. work, feel alone, and be productive

12. Sentence 6: **Having friends at work can make your day more pleasant, and give you energy.**

    Which correction should be made to sentence 6?

    A. change Having to Have
    B. insert a comma after work
    C. remove the comma
    D. change give to giving

13. Sentence 9: **Things get messy, when the friendship unravels in plain view of your boss and coworkers.**

    Which correction should be made to sentence 9?

    A. change get to are getting
    B. remove the comma
    C. insert a comma after unravels
    D. insert a comma after boss

14. Sentence 12: **For instance, don't exchange presents at _________ about your evening out.**

    Choose the option that correctly completes the sentence.

    A. work or talk
    B. work, or talk
    C. work, or talking
    D. working or talking

15. Sentence 14: **Keeping your work life separate from your social life may be hard but it's worth the effort.**

    Which correction should be made to sentence 14?

    A. insert it after social life
    B. insert a comma after hard
    C. insert a comma after but
    D. replace it's with its

Questions 16 through 19 refer to the following paragraphs.

Computer Virus Hoaxes

(A)

(1) If you use email, you've probably received at least one message warning you of a terrible virus that will ruin your computer. (2) Most of these messages are hoaxes. (3) Designed to scare you. (4) Though some messages about viruses are accurate, most are just inaccurate rumors.

(B)

(5) Virus hoax messages are similar to one another. (6) Frequently, they describe viruses that will destroy your hard drive or computer. (7) These hoaxes also claim that a respected authority, such as a government agency, has issued a warning about the virus. (8) You can check a claim like this. (9) Contacting the agency is a good way to check. (10) Finally, hoaxes urge you to send the message to everyone you know, this just creates panic.

(C)

(11) If you receive a virus warning, don't pass it on. (12) However, you don't have to worry about opening the email message itself. (13) Your computer can't get a virus that way. (14) Don't open any suspicious attachments, though, as you might infect your computer with a real virus. (15) By following these guidelines, you can keep your computer equipment safe, and avoid spreading hysteria.

16. Sentences 2 and 3: **Most of these messages are _________ to scare you.**

    Choose the option that correctly completes the sentence.

    A. hoaxes and they are designed
    B. hoaxes and they designed
    C. hoaxes, designing
    D. hoaxes designed

17. Sentences 8 and 9: **You can check a claim like this. Contacting the agency is a good way to check.**

    The most effective combination of sentences 8 and 9 would include which group of words?

    A. Checking a claim like this
    B. To check a claim like this, contact
    C. The agency in question can check
    D. A good way to check, contacting

18. Sentence 10: **Finally, hoaxes urge you to send the message to everyone you _________ just creates panic.**

    Choose the option that best completes the sentence.

    A. know and this
    B. know, this
    C. know. This
    D. know that this

19. Sentence 15: **By following these guidelines, you can keep your computer equipment safe, and avoid spreading hysteria.**

    Which correction should be made to sentence 15?

    A. change By following to To follow
    B. replace these with this
    C. remove the comma after guidelines
    D. remove the comma after safe

STUDY ADVICE

Congratulations on completing another practice set! If you are struggling with a topic and don't feel you have more time to spend on it right this second, flag it for later. Keeping a list of what you should come back to will save time and guide your future studies.

LESSON 1

Organize Ideas into Paragraphs

Effective Paragraphs

A **paragraph** is a group of sentences that relate to one main idea. If the sentences do not help develop the same main idea, the paragraph seems disorganized, and the writer's meaning is unclear.

Incorrect:

> Houseplants make a home more beautiful, but many people find them difficult to take care of. I water my houseplants once a week. There are many different kinds of houseplants. If you are buying a houseplant as a gift, consider how much light the person's home gets.

In the example above, each sentence is about houseplants, but there is no main idea. In the paragraph below, however, each sentence supports one idea: *helping houseplants adjust to a new home.*

Correct:

> Houseplants need help to adjust to a new environment. Your home is probably less bright and humid than a greenhouse or plant store. Therefore, when you get a new houseplant, keep it near a south-facing window at first. Move it away from the light over a period of four weeks. Use a humidifier to make the air in your home more humid. These actions will help avoid the loss of foliage that often occurs when plants change locales.

One paragraph should stop and a new one begin when the main idea shifts. In the example below, the first four sentences describe what road rage is, while the last four sentences tell how to react to road rage. The writer should have started a new paragraph with sentence 5.

Incorrect:

> (1) Road rage is an episode of violent behavior that takes place when one driver's actions anger another driver. (2) Young males are the most likely to lose their cool on the road. (3) Most road rage incidents take place during rush hour, when people often get frustrated. (4) Warm weather is another factor in road rage. (5) If you're a victim of an aggressive driver, try to stay calm. (6) Don't react or make eye contact. (7) Try not to brake or swerve in retaliation. (8) These actions will only infuriate the other driver, and you might lose control of your car.

Sometimes the ideas in two paragraphs really belong in one paragraph:

Incorrect:

> To make chicken broth, boil a pot of water. Take some chicken, onions, parsnips, carrots, and herbs, and wrap them up in cheesecloth.
>
> Make sure it is real cotton cheesecloth, or you won't be able to eat the broth! Simmer the cheesecloth-wrapped vegetables and chicken in the water for several hours; then remove them. Add salt and pepper to taste.

KEY IDEAS

- Each paragraph should have one main idea.
- Each sentence in a paragraph should relate to the main idea.
- Join short paragraphs if they both relate to the same main idea.

HiSET EXAM TIP

If a paragraph is especially long, check to see if the main idea shifts at some point. If so, that is where the paragraph should be divided in two.

PRACTICE 1.1

A. Directions: Read each group of sentences. If there is a main idea, underline it. If there is no main idea, write, "No MI."

____ 1. The pharmacist at the local drugstore is very helpful. She can always get the medicines we need. She arranges deliveries of our prescriptions when we're sick. When we don't have money, she lets us pay the next time. Many people have written to thank her.

____ 2. Keep your toolbox well equipped, and you'll always be able to make home repairs. Common home repairs include replacing lighting fixtures and fixing furniture. The community center offers a class on this subject. You can pay someone to do home repairs.

____ 3. Some people don't vote because they think their vote doesn't count. However, elections have been won by just a few hundred votes. If people don't vote, they are giving up their voice. Every vote counts, so let your voice be heard and vote!

____ 4. When you are traveling, it's a good idea to mark your luggage clearly. Put a luggage tag on every piece you intend to bring, including hand luggage like backpacks. To recognize your luggage quickly, put a brightly colored ribbon on it.

____ 5. Listening to music can benefit you in many ways. When you are feeling stressed, music can help soothe and relax you. When you need energy, rock 'n' roll or hip-hop can give you a boost. If you have a baby or small child, soft music can help lull the child to sleep.

B. Questions 6 and 7 refer to the following paragraphs.

The Common Cold

(A)

(1) How frequently you get colds depends on your age. (2) The average young adult gets two to four colds a year. (3) Adults over 60 have fewer than one cold a year, while children have six to ten colds annually. (4) Colds are caused by viruses. (5) Contrary to popular belief, being cold will not cause you to get a cold. (6) Vitamin C is thought to prevent colds, but there is no proof.

(B)

(7) Because there is no cure for the common cold, prevention is key. (8) Washing your hands is the best way to avoid getting a cold. (9) Encourage others who have colds to sneeze into a tissue and throw it away immediately.

(C)

(10) Refrain from touching your eyes and nose, and stay far from people who have colds.

6. Which revision would improve the effectiveness of the article?

   Begin a new paragraph with

   A. sentence 2
   B. sentence 3
   C. sentence 4
   D. sentence 5

7. Which revision would improve the effectiveness of the article?

   A. remove sentence 1
   B. remove paragraph (B)
   C. remove paragraph (C)
   D. join paragraphs (B) and (C)

Topic Sentences in Paragraphs

Every paragraph should have a **topic sentence** that states the main idea. The other sentences in the paragraph are **supporting details.** These details tell more about the topic sentence. The topic sentence usually appears at the beginning of the paragraph, though it may appear elsewhere.

A topic sentence must do two things:

- Identify the topic, or subject, of the paragraph
- State the central point that the writer wants to make about the topic

In the paragraph below, the topic sentence is underlined. Notice how the topic sentence tells the subject of the paragraph *(graffiti in our neighborhood)* and states the central point about the topic *(graffiti is a serious problem in the neighborhood and should be addressed).*

KEY IDEAS

- A topic sentence states the main idea of a paragraph.
- Each sentence in a paragraph should provide details to support the main idea.
- An essay should have a main idea statement that states the main point of the entire essay.

EXAMPLE

We need to do more to stop the problem of graffiti in our neighborhood. Recently, several bus stops and the exterior walls of many buildings have been defaced with unsightly graffiti. The neighborhood is fast becoming a much less desirable place to live. As a result, prospective renters feel frightened and look elsewhere.

A topic sentence should not be too specific or too general. If it is, readers won't know what the overall point is. A topic sentence like "The market is covered with gang symbols," would be too specific for the paragraph above. "There is graffiti in our neighborhood," would be too general.

Main Idea Statements in Essays

Just as every paragraph should have a topic sentence, every essay should have a **main idea statement**. Whereas a topic sentence states the main idea, or "point," of a single paragraph, a main idea statement expresses the central point of all the paragraphs in an essay. In the essay below, the main idea statement is underlined. Notice that while the main idea statement appears in the first paragraph, it is not the first sentence.

HiSET EXAM TIP

Be sure that every paragraph has a clear topic sentence.

EXAMPLE

While graffiti is indeed a serious problem facing our neighborhood, other issues also need to be addressed. Two of the most pressing neighborhood issues are the crime rate and the lack of decent housing.

In recent months, crime has increased. For example, a number of muggings have occurred. As a result, residents are nervous about going out at night. The number of apartment break-ins has increased as well. We need a stronger police presence to combat the crime problem.

In addition, much of the housing in this neighborhood is in poor condition. Every day, residents are put in danger by loose roof tiles, broken locks, and rundown fences. We must put pressure on landlords to resolve their tenants' complaints, perhaps by showing them that, in the long run, it is in their financial interest to do so.

If we do not act immediately, our neighborhood will decline even more. Therefore, I recommend that we form a community task force to tackle these issues. We should ask our city councilwoman to be an advocate for us. With full participation of community members, we will be on our way to a safer, more livable neighborhood.

PRACTICE 1.2

A. Directions: Write topic sentences for each of the following paragraphs.

1. ____

Weather satellites send us information about weather around the world. Thanks to satellite TV, we have an ever-widening range of programs to choose from. Satellites even play a role in long-distance telephone communication.

2. ____

First of all, stock prices are falling. Second, home sales have slowed to a crawl. Finally, many consumers have cut back on big purchases such as cars, home improvements, and vacations.

3. ____

According to the new dress code, employees of the library may now wear "semi-casual" clothing. Khakis, blue jeans with no holes, and other slacks are acceptable for men and women. Skirts must be knee-length or longer. Sandals are acceptable in the summer. Employees are requested not to wear gym shoes.

B. Questions 4 and 5 refer to the following paragraphs.

Repetitive Strain Injury

(A)

(1) Repetitive strain injury is a problem. (2) The injury can affect factory workers, computer users, and meatpackers, among others. (3) Anyone who uses his or her hands all day may be affected, even if the work does not seem to require a lot of physical effort. (4) When fine hand movements are repeated for many hours a day, they eventually strain the forearms, wrists, and fingers.

(B)

(5) Maintaining a stiff and constrained posture, as is required for working at a computer, places a lot of stress on the body. (6) Likewise, holding muscles still for long periods causes fatigue and discomfort. (7) In addition, many jobs require workers to work at top speed all day long. (8) Consistently working quickly deprives the body of natural rest breaks, forcing workers to push themselves to the limit.

4. Which is the most effective revision of sentence 1?

A. Some workers get repetitive strain injury.
B. Just what, you may ask, is repetitive strain injury?
C. Workers suffer many injuries on the job, and repetitive strain injury is just one of them.
D. Repetitive strain injury is a painful condition resulting from repeated use of the hands.

5. Which sentence would be most effective if inserted at the beginning of paragraph (B)?

A. Repetitive movements cause muscle strain.
B. A number of factors contribute to repetitive strain injury.
C. Watch your posture as you work.
D. Repetitive strain injury is very common.

STUDY ADVICE

Remember that practice has three levels: Learn and Review, Practice and Review, Assess and Review. For each lesson, absorb the concepts on the left side of the page. Then practice using the page on the right, and carefully review the explanations in the back of the book. Afterwards, you'll be able to assess your comprehension by completing the practice set and reviewing the explanations. By following these steps, you'll learn a great deal about how the questions work and what you're doing well.

LESSON 2

Use Logical Order and Relevant Ideas

When you are writing a paragraph, it is important to put your sentences in a logical order. For instance, you may choose to sequence supporting details from most important to least important, from least important to most important, or in time order. All the sentences in the paragraph should follow the same order. If not, your readers may get confused. Look at the sample paragraphs below:

Incorrect:

To clear a clogged drain using a plunger, fill the sink with enough water to cover the plunger cup. Put petroleum jelly on the rim of the cup to form a tight seal. Before you begin, check to make sure that the plunger's suction cup is big enough to cover the drain. Block the sink overflow with rags. Plunge 15 or 20 times.

Correct:

To clear a clogged drain using a plunger, first check to make sure that the plunger's suction cup is big enough to cover the drain. Fill the sink with enough water to cover the plunger cup. Put petroleum jelly on the rim of the cup to form a tight seal. Block the sink overflow with rags. Plunge 15 or 20 times.

The reasons and examples you use to support your points should come immediately after you make each point. If they come later, they will be less effective.

Incorrect:

Don't make a habit of using chemicals to clear your drain. Always wear rubber gloves to protect your hands when using chemical drain cleaners. These powerful cleaners can damage the pipes.

Correct:

Don't make a habit of using chemicals to clear your drain. These powerful cleaners can damage the pipes. Always wear rubber gloves to protect your hands when using chemical drain cleaners.

Sometimes a sentence in a paragraph relates to the topic in a general way but does not support the topic sentence. This mistake is a type of **irrelevant detail**, as shown in the paragraph below:

In many cultures, blonde is considered a desirable hair color. Perhaps blonde hair is valued because few people are naturally blonde. The practice of bleaching one's hair blonde is very old, dating back to ancient Roman times, and it continues to be popular today. My sister dyed her hair last year. A number of hair-bleaching products are sold in drugstores and supermarkets.

The sentence "My sister dyed her hair last year" is an irrelevant detail. While it relates to the topic of bleaching one's hair, it does not support the idea that blonde is a popular hair color in many cultures. This sentence should be deleted.

KEY IDEAS

- The sentences in a paragraph should follow a logical order.
- Keep reasons and examples close to the point you are making with them.
- Eliminate any irrelevant details.

HiSET EXAM TIP

Make sure that every supporting sentence is relevant to the topic sentence. Ask yourself, "Does this support the main idea of the paragraph?" If not, delete it or move it to where it belongs.

PRACTICE 2

A. Directions: Cross out the irrelevant detail in each paragraph.

1. Why do people blame themselves when things go terribly wrong? Some psychologists believe that by blaming themselves, people find a reason for the upsetting event. Getting very ill is one bad thing that could happen. Finding a reason is more comforting than believing that the event took place for no reason at all.

2. It's almost time for the back-to-school rush. This year, come to Wunnzie's to make sure that your child is outfitted with all the things that he or she needs. We have school supplies at rock-bottom prices. Adult students can also use school supplies. Check out our backpacks and lunch boxes in colors your kids will love. At Wunnzie's, we have everything your kids will ever need!

3. Tenants: On Friday, April 23, the boiler in this building will be fixed. This job will be extremely expensive! There will be no water from 8 A.M. to 5 P.M. Please plan in advance, and draw out water the night before to be used the next day. We apologize for the inconvenience.

B. Questions 4 through 6 refer to the following cover letter.

(A)

Dear Mr. Soros:

(1) Thank you very much for taking the time to speak with me about the carpentry position. (2) It was a pleasure to meet you and to learn about your organization. (3) I enjoyed meeting you and learning about your organization.

(B)

(4) As you will see from the enclosed resume, I recently completed a program in carpentry at Dade Community College. (5) I have also worked in the carpentry field. (6) In addition, I held a secretarial job.

(C)

(7) With my education and experience, I believe that I could make a valuable contribution to your company. (8) Thank you for considering me for this position. (9) I look forward to hearing from you soon. (10) I would be honored to take the job if it were offered to me.

Sincerely,

Sandra Barnes

4. Which revision would improve the effectiveness of paragraph (A)?

A. remove sentence 1
B. move sentence 1 to follow sentence 2
C. move sentence 2 to the beginning of paragraph B
D. remove sentence 3

5. Sentence 6: **In addition, I held a secretarial job.**

Which revision should be made to the placement of sentence 6?

A. move sentence 6 to follow sentence 4
B. move sentence 6 to follow sentence 8
C. move sentence 6 to follow sentence 10
D. remove sentence 6

6. Sentence 10: **I would be honored to take the job if it were offered to me.**

Which revision should be made to the placement of sentence 10?

A. move sentence 10 to follow sentence 2
B. move sentence 10 to follow sentence 4
C. move sentence 10 to follow sentence 5
D. move sentence 10 to follow sentence 8

LESSON 3

Relate Sentences and Paragraphs

Good writing flows smoothly and logically from one sentence to the next and from one paragraph to the next. To make your writing flow, use **transitions** to show how ideas are related. Here are some common transitions and their uses.

Transitional Word or Phrase	Use it to . . .
for example, for instance	give an example
also, furthermore, in addition, in the same way, likewise, moreover, similarly	compare ideas or add to an idea
however, nevertheless, on the other hand, in contrast	contrast ideas
first, second, then, next, after that, later, at last, finally, in conclusion	show steps in a process or time order
because	show a cause
as a result, consequently	show a result
therefore, thus	draw a conclusion

KEY IDEAS

- Use transitions to help your writing flow from sentence to sentence and from paragraph to paragraph.
- Choose the transition that expresses the correct relationship between ideas.

You can link two sentences using transitions in the following ways:

EXAMPLES

Begin the second sentence with a transition followed by a comma: Raquel has many hobbies. For example, she paints furniture and sews clothes.

Put the transition within the second sentence and set it off with commas: Raquel has many hobbies. She paints furniture, for example, and sews clothes.

Combine the two sentences into one. Put a semicolon before the transition and a comma after it: Raquel has many hobbies; for example, she paints furniture and sews clothes.

Transitions can also be used to link one paragraph to another, highlighting the relationship between the two paragraphs.

EXAMPLE

> Top performance in sports depends on "mental economy." Mental economy involves focusing the mind on the task at hand. When athletes think too much about what they're doing or worry about the outcome, they interfere with the communication between the brain and the muscles.
>
> In addition, athletes must strive for "physical economy." Although athletes put forth a tremendous amount of effort, they must take care to pace themselves in order to conserve energy for the end of the event.

HiSET EXAM TIP

When you use a transition at the beginning of a sentence, be sure you put a comma after the transition.

To decide which transition to use, see how the paragraph is organized and what you are trying to accomplish. For example, are you comparing two things? If so, you will want to use transitions that compare ideas. Similarly, when choosing transitions to introduce paragraphs, consider the organization of the entire essay.

PRACTICE 3

A. Directions: Rewrite each pair of sentences using a transition from the chart on page 164. Change the punctuation if necessary. Write your answers on a separate sheet of paper.

Example: We have worked very hard this year. Sales are at an all-time high.
We have worked very hard this year. As a result, sales are at an all-time high.

1. Our marketing efforts need to be enhanced. We will soon begin another marketing initiative.
2. Sales representatives say their jobs are extremely demanding. The salary is attractive.
3. The marketing director has instructed sales representatives to try some new ideas. Sales representatives can give away free samples.
4. A new ad campaign will be launched in just a few weeks. We expect sales to increase.

B. Questions 5 through 7 refer to the following paragraphs.

Library Cafés

(A)

(1) Until very recently, eating was not something that most people associated with libraries. (2) A patron would likely be chased out for munching on a sandwich in a corner. (3) Times are changing, and these days patrons can even buy coffee and a croissant in some public libraries.

(B)

(4) Following the lead of successful bookstores, libraries across the country are installing cafés. (5) Some library cafés have menus that offer just as much variety as a regular restaurant. (6) In addition, one of them offers 20 varieties of coffee, hot cider, and muffins. (7) These refreshments make going to the library more pleasant and may therefore increase library patronage.

(C)

(8) To have a café may benefit a library financially. (9) The income from the café adds to library revenues. (10) Also, as more people enjoy coming to the library, they may be more likely to approve tax increases for it.

STUDY ADVICE

The way your ideas relate to each other may be obvious to you, but it won't be to your readers. It's your job to make it clear how sentence 2 relates to sentence 1, and how sentence 3 relates to sentence 2. As you write, think about how you can make it *really easy* for your readers to follow the flow of your ideas.

5. **Sentence 3:** Times are changing, and these days patrons can even buy coffee and a croissant in some public libraries.

   Which correction should be made to sentence 3?

   A. insert however after Times
   B. insert however, after the comma
   C. insert , however after these days
   D. insert , however after coffee

6. **Sentences 5 and 6:** Some library cafés have menus that offer just as much variety as those of a regular ________ one of them offers 20 varieties of coffee, hot cider, and muffins.

   Choose the best option that correctly completes the sentence.

   A. restaurant, in addition,
   B. restaurant. For example,
   C. restaurant. Nevertheless,
   D. restaurant. Thus,

7. **Sentence 8:** To have a café may benefit a library financially.

   Choose the best option that corrects the sentence.

   A. In addition, having a café
   B. On the other hand, having a café
   C. A café, by benefiting a library,
   D. Financially a café

CONNECTING IDEAS PRACTICE QUESTIONS

Questions 1 through 5 refer to the following paragraphs.

The Effects of Lack of Sleep

(A)

(1) Research shows that about 70 million North Americans have experienced the problem of sleep disruption. (2) Losing sleep is more than just an annoyance. (3) In some cases, it can have catastrophic results. (4) In the United States, sleepy drivers are responsible for at least 100,000 car crashes each year. (5) Most people need at least eight hours of shut-eye a night but get only six or seven. (6) Their fast-paced lives leave them little time for sleep. (7) Another factor is poor bedtime habits. (8) Family stresses may also cause sleep loss.

(B)

(9) A study of high school students showed that students with low grades went to bed 40 minutes later and got 25 minutes less sleep than students with high grades. (10) On the other hand, another study shows that when one gets fewer than six to eight hours of sleep, it is harder to learn new skills.

(C)

(11) If you have trouble sleeping, avoid caffeine and alcohol. (12) Get regular exercise during the day, when it won't make you too energized to sleep. (13) Exercise can also help you lose weight.

(D)

(14) Set times for going to bed and getting up each day, and stick to them. (15) Don't watch TV or use a computer late at night, since these stimulate visual response and interfere with sleep. (16) If you find you still can't sleep, get up and do something.

1. Which revision would improve the effectiveness of the article?

   Begin a new paragraph with

   A. sentence 3
   B. sentence 4
   C. sentence 5
   D. sentence 6

2. Which sentence would be most effective if inserted at the beginning of paragraph (B)?

   A. Some high school students get better grades than others.
   B. High-achieving students get more sleep.
   C. Lack of sleep interferes with mathematical ability.
   D. People need more sleep than they used to.

3. Sentences 9 and 10: **A study of high school students showed that students with low grades went to bed 40 minutes later and got 25 minutes less sleep than students with high __________ another study shows that when one gets fewer than six to eight hours of sleep, it is harder to learn new skills.**

   Choose the best option that correctly completes the sentence.

   A. grades. Similarly,
   B. grades, likewise,
   C. grades. As a result,
   D. grades. Therefore,

4. Sentence 13: **Exercise can also help you lose weight.**

   Which revision should be made regarding sentence 13?

   A. move sentence 13 to follow sentence 11
   B. move sentence 13 to follow sentence 14
   C. move sentence 13 to follow sentence 15
   D. remove sentence 13

5. Which revision would improve the effectiveness of the article?

   A. join paragraphs (B) and (C)
   B. move sentence 11 to the end of paragraph (B)
   C. remove sentence 14
   D. join paragraphs (C) and (D)

Questions 6 through 10 refer to the following paragraphs.

Getting Out Those Troublesome Stains

(A)

(1) Have you ever ruined a nice piece of clothing by staining it? (2) If so, the following information on stain removal may interest you. (3) By learning a few simple rules and keeping some household cleaners on hand, you can preserve your clothing. (4) First of all, the faster you act, the better. (5) With time, the stain will set. (6) Be sure to blot the stain rather than scrubbing it. (7) Scrubbing can actually drive the stain into the fabric.

(B)

(8) Use hot water on a grease stain such as salad dressing and cold water on a water-based stain such as wine, pasta sauce, or blood. (9) If you don't know what the stain is or where it came from, use room-temperature water. (10) Otherwise you might set the stain.

(C)

(11) Sometimes other liquids are more effective than water. (12) Lemon juice, for example removes ink, rust, and iodine. (13) White vinegar takes out alcohol, coffee, deodorants, and glue. (14) Liquid shampoo can be used on oil, tar, and grease. (15) Not surprisingly, it works the same way on an oil stain as it does on oil in your hair. (16) Rubbing alcohol removes stains from grass and soft drinks.

(D)

(17) If you find that a stain is not going away or is getting worse, stop and take your clothes to a dry cleaner. (18) Professionals know best. (19) Home remedies may not work on every stain.

6. Which revision would improve the effectiveness of the article?

   Begin a new paragraph with

   A. sentence 3
   B. sentence 4
   C. sentence 5
   D. sentence 6

7. Which sentence would be most effective if inserted at the beginning of paragraph (B)?

   A. Hot and cold water have many uses.
   B. Choose the right water temperature for cleaning each stain.
   C. Hot water takes out tough stains.
   D. The second step is to determine the proper use of hot water.

8. Sentence 12: **Lemon __________ ink, rust, and iodine.**

   Choose the option that correctly completes the sentence.

   A. juice, for example removes
   B. juice, for example. Removes
   C. juice for example removes
   D. juice, for example, removes

9. Which revision would improve the effectiveness of paragraph (C)?

   A. move sentence 11 to follow sentence 12
   B. move sentence 12 to follow sentence 14
   C. remove sentence 14
   D. remove sentence 15

10. Sentence 19: **Home remedies may not work on every stain.**

    Which revision should be made to the placement of sentence 19?

    A. move sentence 19 to the beginning of paragraph (C)
    B. move sentence 19 to follow sentence 13
    C. move sentence 19 to the beginning of paragraph (D)
    D. move sentence 19 to follow sentence 17

Questions 11 through 14 refer to the following memo.

To: All Employees
From: Denise Ellis, Benefits Manager

(A)

(1) Starting on January 1, Allcity will no longer be our insurance carrier. (2) Instead, you will have a choice of two other insurance carriers: HealthPlan and Rainbow Insurance Company.

(B)

(3) HealthPlan is an HMO. (4) You will not have to pay any money to doctors in advance with this plan, but you must go to doctors listed with the insurance company. (5) HMOs are becoming increasingly popular. (6) With Rainbow Insurance, you may choose any doctor you wish. (7) However you must pay the health providers when you receive the service. (8) Afterwards, you submit the receipts to Rainbow Insurance. (9) Representatives of both companies will be here on December 2 to discuss the details of their plans. (10) Please sign up for an informational session on that day. (11) The sign-up sheet is on the door of the conference room, where the meetings will take place.

(C)

(12) At the meeting, you will receive a card on which you must indicate your choice of company. (13) Please mark your choice in the appropriate box and submit it to me by December 5.

(D)

(14) If you do not submit your card in time, you may not be insured for the month of January. (15) If you are not able to attend any of the informational sessions, please let me know right away. (16) Feel free to contact me at ext. 2453 with any questions you may have about this process.

11. Which revision would improve the effectiveness of paragraph (B)?

A. remove sentence 3
B. move sentence 5 to the beginning of paragraph (B)
C. remove sentence 5
D. remove sentence 10

12. Sentence 7: **However you must pay the health providers when you receive the service.**

Which correction should be made to sentence 7?

A. insert a comma after However
B. Insert a comma after pay
C. insert a comma after when
D. change receive to receives

13. Which revision would improve the effectiveness of the memo?

Begin a new paragraph with

A. sentence 7
B. sentence 8
C. sentence 9
D. sentence 10

14. Sentence 14: **If you do not submit your card on time, you may not be insured for the month of January.**

Which revision should be made regarding sentence 14?

A. move sentence 14 to the end of paragraph (C)
B. move sentence 14 to follow sentence 15
C. move sentence 14 to follow sentence 16
D. remove sentence 14

Questions 15 through 19 refer to the following paragraphs.

Repairing a Flat Bicycle Tire

(A)

(1) The first step in fixing a flat bicycle tire is to remove the wheel. (2) Next, release the brake. (3) Before you begin, let out any air in the tire. (4) If you are removing the back wheel, put the derailleur in high gear. (5) Then take off the axle nuts by unscrewing counterclockwise. (6) If your bike has safety washers, remove these also. (7) Then remove the wheel.

(B)

(8) Remove the tire, and mark the valve stem position on it. (9) If possible, remove the tire without using tools, because the inner tube punctures easily. (10) Use tire levers or the backs of forks and spoons if necessary. (11) When you find the leak, scrape the spot with sandpaper. (12) Remove the inner tube and inflate it, listening and feeling for air leaks. (13) Then apply cement to the tube, and let it dry completely before putting the patch on.

(C)

(14) First, inflate the tube and make sure the leak has been fixed. (15) Next, slip the inner tube back into the tire, and put the tire back on the rim. (16) Then inflate the tube to the correct pressure. (17) The pressure is right when there is enough air to steady the tire but not so much air that the tire cannot be squeezed between the brake pads.

(D)

(18) Put the bike back on its wheels, and then tighten the wheel nuts. (19) Moreover, readjust the tire pressure, and you're ready to ride!

15. Which revision would improve the effectiveness of paragraph (A)?

   A. move sentence 2 to follow sentence 3
   B. begin a new paragraph with sentence 5
   C. move sentence 5 to follow sentence 7
   D. remove sentence 6

16. Which revision would improve the effectiveness of paragraph (B)?

   A. move sentence 11 to follow sentence 8
   B. move sentence 11 to follow sentence 9
   C. move sentence 11 to follow sentence 12
   D. move sentence 11 to follow sentence 13

17. Which sentence would be most effective if inserted at the beginning of paragraph (C)?

   A. All you have to do now is take care of the tire pressure.
   B. Fixing a flat tire is a long process that requires a lot of patience.
   C. The next step is to put the tire and tube back onto the rim.
   D. Patching the leak properly is also very important.

18. Which sentence would be most effective if inserted at the beginning of paragraph (D)?

   A. The final step is to reinstall the wheel.
   B. Fixing a flat tire requires careful planning.
   C. Whether you are an experienced cyclist or just a beginner, you can fix a flat tire.
   D. Try not to use sharp tools to fix a flat tire.

19. Sentence 19: **Moreover, readjust the tire pressure, and you're ready to ride!**

   Which correction should be made to sentence 19?

   A. replace Moreover, with Then
   B. change readjust to readjusting
   C. remove the comma after pressure
   D. replace you're with your

LESSON 1

Noun and Pronoun Agreement

KEY IDEAS

- A noun names a person, place, thing, or idea.
- A pronoun takes the place of a noun.
- Use subject, object, and possessive pronouns in the proper places.

Using Nouns and Pronouns

A **noun** names a person (such as *woman* or *Anne*), a place (such as *drugstore* or *Florida*), a thing (such as *car* or *Titanic*), or an idea (*truth* or *Buddhism*). A **proper noun** refers to a specific person, place, thing, or idea; a **common noun** is more general. For example, *Anne* is a proper noun; *woman* is a common noun.

A **pronoun** is a word that replaces a noun. The **antecedent** is the noun that is being replaced, as shown below:

EXAMPLE

Steven lost his address book. It held many important phone numbers.
(address book = antecedent; It = pronoun)

There are three types of pronouns: subject, object, and possessive.

EXAMPLES

A **subject pronoun** replaces the subject of a sentence.

Steven called home. He was very worried.
(Steven = subject; He = subject pronoun)

An **object pronoun** replaces the object of a verb or of a preposition.

Steven's wife called him. She asked him what the problem was.
(him = object pronoun (object of a verb))

She and Steven looked for it.
(it = object pronoun (object of a preposition))

A **possessive pronoun** replaces a possessive noun.
Steven needed Kelly's number. He called 411 to get her number.
(Kelly's = possessive noun; her = possessive pronoun)

Use this chart for help in remembering the three types of pronouns:

Subject Pronoun: replaces subject	Object Pronoun: replaces object	Possessive Pronoun: shows ownership
I	me	my, mine
you	you	your, yours
he	him	his
she	her	her, hers
it	it	its
we	us	ours
they	them	their, theirs

HiSET EXAM TIP

To choose the option with the correct pronoun in a compound like "They went to the party with James and I," take out "James and" and ask yourself whether the sentence still sounds correct.

Avoid these mistakes with pronouns in compound subjects and objects:

Incorrect pronoun in compound subject: Linda and me went to the movies.
Correct: Linda and I went to the movies.

Incorrect pronoun in compound object: We saw Kareem and he at the theater.
Correct: We saw Kareem and him at the theater.

PRACTICE 1.1

A. Directions: Write the correct pronoun to replace each underlined noun.

1. Laurie and Paul just moved to California. ____________________

2. A neighbor told Laurie and Paul that saving water was important there. ____________________

3. He said they should turn the water off when brushing their teeth. ____________________

4. Laurie's sister suggested getting a special shower head that saves water. ____________________

5. Laurie and Laurie's sister will go shopping for it on Sunday. ____________________

B. Questions 6 through 8 refer to the following letter.

To Whom It May Concern:

(A)

(1) I am writing to recommend Bonetta Williams for the position of managerial assistant in your firm. (2) I believe that she is highly qualfied for the position, and I urge you to strongly consider her candidacy.

(B)

(3) Bonetta and me have worked together for three years. (4) As my secretary, she has proven to be responsible and efficient. (5) She always getting her work done on time and looks for ways to help others. (6) In addition, I find her extremely intelligent and likable. (7) I will be sorry to see her go.

(C)

(8) My supervisor, Walter Constantine, has also worked with Bonetta and would be happy to speak with you if necessary. (9) Please contact Walter or I if you need any further information.

Sincerely,

Carol Rhodes

6. Sentence 3: Bonetta and me have worked together for three years.

Which correction should be made to sentence 3?

A. replace me with I
B. replace Bonetta with She
C. insert a comma after me
D. change have worked to been working

7. Sentence 5: She always getting her work done on time and looks for ways to help others.

Which correction should be made to sentence 5?

A. replace She with Her
B. insert a comma after time
C. change looks to looking
D. change getting to gets

8. Sentence 9: Please contact Walter or I if you need any further information.

Which is the best way to write the underlined portion of the sentence?

A. Walter and I
B. Walter or me
C. him or I
D. he or me

KEY IDEAS

- A pronoun should match its antecedent in person and number.
- Make sure it is clear which antecedent a pronoun refers to.
- If necessary, use a noun in place of a pronoun, or construct the sentence differently so that the antecedent is clear.

HiSET EXAM TIP

Take into account the whole passage when you are determining which pronoun is correct. A common error to watch for is when a paragraph begins with the third-person form one *and then shifts to the second-person form* you.

Pronoun-Antecedent Agreement

Pronouns should agree with their antecedents, or the nouns they refer to. For example, a pronoun and its antecedent must agree in number. If the antecedent is singular, the pronoun should be singular. If the antecedent is plural, the pronoun should be plural.

EXAMPLES

Andy's company is very progressive. It pays for his college classes.
company = singular antecedent; It = singular pronoun

Many employees want to learn more skills, so they take classes.
employees = plural antecedent; they = plural pronoun

Incorrect: Any employee who is interested should submit their application.
Correct: Any employee who is interested should submit his or her application.
Correct: Employees who are interested should submit their applications.

Note that for collective nouns (such as *company, jury, family, team, committee, union*), you generally use the singular pronoun *it*.

Incorrect: The committee announced that they will hold weekly meetings.
Correct: The committee announced that it will hold weekly meetings.

A pronoun and its antecedent must agree in person. To agree, they both must be first person (referring to the speaker), second person (the person spoken to), or third person (the person or thing spoken about).

First person	Second person	Third person
I, me, my, mine	you, your, yours	he, him, his
we, us, our, ours		she, her, hers
		it, its
		they, them, their, theirs

The indefinite pronoun *one* is like a third-person personal pronoun. A common error in writing is an incorrect shift between the third-person *one* and the second-person *you.*

Incorrect shift: If one attends college classes, you can be reimbursed.
Correct: If one attends college classes, one can be reimbursed.
Correct: If one attends college classes, he or she can be reimbursed.
Correct: If you attend college classes, you can be reimbursed.

It must be clear which antecedent a pronoun refers to. If necessary, use a noun in place of the pronoun, or reconstruct the sentence.

Unclear: Carlos spoke to his boss, and he told him about the program.
Clear (noun replaces pronoun): Carlos spoke to his boss, and his boss told him about the program.
Clear (different construction): Carlos spoke to his boss, who told him about the program.

Unclear: Michelle helped Shania fill out the financial aid application that she had picked up.
Correct (different construction): After picking up a financial aid application for Shania, Michelle helped her fill it out.

PRACTICE 1.2

A. Directions: Correct any errors in pronoun use. If there are no errors, write *C*. You may also have to change some verbs.

EXAMPLE: People who live in small towns know ~~one has~~ they have access to fewer amenities than big-city dwellers.

___ **1.** Sally is moving to a small town. Her mother is concerned about the healthcare options they offer.

___ **2.** Sally tried to reassure her mother, but it was hard for her to believe her.

___ **3.** Sally asked a friend who lives in the town for information about it's healthcare facilities.

___ **4.** The town has a freestanding clinic where a person can go when they are sick.

___ **5.** There is also a nearby hospital, and they have a very good reputation.

___ **6.** If one is concerned about healthcare, you should sign up for a good insurance plan.

B. Questions 7 through 9 refer to the following paragraphs.

The Best Discipline

(A)

(1) What should parents do when their children act up? (2) Parents often like the idea of punishment, but punishment may not be the most effective solution. (3) If the punishment results from the parent's anger, it won't work. (4) Instead, children will learn only that they shouldn't make one's parents angry.

(B)

(5) One parenting expert feels that they should be clear about their expectations from the outset so that children will not unknowingly violate rules. (6) They should respond to children's misbehavior in a calm and neutral fashion. (7) It's also important to choose a consequence related to the action. (8) If a child hits or bites in a play group, for example, it would be most appropriate not to allow the child to play with them for a short time. (9) He or she will begin to see the connection.

7. Sentence 4: Instead, children will learn only that they shouldn't make one's parents angry.

Which correction should be made to sentence 4?

A. remove the comma after Instead
B. change learn to have learned
C. replace they with you
D. replace one's with their

8. Sentence 5: One parenting expert feels that they should be clear about their expectations from the outset so that children will not unknowingly violate rules.

Which is the best way to write the underlined portion of this sentence?

A. he
B. we
C. one
D. parents

9. Sentence 8: If a child hits or bites in a play group, for example, it would be most appropriate not to allow the child to play with them for a short time.

Which correction should be made to sentence 8?

A. insert a comma after hits
B. replace the child with them
C. replace them with the group
D. change it to you

LESSON 2

Verb Forms and Tenses

Regular Verbs

An important part of writing correctly is using the right verb forms. A **verb** is a word that indicates action or being. Each verb has a base form and four other forms. A **regular verb** follows a consistent pattern to create each verb form.

Base form: look

Tense	Verb form	How to write it
Present	look/looks	with *I, you, we, they:* use the base form
		with *he, she, it:* add *-s* to the base form
Present participle	looking	add *-ing*
Past	looked	add *-ed* (*-d* if verb ends with *e*)
Past participle	looked	add *-ed* (*-d* if verb ends with *e*)

The forms are used to create different **verb tenses**, or times. The table below shows how verb tense and form are related. Notice that when you use certain tenses, you must also use a **helping verb**—often a form of *be* or *have*.

Tense	Verb form	Use
Present	look/looks	a habitual action, general truth, or state of being: *I look at the newspaper every day.*
Past	looked	an action that has been completed: *I looked at it this morning.*
Future	will look	an action that has not yet happened: *I will look at it tonight, too.*
Present progressive	am/is/are looking	an action in progress: *I am looking at it right now.*
Present perfect	have/has looked	an action that began in the past and continues until now: *I have looked at it every day this week.*
Past perfect	had looked	an action that was completed before a specific time in the past: *I had looked at it before it got wet.*
Future perfect	will have looked	an action that will be completed by a specific time in the future: *I will have looked at it by the time I get home.*

Sentences often contain clues that tell you which tense to use. For instance, time words and phrases like *yesterday* or *last week* show that the past should be used, *tonight* and *next month* indicate the future, and *by tonight, since 2000,* and *for seven years* indicate the perfect tenses.

Other verbs in the sentence can be clues: *I look at the newspaper whenever I get the chance.* Finally, verbs in other sentences also can be clues. The verbs in a paragraph or passage are generally in the same tense.

KEY IDEAS

- Each verb has four forms: present, present participle, past, and past participle.
- Verb forms are used to create different tenses, which show time relationships.
- Use clues in the sentence and paragraph to help decide which tense to use.

HiSET EXAM TIP

Some passages on the Writing Test may have a verb-tense question based on the tense of the entire passage. Make sure you select verb forms that are consistent with the tense of the passage.

PRACTICE 2.1

A. Directions: Rewrite each verb in its correct tense. Use clues in each sentence for help in choosing the tense.

EXAMPLE: Between 1892 and 1924, about 12 million immigrants *entered* (enter) the U.S. through Ellis Island in New York.

1. By the 1950s, Ellis Island ____________ (cease) to be an important immigration checkpoint.

2. The government ____________ (close) Ellis Island to immigration in 1954.

3. Now Ellis Island ____________ (function) as a national monument.

4. Since the island was reopened as a museum in 1990, many tourists ____________ (visit) it.

5. Soon, a genealogical center ____________ (open).

6. The island ____________ (look) different than it did originally because 24 acres of landfill have been added.

7. Now we ____________ (think) about taking a trip to Ellis Island next month.

B. Questions 8 through 10 refer to the following advertisement.

Don't Miss Your Chance!

(A)

(1) The Express Lane credit card has offered a fantastic deal right now, for a limited time only. (2) If you are signing up for Express Lane before April 9, you will receive a 20 percent discount on your first five purchases!

(B)

(3) The Express Lane card carries no monthly charge. (4) You'll pay a low $35 fee just once a year. (5) Become an Express Lane member now. (6) Your savings opportunities will be amazing you!

8. Sentence 1: The Express Lane credit card has offered a fantastic deal right now, for a limited time only.

Which is the best way to write the underlined portion of the sentence?

A. offered
B. is offering
C. offers
D. will offer

9. Sentence 2: If you are signing up for Express Lane before April 9, you will receive a 20 percent discount on your first five purchases!

Which correction should be made to sentence 2?

A. change are signing to have signed
B. change you will to one will
C. change will receive to receive
D. change are signing to sign

10. Sentence 6: Your savings opportunities will be amazing you!

Which correction should be made to sentence 6?

A. change Your to You're
B. change Your to One's
C. insert a comma after opportunities
D. change will be amazing to will amaze

STUDY ADVICE

Remembering the *names* of verb tenses (in the first column of the second table on page 174) isn't nearly as important as remembering how to use them. You may want to make flash cards out of the second and third columns of the tables on page 174. On one side of each card, put a time frame and an action word (such as "an action that has been completed; look"). On the other side, put the verb form that matches (in this case, "looked").

Irregular Verbs

Most verbs are regular verbs; their past and participle forms follow the same pattern. Some verbs, however, are **irregular verbs.** Although some irregular verbs follow a pattern, most do not.

KEY IDEAS

- Irregular verb forms do not follow a single pattern.
- Some irregular verbs follow an *i, a, u* pattern.

A common error with irregular verbs is using the past participle in place of the past—for instance, *I been there* instead of *I was there.* Discover which irregular verb forms, if any, give you problems. Then learn the correct forms. Here are some tips for learning the forms of irregular verbs:

- If you find two verbs that rhyme in the present form (for example, *grow* and *throw*), check to see if they have the same forms in the past and past participles (*grew, grown; threw, thrown*). If so, learn them together.
- Learn which verbs follow the *i, a, u* pattern: *sing, sang, sung; drink, drank, drunk; sink, sank, sunk.* However, be aware that there are exceptions (*bring, brought, brought*).

Here is a list of common irregular verbs.

Present Form	Past Form	Past Participle Form
am, are, is	was, were	been
become	became	become
begin	began	begun
blow	blew	blown
break	broke	broken
bring	brought	brought
buy	bought	bought
choose	chose	chosen
come	came	come
do	did	done
drink	drank	drunk
eat	ate	eaten
fall	fell	fallen
fly	flew	flown
freeze	froze	frozen
get	got	gotten
give	gave	given
go	went	gone
grow	grew	grown
have, has	had	had
know	knew	known
leave	left	left
lose	lost	lost
ride	rode	ridden
run	ran	run
see	saw	seen
shake	shook	shaken
show	showed	shown
speak	spoke	spoken
steal	stole	stolen
take	took	taken
throw	threw	thrown
wear	wore	worn
write	wrote	written

HiSET EXAM TIP

When you choose an answer that changes a verb, read the sentence again, with your choice in it. Doing so may help you "hear" whether the verb form is correct.

PRACTICE 2.2

A. Directions: Write the correct form of the verb shown in parentheses.

EXAMPLE: Since November, the school's heating system *has broken* (break) down several times.

1. Yesterday the technician ____________ (come) to resolve the problem once and for all.
2. School employees ____________ (show) him the boiler.
3. The technician said, "If you ____________ (speak) to me about this sooner, it would have been easier to fix."
4. He ____________ (take) parts out of the heating system and replaced them with new ones.
5. He said, "I've never ____________ (see) such a poorly installed system."

B. Questions 6 through 8 refer to the following paragraphs.

TV Rating Systems

(A)

(1) In 1996, television industry representatives announced that the industry had formed TV Parental Guidelines. (2) This rating system, designed to give parents advance warning about the content of TV shows, begun to appear on TV in 1997. (3) The ratings system was broke down into six different categories, ranging from "All Children" to "Mature Audiences Only."

(B)

(4) Six months later, after pressure from advocacy groups, the television industry agreed to include additional labels to advise viewers if a show they were about to view contained violence, sexual activity, coarse language, or sexually suggestive language. (5) These labels now given viewers more specific and therefore more helpful information about an upcoming show.

6. **Sentence 2:** This rating system, designed to give parents advance warning about the content of TV shows, begun to appear on TV in 1997.

   Which correction should be made to sentence 2?

   A. remove the comma after system
   B. change give to be giving
   C. change begun to had begun
   D. change begun to began

7. **Sentence 3:** The ratings system was broke down into six different categories, ranging from "All Children" to "Mature Audiences Only."

   Which is the best way to write the underlined portion of this sentence?

   A. broke itself
   B. broke
   C. was broken
   D. had broken

8. **Sentence 5:** These labels now given viewers more specific and therefore more helpful information about an upcoming show.

   Which correction should be made to sentence 5?

   A. change given to will give
   B. change given to give
   C. insert a comma after information
   D. insert a comma after specific

LESSON 3

Subject-Verb Agreement

KEY IDEAS

- A verb must match its subject in number.
- Collective nouns are singular when they refer to a group as a single unit.
- Indefinite pronouns may be singular, plural, or both.

Agreement with a Simple Subject

In the present tense, subjects and verbs must agree in number. To understand the basics of subject-verb agreement, study the chart below. Notice that present tense verbs take an –*s* ending when they are used with the pronoun subjects *he, she,* and *it* or their noun equivalents.

Verb Forms for Singular Subjects	Verb Forms for Plural Subjects
I jump	*we* jump
you jump	*you* jump
he, she, it jumps	*they* jump

To master subject-verb agreement for the Writing Test, be aware of these special nouns and pronouns:

Collective nouns are usually singular, even though they may seem plural. A collective noun names a group, such as *army, crew, crowd, staff, family, herd,* or *flock.* If the group is considered to be a single unit, it is singular.

EXAMPLES

The army is a good place to learn discipline.
The church choir sings each Sunday.

Some nouns that end in –*s* may look plural, but in fact they are not.

EXAMPLE

Politics is an interesting topic.

HiSET EXAM TIP

To check for correct subject-verb agreement, ask yourself: Does the verb agree with its subject? Is the verb in the right form? Is the verb in the right tense for both the sentence and the passage?

Indefinite pronouns do not refer to a specific person. Some indefinite pronouns are singular, some are plural, and some may be either.

Singular	anyone, everyone, someone, no one, one, anybody, everybody, somebody, nobody, anything, everything, something, nothing, another, other, either, neither, each, much
Plural	many, several, few, both
Singular or plural	all, none, some, any, part, most

EXAMPLES

Singular: These days, it seems as if almost everyone is joining a health club.
Singular: Most of the equipment is easy to use.
Plural: Most of the exercise classes are fun.
Plural: A few are advanced classes for those already in great shape.

PRACTICE 3.1

A. Directions: Underline the correct verb form to complete each sentence.

EXAMPLE: Every Monday, the National Orchestra (perform, performs) live on the radio.

1. The public (is, are) invited to listen free of charge.

2. Free tickets (becomes, become) available one hour before the performance.

3. The performance (is, are) usually held in Barnes Hall.

4. Many well-known musicians (has, have) played there.

5. Everyone (seem, seems) to enjoy these concerts very much.

6. The concert series (is, are) very popular.

B. Questions 7 through 9 refer to the following article.

The Speed of Sound

(A)

(1) Most of us has heard airplane noise that is so loud it sounds like an explosion. (2) That noise occurs when a plane start to fly faster than the speed of sound. (3) Listeners on the ground hear the noise, but it is not audible to passengers.

(B)

(4) The speed of sound is 1,088 feet per second at 32°F at sea level. (5) It is different at other temperatures and in other substances. (6) For example, sound travels faster in water than in air. (7) Sound takes about one second to move a mile under water, but five seconds to move a mile through air. (8) It travels through ice cold vapor at 4,708 feet per second and through ice cold water at 4,938 feet per second. (9) Surprisingly, some other materials conducts sound very well. (10) For instance, sound travels through glass at speeds up to 19,690 feet per second.

STUDY ADVICE

How long are your study sessions at this point? Remember to push yourself, little by little, until you can focus on the material for two to three hours at a time. It may take weeks or months to get there, but don't give up. Remember: You need to train yourself so that you can focus for a few hours on Test Day.

7. Sentence 1: Most of us has heard airplane noise that is so loud it sounds like an explosion.

Which is the best way to write the underlined portion of this sentence?

A. were hearing
B. have heard
C. having heard
D. hears

8. Sentence 2: That noise occurs when a plane start to fly faster than the speed of sound.

Which correction should be made to sentence 2?

A. change occurs to occur
B. change occurs to occurred
C. change start to starts
D. replace than with then

9. Sentence 9: Surprisingly, some other materials conducts sound very well.

Which correction should be made to sentence 9?

A. replace some with any
B. change conducts to conduct
C. change conducts to conducted
D. insert a comma after sound

Agreement with a Compound Subject

A compound subject is made up of two or more subjects joined by *and* or *or.* To make a verb agree with a compound subject, follow these guidelines:

KEY IDEAS

- If a compound subject is joined by *and*, use a plural verb.
- If a compound subject is joined by *or, either . . . or,* or *neither . . . nor,* the verb should agree with the subject closer to it.
- When checking subject-verb agreement, ignore interrupting phrases and watch for inverted structure.

When two or more subjects are joined by *and,* the compound subject is plural. Use the correct verb form for the plural.

EXAMPLE: Tricia and her sister are caring for their mother.

If two subjects are joined by *or,* the verb agrees with the subject closer to it:

EXAMPLE: A health aide or a nurse visits each day.

When subjects are joined by *either . . . or* or *neither . . . nor,* the verb agrees with the subject closer to it.

EXAMPLE: Neither the brother nor his sisters have medical training.

Interrupting Words

Sometimes a word or group of words comes between the subject and the verb. In that case, locate the subject by asking yourself, "What is this sentence really about?" Mentally cross out the interruptor. Then make the verb agree with the subject.

EXAMPLE: The medicine ~~prescribed by the doctors~~ is on a high shelf.
subject interruptor verb

Interrupting phrases often begin with prepositions, such as *of, in, on, from, with, to,* and *for.*

EXAMPLE: A pile ~~of medical supplies~~ rests in the front hallway.

Interrupting phrases may be set off by commas. Watch especially for phrases beginning with words like *along with, as well as, besides,* and *in addition to.*

EXAMPLES

Dr. Silva~~, who is one of the surgeons,~~ consults with the family.
The sisters~~, along with the medical team,~~ keep the patient comfortable.

HiSET EXAM TIP

Read there's *as* there is *and* here's *as* here is.

Inverted Structure

Checking subject-verb agreement can be tricky when the sentence structure is **inverted**—that is, when the subject comes after the verb. Most questions and sentences that begin with *here* or *there* are inverted.

EXAMPLES

Does the pharmacy have enough medicine to fill the prescription?
Here are the hospital supplies that Tricia ordered.

Incorrect: What is Tricia and her family going to do?
Correct: What are Tricia and her family going to do?

Incorrect: Do Tricia want to send her mother to a hospital?
Correct: Does Tricia want to send her mother to a hospital?

Incorrect: There's the bandages. (Remember that *There's* is short for *There is.*)
Correct: There are the bandages.

PRACTICE 3.2

A. Directions: If a sentence contains an interrupting phrase, cross out the interruptor. Then underline the correct verb to complete the sentence.

EXAMPLE: Brushing and flossing ~~with regularity~~ (is, are) key to good dental health.

1. Many toothpastes on the market (carry, carries) a seal of approval from the American Dental Association.
2. Products carrying the seal (are, is) tested to guarantee that they are safe and effective.
3. Fluoride, an important ingredient in many toothpastes, (strengthens, strengthen) teeth and (attacks, attack) bacteria that cause tooth decay.
4. There (is, are) toothpastes that claim to have special benefits, like tartar control or whitening.
5. Some pharmacies and supermarkets (offers, offer) store-brand toothpaste at a low price.
6. Any toothpaste with fluoride and good flavor (is, are) fine to use, even if it's not a brand-name toothpaste.

B. Questions 7 through 9 refer to the following paragraphs.

Unemployment Insurance

(A)

(1) Unemployment insurance provides workers who have lost their jobs with partial replacement of their salary. (2) Each state administers its own program and have its own laws. (3) The amount received is determined by wage level and the length of employment. (4) When the unemployment rate rises above a certain level, states are required to extend the benefits. (5) The state and federal governments share the cost of the additional benefits.

(B)

(6) In most states, employer contributions pay for this program. (7) Unemployed workers who wish to draw benefits reports regularly to their public employment office to learn about job openings.

7. **Sentence 2:** Each state administers its own program and have its own laws.

   Which correction should be made to sentence 2?

   A. change administers to administering
   B. change administers to administer
   C. change have to has
   D. replace its with it's

8. **Sentence 3:** The amount received is determined by wage level and the length of employment.

   If you rewrote sentence 3 beginning with

   Wage level and the length of employment,

   the next word(s) should be

   A. determine
   B. determines
   C. is determined
   D. was determined

9. **Sentence 7:** Unemployed workers who wish to draw benefits reports regularly to their public employment office to learn about job openings.

   Which correction should be made to sentence 7?

   A. change wish to wishes
   B. insert a comma after benefits
   C. change reports to report
   D. replace their with there

LESSON 4

Using Reference Sources

KEY IDEAS

- Referring to trustworthy sources makes a written piece more credible.
- Including bibliographic information is important to avoid plagiarism and to help readers locate and assess the sources.
- Regardless of the format used, references should provide the reader with enough information to identify the source.

HiSET EXAM TIP

A passage that does not cite specific sources of information can be strengthened by adding references, and a passage that provides incomplete bibliographic information can be strengthened by giving more details about its sources.

Simply stating that something is true will not necessarily convince readers that it is true. Informative writing is most credible when the author supports ideas and opinions with specific references to other sources. It is important to cite sources that readers regard as trustworthy.

In addition, writers include **bibliographic information** about their sources for the following reasons:

- It helps readers evaluate the accuracy of the source.
- It allows readers to find the source themselves if they want to read more about the topic.
- It gives credit to the people from whom the writer got the idea. Presenting facts or opinions as one's own when they were actually discovered or conceived of by someone else is **plagiarism**.

Citing sources may be done informally, as in a news article or essay, or formally, as in an academic research paper. There are several widely accepted formats for formal references, such as the *Chicago Manual of Style*. A teacher or publication may ask writers to use a certain format. In any format, when a source is quoted, that text is placed inside quotation marks.

In general, the author should provide the reader with the author(s) and title of the book, article, video, etc., as well as the date of publication or copyright. If the work is an article in a newspaper, magazine, academic journal, or bound collection, then the title of that publication is also given. If the source is online, a website address is often given.

Bibliographic information may be provided entirely within the text, a common approach in less formal writing. More formally, brief citations are provided within the text that allow the reader to cross-reference a list of sources with full information, or the information is provided in footnotes at the bottom of the page or endnotes at the end of the chapter or article.

EXAMPLES

Weak: Everyone knows that getting enough sleep is important, and now science says so, too.

Strong (less formal): An article in the January 11, 2014, *New York Times* by Maria Konnikova describes scientific research that shows getting enough sleep is important.

Strong (more formal): As reported in the *New York Times* (Konnikova, 2014), the journal *Science* published in its October 2013 issue the results of several studies, conducted by a team under Maiken Nedergaard, that show getting enough sleep is important.

REFERENCE LIST

Konnikova, M. (2014, January 11). Goodnight. Sleep clean. *New York Times*. Retrieved from http://www.nytimes.com/2014/01/12/opinion/sunday/goodnight-sleep-clean.html.

Facts that are widely documented as true (e.g., Barack Obama became president on January 20, 2009) and ideas not attributable to a particular person or group (e.g., exercise is important to health) do not need references.

PRACTICE 4

There are several main theories of international relations. One school of thought is realism, which emphasizes the independence of sovereign states and their desire for power needed to maintain that independence. Realists, therefore, see force—especially military force—as the primary factor that determines how nations interact.

1. The author would like to provide support for the ideas in this paragraph. Which of the following would be the best source of this support?

   A. A widely used college textbook on international relations
   B. An online encyclopedia open to contributions by the public
   C. An article in a national news magazine about conflict in the Middle East
   D. A university library's web page about realism in literature

The mastiff is a breed of massive, muscular dog that is popular in the United States. The breed originated in England two thousand years ago, where it was bred as a watchdog and dog of war. The Roman leader Julius Caesar mentioned the courage of mastiffs in his account of his invasion of England. According to the American Kennel Club, the mastiff is courageous and dignified, but good-natured and docile.

2. If the description of the mastiff attributed to the American Kennel Club is taken word for word from that organization's website, what is the best revision of the underlined sentence?

   A. (No change)
   B. "The mastiff is courageous and dignified, but good-natured and docile."
   C. According to the website of the American Kennel Club (akc.org/dog-breeds/mastiff/, accessed December 29, 2015), the mastiff is "courageous and dignified, but good-natured and docile."
   D. Experts on the breed say the mastiff is brave and inspires respect, but friendly and easy to train.

Renovation can add significant value to your home. Many people assume that kitchen and bathroom remodels have the best return on investment. However, you should consider remodeling your basement.

3. The author plans to add a sentence at the end of this paragraph. Which of the following would most strengthen the passage?

   A. According to *REALTOR® Magazine's* 2015 "Cost vs. Value Report," renovated basements add more value to homes than do updated kitchens and bathrooms.
   B. According to contractors who specialize in basements, renovated basements add more value to homes than do updated kitchens and bathrooms.
   C. I remodeled my basement, and I saw a 20 percent gain in my home's value.
   D. *The Wall Street Journal* has reported that remodeled kitchens and bathrooms have a lower return on investment than do renovated basements.

"Despite the growing demand for organic food products, many U.S. farmers are reluctant to switch to organic production methods."[1]

4. The author found this information in a government report. Which of the following would be the best footnote 1?

   A. U.S. Department of Agriculture (Washington, D.C.), *Marketing U.S. Organic Foods: Recent Trends from Farms to Consumers*, 2009, 11.
   B. Carolyn Dimitri and Lydia Oberholtzer, report for the U.S. Department of Agriculture, Washington, D.C., titled *Marketing U.S. Organic Foods: Recent Trends from Farms to Consumers*, 11.
   C. Retrieved from the U.S. Department of Agriculture website at http://www.ers.usda.gov/media/185272/eib58_1_.pdf.
   D. Carolyn Dimitri and Lydia Oberholtzer, *Marketing U.S. Organic Foods: Recent Trends from Farms to Consumers* (Washington, D.C.: U.S. Department of Agriculture, 2009), 11.

USING GRAMMAR CORRECTLY PRACTICE QUESTIONS

Questions 1 through 5 refer to the following paragraphs.

Unorthodox Tennis Stars

(A)

(1) Venus and Serena Williams are not your typical tennis stars. (2) For one thing, they are African Americans in a game that few African Americans have become famous for playing; those who preceded them were Althea Gibson, Arthur Ashe, and Zina Garrison. (3) For another, Venus and Serena are sisters.

(B)

(4) Tennis players often receive hours of instruction from highly paid coaches, but it doesn't happen that way for Venus and Serena. (5) Instead, their father, the former owner of a security-services business, taught them how to play on public courts, after teaching himself through books and films. (6) The family lived in a rough neighborhood, and gang members watched over the girls while she practiced.

(C)

(7) The practice paid off. (8) Venus had won 63 tournaments by the time she turned 12, and she became a professional at 14. (9) In just a few years, she earns millions of dollars in endorsements and prizes. (10) Serena, turning professional a year after Venus, had a slower start. (11) However, some experts think she may now be better than her sister.

(D)

(12) The two sisters, who live in Palm Beach Gardens, Florida, is best friends. (13) Though they sometimes face each other on the court, there been no trace of sibling rivalry.

1. Sentence 4: **Tennis players often receive hours of instruction from highly paid coaches, but it doesn't happen that way for Venus and Serena.**

   Which correction should be made to sentence 4?

   A. change receive to receives
   B. remove the comma
   C. change doesn't to didn't
   D. insert a comma after instruction

2. Sentence 6: **The family lived in a rough neighborhood, and gang members watched over the girls while she practiced.**

   Which is the best way to write the underlined portion of the sentence?

   A. they
   B. the girls
   C. each
   D. them

3. Sentence 9: **In just a few years, she earns millions of dollars in endorsements and prizes.**

   Which is the best way to write the underlined portion of the sentence?

   A. is earning
   B. earned
   C. earn
   D. will earn

4. Sentence 12: **The two sisters, who live in Palm Beach Gardens, Florida, is best friends.**

   Which correction should be made to sentence 12?

   A. remove the comma after sisters
   B. change live to lives
   C. remove the comma after Florida
   D. change is to are

5. Sentence 13: **Though they sometimes face each other on the court, there been no trace of sibling rivalry.**

   Which correction should be made to sentence 13?

   A. change face to faced
   B. remove the comma after court
   C. change been to was
   D. change been to is

Questions 6 through 10 refer to the following paragraphs.

Getting the Best Service for Your Car

(A)

(1) Have you had trouble finding a good mechanic? (2) By following these tips, you can improve your chances of getting quality service.

(B)

(3) Even before your car breaks down, look for a shop you like and trust. (4) Ask people where they will receive good service at a reasonable price. (5) Don't have picked a shop just because it's close to home, for another shop may have a better deal. (6) Be wary of ads that offer rock-bottom prices. (7) Specials like these often comes with restrictions attached.

(C)

(8) Be as specific as possible when you describe your car's problem to the mechanic. (9) If the technician must spend time trying to determine what's wrong, it will cost more. (10) You also need to request information about both estimates and guarantees before the repair work starts. (11) Ask for a price range rather than an exact estimate. (12) Find out how long the guarantee lasts and whether there's any time or mileage limits.

(D)

(13) If you don't understand a repair explanation, ask for clarification right away. (14) In addition, keep records of all repairs and billing in case of a dispute.

6. Sentence 4: **Ask people where they will receive good service at a reasonable price.**

   Which correction should be made to sentence 4?

   A. change Ask to To ask
   B. change will receive to have received
   C. change will receive to receiving
   D. change people to them

7. Sentence 5: **Don't have picked a shop just because it's close to home, for another shop may have a better deal.**

   Which correction should be made to sentence 5?

   A. change have picked to pick
   B. change have picked to be picking
   C. replace it's with its
   D. remove the comma

8. Sentence 7: **Specials like these often comes with restrictions attached.**

   Which correction should be made to sentence 7?

   A. replace these with this
   B. insert a comma after these
   C. change comes to came
   D. change comes to come

9. Sentence 9: **If the technician must spend time trying to determine what's wrong, it will cost more.**

   Which correction should be made to sentence 9?

   A. change must spend to spent
   B. change what's to what are
   C. remove the comma
   D. replace it with the repair job

10. Sentence 12: **Find out how long the guarantee lasts and whether there's any time or mileage limits.**

    Which is the best way to write the underlined portion of the sentence?

    A. there is
    B. there be
    C. there are
    D. there were

Questions 11 through 15 refer to the following letter.

Taxpayer Notification

(A)

(1) We have received your tax return and have noted some inconsistencies in it. (2) We are therefore proposing a number of changes to your return. (3) These changes and its effect on your refund are outlined below.

(B)

(4) First, the amount you claimed for self-employed income differs from our records. (5) If you wish to contest this change, please send photocopies of one's records. (6) Second, you have made an error in your calculations. (7) Please review our calculations, which is appended to this letter.

(C)

(8) These changes having been made to your return, there is an increase in the amount of taxes you owe. (9) Your refund has therefore been reduced accordingly.

(D)

(10) Contact us if you have any questions about these specific problems or about the documents you must send to contest the changes. (11) Be sure to send the last page of this letter when replying by mail. (12) If we determine that your return was correct as filed, we have credited your account.

11. Sentence 3: **These changes and its effect on your refund are outlined below.**

    Which correction should be made to sentence 3?

    A. insert a comma after changes
    B. replace its with their
    C. insert a comma after refund
    D. change are to is

12. Sentence 5: **If you wish to contest this change, please send photocopies of one's records.**

    Which correction should be made to sentence 5?

    A. change wish to wishes
    B. change send to to send
    C. replace one's with your
    D. change you to one

13. Sentence 7: **Please review our calculations, which is appended to this letter.**

    Which correction should be made to sentence 7?

    A. change review to reviewing
    B. replace our with are
    C. remove the comma
    D. change is to are

14. Sentence 8: **These changes having been made to your return, there is an increase in the amount of taxes you owe.**

    If you rewrote sentence 8 beginning with

    Because of these changes to your return, the amount of taxes you owe

    the next words should be

    A. has increased
    B. have increased
    C. is increasing
    D. are increasing

15. Sentence 12: **If we determine that your return was correct as filed, we have credited your account.**

    Which is the best way to write the underlined portion of the sentence?

    A. are crediting
    B. will credit
    C. will have credited
    D. had credited

Questions 16 through 20 refer to the following paragraphs.

Disability Etiquette

(A)

(1) Many of us doesn't know how to act when meeting someone who has a disability. (2) The main thing to remember is that people with disabilities has feelings just like everyone else. (3) They want to be treated with respect and dignity. (4) Beyond that, try the following tips.

(B)

(5) When you meet a person with a disability, speak and act with he or she as you would with anyone else. (6) Use your usual tone of voice. (7) A person who has trouble hearing you will let you know. (8) Don't talk down to the person or stare. (9) Refrain from using a term like handicap, which focuses on the disability rather than on the person. (10) Instead, use a term such as physically disabled or say, "He uses a wheelchair."

(C)

(11) Any assistive equipment, such as a wheelchair, cane, or communication board, are the person's property. (12) Unless you have the person's express permission, you should not touch it. (13) Also, distracting a blind person's guide dog could put the owner in danger, so do not pet it.

(D)

(14) Finally, if you have a child with you, don't prevent him or her from talking to the person or asking questions. (15) Children are often more accepting than adults.

16. Sentence 1: **Many of us doesn't know how to act when meeting someone who has a disability.**

    Which is the best way to write the underlined portion of the sentence?

    A. does not
    B. don't
    C. didn't
    D. never does

17. Sentence 2: **The main thing to remember is that people with disabilities has feelings just like everyone else.**

    Which correction should be made to sentence 2?

    A. add a comma after remember
    B. change is to are
    C. change has to have
    D. change people to them

18. Sentence 5: **When you meet a person with a disability, speak and act with he or she as you would with anyone else.**

    Which is the best way to write the underlined portion of the sentence?

    A. he or her
    B. him or her
    C. him or she
    D. them

19. Sentence 11: **Any assistive equipment, such as a wheelchair, cane, or communication board, are the person's property.**

    Which correction should be made to sentence 11?

    A. remove the comma after wheelchair
    B. change are to is
    C. change person's to persons
    D. insert a comma after assistive

20. Sentence 13: **Also, distracting a blind person's guide dog could put the owner in danger, so do not pet it.**

    If you rewrote sentence 13 beginning with

    Also, don't pet a blind person's guide dog because distracting

    the next word(s) should be

    A. a blind person's guide dog
    B. it
    C. her
    D. them

LESSON 1

Comma Use

As a general rule, **commas** indicate where readers would pause in a sentence if they were reading it aloud. Below are specific guidelines for using commas.

KEY IDEAS

- In a compound sentence, use a comma before the coordinating conjunction.
- Be careful not to use a comma when only two words or phrases are joined by *and*.
- Insert a comma after an introductory word, phrase, or clause.

Commas in Compound Sentences

In a compound sentence, place a comma immediately before the coordinating conjunction.

EXAMPLES

Some people are insecure about hosting a party, but others are relaxed and confident.

Many hosts have years of practice, and they have some organizational tips.

Watch out, though, for sentences that appear to be compound but are not. Some sentences have one main clause but have a compound subject or a compound predicate. If a sentence does not have two independent clauses, a comma is not needed before the coordinating conjunction.

Incorrect: Planning, and list making are two key organizational techniques.
Correct: Planning and list making are two key organizational techniques.

Incorrect: Making a list reduces disorganization, and helps you feel in control.
Correct: Making a list reduces disorganization and helps you feel in control.

HiSET EXAM TIP

Read a sentence out loud to see if you hear a pause. Before you insert a comma, be sure that you can base your decision on a comma rule.

Commas after Introductory Elements

In general, a comma should follow an introductory word, phrase, or clause to separate the introductory element from the main part of the sentence.

EXAMPLES

Introductory words:
Yes, listing your ideas can be very helpful.
However, making a list is only the first step.

Introductory phrases:
Giving it some thought, carefully draw up a guest list.
For a casual feel, have an open house.
On the day of the party, do as much as you can first thing in the morning.
By party time, you should be able to relax.

Introductory clauses:
Before you make a list, decide what kind of party you will have.
If you are a good cook, you might choose to have a dinner party.

Remember that only a subordinate clause at the beginning of a sentence requires a comma after it. A subordinate clause at the end of the sentence generally does not.

No comma: Decide what kind of party you will have before you make a list.

PRACTICE 1.1

A. Directions: Insert commas where needed in the sentences below. If no commas are required, write *NC*.

_____ **1.** Train travel is more pleasant than riding a bus but it can be more expensive.

_____ **2.** When you're on a train you can stand up and stretch if you need to.

_____ **3.** Most trains have club cars where passengers can get snacks and sometimes even sit at tables.

_____ **4.** Unlike buses trains sometimes have seats that face each other.

_____ **5.** Traveling through a scenic area you may find that your train has a double-decker car that offers a better view.

_____ **6.** Lowered air fares and many people's unwillingness to spend long hours in a train have contributed to the declining popularity of rail travel.

B. Questions 7 through 9 refer to the following paragraphs.

Low-Fat Cooking

(A)

(1) To have a more healthful diet, try cooking with less fat. (2) It's not as hard as you think! (3) For starters use cooking methods that require little or no oil or butter, such as steaming, poaching, or baking. (4) When you do include oil in the preparation of your dish, use less of it. (5) Vinegar can be used without oil in salad dressing and the flavor can be enhanced with fresh herbs.

(B)

(6) Another tactic is to cut down on dairy fat. (7) Avoid regular milk, cream, and sour cream. (8) Add low-fat dairy products or another liquid to your dish instead. (9) Many dairy foods come in a low-fat version, and though, not all of them may be pleasing to the palate, some are.

STUDY ADVICE

When you write, don't just make guesses about where to place commas. Use the rules outlined on these pages. People frequently misuse commas in daily life, so what feels right to you may not actually be correct.

7. Sentence 3: For starters use cooking methods that require little or no oil or butter, such as steaming, poaching, or baking.

Which correction should be made to sentence 3?

A. insert a comma after starters
B. remove the comma after butter
C. remove the comma after steaming
D. insert a comma after little

8. Sentence 5: Vinegar can be used without oil in salad dressing and the flavor can be enhanced with fresh herbs.

Which is the best way to write the underlined portion of the sentence?

A. dressing, and
B. dressing and,
C. dressing, or
D. dressing, for example

9. Sentence 9: Many dairy foods come in a low-fat version, and though, not all of them may be pleasing to the palate, some are.

Which correction should be made to sentence 9?

A. remove the comma after version
B. insert a comma after pleasing
C. remove the comma after palate
D. remove the comma after though

Commas in a Series

When three or more items are listed in a series, place commas *between* the items:

KEY IDEAS

- Separate the items in a series with commas.
- Put commas around an appositive only if it gives nonessential details about a noun.
- Don't put a comma between a subject and a verb.
- Don't use a comma between two items joined by *and* or *or*.

EXAMPLES

Keith, Darnelle, Marisol, and Doug are ready to take the HiSET exam.
They have taken a class, studied together, and prepared well.

The comma before the final *and* or *or* is optional (for example, *March 7, March 14, or March 21*), but using one there will help you place commas correctly in the series.

Commas with Appositives

An **appositive** is a word or group of words that gives more information about a noun by renaming it.

EXAMPLES

Marisol, an experienced writer, feels confident about the essay.
Doug's only sister, Gina, was the first in the family to receive a high school equivalency degree.

To decide whether to set off an appositive with commas, mentally cross out the appositive. Then ask, "Can I still identify the person, place, or thing described in the sentence?" If you can, use commas around the appositive.

EXAMPLES

Mann College, a local community college, offers courses for the HiSET exam.
Keith, who attended classes for the HiSET exam, did well on the test.

Here you can identify the noun without the appositive. Each appositive adds more information, but it is not essential to your understanding. Usually when an appositive is renaming a proper noun, it is not essential.

HiSET EXAM TIP

When an option involves removing a comma, see if you can apply a specific rule for using a comma in that place. If you cannot, the comma should probably be removed.

On the other hand, if you cannot identify the person, place, or thing without the appositive, do not set off the appositive with commas.

EXAMPLES

Keith and his friend Antoine plan to work in construction.
Students who study faithfully usually do well on the test.

In these examples, you cannot identify the nouns without the appositives. You would ask, "Which friend?" and "Which students?" The appositives are essential to your understanding and should not be set off by commas.

Comma Errors to Avoid

It is easy to overuse commas. Avoid this error by following these guidelines:

Do not use a comma between the subject and the verb.

Incorrect: Park College, is the school Doug hopes to attend.

Do not use a comma between two subjects, two verbs, or two other items joined by *and* or *or*.

Incorrect: Science, and math are hard subjects for Keith.
Incorrect: Darnell writes practice essays, and reads literature.
Incorrect: They will review his application, and transcript.

PRACTICE 1.2

A. Directions: Insert commas where needed in the sentences below. If no commas are required, write *NC*.

_____ **1.** Kwanzaa is a week-long African American holiday that celebrates culture community and family.

_____ **2.** Kwanzaa a wintertime holiday is based on an ancient African harvest celebration.

_____ **3.** It was developed in modern times by scholar Maulana Karenga.

_____ **4.** Kwanzaa celebrations include rituals such as singing dancing drumming and poetry reading.

_____ **5.** The family lights one candle every day for each of seven principles: unity self-determination responsibility cooperative economics purpose creativity and faith.

_____ **6.** A day during which people consider their moral worthiness marks the end of Kwanzaa.

B. Questions 7 through 9 refer to the following paragraphs.

Childproofing Your Home

(A)

(1) If you have small children, you no doubt appreciate the need to make your home as safe as possible. (2) It is a fact that home accidents, are responsible for more children's injuries than all childhood diseases combined. (3) Taking a few simple measures might reduce the number of times you take your kids to the emergency room.

(B)

(4) Start by putting childproof locks on all cupboards in which medicines poisons, or fragile objects are stored. (5) To keep babies and toddlers from entering dangerous areas, put baby gates in doorways and install sleeves on doorknobs. (6) Install safety locks on doors and windows. (7) Make sure that older children, those ten and up can open them in an emergency. (8) To prevent burns in the bathtub, keep the water temperature below 120°F. (9) Cover unused outlets with outlet plugs.

7. Sentence 2: It is a fact that home accidents, are responsible for more children's injuries than all childhood diseases combined.

Which correction should be made to sentence 2?

A. remove the comma
B. change are to is
C. insert a comma after injuries
D. insert a comma after diseases

8. Sentence 4: Start by putting childproof locks on all cupboards in which medicines poisons, or fragile objects are stored.

Which correction should be made to sentence 4?

A. change Start to Starting
B. insert a comma after medicines
C. insert a comma after objects
D. change are to is

9. Sentence 7: Make sure that older children, those ten and up can open them in an emergency.

Which is the best way to write the underlined portion of this sentence?

A. children those ten and up
B. children, those ten, and up,
C. children, those ten and up,
D. children those ten and up,

Using Writing Mechanics

LESSON 2

Capitalization

To recognize capitalization errors on the Writing Test and to use capital letters correctly in your response, follow these guidelines.

Capitalize proper nouns. A **proper noun** is the name of a specific person, place, thing, or idea. If a proper noun has two or more words, capitalize each word.

EXAMPLES

Claude Normand is a major contributor to Portland Community Hospital.
The hospital is located on Camden Road in Portland, Maine.
The hospital and charities such as the American Cancer Society rely on contributions from citizens.
All major religions, from Islam to Christianity, support giving to charity.

Note that the key words in addresses are proper nouns and are capitalized. The key words include the names of streets, cities, states, and countries.

Do not capitalize common nouns, which do not refer to a specific person, place, or thing.

EXAMPLE

Incorrect: Many Doctors volunteer at Clinics in the City.
Correct: Many doctors volunteer at clinics in the city.

Capitalize the names of proper adjectives. A **proper adjective** is formed from a proper noun.

EXAMPLE

Mr. Normand has a French Canadian heritage.

Capitalize a title before a person's name. Do not capitalize a title when it appears without a person's name unless it is used in direct address.

EXAMPLES

Title before name: Mr. Normand met recently with Dr. Halverson and Mayor Maresky.
Title without name: The doctor and mayor were very receptive to his ideas.
Direct address: He said, "Thank you, Mayor, for listening to my proposal."

Capitalize names of holidays, days of the week, and months. Do not capitalize the names of seasons.

EXAMPLES

Memorial Day is always the last Monday in May and is a paid holiday.
The project will be completed by the end of spring.

Capitalize names of specific school courses and all languages.

EXAMPLE

I am taking Introduction to Computers 101, English, and math.

KEY IDEAS

- Capitalize proper nouns and adjectives.
- Capitalize days of the week, months, and names of holidays but not seasons.
- Capitalize titles if they come before a person's name or are used to address the person.

HiSET EXAM TIP

Use the "proper noun test" to determine if a word should be capitalized. To capitalize, make sure the word or phrase is the name of a person, place, or thing: "my uncle" is fine, and so is "Uncle Leo."

PRACTICE 2

A. Directions: Correct the capitalization errors in the sentences below.

EXAMPLE:

I am writing to thank the ~~S~~s taff of the Waterside Physical Therapy ~~c~~C enter.

1. Last Spring, I broke my arm in a car accident.
2. My internist, doctor claudia McNally, referred me to Waterside.
3. The center's Director, Ilana Harris, assigned me a physical therapist named Ellie Royce.
4. Ellie studied physical therapy in her native London and used british methods of treatment that relieved my pain quite effectively.
5. She also did therapy with me in the pool at Rainbow health club.
6. I finished my treatments just before labor day, and I feel 100 percent better, thanks to Ellie.

B. Questions 7 through 9 refer to the following paragraphs.

An Unusual Breed

(A)

(1) The Akita is a Japanese dog breed that dates to ancient times. (2) The breed has a special spiritual meaning for many. (3) For example, when a child is born, well-wishers give the family small statues of Akitas to express hopes for future happiness and health. (4) In the past, only Emperors and nobles were allowed to own this breed.

(B)

(5) Akitas are massive, powerful dogs, used for hunting game and guarding. (6) Starting in the 17th century, they were trained to hunt game and waterfowl in the Mountains of Japan. (7) In 1937, Akitas were brought to america by author Helen Keller.

7. Sentence 4: In the past, only Emperors and nobles were allowed to own this breed.

Which correction should be made to sentence 4?

A. remove the comma
B. change Emperors to emperors
C. change nobles to Nobles
D. change were to are

8. Sentence 6: Starting in the 17th century, they were trained to hunt game and waterfowl in the Mountains of Japan.

Which correction should be made to sentence 6?

A. change Starting to Started
B. remove the comma
C. change Mountains to mountains
D. insert a comma after game

9. Sentence 7: In 1937, Akitas were brought to america by author Helen Keller.

Which correction should be made to sentence 7?

A. remove the comma
B. change america to America
C. change author to Author
D. change Helen Keller to helen keller

LESSON 3

Possessives and Contractions

KEY IDEAS

- Use apostrophes with possessive nouns but not with possessive pronouns.
- Use an apostrophe to replace the missing letters in a contraction.
- To decide whether to use a possessive or contraction, test to see whether the full form of the contraction makes sense in the sentence.

Some of the most common spelling errors involve possessives and contractions. Follow these guidelines when spelling these words:

A **possessive** shows ownership. Use apostrophes with possessive nouns. Do not use apostrophes with possessive pronouns.

EXAMPLES
Possessive nouns: friend's car Marta's map the dogs' leashes
Possessive pronouns: his, hers, ours, yours, theirs, its
Correct: The car's tires are new. The map is hers.

If a noun is singular or if it is plural but does not end in *s*, add an apostrophe + *s* to form the possessive.

Singular possessive: cat's boss's women's

If a noun is plural and ends in *s*, add an apostrophe after the final *s*.

Plural possessive: workers' ladies'

A singular possessive often sounds like a plural noun. Use an apostrophe only with the possessive.

Correct: My company's benefits (possessive) make it one of the best companies (plural) to work for.

A **contraction** shortens two words by combining the second word with the first and leaving out one or more letters. An apostrophe takes the place of the missing letters. Some contractions combine pronouns with verbs.

EXAMPLES
here is → here's there is → there's I am → I'm

Other contractions combine verbs with the word not.

EXAMPLES
have not → haven't do not → don't will not → won't

Be careful to use the apostrophe in place of the missing letter or letters. Notice that the correct position is not necessarily the point at which the two words come together.

Incorrect: You do'nt have to come with us tonight. (*do'nt* should be *don't*)

Some possessives and contractions sound the same (*your* and *you're*, *its* and *it's*, *their* and *they're*). To determine whether to use a possessive or a contraction, substitute the two words that make up the contraction. If the substitution makes sense, the contraction is correct. If not, use a possessive.

HiSET EXAM TIP

Contractions are acceptable in informal speech and writing. However, try to avoid them in more formal writing situations, such as the essay.

A. Directions: Underline the correct word or words to complete each sentence.

EXAMPLE: I'm (your, you're) downstairs neighbor, and (I've, Iv'e) been having trouble sleeping lately because of noise late at night.

1. (Theirs, There's) a noise that sounds like the thumping beat of rock music.
2. I (ca'nt, can't) be sure (who's, whose) responsible, but (its, it's) coming from your apartment.
3. My roommates and I have discussed this, and (were, we're) running out of patience.
4. You should talk to your children if the stereo is (theirs, there's).
5. Please be considerate of your neighbors just as we are considerate of (our's, ours).

B. Questions 6 through 8 refer to the paragraphs that follow.

Sales Trainees Wanted

(A)

(1) Do you have a warm smile? (2) Do people feel comfortable with you? (3) Do you have a friendly phone manner? (4) Do you have good organizational skills? (5) Are you good at solving problems? (6) If you've answered yes to these questions, we need you're skills at Macro Software.

(B)

(7) Macro Software is one of the industry leaders in software distribution. (8) In addition to our chain of stores, were proud to offer a mail order service that was the first of its kind. (9) We pride ourselves on our high-quality products, quick delivery times, and excellent customer service.

(C)

(10) We are currently hiring sales trainees for our Miami office. (11) Interested parties should send they're resumes to Jim Burns, Macro Software, 904 Ocean Drive, Miami, Florida.

6. **Sentence 6:** If you've answered yes to these questions, we need you're skills at Macro Software.

   Which correction should be made to sentence 6?

   A. insert a comma after yes
   B. remove the comma
   C. change need to needs
   D. replace you're with your

7. **Sentence 8:** In addition to our chain of stores, were proud to offer a mail order service that was the first of its kind.

   Which correction should be made to sentence 8?

   A. replace our with hour
   B. change were to we're
   C. insert a comma after service
   D. replace its with it's

8. **Sentence 11:** Interested parties should send they're resumes to Jim Burns, Macro Software, 904 Ocean Drive, Miami, Florida.

   Which correction should be made to sentence 11?

   A. replace parties with party's
   B. replace they're with their
   C. replace resumes with resume's
   D. replace Burns with Burn's

LESSON 4

Homonyms

Homonyms are words that sound alike but are spelled differently and have different meanings. The following chart lists homonyms and other commonly confused words that people often misspell.

KEY IDEAS

Homonyms are words that sound the same but have different spellings and different meanings.

HiSET EXAM TIP

Possessives, contractions, and homonyms are the kinds of spelling items that appear on the Writing Test. Study the ones that give you problems.

Word	Meaning	Word in Sentence
accept	to receive willingly	I accept responsibility for my actions.
except	excluding	Everyone went except Molly.
affect	to have an impact	Did the medicine affect you?
effect	a result	The effects will wear off soon.
board	a piece of wood	Nail that board to the other one.
bored	not interested	Rami was bored in wood shop class.
brake	to stop; something that stops	Put your foot on the brake!
break	to shatter in pieces	Be careful, or you'll break your arm.
close	to shut	Please close that bag.
clothes	something to wear	I'm going to return those clothes.
desert	to leave behind; arid land	Don't desert a friend in need.
dessert	sweet food served after dinner	They offer dessert to their guests.
fare	money paid by a passenger	The subway fare was just raised.
fair	just, right	A lot of people think it's not fair.
forth	forward	Let's go forth!
fourth	in the 4th position	It is our fourth trip in three days.
grate	to shred	We need to grate some potatoes.
great	fantastic; of large size	It's going to be a great casserole.
hole	opening	There's a hole in the sweater.
whole	entire	Soon the whole thing will fall apart.
know	to understand	I don't know what's wrong with him.
no	opposite of *yes*	He has no sense.
led	past of the verb *lead;* brought	He led the worker to the supply room.
lead	a material in pencils	They gave her some lead pencils.
lessen	to decrease	Will you lessen the sugar in the recipe?
lesson	something you learn; moral	That will teach him a lesson.
male	a boy or man	There are both females and males in the Army.
mail	to send a message through the post office; a message sent	Send the letter through the mail.
passed	went by	Have you passed the post office?
past	opposite of *future*	Yes, in the past.
peace	opposite of *war*	When will there be world peace?
piece	a part	That's only a piece of the problem.
principal	head of a school	The principal has called a meeting.
principle	a guiding rule; a moral	He has no principles.
than	compared with	I used to have more money than you.
then	after that; at that time	Then I spent most of mine.
there	at that place	The car is over there.
their	belonging to them	It is their car.
they're	they are	They're going to sell it.
to	indicates a direction	Go to the grocery store.
too	also, in addition	Sharmaine will go, too.
two	the number 2	Buy me two loaves of bread.

PRACTICE 4

A. Directions: Underline the correct word or words to complete each sentence.

EXAMPLE: The chairman of the (board, bored) has called this meeting.

1. This is our (fourth, forth) meeting on the topic of funding.

2. We don't (no, know) any other sources of funding.

3. The director of the organization brought up this (whole, hole) issue.

4. Next (weak, week), we plan to submit a proposal.

5. We worry that a request for funding may (affect, effect) our nonprofit status.

6. In the (past, passed), we could rely on government funding.

B. Questions 7 through 9 refer to the paragraphs that follow.

Equal Pay for Equal Work?

(A)

(1) In 1963, women earned only 59 percent of the wages men earned. (2) In 1997, the figure was still just 74 percent. (3) Women have logged great achievements in the workforce, so why don't they receive fare pay?

(B)

(4) One explanation is that the statistics include older women. (5) In principal, the age gap could account for the wage gap because older women still work in jobs in which attitudes and conditions of the past prevail. (6) In contrast, women under the age of 25 earn about 92 percent of what men earn. (7) However, upon closer examination, this theory falls flat. (8) Women in entry-level jobs have always earned salaries similar to those of their male peers. (9) The problem is that women don't receive the same raises and promotions that men get. (10) The affect is that, as women get older, the gap between men's and women's salaries becomes greater.

STUDY ADVICE

Homonyms can be tricky. If you are unsure whether you are using the correct word during your practice, be sure to look it up in a dictionary afterward. If you are unsure when writing an essay on Test Day, try to pick a completely different word to avoid an error.

7. Sentence 3: Women have logged great achievements in the workforce, so why don't they receive fare pay?

Which correction should be made to sentence 3?

A. change have to has
B. replace great with grate
C. replace fare with fair
D. replace Women with Woman

8. Sentence 5: In principal, the age gap could account for the wage gap because older women still work in jobs in which attitudes and conditions of the past prevail.

Which correction should be made to sentence 5?

A. change principal to principle
B. change work to working
C. replace past with passed
D. replace for with four

9. Sentence 10: The affect is that, as women get older, the gap between men's and women's salaries becomes greater.

Which correction should be made to sentence 10?

A. replace affect with effect
B. change becomes to become
C. replace greater with grater
D. remove the comma after that

LESSON 5

Idiomatic Usage

KEY IDEAS

- Idioms are combinations of words that are correct because they have been used that way for a long time.
- Many idioms involve selecting the correct preposition to use with a verb.
- Some idioms are colorful figures of speech that, in most contexts, mean something completely different from their component words.

HiSET EXAM TIP

There are far too many idioms to memorize them all. However, by being conscious of idiomatic usage, you can train your "ear" to recognize when words are being used together correctly.

Idioms are word combinations that, due to longstanding usage, are held to be correct. There are many idioms in English, and each idiom has its own "rule" that establishes proper usage. Fortunately, you do not need to memorize all the idioms. Instead, you can usually rely on your "ear" to tell you which combinations of words are correct. In fact, you probably use many idioms correctly every day without even thinking about it.

Idioms often involve a verb and a preposition.

EXAMPLES
Incorrect: He is regarded to be one of the league's best players.
Correct: He is regarded as one of the league's best players.

Incorrect: Some people credit Sir Francis Bacon as writing William Shakespeare's plays.
Correct: Some people credit Sir Francis Bacon with writing William Shakespeare's plays.

Incorrect: The actor is romantically linked with the talk show host.
Correct: The actor is romantically linked to the talk show host.

Some idioms have meanings completely different from those of the individual words.

EXAMPLES
It is raining cats and dogs.
(It is raining heavily.)

We need to go back to the drawing board.
(We need a new plan.)

I wish she wouldn't beat around the bush.
(I wish she would speak her mind directly.)

Here is a list of some common idioms. Note that in certain cases, the lack of a preposition—indicated by [no word]—is idiomatically correct. When you read and listen to people talk, see if you can identify other idioms.

She attributes her success to hard work.	This cake contains less sugar and fewer calories than that one.
The employees were forbidden to enter the manager's office, and they were prohibited from discussing company policies.	The menu offered a choice between two appetizers and among three entrees.
Dogs' personalities are different from cats' personalities.	With practice, one can distinguish between formal and informal writing.
Winters in Florida are warmer than winters in Minnesota.	Some people cannot distinguish red from green.
His formal jacket contrasts with his old jeans.	Many city residents viewed the new regulations as burdensome and perceived their mayor as out of touch. In particular, they considered the parking restrictions [no word] a nuisance and believed the recycling rules to be too difficult to follow.
Economists estimated the average family income to be increasing.	

PRACTICE 5

A. Directions: For each sentence, choose the correct idiom.

1. She had to decide (between/among) many types of breakfast cereal.
2. Many people believe turtles (to be/as) amphibians, but they are reptiles.
3. His father forbade him (to swim/from swimming).
4. Temperatures this summer were higher (from/than) they were last summer.
5. Jenna was disappointed to find (less/fewer) money in her wallet than she expected.

B. <u>Questions 6 through 9</u> refer to the following passage.

(A)

Jon studied the long list of job openings at his company. He wanted to apply for a promotion, and company policy stated that employees could submit only one application at a time. Therefore, he had to choose <u>between</u> the open positions. Jon regarded the warehouse, where he worked now, <u>as</u> a dead end, so he was focusing his search <u>on</u> other departments.

(B)

Abe, his coworker and good friend, came up to him. "You can't squeeze <u>blood</u> from a turnip," Abe said. "Because the company keeps losing money, none of the jobs here pay very well. In fact, our company is <u>considered</u> one of the worst places to work in the industry. I am going to <u>try and</u> get a job someplace else."

(C)

"I understand why you feel that way," Jon said. "However, I credit this company <u>as</u> giving me a <u>leg</u> up when I needed one. Also, there are so many open positions that one of them must be better <u>than</u> my current job."

(D)

Abe looked skeptical. "Well," he said, "___________________________."

6. **Paragraph A:** Which of the following is the best revision?
   A. (No change)
   B. Change "between" to "among"
   C. Change "as" to "as being"
   D. Change "on" to "at"

7. **Paragraph B:** Which of the following is the best revision?
   A. (No change)
   B. Change "blood" to "juice"
   C. Change "considered" to "considered to be"
   D. Change "try and" to "try to"

8. **Paragraph C:** Which of the following is the best revision?
   A. (No change)
   B. Change "as" to "with"
   C. Change "leg" to "lift"
   D. Change "than" to "from"

9. **Paragraph D:** Which of the following is the best sentence to complete the blank?
   A. It's your funeral.
   B. A bird in the hand beats two in the bush.
   C. Don't give up the day job.
   D. It's no use crying over spilled milk.

USING WRITING MECHANICS PRACTICE QUESTIONS

Questions 1 through 5 refer to the following paragraphs.

Single Parents and Relationships

(A)

(1) Children of single parents don't exactly cheer their parents on at the start of a new relationship. (2) Instead, children may have tantrums erase phone messages, and generally try to ruin their parents' chances. (3) If you are a parent in this situation, you need to understand, and show your children that you love them. (4) However, also let your kids know, that you feel you're doing the right thing.

(B)

(5) Your children may become quickly attached to a new date, even within the course of an evening. (6) Alternatively, they may fear that you plan to marry each potential partner you bring home. (7) For these reasons, it makes sense not to introduce all your dates to your children. (8) Try to see your dates at times when your children are'nt at home.

(C)

(9) Once you become committed to a particular person, it's important to include your partner in family events gradually. (10) Don't be surprised if your children have a negative reaction to your new partner. (11) This time may be difficult for your kids. (12) They're not used to seeing you with a new partner, and they may be realizing that a reconciliation with your ex-spouse is impossible. (13) If communication breaks down consider family counseling. (14) Children may be more willing to share their worries and complaints in that setting.

1. Sentence 2: **Instead, children may have tantrums erase phone messages, and generally try to ruin their parents' chances.**

   Which correction should be made to sentence 2?

   A. remove the comma after Instead
   B. insert a comma after tantrums
   C. change their to they're
   D. change have to has

2. Sentence 3: **If you are a parent in this situation, you need to understand, and show your children that you love them.**

   Which is the best way to write the underlined portion of this sentence?

   A. understand, and showing
   B. understand. And show
   C. understand and show
   D. understand, and you show

3. Sentence 4: **However, also let your kids know, that you feel you're doing the right thing.**

   Which correction should be made to sentence 4?

   A. remove the comma after However
   B. replace your with you're
   C. replace you're with your
   D. remove the comma after know

4. Sentence 8: **Try to see your dates at times when your children are'nt at home.**

   Which correction should be made to sentence 8?

   A. replace your with you're
   B. insert a comma after times
   C. change are'nt to aren't
   D. change are'nt to isn't

5. Sentence 13: **If communication breaks down consider family counseling.**

   Which is the best way to write the underlined portion of this sentence?

   A. down will consider
   B. down, consider
   C. down. Consider
   D. down, and consider

Questions 6 through 10 refer to the following paragraphs.

The History of Daylight Saving Time

(A)

(1) We set our clocks forward every spring and back every fall, but few of us stop to think about why we do this. (2) One of the main reasons for daylight saving time, is to save energy. (3) In the evening, we use lights, TVs, and electrical appliances. (4) Daylight saving time makes the period between sunset and bedtime one hour shorter, and therefore less electricity is used.

(B)

(5) With daylight saving time, each time zone changes it's standard time by an hour. (6) Time zones were introduced by the railroads to make schedules standard across the country. (7) In 1918, congress passed a law making the rail time zones official. (8) That same year, a second law put the country on daylight saving time for the rest of World War I. (9) The law was unpopular, however, and it was repealed seven months later. (10) Daylight saving time was also in force during most of World War II.

(C)

(11) From 1945 to 1966, each state and town could decide whether to observe daylight saving time. (12) The resulting inconsistencies created a great deal of confusion. (13) For example radio and TV stations had to put out new schedules every time a state started or ended daylight saving time. (14) Then came the Uniform Time Act of 1966, which established starting and ending dates for daylight saving time, in the spring and fall. (15) This law was amended in 1986, when the starting date was moved almost a month earlier to save energy.

6. Sentence 2: **One of the main reasons for daylight saving time, is to save energy.**

   Which correction should be made to sentence 2?

   A. insert a comma after reasons
   B. remove the comma
   C. change is to are
   D. change main to mane

7. Sentence 5: **With daylight saving time, each time zone changes it's standard time by an hour.**

   Which correction should be made to sentence 5?

   A. remove the comma
   B. replace it's with its
   C. replace hour with our
   D. insert a comma after standard time

8. Sentence 7: **In 1918, congress passed a law making the rail time zones official.**

   Which correction should be made to sentence 7?

   A. remove the comma
   B. change congress to Congress
   C. replace passed with past
   D. change making to made

9. Sentence 13: **For example radio and TV stations had to put out new schedules every time a state started or ended daylight saving time.**

   Which correction should be made to sentence 13?

   A. insert a comma after example
   B. change had to have
   C. change schedules to schedule's
   D. insert a comma after schedules

10. Sentence 14: **Then came the Uniform Time Act of 1966, which established starting and ending dates for daylight saving time, in the spring and fall.**

    Which correction should be made to sentence 14?

    A. change Act to act
    B. replace dates with date's
    C. remove the comma after time
    D. change spring and fall to Spring and Fall

Questions 11 through 15 refer to the following paragraphs.

Rules and Regulations

(A)

(1) Thank you for joining Spring Valley Community center. (2) Before using our facility, please read these rules and regulations carefully.

(B)

(3) Please have your membership card with you at all times when your in the building. (4) When you enter the pool or exercise room, a security guard will request to see your card and will deny you entrance without it.

(C)

(5) Guests are welcome to use the pool and exercise room, but only when accompanied by members. (6) The guest fee is $10 per day. (7) When bringing guests, please have them sign in at the desk in the lobby. (8) They will be given a guest card for the day.

(D)

(9) Pool safety is very important. (10) If you are a week swimmer, life jackets and other flotation devices are available for your use. (11) Do not hesitate to ask lifeguards for help. (12) Children under the age of 12 must swim in the children's pool, unless they're supervised by an adult. (13) Swimming classes are available to help both children and adults improve their skills.

(E)

(14) You must register, and pay for any class you wish to take. (15) Members receive a significant discount. (16) Registration may be limited to a certain number of participants.

11. Sentence 1: **Thank you for joining Spring Valley Community center.**

    Which correction should be made to sentence 1?

    A. insert a comma after you
    B. change Community to community
    C. change center to Center
    D. change you to You

12. Sentence 3: **Please have your membership card with you at all times when your in the building.**

    Which correction should be made to sentence 3?

    A. insert a comma after Please
    B. replace have your with have you're
    C. replace times with times'
    D. replace when your with when you're

13. Sentence 10: **If you are a week swimmer, life jackets and other flotation devices are available for your use.**

    Which correction should be made to sentence 10?

    A. replace week with weak
    B. remove the comma
    C. insert a comma after available
    D. change your to you're

14. Sentence 12: **Children under the age of 12 must swim in the children's pool, unless they're supervised by an adult.**

    Which correction should be made to sentence 12?

    A. insert commas after Children and 12
    B. change children's with childrens'
    C. replace they're to their
    D. remove the comma after pool

15. Sentence 14: **You must register, and pay for any class you wish to take.**

    Which is the best way to write the underlined portion of this sentence?

    A. register, pay
    B. register and pay
    C. register. And pay
    D. register. Pay

Questions 16 through 20 refer to the following paragraphs.

Racial Profiling

(A)

(1) African American and Hispanic motorists are much more likely to be stopped by police then their white counterparts, often for no apparent reason. (2) What's their offense? (3) It may be that these individuals have been targeted because of their race.

(B)

(4) Blacks and Hispanics, who some police officers believe are more likely to commit crimes, have been systematically targeted by police. (5) Police statistics from 23 states show that this policy, called racial profiling occurs in every geographic location. (6) Motorists, pedestrians, and airline passengers have been searched. (7) The police do not make class distinctions for nonwhites of every station in life have been victims of this practice.

(C)

(8) The statistical evidence shows a clear pattern. (9) On one Maryland highway, 73 percent of those stopped by police were African American, even though blacks represented only 17 percent of all drivers. (10) Hispanics make up only 8 percent of the population in illinois, yet 30 percent of drivers stopped there are Hispanic. (11) However, police superintendents chiefs of police, and other law enforcement officials dispute the studies that document racial profiling. (12) They maintain that the problem has been confined to a small number of officers and can be remedied easily.

16. Sentence 1: **African American and Hispanic motorists are much more likely to be stopped by police then their white counterparts, often for no apparent reason.**

    Which correction should be made to sentence 1?

    A. change motorists to Motorists
    B. insert a comma after then
    C. replace then with than
    D. replace for with four

17. Sentence 5: **Police statistics from 23 states show that this policy, called racial profiling occurs in every geographic location.**

    Which correction should be made to sentence 5?

    A. change states to States
    B. insert a comma after states
    C. insert a comma after profiling
    D. remove the comma

18. Sentence 7: **The police do not make class distinctions for nonwhites of every station in life have been victims of this practice.**

    Which is the best way to write the underlined portion of this sentence?

    A. distinctions. For nonwhites
    B. distinctions, for nonwhites
    C. distinctions moreover nonwhites
    D. distinctions nonwhites

19. Sentence 10: **Hispanics make up only 8 percent of the population in illinois, yet 30 percent of drivers stopped there are Hispanic.**

    Which correction should be made to sentence 10?

    A. change make to makes
    B. change illinois to Illinois
    C. remove the comma
    D. replace yet with and

20. Sentence 11: **However, police superintendents chiefs of police, and other law enforcement officials dispute the studies that document racial profiling.**

    Which correction should be made to sentence 11?

    A. remove the comma after However
    B. insert a comma after superintendents
    C. insert a comma after officials
    D. change studies to studies'

LESSON 1

Unpack the Writing Prompt

On the Writing Test, you will write an essay in response to a pair of passages and a **prompt,** or assignment. You will want to spend 45 minutes on this task. To master this portion of the exam, you need to employ **evidence-based writing.** This type of writing requires that you develop an argument or explanation by using evidence and details from the text(s). The passages may discuss topics from science, history, or any other field. However, you do not need to have any prior knowledge about the topics. All the information you need will be provided for you in the passage(s).

The prompt will ask you to write a particular kind of essay, an Argument essay. Your task is to take a position on the issue discussed in the passages and support your position with logical reasons and relevant examples. To earn a high score, you will also consider a reason why someone might support the other side of the issue and rebut that argument.

Your task will be to write a few paragraphs (three or four) that clearly develop a line of thought. You will introduce your essay with a thesis statement; organize it into paragraphs, each of which develops one idea in support of that thesis statement; and conclude it with a summary of your argument.

Unpack the writing prompt to determine what your task is. What does it mean to "unpack" a prompt? When you unpack a suitcase, you take things out and think about what you are going to do with them—wash them, fold them, hang them up, or put them in a drawer. Similarly, with a writing prompt, you will take it apart in your mind and plan how you are going to accomplish the task.

Unpack the prompt by asking yourself these questions:

1. What is the writing assignment about?
2. Based on the prompt, how many passages will I be given, and what will they contain?
3. What does the prompt ask me to do?
4. What am I being asked to include in my response?

KEY IDEAS

- The essay will require reading two passages and writing a response to a prompt.
- To draft an acceptable response to the text, the first step is to "unpack" the prompt—to focus on the specific question you need to address.
- Your response must be evidence based, which means that it needs to be grounded in facts, details, and examples from the text.

HiSET EXAM TIP

It is advisable to read the prompt *before you read the passages. That will help you to focus on the argument and the supporting evidence in the passages.*

PRACTICE 1

Practice using the following prompt. (This prompt does not have passages associated with it, and you will not be writing an essay in response to it.)

Hydraulic fracturing is currently used in many parts of the United States to extract natural gas from deep in the ground. There is an ongoing debate about whether hydraulic fracturing (or "fracking") should be allowed. Read the two passages, weigh the arguments on both sides, and write an argumentative essay in which you argue for or against allowing hydraulic fracturing. Use details and evidence from both passages in your essay.	Make sure that you: • Include your thesis statement early. • Give reasons and evidence from the passages to support your thesis statement. • Argue against the opposite side. • Organize your ideas, and show how the ideas relate to each other. • Use a businesslike style. • Conclude with a short summary of your argument.

1. What is the writing assignment about? *Whether hydraulic fracturing should be allowed*

2. Based on the prompt, how many passages will I be given, and what will they contain? *Two passages, which present the two sides of the argument about hydraulic fracturing*

3. What does the prompt ask me to do? *Pick a side and argue for it. Should hydraulic fracturing be allowed and why?*

4. What am I being asked to include in my response? *Introduction, details from the passages, logical reasons why my argument is right, argument against the opposing view, good organization, concluding statement*

In response to the prompt below, answer the four questions listed on page 204.

Most people probably don't think about where the calendar came from, but it actually has a long and fascinating history. Read the passages describing the history of the Gregorian calendar (the one used by most people in the United States) and the development of other calendars used in other parts of the world. Write an essay arguing for or against the idea that the Gregorian calendar differs significantly from other calendars. Use details, facts, and definitions from the passage in your essay.	Make sure that you: • State your position clearly. • Give details, facts, and definitions from the passage to develop your explanation. • Organize your ideas, and show how the ideas relate to each other. • Use a businesslike style. • Conclude with a short summary of your argument.

LESSON 2

Read the Passages with the Prompt in Mind

Before writing your essay, you will first analyze the passages while keeping the prompt in mind. The writing prompt asks you to make an argument. Thus, as you read, ask yourself some questions that will equip you to perform that task. Take brief notes about these questions as you read.

First, identify the topic of each passage. Then ask: Is the author neutral about the topic—that is, is she merely giving you the history of something, explaining how something works, or describing something? Or does the author have an opinion about the topic?

If the author has an opinion, is she arguing for a certain policy or method, or is she countering someone else's argument? What evidence does she use to support her argument?

If she does not have an opinion, why did she write the passage? Your answer to that might sound like one of these examples:

- "The author wrote the passage to explain the history of the civil rights movement."
- "The author wrote the passage to describe the two sides of a debate, but she herself doesn't take a side."
- "The author wrote the passage to introduce a new way of thinking about her topic."
- "The author wrote the passage to compare and contrast two new products."

Read the following short passage. Consider whether the author is neutral or whether she has an opinion.

> Secondhand smoke is the smoke that comes either from the lighted end of a cigarette, pipe, or cigar or from the exhalation of a smoker. Most people consider secondhand smoke to be less dangerous than the nicotine that a cigarette user intakes. However, the particles that come from the smoke of the lighted end of a cigarette, called sidestream smoke, contain higher concentrations of carcinogens, which are chemicals that cause cancer. These particles can be breathed in easily by people around smokers, especially in enclosed areas. Therefore, all restaurants should ban smoking inside.

1. What is the writer's topic?
   (1) Secondhand smoke and its effects
   (2) The most common carcinogens
2. What is the writer's opinion about the topic?
   (1) Sidestream smoke contains high concentrations of carcinogens.
   (2) Smoking should be banned inside restaurants.

In question 1, choice **(1)** is correct. The writer focuses on secondhand smoke throughout the passage. In question 2, choice **(2)** is correct. The writer uses the information about secondhand smoke as support for the claim that smoking should be banned inside restaurants.

KEY IDEAS

- As you read passages on the Writing Test, keep the writing prompt in mind. Gather information that will allow you to complete the writing task.
- As you read, ask yourself, "What is the writer's topic? Does the writer have an opinion about that topic?"
- If the writer has an opinion, ask yourself what evidence she uses to support that opinion. If she does not have an opinion, ask yourself why she wrote the passage.

HiSET EXAM TIP

When you are reading the passages for the essay, ask yourself: What is the writer's conclusion?

PRACTICE 2

Directions: For each passage, answer the questions about topic, opinion, and evidence.

Passage 1

Some U.S. representatives advocate a bill requiring all young people to perform two years of military service by the age of 25. Proponents of the bill argue that this will not only prepare the U.S. military for any potential threat from other nations but will also build a greater spirit of patriotism among U.S. citizens. Citizens, they argue, will be able to appreciate the service of the military and acquire a deeper respect toward honoring their country. On the other side of the debate, opponents of the bill argue that requiring military service would lead people to feel resentful toward their government. They argue that, instead of requiring military service, the government should more heavily promote volunteer programs. Then young people could serve their countries by helping the poor or marginalized in their communities. At the present time, the bill's proponents and opponents continue to debate without reaching an agreement.

1. What is the writer's topic?

____

____

2. Does the writer have an opinion, or is she neutral?

____

3. If the writer has an opinion, how does she support it? If she's neutral, what was her purpose in writing the passage?

____

____

____

Passage 2

To best protect children from being subjected to portrayals of violence, we must reduce the amount of violence that is present in video games. Numerous studies done by various groups show a positive correlation between video game usage and violence.

Many people consider violence in video games a recent trend, but one of the earliest and most controversial video games was Death Race, released in 1976. In this game, the players controlled cars that ran over gremlins. The game was later pulled from stores due to public outcry. With the successful protest against Death Race as a model, we should be as proactive now to reduce or eliminate violence in video games.

4. What is the writer's topic?

____

____

5. Does the writer have an opinion, or is he neutral?

____

6. If the writer has an opinion, how does he support it? If he's neutral, what was his purpose in writing the passage?

____

____

____

STUDY ADVICE

Remember to build up your study time in increments. If writing tends to tire you out in the beginning, don't worry! You can spend an entire study session on the essay sample and then take a break. Over time, you can work up to longer study sessions.

LESSON 3

Develop a Thesis Statement

You have been reading and analyzing writers' arguments. Now it is your turn to develop a response to what writers have to say. Once you have unpacked the prompt and read the reading passages, you will construct a **thesis statement** for your writing. The thesis statement either states your central claim, or the position that you will be arguing for and supporting with evidence.

A thesis statement does the following:

- Makes your main point clear
- Provides the reader with a preview of what you will be discussing

KEY IDEAS

- A thesis statement makes a claim and indicates that the passage will support the claim with specific and relevant information.
- A thesis statement differs from an opinion, which is a feeling or belief about the topic of the passage.
- A thesis statement should introduce the topic that will be discussed in the essay.

Example 1: Hydraulic Fracturing Essay

Compare the following two sentences, written in response to the prompt about hydraulic fracturing on page 205. Put a *T* next to the one sentence that fulfills the purpose of a thesis statement as described previously.

____ Hydraulic fracturing has some good points and bad points, though the bad points can threaten to outweigh the good points.

____ Hydraulic fracturing should not be allowed because of the threats it poses to the environment.

If you put a *T* next to the second sentence, you are correct. The first sentence does not clearly state its claim, and it does not preview what the rest of the essay will discuss. The second sentence states its claim very clearly and also tells the reader that the rest of the essay will discuss the environmental threats posed by hydraulic fracturing.

Example 2: Gregorian Calendar Essay

Now compare the following two sentences, written in response to the prompt about calendars on page 205. Put a *T* next to the one that fulfills the purpose of a thesis statement.

____ The Gregorian calendar differs from other calendars in many ways for a variety of complex reasons.

____ The Gregorian calendar is guided by the sun rather than the moon, has a Leap Day, and uses 12 months because this arrangement suited religious and business needs in Europe several centuries ago.

You should have placed a *T* next to the first sentence, because it states a clear position on the issue—the calendar *is* different. The second sentence provides a lot of details about the Gregorian calendar, but the reader does not know what position the essay will take.

HiSET EXAM TIP

Although writers have different approaches, it is best to introduce your essay response with your thesis. This will let a reader know your position right away. Also, periodically review your thesis statement as you write. This will keep you on track.

PRACTICE 3

Directions: Read each paragraph and answer the questions that follow.

DIRECT-TO-CONSUMER ADVERTISING

Sit down to enjoy any television show today, and you'll find that almost every other commercial seems to be pushing a prescription drug. Although this form of direct-to-consumer (DTC) advertising of prescription medication has become commonplace in American programming, it remains a relatively new development in the medical world. In fact, the practice is currently legal in only two countries, the United States and New Zealand. Patient advocates and those who wish to maintain high standards of healthcare argue that DTC advertising should be eliminated altogether. Advertising prescription medications on television creates a popular demand for the drugs, and it may lead individuals to pressure their healthcare providers for treatments that are inappropriate or even dangerous. At the same time, because prescription commercials must name all potential side effects of a certain medication, the ads may frighten other individuals away from using drugs that are both safe and effective for the general public. While such DTC advertisements serve to increase the profits of drug companies, they do little to ensure that the public is better educated about its healthcare choices.

1. Is the writer neutral (giving a history, explaining something, etc.), or does he make an argument?

 ____

2. What is the writer's argument about prescription drug advertising on TV?

 ____

3. Write a thesis statement in which you take a stand for or against advertising prescription drugs on TV. State your position and preview how you will support it.

 ____

 ____

HOW DID THE MOON FORM?

There are several theories about how the Moon formed. Some scientists have suggested that the Moon was originally part of Earth and somehow broke off early in the history of the solar system. Others have suggested that the Moon was formed separately from Earth and then at some point was drawn into Earth's gravitational field, where it remains. Another possible answer involves rings. Earth (and other planets with a moon or moons) may have originally had rings like those of the planet Saturn. According to this idea, a moon begins to come together out of debris near the outer edges of a planet's rings. At those outer edges, the newly formed moon has a better chance of holding together without being broken up again by the planet's gravity. (Small objects orbiting close to a planet tend to be pulled toward the planet by gravity; they often ultimately crash into the planet.) The initial products of this process are small "moonlets" that spin outward from the planet. The moonlets collide and fuse with other moonlets as they travel. The process would be somewhat similar to that of a snowball rolling downhill, gathering more material as it rolls.

4. Is the writer neutral (giving a history, explaining something, etc.), or does she make an argument?

 ____

5. What does the author explain in this passage?

 ____

6. Write a thesis statement in response to this question: Which theory about the formation of the Moon is more credible? Make sure your thesis statement states your position and previews the rest of the essay.

 ____

LESSON 4

Collect Supporting Evidence

Once you have formulated your thesis statement, you need to use **evidence** and **details** from the passage or passages to support your claim. You should preview the **prompt** before you read the passage or passages. That benefit of this strategy is that you can:

- Formulate your thesis statement while you are reading
- Gather specific and relevant evidence and details to support your thesis

How can you gather evidence while you read? Whether you are taking the paper version or the computer version of the test, you can take notes on scratch paper, which will be provided.

KEY IDEAS

- Formulate your thesis statement and collect supporting evidence or relevant details while you read.
- As you read, take notes about which details you can use to support your thesis statement.

Thesis statement: Family time is a thing of the past because too many distractions interfere with conversation and other interactions.

Practice gathering evidence with the passage below. Circle specific pieces of evidence that support the thesis statement above.

I know it sounds corny, but I miss the way my family was together when I was growing up. Even though Mom and Dad worked, we usually had breakfast together. Now, I work the night shift and sleep in the morning, while my husband is too harried with getting the kids to eat and making their lunches to get a preview of their day.

After school, our kids have part-time jobs, and everyone gets home at different times. Even though I have dinner ready before I leave at 8:00 P.M., someone is doing homework, someone is on the Internet, and someone is texting friends that he or she saw an hour before. I can't remember the last time we all ate together and had a conversation. Even when I try to organize a movie night, it seems that one of us has social or work obligations. We all love each other, but it is hard to have what we can call family time. Thank goodness for holidays and vacations when we can slow down and enjoy each other.

HiSET EXAM TIP

When you cite the writer's evidence, use phrases such as "The passage stated . . ."; "In the text . . ."; and "One example from the text is . . ."

Evidence statements that support the thesis statement:

- Breakfast time is hectic and one parent is asleep.
- After school, people are working or engaged in distractions.
- Family members don't eat dinner together.
- Not everyone is available for common activities, like movie night.

PRACTICE 4

Directions: Read the prompt, the reading selection, and the writer's conclusion. List three pieces of supporting evidence from the passage that you could use in a response to the prompt. Add one piece of supporting evidence from your own experience or observations. <u>You will not be writing a response to this prompt</u>.

> **Drinking Age Prompt**
>
> The writer of this passage has a position on keeping the minimum legal drinking age at 21. Take a position in response to the writer's argument, using relevant and specific information from the selection to support your response.

The Case for Keeping the Minimum Drinking Age at 21

We owe it to young adults, teens, and children to keep the minimum drinking age right where it is: at 21. The dangers of alcohol are often overlooked due to the fact that it is not a prohibited substance, but make no mistake: it is eminently dangerous, particularly to our youth.

In larger doses—consistent with binge drinking— alcohol wreaks havoc on the sensitive chemistry of the brain. The feast-and-famine pattern of drinking that is typical of teenage drinkers can lead to permanent damage to the prefrontal cortex, the part of the brain responsible for planning and decisions. Since this portion of the brain continues to develop later in life, younger brains are particularly vulnerable to the effects of alcohol. Even in moderate doses, it causes long-term damage to the heart, the liver, and the stomach.

Proponents of a lower drinking age maintain that the allure of the taboo of alcohol encourages abuse among youth. The United Kingdom, however, has a long history of social drinking, and the legal drinking age is 18 in bars and 16 in restaurants; despite this, alcohol-related deaths had doubled in the U.K. in the decade before 2008. Indeed, a 2008 BBC documentary ranked alcohol as the fifth most dangerous drug in the U.K., ahead of speed, LSD, ecstasy, and cannabis.

As a nation, we recognized the dangers that alcohol represented to our citizens and communities when we united to pass a constitutional amendment against it a century ago. That experiment was abandoned only due to challenges of enforcement, but Al Capone could never have built a crime empire on the dimes of 18- to 20-year-olds alone. We owe it to our youth—and the future of our nation—to protect their brains and their lives.

Writer's Conclusion

The conclusion is that despite some logical reasons for lowering the legal drinking age, it should remain at 21.

1. Three pieces of evidence used in the passage to support this conclusion are . . .

a. The passage states that ______________________________

____

____

b. Another fact from the passage is

____

____

c. In support of this position, the text further says that ______________________________

____

____

2. I (agree/disagree) with the position of this piece.

3. One piece of evidence I would use to support my position is ______________________________

____

____

____

____

LESSON 5

Plan Your Response

You will want to spend about 45 minutes to complete the essay. You need to use that time wisely, and the best thing you can do is to take 10 minutes for **prewriting**, or planning, what you are going to write.

Successful test takers do this type of planning. It ensures that you understand the prompt, write a thesis statement, gather the relevant evidence, and have your ideas in place before you begin to write.

Essay-Writing Strategy

This **Essay-Writing Strategy** will maximize your ability to use the 45 minutes efficiently and effectively. As you work through the rest of this unit, practice managing each stage of the strategy.

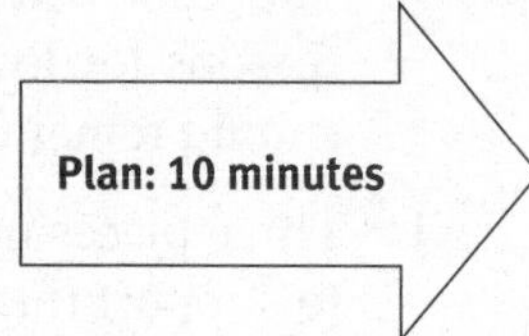

- Preview the writing prompt.
- Read the passage(s), making notes of key details on scratch paper.
- Use scratch paper to write your thesis statement and plan your response with either an outline or an idea map.

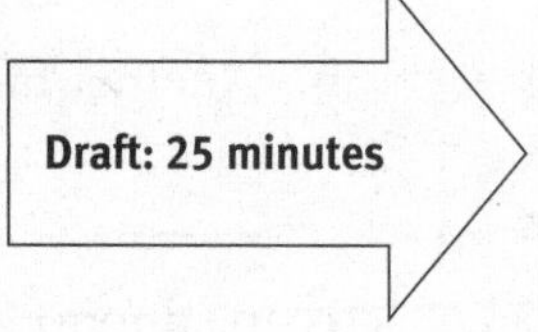

- Write a thesis statement as the introduction to your response.
- Use your plan, citing specific evidence from the text to support your ideas.
- Provide other relevant information based on your own knowledge and perspective.
- Write a closing that summarizes your position or restates the thesis statement in another way.

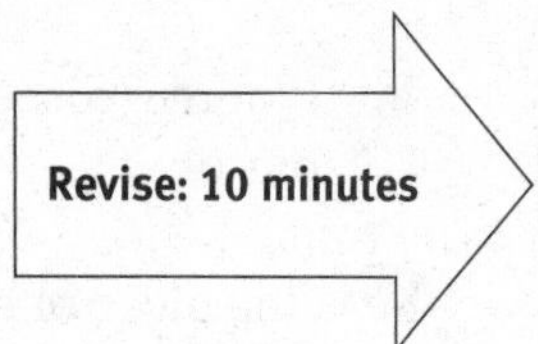

- Reread your thesis statement and review your response to make sure your response stayed focused on the prompt.
- Use the **Revision Questions** on page 222 to improve the response.
- Use the **Editing Questions** on page 224 to correct errors.

KEY IDEAS

- Take ten minutes to unpack the prompt, read the passages, and plan your response.
- As you read the passages, develop your thesis statement and collect supporting evidence by taking notes.
- Plan your response by either outlining or mapping the key ideas that you will use in the response.

HiSET EXAM TIP

Follow through on all of the planning steps before you write. You will have plenty of time to execute your plan, and your score will be higher if you have thought your response through and mapped it out.

Prewriting Strategies

Two of the most useful prewriting strategies for any kind of writing, including evidence-based writing, are outlining and mapping. Look at both methods of grouping ideas based on the same thesis statement.

> **Thesis statement:** *People need both close friends and acquaintances because they meet our social needs in different ways.*

An **outline** depicts each main topic by using a system of numbers and letters stressing a logical progression of ideas. Here is an outline based on the thesis statement above.

I. Benefits of close friends

   a. Will always be there for you

   b. Can always be yourself with them

   c. Can have intimate conversations that are satisfying but confidential

   d. Stand the test of time

II. Benefits of acquaintances

   a. Add variety to your life

   b. Expand your world

III. Acquaintances fulfill some special needs

   a. Social needs—if you can't see closest friends every day

   b. Networking needs—when you need to search for a job, find a new day care provider, etc.

   c. Can make a party or other social event more interesting

An **idea map** uses a drawing to visually group ideas. To make a map, write your main idea in the center. Then draw lines from there to your main topics. From there, you attach the supporting ideas.

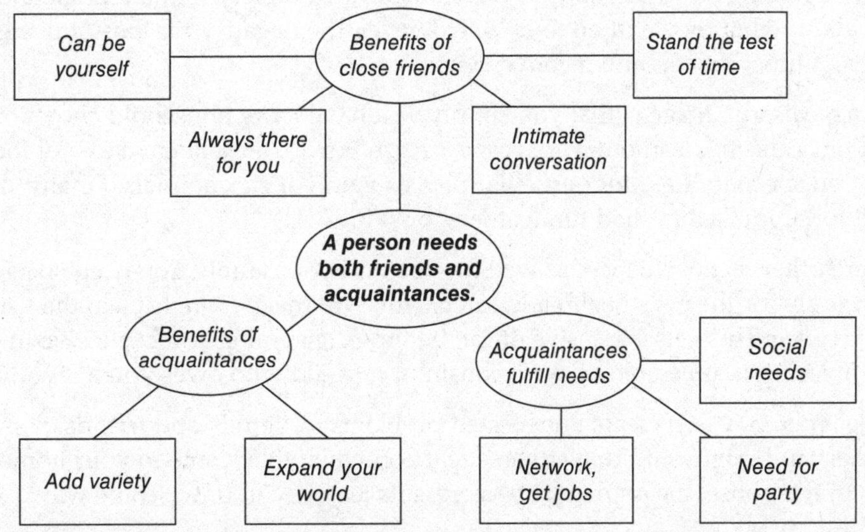

STUDY ADVICE

You won't write a good essay if you don't have a good plan for it. If this is something you struggle with, spend some time working on just the planning step. With practice you will get the hang of it!

PRACTICE 5

Directions: Follow these steps to plan a response.

- Read the writing prompt to understand your task.
- Read the passage. Think about your thesis statement. Underline and take notes on key points that you will want to summarize or respond to.
- Write a thesis statement based on responding to the prompt and the passage.
- Make an outline and an idea map based on the selection.

Family Pets Writing Prompt

The writer of this passage explains the reasons a family should not own a pet. Read the selection and take a stand for or against the author's viewpoint.

Use details and evidence from the passage in your essay.

Make sure that you:

- Include your thesis statement early.
- Give reasons and evidence from the passages to support your thesis statement.
- Argue against the opposite side.
- Organize your ideas and show how the ideas relate to each other.
- Use a businesslike style.
- Conclude with a short summary of your argument.

When you are trying to decide whether or not to buy a household pet, you need to weigh the pros and cons of doing so. Your children will make heartfelt pleas for an animal and will make wild claims about what they will do to help. However, the negative reasons outweigh the positive ones in terms of time, money, and inconvenience.

One major disadvantage is that you simply will have more household chores. You will need to take the pet on walks or clean out a box, cage, or fish bowl. You will have to buy food regularly, sometimes even specialty food for particular pets or aging or sick animals. Finally, ongoing cleanup is needed for animals that shed fur, feathers, or skin.

There are other inconveniences as well for you and your family. You need specialized knowledge to care properly for the pet's health and safety. You will make more trips to the vet than you do to the doctor's office. This gets expensive. It can be time-consuming and expensive to go away for a weekend or a vacation, unless you have a cousin or a friend who owes you a favor.

Owning a pet may also create unexpected problems for family and friends. Some people are allergic to animals and might suffer an adverse reaction when they come to your home. Also, if a new baby arrives in the house, the animal may express its jealousy in unwelcome ways.

Owning a pet does have a positive side. Animals can be great companions and return your love unconditionally. They can provide security (or at least a sense of security). Also, that walking I belittled at the outset can actually be good exercise. Finally, I have to admit that with all of the work involved, caring for an animal is still less work than caring for a child.

On balance, however, I think the wisest course of action for a family is to forgo the joys of pet ownership. The time and money saved can be put to different uses, which hopefully will give you satisfaction and companionship as well.

1. **Thesis Statement** According to the prompt, you are to take a position in agreement or disagreement with the writer of "Family Pets." Decide what you think and write your thesis statement below.

   I. I think that the writer's position on owning a family pet is correct/incorrect (circle one) because

   ____

   ____

On Test Day, you may write an outline or make an idea map. Practice both approaches on this page.

2. **Outline** Write an outline, using this as a model. **Keep your outline; you will use it in Lesson 6.**

Also address related reasoning issues, either by stating and contradicting the **counterargument** (main argument against your position) *or* by addressing the writer's **faulty reasoning** (if any).

I. Thesis statement
II. Main supporting reason related to the text
III. Another supporting reason related to the text
IV. Another supporting reason related to the text
V. Related arguments
   A. Counterargument
      i. Argument against my position
      ii. My rejection of the counterargument, with example
   B. Writer's faulty reasoning (if any)
      i. Why the writer's reasoning is faulty
      ii. Supporting example

3. **Idea Map** Make a map of your response to the passage. Use facts and evidence from the passage as well as your own ideas. Draw it on a sheet of paper. **Keep your map; you will use it in Lesson 6.**

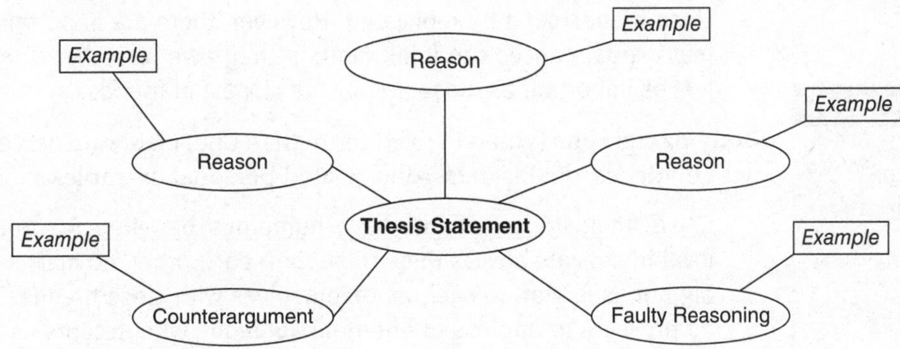

4. **Reflect** Which way worked better for you—outline or map? Practice both until you find the method that will work best for you on the test.

LESSON 6

Draft Your Response

You have practiced the first part of the **Essay-Writing Strategy: Planning**. Once you have planned your writing, the next stage is to **draft** your response. You should take about 30 minutes to do the following:

- Use your thesis statement to **introduce** your argument and how you intend to support it.
- Use your plan to write the **body** of your response, **citing specific evidence and details from the text** to support your ideas.
- Provide **additional relevant information** based on your own knowledge and perspective.
- Consistently **refocus** on your thesis statement to make sure that you are staying on track.
- Write a **closing** that summarizes your position or restates the thesis statement in another way.

Review the planning on page 213 for writing on the topic of close friends and acquaintances. See how that planning was used to draft the writing below. (Note that an underlined **topic sentence** introduces each paragraph.)

An **introduction** lays out your argument and how you will support it:

> People need both close friends and acquaintances because they meet our social needs in different ways. The special bond a person has with close friends can't be replicated. However, there are important needs that acquaintances can fulfill, and, in their own way, these needs are just as important as those met by the closest of friends.

Body paragraphs (you will need more than one) elaborate on your support with evidence, details, facts, and related personal examples.

> Close friendships certainly have numerous benefits. For one thing, loyal friends are always there to support each other, no matter what. A big bonus is that we can just be ourselves with close friends. There is no pressure to impress or entertain someone who accepts us for who we are. Some friendships last years, becoming deeper and more meaningful with time. For example, even though I am now 35, my best friend from high school and I are still in touch, sharing stories about our two-year-old boys.

A **closing paragraph** restates your main point to reinforce it.

> Therefore, while it is important to have close friends, it is really rewarding to have a wide circle of acquaintances as well. Even though the quality of the relationship may not be as deep, these people broaden our lives and networks to enrich our experiences and help us to grow.

KEY IDEAS

- Use your thesis statement to begin your introductory paragraph and to keep you focused as you write.
- Write several body paragraphs based on the facts, details, and evidence in your outline or idea map.
- Wrap up the response with a concluding paragraph that reinforces your thesis.

HiSET EXAM TIP

One key to a good score on the essay is to cite specific evidence from the reading passages. This is called an "evidence-based" writing activity because you are expected to base your response on evidence from the text.

PRACTICE 6.1

Part A: Introduction

Directions: Practice writing an introduction based on the prompt and passage from page 214 and your planning from page 215. If you are taking the HiSET exam on paper, complete this exercise on paper. If you are taking the computer version of the HiSET exam, try to write your introduction on a computer if possible. Save the file as *Family Pets Introduction.*

Family Pets Writing Prompt

The writer of this passage explains the reasons a family should not own a pet. Read the selection and take a stand for or against the author's position. Use details and evidence from the passage in your essay.

Make sure that you:

- Include your thesis statement early.
- Give reasons and evidence from the passages to support your thesis statement.
- Argue against the opposite side.
- Organize your ideas and show how the ideas relate to each other.
- Use a businesslike style.
- Conclude with a short summary of your argument.

- Begin with a topic sentence that summarizes your thesis statement from page 215.
- Support your topic sentence with either:
  - a preview of the main points you will be covering based on your outline or idea map; or
  - an example, description, or personal story—tied to the thesis statement—that will interest the reader.

Part B: Concluding Statement

Directions: Practice writing a concluding statement based on the prompt above and your planning from page 215. If you are taking the HiSET exam on paper, complete this exercise on paper. If you are taking the computer version of the HiSET exam, try to write your conclusion on a computer if possible. Save the file as *Family Pets Conclusion.*

- Restate your thesis statement from page 215 in different words. (Don't just repeat what your reader has already read.)
- Make a statement that answers the question "So what?" Give your reader a reason to care about your argument.
- Don't introduce new arguments but leave the reader with something to think about that wraps up the paper.

STUDY ADVICE

If you can, enlist a partner to help you with the essay portion of the exam. This may be a friend or family member with good writing skills. Ask that person to read this chapter so that he or she will understand what the essay requires. Then ask that person to give you feedback about your practice essays.

PRACTICE 6.2

Directions: Plan and draft an essay in response to the prompt below and the passage on the facing page. If you will be taking the HiSET exam on paper, practice writing your essay on paper. If you will be taking the HiSET exam on a computer, try to practice writing your essay on a computer if possible.

Step 1—Plan: Take 10 minutes to read the prompt and the passage. Under the prompt, make an outline *or* draw an idea map to organize the following:

- Your thesis statement
- Your main points and supporting evidence from the passage
- Counterarguments and your response *or* faulty reasoning in the passage

Step 2—Draft: Take 25 minutes to draft your response, which will include the following:

- An introductory statement with your thesis statement as the topic sentence
- Body paragraphs, with your reasons accompanied by supporting evidence from the text
  - Use phrases such as "As the writer says . . . ," "The information in the passage states . . . ," "This is supported in the passage by . . ."
- A concluding statement wrapping up the piece

Save your response, since you will be revising and editing it in Lesson 7.

Cell Phone Writing Prompt

The writer of the passage on the next page discusses the "risks and unknowns" of cell phone use. Read the passage and write an essay in which you argue for or against the idea that cell phones are too dangerous for daily use. You might focus on the known risks or benefits of cell phone use, as well as the gaps in our current scientific knowledge about these devices. Use details, facts, and definitions from the passage in your essay.

Make sure that you:

- Include your topic clearly.
- Give details, facts, and definitions from the passage to develop your explanation.
- Organize your ideas and show how the ideas relate to each other.
- Use a businesslike style.
- Conclude with a short summary of your explanation.

Cell Phones: Risky or Safe?

The Federal Communications Commission has determined that there is not enough evidence to link cell phones to cancer. But a lack of evidence does not mean that such a risk does not exist. Moreover, cell phones carry other safety hazards. You should be aware of the risks and unknowns associated with mobile phones and take steps to protect yourself.

Cell phones emit types of radiation that can penetrate several inches into the brain. These types of radiation are not normally associated with cancer, and most scientific studies show that frequent cell phone users do not have an increased risk of tumors. But a few scientists claim to have found a connection between mobile phones and a type of brain cancer known as glioma. Even a small chance of brain cancer should make you very nervous.

Also, we may eventually discover that the cancer risk is greater than it currently appears. Mobile phones were very rare before the late 1990s. If the risk of phone-related disease increases sharply after 20 or 30 years of constant use, we might only find out after millions of people get sick. It's true that there is no increased illness observed among people who have worked at radio towers for 30 years or more, but cell phones are held much closer to the body than radio equipment is.

Finally, in addition to the possible cancer risk, cell phones come with a much more obvious safety issue. While being able to contact emergency services from anywhere is a major advantage of modern technology, being distracted by that technology can cause accidents. Calling or texting while driving or operating machinery is dangerous.

Be cautious with your cell phone. You may find that you need it to function in today's modern society, but your health and well-being are too important to risk through careless use of this technology. Do not assume that your phone is completely free of danger.

PRACTICE 6.3

Directions: Plan and draft an essay in response to the prompt and the paired passages on the facing page. If you will be taking the HiSET exam on paper, practice writing your essay on paper. If you will be taking the HiSET exam on a computer, try to practice writing your essay on a computer if possible.

Step 1—Plan: Take 10 minutes to read the prompt below and the passages. Take notes as you read, or underline evidence that you will want to use. Make an outline *or* an idea map to organize:

- Your thesis statement
- Your main points and supporting evidence from the passages
- Counterarguments and your response *or* faulty reasoning in either of the passages

Step 2—Draft: Take 25 minutes to draft your response with:

- An introductory statement with your thesis statement as the topic sentence
- Body paragraphs, with your reasons accompanied by supporting evidence from the text
- A concluding statement wrapping up the piece

Save your response, since you will be revising and editing it later.

Gettysburg Address Writing Prompt

Abraham Lincoln's Gettysburg Address is renowned as one of the most significant speeches of all time. Delivered in the midst of a brutal civil war, this address places that war in the context of U.S. history—past, present, and future. However, it was not universally acclaimed at the time, as shown by the excerpt from the *Chicago Times* newspaper.

Read both of the passages closely. Take a stand on which passage does a better job of explaining the significance of the Battle of Gettysburg's casualties. There were a total of more than 45,000 casualties on both sides, Union and Confederacy.

Make sure that you:

- Include your thesis statement early.
- Give reasons and evidence from the passages to support your thesis statement.
- Argue against the opposite side.
- Organize your ideas and show how the ideas relate to each other.
- Use a businesslike style.
- Conclude with a short summary of your argument.

STUDY ADVICE

Some people don't enjoy writing essays. However, it's important to practice before Test Day. Discipline yourself to write each essay when it's assigned in this book. The only way to get better at writing is to *write.*

Abraham Lincoln's Gettysburg Address

Fourscore and seven years ago our fathers brought forth on this continent a new nation, conceived in Liberty, and dedicated to the proposition that all men are created equal. Now we are engaged in a great civil war, testing whether that nation, or any nation so conceived and so dedicated, can long endure. . . . But, in a larger sense, we cannot dedicate—we cannot consecrate—we cannot hallow—this ground. The brave men, living and dead, who struggled here, have consecrated it, far above our poor power to add or detract. The world will little note, nor long remember what we say here, but it can never forget what they did here. It is for us the living, rather, to be dedicated here to the unfinished work which they who fought here have thus far so nobly advanced. It is rather for us to be here dedicated to the great task remaining before us—that from these honored dead we take increased devotion to that cause for which they gave the last full measure of devotion—that we here highly resolve that these dead shall not have died in vain—that this nation, under God, shall have a new birth of freedom—and that government of the people, by the people, for the people, shall not perish from the earth.

—Abraham Lincoln, November 19, 1863

Critical Review of the Gettysburg Address

. . . The President's exhibition . . . was an insult at least to the memories of a part of the dead, whom he was there professedly to honor—in its misstatement of the cause for which they died, it was a perversion of history so flagrant that the most extended charity cannot regard it as otherwise than willful. As a refutation . . . we copy certain clauses in the Federal constitution:

"Representatives and direct taxes shall be apportioned among the several States which may be included in this Union, according to their respective numbers, which shall be determined by adding to the whole number of free persons, including those bound to service for a term of years, and excluding Indians not taxed, three-fifths of all other persons.

"The migration or importation of such persons as any of the States now existing shall think proper to admit shall not be prohibited by the Congress prior to the year 1808, but a tax or duty may be imposed on such importation, not exceeding ten dollars for each person.

"No amendment to the constitution, made prior to 1808, shall affect the preceding clause.

"No person held to service or labor in one State under the laws thereof, escaping into another, shall, in consequence of any law or regulation therein, be discharged from such service or labor, but shall be delivered up on claim of the party to whom such service or labor may be due."

Do these provisions in the constitution dedicate the nation to "the proposition that all men are created equal"? Mr. Lincoln occupies his present position by virtue of this constitution, and is sworn to the maintenance and enforcement of these provisions. It was to uphold this constitution, and the Union created by it, that our officers and soldiers gave their lives at Gettysburg. How dared he, then, standing on their graves, misstate the cause for which they died, and libel the statesmen who founded the government? . . .

Excerpted from the *Chicago Times*, November 23, 1863

LESSON 7

Revise and Edit Your Response

KEY IDEAS

- Take about ten minutes to revise and edit your response.
- Reread the response to improve the clarity of your arguments; sufficiency of evidence from the text; and organization of sentences, paragraphs, and the entire piece.
- If you are taking the computer version of the HiSET exam, you can use the insert and delete, cut and paste, and undo functions to make revisions. Otherwise, use your pencil and neatly erase or strike out text you are changing.

HiSET EXAM TIP

Reviewing your essay allows you to double-check that you stayed on track the entire time.

Revising Your Work

Once you have completed your draft, you need to **revise**. You should take about ten minutes to read over your response and make improvements. If you are taking the paper version of the HiSET exam, use your pencil to erase or strike out portions you would like to change. If you are taking the computer version of the HiSET exam, use the insert and delete, cut and paste, and undo functions on the computer. As you edit your essay, ask yourself:

- Does the introductory paragraph contain the **thesis statement** and lay out the main point of my response?
- Does each paragraph have **one main idea**, begin with a **topic sentence**, and support the thesis statement?
- Is there **specific and relevant supporting evidence from the text** for each main idea?
- Have I assessed the **validity** of the arguments in the passages?
- Is there a **clear flow of ideas** from one paragraph to the next, using transitional words, phrases, and ideas?
- Are there any **irrelevant ideas or sentences** that can be removed?
- Are there any **short, choppy sentences** that could be combined?
- Can I improve my **word choice** to be more specific or interesting?
- Is there a concluding paragraph that **restates and reinforces** the thesis?

Read the writing sample below and review the revisions that were made by hand to improve the draft. Think about why each change was made.

A job is much more pleasant when you like and admire your supervisor. A good supervisor must have excellent communication skills and must make it a priority to help workers get ahead.

Communication is a key part of management. ^ Supervisors need to give clear directions to spare the workers many hours of frustration. In addition, supervisors should be confident ^ *and decisive.* ~~They should also be decisive.~~ Finally, supervisors should be as honest as possible. Once they make a decision, they should stick to it, so ^ *that* everyone knows what the policy is. ^

Good bosses want to see their workers progress. Therefore, supervisors should give lots of encouragement and reward workers who display initiative and problem-solving abilities. ^ *Also,* ~~S~~upervisors should offer opportunities for workers to improve their skills ^ *and education*.

A. Directions: Read the response below, and revise the problems in sentence structure and organization. Try to complete your revisions in five minutes, but use more time if needed.

Most of us are aware of the consequences of speeding, which range from receiving a speeding ticket to getting into an accident. A quick survey of any highway will show that many drivers exceed the speed limit, showing that speed limit laws need to be more strictly enforced. Why do people speed? One common reason is that people do not think they will suffer any consequences. If they have never been stopped by the police or crashed their car, they don't see any reason to worry.

People simply need to get somewhere in a hurry. They realize that they are speeding but they have such a need to arrive on time that they don't care. They've got ants in their pants. A final reason is lack of respect for other drivers, one driver who is speeding makes road conditions less safe for everyone. Drivers who act as though they are in the Indy 500 they have no regard for the safety of others.

We know that people speed because of impatience and they don't fear the consequences. Another reason is no respect. Let's figure out what will make them stop.

B. Directions: Revise the response that you wrote on the topic from page 218, reprinted below. Time yourself. Try to complete the revision in five minutes. Save your work. You will use the response again.

Cell Phone Writing Prompt

The writer of the passage on the next page makes an argument about the safety of cell phones. Read the passage and write an essay in which you explain what additional information would be necessary before we determine whether or not cell phones are safe. Use details, facts, and definitions from the passage in your essay.

Make sure that you:

- Include your topic clearly.
- Give details, facts, and definitions from the passage to develop your explanation.
- Organize your ideas and show how the ideas relate to each other.
- Use a businesslike style.
- Conclude with a short summary of your explanation.

C. Directions: After you check your answers to the exercises above, complete the strategy box below. If you need more practice with specific skills and concepts, study "Connecting Ideas" on pages 158–169 and "Polishing Your Writing" on pages 230–243.

MY TEST-TAKING STRATEGY

I need to pay special attention to these areas of revising. (Check all that apply.)

- ❑ Writing introductory paragraphs
- ❑ Writing concluding paragraphs
- ❑ Writing topic sentences
- ❑ Adding support to body paragraphs
- ❑ Putting sentences in logical places
- ❑ Putting in paragraph breaks
- ❑ Remembering to use transitions
- ❑ Deleting irrelevant details
- ❑ Combining short, choppy sentences
- ❑ Making sure each sentence makes sense

Editing Your Work

Once you're satisfied with the organization and clarity of your essay, check for other errors in sentence structure, as well as errors in grammar, usage, and mechanics. To edit your response, take another five minutes to reread your response and ask yourself these questions:

- Are all the sentences complete?
- Are there any run-ons or comma splices that should be corrected?
- Are all lists parallel in structure?
- Are nouns and pronouns used correctly?
- Are verb forms and tenses used correctly?
- Does the subject of each sentence match the verb?
- Is the punctuation correct?
- Is capitalization used correctly?
- Are all words correctly spelled?
- Are there any inappropriate word choices?

KEY IDEAS

- Edit your work to make sure there are no errors in sentence structure, grammar, usage, or mechanics.
- An editing checklist can help you find errors as you practice for the Writing Test.

► Read the paragraph below and notice how the errors were corrected.

A job is much more pleasant when you like and admire your supervisor. A good supervisor must have excellent communication skills, and must make it a priority to help workers get ahead. In addition, a supervisor should be a fair and moral person.

Clear communication is a key part of Management. Supervisors need to give clear directions. To spare the workers many hours of frustration. In addition, supervisors should be confident and decisive. Once they made a decision, they should stick to it so everyone knows what the policy is. Finally, supervisors should be as honest as possible.

Good bosses want to see their workers progress. Therefore, supervisors should ~~give lots of~~ encourage~~ment~~ and reward workers who display initiative, and problem-solving abilities. Also, supervisors should offer opportunities for workers to improve their skills, and education.

Top-notch supervisors ~~has~~ have a high level of moral character. They reward honesty and fire workers who have lied or cheated. Some bosses keep employees who lie if ~~his~~ their skills are valuable to the Company, but I feel that this is an example of poor management.

Knowing the qualities of a good supervisor is important for both bosses and workers. The next time you apply for a job, think about whether ~~you're~~ your prospective boss is a moral person and a clear communicator who want s you to succeed.

HiSET EXAM TIP

Whether you take the paper or computer version of the HiSET exam, there will be no spell-check or grammar-check tools available to you. Practice spotting spelling and grammar mistakes on your own. If you are practicing the essay on a computer, turn off the spell-check and grammar-check features while you practice and turn them back on when you review your work.

PRACTICE 7.2

A. **Directions: Read the body of the writing sample. Correct errors in sentence structure, grammar, usage, mechanics, and word choice. Try to finish editing in five minutes, but use more time if needed.**

One common reason for speeding is that people don't think they will suffer any consequences. If they have never been stopped by the Police or crashed there car they don't see any reason too worry.

Another reason is that people simply are needing to get somewhere in a hurry. They realize that they are speeding, but they have such a need to arrive on time that they dont care. There impatience get the better of them.

A final reason is lack of respect for other drivers, one driver who is speeding make road conditions less safe for everyone. Drivers who act as though they are in the indy 500 got no regard for the safety of others.

B. **Directions: Edit the response that you wrote on the topic below, which you saw on page 218. Time yourself and try to complete the edit in five minutes.**

Cell Phone Writing Prompt

The writer of the passage on the next page makes an argument about the safety of cell phones. Read the passage and write an essay in which you argue either that we need additional information before we can determine whether cell phones are safe or that we have all the information we need to answer that question. Use details, facts, and definitions from the passage in your essay.

C. **Directions: After you check your answers to the exercises above, complete the strategy box below. If you need more practice with specific skills and concepts, review the sections in the book that correspond to these skills.**

MY TEST-TAKING STRATEGY

I need to pay special attention to these areas of editing. (Check all that apply.)

- ❑ Making sure my sentences are complete
- ❑ Correcting run-ons and comma splices
- ❑ Using parallel structure
- ❑ Using nouns and pronouns correctly
- ❑ Using verb forms and tenses correctly
- ❑ Matching subjects and verbs
- ❑ Making sure punctuation is correct
- ❑ Using capitalization correctly
- ❑ Making sure words are spelled correctly
- ❑ Choosing appropriate words

STUDY ADVICE

Often when you are writing, ideas might come into your head in an illogical order. That's okay. For one thing, taking the time to plan will help with that. But also be sure to practice rereading your writing and moving sentences around as necessary.

Writing the Essay Practice Questions

Part A

Directions: Plan and draft an essay in response to the prompt below and the passage on the facing page. If you will be taking the HiSET exam on paper, practice writing your essay on paper. If you will be taking the HiSET exam on a computer, try to practice writing your essay on a computer if possible.

Step 1—Plan: Take 10 minutes to read the prompt and the passage. Under the prompt, make an outline *or* draw an idea map to organize:

- Your thesis statement
- Your main points and supporting evidence from the passage
- Counterarguments and your response *or* faulty reasoning in the passage

Step 2—Draft: Take 25 minutes to draft your response, which will include the following:

- An introduction, with your thesis statement as the topic sentence
- Body paragraphs, with your reasons accompanied by supporting evidence from the text
  - Use phrases such as "As the writer says . . . ," "The information in the passage states . . . ," "This is supported in the passage by . . ."
- A concluding statement wrapping up the piece

Step 3—Revise and Edit: Take 10 minutes to reread your response to:

- Revise to improve organization, cohesion, and clarity of sentences, paragraphs, and the entire piece
- Edit to correct errors in sentence structure, grammar, punctuation, capitalization, and spelling

Social Networking on the Internet—Positive or Negative?

The passage addresses the serious impact that the explosion of social networking has had on our lives. In recent years, social relations have developed online that allow us to connect with friends or create communities around common interests. Supporters feel that these networks create greater interaction and increased information. Critics say that this trend actually limits social interactions and creates short- and long-term risks for the users.

In your response, compare the arguments in the reading selection and take a position favoring either the benefits or the drawbacks of social networking. Use relevant and specific information to support your response.

Make sure that you:

- Include your thesis statement early.
- Give reasons and evidence from the passages to support your thesis statement.
- Argue against the opposite side.
- Organize your ideas and show how the ideas relate to each other.
- Use a businesslike style.
- Conclude with a short summary of your argument.

"Social Networking on the Internet—Positive or Negative?"

In a hundred years, humanity will look back and try to pinpoint the moment in its history when it overcame the clumsy limits of flesh-and-blood existence. When it does, Internet social networking will stand out as an important change, not just in the ways in which we communicate with each other but also, and perhaps more importantly, in the ways in which we perceive ourselves.

At this primitive moment, our contacts on social networks are still people we have met in person, for the most part. And there was a time when this was natural: you have to choose your friends from the selection available to you. But the menu has changed. The great promise of Internet socialization is that congregation is no longer at the mercy of geography. If I join an online community of checkers enthusiasts whose members are scattered across four continents, our interactions will be little different than if we all lived in the United States. Our shared interest, rather than where our bodies happen to live, is what brings us together.

As our online friendships increasingly supplant our in-person friendships, our online personalities begin to replace our old selves, too. What happens when two-thirds of my acquaintances know me by an invented username rather than by my real name, or by an animated icon of a dancing stick-figure rather than by my face? The answer: I learn that I can essentially define myself for this group of people. I can be exactly who I want to be.

With time, we will all come to shift to interest-based interactions almost exclusively. If you've always felt alone because you've never been able to find anyone who shares your greatest passion—and that passion happens to be watching macramé competitions—then the Internet opens up a new world of like-minded individuals to you. You'll share experiences, pictures, and tips and live as you never could have 30 years ago, when you would have been forced to endure your isolation.

At the same time, we must ask ourselves: Is this something we want to encourage? One of the great protective mechanisms of the flesh-and-blood version of human communities is shame. As unfair as it may sound to ridicule our poor macramé enthusiast, social disapproval is an important tool for discouraging destructive behavior and extremism. When online communities offer a meeting place for outcasts, the shunning of these tendencies loses its force. It is no coincidence that online communities are the single most fertile recruiting ground for terrorism. And isn't accepting differences in others—rather than surrounding ourselves with homogeneous communities of like-minded friends—an important part of the human experience?

For children of the 20th century, there is something else very alarming in the idea of channeling so many of our interactions through the Internet. In the heyday of the Soviet Union, a video camera in every home was presented as the greatest tool a totalitarian state could wish for. If all my interactions pass through the Internet, won't the government be watching me? Regardless of whether it will or won't, it certainly seems now to have that option.

We also must wonder what will become of our most cherished traits as we transition to an existence of ones and zeros. As biological beings, we have emotional needs tied to touch and warmth. None of my online friends can give me a hug!

Ultimately, the new possibilities that the online world opens up to us are irresistible and herald a new era of finely tuned communities with unprecedented potential. The challenge will lie in making the most of this new world without losing the vital elements of our nonelectronic human experience.

Part B

Directions: Develop an essay in response to the prompt below and the paired passages on the facing page. If you will be taking the HiSET exam on paper, practice writing your essay on paper. If you will be taking the HiSET exam on a computer, try to practice writing your essay on a computer if possible.

Step 1—Plan: Take 10 minutes to read the prompt and the passages. Under the prompt, make an outline *or* draw an idea map to organize:

- Your thesis statement
- Your main points and supporting evidence from the passage
- Counterarguments and your response *or* faulty reasoning in the passage

Step 2—Draft: Take 25 minutes to draft your response, which will include the following:

- An introductory statement, with your thesis statement as the topic sentence
- Body paragraphs, with your reasons accompanied by supporting evidence from the text
  - Use phrases such as "As the writer says . . . ," "The information in the passage states . . . ," "This is supported in the passage by . . ."
- A concluding statement wrapping up the piece

Step 3—Revise and Edit: Take 10 minutes to reread your response and do the following:

- Revise to improve organization, cohesion, and clarity of sentences, paragraphs, and the entire piece.
- Edit to correct errors in sentence structure, grammar, punctuation, capitalization, and spelling.

Health and Safety on the Job

The first passage presents regulations of the U.S. Occupational Safety and Health Administration (OSHA). The second passage is a newspaper article about workers who successfully sued their employer, claiming that they were fired because they had reported injuries on the job.

Read both the OSHA regulations and the news report carefully. Take a position on whether or not you think that the court decision was correct based on the OSHA guidelines.

Use relevant and specific information from both passages to support your response.

Make sure that you:

- Include your thesis statement early.
- Give reasons and evidence from the passages to support your thesis statement.
- Argue against the opposite side.
- Organize your ideas and show how the ideas relate to each other.
- Use a businesslike style.
- Conclude with a short summary of your argument.

STUDY ADVICE

If you aren't taking the Writing Test for a while, be sure not to let your writing skills rust. Every couple of weeks, write an essay (you can rewrite one of the essays from this chapter if you like). Continue to practice using the method outlined in this chapter so that it will be second nature on Test Day.

OSHA Standards and Worker Protection

OSHA standards are rules that describe the methods that employers must use to protect their employees from hazards. There are OSHA standards for Construction work, Agriculture, Maritime operations, and General Industry, which are the standards that apply to most worksites. These standards limit the amount of hazardous chemicals workers can be exposed to, require the use of certain safe practices and equipment, and require employers to monitor hazards and keep records of workplace injuries and illnesses. Examples of OSHA standards include requirements to: provide fall protection, prevent trenching cave-ins, prevent some infectious diseases, assure that workers safely enter confined spaces, prevent exposure to harmful substances like asbestos, put guards on machines, provide respirators or other safety equipment, and provide training for certain dangerous jobs.

You Cannot Be Punished or Discriminated Against for Using Your OSHA Rights

The OSHA Act protects workers who complain to their employer, OSHA, or other government agencies about unsafe or unhealthful working conditions in the workplace or environmental problems. You cannot be transferred, denied a raise, have your hours reduced, be fired, or punished in any other way because you used any right given to you under the OSHA Act. Help is available from OSHA for whistleblowers.

If you have been punished or discriminated against for using your rights, you must file a complaint with OSHA within 30 days of the alleged reprisal for most complaints.

Source: U.S. Occupational Safety and Health Administration

OSHA fines Norfolk Southern $802K for firing workers

The U.S. Occupational Safety and Health Administration announced Monday that it was fining a Norfolk Southern Corp. subsidiary more than $800,000 for firing three workers who had reported injuries on the job.

OSHA, a division of the U.S. Department of Labor, ordered Norfolk Southern Railway Co. to pay the former workers a total of $802,169 in damages. The agency also said the railroad company must clear the workers' disciplinary records and post workplace notices and offer training on whistleblower rights.

"OSHA's investigations have found that the company continues to retaliate against employees for reporting work-related injuries and has effectively created a chilling effect in the railroad industry," the Labor Department said in a news release.

Norfolk Southern spokesman Robin Chapman said the company would appeal the decisions on all three workers before an administrative law judge at the Labor Department.

Two of the three incidents occurred in 2010, according to the agency's release. An engineer in Louisville, Ky., and a conductor in Harrisburg, Pa., were fired after reporting injuries from falls in or near company bathrooms.

Norfolk Southern accused the employees of falsifying their injuries, the agency said. The company also accused the conductor of failing to promptly report the injury. "The day before the injury, the employee had been lauded for excellent performance, highlighted by no lost work time due to injuries in his 35-year career," according to the Labor Department release.

OSHA found that the company hearings for both workers were "flawed." In the case of the engineer, the hearing "was orchestrated to intentionally support the decision to terminate the employee," the release said.

In the third incident, an employee in Greenville, S.C., was fired after he reported being hit by a company truck. Norfolk Southern accused him of "improper performance of duties." The agency found he was treated "disparately in comparison to four other employees involved in the incident," none of whom had reported injuries.

"Firing workers for reporting an injury is not only illegal, it also endangers all workers," David Michaels, an assistant U.S. secretary of labor, said in a statement. "To prevent more injuries, railroad workers must be able to report an injury without fear of retaliation."

Reprinted with permission from *The Virginian-Pilot*.

LESSON 1

Strengthen Sentences

Revising Unclear and Incorrect Sentences

When you write your response, your first step is to get your ideas down. To do this, you follow a prewriting and drafting plan like the ones in the previous chapter. When you are finished drafting, go back and reread what you have written. As you read each sentence, ask yourself:

- Do the ideas in the sentence make sense? If not, how can I make the sentence clearer? Add some words? Drop or move a confusing word or phrase? Insert or delete punctuation? Change the words?
- Is the sentence structure correct? If not, how can I correct it?

Read the paragraph below and think about how you would revise the errors in clarity and sentence structure. Then compare it with the revised paragraph.

Paragraph with unclear and incorrect sentences:

Working outdoors has many advantages over working indoors. When you are outside you are in contact with nature. You can enjoy the sunshine on your face, hear the birds, and to smell the flowers. You don't have to consult the weather forecast on TV. In contrast, sitting in a climate-controlled cubicle, it is not known whether the sky is sunny or cloudy. Also, most outdoor jobs require you to use your body, that can be a huge advantage. Finally, if you work indoors, you might be sitting down at a desk, and typing all day long. After work, instead of relaxing. You'll probably have to go to the gym to work out.

Paragraph with revised sentence structure:

Working outdoors has many advantages over working indoors. When you are outside, you are in contact with nature. You can enjoy the sunshine on your face, hear the birds, and smell the flowers. You don't have to consult the weather forecast on TV. In contrast, when you sit in a climate-controlled cubicle, you don't know whether the sky is sunny or cloudy. Also, most outdoor jobs require you to use your body, and that can be a huge advantage. Finally, if you work indoors, you might be sitting down at a desk and typing all day long. After work, instead of relaxing, you'll probably have to go to the gym to work out.

Use these **revision marks** when you revise your sentences on paper:

- To delete a word or punctuation mark, cross it out.
- To add a word or punctuation mark, insert a caret (^) in the line where you want it to go, and then write it in above the line.
- To change a word, cross it out and write the new word above it.
- To move a word or phrase, circle it and draw an arrow to its new position.
- To capitalize a letter, draw three lines under it.

KEY IDEAS

- Read your work as a whole to make sure that it is clear and logical.
- Imagine that you are reading your work for the first time.
- Correct any sentences that have errors in structure or punctuation.

HiSET EXAM TIP

To prepare for the essay, practice prewriting, drafting, and revising often. Frequent practice will help you feel more comfortable and confident as a writer.

PRACTICE 1

A. Directions: Read and revise the sentences. Correct these problems by using revision marks.

☑ fragments, run-ons, and comma splices
☑ incorrect coordination and subordination
☑ misplaced or dangling modifiers
☑ problems in parallel structure

EXAMPLE: It's fun to do a family tree, you can learn a lot.

1. First, write down what you know about your family then interview relatives.
2. Videotaping or to record the interviews is a good idea.
3. Ask relatives to provide exact names, dates, and give other details.
4. Making copies of documents such as birth certificates and marriage licenses.
5. Interviewing older family members, they'll often tell you stories you never heard.
6. Record all the information you get and put it in a three-ring binder carefully.
7. Some people use their computers to do genealogy searches, they get very good results.
8. However, one must have the time, the patience, and know-how to use the Internet.
9. If you decide to learn more about your roots don't be surprised to find yourself at a huge family reunion.
10. The whole process of putting together a family tree and contacting long-lost family members.

B. Directions: Read the paragraphs below. Use revision marks to correct problems with sentences.

It was a beautiful day, the blue ocean sparkled in the sunlight. A perfect day for going to the beach. Looking across the sand, two little girls were building a sandcastle and made a moat next to it. Renelle spread out her towel she anchored it with her shoes and beach bag and began to read a magazine. Suddenly she heard a voice. "Are you going to get in the water, or are you just going to lie there?" Renelle looked up, and saw her friend Terry. She laughed softly and she got up and she greeted Terry. Putting on her sandals, the two of them walked across the burning sand to the water's edge.

Renelle loved going to the beach. Going to the beach relaxed her. Going to the beach helped her forget about her problems. It didn't cost money like most other forms of entertainment. Most of Renelle's friends also spent a lot of time at the beach so that was another incentive.

LESSON 2

Improve Organization

KEY IDEAS

- Revise your response so that the organization is clear to the reader.
- Make sure that paragraph breaks fall in the right places.
- Check for faulty transitions and irrelevant details.

HiSET EXAM TIP

When you practice writing essays on paper, leave wide margins and space between the lines so that you can more easily revise your work. If you are taking the HiSET exam on a computer, try to practice writing your essays on a computer.

Revising Problems in Organization

When you reread your response, you may also need to make changes in organization to make the response clearer to the reader. As you read, ask yourself:

- Is my main idea clear?
- Are there a clear introduction, body of support, and conclusion?
- Is the paragraphing correct? Does each paragraph relate to only one main idea? Should any paragraphs be split into two? Should any be combined?
- Does each paragraph have a topic sentence that tells the main idea? Are any of the other sentences in a place that doesn't make sense? Are there any irrelevant details that should be removed?
- Does the writing flow smoothly from sentence to sentence and from paragraph to paragraph? If not, where can I add transitions?

Read the sample paragraph below. Think about how you would correct the errors in organization. Then compare it with the revised paragraph.

Paragraph with problems in organization:

(1) Many people believe that changes in technology have improved our communication with others. (2) I believe that the opposite is true. (3) So-called technological improvements have led to a marked decline in the quality of interpersonal communication. (4) In the old days, when you called someone, the person was likely to pick up the phone to find out who was calling. (5) Nowadays, caller ID makes that unnecessary. (6) The person you call can simply decide not to pick up once she sees that you are the caller. (7) This encourages long games of "phone tag." (8) Television is another example—you can barely get a word out of someone who is glued to the tube.

Paragraphs with revised organization:

(1) Many people believe that changes in technology have improved our communication with others. (2) <u>However,</u> I believe that the opposite is true. (3) So-called technological improvements have led to a marked decline in the quality of interpersonal communication.

<u>(*) Phone use is one area in which communication has suffered.</u> (4) In the old days, when you called someone, the person was likely to pick up the phone to find out who was calling. (5) Nowadays, screening devices make that unnecessary. (6) The person you call can simply decide not to pick up once she sees that you are the caller. (7) This encourages long games of "phone tag."

In the revised paragraphs, the transition *however* was added to sentence 2. The piece was divided into two paragraphs—an introductory paragraph and a body paragraph about phone use. A topic sentence (marked with *) was added. Sentence 8 of the original, which was not related to telephones, was deleted.

Use these symbols to revise essay organization:

- To change whole sentences, use the same marks you used to change words.
- To start a new paragraph, use the paragraph symbol (¶).

A. Directions: Using the revision marks, revise the paragraphs below. One revision has been made for you.

We've all heard countless advertising campaigns warning us not to litter. Yet some people still think nothing of throwing a soda can out of their car window onto the highway or dropping a candy wrapper on the sidewalk. Most of us realize that we are upsetting a delicate ecological balance when we don't dispose of our trash properly. ¶ Why do people continue to litter? One reason people litter is that they just don't care about others. It doesn't bother them to leave their trash in front of someone else's apartment building, forcing another person to deal with the problem.

This inconsiderate attitude is also reflected in the refusal to recycle plastic, glass, and newspapers. People figure that they won't be around in the future when the landfills are used up, so who cares? Another possible reason for littering is low self-esteem. If people don't feel good about themselves, they won't be motivated to keep their environment looking attractive. Low self-esteem can cause many other problems, including depression and lack of self-confidence. People who have high self-esteem believe that it's important to keep their home, the planet Earth, clean and beautiful.

B. Directions: Revise the response that you wrote to the Gettysburg Address writing prompt on page 220.

Be sure to check for:

- ☑ clear main idea
- ☑ introduction, body, and conclusion
- ☑ correct paragraphing
- ☑ topic sentences
- ☑ logical placement of sentences
- ☑ irrelevant details that should be removed
- ☑ clear transitions

Save your work. You will use it in the next step of the writing process, editing.

LESSON 3

Word Choice

After you have written and revised your response, you will need to edit it. In the editing stage of the writing process, you check for correct grammar, usage, and word choice. You may already have made some organizational changes. The kinds of changes you make when you are editing will be smaller—more like fine-tuning.

KEY IDEAS

- Use precise words instead of vague ones.
- Express your ideas in as few words as possible.
- When writing a response, use formal language instead of slang.

Word choice is an important aspect of writing. There are several aspects of word choice to look at when you are editing: using precise words, avoiding wordiness, and avoiding slang.

People often use vague terms when they are speaking. They say things like, "It was a great party!" or "The weather is nice today." General words like *great* and *nice* are okay in conversation because the listener can ask questions such as, "What was so great about the party?" In writing, however, you should try to write specific words that create a clear picture for the reader.

With vague words: Tim took a long hike in the beautiful mountains.
With precise words: Tim took a 12-mile hike in the rocky, snowy mountains.

With vague words: He walked through a forest where the ground was covered with pine needles.
With precise words: He meandered through a forest where the ground was carpeted with pine needles.

HiSET EXAM TIP

When you read your draft, focus on the specific words and ask yourself, "Can I make this clearer or more concise?" If so, revise accordingly to improve your score on the response.

It's also helpful to your reader if you write concisely and avoid wordiness. Being brief helps the reader focus on your message. If you notice that you have said the same thing twice, cut out the extra words.

Too wordy: Tim's dream and the thing he hopes for most of all is to make a home for himself and live in a cabin in the woods.
More concise: Tim's most cherished dream is to live in a cabin in the woods.

Too wordy: The only thing getting in the way of his having this dream come true is that his wife isn't so sure that it's such a fantastic idea.
More concise: The only obstacle to realizing his dream is his wife's resistance.

Finally, avoid using slang when writing your essay. Though people sometimes use informal language when speaking, essay writing calls for more formal language. Take care to express yourself appropriately.

With slang: Tim is going to hit the road at seven tonight.
With more formal language: Tim is going to leave town at seven tonight.

With slang: He needs a better map because he's totally clueless about directions.
With more formal language: He needs a better map because he has difficulty understanding directions.

PRACTICE 3.1

A. Directions: Replace each of the underlined words or phrases with more appropriate language. Write your answers on a separate sheet of paper.

1. Families International is a nonprofit organization that does not make any money.
2. We give aid to many children in the Third World every year.
3. These children must endure lousy living conditions.
4. Your donation, even if it is only five bucks, will help a child get food and clothing.
5. Please send your donation as soon and as quickly as possible to the following address.

B. Directions: Edit the paragraphs below for correct grammar and usage, paying special attention to nouns and pronouns, subject-verb agreement, and regular and irregular verbs.

If you ever order merchandise from a catalog, you should be aware of your rights. All companies, regardless of what state they are located in, is required to ship your order within 30 days unless they have advertise a different shipping time. If a company is unable to meet the shipping deadline, they must send you an "Option Notice." You can choose to wait longer or get a refund.

Some consumers complaining about receiving merchandise that they did not order. They were told that companies that engaged in this practice broken the law. If they send you a product you haven't order, it is yours to keep.

If you receive a package that been damaged, don't open it. Write "REFUSED" on the package, and return it to the seller. There's no need to add new postage as long as the package come by regular mail.

C. Directions: Revise the response you wrote to the Gettysburg Address writing prompt on page 220.

Be sure to check for:

☑ Correct use of nouns and pronouns
☑ Correct use of regular and irregular verbs
☑ Subject-verb agreement
☑ Word choice

Words with Similar Meanings

To express your ideas clearly, it is important to use the word that means precisely the type or extent of the idea you wish to communicate. Knowing the shades of meaning of different words also helps you understand exactly what other people are saying (see Lesson 7: Word Choice in the Reading unit on page 84).

Here is a group of words that all mean "very happy":

bliss	ultimate, serene happiness
ecstasy	extreme, even frenzied joy
elation	very happy with pride or optimism
euphoria	strong, even disproportionate sense of well-being and confidence
rapture	intense, love-filled joy

Note, for example, that *bliss* is happiness accompanied by a sense of calm, while *ecstasy* is happiness along with great excitement.

EXAMPLES

1. Richard had studied very hard for the test, so when he found out that he had scored well, he felt elated.

Richard worked hard to achieve this excellent result, so to communicate the pride Richard feels, the writer chooses the word *elated*.

2. Some medications used to treat allergies can produce a feeling of euphoria in patients, causing them to make poor decisions.

The writer uses the word *euphoria* because people who take these medicines can feel extremely confident, as though nothing can hurt them.

3. When Stacy found out that she was finally pregnant, she felt rapture and began to think about names for a boy or a girl.

Stacy's happiness concerns love for her future child, so the author has chosen the word *rapture* to communicate Stacy's emotional state.

Writers also select words to communicate the degree of something. The following words could all be used to describe a "small" house:

modest	not lavish or impressive
cramped	not having as much room as one needs
diminutive	much smaller than normal
miniature	so small as to be a model of the real thing

Most people would probably enjoy living in a *modest* home, even if they would prefer a larger one, but a *miniature* house would be one that children would play in or even a dollhouse.

Here are some examples using words that mean "to disagree."

EXAMPLES

4. The two politicians held opposite views, so they clashed repeatedly during debates.

To clash means "to argue or fight," and the writer uses this word to indicate how strongly these politicians disagreed with each other.

5. Marcos wanted to stay on good terms with his manager, so when his manager made outrageous demands, he only occasionally demurred.

Here the writer chooses the word *demurred* ("politely disagreed") to fit the relationship Marcos was trying to maintain with his boss.

KEY IDEAS

- English has many words that express approximately the same idea.
- Choose the word that most precisely conveys the quality or characteristic of a thing or action.
- Choose the word that most accurately communicates the extent or degree of a thing or action.

HiSET EXAM TIP

When asked to revise a passage, pay careful attention to clues that tell you exactly what idea the author intends to communicate. Doing so will help you select the best word or phrase among the answer choices.

PRACTICE 3.2

A. Directions: For each sentence, choose the word that better fits the context.

1. The comedian was extremely funny, and the audience (chuckled/roared) after every joke.
2. Tyler's aunt knitted him a (red/crimson) sweater that was unique in style and color.
3. When the student answered a question correctly, the tutor would then ask a more difficult one, making the student feel (uncomfortable/miserable).
4. Xiu was proud of her promotion at work, and she (strode/shuffled) through the hallways with a smile on her face.
5. Kelsey (asked/interrogated) her five-year-old son about whether he had said thank you for the gift.

B. <u>Questions 6 through 8</u> refer to the following passage.

(1) The children could not believe their good fortune. (2) The snow had fallen <u>steadily</u> all night, and now it lay in <u>huge</u> piles around the house and <u>blockaded</u> the driveway. (3) "No school!" they shouted.

(4) Their parents were less <u>agitated</u> and looked at each other across the breakfast table with <u>anxious</u> expressions, wondering which of them would have to <u>stay</u> at home with the children. (5) "If I call in sick to work again," their father said, "my boss will be angry." (6) Their mother said, "But I'm supposed to give an important sales presentation today. My company is counting on me."

(7) Bella, the oldest, overheard her parents talking and had an idea. (8) "Why don't we ask our neighbor if we can stay with her?" she asked. (9) "Mrs. Alvarez has trouble shoveling her sidewalk, so we can do that for her in exchange."

(10) "That's a wonderful idea, Bella!" her mother exclaimed. (11) Her father added, "Our daughter certainly is ________."

6. **Sentence 2:** Which of the following is the best revision?

   A. (No change)
   B. Change "steadily" to "smoothly"
   C. Change "huge" to "monstrous"
   D. Change "blockaded" to "blocked"

7. **Sentence 4:** Which of the following is the best revision?

   A. (No change)
   B. Change "agitated" to "excited"
   C. Change "anxious" to "tormented"
   D. Change "stay" to "reside"

8. **Sentence 11:** Which of the following is the best word for the blank?

   A. intelligent
   B. enlightened
   C. imaginative
   D. perceptive

LESSON 4

Expression and Voice

Writing is most engaging when the author uses distinctive language that reveals his or her personality and perspective. An author's unique way of using language is the author's **voice**. Writers with a strong voice use fresh, striking language rather than flat, matter-of-fact wording or trite phrases, and they express heartfelt emotions, either their own (nonfiction) or a character's (fiction).

KEY IDEAS

- Voice is the unique way in which an author uses language.
- Writing is most expressive when it conveys authentic emotions.
- Writers have a strong voice when they choose words that create vivid pictures in the reader's mind.

EXAMPLES

Weak voice: I had an idea that seemed inadequate but had potential if I continued to think about it.
Strong voice: "Alas, laid on the grass how small, how insignificant this thought of mine looked; the sort of fish that a good fisherman puts back in the water so that it may grow fatter and be one day worth cooking and eating."

In her treatise *A Room of One's Own* (1929), Virginia Woolf uses the metaphor of a fish to represent the creative process as she describes how she struggled to write a lecture she'd been asked to give. The reader can relate to the patience required to throw back a too-small fish so it can mature.

Weak voice: I was very nervous and still am, but I don't understand why people think I'm crazy.
Strong voice: "TRUE!—nervous—very, very dreadfully nervous I had been and am; but why *will* you say that I am mad?"

HiSET EXAM TIP

When asked how best to revise a passage, or when revising your own work, choose precise language that conveys the intended thought in a way that is consistent with the author's voice in the rest of the passage.

In the opening line of Edgar Allan Poe's short story "The Tell-Tale Heart" (1843), the repetition of the words *very* and *nervous*, as well as the accentuation with an exclamation mark and interruptions with dashes, create on the page the jittery anxiety the character feels. The question opens the possibility that this is an unreliable narrator who is insane, as people say, but does not realize it.

Weak voice: Merry was so surprised that despite being frightened, he opened his eyes. The Nazgûl Lord rode a large animal that cast a shadow in all directions, and he was very scary.
Strong voice: "Very amazement for a moment conquered Merry's fear. He opened his eyes. . . . There some paces from him sat the great beast, and all seemed dark about it, and above it loomed the Nazgûl Lord like a shadow of despair."

This description of physical action from J. R. R. Tolkien's *The Lord of the Rings* (1954–1955) captures the otherworldliness of Merry's foe (the word "seemed" rather than "was" conveys a scene that can't quite be captured by ordinary senses) and the terror Merry feels ("loomed" and "shadow of despair").

PRACTICE 4

<u>Questions 1 through 3</u> refer to the following passage.

(A)

The average age of the U.S. population is increasing. Of course, it is good news that people are living longer. However, old age is often accompanied by some degree of disability. One result of the aging population is that more middle-aged adults need to care for both their children and one or more parents. The individuals with these responsibilities have been called the "sandwich generation."

(B)

One of the most challenging illnesses that can afflict elderly people is Alzheimer's disease. This condition begins with deterioration of short-term memory. People with the disease may notice that they have more trouble than usual remembering where they put their keys, recalling names of acquaintances, and planning daily activities. In this early stage of the disease, many sufferers, as well as their family and friends, attribute memory lapses to "senior moments" or the natural aging process. Therefore, individuals with Alzheimer's are often not diagnosed in the early stage.

(C)

In the middle stage of the disease, people have trouble remembering what day it is and important personal details such as their address. They may also become highly suspicious of others and withdraw from social situations. The final stage brings an inability to speak, loss of control over the body, and—eventually—death.

The author wants to use a personal example to illustrate the ideas in this essay. To do so, the author will add a sentence to the end of each paragraph. For each question, choose the sentence that is most expressive of the author's voice.

1. Which sentence is best to add to paragraph A?

   A. I am a member of the sandwich generation because I am caring for my 77-year-old mother and two children.
   B. As a member of this sandwich generation, I experience the occasional joys and many challenges of caring for my 77-year-old mother and two children.
   C. Caring for my 77-year-old mother and two children makes me a member of the sandwich generation.
   D. Because I care for my 77-year-old mother and two children, I am part of the sandwich generation.

2. Which sentence is best to add to paragraph B?

   A. To my shame, I ignored my mother's increasing disorganization and failed to support her.
   B. I laughed off my mother's increasing disorganization for a long time.
   C. I did not recognize my mother's symptoms of Alzheimer's at first, so I did not help her.
   D. My mother had annual physical examinations, but the doctor never diagnosed Alzheimer's disease.

3. Which sentence is best to add to paragraph C?

   A. When my mother enters the late stage, I will need to determine whether she stays in an assisted-living facility.
   B. My mother's disease will soon progress to the final stage.
   C. The late stage of the disease in my mother will place even greater demands on me.
   D. I dread the decisions I will have to make as my mother's mind betrays her, such as whether I can care for her at home.

STUDY ADVICE

How's your stress level at this point? Remember to manage your stress just as you manage other aspects of the HiSET exam. Stay on a regular sleep schedule, exercise, and eat right. Whenever you're feeling stressed, step away. Remember: You *can* do this.

Polishing Your Writing Practice Questions

<u>Questions 1 through 5</u> refer to the following paragraphs.

Gardening for success

(A)

(1) Flowers, herbs, and shrubs can beautify both small and large spaces in your home or yard. (2) If you want to be a successful gardener. (3) It's important that you follow some simple guidelines.

(B)

(4) First, determine whether you'll be gardening indoors or outdoors. (5) This might depend on what type of home you live in, or it might depend on the climate. (6) If you live in an apartment building and don't have access to a community garden, an indoor garden might be right for you. (7) An indoor garden is also an option if you live in a climate that is not good for the plants that you'd like to grow.

(C)

(8) Indoors, you'll need to place your plants near a window where they'll get some sunlight each day. (9) Choose your growing space carefully, whether indoors or outdoors. (10) Outdoors, find a spot that doesn't have a lot of rocks or clay. (11) Likewise, you should choose your plants carefully.

(D)

(12) Investigate various plants, find out how much sunlight and water they need and what temperature they prefer. (13) You might be surprised to find, for instance, that you shouldn't try to grow basil in a shady side yard or impatiens in full sun. (14) A little extra effort up front will help you avoid common gardening pitfalls and enjoy your garden more.

1. Sentences 2 and 3: **If you want to be a successful <u>gardener. It's important that</u> you follow some simple guidelines.**

   Which is the best way to write the underlined portion of these sentences?

   A. gardener, importantly
   B. gardener, but it's important that
   C. gardener, it's important that
   D. gardener. And it's important that

2. Sentence 7: **An indoor garden is also an option if you live in a climate that is not good for the plants that you'd like to grow.**

   Which revision would improve the effectiveness of sentence 7?

   A. replace <u>not good</u> with <u>too extreme</u>
   B. replace <u>you live</u> with <u>one lives</u>
   C. insert a comma after <u>option</u>
   D. replace <u>also</u> with <u>additionally</u>

3. Which revision would improve the effectiveness of paragraph (C)?

   A. move sentence 11 to the beginning of paragraph (C)
   B. move sentence 8 to follow sentence 9
   C. move sentence 8 to follow sentence 10
   D. move sentence 8 to follow sentence 11

4. Which revision would improve the effectiveness of the article?

   A. move sentence 12 to the end of paragraph (C)
   B. move sentence 3 to the beginning of paragraph (B)
   C. move sentence 7 to the beginning of paragraph (C)
   D. move sentence 11 to the beginning of paragraph (D)

5. Sentence 12: **Investigate various <u>plants,</u> find out how much sunlight and water they need and what temperature they prefer.**

   Which is the best way to write the underlined portion of the sentence?

   A. plants, but
   B. plants or
   C. plants to
   D. plants, and then

<u>Questions 6 through 10</u> refer to the following paragraphs.

Rowing Across the Atlantic

(A)

(1) When I was a child, my grandmother often told me stories about her father. (2) He was born in Wales which had come to the United States when he was 2 years old. (3) His trip to this country was a mystery to me.

(B)

(4) "Dad always said he came over in a rowboat," Granny explained. (5) I tried to imagine a 2-year-old boy rowing across the ocean it seemed impossible that he could have done that. (6) Could he have crossed the really big Atlantic Ocean *in a rowboat*?

(C)

(7) I had many questions for Granny. (8) "Were his parents with him?" I asked. (9) "No, I think he came by himself," she explained, laughing. (10) Was she totally pulling my leg? (11) The stories always ended with Granny wiping tears from her eyes. (12) She had several grandchildren. (13) "Oh, how I wish you had known him," she cried.

6. Sentence 2: **He was born in Wales which had come to the United States when he was 2 years old.**

   Which correction should be made to sentence 2?

   A. change <u>which had come</u> to <u>and had come</u>
   B. change <u>had come</u> to <u>coming</u>
   C. change <u>He was born</u> to <u>Having been born</u>
   D. insert a comma after <u>Wales</u>

7. Sentence 5: **I tried to imagine a 2-year-old boy rowing across the <u>ocean it</u> seemed impossible that he could have done that.**

   Which is the best way to write the underlined portion of the sentence?

   A. ocean however it
   B. ocean, thus it
   C. ocean. Thus it
   D. ocean; it

8. Sentence 6: **Could he have crossed the really big Atlantic Ocean *in a rowboat*?**

   Which correction should be made to sentence 6?

   A. replace <u>have crossed</u> with <u>had crossed</u>
   B. change <u>Could he</u> to <u>He could</u>
   C. replace <u>really big</u> with <u>vast</u>
   D. remove <u>have</u>

9. Sentence 10: **Was she <u>totally pulling my leg</u>?**

   Which is the best way to write the underlined portion of the sentence?

   A. totally pulling the leg of mine
   B. kidding me
   C. totally joking
   D. for real

10. Sentence 12: **She had several grandchildren.**

    Which correction should be made to sentence 12?

    A. replace <u>had</u> with <u>have</u>
    B. remove the sentence
    C. remove <u>several</u>
    D. replace <u>grandchildren</u> with <u>grandkids</u>

Questions 11 through 14 refer to the following paragraphs.

Southern Gothic Writer

(A)

(1) Flannery O'Connor was a gifted Southern writer. (2) She wrote many short stories and two novels. (3) She is known for writing in a Southern gothic style and exploring topics of religion, ethics, and morality she also frequently explored the dark side of human nature.

(B)

(4) One of O'Connor's most popular stories, "A Good Man Is Hard to Find" was written in 1953 and focuses on a man called The Misfit. (5) Many reckon this is her most shocking story. (6) It raises important questions of good and evil, morality and immorality, and Southern historical issues.

(C)

(7) When Flannery was just 26, she was diagnosed with lupus. (8) The disease that had killed her father. (9) To manage her health, she returned to her family's farm, Andalusia, in Milledgeville, Georgia. (10) There, she lived with her mother Regina and wrote many of her most important works. (11) She delighted in raising birds of all varieties, including peafowl.

(D)

(12) During her time at Andalusia, Flannery also maintained many fulfilling correspondences with friends, family, and other writers which is why she is believed to have had a special insight into human behavior that is displayed in her writing. (13) Although she was only expected to live for five years after her lupus diagnosis, she managed to survive for fourteen.

11. Sentence 3: **She is known for writing in a Southern gothic style and exploring topics of religion, ethics, and morality she also frequently explored the dark side of human nature.**

    Which correction should be made to sentence 3?

    A. place a comma after morality
    B. place a comma after also
    C. remove she also
    D. place a period after morality and begin a new sentence with She

12. Sentence 5: **Many reckon this is her most shocking story.**

    Which is the best way to rewrite this sentence?

    A. Many reckon this is her most shockingest story.
    B. Many consider this her most shocking story.
    C. Many think it ought to be a most shocking story.
    D. Many reckon this ought to be her most shocking story.

13. Sentences 7 and 8: **(7) When Flannery was just 26, she was diagnosed with lupus. (8) The disease that had killed her father.**

    Which is the best way to revise these two sentences?

    A. move sentence 8 to before sentence 7
    B. move sentence 8 to after the comma in sentence 7
    C. change lupus. The to lupus, the
    D. change with lupus. The disease that to with the disease, lupus, that

14. Sentence 12: **During her time at Andalusia, Flannery also maintained many fulfilling correspondences with friends, family, and other writers which is why she is believed to have had a special insight into human behavior that is displayed in her writing.**

    Which is the best way to rewrite the underlined portion of this sentence?

    A. Flannery maintained many fulfilling correspondences that gave her the insight into human behavior that is evident in her writing.
    B. Flannery also maintained many correspondences with friends, family, and other writers, which is why she had a special insight into human behavior that is displayed in her writing.
    C. Flannery also maintained many fulfilling correspondences with friends, family, and other writers which is why she is believed to have had a special insight into human behavior that is in her writing.
    D. Flannery maintained many correspondences with friends, family, and other writers which is why she is believed to have had a special insight into human behavior.

Questions 15 through 19 refer to the following paragraphs.

Notification of Utility Repairs

(A)

(1) Universal Utilities will soon begin repairs of the underground lines in your neighborhood. (2) This will ensure you always continue to receive the exceptional service you have come to expect from us.

(B)

(3) We will begin by installing a new pipeline under your street. (4) Then next we will replace the smaller line that runs from the street to your home. (5) Lastly we will install a new meter at your home.

(C)

(6) This work will require our company's trucks to be in your neighborhood. (7) We apologize for any inconvenience this may cause during peak travel times and you may experience a temporary disruption in your utility service. (8) However we will adjust your bill accordingly if your service is interrupted.

(D)

(9) If you have any questions about the scheduled repairs. (10) Please contact our office. (11) We can be reached by telephone, or you may visit our website. (12) Thank you for allowing us to serve your utility needs.

15. Sentence 2: **This will ensure you always continue to receive the exceptional service you have come to expect from us.**

    Which correction should be made to sentence 2?

    A. remove always
    B. insert a comma after service
    C. change will ensure to is ensuring
    D. replace you with they

16. Sentence 4: **Then next we will replace the smaller line that runs from the street to your home.**

    Which correction should be made to sentence 4?

    A. change then to than
    B. remove next
    C. insert a comma after line
    D. change replace to have replaced

17. Sentence 7: **We apologize for any inconvenience this may cause during peak travel times and you may experience a temporary disruption in your utility service.**

    What is the best way to write the underlined portion of the sentence?

    A. times, you
    B. times but you
    C. times. You
    D. times, and so you

18. Sentence 8: **However we will adjust your bill accordingly if your service is interrupted.**

    Which correction should be made to sentence 8?

    A. change interrupted to interrupts
    B. change accordingly to according
    C. replace if with thus
    D. insert a comma after However

19. Sentences 9 and 10: **If you have any questions about the scheduled repairs. Please contact our office.**

    Which correction should be made to sentences 9 and 10?

    A. change If you have to Having
    B. change repairs. Please to repairs, please
    C. place sentence 10 before sentence 9
    D. insert a comma after questions

Language Arts: Writing Answers and Explanations

Writing Effective Sentences

Lesson 1: Simple Sentences

Practice 1

A. The revisions are samples. Your rewrites may differ.

1. **F** It drives his girlfriend crazy.
2. **F** As soon as he comes home from work, he starts talking on the telephone.
3. **C**
4. **F** Dave's sister and his best friend like to talk on the telephone, too.

B. 5. **C. call from** Choice (C) joins a sentence fragment to a complete sentence. "A calling conference" in choice (D) is badly worded.

6. **C. insert you before can** Choice (C) adds a subject to a sentence fragment, thus creating a complete sentence.
7. **C. service can** Choice (C) joins a sentence fragment to a complete sentence and makes sense.

Lesson 2: Compound and Complex Sentences

Practice 2.1

A. 1. It was late, and I was walking home from work.

2. My co-worker, Judy, had offered to drive me, but I had refused.
3. It was a warm night, so I decided to get some fresh air.
4. It was really my choice. I could have taken a cab, or I could have walked.
5. I heard a loud noise, so I ran the last block to my house. Later, I learned that it was only a car backfiring.

B. 6. **B. remove the comma** A comma is required when two independent clauses are joined but not when two verbs are joined (*carries . . . gets*).

7. **A. airlines, but** *But* is the most logical coordinating conjunction here. Most travelers on major airlines can check baggage. Because there are two clauses (*couriers . . . fly, . . . they can't check*), a comma is needed.
8. **B. insert a comma after advance** A comma precedes a coordinating conjunction joining two independent clauses.

Practice 2.2

A. 1. Most fatal fires occur when a family is asleep.

2. Because a smoke alarm wakes you up, it can allow you to escape.
3. Try to replace the smoke detector's battery before it goes dead.
4. Although smoke detectors cost money, the expense is worth it.

B. 5. **B. insert a after making** An indefinite article is needed.

6. **A. replace Whenever with After** *Whenever* is used inappropriately; it does not convey the intended meaning.
7. **D. up, thank** Choice (D) correctly combines a sentence fragment and an independent clause to form a complex sentence.

Lesson 3: Run-Ons and Comma Splices

Practice 3

A. There are several possible correct answers. There may be other correct answers in addition to those listed.

1. Jeff just got his driver's license, and he's very excited. OR Jeff just got his driver's license. He's very excited.
2. He bought a car that has a lot of miles on it, so it wasn't very expensive. OR Because he bought a car that has a lot of miles on it, it wasn't very expensive.
3. He doesn't have a lot of free time, but he'd like to take a car trip. OR Although he doesn't have a lot of free time, he'd like to take a car trip.
4. He needs to find out about car insurance, get a good map, and join an auto club.

B. 5. **A. pictures if you just** Choice (A) turns a run-on sentence into a complex sentence by adding a subordinating conjunction. The comma in choice (C) is unnecessary because the subordinate clause is the second half of the sentence.

6. **B. insert and after the comma** Choice (B) turns a comma splice into a compound sentence by adding a coordinating conjunction. Don't be misled by the apparent lack of a subject; both clauses are commands, meaning the subject, *you*, is implied but unstated.
7. **C. insert because in place of the comma** Choice (C) turns a run-on sentence into a complex sentence with both an independent and a dependent clause.

Lesson 4: Subordinate Ideas

Practice 4

A. There are several possible answers for each question. Sample answers:

1. Tornadoes and earthquakes can cause a lot of damage.
2. Earthquakes are somewhat common in California, but many Californians do not seem to mind.
3. On May 20, 2013, a tornado in Oklahoma killed twenty-three people and injured almost 400.
4. Tornadoes can occur anywhere in the United States and at any time of year.

B. 5. **D. repaired up** Choice (D) combines two short, choppy sentences into one smooth sentence. The other choices are run-ons, excessively wordy, or both.

6. **A. brought or mailed to** Choice (A) forms a compound predicate and combines two short, choppy sentences into one smooth, effective sentence.
7. **D. accidents, mishandling, or faulty installation** Choice (D) combines two wordy, repetitive sentences into one smooth, detailed sentence by forming a compound predicate.

Lesson 5: Modify Ideas

Practice 5

A. There are several possible answers for each question. Sample answers:
   1. Trent's sister, who is a health professional, encouraged him to become a nurse.
   2. When he wakes up the patients to take their blood pressure, they get rather annoyed.
   3. He carefully writes their temperature and blood pressure on their charts.
   4. It is hard to make visitors who are talking with patients leave at 9:00 P.M.

B. 5. **B. a person who is not the birth child** *not the birth child* is a misplaced modifier in the original sentence; choice (B) moves the modifier so it modifies the correct noun.
   6. **C. An agency requires a "home study"** In the original sentence, it is not clear who is going through an agency.
   7. **D. move frequently to follow Lawyers** Choice (D) moves the modifier to show that it is the lawyers who frequently handle adoptions, not the parents who frequently ask about them.

Lesson 6: Parallel Structure

Practice 6

A. There are multiple ways to revise these sentences. An example of each is listed below.
   1. Jenna has worked in a factory, a store, and a restaurant.
   2. She would like to put her kids in a better school and to get a better job.
   3. She thinks the kids' father is irresponsible, lazy, and uncaring.
   4. He doesn't have the time, the energy, or the money to give them what they deserve.

B. 5. **C. insert more before pleasant** Choice (C) correctly makes all the adjectives into comparatives (*safer, more comfortable*, and *more pleasant*).
   6. **D. computers, and** The original sentence combined single words and clauses in the same series. Choice (D) corrects the error by turning the last item in the list from a clause to a noun phrase (*lights, computers, and coffee makers*).
   7. **C. change be leaving to leave** Choice (C) makes all the verbs in the sentence (*punch, press*, and *leave*) parallel.

Lesson 7: Writing Style

Practice 7.1

1. **B. While different attitudes toward slavery were an obvious cause of the American Civil War,** This choice succinctly expresses one cause (the "obvious" one) of the war. Choice (D)'s "It is clear as day" is too informal.
2. **A. because this law unfairly restricts the property rights of some citizens** This choice concisely expresses the reason the city council should lift the ban. The other choices are wordy or awkward.
3. **D. watch out when someone makes promises that seem too good to be true** The syntax and word choice are consistent with that of the dialogue.
4. **B. employees with more than three weeks of vacation saved up at the end of September** This wording is appropriate for a business communication. Choice (C)'s "swimming in" is too informal; choice (D)'s "accrued in excess" is needlessly complicated.

Practice 7.2

1.

The letters *z* and *q* are the most infrequently used in the English language.	c. 7.59 Individual letters and combinations of letters of the Latin alphabet are usually italicized.
When viewing a solar eclipse, it is important not to look at the sun directly.	a. 8.140 The words *sun* and *moon* are usually lowercased in nontechnical contexts and always lowercased in the plural.
Many early civilizations arose in the Fertile Crescent, an area that today includes the nations of Egypt and Iraq.	d. 8.47 Popular names of places, or epithets, are usually capitalized [in contexts where they will be readily understood].
He was not sure whether he should apply to college or not, but if he did, he would ask Mr. Robson for a letter of recommendation.	b. 5.220 While *if* is conditional, *whether* introduces an alternative.

2.

They asked an impartial mediator to help them resolve their dispute, but the mediator was uninterested in the case.	b. Use *disinterested* to mean impartial. Use *uninterested* to mean that someone lacks interest.
The smokejumpers who fight fires in national forests undergo extensive training.	a. The job titles *firefighter, smokejumper*, and *bookbinder* are written as one word and are not capitalized.
Before she signed up for Psychology 101, she read that it must be taken prior to Psychology 102.	d. In general, *before* is preferable to *prior to*. *Prior to* is appropriate, however, when something is required for something else to happen.
The president is the commander in chief of the armed forces.	c. In general, only capitalize titles when they are used directly before an individual's name.

3. **A. veterans with disabilities** This wording puts the people first.
4. **C. 1:00 p.m. (GMT)** *p.m.* is correctly lowercase and includes periods, and the time zone is abbreviated inside parentheses.

Writing Effective Sentences Practice Questions

1. **B. remove the comma** When an independent clause comes before a subordinate clause in a complex sentence, there is no need to use a comma.

2. **B. during the day and 62°F** Choice (B) is the most concise.
3. **D. sunlight, keep** Choice (D) combines a subordinate clause sentence fragment and an independent clause to form a complex sentence.
4. **D. home. Do change** Choice (D) corrects the comma splice by adding a period, and is consistent with the theme of the paragraph as a list of recommendations.
5. **A. Your home will not cool down any faster.** *Any faster* should be placed next to the phrase it modifies, *cool down.*
6. **B. insert a comma after home** In this sentence, *When* begins a subordinate clause. A comma should be placed after a subordinate clause that begins a complex sentence.
7. **A. replace Returning with I returned** Choice (A) adds a subject to a sentence fragment and corrects the verb form to make a complete sentence.
8. **A. He claimed that because** There is no clear subject for the verb phrase at the beginning of the sentence to modify. By adding the subject *He,* choice (A) makes it clear who was claiming that the TV had been used.
9. **A. angry and frustrated about the** Choice (A) makes a smooth complex predicate out of a choppy run-on sentence.
10. **C. refund or get** Choice (C) puts both verbs in the same form. Choice (A) is grammatically correct but illogically suggests that Jeffrey will return *and* repair the TV.
11. **A. work productively if you** This choice moves the idea of being productive closer to the word it modifies, *work.* It also reduces wordiness by using the adverb form *productively.*
12. **C. remove the comma** A comma is not required before a coordinating conjunction that joins two verbs.
13. **B. remove the comma** A comma is not required in a complex sentence when the subordinate clause follows the independent clause.
14. **A. work or talk** Both verbs in the sentence should be in the same form. There is no need for a comma when a coordinating conjunction joins two verbs.
15. **B. insert a comma after hard** A comma is required before the coordinating conjunction that joins the two independent clauses in a compound sentence.
16. **D. hoaxes designed** This choice joins a sentence fragment to an independent clause.
17. **B. To check a claim like this, contact** Choice (B) combines two choppy sentences into one smooth, effective sentence.
18. **C. know. This** Choice (C) splits a comma splice into two independent, correct sentences.
19. **D. remove the comma after safe** A comma is not needed in a compound predicate.

Connecting Ideas

Lesson 1: Organize Ideas into Paragraphs

Practice 1.1

A. 1. The pharmacist at the local drugstore is very helpful.
2. No MI
3. Every vote counts, so let your voice be heard and vote!
4. When you are traveling, it's a good idea to mark your luggage clearly.
5. Listening to music can benefit you in many ways.

B. 6. **C. sentence 4** Sentences 1–3 explain who gets colds and how frequently. Sentences 4–6 are about the causes and prevention of colds.
7. **D. join paragraphs B and C** Sentence 10 in paragraph C is related to the main idea of paragraph B, the prevention of colds.

Practice 1.2

A. Your topic sentences should be similar to these:
1. Satellites have many different functions in today's world.
2. All signs show that the economy is headed for a slump.
3. The library has adopted a new dress code for employees.

B. 4. **D. Repetitive strain injury is a painful condition resulting from repeated use of the hands.** The original topic sentence is too general. The other options don't tell the central point: what repetitive strain injury is.
5. **B. A number of factors contribute to repetitive strain injury.** This sentence covers the three causes of repetitive strain injury mentioned in the paragraph.

Lesson 2: Use Logical Order and Relevant Ideas

Practice 2

A. 1. Irrelevant detail: Getting very ill is one bad thing that could happen.
2. Irrelevant detail: Adult students can also use school supplies.
3. Irrelevant detail: This job will be extremely expensive!

B. 4. **D. remove sentence 3** This sentence adds no new information to what was given in the previous sentences.
5. **D. remove sentence 6** The information about the secretarial job is not relevant to getting a job in carpentry.
6. **D. move sentence 10 to follow sentence 8** It would be more logical to place sentence 9 at the end of the letter.

Lesson 3: Relate Sentences and Paragraphs

Practice 3

A. Your transitions should be similar to these:

1. Our marketing efforts need to be enhanced. Therefore, we will soon begin another marketing initiative.
2. Sales representatives say that their jobs are extremely demanding. However, the salary is attractive.
3. The marketing director has instructed sales representatives to try some new ideas. For example, sales representatives can give away free samples.
4. A new ad campaign will be launched in just a few weeks. As a result, we expect sales to increase.

B. 5. **B. insert however, after the comma** This position is the most logical for the transition. Also, because it is in the middle of a sentence, it should be set off by commas.

6. **B. restaurant. For example,** Sentence 6 offers an example of the broad menu described in sentence 5.
7. **A. In addition, having a cafe** This option inserts a helpful transition to move the reader smoothly from paragraph B to paragraph C.

Connecting Ideas Practice Questions

1. **C. sentence 5** Sentences 1–4 are about the general problem of sleep disruption, whereas sentences 5–8 are about reasons why people don't get enough sleep.
2. **B. High-achieving students get more sleep.** Both studies relate to the impact of lack of sleep on learning.
3. **A. grades. Similarly,** The ideas in the two sentences are similar, so they can be connected this way.
4. **D. remove sentence 13** The paragraph is about sleep, not losing weight.
5. **D. join paragraphs (C) and (D)** Both paragraphs contain tips for getting more sleep.
6. **B. sentence 4** Sentences 1–3 introduce the purpose of the passage. Sentences 4–7 contain general rules for stain removal.
7. **B. Choose the right water temperature for cleaning each stain.** This sentence is appropriate since the paragraph discusses hot, cold, and room-temperature water.
8. **D. juice, for example, removes** When a transition is placed in the middle of a sentence, commas should both precede and follow it.
9. **D. remove sentence 15** Sentence 15 explains a minor detail and moves away from the main idea of the paragraph.
10. **C. move sentence 19 to the beginning of paragraph D** Putting sentence 19 at the beginning of the paragraph lets readers know in advance what point the paragraph will make.
11. **C. remove sentence 5** Sentence 5 is a general statement about HMOs. It is not relevant to the explanation of which insurance carriers are being made available.
12. **A. insert a comma after However** A comma should follow when a transition begins a sentence.
13. **C. sentence 9** Until sentence 9, paragraph B is about the differences between the two insurance plans. Sentence 9 introduces the idea of the informational sessions.
14. **A. move sentence 14 to the end of paragraph C** Sentence 14 refers to the card that was mentioned in paragraph C and so continues that idea.
15. **A. move sentence 2 to follow sentence 3** The description of removing the wheel should start with the initial step.
16. **C. move sentence 11 to follow sentence 12** Sentence 11 tells what to do with the spot where there is a leak, so it should follow the information on finding that spot.
17. **C. The next step is to put the tire and tube back onto the rim.** Paragraph C describes the process of putting the tire and tube back on the rim.
18. **A. The final step is to reinstall the wheel.** Paragraph D describes the final step in the process; putting the wheel back on the bike.
19. **A. replace Moreover, with Then** *Then* is a more appropriate transition for describing steps in a process.

Using Grammar Correctly

Lesson 1: Noun and Pronoun Agreement

Practice 1.1

A. 1. They

2. him
3. it
4. Her
5. she

B. 6. **A. replace me with I** *Bonetta and I* is a compound subject, so a subject pronoun is required.

7. **D. change getting to gets** The simple present tense is appropriate here.
8. **B. Walter or me** The phrase *Walter or me* is an object, so an object pronoun is required.

Practice 1.2

A. 1. Sally is moving to a small town. Her mother is concerned about the healthcare options it offers.

2. Sally tried to reassure her mother, but it was hard for her mother to believe Sally.
3. Sally asked a friend who lives in the town for information about its healthcare facilities. OR the town's healthcare facilities.
4. The town has a freestanding clinic where a person can go when he or she is sick. OR where people can go when they are sick.
5. There is also a nearby hospital, and it has a very good reputation.
6. If one is concerned about healthcare, one should sign up for a good insurance plan. OR If you are concerned about healthcare, you should sign up for a good insurance plan.

B. 7. **D. replace one's with their** The word *children* earlier in the sentence is the antecedent to the pronoun;

their agrees correctly with that antecedent, while the singular *one's* does not.

8. **D. parents** Only choice (D) correctly identifies who should be clear about their expectations.
9. **C. replace them with the group** The term *play group* is a collective noun, so the plural *them* should not be used to refer to it. In this case, repeating the word *group* is the best way to make the meaning clear.

Lesson 2: Verb Forms and Tenses

Practice 2.1

A. 1. had ceased
2. closed
3. functions
4. have visited
5. will open
6. looks
7. are thinking

B. 8. **B. is offering** The action is taking place right now, so the present progressive is the correct tense.
9. **D. change are signing to sign** The present-tense verb *sign* in the subordinate clause is appropriate, given the the future-tense verb *will receive* in the main clause.
10. **D. change will be amazing to will amaze** The verb *will amaze* is in the simple future tense. The future progressive tense in *will be amazing you* is incorrect and overcomplicated.

Practice 2.2

A. 1. came
2. showed
3. had spoken
4. took
5. seen

B. 6. **D. change begun to began** The action takes place in the past tense, so the verb should be in its past form, *began. Begun* is the past participle.
7. **C. was broken** *Broken* is the correct past participle.
8. **B. change given to give** The clue word *now* tells you that the action is still true, so the present-tense form of *give* is correct.

Lesson 3: Subject-Verb Agreement

Practice 3.1

A. 1. is
2. become
3. is
4. have
5. seems
6. is

B. 7. **B. have heard** In this sentence, the indefinite pronoun *most* is plural ("most of us"). The verb *have heard* agrees with the plural subject.
8. **C. change start to starts** The verb *starts* agrees with the singular subject *plane*.
9. **B. change conducts to conduct** The verb *conduct* agrees with the plural subject *materials*.

Practice 3.2

A. 1. ~~on the market~~ carry
2. ~~carrying the seal~~ are
3. ~~an important ingredient in many toothpastes~~ strengthens, attacks
4. are
5. offer
6. ~~with fluoride and good flavor~~ is

B. 7. **C. change have to has** The verb *has* agrees with the singular subject *state*.
8. **A. determine** The verb *determine* agrees with the compound subject *Wage level and the length of employment*.
9. **C. change reports to report** The verb *report* agrees with the plural subject *workers*.

Lesson 4: Using Reference Sources

Practice 4

1. **A. A widely used college textbook on international relations** An international relations textbook would be an authoritative source for this passage. A source open to contributions by the public (B) may or may not be properly vetted for accuracy. The news magazine article (C) is focused on a particular conflict, not on theories about why nations engage in conflict. The university's web page (D) discusses realism in a different field of study.
2. **C. According to the website of the American Kennel Club (akc.org/dog-breeds/mastiff/, accessed December 29, 2015), the mastiff is "courageous and dignified, but good-natured and docile."** Quoted text must be enclosed in quotation marks, and the source must be provided. Choice (D) avoids the need for quotation marks by paraphrasing the text, but it is less authoritative because it refers to the vague "experts on the breed" instead of the specific "American Kennel Club."
3. **A. According to *REALTOR® Magazine's* 2015 "Cost vs. Value Report," renovated basements add more value to homes than do updated kitchens and bathrooms.** The reference to a recent real estate industry report to support data on home values is most credible. In choice (D), the articles in *The Wall Street Journal*, a national financial newspaper, may be authoritative sources, but the sentence does not provide enough information, such as the dates of the articles, to evaluate them—they may not be current.
4. **D. Carolyn Dimitri and Lydia Oberholtzer, *Marketing U.S. Organic Foods: Recent Trends from Farms to Consumers* (Washington, D.C.: U.S. Department of Agriculture, 2009), 11.** This footnote contains the authors, title, publisher, date, and page number of the information in the sentence. The website address in (C) would also be useful, but it is not sufficient by itself; for one thing, if the link no longer works when the reader accesses it, the reader does not have enough information to search for the report. Choice (A) does not provide the authors, and choice (B) does not contain the year of publication.

Using Grammar Correctly Practice Questions

1. **C. change doesn't to didn't** The past tense is required because the second clause in the sentence is discussing what happened in the past.
2. **A. they** The antecedent of the underlined pronoun is *girls*, so it should be plural. *They* is clear; repeating *the girls* (as in choice (B)) is unecessary. Choice (D) *them* is incorrect because the pronoun is the subject of the dependent clause *while they practiced*.
3. **B. earned** The past tense is correct here because the action happened in the past over the course of a few years.
4. **D. change is to are** The verb *are* agrees with the plural subject *sisters*.
5. **D. change been to is** The main clause needs the present tense verb *is* because the introductory subordinate clause has a present-tense verb, *face*. *Been* is an incomplete verb form.
6. **B. change will receive to have received** The present perfect is correct here because the point is to find out about other people's past experiences with auto shops, not their predictions about them.
7. **A. change have picked to pick** Because this sentence is a command, the simple present tense is necessary.
8. **D. change comes to come** The verb *come* agrees with the plural subject *specials*. The agreement error could also be fixed with *came*, choice (C), but doing so would introduce a tense error in its place.
9. **D. replace it with the repair job** The pronoun *it* had no clear antecedent, so replacing it with a noun corrects the sentence.
10. **C. there are** The verb *are* agrees with the plural subject *limits*. The present tense is correct and should not be changed.
11. **B. replace its with their** The antecedent *changes* is plural, so the plural possessive *their* should be used.
12. **C. replace one's with your** *Your* is used in the rest of the paragraph, so it is appropriate here.
13. **D. change is to are** The word *which* is the subject of a subordinate clause. It refers to the plural noun *calculations*. Therefore, the verb *are*, not *is*, is required.
14. **A. has increased** The interrupting phrase *of taxes* does not change the fact that the subject of the new independent clause is *amount*, which is singular. The verb *has increased* therefore agrees with it.
15. **B. will credit** The future tense indicates an action that will take place at a later time, which is appropriate in this sentence.
16. **B. don't** The plural indefinite pronoun *many* is the subject of the sentence; the verb *don't* (don't = do + not) agrees with it. Changing to the past tense, choice (C), would be incorrect.
17. **C. change has to have** The verb *have* agrees with the plural subject *people*.
18. **B. him or her** The pronouns are objects of the preposition *with*, so the objective forms *him* and *her* are needed. The antecedent is *a person*, so the plural *them* in choice (D) cannot be used.
19. **B. change are to is** The verb *is* agrees with the singular subject *equipment*, and the interrupting phrase listing examples of assistive equipment is properly punctuated.
20. **B. it** *It* is the proper pronoun to use to refer to a dog.

Using Writing Mechanics

Lesson 1: Comma Use

Practice 1.1

A. 1. Train travel is more pleasant than riding a bus, but it can be more expensive.
2. When you're on a train, you can stand up and stretch if you need to.
3. NC
4. Unlike buses, trains sometimes have seats that face each other.
5. Traveling through a scenic area, you may find that your train has a double-decker car that offers a better view.
6. NC

B. 7. **A. insert a comma after starters** A comma is required after an introductory phrase.
8. **A. dressing, and** A comma should come before a coordinating conjunction in a compound sentence.
9. **D. remove the comma after though** The words *though not all of them may be pleasing to the palate* form a subordinate clause, and no commas are necessary in that clause.

Practice 1.2

A. 1. Kwanzaa is a week-long African American holiday that celebrates culture, community, and family.
2. Kwanzaa, a wintertime holiday, is based on an ancient African harvest celebration.
3. NC
4. Kwanzaa celebrations include rituals such as singing, dancing, drumming, and poetry reading.
5. The family lights one candle every day for each of seven principles: unity, self-determination, responsibility, cooperative economics, purpose, creativity, and faith.
6. NC

B. 7. **A. remove the comma** The subject and verb of a sentence should not be separated by a comma.
8. **B. insert a comma after medicines** Commas should be placed between items in a series.
9. **C. children, those ten and up,** You can mentally omit the phrase *those ten and up* and still understand the meaning of *older children*. Therefore, the appositive *those ten and up* should be set off by commas.

Lesson 2: Capitalization

Practice 2

A. 1. Last spring, I broke my arm in a car accident.
2. My internist, Doctor Claudia McNally, referred me to Waterside.

3. The center's director, Ilana Harris, assigned me a physical therapist named Ellie Royce.
4. Ellie studied physical therapy in her native London and used British methods of treatment that relieved my pain quite effectively.
5. She also did therapy with me in the pool at Rainbow Health Club.
6. I finished my treatments just before Labor Day, and I feel 100 percent better, thanks to Ellie.

B. 7. **B. change Emperors to emperors** A title should be capitalized only when it comes directly before a person's name or is used in direct address.
8. **C. change Mountains to mountains** A geographic feature is capitalized only when it is part of the name of a specific place, like *Rocky Mountains.*
9. **B. change america to America** Proper nouns should be capitalized.

Lesson 3: Possessives and Contractions

Practice 3

A. 1. There's
2. can't, who's, it's
3. we're
4. theirs
5. ours

B. 6. **D. replace you're with your** In this sentence, the pronoun in question is showing ownership, so *your* is correct.
7. **B. change were to we're** *Were* is a verb and is incorrect in this sentence. Rather, an apostrophe should be inserted to create the contraction *we're*, the combined form of *we are.*
8. **B. replace they're with their** In this sentence, the pronoun is possessive, so *their* is correct.

Lesson 4: Homonyms

Practice 4

A. 1. fourth
2. know
3. whole
4. week
5. affect
6. past

B. 7. **C. replace fare with fair** A *fare* is what you pay to get on the subway; *fair* means *just.*
8. **A. change principal to principle** A *principal* is the head of a school; *principle* means *a guiding rule.*
9. **A. replace affect with effect** *Affect* is a verb meaning *to influence*; *effect*, which means *result*, is required here.

Lesson 5: Idiomatic Usage

Practice 5

A. 1. **among** There are more than two types of cereal, so *among* is correct. The idiom *between [something] and [something]* is used to compare two items.
2. **to be** The idiom is *believe [something] to be [something else].*
3. **to swim** The idiom is *forbid [someone] to do [something].*
4. **than** Comparisons use *than.*
5. **less** Money is not individually countable, so *less* is correct. However, Jenna would find *fewer* dollar bills in her wallet, because dollar bills are countable.

B. 6. **B. Change "between" to "among"** The list of job openings is "long," so there are more than two openings, making *among* the correct idiom. To *regard [something] as [something]* and to *focus on [something]* are correct idioms.
7. **D. Change "try and" to "try to"** One does not *try and do [something]*. The idiom is *try to do* [*something*]. The customary expression is *squeeze blood from a turnip* (to try to get some benefit when that is impossible), and *consider* is followed directly by the noun or pronoun.
8. **B. Change "as" to "with"** The idiom is *credit [someone] with [doing something]*. The customary expression is *to give [someone] a leg up* (to help someone or give a person an advantage), and a comparison uses *than.*
9. **A. It's your funeral.** Abe is "skeptical" that Jon's approach is a good one, so this is the appropriate idiom for Abe to use. If Jon were going to quit his current job without having a new one, Abe might say, "A bird in the hand beats two in the bush." If Abe felt Jon would not be very good at the new career he was considering, Abe might say, "Don't give up the day job," and if something bad had happened that could not be made better, Abe might say, "It's no use crying over spilled milk."

Using Writing Mechanics Practice Questions

1. **B. insert a comma after tantrums** The phrase *have tantrums* is the first item in series, so it should be followed by a comma.
2. **C. understand and show** A comma should not be used between two verbs, and removing the comma is simpler and cleaner than adding a new subject as in incorrect choice (D).
3. **D. remove the comma after know** All the possessives, contractions, and homonyms in the sentence are spelled correctly. The comma following the introductory transition *However* cannot be removed, but the comma after *know* is incorrect.
4. **C. change are'nt to aren't** The apostrophe in a contraction must be placed in the spot where a letter has been removed.
5. **B. down, consider** An introductory subordinate clause should be followed by a comma.
6. **B. remove the comma** The subject (*One*) and its verb (*is*) should not be separated by a comma.
7. **B. replace it's with its** The sentence is about ownership: each time zone has its own standard time. The possessive form *its* is correct.

8. **B. change congress to Congress** The name *Congress* refers to a specific body of lawmakers and should therefore be capitalized.
9. **A. insert a comma after example** An introductory phrase must be followed by a comma.
10. **C. remove the comma after time** There is no need to separate the final phrase from the rest of the sentence with a comma.
11. **C. change center to Center** When a proper name consists of more than one word, all the words should be capitalized.
12. **D. replace when your with when you're** The sentence is saying, "when you are in the building," so the contraction *you're* is needed.
13. **A. replace week with weak** A *week* is seven days. *Weak,* meaning *not strong,* is appropriate for this sentence.
14. **D. remove the comma after pool** The clause beginning with *unless* does not need to be set off with commas.
15. **B. register and pay** Two items joined by *and* do not require a comma unless both are independent clauses.
16. **C. replace then with than** The word needed in the sentence is *than,* meaning *compared with. Then* means *after that* or *at that time.*
17. **C. insert a comma after profiling** The phrase *called racial profiling* is an appositive but is not essential to understanding the sentence. It needs a comma before (which is already given) and after it.
18. **B. distinctions, for nonwhites** The conjunction *for* is connecting two independent clauses in a compound sentence, so it must be preceded by a comma.
19. **B. change illinois to Illinois** Names of states should be capitalized.
20. **B. insert a comma after superintendents** Three items are listed in the series: *police superintendents, chiefs of police, and other law enforcement officials.* There should be commas separating them.

Writing the Essay

Lesson 1: Unpack the Writing Prompt

Practice 1

1. The writing assignment is about whether the Gregorian calendar is significantly different from other calendars.
2. Based on the prompt, I will be given two passages containing the history of the development of various types of calendars.
3. Argue that the Gregorian calendar is similar to or different from other calendars.
4. I am being asked to include details from the passages.

Lesson 2: Read the Passages with the Prompt in Mind

Practice 2

Your answers should be similar to this, but your wording may vary.

1. Mandatory military service.
2. The writer remains neutral in this essay.
3. The author's purpose was to explain two differing viewpoints on the topic of mandatory military service.
4. Violence in video games
5. The writer has an opinion.
6. The writer supports his opinion in numerous ways. He cites studies linking violence to video games and he gives an example of the public making a change in the video game marketplace.

Lesson 3: Develop a Thesis Statement

Practice 3

These answers are samples; your answers may vary.

1. The author makes an argument.
2. Prescription drug advertising on TV is harmful because it can lead patients to request or refuse medication for reasons that are not medically sound.
3. Advertising prescription drugs on TV is not in the public's best interest. The advertising can cause consumers to make poorly informed decisions regarding their healthcare.
4. The writer is neutral.
5. The author explains various theories of how the Moon was formed.
6. Of the two theories of lunar formation presented, the one with more support is the idea that Earth originally had rings of debris that eventually became the Moon.

Lesson 4: Collect Supporting Evidence

Practice 4

These answers are samples; your answers may vary.

1. The passage states that alcohol is particularly harmful to parts of the brain that grow later in life.
   Another fact from the passage is that alcohol causes long-term damage to the heart and liver.
   In support of this position, the text further says that the United Kingdom allows younger individuals to drink and also has high rates of alcohol-related death.
2. Choose either agree or disagree.
3. You might have written something like this:
   (Agree) One piece of evidence I would use to support my position is that teenagers are already at higher risk of accidents when driving, and alcohol would only exacerbate the danger they pose to themselves and others.
   (Disagree) One piece of evidence I would use to support my position is that 18-year-olds can enter combat in the military and can vote for the president. Claiming they are not responsible enough for alcohol is inconsistent with the responsibilities and privileges we otherwise give 18-year-olds.

Lesson 5: Plan Your Response

Practice 5

The following is a sample response. There is no objectively correct answer to the writing prompt. You may write your essay either for or against the author's position. Thus, answers to the following questions may vary.

1. **Sample thesis statement:** I think that the writer's position on owning a family pet is correct because the inconvenience and expenses cited outweigh the benefits, and because as someone allergic to cats, I agree with the writer's point that having pets can make it difficult for friends who visit.

2. **Sample outline:**
   I. The writer is correct that pets have more downsides than benefits and that families should not have pets.
   II. Monetary expenses; food, pet sitters, veterinary care, cleaning.
   III. Chores and time involved; kids may promise to help, but likely would not.
   IV. Friend can't visit; allergies, difficult with overnight guests.
   V. Pets are good friends and can be a calming influence when people are stressed.
      A. Some people think this justifies any expense and difficulty in keeping animals.
         i. But pets can keep away real friends and introduce stress as well, countering benefits.
         ii. Instead of petting a cat to relieve stress over money, it would be better to save the money you would spend on the cat's food and vet bills.

3. **Sample idea map:**
The idea map shown demonstrates how you might organize your thoughts to argue for pet ownership. Your idea map may vary.

Lesson 6: Draft Your Response

Practice 6.1

Your answers may vary.

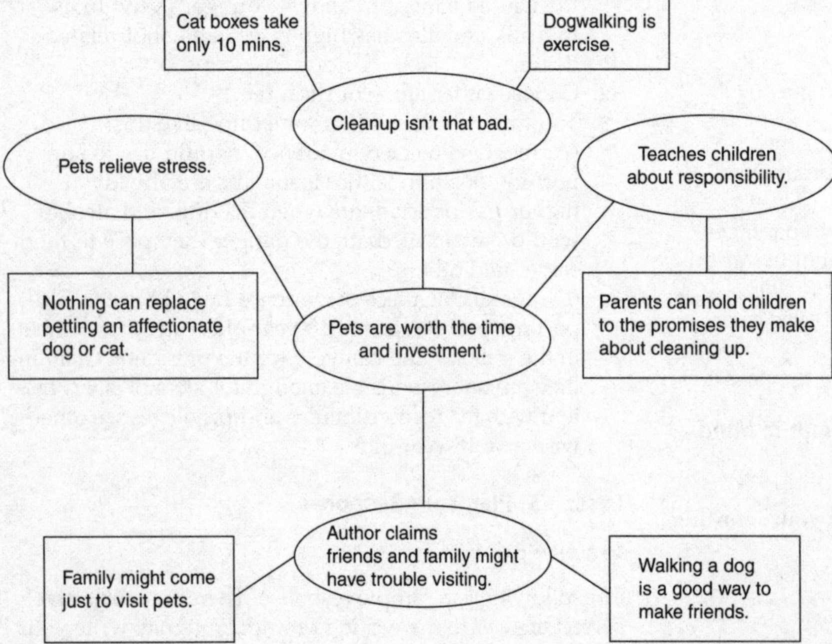

A. Sample topic sentences:
Pet ownership is a major burden, and the time and money people invest in pets could be better spent elsewhere.

The author of the passage says that keeping a pet is not worth the trouble, but he fails to consider all of the many benefits of pet ownership.

Your supporting statements may vary quite a bit, so no samples are given here. Check to make sure that your supports are relevant to your topic statement.

B. Sample concluding statements:
And so, when all is taken into consideration, the conclusion is clear: the cost of a pet far outweighs the benefit.

Don't let the long list of difficulties listed by the author scare you away, because a pet can be a friend to you and your children, one whose value can't be measured against time and money.

Practice 6.2

Refer to the Essay Scoring Guide on pages 761–762 to evaluate your response.

Practice 6.3

Refer to the Essay Scoring Guide on pages 761–762 to evaluate your response.

Lesson 7: Revise and Edit Your Response

Practice 7.1

A.

Most of us are aware that speeding has consequences, which range from receiving a speeding ticket to getting into an accident. Nonetheless, a quick survey of any highway will show that many drivers exceed the speed limit, showing that speed limit laws need to be more strictly enforced. This raises the question: why do people speed despite the fact that doing so is illegal?

One common reason is that people do not think they will suffer any consequences. If they have never been stopped by the police or ~~crashed their car,~~ been involved in a car crash, they don't see any reason to worry.

Another reason is that people simply need to get somewhere in a hurry. They realize that they are speeding^ but ~~they have such a need to arrive on time that they don't care~~ their impatience gets the better of them. ~~They've got ants in their pants.~~

¶A final reason is lack of respect for other drivers~~, one~~. One driver who is speeding makes road conditions less safe for everyone. Drivers who act as though they are in the Indy 500 ~~they~~ have no regard for the safety of others.

We know that people speed because ~~of impatience and they don't fear the consequences~~. they're impatient and don't fear the consequences. ~~Another reason is no respect~~. They also don't respect other drivers. Let's figure out what will make them stop speeding.

B. Refer to the Essay Scoring Guide on pages 761–762 to evaluate your response.

Practice 7.2

Your revised paragraphs should be similar to the following.

One common reason for speeding is that people don't think they will suffer consequences. If they have never been stopped by the police or been involved in a car crash, they've never experienced the dangers of speeding firsthand.

Another reason is that people simply need to get somewhere in a hurry. They realize that they are speeding, but their impatience gets the better of them.

A final reason is lack of respect for other drivers. One driver who is speeding makes road conditions less safe for everyone. Drivers who act as though they are in a race have no regard for the safety of other drivers.

Writing the Essay Practice Questions

A. Refer to the Essay Scoring Guide on pages 761–762 to evaluate your response.

B. Refer to the Essay Scoring Guide on pages 761–762 to evaluate your response.

Polishing Your Writing

Lesson 1: Strengthen Sentences

Practice 1

A. Your revised sentences should be similar to the following. The underlined parts show where your revision marks should be:

1. First, write down what you know about your family. Then interview relatives. (Run-on sentence)
2. Videotaping or recording the interviews is a good idea. (Structure not parallel)
3. Ask relatives to provide exact names, dates, and other details. (Structure not parallel)
4. Make copies of documents such as birth certificates and marriage licenses. (Sentence fragment)
5. When older family members are interviewed, they'll often tell you stories you never heard. (Dangling modifier)
6. Carefully record all the information you get and put it in a three-ring binder. (Misplaced modifier)
7. Some people use their computers to do genealogy searches, and they get very good results. (Comma splice; coordinating conjunction needed)
8. However, one must have the time, the patience, and the know-how to use the Internet. (Structure not parallel)
9. If you do decide to learn more about your roots, don't be surprised to find yourself at a huge family reunion. (Comma needed after subordinate clause)
10. The whole process of putting together a family tree and contacting long-lost family members is rewarding. (Sentence fragment)

B. Sample revisions:

It was a beautiful day, and the blue ocean sparkled in the sunlight. It was a perfect day for going to the beach. As Renelle looked across the sand, she saw two little girls building a sandcastle and making a moat next to it. Renelle spread out her towel, anchored it with her shoes and beach bag, and began to read a magazine. Suddenly she heard a voice say, "Are you going to get in the water, or are you just going to lie there?" Renelle looked up and saw her friend Terry. She laughed softly and got up to greet Terry. Putting on her sandals, she walked with Terry across the burning sand to the water's edge.

Renelle loved going to the beach. It relaxed her and helped her forget about her problems. It didn't cost money like most other forms of entertainment. Most of Renelle's friends also spent a lot of time at the beach, so that was another incentive.

Lesson 2: Improve Organization

Practice 2

A. Your revised paragraphs should be similar to the following (starting after the first revision made for you):

Why do people continue to litter? One reason people litter is that they just don't care about others. It doesn't bother them to leave their trash in front of someone else's apartment building, forcing another person to deal with the problem. This inconsiderate attitude is also reflected in the refusal to recycle plastic, glass, and newspapers. People figure that they won't be around in the future when the landfills are used up, so who cares?

¶Another possible reason for littering is low self-esteem. If people don't feel good about themselves, they won't be motivated to keep their environment looking attractive. ~~Low self-esteem can cause many other problems, including depression and lack of self-confidence.~~ People who have high self-esteem believe that it's important to keep their home, the planet Earth, clean and beautiful.

B. Ask a friend or family member to evaluate your work.

Lesson 3: Word Choice

Practice 3.1

Sample answers:

A. 1. nonprofit organization
2. thousands of
3. substandard
4. dollars
5. as soon as possible

B. If you ever order merchandise from a catalog, you should be aware of your rights. All companies, regardless of the state in which they are located, are required to ship your order within 30 days unless they have advertised a different shipping time. If a company is unable to meet the shipping deadline, it must send you an "Option Notice." You can choose to wait longer or get a refund.

Some consumers have complained about receiving merchandise that they did not order. Companies that engage in this practice are breaking the law. If you receive a product you haven't ordered, it is yours to keep.

If you receive a package that has been damaged, don't open it. Write "REFUSED" on the package, and return it to the seller. There's no need to add new postage as long as the package came by regular mail.

C. Have a friend or family member evaluate your work.

Practice 3.2

A. 1. roared The comedian was "extremely" funny, so the audience would laugh loudly, not softly.

2. crimson The author is pointing out that the sweater is "unique," so the word for a specific shade of red (purplish-red) is more appropriate.

3. uncomfortable A student who has already successfully answered a question may feel uneasy when asked a harder one, but is unlikely to be very unhappy.

4. strode Given that Xiu feels proud of herself, walking with big steps makes more sense than barely lifting her feet off the floor.

5. asked The child is only five years old and the situation is not that serious, so his mother would not formally or forcefully demand an answer.

B. 6. D. Change "blockaded" to "blocked." *To blockade* is to block in a very specific way—to block goods from entering or leaving a country. Snow always falls *smoothly* (without difficulty), so there is no need to say so; the author's point is that it fell *steadily* (continuously) so there was a lot of it. *Monstrous* means "large" but has a negative connotation that would not fit the sentence; *huge* is better.

7. B. Change "agitated" to "excited." The word needs to describe the happy enthusiasm of the children, in contrast to their parents, and *excited* works well; *agitated* has a negative connotation. The parents are worried, not *tormented* (in severe physical or mental pain), so *anxious* is correct. *To reside* refers to living somewhere, and the parents already live at home with their children, so *stay* is correct.

8. A. intelligent All these words mean positive intellectual qualities. Bella's father is remarking on her good idea, so a word meaning "smart" is correct. The other choices are too specific for this situation.

Lesson 4: Expression and Voice

Practice 4

1. **B. As a member of this sandwich generation, I experience the occasional joys and many challenges of caring for my 77-year-old mother and two children.** With words like "joys" and "challenges," this sentence conveys the author's mind-set.
2. **A. To my shame, I ignored my mother's increasing disorganization and failed to support her.** The words "shame," "ignored," and "failed" communicate the author's emotions about the situation.
3. **D. I dread the decisions I will have to make as my mother's mind betrays her, such as whether I can care for her at home.** The verbs "dread" and "betray" are vivid and emphasize the concern the author feels.

Polishing Your Writing Practice Questions

1. **C. gardener, it's important that** Sentence 2 is a subordinate clause, not a complete sentence. Use a comma to combine it with the independent clause in sentence 3, creating a complex sentence.
2. **A. replace not good with too extreme** The phrase *not good* is vague, since it provides no information about how a climate might be unsuitable. *Too extreme* allows the reader to anticipate the temperature and moisture requirements discussed in paragraph D.
3. **B. move sentence 8 to follow sentence 9** Sentence 9 is the topic sentence—it gives the main idea—for paragraph C. As such, it should be the first sentence of the paragraph.
4. **D. move sentence 11 to the beginning of paragraph D** The topic of paragraph C is choosing a garden spot, whereas the topic of paragraph D is choosing plants. Therefore, sentence 11, which is about choosing plants, should appear in paragraph D.
5. **C. plants to** Sentence 12 contains a comma splice joining two independent clauses. These clauses should instead be joined with a word or phrase that expresses the relationship between them.
6. **A. change which had come to and had come** The phrase *which had come* implies that Wales had come to the United States, not the boy. Replace *which* with *and* to clarify.
7. **D. ocean; it** A semicolon is required to separate two independent clauses, correcting the run-on sentence.
8. **C. replace really big with vast** Describing the ocean as *vast* conveys the sense of size more precisely.
9. **B. kidding me** The adverb *totally* is used informally here, and *pulling my leg* is slang that should be avoided.
10. **B. remove the sentence** Sentence 12 is unnecessary and should be removed.

11. **D. place a period after morality and begin a new sentence with She** Doing so corrects the run-on sentence.
12. **B. Many consider this her most shocking story.** Replacing "reckon" with "consider" replaces slang with more formal language.
13. **C. change lupus. The to lupus, the** As written, sentence 8 is not a sentence at all. It should serve as an appositive describing *lupus* in the previous sentence.
14. **A. Flannery maintained many fulfilling correspondences that gave her the insight into human behavior that is evident in her writing.** This construction eliminates wordiness while maintaining the original meaning of the sentence.
15. **A. remove always** The adverb *always* is unnecessary when paired with the verb *continue*.
16. **B. remove next** The adverbs *then* and *next* are redundant when used together.
17. **C. times. You** Insert a period and remove *and* between the two independent clauses.
18. **D. insert a comma after However** Unless *However* is followed by a comma, it seems that it is being used to modify the adjustment. Insert a comma to clarify that *However* introduces the sentence.
19. **B. replace repairs. Please with repairs, please** Sentence 9 is a fragment and must be joined to sentence 10 with a comma to present a complete thought.

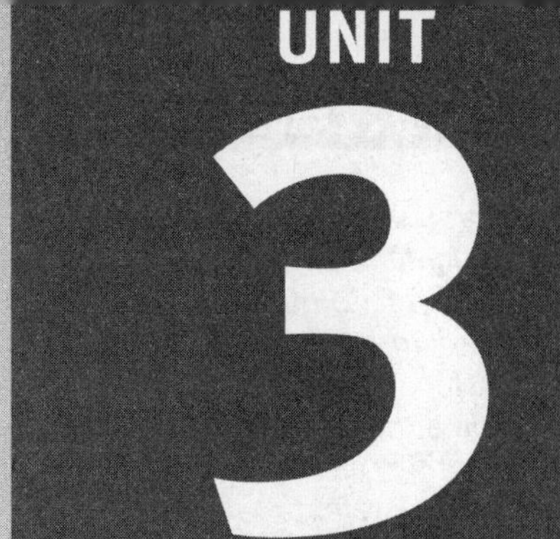

ABOUT THE TEST

Mathematics

The HiSET Mathematics Test assesses your ability to reason with numbers. You will have 90 minutes to answer 50 multiple-choice questions that will target skills such as:

- Performing number operations to solve problems
- Solving word problems
- Understanding proportions and percentages
- Interpreting graphic representations of data
- Finding averages
- Understanding and performing operations with algebraic expressions
- Solving linear and quadratic equations
- Solving problems using geometric formulas

Tools

On the Mathematics Test, two tools will be available to you to help you answer questions.

Calculator: Whether you take the paper or computer version of the HiSET exam, you will have access to a calculator for the Mathematics Test. See below for more information.

Formula sheet: You will also be provided with a formula sheet that lists common mathematical formulas. Become familiar with this sheet, which is reproduced on page 259. If a formula is discussed in this book but not listed on the formula sheet, you will need to memorize it.*

A Note about Calculators

The Mathematics test is calculator neutral. This means that a calculator is not required and you are NOT allowed to bring one with you on Test Day. If you are taking the paper version of the test and request a calculator, however, the test center is required to provide either a four-function or scientific calculator (the type of calculator provided is at the testing center's discretion). Please refer to the state policies for the state in which you are testing. If you are taking the computer version of the test, an on-screen calculator is available to you that you can access at any time during the test. It contains all of the basic functions you'll need: addition, subtraction, multiplication, division, and square root.

While it is unknown which calculator you will receive on Test Day (if taking the paper version of the test), for illustrative purposes, this lesson will walk you through how to use one sample scientific calculator, the Texas Instruments TI-30XS MultiView™. On this calculator, you use the white numeric keypad to enter numbers, the decimal point, and the negative sign (–) for a negative number such as –213. The operation keys, on the right, allow you to add, subtract, multiply, and divide. The four arrows at the top right of the calculator allow you to move the on-screen cursor up, down, left, or right as needed. The delete key to the left of the arrows allows you to correct mistakes as you work.

* Note: The information given here was the latest information available as of December 2018. It is possible that changes were made between this printing and your test date. For updates, visit http://hiset.ets.org.

HiSET EXAM TIP

While you may NOT bring your own calculator with you on Test Day, feel free to utilize one as you work through this book. If requested, your test center will provide either a four-function or scientific calculator on Test Day. Please refer to the state policies for the state in which you are testing.

The following Casio® calculators have the same basic key functions as the TI-30XS MultiView™, but some of the keys are in different locations and/or have slightly different symbolic representation for various functions. For example, the Casio® calculators use an "equals" key, whereas the TI-30XS MultiView™ has a button that says "enter," which performs the same function.

- **Casio FX-115ES PLUS**
- **Casio FX-115MS PLUS**
- **Casio FX-300ES PLUS**

A Note about the Mathematics Formula Sheet

Some test questions require the use of formulas. The formulas needed to answer certain questions will be provided via a formula sheet, which can be found on page 259. While this document will be available to you during the Mathematics test, you should also know some formulas prior to testing as these will not be provided to you. Some of these include: distance-rate-time, the Pythagorean theorem, and the quadratic formula.

Do not attempt to absorb and memorize these formulas here and now. Skip to page 260 to begin your math studies. Periodically you will refer back to these pages as you work through practice problems.

MATHEMATICS FORMULA SHEET

This page displays formulas that you will be given when you take the HiSET exam.

Perimeter / Circumference

Rectangle

Perimeter = 2(*length*) + 2(*width*)

Circle

Circumference = 2π(*radius*)

Area

Circle

Area = $\pi(radius)^2$

Triangle

Area = $\frac{1}{2}$(*base*)(*height*)

Parallelogram

Area = (*base*)(*height*)

Trapezoid

Area = $\frac{1}{2}(base_1 + base_2)(height)$

Volume

Prism/Cylinder

Volume = (*area of the base*)(*height*)

Pyramid/Cone

Volume = $\frac{1}{3}$(*area of the base*)(*height*)

Sphere

Volume = $\frac{4}{3}\pi(radius)^3$

Length

1 foot = 12 inches

1 yard = 3 feet

1 mile = 5,280 feet

1 meter = 1,000 millimeters

1 meter = 100 centimeters

1 kilometer = 1,000 meters

1 mile ≈ 1.6 kilometers

1 inch = 2.54 centimeters

1 foot ≈ 0.3 meter

Capacity / Volume

1 cup = 8 fluid ounces

1 pint = 2 cups

1 quart = 2 pints

1 gallon = 4 quarts

1 gallon = 231 cubic inches

1 liter = 1,000 milliliters

1 liter ≈ 0.264 gallon

Weight

1 pound = 16 ounces

1 ton = 2,000 pounds

1 gram = 1,000 milligrams

1 kilogram = 1,000 grams

1 kilogram ≈ 2.2 pounds

1 ounce ≈ 28.3 grams

Number and Quantity Part I: Problem Solving

LESSON 1

Compare and Order Numbers

KEY IDEAS

- When ordering numbers, compare the same place values between numbers.
- Round numbers to estimate answers or eliminate answer choices in multiple-choice questions.

HiSET EXAM TIP

It's important to know the inequality symbols below.
$<$ means "is less than"
$\leq$ means "is less than or equal to"
$>$ means "is greater than"
$\geq$ means "is greater than or equal to"

Place Value

Numbers are part of your everyday life. Whether you're paying with cash, reading bus schedules, or changing television channels, you're using whole numbers.

The value of a number depends on the **place value** of its digits. On the place-value chart below, note that the value of a digit increases as you move to the left.

___ , ___ ___ ___ 1 , 4 7 9

millions, hundred thousands, ten thousands, thousands, hundreds, tens, ones

In the whole number shown on the chart, 1 has the greatest value. The number would be read as "one thousand four hundred seventy-nine."

Comparing and Ordering Values

To **order** numbers, you need to compare the value of their digits. Align the place values of the numbers you are comparing. Start at the left and compare the value of the first digit of each number.

Example 1: Place the numbers 342, 98, and 317 in order from least to greatest.

1. Compare the first digit in each number. Since 98 is a two-digit number, and the other numbers are three-digit numbers, 98 has the smallest value.
2. Next, compare the first digit of the remaining numbers. Since both numbers have the same digit (3) in the hundreds place, compare the digits in the tens place. Since 1 is less than 4, 317 is less than 342.

hundreds tens ones

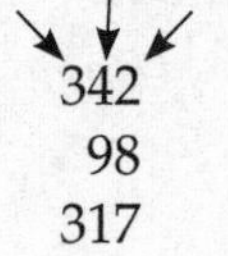

From least to greatest:
98, 317, 342

Rounding Numbers

Place value is also essential to **rounding** numbers.

Example 2: Round 2451 to the nearest hundred.

1. Locate the place value that you want to round to. Then look at the place value to the right. If the digit to the right is 5 or greater, round up. If the digit to the right is less than 5, then don't change the number in the hundreds place.
2. Round up the digit in the hundreds place. Then change the digits to the right of the hundreds place to zeros.

24[5]1

The value to the right of the hundreds place is a 5. Round up.

2451 rounds up to **2500.**

PRACTICE 1

A. Write the digit from the number below that corresponds to the listed place value. The first one is done for you.

1,436,879

_4_ **1.** hundred thousands

____ **2.** hundreds

____ **3.** ones

____ **4.** millions

____ **5.** thousands

____ **6.** tens

____ **7.** ten thousands

B. Round these numbers as directed.

8. Round 544 to the nearest hundred.

9. Round 76 to the nearest ten.

10. Round 1058 to the nearest hundred.

11. Round 11,632 to the nearest thousand.

12. Round 1525 to the nearest thousand.

13. Round 84 to the nearest hundred.

C. In each of the following pairs, which number is greater?

14. 100 or 89

15. 339 or 341

16. 1099 or 1145

17. 125,391 or 119,450

D. Write these numbers in order from least to greatest.

18. 23 18 45 39

19. 111 89 109 91

20. 1087 932 909 1139

21. 1429 1420 1432 1425

22. 12,071 11,098 12,131

23. 15,356 15,309 15,298

E. Choose the one best answer to each question.

24. When stacking items, the heaviest items should be placed at the bottom. Starting at the bottom, in what order should items weighing 45 pounds, 40 pounds, 50 pounds, and 48 pounds be stacked?

A. 40, 45, 48, 50
B. 45, 50, 40, 48
C. 45, 48, 50, 40
D. 50, 48, 45, 40
E. 50, 40, 45, 48

25. Which of the following correctly shows 1,543,976 rounded to the nearest hundred thousand?

A. 2,000,000
B. 1,600,000
C. 1,500,000
D. 1,540,000
E. 1,544,000

STUDY ADVICE

Not a math person? Have no fear! The math concepts tested on the Mathematics Test are covered in this book; you just need to plan your study schedule to include plenty of time to master these topics.

Number and Quantity Part I: Problem Solving

LESSON 2

Whole Number Operations

Addition and Subtraction

You use **addition** when you need to combine amounts. The answer in an addition problem is called the **sum,** or **total.** When you are adding, it's helpful to stack the numbers in a column. Be sure to line up the place-value columns and then work from right to left, starting with the ones column.

Sometimes the digits in a place-value column add up to 10 or more. When this happens, you will need to **regroup** to the next place value.

Example 1: Add 40 + 129 + 24.

1. Align the numbers you want to add on the ones column. Working from right to left, add the ones column first. Since the ones column totals 13, write the 3 in the ones column and regroup, or **carry**, the 1 ten to the tens column.

$$\begin{array}{r} 1 \\ 40 \\ 129 \\ +\ 24 \\ \hline 3 \end{array}$$

2. Add the tens column, including the regrouped 1.

$$\begin{array}{r} 1 \\ 40 \\ 129 \\ +\ 24 \\ \hline 93 \end{array}$$

3. Then add the hundreds column. Since there is only one value, write the 1 hundred in the answer.

$$\begin{array}{r} 1 \\ 40 \\ 129 \\ +\ 24 \\ \hline \mathbf{193} \end{array}$$

KEY IDEAS

- Add when combining amounts and subtract when finding the difference.
- Align place-value columns when adding or subtracting.
- Always look to the next place-value column to regroup.

HiSET EXAM TIP

Another way to check answers is to round the numbers in a problem and find an approximate answer.

You **subtract** when you want to find the **difference** between amounts. Write the greater number on top, and align the amounts on the ones column. You may also need to regroup as you subtract.

Example 2: If Sue is 57 and Kathy is 38, how many years older is Sue?

1. Find the difference in their ages. Start with the ones column. Since 7 is less than the number being subtracted (8), regroup, or **borrow**, 1 ten from the tens column. Add the regrouped amount to the ones column. Now subtract 17 − 8 in the ones column.

$$\begin{array}{r} 4\,17 \\ \not{5}\not{7} \\ -\ 38 \\ \hline 9 \end{array}$$

2. Regrouping 1 ten from the tens column left 4 tens. Subtract 4 − 3 and write the result in the tens column of your answer. Check: 19 + 38 = 57.

$$\begin{array}{r} 4\,17 \\ \not{5}\not{7} \\ -\ 38 \\ \hline \mathbf{19} \end{array}$$

Sue is **19 years older** than Kathy.

PRACTICE 2.1

Example 3: Find the difference between 205 and 67.

1. Subtract. Start with the ones column. Since 5 is less than the number being subtracted (7), regroup. Since there are 0 tens in the tens column, regroup 1 hundred from the hundreds column. From 10 tens, regroup 1 ten to the ones column. Now subtract 15 − 7 in the ones column.

$$\begin{array}{r} \scriptstyle 9 \\ \scriptstyle 1\ \not{10}\ 15 \\ \not{2}\,\not{0}\,\not{5} \\ -\ 6\ 7 \\ \hline 8 \end{array}$$

2. Regrouping 1 ten from the tens column left 9 tens. Subtract 9 − 6, and write the result in the tens column of your answer.

$$\begin{array}{r} \scriptstyle 9 \\ \scriptstyle 1\ \not{10}\ 15 \\ \not{2}\,\not{0}\,\not{5} \\ -\ 6\ 7 \\ \hline 3\ 8 \end{array}$$

3. Regrouping 1 hundred from the hundreds column left 1 hundred. Subtract the hundreds column: 1 − 0. Check: 138 + 67 = 205.

$$\begin{array}{r} \scriptstyle 9 \\ \scriptstyle 1\ \not{10}\ 15 \\ \not{2}\,\not{0}\,\not{5} \\ -\ 6\ 7 \\ \hline \mathbf{1\ 3\ 8} \end{array}$$

A. Solve.

1. $\begin{array}{r} 54 \\ +23 \\ \hline \end{array}$

2. $\begin{array}{r} 46 \\ +54 \\ \hline \end{array}$

3. $\begin{array}{r} 73 \\ -21 \\ \hline \end{array}$

4. $\begin{array}{r} 55 \\ -19 \\ \hline \end{array}$

5. $\begin{array}{r} 105 \\ +85 \\ \hline \end{array}$

6. $\begin{array}{r} 2386 \\ +1692 \\ \hline \end{array}$

7. $\begin{array}{r} 100 \\ -57 \\ \hline \end{array}$

8. $\begin{array}{r} 2500 \\ -383 \\ \hline \end{array}$

B. Rewrite the problems in columns before solving.

9. 20 + 12 + 33 =
10. 245 − 131 =
11. 30 + 75 + 75 =
12. 378 − 85 =
13. 144 + 238 + 101 =
14. 545 − 89 =
15. 2095 + 324 =
16. 1250 − 350 =
17. 10,326 + 982 =
18. 15,890 − 705 =
19. 108,755 + 22,442 =
20. 44,789 − 13,890 =

C. Choose the <u>one best answer</u> to each question.

21. What is the total weight of the boxes below?

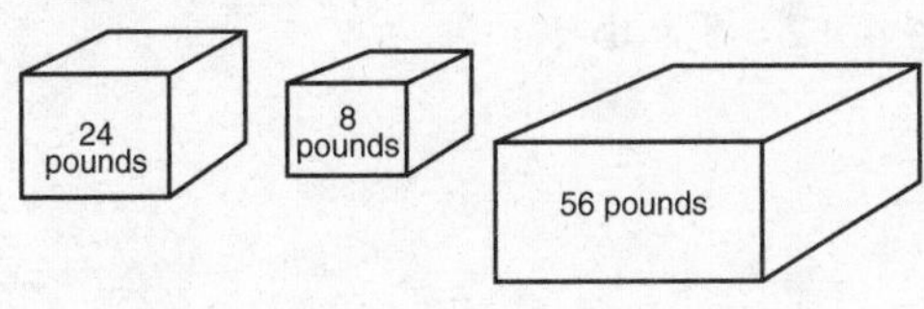

A. 78
B. 88
C. 150
D. 160
E. 188

22. Celia's share for lunch is $7. If she pays with a $20 bill, how much change should she get?

A. $3
B. $7
C. $10
D. $13
E. $27

Multiplication and Division

You **multiply** to combine the same amount multiple times. For example, instead of adding 24 + 24 + 24, you could multiply 24 by 3. If a problem asks you to find the **product** of two or more numbers, you should multiply.

Example 4: Find the product of 24 and 63.

1. Align place values as you rewrite the problem in a column. Multiply the ones place of the top number by the ones place of the bottom number: $4 \times 3 = 12$. Write the 2 in the ones place in the first partial product. Regroup the 1 ten.

$$\begin{array}{r} {\scriptstyle 1} \\ 24 \\ \times 63 \\ \hline 2 \end{array}$$

2. Multiply the tens place in the top number by 3: $2 \times 3 = 6$. Then add the regrouped amount: $6 + 1 = 7$. Write the 7 in the tens place in the partial product.

$$\begin{array}{r} {\scriptstyle 1} \\ 24 \\ \times 63 \\ \hline 72 \end{array}$$

3. Now multiply by the tens place of 63. Write a **placeholder** 0 in the ones place in the second partial product, since you're really multiplying by 60. Then multiply the top number by 6: $4 \times 6 = 24$. Write 4 in the partial product and regroup the 2. Multiply $2 \times 6 = 12$. Add the regrouped 2: $12 + 2 = 14$.

$$\begin{array}{r} {\scriptstyle 2} \\ 24 \\ \times 63 \\ \hline 72 \\ 1440 \\ \hline \mathbf{1512} \end{array}$$

4. Add the partial products to find the total product: $72 + 1440 =$ **1512.**

To **divide** means to find how many equal parts an amount can be divided into. The amount being divided is called the **dividend.** The number you are dividing by is the **divisor,** and the answer to a division problem is the **quotient.**

Example 5: At a garage sale, 3 children sold their old toys for a total of $54. If they share the money equally, how much money should each child receive?

1. Divide the total amount ($54) by the number of ways the money is to be split (3). Work from left to right. How many times does 3 go into 5? Write the answer 1 directly above the 5 in the dividend. Since $3 \times 1 = 3$, subtract $5 - 3 = 2$.

$$\begin{array}{r} 1 \\ 3\overline{)\$54} \\ -3 \\ \hline 2 \end{array}$$

2. Continue dividing. Bring down the 4 from the ones place in the dividend. How many times does 3 go into 24? Write the answer 8 directly above the 4 in the dividend. Since $3 \times 8 = 24$, subtract $24 - 24 = 0$.

   Each child should receive **$18.**

$$\begin{array}{r} 18 \\ 3\overline{)\$54} \\ -3 \\ \hline 24 \\ -24 \\ \hline 0 \end{array}$$

Example 6: Divide $1006 \div 4$.

1. Divide the total amount (1006) by 4. Work from left to right. Since 4 doesn't divide into 1, use the next place value in the dividend. How many times does 4 go into 10? Write the answer 2 directly above the first 0 in the dividend. Since $4 \times 2 = 8$, subtract $10 - 8 =$ **2**.

$$\begin{array}{r} 2 \\ 4\overline{)1006} \\ -8 \\ \hline 2 \end{array}$$

2. Continue dividing. Bring down the 0 from the tens place in the dividend. How many times does 4 go into 20? Write the answer 5 directly above the second 0 in the dividend. Since $4 \times 5 = 20$, subtract $20 - 20 = 0$. Bring down the 6 from the ones place in the dividend. How many times does 4 go into 6? Write the answer 1 above the 6 in the dividend. Since $4 \times 1 = 4$, subtract $6 - 4 = 2$. Write the **remainder** of 2 as part of the quotient.

$$\begin{array}{r} 251\text{ r2} \\ 4\overline{)1006} \\ -8 \\ \hline 20 \\ -20 \\ \hline 06 \\ -4 \\ \hline 2 \end{array}$$

By reviewing and memorizing multiplication tables, you can save yourself precious time on the Mathematics Test.

A. Solve.

1. $\begin{array}{r} 121 \\ \times 4 \\ \hline \end{array}$
2. $\begin{array}{r} 250 \\ \times 4 \\ \hline \end{array}$
3. $\begin{array}{r} 342 \\ \times 8 \\ \hline \end{array}$
4. $5\overline{)65}$
5. $7\overline{)735}$
6. $9\overline{)189}$
7. $\begin{array}{r} 45 \\ \times 30 \\ \hline \end{array}$
8. $\begin{array}{r} 105 \\ \times 25 \\ \hline \end{array}$
9. $\begin{array}{r} 211 \\ \times 16 \\ \hline \end{array}$
10. $10\overline{)280}$
11. $15\overline{)225}$
12. $19\overline{)114}$

B. Solve. If multiplying more than two numbers, find the product of two numbers before multiplying by the next number, and so on.

13. $50 \times 5 =$
14. $179 \div 4 =$
15. $5 \times 6 \times 10 =$
16. $1004 \div 5 =$
17. $25 \times 3 \times 2 =$
18. $7452 \times 9 =$
19. $10,760 \div 20 =$
20. $12 \times 8 \times 4 =$
21. $144,140 \div 12 =$

C. Choose the one best answer to each question.

22. A fruit juice container holds 16 servings. If the serving size is 6 ounces, how many ounces does the container hold in all?

A. 10
B. 22
C. 64
D. 76
E. 96

23. A cashier has fifteen $5 bills. How much money does he have?

A. $15
B. $25
C. $75
D. $150
E. $175

24. How many 2-foot lengths can be cut from the string shown below?

12 ft

A. 2
B. 4
C. 6
D. 12
E. 24

LESSON 3

HiSET Exam Calculator Skills

KEY IDEAS

- This lesson walks you through how to utilize one sample scientific calculator, the Texas Instruments TI-30XS MultiView™. It is important to note that this may NOT be the type of calculator provided to you by your testing center. Regardless, it will give you practice to become familiar with scientific calculators and their keys.
- Use the calculator when you think it will save you time or improve your accuracy.

If you take the paper version of the HiSET exam, you will be able to use a handheld four-function or scientific calculator provided to you by your testing center. You may NOT bring your own calculator with you on Test Day. If you take the computer version of the HiSET exam, you will have access to an on-screen calculator that contains all of the basic functions you'll need: addition, subtraction, multiplication, division, and square root. See pages 257–258 for more information regarding calculators for both the paper and computer tests.

For illustrative purposes, this lesson will walk you through how to use one sample scientific calculator, the Texas Instruments TI-30XS MultiView™. Some things to keep in mind when using this calculator (or a scientific calculator in general):

- When you are finished with a calculation, use the enter button. (There is no "equals sign" button on this calculator.)
- Every time you begin a calculation, press the clear button above the operation keys to clear the calculator's memory.

Look at the reproduction of the calculator below and follow the examples that demonstrate how to use the calculator's **operation keys**.

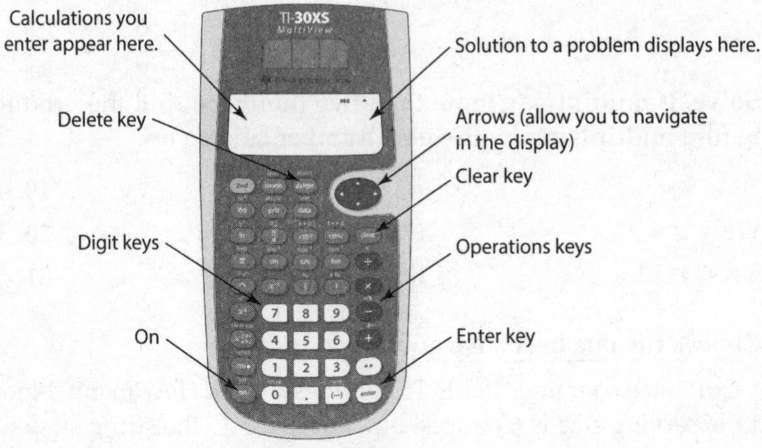

Example 1: Add 63 + 97 + 58 + 32 + 81.

1. Always clear a calculator before starting a new computation. On the TI-30XS MultiView™, use the *clear* key.	clear
2. Enter each number followed by the plus sign. As you type, the numbers and plus signs will appear on the calculator's screen. If you make a mistake, press *delete* to go back and reenter a number.	63 + 97 + 58 + 32 + 81
3. Press *enter* to find the total.	enter
The total, **331**, will appear on the right-hand side of the display:	**331**

Example 2: Find the difference between 15,789 and 9,332.

1. Always clear a calculator before starting a new computation.	clear
2. Enter the greater number first, followed by the minus operator. Note: Use the minus key that is on the right side of the calculator with the other operation symbols. Don't use the (–) key at the bottom of the calculator; that key is used to enter a negative number.	15789 −
3. Enter the number being subtracted.	9332
4. Press the *enter* key to find the answer.	enter
The answer **6457** will appear on the right-hand side of the display.	**6457**

Example 3: Find the product of 309 and 68.

1. Always clear a calculator before starting a new computation.	clear
2. Enter the first number, followed by the multiplication operator. (The multiplication sign will appear in the display as an asterisk rather than an ×, but the *multiplication key* looks like an ×.)	309 ×
3. Enter the next number.	68
4. Press the *enter* key to find the product.	enter
The answer **21012** will appear on the right-hand side of the display.	**21012**

Example 4: Divide 12,456 by 12.

1. Always clear a calculator before starting a new computation.	clear
2. Enter the number to be divided first, followed by the division operator.	12456 ÷
3. Enter the number you are dividing by.	12
4. Press the *enter* key to find the quotient.	enter
The answer **1038** will appear on the right-hand side of the display.	**1038**

A. Practice solving the following problems on your calculator.

1. 19 + 26 + 85 + 23 =

2. 2,579 – 1,392 =

3. 4 × 28 × 7 =

4. 2,568 ÷ 107 =

5. 12,356 + 14,728 =

6. 107,899 – 93,457 =

7. 209 × 56 =

8. 972 ÷ 18 =

9. 20,540 ÷ 13 =

B. Choose the one correct answer to each question.

10. Dan bought a used car with 16,741 miles on it. If the car now has 42,920 miles on it, how many miles has Dan put on the car?

A. 16,741
B. 25,821
C. 26,179
D. 42,920
E. 59,661

11. A shipment of 20 computers arrived at a warehouse. If each computer is valued at $995, what is the total value of the shipment?

A. $995
B. $1,015
C. $1,990
D. $19,900
E. $19,990

Using the 2nd Key for a Second Function

To access some of the functions on the TI-30XS MultiView™, you need to press the 2nd key in the upper left corner of the keypad. This bright green key will activate the second function also shown in green above the corresponding key. To access the second function of a key, press the 2nd key first—do not press it at the same time as the function key. Highlighted below are two commonly used second functions—square root and percent. Use the process shown here for all 2nd function keys.

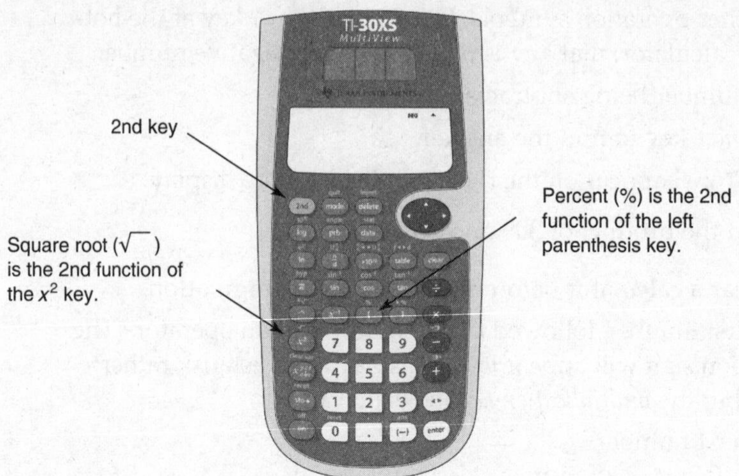

Example 5: Find the square root of 169.	**Keys to Press**	**On the Display**
1. Always clear a calculator before starting a new computation.	clear	
2. Recognize that square root is a 2nd function over the x^2 key. Press the 2nd key. (Note that the term 2nd now appears in the upper left corner of the display.)	2nd	2nd
3. Next, press the x^2 key to activate the square root function in green over the key. You will see a blinking cursor under the square root.	$\sqrt{}$ / x^2	$\sqrt{\square}$
4. Now that you have the square root function, enter the number. The number will appear under the square root symbol in the display.	169	$\sqrt{169}$▶
5. Press the enter key to find the square root. The answer, **13**, will appear on the right-hand side of the display.	enter	$\sqrt{169}$ 13

For more information about square roots, see pages 372–373.

Remember: For all 2nd functions, (1) press the 2nd key first to activate the 2nd function, (2) press the key, and (3) enter the numbers.

PRACTICE 3.2

Example 6: Find the part if you are given the percent and the whole. Find 10 percent of 500.

1. Always clear a calculator before starting a new computation. — clear
2. Enter the number you want to find the percent of. — 500
3. Press the multiplication sign. — ×
4. Enter the percent number. — 10
5. Press the *2nd* key and then press the open, or left, parenthesis key to activate the percent function. 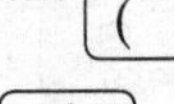
6. Press the *enter* key to find the answer. — enter

The answer, **50**, will appear on the right-hand side of the display. Ten percent of 500 is 50. — **50**

Example 7: Find the percent if you are given the whole and the part. What percent of 240 is 60?

1. Always clear a calculator before starting a new computation. — clear
2. Enter the part. — 60
3. Press the division sign. 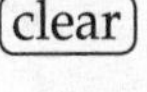
4. Enter the whole. — 240
5. Press the *2nd* key and then press the close, or right, parenthesis symbol. This tells the calculator to translate the answer into a percent. 
6. Press the *enter* key to find the answer. — enter

The answer, 25%, will appear on the right-hand side of the display. Sixty is 25% of 240. — **25%**

For more information about percents, see pages 314–315.

A. Practice solving the following problems on your calculator.

1. $\sqrt{625}$

2. $\sqrt{324}$

3. $\sqrt{1225}$

4. Find 20% of 680.

5. Find 10% of 1250.

6. 15 is what percent of 300?

7. Find 5% of 40.

8. Find 30% of 450.

9. 20 is what percent of 400?

B. Choose the <u>one best</u> answer to each question.

10. Tanya paid 20% of $1,680 as a down payment. How much was the down payment?

A. $20
B. $168
C. $336
D. $840
E. $3,360

11. Aaron received a credit of $48 on a purchase of $960. What percent of $960 is $48?

A. 2%
B. 5%
C. 20%
D. 48%
E. 912%

Number and Quantity Part I: Problem Solving

LESSON 4

Word Problems

KEY IDEAS

- Successful math problem solvers use a five-step process.
- Read carefully to understand the question and select only the information needed to answer it.
- When you have found an answer, check that it makes sense.

To pass the Mathematics Test, you will need to solve word problems. These questions are easier to manage if you use a **five-step problem-solving process**. Practice this process with word problems in this book.

Step 1. What is the **question** asking me to find?

Read the problem carefully. State the question in your own words.

Step 2. What **information** from the problem do I need?

Select only *the information you need to answer the question.*

Step 3. Which **operation** do I need to perform—addition, subtraction, multiplication, or division?

Choose from one of the four operations above based on your understanding of the question.

Step 4. What is my **solution**?

Carry out the operation with the numbers you chose in step 2.

Step 5. Does my answer **make sense**?

Look back to make sure that you answered the question. Check that your answer makes sense.

To help you decide which operation to use, keep the following ideas in mind.

You...	in order to...
add	combine amounts of different sizes
subtract	find the difference between amounts
multiply	combine the same amount multiple times
divide	separate one amount into equal-sized groups

HiSET EXAM TIP

Some questions on the Mathematics Test may include information that is not needed to answer the specific question. In multiple-choice questions, wrong answer choices may be based on mistakenly using this "extra" information, so read carefully.

Example 1: To cover a sofa, Sophia needs 12 yards of fabric that costs $14 per yard. How many yards does Sophia need for 3 sofas?

A. 4
B. 36
C. 42
D. 168
E. 504

The correct answer is **(B) 36 yards** of fabric. The question asked you to find the total number of yards of fabric Sophia needs for 3 sofas. Note that the cost of a yard of fabric is not needed to answer the question.

Since you were asked to find the amount of fabric for 3 sofas, you should multiply 12 yards × 3 sofas = 36 yards. Here are three common errors to avoid:

- If you had mistakenly divided, you would have gotten the incorrect answer of 4 yards of fabric for 3 sofas.
- If you had used the $14 price per yard and multiplied by either 3 sofas or 12 yards, you would have been tempted by wrong answers 42 or 168. However, the cost per yard is not needed.
- If you had multiplied all 3 numbers together (12 × 14 × 3), you would have chosen incorrect answer choice (E).

PRACTICE 4.1

1. Peter wants to repaint his 700-square-foot apartment. He calculates that he has 3500 square feet of wall space to paint. (He will not paint the floor or the ceiling.) If each gallon of paint will cover 350 square feet of wall space, how many gallons will Peter need?

   A. 2
   B. 5
   C. 10
   D. 15
   E. 20

2. For a family get-together, Darryl wants to be sure that each child gets 2 party favors. The party favors cost $3 each, and there are 11 children coming. How many party favors will Darryl need?

   A. 9
   B. 11
   C. 18
   D. 22
   E. 33

3. Sarah and Kate live 18 miles apart, and they both work at the same office. If Sarah lives 25 miles from the office and Kate lives 30 miles from the office, how many miles farther from the office does Kate live than Sarah?

   A. 5
   B. 7
   C. 12
   D. 15
   E. 18

4. The Navarro family uses an average of 225 gallons of water per day, 5 gallons of which goes through the family's water filter. The Navarros' water filter can process 450 gallons before it needs to be replaced. After how many days of average water use will the family need to replace their filter?

   A. 2
   B. 9
   C. 45
   D. 90
   E. 225

Questions 5 and 6 are based on the following information.

Joyce owns a beauty salon, and she has posted the following information in her salon.

Service	Minutes to Complete	Price
Manicure	30	$15
Pedicure	30	$25
Manicure & Pedicure	45	$35
Facial	45	$45
Makeover	60	$60

5. How many minutes will it take Joyce to give 3 pedicures?

   A. 30
   B. 55
   C. 60
   D. 75
   E. 90

6. How much more does a customer pay for the makeover than for the manicure & pedicure combination?

   A. $15
   B. $20
   C. $25
   D. $30
   E. $35

---

7. Brandon is planning his part of the local community garden. He has calculated that he can plant 6 seedlings per row, and the garden allots 7 rows to each gardener. What is the maximum number of seedlings Brandon could plant?

   A. 6
   B. 7
   C. 13
   D. 24
   E. 42

Multi-Step Word Problems

The word problems on the previous two pages involved only one operation to solve. However, on the Mathematics Test and other tests, you may need to do several math processes to solve a problem. These are called **multi-step problems**.

When you are working on multi-step problems, there are two important ideas to keep in mind. *What is the question asking me to find?* and *Did I answer the question?*

Review this example of a multi-step problem and the problem-solving process below.

Example 1: To win a prize, Sarah's daughter has to sell 75 boxes of cookies in 3 days. If she sold 16 boxes on day 1 and 34 boxes on day 2, how many boxes would she need to sell on day 3 to win the prize?

(1) 18
(2) 25
(3) 50

Step 1. What is the question asking me to find?

The question asks me to find how many boxes Sarah's daughter needs to sell on the third day to make her goal of 75 boxes.

Step 2. What information from the problem do I need?

I know the total number of boxes she needs to sell (75 boxes).

I know how many boxes she sold on day 1 (16 boxes) and day 2 (34 boxes).

Step 3. Do I need to do only one operation, or do I need to do more than one?

I can add to find how many boxes Sarah's daughter has sold so far: 16 + 34 = 50.

However, that doesn't tell me how many boxes she needs to sell on day 3. I need one more step.

Step 4. What is my solution?

75 boxes total – 50 boxes sold = 25 boxes for day 3. The correct answer is (2) ***25.***

Step 5. Does my answer make sense? Did I answer the question?

By taking the additional step, I answered the question of how many boxes need to be sold on day 3.

This sample multi-step problem involved only two operations: adding and subtracting. On the actual test, you may need to do three or more operations to answer a question, so read and think carefully about each problem.

As you think about the example, note the most common mistake people make with multi-step problems. Often they stop short of answering the question. Notice that choice (3) 50 is a **partial solution**, but it is not the answer to the question. Using the five-step problem-solving process will help you avoid that mistake.

PRACTICE 4.2

<u>Questions 1–3</u> **are based on the information below.**

Farhana's produce company distributes to several restaurants. The table below shows how many cases of different produce each restaurant ordered from Farhana's company in July.

Produce Orders in July					
	Asparagus	Boston Lettuce	Carrots	Romaine Lettuce	Tomatoes
Restaurant A	2	3	1	4	3
Restaurant B	4	4	2	2	1
Restaurant C	0	0	3	4	3
Restaurant D	1	2	2	3	4
Restaurant E	3	0	3	2	1

1. If Boston lettuce costs $17 per case and romaine lettuce costs $23 per case, how much did Restaurant D spend on lettuce ordered from Farhana in July?

A. $85
B. $93
C. $97
D. $103
E. $143

2. Delivery costs $2 per case for the first 5 cases and $1 per case for each additional case of produce. What was Restaurant B's delivery charge in July?

A. $10
B. $13
C. $18
D. $20
E. $26

3. If asparagus costs $22 per case and tomatoes cost $15 per case, which of the following restaurants spent the most on asparagus and tomatoes combined?

A. Restaurant A
B. Restaurant B
C. Restaurant C
D. Restaurant D
E. Restaurant E

4. At a certain store, loose-leaf paper comes only in packages of 400 sheets. If a student buys enough paper at this store to fill 3 binders with 150 sheets of paper each, how many sheets will be left over?

A. 17
B. 50
C. 150
D. 350
E. 450

5. Three friends are baking cupcakes for a bake sale. Each batch of 24 cupcakes requires 2 cups of flour. The friends have a single 5-pound bag of flour that contains 19 cups of flour. How many whole batches of cupcakes can they bake?

A. 5
B. 9
C. 38
D. 216
E. 228

6. A certain health insurance plan costs $3,000 per year for a family of six. If each member of the family has $750 in medical expenses in a year, and the plan pays 100% of those expenses, how much will the family save by purchasing the plan?

A. $1,000
B. $1,500
C. $2,000
D. $2,500
E. $3,000

Number and Quantity Part I: Problem Solving

LESSON 5

Distance and Cost

Distance

On the Mathematics Test, you'll see questions that will require you to apply formulas. When a relationship is constant, use a formula to set up the information about how the different parts relate to each other. One of the most commonly tested formulas deals with distance, rate, and time. Distance is a product of the rate at which something travels and the amount of travel time:

$$\text{distance} = \text{rate} \times \text{time}, \quad \text{or} \quad d = rt$$

Notice that letters, or variables, can be used to represent the different parts of a formula. A formula allows you to substitute known values for certain variables and solve for the unknown variable.

Example 1: How many miles can you travel if you drive at an average speed of 55 miles per hour for 3 hours?

1. You know the rate (55 miles per hour) and the time (3 hours). Substitute the values in the distance formula. — distance = 55×3

2. Multiply to find the distance. — $55 \times 3 =$ **165 miles**

Cost

Another helpful formula is the cost formula. It expresses the relationship between cost, the number of units, and rate (price per unit). Note: The word *per* means "for every one unit." The cost formula can be written as follows:

$$\text{total cost} = (\text{number of units}) \times (\text{price per unit}), \quad \text{or} \quad c = nr$$

Example 2: At a bakery, a package of frosted cookies is priced at $3 per package. If a teacher treats her class by buying 4 packages, how much would the cookies cost before tax?

1. You know the number of units (4 packages) and the price per unit ($3 per package). Substitute the values in the cost formula. — $c = nr$; total cost $= 4 \times \$3$

2. Multiply to find the total cost. — $4 \times \$3 =$ **$12**

If you know any two of the three variables in a formula, you can solve for the third variable.

Example 3: Max bought a set of 4 floor mats for $44. How much was the price per floor mat?

1. You know the total cost ($44) and the number of units (4 floor mats). Rewrite the formula to solve for the price per unit (r). — $c = nr$; $r = \frac{c}{n}$

2. Substitute the known values in the cost formula. Divide to find the price per unit. — $\frac{\$44}{4} =$ **$11**

KEY IDEAS

- The following all indicate multiplication:

  $n \times r \quad nr \quad n(r) \quad n \cdot r$

- The following indicate division:

  $c \div n \quad \frac{c}{n}$

- A formula can be rewritten to solve for each of its variables:

  $c = nr \quad \frac{c}{n} = r \quad \frac{c}{r} = n$

  $d = rt \quad \frac{d}{r} = t \quad \frac{d}{t} = r$

HiSET EXAM TIP

Substitute all of the values for variables back into a formula to check your answer.

PRACTICE 5

A. Each problem below includes two of the three variables from either the distance formula or the cost formula. Write the missing variable you need to solve for. Then decide which of the following formula variations you would use in each situation. The first one is done for you.

$d = rt \qquad \frac{d}{r} = t \qquad \frac{d}{t} = r \qquad c = nr \qquad \frac{c}{n} = r \qquad \frac{c}{r} = n$

1. Given: distance and time
   Solve for: rate
   Formula: $\frac{d}{t} = r$
2. Given: rate and time
   Solve for: ___________
   Formula: ___________
3. Given: distance and rate
   Solve for: ___________
   Formula: ___________
4. Given: cost and number of units
   Solve for: ___________
   Formula: ___________
5. Given: number of units and price per unit
   Solve for: ___________
   Formula: ___________
6. Given: cost and price per unit
   Solve for: ___________
   Formula: ___________

B. Use the formulas provided in part A above to help you set up the problems. Solve for the unknown variable.

7. Find the total cost of 4 flats of plants at $12 each.
8. Find the total cost of 12 boxes of cookies if each box costs $3.
9. If 4 tires cost $320, how much does a single tire cost?
10. How many tickets would you get for $25 if raffle tickets cost $5 apiece?
11. If you paid $20 for 10 bus transfer tickets, how much did you pay per ticket?
12. Find the distance traveled by a car averaging 60 miles per hour for 3 hours.
13. Find the distance traveled by a train averaging 50 miles per hour for 4 hours.
14. How long does it take for a bus to travel 25 miles at an average rate of 25 miles per hour?
15. If a train travels 270 miles in 3 hours, what is the train's average speed?
16. How long does it take to complete a delivery route of 75 miles at a rate of 25 miles per hour?

C. Choose the one best answer to each question.

17. A company sold a total of $640 in gift boxes. If the gift boxes cost $20 apiece, how many gift boxes did the company sell?
    A. 32
    B. 120
    C. 320
    D. 660
    E. 1280
18. A truck driver traveled 275 miles in 5 hours. What was his average speed in miles per hour?
    A. 1,375
    B. 280
    C. 270
    D. 75
    E. 55

Number and Quantity Part I: Problem Solving

LESSON 6

Measurement

The English System of Measurement

Measurements are used to describe an object's length, weight, or volume. We also use measurement to describe a quantity of time. Many people and institutions in the United States use the English system of measurement.

KEY IDEAS

- Multiply to change from a larger unit of measure to a smaller one.
- Divide to change from a smaller unit of measure to a larger one.
- When dividing, the remainder is the same unit of measure as the number you are dividing by.

Measurement Equivalencies	
Length 1 foot (ft) = 12 inches (in) 1 yard (yd) = 3 ft 1 mile (mi) = 5280 ft	**Weight** 1 pound (lb) = 16 ounces (oz) 1 ton (t) = 2000 lb
Time 1 minute (min) = 60 seconds (sec) 1 hour (hr) = 60 min 1 day = 24 hr 1 week = 7 days 1 year (yr) = 12 months (mo)	**Volume** 1 cup (c) = 8 fluid ounces (fl oz) 1 pint (pt) = 2 c 1 quart (qt) = 2 pt 1 gallon (gal) = 4 qt

To solve problems, you will need to change from one unit of measure to another. If you need to *change a larger unit of measure to a smaller one,* you need to *multiply.* To change a *smaller unit of measure to a larger one,* you *divide.* Use the measurement equivalencies provided in the chart.

Example 1: A picture frame is 3 ft 8 in long. What is the length of the frame in inches?

1. Change 3 feet to inches using the fact that 1 foot = 12 inches. $3 \text{ ft} \times 12 = 36 \text{ in}$
2. Add the remaining 8 inches. $36 + 8 = 44 \text{ in}$

The picture frame is **44 inches** in length.

Example 2: A package weighs 84 ounces. What is the weight of the package in pounds?

$$\begin{array}{r} 5 \\ 16\overline{)84} \\ -80 \\ \hline 4 \end{array}$$

1. Change 84 ounces to pounds. Because 1 pound = 16 ounces, divide by 16.
2. The remainder is in ounces, the same unit you started with. Therefore, the package weighs **5 lb 4 oz**, or you can express the remainder as a fraction, $5\frac{4}{16} = \mathbf{5\frac{1}{4}}$ **lb.**

You may need to do a series of conversions.

Example 3: A container holds 1.5 gallons. How many cups does the container hold?

1. Change 1.5 gallons to quarts. (Use the fact that 1 gal = 4 qt.) $1.5 \text{ gal} \times 4 = 6 \text{ qt}$
2. Change 6 quarts to pints. (Use the fact that 1 qt = 2 pt.) $6 \text{ qt} \times 2 = 12 \text{ pt}$
3. Change 12 pints to cups. (Use the fact that 1 pt = 2 c.) $12 \text{ pt} \times 2 = 24 \text{ c}$

The container holds **24 cups.**

PRACTICE 6.1

In a measurement problem, you may need to add, subtract, multiply, or divide measurements. You can only perform mathematical operations on measurements that use the same unit.

Example 4: A deck requires pieces of railing that are 5 ft 9 in, 15 ft 4 in, and 8 ft 6 in. What is the total length of railing needed?

1. Write the measurements in a column, aligning like units of measure.
2. Add like units.
3. Simplify the answer. (Change 19 in to 1 ft 7 in, and add to 28 ft.)

5 ft	9 in
15 ft	4 in
8 ft	6 in
28 ft	19 in

28 ft + 1 ft 7 in = 29 ft 7 in

The deck requires **29 ft 7 in** of railing.

To multiply a measurement by a whole number, multiply the units of measure separately. Then simplify the result.

Example 5: Tony has five lengths of plastic pipe, each measuring 6 ft 10 in. What is the combined length of the pipe?

1. Multiply each part of the measurement by 5.
2. Simplify using the fact that 1 ft = 12 in.

The combined length is **34 ft 2 in.**

6 ft 10 in
× 5
30 ft 50 in = 30 ft + 4 ft 2 in = 34 ft 2 in

A. Solve.

1. How many inches are equal to 4 feet?

2. How many minutes are equal to 420 seconds?

3. How many hours are in 3 days?

4. Convert 40 fluid ounces to pints.

5. Five gallons are equal to how many quarts?

6. How many tons is 11,000 pounds?

7. Four yards equal how many inches?

8. How many hours are equal to 720 minutes?

9. How many cups are in two gallons?

B. Choose the one best answer to each question.

Questions 10 and 11 refer to the following information.

> **Portable Air Cooler**
> Duracool R612
> 3.75 gallon capacity
> Runs 6 hours without refilling
> width: 27 in; depth: 16 in
> height: 13 3/4 in
> shipping weight: 26 lb

10. Bob wants to buy an air cooler. He knows the capacity of several other models in quarts. Which of the following expressions could he use to find the capacity for this model in quarts?

A. 3.75 × 2
B. 3.75 ÷ 2
C. 3.75 × 3
D. 3.75 × 4
E. 3.75 ÷ 4

11. Which of these measurements is equal to the width of the Duracool R612?

A. 1 ft $1\frac{3}{4}$ in
B. 2 ft 1 in
C. 2 ft 3 in
D. 213 ft
E. 2 ft 7 in

---

12. Max needs to ship six identical packages, each weighing 3 lb 12 oz. What is the total weight of the shipment?

A. 15 lb 6 oz
B. 19 lb 2 oz
C. 22 lb 8 oz
D. 24 lb 12 oz
E. 25 lb 2 oz

The Metric System

The metric system is the measurement system used in most of the countries of the world. The main unit of length in the metric system is the **meter** (m). The **gram** (g) is the basic metric measure of mass (or weight). The basic unit of volume is called the **liter** (*l*). To form units of measure, add prefixes to the basic units described above.

milli- (m) means one-thousandth *centi-* (c) means one-hundredth *deci-* (d) means one-tenth	*deka-* (da) means ten *hecto-* (h) means one hundred *kilo-* (k) means one thousand

Therefore, a kilometer (km) equals 1,000 meters, a milligram (mg) equals one one-thousandth gram, and a centiliter (cl) equals one one-hundredth liter.

Memorize the following chart. As in our decimal place-value system, each column on the chart is 10 times the column to its right. To convert between metric units, count the spaces from the unit you are converting from to the unit you are converting to. Then move the decimal point that number of place values in the same direction.

kilo-	*hecto-*	*deka-*	*meter*	*deci-*	*centi-*	*milli-*
(km)	(hm)	(dam)	(m)	(dm)	(cm)	(mm)
1000 m	100 m	10 m	1 m	0.1 m	0.01 m	0.001 m

Although the chart uses the meter as the basic unit, the chart can also be used with liters (*l*) and grams (g).

Example 1: How many millimeters (mm) are equal to 3 centimeters (cm)?

1. Find *milli-* and *centi-* on the chart. The prefix *milli-* is one place to the right of the prefix *centi-*; therefore, you need to move the decimal point one place to the right to convert from centimeters to millimeters.

2. For example, 3 cm = 3.0 cm = **30 mm.**

Example 2: How many grams (g) are equal to 6,400 milligrams (mg)?

1. Start in the *milli-* column. The basic unit (or ones column) is three columns to the left. Move the decimal point three place-value columns to the left.

2. For example, 6,400 mg = 6,400. mg = **6.4 g.**

You may want to memorize the following common conversions:

1,000 meters = 1 kilometer — 1 meter = 1,000 millimeters

1 meter = 100 centimeters — 1 centimeter = 10 millimeters

Solving Problems with Metric Measurement

Metric measurements are written as decimal numbers. Therefore, you can perform operations with metric measurements using the rules for adding, subtracting, multiplying, and dividing decimals.

Example 3: Three metal rods measure 1.5 meters, 1.85 meters, and 450 centimeters. What is the total length of the rods in meters?

1. Read the question carefully. You are asked to find the total length in *meters*.

2. The first two measures are written in meters. Convert the third measure to meters.
450 cm = 4.5 m

3. Add using the rules for adding decimals. The total is **7.85 m.**

PRACTICE 6.2

Example 4: Alex is a buyer for a rug retail store. He plans to order 25 acrylic rugs to sell in the store. The shipping weight for each rug is 7.8 kilograms. What is the shipping weight in kilograms of the entire order?

1. Multiply the weight of one rug (7.8 kg) by 25.
2. The weight of 25 rugs is **195 kilograms.** Notice that the answer has the same unit of measure as the number you multiplied.

Note: A common mistake when solving metric problems is putting the decimal point in the wrong place. To avoid errors, estimate before you work the problem. Compare your answer to the estimate.

A. Solve.

1. How many meters equal 5 kilometers?

2. 600 centimeters equal how many meters?

3. How many milligrams equal 4 grams?

4. Eight kilograms equal how many grams?

5. How many centiliters is 40.5 liters equal to?

6. How many liters are equal to 1500 ml?

7. How many grams is 250 milligrams equal to?

8. How many meters are in 30 kilometers?

9. How many cl is 0.75 *l* equal to?

10. Fifty grams equal how many kilograms?

11. How many liters is 35,200 milliliters equal to?

12. How many centimeters are in 15 meters?

B. Choose the <u>one best answer</u> to each question.

13. A can of machine oil holds 118.3 ml. How many liters of machine oil does the can hold?

A. 0.001183
B. 0.01183
C. 0.1183
D. 1.183
E. 11.83

14. In a vitamin supplement, each capsule contains 500 milligrams of vitamins. How many grams of vitamins are found in each capsule?

A. 5,000
B. 500
C. 50
D. 5
E. 0.5

15. A type of bonding gel comes in a small container that holds 4 g of the gel. How many of the small containers could be filled from 2.5 kg of the gel?

A. 6,250
B. 625
C. 62
D. 10
E. 6

16. Sharon buys 4.8 meters of ribbon to use as trim on a set of kitchen curtains. She actually uses 350 centimeters. How many centimeters of the ribbon are left?

A. 13
B. 44.5
C. 130
D. 302
E. 445

LESSON 7

Measurement Accuracy

KEY IDEAS

- A good test for the level of accuracy to use in measurement is "what makes sense."
- As the unit of measure increases, the accuracy in measurement decreases.
- The right method of measurement is representative of what's being measured and appropriate in scale.

In the previous section, you saw different units of measurement for length, time, weight, and volume. When determining the weight of, say, a taco, you could say that it weighs about 2.9 ounces, 0.18125 pounds, or 0.00008221 metric tons. However, in everyday life, it doesn't make sense to use the larger units of measure for something as small as a taco.

As you practice converting measurements into their equivalents, be sure to take notice of whether one unit of measure or the other makes sense for use in the real world. The HiSET exam can test this both directly and indirectly—in the latter case, being mindful of "what makes sense" can often help you avoid errors that you would otherwise make.

Example 1: On Wednesday afternoon, Bob purchased a small bag of gummy bears at a local candy store. Which of the following could be the weight listed on the package?

A. 1.42 g
B. 142 g
C. 1,420 g
D. 0.0142 kg
E. 14.2 kg

The correct answer is **(B)**, which is about 5 oz worth. (A) is roughly the weight of half of one bear, (C) is about 3.13 lb (hardly a small bag), and (E) would be ten times that, or over 31 lb! (D) may have been tempting, as 0.0142 kg is about half an ounce, but a bag that small would not list the weight in kg.

Determining an Appropriate Method of Measurement

HiSET EXAM TIP

Determining an appropriate level of accuracy is similar to using estimation, a skill that helps tremendously throughout the math section in making problems quicker and easier to solve.

To choose an appropriate measurement, you'll need the right tool or method, depending on what you're trying to measure. It would be very appropriate to measure the taco referenced earlier with a kitchen scale but not with a roadside scale used to weigh trucks. The examples below illustrate a couple of ways you can be tested on this concept.

Example 2: Samantha plans to paint her bedroom over the summer and needs to figure out how much paint to buy. Which of the following tools would allow her to do so most effectively?

A. Ruler
B. Bathroom scale
C. Tape measure
D. Measuring cup
E. Global positioning system (GPS)

The correct answer is (C). While paint can be measured in a measuring cup, the critical information needed here is the size of the room. A ruler would work but it wouldn't be as effective as a tape measure since a room is a number of feet long and wide and a tape measure is longer than a ruler.

PRACTICE 7

Example 3: For this year's community talent show, Cindy wants to order the contestants so that the most anticipated act appears last. Which of the following would be the best way for Cindy to determine the most anticipated act?

A. Flip a coin several times
B. Ask her family members
C. Poll all of her friends and coworkers
D. Randomly survey 500 people from the community
E. Ask the talent show participants

The correct answer is **(D)**. In this type of problem, the key to getting an appropriate measurement is ensuring that the sample selected is representative of what you're trying to measure. Since the show is for the community, a random sample of 500 will give a good indication of the community's preference as a whole.

A. Would ounces, pounds, or tons be the most appropriate unit of measure?

1. A bookcase full of books
2. A small bag of potato chips
3. An oven-roasted turkey
4. A minivan
5. A commercial plane
6. One serving of orange juice
7. The amount of seafood sold on a single day at a busy restaurant
8. The amount of spice used in a pot of chicken noodle soup

B. Choose the <u>one best answer</u> to each question.

9. The gas tank in Madeline's car holds 11 units of gasoline. A unit is most likely a(n)

A. ounce
B. cup
C. quart
D. gallon
E. barrel

10. Jeremy is trying to measure his dog with a ruler. Which of the following is the **smallest** unit he can expect to be accurate to?

A. millimeter
B. centimeter
C. meter
D. yard
E. kilometer

11. Susan is preparing an antique box two inches in length for an online auction. If she wants to give bidders an accurate sense of its size, the best item to photograph it next to is

A. a similar antique box that is one inch in length
B. a US quarter
C. a chocolate chip cookie
D. her purse
E. a celery stalk

12. The tree in Judy's backyard is roughly the height of her house. Which of the following is most likely the tree's height?

A. 7 in
B. 4 ft
C. 6 yd
D. 25 yd
E. 1 mi

Number and Quantity Part I: Problem Solving Practice Questions

Directions: Choose the best answer to each question.

1. A beverage container holds 12 servings. If the serving size is 8 ounces, how many ounces does the container hold in all?

   A. 20
   B. 32
   C. 64
   D. 48
   E. 96

2. Sales at 3 concession stands are $839, $527, and $726. What is the total amount in sales?

   A. $1,581
   B. $2,092
   C. $2,178
   D. $2,517
   E. $3,092

3. If you want to cut 24 two-foot braces, how many boards of the length shown below would you need?

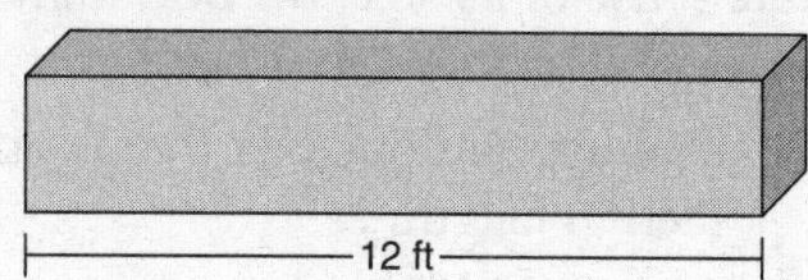

   A. 2
   B. 4
   C. 6
   D. 12
   E. 24

4. Using your calculator, find the value of $\sqrt{441}$.

   A. 11
   B. 19
   C. 21
   D. 221
   E. 441

5. Angelo bought a used car with 39,451 miles on it. If the car now has 70,040 miles on it, how many miles has Angelo driven the car?

   A. 30,589
   B. 39,459
   C. 41,549
   D. 70,040
   E. 109,491

6. Use your calculator to solve this problem. If Emory paid 20% of $3,280 as a down payment, how much was the down payment?

   A. $164
   B. $328
   C. $656
   D. $1,640
   E. $6,560

7. Inventory shows that a warehouse has 45 printers in stock. If each printer is valued at $125, what is the total value of the printer inventory?

   A. $5,625
   B. $4,750
   C. $170
   D. $80
   E. $45

8. Linda can drive 180 miles in 3 hours. On Tuesday, she drove for 7 hours at that rate. How many miles did she drive on Tuesday?

   A. 60
   B. 360
   C. 420
   D. 600
   E. 1,260

9. Janelle wants to drive from Danville to Brownsville. If she averages 60 miles per hour, how many hours will it take her to drive the distance?

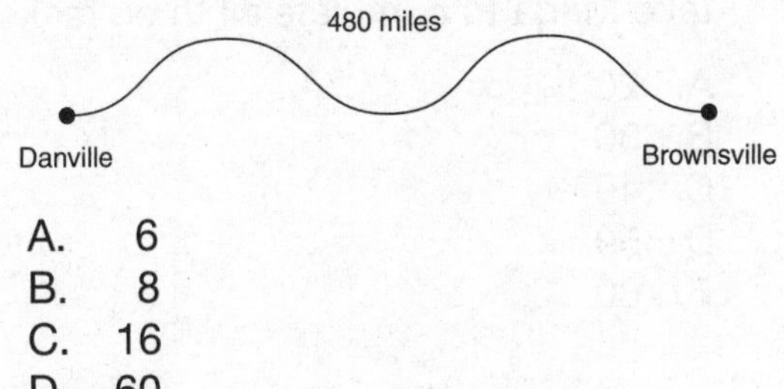

A. 6
B. 8
C. 16
D. 60
E. 540

10. A company sold a total of $1,440 in gift bears for Valentine's Day. If the gift bears cost $15 apiece, how many gift bears did it sell?

A. 15
B. 96
C. 144
D. 720
E. 1,440

11. In addition to interest charges, Richard's credit card company charges a $25 late fee for payments made after the payment due date. If he was charged a late fee for 8 monthly bills, how much could he have saved by paying the bills on time?

A. $200
B. $100
C. $80
D. $33
E. $25

12. A waiter has seven $5 bills and eighteen $1 bills from tips. In all, how much does he have in tips?

A. $18
B. $25
C. $35
D. $43
E. $53

13. April has taken her car in for the recommended oil and filter change every 3,500 miles. If April bought her car brand-new, and the odometer now shows just over 17,500 miles, how many oil changes has her car received?

A. 3
B. 5
C. 14
D. 123
E. 1,236

14. A clinic treated 536 children over a 4-month period. At this rate, how many children did the clinic treat in 1 month?

A. 134
B. 159
C. 536
D. 540
E. 2,144

15. Attendance at a local play was 438 Friday night, 820 Saturday night, and 636 Sunday afternoon. How many more people attended the play on Sunday than on Friday?

A. 198
B. 278
C. 382
D. 438
E. 636

16. Raquel has 4 payments left on her car. If each payment is $268, how much does she still owe on her car?

A. $268
B. $536
C. $668
D. $972
E. $1072

17. In what order should items weighing 51 pounds, 40 pounds, 48 pounds, and 44 pounds be stacked if you want them in order from heaviest to lightest?

A. 51, 44, 40, 48
B. 48, 44, 40, 51
C. 40, 44, 48, 51
D. 51, 48, 44, 40
E. 51, 40, 44, 48

18. Which of the following correctly shows 2,354,769 rounded to the nearest ten thousand?

A. 2,400,000
B. 2,355,000
C. 2,350,000
D. 2,300,000
E. 2,000,000

19. What is the total weight in pounds of the packages below?

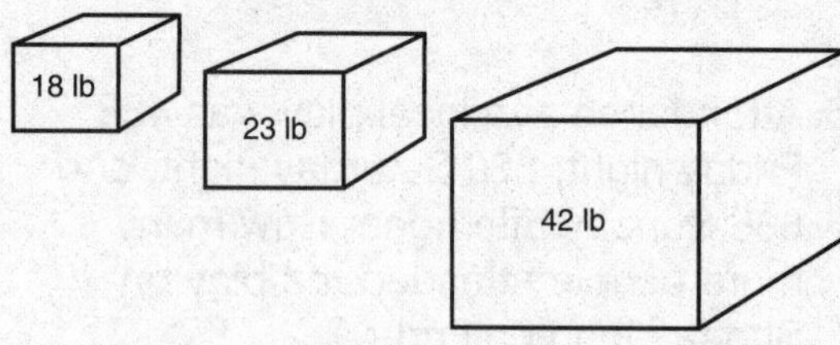

A. 93
B. 83
C. 65
D. 60
E. 42

20. Jason paid a $14 dinner bill with a $20 bill. How much change should he receive?

A. $6
B. $7
C. $12
D. $14
E. $34

21. Maria spent 8 minutes installing a new showerhead, 33 minutes rodding out a drain, and 18 minutes fixing a leaking faucet. About how many minutes did it take Maria to complete all three tasks?

A. 20
B. 30
C. 40
D. 50
E. 60

22. Carla drove 248 miles in 4 hours. What was her average rate of speed, in miles per hour?

A. 42
B. 48
C. 52
D. 58
E. 62

23. A bulk bag of nuts contains 144 ounces of nuts. If the nuts are packaged in smaller 8-ounce bags, how many bags will there be?

A. 6
B. 8
C. 12
D. 16
E. 18

24. If you drove 299 miles on 9 gallons of gasoline, about how many miles per gallon did the car get?

A. 10
B. 20
C. 30
D. 270
E. 300

25. Nydia works in a photo lab. She uses 1 pt 6 fl oz of film developer from a full container. If the capacity of the container is 3 qt, how much developer is left in the container?

A. 1 qt 6 fl oz
B. 1 qt 10 fl oz
C. 2 qt 2 fl oz
D. 2 qt 6 fl oz
E. 2 qt 10 fl oz

26. A shipment of 33 crates like the one shown below is delivered. Approximately how many pounds did workers unload?

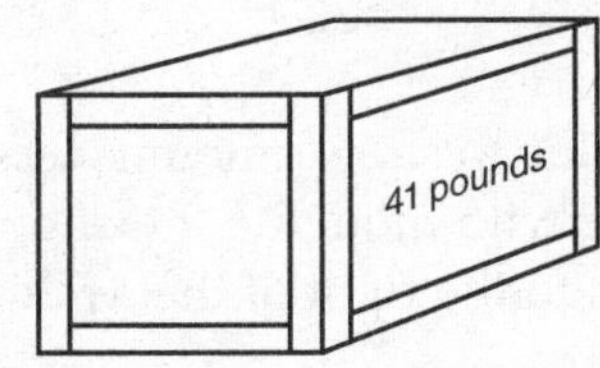

A. 40
B. 120
C. 720
D. 1200
E. 2,000

27. Four friends bought a birthday cake for $21 and balloons for $15. If they divided the cost equally, how much did each friend pay toward the birthday party?

A. $4
B. $5
C. $9
D. $12
E. $36

28. David paid $20 toward a dinner bill of $128. If the remainder of the bill is divided equally among the remaining 9 people in the group, how much should each person other than David pay?

A. $12
B. $16
C. $18
D. $20
E. $108

29. A driver traveled 4 hours at an average rate of 65 miles per hour. How many miles did the person drive?

A. 61
B. 69
C. 130
D. 240
E. 260

30. Using the following information, how much would a large pizza with 3 toppings cost?

Large 1-Topping Pizza for $14 $2 for Each Additional Topping

A. $20
B. $18
C. $16
D. $14
E. $6

31. Bagels are 2 for $1. What is the maximum number of bagels you could buy for $7?

A. 7
B. 10
C. 14
D. 15
E. 16

32. How many months would it take to save $1800 at $75 per month?

A. 12
B. 16
C. 18
D. 20
E. 24

33. How many 45-page documents would a binder hold if its maximum capacity is 630 sheets of paper?

A. 10
B. 11
C. 12
D. 13
E. 14

STUDY ADVICE

How did these practice questions go? If you understood the concepts but made simple addition or subtraction mistakes, congratulate yourself and try to be more careful about small math errors. If this practice set did not go well, review the examples in this chapter.

Number and Quantity Part II: Decimals and Fractions

LESSON 1

Decimal Basics

KEY IDEAS

- The decimal point separates the whole number from the decimal part.
- To round decimals, use the same rules as with rounding whole numbers.
- Adding zeros to the right of the last digit after the decimal does not change the number's value.

HiSET EXAM TIP

The Mathematics Test may show a zero written before the decimal point. The zero does not change the value of the number. Example: 0.75 = .75

The Decimal System

Decimals are numbers that use place value to show amounts less than 1. You already use decimals when working with money. For example, in the amount $10.25, you know that the digits to the right of the **decimal point** represent cents, or hundredths of a dollar.

The first four decimal place values are labeled on the chart below.

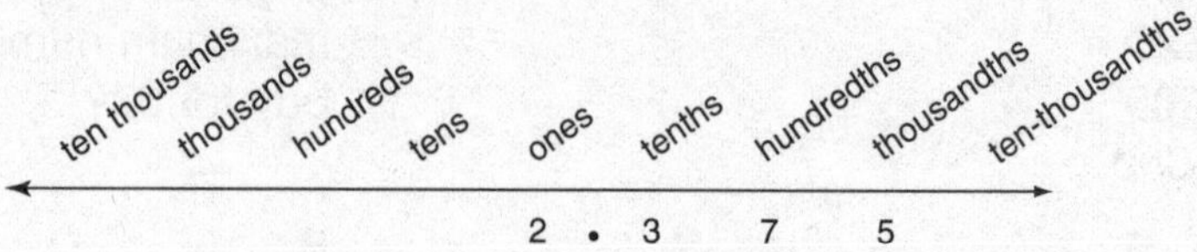

The number 2.375 is shown on the chart. Read *and* in place of the decimal point. After reading the decimal part, say the place value of the last decimal digit. This number would be read "two *and* three hundred seventy-five *thousandths*."

Rounding

Round decimals the same way you round whole numbers.

Example 1: A calculator display reads 3.62835. Round to the hundredths place.

1. Look at the digit to the right of the hundredths place.	3.62[8]35
2. If the digit to the right is 5 or greater, round up. If the digit is less than 5, don't change the number. Then drop all digits to the right of the place you are rounding to.	Since 8 is greater than 5, round up. 3.62835 rounds to **3.63.**

Comparing and Ordering

Comparing decimals is similar to comparing whole numbers.

Example 2: Matt ran the 400-meter race in 45.8 seconds. Alonzo ran the same race in 45.66 seconds. Which runner had the faster time?

1. Line up the decimal points. Add a zero at the **end** of 45.8 so that both times have the same number of digits after the decimal.	45.80 45.66
2. Compare the decimal parts of the numbers as though they were whole numbers. **Alonzo's time was faster.**	80 is greater than 66, so 45.8 is greater than 45.66.

PRACTICE 1

When you compare more than two numbers, it is helpful to compare one place-value column at a time, working from left to right.

Example 3: Arrange the numbers 0.85, 1.8, 0.8, and 0.819 in order from greatest to least.

1. Write the numbers in a column, lining up the decimal points. Add zeros so that the numbers have the same number of decimal places.

   0.850
   1.800
   0.800
   0.819

2. Compare the digits, working from left to right. Only 1.8 has a whole number part, so it is greatest. The remaining numbers each have 8 in the tenths column. Looking at the hundredths column, 0.85 is next, followed by 0.819. The least number is 0.8.

   In order: **1.8**
   0.85
   0.819
   0.8

A. Round these numbers as directed.

1. Round 3.75 to the tenths place.

2. Round 5.908 to the ones place.

3. A calculator display reads 0.4285714. Round to the nearest hundredth.

4. Round 0.66667 to the nearest thousandth.

5. Round 8.125 to the nearest tenth.

6. A calculator display reads 2.7142857. Round to the nearest thousandth.

B. In each of the following pairs, which number is greater?

7. 0.45 or 0.449

8. 0.008 or 0.08

9. 4.68 or 4.086

10. 0.75 or 1.85

11. 1.0275 or 1.029

12. 0.14 or 0.104

C. Write these numbers in order from least to greatest.

13. 5.6 5.08 5.8 5.802

14. 0.1136 0.12 0.2 0.115

15. 14.005 4.52 4.8 4.667

16. 0.8023 0.8 0.803 0.823

D. Choose the one best answer to each question.

17. In a circuit board assembly, the weights of three parts are 0.572 grams, 0.0785 grams, and 0.6 grams. Which of the following lists the weights in order from greatest to least?

A. 0.0785 g, 0.572 g, 0.6 g
B. 0.6 g, 0.0785 g, 0.572 g
C. 0.0785 g, 0.6 g, 0.572 g
D. 0.572 g, 0.6 g, 0.0785 g
E. 0.6 g, 0.572 g, 0.0758 g

18. Which of the following correctly shows 1.3815 rounded to the nearest hundredth?

A. 1.5
B. 1.4
C. 1.382
D. 1.381
E. 1.38

Number and Quantity Part II: Decimals and Fractions

LESSON 2

Decimal Operations

Addition and Subtraction

Adding decimals is much like adding whole numbers. The trick is to make sure you have lined up the place-value columns correctly. You can do this by writing the numbers in a column and carefully lining up the decimal points.

Example 1: Add $0.37 + 13.5 + 2.638$.

1. Write the numbers in a column, lining up the decimal points.
2. You may add placeholder zeros so that the decimals have the same number of decimal places.

$$\begin{array}{r} 0.370 \\ 13.500 \\ +\,2.638 \\ \hline \end{array}$$

3. Add. Start on the right and add each column. Regroup, or carry, as you would with whole numbers.
4. Place the decimal point in the answer directly below the decimal points in the problem.

$$\begin{array}{r} {\scriptstyle 1\,1} \\ 0.370 \\ 13.500 \\ +\,2.638 \\ \hline \mathbf{16.508} \end{array}$$

To subtract decimals, write the numbers in a column with the greater number on top. Make sure the decimal points are in a line.

Example 2: Find the difference between 14.512 and 8.7.

1. Write the numbers in a column, lining up the decimal points. Add placeholder zeros so that the numbers have the same number of decimal places.

$$\begin{array}{r} 14.512 \\ -\,8.700 \\ \hline \end{array}$$

2. Subtract. Regroup, or borrow, as needed. Place the decimal point in the answer directly in line with the decimal points in the problem.

$$\begin{array}{r} {\scriptstyle 13\ 15} \\ 14.512 \\ -\,8.700 \\ \hline \mathbf{5.812} \end{array}$$

The greater number may have fewer or no decimal places. In the next example, a decimal is subtracted from a whole number.

Example 3: What does 9 minus 3.604 equal?

1. Line up the place-value columns. Put a decimal point after the whole number 9 and add placeholder zeros.

$$\begin{array}{r} 9.000 \\ -3.604 \\ \hline \end{array}$$

2. Subtract, regrouping as needed. Place the decimal point in the answer.

$$\begin{array}{r} {\scriptstyle 8\ \ 9\ \ 9\ 10} \\ 9.000 \\ -3.604 \\ \hline \mathbf{5.396} \end{array}$$

KEY IDEAS

- Always add and subtract like place-value columns.
- Always line up the decimal points when you write a problem in columns.
- When adding or subtracting, place the decimal point in the answer directly below the decimal point in the problem.

HiSET EXAM TIP

To make sure that your answer makes sense, mentally round the numbers to the nearest whole number and then add or subtract. The result should be close to your answer.

PRACTICE 2.1

A. Solve.

1. $\begin{array}{r} 4.025 \\ +\,3.971 \\ \hline \end{array}$

2. $\begin{array}{r} 6.5 \\ +\,4.008 \\ \hline \end{array}$

3. $\begin{array}{r} 2.8 \\ +\,9.46 \\ \hline \end{array}$

4. $\begin{array}{r} 8.04 \\ -\,2.19 \\ \hline \end{array}$

5. $\begin{array}{r} 8.5 \\ -\,1.074 \\ \hline \end{array}$

6. $\begin{array}{r} 10 \\ -\,7.89 \\ \hline \end{array}$

7. $\begin{array}{r} 17.294 \\ +\,0.8 \\ \hline \end{array}$

8. $\begin{array}{r} 4.07 \\ +\,1.047 \\ \hline \end{array}$

9. $\begin{array}{r} 17.52 \\ +\,3.8 \\ \hline \end{array}$

10. $\begin{array}{r} 3.8 \\ -\,2.905 \\ \hline \end{array}$

11. $\begin{array}{r} 14.64 \\ -\,10.8 \\ \hline \end{array}$

12. $\begin{array}{r} 100.5 \\ -\,98.15 \\ \hline \end{array}$

13. $0.236 + 2.4 + 2.87 =$
14. $38.06 - 16.9 =$
15. $0.006 + 0.09 + 0.549 =$
16. $8.5 - 6.074 =$
17. $1.02 - 0.87 =$
18. $0.45 + 1.8 + 0.07 + 2.56 =$
19. $12.5 - 0.7 =$
20. $25 - 10.984 =$
21. $0.01 + 2.052 + 0.96 + 1.5 =$
22. $12.9 - 10.54 =$
23. $0.68 + 12.3 + 4.9 =$
24. $32.9 - 15.675 =$

B. Choose the one best answer to each question.

25. James ran 3 miles. His times for the individual miles were 7.2 minutes, 6.8 minutes, and 8.25 minutes. How long did it take him, in minutes, to run the 3-mile distance?

A. 22.25
B. 22.7
C. 23.35
D. 32.25
E. 96.5

26. Claudia earns overtime pay when she works more than 40 hours in one week. How many hours of overtime pay did she work for the week of March 4?

Work Record for March 4–10

March 4	8.5
March 5	Off
March 6	9.25
March 7	8.75
March 8	10
March 9	Off
March 10	7.75

A. 44.25
B. 40.0
C. 8.5
D. 4.25
E. 2.25

27. A plumber cut two lengths of pipe measuring 2.8 and 1.4 meters from a 6-meter length.

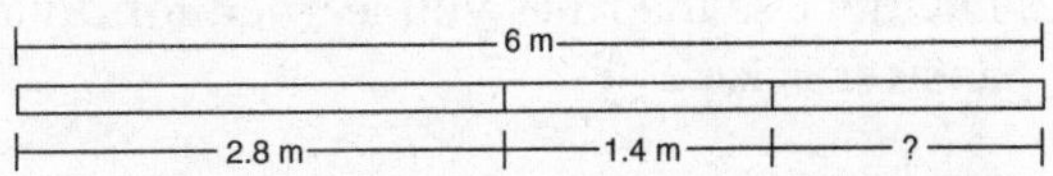

Assuming there was no waste when the cuts were made, what is the length in meters of the remaining piece?

A. 1.8
B. 3.2
C. 4.2
D. 5.2
E. 7.4

28. Mona purchased the following art supplies: a storage box for \$16.98, a set of art markers for \$31.78, and a pad of paper for \$6.50. What was the cost of the three items?

A. \$48.76
B. \$53.26
C. \$55.26
D. \$61.76
E. \$65.26

Multiplication and Division

The rules you used to multiply whole numbers can be used to multiply decimals. You don't have to line up the decimal points. You will wait until you are finished multiplying before you place the decimal point in the answer. The number of decimal places in the answer equals the total number of decimal places in the numbers you are multiplying.

Example 4: Find the product of 2.6 and 0.45.

$$\begin{array}{r} 2.6 \\ \times .45 \\ \hline \end{array}$$

1. Set up the problem as though you were multiplying the whole numbers 26 and 45.
2. Ignore the decimal points while you multiply.
3. Now count the decimal places in the numbers you multiplied. The number 2.6 has one decimal place, and 0.45 has two decimal places, for a total of three.
4. Starting from the right, count three places to the left and insert the decimal point. Thus, the answer is **1.17**.

$$\begin{array}{r} 2.6 \\ \times .45 \\ \hline 130 \\ 1\,040 \\ \hline 1.170 \\ \hline \end{array}$$

When you divide decimals, you must figure out where the decimal point will go in the answer before you divide.

Example 5: Divide 14.4 by 6.

1. Set up the problem. Since the divisor (the number you are dividing by) is a whole number, place the decimal point in the answer directly above the decimal point in the dividend (the number you are dividing).
2. Divide. Use the rules you learned for dividing whole numbers. The answer is **2.4**.

$$\begin{array}{r} 2.4 \\ 6\overline{)14.4} \\ -12 \\ \hline 24 \\ -24 \\ \hline 0 \end{array}$$

If the divisor is a decimal, you must move the decimal points in both the divisor and the dividend before you divide.

Example 6: Divide 4.9 by 0.35.

$$.35\overline{)4.90}$$

1. Set up the problem. There are two decimal places in the divisor. Move the decimal point in *both* the divisor and the dividend two places to the right. Note that you need to add a zero in the dividend in order to move the decimal two places.
2. Place the decimal point in the quotient directly above the decimal point in the dividend.
3. Divide. The correct answer is **14**.

$$\begin{array}{r} 14. \\ 35\overline{)490.} \\ -35 \\ \hline 140 \\ -140 \\ \hline 0 \end{array}$$

Note: You may not need to finish dividing in order to choose the correct answer. You may be able to eliminate all but one of the answer choices after only one or two division steps.

PRACTICE 2.2

A. Solve.

1. 5.3×0.5

2. 64×0.2

3. 12.4×0.04

4. $6\overline{)3.12}$

5. $8\overline{)28.8}$

6. $5\overline{)20.45}$

7. 6.25×1.4

8. 13.5×0.25

9. 9.62×1.005

10. $1.25\overline{)30}$

11. $2.8\overline{)39.76}$

12. $0.003\overline{)47.4}$

13. $15.5 \times 2.2 =$

14. $0.944 \div 0.4 =$

15. $2.05 \times 0.32 =$

16. $1.32 \div 0.5 =$

17. $2.75 \times 0.6 =$

18. $12.825 \div 3 =$

19. $3.36 \times 1.1 =$

20. $15.03 \div 15 =$

21. $0.12 \times 0.06 =$

B. Choose the one best answer to each question.

22. One container of floor cleaner holds 3.79 liters. If Zachary bought 4 containers, how many liters of cleaner did he buy?

A. 0.9475
B. 7.79
C. 12.83
D. 13.79
E. 15.16

23. Ribbon costs $0.45 per foot. A sewing project calls for 20.5 feet of ribbon. To the nearest cent, what will be the cost of the ribbon for the project?

A. $0.92
B. $9.23
C. $9.90
D. $18.50
E. $45.56

24. Armando drove 278.7 miles over a 3-day period. On average, how many miles did he drive each day?

A. 9.3
B. 90.3
C. 92.9
D. 278.7
E. 836.1

Questions 25 and 26 are based on the following information.

Cereal	Net Weight	Servings per Box
Toasted Oats	22.8 oz	19
Crisp Rice	16.9 oz	13
Honey Mix	12.5 oz	10

25. A box of Toasted Oats cereal is priced at $4.94. What is the cost per serving? (*Hint:* Divide the price by the number of servings.)

A. $0.49
B. $0.29
C. $0.26
D. $0.22
E. $0.20

26. Lee bought 4 boxes of Honey Mix cereal. How many ounces of cereal did she buy?

A. 31.25
B. 50.0
C. 67.6
D. 91.2
E. 100.0

STUDY ADVICE

You work with decimals in real life almost every day, because amounts of money are usually expressed in decimal form. *So don't be intimidated* by decimal problems: If you can understand prices, you can work with decimals!

Number and Quantity Part II: Decimals and Fractions

LESSON 3

Fraction Basics

A **fraction** uses two numbers to represent part of a whole. The bottom number, called the **denominator,** tells how many equal parts are in the whole group or item. The top number, called the **numerator,** tells how many parts you are working with.

There are 4 equal parts in this rectangle. Since 3 are shaded, we say that $\frac{3}{4}$ of the rectangle is shaded.

In a proper fraction, the numerator is less than the denominator. A **proper fraction** represents a quantity less than 1. An **improper fraction** is equal to or greater than 1.

There are 6 equal parts in the figure, and 6 are shaded; therefore, $\frac{6}{6}$ of the figure is shaded. $\frac{6}{6} = 1$

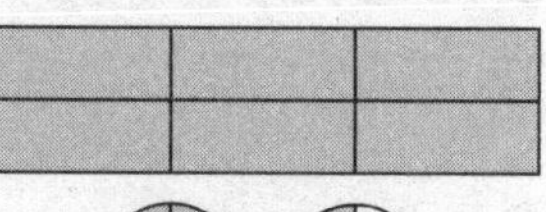

In this grouping, each figure is divided into 2 equal parts. A total of 3 parts are shaded, so $\frac{3}{2}$ are shaded.

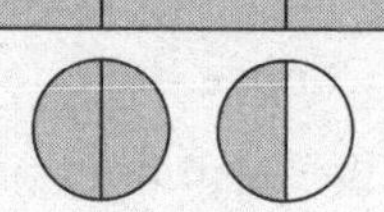

A **mixed number** is another way to show an amount greater than 1. It consists of a whole number and a proper fraction. Another name for the shaded portion in the last figure is $1\frac{1}{2}$. The improper fraction $\frac{3}{2}$ equals $1\frac{1}{2}$.

You can also change an improper fraction to a whole or mixed number.

Example 1: Change $\frac{16}{5}$ to a mixed number.

1. Divide the numerator (16) by the denominator (5). Since 16 is not evenly divisible by 5, there is a remainder of 1. $16 \div 5 = 3 \text{ r } 1.$
2. The answer becomes the whole number, and the remainder becomes the numerator of the proper fraction. The denominator is the same as the one in the original fraction. $\frac{16}{5} = \mathbf{3\frac{1}{5}}$

You can also change a mixed number to an improper fraction.

Example 2: Change $7\frac{2}{3}$ to an improper fraction.

1. Multiply the whole number (7) by the denominator of the fraction (3), and add the numerator (2). $7 \times 3 = 21$; $21 + 2 = 23$
2. Write the sum over the denominator of the original fraction. $7\frac{2}{3} = \mathbf{\frac{23}{3}}$

KEY IDEAS

- The bottom number of a fraction tells how many parts the group or object has.
- The top number tells how many parts you are working with.
- When the top number is greater than the bottom number, the fraction is greater than 1.

HiSET EXAM TIP

If you have trouble visualizing the fractions in a problem, draw a quick sketch of the information presented in the problem similar to the ones on this page.

To perform operations with fractions, you need to be able to write equal fractions in higher or lower terms. The **terms** are the numerator and the denominator. A fraction is **reduced to lowest terms** when the two terms do not have any common factor except 1.

To **raise** a fraction, multiply both terms by the same number: $\frac{3}{4} = \frac{3 \times 3}{4 \times 3} = \frac{9}{12}$.

To **reduce** a fraction, divide both terms by the same number: $\frac{10}{15} = \frac{10 \div 5}{15 \div 5} = \frac{2}{3}$.

A. Write a proper fraction for the shaded portion of each figure.

1. 

2. 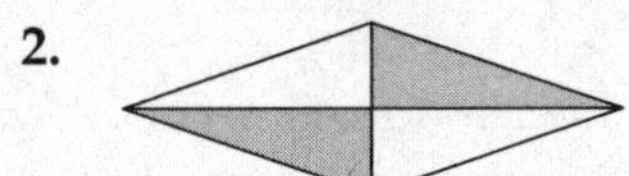

3.

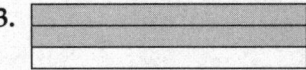

B. Write an improper fraction and a mixed number for the shaded portion of each figure.

4. 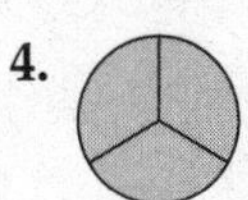 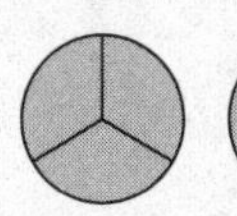 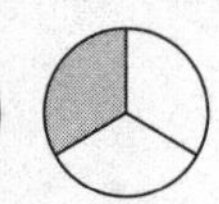

5. 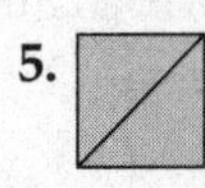 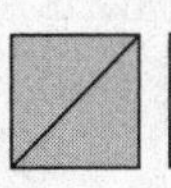 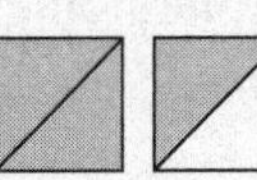

6. 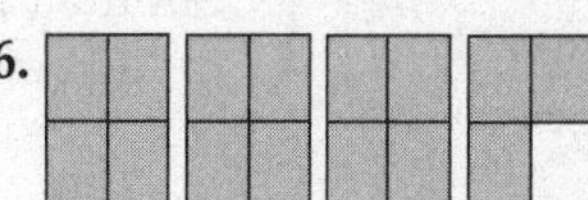

C. Write improper fractions as mixed numbers and mixed numbers as improper fractions.

7. $\frac{17}{3} =$ **9.** $\frac{24}{6} =$ **11.** $\frac{19}{4} =$ **13.** $\frac{43}{9} =$ **15.** $\frac{33}{4} =$

8. $3\frac{3}{5} =$ **10.** $5\frac{2}{9} =$ **12.** $2\frac{5}{12} =$ **14.** $1\frac{3}{4} =$ **16.** $5\frac{7}{10} =$

D. Write an equal fraction with the given denominator.

17. $\frac{3}{4} = \frac{}{16}$ **18.** $\frac{1}{3} = \frac{}{21}$ **19.** $\frac{4}{5} = \frac{}{60}$ **20.** $\frac{3}{8} = \frac{}{40}$ **21.** $\frac{6}{25} = \frac{}{100}$

(*Hint for question 17:* $4 \times ? = 16$)

E. Reduce each fraction to lowest terms.

22. $\frac{21}{28} =$ **23.** $\frac{4}{24} =$ **24.** $\frac{12}{20} =$ **25.** $\frac{26}{30} =$ **26.** $\frac{60}{90} =$

F. Choose the one best answer to each question.

27. Eighteen out of every 24 people surveyed say they went to at least one movie in December. What fraction of the people surveyed went to at least one movie in December?

A. $\frac{3}{4}$

B. $\frac{2}{3}$

C. $\frac{1}{2}$

D. $\frac{1}{3}$

E. $\frac{1}{4}$

28. Which of the following fractions equals $\frac{2}{5}$?

A. $\frac{15}{100}$

B. $\frac{30}{100}$

C. $\frac{40}{100}$

D. $\frac{60}{100}$

E. $\frac{80}{100}$

Number and Quantity Part II: Decimals and Fractions

LESSON 4

Fraction Operations

KEY IDEAS

- You can add or subtract fractions, but they must have the same denominator.
- If denominators are not the same, find a common denominator and raise one or both fractions.
- Always reduce answers to lowest terms and change improper fractions to mixed numbers.

HiSET EXAM TIP

If your solution to a fraction problem is not one of the given answer choices, make sure that you reduced your answer to lowest terms. On the Mathematics Test, answer choices are always written in lowest terms.

Addition and Subtraction

You can add or subtract **like fractions.** Like fractions have a **common denominator.** In other words, their denominators are the same.

Example 1: Add $\frac{3}{10}+\frac{5}{10}$.

1. Since the denominators are the same, add the numerators. $\frac{3}{10}+\frac{5}{10}=\frac{8}{10}$
2. Reduce the answer to lowest terms. $\frac{8}{10}=\frac{8\div 2}{10\div 2}=\frac{4}{5}$

Example 2: Subtract $\frac{2}{9}$ from $\frac{7}{9}$.

Subtract the numerators. The answer is already in lowest terms. $\frac{7}{9}-\frac{2}{9}=\frac{5}{9}$

If the denominators are not the same, raise one or both fractions to higher terms so that they become like fractions.

Example 3: Add $\frac{5}{6}+\frac{1}{4}$.

1. One way to find a common denominator is to think of the multiples of both denominators. The lowest is 12.
   Multiples
   of 6: 6, [12], 18
   of 4: 4, 8, [12], 16
2. Raise each fraction to higher terms with a denominator of 12. $\frac{5\times 2}{6\times 2}=\frac{10}{12}, \frac{1\times 3}{4\times 3}=\frac{3}{12}$
3. Add the like fractions. Rewrite the sum as a mixed number. $\frac{10}{12}+\frac{3}{12}=\frac{13}{12}=\mathbf{1\frac{1}{12}}$

Use the same process to add or subtract mixed numbers. Example 4 shows how to regroup when subtracting mixed numbers.

Example 4: Subtract $4\frac{1}{16}-1\frac{3}{8}$.

1. Raise the second fraction so that it also has a denominator of 16. $\frac{3\times 2}{8\times 2}=\frac{6}{16}$
2. Set up the problem. To subtract the fractions, you need to regroup 1 from the whole number column and add it to the top fraction. $4\frac{1}{16}=3\frac{16}{16}+\frac{1}{16}=3\frac{17}{16}$
3. Subtract the fractions and then the whole numbers. $3\frac{17}{16}-1\frac{6}{16}=\mathbf{2\frac{11}{16}}$

PRACTICE 4.1

A. Solve. Reduce answers to lowest terms. Simplify improper fractions as mixed numbers.

1. $\frac{3}{8} + \frac{1}{8}$

2. $\frac{1}{6} + \frac{5}{6}$

3. $\frac{8}{9} - \frac{5}{9}$

4. $\frac{7}{12} - \frac{5}{12}$

5. $\frac{1}{4} + \frac{2}{3}$

6. $\frac{1}{2} + \frac{5}{8}$

7. $\frac{9}{10} - \frac{3}{5}$

8. $\frac{7}{9} - \frac{1}{2}$

9. $2\frac{1}{5} + 1\frac{2}{3}$

10. $4\frac{1}{2} - 2\frac{3}{4}$

11. $5\frac{5}{6} + 2\frac{2}{3} =$

12. $6\frac{7}{8} + 4\frac{3}{4} =$

13. $12\frac{1}{10} + 9\frac{3}{5} =$

14. $2\frac{2}{9} + \frac{2}{3} + 4\frac{5}{6} =$

15. $3\frac{1}{3} + 5\frac{2}{3} + 3\frac{5}{6} =$

16. $\frac{3}{8} + \frac{7}{12} + 1\frac{2}{3} =$

17. $16\frac{2}{3} + 25\frac{3}{4} =$

18. $10\frac{1}{2} + 8\frac{4}{5} + 3\frac{1}{4} =$

19. $8\frac{1}{2} - 3\frac{4}{9} =$

20. $15 - 3\frac{7}{8} =$

21. $14\frac{1}{4} - 10\frac{3}{7} =$

22. $9\frac{11}{12} - 8\frac{5}{8} =$

23. $6 - 3\frac{4}{7} =$

24. $13\frac{1}{3} - 4\frac{4}{9} =$

25. $5\frac{5}{7} - 4\frac{4}{5} =$

B. Choose the <u>one best answer</u> to each question.

26. To make the top of a dining room table, Craig glues a piece of oak that is $\frac{5}{16}$ inch thick to a piece of pine that is $\frac{7}{8}$ inch thick. What is the total thickness, in inches, of the tabletop?

A. $\frac{9}{16}$
B. $1\frac{3}{16}$
C. $1\frac{1}{4}$
D. $1\frac{9}{16}$
E. $2\frac{1}{4}$

27. Carol will use the two bolts shown below to assemble a book cart. How much longer, in inches, is bolt A than bolt B?

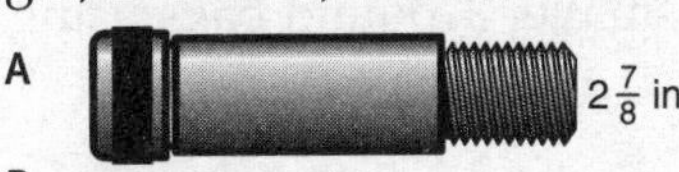

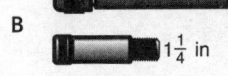

A. $\frac{5}{8}$
B. $1\frac{3}{8}$
C. $1\frac{5}{8}$
D. $1\frac{3}{4}$
E. $2\frac{5}{8}$

28. At a fabric store, Melissa sold $8\frac{7}{8}$ yards of cloth to a customer. If the material was cut from a bolt of fabric containing $23\frac{1}{4}$ yards, how many yards are left on the bolt?

A. $14\frac{3}{8}$
B. $15\frac{3}{8}$
C. $15\frac{3}{4}$
D. $17\frac{3}{4}$
E. $31\frac{7}{8}$

29. A batch of salad dressing requires $1\frac{2}{3}$ cups of olive oil, $\frac{1}{2}$ cup of vinegar, and $\frac{3}{4}$ cup of water. How many cups of salad dressing will this recipe produce?

A. $1\frac{2}{3}$
B. $2\frac{5}{6}$
C. $2\frac{11}{12}$
D. $3\frac{7}{12}$
E. $3\frac{2}{3}$

STUDY ADVICE

Remember that practice has three levels: Learn and Review, Practice and Review, Assess and Review. For each lesson, absorb the concepts on the left page, practice using the page on the right, and carefully review the explanations in the back of the book. Finally, use the question sets at the end of each chapter to assess your progress. Don't forget to review the explanations for those question sets, too.

Multiplication and Division

It isn't necessary to find a common denominator to multiply and divide fractions. To multiply fractions, simply multiply the numerators and then the denominators. Reduce the answer, if necessary.

Example 5: What is the product of $\frac{7}{8}$ and $\frac{1}{2}$?

Multiply the numerators together, and then the denominators. The answer is in lowest terms.

$$\frac{7}{8} \times \frac{1}{2} = \frac{7 \times 1}{8 \times 2} = \frac{7}{16}$$

Before multiplying a mixed number, change it to an improper fraction.

Example 6: What is $\frac{1}{3}$ of $3\frac{3}{4}$?

1. Change $3\frac{3}{4}$ to an improper fraction. $3\frac{3}{4} = \frac{15}{4}$
2. Multiply the numerators and the denominators. $\frac{15}{4} \times \frac{1}{3} = \frac{15 \times 1}{4 \times 3} = \frac{15}{12}$
3. Change to a mixed number and reduce to lowest terms. $\frac{15}{12} = 1\frac{3}{12} = \mathbf{1\frac{1}{4}}$

You can use a shortcut called **canceling** to reduce the fractions as you work the problem. To cancel, divide both a numerator and a denominator by the same number. The numerator and the denominator can be in different fractions.

Example 7: Multiply $1\frac{1}{2}$ by $1\frac{1}{5}$.

1. Change to improper fractions. $1\frac{1}{2} = \frac{3}{2}$ and $1\frac{1}{5} = \frac{6}{5}$
2. Set up the multiplication problem. Both 6 (a numerator) and 2 (a denominator) are evenly divisible by 2. Divide them by 2. Then multiply using the new numerator and denominator. Finally, change the improper fraction to a mixed number.

$$\frac{3}{2} \times \frac{6}{5} = \frac{3}{\cancel{2}_1} \times \frac{\cancel{6}^3}{5} = \frac{9}{5} = \mathbf{1\frac{4}{5}}$$

The slash marks show that the numbers have been divided.

You will need two additional steps to divide fractions. Before dividing, **invert** the divisor (the fraction you are dividing by). To invert the fraction, switch the numerator and the denominator. Finally, change the division symbol to a multiplication symbol and multiply.

Example 8: Jim has an 8-pound bag of nuts. He wants to fill smaller $\frac{1}{2}$-pound bags using the nuts. How many small bags can he make?

1. Divide 8 by $\frac{1}{2}$. Set up the division problem. Always write whole or mixed numbers as improper fractions. $8 \div \frac{1}{2} = \frac{8}{1} \div \frac{1}{2} =$
2. Invert the fraction you are dividing by. Then change the operation sign to multiplication. Multiply, following the rules for multiplying fractions. **Jim can make 16 small bags.** $\frac{8}{1} \times \frac{2}{1} = \frac{16}{1} = \mathbf{16}$

Note: When you multiply by a fraction less than 1, the answer is smaller than the number you started with because you are finding a "part of." When you divide by a fraction less than 1, the answer is greater than the number.

PRACTICE 4.2

A. Solve. Reduce answers to lowest terms. Simplify improper fractions as mixed numbers.

1. $\frac{2}{3} \times \frac{1}{4} =$

2. $1\frac{5}{6} \times \frac{1}{2} =$

3. $\frac{2}{3} \times 21 =$

4. $50 \times \frac{3}{8} =$

5. $3\frac{1}{2} \times \frac{1}{4} =$

6. $\frac{3}{4} \times \frac{7}{8} =$

7. $2\frac{1}{3} \times 3\frac{2}{5} =$

8. $15 \times 2\frac{3}{4} =$

9. $\frac{5}{8} \times 3\frac{1}{4} =$

10. $\frac{7}{8} \div \frac{1}{16} =$

11. $\frac{4}{5} \div \frac{4}{9} =$

12. $12 \div \frac{1}{4} =$

13. $6 \div 2\frac{1}{2} =$

14. $3\frac{3}{4} \div 1\frac{2}{3} =$

15. $9 \div \frac{1}{3} =$

16. $26\frac{2}{3} \div 3\frac{1}{3} =$

17. $40\frac{3}{8} \div 4\frac{1}{4} =$

18. $3\frac{7}{8} \div 5\frac{1}{6} =$

B. Choose the <u>one best answer</u> to each question.

19. A city is considering raising taxes to build a football stadium. A survey of registered voters yielded the following results:

Position	Fraction of Those Surveyed
Against Tax Hike	$\frac{7}{16}$
For Tax Hike	$\frac{3}{16}$
Undecided	$\frac{3}{8}$

If 400 people were surveyed, how many support the tax hike?

A. 48
B. 75
C. 150
D. 175
E. 200

20. A tailor has 20 yards of shirt fabric. How many shirts can she <u>complete</u> if each shirt requires $2\frac{3}{4}$ yards of fabric?

A. 6
B. 7
C. 8
D. 10
E. 20

21. An insurance agent estimates that it takes $\frac{2}{3}$ hour to process a customer's claim. If the agent spends 22 hours per week processing claims, about how many claims does he process in a week?

A. $14\frac{2}{3}$
B. 33
C. 44
D. 66
E. 88

22. A fluorescent lighting panel is $12\frac{5}{8}$ inches wide. If three of the panels are installed as shown below, what will be the width in inches of the combined panels?

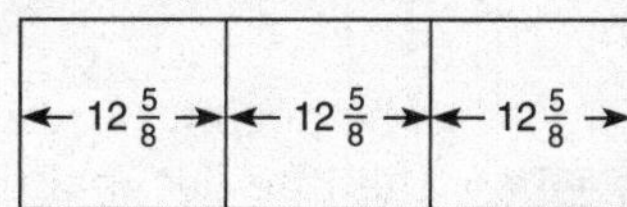

A. $13\frac{7}{8}$
B. $36\frac{5}{8}$
C. $37\frac{7}{8}$
D. $42\frac{7}{8}$
E. $50\frac{1}{4}$

Number and Quantity Part II: Decimals and Fractions

LESSON 5

Fraction and Decimal Equivalencies

Fractions and decimals are two ways to show part of a whole. You can change fractions to decimals by dividing.

Example 1: Change $\frac{3}{8}$ to a decimal.

The fraction $\frac{3}{8}$ means $3 \div 8$. Use a calculator to divide. $3 \div 8 = \mathbf{0.375}$

You can also change a decimal to a fraction.

Example 2: Change 0.35 to a fraction.

Write the decimal number over the place-value name of the last decimal digit on the right. The last digit, 5, is in the hundredths column. Reduce to lowest terms. $\frac{35}{100} = \frac{35 \div 5}{100 \div 5} = \mathbf{\frac{7}{20}}$

You will find it useful to memorize the most common fraction and decimal equivalents. These equivalents will also help you solve percent problems.

Decimal	Fraction	Decimal	Fraction	Decimal	Fraction
0.1	$\frac{1}{10}$	0.375	$\frac{3}{8}$	0.7	$\frac{7}{10}$
0.125	$\frac{1}{8}$	0.4	$\frac{2}{5}$	0.75	$\frac{3}{4}$
0.2	$\frac{1}{5}$	0.5	$\frac{1}{2}$	0.8	$\frac{4}{5}$
0.25	$\frac{1}{4}$	0.6	$\frac{3}{5}$	0.875	$\frac{7}{8}$
0.3	$\frac{3}{10}$	0.625	$\frac{5}{8}$	0.9	$\frac{9}{10}$
$0.33\overline{3}$	$\frac{1}{3}$	$0.66\overline{6}$	$\frac{2}{3}$		

The decimal equivalents for $\frac{1}{3}$ and $\frac{2}{3}$ are marked with a bar. The bar shows that the decimal repeats indefinitely.

You can use fraction and decimal equivalents to save time when solving math problems.

Example 3: Each dose of cough medicine contains 0.25 ounce of medication. How many ounces of medication are in 48 doses?

To solve the problem, you need to multiply 48 by 0.25, a time-consuming calculation. However, since $0.25 = \frac{1}{4}$ you can find $\frac{1}{4}$ of 48 to solve the problem. The answer is **12 ounces.** $48 \times \frac{1}{4} = \frac{48}{4} = \mathbf{12}$

KEY IDEAS

- To change a fraction to a decimal, divide the numerator by the denominator.
- To change a decimal to a fraction, write the number without the decimal point over the place value of the last decimal digit. Reduce.
- Avoid time-consuming calculations by using fraction-decimal equivalents.

HiSET EXAM TIP

Look at the answer choices before you begin working a multiple-choice problem. Knowing whether you need an answer in fraction or decimal form may affect how you approach the problem.

PRACTICE 5

Knowing fraction-decimal equivalents can also help you interpret remainders when using a calculator.

Example 4: Ray inspects machine assemblies. He must inspect 12 assemblies during his 40-hour workweek. On average, how many hours can he spend on each inspection?

Using a calculator, divide 40 by 12: 40 [÷] 12 [enter]. The right side of the display reads 3.333333333.

Since you know that $0.33\overline{3} = \frac{1}{3}$, the answer is **$3\frac{1}{3}$ hours.**

Solve. When possible, use fraction and decimal equivalents to make the work easier.

1. During a 25%-off sale, store clerks find the amount of the discounts by multiplying the regular price by 0.25. What is the discount on an item with a regular price of $80?

A. $32.00
B. $25.00
C. $20.00
D. $16.40
E. $2.00

2. At Linton Products, $\frac{3}{10}$ of the workers are in the company's ride-share program. If there are 480 workers, which of the following expressions could be used to find the number in the ride-share program?

A. 480×0.7
B. $480 \div 0.7$
C. 480×0.5
D. 480×0.3
E. $480 \div 0.3$

3. Sharon is using a calculator to find out how many hours she has spent on a certain job. She divides, and her display reads:

[4.666666666]

Assuming her calculations are correct, how many hours did she spend on the job?

A. $4\frac{1}{6}$
B. $4\frac{2}{3}$
C. $4\frac{6}{7}$
D. 46
E. $46\frac{2}{3}$

4. A gourmet candy company charges the following prices per pound.

Jelly Beans	$9.60
Peanut Brittle	$12.00
Almond Toffee	$28.50

How much would a customer pay for 1.5 pounds of peanut brittle?

A. $6.00
B. $14.40
C. $15.00
D. $18.00
E. $42.75

5. At 1 P.M., the amount of rain in a rain gauge is 1.125 inches. At 3 P.M., the gauge holds 1.875 inches. What fraction of an inch of rain fell between 1 P.M. and 3 P.M.?

A. $\frac{7}{8}$
B. $\frac{3}{4}$
C. $\frac{7}{10}$
D. $\frac{3}{8}$
E. $\frac{1}{8}$

6. A steel rod, 3 meters in length, is cut into 8 equal pieces. What is the length in meters of each piece?

A. 0.125
B. 0.333
C. 0.375
D. 2.333
E. 3.000

STUDY ADVICE

Memorizing some basic fraction-decimal equivalencies can save you time on the Mathematics Test. Consider making flash cards to help you memorize them.

Number and Quantity Part II: Decimals and Fractions

LESSON 6

Decimals and Fractions on the Number Line

KEY IDEAS

- A number line is a picture that helps you compare the sizes of numbers. Numbers on the left are smaller than numbers on the right.
- Number lines can also be used to represent and compare decimals.
- Fractions and mixed fractions can also be represented on a number line.

On the Mathematics Test you may need to recognize or locate fractions, mixed fractions, or decimals on a **number line**. A number line represents numbers in order from least to greatest. As you move to the left along a number line, numbers decrease in value. As you move to the right, numbers increase in value.

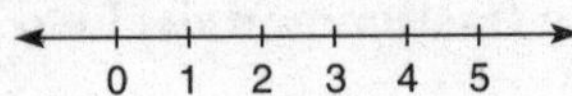

The arrows on the ends indicate that numbers continue forever in both directions. If you imagine zooming in on a portion of that number line, it might look like this:

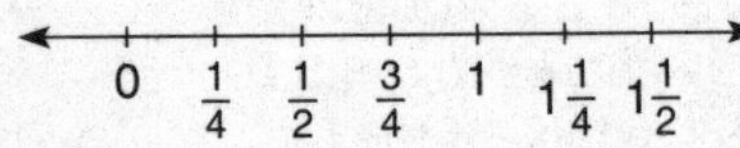

Thus, a number line can include decimals and whole numbers. For example, the point represents 0.75, which is greater than 0.5 and less than 1.

A number line can also represent fractions and mixed fractions in order from least to greatest:

$$0 \quad \frac{1}{4} \quad \frac{1}{2} \quad \frac{3}{4} \quad 1 \quad 1\frac{1}{4} \quad 1\frac{1}{2}$$

Use this question to practice working with number lines:

Example 1: John works five shifts per week. His boss asks him to spend exactly half of his time this week working on a specific project. How many work shifts will John devote to that project? Circle the answer on the number line below.

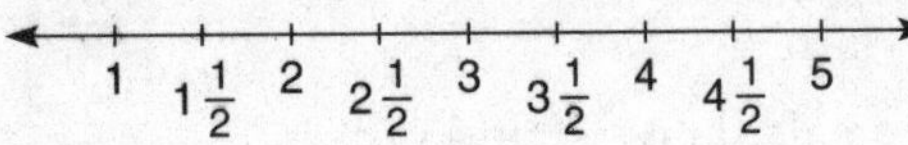

If you circled $\mathbf{2\frac{1}{2}}$, you are correct. Multiply 5 by $\frac{1}{2}$ to determine that John will spend $\mathbf{2\frac{1}{2}}$ shifts on the project.

PRACTICE 6

A. Choose the one best answer to each question.

1. What is the value of the point on the number line below?

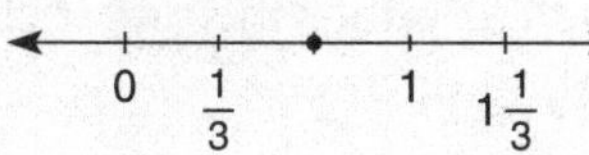

A. 0
B. $\frac{1}{2}$
C. $\frac{2}{3}$
D. $\frac{5}{6}$
E. $1\frac{1}{3}$

2. What is the value of the point on the number line below?

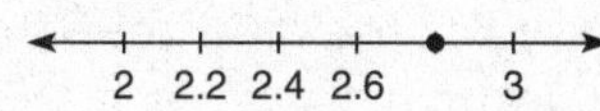

A. 2
B. 2.2
C. 2.5
D. 2.7
E. 2.8

3. On the number line below, what is the value of A minus B?

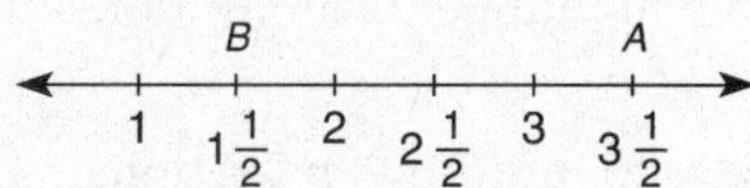

A. 1
B. $1\frac{1}{2}$
C. 2
D. $3\frac{1}{2}$
E. 5

4. Angela baked 24 cookies and gave 16 of them to her neighbor. On the number line below, circle the fraction of Angela's cookies that she gave to her neighbor.

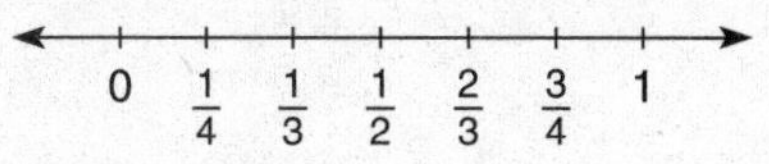

B. Write the decimal values of the points on the number lines.

For each of the number lines below, fill in the value of the point using decimals.

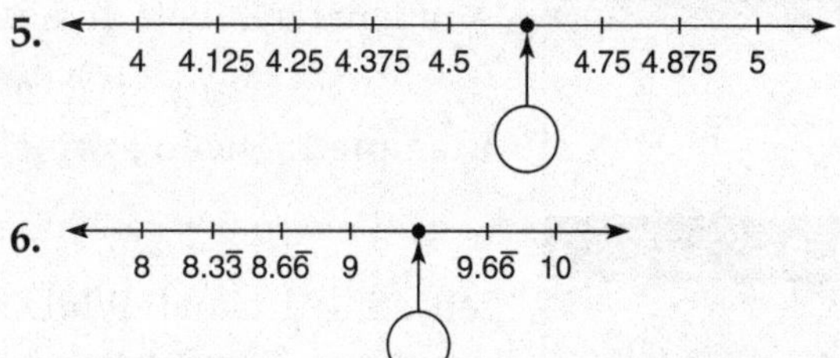

C. Write the fraction values of the points on the number lines.

For each of the number lines below, fill in the value of the point using mixed fractions.

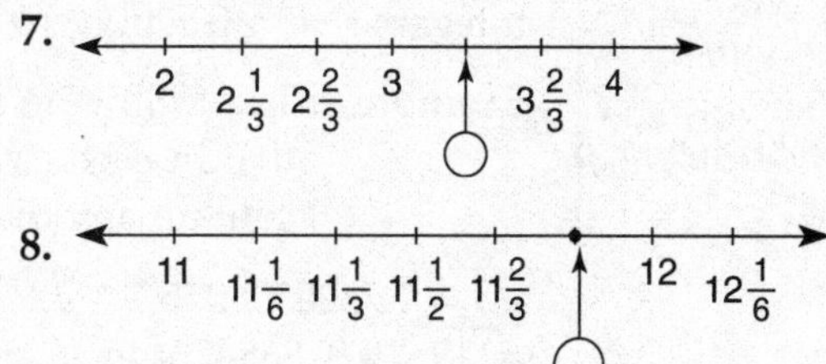

Number and Quantity Part II: Decimals and Fractions

LESSON 7

Rational and Irrational Numbers

A rational number can always be expressed as either the ratio between two integers (i.e., a fraction) or as a repeating decimal.

Example 1: The following are all examples of rational numbers. In each case, the number can either be expressed as a fraction ($17 = \frac{17}{1}$) or a repeating decimal. While many square roots tend to be irrational when evaluated, 25 is a perfect square, so $\sqrt{25}$ is rational.

5 0.333333... 17 0.4714714714714... $\frac{7}{2}$ $\sqrt{25}$ 0.5

Note that a number such as 0.5 can be written as a repeating decimal like so: 0.50000000000...

An irrational number can never be expressed as the ratio between two integers (i.e., a fraction) or as a repeating decimal.

Example 2: The following are all examples of irrational numbers. Note that in each case, the decimal is nonrepeating and does not contain any discernable pattern.

$\sqrt{3} = 1.73205080757\ldots$ $\sqrt{2} = 1.41421356237\ldots$ $\pi = 3.14159265359\ldots$ $\sqrt[3]{119} = 4.91868473446\ldots$

Operations Between a Rational and an Irrational Number

The product of a rational and an irrational number is an irrational number (as long as the rational number is not zero).

Example 3: The easiest way to see this is to multiply an irrational number, such as $\sqrt{3} = 1.73205080757\ldots$, by the rational number 10. Since multiplying any number by 10 can be done by moving the decimal point one place to the right, the answer would be 17.3205080757....

While the *value* of the irrational number has changed, the pattern's randomness has not. In fact, as you will see, you need very specific random patterns (i.e., irrational numbers) to change the unpredictable pattern of an irrational number into the predictable pattern of a rational one.

A rational number plus or minus an irrational number is an irrational number.

KEY IDEAS

- The difference between rational and irrational numbers is predictability: Rational numbers conform to a pattern whereas irrational numbers do not.
- Multiplying or dividing one irrational number by another *might* result in a rational number. All other basic operations with at least one irrational number (except multiplying by 0) will result in an irrational number.

HiSET EXAM TIP

Familiarity with perfect squares and perfect cubes will allow you to quickly identify rational numbers that you might otherwise mistake for irrational.

Example 4: Using $\sqrt{3}$ = 1.73205080757… as an example of an irrational number, see what happens when various rational numbers are added or subtracted:

1.73205080757… + 4 = 5.73205080757… 1.73205080757… – 0.53 = 0.20205080757…

1.73205080757… – 0.111 = 1.62105080757… 1.73205080757… + 6.268 = 8.00005080757…

The values changed, and even the patterns changed a little. However, the *unpredictability* of the pattern did not change. In the final example, we came much closer to changing the pattern to something predictable and repeating, but notice how the effect stopped once we ran out of digits and that the digits themselves needed to be pretty specific to achieve this. To end up with a rational number, you would need to add or subtract two irrational numbers that happen to complement each other *exactly*.

Operations Between Irrational Numbers

The sum or product of two irrational numbers can be rational or irrational.

Example 5: Note the outcomes in the following examples:

$\sqrt{5} + \sqrt{5} = 2\sqrt{5} = 4.47213595499\ldots$ (irrational) $\pi \times \pi = \pi^2 = 9.86960440108\ldots$ (irrational)

$\sqrt{5} + -\sqrt{5} = 0$ (rational) $\sqrt{2} \times \sqrt{2} = 2$ (rational)

A. Label each of the following as rational or irrational.

1. 23 **2.** $\sqrt{7}$ **3.** $\frac{5}{16}$ **4.** $0.\overline{6}$ **5.** 0 **6.** $\sqrt[3]{27}$ **7.** $\sqrt{13}$

B. Will the result be rational or irrational?

8. $0.1\overline{6} + \frac{7}{6}$ **9.** $\sqrt{2} + \sqrt{121}$ **10.** $\sqrt{265} \times \sqrt{265}$ **11.** $\frac{4}{5} \times \pi$ **12.** $\sqrt[3]{64} \times \sqrt{64}$ **13.** $\sqrt{49} + \sqrt{16}$

Number and Quantity Part II: Decimals and Fractions

LESSON 8

Decimal and Fraction Calculator Skills

Several important calculator keys are used to work with decimals and fractions. Remember, for illustrative purposes, this lesson will walk you through how to use one sample scientific calculator, the Texas Instruments TI-30XS MultiView™. For more information regarding the use of calculators on the HiSET exam, see pages 257–258.

KEY IDEAS

- Fraction and decimal operations are entered in the same order as whole-number operations.
- On the TI-30XS MultiView™ calculator, use the decimal point key (.) for decimals and the fraction key, $\frac{n}{d}$, for fractions.
- To work with mixed fractions, use the 2nd function, $U\frac{n}{d}$, which is in green over the fraction key.

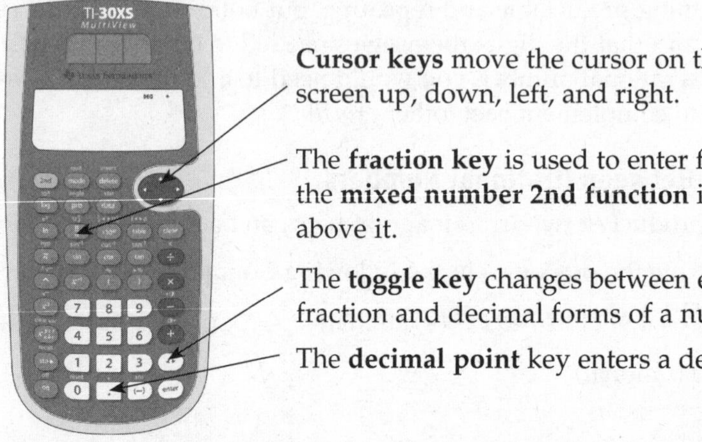
TI-30XS
MultiView
Cursor keys move the cursor on the screen up, down, left, and right.
The **fraction key** is used to enter fractions; the **mixed number 2nd function** is in green above it.
The **toggle key** changes between equivalent fraction and decimal forms of a number.
The **decimal point** key enters a decimal point.

Calculator **decimal operations** are performed in the same way that you use operations with whole numbers. You need to use the **decimal point key** (•) under the 2 in the white **numeric keypad**. Practice with these examples:

To solve this problem...	Press these keys...	The right-hand side of the display reads...
$3.89 + 2.5$	3.89(+)2.5(enter)	6.39
$5.2 - 0.78$	5.2(−).78(enter)	4.42
0.9×15	.9(×)15(enter)	13.5
$1.7 \div 2$	1.7(÷)2(enter)	0.85

HiSET EXAM TIP

A fraction answer may appear in the form of an improper fraction. In order to change to an equivalent mixed number on the TI-30XS MultiView™, use the green 2nd function over this key:

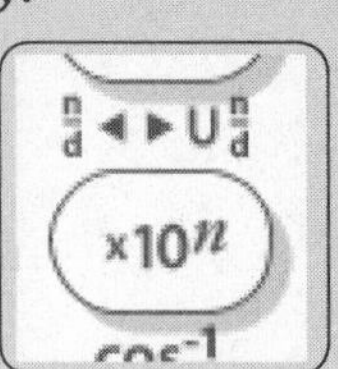
×10ⁿ

You will use several calculator functions to work with **fractions** and **mixed fraction operations**. First practice entering fractions and converting to decimals.

Example 1: Reduce $\frac{56}{448}$ to lowest terms and then convert to a decimal.

<u>On the Display</u>

1. Clear the calculator.
2. Press the $\frac{n}{d}$ button to enter a fraction. Enter 56 at the blinking cursor, in the numerator.

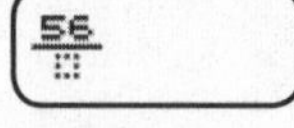

3. Use the down cursor key (▼) to enter 448 in the denominator.

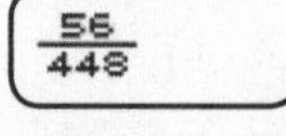

4. Press (enter) to reduce the fraction to lowest terms, which appears on the right of your screen: $\frac{1}{8}$

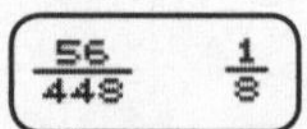

5. To express the fraction as a decimal, press the *toggle* button: (◄►). The decimal **0.125** appears on the right display.

$\frac{1}{8}$ ▸◂ 0.125

Now practice operations with **mixed fractions** using the 2nd function key.

Example 2: A plastic pipe is to be cut into pieces measuring $1\frac{7}{8}$ feet. The original pipe was $20\frac{5}{8}$ feet long. How many pieces can be cut from the pipe?

	Keys to Press	On the Display
1. Clear the calculator.	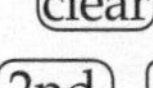	
2. Recognize that a mixed fraction is a green 2nd function: (U $\frac{n}{d}$) over the $\frac{n}{d}$ key. Press the (2nd) key and the $\frac{n}{d}$ key. Note both a whole number and a blinking fraction cursor on the display.	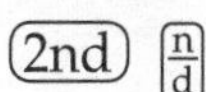	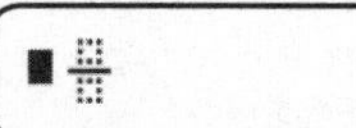
3. Enter the number being divided first—the whole pipe: $20\frac{5}{8}$. Enter 20, then follow the direction of the on-screen arrow and press the right arrow button to move to the fraction cursors. Enter 5 and then use the down arrow to enter the 8. Exit the fraction by pressing the right arrow again.	20 ▶ 5 ▼ 8 ▶	$20\frac{5}{8}$
4. Press the division key. Then follow the same process with the second number: $1\frac{7}{8}$, starting with the 2nd function: (U $\frac{n}{d}$)	(÷) (2nd) $\frac{n}{d}$ 1 ▶ 7 ▼ 8 ▶	$20\frac{5}{8}\div1\frac{7}{8}$
5. Press the (enter) button for the solution. The answer 11 for **11 pieces** appears on the right side of the screen.	(enter)	$20\frac{5}{8}\div1\frac{7}{8}$ 11

A. Solve the following problems.

1. $3.5 + 1.87 + 2.009$ **2.** $3\frac{2}{3} - 1\frac{5}{12}$ **3.** $\$25.35 \times 15$ **4.** $10\frac{1}{2} \div \frac{1}{4}$

5. Linda earns \$95 per day. If she works $\frac{8}{9}$ of a day, how much will she earn?

6. Aaron bought a refrigerator for \$956.88. The price includes tax and interest charges. If he makes 12 equal monthly payments, how much will he pay each month?

7. An insurance agent estimates the annual cost of insurance on a home by multiplying the sale price of the home by 0.0125. What will be the yearly cost of insurance on a home priced at \$118,000?

8. In a recipe, the total liquid added to a mixture is $1\frac{1}{2}$ cups of water and $2\frac{3}{4}$ cups of chicken broth. How many cups of liquid are used in the recipe?

9. A quilt costs \$84.99 and weighs 5.56 pounds. The shipping charge is \$1.20 per pound. To the nearest cent, what would be the shipping charge on the quilt?

A. \$5.56
B. \$6.67
C. \$8.26
D. \$48.49
E. \$10.20

10. A state park contains 64 acres. A wildlife preserve makes up $\frac{3}{8}$ of the park. How many acres are in the preserve?

A. 8
B. 21
C. 24
D. 27
E. 32

DECIMALS AND FRACTIONS PRACTICE QUESTIONS

Directions: Choose the best answer to each question.

1. A wooden flooring strip is $20\frac{1}{2}$ inches long. If you cut off $4\frac{3}{4}$ inches from one end, what will be the new length of the strip in inches?

   A. $16\frac{3}{4}$
   B. $16\frac{1}{4}$
   C. $15\frac{3}{4}$
   D. $15\frac{1}{4}$
   E. $14\frac{3}{4}$

2. A box of cereal costs $4.69. The package label says that the box contains 19 servings. What is the cost of 1 serving to the nearest cent?

   A. $0.02
   B. $0.22
   C. $0.25
   D. $0.47
   E. $2.46

3. How much would a computer system cost if it is priced as shown below?

Pay $200 down and make 12 monthly payments of only $98.85.

   A. $3,586.20
   B. $2,400.00
   C. $1,386.20
   D. $1,186.20
   E. $988.50

4. Unleaded gasoline sells for $2.869 per gallon. How much would $10\frac{1}{2}$ gallons cost? Round your answer to the nearest cent.

   A. $13.40
   B. $28.69
   C. $30.12
   D. $31.56
   E. $301.20

5. Three packages weigh $1\frac{1}{2}$ pounds, $4\frac{3}{4}$ pounds, and $2\frac{3}{10}$ pounds. What is the average weight, in pounds, of the packages? (*Hint:* Add the weights, then divide by the number of packages.)

   A. 2.14
   B. 2.85
   C. 4.75
   D. 6.75
   E. 8.55

6. Gina is paid $8 an hour. If she earned $258 in 1 week, how many hours did she work?

   A. $34\frac{1}{2}$
   B. $33\frac{1}{4}$
   C. $32\frac{1}{3}$
   D. $32\frac{1}{4}$
   E. $32\frac{1}{5}$

7. A developer plans to build homes on $20\frac{1}{2}$ acres. She estimates that $6\frac{1}{4}$ acres will be used for roads. The remaining land will be divided into $\frac{1}{4}$-acre lots. How many lots can the subdivision include?

   A. 7
   B. 57
   C. 81
   D. 107
   E. 125

8. A school buys 1,000 white-board markers. Below is the price per marker for two brands. How much did the school save by buying Brand A instead of Brand B?

   Brand A: $0.27 each
   Brand B: $0.36 each

   A. $0.09
   B. $0.90
   C. $9.00
   D. $63.00
   E. $90.00

Questions 9 and 10 refer to the following information.

Madison Small Animal Clinic Scheduling Guidelines	
New-Patient Appointment	$\frac{3}{4}$ hr
Immunizations	$\frac{1}{4}$ hr
Routine Physical	$\frac{1}{3}$ hr
Dental Scaling	$\frac{3}{4}$ hr
Sick Animal Visit	$\frac{1}{2}$ hr
Serious-Injury Visit (includes X-rays)	$1\frac{1}{4}$ hr

9. Ray is a veterinarian at the small-animal clinic. He has four appointments scheduled for Monday morning: two new-patient appointments, a serious-injury visit, and a dental scaling. In hours, how much time should these appointments take?

   A. $2\frac{3}{4}$
   B. $3\frac{1}{2}$
   C. $3\frac{3}{4}$
   D. 4
   E. $4\frac{1}{2}$

10. Jennifer works $3\frac{1}{2}$ hours each morning at the clinic. How many routine physicals could she complete in one morning?

    A. 4
    B. 9
    C. 10
    D. 11
    E. 15

---

11. A minor-league baseball stadium has 6000 seats. On Beach Towel Night, the stadium sold 5500 of its available seats. What fraction of the seats were sold?

    A. $\frac{5}{6}$
    B. $\frac{6}{7}$
    C. $\frac{8}{9}$
    D. $\frac{9}{10}$
    E. $\frac{11}{12}$

12. The City Center parking garage charges $3.50 for the first hour and $1.25 for each additional $\frac{1}{2}$ hour. How much would it cost to park at the garage for $2\frac{1}{2}$ hours?

    A. $4.75
    B. $6.25
    C. $7.25
    D. $9.75
    E. $10.50

13. Susan scheduled 84 appointments for patients at a hospital outreach clinic. Only 56 patients kept their appointments. What fraction of the scheduled appointments were kept?

    A. $\frac{1}{4}$
    B. $\frac{1}{3}$
    C. $\frac{1}{2}$
    D. $\frac{5}{8}$
    E. $\frac{2}{3}$

14. This portion of a gas bill compares a household's natural gas usage for December of this year and last year.

Gas Bill Comparison Average Daily Usage			
This Year		Last Year	
Dec	3.13 therms	Dec	3.97 therms

How many more therms of natural gas did the household use in December of last year than December of this year? Express your answer as a decimal.

A. 0.74
B. 0.84
C. 0.94
D. 0.97
E. 1.04

15. Jim and Carl have until 1 P.M. to load 250 boxes. By 12:30 P.M., 175 of the boxes are loaded. What fraction of the boxes has not been loaded?

A. $\frac{1}{5}$
B. $\frac{3}{10}$
C. $\frac{3}{5}$
D. $\frac{7}{10}$
E. $\frac{3}{4}$

16. On the number line below, what is the value of *A* minus *B*?

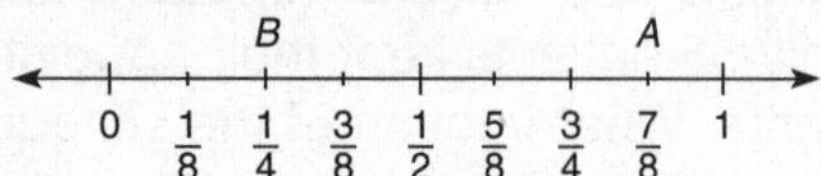

A. $\frac{1}{4}$
B. $\frac{5}{8}$
C. $\frac{7}{8}$
D. $1\frac{1}{8}$
E. $1\frac{3}{8}$

17. Scott is driving about 380 miles from Los Angeles to San Francisco. He plans to cover $\frac{3}{4}$ of the distance before noon. How many miles does he plan to drive before noon?

A. 285
B. 254
C. 126
D. 95
E. 65

18. A cookie recipe calls for $1\frac{2}{3}$ cups of sugar. If you wanted to make half the quantity shown in the recipe, how many cups of sugar would you use?

A. $\frac{2}{5}$
B. $\frac{2}{3}$
C. $\frac{5}{6}$
D. $1\frac{1}{6}$
E. $1\frac{1}{4}$

19. How many miles would a map distance of $\frac{5}{8}$ inch represent if 1 in = 240 mi?

A. 40
B. 130
C. 150
D. 200
E. 250

Question 20 is based on the following information.

Carbide Steel Drill Bits		
Description	**Size (inches)**	**Price**
Cutter	$\frac{9}{16}$	$6.19
Core Box	$\frac{5}{32}$	$16.40
Classic	$\frac{3}{8}$	$17.85
Bevel	$\frac{1}{2}$	$10.50

20. Which of the following shows the drill bits arranged in order from least to greatest in size?

A. cutter, bevel, classic, core box
B. core box, bevel, classic, cutter
C. bevel, classic, cutter, core box
D. bevel, cutter, core box, classic
E. core box, classic, bevel, cutter

21. Joe is going to order a pizza. He will eat at least $\frac{1}{2}$ of it. If he's very hungry, he might eat as much as $\frac{7}{8}$ of it. Identify the two points on the number line below that represent the minimum fraction of the pizza Joe might have left over and the maximum fraction of the pizza Joe might have left over.

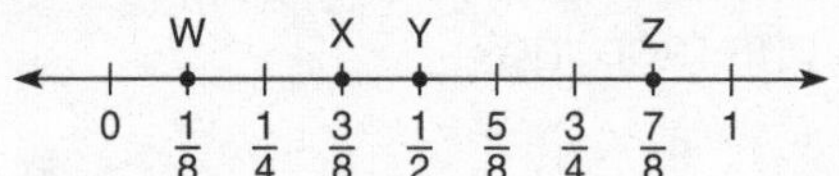

A. W and Z
B. W and Y
C. X and Z
D. Y and Z
E. Y and X

22. A project should take no more than 60 hours. If John can spare 7.5 hours per day to work on the project, what is the maximum number of days it will take him to finish?

A. 6
B. 7
C. 8
D. 9
E. 10

23. A survey shows that $\frac{2}{3}$ of all homeowners have a pet. Of those, $\frac{3}{4}$ have either a dog or cat. Of the homeowners surveyed, what fraction has either a dog or a cat?

A. $\frac{1}{2}$
B. $\frac{2}{3}$
C. $\frac{3}{4}$
D. $\frac{5}{7}$
E. $\frac{6}{7}$

24. At Wyman Shipping, 140 employees work during the day shift. At night, the crew is $\frac{2}{5}$ the size of the day shift. How many workers are scheduled to work the night shift?

A. 28
B. 56
C. 70
D. 94
E. 196

Question 25 refers to the following map.

The map below shows the distance, in miles, between four stores.

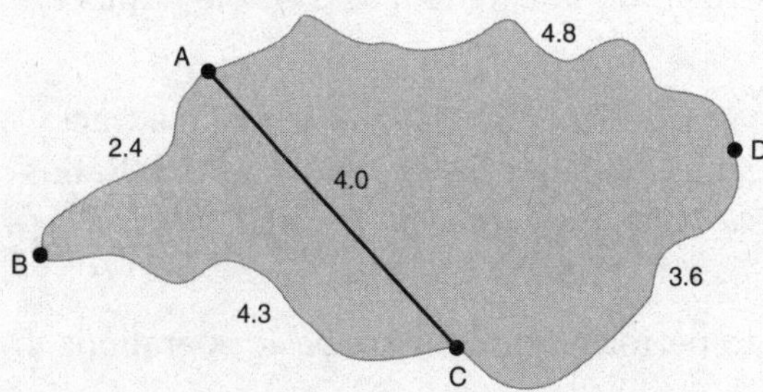

25. Maya drives a van that delivers supplies to each of the stores. On Friday, she traveled the following route.

Store A to Store B
Store B to Store C
Store C to Store D
Store D to Store C
Store C to Store A

How many miles did she drive in all?

A. 13.9
B. 15.1
C. 17.9
D. 19.1
E. 21.5

26. From a wooden dowel $12\frac{1}{2}$ feet long, Jamie cut two pieces, each $3\frac{3}{4}$ feet long. How long, in feet, is the remaining piece?

A. $8\frac{3}{4}$
B. $7\frac{1}{2}$
C. $6\frac{1}{2}$
D. 6
E. 5

27. Luis bought 20 shares of stock, priced at $26.38 per share. He also paid an $8 transaction fee. How much did he pay?

A. $687.60
B. $535.60
C. $527.60
D. $519.60
E. $435.60

28. A mat board is 60 inches wide. How many strips measuring 0.75 inches wide can be cut from the board? (Assume no waste from the cuts.)

A. 45
B. 50
C. 60
D. 75
E. 80

29. Of his take-home pay each month, Jerry spends $\frac{1}{6}$ on a car payment and $\frac{1}{4}$ on food. What fraction of his take-home pay is left after paying for these two items?

A. $\frac{1}{12}$
B. $\frac{1}{6}$
C. $\frac{1}{4}$
D. $\frac{5}{12}$
E. $\frac{7}{12}$

Number and Quantity Part III: Ratio, Proportion, and Percent

LESSON 1

Ratio and Proportion

Ratio

A **ratio** compares two numbers. You can write a ratio using the word *to,* using a colon (:), or using fraction form.

Example 1: A softball pitcher strikes out four batters for every one batter that she walks. What is the ratio of strikeouts to walks?

Always write the numbers in the ratio in the same order in which they appear in the question. **4 to 1** **4:1** $\mathbf{\frac{4}{1}}$

Ratios are similar to fractions. They have two terms, and they can be simplified by reducing to lowest terms.

Example 2: Frank manages a small drugstore. During a two-hour period, he counts 25 cash sales and 15 credit card sales. What is the ratio of credit card to cash sales?

1. Write the ratio as a fraction with the terms in the correct order: credit card to cash sales. $\frac{\text{credit card sales}}{\text{cash sales}} = \frac{15}{25}$

2. Reduce to lowest terms. The ratio of credit card to cash sales is **3 to 5.** $\frac{15 \div 5}{25 \div 5} = \frac{3}{5}$

There are some fraction rules that ratios do not follow. Do not change a ratio that is an improper fraction to a mixed number. Also, if a ratio in fraction form has a denominator of 1, do not write it as a whole number. Leave it in fraction form.

Another important difference is in the use of labels. The terms in a fraction have the same unit labels: $\frac{5}{6}$ *of a pie means 5 slices out of 6 slices.* Ratios may have different labels: *The sale advertised 6 cans for $1, a 6:1 ratio.*

To write a ratio, you may need to perform one or more basic operations to find one of the terms.

Example 3: A football team won 12 games and lost 8. There were no tied games. What is the ratio of games won to games played?

1. The problem does not tell you the number of games played. Add the games won to the games lost to find the games played. 12 won + 8 lost = 20 played

2. Write the ratio in the correct order and simplify. **The team won 3 games for every 5 games it played, a 3:5 ratio.** $\frac{\text{games won}}{\text{games played}} = \frac{12}{20} = \frac{12 \div 4}{20 \div 4} = \frac{3}{5}$

KEY IDEAS

- A ratio has two terms and can be written in words, with a colon, or as a fraction.
- Ratios are simplified by reducing to lowest terms.
- The terms in a ratio can have different labels.

HiSET EXAM TIP

The terms in a ratio must be written in the order given by the words of the question. Don't be fooled by an answer choice on a multiple-choice question that reverses the order of the numbers.

PRACTICE 1.1

A. Write each ratio as a fraction in lowest terms.

1. Stan made 24 sales in 6 hours. What is the ratio of sales to hours?
2. Carol's monthly take-home pay is $1500. She spends $250 a month on food. What is the ratio of food costs to take-home dollars?
3. A toy rocket travels 180 ft in 15 sec. What is the ratio of feet to seconds?
4. At Phil's work, there are 12 part-time workers and 18 full-time workers. What is the ratio of part-time workers to total workers?
5. Juanita drove 336 miles on 14 gallons of gasoline. What is the ratio of miles to gallons?
6. Lynn estimates that a roofing job will cost $1500. Bo estimates that the same job will cost $2400. What is the ratio of Lynn's estimate to Bo's estimate?
7. A basketball player attempted 32 free throws and made 20. What is the ratio of free throws made to free throws missed?
8. There are 10 men and 14 women in Kathleen's math class. What is the ratio of women to the total number of students in the class?
9. To paint his apartment, Alex bought 6 gallons of paint to cover 1440 square feet. What is the ratio of square feet to gallons of paint?

B. Choose the one best answer to each question.

Questions 10 through 12 refer to the following information.

Three candidates are running for mayor. Below are the results of a survey of 600 registered voters.

Candidate	Number of Supporters
Stothard	220
Mesa	180
Newmark	50
Undecided	150

10. What is the ratio of Mesa's supporters to Stothard's supporters?
    A. 9:11
    B. 11:9
    C. 11:20
    D. 20:11
    E. 30:11

11. What is the ratio of voters who prefer Mesa to the total number surveyed?
    A. 3 to 7
    B. 3 to 10
    C. 3 to 13
    D. 11 to 30
    E. 13 to 30

12. What is the ratio of undecided voters to voters who have made a decision?
    A. $\frac{1}{4}$
    B. $\frac{1}{3}$
    C. $\frac{3}{1}$
    D. $\frac{4}{1}$
    E. $\frac{8}{1}$

13. Soan made a $400 down payment on a washer and dryer that cost a total of $1200. What is the ratio of the amount Soan has paid to the amount he still owes?
    A. 1 to 4
    B. 1 to 3
    C. 1 to 2
    D. 2 to 3
    E. 2 to 1

14. A team played 77 games and won 56 of them. There were no tied games. What is the ratio of wins to losses?
    A. 3:8
    B. 8:11
    C. 11:8
    D. 7:5
    E. 8:3

Proportion

A **proportion** is an equation that shows that two ratios are equal. The **cross products** in a true proportion are equal. In other words, when you multiply diagonally across the equals sign, the products are equal.

Example 4: The directions on a can of powdered drink mix say to add 3 cups of water to every 2 scoops of drink mix. Matt adds 12 cups of water to 8 scoops of drink mix. Did he make the drink correctly?

1. Write a proportion, making sure the terms of the ratios are in the same order. $\frac{\text{cups}}{\text{scoops}}\ \frac{3}{2} \times \frac{12}{8}$

2. Cross multiply and compare the products. Since the products are the same, the ratios are equal. **Matt made the drink correctly.** $3 \times 8 = 24$; $2 \times 12 = 24$

In most proportion problems, you are asked to solve for a missing term.

Example 5: A map scale says that 2 inches = 150 miles. What actual distance would a map distance of 5 inches represent?

1. Write a proportion with both ratios in the same form: inches to miles. The variable x represents the unknown distance. $\frac{\text{inches}}{\text{miles}}\ \frac{2}{150} = \frac{5}{x}$

2. Locate the term in the first ratio that is diagonal from the known term in the second ratio. Cross multiply. $\frac{2}{150} = \frac{5}{x}$; $150 \times 5 = 750$

3. Divide the result by the remaining known term to find the value of x. $750 \div 2 =$ **375 miles**

Some proportion problems ask you to find a **rate.** A rate compares a quantity to 1. When a rate is written in fraction form, its denominator is always 1. In word form, rates are often expressed using the word *per.*

Example 6: Connie drove 276 miles on 12 gallons of gasoline. How many miles per gallon did she get on the trip?

1. Gas mileage is one kind of rate. You need to find how many miles Connie drove on one gallon of gasoline. $\frac{\text{miles}}{\text{gallons}}\ \frac{276}{12} = \frac{x}{1}$

2. Solve. $276 \times 1 = 276$; $276 \div 12 =$ **23 miles per gallon**

Using your calculator, you can solve proportion problems in one series of calculations.

Example 7: Find the value of x in the proportion $\frac{6}{16} = \frac{21}{x}$.

You need to multiply 16 and 21, then divide by 6. On the TI-30XS MultiView™ calculator:

1. Press 16 [×] 21 [÷] 6.

2. Then press [enter]. The right side of the display will read 56.

The missing term is **56.**

Note: When working a problem, ask yourself if it can be solved using proportion. This may be possible when two quantities are compared or when three values are given and you are asked to find a fourth.

PRACTICE 1.2

A. Solve for the missing term in each proportion problem. *Note*: Answers will not always be whole numbers.

1. $\frac{2}{3} = \frac{x}{18}$
2. $\frac{3}{5} = \frac{27}{x}$
3. $\frac{6}{5} = \frac{3}{x}$
4. $\frac{15}{2} = \frac{x}{8}$
5. $\frac{4}{\$212} = \frac{7}{x}$
6. $\frac{25}{6} = \frac{400}{x}$
7. $\frac{7}{30} = \frac{x}{9}$
8. $\frac{0.5}{12} = \frac{3}{x}$
9. $\frac{20}{2.5} = \frac{100}{x}$
10. $\frac{\$5.96}{2} = \frac{x}{3}$
11. $\frac{12}{5} = \frac{3}{x}$
12. $\frac{4}{60} = \frac{2.5}{x}$
13. $\frac{3}{19} = \frac{x}{114}$
14. $\frac{9}{\$80.10} = \frac{x}{\$284.80}$
15. $\frac{\$26.00}{4} = \frac{x}{7}$
16. $\frac{24}{96} = \frac{7}{x}$

B. Choose the one best answer to each question.

17. A store is advertising the following sale:

Tomato Soup 4 cans for $0.98

To the nearest cent, how much would five cans of tomato soup cost?

A. $0.25
B. $1.23
C. $2.45
D. $2.75
E. $4.90

18. The Bay City Cardinals have won 5 out of 8 games. At the same rate, how many games will they have to play to win 60 games?

A. 180
B. 150
C. 120
D. 108
E. 96

19. Carla drove her truck 414 miles on 18 gallons of gasoline. How many miles did she drive per gallon?

A. 18
B. 23
C. 54
D. 74
E. 95

20. The scale on a map reads, "2 cm = 150 km." How many kilometers would be represented by a distance of 4.6 centimeters?

A. 300
B. 345
C. 690
D. 830
E. 1,380

21. Two ingredients in a recipe are $2\frac{1}{2}$ cups of flour and $1\frac{1}{2}$ cups of sugar. If June keeps the proportion the same, how many cups of flour should she add to 4 cups of sugar?

A. $6\frac{2}{3}$
B. 6
C. 5
D. $3\frac{3}{4}$
E. 3

22. Claudia drove 155 miles in 2.5 hours. Which of the following expressions could be used to find how many miles she can drive in 7 hours?

A. $155 \times 7 \div 2.5$
B. $2.5 \times 7 \div 155$
C. $155 \times 2.5 \div 4 7$
D. $7 \times 2.5 \times 155$
E. 7×155

STUDY ADVICE

Proportions are useful in many ways. If you've ever doubled a recipe or thought about how much it would cost to fill up your car with gas, you've used proportions:

$$\frac{2\text{ c flour}}{1\text{ batch}} = \frac{4\text{ c flour}}{2\text{ batches}} \quad \text{or} \quad \frac{\$3.99}{1\text{ gallon}} = \frac{\$39.90}{10\text{ gallons}}$$

Proportions simply ask you to apply these real-world concepts.

Number and Quantity Part III: Ratio, Proportion, and Percent

LESSON 2

Percents

Percent means "per hundred" or "out of one hundred." For example, if you have $100 and you spend $25, you spent $25 out of $100, or 25% of your money.

Since percent is a way of showing part of a whole, it has much in common with fractions and decimals. To convert a percent to a fraction, write the percent over 100 and reduce. To convert percents to decimals, drop the percent symbol and move the decimal point two places to the left.

Percent to Fraction	**Percent to Decimal**
$25\% = \frac{25}{100} = \frac{1}{4}$	$25\% = .25 = 0.25$

In any percent problem, there are three elements: the base, the part, and the rate. The **base** is the whole quantity, or amount, that the problem is about. The **part** (also called a **percentage**) is a portion of the base. The **rate** is a number followed by the percent symbol (%).

Example 1: At a restaurant, Janice's bill is $20. She gives the waiter a tip of $3, which is 15% of her bill. Identify the base, part, and rate in this situation.

The entire bill of $20 is the base. The $3 tip is part of the base, and the rate is 15%.

One way to think of a percent problem is as a proportion. In Example 1, there are two ratios. The $3 tip is part of the $20 total bill, and 15% is the same as $\frac{15}{100}$. Since the two ratios are equal, they can be written as a proportion.

$$\frac{\text{part}}{\text{base}} \quad \frac{3}{20} = \frac{15}{100}$$

Cross multiply to prove the ratios are equal.

$$20 \times 15 = 300$$
$$3 \times 100 = 300$$

You can solve percent problems by setting up a proportion and solving for the missing elements. Just remember to express the percent as a number over 100.

Example 2: At a plant that manufactures lighting fixtures, it is expected that about 2% of the fixtures assembled each day will have some type of defect. If 900 fixtures are completed in one day, how many are expected to be defective?

1. Write a proportion. Remember that 2% means 2 out of 100. Use the variable x to stand for the number of defective fixtures.

$$\frac{\text{part}}{\text{base}} = \frac{\text{rate}}{100}$$
$$\frac{x}{900} = \frac{2}{100}$$

2. Solve for x. Cross multiply and divide by the remaining number. **The company can expect about 18 defective fixtures.**

$$900 \times 2 = 1800$$
$$1800 \div 100 = \mathbf{18}$$

KEY IDEAS

- The percent symbol (%) means "out of 100."
- The three elements of a percent problem are the base, the part, and the rate.
- Percent problems can be solved by writing a proportion that has a denominator of 100.

HiSET EXAM TIP

The word "of" often comes before the base in a percent problem. For example, if you are asked to find 75% of 250, you know that 250 is the base.

PRACTICE 2

A. For each situation, identify and label the base, part, and rate.

1. Victor owes his uncle $1000. Recently, he gave his uncle $200. The payment was 20% of the money he owes.
2. On a test with 80 problems, Sophie got 72 problems right. In other words, she answered 90% of the problems correctly.
3. The Kang family made a down payment of $2,740 on a new car. The down payment was 20% of the purchase price of $13,700.
4. Zoe's take-home pay each month is $2000. She spends $500 on rent each month, which is 25% of her take-home pay.
5. This year, Rafael has 60 regular customers, which is 150% of the 40 regular customers he had last year.
6. Kayla bought a dress for $38. She paid $3.23 in sales tax. The sales tax rate in her state is 8.5%.
7. Misako's employer withholds 15% of her salary each paycheck for taxes. Misako earns $900 each week, and her tax withholding is $135.
8. Harrison got a 10% raise. Before the raise, his hourly wage was $10.70. Now he earns an additional $1.07 per hour.
9. Kim Industries has 800 employees. Of those, 200 workers, or 25%, work part-time.
10. In an election, 5,000 of the 12,500 registered voters actually voted. Only 40% of the registered voters actually voted.

B. Choose the one best answer to each question. Use the proportion $\frac{\text{part}}{\text{base}} = \frac{\text{rate}}{100}$ to solve each problem.

Questions 11 and 12 refer to the following information.

A local newspaper printed the following high school basketball standings:

Team	Wins	Losses
Fairfax	9	3
Hamilton	8	4
Bravo	6	6
Mountain View	4	8
Lincoln	3	9

11. Which of the following expressions could be used to find what percent of its total games Fairfax has won?

A. $\frac{9 \times 100}{12}$
B. $\frac{3 \times 100}{12}$
C. $\frac{12 \times 100}{9}$
D. $\frac{6 \times 100}{12}$
E. $\frac{(6 \times 100)}{9}$

12. What percent of its games did Bravo win?

A. 100%
B. 80%
C. 75%
D. 60%
E. 50%

13. A jacket with a price tag of $128 is on a rack with the following sign:

All Items:
25% off marked price
Discount taken at register

By how much will the price be reduced when the jacket is taken to the register?

A. $4
B. $25
C. $32
D. $64
E. $96

Number and Quantity Part III: Ratio, Proportion, and Percent

LESSON 3

Using the Percent Formula

KEY IDEAS

- You can use a formula to solve percent problems: *Base × Rate = Part*.
- To change a percent to a decimal, drop the % sign and move the decimal point two places to the left.
- To change a decimal to a percent, move the decimal point two places to the right and add the % sign.

HiSET EXAM TIP

When you take the Mathematics Test, make a quick sketch of the percent diagram on the scratch paper to help you analyze percent problems.

Solving for Part

You have seen how to use proportion to solve percent problems. You can also solve percent problems using the formula ***Base × Rate = Part.***

Study the diagram at the right to learn how to use the formula. To use the diagram, cover the element you need to solve for: B = Base, R = Rate (percent), and P = Part. Then perform the operation that connects the remaining elements.

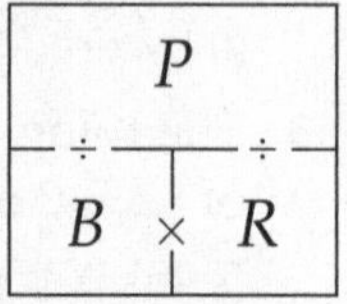

Example 1: A company offers its employees two health plans. In a recent newsletter, the personnel department stated that 70% of the employees chose Plan A. If the company has 320 workers, how many chose Plan A?

1. The rate is 70%, and the base is 320, the total number of workers. You need to solve for the part. Using the diagram, cover P for part. You can see that you need to multiply to solve the problem.

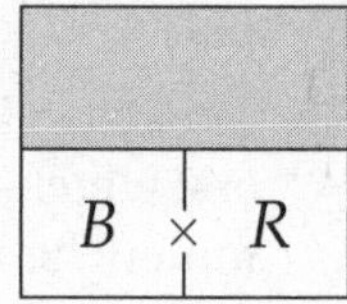

2. Change the percent to a decimal and multiply. **Out of 320 workers, 224 chose Plan A.**

$70\% = 0.7$

$320 \times 0.7 = \mathbf{224}$

Solving for Rate

Rewrite the percent formula to solve for rate. Use the formula *Part ÷ Base = Rate*. You can use the diagram to help you remember the formula.

Example 2: A computer system is regularly priced at $1600. On Friday, the manager reduced the price by $640. By what percent did the manager discount the computer system?

1. The base is $1600, the regular price. The part is $640, the amount the price was reduced. You are asked to find the rate of the discount. Cover R for rate (percent). You need to divide the part by the base to solve the problem.

P
÷
B

2. Divide 640 by 1600.

3. Convert the decimal answer to a percent by moving the decimal point two places to the right and adding the percent sign. The price reduction was a **40% discount.**

$$1600\overline{)640.0} = 0.4$$

640.0

$0.4 = 40 = \mathbf{40\%}$

Always ask yourself whether your answer seems reasonable. For example, you know that 40% is a little less than $\frac{1}{2}$, and $\frac{1}{2}$ of $1600 is $800. Since $640 is a little less than $800, it is a reasonable answer.

PRACTICE 3.1

A. Solve.

1. What is 20% of \$25?
2. Find 90% of 200.
3. What is 35% of 400?
4. What percent is 19 out of 20?
5. 42 is what percent of 168?
6. What percent is \$18 out of \$600?
7. Find $33\frac{1}{3}\%$ of 51. (*Hint:* $33\frac{1}{3}\% = \frac{1}{3}$)
8. What is 125% of \$48?
9. 240 is what percent of 120?
10. What percent is 3 out of 60?
11. \$52 is what percent of \$650?
12. Find $8\frac{1}{2}\%$ of \$46.
13. \$0.65 is what percent of \$10.00?
14. Find 28% of \$1300.
15. What percent is 2.5 out of 4?
16. Find $66\frac{2}{3}\%$ of 108. (*Hint:* $66\frac{2}{3}\% = \frac{2}{3}$)

B. Choose the one best answer to each question.

17. Pat called 120 customers to offer a software upgrade. Of those he called, 72 purchased the upgrade. What percent agreed to the purchase?

A. 40%
B. 48%
C. 60%
D. $66\frac{2}{3}\%$
E. 72%

18. Douglas received a 6% raise. If his old monthly salary was \$2,250, what is his monthly salary now? (*Hint:* Find the amount of the raise. Then add the raise to the previous monthly salary.)

A. \$2,256
B. \$2,385
C. \$2,850
D. \$3,600
E. \$13,500

19. At a restaurant, Levy's total bill is \$46. If he wants to tip 15%, how much should he leave as a tip?

A. \$690.00
B. \$31.00
C. \$15.00
D. \$6.90
E. \$4.60

20. The following advertisement for sporting goods appeared in the newspaper. What percent of the original price is the sale price?

Little League Package
Magnum bat, tote bag, and youth cleats
Only \$45.50
Originally \$65

A. 20%
B. 31%
C. 44%
D. 60%
E. 70%

21. Lydia pays \$3 sales tax on a \$50 purchase. Which of the following expressions could be used to find the sales tax rate in her state?

A. $\frac{\$3 \times 100}{\$50}$
B. $\frac{\$3 \times \$50}{100}$
C. $\$3 \times \$50 \times 100$
D. $\$3 \div \$50$
E. $\$3 \times 0.5$

STUDY ADVICE

Remember as you study to pay particular attention to words in bold and the Key Ideas on each page on the left. Also, study each worked example to see how to apply the concepts in your own practice.

Solving for Base

Some problems on the Mathematics Test may require you to solve for the base in a percent situation. Remember, the base represents the whole item or group. Read each situation carefully to figure out which element is missing. Then choose the correct method for solving the problem.

Example 3: In a math class, 75% of the students got at least a B grade on the final exam. If 18 students got at least a B, how many students are in the class?

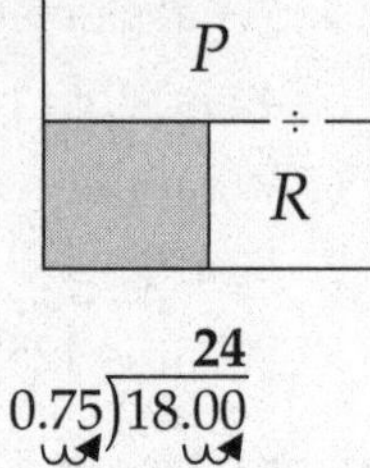

1. Analyze the situation. The 18 students are part of the larger class. You know that the 18 students are 75% of the whole group, so 75% is the rate and the base is unknown.

   Use the diagram. Cover *B* for base. You need to divide the part by the rate to solve the problem.

2. Convert the rate to a decimal (75% = 0.75) and divide. There are **24 students** in the class.

$$0.75\overline{)18.00} = \mathbf{24}$$

$$\begin{array}{r} 150 \\ \hline 300 \\ 300 \\ \hline \end{array}$$

Most of the time, we work with percents that are less than 100%. When a percent is less than 100%, the part is less than the base. However, it is possible to have a situation in which the part is greater than the base. When this occurs, the percent will be greater than 100%.

Example 4: The workforce at Eastland Inc. is growing rapidly. The number of employees this year is 225% of the number last year. If there are 135 employees this year, how many employees did the company have last year?

P
÷
R

1. The base is the number of employees the company had last year. This year's number is a percent of last year's number. Therefore, the rate is 225%, the part is 135, and the base is unknown.

2. Convert 225% to a decimal. Drop the % sign and move the decimal point two places to the left.

$$225\% = 2.25 = 2.25$$

3. Divide the part (135) by the rate (2.25). Last year, there were only **60 employees.**

$$2.25\overline{)135.00} = \mathbf{60}$$

$$\begin{array}{r} 135.0 \\ \hline \end{array}$$

There is often more than one way to approach the solution to a problem. Both the percent formula presented in this lesson and the proportion method from Lesson 1 can be used to solve Example 4.

Formula method: $\frac{135}{2.25}$ Proportion method: $\frac{135 \times 100}{225}$

If you evaluate both methods using a calculator, both expressions equal 60, the correct solution.

Note: Don't begin calculations before you completely analyze a situation. Every percent problem has three elements. Make sure you know which one is missing before you multiply or divide.

PRACTICE 3.2

A. Find the missing element in each set.

1. $35 is 20% of what amount?
2. 5% of what number is 14?
3. 3.2 is 50% of what number?
4. $170 is 85% of what amount?
5. 24 is 80% of what number?
6. $105 is 125% of what amount?
7. 190 is 95% of what number?
8. What number is 15% of 60?
9. 90% of $15 is what number?
10. $42 is what percent of $168?
11. $150 is 200% of what amount?
12. 15% of $62 is what amount?
13. 9 is 1% of what number?
14. What percent is 126 of 140?
15. 65% of $1200 is what amount?
16. 5% of an amount is $156. What is the amount?
17. $2\frac{1}{2}$% of a number is 100. What is the number?
18. What percent is $15.60 of $156.00?

B. Choose the one best answer to each question.

19. Kevin's total payroll deductions are 30% of his earnings. If his deductions add up to $369 for a two-week period, how much were his earnings for the period?

 A. $110.70
 B. $123.00
 C. $1,230.00
 D. $1,369.00
 E. $11,070.00

20. A city council established the following budget to improve public transportation.

	Project Budget
Salaries	50%
Office lease	35%
Equipment	6%
Supplies	2%
Miscellaneous	7%

If $72,000 is allotted for equipment, what is the total budget for the project?

 A. $432,000
 B. $940,000
 C. $1,200,000
 D. $12,000,000
 E. $120,000,000

21. Jack earns a 5% commission on each sale. If he is paid a $160 commission, which of the following expressions could be used to find the amount of the sale?

 A. $\frac{5 \times 100}{160}$
 B. $\frac{160 \times 100}{5}$
 C. $\frac{5 \times 160}{100}$
 D. $5 \times 100 \times 1.60$
 E. 0.5×160

22. American Loan Company mailed 3600 customers an application for a new credit card. Only 20% of the customers returned the application. How many customers returned the application?

 A. 72
 B. 200
 C. 180
 D. 720
 E. 180,000

Number and Quantity Part III: Ratio, Proportion, and Percent

LESSON 4

Percent Calculator Skills

By changing a percent to either a fraction or decimal, you can use a calculator to solve percent problems. The following examples are worked out using the keys on the TI-30XS MultiView™. Remember, your calculator may differ if you are taking the HiSET exam on paper.

Example 1: What is 25% of 120? Try both decimals and fractions.

<u>On the Display</u>

Change 25% to the decimal (.25), multiply times 120, and press [enter]. **30** is on the right of the display.

`.25*120   30`

Change 25% to the fraction $\frac{25}{100}$ using the [n/d] key, multiply times 120, and press [enter]. **30** is on the right of the display.

`25/100*120   30`

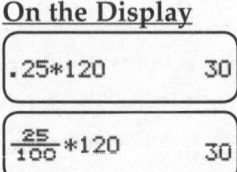

Using either decimals or fractions, you can find that **30** is 25% of 120.

When you use the *percent 2nd* function, you don't have to convert the percent to a fraction or decimal. Practice this function below to multiply to find the **part** when you are given the rate (percent).

Example 2: What is 65% of $360?

<u>Keys to Press</u> | <u>On the Display</u>

1. Type the base, 360, and press the multiplication sign.
2. Type the rate (65). Press the 2nd function key and engage the percent 2nd function—over the [(] key. Then press [enter].

The amount **$234** is 65% of $360.

You can use the percent function to divide to find the **base** when given the rate.

Example 3: Ned paid $150 for a stereo. The amount Ned paid was 20% of the original cost. What was the original cost of the stereo?

<u>Keys to Press</u> | <u>On the Display</u>

1. Enter the base, 150, and press the division sign. — 150 [÷] — `150÷`
2. Enter 20 and press the 2nd function key and the [(] key. Then press *enter*. — 20 [2nd] [% (] [enter] — `150÷20%   750`

The original cost of the stereo appears on the right of the display: **$750**.

KEY IDEAS

- One way to solve percent problems on the calculator is to change the percent to a decimal or a fraction.
- On the TI-30XS MultiView™ calculator, you can use the percent 2nd function to find the part and the base.
- To create a percent, use the 2nd function, %, which is in green over the left parenthesis [(] key.

HiSET EXAM TIP

If you are using the TI-30XS MultiView™, practice using the Delete *key when you make a mistake in a problem. That will erase your latest entry. The* Clear *key will erase the entire entry. If you are using a different calculator, find the appropriate keys for these two functions and practice using them.*

PRACTICE 4

A. Solve.

1. Find 46% of $130.
2. 14% of what amount is $13.44?
3. What is 12% of $126?
4. What number is $62\frac{1}{2}$% of 64?
5. 12 is what percent of 400?
6. A number is 32% of 6500. What is the number?
7. 36 is what percent of 144?
8. 90% of what number is 63?
9. Find 7% of 360.
10. What number is $33\frac{1}{3}$% of 237?
11. 25 is what percent of 1000?
12. What is $12\frac{1}{2}$% of 384?
13. 390 is what percent of 500?
14. Find 2% of $800.
15. 32% of what number is 80?
16. What number is $87\frac{1}{2}$% of 16?
17. $112 is what percent of $1600?
18. A number is $66\frac{2}{3}$% of 414. What is the number?

B. Choose the one best answer to each question.

Questions 19 and 20 refer to the following chart.

Shipping and Handling Information	
For items costing:	**% of order + handling:**
$20 or less	3% + $1.50
$20.01 to $50	4% + $2.50
$50.01 to $100	5% + $4.00
$100.01 or more	8%

19. Chanel placed an $84 order. How much shipping and handling will she be charged on her order?

 A. $4.20
 B. $4.40
 C. $8.20
 D. $8.36
 E. $9.00

20. Jason placed an order totaling $110. Zola placed a $90 order. How much more did Jason pay in shipping and handling than Zola?

 A. $0.30
 B. $4.30
 C. $4.50
 D. $5.00
 E. $20.00

21. In an election, 3190 out of 3625 registered voters voted against a tax increase. What percent of the registered voters voted against the increase?

 A. 43%
 B. 83%
 C. 88%
 D. 93%
 E. 98%

22. A baseball player has the following statistics. To the nearest percent, what percent of the player's at bats were strikeouts?

At Bats	Hits	Home Runs	Walks	Strikeouts
410	108	2	70	63

 A. 90%
 B. 58%
 C. 26%
 D. 20%
 E. 15%

STUDY ADVICE

Remember not to rely too much on the calculator during the Mathematics Test. Not all questions will require you to do lots of math, so don't just start plugging numbers into the calculator. First think about what the problem is asking for.

LESSON 5

Interest

KEY IDEAS

- Simple interest is found by multiplying principal, rate, and time: $I = prt$.
- The time must be written in terms of years. Write months as a fraction of a year.
- To find the amount paid back, add the principal and the interest.

Interest is a fee paid for the use of someone else's money. If you put money in a savings account, you receive interest from the bank. If you borrow money, you pay interest. In each case, the amount that you invest or borrow is called the **principal.**

Simple interest is a percent of the principal multiplied by the length of the loan. This is how simple interest is calculated:

$$\text{Interest} = \text{principal} \times \text{rate} \times \text{time}$$

Or, using abbreviations: $I = prt$.

Example 1: Asher borrows $2500 from his uncle for three years at 6% simple interest. How much interest will he pay on the loan?

1. Write the rate as a decimal. $6\% = 0.06$

2. Substitute the known values in the formula. Multiply.

$$\begin{aligned} I &= prt \\ &= \$2500 \times 0.06 \times 3 \\ &= \mathbf{\$450} \end{aligned}$$

Asher will pay **$450** in interest.

Some problems ask you to find the **amount paid back.** This adds an additional step to an interest problem. In Example 1, Asher will owe $450 in interest at the end of three years. However, he will pay back the interest ($450) plus the principal ($2500): $2500 + $450 = $2950. When he has finished paying the loan, Asher will have paid his uncle $2950.

Most bank accounts, loans, and credit cards do not use simple interest. Instead, they use **compound interest,** which means that the interest is periodically added to the principal. That new total is then used to calculate the interest for that period. The formula for compound interest is as follows:

$$A = p\left(1 + \tfrac{r}{n}\right)^{nt}$$

In the formula, A is the amount that will be in the account or owed on the loan after t years. Again, p is the principal and r is the annual interest rate expressed as a decimal. The letter t stands for the number of years since the principal started earning interest. The letter n represents the number of times per year the interest is **compounded**, or added to the principal.

HiSET EXAM TIP

A formula sheet is provided when you take the Mathematics Test (see page 259). Every time you see a formula in this book, check to see if it is on the formula sheet. If the formula is not there, you will need to memorize it.

That formula may look intimidating, but just remember: When you see a compound interest problem, simply figure out which pieces of information in the problem represent p, r, n, and t. Then plug those values into the formula. (Your calculator will be handy here. For more information about exponents, see page 372.)

Notice that the simple interest formula at the top of this page allows you to calculate the interest. The compound interest formula allows you to calculate the total amount of the loan or investment after interest has been added. If a question asks you for just the interest on a loan or investment that has compound interest, use the compound interest formula and subtract the principle from the result.

Example 2: Malik takes out a bank loan for \$2,000 for a period of two years. The bank will charge him 10% interest, compounded quarterly (that is, four times per year). How much will Malik have to pay the bank back two years from now? Round your answer to the nearest dollar.

Step 1: You are asked to solve for A. Identify the other values.

$p = 2{,}000$ $\quad r = 0.05$

$n = 4$ $\quad t = 2$

Step 2: Plug those values into the formula and solve.

$$A = 2{,}000\left(1+\tfrac{.05}{4}\right)^{(4\times2)}$$

$$A = 2{,}000(1.0125)^8$$

$$A = 2{,}000(1.1045) = 2{,}208.97$$

Malik will pay the bank **\$2209** two years from now.

A. Solve these problems using the interest formulas on the previous page. Round your answers to the nearest dollar.

1. Leah borrows \$1500 for 2 years at a 12% *simple* interest rate. Find the interest on the loan.
2. Ricardo borrows \$1850 for 8 months at 12% *simple* interest. What is the total amount he will pay back at the end of the loan period?
3. Dominica invested \$2000 for 3 years at an interest rate of 7%, compounded annually. How much interest did she earn on her money?
4. If you take out a loan of \$800 at 14% interest, compounded annually, for 2 years, how much will you have to pay back at the end of the 2 years?

B. Choose the one best answer to each question.

5. Jean borrowed \$1,300 to buy tools for her job as an auto mechanic. The loan is for 1 year 6 months at 9% simple interest. Which of the following expressions could be used to find the amount she will pay back at the end of the loan period?

A. \$1,300 × 0.09 × 1.5
B. \$1,300 × 1.5 × 0.09
C. \$1,300 × 1.5 × 9
D. \$1,300 + (\$1,300 × 9 × 1.5)
E. \$1,300 + (\$1,300 × 0.09 × 1.5)

Question 6 refers to the following information.

Option	Length of Loan	Simple Interest Rate
A	$2\frac{1}{2}$ years	12%
B	3 years	10%
C	4 years	9%

6. Charlotte needs to borrow \$2,400. She is considering the three loan options shown above. How much more interest would Charlotte pay if she takes loan option C instead of option A?

A. \$108
B. \$144
C. \$720
D. \$864
E. \$1,440

LESSON 6

Percent of Change

Percent is often used to show change.

Example 1: Michelle recently started her own business. Last month, she earned \$1000. This month, she earned \$2000. How could she describe the increase in her earnings?

All of the following statements accurately describe the change:

- Michelle's earnings doubled from last month to this month.
- This month, her earnings increased by 100%.
- This month's earnings are 200% of last month's earnings.

Percent of change compares a new number, which shows an **increase** or a **decrease**, to the original number—the number before the change.

Example 2: Before her raise, Lisa earned \$10.50 per hour. Now she earns \$11.34 per hour. What percent raise did her boss give her?

1. Subtract to find the amount of change. $\$11.34 - \$10.50 = \$0.84$
2. Divide the amount of change by \$10.50, Lisa's wage before the change. Convert the decimal to a percent. Lisa's hourly wage **increased by 8%.** $\frac{\$0.84}{\$10.50} = 0.08 = \mathbf{8\%}$

Think carefully about a situation to decide which number is the original amount.

Example 3: A jacket is on sale for \$90. Three days ago, the jacket was on sale for \$120. By what percent was the price of the jacket reduced?

1. Subtract to find the amount of change. $\$120 - \$90 = \$30$
2. The price of the jacket was \$120 before it was \$90, so \$120 is the original price. Divide the amount of change by \$120. The new price is **25% less** than the price three days ago. $\frac{\$30}{\$120} = 0.25 = \mathbf{25\%}$

Percent of increase may be greater than 100%.

Example 4: Calvin started his business with 10 employees. Now he has 60 employees. By what percent has his workforce increased?

1. Subtract to find the amount of change. $60 - 10 = 50$
2. Divide by the original number. Convert the number to a percent. Calvin's workforce has **increased by 500%.** $\frac{50}{10} = 5.0 = \mathbf{500\%}$

KEY IDEAS

- The amount of change is the difference between the new number and the original number.
- Find the percent of change by dividing the amount of change by the original number.
- Percent of increase may be greater than 100%.

HiSET EXAM TIP

You can work backward to check your answers. For example, if a price has decreased by 25%, the new price should be 75% of the original price, since 25% + 75% = 100%.

PRACTICE 6

A. Solve as directed. If necessary, round your answer to the nearest percent.

1. Find the percent of increase from 2000 to 3000.
2. Find the percent of decrease from $2.00 to $1.25.
3. What is the percent of increase from 30 to 90?
4. Find the percent of decrease from 20 to 11.
5. Find the percent of increase from $25 to $30.
6. What is the percent of decrease from 500 to 340?
7. Find the percent of increase from $1.89 to $2.29.
8. What is the percent of decrease from 21 to 3?
9. Find the percent of increase from 65 to 338.
10. What is the percent of decrease from $1550 to $1025?

B. Choose the one best answer to each question.

11. Justin recently moved from a part-time to a full-time job. Because of the change, his weekly pay increased from $280 to $448. To the nearest percent, by what percent did his income increase?

    A. 38%
    B. 60%
    C. 75%
    D. 168%
    E. 267%

12. David bought a computer game on sale for $36. The game was originally $48. What was the percent of decrease in the game's price?

    A. 12%
    B. 25%
    C. $33\frac{1}{3}\%$
    D. 50%
    E. 75%

13. The Utleys' rent increased from $600 to $636 per month. By what percent did the rent increase?

    A. 3%
    B. 4%
    C. 5%
    D. 6%
    E. 7%

Questions 14 and 15 refer to the following information.

Marc sells computer equipment. He buys printers at wholesale and sells them at retail price. Customers who join his discount club pay the member's price.

Printer Pricing Chart

Model Number	Wholesale Price	Retail Price	Member's Price
L310	$63.00	$141.75	$92.15
L1430	$86.00	$150.50	$105.35

14. What is the percent of increase from wholesale to retail price of the L310 model?

    A. 56%
    B. 78%
    C. 125%
    D. 225%
    E. 250%

15. For the L1430 model, what is the percent of decrease from retail price to member's price?

    A. 26%
    B. 30%
    C. 33%
    D. 43%
    E. 53%

STUDY ADVICE

Here's a quick rule to remember: When determining percent of change—either increase or decrease—the denominator is always the original value. Study these examples to see percent of change in action.

Ratio, Proportion, and Percent Practice Questions

Directions: Choose the one best answer to each question.

1. From a total yearly budget of $360,000, the Kimball Foundation spends $30,000 on leasing office space. What is the ratio of dollars spent on office space to dollars spent on other costs?

   A. 12:1
   B. 11:1
   C. 1:11
   D. 1:12
   E. 1:36

2. A worker can assemble 5 motors in 2 hours. Which of the expressions below could be used to find how long it would take the worker to assemble 50 motors?

   A. $2 \times \frac{50}{5}$
   B. $\frac{5 \times 50}{2}$
   C. $\frac{5}{2 \times 50}$
   D. $2 \times 5 \times 50$
   E. 50×2

3. Frank owns a discount music store. The table below shows how much Frank pays for certain merchandise items.

Item	Wholesale Price
CDs	$7.20
Posters	$5.60

   To find his selling price, Frank increases each price by 35%. What is the selling price of a poster?

   A. $9.72
   B. $7.56
   C. $5.95
   D. $4.68
   E. $1.96

4. Neva's car is now worth $12,000. This is 60% of what she paid for it. How much did she pay for the car?

   A. $7,200
   B. $16,000
   C. $18,000
   D. $19,200
   E. $20,000

5. At a shop, the ratio of union to non-union workers is 7 to 3. If there are 18 nonunion workers at the shop, how many union workers are there?

   A. 21
   B. 25
   C. 42
   D. 63
   E. 126

6. Camilla earned $954 in commission on $15,900 in sales. What is her rate of commission?

   A. 6%
   B. 9%
   C. $16\frac{2}{3}$%
   D. 25%
   E. 60%

7. John spent the following amounts of time building a workbench:

drawing the plans:	2 hours
cutting the wood:	$1\frac{1}{2}$ hours
assembling the workbench:	2 hours
sanding and sealing:	$3\frac{1}{2}$ hours

   What is the ratio of time spent cutting wood to total time spent on the project?

   A. 1:9
   B. 1:6
   C. 1:5
   D. 3:7
   E. 6:1

Questions 8 and 9 refer to the following information.

Ford County Farmland Usage Total Acreage: 40,000	
Usage	**Number of Acres**
Dairy	22,000
Nursery/greenhouse	3,600
Vegetables/fruits	5,200
Grains	9,200

8. What percent of Ford County farmland is used for the growing of grains, vegetables, or fruits?

A. 23%
B. 36%
C. 57%
D. 64%
E. 80%

9. One dairy farmer in Ford County is considering selling her farm to developers, who will convert it from a dairy farm to a resort. If this happens, the amount of farmland devoted to dairy in Ford County will decrease by 20%. How many total acres of farmland will Ford County then have if the dairy farmer decides to sell?

A. 35,600
B. 32,000
C. 16,600
D. 17,600
E. 4,400

---

10. A serving of peanut butter contains 3 grams of saturated fat and 13 grams of unsaturated fat. This amount of fat is 25% of the recommended amount of fat in a 2000-calorie diet. What is the ratio of grams of saturated fat to total fat in a serving of peanut butter?

A. $\frac{3}{16}$
B. $\frac{3}{13}$
C. $\frac{13}{16}$
D. $\frac{16}{3}$
E. $\frac{3}{19}$

11. A drawing of a company logo is 4 inches wide and 5 inches long. If the drawing is enlarged so that it is 12.5 inches long, and the original proportions remain unchanged, how many inches wide will the enlarged drawing be?

A. 7.5
B. 10
C. 15.625
D. 20
E. 25

12. A local hospital currently has 184 male patients. If the ratio of male to female patients is 4:3, how many female patients are there in the hospital?

A. 245
B. 225
C. 184
D. 144
E. 138

13. A newspaper advertisement contains the following information.

Busy Body Fitness Center Inventory Reduction Blowout! All sale prices are 20% off original price!	
Equipment	**Sale Price**
Treadmill	$1,512
Upright bike	$720
Home gym	$3,148

In dollars, what was the original price of the upright bike?

A. $566
B. $744
C. $900
D. $1,110
E. $1,890

14. The Tigers' ratio of wins to losses is 5 to 4. If the team continues winning at the same rate, how many games will the Tigers win in a 72-game season?

A. 20
B. 30
C. 36
D. 40
E. 52

15. A television station called 400 adults and asked the following question: "Do you approve of the governor's new education program?" The table below shows the results of the survey:

Response	Percentage
Undecided	16%
Yes	32%
No	52%

Of the people called, how many did not answer "no"?

A. 64
B. 128
C. 192
D. 208
E. 272

16. The price of a carton of computer paper decreased from $25 to $20. What was the percent decrease in the price?

A. 80%
B. 50%
C. 20%
D. 10%
E. 5%

17. Six months ago, Sandra had 55 regular customers. Now, she has 220% as many regular customers as she had six months ago. How many regular customers does Sandra have now?

A. 220
B. 121
C. 90
D. 66
E. 25

18. If 1 gram of fat equals 9 calories, what percent of the calories in a Munchies roast beef sandwich come from fat?

Munchies Sandwich Facts		
Sandwich	**Fat (grams)**	**Calories**
Roast Beef	6	300
Club Classic	5	335

A. 2%
B. 3%
C. 6%
D. 12%
E. 18%

19. For every $8 in their budget, the Parks spend $3 on food. If their weekly budget is $704, how much do they spend on food each week?

A. $88
B. $192
C. $235
D. $264
E. $352

20. Suddeth Travel estimates that 80% of its employees have more than 12 days of unused sick leave. If 140 employees have more than 12 days of unused sick leave, how many employees work at the agency?

A. 112
B. 164
C. 175
D. 280
E. 700

21. The Gladstone Theater has 900 seats. At a recent show, the ratio of tickets sold to tickets unsold was 11 to 1. How many tickets were sold?

A. 75
B. 90
C. 810
D. 818
E. 825

22. Matthew put $2,200 in a savings account for one year and six months. If he earns simple interest at an annual rate of 8%, how much will he have in the account at the end of the time period?
    A. $2,212
    B. $2,376
    C. $2,464
    D. $2,552
    E. $2,640

23. A television set that is regularly priced at $410 is on sale for 20% off. What is the sale price of the television set?
    A. $82
    B. $328
    C. $358
    D. $390
    E. $492

24. On a county map shown below, the map scale reads, "0.5 in = 60 mi."
    What is the actual distance in miles between Lakeview and Riverside?

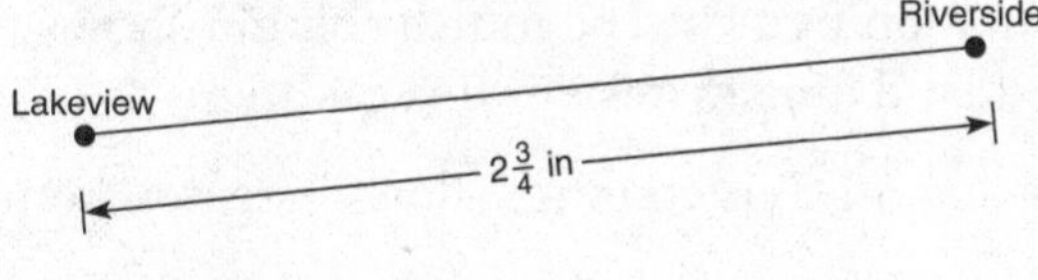

    A. 23
    B. 120
    C. 165
    D. 300
    E. 330

STUDY ADVICE

Congratulations! You've done a ton of work learning the "number and quantity" skills tested by the HiSET exam. While 19% of the questions on the Mathematics Test directly test number and quantity skills, you will also need these skills to work algebra, geometry, and statistics problems. Keep periodically reviewing the first three chapters of this unit as you work through the remaining chapters.

Question 25 refers to the following information.

Leo's Bookstore kept track of the number of customers who visited the store over a 3-day period and the number of those who made a purchase.

Day	Number of Customers	Number of Customers Who Made a Purchase
Friday	112	83
Saturday	138	45
Sunday	140	91

25. Which of the following could be used to find what percent of Sunday's customers did <u>not</u> make a purchase?
    A. $\frac{91}{140}$
    B. $\frac{(140+91)}{140}$
    C. $\frac{91}{140}\times 100$
    D. $\frac{(140-91)}{140}\times 100$
    E. $\frac{(140-91)}{91}\times 100$

26. A school admits 9 out of every 14 who apply. At that rate, how many students will be admitted if 420 apply?
    A. 90
    B. 140
    C. 180
    D. 210
    E. 270

27. In a 40-hour workweek, Marcie spends 15 hours answering telephones. What is the ratio of hours spent answering telephones to hours doing other types of work? (Record your answer as a fraction.)
    A. $\frac{1}{5}$
    B. $\frac{3}{8}$
    C. $\frac{1}{2}$
    D. $\frac{3}{5}$
    E. $\frac{3}{4}$

LESSON 1

Tables and Pictographs

Data are facts and information. By analyzing data, we can make predictions, draw conclusions, and solve problems. To be useful, data must be organized in some way. A **table** organizes data in columns and rows. The labels on the table will help you understand what the data mean.

KEY IDEAS

- Tables and graphs are often used to display data.
- Always read all labels to understand what data are presented in the table or graph.
- If symbols are used in a graph, a key will explain what each symbol represents.

Example 1: The table below shows population figures for selected counties in 2000 and 2010 and the land area in square miles for each county.

County	2000 Pop.	2010 Pop.	Land Area in sq. mi.
Adams	11,128	15,295	4,255
Bell	25,199	22,707	2,523
Cook	6,532	6,518	2,398
Davis	82,204	90,834	1,139
Evans	139,510	130,748	921

Which county showed the greatest percent of increase in population from 2000 to 2010?

1. **Read the labels.** The first column shows the county names. The second and third columns show population figures. The fourth column shows land area data. You don't need land area to answer this question.

2. **Analyze the data.** Only Adams and Davis counties show increases from 2000 to 2010.

3. **Use the data.** Find the percent of increase for Adams and Davis counties.

$$\text{Adams: } \frac{15,295-11,128}{11,128} \approx 0.374 \approx 37\%; \text{ Davis: } \frac{90,834-82,204}{82,204} \approx 0.105 \approx 10\%$$

Adams County shows the greatest percent of increase in population from 2000 to 2010.

HiSET EXAM TIP

Tables provide a lot of information. When you are answering a question based on a table, use only the information that is needed to answer the question. As Example 1 shows, the question is about population, so you do not need to use information from the last column.

A **pictograph** is another way to display data. Pictographs use symbols to compare data. A key shows what value each symbol represents.

Example 2: A city has three public library branches. A librarian kept track of the numbers of books checked out from each branch in a week. He used the data to create the pictograph below.

Branches	Books checked out from March 4 to March 10
North	
South	
West	

Key
= 150 books

PRACTICE 1

From March 4 to March 10, how many books were checked out from the South and West branches combined?

1. There are $4\frac{1}{2}$ symbols for the South Branch and 9 symbols for the West branch. Add: $4\frac{1}{2}+9=13\frac{1}{2}$ symbols.
2. Find the value of the symbols. The key states that each symbol equals 150 books. Multiply by 150: $13\frac{1}{2}\times 150=$ **2025 books.**

A. Use the table on page 330 to answer questions 1 and 2. Use the pictograph on page 330 to answer questions 3 and 4.

1. On average, how many people were there per square mile in Bell County in 2010?
2. To the nearest percent, what was the percent of decrease in Evans County's population from 2000 to 2010?
3. How many more books were checked out from North Branch than from South Branch during the week of March 4?
4. How many books were checked out from all three branches combined?

B. Choose the one best answer to each question.

Questions 5 and 6 refer to the following table.

Percentage of 3-year-old children with school-readiness skills for the years 2004 and 2010

	2004	2010
Recognizes all letters	11%	17%
Counts to 20 or higher	37%	47%
Writes own name	22%	34%
Reads or pretends to read	66%	67%

5. If 100,000 children were surveyed in each year, which category showed the least percent of increase from 2004 to 2010?
   A. Recognizes all letters
   B. Counts to 20 or higher
   C. Writes own name
   D. Reads or pretends to read
   E. No category increased

6. A community had 350 three-year-old children in 2010. If the chart is representative of the community, how many were able to write their own name?
   A. 34
   B. 97
   C. 119
   D. 134
   E. 175

Questions 7 and 8 refer to the following graph.

Mayfair Parking Garage
Daily Average of Parked Cars by Timed Period

Time of Day	Average Number of Cars
8:00 A.M.–noon	
12:01–4:30 P.M.	
4:31–8:00 P.M.	

Key

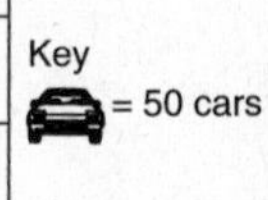

7. How many cars are parked in the garage from 12:01 to 4:30 P.M.?
   A. 275
   B. 350
   C. 375
   D. 425
   E. 650

8. How many more cars are parked from 8 A.M. to noon than are parked after 4:30 P.M.?
   A. 75
   B. 100
   C. 175
   D. 200
   E. 225

Bar and Line Graphs

KEY IDEAS

- A bar graph uses bars to represent numbers.
- To find the value of a bar, compare its length to the scale shown on one of the axis lines. Estimate the value.
- A double-bar graph compares groups of data. Read the key to find the meaning of the bars.

Working with Bar Graphs

A **bar graph** uses bars to represent values. Bar graphs have two axis lines. One line shows a number scale, and the other shows labels for the bars. By comparing the length of a bar to the scale, you can estimate what value the bar represents.

Example 1: A national corporation made a bar graph (shown below) to show the number of discrimination complaints made by employees during a six-year period. About how many more complaints were made in 2010 than in 2009?

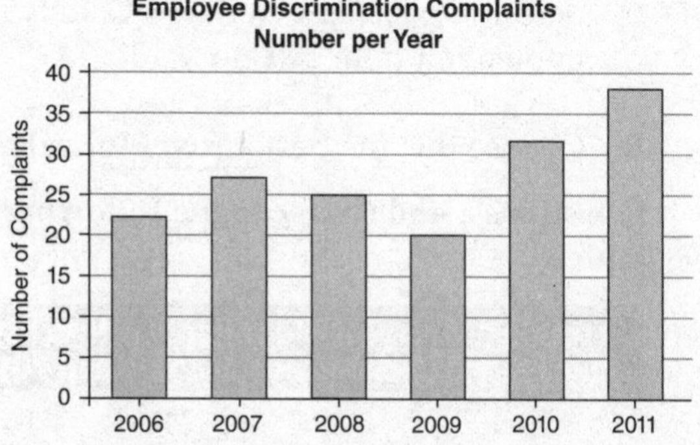

1. **Read the labels.** Each bar represents the number of complaints made within a year. The years are shown beneath the bars.
2. **Analyze the data.** Compare the bars for 2009 and 2010 to the scale. There were 20 complaints in 2009 and about 32 complaints in 2010.
3. **Use the data.** Subtract: $32 - 20 = 12$. There were **about 12 more** complaints in 2010 than in 2009.

A **double-bar graph** compares more than one type of data.

Example 2: A studio released four films in one year. The graph below compares the cost of making each movie to its box-office receipts, or ticket sales. Film B's cost is what percent of its box-office receipts?

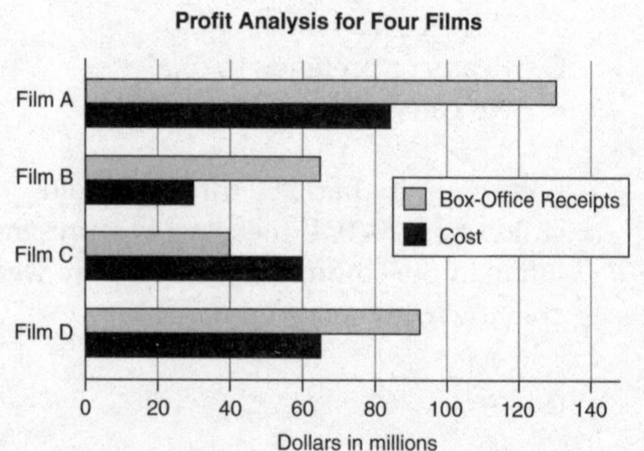

1. **Read the labels.** Read the key to find the meaning of the bars. Notice that the scale represents millions of dollars.
2. **Analyze the data.** Film B's cost is about \$30 million. It brought in about \$65 million in receipts.
3. **Use the data.** Find what percent \$30 is of \$65.
$\frac{\$30}{\$65} \approx 0.462 \approx$ **46%**

HiSET EXAM TIP

You may not be able to find the exact value of a bar. If the bar falls about halfway between two numbers on the scale, use a whole number that lies in the middle.

PRACTICE 2.1

A. For questions 1 through 3, use the bar graph entitled "Employee Discrimination Complaints" on page 332. For questions 4 through 6, use the bar graph entitled "Profit Analysis for Four Films" on page 332.

1. To the nearest ten, how many employee discrimination complaints were there in 2006 and 2007?

2. To the nearest five, how many more complaints were there in 2011 than in 2006?

3. By what percent did the number of complaints decrease from 2008 to 2009?

4. About how much more did it cost to make Film A than Film D?

5. Which film made the greatest amount of profit? (*Hint:* profit = receipts − cost)

6. Film C's cost was what percent of its box-office receipts?

B. Choose the one best answer to each question.

Questions 7 and 8 refer to the following graph.

Items Sold for the Week of Sept 20

Games
Toys
Books
Movies
T-shirts
0 20 40 60 80 100 120
Number sold

7. Approximately how many more T-shirts were sold than books and toys combined?
   A. 40
   B. 70
   C. 80
   D. 90
   E. 110

8. One-half of the games sold during the week of September 20 were on sale for \$16. The rest sold for the full price of \$24. Approximately how much money did the store take in for games sold during the week of September 20?
   A. \$400
   B. \$600
   C. \$800
   D. \$1,000
   E. \$1,200

Questions 9 and 10 refer to the following graph.

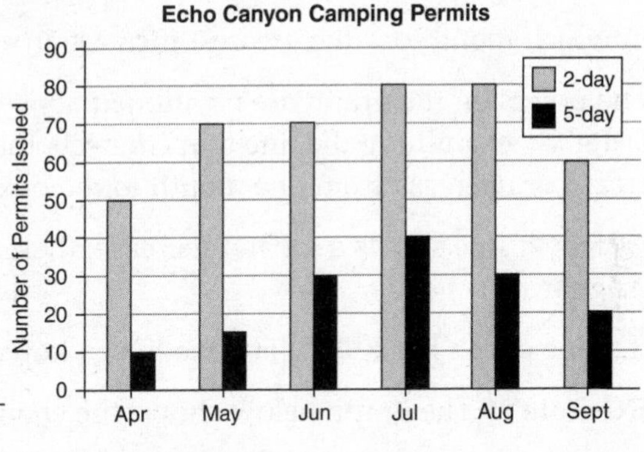

9. In May, what was the ratio of the number of 2-day permits to the number of 5-day permits?
   A. 2:5
   B. 3:17
   C. 14:3
   D. 14:17
   E. 7:3

10. In which month was there a total of 80 permits issued?
    A. May
    B. June
    C. July
    D. August
    E. September

Working with Line Graphs

A **line graph** is useful for showing changes over time. By analyzing the rise and fall of the line, you can tell whether something is increasing, decreasing, or staying the same. Like a bar graph, a line graph has two axis lines. One is marked with a scale; the other is marked in regular time intervals.

Example 3: The graph below shows the number of patients who visited an emergency room for the treatment of scooter-related injuries.

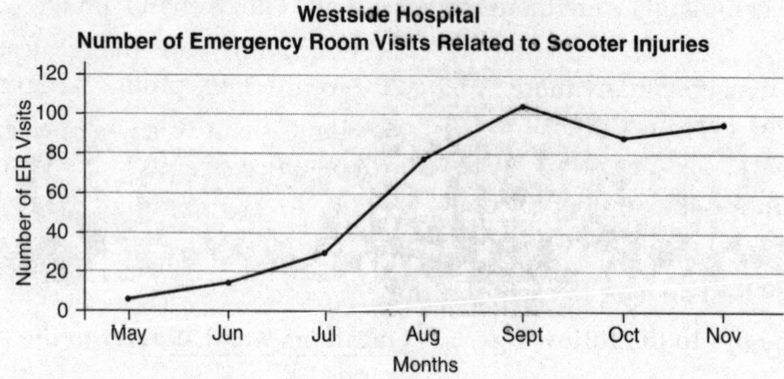

In which month did the greatest increase in scooter-related injuries occur?

The points on the graph are positioned above the months, which are arranged in calendar order. By examining the line that connects the points, you can tell whether there was an increase or decrease from one month to the next.

A steeper line shows a greater increase; therefore, the **greatest increase was from July to August**.

If a line graph has more than one line, a key will tell you what the lines represent.

Example 4: The graph below shows the changes in ticket prices for two amusement parks.

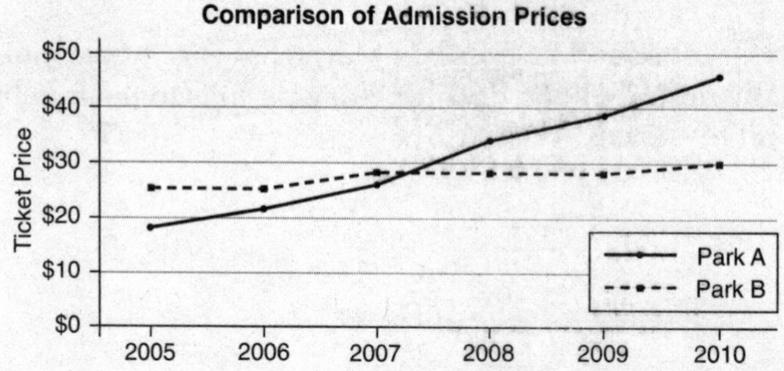

What was the last year in which the admission price to Park B was greater than the admission price to Park A?

The admission prices for Park A are represented by a solid line. Park B's prices are shown with a dotted line. The graph begins in 2005. In 2005, Park B's ticket price is greater than Park A's. Follow the two lines to the right. Between 2007 and 2008, the lines cross, and Park A's prices climb higher than Park B's. **The year 2007** was the last time that Park B charged more than Park A for a ticket.

Note: The steepest line shows the greatest increase or decrease, but it may not show the greatest *percent* of change. When the original value is small, a small change may result in a high percent of change.

PRACTICE 2.2

A. For questions 1 through 3, use the graph from Westside Hospital on page 334. For questions 4 through 6, use the graph "Comparison of Admission Prices" on page 334.

1. In which month did the number of scooter-related injuries decrease?
2. To the nearest 10, how many emergency room visits were due to scooter injuries in August, September, and October combined?
3. Which of the following shows the greater percent of increase: the change in injuries from June to July or the change from August to September?
4. About how much more did it cost to buy a ticket to Park A than a ticket to Park B in 2009?
5. What was the percent of increase in the ticket prices at Park B from 2005 to 2010?
6. To the nearest 10, how much more did it cost to buy a ticket to Park A in 2010 than in 2005?

B. Choose the one best answer to each question.

Questions 7 and 8 refer to the graph below.

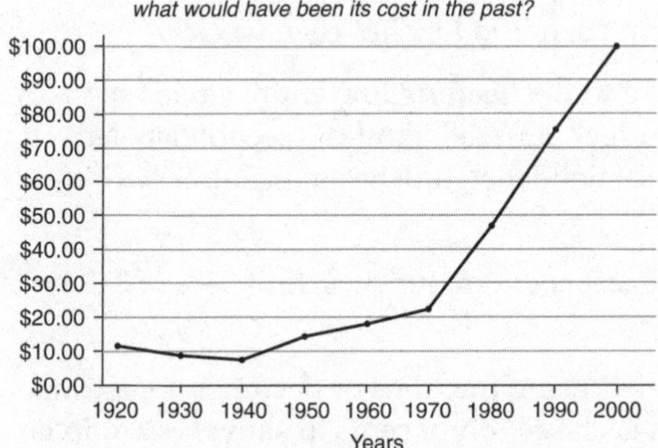

7. Over what period of time did the price of goods actually decrease?
   A. 1930 to 1940
   B. 1940 to 1950
   C. 1960 to 1970
   D. 1970 to 1980
   E. 1980 to 1990

8. Goods purchased in 1970 were about what fraction of their cost in the year 2000?
   A. $\frac{4}{5}$
   B. $\frac{1}{2}$
   C. $\frac{1}{3}$
   D. $\frac{1}{4}$
   E. $\frac{1}{5}$

Questions 9 and 10 refer to the graph below.

Lamp Depot has two stores. The graph shows the sales data from the two stores for an 8-week period.

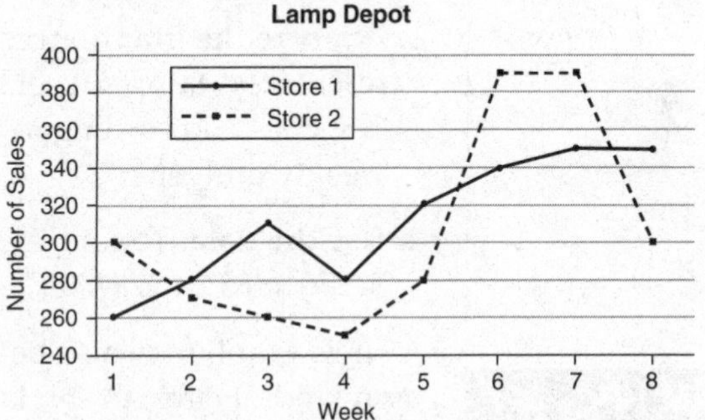

9. About how many more sales were there at Store 2 than at Store 1 in week 6?
   A. 110
   B. 50
   C. 40
   D. 25
   E. 5

10. During which week did Store 1 experience the greatest increase in sales from the week before?
    A. Week 1
    B. Week 2
    C. Week 3
    D. Week 4
    E. Week 5

LESSON 3

Circle Graphs

KEY IDEAS

- In a circle graph, the circle represents a whole amount, and the sections represent parts of the whole.
- Sections are usually labeled with percentages, but they can show amounts.
- The size of each section of a circle graph is equal to the fraction or percentage it represents.

A **circle graph** is used to show how a whole amount is broken into parts. The sections of a circle graph are often labeled with percentages. The size of each section corresponds to the fraction it represents. For example, a section labeled 25% is $\frac{1}{4}$ of the circle.

Example 1: A graph below shows how a children's sports camp spends its weekly budget.

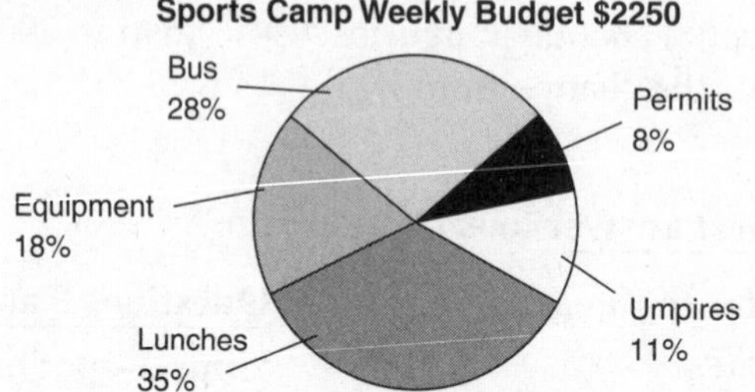

How much does the sports camp spend on lunches each week?

1. **Analyze the graph.** According to the heading, the entire circle represents the camp's weekly budget of $2250. Find the section labeled "lunches." According to the section label, lunches make up 35% of the weekly budget.
2. **Use the data.** To find the amount spent on lunches, find 35% of $2250: $\$2250 \times 0.35 =$ **$787.50.**

HiSET EXAM TIP

Since a circle graph represents a whole, or 100%, amounts can easily be converted to percentages. For example, $0.05 on a circle graph can also represent 5%.

A circle graph may also be labeled using fractions or decimals. One common kind of circle graph labels each section in cents to show how a dollar is used.

Example 2: According to the graph, what percent of the average energy bill is spent on drying clothes, lighting, and heating water?

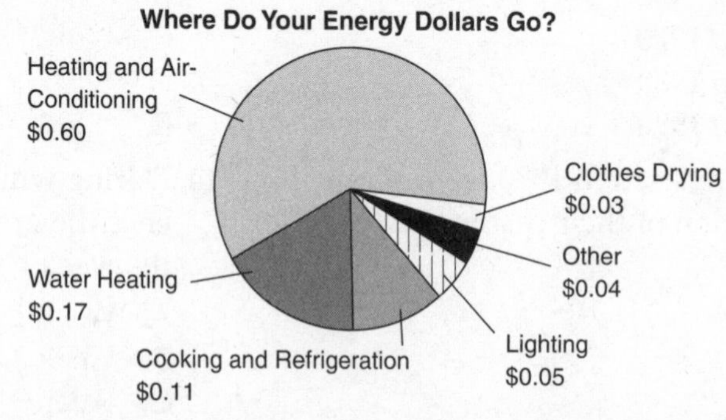

1. **Analyze the graph.** The entire circle represents $1. The amounts in the sections mentioned in the problem are $0.03, $0.05, and $0.17.
2. **Use the data.** Add the amounts: $\$0.03 + \$0.05 + \$0.17 = \$0.25$. Since $0.25 is 25% of a dollar, **25%** of an average bill is spent on these items.

PRACTICE 3

A. For questions 1 through 3, use the sports camp budget on page 336. For questions 4 through 6, use the circle graph on energy on page 336.

1. What percent of the total sports camp budget is spent on equipment and umpires?
2. What fraction of the sports camp budget is spent on permits?
3. What amount does the camp spend each week on busing?
4. A family's energy bill is $180. Assuming the family's energy use is typical, how much did the family spend on water heating?
5. Which section is greater than 50% of an energy dollar?
6. Which energy cost is about $\frac{1}{10}$ of the energy dollar?

B. Choose the one best answer to each question.

Questions 7 and 8 refer to the following graph.

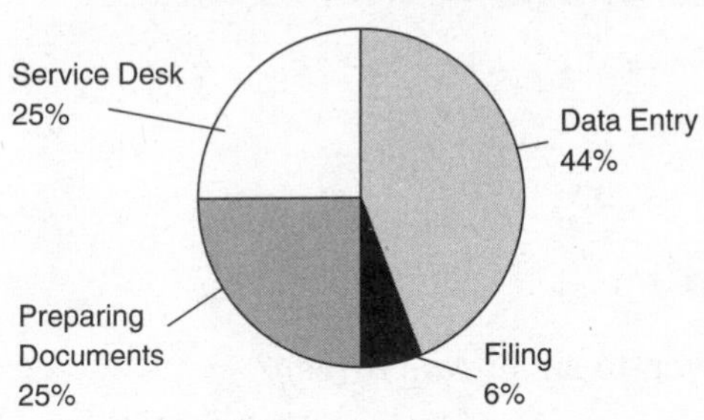

7. During a 40-hour workweek, how many hours does a records clerk spend preparing documents?
   A. 10
   B. 15
   C. 20
   D. 25
   E. 30

8. What percent of a records clerk's time is spent on tasks other than data entry?
   A. 25%
   B. 31%
   C. 44%
   D. 50%
   E. 56%

Questions 9 and 10 refer to the following graph.

The employees of National Bank are given the following graph to explain how their retirement fund is invested.

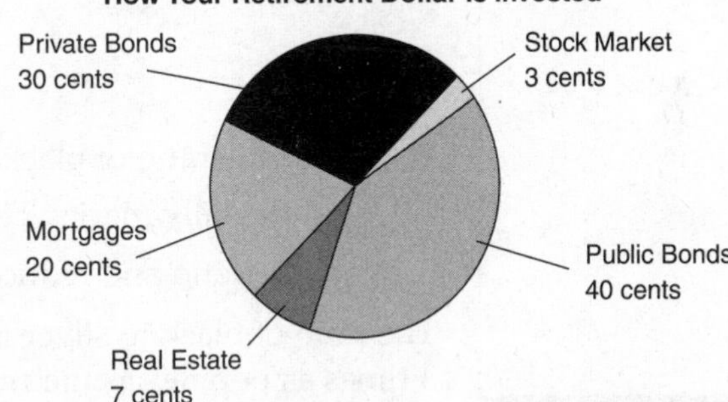

9. What percent of each retirement dollar is invested in real estate and the stock market?
   A. 4%
   B. 10%
   C. 24%
   D. 40%
   E. 90%

10. Steve contributes $120 of each paycheck to his National Bank retirement fund. How much of each contribution is invested in public bonds?
    A. $36
    B. $40
    C. $48
    D. $64
    E. $84

LESSON 4

Measures of Central Tendency

Using a Frequency Table

KEY IDEAS

- A frequency table is used to show how often data occurs.
- Tally marks are made next to a list to record the data.
- Numerical data is often grouped in intervals.

A **frequency table** shows how often an item appears in a data set. The data is in the form of tally marks next to a list of items.

Example 1: The sales manager at Montana Motors asked her sales staff to keep a record of the color of the cars that were chosen for test-drives in one month. Then she combined the data to make the frequency table shown below.

Montana Motors—Car Color Preferences	
white	𝍸 𝍸 𝍸 𝍸 𝍸 𝍸
black	𝍸 𝍸 𝍸 𝍸 𝍸 𝍷𝍷
red	𝍸 𝍸 𝍸
green	𝍸 𝍸 𝍷
silver	𝍸 𝍷𝍷𝍷𝍷
other	𝍸 𝍸 𝍸 𝍷

What was the ratio of black cars driven to silver cars driven?

1. Count the tally marks. There are 27 marks for black and 9 for silver.
2. Write the ratio and reduce to lowest terms. $\frac{27}{9} = \frac{3}{1}$

The ratio of black to silver is **3 to 1**. You can also say that the black cars are 3 times as popular as the silver cars.

HiSET EXAM TIP

If several problems refer to a frequency table, you may want to count the tally marks for each line and record the numbers on your scratch paper. Then use the numbers to solve all related problems.

Numerical data is often grouped in intervals. The table below shows data grouped in intervals of 18 to 24, 25 to 40, and so on. This way of presenting data is called a **grouped frequency table**.

Example 2: The table below shows the ages of the customers at Louise's Diner for a four-day period. What percent of the customers were from 25 to 40 years old?

Louise's Diner Customers by Age Group, February 19–22	
under 18	𝍸 𝍷
18–24	𝍸 𝍸 𝍸 𝍷𝍷𝍷
25–40	𝍸 𝍸 𝍸 𝍸 𝍸 𝍷𝍷𝍷
41–55	𝍸 𝍸
over 55	𝍸 𝍷𝍷𝍷

1. Find the data you need. There are 28 marks for the 25–40 age group. Add the tally marks for all age groups to find the total number of customers for the three-day period: $6 + 18 + 28 + 10 + 8 = 70$.
2. Find the percent. The base is 70, the total number of customers. The part is 28, the number of customers in the desired age group. Solve for the rate: $\frac{28}{70} = \frac{4}{10} = 0.4 =$ **40%**.

PRACTICE 4.1

A. For questions 1 through 3, use the frequency table from Montana Motors on page 338. For questions 4 through 6, use the frequency table from Louise's Diner on page 338.

1. What was the total number of test drives of black and white cars combined?
2. How many more drivers chose red than silver cars?
3. What was the ratio of red cars to white cars chosen for test drives?
4. What is the ratio of customers under 18 to those over 55?
5. What was the total number of customers from 18 to 40 years of age?
6. What percent of the total customers were from 41 to 55 years of age? (Round your answer to the nearest whole percent.)

B. Choose the <u>one best answer</u> to each question.

<u>Questions 7 and 8</u> refer to the following information.

The frequency table shows the reasons customers gave for returning clothing merchandise to a store.

Reason	Number
Wrong size	𝍸 𝍸 𝍸 𝍷
Unwanted gift	𝍸 𝍸 𝍸 𝍸
Found flaw after purchase	𝍷𝍷𝍷
Changed mind	𝍸

7. What is the ratio of customers saying the clothes were the wrong size to all the returns represented?
   A. $\frac{4}{15}$
   B. $\frac{4}{11}$
   C. $\frac{4}{7}$
   D. $\frac{2}{3}$
   E. $\frac{4}{5}$

8. Approximately what percent of the customers who returned clothing said that the clothes were an unwanted gift?
   A. 20%
   B. 25%
   C. 45%
   D. 50%
   E. 60%

<u>Questions 9 and 10</u> refer to the following information.

A personnel office gives typing tests to people applying for a job. The test shows how many words per minute (wpm) a job applicant can enter correctly. After testing 90 applicants, the manager made the following table.

Typing Speed	Number
Under 30 wpm	𝍸 𝍸 𝍸 𝍸 𝍸 𝍸 𝍸
30–45 wpm	𝍸 𝍸 𝍸 𝍸 𝍸
46–60 wpm	𝍸 𝍸 𝍸 𝍷𝍷𝍷
Over 60 wpm	𝍸 𝍸 𝍷𝍷

9. What percent of the applicants had a speed of under 30 wpm?
   A. 14%
   B. 25%
   C. 28%
   D. 39%
   E. 44%

10. What is the ratio of applicants who could type at a speed above 45 wpm to those who could type at a speed of 45 wpm or less?
    A. 1:3
    B. 1:2
    C. 2:3
    D. 6:5
    E. 7:5

STUDY ADVICE

Remember that practice has three levels: Learn and Review, Practice and Review, Assess and Review. For each lesson, absorb the concepts on the left page, practice using the page on the right, and carefully review the explanations in the back of the book. Finally, use the question sets at the end of each chapter to assess your progress.

Mean, Median, and Mode

Suppose you were asked how much money you usually spend on groceries in a week. Some weeks, you may spend a great deal; other weeks, much less. You would probably choose an amount in the middle to represent what you typically spend. This middle value is called an **average**, or **measure of central tendency**.

The most common type of average is the **mean**, or the arithmetic average.

Example 3: In five football games, a team scored 14, 21, 3, 20, and 10 points. What is the mean, or average, score per game?

1. Add the values. $14 + 21 + 3 + 20 + 10 = 68$
2. Divide by the number of items in the data set. $68 \div 5 =$ **13.6 points per game**

Although it is impossible for a football team to score 13.6 points in a game, the number represents the center of the scores from the five games.

A calculator is useful for finding the mean. Do the calculations in two steps. Enter the addition operations. Then, if you are using the TI-30XS MultiView™, press *enter* to find the sum. Then key in the division operation. Try Example 3 above with a calculator.

Another measure of average is the median. The **median** is the middle value in a set of data.

Example 4: During a 7-hour period, a bookstore recorded the following numbers of sales. Find the median number of sales.

Hour 1	Hour 2	Hour 3	Hour 4	Hour 5	Hour 6	Hour 7
43	28	24	36	32	37	48

1. Arrange the values by size. 24, 28, 32, 36, 37, 43, 48
2. Find the middle number. 24, 28, 32, **36**, 37, 43, 48

If there is an even number of values, the median is the mean of the two middle values.

Example 5: Robert has the following test scores in his math class: 90, 72, 88, 94, 91, and 80. What is the median score?

1. Arrange the values by size and find the middle. 72, 80, **88, 90,** 91, 94
2. Find the mean of the two middle values. The median score is **89**. Add: $88 + 90 = 178$ Divide by 2: $178 \div 2 =$ **89**

The **mode** is the value that occurs most often in a set of data. A set of data could have more than one mode if several items occur the same number of times. If each item of data occurs only once, there is no mode.

Example 6: Six weather stations recorded the following temperatures at 3:00 P.M.: 45°, 44°, 45°, 47°, 46°, and 45°. What is the mode of the data?

The temperature 45° occurs most often (3 times). The mode is **45°**.

PRACTICE 4.2

A. For each data set, find the mean, median, and mode. Round calculations to the nearest hundredth or cent.

1. Golf scores for 7 rounds:
76, 82, 75, 87, 80, 82, and 79
2. Sales totals for 6 weeks:
$5,624; $10,380; $8,102; $6,494; $12,008; and $8,315
3. Cost of lunch for 8 days:
$4.50, $5.25, $4.50, $3.75, $4.50, $5.25, $6.10, and $4.25
4. Miles driven per day for 5 days:
330, 286, 342, 300, and 287
5. Grocery bills for 4 weeks:
$97.48, $106.13, $110.98, and $92.74
6. Scores on 7 quizzes:
90, 72, 86, 100, 88, 78, and 88
7. High temperatures for 10 days:
96°, 103°, 98°, 101°, 98°, 100°, 100°, 97°, 98°, and 100°
8. Inches of rainfall over 3-day period:
2.5, 1.8, and 1.4
9. Attendance figures at a play for 7 performances:
305, 294, 328, 296, 305, 315, and 292
10. Hours worked per week for 5 weeks:
36, 40, 38, 40, and 40

B. Choose the one best answer to each question.

Questions 11 and 12 refer to the following information.

Homes Sold in Fairfield Heights in June

Home	Asking Price	Selling Price
#1	$124,600	$116,500
#2	$132,400	$124,800
#3	$118,900	$116,500
#4	$98,500	$103,600
#5	$105,800	$109,000
#6	$122,400	$118,400

11. What was the mean asking price of the homes sold in Fairfield Heights in June?

A. $117,100
B. $116,500
C. $115,450
D. $114,800
E. $109,800

12. What was the median selling price of the homes sold in Fairfield Heights in June?

A. $112,750
B. $114,800
C. $116,500
D. $117,450
E. $118,900

13. The numbers of patients enrolled at four health clinics are 790, 1,150, 662, and 805. Which expression could be used to find the mean number of patients per clinic?

A. $\dfrac{790+1{,}150+662+805}{4}$
B. $790+1{,}150+662+805$
C. $\dfrac{662+1{,}150}{2}$
D. $(790+1{,}150+662+805)\div 2$
E. $(790+805)\times 2$

14. What is the median value of $268, $1,258, $654, $1,258, $900, $1,558, and $852?

A. $1,258
B. $964
C. $900
D. $852
E. $654

15. What is the mode of the following points scored: 14, 17, 14, 12, 13, 15, 22, and 11?

A. 13.5
B. 14
C. 14.75
D. 16.5
E. 17

LESSON 5

Line Plots

The same kind of information that can be expressed in a frequency table (see page 338) can also be expressed in a **line plot**. A line plot shows the frequency of data along a number line. Study the following example.

KEY IDEAS

- A line plot is a graph that shows the frequency of data along a number line.
- Based on frequency tables, line plots consist of a horizontal scale and points or x's placed over corresponding numbers.
- Line plots help us to interpret the distribution of data.

Example 1: The student health services department at a university surveyed several students and asked them how many times per week they visited the school's gym. The following frequency table shows the results for several students.

Weekly Gym Visits	Number of Students
0	I
1	II
2	II
3	III
4	0
5	I
6	0
7	I

Next, the health services department decided to create a line plot in order to see the distribution of gym visits. Each x represents a student.

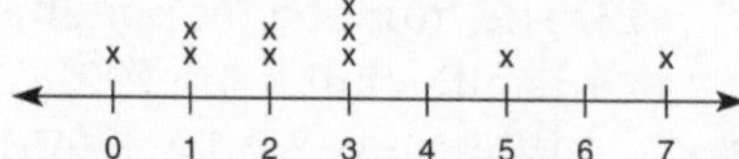

You can see from this line plot that there is an uneven **distribution**, or arrangement, of students across the numbers of possible gym visits. Three visits per week has the **highest frequency**, meaning that more students go to the gym three times per week than any other number of visits. You can also see that the data **range** extends from zero visits per week to seven visits per week—no student visits the gym more often than that. The data point showing the one student who visits the gym seven times per week is an **outlier**—that is, a data point that is distant from where most of the data is clustered.

The Mathematics Test may ask you to identify highest frequency, range, and outliers, or it may give you some data and ask you to place x's or dots on a number line to create a line plot.

HiSET EXAM TIP

One type of question may ask you to analyze data on a line plot. Another type of question could ask you to use a frequency table to place an element on a line plot.

Use the following example to study these concepts further.

Example 2: Students in Ms. Jones's class took a math test. Their scores on the test are displayed on the line plot below. Each dot represents a student. Which grade displayed the highest frequency?

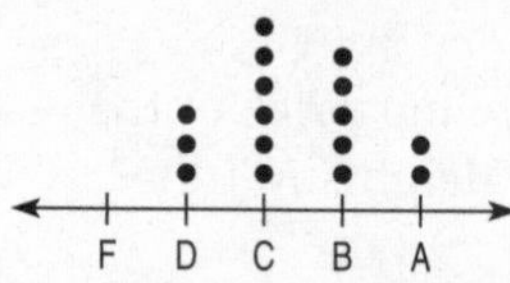

More students received a C than received any other grade. Therefore, grade **C** has the highest frequency of any grade on the line plot.

The range of grades on the math test was from D (the lowest grade received by any student) to A (the highest grade received by any student).

PRACTICE 5

For questions 1 and 2, choose the line plot that matches each frequency table. Use choices A–E below for both questions.

1. Zoologists have counted the number of stripes on certain zebras in a zoo. The set of data from these observations is represented by the following frequency table:

Number of stripes per side	Number of zebras with that many stripes
24	I
25	0
26	II
27	0
28	II
29	0
30	II
31	0
32	I

Which line plot represents this data?

2. At a certain elementary school, classes may have different numbers of students. The following frequency table represents how many students are in the classes this year:

Number of students	Number of classes with that many students
24	0
25	0
26	0
27	I
28	I
29	III
30	0
31	I
32	II

Which line plot represents this data?

A.

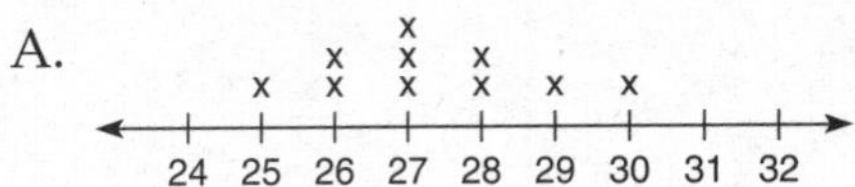

B.

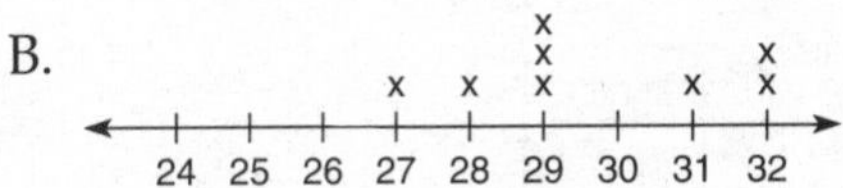

C.

X X X X X X X X

24 25 26 27 28 29 30 31 32

D.

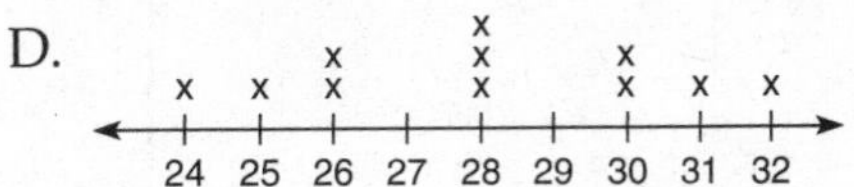

E.

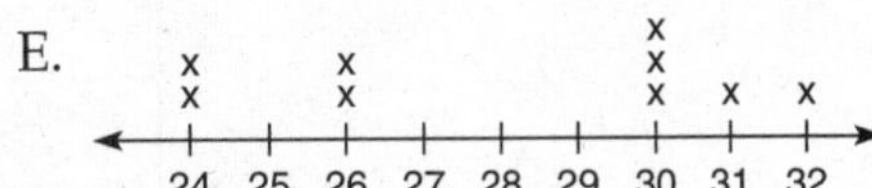

Question 3 is based on the following information.

Juana runs a community garden. She records how many different types of vegetables garden members are planting. The following line plot is based on Juana's data. Each point represents a member of the community garden. The values on the line plot represent the number of types of vegetables planted by each person.

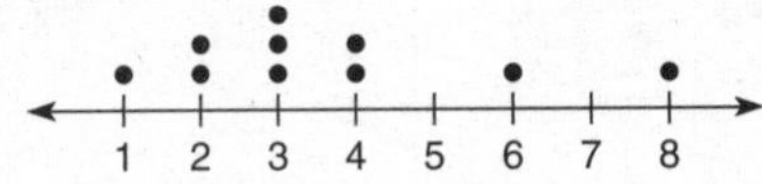

3. Which of the following can be described as (an) outlier(s)?
   - A. the member who plants one type of vegetable
   - B. the members who plant two types of vegetables
   - C. the members who plant three types of vegetables
   - D. the members who plant four types of vegetables
   - E. the member who plants eight types of vegetables

Statistics and Probability

LESSON 6

Scatter Plots

KEY IDEAS

- Scatter plots make it easier to spot trends in data that is non-linear.
- They illustrate correlations in data, whether positive, negative, or null.
- A line of best fit does not need to connect every point of data.

A scatter plot shows the correlation between two variables as a series of dots plotted on the coordinate plane. While line graphs can do the same thing in a far less complex manner, their use is limited to data that have a direct linear relationship between variables. If your watch ticks 60 times per minute, you should expect it to tick exactly 60 times every minute (as long as it works correctly), and a line graph would be a great tool to plot the number of ticks over time. However, if 60 students each studied exactly 100 hours for the HiSET exam, you would not expect exactly the same improvement from each of them. For a variety of reasons, some will see more improvement than others despite studying the same amount of time. While a line graph would be useless for this type of data, a scatter plot would be ideal.

Despite not having a strict correlation from point to point, data on a scatter plot can show either a positive correlation (rising trend) or a negative correlation (falling trend). It can also have a null correlation (no trend). The following are examples of each.

Example 1: Scatter plot with a positive correlation

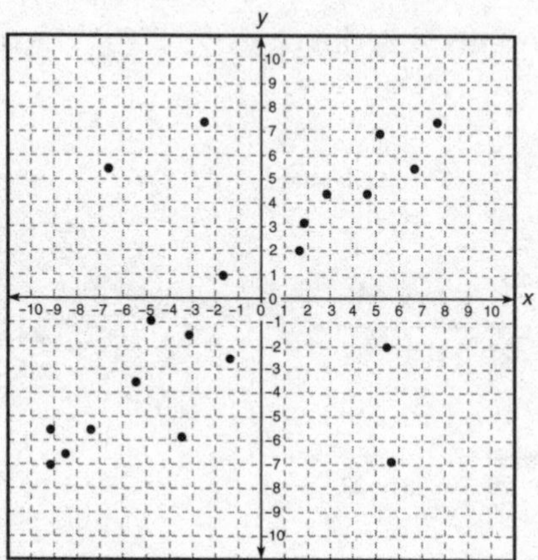

Example 2: Scatter plot with a negative correlation

HiSET EXAM TIP

When the format of a line graph would be the more useful depiction yet the data provided make such a graph impossible to draw, scatter plots are the solution.

PRACTICE 6.1

Example 3: Scatter plot with a null correlation

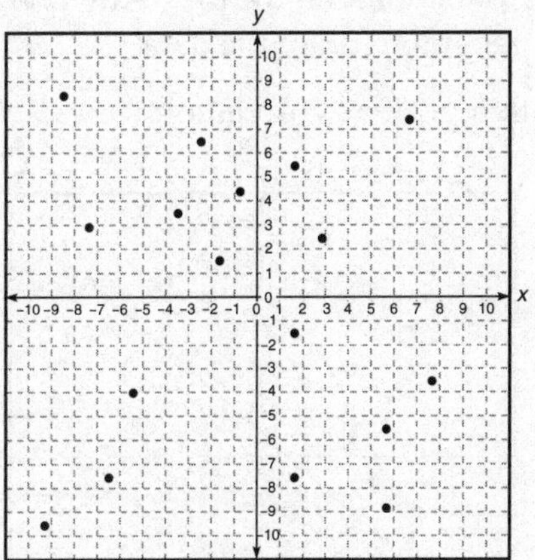

Would a positive, negative, or null trend among the given data points be the most likely?

1. Average daily temperature and ice cream sales
2. Average daily sales at a barber shop over the course of a month
3. Cronut prices and number of cronuts sold
4. Number of working doctors in Fluville and the average wait time to see a doctor in Fluville
5. Number of invited guests for a holiday party and size of the room booked for that party

Line of Best Fit

The primary use of a scatter plot, once drawn, is to more easily locate a general trend (if one exists) among the data. When a trend does exist, a **line of best fit**, also known as a *trend line*, can be drawn to bring this trend to light. As the name suggests, a line of best fit will usually *not* connect every data point on the plot—it will instead aim to connect as many points as possible that fit the general trend of the data.

Example 4: Line of best fit with a positive correlation

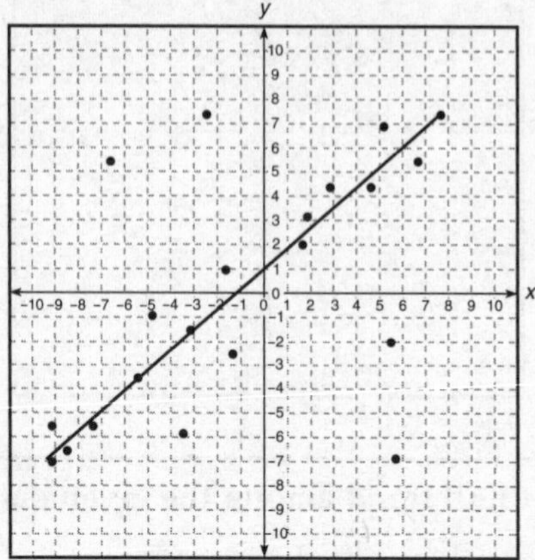

Example 5: Line of best fit with a negative correlation

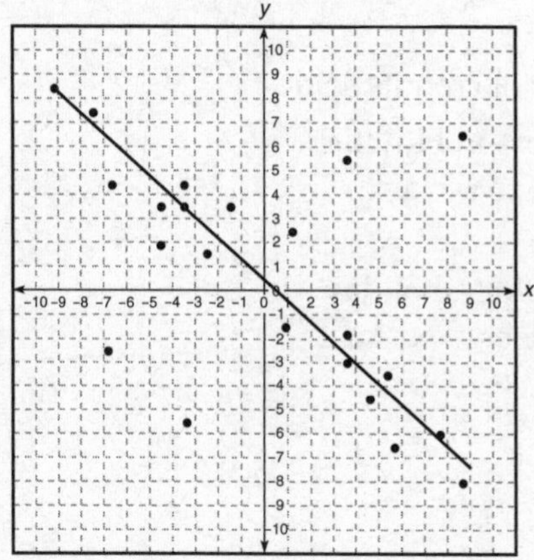

Note that no line of best fit can be drawn when a scatter plot has a null correlation.

PRACTICE 6.2

Choose the one best answer to each question. Questions 1–3 refer to the following graph.

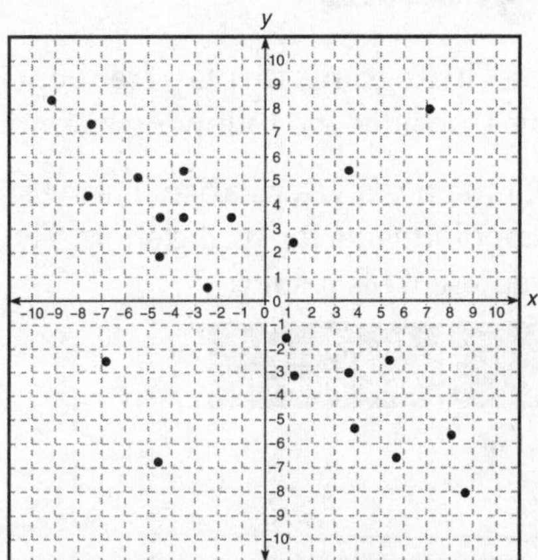

1. Which of the following is true of the graph?
   A. A line of best fit with a positive correlation can be drawn.
   B. A line of best fit with a negative correlation can be drawn.
   C. A line of best fit with a positive or a negative correlation can be drawn.
   D. A line of best fit with a null correlation can be drawn.
   E. No line of best fit is possible as no single line will connect every dot.

2. Which of the following are the most likely labels for the *x*- and *y*-coordinates, respectively?
   A. Number of hours spent studying and grades of students in a math class
   B. Number of hours the average person in Metroville works and average hourly wage
   C. Amount of candy consumed and number of cavities
   D. Average daily temperatures and number of people at the beach
   E. Annual winter temperatures and sales of winter gear

3. If an additional data point that conforms closely to the trend appeared on the graph, that point would most likely be at
   A. (–5, –5)
   B. (–1, 9)
   C. (0, –8)
   D. (6, 6)
   E. (9, –9)

Histograms

Like line plots, **histograms** display **frequencies**, but they do so in a very different way. Consider the following example:

KEY IDEAS

- A histogram is another form of data display based on utilizing groups and counts within a group.
- Groups are plotted on the horizontal axis, and frequencies are plotted on the vertical axis.

Example 1: Graham is a veterinarian. Last year, he decided to track client appointments for spring shots. The following table and histogram represent his results:

Week of	Number of Appointments
March 1–7	2
March 8–14	4
March 15–21	8
March 22–28	11
March 29–April 4	14
April 5–11	17
April 12–18	13
April 19–25	7
April 26–May 2	5

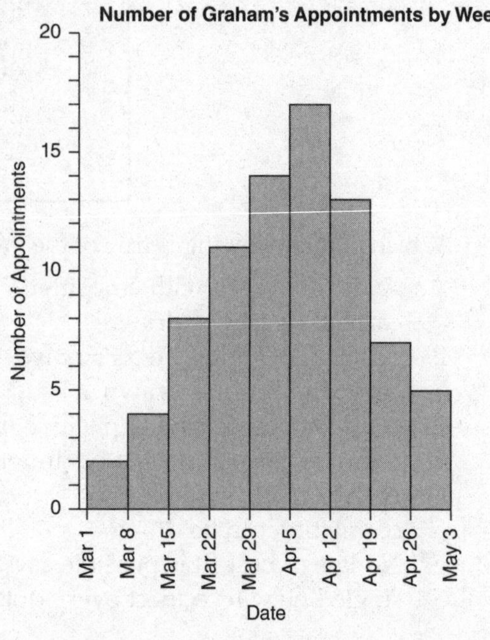

The **histogram** above on the right has two axes: a **vertical axis** (or y-axis) representing numbers of appointments and a **horizontal axis** (also called an x-axis) that has increments representing the weeks. The **height** of each bar represents the number of appointments for that week. Thus, you can see not only how many appointments were in any given week but also how the **frequency** of appointments changed over the weeks in the chart.

HiSET EXAM TIP

Some multiple-choice questions may ask you to identify graphs that represent different types of data collection. You may be given some data and asked which graph represents that set of data.

Finally, histograms can also be used to show percentages. If we alter the histogram about Graham's appointments so that each bar represents the *percentage* of total appointments each week, it will look like the one on the right.

Because the percentages add up to 100%, the heights of all the bars add up to 100.

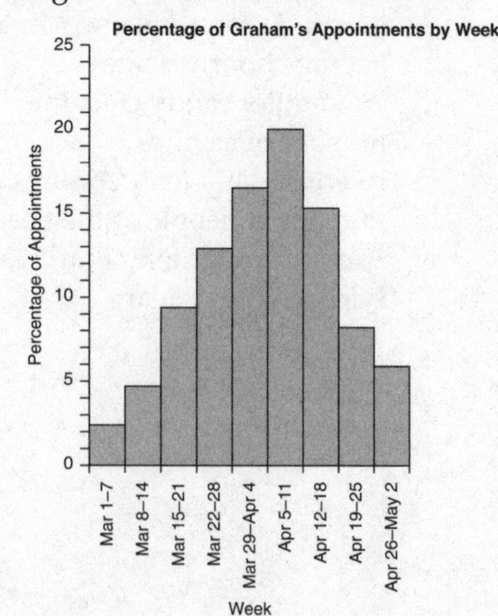

Example 2: What percent of appointments for spring shots occurred during the first two weeks of March?

You can figure this out by adding the percentages for those weeks (you can approximate based on the histogram): for March 1–7, about 2%; for March 8–14, about 5%. Approximately 7% of appointments for spring shots occurred during those two weeks.

A. Choose the histogram that matches each frequency table. Use choices A–E below for both questions 1 and 2.

1. Josefina runs a retail business. She posted a coupon to a social media site from 9:00 A.M. to 5:00 P.M. The table shows how many people downloaded or printed the coupon.

Hour beginning with:	Number of people who downloaded or printed coupon:
9:00 A.M.	30
10:00 A.M.	56
11:00 A.M.	80
12:00 P.M.	71
1:00 P.M.	56
2:00 P.M.	31
3:00 P.M.	22
4:00 P.M.	14

2. Mike administered a skills assessment to his employees. Possible scores on the skills assessment ranged from 200 to 1800. The following table shows how his employees performed on the assessment:

Score range	Number of employees
200–399	15
400–599	22
600–799	35
800–999	62
1000–1199	80
1200–1399	69
1400–1599	47
1600–1800	20

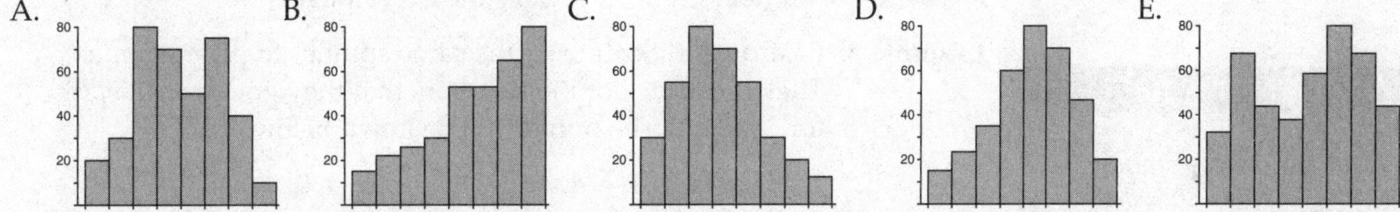

B. Choose the one best answer to the following question.

Question 3 refers to the following histogram and information.

Influenza, or "flu," season in the United States tends to last from fall through spring.

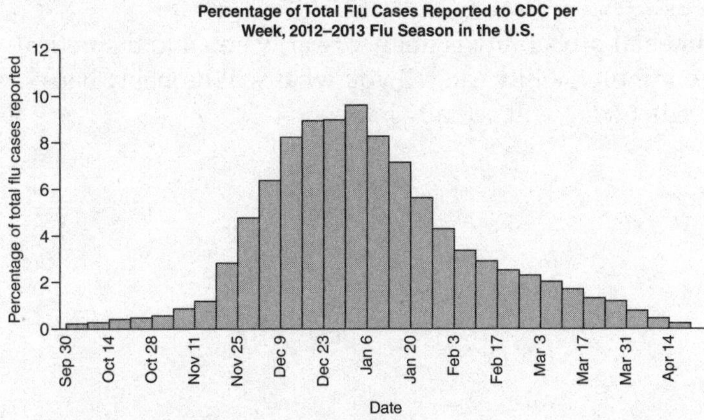

Source: Centers for Disease Control and Prevention

3. Approximately what percent of flu cases was reported to the CDC during the 2012–2013 season during the time period of December 9 to January 5?

A. 7%
B. 15%
C. 36%
D. 50%
E. 58%

LESSON 8

Probability

KEY IDEAS

- Probability is a ratio. It can be expressed as a ratio, fraction, decimal, or percent.
- Theoretical probability is the ratio of favorable outcomes to possible outcomes.
- Experimental probability is the ratio of favorable outcomes to the number of trials in an experiment.

Simple Probability

Probability tells whether something is likely or unlikely to happen. The probability of any event can be expressed by a number from 0 to 1. If an event has 0 probability, the event is impossible. An event with a probability of 1 is certain to happen. Most events are somewhere in between.

To find the probability of a simple random event, we must identify favorable and possible outcomes. A **favorable outcome** is the event that we are interested in. The **possible outcomes** are all the possible events that could occur. **Theoretical probability** (sometimes called **simple probability**) is the ratio of favorable outcomes to possible outcomes.

Example 1: The spinner is divided into 8 equal sections. What is the probability of spinning a 4 on the spinner?

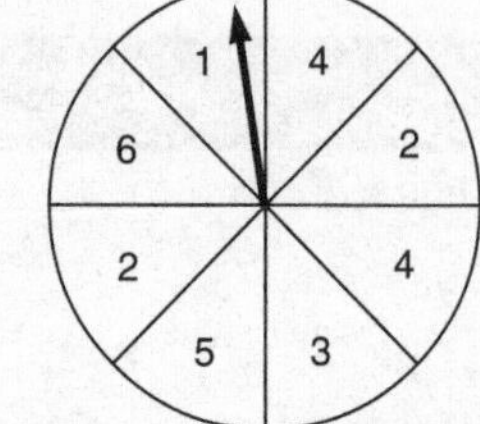

1. There are two sections labeled 4 on the spinner, and there are 8 sections in all.
2. Use the probability ratio: $\frac{\text{favorable outcomes}}{\text{possible outcomes}} = \frac{2}{8} = \frac{1}{4}$.

The probability of spinning a 4 on the spinner is **1 out of 4, $\frac{1}{4}$, 0.25, or 25%.**

In Example 1, probability was based on what we knew could happen. Another type of probability, called **experimental probability**, is based on what actually happens during the trials of an experiment. The number of trials are the number of times you try the experiment.

Example 2: Ricardo and Scott used the same spinner to play a game. They kept track of the numbers that they got on each spin for 20 spins. The numbers are shown below.

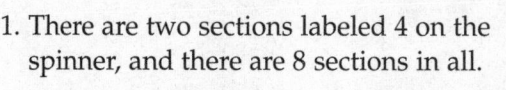

2, 4, 4, 6, 4, 3, 4, 6, 4, 3, 1, 6, 2, 2, 5, 2, 4, 2, 1, 2

Based on their results, what is the experimental probability of spinning a 4?

1. Ricardo and Scott spun a 4 six times out of twenty.
2. Use this ratio: $\frac{\text{favorable outcomes}}{\text{number of trials in experiment}} = \frac{6}{20} = \frac{3}{10}$, **0.3, or 30%.**

Notice that experimental probability is not necessarily equal to theoretical probability. Theoretical probability can tell you what will probably happen, but it can't predict what will actually happen.

HiSET EXAM TIP

In a multiple-choice probability problem, skim the answer choices to see if they are in fraction, percent, or ratio form. Knowing the answer form will help you decide how to do your calculation.

PRACTICE 8.1

A. Express probability as a fraction, decimal, <u>and</u> percent for questions 1 through 5.

1. A game has 50 wooden tiles. Players draw tiles to spell words. If 20 of the tiles are marked with vowels, what is the probability of drawing a vowel from the tiles?

2. A spinner has five equal sections colored either red, white, or blue. After 40 spins, a player has the following results:

Color	Frequency
red	卌
white	卌 II
blue	卌 卌 卌 卌 卌 III

What is the experimental probability of not spinning blue on the spinner?

3. There are four red, four blue, and two green marbles in a bag. If one marble is chosen at random from the bag, what is the probability that the marble will be green?

4. A movie theater sells 180 adult tickets and 60 children's tickets to a movie. As part of a special promotion, one ticket will be chosen at random, and the winner will receive a prize. What is the probability that the winner will be a child?

5. A spinner has six equal sections numbered from 1 to 6. What is the probability of spinning either a 5 or 6?

B. Choose the <u>one best answer</u> to each question.

<u>Questions 6 and 7</u> refer to the following information.

A deck of 12 cards is marked with the following symbols.

6. If a card is chosen at random, what is the probability of selecting a diamond (♦)?

A. 6%
B. 12%
C. 33%
D. 50%
E. 60%

7. If a card is chosen at random, what is the probability of selecting something other than a club (♣)?

A. $\frac{3}{4}$
B. $\frac{2}{3}$
C. $\frac{1}{3}$
D. $\frac{1}{4}$
E. $\frac{9}{100}$

<u>Questions 8 and 9</u> refer to the following information.

Erin flipped a coin 40 times and made this table to show how many outcomes were "heads" and how many were "tails."

heads	卌 卌 卌 卌 IIII
tails	卌 卌 卌 I

8. Based on Erin's data, what is the experimental probability of getting tails on a coin flip?

A. 3 out of 5
B. 3 out of 4
C. 1 out of 2
D. 2 out of 3
E. 2 out of 5

9. Based on Erin's data, what is the experimental probability of getting heads on a coin flip?

A. 3 out of 5
B. 3 out of 4
C. 2 out of 3
D. 1 out of 2
E. 2 out of 5

Dependent and Independent Probability

You know how to find the probability of a single event. You can use this knowledge to find the probability of two or more events.

Example 3: Brad tosses two quarters into the air. What is the probability that both will land so that the heads sides are showing?

One way to solve the problem is to list or diagram all the possible outcomes.

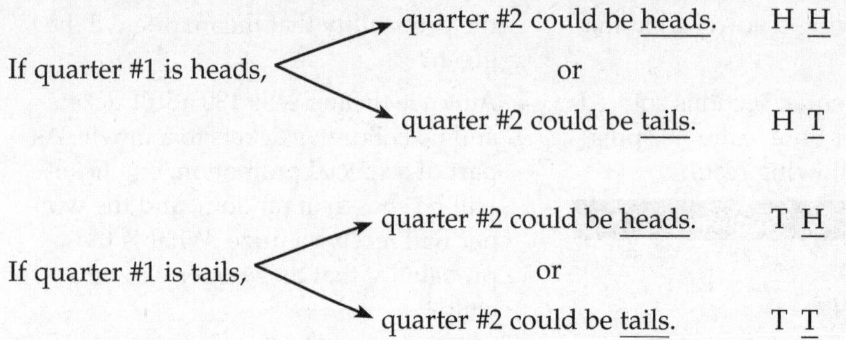

There are four possible outcomes, and only one is favorable (HH). Therefore, the probability of having both land with the heads side up is $\frac{1}{4}$, or **25%**.

You can also use multiplication to find the probability.

1. Find the probability of the individual events. The probability that one coin will be heads is $\frac{1}{2}$, and the probability that the other will be heads is $\frac{1}{2}$.
2. Multiply to find the probability of both events. $\frac{1}{2} \times \frac{1}{2} = \frac{1}{4}$

The two coin tosses in Example 3 are **independent events**. When events are independent, one does not affect the probability of another. In Example 4 below, the events are **dependent**. Once the first event takes place, the probability of the second event is changed.

Example 4: A box contains four blue marbles and two red marbles. If you select two marbles, what is the probability that both will be blue?

(*Hint:* Even though the marbles in the box are taken out at the same time, think of one as the first marble and the other as the second marble.)

1. There are six marbles in the box, and four are blue. The probability that the first marble will be blue is $\frac{4}{6}$, which reduces to $\frac{2}{3}$.
2. Assume the first marble selected is blue. Now there are only five marbles in the box, and three are blue. The probability that the second marble will be blue is $\frac{3}{5}$.

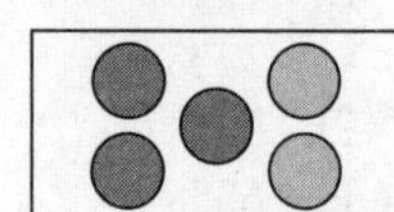

3. Multiply to find the probability of the two events. $\frac{2}{3} \times \frac{3}{5} = \frac{6}{15}$, or $\frac{2}{5}$

The probability that both marbles will be blue is **2 out of 5**.

Note: The events in Example 4 would not be dependent if the first marble were replaced before the second marble was selected. Always think carefully about the situation to decide whether two events are dependent or independent.

PRACTICE 8.2

A. Solve as directed. Express answers as fractions.

1. Kim rolls two standard six-sided dice. What is the chance that both will be 4s?
2. Ten cards are numbered from 1 to 10. Toni draws out a card, replaces it, and then draws another card. What is the probability that both cards will be numbers greater than 5?
3. A spinner has four equal sections. Two sections are red, one is green, and one is blue. If the spinner is spun three times, what is the probability that all three spins will be red?
4. Twenty marbles are placed in a bag. Ten are red and ten are black. One marble is drawn from the bag and set aside. Another marble is drawn from the bag. What is the chance that both marbles will be red?
5. Allison tosses a coin four times. What is the chance that the coin will be heads all four times?
6. If you roll two standard dice, what is the probability that both will be an odd number?

B. Choose the one best answer to each question.

Questions 7 and 8 refer to the following information.

In a game a player rolls a die, numbered from 1 to 6, and spins a spinner. The spinner is shown below.

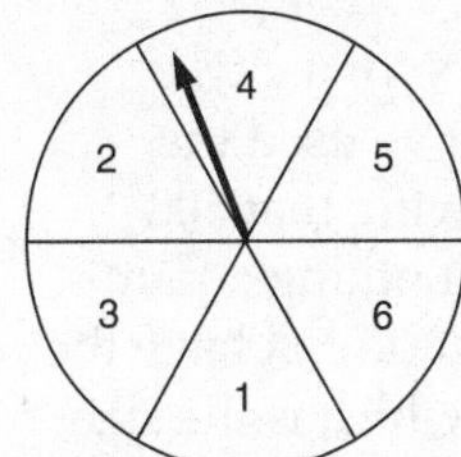

7. What is the probability of rolling a 5 and then spinning an even number?
   A. $\frac{1}{9}$
   B. $\frac{1}{6}$
   C. $\frac{1}{2}$
   D. $\frac{2}{3}$
   E. $\frac{5}{6}$

8. What is the chance that a player will get the same number on both the die and the spinner?
   A. $\frac{5}{6}$
   B. $\frac{2}{3}$
   C. $\frac{1}{2}$
   D. $\frac{1}{6}$
   E. $\frac{1}{36}$

Daniel uses the ten cards below in a magic trick.

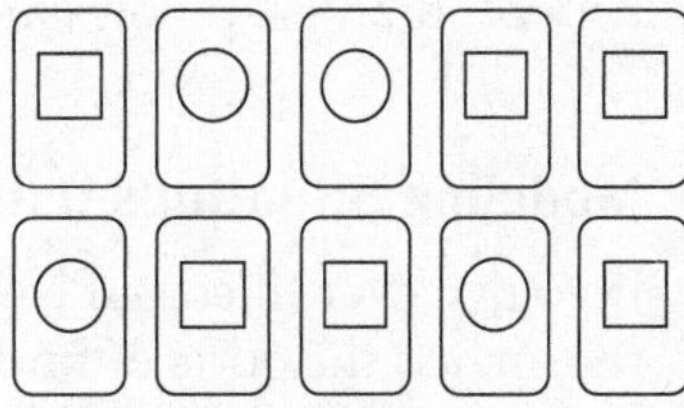

9. Daniel shuffles the cards and asks an audience member to choose and hold two cards. If the cards are chosen randomly, what is the chance that both will be marked with a square?
   A. 8 out of 14
   B. 3 out of 5
   C. 1 out of 3
   D. 1 out of 5
   E. 1 out of 6

10. There are 15 colored chips in a bag. Eight are green, and seven are white. Five white chips are removed. What is the probability that the next chip selected will be green?
   A. 100%
   B. 80%
   C. 75%
   D. 50%
   E. 25%

STUDY ADVICE

Consider making flash cards for some of the mathematical formulas presented in this unit. Then ask a friend to help you do drills using the flash cards.

LESSON 9

Density

KEY IDEAS

- Density is a measure of concentration in a given space. The higher the density, the more of something you have in the same area.
- Since *density is x units per y area*, knowing two of the values of density, *x* and *y*, allows you to figure out the third.

Density is a measure of concentration. In science, it is specifically the mass of an object per unit volume. A block of lead is much heavier than an equal-sized block of wood because the former contains a lot more "stuff" than the latter in the same amount of space. Thus, we say that lead is denser than wood.

Example 1: A local bedding store sells brand A memory foam pillows that weigh 5 lb and brand B memory foam pillows that weigh 7 lb. If the brand A pillows are 2 cu ft in volume and the brand B pillows are 3 cu ft in volume, which brand has the denser pillow?

Brand A pillows weigh 5 lb for 2 cu ft of volume, so their density is $\frac{5}{2} = 2\frac{1}{2}$ lb of pillow per cu ft of volume. Brand B pillows weigh 7 lb for 3 cu ft of volume, so their density is $\frac{7}{3} = 2\frac{1}{3}$ lb of pillow per cu ft of volume. Because $2\frac{1}{2} > 2\frac{1}{3}$, brand A pillows are denser.

HiSET EXAM TIP

The concept of density is very similar to that of ratios and proportions. An understanding of one can greatly help you with the other.

Modeling Situations Using Density

If you've ever filled out a census, checked crime statistics for a city, or researched the odds of finding a job where you live, you've used the concept of density to model a real-world situation. Knowing that 500 people in your town ride bikes on a given day tells you nothing about your likelihood of running into someone on a bike if you do not have the remaining key elements of the density equation, one of which is the size of your town.

Example 2: In an effort to clean up their streets, volunteers in each of sectors A, B, and C of a certain city instituted a weeklong trash pickup program in their corresponding sector. At the end of the week, sector A has 7 tons of trash remaining on its streets while sectors B and C have 5 tons and 15 tons, respectively. If sectors A and B are each 100 sq mi while sector C is 150 sq mi and all trash is of the same type, which of the three sectors would look the cleanest if you walked through it?

The type of trash isn't different, so the key will be the quantity per square mile. Sectors A and B are the same size, but the latter has 2 fewer tons of total trash, so sector B is cleaner than sector A per square mile. Sector C has 3 times the total trash tonnage as sector B, so it would need more than 3 times the total square mileage to be cleaner. Because it only has 1.5 times the square mileage, sector C will be roughly twice the dump that sector B is. Therefore, sector B would look the cleanest in a walkthrough.

PRACTICE 9

A. In questions 1–7, which has the higher density?

1. An ounce of feathers in a 1 gallon storage bag or an ounce of feathers in a 2 gallon storage bag
2. A rectangular section of a lawn measuring 6 ft by 4 ft with 4 lb of weeds or a square section of a lawn measuring 5 ft by 5 ft with 4 lb of weeds
3. A 1,000 sq ft apartment with 2 occupants or a 2,100 sq ft apartment with 3 occupants
4. 4 chocolate chips in a 1-oz cookie or 7 chocolate chips in a 2-oz cookie
5. 15 g of sugar in a 20-oz glass of water or 50 g of sugar in a 30-oz glass of water
6. 460 new births per year in a town of 100,000 or 1,100 new births per year in a town of 300,000
7. The juice of 4 standard-size oranges in a 32-oz pitcher or the juice of 3 standard-size oranges in a 15-oz pitcher

B. Choose the <u>one best answer</u> to each question.

8. Bob has two jars of marmalade, one orange and one peach. With a kitchen scale, he notes that the contents of the jar of orange marmalade weigh 2 lb. If the contents of the jar of peach marmalade also weigh 2 lb and peach marmalade is half as dense as orange marmalade, then

   A. the orange marmalade's jar is twice the volume of the peach marmalade's jar
   B. the orange marmalade's jar is four times the volume of the peach marmalade's jar
   C. the peach marmalade's jar is twice the volume of the orange marmalade's jar
   D. the peach marmalade's jar is four times the volume of the orange marmalade's jar
   E. the two jars have the same volume

9. In Springville Township, roughly 1 in every 4 citizens is a moviegoer. If Summerville Township has 200,000 more citizens than Springville Township and the same proportion of citizens to moviegoers, how many more moviegoers does Summerville Township have?

   A. 20,000
   B. 50,000
   C. 200,000
   D. 500,000
   E. 800,000

10. In a 50-oz retail package of Very Fruity Fruit Punch, 10 oz is water. In a 50-oz retail package of Somewhat Fruity Fruit Punch, 20 oz is water. Cindy pours a package of each brand into a separate pitcher and adds 10 oz of water to the pitcher of Very Fruity Fruit Punch. If each package contained only water and fruit juice, then which of the following must be true?

    A. The pitcher with Very Fruity Fruit Punch has a lower concentration of fruit juice than the pitcher of Somewhat Fruity Fruit Punch.
    B. The pitcher with Somewhat Fruity Fruit Punch has a lower concentration of fruit juice than the pitcher with Very Fruity Fruit Punch.
    C. The two pitchers now have the same concentration of fruit juice.
    D. The pitcher containing Very Fruity Fruit Punch is larger than the pitcher containing Somewhat Fruity Fruit Punch.
    E. The pitcher containing Somewhat Fruity Fruit Punch is larger than the pitcher containing Very Fruity Fruit Punch.

LESSON 10

Combinations

Combinations with One Type of Item

KEY IDEAS

- Combinations are used to select several things out of a larger group when the order doesn't matter.
- If you are asked to find how many ways to combine items from one group, use an organized list or table.
- If you are asked to find how many ways to combine one item from each of a number of different types of items, use a tree diagram or the fundamental counting principle.

Sometimes the Mathematics Test will ask you how many ways you can combine a set of items. Sometimes you may have only one type of item to combine, and sometimes you may have more than one type to combine. This difference will determine your problem-solving strategy.

Consider an example with *only one type of item:*

Example 1: Pablo is going shopping at a fruit stand that sells apples, bananas, grapes, and pears. Pablo will buy two different kinds of fruit. How many combinations of two kinds of fruit could Pablo buy?

The question is asking you to list possible groups of two out of the overall set of four. Notice that order doesn't matter—that is, *apples and bananas* is no different from *bananas and apples.* To solve this problem, you can make a list. Start with apples, and list all of the **combinations** that include apples: AB, AG, AP. Then make a list of groups that start with bananas and include the remaining fruits: BG, BP. Don't include BA because that's the same as AB. Then make a list of groups that start with grapes and include only the remaining fruits: GP. There are no remaining groups that start with P. You may find it easier to make this list in columns, as follows:

AB

AG BG

AP BP GP

There are **6** possible combinations.

HiSET EXAM TIP

You can use your scratch paper to make a tree diagram or other diagrams to help you visualize problems.

You can also draw a quick table like the following. Include a column for each of the fruits, and let each row represent a possible combination. Place two *x*'s in each row to represent a combination of two fruits.

Apples	Bananas	Grapes	Pears
x	x		
x		x	
x			x
	x	x	
	x		x
		x	x

Notice that you could not draw any more rows with two *x*'s without duplicating some of the existing rows. Count the rows: there are **6** possible combinations of two fruits.

PRACTICE 10.1

If you are asked to find the number of possible combinations ($_nC_r$) in a problem that uses larger numbers, you can use this formula:

$$_nC_r = \frac{n!}{(n-r)!r!}$$

In the formula, *n* is the number of items in the group. The letter *r* represents the number of items you are asked to combine. The exclamation point indicates a **factorial,** which works like this: Multiply the number by all the smaller whole numbers greater than zero: $6! = 6 \times 5 \times 4 \times 3 \times 2 \times 1$.

Example 2: Maclellan will take 7 of her 9 friends for a fishing weekend. How many combinations of her 9 friends are possible?

Step 1: Plug in the values given in the problem.

$$C = \frac{9!}{(9-7)!7!}$$

Step 2: Either use your calculator, or write out the factorials and cancel.

$$C = \frac{9 \times 8 \times 7 \times 6 \times 5 \times 4 \times 3 \times 2 \times 1}{(2 \times 1)(7 \times 6 \times 5 \times 4 \times 3 \times 2 \times 1)}$$

$$C = \frac{9 \times 8 \times \cancel{7 \times 6 \times 5 \times 4 \times 3 \times 2 \times 1}}{(2 \times 1)(\cancel{7 \times 6 \times 5 \times 4 \times 3 \times 2 \times 1})}$$

$$C = \frac{(9 \times 8)}{2} = 36$$

A. Solve.

1. As a supervisor, Rob is choosing four of his employees to work on a special project. The employees are Angela, Barbara, Colin, David, and Elizabeth. Of those five employees, how many teams of four are possible?
2. Jessica wants to take three books on vacation with her. She has five books to choose from. How many possible combinations of three books could she take on vacation?
3. Grant is cooking a homemade pizza, and he has the following toppings available: anchovies, ham, mushrooms, and sausage. He will choose three of those toppings. How many ways could Grant combine those toppings?

B. Choose the <u>one best answer</u> to each question about combinations.

4. Celia is going to plant a small flower bed with four flowers. She can choose from begonias, fuchsias, hellebore, daisies, and salvia. How many combinations of four flowers are possible?

   A. 5
   B. 20
   C. 24
   D. 48
   E. 120

5. The Sarkesian brothers own a hardware store. There are five items the owners might display in the window. Joe Sarkesian thinks that the window should have two items, but his brother Rick thinks the window should have three items. Counting both Joe's ideas and Rick's ideas for the window, how many possible combinations of the five items are there?

   A. 10
   B. 20
   C. 30
   D. 60
   E. 120

Combinations with More Than One Type of Item

Sometimes you may be asked to count possible combinations with more than one type of item. Consider the following example:

Example 3: Sarah is deciding what to wear. She has three shirts, two pairs of pants, and two pairs of shoes. How many possible outfits does she have, if an outfit is one shirt, one pair of pants, and one pair of shoes?

This question differs from the question about Pablo on page 356. In that question, Pablo was choosing from one overall group of fruits. Here, Sarah is choosing one out of each of three groups—shirts, pants, and shoes. If you are given more than one type of item and must choose one of each type, you can use a tree diagram to figure out all the possible combinations. Study the following example:

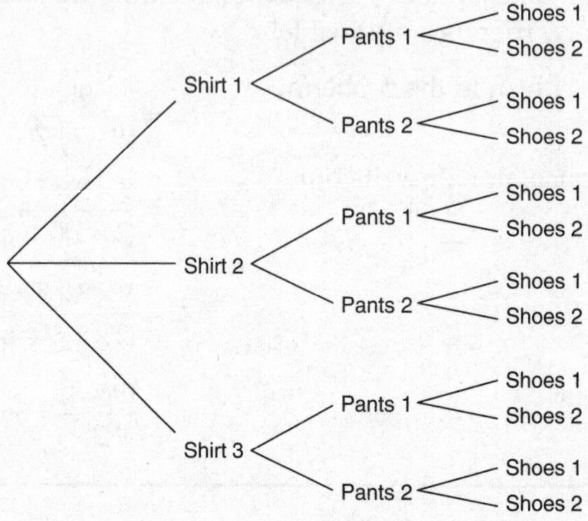

Each "branch" of the tree represents a possible combination. The number of branches on the right-hand side represents the possible number of combinations; in this case, there are **12** possible outfits.

However, you can solve the same type of problem (where you have more than one type of item and are choosing one of each type) using the **fundamental counting principle,** which works like this:

Start with shirts: for each shirt, Sarah has two pants options. That's $3 \times 2 = 6$. Additionally, for each of those six options, she has two options for shoes. That's $3 \times 2 \times 2 = \mathbf{12}$.

Use the fundamental counting principle to solve the following problem:

Example 4: Gordon is at a restaurant that serves a three-course meal: an appetizer, an entrée, and a dessert. There are three appetizers, six entrées, and four desserts to choose from. Gordon will order one of each. How many different meals could he order?

Multiply three appetizers by six entrées by four desserts: $3 \times 6 \times 4 = 72$. There are **72** possible ways Gordon could order his meal.

PRACTICE 10.2

A. Use a tree diagram or the fundamental counting principle to solve the following problems.

1. Frank is making a sandwich. His sandwich will have one type of bread, one type of meat, and one condiment. He has four types of bread: white, wheat, rye, and a Kaiser roll. Meats he can choose from are chicken, turkey, and roast beef. For condiments, Frank can choose mayonnaise, mustard, vinaigrette, or horseradish. How many ways can Frank make his sandwich?
2. Van Ahn attended a trivia contest and won three rounds. For the first round she won, she could choose one of three restaurant gift certificates. The prize for another round was one of two T-shirts. Winning the third round allowed her to choose one of four souvenir hats. How many possible combinations of prizes were available to Van Ahn?
3. Henry is wrapping a gift for his daughter. He will use one type of wrapping paper, one type of ribbon, and one bow. He has three different types of wrapping paper, three different types of ribbon, and three different bows. How many ways can Henry wrap the gift?
4. Julio is looking forward to a three-day weekend. On Friday, he will either go to the beach or attend a street festival. On Saturday, he plans to visit a museum, but he is trying to decide among three different museums. On Sunday, he will try one of four new restaurants. How many ways could Julio combine these weekend activities?

B. Choose the one best answer to each question about combinations. Determine whether you are being asked to find possible combinations from one type of item or from multiple types of items.

5. The Nu Mu Beta fraternity is deciding what secret passphrase it should require its members to say before being admitted to meetings. The first and third words of the passphrase will be the names of Greek letters. There are 24 letters in the Greek alphabet. The second word will be a number from one to nine. How many possible passphrases are there?

A. 24
B. 57
C. 576
D. 5,184
E. 5,760

6. A video game designer is creating a new superhero, who will have three of five potential superpowers. How many combinations of superpowers could the new superhero have?

A. 10
B. 15
C. 50
D. 100
E. 125

7. A chef will make a soup with five ingredients: one of four meats, one of four vegetables, one of four kinds of noodles, one of four kinds of broth, and one of four spices. How many possible combinations of ingredients could the chef put into the soup?

A. 20
B. 256
C. 1,024
D. 2,048
E. 3,125

8. A doctor is deciding how to treat a given disease. The doctor will prescribe one medication, one dietary change, and one type of vitamin supplement. There are five medications, five dietary changes, and five types of vitamins the doctor might prescribe. How many combinations are possible?

A. 125
B. 625
C. 1,250
D. 3,125
E. 5,000

LESSON 11

Permutations

KEY IDEAS

- Permutations are used to find the number of possible outcomes when the order does matter.
- Use the total number of people or items and the number of possible outcomes to find the number of permutations that are possible.

On the Mathematics Test, you may be asked how many permutations, or sequences, are possible given a group of items. Consider the following example:

Example 1: Eliza is planning her day off. She wants to visit the art museum, try the new coffee shop, call her mom, and take a walk, but not necessarily in that order. How many possible sequences of those four activities are there?

This question asks you for all possible permutations, or ways to sequence the items. Thus, *coffee-art-mom-walk* and *art-coffee-mom-walk* are two different possible outcomes. Consider how this problem differs from the combinations problems on pages 356–359. In those cases, order did not matter; in a permutations problem, order does matter.

Start with how many things could go first: here, there are four possibilities for Eliza's first activity. Once she has done that first activity, three possibilities remain. After she has done a first and second activity, two possibilities remain, and then only one. So you simply multiply: $4 \times 3 \times 2 \times 1$. There are **24** possible permutations.

Some permutations questions may ask you to determine the possible orderings for only some of the items in a list. Consider this example:

Example 2: Ten runners are competing in a race. There are prizes for first, second, and third place. How many possible sequences of the top three prize winners are there?

Notice that you are not simply figuring out how many groups of three can be made out of the ten. Rather, you are figuring out how many sequences of three can be made out of the ten.

Now, multiplying $10 \times 9 \times 8 \times 7 \times 6 \times 5 \times 4 \times 3 \times 2 \times 1$ would give you all the possible permutations of all ten runners, so that approach will not work here. Instead, start with how many people could win first place: here, ten. Once someone has won first, there are nine possibilities for second place. Once someone has won first and someone else has won second, there are eight possibilities for third place. And then you stop multiplying: $10 \times 9 \times 8 = 720$. There are **720** possible ways that the runners could be arranged in the top three prize-winning slots. (Note that simply multiplying 10 by 3 will not work.)

To find the number of possible permutations $({}_nP_r)$:

$${}_nP_r = \frac{n!}{(n-r)!}$$

In that formula, n is the number of items in the group, and r is the number of items you are asked to include in the permutations. To solve Example 2 using the formula, plug in the values and cancel out the values that appear in both the numerator and the denominator:

$$P = \frac{10!}{(10-3)!} = \frac{10\times9\times8\times\cancel{7\times6\times5\times4\times3\times2\times1}}{\cancel{7\times6\times5\times4\times3\times2\times1}} = 10\times9\times8$$

HiSET EXAM TIP

When you are reading a question that suggests that you may want to find a combination or a permutation, ask yourself, "Am I finding a number of groups (combinations), or am I finding the number of possible sequences (permutations)?"

PRACTICE 11

A. Read the problems and decide whether you are being asked to find combinations or permutations. Then solve.

1. Noemi is trying to remember the password for her email. She knows that it has the following characters in it: M, Q, $, L, 7. But she can't remember the order they go in. How many possible sequences of those five characters are there?
2. Five students in a class have volunteered for a special project. Only three can actually help with the project. How many possible groupings of three out of the five are possible?
3. Tyrell is the curator at a gallery and is deciding how to arrange six paintings that will be displayed in a line along one wall. All six paintings will be included. How many possible sequences could Tyrell choose?

B. Choose the <u>one best answer</u> to each question about combinations or permutations.

4. Soraya has been given six tasks to do at work, but she has time to complete only four of them. She must decide in what order to do the tasks. How many possible orderings of four tasks are available to Soraya?

A. 24
B. 36
C. 360
D. 720
E. 1,440

5. In a certain public garden, the gardener wanted to show the different visual effects that arranging flowers in different sequences can have. So he chose three kinds of flowers and planted flower beds showing each of the possible sequences of the three kinds. How many such flower beds did the gardener plant?

A. 3
B. 6
C. 9
D. 12
E. 15

6. Ten people hope to become extras in a movie. The movie's casting director will choose four people to fill the following specific roles in the movie: Bystander #1, Bystander #2, Bystander #3, and Bystander #4. How many ways could those four roles be filled?

A. 24
B. 40
C. 540
D. 1,024
E. 5,040

<u>Questions 7 and 8</u> refer to the following information.

Clark and his daughter are at the amusement park, and Clark is offering his daughter a choice. They don't have time to ride all six rides at the amusement park, but they can ride three of them.

7. How many combinations of three rides could Clark's daughter choose?

A. 720
B. 120
C. 36
D. 20
E. 18

8. Clark's daughter can also choose the order in which she wants to enjoy the rides. How many possible orderings of three out of the six rides are possible?

A. 18
B. 20
C. 120
D. 360
E. 720

STATISTICS AND PROBABILITY PRACTICE QUESTIONS

Directions: Choose the one best answer to each question.

Questions 1 and 2 refer to the following graph.

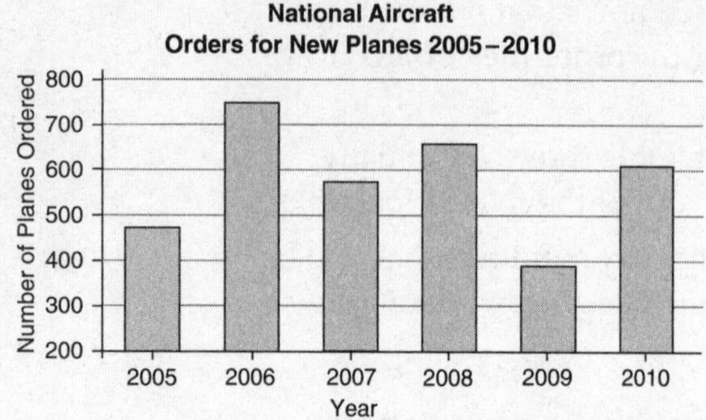

1. The mean number of aircraft orders for the six years shown on the graph is 573 planes. In which year was the number of orders closest to the mean?

   A. 2006
   B. 2007
   C. 2008
   D. 2009
   E. 2010

2. By about what percent did orders at National Aircraft decrease from 2008 to 2009?

   A. 30%
   B. 40%
   C. 50%
   D. 68%
   E. 75%

---

3. At a convention, Jim and his three friends each bought three raffle tickets. At the time of the drawing, 400 tickets had been sold. What is the probability that either Jim or one of his friends will win?

   A. $\frac{3}{100}$
   B. $\frac{1}{25}$
   C. $\frac{3}{50}$
   D. $\frac{9}{100}$
   E. $\frac{6}{50}$

Questions 4 through 6 are based on the following table.

Southland Weather March 9			
Area	**High Temp.**	**Low Temp.**	**Precipitation (in inches)**
Downtown	65° F	53° F	0.45
Airport	62° F	50° F	0.63
Woodland Hills	68° F	50° F	1.34
East Village	56° F	48° F	3.53
Ventura	62° F	49° F	2.57
Highland Park	64° F	55° F	0.84

4. Based on the data in the table, what was the median low temperature for March 9?

   A. 62.8°
   B. 53°
   C. 51.5°
   D. 50.8°
   E. 50°

5. What was the mean amount of precipitation (in inches) on March 9 for the areas listed in the table?

   A. 0.65
   B. 1.09
   C. 1.56
   D. 1.99
   E. 1.87

6. For which area on the table was there the greatest range, or difference, between the high and low temperatures?

   A. Ventura
   B. East Village
   C. Woodland Hills
   D. Downtown
   E. Highland Park

STUDY ADVICE

On the next few pages, you'll practice the statistics and probability skills you learned in this chapter. Remember, only about 18% of questions on the Mathematics Test will be about statistics and probability. So, definitely review these concepts if you need to, but also leave yourself time to study algebra, functions, and geometry (the next three chapters) in depth.

Questions 7 and 8 refer to the graph.

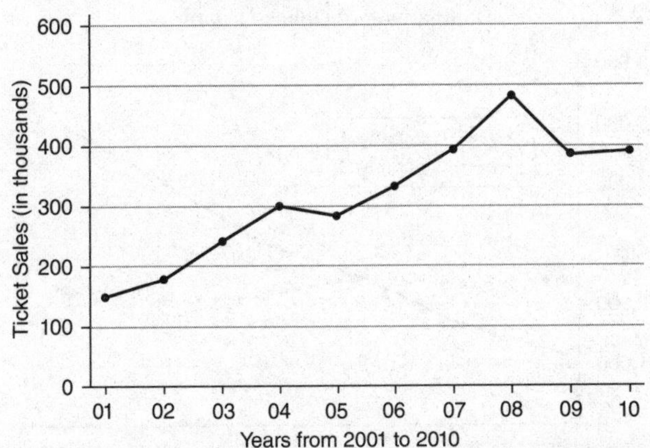

7. Platinum Cinemas opened its first theaters in 2001. The company's ticket sales increased steadily until what year, when there was a drop in sales?

A. 2004
B. 2005
C. 2008
D. 2009
E. 2010

8. Which year had the sharpest increase in ticket sales over the previous year?

A. 2002
B. 2005
C. 2006
D. 2008
E. 2009

---

9. At Nelson Stationers, the first 25 customers who visited the store on Monday morning received their choice of a gift. The table below shows how many customers chose each gift.

pen and pencil set	~~||||~~
calculator	~~||||~~ ~~||||~~ ||
mouse pad	~~||||~~ |||

What percent of the customers chose a mouse pad?

A. 17%
B. 20%
C. 25%
D. 32%
E. $33\frac{1}{3}\%$

10. A standard deck of playing cards has 52 cards, with 13 cards each of hearts, diamonds, clubs, and spades. If a card is drawn randomly from the deck, what is the probability that it will be either hearts or diamonds?

A. 1 in 2
B. 1 in 4
C. 1 in 8
D. 1 in 13
E. 1 in 16

11. Nita worked the following overtime hours over a six-week period.

Week 1: 5 hours

Week 2: $3\frac{1}{2}$ hours

Week 3: 4 hours

Week 4: 0 hours

Week 5: $1\frac{1}{2}$ hours

Week 6: 7 hours

What is the mean number of overtime hours Nita worked each week?

A. 2
B. 3
C. 3.5
D. 4
E. 4.5

12. A spinner has five equal sections, and they are numbered from 1 to 5. What is the probability of spinning a number greater than 3? (Express the answer as a fraction.)

A. $\frac{4}{5}$
B. $\frac{3}{5}$
C. $\frac{1}{2}$
D. $\frac{2}{5}$
E. $\frac{1}{5}$

Questions 13 through 15 refer to the following graph.

In a recent election, five candidates ran for the city council seat from District 11. The results of the race are shown in the graph below.

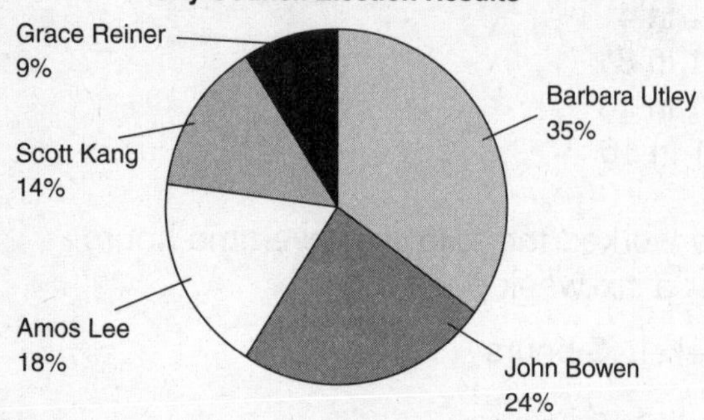

13. The three city council candidates who received the fewest votes received what percent of the total vote?

A. 23%
B. 41%
C. 56%
D. 65%
E. 77%

14. Which two candidates combined received about $\frac{3}{5}$ of the votes cast?

A. Grace and Utley
B. Kang and Utley
C. Bowen and Utley
D. Lee and Bowen
E. Lee and Utley

15. If 5,100 votes were cast in the election, which of the following expressions could be used to find out how many votes Grace Reiner received?

A. $5{,}100 \times 0.9$
B. $\frac{5{,}100}{0.9}$
C. $\frac{5{,}100}{0.09}$
D. $5{,}100 \times 0.09$
E. $5{,}100 \times 0.91$

Questions 16 through 18 refer to the following graph.

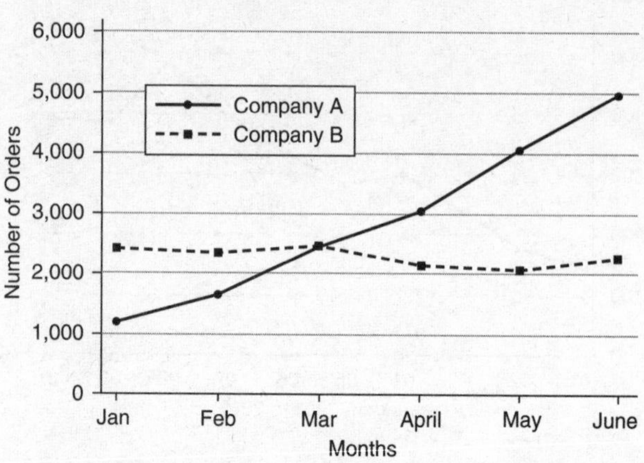

16. In which month did Company A and Company B receive about the same number of online orders?

A. January
B. February
C. March
D. April
E. May

17. Based on the trends shown by the data, what would be the best prediction for the number of online orders in July for Company A?

A. 7,200
B. 6,500
C. 5,900
D. 5,200
E. 4,900

18. About 18% of the online orders in April at Company A are returned for credit or exchange. How many orders at Company A were returned for credit or exchange in the month of April?

A. 180
B. 360
C. 540
D. 600
E. 720

Questions 19 and 20 are based on the following information.

A basketball player's statistics for an eight-game series are shown in the table below.

Game	Shots Attempted	Shots Made
1	25	10
2	23	12
3	26	10
4	24	13
5	29	15
6	18	7
7	24	12
8	27	10

19. What was the median number of shots attempted by this player in the series?

A. 24
B. 24.5
C. 25
D. 26.5
E. 27

20. What is the mode of the shots made by this player during the series?

A. 13
B. 12
C. 11
D. 10 and 12
E. 10

21. A bag contains 24 marbles. Eight are red, six are blue, and ten are white. A marble is drawn from the bag and replaced. A second marble is chosen at random from the bag. What is the probability that the first marble is red and the second is white?

A. $\frac{2}{5}$
B. $\frac{5}{24}$
C. $\frac{5}{36}$
D. $\frac{5}{48}$
E. $\frac{1}{48}$

22. A company has 36 employees. For three months, the owner has kept track of the number of sick days used by her employees per month.

Month	Sick Days
Sept.	34
Oct.	31
Nov.	42

Which expression could be used to find the average number of sick days taken each month?

A. $\frac{34+31+42}{36}$
B. $\frac{34+31+42}{3}$
C. $\frac{34+31+42+36}{4}$
D. $(34+31+42)\times 3$
E. $\frac{34+31+42}{12}$

23. Andy rolls two standard six-sided dice. What is the probability of rolling two 1s? Express your answer as a fraction.

A. $\frac{1}{6}$
B. $\frac{1}{9}$
C. $\frac{1}{12}$
D. $\frac{1}{24}$
E. $\frac{1}{36}$

24. Angelique, a teacher, is making a reading list for her students. She wants to include one historical novel, one work of science fiction, one book of poetry, and one graphic novel. She has five of each type of book to choose from. How many possible combinations of books could she include in her reading list?

A. 4
B. 20
C. 125
D. 625
E. 2,500

25. A charity's board has ten members. One of the members will be elected president, then another will be elected treasurer, and then a third will be elected secretary. If no member can hold more than one position, how many ways can the members fill those positions?

A. 27
B. 30
C. 720
D. 2,048
E. 5,040

<u>Questions 26 and 27</u> are based on the following information.

The frequency table below displays the reasons why patients visited a walk-in clinic during a certain week.

Reason	Number of patients
Colds and flu	卌 卌 卌 I
Cuts and scrapes	卌 卌 III
Sprained muscles	卌 卌 II
Tetanus shots	卌 II
Severe headaches	卌 卌 II

26. What percent of the patients represented in the table visited the walk-in clinic because of sprained muscles?

A. 17%
B. 20%
C. 24%
D. 40%
E. 75%

27. In the week represented in the table, what was the ratio of the number of patients with colds or flu to the number of patients with severe headaches?

A. 4:15
B. 4:3
C. 3:4
D. 2:3
E. 1:5

<u>Questions 28 and 29</u> are based on the following information and graph.

A hundred people are participating in a medical study. As a first step, the researchers collected information about participants' weight. The graph below represents how many people fell into each weight category.

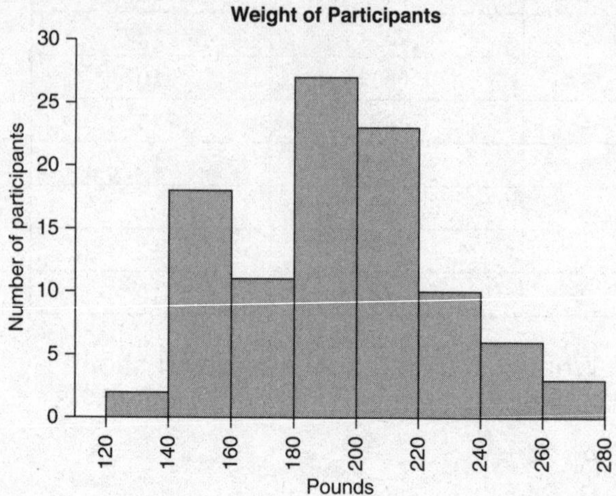

28. Which weight category displays the highest frequency?

A. 120–139 lb
B. 140–159 lb
C. 180–199 lb
D. 200–219 lb
E. 260–279 lb

29. Consider only the 100 individuals represented in the graph. Which one of the following groups contains the most people?

A. Participants weighing 200 lb or more
B. Participants weighing less than 200 lb
C. Participants weighing 180–199 lb
D. Participants weighing less than 180 lb
E. Participants weighing less than 180 lb or more than 220 lb

30. There are four children in Mr. Martin's class. Three of them will be selected to be hall monitors. How many combinations of hall monitors are possible?

A. 3
B. 4
C. 6
D. 9
E. 12

Questions 31 through 33 refer to the following information and table.

The owner of a taxi company measures the gas mileage of each of the cars in her fleet. The frequency table below shows her results.

Average miles per gallon	Number of cars
15	II
20	𝍸 II
25	𝍸
30	𝍸 I
35	I

31. Which of the values (average miles per gallon) displays the highest frequency?
A. 15 miles per gallon
B. 20 miles per gallon
C. 25 miles per gallon
D. 30 miles per gallon
E. 35 miles per gallon

32. What is the ratio of taxis that get 35 miles per gallon on average to the number of taxis that get 15 miles per gallon on average?

A. $\frac{1}{2}$

B. $\frac{1}{5}$

C. $\frac{3}{2}$

D. $\frac{4}{5}$

E. $\frac{1}{10}$

33. Choose the line plot that represents the information in the table.

A.

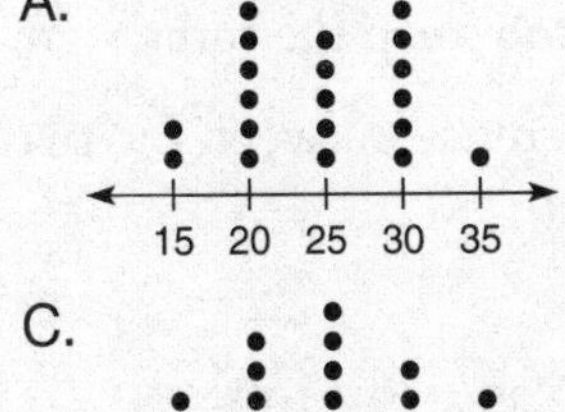

B.

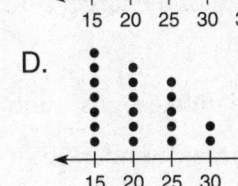

C.

D.

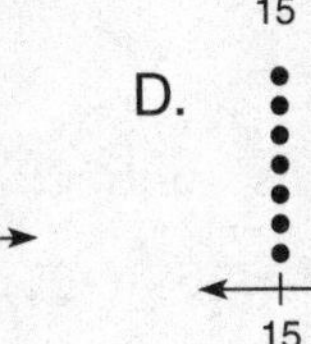

E.

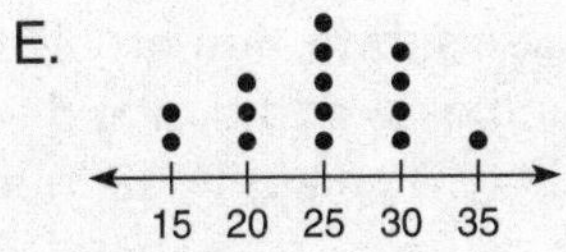

34. Ahmed works at the ticket window of a theater, and one night he decides to track when the patrons arrive for a 7:30 P.M. show. The table below represents his data.

Time period	Percent of patrons who arrive
5:30 to 5:59 P.M.	2%
6:00 to 6:29 P.M.	14%
6:30 to 6:59 P.M.	25%
7:00 to 7:29 P.M.	48%
7:30 to 8:00 P.M.	11%

Which one of the histograms below accurately represents Ahmed's data?

A.

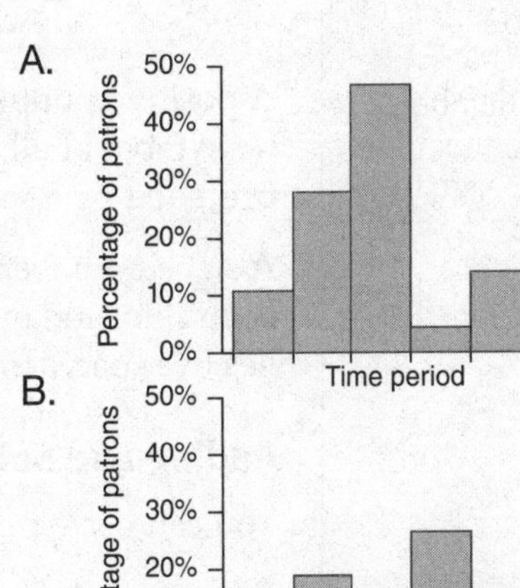

B.

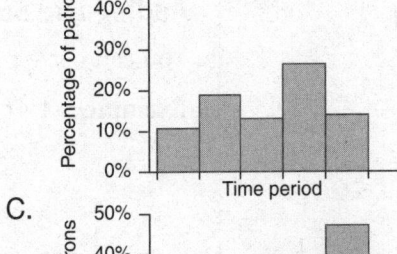

C.

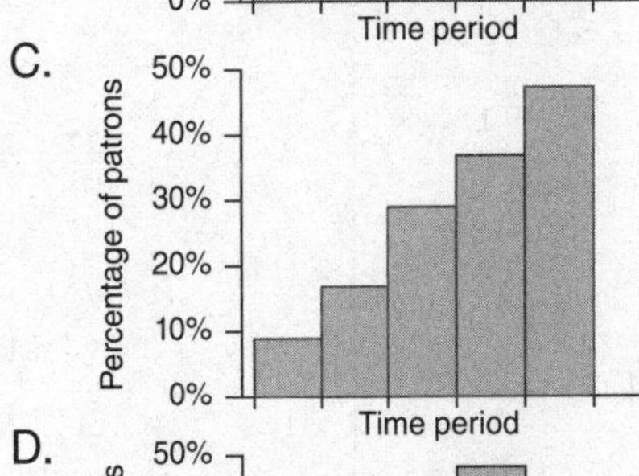

D.

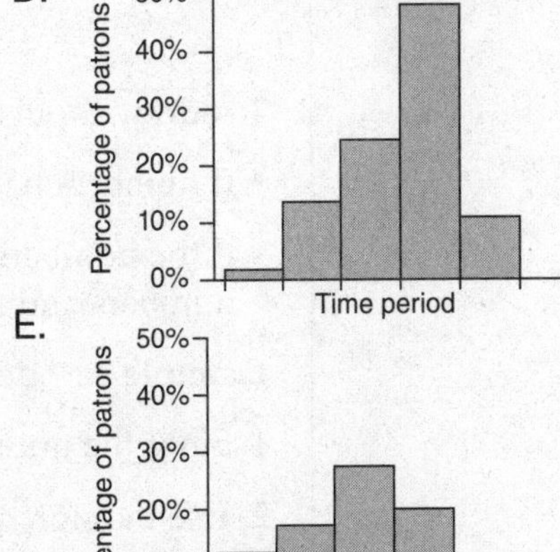

E.

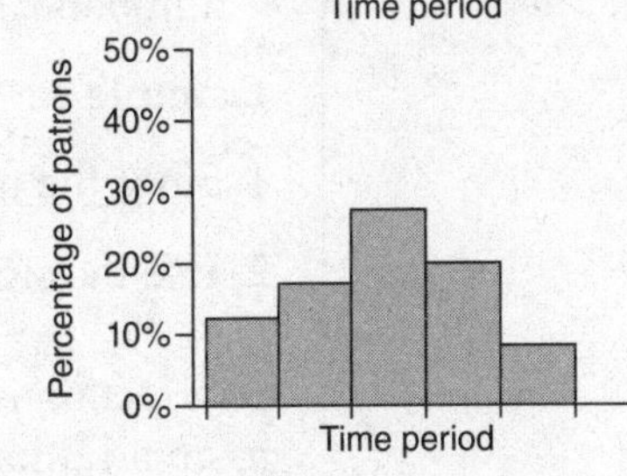

LESSON 1

The Number Line and Signed Numbers

KEY IDEAS

- If numbers have like signs, add and keep the same sign.
- If numbers have unlike signs, find the difference and use the sign from the larger number.
- To subtract signed numbers, change the operation to addition and change the sign of the number you are subtracting.

Understanding Signed Numbers

Signed numbers include zero, all positive numbers, and all negative numbers. Zero is neither positive nor negative. On a number line, the positive numbers are shown to the right of zero, and the negative numbers are shown to the left.

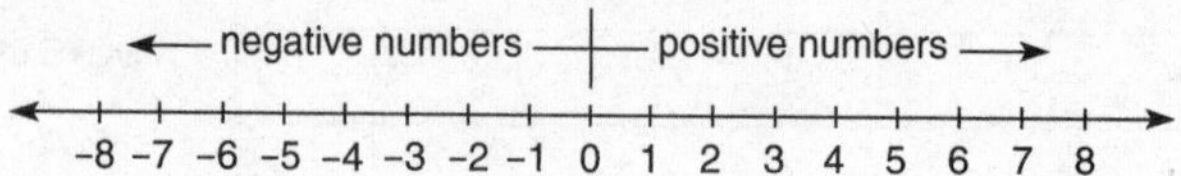

A positive number may be written with a plus (+) symbol. If a number has no symbol at all, we assume that it is positive. A negative number *must* be preceded by a minus (–) symbol.

A signed number provides two important facts. The sign tells the direction from zero, and the number tells you the distance from zero. For example, –5 lies five spaces to the left of zero, and +4 lies four spaces to the right of zero.

Adding and Subtracting Signed Numbers

You can use a number line to model the addition of signed numbers.

Examples: $1 + (-4) = -3$ Begin at +1; move 4 in a negative direction (left).

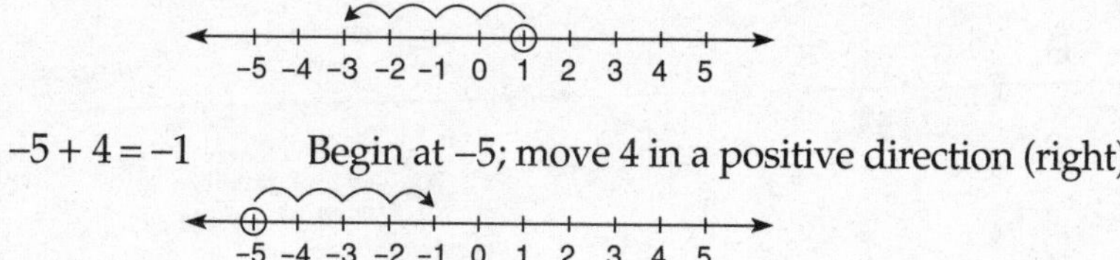

$-5 + 4 = -1$ Begin at –5; move 4 in a positive direction (right).

$-2 + (-3) = -5$ Begin at –2; move 3 in a negative direction (left).

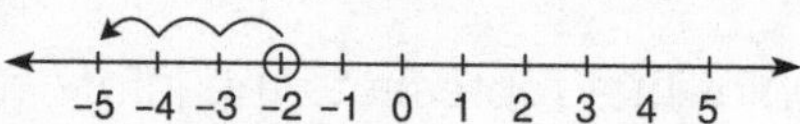

To add without a number line, follow these steps:

- If numbers have like signs, add the numbers and keep the same sign.
- If the numbers have unlike signs, find the difference between the two numbers and use the sign of the larger number.

Example 1: Add $15 + (-25)$.

1. Since the numbers have unlike signs, subtract. $25 - 15 = 10$.
2. Use the sign from the larger number. $15 + (-25) = \mathbf{-10}$.

Subtraction is the opposite of addition. To rewrite a subtraction problem as an addition problem, change the operation symbol to addition and change the sign on the number you are subtracting. Then apply the rules for adding signed numbers.

PRACTICE 1.1

Example 2: Subtract $3 - 8$.

1. Change the operation symbol and the sign of the number you are subtracting. — $3 - 8$ becomes $3 + (-8)$.

2. Add. — $3 + (-8) = -5$

You can use the same rules to combine several signed numbers.

Example 3: $(-5) + 6 - 4 - (-2) = ?$

1. Rewrite each subtraction as addition. — $(-5) + 6 + (-4) + 2$

2. Add the positive terms. — $6 + 2 = 8$

   Add the negative terms. — $-5 + (-4) = -9$

3. Combine the results. — $8 + -9 = -1$

A. Solve.

1. $8 + (-3)$
2. $50 - 5$
3. $11 - (-2)$
4. $-1 + 2$
5. $-4 - (-5)$
6. $8 - (-2)$
7. $6 - 9$
8. $2 + 11$
9. $(-7) - (-3)$
10. $(-4) + 6$
11. $-15 + (-7)$
12. $36 - 4$
13. $-60 - (-10)$
14. $-5 - 6$
15. $12 + 13$
16. $-55 + 20$
17. $7 + (-3) + (-5) - 10$
18. $66 + (-22) - 33$
19. $-14 - (-6) + 18$
20. $80 - (-15) - 20$
21. $6 - (-3) + (-5) + 8$
22. $-23 + (-11) - (-15) + 21$
23. $3 + 9 - 5 + 12 - 9 - 11$
24. $-7 - 20 - (-14)$

B. Choose the one best answer to each question.

Question 25 refers to the following number line.

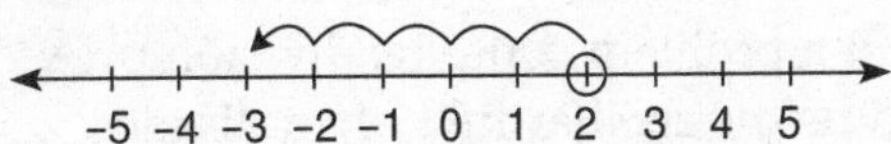

25. The number line above shows which of the following expressions?
   A. $2 + (-3)$
   B. $2 + (-5)$
   C. $-3 + 2$
   D. $-3 - (+2)$
   E. $-3 + 5$

26. At noon, the temperature in the high desert was 92°F. A scientist observed the following temperature changes over the course of the next two hours: +12°, –5°, +6°, –3°, and +13°. What was the temperature in degrees Fahrenheit at the end of the two-hour period?
   A. 95°
   B. 99°
   C. 103°
   D. 115°
   E. 131°

STUDY ADVICE

Number lines are very useful for understanding numerical information. They help you visualize the relationship between numbers and quantities. To review and learn about other uses for number lines, turn to pages 368–371.

Multiplying and Dividing Signed Numbers

In algebra, multiplication is not shown using the times sign (×) because the symbol could be easily mistaken for the variable x. Instead, multiplication is shown using a dot or by placing two numbers next to each other. To avoid confusion, one or both of the numbers may be enclosed in parentheses. For example, the expressions $-5 \cdot 6$ and $-5(6)$ and $(-5)(6)$ all mean "–5 times 6."

In algebra, division can be written with the ÷ symbol, but it is usually shown with a line that means "divided by." The expression $\frac{20}{-5}$ means "20 divided by –5," as does 20/–5.

When multiplying or dividing signed numbers, use the following rules:

- If the signs are the same, the answer is positive.
- If the signs are different, the answer is negative.

Example 4: Multiply $4(-25)$.

1. Multiply the numbers only. $4 \times 25 = 100$.
2. Determine the sign. Since the signs on the numbers are different, the answer is negative: $4(-25) = \mathbf{-100}$.

Example 5: Divide $\frac{-160}{-8}$.

1. Divide the numbers only. $160 \div 8 = 20$.
2. Determine the sign. Since the signs on the numbers are the same, the answer is positive: $\frac{-160}{-8} = \mathbf{20}$.

A problem may contain more than two factors. Remember that each pair of negative factors will equal a positive product. Therefore, if there is an even number of negative terms, the product will be positive. If there is an odd number of negative terms, the product will be negative.

Example 6: $(-5)(6)(-1)(-2)(2) = ?$

1. Multiply. $5 \times 6 \times 1 \times 2 \times 2 = 120$.
2. There are three negative terms. Since 3 is an odd number, the product is negative: **–120.**

When a problem contains more than one operation, follow this **order of operations**. Do multiplication and division operations first, working from left to right. Do addition and subtraction operations last, also working from left to right. If a problem contains division presented with a division bar, do any operations above and below the bar first, then divide.

Example 7: $(-4)(6) - \frac{3+(-9)}{-2}$

1. Multiply. $-24 - \frac{3+(-9)}{-2}$.
2. Do the operation above the fraction bar. $-24 - \frac{-6}{-2}$.
3. Divide. $-24 - (+3)$.
4. Subtract. $-24 - (+3) = -24 + (-3) = \mathbf{-27}$.

Note: *Notice how parentheses clarify meaning:* 4 – 5 means "four minus five," but 4(–5) means "four times negative five."

PRACTICE 1.2

A. Solve.

1. (5)(4)
2. (7)(−3)
3. (−8)(6)
4. (−2)(−9)
5. (−10)(1)
6. 9 ÷ 3
7. 12 ÷ (−4)
8. −25 ÷ 5
9. (−18) ÷ (−9)
10. $\frac{40}{-8}$
11. (14)(−2)
12. (−75) ÷ 25
13. 13 ÷ (−13)
14. (−5)(15)
15. $\frac{18}{3}$
16. $\frac{25(4)}{-5}$
17. (−3)(−5)(2)(−10)
18. 20 ÷ (−5) ÷ (−2)
19. $\frac{6(5)}{(-3)(2)}$
20. (−11)(2)(−5)(6)
21. (12)(−2) ÷ (−2)
22. (−4)(−6)(−5)
23. 50 ÷ (2)(−5)
24. (−1)(2)(−3)(2)(−1)
25. $\frac{(3)(-4)(2)(5)}{-6}$
26. $\frac{4(-4)}{-8(-2)}$
27. (−5)(−2)(0)(−1)

B. Choose the <u>one best answer</u> to each question.

28. Janice is creating a computer spreadsheet. A portion of her work is shown below.

	A	B	C
1	−3	4	7
2	2	−5	−8
3	−1	3	−2

Using the information from the spreadsheet, what is the value of the expression A1*C1*A3/(B3*A3)? (*Hint*: In a spreadsheet, the symbol * means multiplication.)

A. −21
B. −7
C. $\frac{-1}{7}$
D. 7:5
E. 21

29. The product of 2 and 8 is divided by −8. Which of the following expressions could be used to find the value of the statement?

A. $\frac{\frac{2}{8}}{-8}$
B. 2(8)(−8)
C. $\frac{2(8)}{(-8)}$
D. $\frac{2(-8)}{8}$
E. 2 × 8 − 8

30. Which of the following is a true statement about the value of the expression (52)(−103)(−45)(−8)(3)?

A. The result is a fraction.
B. The result is greater than 1.
C. The result is a negative number.
D. The result is a positive number.
E. The result is a prime number.

STUDY ADVICE

Approximately 45% of questions on the Mathematics Test will target algebra skills. Therefore, even though this chapter is long, working your way through it will really pay off on Test Day. Concepts covered in the chapter will increase in difficulty as you go, but be sure to review previous lessons anytime you need to.

LESSON 2

Powers and Roots

KEY IDEAS

- In the expression 2^3, the base is 2 and the exponent is 3.
- To raise a number to a certain power, write the base the number of times shown by the exponent and then multiply.
- To find a square root, think, "What number times itself equals this number?"

Powers are a special way to show repeated multiplication. For example, suppose you needed to multiply $5 \times 5 \times 5 \times 5$. This series of operations can be expressed as "five to the fourth power." In other words, the number 5 appears in the multiplication problem four times.

We can write the operations algebraically using **exponents**. In the expression $5 \times 5 \times 5 \times 5$ above, the number 5 is the base. The exponent, a small number written above and to the right of the **base**, tells how many times the base is repeated: $5 \times 5 \times 5 \times 5 = 5^4$.

To evaluate an expression, perform the multiplication indicated by the exponent.

Example 1: Find the value of 2^5.

Write the base the number of times indicated by the exponent and then multiply:

$2^5 = 2 \times 2 \times 2 \times 2 \times 2 = \mathbf{32}$.

You may encounter some special uses of exponents on the Mathematics Test. An exponent can be any positive number, or it can be 0, or a negative number. Memorize the situations described below.

1. A number raised to the first power equals itself: $8^1 = 8$.
2. A number other than zero raised to the power of zero equals 1: $6^0 = 1$.
3. A number raised to a negative exponent is equal to a fraction with a numerator of 1: $4^{-2} = \frac{1}{4^2} = \frac{1}{4 \times 4} = \frac{1}{16}$.

HiSET EXAM TIP

Make a list of common square roots by squaring the numbers from 1 to 15. Memorize them. You will need to know common square roots to solve geometry problems about area and right triangles.

You can use a calculator to raise numbers to any power. Use the [x^2] or [^] key. The following examples are worked out using the keys on the TI-30XS MultiView™. Remember, your calculator may differ if you are taking the HiSET exam on paper.

Example 2: What is the value of 24^2?

Press: 24 [x^2] [enter]. The right side of the display reads 576.

The square of 24 is **576**.

Example 3: Find the value of 9^4.

Enter the base, press [^], and enter the exponent. Then press [enter].

Press 9 [^] 4 [enter]. The right side of the display reads 6561.

Nine raised to the fourth power is **6561**.

Note: To raise a negative number to a power using the TI-30XS MultiView™ calculator, you must enter that number in parentheses: [(] [(−)] 4 [)] [x^2] [enter].

To **square** a number, multiply the number by itself. For example, $6^2 = 6 \times 6 = 36$. In the expression $6 \times 6 = 36$, the number 36 is the **square**, and the number 6 is the **square root** of 36.

PRACTICE 2

The symbol for square root is $\sqrt{\ }$. To find a square root, think, "What number multiplied by itself is equal to the number beneath the square root symbol?"

Example 4: Find the value of $\sqrt{144}$.

You know that $12 \times 12 = 144$, so the square root of 144 is **12**. Although $(-12) \times (-12)$ also equals 144, you will only be expected to find positive roots on the Mathematics Test.

You may have to approximate the value of a square root.

Example 5: What is the square root of 90?

You know that $9 \times 9 = 81$ and $10 \times 10 = 100$. Therefore, the square root of 90 is **between 9 and 10**.

You can also use your calculator to find a square root. On the TI-30SX MultiView™, you must first press the (2nd) key to access the square root function. The $\sqrt{\ }$ function is directly above the $[x^2]$ key. (Other calculators may not require the use of the (2nd) key.)

Example 6: Use your calculator to find $\sqrt{90}$ to the nearest tenth.

On the TI-30SX MultiView™, press (2nd) $[x^2]$ 90 (enter). The right side of the display reads $3\sqrt{10}$.

Press the toggle key, ◀▶, to change the format of the answer into a decimal. The right side of the display now reads 9.486832981. Rounding to the tenths place, $\sqrt{90} \approx$ **9.5**.

A. Solve each expression.

1. 3^2
2. 4^1
3. $\sqrt{9}$
4. 25^0
5. $(-3)^2$
6. $\sqrt{49}$
7. 5^3
8. 4^{-2}

B. Solve each expression below. Round your answer to the nearest tenth.

9. 3^8
10. $(-6)^4$
11. $\sqrt{150}$
12. 20^3
13. 1^{15}
14. $(-4)^{-2}$
15. $\sqrt{242}$
16. $(3.3)^2$
17. $\sqrt{57}$
18. $\sqrt{536}$
19. 112^0
20. $(-2)^8$

C. Choose the <u>one best answer</u> to each question.

21. The cube shown below measures 6 inches on each side. You can find the volume of the cube by multiplying length × width × height. Which of the following expressions represents the volume of the cube?

    A. 18
    B. 6^1
    C. 6^2
    D. 6^3
    E. 6^6

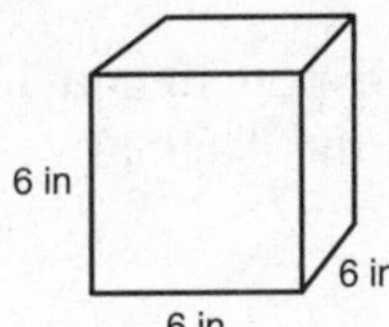

22. Which of the following expressions has the least value?

    A. 3^{-3}
    B. 4^0
    C. 4^1
    D. 2^{-4}
    E. 5^{-1}

LESSON 3

Scientific Notation

KEY IDEAS

- In scientific notation, a number equal to or greater than 1 and less than 10 is multiplied by a power of ten.
- Very small numbers are expressed by multiplying by a negative power of ten.
- In scientific notation, the number with the greatest power of ten has the greatest value.

HiSET EXAM TIP

Always try to save time. Suppose the multiple-choice answers are written in scientific notation. Instead of changing each choice to standard notation, change your answer to scientific notation.

Scientific notation uses the powers of ten to express very small and very large numbers. In scientific notation, a decimal number (greater than or equal to 1 and less than 10) is multiplied by a power of ten.

Look for patterns as you review these powers of ten.

$10^1 = 10$ $\quad 10^2 = 100$ $\quad 10^3 = 1,000$ $\quad 10^4 = 10,000$ and so on.

$10^{-1} = 0.1$ $\quad 10^{-2} = 0.01$ $\quad 10^{-3} = 0.001$ $\quad 10^{-4} = 0.0001$ and so on.

Did you find the patterns? In the row with positive exponents, the exponent is the same as the number of zeros in the number written in standard form. In the row with negative exponents, the exponent is the same as the number of decimal places in the number.

You can use these patterns to change scientific notation to standard form.

Example 1: Write 6.2×10^5 in standard form. 6.20000

Move the decimal point five places to the *right* (the same number as the exponent). Add zeros as needed. **620,000**

Example 2: Write 3.82×10^{-3} in standard form.

Move the decimal point three places to the *left* (the same number as the exponent). Add zeros as needed. **0.00382**

Work backward to write large and small numbers in scientific notation.

Example 3: To reach Mars, the Viking 2 spacecraft traveled 440,000,000 miles. What is the distance traveled in scientific notation?

1. Move the decimal point to the left until there is only a single digit in the ones place. 4.40000000
2. Multiply by 10 raised to a power equal to the number of places you moved the decimal point. $\mathbf{4.4 \times 10^8}$

Example 4: Scientists find that a kind of bacteria moves at a rate of 0.00016 kilometers per hour. Write the measurement in scientific notation.

1. Move the decimal place to the right until there is a single digit in the ones place. 0001.6
2. Multiply by 10 raised to a negative exponent equal to the number of places you moved the decimal point. $\mathbf{1.6 \times 10^{-4}}$

PRACTICE 3

You may be asked to compare numbers in scientific notation.

Example 5: Which is greater: 4.5×10^3 or 9.8×10^4?

You don't need to change the numbers to standard notation. Simply consider the powers of ten. Multiplying by 10^4, or 10,000, must have a greater result than multiplying by 10^3, which equals 1,000. In scientific notation, the number with the greater power of 10 has the greater value. Therefore, **9.8×10^4 is greater than 4.5×10^3.**

A. Write each number in scientific notation.

1. 2300
2. 0.00042
3. 12,400,000
4. 14,320,000,000
5. 36,000,000
6. 0.0095
7. 0.00000058
8. 150,000,000,000
9. 0.000000009

B. Convert from scientific notation to standard notation.

10. 5.173×10^{-4}
11. 3.7×10^6
12. 4.8×10^8
13. 1.7×10^{-5}
14. 7.2×10^{-3}
15. 9.16×10^5
16. 8.591×10^7
17. 9.56×10^{-6}

C. Answer the following questions.

18. Many domestic satellites maintain an orbit approximately 23,500 miles above Earth. What is that distance in miles in scientific notation?

19. Modern technology measures very fast transactions in nanoseconds. One nanosecond equals 1.0×10^{-9} of a second. How many seconds is a nanosecond, in standard notation?

20. The average distance of Neptune from Earth is 2.67×10^9 miles. Write the distance, in miles, in standard notation.

21. Light in the vacuum of space travels at a speed of nearly 300 million meters per second. Write the speed, in meters per second, in scientific notation.

D. Choose the <u>one best answer</u> to each question.

<u>Questions 22 and 23</u> refer to the following table.

Unit	U.S. Equivalent	Metric Equivalent
1 ton	2,000 lb	0.907 metric ton
1 acre	43,560 sq ft	4,047 square m

22. What is the number of square feet in an acre, written in scientific notation?

A. 0.4356×10^6
B. 4.356×10^5
C. 4.356×10^4
D. 4.356×10^3
E. 43.56×10^3

23. A shipment of goods weighs 5 tons. Which of the following expressions could be used to express the weight in metric tons?

A. $5 \times 0.907 \times 10^{-1}$
B. $5 \times 9.07 \times 10^1$
C. $5 \times 9.07 \times 10^{-2}$
D. $5 \times 9.07 \times 10^{-1}$
E. 5×9.07

LESSON 4

Order of Operations

When a mathematical expression contains more than one operation, its value may depend upon the order in which the operations are performed. To avoid confusion, mathematicians have agreed to perform operations in a certain order.

KEY IDEAS

- To evaluate an expression correctly, you must follow the order of operations.
- If an expression uses more than one set of grouping symbols, start with the inside set and work to the outside.
- The division bar may be used as a grouping symbol.

The Order of Operations

1. Parentheses or any other grouping symbols that enclose operations
2. Exponents and roots
3. Multiplication and division, working from left to right
4. Addition and subtraction, working from left to right

Study the following example to see how to apply the order of operations. Notice that parentheses are used in two places in the expression; however, only the first set of parentheses encloses an operation.

Example 1: Evaluate the expression $\frac{(5+3)^2}{4}+3(-1)$.

1. Perform the addition operation in parentheses.	$\frac{(8)^2}{4}+3(-1)$
2. Raise 8 to the second power.	$\frac{64}{4}+3(-1)$
3. Divide, then multiply.	$16+(-3)$
4. Add.	13

The value of the expression $\frac{(5+3)^2}{4}+3(-1)$ is **13**.

HiSET EXAM TIP

If using a scientific calculator, you can use the parentheses keys to help you follow the order of operations.

In more complicated expressions, one set of grouping symbols may be nested within another set. To avoid confusion, you can also use brackets [ ] or braces { } to group operations. To evaluate an expression with more than one set of grouping symbols, work from the inside to the outside.

Example 2: Evaluate the expression $4[5(-4+3)+2]$.

1. Perform the operation in the inner set of grouping symbols: $(-4+3)$.	$4[5(-4+3)+2]$ $4[5(-1)+2]$
2. Do the operations inside the brackets. Since multiplication comes before addition in the order of operations, multiply 5 and −1 and then add 2.	$4[-5+2]$ $4[-3]$
3. Multiply 4 and −3.	**−12**

The division bar is also a grouping symbol. Before you divide, perform any operations shown above and below the bar.

Example 3: Evaluate the expression $\frac{15+25}{2(5)}+6$.

1. Perform the operations above and below the fraction bar. $\frac{15+25}{2(5)}+6$

2. Divide, then add. $\frac{40}{10}+6$

$4+6=\mathbf{10}$

A. Solve.

1. $4(3)-2+(6+4\cdot 2)$
2. $16\div(10-6)^2$
3. $5^2-(5-7)(2)$
4. $3(-3)+(7+4)$
5. $\frac{3^3}{5-2}-\frac{(4-2)^2}{2}$
6. $\frac{25}{(4+1)}\cdot 3+(6-1)$
7. $2^3+(8-5)^2-3$
8. $(4-12)(-6)+(10-3)$
9. $30\div 3(5-4)$
10. $15+(4)(3)-2^2$
11. $(4+2)^2+(7-2)^3$
12. $7^2\div(11-4)+(9+14)$
13. $2\left[(17-11)^2\cdot\frac{(15-5)}{2}\right]$
14. $(5^2+6-3)\div(16-3^2)$
15. $150-4\left[\frac{3+9}{4-1}\cdot(14-11)^2\right]$

B. Choose the one best answer to each question.

Question 16 refers to the following information.

Susan is in charge of planning Midvale Hospital's parent education classes. The table below shows the cost of each class to the hospital.

Type of Workshop	Cost per Participant
Childbirth Classes	$35 per couple
Infant Care	$30 per person
Teaching Your Child to Read	$60 per person

16. A local foundation has offered to pay 75% of the cost of infant care classes. The hospital will cover any remaining costs. There are 28 parents enrolled in the upcoming infant care class. Which of the following expressions could be used to find the amount the hospital will pay?

A. (75)(28)(30)
B. (28)(30) – (0.75)(30)
C. (1 – 0.75)(28)(30)
D. (1 – 0.75)(30) + 28
E. (25)(28) – 30

17. In the expression

$$5+2\left[7\left(\frac{10^2}{10}\right)+(6-2)(3)\right],$$

what is the last operation you should perform to find the value of the expression?

A. Subtract 2 from 6.
B. Add 5.
C. Multiply by 2.
D. Find the square of 10.
E. Multiply by 7.

18. Find the value of the expression $22+6[(14-5)\div 3(17-14)]$.

A. 2.73
B. 28
C. 76
D. 76
E. 111

STUDY ADVICE

An easy way to remember the order of operations is to memorize the phrase *"Please excuse my dear Aunt Sally. Love, Ron."* The first letters of that phrase correspond to the order of operations: Parentheses, Exponents, Multiply, Divide, Add, Subtract, and work Left to Right.

LESSON 5

Absolute Value

The **absolute value** of a number is its distance from zero on the number line. For example, the absolute value of 5 is 5, since 5 is five spaces away from zero on the number line. But the absolute value of –5 is also 5, since –5 is also five spaces away from zero on the number line. Because **distance** is always **positive**, the absolute value of any positive or negative number is always positive.

Absolute value is written as two straight lines around a number, like this: |–5|.

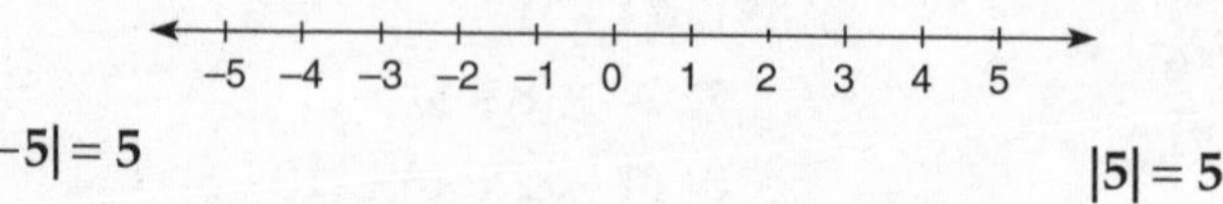

|–5| = 5

|5| = 5

Example 1: Which of the following is equal to |–13|?

(1) 13

(2) –13

The correct answer is **(1)**. Absolute value is always positive.

Treat the absolute value sign as you would treat parentheses in the order of operations. If numbers inside the absolute value sign are being added, subtracted, multiplied, or divided, then do that operation before you do anything else.

Example 2: Which of the following is equal to –20 | 17 – 34 |?

(1) 340

(2) –340

The correct answer is **(2)**. First perform the subtraction within the absolute value sign. Because you first found the absolute value, change –17 to 17. Then multiply by –20, like this:

$-20\,|17-34| = -20\,|-17| = -20\,(17) = \mathbf{-340.}$

We often think in terms of absolute value in real life, though we might not bother to call it that. For example, imagine that you have $314 in a checking account but you write a check for $400. You've overdrawn your account by $86. The bank will record your balance as –$86. But you'll think, "I'm $86 short." You'll just think of the absolute value, or **magnitude**, of the overdraft, without the negative sign.

KEY IDEAS

- The magnitude of a number, without a sign, is called the absolute value.
- Absolute value is used to determine distance of a positive or negative number from zero.
- In the order of operations, absolute value is treated the same as a set of parentheses.

HiSET EXAM TIP

A signed number, positive or negative, is used to show its direction in relation to zero. However, when you see a number inside two straight lines, you are working with its distance from zero—which is always positive.

PRACTICE 5

A. Find the absolute values.

1. $\lvert 18 \rvert$	**4.** $\lvert 95 \rvert$	**7.** $\lvert -5{,}708{,}432 \rvert$	**10.** $\lvert 10.5 \rvert$
2. $\lvert -107 \rvert$	**5.** $\lvert -7026 \rvert$	**8.** $\lvert -85.6 \rvert$	**11.** $\lvert -163.24 \rvert$
3. $\lvert 423 \rvert$	**6.** $\lvert -18 \rvert$	**9.** $\lvert 42 \rvert$	**12.** $\lvert -3.14 \rvert$

B. Use absolute value to find the solutions.

13. $5+\lvert -6 \rvert$	**17.** $-\lvert 110-201 \rvert$	**21.** $-5\lvert -4 \rvert$
14. $-3\lvert 52 \rvert$	**18.** $-14+\lvert -28 \div 2 \rvert$	**22.** $\lvert -6 \rvert - \lvert -7 \rvert$
15. $3\lvert -52 \rvert$	**19.** $706.2-\lvert -86.4+0.2 \rvert$	**23.** $\lvert 17 \rvert \div \lvert -8 \rvert$
16. $12 \div \lvert -4 \rvert$	**20.** $49 \div (-\lvert -7 \rvert)$	**24.** $\lvert -5.5 \rvert \times (-2)$

C. Choose the one best answer to each question.

25. The temperature in Northville at 9:00 P.M. was –5°F. By 5:00 A.M. the following morning, the temperature was –15°F. By how many degrees did the temperature change?

A. –15 degrees
B. –5 degrees
C. 5 degrees
D. 10 degrees
E. 15 degrees

26. Bob has errands to run. He walks 5 blocks east from his apartment to the barber shop, then walks 6 blocks west to the grocery store, then walks another 2 blocks west to the post office, and finally walks back home. Assuming that Bob's apartment, the barber shop, the grocery store, and the post office are all located on the same street, how many blocks did Bob walk in completing his errands?

A. 6
B. 9
C. 11
D. 13
E. 16

27. Milania has a score of –65 points, and Chris has a score of 55 points. By how many points is Milania losing to Chris?

A. 10
B. 55
C. 65
D. 120
E. 150

28. Absolute error is the absolute value of the difference between an actual value and its measurement. A deli scale gives a measurement of 25 ounces for a cut of meat that actually weighs only 23.5 ounces. What is the absolute error, in ounces, of the deli scale in this instance?

A. 1.5
B. 15.0
C. 23.5
D. 25
E. 48.5

LESSON 6

Algebraic Expressions

Writing Algebraic Expressions

An **algebraic expression** uses numbers, operations, and variables to show number relationships. **Variables** are letters (such as x and y) that represent unknown numbers. Each time a letter is used within the same expression, it represents the same number.

To solve algebra problems, you will need to be able to translate number relationships described in words into algebraic expressions. Study the following examples.

Algebraic expressions in words	In symbols
the product of 5 and a number	$5x$
a number decreased by 12	$x - 12$
the sum of 3 and the square of a number	$3 + x^2$
6 less than the quotient of a number and 2	$\frac{x}{2} - 6$
one-half a number increased by 15	$\frac{1}{2}x + 15$
4 times the difference of −3 and a number	$4(-3 - x)$
a number less another number	$x - y$
10 less the square root of a number plus 3	$10 - \sqrt{x + 3}$

KEY IDEAS

- Algebraic expressions show mathematical relationships using numbers, symbols, and variables.
- Variables are letters that take the place of unknown numbers.

To do well on algebra questions on the Mathematics Test, you must be able to translate a common life situation into mathematical symbols. You will use this skill to write equations and functions, to apply formulas, and to solve word problems.

HiSET EXAM TIP

To check whether the expression you have chosen is correct, substitute easy numbers into the expression and complete the operations. Then see if the result is reasonable for the situation.

Example 1: Kyle processes sales for an online bookstore. The shipping and handling on an order is equal to 4% of the total cost of the order plus $0.95 per book. If c represents total cost and n represents the number of books in an order, which of the following expressions could be used to find the shipping and handling for an order?

(1) $\frac{4}{100}nc + 0.95$
(2) $(0.04 + 0.95)n + c$
(3) $0.04c + 0.95n$

This kind of problem is called a **setup problem.** You need to recognize the correct way to find the shipping and handling based on the total cost and number of items. The relationship is described in the second sentence.

shipping and handling = 4% of total cost (c) plus \$0.95 per book (n)

$$= 0.04c + 0.95n$$

The correct answer is option **(3), $0.04c + 0.95n$.**

PRACTICE 6.1

A. Write an algebraic expression for each description. Use the variables x and y.

1. a number decreased by 7
2. the product of 3 and the square of a number increased by that number
3. the product of 8 and a number less 10
4. the difference of −3 multiplied by a number and the product of 2 and another number
5. 5 less than the quotient of 10 and a number
6. the sum of −8 and the product of 7 and a number
7. the sum of 16 times a number and the number decreased by 3 times another number
8. a number squared plus the number raised to the fourth power
9. the square of a number plus the quotient of 4 and 7
10. 6 subtracted from the sum of 15 and the square root of a number
11. a number less the sum of another number and 13
12. the square of the sum of a number and 6
13. 17 less the sum of 2 times a number plus another number
14. a number increased by the quotient of 24 and the number
15. the difference of the product of 2 and a number and 15
16. 4 times the difference of two different numbers
17. 5 multiplied by the difference of a number squared and 3
18. the product of a number and the difference of 11 and the square root of 100

B. Choose the one best answer to each question.

19. A minor-league baseball team is giving a local charity the sum of \$1,500 and \$0.50 for each ticket over 2,000 sold for one game. Let x represent the number of tickets sold. If the team sells more than 2,000 tickets, which of the following expressions could be used to find the amount of the donation?

A. \$1,500 + \$0.50x
B. \$1,500 + \$0.50(2,000 − x)
C. \$1,500 + \$0.50(x − 2,000)
D. \$1,500(2,000 − x)(\$0.50)
E. (x − 2,000)(\$1,500)

20. The sum of 3 times a number and 4 times a second number is divided by the sum of 2 and a third number. Which of the following expressions represents this series of operations?

A. $(3x + 4y) \div 2$
B. $(3x + 4y) \div (2 + z)$
C. $3x + 4y \div (2 + z)$
D. $3x + 4y \div 2 + z$
E. $(3x + 4y) \div 2z$

Question 21 refers to the following information.

Appliance City employees earn an hourly wage plus commission. Wage options are shown below.

Option	Hourly Wage	Commission on Sales
A	\$7.50	1%
B	\$6.00	3%

21. Chandra is paid under Option B. If h represents the number of hours worked and s represents Chandra's total sales, which of the following expressions could be used to find her weekly pay?

A. $6 + h + 0.03s$
B. $6h + 0.03s$
C. $6s + 0.03h$
D. $0.03(h)(s)$
E. $0.03(h)(s) + 6s$

Simplifying and Evaluating Expressions

Simplifying an expression means to perform all the operations you can within an expression. When working with variables, you must remember an important rule: You can add or subtract like terms only.

A **term** is a number, a variable, or the product or quotient of numbers and variables. A term cannot include a sum or a difference.

Examples: $5x$ $3y^2$ 13 x^3 $\frac{x}{2}$

Like terms have the same variable raised to the same power. For example, $3x^2$ and $5x^2$ are like terms. $8y$ and $4y$ are also like terms. However, $6x$ and $2x^2$ are not like terms because the variables are not raised to the same power.

To simplify an expression, combine like terms.

Example 2: Simplify $2x-5+4x^2-8+6x$.

Combine like terms. It is customary to write the term with the greatest exponent first and to continue in descending order.

$$2x-5+4x^2-8+6x$$
$$=(2x+6x)+(-5+-8)+4x^2$$
$$=8x+(-13)+4x^2$$
$$=\mathbf{4x^2+8x-13}$$

The **distributive property** allows you to remove grouping symbols to simplify expressions. We can state the distributive property using symbols.

$$a(b+c)=ab+ac \quad \text{and} \quad a(b-c)=ab-ac$$

In other words, each term inside the parentheses is multiplied by the term outside the parentheses, and the results are added or subtracted depending on the operation inside the parentheses. Example 3 applies the distributive property.

Example 3: Simplify $4x-3(x+9)+15$.

1. Change subtracting to adding a negative number.
2. Use the distributive property. Multiply -3 by each term in the parentheses.
3. Combine like terms. (**Note:** $1x$ means x.)

$$4x-3(x+9)+15$$
$$=4x+-3(x+9)+15$$
$$=4x+(-3x)+(-3)(9)+15$$
$$=4x+(-3x)+(-27)+15$$
$$=(4x+-3x)+(-27+15)$$
$$=\mathbf{x-12}$$

Evaluating an expression means finding its value. To evaluate an expression, substitute a given number for each variable. Follow the order of operations.

Example 3: Find the value of the expression $\frac{3x+2y}{4}$ when $x=6$ and $y=5$.

1. Replace the variables with the values given in the problem.

$$\frac{3x+2y}{4}=\frac{3(6)+2(5)}{4}$$

2. Perform the operations above the fraction bar. Then divide.

$$\frac{3(6)+2(5)}{4}=\frac{18+10}{4}=\frac{28}{4}=\mathbf{7}$$

Note: To remove parentheses from an operation that follows a minus sign, imagine that the parentheses are preceded by 1. Then use the distributive property.

$$-(2x+3)$$
$$=-1(2x+3)$$
$$=-1(2x)+(-1)(3)$$
$$=\mathbf{-2x+(-3)\ or\ -2x-3}$$

PRACTICE 6.2

A. Simplify.

1. $5 + x^2 - 3 + 3x$
2. $2y + 5 + 17y + 8$
3. $3x - 6(x - 9)$
4. $6x^3 + 4 + 2x^2(15) + x^2$
5. $4(y + 8) + 3(y - 6)$
6. $5 - (x - 3) + 4x$
7. $16x + 6(x - 2)$
8. $5y^2 + 4 - 3y^2 + 5 + y$
9. $-3(x + 3) - 2(x + 4)$
10. $5x - (x + 4) - 3$

B. Evaluate each expression as directed.

11. Find the value of $6(x + 2) + 7$ when $x = 2$.
12. Find the value of $3x^2 + 3(x + 4)$ when $x = 3$.
13. Find the value of $\frac{(x + y)^2}{2} - 10$ when $x = 2$ and $y = 4$.
14. Find the value of $y^2 + 16 - (y - 5)^2$ when $y = 3$.
15. Find the value of $8x + 9y - (2x + y)$ when $x = 4$ and $y = 6$.
16. Find the value of $x^2 + 3y - 4 + 2(x - z)$ when $x = 7$, $y = 5$, and $z = -3$.
17. Find the value of $(14 - x)^2 + 20\sqrt{x}$ when $x = 9$.
18. Find the value of $\frac{3(2x - y)}{3} + 6(y - 5)$ when $x = -2$ and $y = 3$.
19. Find the value of $x^2 - (x^3 + 3)$ when $x = -2$.
20. Find the value of $30x + 2 + 2y^2 - 3(x - 2)^2$ when $x = 1$ and $y = 4$.

C. Choose the <u>one best answer</u> to each question.

21. Which of the following expressions is equal to $3x^2 + 3(x - 3) + x + 10$?

A. $x^2 + 9x + 1$
B. $3x^2 + 4x + 19$
C. $3x^2 - 2x + 19$
D. $3x^2 + 4x + 1$
E. $4x^2 + 2x - 1$

22. Given the expression $4x^2 - 3(y + 6)$, which of the following values for x and y will result in a value of -11?

A. $x = 2, y = 3$
B. $x = -2, y = 4$
C. $x = -1, y = 2$
D. $x = 1, y = 0$
E. $x = 3, y = 1$

<u>Question 23</u> refers to the following information.

Temperature Conversion Formulas	
To convert Fahrenheit (F) to Celsius (C)	$C = \frac{5}{9}(F - 32)$
To convert Celsius (C) to Fahrenheit (F)	$F = \frac{9}{5}C + 32$

23. If the temperature is 68° Fahrenheit, what is the temperature in Celsius?

A. 20°
B. 36°
C. 54°
D. 154.4°
E. 180°

STUDY ADVICE

Algebraic expressions are the foundation for much of the Mathematics Test. In the next chapter, you'll take these skills one step further by working with expressions in word problems, equations, and functions. So, make sure you understand the material so far before moving on.

LESSON 7

Expressions and Calculator Skills

KEY IDEA

- If using a scientific calculator, use the *change sign* key to enter a negative number and the *grouping symbol* keys to change the order of operations.

Sometimes a calculator may be helpful when you work algebra problems. The following examples are worked using the TI-30XS MultiView™; however, remember your calculator may vary on Test Day. Please see pages 257–258 for more information about calculators. The TI-30XS MultiView™, like most scientific calculators, uses algebraic logic, which means that it follows the order of operations that you saw on page 376.

You need to practice using a scientific calculator with algebraic logic. You can find out whether your calculator uses algebraic logic by running this simple test.

Press: 4 [×] 3 [x^2] [enter]. (Your calculator may have an equal sign instead of an *enter* button.) If the display reads **36**, your calculator uses algebraic logic. If the display reads **144**, your calculator does not use algebraic logic. You should find another calculator to practice with for the Mathematics Test.

You can use a calculator to evaluate an expression that contains several operations.

Example 1: Find the value of the expression $2x^2 + 3x - 5$ when $x = -4$.

When you come to the variable x, enter -4 by pressing [(−)] 4. The [(−)] key is called the **change sign key**.

Press: 2 [×] [(−)] 4 [x^2] [+] 3 [×] [(−)] 4 [−] 5 [enter].

The right side of the display reads **15**.

The value of the expression is 15.

HiSET EXAM TIP

To check your work when using a calculator, enter each calculation twice. If the results are the same, you probably pressed the keys that you intended.

Expressions sometimes contain grouping symbols to show a different order of operations. You can enter grouping symbols on a scientific calculator. On the TI-30XS MultiView™, the grouping symbols [(] and [)] are found above the [8] and [9], respectively. When you enter the left, or open, parenthesis, [(], the calculator waits until you enter the right, or closing, parenthesis, [)], before it calculates what is inside the symbols.

Example 2: Find the value of the expression $2(x+4)+\frac{5x}{3}$ when $x = 6$.

Press: 2 [×] [(] 6 [+] 4 [)] [+] 5 [×] 6 [÷] 3 [enter].

The right side of the display reads **30**.

The value of the expression is **30**.

You can also use your calculator for only part of an expression.

Example 3: Find the value of the expression $\frac{3x+6}{2}+\sqrt{225}$ when $x = 4$.

Substitute 4 for x in the first part of the expression and calculate the results by hand or using your calculator: $\frac{3(4)+6}{2}=\frac{12+6}{2}=\frac{18}{2}=9$.

Now use your calculator to find the square root of 225.

Press: [2nd] [x^2] 225 [enter]. The right side of the display reads 15.

Add the results of the two steps: $9 + 15 =$ **24**.

PRACTICE 7

A. Use a calculator as needed to find the value of the expressions as directed.

1. What is the value of $5x^2 - 3x + 5$ when $x = 2$?
2. Find the value of $\sqrt{7x} + 2x$ to the nearest tenth when $x = 5$.
3. If $x = -3$, what is the value of $7x^2 + 2x - 6$?
4. What is the value of $\frac{1}{2}x + 15$ when $x = 3$?
5. Find the value of $3(2x + 3 + y) - 14$ when $x = -2$ and $y = 9$.
6. If $y = -3$, what is the value of $4y^3 + 2(y^2 - 4)$?
7. What is the value of $2(x^2 + 6) + 3(x - 1)$ when $x = 5$?
8. If $x = 4$ and $y = -4$, what is the value of the expression $6x^2 + 3y^2 + 2$?
9. Find the value of $-2(x^3 + 3) + 16x + 2$ when $x = 2$.
10. If $x = 7$, what is the value of the expression $7 + 3(x - 2) - 2x^2$?
11. Find the value of $-(x + y) + 3(2z - y)$ if $x = -5$, $y = -7$, and $z = 4$.
12. What is the value of the expression $x^2 - 7(3 - y) + 4$ when $x = 5$ and $y = 4$?
13. If $x = -2$ and $y = 8$, what is the value of $x^2 + y - 6(y + 3)$?
14. What is the value of $\sqrt{760 - 4x^2}$ to the nearest tenth when $x = 6$?
15. If $x = 20$, what is the value of the expression $4(x + 7) - 3(x - 2)$?
16. Find the value of $\dfrac{x(25 + 2x - y)}{-z}$ when $x = -3$, $y = 4$, and $z = -1$.
17. What is the value of $5y^2 + 4x^2 - 6(x - y)$ when $x = 5$ and $y = -2$?
18. Find the value of $3x^2 \cdot \dfrac{2(x - 3y)}{6}$ when $x = 6$ and $y = 1$.
19. What is the value of the expression $(x^2 + 5)(x^2 - x + 2) - 3$ when $x = -4$?
20. Find the value of $(x + y)(x - y)(2x + y)$ when $x = 9$ and $y = 4$.

B. Choose the <u>one best answer</u> to each question.

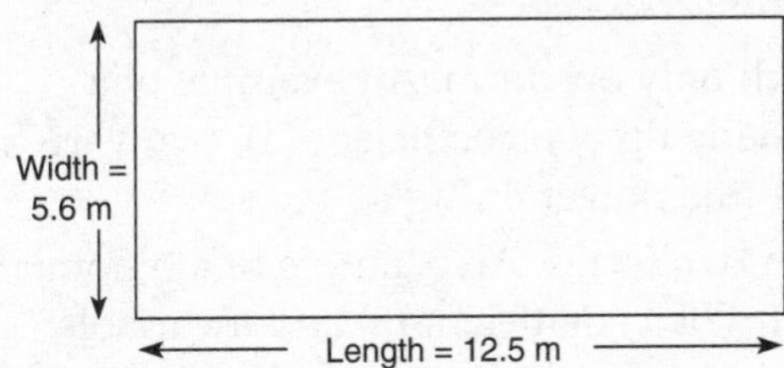

21. Jake has to buy enough fencing to enclose the rectangular garden shown above. The formula for finding the perimeter of (or distance around) a rectangle is $P = 2l + 2w$, where P = perimeter, l = length, and w = width. Using the values from the drawing, what is the perimeter in meters of the garden?
    A. 18.1
    B. 36.2
    C. 70
    D. 72.4
    E. 140
22. If $x = -5$ and $y = 2$, which of the following expressions has the greatest value?
    A. $x + y$
    B. $-x + y$
    C. xy
    D. $-2xy$
    E. $(-x)(-y)$
23. What is the value of the expression $2 \div x^{-4}$ when $x = 2$?
    A. 32
    B. 16
    C. 8
    D. −16
    E. $\frac{1}{8}$

LESSON 8

Understand Polynomials

The Mathematics Test will expect you to understand polynomials. A **polynomial** is made up of terms, and since the prefix *poly-* means "many," a polynomial is a term in which many parts are being combined. Each term in a polynomial may be made up of a combination of coefficients, variables, exponents, and constants.

Coefficients include numbers such as 4, –25, or $\frac{1}{2}$ and will come before the variables. Coefficients can be negative, like –25. If there is no coefficient next to a variable, assume the coefficient is 1. In the expression $x + y + z$, the coefficient in front of each variable is equal to 1.

Variables are letters such as x and y in polynomial terms. In the polynomial $45a^2b$, the variables are a and b.

Exponents, or powers, are a way of showing repeated multiplication. This is also known as raising a number or variable to a power. Polynomials must be raised to whole number exponents. There are no negative or fractional powers in polynomials. In the polynomial $6x^3y^4$, the exponents are 3 and 4. The **degree** of a polynomial with only one variable is the largest exponent of that variable. For example, in the expression $4x^3 + 3x^2 - 5$, the degree is 3 (the largest exponent of x).

A **constant** is a number on its own that will always remain the same. It is not next to a variable. A constant can be either positive or negative, depending on whether it is being added or subtracted. In the expression $4x^3 + 3x^2 + 5$, the constant is 5. No matter what value you substitute for x, 5 will always be just 5.

Polynomials are built out of all of the components above, and there are different types of polynomials, including monomials, binomials, and trinomials. These are important to know.

- A **monomial** is a polynomial with only one term. An example of a monomial is $4xy^2$. This term is made up of a coefficient (4), two variables (x and y), and an exponent (the power of 2).
- A **binomial** is a polynomial with two terms. An example of a binomial is $3x + 2$. The first term is made up of a coefficient (3) and a variable (x), and the second term consists of a constant (2).
- A **trinomial** is a polynomial with three terms. An example of a trinomial is $4x + 3y^2 - 4$. The first term is made up of a coefficient (4) and a variable (x). The second term is made up of a coefficient (3), a variable (y), and an exponent (the power of 2). The third term is made up of a constant, and this time it is a negative number (–4).

A few types of numbers are not categorized as polynomials and cannot be present in polynomial terms. These include the following:

- Division by a variable, such as $\frac{3}{x+3}$ or $\frac{1}{x}$
- Negative exponents, such as $4xy^{-2}$ (exponents can only be 0, 1, 2, etc.)
- Fractional exponents, such as $3a^{\frac{1}{2}}$
- Variables inside radicals, such as $\sqrt{x}$

In a polynomial term, however, you can divide by a constant or have numbers inside a radical. For example, $\frac{4x}{12}$ is allowed, as is $\sqrt{10}$.

KEY IDEAS

- A polynomial is an expression with more than one term—any combination of coefficients, variables, exponents, and constants.
- Specific types of polynomials include monomials, binomials, and trinomials.

HiSET EXAM TIP

If there is no coefficient next to a variable, assume the coefficient is 1.

PRACTICE 8

A. Identify whether each of the following is a monomial, binomial, or trinomial.

1. $25a$
2. $2xy^2z$
3. $x-4$
4. x^3+y-1
5. $7y-1$
6. $2x^4+3x+4$
7. $\frac{x}{3}$
8. y^2
9. $g^2h^2i^2j^2$
10. x^2+x^2
11. $x^2+14x+3$
12. x^2y+x^2+y
13. $g+h$
14. $\sqrt{49}$
15. $3x^2-5$

B. For each polynomial, identify the terms. Remember that a coefficient can be positive or negative.

16. $3x^4-2x^2+3$
17. $12a^2bc$
18. $3g-4h$
19. x^2+y
20. $-4a-3b^2+c$
21. 25
22. $4x^2+3x-7$
23. $\frac{3x}{8}$
24. $\sqrt{25}$
25. $\frac{x^2}{9}$
26. $49x^2y^2z^2$
27. $18y^2-4y^2+8$
28. $3h-4$
29. x^2-x+y^2-2
30. $ab+ab^2+b^2-4$

C. Choose the <u>one best answer</u> to each question.

31. What is the sum of the exponents in the expression $4x^3+3x^2+5$?
   A. 3
   B. 4
   C. 5
   D. 12
   E. 17

32. What is the sum of the coefficients in the expression $a-3b-c+2d$?
   A. −3
   B. −1
   C. 1
   D. 2
   E. 3

STUDY ADVICE

If you're having trouble sticking to your study schedule, consider finding a study partner. The two of you can remind each other to stick to your study schedules, encourage each other, and even have study sessions together.

LESSON 9

Simplify Polynomials

Combine Like Terms

When working with polynomials, you must work to combine like terms. **Like terms** have variables that are the same or are terms that have the same variable raised to the same power, or exponent. For example, $8x^3$ and $4x^3$ are like terms, and $5y$ and $3y$ are also like terms.

Unlike terms have variables that are different or have the same variable raised to different powers. For example, $3a$ and $5b$ are unlike terms. The terms $9x$ and $7x^2$ are also unlike terms because the variables are raised to different powers.

You can only combine like terms when simplifying polynomials. Unlike terms cannot be combined. For example, in the polynomial $7x^2 + 4x^3$, you cannot combine the terms because x is raised to different powers in each term. However, in the polynomial $7x^2 + 4x^2$, you can combine terms that all have the same variable and the same exponent: $7x^2 + 4x^2 = 11x^2$.

Example 1: Combine like terms in the polynomial $4y^3 + 2x^3 - 7y^3$.
1. First, identify and group the like terms. $4y^3 - 7y^3 + 2x^3$

The two y^3 terms are alike; the x^3 term cannot be combined with them.

2. Combine the like terms. $\mathbf{-3y^3 + 2x^3}$

Simplify Polynomials

Some polynomials may contain both like and unlike terms. The following example shows how like and unlike terms are handled when you have to simplify a polynomial. Start by combining like terms from the exponent with the largest number, or degree, and proceed to the exponent with the smallest number.

Example 2: Simplify the polynomial $7x^4 - 13x^2 + x^4 + 2x^2 + 5x + 3 + x$.

1. Combine like terms with the largest degree, which is 4. Add: $7x^4 + x^4 = 8x^4$.
2. You now have $8x^4 - 13x^2 + 2x^2 + 5x + 3 + x$. Combine like terms from the exponent with the next largest degree, which is 2. Add: $-13x^2 + 2x^2 = -11x^2$.
3. You now have $8x^4 - 11x^2 + 5x + 3 + x$. Finally, combine like terms with the next largest degree, which is 1. Add: $5x + x = 6x$.
4. You now have $\mathbf{8x^4 - 11x^2 + 6x + 3}$.

This is as much as you can simplify this polynomial by combining like terms. The simplified polynomial has no more like terms and must remain as is.

KEY IDEAS

- Like terms can be combined; unlike terms cannot.
- Like terms are either numbers—positive or negative—or variables with the same degree of exponents.
- Polynomials with unlike terms cannot be simplified.

HiSET EXAM TIP

When working with polynomials, treat the minus sign before a coefficient or constant as an indicator of a negative number. This will help you to combine like terms using the rules of signed numbers that you learned on pages 368–371.

PRACTICE 9

A. For each pair of terms, indicate if they are like terms or unlike terms.

1. $4x^3, x^3$ __________ terms
2. $3x, x$ __________ terms
3. b, b^2 __________ terms
4. $-2x, 7y$ __________ terms
5. $-2x, 7x$ __________ terms
6. $4a, 4$ __________ terms
7. g^2, g^2hi __________ terms
8. $2x^2y, 8x^2y$ __________ terms
9. $-5m, -5m^2$ __________ terms
10. x^2y, xy^2 __________ terms
11. $ab, 8ab$ __________ terms
12. $3y, 3y^2$ __________ terms
13. $14g, \frac{1}{3}g$ __________ terms
14. $12x^2, x^2$ __________ terms
15. a, ab^2 __________ terms
16. $15x^2, -x^2$ __________ terms
17. $10y, 11yz$ __________ terms
18. $x^2, \frac{x^2}{2}$ __________ terms
19. $g, -g^2$ __________ terms
20. $\frac{x}{8}, x^2$ __________ terms

B. Simplify each expression by combining like terms.

21. $3x^2y + 4x^2y$
22. $3b + b$
23. $a - 7a + 3$
24. $14ab + ab^2 + 2ab + 3$
25. $x^2 - 3x^2 + 7$
26. $ab + 2ab + ab$
27. $7g + 7gh + 7g + 7gh$
28. $g^2 + h^2 - 4g^2h^2 + g^2 + h^2 - 4$
29. $9y + y - y^2 - y$
30. $x^2 - 8x^2 + y - 3$
31. $11y + 11y - 7$
32. $9x^2y - 3x^2y + 4y^2 - 21 + y^2 - 2$
33. $8x^2 - 4x + 7 + 4x^3 - x^2 + 7x - 2$
34. $-3x^2 + 6x - 2x^2 - 10x + 5$
35. $9x^2 - 3x^3 + x - 2x^2$

C. Choose the one best answer to each question.

36. What is the simplified form of the expression $3a^2b + 4ab + 3a^2b + 5ab$?
    A. $6a^3b^2 + 8a^3b^2$
    B. $6a^2b + 9ab$
    C. $6a^2b + 8ab$
    D. $9a^2b - 6ab$
    E. $15a^6 + b^4$

37. When simplified, how many terms are in the polynomial $j^2 + k^3 - 2j^3 + 5k^3 - 2j^2$?
    A. 2
    B. 3
    C. 4
    D. 5
    E. 6

LESSON 10

Add and Subtract Polynomials

Add Polynomials with One Variable

On the Mathematics Test, you may be required to add polynomials that have one variable. You can add polynomials when they have like terms, including variables and exponents. When you see polynomials within parentheses linked by an addition sign, add them by combining the like terms across the polynomials.

Example 1: Add $(3x^2 + x + 4) + (2x^2 + 2x - 16)$.

1. To add these polynomials, simply combine like terms. Add: $3x^2 + 2x^2 = 5x^2$.
2. Add: $x + 2x = 3x$.
3. Add: $4 + (-16) = -12$.
4. Combine the results into one polynomial: $\mathbf{5x^2 + 3x - 12}$.

Sometimes, an expression needs to be simplified before you add and combine like terms.

Example 2: Add $(5x^2 + 8x - 4) + (2x^2 - 6x + 14x)$.

1. Simplify within the second parentheses. Add: $-6x + 14x = 8x$.
2. Combine like terms across the polynomials. Add: $5x^2 + 2x^2 = 7x^2$.
3. Use the simplified expression from step 1. Add: $8x + 8x = 16x$.
4. Combine the results into one polynomial: $\mathbf{7x^2 + 16x - 4}$.

Subtract Polynomials with One Variable

The only difference between adding and subtracting polynomials is the minus sign between the parentheses. You must distribute the negative sign across the second polynomial. To distribute the negative sign across the second polynomial, simply reverse the signs of each term. Then drop the parentheses and combine like terms across both polynomials.

Example 3: Subtract $(3x^2 + x + 4) - (7x^2 + 2x - 16)$.

1. Distribute the negative sign to everything in the second set of parentheses by reversing the sign of each term: $-7x^2 - 2x + 16$.
2. Drop the parentheses from the entire expression and combine like terms:
   $3x^2 + x + 4 - 7x^2 - 2x + 16$
   $-4x^2 + x + 4 - 2x + 16$
   $-4x^2 - x + 4 + 16$
   $\mathbf{-4x^2 - x + 20}$

Note that subtracting a negative constant or coefficient is the same as adding a positive. In the next example, watch what happens to the negative coefficient inside the second set of parentheses when the sign is distributed.

KEY IDEAS

- Monomials, binomials, or trinomials can be added or subtracted.
- In some cases, a polynomial needs to be simplified before it can be added or subtracted.
- When subtracting polynomials, distribute the minus sign across the second polynomial, changing the signs for coefficients, and then combine all the like terms.

HiSET EXAM TIP

When you subtract, you are simply reversing the signs within the second polynomial. Be careful to make all negative signs positive. Study Examples 3 and 4 carefully to avoid common errors.

PRACTICE 10.1

Example 4: Subtract $(x^2 + 2x + 3) - (4x^2 - x + 6)$.

1. Distribute the negative sign to everything in the second set of parentheses by reversing the sign of each term. $-4x^2 + x - 6$

2. Drop the parentheses and combine like terms.

$$x^2 + 2x + 3 - 4x^2 + x - 6$$
$$x^2 - 4x^2 + 2x + x + 3 - 6$$
$$\mathbf{-3x^2 + 3x - 3}$$

A. Add the following polynomials.

1. $(3x + 4) + (2x + 2)$
2. $(17y - y + 3) + (4y + 3y + 3)$
3. $(5x^2 - 3x - 4) + (3x^2 - 2x + 6)$
4. $(-a^2 + 2a) + (16a^2 + 6a)$
5. $(9x^2 - 3x - 2) + (2x^2 + 5x + 5)$
6. $(6a + 6) + (-5a - 5)$
7. $(-8g^2 + 7g + 6) + (8g^2 - 7g - 5)$
8. $(2x^2 + 5x) + (2x^2 + 4x + 7x - 9)$
9. $(13y + 4y + 4) + (7y - 7)$
10. $(-a^2 - a^2 - a - 4) + (-a^2 - a^2 - a - 5)$

B. Subtract the following polynomials.

11. $(3y - 4) - (2y - 2)$
12. $(x + 16) - (4x + 3)$
13. $(2a + 1) - (-a - 1)$
14. $(5x^2 + 2x + 4) - (2x^2 + x + 2)$
15. $(7y + 5y + 5) - (2y - 2)$
16. $(9x^2 + 4x + 5x + 4) - (7x^2 + 6x - 9)$
17. $(-g + g - 1) - (-g - g - 2)$
18. $(17a^2 - 4a - 4) - (16a^2 + 6a - 6)$
19. $(7b^2 + b - 8) - (7b^2 + b + 8)$
20. $(21x^2 + 3x^2 - 2x - 4 - 1) -$
$(3x^2 + x^2 + x + 2x - 5 - 1)$

C. Choose the one best answer to each question.

21. What is the sum of the polynomials $(2xy + 3xy^2 - 4x^2y) + (5x^2y - 3xy^2 + 2xy)$?

A. $5x^2y - xy + xy^2$
B. $x^2y + 4xy$
C. $4xy + 3x + y$
D. $7x - 2y$
E. $7x^2y - 2xy$

22. Which of the following equals $(5x^2 - 2x + 1) - (3x^2 - 3x - 2)$?

A. $x - 5x - 1$
B. $2x^2 - x + 3$
C. $2x^2 + x + 3$
D. $2x^2 - 5x + 3$
E. $8x^2 - 5x + 3$

STUDY ADVICE

Look back over your work. If you understood how to add or subtract polynomials, but you made small or careless errors in doing so, give yourself a pat on the back! You've learned the concept, and now you know to watch for small math errors.

Simplifying Polynomials with More Than One Variable

Some polynomials contain terms with different variables—for example, the binomial $2x + 3y$ contains an x term and a y term. You add, subtract, and simplify polynomials with more than one variable just as you do polynomials with just a single variable. However, you have to be careful to add and subtract only like terms. Remember that in all polynomials, like terms have the *same variable* and the *same exponent*. For example, in the polynomial $x^2 + 2x + y^2 + 3x + 2y$, the only like terms are the two x^1 terms. You can combine the $2x$ and the $3x$, but you cannot combine x^2 with any other term, nor can you combine the y^2 or the $2y$ with any other term. The most simplified version of this polynomial is $x^2 + 5x + y^2 + 2y$.

A term that consists of two or more variables multiplied together cannot be combined with terms that contain only one of those variables. For example, you cannot combine $2xy + 7x$. However, you can combine $2xy + 7xy$ to get $9xy$.

Example 5: Simplify $6xy^4 - 20x^2 - 3 + xy^4 + 12x^2 - 30$.

Start by grouping the like terms together. Then add and subtract as appropriate.

$$6xy^4 - 20x^2 - 3 + xy^4 + 12x^2 - 30$$
$$= 6xy^4 + xy^4 - 20x^2 + 12x^2 - 3 - 30$$
$$= \mathbf{7xy^4 - 8x^2 - 33}$$

Adding Polynomials with More Than One Variable

Adding polynomials that contain more than one variable requires the same process as adding polynomials that have only one variable. Just remove the parentheses and combine like terms across both polynomials. Remember that only like terms can be combined.

Example 6: Add $(3x^2 + 6x + 3xy) + (5x^2 - 6xy + 14y)$.

$$(3x^2 + 6x + 3xy) + (5x^2 - 6xy + 14y)$$
$$= 3x^2 + 5x^2 + 6x + 3xy - 6xy + 14y$$
$$= \mathbf{8x^2 + 6x - 3xy + 14y}$$

Subtracting Polynomials with More Than One Variable

Subtracting polynomials that contain more than one variable is exactly the same as subtracting polynomials that contain only a single variable. Remember to distribute the minus sign across the second polynomial when you remove the parentheses. Also remember that only like terms can be combined.

Example 7: Subtract $(3xy^2 + x + 2xy + 4) - (7xy^2 + 2xy - 16)$.

$$(3xy^2 + x + 2xy + 4) - (7xy^2 + 2xy - 16)$$
$$= 3xy^2 + x + 2xy + 4 - 7xy^2 - 2xy + 16$$
$$= \mathbf{-4xy^2 + x + 20}$$

Notice that there is no xy term in the final simplified expression because $2xy - 2xy = 0$.

PRACTICE 10.2

A. Simplify the following polynomials.

1. $a^2 + 2a + b^2 + 3a + 3b^2$
2. $x + 3xy + y + 16 - 5x - 4xy$
3. $yz^2 - z^2 + 5 + 3yz - 3z^2 + 4yz$
4. $ab - b + c + 17 + 6ab - 34$
5. $a^4 + c^2 + 3ac - 5a^4 - 2c^2 + 5$
6. $19xyz + x - y + 3xyz + 6 + y$
7. $ef + ef^2 - 10 + 6ef + f$
8. $p + pq - q - p + 3pq - 3 - q + 7$

B. Add the following polynomials.

9. $(ab + b - c + 6) + (3ab - b + c - 6)$
10. $(x^2 + xy - y - 3) + (-x^2 - xy + y + 3)$
11. $(p^6 + p^5 + pq - p^2) + (2p^6 - p^5 + 3pq - q^2)$
12. $(x + xy + 7) + (y - xy + 8)$
13. $(9a + bc + c^2) + (-9a - b + bc - c^2)$
14. $(4xyz + 4x - 4y) + (6xyz - 4x - 4y + 16)$
15. $(5a + 5b + 4c - 6) + (a - b - 4c + d + 6)$
16. $(pq - q + 15) + (6pq - 15)$

C. Subtract the following polynomials.

17. $(ab + a + b + 6) - (8ab + a - b - 6)$
18. $(xy + x + y) - (xy + x + y)$
19. $(p^2 + q^2 + 14) - (3p^2 - 4q^2 + 7)$
20. $(x^4 + yz + z^4) - (yz + z^5)$
21. $(bc^2 + bc + c - 7) - (2bc - c - 7)$
22. $(xy + xz - xyz) - (4xy + xyz)$
23. $(c^3d^7 + c^2 - d + 35) - (2c^2 - 3d + 35)$
24. $(ef^2g - fg + 16) - (ef^2 + fg + 8)$

D. Choose the <u>one best answer</u> to each question.

25. Which of the following equals $(x + y + z) - (-2x + 2y + z)$?

A. $-x + 3y + 2z$
B. $-2x - y + 2z$
C. $3x - 2y + 2z$
D. $-3x + 2y - 2z$
E. $3x - y$

26. Which of the following equals $(2g^2 + 3h - 5k) + (g^2 + 2h + 3k)$?

A. $g^2 + h - 8k$
B. $3g^2 + 5h - 2k$
C. $2g^2 + 6h^2 - 15k^2$
D. $2g^4 + 5h - 2k$
E. $3g^2 + h + 2k$

Multiply Polynomials

KEY IDEAS

- There are a number of ways to multiply polynomials.
- The basic concepts in all involve learning procedures for multiplying constants, variables, and exponents.
- A common method for multiplying binomials is called FOIL for short.

Multiply a Monomial by a Monomial

To multiply two monomials, multiply each component separately. Start by multiplying the coefficients (or numbers). If there is no coefficient given, assume that the coefficient is 1 (for example, $xy = 1xy$). Then, multiply each variable separately by adding the exponents of like variables. Remember that a variable with no exponent is a variable raised to the first power (for example, $x = x^1$). So $x\left(x^3\right) = x^1\left(x^3\right) = x^4$.

Example 1: Multiply $(2ab)(4b)$.

$$2 \times 4 \times a \times b^1 \times b^1 = \mathbf{8ab^2}$$

Multiply a Monomial by a Binomial

To multiply a monomial by a binomial, multiply the monomial by the first term in the binomial, then multiply the monomial by the second term in the binomial. Finally, add the resulting terms.

Example 2: Multiply $-2z^2(z + 3yz)$.

1. Distribute the negative sign:
   $-2z^2(z + 3yz) = 2z^2(-z - 3yz)$.
2. Multiply the monomial by each term in the binomial:
   $2z^2(-z - 3yz) = [2 \times (-1) \times z^2 \times z^1] + [2 \times (-3) \times z^2 \times y^1z^1]$.
3. Add: $-2z^3 + (-6yz^3) = \mathbf{-2z^3 - 6yz^3}$.

Multiply Two Binomials

To multiply two binomials, multiply the first terms, then the outer terms, then the inner terms, and, finally, the last terms. Add the results and combine like terms. You can remember this process by the acronym **FOIL**, which stands for First, Outer, Inner, Last.

HiSET EXAM TIP

Always finish the FOIL method by combining like terms after you have multiplied.

Example 3: Multiply $(2g^2 + 9)(3g^2 - 4)$.

1. Multiply using FOIL:
   $(2g^2 + 9)(3g^2 - 4) = \overbrace{(2g^2)(3g^2)} + \overbrace{(2g^2)(-4)} + \overbrace{(9)(3g^2)} + \overbrace{(9)(-4)}$.
2. Add: $6g^4 - 8g^2 + 27g^2 - 36$.
3. Combine like terms:
   $6g^4 - 8g^2 + 27g^2 - 36 = \mathbf{6g^4 + 19g^2 - 36}$.

A. Multiply the monomials.

1. $(6x)(5x)$
2. $(2xy)(3y)$
3. $(7abc)(4bc)$
4. $(12y)(z)$
5. $(a)(9bc)$
6. $(5xyz)(2xy^2z^4)$
7. $(4ab)(bc^2)$
8. $(17f^2gh^3)(2fh^4)$

B. Multiply the binomials by the monomials.

9. $3z^2(6xy+4z)$
10. $6x(7x-6z)$
11. $-5ab(3b+11c)$
12. $-3f^3(6h-8fgh^2)$
13. $10z(7x^7-5z)$
14. $-z(-z-6xy)$
15. $8b(9ab+8a)$
16. $-9(-2x^4+3xy^2)$

C. Multiply the binomials by using FOIL. Remember to complete by combining like terms wherever possible.

17. $(x+5)(x-6)$
18. $(x+y)(x+y)$
19. $(z+9)(z-9)$
20. $(yz^2+x)(yz^2-3x)$
21. $(3x+3)(3x+5)$
22. $(x+y)(x-y)$
23. $(y^2-6)(y^4+10)$
24. $(ab+3)(ab-4)$

D. Choose the one best answer to each question.

25. Which of the following expressions is equal to $(4a^3b^2)(3a^2c)$?
    A. $12a^5b^2c$
    B. $7a^5b^2c$
    C. $12a^6bc$
    D. $7a^6b^2c$
    E. $12a^5bc$

26. Martha has $2pc^2$ board games, and John has $6p^2c$ board games. Which of the following expressions represents the product of the number of board games that Martha and John have?
    A. $4p^2c^2$
    B. $8p^3c^3$
    C. $8p^2c^2$
    D. $12p^2c^2$
    E. $12p^3c^3$

27. Which of the following expressions is equal to $(4ab+2)(3ab-7)$?
    A. $7a^2b^2+22ab+5$
    B. $12a^2b^2-22ab-14$
    C. $12a^2b^2+22ab+14$
    D. $7a^2b^2-22ab-5$
    E. $a^2b^2+2ab-14$

STUDY ADVICE

How's your stress level? As you're working through difficult content, it's especially important to manage your stress. Stay on a regular sleep schedule, exercise, and eat right. Whenever you're stressing out, step away. Remember: You can do this. Just don't let stress get in your way.

Divide Polynomials

KEY IDEAS

- You can divide a polynomial by numbers, expressions, or other polynomials.
- The key to dividing a polynomial is to isolate a common factor that divides into the numerator and denominator.
- Common factors can be numbers, variables, or a combination of the two such as addition, subtraction, or multiplication expressions.

HiSET EXAM TIP

One algebraic expression divided by another is called a rational expression. If you are asked to simplify a rational expression, you are simply dividing.

Divide Polynomials by a Number

The Mathematics Test will sometimes ask you to simplify a polynomial that is written as a fraction. To simplify, divide the numerator and denominator by a common term. A common term can be the following:

- A number
- A variable with a number as a coefficient
- A more complicated expression

You may need to factor the common term out of the numerator or denominator before you can do the division.

Example 1: Simplify $\frac{3x+6}{3}$.

$$\frac{3x+6}{3}=\frac{3(x+2)}{3}=\frac{\cancel{3}(x+2)}{\cancel{3}}=\boldsymbol{x+2}$$

Divide Polynomials by an Expression

Dividing a polynomial by an expression is really no different from dividing by a number. You need a common term in the numerator and denominator, and you may have to factor out that common term (including any variables) before you can do the division.

Example 2: Simplify $\frac{25x^3-45x^2}{5x}$.

$$\frac{25x^3-45x^2}{5x}=\frac{5x(5x^2-9x)}{5x}=\frac{\cancel{5x}(5x^2-9x)}{\cancel{5x}}=\boldsymbol{5x^2-9x}$$

When the numerator has two added or subtracted expressions that both include the common term, it may be easier to split the polynomial into two separate fractions and simplify them separately. Doing it this way will help you keep straight exactly which terms you can cancel.

Example 3: Simplify $\frac{x(x+7)-3(x+7)}{x+7}$.

$$\frac{x(x+7)-3(x+7)}{x+7}=\frac{x(x+7)}{x+7}-\frac{3(x+7)}{x+7}$$

$$=\frac{x\cancel{(x+7)}}{\cancel{x+7}}-\frac{3\cancel{(x+7)}}{\cancel{x+7}}=\boldsymbol{x-3}$$

A fraction that has an algebraic expression in both its numerator and its denominator, as in the previous examples, is sometimes called a rational expression. Do not be confused if you see this term on the HiSET exam: It simply means that you are being asked to simplify by dividing one expression by another.

PRACTICE 12

A. To simplify, divide each polynomial by a number. (You may need to factor the numerator and/or denominator to find the common term.)

1. $\frac{2y+30}{2}$
2. $\frac{7x+21}{7}$
3. $\frac{4x+20}{4}$
4. $\frac{3a+3b}{3}$
5. $\frac{11x^2+22x}{11}$
6. $\frac{26x^2+39x+13}{13}$
7. $\frac{5x+10y}{5}$
8. $\frac{21a+14b}{7}$
9. $\frac{48x+32y}{32}$
10. $\frac{9a-15b}{12}$
11. $\frac{6b+24c}{18}$
12. $\frac{25a+5b+15c}{10}$

B. Divide each polynomial. Decide whether it is easier for you to divide the original numerator by the common term (as in Example 2) or whether to split the numerator first (as in Example 3).

13. $\frac{18x^2+6x}{3x}$
14. $\frac{10x^2+6x}{2x}$
15. $\frac{40y^2+10y}{5y}$
16. $\frac{42xy+49x}{7x}$
17. $\frac{38xy+38x}{19x}$
18. $\frac{3x+18}{x+6}$
19. $\frac{x(x+4)-6(x+4)}{x+4}$
20. $\frac{y(y+3)+7(y+3)}{y+3}$
21. $\frac{z(z+2)-5(z+2)}{z+2}$
22. $\frac{22x^2+66x}{11x}$
23. $\frac{x(y-2)-6(y-2)}{y-2}$
24. $\frac{a(b+3)+3(b+3)}{b+3}$

C. Choose the <u>one best answer</u> to each question.

25. Which of the following is equal to $\frac{21a+14b}{7}$?

   A. $5a+5b$
   B. $3a+14b$
   C. $3a+2b$
   D. $21a+2b$
   E. $14a+7b$

26. James has $27x$ apples, Rachel has $51y$ oranges, and Glen has $60z$ peaches. Which of the following expressions represents the average number of pieces of fruit that James, Rachel, and Glen have in their baskets?

   A. $9x+51y+60z$
   B. $46x+46y+46z$
   C. $9x+17y+60z$
   D. $9x+17y+20z$
   E. $81x+151y+180z$

ALGEBRAIC EXPRESSIONS PRACTICE QUESTIONS

1. Which of the following expressions is equal to $6 - 4(x + 3)$?

   A. $4x + 3$
   B. $4x - 3$
   C. $4x - 9$
   D. $-4x + 9$
   E. $-4x - 6$

2. If Kris makes d dollars and Heidi makes 75 dollars less than 3 times Kris's wage, what does Heidi make in terms of d?

   A. $d + 75$
   B. $d - 225$
   C. $3d - 75$
   D. $3d - 225$
   E. $\dfrac{d}{3-75}$

3. What is the product of 700 and 180,000 written in scientific notation?

   A. 12.6×10^9
   B. 1.26×10^8
   C. 1.26×10^9
   D. 1.26×10^{10}
   E. 126,000,000

4. If there are $4x$ identical schools in a region and each school has $3y$ classrooms each with $7x$ desks, how many desks are there in the region?

   A. $11x + 3y$
   B. $28x + 3y$
   C. $84xy^2$
   D. $84x^2y$
   E. $11x(3y)$

5. Which of the following is equivalent to $x^2 - 25$?

   A. $x(x - 25)$
   B. $(x - 5)^2$
   C. $(x + 5)(x - 5)$
   D. $(x - 25)^2$
   E. $\dfrac{(x+y)}{(x-y)}$

6. If Tom has $9x$ baseball cards, Adam has 13 more than Tom, and Dave has $2y$ baseball cards, together they would have how many cards?

   A. $9x + 2y + 13$
   B. $18xy + 13$
   C. $18xy + 2y$
   D. $18y + 2x + 13$
   E. $18x + 2y + 13$

Questions 7 and 8 refer to the figure below.

The figure below is a multiplication box. Each place represents the horizontal number multiplied by the vertical number; for example, the 9 in the lower right corner equals 3 multiplied by 3.

	5	***r***	**3**
1	5		3
****	20	*a*	
3	*b*	*d*	9

7. Which of the following is equal to ab?

   A. $5y$
   B. $60y$
   C. $100y$
   D. $500y$
   E. $180d$

8. Which of the following is equal to $a - d$?

   A. a
   B. b
   C. c
   D. x
   E. y

9. Multiply $7c^2(a^2 + 5b + 7c^2)$.

A. $(7a^2 + c^2)(a^2 - b^2)$
B. $7a^2c^2 + 35bc^2 + 49c^4$
C. $7(ac)^2 + 35(bc)^2 + 49c^4$
D. $7a^2 + 35b + 49c^4$
E. $a^2 + 5b + 14c^2$

10. A Little League pie sale fundraiser generated $900. If there were 6*x* pies sold, how much did each pie cost?

A. $10
B. $15
C. $15*x*
D. $\$\frac{x}{150}$
E. $\$\frac{150}{x}$

11. Simplify the expression $\frac{(a-4)^2\,(6b)}{2(3b)\,(a+4)\,(a-4)}$.

A. $\frac{a-4}{a+4}$
B. $\frac{a+4}{a-4}$
C. $\frac{a-2}{2}$
D. 1
E. $2a - 4$

12. Emilie buys *x* ounces of chicken for each of her guests at a dinner party. There are 8*y* people coming, and chicken is $*z* a pound. How much will the total amount of chicken cost in dollars? (*Hint*: There are 16 ounces in one pound.)

A. $8xyz$
B. $16xyz$
C. $\frac{xyz}{2}$
D. $\frac{xyz}{8}$
E. $\frac{xy}{8z}$

13. What is the value of the expression $6(x - y) - 8x$ when $x = -2$ and $y = 5$?

A. −58
B. −26
C. 2
D. 34
E. 54

14. Which of the following would be equal to $x^2 + 6z$ multiplied by $2y - 4z$ if $x = 2$, $y = 4$, and $z = 3$?

A. 104
B. 88
C. 0
D. −72
E. −88

15. What is the value of the following expression?

$$\frac{4^3 - [3(12 + 2^2)]}{6 + 5(4) - 15}$$

A. 0
B. $\frac{9}{11}$
C. $\frac{16}{41}$
D. $1\frac{5}{11}$
E. $3\frac{4}{11}$

16. If every member of a team is paid 5*p* dollars for his or her participation, and Team Alpha has 6*k* members, Team Beta has 4*p* members, and Team Delta has 9*h* members, which of the following represents the total amount paid to the members of all three teams?

A. $1080hkp$
B. $1080hkp^2$
C. $120p^2k + 45ph$
D. $30kp + 20p^2 + 45hp$
E. $120(h + k + p)$

17. Which of the following is equal to $7x - [(5y)2x - 9y + 8x]$?

A. $x - 9y + 10xy$
B. $-3x - 4y$
C. $-x + 9y - 10xy$
D. $15x - 9y + 10xy$
E. $9x - 10xy + 12y$

18. If Stephanie has 5*c* CDs for every DVD Alyshia has, and Jeff has 4*d* DVDs, which is 15 more than Alyshia has, how many CDs does Stephanie have?

A. $20cd - 75c$
B. $20cd + 15$
C. $80cd - 15$
D. $80cd - 75c$
E. $160cd - 75cd$

19. Divide $\dfrac{56x^4 + 49x^3y^3 - 84x^3 - 7x^2}{7x^2}$.

A. $8x^2 - 7xy^3 + 12x - 1$
B. $8x^2 + 7xy^3 - 12x - 1$
C. $8x^4 + 7x^3y^3 - 12x^3 - x^2$
D. $8x^4 + 7y^3 - 5x^3 - 1$
E. $49x^2 + 42xy^3 - 77x$

20. A charity with a yearly budget of 80*d* gets all of its money from either its yearly ball or from private donations. If the charity raised 64*d* from the silent auction at the ball and 4*a* from ticket sales at the ball, how much will need to be raised in private donations to meet the budget?

A. $16d$
B. $16d - 4a$
C. $16d + 4a$
D. $144d - 4a$
E. $144d + 4a$

21. Divide $\dfrac{x^4 + 4x^2y^4 - 8x - y^2}{2y^2}$.

A. $\dfrac{x^4}{2y^2} + 2x^2y^2 - \dfrac{4x}{y^2} - \dfrac{1}{2}$

B. $\dfrac{x^2}{2y} + \dfrac{2x^2y^2 - 4x}{y^2 - \frac{1}{2}}$

C. $\dfrac{2x^4y^2 + 8x^2y^2 - 16x}{y^2 + 2y^4}$

D. $\dfrac{x^4 - 4x}{2y^2 + 2x^2y^2 - \frac{1}{2}}$

E. $(x - 2y)(2x + y)$

22. If 12*k* privates, 8*f* lieutenants, and 6*r* captains are divided into 2*r* equal squads, which of the following would express the number of members of one squad?

A. $6k + 4f + 3r$
B. $6k + 4f + 3r^2$
C. $\dfrac{6k + 4f}{r} + 3$
D. $12k + 8f + 4r$
E. $12k + 8f + 3r$

23. If $q = 2$ and $r = 4$, which of the following would equal $\dfrac{r^2x^2 + q^3x}{(q^2x)}$?

A. $4x + 2$
B. $4x^2 + 2$
C. $8x + 4$
D. $16x^2 + 8x - 2$
E. $16x^2 + 2$

24. Simplify:

$$\frac{44x^6 + 55x^3y^4 + 88x^2 - 11y^2}{11x^2} - 6x^4 - 8$$

A. $4x^4 + 5xy^2 + 8x - 1$

B. $2x^4 + 5xy^3 - y^2 - 8$

C. $-2x^4 + 5xy^4 - \dfrac{y^2}{x^2}$

D. $10x^4 + 5y^4 - \dfrac{y^2}{x^2} - 8$

E. $2x^3y + 5xy^3 - 19$

25. Simplify:

$$(6x^2 + 5xy^2)(y) - (4xy - 9x)(4xy)$$

A. $5xy^3 - 16x^2y^2 + 42x^2y$
B. $5xy^3 - 16x^2y^2 - 30x^2y$
C. $6x^2y - 11x^2y^2 - 36xy^2$
D. $6x^2y + 5x^2y^2 - 36xy^2 + 16xy$
E. $30x^2y^2 - 36$

26. There are $4x$ workers, including managers, in an office. If the salaries of the 3 managers are not included, the average salary of each employee is $5x - 6$. What do the nonmanagerial employees earn in total?

A. $20x^2 - 24x$
B. $20x^2 - 24x - 3$
C. $20x^2 - 9x + 18$
D. $20x^2 - 39x + 18$
E. $20x^2 + 39x - 18$

27. What is the value of $\dfrac{45xy + 63y^2}{9y}$ if $x = 6$ and $y = 3$?

A. 180
B. 156
C. 108
D. 64
E. 51

28. Simplify:

$$\frac{3x(x^2 + 3) - 2x\,(x^2 + 3) - (x^2 + 3)}{x^2 + 3}$$

A. $x^3 - 1$
B. $x^3 - 3x - 1$
C. $3x - 1$
D. $2x - 1$
E. $x - 1$

29. If the $3h$ people in one country and the $4k$ people in the neighboring country each consume $h - 17$ pounds of rice per year on average, how much rice would be consumed by both countries in one year?

A. $4h + 4k - 17$
B. $4h^2 + 4k - 68k$
C. $12hk + h - 17$
D. $3h^2 + 4hk - 51h - 68k$
E. $2h^2 + 3hk - 17h + 68k$

30. Simplify:

$$\frac{4x^2(x + y) - 2(x + y)^2(x - y) - xy(x + y)}{x + y}$$

A. $2x^2 + 2y^2 - xy$
B. $4x^2 + xy - 2x - 2y$
C. $4x^2 - xy - 2x - 2y$
D. $3x^2 - 2xy^2 - xy$
E. $4x^2 + 2x + 2y - xy$

Questions 31 and 32 refer to the figure below.

The figure below is a multiplication box. Each place represents the horizontal number multiplied by the vertical number; for example, the 20 in the lower right corner equals 5 multiplied by 4.

	a^2	Z[	5
Z			ab
\	$8b$		
-		40	20

31. Which of the following is equal to a?

A. 2
B. 4
C. 5
D. 10
E. 12

32. Which of the following is equal to a^2c?

A. 5
B. 8
C. 20
D. 32
E. 40

LESSON 1

Equations

Writing and Solving One-Step Equations

An **equation** is a mathematical statement that two expressions are equal.

Examples: $3+5=4\cdot 2$ $\quad 10-1=3^2$ $\quad 5(3+4)=35$

An equation can contain one or more variables. Solving an equation means finding a value for the variable that will make the equation true.

Examples: $4+x=11$ $\quad 3x=24$ $\quad x-5=-2$

$\mathbf{x=7}$ $\quad \mathbf{x=8}$ $\quad \mathbf{x=3}$

KEY IDEAS

- An equation states that two expressions are equal.
- To solve an equation, isolate the variable by applying inverse operations to both sides of the equation.
- Check your work by substituting your solution for the variable in the original equation and simplifying.

The basic strategy in solving an equation is to isolate the variable on one side of the equation. You can do this by performing **inverse**, or opposite, operations. However, you must always follow one basic rule: whatever you do to one side of the equation, you must also do to the other side.

Example 1: Solve $x-23=45$.

On the left side of the equation, the number 23 is subtracted from x. The inverse of subtraction is addition. Add 23 to both sides of the equation.

$$x-23=45$$
$$x-23+\mathbf{23}=45+\mathbf{23}$$
$$\mathbf{x=68}$$

To check your work, replace the variable with your solution and simplify.
When $x=\mathbf{68}$, the equation is true.

Check: $x-23=45$
$$68-23=45$$
$$45=45$$

The following examples use the inverse operations of multiplication and division.

HiSET EXAM TIP

If you are unsure about a multiple-choice algebra problem, substitute each of the answer choices for the variable in the equation. You may be able to do this quickly using your calculator.

Example 2: Solve $\frac{x}{2}=17$.

The variable x is divided by 2. Since multiplication is the inverse of division, you must multiply each side of the equation by 2.

$$\tfrac{x}{2}=17$$
$$2\left(\tfrac{x}{2}\right)=2(17)$$
$$\mathbf{x=34}$$

When $x=\mathbf{34}$, the equation is true.

Check: $\frac{34}{2}=17$
$$17=17$$

Example 3: Solve $5x=75$.

Since the variable x is multiplied by 5, divide both sides of the equation by 5.

$$5x=75$$
$$\tfrac{5x}{5}=\tfrac{75}{5}$$
$$\mathbf{x=15}$$

When $x=\mathbf{15}$, the equation is true.

Check: $5(15)=75$
$$75=75$$

PRACTICE 1.1

A. Solve for the variable in each equation.

1. $7x = 63$
2. $23 + m = 51$
3. $-13 = y - 12$
4. $\frac{x}{4} = -16$
5. $5a = 625$
6. $y - 17 = -30$
7. $x + 6 = 33$
8. $4c = 28$
9. $\frac{12}{x} = -3$
10. $26 = b + 33$
11. $93 = 3x$
12. $s + 16 = 8$
13. $36 = \frac{x}{3}$
14. $t + 14 = 53$
15. $\frac{x}{6} = 8$
16. $16y = -48$
17. $r - 35 = 75$
18. $24 = \frac{120}{x}$
19. $5y = -45$
20. $d + 45 = 20$
21. $16 = 4x$
22. $-4x = 24$
23. $19 = h - 7$
24. $\frac{x}{11} = 6$
25. $m + 24 = 14$
26. $5y = 45$
27. $14 - w = 42$
28. $18 = \frac{y}{4}$

B. Choose the one best answer to each question.

Questions 29 and 30 refer to the following table.

April Time Sheet Summary
Hours Worked per Week

Week	1	2	3	4
Kayla Sax	36	40	40	
Erin Grady		24	28	38

29. Kayla and Erin worked a total of 77 hours during Week 1. Let x = Erin's hours for Week 1. Which of the following equations could be used to solve for Erin's hours during Week 1?
A. $x - 36 = 77$
B. $x + 77 = 36$
C. $x + 36 = 77$
D. $x - 77 = 36$
E. $x = 77 + 36$

30. Erin worked twice as many hours as Kayla did during Week 4. Let y = Kayla's hours for Week 4. Which of the following equations could be used to solve for Kayla's hours during Week 4?
A. $\frac{y}{2} = 38$
B. $38y = 2$
C. $2y = \frac{38}{y}$
D. $2y = 38$
E. $\frac{1}{2y} = 38$

31. The quotient of a number divided by 4 is 32. What is the number?
A. 8
B. 28
C. 64
D. 128
E. 512

32. The solution $x = -5$ makes which of the following equations true?
A. $14 - x = 9$
B. $\frac{x}{5} = 1$
C. $x + 3 = 8$
D. $12x = -60$
E. $12 - x = 7$

33. Mike had $572.18 in his checking account. After writing a check, he had $434.68. Which of the following equations could be used to find the amount of the check (c)?
A. $\$572.18 + c = \$434.68$
B. $\$572.18 - c = \$434.68$
C. $\$572.18c = \$434.68$
D. $\frac{\$572.18}{c} = \$434.68$
E. $\$572.18 = \$434.68(c)$

Solving Multi-Step Equations

Most equations require more than one operation in order to find a solution. Follow these basic steps:

- Simplify by combining like terms.
- Perform addition and subtraction steps.
- Perform multiplication and division steps.

Example 4: Solve $6x + 5 - 2x = 25$.

1. Combine like terms ($6x - 2x = 4x$).

$$6x + 5 - 2x = 25$$
$$4x + 5 = 25$$

2. Subtract 5 from both sides.

$$4x + 5 - 5 = 25 - 5$$
$$4x = 20$$

3. Divide both sides by 4.

$$\frac{4x}{4} = \frac{20}{4}$$
$$\mathbf{x = 5}$$

4. Check by substituting the solution for x in the original equation.

$$6(5) + 5 - 2(5) = 25$$
$$30 + 5 - 10 = 25$$
$$25 = 25$$

In this example, the distributive property is used to simplify an expression. Notice that not every step is written out. As you gain experience, you can perform an operation on both sides of an equation mentally.

Example 5: Solve $-4(x - 6) = 2x$.

1. Use the distributive property to remove the grouping symbols.
2. Add $4x$ to each side.
3. Divide each side by 6.

$$-4(x - 6) = 2x$$
$$-4x + 24 = 2x$$
$$24 = 6x$$
$$\mathbf{4 = x}$$

4. Check.

$$-4(4 - 6) = 2(4)$$
$$-4(-2) = 8$$
$$8 = 8$$

Some of the time you will be expected to write an equation from information given in the problem. The problem will describe two expressions that are equal. Write each expression in symbols and connect the expressions with the equal sign (=). In many problems, the word *is* indicates the = symbol.

Example 6: The product of a number and 6 is 44 more than twice the number. What is the number?

1. Write an equation. The word *is* represents the equal sign.
2. Subtract $2x$ from both sides.
3. Divide both sides by 4.

$$6x = 44 + 2x$$
$$4x = 44$$
$$\mathbf{x = 11}$$

4. Check.

$$6(11) = 44 + 2(11)$$
$$66 = 44 + 22$$
$$66 = 66$$

The number described in the problem is **11**.

Note: Subtraction and division operations must be written in the order indicated by the words. "The difference between x and y" must be written $x - y$, not $y - x$. "The quotient of x and y" must be written $\frac{x}{y}$, not $\frac{y}{x}$.

PRACTICE 1.2

A. Solve for the variable in each equation.

1. $3x - 20 = 130$
2. $2y - 8 = -3y - 18$
3. $6m = 14m - 16$
4. $2x + 5 + 6x = -27$
5. $5y + 3(y + 2) = 54$
6. $17 - 4z + 2z = 13$
7. $6m - 4 = m + 11$
8. $35 = x + 7 + 6x$
9. $5p - 2 = 6p - 9$
10. $50 = 3(s + 16) - 2(s - 2)$
11. $\frac{5(2x - 10)}{2} + 14 = 19$
12. $3(3 + r) = 2r + 4$
13. $5y = 2y + 22 + y$
14. $38 = 5(2b - 3) + 3b + 1$
15. $-5 - x = 2x - (4x + 6)$
16. $\frac{3h}{2} = 30$
17. $4(3 + 2x) + 8 = 92$
18. $-5(3 - z) = z + 1$
19. $10 - 3b + 3 = -1 + (b + 2)$
20. $5n + 8 - n = 6(n - 1)$

B. Choose the one best answer to each question.

21. Three times a number increased by 9 is 15 less than six times the number. Let x = the unknown number. Which of the following equations could be used to find the value of x?

A. $3(9x) = 6(15x)$
B. $3x(9) = 6x - 15x$
C. $3x + 9 = 15 - 6x$
D. $3x + 9 = 6x - 15$
E. $3x + 9 = \frac{x}{6} - 15$

22. Dave has 500 baseball cards, which is as many as Eric and Travis have combined. Eric has three times as many cards as Travis has.

Dave	Eric	Travis
500	$3x$	x

From the information, you can write the equation $3x + x = 500$. How many cards does Eric have? (*Hint:* Solve for x. Then find how many cards Eric has.)

A. 150
B. 250
C. 350
D. 375
E. 450

23. The difference of four times a number and 7 is 15 plus the quotient of the number and 3. Which of the following equations could be used to find the value of x?

A. $3(9) = 6(15x)$
B. $4x - 7 = \frac{x}{3} + 15$
C. $7 - 4x = \frac{x}{3} + 15$
D. $7 - 4x = \frac{3}{x} + 15$
E. $4x - 7 = \frac{3}{x} + 1$

24. Kim earned x dollars at his part-time job on Friday. His wife earned $12 more than twice Kim's pay $(2x + 12)$. Together, they earned $174. How much did Kim earn on Friday? (*Hint:* Use the equation $x + (2x + 12) =$ \$174.)

A. $54
B. $87
C. $108
D. $120
E. $174

STUDY ADVICE

Remember to include rewards and breaks in your study schedule. Celebrate a job well done with a fun outing. Don't try to study seven days a week—this can lead to burnout. Plan a day off to rest, relax, and reward yourself for the focused studying you have done!

LESSON 2

Equation Word Problems, Part I

Algebra problems describe how several numbers are related. One number is the unknown, which you will represent with a variable. Using the relationships described in the problem, you can write an equation and solve for the variable.

KEY IDEAS

- To solve a word problem, decide what quantity will be represented by *x*. Then write expressions for the other quantities in terms of *x*.
- Write and solve an equation. Answer the question asked in the problem.

Example 1: There are twice as many women as men in a class on auto repair. If there are 24 students in the class, how many are women?

1. Express the numbers in the problem in terms of the same variable. Let x represent the number of men. Since there are twice as many women, let $2x$ represent the number of women.

2. Write and solve an equation. The total number of men and women is 24, so $x+2x=24$. Solve:
$$x+2x=24$$
$$3x=24$$
$$x=8$$

Since $x=8$, $2x=2(8)=16$. There are 8 men and **16 women** in the class.

Consecutive numbers are numbers that follow in counting order. For example, 1, 2, and 3 are consecutive numbers. The numbers 2, 4, and 6 are consecutive even numbers, and 1, 3, and 5 are consecutive odd numbers.

Example 2: The sum of three consecutive numbers is 105. What is the greatest of the three numbers?

1. Let x represent the first number and $x+1$ and $x+2$ represent the other numbers.

2. Write an equation and solve.
$$x+(x+1)+(x+2)=105$$
$$3x+3=105$$
$$3x=102$$
$$x=34$$

3. Find the answer. The variable x represents the first number in the sequence, so the three numbers are 34, 35, and 36. The problem asks for the greatest number, which is **36**.

HiSET EXAM TIP

When you find x, you may not be finished solving a problem. Always reread the question. As shown in Example 2, you may need to use the value of x to calculate the solution in a multi-step problem.

You may need to use the difference between numbers to write equations.

Example 3: The ticket prices for a play are \$12 for adults and \$8 for children. One evening, the box office sold 200 tickets. If the total box office receipts were \$2240, how many adult tickets were sold?

1. Let x represent the number of adult tickets. Since 200 tickets were sold, the number of children's tickets sold can be written as $200-x$.

2. Multiply each term by the cost for that type of ticket. Set the total equal to \$2240, and solve for x.
$$12x+8(200-x)=2240$$
$$12x+1600-8x=2240$$
$$4x+1600=2240$$
$$4x=640$$
$$x=160$$

3. There were **160 adult tickets** sold.

PRACTICE 2

A. Solve.

1. Two houses are for sale on the same street. The second house has 1000 square feet less than twice the square feet of the first house. Together, the houses have 4400 square feet. What is the square footage of the first house?
2. Julia has 24 coins in her pocket. The coins are either dimes or quarters. The total value of the coins is $4.50. How many coins are dimes? (*Hint:* The value of the dimes is $0.10x$, and the value of the quarters is $0.25(24 - x)$.)
3. The Bulldogs won twice as many games as they lost. If they played a total of 36 games, how many did they win? (There were no tied games.)
4. The sum of four consecutive even numbers is 212. What is the third number? (*Hint:* Let $x =$ the first number, $x + 2 =$ the second number, $x + 4 =$ the third, and so on.)
5. A children's store is selling pants for $6 each and shirts for $4. Brenda bought 13 items and paid $62. How many shirts did she buy?
6. The sum of three consecutive numbers is 180. What is the least number in the series?
7. In a month, Andrew spends twice as much on rent as he does on food for his family. Last month, he spent $1650 on rent and food. How much did he spend on rent?
8. George spends four times as much time helping customers as he does stocking shelves. Last week, he spent 35 hours on the two tasks. How many hours were spent helping customers?

B. Choose the <u>one best answer</u> to each question.

9. Sylvia scored 10 points better than Wiley on their science exam. Greg scored 6 points less than Wiley. Altogether, the students earned 226 points. How many points did Sylvia earn?

   A. 74
   B. 78
   C. 84
   D. 88
   E. 94

10. Two adults and four children paid $48 to get into the fair. A child's ticket is $6 less than an adult's ticket. What is the cost of an adult's ticket?

    A. $18
    B. $15
    C. $12
    D. $9
    E. $6

11. Jenny is four times as old as her niece Tina. In 12 years, Jenny will be only twice as old as Tina. The chart shows expressions for Tina and Jenny's ages now and in 12 years.

	Jenny's Age	Tina's Age
Now	$4x$	x
In 12 Years	$4x + 12$	$x + 12$

How old is Tina now?

   A. 4
   B. 6
   C. 8
   D. 10
   E. 12

Inequalities

An **inequality** is a mathematical statement that connects two unequal expressions. The inequality symbols and their meanings are:

$>$ greater than	$\geq$ greater than or equal to
$<$ less than	$\leq$ less than or equal to

An inequality is solved much like an equation. Use inverse operations to isolate the variable.

Example 1: Solve for x in the inequality $3x + 2 < 8$.

1. Subtract 2 from both sides. $\quad 3x + 2 < 8$, $\quad 3x < 6$
2. Divide both sides by 3. $\quad \boldsymbol{x < 2}$

The solution $x < 2$ states that any number less than 2 makes the inequality true. Check by substituting 1 (a number less than 2) for x: $3(1) + 2 < 8$, which simplifies to $5 < 8$, a true statement.

There is one important difference between solving equalities and inequalities. Whenever you multiply or divide both sides of an inequality by a *negative* number, you must *reverse* the inequality symbol.

Example 2: Solve for n in the inequality $-2n - 5 \geq 3$.

1. Add 5 to both sides to remove -5 from the left side of the equation. $\quad -2n - 5 + 5 \geq 3 + 5$, $\quad -2n \geq 8$
2. Divide both sides by -2 and *reverse the inequality symbol.* $\quad \frac{-2n}{-2} \geq \frac{8}{-2}$, $\quad \boldsymbol{n \leq -4}$

Check your work by substituting a number that is less than or equal to -4 into the *original* inequality. Here -5 is used for n. Since $5 \geq 3$ is a true statement, the answer is correct.

$$-2n - 5 \geq 3$$
$$-2(-5) - 5 \geq 3$$
$$5 \geq 3$$

When an inequality contains a variable, there is usually a range of numbers that make the inequality true. For that reason, we often graph the solution. In the examples below, a closed dot means that the number is included in the solution set. An open dot means the number is not included.

Examples:

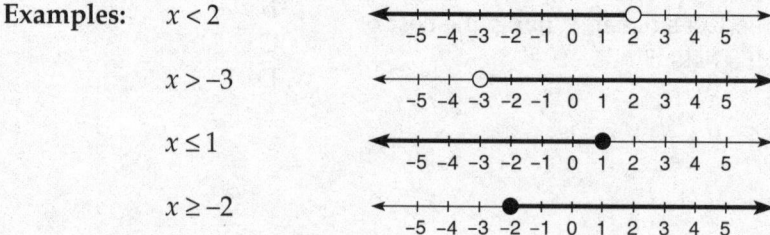

$x < 2$

$x > -3$

$x \leq 1$

$x \geq -2$

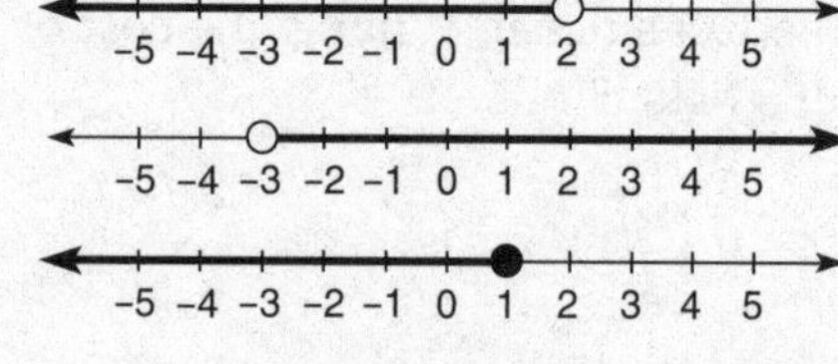

KEY IDEAS

- Use <, >, ≤, and ≥ to show the relationship between two unequal expressions.
- The symbol always points to the smaller expression.
- Use inverse operations to solve inequalities. Reverse the inequality sign if you multiply or divide by a negative number.

HiSET EXAM TIP

Avoid the most common mistake with inequalities: reversing the symbol accidentally. Always check your work by substituting any number that fits the solution into the original inequality.

PRACTICE 3

A **compound inequality** combines two inequalities. To solve a compound inequality, separate the inequalities and solve both. Then combine the solutions.

Example 3: Solve $3x+4<5x<16+x$.

1. Write two inequalities and solve each separately.	$3x+4<5x$	$5x<16+x$
2. Write the result as a compound inequality. $\mathbf{2<x<4}$	$4<2x$	$4x<16$
	$2<x$	$x<4$

In other words, any quantity that is greater than 2 *and* less than 4 will make the compound inequality true.

A. Solve.

1. $3x-7>5$

2. $13<2x-1$

3. $4+2x\le -2$

4. $\dfrac{4+x}{5}\le 8$

5. $2(x+3)<4$

6. $3+9x\ge 4(x+7)$

7. $-4(x+2)<24$

8. $-2x+9<1$

9. $\dfrac{x-2}{3}>2x+11$

10. $6x<5x+2$

11. $x+6\le 8x-15$

12. $5x+14>2+7x$

13. $13x-7\ge 25-3x$

14. $x-6<2(x+2)$

15. $-5+3x\ge 4(3x-8)$

16. $36>4(x-12)$

17. $6\le 3(x+3)$

18. $\dfrac{4x}{3}>8x-20$

19. $x-2<\dfrac{2x+6}{4}$

20. $x\ge 4x-9$

21. $30\ge 5(x+4)\ge 10$

22. $-7x>-2(x+15)<10$

23. $3<5x-27<53$

24. $22\le 6x-2\le 4x+16$

B. Choose the <u>one best answer</u> to each question.

25. The perimeter of a square can be found using the formula $P=4s$, where s is one side of the square.

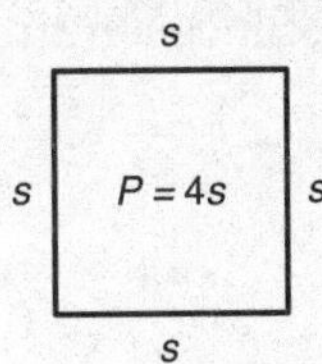

The perimeter of a square is less than or equal to 64 inches. Which of the following represents the possible measures of the side of the square in inches?

A. $s\le 16$
B. $s\ge 16$
C. $s\ge 8$
D. $s\le 64$
E. $s\ge 32$

26. Three added to the product of –4 and a number (x) is less than 5 added to the product of –3 and the number. Which of the following is a graph of the solution set of x?

A. 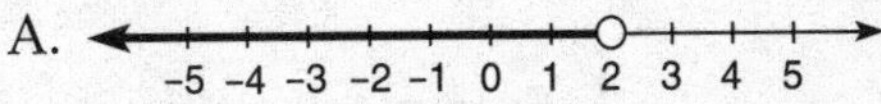

B. -5 -4 -3 -2 -1 0 1 2 3 4 5

C. -5 -4 -3 -2 -1 0 1 2 3 4 5

D. -5 -4 -3 -2 -1 0 1 2 3 4 5

E. -5 -4 -3 -2 -1 0 1 2 3 4 5

STUDY ADVICE

Remember to take frequent breaks when studying, at least 10 minutes out of each hour. During your breaks, stand up and move around so you come back to studying refreshed.

LESSON 4

Quadratic Equations

KEY IDEAS

- A quadratic equation can have two solutions.
- Set the quadratic equation equal to 0 and factor.
- Find the values for x that will make each factor equal 0.

A **quadratic equation** contains a squared variable, such as $x^2 - 3x = 4$. One way to solve quadratic equations is by factoring. This is the simplest method and the one you should use on the Mathematics Test. When you factor an expression, you find the terms that divide evenly into the expression.

Example 1: Factor the expression $15x^2 + 9x$.

1. Look for a term that divides evenly into both $15x^2$ and $9x$. Both terms can be divided by $3x$. — $15x^2 \div 3x = 5x$; $9x \div 3x = 3$
2. Factor out $3x$. Write the terms as factors. — $15x^2 + 9x = \mathbf{3x(5x+3)}$

Study Example 2 to learn how to multiply factors with more than one term.

Example 2: Multiply $\underbrace{\overset{\text{(factor)}}{(2x+3)}\overset{\text{(factor)}}{(x-4)}}_{\text{four terms}}$.

1. Multiply each term in the first factor by each term in the second factor.
   $2x \cdot x = 2x^2$
   $2x \cdot -4 = -8x$
   $3 \cdot x = 3x$
   $3 \cdot -4 = -12$
2. Combine the results.
   $2x^2 + (-8x) + 3x + (-12) =$
   $\mathbf{2x^2 - 5x - 12}$

This method of multiplying factors is called the FOIL method. The letters in FOIL stand for First, Outer, Inner, and Last. Use the word FOIL to make sure you have performed all the necessary operations.

You factor a quadratic equation to solve it. A quadratic equation may have two solutions. Find values that make the factors equal to 0. Since a number multiplied by 0 is 0, each of the values is a solution.

Example 3: Solve $x^2 - 3x = 4$.

1. Set the equation equal to 0 by subtracting 4 from both sides.
   $x^2 - 3x = 4$
   $x^2 - 3x - 4 = 0$
2. Factor by trial and error. Think: What factors of the last term, –4, when added, will equal –3, the number part of the middle term?
   $-4 \cdot 1 = -4$ and $-4 + 1 = -3$
   $(x \quad)(x \quad) = 0$
   $(x+1)(x-4) = 0$
3. If either one of the factors equals 0, then the product of the factors will be 0. Set each factor equal to 0 and solve for x.
   $x + 1 = 0$
   $\mathbf{x = -1}$
   $x - 4 = 0$
   $\mathbf{x = 4}$

The solutions to the quadratic equation are **–1 and 4.**

PRACTICE 4

A. Multiply.

1. $(x+4)(x+2)$

2. $(x-3)(x+5)$

3. $(x-1)(x+4)$

4. $(x-6)(x-3)$

5. $(x+8)(x-2)$

6. $(2x+1)(x-2)$

7. $(x-9)(x-5)$

8. $(x+1)(3x-2)$

9. $(x-2)(x+7)$

10. $(3x+8)(x+2)$

11. $(x-6)(x+5)$

12. $(x-10)(x-3)$

13. $(2x+1)(2x+2)$

14. $(x+9)(x-4)$

15. $(x-5)(x-5)$

B. Factor each expression.

16. x^2+4x+3

17. x^2+4x-5

18. $x^2+8x+12$

19. x^2-x-6

20. $x^2+5x-14$

21. x^2-x-12

22. $x^2+2x-35$

23. $x^2-12x+36$

24. x^2-6x-7

25. $x^2+4x-32$

26. $2x^2+5x-3$

27. $2x^2-8x-10$

28. $x^2+5x-50$

29. $4x^2+4x-3$

30. x^2+x-56

C. Choose the one best answer to each question.

31. What are two solutions for the equation $x^2-x=20$?

A. 4 and 5
B. –4 and 5
C. 4 and –5
D. –10 and 2
E. –2 and 10

32. For which of the following equations is $x=-4$ a solution?

A. $2x^2-8=0$
B. $x^2-8x+64=0$
C. $x^2-2x-15=0$
D. x^2-x-12
E. $2x^2+2x-24=0$

33. What is the only positive solution for the equation $2x^2-7x-30=0$?

A. 5
B. 6
C. 7
D. 8
E. 9

34. The area of a rectangle is found by multiplying the length by the width. In the rectangle below, the area of the rectangle is equal to the expression $2x^2-27x+70$.

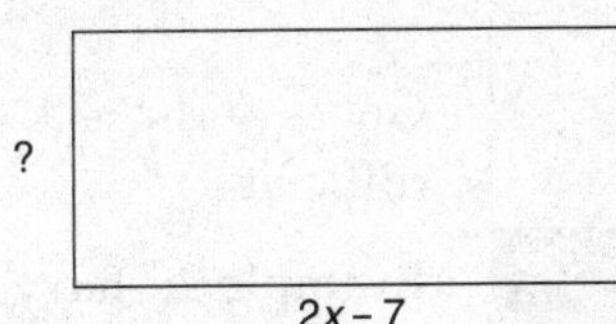

An expression equal to the length is shown on the diagram. Which of the following expressions is equal to the width of the rectangle?

A. $4x-14$
B. $2x+10$
C. $2x-10$
D. $x-10$
E. $x-10$

LESSON 5

Algebra Problem Solving

One strategy that can help you save time on the more complicated algebra problems is **guess-and-check.** Guess-and-check means selecting one of the answer choices and trying that value in the problem. If you guess correctly, you can move on to the next question. If not, guess again. Guess-and-check is a good strategy for problems involving quadratic equations and expressions.

KEY IDEAS

- Guess-and-check is a strategy for answering complicated multiple-choice problems.
- Choose an answer from the options and try the value in the problem. If it works, you have found the correct answer.

Example 1: Which of the following is a solution for the equation $2x^2 - 12 = 2x$?

A. 4
B. 3
C. 0
D. –1
E. –3

To solve the problem, you would have to rewrite the equation so that the quadratic expression equals zero, factor the expression, and solve.

Instead, substitute each answer choice into the equation.

Option (A): $2x^2 - 12 = 2x$

$$2(4)^2 - 12 = 2(4)$$
$$20 \neq 8$$

Option (B): $2x^2 - 12 = 2x$

$$2(3)^2 - 12 = 2(3)$$
$$6 = 6$$

Option (B) 3 makes the equation true.

Guess-and-check can also save time when writing an equation seems difficult.

HiSET EXAM TIP

Use your judgment. Do not use guess-and-check if you can quickly see how to solve the problem. Trying each answer choice may take longer than simply solving the problem.

Example 2: Terry is ten years older than his brother Tomas. Twenty years ago, Terry was twice as old as Tomas. How old is Terry now?

A. 25
B. 30
C. 40
D. 45
E. 50

Instead of writing an equation, try each age in the answer choices for Terry.

A. If Terry is 25 now, Tomas is 15. Twenty years ago, Tomas would not have been born.
B. If Terry is 30 now, Tomas is 20. Twenty years ago, Tomas would have been 0 years old, and Terry would have been 10.
C. If Terry is 40 now, Tomas is 30. Twenty years ago, Tomas would have been 10, and Terry would have been 20, which is twice as old as 10.

Therefore, option **(C) 40** is correct.

PRACTICE 5

A. Use guess-and-check to solve the following problems.

1. A number divided by 2 is equal to 12 less than the original number. What is the number?

A. 12
B. 20
C. 24
D. 28
E. 32

2. For a fund-raiser, Sandra raised three times as much money as Barbara, and Barbara raised $50 more than Matt. Together they raised $950. How much money did Barbara raise?

A. $150
B. $175
C. $200
D. $325
E. $500

3. The three packages below weigh a total of 15 pounds.

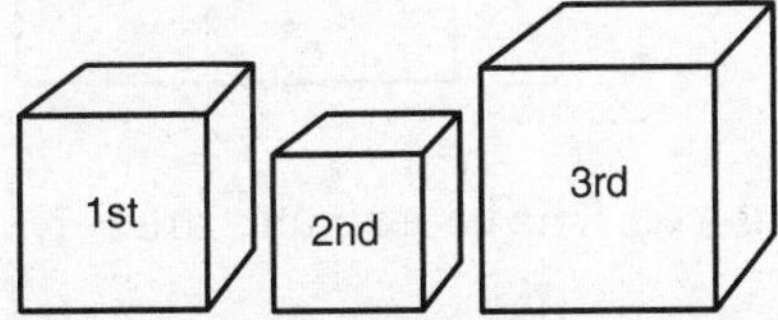

The first package weighs twice as much as the second package. The third package weighs three times as much as the second package. How many pounds does the first package weigh?

A. 2
B. 4
C. 5
D. $6\frac{1}{2}$
E. 8

4. Hannah scored a total of 170 points on two math tests. The score of the first test was 6 points lower than the score of the second test. How many points did Hannah score on the first test?

A. 100
B. 96
C. 90
D. 88
E. 82

5. Nelson is twice as old as Maria. Six years ago, Nelson was five times as old as Maria. How old was Nelson six years ago?

A. 5
B. 10
C. 15
D. 20
E. 24

6. Which of the following is a solution for the quadratic equation $2x^2 + x - 15 = 0$?

A. -3
B. -1
C. 2
D. 3
E. 4

7. An amusement park sells adults' and children's passes. An adult's pass is $25, and a child's pass is $15. A group spent $440 on 20 passes. How many children's passes did the group purchase?

A. 5
B. 6
C. 9
D. 14
E. 18

8. The rectangular garden below is twice as long as it is wide. If the total distance around the garden is 120 feet, what is the width of the garden in feet?

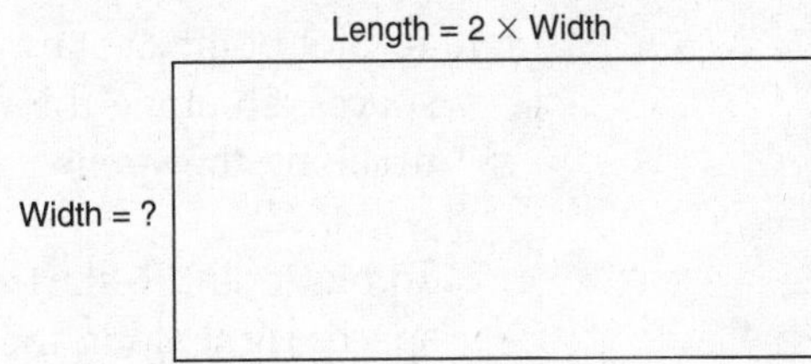

A. 15
B. 20
C. 30
D. 40
E. 50

Functions

LESSON 6

The Coordinate Plane

A **coordinate grid** is a way to locate points that lie in a **plane,** or flat surface. The grid is formed by two intersecting lines, an *x*-axis and a *y*-axis. The *x*-axis is actually a horizontal number line, and the *y*-axis is a vertical number line. The point at which the two axes intersect is called the **origin.**

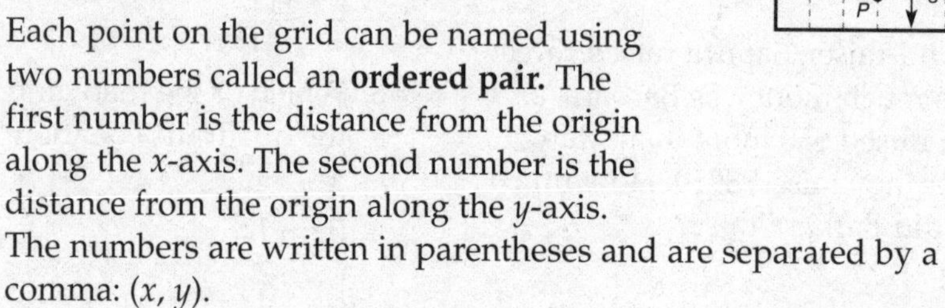

Each point on the grid can be named using two numbers called an **ordered pair.** The first number is the distance from the origin along the *x*-axis. The second number is the distance from the origin along the *y*-axis. The numbers are written in parentheses and are separated by a comma: (x, y).

KEY IDEAS

- A coordinate grid is formed by two intersecting axes, or number lines.
- The *x*-axis is horizontal and the *y*-axis is vertical.
- The location of a point is shown by two numbers called an ordered pair: (x, y).

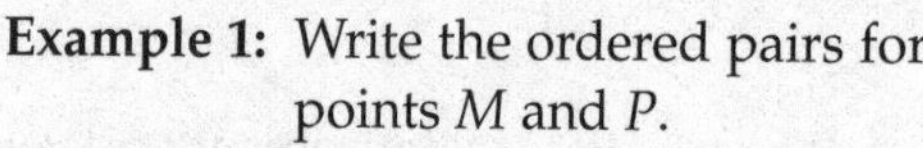

Example 1: Write the ordered pairs for points *M* and *P*.

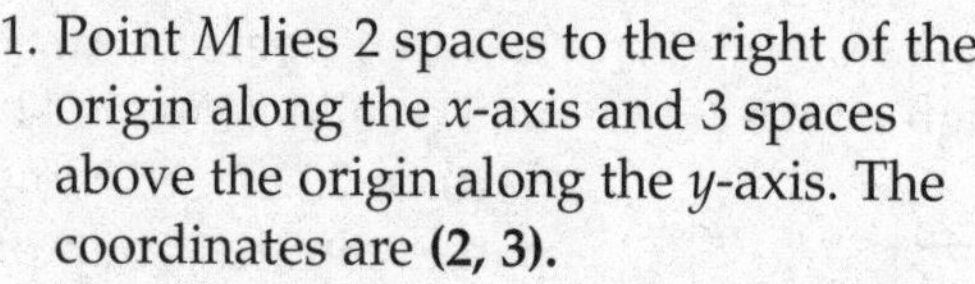

1. Point *M* lies 2 spaces to the right of the origin along the *x*-axis and 3 spaces above the origin along the *y*-axis. The coordinates are **(2, 3).**

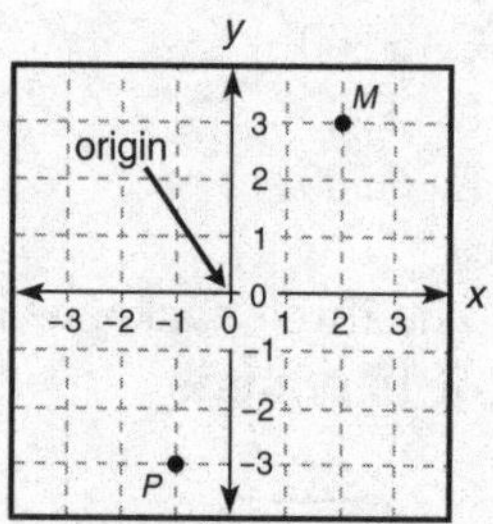

2. Point *P* lies 1 space to the left along the *x*-axis and 3 spaces down along the *y*-axis. The coordinates are **(–1, – 3).**

HiSET EXAM TIP

If you are given a coordinate grid that is not labeled, remember that the origin is at (0,0). Starting at the origin, count either right or left first, then up or down.

To plot points on the grid, use the number lines located at the axes. Remember that right and up are the directions for positive numbers and left and down are the directions for negative numbers.

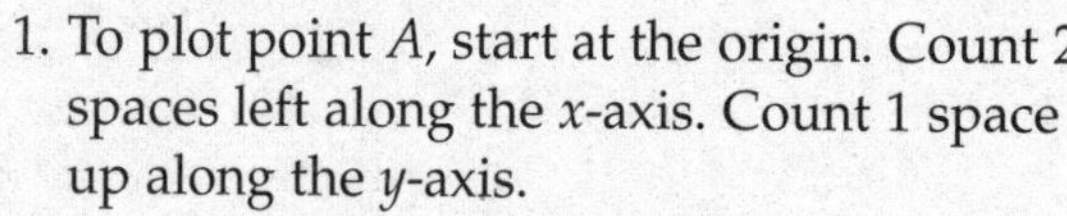

Example 2: Point *A* is located at (–2, 1), and point *B* is located at (3, – 2). Plot these points on a coordinate grid.

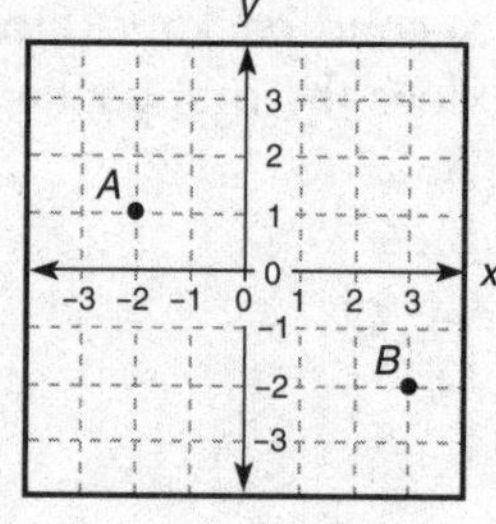

1. To plot point *A*, start at the origin. Count 2 spaces left along the *x*-axis. Count 1 space up along the *y*-axis.
2. To plot point *B*, start at the origin. Count 3 spaces right along the *x*-axis. Count 2 spaces down along the *y*-axis.

PRACTICE 6

A. Write the ordered pair for each point.

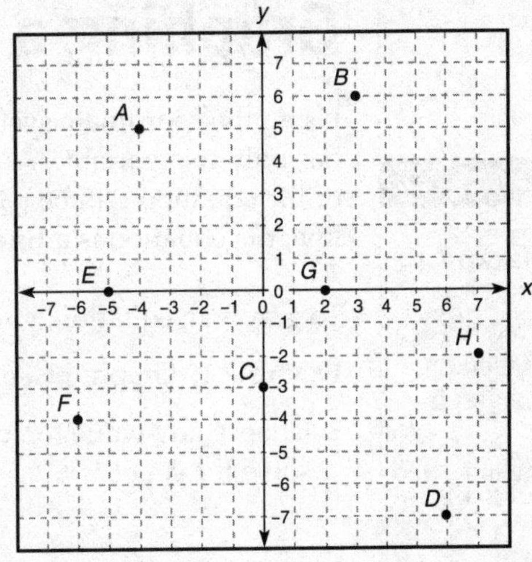

1. Point A
2. Point B
3. Point C
4. Point D
5. Point E
6. Point F
7. Point G
8. Point H

B. Plot the points on the coordinate grid.

9. Plot the following points:

J at (–3, – 2)

K at (4, 0)

L at (1, – 3)

M at (–4, 2)

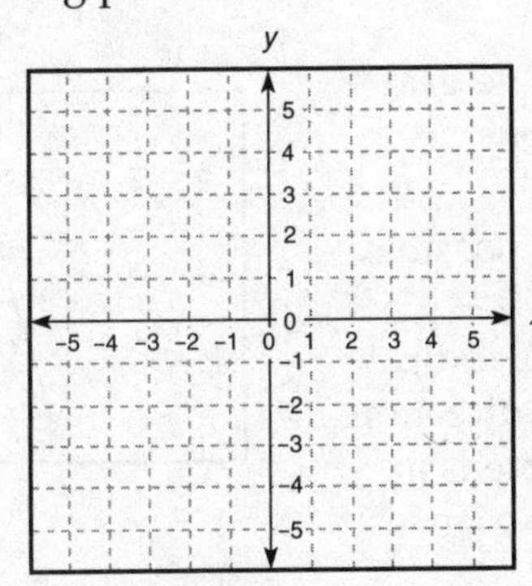

10. Plot the following points:

N at (0, – 1)

O at (–4, –4)

P at (3, 1)

Q at (–3, 0)

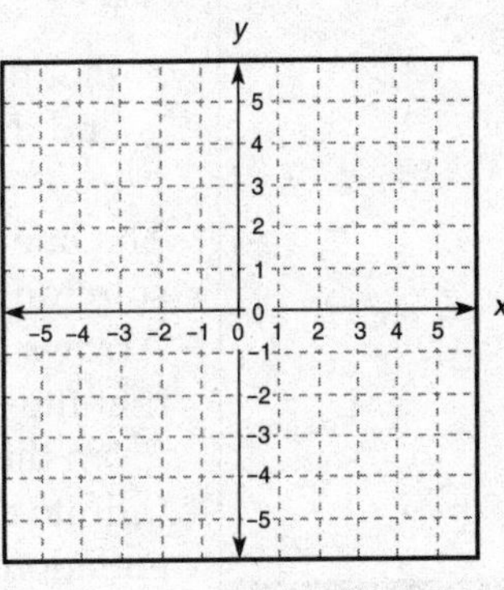

C. Choose the one best answer to each question.

11. On the coordinate grid below, a line passes through points A and B.

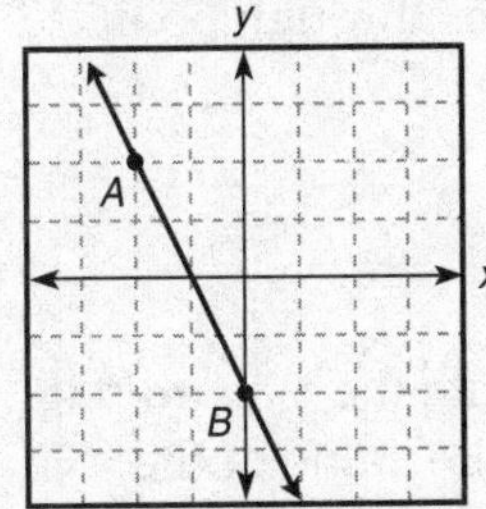

Which of the following ordered pairs also lies on the line?

A. (0, –2)
B. (1, 0)
C. (1, –1)
D. (0, –1)
E. (–1, 0)

12. Two of the corners of a triangle are located at (3, –3) and (2, 3). What is the location of the third corner as shown in the diagram below?

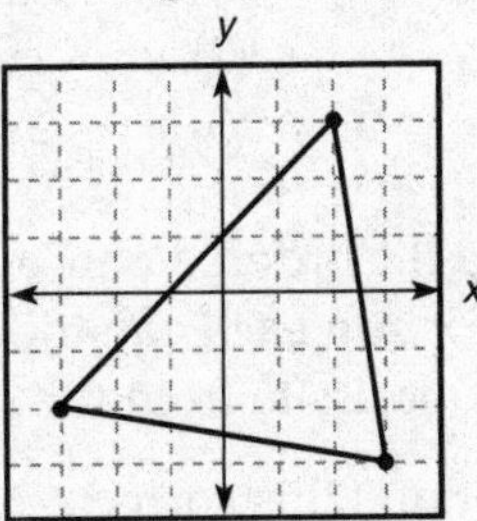

A. (–3, –2)
B. (–3, 2)
C. (–2, –3)
D. (3, –2)
E. (3, 2)

LESSON 7

Graphing a Line

Using the coordinate system, we can graph equations. When an equation has only two variables, x and y, and neither is raised to a power, the graph of the equation will be a line. When the graph of an equation is a straight line, the equation is a **linear equation.**

To graph an equation, you need to solve for two points on the line.

Example 1: Graph the equation $y = 3x - 4$.

1. Choose any value for x and solve for y. Let $x = 1$.

$y = 3(1) - 4$
$y = 3 - 4$
$y = -1$

If $x = 1$, then $y = -1$. The ordered pair for the first point is $(1, -1)$.

2. Choose another value for x and solve for y. Let $x = 2$.

$y = 3(2) - 4$
$y = 6 - 4$
$y = 2$

If $x = 2$, then $y = 2$. The ordered pair for the second point is $(2, 2)$.

3. Plot the points on a coordinate grid and draw a line through them.

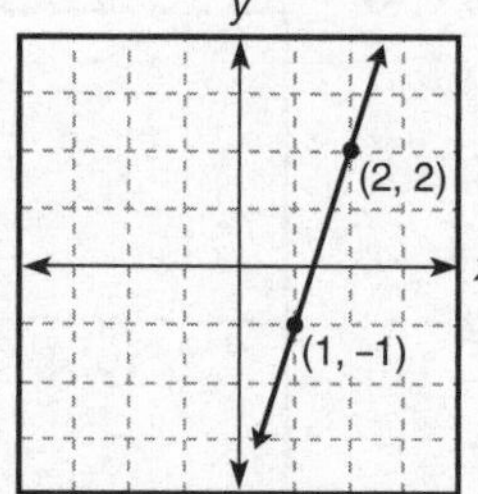

The line is the graph of all the possible solutions for the equation $y = 3x - 4$. Arrows at both ends of the line indicate that the line continues in both directions. From this, you can see that there is an infinite number of solutions to a linear equation.

Some linear equation problems don't require you to draw a graph.

Example 2: Point A lies at $(5, -6)$ on a coordinate grid. The graph of which of the following equations passes through point A?

(1) $y = -5x + 18$
(2) $y = -4x + 14$
(3) $y = -2x - 13$

Use the ordered pair given in the problem. Substitute the x-coordinate, 5, for x in each equation and solve for y. If $y = -6$, the value of the y-coordinate from the ordered pair, you have found the correct equation.

Option **(2)** is correct.

$y = -4x + 14$
$y = -4(5) + 14$
$y = -20 + 14 = -6$

KEY IDEAS

- A linear equation has two variables, x and y.
- When the solutions to a linear equation are graphed on a coordinate grid, the graph forms a line.
- To find a point on the line, substitute a value for x and solve for y.
- You must solve for at least two points in order to draw the line.

HiSET EXAM TIP

If a linear equation is not written with y on one side of the equation, use inverse operations to isolate y.
Example: $2x + y = 15$.
Subtract 2x from each side.
$y = -2x + 15$.

PRACTICE 7

A. Fill in the y column in each table and graph the equation.

1. $y = \frac{1}{2}x + 3$

If $x =$	then $y =$
–2	
0	
2	

2. $y + 3x = -1$

If $x =$	then $y =$
–1	
0	
1	

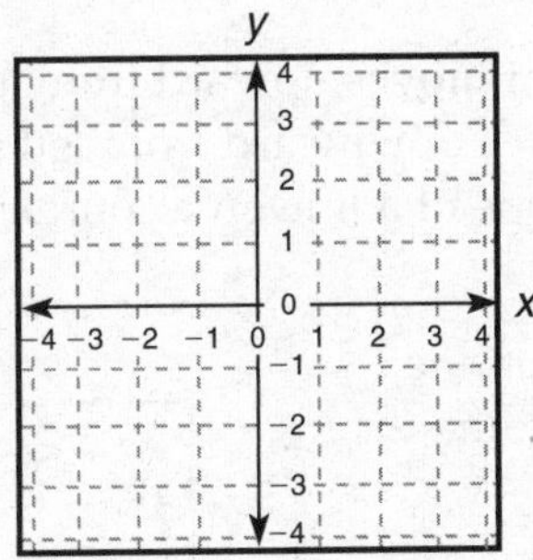

3. $-2 + y = -x$

If $x =$	then $y =$
1	
2	
3	

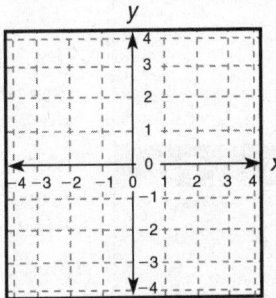

4. $y = 3 - 2x$

If $x =$	then $y =$
0	
1	
2	

B. Choose the one best answer to each question.

Questions 5 and 6 refer to the following coordinate grid.

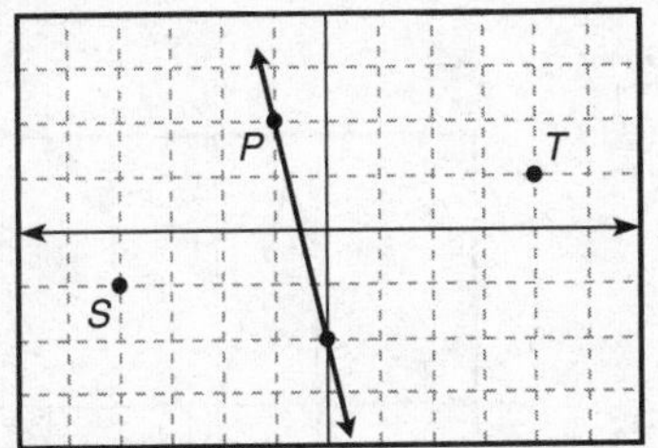

5. The graph of the equation $y = \frac{1}{4}x$ will pass through which of the following pairs of points?
   A. point S and (–1, 2)
   B. point S and (0, –2)
   C. Point P and Point S
   D. point T and (0, –2)
   E. point T and (0, 0)

6. Line P is the graph of which of the following equations?
   A. $y = 4x + 1$
   B. $y = -4x - 1$
   C. $y = 4x + 2$
   D. $y = 4x - 2$
   E. $y = -4x - 2$

7. Point C is located at (–3, 5). A graph of which of the following equations would pass through point C?
   A. $3x + 2y = 5$
   B. $2x + 3y = 9$
   C. $4x - 2y = 8$
   D. $3x - 3y = 6$
   E. $3x - 5y = 0$

STUDY ADVICE

Hang in there: You're more than halfway through the Mathematics unit! It may feel like a long haul until Test Day, but keep thinking about how good it will feel to have your high school equivalency degree in hand!

Slope of a Line

KEY IDEAS

- Slope is the ratio of rise to run.
- Moving from left to right, a line that goes upward has a positive slope, and a line that moves downward has a negative slope.
- You can find slope by counting spaces and writing a ratio or by using the slope formula.

HiSET EXAM TIP

Think of the slope formula this way: write the difference of the y's over the difference of the x's. Just make sure that you always subtract the coordinates in the same order.

Slope is the measurement of the steepness of a line. Imagine a road going up a hill. If the road must reach the top of the hill over a short distance, the road will be very steep. Slope measures the relationship between **rise** (how high the road must climb) and **run** (the distance the road goes forward).

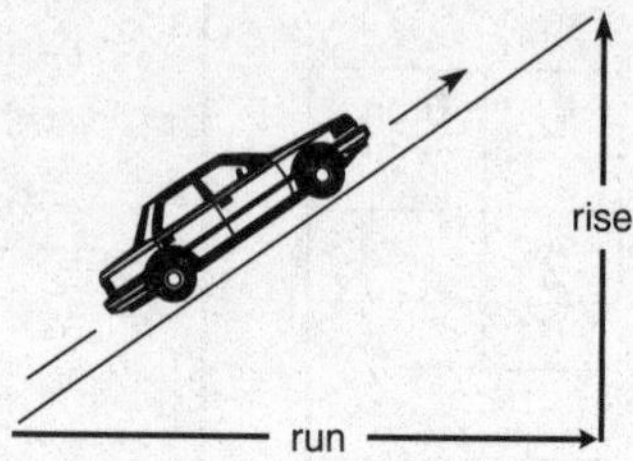

On a coordinate grid, a line that moves upward from left to right has a **positive slope.** A line that moves downward from left to right has a **negative slope.** You can find the slope of a line on a coordinate grid by writing the ratio of rise to run.

Example 1: What is the slope of line P shown on the coordinate grid?

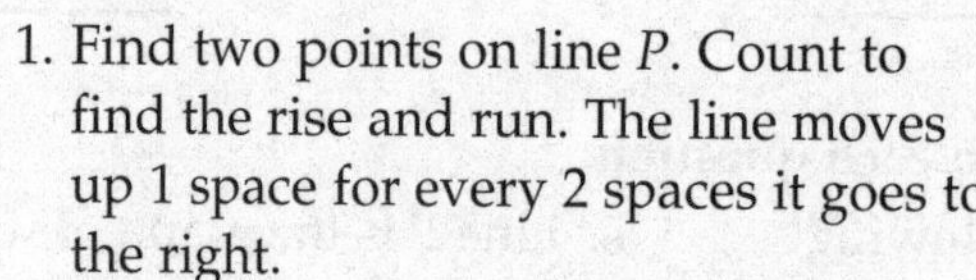

1. Find two points on line P. Count to find the rise and run. The line moves up 1 space for every 2 spaces it goes to the right.

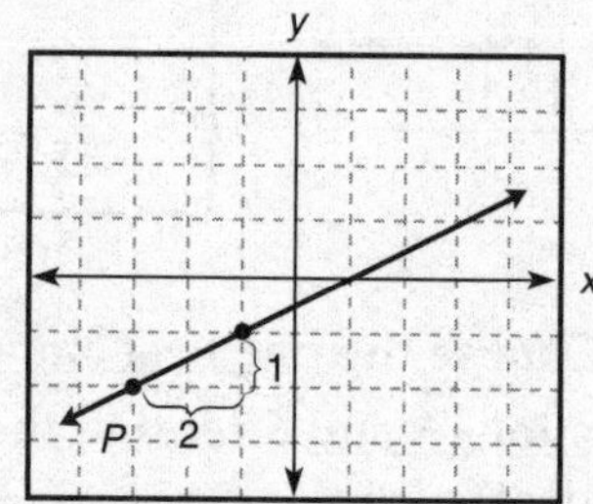

2. Write the ratio: $\frac{\text{rise}}{\text{run}} = \frac{1}{2}$. The slope is $\frac{1}{2}$.

Example 2: What is the slope of line S shown on the coordinate grid?

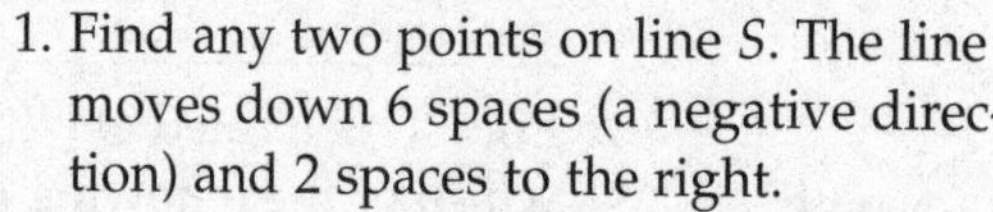

1. Find any two points on line S. The line moves down 6 spaces (a negative direction) and 2 spaces to the right.

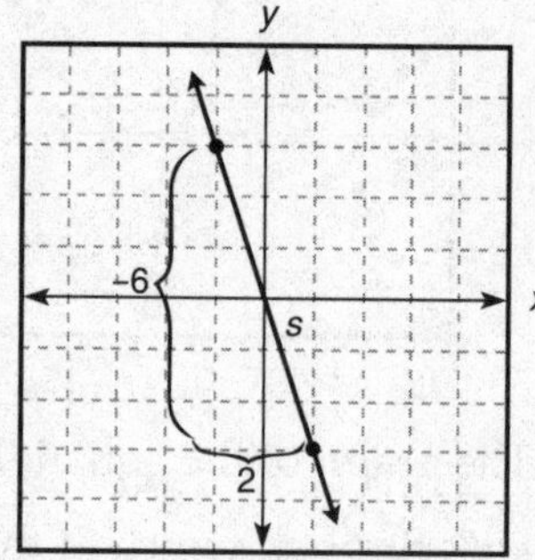

2. Write the ratio: $\frac{\text{rise}}{\text{run}} = \frac{-6}{2} = -3$.

The slope of line S is **−3.**

You can also find slope using the slope formula:

slope of a line $= \frac{y_2 - y_1}{x_2 - x_1}$, where (x_1, y_1) and (x_2, y_2) are two points on a line.

Example 3: A line passes through points at coordinates (1, 4) and (−5, 2). What is the slope of the line?

1. Choose one point to be (x_1, y_1). The other will be (x_2, y_2). It doesn't matter which you choose. For this example, $(x_1, y_1) = (1, 4)$ and $(x_2, y_2) = (-5, 2)$.

2. Substitute the values into the slope formula and solve:

$$\frac{y_2 - y_1}{x_2 - x_1} \qquad \frac{2-4}{-5-1} = \frac{-2}{-6} = \frac{1}{3} \quad \text{The slope is } \tfrac{1}{3}.$$

Since the slope is positive, you know that the line rises from left to right. You also know that it goes up 1 space for every 3 spaces it moves to the right.

In working with slope, there are a few special circumstances that you should memorize. A horizontal line, just like a flat stretch of roadway, has a **slope of 0**. The slope of a vertical line is **undefined**; in other words, our definition of slope will not work for a line that has no run at all.

A. Find the slope of each line.

1.

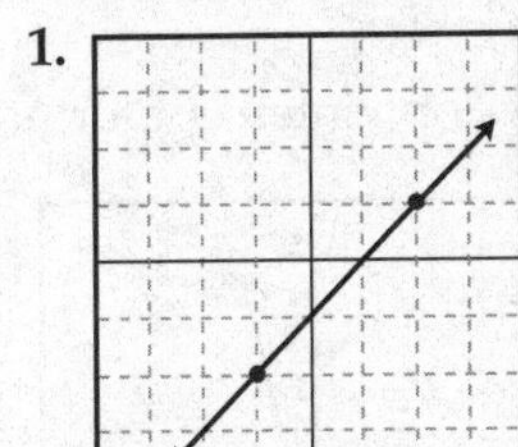

2.

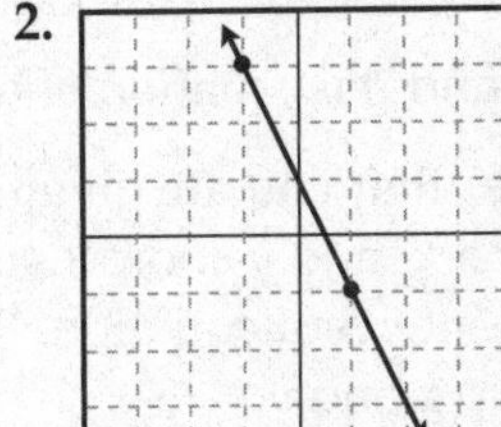

3.

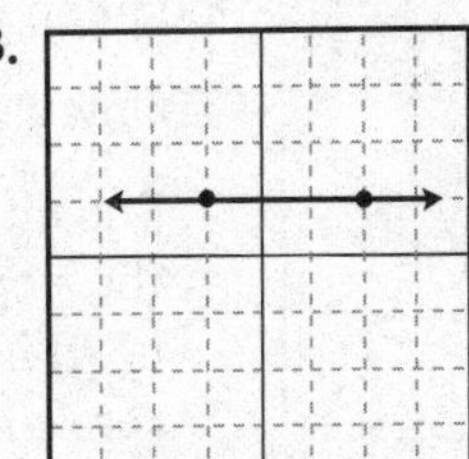

B. Use the slope formula to find the slope of a line that passes through the following pairs of points.

4. (3, 5) and (–1, 2)

5. (0, 2) and (4, 0)

6. (4, 2) and (2, 2)

7. (6, 1) and (0, 3)

8. (1, 4) and (–2, –2)

9. (4, –2) and (2, 4)

C. Choose the one best answer for each question.

Question 10 refers to the following graph.

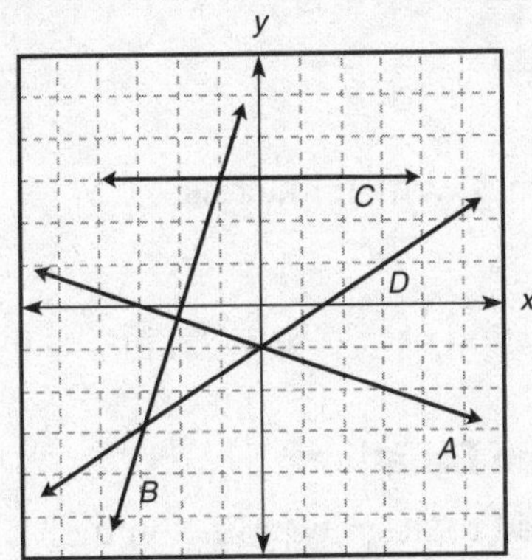

10. Which of the following lines shown on the graph has a slope of $-\frac{1}{3}$?

A. line *A*
B. line *B*
C. line *C*
D. line *D*
E. None of the above

11. Line *N* passes through the following points: (0, 4), (1, 2), (2, 0), and (3, –2). What is the slope of line *N*?

A. –4
B. –2
C. 2
D. 4
E. 6

12. Line *L* passes through point (1, 0) and has a slope of 3. Which of the following points also lies on line *L*?

A. (0, 3)
B. (1, 3)
C. (2, 3)
D. (2, 5)
E. (3, 9)

Slope and Equations

Use the Slope-Intercept Form to Find an Equation

KEY IDEAS

- There are two ways to find an equation if you are given the slope of a line and a point.
- One method is the slope-intercept form.
- The other method is the point-slope form.

Lesson 8 showed how to find the slope of a line and graph it. The examples in this lesson show how you can use the slope and a point on the line to find the equation of a line in two different forms. (You might also need to find the equation of a line from two points. In this case, you would calculate the slope first, then use the slope and one of the points to find the equation.)

The first of these forms is the **slope-intercept form:** $y = mx + b$. In this form of the equation, the variable m stands for the **slope** of the line. The variable b stands for the ***y*-intercept,** which is the y-value at the point where the line crosses the y-axis. The variables x and y are the x- and ***y*-coordinates** of any point on the line and are usually written as an ordered pair.

Follow these steps to find the equation of a line in the slope-intercept form.

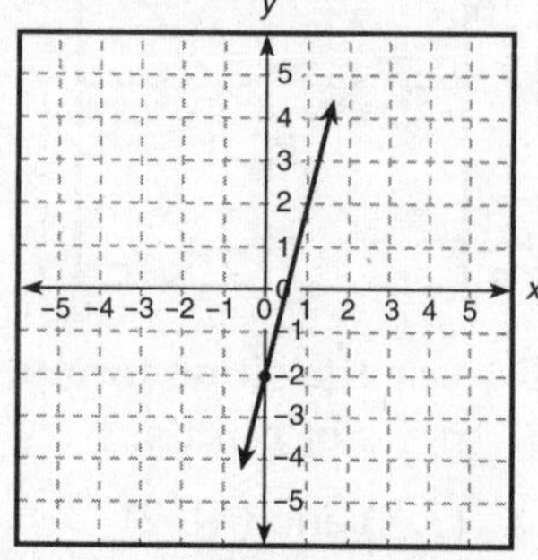

1. Substitute the values that you are given for the slope (m) and the x- and y-coordinates (x, y) into the slope-intercept equation. Be careful not to mix up x and y.
2. Use inverse operations to isolate b.
3. Rewrite the equation in slope-intercept form, leaving x and y as variables and substituting values for m and b.

Example 1: Use the slope-intercept form to find the equation of a line that has the slope $m = 4$ and passes through the point (–1, –6).

1. $-6 = (4) \times (-1) + b$

   $-6 = -4 + b$
2. $-2 = b$
3. $\mathbf{y = 4x - 2}$

HiSET EXAM TIP

Memorize the formulas for the slope-intercept form and the point-slope form to save time on Test Day.

Note that linear equations are sometimes written like this:

$f(x) = mx + b$

The symbol $f(x)$ simply means "a function of x." Treat $f(x)$ just as though it were the variable y.

Use the Point-Slope Form to Find an Equation

The second important form that is used to describe a line on the Mathematics Test is the **point-slope form:** $y - y_1 = m(x - x_1)$. In this form, (x_1, y_1) is an ordered pair that corresponds to a point on the line. As in the slope-intercept form, m stands for the slope. If you simplify an equation in point-slope form by solving for y, you will get the slope-intercept form of the equation.

Follow these steps to find the equation of a line in the point-slope form.

1. Call the point that you are given (x_1, y_1).
2. Put the x_1 and y_1 values into the point-slope equation.
3. Put the slope value in the point-slope equation for m.

Example 2: Use the point-slope form to find the equation of the line that passes through the point (4, 3) and has a slope of 2.

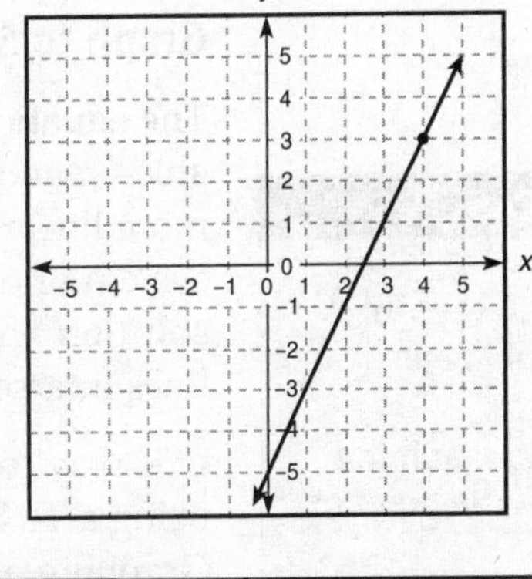

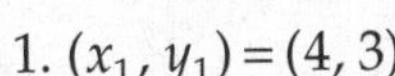

1. $(x_1, y_1) = (4, 3)$
2. $y - 3 = m(x - 4)$
3. $\mathbf{y - 3 = 2(x - 4)}$

Notice that you can simplify the equation to find the slope-intercept form:

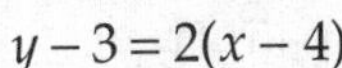

$y - 3 = 2(x - 4)$

$y - 3 = 2x - 8$

$y = 2x - 5$

A. Use the slope-intercept form, $y = mx + b$, to find the equation of the line that passes through the given point and has the given slope.

1. $(1, -2); m = -4$ **2.** $(-1, -4); m = 2$ **3.** $(-4, 2); m = -\frac{1}{3}$

B. Use the point-slope form, $y - y_1 = m(x - x_1)$, to find the equation of the line that passes through the given point and has the given slope.

4. $(2, 0); m = -\frac{1}{3}$ **5.** $(2, 0); m = -\frac{1}{3}$ **6.** $(1, -2); m = 1$

C. Find the equation of the line that passes through the given points. Write your answer in slope-intercept form.

7. $(-5, 3), (1, 1)$ **8.** $(-3, 0), (-2, 4)$ **9.** $(-3, -4), (7, 1)$

D. Choose the <u>one best answer</u> for each question.

10. Which of the following is an equation for the line that passes through $(-1, 0)$ and $(2, -3)$?

A. $y = 3x + 3$
B. $y = x^2 - 2$
C. $y = -3x + 9$
D. $y = -x - 1$
E. $y = x - 5$

11. Which of the following equations describes the same line as $y - 2 = \frac{1}{2}(x - 6)$?

A. $y = 3x + 2$
B. $y = \frac{1}{2}x - 4$
C. $y = -x + 12$
D. $y = 2x - 3$
E. $y = \frac{1}{2}x - 1$

Question 12 refers to the following graph.

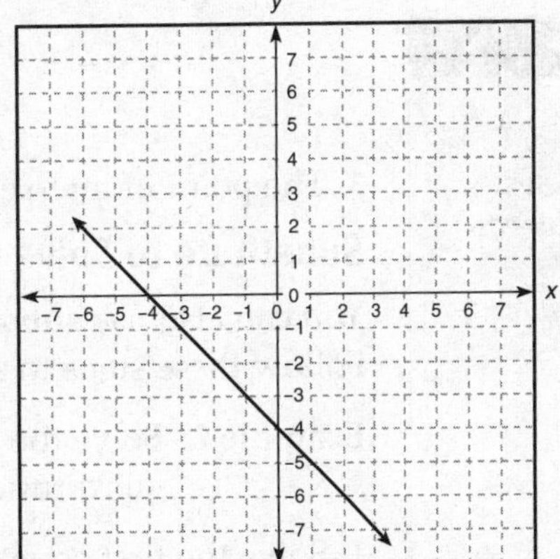

12. Which of the following equations correctly describes the line on the graph?

A. $y = x - 4$
B. $y = -x - 4$
C. $y = x + 4$
D. $y = -x + 4$
E. $y = 2x - 4$

LESSON 10

Systems of Linear Equations

KEY IDEAS

- There are several ways to solve a system of linear equations.
- One method is to graph the equations to see the point of intersection.
- Another method is to find one value (x or y) and substitute it into the other equation to find the solution.

HiSET EXAM TIP

You may be asked whether a point is a solution to a system of equations, and you can use either of the methods shown here to find the answer.

Graph to Solve the System of Equations

The equations in Lessons 7 and 9 are **linear equations:** they have two variables, x and y, and represent straight lines in the coordinate plane. Two or more linear equations make up a **system of linear equations**. Solving a system of two equations means finding the values of both variables. The **solution** will give the x- and y-coordinates of the point at which the two lines intersect. You can express this solution as an ordered pair: (x, y).

One way to solve a system of equations is by graphing each equation using a **T-chart**—like those that you filled in for the Lesson 7 practice. Graphing a system of linear equations provides a picture of the intersection. Follow these steps to solve a system of equations by graphing.

1. Set up an x and y T-chart for each equation. Find two ordered pairs for each equation: use $x = 0$ and find y, and then use $y = 0$ and find x.
2. Graph both lines, using the ordered pairs that you generated in step 1.
3. Find the point of intersection and express it in the form (x, y).

Example 1: Graph the equations $6x + 3y = 12$ and $5x + y = 7$ to find the solution.

1. $6x + 3y = 12$

x	y
0	4
2	0

$5x + y = 7$

x	y
0	7
$\frac{7}{5}$	0

2.

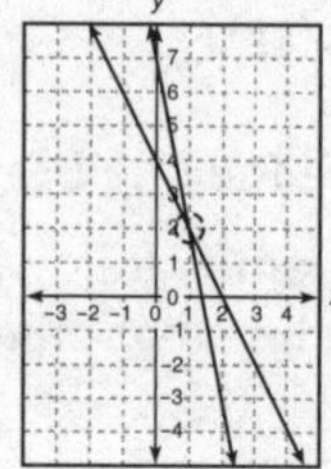

3. The point of intersection—that is, the solution—is **(1, 2)**.

Substitute to Solve the System of Equations

You can also use **substitution** to solve a system of linear equations. Follow these steps to solve a system of linear equations by substitution.

Example 2: Solve the equations $6x + 3y = 12$ and $5x + y = 7$ by substitution.

1. Solve the first equation so that y is expressed in terms of x.

$$6x + 3y = 12$$
$$3y = 12 - 6x$$
$$y = 4 - 2x$$

2. Substitute that value of y into the second equation and solve for x.

$$5x + (4 - 2x) = 7$$
$$3x + 4 = 7$$
$$3x = 3$$
$$x = 1$$

3. Substitute that value of x into the first equation and solve for y.

$$6(1) + 3y = 12$$
$$6 + 3y = 12$$
$$3y = 6$$
$$y = 2$$

The solution is **(1, 2)**.

PRACTICE 10

A. Find two pairs of coordinates for each equation by making a T-chart. Use the coordinates to graph the lines and find the solution.

1. $y = 3x - 15$
   $x + y = 13$

2. $4x + 2y = 10$
   $y = -5x - 4$

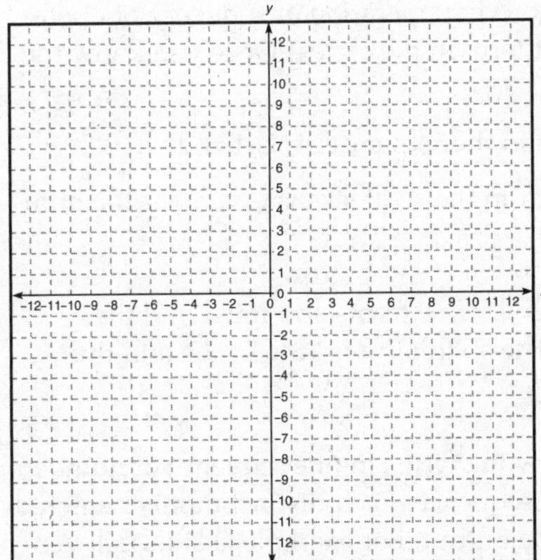

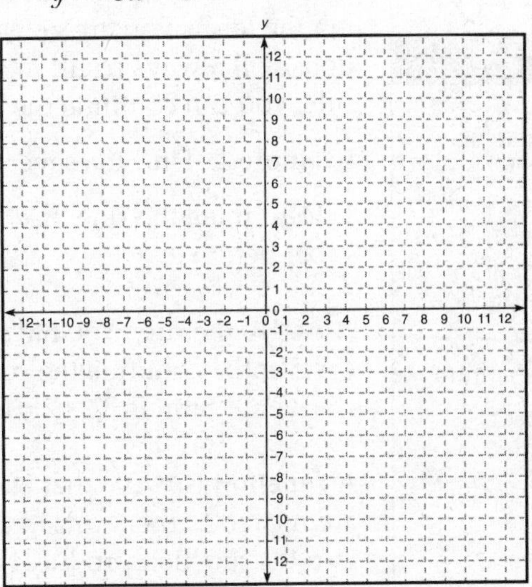

B. Find the solution for the two equations by substitution. Express as an ordered pair in the form (*x*, *y*).

3. $-7x - y = 22$
   $4x + 2y = 10$

4. $x + y = 9$
   $2x - 3y = 8$

5. $y = 3x + 15$
   $5x - 2y = -26$

6. $10x - y = -1$
   $y = 12x$

C. Choose the one best answer for each question.

7. Where does the line with the equation $x - 2y = 4$ intersect with the line with the equation $6y + 5x = 4$?
   A. (2, −1)
   B. (3, −2)
   C. (−2, 1)
   D. (−1, 2)
   E. (2, 1)

8. Where does the line with the equation $y = x$ intersect with the line with the equation $y = -x$?
   A. (1, −1)
   B. (−1, 1)
   C. (0, 0)
   D. (1, 0)
   E. (0, 1)

9. Where does the line with the equation $y = -2$ intersect with the line with the equation $3y = 2x + 3$?
   A. $(-\frac{2}{9}, -2)$
   B. $(-\frac{1}{3}, -2)$
   C. $(\frac{1}{3}, 2)$
   D. $(\frac{9}{2}, 2)$
   E. $(-\frac{9}{2}, -2)$

10. Which of the following is the equation of a line that intersects $y = 4x + 2$?
    A. $2y = 8x + 2$
    B. $y = 4x - 2$
    C. $y = -4x + 2$
    D. $\frac{1}{2}y = 2x - 7$
    E. $-y = -1(-4x + 4)$

LESSON 11

Patterns and Functions

KEY IDEAS

- A pattern is a sequence of numbers determined by a mathematical rule.
- A function is a rule that shows how one set of numbers is related to another set of numbers.
- To use a function, substitute values for variables and solve.

HiSET EXAM TIP

To figure out what rule has been used to form a pattern, begin by finding the difference between each term and the term that follows it in the sequence.

A **pattern** is a series of numbers or objects whose sequence is determined by a particular rule. You can figure out what rule has been used by studying the terms you are given. Think: What operation or sequence of operations will always result in the next term in the series? Once you know the rule, you can continue the pattern.

Example 1: Find the seventh term in the sequence: 1, 2, 4, 8, 16, . . .

1. Determine the rule. Each number in the sequence is two times the number before it.

2. Apply the rule. You have been given five terms and must find the seventh. Continue the pattern. The sixth term is $16 \times 2 = 32$, and the seventh term is $32 \times 2 = \mathbf{64}$.

A **function** is a rule that shows how the terms in one sequence of numbers are related to the terms in another sequence. Each distinct number entered into the function produces a unique output. For example, a sidewalk vendor charges $1.50 for a slice of pizza. The chart below shows how much it would cost to buy one to six slices.

Number of Pizza Slices	1	2	3	4	5	6
Cost	$1.50	$3.00	$4.50	$6.00	$7.50	$9.00

Each number in the first row corresponds to a price in the second row. We could say that the amount a customer will pay is a function of (or depends upon) the number of slices the customer orders. This function could be written:

Cost = number of slices × $1.50, or $C = n(\$1.50)$.

If you know the function and a number in the first set of numbers, you can solve for its corresponding number in the second set.

Example 2: Using the function $y = 3x + 5$, what is the value of y when $x = -3$?

1. Substitute the given value of x. $\quad y = 3(-3) + 5$
2. Solve for y. $\quad y = -9 + 5$

$y = \mathbf{-4}$

Example 3: Using the function $n = 100 - 4(3 + m)$, what is the value of n when $m = 6$?

1. Substitute the given value of m. $\quad n = 100 - 4(3 + 6)$
2. Solve for n. $\quad n = 100 - 4(9)$

$n = 100 - 36$

$n = \mathbf{64}$

PRACTICE 11

A. Solve.

1. Which number should come next in the following pattern?

$-12, -9, -6, -3,$ ______

2. What is the next number in the sequence?

21, 26, 31, 36, ______

3. In the function $y = 4x + 10$, if $x = -2$, what is the value of y?

4. In the function $y = 2x(4 + x) - 2$, if $x = 3$, what is the value of y?

5. Each term in the second row is determined by the function $y = 2x - 1$.

x	1	2	3	4	5	. . .	12
y	1	3	5	7	9	. . .	

What number belongs in the shaded box?

6. In the function $y = \frac{x+3}{6} - 8$, if $x = 21$, what is the value of y?

7. What is the next term in the pattern below?

1000, 500, 250, 125, 62.5, ______

8. What is the next number in the sequence?

$3, -5, 7, -9, 11,$ ______

9. Each term in the second row is determined by the function $y = 3x + 5$.

x	−2	−1	0	1	2	. . .	9
y	−1	2	5	8	11	. . .	

What number belongs in the shaded box?

10. In the function $y = (x - 7) + 12$, if $x = -10$, what is the value of y?

B. Choose the one best answer to each question.

Question 11 refers to the following drawing.

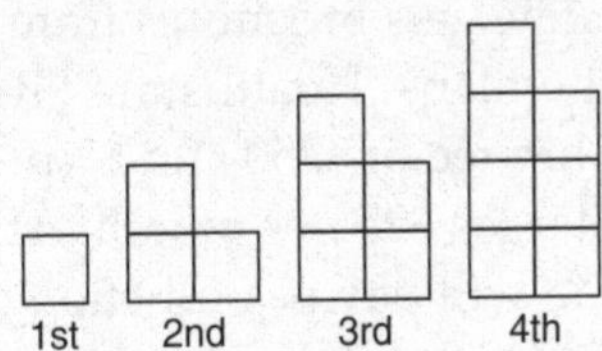

11. How many blocks would be needed to build the 25th construction in the sequence?

A. 55
B. 54
C. 53
D. 51
E. 49

12. What is the sixth term in the sequence below?

$-14, -8, -2, 4, \ldots$

A. 10
B. 14
C. 16
D. 22
E. 26

13. The price per scarf is a function of the number of scarves purchased. The table shows the price per scarf for purchases of up to four scarves.

number (n) of scarves	1	2	3	4
cost (c) per scarf	\$5.00	\$4.75	\$4.50	\$4.25

Which of the following functions was used to determine the prices shown in the table?

A. $c = n(\$5.00 - \$0.25)$
B. $c = \$5.00 - \$0.25(n - 1)$
C. $c = \$5.00 - \$0.25n$
D. $c = \$5.00n - \$0.25n$
E. $c = \$5.25(n - 1)$

14. Which of the following sequences of values of y could be created using the function $y = 4x - 3$?

A. 1, 4, 7, 10, 13, . . .
B. 1, 5, 9, 13, 17, . . .
C. 1, 4, 8, 13, 19, . . .
D. 1, −1, −3, −5, −7, . . .
E. −1, 3, 7, 11, 15, . . .

LESSON 12

Function Applications

Functions are used in many business applications. For instance, they can be used to calculate profit, cost, employee wages, and taxes. On the Mathematics Test, you will read about common work and life situations. The problems may contain or describe a function that you can use to solve the problem.

KEY IDEAS

- Functions are used to make many common work calculations.
- Functions can be used to make comparisons.
- To use a function, you must know the meaning of the variables. This information should be given in the text of the problem.

Example 1: Celino Advertising is finishing a series of print ads for a client. Finishing the project will cost \$2000 per day for the first seven days and \$3500 per day after seven days. The finishing costs can be found using the function $C = \$2000d + \$1500(d-7)$, where C = the cost of finishing the project and d = the number of days. If the project takes 12 days to complete, what will the project cost?

Use the function to solve the problem.

$$\begin{aligned} C &= \$2000d + \$1500(d-7) \\ &= \$2000(12) + \$1500(12-7) \\ &= \$24{,}000 + \$1500(5) \\ &= \$24{,}000 + \$7500 \\ &= \$31{,}500 \end{aligned}$$

You may be asked to use functions to make comparisons.

Example 2: Nita decides to join a health club. She gets brochures from two health clubs and compares the plans. Healthstars Fitness charges a one-time membership fee of \$250 and \$8 per month. Freedom Health Center charges \$25 per month. At both health clubs, the price (P) Nita will pay is a function of the number of months (m) she attends the club. The functions are:

Healthstars Fitness	$P = \$250 + \$8m$
Freedom Health Center	$P = \$25m$

HiSET EXAM TIP

There is often more than one way to work a problem, even when a function is given. Solve using the function. If you see another way to solve the problem, use it to check your answer.

Nita plans to move in 18 months. If she attends a health club until she moves, which one offers the better price?

1. Find the price at Healthstars Fitness:

$$\begin{aligned} P &= \$250 + \$8m \\ &= \$250 + \$8(18) \\ &= \$250 + \$144 \\ &= \$394 \end{aligned}$$

2. Find the price at Freedom Health Center:

$$\begin{aligned} P &= \$25m \\ &= \$25(18) \\ &= \$450 \end{aligned}$$

3. Compare the results. Even though Nita will have to pay a large amount up front, **Healthstars Fitness** offers the better price.

PRACTICE 12.1

A. Solve.

1. The Chimney Sweep charges \$25 for a chimney inspection. If the customer purchases additional services, \$15 of the inspection fee is deducted. Let s = the cost of any additional services. The total cost (C) of an inspection and services can be determined by the function $C = \$25 + (s - \$15)$, where s is not 0.
   a. Jan has her chimney inspected and purchases a smoke guard for \$89. How much will she be charged?
   b. After an inspection, Ahmed decides to have a new damper installed for \$255. How much will he pay?

2. Ricardo does a great deal of driving for his work. He generally estimates his driving time in hours (t) using the function $t = \frac{m}{60}$, where m = the number of miles.
   a. How many hours will it take Ricardo to drive 330 miles?
   b. How many hours will it take Ricardo to drive 255 miles?

3. A customer's phone charges are a function of the number of minutes of long-distance calls made. The graph shows a comparison of two plans available.

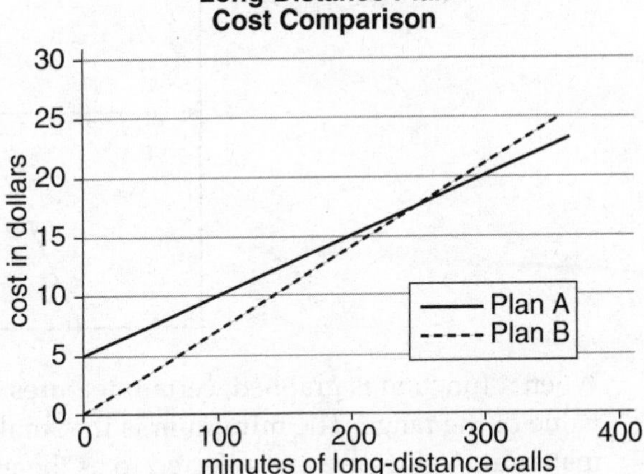

   a. Michelle looks at her previous phone bills and finds that she makes about 350 minutes of long-distance calls per month. Which plan is better for her?
   b. Craig usually makes about 150 minutes of long-distance calls per month. Which plan is better for him?

B. Choose the one best answer to each question.

Questions 4 and 5 refer to the following information.

Alicia is considering three job opportunities. At all three jobs, weekly pay (P) is a function of the number of hours (h) worked during the week. The functions are shown below:

Job 1	$P = \$9.75h$
Job 2	$P = \$70 + \$8.40h$
Job 3	$P = \$380 \times \frac{h}{38}$

4. If Alicia works 30 hours in a week, how much more will she earn at Job 2 than at Job 1?
   A. \$5.33
   B. \$29.50
   C. \$40.50
   D. \$59.00
   E. \$68.00

5. If Alicia works 40 hours per week, which of the following is a true statement?
   A. Alicia will earn the least at Job 3.
   B. Job 1 will pay more than Job 3.
   C. Job 3 will pay more than Job 2.
   D. Alicia will earn the least at Job 2.
   E. Alicia will earn the most at Job 2.

6. A company is awarded a \$95,000 job that will cost \$5,400 per day in expenses. Profits (P) can be calculated using $P = \$95{,}000 - \$5{,}400d$, where d = number of days. What is the company's profit if the job takes 14 days to complete?
   A. \$10,800
   B. \$19,400
   C. \$66,100
   D. \$75,600
   E. \$84,400

Graphing Functions

A function can be graphed on the coordinate plane. The input values become the x-coordinates, and the output values are the y-coordinates. As a mental shortcut, you can remember that $f(x)$ or $g(x)$ is just like y in the linear equations you've seen.

Example 3: Graph $f(x) = 2x - 1$ for $-2 \le x \le 2$.

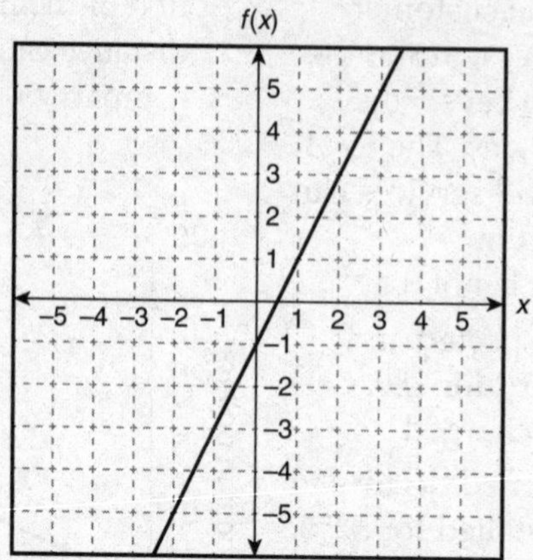

When a function is graphed, certain features become apparent. The **maximum** is the largest value of the range. The **minimum** is the smallest value of the range. The minimum and maximum values are also referred to as the **extreme values** of the function. The ***y*-intercept** is the point(s) where the line or curve crosses the y-axis, or where $x = 0$. The ***x*-intercept** is the point(s) where the line or curve crosses the x-axis, or where $y = 0$.

In Example 3, the maximum of $f(x)$ is 3, the minimum is –5, the x-intercept is $\frac{1}{2}$, and the y-intercept is –1.

A function can be described as **increasing** between two points on the x-axis or as **decreasing** between two points on the x-axis. It can also be described as **symmetrical** about a point or a line, such as "symmetrical about the y-axis." That statement would mean that the graph to the left of the y-axis and the graph to the right of it are mirror images.

Example 4: The function $g(x)$ increases from $x = 0$ to $x = 2$ and decreases from $x = 2$ to $x = 4$. The y-intercept is 0. The function is symmetrical about the line $x = 2$, and its maximum is $y = 2$. Given this information, graph the function.

Here is a graph that satisfies the given information. This graph represents the function $g(x) = -|x - 2| + 2$.

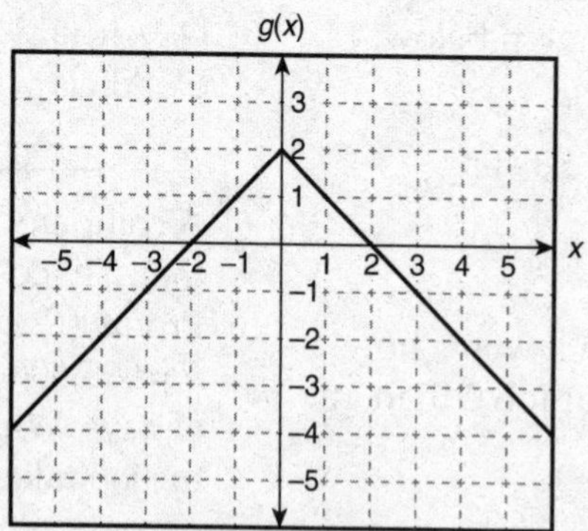

PRACTICE 12.2

A. Draw a rough graph of each of the following functions.

1. $f(x) = 2x - 8$

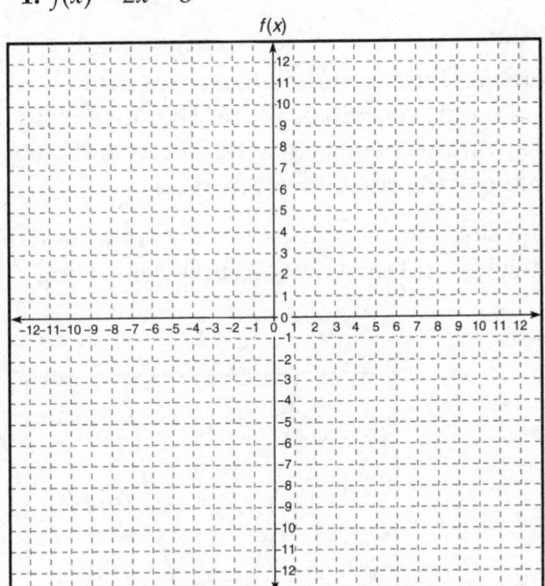

2. $f(x) = -|x|$

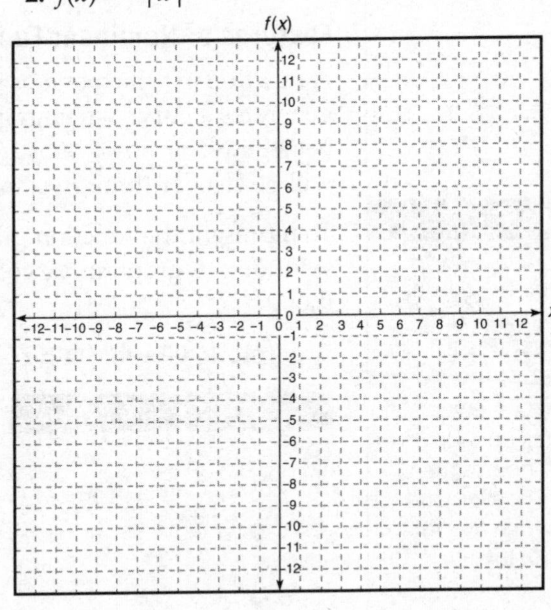

B. Mark the graph or answer the question as directed.

3. On the coordinate plane below, place a dot on the x-intercept and the y-intercept of the function $f(x) = -4x + 4$.

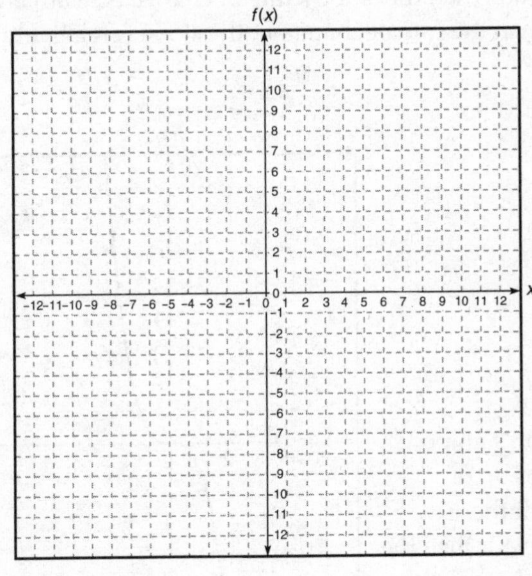

4. The graph below represents which of the following functions?

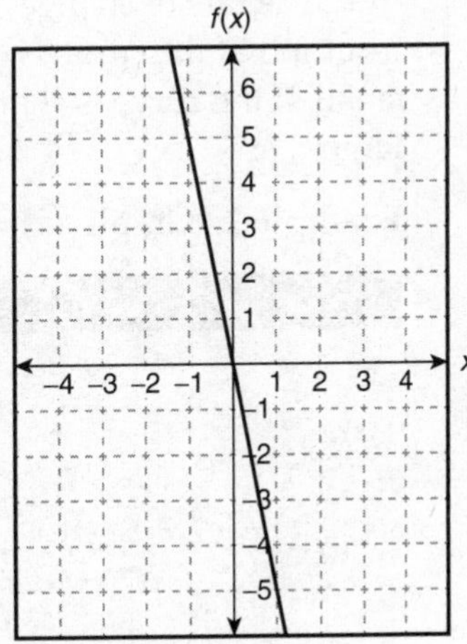

A. $f(x) = x + 5$
B. $f(x) = x - 5$
C. $f(x) = -5x$
D. $f(x) = \frac{x}{5}$
E. $f(x) = 5 - x$

LESSON 13

Nonlinear Functions

Features of Nonlinear Functions

A function in which one or more variables are raised to an exponent generates a curve when graphed on the coordinate plane. The slope may be negative or positive or zero at various points along the curve, and it will be steeper through some parts of the curve than others.

To represent the function graphically, you can calculate a few points in the solution set, graph those coordinates, and then draw a curve connecting them.

KEY IDEAS

- When graphed on the coordinate plane, a function with an exponent generates a curved line—that is, the slope of the line changes.
- The shape of the curve is determined by whether the exponent is odd or even and whether the coefficient with the variable is positive or negative.
- You may be asked about specific aspects of a nonlinear function, such as its minimum or maximum, a local minimum or maximum, or its periodicity.

Example 1: Graph $f(x) = x^2$.

x	$f(x)$
−2	4
−1	1
0	0
1	1
2	4

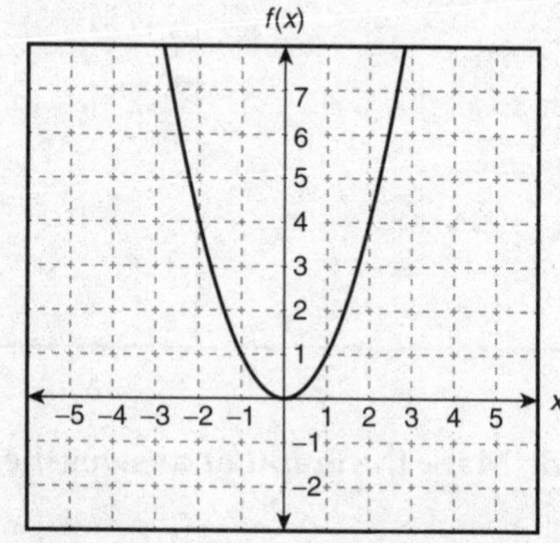

In the graph above, note that the slope at the point (0, 0) is zero, while the slope at (2, 4) is much steeper. The slope at any negative x-value is negative. The rate of change of a function's slope can be estimated from looking at its graph. If the curve is gradual, then the slope's rate of change is relatively small. If the curve is sharp, then the rate of change in the slope is relatively large.

Example 2: Graph $f(x) = x^3$.

x	$f(x)$
−2	−8
−1	−1
0	0
1	1
2	8

The **end behavior** of a function's graph refers to whether its "arms" go up or down. Memorize these rules: If the exponent is even, as in Example 1, then the arms extend either both up or both down. If the exponent is odd, as in Example 2, then one arm extends upward while the other extends downward.

HiSET EXAM TIP

Graphing a few points of a function often gives you enough information to figure out how the function behaves throughout its domain. Start with a table of x- and y-values, just as you would with a linear function. Then you can roughly sketch the curve that would connect those lines.

The right arm of the graph travels upward if the coefficient of the variable with the exponent is positive, as in both Examples 1 and 2 above. The right arm of the graph travels downward if the coefficient of the variable with the exponent is negative.

Example 3: Graph $f(x) = -x^2 + 3$.

x	$f(x)$
−2	−1
−1	2
0	3
1	2
2	−1

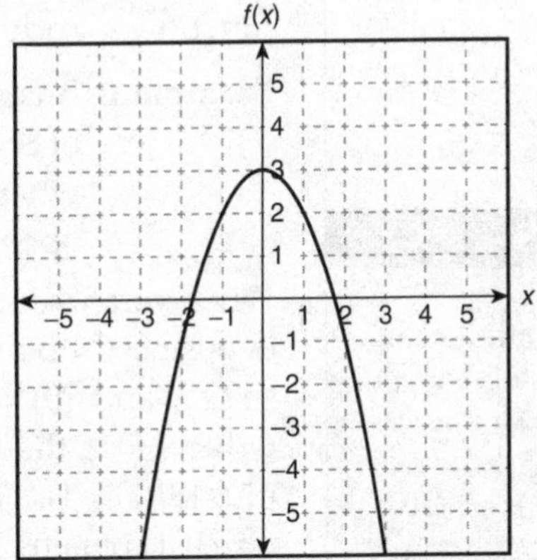

Because the coefficient of the variable is −1, and the exponent is even, both arms of the graph point downward.

A. Choose the one best answer to each question.

1. Which of the following describes the end behavior of $f(x) = 5x^3 + x - 10$?

A. The left arm goes down, and the right arm goes up.
B. The left arm goes up, and the right arm goes down.
C. Both arms go up.
D. Both arms go down.
E. The left arm goes up, and the right arm could go up or down.

2. Which of the following describes the end behavior of $f(a) = -7a^4 - 11$?

A. The left arm goes down, and the right arm goes up.
B. The left arm goes up, and the right arm goes down.
C. Both arms go up.
D. Both arms go down.
E. The left arm goes up, and the right arm could go up or down.

3. The graph of $f(x) = Ax^2 - 3.25$ has a maximum and no minimum. The coefficient A must be

A. positive
B. negative
C. even
D. odd
E. zero

B. Solve.

4. $f(x) = -\frac{x^2}{2}$. Match the value of x to the slope of the curve at that point. (*Hint:* You do not have to actually calculate the slope. You can make inferences about where the curve is steeper and which way the "arms" are pointing in order to complete this question.)

$x = -3$	
$x = 0$	
$x = 1$	
$x = 4$	

−4
−1
0
3

5. $f(x) = x^3 - 3x + 2$. Match the value of x to the slope of the curve at that point. (*Hint:* You do not have to actually calculate the slope. You can make inferences about where the curve is steeper and which way the "arms" are pointing in order to complete this question.)

$x = -2$	
$x = -1$	
$x = 0$	

−3
0
9

LESSON 14

Modeling with Functions

The Mathematics Test may ask you to model real-life situations using functions. Study the example below.

Example 1: Imagine that you open a checking account with an initial deposit of \$60. Each month you add \$100. Create a function called $f(t)$, where t represents the number of months the account has been open, to calculate the amount of money in the account.

When you first open the account and deposit \$60, no time at all has passed yet, so $t = 0$ and $f(0) = 60$. The first month (when $t = 1$), the account contains \$60 plus (\$100 × 1). The second month (when $t = 2$), it contains \$60 plus (\$100 × 2), or \$260. The third month (when $t = 3$), it contains \$60 plus (\$100 × 3), or \$360, and so on. So $f(t) = \$60 + \$100t$.

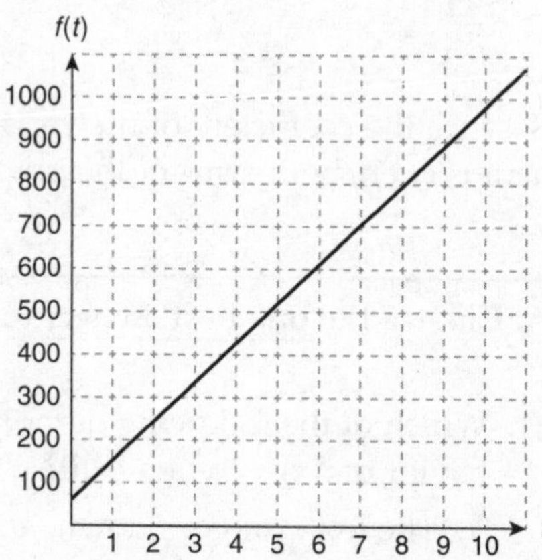

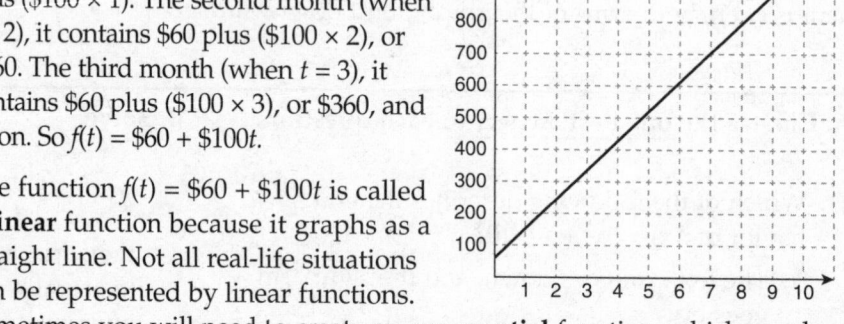

The function $f(t) = \$60 + \$100t$ is called a **linear** function because it graphs as a straight line. Not all real-life situations can be represented by linear functions. Sometimes you will need to create an **exponential** function, which graphs as a curve.

Example 2: Imagine a carton of milk going sour. The souring process is caused by bacteria that produce lactic acid. At optimal temperature and pH, these bacteria tend to double once per hour. If there are 100 lactic acid bacteria in a carton of milk initially, create a function $L(t)$ to model the bacterial population as a function of time.

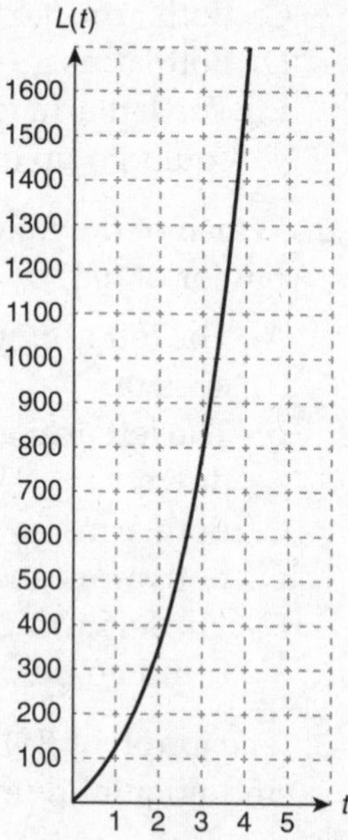

At the end of one hour, that is, when $t = 1$, the bacteria have doubled, so there are now $2(100) = 200$. At the end of the next hour, when $t = 2$, they have doubled again, so there are now $2(2)(100) = 400$. Each hour, the population is multiplied by 2 so that at the end of the tenth hour (when $t = 10$), there will be $2^{10}(100)$ bacteria, and at the end of the twentieth hour (when $t = 20$), there will be $2^{20}(100)$ bacteria, and so on. So we can write $L(t)$ like this:

$$L(t) = 2^t \times 100$$

Note that $L(0) = 100$, which is the number of bacteria at $t = 0$. The graph shows what $L(t)$ looks like when graphed (notice the units on each axis).

KEY IDEAS

- Some real-life situations can be modeled using linear functions. Others require nonlinear functions.
- You can tell whether you need to use a linear or nonlinear function by looking at a few *x*- and *y*-values. If *y* changes by a constant value for each corresponding constant change in *x*, then the function is linear; if not, it is nonlinear.
- The Mathematics Test may describe a real-life situation and ask you to determine whether it would be modeled with a linear function or a nonlinear function.

HISET EXAM TIP

When modeling something as a function of time, start by noting the initial situation (at $t = 0$). Then think about what happens when $t = 1$, $t = 2$, $t = 3$, and so on. Use the pattern you notice to construct the function.

PRACTICE 14.1

You can determine whether a function is linear or not if you are given sets of data points or if you use the equation to generate some values for x and y. In a linear function, as the x-value changes by a constant, the y-value also changes by a constant. For example, consider the line represented by the function $f(x) = 2x$. Every time x increases by 1, y increases by 2:

x-value	y-value
1	2
2	4
3	6

However, in a function involving an exponent, each time the x-value increases by a constant, the y-value changes by a non-constant amount. For instance, here are a few x- and y-values for the function $f(x) = x^2$:

x-value	y-value
1	1
2	4
3	9
4	16

Solve.

1. Consider the x- and y-values for a function, given in the chart below. Is this function linear?

x-value	y-value
−2	−8
−1	−1
0	0
1	1
2	8

____

Questions 2 and 3 refer to the following situation:

A small business has an expense account that contains \$6,000 on January 2 of the year. On the first day of each month, the business pays \$500 for equipment rental from this account. The expense account does not have overdraft protection, so the business does not allow the account to dip below zero.

2. If the business does not put any money into the account during the year, then which of the following equations, where t represents the number of months that have passed, describes the expense account balance as a function of time?

   A. $B(t) = \$6{,}000 + \$500t$
   B. $B(t) = \$6{,}000 \times t^2$
   C. $B(t) = \$6{,}000 \times \$500t^2$
   D. $B(t) = \$6{,}000 - \$500t$
   E. $B(t) = \$6{,}000t + \$500$

3. What is the maximum possible value for t? Write your answer on the line below.

____

Questions 4 and 5 refer to the following situation:

Ten rabbits are accidentally introduced to a large island that previously had no rabbits at all. The rabbit population triples every four months.

4. Which of the following functions correctly describes the rabbit population as it grows over time, where y represents the number of years that have passed since the rabbits were first introduced?

   A. $P(y) = 10 \times 3^{3y}$
   B. $P(y) = 10 \times 3^y$
   C. $P(y) = 10 \times 4y$
   D. $P(y) = 10 + 30y$
   E. $P(y) = 10 + 4y$

5. If the island can sustain a maximum of 7,300 rabbits before they begin to die due to lack of resources, what is the maximum possible integer value for y?

   A. 0
   B. 1
   C. 2
   D. 3
   E. 4

Parameters of Functions in a Modeling Context

The Mathematics Test may provide you with a function used to model a real-life situation and ask you to interpret the function's parameters, or constants. Study the example below.

Example 3: The rate a certain taxi company charges is given by the function $C(m) = \$2m + \$3$, where m represents length of the trip in miles and $C(m)$ represents the cost of the trip. The \$3 (which is the y-intercept on the graph of this function) represents the flat charge already on the meter before the taxi starts moving. The \$2 (which is the slope of the graph of this function) represents the rate per mile. Look at the graph below and think about what would happen to the graph if the taxi company charged a different flat fee, or if it charged more or less per mile.

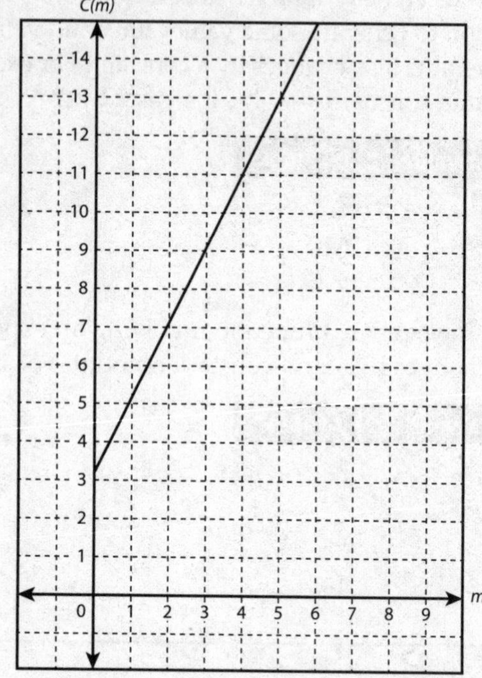

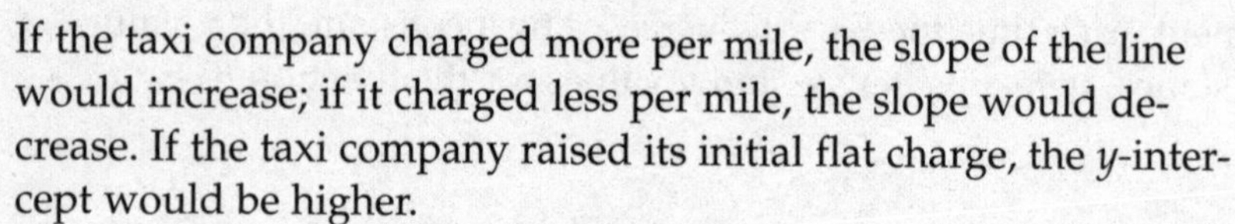

If the taxi company charged more per mile, the slope of the line would increase; if it charged less per mile, the slope would decrease. If the taxi company raised its initial flat charge, the y-intercept would be higher.

The example to the right is a linear function. Some situations must be modeled using a **nonlinear function**.

Example 4: If a ball is thrown straight up, you need a quadratic function to calculate when the ball will hit the ground given its initial position and velocity. Imagine that a ball is tossed into the air from a height of 3 meters at an initial velocity of 2 m/s. Three things must be included in this model: the ball's initial height, the velocity produced by its being thrown upward (which causes a change in the ball's height), and gravity. Gravity causes objects to fall toward the ground and to accelerate as they do so. Adding its initial height plus its change in height due to its initial velocity plus its change in height due to its acceleration due to gravity (which is approximately -5m/s^2) gives its height h at any point in time t:

The ball will hit the ground when $h = 0$:

$$0 = -5t^2 + 2t + 3$$

Divide by -1 and solve for t:

$$0 = 5t^2 - 2t - 3$$

$$0 = (5t + 3)(t - 1)$$

$$t = -\frac{3}{5} \text{ or } t = 1$$

A negative value for t would mean a time before the ball was tossed into the air, and that doesn't make sense. So only the positive value, $t = 1$, makes sense. The ball will hit the ground after 1 second.

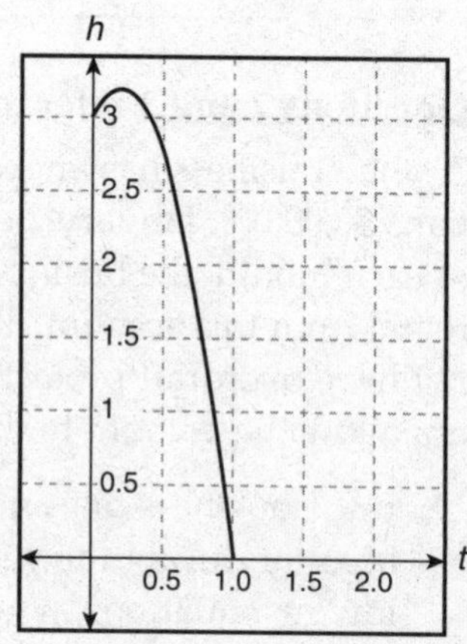

Consider the graph of this function and think about what would happen to the curve if the ball were thrown from a different height, or if it were thrown with a different velocity.

Both of the examples above involve equations. But sometimes, real-life constraints are not equations, but inequalities. Study the following example.

PRACTICE 14.2

Example 5: Imagine that a high school theater club needs to raise money to buy costumes, so the club opens a lemonade stand in the school cafeteria at lunch hour. Each day for a week, the theater club sells both iced tea (i, at \$2.00 per cup) and lemonade (l, at \$1.50 per cup). The club members have a total of 500 drink cups, so they can sell a maximum of 500 drinks. They must raise a minimum of \$850. Which of the following represents the system of inequalities that describes the theater club's constraints?

(1) $2i + 1.5l \geq 850$; $i + l \leq 500$

(2) $2i + 1.5l \leq 850$; $i + l \geq 500$

Choice **(1)** is correct. The amount of money the students need to make must be greater than or equal to \$850, and the total number of drinks sold must be less than or equal to 500.

Solve.

1. A bakery makes peanut butter cookies according to the following cost function, where d represents the number of cookies in dozens and $C(d)$ represents the total cost of making cookies: $C(d) = \$10 + \$7(d - 1)$. What is the y-intercept of this function, and what does the y-intercept represent?
   A. The y-intercept is 10, which represents the number of cookies in the first dozen made.
   B. The y-intercept is 7, which represents the cost per dozen after the first dozen.
   C. The y-intercept is 7, which represents the cost per dozen for the first dozen.
   D. The y-intercept is 3, which represents the bakery's fixed costs incurred before any cookies are made.
   E. The y-intercept is 3, which represents the bakery's costs after the first dozen.

2. If a certain rodent population is allowed to grow without constraints, that population growth can be modeled by the function $P(t) = 100 \times 2^{5t}$, where 100 is the starting population and t represents years. What does the 5 in the exponent signify?
   A. It means that the population study went on for 5 years.
   B. It means that the population doubles 5 times per year.
   C. It means that the population quintuples every year.
   D. It means that the population quintuples every two years.
   E. It means that the population doubles for the first five years.

3. Sascha has at most \$30 to spend on chocolate. Her favorite mint chocolate bars (m) cost \$3.50 each, while her favorite dark chocolate bars (d) cost \$4.50 each. She knows that she will purchase at least one dark chocolate bar and at least two mint chocolate bars. Which system of inequalities best models this situation?
   A. $3.5m + 4.5d \leq 30$; $d \geq 1$; $m \geq 2$
   B. $3.5d + 4.5m \leq 30$; $d \geq 1$; $m \geq 2$
   C. $3.5m + 4.5d \geq 30$; $d \geq 2$; $m \geq 1$
   D. $3.5d + 4.5m \geq 30$; $d \geq 2$; $m \geq 1$
   E. $3.5m + 4.5d \leq 30$; $d \geq 2$; $m \geq 2$

4. A rectangular lawn is 10 feet longer than it is wide and has an area of 1,200 square feet. What is the width (that is, the shorter dimension) of the lawn? Write your answer in the space below.

   ____

LESSON 15

Equation Word Problems, Part II

Now that you have learned more about equations and systems of equations, you are ready to apply those skills to solve word problems.

KEY IDEAS

- Some questions on the Mathematics Test may give you a word problem that portrays a linear equation or system of equations.
- You may be asked to infer an equation from a graphic.
- Carefully write out the equation(s) from the word problem, then solve as usual.

Example 1: Two companies, A and B, charge for shipping by the pound. Company A charges a fixed fee of \$3 for any shipment plus \$1.50 for each pound in the shipment. Company B charges a fixed fee of \$6 for any shipment plus \$1 for each pound in the shipment. For what number of pounds would the two companies' shipping charges be the same?

This word problem gives you two equations: one for Company A and one for Company B. Let y represent the shipping charge and x represent pounds in the shipment, and write out the equations:

Company A: $y = 1.5x + 3$ Company B: $y = 1x + 6$

The question asks you what value of x will give the same value of y in both equations. In other words, what is the solution of the system of equations?

Solve by substitution:

$1x + 6 = 1.5x + 3$

$3 = 0.5x$

$\mathbf{6 = x}$

The companies would charge the same amount for shipping a **6-pound order.**

HiSET EXAM TIP

When working on word problems, use your scratch paper to write out the information given in the form of a mathematical equation.

You may also be asked to infer an equation from a graphic. Study the following example.

Example 2: A charity was struggling to raise funds. In November of last year, it raised only \$1500. It then decided to launch a social media campaign. The following graph shows how much money the charity raised for several months, starting with November of last year.

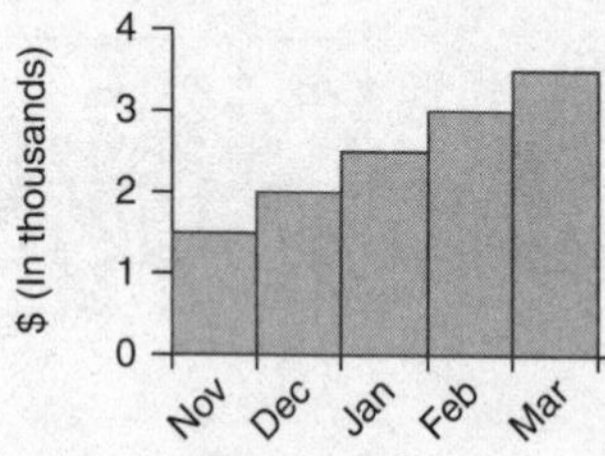

Which of the following equations could be used to find the money raised by the charity in the month x months after November last year? Here, y represents the money raised by the charity.

(1) $y = 1{,}500x + 500$

(2) $y = 500x + 1{,}500$

Choice **(2)** is correct: **\$1500** is the charity's starting place at the end of November. Each month after that it raises \$500 more. In February, which was three months after November, it raised \$3000: $500(3) + 1500 = 3000$.

You may also be asked to solve word problems using quadratic equations. Study the following example.

Example 3: Xavier's age times Yelena's age is 120. Xavier is 2 years older than Yelena. How old are Xavier and Yelena?

Write two equations to represent the information given: $xy = 120$ $x - y = 2$

Solve using substitution.

1. Isolate a variable in the second equation: $x = 2 + y$

2. Substitute and simplify: $(2 + y)y = 120$

$y^2 + 2y = 120$

3. Make the equation equal zero and solve by factoring: $y^2 + 2y - 120 = 0$

$(y - 10)(y + 12) = 0$

$y = 10$ or -12

Now, it doesn't make sense for Yelena to have a negative age. So she must be **10 years old.** Substitute that value back into one of the original equations: $x - 10 = 2$

Therefore, Xavier is **12 years old.**

Choose the one best answer to each question.

1. Marguerite, a salesperson, earns a base salary plus a commission based on how much she sells. The following graph represents how much Marguerite can make.

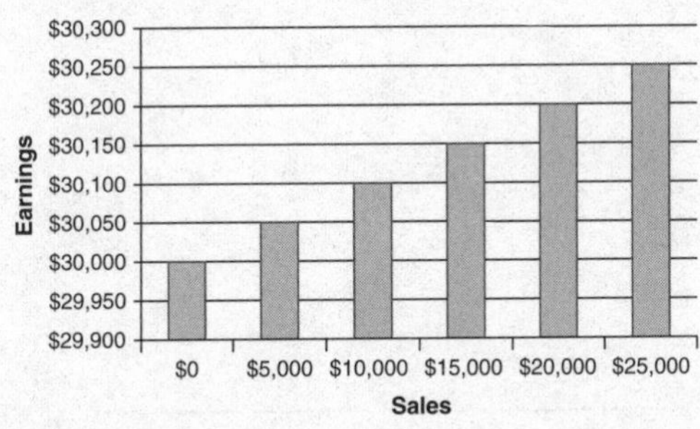

Which of the following equations accurately expresses Marguerite's earnings (e) in terms of her sales (s)?

A. $e = 30{,}000s$
B. $e = 0.3s + 5{,}000$
C. $e = 30{,}250 - 50s$
D. $e = 0.01s + 30{,}000$
E. $e = 0.02s + 30{,}000$

2. A car dealership is offering a discount on used cars. For sedans, the discount is $1,000 plus $100 for each year of the vehicle's age. For minivans, the discount is $1,500 plus $50 for each year of the vehicle's age. At what age would a vehicle have the same discount whether it were a sedan or minivan?

A. 18
B. 16
C. 14
D. 12
E. 10

3. A zoo has contacted two stroller manufacturers to replace its current strollers with upgraded versions. Company A will charge $2,000 initially and $40 per stroller. Company B will only charge $1,550 initially, but $55 per stroller. For what number of strollers will the two companies charge the same price?

A. 15
B. 20
C. 30
D. 35
E. 40

FUNCTIONS PRACTICE QUESTIONS

Directions: Choose the one best answer to each question.

1. Which of the following expressions is equal to $6 - 4(x + 3)$?

   A. $4x + 3$
   B. $4x - 9$
   C. $-4x - 3$
   D. $-4x - 6$
   E. $6x - 12$

2. Three increased by the product of 4 and a number is equal to the same number decreased by 6. What is the number?

   A. –3
   B. –1
   C. 1
   D. 3
   E. 6

3. What is the equation of a line with a slope of –4 that passes through the point (1, 2)?

   A. $y = -4x + 2$
   B. $y = -4x + 6$
   C. $y = 4x + 1$
   D. $y = 4x + 6$
   E. $y = 6x + 4$

4. The ordered pair (–2, –1) is a solution to which of the following equations?

   A. $-4x - y = 7$
   B. $4x + y = -7$
   C. $4x - y = -7$
   D. $-4x + y = -7$
   E. $-2x - y = 0$

5. For a two-week period, Jan earned $150 less than twice Tom's earnings. Together Jan and Tom earned $1380. How much did Tom earn?

   A. $720
   B. $660
   C. $510
   D. $360
   E. $300

Questions 6 and 7 refer to the following graph.

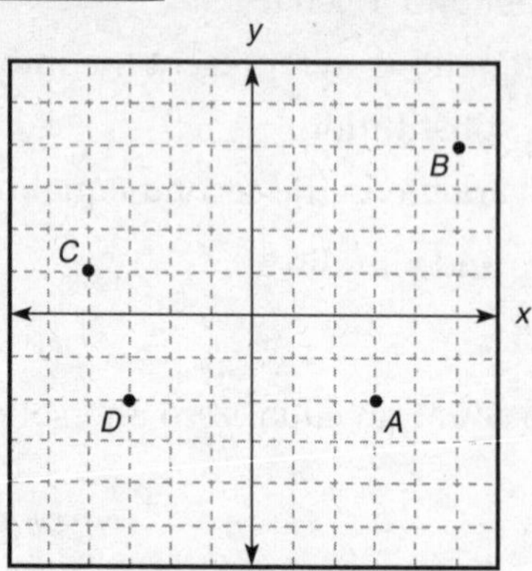

6. If the graph of the equation $y = -x - 5$ were drawn on the grid, which of the points would be on the line?

   A. *A*
   B. *B*
   C. *C*
   D. *D*
   E. None of the above

7. If a line were drawn through points *B* and *C*, what would be the slope of the line?

   A. –3
   B. $-\frac{1}{3}$
   C. $\frac{1}{3}$
   D. 3
   E. 6

8. Samuel is paid $350 per month plus a 10% commission on his total sales for the month. If he needs to earn at least $2100 per month, which of the following expressions represents the total sales for the month (s) Samuel needs to achieve?

   A. $s = \$2,450$
   B. $s \leq \$14,500$
   C. $s \geq \$14,500$
   D. $s \leq \$17,500$
   E. $s \geq \$17,500$

9. For its Checking Plus account, a bank charges \$3.95 per month plus \$0.10 for each check written after the first ten checks written that month. The function to find the total monthly fee (F) is $F = \$3.95 + \$0.10(n - 10)$, where n = number of checks written.

Greg writes 24 checks in March. How much will he pay in fees for the month?

A. \$6.35
B. \$5.35
C. \$4.35
D. \$2.40
E. \$1.40

10. The sum of four consecutive odd numbers is 104. What is the largest number?

A. 23
B. 25
C. 27
D. 29
E. 31

11. Which value for x makes the inequality $x > 400$ true?

A. 7^3
B. 4^4
C. 3^6
D. 6^3
E. 19^2

12. Four less than the product of a number (x) and 5 is equal to 8 more than 2 added to 3 times the number. Which of these equations could be used to find the value of x?

A. $4 - 5x = 8 + 2 + 3x$
B. $5x - 4 = 8 + 2 + 3x$
C. $5x = 4 - 8 + 2 + 3x$
D. $5x - 4 = 8 + 2 + 3$
E. $5x - 4 = 10x + 3$

13. What is the slope of a line that passes through the points (2, 4) and (4, 6)?

A. −2
B. 1
C. $\frac{3}{2}$
D. 2
E. 4

14. What is the next number in the sequence?
1, 7, 14, 22, . . .

A. 30
B. 31
C. 32
D. 33
E. 34

15. What is the y-intercept of the line with a slope of 2 that passes through the point (1, 2)?

A. −2
B. $-\frac{1}{2}$
C. 0
D. $\frac{1}{2}$
E. 1

16. If the graphs of the equations $y = x + 3$ and $y = -2x - 3$ are drawn on a coordinate grid, at which point do the two lines intersect?

A. (−3, 2)
B. (−2, 1)
C. (−2, −1)
D. (2, 3)
E. (0, 3)

17. A hotel is installing a swimming pool that gets deeper as you approach the center. The following graph shows the depth of the pool in relation to the distance from the edge.

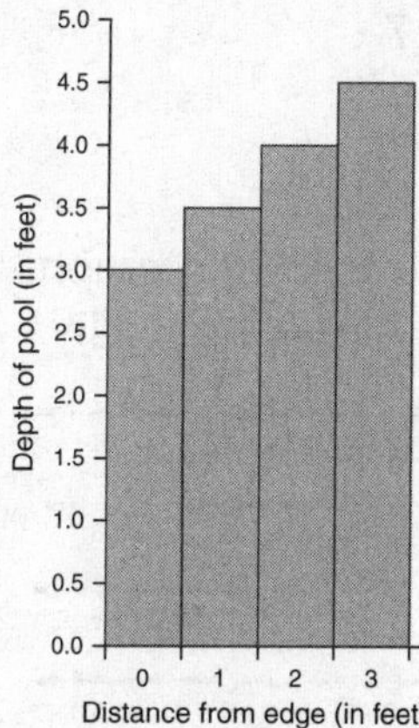

Which equation properly represents this relationship if x is the distance from the edge of the pool and y is the depth of the pool?

A. $y = 4.5 + 0.5x$
B. $y = 4.5 + x$
C. $y = 3 + x + 1.5x$
D. $y = 3 + x$
E. $y = 3 + 0.5x$

18. Which of the following shows the product of −7 and x decreased by the sum of 8 and y?

A. $-7x - (8 + y)$
B. $-7x - 8 + y$
C. $(8 + y) - 7x$
D. $(-7 + x) - (8 + y)$
E. $-7x - 8y$

19. What are the possible solutions for the quadratic equation $x^2 - 5x = 24$?

A. −8 and 3
B. −6 and 4
C. 8 and −3
D. 4 and −6
E. −5 and 24

20. Cynthia is 6 times as old as Rebecca. In 6 years, Cynthia will be only 3 times as old as Rebecca. How old is Rebecca now?

A. 3
B. 4
C. 8
D. 12
E. 18

21. The graph of which equation will pass through points (0, −3) and (5, 7)?

A. $y = \frac{1}{2}x - 3$
B. $y = 2x - 3$
C. $y = 2x + 7$
D. $y = -2x + 3$
E. $y = 5x - 7$

22. Which of the following graphs represents the solution set of the inequality $-2(x - 6) > 8$?

A. 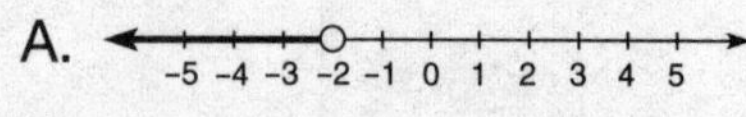

B. -5 -4 -3 -2 -1 0 1 2 3 4 5

C. -5 -4 -3 -2 -1 0 1 2 3 4 5

D. -5 -4 -3 -2 -1 0 1 2 3 4 5

E. -5 -4 -3 -2 -1 0 1 2 3 4 5

Questions 23 and 24 refer to the following graph.

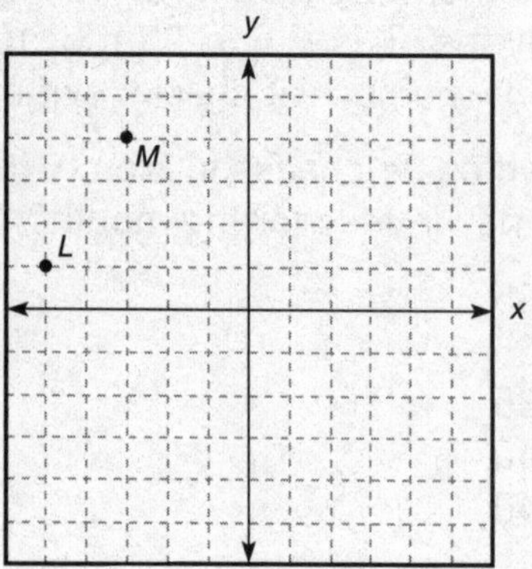

23. Which of the following ordered pairs shows the location of point L?

A. (−5, −1)
B. (−5, 1)
C. (−1, 5)
D. (1, −5)
E. (−3, 4)

24. What is the slope of the line that passes through points L and M?

A. $\frac{-3}{2}$
B. $\frac{-2}{3}$
C. $\frac{2}{3}$
D. 1
E. $\frac{3}{2}$

25. Bob, Celia, Sam, and Daniel contributed money to buy their boss a retirement gift. Sam and Daniel each gave the same amount of money. Celia gave $12 more than Daniel. Bob gave half as much as Celia gave. If the four workers gave a total of $81, how much did Sam give?

A. $9
B. $15
C. $18
D. $21
E. $25

STUDY ADVICE

On Test Day, you will likely see several questions that give you a word problem, a table, or a graph and ask you to apply an equation or infer an equation from the situation. Carefully review the last three lessons to master those skills.

26. What is the solution set of the inequality $-7x - 4 \geq x - 28$?

A. $x \leq 3$
B. $x \geq 3$
C. $x \leq -3$
D. $x \geq -4$
E. $x = 3$

27. A line goes through the points (0, 2) and (1, 3). What is the equation of the line?

A. $y = -\frac{1}{2}x + 3$
B. $y = \frac{1}{2}x + 2$
C. $y = x + 2$
D. $y = x + 3$
E. $y = 2x + 1$

28. In a recent election, Perez got 5512 more votes than $\frac{1}{3}$ of the leading candidate's votes. Together the two candidates received 18,072 votes. How many people voted for Perez?

A. 6,024
B. 8,652
C. 9,420
D. 10,240
E. 12,560

29. What is the value of x in the equation $-4(x + 2) - 10 = 5x$?

A. $x = -18$
B. $x = -2$
C. $x = 2$
D. $x = 18$
E. $x = 36$

30. Marcia counts the \$5 bills and \$10 bills in her cash register drawer. She counts a total of 35 bills with a total value of \$240. If x = the number of \$5 bills in the drawer, which of the following equations could be used to find the number of \$5 bills in the drawer?

A. $\$5x + \$10x = 35$
B. $\$5x + \$10x + 35 = \$240$
C. $\$5(35 - x) + \$10x = \$240$
D. $\$5x + \$10(35 - x) = \$240$
E. $\$5x + \$10(x - 35) = \$240$

31. The sum of five consecutive numbers is 370. What is the fourth number in the sequence?

A. 73
B. 74
C. 75
D. 76
E. 77

32. A baseball pitcher's earned run average (E) is a function of the number of earned runs (r) given up and innings pitched (i). The function is written $E = \frac{9r}{i}$. What is the earned run average of a pitcher who gives up 8 runs in 18 innings?

A. 2
B. 3
C. 4
D. 6
E. 8

33. Tonya is selling boxes of cookies for charity. She will purchase five boxes of cookies herself and then try to sell more at her office. The following graph represents how many cookies she can sell as a function of how many of her coworkers are willing to purchase cookies.

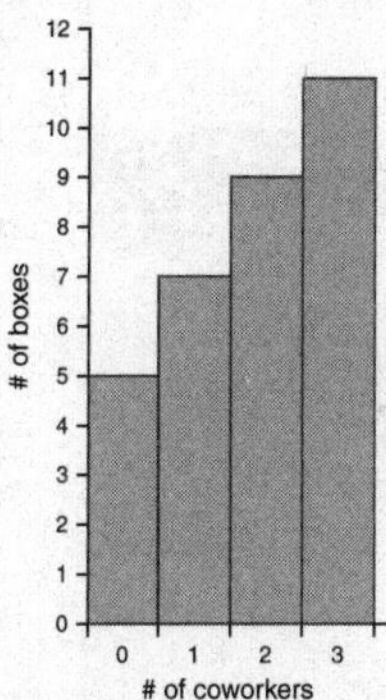

If x is the number of Tonya's coworkers who are willing to buy cookies and y is the number of boxes of cookies sold, which formula can be used to find the number of boxes of cookies Tonya will sell?

A. $y = 5 + x$
B. $y = 5 + 2x$
C. $y = 7 + x$
D. $y = 7 + 2x$
E. $y = 7x + 2$

Geometry

LESSON 1

Points, Lines, and Angles

KEY IDEAS

- Most geometric figures are named by points that lie on the figure.
- Angles are measured in degrees and are classified by their measures.
- The sum of two complementary angles is 90°. The sum of two supplementary angles is 180°.

Basic Definitions

A **point** is a single location in space. We assign a name to a point by writing a letter next to it. A **plane** is a collection of points that extends to form a flat surface. In the drawing, point A lies on plane P.

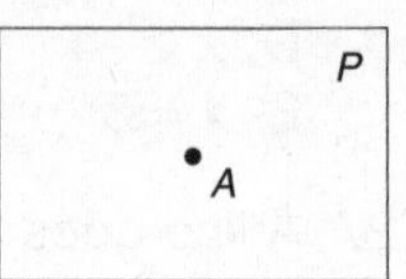

Much of your work in geometry will be concerned with lines and angles. A **line** is a straight pathway of points that extends indefinitely in two directions. A line may be named by a single letter or by two points on the line.

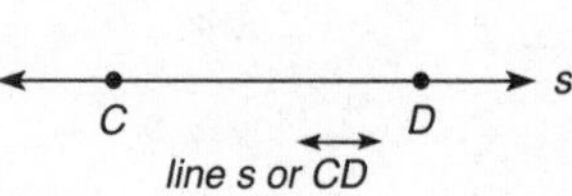

A **ray** is part of a line that begins at an endpoint and extends indefinitely in one direction. A portion of a line with two endpoints is called a **line segment.** Both rays and line segments are named using two points.

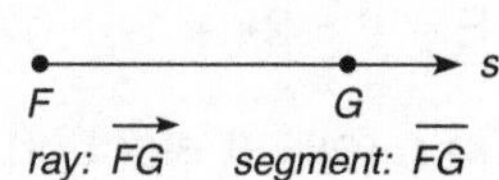

When two rays share an endpoint, they form an **angle.** The shared endpoint is the vertex of the angle. An angle can be named in different ways: by a number written in degrees inside the angle, by the vertex, or by the points on the angle. The symbol ∠ means angle.

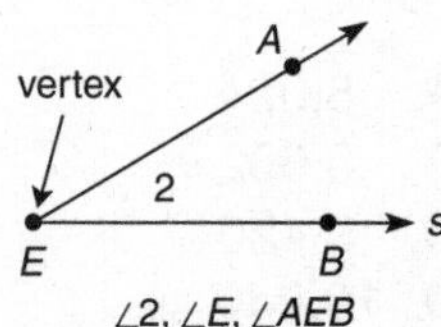

Angles are measured in degrees, indicated by a number and the symbol °. We classify angles by their measurement.

A **right angle** forms a square corner and measures 90°. A right angle is often identified by a small square drawn inside it, as shown here.

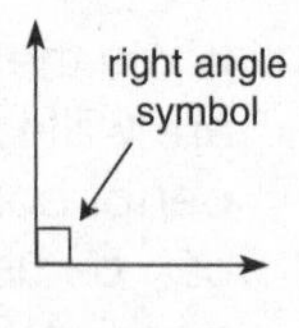

An **acute angle** is less than 90°.

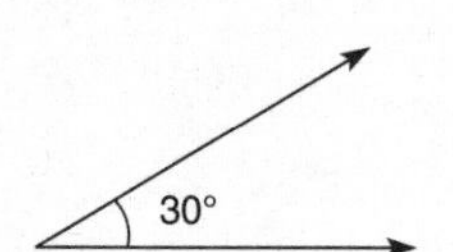

An **obtuse angle** is greater than 90° but less than 180°.

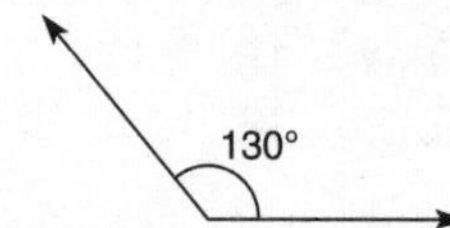

A **straight angle** measures 180°.

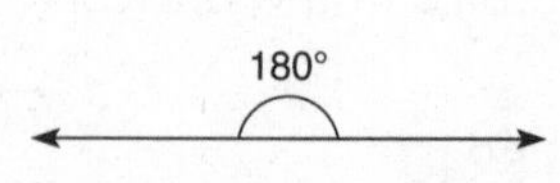

A **reflex angle** has a measure greater than 180° but less than 360°.

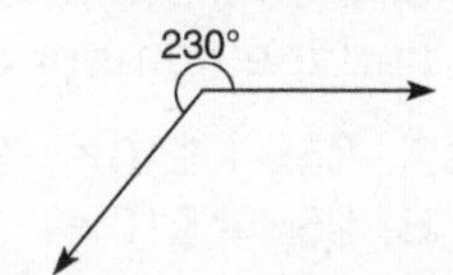

HiSET EXAM TIP

A geometric drawing may show several figures at once. As you read a problem, find each figure named in the problem.

Some Mathematics Test problems are about angle relationships. When the sum of two angles is 90°, a right angle, the angles are **complementary.** When the sum of two angles is 180°, a line or straight angle, the angles are **supplementary.** You can use this information to solve for a missing angle measure.

PRACTICE 1

Example 1: In the drawing, $\angle AOB$ and $\angle BOC$ are complementary. What is the measure of $\angle AOB$?

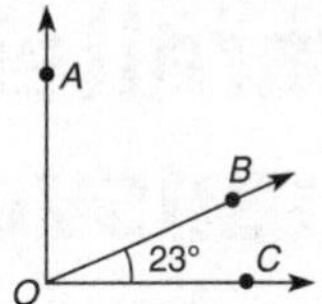

The measure of angle BOC is given as 23°, or $m\angle BOC = 23°$. The sum of the angles is 90°. Therefore, $\angle AOB$ measures **67°**.

$$m\angle AOB + 23° = 90°$$
$$m\angle AOB = 90° - 23°$$
$$m\angle AOB = 67°$$

Example 2: In the drawing, $\angle 1$ and $\angle 2$ are supplementary. What is the measure of $\angle 1$?

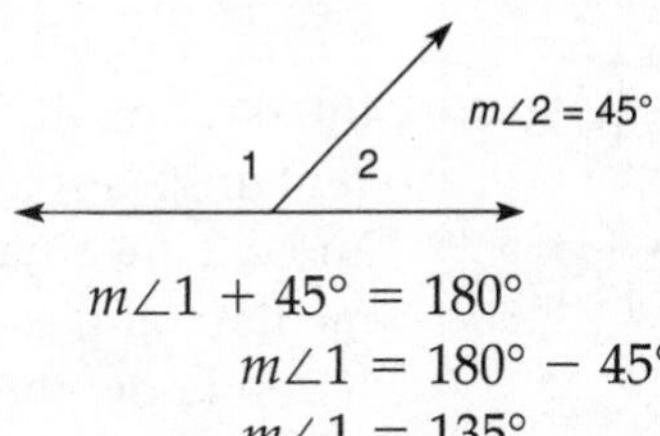

The measure of $\angle 2$ is 45°. The sum of the angles is 180°. $\angle 1$ measures **135°**.

$$m\angle 1 + 45° = 180°$$
$$m\angle 1 = 180° - 45°$$
$$m\angle 1 = 135°$$

A. Classify each angle based on its angle measure.

1. 55°
2. 95°
3. 180°
4. 18°
5. 270°
6. 90°
7. 30°
8. 110°

B. Choose the <u>one best answer</u> to each question.

<u>Questions 9 and 10</u> refer to the drawing below.

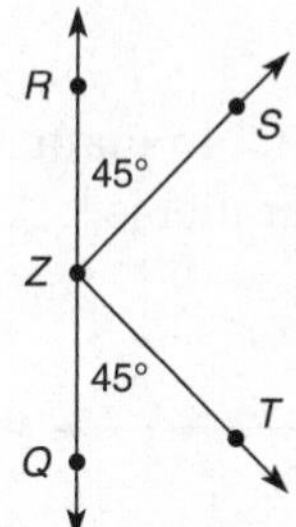

9. $\angle QZR$ is a straight angle. What is the measure of $\angle QZS$?

A. 45°
B. 60°
C. 90°
D. 125°
E. 135°

10. What kind of angle is $\angle SZT$?

A. acute
B. obtuse
C. right
D. straight
E. reflex

<u>Questions 11 and 12</u> refer to the following drawing.

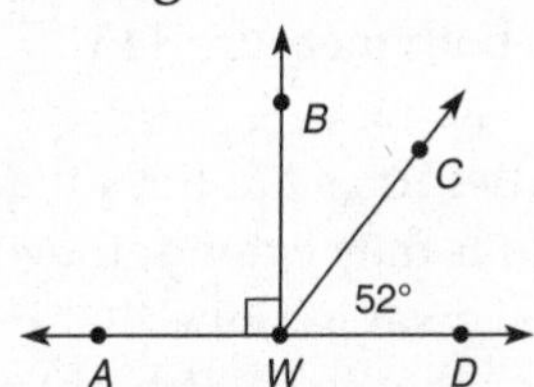

11. $\angle AWD$ is a straight angle. What is the measure of $\angle BWC$?

A. 38°
B. 52°
C. 128°
D. 138°
E. 142°

12. What type of angle is $\angle AWC$?

A. right
B. acute
C. obtuse
D. straight
E. reflex

LESSON 2

Parallel Lines and Transversals

KEY IDEAS

- Vertical angles, which are equal in measure, are formed when two lines intersect.
- When a transversal crosses two parallel lines, special angle relationships form.
- You can find the measure of any angle formed by the transversal if the measure of one angle is known.

Working with Vertical Angles and Transversals

When two lines intersect, they form two pairs of vertical angles. **Vertical angles** have the same angle measure. In the drawing, $\angle 1$ and $\angle 3$ are vertical angles, as are $\angle 2$ and $\angle 4$.

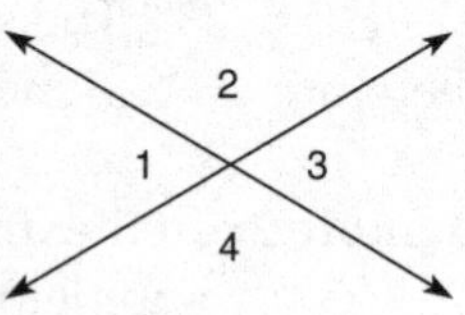

Intersecting lines also form adjacent angles. **Adjacent angles** share the same ray. For example, $\angle 1$ and $\angle 2$ are adjacent angles. The adjacent angles in this figure are supplementary angles because their sum is 180°, the measure of a straight angle. If you know the measure of one angle, you can find the measures of the other three angles.

Example 1: In the figure above, $m\angle 1 = 35°$. What are the measures of $\angle 2$, $\angle 3$, and $\angle 4$?

1. The measures of $\angle 1$ and $\angle 2$ are supplementary so their sum equals 180°. Solve for $\angle 2$.

   $m\angle + 35° = 180°$
   $m\angle 2 = 145°$

2. Angles 1 and 3 are vertical, so both measure 35°. Angles 2 and 4 are vertical, so both measure 145°.

   $\mathbf{m\angle 1 = 35°, m\angle 3 = 35°,}$
   $\mathbf{m\angle 2 = 145°, m\angle 4 = 145°}$

Parallel lines are lines that are exactly the same distance apart. No matter how far they extend, they will never touch. The symbol for parallel is ‖. A **transversal** is a line that intersects two or more other lines. When a transversal intersects two parallel lines, special angle relationships are formed.

In the drawing, $M \parallel N$. The transversal, line P, forms eight angles.

Each angle matches another angle in the same position on the transversal. These angles, called **corresponding angles,** always have the same measure. The corresponding angles are $\angle 1$ and $\angle 5$, $\angle 2$ and $\angle 6$, $\angle 3$ and $\angle 7$, and $\angle 4$ and $\angle 8$.

HiSET EXAM TIP

You can often tell which angles are equal by looking at a figure. However, you must be able to prove two angles are equal to answer setup questions and problems on logical reasoning.

Alternate exterior angles, which are also equal in measure, are on opposite sides of the transversal and are on the outside of the parallel lines. One pair of alternate exterior angles is $\angle 1$ and $\angle 7$. The other is $\angle 2$ and $\angle 8$.

Alternate interior angles are on opposite sides of the transversals and are inside the parallel lines. One pair of alternate interior angles is $\angle 3$ and $\angle 5$. The other is $\angle 4$ and $\angle 6$. Alternate interior angles are always equal in measure.

PRACTICE 2

Example 2: In the figure, $C \parallel D$. If $m\angle 4 = 48°$, what is the measure of $\angle 5$?

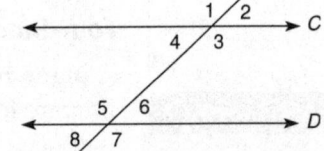

1. There are many ways to solve the problem. Here is one way: $\angle 4$ and $\angle 8$ are corresponding angles, so $m\angle 8 = 48°$.

2. $\angle 8$ and $\angle 5$ are supplementary angles, so $m\angle 5 + 48° = 180°$, and $\mathbf{m\angle 5 = 132°}$.

A. Using the figure shown at the right, solve as directed.

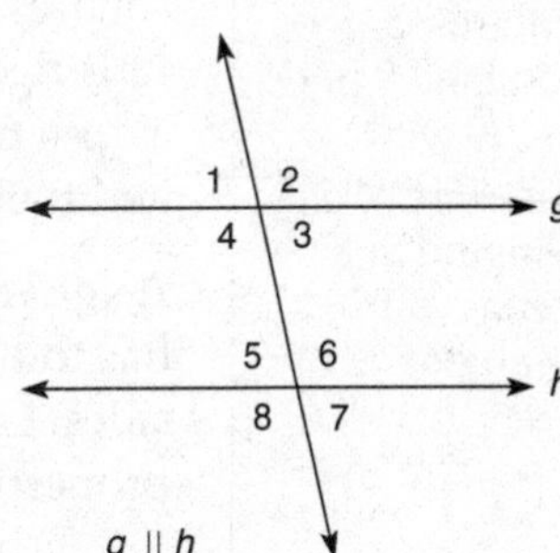

1. List one pair of alternate interior angles.
2. Which angle corresponds to $\angle 7$?
3. If $m\angle 3 = 80°$, what is $m\angle 8$?
4. List one pair of alternate exterior angles.
5. List one pair of vertical angles.
6. Which angle corresponds to $\angle 8$?

B. Choose the <u>one best answer</u> to each question.

<u>Question 7</u> refers to the following figure.

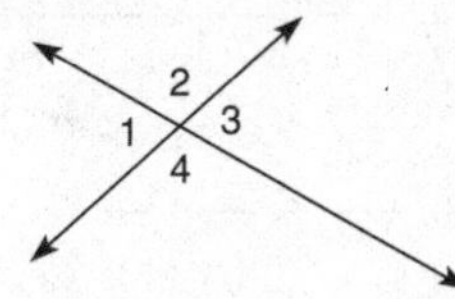

7. The measure of $\angle 3$ is 75°. What is the measure of $\angle 1$?

   A. 15°
   B. 75°
   C. 105°
   D. 115°
   E. 165°

8. Which of the following is a true statement about corresponding angles?

   A. They are also supplementary angles.
   B. They are in the same position with respect to both parallel lines.
   C. They are also alternate interior angles.
   D. They are also alternate exterior angles.
   E. They are also complementary angles.

STUDY ADVICE

About 18% of questions on the Mathematics Test are about geometry. If these concepts seem new, take your time absorbing the basics. Geometry is challenging for a lot of people, but you can master these skills with practice.

<u>Questions 9 and 10</u> refer to the following figure.

9. The measure of $\angle 7$ is 115°. What is the measure of $\angle 4$?

   A. 25°
   B. 65°
   C. 115°
   D. 245°
   E. 295°

10. Which of the following angles is equal in measure to $\angle 2$?

   A. $\angle 1$
   B. $\angle 3$
   C. $\angle 5$
   D. $\angle 7$
   E. $\angle 8$

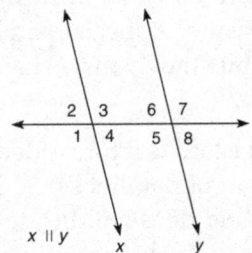

Plane Figures

KEY IDEAS

- Plane figures are classified by the properties of their sides and angles.
- The sum of the interior angles of any four-sided plane figure is 360°.
- By using the properties of any four-sided plane figure and algebraic reasoning, you can find missing angle measures.

HiSET EXAM TIP

Don't rely on sight alone to identify a geometric figure. Read carefully to see which properties are given. Then identify the figure based on the properties.

Four-Sided Plane Figures

A **plane figure** is a set of line segments, all lying on a single plane. To prepare for the Mathematics Test, learn the properties of each shape. You will need to identify the characteristics of different types of four-sided plane figures and draw conclusions about their angles and sides.

Sides with the same markings are equal.

You are already familiar with rectangles and squares. A **rectangle** is a four-sided figure with four right angles. The opposite sides (sides across from each other) are the same length, and they are parallel.

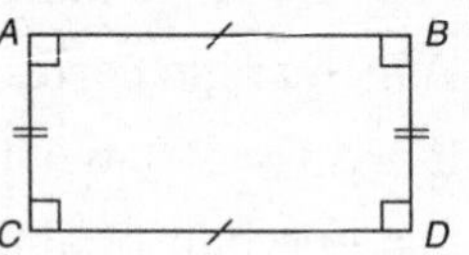

A **square** is actually a kind of rectangle. It, too, has four right angles with parallel opposite sides. However, a square has one additional property: its four sides are all the same length.

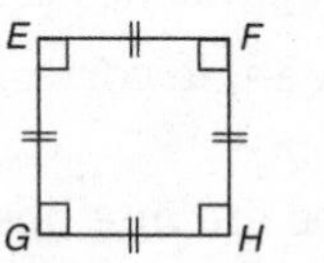

A **parallelogram** is a four-sided figure whose opposite sides are parallel and the same length. In addition, its opposite angles (the angles diagonally across from each other) are also equal in measure. A special parallelogram, called a **rhombus** (not shown), has four sides of equal length.

A **trapezoid** is a four-sided figure with exactly one pair of parallel sides. The definition of a trapezoid does not dictate the measure of the angles or the lengths of the sides.

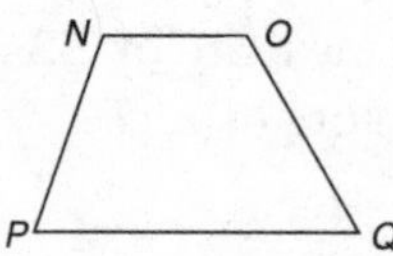

All four-sided plane figures have one important property in common. The sum of the measures of the interior angles is 360°. You can use this fact to find a missing angle measure.

Example 1: In figure $ABCD$, the opposite sides are parallel. What is the measure of $\angle A$?

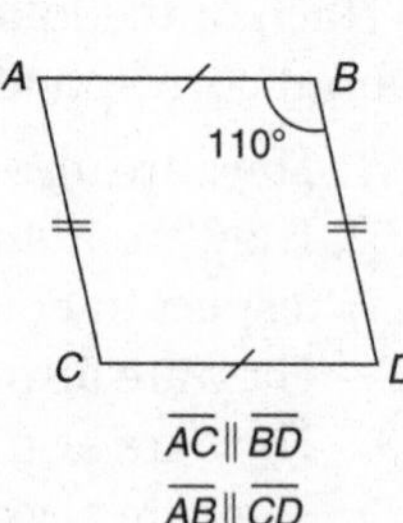

$\overline{AC} \parallel \overline{BD}$

$\overline{AB} \parallel \overline{CD}$

1. Identify the figure. The notation on the drawing tells you that the opposite sides are equal in measure. Since they are also parallel, the figure is a parallelogram.

2. Find the measure of $\angle C$. The opposite angles of a parallelogram are equal in measure; therefore, $m\angle C = m\angle B$. Both $\angle B$ and $\angle C$ measure 110°.

3. Find the measure of $\angle A$. You know the measures of $\angle A$ and $\angle D$ are equal and that the sum of all four angles equals 360°. Let $x = m\angle A$. Therefore, $2x$ = the sum of $m\angle A$ and $m\angle D$. Write an equation and solve.

$$2x + 110° + 110° = 360°$$
$$2x + 220° = 360°$$
$$2x = 140°$$
$$x = \mathbf{70°}$$

The measure of $\angle A$ is **70°**.

A. List the names of four-sided plane figures introduced on page 446 that can exhibit the following properties. Write *None* if no four-sided plane figure has the given property.

1. four right angles
2. opposite sides are equal in length
3. exactly one pair of parallel sides
4. all angles are equal in measure
5. only three right angles
6. opposite angles are equal in measure
7. all four sides are equal in length
8. sum of interior angles is 360°
9. sides are all of different lengths
10. four equal angles and four equal sides

B. Choose the <u>one best answer</u> to each question.

<u>Question 11</u> refers to the following figure.

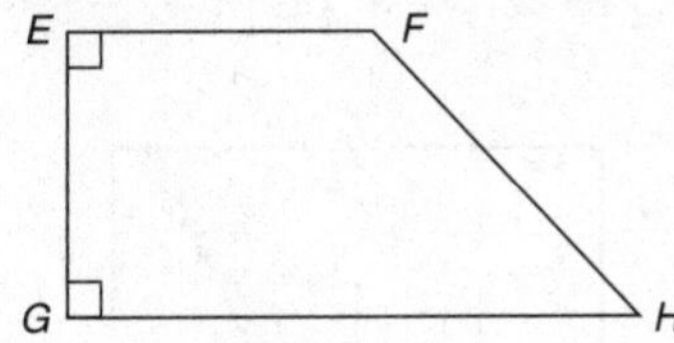

11. Angle F is 20° more than three times the measure of $\angle H$. What is the measure of $\angle F$?

A. 40°
B. 120°
C. 140°
D. 180°
E. 220°

<u>Question 12</u> refers to the following figure.

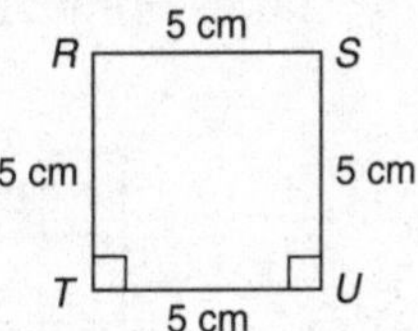

12. If the opposite sides in figure $RSUT$ are parallel, what is the measure of $\angle R$?

A. 5°
B. 20°
C. 90°
D. 180°
E. 270°

---

13. A four-sided plane figure has sides measuring 10, 15, 10, and 15. The opposite angles are equal, but there are no right angles. What is the figure?

A. rhombus
B. rectangle
C. square
D. trapezoid
E. parallelogram

Transformations in the Plane

KEY IDEAS

- Translation moves an object left/right and up/down.
- Reflection flips an object over a line.
- Rotation moves an object in a circular motion around a fixed point.
- Dilation stretches or shrinks an object about a fixed point.

HiSET EXAM TIP

A complex series of transformations can be made much more manageable if you visualize each step before moving on to the next one.

Transformation Basics

A **transformation** is a set of instructions for moving a shape in the plane. Transformations have many real-world applications, one of which is in the creation of video games, as the instructions let the computer know how it should move the images around.

There are four basic types of transformations: translation, reflection, rotation, and dilation. The first three may also be referred to as rigid motions because they relocate the object without changing its size or shape.

Translation

A **translation** is a set of instructions to move things left or right and/or up or down. Translating an object essentially "slides" it a fixed distance in a given direction.

Reflection

Reflection is the act of "flipping" an object over a line.

Example 1: The translation (–3, –2) takes point A to point B.

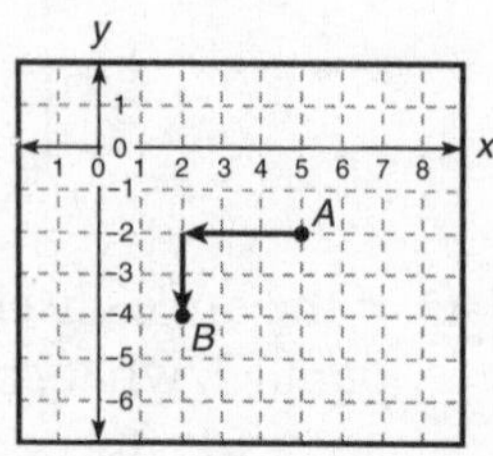

A translation of (–3, –2) means "move three to the left and two down."

Example 2: Reflect point A over line Q to arrive at point B.

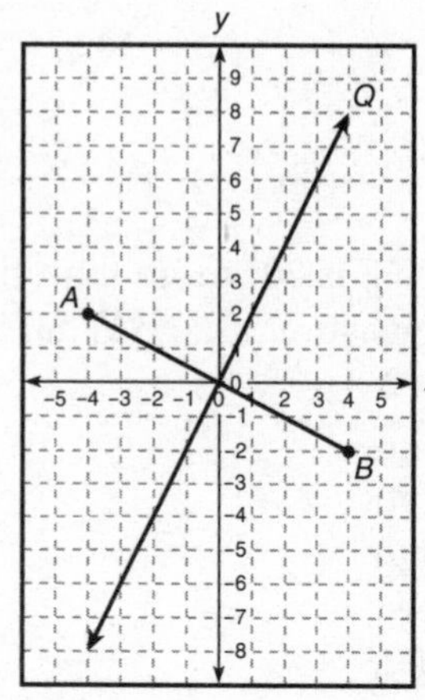

The reflection of point A at (–4, 2) about line Q is point B at (4, –2). For Test Day, the critical takeaway here is that the newly formed line $\overline{AB}$ is perpendicular to—that is, it forms a 90° angle with—line Q, so the two have negative reciprocal slopes. Line Q has a slope of 2, so $\overline{AB}$ has a slope of $-\frac{1}{2}$. For more information on slope, please see Functions: Lessons 8 and 9.

Solve.

1. Translating a point (4, –4) does which of the following?

   A. The point moves four units up, then four units down.
   B. The point moves four units up, then four units left.
   C. The point moves four units right, then four units down.
   D. The point moves four units right, then four units left.
   E. The point moves four units left, then four units down.

2. The translation (5, 7) takes point A to point B. If the coordinates of point A are (–4, 0), then what are the coordinates of point B?

3. A reflection acting on the coordinate plane takes point E to point F. What is the equation for the line of reflection?

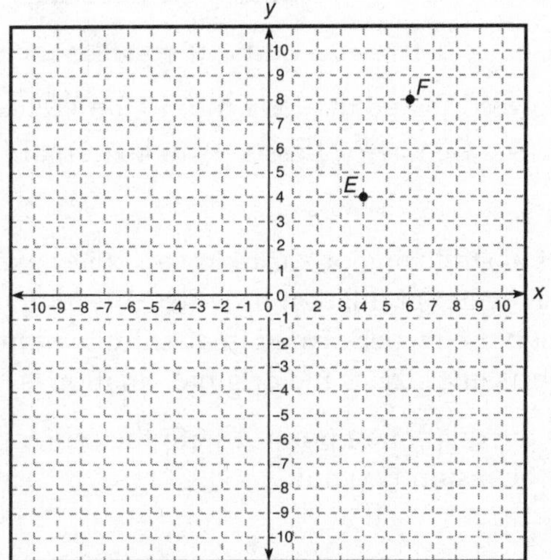

4. A translation takes point C to point D. If the same translation takes point A to point B, and the coordinates of points B, C, and D are (–2, 3), (8, 3), and (5, 7), respectively, what are the coordinates of point A?

Rotation

Rotation is the act of moving in a circular arc around a fixed point.

Example 3: Rotate point G 90° clockwise around point R to arrive at point H.

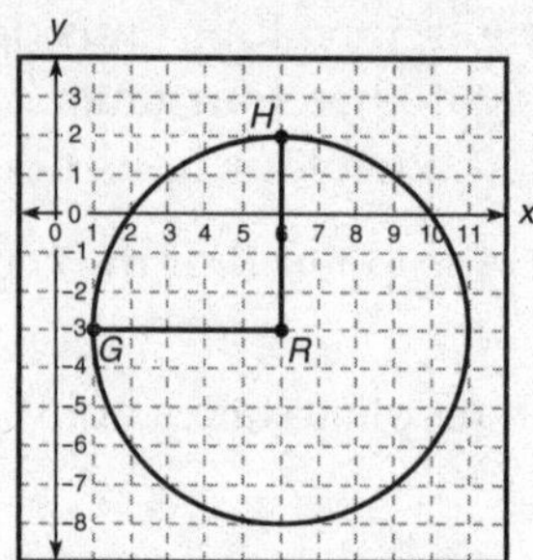

Notice that the distance between G and R is equal to the distance between H and R. Since we essentially relocated the point along the circumference of a circle, $\overline{GR}$ and $\overline{HR}$ are both radii of the circle. (See Geometry, Lesson 9, to learn more about circles.)

Dilation

Dilation is the act of stretching or shrinking an object about a fixed point known as the center of dilation. This center of dilation provides direction for the action, as without it a given dilation could otherwise be performed in an infinite number of directions. Note that, as the end result is *not* the same size as the original, dilation is not a rigid motion.

Example 4: Draw the dilation of point A with the center of dilation at the origin and a scale factor of 3. Label the resulting point B.

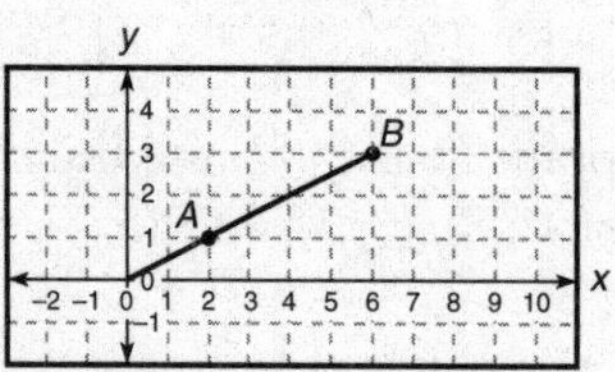

A's position relative to the center of dilation tells us that the dilation needs to be performed up and to the right. Point A was two to the right and one up from the origin, at point (2, 1), so to get a scale factor of 3, repeat those directions two more times (for a total of three times) to arrive at point (6, 3).

Example 5: Draw the dilation of square $ABCD$ with the center of dilation at point E and a scale factor of $\frac{1}{2}$.

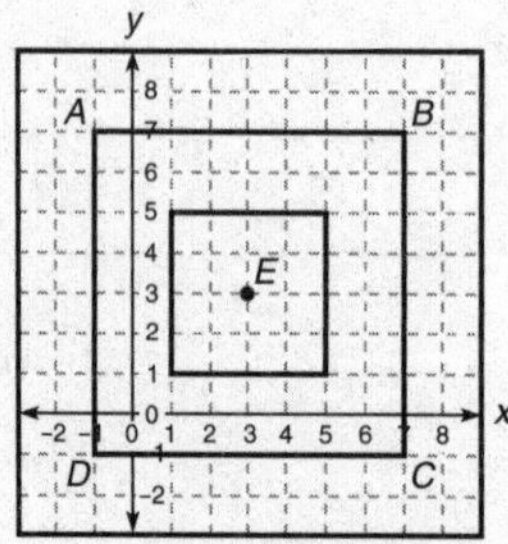

A scale factor of $\frac{1}{2}$ shrinks the figure in half.

PRACTICE 4.2

Solve.

1. Point M is at (3, 3). A dilation of point M with the center of dilation at (−1, −1) and a scale of 2 would result in which of the following points?

   A. (−3, −3)
   B. (−2, −2)
   C. (5, 5)
   D. (6, 6)
   E. (7, 7)

2. Which of the following represents a dilation of square $ABCD$ with a scale of $\frac{1}{2}$ and a center of dilation at point B?

A.
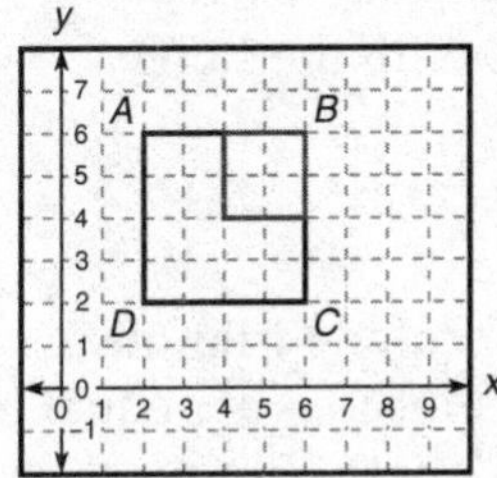

B.
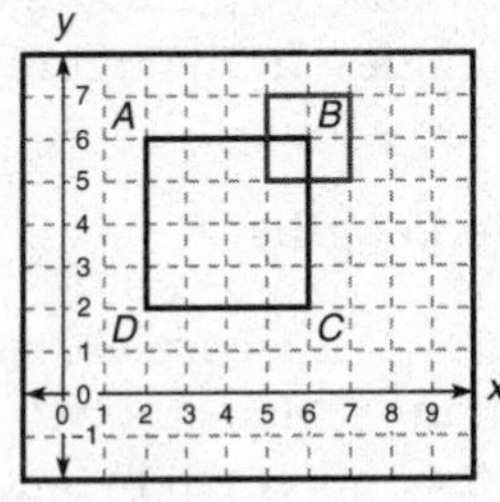

C.
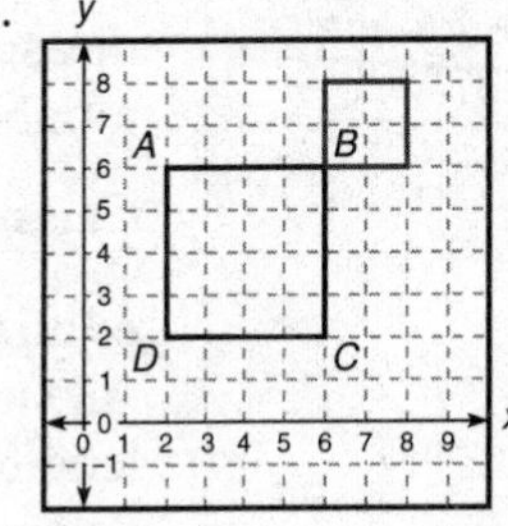

D.
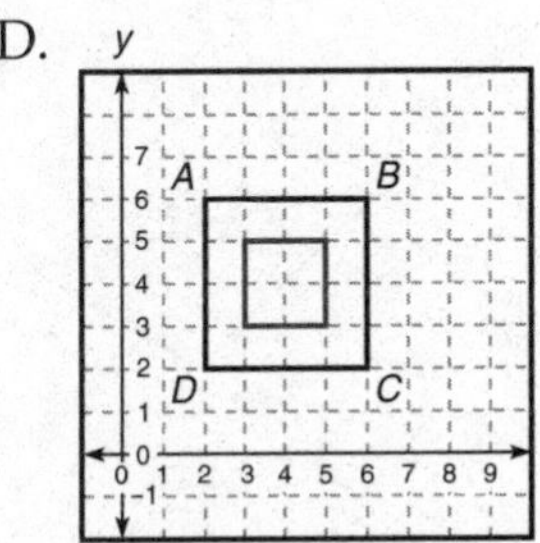

E.
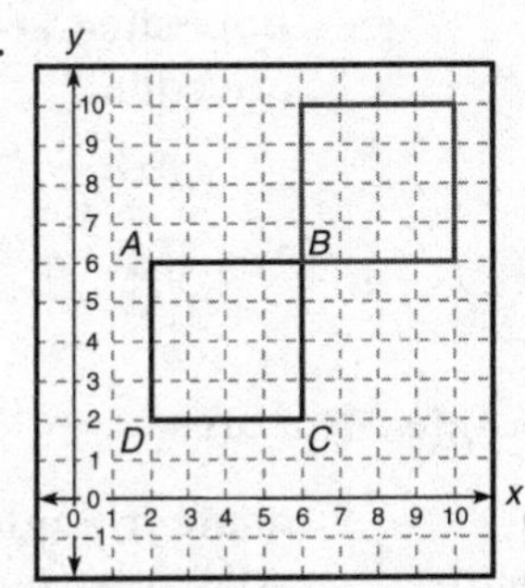

3. A 180° rotation around point R takes point P to point Q. What are the coordinates of point R?

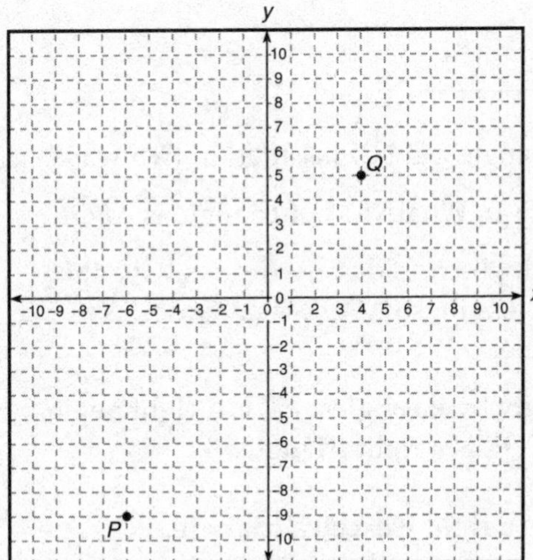

LESSON 5

Triangles

KEY IDEAS

- Triangles are named by their vertices.
- They are classified in two ways: by their side lengths and by their angle measures.
- The sum of the interior angles of any triangle is 180°.

The Properties of Triangles

A **triangle** is a closed three-sided plane figure. From the definition, we can infer other properties. Since a triangle has three sides, it must also have three interior angles and three vertices.

A triangle is named by writing its vertices in any order. The triangle shown at right could be named ΔDEF. Its sides are DE, EF, and DF.

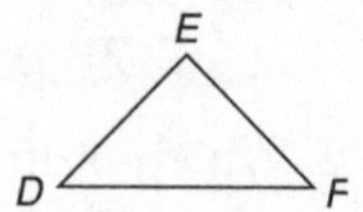

Triangles can be classified by the lengths of their sides and by the measures of their angles. In the figures below, sides with the same number of marks are equal.

Classified by Side Lengths

equilateral triangle
All sides are equal in length. Note that the angles also are equal.

isosceles triangle
Exactly two sides are equal in length. Note that the two angles opposite these sides are equal.

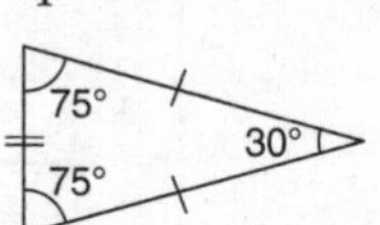

scalene triangle
No sides are equal in length, and no angles are equal.

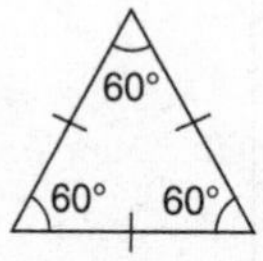

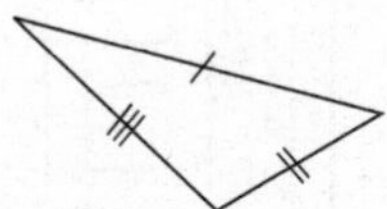

Classified by Angle Measures

HiSET EXAM TIP

Classify triangles by their properties, not by how they look. For example, the triangle in Example 1 may not immediately look like a right triangle because the right angle is at the top.

right triangle
One angle measures 90°.

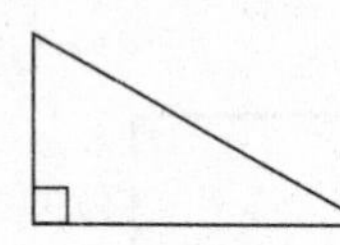

acute triangle
All angles measure less than 90°.

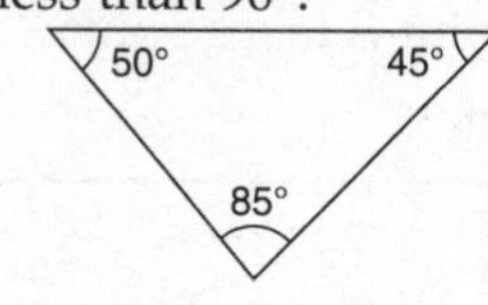

obtuse triangle
One angle is greater than 90°.

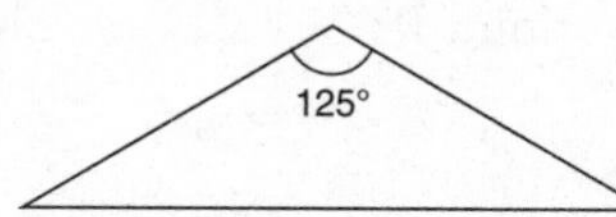

Each triangle can be classified in two ways.

Example 1: What kind of triangle is ΔPQR?

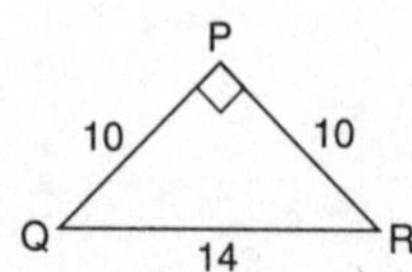

1. Classify by its sides: Two sides have the same length, so ΔPQR is an isosceles triangle.
2. Classify by its angles: $\angle P$ is a right angle, so ΔPQR is a right triangle.

ΔPQR is a **right isosceles triangle**.

PRACTICE 5

The sum of the measures of the interior angles of any triangle is 180°. We can use this fact to solve for a missing angle.

Example 2: In ΔABC, $\angle A$ measures 55° and $\angle B$ measures 100°. What is the measure of $\angle C$?

Write an equation and solve.

$$55° + 100° + \angle C = 180°$$
$$155° + \angle C = 180°$$
$$\angle C = 25°$$

The measure of $\angle C$ is **25°**.

A. Classify each triangle in two ways.

1. 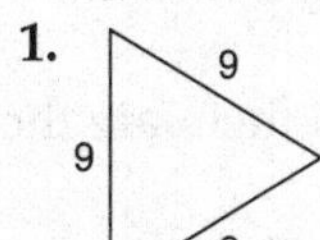

2. 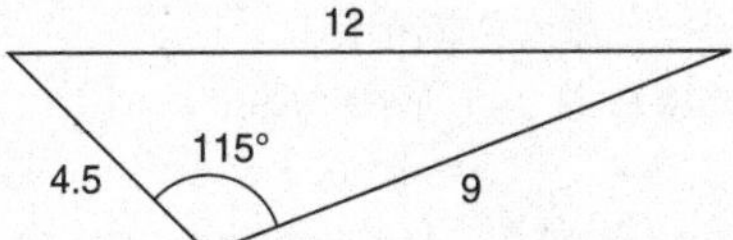

3. 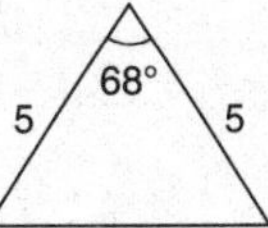

B. Find the measure of the unknown angle in each triangle.

4. 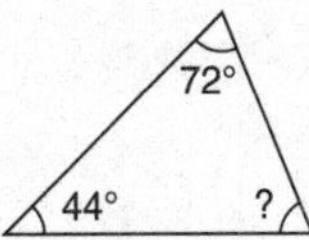

5. 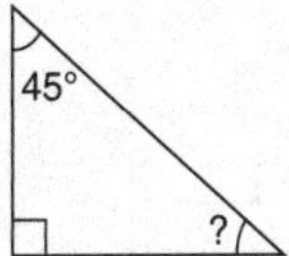

6. 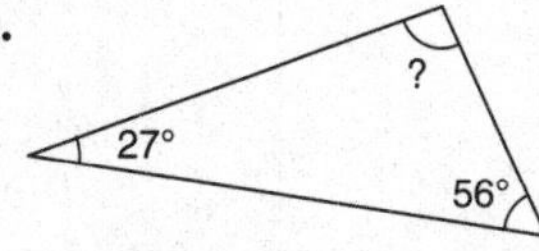

C. Choose the <u>one best answer</u> to each question.

<u>Questions 7 and 8</u> refer to the following figure.

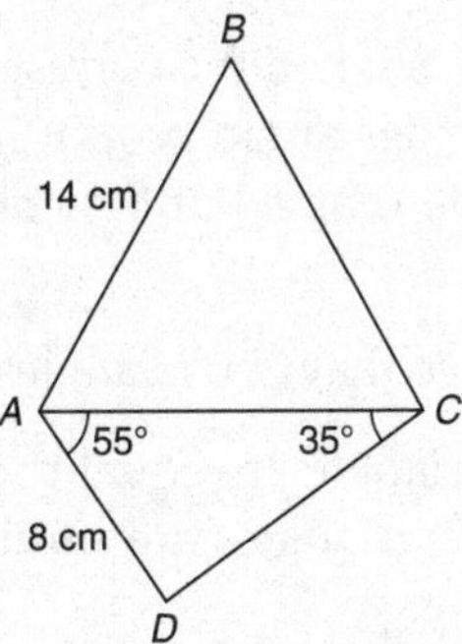

7. If $\angle DAB$ measures 115° and $\angle DCB$ measures 95°, what is the length of side AC in centimeters? (*Hint*: Use the facts in the problem to find $m\angle BAC$ and $m\angle BCA$.)
   A. 6
   B. 8
   C. 14
   D. 22
   E. 26

8. What kind of triangle is ΔACD?
   A. isosceles
   B. acute
   C. scalene
   D. obtuse
   E. right

9. One angle in a scalene triangle measures 38°, and another angle measures 56°. What is the measure of the third angle?
   A. 38°
   B. 56°
   C. 86°
   D. 94°
   E. 124°

LESSON 6

Congruent and Similar Triangles

KEY IDEAS

- Congruent figures are the same size and shape. Similar figures are the same shape, but they do not have to be the same size.
- Prove triangles are congruent using the rules SSS, SAS, or ASA.
- Triangles are similar if two angles are congruent or if all corresponding sides are in proportion.

Comparing Triangles

Figures are **congruent** (indicated by the symbol ≅) when they have exactly the same size and shape. In other words, two figures are congruent if their corresponding parts (the angles and sides) are congruent. You can often tell that two geometric shapes are congruent by looking. However, in geometry, you must be able to prove that figures are congruent.

Two triangles are congruent if the following corresponding parts are congruent:

Side-Side-Side (SSS)	The side measures for both triangles are the same.
Side-Angle-Side (SAS)	Two sides and the angle between them are the same.
Angle-Side-Angle (ASA)	Two angles and the side between them are the same.

Example 1: Are triangles *ABD* and *BCD* congruent?

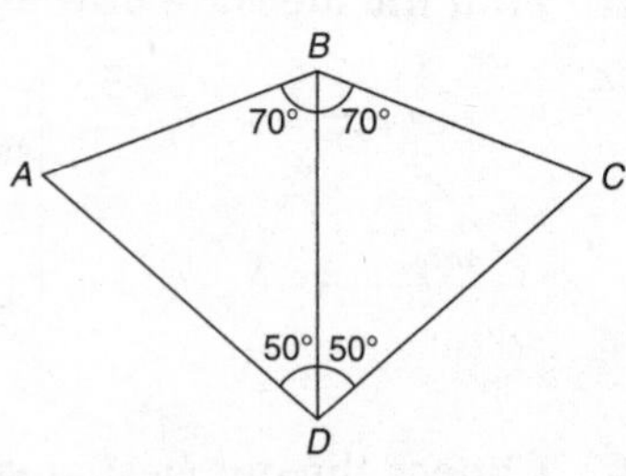

1. Find the known corresponding parts: $\angle ABD \cong \angle CBD$ and $\angle ADB \cong \angle CDB$. Both triangles share side *BD*.
2. Is this enough information to prove the triangles are congruent? Yes, two angles and the side between them are equal. Using the ASA rule, $\Delta ABD \cong \Delta BCD$.

Understanding Similarity

Figures are **similar** (shown by the symbol ~) when the corresponding angles are congruent and the corresponding sides are in proportion. In other words, similar figures always have the same shape, but they do not have to be the same size.

There are two rules that you can use to prove that two triangles are similar:

Rule 1: If two angle measures in the first triangle are equal to two angle measures in the second triangle, the triangles are similar.

Rule 2: If all corresponding sides have the same ratio, the triangles are similar.

Example 2: Are triangles *JKL* and *MNO* similar?

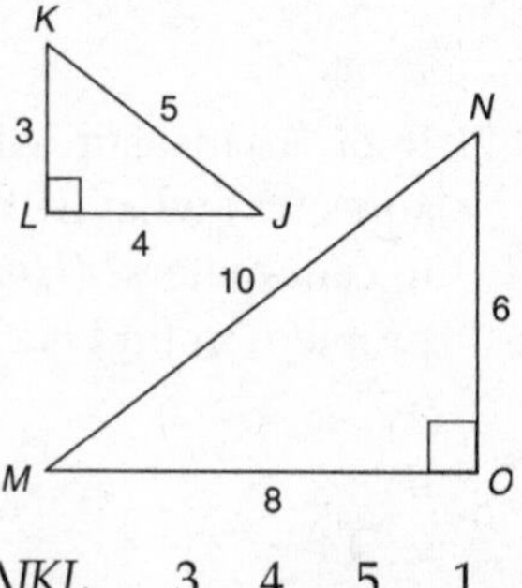

1. Compare corresponding angles. Since only one angle measure is given, you cannot use Rule 1 to prove the triangles are similar.
2. Write ratios comparing the sides in the first triangle to the corresponding sides in the second triangle. Each ratio is equal to $\frac{1}{2}$.

$$\frac{\Delta JKL}{\Delta MNO} \quad \frac{3}{6}=\frac{4}{8}=\frac{5}{10}=\frac{1}{2}$$

Because the ratios are equal, the triangles are similar: **ΔJKL ~ ΔMNO.**

HiSET EXAM TIP

When a figure is flipped or turned, it may be difficult to identify corresponding parts. Try redrawing one of the figures so that it is turned to match the first figure. Always label your sketch carefully.

If you know that two triangles are similar, you can use proportion to find an unknown measure.

Example 3: $\Delta XYZ \sim \Delta STU$. What is the measure of side ST?

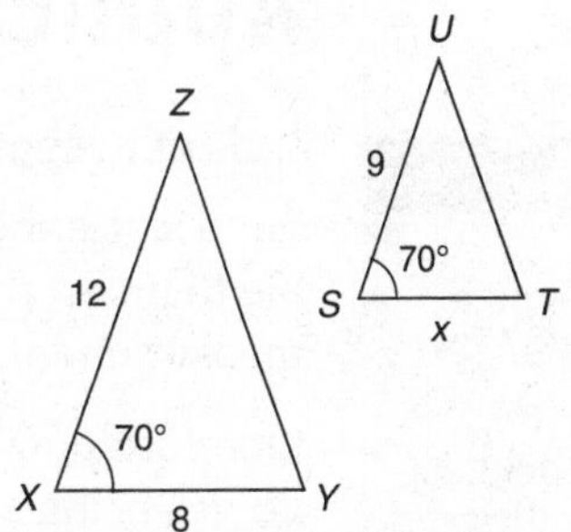

Side SU corresponds to side XZ, and side ST corresponds to side XY. Set up a proportion and solve.

$$\frac{SU}{XZ} = \frac{ST}{XY} \quad \frac{9}{12} = \frac{x}{8} \qquad 12x = 72 \quad x = 6$$

Side ST measures **6 units.**

A. For these items, the figures are not drawn to scale. Decide whether the triangles are congruent. Write *Yes, No,* or *Not Enough Information.*

1.

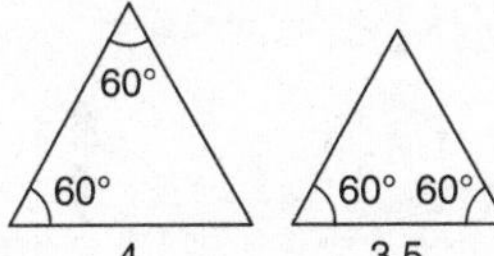

2.

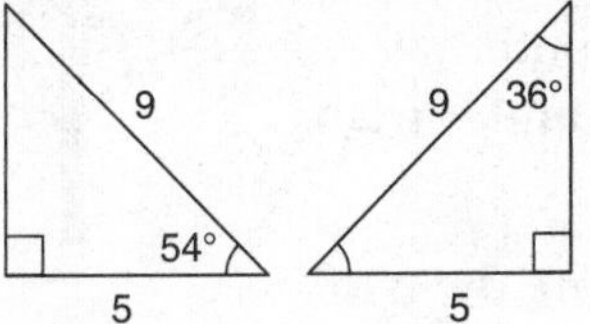

3.

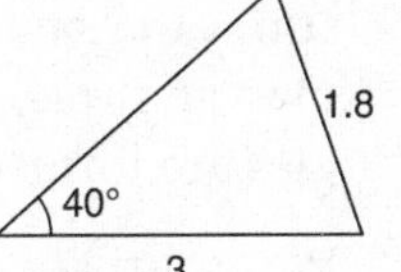

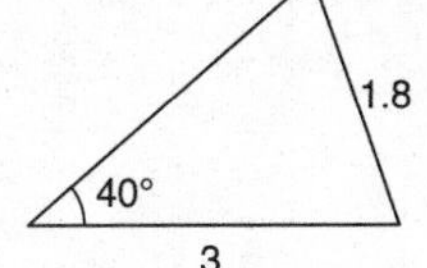

B. Choose the <u>one best answer</u> to each question.

<u>Questions 4 and 5</u> refer to the following figure.

R, X, 40, 25, T, S, Y

$\Delta RST \sim \Delta XYT$

4. What is the measure of side ST if side YT measures 30 units?

A. 40
B. 45
C. 48
D. 55
E. 65

5. If $m\angle S = 68°$ and $m\angle T = 48°$, what is the measure of $\angle TXY$?

A. 48°
B. 64°
C. 68°
D. 88°
E. 116°

<u>Question 6</u> refers to the following figure.

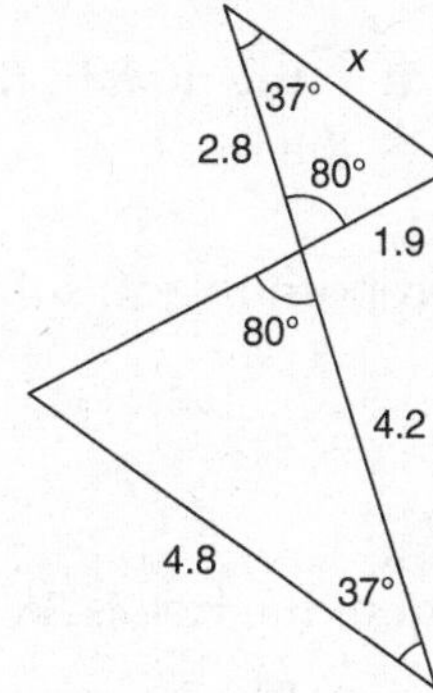

6. What is the measure of the side labeled x?

A. 2.5
B. 2.9
C. 3.2
D. 3.8
E. 4.2

LESSON 7

Similar Triangle Applications

KEY IDEAS

- Use triangle relationships to indirectly measure distances.
- Objects and their shadows form similar triangles because the sun strikes both at the same angle.
- Use the corresponding angles and sides in similar triangles to measure the distance across a large object.

HiSET EXAM TIP

Sometimes you can easily see the scale used in a problem. In Example 1, the tree's shadow is six times the man's shadow; therefore, the tree's height must be six times the man's height: 6 × 6 = 36 ft.

Indirect Measurement

Similar triangles are often used to measure objects that would be impossible to measure using ordinary tools. This process is called **indirect measurement.**

One common application involves using shadows to find the height of a tall object. In the diagram, both a man and a tree cast shadows at the same time of day. Since the angle of the sun is the same for both the man and tree, two similar triangles are formed.

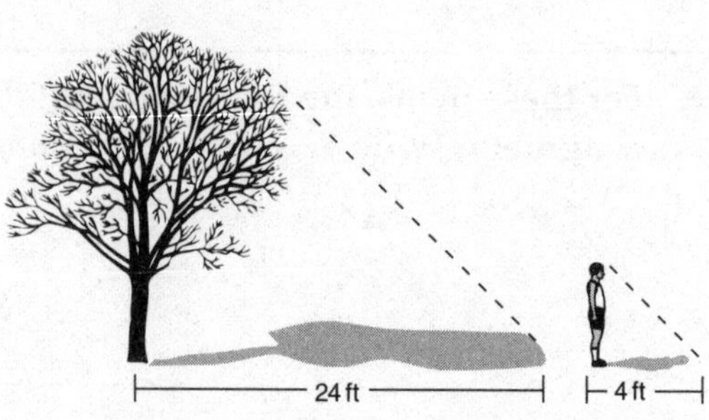

We can easily measure the two shadows using ordinary tools. We can also measure the man's height. Using these facts, we can solve for the height of the tree.

Example 1: If the man in the diagram is 6 feet tall, what is the height of the tree?

Write a proportion and solve. $\frac{\text{man's shadow}}{\text{tree's shadow}} \quad \frac{4}{24} = \frac{6}{x} = \frac{\text{man's height}}{\text{tree's height}}$

$$24(6) = 4x$$
$$144 = 4x$$
$$36 = x$$

The height of the tree is **36 feet.**

We also use indirect measurement to measure distance across a large object.

Example 2: An engineer needs to know the width of a small lake. Using surveyor's tools, she marks off two similar triangles. She measures the distances shown on the diagram. Using her findings, what is the width of the lake?

The 10-ft side corresponds to the 25-ft side. The 24-ft side of the small triangle corresponds to the lake's width.

$\frac{10}{25} = \frac{24}{x}$

$$25(24) = 10x$$
$$600 = 10x$$
$$60 = x$$

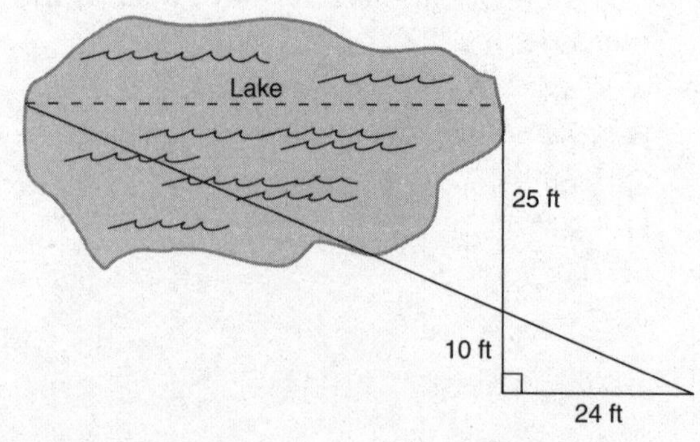

The lake is **60 feet wide.**

PRACTICE 7

Choose the one best answer to each question.

1. An 8-foot-tall street sign casts a 6-foot shadow at the same time that a building casts a 48-foot shadow. How many feet tall is the building?

   A. 36
   B. 54
   C. 64
   D. 96
   E. 144

Question 2 refers to the following diagram.

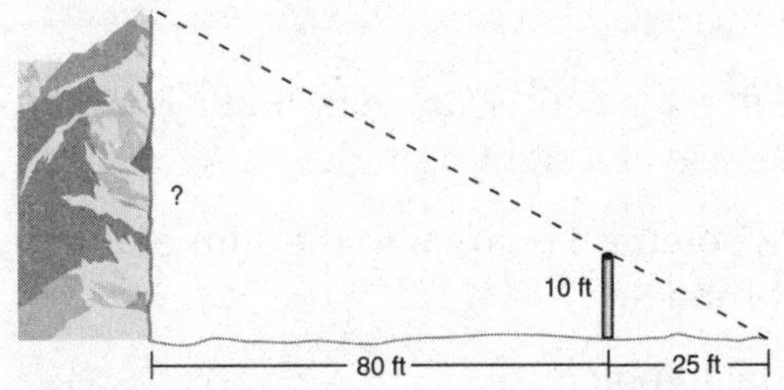

2. To find the height of a cliff, a surveyor puts a 10-foot pole in the ground, 80 feet from the base of the cliff. He then determines the point on the ground from which he can sight both the top of the pole and top of the cliff. Using the distances shown in the diagram, what is the height of the cliff?

   A. 32
   B. 42
   C. 105
   D. 200
   E. 224

3. A meter stick is placed in the ground near a flagpole. At the time that the meter stick casts a shadow 2.5 meters in length, the flagpole casts a shadow 22.5 meters long. Which of the following proportions can be used to find the height of the flagpole (x) in meters?

   A. $\frac{2.5}{22.5} = \frac{1}{x}$
   B. $\frac{22.5}{2.5} = \frac{1}{x}$
   C. $\frac{1}{2.5} = \frac{22.5}{x}$
   D. $\frac{22.5}{1} = \frac{x}{2.5}$
   E. $\frac{2.5}{1} = \frac{22.5}{x}$

Question 4 refers to the following diagram.

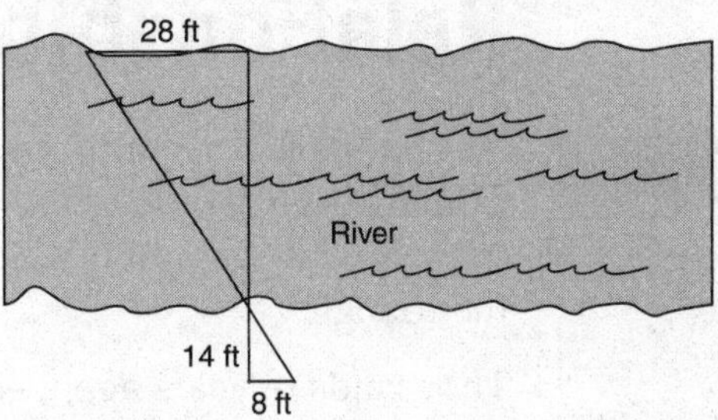

4. To find the distance across a river, a surveyor marks off two similar right triangles. Using the distances shown in the diagram, what is the distance, in feet, from one bank of the river to the other?

   A. 36
   B. 39
   C. 42
   D. 49
   E. 54

5. Phil is building a frame to hold a hammock. He wants to place a metal brace across the frame as shown in the drawing below. If he places the brace as shown in the diagram, what will be the length of the brace in feet?

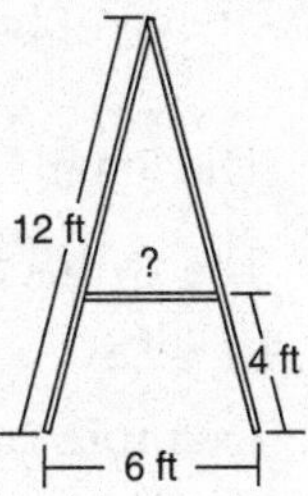

   A. 3
   B. 4
   C. 6
   D. 8
   E. 10

LESSON 8

Pythagorean Relationship

KEY IDEAS

- The hypotenuse is the longest side of a right triangle. It is found opposite the right angle.
- The sum of the squares of the legs of a right triangle equals the square of the hypotenuse.

As you know, a right triangle has one right angle. The side directly across from the right angle, called the **hypotenuse**, is the longest side of the right triangle. The remaining sides, the rays of the right angle, are the **legs** of the triangle.

Thousands of years ago, people found a special relationship, called the **Pythagorean relationship**, among the sides of a right triangle. You can use this relationship to find the measure of any side of a right triangle if the other two side measures are known.

Pythagorean relationship $a^2 + b^2 = c^2$; a and b are legs, and c is the hypotenuse of a right triangle

In other words, the square of the hypotenuse is equal to the sum of the squares of the two legs of the right triangle.

Example 1: What is the length of the hypotenuse of the right triangle shown in the diagram?

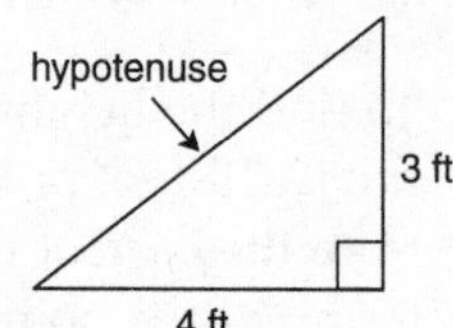

1. The lengths of the legs are 3 ft and 4 ft. Let one leg equal a and the other equal b.
2. Solve for c. Substitute the values.
3. When one side of an equation equals a squared variable, isolate the variable by finding the square root of both sides.

$$a^2 + b^2 = c^2$$
$$3^2 + 4^2 = c^2$$
$$9 + 16 = c^2$$
$$25 = c^2$$
$$\sqrt{25} = c$$
$$5 = c$$

The length of the hypotenuse is **5 feet**.

HiSET EXAM TIP

Watch for right triangles with sides in a 3-4-5 or 5-12-13 ratio. These triangles often appear on math tests because the measures of the sides are all whole numbers.

The Pythagorean relationship can also be used to solve for the length of a leg.

Example 2: If John places a 13-foot ladder 3 feet from the base of a wall, how far up the wall will the ladder reach to the nearest tenth foot?

The wall, ground, and ladder form a right triangle. The hypotenuse is 13 ft in length. One leg is 3 ft. You need to find the length of the other leg.

$$a^2 + b^2 = c^2$$
$$3^2 + b^2 = 13^2$$
$$9 + b^2 = 169$$
$$b^2 = 160$$
$$b = \sqrt{160}$$
$$b \approx 12.6$$

The ladder will extend **12.6 feet** up the wall.

Note: Most of the time, you will need to use your calculator for the final step when using the Pythagorean relationship. To find the square root of 160 on the TI-30XS MultiView™ calculator, press: [2nd] [x^2] 160 [enter] (use [◄►] to convert the result from a radical to a decimal format).

PRACTICE 8

Some right triangles display special proportions, which are worth memorizing.
A right triangle whose angles are 45°, 45°, and 90° displays the following relationship: leg:leg:hypotenuse = x:x:x.
A right triangle whose angles are 30°, 60°, and 90° displays the following relationship: leg:leg:hypotenuse = x:x:$2x$.

A. The lengths of two sides of a right triangle are given. Find the length of the remaining side to the nearest tenth unit.

1. leg a: 8 in
leg b: 8 in
hypotenuse c: ? in

2. leg a: 9 yd
leg b: 12 yd
hypotenuse c: ? yd

3. leg a: 1.5 cm
leg b: 2 cm
hypotenuse c: ? cm

4. leg a: ? m
leg b: 3 m
hypotenuse c: 6 m

5. leg a: 6 mm
leg b: ? mm
hypotenuse c: 10 mm

6. leg a: ? ft
leg b: 5 ft
hypotenuse c: 18 ft

7. leg a: 7 cm
leg b: 10 cm
hypotenuse c: ? cm

8. leg a: 15 in
leg b: ? in
hypotenuse c: 30 in

9. leg a: 4 km
leg b: 5 km
hypotenuse c: ? km

B. Choose the one best answer to each question.

10. On a coordinate plane, points A, B, and C can be connected to form a right triangle.

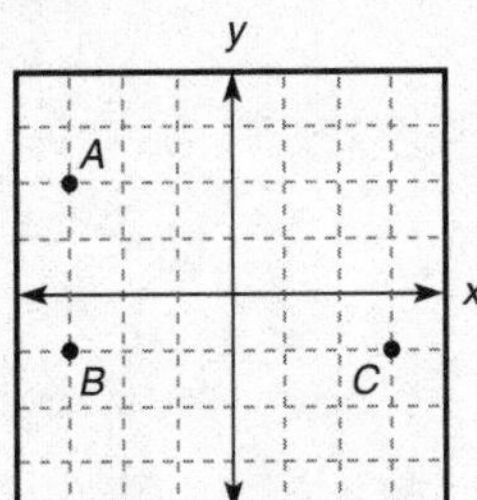

What is the distance from A to C, to the nearest tenth unit? (*Hint:* Count units to find the lengths of the sides, and use the Pythagorean relationship to find the distance between the points.)

A. 5.2
B. 6.7
C. 8.4
D. 10.1
E. 11.3

11. The two shorter sides of a right triangle measure 18 ft and 24 ft. What is the measure in feet of the third side?

A. 25
B. 28
C. 30
D. 42
E. 48

12. Jan has built a rectangular frame out of wood to use for the bottom of a platform. He wants to add a diagonal brace as shown in the drawing below.

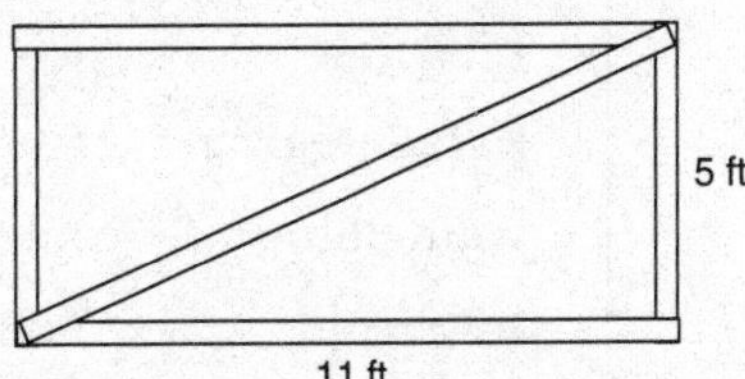

What will the length of the brace be, to the nearest tenth of a foot?

A. 16.0
B. 14.2
C. 13.7
D. 12.8
E. 12.1

13. The hypotenuse of a right triangle measures 39 inches. If one leg measures 15 inches, what is the measure of the other leg, in inches?

A. 12
B. 15
C. 18
D. 24
E. 36

Geometry

LESSON 9

Perimeter and Area

KEY IDEAS

- Perimeter is the distance around a figure.
- Area is the measure of the space inside a flat figure. It is measured in square units.
- You need to memorize the formulas on this page except those for area of a parallelogram, area of a triangle, and area of a trapezoid.

Perimeter is the distance around a figure. To find perimeter, simply add the lengths of the sides. For common figures, you can apply a formula to find the perimeter. You need to memorize these formulas.

square	Perimeter = 4 × side	$P = 4s$
rectangle	Perimeter = 2 × length + 2 × width	$P = 2l + 2w$
triangle	Perimeter = $\text{side}_1 + \text{side}_2 + \text{side}_3$	$P = a + b + c$

Example 1: A rectangle is 16 inches long and 9 inches wide. What is the perimeter of the rectangle?

Use the formula: Perimeter = 2 × length + 2 × width

$= 2 \times 16 + 2 \times 9$

$= 32 + 18$

$= \mathbf{50\ in}$

Area is the measure of the space inside a flat figure. Area is measured in square units. For example, if the sides of a figure are measured in inches, its area will be measured in square inches. The formulas for finding area are shown below.

square	Area = side^2	$A = s^2$
rectangle	Area = length × width	$A = lw$
parallelogram	Area = base × height	$A = bh$
triangle	Area = $\frac{1}{2}$ × base × height	$A = \frac{1}{2}bh$
trapezoid	Area = $\frac{1}{2}$ × height $(\text{base}_1 + \text{base}_2)$	$A = \frac{1}{2}h(b_1 + b_2)$

HiSET EXAM TIP

Formulas for the area of a circle, triangle, parallelogram, and trapezoid will appear on the Mathematics formula sheet.

Three of the formulas mention two new measures: base and height. The **base** is one side of the figure. The **height** is the length from the vertex to the base, forming a right angle to the base.

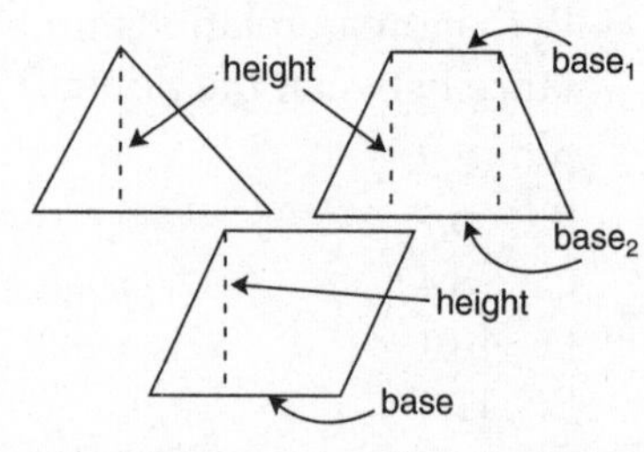

Example 2: Find the area of figure *ABCD*.

1. Identify the figure. *ABCD* is a parallelogram.
2. Find the facts you need. To use the formula for finding the area of a parallelogram, you need to know the height and the length of the base. Ignore the length of side *BD*.
3. Use the formula Area = base × height.

   Area = 12 × 7

   = **84 sq cm or 84 cm²**

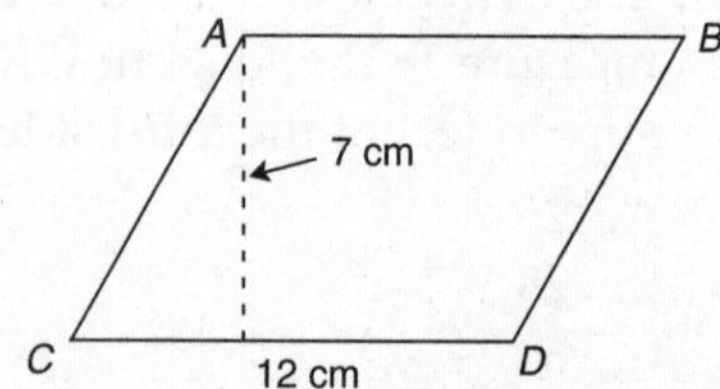

PRACTICE 9

A. Find the area and perimeter of each figure.

1\. 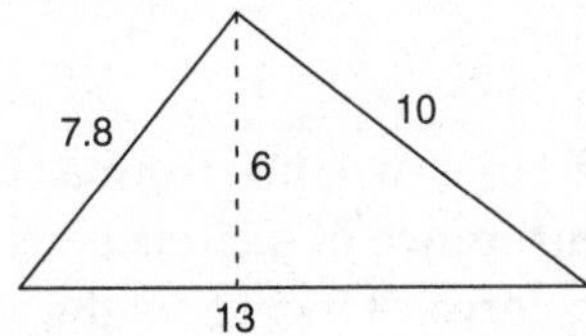

3\. 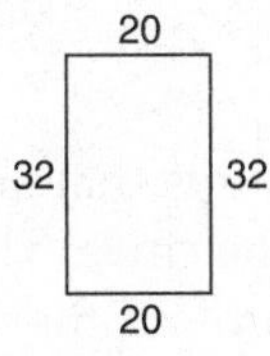

5\. 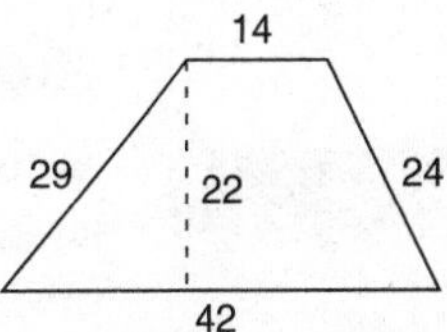

2\. 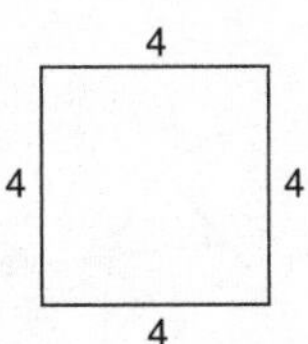

4\. 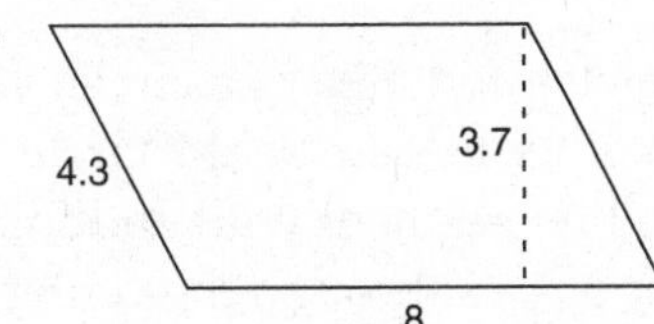

6\. 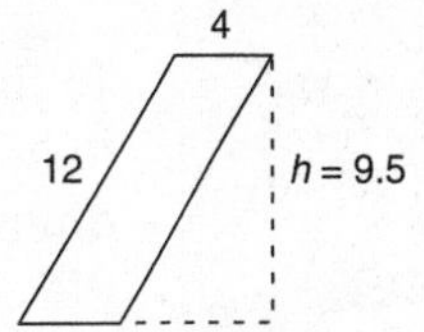

B. Choose the one best answer to each question.

Question 7 refers to the following figure.

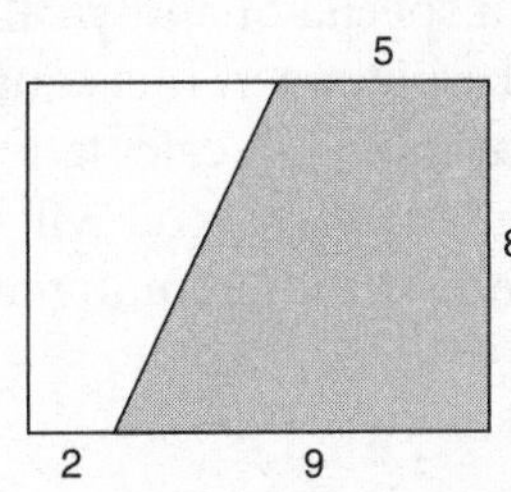

7\. What is the area in square inches of the shaded portion of the rectangle?

A. 38
B. 40
C. 56
D. 65
E. 88

8\. The four sides of a rectangle measure 9 feet, 6 feet, 9 feet, and 6 feet. What is the area of the rectangle in square feet?

A. 30
B. 36
C. 54
D. 81
E. 108

9\. Martin is building a rectangular patio centered on one side of his yard. The rest of his yard, shown in the diagram, is planted in grass.

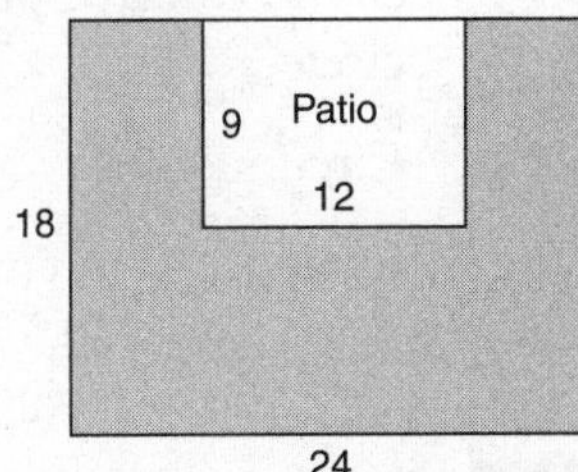

If the measurements in the diagram are in feet, what is the square footage of the grass portion of Martin's yard?

A. 108
B. 162
C. 216
D. 324
E. 432

10\. A square measures 6 centimeters on one side. What is the perimeter of the square in centimeters?

A. 12
B. 24
C. 36
D. 60
E. 216

Geometry

LESSON 10

Circles

Circumference and Area

A **circle** is a closed set of points that are all the same distance from a single point, the center of the circle. The **circumference** of a circle is its perimeter, or the distance around the circle. The **area** of a circle is the space inside the circle.

To find perimeter and area of a circle, you need to know two other measures of a circle. The **diameter** is a line segment with endpoints on the circle that passes through the center of the circle. The **radius** is a line segment that connects the center of the circle to any point on the circle. As you can see from the diagram, the radius is one-half the diameter.

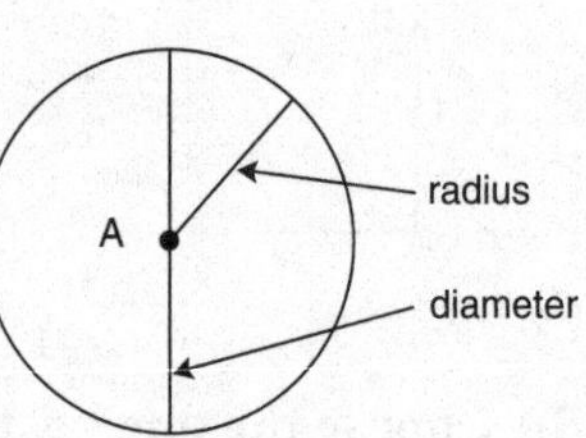

The formulas for circumference and area use a special quantity called **pi** (π). Pi is the ratio of the circumference to the diameter. It is equal to approximately 3.14. The digits for pi continue infinitely, so calculations with pi are always approximations. For the Mathematics Test, you will use 3.14 as the value of pi. Below is the formula for finding the circumference of a circle.

Circumference = $\pi \times$ diameter, or $C = \pi d$

Example 1: A china plate has a gold rim. If the plate's diameter is 10.5 inches, what is the distance around the rim to the nearest tenth of an inch?

Use the formula: $C = \pi d$

$= 3.14(10.5)$

$= 32.97$, which rounds to **33.0 inches**

Use this formula to find the area of a circle: Area = $\pi \times$ radius^2, or $A = \pi r^2$.

Example 2: The circular surface of a satellite component must be covered with heat-resistant tiles. If the radius of the component is 4 meters, what is the area in square meters?

Use the formula: $A = \pi r^2$

$= 3.14(4^2)$

$= 3.14(16)$

$=$ **50.24 square meters**

In some situations, you may need to solve for either the diameter or radius. Remember, the diameter is twice the radius ($d = 2r$), and the radius is one-half the diameter: $r = \frac{1}{2}d$.

KEY IDEAS

- Pi, expressed as 3.14, is the ratio of the circumference of a circle to its diameter.
- To find circumference, multiply pi by the diameter (distance across) the circle.
- The radius is the distance from the center to the edge of the circle. To find area, multiply pi by the square of the radius.

HiSET EXAM TIP

Formulas for circumference, perimeter, and area will appear on the Mathematics formula sheet.

Example 3: What is the circumference of circle B to the nearest tenth of a centimeter?

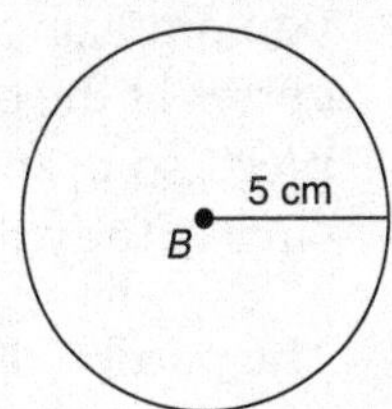

1. The radius of the circle is 5 cm. Therefore, the diameter is 2×5, or 10 cm.

2. Use the formula: $C = \pi d$
$= 3.14(10)$
$= \mathbf{31.4\ cm}$

A. Find the circumference and area of each circle. Round answers to the nearest tenth.

1.

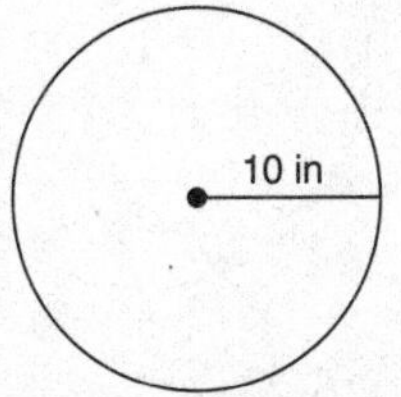

2.

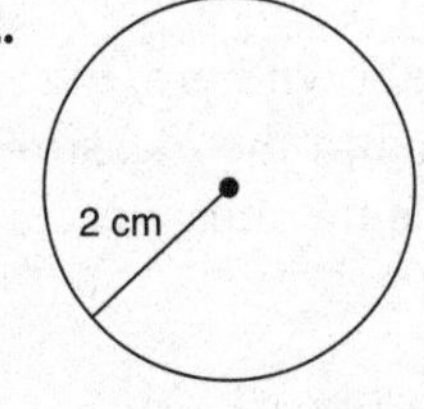

3.

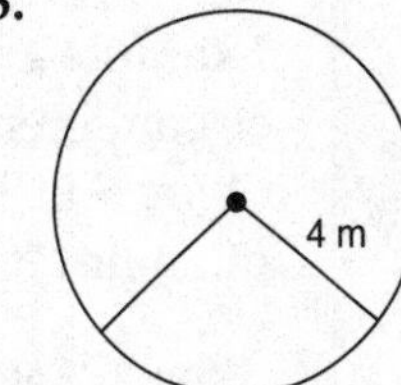

B. Choose the one best answer to each question.

Questions 4 and 5 refer to the following drawing.

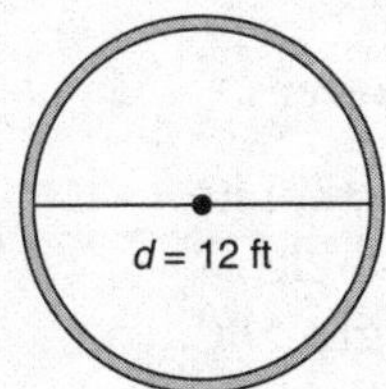

4. If workers lay a tile border around the edge of the fountain shown in the diagram, how many feet long will the border be to the nearest foot?

A. 19
B. 36
C. 38
D. 57
E. 144

5. Which of the following expressions could be used to find the area of the bottom surface of the fountain?

A. 3.14×6
B. 3.14×6^2
C. 3.14×12
D. 3.14×12^2
E. 3.14×6^3

6. The radius of a circle is 6.5 cm. What is the diameter of the circle in centimeters?

A. 3.25
B. 13.0
C. 20.4204
D. 33.16625
E. 132.665

7. On the target below, the 5- and 10-point bands are each 2 inches wide, and the inner circle has a diameter of 2 inches.

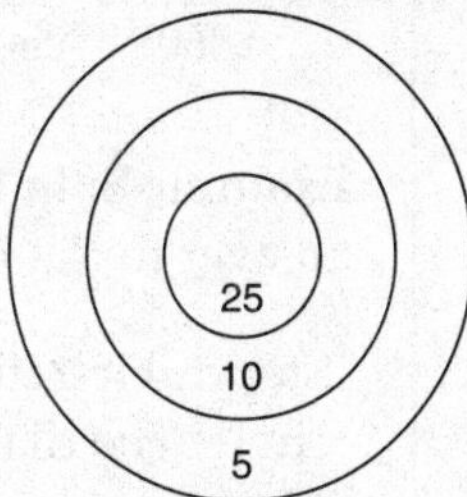

To the nearest inch, what is the outer circumference of the 10-point band?

A. 6
B. 13
C. 19
D. 25
E. 31

KEY IDEAS

- A circle represents 360 degrees.
- An arc is a portion of the circumference of a circle. Its length can be calculated if you know the circumference of the circle and the degree measure of the angle that defines that arc.
- A chord is a straight line whose end points fall on the circumference of a circle.

HiSET EXAM TIP

The Mathematics formula sheet does NOT contain formulas related to chords and arcs so you will have to memorize these.

Interior Angles, Arcs, and Chords

You have learned that angles are measured in degrees. A circle represents 360 degrees. If you draw an angle of x degrees with the vertex at the center of the circle, that pie piece, so to speak, will take up $\frac{x}{360}$ of the circle. Study the following diagram:

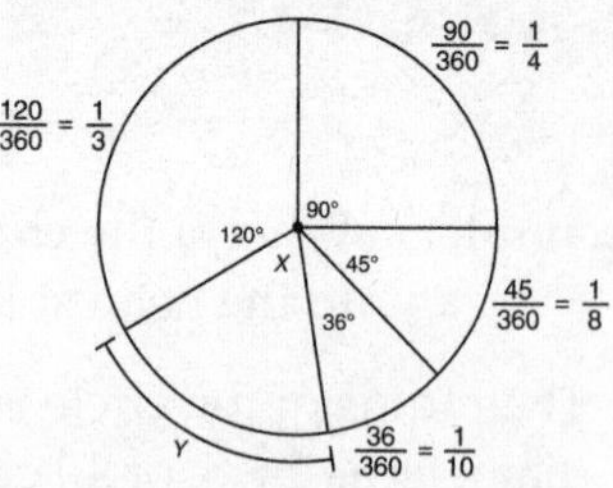

The portion of a circle's circumference that forms the outside of a "pie piece" is called an **arc.** The length of an arc has the same proportional relationship to the circumference that its angle does to 360. In the previous diagram:

$$\frac{\text{length of } Y}{\text{circumference}} = \frac{m\angle X}{360}$$

Example 4: In the circle shown here, the circumference is 400 feet and the measure of arc S is 50 feet. What is the measure of angle AOB?

Step 1: Set up the proportion. $\quad \frac{50}{400} = \frac{mAOB}{360}$

Step 2: Cross multiply and divide to solve the proportion. $\quad 400 \times mAOB = 50 \times 360$

The measure of angle AOB is **45 degrees.** $\quad mAOB = \frac{18{,}000}{400} = 45$

Now suppose you drew an angle so that its vertex was not on the center of the circle but on one side of the circle, like angle ABC. You could still use a proportion to find the length of arc Q. However, the proportion is different:

$$2 \times \frac{mABC}{360} = \frac{\text{length of arc } Q}{\text{circumference of circle}}$$

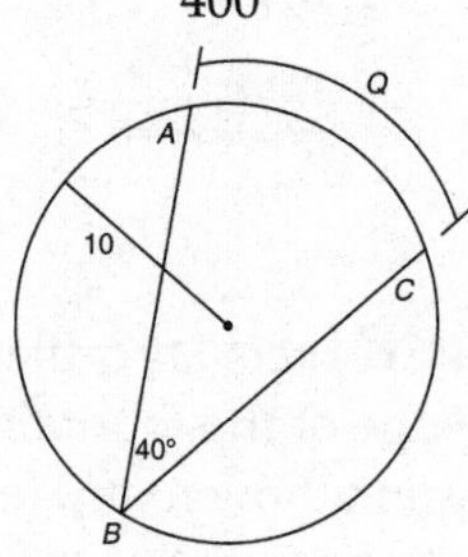

Example 5: In the circle shown, what is the length of arc Q? Round your answer to the nearest tenth.

Step 1: First, find the circumference of the circle. The diagram shows that the radius is 10 units. $\quad C = 20\pi \approx 62.8$

Step 2: Set up the proportion. Simplify.

$$2 \times \frac{40}{360} = \frac{\textit{length of arc } Q}{62.8}$$

$$\frac{2}{9} = \frac{\textit{length of arc } Q}{62.8}$$

Step 3: Cross multiply to solve. $\quad 62.8 \times 2 \div 9 \approx \mathbf{14}$

Arc Q is **14 units** long.

PRACTICE 10.2

A **chord** is a straight line that has its endpoints on the circumference of a circle. You can find the length of a chord if you know the circle's radius and how far the midpoint of the chord is from the center of the circle. That's because the radius forms the hypotenuse of a right triangle, as shown in the diagram.

Example 6: In the circle shown, what is the length of chord *AB*?

Step 1: One leg of the right triangle is 3, and the hypotenuse is 5. Set up an equation based on the Pythagorean relationship.	$(\text{length of } XB)^2 + 3^2 = 5^2$
Step 2: Solve for the length of *XB*.	$(\text{length of } XB)^2 = 16$ $(\text{length of } XB) = 4$
Step 3: Because *XB* is only half of chord *AB*, double the result to find the length of chord *AB*. Chord *AB* is **8 units** long.	$4 \times 2 = 8$

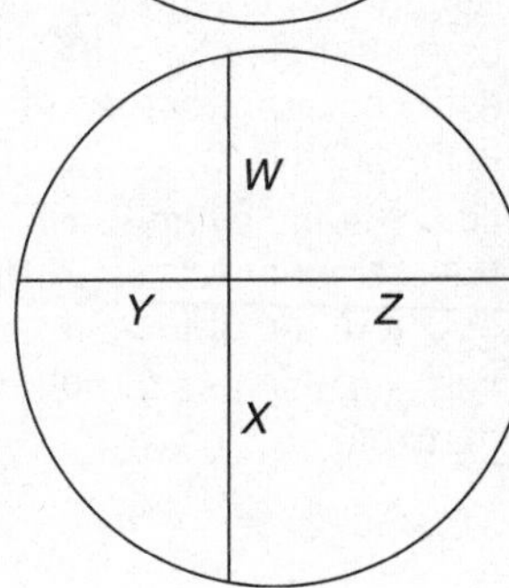

Two chords that intersect have the following relationship:

length of $W \times$ length of $X =$ length of $Y \times$ length of Z

A. For each of the following circles, find either the measure of the angle marked X or the length of the chord marked Y. Use 3.14 for pi, and round your answer to the nearest unit.

1.

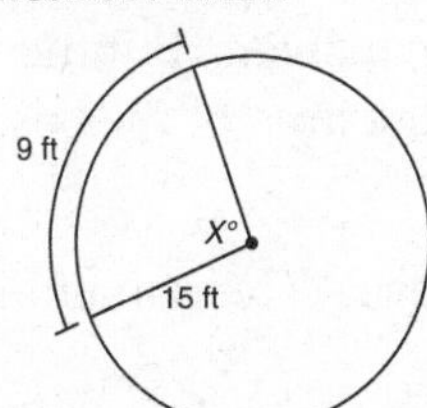

2.

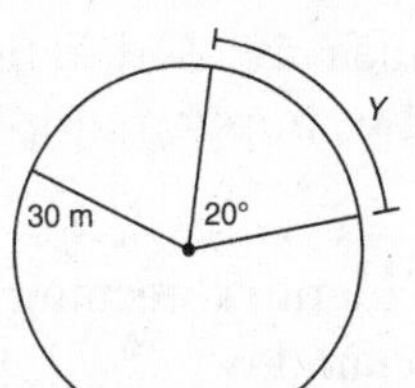

3.

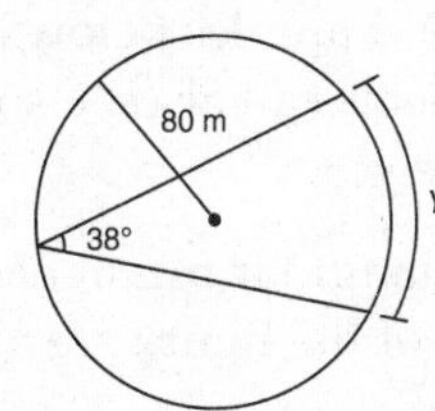

B. Choose the <u>one best answer</u> to each question.

4. In the following circle, what is the length of A in meters?

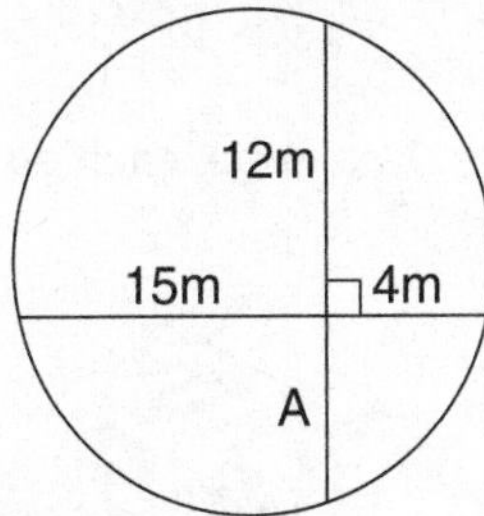

A. 4
B. 5
C. 6
D. 10
E. 12

5. In the following circle, what is the length of chord *LM*?

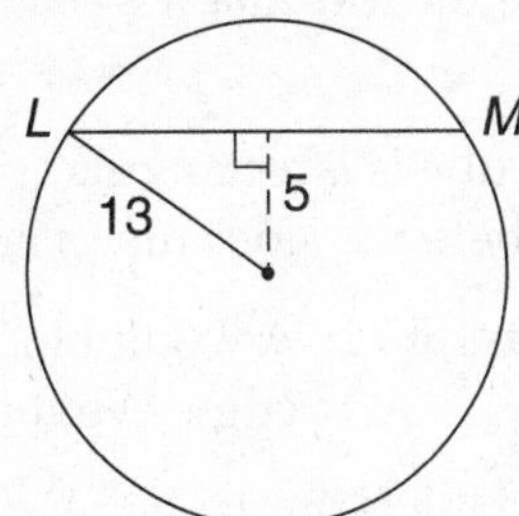

A. 12
B. 14
C. 24
D. 26
E. 36

LESSON 11

Volume

Rectangular Solids, Cubes, Cylinders, and Spheres

Volume, also called **capacity**, is the measure of space inside a three-dimensional object. You measure volume in cubic units. In other words, if the sides of an object are measured in inches, the volume is the number of cubes (one inch per side) you would need to fill the object.

Many common three-dimensional objects have at least two identical and parallel faces. Think of a cereal box or a soup can. Both objects have identical faces at the top and bottom of the container. Either of these faces can be called the base of the object. To find the volume of any container with identical bases, multiply the area of one base by the height of the object: Volume = area of base × height.

Another way to find the volume of an object is to use the formula that applies specifically to that object.

rectangular prism	Volume = base × height	$V = Bh$
cube	Volume = edge^3	$V = e^3$
cylinder	Volume = pi × radius^2 × height	$V = \pi r^2 h$
sphere	Volume = $\frac{4}{3}$ × pi × radius^3	$V = \frac{4}{3}\pi r^3$

In the examples below, formulas are used to find the answers, but the problems can also be solved by simply multiplying the area of the base by the height.

A **rectangular prism** has two identical rectangular bases. The remaining sides of the figure are also rectangles.

Example 1: A cardboard box has the dimensions shown in the diagram. What is the volume of the box in cubic feet?

3 ft
5 ft
4 ft

Use the formula: $V = Bh$, where B is *length* × *width*
$= (4 \times 5)(3) =$ **60 cubic feet**

A **cube** is a rectangular prism with six identical faces. In a cube, each edge (where the sides meet) is the same length.

Example 2: A wood block measures 2 inches per edge. What is the volume of the block?

E
A B

Use the formula: $V = e^3$
$= 2^3 =$ **8 cubic inches**

A **cylinder** has two circular bases. The bases are connected by a curved surface. Cans, barrels, and tanks are often in the shape of cylinders.

KEY IDEAS

- Volume is measured in cubic units that may be written using an exponent: 6 cubic inches or 6 in^3.
- Find volume by multiplying the area of one base by the height of the object.
- You can also use formulas to find volume.

HiSET EXAM TIP

Learn which area formula goes with which shape. Once you know the area formulas for rectangular prisms, cubes, and cylinders, you can change them to volume by putting an h at the end. Compare:
Area of circle: πr^2
Volume of cylinder: $\pi r^2 h$

PRACTICE 11.1

Example 3: A storage tank has a radius of 1.5 meters and a height of 3 meters. What is the volume of the tank to the nearest cubic meter?

1.5 m
3 m

Use the formula: $V = \pi r^2 h$

$= 3.14(1.5^2)(3) = 21.195 \text{ m}^3$,

which rounds to **21 cubic meters**

A. Find the volume of each object to the nearest whole unit.

1.

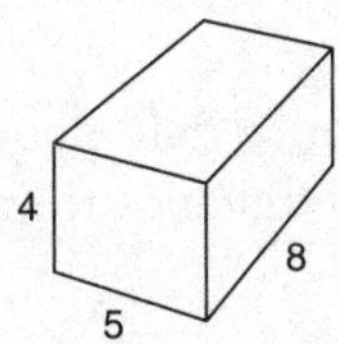

2.

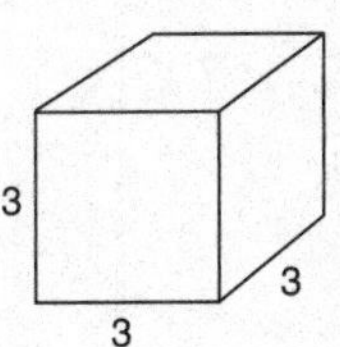

3.

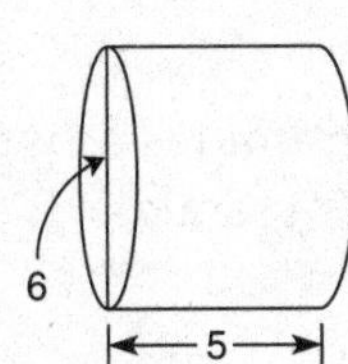

4.

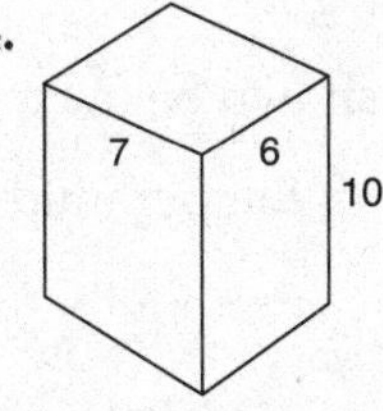

5.

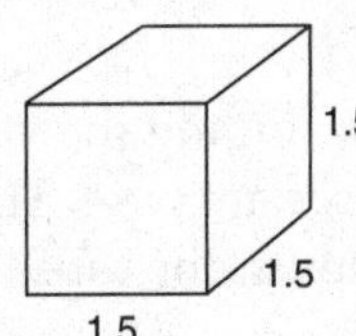

6.

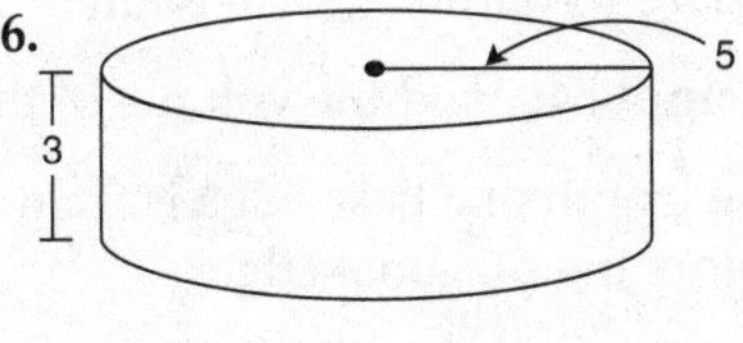

B. Choose the <u>one best answer</u> to each question.

<u>Question 7</u> refers to the following drawing.

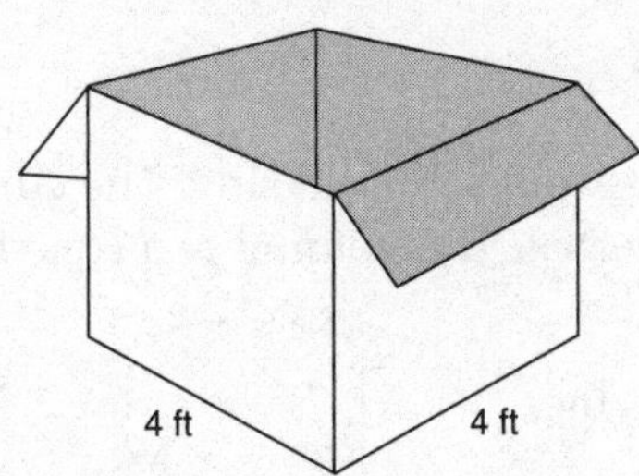

7. A rectangular box with a volume of 80 cubic feet has the length and width shown in the drawing. What is the height of the box?

   A. 5
   B. 10
   C. 16
   D. 20
   E. 24

8. A wooden crate measures 5 feet along each edge. What is the crate's volume in cubic feet?

   A. 15
   B. 25
   C. 125
   D. 150
   E. 225

<u>Question 9</u> refers to the following drawing.

9. Linda adds a water stabilizer to her children's swimming pool once a week. The instructions tell her to add one scoop of the product for every 20 cubic feet of water. About how many scoops should she add per week?

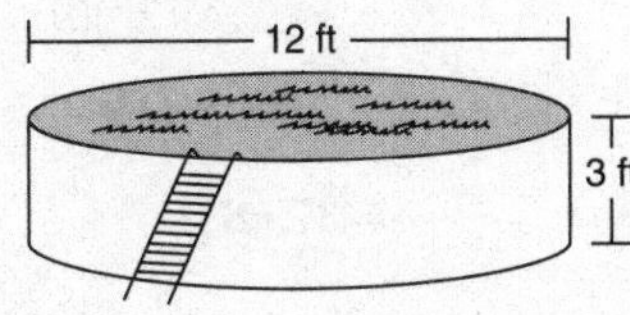

   A. 3
   B. 6
   C. 9
   D. 17
   E. 36

Volume of Pyramids and Cones

A **pyramid** is a three-dimensional object with four triangle faces that connect to the same vertex. The base of a pyramid can be any closed figure, but you will likely not see pyramids with complicated bases on the HiSET exam. Here, we will focus on pyramids with square bases. But remember: If you can find the area of the base, you can find the volume of the pyramid.

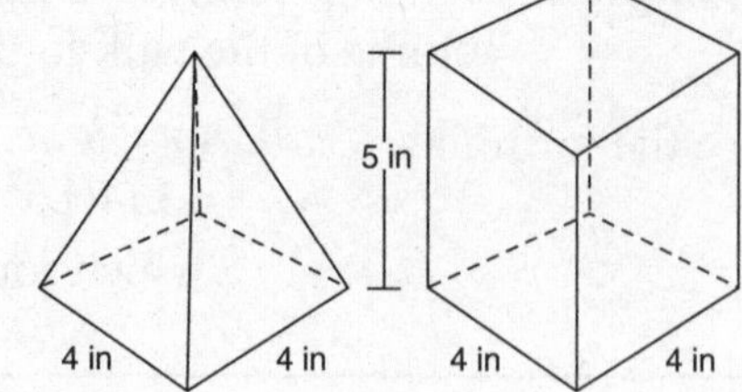

The rectangular prism and the pyramid shown here both have identical square bases and the same height. Compare the two figures. As you can see, the pyramid holds much less than the rectangular prism. In fact, it holds only one-third of the rectangular prism's volume.

The formula for finding the volume of a pyramid is as written below. Notice that *B* equals the area of the square base. The height of a pyramid is the perpendicular distance from the base to the vertex at the top.

square pyramid Volume $= \frac{1}{3} \times \text{base} \times \text{height}$

Example 4: Find the volume of the pyramid shown below.

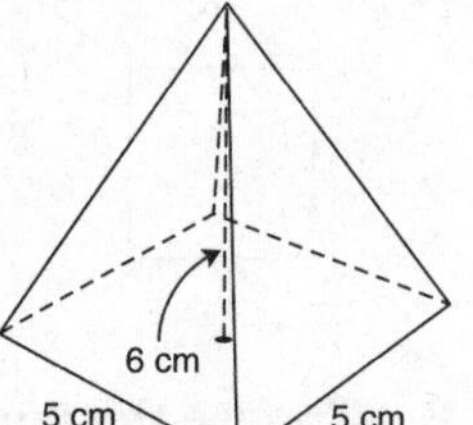

The length of a base edge is 5 cm. The height of the pyramid is 6 cm. Ignore the diagonal edges.

Apply the formula: $V = \frac{1}{3}Bh$

$$= \frac{1}{3}(5^2)(6)$$

$$= \frac{1}{3}(25)(6)$$

$$= \mathbf{50\ cm^3}$$

A **cone** is similar to a cylinder. Both have a circular base and a curved side. The curved side of a cone slants inward so that it meets at a point, or vertex. The volume of a cone is $\frac{1}{3}$ of the volume of a cylinder with the same size base and height.

Notice that the formula for the volume of a cone contains the formula for finding the area of a circle (πr^2).

cone Volume $= \frac{1}{3} \times \pi \times \text{radius}^2 \times \text{height}$

Example 5: Find the volume of the cone shown below.

The radius of the base is 2 inches, and the height is 9 inches.

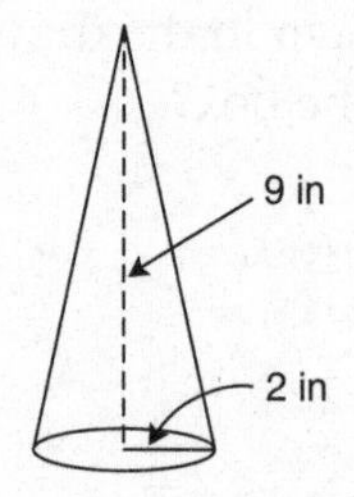

Apply the formula: $V = \frac{1}{3}\pi r^2 h$

$$= \frac{1}{3}(3.14)(2^2)(9)$$

$$= \frac{1}{3}(3.14)(4)(9)$$

$$= \mathbf{37.68\ in^3}$$

Note: In volume formulas for cones and square pyramids, the factor $\frac{1}{3}$ is shown first. However, do not begin with this factor. Multiply the other factors first and then divide by 3, unless one of the numbers is easily divided by 3.

PRACTICE 11.2

A. Find the volume of each object to the nearest unit.

1.

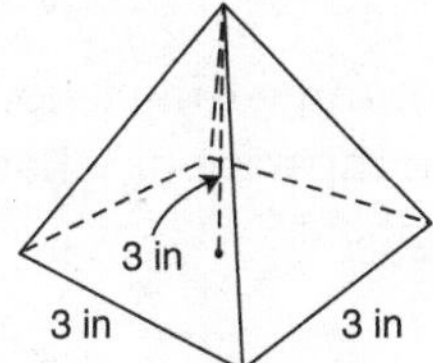

2.

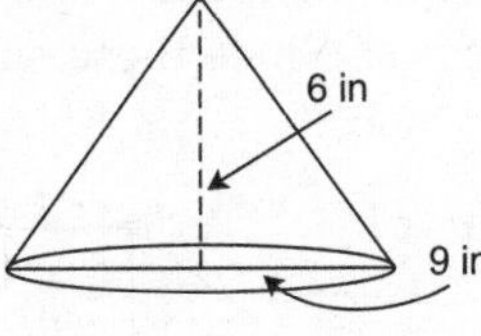

3.

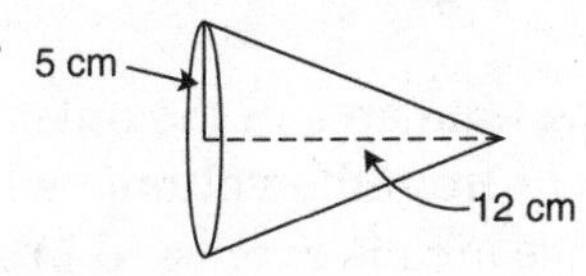

4.

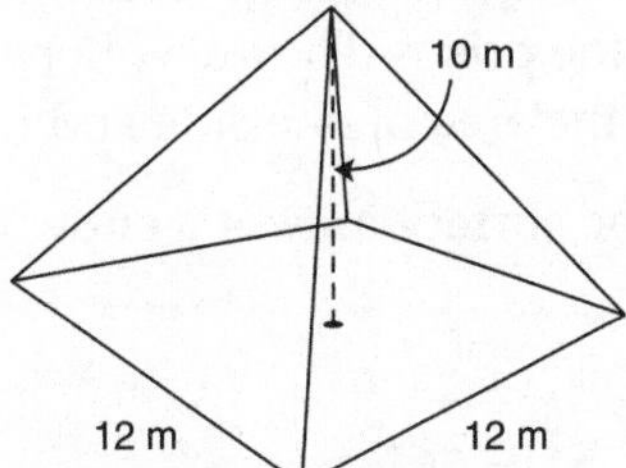

5.

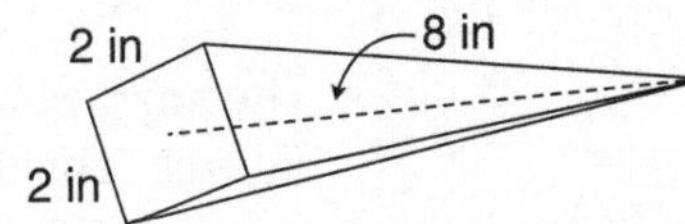

6.

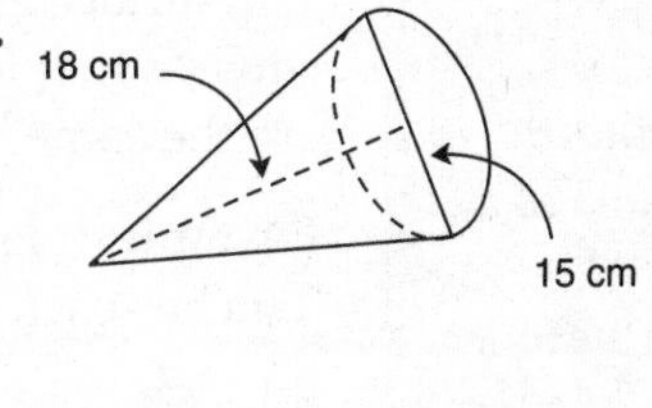

B. Choose the <u>one best answer</u> to each question.

7. Advertisers have designed this pyramid-shaped package to hold action figures.

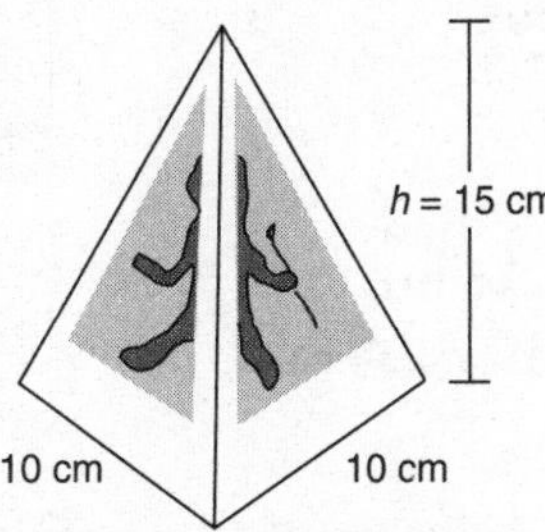

After testing the design, the manufacturer decides to increase both the length and width of the base by 4 cm. How many more cubic centimeters will the new package hold than the package shown above?

A. 480
B. 500
C. 980
D. 1,460
E. 2,940

8. The height of a cone is half the diameter of its base. If the cone's height is 4 inches, what is the cone's volume to the nearest cubic inch?

A. 21
B. 48
C. 67
D. 81
E. 201

9. Which of the following is a true statement about the figures shown below?

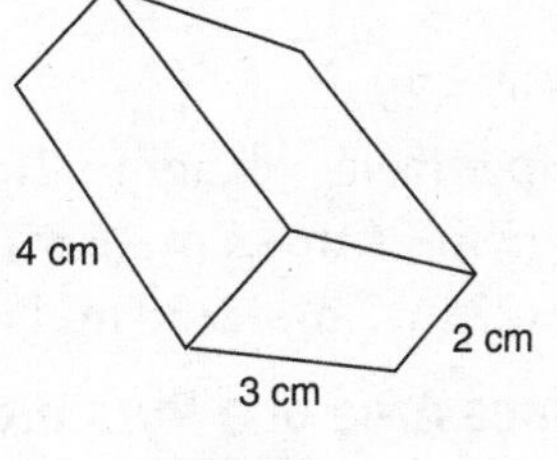

Figure A

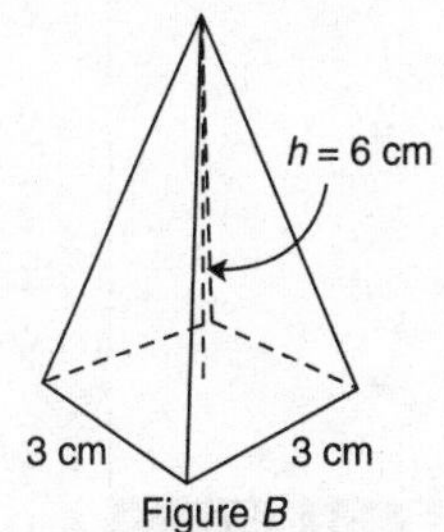

Figure B

A. The volume of *A* equals the volume of *B*.
B. The volume of *B* is greater than the volume of *A*.
C. Both *A* and *B* have a volume greater than 20 cubic centimeters.
D. Both *A* and *B* have a volume less than 20 cubic centimeters.
E. The volume of *B* is less than the volume of *A*.

10. A cone's base is a circle with a radius of 8 inches. The cone's height is 15 inches. What is the cone's approximate volume in cubic inches?

A. 125
B. 250
C. 500
D. 750
E. 1,000

Surface Area

The **surface area** is the total area of the outside **faces** of three-dimensional figures. This is different from the **volume**, which is the capacity of what a figure can hold. Surface area is expressed in square units.

Surface Area of a Square Prism

The surface area of a **square prism (cube)** is the sum of the areas of the six squares that form the prism. The area of one square is s^2. Since these sides are the same, find the area of one side and multiply by 6.

Example 1: Find the surface area of a cube with sides of 3 inches each.

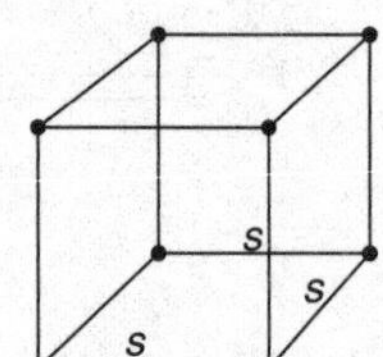

$SA = 6s^2$

$SA = 6(3\text{ in})^2 = 6(9\text{ in}^2) = \mathbf{54\text{ in}^2}$

Surface Area of a Rectangular Prism

The surface area of a **rectangular prism** is the sum of the areas of the six rectangles that form the prism.

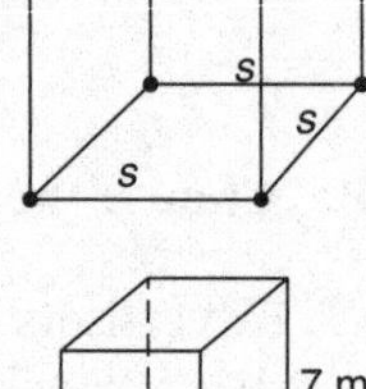

Example 2: Find the surface area of this box.

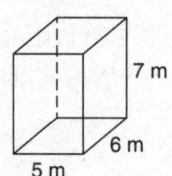

$SA = ph + 2B$

$SA = \text{perimeter} \times \text{height} + 2(\text{area of base})$

$SA = (5\text{ m} + 6\text{ m} + 5\text{ m} + 6\text{ m}) \times 7\text{ m} + 2(6\text{ m} \times 5\text{ m})$

$SA = (22\text{ m})7\text{ m} + 2(30\text{ m}^2) = 154\text{ m}^2 + 60\text{ m}^2 = \mathbf{214\text{ m}^2}$

Surface Area of a Pyramid

The surface area of a **pyramid** is $\frac{1}{2}$ the perimeter of the base (p) times the **slant height** (s) plus the area of the base (B). The slant height is the length of a line segment from the **apex** (top) to the **base**.

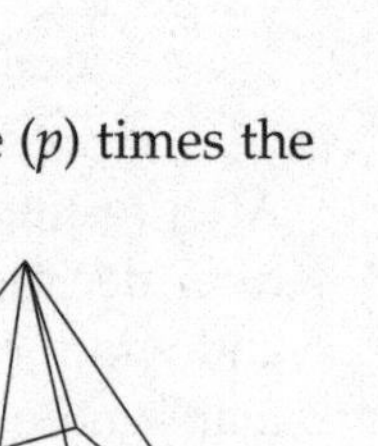

Example 3: What is the surface area of a pyramid with a slant height of 5 feet, a base with a perimeter of 14 feet, and a base with an area of 12 feet?

$SA = \frac{1}{2}ps + B$

$SA = \frac{1}{2}\text{ perimeter} \times \text{slant height} + \text{base area}$

$SA = \frac{1}{2}(14\text{ ft})(5\text{ ft}) + 12\text{ ft}^2$

$SA = \frac{1}{2}(70\text{ ft}^2) + 12\text{ ft}^2 = 35\text{ ft}^2 + 12\text{ ft}^2 = \mathbf{47\text{ ft}^2}$

KEY IDEAS

- The surface area is the area of the total surface of a three-dimensional object.
- To find the surface area of a cube, you need to multiply the area of one side by 6.
- To find the surface area of a rectangular prism and a pyramid, you need to use formulas to find several dimensions and combine them.

HiSET EXAM TIP

No surface area formulas will appear on the formula sheet provided on the HiSET exam. You will need to memorize the formulas on this page.

PRACTICE 12.1

A. Find the surface area of each object in square units. Use the formulas on page 470.

1.

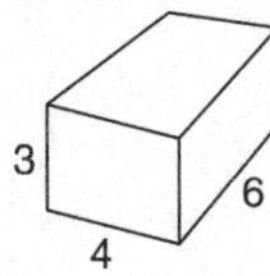

2.

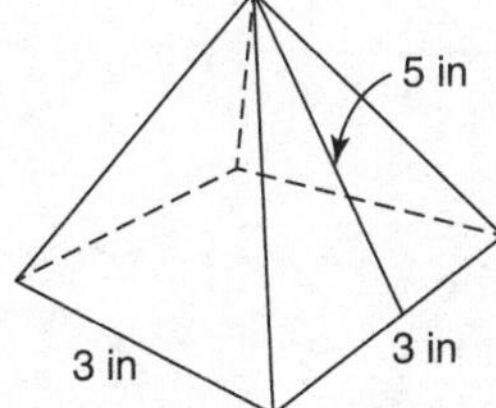

3.

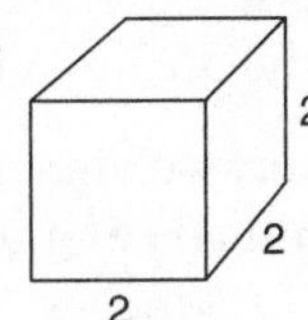

4.

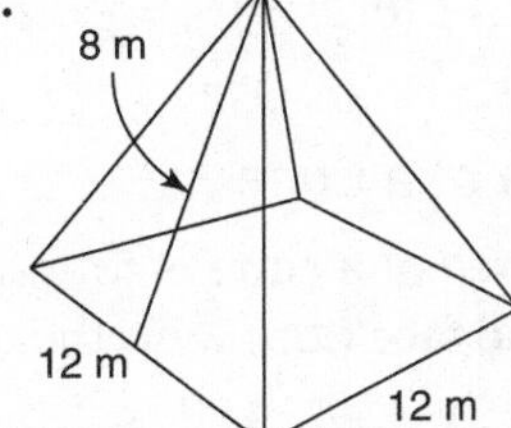

5.

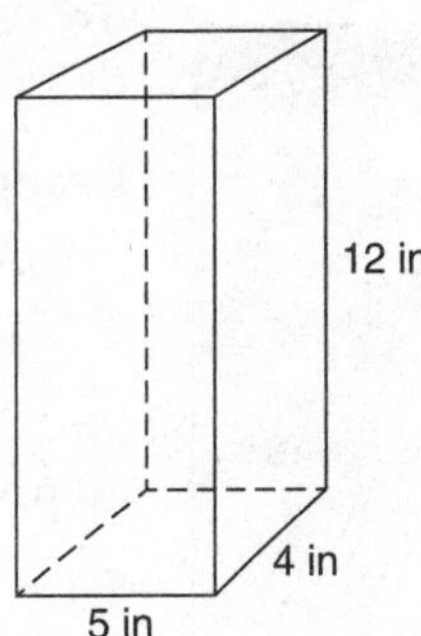

6.

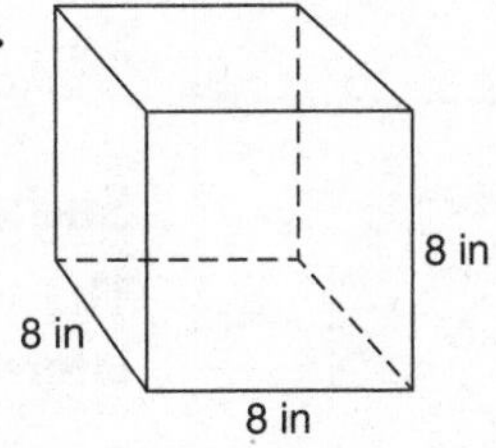

B. Choose the <u>one best answer</u> to each question. Use the formulas on page 470.

7. Which of the following is a true statement about the figures shown below? (Measurements indicated are all in the same units.)

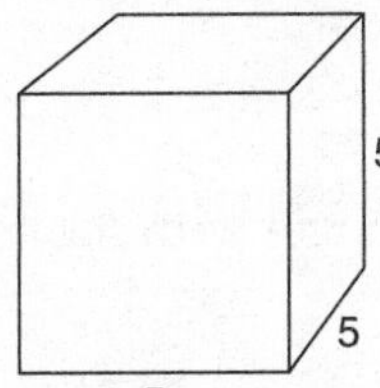

Figure *A*

Figure *B*

A. The surface area of Figure *A* is equal to the surface area of Figure *B*.
B. The surface area of Figure *A* is half of the surface area of Figure *B*.
C. The surface area of Figure *A* is greater than the surface area of Figure *B*.
D. The sum of the surface areas of both Figure *A* and Figure *B* is greater than 300.
E. The surface area of Figure *A* is less than the surface area of Figure *B*.

8. If the dimensions of the box below are doubled, by how many square centimeters does the surface area increase?

A. 8
B. 54
C. 108
D. 162
E. 216

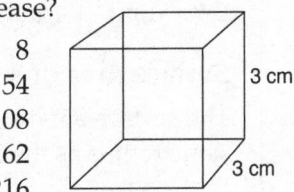

9. All the edges of a metal box are of equal length. If the surface area is 150 square inches, what is the length, in inches, of each edge of the box?

A. 5
B. 6
C. 25
D. 50
E. 75

STUDY ADVICE

Understanding surface area can be challenging. Be sure to allot ample study time to this important topic!

Finding the surface areas of cylinders, cones, and spheres involves using some dimensions of circles.

Surface Area of a Cylinder

To find the surface area of a **cylinder**, multiply the **circumference** ($2\pi r$) by the **height** (h) and add the product to the area of the two ends of the cylinder, each of which is the area of a circle (πr^2).

KEY IDEAS

- The formulas for surface area of cylinders, cones, and spheres all use dimensions of a circle.
- All of the formulas use π and the radius of a circle.

Example 4: Find the surface area of a cylinder with a radius (r) of 4 inches and a height (h) of 3 inches.

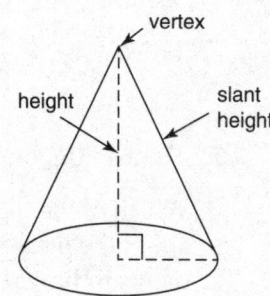

You may find the on-screen calculator helpful to complete these calculations effectively.

$SA = 2\pi rh + 2\pi r^2$
$SA = (2 \times 3.14 \times 4 \times 3) + (2 \times 3.14 \times 4^2)$
$SA = (6.28 \times 12) + (6.28 \times 16) = 75.36\ \text{in}^2 + 100.48\ \text{in}^2$
$= \mathbf{175.84\ in^2}$

Surface Area of a Cone

The surface area of a **cone** is found by combining the **lateral side surface** (πrs) with the area of its **base** (πr^2).

Example 5: Find the surface area of a cone with a radius of 2 feet and a slant height of 5 feet.

$SA = \pi rs + \pi r^2$
$SA =$ lateral side surface with slant height + area of base
$SA = \pi(2)(5) + \pi(2^2)$
$SA = 10\pi \text{ft}^2 + 4\pi \text{ft}^2 = 14\pi \text{ft}^2 = 14\ \text{ft}^2 \times 3.14 \cong \mathbf{43.96\ ft^2}$

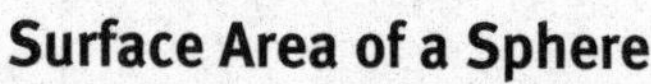

Surface Area of a Sphere

The surface area of a **sphere** is four times the area of a circle with the same radius as the sphere.

Example 6: What is the surface area of this sphere with a radius of 10 feet?

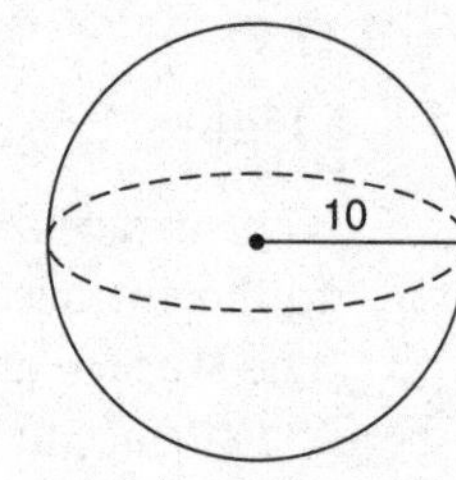

$SA = 4\pi r^2$
$SA \approx 4 \times 3.14 \times 10^2 \approx \mathbf{1256\ ft^2}$

PRACTICE 12.2

A. Find the surface area of each object in square units. Use the formulas on page 472.

1.
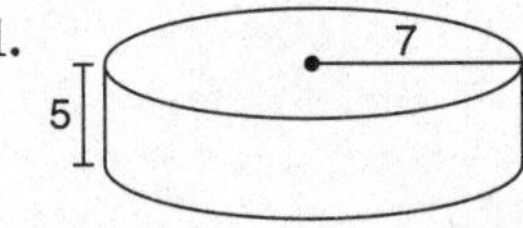

2.
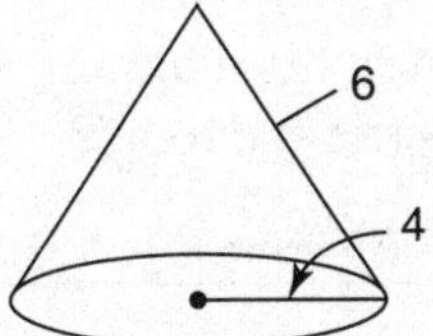

3.
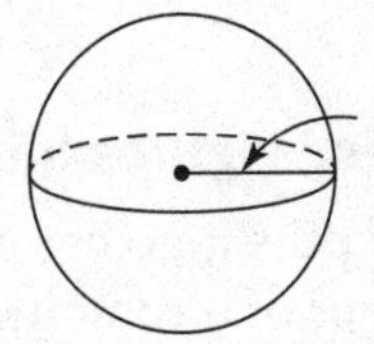

4.
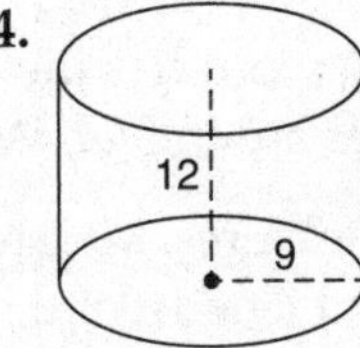

5.
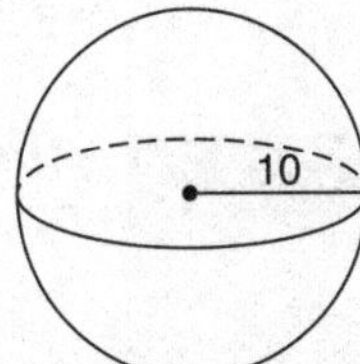

6.
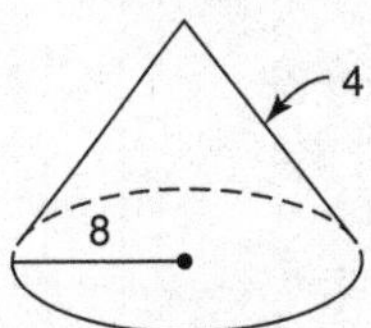

B. Choose the <u>one best answer</u> to each question. Use the formulas on page 472.

7. If the length of the diameter of a sphere is 8, how many square units is its surface area?

   A. 16π
   B. 64π
   C. 256π
   D. 512π
   E. 768π

8. A cone, pictured below, has a slant height of 8 inches and a diameter of 8 inches. If the cone's slant height is doubled, and the diameter is halved, which of the following statements must be true?

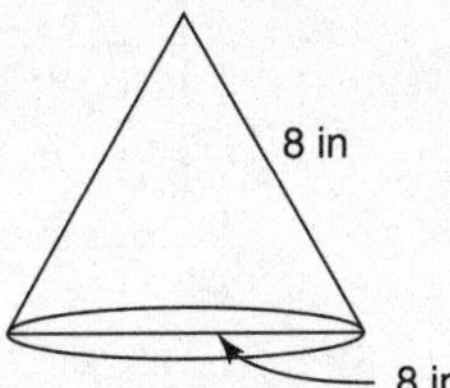
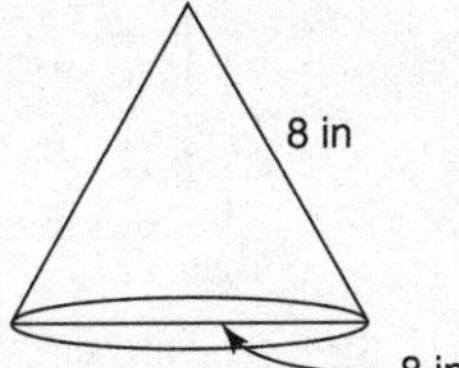

   A. The new cone will have the same surface area as the original cone.
   B. The new cone will have a surface area exactly half of the surface area of the original cone.
   C. The new cone will have a surface area exactly double that of the surface area of the original cone.
   D. The new cone will have a surface area greater than the surface area of the original cone.
   E. The new cone will have a surface area less than the surface area of the original cone.

9. In the cylinder below, the diameter of the circular base is equal to the height of the cylinder. What is the surface area of the cylinder, to the nearest square inch?

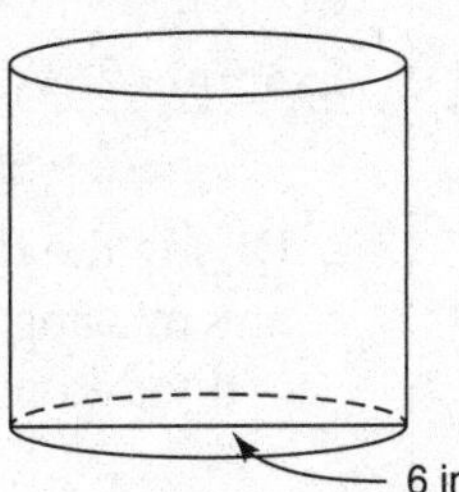

   A. 57
   B. 113
   C. 170
   D. 339
   E. 361

LESSON 13

Combined Figures

KEY IDEAS

- Combined figures are made from two or more regular figures.
- To find the perimeter of a combined figure, add the lengths of all the sides.
- To find area or volume of a combined figure, break the figure into parts and find the area or volume of each part; then combine the results.

HiSET EXAM TIP

There is usually more than one way to break down a combined figure. Solve the problem the way that seems easiest to you. The answer will be the same.

Breaking Combined Figures into Parts

A combined figure puts together geometric figures to form a new shape. To find the perimeter of a combined figure, simply add the lengths of the sides. You may need to solve for one or more missing lengths.

Example 1: A family room has the dimensions shown in the diagram. All measures are in feet. What is the perimeter of the room?

1. Find the missing measures. Measurement x equals the combined lengths of the two opposite walls: $x = 8 + 4 = 12$ ft. You also know that $18 - 10 = y$, so $y = 8$ ft.

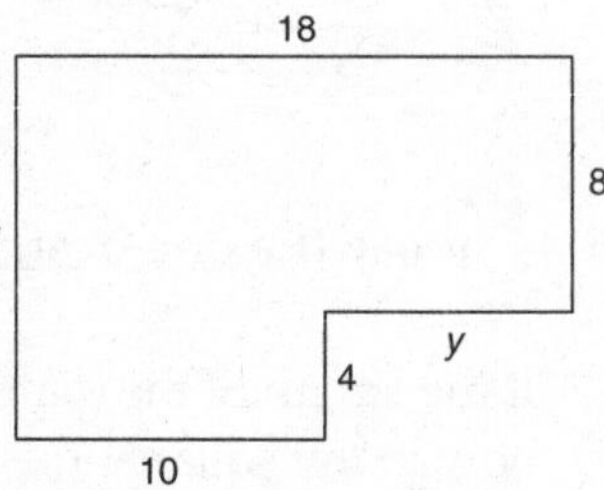

2. Add all distances to find the perimeter: $12 + 18 + 8 + 8 + 4 + 10 =$ **60 ft.**

To find the area or volume of a combined figure, break the figure into parts. Then apply the correct formula to each part.

Example 2: What is the area of the figure in square centimeters?

1. Divide the figure into two shapes, and find any missing measurements. Here the figure is divided into a trapezoid and a rectangle.

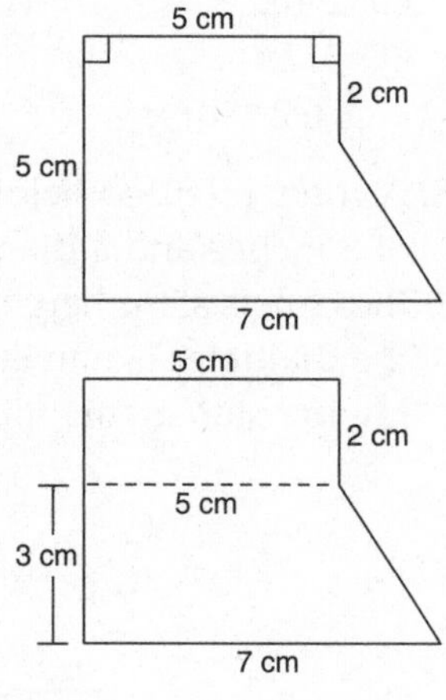

2. Calculate the area of each shape.

Rectangle: $A = lw$
$= 2(5) = 10 \text{ cm}^2$

Trapezoid: $A = \frac{1}{2}h(b_1 + b_2)$
$= \frac{1}{2}(3)(5 + 7) = 18 \text{ cm}^2$

3. Combine: $10 + 18 =$ **28 cm^2.**

Example 3: Find the volume of the container shown below.

Break the figure into a cylinder and a cone and find the volume of each.

1. Cylinder: $V = \pi r^2 h$
$= (3.14)(1^2)(2) = 6.28 \text{ m}^3$

2. Cone: $V = \frac{1}{3}\pi r^2 h$
$= \frac{1}{3}(3.14)(1^2)(1.5) = 1.57 \text{ m}^3$

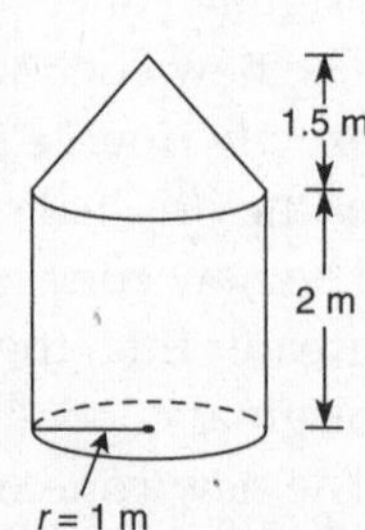

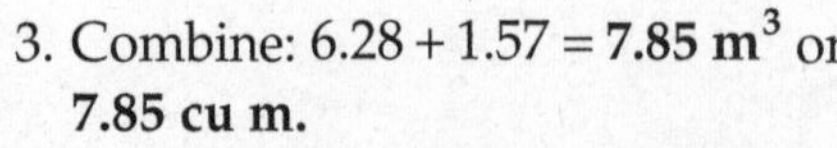
3. Combine: $6.28 + 1.57 =$ **7.85 m^3** or **7.85 cu m.**

PRACTICE 13

A. Find the perimeter and area of each figure.

1.

2.

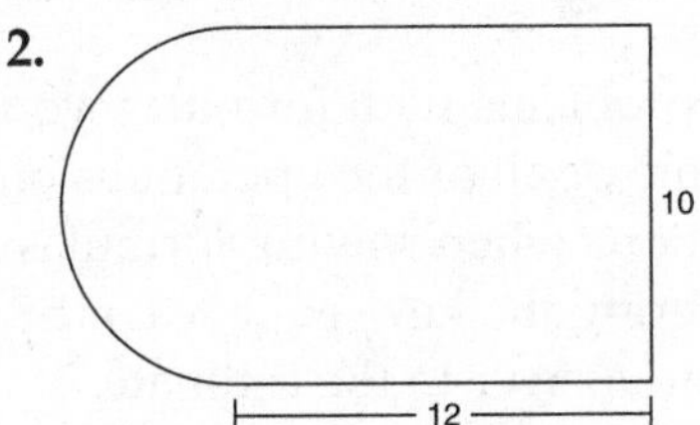

(*Hint:* Think of the figure as a rectangle and a half circle.)

3.

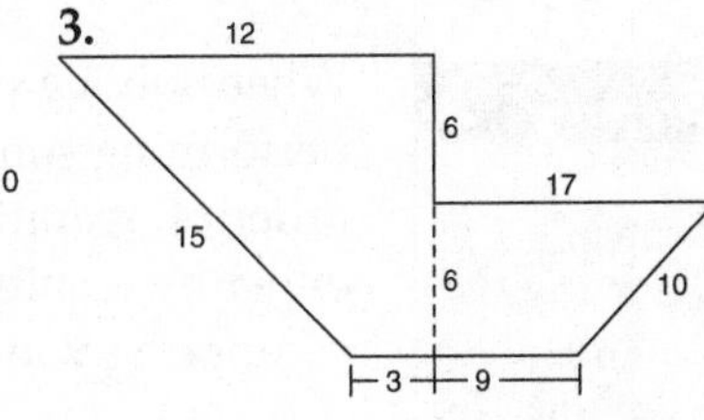

B. Find the volume of each figure to the nearest cubic unit.

4.

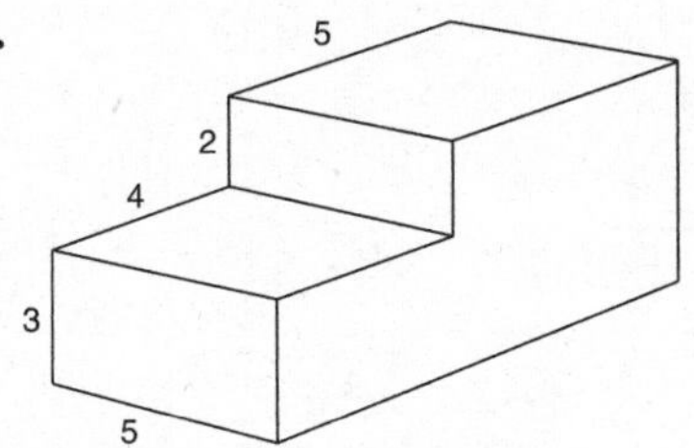

5.

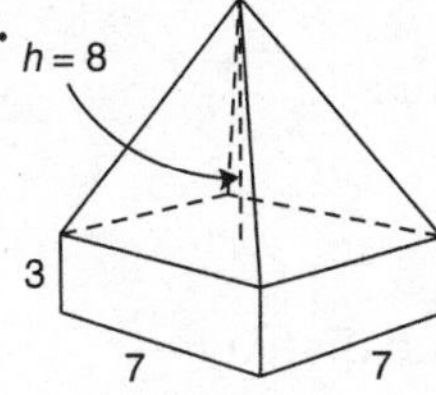

6.

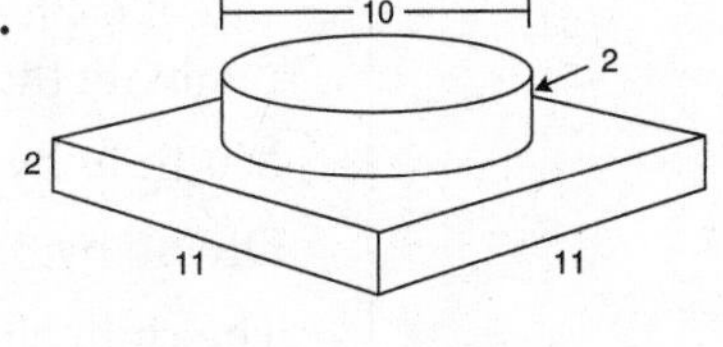

C. Choose the <u>one best answer</u> to each question.

7. A slab of concrete will have four concrete blocks in each corner as shown in the drawing below.

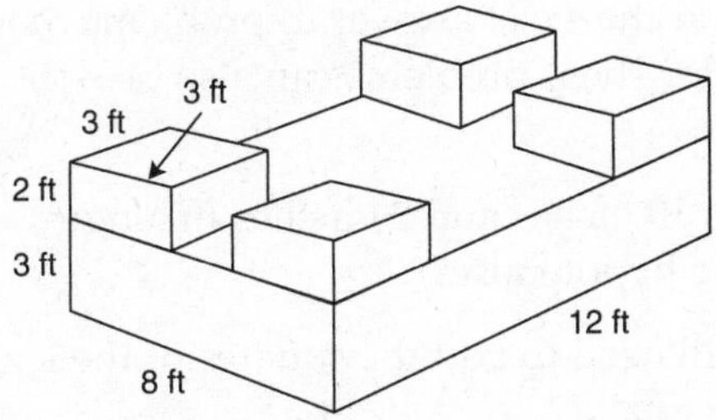

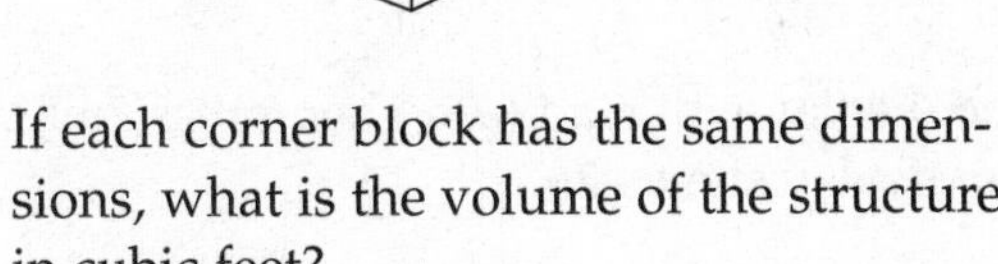

If each corner block has the same dimensions, what is the volume of the structure in cubic feet?

A. 72
B. 168
C. 288
D. 360
E. 384

8. A candy package is in the shape of a cylinder with a cone on each end.

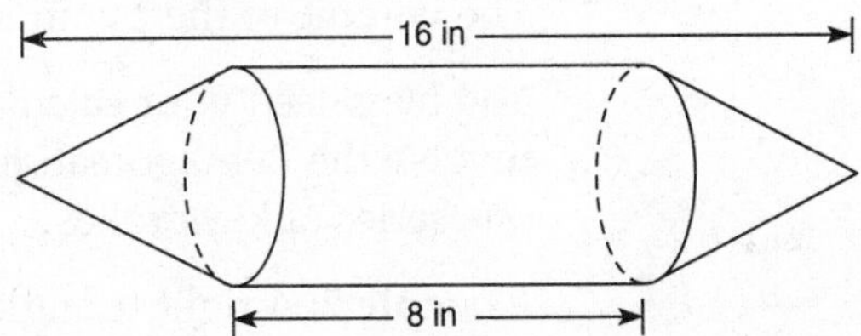

If the radius of the cylinder is 2 inches and the cones are identical, what is the capacity of the container to the nearest cubic inch?

A. 33
B. 100
C. 134
D. 201
E. 212

STUDY ADVICE

Any time you are feeling overwhelmed, step away and take a walk (or play basketball, or work on a hobby). Even though there is a great deal of information to absorb to do well on the HiSET exam, you can do it if you maintain focus and are patient with yourself.

Geometry

LESSON 14

Geometry Calculator Skills

KEY IDEAS

- When a problem involves many calculations, use the order of operations to decide which operation to do first.
- Check your work by estimating an answer or by quickly repeating the keystrokes to see if the result is the same.

When solving problems with formulas, you can generally save time by performing some or all of the operations on a calculator. Remember the order of operations when solving formulas and always check your work, either by reentering the key sequence or by estimating an answer and comparing your answer to the estimate.

Example 1: A pyramid has a height of 81 feet. The base is in the shape of a square with each side measuring 40 feet. What is the volume in cubic feet of the pyramid?

Use the formula for the volume of a pyramid: $\frac{1}{3}Bh$. Begin by calculating the area of the base: 40×40, or 40^2. Multiply that by the height, 81. In the last step, dividing by 3 is the same as multiplying by $\frac{1}{3}$.

Evaluate the exponent.	40 [x^2]
Multiply by 81.	[×] 81
Divide by 3.	[÷] 3 [enter]
The right side of the display shows the correct answer, **43,200**.	**43200**

To enter this formula using a fraction using one series of keystrokes on the TI-30XS MultiView™ calculator, enter the following: [$\frac{n}{d}$] 1 [▼] 3 [×] 40 [x^2] [×] 81 [enter].

The right side of the display shows **43200**.

The volume of the pyramid is **43,200 square feet.**

You may need your calculator to find the exact answer to problems that involve the Pythagorean relationship. These problems can also be done in one series of keystrokes.

Example 2: A right triangle has legs 10 inches and 24 inches in length. What is the length of the hypotenuse?

Use the formula $a^2 + b^2 = c^2$. You will need to add the squares of the legs and then find the square root of the total.

Press: 10 [x^2] [+] 24 [x^2] [enter]. The display will read 676. Then press [2nd] [x^2] 676 [enter]. The right side of the display shows **26.**

The hypotenuse is **26 inches** in length.

If you need to include the quantity pi (π) in a calculation, the TI-30XS MultiView™ calculator includes a *pi* key, located three keys below the *2nd* key on the left-hand side of the keypad.

Example 3: What is the area of a circle with radius 2.4 cm? Round your answer to the nearest tenth.

Use the formula Area $= \pi r^2$. Press [π] [×] 2.4 [$\sqrt{}$ / x^2] and then press [enter]. The right side of the display reads 18.09557368. Round that to find the answer: **18.1 cm²**.

HiSET EXAM TIP

Watch the calculator display while you are entering all of these keystrokes. If you make a mistake, use the delete key to remove that mistake and then replace it with the correct number or function. Practice that with these examples.

A. Use your calculator to evaluate each formula.

1. Find the perimeter of a rectangle with a length of 16 inches and a width of 5 inches.
   Perimeter = 2 × length + 2 × width
2. Find the area of a triangle with a base of 26 centimeters and a height of 15 centimeters. Area = $\frac{1}{2}$ × base × height
3. What is the volume of a cube if the edge measures 3.5 feet? Round to the nearest cubic foot. Volume = edge^3
4. What is the measure of the hypotenuse of a right triangle when the legs measure 13 cm and 9 cm? Round your answer to the nearest tenth.
   Pythagorean relationship: $a^2 + b^2 = c^2$
5. Find the circumference of a circle with a diameter of 12 inches. Round to the nearest tenth.
   Circumference = π × diameter
6. Find the volume of a cone with a radius of 12 cm and a height of 20 cm. Round to the nearest cm^3.
   Volume = $\frac{1}{3}$ × π × radius^2 × height

B. Choose the one best answer to each question.

Question 7 refers to the following drawing.

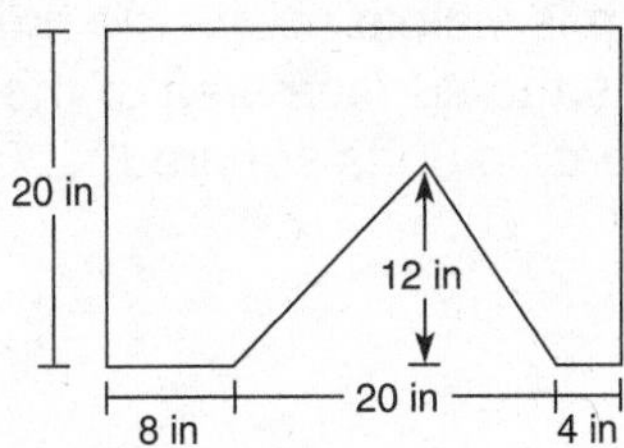

7. For a woodworking project, Paul cuts the shape shown above from plywood. What is the area in square inches of the piece? (*Hint:* Think of the shape as a triangle removed from a rectangle.)
   A. 400
   B. 480
   C. 520
   D. 640
   E. 720

8. To the nearest cubic meter, what is the volume of a cylinder with a radius of 1.5 meters and a height of 5 meters?
   A. 24
   B. 35
   C. 45
   D. 77
   E. 141

Questions 9 and 10 refer to the drawing.

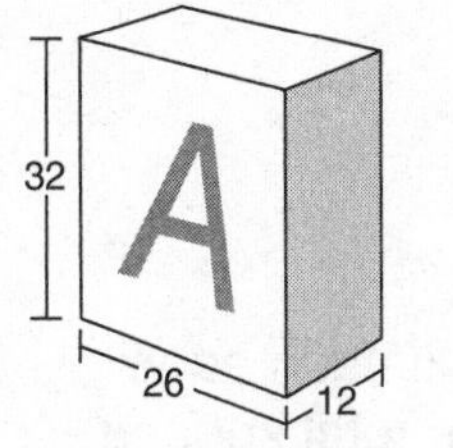

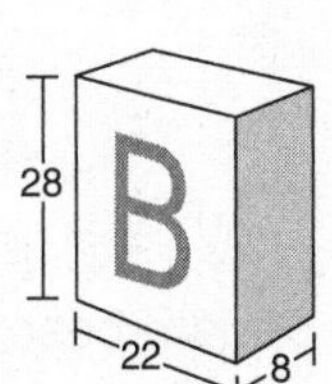

All measurements are in centimeters.

9. How many cubic centimeters greater is the volume of Box A than the volume of Box B?
   A. 64
   B. 1,448
   C. 2,464
   D. 4,928
   E. 5,056

10. An advertiser plans to print advertisements on one side panel of each of the boxes (the shaded faces in the drawing). What is the total area, in square centimeters, that the advertiser will cover?
    A. 224
    B. 384
    C. 608
    D. 836
    E. 1,448

GEOMETRY PRACTICE QUESTIONS

1. What is the surface area, in square centimeters, of a cube with each edge length of 5 cm?

   A. 15
   B. 25
   C. 125
   D. 150
   E. 225

2. What is the surface area, in square centimeters, of a cylinder with a height of 10 cm and a radius of 6 cm?

   A. 136π
   B. 160π
   C. 192π
   D. 256π
   E. 324π

3. What is the surface area, in square centimeters, of a cylinder that measures 8 cm tall with a diameter of 6 cm on its base?

   A. 48π
   B. 57π
   C. 66π
   D. 132π
   E. 144π

4. A pyramid has a square base. If each edge of the pyramid is 4, what is the total surface area of the entire pyramid?

   A. $8\sqrt{3}$
   B. $8\sqrt{3}+16$
   C. $16\sqrt{3}+16$
   D. $64\sqrt{3}$
   E. $16\sqrt{3}+16$

Question 5 refers to the following figure.

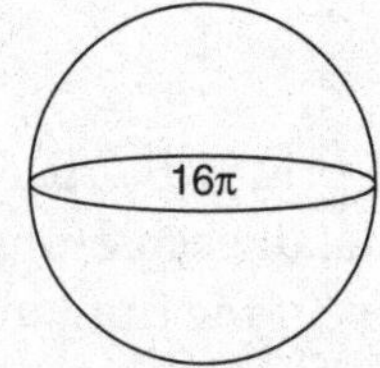

5. A toy factory paints all of its rubber balls with 2 coats of latex for durability. How many square centimeters of latex are needed to cover a rubber ball with a circumference of 16π cm?

   A. 64π
   B. 128π
   C. 256π
   D. 512π
   E. 1024π

6. The floor of a walk-in closet measures 7 feet by 4 feet. If the ceiling height is 8 feet, what is the volume in cubic feet of the closet?

   A. 28
   B. 56
   C. 112
   D. 140
   E. 224

Question 7 refers to the following figure.

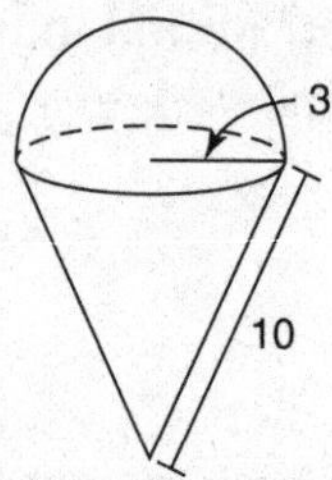

7. An ice cream cone has a spherical scoop of ice cream placed inside. Exactly one-half of the ice cream is visible above the rim of the cone. What is the surface area of the entire ice cream treat, in units squared?

   A. 24π
   B. 30π
   C. 48π
   D. 60π
   E. 72π

---

8. The radius of Sphere A is 2, and the radius of Sphere B is 1. What is the ratio of the volume of Sphere A to that of Sphere B? (*Hint*: Use the formula for the volume of a sphere on page 472.)

   A. 1:2
   B. 4:1
   C. 8:1
   D. 8:3
   E. 2:1

Question 9 refers to the following figure.

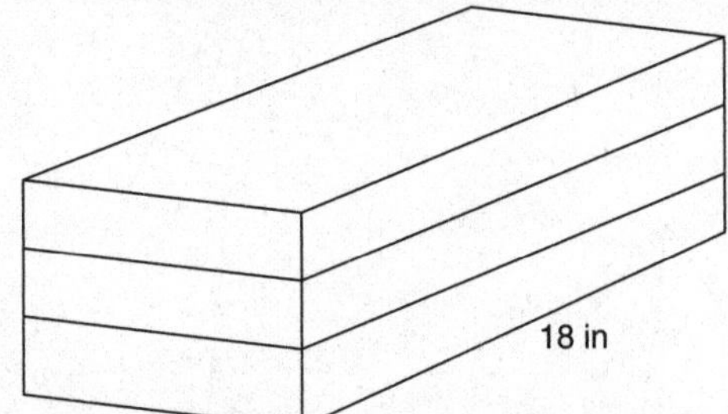

9. Three identical rectangular boxes are stacked one on top of another. The total height of all three boxes is the same as the width of one box. The length of the boxes is 18 in, and the width is half the length. What is the combined volume, in cubic inches, of all three boxes?

A. 1,458
B. 1,800
C. 2,124
D. 3,136
E. 3,248

---

10. Using a compass, Max hikes 300 yards due north of his campsite. From that point, he hikes 400 yards due east. If he were to hike directly to his campsite from this point, how many yards would he have to hike?

A. 300
B. 400
C. 500
D. 600
E. 700

11. The rectangular base of a container is 9 inches long and 7 inches wide. By how many cubic inches will the volume of the container increase if you increase the length of the base by 2 inches?

A. 84
B. 126
C. 168
D. 216
E. 224

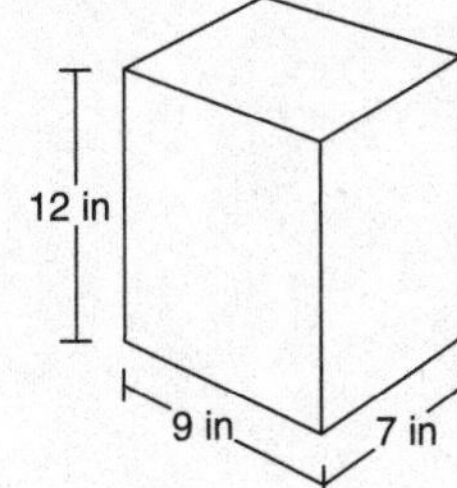

12. In a right triangle, the hypotenuse measures 15 inches. If one leg of the triangle measures 6 inches, which of the following equations could be used to find the length of the other leg (x) in inches?

A. $x = \sqrt{15-6}$
B. $x = 15 - 6$
C. $x^2 = 15^2 + 6^2$
D. $x^2 = 15^2 - 6^2$
E. $x = 15^2 + 6^2$

13. The length of a rectangle is three times its width. If the perimeter of the rectangle is 96 inches, what is its length in inches?

A. 6
B. 9
C. 12
D. 24
E. 36

Question 14 refers to the following figure.

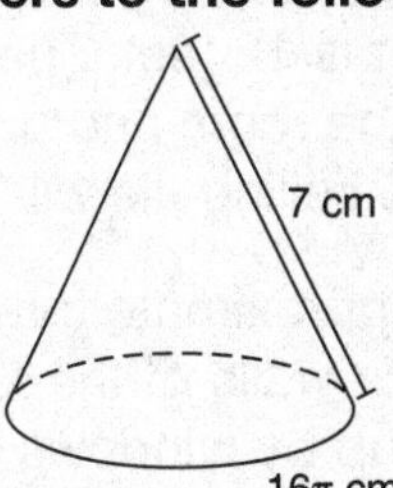

14. Sarah is making party hats for a birthday party. Each hat is in the shape of a cone and will have a circumference of 16π cm and a slant height of 7 cm. She will be making 20 hats. What is the total surface area, in square centimeters, of all 20 hats combined?

A. 32π
B. 56π
C. 112π
D. 336π
E. 1120π

Question 15 refers to the following figure.

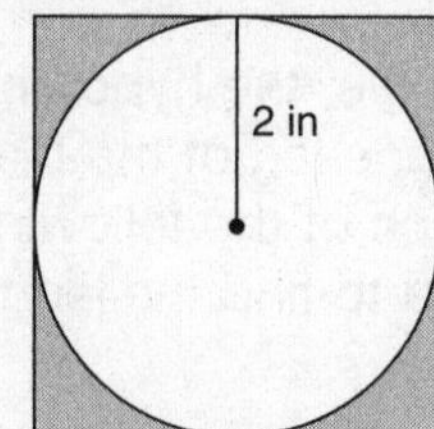

15. Use your calculator to make the following calculation. In the figure above, a square contains a circle such that each of the sides of the square is touching a point on the circle. What is the area, in square inches, of the shaded portion?

A. 3.43
B. 12.57
C. 16.00
D. 28.57
E. 32.14

Questions 16 and 17 refer to the following.

A classroom is 40 feet long and 25 feet wide. The ceiling height is 12 feet. The school district plans to repaint the room and put in air-conditioning. The ceiling tile will not be painted.

16. What is the approximate total square footage of the four walls of the room? Ignore space taken up by windows and doors.

A. 1,200
B. 1,560
C. 1,920
D. 2,240
E. 4,000

17. To choose an air-conditioning system, the school district must know the volume of the room. What is the volume in cubic feet?

A. 1,000
B. 3,120
C. 12,000
D. 15,625
E. 18,000

Question 18 refers to the following figures.

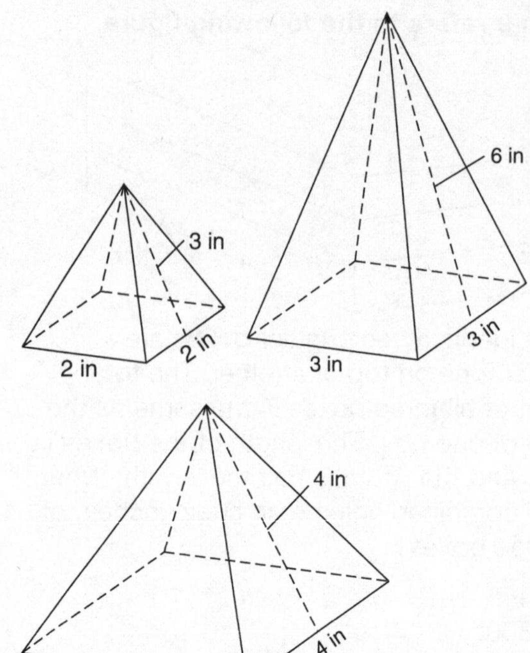

18. Laura is painting model pyramids for an art project. She needs one tube of paint for every 30 square inches of surface area. If Laura paints each pyramid and its base, approximately how many tubes of paint should she buy?

A. 4
B. 16
C. 48
D. 109
E. 127

19.

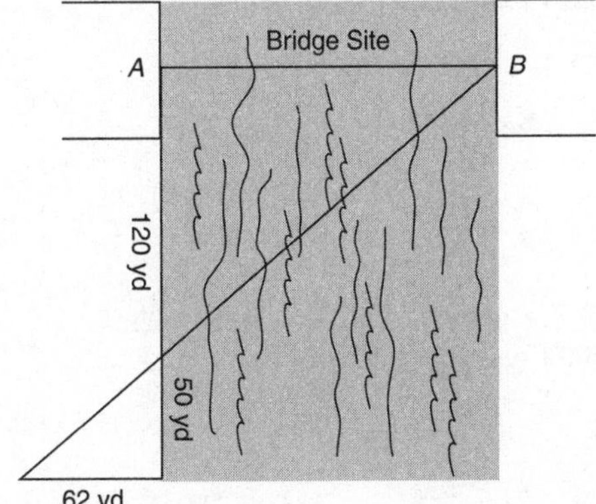

A city plans to build a bridge across a local river. To find the width the bridge will span, an engineer stakes out two similar triangles. What is the distance in yards from point A to point B?

A. 2.4
B. 25.8
C. 148.8
D. 170
E. 196.2

Questions 20 and 21 are based on the following figure.

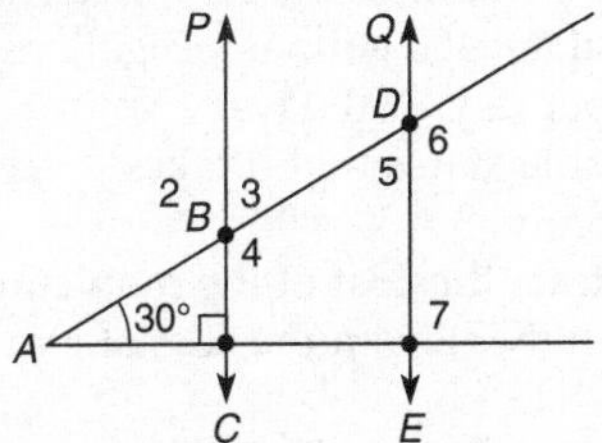

line $P \parallel$ line Q

20. Which of the following conclusions can you draw based on the information given in the drawing?

A. $m\angle 5 = 60°$
B. $\angle 7$ is an obtuse angle
C. $m\angle 3 = 30°$
D. $\angle 2$ must be a right angle
E. $m\angle 5$ must be a right angle

21. Which of the following is a true statement about the figure?

A. $m\angle 2 + m\angle 7 = 180°$
B. $m\angle 4 = m\angle 7$
C. $m\angle 3 + m\angle 4 = 90°$
D. $m\angle 3 + m\angle 6 = 180°$
E. $m\angle 3 = m\angle 6$

22. The following diagram shows the length of the shadows of a man and a building at 4 P.M.

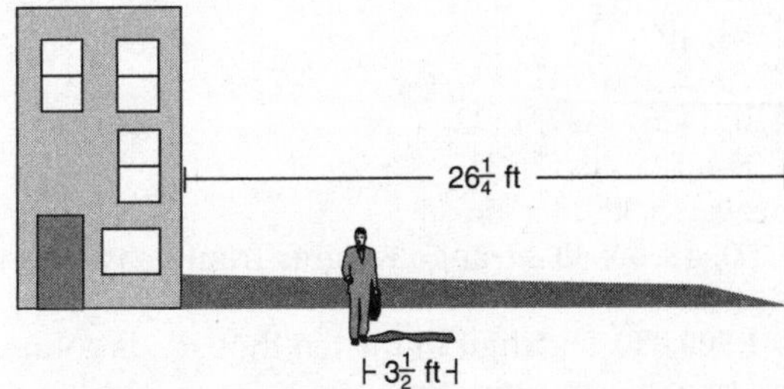

If the man in the drawing is 6 feet in height, what is the height of the building in feet?

A. 20
B. 24
C. 37
D. 42
E. 45

23. A parallelogram has a base of 6 centimeters and a height of 10 centimeters. This parallelogram has the same area as a triangle with a height of 5 centimeters. What is the measure, in centimeters, of the base of the triangle?

A. 11
B. 16
C. 21
D. 24
E. 30

STUDY ADVICE

Congratulations! You've made it through the Mathematics unit. Reward yourself! And remember to review these concepts periodically as you continue to study, up until you take the Mathematics Test.

Mathematics Answers and Explanations

Number and Quantity I: Problem Solving

Lesson 1: Compare and Order Numbers

Practice 1

1. 4
2. 8
3. 9
4. 1
5. 6
6. 7
7. 3
8. 500
9. 80
10. 1100
11. 12,000
12. 2000
13. 100
14. 100
15. 341
16. 1145
17. 125,391
18. 18, 23, 39, 45
19. 89, 91, 109, 111
20. 909, 932, 1087, 1139
21. 1420, 1425, 1429, 1432
22. 11,098, 12,071, 12,131
23. 15,298, 15,309, 15,356
24. **D. 50, 48, 45, 40** Arrange weights from heaviest to lightest.
25. **C. 1,500,000** The digit in the ten thousands column is less than 5, so round down.

Lesson 2: Whole Number Operations

Practice 2.1

1. 77
2. 100
3. 52
4. 36
5. 190
6. 4078
7. 43
8. 2117
9. 65
10. 114
11. 180
12. 293
13. 483
14. 456
15. 2419
16. 900
17. 11,308
18. 15,185
19. 131,197
20. 30,899
21. **B. 88** Calculate: 24 + 8 + 56 = 88
22. **D. $13** Calculate: $20 – $7 = $13.

Practice 2.2

1. 484
2. 1000
3. 2736
4. 13
5. 105
6. 21
7. 1350
8. 2625
9. 3376
10. 28
11. 15
12. 6
13. 250
14. 44 r3
15. 300
16. 200 r4
17. 150
18. 67,068
19. 538
20. 384
21. 12,011 r8
22. **E. 96** Calculate: 16 × 6 = 96.
23. **C. $75** Calculate: 15 × 5 = 75.
24. **C. 6** Calculate: 12 ÷ 2 = 6.

Lesson 3: HiSET Exam Calculator Skills

Practice 3.1

1. 153
2. 1187
3. 784
4. 24
5. 27,084
6. 14,442
7. 11,704
8. 54
9. 1580
10. **C. 26,179** Press (clear) 42920 (−) 16741 (enter).
11. **D. $19,900** Press (clear) 995 (×) 20 (enter).

Practice 3.2

1. 25
2. 18
3. 35
4. 136
5. 125
6. 5%
7. 2
8. 135
9. 5%
10. **C. $336** Press (clear) 1680 (×) 20 (2nd) (() (enter).
11. **B. 5%** Press (clear) 48 (÷) 960 (2nd) ()) (enter). The right side of the screen will display 5%.

Lesson 4: Word Problems

Practice 4.1

1. **C. 10** No paint is needed for the floor, so ignore the 700 square feet. 3500 square feet of wall space ÷ 350 square feet per gallon = 10 gallons.
2. **D. 22** 11 children × 2 party favors per child = 22.
3. **A. 5** Calculate: 30 – 25 = 5. The information that Sarah and Kate live 18 miles apart is not needed.
4. **D. 90** Calculate: 450 gallons ÷ 5 gallons of *filtered* water use per day = 90 days.
5. **E. 90** The table states that it takes Joyce 30 minutes to give a pedicure. 3 × 30 = 90
6. **C. $25** Subtract the cost of the manicure & pedicure combination ($35) from the cost of a makeover ($60). $60 – $35 = $25
7. **E. 42** Calculate: 7 × 6 = 42

Practice 4.2

1. **D. $103** Restaurant D ordered 2 cases of Boston lettuce and 3 cases of romaine lettuce in July. (2 × $17) + (3 × $23) = $103.
2. **C. $18** Calculate: 4 + 4 + 2 + 2 + 1 = 13 total cases, and delivery for the first 5 cases costs $2 each. 13 – 5 = 8 cases remained after the first 5, so delivery for those 8 cases costs $1 each. (5 × $2) + (8 × $1) = $18.
3. **C. Restaurant B** Calculate the totals for each restaurant:

Rest.	Asparagus	Tomatoes	Asparagus + Tomatoes
A	2 × $22	3 × $15	$44 + $45 = $89
B	4 × $22	1 × $15	$88 + $15 = $103
C	0 × $22	3 × $15	$0 + $45 = $45
D	1 × $22	4 × $15	$22 + $60 = $82

4. **D. 350** Calculate: $3 \times 150 = 450$ sheets will be used. Since the paper sells in packages of 400 sheets, 2 packages are needed, and $2 \times 400 = 800$. $800 - 450 = 350$ sheets left over.
5. **B. 9** Calculate: $19 \div 2 = 9$ r1, so the friends can make 9 whole batches using 2 cups of flour for each batch (and 1 cup will be left over).
6. **B. $1500** Calculate: $(6 \times \$750) - \$3000 = \$1500$.

Lesson 5: Distance and Cost

Practice 5

1. rate; $\frac{d}{t} = r$
2. distance; $d = rt$
3. time; $\frac{d}{r} = t$
4. price per unit; $\frac{c}{n} = r$
5. cost; $c = nr$
6. number of units; $\frac{c}{r} = n$
7. **$48** $c = nr$
   $4 \times \$12 = \$48$
8. **$36** $c = nr$
   $12 \times \$3 = \$36$
9. **$80** $\frac{c}{n} = r$
   $\frac{\$320}{4} = \$80$
10. **5** $\frac{c}{r} = n$
    $\frac{\$25}{\$5} = 5$
11. **$2** $\frac{c}{n} = r$
    $\frac{\$20}{10} = \$2$
12. **180 miles** $d = rt$
    $60 \times 3 = 180$
13. **200 miles** $d = rt$
    $50 \times 4 = 200$
14. **1 hour** $\frac{d}{r} = t$
    $\frac{25}{25} = 1$
15. **90 miles per hour** $\frac{d}{t} = r$
    $\frac{270}{3} = 90$
16. **3 hours** $\frac{d}{r} = t$
    $\frac{75}{25} = 3$
17. **A. 32** $\frac{c}{r} = n$
    $\frac{\$640}{\$20} = 32$
18. **E. 55** $\frac{d}{t} = r$
    $\frac{275}{5} = 55$

Lesson 6: Measurement

Practice 6.1

1. 48 in
2. 7 min
3. 72 hr
4. $2\frac{1}{2}$ pt
5. 20 qt
6. $5\frac{1}{2}$ tons
7. 144 in
8. 12 hr
9. 32 c
10. **D. 3.75 × 4** 4 qt = 1 gal, so multiply the number of gallons by 4 to find the number of quarts.
11. **C. 2 ft 3 in** 12 in = 1 ft Divide. $27 \div 12 = 2$ r3, or 2 ft 3 in
12. **C. 22 lb 8 oz** Multiply: 3 lb 12 oz × 6 = 18 lb 72 oz. To simplify, divide. Use the fact that 1 lb = 16 oz. $72 \div 16 = 4$ r8. 18 lb + 4 lb 8 oz = 22 lb 8 oz.

Practice 6.2

1. 5,000 m
2. 6 m
3. 4,000 mg
4. 8,000 g
5. 4,050 cl
6. 1.5 l
7. 0.25 g
8. 30,000 m
9. 75 cl
10. 0.05 kg
11. 35.2 l
12. 1500 cm
13. **C. 0.1183** There are 1,000 milliliters in 1 liter. 118.3 ml ÷ 1,000 = 0.1183 l
14. **E. 0.5** There are 1000 milligrams in 1 gram. 500 ÷ 1,000 = 0.5 g
15. **B. 625** Convert 2.5 kg to grams. 2.5 ÷ 1,000 = 2500 g Divide. 2,500 g ÷ 4 g = 625 containers
16. **C. 130** Convert 4.8 meters to centimeters. 4.8 × 100 = 480 cm Subtract. 480 – 350 = 130 cm

Lesson 7: Measurement Accuracy

Practice 7

1. pounds
2. ounces
3. pounds
4. tons
5. tons
6. ounces
7. pounds
8. ounces
9. **D. gallon**
10. **B. centimeter**
11. **B. a US quarter** While many of the given items are of the right size, only the US quarter is a standard size that would be recognized by all viewers, so it is the best choice.
12. **C. 6 yd** The tree is about as tall as Judy's house, and a two-story house is about 6 yd (18 ft) high; 25 yd is far too tall for a house.

Problem Solving Practice Questions

1. **E. 96** Multiply: 12 servings × 8 ounces = 96.
2. **B. $2092** Add to find the total: $839 + $527 + 726 = $2092.
3. **B. 4** Divide the length of the sample board by the length of the brace you want: 12 foot board ÷ 2 feet per brace = 6 braces per board. Since you can get 6 braces from each board, divide the total number of braces you want by 6: 24 ÷ 6 = 4 boards.

4. **C. 21** Use the square root function on your calculator or multiply each answer option by itself to find the square root of 441.
5. **A. 30,589** Subtract to find the difference in mileage: 70,040 – 39,451 = 30,589.
6. **C. $656** You can use your calculator. Multiply: $3280 × 20% = $656.
7. **A. $5625** Multiply: $125 × 45 = $5625.
8. **C. 420** Divide distance by time to find Lydia's speed per hour: 180 ÷ 3 = 60. Then multiply by the number of hours she drove on Tuesday: 60 × 7 = 420.
9. **B. 8** Divide the distance by the speed to find the time: 480 ÷ 60 = 8 hours.
10. **B. 96** Divide the total cost by price per item to find the number of items: $1440 ÷ 15 = $96.
11. **A. $200** Multiply the late fee by the number of times Richard has paid his bill late: $25 × 8 = $200
12. **E. $53** Multiply: 7 × $5 = $35 and 18 × $1 = $18. Add the two amounts: $35 + $18 = $53
13. **B. 5** Divide: 17,500 total miles ÷ 3,500 miles between oil changes = 5 oil changes.
14. **A. 134** Divide: 536 total children ÷ 4 months = 134 children per month
15. **A. 198** Subtract to find the difference: 636 – 438 = 198
16. **E. $1072** Multiply: $268 per payment × 4 payments left = $1072
17. **D. 51, 48, 44, 40**
18. **C. 2,350,000** Since the digit to the right of the ten thousands place is less than 5, the digit in the ten thousands place remains the same.
19. **B. 83** Add: 18 + 23 + 42 = 83
20. **A. $6** Subtract: $20 – $14 = $6
21. **E. 60** Since the question says "about," you can use approximate, or rounded, figures. Round the amounts and add: 8 + 33 + 18 ≈ 10 + 30 + 20 = 60
22. **E. 62** Divide distance by time to find the rate of speed: 248 ÷ 4 = 62
23. **E. 18** Divide: 144 ÷ 8 = 18
24. **C. 30** Since the question says "about," you can use approximate figures. Round 299 to 300 and 9 to 10 and then divide: 300 ÷ 10 = 30
25. **E. 2 qt 10 fl oz** 3 qt = 2 qt 2 pt = 2 qt 1 pt 16 fl oz Subtract.

	2 qt 1 pt 16 fl oz
–	1 pt 6 fl oz
	2 qt 10 fl oz

26. **D. 1200** Use rounded figures: 33 rounds to 30, and 41 pounds rounds to 40: 30 × 40 = 1200.
27. **C. $9** Find the total and divide by 4: $21 + $15 = $36, then $36 ÷ 4 = $9
28. **A. $12** Subtract the amount David paid from the total: $128 – $20 = $108. Then divide the remaining amount by the remaining number of people in the group: $108 ÷ 9 = $12.
29. **E. 260** 65 miles per hour × 4 hours = 260 miles.
30. **B. $18** Add the cost of a 1-topping pizza and $2 for each of the 2 additional toppings: $14 + $2 + $2 = $18
31. **C. 14** Multiply by 2 for each dollar: 2 × 7 = 14.
32. **E. 24** Divide: $1800 ÷ $75 per month = 24 months.
33. **E. 14** Divide the maximum capacity by the number of pages per document: 630 ÷ 45 = 14.

Number and Quantity II: Decimals and Fractions

Lesson 1: Decimal Basics

Practice 1

1. 3.8
2. 6
3. 0.43
4. 0.667
5. 8.1
6. 2.714
7. 0.45
8. 0.08
9. 4.68
10. 1.85
11. 1.029
12. 0.14
13. 5.08, 5.6, 5.8, 5.802
14. 0.1136, 0.115, 0.12, 0.2
15. 4.52, 4.667, 4.8, 14.005
16. 0.8, 0.8023, 0.803, 0.823
17. **E. 0.6 g, 0.572 g, 0.0785 g** The correct answer lists the weights from greatest to least. Since none of the weights has a whole number part, compare the tenths places.
18. **E. 1.38** This is the only choice that is rounded to the hundredths place. Since the number in the thousandths place of 1.3815 is less than 5, round down.

Lesson 2: Decimal Operations

Practice 2.1

1. 7.996
2. 10.508
3. 12.26
4. 5.85
5. 7.426
6. 2.11
7. 18.094
8. 5.117
9. 21.32
10. 0.895
11. 3.84
12. 2.35
13. 5.506
14. 21.16
15. 0.645
16. 2.426
17. 0.15
18. 4.88
19. 11.8
20. 14.016
21. 4.522
22. 2.36
23. 17.88
24. 17.225
25. **A. 22.25** Add the times: 7.2 + 6.8 + 8.25 = 22.25 minutes. You do not need to use the 3-mile distance to solve the problem.
26. **D. 4.25** Add to find Claudia's total hours for the week: 8.5 + 9.25 + 8.75 + 10 + 7.75 = 44.25. Then subtract 40 to find the number of overtime hours: 44.25 – 40 = 4.25 hours.
27. **A. 1.8** Add the lengths cut from the pipe: 2.8 + 1.4 = 4.2. Then subtract from 6: 6 – 4.2 = 1.8 meters.
28. **C. $55.26** Add the amounts: $16.98 + $31.78 + $6.50 = $55.26

Practice 2.2

1. 2.65
2. 12.8
3. 0.496
4. 0.52
5. 3.6
6. 4.09
7. 8.75
8. 3.375
9. 9.6681
10. 24
11. 14.2
12. 15,800
13. 34.1
14. 2.36
15. 0.656
16. 2.64
17. 1.65
18. 4.275
19. 3.696
20. 1.002
21. 0.0072
22. **E. 15.16** Multiply 3.79 liters by 4: $3.79 \times 4 = 15.16$ liters.
23. **B. $9.23** Multiply $0.45 × 20.5: $0.45 × 20.5 = $9.225, which rounds to $9.23.
24. **C. 92.9** Divide to find the average daily miles: $278.7 \div 3 = 92.9$ miles.
25. **C. $0.26** There are 19 servings in a box of Toasted Oats. Divide: $4.94 ÷ 19 = $0.26.
26. **B. 50.0** Find the weight in the table and multiply: $12.5 \times 4 = 50$ ounces.

Lesson 3: Fraction Basics

Practice 3

1. $\frac{3}{5}$
2. $\frac{2}{4}$; $\frac{1}{2}$
3. $\frac{2}{3}$
4. $\frac{7}{3}$; $2\frac{1}{3}$
5. $\frac{7}{2}$; $3\frac{1}{2}$
6. $\frac{15}{4}$; $3\frac{3}{4}$
7. $5\frac{2}{3}$
8. $\frac{18}{5}$
9. 4
10. $\frac{47}{9}$
11. $4\frac{3}{4}$
12. $\frac{29}{12}$
13. $4\frac{7}{9}$
14. $\frac{7}{4}$
15. $8\frac{1}{4}$
16. $\frac{57}{10}$
17. $\frac{12}{16}$
18. $\frac{7}{21}$
19. $\frac{48}{60}$
20. $\frac{15}{40}$
21. $\frac{24}{100}$
22. $\frac{3}{4}$
23. $\frac{1}{6}$
24. $\frac{3}{5}$
25. $\frac{13}{15}$
26. $\frac{2}{3}$
27. **A.** $\frac{3}{4}$ Of those surveyed, $\frac{18}{24}$ went to at least one movie. Reduce the fraction to lowest terms: $\frac{18 \div 6}{24 \div 6} = \frac{3}{4}$.
28. **C.** $\frac{40}{100}$ Raise $\frac{2}{5}$ to an equivalent fraction with a denominator of 100 by multiplying both numbers by 20: $\frac{2 \times 20}{5 \times 20} = \frac{40}{100}$.

Lesson 4: Fraction Operations

Practice 4.1

1. $\frac{1}{2}$
2. 1
3. $\frac{1}{3}$
4. $\frac{1}{6}$
5. $\frac{11}{12}$
6. $1\frac{1}{8}$
7. $\frac{3}{10}$
8. $\frac{5}{18}$
9. $3\frac{13}{15}$
10. $1\frac{3}{4}$
11. $8\frac{1}{2}$
12. $11\frac{5}{8}$
13. $21\frac{7}{10}$
14. $7\frac{13}{18}$
15. $12\frac{5}{6}$
16. $2\frac{5}{8}$
17. $42\frac{5}{12}$
18. $22\frac{11}{20}$
19. $5\frac{1}{18}$
20. $11\frac{1}{8}$
21. $3\frac{23}{28}$
22. $1\frac{7}{24}$
23. $2\frac{3}{7}$
24. $8\frac{8}{9}$
25. $\frac{32}{35}$
26. **B.** $1\frac{3}{16}$ Add to find the total: $\frac{5}{16} + \frac{7}{8} = \frac{5}{16} + \frac{14}{16} = \frac{19}{16} = 1\frac{3}{16}$ inches.
27. **C.** $1\frac{5}{8}$ Subtract to find the difference in the lengths: $2\frac{7}{8} - 1\frac{1}{4} = 2\frac{7}{8} - 1\frac{2}{8} = 1\frac{5}{8}$ inches.
28. **A.** $14\frac{3}{8}$ Subtract the amount sold from the amount on the bolt: $23\frac{1}{4} - 8\frac{7}{8} = 23\frac{2}{8} - 8\frac{7}{8} = 22\frac{10}{8} - 8\frac{7}{8} = 14\frac{3}{8}$ yards.
29. **C.** $2\frac{11}{12}$ Add the amounts: $1\frac{2}{3} + \frac{1}{2} + \frac{3}{4} = 1\frac{8}{12} + \frac{6}{12} + \frac{9}{12} = 1\frac{23}{12} = 2\frac{11}{12}$ cups.

Practice 4.2

1. $\frac{1}{6}$
2. $\frac{11}{12}$
3. 14
4. $18\frac{3}{4}$
5. $\frac{7}{8}$
6. $\frac{21}{32}$
7. $7\frac{14}{15}$
8. $41\frac{1}{4}$
9. $2\frac{1}{32}$
10. 14
11. $1\frac{4}{5}$
12. 48
13. $2\frac{2}{5}$
14. $2\frac{1}{4}$

15. 27

16. 8

17. $9\frac{1}{2}$

18. $\frac{3}{4}$

19. **B. 75** Find $\frac{3}{16}$ of 400 by multiplying:
$400 \times \frac{3}{16} = \frac{\overset{25}{\cancel{400}}}{1} \times \frac{3}{\underset{1}{\cancel{16}}} = \frac{75}{1} = 75.$

20. **B. 7** Divide: $20 \div 2\frac{3}{4} = \frac{20}{1} \div \frac{11}{4} = \frac{20}{1} \times \frac{4}{11} = \frac{80}{11} = 7\frac{3}{11}$. Ignore the remainder since the problem asks how many shirts can be completed.

21. **B. 33** You need to find how many $\frac{2}{3}$ hours there are in 22 hours. Divide: $22 \div \frac{2}{3} = \frac{22}{1} \div \frac{2}{3} = \frac{11}{1} \times \frac{3}{1} = \frac{33}{1}$.

22. **C. $37\frac{7}{8}$** Multiply $12\frac{5}{8}$ inches by 3, the number of panels: $12\frac{5}{8} \times 3 = \frac{101}{8} \times \frac{3}{1} = \frac{303}{8} = 37\frac{7}{8}$.

Lesson 5: Fraction and Decimal Equivalencies

Practice 5

1. **C. $20.00** Instead of multiplying $80 by 0.25, you can also find $\frac{1}{4}$ of $80.
2. **D. 480 × 0.3** Find $\frac{3}{10}$ of 480. "Of" in "of the workers" indicates multiplication, and the decimal equivalent of $\frac{3}{10}$ is 0.3.
3. **B. $4\frac{2}{3}$** The decimal part of the calculator display equals the fraction $\frac{2}{3}$.
4. **D. $18.00** Multiply 12 by 1.5. The decimal $1.5 = 1\frac{1}{2}$. Convert that fraction to an improper fraction: $\frac{3}{2}$ Now multiply: $12 \times \frac{3}{2} = \frac{36}{2} = 18$.
5. **B. $\frac{3}{4}$** Subtract: $1.875 - 1.125 = 0.75$, which equals $\frac{3}{4}$ inch.
6. **C. 0.375** Instead of dividing 3 by 8, think: $3 \div 8$ means $\frac{3}{8}$, which equals 0.375.

Lesson 6: Decimals and Fractions on the Number Line

Practice 6

1. **C. $\frac{2}{3}$** The number line is in increments of $\frac{1}{3}$, and the value you are asked to identify comes halfway between $\frac{1}{3}$ and 1.
2. **E. 2.8** The number line is in increments of 0.2, and the value you are asked to identify comes halfway between 2.6 and 3.
3. **C. 2** A minus B is $3\frac{1}{2} - 1\frac{1}{2} = 2$.
4. $\frac{2}{3}$ Angela gave 16 of 24 cookies to her neighbor: $\frac{16}{24} = \frac{2}{3}$.
5. **4.625** Each increment on this number line is 0.125 greater than the previous increment.
6. **$9.3\overline{3}$** Each increment on the number line is $0.3\overline{3}$ greater than the previous increment.
7. **$3\frac{1}{3}$** Each increment on the number line is $\frac{1}{3}$ greater than the previous increment.
8. **$11\frac{5}{6}$** Each increment on the number line is $\frac{1}{6}$ greater than the previous increment.

Lesson 7: Rational and Irrational Numbers

Practice 7

1. Rational
2. Irrational: $\sqrt{7} = 2.64575131106...$
3. Rational
4. Rational: (also: $\frac{2}{3}$)
5. Rational
6. Rational: $\sqrt[3]{27} = 3$
7. Irrational: $\sqrt{13} = 3.60555127546...$
8. Rational: $0.1\overline{6} + \frac{7}{6} = \frac{1}{6} + \frac{7}{6} = \frac{8}{6}$
9. Irrational: $\sqrt{2} + \sqrt{121} = \sqrt{2} + 11$
10. Rational: $\sqrt{265} \times \sqrt{265} = 265$
11. Irrational: rational × irrational = irrational
12. Rational: $\sqrt[3]{64} \times \sqrt{64} = 4 \times 8 = 32$
13. Rational: $\sqrt{49} + \sqrt{16} = 7 + 4 = 11$

Lesson 8: Decimal and Fraction Calculator Skills

Practice 8

1. **7.379**
2. **$2\frac{1}{4}$** To work with mixed fractions on the TI-30XS MultiView™, use the (2nd) function above the [n/d] key: (2nd) [n/d] 3 ▶ 2 ▼ 3 ▶ ⊖ (2nd) [n/d] 1 ▶ 5 ▼ 12 (enter). The number $\frac{9}{4}$ will appear on the right-hand side of the display.
3. **$380.25**
4. **42**
5. **$84.44** Multiply: $\$95 \times \frac{8}{9} = 84.44\overline{4}$. Round to get $84.44.
6. **$79.74** Divide: $956.88 ÷ 12 = $79.
7. **$1,475** Multiply: $118,000 ×0.0125 = $1,475
8. **$4\frac{1}{4}$ cups** Add: $1\frac{1}{2} + 2\frac{3}{4} = 4\frac{1}{4}$
9. **B. $6.67** Multiply the weight of the quilt by $1.20: 5.56 × $1.20 = $6.672, which rounds to $6.67.
10. **C. 24** You need to find $\frac{3}{8}$ of 64. Multiply. $64 \times \frac{3}{8} = 24$ acres.

Decimals and Fractions Practice Questions

1. **C. $15\frac{3}{4}$** Subtract: $20\frac{1}{2} - 4\frac{3}{4} = 20\frac{2}{4} - 4\frac{3}{4} = 19\frac{6}{4} - 4\frac{3}{4} = 15\frac{3}{4}$
2. **C. $0.25** Divide the cost by the number of servings: $4.69 ÷ 19 ≈ 0.247, which rounds to $0.25.
3. **C. $1386.20** To find the amount the 12-month plan will cost a customer, multiply $98.85 by 12 and add $200: ($98.85 × 12) + $200 = $1386.20.
4. **C. $30.12** Multiply using your calculator. Use 10.5 for $10\frac{1}{2}$: $2.869 × 10.5 = $30.1245, which rounds to $30.12.
5. **E. 2.85** Since the answer choices are decimals, use your calculator. Use decimals instead of fractions:

$1\frac{1}{2} = 1.5$, $4\frac{3}{4} = 4.75$, and $2\frac{3}{10} = 2.3$. To find the average, add the three weights and divide the total by 3: $\frac{1.5+4.75+2.3}{3} = \frac{8.55}{3} = 2.85$,

6. **D. $32\frac{1}{4}$** Divide: $\$258 \div \$8 = 32.25$, which equals $32\frac{1}{4}$.
7. **B. 57** Subtract $6\frac{1}{4}$ from $20\frac{1}{2}$ and divide the difference by $\frac{1}{4}$. To do the work quickly, use the fraction keys on your calculator or change the fractions to decimals: $20\frac{1}{2} - 6\frac{1}{4} = 14\frac{1}{4}$; $14\frac{1}{4} \div \frac{1}{4} = 57$.
8. **E. $90.00** Brand B costs $0.09 more than Brand A, so the school will save $0.09 on each marker. Multiply the savings by 1000: $\$0.09 \times 1000 = \$90.00$.
9. **B. $3\frac{1}{2}$** Add the times for the appointments:
$\frac{3}{4} + \frac{3}{4} + 1\frac{1}{4} + \frac{3}{4} = 1\frac{10}{4} = 3\frac{2}{4} = 3\frac{1}{2}$
10. **C. 10** Divide $3\frac{1}{2}$ hours by the amount of time needed for a routine physical: $3\frac{1}{2} \div \frac{1}{3} = \frac{7}{2} \div \frac{1}{3} = \frac{7}{2} \times \frac{3}{1} = \frac{21}{2} = 10\frac{1}{2}$. Therefore, Jennifer can complete 10 physicals. Ignore the fraction remainder.
11. **E. $\frac{11}{12}$** Write the fraction and reduce it to lowest terms. You can save time by using the fraction key on your calculator, which automatically reduces a fraction to lowest terms. Press 5500 [n/d] [▼] 6000 (enter). The right-hand side of the display will read $\frac{11}{12}$.
12. **C. $7.25** The first hour costs $3.50, and there are $1\frac{1}{2}$ hours left. There are 3 half hours, or $1\frac{1}{2}$ hours, so you will pay $\$3.50 + (3 \times \$1.25) = \$7.25$.
13. **E. $\frac{2}{3}$** Write a fraction and reduce: $\frac{56}{84} = \frac{56 \div 28}{84 \div 28} = \frac{2}{3}$
14. **B. 0.84** Subtract to compare: $3.97 - 3.13 = 0.84$
15. **B. $\frac{3}{10}$** Subtract: $250-175=75$. Thus, 75 out of 250, or $\frac{75}{250}$, have not been loaded. Reduce: $\frac{75 \div 25}{250 \div 25} = \frac{3}{10}$.
16. **B. $\frac{5}{8}$** $A - B = \frac{7}{8} - \frac{1}{4}$. Find a common denominator and subtract: $\frac{7}{8} - \frac{2}{8} = \frac{5}{8}$.
17. **A. 285** To find $\frac{3}{4}$ of 380, multiply. Change $\frac{3}{4}$ to 0.75. Then $380 \times 0.75 = 285$.
18. **C. $\frac{5}{6}$** To find half of $1\frac{2}{3}$, either multiply by $\frac{1}{2}$ or divide by 2. Both results are the same: $1\frac{2}{3} \times \frac{1}{2} = \frac{5}{3} \times \frac{1}{2} = \frac{5}{6}$.
19. **C. 150** You need to find $\frac{5}{8}$ of 240. Multiply:
$240 \times \frac{5}{8} = \frac{\overset{30}{\cancel{240}}}{1} \times \frac{5}{\underset{1}{\cancel{8}}} = \frac{150}{1} = 150$.
20. **E. core box, classic, bevel, cutter** You could change the fractions to decimals to solve the problem, but the quickest method is to rewrite the fractions with a common denominator of 32:
cutter: $\frac{9}{16} = \frac{18}{32}$;
core box: $\frac{5}{32}$;
classic: $\frac{3}{8} = \frac{12}{32}$;
bevel: $\frac{1}{2} = \frac{16}{32}$.
Then arrange the like fractions from least to greatest by their numerators.
21. **B. W and Y** The most Joe will eat will be $\frac{7}{8}$ of his pizza, so the minimum he'll have left over will be $\frac{1}{8}$ of it. The least Joe will eat will be $\frac{1}{2}$, so the maximum he'll have left over will be $\frac{1}{2}$ of the pizza.
22. **C. 8** Divide: $60 \div 7.5 = 8$ days.
23. **A. $\frac{1}{2}$** Multiply: $\frac{2}{3} \times \frac{3}{4} = \frac{\overset{1}{\cancel{2}}}{\underset{1}{\cancel{3}}} \times \frac{\overset{1}{\cancel{3}}}{\underset{2}{\cancel{4}}} = \frac{1}{2}$.
24. **B. 56** Multiply: $140 \times \frac{2}{5} = \frac{\overset{28}{\cancel{140}}}{1} \times \frac{2}{\cancel{5}} = \frac{56}{1} = 56$.
25. **C. 17.9** Maya travels five segments of the route. Add to find the total distance: $2.4 + 4.3 + 3.6 + 3.6 + 4.0 = 17.9$.
26. **E. 5** Add to find the total amount to be cut off:
$3\frac{3}{4} + 3\frac{3}{4} = 6\frac{6}{4} = 7\frac{1}{2}$. Subtract from $12\frac{1}{2}$: $12\frac{1}{2} - 7\frac{1}{2} = 5$.
27. **B. $535.60** Multiply $26.38 by 20 and add $8 to the result: $\$26.38 \times 20 = \$527.60$. Then: $\$527.60 + \$8.00 = \$535.60$.
28. **E. 80** Divide: $60 \div 0.75 = 80$.
29. **E. $\frac{7}{12}$** Add the fractions and subtract the total from 1:
$\frac{1}{6} + \frac{1}{4} = \frac{2}{12} + \frac{3}{12} = \frac{5}{12}$. Then: $1 - \frac{5}{12} = \frac{12}{12} - \frac{5}{12} = \frac{7}{12}$.

Number and Quantity III: Ratio, Proportion, and Percent

Lesson 1: Ratio and Proportion

Practice 1.1

1. $\frac{24}{6} = \frac{4}{1}$
2. $\frac{\$250}{\$1500} = \frac{1}{6}$
3. $\frac{180}{15} = \frac{12}{1}$
4. $\frac{12}{30} = \frac{2}{5}$ Add $12 + 18 = 30$ to find the total workers.
5. $\frac{336}{14} = \frac{24}{1}$
6. $\frac{\$1500}{\$2400} = \frac{5}{8}$
7. $\frac{20}{12} = \frac{5}{3}$ Subtract $32 - 20 = 12$ to find the free throws missed.
8. $\frac{14}{24} = \frac{7}{12}$ Add $10 + 14 = 24$ to find the total students.
9. $\frac{1440}{6} = \frac{240}{1}$
10. **A. 9:11** Write the ratio in fraction form and reduce: $\frac{180}{220} = \frac{9}{11}$.
11. **B. 3 to 10** Calculate: $\frac{180}{600} = \frac{3}{10}$.
12. **B. $\frac{1}{3}$** Subtract to find the voters who have made a decision: $600 - 150 = 450$. Write the ratio and reduce: $\frac{150}{450} = \frac{1}{3}$.
13. **C. 1 to 2** Subtract to find the amount owed: $\$1200 - \$400 = \$800$. Write the ratio and reduce: 400 to 800 = 1 to 2.
14. **E. 8:3** Subtract to find the number of losses: $77 - 56 = 21$. Write the ratio and reduce: $\frac{56}{21} = \frac{8}{3}$.

Practice 1.2

1. 12
2. 45

3. 2.5 or $2\frac{1}{2}$
4. 60
5. $371
6. 96
7. 2.1 or $2\frac{1}{10}$
8. 72
9. 12.5 or $12\frac{1}{2}$
10. $8.94
11. 1.25 or $1\frac{1}{4}$
12. 37.5 or $37\frac{1}{2}$
13. 18
14. 32
15. $45.50
16. 28
17. **B. $1.23** Calculate: $\frac{4}{\$0.98} = \frac{5}{x}$ $0.98 × 5 ÷ 4 = $1.225, which rounds to $1.23.
18. **E. 96** Calculate: $\frac{5}{8} = \frac{60}{x}$; 8 × 60 ÷ 5 = 96.
19. **B. 23** Calculate: $\frac{414}{18} = \frac{x}{1}$; 414 × 1 ÷ 18 = 23.
20. **B. 345** Calculate: $\frac{2\text{ cm}}{150\text{ km}} = \frac{4.6\text{ cm}}{x\text{ km}}$; 150 × 4.6 ÷ 2 = 345.
21. **A. $6\frac{2}{3}$** Write the proportions using fractions. The process is the same: $\frac{2\frac{1}{2}}{1\frac{1}{2}} = \frac{x}{4}$; $2\frac{1}{2} \times 4 \div 1\frac{1}{2} = 6\frac{2}{3}$.
22. **A. 155 × 7 ÷ 2.5** Set up the proportion and think about the order of operations you would need to solve for *x*: $\frac{155}{2.5} = \frac{x}{7}$; 155 × 7 ÷ 2.5 = *x*.

Lesson 2: Percents

Practice 2

1. base = $1000
part = $200
rate = 20%
2. base = 80
part = 72
rate = 90%
3. base = $13,700
part = $2,740
rate = 20%
4. base = $2000
part = $500
rate = 25%
5. base = 40
part = 60
rate = 150%
60 is 150% *of* 40. The word *of* indicates that 40 is the base.
6. base = $38
part = $3.23
rate = 8.5%
7. base = $900
part = $135
rate = 15%
8. base = $10.70
part = $1.07
rate = 10%
9. base = 800
part = 200
rate = 25%
10. base = 12,500
part = 5,000
rate = 40%
11. **A. $\frac{9 \times 100}{12}$** Add the wins and losses to find the total games played: 9 + 3 = 12; then write the proportion: $\frac{9}{12} = \frac{x}{100}$. To solve the proportion, you need to find the expression that multiplies 9 and 100 and divides by 12. Only choice (A) does this.
12. **E. 50%** Bravo played 12 games (6 + 6 = 12). Then $\frac{6}{12} = \frac{x}{100}$ and 6 × 100 ÷ 12 = 50.
13. **E. $32** To find 25% of $128, solve the proportion: $\frac{x}{\$128} = \frac{25}{100}$; $128 × 25 ÷ 100 = $32. Since 25% = $\frac{1}{4}$, you can also find the answer by dividing $128 by 4.

Lesson 3: Using the Percent Formula

Practice 3.1

1. $5
2. 180
3. 140
4. 95%
5. 25%
6. 3%
7. 17
8. $60
9. 200%
10. 5%
11. 8%
12. $3.91
13. $6\frac{1}{2}$% or 6.5%
14. $364
15. 62.5% or $62\frac{1}{2}$%
16. 72
17. **C. 60%** Calculate: 72 ÷ 120 = 0.6 = 60%.
18. **B. $2,385** Calculate: $2,250 × 0.06 = $135, and $2,250 + $135 = $2,385.
19. **D. $6.90.** Calculate: $46 × 0.15 = $6.90.
20. **E. 70%** Find what percent $45.50 is of $65 by dividing: $45.50 ÷ $65 = 0.7, which equals 70%.
21. **A. $\frac{\$3 \times 100}{\$50}$** You need to divide the part ($3) by the whole ($50) to find the rate; however, choice (D) states $3 ÷ $50, which equals 0.06. You still need to change 0.06 to a percent, which you can do by multiplying by 100. If you write a proportion to solve the problem, you will see that choice (A) is correct.

Practice 3.2

1. $175
2. 280
3. 6.4
4. $200
5. 30
6. $84
7. 200
8. 9
9. $13.50
10. 25%
11. $75
12. $9.30
13. 900
14. 90%
15. $780
16. $3120
17. 4000
18. 10%
19. **C. $1,230.00** Solve for the base: $\frac{\$369}{0.3}$ = $1,230.
20. **C. $1,200,000** Solve for the base. $\frac{\$72{,}000}{0.06}$ = $1,200,000.
21. **B. $\frac{160 \times 100}{5}$** Set up the problem as a proportion: $\frac{160}{x} = \frac{5}{100}$. To solve the proportion, you would multiply 160 × 100 and divide by 5. Only choice (B) carries out those operations.
22. **D. 720.** The base is 3600, the total number who received the application. The part is the unknown number who returned the application. Since 20% = 0.2, you can solve for the part by multiplying the base by the rate: 3600 × 0.2.

Lesson 4: Percent Calculator Skills

Practice 4

1. $59.80
2. $96
3. $15.12
4. 40
5. 3%
6. 2080
7. 25%
8. 70
9. 25.2
10. 79
11. 2.5% or $2\frac{1}{2}$%
12. 48
13. 78%
14. $16
15. 250
16. 14
17. 7%
18. 276
19. **C. $8.20** Chanel's order falls between $50.01 and $100. Find 5% of $84: press: 0.05 ⊗ 84 (enter). The right side of the display reads 4.2, or $4.20. Add $4: $4.20 + $4 = $8.20.
20. **A. $0.30** Find the shipping and handling for Jason's order: 8% of $110 = $8.80. Find the shipping and handling for Zola's order: 5% of $90 = $4.50, and $4.50 + $4.00 = $8.50. Then find the difference: $8.80 – $8.50 = $0.30.
21. **C. 88%** Press: 3190 ⊕ 3625 (2nd) () (enter). The right side of the display reads 0.88. You could also simply divide: 3190 ÷ 3625 = .88. Then mentally translate .88 into 88%.
22. **E. 15%** Divide strikeouts (63) by at bats (410): press: 63 ⊕ 410(enter). The right side of the display reads 0.153658537, which rounds to 15%.

Lesson 5: Interest

Practice 5

1. **$360**
2. **$1,998** Because 8 months is $\frac{2}{3}$ of a year, use $\frac{2}{3}$ for t in the formula.
3. **$420**
4. **$1,024**
5. **E. $1,300 + ($1,300 × 0.09 × 1.5)** Find the interest by multiplying the amount borrowed ($1300) by the interest expressed as a decimal (0.09) by the time period in years (1.5). To find the amount paid back, the amount borrowed must be added to the interest. Only choice (E) shows this series of operations.
6. **B. $144** Find the interest for each loan option: Option A: $2,400 × 0.12 × 2.5 = $720; Option C: $2,400 × 0.09 × 4 = $864. Subtract to find the difference: $864 – $720 = $144.

Lesson 6: Percent of Change

Practice 6

1. 50%
2. 38%
3. 200%
4. 45%
5. 20%
6. 32%
7. 21%
8. 86%
9. 420%
10. 34%
11. **B. 60%** Subtract: $448 – $280 = $168. Divide by the original weekly pay: $168 ÷ $280 = 0.6, which equals 60%.
12. **B. 25%** Subtract: $48 – $36 = $12. Divide by the original price: $12 ÷ $48 = 0.25, which equals 25%.
13. **D. 6%** Subtract: $636 – $600 = $36. Divide by the original rent: $36 ÷ $600 = 0.06, which equals 6%.
14. **C. 125%** The wholesale price of the model is $63, and the retail price is $141.75. Subtract: $141.75 – $63 = $78.75. Divide by the wholesale price: $78.75 ÷ $63 = 1.25, which equals 125%.
15. **B. 30%** The retail price of the model is $150.50, and the member's price is $105.35. Subtract: $150.50 – $105.35 = $45.15. Divide by the retail price: $45.15 ÷ 150.50 = 0.3, which equals 30%.

Ratio, Proportion, and Percent Practice Questions

1. **C. 1:11** Subtract to find the dollars spent on other costs: $360,000 – $30,000 = $330,000. Write a ratio and reduce: $\frac{\$30,000}{\$330,000} = \frac{1}{11}$.
2. **A. 2 × $\frac{50}{5}$** Write a proportion: $\frac{5}{2} = \frac{50}{x}$. To solve it, multiply 2 × 50 and divide by 5. Only choice (A) performs these operations.
3. **B. $7.56** Find 35% of $5.60: $5.60 × 0.35 = $1.96; add: $1.96 + $5.60 = $7.56. Another way to get the answer is to find 135% of $5.60. $5.60 × 1.35 = $7.56.
4. **E. $20,000** The current worth of the car ($12,000) is part of the base. Solve for the base: $12,000 ÷ 0.6 = $20,000.
5. **C. 42** Solve the proportion: $\frac{7}{3} = \frac{x}{18}$; 7 × 18 ÷ 3 = 42.
6. **A. 6%** The commission is part of the base. Solve for the part: $954 ÷ $15,900 = 0.06 = 6%.
7. **B. 1:6** Add to find the total time spent on the project: $2 + 1\frac{1}{2} + 2 + 3\frac{1}{2} = 9$ hours. $1\frac{1}{2}$ hours = 1.5 hours. Write a ratio using decimals and reduce: $\frac{1.5}{9} = \frac{1}{6}$.
8. **B. 36%** Add to find the acres used for grains, vegetables, or fruits: 5,200 + 9,200 = 14,400. Solve for percent: 14,400 ÷ 40,400 = 0.36 = 36%.
9. **A. 35,600** Calculate the decrease in acres of dairy farmland: 22,000 × 20% = 4,400. Subtract that amount from the total acreage of farmland to determine how many acres of farmland will remain: 40,000 – 4,400 = 35,600.
10. **A. $\frac{3}{16}$** The total fat is 3 + 13 = 16 grams. Write the ratio of saturated fat (3 grams) to the total (16 grams). The ratio cannot be simplified.
11. **B. 10** Write a proportion and solve: $\frac{4}{5} = \frac{x}{12.5}$. Then 4 × 12.5 ÷ 5 = 10 inches.
12. **E. 138** Write a proportion and solve: $\frac{4}{3} = \frac{184}{x}$. Then 3 × 184 ÷ 4 = 138 female patients.
13. **C. $900** If 20% is the amount of the discount, then the sale price must be 80% of the original price. The sale price is the part, and the original price is the base. Solve for the base: $720 ÷ 0.8 = $900.
14. **D. 40** If the ratio of wins to losses is 5:4, then the ratio of wins to games played is 5:9. Write a proportion and solve: $\frac{5}{9} = \frac{x}{72}$; 5 × 72 ÷ 9 = 40 games won.
15. **C. 192** Add to find the number that did not answer "no": 16% + 32% = 48%. Find 48% of 400: 400 × 0.48 = 192.

16. **C. 20%** To find the percent decrease, subtract the lower price from the higher price and divide the difference by the original price. In this case, the original price is \$25, the higher price. To change the answer to a percent, you must move the decimal point two places to the right or multiply by 100.
17. **B. 121** When the rate is greater than 100%, the part will be greater than the base. Solve for the part: $55 \times 2.2 = 121$.
18. **E. 18%** There are 6 grams of fat in the roast beef sandwich, so there are $6 \times 9 = 54$ calories in the sandwich from fat. The total number of calories in the sandwich is 300. Find what percent 54 is of 300: $54 \div 300 = 0.18 = 18\%$.
19. **D. \$264** Write a proportion and solve: $\frac{\$8}{\$3} = \frac{\$704}{x}$; $\$3 \times \$704 \div \$8 = \$264$.
20. **C. 175** The 140 employees who have more than 12 days of sick leave are part of the whole workforce. You need to solve for the base: $140 \div 0.8 = 175$.
21. **E. 825** If the ratio of sold to unsold tickets is 11 to 1, then the ratio of sold to total tickets is 11 to 12. Write a proportion and solve: $\frac{11}{12} = \frac{x}{900}$; $11 \times 900 \div 12 = 825$.
22. **C. \$2464** Use the formula for finding simple interest: $i = prt$: $\$2200 \times 0.08 \times 1.5 = \$264$. To find the amount in the account at the end of the time, add the interest to the original investment: $\$2200 + \$264 = \$2464$.
23. **B. \$328** Once you find the discount by multiplying 0.2 by \$410, you will need to subtract the discount from \$410 to find the sale price.
24. **E. 330** After changing $2\frac{3}{4}$ to the decimal 2.75, write a proportion and solve: $\frac{0.5}{60} = \frac{2.75}{x}$; $60 \times 2.75 \div 0.5 = 330$.
25. **D.** $\frac{(140-91)}{140} \times 100$ There were 140 customers on Sunday, and 91 made a purchase. Therefore, 140 – 91 did not make a purchase. To find the percent rate, divide the difference by 140, the total number of customers on Sunday (the base). Then move the decimal point two places to the right or multiply by 100 to change the answer to a percent. Only choice (D) shows this sequence of operations.
26. **E. 270** Write a proportion and solve: $\frac{9}{14} = \frac{x}{420}$.
27. **D.** $\frac{3}{5}$ If Marcie spends 15 hours answering telephones, she spends 40 – 15, or 25 hours doing other tasks. Write a ratio and reduce: $\frac{15}{25} = \frac{3}{5}$.

Statistics and Probability

Lesson 1: Tables and Pictographs

Practice 1

1. **9** Calculate: $22{,}707 \div 2523 = 9$
2. **6%** Calculate: $(139{,}510 - 130{,}748) \div 139{,}510 \approx 0.06$, or 6%.
3. **300** There are $6\frac{1}{2}$ symbols in the "North" row and $4\frac{1}{2}$ in the "South" row. Two more symbols translates to 300 more books.
4. **3000** Count the number of symbols, 20, and multiply by 150.
5. **D. Reads or pretends to read** If 100 children were surveyed in each year, then the number of children who recognized all letters increased from 11 to 17. To find the percent change, use the percent change formula: $\frac{\text{amount of change}}{\text{original value}} = \frac{17-11}{11} = \frac{6}{11}$, or a roughly 55% increase. Performing similar calculations for all categories will reveal that "reads or pretends to read" showed the least percent increase: $\frac{67-66}{66} = \frac{1}{66} \approx 2\%$. Note that simply subtracting 66 from 67 does not give you the percent of change.
6. **C. 119** In 2010, 34% of 3-year-old children could write their own names. Find 34% of 350: $350 \times 0.34 = 119$.
7. **C. 375** There are $7\frac{1}{2}$ car symbols. Each symbol represents 50 cars. Multiply: $7\frac{1}{2} \times 50 = 375$
8. **A. 75** Compare the symbols for the two rows. There are $1\frac{1}{2}$ more symbols for 8 A.M. to noon than there are after 4:30 P.M. Multiply: $1\frac{1}{2} \times 50 = 75$

Lesson 2: Bar and Line Graphs

Practice 2.1

1. **50**
2. **about 15** Estimate 38 complaints in 2011 and 22 complaints in 2006. Subtract and round.
3. **20%** The number of complaints decreased by 5, from 25 to 20. This represents a $\frac{5}{25} = 20\%$ decrease.
4. **about \$20 million** Estimate values from the graph and subtract. Be sure to use the black bars that represent cost.
5. **Film A** Film A has the biggest difference in size between the bar representing box-office receipts and the bar representing cost.
6. **150%** Calculate: $\frac{60}{40} = \frac{3}{2} = 150\%$
7. **A. 40** There are approximately 110 T-shirts, more than 40 books, and a little fewer than 30 toys sold. Combined, about 70 books and toys were sold. Subtract 70 from 110, and you have about 40.
8. **D. \$1000** There were about 50 games sold, so 25 sold for \$16 and 25 sold for \$24. Calculate: $(25 \times 16) + (25 \times 24) = 1000$.
9. **C. 14:3** Write a ratio and simplify: $\frac{70}{15} = \frac{14}{3}$
10. **E. September** Add the 2-day and 5-day permits for each month. Only September's permits equal 80.

Practice 2.2

1. **October** The point representing October is lower than the point representing the previous month, and the line leading to it slopes downward. This indicates a decrease.
2. **270** Estimate totals for the three months and add.
3. **from June to July** The number of visits increased more from August to September, but because the number in June was so low, the percentage increase from June to July is nearly 100%.
4. **\$10** Estimate values and subtract.

5. **20%** The price increased from about \$25 to about \$30, an increase of \$5. $\frac{5}{25}$ = 20%.
6. **\$30** The price increased from about \$18 to about \$45. This increase is almost \$30.
7. **A. 1930 to 1940** The price of goods decreased over two decades, 1920 to 1940. Note the downward movement of the line. Only the time period 1930 to 1940 is included among the answer options.
8. **E. $\frac{1}{5}$** The price of the same goods was about \$20 in 1970 and \$100 in 2000. Write a ratio and simplify: $\frac{\$20}{\$100} = \frac{1}{5}$
9. **B. 50** There were about 390 sales in Store 2 and 340 sales in Store 1 in the sixth week: 390 – 340 = 50.
10. **E. Week 5** The steepest line segment leads from week 4 to week 5, indicating the largest increase in sales from the previous week.

Lesson 3: Circle Graphs

Practice 3

1. **29%** Find those two categories on the circle graph and add.
2. $\frac{2}{25}$ 8% = $\frac{8}{100} = \frac{2}{25}$
3. **\$630** Use the total budget. \$2250 × 28% = \$630.
4. **\$30.60** 17 cents of every dollar are spent on water heating: \$180 × 0.17 = \$30.60.
5. **Heating and Air-Conditioning** The section labeled "Heating and Air-Conditioning" takes up more than half the circle.
6. **Cooking and Refrigeration** This section is 11 cents of every dollar, which is about 10%.
7. **A. 10** According to the graph, a records clerk spends 25%, or $\frac{1}{4}$, of his or her time preparing documents. Then 25% of 40 hours is 10 hours.
8. **E. 56%** If 44% of the time is spent on data entry, then 100% – 44% = 56% spent on other tasks.
9. **B. 10%** Add: 3 cents plus 7 cents in 10 cents. Then 10 cents out of 100 cents is $\frac{10}{100}$, or 10%.
10. **C. \$48** 40 cents out of every dollar, or 40%, is spent on public bonds. Then 40% of \$120 is found by multiplying: \$120 × 0.4 = \$48.

Lesson 4: Measures of Central Tendency

Practice 4.1

1. **57** Count the number of tally marks and add.
2. **6** Count the number of tally marks and subtract.
3. **1:2** Calculate: $\frac{15}{30} = \frac{1}{2}$
4. **3:4** Calculate: $\frac{6}{8} = \frac{3}{4}$
5. **46** Count the tally marks and add.
6. **14%** Count the total number of tally marks, then divide: $\frac{10}{70} \approx 0.14 = 14\%$.
7. **B. $\frac{4}{11}$** There are 16 tally marks next to the reason "wrong size." Add all the tally marks: 16 + 20 + 3 + 5 = 44. Write a ratio and reduce. $\frac{16}{44} = \frac{4}{11}$.
8. **C. 45%** Adding all the tally marks, you find that there were 44 clothing returns in all. Since there are 20 tally marks by "unwanted gift," $\frac{20}{44}$ or ≈ 45% of the total reasons given were "unwanted gift."
9. **D. 39%** Calculate: 35 applicants had a speed under 30 wpm, out of a total of 90 applicants, so $\frac{35}{90} \approx 39\%$.
10. **B. 1:2** To find those who could type above 45 wpm, add: 18 + 12 = 30. The number typing below 45 wpm is found by adding 35 + 25 = 60. Write a ratio and reduce: $\frac{30}{60} = \frac{1}{2}$.

Practice 4.2

1. mean: 80.14
   median: 80
   mode: 82
2. mean: \$8,487.17
   median: \$8,208.50
   mode: none
3. mean: \$4.76
   median: \$4.50
   mode: \$4.50
4. mean: 309 miles
   median: 300 miles
   mode: none
5. mean: \$101.83
   median: \$101.81
   mode: none
6. mean: 86
   median: 88
   mode: 88
7. mean: 99.1°
   median: 99°
   mode: 98° and 100°
8. mean: 1.9 inches
   median: 1.8 inches
   mode: none
9. mean: 305
   median: 305
   mode: 305
10. mean: 38.8 hours
    median: 40 hours
    mode: 40 hours
11. **A. \$117,100** Add the amounts in the column labeled "Asking Price" and divide by 6, the number of prices listed.
12. **C. \$116,500** Arrange the selling prices in order: \$124,800; \$118,400; \$116,500; \$116,500; \$109,000; \$103,600. Since the number of items is even, there are two in the middle: \$116,500 and \$116,500. Since these are the same amount, the average of the two is also \$116,500.
13. **A.** $\frac{790 + 1150 + 662 + 805}{4}$ To find the mean, add the numbers and divide by the number of items in the set. In this case, there are 4 numbers.
14. **C. \$900** The median is the middle amount. Arrange the amounts in order and find the middle amount.
15. **B. 14** The mode is the number that occurs most often. Only 14 occurs more than once in the data.

Lesson 5: Line Plots

Practice 5

1. **C.** Look for a line plot that reflects that two zebras have 26 stripes, two have 28, two have 30, etc.
2. **B.** Look for a line plot that reflects three classes with 29 students, two classes with 32, etc.
3. **E. the member who plants eight types of vegetables** Most of the data points are clustered around the quantities 1 through 4. The member who planted 8 types of vegetables is distant from that cluster of data and so is an outlier.

Lesson 6: Scatter Plots

Practice 6.1

1. Positive
2. Null
3. Negative
4. Negative
5. Positive

Practice 6.2

1. **B. A line of best fit with a negative correlation can be drawn.** Note that a null correlation cannot have a line of best fit and that a line of best fit usually will not connect every dot.
2. **E. Annual winter temperatures and sales of winter gear.** The data in (B) would have a null correlation while the remaining choices would have positive correlations. Only (E) has a negative correlation—as temperatures go *down*, winter gear sales should generally trend *up*.
3. **E. (9, –9)** A point that conforms closely to the trend would be closest to the line of best fit. To see why (E) is correct, draw the line of best fit and plot each of the choices:

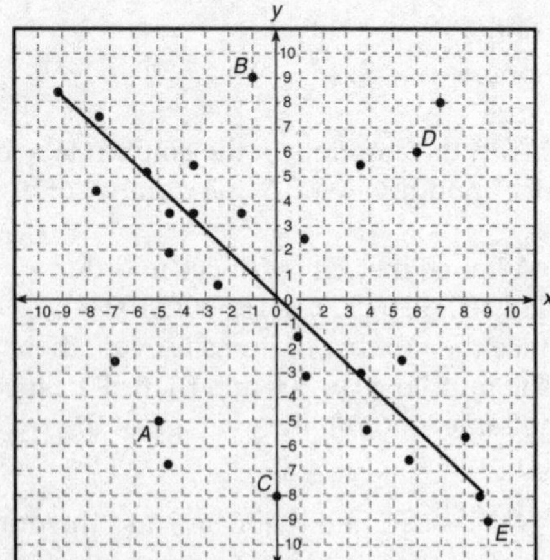

Lesson 7: Histograms

Practice 7

1. **C.** Look for the histogram that begins with 30 and that has a second bar at 56, a third bar at 80, etc.
2. **D.** Look for the histogram that begins with 15 and that has a second bar at 22, a third bar at 35, etc.
3. **C. 36%** Estimate the percentages represented by the four bars that cover the time period of December 9 through January 5: 8%, 9%, 9%, and 10%. Add those estimates to find the approximate percentage of cases reported during that entire time period, resulting in 35%.

Lesson 8: Probability

Practice 8.1

1. **$\frac{2}{5}$, 0.4, 40%** Calculate: $\frac{20}{50} = \frac{2}{5}$
2. **$\frac{3}{10}$, 0.3, 30%** There were 12 non-blue spins out of 40 total spins: $\frac{12}{40} = \frac{3}{10} = 30\%$.
3. **$\frac{1}{5}$, 0.2, 20%** Calculate: $\frac{2}{2+4+4} = \frac{2}{10} = \frac{1}{5} = 20\%$
4. **$\frac{1}{4}$, 0.25, 25%** Calculate: $\frac{60}{180+60} = \frac{60}{240} = \frac{1}{4} = 25\%$
5. **$\frac{1}{3}$, 0.33, $33\frac{1}{3}\%$** Calculate: $\frac{2}{6} = \frac{1}{3}$
6. **D. 50%** There are 12 cards in the deck, and 6 are diamonds: $\frac{6}{12} = \frac{1}{2} = 50\%$
7. **A. $\frac{3}{4}$** There are 3 clubs, so 9 are not clubs: $\frac{9}{12} = \frac{3}{4}$.
8. **E. 2 out of 5** Sixteen out of 40 trials resulted in tails: $\frac{16}{40} = \frac{2}{5}$.
9. **A. 3 out of 5** Twenty-four out of 40 trials resulted in heads: $\frac{24}{40} = \frac{3}{5}$.

Practice 8.2

1. **$\frac{1}{36}$** The events are independent, so multiply: $\frac{1}{6} \times \frac{1}{6} = \frac{1}{36}$
2. **$\frac{1}{4}$** Because the first card is replaced, the two choices are independent. The cards greater than 5 are 6, 7, 8, 9, 10. Multiply: $\frac{5}{10} \times \frac{5}{10} = \frac{1}{2} \times \frac{1}{2} = \frac{1}{4}$
3. **$\frac{1}{8}$** Half of the sections are red, so there is a $\frac{1}{2}$ chance that the result will be red. Each spin is independent. Multiply: $\frac{1}{2} \times \frac{1}{2} \times \frac{1}{2} = \frac{1}{8}$
4. **$\frac{9}{38}$** The marble is *not* replaced, so the probabilities are not the same. There is a $\frac{1}{2}$ chance the first marble is red. But once one red marble is removed, the odds of a second red become $\frac{9}{19}$. Multiply: $\frac{1}{2} \times \frac{9}{19} = \frac{9}{38}$.
5. **$\frac{1}{16}$** Each flip is independent and has a $\frac{1}{2}$ chance of coming up heads: $\frac{1}{2} \times \frac{1}{2} \times \frac{1}{2} \times \frac{1}{2} = \frac{1}{16}$.

6. $\frac{1}{4}$ Half of the numbers on a standard die are odd: $\frac{1}{2} \times \frac{1}{2} = \frac{1}{4}$.
7. **A.** $\frac{1}{9}$ The probability of rolling a 5 is $\frac{1}{6}$. Of the six equal sections on the spinner, four are even numbers, so there is a $\frac{4}{6}$, or $\frac{2}{3}$, chance of spinning an even number. Multiply the probability of each outcome: $\frac{1}{6} \times \frac{2}{3} = \frac{2}{18} = \frac{1}{9}$.
8. **E.** $\frac{1}{36}$ The chance of spinning a specific number and then rolling the same number is $\frac{1}{6} \times \frac{1}{6}$, which equals $\frac{1}{36}$.
9. **C. 1 out of 3** Of the 10 cards, 6 are marked with a square; therefore, there is a 6 in 10, or $\frac{3}{5}$, chance of getting a square on the first pick. Now there are only 9 cards left, and 5 are squares, so there is a a $\frac{5}{9}$ chance of getting a square on the second pick. Multiply: $\frac{3}{5} \times \frac{5}{9} = \frac{15}{45} = \frac{1}{3}$.
10. **B. 80%** After the five white chips are removed from the bag, the bag contains 10 chips, with 8 green and 2 white. The probability of getting green is $\frac{8}{10}$, which equals 80%.

Lesson 9: Density

Practice 9

1. The 1 gallon storage bag is smaller, so the same quantity of feathers in it will have a higher density.
2. The rectangular section is $6 \times 4 = 24$ sq ft while the square section is $5 \times 5 = 25$ sq ft. There is the same amount of weeds in both, so the rectangular section (with the smaller area) is denser.
3. The first apartment with 500 sq ft per occupant is denser than the second, which has 700 sq ft per occupant.
4. The second cookie has fewer than twice the chips but is twice the size, so the 1-oz cookie with four chips has the higher density.
5. 15 g of sugar in 20 oz of water is less than 1 g per oz, while 50 g of sugar in 30 oz of water is more than 1 g per oz, so the second glass has a higher density of sugar.
6. The larger town has three times the population but less than three times the new births, so the town with 100,000 people has the higher density of new births.
7. The juice of 4 oranges in the 32-oz pitcher is 1 orange per 8 oz, while the juice of 3 oranges in the 15-oz pitcher is 1 orange per 5 oz, so the second pitcher has the higher density.
8. **C. the peach marmalade's jar is twice the volume of the orange marmalade's jar** Peach is half the density of orange, so there must be twice as much peach to weigh the same as orange.
9. **B. 50,000.** The two townships have the same density of moviegoers, so 1 in 4 of the 200,000 additional citizens in Summerville Township will also be moviegoers. That's 50,000 people.
10. **B. The pitcher with Somewhat Fruity Fruit Punch has a lower concentration of fruit juice than the pitcher with Very Fruity Fruit Punch.** Adding 10 oz of water to Very Fruity means both pitchers have 20 oz of water each. However, their concentrations aren't equal: The pitcher with Very Fruity has 40 oz of juice, while the pitcher with Somewhat Fruity only has 30 oz of juice, so Somewhat Fruity still has a lower concentration of juice than Very Fruity. Be careful with choices (D) and (E) as nothing was said about the size of the pitchers (each could hold 100 oz for all we know).

Lesson 10: Combinations

Practice 10.1

1. **5** Since Rob is choosing 4 team members, each possible team leaves out exactly 1 employee. There are 5 possible employees Rob could leave out, so there are 5 possible teams.
2. **10** Either an organized list or a table will work. To solve this problem using a list organized in columns, assign the books letters: A, B, C, D, and E. Count possible combinations:

A and B combinations	A and C combinations	A and D combinations	B and C combinations	B and D combinations	C and D combinations
ABC	ACD	ADE	BCD	BDE	CDE
ABD	ACE		BCE		
ABE					

3. **4** Use either a table or an organized list, as above.
4. **A. 5** Use a table, an organized list, or the formula.
5. **B. 20** This question asks you to add the number of possible groups of two out of five to the number of possible groups of 3 out of 5. Perform each of those tasks separately, or realize that they will have the same solution because choosing 3 to be in the group is the same as choosing 2 to be out of the group. Then, add the possible combinations together.

Practice 10.2

1. **48** Use the fundamental counting principle: 4 (types of bread) × 3 (types of meat) × 4 (condiments) = 48.
2. **24** Use the fundamental counting principle: 3 (restaurant certificates) × 2 (T-shirts) × 4 (hats) = 24.
3. **27** Use the fundamental counting principle: $3 \times 3 \times 3 = 27$.
4. **24** On Friday, Julio has 2 choices. On Saturday, he has 3. On Sunday, he has 4 choices. Use the fundamental counting principle: $2 \times 3 \times 4 = 24$
5. **D. 5,184** There are three words in the passphrase: 24 choices for the first, 9 for the second, 24 for the third. Use the fundamental counting principle: $24 \times 9 \times 24 = 5184$.

6. **A. 10** You are asked for combinations from one set of items. Use either a table or an organized list. You can assign the superpowers letters A–E to make it easier to see how to combine them.
7. **C. 1,024** Use the fundamental counting principle: 4 (meats) × 4 (vegetables) × 4 (noodles) × 4 (broth) × 4 (spices) = 1024.
8. **A. 125** Use the fundamental counting principle: 5 (medications) × 5 (dietary changes) × 5 (vitamins) = 125.

Lesson 11: Permutations

Practice 11

1. **120** This is a permutations problem, because order matters. The question asks how many sequences of five items are possible. 5 × 4 × 3 × 2 × 1 = 120.
2. **10** This is a combinations problem: you are being asked how many groups of three are possible, given five students. Order does not matter. Use a table or an organized list; you may name the students A–E if that is easier.
3. **720** This is a permutations problem, because order matters. 6 × 5 × 4 × 3 × 2 × 1 = 720.
4. **C. 360** This is a permutations problem, in which you are counting possible sequences of four out of six tasks. 6 × 5 × 4 × 3 = 360.
5. **B. 6** This is a permutations problem: the question asks you how many possible sequences of three types of flowers are possible. 3 × 2 × 1 = 6.
6. **E. 5,040** This is a permutations problem, because you are told that the role of Bystander #1 is different from the role of Bystander #4. (Notice the phrase "specific roles" in the question.) Thus, order matters. The question is asking how many sequences of four are possible given ten people. 10 × 9 × 8 × 7 = 5040.
7. **D. 20** This is a combinations problem asking how many groups of three out of six are possible. Use a table or an organized list.
8. **C. 120** This is a permutations problem asking how many sequences of three out of six are possible. 6 × 5 × 4 = 120.

Statistics and Probability Practice Questions

1. **B. 2007** Only the bar for 2007 falls between 500 and 600 on the scale.
2. **B. 40%** Estimate the values for 1998 and 1999. Then find the percent of decrease. Estimate roughly 650 and 390 for 1998 and 1999. Subtract. 650 − 390 = 260. Divide by the original number. 260 ÷ 650 = 0.4 = 40%
3. **A. $\frac{3}{100}$** Jim and his friends bought a total of 12 tickets (4 people × 3 tickets). Then 12 out of 400 = $\frac{12}{400} = \frac{3}{100}$
4. **E. 50°** Arrange the low temperatures in order: 55°, 53°, 50°, 50°, 49°, and 48°. Find the middle of the list. Since there are two temperatures in the middle and both are 50°, the mean of the two must be 50°.
5. **C. 1.56** Add the six amounts, and divide by 6: 0.45 + 0.63 + 1.34 + 3.53 + 2.57 + 0.84 = 9.36, and 9.36 ÷ 6 = 1.56 inches. It makes sense to use your calculator on this question.
6. **C. Woodland Hills** Mentally subtract the low temperature from the high temperature for each area. The greatest difference is in Woodland Hills. 68° − 50° = 18°.
7. **B. 2005** Ticket sales increased each year from 2001 through 2004. The first year in which they declined was 2005.
8. **D. 2008** The line graph shows the steepest increase (line rising from left to right) from 2007 to 2008.
9. **D. 32%** Eight customers chose a mouse pad. 8 ÷ 25 = 0.32 = 32%
10. **A. 1 in 2** Of the 52 cards, 26 are either hearts or diamonds. $\frac{26}{52} = \frac{1}{2}$
11. **C. 3.5 or $\frac{7}{2}$** Add the hours, and divide by 6, the number of weeks: 5 + 3.5 + 4 + 0 + 1.5 + 7 = 21 hours, and 21 hours ÷ 6 = 3.5 hours.
12. **D. $\frac{2}{5}$** Only the numbers 4 and 5 are greater than 3. The probability is 2 out of 5, $\frac{2}{5}$, or 0.4.
13. **B. 41%** The three candidates who received the smallest percentages of the vote also received the smallest number of votes. Add. 9% + 14% + 18% = 41%
14. **C. Bowen and Utley** Since $\frac{3}{5}$ = 60%, look for two candidates whose combined percent is close to 60%. Since 24% + 35% = 59%, the correct answer is choice (C).
15. **D. 5100 × 0.09** Grace Reiner received 9%, which equals 0.09. You know the percent and the base. Multiply to find the part.
16. **C. March** The lines for both companies cross in March.
17. **C. 5900** Company A's orders continue to climb at about the same rate. Imagine extending the solid line to the next month. The line would reach to almost 6000. Choices (A) and (B) are too high an increase.
18. **C. 540** The graph indicates that about 3000 orders were placed in April. Multiply: 3000 × 18% = 540.
19. **B. 24.5** Use only the Shots Attempted column. Put the numbers in order, and find the middle: 29, 27, 26, 25, 24, 24, 23, 18. The two in the middle are 25 and 24. Find the mean of those numbers: 25 + 24 = 49, and 49 ÷ 2 = 24.5.
20. **E. 10** Use the Shots Made column. The mode is the number that occurs most often. In this case, the mode is 10, which occurs three times.
21. **C. $\frac{5}{36}$** The probability that a marble is red is $\frac{8}{24}$, or $\frac{1}{3}$. The chance that a marble is white is $\frac{10}{24}$, or $\frac{5}{12}$. Because the first marble is replaced, the two events are independent. Multiply: $\frac{1}{3} \times \frac{5}{12} = \frac{5}{36}$.
22. **B. $\frac{34+31+42}{3}$** To find the mean, add the three numbers and divide by 3, the number of months in the list. There are 36 employees, but you don't need this number to solve the problem.

23. **E.** $\frac{1}{36}$ The probability of rolling one 1 is $\frac{1}{6}$. Multiply to find the chance of rolling two 1s: $\frac{1}{6}\times\frac{1}{6}=\frac{1}{36}$.
24. **D. 625** Use the fundamental counting principle: $5\times5\times5\times5=625$.
25. **C. 720** This is a permutations question, because the board is not simply picking three members. Rather, those members will also be ordered in a specific way. Multiply: 10 options for president × 9 options for secretary × 8 options for treasurer = 720.
26. **B. 20%** First find the total number of patients: 16 (colds and flu) + 13 (cuts and scrapes) +12 (sprained muscles) + 7 (tetanus shots) + 12 (severe headches) = 60. Now find what percent of 60 is represented by 12: $\frac{12}{60}\times100=20\%$
27. **B. 4:3** The ratio of patients with colds or flu to the number of patients with severe headaches is 16:12, which simplifies to 4:3.
28. **C. 180–199 lb** The bar corresponding to this weight range is the tallest bar on the graph.
29. **B. Participants weighing less than 200 lb** Choices (C) and (D) are both subsets of choice (B), and so cannot be correct. Add the totals of the columns in the graph to reveal that the total for choice (B) is greater than that of (A). The easiest way to evaluate and eliminate choice (E) is to add the two columns that are not included and subtract that amount from 100. The result is less than choice (B).
30. **B. 4** In each combination, one child is left out. There are 4 ways to leave out one child.
31. **B. 20 miles per gallon** Seven cars got 20 miles per gallon on average, more than in any other line of the table.
32. **A.** $\frac{1}{2}$ One car got 35 miles per gallon, and two got 15 miles per gallon.

33. **A.**

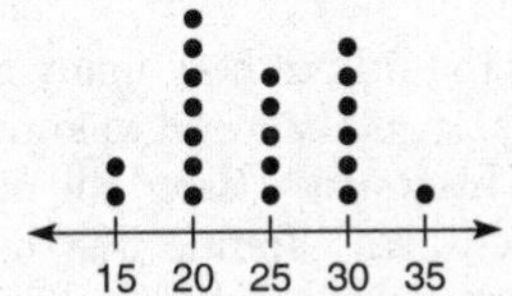

34. **D.**

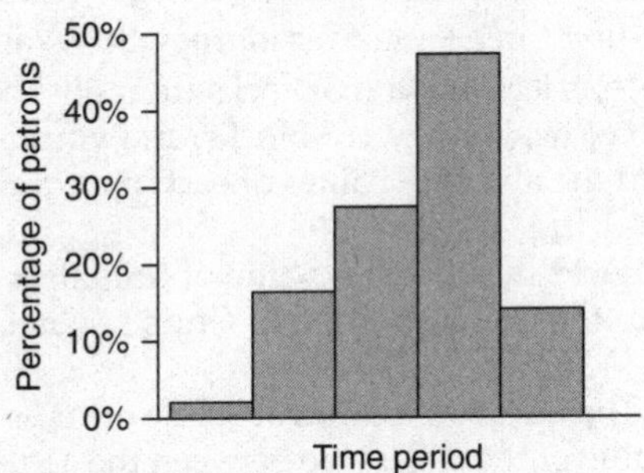

Only choice (D) reflects that 48% of visitors arrived during the fourth time period listed.

Algebraic Expressions

Lesson 1: The Number Line and Signed Numbers

Practice 1.1

1. 5
2. 45
3. 13
4. 1
5. 1
6. 10
7. –3
8. 13
9. –4
10. 2
11. –22
12. 32
13. –50
14. –11
15. 25
16. –35
17. –11
18. 11
19. 10
20. 75
21. 12
22. 2
23. –1
24. –13
25. **B. 2 + (–5)** The operation starts on +2 and moves 5 units to the left (a negative direction).
26. **D. 115°** Begin with 92°. Then perform the following operations: 92° + 12° – 5° + 6° – 3° + 13° = 115°

Practice 1.2

1. 20
2. –21
3. –48
4. 18
5. –10
6. 3
7. –3
8. – 5
9. 2
10. –5
11. –28
12. –3
13. –1
14. –75
15. 6
16. –20
17. –300
18. 2
19. –5
20. 660
21. 12
22. –120
23. –125
24. –12
25. 20
26. –1
27. 0

28. **B. –7** Substitute the numbers from the spreadsheet for the cells in the expression and solve. Note that A1 is column A, row 1; A3 is column A, row 3; and so on. $\frac{(-3)(7)(-1)}{(3)(-1)}=\frac{21}{-3}=-7$
29. **C.** $\frac{2(8)}{(-8)}$ To find the product of two numbers, multiply: 2(8). Then divide by –8, as directed in the problem.
30. **C. The result is a negative number.** Do not do any calculations. Instead, examine the factors. Since there is an odd number of negative factors, the answer will be negative. This is the only possible option.

Lesson 2: Powers and Roots

Practice 2

1. 9
2. 4
3. 3
4. 1
5. 9
6. 7
7. 125
8. $\frac{1}{16}$
9. 6561
10. 1296
11. 12.2
12. 8000
13. 1
14. $\frac{1}{16}$
15. 15.6
16. 10.9
17. 7.5
18. 23.2
19. 1
20. 256
21. **D. 6^3** To find the volume, you would need to solve 6 × 6 × 6, which can be written as 6^3.
22. **A. 3^{-3}** Examine the choices. Choices (A), (D), and (E) will result in a fraction, a value less than 1. Choices (B) and (C) will each have a value of 1 or greater.

    Choice (A): $3^{-3} = \frac{1}{3^3} = \frac{1}{27}$

    Choice (D): $2^{-4} = \frac{1}{2^4} = \frac{1}{16}$

    Choice (E): $5^{-1} = \frac{1}{5}$

    Since $\frac{1}{27} < \frac{1}{16} < \frac{1}{5}$, choice (A) is correct.

Lesson 3: Scientific Notation

Practice 3

1. 2.3×10^3
2. 4.2×10^{-4}
3. 1.24×10^7
4. 1.432×10^{10}
5. 3.6×10^7
6. 9.5×10^{-3}
7. 5.8×10^{-7}
8. 1.5×10^{11}
9. 9×10^{-9}
10. 0.0005173
11. 3,700,000
12. 480,000,000
13. 0.000017
14. 0.0072
15. 916,000
16. 85,910,000
17. 0.00000956
18. 2.35×10^4
19. 0.000000001
20. 2,670,000,000
21. 3×10^8
22. **C. 4.356×10^4** In scientific notation, the whole-number portion must be a digit from 1 to 9. Choice (C) is correct because the decimal place must be moved 4 places.
23. **D. $5 \times 9.07 \times 10^{-1}$** In scientific notation, a ton = 9.07×10^{-1} metric tons. Multiply this by 5 to find the equivalent weight of five tons.

Lesson 4: Order of Operations

Practice 4

1. 24
2. 1
3. 29
4. 2
5. 7
6. 20
7. 14
8. 55
9. 10
10. 23
11. 161
12. 30
13. 360
14. 4
15. 6
16. **C. (1 – 0.75)(28)(30).** The total cost of the class can be found by multiplying 28 members by \$30. Since the foundation pays 75%, or 0.75, the hospital will pay 100% – 75%, or (1 – 0.75). You must multiply the amount the class will cost by the percent that the hospital will pay. Only choice (C) performs these operations.
17. **B. Add 5.** The operations in the brackets must be performed first. Once these are completed, multiply by 2 and then add 5. Notice that it is not necessary to find the value of the expression to answer the question.
18. **B. 28**

    $22 + 6[(14 - 5) \div 3(17 - 14)]$
    $= 22 + 6[9 \div 3(3)]$
    $= 22 + 6[9 \div 9]$
    $= 22 + 6[1]$
    $= 22 + 6 = 28$

Lesson 5: Absolute Value

Practice 5

1. 18
2. 107
3. 423
4. 95
5. 7,026
6. 18
7. 5,708,432
8. 85.6
9. 42
10. 10.5
11. 163.24
12. 3.14
13. 11
14. –156
15. 156
16. 3
17. –91
18. 0
19. 620
20. –7
21. –20
22. –1
23. 2.125
24. –11
25. **D. 10 degrees** The change in temperature is the absolute value of the result of the new temperature minus the old temperature: $|(-5)-(-15)| = |10|$, or 10 degrees.
26. **E. 16** In order to find out how many blocks Bob walked in total, you also need to know how long the last leg of his journey (from the post office back to his apartment) was. To find this distance, you can think of movement east as having a positive value and movement west as having a negative value. So, on the first three legs of his journey Bob walked 5 + (–6) + (–2), leaving him 3 blocks from his house. The last leg of his journey is 3 blocks, and you can simply add the absolute values of each part of the trip: $|5|+|-6|+|-2|+|3| = 16$
27. **D. 120** Add the absolute value of Milania's score to the absolute value of Chris's score: $|-65|+|55| = 65 + 55 = 120$
28. **A. 1.5** The question defines absolute error as the absolute value of the difference between the actual and approximate values: $23.5 - 25 = -1.5$, and $|-1.5| = 1.5$.

Lesson 6: Algebraic Expressions

Practice 6.1

1. $x - 7$
2. $3x^2 + x$
3. $8x - 10$
4. $-3x - 2y$
5. $\frac{10}{x} - 5$
6. $-8 + 7x$
7. $16x + x - 3y$
8. $x^2 + x^4$
9. $x^2 + \frac{4}{7}$
10. $15 + \sqrt{x} - 6$
11. $x - (y + 13)$
12. $(x + 6)^2$
13. $17 - (2x + y)$
14. $x + \frac{24}{x}$
15. $2x - 15$
16. $4(x - y)$
17. $5(x^2 - 3)$
18. $x(11 - \sqrt{100})$
19. **C. $1500 + $0.50($x$ – 2000)** Let x represent the number of tickets sold. The expression $x - 2000$ is the number of tickets over 2000 sold. Multiply this expression by $0.50 to find the amount donated based on ticket sales. Then add $1500. Only choice (C) shows this sequence of operations.
20. **B. $(3x + 4y) \div (2 + z)$** The sum of 3 times a number and 4 times a second number is represented by the expression $3x + 4y$. The sum of 2 and a third number is represented by $2 + z$. The first expression is divided by the second. Parentheses are necessary to clarify the order of operations.
21. **B. $6h + 0.03s$** The correct sequence of operations shows the sum of 6 multiplied by the number of hours ($6h$) and 3% of the sales, or $0.03s$. Only choice (B) adds these two expressions.

Practice 6.2

1. $x^2 + 3x + 2$
2. $19y + 13$
3. $-3x + 54$
4. $6x^3 + 31x^2 + 4$
5. $7y + 14$
6. $3x + 8$
7. $22x - 12$
8. $2y^2 + y + 9$
9. $-5x - 17$
10. $4x - 7$
11. 31
12. 48
13. 8
14. 21
15. 72
16. 80
17. 85
18. –19
19. 9
20. 61
21. **D. $3x^2 + 4x + 1$** Simplify the expression.
$3x^2 + 3(x - 3) + x + 10$
$= 3x^2 + 3x - 9 + x + 10$
$= 3x^2 + 4x + 1$
22. **A. $x = 2$, $y = 3$** Substitute the values in the choices into the expression. Choice (A) equals –11.
$4x^2 - 3(y + 6)$
$= 4(2^2) - 3(3 + 6)$
$= 4(4) - 3(9)$
$= 16 - 27$
$= -11$
23. **A. 20°** You need to convert a Fahrenheit temperature to Celsius.
$C = \frac{5}{9}(F - 32)$
$C = \frac{5}{9}(68 - 32) = 20$

Lesson 7: Expressions and Calculator Skills

Practice 7

1. 19
2. 15.9
3. 51
4. $16\frac{1}{2}$
5. 10
6. –98
7. 74
8. 146
9. 12
10. –76
11. 57
12. 36
13. –54
14. 24.8
15. 54
16. –45
17. 78
18. 108
19. 459
20. 1430
21. **B. 36.2** Use the formula stated in the problem.
$P = 2l + 2w$
$= 2(12.5) + 2(5.6)$
$= 25 + 11.2$
$= 36.2$
22. **D. $-2xy$** Try each expression: $x + y = -3$; $-x + y = 7$; $x - y = 3$; $xy = -10$; and $-2xy = 20$. The value of choice (D) is greatest.
23. **A. 32** If $x = 2$, then $2 \div x^{-4} = 2 \div \frac{1}{2^4} = 2 \div \frac{1}{16} = 32$.

Lesson 8: Understand Polynomials

Practice 8

1. Monomial
2. Monomial
3. Binomial
4. Trinomial
5. Binomial
6. Trinomial
7. Monomial
8. Monomial
9. Monomial
10. Binomial
11. Trinomial
12. Trinomial
13. Binomial
14. Monomial
15. Binomial
16. First term: $3x^4$, second term: $-2x^2$, third term: -3
17. First term: $12a^2bc$
18. First term: $3g$, second term: $-4h$
19. First term: x^2 second term: y
20. First term: $-4a$, second term: $-3b^2$, third term: c
21. First term: 25
22. First term: $4x^2$, second term: $3x$, third term: -7
23. First term: $\frac{3x}{8}$
24. First term: $\sqrt{25}$
25. First term: $\frac{x^2}{9}$
26. First term: $49x^2y^2z^2$
27. First term: $18y^2$, second term: $-4y^2$, third term: 8
28. First term: $3h$, second term: -4
29. First term: x^2, second term: $-x$ third term: y^2, fourth term: -2
30. First term: ab, second term: ab^2, third term: b^2, fourth term: -4
31. **C. 5** Two variables in the expression have exponents: x^3 and x^2. Add the values of the exponents: $3 + 2 = 5$
32. **B. –1** The coefficients in this expression are 1, –3, –1, and 2. Add those values: $1 + (-3) + (-1) + 2 = -1$

Lesson 9: Simplify Polynomials

Practice 9

1. Like
2. Like
3. Unlike
4. Unlike
5. Like
6. Unlike
7. Unlike
8. Like
9. Unlike
10. Unlike
11. Like
12. Unlike
13. Like
14. Like
15. Unlike
16. Like
17. Unlike
18. Like
19. Unlike
20. Unlike
21. $7x^2y$
22. $4b$
23. $-6a + 3$
24. $ab^2 + 16ab + 3$
25. $-2x^2 + 7$
26. $4ab$
27. $14g + 14gh$
28. $-4g^2h^2 + 2g^2 + 2h^2 - 4$
29. $-y^2 + 9y$
30. $-7x^2 + y - 3$
31. $22y - 7$
32. $6x^2y + 5y^2 - 23$
33. $4x^3 + 7x^2 + 3x + 5$
34. $-5x^2 - 4x + 5$
35. $-3x^3 + 7x^2 + x$
36. **B. $6a^2b + 9ab$** Identify and group like terms. Then combine:
    $3a^2b + 4ab + 3a^2b + 5ab$
    $= 3a^2b + 3a^2b + 4ab + 5ab$
    $= 6a^2b + 9ab$
37. **B. 3** Identify and group like terms. Then combine:
    $j^2 + k^3 - 2j^3 + 5k^3 - 2j^2$
    $= j^2 - 2j^2 + k^3 + 5k^3 - 2j^3$
    $= -j^2 + 6k^3 - 2j^3$
    The expression has three terms.

Lesson 10: Add and Subtract Polynomials

Practice 10.1

1. $5x + 6$
2. $23y + 6$
3. $8x^2 - 5x + 2$
4. $15a^2 + 8a$
5. $11x^2 + 2x + 3$
6. $a + 1$
7. 1
8. $4x^2 + 16x - 9$
9. $24y - 3$
10. $-4a^2 - 2a - 9$
11. $y - 2$
12. $-3x + 13$
13. $3a + 2$
14. $3x^2 + x + 2$
15. $10y + 7$
16. $2x^2 + 3x + 13$
17. $2g + 1$
18. $a^2 - 10a + 2$
19. -16
20. $20x^2 - 5x + 1$
21. **E. $x^2y + 4xy$** Identify, group, and combine like terms:
    $(2xy + 3xy^2 - 4x^2y) + (5x^2y - 3xy^2 + 2xy)$
    $= 2xy + 2xy - 4x^2y + 5x^2y + 3xy^2 - 3xy^2$
    $= 4xy + x^2y$
22. **C. $2x^2 + x + 3$** Distribute the negative sign to everything in the second polynomial. Then group and combine like terms:
    $(5x^2 - 2x + 1) - (3x^2 - 3x - 2)$
    $=5x^2 - 2x + 1 - 3x^2 + 3x + 2$
    $=5x^2 - 3x^2 - 2x + 3x + 1 + 2$
    $=2x^2 + x + 3$

Practice 10.2

1. $a^2 + 5a + 4b^2$
2. $-4x - xy + y + 16$
3. $yz^2 - 4z^2 + 7yz + 5$
4. $7ab - b + c - 17$
5. $-4a^4 - c^2 + 3ac + 5$
6. $22xyz + x + 6$
7. $7ef + ef^2 + f - 10$
8. $4pq - 2q + 4$
9. $4ab$
10. 0
11. $3p^6 + 4pq - p^2 - q^2$
12. $x + y + 15$
13. $2bc - b$
14. $10xyz - 8y + 16$
15. $6a + 4b + d$
16. $7pq - q$
17. $-7ab + 2b + 12$
18. 0
19. $-2p^2 + 5q^2 + 7$
20. $x^4 + z^4 - z^5$
21. $bc^2 - bc + 2c$
22. $-3xy + xz - 2xyz$
23. $c^3d^7 - c^2 + 2d$
24. $ef^2g - ef^2 - 2fg + 8$
25. **E. $3x - y$** Distribute the negative sign. Then identify, group, and combine like terms:
    $(x + y + z) - (-2x + 2y + z)$
    $= x + y + z + 2x - 2y - z$
    $= x + 2x + y - 2y + z - z$
    $= 3x - y$
26. **B. $3g^2 + 5h - 2k$** Identify, group, and combine like terms:

    $(2g^2 + 3h - 5k) + (g^2 + 2h + 3k)$
    $= 2g^2 + g^2 + 3h + 2h - 5k + 3k$
    $= 3g^2 + 5h - 2k$

Lesson 11: Multiply Polynomials

Practice 11

1. $30x^2$
2. $6xy^2$
3. $28ab^2c^2$
4. $12yz$
5. $9abc$
6. $10x^2y^3z^5$
7. $4ab^2c^2$
8. $34f^3gh^7$
9. $18xyz^2 + 12z^3$
10. $42x^2 - 36xz$
11. $-15ab^2 - 55abc$
12. $-18f^3h + 24f^4gh^2$
13. $70x^7z - 50z^2$
14. $z^2 + 6xyz$
15. $72ab^2 + 64ab$
16. $18x^4 - 27xy^2$
17. $x^2 - x - 30$
18. $x^2 + 2xy + y^2$
19. $z^2 - 81$
20. $y^2z^4 - 2xyz^2 - 3x^2$
21. $9x^2 + 24x + 15$
22. $x^2 - y^2$
23. $y^6 - 6y^4 + 10y^2 - 60$
24. $a^2b^2 - ab - 12$
25. **A. $12a^5b^2c$** The coefficients of each term are 4 and 3, so the coefficient of their product is 12. The product of a^3 and a^2 is a^5. Only choice (A) contains both of these elements.
26. **E. $12p^3c^3$** You need the product of $2pc^2$ and $6p^2c$, which can be calculated as $(2pc^2)(6p^2c)$. The product of the coefficients 2 and 6 is 12, the product of p and p^2 is p^3, and the product of c and c^2 is c^3. Only choice (E) has all three of these elements.
27. **B. $12a^2b^2 - 22ab - 14$** Use FOIL:
$(4ab \times 3ab) + (4ab \times [-7]) + (2 \times 3ab) + (2 \times [-7])$
$= 12a^2b^2 - 28ab + 6ab - 14$
$= 12a^2b^2 - 22ab - 14$

Lesson 12: Divide Polynomials

Practice 12

1. $y + 15$
2. $x + 3$
3. $x + 5$
4. $a + b$
5. $x^2 + 2x$
6. $2x^2 + 3x + 1$
7. $x + 2y$
8. $3a + 2b$
9. $\frac{3x}{2} + y$
10. $\frac{3a}{4} - \frac{5b}{4}$
11. $\frac{b + 4c}{3}$
12. $\frac{5a + b + 3c}{2}$
13. $6x + 2$
14. $5x + 3$
15. $8y + 2$
16. $6y + 7$
17. $2y + 2$
18. 3
19. $x - 6$
20. $y + 7$
21. $z - 5$
22. $2x + 6$
23. $x - 6$
24. $a + 3$
25. **C. $3a + 2b$** Break the fraction up into two separate fractions: $\frac{(21a + 14b)}{7} = \frac{21a}{7} + \frac{14b}{7}$
Then divide each numerator by 7 to get $3a + 2b$.
26. **D. $9x + 17y + 20z$** The average of a set of terms is equal to the sum of terms divided by the number of terms in the set. In this case, that can be represented by the expression:
$\frac{(27x + 51y + 60z)}{3}$
Break this up into three separate fractions:
$\frac{27x}{3} + \frac{51y}{3} + \frac{60z}{3}$
Then divide each numerator by 3 to get $9x + 17y + 20z$.

Algebraic Expressions Practice Questions

1. **E.** $-4x - 6$
2. **C. $3d - 75$** Since Heidi makes 75 less than 3 times Kris's wage, multiply Kris's wage, d, by 3 and subtract 75 to get $3d - 75$.
3. **B. 1.26×10^8** Calculate: $700 \times 180{,}000 = 126{,}000{,}000$. Scientific notation reduces to a single digit in front of the decimal, and to do this requires moving up 8 digits, so it would be 1.26×10^8.
4. **D. $84x^2y$** Total desks = schools × rooms per school × desks per room. $4x \times 3y \times 7x = (4)(3)(7)(x)(x)(y) = 84x^2y$.
5. **C. $(x + 5)(x - 5)$** Multiply the monomials and polynomials in the answer choices until you find an answer choice that results in the expression in the question stem. For answer choice (C), use FOIL: $(x + 5)(x - 5) = x^2 - 5x + 5x - 25 = x^2 - 25$.
6. **E. $18x + 2y + 13$** Tom has $9x$, Adam $9x + 13$, and Dave $2y$: $9x + (9x + 13) + 2y = 18x + 2y + 13$.
7. **B. $60y$** The diagram shows multiplication problems done using a table, so the horizontal number times the vertical number will yield the value in the table. The table tells you that $a = yc$ and $b = 5 \times 3 = 15$. So $ab = 15yc$. Now look for a value for c. Since $20 = 5c$, c must equal 4, and you have $ab = (15)(4)y = 60y$. There is not enough information to deduce the value of y, but since y appears in all the answer choices, you do not need to try to find its value.
8. **E. y** The diagram shows multiplication problems done using a table, so the horizontal number times the vertical number will yield the value in the table. $d = 3y$ and $a = 4y$, so $a - d = 4y - 3y = y$.

9. **B. $7a^2c^2 + 35bc^2 + 49c^4$** Multiply each term by $7c^2$. $7c^2(a^2) + 7c^2(5b) + 7c^2(7c^2) = 7a^2c^2 + 35bc^2 + 49c^4$.

10. **E. $\$\frac{150}{x}$** To figure out the individual pie cost, divide \$900 by the number of pies, $6x$: $\frac{900}{6x} = \frac{150}{x}$.

11. **A. $\frac{a-4}{a+4}$** Cancel out $6b$ in the numerator and $2(3b)$ (which equals $6b$) in the denominator. Then, one $(a - 4)$ will cancel, leaving $\frac{a-4}{a+4}$.

12. **C. $\frac{xyz}{2}$** To find the total cost, multiply ounces per guest by the number of guests by the cost per ounce. Since \$z is the cost per pound, the result needs to be divided by 16. $\frac{(x)(8y)(z)}{16} = xyz\left(\frac{8}{16}\right) = \frac{xyz}{2}$.

13. **B. –26** Substituting –2 for x and 5 for y leads to $6(-2 - 5) - 8(-2) = 6(-7) - (-16) = -42 + 16 = -26$.

14. **E. –88** Substituting 2 for x, 4 for y, and 3 for z leads to a product of $[2^2 + 6(3)] \times [2(4) - 4(3)] = (4 + 18) \times (8 - 12) = 22 \times -4 = -88$.

15. **D. $1\frac{5}{11}$** Calculate: $\frac{4^3 - [3(12 + 2^2)]}{6 + 5(4) - 15} =$

$\frac{64 - [3(12 + 4)]}{6 + 5(4) - 15} = \frac{64 - [3(16)]}{6 + 20 - 15} = \frac{64 - 48}{6 + 20 - 15} = \frac{16}{11} = 1\frac{5}{11}$

16. **D. $30kp + 20p^2 + 45hp$** Because $5p$ is paid to every member, each number of team members would be multiplied by $5p$, and the team totals would be added. $5p(6k) + 5p(4p) + 5p(9h) = 30kp + 20p^2 + 45hp$

17. **C. $-x + 9y - 10xy$** Solve: $7x - [(5y)2x - 9y + 8x] = 7x - [10xy - 9y + 8x] = 7x - 10xy + 9y - 8x = -x - 10xy + 9y$.

18. **A. $20cd - 75c$** Alyshia has $4d - 15$ DVDs. Multiply $5c$ by Alyshia's DVD total: $(4d - 15)$: $5c(4d - 15) = 5c(4d) - (5c)(15) = 20cd - 75c$

19. **B. $8x^2 + 7xy^3 - 12x - 1$** Factor out $7x^2$:

$\frac{56x^4 + 49x^3y^3 - 84x^3 - 7x^2}{7x^2}$

$= \frac{(7x^2)(8x^2 + 7xy^3 - 12x - 1)}{7x^2}$

$= 8x^2 + 7xy^3 - 12x - 1$

20. **B. $16d - 4a$** The amount $80d$ is needed. Anything earned at the ball will be subtracted, and $64d$ and $4a$ were both earned: $80d - 64d - 4a = 16d - 4a$ left to raise.

21. **A. $\frac{x^4}{2y^2} + 2x^2y^2 - \frac{4x}{y^2} - \frac{1}{2}$** Split the fraction:

$\frac{x^4 + 4x^2y^4 - 8x - y^2}{2y^2}$

$= \frac{x^4}{2y^2} + \frac{4x^2y^4}{2y^2} - \frac{8x}{2y^2} - \frac{y^2}{2y^2}$

$= \frac{x^4}{2y^2} + 2x^2y^2 - \frac{4x}{y^2} - \frac{1}{2}$.

22. **E. $\frac{6k + 4f}{r} + 3$** The total of the three groups $(12k + 8f + 6r)$ should be divided by the number of squads, $2r$:

$\frac{12k + 8f + 6r}{2r} = \frac{12k}{2r} + \frac{8f}{2r} + \frac{6r}{2r}$

$= \frac{6k}{r} + \frac{4f}{r} + 3$

$= \frac{6k + 4f}{r} + 3$.

23. **A. $4x + 2$** Substitute 2 for q and 4 for r in the expression: $\frac{4^2x^2 + 2^3x}{2^2x} = \frac{16x^2 + 8x}{4x} = 4x + 2$.

24. **C. $-2x^4 + 5xy^4 - \frac{y^2}{x^2}$** Split the fractions and then simplify by factoring out $11x^2$:

$\frac{11x^2(4x^4 + 5xy^4 + 8)}{11x^2} - \frac{11y^2}{11x^2} - 6x^4 - 8$

$= 4x^4 + 5xy^4 + 8 - \frac{y^2}{x^2} - 6x^4 - 8$

$= -2x^4 + 5xy^4 - \frac{y^2}{x^2}$

25. **A. $5xy^3 - 16x^2y^2 + 42x^2y$** Distribute:

$(6x^2 + 5xy^2)(y) - (4xy - 9x)(4xy)$

$= 6x^2(y) + 5xy^2(y) - (4xy(4xy) - 9x(4xy))$

$= 6x^2y + 5xy^3 - (16x^2y^2 - 36x^2y)$

$= 42x^2y + 5xy^3 - 16x^2y^2$

26. **D. $20x^2 - 39x + 18$** The question states that the average salary of the non-managerial employees is $(5x - 6)$. That means that

$5x - 6 = \frac{\text{Total of non-managers' salaries}}{\text{Number of non-managers}}$

The question also states that the number of non-managers in the office is $4x - 3$. So,

$5x - 6 = \frac{\text{Total of non-managers' salaries}}{4x - 3}$

Then $(5x - 6)(4x - 3)$ = total of non-managers' salaries = $20x^2 - 39x + 18$

27. **E. 51** Factor before substituting.

$\frac{45xy + 63y^2}{9y} = \frac{(9y)(5x + 7y)}{9y} = (5x + 7y)$.

Substitute 6 for x and 3 for y: $5(6) + 7(3) = 30 + 21 = 51$.

28. **E. $x - 1$** Split the fraction:

$\frac{3x(x^2 + 3) - 2x(x^2 + 3) - (x^2 + 3)}{x^2 + 3}$

$= \frac{3x(x^2 + 3)}{x^2 + 3} - \frac{2x(x^2 + 3)}{x^2 + 3} - \frac{x^2 + 3}{x^2 + 3}$

$= 3x - 2x - 1 = x - 1$.

29. **D. $3h^2 + 4hk - 51h - 68k$** Add the populations of both countries $(3h + 4k)$ and multiply by the rice consumption: $(h - 17)$: $(3h + 4k)(h - 17)$

$= (3h)(h) + (3h)(-17) + (4k)(h) + (4k)(-17)$

$= 3h^2 - 51h + 4hk - 68k$.

30. **A. $2x^2 + 2y^2 - xy$** Split the fraction:

$\frac{4x^2(x+y)}{(x+y)} - \frac{2(x+y)^2(x-y)}{(x+y)} - \frac{xy(x+y)}{(x+y)}$

$= 4x^2 - 2(x + y)(x - y) - xy$

$= 4x^2 - 2(x^2 - y^2) - xy$

$= 2x^2 + 2y^2 - xy$

31. **A. 2** The diagram shows multiplication problems done using a table, so the horizontal number times the vertical number will yield the value in the table. To figure out a, first look at the top right term. Since $5 \times a = ab$, $b = 5$. Another term with only a and b is the bottom middle, $4 \times ab = 40$. Substituting 5 for b shows that $20a = 40$, so $a = 2$.

32. **E. 40** The table tells you that $a^2 \times c = 8b$. Use the table to find a value for b. Since the top right cell of the table shows that $5 \times a = ab$, b must equal 5, and $8b = 40$.

Functions

Lesson 1: Equations

Practice 1.1

1. $x = 9$
2. $m = 28$
3. $y = -1$
4. $x = -64$
5. $a = 125$
6. $y = -13$
7. $x = 27$
8. $c = 7$
9. $x = -4$
10. $b = -7$
11. $x = 31$
12. $s = -8$
13. $x = 108$
14. $t = 39$
15. $x = 48$
16. $y = -3$
17. $r = 110$
18. $x = 5$
19. $y = -9$
20. $d = -25$
21. $x = 4$
22. $x = -6$
23. $h = 26$
24. $x = 66$
25. $m = -10$
26. $y = 9$
27. $w = -28$
28. $y = 72$
29. **C. $x + 36 = 77$** Erin's hours (x) plus Kayla's hours (36) = 77 hours.
30. **D. $2y = 38$** Erin worked twice as many hours as Kayla ($2y$), and Erin worked 38 hours, so $2y = 38$.
31. **D. 128** A number (x) divided by 4 is 32. Solve for x: $\frac{x}{4} = 32$, $x = 128$.
32. **D. $12x = -60$** Try –5 for x in each equation. Only choice (D) is true when –5 is substituted for x.
$$12x = -60$$
$$12(-5) = -60$$
$$-60 = -60$$
33. **B. $572.18 – c = $434.68** When you subtract the check from the amount in the checking account, the result will be the current balance.

Practice 1.2

1. $x = 50$
2. $y = -2$
3. $m = 2$
4. $x = -4$
5. $y = 6$
6. $z = 2$
7. $m = 3$
8. $x = 4$
9. $p = 7$
10. $s = -2$
11. $x = 6$
12. $r = -5$
13. $y = 11$
14. $b = 4$
15. $x = -1$
16. $h = 20$
17. $x = 9$
18. $z = 4$
19. $b = 3$
20. $n = 7$
21. **D. $3x + 9 = 6x - 15$** "Three times a number" is $3x$ and "increased by 9" means to add 9. "Six times the number" is $6x$, and "15 less than" means to subtract 15. The word "is" shows that the two expressions should be connected by the = symbol.
22. **D. 375** Solve:
$$3x + x = 500$$
$$4x = 500$$
$$x = 125$$
The variable x is the number of cards that Travis has. Eric has $3x$, or 3×125, which equals 375.
23. **E. $4x - 7 = \frac{x}{3} + 15$** Remember that differences and quotients must be written in the order stated in the problem. The difference of four times a number and 7 is $4x - 7$. The quotient of the number and 3 plus 15 is $\frac{x}{3} + 15$.
24. **A. $54** Solve:
$$x + (2x + 12) = \$174$$
$$3x + 12 = \$174$$
$$3x = \$162$$
$$x = \$54$$

Lesson 2: Equation Word Problems, Part I

Practice 2

1. **1800 sq ft** Let the square footage of the first house be h, and the second house's square footage will then be $(2h - 1000)$. Then write an equation that combines both houses. The equation is $h + (2h - 1000) = 4400$. Solve for h.
2. **10 dimes** Let x equal the number of dimes in Julia's pocket. The equation is $0.10x + 0.25(24 - x) = 4.50$.
3. **24 games** Let w represent the number of wins, and then the number of losses will be half of w. Write an equation:
$$w + \tfrac{1}{2}w = 36$$
$$1\tfrac{1}{2}w = 36$$
$$\tfrac{3}{2}w = 36$$
$$3w = 72$$
$$w = 24$$
Alternatively, you could solve the equation by calculating the number of losses. Let l = losses. Wins will be twice that much. Then the equation would read $l + 2l = 36$. Once you find l, remember to multiply it by two to find the number of wins.
4. **54** The equation is $x + (x + 2) + (x + 4) + (x + 6) = 4x + 12 = 212$. Solve for $x + 4$, the third number.
5. **8 shirts** Let s represent the number of shirts Brenda bought, and then the number of pants she bought will be equal to $13 - s$. Then, write an equation using the dollar amount she spent: $\$6(13 - s) + \$4s = \$62$. Solve for s.
6. **59** Let x equal the smallest of the three consecutive numbers. Then: $x + (x + 1) + (x + 2) = 180$. Solve for x.
7. **$1100** Andrew spends twice as much on rent, which means he spends half as much as his rent on food. The equation is $r + \frac{1}{2}r = \$1650$. Solve for r.
8. **28 hours** Let h represent the time he spends helping customers, and then stocking shelves will be one-fourth of h. Write an equation:
$$h + \tfrac{1}{4}h = 35$$
$$1\tfrac{1}{4}h = 35$$
$$\tfrac{5}{4}h = 35$$
$$5h = 140$$
$$h = 28$$

9. **C. 84** Let w = Wiley's points, $w + 10$ = Sylvia's points, and $w - 6$ = Greg's points. Write and solve an equation:

$w + w + 10 + w - 6 = 226$
$3w + 4 = 226$
$3w = 222$
$w = 74$

Wiley scored 74 points, so Sylvia scored 74 + 10 = 84 points.

10. **C. $12** Let a = the price of an adult's ticket and a – $6 = the price of a child's ticket. The question states that the cost of 2 adults' tickets and 4 children's tickets is $48. Write and solve an equation:

$2a + 4(a - 6) = 48$
$2a + 4a - 24 = 48$
$6a - 24 = 48$
$6a = 72$
$a = 12$

11. **B. 6** You know that in 12 years, Jenny will be twice as old as Tina. Therefore, if you multiply Tina's age in 12 years by 2, it will equal Jenny's age in 12 years. Write and solve an equation:

$4x + 12 = 2(x + 12)$
$4x + 12 = 2x + 24$
$2x = 12$
$x = 6$

Lesson 3: Inequalities

Practice 3

1. $x > 4$
2. $x > 7$
3. $x \leq -3$
4. $x \leq 36$
5. $x < -1$
6. $x \geq 5$
7. $x > -8$
8. $x > 4$
9. $x < -7$
10. $x < 2$
11. $x \geq 3$
12. $x < 6$
13. $x \geq 2$
14. $x > -10$
15. $x \leq 3$
16. $x < 21$
17. $x \geq -1$
18. $x < 3$
19. $x < 7$
20. $x \leq 3$
21. $-2 \leq x \leq 2$
22. $-20 < x < 6$
23. $6 < x < 16$
24. $4 \leq x \leq 9$
25. **A. $s \leq 16$** The perimeter must be less than or equal to 64, so solve the inequality: $4s \leq 64$, which leads to $s \leq 16$.
26. **D.**

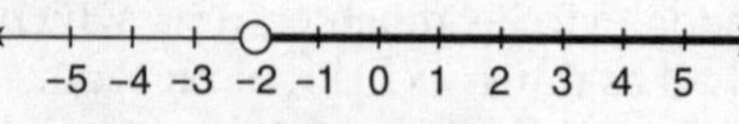

Solve the inequality:

$-4x + 3 < -3x + 5$
$-x < 2$
$x > -2$

To graph the solution $x > -2$, place an open circle at –2, because –2 is not included in the solution. Then, extend the line to the right to include all values greater than –2.

Lesson 4: Quadratic Equations

Practice 4

1. $x^2 + 6x + 8$
2. $x^2 + 2x - 15$
3. $x^2 + 3x - 4$
4. $x^2 - 9x + 18$
5. $x^2 + 6x - 16$
6. $2x^2 - 3x - 2$
7. $x^2 - 14x + 45$
8. $3x^2 + x - 2$
9. $x^2 + 5x - 14$
10. $3x^2 + 14x + 16$
11. $x^2 - x - 30$
12. $x^2 - 13x + 30$
13. $4x^2 + 6x + 2$
14. $x^2 + 5x - 36$
15. $x^2 - 10x + 25$

For questions 16–30, the order of the factors does not matter: $(2x - 1)(x + 3) = (x + 3)(2x - 1)$

16. $(x + 1)(x + 3)$
17. $(x - 1)(x + 5)$
18. $(x + 2)(x + 6)$
19. $(x - 3)(x + 2)$
20. $(x - 2)(x + 7)$
21. $(x - 4)(x + 3)$
22. $(x - 5)(x + 7)$
23. $(x - 6)(x - 6)$
24. $(x - 7)(x + 1)$
25. $(x - 4)(x + 8)$
26. $(2x - 1)(x + 3)$
27. $(2x - 10)(x + 1)$ or $(2x + 2)(x - 5)$ or $(2)(x - 5)(x + 1)$
28. $(x - 5)(x + 10)$
29. $(2x - 1)(2x + 3)$
30. $(x - 7)(x + 8)$
31. **E. –4 and 5** Get 0 on one side of the equation: $x^2 - x - 20 = 0$. Then, factor: $(x + 4)(x - 5) = 0$. Determine which values of x will make each factor equal to 0. The solutions 5 and –4 will make the equation true.
32. **E. $2x^2 + 2x - 24 = 0$** Substitute –4 for x in the answer choices. Only choice (E) works. $2(-4)^2 + 2(-4) - 24 = 2(16) + (-8) - 24 = 32 - 32 = 0$
33. **B. 6** Substitute the answer choices for x in the equation. Only choice (B) makes the equation true: $2(6)^2 - 7(6) - 30 = 2(36) - 42 - 30 = 72 - 72 = 0$. You can also factor the original equation: $(x - 6)(2x + 5)$, so $x = 6$ or $x = -\frac{5}{2}$.
34. **E. $x - 10$** You know that length × width = area. You need to factor the expression $2x^2 - 27x + 70$, and you know that one of the factors is the length, $(2x - 7)$. So $2x^2 - 27x + 70 = (2x - 7)(x - 10)$. The width is $(x - 10)$.

Lesson 5: Algebra Problem Solving

Practice 5

1. **C. 24** Take each answer choice and divide it by 2. Then, check to see if the resulting number is 12 less than the answer choice. For example, choice (A) 12: $12 \div 2 = 6$. And 6 is not 12 less than 12. Thus, choice (A) is incorrect. Only choice (C) works: $24 \div 2 = 24 - 12$.
2. **C. $200** Try each number. Choice (A) says Barbara raised $150. If she did, Sandra would have raised $450, and Matt would have raised $100. Also, the three of them together would have raised $150 + $450 + $100 ≠ $950. Since those numbers don't total to

$950, (A) must be incorrect. Only (C) works: $200 + $600 + $150 = $950.

3. **C. 5** The answer choices represent possible weights for the first package. Try (A): if the first package weighs 2, the second package would weigh 1, and the third package would weigh 3. Add them together to see if they total 15: $2 + 1 + 3 \neq 15$. So (A) is incorrect. Only (C) works: $5 + 2.5 + 7.5 = 15$.
4. **E. 82** The answer choices represent possible scores for the first test. If (A) 76 is Hannah's score on the first test, then her score on the second test would be 82, and $76 + 82 \neq 170$. Only choice (E) works: $82 + 88 = 170$.
5. **B. 10** The answer choices represent how old Nelson might have been six years ago. If (A) were correct, then Nelson would have been 5 six years ago, and he would be 11 now. Also, six years ago Maria would have been 1 year old, and today she would be 7. Now, the question is, is Nelson's current age twice Maria's age? $11 \neq 2 \times 7$. So (A) is incorrect. Choice (B) does work: if Nelson was 10 six years ago, then Maria would have been 2. Today Nelson would be 16 and Maria would be 8, and 16 is two times 8.
6. **A. –3** To solve by guessing, plug each answer choice into the equation. Try (A):
$$2(-3)^2 + (-3) - 15 = 0$$
$$2(9) - 18 = 0$$
$$18 - 18 = 0$$
7. **B. 6** If the group purchased 5 children's passes, as (A) suggests, then they would have purchased 15 adult's passes. Multiply each amount by the cost of that type of ticket, to see if the total equals $440: (5 × $15) + (15 × $25) = $450. Thus, (A) is incorrect. Choice (B) works: (6 × $15) + (14 × $25) = $440.
8. **B. 20** The answer choices represent possible values for the width. If (A) were correct, then the width would be 15 and the length would be 30. Add to find out whether choice (A) would give the value of 120 for the perimeter: $15 + 15 + 30 + 30 = 90$. Thus, (A) is incorrect. Choice (B) works: $20 + 20 + 40 + 40 = 120$.

Lesson 6: The Coordinate Plane

Practice 6

1. (–4, 5)
2. (3, 6)
3. (0, –3)
4. (6, –7)
5. (–5, 0)
6. (–6, –4)
7. (2, 0)
8. (7, –2)
9.

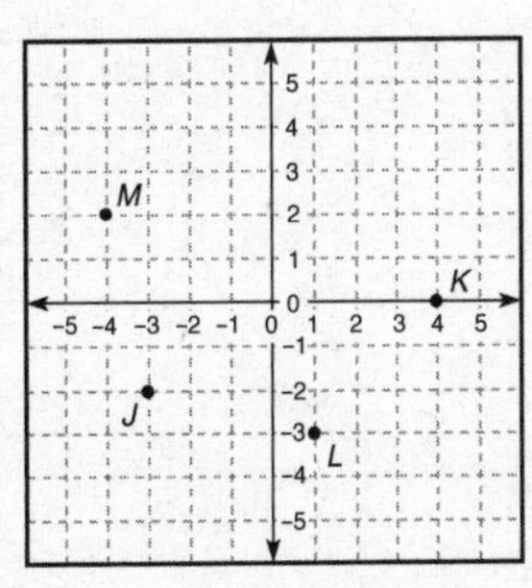

10.

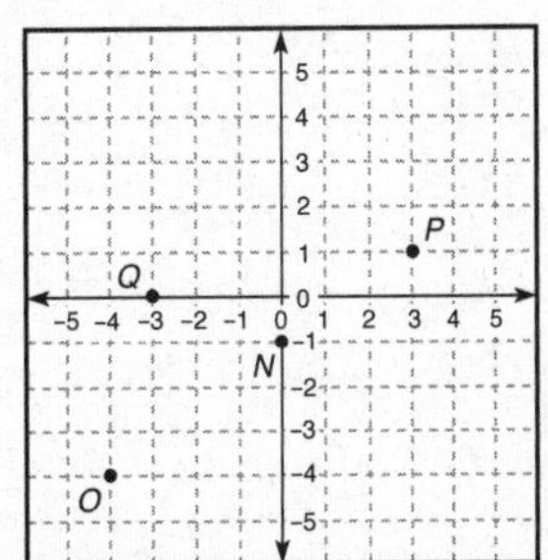

11. **E. (–1, 0)** Plot each point in the answer choices. Only choice (E) lies on the line that passes through points A and B.
12. **A. (–3, –2)** Find the two points discussed in the problem. Then locate the third corner of the triangle, and find the coordinates of the corner. The missing corner is 3 spaces to the left of the origin and 2 spaces down: (–3, –2).

Lesson 7: Graphing a Line

Practice 7

1.

If $x =$	Then $y =$
–2	**2**
0	**3**
2	**4**

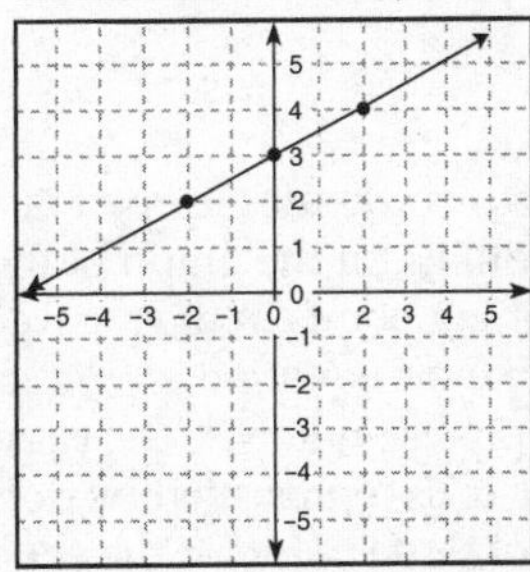

2.

If $x =$	then $y =$
–1	**2**
0	**–1**
1	**–4**

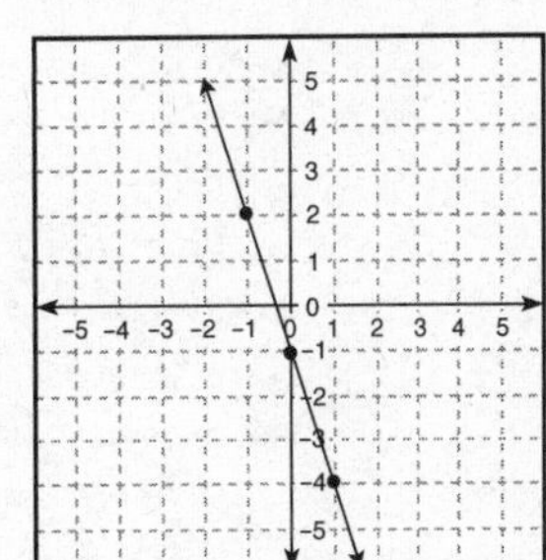

3.

If $x =$	then $y =$
1	**1**
2	**0**
3	**–1**

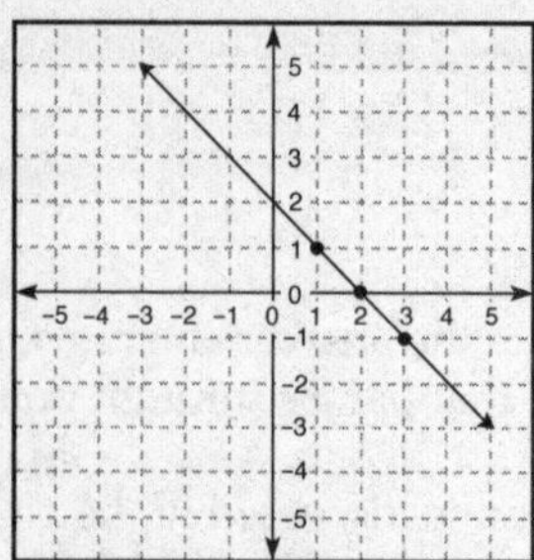

4.

If $x =$	then $y =$
0	**3**
1	**1**
2	**–1**

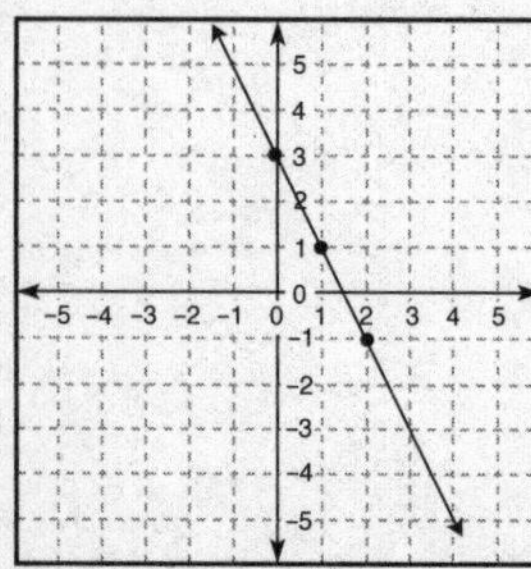

5. **E. point *T* and (0, 0)** Try the coordinates for points *S* and *T* in the equation. Both lie on the graph of the equation. Check the remaining points in the answer choices. Only (0,0) will make the equation $y = \frac{1}{4}x$ true.
6. **E. $y = -4x - 2$** Choose two points on line *P*. The easiest points to work with are the ones represented by dots: (–1, 2) and (0, –2). Try one of those points in the equations. If the point works in the equation, try the other point as well. (You must try both because any number of lines may pass through a single point. To establish that the equation represents line *P*, it must fit both points.) Both points work only in choice (E): $y = -4x - 2$.
7. **B. $2x + 3y = 9$** Try the coordinates (–3, 5) in each equation. Only choice (B) is true.

$$2x + 3y = 9$$
$$2(-3) + 3(5) = 9$$
$$-6 + 15 = 9$$
$$9 = 9$$

Lesson 8: Slope of a Line

Practice 8

1. 1
2. –2
3. 0
4. $\frac{3}{4}$
5. $-\frac{1}{2}$
6. 0
7. $-\frac{1}{3}$
8. 2
9. –3
10. **A. line *A*** Of the answer choices, only line *A* has a negative slope, so it must be the correct answer. Line *A* moves down 1 space each time it goes 3 spaces to the right, a ratio of –1 to 3 or $-\frac{1}{3}$.
11. **B. –2** You have more information than you need. Choose any two points and use the slope formula to solve for the slope. For example, if you choose points (0, 4) and (1, 2), your calculations would be: $\frac{2-4}{1-0} = -\frac{2}{1} = -2$.
12. **C. (2, 3)** The best way to solve the problem is probably to make a quick sketch. Because the line has a slope of 3, start at point (1, 0) and count 3 spaces up and 1 space to the right. You are now at point (2, 3), which is choice (C). You can check your work using the slope formula.

Lesson 9: Slope and Equations

Practice 9

1. $\mathbf{y = -4x + 2}$
   $x = 1; y = -2; m = -4$
   $-2 = -4(1) + b$
   $b = 2$
2. $\mathbf{y = 2x - 2}$
   $x = -1; y = -4; m = 2$
   $-4 = 2(-1) + b$
   $b = -2$
3. $\mathbf{y = -\frac{1}{3}x + \frac{2}{3}}$
   $x = -4; y = 2; m = -\frac{1}{3}$
   $2 = -\frac{1}{3}(-4) + b$
   $b = \frac{2}{3}$
4. $\mathbf{y - 1 = 3(x - 2)}$
   $x_1 = 2; y_1 = 1; m = 3$
5. $\mathbf{y = -\frac{1}{3}(x - 2)}$
   $x_1 = 2; y_1 = 0; m = -\frac{1}{3}$
6. $\mathbf{y + 2 = x - 1}$
   $x_1 = 1; y_1 = -2; m = 1$
7. $\mathbf{y = -\frac{1}{3}x + \frac{4}{3}}$
   First, find the slope:
   $m = \frac{3-1}{-5-1} = -\frac{1}{3}$
   Choose either ordered pair to substitute for x and y:
   $m = -\frac{1}{3}; x = 1; y = 1$
   Follow the steps to find the equation of a line in the slope-intercept form:
   $1 = -\frac{1}{3}(1) + b$
   $b = \frac{4}{3}$
8. $\mathbf{y = 4x + 12}$
   $m = \frac{4-0}{-2-(-3)} = 4$
   $0 = 4(-3) + b$
   $b = 12$
9. $\mathbf{y = \frac{1}{2}x - \frac{5}{2}}$
   $m = \frac{1-(-4)}{7-(-3)} = \frac{1}{2}$
   $1 = \frac{1}{2}(7) + b$
   $b = -\frac{5}{2}$

10. **E. $y = -x - 1$** Plug both points into the slope formula. $m = \frac{-3-0}{2-(-1)} = -1$. Then, use m and one of the points to solve for b:
$0 = -1(-1) + b$
$b = -1$

11. **E. $y = \frac{1}{2}x - 1$** To answer this question, simplify the equation in the question to find an answer that matches:
$y - 2 = \frac{1}{2}(x - 6)$
$y - 2 = \frac{1}{2}x - 3$
$y = \frac{1}{2}x - 1$

12. **B. $y = -x - 4$** Because the line on the graph slopes down from left to right, its slope is negative, so you can eliminate choices (A) and (C) immediately. Then note that the line crosses the y-axis at (0, –4), so the y-intercept is –4. Therefore, the correct choice is (B).

Lesson 10: Systems of Linear Equations

Practice 10

1. **(7, 6)**

$y = 3x - 15$

x	y
0	–15
5	0

$x + y = 13$

x	y
0	13
13	0

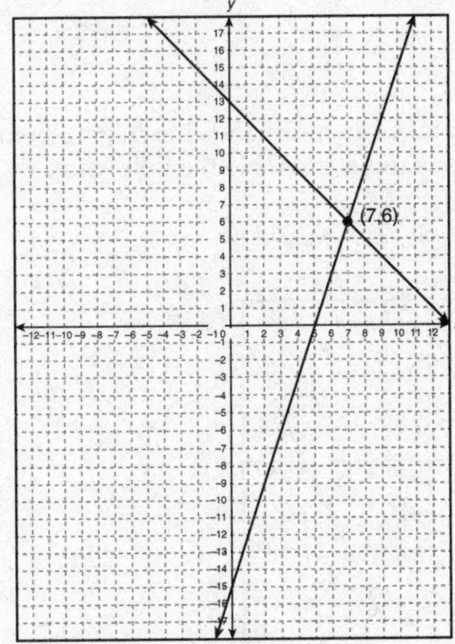

2. **(–3, 11)**

$4x + 2y = 10$

x	y
0	5
$\frac{5}{2}$	0

$y = -5x - 4$

x	y
0	–4
$-\frac{4}{5}$	0

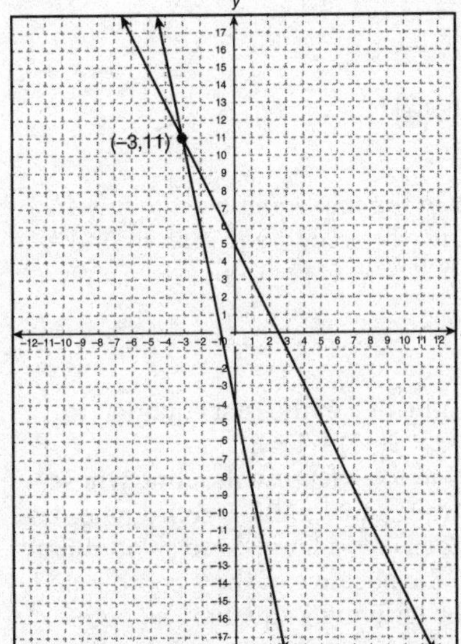

3. **(3, –1)**
Isolate y:
$-y = -7x + 22$
$y = 7x - 22$
Substitute:
$4x + 2(7x - 22) = 10$
$4x + 14x - 44 = 10$
$18x = 54$
$x = 3$
Substitute back:
$y = 7(3) - 22$
$y = -1$

4. **(7, 2)**
Isolate y:
$y = 9 - x$
Substitute:
$2x - 3(9 - x) = 8$
$2x - 27 + 3x = 8$
$5x = 35$
$x = 7$
Substitute back:
$y = 9 - 7$
$y = 2$

5. **(–4, 3)**
y is already isolated.
$y = 3x + 15$
Substitute:
$5x - 2(3x + 15) = -26$
$5x - 6x - 30 = -26$
$-x = 4$
$x = -4$
Substitute back:
$y = 3(-4) + 15$
$y = 3$

6. **$(\frac{1}{2}, 6)$**
y is already isolated.
$y = 12x$
Substitute:
$10x - (12x) = -1$

$$-2x = -1$$
$$x = \frac{1}{2}$$

Substitute back:

$$y = 12\left(\frac{1}{2}\right)$$
$$y = 6$$

7. **A. (2, –1)** Isolate x in the first equation. $x = 2y + 4$. Then, substitute into the second equation to find a value for y:
   $6y + 5(2y + 4) = 4$
   $16y + 20 = 4$
   $y = -1$
   Finally, use that value of y in the first equation to find a value for x. $x = 2(-1) + 4 = 2$
8. **C. (0,0)** The equation $y = x$ represents a line whose x-coordinate is always equal to the y-coordinate. The equation $y = -x$ represents a line whose y-coordinate is always equal to the negative of the x-coordinate. Neither line has a b term in its equation, so both lines have a y-intercept of zero, meaning that they both cross the y-axis at (0, 0).
9. **E.** $\left(-\frac{9}{2}, -2\right)$ Since the only possible y-value for the line $y = -2$ is –2, simply substitute that value for y in the equation $3y = 2x + 3$ to find the intersection:
   $3(-2) = 2x + 3$
   $-9 = 2x$
   $x = -\frac{9}{2}$
10. **C.** $y = -4x + 2$ Two different lines cannot intersect if they are parallel. Lines are parallel if they have the same slope. Only choice (C) does not have a slope of 4, so this is the correct choice.

Lesson 11: Patterns and Functions

Practice 11

1. 0
2. 41
3. 2
4. 40
5. 23
6. –4
7. 31.25
8. –13
9. 32
10. –5
11. **E. 49** To highlight the pattern, it might be useful to make a table or list:

1st	2nd	3rd	4th
1 block	3 blocks	5 blocks	7 blocks

   The number of blocks in each construction equals $2n - 1$, where n is the number in the sequence. The 25th construction would require $2(25) - 1 = 49$ blocks.
12. **C. 16** Each term is 6 greater than the term before it. The next (that is, the fifth) term in the sequence is 10, and the sixth term is 16.
13. **B.** $c = \$5.00 - \$0.25\ (n - 1)$ The original price per scarf ($5) is reduced by 25 cents starting with the second scarf.
14. **B. 1, 5, 9, 13, 17, . . .** Try the numbers 1, 2, and 3 for x in the function. This will result in the first three terms of the pattern: 1, 5, and 9. Only choice (B) contains these three terms.

Lesson 12: Function Applications

Practice 12.1

1. a. $99
   b. $265
2. a. 5.5 hours
   b. 4.25 hours
3. a. Plan A
   b. Plan B
4. **B. $29.50** Use the functions for the two jobs, substituting 30 hours for h:
   Job 1: $P = \$9.75h = \$9.75(30) = \$292.50$
   Job 2: $P = \$70 + \$8.40h = \$70 + \$8.40(30) = \$70 + \$252 = \$322$
   Subtract: $\$322 - \$292.50 = \$29.50$
5. **E. Alicia will earn the most at Job 2.** Use the functions to find Alicia's wages at all three jobs based on 40 hours:
   Job 1: $P = \$9.75h = \$9.75(40) = \$390$
   Job 2: $P = \$70 + \$8.40h = \$70 + \$8.40(40) = \$70 + \$336 = \$406$
   Job 3: $\$380 \times \frac{h}{38} = \$380 \times \frac{40}{38} = \$10 \times 40 = \$400$
   Compare the three results. Alicia will earn the most at Job 2.
6. **B. $19,400** Use the function to calculate the profit:
   $P = \$95{,}000 - \$5{,}400d$
   $P = \$95{,}000 - \$5{,}400(14)$
   $P = \$95{,}000 - \$75{,}600$
   $P = \$19{,}400$

Practice 12.2

For questions 1 and 2, your hand-drawn graphs may be rougher but should resemble the following.

1. The graph of $f(x) = 2x - 8$ is below.

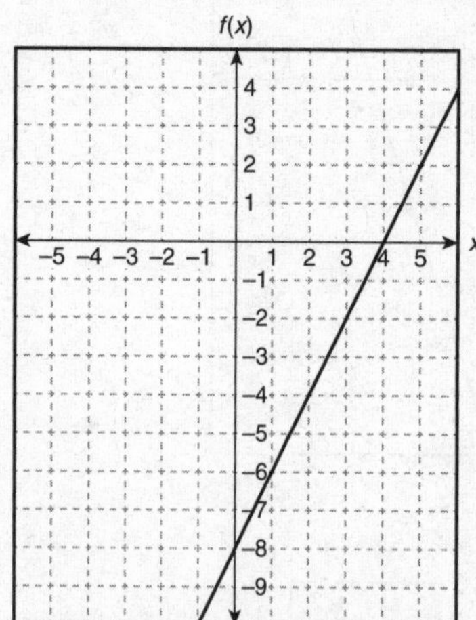

2. The graph of $f(x) = -|x|$ is below.

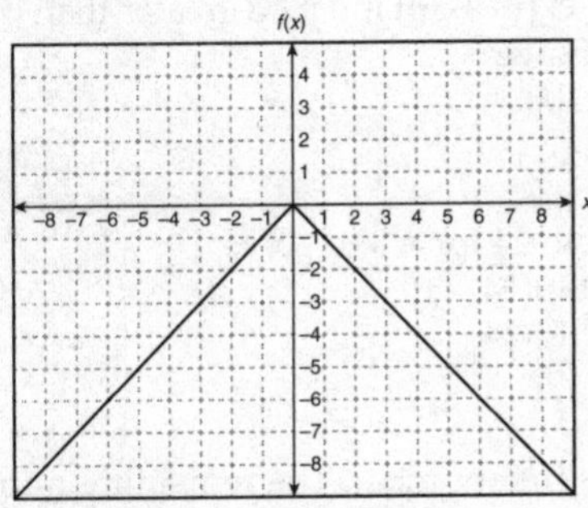

3. **x-intercept = (1, 0); y-intercept = (0, 4)**

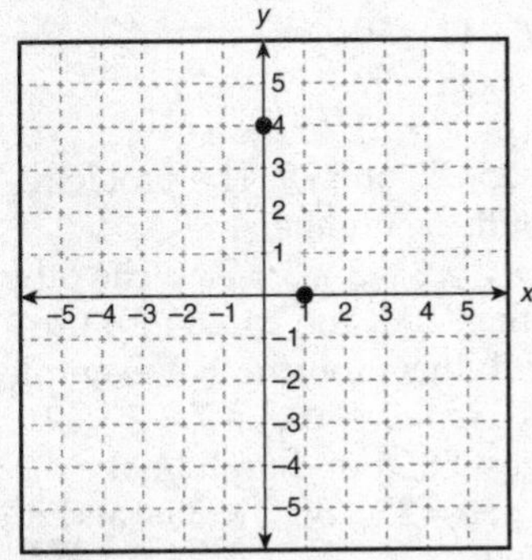

4. **C. $f(x) = -5x$** First look for the function's y-intercept. The line crosses the y-axis at 0, so that allows you to eliminate answer choices (A) and (B). Then look for the slope. The slope is negative, and that eliminates answer choice (D).

Lesson 13: Nonlinear Functions

Practice 13

1. **A. The left arm goes down, and the right arm goes up.** The odd exponent 3 means the arms go in opposite directions; the positive coefficient 5 means the right arm goes up.
2. **D. Both arms go down.** The even exponent 4 means the arms go in the same direction; the negative coefficient –7 means the arms go down.
3. **B. negative** The even exponent 2 means both arms go in the same direction. The fact that the function has a maximum means the arms go down. The coefficient of the squared term must be negative.
4.

$x = -3$	3
$x = 0$	0
$x = 1$	–1
$x = 4$	–4

5.

$x = -2$	9
$x = -1$	0
$x = 0$	–3

Lesson 14: Modeling with Functions

Practice 14.1

1. **No** From the first to the second data point, x increases by 1, while y increases by 7. After that, each time x increases by 1, y increases by 1 as well. So the change in y is not constant, and this cannot be a linear function.
2. **D. $B(t) = \$6{,}000 - \$500t$** At $t = 0$, there is \$6,000 in the account. Start with \$6,000 and subtract \$500 for each month.
3. **12** The question states that the small business does not allow its account balance to dip below zero. The amount of money in the account decreases each month and becomes zero when $t = 12$. $B(12) = \$6{,}000 - \$500 \times 12 = \$6{,}000 - \$6{,}000 = 0$.
4. **A. $P(y) = 10 \times 3^{3y}$** The population is 10 initially, and it triples 3 times each year. When $y = 1$, it will have tripled three times, or increased by a factor of 3^3. When $y = 2$, it will have tripled 6 times, or increased by a factor of $3^{3 \times 2}$, and so on.
5. **C. 2** $10 \times 3^{3 \times 2} = 7{,}290$, which is less than 7,300. $10 \times 3^{3 \times 3} = 196{,}830$, which is far too big. So the greatest possible value for y is 2. Notice that the question called for the greatest possible *integer* value, but even if it had not, you could have inferred that the answer would be a whole number. After all, it does not make sense to speak in terms of fractions of rabbits.

Practice 14.2

1. **D. The y-intercept is 3, which represents the surcharge for the first dozen cookies sold.** To find the y-intercept, rewrite the function in the form $y = mx + b$:
$C(d) = 10 + 7(d - 1)$
$C(d) = 10 + 7d - 7$
$C(d) = 7d + 3$
The y-intercept is 3. Each dozen cookies costs \$7, but there is a surcharge of \$3 no matter how many dozens one buys. So the y-intercept represents the flat fee added to the cost of the first dozen cookies.
2. **B. It means that the population doubles 5 times per year.** The base 2 means that the population is multiplied by 2, or doubles, at certain intervals. The exponent signifies how often the population doubles. The exponent is $5y$, so the population doubles 5 times each year.
3. **A. $3.5m + 4.5d \leq 30$; $d \geq 1$; $m \geq 2$** The mint chocolate bars cost \$3.50 each and the dark chocolate bars cost \$4.50 each, and the total expenditure must be less than or equal to \$30. The correct way to express this situation is $3.5m + 4.5d \leq 30$. The second and third inequalities in the answer choice give Sascha's stated constraints: she will buy at least one dark chocolate bar and at least two mint chocolate bars. Only choice (A) gives this inequality.
4. **30 feet** Call the width of the lawn x and the length $x + 10$. $A = wl = x(x + 10) = 1{,}200$, so $x^2 + 10x - 1{,}200 = 0$. Factor: $(x + 40)(x - 30) = 0$. So $x = -40$ or $x = 30$.

Because distances are always positive, the natural constraint in this situation is that $x > 0$. There is only one solution that meets this constraint, so the width of the lawn is 30 feet.

Lesson 15: Equation Word Problems, Part II

Practice 15

1. **D. $e = 0.01s + 30{,}000$** Marguerite's base salary is $30,000 and increases by 0.01 times the amount of her sales.
2. **E. $10** Set up two equations using the given information: $1,000 + 100x$ for sedans and $1,500 + 50x$ for minivans, where x represents the vehicle's age. Set the two equations equal to each other $1,000 + 100x$ = $1,500 + 50x$. Then subtract 50x$ from both sides: $1,000 + 50x$ = $1,500. Next, subtract $1,000 from each side: 50x$ = $500. Divide both sides by $50 to solve.
3. **C. $30** Set up two equations using the given information. For company A, the cost is $2,000 + 40x$ where x represents the number of strollers. For company B, the cost is $1,550 + 55x$. Set the two equations equal to each other $2,000 + 40x$ = $1,550 + 55x$. Subtract 40x$ from both sides: $2,000 = $1,550 + 15x$. Next, subtract $1,550 from each side: $450 = 15x$. Divide both sides by $15 to solve.

Functions Practice Questions

1. **D. $-4x - 6$** Use the order of operations: $6 - 4(x + 3) = 6 - 4x - 12 = -4x - 6$
2. **A. -3**
   $3 + 4x = x - 6$
   $3x = -9$
   $x = -3$
3. **B. $y = -4x + 6$** Choices (A) and (B) are the only two choices with the correct slope. Plug in $x = 1$ and $y = 2$ into both equations; only (B) works.
4. **C. $4x - y = -7$** Try $x = -2$ and $y = -1$ in each equation. Only choice (C) is true: $4(-2) - (-1) = -8 + 1 = -7$
5. **C. $510** Let t = Tom's earnings and $2t$ – $150 = Jan's earnings.
   $2t - \$150 + t = \$1380$
   $3t - \$150 = \$1380$
   $3t = \$1530$
   $t = \$510$
6. **D. D** The coordinates of D are $(-3, -2)$, which make the equation $y = -x - 5$ true.
   $y = -x - 5$
   $-2 = -(-3) - 5$
   $-2 = 3 - 5$
   $-2 = -2$
7. **C. $\frac{1}{3}$** Count the rise and run from C to B. The line moves up 3 spaces as it moves 9 to the right: $\frac{3}{9} = \frac{1}{3}$.
8. **E. $s \geq \$17{,}500$** Samuel's earnings can be represented by the expression $350 + 0.1$s$, where s represents total sales for the month. Since Samuel needs to earn at least $2,100, this expression must be greater than or equal to $2,100. Solve:
   $\$350 + 0.1s \geq \$2{,}100$
   $0.1s \geq \$1{,}750$
   $s \geq \$17{,}500$
9. **B. $5.35** Substitute 24 for n and solve:
   $F = \$3.95 + \$0.10(24 - 10)$
   $F = \$3.95 + \$0.10(14)$
   $F = \$3.95 + \$1.40$
   $F = \$5.35$
10. **D. 29** Let x = the first number. The remaining numbers are $x + 2$, $x + 4$, and $x + 6$. Solve:
    $x + (x + 2) + (x + 4) + (x + 6) = 104$
    $4x + 12 = 104$
    $4x = 92$
    $x = 23$
    The numbers are 23, 25, 27, and 29. The problem asks for the largest of these numbers.
11. **C. 3^6** Calculate: $3 \times 3 \times 3 \times 3 \times 3 \times 3 = 729$. The other expressions are less than 400. You could also use estimation to help with this problem. For example, to evaluate choice (A), remember that $7 \times 7 = 49$. Then, since 49 is almost 50, round up to make the calculation easier: $7 \times 50 = 350$. So $7^3 < 350$, and it is definitely less than 400.
12. **B. $5x - 4 = 8 + 2 + 3x$** Translate each part of the problem to numbers and symbols and then connect the parts with the = symbol.
13. **B. 1** To find the slope of a line that crosses two points, find the difference between the y-coordinates and then divide by the difference in the x-coordinates: $\frac{6-4}{4-2} = \frac{2}{2} = 1$.
14. **B. 31** From 1 to 7, there is a difference of 6. From 7 to 14, there is a difference of 7. From 14 to 22, there is a difference of 8. To find the next term, add 9 to 22: $22 + 9 = 31$.
15. **C. 0** To find the y-intercept of a line when given the slope and a point, plug the x- and y-coordinates and the slope into the slope-intercept form, $y = mx + b$. This results in $2 = 2(1) + b$. Solve for b.
16. **B. $(-2, 1)$** Create tables for each linear equation to find values of y when substituting values for x:
    $y = x + 3$

x	y
0	3
−3	0

    $y = -2x - 3$

x	y
0	−3
$-\frac{3}{2}$	0

17. **E. $y = 3 + 0.5x$** Start with what is given: around the edge the pool is 3 feet deep. Then add another 0.5 feet of depth for every foot you walk from the edge, which is represented by $0.5x$. Putting the two pieces of information together yields the equation $y = 3 + 0.5x$
18. **A. $-7x - (8 + y)$** The word *product* indicates multiplication, and the word *sum* indicates addition. Choice (B) means that y is added, rather than subtracted,

from the product (due to order of operations), so it is incorrect.

19. **C. 8 and –3** Either solve by factoring or by trying each option in the equation. The correct factorization is as follows:
$x^2 - 5x - 24 = 0$
$(x - 8)(x + 3) = 0$
$x = 8$ or $x = -3$

20. **B. 4** Cynthia's age right now is six times Rebecca's, or $6r$. Thus, in six years, Cynthia will be $6r + 6$ years old, and Rebecca will be $r + 6$ years old. Write an equation and solve for r:
$6r + 6 = 3(r + 6)$.

21. **B. $y = 2x - 3$** Try the given points in the equations in the answer options. Only choice (B) works with both points.

22. **B.**
$-2(x - 6) > 8$
$-2x + 12 > 8$
$-2x > -4$
$x < 2$

Remember to reverse the inequality symbol when you divide both sides by a negative number.

23. **B. (–5, 1)** Point L is 5 spaces to the left of the origin along the x-axis and 1 space above the origin along the y-axis.

24. **E. $\frac{3}{2}$** The coordinates of point L are (–5, 1), and the coordinates of point M are (–3, 4). Find the slope by finding the difference of the y-coordinates, and divide by the difference of the x-coordinates: $\frac{1-4}{-5-(-3)} = \frac{-3}{-2} = \frac{3}{2}$.

25. **C. $18** Let s = Sam's gift. Then:
Daniel's gift = s.
Celia's gift = $s + 12$ (since Sam and Daniel gave the same amount).
Bob's gift = $0.5(s + 12)$ (that is, one-half of Celia's gift).
Add those four quantities together and set the sum total to $81:
$s + s + (s + 12) + .5(s + 12) = 81$
$3.5s + 18 = 81$
$3.5s = 63$
$s = 18$

26. **A. $x \leq 3$** Remember to reverse the inequality sign when dividing by a negative number.
$-7x - 4 \geq x - 28$
$-8x \geq -24$
$x \leq 3$

27. **C. $y = x + 2$** Start by finding the slope: $\frac{3-2}{1-0} = 1$. Now you know that the equation will be $y = x + b$, and you can eliminate choices (A) and (B). And in this case, no calculations are required to find the y-intercept, because one of the points given in the question is (0, 2)—the point where the line crosses the y-axis.

28. **B. 8,652** Let x = votes for the leading candidate and p = votes for Perez. Write an equation: $p = \frac{1}{3}x + 5{,}512$. Additionally, you can say that $p + x = 18{,}072$, or $p = 18{,}072 - x$. Substitute for p:
$18{,}072 - x = \frac{1}{3}x + 5{,}512$
$12{,}560 = \frac{4}{3}x$
$x = 9420$
That number represents the number of votes the opposing candidate received. Now, substitute that value back into the simpler of the two original equations:
$p + 9{,}420 = 18{,}072$
$p = 8{,}652$

29. **B. $x = -2$** Simplify:
$-4(x + 2) - 10 = 5x$
$-4x - 8 - 10 = 5x$
$-4x - 18 = 5x$
$-18 = 9x$
$-2 = x$

30. **D. $5x + $10(35 – x) = $240** The total value of the $5 bills is 5x$. Since there are 35 bills, the number of $10 bills must be $35 - x$. The value of the $10 bills is $10($35 - x$). The sum of the value of the $5 bills plus the value of the $10 bills is $240.

31. **C. 75** Let x = the first number in the sequence. Then write an equation:
$x + (x + 1) + (x + 2) + (x + 3) + (x + 4) = 370$
$5x + 10 = 370$
$x = 72$
The first number in the sequence is 72. That means the fourth number (which equals $x + 3$) is 75.

32. **C. 4** Substitute and solve: $E = \frac{9(8)}{18} = 4$.

33. **B. $y = 5 + 2x$** Because Tonya initially purchases five boxes of cookies, the equation will start out with 5. Each coworker can be counted on to purchase two boxes, written as $2x$. Thus, the amount of cookies sold can be represented with the function $y = 5 + 2x$.

Geometry

Lesson 1: Points, Lines, and Angles

Practice 1

1. acute
2. obtuse
3. straight
4. acute
5. reflex
6. right
7. acute
8. obtuse
9. **E. 135°** $m\angle RZS + m\angle QZS = 180°$. Because $\angle RZS$ measures 45°, $\angle QZS$ must measure 135°.
10. **C. right** Because $m\angle RZQ = 180°$, subtract the two known angles to find the measure of $\angle SZT$. $180° - 45° - 45° = 90°$. Because $\angle SZT$ measures 90°, it is a right angle.
11. **A. 38°** $\angle AWB + \angle BWC + \angle CWD = \angle AWD$, a straight angle with a measure of 180°. You know that $m\angle AWB = 90°$ and $m\angle CWD = 52°$, so substitute those values in the first equation: $90° + m\angle BWC + 52° = 180°$, which results in $\angle BWC = 38°$.

12. **C. obtuse** $m\angle AWC$ is greater than the right angle $\angle AWB$ and less than the straight angle $\angle AWD$. $\angle AWC$ must be obtuse.

Lesson 2: Parallel Lines and Transversals

Practice 2

All possible answers are shown.

1. $\angle 4$ and $\angle 6$, $\angle 3$ and $\angle 5$
2. $\angle 3$
3. 100°
4. $\angle 1$ and $\angle 7$, $\angle 2$ and $\angle 8$
5. $\angle 1$ and $\angle 3$, $\angle 2$ and $\angle 4$, $\angle 5$ and $\angle 7$, $\angle 6$ and $\angle 8$
6. $\angle 4$
7. **B. 75°** $\angle 3$ and $\angle 1$ are vertical angles. Therefore, $m\angle 3 = m\angle 1$. $m\angle 3 = 75°$, so $m\angle 1 = 75°$.
8. **B. They are in the same position from one parallel line to the other.** The transversal and the parallel lines form eight angles. Corresponding angles lie on the same side of the transversal and have the same relationship to the nearest parallel line.
9. **B. 65°** Angles $\angle 7$ and $\angle 3$ are corresponding angles, so $m\angle 7 = m\angle 3$; therefore, $m\angle 3 = 115°$. Angles $\angle 3$ and $\angle 4$ are adjacent angles, which means 115°+ $m\angle 4 = 180°$ and $m\angle 4 = 65°$.
10. **E. $\angle 8$** Angles $\angle 2$ and $\angle 8$ are alternate exterior angles. Therefore, they are equal.

Lesson 3: Plane Figures

Practice 3

1. rectangle, square
2. parallelogram, rectangle, square, rhombus
3. trapezoid
4. rectangle, square
5. none
6. rectangle, square, parallelogram, rhombus
7. square, rhombus
8. rectangle, square, parallelogram, rhombus, trapezoid
9. trapezoid
10. square
11. **C. 140°** Let h = the measure of $\angle H$. Then $3h + 20° = m\angle F$. The sum of the angles of a quadrilateral is 360°, so $3h + 20° + h + 90° + 90° = 360°$.
    Solve the equation:
    $4h + 200° = 360°$, so $4h = 160°$, $h = 40°$, and $3h + 20° = 140°$.
12. **C. 90°** If the opposite sides of a figure are parallel and all four sides are equal, then the figure is either a square or rhombus. Since $\angle T$ is a right angle, the figure is square. Therefore, all the angles measure 90°.
13. **E. parallelogram** This quadrilateral has opposite sides that are equal and opposite angles that are equal. It has no right angles, and the two sets of sides are different lengths. The quadrilateral must be a parallelogram.

Lesson 4: Transformations in the Plane

Practice 4.1

1. **C. The point moves four units right, then four units down.**
2. **(1, 7)** A translation of (5, 7) would move the point five units right, then seven units up. So add 5 to the –4 and 7 to the 0 to arrive at point (1, 7).
3. $y = -\frac{1}{2}x + \frac{17}{2}$ This is a difficult problem that involves multiple steps, so let's take them one at a time. First, you need the slope of $\overline{EF}$. Traveling from E to F requires moving four spaces up and two spaces to the right, so the slope is $\frac{4}{2} = 2$. The line of reflection is perpendicular to $\overline{EF}$, so its slope is the negative reciprocal of 2, or $-\frac{1}{2}$. To find the equation for the line of reflection, you need a point on that line to combine with the slope in the point-slope formula. Fortunately, since the line of reflection by definition goes through the midpoint of $\overline{EF}$, $\overline{EF}$'s midpoint is a point on the line. Point E starts at (4, 4), and you went four units up and two units right to reach point F, so going half that distance, or two units up and one unit to the right, gets you to the midpoint. That's point (5, 6). Now use the point-slope formula to solve:
$$y - y_1 = m(x - x_1)$$
$$y - 6 = -\frac{1}{2}(x - 5)$$
$$y - \frac{12}{2} = -\frac{1}{2}x + \frac{5}{2}$$
$$y = -\frac{1}{2}x + \frac{17}{2}$$
4. **(1, –1)** Begin by determining the translation from C to D. Going from (8, 3) to (5, 7) requires going left three ($8 \rightarrow 5$), then up four ($3 \rightarrow 7$), for a translation of (–3, 4). At this point, be wary of the trap: You are given the *result* of the other translation, not the starting point, so apply the reverse of the translation, or (3, –4), to arrive at point A. Point B is at (–2, 3). Three units to the right and four units down is (1, –1).

Practice 4.2

1. **E. (7, 7)** Dilating a point with a scale of 2 doubles the initial distance from the center of dilation. Point M is at (3, 3) and the center of dilation is (–1, –1), so traveling from the center of dilation to point M requires moving four units to the right and four units up. Dilating with a scale of 2 changes that to eight units right, eight units up. That's (7, 7).
2. **A.** Dilating with point B as the center means that scale is applied to the distance from B to each of the other points. A and C are currently four units left and four units down from B, respectively, so their dilated points at a scale of $\frac{1}{2}$ would be two left and two down, respectively. Point D is directly opposite

point B, so its dilated point would be two left and two down from B. That's the square in choice (A).

3. **(–1, –2)** Moving 180° around a point takes you to the opposite side of a circle, so points P and Q are actually the endpoints of a diameter of this circle. You can draw this to help visualize the solution:

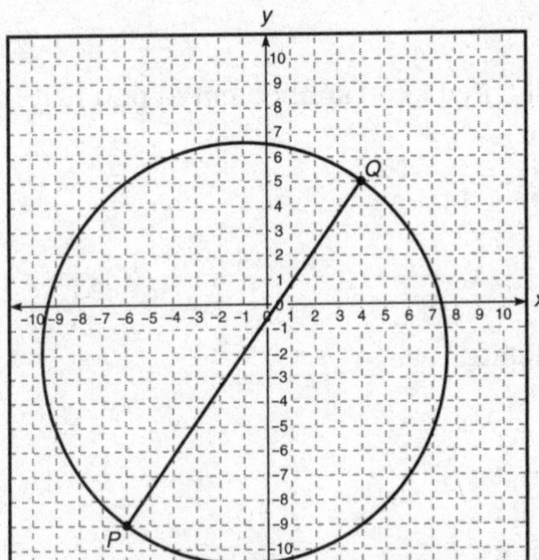

Now, to find the missing point R, all you need is the midpoint of $\overline{PQ}$. To go from P to Q, you moved 14 units up and 10 units to the right, so moving half that much, or 7 up and 5 right, will get you to point R. Point P is at (–6, –9), so point R is (–1, –2).

Lesson 5: Triangles

Practice 5

1. equilateral, acute
2. scalene, obtuse
3. isosceles, acute
4. 64°
5. 45°
6. 97°
7. **C. 14** Solve for $\angle BAC$: $m\angle BAC + 55° = 115°$, so $m\angle BAC = 60°$. Solve for $\angle BCA$: $\angle BCA + 35° = 95°$, so $\angle BCA = 60°$. If two of the angles of ΔABC each measure 60°, the third angle also measures 60°. The triangle is equilateral, and all the sides of ABC are equal to side AB.
8. **E. right** $55° + 35° + m\angle D = 180°$. Solve for the missing angle: $m\angle D = 90°$. Therefore, the triangle is a right triangle.
9. **C. 86°** The angles of a triangle add up to 180°. 38° + 56° = 94°, so the third angle can be found by subtracting 94° from 180°: 180° – 94° = 86°.

Lesson 6: Congruent and Similar Triangles

Practice 6

1. No
2. Yes
3. Not enough information
4. **C. 48** Because the triangles are similar, the sides must be proportional. Set up the ratio $\frac{25}{40} = \frac{30}{x}$ where x equals the length of ST. Solve: $x = 48$
5. **B. 64°** Similar triangles have equal angle measures. If $m\angle S = 68°$, then $m\angle TYX = 68°$. $m\angle TYX + m\angle T + m\angle TXY = 180°$. Substitute and solve: $68° + 48° + m\angle TXY = 180°$, so $m\angle TXY = 64°$.
6. **C. 3.2** The two triangles are similar because two of the angle measures in one triangle are equal to two of the angle measures in the other triangle. The side labeled x corresponds to the side with length 4.8. The side of length 2.8 corresponds to the side with length 4.2. Solve the ratio $\frac{x}{4.8} = \frac{2.8}{4.2}$: $x = 3.2$.

Lesson 7: Similar Triangle Applications

Practice 7

1. **C. 64** Set up a proportion comparing the sign's shadow to the building's shadow and the sign's height to the building's height. $\frac{6}{48} = \frac{8}{x}$: so $x = 64$.
2. **B. 42** The 10-ft pole is 25 ft from the vertex of the angle; the base of the cliff is 80 + 25, or 105 ft from the vertex of the angle. Set up a proportion. $\frac{105}{25} = \frac{x}{10}$: so $x = 42$.
3. **A.** $\frac{2.5}{22.5} = \frac{1}{x}$ Set up a proportion comparing the meter stick's shadow to the flagpole's shadow and the meter stick's height to the flagpole's height.
4. **D. 49** Examine the two triangles to find corresponding sides. The 8-ft side of the smaller triangle corresponds to the 28-ft side of the larger triangle. Write a proportion and solve. $\frac{8}{28} = \frac{14}{x}$: so $x = 49$.
5. **B. 4** If you imagine a line drawn at the bottom of the frame, you will have two similar triangles. The base of the large triangle is 6 ft, and the base of the small triangle is unknown. The side of the large triangle is 12 ft and the side of the small one is 12 – 4 = 8 ft. Write a proportion and solve: $\frac{8}{12} = \frac{x}{6}$, so $x = 4$.

Lesson 8: Pythagorean Relationship

Practice 8

1. $c = 11.3$ in
2. $c = 15$ yd
3. $c = 2.5$ cm
4. $a = 5.2$ m
5. $b = 8$ mm
6. $a = 17.3$ ft
7. $c = 12.2$ cm
8. $b = 26.0$ in
9. $c = 6.4$ km
10. **B. 6.7** The distance from A to C is 3 units, and the distance from B to C is 6 units.
$c^2 = a^2 + b^2$
$c^2 = 3^2 + 6^2$
$c^2 = 9 + 36$
$c^2 = 45$
$c = \sqrt{45} \cong 6.7$
11. **C. 30** The shorter sides are the legs. Solve for the hypotenuse.
$c^2 = a^2 + b^2$
$c^2 = 18^2 + 24^2$
$c^2 = 324 + 576$
$c^2 = 900$
$c = \sqrt{900} = 30$
12. **E. 12.1** The brace divides the rectangle into two right triangles with the brace as the hypotenuse of each.

Solve for the hypotenuse of one of the triangles:
$c^2 = a^2 + b^2$
$c^2 = 5^2 + 11^2$
$c^2 = 25 + 121$
$c^2 = 146$
$c = \sqrt{146} \cong 12.08$, which rounds to 12.1.

13. **E. 36** Calculate:
$c^2 = a^2 + b^2$
$39^2 = 15^2 + b^2$
$1{,}521 = 225 + b^2$
$1{,}296 = b^2$
$b = \sqrt{1{,}296} = 36$

Lesson 9: Perimeter and Area

Practice 9

1. area: 39 sq units
perimeter: 30.8 units
2. area: 16 sq units
perimeter: 16 units
3. area: 640 sq units
perimeter: 104 units
4. area: 29.6 sq units
perimeter: 24.6 units
5. area: 616 sq units
perimeter: 109 units
6. area: 38 sq units
perimeter: 32 units
7. **C. 56** The shaded portion is a trapezoid: $\frac{1}{2} \times (5 + 9) \times 8 = 56$.
8. **C. 54** The area of a rectangle is its base times its height. $9 \times 6 = 54$.
9. **D. 324** Subtract the area of the patio from the area of the entire yard. Both are rectangles, so multiply length and width to find the area: $(24 \times 18) - (12 \times 9) = 324$.
10. **B. 24** Add all four sides: $6 + 6 + 6 + 6 = 24$ centimeters.

Lesson 10: Circles

Practice 10.1

1. $C = 62.8$ in; $A = 314.2$ in^2
2. $C = 12.6$ cm; $A = 12.6$ cm^2
3. $C = 25.1$ m; $A = 50.2$ m^2
4. **C. 38** Use the formula $C = \pi d$, where $d = 12$. $12 \times 3.14 = 37.7$
5. **B. 3.14×6^2** The formula for the area of a circle is $A = \pi r^2$. The radius of a circle is half of the diameter. Half of 12 is 6. Substitute 6 for r and 3.14 for π. $A = 3.14 \times 6^2$.
6. **B. 13.0** The diameter of a circle is twice the radius. $6.5 \times 2 = 13$.
7. **E. 31.** Find the circumference of the 10-point band. First find the diameter, which passes through the 10-point band, the inner circle, and the 10-point band a second time on its way from one edge of the circle to the other. Add the width of the 10-point band twice and the diameter of the inner circle: $2 + 2 + 2 + 2 + 2 = 10$ inches. Now you can use the formula for circumference: $10 \times 3.14 = 31.4$, which rounds to 31 inches.

Practice 10.2

1. 34.4°
2. 10.5 m
3. 106.1 m
4. **B. 5** To solve for A, use the formula at the top of the practice page.
$12 \times A = 15 \times 4$
$A = \frac{60}{12} = 5$
5. **C. 24** Use the Pythagorean theorem to find half the length of LM:
$(\text{half of } LM)^2 + 5^2 = 13^2$
$(\text{half of } LM)^2 = 144$
half of $LM = 12$
$LM = 24$

Lesson 11: Volume

Practice 11.1

1. 160 cubic units
2. 27 cubic units
3. 141 cubic units
4. 420 cubic units
5. 3 cubic units
6. 236 cubic units
7. **A. 5.** $V = lwh$ You know that the length and width of the box both equal 4 and that the volume equals 80. Solve the equation:
$80 = 4 \times 4 \times h$
$80 = 16h$
$5 = h$
8. **C. 125** If each edge measures 5 feet, then the figure is a cube. $5^3 = 125$.
9. **D. 17** First, you must find the volume of the pool. The radius of the pool is 6 and the height is 3.
$V = \pi r^2 h$
$\approx 3.14 \times 6^2 \times 3$
$\approx 3.14 \times 36 \times 3$
≈ 339.12
Therefore, the volume is about 339. Solve the proportion $\frac{1}{20} = \frac{x}{339}$, where x equals the number of scoops Linda must add: $20x = 339$; $x = 16.95$, about 17.

Practice 11.2

1. 9 in^3
2. 127 in^3
3. 314 cm^3
4. 480 m^3
5. 11 in^3
6. 1060 cm^3
7. **A. 480** First, find the volume of the original package. Substitute the numbers given into the volume equation: $V = \frac{1}{3} \times 10^2 \times 15 = 500$. Then find the volume of the new package. Add 4 to the length and width of the base to get 14. Substitute into the volume equation again and solve: $V = \frac{1}{3} \times 14^2 \times 15 = 980$. Find the difference of the two volumes: $980 - 500 = 480$.

8. **C. 67** You know that the height of the cone is half of the diameter of the base. Since the radius of the base is also half of the diameter, the radius must equal the height. Therefore, the radius is 4. Now solve the equation:
$V = \frac{1}{3} \times \pi \times 4^2 \times 4 \approx 67$.
9. **E. The volume of *B* is less than the volume of *A*.** First, find the volumes of the two figures. Figure *A* is a rectangular solid. Use the formula $V = lwh = 4 \times 3 \times 2 = 24$. Figure *B* is a pyramid. Use the formula $V = \frac{1}{3}Bh = \frac{1}{3} \times 3^2 \times 6 = 18$. Now compare the two volumes. Since $24 > 18$, choice (D) must be the answer.
10. **E. 1,000** Use the formula $V = \frac{1}{3}\pi r^2 h = \frac{1}{3} \times \pi \times 8^2 \times 15 \approx$ 1,005, which is about 1,000.

Lesson 12: Surface Area

Practice 12.1

1. 108
2. 39
3. 24
4. 336
5. 256
6. 384
7. **C. The surface area of Figure *A* is greater than the surface area of Figure *B*.** Calculate both surface areas. Figure *A*: $25 \times 6 = 150$. Figure *B*: $(30 \times 4) + (9 \times 2) = 138$. Therefore, Figure *A*'s surface area is greater than Figure *B*'s.
8. **D. 162** The original box has a side length of 3 centimeters, so the surface area is 54 square centimeters. When the dimensions are doubled, the new box has a side length of 6 centimeters, so the surface area is 216 square centimeters. The difference in surface areas is 216 cm – 54 cm, which is 162 square centimeters.
9. **A. 5** If all the edges are the same length, then the box must be a cube, and each square face has the same area. There are 6 faces. Divide 150 by 6 to get an area of 25 for each face. Then $\sqrt{25} = 5$, so each side has a length of 5 in.

Practice 12.2

1. 168π	4. 378π
2. 40π	5. 400π
3. 36π	6. 96π

7. **B. 64π** The formula for the surface area of a sphere uses the radius, and the radius is half the diameter, so $8 \div 2 = 4 = r$. Now use the formula for the surface area of a sphere: $SA = 4\pi r^2 = 4 \times \pi \times 4^2 = 64\pi$.
8. **E. The new cone will have a surface area less than the surface area of the original cone.** The original cone has a radius of 4, so its surface area is $\pi(4)(8) + \pi(4^2) = 32\pi + 16\pi = 48\pi$. The new cone will have a slant height of 16, a diameter of 4, and a radius of 2, so its surface area is: $\pi(2)(16) + \pi(2^2) = 32\pi + 4\pi = 36\pi$, which is less than 48π.
9. **C. 170** The surface area of the cylinder is $2\pi(3)(6) + 2\pi(3^2) = 36\pi + 18\pi = 54\pi = 54(3.14) \approx 170$ square inches.

Lesson 13: Combined Figures

Practice 13

1. $P = 150$ units
   $A = 1050$ sq units
2. $P = 49.7$ units
   $A = 159.3$ sq units
3. $P = 72$ units
   $A = 168$ sq units
4. $V = 185$ cubic units
5. $V = 278$ cubic units
6. $V = 399$ cubic units
7. **D. 360** Find the volume of the main rectangular slab: $V = lwh$, so $V = 3 \times 8 \times 12 = 288$ cubic feet. Find the volume of one of the blocks: $V = lwh$, so $V = 3 \times 3 \times 2 = 18$ cu ft. Multiply by 4, the number of blocks: $18 \times 4 = 72$ cu ft. Finally, add the main slab to the blocks: $288 + 72 = 360$ cu ft.
8. **C. 134** The radius of both the cones and the cylinder is 2. The height of one cone is 4 inches. Find the volume of one cone: $V = \frac{1}{3}\pi r^2 h = \frac{1}{3} \times 3.14 \times 2^2 \times 4 \approx 16.7$ cu in. Multiply by 2 to find the volume of both cones: $16.7 \times 2 = 33.4$ cu in. Find the volume of the cylinder: $V = \pi r^2 h \approx 3.14 \times 2^2 \times 8 \approx 100.48$ cu in. Add to find the total volume: $33.4 + 100.48 = 133.88$ cu in, which rounds to 134 cu in.

Lesson 14: Geometry Calculator Skills

Practice 14

1. 42 in	4. 15.8 cm
2. 195 cm^2	5. 37.7 in
3. 43 ft^3	6. 3016 cm^3

7. **C. 520** Use the formulas for finding the area of a rectangle and the area of a triangle, and subtract the area of the cut-out triangle from the area of the rectangle. On the TI-30XS MultiView™ calculator, enter the following: 32 ⊗ 20 ⊖ 20 ⊗ 12 ⊗ .5 (enter). The right side of the display will read **520.** You can enter the entire calculation in this fashion because the TI-30XS™ MultiView understands the algebraic order of operations. If you press enter after each of those operations, your answer will be incorrect.
8. **B. 35** Use the formula for finding the volume of a cylinder. Press: (π) ⊗ 1.5 (x^2) ⊗ 5 (enter). The right side of the display will read **35.34291735**, which rounds to 35 meters
9. **E. 5,056** Use the formula for finding the volume of a rectangular solid. Subtract the volume of Box B from the volume of Box A. Press: 26 ⊗ 12 ⊗ 32 ⊖ 22 ⊗ 8 ⊗ 28 (enter). The right side of the display will read **5056.**
10. **C. 608** Work carefully to make sure you find the area of the correct sides of the boxes. The shaded sides have dimensions of 32 cm × 12 cm and 28 cm × 8 cm. To find the area of one rectangle, use the formula for finding the area of a rectangle: $A = b \times h$. To find the total area, find the area of each side and add these areas together: $(32 \times 12) + (28 \times 8)$. Press: 32 ⊗ 12 ⊕

28 ⊗ 8 (enter). The right side of the display will read **608.** The total area that the advertiser will cover is 608 cm^2, so choice (C) is correct.

Geometry Practice Questions

1. **D. 150** If the edge length is 5 cm, then each square surface has an area of 25 cm^2. There are 6 faces, so multiply by 6 to get 150 cm^2.
2. **C. 192π** Substitute the values given in the question into the formula for the surface area of a cylinder:
   $SA = 2\pi rh + 2\pi r^2$
   $SA = 2\pi(6)(10) + 2\pi(6^2)$
   $SA = 120\pi + 72\pi = 192\pi$
3. **C. 66π** The surface area of a cylinder is calculated with the formula $SA = 2\pi rh + 2\pi r^2 = (2 \times \pi \times 3 \times 8) + (2 \times \pi \times 9) = 48\pi + 18\pi = 66\pi$.
4. **C. $16\sqrt{3} + 16$** The surface area of a pyramid with a four-sided base is $SA = \frac{1}{2}ps + B$, where p is the perimeter of the base, s is the slant height of a face of the pyramid, and B is the area of the base. The pyramid described in this problem has a square base with sides of length 4, so both the perimeter (p) and the area of its base (B) are 16. Each face of the pyramid is an equilateral triangle, the height of which represents the slant height (s) of the pyramid. Divide one of the equilateral triangles into two 30:60:90 triangles and use the side length ratio x:$x\sqrt{3}$:$2x$ to determine the slant height of the pyramid. Since the base of one of these 30:60:90 triangles is 2 (half the length of a side of the pyramid's base) and the hypotenuse is 4 (the length of a side of the equilateral triangles making up the faces of the pyramid), the height of each 30:60:90 triangle (and, therefore, of each equilateral triangle face of the pyramid) is $2\sqrt{3}$. That is the slant height (s) of the pyramid as well. Now, plug in all of the relevant measures and solve: $\frac{1}{2}ps + B = \frac{1}{2} \times (16 \times 2\sqrt{3}) + 16 = 16\sqrt{3} + 16$.
5. **D. 512π** The circumference is 16π so the diameter is 16, and the radius is 8. The surface area is $4\pi r^2 = 256\pi$. The paint covers the ball twice, so multiply by 2 to get 512π.
6. **E. 224** A closet is in the shape of a rectangular solid. To find the volume, multiply: $V = lwh = 7 \times 4 \times 8 = 224$ cubic feet.
7. **C. 48π** The cone has a surface area of $\pi rs = \pi \times 3 \times 10 = 30\pi$ (don't include the base of the cone). A sphere with radius 3 has a surface area of $4\pi r^2 = 4 \times \pi \times 3^2 = 36\pi$. The surface area of the ice cream is half of that, or 18π. Add to get $30\pi + 18\pi = 48\pi$.
8. **C. 8:1** The formula for the volume of a sphere is $V = \frac{4}{3}\pi r^3$. Find the volumes of both spheres and simplify the ratio between those volumes. Or think about it this way: the ratio of the volume of Sphere A to that of Sphere B would be as follows:
   $(\frac{4}{3}\pi \times 2^3)$ to $(\frac{4}{3}\pi \times 1^3)$
   Find the value of the exponents:
   $(\frac{4}{3}\pi \times 8)$ to $(\frac{4}{3}\pi \times 1)$
   You know that you can simplify a ratio by dividing both sides of the ratio by a number. Here, divide both sides by $\frac{4}{3}\pi$ to get: 8 to 1.
9. **A. 1458** The height of all three boxes is 9 in, the length is 18 in, and the width is 9 in. The total volume is $18 \times 9 \times 9 = 1458$.
10. **C. 500** Since Max hikes directly east after hiking directly due north, he has made a 90° turn. The distances hiked therefore form a right triangle. The legs are 300 and 400 yards. To solve for the hypotenuse, use the Pythagorean relationship:
    $$a^2 + b^2 = c^2$$
    $$300^2 + 400^2 = c^2$$
    $$90{,}000 + 160{,}000 = c^2$$
    $$250{,}000 = c^2$$
    $$500 = c$$
    A quicker solution would be to notice that the distances form a large triangle with sides in the 3:4:5 ratio. Then it is easy to see that the hypotenuse of a triangle with legs of 300 and 400 yards is 500 yards.
11. **C. 168** The volume of the container as drawn in the diagram is $V = lwh = 9$ in $\times$ 7 in $\times$ 12 in = 756 in^3. If you increase the length by 2 inches, the volume is 11 in $\times$ 7 in $\times$ 12 in = 924 in^3. Find the difference: 924 in^3 – 756 in^3 = 168 in^3. You can solve the problem more easily by multiplying the added length by the width and height: 2(7)(12) = 168.
12. **D. $x^2 = 15^2 - 6^2$** Use the Pythagorean relationship. If $a^2 + b^2 = c^2$ and c is the hypotenuse, then $b^2 = c^2 - a^2$, and $x^2 = 15^2 - 6^2$.
13. **E. 36** Use the formula for finding the perimeter of a rectangle. Let $3w$ = length.
    $P = 2l + 2w$
    $96 = 2(3w) + 2w$
    $96 = 8w$
    $w = 12$
    So the width is 12 inches, and the length is $3 \times 12 = 36$ inches.
14. **E. 1120π** The circumference is 16π, so $r = 8$ cm. A cone-shaped party hat does not have a base, so $SA = \pi rs = 56\pi$. Multiply by 20 to get 1120π.
15. **A. 3.43** To find the area of the shaded region, subtract the area of the circle from the area of the square. One side of the square is equivalent to the diameter of the circle. The radius is 2, so the diameter—and each side of the square—is 4. So $A = 4^2 - \pi \times 2^2 \approx 3.43$.
16. **B. 1,560** You may find it helpful to draw a sketch of the room. Two walls measure 40 by 12 feet. Two measure 25 by 12 feet. Find the total area: $2 \times 40 \times 12 + 2 \times 25 \times 12 = 960 + 600 = 1{,}560$.
17. **C. 12,000** Use the formula $V = lwh$. Multiply: $40 \times 25 \times 12 = 12{,}000$.
18. **A. 4** Begin by finding the total surface area of all three pyramids. The formula for the surface area of a pyramid is $SA = \frac{1}{2}ps + B$. For each pyramid, plug in the values and calculate:

Top left pyramid:
$SA = \frac{1}{2}(2+2+2+2)(3)+(2\times 2)$
$= 16$
Top right pyramid:
$SA = \frac{1}{2}(3+3+3+3)(6)+(3\times 3)$
$= 45$
Bottom pyramid:
$SA = \frac{1}{2}(4+4+4+4)(4)+(4\times 4)$
$= 48$
Thus, the total surface area for all three pyramids is:

$16 + 45 + 48 = 109$

The problem states that Laura needs one tube of paint for each 30 square inches. Thus, she needs $109 \div 30 \approx 3.6$. In order to finish her project, she should buy four tubes of paint.

19. **C. 148.8** Because the triangles are similar, the lengths of their legs are proportional. Set up a proportion: $\frac{50}{120}=\frac{62}{x}$, where x is the length of the bridge. Then cross multiply and solve: $x = 120 \times 62 \div 50 = 148.8$.
20. **A. $m\angle 5 = 60°$** $m\angle ABC$ must equal 60° because the sum of the interior angles of a triangle is 180°, and you know that $\angle BAC$ measures 30° and $\angle ACB$ measures 90°. 180° = 30° + 90° + 60°. Since lines P and Q are parallel, triangles ABC and ADE are similar. Angle 5, or $\angle ADE$, corresponds to $\angle ABC$; therefore, $\angle 5$ measures 60°.
21. **D. $m\angle 3 + m\angle 6 = 180°$** Lines P and Q are parallel, so AD is a transversal. You know that $\angle 3$ and $\angle 4$ are adjacent supplementary angles, so their sum is 180°. $\angle 4$ and $\angle 6$ are corresponding angles, so they have equal measures. Since the sum of $m\angle 3$ and $m\angle 4$ is 180° and $m\angle 6 = m\angle 4$, the sum of $m\angle 3$ and $m\angle 6$ must be 180° as well.
22. **E. 45** Imagine drawing a line from the top of the man to the end of his shadow and another line from the top of the building to the end of the building's shadow. Once you do so, you have two similar right triangles. Let x equal the height of the building, and set up a proportion: $\frac{3.5}{26.25}=\frac{6}{x}$. Cross multiply and solve: $26.25 \times 6 \div 3.5 = 45$.
23. **D. 24** It may help to make a sketch. The area of the parallelogram is 6(10) = 60 sq cm, so the area of the triangle is also 60 sq cm. To find the base of the triangle, use the formula for finding the area of a triangle and solve for base:
$60 = \frac{1}{2}b(5)$
$60 = 2.5b$
$24 = b$

UNIT 4

ABOUT THE TEST

Social Studies

The HiSET Social Studies Test evaluates your ability to understand, interpret, and apply information. You will have 70 minutes to answer 50 multiple-choice questions.*

Content Areas

Civics and Government (38%) topics may include the civic ideals of a democratic society; the practice, role, and meaning of informed citizenship; concepts of power and authority; the characteristics of modern and historic systems of governance, with an emphasis on the U.S. constitution and government; and the relationship between individuals rights and society.

History (38%) topics may include historical sources and perspectives; the relationship between past and present events; U.S. history from colonialism to present; and world history and the political, economic, and cultural characteristics of different eras.

Economics (18%) topics include basic economics concepts and systems; the difference between needs and wants; the interdependent nature of economies; and how economies are affected by government.

Geography (6%) topics may include concepts and terminology of physical and human geography; and interpretations of maps and the use of spatial analysis to describe economic, political, and social factors.

Social Studies Skills

In addition to testing your understanding of social studies passages and graphics, questions are based on your understanding of major skills, which introduce this unit on pages 518–541. After you study these skills, you will reinforce them as you work through the unit. They include:

- Determining **central ideas and making inferences**
- Analyzing **relationships within and between social studies materials**
- Analyzing **facts, opinions,** and **values** in social studies contexts
- Analyzing authors' **purposes, assumptions, and arguments**
- Evaluating authors' **reasoning** and **reliability of evidence**
- Interpreting data and statistics in **graphs** and **charts**
- Determining the adequacy of information for **reaching valid conclusions**

(While you will be expected to interpret data, you will not have to perform extensive calculations during the HiSET Social Studies Test.)

* Note: The information given here was the latest information available as of December 2018. It is possible that some of this information may change between this printing and your test date. For updates, visit http://hiset.ets.org.

LESSON 1

Determine Central Idea and Draw Conclusions

The **central idea** of a passage or graphic is the main idea it is intended to convey. This is supported by **details** or **examples**.

> At the outset of the Revolutionary War, the American colonies had a small navy of only 31 ships. To contest the far superior number of vessels in the British fleet, the colonies employed privateers, independent ships authorized to harass and capture enemy merchant and cargo ships. Armed with more than 14,000 guns, American privateers captured well over 2,000 enemy ships. These figures demonstrate how difficult it would have been, without the aid of privateers, for the colonies to win their independence against a larger, better equipped British Navy.

▶ What is the topic of this passage?

(1) the importance of colonial privateers to winning the Revolutionary War

(2) the fact that American privateers captured well over 2,000 enemy ships

Choice **(1)** is correct. The main point of the passage is that privateers were crucial to the colonies' success in their war for independence. The number of ships captured by privateers, referred to in choice (2), is used to support that point.

One skill needed to understand social studies information is the ability to **draw conclusions** from what you read or see. This skill requires you to go beyond what is directly stated and make an inference about what is meant or implied.

▶ Which of the following conclusions can be drawn based on this graph?

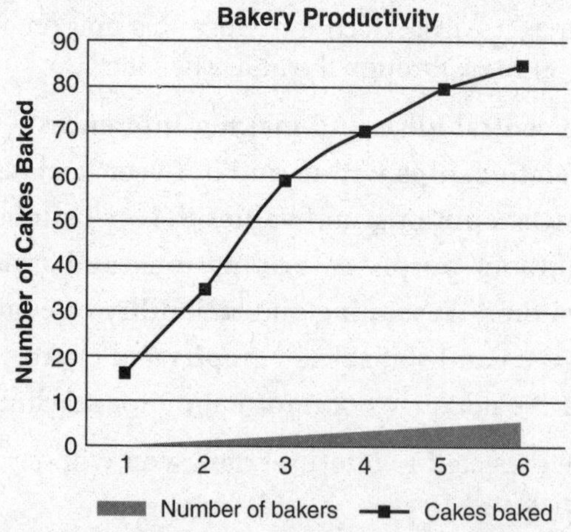

(1) The productivity of a bakery is based on a number of factors.

(2) The productivity of the bakery rises when more bakers are added.

You were correct if you selected choice **(2)**. As you look at the graph, the line—the number of cakes baked—rises steeply when more bakers are added. This associates the productivity of the bakery with the number of bakers. Choice (1) may well be true, but it is not a conclusion based on this graph.

KEY IDEAS

- Social Studies Test presentations consist of text, graphics, or a combination of the two.
- Comprehending social studies material requires understanding the central idea or point and its supporting details.
- The Social Studies Test questions also require you to make inferences in order to draw conclusions.

HiSET EXAM TIP

To answer questions based on a passage or graphic, ask yourself, "What is the main point? What evidence or details are used to support it? What conclusion can I draw?"

PRACTICE 1

Questions 1 through 3 are based on the following passage.

Theater was one of the most popular forms of art in ancient Greece, and one form of drama—tragedy—was central to Greek culture. Tragedies told familiar stories from Greek myths and epics, but actors portrayed the main roles, and a chorus narrated the background of the story and commented on the action. These serious dramas centered on a main character who displayed exceptional attributes but also had a tragic flaw that caused his downfall. This flaw was often hubris, which is excessive pride or overconfidence.

1. Which of the following is the topic of the paragraph?
   A. the superiority of Greek theater
   B. the standard forms of Greek drama
   C. the characteristics of Greek tragedy
   D. the most popular Greek tragedies

2. Which of these details supports the central idea?
   A. Theater was one of the most popular Greek art forms.
   B. Tragedies were more important than comedies in ancient Greece.
   C. Greeks thought flaws other than hubris were not tragic.
   D. The main character in Greek drama has a tragic flaw that causes his downfall.

3. Which of these conclusions is supported by the paragraph?
   A. Ancient Greeks did not expect to see an original story each time they attended the theater.
   B. Playwrights in ancient Greece also wrote myths and epics.
   C. Tragedies in ancient Greece were judged on the basis of how serious their stories were.
   D. Only highly cultured people attended tragedies in ancient Greece.

Questions 4 and 5 are based on this graphic.

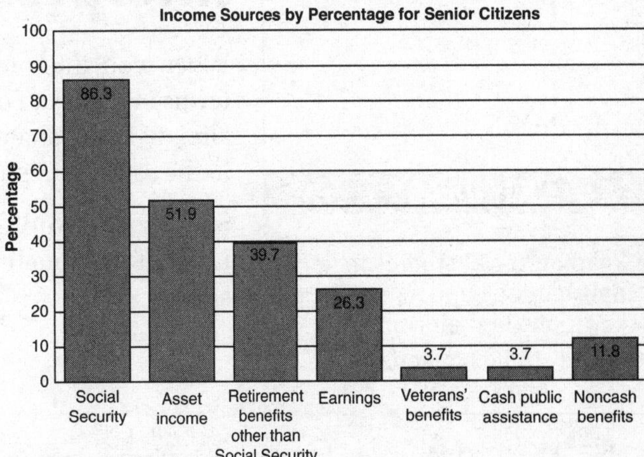

Source: Social Security Administration

4. The graph answers which of the following questions?
   A. What is the dollar value of the income for senior citizens?
   B. How much do senior citizens have in savings accounts?
   C. How many senior citizens are dependent on veterans' benefits for their retirement income?
   D. Where do the incomes of senior citizens come from?

5. Which of the following conclusions can be drawn from this graph?
   A. More senior citizens need to continue to work in order to make ends meet now than in the past.
   B. Social Security benefits are the most widespread means of support for most senior citizens.
   C. Senior citizens who receive income from veterans' benefits also receive benefits from public assistance.
   D. Senior citizens who do not receive Social Security benefits get income from one or more other sources.

STUDY ADVICE

If you have trouble identifying the central idea of social studies passages, review the Language Arts: Reading lessons on pages 70–71. Identifying the main idea of a passage works the same way no matter what type of passage you are reading.

LESSON 2

Interpret Words and Ideas

When you interpret social studies materials, you need to understand **key terms** in context. For instance, on page 558, the word *articles* is presented. You already know an everyday use of the word, such as "articles of clothing," but in the context on page 558, an *article* refers to a section of the U.S. Constitution.

Some social studies material is organized in **chronological** or time order. Look at the timeline below and answer a question about the sequence of events.

Inventions in the 1870s

1875	1876	1877	1879
Blasting gel	Telephone	Cylinder phonograph Carbon arc light bulb	Cash register Carbon filament light bulb

▶ Which of the following events preceded the invention of the carbon arc light bulb?

(1) invention of the telephone
(2) invention of the carbon filament light bulb

Timelines are read left to right, from oldest to most recent, so choice **(1)** is correct. Choice (2) refers to the carbon filament light bulb, invented in 1879, a year after the carbon arc light bulb.

Another way that social studies material is organized is by **cause and effect,** which is another way of asking "What resulted from this action?" or "What made this event happen?" Read the following paragraph to practice this skill.

The prices of goods and services are determined by the relationship between supply and demand. When supply exceeds demand, sellers must lower prices to stimulate sales; on the other hand, when demand exceeds supply, consumers bid up prices as they compete to purchase items or services that they desire.

▶ Based on the theory of supply and demand, under which of the following scenarios would prices be most likely to rise?

(1) The demand for a product exceeds that product's supply.
(2) Producers and sellers advertise a product in order to stimulate demand for that product.

Choice **(1)** is correct. According to the law of supply and demand, prices rise when demand outpaces supply. Choice (2) describes a situation in which producers and sellers advertise to stimulate demand for their product, but without knowing whether the supply is limited, we cannot conclude that this would cause the price to increase.

Some questions may require you to understand that the fact that two events **correlate,** or happen at the same time, does not necessarily mean that one **caused** the other. Remember that causation can never be deduced from correlation alone.

KEY IDEAS

- Reading social studies materials requires understanding key terms in their context.
- Social studies material is often organized as a sequence of events or as steps in a process.
- Analyzing social studies materials often involves relating causes to effects.

HiSET EXAM TIP

To learn key social studies terms, pay close attention to the meaning of the words in ***bold type*** *throughout this unit.*

PRACTICE 2

Questions 1 through 3 are based on this passage.

From 1820 to 1870, more than 7.5 million immigrants arrived on U.S. shores. That was more people than the entire U.S. population in 1810. Almost all of these immigrants came from Northern Europe, and a majority were Catholic. Historians have often focused on what pushed these emigrants out of Europe. During the 1840s, for example, Germany experienced a series of crop failures that, combined with social upheaval triggered by rapid industrialization in urban areas, produced riots, civil unrest, and open rebellion. During the same years, Ireland saw the infamous potato famine strike poor and working-class Irish families, killing an estimated 700,000 people.

While those crises spurred Europeans to emigrate, a variety of factors created a simultaneous pull to immigrate to the United States. Letters home from friends and family members who had immigrated earlier often described the United States as a "land of plenty" and related stories of successful employment and plentiful land. Steamship companies offering passage across the Atlantic advertised with posters that showed majestic scenes of American abundance.

1. According to the passage, which of the following was a cause of Northern European immigration to the United States in the 1840s and 1850s?

   A. Americans' desire to double the population of the United States
   B. efforts by Northern European governments to reduce the number of people living in poverty
   C. political and social instability in some Northern European countries
   D. efforts to spread Catholicism to the United States

2. Based on the passage, which one of the following was most likely to have been featured on a steamship company poster?

   A. a folk-art painting depicting the life of the rural poor in the United States
   B. a portrait of an American politician from the 1840s
   C. a poster advertising an American product
   D. a painting of pioneers settling and farming productive prairie land

3. Which of the following results of Northern European immigration to the United States in the mid-1800s can be inferred from the passage?

   A. a spread of poverty in the United States
   B. a decline in political upheaval in Northern Europe
   C. a growth in the population of the United States
   D. a number of Americans converting to the Catholic faith

Questions 4 and 5 are based on this timeline.

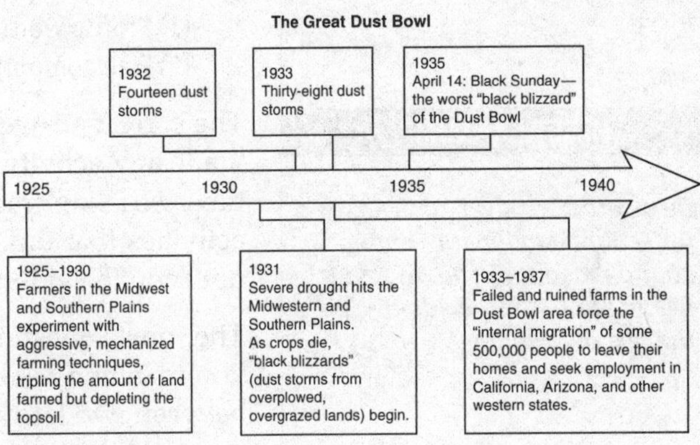

Source: www.pbs.org

4. Given the information in the timeline, which of the following would be a flawed inference?

   A. Mechanized farming contributed to dust storms.
   B. Internal migration led to overgrazing.
   C. Severe drought contributed to "black blizzards."
   D. Some farmers left the Dust Bowl before the worst dust storm hit the region.

5. Which of the following could have been a cause of the Great Dust Bowl?

   A. "black blizzards"
   B. internal migration
   C. depleted topsoil
   D. failed farms

Make Inferences

An **inference** is a statement based on facts and reasoning that must be true but that is not explicitly stated. Inferring an author's intended meaning or determining what a quote implies is a similar process to drawing a conclusion. Inference questions may ask you directly about the relationship between two factors, or they may ask you to interpret a specific element of the data or text. In all cases, you must base your answer on the evidence provided.

KEY IDEAS

- Inferences are logical conclusions that aren't directly stated but can be supported with evidence.
- Questions requiring you to make inferences may ask about the author's attitude or point of view, or they may ask you to look for trends or patterns in a set of data.

HiSET EXAM TIP

Be aware of answer choices presenting statements that sound reasonable but lack sufficient supporting evidence in the text or graphic.

Read and answer the following question asking for an interpretation:

> The Sherman Antitrust Act, passed by Congress in 1890, states, "Every contract, combination in the form of trust or otherwise, or conspiracy, in restraint of trade or commerce [. . .] is declared illegal."

► What does the passage reveal about U.S. society during that time period?

(1) Profits were thought to be more likely if trusts were disbanded.
(2) Free competition in trade and commerce was thought to be desirable.

The correct answer is **(2)**. The text reveals that the Sherman Antitrust Act made any activity "in restraint of trade" illegal. This suggests that activities restricting trade or commerce were viewed negatively, and therefore activities that did not restrict trade would be viewed positively. There is not enough evidence to support choice (1) because profit is not mentioned.

The next question asks you to infer a relationship between two factors.

Women in the Labor Force

Number of Women in the Labor Force (thousands): 14.0, 15.4, 16.8, 18.2, 19.6

Year: 1940, 1941, 1942, 1943, 1944, 1945

Source: Historical Statistics of the United States 1789–1945: A Supplement to the Statistical Abstract of the United States. Series D 11-31, p. 63, Bureau of the Census.

► Consider the following true statement in conjunction with the graph:

> In 1942, the Office of War Information (OWI) began its poster campaign to mobilize the nation's war effort. Suppose a relationship exists between the OWI campaign and the number of women entering the labor force.

► Which of the following most likely represents this relationship?

(1) The campaign had a positive impact on the number of women joining the labor force.
(2) The campaign was created in response to an increased number of women joining the labor force.

The correct answer is **(1)**. The data show the largest increase in the number of women entering the labor force after the OWI began the poster campaign. Therefore, you can infer that the campaign affected the number of women in the workforce, not the other way around. The impact was positive because the number of women entering the labor force increased.

PRACTICE 3

Questions 1 through 3 are based on the information below.

Following the 1941 attack on Pearl Harbor, President Roosevelt signed Executive Order 9066, authorizing the removal of over 100,000 Japanese and Japanese Americans from their West Coast homes in order to be transferred to internment camps after being vetted by the FBI. Below are two editorials published following the announcement that Japanese Americans would be allowed to return to the West Coast.

University Daily

We stand up for the constitutional rights of the Japanese Americans, just as we stand in support of our armies who are protecting the Constitution and human freedom wherever they are fighting. These are our fellow citizens.

The governor claims that we cannot predict the works of espionage these people might commit, but among the 100,000 persons displaced, the majority love this nation as their home. Those slated to be released have been cleared by the Federal Bureau of Investigation. To question the motives of these individuals is to question the soundness of the FBI. Without a doubt, they are loyal citizens.

West Coast Tribune

We are emphatically and unalterably opposed to the return of any individual of Japanese ancestry now or for the duration of the war. Our sons are fighting in Japan, and we do not want them to return home to find the reminders of war in their backyards.

These objections are based purely on military considerations and have nothing to do with racial matters as others might suggest. The public has not been fully informed of the extent to which Japanese Americans have been collaborating with Japan. There is more potential danger from Japanese who are born here than who are born in Japan, as there is no way of knowing where their loyalties lie.

1. It can be inferred that the author of the *West Coast Tribune* editorial

A. believed all individuals of Japanese ancestry should return to Japan
B. did not trust the investigations of the FBI into this matter
C. had a family member fighting in the military
D. was aware of potential threats that the FBI had not discovered

2. The author of the *University Daily* editorial apparently supported

A. the abolition of internment camps
B. the repeal of Executive Order 9066
C. expanding the power of the FBI
D. the return of Japanese Americans

3. What is implied by the fact that the *West Coast Tribune* editorial writer believes that the "public has not been fully informed" of Japanese-American activities?

A. The public has a right to know about collaborative activity.
B. The FBI has not conducted a thorough investigation.
C. The constitutional rights of Japanese Americans are unclear.
D. The public does not believe Japanese Americans pose a credible danger.

Question 4 is based on this photograph of a woman hanging a billboard in the early 20th century.

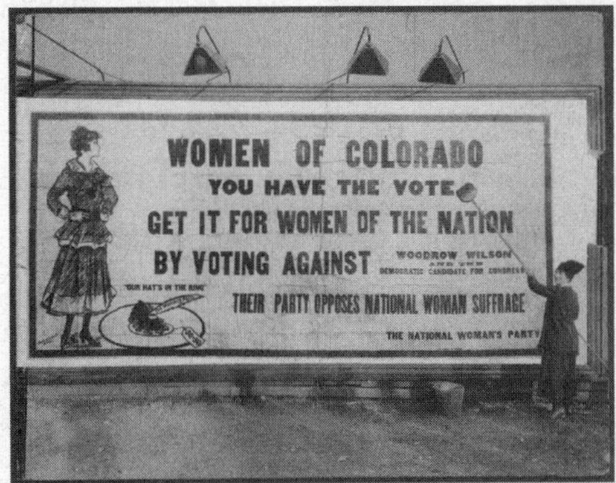

Source: Part of the Vast Billboard Campaign of the Woman's Party. Putting up billboard in Denver—1916. Records of the National Woman's Party, Manuscript Division, Library of Congress, Washington, D.C.

4. It can be inferred that at the time of this billboard

A. Woodrow Wilson supported the suffrage movement
B. only some women had the right to vote
C. the Democratic Party was poised to lose the election
D. women of Colorado could ratify the Nineteenth Amendment

LESSON 4

Form and Apply Valid Conclusions

KEY IDEAS

- A valid conclusion must be supported by evidence in the text or graphic.
- A generalization is a conclusion based on a specific event that can be applied to other situations.

In addition to drawing conclusions, you may be asked to assess whether a given conclusion is valid or to identify the weaknesses of a flawed conclusion. Valid conclusions are most often inferences that can be made by using details, key terms, tone, and/or visual symbols as context clues.

Read the example below and answer the question that follows:

> In 1867, Secretary of State William H. Seward agreed to purchase the territory of Alaska from Russia. This decision was ridiculed by Congress, and for thirty years after the purchase, critics seemed justified in their belief that the United States had acquired little more than a "polar bear garden." Initial attempts at settlement were slow, until the discovery of gold in the Klondike region ushered in waves of prospectors. The frenzy for gold would last until 1899.

▶ Is it reasonable to conclude that critics of the Alaskan Purchase had reversed their position by the early 20th century?

(1) Yes, because gold had been discovered in the region.
(2) No, because the opinion of the critics and the actions of the prospectors are unrelated.

The correct answer is **(2)**. The passage implies that the critics' opinion was no longer justified after the discovery of gold. However, it never states that they changed their mind as a result. The discovery of gold *may* have led some to view the purchase more favorably, but this outcome is speculative as the passage provides no evidence that this is true.

HiSET EXAM TIP

When asked to determine a reasonable conclusion or to define the most likely outcome, look for evidence in the text to support your answer.

Conclusions are also used to make generalizations. A **generalization** is an idea or statement based on a specific instance that can be applied to other similar or related instances. Making generalizations is a way to apply the information you've learned in one situation to reasonably predict what will likely happen in other situations.

Read the information below and answer the following question:

> In her magazine series "The History of the Standard Oil Company," Ida Tarbell exposed the unethical tactics of the oil monopoly and called for reforms, earning her and her generation of investigative journalists the moniker of "muckraker" from President Theodore Roosevelt.

▶ In which of the following projects would a "muckraker" journalist most likely be involved?

(1) Filming a documentary deploring the unsafe working conditions of a steel mill
(2) Writing a biography of oil tycoon John D. Rockefeller

The correct answer is **(1)**. Based on the information, we can conclude that a general definition of a "muckraker" is an investigative journalist who calls for reform. Applying this general definition to a new scenario, we choose filming a documentary that exposes unsafe working conditions as the activity that best fits.

PRACTICE 4

Questions 1 and 2 are based on the following except from a campaign speech that Franklin D. Roosevelt delivered in October 1932.

"During these weeks I have made it abundantly clear that I propose a national agricultural policy which will direct itself not only to the better use of our hundreds of millions of acres of every type of land in the United States, but also to the rehabilitation of that half of our population which is living on or directly concerned with the products of the soil. Our object must be the rebuilding of the rural civilization of America. Our object must be all-inclusive—a constructive program attacking the enemy on every front."

1. Based on the speech and on Roosevelt's landslide victory in the 1932 presidential race, which idea was *most likely* supported by the majority of U.S. voters?

   A. repealing New Deal policies
   B. reducing crop surpluses through farm subsidies
   C. establishing mandatory rehabilitation programs for violating Prohibition laws
   D. conducting military interventions in foreign countries

2. It is reasonable to conclude that the "enemy" Roosevelt mentions is most likely

   A. responsible for the destruction of rural civilization
   B. attacking citizens on American soil
   C. opposed to legislative relief for farmers
   D. interested in a new national agricultural policy

Questions 3 and 4 are based on the 1896 Supreme Court ruling in *Plessy v. Ferguson* (1896).

JUSTICE HARRY BROWN: "The enforced separation of the races [. . .] neither abridges the privileges or immunities of the colored man, deprives him of his property without due process of law, nor denies him the equal protection of the laws."

JUSTICE JOHN MARSHALL HARLAN: "The Constitution of the United States does not [. . .] permit any public authority to know the race of those entitled to be protected [. . .] [S]uch legislation as that here in question is inconsistent not only with that equality of rights which pertains to citizenship, National and State, but with the personal liberty enjoyed by everyone within the United States."

3. Based on the information above, how would Justice Brown most likely have responded to the assertion that schools should be desegregated?

   A. It is beyond the power of the Supreme Court to legislate the desegregation of public facilities.
   B. Segregation is inherently unequal and thus denies citizens political equality.
   C. As long as separate segregated schools are provided, no constitutional rights are being denied.
   D. Desegregation is inconsistent with the equality of rights all citizens should enjoy.

4. It is reasonable to conclude that

   A. both justices supported a strict interpretation of the Constitution
   B. the ruling was widely praised by the American public
   C. neither justice had focused on civil rights before this trial
   D. Supreme Court rulings are not always unanimous

LESSON 5

Analyze Author's Purpose and Point of View

Any author of social studies material has a viewpoint and a purpose. Social studies material can have many purposes, such as to inform or educate (for example, a textbook or magazine article). Other materials, such as newspaper editorials and online blogs, are used to convince people of a point of view.

An author's **point of view** is his or her way of looking at the world. Some social scientists follow a method of examining the facts and coming to a conclusion. In other cases, an author may start with a point of view and assemble facts or evidence to support it.

When you read social studies materials, determine whether an author has a **bias**, a tendency to see one point of view. A bias is not a bad thing in and of itself (after all, we all have biases), but you should take the author's bias into account. One kind of material that displays extreme bias is **propaganda**, in which an author tries to convince people to act and think as the author wants. Authors of propaganda selectively include certain facts and ignore others, or they use loaded words to trigger emotional responses. Use the following example to practice finding the author's point of view.

> Until the 1980s, most anthropologists mistakenly estimated the native population in North America at the time of Columbus's expedition in 1492 to be somewhere between 2 million and 7 million people. They based these estimates on the number of Native Americans alive at the time of their first contact with European explorers and settlers. However, the estimates ignored the impact of infectious diseases, such as smallpox, which traveled much faster than humans did and would have decimated the native population before Europeans made contact with native people.

► What is the author's point of view about the population of North America in 1492?

(1) that it was not exactly 2 million people or 7 million people but was somewhere in between those two numbers
(2) that it was probably much larger than 7 million people

Choice **(2)** is correct. The author points out a reason to think that anthropologists prior to the 1980s undercounted the native population. Answer (1) gives the estimate of most anthropologists prior to the 1980s.

► Which of the following words is a clue to the author's viewpoint?

(1) ignored
(2) estimated

The correct choice is **(1)**. The author believes that the anthropologists' estimates were flawed because they ignored relevant information about the impact of diseases on the native population. Answer (2) misses the author's point; he doesn't fault them for estimating, but rather for ignoring evidence when they made their estimates.

KEY IDEAS

- Social studies material may be written to inform or to persuade.
- Thoughtful readers need to take an author's purpose and point of view into account.
- Some authors may express a bias or point of view by the selection of supporting details or use of loaded words.

HiSET EXAM TIP

You may be provided with a newspaper editorial, an online blog commentary, or a speech. Ask yourself, "What is the author's viewpoint? How are facts and evidence organized to be convincing? How are words chosen to have an impact?"

Questions 1 through 3 are based on the paragraph and poster below.

During World War I, the U.S. National War Garden Commission began a campaign to encourage private citizens to grow their own food as a means of supporting the war effort. This practice became very popular. With increased private food production, the government could reserve much of the cheaper, mass-produced food for the troops. The money saved in feeding soldiers freed up resources for other military needs. In addition, planting war gardens, also known as victory gardens, gave American citizens a sense of empowerment.

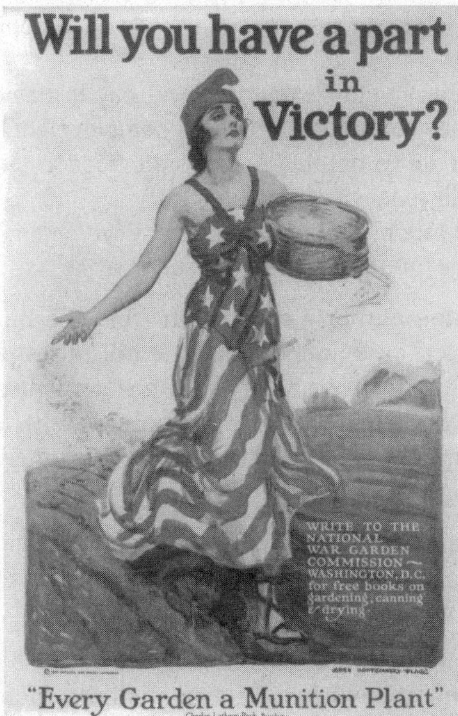

Source: Library of Congress Poster by James Montgomery Flagg

1. Which of the following best describes the poster's use of the word *Victory*?

   A. ambiguous
   B. informative
   C. propagandistic
   D. impersonal

STUDY ADVICE

If you find it difficult to identify an author's point of view, review the Language Arts: Reading lesson on pages 86–87.

2. What is meant by the poster's caption "Every Garden a Munition Plant"?

   A. War gardens require a great deal of time to cultivate.
   B. Citizens who plant war gardens encourage a sense of community in their hometowns.
   C. Citizens who plant war gardens help supply the war effort with essential resources.
   D. War gardens provide an excellent opportunity to learn about gardening, canning, and food drying.

3. The author's primary purpose in writing the paragraph accompanying the poster is most likely to

   A. describe war gardens and explain their popularity in the United States
   B. encourage patriotism and continued support for a strong United States military
   C. distinguish the efforts of American citizens during World War I from those of citizens in other countries
   D. rebut the accusations of those who claimed that civilians did not do enough to support the U.S. war effort in World War I

Question 4 is based on the following dialogue.

Congresswoman Burns: The new organic food safety regulations are likely to increase the average cost of some food staples. The costs are justified, however, by the peace of mind that comes from knowing your food is safe and healthy.

Concerned Citizen: Rising prices are a cancer eating away at our families. High costs will drive people away from healthy foods and wind up harming our children's diets. Instead of buying wholesome, natural products, parents will feed their kids fast food.

4. Which of the following constitute "loaded" words the Concerned Citizen uses to support her point?

   A. high costs
   B. fast food
   C. a cancer
   D. our children's diets

LESSON 6

Evaluate Author's Reasoning and Evidence

Social studies authors in print and online publications use a variety of strategies to support their viewpoints. They may use the following:

- **Facts**—information that can be proven to be true
- **Opinions**—beliefs about a concept or situation
- **Judgments**—conclusions that are supported by reasons and evidence

On the Social Studies Test, you need to read carefully to distinguish among these three concepts.

KEY IDEAS

- An author's point of view may be supported by facts, opinions, and reasoned judgment.
- While reading, analyze whether information is a fact, an opinion, or a conclusion based on reasoning or evidence.
- A careful reader evaluates whether an author supports his or her claims with evidence.

► Indicate whether each of the following statements is a fact (F), an opinion (O), or a judgment (J).

(1) ___ Because it raises the amount employers will pay in payroll taxes, the new tax bill may contribute to higher unemployment.

(2) ___ Last year, manufacturing output in our state rose by 4.6 percent over the previous year.

(3) ___ We should limit the role played by the federal government in formulating energy policy for our region of the country.

Statement (1) is a judgment; the author's conclusion (that the bill may increase unemployment) is based on evidence (that the bill raises payroll taxes). Statement (2) is a fact; the truth or falsity of the statement can be checked against empirical data. Statement (3) is an opinion; the author makes a recommendation (limit the role of the federal government) but offers no evidence or reasoning to support it.

To be credible, an author needs to support his or her claims with evidence. Part of your job on the Social Studies Test is to answer questions about whether or not an author's claims are supported.

HiSET EXAM TIP

When you read social studies material, ask yourself, "What is the claim being made? Is evidence provided to support this claim? Is the evidence relevant to the claim and sufficient and credible enough to support it?"

Delaware was the first state to ratify the U.S. Constitution. Because of its history of favorable corporate tax policies, Delaware is today home to 63 percent of Fortune 500 corporations. There is no doubt then that Delaware's Freedom of Information Act, requiring the state government to respond within 15 days of a request, should serve as a model for similar acts in other U.S. states.

► Does the author support the claim of the passage?

(1) Yes, because he believes and asserts that there is no doubt about the truth of the claim.

(2) No, because he asserts the truth of the claim without offering evidence relevant to the claim.

Choice **(2)** is correct. The author's claim is that Delaware's Freedom of Information Act should serve as a model for similar acts in other states, but the other statements in the passage are irrelevant to that claim. Choice (1) is incorrect because stating a claim firmly ("no doubt") does not provide *support* for the claim.

PRACTICE 6

1. Consultant: Finding a reliable energy supply is vital to Cambodia, a country still recovering from decades of civil war and genocide in the late 1970s. Damming the Mekong River could solve Cambodia's energy supply problems. However, since the Mekong flows through China, Myanmar, Laos, and Thailand before it reaches Cambodia, regional cooperation will be necessary.

   Which of the following is an opinion, and not a fact, presented by the consultant?

   A. Damming the Mekong could solve Cambodia's energy problems.
   B. The Mekong River flows through several countries before reaching Cambodia.
   C. Cambodia experienced civil war.
   D. Many Cambodians were killed in the late 1970s.

Question 2 is based on this cartoon referencing the labor movement of the early 20th century.

Protected by George Matthew Adams.
SPITING HIMSELF.
—Morris for the George Matthew Adams Service.

Source: Literary Digest 9/6/1919. Originally from the George Matthew Adams Service (Morris).

2. Which of the following represents the viewpoint of the cartoonist?

   A. Strikes can achieve better working conditions.
   B. Strikes have a detrimental impact on workers.
   C. Farmworkers are more likely to engage in strikes than are factory workers.
   D. Strikes should hamper production.

3. Historian: Ancient Greece was the greatest of the early civilizations. While the Babylonians may have had arithmetic and ancient Egypt built the pyramids, ancient Greece gave us our first taste of democracy.

   Which of the following is a fact that the historian uses to support her opinion?

   A. Ancient Greece was the greatest early civilization.
   B. Babylonians made use of arithmetic.
   C. The pyramids were built in ancient Egypt.
   D. Ancient Greece pioneered democracy.

Question 4 is based on the following chart.

The Articles of Confederation were the predecessor to the United States Constitution.

	The Articles of Confederation	The Constitution
Federal Court System	No system of federal courts	Court system exists to deal with issues between citizens, states
Regulating Trade	No provision to regulate interstate trade	Congress has the right to regulate trade between states
Executive Power	No executive with power; president merely presided over Congress	Executive branch is headed by president who chooses Cabinet and has checks on power of judiciary and legislature
Raising an Army	Congress could not draft troops; depended on states to contribute forces	Congress can raise an army to deal with military situations
Sovereignty	Sovereignty resides in states	The Constitution is the supreme law of the land
Taxes	Congress could ask states to pay taxes	Congress has the right to levy taxes on individuals

4. Which of the following is a conclusion supported by the table above, rather than a detail stated in the table?

   A. The Constitution allows Congress to enforce collection of taxes, whereas the Articles of Confederation did not.
   B. The Constitution grants more power to the federal government than did the Articles of Confederation.
   C. There were no national armed forces before the Constitution was drafted.
   D. Trade was not nationally regulated by the Articles of Confederation.

LESSON 7

Source Reliability

Social studies information is obtained from a variety of sources, which are classified according to the type of information they contain.

Firsthand accounts and original documents, such as newspaper articles, survey data, and interviews, are **primary sources**. Primary sources are created in the time period being studied, and they reflect the point of view of witnesses to the event or those affected by it. **Secondary sources**, like biographies and reports, summarize and interpret primary sources. Secondary sources are written for a specific purpose and may reflect the biases of the author or sponsor or a loss of data since the events described. **Tertiary sources** are collections of information gathered to provide facts. Examples include encyclopedias and textbooks. Tertiary sources are often designed to convey a neutral point of view, defined as facts and interpretations that are widely accepted.

Some questions ask you to to identify which source is best to use in a given scenario. Other questions may ask you to compare or contrast multiple sources, identifying their strengths and weaknesses. Primary sources such as letters or diaries can offer insight into the emotions of those experiencing a time period or event, but they only reflect the limited personal viewpoint of the author. Other primary sources, such as property deeds and birth certificates, provide unbiased data but lack context. Secondary and tertiary sources are easier to access than primary sources and are useful for understanding varying perspectives or interpretations. However, it is important to verify the credibility of the author to ensure the information is reputable.

Answer the following question that asks you to explain why one source is more useful than another:

► Suppose you wanted to learn about the living conditions of pioneers on the Oregon Trail. Why would diaries written by settlers who traveled this route be a more credible source of information than a description in a recent history book of the hardships settlers faced?

(1) The diarists are more likely to be experts on the history of the Oregon Trail.

(2) The diaries are more likely to contain firsthand accounts of living conditions.

The correct answer is **(2)**. Diaries are a primary source, which means they contain descriptions from those who lived through or witnessed an event. Pioneers who traveled the Oregon Trail would not be considered experts on its history as their knowledge would be limited to personal experience.

KEY IDEAS

- Primary sources contain firsthand accounts of an event or are original documents.
- Secondary and tertiary sources provide analysis and interpretation of one or more primary sources.
- Credible sources are written by an expert or authority on the subject.

HiSET EXAM TIP

On the Social Studies Test, consider what type of source—primary, secondary, or tertiary—is presented. Match the type of source to the type of information it contains.

PRACTICE 7

<u>Questions 1 through 4</u> **are based on the information below.**

Source 1: Excerpt from the diary of Orville Wright, December 14, 1903

A couple small boys, who had come with the men from the station, made a hurried departure over the hill for home on hearing the engine start. We tossed up coin to decide who should make first trial, and Will won. After getting adjustments of engine ready I took right end of machine. Will got on. When all was ready Will attempted to release fastening to rail, but the pressure due to the weight of machine and thrust of screws was so great that he could not get it loose. We had to get a couple of the men to help push machine back till rope was slipped loose. While I was signaling man at other end to leave go, but before I myself was ready, Will started machine. I grabbed the upright the best I could and off we went.

Source 1: Wilbur and Orville Wright Papers, Manuscript Division, Library of Congress, Washington, D.C., https://www.loc.gov/resource/mwright.01007/?sp=26

Source 2: Excerpt from an article on the history of flight

The Wright brothers made their first attempt at powered flight at Kitty Hawk, North Carolina, on December 14, 1903. The engine stalled upon takeoff, and though they gained a short distance, they did not consider it a successful flight, as the flying machine only made it less than a dozen feet off the ground. Three days later, after all the damage of the earlier trial had been repaired, both Wilbur and Orville successfully flew the aircraft in front of five witnesses before a gust of wind overturned the machine, damaging it beyond repair. The brothers telegrammed their father with the news, and the modern age of aviation was born.

1. Compared to source 1, source 2

   A. contains only personal details
   B. is written with a clear personal bias
   C. does not provide any interpretation
   D. is written from a more objective point of view

2. Consider the following statement:

Source 2 provides a more credible source of information than source 1 on the impact of the first attempt at flight.

   This statement is

   A. true, because the author of source 2 is an expert on aviation history
   B. true, because the author is analyzing an event after it has happened
   C. false, because the author was not there during the first flight attempt
   D. false, because the author is not qualified to write about aviation history

3. Which of the following statements correctly compares the two sources?

   A. Source 1 contains reliable information on early attempts at flight, while source 2 does not.
   B. Source 1 contains a firsthand account of the first attempt at flight, and source 2 provides an interpretation of why the first attempt was considered unsuccessful.
   C. Source 1 describes what it felt like to fly, and source 2 describes multiple attempts at flight.
   D. Source 1 and source 2 both contain accounts with such a degree of bias that a historian could not rely on them.

4. Which of the following would be the least reliable source to learn more about the Wright brothers?

   A. an article in an aviation magazine, written by a historian
   B. letters written by one of the witnesses of the first flight
   C. a biography of the Wright brothers
   D. an instruction manual for pilots, published by the Federal Aviation Administration

LESSON 8

Analyze Relationships Between Materials

KEY IDEAS

- Social studies materials may use graphics to illustrate key concepts.
- Circle, bar, and line graphs visually portray social studies information.
- Maps are drawings that show places and regions with keys, compasses, and scales.

HiSET EXAM TIP

When you interpret a social studies graphic, carefully read the title and all labels and keys to make sure that you correctly understand the main idea and the type of information being displayed.

Content Presented in Graphic Format

Social studies content is often presented in graphic form. Two of the most useful displays are graphs and maps.

Circle graphs are used to show how a whole is divided into parts; they show fractions or percentages.

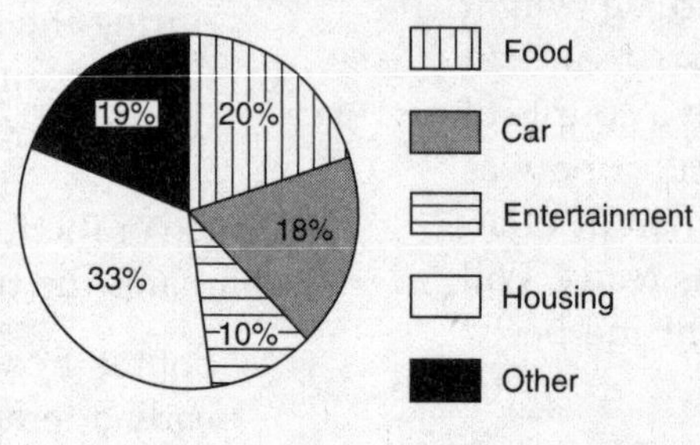

Line graphs and **bar graphs** organize material by using labels on the bottom axis and values on the side.

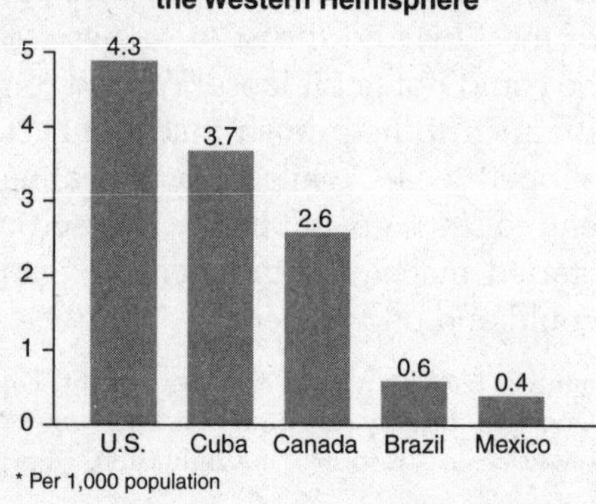

Maps use a **legend** (also called the **key**) to explain symbols, a **compass rose** to indicate directions, and **scales** to determine distances. To interpret information on a map, note any labels printed directly on the map. Then, check the legend to see whether the color, shading, or symbols shown give additional information.

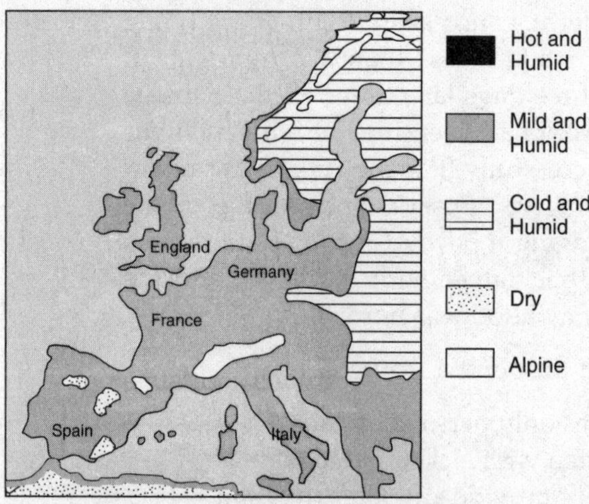

► According to the map, what is England's climate?

(1) mild and humid
(2) cold and humid

In this map, England appears just to the left and slightly above the center. It is shown in gray, indicating that its climate is "mild and humid." The correct answer here is choice **(1)**.

PRACTICE 8.1

1. According to the circle graph on page 532, the greatest portion of the Sanchez family's budget is spent on which two items?

   A. housing and food
   B. housing and entertainment
   C. food and car
   D. entertainment and other

2. Which of the following statements is supported by the bar graph on page 532?

   A. Cuba has the highest divorce rate in the hemisphere.
   B. Mexico has the lowest divorce rate in the hemisphere.
   C. Mexico's divorce rate is decreasing.
   D. Brazil has a higher divorce rate than Mexico.

Questions 3 and 4 refer to the following graph.

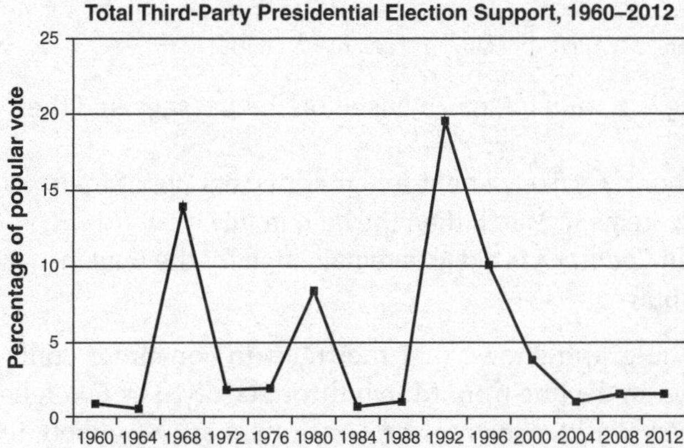

3. Based on the graph, you may validly infer that support for third-party candidates ________ during the 1980s and 1990s.

   A. steadily increased
   B. steadily decreased
   C. neither increased nor decreased
   D. fluctuated

4. The graph can be used to disprove which one of the following claims?

   A. Third-party candidates have not enjoyed significant support in the 21st century.
   B. The third-party candidate who garnered the most support since 1960 was Ross Perot in 1992.
   C. Third-party candidates have never captured more than 10 percent of the popular vote in any presidential election.
   D. In most elections, all third-party candidates combined get less than 5 percent of the popular vote.

Questions 5 and 6 are based on the following map.

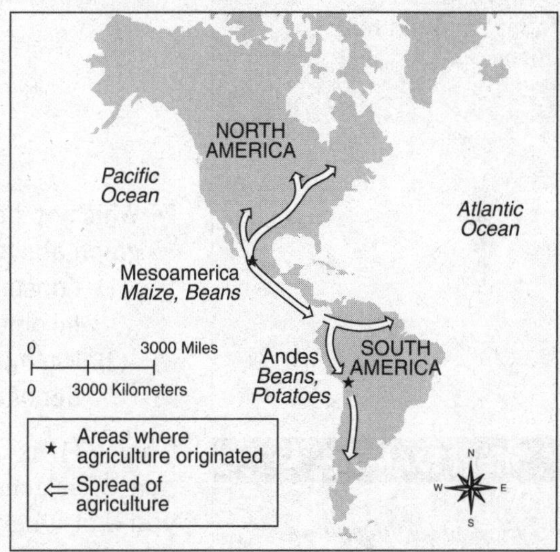

5. What does this map show?

   A. political boundaries in the ancient Americas
   B. physical features of the Americas
   C. how agriculture spread in the Americas
   D. all ancient civilizations of the Americas

6. Which of the following statements is supported by the information on the map?

   A. Both the Andes civilization and Mesoamerica domesticated maize.
   B. Both the Andes civilization and Mesoamerica domesticated beans.
   C. Agriculture developed in the Andes civilization before it did in Mesoamerica.
   D. Agriculture spread more rapidly northward than southward.

Integrating Text and Graphic Content

In reading social studies materials and the materials you encounter in daily life, you often have to combine text information with a graphic. For example, an online article about a conflict in Africa may have a map. A newspaper graph with information about new immigrants in your community may accompany a story about their contributions to local healthcare and manufacturing industries.

Practice combining information with the passage and graphic below.

> Consumer confidence is an economic indicator that reflects how optimistic consumers are about their personal finances, given the state of the economy. When consumer confidence shows a monthly trend of decline month after month, consumers are pessimistic about their chances of finding and keeping good jobs. When their confidence is low, consumers spend less—especially on nonessential items—and tend to save more of their money. On the other hand, when confidence is high, consumers will make more discretionary, or optional, purchases.

KEY IDEAS

- Some situations combine text information with a graphic.
- To better understand the main point or supporting evidence, you need to combine information from both sources.

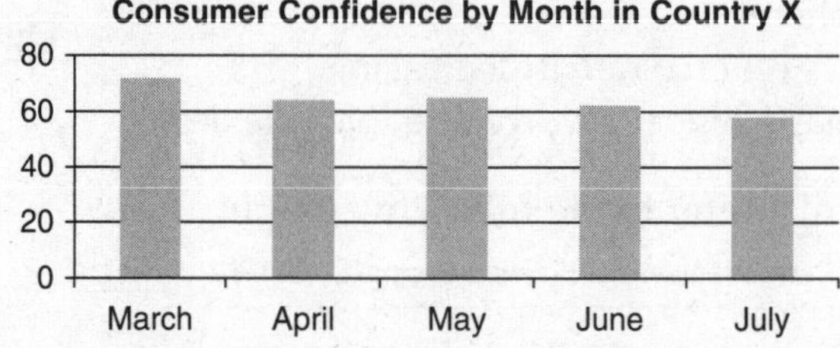

► Which of the following is a valid inference based on the passage and the graph above?

(1) Consumers in Country X likely spent a higher percentage of their income on luxury items in March than they did in July.
(2) Unemployment in Country X is likely to remain high for the remainder of the year shown.

HiSET EXAM TIP

When you see text accompanied by a graphic, read the questions carefully. Some questions may ask about the text or the graphic individually. Others may ask you to combine information from both sources.

Choice **(1)** is correct. The graph shows that the trend in consumer confidence has generally been in decline from March through July. The text tells you that when consumer confidence is lower, consumers are less likely to spend, especially on nonessential goods. These two statements combined support choice (1). Choice (2) cannot be inferred from the information in the passage or the graph. Neither of those sources provides a basis to make a prediction about future unemployment.

PRACTICE 8.2

Questions 1 through 3 relate to the following passage and map.

The sea otter (*Enhydra lutris*) is a marine mammal native to the coasts of the northern and eastern North Pacific Ocean. At one time, southern sea otters populated the entire coast of what is now the state of California and farther south along Mexico's Baja California coastline. Prior to 1741, the sea otter population worldwide is estimated to have been 150,000–300,000.

Between 1741 and 1930, however, sea otters were hunted extensively for their fur, and the world population fell to around 2,000 individuals. By 1930, the wild sea otter population in California was limited exclusively to about 50 living in a small area between Big Sur and Monterey Bay.

Fortunately, the 1911 international ban on hunting and conservation efforts and programs to reintroduce the sea otter into previously populated areas have contributed to rebounding numbers. The Monterey Bay National Marine Sanctuary (MBNMS) was created to protect otters and other marine life at risk of extinction, and California sea otters now occupy about one-fourth of their former range. Despite these successes, sea otter populations in California have remained steady at around 3,000 individuals, and the sea otter continues to be classified as an endangered species.

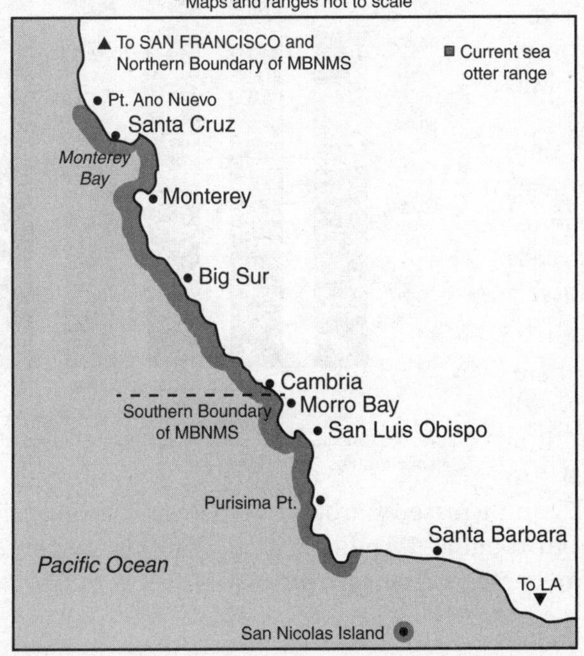

1. According to the passage, which one of the following statements about the sea otter is true?
   A. Sea otter conservation efforts have been more successful in areas outside of California than they have been within California.
   B. Sea otter populations were threatened by water pollution as well as by extensive hunting.
   C. The sea otter population is now about one-fourth of its pre-1741 number.
   D. Sea otters have been able to live in habitats from which they were once eliminated.

2. Which of the following conclusions can be drawn from the information in the passage and the map?
   A. Sea otters will soon have the same range they had prior to 1741.
   B. Sea otter habitat has been restored only within the boundaries of the MBNMS.
   C. Sea otters are still hunted in the area north of Point Ano Nuevo.
   D. The current range of the sea otter in California is larger than it was in 1911.

3. The author of the passage would be most likely to agree with which of the following statements about the information in the map?
   A. The range of sea otters shown on the map indicates that sea otter conservation programs are no longer needed.
   B. The range of sea otters shown on the map is identical to the range of sea otters prior to 1741.
   C. Without conservation efforts and reintroduction programs, the range of sea otters in California would be smaller than what is shown on the map.
   D. Ten years from now, the range of sea otters in California will be larger than what is currently shown on the map.

Interpret Data and Statistics

Social studies materials often involve data or statistics. The Social Studies Test will not require you to perform extensive calculations; however, you may be asked to interpret data to spot **trends,** make **comparisons** or **contrasts**, or make **inferences** from data.

KEY IDEAS

- Tables and graphs are commonly used to present data in social studies materials.
- A measure of central tendency is used to summarize data with one number.
- Bar graphs are used to compare data, and line graphs are used to show trends.

Franklin County Family Finances

Year	Median income (family of 4)	Average % to taxes	Average % to savings
2009	$40,800	27%	5.2%
2010	$41,500	28%	6.0%
2011	$42,300	29%	5.5%
2012	$44,100	29%	5.1%

▶ Which of the following statements about Franklin County families is supported by the table?

(1) An increase in their median income over the last few years has caused those families to save less.

(2) An increase in their median income has not necessarily resulted in an increase in the percentage of their income saved by those families.

Choice **(2)** is correct. As the median income has increased over the last few years, the rate of savings has not, on average, increased. Choice (1) is not supported because the table contains no information about what causes Franklin County families to behave in any way.

Some questions may ask you to use graphs to make comparisons or to identify trends.

HiSET EXAM TIP

On the Social Studies Test, you may be asked to interpret data in ways that do not involve calculations. Ask yourself, "What can I infer from this graph or table?" And also, "What can't I infer from it?"

▶ What of the following trends is indicated by the data in the chart?

(1) Between 2003 and 2007, foreign arrivals from overseas grew at a faster pace than foreign arrivals from North America.

(2) Between 2003 and 2007, foreign arrivals from North America grew at a faster pace than foreign arrivals from overseas.

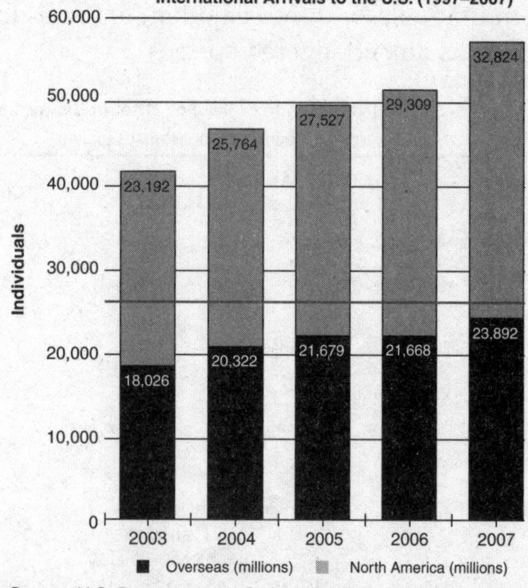

Source: U.S. Department of Commerce, Office of Travel and Tourism Industries

Choice **(2)** is correct here. Foreign arrivals from North America grew from a little over 23 million in 2003 to almost 33 million in 2007, an increase of around 41 percent. Meanwhile, overseas arrivals rose from roughly 18 million in 2003 to just under 24 million, a change of approximately 33 percent growth.

PRACTICE 9

Question 1 is based on the following table.

New Mexico: Population by Age, 2010	
Under 18	518,672
18–19	61,169
20–24	142,370
25–34	267,245
35–49	393,362
50–64	404,106
65 & over	272,255
Total	**2,059,179**

Adapted from U.S. Census Bureau

1. The table provides data that will allow you to answer which one of the following questions about New Mexico in 2010?

   A. What specific age was the median age?
   B. How many residents were teenagers?
   C. What percentage of residents were 50 or older?
   D. Why were individuals over 65 such a small part of the population?

Question 2 is based on the following line graph.

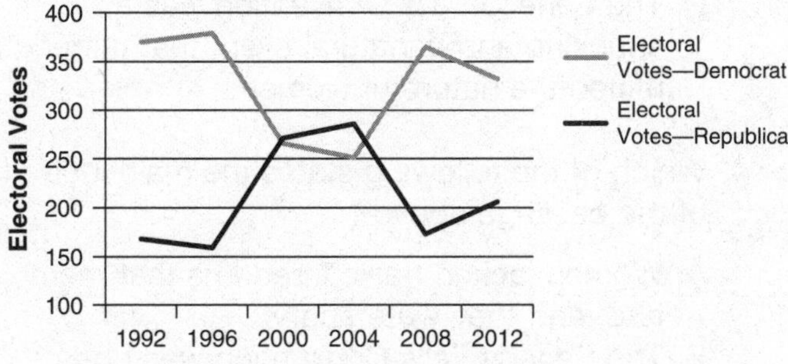

2. The information in the graph supports the conclusion that in the presidential elections from 1992 to 2012,

   A. Democrats and Republicans won the presidency an equal number of times.
   B. the average margin of victory was higher in years when a Democrat won than in years when a Republican won.
   C. the average margin of victory was higher in years when a Republican won than in years when a Democrat won.
   D. more electoral votes were cast in the 2008 presidential election than were cast in the 1996 presidential election.

Questions 3 and 4 are based on the following chart.

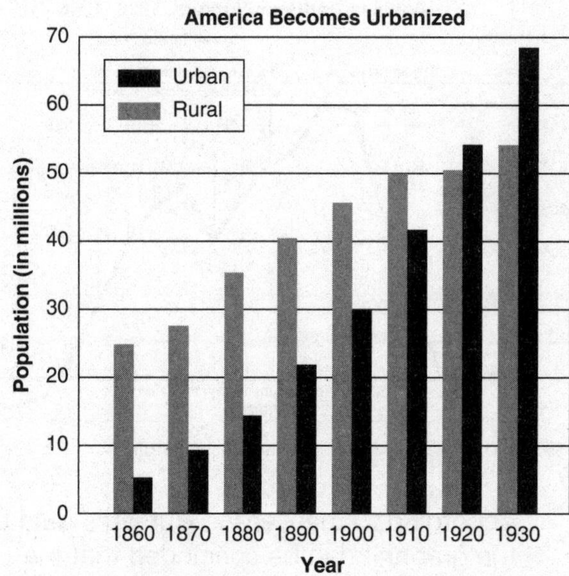

Source: U.S. Census (adapted)

3. According to the bar graph, in what year were there approximately as many Americans living in rural locations as there were in urban settings?

   A. 1860
   B. 1910
   C. 1920
   D. 1930

4. During the decades represented in the graph, the urban population of the United States grew at increasing rates, while the rural population

   A. continued to grow at a steady rate.
   B. grew and then shrank.
   C. continued to grow, but at decreasing rates.
   D. grew at first and then stopped growing.

Social Studies Skills Practice Questions

Questions 1 and 2 are based on the following line graph and timeline.

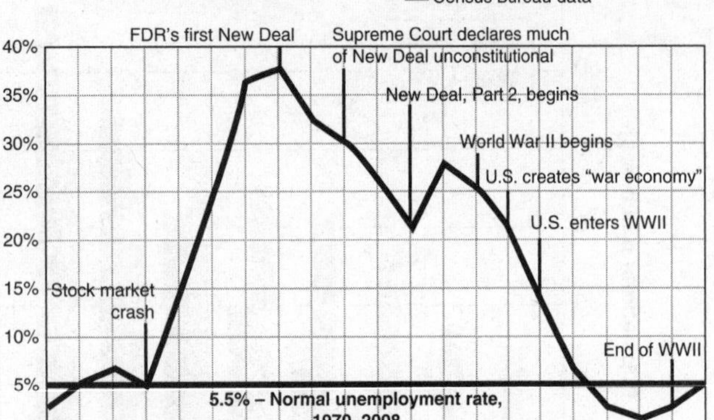

Source: U.S. Census Bureau, Bureau of Labor Statistics

1. According to the Census Bureau's data on the graph, it can be concluded that the onset of World War II contributed to which change in the U.S. unemployment rate?

   A. The unemployment rate stabilized at the beginning of World War II and remained stable until the war's end.
   B. The unemployment rate declined consistently until shortly before the war's end.
   C. The unemployment rate decreased during World War II but remained above the normal rate throughout the war.
   D. The unemployment rate increased gradually throughout the war.

2. According to the graph, the most significant and uninterrupted change in the U.S. unemployment rate between 1926 and 1946 occurred immediately after

   A. the stock market crash
   B. FDR's first New Deal
   C. the New Deal, Part 2, began
   D. the U.S. entered World War II

Questions 3 and 4 are based on the following passage.

The women's rights movement in the United States gained strength with the 1848 Seneca Falls Convention. The defining document of this gathering was the Declaration of Sentiments, which was patterned after the Declaration of Independence but focused on the fact that women lacked basic freedoms that men enjoyed. The revolutionary nature of the Seneca Falls Convention was apparent in the public's response to the event. One newspaper described Seneca Falls as "the most shocking and unnatural event ever recorded in the history of womanity."

3. Which of the following statements based on the passage is an opinion, not a fact?

   A. The Seneca Falls Convention helped the women's rights movement gain strength.
   B. The Declaration of Sentiments was modeled on the Declaration of Independence.
   C. The Declaration of Sentiments described how women's rights were limited.
   D. The Seneca Falls Convention was a shocking and unnatural event that undermined the nature of women.

4. Which of the following states the main idea of the passage above?

   A. Women lacked basic freedoms that men had, and they were angry.
   B. The Seneca Falls Convention was open to both men and women.
   C. The women's rights movement was stronger in Seneca Falls than in the rest of the United States.
   D. The Seneca Falls Convention was important in the fight for women's rights.

Questions 5 and 6 refer to the following map.

Reported Cases of Human Plague—United States, 1970–2010

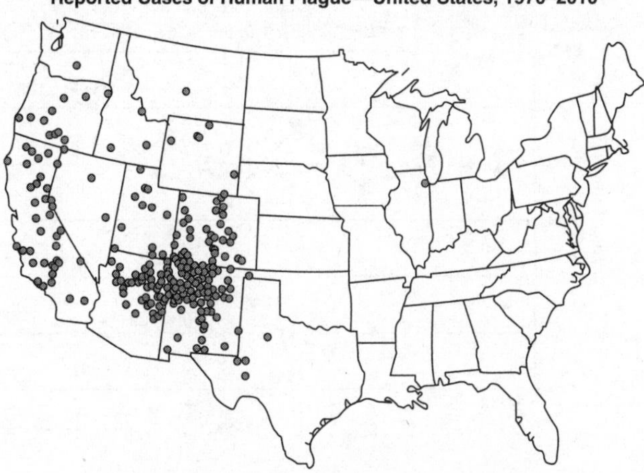

1 dot placed in county of exposure for each plague case

Source: Centers for Disease Control and Prevention

5. Which of the following conclusions is supported by this map?

   A. More than half of the reported cases of human plague in the United States between 1970 and 2010 were reported in four states.
   B. More than 99 percent of diphtheria-related deaths in the United States between 1970 and 2010 occurred in the western half of the United States.
   C. The majority of reported cases of plague in the American Southwest spread from one infected person.
   D. In the United States, human plague most frequently occurs within larger cities, where the risk of contagion is greatest.

6. The map above could be used to disprove which of the following claims?

   A. There were more cases of plague in the United States between 2000 and 2010 than there were between 1990 and 2000.
   B. Although many cases of plague have been reported in the United States since 1970, no deaths have been reported.
   C. Several cases of plague were reported on the East Coast of the United States between 1970 and 2010.
   D. Plague is less virulent in colder climates than it is in warmer climates.

Question 7 is based on the following passage and chart.

The invention of the cotton gin by Eli Whitney in 1784 revolutionized the cotton industry in the American South. The separation of the cotton seeds and fibers, once a painstaking task that slaves performed by hand, could now be done quickly by machine. This made cotton goods more affordable, thereby increasing international demand for these goods and, consequently, the profits of cotton farmers. Ironically, however, the cotton gin did not reduce the South's reliance on slavery. In fact, with the boom of the cotton industry, more slaves were used to pick the cotton at a faster rate to keep up with the increasing demand for cotton.

Growth of Slavery and Cotton in America

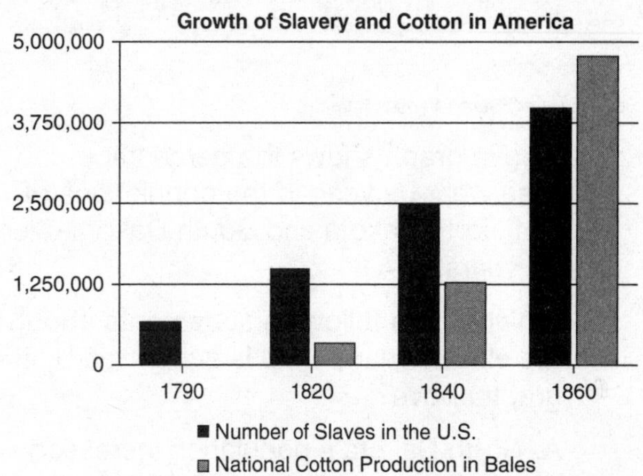

7. Which of the following conclusions is supported by the passage?

   A. Eli Whitney invented the cotton gin with the hope that it would reduce slavery.
   B. The cotton gin had little impact on the cotton industry in the South.
   C. After the invention of the cotton gin, many plantation owners found that they needed fewer slaves.
   D. The effects of the cotton gin on the cotton industry actually led to an increased demand for slaves in the South.

<u>Question 8</u> is based on the following graph.

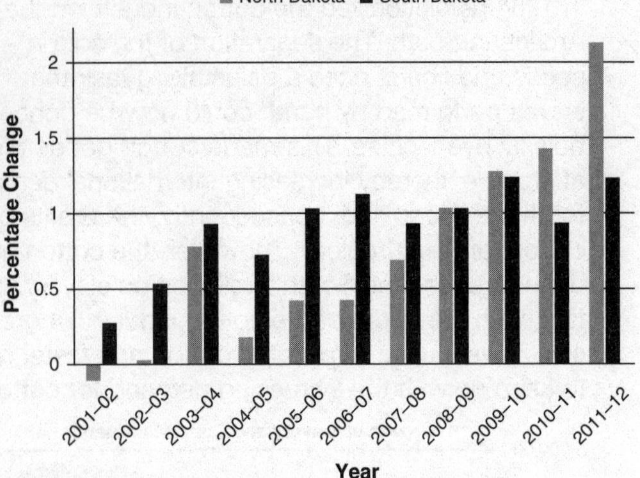

Source: United States Census Bureau

The above graph shows the percentage increase, year by year, in the populations of each of North Dakota and South Dakota over eleven years.

8. Which of the following statements about the eleven-year period is supported by the graph above?

   A. North Dakota's population increased every year, while South Dakota's stayed the same.
   B. The population of South Dakota was originally greater than that of North Dakota, but in 2012, the population of North Dakota was greater than that of South Dakota.
   C. In most years, the percentage population increase in South Dakota was greater than that in North Dakota.
   D. In most years, the percentage population increase in North Dakota was greater than that in South Dakota.

<u>Questions 9 and 10</u> are based on the following graphic.

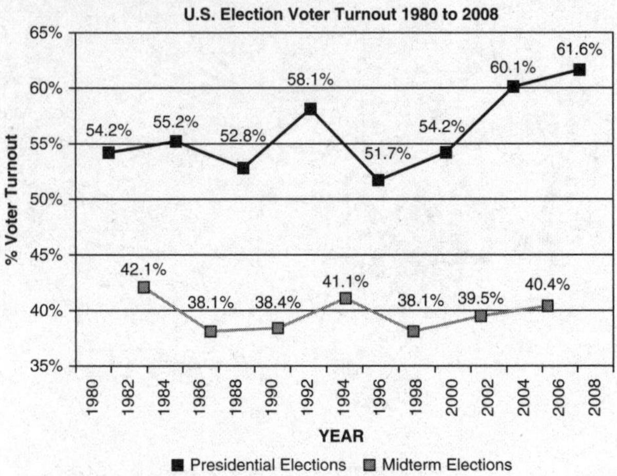

Source: weathertrends360.com

9. Which one of the following statements about elections in the years 1980–2008 is supported by the graph?

   A. Voter turnout for midterm elections displayed a greater range than voter turnout for presidential elections.
   B. The data for voter turnout for presidential elections displayed no mode.
   C. On average, half as many voters turned out for midterm elections as turned out for presidential elections.
   D. A smaller percentage of voters turned out for each midterm election than turned out for each presidential election.

10. The graph provides information that would allow you to answer which one of the following questions?

   A. Why did a greater percentage of voters turn out for the 1994 midterm election than for other midterm elections?
   B. The average voter turnout for midterm elections was approximately how much lower than that for presidential elections for the years 1980–2008?
   C. How does voter turnout for a presidential election affect voter turnout for the midterm election two years later?
   D. How did the presence of a high-profile third-party candidate in the 1992 presidential election affect voter turnout?

Questions 11 and 12 are based on the following excerpt from a speech.

Today, 8 million adult Americans, more than the entire population of Michigan, have not finished five years of school. Nearly 20 million have not finished eight years of school. Nearly 54 million—more than one-quarter of all America—have not . . . finished high school.

Each year more than 100,000 high school graduates, with proved ability, do not enter college because they cannot afford it. And if we cannot educate today's youth, what will we do in 1970 when elementary enrollment will be 5 million greater than 1960? . . .

In many places, classrooms are overcrowded and curricula are outdated. Most of our qualified teachers are underpaid, and many of our paid teachers are unqualified. So we must give every child a place to sit and a teacher to learn from. Poverty must not be a bar to learning, and learning must offer an escape from poverty.

—President Lyndon Johnson, May 22, 1964
Great Society Speech, University of Michigan

11. Which of the following statements from the speech is an opinion rather than a fact?
    A. Each year more than 100,000 high school graduates do not enter college.
    B. Eight million adult Americans have not finished five years of school.
    C. Most of our qualified teachers are underpaid.
    D. More than one-quarter of Americans have not finished high school.

12. Which of the following would be the best title for this excerpt?
    A. "A History of Educational Problems"
    B. "Why Michigan Is Falling Behind"
    C. "Why College Is Unaffordable"
    D. "Our Duty Is to Educate Our Children"

STUDY ADVICE

Many questions on the Social Studies Test will reward you for the skills you just learned. You may sometimes need to combine those skills with some basic knowledge of social studies content. The next five chapters will provide you with an overview of that content.

Questions 13 and 14 are based on the following information and graph.

From 1861 to 1865, the United States fought a devastating Civil War. The Union (the North) eventually defeated the Confederates (the South). The following chart gives facts about the population in both Union and Confederate states in 1860.

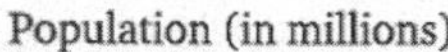

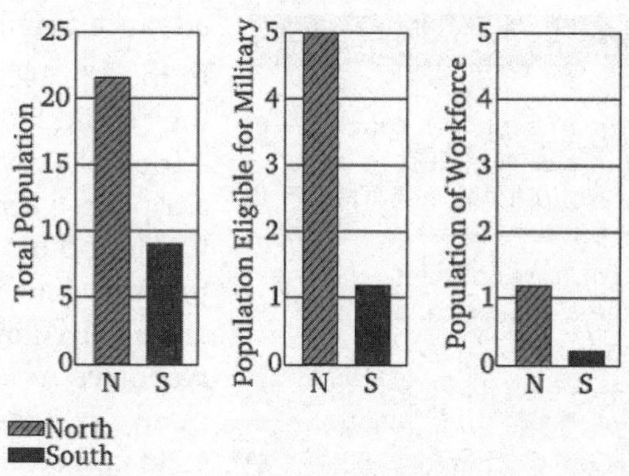

13. Which of the following statements is supported by the information and graph?
    A. The war was likely to end in a stalemate.
    B. Population differences would have no effect on the war's outcome.
    C. The Union states had significant population advantages in the war.
    D. The population in the Union states grew substantially during the war.

14. The graph provides information that allows you to answer which one of the following questions about the Civil War?
    A. What percentage of the total population in the United States fought in the military?
    B. What percentage of the total population of the United States was eligible for the military?
    C. Why was the population in the workforce much lower than the population eligible for the military?
    D. How did differences in skills held by people in the workforce affect the outcome of the Civil War?

LESSON 1

Exploration, Colonialism, and the American Revolution

The first Americans traveled from Asia across the Bering Strait into North America and, over many generations, down to South America. Called **Native Americans**, they established extensive tribal cultures and several advanced civilizations.

In the late 1400s, **explorers** from Europe searched for a sea route to Asia so they could trade for Asian gold and spices. They traveled around the tip of Africa. However, in 1492, Christopher Columbus convinced Spain to finance a trip west, across the Atlantic Ocean. When he reached land, he thought he had found India and called the inhabitants Indians. Later explorers realized that they had found a "New World," and many European nations set out to establish **colonies** there. The first explorers were searching for valuable resources and for the glory of conquest. This colonization led to tragedy for many Native Americans, who died from diseases or were killed, enslaved, or forced off their lands.

In the 1500s and 1600s, European nations, including Spain, France, England, and the Netherlands, established settlements in North America. Settlements were established to gain power and wealth or to provide colonists a place for permanent residence. The first permanent English settlement was established in Jamestown, Virginia, in 1607. In 1620, the **Pilgrims** sailed to the Americas aboard the *Mayflower* and established a second English colony in Massachusetts. Beginning about 1675, colonists began importing a large number of slaves who had been forcibly taken from Africa. Many were put to work on the plantation system in the Southern colonies.

The colonies grew rapidly in the early 1700s. When England defeated France in the French and Indian War (1754–1763), England acquired many of France's American colonies. After the war, England sought to regain more control over the Thirteen Colonies. It also sought to recover economically from the debts caused by the costly war. New British taxes and policies troubled the colonists; however, it was not until 1775 that a war for independence seemed inevitable. After a series of skirmishes, the **Continental Congress** assigned George Washington to lead the Continental Army and ordered publication of the **Declaration of Independence** on July 4, 1776.

Despite the superiority of the well-trained British forces, the Americans had the advantage of defending their own land and eventually forged a fighting force with strong military leaders. The **American Revolution** lasted until the surrender of the British at Yorktown in 1781. In 1783, the final treaty to end the war resulted in the recognition of American independence. The new nation initially formed a weak national government through the **Articles of Confederation**. This first effort stressed a loose confederation of the states with strong local control. Over time, many colonial leaders recognized the need for a centralized government. The principles of this government were established in the **U.S. Constitution**, which was ratified in 1788. To counter fears of an overly powerful government, the first ten amendments to the Constitution, the **Bill of Rights**, promised many individual freedoms, such as freedom of speech and assembly.

KEY IDEAS

- European explorers sought wealth and conquest in the New World from the 1400s to the 1600s.
- The Thirteen Colonies declared independence from England in 1776.
- America won its independence in 1783 and ratified the U.S. Constitution in 1788.

HiSET EXAM TIP

*Reviewing key vocabulary can help you prepare for the HiSET exam. As you review, look up any words that you do not understand. Pay special attention to the words in **bold type**.*

PRACTICE 1

<u>Questions 1 and 2</u> refer to the following map.

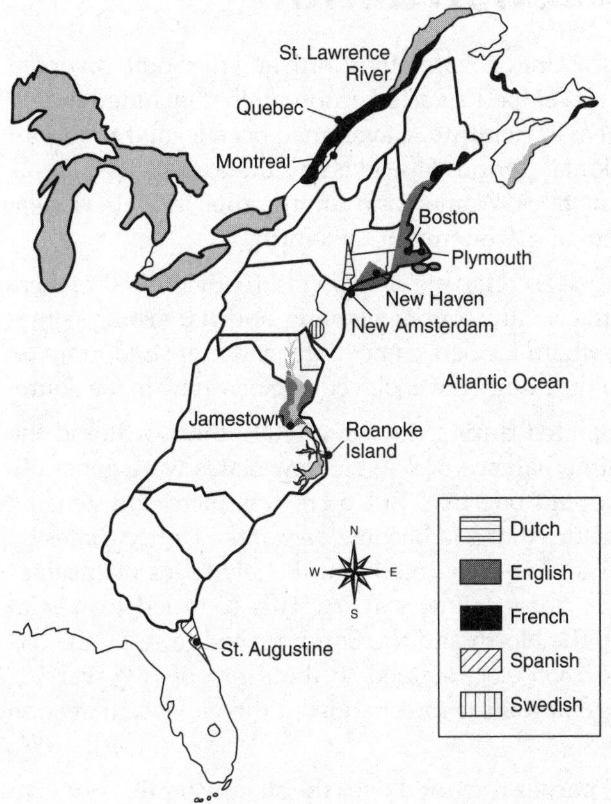

1. Choose the correct phrase that would fill in the blank.
Based on the map, __________________ had the southernmost colony in 1650.

A. the Dutch
B. the English
C. the Spanish
D. the Swedish

2. Which of the following conclusions is supported by the map?

A. By 1650, Spain had conquered most of North America.
B. The English established several colonies in the New World.
C. The Dutch established their colonies in the western part of North America.
D. French colonies extended along the East Coast between Boston and Jamestown.

3. Some of the early colonists did not come to the New World to gain power and wealth. These groups came seeking freedom from persecution.

Which immigrant group is most similar to those early colonists?

A. African slaves who were involuntarily brought to work on plantations
B. Mexican workers who came to the U.S. to earn better wages than they could at home
C. British businessmen who visited the U.S. to invest in media companies
D. Haitian refugees who fled to the U.S. to escape a dictatorship

4. Which of the following was a cause of the American Revolution?

A. France's defeat in the French and Indian War
B. increased British taxes and restrictions on the colonies
C. Britain's acquisition of France's colonies in North America
D. the publication of the Declaration of Independence

5. The first amendment to the U.S. Constitution states: "Congress shall make no law abridging the right of the people peaceably to assemble, and to petition the government for a redress of grievances."

Based on the passage on page 542, what is the most likely reason the framers of the Constitution included these guarantees?

A. They were planning to organize assemblies.
B. They were concerned about the government becoming tyrannical.
C. They were hoping to petition the government.
D. They were attempting to prevent a redress of grievances.

LESSON 2

Westward Expansion, the Civil War, and Reconstruction

KEY IDEAS

- The economy of the South was based on slavery. The Northern economy was based on paid labor.
- Conflict over whether slavery should be allowed in the nation's new western territories led to the Civil War.
- The North won the war and ended slavery. During Reconstruction, the South was rebuilt.

HiSET EXAM TIP

As you study for the Social Studies Test, focus on analyzing events to understand causes and effects, rather than memorizing names and dates.

Early on in the history of the United States, the North and the South diverged economically. The North developed a varied economy that included industry and commerce as well as agriculture. Slavery had been legal throughout the North during the colonial period. However, by the early 1800s, it was **abolished** in all Northern states. Women and **immigrants**, as well as men, provided labor for the growing economy in the North.

The Southern economy was based largely on agriculture. By the 1800s, there was one major crop in the South: cotton. Planting and harvesting cotton required a lot of labor. Southern farmers came to depend more and more on slaves to do the work, and the number of enslaved persons grew in the South.

As the United States expanded during the early 1800s, the North and the South worked to maintain a balance of power. New states were generally added in pairs, one slave and one free. But there was increasing tension over the vast western territory that had become part of the United States by the mid-1800s. In the 1850s, Congress voted that the territories themselves should decide whether or not to allow slavery. This soon led to war in Kansas. People from both the North and the South rushed to settle the territory. Voter fraud in the 1855 elections led to the setup of two warring governments. The violence in Kansas foreshadowed the violence that soon tore up the nation.

In the late 1850s, political parties fractured over the slavery issue. Four candidates ran for president in 1860. Abraham Lincoln, who promised to halt the spread of slavery (although not abolish it where it already existed) won. Opposed to Lincoln's policies, most slave states **seceded** from the United States. They set up their own government, called the **Confederacy**. By April 1861, the United States (called the **Union**) and the Confederacy were at war.

At first it seemed as if the Confederacy might win. They had well-trained military leaders and soldiers who were willing to fight hard to hold onto their way of life, so the Confederacy won many early battles. However, by the summer of 1863, the Confederacy began to wear down. Ammunition, uniforms, and shoes were in short supply for Confederate soldiers, because the South lacked industry. There were food shortages for soldiers and civilians alike. The war was fought mostly in the South, and the destruction was terrible. After four long years, in 1865, Confederate general Robert E. Lee surrendered to Union general Ulysses S. Grant. The Civil War ended.

For the next 12 years, federal troops oversaw the rebuilding of the South. This period was called **Reconstruction**. Schools were established for former slaves, who were all freed when the war ended. However, the **sharecropping** system, which kept black farmers enslaved economically, soon came into being. Whites who came back to power as Reconstruction ended in the South in the 1870s prevented African Americans from exercising their right to vote. The Civil War ended slavery, but it did not end racism.

1. Which of the following disagreements was a main cause of the Civil War?

   A. whether cotton should be the main crop in the South
   B. whether slavery should continue to exist
   C. whether the United States should expand westward
   D. whether slavery should be permitted in territories in the West

2. In 1820, Missouri proposed to enter the Union as a slave state. Based on the passage, what do you think was the response of Northerners in Congress?

   A. They supported having another slave state join the Union.
   B. They lobbied against having Missouri join the Union at all.
   C. To balance the admission of Missouri, they agreed to a compromise in which Maine was admitted as a free state.
   D. They started a war to prevent Missouri from attaining statehood.

3. In the mid-1950s, the country of Vietnam was divided. There was a communist government in the North and a noncommunist government in the South. The two fought for control of Vietnam. In 1975, the communists won. Vietnam was united under this form of government.

   Because both wars __________, the Vietnam War and the U.S. Civil War can be said to share some similarities.

   A. involved racial conflict
   B. saw the addition of new territory upset the balance of power
   C. concluded with the formation of new nations
   D. concluded with the reunification of the nation

STUDY ADVICE

If you find that Social Studies is your favorite subject so far, wonderful! You won't have trouble staying focused and motivated. However, if you find this material boring, do short study sessions with breaks in between. Four half-hour sessions can be more efficient than one two-hour session if you are having trouble concentrating on this material.

Questions 4 and 5 refer to the following photographs of people who served in South Carolina's state government in 1868.

Photography by Katherine Wetzel. Reprinted with the permission of The Museum of the Confederacy, Richmond, Virginia.

4. Which of the following is a fact confirmed by information in the photographs?

   A. Southern Democrats were treated very well during Reconstruction.
   B. It was unfair that former Confederate soldiers could vote during Reconstruction.
   C. In 1868, many African Americans served in the government of South Carolina.
   D. The most qualified leaders in South Carolina government in 1868 were African Americans.

5. Which of the following conclusions is supported by the photographs and the passage?

   A. Over the course of Reconstruction, African Americans in the South gained and then lost political power.
   B. Over the course of Reconstruction, African Americans in the South lost and then gained political power.
   C. Over the course of Reconstruction, whites in the South gained and then lost political power.
   D. In the early years of Reconstruction, African Americans served in government in each Southern state.

LESSON 3

Industrialization, Immigration, and the Progressive Era

KEY IDEAS

- The U.S. underwent rapid industrialization starting in the mid-1800s.
- Immigrants came from many places to work in the expanding American industries.
- Rapid industrialization brought problems, which labor unions and reformers tried to solve, especially during the Progressive Era.

HiSET EXAM TIP

The Social Studies Test examines your ability to interpret graphs, charts, maps, and other visual sources of information.

In the mid-1800s, American industries, which had been growing steadily since the late 1700s, began a period of extremely fast growth. This rapid **industrialization** occurred for several interconnected reasons. With the addition of the vast western territories, the United States gained plentiful **natural resources**. Among these resources were materials, such as metals, needed to manufacture new products and machines, and fuels, such as coal, needed to run these machines. Another reason for rapid industrialization was the invention of many new machines and new industrial processes. With these new inventions and processes, manufactured goods could be produced more easily, more efficiently, and less expensively. A third reason for the rapid industrialization was the nation's booming population. The U.S. population more than doubled in the last 40 years of the 1800s. There were more people to buy more goods, spurring commerce and further industrial growth.

Rapid industrialization meant that many new factories were built in the mid- and late-1800s. Most were built in or near the nation's large cities, including New York, Boston, Chicago, Philadelphia, and Pittsburgh. These urban centers had large groups of people who could work in the factories and large groups of people who would buy the goods the factories produced.

U.S. factory jobs drew many **immigrants** to American cities. Although the United States has always been a "nation of immigrants," the late 1800s saw a sharp rise in the number of people moving here from foreign countries. The majority came from Europe, including Germany, Italy, Russia, and Eastern European countries. Many also came from Mexico and Central America. Asian immigration was declining because the government had passed laws barring Chinese from moving to the United States. However, thousands of Japanese came to this country, taking jobs in farm fields and mines.

America's factory workers, whether native- or foreign-born, worked very hard at grueling, dangerous work. Many received low pay for long hours on the job. Over time, workers began to unionize. By joining a **union**, workers pledged to work together for better and safer working conditions and higher wages. They called **strikes** when their employers cut their pay or refused to grant raises. Many of the laws we have today, including the eight-hour workday and the five-day workweek, came about through the bitter struggles for better working conditions that unions waged in the late 1800s and the early 1900s.

Unions weren't the only groups working to solve problems brought on by America's rapid industrialization. Some reformers worked to clean up slums, improve healthcare, and stop child labor. Others worked to preserve the nation's natural beauty by creating national parks. Still others worked to give more people a voice in government. For example, many women lobbied to gain the right to vote. In the early 1900s, groups were working toward so many sweeping social and political improvements that the time is called the **Progressive Era**.

PRACTICE 3

1. Which of the following likely occurs during a period of rapid industrialization?

   A. the annexation of new territory
   B. an increase in manufacturing
   C. an increase in population
   D. an increase in immigration

2. Which event most likely contributed to the growth of American industries in the mid-1800s?

   A. the passage of the Chinese Exclusion Act, which banned Chinese immigration
   B. the passage of the Sherman Antitrust Act, which helped prevent businesses from forming monopolies
   C. the development of the Bessemer process, which made it easier to produce steel
   D. the development of settlement houses to aid impoverished immigrants and city dwellers

3. Based on the passage, which of the following would early union workers have valued the most?

   A. productivity in the workplace
   B. contact with people of all different backgrounds
   C. cooperation with others to improve worker safety
   D. the freedom to work whenever they pleased

4. What was a strong ideal held by people working toward reforms during the Progressive Era?

   A. efficiency
   B. wealth
   C. artistic beauty
   D. fairness

Questions 5 and 6 refer to the following graphs.

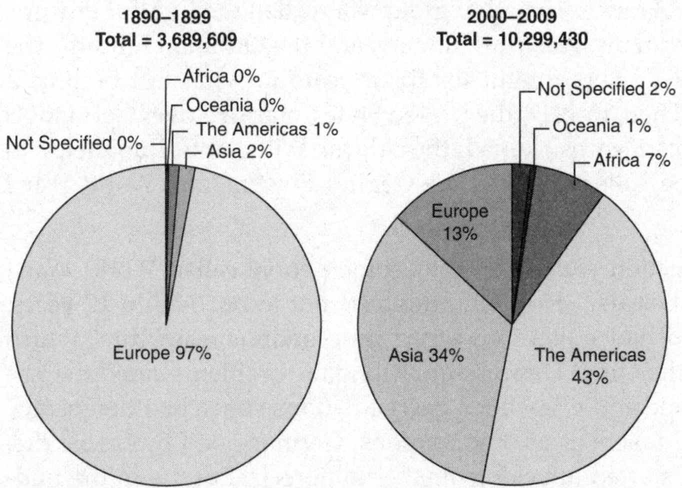

5. Which of the following best completes this statement? In the 1890s, the vast majority of persons gaining permanent legal residency came from Europe, whereas in the early 2000s, a majority of such persons came from _________.

   A. Europe and Asia
   B. Asia and the Americas
   C. Africa, Oceania, and Europe
   D. Africa and the Americas

6. A student looked at these graphs and said, "So I see that, in the years 1890–1899, roughly seven times as many people came to the United States from Europe than did in the years 2000–2009. After all, 97 is roughly seven times 13."

   Which of the following best describes the flaw in the student's reasoning?

   A. The student failed to differentiate between northern Europe and southern Europe.
   B. The student failed to consider the reasons why people immigrate to the United States.
   C. The student failed to consider the different totals represented by each pie chart.
   D. The student failed to explain what led to a decrease in immigration from Europe.

LESSON 4

The United States as an Emerging World Power

The expansion of U.S. industries in the mid-1800s had an effect not only on the nation's economy but also on its politics. Business and government leaders wanted access to more natural resources, which industries needed to continue growing. They also wanted to be able to sell more goods overseas. Regions in Africa, Asia, and Latin America had rich natural resources. People in these regions might buy what Americans wanted to sell. To promote industrial growth and increase its power, the United States became imperialistic. **Imperialism** is the policy by which a stronger nation extends economic, military, and/or political control over a weaker nation or region.

KEY IDEAS

- Industrialization spurred U.S. interest in gaining access to the raw materials and markets of other countries.
- The U.S. pursued imperialist policies in the late 1800s.
- The U.S. entered both WWI and WWII on the side of the Allies and contributed to their winning both wars.

European nations had been engaging in imperialism for many centuries. In the late 1800s, the United States joined in. In 1898, the United States fought the Spanish-American War. Ostensibly, the United States declared war on Spain because of Spain's mistreatment of Cuba, which was a Spanish colony. Yet, after winning the war, the United States took over Spain's colonies of Cuba, Puerto Rico, the Philippines, and Guam. It granted independence to none of them.

The next war the United States was involved in was World War I, which began in Europe in 1913. It pitted two groups of nations against each other. One group was called the **Allies;** the leading Allied nations included Great Britain, Russia, and France. The other group was called the **Central Powers,** which included Germany, Austria-Hungary, and the Ottoman Empire. The Allies and Central Powers fought for three years in what fast became a deadly stalemate. Then, in 1917, the United States, alarmed over Germany's sinking of American ships, joined the Allies. With American help, in November 1918 the Allies defeated the Central Powers, and World War I ended.

HiSET EXAM TIP

When weighing answer choices, immediately eliminate ones that are directly contradicted by information in the passage or graphic.

Because the destruction was so terrible, some people called World War I "the war to end all wars." However, this was not to be. Within 12 years, by 1929, the world had fallen into a serious economic downturn, which Americans called the **Great Depression**. Economic problems aided the rise of **fascism** in Europe and elsewhere. Fascist nations squelched democracy and advocated the takeover of other nations. Germany, led by fascist dictator Adolf Hitler, started attacking smaller nations in Europe in the mid-1930s. Italy fought to take over Ethiopia, in Africa. Japan attacked China. Hitler built an alliance with Italy and Japan, which came to be called the **Axis**. By 1939, war again broke out between the Axis and the Allies.

The United States did not enter World War II until 1941, when the Japanese bombed the U.S. naval base at Pearl Harbor in Hawaii. This time, Americans fought not only in Europe but also in Africa and Asia. With its horrific battles, the fire-bombing of cities, the **Holocaust**, and the dropping of two atomic bombs on Japan, World War II led to massive destruction. The United States, which played a major part in the Allied victory in World War II in 1945, also played a major part in helping to rebuild war-scourged nations after the war was over.

PRACTICE 4

Question 1 refers to the following chart.

Factors Related to the Growth of Imperialism

Economic	Desire for greater access to natural resources or new markets
Military	Desire for control of ports that could serve as refueling stations for long sea voyages or air flights
Political	Desire to spread the institutions of democracy or other political systems
Religious	Desire to spread Christianity or other faith
Cultural/Racial	Lack of respect for different cultures or races

1. Cuba lies about 90 miles off the coast of Florida. After the United States freed Cuba from Spanish rule in 1898, the U.S. Navy built an important base there.

   Which of the following factors from the chart best explains the situation in Cuba after 1898?

   A. economic
   B. religious
   C. political
   D. military

---

2. What assumption do you need to make to fully understand the last sentence in paragraph 4 on page 548?

   A. In World War I, the Allies fought the Central Powers.
   B. In World War II, the Allies included England, France, and Russia.
   C. In World War II, the Allies included the Germans, Austrians, and Ottoman Turks.
   D. In World War II, the Axis included Germany, Italy, and Japan.

3. Franklin D. Roosevelt became president during the height of the Great Depression, in 1933. He soon instituted a set of federal programs called the New Deal to try to lower unemployment.

   Which conclusion about the effectiveness of New Deal programs does the text on page 548 and graph below support?

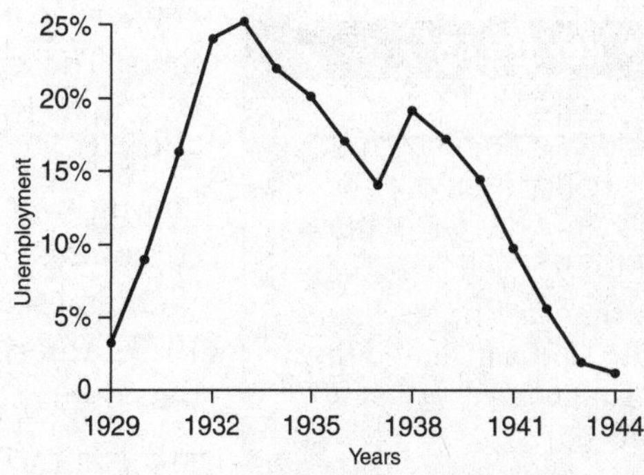

Source: *Historical Statistics of the United States*

   A. Within a year, the New Deal had raised unemployment to its pre-Depression level.
   B. Within a year, the New Deal had lowered unemployment to its pre-Depression level.
   C. Unemployment fell after the start of the New Deal and continued to fall sharply as the U.S. entered World War II.
   D. The New Deal lowered unemployment, but the Allied victory in World War II lowered it further.

4. Which statement best summarizes the main idea of paragraph 5 on page 548?

   A. America entered World War II in 1941.
   B. Americans fought in Europe, Africa, and Asia.
   C. World War II involved more nations than any other war ever fought.
   D. America took a strong leadership role during and after World War II.

STUDY ADVICE

If you feel like you have a good handle on U.S. History topics from the past 100 years, great! The Social Studies Test emphasizes these. If not, don't worry. Spend a little more of your time studying these lessons.

LESSON 5

The Cold War and the Civil Rights Era

KEY IDEAS

- The Cold War dominated U.S. foreign policy from the end of WWII until the fall of the Soviet Union.
- Social changes in the U.S. in the mid-1900s included the expansion of civil rights for minorities.
- Technological advances have introduced benefits but also caused problems.

HiSET EXAM TIP

The Social Studies Test will include some questions that focus on the role of the United States in the world.

After World War II ended, the capitalist and communist nations soon began engaging in a power struggle called the **Cold War**. Leading the capitalist nations was the United States; leading the communist nations was the Soviet Union. The Cold War never led to direct fighting between these two superpowers, although there was a constant threat of nuclear war. Clashes between communism and capitalism did lead to numerous smaller conflicts. These included the Korean War of the early 1950s and the Vietnam War, which lasted from 1954 to 1975. The United States sent soldiers to both. The Vietnam War was long and difficult and caused deep divisions among Americans. The United States sent massive military aid to the noncommunist South Vietnamese, but they kept losing to the communist North Vietnamese. Although a few Americans wanted to continue fighting, in 1973, America pulled out of Vietnam. In 1975, the communists took over the country.

The Cold War ended in 1991 with the breakup of the Soviet Union and the end of communism there. In the late 1980s, Soviet leader Mikhail Gorbachev had tried to reform the communist government. But the loosening of Soviet control led to the collapse of many communist governments of Eastern Europe. The Berlin Wall, which had separated East and West Germany, was torn down. With communism no longer so threatening, world politics became less tense but also more unpredictable.

During the second half of the 20th century, the United States continued to face many challenges. In the 1950s, African American leaders launched the **civil rights movement** to try to end segregation and discrimination in the United States. Their victories included the integration of public schools and other public facilities, the passage of laws protecting the voting rights of minorities, and the striking down of laws that permitted overt discrimination based on race or cultural background. However, minority groups and people of all backgrounds concerned about fair application of the law have continued to be vigilant in insisting that civil rights laws be upheld.

Another area of challenge in recent decades has been **technology**. Technology has led to many advances in science, medicine, and our personal lives. Computers, for instance, make many jobs easier and more productive. They allow almost instantaneous communication with coworkers, family, and friends. Furthermore, they allow people from around the world to share information quickly and easily, giving us the sense that we live in a "global village." However, our reliance on the use of technology has led us to pollute the air with exhaust from a growing number of cars. It has led us to pollute the water with acid rain, resulting from burning coal to generate increased electricity. It has led us to pollute our land with mountains of trash and tons of hazardous wastes.

PRACTICE 5

1. The conflict during the second half of the 20th century between the United States and the Soviet Union was called the Cold War because it involved _________.

   A. communists and capitalists
   B. two countries at the far north of Earth
   C. the threat of nuclear war
   D. no direct combat

2. Which of the following best summarizes the message of the cartoon below?

   A. Nuclear bombs are extremely destructive.
   B. Expanding U.S. nuclear capabilities is a good idea.
   C. The buildup of nuclear arms increases fear and instability, not peace.
   D. The threat of nuclear war is lessened if both superpowers have equally powerful weapons.

3. Which of the following statements about the Vietnam War is a false generalization?

   A. Some Americans served in both Korea and Vietnam.
   B. The United States sent massive military aid to South Vietnam.
   C. Americans were in complete agreement about pulling out of Vietnam.
   D. The Vietnam War lasted much longer than the Korean War.

4. Which of the following goals would a civil rights activist be most likely to pursue?

   A. getting Congress to enact laws to restrict the sale of firearms
   B. petitions for a city ordinance requiring those selling real estate to select a buyer without regard to race
   C. getting local companies to stop polluting the environment
   D. working with local clergy to publicize a worship service open to people of all religions

5. Which of the following is a conclusion about technology rather than a supporting detail?

   A. Reliance on technology has increased pollution.
   B. Cars cause air pollution.
   C. Coal-generating power plants cause acid-rain pollution.
   D. The ease of manufacturing disposable items has led to land pollution at landfill sites.

U.S. History Practice Questions

Questions 1 and 2 refer to the timeline below.

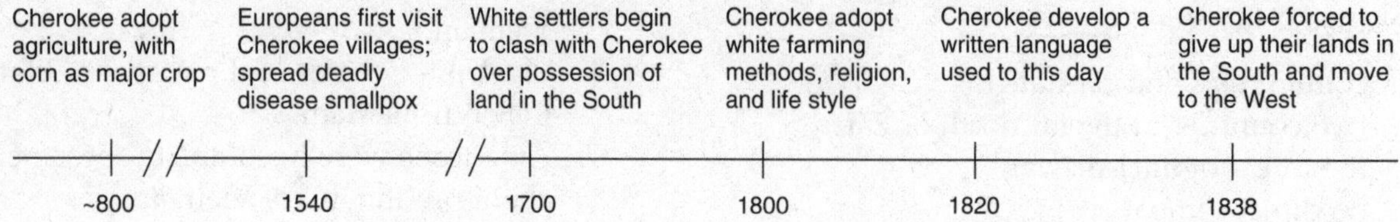
Important Events in Early Cherokee History
Cherokee adopt agriculture, with corn as major crop
Europeans first visit Cherokee villages; spread deadly disease smallpox
White settlers begin to clash with Cherokee over possession of land in the South
Cherokee adopt white farming methods, religion, and life style
Cherokee develop a written language used to this day
Cherokee forced to give up their lands in the South and move to the West
~800
1540
1700
1800
1820
1838

1. Which of the following is a conclusion based on multiple details in the timeline?
   A. The Cherokee had begun farming around 800, before Europeans came to America.
   B. Although the Cherokee adopted many aspects of white culture, they were driven off their ancestral lands.
   C. The Cherokee traditionally considered land ownership to be a tribal matter rather than a right of individuals acting on their own.
   D. The Bible was one of the first books the Cherokee translated into their written language.

2. When President Andrew Jackson mandated that the Cherokee move west in 1830, he claimed that the U.S. government would be better able to protect the Cherokee from whites who might try to get their new land in the West. The Cherokee considered this to be illogical.

   Which of the following summarizes the logical fallacy?
   A. If the government can't protect us from white settlers here, now, how could it protect us from whites moving west in the future?
   B. If you ask us to move to the West now, how do we know you won't ask us to move back to the South in the future?
   C. If the land we have in the South is good, why wouldn't the land in the West be better?
   D. If the state governments are protecting us now, why can't the U.S. government help later?

---

3. In the late 1700s, Abigail Adams—wife of John Adams, who was our nation's second president—wrote the following in a letter to her sister:

   I will never consent to have our sex considered in an inferior point of light. Let each planet shine in their own orbit . . . if man is Lord, woman is Lordess—that is what I contend for.

   Based on this letter, which of the following principles was Abigail Adams advocating?
   A. the separation of church and state
   B. the abolition of slavery
   C. the promotion of scientific learning
   D. equal rights and opportunities for women

Questions 4 and 5 refer to the following map.

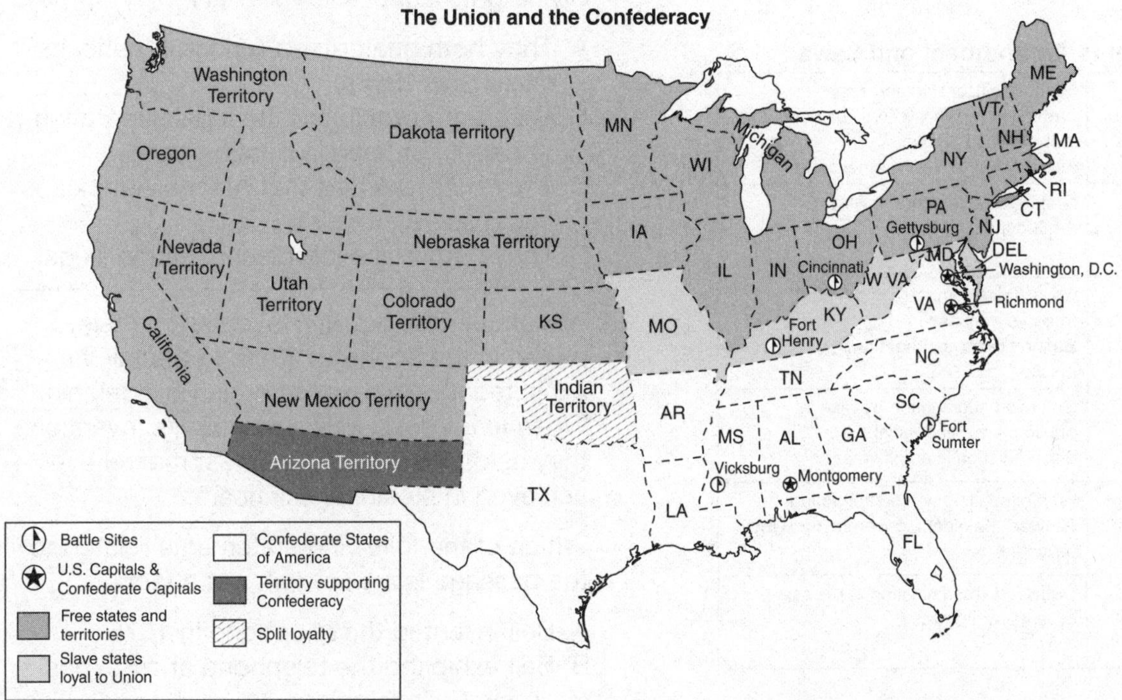

4. Which state permitted slavery but did not join the Confederacy?

   A. West Virginia
   B. Arkansas
   C. Kansas
   D. Tennessee

5. The loyalty of Maryland was of crucial importance to the Union. Based on the map, which statement best explains why this was so?

   A. The nation's capital was located nearby.
   B. The Confederate capital was located there.
   C. It was close to Fort Sumter, where the Civil War began.
   D. Important rail lines ran through Baltimore, Maryland.

---

6. In the Emancipation Proclamation, issued in 1863, President Lincoln freed all people enslaved in the states that had seceded from the Union. This proclamation was explicitly not to be put into effect in slave states that had remained in the Union. The proclamation went on to say:

   "I hereby enjoin upon the people so declared to be free to abstain from all violence . . . and make known that such persons of suitable condition will be received into the armed services of the United States to garrison forts, positions, stations, and other places, and to man vessels of all sorts."

   Based on the information given about the Emancipation Proclamation and the text of the order itself, which of the following was a major reason Lincoln issued the proclamation?

   A. to encourage states to secede from the Union
   B. to punish slaveholders throughout the South
   C. to weaken the North by enlisting former slaves in the Confederate army
   D. to weaken the South by enlisting former slaves in the Union army

Questions 7 through 9 refer to the following chart.

Civil Rights Amendment and Laws

14th Amendment (1868)	Granted citizenship and equal protection of the law to all persons born in the United States (not applied to Native Americans)
15th Amendment (1870)	Granted voting rights to African Americans
Civil Rights Act of 1875	Gave African Americans the right to serve on juries Banned racial segregation in public places
Civil Rights Act of 1964	Outlawed segregation by race in public places and racial discrimination in employment
Voting Rights Act of 1965	Prohibited literacy tests for voting Allowed the federal government to register voters
Civil Rights Act of 1968	Outlawed discrimination in the sale or rental of homes

7. An Asian American registers to vote and is given a reading test. Which of the following is the civil rights amendment or law relevant to this situation?

   A. Civil Rights Act of 1875
   B. Civil Rights Act of 1964
   C. Voting Rights Act of 1965
   D. Civil Rights Act of 1968

8. Which statement best summarizes what this chart shows about voting rights?

   A. African Americans were granted the vote five years after the Civil War ended.
   B. African Americans were granted the vote 100 years after the Civil War ended.
   C. African Americans were granted the vote soon after the Civil War, but laws enforcing these rights had to be passed a century later.
   D. African Americans were granted the vote in 1870, but Native Americans were never granted these same rights.

9. How are the Civil Rights Act of 1875 and the Civil Rights Act of 1964 similar?

   A. They both guaranteed African Americans citizenship rights.
   B. They both prohibited the legal separation of people by race in public places.
   C. They both ensured that African Americans could serve on juries.
   D. They both make job discrimination illegal.

10. Alexander Graham Bell invented the telephone in the spring of 1876. In the fall, he exhibited it at an exposition in Philadelphia. When leading scientists saw Bell's invention, they said, "Here is the greatest marvel ever achieved in electrical science."

    Which of the following statements related to the passage is an opinion, not a fact?

    A. Bell invented the telephone in 1876.
    B. Bell exhibited the telephone at an exposition in Philadelphia.
    C. Scientists admired Bell's invention.
    D. The telephone was the greatest electrical invention ever.

Questions 11 through 13 are based on the paragraph and the political cartoon below.

In 1974, President Richard Nixon resigned from office. He had been involved in a scandal known as Watergate. The Watergate scandal implicated Nixon in covering up crimes committed by members of his reelection committee. These crimes ranged from illegally harassing political opponents to burglary and bribery. With Congress investigating him, he was sure to be impeached. This cartoon was published before Nixon resigned to avoid impeachment.

Hey guys, do you really think we need that clause about impeachment in there?

Cartoon by Robert Lawlor. Reprinted with permission of the *Philadelphia Daily News.*

11. In this cartoon, whom is Nixon addressing?

    A. the writers of the Declaration of Independence
    B. the framers of the U.S. Constitution
    C. the past presidents of the United States
    D. the present session of Congress

12. Which value was Congress furthering by investigating Nixon and Watergate?

    A. the pursuit of justice
    B. the duty of obedience
    C. loyalty to a friend
    D. love of mercy

STUDY ADVICE

How did this practice set go? If you missed a few questions, go back and review those lessons. Remember as you study to pay particular attention to words in bold and the Key Ideas in each lesson.

13. About Watergate, one historian has written, "In a society in which distrust of leaders and institutions of authority was already widespread, the fall of Richard Nixon seemed to confirm the most cynical assumptions about the character of American public life."

    Which of the following was most likely a reason for Americans' growing distrust of their government in the years just prior to Watergate?

    A. mismanagement of the New Deal
    B. the beginning of rock music
    C. the escalation and failure of the Vietnam War
    D. the scandals of previous presidents, including John Kennedy and Bill Clinton

Questions 14 and 15 refer to the graph below.

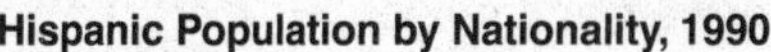

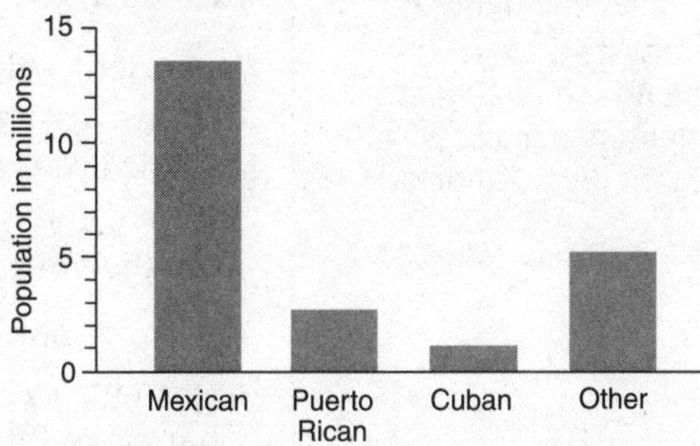

Source: U.S. Census Bureau

14. In 1990, approximately how many people of Cuban nationality lived in the United States?

    A. 100
    B. 100,000
    C. 1,000,000
    D. 5,000,000

15. A Hispanic family moved into an apartment next door to yours in 1990. Based solely on the bar graph, which place was the family most likely to be from?

    A. Cuba
    B. Mexico
    C. Puerto Rico
    D. Spain

LESSON 1

Historic Basis for U.S. System

The system of government in the United States is known as **representative democracy**. In this form of government, the citizens vote to elect representatives who make and execute laws. To understand this form of democracy, it is helpful to first distinguish democracy from other types of government. Then, you can trace the historical development of democracy and see how representative democracy differs from other types of democracy employed over time and around the globe.

The origins of **democracy** are ancient. The term *democracy,* which means "rule of the people" in Greek, arose in approximately 500 B.C.E in the Greek city-state of Athens. This distinguishes democracy from **monarchy**, the "rule of one person" (such as a king or queen); **aristocracy**, the "rule of an elite class" (lords or barons, for example); **theocracy**, the "rule of the church"; and **anarchy**, the "rule of the mob" (arguably not a form of government at all). Democracy is also distinct from forms of **authoritarian rule**, such as dictatorship, military rule, and fascism.

In ancient Athenian democracy, laws were voted on by a council of all citizens, a system known as **direct democracy**. In ancient Athens, however, a "citizen" was defined as a free male landowner over the age of 20. Women, foreigners, slaves, non-landowners, and minors were excluded from the vote.

For the eventual development of democracy in the U.S., one of the most important events was the signing of the **Magna Carta** (Latin for Great Charter) in England in 1215. England was a monarchy, but some protested the king's absolute power. The result was the signing of the Magna Carta, a document limiting the king's rule and subjecting his decisions to review. This same period also saw the development of the legal doctrine of **habeas corpus**, which made it illegal for the government to hold or imprison individuals without granting them trials.

Over time, the group allowed by the Magna Carta to review the king's decisions developed into a **parliament** of lawmakers appointed by title and/or elected by citizens. As the power of the parliament grew, England transformed into a **parliamentary democracy**. In this system, a government is formed by the party holding a majority of seats in the parliament. In most parliamentary democracies, the majority party appoints or authorizes the chief executive, such as the president.

Known as the Age of Enlightenment, the 17th and 18th centuries saw the spread of democracy to many other European countries. England, France, Holland, and other European powers also adopted **bills of rights** for individuals during this period. The philosophies dominant in this era emphasized reason and individual rights and encouraged government by the people. Enlightenment philosophers such as Adam Smith, John Locke, and Voltaire strongly influenced the founders of the United States.

KEY IDEAS

- The idea of democracy originated with the ancient Greeks, who spoke of the "rule of the people."
- The historic basis of the U.S. government came from the British system that limited the king's powers and protected individual rights.
- The U.S. system evolved from the British idea of a parliamentary democracy to a representative democracy.

HiSET EXAM TIP

*While you will be tested on the dates of major events, you should also be familiar with key terms, such as the ones in **bold type**.*

PRACTICE 1

1. Which of the following is a form of government in which laws are made and administered by lords who inherit their lands and titles?
   A. monarchy
   B. direct democracy
   C. representative democracy
   D. aristocracy

2. Which of following can be inferred about the Founding Fathers of the United States?
   A. They sought to establish the power of the king of England in the United States.
   B. They were concerned about protecting the rights of individuals.
   C. They argued that the United States should adopt a system of direct democracy.
   D. They thought representatives from the United States should sit in Parliament.

3. In the United States, laws are enacted by Congress, a group of representatives elected by the people. Which of the following was most likely the chief historical model for the U.S. Congress?
   A. Athenian council of citizens
   B. Magna Carta
   C. Parliament of England
   D. Declaration of the Rights of Man and the Citizen adopted in France in 1789

4. Some nations have been ruled by a form of government known as constitutional monarchy. While a king or queen is the single, sovereign ruler of the country, his or her power is limited by a constitution, a formal document outlining which of the monarch's decisions are subject to review or may be overruled by a court of law.

   Which of the following was most likely a constitutional monarchy?
   A. the ancient city-state of Athens
   B. any country ruled by fascism
   C. the United States at the time of its founding
   D. England during the Age of Enlightenment

5. If the United States were a parliamentary democracy, which of the following would be most likely to occur?
   A. The office of the president would decrease in power.
   B. The office of the president would increase in power.
   C. The president would be elected by a majority vote of all citizens.
   D. The president would be appointed by the majority party in the parliament.

Constitutional Government

KEY IDEAS

- The U.S. Constitution is the basis for our government structure and legal system.
- The Bill of Rights—the first ten constitutional amendments—define the rights of citizens.
- Amendments to the Constitution require wide support, but many important amendments have gained enough support to be ratified.

HiSET EXAM TIP

The Social Studies Test may include an excerpt from or a reference to one of the following U.S. historical documents:

- *Declaration of Independence*
- *U.S. Constitution, including the Bill of Rights and other amendments*
- *Landmark Supreme Court cases*

The Constitution of the United States is the foundation of our national government and legal system. The United States is a **republic**, a form of government in which citizens elect the people who will govern them. A republic is very different from a government system in which citizens do not choose their political leaders, such as a **monarchy** or **dictatorship**.

The people who wrote the Constitution set particular goals for the new nation, which they stated in the **preamble**, or introduction. They wanted to unite the states under one government, establish a nation where people could live peacefully and safely under the rule of law, and make prosperity and freedom possible for all citizens.

Following the preamble are the original seven **articles** of the U.S. Constitution. These articles provide for the three branches of government (see page 560), establish the rights of states, and set forth procedures for ratifying and amending the Constitution. Article 6 states that all government officials must uphold the Constitution as "the supreme law of the land" and that no other laws can contradict any part of the Constitution.

According to Article 5, a constitutional **amendment** can be proposed by Congress if it is supported by two-thirds majorities in both the House and Senate. The proposed amendment then must be ratified by three-fourths of the states. This process ensures that amendments have very broad national support.

The original Constitution did not specifically describe citizens' rights. Even as the Constitution was being written, some political leaders insisted that a bill of rights was needed to help develop citizens' trust in the new government. However, they agreed to wait to make amendments to the Constitution until after it was **ratified**. As a result of this compromise, the first ten amendments to the U.S. Constitution, passed in 1791, became the **Bill of Rights**. These rights are well known to many Americans. The First Amendment, for example, guarantees freedom of religion, freedom of speech, and freedom of the press. The Sixth and Seventh Amendments guarantee citizens' rights to trial by jury.

As Americans' ideas about citizenship and government have evolved, the amendment process has allowed the Constitution to evolve as well. The Thirteenth Amendment (1865) outlawed slavery; the Fifteenth Amendment (1870) established that the rights of citizens "shall not be denied or abridged . . . on account of race, color, or previous condition of servitude."

A number of constitutional amendments have extended voting rights to citizens. The Nineteenth Amendment (1920) gave women the right to vote. The Twenty-fourth Amendment (1964) banned poll taxes, which some states were using to prevent African Americans from voting. The Twenty-sixth Amendment (1971) lowered the voting age to 18.

1. Which of the following is the main characteristic of a republic?

   A. voting rights extended to few adult citizens
   B. elected representatives exercising government power on behalf of citizens
   C. people governing themselves by voting directly on all issues
   D. power concentrated among a small group

2. The Constitution is a relatively brief document containing only about seven thousand words. It establishes the structure and powers of the U.S. government but does not give many specifics.

   What assumption were the drafters of the Constitution working under as they kept the document general and brief?

   A. There was not enough time to draft a long, detailed document before the states had to ratify it.
   B. Most of the power of the federal government would be reserved to the president, who could govern as he saw fit.
   C. The details of government would be worked out in the future, as the need arose, within the framework of the Constitution.
   D. Written constitutions were an untested basis for democratic government, so it was better to keep such a document brief.

3. Franklin Delano Roosevelt was elected to the presidency four times between 1933 and 1945. In reaction to this, the Twenty-second Amendment, ratified in 1951, allowed presidents a maximum of two terms in office.

   People who favored presidential term limits would most likely have valued which of the following?

   A. responsibility but no authority
   B. authority but no responsibility
   C. the power of an office, not an individual
   D. the power of an individual, not an office

4. The third paragraph of the passage on page 558 includes a summary of Article 6 of the Constitution, also called the supremacy clause.

   ____________ is an example of the supremacy clause in action.

   A. Congress voting to appropriate $2 billion for a federal highways program
   B. The Environmental Protection Agency issuing new regulations on a pollutant
   C. The U.S. Supreme Court refusing to hear a case
   D. The U.S. Supreme Court declaring an Illinois state law unconstitutional

Question 5 refers to the following chart.

Methods of Amending the Constitution

Proposal	Ratification Method	When Used
Two-thirds vote in both houses of Congress to propose an amendment	By three-quarters of the state legislatures	For every amendment except one
	By special conventions in three-fourths of the states	Twenty-first Amendment (repealing Prohibition)
Two-thirds of states request Congress to call a constitutional convention to consider an amendment	By three-quarters of the state legislatures	Never used
	By special conventions in three-fourths of the states	Never used

5. Which of the following would best explain why the third and fourth methods of amending the Constitution have never been used?

   A. State governments do not usually act together.
   B. Only Congress can propose amendments.
   C. State legislatures can vote on an amendment.
   D. Conventions meet more frequently than Congress and state legislatures do.

STUDY ADVICE

The Social Studies Test may present you with primary source documents from the founding of the American political system, such as the U.S. Constitution. If you have a solid understanding of this era, congratulations! If you still feel a bit shaky, review the key terms presented in this chapter.

LESSON 3

Levels and Branches of Government

KEY IDEAS

- Under our Constitution, the federal government must share power with the states.
- The federal government has three major branches—executive, legislative, and judicial.
- The three branches of the government balance each other's power.

HiSET EXAM TIP

Editorial cartoons like the one on page 561 use pictures and humor to make a political point.

The U.S. government works in layers with different responsibilities at the national, or **federal**, level; the state level; and local levels, including cities, villages, and counties. The federal government works across all 50 states, and its decisions and actions affect everyone. States have their own constitutions, similar to the U.S. Constitution. State governments also are quite powerful in shaping the lives of people in their states.

Federalism, which is a basic principle of the U.S. Constitution, means that power is shared between the national and state levels of government. Dividing power between federal and state government protects the rights of individual states, but also allows our national government to enforce certain rights of citizenship. The Constitution gives some powers only to the national government, some only to state government, and some to both. For example, only the federal government can declare war. States are given the power to establish schools. Both federal and state governments can levy taxes and set up court systems.

There are three branches of government at the federal level, each with different roles to play. The powers of each branch are described in the Constitution. The **executive branch** consists of the president and various advisors (including the president's cabinet) and government departments, such as the State Department. The executive branch enforces the nation's laws and provides national leadership, setting goals and policies. The **legislative branch** consists of two houses of **Congress**: the **Senate** and the **House of Representatives**. Congress is responsible for making laws that all citizens, organizations, and businesses must follow. The **judicial branch**, made up of the federal court system including the Supreme Court, decides disputes related to laws, including the U.S. Constitution.

U.S. citizens vote for the president and all members of Congress. As a result, these politicians have a responsibility to represent and serve their **constituents**—the people who elected them. The president may be elected to only two terms of four years each. Representatives are elected for two years and Senators for six years; these members of Congress may be reelected for any number of terms.

Federal judges, in contrast, are appointed by the president and **confirmed** by the Senate. They can serve in these positions for life. As citizens, we have a right to expect our federal judges to make **impartial** decisions based on the Constitution and the laws of the United States.

The people who wrote the U.S. Constitution were afraid to give any government body too much power. Therefore, the Constitution limits the power of each branch of the federal government. Each branch has separate powers. Each branch also has the power to act in ways that affect the other branches, in a system called **checks and balances**. For example, the president can **veto** laws made by Congress. Congress can override a presidential veto by repassing the law with a two-thirds majority. The Constitution is also now interpreted to mean that judges can review laws and declare them **unconstitutional**.

PRACTICE 3

1. What is the key characteristic of federalism?

   A. division of power between national and state governments
   B. concentration of power in one government
   C. concentration of power at the local level
   D. a judicial system with trial, appellate, and supreme courts

2. Which of the following is an example of a government entity that is part of the executive branch?

   A. the Democratic National Committee
   B. Congress's House Rules Committee
   C. the U.S. Court of Appeals
   D. the State Department

3. Why do lifetime appointments help ensure that federal judges rule impartially on legal issues?

   A. Federal judges need not worry about pleasing their constituents in order to be reelected.
   B. Only people who demonstrate loyalty to the ruling political party are appointed.
   C. Lifetime appointments mean that federal judges acquire a great deal of experience.
   D. A federal judge must be impartial or he or she will not be reelected.

4. Senators serve ____________ year terms in Congress, and representatives serve ____________ year terms, with the option to be reelected for any number of terms.

   A. two; four
   B. six; two
   C. two; six
   D. four; two

Question 5 refers to the following cartoon.

"Let's never forget that the constitution provides for three equally important branches of government: the legislative and the other two."

5. Which of the following people is most likely depicted in the cartoon?

   A. the president
   B. a member of Congress
   C. the head of a government department
   D. a federal judge

LESSON 4

The Electoral System

At the national level in particular, two **political parties** dominate the political arena in the United States: the **Democrats** and the **Republicans**. These parties represent different ideas about the role of government in our nation. In each election season, the parties and candidates work to promote their views, or **platforms**—their positions on issues like tax reform, Social Security, education spending, environmental protection, and so on.

The political parties have developed large organizations for raising money and getting their candidates elected. Each party runs its own **primary** election, in which candidates within the party compete with each other for the party's **nomination**. After the primary elections, the winners from each party's primary face off in the general election. In presidential elections, the primary season ends with a party **convention**, where delegates from each state gather to select the party's candidate. Citizens vote in a general election, and the results are tallied by state. Following the general election, electors from each state cast their state's votes in the **Electoral College**. The electors generally must cast their votes for the candidate who won the general election in their state. The candidate who wins the greatest number of electoral votes becomes president.

Although Democrats and Republicans are by far the largest political parties, there are small parties as well. At times, a third-party candidate like Ralph Nader or Ross Perot attracts enough support to influence the outcome of the national election. Even when small parties offer interesting new ideas or solutions to problems, they have great difficulty attracting money and public attention because the Democratic and Republican parties are so well established.

Although many voters consider themselves to be either Republicans or Democrats, many others are **independent**. Candidates and their political parties rely heavily on **opinion polls** to find out what voters think; they try to tailor their campaign messages to appeal to large numbers of voters. Groups of voters who might "swing" an election one way or another are particularly important targets for political campaigns. Sometimes opposing candidates participate in public **debates**.

Political campaigns can be very expensive, and the higher the office, the more expensive the campaign. To reach the public, candidates pay for mailings, TV ads, and events, including personal appearances. They need campaign staff and offices; they must pay for travel expenses. As a result, fund-raising has become a very important part of running for office.

In recent decades, Americans have become more and more concerned about the high cost of running for office. Many Americans believe that a candidate should not have to be wealthy to begin with, or be overly obligated to contributors, in order to gain political office. We now have laws that restrict the size of campaign contributions directly to politicians. We also have restrictions on how **political action committees** (PACs) operate. However, many people believe that more reforms are needed.

KEY IDEAS

- U.S. politics are dominated by the Democratic and Republican parties.
- Political parties hold primaries to select candidates for the general election.
- Political campaigns are very expensive, and many people believe that we must reform our campaign finance laws.

HiSET EXAM TIP

When you are asked a question about a circle graph, remember that it represents a whole, or 100%.

PRACTICE 4

1. Which of the following is necessary for a candidate to win the presidency?

   A. earning a majority of primary wins
   B. receiving a majority of the popular vote
   C. receiving a majority in the Electoral College
   D. having no third-party opponent

2. An exit poll is one that surveys people as they leave a voting location. Instead of waiting for votes to be counted, the media often announce the winners of elections based on exit polls.

   Which of the following is an important drawback of using exit polls?

   A. Exit polls may be inaccurate if the people polled are not representative of the political unit as a whole or if the election is very close.
   B. Exit polls allow the media to present election results during prime time on election night instead of waiting until later in the evening.
   C. Exit polls have undue influence on the way politicians running for office conduct their campaigns.
   D. Exit polls are likely to be unreliable when there is a wide margin between the candidates.

3. Which of the following is an example of a primary election?

   A. A Democrat and a Republican oppose one another in a race for the U.S. Senate.
   B. A Republican and an independent candidate oppose one another in a race for the state senate.
   C. Once presidential candidates are chosen, they select their running mates.
   D. Two city council members are on a ballot to determine which one will run for mayor as a Democrat.

STUDY ADVICE

If you've been working through this book in order, it might be time to review the Reading and Writing units. Don't forget to do periodic reviews of material you haven't seen in a while so that those skills don't get rusty.

Questions 4 and 5 refer to the following graphs.

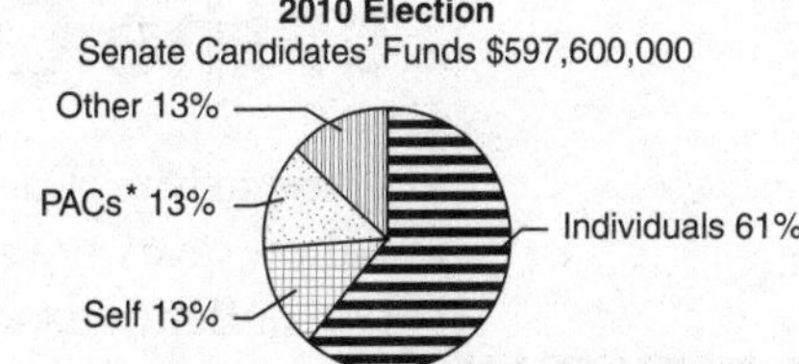

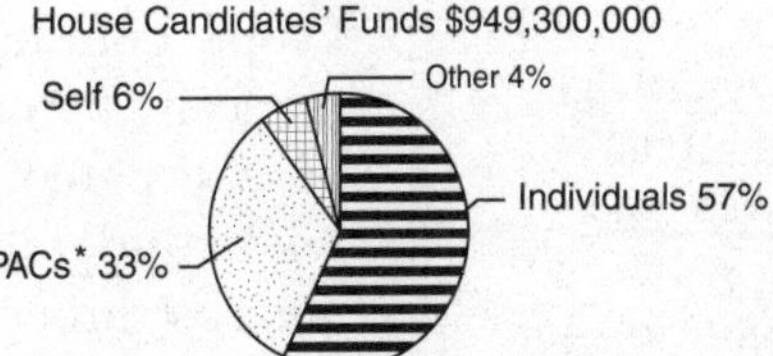

*PACs are Political Action Committees—groups that raise money for candidates.

Source: Federal Election Commission

4. How do the campaign funding sources of Senate and House candidates compare?

   A. Individual donations provided a larger percentage of funds raised by House candidates than of those raised by Senate candidates.
   B. In total, individuals contributed a greater dollar amount to House candidates than they did to Senate candidates.
   C. Political parties provided a greater percentage of the funds raised by Senate candidates than they did of funds raised by House candidates.
   D. On average, Senate candidates received a greater percentage of their funds from PACs than did House candidates.

5. Which of the following statements is supported by the graphs?

   A. In 2010, self-funding was a larger source of funds for Senate candidates than it was for House candidates.
   B. In 2010, individual donations were the largest source of funds for Senate candidates but not for House candidates.
   C. In 2010, PACs were the largest source of funds for House candidates but not for Senate candidates.
   D. Fund-raising accounts for most of the work on a congressional campaign.

LESSON 5

The Role of the Citizen

KEY IDEAS

- U.S. citizens have the right to vote and to hold public office, as well as to enjoy many freedoms.
- Citizens are responsible for contributing to the general welfare of the nation.
- In our court system, citizens serve on juries in order to protect the rights of other citizens.

HiSET EXAM TIP

The Social Studies Test will ask you about the citizen's role in government. You may be asked to interpret materials about "civic life," such as election information or a voter registration document.

Citizenship is a special relationship between a person and a nation: the nation owes the person certain rights and guarantees; the person has certain obligations to the nation. Thus, citizens of the United States have both rights and responsibilities.

People born in the United States, no matter what the circumstances, automatically become U.S. citizens. Regardless of where you were born, if one of your parents was a U.S. citizen, then you are also a U.S. citizen. People who **immigrate** to the United States from other countries can become U.S. citizens through a legal process called **naturalization**; underage children are naturalized along with their parents.

Our rights of citizenship are established in the first ten amendments to the U.S. Constitution—the Bill of Rights (see page 558)—and in other sections of the Constitution. One of the most fundamental rights of U.S. citizens is our right to participate in our nation's political life. We are eligible to vote and to hold public office, and we elect representatives to govern us. In a famous phrase in the Gettysburg Address, Abraham Lincoln said that we have a government "of the people, by the people, and for the people."

As Lincoln's famous remark implies, a government "by the people" requires that citizens take responsibility. First and foremost, we must uphold the laws of our country. As citizens, we also make contributions to the national welfare. Our taxes pay for services that the government provides to benefit everyone. By voting, we not only choose our government representatives, but we also help to make the political process meaningful for everyone. Through national service—such as military service, holding public office, or participating in intensive volunteer programs like Teach for America—citizens may devote years of their lives to the responsibilities of citizenship.

Our **jury** system is an important example of the give-and-take of citizenship. Each of us is guaranteed the right to a fair and speedy trial, heard by "a jury of peers," if we are accused of a crime. However, we are also obligated to serve on juries or as **witnesses** when we are called by the court system. The fairness of our legal system depends on citizens participating in that system. Therefore, our employers are obligated to release us from work at the request of the courts.

In addition to the rights and responsibilities established by law, many citizens contribute their time and money in other ways that serve society as a whole. People volunteer to serve organizations in their communities or within their professions—serving meals in shelters, fund-raising for schools, offering free medical services, and so on. People also give money to causes they think are important, from political campaigns to food pantries to environmental organizations. Many citizens also work hard to conduct their daily lives in ways that contribute to the general welfare: by recycling, cleaning up trash, and looking out for their neighbors and family members.

1. _______________ outlines the rights of U.S. citizens.

   A. The Declaration of Independence
   B. The U.S. Constitution
   C. A U.S. passport
   D. A person's naturalization papers

Questions 2 and 3 refer to the following information.

Aliens are individuals who are neither U.S. citizens nor U.S. nationals; they can be classified into five groups:

Immigrant/Legal Permanent Resident (LPR) An alien who has established legal permanent residence in the United States.

Nonimmigrant A documented alien who is staying in the United States for a brief, specified period.

Enemy alien An alien who is a native or citizen of a nation at war with the United States.

Refugee A nonimmigrant fleeing his or her country to escape persecution or danger.

Undocumented alien An alien who comes to the United States without legal documentation.

2. Louvina married an American and moved to the United States from Trinidad in 2010. Three years later, she filed a legal petition requesting U.S. citizenship. In what category of alien does Louvina most likely belong?

   A. immigrant
   B. nonimmigrant
   C. enemy alien
   D. refugee

3. What would happen to the legal status of noncitizens living in the United States if their country declares war on the United States?

   A. They would become nonimmigrants.
   B. They would become immigrants.
   C. They would become enemy aliens.
   D. They would become refugees.

4. The United States must balance the right of society to protect itself against the rights of an accused criminal. One aspect of this tension is the Fourth Amendment guarantee of "the right of people to be secure in their persons, houses, papers, and effects, against unreasonable searches and seizures."

   Which of the following values is supported by the Fourth Amendment?

   A. free speech
   B. privacy
   C. civic duty
   D. volunteerism

Question 5 refers to the following graph.

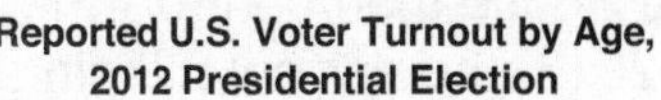

Reported U.S. Voter Turnout by Age,
2012 Presidential Election

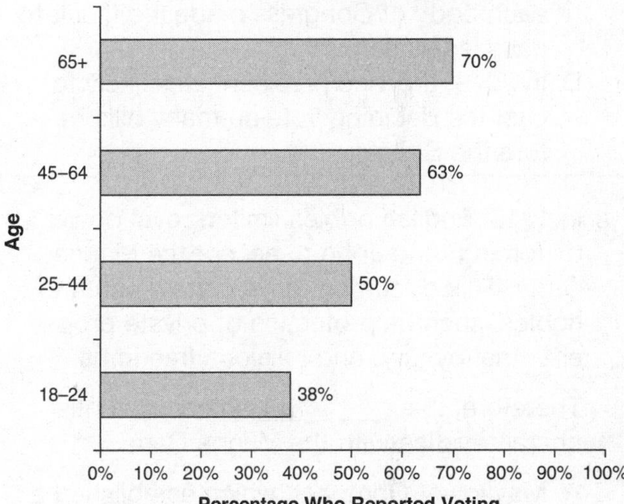

Source: United States Census Bureau

5. Which of the following is a conclusion based on the graph rather than a detail of the graph?

   A. About 63 percent of people aged 45 to 64 reported voting in the 2012 presidential election.
   B. Those aged 65+ reported the highest voter turnout in the 2012 presidential election, at 70 percent.
   C. If the 2012 presidential election is representative of elections generally in the United States, voter turnout increases with age.
   D. Only about 38 percent of young people reported voting in the 2012 presidential election.

Civics and Government Practice Questions

Question 1 refers to the following chart.

Political Divisions in the 113th Congress, 2013

Party	House	Senate
Republicans	234	45
Democrats	201	53
Others	—	2 (In case of a tie, Vice President Joe Biden (D) votes.)
Vacant	—	—

1. Which of the following is the best summary of the chart above?

   A. Congress is made up of the House and the Senate.
   B. In 2013, a different major party controlled the House than controls the Senate.
   C. In 2013, the narrow margin of control in each body of Congress made it difficult to pass legislation.
   D. In 2013, the vice president was likely to cast the deciding vote on many bills before the Senate.

---

2. In 1215, English nobles limited royal power by forcing King John to accept the Magna Carta. This document gave certain rights to nobles, such as protection of private property, trial by jury, and religious freedoms.

   Therefore, the __________ shares essential characteristics with the Magna Carta.

   A. Mayflower Compact, which established a government for Plymouth colony,
   B. Bill of Rights of the U.S. Constitution, which guarantees citizens certain rights,
   C. Albany Plan of Union, which called for a colonial confederation,
   D. *Federalist Papers*, which encouraged ratification of the U.S. Constitution,

Questions 3 and 4 refer to the following passage.

In 1979, Congress passed legislation to allow political parties to raise unlimited amounts of general-purpose money not designated for particular candidates. In 1991, a lawsuit forced disclosure of such "soft money" contributions, and concern grew about the size of individual donations, the extent of total donations, and the ways in which the money was being spent. During the presidential elections of 1996 and 2000, campaign fund-raising, especially the raising and spending of soft money, was an issue, with the candidates promising reform. Finally, in 2001, after several years of hearings, the Senate passed the McCain-Feingold bill, which would eliminate the unregulated soft money contributions that make up a large proportion of the parties' budgets.

3. Which of the following is an example of a soft money contribution?

   A. a $250 ticket to a fund-raising dinner-dance to benefit a mayoral candidate
   B. a $3,000 donation to the campaign fund of an incumbent senator
   C. a $3,000 contribution to a party fund for TV ads on political issues
   D. a $1,000 gift to a senator's campaign fund in response to a direct mail solicitation

4. Which of the following is the most likely reason soft money was not a major issue in the 1980s?

   A. People were less aware of soft money because disclosure was not required at that time.
   B. Political campaigns were publicly financed, so soft money was not needed.
   C. Most candidates spent part of their campaign funds on television ads.
   D. McCain and Feingold had not submitted their campaign finance reform bill.

Questions 5 and 6 refer to the following paragraph and graphs.

In order to win a presidential election, a candidate must win a majority of the votes in the Electoral College. Each state has as many electors as it has senators and representatives in Congress. In most states, the winner of the popular vote gets all the electoral votes of the state. These graphs show the popular and Electoral College votes in the election of 2012.

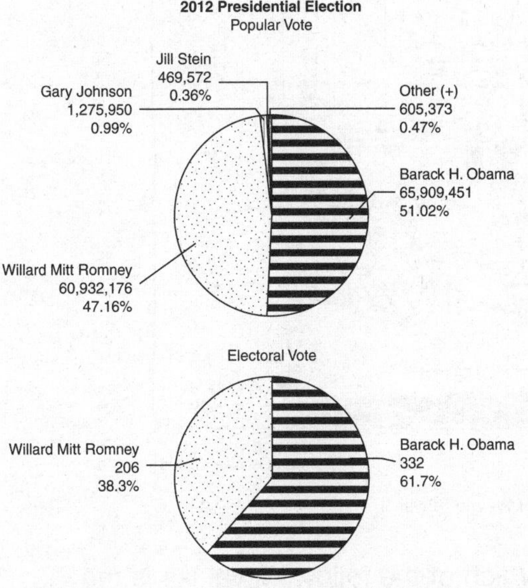

5. Which one of the following statements is supported by the information in the paragraph and the graphs?

   A. A presidential candidate will receive the same percentage of electoral votes as he or she received of the popular vote.
   B. Romney won a greater percentage of the electoral vote than of the popular vote in 2012.
   C. Jill Stein won a greater percentage of the popular vote than of the electoral vote in 2012.
   D. The total of popular votes cast for all candidates other than Barack Obama was greater than the total of those cast for Barack Obama.

6. Which of the following would be the best title for the paragraph and the graphs?

   A. 2012 Presidential Election: How Obama Defeated Romney
   B. 2012 Presidential Election: Third-Party Influence
   C. 2012 Presidential Election: Winning the Electoral College
   D. 2012 Presidential Election: Popular and Electoral Votes

Question 7 refers to the following passage.

Where do I vote? Your voting district is determined by your place of residence. Watch your local newspaper for an announcement indicating polling locations and times, or contact your local board of election to determine your voting location.

You may also obtain your polling place location by accessing the website of the Office of the Secretary of State for your state, or call the Office of the Secretary of State for assistance.

7. Which of the following is assumed but not stated outright in the voter guide above?

   A. The board of election is the county, city, or town office responsible for local voting.
   B. A voter's polling place is determined by his or her address.
   C. A voter can find his or her polling place on the Internet.
   D. A voter can call the Office of the Secretary of State to find out where to vote.

---

8. An interest group is an organization with specific goals that seeks to influence government policies. Which of the following entities constitutes an interest group?

   A. the Democratic Party, which nominates candidates and tries to win elections
   B. the National Association of Manufacturers, which lobbies for businesses
   C. the Federal Communications Commission, which regulates broadcasters
   D. the Cabinet, an advisory body for the president

Questions 9 and 10 refer to the following cartoon.

9. What is the main idea of this cartoon?

   A. Most voters are working people.
   B. Most registered voters don't vote.
   C. Voters should establish another political party.
   D. A non-voters' party would lose every election.

10. Which of the following values is the cartoonist appealing for?

   A. the work ethic
   B. majority rule
   C. civic duty
   D. national pride

11. An oligarchy is a system of government in which a small group of people holds power.

    Which of the following is an oligarchy?

   A. China, where the top leaders of the communist party control the government
   B. Iraq, when it had a dictator, Saddam Hussein
   C. Great Britain, with a monarch, a prime minister, and an elected parliament
   D. Greece, with a prime minister and an elected parliament

12. Three typical laws from the code of Hammurabi, written about 1700 B.C.E., are "If a son strike his father, his hands shall be hewn off. If a man put out the eye of another man, his eye shall be put out. If he break another man's bone, his bone shall be broken."

    What principle underlies these laws?

   A. retribution
   B. rehabilitation
   C. incarceration
   D. mediation

Questions 13 and 14 refer to the following map and table.

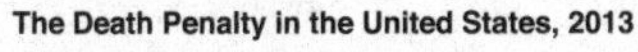
The Death Penalty in the United States, 2013

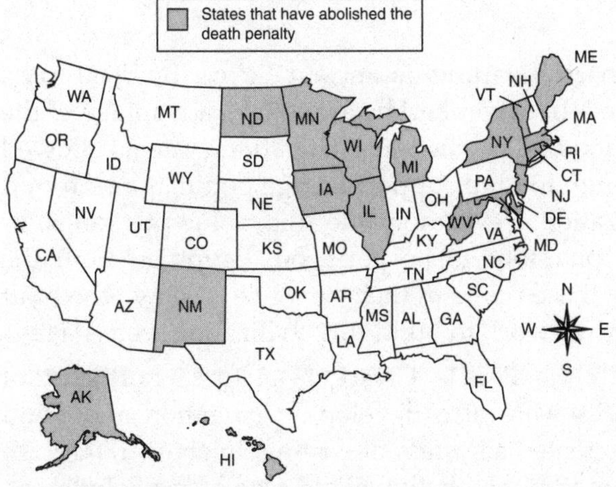

NOTE: Connecticut, Maryland, and New Mexico have abolished the death penalty prospectively. Anyone convicted of a capital offense that occurred prior to abolition of the death penalty in these states may be legally executed.

Homicide Rate per 100,000 Population, 2010

Highest	Lowest
Louisiana, 11.9	Vermont, 1.3
Mississippi, 9.6	New Hampshire, 1.4
Alabama, 8.2	Idaho, 1.5
Maryland, 7.6	Wyoming, 1.6
New Mexico, 7.4	Hawaii, 1.8

Source: National Center for Health Statistics and U.S. Bureau of the Census

13. How many states have the death penalty?

 A. 12
 B. 18
 C. 32
 D. 40

14. People who favor capital punishment usually argue that it prevents serious crimes like homicide. Based on the map and chart, what is a logical flaw with this argument?

 A. A life sentence without parole costs taxpayers more than executing an inmate.
 B. Some executed inmates turn out to have been innocent based on newly discovered evidence.
 C. Two of the five states with the highest per capita homicide rates have abolished the death penalty.
 D. Two of the five states with the lowest per capita homicide rates have abolished the death penalty.

15. The U.S. Constitution gives the president the power to make treaties with foreign nations, and it gives the Senate the power to "advise and consent" on all treaties. Thus, a two-thirds majority of the Senate must ratify any treaty presented by the president. In 1978, President Jimmy Carter persuaded the Senate to ratify treaties with Panama that transferred control of the Panama Canal from the United States to Panama. Many Americans were outraged and believed that U.S. interests had been given away.

 Which of the following is an opinion rather than a statement of fact?

 A. Presidents have the power to enter into treaties with foreign nations.
 B. A two-thirds majority of the Senate is needed to ratify a treaty.
 C. The 1978 Panama treaties sold out U.S. interests to Panama.
 D. The 1978 Panama treaties gave control of the Panama Canal to Panama.

16. In the mayor-council form of city government, voters elect both a mayor and a city council. The mayor is the city's chief executive, operating the city on a day-to-day basis and also serving a ceremonial function. The city council is a legislative body, in charge of the city's finances and passing city laws. In the council-manager form of city government, voters elect a city council that makes city policies and laws. The council may elect a mayor who has a largely ceremonial function. It appoints a professionally trained city manager to oversee day-to-day operations.

 What is the main similarity between the mayor's role in the mayor-council and in the council-manager forms of city government?

 A. The mayor sets policy.
 B. The mayor runs day-to-day operations.
 C. The mayor is elected by voters.
 D. The mayor has ceremonial duties.

LESSON 1

Early Civilizations

KEY IDEAS

- Ancient civilizations developed where people could settle in one place with a secure food supply.
- The ancient republics of Greece and Rome were incubators for important ideas in modern government.
- Ancient civilizations also left legacies in art, architecture, science, and astronomy.

HiSET EXAM TIP

The world history questions require that you have familiarity with major topics in world history.

One of the earliest known **civilizations** is ancient Egypt. By 5000 B.C.E., people who lived along the **Nile River** had begun to take advantage of the fertile soil left behind by floods. The river and irrigation systems allowed the Egyptians to grow enough food to support a large population. Around 3000 B.C.E., Egyptian civilization grew under the rule of Egypt's kings, or **pharaohs**. Believing their pharaohs to be part god, Egyptians built the famous **pyramids** to house these rulers in their next lives. Many who built the pyramids and did the hard work to build this civilization were slaves.

Around the same time, in the **Fertile Crescent**—an area northeast of Egypt—**Sumerian** city-states were also developing irrigation and flood control methods, and they created a system of writing. In about 1800 B.C.E., the Sumerians were conquered by the Babylonians. One of the Babylonian kings, Hammurabi, is remembered for codifying laws. The **Code of Hammurabi** was written on a huge stone in a public place so all Babylonians could know and follow the law.

The civilization of **ancient Greece** did not develop around a river, but around the sea. The Greeks built an **empire**: they established colonies on the Mediterranean Sea and the Black Sea; then they imported food from the colonies. However, Greece itself was not politically unified. As its city-states fought for control of each other's land, Sparta, a particularly warlike state, took over a number of other city-states. Athens, another city-state, is known as the first political **democracy**. All Athenian citizens could vote—but less than half of Athenians were citizens. Women could not vote, nor could the many slaves. The Greek Empire lasted only a few hundred years, but its original ideas, such as democracy, and its stunning arts, including architecture and literature, remain influential even now.

Eventually, the Greek Empire fell to **Roman** conquerors. Rome began as a city on the Italian Peninsula, governed by its wealthy citizens through an elected Senate. Roman citizens were governed by a system of laws that is still influential in the United States. For example, the Romans believed that a person accused of a crime was innocent until proven guilty. The power of Rome grew, and the Romans took over many lands surrounding the Mediterranean Sea, pushing north as far as England and east into Asia by about 100 C.E. Roman leaders built systems and infrastructure to make their empire strong: schools, roads and bridges, hospitals, a tax system, and an army. The ancient Roman Empire lasted until 476 C.E.

Ancient Egypt, Greece, and Rome were only a few of the early civilizations in which people made important scientific discoveries and developed enduring ideas. In Central America, the **Maya**, whose culture was strongest from 300 to 900 C.E., invented a pictographic writing system in which they recorded remarkable discoveries in mathematics and astronomy. The **Inca Empire** in South America had a sophisticated system of government. The Incas built amazing roads and bridges in their rugged mountain lands. In Mexico, the **Aztecs** invented a written language and a calendar system and expanded their farmlands by dredging mud from lakes.

PRACTICE 1

1. Which of the following Central American civilizations is particularly noted for achievements in both mathematics and astronomy?

   A. the Sumerians
   B. the Maya
   C. the Aztecs
   D. the Incas

2. According to the information on page 570, two ancient civilizations were particularly influential on the form of government adopted by the United States of America. Select the answer choice that correctly lists the two civilizations that had the greatest impact on America's systems of law and government.

   A. Sumer and Ancient Greece
   B. Ancient Greece and Ancient Rome
   C. Incas and Ancient Egypt
   D. Ancient Egypt and Ancient Rome

3. What did the ancient civilizations of Egypt and the Fertile Crescent have in common?

   A. Both developed flood control and irrigation technologies to boost food production.
   B. Both had a public code of law engraved on a huge stone.
   C. Both were centered on the shores of the Mediterranean Sea.
   D. Both developed systems of political democracy in which citizens could vote.

4. Once a society developed agriculture and domesticated animals, food surpluses and rising populations made possible which of the following developments?

   A. a nomadic lifestyle
   B. towns
   C. stone tools
   D. stone carvings

STUDY ADVICE

You should be familiar with the broad themes of world history. Pay particular attention to the Key Ideas and the terms in bold on each page on the left.

Questions 5 and 6 refer to the following map.

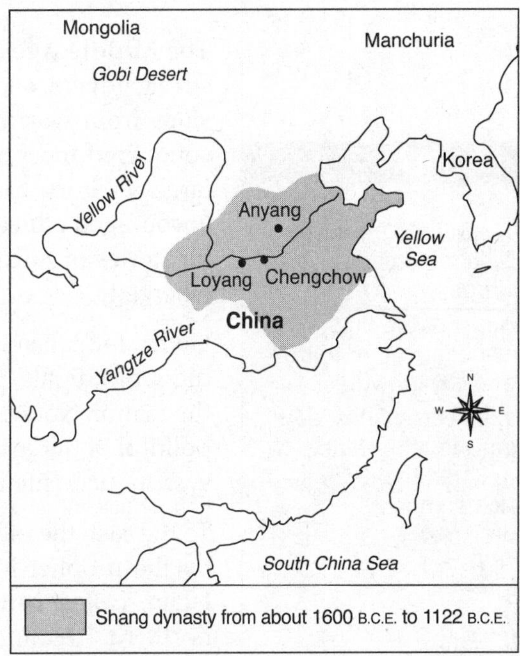

5. In the Yellow River valley, floods deposit a fertile yellow soil called loess that is easily worked by farmers.

   Which of the following civilizations arose under geographic conditions similar to those in ancient China?

   A. the Aztecs
   B. ancient Greece
   C. ancient Rome
   D. ancient Egypt

6. Which of the following statements is supported by the information in the map?

   A. The Yellow River is the only major river in China.
   B. The Shang dynasty, or ruling family, controlled China for almost a thousand years.
   C. The Yellow River was probably the main trade route between Loyang and Chengchow.
   D. The Shang civilization traded more with Korea than with Manchuria.

LESSON 2

Feudalism to Nation States

The **Middle Ages** in Europe lasted from about 500 to 1500 C.E. As the once strong government of Rome weakened, Europe became vulnerable to invasions from warring groups or tribes. A tribal ruler named **Charlemagne** conquered most of Europe by 800. Charlemagne was able to stabilize this large territory for a time. He established laws, spread Christianity, and encouraged education and commerce. When Charlemagne died in 814, the territories of Europe became unstable again, and the system of **feudalism** emerged.

KEY IDEAS

- During the Middle Ages, the feudal system helped to stabilize Europe.
- A by-product of the Crusades was the opening up of trade routes and city growth.
- During the Renaissance, education grew in importance, and people left the Catholic Church to establish Protestantism.

Under feudalism, kings granted control of land to nobles. A noble's soldiers, or knights, protected the noble's estate, or manor. **Peasants** farmed at the manor. Nobles paid taxes to kings; peasants paid taxes to nobles. As the political boundaries among the kings' lands became established, the feudal system made life in Europe more peaceful over several hundred years.

To the east, the religion of **Islam** was founded during the early Middle Ages by the prophet Muhammad, who was born in 570 C.E. The followers of Islam, called **Muslims**, conquered large territories in the Middle East, northern Africa, Spain, Persia, and India. They established a series of empires. Many people in these conquered lands converted to Islam while contributing their own knowledge and arts to the Muslim culture. Although the Islamic empires did not last, Islam and its culture have remained strong.

HiSET EXAM TIP

To summarize a graph such as the one on page 573, ask yourself: What is the topic of the graph? What is the main point of the data? How could I say this in a sentence or two?

During the late Middle Ages, Christians and Muslim Turks fought over the holy city of Jerusalem in a series of wars called the **Crusades**. Christians gained control of Jerusalem from the Turks, but they ruled the city for less than 90 years. A more lasting effect of the Crusades was to open up trade between Europe and the Middle East and even China. As trade, money, and merchants grew in importance in Europe, feudalism declined. People left the manors and went to live and work in cities, where opportunities were greater. Cities gained political, economic, and cultural importance.

During the Middle Ages, European nations began to form as **monarchs** combined territories of small rulers and took advantage of the wealth of cities. England's monarchy was established by 1100. France won the Hundred Years' War against England and emerged as a strong nation under its monarch. Spain united through the marriage of two rulers, Ferdinand and Isabella, who had each controlled smaller states.

The **Renaissance**, which spread from Italy across Europe between 1300 and 1600, brought growth in education, science, and the arts. The Renaissance also led to changes in the Catholic Church. During the **Reformation** in the 1500s, reformers criticized the church for abusing its power. Those who believed that people should read the Bible themselves rather than follow the pope split from the Catholic Church and formed the **Protestant** religion. King Henry VIII of England broke from the Catholic Church and formed the Church of England so he would not have to obey the pope.

PRACTICE 2

1. What was the role of the knights in feudal Europe?

   A. to collect taxes for the king
   B. to take care of livestock
   C. to protect their noble's land from attack
   D. to administer justice

2. Given the information on page 572, in which of the following modern European nations are you most likely to find evidence of Muslim arts and culture?

   A. Spain
   B. France
   C. Germany
   D. Italy

3. During the late Middle Ages, the growth of trade spurred a migration of peasants from the manors to the towns. To which of the following events is this most similar?

   A. the migration of Puritans to the New World to escape religious persecution in the 1600s
   B. the migration of people from farms to industrial cities in the 1800s
   C. the migration of political refugees to the United States in the 1900s
   D. the migration of individuals with health problems from cold, damp regions to warm, dry regions

4. At the time of the Reformation, which of the following was one of the main differences between Roman Catholics and Protestants?

   A. Roman Catholics accepted the authority of the pope and Protestants did not.
   B. Roman Catholics lived on the manors and Protestants lived in the towns.
   C. Roman Catholics supported the monarchies in their nations and Protestants did not.
   D. Roman Catholics led the Church of England under Henry VIII and Protestants did not.

5. In England in the 1100s, any free man could bring a case before a royal court headed by a circuit judge, who formed juries of local people. The decisions of these courts were recorded and formed the basis for common law, which was applied to everyone in the kingdom. In contrast, justice in the manor courts, which were run by the nobles, could be fickle. There were few written laws, and the verdicts could be overturned by the lord.

   People usually preferred to be tried in royal courts rather than manor courts because the royal courts valued which of the following?

   A. accepted legal principles
   B. harsh punishment
   C. power for the local lord
   D. fines rather than imprisonment

Question 6 refers to the following graph.

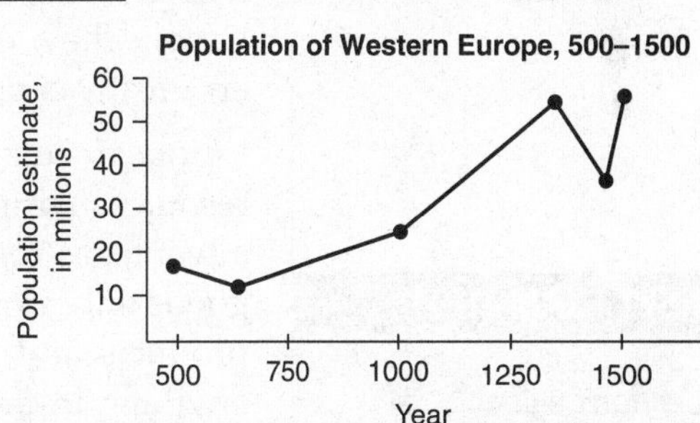

Source: Carlo M. Cippola, ed. *The Fontana Economic History of Europe: The Middle Ages* and Carlo M. Cippola *Before the Industrial Revolution: European Society and Economy, 1000–1700*

6. Which of the following best summarizes the information shown on the graph?

   A. The population of western Europe showed the most growth between the years 750 and 1000.
   B. There were fewer than 50 million people living in western Europe at any given time.
   C. The population of western Europe showed almost constant growth with only brief periods of decline.
   D. The population of western Europe fell to its lowest around the year 1450.

LESSON 3

Exploration and Colonialism

KEY IDEAS

- European explorers sought new sailing routes to make trading easier with India and Asia.
- European rulers set up colonies to extend their territories and gain new wealth.
- Native peoples and cultures were exploited by colonization.

HiSET EXAM TIP

Some questions will ask, "Which of the following statements is supported by the graph (or the map)?" Read the choices and carefully check each against the graphic.

About 500 years ago, explorers from European nations such as Spain and France sailed on risky voyages all over the world. Europeans had many reasons for leaving the shores of their own continent. Some were looking for trade routes and valuable goods, such as spices, to bring back. Others were missionaries bent on spreading the Christian religion. Still others were paid by their rulers to find new lands to conquer. No matter what the reasons for their journeys, they faced real dangers and uncertain rewards, and many left the lands they reached in ruins. Most Americans know the story of Christopher Columbus, who sailed west from Spain in 1492, expecting to reach Asia. Instead, he reached the **New World**—the Americas. In 1498, Vasco da Gama, a Portuguese explorer, sailed south around Africa to reach India. His journey took two years, but it was profitable: His four ships returned full of spices. In 1519, Ferdinand Magellan and his crew left Spain to sail around the southern tip of South America en route to India. Of Magellan's five ships, only one made it back to Spain; Magellan himself died in the Pacific. However, the ship that returned to Spain is believed to be the first ship to circumnavigate the globe. Not long after, French explorer Jacques Cartier tried and failed to find a river route through North America to the Pacific. Despite the sometimes negative consequences of their journeys, these explorers greatly expanded the Europeans' knowledge of geography.

European rulers turned to distant lands to expand their own power and resources, primarily for economic gain. **Colonies** offered a number of advantages to their ruling nations. Colonies could be required to **import** goods only from the ruling nation, and they could be forced to export their products and natural resources only to the ruling nation. Furthermore, anything in the colonized area was considered the property of the ruling nation. In the 1500s, Spain gained great wealth from its colonies in the New World by stealing valuable objects from the native civilizations and by mining and removing gold, silver, and other minerals from their lands. Colonialism could be utterly devastating to native cultures, economies, and populations, as colonizers brought not only weapons but also deadly diseases. Not only North America but also large parts of South America, Africa, and Asia suffered during the age of colonialism.

Historians distinguish among different types of colonies, depending on the relationship between the ruling nation and the colony. In colonies of **settlement,** people from the ruling nation migrated to the colony and established a government under the authority of the ruling nation. The English colonies in North America were colonies of settlement. Although Native Americans had long-established societies and territories of their own, the English settlers disregarded these. From the point of view of the British government, the lands belonged to England, and the Native Americans were subject to British law and had to obey the British colonial government.

Colonies of **exploitation** were common in tropical climates, where Europeans did not want to establish their own settlements. In these colonies, the ruling nation established a government to exploit the local labor force and natural resources. The native people were forced to produce goods and crops to benefit the ruling nation.

PRACTICE 3

1. For what is Magellan best known?
   A. discovering a route north of North America to the Pacific Ocean
   B. discovering a route to India around the southern tip of Africa
   C. exploring North America's rivers
   D. leading the first expedition to result in an around-the-world voyage

2. According to the passage on page 574, what is the main reason European rulers explored the New World and established colonies?
   A. to convert people to Christianity
   B. to establish democratic governments
   C. to gain economic benefits
   D. to find a river route through North America

3. Which of the following is an example of a colony of exploitation?
   A. Pennsylvania, where Quakers and other religious minorities settled to escape religious persecution in Europe
   B. Malaya, where the British set up and ran rubber plantations worked by the native peoples
   C. the island of Manhattan and areas north along the Hudson River, where the Dutch established the settlement of New Netherlands
   D. Brazil, where the King of Portugal gave large parcels of land to loyal subjects, who enlisted others to settle on the land

4. Based on the passage, what was the main cause of population decline among native colonized peoples?
   A. emigration to other colonies
   B. slavery
   C. war and disease
   D. low birthrate

Question 5 refers to the following map.

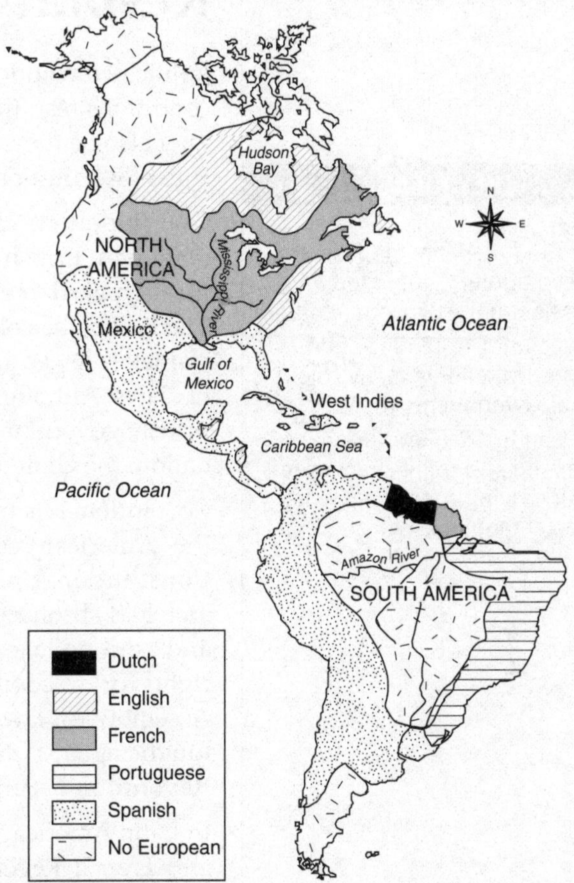

5. Which of the following statements is supported by information on the map?
   A. In 1700, most of the Amazon River valley was claimed by Portugal.
   B. The Dutch had the smallest claim in the Americas in 1700.
   C. By 1700, the English had claimed the west coast of North America.
   D. In 1700, Mexico was claimed by both the Portuguese and the Spanish.

LESSON 4

The Age of Revolutions

Political revolutions often happen when people are unhappy about the conditions resulting from their system of government. Political revolutions may also be fueled by new ideas about who is best suited to govern. In the Age of Revolutions, many people wanted more political power.

One important cause of the **American Revolution** was British taxation. Although British citizens in England were represented in government through **Parliament**, the American colonists did not have representatives in that body. The colonists believed that they should not have to pay the special taxes levied on them, since they had had no voice in determining the tax laws. Although the colonists began by arguing for representation in the British government, by 1776 they had declared themselves a sovereign nation, the United States of America.

Revolutionaries in France were inspired by democratic ideas expressed in the American colonies' **Declaration of Independence** and the **U.S. Constitution**. Unlike England, France had no Parliament; the French monarch had absolute power. The nobility and the Church had many privileges and paid no taxes, while ordinary citizens paid heavy taxes and had few rights or freedoms. In 1789, the French people organized a National Assembly—a law-making body to represent them. When King Louis XVI fought against the establishment of the National Assembly, the **French Revolution** began. Its turmoil lasted for ten years.

In Latin America, many colonized people, inspired in part by the American and French Revolutions, began to shake off European rule. In Haiti, an island in the Caribbean Sea, slaves led by Toussaint L'Ouverture overturned French rule and established an independent nation in 1804. Mexican revolutionaries finally won their independence from Spain in 1821. In South America, revolutions rocked the continent until 1824, by which time most countries had gained their independence.

Important revolutions are not always political. The **Industrial Revolution** started in the late 1700s in the textile industry, when new equipment was invented for spinning thread and weaving cloth. Instead of workers using their own tools at home, factories could house many workers using machines to produce much greater quantities. This factory model for large-scale production spread along with **steam engines** and electricity. Workers moved into factory towns and cities to work for wages. The Industrial Revolution brought a mixture of benefits and problems—useful inventions, increasing wealth, and new **social mobility** were offset by dangerous factory jobs, **child labor**, crowded cities, and **pollution**.

The Industrial Revolution also brought sweeping social changes. The economic mainstay of the European **aristocracy** had been farmland. After the Industrial Revolution, manufacturing and trade became more important economically than agriculture. Thus, the merchant classes became more powerful. New ideas about political equality affected how people thought about social equality as well.

KEY IDEAS

- In the American and French Revolutions, people fought against unjust governments.
- Revolution spread to Latin America, ending many colonial governments there.
- The Industrial Revolution caused sweeping changes in work, living conditions, and social mobility.

HiSET EXAM TIP

As part of the Social Studies Test, you may be provided with basic historic information and asked to make comparisons—such as the similarities and differences between two revolutions.

PRACTICE 4

1. Which of the following had a great influence on the French Revolution?

   A. the Industrial Revolution
   B. the Mexican Revolution
   C. the U.S. Declaration of Independence
   D. the British monarchy

Question 2 refers to the following paragraph and graph.

Before the French Revolution, the French were divided into three groups by law, each with different privileges. In the First Estate were the higher clergy, who were nobles, and the parish priests, who were commoners. The Second Estate consisted of nobles who were not members of the clergy. The Third Estate was made up of commoners, including the middle class and peasants.

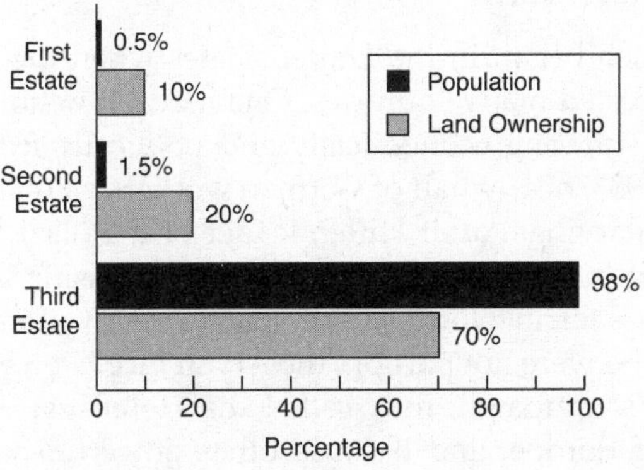

2. Which of the following statements is supported by the paragraph and the graph?

   A. All members of the nobility belonged to the First Estate.
   B. The members of the First Estate owned more property than members of the Second Estate.
   C. The distribution of wealth in prerevolutionary France favored the Third Estate.
   D. Members of the Third Estate owned the least amount of land per person.

STUDY ADVICE

How are you feeling about the Social Studies Test at this point? If you're feeling encouraged, that's fantastic. If you're feeling discouraged, don't give up. Most people have to work very hard to get their high school equivalency degree. Stick with it—you'll get there!

3. According to the information on page 576, what is the main difference between the English and French governments before 1789?

   A. England was a monarchy, while France was not a monarchy.
   B. England had a parliament, while France did not have a parliament.
   C. England was a democratic republic, while France was not a direct democracy.
   D. England was not a monarchy, while France was a monarchy.

4. On what was the economic power of the aristocracy based in 18th-century Europe?

   A. moral superiority
   B. attaining a high level of education
   C. possessing large landholdings
   D. belonging to the Church bureaucracy

5. Which of the following does the writer of the text on page 576 take for granted that you know, but does not state outright?

   A. The American colonists demanded representation in the British government before they declared independence.
   B. A sovereign nation is independent, having the power to govern itself.
   C. Many colonies were influenced by the American and French revolutions to seek independence.
   D. As manufacturing and trade became more important, the merchant classes gained power.

6. The Information Revolution of the late 20th century, spurred by the availability of personal computers and the Internet, is most similar to which of the following revolutions?

   A. the American Revolution
   B. the French Revolution
   C. the Mexican Revolution
   D. the Industrial Revolution

LESSON 5

The Twentieth Century

World War I resulted from **nationalism** and **imperialism**—the desire of nations to extend their empires. This desire for expansion led to military buildup. When war broke out in 1914 between Serbia and Austria-Hungary over the assassination of an Austrian leader visiting Serbia, a chain reaction started as other countries also declared war. Germany and Austria-Hungary were the mainstays of the **Central Powers**, who fought against the **Allies**—England, France, Russia, Serbia, and eventually the United States. When the Central Powers finally lost the war, millions of people had been killed. The war devastated Europe, leaving many people jobless and homeless. In the 1918 **Treaty of Versailles**, Germany was blamed for the war and forced to pay **reparations** to the Allies.

KEY IDEAS

- Two devastating world wars occurred during the first half of the 20th century.
- The United States and Soviet Union emerged as superpowers after World War II.
- The superpowers faced off during the Cold War, which ended with the breakup of the Soviet Union in 1991.

Revolution in Russia began during World War I. The Russian **Czar** refused to pull out of the war, even though most Russians did not support involvement. In 1917, the Czar and his family were assassinated, and the **Russian Revolution** ended with Bolshevik leader Vladimir Lenin in power. The Bolsheviks founded the Soviet Union as a **communist** nation with one political party—the Communist Party.

The Great Depression, which began in the United States when the stock market crashed in 1929, affected many countries. One hard-hit nation was Germany, which was still suffering economically and politically from its defeat in World War I. By 1933, nearly half of German workers were unemployed, and people were starving. Adolf Hitler, leader of the Nazi Party, rose to power by appealing to German nationalism and promising to put people back to work. Hitler's terrible form of nationalism involved imprisoning and killing people who were not part of "the Aryan race." Jews were the main targets of Hitler's campaign, now called the **Holocaust**. Hitler wanted to take over all of Europe, and because other powerful nations wanted to avoid war, they let him annex Austria, then Czechoslovakia. But when Hitler invaded Poland in 1939, England and France declared war on Germany, and **World War II** began. Many nations went to war, including the United States. Once again, Germany and the other **Axis Powers** (including Italy and Japan) were defeated by the Allies. The United States dropped the first **atomic bomb** on Hiroshima to end the war.

HiSET EXAM TIP

You may be familiar with some of the world events covered on the test. However, answer questions based on the information provided on the test, even if it differs from what you remember.

After World War II, the United States and the Soviet Union emerged as **superpowers**. Former allies, they each led opposing groups of countries, one group democratic, the other group communist. The two groups of nations so distrusted each other that the period following World War II was called the **Cold War**—a war fought through political and diplomatic contests instead of battles. To catch up with the United States, the Soviet Union started to build its own nuclear weapons, and the **arms race** began, soon followed by the "space race."

However, by 1990 the Soviet bloc was falling apart. The Soviet Union itself split into 15 countries in 1991. People who had lived under repressive governments for many years struggled to establish democracy—not only in the former Soviet bloc, but also in Africa, Latin America, and Asia.

PRACTICE 5

1. As a result of the 1918 Treaty of Versailles, what did Germany have to do?

A. pay the Allies money to repair war damages
B. develop its military forces to protect Europe
C. adopt a communist government
D. promote nationalism among its people

2. What event was the immediate cause of England and France declaring war on Germany at the beginning of World War II?

A. the annexation of Austria
B. the annexation of Czechoslovakia
C. the invasion of Poland
D. the invasion of France

3. Before the atomic bomb was dropped on Hiroshima, the Allies warned Japan they would suffer "complete and utter destruction" unless they surrendered. Despite the fact that 80,000 people were killed and 40,000 wounded by the bombing of Hiroshima, Japan still refused to surrender. The United States then dropped a second atomic bomb on the city of Nagasaki, killing 40,000 more people. After the second bombing, the Japanese surrendered.

Japan's refusal to surrender after the bombing of Hiroshima suggests that the Japanese placed a high value on which of the following?

A. negotiation
B. national pride
C. the lives of military personnel
D. a lasting peace

4. Which of the following is a similarity between World War I and World War II?

A. Both were confined to Europe.
B. Both occurred after the Russian Revolution.
C. Both involved the use of atomic weapons.
D. Both were won by the Allies.

Questions 5 and 6 refer to the following chart.

Casualties in World War II

Nation	Military Dead	Military Wounded	Civilian Dead
Great Britain	398,000	475,000	65,000
Soviet Union	7,500,000	14,102,000	15,000,000
United States	292,000	671,000	very few
Germany	2,850,000	7,250,000	5,000,000
Japan	1,576,000	500,000	300,000

Source: *The Second World War* by Henri Michel

5. What was the main difference between the casualties sustained by the United States and those sustained by other nations in World War II?

A. The United States had more military dead than wounded.
B. The United States sustained only a few civilian casualties.
C. The United States had the fewest wounded.
D. The United States had more civilian than military casualties.

6. The main reason that the Soviet Union had so many casualties is that it was invaded by the German army, which got as far as the outskirts of Moscow and Leningrad. There, the Germans halted in 1941. Severe winters, long supply lines back to Germany, and stiff resistance from the Soviets ultimately defeated the Germans.

Which of the following events is most similar to the German invasion of the Soviet Union?

A. the 1812 French invasion of Russia, which failed due to harsh weather and lack of supplies
B. the occupation of Singapore by Japan in World War II, which gave Japan control of Malaya
C. the 1941 Japanese attack on Pearl Harbor, which drew the United States into World War II
D. the 1945 Allied invasion of Europe, which liberated Europe from German control

WORLD HISTORY PRACTICE QUESTIONS

1. The Germanic tribes that invaded the Roman Empire had relatively simple governments. There were few government officials and taxes. Rulers depended on the loyalty of their warriors rather than on a government bureaucracy. Germanic laws were based on custom and designed to prevent warfare between families.

   Which of the following is the best title for this passage?

   A. How Germanic Tribes Governed
   B. Germanic Tribes and the Roman Empire
   C. The Invasion of the Roman Empire
   D. Loyalty Among the Germanic Tribes

2. The mechanization of the textile industry, the invention of the steam engine, and the development of the coal and iron industries contributed to Great Britain's lead in the Industrial Revolution. However, after 1850, other nations began to challenge Great Britain's lead. Belgium, France, and Germany all industrialized quickly. By 1900, natural resources and railroad building helped make the United States the leading industrial nation.

   Which of the following is the best summary of this passage?

   A. The development of natural resources made Great Britain the leader in the Industrial Revolution.
   B. The Industrial Revolution started in Great Britain and spread throughout the world.
   C. The Industrial Revolution started in Great Britain and spread to Europe, but by 1900 the United States was the leading industrialized nation.
   D. Plentiful natural resources and a vast railroad system were the underpinnings of the Industrial Revolution in the United States.

Questions 3 and 4 refer to the following map.

Early Civilizations in Africa

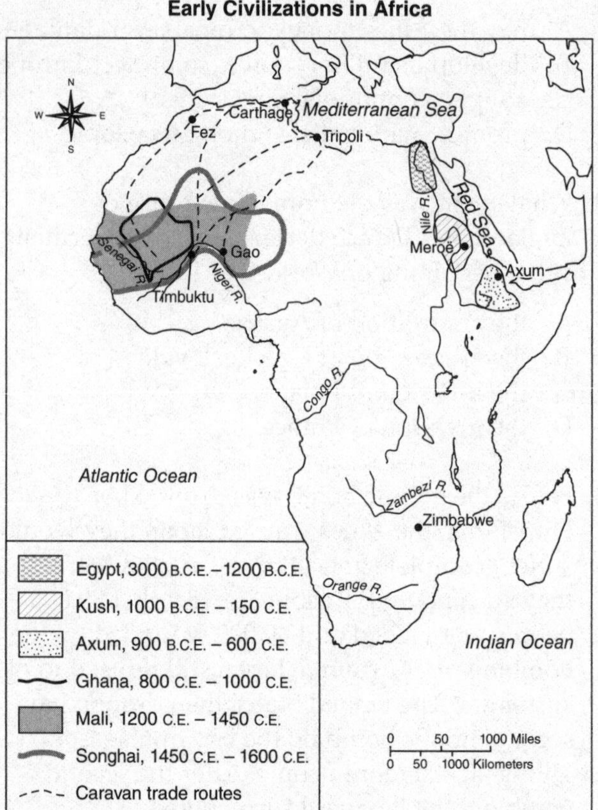

3. Which area on the map shows where the earliest civilizations in Africa developed?

   A. Egypt
   B. Kush
   C. Axum
   D. Mali

4. Which of the following statements is supported by information on the map?

   A. Over 800 years, several civilizations succeeded one another in western Africa.
   B. The Kingdom of Mali dominated western Africa for more than 500 years.
   C. Timbuktu was an important center of learning in Songhai.
   D. Gold and salt were transported along caravan trade routes in western Africa.

Questions 5 through 8 refer to the following timeline.

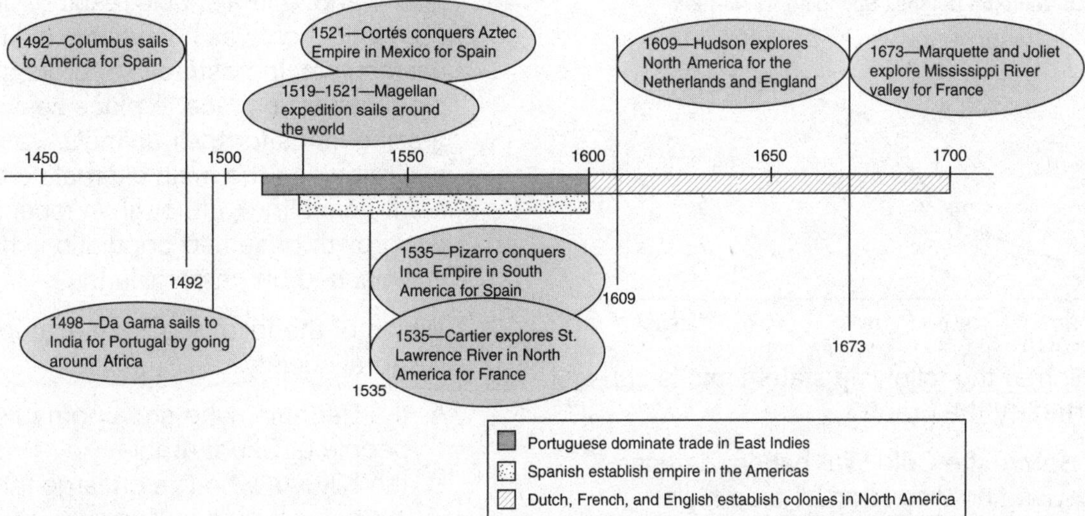

5. Portugal dominated trade in the East Indies for most of the 1500s. Which event from the timeline most likely first triggered Portugal's superiority in the region?

   A. 1492—Columbus sails to America for Spain
   B. 1498—Da Gama sails to India for Portugal by going around Africa
   C. 1519–1521—Magellan expedition sails around the world
   D. 1535—Pizarro conquers the Inca Empire in South America for Spain

6. Which of the following statements is supported by information on the timeline?

   A. Spanish and Portuguese domination of exploration gave way to that of the Dutch, French, and English.
   B. Henry Hudson discovered more places in North America than did Marquette and Joliet and Cartier.
   C. Both Cartier and Da Gama explored North America on behalf of France.
   D. French explorers cooperated with Native Americans in establishing trade.

7. Instead of financing expeditions themselves, the rulers of Spain allowed conquistadors to establish outposts in the Americas. The conquistador financed his own expedition, but if he succeeded, he was allowed to keep four-fifths of any treasure he found. Cortés was a conquistador who became rich by conquering the Aztecs in Mexico.

   ________ was also a conquistador.

   A. da Gama
   B. Pizarro
   C. Cartier
   D. Hudson

8. Which of the following is the best title for this timeline?

   A. The Spanish Explorers and Empire
   B. The Age of Exploration
   C. History of the 16th and 17th centuries
   D. European Colonies in the Americas

Question 9 refers to the following graph.

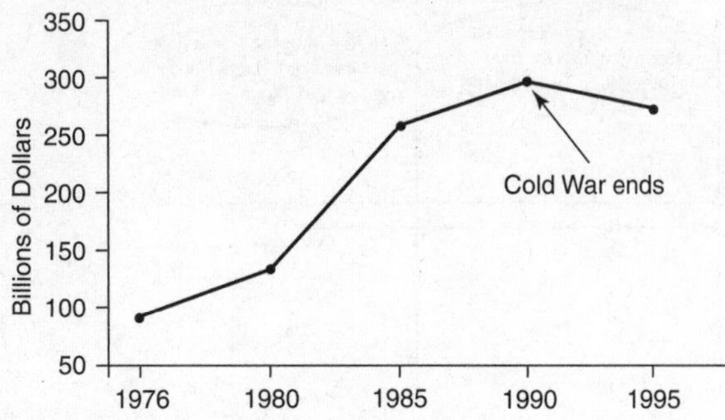

9. Which of the following statements is supported by the graph?

   A. Before the Cold War began, defense spending was at an all-time high.
   B. Defense spending remained steady throughout the Cold War.
   C. Defense spending declined steadily during the period 1976 to 1990.
   D. After the Cold War ended, defense spending began to fall.

10. When establishing colonies, European nations wanted their colonies to be economically self-sufficient. That meant that each colony paid for its government salaries and the cost of building and maintaining roads, railroads, and government buildings. To do this, European colonists or the colonial governments exported natural resources such as gold or copper or grew cash crops such as sugar or rubber.

    Which of the following statements is an opinion rather than a fact?

    A. European countries had similar goals in establishing their colonies.
    B. Colonies should be economically independent.
    C. European nations built railroads, roads, and government buildings in their colonies.
    D. Colonies provided natural resources that colonists could export.

11. During the Neolithic Age (about 8000 B.C.E. to 3500 B.C.E.), many societies domesticated plants and animals. One result of animal domestication was a new way of life called *pastoralism*. In pastoralism, groups of people move from place to place seeking new grazing lands for their animals. Pastoralism has remained the main alternative to settlement agriculture, although in recent times the growth of settled populations has encroached on pastoral lands.

    Which of the following is an example of a pastoral society?

    A. the Bedouin, who are a nomadic herding people of Saudi Arabia
    B. the Kikuyu, who live on large family farming homesteads in Kenya
    C. the Amish, who preserve traditional farming methods in the United States
    D. the Palestinian Arabs, many of whom live in refugee camps

12. During the Age of Imperialism (1870–1914), the nations of Europe and the United States dominated the political, economic, and cultural life of many countries in Africa, Asia, and Latin America.

    Which of the following is an example of imperialism?

    A. Communists under Mao Zedong won control of mainland China after World War II.
    B. Fifteen independent nations, of which Russia is the largest, were formed after the breakup of the Soviet Union.
    C. The United States gained influence over Panama through the building and running of the Panama Canal.
    D. After gaining independence from Great Britain, East Pakistan broke away from West Pakistan and formed the nation of Bangladesh.

Questions 13 and 14 refer to the following map.

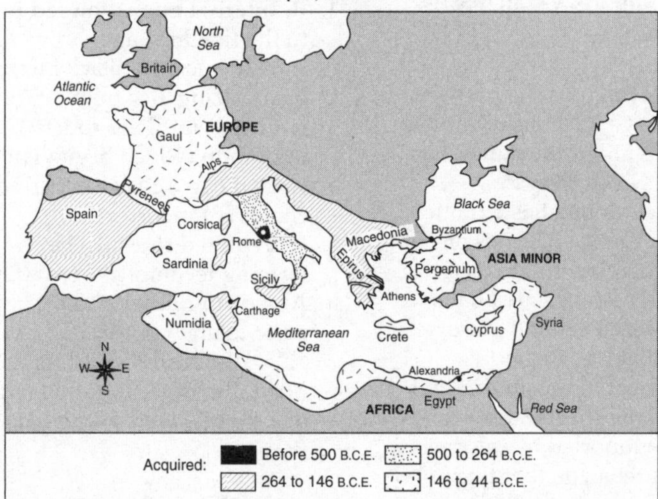

13. During which time period did the Roman Empire gain the most territory in Asia Minor?
    A. before 500 B.C.E.
    B. between 500 and 264 B.C.E.
    C. between 264 and 146 B.C.E.
    D. between 146 and 44 B.C.E.

14. Which of the following conclusions is supported by the information on the map?
    A. Before 264 B.C.E., Rome conquered through overland military campaigns; later conquests were made by navies as well.
    B. Numidia was added to the Roman Empire before the island of Sicily was.
    C. Corsica, Crete, and Cyprus were conquered by the Romans during the same military campaign.
    D. Hannibal marched from Carthage to Italy by way of Spain, crossing the Pyrenees into Gaul and the Alps into northern Italy.

Questions 15 and 16 refer to the following passage.

Society under Japanese feudalism had a class of warrior leaders, the *bushi*, at the top. Bushi possessed the responsibilities of enforcing laws, supervising the construction of public works, and collecting taxes. To assist them in the protection of their property, they built up their own armies of soldiers called *samurai*. The samurai lived by a code called *bushido*, which stressed absolute loyalty to one's lord. Bushido was followed by both men and women of the samurai class who, in addition to protecting their lord, were expected to protect the emperor. The code of bushido emphasized the preservation of family honor and willingness to face death rather than the acceptance of defeat or retreat. Because they were expected to provide the lord with military services, the samurai were released from agricultural responsibilities and were allowed a portion of the produce grown by peasants. The bushi and samurai depended on peasants to supply them with food while they devoted themselves to activities preparing them for war, such as archery and riding. Japanese peasants were placed in a subordinate position similar to that of serfs in medieval Europe. Unlike serfs, who were bound only to the land they worked, Japanese peasants were bound to both the land and their lord.

15. Aspects of the warrior's code of bushido resemble which of the following?
    A. the European ideal of chivalry
    B. the star player on a sports team
    C. neighborhood watch duty in a subdivision
    D. the death sentence

16. Agricultural responsibilities in feudal Japan fell to
    A. the bushi.
    B. the samurai.
    C. the peasants.
    D. the serfs.

Social Studies Answers and Explanations

Social Studies Skills

Lesson 1: Determine Central Idea and Draw Conclusions

Practice 1

1. **C. the characteristics of Greek tragedy** The passage describes tragedy as "central to Greek culture" and supports this point with details about the plots, staging, characters, and themes of Greek tragedy.
2. **D. The main character in Greek drama has a tragic flaw that causes his downfall.** Choice (D) cites one of the details the author uses to describe the characteristics of Greek tragedy. The other choices are all too broad (choice (A)) or misrepresent what the passage actually said (choices (B) and (C)).
3. **A. Ancient Greeks did not expect to see an original story each time they attended the theater.** Choice (A) is the only answer choice supported by information in the passage. The writer tells you that tragedies "told stories familiar from myths and epics," so it must have been the case that theatergoers knew the general story that would be acted out.
4. **D. Where do the incomes of senior citizens come from?** Choice (D) is correct because the graph tells you the sources of income for American senior citizens. The graph doesn't give any actual dollar amounts, nor does it state how many senior citizens there are in the U.S. You would need those numbers to answer the questions in choices (A), (B), and (C).
5. **B. Social Security benefits are the most widespread means of support for most senior citizens.** Each bar in the graph represents the percentage of all seniors who receive some of their income from that source. Since the Social Security bar is the tallest (representing more than 86% of all seniors), choice (B) must be true based on the graph.

Lesson 2: Interpret Words and Ideas

Practice 2

1. **C. political and social instability in some Northern European countries** In the first paragraph of the passage, the author mentions "riots, civil unrest, and open rebellion" as some of the factors that pushed German citizens to migrate. Those events are examples of "political and social instability," so choice (C) is correct.
2. **D. a painting of pioneers settling and farming productive prairie land** In the passage, the author discusses "abundance" in the second paragraph, giving examples of the kinds of optimistic messages that attracted people to the U.S. The image of pioneers opening up productive farmland is symbolic of the economic opportunity promised to 19th century immigrants to the U.S., so choice (D) is correct.
3. **C. a growth in the population of the United States** In the first paragraph, the author tells you that the number of immigrants arriving in the U.S. between 1820 and 1870 was greater than the entire U.S. population just 10 years before that time period. You can conclude from the passage that the U.S. population grew.
4. **B. Internal migration led to overgrazing.** According to the timeline, aggressive agriculture occurred prior to 1930 and the "black blizzards," caused in part by overgrazing, began in 1931. Internal migration did not begin until around 1933. Inferring that internal migration (which began later) caused overgrazing (which had already occurred) would be illogical, so choice (B) is correct.
5. **C. depleted topsoil** The "aggressive, mechanized farming techniques" that depleted the topsoil in the American Midwest and Southern plains occurred prior to and contributed to the dust storms and "black blizzards" that characterize the Great Dust Bowl. Internal migration (choice (B)) and failed farms (choice (C)) were results, not causes, of the Dust Bowl.

Lesson 3: Make Inferences

Practice 3

1. **B. did not trust the investigations of the FBI into this matter** The author of the *West Coast Tribune* editorial stated "there is no way of knowing where their loyalties lie." This contradicts the findings of the FBI, which has cleared each individual slated to return.
2. **D. the return of Japanese Americans** The tone of the *University Daily* editorial is positive; the author describes Japanese Americans as "without a doubt [. . .] loyal citizens." The text does not support choices (A) or (B), as the author is only addressing the release of certain internees and not the existence of the internment camps in general. While this writer expresses confidence in the FBI, no opinion is given about whether its power should be expanded.
3. **A. The public has a right to know about collaborative activity.** The author uses the reasoning that "[t]he public has not been fully informed" as support for the claim that Japanese Americans should not be released because of the danger they pose. The author's tone suggests that the public deserves to know about possible collaborative activity.
4. **B. only some women had the right to vote** The poster indicates that Colorado women already have the right to vote but that they can "get it for women of the nation." Answer choice (A) is the opposite of what the poster indicates.

Lesson 4: Form and Apply Valid Conclusions

Practice 4

1. **B. reducing crop surpluses through the farm subsidies** Roosevelt proposes "a national agricultural policy" that will rebuild rural American by supporting those who work with "products of the soil." Choice (B) is the only option that proposes a change to agricultural policy.
2. **C. opposed to legislative relief for farmers** The focus of the speech is on agricultural reforms that

will help the American farmer. The "enemy" therefore would be anyone who opposed this course of action. Choice (D) indicates the opposite.

3. **C. As long as separate segregated schools are provided, no constitutional rights are being denied.** Justice Brown states that "enforced separation" does not deny an individual equal protection. This "separate but equal" ruling in *Plessy v. Ferguson* is seen in choice (C). Choices (B) and (D) are the opposite of what Justice Brown implies (though Justice Harlan might agree), whereas choice (A) is untrue. The Supreme Court was ruling on the issue of segregation of public facilities in *Plessy v. Ferguson*, and if the Court did not have this power, the justices would not have written opinions in the case.
4. **D. Supreme Court rulings are not always unanimous** Justices Brown and Harlan present opposing views on the ruling of the case. This provides clear evidence for answer choice (D). Answer choices (A), (B), and (C) are not supported by the provided information.

Lesson 5: Analyze Author's Purpose and Point of View

Practice 5

1. **C. propagandistic** Page 526 explains that propaganda uses emotional language to influence readers' behavior. Here, asking the readers to "have a part in Victory" is just such language.
2. **C. Citizens who plant war gardens help supply the war effort with essential resources.** As the passage explains, war gardens were encouraged so that, with citizens supplying more of their own food, the government could use its limited resources to feed and equip soldiers, sailors, and airmen. Choice (C) paraphrases this nicely.
3. **A. describe war gardens and explain their popularity in the United States** The author's tone is neutral and explanatory; he or she simply wants to explain what war gardens were and why they were popular during the two world wars. The author is not advocating a point of view (choice (B)), trying to compare or contrast the U.S. with any other country (choice (C)), or arguing against anyone else's position (choice (D)).
4. **C. a cancer** By using a frightening and often fatal disease such as "cancer" to describe the impact of the proposed regulations, the citizen is making an emotional comparison. The analogy is especially aggressive given that the issue addresses health and safety.

Lesson 6: Evaluate Author's Reasoning and Evidence

Practice 6

1. **A. Damming the Mekong could solve Cambodia's energy problems.** The author argues for cooperation among Cambodia and its neighboring countries, all of which share the Mekong river. The reason this is important, the author asserts, is because hydroelectric power from the Mekong would help solve Cambodia's energy problems. Nowhere in the argument, however, does the author support this contention.
2. **B. Strikes have a detrimental impact on workers.** The cartoon shows a laborer using a strike as a means of "cutting off" production, depicted as a tree branch. The joke is that the worker sits on the wrong side of the branch he's cutting. Once the worker is successful in cutting off production, the cartoonist implies, he will fall to the ground along with production. Choice (B) neatly sums up the cartoonist's point.
3. **D. Ancient Greece pioneered democracy.** The one reason the author gives for believing that ancient Greece was the greatest of the early civilizations is that it was the birthplace of democracy. Thus, choice (D) is correct. Choice (A) is the author's opinion, not a fact supporting that opinion. Choices (B) and (C) are both reasons that ancient Babylon and Egypt (and not the author's favorite, Greece) might be considered great.
4. **B. The Constitution grants more power to the federal government than did the Articles of Confederation.** In each category compared in the chart, the federal government has more power under the Constitution than it had under the Articles of Confederation, so choice (B) is a valid inference, though it is not explicitly stated anywhere on the chart. All three wrong answers cite specific facts stated in the chart.

Lesson 7: Source Reliability

Practice 7

1. **D. is written from a more objective point of view** Source 2 describes the events of the first attempt of flight using a neutral, matter-of-fact tone. It does not contain only personal details (choice (A)), is not strongly biased (choice (B)), and does provide interpretation (choice (C)).
2. **B. true, because the author is analyzing an event after it has happened** Source 2 is a secondary source that interprets and analyzes the event described from a singular eyewitness perspective in Source 1. The author of Source 2 can describe the impact as defining when "the modern age of aviation was born" because this writer can see the event in the context of subsequent events.
3. **B. Source 1 contains a firsthand account of the first attempt at flight and source 2 provides an interpretation of why the first attempt was considered unsuccessful.** Source 1 contains Orville Wright's eyewitness description of the first attempt at flight, on December 14, 1903, and Source 2 interprets why that attempt was deemed unsuccessful, stating that they did "not consider it a successful flight, as the flying machine only made it less than a dozen feet off the ground." Both sources provide relevant, reliable information, so choice (A) is false. Although source 1 does contain personal thoughts, it does not provide any information on how it felt to fly (choice (C)).

4. **D. an instruction manual for pilots, published by the Federal Aviation Administration** An instruction manual for pilots may be a credible source to learn how to fly a plane or about the training of pilots, but it would not contain relevant information on the Wright brothers. The sources in choices (A), (B), and (C) are all credible for this purpose.

Lesson 8: Analyze Relationships Between Materials

Practice 8.1

1. **A. housing and food** Study the circle graph (pie chart) to see that the two largest portions are labeled with white (33%) and vertical lines (20%). Checking the legend to the right shows that these "slices" correspond to housing and food, respectively.
2. **D. Brazil has a higher divorce rate than Mexico.** This bar chart directly supports choice (D): Brazil's divorce rate is 0.6 per thousand, while Mexico's is 0.4 per thousand. Choice (B) is incorrect because this chart shows five countries in the Western Hemisphere, not all of them. One of the countries not shown on the chart may have a divorce rate even lower than Mexico's. Choice (C) is incorrect because this chart conveys nothing about how divorce rates have changed over time.
3. **D. fluctuated** As you read the line graph left to right, showing the change over time, you see that percentage of votes for third-party presidential candidates went up and down multiple times, so "fluctuated" is accurate.
4. **C. Third-party candidates have never captured more than 10 percent of the popular vote in any presidential election.** The statement in choice (C) is disproved by 1968 (14 percent) and 1992 (more than 19 percent).
5. **C. how agriculture spread in the Americas** The map shows two places at which agriculture originated independently (indicated by black stars) and where agriculture spread out from those two points (indicated by the white arrows). The map shows no political boundaries (choice (A)) or physical features (choice (B)) of the Americas, nor does it claim to name all of the ancient civilizations on the two continents (choice (D)).
6. **B. Both the Andes civilization and Mesoamerica domesticated beans.** Check right below the names of the two civilizations named on the map and you'll find the crops they learned to grow. "Beans" is the only crop listed for both the Andes and Mesoamerican groups.

Practice 8.2

1. **D. Sea otters have been able to live in habitats from which they were once eliminated.** Choice (D) is directly supported by the third paragraph of the passage, which refers to successful "programs to reintroduce the sea otter into previously populated areas." Choice (C) is incorrect because the passage does not indicate that they have reached one-fourth of their former population numbers. Choices (A) and (B) are not mentioned at all in the passage.
2. **D. The current range of the sea otter in California is larger than what it was in 1911.** According to the passage, the sea otter's range in 1911 "was limited . . . to about 50 living in a small area between Big Sur and Monterey Bay." The map makes it clear that the sea otter's range now extends significantly to both the north and south of Monterey Bay. Putting the information from the passage together with that from the map shows that choice (D) must be true.
3. **C. Without conservation efforts and reintroduction programs, the range of sea otters in California would be smaller than what is shown on the map.** In the third paragraph of the passage, the author states that conservation and reintroduction programs "have contributed to" the expansion of the sea otter's habitat range in California. This directly supports the statement in choice (C).

Lesson 9: Interpret Data and Statistics

Practice 9

1. **C. What percent of residents were 50 or over?** To calculate the percentage of New Mexico residents age 50 and over, you first find the number of residents 50 and over and divide that by the total number of residents. You can find the total number of residents who are at least age 50 by adding the categories for 50–64 and 65 & over. You are given the total number of residents so you can solve for this question. Because age brackets are grouped and exact ages aren't given, it is not possible to solve for choice (A). You cannot solve for choice (B) because the bracket "under 18" contains teenagers and nonteenagers with no distinction between the two. The chart gives no reasoning, only numerical information, so choice (D) is also incorrect.
2. **B. the average margin of victory was higher in years when a Democrat won than in years when a Republican won.** In both years in which a Republican won the presidential election (2000 and 2004) the final electoral vote count was very close. In each of the four years in which a Democrat won (1992, 1996, 2008, and 2012) the Democratic candidate captured a much larger portion of the electoral vote. Thus, choice (B) is supported by the graph.
3. **C. 1920** Of the years shown on the graph, 1920 is the point when the rural and urban populations are closest in number. Prior to 1920, the rural population was much larger than the urban population. After 1920, the urban population begins to be much larger than the rural population.
4. **C. continued to grow, but at decreasing rates** The rural population continued to increase during every decade shown in the graph. However, the increase in

population growth was less in the later decades than in the earlier decades, as evidenced by the smaller differences between the heights of the bars in the later decades than the earlier ones.

Social Studies Skills Practice Questions

1. **B. The unemployment rate declined consistently until shortly before the war's end.** Checking the timeline, you can see that World War II began in 1939 and ended in 1945. Unemployment went down every year between 1939 and 1944, and rose just slightly in 1945. Thus, choice (B)'s description of the war's impact on unemployment is correct.
2. **A. the stock market crash** Immediately after the stock market crash in 1929, unemployment increases dramatically and directly until 1933. That makes choice (A) correct. After 1933, unemployment declines gradually until the end of the war, and the decline is interrupted by a small increase during 1937–1938.
3. **D. The Seneca Falls Convention was a shocking event that undermined the nature of women.** There is no objective way to prove that something is "shocking and unnatural." Those words reveal that the statement in choice (D) was the opinion of one newspaper's editors.
4. **D. The Seneca Falls Convention was important in the fight for women's rights.** The passage's primary purpose is to explain how the women's movement "gained strength" at the Seneca Falls Convention.
5. **A. More than half of the reported cases of human plague in the United States between 1970 and 2010 were reported in four states.** Even if you don't recognize the four states in question as Arizona, California, Colorado, and New Mexico, the map clearly shows the overwhelming concentration of reported plague cases as occurring there. Choice (A) is justified by the information in the map.
6. **C. Several cases of plague were reported on the East Coast of the United States between 1970 and 2010.** The statement in choice (C) is clearly false given the information in the map. No cases of plague were recorded east of Illinois during the time period depicted by the map.
7. **D. The effects of the cotton gin on the cotton industry actually led to an increased demand for slaves in the South.** The fact stated in choice (D) is directly supported by the end of the passage where the writer explains the effects of the cotton gin: "with the boom in the cotton industry, more slaves were used to pick cotton at a faster rate."
8. **C. In most years, the percent population increase in South Dakota was greater than that in North Dakota.** Choice (C) is correct. In seven of the eleven years shown (every year from 2001–2002 to 2007–2008), South Dakota's annual population increase was greater than that of North Dakota. The increases were approximately equal in 2008–2009, and North Dakota's increase was greater in the remaining three years. Choices (A) and (B) make statements about the populations of these states, but the graph only contains information about *percent increase,* or proportional increase, of the population.
9. **D. A smaller percentage of voters turned out for each midterm election than turned out for each presidential election.** The entire midterm election line graph falls below the line graph for the presidential elections, meaning that in each instance, the percentage of voters who turned out for the midterm election was smaller than the percentage that turned out for the presidential election.
10. **B. The average voter turnout for midterm elections was approximately how much lower than that for presidential elections for the years 1980–2008?** You can find the average voter turnout for each type of election by taking the average of each line graph. Dividing the average voter turnout for midterm elections by the average voter turnout for presidential elections and multiplying by 100 will answer the question in choice (B). The remaining answer choices all ask for the reasoning behind a given circumstance, and no rationale for the numbers can be determined using only the numbers themselves.
11. **C. Most of our qualified teachers are underpaid.** Choice (C) is a value judgment. A fact is a statement that can be proven or disproven by direct experience or objective verification. An opinion is a statement of belief or judgment. President Johnson uses both facts and opinions to support his contention that there is a crisis in education, including statistical facts (choices (A), (B), and (D)) and the value judgment that teachers should be paid more.
12. **D. "Our Duty Is to Educate Our Children"** The excerpt is about the importance of educating every child in the country. It does not give a history of education, as stated in choice (A), nor does it mention the specifics of education in Michigan, as stated in choice (B). While the cost of college education is briefly mentioned in the second paragraph, it is simply a detail, not the main topic of the passage, so choice (C) is incorrect.
13. **C. The Union states had significant population advantages in the war.** It is clear that in all three graphs, the Confederate states were at a population disadvantage in comparison to the North at the start of the Civil War.
14. **B. What percentage of the total population of the United States was eligible for the military?** The percentage of the total population eligible for the military can be found by obtaining the total population and the total population eligible for the military. Both can be found by using the charts. There is no information given about the total number of people that actually fought in the military, so answer choice (A) cannot be determined. Choices (C) and (D) both ask for reasoning behind something, which cannot be determined from the numbers alone.

U.S. History

Lesson 1: Exploration, Colonialism, and the American Revolution

Practice 1

1. **C. the Spanish** According to the map and the key, Spain had the southernmost colony along the east coast of what would eventually become the United States.
2. **B. The English established several colonies in the New World.** The map shows several English colonies along the New England coast and in what is now Virginia and Maryland.
3. **D. Haitian refugees who fled to the U.S. to escape a dictatorship** Like the early colonists, the Haitian refugees of the mid- and late 1900s came to the United States seeking freedom from political persecution.
4. **B. increased British taxes and restrictions on the colonies** The fourth and fifth sentences of paragraph 4 link increased taxes and restrictions to the outbreak of the American Revolution.
5. **B. They were concerned about the government becoming tyrannical.** The first amendment guarantees citizens' rights to pressure their government. The passage explains that the framers of the U.S. Constitution did not want the government to become overly powerful. While choices (A) and (C) were both rights listed amongst the guarantees of the First Amendment, they do not explain *why* the framers listed them. Choice (B) discusses their motivations and is correct.

Lesson 2: Westward Expansion, the Civil War, and Reconstruction

Practice 2

1. **D. whether slavery should be permitted in territories in the West** This is implied in the third and fourth paragraphs of the passage. Choice (B) is incorrect because the fourth paragraph says that Abraham Lincoln promised to halt the spread of slavery, not to end it where it already existed.
2. **C. To balance the admission of Missouri, they agreed to a compromise in which Maine was admitted as a free state.** The third paragraph of the passage describes how the U.S. government tried to maintain a balance of power between the North and the South by adding states in pairs: one slave state and one free state. Since Missouri was a slave state, the most likely response of Northerners would be to propose the addition of a free state. (Indeed, Maine and Missouri were the 23rd and 24th states to join the United States.)
3. **D. concluded with the reunification of the nation** The information in the question indicates that North and South Vietnam were reunited under the Communists at the end of the Vietnam War. The passage implies that at the end of the U.S. Civil War, the North and the South again were united under the United States federal government.
4. **C. In 1868, many African Americans served in the government of South Carolina.** There are more than 20 African Americans included in this composite photograph of the South Carolina legislature. The other choices are opinions that cannot be confirmed by the photograph.
5. **A. Over the course of Reconstruction, African Americans in the South gained and then lost political power.** The number of African Americans in the composite photograph of the South Carolina state legislature of 1868 indicates that near the beginning of the Reconstruction period, African Americans had considerable political power. The last paragraph of the passage on page 544 states that by the 1870s, whites were preventing African Americans from exercising their newly won right to vote. This indicates that African Americans were losing political power as Reconstruction ended.

Lesson 3: Industrialization, Immigration, and the Progressive Era

Practice 3

1. **B. an increase in manufacturing** By definition, industrialization is related to increased manufacturing. This meaning is implied in the passage in paragraphs one and two.
2. **C. the development of the Bessemer process, which made it easier to produce steel** The first paragraph of the passage relates rapid industrialization to the invention of new industrial processes. The Bessemer process was one such process. It made steel more readily available for tools, railroads, construction, and other uses.
3. **C. cooperation with others to improve worker safety** The fourth paragraph indicates that union workers pledged to work together (cooperate) for better working conditions. The passage states that better working conditions include improved worker safety.
4. **D. fairness** The fifth paragraph discusses the Progressive Era. The fact that reformers were working to improve conditions for poor people and to give people a greater voice in government indicates that fairness was a strong ideal for them.
5. **B. Asia and the Americas** The second circle graph indicates that, in the years 2000–2009, 77 percent of persons obtaining legal resident status came from Asia and the Americas.
6. **C. The student failed to consider the different totals represented by each pie chart.** When comparing percentages that are based on two different totals, the percentages cannot be directly compared.

Lesson 4: The United States as an Emerging World Power

Practice 4

1. **D. military** The building of a naval base indicates that the correct category is "military."
2. **B. In World War II, the Allies included England, France, and Russia.** The author assumes that you

realize that the Allies of World War II included the same major powers as the Allies in World War I. If you do not recognize this unstated assumption, you will not understand who fought whom in World War II.

3. **C. Unemployment fell after the start of the New Deal and continued to fall as the U.S. entered World War II.** The graph shows a decline in the unemployment rate after the New Deal went into effect in 1934. It shows that unemployment went up in 1938 but then dropped after that and dropped considerably after the U.S. entry into World War II in 1941.
4. **D. America took a strong leadership role during and after World War II.** The paragraph focuses on the role the United States played during and after World War II. The other choices are details from the paragraph or they bring up information not included in the paragraph.

Lesson 5: The Cold War and the Civil Rights Era

Practice 5

1. **D. no direct combat** The first paragraph of the passage implies that the name "Cold War" was used because there was no direct fighting.
2. **C. The buildup of nuclear arms increases fear and instability, not peace.** The statement about peace and stability made by the man on the right in the bottom frame of the cartoon is supposed to be ironic. The cartoonist's mention of the man's trembling arms suggests that the situation is not stable, and that perhaps we should be afraid.
3. **C. Americans were in complete agreement about pulling out of Vietnam.** Paragraph one states that even when defeat for South Vietnam seemed fairly certain, a few Americans still wanted to continue contributing to the fighting. Therefore, it is an overstatement to say that Americans were in complete agreement that pulling out of Vietnam was the right thing to do.
4. **B. petitioning for a city ordinance requiring those selling real estate to select a buyer without regard to race** Paragraph three states that the aim of the civil rights movement was to end segregation and discrimination in the United States. Preventing the selective selling of real estate was one important way civil rights activists worked to end discrimination, making decreased segregation possible.
5. **A. Reliance on technology has increased pollution.** This is a conclusion—a general statement about a topic. The other choices are details—facts or examples—that support this conclusion.

U.S. History Practice Questions

1. **B. Although the Cherokee adopted many aspects of white culture, they were driven off their ancestral lands.** This statement is the only one with a large enough scope to be considered a conclusion. The other choices are details that are either included in, related to, or not based on the timeline.
2. **A. If the government can't protect us from white settlers here, now, how could it protect us from whites moving west in the future?** This question shows the lack of logic in the government's claim that location was what made it difficult to protect Cherokee rights. Location had nothing to do with the government's lack of protection of Cherokee land in the South. The government did not have the political will to enforce laws protecting the Cherokee.
3. **D. equal rights and opportunities for women** Adams's statements that women are not inferior and her invention of the term *Lordess* both indicate that she advocated equality for women.
4. **A. West Virginia** The map shows that West Virginia was a slave state loyal to the Union.
5. **A. The nation's capital was located nearby.** If the nation's capital, located adjacent to the state of Maryland, had been surrounded by Confederate states, it would have been extremely difficult for the U.S. army to defend it. This would have given a great edge to the Confederacy during the Civil War. The other choices are untrue, irrelevant, or not verifiable by the map.
6. **D. to weaken the South by enlisting former slaves in the Union army** This was implied by the text of the Proclamation that is quoted. None of the other choices are supported by the text.
7. **C. Voting Rights Act of 1965** The chart explains that this act prohibited literacy (reading) tests for voting.
8. **C. African Americans were granted the vote soon after the Civil War, but laws enforcing these rights had to be passed a century later.** This is implied by the passage of the 15th Amendment in 1870 and by the passage of the Voting Rights Act of 1965. Congress would not have passed the later law if the 15th Amendment were being upheld and enforced. Choice (A) is true, based on the chart, but is not a summary of the information in the chart.
9. **B. They both prohibited the legal separation of people by race in public places.** The chart shows that both the 1875 and the 1964 Civil Rights Acts banned racial segregation in public places.
10. **D. The telephone was the greatest electrical invention ever.** This statement is said to have been made by leading scientists of the time; this is not in the author's voice. It is the only opinion. Choices (A), (B), and (C) are all facts stated in the passage.
11. **B. the framers of the U.S. Constitution** The clothes of the men in the picture indicate that this cartoon is set in the late 1700s. Impeachment is discussed in the caption. Impeachment was a provision that the framers of the Constitution included in order to prevent the kind of abuse of presidential power carried out by Nixon. Impeachment of elected officials was not discussed in the Declaration of Independence, which laid out the reasons for the United States' independence from Great Britain, so choice (A) is incorrect.
12. **A. the pursuit of justice** By investigating the circumstances of Watergate, Congress was trying to make sure that the nation's laws were carried out.

13. **C. the escalation and failure of the Vietnam War** Of the choices listed, only (C) describes an event just prior to the Watergate scandal. The bloodshed and failure of the Vietnam War caused many people to question authority, including the government, and to question decisions made by the government.
14. **C. 1,000,000** The scale on the vertical axis of the bar graph shows that population is measured in millions. The bar for Cuba stands one unit high. This means that about 1,000,000 people of Cuban descent lived in the U.S. in 1990.
15. **B. Mexico** The bar graph shows that most people in the U.S. who are Hispanic originally came from Mexico. Therefore, Mexico is the most likely nation of origin of the unknown family.

Civics and Government

Lesson 1: Historic Basis for U.S. System

Practice 1

1. **D. aristocracy** In an aristocracy, the laws are made by members of the ruling class, who acquire their land, titles, and power through inheritance.
2. **B. They were concerned about protecting the rights of individuals.** According to the passage on the previous page, the Founding Fathers were influenced by the Enlightenment philosophers, who did place importance on the rights of the individual.
3. **C. Parliament of England** Similar to the United States Congress, the parliamentary system in England allows for citizens to elect representatives to a lawmaking body.
4. **D. England during the Age of Enlightenment** According to the passage on page 556, England adopted a bill of rights for the individual during the Enlightenment. This action limited the monarchy's power over the individual.
5. **D. The president would become the chief lawmaker.** In a parliamentary democracy, the majority party in the Parliament appoints the president. Since the Parliament is the lawmaking body of government, the President would become the chief lawmaker. Nothing in the text indicates whether this would make the office of the president more or less powerful than it currently is, so choices (A) and (B) are unsupported.

Lesson 2: Constitutional Government

Practice 2

1. **B. elected representatives exercising government power on behalf of citizens** According to the first paragraph of the passage, the key characteristic of a republic is elected officials governing for the voters.
2. **C. The details of government would be worked out in the future, as the need arose, within the framework of the Constitution.** The leaders who drafted the Constitution were wise enough to realize that they could not anticipate every eventuality, so instead of trying to cover everything in the Constitution, they made it a general framework within which specific future decisions and laws could be made.
3. **C. the power of an office, not an individual** Roosevelt's long tenure worried many people as they saw his power growing with time. They pursued term limits to prevent any individual from amassing too much power as president.
4. **D. The U.S. Supreme Court declaring an Illinois state law unconstitutional** The supremacy clause asserts the supremacy of federal law when it conflicts with state law. Therefore, the declaration that a state law is unconstitutional is an exercise of the supremacy clause.
5. **A. State governments do not usually act together.** The third and fourth methods of passing a constitutional amendment both require concerted action by state governments. Therefore, choice (A) would explain why those methods have never been used. Choices (B) and (D) are contradicted by information in the chart. Choice (C) repeats information in the chart, but does not provide a useful explanation.

Lesson 3: Levels and Branches of Government

Practice 3

1. **A. division of power between national and state governments** According to the second paragraph of the passage on page 560, a federalist form of government divides power between the national and state levels of government.
2. **D. the State Department** The State Department is part of the executive branch; its head is a member of the president's cabinet. The Democratic National Committee, choice (A), is not part of the government at all. Choice (B) is part of Congress, and therefore part of the legislative branch. Courts, choice (C), are in the judicial branch.
3. **A. Federal judges need not worry about pleasing their constituents in order to be reelected.** Because they do not need to please any constituents in order to be reelected, federal judges can preside without worrying about making unpopular decisions. This leaves them freer to be impartial judges of the law.
4. **B. six; two** A senator is a legislator who serves a six-year term. A representative is a legislator who serves a two-year term.
5. **B. a member of Congress** Although this person subscribes to the idea that the government is divided into three branches, he can only think of one of them—the one to which he belongs. Since he is probably in the legislative branch, he is likely to be a member of Congress. The way the desks are arranged and the way the man is standing to make his point are visual cues that the setting of the cartoon is Congress.

Lesson 4: The Electoral System

Practice 4

1. **C. receiving a majority in the Electoral College** According to the second paragraph of the passage on page 562, a president must have a majority in the Electoral College to be elected.
2. **A. Exit polls may be inaccurate if the people polled are not representative of the political unit as a whole or if the election is very close.** It is more likely that a poll will be wrong if an unrepresentative sample is used or if the election is very close. Under those circumstances, it is hazardous to call an election based on exit poll results, as was shown in the 2000 presidential election, in which the media gave Florida's vote first to Gore, then to Bush, and only hours later declared the state too close to call.
3. **D. Two city council members are on a ballot to determine which one will run for mayor as a Democrat.** A primary is an election to choose among candidates of the same party. The winner of the primary then faces an opponent of another political party in the general election.
4. **B. In total, individuals contributed a greater dollar amount to House candidates than they did to Senate candidates.** Although Senatorial candidates received a higher percentage (greater by 4%) of their contributions from individual donors, the total dollar amount received by the House candidates was much higher (greater by approximately $350,000,000). Therefore, the total dollar amount of individual contributions received by the House candidates was ultimately greater than that received by the Senate candidates.
5. **A. In 2010, self-funding was a larger source of funds for Senate candidates than it was for House candidates.** The Senate candidates' own contributions accounted for 13% of the total Senate Candidates' Funds while the House Candidates' own contributions accounted for only 6% of the total House Candidates' Fund. In addition, calculations based on the total amount of funds reveal that Senate candidates spent more total dollars on self-funding than did House candidates.

Lesson 5: The Role of the Citizen

Practice 5

1. **B. The U.S. Constitution** According to the third paragraph of the passage, the Constitution sets forth the rights of citizens.
2. **A. immigrant** Because she moved here permanently as the wife of an American citizen, Louvina is an immigrant and will remain so until she qualifies for citizenship through naturalization.
3. **C. They would become enemy aliens.** If the country of aliens residing in the United States declares war on the United States, that nation becomes an enemy state, and the aliens become enemy aliens.
4. **B. privacy** The protection against unreasonable search and seizure is essentially a protection of citizens' privacy rights. The government must demonstrate a good reason before it is allowed to search or seize property.
5. **C. If the 2012 presidential election is representative of elections generally in the United States, voter turnout increases with age.** This is the only statement general enough to be a conclusion. All the other options are details from the graph that support this conclusion.

Civics and Government Practice Questions

1. **B. In 2013, a different major party controlled the House than controlled the Senate.** According to the numbers of the 113th Congress, the Republicans had majority control in the House and the Democrats had majority control in the Senate. Choice (A) is too broad to be a summary of this chart, which focuses on political divisions. The conclusions in choices (C) and (D) require more information than the chart provides.
2. **B. Bill of Rights of the U.S. Constitution, which guarantees citizens certain rights,** Like the Magna Carta, the Bill of Rights of the U.S. Constitution accords citizens certain rights and protections. Note that the scope of the Bill of Rights is broader in that it protects the rights of all citizens, not just a special group, as the Magna Carta did.
3. **C. a $3,000 contribution to a party fund for TV ads on political issues** Of all the choices, this is the only donation that is going to a political party fund rather than to a specific candidate, so it is a "soft money" contribution.
4. **A. People were less aware of soft money because disclosure was not required.** During the 1980s, political parties did not have to reveal the amount and sources of their soft money contributions, so the extent of this type of campaign financing was not generally known. Only when a law was passed requiring disclosure did people become aware of the scale of soft money donations and so began to raise their concerns about the issue.
5. **C. Jill Stein won a greater percentage of the popular vote than of the electoral vote in 2012.** Jill Stein won 0.36% of the popular vote, but she did not win any electoral votes in the 2012 election.
6. **D. 2012 Presidential Election: Popular and Electoral Votes** This is the only option that covers the topic of the paragraph as well as that of the graphs.
7. **A. The board of election is the county, city, or town office responsible for local voting.** Nowhere in this excerpt from the voter's guide is the board of election defined or explained; the writer assumes that the reader knows what it is.
8. **B. The National Association of Manufacturers, which lobbies for businesses** This is the only answer choice that contains a group with common interests and goals that works to influence government policies. The other choices are either political parties or part of the executive branch.

9. **B. Most registered voters don't vote.** Despite the fact that voting is one of the obligations of citizens, in most elections, less than half of the nation's registered voters actually vote.
10. **C. civic duty** The cartoonist is appealing to voters to take their civic duty to vote more seriously.
11. **A. China, where the top leaders of the Communist party control the government** Of the national governments described, only China is an oligarchy, a government with rule by a small group of people. The other options are not oligarchies; they are either democracies or autocracies.
12. **A. retribution** These laws all embody the urge to take revenge on wrongdoers, or to exact retribution. The other principles underlie the modern criminal justice system and other modern legal systems.
13. **C. 32** Look for the map key to determine the symbol for death penalty states. According to the map, 18 states do not have the death penalty, so 32 out of 50 states have the death penalty.
14. **D. Two of the five states with the lowest per capita homicide rates have abolished the death penalty.** If that argument were correct, then the states with the lowest homicide rates should all be death penalty states, but that is not the case. Two states—Vermont and Hawaii—that have homicide rates among the lowest in the nation do not have the death penalty.
15. **C. The 1978 Panama treaties sold out U.S. interests to Panama.** Choice (C) states an opinion about the Panama treaties, not a fact that can be tested or proved. The word in the passage that signals an opinion is "believed."
16. **D. The mayor has ceremonial duties.** In both the mayor-council and the council-manager forms of city government, at least part of the time, the mayor plays a ceremonial role.

World History

Lesson 1: Early Civilizations

Practice 1

1. **B. the Maya** According to the passage, the Maya recorded their discoveries about mathematics and astronomy in a pictographic writing system.
2. **B. Ancient Greece and Ancient Rome** As stated in the passage, the Greek idea of democracy, in which citizens voted, and the representative government and laws of ancient Rome were great influences on the founders of the United States.
3. **A. Both developed flood control and irrigation technologies to boost food production.** Both ancient Egypt and the civilizations of the Fertile Crescent grew up along rivers. The passage points out that in both areas, people learned to control floods and irrigate fields in order to improve food production.
4. **B. towns** The food surpluses that result from agriculture mean that not everyone must grow or gather their own food. Therefore, some people are free to live in towns where they can pursue a craft or business in exchange for food from farmers. The other options occur without the gathering together of people in settlements.
5. **D. ancient Egypt** Ancient China developed along a great river, the Yellow River. Of the civilizations listed, only ancient Egypt also grew up along a river, the Nile. In both ancient China and ancient Egypt, the river kept the soil rich and damp.
6. **C. The Yellow River was probably the main trade route between Loyang and Chengchow.** Not only were rivers the source of water for irrigation, they were major thoroughfares for the transport of goods. Since both cities are on the Yellow River, trade between them most likely took place by river at that time.

Lesson 2: Feudalism to Nation States

Practice 2

1. **C. to protect their noble's land from attack** According to the passage, the role of the knights in feudal society was to protect their noble's estate, or land.
2. **A. Spain** Of the lands mentioned in the passage that were conquered by the Muslims, only Spain is in Europe. Thus, of the European nations marked for selection in the map, Spain is the one in which you would most expect to find evidence of Muslim culture.
3. **B. the migration of people from farms to industrial cities in the 1800s** Like the migration to the cities in the 1800s, the migration from manors to towns in the late Middle Ages resulted from economic causes. In both migrations, people were seeking better economic opportunities than farming offered.
4. **A. Roman Catholics accepted the authority of the pope and Protestants did not.** According to the passage, this was one of the main differences between the two branches of Christianity.
5. **A. accepted legal principles** Since the manor court did not rely on a written body of legal rulings, its actions were unpredictable. Most people felt they would get a fairer ruling in the royal courts, which were bound by written common law that applied to everyone in the kingdom.
6. **C. The population of western Europe showed almost constant growth with only brief periods of decline.** This is the best summary because it contains the main idea (Europe's population rose from 500 to 1500) and important details (two brief periods of decline).

Lesson 3: Exploration and Colonialism

Practice 3

1. **D. leading the first expedition to result in an around-the-world voyage** The passage states that, although Magellan himself did not circumnavigate the globe, one of his ships did. The crew members of that ship are believed to be the first people to sail completely around the world.

2. **C. to gain economic benefits** According to the second paragraph of the passage, the main goal of European colonization was economic gain.
3. **B. Malaya, where the British set up and ran rubber plantations worked by the native peoples** Of all the options, only Malaya was a colony of economic exploitation rather than of settlement.
4. **C. war and disease** The second paragraph of the passage indicates that war and disease, more than economic exploitation, were primary causes of the population decline among native colonized peoples.
5. **B. The Dutch had the smallest claim in the Americas in 1700.** The map shows that by 1700, the Dutch had only a small claim on the northern coast of South America, and the other nations had much larger claims.

Lesson 4: The Age of Revolutions

Practice 4

1. **C. the U.S. Declaration of Independence** According to the passage, the American Revolution and its goals of democracy (as expressed in the Declaration of Independence and the Constitution) were big influences on the French.
2. **D. Members of the Third Estate owned the least amount of land per person.** With 98 percent of the population but only 70 percent of the land, the Third Estate owned the least land in proportion to its numbers. Members of the First and Second Estates owned more land in proportion to their percentage of the population.
3. **B. England had a Parliament; while France did not have a parliament** This contrast is stated in the third paragraph of the passage. It is one of the reasons French citizens were dissatisfied with their lack of representation in the monarchy of Louis XVI.
4. **C. possessing large landholdings** The last paragraph of the passage on page 576 states that farmland had been the economic mainstay of the aristocracy up until the time of the Industrial Revolution, which began late in the eighteenth century.
5. **B. A sovereign nation is independent, having the power to govern itself.** In the passage, the word *sovereign* is used but not explained; the author takes for granted you know what it means. The remaining options are all stated in the passage.
6. **D. the Industrial Revolution** Like the Industrial Revolution, the Information Revolution is an economic revolution that has brought about social change. The other revolutions are all political in nature.

Lesson 5: The Twentieth Century

Practice 5

1. **A. pay the Allies money to repair war damages** According to the passage, paying reparations was one of the provisions of the Treaty of Versailles.
2. **C. the invasion of Poland** The third paragraph of the passage indicates that to avoid going to war, the Allies permitted Germany to take over, or annex, Austria and Czechoslovakia. However, Germany's invasion of Poland spurred England and France to declare war.
3. **B. national pride** The Japanese had a great deal of national pride, which they found difficult to put aside. Thus, it took the destruction of two cities and thousands of deaths to overcome their reluctance to surrender.
4. **D. Both were won by the Allies.** Of the options listed, the fact that the Allies won both wars is the only similarity. Choices (B) and (C) are true only of World War II, and choice (A) is not true: both wars involved other parts of the world.
5. **B. The United States sustained only a few civilian casualties.** The chart indicates "very few" civilian dead in the United States; every other cell in the chart has a number in the thousands or millions.
6. **A. the 1812 French invasion of Russia, which failed due to harsh weather and lack of supplies** Both the French and German invasions failed due to weather and lack of supplies, making them similar. The campaigns and actions mentioned in the other answer choices failed for different or unspecified reasons.

World History Practice Questions

1. **A. How Germanic Tribes Governed** The focus of the passage is the minimal governmental structure of the Germanic tribes.
2. **C. The Industrial Revolution started in Great Britain and spread to Europe, but by 1900 the United States was the leading industrialized nation.** This summary statement has all the major details from the paragraph—the start of the Industrial Revolution in Great Britain, its spread to Europe, and the lead taken by the United States. The other choices either focus too narrowly on a couple of details or are too broad to be an effective summary.
3. **A. Egypt** The map key gives the dates of each civilization shown on the map. Egypt, Kush, and Axum were the earliest civilizations. They are all located along the Nile River in the northeast part of Africa.
4. **A. Over 800 years, several civilizations succeeded one another in western Africa.** The civilizations of Ghana, Mali, and Songhai developed one after the other in the same region of Africa. None of the other choices is supported by information on the map.
5. **B. 1498—Da Gama sails to India for Portugal by going around Africa.** Da Gama's voyage opened up new trading opportunities for the Portuguese. Note from the timeline that the Portuguese dominated trade in the East Indies from about 1510 to 1600.
6. **A. Spanish and Portuguese domination of exploration gave way to that of the Dutch, French, and English.** According to the timeline, most Spanish and Portuguese exploration and conquest took place during the 1500s. From the 1600s on, other nations such as England, France, and the Netherlands

increased their activity considerably. The other choices are incorrect or cannot be determined from the information in the timeline.

7. **B. Pizarro** Like Cortés, Pizarro explored on behalf of the Spanish rulers. He conquered the Inca Empire in South America.
8. **B. The Age of Exploration** This title describes the era and events shown. The other choices are too narrow, too broad, or simply incorrect.
9. **D. After the Cold War ended, defense spending began to fall.** The graph shows defense spending decreasing in the period 1990–1995, after the Cold War ended in 1990. None of the other choices is supported by data on the graph.
10. **B. Colonies should be economically independent.** Of all the choices, only this one is an opinion. The other choices are facts that are stated in the paragraph.
11. **A. the Bedouin, who are a nomadic herding people of Saudi Arabia** The Bedouin follow a pastoral lifestyle, moving their herds of animals and temporary settlements from place to place in search of good grazing.
12. **C. The United States gained influence over Panama through the building and running of the Panama Canal.** Among the choices, this is the only example of imperialism—the takeover of aspects of one nation by another. The other options involve either internal events or the independence of one nation from another.
13. **D. between 146 and 44 B.C.E.** First locate Asia Minor on the map and see how it is shaded or patterned. Then consult the map key to see when land in Asia Minor was acquired by the Roman Empire. The map shows that most of the land was acquired between 146 and 44 B.C.E.
14. **A. Before 264 B.C.E., Rome conquered through overland military campaigns; later conquests were made by navies as well.** The map shows that up to 264 B.C.E., all of Rome's conquests were located on the Italian peninsula, reachable by land-based military units. After that time, as Rome sought to expand beyond the peninsula, it built navies to help conquer overseas areas.
15. **A. the European ideal of chivalry** The ideals of loyalty, devotion, and service are similar in both bushido and chivalry.
16. **C. the peasants** The passage mentions that the bushi and samurai were released from agricultural responsibilities because they were preparing for war, and the peasants provided them with a supply of the food they grew.

UNIT 5

ABOUT THE TEST

Science

The HiSET Science Test assesses your ability to understand, interpret, and apply scientific information. You will have 80 minutes to answer 50 multiple-choice questions.*

Each question will assess both your familiarity with a content area and your ability to perform a skill related to understanding and interpreting scientific information.

Science Content Areas

Life Science (50%) topics may include fundamental biological concepts, including the life cycle and environment of organisms; cellular processes and body systems; interdependence of organisms in an ecosystem; and the relationship between the structure and function in living systems.

Earth Science (21%) topics may include properties of earth materials; plate tectonics; Earth's movements in the solar system; and geologic structures, cycles, and processes over time.

Physical Science (29%) topics may include observable properties of matter such as size, weight, shape, color and temperature; forces and concepts relating to the position and motion of objects; and the principles of light, heat, electricity, and magnetism.

Science Skills

In addition to testing your understanding of science passages and graphics, the questions are based on your understanding of skills that are used in scientific study and investigation. After you study these skills, you will reinforce them as you work through the unit. The science skills include:

- **Comprehending scientific presentations** to interpret passages and graphics
- **Using the scientific method** to design investigations, reason from data, and work with findings
- **Evaluating experimental design** to identify reasons for a procedure, analyze the limitations, and select the best procedure
- **Reasoning with scientific information** to evaluate conclusions with evidence
- **Applying concepts and formulas** to express scientific information and apply scientific theories
- **Using statistics and probability** in a science context
- **Assessing the credibility** of sources

*Note: The information given here was the latest information available as of December 2018. It is possible that some of this information may change between this printing and your test date. For updates, visit http://hiset.ets.org.

LESSON 1

Comprehend Scientific Presentations

KEY IDEAS

- The Science Test presentations consist of text, graphics, or a combination of the two.
- Understanding science presentations on the Science Test requires understanding the main idea or point.
- Main ideas in science materials are supported by specific facts, details, or evidence.

HiSET EXAM TIP

To answer questions based on a passage or graphic, ask yourself, "What is the main point? What evidence or details are used to support it?"

The Science Test consists of questions based on science passages and graphics. To comprehend science presentations, you need to understand main ideas and their supporting details.

The **main idea** of a science presentation or graphic is its topic or the writer's point. Use this science diagram to practice finding the main idea.

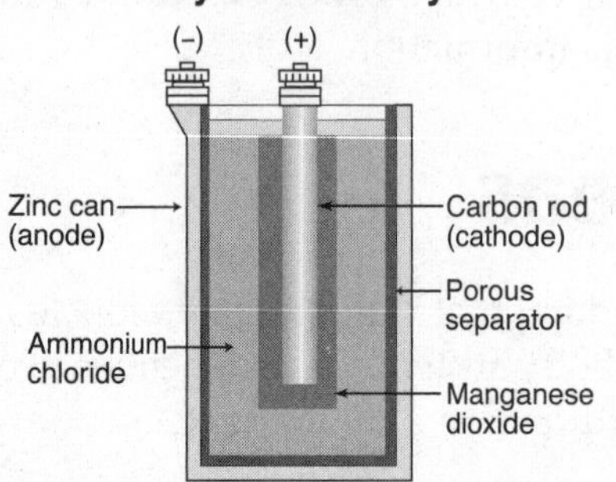

► What is the topic of this diagram?

(1) the components of a dry cell battery

(2) how a dry cell battery powers machinery

The correct answer is choice **(1)**. The diagram displays the different components (that is, the parts) of a dry cell battery. It does not show the process by which the battery actually operates or powers machinery, so (2) is incorrect.

Science writers support their main ideas with **details**, **facts**, and **evidence**.

Read the paragraph below and answer the question.

> Earthquakes can be classified as either surface earthquakes or deep-focus earthquakes. Scientists agree that surface earthquakes occur when rock in Earth's crust fractures to relieve stress. Deep-focus earthquakes originate from seismic activity more than 300 kilometers below Earth's surface. The causes of deep-focus earthquakes remain a subject of debate, but scientists believe they may be caused by the pressure of fluids trapped in Earth's tectonic plates.

► Which of the following details supports the main point of this paragraph?

(1) The causes of deep-focus earthquakes remain a subject of debate among scientists.

(2) Surface earthquakes are caused by stress in Earth's crust, while deep-focus earthquakes may be caused by pressure.

The correct answer is choice **(2)**. The main point of the paragraph is that earthquakes can be classified into two types based on their causes, and **(2)** provides supporting details that illustrate the differences between the two types. While (1) is mentioned in the paragraph, it is not a fact that supports the main point about the classification of earthquakes.

PRACTICE 1

Questions 1 through 3 are based on the passage below.

Despite the prevalence of type 2 diabetes, the causes of the disease remain somewhat uncertain. It is likely that some combination of genetics and lifestyle contributes to the development of type 2 diabetes. However, scientists have not fully determined the roles played by various lifestyle factors (such as diet and exercise).

For Americans, one contributing factor may be high sugar consumption. Sugar from food is broken down and absorbed into the bloodstream, and insulin is required for the body to be able to use that sugar. In a study of individuals 18–25 years old who consumed more than the recommended amount of sugar daily, it was shown that the majority had significantly elevated levels of glucose (that is, sugar) in their blood but normal levels of insulin. In other words, these subjects could not produce enough insulin to allow their bodies to use the amount of sugar they were consuming. Elevated blood glucose levels may put individuals consuming high amounts of sugar at higher risk of developing type 2 diabetes.

1. Which one of the following is the topic of the entire passage?

A. sources of sugar in Americans' diet
B. the role of insulin in metabolizing sugar from food
C. the causes of type 2 diabetes
D. how to prevent type 2 diabetes

2. Which of the following is the main idea of the first paragraph?

A. It is likely that sugar consumption contributes to the development of type 2 diabetes.
B. It is likely that genetics plays a role in the development of type 2 diabetes.
C. Researchers have discovered the causes of type 2 diabetes.
D. The causes of type 2 diabetes are not fully understood.

3. The main idea of the second paragraph is that high sugar consumption may put individuals at greater risk of developing type 2 diabetes. Which of the following details supports that main idea?

A. Sugar from food is absorbed into the bloodstream.
B. A study of 18- to 25-year-olds showed that a majority did not produce enough insulin to offset the high amounts of sugar they were consuming.
C. A study of 18- to 25-year-olds showed that high sugar consumption interacted with genetic factors in a majority of those individuals in order to suppress insulin production.
D. It has not been proven that sugar is a contributing factor to the development of type 2 diabetes.

Question 4 is based on this graphic.

How Topography Contributes to Precipitation

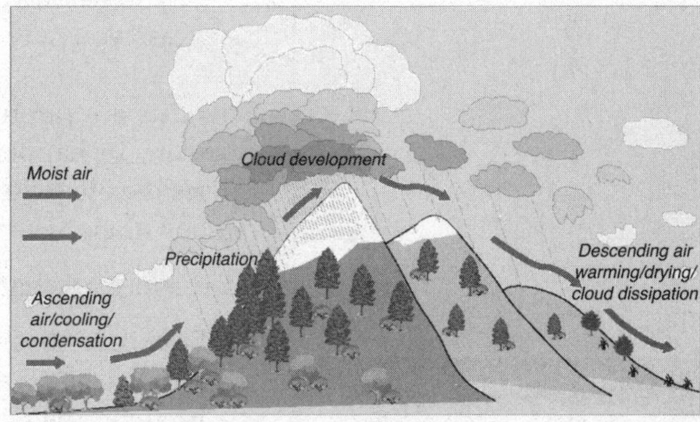

Source: U.S. Geological Survey

4. Which statement correctly describes the process depicted in the graphic above?

A. As moist, flowing air encounters rising elevations, it cools, which causes condensation, a stage that precedes precipitation and cloud development.
B. Once above the tree line, flowing air is likely to slow down and stop moving, and then collect in the form of snow.
C. Clouds dissipate before encountering mountain peaks.
D. Moist air flows from the west, while drier air usually flows from the east.

LESSON 2

Use the Scientific Method

KEY IDEAS

- The scientific method is used to investigate events and to acquire knowledge.
- Scientists follow a series of procedures involving observing, collecting information, and forming a hypothesis.
- After the hypothesis has been tested in an experiment or study, scientists draw a conclusion.

HiSET EXAM TIP

The Science Test may present an experiment and ask you to answer multiple-choice questions interpreting it.

The **scientific method** is a set of techniques that scientists use to investigate observable facts and occurrences and to acquire new knowledge. Here are the steps in the scientific method:

1. **Observe a phenomenon** and **formulate a question** about it. Formulate the question about something that you can observe and measure.
2. **Collect data** about the phenomenon you are studying. Scientific study is founded on **data**, or observable facts.
3. **Form a hypothesis**. A **hypothesis** is an educated guess about the answer to your question.
4. **Test the hypothesis through an experiment**. Your experiment should be a fair test of the hypothesis. You may need to adjust the experiment. You would do so by changing only one factor at a time while **controlling** other factors. You should also repeat the experiment to make sure the first results are valid.
5. **Draw a conclusion** about the hypothesis based on the experiment. When the experiment is complete, you may conclude that your hypothesis was supported by the data or that it was not, in which case you may formulate a new hypothesis.

Scientists are careful when drawing conclusions. The fact that two events **correlate**, or happen at the same time, does not necessarily mean that one **causes** the other. Remember that causation can never be deduced from correlation alone.

Read about a scientific observation and answer the question below.

> Scientists observed unusual plant and algae growth in a pond. They sampled the water and also discovered very high concentrations of bacteria. The pond was fairly close to neighboring farmland, and two streams carried water from the farm to the pond.

► *What could be a sound hypothesis about the growth in the pond?*

(1) Runoff from the neighboring farm may be carrying excessive phosphates and nitrates from fertilizers into the pond.
(2) Proximity to farmland is the cause of plant and algae growth in ponds and other bodies of water.

Choice **(1)** is correct. That hypothesis is an educated guess about the reason for the unusual plant and algae growth in the pond. It could be tested by an experiment that compares samples from the pond water to samples from streams coming from neighboring fields. Choice (2) is an assertion that is very general and cannot be measured in this specific situation.

The phenomenon you are studying is called the **dependent variable**. A factor that you believe might be affecting that phenomenon is called the **independent variable**. In the example above, the unusual plant and algae growth would be the dependent variable. The runoff from the neighboring farm would be the independent variable.

PRACTICE 2

<u>Questions 1 through 3</u> **are based on this passage.**

A majority of teenagers develop acne, but scientists still struggle to explain its cause. It has long been thought that bacteria play a role, although until recently it was assumed that role was purely detrimental—contributing to acne. However, a team of researchers began to wonder whether different strains of bacteria might impact acne in different ways.

The research team studied 49 individuals with acne and 52 individuals without acne, and the researchers collected samples of bacteria from the nasal pores of all those individuals. The researchers found that some combinations of bacterial strains were highly likely to be found in clear-skinned individuals, while other combinations were highly likely to be found in individuals with acne.

After carefully analyzing their data, the scientists concluded that, while some bacterial combinations likely contribute to acne, other bacterial combinations may actually help to ward it off. The researchers suggested that, if further studies confirm these findings, we may want to treat acne by encouraging the growth of helpful bacteria.

1. What question is being investigated in this experiment?

A. What causes bacteria to collect in people's facial pores?
B. What are all the contributing factors to the development of acne?
C. What role do bacteria play in the development of acne?
D. What is the best way to treat acne?

2. What was the researchers' hypothesis?

A. Combinations of bacteria are a major cause of acne.
B. Different kinds of bacteria may impact acne differently.
C. We may want to change the way we treat acne, treating it by encouraging the growth of beneficial bacteria.
D. Some combinations of bacteria may actually help ward off acne.

3. What conclusion did the researchers reach based on their data?

A. Combinations of bacteria are a major cause of acne.
B. Acne sufferers have more types of bacterial strains in their facial pores than do non-sufferers.
C. The way we currently treat acne is misguided.
D. Some combinations of bacteria may actually help ward off acne.

<u>Questions 4 and 5</u> **are based on the following information.**

Suppose that you notice your right knee hurts every time you play softball. You suspect that one of the movements involved in playing softball is causing your knee to hurt, but you are not sure which movement is the culprit. You decide to do a scientific investigation to find out more. That is, you form a hypothesis, design an experiment to test that hypothesis, perform your experiment and record your data, and draw a conclusion based on that data.

4. Which of the following steps in your investigation corresponds to forming your hypothesis?

A. You make a list of each of the movements involved in softball. In the off season (when you are not playing entire games), you plan to perform each movement several times without performing the others.
B. Based on the data you collected in your experiment, you think it is likely that stopping suddenly after running a short distance is indeed the cause of your knee pain.
C. Based on your experience, you make a guess about which of the movements involved in playing softball puts the greatest stress on the knees. You suspect that it may be stopping suddenly after running a short distance.
D. After performing each movement in isolation, you record how your knee feels, letting your knee recover between tests of each type of movement.

5. Which of the following is the dependent variable in your experiment?

A. playing softball
B. your knee pain
C. running and then stopping
D. your recorded data

LESSON 3

Evaluate Experimental Design

KEY IDEAS

- *Well-designed scientific experiments eliminate the effect of confounding variables.*
- *A control group provides scientists with a baseline from which to compare experimental groups.*
- *The only factor that will change in a scientific experiment is the factor being tested.*

In the previous lesson, you saw that scientists test hypotheses with experiments by following a certain procedural format. You may be asked to identify the scientist's reasoning behind certain procedures in a given experiment.

You may recall that for an experiment to achieve valid results, only one factor may be changed at a time. Scientists have several ways to eliminate the effect of **confounding variables**, external factors that can interfere with the results. One way is to establish a control group. A **control group** does not receive the experimental treatment that is being tested. This allows scientists to observe what happens under normal conditions and to eliminate the effect of variables such as time.

Another way to control for confounding variables is randomization, or making sure that each independent sample has an equal chance of being selected for a particular experimental condition. Yet another way is to adjust the procedure to account for biases that may result from the order, sequence, or placement of experimental factors.

Read the experiment below and answer the question that follows:

> Anthocyanins are plant pigments sensitive to changes in pH, and they are found in red cabbage leaves. To test the effect of acid on anthocyanin pigment, a student prepared four identical test tubes each containing identical quantities of red cabbage and distilled water. He then added concentrated HCl solution to three test tubes until the pH was 5, 3, and 1, respectively, and measured the color of the cabbage in all four test tubes using a colorimeter.

► *Which of the following best explains why the student added only distilled water to the cabbage in one test tube?*

(1) Water is needed to dilute the anthocyanin pigment.
(2) Distilled water has a neutral pH.

The correct answer is **(2)**. Because this experiment is testing the effect of acid (independent variable) on color change (dependent variable), a baseline color of anthocyanin at a pH that is neither acidic nor basic must first be established. Distilled water has a pH of 7 and therefore serves as a control group for evaluating color change. Choice (1) suggests a reason for adding liquid to *all* test tubes, but it doesn't address the question of why distilled water was the only liquid added to one test tube.

Other questions may ask you to select the proper procedure needed to test a new idea.

HiSET EXAM TIP

When you are asked about the reasoning behind an experimental procedure, identify which factor is being addressed. Are you being asked about a procedure related to the independent variable, the dependent variable, or a confounding variable?

Questions 1 through 3 are based on the information below.

Catalase is an enzyme found in living cells that decomposes hydrogen peroxide into water and oxygen.

Kristina is interested in the environmental conditions that affect catalase enzyme activity. Because extreme temperatures can cause proteins, including enzymes, to unfold into random configurations (denaturation), she has hypothesized that high temperatures will cause a decrease in the catalase reaction rate. She heated a water bath to 20°C. Then she inserted a test tube containing hydrogen peroxide and a pH buffer, which stabilizes a solution's pH. She immediately added turnip extract (the source of catalase) and measured the number of oxygen bubbles released over 10 seconds. She repeated the procedure at 5-degree intervals up to 65°C.

The results are shown in the following graph:

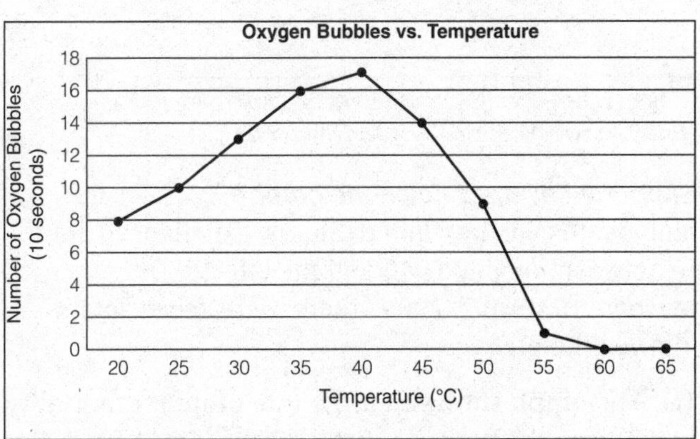

1. What is the most likely reason that Kristina added a pH buffer to each of the test tubes?
   A. To prevent the early release of oxygen
   B. To ensure that the pH of each trial was the same
   C. To stabilize the activity of the enzyme
   D. To control the amount of oxygen being released

2. The upper temperature limit used in the experiment was most likely chosen for which of the following reasons?
   A. Hydrogen peroxide only decomposes between 20°C and 65°C.
   B. The enzyme had likely denatured at 60°C, so further temperature increases would yield no new data.
   C. At 60°C, the enzyme had already converted all the hydrogen peroxide into water and oxygen.
   D. Oxygen gas does not form bubbles at temperatures greater than 65°C.

3. Suppose that catalase can be extracted from potatoes in double the concentration per gram as from turnips. If Kristina wanted to test how catalase concentration affects reaction rate, how could this idea best be tested?
   A. Repeat the experiment, replacing turnip extract with an equal quantity of potato extract, and compare the results.
   B. Repeat the experiment, adding equal quantities of turnip extract and potato extract, and compare the results.
   C. Replace the potato extract with an equal quantity of turnip extract and continue heating the water bath in 5-degree intervals from 65°C to 130°C.
   D. Double the amount of potato extract added and continue the experiment, heating the water bath in 5-degree intervals from 65°C to 130°C.

---

4. Davis wants to test Newton's Second Law of Motion on objects in free fall, and hypothesizes that heavier objects will take less time to fall to earth than lighter objects because they have different masses. How could this idea best be tested?
   A. Drop identical spheres that only differ in mass from the same height and record the time it takes for each sphere to hit the ground.
   B. Drop identical spheres that only differ in mass from different heights and record the time it takes for each sphere to hit the ground.
   C. Drop different objects of varying sizes from the same height and record the time it takes for each object to hit the ground.
   D. Drop different objects of varying sizes from different heights and record the time it takes for each object to hit the ground.

LESSON 4

Reason with Scientific Information

KEY IDEAS

- Reasoning with scientific information requires citing specific evidence to support a conclusion.
- In some cases, an existing theory can be challenged by new data or evidence.
- One of the ways scientists use information is in making predictions.

Some questions require recognizing or citing specific evidence to support a conclusion. Another type of question may ask you to judge whether a **conclusion** or a **scientific theory**—a substantiated explanation of the natural world—is challenged by particular data or evidence.

Use the graph below to practice scientific reasoning.

Rates of Infant Mortality, 1940–2009

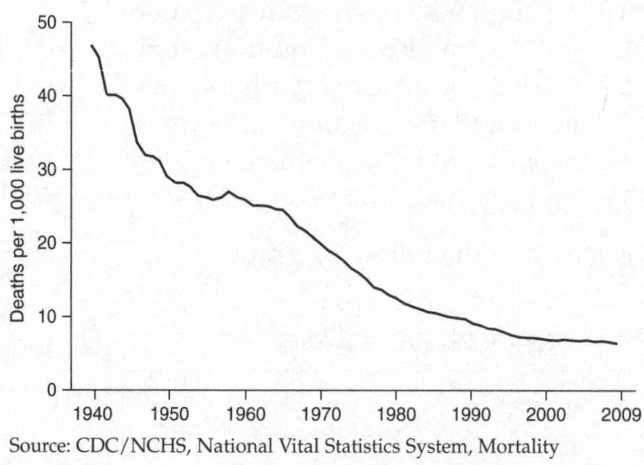

Source: CDC/NCHS, National Vital Statistics System, Mortality

► *Which conclusion is supported by the data on the graph?*

(1) The rate of infant deaths in the United States experienced its sharpest decline between roughly 1940 and the late 1950s.

(2) In each year between 1940 and 2009, there were fewer infant deaths than in the year before.

HiSET EXAM TIP

When you interpret a line graph, carefully follow the direction of each line to see its trend. You can use trends to make predictions.

The correct answer is **(1)**. The graph shows that the rate of infant mortality decreased most sharply between the years of 1940 and the late 1950s. After the late 1950s, it continued to decrease, but more gradually. Choice (2) is not a true statement based on the graph: around 1960, there was an uptick in the rate of infant deaths.

Other questions will ask you to make a **prediction** based on evidence or data that the test provides to you. Based on the **trend** observed, scientists use data to predict, or forecast, what they think may happen in the future.

► *Which of the following predictions is based on the graph above?*

(1) Since there has not been an increase in infant deaths since 1960, there will likely be such an increase sometime soon.

(2) The rate of infant deaths is unlikely to experience sharp declines in the near future.

Choice **(2)** is correct: the line on the graph shows the trend in infant mortality has been one of very gradual decrease since the 1950s. A good prediction based on that pattern would be that the trend of gradual decline is likely to continue. The graph shows a downward trend, but gives no information to suggest a future increase, so choice (1) is incorrect.

PRACTICE 4

1. Inertia causes an object to resist changes in its state of motion. In other words, inertia causes an object at rest to resist any attempt to set it in motion. Similarly, inertia causes an object in motion to resist any attempt to stop its motion. Objects with greater mass have greater inertia.

   These figures represent the mass of two objects:

Brick:	100 grams
Block of wood:	70 grams

   Which of the following is supported by the information above?

   A. It would require more effort to break the brick than to break the block of wood.
   B. If both objects were currently sitting still, it would require more effort to push the block of wood across the floor than it would to push the brick across the floor.
   C. If both objects were currently sitting still, it would require more effort to push the brick across the floor than it would to push the block of wood across the floor.
   D. The brick would absorb water more readily than would the block of wood.

2. In the last several decades, the spider population has exploded on the island of Guam: parts of the island have as many as 40 times more spiders than nearby islands do. One scientist has concluded that the explosion in the Guam spider population is due to an increase in the population of an invasive species of brown tree snake. The snake was introduced into Guam in the 1940s but was not introduced into the neighboring islands. The brown tree snake preys on birds.

   Which one of the following, if true, makes the scientist's conclusion more likely?

   A. The birds that the brown tree snake eats are the primary predators of spiders on Guam.
   B. The brown tree snake is typically introduced into islands via ships carrying tourists. Guam and the islands nearby have long been popular tourist spots.
   C. Brown tree snakes eat spiders as well as birds.
   D. In the rainy season, the island of Guam can have more than 40 times as many spiders as it did ten years ago.

Questions 3 and 4 are based on the following passage.

Melting ice sheets in Greenland and Antarctica have the potential to contribute significantly to rising sea levels in the next century. Some ice sheets melt more quickly than others, and scientists have wondered why. A team of researchers recently used data from both satellites and radar to study the composition of many of the ice sheets in Greenland and Antarctica. They found that some of the ice sheets formerly thought to sit on rock actually sit on water. This finding could be significant because it may be the case that ice sheets sitting on water tend to melt more quickly than those sitting on rock.

3. Which of the following is a prediction scientists might make based on the information above?

   A. If large areas of ice sheets sit on rock, the rising of sea levels may proceed more quickly than had previously been predicted.
   B. If large areas of ice sheets sit on water, the rising of sea levels may proceed more quickly than had previously been predicted.
   C. Ice sheets in Greenland will likely melt more quickly than ice sheets in Antarctica.
   D. All the ice sheets that are melting more quickly will be found to be sitting on water.

4. A scientist predicts that the ice sheets sitting on water will collectively discharge more water into the ocean than will those sitting on rock. Which of the following facts, if true, might weaken that prediction?

   A. Most of the ice sheets sitting on water are covering inland lakes with no access to the ocean.
   B. Water sitting under ice sheets flows directly into the ocean.
   C. Ice in a glass of water will melt even if the room is very cold.
   D. Radar used alone is an unreliable way to assess the composition of ice sheets.

LESSON 5

Synthesize Relevant Information

KEY IDEAS

- *Explanations for given scenarios will be based on relevant information in the text.*
- *The phrase "most likely" indicates that you are being asked to evaluate multiple pieces of information in order to make a prediction.*
- *Identify the relationship between different pieces of information to predict likely outcomes.*

HiSET EXAM TIP

Strategically eliminate answer choices that are extreme or that have no basis in the passage. The right answer will be supported with relevant information in the text or data.

Think of a passage and accompanying data as providing you with a frame in which to view a particular issue. Science passages contain numerous details, but they focus on a central idea or hypothesis. When asked about the details a passage does or does not provide, focus on what the text actually says.

Read and answer the following question to see how relevant information is used:

> A cover crop is a plant sown, typically in fall or winter, to manage soil erosion and increase soil quality. Certain cover crops also increase soil fertility by adding nutrients back into the soil. One such species is crimson clover. Crimson clover maintains a symbiotic relationship with nitrogen-fixing bacteria in its root nodules. These bacteria convert atmospheric nitrogen into a form that plants can use to grow.

▶ *Which of the following questions CANNOT be answered based on the text?*

(1) How does crimson clover increase soil quality?
(2) When should a farmer plant a cover crop?

The correct answer is **(2)**. While the text states that cover crops are typically sown in fall or winter, this only tells us when the plants are usually sown, not when a farmer *should* plant them. The fourth and fifth sentences give an example of how crimson clover increases soil quality: it promotes the growth of bacteria that add nitrogen back into the soil.

This same logic applies to questions that ask you to propose likely explanations or predict a likely result for a given scenario in context. Unlike questions that test your ability to locate a particular fact, these test your ability to synthesize the relevant data in order to demonstrate an understanding of the relationship between two or more pieces of information.

> The unique physical properties of water have a direct influence on the prosperity of aquatic ecosystems. Water has a very high specific heat, meaning that a larger amount of heat is required to increase the temperature of water 1°C compared to other liquids.
>
> Some aquatic organisms that lack internal thermoregulation rely on this stable thermal environment to survive. Brook trout, for example, are particularly susceptible to environmental fluctuations. Other species, like the carp, have adapted to a wide range of external temperatures.
>
> ▶ *Suppose the specific heat of water were to suddenly decrease. What would be the most likely result?*
>
> (1) The brook trout population would decrease.
> (2) The carp population would increase.

The correct answer is **(1)**. The text describes the relationship between the high specific heat of water and the stable thermal environment. If the specific heat of water were to decrease, the thermal environment would be more prone to changes. This would most likely be problematic for species like brook trout, which is susceptible to environmental fluctuations.

PRACTICE 5

Questions 1 through 3 are based on the information below.

Pneumonia is a lung infection that can cause severe breathing difficulty. Inhaling either a bacterium or a virus into the lungs can lead to pneumonia, and because many of its symptoms—such as coughing, chest pain, and fatigue—are the same as those of the common cold, a chest X-ray is often needed to make a diagnosis.

The most common treatment for bacterial pneumonia is a prescription for antibiotics. Antibiotics destroy harmful bacterial pathogens in the body by disrupting vital cellular processes. Penicillin is one such antibiotic. It blocks an enzyme necessary for building the cell wall. Another antibiotic is azithromycin. Azithromycin binds to the ribosome and prevents proteins from being synthesized.

While the discovery of antibiotics has revolutionized the fight against infectious disease, many medical professionals warn against prescribing them unnecessarily. If an individual does not have a bacterial infection, a prescription for antibiotics will be ineffective and could create drug-resistant germs that will be more difficult to treat in the future.

1. Consider the following statement:

An individual with a lung infection should always receive a prescription for antibiotics.

How does the information provided relate to this statement?

A. The information proves that the statement is true.
B. The information supports the statement but does not prove it.
C. The information proves that the statement is false.
D. There is not enough relevant information to evaluate the statement.

2. Which of the following questions CANNOT be answered by the passage?

A. How does a doctor distinguish bacterial pneumonia from viral pneumonia?
B. Why is a chest X-ray needed to make a diagnosis of pneumonia?
C. What is a risk associated with overprescribing antibiotics?
D. How does azithromycin treat bacterial infections?

3. Suppose an individual is diagnosed with bacterial pneumonia and begins taking penicillin. What would be the most likely result?

A. The pneumonia bacteria would be weakened because cell walls couldn't form properly.
B. The pneumonia bacteria would be weakened because ribosomes would not be able to synthesize proteins.
C. The pneumonia bacteria would become resistant to future drug treatment.
D. Nothing, because penicillin is ineffective at treating bacterial pneumonia.

4. According to the information, which of the following actions could you take to help prevent the creation of drug-resistant bacteria?

A. Stop taking prescribed antibiotics once you start to feel better.
B. Take antibiotics only when a doctor necessarily prescribes them for you.
C. Only take antibiotics if your life is in danger.
D. Save leftover antibiotics for a future illness to avoid needing a second prescription.

LESSON 6

Assess the Credibility of Sources

KEY IDEAS

- *Reliable sources of scientific knowledge support their claims with evidence and facts.*
- *Scientists review each other's work for sources of error or false claims in a process called peer review.*
- *An idea may be popular, but that does not necessarily mean that it is true.*

HiSET EXAM TIP

When determining credibility of a source, ask yourself: Does the author have a reason to favor one side over the other? Does the evidence support the claim being made?

Much as an experiment doesn't provide reliable data unless it adheres to specific procedures, scientific articles or news reports must adhere to certain guidelines in order to be viewed as reliable sources of information. This is often referred to as "being credible." **Credible sources** contain claims that are supported with valid, verifiable evidence and contain accurate, relevant facts.

Just because an idea is published does not make it true. Scientists have a system for establishing credibility called **peer review**. Before a study is published, it is reviewed by other experts and authorities in the field. Studies should also be **objective**, meaning that they are free of bias and do not rely on a reader's emotional reaction to make a point. An article may be biased yet still contain other useful information; however, the presence of bias means that more research is necessary to verify the accuracy of any claims.

You may be asked to identify sources of error or flaws in an argument's reasoning, analyze claims drawn from evidence, or determine whether a source is credible and provide a basis for your reasoning.

Read the example below and answer the question that follows:

> Andras is writing a report on the environmental impact of hydroelectric power, but two of his resources present conflicting ideas. An article published on the River Rafters United website claims that because hydroelectric power plants reduce water flow, they are an environmental nightmare. The article cites a study linking extreme drought conditions to the disappearance of several plant species. A separate article accessed from an online library database and written by an independent research ecologist claims that the effect of hydroelectric power plants can be minimized with appropriate modifications and thus do not pose an unnecessary environmental threat. He cites a recent study documenting that the number of fish migrating upstream remained the same after a hydroelectric dam with a fish ladder was built across a local river.

► *Which of the following provides the most credible source of information?*

(1) The article on the River Rafters United website
(2) The article by the unaffiliated ecologist

The correct answer is **(2)**. The article by the unaffiliated ecologist cites a study directly related to his claim that modifications can reduce the environmental impact of the dam. The article by River Rafters United cites a study unrelated to its claim; there is no evidence presented that the drought conditions that led to the disappearance of the plant species were created by a dam. Furthermore, articles on a website for river-rafting enthusiasts are more likely to be biased toward keeping rivers free-flowing, whereas the independent research ecologist is likely to approach the topic objectively.

PRACTICE 6

Questions 1 and 2 are based on the information below.

After Joanie eats a triple bacon cheeseburger for lunch her stomach begins to hurt. She recalls learning in science class that hamburger, bacon, and cheese all contain saturated fat, so she starts to wonder whether her lunch is causing her stomach pain. She does an Internet search for "Does eating saturated fat cause stomach pain?" The top result is from a website selling a fat–blocking supplement. The site claims that eating meals high in saturated fat can cause digestion problems. The second result is a blog post that describes how the author had stomach pain after eating a grilled cheese sandwich.

1. Does Joanie have reliable evidence to claim that saturated fats are the cause of her stomach pain?

A. Yes, because both websites confirmed that stomach pain occurs after eating saturated fat.
B. Yes, because the author of the blog also experienced stomach pain after eating cheese.
C. No, because only a doctor can know whether saturated fat is related to stomach pain.
D. No, because neither website is a source of credible information on this topic.

2. The website claiming saturated fat can cause digestive problems is

A. credible, because it is the top result of the Internet search engine.
B. credible, because a study could later show that the claim is true.
C. not credible, because the authors have a personal motive to make their claim.
D. not credible, because not everyone experiences stomach pain after eating cheeseburgers.

3. Alfred Wegener proposed continental drift in 1912 to explain how land masses separated by an ocean nonetheless contain similar fossils and shoreline characteristics. Which of the following is the most credible evidence to support this theory?

A. A student notices that the shorelines of eastern South America and western Africa fit together.
B. *Mesosaurus* fossils have been found on different continents, oceans apart.
C. A poll of leading geographers concluded that the majority believe in continental drift.
D. A peer-reviewed study demonstrates that magnetic fields in the ocean bedrock push the continents apart.

4. Which of the following is least likely to be a reliable source of information about climate change?

A. A newspaper opinion piece by a respected political leader
B. An article published in an academic journal
C. A quarterly report from a global research institution
D. A science textbook cowritten by several authors

LESSON 7

Express and Apply Scientific Information

Scientific information can be expressed in different forms. On the Science Test, you may be asked to find relationships among science passages, graphics, formulas, or equations.

Scientific equations for **chemical reactions** often use these symbols:

Symbol	Meaning
+	Positive symbol separates two or more **reactants** or **products** from one another.
→	Yield symbol separates reactants from products and shows the reaction direction.
⇆	Reversible reaction symbol indicates that the reaction can proceed in both directions.

For example, here is the general chemical equation for what happens when carbon (C) is burned:

$$C + O_2 \rightarrow CO_2$$

▶ *Which statement describes the process in the equation?*

(1) Carbon combines with oxygen to produce carbon dioxide.

(2) Carbon creates oxygen, which takes on another oxygen atom in order to produce carbon dioxide.

The correct answer is **(1)**. In this case, carbon and oxygen (O_2) combine without losing any of their components. The result is carbon dioxide, a molecule made up of one carbon atom and two oxygen atoms. (The prefix *di-* means "two," so *carbon dioxide* means "a C and two Os.") The plus sign on the left-hand side of the equation indicates that carbon and oxygen are separate reactants, not that carbon creates oxygen. Thus, statement (2) is incorrect.

Other questions may ask you to understand a science concept and **relate** it to a specific situation.

> The term *desertification* describes a chain of events in which so much soil erodes from land that the land can no longer support plant or animal life. The lack of plant life allows for further soil erosion, making the land even more barren. It is very difficult to reverse desertification.

▶ Which of the following could be an example of the early stages of desertification?

(1) In a certain valley, overgrazing has nearly eliminated plant life. This lack of vegetation has led to rapid soil erosion.

(2) In a certain valley, the climate is arid, and soil erosion has occurred when the infrequent rains arrive. Farmers have devised an irrigation system to grow crops and thus reverse the rate of soil erosion.

Choice **(1)** is correct. Soil erosion is the cause of desertification, so the valley may be in the early stages of desertification. In choice (2), farmers have found a way to combat erosion, so this valley does not appear to be undergoing desertification.

KEY IDEAS

- Scientific information can be conveyed in multiple forms: in words, graphics, or formulas.
- Scientific formulas use numbers, letters, and symbols to represent a relationship or process.
- An important science reasoning concept is the ability to apply a scientific concept to a different situation.

HiSET EXAM TIP

When you are given a science concept and asked which one of the choices is the best example, carefully eliminate the three that do not have all the same characteristics.

PRACTICE 7

Questions 1 through 4 are based on the information below.

Imagine a substance (such as salt or sugar) dissolved in a liquid (such as water or alcohol). The liquid in which the substance is dissolved is called the *solvent*. *Osmosis* is the diffusion (movement) of a solvent across a semipermeable membrane (a barrier that allows some substances to pass through it). The solvent moves from the side of the membrane with less dissolved material to the side of the membrane with more dissolved material. The result of osmosis is an equilibrium: that is, the rate the solvent flows across the membrane is the same in both directions.

Gillian conducted an experiment to see how quickly various liquids with a specific amount of sugar dissolved in them would undergo osmosis. She used vats of the same size with semipermeable membranes separating one side of the vat from the other, and she put equal quantities of various liquids in both sides:

Container Used for Studying Osmosis

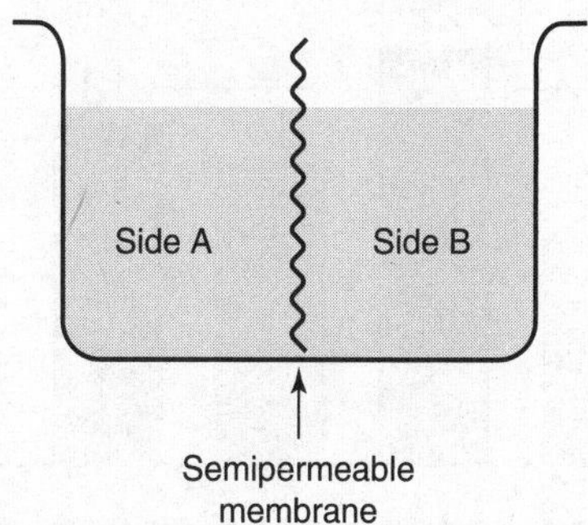

1. Gillian used one of the vats to test the rate of diffusion of liquid acetone in the process of osmosis. What did she most likely put on the two sides of the semipermeable membrane in that vat?

	Side A	Side B
A.	Pure acetone	Sugar in a glass container, submerged in acetone
B.	A 50 percent solution of sugar in acetone	A 50 percent solution of sugar in acetone
C.	Pure acetone	A solution of sugar in acetone
D.	Pure acetone	Pure acetone

Gillian's experiment yielded the following results:

Solvent	Time Required to Reach Equilibrium
Water	20 minutes
Acetone	25 minutes
Acetic acid	18 minutes
Formic acid	15 minutes

2. Based on the table above, which solvent had the highest rate of diffusion?

   A. water
   B. acetone
   C. acetic acid
   D. formic acid

3. Based on the table, what was the median time required for the solvents to reach equilibrium?

   A. 15 minutes
   B. 16 minutes
   C. 18 minutes
   D. 19 minutes

4. Osmosis is the reason why it is unhealthy and potentially dangerous to drink seawater. If you drink seawater, which contains a high concentration of salts and other dissolved material, some of the dissolved material will be absorbed into your bloodstream, causing your blood to have a higher-than-normal concentration of dissolved material. As that blood circulates through your body, water will move from your body's tissues into your blood vessels, causing your tissues to lose water and dry out.

   Choose the choice that best completes the sentence: Based on the information given, your tissues would begin to lose water and dry out when your blood has a level of dissolved material __________ that of your body's tissues.

   A. greater than
   B. slightly less than
   C. much less than
   D. equivalent to

Use Statistics and Probability

Because scientists often need to perform calculations, you will do some math on the Science Test. This math work will include the following:

- Central tendency: average (mean), median, mode, and range
- Independent and dependent probabilities
- Combinations and permutations

You may want to review these topics on pages 330–361 of the unit on Mathematics.

KEY IDEAS

- A measure of central tendency is used to summarize data.
- Probabilities are used to make predictions.
- Combinations and permutations are used to calculate numbers of ordered and unordered arrangements, respectively.

Scientists use **measures of central tendency** (mean, median, mode, and range) to summarize many pieces of data with one number.

Use the graph below to answer a question about central tendency.

Annual Tornadoes, 2000–2006, Goodland (Kansas) 19-County Warning Area

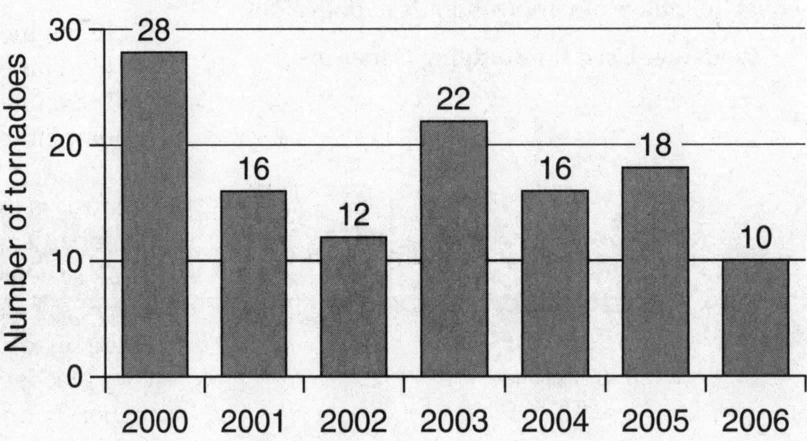

Source: National Oceanic and Atmospheric Administration

► *Calculate the mean (arithmetic average) number of tornadoes that struck the Goodland area per year in the years 2002 through 2005.* __________

To find the mean of a set of quantities, sum the quantities and divide by the number of items in the set. The list from 2002 to 2005 is 12, 22, 16, and 18. The sum of those numbers is 68. Divide by the number of items in the list (4), and the result is **17**.

Scientists frequently use data to investigate the **probability** that an event will happen. You may wish to review pages 350–353 to refresh your memory about working with probability.

PRACTICE 8

Questions 1 through 4 are based on the following information.

Metabolism is a set of chemical processes that occur in the tissues of living organisms. One example of a metabolic process in animals is the breaking down of carbohydrates from food into substances the body can store. Another example is the transformation of those same substances into energy that the animal can use. The *rate of metabolism* describes the speed at which these processes take place. Metabolic rate varies among different species. The graph below compares several animal species by both average metabolic rate and average body weight.

Metabolic Rates of Seven Species

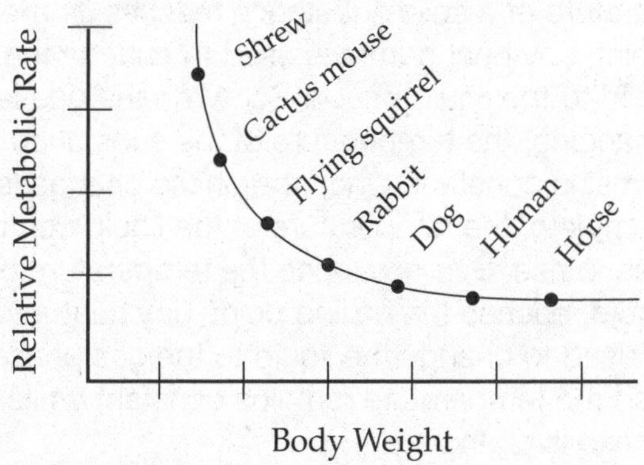

1. Of the species in this graph, which has the median body weight?

   A. shrew
   B. cactus mouse
   C. flying squirrel
   D. rabbit

2. Of the species in this graph, which has the median metabolic rate?

   A. rabbit
   B. dog
   C. human
   D. horse

STUDY ADVICE

When you see a figure, remember to ask:

What does the figure show?

What are the units of measurement?

When you see a figure with text, ask yourself how the text and the figure relate to one another.

3. Imagine that you could calculate the average (mean) of metabolic rates of all the animal species in this graph. Now imagine that the shrew were removed from the graph and that you recalculated the average of the remaining species. Without the shrew, the new average metabolic rate would be

   A. higher than the previous average.
   B. lower than the previous average.
   C. the same as the previous average.
   D. equal to the average of the metabolic rates of the horse and cactus mouse.

4. Adult elephants weigh more than adult horses. Based on the graph, what would you predict would be true of elephants?

   A. Their metabolic rate would resemble that of cactus mice, which, like elephants, live in warm climates.
   B. Their metabolic rate would be equivalent to that of horses.
   C. Their metabolic rate would be slightly lower than that of horses.
   D. Their metabolic rate would be significantly higher than that of horses.

5. Growing the same crop on a field year after year can cause crop yields to decline as the soil becomes depleted and insect populations become firmly established. Crop rotation, or growing different crops in different years, is one way to avoid these problems. However, discovering the most effective rotation of a number of different crops is difficult, because there are so many possible orders in which to grow them and testing any given crop rotation takes several years.

   For example, imagine a proposed rotation of corn, peanuts, onions, beets, and carrots, with a different crop grown each year for five years. How many different orderings of these five crops are possible?

   A. 15
   B. 25
   C. 120
   D. 125

Science Skills Practice Questions

Questions 1 through 3 are based on the following passage.

The 1543 publication of Nicolaus Copernicus's heliocentric, or sun-centered, theory of the universe marked a crucial moment in the history of science. Copernicus's theory that the planets revolve around the sun was controversial: at first, many refused to accept that Earth could be hurtling through space. However, we now know that Copernicus's theory was accurate in many ways.

Despite its importance as a breakthrough, Copernicus's theory contained a number of ideas that today seem primitive. For example, Copernicus maintained that the planets were embedded in crystalline spheres. Additionally, while Copernicus developed the novel, and later widely accepted, idea that Earth rotates on its axis, he also believed that the planets orbit around the sun in perfect circles. We now know that the planets move in elliptical orbits.

1. Which of the following is the main idea of the second paragraph?

   A. Primitive astronomers accepted Copernicus's theory when it was first published.
   B. While Copernicus's theory was an important development, it included elements that are outdated today.
   C. Copernicus believed that Earth moved around the sun, rather than the other way around.
   D. Earth does not hurtle through space.

2. Which of the following would be an appropriate title for this passage?

   A. "Important Landmarks in 16th-Century Science"
   B. "Copernicus: The Life of an Astronomer"
   C. "The Significance and Limitations of the Copernican Theory"
   D. "The Earth-Centered Universe"

3. Which of the following can be inferred from the passage?

   A. Astronomers now believe that the planets are not embedded in crystalline spheres.
   B. Astronomers now know that Earth does not move around the sun in an ellipse.
   C. All aspects of the Copernican theory have now been disproven.
   D. Copernicus took inspiration from the primitive astronomers who came before him.

4. Matter is generally found in one of three phases: solid, liquid, or gas. A substance can be converted from a solid to a liquid and then from a liquid to a gas by adding heat. Once the temperature of a solid substance reaches its melting point, any heat added is used to change the solid to the liquid phase. So, while the phase is changing, the temperature of the substance remains constant. Once the phase change is complete, the temperature of the liquid continues to rise. Similarly, once the temperature of a liquid reaches the boiling point, any heat added is used to change the liquid to the gas phase, and the temperature remains constant while the phase is changing.

   Temperature and Phase Changes of a Substance

   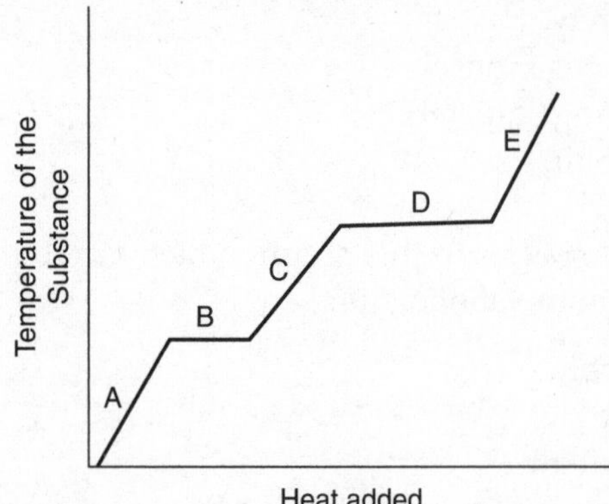

   At which points are phase changes occurring in the graph above?

   A. A and E
   B. A, C, and E
   C. B and D
   D. C, D, and E

5. While all types of cancer share the common trait of uncontrolled cell growth, the causes of that uncontrolled growth are complex and varied. Nevertheless, a number of specific causes of several types of cancer are known. For example, long-term asbestos exposure can result in mesothelioma (a cancer that can affect multiple organs), while long-term regular inhalation of tobacco smoke can lead to lung cancer. In addition to such chemical causes, viruses are also responsible for a number of types of cancer: human papillomavirus precipitates cervical cancer, while the hepatitis B virus causes liver cancer.

   Given the previous information, which of the following medical procedures could potentially prevent a specific type of cancer from forming?

   A. surgery to remove a brain tumor
   B. chemotherapy to treat lung cancer
   C. annual mammography screenings for breast cancer
   D. a vaccine to prevent infection with the hepatitis B virus

6. The phalarope, a North American shorebird, feeds on tiny crustaceans. To catch them, the phalarope swims in rapid circles, creating a vortex that raises prey to the surface of shallow water. The bird then opens and shuts its long, narrow beak to draw water droplets containing its prey up to its mouth. Because drawing up the water droplets depends upon the surface tension of water, the phalarope is exceptionally vulnerable to oil spills; the phalarope cannot remove oil from its beak on its own, so once it is exposed to oil-covered water, it cannot feed.

   Which of the following must be true based on the passage?

   A. The phalarope prefers salt water to brackish water or fresh water.
   B. At least some of the phalarope's prey is smaller than a water droplet.
   C. A phalarope whose beak becomes coated in oil will be able to feed if it can find clean water, not coated in oil, that contains tiny crustaceans.
   D. In addition to crustaceans, the phalarope feeds on small saltwater fish.

Questions 7 through 9 are based on the following paragraph and graphic.

Record high temperatures were recorded in numerous Australian cities in the summer of 2012. The chart below indicates current and former record temperatures for seven of those cities. For instance, Hobart's previous record was a little below 41°C, and its current record is a little above 41°C.

Record High Temperatures in Australian Cities

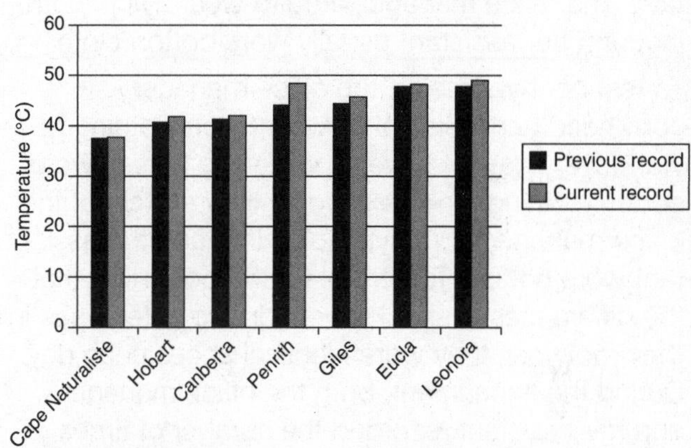

7. According to the chart, which city experienced the largest increase from its previous record to its current record?

   A. Hobart
   B. Penrith
   C. Eucla
   D. Leonora

8. Which of the following cities had a previous record equal to the median of all the cities' previous records?

   A. Cape Naturaliste
   B. Canberra
   C. Penrith
   D. Eucla

9. According to the chart, which of the following statements is true?

   A. Temperatures will likely continue to increase.
   B. Temperatures increased 5 degrees or less.
   C. Temperatures increased more than 5 degrees.
   D. Temperatures usually increase 2–5 degrees in the summer.

Questions 10 through 13 are based on the following passage.

An office manager noticed that each time she touched the metal filing cabinet next to her desk, she experienced an electrostatic shock (commonly known as "static"). Her assistant, however, only rarely experienced such shocks when touching the cabinet. The office manager wondered why this might be.

The office manager developed a hypothesis: perhaps differences in clothing could explain why she was experiencing more shocks than her assistant. The office manager liked to wear nylon clothing, and her assistant usually wore cotton clothing.

To test her hypothesis, the office manager convinced her assistant to wear nylon clothing to work every day for a week, while she herself wore cotton clothing. The next week, they switched: the office manager wore nylon clothing, and the assistant wore cotton. To control for the possibility that the differences in shocks were due to differences in their footwear, they wore identical shoes each day. During the experiment, both the office manager and her assistant recorded the number of times they touched the metal filing cabinet each day, and they also recorded the number of times they experienced electrostatic shocks when doing so.

At the end of the first week, they found that the assistant had experienced 73 electrostatic shocks, while the office manager had experienced 10. During the second week, the office manager experienced 68 shocks, and her assistant 12. The office manager concluded that these results supported her hypothesis, and as a result she decided to switch to wearing mostly cotton clothing.

10. Scientific investigations begin with a question. Which of the following is the question that formed the basis for the office manager's experiment?

   A. Is it better to wear cotton clothing or nylon clothing?
   B. Why does touching the metal filing cabinet produce more electrostatic shocks than touching other office furniture?
   C. Why, when I touch the metal filing cabinet, do I experience more electrostatic shocks than my assistant does when she touches it?
   D. Could my shoes be causing me to experience more electrostatic shocks than my assistant experiences?

11. Which of the following best summarizes how the office manager conducted her experiment?

   A. The office manager suspected that her nylon clothing was causing her to experience electrostatic shocks.
   B. The office manager switched to cotton clothing after seeing that her hypothesis was supported by her data.
   C. The office manager wore shoes of a different material than those of her assistant.
   D. The office manager wore one type of clothing, while her assistant wore another type of clothing, and they recorded the number of shocks they experienced.

12. Why did the office manager and her assistant wear the same type of shoes while conducting the experiment?

   A. They wanted to test the effect of their clothing on the number of shocks they experienced, and wearing different types of shoes might have confused their results.
   B. They wanted to test whether the office manager's shoes were causing the high number of electrostatic shocks she was experiencing.
   C. They believed that wearing cotton might cause the wearer to experience more electrostatic shocks.
   D. They wanted to protect themselves from the effects of electrostatic shock.

13. Imagine that the results of the office manager's experiment had demonstrated that her clothing was not in fact responsible for the large number of electrostatic shocks she was experiencing. After reviewing those findings, the office manager then wondered if her footwear might be responsible, and she decided to conduct a new experiment to test this idea. Before she conducted that experiment, the idea that her shoes might be responsible would be which of the following?

   A. a new conclusion based on findings
   B. a general principle from the study of physics
   C. a new hypothesis
   D. an experiment design

14. Common garden snails are hermaphroditic. That is, each individual snail produces both sperm and eggs. Mating between two garden snails involves the transfer of sperm from each partner to the other. A high school science teacher has created a large terrarium for his classroom that contains 6 adult garden snails. Assuming that all 6 snails are healthy, how many different mating pairs are possible?

A. 2
B. 12
C. 15
D. 36

15. The sun is a class G star, which is a type of main-sequence star. Approximately 90 percent of all stars in the Milky Way galaxy are main-sequence stars, and approximately 7 percent of all main-sequence stars are class G stars. What is the probability, expressed as a percentage, that any given star in the Milky Way galaxy is a class G star?

A. 6.3%
B. 9.7%
C. 63%
D. 97%

Questions 16 and 17 refer to the information and table below.

The table below contains data observed in a group of 58-year-old men. The study examined the relationship between tobacco use and formations called plaques that build up on the walls of arteries, which are blood vessels that carry blood from the heart to the body's tissues. The carotid and femoral arteries are two large and very important arteries.

Average Characteristics of 58-Year-Old Men, by Smoking Status

	Never Smokers	Ex-Smokers	Current Smokers
Waist circumference (cm)	93.8	99.1	95.4
Carotid plaques (%)			
None	62	55	53
Small	15	23	16
Large	23	22	31
Femoral plaques (%)			
None	80	54	45
Small	10	13	14
Large	10	33	41

16. In the study described, current smokers showed the highest percentage of which of the following kinds of plaques?

A. small carotid plaques
B. large carotid plaques
C. small femoral plaques
D. large femoral plaques

17. Why might the ex-smokers have the highest waist circumference of the groups listed in the chart?

A. People who have never smoked tend to consume more high-calorie foods than do those who smoke currently.
B. People who have never smoked tend to consume more high-calorie foods than do those who have smoked in the past.
C. People who quit smoking tend to substitute snacking for smoking.
D. Ex-smokers tend to exercise more than do current smokers.

LESSON 1

Cell Structures and Functions

KEY IDEAS

- The basic unit of all living things is the cell, which carries out the life functions, including movement, growth, and reproduction.
- All cells have a cell membrane, cytoplasm, and genetic material.
- Unlike an animal cell, a plant cell contains a cell wall—a structure that gives the cell rigidity and shape.

HiSET EXAM TIP

The title and labels of a diagram usually tell you the main idea of the diagram. Here, the main idea is that plant cells have cell structures with specialized functions.

All living things are made of **cells**, the basic unit of life. Some organisms, such as bacteria and protozoa, are **unicellular**—they consist of a single cell. Others, such as plants and animals, are **multicellular**, consisting of many different types of specialized cells. For example, humans have skin cells, blood cells, and nerve cells, to name just a few. All cells carry out the basic life functions: movement, growth, cell maintenance, reproduction, and the manufacture of specialized substances.

Although cells differ widely in size and appearance, they all have basic structures in common. All cells have a **cell membrane**, a structure that keeps the cell's contents separate from its external environment. The cell membrane is selectively permeable, which means that it allows certain substances, such as water, nutrients, and wastes, to pass between the cell's interior and the surrounding environment. Inside the cell membrane is the **cytoplasm**, a watery, jellylike substance that can include other cell structures. Finally, all cells have **genetic material**, which contains coded instructions for carrying out the cell's activities. In bacteria, the genetic material consists of a single molecule suspended in the cytoplasm. Bacteria are called **prokaryotes**. In all other cells, the genetic material is contained within a **nucleus**. Such cells are called **eukaryotic cells**. All plant and animal cells are eukaryotic. A typical plant cell is shown below. Note that a plant cell has a **cell wall**, which gives the cell shape and rigidity, and an animal cell does not.

A Plant Cell

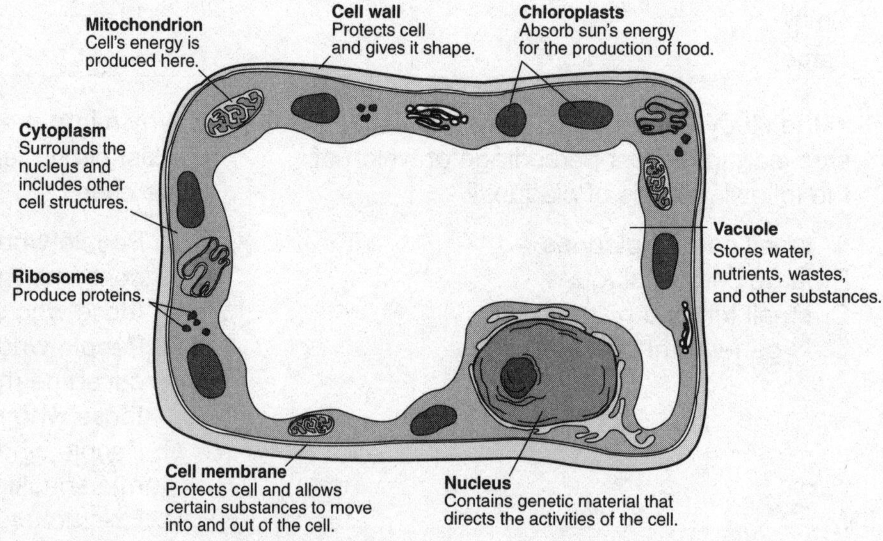
Mitochondrion
Cell's energy is produced here.
Cell wall
Protects cell and gives it shape.
Chloroplasts
Absorb sun's energy for the production of food.
Cytoplasm
Surrounds the nucleus and includes other cell structures.
Vacuole
Stores water, nutrients, wastes, and other substances.
Ribosomes
Produce proteins.
Cell membrane
Protects cell and allows certain substances to move into and out of the cell.
Nucleus
Contains genetic material that directs the activities of the cell.

PRACTICE 1

1. According to the diagram on page 616, the function of the _________ is to supply energy to the cell.

   A. nucleus
   B. ribosomes
   C. mitochondrion
   D. vacuole

2. In addition to the cell wall, the water stored in a plant cell's vacuole helps give the plant firmness and shape. When a plant is not taking in enough water from the soil through its roots, it uses up its stored water and its vacuoles shrink. When the vacuoles shrink, the plant wilts.

   Which of the following is a conclusion based on the paragraph above rather than a given fact?

   A. Cell walls help give a plant cell firmness and shape.
   B. Vacuoles help give a plant cell firmness and shape.
   C. Plants take in water from the soil through their roots.
   D. Cell walls cannot maintain a plant's shape and rigidity when the plant lacks water.

3. A student is examining a cell using a microscope. She is able to identify the cell membrane, the cytoplasm, a small vacuole, and the nucleus, but she does not see a cell wall or any chloroplasts. She concludes that the cell is a eukaryotic cell.

   Which of the following is evidence that her conclusion is correct?

   A. the presence of a nucleus
   B. the presence of cytoplasm
   C. the absence of chloroplasts
   D. the absence of a cell wall

4. Cells were first seen during the 1600s, when English scientist Robert Hooke observed cork cell walls through a microscope that could magnify a specimen a couple of hundred times its original size. In the 1800s, the compound light microscope, which magnifies up to a thousand times, was developed. Electron microscopes, which can magnify up to a million times, were invented during the 1900s.

   Which of the following best explains why our knowledge of cells has grown with improvements in microscope technology?

   A. Each time the microscope is improved, scientists can see cell structures more clearly.
   B. With the first microscopes, all cell structures were clearly visible.
   C. Compound light microscopes can magnify cells up to a thousand times.
   D. Robert Hooke's microscope only allowed him to see the largest cell structures.

5. Diffusion is a process by which particles move from an area of higher concentration to an area of lower concentration. For example, oxygen diffuses through the cell membrane of a unicellular pond organism from the water, where there is lots of oxygen, into the cell, where there is less oxygen. Eventually, the concentration of oxygen inside and outside the unicellular organism is the same.

   What would happen if the concentration of oxygen were greater in the unicellular organism than in its watery environment?

   A. Water would diffuse from the unicellular organism into the pond water.
   B. Oxygen would diffuse from the unicellular organism into the pond water.
   C. Oxygen would diffuse from the pond water into the unicellular organism.
   D. Diffusion of oxygen between the organism and the pond water would stop entirely.

STUDY ADVICE

You don't have to know a lot of science vocabulary or facts in order to do well on Science Test questions. You just need a basic familiarity with the science concepts discussed in this book. Remember to pay particular attention to the Key Ideas and the **words in bold**.

LESSON 2

Cell Processes and Energy

KEY IDEAS

- In photosynthesis, plants use light energy to form glucose from carbon dioxide and water. Oxygen is a by-product.
- In cellular respiration, glucose is broken down in the presence of oxygen to release energy. Carbon dioxide is a by-product.
- These two processes help maintain oxygen and carbon dioxide levels in the atmosphere.

HiSET EXAM TIP

About 50% of the questions on the Science Test are about life science topics.

All cells need energy to carry out the life functions, such as growth and reproduction. Green plants, some algae, and some bacteria use energy from sunlight to make food in a process called **photosynthesis**.

In photosynthesis, plants use sunlight to power chemical reactions that convert carbon dioxide gas and water into oxygen and the simple sugar **glucose**. In the first stage of photosynthesis, light energy is captured by chloroplasts inside plant cells. Chloroplasts contain **chlorophyll**, a pigment that gives plants their green color. Chlorophyll absorbs light energy for photosynthesis. In the second stage, water (H_2O) that the plant gets from the soil and carbon dioxide (CO_2) that the plant gets from the air undergo a complex series of chemical reactions inside the chloroplasts. The products of these reactions are oxygen (O_2) and glucose $(C_6H_{12}O_6)$. Plant cells use the energy that is stored in glucose to power cell processes. Photosynthesis can be summarized in the chemical equation shown below:

$$6CO_2 + 6H_2O \xrightarrow{\text{light energy}} C_6H_{12}O_6 + 6O_2$$

In words, this means that carbon dioxide plus water, in the presence of light energy, yields glucose plus oxygen.

As a result of photosynthesis, energy is stored in sugars and other **carbohydrates** in the plant. To meet their energy needs, other organisms eat plants or eat organisms that eat plants. When energy is needed in a cell, carbohydrates are broken down to release the energy in a process called **cellular respiration**. In this process, oxygen from the air reacts with glucose from food to yield carbon dioxide, water, and energy. Cellular respiration can be summarized in the following chemical equation:

$$C_6H_{12}O_6 + 6O_2 \rightarrow 6CO_2 + 6H_2O + \text{energy}$$

In words, this means that glucose plus oxygen yields carbon dioxide, water, and energy.

If you examine the two equations, you will notice that the products of photosynthesis are the raw materials of cellular respiration, and the products of cellular respiration are the raw materials of photosynthesis. These two processes are part of a cycle. Plants release oxygen, a waste product of photosynthesis, into the atmosphere. Animals breathe in the oxygen and use it in cellular respiration. They breathe out carbon dioxide, a waste product of cellular respiration. The carbon dioxide is then used by plants in photosynthesis, and the cycle repeats. Between them, photosynthesis and cellular respiration help keep the amounts of oxygen and carbon dioxide in the atmosphere fairly constant.

PRACTICE 2

1. Which of the following are the products of cellular respiration?

   A. glucose and light energy
   B. carbon dioxide and oxygen
   C. glucose, oxygen, and energy
   D. carbon dioxide, water, and energy

2. A horticulturist wants to grow large, healthy plants by maximizing the rate of photosynthesis.

   Which of the following actions would be most likely to get the results she wants?

   A. increasing the amount of light the plants receive each day
   B. increasing the amount of oxygen the plants receive each day
   C. decreasing the amount of oxygen the plants receive each day
   D. decreasing the amount of carbon dioxide the plants receive each day

3. Carbon dioxide is one of the "greenhouse gases" that help keep Earth warm by trapping radiated heat in the atmosphere. Global warming is thought to be caused in part by increased amounts of carbon dioxide in the atmosphere.

   Which of the following would help reduce the level of carbon dioxide in the atmosphere and thus perhaps slow the global warming trend?

   A. increasing the population of domestic animals
   B. increasing the number of green plants
   C. increasing the harvest of trees
   D. increasing the amount of glucose in our food

Questions 4 and 5 refer to the following information and diagram.

In most plants, photosynthesis takes place primarily in the palisade cells of leaves.

Cross Section of a Leaf

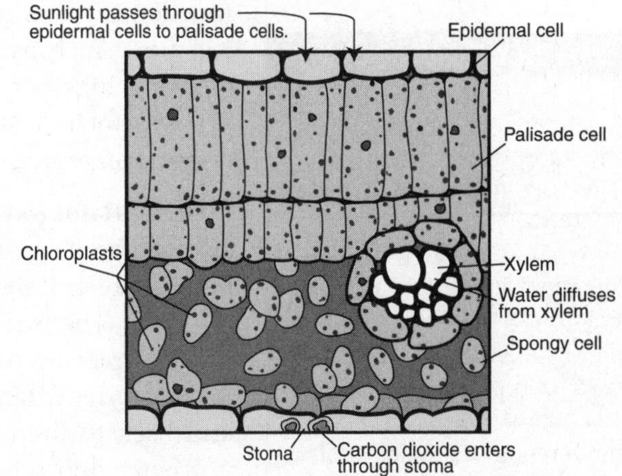

4. Which of the following is an opening in the lower surface of the leaf through which gases such as carbon dioxide can pass?

   A. palisade cell
   B. chloroplast
   C. xylem
   D. stoma

5. Chloroplasts are structures found within some of the cells in a leaf. They help in the process of photosynthesis. In the diagram, they are represented by small gray spots on the cells.

   Which of the following statements is supported by the information in the diagram?

   A. Palisade cells provide a means of transporting water through a plant.
   B. Most of a leaf's chloroplasts are found in its palisade cells.
   C. The spongy cells are soft, like a sponge.
   D. The epidermis blocks light from reaching the palisade cells.

LESSON 3

Human Body Systems

KEY IDEAS

- The circulatory system moves blood around the body, delivering and taking away substances.
- The respiratory system brings oxygen into the body and gets rid of carbon dioxide.
- The digestive system breaks down food into nutrients that cells can use.
- The nervous system controls body activities.

There are four levels of organization in the human body: (1) cells, the smallest unit of life; (2) **tissues**, groups of similar cells that perform a specific function, such as muscle tissue; (3) **organs**, groups of tissues that perform a function, such as the stomach; and (4) body systems, groups of organs working together to perform a function, such as digestion. Human body systems include the circulatory, respiratory, digestive, nervous, immune, endocrine, reproductive, urinary, skeletal, and muscular systems.

The **circulatory system**, sometimes called the cardiovascular system, consists of the heart and the blood vessels. Its main function is to move the blood, which transports substances like oxygen and nutrients, throughout the body. The major **organ** of the circulatory system is the **heart**, a muscle that contracts to pump blood. Blood moves through the blood vessels from large **arteries** to smaller arteries, to **capillaries**, to small **veins**, to large veins, and back to the heart. Through the thin walls of the capillaries, oxygen, nutrients, and other substances pass from the blood into the body's cells, and carbon dioxide and other wastes pass from the cells into the blood.

The **respiratory system** consists of the nose, throat, **trachea** (windpipe), and **lungs**. Its function is to take oxygen from the air into the body when we inhale and to get rid of waste in the form of carbon dioxide when we exhale. The trachea branches into two tubes called the **bronchi**, one of which goes into each lung. The bronchi branch into smaller tubes called **bronchioles**, each of which ends in an **alveolus**, a tiny spherical sac. Inside the capillaries of the alveoli, oxygen diffuses into the blood and carbon dioxide diffuses out of the blood.

HiSET EXAM TIP

On the Science Test, you will have to answer questions that require you to use information from both text and a graphic, as in questions 4 and 5 on page 621.

The **digestive system** consists of the mouth, **esophagus**, **stomach**, **small intestine**, and **large intestine**. Its function is to break down food into nutrients, which are used for cell processes including the production of energy, and to get rid of digestive wastes. Digestion begins in the mouth, where the teeth grind food into smaller pieces, and **saliva** begins to break it down chemically. Food is pushed by muscular action down through the esophagus into the stomach, where it is churned and further broken down by **enzymes** and stomach acids. From the stomach it travels to the small intestine, where most of the nutrients are absorbed into the blood through tiny capillaries in the **villi**. What remains goes to the large intestine, which removes water, leaving solid waste to be excreted through the **rectum**.

The **nervous system** consists of the **brain**, **spinal cord**, and **nerves**. Its function is to receive, process, and transmit information, controlling body activities. The brain has three main parts: the **cerebrum**, which controls functions such as thinking, seeing, and speaking; the **cerebellum**, which coordinates movement and position; and the **brainstem**, which controls breathing and heart rate. Information is transmitted to and from the brain through the nerves, which are bundled in the spinal cord and branch out from there into all parts of the body.

PRACTICE 3

1. Which human body system interacts with each cell of the body?

   A. the circulatory system
   B. the digestive system
   C. the muscular system
   D. the skeletal system

2. How are the alveoli in the lungs and the villi in the small intestine similar?

   A. Both are structures located in the respiratory system.
   B. Both are structures located in the digestive system.
   C. Both are structures in which substances pass through capillary walls into the blood.
   D. Both are structures involved in coordination and movement.

3. In the 17th century, English physician William Harvey concluded that blood in the veins flows toward the heart.

   Which of the following facts helps support Harvey's conclusion?

   A. The heart pumps about 1,800 gallons of blood per day.
   B. The heart has four chambers: two atria and two ventricles.
   C. Large veins branch into smaller blood vessels called capillaries.
   D. Veins have valves that allow blood to flow in one direction only.

Questions 4 and 5 refer to the following information and diagram.

The kidneys of the urinary system remove cellular wastes and excess water from the blood. This material, called urine, is stored in the bladder until it is excreted from the body.

The Urinary System

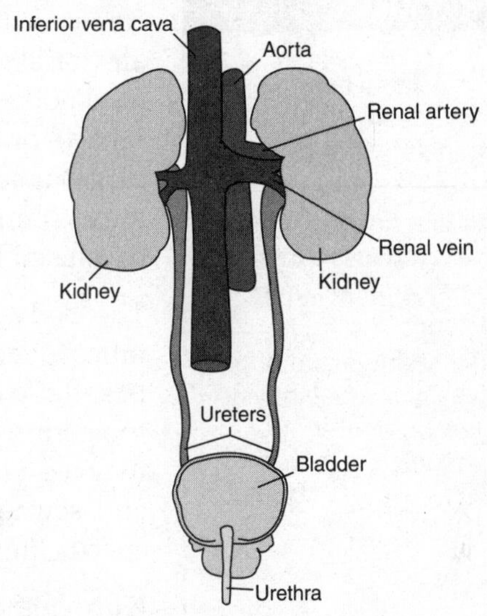

4. Which of the following is the name of the structure(s) through which urine passes from each kidney to the bladder?

   A. ureter
   B. urethra
   C. renal veins
   D. aorta

5. A urologist is a doctor who specializes in disorders of the urinary system.

   Which of the following patients is most likely to be treated by a urologist?

   A. a patient with low levels of iron in her blood
   B. a patient with a painful kidney stone
   C. a patient with swollen veins in the anus, called hemorrhoids
   D. a patient with chronic indigestion

STUDY ADVICE

Speaking of health, how's your stress level? Remember that you have to manage your stress just as you manage any other aspect of your studies. Keep yourself on a regular sleep schedule, eat right, exercise, and find other healthy ways to manage your stress.

LESSON 4

Health Issues

Health can be affected by infections, nutrition, and substance abuse.

An **infection** is the invasion of the body by germs—microorganisms that cause disease. It is often characterized by fever and other symptoms. Germs can enter the body through breaks in the skin (for example, tetanus), with air (for example, influenza), in contaminated food and water (for example, food poisoning), by contact with contaminated blood or saliva (for example, rabies), or through sexual activity (for example, gonorrhea). Infections can be grouped according to the type of microorganisms that cause them. The most common germs are **bacteria** and **viruses**, although infections can also be caused by fungi, protozoans, and worms.

The body has natural defenses against infection, such as the skin, the mucous membranes in the nose, tears, and acid in the stomach. If germs get past these defenses, the **immune system** produces **antibodies** that destroy the germs. In developed nations, infectious diseases are less common than they used to be because of better nutrition and living conditions, safer water and sewage systems, **immunization** (which provides protection against specific infectious diseases), and **antibiotics**, drugs that fight bacteria.

Nutrients are substances that are needed for growth, normal functioning, and maintenance of cells. The body does not produce nutrients; instead, we get them from the food we eat. The nutrients that humans need for good health include **proteins**, **carbohydrates** (sugars and starches), **fats**, **vitamins**, **minerals**, and water. In a well-balanced diet, people get enough nutrients to provide energy as well as the right nutrients needed for all the body's functions. Too much or too little of a nutrient can cause problems. For example, a diet with too much fat can lead to obesity and contribute to heart disease. Too little vitamin C can cause scurvy, a painful disease.

Drugs are substances that affect the structure or function of the body. They are usually used to treat disease or relieve its symptoms, although some drugs, like nicotine in tobacco, have no medicinal purpose. The nonmedical use of a drug to the point that it interferes with a person's normal functioning is called **drug abuse**, or substance abuse. Drug abuse can lead to **addiction**, a severe form of dependence that causes physical changes in the body so that when the drug wears off or is stopped, withdrawal symptoms such as nausea and pain occur. Heroin, speed, alcohol, nicotine, and barbiturates are frequently abused addictive drugs. A milder form of dependence than addiction is **psychological dependence**, or **habituation**. In this type of dependence, the urge to take the drug is strong, even though there are no withdrawal symptoms. Examples of drugs that can cause habituation in humans are marijuana and hallucinogens. People also abuse substances that are not drugs, like glue, gasoline, and aerosols. Most of these substances are **inhalants**—they are sniffed for their effect on the nervous system. Inhalants generally depress, or slow, the functioning of the nervous system, sometimes causing their users to lose control or become unconscious.

KEY IDEAS

- Infections occur when the body is invaded by germs—microorganisms that cause disease.
- A healthy diet has the right nutrients—proteins, carbohydrates, fats, vitamins, minerals, and water.
- The abuse of drugs and other substances can cause physical changes and interfere with a person's daily functioning.

HiSET EXAM TIP

All questions on the Science Test are in multiple-choice format. For each question, you must pick the one correct answer from the four options that are given.

PRACTICE 4

1. Which of the following is among the body's first barriers against germs?

   A. the immune system
   B. antibiotics
   C. antibodies
   D. the skin

2. Each evening, Sara has a glass of wine. If there is no wine in the house, she feels a strong urge to get some, although she feels no ill effects if she does not.

   What is Sara's relationship to alcohol?

   A. addiction
   B. physical dependence
   C. habituation
   D. withdrawal

Questions 3 and 4 are based on the following table.

Nutrients in the Diet

Nutrient	Description	Function	Source
Proteins	Complex molecules of amino acids made of oxygen, carbon, nitrogen, hydrogen	Growth and maintenance of cells and metabolism	Meat, fish, eggs, dairy products, legumes, nuts, seeds
Carbohydrates	Molecules containing oxygen, carbon, and hydrogen	Body's main energy source, providing 4 calories of energy per gram; roughage for digestion	Bread, pasta, cereal, rice, fruits, potatoes
Fats	Fatty acids containing oxygen, carbon, and hydrogen	Concentrated source of energy, providing 9 calories of energy per gram; insulation; cell maintenance	Fish oils, vegetable oils, and animal fats
Vitamins	Substances used in very small quantities that are vital for body chemistry	Growth, maintenance, repair of cells; protein synthesis; metabolism; and other functions	Various foods, sunlight on skin (vitamin D), microorganisms in the bowel (vitamin K)
Minerals	Substances, such as iron and calcium, necessary for normal development	Many functions, including making red blood cells and building strong bones	Various foods
Water	A liquid made of oxygen and hydrogen atoms	Involved in almost all body processes	Beverages, soups, foods

3. Which of the following statements is supported by the information in the table?

   A. Fats are a more concentrated source of energy than carbohydrates.
   B. Vitamins are more important in the diet than minerals.
   C. A good source of vitamin C is citrus fruits.
   D. Minerals provide a low-fat source of energy.

4. Which of the following is a fact, rather than an opinion, based on the table?

   A. Eating meat is the best way to get sufficient protein in your diet.
   B. Carbohydrates come from fruits as well as from bread and rice.
   C. Iron is the only mineral you need.
   D. Everyone should drink eight glasses of water each day.

LESSON 5

Reproduction and Heredity

All **species** of organisms reproduce in some way. There are two types of reproduction. In **asexual reproduction**, an individual organism produces offspring identical to the parent. For example, in a type of asexual reproduction called budding, a tiny freshwater animal called a hydra grows buds that develop into offspring. In **sexual reproduction**, two sex cells combine to form unique offspring with characteristics from both parent cells. In humans and many other species, those specialized sex cells are called **sperm** and **ova**.

Physical characteristics of organisms are called **traits**. The passing of traits from parents to offspring in sexual reproduction is called **heredity**. The first person to study heredity in a systematic way was an Austrian monk, **Gregor Mendel** (1822–1884). He bred plants and observed that sometimes offspring plants had the same traits as the parents and sometimes they did not. Mendel experimented with **purebred** pea plants—plants that always produced offspring with the same form of a trait as the parent. For example, purebred short plants always produced short offspring. First he crossed purebred short plants with purebred tall plants. In the first generation of offspring, all the plants were tall—the shortness trait had vanished. When the first-generation offspring reproduced, about three-quarters of the next generation of plants were tall, and one-quarter were short. The shortness trait had reappeared.

Mendel repeated his pea plant experiments with other traits over a ten-year period. Eventually he concluded that individual factors from each parent plant control the **inheritance** of specific traits. An offspring plant inherited one factor from the female parent and one from the male parent. Mendel concluded that one factor in a pair can hide the other factor. For example, the tallness factor hid the shortness factor in the first generation of offspring.

The factors that control traits are called **genes**. Different forms of a gene are called **alleles**. The gene that controls pea plant height, for example, has one allele for tallness and one allele for shortness. Each pea plant inherits one allele for the height gene from each parent. Therefore, any particular pea plant may have (1) two alleles for tallness, (2) two alleles for shortness, or (3) one allele for shortness and one for tallness. In the third case, the **dominant allele**, the tallness allele, controls the appearance of the trait. The **recessive allele**, the shortness allele, is hidden. For a recessive trait to appear in an individual, the individual must inherit two recessive alleles.

In Mendel's original experiment, the parent plants were purebred tall and purebred short. Thus, one parent had two dominant alleles for tallness, and the other parent had two recessive alleles for shortness. All the offspring in the first generation were **hybrid**—each had one allele for tallness and one for shortness. Because the tallness allele is dominant, all of the first generation plants were tall. In the next generation, some plants inherited two dominant alleles, some inherited two recessive alleles, and some inherited one dominant and one recessive allele, producing a mix of plants.

KEY IDEAS

- In asexual reproduction, an offspring is identical to its parent; in sexual reproduction, an offspring is unique, inheriting traits from each parent.
- Gregor Mendel was the first to observe patterns of trait inheritance.
- Traits are controlled by genes, which come in forms called alleles. A dominant allele hides a recessive allele.

HiSET EXAM TIP

As you take the test, pace yourself. If you are unsure of an answer, do your best and make a note to yourself to revisit that question. At the end of the test, you may have time to review those questions.

PRACTICE 5

Questions 1 through 3 refer to the following paragraph and diagram.

The Punnett square below shows all the possible combinations of alleles for height in offspring pea plants when two tall hybrid pea plants are crossed. A capital *T* represents the dominant tallness allele, and a lowercase *t*, the recessive shortness allele. One parent's alleles are shown along the top of the square; the other's are shown on the left side. The **genotypes** of the offspring are shown in the boxes.

	T	t
T	TT	Tt
t	Tt	tt

1. Of the parent pea plants,

A. both are tall.
B. both are short.
C. both are of medium height.
D. one is tall and one is short.

2. What chance is there that an offspring will be short?

A. 0 out of 4
B. 1 out of 4
C. 2 out of 4
D. 3 out of 4

3. If you wanted to grow only tall pea plants in your garden over several growing seasons, which of the following genotypes would give you the best results?

A. tt
B. Tt
C. tT
D. TT

4. To show a recessive trait, an organism must inherit how many recessive alleles for that trait?

A. none
B. at least one
C. at most one
D. two

5. Why are organisms that reproduce sexually more genetically diverse than organisms that reproduce asexually?

A. Organisms that reproduce sexually tend to produce more offspring than those that reproduce asexually.
B. Organisms that reproduce sexually produce offspring that inherit diverse traits from only one parent.
C. Organisms that reproduce sexually produce offspring with entirely new traits unlike those of either parent.
D. Organisms that reproduce sexually produce offspring that have inherited a mix of traits from their parents.

6. A student is trying to repeat Mendel's experiments using the trait of fur color in rabbits. Black fur is dominant and white fur is recessive. She starts with what she assumes is a purebred white female rabbit and a purebred black male rabbit. She crosses them and is surprised when one of the offspring has white fur.

What probably was wrong with the student's experiment?

A. The white female was actually a hybrid.
B. The black male was actually a hybrid.
C. Most of the offspring were hybrids.
D. Most of the offspring were purebred.

LESSON 6

Modern Genetics

Years after Mendel died, scientists identified **chromosomes**, rod-shaped structures in the nucleus of each cell, as responsible for carrying genes from parent organisms to their offspring. Reproductive cells have half the number of chromosomes of an organism's other cells. When a sperm cell and an ovum unite, the resulting offspring has a full set of chromosomes. For example, human sex cells have 23 chromosomes and our other cells have 46.

KEY IDEAS

- Chromosomes are structures in a cell's nucleus that are composed mostly of genes, which are located on long molecules of DNA.
- DNA contains the genetic code for making proteins in the cell.
- Knowledge of genetics has led to advances in many fields but especially in medicine.

One chromosome can contain thousands of genes on a single long molecule of **deoxyribonucleic acid (DNA)**. A DNA molecule is shaped like a spiral ladder. The sides of the ladder are made of deoxyribose—a sugar—and phosphate. Each rung of the ladder is made of a pair of nitrogen bases. There are four of these bases: adenine (A), guanine (G), thymine (T), and cytosine (C). The four bases pair up in a specific way: A always pairs with T, and C always pairs with G.

DNA

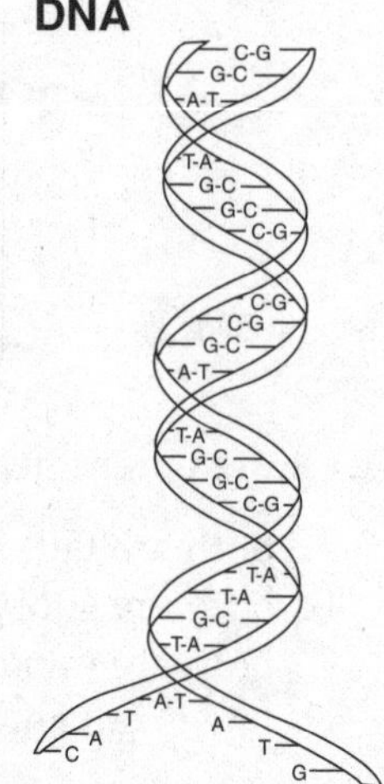

DNA controls the cell's production of proteins, which help determine all the characteristics and processes of the organism. During **protein synthesis**, the information from a gene in the cell's nucleus is used to produce a protein on ribosomes in the cytoplasm. Messenger **ribonucleic acid (RNA)** transmits the code from the DNA. Each set of three base pairs on the messenger RNA, called a **codon**, contains instructions for creating an **amino acid**—a protein building block. The sequence of codons determines the sequence of amino acids in the protein and thus the specific protein to be made. So, the order of bases on the gene forms a **genetic code** for the synthesis of a particular protein.

HiSET EXAM TIP

Some questions on the Science Test are based entirely on a graphic. Read the title of the diagram, chart, or graph to make sure you understand its main idea before you answer questions based on it.

There have been many recent advances in genetics, some controversial. Dolly the sheep and other animals have been cloned from single cells. Cloning bypasses sexual reproduction, raising the possibility that one day humans will be cloned—an idea that many find unethical. Through genetic engineering, the DNA of one organism can be introduced into the DNA of another organism, changing the second organism's traits. Genetic engineering has been used to produce medicines, such as insulin. It has been more controversial when used to improve foods. Finally, the entire **human genome**, or genetic code, has been decoded, making possible many advances in medicine. Scientists have identified genes involved in genetic disorders such as cystic fibrosis. They have also identified genes that predispose people to diseases such as breast cancer and Alzheimer's disease. Through genetic testing, people can find out whether they have any of these disease-related genes. In some cases, they can take steps to prevent the disease or to seek early treatment. In recent years, scientists have also succeeded in correcting certain genetic disorders through gene therapy.

PRACTICE 6

1. Which of the following provides the code needed for a cell to make proteins?

   A. the number of chromosomes in the cell
   B. the amino acids in the cytoplasm
   C. the sequence of base pairs in a gene
   D. the pairing of adenine with thymine

2. A mutation is any change in the DNA of a gene. Which of the following is the most likely result of a mutation?

   A. the loss of one or more chromosomes
   B. an extra chromosome
   C. too much RNA in the cytoplasm
   D. a change in protein synthesis

3. Some animals have been genetically engineered to grow larger. Plants have been engineered to resist diseases or insects. Some fruits have been engineered to ripen more slowly. Genetic engineering of domesticated plants and animals is controversial. According to some people, these foods pose a risk because their effects on consumers and the environment are unknown. Others claim that genetically engineered foods are safe.

   Which of the following statements is an opinion about genetic engineering rather than a fact?

   A. Scientists have used genetic engineering to produce animals that grow larger.
   B. Disease-resistant plants have been produced by genetic engineering.
   C. Some genetically engineered fruit takes longer to ripen than its unaltered counterpart.
   D. Genetically engineered foods are safe for consumers and the environment.

4. When a cell reproduces through cell division, scientists call the reproducing cell the parent cell, and the two cells that result from the division are called daughter cells. The daughter cells are genetically identical to the parent cells. Before a parent cell starts to divide, the DNA in its nucleus replicates, or makes a complete copy of itself.

   Why is this process necessary?

   A. so that the parent cell will have an extra copy of DNA
   B. so that each daughter cell receives a complete set of DNA
   C. so that each daughter cell will not need to synthesize proteins
   D. so that each daughter cell will receive half its DNA from each parent cell

5. Which of the following statements is supported by the diagram and the passage on page 626?

   A. The DNA molecule unzips between the sugar and phosphate segments.
   B. The base guanine pairs only with the base cytosine.
   C. In a sequence of DNA bases, guanine always comes before adenine.
   D. About 10 percent of DNA contains genes; the remainder is "junk" DNA.

6. Proteins, which perform a variety of functions, are built from chains of _________.

   A. amino acids
   B. RNA
   C. codons
   D. enzymes

STUDY ADVICE

On Test Day, you may see some questions about inheritance and how traits can vary from one generation to the next. Be sure you've absorbed this lesson, and, as you read the next lesson, think about how heredity and evolution relate to each other.

LESSON 7

Evolution and Natural Selection

In 1831, the British ship the *Beagle* set sail with naturalist Charles Darwin (1809–1882) aboard. Darwin's job was to observe living things he encountered. His observations during this five-year trip around the world led him to formulate an important scientific theory, the theory of **evolution**.

One of the *Beagle*'s stops was the Galápagos Islands, a group of islands in the Pacific Ocean off the South American coast. There, Darwin saw great diversity of life forms. He noticed that many of the plants and animals resembled those he had seen on the South American mainland. However, there were also important differences between mainland and island organisms. For example, the iguanas on the mainland had small claws that allowed them to climb trees to eat leaves. On the Galápagos, iguanas had large claws that allowed them to grip wet, slippery rocks and eat seaweed. As Darwin traveled among the Galápagos Islands, he also observed that similar species of organisms sometimes differed from island to island. For example, small birds called ground finches had strong, wide beaks well-suited for breaking and eating seeds. However, different species of ground finches had different sized beaks, depending on which island they lived on. The sizes of the iguanas' claws and the birds' beaks are examples of **adaptations**, traits that help an organism survive in its environment. From these observations, Darwin concluded that organisms had originally come from the mainland and had changed, or evolved, over many generations to become better adapted to their new island environments.

Darwin explained that species evolve because of **natural selection**. By this process, individuals that are better adapted to their environments are more likely to survive and reproduce, passing their favorable adaptations to their offspring. Several factors are involved in natural selection:

1. Most species produce far more offspring than can survive.
2. These offspring compete with one another for scarce resources in their environment.
3. Members of a species have different traits, called **variations**. Some variations make individuals better adapted to survive in their environment.
4. Individuals with favorable variations are more likely to survive, reproduce, and pass the favorable traits to their offspring.
5. Over generations, helpful variations spread through a species, causing the species to change, or evolve.

Evolution through natural selection explains how species change over time. But how do new species evolve? Geographic isolation seems to play a big role in the evolution of new species. When a group of individuals remains separated from the rest of its species long enough, it may become a new species. This means that members of the new species will be unable to interbreed with members of the original species. For example, there are 13 species of finches on the various Galápagos Islands. They all probably evolved from a single ancestral species.

KEY IDEAS

- Charles Darwin's observations in the Galápagos Islands led him to formulate the theory of evolution.
- Adaptations are traits that help an organism survive in its environment.
- Natural selection is the process by which individuals with favorable variations survive, reproduce, and pass the variations to their offspring.

HiSET EXAM TIP

The Science Test will likely not test memorized definitions of terms such as "adaptation" and "natural selection." However, you could be asked a question about the meaning of a term in the context of a science passage.

PRACTICE 7

Questions 1 and 2 refer to the following paragraph and diagram.

The forelimbs of humans, penguins, birds that fly, and alligators are similar. The similar pattern of the bones may be evidence that these animals evolved from a common ancestor. Similar structures that organisms may have inherited from a common ancestor are called homologous structures.

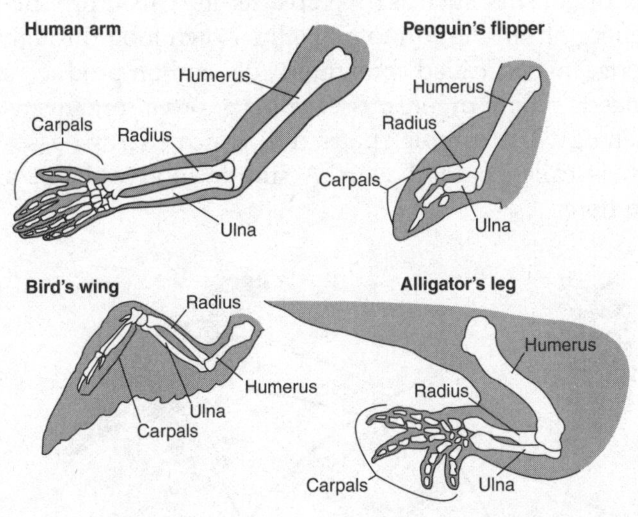

1. The forelimbs of frogs are homologous to those of human arms, penguins' flippers, birds' wings, and alligators' legs. Based on the diagram and paragraph, which of the following is likely to be true of frogs' forelimbs?

   A. Frogs use their forelimbs for swimming.
   B. Frogs' forelimbs contain carpal bones.
   C. Frogs' forelimbs resemble wings more than they resemble human arms.
   D. Frogs are more closely related to humans than they are to alligators.

2. Which of the following statements is supported by the paragraph and the diagram?

   A. The tip of a bird's wing is homologous to the upper arm of a human.
   B. Penguins are more closely related to humans than they are to birds.
   C. In penguins, flying birds, humans, and alligators, the forelimbs have similar structures despite performing different functions.
   D. Homologous structures have similar functions in modern organisms but had different functions in modern organisms' ancestors.

3. What are **adaptations**, according to the passage on page 628?

   A. traits that make an organism better able to survive in its environment
   B. traits that all members of a species possess
   C. traits that are learned and not inherited
   D. traits that appear only when two recessive alleles are inherited

4. The more similar the DNA of two species, the more closely related they are. Scientists have used modern DNA analysis to trace the evolutionary relationships among Darwin's 13 species of finches. DNA analysis revealed that the finch species all had very similar DNA. Thus, Darwin was correct when he proposed that they had evolved from a common ancestor.

   Which of the following best explains why DNA analysis provides better evidence to support the hypothesis that Darwin's finches evolved from a common ancestor than the scientific methods that Darwin used?

   A. DNA analysis takes less time than observation.
   B. DNA analysis is easier to do than observing birds in the wild.
   C. DNA analysis provides more objective data than observation does.
   D. Technological methods of obtaining evidence are inferior to observation.

LESSON 8

Organization of Ecosystems

An **ecosystem** is an area consisting of a community of organisms—plants, animals, fungi, bacteria—and the physical environment in which they live—soil, air, water, and climate. Earth as a whole is an enormous ecosystem called the **biosphere**. Smaller ecosystems include meadows, ponds, wetlands, and tidal zones. A healthy ecosystem contains a diversity of organisms. Some of the organisms, such as green plants, are called **producers** because they use energy from the sun to make their own food through photosynthesis. Other organisms, called **consumers**, depend on producers to meet their energy needs. These organisms eat plants, or eat organisms that eat plants, to get energy. The complex pattern in which energy passes through an ecosystem is called a **food web**. A simple food web for a wooded area is shown here.

KEY IDEAS

- An ecosystem is a community of organisms and their physical environment.
- Energy passes through an ecosystem from the sun, to producers (green plants), to consumers.
- Carbon, oxygen, nitrogen, and water cycle through the biosphere from the living to the nonliving components and back again.

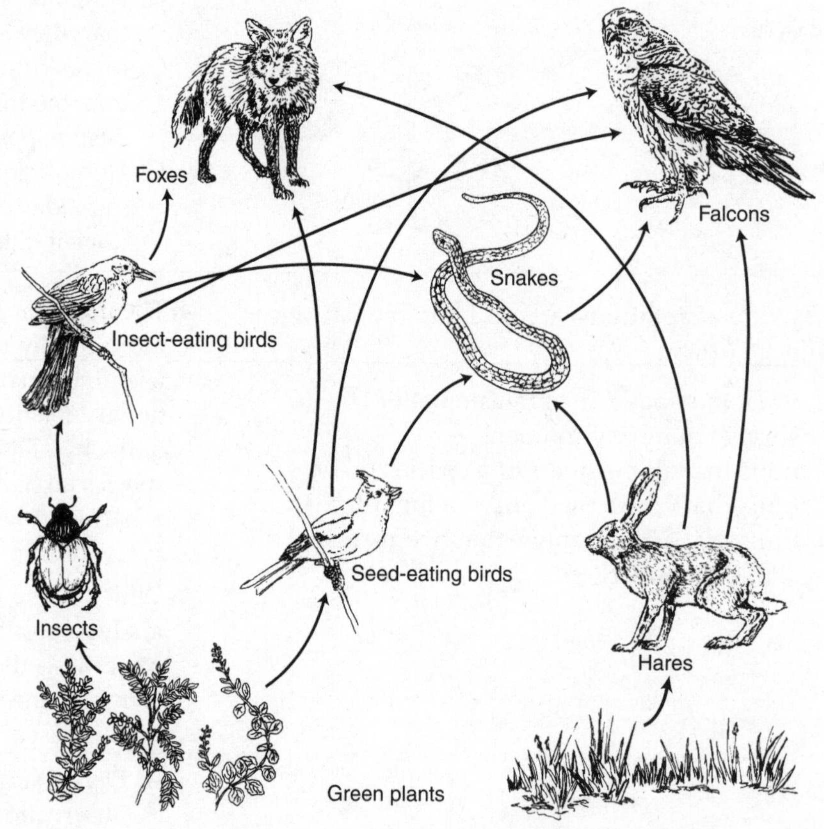

HiSET EXAM TIP

You may see diagrams, like the one on this page, which contain arrows. Follow the directions of the arrows to understand the process.

Carbon, oxygen, nitrogen, and water also cycle through ecosystems from the living to the nonliving components and back again. As discussed in Lesson 2, carbon and oxygen cycle through the biosphere as a result of photosynthesis and cellular respiration. Nitrogen cycles between the land, organisms, and the air through chemical processes. Water cycles between the oceans and other surface water, the air, land, and organisms through evaporation, condensation, precipitation, and transpiration from plants.

PRACTICE 8

1. According to the passage, what is the ultimate source of energy for the food web on page 630?

   A. green plants
   B. mammals
   C. soil, air, and water
   D. the sun

2. Suppose most of the foxes in the woodland ecosystem on page 630 were hunted and killed. Which of the following is most likely to happen as a result?

   A. The amount of plant life in the woodland would increase.
   B. The populations of hares and seed-eating birds would increase.
   C. The populations of insects and insect-eating birds would decrease.
   D. The population of snakes would decrease.

3. Which of the following is most similar to a naturally occurring ecosystem?

   A. a diorama with dried vegetation and stuffed animals
   B. an aquarium with aquatic plants and herbivorous tropical fish
   C. a house with central air conditioning and heating
   D. a supermarket with a large section of fresh fruits and vegetables

4. In most cases, changes in one aspect of an ecosystem result in reactions in other parts of the ecosystem, restoring balance. In some cases, however, changes can be so great that the original ecosystem is replaced with another. When this occurs naturally, as when grasses are replaced by taller plants, shrubs, and eventually trees, it is called succession.

   Which of the following statements is supported by the information above?

   A. When changes are introduced into an ecosystem, its balance is permanently disrupted.
   B. Succession is usually caused by human destruction of an ecosystem.
   C. The intentional replacement of a wooded area by a field of cultivated wheat is an example of succession.
   D. The natural replacement of lichens by mosses and ferns, and then shrubs, is an example of succession.

5. Although more than three-quarters of the atmosphere is nitrogen, atmospheric nitrogen cannot be used directly by plants and animals. Instead, certain bacteria and blue-green algae take nitrogen from the air and, through a process called nitrogen fixation, turn it into compounds that plants can use. Nitrogen-fixing bacteria are found in the roots of some plants such as peas and beans. When these plants are present, the nitrate content of the soil is increased. Nitrates are absorbed by plants, which are eaten by consumers. Eventually the nitrogen returns to the soil in excrement and when organisms die.

   What is the role of nitrogen-fixing bacteria in the nitrogen cycle?

   A. to decompose dead plants and animals
   B. to add nitrogen to the atmosphere
   C. to turn atmospheric nitrogen into compounds plants and animals can use
   D. to take nitrogen from blue-green algae and turn it into compounds plants can use

Life Science Practice Questions

1. Cell membranes are selectively permeable, allowing some substances to pass through and blocking others. The movement through the cell membrane takes place by means of passive or active transport. In passive transport, materials like water move through the cell's membrane without using any of the cell's energy. Active transport is the movement of materials in the cell from areas of low concentration to areas of high concentration. In active transport, the cell uses energy to move substances in and out. For example, transport proteins use energy when they carry molecules into and out of the cell.

   What is the main difference between passive transport and active transport?

   A. Active transport involves the passage of water, and passive transport does not.
   B. Active transport requires the cell to use energy, and passive transport does not.
   C. Active transport is used by animal cells, and passive transport is used by plant cells.
   D. Active transport takes substances out of the cell, and passive transport brings them in.

2. Ben set up an experiment to prove that ivy plants take in water through their roots. He took a jar, put an ivy plant in the open jar, and filled the jar with water to cover only the roots of the ivy. After a week, he checked the water level in the jar and found it had gone down. Ben concluded that the plant had absorbed water through its roots.

   Why does Ben have insufficient proof for his conclusion?

   A. Ben should have put more ivy plants in the open jar.
   B. Ben should have put several plants of different species in the open jar.
   C. The water level in the jar might have gone down because of evaporation.
   D. There should have been soil in the jar rather than water.

Questions 3 and 4 refer to the following information and diagram.

A pedigree shows the pattern of inheritance of a trait in a family. In a pedigree, circles represent females; squares represent males. A completely shaded shape indicates that the person has the trait. A half-shaded shape indicates the person carries the recessive form of the gene for the trait but does not have the trait. An unshaded shape indicates the person neither has nor carries the trait. In the following pedigree, Megan is a carrier of the genetic disorder cystic fibrosis, although she is healthy.

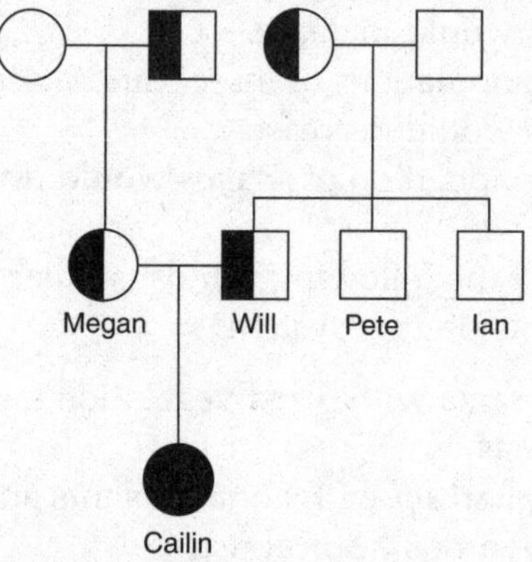

3. Which of the following people is a carrier of cystic fibrosis?

   A. Megan's mother
   B. Megan's father
   C. Will's father
   D. Pete

4. Which of the following best explains why Megan's and Will's families were surprised to learn Cailin had inherited cystic fibrosis?

   A. Megan and Will are carriers of cystic fibrosis.
   B. Some of Will's distant ancestors had cystic fibrosis.
   C. Megan's father and Will's mother are carriers of cystic fibrosis.
   D. No one in either Megan's or Will's immediate family has cystic fibrosis except Cailin.

Questions 5 through 7 refer to the following paragraph and diagram.

Mitosis is a type of cell division in which two daughter cells are formed that have the same genetic material as the parent cell. Before mitosis starts, each chromosome in the nucleus duplicates itself to produce two sections, called chromatids, which are linked. Those chromatids then split, so that each daughter cell has DNA identical to that of the parent cell and to that of the other daughter cell. The function of the spindle fiber in mitosis is to control the movement of chromatids during mitosis. During metaphase, for example, the spindle fiber helps to align the chromatids in a line across the middle of the cell so that the chromatids can divide evenly. The spindle fibers then direct the movement of the chromatids after they split, ensuring that each daughter cell has a full set of identical chromatids.

The Process of Mitosis

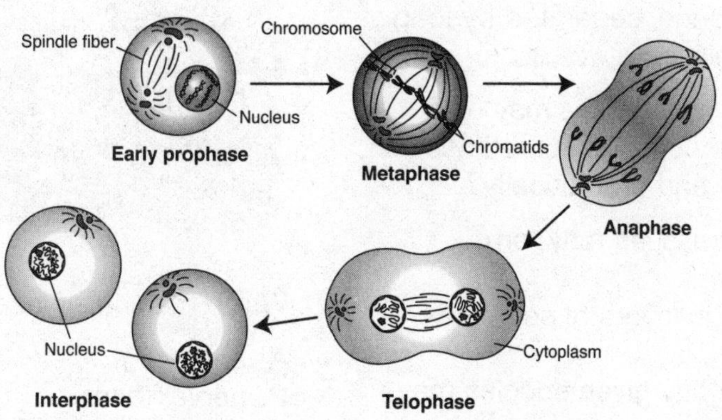

5. During which stage do the chromosomes line up across the middle of the cell?
   A. early prophase
   B. metaphase
   C. telophase
   D. interphase

6. Which of the following is true based on the paragraph and diagram?
   A. After mitosis, one of the resulting daughter cells is larger than the other one.
   B. After mitosis, the two daughter cells have their own nuclei.
   C. The first stage of mitosis is the division of the cell into two separate cells.
   D. The first stage of mitosis involves the formation of cytoplasm.

7. What is the function of the spindle during mitosis?
   A. to duplicate the chromosomes
   B. to control the movement of chromosomes
   C. to dissolve the nuclear membrane
   D. to help divide the cytoplasm for the two daughter cells

8. Charles Darwin thought that evolution took place gradually, with tiny changes eventually adding up to major change in a species. If this view is right, then there should be fossils, remains of long-dead organisms, that show the intermediate stages of evolution in a species. However, the fossil record often shows no intermediate forms for long periods of time. Instead, fossils of a species appear to suddenly become distinctly different. To account for this, some modern scientists have hypothesized that species evolve during short periods of rapid, major change, separated by long periods of relative stability.

   Which of the following hypotheses may also explain why evolutionary change sometimes seems to occur rapidly and dramatically?

   A. Organisms with soft tissues may form fossils.
   B. Fossils usually form in layers of sedimentary rock.
   C. The fossil record for any given species may be incomplete.
   D. Fossils do not provide evidence for evolution.

9. Blood consists of blood cells and proteins suspended in a yellowish liquid called plasma. Red blood cells carry oxygen to the body. White blood cells protect the body against infection. Plasma transports nutrients and hormones to the body's cells and removes waste.

   Which answer choice below describes some of the main functions of blood?

   A. energy production and movement
   B. movement and cell repair
   C. cell repair and respiration
   D. nutrient transport and immune defense

Questions 10 and 11 refer to the following diagram.

Tooth Cross Section

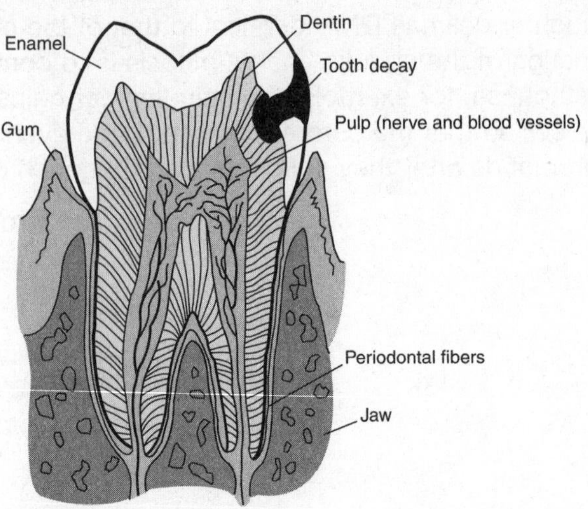

10. Which material covers the tooth's top surface?

    A. enamel
    B. nerve fibers
    C. blood vessels
    D. periodontal fibers

11. Tooth decay can eat away at the structure of a tooth. Tooth decay begins at the surface, but it must reach the pulp, which contains many nerve endings, before it will cause extreme pain. That suggests that the dentin contains __________.

    A. few or no nerve endings
    B. many nerve endings
    C. more minerals than the enamel
    D. fewer minerals than the enamel

12. The carrying capacity of an ecosystem is the maximum number of organisms it can support. If the carrying capacity is exceeded, there will not be enough resources, and one or more species will decline until a balance of organisms and resources is reached.

    Which of the following is an example of people overloading the carrying capacity of an ecosystem?

    A. using a park for recreation
    B. grazing too many cattle on grassland
    C. adding a room to a suburban house
    D. banning shellfishing in polluted waters

13. Classification is the grouping of organisms based on similarities in their traits and their evolutionary histories. In the past, scientists classified organisms based primarily on a visual analysis of their structures and on the fossil record. Today, DNA analysis of selected genes is overturning many traditional classifications. For example, it was thought that sperm whales and dolphins, both of which have teeth, were closely related. However, DNA analysis revealed that sperm whales are actually more closely related to baleen whales, which do not have teeth.

    What is the reason that DNA analysis has led to changes in the classification of organisms?

    A. DNA analysis provides more fundamental, accurate data than does a visual analysis of structures and fossils.
    B. Traditional classification was based on the erroneous assumption that organisms could be grouped by similarities.
    C. When organisms possess similar structures, it always means that they are closely related.
    D. When data from DNA analysis conflict with data from structural analysis, usually the structural data are correct.

14. *Homeothermy* refers to the maintenance of a constant body temperature in warm-blooded animals, such as dogs and human beings. Warm-blooded animals have specific body processes to help them gain or lose heat. For example, sweating helps cool the body through the evaporation of water, and shivering helps generate heat in cold environments.

    Which of the following is most likely an example of a homeothermic process in dogs?

    A. panting
    B. healing after a wound
    C. reproduction
    D. grooming

Questions 15 through 17 refer to the following graph.

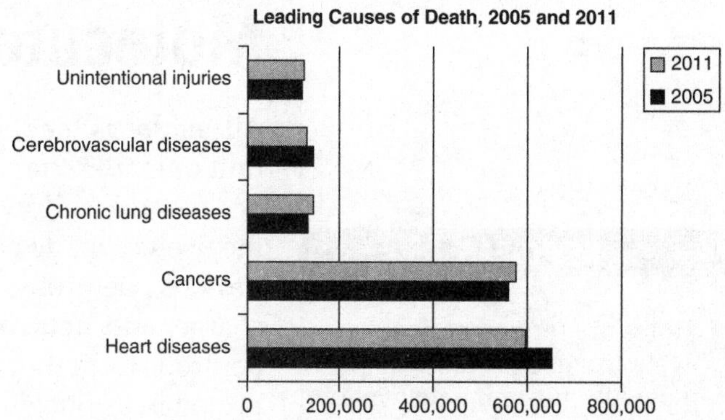

Source: National Center for Health Statistics

15. How many of the five causes of death depicted in the graph produced more deaths in 2011 than in 2005?

    A. 2
    B. 3
    C. 4
    D. 5

16. Compare the number of deaths from heart disease in 2005 to the number of deaths from heart disease in 2011. Of the causes of death depicted in the graph, that difference represents the

    A. biggest increase
    B. biggest decrease
    C. smallest increase
    D. smallest decrease

17. Which of the following approximately expresses the percentage change in deaths from heart diseases from 2005 to 2011? You MAY use your calculator.

    A. 8% increase
    B. 8% decrease
    C. 92% increase
    D. 92% decrease

Physical Science

LESSON 1

Atoms and Molecules

All matter is made of tiny particles called atoms. An **atom** is the smallest unit of matter that can combine chemically with other matter and that cannot be broken down into smaller particles by chemical means. Atoms are themselves made of **subatomic particles**. The major subatomic particles are protons, neutrons, and electrons. **Protons** are particles with a positive charge, and **neutrons** are particles with no charge. Together, protons and neutrons form the nucleus of all atoms except hydrogen, which has just one proton in its nucleus. **Electrons** are particles with negative charge. Electrons orbit the nucleus of an atom. When an atom has an equal number of protons and electrons, it is electrically neutral. When an atom gains or loses electrons, it becomes a negatively charged or positively charged **ion**.

KEY IDEAS

- Atoms are formed of positively charged protons, neutral neutrons, and negatively charged electrons.
- All matter can be classified as elements, compounds, or mixtures.
- Atoms are held together in molecules and compounds by bonds.

Matter can be classified as elements, compounds, or mixtures.

- **Elements** are substances that cannot be broken down into other substances. They are made of a single type of atom. Gold, iron, hydrogen, sodium, oxygen, and carbon are some familiar elements. Each element has a **chemical symbol**. For example, gold is Au, iron is Fe, hydrogen is H, sodium is Na, oxygen is O, and carbon is C.
- **Compounds** are substances formed of two or more elements chemically combined in a definite proportion. Compounds have properties that differ from the properties of the elements that they contain. For example, at room temperature, water is a liquid compound made of the elements hydrogen and oxygen, which, uncombined, are both gases. Compounds are represented by **chemical formulas**. The chemical formula for water is H_2O, indicating that a water molecule is made of two atoms of hydrogen and one atom of oxygen.
- **Mixtures** are physical combinations of two or more substances that keep their own properties. For example, salt water is a mixture.

HiSET EXAM TIP

If you are having trouble choosing the correct answer to a multiple-choice question, eliminate the options that are clearly wrong. Of the remaining options, choose the one that makes the most sense.

When elements combine to form **molecules** or ionic compounds, their constituents are held together by **bonds**. There are two main types of bonds: covalent and ionic. In a **covalent bond**, atoms share a pair of electrons, each atom contributing one electron. For example, the compound water is held together by covalent bonds. In an **ionic bond**, atoms gain or lose electrons to become ions, and the attraction between positively (+) and negatively (–) charged ions holds the compound together. For example, sodium chloride (NaCl), commonly called table salt, is an ionic compound.

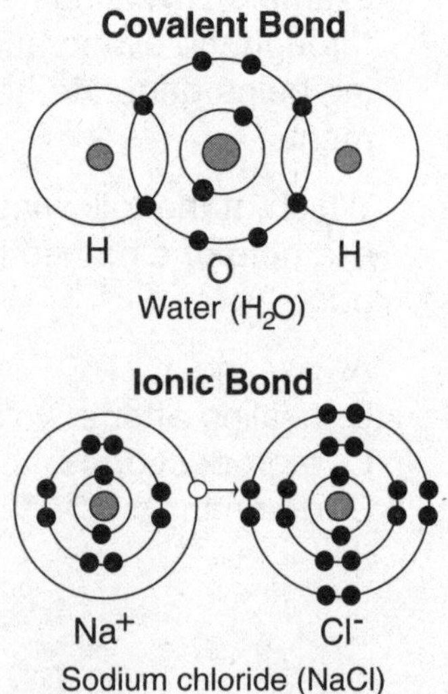

PRACTICE 1

1. Sodium is represented by the chemical symbol Na, and chlorine is represented by the chemical symbol Cl. According to the text and the diagram on page 636, what happens when sodium chloride forms?

   A. The sodium atom loses an electron, becoming positively charged, and the chlorine atom gains an electron, becoming negatively charged.
   B. The sodium atom gains an electron, becoming negatively charged, and the chlorine atom loses an electron, becoming positively charged.
   C. The sodium atom gains an electron, becoming positively charged, and the chlorine atom loses an electron, becoming negatively charged.
   D. The sodium and chlorine atoms share a pair of electrons, becoming ions and forming a covalent bond.

2. Water is composed of two atoms of hydrogen and one atom of oxygen and has the formula H_2O. Glucose, a simple sugar, consists of 6 atoms of carbon, 12 atoms of hydrogen, and 6 atoms of oxygen.

   Which of the following is the chemical formula for glucose?

   A. CHO
   B. ${}_6C_{12}H_6O$
   C. $C^6H^{12}O^6$
   D. $C_6H_{12}O_6$

3. Based on the information on page 636, ions are

   A. electrically neutral atoms.
   B. atoms that have gained electrons to become positively charged.
   C. atoms that have lost electrons to become negatively charged.
   D. atoms that have either gained electrons to become negatively charged or lost electrons to become positively charged.

4. In 1911, British scientist Ernest Rutherford performed experiments that increased our knowledge of atomic structure. He bombarded an extremely thin sheet of gold foil with helium nuclei. (Helium nuclei, also called alpha particles, consist of two protons and two neutrons). He found that most of the helium nuclei passed right through the foil. Only a few were deflected back toward the source. On the basis of this experiment, Rutherford concluded that an atom has a dense nucleus with electrons orbiting it, but consists mostly of empty space.

   Which of the following is evidence that atoms consist mostly of empty space?

   A. Helium nuclei consist of two protons and two neutrons.
   B. Most of the alpha particles passed right through the gold foil.
   C. A few alpha particles were deflected off the gold foil and bounced back toward the source.
   D. Electrons orbit a dense nucleus consisting of protons and neutrons.

5. The number of protons in the nucleus of an atom is called the atomic number. Each element has a unique number of protons in its nucleus and therefore a unique atomic number.

   The atomic number of the element sodium is 11. How many electrons does a non-ionic sodium atom have?

   A. 10
   B. 11
   C. 12
   D. 22

LESSON 2

Properties and States of Matter

KEY IDEAS

- Matter has mass and occupies space.
- The three states of matter include solid, liquid, and gas. A substance's state of matter can be changed by adding or removing heat.
- Solutions are a type of mixture. The solute is the dissolved substance. The solvent is what the solute is dissolved in. Solvents and solutes can be any of the states of matter.

HiSET EXAM TIP

Approximately 29% of the questions on the Science Test are about physical science topics.

Matter is anything that has mass and takes up space. The **mass** of an object is the amount of matter that it contains, and its **weight** is a measure of the gravitational force exerted on it. The mass of an object like a shovel never changes, but its weight can change. For example, a shovel weighs less on the moon than it does on Earth because the gravitational pull of the moon is less than that of Earth.

Under most conditions, there are three **states of matter**, as described below:

- **Solids** have a definite shape and volume because the molecules of which they are made occupy fixed positions and do not move freely. In some solids, such as minerals, the molecules form an orderly pattern called a **crystal**.
- **Liquids** have a definite volume but no definite shape because the molecules in a liquid are loosely bound and move freely. For this reason, a liquid conforms to the shape of its container.
- **Gases** have no definite shape or volume. The attraction between the molecules of a gas is very weak. In consequence, the molecules of a gas are far apart and are always in motion, colliding with one another and with the sides of the container.

The states of matter can be changed by adding or removing heat energy. When heat is applied to a solid, it melts. This happens because the motion of the solid's molecules increases until the bonds between them are loosened, allowing them to flow freely. The temperature at which a solid becomes a liquid is its **melting point**. When heat is applied to a liquid, it boils and evaporates, turning into a gas as the motion of its molecules increases. The temperature at which a liquid becomes a gas is called its **boiling point**. When heat is removed from a gas, the motion of its molecules decreases and it turns into a liquid. The temperature at which a gas becomes a liquid is its **condensation point**. When heat is removed from a liquid, the motion of its molecules slows until it solidifies. The temperature at which a liquid becomes a solid is its **freezing point**. The temperatures at which a substance changes state are unique properties of that substance. For example, water boils at 100°C (212°F) and freezes at 0°C (32°F). Water is also the only substance that is found naturally in all three states on Earth.

As you learned in Lesson 1, mixtures are physical combinations of two or more substances that keep their original properties. A **solution** is a mixture (such as salt water) that is uniform throughout and that contains ions, atoms, or molecules of two or more substances. The substance in a solution that is dissolved is called the **solute**. The substance in which the solute is dissolved is the **solvent**. In salt water, for example, salt is the solute and water is the solvent. Water is called the universal solvent because so many substances dissolve in it. However, solutions are not always liquids. They can be solids, as when two or more metals are combined in an **alloy**, or they can be gases, as when oxygen and nitrogen are combined in the air.

PRACTICE 2

1. Which of the following physical changes involve adding heat to a substance?

   A. melting and boiling
   B. boiling and condensing
   C. condensing and freezing
   D. evaporating and condensing

2. Density is the amount of mass in a particular volume of a substance. It can be expressed in grams per cubic centimeter. The chart shows the densities of some common substances.

Densities of Substances

Substance	Density (g/cm^3)
Solids	
Lead	11.35
Iron	7.87
Aluminum	2.70
Liquids	
Chloroform	1.49
Water	1.00
Ethyl alcohol	0.79
Gases	
Oxygen	0.0013
Nitrogen	0.0012
Helium	0.0002

   Which of the following statements is supported by the information provided?

   A. Water is the least dense liquid on Earth.
   B. Solids are usually denser than liquids and gases.
   C. Density increases as the volume of a substance increases.
   D. Density decreases as the force of gravity decreases.

3. It is well known that the boiling point of water is 100° Celsius. More viscous, or thicker, substances often have higher boiling points. Glycerin, for example, boils at 290° Celsius, while olive oil boils at 300° Celsius.

   By what percentage is the boiling point of glycerin greater than that of water?

   A. 150%
   B. 190%
   C. 200%
   D. 290%

4. Water is different from most other substances. It changes from gas to liquid to solid at temperatures that are common on Earth. When it freezes, its molecules form a crystal lattice, so that its solid form is less dense than its liquid form. It is the most common solvent.

   Which of the following is a conclusion about water rather than a supporting statement?

   A. Water is a unique substance on Earth.
   B. Water changes state at temperatures typical on Earth.
   C. Frozen water is less dense than liquid water.
   D. Water is Earth's most common solvent.

5. When a solute is dissolved in a liquid solvent, the freezing point of the solution is lower than the freezing point of the pure liquid.

   In which of the following situations is this property of liquid solutions applied?

   A. Sugar dissolves in water more quickly if the solution is heated.
   B. Antifreeze added to water in a car's radiator lowers the freezing point below 0°C.
   C. The oil and vinegar in salad dressing is mixed more thoroughly by shaking.
   D. Spherical ice "cubes" freeze more quickly than regular ice cubes do.

6. A suspension is a mixture in which the distributed particles are larger than those of the solvent and in which the particles, in time, will settle out.

   Which of the following is a suspension?

   A. pure gold
   B. pure oxygen
   C. salt water
   D. dusty air

Physical Science

LESSON 3

Chemical Reactions

In a **chemical reaction,** the atoms or ions of one or more substances, called the **reactants,** are rearranged, resulting in one or more different substances, called the **products.** For example, iron, water, and oxygen react to form hydrated iron oxide, or rust. Matter is neither created nor destroyed during a chemical reaction, so the mass of the products always equals the mass of the reactants. This principle is known as the **law of conservation of mass.**

KEY IDEAS

- In a chemical reaction, the atoms or ions of one or more reactants are rearranged, yielding one or more products. Mass is conserved during chemical reactions.
- Chemical reactions can be represented by chemical formulas.
- Chemical reactions are either endothermic or exothermic.

Chemical reactions can be represented by **chemical equations**. Chemical equations show the reactants on the left side and the products on the right side. They also show the proportions of the reacting substances—how many units of each reactant and each product are involved. Because of the law of conservation of mass, a chemical equation must balance. That is, the total number of atoms of an element on the left side must be equal to the total number of atoms of the element on the right side. Here is the chemical equation that represents the burning of hydrogen and oxygen to yield water:

$$2H_2 + O_2 \rightarrow 2H_2O$$

Restated in words: two molecules of hydrogen (H_2) combine with one molecule of oxygen (O_2) to form two molecules of water (H_2O). The equation balances because there are four hydrogen atoms on the left side and four on the right; there are two oxygen atoms on the left side and two on the right. To balance a chemical equation, you can change the coefficients—the number of units of any reactant or product. However, you *cannot* change the subscripts of any reactant or product.

HiSET EXAM TIP

There is no penalty for getting a wrong answer on the test. If you are not sure of your answer, make your best guess, flag the question, and come back to it if you complete the test before time is up.

Energy is involved in all chemical reactions. A reaction in which the reactants absorb energy from their surroundings is an **endothermic reaction**. For example, when you scramble an egg, you add heat energy and the egg solidifies. A reaction in which energy is given off with the products, usually in the form of heat or light, is an **exothermic reaction**. When you burn wood in a fireplace, for example, heat and light energy are given off. **Activation energy** is the amount of energy needed to get a reaction going. These energy relationships can be shown in graphs like those below.

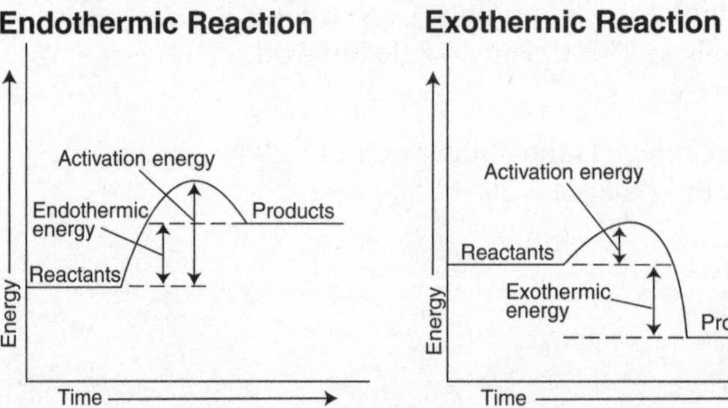

1. Which of the following chemical formulas represents the reaction in which copper (Cu) and oxygen gas (O_2) combine to form copper oxide (CuO)?

   A. $2CuO \rightarrow 2Cu + O_2$
   B. $Cu + O_2 \rightarrow 2CuO$
   C. $2Cu + O_2 \rightarrow 2CuO$
   D. $Cu + 2O_2 \rightarrow 2CuO$

2. Which of the following procedures would provide evidence for the law of conservation of mass?

   A. Weigh the reactants, conduct the reaction in an open container, and weigh the products.
   B. Weigh the reactants, conduct the reaction in a sealed container, and weigh the products.
   C. Measure the volume of the reactants, conduct the reaction in a sealed container, and measure the volume of the products.
   D. Write the chemical formula for the reaction and balance it.

3. Juanita would like to cook a scrambled egg on her gas stove. When she first turns on the stove's burner, the electronic ignition produces a spark that sets the gas burning. As the gas burns, it heats the frying pan. As the egg cooks, it absorbs the heat energy from the pan and solidifies.

   Which form of energy is needed for each step of Juanita's cooking process?

   A. Igniting the gas requires endothermic energy, the gas burning releases activation energy, and the egg solidifying requires exothermic energy.
   B. Igniting the gas requires activation energy, the gas burning releases endothermic energy, and the egg solidifying requires exothermic energy.
   C. Igniting the gas requires activation energy, the gas burning releases exothermic energy, and the egg solidifying requires endothermic energy.
   D. Igniting the gas requires endothermic energy, the gas burning releases exothermic energy, and the egg solidifying requires activation energy.

4. In the graphs on page 640, what does the horizontal axis represent?

   A. the instant the reaction starts
   B. the instant the reaction stops
   C. the time during which the reaction occurs
   D. the energy level in the reaction

5. Organic compounds are those containing linked carbon atoms that form bonds with other atoms, usually hydrogen, oxygen, nitrogen, and/or sulfur. Organic compounds consist of chains, branching chains, rings, and other complex arrangements of carbon atoms with which other atoms bond. One type of organic compound is a polymer, a large long-chain or branching structure made up of many repeated simple units, called monomers. Natural polymers include cellulose. Synthetic polymers include polyethylene and other types of plastics.

   Which of the following is taken for granted and not stated by the writer of the paragraph above?

   A. Compounds are substances consisting of two or more elements chemically combined in a definite proportion.
   B. Organic compounds have linked carbon atoms forming bonds with other atoms, usually hydrogen, oxygen, nitrogen, and/or sulfur.
   C. Chains are among the arrangements carbon atoms in an organic compound can take.
   D. Plastics are synthetic polymers and cellulose is a natural polymer.

6. An acid is a compound that releases hydrogen ions (H^+), or protons, in the presence of water. Strong acids, like battery acid and stomach acid, are corrosive. Most dilute acids, like lemon juice, have a sour taste.

   A base is a compound that accepts hydrogen ions, or protons. Household cleaners like ammonia, lye, and bleach are bases. When an acid reacts with a base, the product is a salt and water. This reaction is called neutralization.

   Which of the following is the best title for this passage?

   A. Corrosive Substances
   B. Acids and Bases
   C. Acids and Bases in the Lab
   D. Neutralization Reactions

LESSON 4

The Nature of Energy

Energy is defined as the capacity to do work. **Work** is done whenever a force is applied to an object to set it in motion. Thus, anything that can force matter to move, change direction, or change speed has energy.

Energy comes in many forms. **Heat energy** can change a solid to a liquid and a liquid to a gas. It is also involved in most chemical reactions. **Light energy** can create an image by causing the chemicals on a piece of film to react. It provides the energy needed for the process of photosynthesis in green plants. **Electrical energy** can turn a motor, plate a set of flatware with a layer of silver, or store data on a hard drive. **Chemical energy** in food provides the energy humans need for life functions. It heats our buildings when we burn oil, gas, coal, or wood. Chemical energy in batteries provides electricity when the batteries are connected in a circuit. **Nuclear energy** from breaking apart the nuclei of atoms provides energy to produce electricity or power a submarine. **Mechanical energy** turns the axles of a car or the blades of a fan.

Energy can be converted from one form to another. Consider the production and use of electricity. In most electric plants, a fossil fuel (chemical energy) is burned, producing heat energy that turns water to steam. The energy in the steam turns the blades of a turbine, producing mechanical energy. The turbine powers the generator, which produces electrical energy. Electrical energy is used in homes to provide heat energy (in stoves and toasters), light energy (in light bulbs), sound energy (in the stereo), and mechanical energy (in a blender). Even though energy undergoes changes in form, the amount of energy in a closed system remains the same. This principle is known as the **law of conservation of energy**.

Two basic types of energy are **potential energy** and **kinetic energy**. An object has potential energy because of its position; it has kinetic energy when it moves. For example, when you raise a hammer, at the top of your upswing the hammer has potential energy. When you lower the hammer to hit a nail, the hammer has kinetic energy, the energy of motion. When the hammer hits the nail, it transfers energy to the nail. The energy transferred is equal to the work done by the hammer on the nail, and it can be measured in **joules**. The rate of doing work or consuming energy is called **power**, and it can be measured in horsepower (in the English system) or **watts** (joules per second in the metric system).

Physicist Albert Einstein discovered the relationship between energy and mass and expressed it in the equation $E = mc^2$, in which E represents energy, m represents mass, and c represents the speed of light. Since the speed of light is a very large number, the equation indicates there is a great deal of energy in even the tiniest bit of matter. So, for example, in nuclear bombs and nuclear power plants, mass is changed to energy when large atoms are split into two or more smaller atoms with less mass than the original large atom.

KEY IDEAS

- Anything that can force matter to move, change direction, or change speed has energy.
- Energy comes in many forms and can be converted from one form to another.
- The law of conservation of energy states that energy can neither be created nor destroyed, only changed in form.

HiSET EXAM TIP

It is important to carefully read the titles and all of the other information on all graphics. Make sure you understand a graphic before answering questions based on it.

PRACTICE 4

1. Which of the following states the law of conservation of energy?

 A. Potential energy is the energy of position; kinetic energy is the energy of motion.
 B. Energy can be created and destroyed as well as changed in form.
 C. Energy cannot be created or destroyed, but can only change in form.
 D. Energy cannot be created, destroyed, or changed in form.

2. During a power outage, George relied on his flashlight to move around his home. The flashlight is constructed with wires and a light bulb enclosed in a plastic casing. It requires batteries to operate.

 Which one of the following types of energy powers George's flashlight?

 A. nuclear
 B. light
 C. mechanical
 D. chemical

3. An oak tree may grow very tall very slowly. It may take the tree a hundred years to absorb light energy and store it as chemical energy, yet only a single winter to be turned into heat energy in someone's wood stove. Which concept does this fact best relate to?

 A. work
 B. power
 C. force
 D. kinetic energy

4. What does Einstein's equation $E = mc^2$ express?

 A. the relationship between electricity and magnetism
 B. the relationship between energy and mass
 C. the speed of light in a vacuum
 D. the relationship between electrical energy and nuclear energy

Question 5 refers to the following diagram.

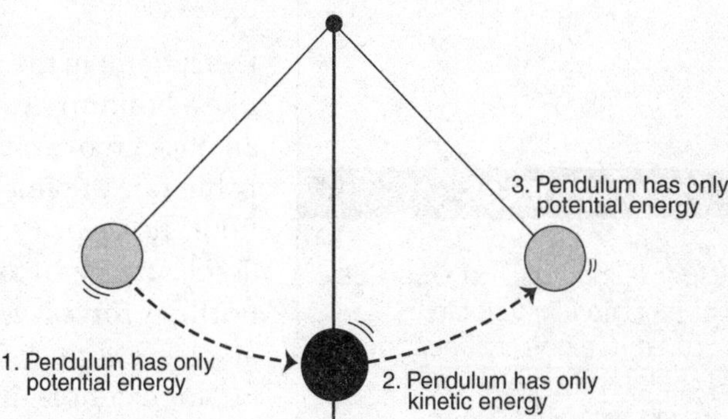
A Pendulum's Energy
3. Pendulum has only potential energy
1. Pendulum has only potential energy
2. Pendulum has only kinetic energy

5. Which of the following statements is supported by the information in the diagram?

 A. At the high point of its swing, a pendulum has kinetic energy.
 B. At the high point of its swing, a pendulum has potential energy.
 C. As a pendulum swings through one arc, it loses all its energy.
 D. A pendulum can swing forever because of kinetic energy.

---

6. Heat energy is present in all matter in the form of the kinetic energy of its atoms and molecules. Heat energy can pass from one place to another through conduction: the transfer of kinetic energy from molecules in greater motion (hot areas) to molecules of lesser motion (cold areas). Solid metals like silver and copper are good conductors of heat energy; gases like air are poor conductors.

 What is the reason that air is a poor conductor of heat?

 A. The molecules in air are far apart.
 B. The molecules in air are very large.
 C. The molecules in air do not move.
 D. The molecules in air are very small.

LESSON 5

Motion and Forces

KEY IDEAS

- Speed is the rate at which an object moves; velocity is speed in a given direction; acceleration is the rate at which velocity changes.
- A force is anything that changes the state of rest or motion of an object.
- Newton stated three laws of motion that explain the inertia, acceleration, and momentum of objects.

HiSET EXAM TIP

If you are asked to apply a general law or principle of science to a particular situation, ask yourself: "What is similar about this situation and the general principle?"

Everything in the universe is in motion. Even objects that seem to be at rest, like a building, are moving with Earth's rotation. **Speed** is the rate at which an object moves; **velocity** is its speed in a particular direction. **Acceleration** is the rate at which velocity changes. So a car's speed may be 40 miles per hour; its velocity may be 40 miles per hour toward the north; and it may accelerate by 10 feet per second until its velocity is 50 miles per hour to the north. A **force** is anything that tends to change the state of rest or motion of an object. A push or a pull on an object is a force, as are gravity and friction. So, for example, if you allow a car to coast on a level road, the force of friction will eventually bring it to a stop.

Sir Isaac Newton (1642–1727), an English physicist and mathematician, set down three laws by which the planets and all other objects move when acted upon by a force. These are called the **laws of motion**.

Newton's first law of motion, the **law of inertia**, states that an object at rest will stay at rest until a force acts upon it, and an object in motion will stay in motion at a constant speed in a straight line until a force acts upon it. Objects moving on Earth eventually slow down and stop because of the forces of friction and gravity. A bullet, for example, would continue its forward motion in a straight line, but friction from the air slows it down and the force of gravity pulls it toward the ground.

The second law of motion, sometimes called the **law of motion** or **acceleration**, states that the acceleration of an object depends on its mass and the force acting upon it. The greater the force, the greater the acceleration. The more massive the object, the more force it takes to accelerate it. Additionally, if a constant force acts upon an object, the object will move with constant acceleration in the direction of the force. This is why truck engines are more powerful than car engines: it takes more force to accelerate an object with more mass (a truck) than an object with less mass (a car).

Newton's third law of motion states that for every action, there is an equal and opposite reaction. This law was used to derive the law of conservation of momentum. **Momentum** is related to the amount of energy that a moving object has, and it depends on the mass of the object and its velocity. In fact, momentum is defined as an object's mass multiplied by its velocity. Newton's third law states that when an object is given a certain amount of momentum in a particular direction, some other object must receive an equal momentum in the opposite direction. Another way to state this is to say that all forces exist in pairs, and that all forces are interactions between objects. So, for example, when a bullet is fired out of a gun, the bullet's forward momentum causes the gun to recoil, or move backward.

PRACTICE 5

1. What is a force?

A. the rate at which an object moves in a particular direction
B. any change in an object's acceleration or deceleration
C. the inertia and momentum of an object at rest
D. anything that changes the rest or motion of an object

2. What is inertia?

A. the speed at which an object is moving
B. changes in an object's speed or direction
C. the force needed to move an object a certain distance
D. the tendency of an object to remain at rest or in motion

3. The force that is needed to keep an object moving in a circular path is called centripetal force.

Which of the following is an example of motion that requires centripetal force?

A. the tides occurring as a result of the moon's gravitational pull
B. the International Space Station orbiting Earth
C. a parachute slowing as it falls to the ground
D. a gun recoiling as a bullet is fired

4. A car is traveling at a velocity of 30 miles per hour across a narrow bridge when it is approached on a collision course by another car traveling at 30 miles per hour. The momentum of each car is propelling it forward, and there is no way to completely avoid an impact. Each driver should attempt to decrease his car's speed to lessen the severity of impact because

A. the momentum of the car decreases when its velocity decreases.
B. the momentum of the car increases when its velocity decreases.
C. the momentum of the car decreases when its velocity increases.
D. the momentum of the car remains the same whether its velocity increases or decreases.

Question 5 refers to the following graph, the paragraph below, and the information on page 644.

Graphs are often used to convey information about motion. One type of motion graph shows distance and time. Distance is measured from a particular starting point. If the distance graph has a straight, horizontal line, the distance is unchanging and the object is not moving. If the distance graph has a straight line with an upward slope, the distance is changing at a constant rate; this means that the object is moving at a constant speed. If the distance graph is a curve, the object is accelerating or decelerating, depending on the shape of the curve.

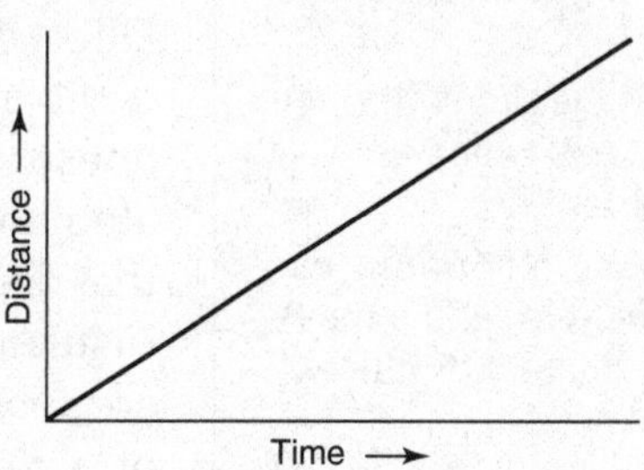

5. What does the graph above show?

A. an object that is not moving
B. an object that has a constant speed
C. an object that is accelerating
D. an object that is decelerating

---

6. A machine is a device that transmits a force, changing the direction or size of the force and doing work. The force applied to a machine is the effort force; the force it overcomes is the load. Types of simple machines include the inclined plane, wedge, lever, pulley, and wheel-and-axle.

Which of the following statements is supported by the information given?

A. The force a machine overcomes is called the effort force.
B. Work can be done only with machines.
C. Some machines simply change the direction of a force.
D. All machines change both the direction and size of a force.

LESSON 6

Electricity and Magnetism

As you recall from your study of atoms, electrons have a negative charge (–), and protons have a positive charge (+). This **electric charge** causes them to exert forces on one another. Particles with like charges repel one another, and particles with unlike charges attract one another. Sometimes electrons are temporarily pulled away from atoms, creating stationary areas of positive and negative charge. This can happen when two objects, like a balloon and a rug, are rubbed together, creating **static electricity**.

The movement of charged particles, usually electrons, is an **electric current**. Direct current flows in one direction only, and it is used in battery-operated devices. Alternating current flows back and forth rapidly, and it is used in household wiring. A material that allows electrons to move freely from atom to atom is called a **conductor**. Metals are good conductors. A material that does not allow electrons to move freely from atom to atom is called an **insulator**. Rubber and plastic are examples of insulators. **Semiconductors** are substances whose ability to conduct electricity is midway between that of a conductor and an insulator. Semiconductors like silicon are used in electronic devices.

An electric current produces a **magnetic field** that affects magnetic substances such as iron in the same way a permanent magnet does. Magnetic fields are produced by moving charged particles. In an **electromagnet**, the charged particles move along a coil of wire connected to a battery or other power source. In a **permanent magnet**, the spinning of electrons creates a magnetic field. Every magnet has two ends, called the north and south poles. The north pole of one magnet attracts the south pole of another magnet; like poles repel one another.

Just as an electric current produces a magnetic field, a moving magnetic field produces an electric current. This principle underlies electric motors, generators, and transformers. In an **electric motor**, for example, magnetic fields are produced by electric currents. The magnetic fields push against one another, turning the shaft of the motor. In a **generator**, a moving magnetic field produces electric current. In a **transformer**, an incoming electric current in coiled wire produces fluctuating magnetic fields, which in turn produce an outgoing electric current of a different **voltage**. The difference in voltage is caused by the differing sizes of the wire coils.

Magnetic Fields

Bar magnet

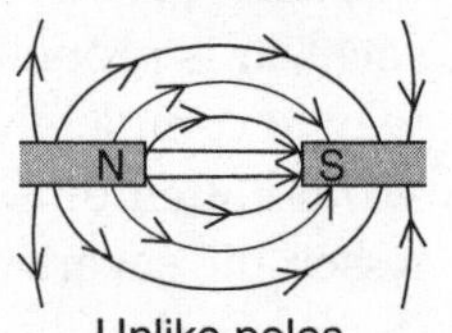

Unlike poles

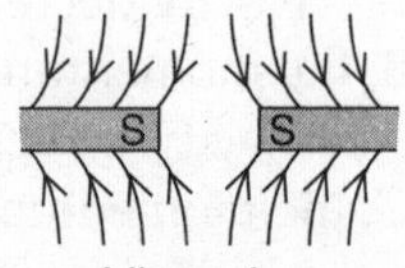

Like poles

KEY IDEAS

- Particles with like electric charges repel one another, and particles with unlike electric charges attract one another.
- The flow of electrons through a substance is called an electric current.
- An electric current produces a magnetic field, and a moving magnetic field produces an electric current.

HiSET EXAM TIP

You can use your knowledge of everyday things like electricity and motors to help you answer questions on the Science Test.

PRACTICE 6

1. Suppose a drawing of two magnets with their north poles facing one another were added to the diagram on page 646. What would the new drawing show?

   A. two poles attracting one another
   B. two poles repelling one another
   C. magnetic lines of force connecting the poles
   D. magnetic lines of force flowing southward

2. What is the reason copper and aluminum are used for electrical wiring?

   A. Copper and aluminum are conductors.
   B. Copper and aluminum are insulators.
   C. Copper and aluminum are semiconductors.
   D. Copper and aluminum are magnetic.

3. Based on the information on page 646, which of the following devices is most likely to use direct current?

   A. a washing machine
   B. a desktop computer
   C. a toaster
   D. a flashlight

4. In an electric power plant, generators may produce electric current at about 10,000 volts. The current may be stepped up and transmitted along high voltage lines at 230,000 volts, and then stepped down to about 2,300 volts for transmission in a city. Finally, before it enters houses, the current is stepped down to 110 volts.

   Based on the information above and that on page 646, which of the following devices steps current up and down for efficient transmission?

   A. a conductor
   B. an electromagnet
   C. an electric motor
   D. a transformer

Questions 5 and 6 refer to the following paragraph and diagram.

An electric circuit is a complete pathway for the flow of electric current. It consists of a source of electricity, such as a battery, wires along which the current travels, devices called resistors powered by the current, and often a switch to start and stop the flow of current.

A Series Circuit

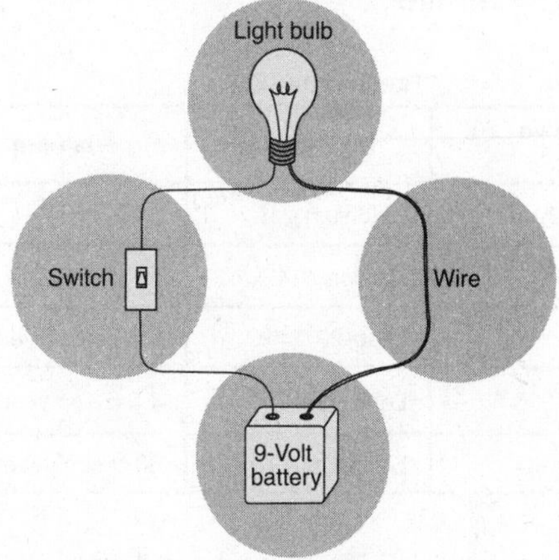

5. Which element in the diagram acts as a resistor in the circuit?

   A. the light bulb
   B. the switch
   C. the wire
   D. the 9-volt battery

6. A student was asked how the current in the circuit shown above could be stopped without using the switch. He answered that the only way to stop the current was to disconnect the battery.

   What was wrong with the student's response?

   A. Disconnecting the battery will not stop the current.
   B. Removing the fuse will also stop the current.
   C. Disconnecting the light bulb will also stop the current.
   D. There is no way to stop the current without using the switch.

STUDY ADVICE

Congratulations! Only one more practice set to go. If you've been working through the book in order, you've covered all of the concepts, and all that remains is to continue to review and practice them up until Test Day. Reward yourself for all your hard work!

PHYSICAL SCIENCE PRACTICE QUESTIONS

Questions 1 and 2 refer to the following paragraph and chart.

When the nuclei of unstable elements disintegrate, emitting radioactive radiation, the unstable elements change into other elements, becoming more stable. The amount of time it takes for half of a sample of a radioactive element to decay into its stable product is called the radioactive element's half-life.

Radioactive Decay

Radioactive element	Decays into	Half-life
Radon-222	Polonium-218	3.82 days
Carbon-14	Nitrogen-14	5,730 years
Uranium-235	Lead-207	713 million years
Uranium-235	Lead-206	4.5 billion years
Rubidium-87	Strontium-87	50 billion years

1. What is the half-life of carbon-14?

   A. 3.82 days
   B. 5,730 years
   C. 713 million years
   D. 4.5 billion years

2. Uranium is used as fuel in nuclear power plants, resulting in radioactive waste, which is dangerous to living things.

   Which of the following arguments is likely to be used by opponents of nuclear power?

   A. Uranium is a plentiful source of fuel for generating electricity.
   B. Uranium is a renewable resource, and therefore its use is limitless.
   C. During the three days that radioactive waste is unstable, it may harm living things.
   D. Uranium produces radioactive waste that may harm living things for millions of years.

Questions 3 and 4 refer to the following paragraph and diagram.

An oscillation is a back-and-forth or up-and-down movement. When an oscillation travels through matter or space and transfers energy, it is called a wave.

Longitudinal Wave

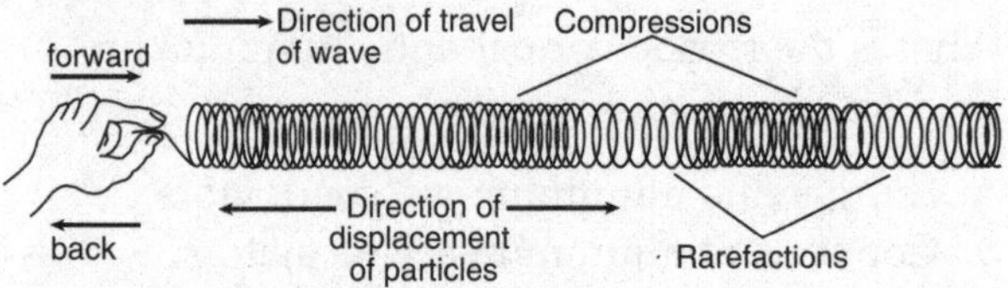

Transverse Wave

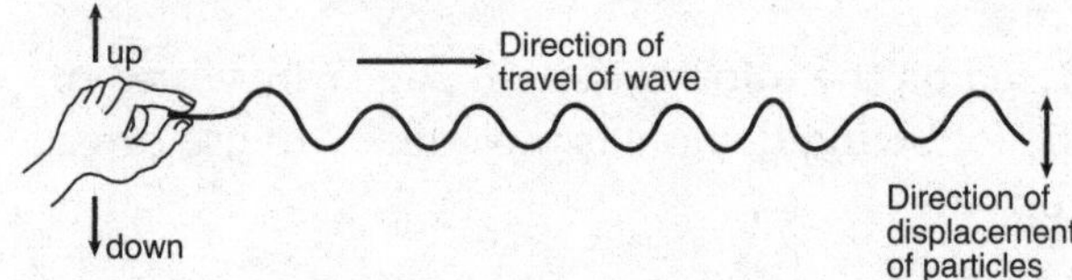

3. What is the main similarity between longitudinal and transverse waves?

   A. Both involve up-and-down displacement of particles.
   B. Both involve back-and-forth displacement of particles.
   C. Both involve compressions in which particles are pushed together.
   D. Both involve the transfer of energy through matter or space.

4. After a transverse wave passes through a substance, no particle ever ends up far from its original position.

   Which of the following illustrates this principle?

   A. A cork in water bobs up and down as waves pass.
   B. Sound waves travel through air.
   C. When two waves overlap, they interfere with one another.
   D. A stone dropped into a pond causes ripples to radiate outward.

5. According to the kinetic theory of matter, all matter is made up of molecules in a state of constant motion. The motion of molecules can be inferred by observing particles in a fluid (a liquid or a gas) as they are hit by molecules of the fluid. The random, zigzag movement of the particles is called Brownian motion.

   Which of the following is an example of Brownian motion?

   A. dust motes dancing in a shaft of sunlight
   B. the ground vibrating as a truck passes
   C. water evaporating from a puddle
   D. an inflatable raft floating on a lake

6. In a chemical reaction, the surface area of the reactants affects the rate at which the reaction occurs. The greater the surface area of the reactants, the faster the reaction rate will be.

   When dilute sulfuric acid reacts with marble, carbon dioxide gas is produced. Which of the following would increase the rate at which carbon dioxide gas is produced?

   A. increasing the size of the container in which the reaction is taking place
   B. decreasing the size of the container in which the reaction is taking place
   C. using larger chunks of marble
   D. using powdered marble

7. Boyle's law states that at a constant temperature, the volume of a fixed amount of gas varies inversely with the pressure exerted on the gas. Therefore, the volume of a gas ________ when the pressure on the gas increases.

   A. increases
   B. decreases
   C. increases initially but then decreases
   D. decreases initially but then increases

Questions 8 and 9 refer to the following paragraph and chart.

All of the elements are arranged in the periodic table according to atomic number—the number of protons in an atom of each element. The rows of the periodic table show elements according to the structure of their electron orbits. The columns, or groups, show elements with similar properties. A portion of the periodic table is shown below.

Part of the Periodic Table

13	14	15	16	17	18
					He 2
B 5	C 6	N 7	O 8	F 9	Ne 10
Al 13	Si 14	P 15	S 16	Cl 17	Ar 18
Ga 31	Ge 32	As 33	Se 34	Br 35	Kr 36
In 49	Sn 50	Sb 51	Te 52	I 53	Xe 54
Tl 81	Pb 82	Bi 83	Po 84	At 85	Rn 86

8. Group 18 is also called the noble gases. Their electron orbits are completely filled, and they rarely react with other elements. Which of the following is a noble gas?

   A. nitrogen (N)
   B. chlorine (Cl)
   C. xenon (Xe)
   D. fluorine (F)

9. Which of the following statements is supported by the information given?

   A. Silicon (Si) is a very common element.
   B. Chlorine (Cl) and iodine (I) have similar properties.
   C. Arsenic (As) and antimony (Sb) have very different properties.
   D. Arsenic (As) has 85 protons in its nucleus.

Questions 10 and 11 refer to the following paragraph and diagram.

Electromagnetic radiation consists of electric and magnetic fields that oscillate back and forth. There is a wide range of types of electromagnetic radiation, which together form the electromagnetic spectrum.

The Electromagnetic Spectrum

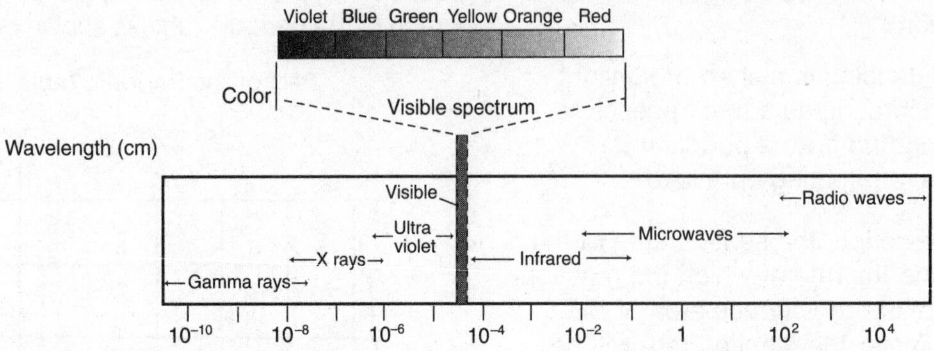

10. Which of the following types of electromagnetic radiation has a wavelength longer than those in the visible spectrum?

    A. microwaves
    B. ultraviolet light
    C. X-rays
    D. colored light

11. Which of the following generalizations is supported by the diagram?

    A. Unlike people, some insects can see ultraviolet light.
    B. Warm colors like yellow have a shorter wavelength than cool colors like blue.
    C. People can see only a small portion of the electromagnetic spectrum.
    D. In medicine, X-rays are used to make images of bones.

12. Objects are attracted to one another by the force of gravity. Gravity is proportional to the mass—the amount of matter—objects have; gravity decreases as the distance between the objects increases. An object's weight is a measurement of the Earth's gravitational pull on the object.

    What happens to the mass and weight of a rocket as it travels beyond Earth's orbit?

    A. Its mass remains the same, and its weight increases.
    B. Its mass remains the same, and its weight decreases.
    C. Its mass decreases, and its weight decreases.
    D. Its mass increases, and its weight remains the same.

13. Heat energy can be transferred from one object to another. In summer, when you hold an ice-cold can of soda against your face, your face feels cooler. However, what is really happening is that the can is being warmed by heat from your body. You are actually losing a little body heat.

    Which of the following is an unstated assumption related to the paragraph?

    A. Heat can be transferred.
    B. Coldness cannot be transferred.
    C. A cool object can be warmed by your body.
    D. You can lose body heat.

Questions 14 and 15 refer to the following table and paragraph.

An aviation engineer tests five newly developed airplanes by measuring and recording the top speed of each plane. Unbeknownst to the engineer, the radar she used to measure the planes' speeds is faulty: it gives the speed of any object in motion as 3.7 km/hour faster than it really is. The following table shows the speeds that the engineer recorded using the faulty radar and the actual speed of each plane:

Airplane	Recorded speed (km/hour)	Actual speed (km/hour)
1	214.4	210.7
2	362.1	358.4
3	410.0	406.3
4	214.4	210.7
5	359.6	355.9

Using the speeds recorded from the faulty radar, the engineer then calculated the mean, median, mode, and range of the planes' speeds.

14. Which one of the engineer's calculations using the recorded speed is identical to what it would have been had the engineer made the same calculation using the actual speed of each plane?

    A. the mean
    B. the median
    C. the mode
    D. the range

15. After completing her measurements, the engineer selects at random two planes to demonstrate at an upcoming air show. What is the probability that the actual speeds of both planes selected are less than 360 km/hour?

    A. $\frac{1}{5}$
    B. $\frac{3}{10}$
    C. $\frac{3}{5}$
    D. $\frac{4}{5}$

16. Collisions can be elastic, inelastic, or totally inelastic depending on how much energy is transferred between objects. During elastic collisions, the objects bounce off of each other perfectly and there is no net change in momentum or energy. During inelastic collisions, there is a loss of energy. An experiment was conducted to verify these facts.

    Consider the following data:

Measurements of Momentums and Kinetic Energies

Trial	Initial Momentum (kg*m/s)	Initial Kinetic Energy (J)	Final Momentum (kg*m/s)	Final Kinetic Energy (J)
1	10	50	10	50
2	15	75	15	50
3	20	100	20	75

    From the information in the chart, you can see that the type of collision that occurred during Trial 1 was a(n) ______ collision.

    A. elastic
    B. inelastic
    C. totally inelastic
    D. plastic

17. The following graph illustrates the effect of temperature change on 1 gram of ice. Which point on the graph corresponds to the temperature at which the substance freezes?

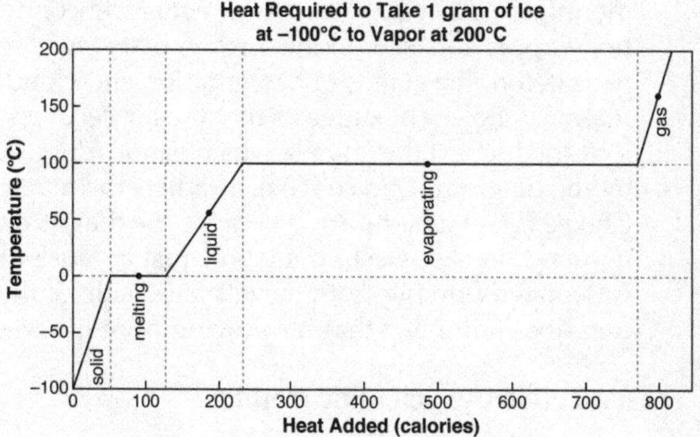

    A. –100°
    B. 0°
    C. 100°
    D. 200°

Science Answers and Explanations

Science Skills

Lesson 1: Comprehend Scientific Presentations

Practice 1

1. **C. the causes of type 2 diabetes** The passage as a whole discusses the causes of type 2 diabetes. Choices (A) and (D) are not discussed in the passage. Choice (B) is mentioned in the second paragraph but is only a supporting detail.
2. **D. The causes of type 2 diabetes are not fully understood.** This question asks for the main point of just the first paragraph, which explains that scientists do not fully understand the role played by various factors in causing diabetes. Choices (A) and (B) both commit the same error: that is, they mention a specific detail from the first paragraph while missing the big picture. Choice (C) contradicts the paragraph.
3. **B. A study of 18- to 25-year-olds showed that a majority did not produce enough insulin to offset the high amounts of sugar they were consuming.** The question asks for a detail that serves to support the idea that high sugar consumption may contribute to the development of type 2 diabetes. Only choice (B) does so. Choice (A) is a detail that is indeed mentioned in the paragraph, but only as background information. It does not serve to support the author's point that sugar consumption may contribute to diabetes. Choice (C) brings in "genetic factors," which are not mentioned in paragraph two. Although choice (D) may be implied by the author's use of hesitant language, such as "one contributing factor *may* be high sugar consumption," this does not support the paragraph's main idea.
4. **A. As moist, flowing air encounters rising elevations, it cools, which causes condensation, a stage that precedes precipitation and cloud development.** In interpreting this diagram, follow the arrows. The diagram depicts air flowing toward hills or mountains. As it does so, the air cools and condensation happens. Based on the arrows, that stage happens before the stages of precipitation and cloud formation. Choice (B) suggests that the air becomes static at the highest elevations, which is not supported by the diagram. Choice (C) contradicts the diagram. Choice (D) is unsupported because the diagram does not have an east-west orientation: just because the air is depicted flowing from the left-hand side of the picture does not mean that it's flowing from the west.

Lesson 2: Use the Scientific Method

Practice 2

1. **C. What role do bacteria play in the development of acne?** The researchers were studying the question of how different combinations of bacteria affect acne symptoms. Because the researchers thought acne symptoms might depend on differences in bacteria, acne was the researchers' dependent variable. Combinations of bacteria are not affected by acne symptoms, but the researchers thought bacteria might affect those acne symptoms. Therefore, combinations of bacteria were the researchers' independent variable.
2. **B. Different kinds of bacteria may impact acne differently.** The last sentence of the first paragraph provides this answer as well. The researchers "began to wonder whether different strains of bacteria might impact acne in different ways": that statement represents the idea they sought to test—that is, their hypothesis. Choice (A) describes an assumption that was widely held before the researchers began their study. Choice (C) is a suggestion the researchers made after concluding their study, and choice (D) is their conclusion—not their starting hypothesis.
3. **D. Some combinations of bacteria may actually help ward off acne.** This question asks for the researchers' conclusion—that is, the idea they embraced after concluding their study. That idea is described by choice (D). Choice (A) is an assumption many people held before the research began. Choice (B) is not supported by the passage. Choice (C) is not supported by the passage: after drawing their conclusions, the researchers suggested a way to treat acne in the future, but they did not suggest that current treatments are misguided.
4. **C. Based on your experience, you make a guess about which of the movements involved in playing softball puts the greatest stress on the knees. You suspect that it may be stopping suddenly after running a short distance.** Forming a hypothesis occurs before the actual experiment takes place. All of the other answer choices occur during the experiment itself or afterward.
5. **B. your knee pain** A dependent variable depends on the various factors in the experiment. In this experiment, your knee pain is dependent on the actions taken.

Lesson 3: Evaluate Experimental Design

Practice 3

1. **B. To ensure that the pH of each trial was the same** Change in pH could be a confounding variable that would affect the outcome, so a pH buffer was used to keep the pH constant across trials. The turnip extract was added to the test tube last to prevent the early release of oxygen (choice (A)). The amount of oxygen being released is the dependent variable and thus is not controlled by the scientist (choice (D)).
2. **B. The enzyme had likely denatured at 60°C, so further temperature increases would yield no new data.** The passage indicates that proteins unfold at high temperatures, which decreases enzyme activity. The graph illustrates that after 60°C, no bubbles are formed; thus, it can be inferred that the enzyme is no longer active at this, or higher, temperatures.
3. **A. Repeat the experiment, replacing turnip extract with an equal quantity of potato extract, and com-**

pare the results. To test the effect of concentration on reaction rate, only catalase concentration should be varied. This is accomplished with choice **(A)**, which keeps everything else about the experiment the same. Choice (B) introduces the confounding variable of turnip and potato extract interaction, and choices (C) and (D) also change the temperature.

4. **A. Drop identical spheres that only differ in mass from the same height and time how long it takes for each sphere to hit the ground.** Because this experiment is testing the relationship between mass and time, only the mass of the dropped objects should change. Choices (B) and (D) incorrectly change the height for each trial, and choice (C) changes the objects' size, not their mass.

Lesson 4: Reason with Scientific Information

Practice 4

1. **C. If both objects were currently sitting still, it would require more effort to push the brick across the floor than it would to push the block of wood across the floor.** According to the passage, a heavier object has more inertia, and the brick is heavier than the block. Therefore, you can conclude that it would be harder to move the brick across the floor. Choice (A), breakage, and choice (D), absorbing water, are not mentioned and are irrelevant to this question. Choice (B) is the opposite of the correct answer.
2. **A. The birds that the brown tree snake eats are the primary predators of spiders on Guam.** The scientist's conclusion is that the brown tree snake is the reason there are so many spiders on Guam. The question asks for a piece of information that makes that conclusion more likely—that is, a choice that makes the scientist's conclusion more reasonable or believable. Choice (A) explains why more brown tree snakes would lead to more spiders. Choices (B) and (D) don't link the spiders and snakes at all. Choice (C) describes a relationship between them, but it suggests that more brown tree snakes would lead to *fewer* spiders.
3. **B. If large areas of ice sheets sit on water, the rising of sea levels may proceed more quickly than had previously been predicted.** The main idea of the passage is that some ice sheets may be sitting on water and that those ice sheets may melt more quickly than ice sheets sitting on rock. The passage also states that melting ice sheets contribute to rising sea levels. Putting those two ideas together, a scientist could predict that ice sheets sitting on water might send more melted water into the oceans than would ice sheets on rock. Choice (A) expresses the opposite of that idea. Choice (C) introduces a comparison that is not supported by the passage. Choice (D) goes too far by insisting that *all* of the quickly melting ice sheets are sitting on water.
4. **A. Most of the ice sheets sitting on water are covering inland lakes with no access to the ocean.** Choice (A) would make the prediction less likely, because if most ice sheets sitting on water have no way to send water into the ocean, then the link between the ice sheets and rising sea levels would be undermined. Choices (B) and (C) actually make the scientist's prediction more likely. Choice (D) may seem to undermine the information in the passage—until you notice that choice (D) criticizes the use of "radar alone" to assess ice sheets. The passage indicates that researchers used both satellite and radar data, which makes choice (D) irrelevant to the prediction.

Lesson 5: Synthesize Relevant Information

Practice 5

1. **C. The information proves that the statement is false.** This question asks about all lung infections, but the focus of the passage is on one specific lung infection—pneumonia. The relevant information in the passage also informs us that a lung infection like pneumonia can be caused by either a bacterial or a viral infection. Since paragraph 2 states that antibiotics work by destroying harmful bacteria, antibiotics would not be effective if an individual had a lung infection that was caused by a virus.
2. **A. How does a doctor distinguish bacterial pneumonia from viral pneumonia?** The passage indicates that pneumonia can be caused by either a bacterium or a virus, but it never indicates how a doctor distinguishes between the two. Choice (B) is explained in the second sentence: chest X-rays are used because symptoms of pneumonia are similar to those of the common cold. Choice (C) is answered in the last sentence: overprescribing antibiotics when there isn't a need could lead to drug-resistant germs. Choice (D) is answered in the second paragraph.
3. **A. The pneumonia bacteria would be weakened because cell walls couldn't form properly.** The relevant information can be found in the second paragraph. Antibiotics, like penicillin, treat pneumonia by "disrupting vital cellular processes." Specifically, penicillin "blocks an enzyme necessary for building the cell wall."
4. **B. Take antibiotics only when a doctor necessarily prescribes them for you.** The relevant information can be found in the third paragraph, which states that "medical professionals warn against prescribing [antibiotics] unnecessarily."

Lesson 6: Assess the Credibility of Sources

Practice 6

1. **D. No, because neither website is a source of credible information on this topic.** The website selling the supplement is biased toward claims that improve sales, and the blog entry is a personal anecdote. Neither source refers to verifiable facts nor is written by an expert. Just because the websites confirm Janie's prediction does not make the information

they contain true (choice (A)). The blog in choice (B) only describes a similar situation, without providing evidence of causation.

2. **C. not credible, because the authors have a personal motive to make their claim.** The authors of a website selling a fat-blocking supplement would be biased toward a claim that would increase sales of their supplement, such as one that linked saturated fat to digestive problems. Choice (A) is incorrect because the location of an Internet search result is not necessarily related to credibility. Choice (B) is incorrect because a study showing the claim to be true would only help the website's credibility if the study already existed and if the website had referenced it. Choice (D) is incorrect because its reasoning refers to anecdotal evidence.
3. **D. A peer-reviewed study demonstrates that magnetic fields in the ocean bedrock push the continents apart.** Answer choice (D) provides a peer-reviewed explanation for what causes continental drift. Choice (A) is an observation with no explanatory value; it provides some evidence that the two continents may once have been one, but it does not support the theory of continental drift. Choice (B) provides no more evidence than there was before Wegener proposed his theory; people already knew similar fossils were found on continents an ocean apart. Choice (C) only provides evidence that the theory is popular, not evidence to support that it is true.
4. **A. A newspaper opinion piece by a respected political leader.** Essays stating an opinion, or op-eds, express the personal views of the author and do not undergo rigorous review. The author in choice (A) is not a scientist, and is therefore the least likely to be a credible source. Choices (B), (C), and (D) all contain credible sources that are written by experts, are peer reviewed, and contain verifiable evidence, data, and facts. Note that this does not mean the op-ed is incorrect, only that it cannot be relied upon for accuracy.

Lesson 7: Express and Apply Scientific Information

Practice 7

1. **C. pure acetone; a solution of sugar in acetone** The passage states that, during osmosis, a liquid moves from a place where there is a higher concentration of dissolved material to where there is a lower concentration of dissolved material. Thus, to test the rate of osmosis of a liquid, Gillian would want to put that same liquid on two sides of the vat, with more dissolved material on one side than on the other. Only choice (C) describes that arrangement.
2. **D. formic acid** The solvent with the highest rate of diffusion would be the solvent that took the least time to reach equilibrium. Here it took formic acid the least time to do so.
3. **B. 19** Put the numbers in order: 15, 18, 20, 25. The median is the middle number. Because there are an even number of values given, take the average of the two middle numbers by adding them together: 18+20=38 and dividing by 2: $\frac{38}{2}=19$.
4. **A. greater than** If your blood has more dissolved material than your tissues, water will move from the tissues into the blood, causing the tissues to dry out.

Lesson 8: Use Statistics and Probability

Practice 8

1. **D. rabbit** The median is the middle number of a set of numbers, and in this graph, the rabbit has a lower body weight than the dog, human, and horse and a higher body weight than the shrew, cactus mouse, and flying squirrel. It isn't necessary to know the animals' actual body weights to determine this.
2. **A. rabbit** Similarly, the graph shows that the rabbit has the middle metabolic rate of the seven species in the graph.
3. **B. lower than the previous average** To find an average, you add up all the numbers in a list and divide by the number of items in the list, like this:

$$\frac{\text{shrew} + \text{c.mouse} + \text{f.squirrel} + \text{rabbit} + \text{dog} + \text{human} + \text{horse}}{7}$$

The shrew is the largest of those numbers: it has the highest metabolic rate. Therefore, if you removed it and recalculated the average, the new average would be lower than the previous average.

4. **C. Their metabolic rate would be slightly lower than that of horses.** The question states that elephants weigh more than horses. Thus, elephants would be to the right of horses on the line graph. Based on the curve of the line, you can guess that elephants would have a slightly lower metabolism than that of horses. Because the line continues to decrease slightly, choice (B) is unsupported.
5. **C. 120** The question asks how many different orderings, or sequences, of the five crops are possible. This is a permutations question, because order matters. Thus, multiply to find the number of permutations: $5 \times 4 \times 3 \times 2 \times 1 = 120$

Science Skills Practice Questions

1. **B. While Copernicus's theory was an important development, it included elements that are outdated today.** The first sentence of the second paragraph provides the main idea. The words "[f]or example" help to make clear that the second and third sentences are details supporting that main idea.
2. **C. "The Significance and Limitations of the Copernican Theory"** The title of a passage should reflect its topic or main idea. The topic of this passage is the importance, or significance, of Copernicus's theory, as well as the fact that Copernicus's theory was not completely correct. Choices (A) and (D) are both too broad, while choice (B) is incorrect because the passage is not about Copernicus's life.
3. **A. Astronomers now believe that the planets are not embedded in crystalline spheres.** The question asks

for something that can be inferred, or deduced, from the passage. Choice (A) is supported by the passage. Copernicus's idea that the planets are embedded in crystalline spheres is mentioned in the second paragraph as an example of an idea that is today considered "primitive." This implies that astronomers today no longer believe this to be true. Choices (B) and (C) are contradicted by the passage. Choice (D) is not supported by the passage: primitive astronomers who came before Copernicus are not discussed.

4. **C. B and D** The passage describes what happens when you add heat to a substance: the temperature of the substance increases, up to the point when the substance starts to change from a solid to a liquid or from a liquid to a gas. Then the temperature of the substance holds steady while the substance is undergoing that change. When more heat is added but the temperature of a substance remains constant, it must be undergoing a phase change. The places in the diagram where the temperature is flat—B and D—thus represent the two places where the substance is changing from solid to liquid or from liquid to gas.

5. **D. a vaccine to prevent infection with the hepatitis B virus** According to the passage, hepatitis B virus causes liver cancer. A vaccine that prevents infection with the hepatitis B virus would therefore also prevent liver cancer.

6. **B. At least some of the phalarope's prey is smaller than a water droplet.** If the phalarope feeds on prey that it draws into its beak via water droplets, the prey must be smaller than a water droplet.

7. **B. Penrith** The black bars on the graph represent each city's previous record, and the gray bars represent its current record. Find the city for which the gray bar is furthest above the black bar: Penrith.

8. **C. Penrith** The median number is the middle of a list of numbers. Here, because there are seven cities, the city with the "previous record equal to the median of all the cities' previous records" simply means the city with the middle value (among the previous record values). Fortunately, the cities are represented in the graph in such a way that their previous records are in ascending order, and the median previous record belongs to Penrith.

9. **B. Temperatures increased 5 degrees or less** The largest increase was in the city of Penrith and was approximately 5 degrees.

10. **C. Why, when I touch the metal filing cabinet, do I experience more electrostatic shocks than my assistant does when she touches it?** The first paragraph of the passage explains that the office manager "wondered why" she experienced more static shocks than her assistant. That's the question that prompted her experiment. While it is true that the office manager decided to switch to cotton clothing, she didn't begin by wondering whether it was better, so choice (A) is incorrect. Choice (B) distorts the office manager's thoughts. Choice (D) places too much emphasis on shoes, which were not the subject of the office manager's experiment.

11. **D. The office manager wore one type of clothing, while her assistant wore another type of clothing, and they recorded the number of shocks they experienced.** The office manager wanted to test her hypothesis that her nylon clothing was causing her to experience shocks when touching a metal filing cabinet. To do so, she conducted an experiment in which she wore cotton clothing for a week, while her assistant wore nylon clothing; both wore identical shoes. Then the manager and assistant recorded the number of shocks they each experienced during the course of a week. Choice (D) correctly describes this experiment. Choice (A) describes the office manager's hypothesis. Choice (B) describes the office manager's course of action after she had completed her experiment, while choice (C) is the opposite of what actually occurred during the experiment (both the manager and the assistant wore identical shoes).

12. **A. They wanted to test the effects of their clothing on the number of shocks they were experiencing, and wearing different types of shoes might have confused their results.** In an experiment, it is important to control factors other than the one thing the experimenter wants to study. In this case, the office manager wanted to study the effect of clothing on the number of static shocks she was receiving. Choice (B) wrongly suggests that shoes were the subject of the office manager's experiment. Choices (C) and (D) distort the passage: the two individuals had the opposite hypothesis about cotton clothes, and, during her experiment, the office manager was trying to study static shocks—not avoid them.

13. **C. a new hypothesis** Remember, a hypothesis is a guess that a researcher starts with and then tests through an experiment. If the office manager formed a new guess about what was causing the static shocks, and she intended to study that new guess through an experiment, that would be a new hypothesis. It would not, at that point, be (A), a new conclusion based on findings. While she might, as choice (D) suggests, design an experiment to test this idea, the idea itself is not an experiment design. And the idea is certainly not (B), a general principle from the study of physics; rather, the office manager is making a guess based on observation.

14. **C. 15** This is a combinations question: you are asked for all possible groupings of two out of the six snails, and the order of snails within each group does not matter. Use a table or an organized list to find the number of possible groupings. Name the snails A–F if that makes it easier.

AB				
AC	BC			
AD	BD	CD		
AE	BE	CE	DE	
AF	BF	CF	DF	EF

Count the possible pairs: there are 15.

15. **A. 6.3%** The question asks for the probability that any given star is a class G star, and we have to combine two probabilities to find it. We know that there is a 90 percent chance, or a .9 probability, that a star will be a main sequence star. We also know that, if it is a main sequence star, there is a 7 percent chance, or a .07 probability, that it will be a class G star. Multiply those two probabilities to find the probability of *both* of them happening: $.9 \times .07 = .063$. Express your answer as a percentage: 6.3%.
16. **D. large femoral plaques** Forty-one percent of current smokers had large femoral plaques. That is a higher percentage than any other type of plaque listed in the chart.
17. **C. People who quit smoking tend to substitute snacking for smoking.** This is a plausible reason why those who quit smoking tend to gain weight and why they consequently have a higher waist circumference.

Life Science

Lesson 1: Cell Structures and Functions

Practice 1

1. **C. mitochondrion** The diagram indicates that the mitochondria produce a cell's energy.
2. **D. Cell walls cannot maintain a plant's shape and rigidity when the plant lacks water.** Even though cell walls contribute to keeping a plant firm and rigid, they cannot do the job without water-filled vacuoles. This conclusion follows from the fact that a plant that lacks water will wilt.
3. **A. the presence of a nucleus** According to the passage, the presence of a cell nucleus defines a cell as eukaryotic.
4. **A. Each time the microscope is improved, scientists can see cell structures more clearly.** Since cell structures are tiny, the more a cell is magnified, the more detail can be seen.
5. **B. Oxygen would diffuse from the unicellular organism into the pond water.** Since diffusion is the movement of molecules toward areas of lower concentration, if the organism had more oxygen than the surrounding water did, oxygen would pass out of the organism into the water until the concentrations were equalized.

Lesson 2: Cell Processes and Energy

Practice 2

1. **D. carbon dioxide, water, and energy** According to the equation that summarizes cellular respiration, the products of this process are carbon dioxide, water, and energy.
2. **A. increasing the amount of light the plants receive each day** Because light is required for photosynthesis, increasing light is the best choice for increasing the rate of photosynthesis. The other options either would have no effect or would decrease the rate of photosynthesis.
3. **B. increasing the number of green plants** Because green plants use up carbon dioxide during photosynthesis, increasing the amount of greenery on Earth would help reduce the amount of carbon dioxide in the atmosphere.
4. **D. stoma** According to the diagram, carbon dioxide enters the leaf through the stomata (the plural form of *stoma*).
5. **B. Most of a leaf's chloroplasts are found in its palisade cells.** The diagram shows that most of the leaf's chloroplasts are in the palisade cells. Evidence to support the other choices cannot be found in the diagram.

Lesson 3: Human Body Systems

Practice 3

1. **A. the circulatory system** According to the passage on the page before this practice set, the circulatory system transports blood to all the cells of the body.
2. **C. Both are structures in which substances pass through capillary walls into the blood.** Both alveoli and villi are tiny structures containing capillaries in which substances pass to and/or from the blood. In the alveoli of the respiratory system, oxygen and carbon dioxide pass into and out of blood; in the villi of the digestive system, nutrients pass into the blood.
3. **D. Veins have valves that allow blood to flow in one direction only.** Of the four facts given, this is the only one that involves the direction of flow of the blood. Therefore, it helps to support Harvey's conclusion that blood in the veins flows toward the heart.
4. **A. ureter** According to the diagram, the ureter is the only structure connecting the kidney to the bladder, so urine must flow through the ureters to reach the bladder.
5. **B. a patient with a painful kidney stone** Because a kidney stone forms in the urinary system, the patient is most likely to be treated by an urologist.

Lesson 4: Health Issues

Practice 4

1. **D. the skin** As implied by the passage, the skin is one of the first defenses against germs, along with mucous membranes, tears, and stomach acid.
2. **C. habituation** Although Sara feels an urge to drink wine, she feels no ill effects if she does not; this indicates that she is habituated to alcohol. She has a psychological dependence rather than a physical dependence on alcohol. If her dependence were physical, she would feel the effects of skipping her daily drink.
3. **A. Fats are a more concentrated source of energy than carbohydrates.** According to the table, carbohydrates provide 4 calories per gram while fats provide 9 calories per gram. None of the other statements is supported by the information in the table.
4. **B. Carbohydrates come from fruits as well as from bread and rice.** According to the table, bread and rice are not the only foods that provide carbohydrates;

fruits and at least one type of vegetable (potatoes) also do. Choices (A) and (D) are opinions, not facts. Choice (C) is contradicted by the table.

Lesson 5: Reproduction and Heredity

Practice 5

1. **A. both are tall** Each parent pea plant has one dominant tallness allele and one recessive shortness allele. The dominant allele is the one that will be expressed, so both parent pea plants will be tall.
2. **B. 1 out of 4** According to the Punnett square, only one out of four possible combinations yields a short plant (one with two recessive alleles for height: tt).
3. **D. TT** If you want to grow only tall plants, then it is better to use purebred tall plants (TT). If you use hybrid tall plants—(Tt) or (tT)—then in the next generation, you will likely get some short plants in your garden.
4. **D. 2** The passage states that if even one dominant allele is present, the dominant trait will be expressed. For a recessive trait to be expressed, both alleles must be recessive.
5. **D. Organisms that reproduce sexually produce offspring that have inherited a mix of traits from their parents.** Because they are inheriting a mix of genes from two parents, the offspring of organisms that reproduce sexually are different from the parents and from each other, creating a more diverse population. When an organism reproduces asexually, the offspring are identical to the parent and to each other, which means less diversity in the population.
6. **B. The black male was actually a hybrid.** The only way a white rabbit and a black rabbit could produce a white offspring is if the black rabbit is carrying the recessive allele for white fur. That means the black rabbit was actually a hybrid, not purebred as the student had assumed.

Lesson 6: Modern Genetics

Practice 6

1. **C. the sequence of base pairs in a gene** According to the third paragraph of the passage on page 626, particular sequences of base pairs code for particular amino acids, which are the building blocks of proteins. Therefore, as the paragraph concludes, the order of bases on a gene forms a code for making a particular protein.
2. **D. a change in protein synthesis** Since DNA provides the blueprint for protein synthesis, any change in DNA may affect protein synthesis.
3. **D. Genetically engineered foods are safe for consumers and the environment.** This is an opinion; it is not a fact that can be proved true from the information in the text. All the other statements are facts, based on information given in the paragraph.
4. **B. so that each daughter cell receives a complete set of DNA** Cell division produces two daughter cells with genetic material, or DNA, that is identical to that of the parent cell. The DNA must be replicated in the parent cell first so that each daughter cell can receive an exact copy of it.
5. **B. The base guanine pairs only with the base cytosine.** According to both the diagram and the passage, in DNA sequences, the base guanine always pairs with the base cytosine. (Note that in the diagram, each base is represented by its initial.) The remaining statements are not supported by the passage or the diagram.
6. **A. amino acids** Proteins are composed of chains of amino acids.

Lesson 7: Evolution and Natural Selection

Practice 7

1. **B. Frogs' forelimbs contain carpal bones.** All four homologous structures in the diagram include the same layout of bones: humerus, radius, ulna, and carpal bones. Since frogs' limbs are homologous to those of the other animals, they will likely have the same bones. Choices (A), (C), and (D) may be true, but they are not supported by the diagram.
2. **C. In penguins, flying birds, humans, and alligators, the forelimbs have similar structures despite performing different functions.** Even though the forelimbs of these organisms look alike, they all perform different functions. The arm helps to lift and hold things, the penguin's flipper helps it to swim, the bird's wing helps it to fly, and the alligator's foreleg helps it to walk.
3. **A. traits that make an organism better able to survive in its environment** According to the passage on the page before this practice set, adaptations are traits that some individuals possess that enable them to compete successfully in their environment.
4. **C. DNA analysis provides more objective data than observation does.** DNA analysis is more objective than observation, because the person doing the observing must interpret what he or she sees.

Lesson 8: Organization of Ecosystems

Practice 8

1. **D. the sun** The ultimate source of energy for the food web on the previous page is the sun. This is implied by the first paragraph, which explains that the green plants at the bottom of the food web produce their own energy from the sun. The other species in the food web ultimately depend on those producers for food.
2. **B. The populations of hares and seed-eating birds would increase.** With fewer foxes to hunt them, more hares and seed-eating birds would survive long enough to reproduce, increasing the populations of these organisms.
3. **B. an aquarium with aquatic plants and herbivorous tropical fish** An aquarium is a human-made ecosystem with living organisms in balance with

one another and with their physical environment. It includes both producers (the aquatic plants) and consumers (the herbivorous, which means plant-eating, fish).

4. **D. The natural replacement of lichens by mosses and ferns, and then shrubs, is an example of succession.** According to the information, succession is a naturally occurring replacement of one ecosystem by another.
5. **C. to turn atmospheric nitrogen into compounds plants and animals can use** According to the information, nitrogen-fixing bacteria on the roots of plants like peas and beans take nitrogen and use it to form compounds that plants and animals can use.

Life Science Practice Questions

1. **B. Active transport requires the cell to use energy, and passive transport does not.** According to the information given, the key difference between active and passive transport is the use of the cell's energy.
2. **C. The water level in the jar might have gone down because of evaporation.** Because the experiment did not control for evaporation, it does not prove that the water was absorbed by the ivy.
3.

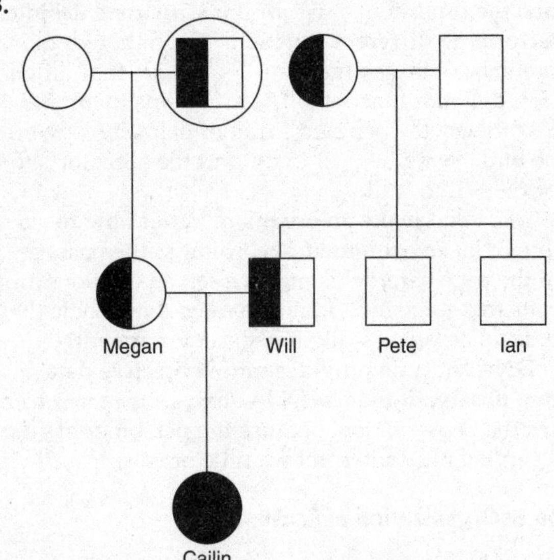

B. Megan's father The paragraph indicates that squares stand for males and half-shading represents genetic carriers. Of all the choices, only the square that represents Megan's father is half-shaded, indicating that Megan's father is a carrier of cystic fibrosis.

4. **D. No one in either Megan's or Will's immediate family has cystic fibrosis except Cailin.** Since everyone in the pedigree except for Cailin has only the recessive gene for cystic fibrosis, no one else suffers from the disease. Thus, Cailin's family members were probably unaware that some of them were carriers for cystic fibrosis.
5. **B. metaphase** According to the diagram, the chromosomes line up across the middle of the cell during metaphase.
6. **B. After mitosis, the two daughter cells have their own nuclei.** The two daughter cells in the interphase section of the diagram each have their own nuclei.
7. **B. to control the movement of chromosomes.** The spindle fibers help the chromatids move to different locations during mitosis.
8. **C. The fossil record for any given species may be incomplete.** Because fossils are found at random, scientists cannot be sure they have a complete fossil record for many species. An incomplete fossil record would also explain why evolution sometimes seems to take place in bursts rather than gradually.
9. **D. nutrient transport and immune defense** According to the information, plasma transports nutrients. White blood cells defend against infection.
10. **A. enamel** The diagram shows that the top surface of the tooth is made of enamel.
11. **A. few or no nerve endings** Pain is caused by nerves sending signals to the brain. If a decaying tooth does not become painful until the decay reaches the pulp, the outer parts of the tooth—the enamel and dentin—must not contain many nerve endings.
12. **B. grazing too many cattle on grassland** Overgrazing of domestic animals like cattle can destroy much plant life in grassland ecosystems. When that happens, the number of cattle the grassland can support decreases, as described in the paragraph.
13. **A. DNA analysis provides more fundamental, accurate data than does a visual analysis of structures and fossils.** Because DNA analysis involves genetic data at the molecular level, it is a better indicator of the relationships among organisms than visible similarities such as teeth. Thus, DNA analysis has changed the way scientists previously classified some organisms.
14. **A. panting** A dog's panting and a human being's sweating are both processes that cause loss of body heat through the evaporation of water. In other words, they are body processes that function to cool off an overheated animal.
15. **B. 3** According to the graph, unintentional injuries, chronic lung diseases, and cancers caused more deaths in 2011 than in 2005.
16. **B. biggest decrease** The number of deaths caused by heart disease decreased between 2005 and 2011. Of the remaining causes of death, only cerebrovascular disease caused fewer deaths in 2011 than in 2005, but this decrease is much smaller than that for heart disease.
17. **B. 8% decrease** To find the percent change, first subtract to find the amount of the change. The number of deaths from heart diseases in 2005 was roughly 650,000, and the number in 2011 was roughly 600,000. So the amount of change was 50,000. Now, divide that by the original value: $\frac{50,000}{650,000} \approx .08$. To convert that number to a percentage, multiply by 100: 8%. Since the number of deaths from heart diseases in 2011 was lower than in 2005, there was an 8% decrease.

Physical Science

Lesson 1: Atoms and Molecules

Practice 1

1. **A. The sodium atom loses an electron, becoming positively charged, and the chlorine atom gains an electron, becoming negatively charged.** According to the diagram, the sodium atom gives up an electron to the chlorine atom. With one fewer electron than protons, the sodium becomes a positively charged ion. When the chlorine atom gains an electron, it has one more electron than protons, making it a negatively charged ion. The sodium and chloride ions are attracted to each other, forming an ionic bond.
2. **D. $C_6H_{12}O_6$** According to the passage on the previous page and the question text, a chemical formula represents the number of atoms of each element in a compound. Chemical symbols, which are letters, represent the elements, followed by subscripts, which represent the number of atoms.
3. **D. atoms that have either gained electrons to become negatively charged, or atoms that have lost electrons to become positively charged** An ion is defined as an atom that carries a charge. The only way for an atom's charge to change is for it to gain or lose electrons.
4. **B. Most of the alpha particles passed right through the gold foil.** Because most of the alpha particles passed right through the foil without being stopped or deflected, Rutherford concluded that atoms must consist mostly of empty space.
5. **B. 11** The atomic number of sodium refers to how many protons the atom has. An atom that is not an ion has the same number of protons as electrons. Therefore, a sodium atom has 11 electrons.

Lesson 2: Properties and States of Matter

Practice 2

1. **A. melting and boiling** According to the passage on the previous page, adding heat to a solid melts the solid, and adding heat to a liquid causes it to boil, or change to a gas.
2. **B. Solids are usually denser than liquids and gases.** If you compare the densities of the solids, liquids, and gases in the chart, you will see that the solids are denser than the liquids and the gases.
3. **B. 190%** According to the paragraph, glycerin's boiling point is 190° greater than water's boiling point. To find the percentage by which glycerin's boiling point is greater than that of water, divide the difference between the two substances' boiling points by the boiling point of water and multiply the quotient by 100%. Thus, $\frac{190}{100} \times 100\% = 190\%$. Always read questions carefully. Glycerin's boiling point is 290% of water's boiling point, but this question asks for the percentage by which glycerin's boiling point is *greater than* water's.
4. **A. Water is a unique substance on Earth.** This statement is a conclusion (a general statement) that is supported by the statements that give details about the properties of water.
5. **B. Antifreeze added to water in a car's radiator lowers the freezing point below 0°C.** Adding antifreeze (a solute) to water (a solvent) lowers the freezing point of the solution, the liquid in the radiator.
6. **D. dusty air** Dusty air is the only choice with large suspended particles. Gold and oxygen are elements, not mixtures. Salt water is a solution; it has small particles that do not settle out of the mixture.

Lesson 3: Chemical Reactions

Practice 3

1. **C. $2Cu + O_2 \rightarrow 2CuO$** You can eliminate choice (A) because the product (CuO) is on the left side of the equation rather than on the right side. To determine which of the remaining answer choices is correct, you must look for the equation that has two copper atoms and two oxygen atoms on the left side to balance the two copper atoms and two oxygen atoms on the right side.
2. **B. Weigh the reactants, conduct the reaction in a sealed container, and weigh the products.** This procedure should result in the weights of the reactants and products being equal, because none of the products would escape from the sealed container. The weight measurements would provide evidence for the law of the conservation of mass.
3. **C. Igniting the gas requires activation energy, the gas burning releases exothermic energy, and the egg solidifying requires endothermic energy.** Activation energy is the energy needed to start a chemical reaction. Exothermic energy is the energy given off by a chemical reaction, while endothermic energy is energy absorbed by a system.
4. **C. the time during which the reaction occurs** The horizontal axis is labeled "Time," so you can eliminate choice (D). The graph shows the progress of the reaction, which takes place over time, not just one instant of the reaction, so you can eliminate choices (A) and (B).
5. **A. Compounds are substances consisting of two or more elements chemically combined in a definite proportion.** The writer of the paragraph takes for granted that you know what a compound is and does not define the term *compound* in the paragraph. The other answer choices are stated explicitly in the paragraph.
6. **B. "Acids and Bases"** The passage gives an overview of acids and bases and describes what happens when they react with one another.

Lesson 4: The Nature of Energy

Practice 4

1. **C. Energy cannot be created or destroyed, but can only change in form.** According to the third paragraph on the previous page this is the law of conservation of energy.
2. **D. chemical** The potential energy stored in the batteries is chemical energy. This energy is used to power the flashlight.
3. **B. power** Power is the rate at which work is done or, in this case, the rate at which energy is consumed. The wood stove has greater power than the oak tree because it consumes the tree's energy in much less time than it takes the tree to consume the sun's energy.
4. **B. the relationship between energy and mass** According to the passage, Einstein's equation explains how energy can be converted to mass, and vice versa.
5. **B. At the high point of its swing, a pendulum has potential energy.** The diagram shows that at the high point of its swing, the pendulum has potential energy, the energy of position. The information in the diagram does not support any of the other statements.
6. **A. The molecules in air are far apart.** Because the molecules of a gas like air are far apart, they are in contact with one another less frequently than are the molecules of a liquid or solid, since liquids and solids are much denser. That is why gases have lower conductivity than liquids and solids do.

Lesson 5: Motion and Forces

Practice 5

1. **D. anything that changes the rest or motion of an object** According to the passage on the previous page, this is the definition of a force.
2. **D. the tendency of an object to remain at rest or in motion** According to the third paragraph on the previous page, inertia is described in Newton's first law of motion as the tendency of objects to remain at rest or keep moving until acted upon by a force.
3. **B. the International Space Station orbiting Earth** The key concept regarding centripetal force is circular motion, and the orbit of the space station is the only example of circular motion among the options given.
4. **A. the momentum of the car decreases when its velocity decreases.** Momentum is the product of mass and velocity. The mass of each car does not change, but each car's momentum will be directly proportional to its velocity.
5. **B. an object that has a constant speed** The graph shows a straight line that slopes upward. According to the paragraph, this type of graph shows an object that is moving at a constant speed.
6. **C. Some machines simply change the direction of a force.** According to the information given, a machine is a device that changes the direction *or* the size of a force, which means that some machines change only the direction of the force. An example is a simple pulley, which allows you to push down, rather than pull up, to lift a load.

Lesson 6: Electricity and Magnetism

Practice 6

1. **B. two poles repelling one another** According to the diagram, like poles repel, so a drawing of two north poles facing each other would look the same as the diagram of two south poles facing each other.
2. **A. Copper and aluminum are conductors.** Electrical wires need to be made of something that carries electricity easily, which is what conductors do.
3. **D. a flashlight** According to the passage, direct current is used in battery-powered devices. Choice (D) is correct because flashlights typically run on batteries.
4. **D. a transformer** According to the passage, transformers change the voltage of an incoming electric current.
5. **A. the light bulb** An incandescent light bulb is basically a thin tungsten filament through which current flows. This filament has resistance and thus functions as a resistor in a circuit.
6. **C. Disconnecting the light bulb will also stop the current.** To have current, you need to have a loop. Getting rid of any piece of the circuit—the battery, the switch, the light bulb, or the wire—would break the loop and thus stop the current.

Physical Science Practice Questions

1. **B. 5,730 years** This information is in the table, in the row for carbon-14 and the column for half-life.
2. **D. Uranium produces radioactive waste that may harm living things for millions of years.** Since the question asks what an *opponent* of nuclear power would say, the correct answer should be a negative fact about uranium. According to the table, uranium is unstable for millions or even billions of years, so choice (D) is both negative and true. Choice (C) is a negative claim about uranium, but it's a false one—uranium is unstable for much longer than three days.
3. **D. Both involve the transfer of energy through matter or space.** According to the paragraph, a wave is something that transfers energy through matter or space, so both types of waves would have that in common. Longitudinal waves have forward-and-back displacement, while transverse waves have up-and-down displacement, so choices (A) and (B) are incorrect. Choice (C) is incorrect because only longitudinal waves involve compressions.
4. **A. A cork in water bobs up and down as waves pass.** The question asks for an example in which something stays in roughly the same place after a wave passes through it. If a cork merely bobs up and down as waves pass, then the cork will be in its

original position after the waves stop. Thus, choice (A) is the right example.

5. **A. dust motes dancing in a shaft of sunlight** Brownian motion is the random movement of particles in a liquid or a gas. Choice (A) is correct because dust motes move about randomly in the air, which is a gas. Choice (C) is wrong because it doesn't involve movement, choice (D) is wrong because the raft is *on* a lake (not *in* it), and choice (B) is wrong because the ground is a solid.
6. **D. Using powdered marble** The smaller the pieces of marble used, the greater their surface area will be and, therefore, the faster the reaction rate will be.
7. **B. decreases** "Varies inversely" means "is inversely proportional to." So as pressure increases, volume does the opposite—it decreases.
8. **C. xenon (Xe)** According to the chart, the noble gases are in column 18. Choice (C) xenon is the only choice in this column.
9. **B. Chlorine (Cl) and iodine (I) have similar properties.** According to the information given, elements in the same column have similar properties. Since chlorine and iodine are in the same column, choice (B) is correct. There is no mention in the paragraph or chart of common elements, so choice (A) is incorrect. Choice (C) is false because arsenic (As) and antimony (Sb) are in the same column and thus are similar, not different. Arsenic (As) is number 33, so there are 33 protons in its nucleus, not 85 as stated in choice (D).
10. **A. microwaves** According to the diagram, wavelengths increase as you go left to right. Since microwaves are to the right of the visible spectrum, choice (A) is correct.
11. **C. People can see only a small portion of the electromagnetic spectrum.** In the diagram, the visible spectrum—the section that people can see—is only a small piece of the entire electromagnetic spectrum.
12. **B. Its mass remains the same, and its weight decreases.** The mass of an object doesn't depend on anything; rather, mass is a property of the object. By contrast, the weight of an object gets smaller as the object gets farther from Earth. So, as a rocket travels away from Earth, its mass won't change, but its weight will get smaller.
13. **B. Coldness cannot be transferred.** The paragraph directly states that heat can be transferred (A), a cold object can be warmed by your body (C), and that your body heat can be lost (D). What the passage assumes but doesn't say is that *only* heat can be transferred; coldness can't be. This is choice (B).
14. **D. the range** All of the engineer's recorded speeds are off by 3.7 km/hour, which skews the mean, mode, and median upward. However, the range is unchanged, because the difference between the largest value and the smallest value is the same in both columns (195.6 km/hour).
15. **C. $\frac{3}{5}$** This question asks about the planes' actual speeds, so be sure to use the "actual speed" column. Four of the five planes have a speed less than 360 km/hour, and once one of those planes is chosen, three of the four remaining planes will have a speed less than 360 km/hour. Thus, the probability that both chosen planes have a speed less than 360 km/hour is $\frac{4}{5} \times \frac{3}{4} = \frac{3}{5}$.
16. **A. Elastic** In trial 1, both the final momentums and kinetic energies are equal to their initial values. Because momentum and kinetic energy are conserved, the collision that occurred in trial 1 must be elastic.
17. **B. 0°** The freezing point of water is 0°C.

Practice Tests

STEP 1: To practice for the actual HiSET exam, you can take the following five practice tests. When you take the practice tests, follow the same time limits you will face on the actual tests.

Language Arts: Reading, 65 minutes, pages 664–677
40 multiple-choice questions

Language Arts: Writing, 120 minutes, pages 678–695
Part I: 51 multiple-choice questions, 75 minutes
Part II: 1 essay, 45 minutes

Mathematics, 90 minutes, pages 696–707
50 multiple-choice questions

Social Studies, 70 minutes, pages 708–724
50 multiple-choice questions

Science, 80 minutes, pages 725–739
50 multiple-choice questions

For the multiple-choice questions, you can fill in the circles next to the correct answers in this book, or you can write your answers on a separate piece of paper.

You may use your calculator on the Mathematics Test and as needed during the rest of the test.

STEP 2: Review your work using the Practice Test Answers and Explanations that begin on page 740, and fill in the Practice Test Evaluation Charts. These charts will allow you to see which study areas may still need work.

STEP 3: Confirm your readiness to take the actual HiSET exam.

LANGUAGE ARTS: READING PRACTICE TEST

Directions: Use 65 minutes to answer the following 40 questions.

Questions 1 through 7 refer to the following excerpt from a short story.

Excerpted from *The Living Is Easy*

1 He gave them each a copper, too, though he could hardly spare it, what with four of them to feed and Mama wanting yard goods and buttons and ribbons to keep herself feeling proud of the way she kept her children. Time was, he gave them kisses for toting his bucket. But the day Cleo brazenly said, I don't want a kiss, I want a copper, the rest of them shamefacedly said it after her. Most times Pa had a struggle to dig down so deep. Four coppers a day, six days a week, was half a day's pay gone up in smoke for candy.

2 Pa couldn't bring himself to tell Mama. She would have wrung out of him that Cleo had been the one started it. And Cleo was his eldest. A man who loved his wife couldn't help loving his first-born best, the child of his fiercest passion. When that first-born was a girl, she could trample on his heart, and he would swear on a stack of Bibles that it didn't hurt.

3 The sisters put their coppers in their pinafore pockets and skipped back through the woods. Midway Cleo stopped and pointed to a towering oak. "You all want to bet me a copper I can't swing by my feet from up in that tree?"

4 Lily clapped her hands to her eyes. "I doesn't want to bet you," she implored. "I ain't fixing to see you fall."

5 Serena said severely, "You bust your neck, you see if Mama don't bust it again."

6 Charity said tremulously, "Cleo, what would us do if our sister was dead?"

7 Cleo saw herself dressed up fine as Josie Beauchamp, stretched out in a coffin with her sisters sobbing beside it, and Pa with his Sunday handkerchief holding his tears, and Mama crying, I loved you best, Cleo. I never said it when you were alive. And I'm sorry, sorry, I waited to say it after you were gone.

8 "You hold my copper, Charity. And if I die, you can have it."

9 Lily opened two of her fingers and peeped through the crack. "Cleo, I'll give you mine if you don't make me see you hanging upside down." It was one thing to hear Cleo tell about herself. It was another thing to see her fixing to kill herself.

10 "Me, too," said Serena, with a little sob, more for the copper than for Cleo, whom she briefly hated for compelling unnecessary sacrifice.

1. Which of the following would Cleo probably enjoy?

   - A. Jumping from a roof before an audience
   - B. Sewing clothes with her mother
   - C. Reading a good book
   - D. Treating her sisters to candy

2. Whose point of view is explained by this quote from paragraph 2? "A man who loved his wife couldn't help loving his first-born best, the child of his fiercest passion."

   - A. Cleo's
   - B. Mama's
   - C. The narrator's
   - D. Pa's

3. Which one of the following happened before the day described in the excerpt?

   - A. Cleo envisions her own funeral.
   - B. Cleo's sisters offer her their coppers.
   - C. Cleo says that she does not want a kiss but wants a copper instead.
   - D. Cleo asks her sisters to bet on whether she can swing from her feet in an oak tree.

4. Why did Serena offer Cleo her own copper?

   - A. Serena wanted Cleo to get in trouble for taking the others' money.
   - B. Serena had placed a bet that Cleo could not swing from the oak tree.
   - C. Serena felt that she had no choice but to give Cleo her copper to stop Cleo from doing something unsafe.
   - D. Serena wanted to show how much she loved her sister.

5. What is meant by the following quote from paragraph 1? "Most times Pa had a struggle to dig down so deep."

   - A. It was difficult for Pa to find it within himself to be generous.
   - B. Pa had so few coins that they were usually far down in his pockets.
   - C. Pa often searched for reasons not to give coppers to Cleo and her sisters.
   - D. Pa could not really afford to give Cleo and her sisters money.

6. Which of the following statements best describes the theme of the passage?

   - A. Cleo is wrong to take advantage of her sisters and her father.
   - B. Cleo's boldness and her family's love for her sometimes make them feel powerless to resist her.
   - C. Cleo's longing to be loved makes her vulnerable.
   - D. Cleo and her sisters are becoming greedy as they learn how to extract money from each other and from their parents.

7. What is the "copper" that Pa gave each of the girls?

   - A. A coin
   - B. A piece of candy
   - C. A kiss
   - D. A piece of copper tubing

Questions 8 through 13 refer to the following book excerpt.

Excerpt from *Small Business for Dummies*

1 The domestic automakers had a huge market share coming into the 1970s but, unfortunately, were upsetting customers left and right. The Detroit auto manufacturers were able to keep their costs low and profits high in part by producing sub-par cars. Sure, their cars looked nice on the auto dealer's lot, but after a short time in use, many of the U.S.-manufactured cars developed far more problems than their foreign equivalents. And, to add insult to injury, U.S. auto customers didn't get particularly good customer service when they brought their cars in for needed tune-ups and repairs.

2 The chief bean counters and the management of the major U.S. automakers weren't considering the bigger picture when they analyzed their companies' financial statements during the 1970s. These companies were too focused on their short-term profitability and weren't considering the after-sales service that was required as a result of their initially shoddy products.

3 Not surprisingly, the U.S. automakers lost tremendous market share at the expense of the best foreign automakers during the 1970s and 1980s. In fact, one of the big four U.S. automakers—Chrysler—nearly went bankrupt and was saved only because of a government bailout.

4 In the long run, the Detroit automakers learned the hard way that getting your product right the first time is less costly and more profitable than retrenching to play catch-up. Customers aren't stupid, and if you continually sell them shoddy merchandise (especially when better merchandise is available from other sources), they won't come back the next time they're in the market for the products and services you have to offer. What's more, they'll tell others of their lousy experience with your company.

5 Although the major U.S. automakers ultimately got their act together in the 1990s and have stopped the erosion of market share, they still feel the financial pain from the millions of customers they alienated and lost to foreign competitors in the two preceding decades.

From *Small Business for Dummies* by Eric Tyson and Jim Schell, Foster City, CA: IDG Books, 2000.

8. The passage states that in the 1970s and 1980s, the management of the major U.S. automakers was too focused on which of the following?
   - A. Attractiveness of the cars they manufactured
   - B. After-sales service
   - C. Manufacturing shoddy merchandise
   - D. Short-term profitability
9. According to the passage, which of the following is a lesson learned by the Detroit automakers?
   - A. Getting your product right the first time is more profitable than fixing mistakes later.
   - B. Servicing your product is not profitable and therefore unimportant.
   - C. Bankruptcy is profitable for large companies due to government bailouts.
   - D. It is easy to win back customers a company has lost to a competitor.
10. What do the authors suggest was one of the goals of foreign automakers?
   - A. They studied and then improved on the design of U.S. cars.
   - B. They deliberately underpriced their cars to get a share of the U.S. market.
   - C. They wanted to build quality cars with few repair problems.
   - D. They put short-term profitability above all else.
11. The author uses the phrase "chief bean counters" most probably in order to
   - A. underscore the fact that customers will not return once they have had a poor experience with a certain company.
   - B. argue that foreign automakers provided better customer service than U.S. automakers.
   - C. emphasize U.S. automakers' preoccupation with keeping costs low and profits high in the short term, at the expense of their long-term outlook.
   - D. indicate that domestic automakers enjoyed tremendous market share at the beginning of the 1970s.
12. Which of the following best describes the authors' tone toward U.S. automakers?
   - A. Critical
   - B. Proud
   - C. Approving
   - D. Arrogant
13. Later, the authors advise: "As a small-business owner, remember that if you don't get your product right the first time, you may not have a second chance."

   Based on this information and the excerpt, who did get a second chance?
   - A. U.S. automakers
   - B. Foreign automakers
   - C. Small-business owners
   - D. The government

<u>Questions 14 through 21</u> refer to the following passage from a short story.

Excerpted from "The Twins"

1 After a while, there was a ring at the back door. The children scampered in from the garden, while Jennie answered the ring.

2 "Baker," said the man.

3 "Oh, yes," said Jennie: "wait, I'll get my purse."

4 I went on writing my letter, only half hearing the sound of Jennie's small-change as she, presumably, paid the baker's man.

5 In a moment, Marjie was by my side.

6 "Hallo," I said.

7 Marjie did not answer.

8 "Hallo, Marjie," I said. "Have you come to keep me company?"

9 "Listen," said little Marjie in a whisper, looking over her shoulder. "Listen."

10 "Yes," I said.

11 She looked over her shoulder again, as if afraid her mother might come in.

12 "Will you give me half-a-crown?" whispered Marjie, holding out her hand.

13 "Well," I said, "what do you want it for?"

14 "I want it," said Marjie, looking furtively behind her again.

15 "Would your mummy want you to have it?" I said.

16 "Give me half-a-crown," said Marjie.

17 "I'd rather not," I said. "But I'll tell you what, I'll buy you a—"

18 But Marjie had fled, out of the door, into the kitchen. "She'd rather not," I heard her say to someone.

19 Presently, Jennie came in, looking upset.

20 "Oh," she said, "I hope you didn't feel hurt. I only wanted to pay the baker, and I hadn't enough change. He hadn't any either; so just on the spur of the moment I sent Marjie for a loan of half-a-crown till tonight. But I shouldn't have done it. I never borrow anything as a rule."

21 "Well, of course!" I said. "Of course I'll lend you half-a-crown. I've got plenty of change. I didn't understand and I got the message all wrong; I thought she wanted it for herself and that you wouldn't like that."

22 Jennie looked doubtful. I funked explaining the whole of Marjie's act. It isn't easy to give evidence against a child of five.

23 "Oh, they never ask for money," said Jennie. "I would never allow them to ask for anything. They never do that."

24 "I'm sure they don't," I said, floundering a bit.

14. What does Marjie's looking over her shoulder suggest to the narrator?

    The narrator thinks Marjie

    - A. is imagining what she'll do with the money.
    - B. has forgotten something in the other room.
    - C. is shy and lacks confidence.
    - D. is hoping her mother won't hear her asking for money.

15. Which of the following becomes evident during the discussion between Jennie and the narrator?
    - A. Jennie knows the narrator wanted to lend her the money.
    - B. Jennie can't believe that the narrator wouldn't lend her the money.
    - C. Jennie is perplexed when the narrator blames Marjie.
    - D. The narrator and Jennie eventually forget the misunderstanding.

16. If Jennie were criticized by her boss at work, what would she most likely do?
    - A. Resent it in silence
    - B. Discuss it defensively
    - C. Not take it seriously
    - D. Argue forcefully

17. The first person point of view allows the reader to know
    - A. the narrator's thoughts.
    - B. the thoughts and actions of all characters.
    - C. only the actions of the narrator.
    - D. Marjie's opinions about the narrator.

18. What kind of relationship do Jennie and the narrator have?
    - A. They are cool and indifferent to each other.
    - B. They frequently disagree on matters.
    - C. They know each other but are not close.
    - D. Jennie takes advantage of the narrator.

19. Which of the following best describes the situation presented in this excerpt?
    - A. Humorous
    - B. Sad
    - C. Uncomfortable
    - D. Sentimental

20. Which one of the following best describes Jennie?
    - A. Obedient
    - B. Untidy
    - C. Proud
    - D. Furtive

21. What does "funked" mean in paragraph 22?
    - A. Had a bad odor
    - B. Lied about
    - C. Shied away from
    - D. Agreed with

Questions 22 through 26 refer to the following passage and graphic.

How Should We Measure the Rate of Poverty?

1 The rate of poverty appears to be increasing. Each year, the U.S. Census Bureau estimates the rate of poverty, or how many people in the U.S. are living in poverty. According to the Census Bureau, about 15.9 percent of the U.S. population was poor in 2011. That was a 15.3 percent increase over 2010. Moreover, the rate of poverty rose each year from 2007 to 2011.

2 It has been argued that the estimated rate of poverty is too low—that, in fact, more Americans are poor. To understand this, it is important first to understand how the Census Bureau determines who is poor. The Bureau surveys people about their income and then compares that income to the official "poverty threshold" (often called the "poverty line"). This poverty threshold varies depending on age, family size, and number of children. For example, in 2011 the poverty threshold for a single individual under 65 was $11,702. For a family of four, it was $23,021.

3 Some researchers have argued that these poverty thresholds do not account for taxes, living expenses, medical costs, or differences in cost of living. For example, in a major city, higher rents may leave individuals with less money for food. If the poverty thresholds were adjusted to account for these considerations, the estimated rate of poverty might be higher.

4 A panel of experts has proposed a different measure of poverty, which they call the Supplemental Poverty Measure, or SPM. The graph below shows what percentage of people are living in poverty as measured by the official poverty threshold and compares it to the percentage of people who would be considered poor by the SPM.

5 Why does it matter how many people are considered poor by the Census Bureau? One answer is that the Bureau's estimate of the rate of poverty is used by the federal government to allot resources to states and local communities. Local governments also use the estimate to figure out how many people are eligible for anti-poverty programs.

Poverty Rates Using Two Measures for Total Population and by Age Group, 2011

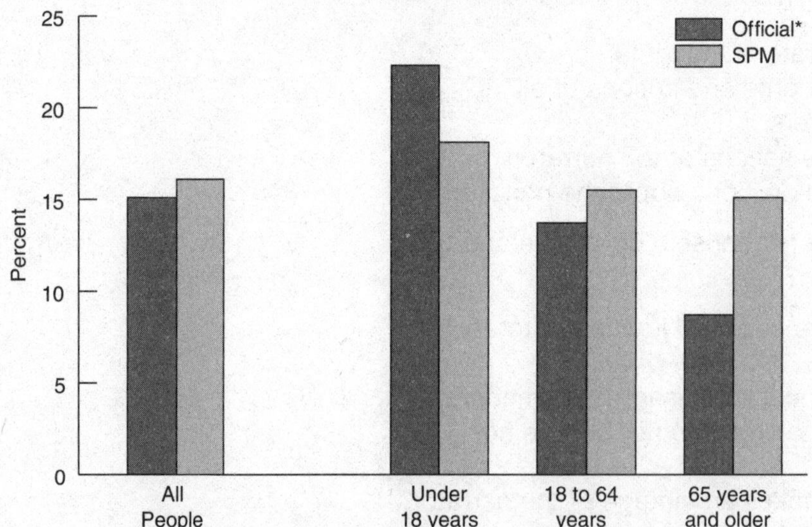

*Includes unrelated individuals under age 15.
Source: U.S. Census Bureau, Current Population Survey, 2012 Annual Social and Economic Supplement

Adapted information from the U.S. Census Bureau

22. Which of the following best states the main idea of the passage and graph?

- A. The Census Bureau uses a set of poverty thresholds to determine the rate of poverty.
- B. If the Census Bureau adopted the SPM, the estimate of the rate of poverty among seniors would increase.
- C. There may be more people in poverty than the Census Bureau's official estimate suggests.
- D. It is important that the government take action to combat poverty.

23. How does the bar graph support the main idea of the passage?

- A. The bar graph supports the claim that some people who do not think they are poor may actually be poor.
- B. The bar graph supports the claim that the government should do more to combat poverty.
- C. The bar graph supports the claim that a different way to measure poverty would produce a different estimate of the rate of poverty.
- D. The bar graph supports the claim that 15.9% of people in the U.S. were poor in 2011.

24. Which of the following describes a cause-and-effect relationship mentioned in the passage?

- A. The poverty thresholds cause individuals to have lower income.
- B. The Census Bureau's estimated rate of poverty can cause government officials to care about poverty.
- C. Higher rents can cause people to have less money for food.
- D. The SPM would cause more money to be spent on programs for senior citizens.

25. If the SPM were adopted, the official estimate of __________ living in poverty would be higher, and the official estimate of ________ living in poverty would be lower.

- A. people over 65; people under 18
- B. people under 18; people over 65
- C. people under 18; all people
- D. all people; people aged 18 to 64

26. A student reviewed this passage and graph and then said: "It's clear to me that if the Census Bureau adopted the SPM, then local governments would get significantly more federal money to spend on anti-poverty programs." Which of the following best describes the flaw in the student's reasoning?

- A. The student has confused the causes of poverty with the effects of poverty.
- B. The student has overlooked the fact that other factors might impact how much money local governments receive from the federal government.
- C. The student has overlooked the possibility that not all local governments work to combat poverty.
- D. The student has overlooked the fact that other countries have even higher rates of poverty.

Questions 27 through 31 refer to the following two passages.

Glenwood Community Improvement Council Member:

As a member of the Glenwood Community Improvement Council, I fully support spending money to beautify our public parks. Over the last few years, several of our community parks have fallen into disrepair. Walking paths through the parks are not clearly marked, graffiti is visible on picnic shelters, and garden areas are overgrown with weeds. My neighbors tell me that they do not visit our parks because of the parks' condition. Some even said that they worry the parks are dangerous! We should spend money to ensure that our parks are good places to spend time with your family.

Improving and maintaining the parks would have a positive effect on crime and vandalism. If the parks are established as a source of pride for all of the community, vandals will be less likely to deface them. Well-maintained basketball and volleyball courts, picnic areas, and special events such as concerts in the parks would provide activities for the whole town and help neighbors spend time together.

Furthermore, beautiful public spaces are essential to community pride. Without community pride, Glenwood residents and others are unlikely to invest in creating and supporting small businesses. And small businesses are the heart of a thriving community. We must present Glenwood as a beautiful place to live in order to attract successful entrepreneurs from the surrounding area. If we do so, our investment in the parks will quickly pay for itself. Thus, we must improve our public parks.

Concerned Local Business Owner:

I think I speak for most of the business owners in Glenwood when I say that spending money to improve parks would be a complete waste of resources. The parks are not popular, and we do not know that they would become popular after being improved.

If we want a shining example of our town's successes to attract businesses, our growing business district is all we need! In the last four years, six new businesses have moved into vacant locations on Main Street. On top of that, several restaurants and shops downtown have survived the recent economic downturn and are now seeing more customers.

The city should do more to support these businesses. We should spend money to improve the infrastructure and appearance of the downtown business district. Improvements could be made to streetlights, signs, and building exteriors along our historic Main Street. We also currently are not able to plant public flower beds or clean and maintain the sidewalks. Investments in these areas would make downtown inviting to both customers and small business owners.

Beautifying our town is important if we want economic growth. But we should make sure that our beautification efforts are in the most important places. Clearly, beautifying downtown would help us build a healthy local economy. And once we have done so, then we can put money toward our parks.

27. The topic of both passages is
   - A. the best way to enjoy public spaces.
   - B. what businesses should exist in Glenwood.
   - C. whether beautification projects create economic growth.
   - D. how best to spend public money.

28. The writers of the passages disagree about which of the following claims about Glenwood Public Parks?
   - A. They are in a state of disrepair.
   - B. They are a current source of pride for the community.
   - C. Improving them is a good use of funds right now.
   - D. Park activities can lower the amount of crime.

29. Which of the following is a detail used by the business owner to support her claim that the town's business district will attract new businesses?
   - A. The city's parks are currently unpopular.
   - B. Public flowerbeds have not been maintained.
   - C. Money could be put toward the parks later.
   - D. Several restaurants downtown have survived the bad economy.

30. Which of the following would the two writers most likely agree on?
   - A. Improving Glenwood Public Parks will have an immediate impact on local business.
   - B. Investing in our community is important for the future of Glenwood.
   - C. The parks would be used regularly if they were in better repair.
   - D. Public activities are more important than encouraging new local business.

31. What can you infer happened before these passages were written?
   - A. The council member and business owner argued publicly at a town meeting.
   - B. Glenwood initially invested in building parks but then did not spend enough to maintain them.
   - C. Glenwood had never invested any money in its parks and public spaces.
   - D. The business owner conducted a survey of small business owners.

Questions 32 through 35 are based on the following passage.

Excerpted from *The Tale of Genji*

The Tale of Genji *is a Japanese novel written around 1000* AD *by a woman in the imperial court at the time. The novel is considered a great work of classical Japanese literature. It is about a concubine—that is, a woman who lives in the palace with the Emperor. This excerpt is from the very beginning of the novel.*

1 In the reign of a certain Emperor, whose name is unknown to us, there was . . . one who, though she was not of high birth, enjoyed the full tide of Royal favor. Hence her superiors [other concubines], each one of whom had always been thinking—"I shall be the one," gazed upon her disdainfully with malignant eyes, and her equals and inferiors were more indignant still.

2 Such being the state of affairs, the anxiety which she had to endure was great and constant, and this was probably the reason why her health was at last so much affected, that she was often compelled to absent herself from Court, and to retire to the residence of her mother.

3 In due course . . . a jewel of a little prince was born to her. The first prince who had been born to the Emperor was the child of Koki-den-Niogo, the daughter of the Udaijin (a great officer of State). Not only was he first in point of age, but his influence on his mother's side was so great that public opinion had almost unanimously fixed upon him as heir-apparent. Of this the Emperor was fully conscious, and he only regarded the new-born child with that affection which one lavishes on [a favorite servant] . . .

4 When the young Prince [that is, the favored woman's son] was three years old [an important ceremony celebrating the child] took place. It was celebrated with a pomp scarcely inferior to that which adorned the investiture of the first Prince. . . . And again the public [showed its displeasure]. In the summer of the same year the [favored concubine] became ill, and wished to retire from the palace. . . . [H]er illness increased day by day; and she had drooped and pined away until she was now but a shadow of her former self.

5 . . . [One night her death was near.] To the Emperor the night now became black with gloom. He sent messenger after messenger to make inquiries, and could not await their return with patience. Midnight came, and with it the sound of lamentation. The messenger, who could do nothing else, hurried back with the sad tidings of the truth. From that moment the mind of the Emperor was darkened, and he confined himself to his private apartments.

6 He would still have kept with himself the young Prince now motherless, but there was no precedent for this, and it was arranged that he should be sent to his grandmother for the mourning. The child, who understood nothing, looked with amazement at the sad countenances of the Emperor, and of those around him. All separations have their sting, but sharp indeed was the sting in a case like this.

7 Now the funeral took place. During the ceremony, an Imperial messenger came from the Palace, and invested the dead with [a title of honor]. . . . Once more [some people showed their displeasure]. But, in other respects, the beauty of the departed, and her gracious bearing, which had ever commanded admiration, made people begin to think of her with sympathy. It was the excess of the Emperor's favor which had created so many detractors during her lifetime; but now even rivals felt pity for her. . . . "When one is no more, the memory becomes so dear," may be [a description] of a case such as this.

Excerpted from *The Tale of Genji* by Murasaki Shikibu, translated into English by Suematsu Kencho.

32. Why does the author include the sentence, "All separations have their sting, but sharp indeed was the sting in a case like this"?
   - A. To show that the young Prince understood what was going on
   - B. To illustrate the public's devotion to the young Prince
   - C. To underscore the serious consequences his mother's death will have on the young Prince's future
   - D. To emphasize the young Prince's sadness at losing his mother

33. In paragraph 5, what is the meaning of the phrase "sad tidings of the truth"?
   - A. A report of the illness of the young Prince
   - B. News of the death of the Emperor's favorite concubine
   - C. The unmasking of the young Prince's chief rival
   - D. An unfounded report of the young Prince's death

34. What tone is created by the sentence, "When one is no more, the memory becomes so dear"?
   - A. Comic
   - B. Ominous
   - C. Cheerful
   - D. Ironic

35. Why does the public resent the son of the favorite concubine?
   - A. The public believes that the Emperor's younger son is not yet old enough for the ceremony held in his honor.
   - B. Holding a lavish ceremony is seen as a wasteful expenditure.
   - C. The public believes that the Emperor's younger son should be sent to live with his grandmother.
   - D. Public opinion is that the Emperor's older son, born to a woman with greater influence than the younger Prince's mother, should be the Emperor's heir.

Questions 36 through 40 are based on the passage below.

Excerpt from *A Raisin in the Sun*

This play, first performed in 1959, is about a family living on the South Side of Chicago. Walter Younger has died, and his wife, referred to here as "Mama," is expecting a check from his life insurance. Mama and her family have been discussing what she should do with the money.

1 RUTH Well—what are you going to do with it then?

2 MAMA I ain't rightly decided. (*Thinking. She speaks now with emphasis*) Some of it got to be put away for Beneatha and her schoolin'—and ain't nothing going to touch that part of it. Nothing. (*She waits several seconds, trying to make up her mind about something, and looks at RUTH a little tentatively before going on*) Been thinking that we maybe could meet the notes on a little old two-story somewhere, with a yard where Travis could play in the summertime, if we use part of the insurance for a down payment and everybody kind of pitch in. I could maybe take on a little day work again, few days a week—

3 RUTH (*Studying her mother-in-law furtively and concentrating on her ironing, anxious to encourage without seeming to*) Well, Lord knows, we've put enough rent into this here rat trap to pay for four houses by now...

4 MAMA (*Looking up at the words "rat trap" and then looking around and leaning back and sighing in a suddenly reflective mood—*) "Rat trap"—yes, that's all it is. (*Smiling*) I remember just as well the day me and Big Walter moved in here. Hadn't been married but two weeks and wasn't planning on living here no more than a year. (*She shakes her head at the dissolved dream*) We was going to set away, little by little, don't you know, and buy a little place out in Morgan Park. We had even picked out the house. (*Chuckling a little*) Looks right dumpy today. But Lord, child, you should know all the dreams I had 'bout buying that house and fixing it up and making me a little garden in the back—(*She waits and stops smiling*) And didn't none of it happen.

5 (*Dropping her hands in a futile gesture*)

6 RUTH (*Keeps her head down, ironing*) Yes, life can be a barrel of disappointments, sometimes.

7 MAMA Honey, Big Walter would come in here some nights back then and slump down on that couch there and just look at the rug, and look at me and look at the rug and then back at me—and I'd know he was down then . . . really down. (*After a second very long and thoughtful pause; she is seeing back to times that only she can see*) And then, Lord, when I lost that baby—little Claude—I almost thought I was going to lose Big Walter too. Oh, that man grieved hisself! He was one man to love his children.

8 RUTH Ain't nothin' can tear at you like losin' your baby.

9 MAMA I guess that's how come that man finally worked hisself to death like he done. Like he was fighting his own war with this here world that took his baby from him.

10 RUTH He sure was a fine man, all right. I always liked Mr. Younger.

11 MAMA Crazy 'bout his children! God knows there was plenty wrong with Walter Younger—hard-headed, mean, kind of wild with women—plenty wrong with him. But he sure loved his children. Always wanted them to have something—be something. That's where Brother gets all these notions, I reckon. Big Walter used to say, he'd get right wet in the eyes sometimes, lean his head back with the water standing in his eyes and say, "Seem like God didn't see fit to give the black man nothing but dreams—but He did give us children to make them dreams seem worthwhile." (*She smiles*) He could talk like that, don't you know.

Excerpted from *A Raisin in the Sun*, a play by Lorraine Hansberry.

36. Which of the following is a central idea of this passage?

- A. The house Mama might buy now would give the family more space.
- B. The grief one experiences over the death of a child is unlike any other grief.
- C. Mr. Younger may have been flawed, but he was a hard-working man and a loving father.
- D. The family has experienced many disappointments and tragedies.

37. Even though Mr. Walter Younger (Mama's late husband) is not present in this scene, the reader learns quite a bit about him. Which of the statements below about Mr. Younger are supported by this passage?

- A. He thought the house in Morgan Park was a bad investment.
- B. He taught his son to dream of one day owning a house.
- C. His love for his children helped keep his dreams alive.
- D. He finally gave up on his attempts to improve his family's situation.

38. Ruth and Mama both describe their apartment as a "rat trap." Which of the following best describes the impact of that phrase in this passage?

- A. It means that the apartment building is a hangout for criminals.
- B. It suggests that the family see themselves as undesirable, like rats.
- C. It suggests that the apartment is very run-down, and that the family feels trapped there.
- D. It means that the apartment has rats, and the phrase has no other meaning.

39. Mama quotes her late husband as saying, "Seem like God didn't see fit to give the black man nothing but dreams, but He did give us children to make them dreams seem worthwhile." What theme from the passage does this quote summarize?

- A. The contrast between how hard it has been for the family to improve its situation and how much Mama would still like to try
- B. The contrast between the child that survived ("Brother") and the one that died (Claude)
- C. The contrast between the dreams of black people with children and the dreams of other people with children
- D. The contrast between Walter Younger's religious doubts and Mama's unshakeable faith

40. Imagine that you are a director, putting on a performance of this play with a group of actors. The actor playing Mama says to you, "I think I should have my back to Ruth for most of this scene and face outward like I'm talking to thin air." If the actor playing Mama did so, what effect would that have on the scene?

- A. It would suggest that Ruth has to struggle to win Mama's approval.
- B. It would suggest that it's none of Ruth's business what Mama does with the money.
- C. It would suggest that Mama is lost in her own powerful memories.
- D. It would suggest that Ruth is not a strong person and is controlled by Mama.

STOP. You have completed the Language Arts: Reading Test.

Language Arts: Writing Practice Test
Part I: Language Skills

Directions: Use 75 minutes to answer the following 51 questions.

Questions 1 through 6 refer to the following paragraphs.

Painting a Room

(A)

(1) Would you like to redecorate a room in your home? (2) Painting is a fast and inexpensive way to give that room a hole new look. (3) First, remove the furniture, or move it to the center of the room and cover it with drop cloths. (4) Prepare the room by stripping paint and extra layers of wallpaper, filling cracks, and add a coat of primer if necessary.

(B)

(5) Now you're ready to paint. (6) Use a brush to paint a clean line along all edges where paint stops, such as where the wall meets the door frame, and in places where the ceiling meet a wall of a different color. (7) This is called "cutting in."

(C)

(8) The next step was to paint the room in the following order: ceiling, walls, trim, doors, and windows. (9) Put no more than $\frac{3}{4}$ of an inch of paint, in the paint pan. (10) Run your roller through the paint, being careful not to overload the roller. (11) Apply paint to the ceiling and walls in a "W" or "Z" zigzag pattern.

(D)

(12) Spread the paint evenly by rolling either side to side or up and down, using gentle strokes so as not to leave roller marks. (13) After finishing an area, look for spots you missed, go over them with your relatively dry roller.

1. Sentence 2: **Painting is a fast and inexpensive way to give that room a hole new look.**

   Which correction should be made to sentence 2?

   - A. change is to are
   - B. insert a comma after fast
   - C. change to give to giving
   - D. replace hole with whole

2. Sentence 4: **Prepare the room by stripping paint and extra layers of wallpaper, filling cracks, and add a coat of primer if necessary.**

   Which correction should be made to sentence 4?

   - A. change Prepare to Preparing
   - B. insert a comma after paint
   - C. remove the comma after wallpaper
   - D. change add to adding

3. Sentence 6: **Use a brush to paint a clean line along all edges where paint stops, such as where the wall meets the door frame, and in places where the ceiling meet a wall of a different color.**

   Which correction should be made to sentence 6?

   - A. change ceiling meet to ceiling meets
   - B. remove the comma after stops
   - C. remove the comma after frame
   - D. change ceiling meet to ceiling met

4. Sentence 8: **The next step was to paint the room in the following order: ceiling, walls, trim, doors, and windows.**

   Which is the best way to write the underlined portion of this sentence?

   - A. was
   - B. being
   - C. is
   - D. had been

5. Sentence 9: **Put no more than $\frac{3}{4}$ of an inch of paint, in the paint pan.**

   Which correction should be made to sentence 9?

   - A. change pan to pans
   - B. change no more to anymore
   - C. remove the comma after paint
   - D. insert a comma after Put

6. Sentence 13: **After finishing an area, look for spots you missed, go over them with your relatively dry roller.**

   Which is the best way to write the underlined portion of this sentence?

   - A. missed, and go
   - B. missed, and going
   - C. missed go
   - D. missed, but go

Questions 7 through 12 refer to the following passage.

Starting a Community Garden

(A)

(1) In many cities, neighborhood groups are forming community gardens in vacant lots, in parks, or on rooftops. (2) These gardens is an ideal way for both children and adults to work with nature while making the neighborhood more beautiful. (3) If you would like to start a community garden first determine whether people are truly interested in the project. (4) If they are, organize a meeting of interested people, and choose someone to be the garden coordinator. (5) Form committees for tasks like finding money for the garden.

(B)

(6) Once your group is organized, approach a sponsor this could be a group or individual who can support your garden. (7) Keep in mind that contributions of seeds, tools, and land are just as important as money. (8) Schools, churches, citizen groups, and private businesses are all potential sponsors.

(C)

(9) Find out how the land has been used in the past to avoid places that may be contaminated. (10) Pick a site that gets at least six hours of direct sunlight a day, and make sure that water is available. (11) Contact the owner of the site try to get a lease that allows you to use the land for at least three years.

(D)

(12) After choosing a site, the group of gardeners needs to decide how to organize the garden. (13) What size should each plot be, and how will plots be assigned? (14) Finally, establish a procedure to follow to maintain tidiness and piece in the garden.

7. Sentence 2: **These gardens is an ideal way for both children and adults to work with nature while making the neighborhood more beautiful.**

   Which correction should be made to sentence 2?

   - A. change gardens to garden
   - B. change is to are
   - C. replace way with weigh
   - D. insert a comma after children

8. Sentence 3: **If you would like to start a community garden first determine whether people are truly interested in the project.**

   Which correction should be made to sentence 3?

   - A. change would to will
   - B. insert a comma after garden
   - C. replace whether with weather
   - D. change are to is

9. Sentence 6: **Once your group is organized, approach a sponsor this could be a group or individual who can support your garden.**

   Which correction should be made to sentence 6?

   - A. insert a comma after sponsor
   - B. insert a period after sponsor and capitalize this
   - C. remove the comma after organized
   - D. insert a comma after group

10. Which sentence would be most effective if inserted at the beginning of paragraph C?

    - A. Next, choose a site for the garden.
    - B. Land use is a very significant factor.
    - C. We all know that you are going to need land for your garden.
    - D. Learn about the history of your site.

11. Which of the following would improve the effectiveness of paragraph A?

    - A. Start a new paragraph before sentence 2.
    - B. Start a new paragraph before sentence 3.
    - C. Combine sentences 2 and 3 into a compound sentence.
    - D. Combine paragraphs A and B.

12. Sentence 14: **Finally, establish a procedure to follow to maintain tidiness and piece in the garden.**

    Which correction should be made to sentence 6?

    - A. change to follow to to be following
    - B. change piece to peace
    - C. change tidiness to tidyness
    - D. change establish to establishing

Questions 13 through 18 refer to the following paragraphs.

Sick Building Syndrome

(A)

(1) Do you often feel sick when at you're workplace? (2) Do you experience symptoms such as coughing, sneezing, nausea, headaches, and difficulty breathing? (3) Do these symptoms seem to disappear once you leave work magically? (4) If so, we may be working in a sick building.

(B)

(5) "Sick building syndrome" is a term that refers to working in a building that makes you sick. (6) The syndrome may be caused by improper building design. (7) Over the past 20 years, architects have designed office buildings with an eye to saving energy. (8) The buildings are tightly sealed so that little heat escapes, and the air inside the buildings is recirculated to avoid the cost of heating fresh air. (9) Although this design reduces energy costs, the lack of ventilation causes a buildup of toxins in the air. (10) On the other hand, an older isn't necessarily immune to the syndrome. (11) Even if they originally opened to let in fresh air, adding insulation, caulking, and weather stripping at a later date may have made the windows airtight.

(C)

(12) Toxins in the air come from a variety of sources. (13) Biological agents, including bacteria, viruses, fungi, and pollen, may be found in poorly maintained air circulation systems and dirty washrooms. (14) The deadly gas, carbon monoxide can seep into a building's air through an improperly ventilated garage or a leaky duct. (15) Formaldehyde is frequently found in furniture, paneling, draperies, glues, and upholstery.

(D)

(16) It is possible to "cure" a sick building. (17) Steps to take include eliminating tobacco smoke, providing good ventilation, keeping the ventilation system in good repair, and removing all sources of pollution.

13. Sentence 1: **Do you often feel sick when at you're workplace?**

    Which correction should be made to sentence 1?

    - A. insert a comma after sick
    - B. change sick to sickly
    - C. replace you're with your
    - D. change Do to Are

14. Sentence 3: **Do these symptoms seem to disappear once you leave work magically?**

    The most effective revision of sentence 3 would include which group of words?

    - A. disappear magically once you leave
    - B. once you disappear magically
    - C. upon leaving work magically
    - D. seem to disappear, once you leave

15. Sentence 4: **If so, we may be working in a sick building.**

    Which correction should be made to sentence 4?

    - A. replace a with the
    - B. insert a comma after working
    - C. replace we with you
    - D. replace may with are

16. Sentence 10: **On the other hand, an older isn't necessarily immune to the syndrome.**

    Which correction should be made to sentence 10?

    - A. change older to older building
    - B. change isn't to aren't
    - C. insert a comma after immune
    - D. replace to with too

17. Sentence 11: **Even if they originally opened to let in fresh air, adding insulation, caulking, and weather stripping at a later date may have made the windows airtight.**

    Which is the best way to write the underlined portion of this sentence?

    - A. them
    - B. it
    - C. the building
    - D. the windows

18. Sentence 14: **The deadly gas, carbon monoxide can seep into a building's air through an improperly ventilated garage or a leaky duct.**

    - A. delete the comma after gas
    - B. insert a comma after monoxide
    - C. replace can seep with is seeping
    - D. replace improperly with improper

Questions 19 through 24 refer to the following flyer.

Save Compton Point!

(A)

(1) Compton Point, home to many animal species that are threatened with extinction, now faces a threat of its own. (2) Developers are attempting to change the zoning in order to build a hotel, a tourist center, and an observation tower. (3) If they succeed in getting the rights to build, construction will begin next August.

(B)

(4) Sam Wanamaker, director of the Society for the Protection of Nature, warns that construction of the development is likely to drive out more than 30 animal species that live on the point. (5) Air pollution from tourist traffic will further reduce the animals' chances for survival, not to mention litter left behind by floods of tourists wandering through the area.

(C)

(6) The Compton Point area is zoned as natural parkland. (7) There are several other areas in the county that are zoned as natural parkland. (8) However, because this project is potentially so lucrative for the city, the zoning board seems to be bending to the will of the developer's.

(D)

(9) Developers argue that the new jobs resulting from their development would boost the region's sagging economy. (10) The influx of tourism would, too. (11) Certainly, everyone in the community agrees that the economy around here could use a lift, but this is not the way to do it.

(E)

(12) Register your opposition to the development of Compton Point! (13) Come to a demonstration at 10 A.M. on Saturday, May 7, in front of the mayor's office, 34 Wilton road. (14) Bring signs with slogans that tell how you feel. (15) A strong turnout at this demonstration did send a message to developers.

19. Sentence 5: **Air pollution from tourist traffic will further reduce the animals' chances for survival, not to mention litter left behind by floods of tourists wandering through the area.**

The most effective revision of sentence 5 includes which group of words?

- A. Tourism increases both air pollution and litter, which will
- B. Litter, which tourists leave behind, and besides
- C. Animals will have less chance for survival when air pollution
- D. Air pollution and litter, having been caused by tourists,

20. Sentence 8: **However, because this project is potentially so lucrative for the city, the zoning board seems to be bending to the will of the developer's.**

Which correction should be made to sentence 8?

- A. remove the comma after <u>However</u>
- B. insert a comma after <u>will</u>
- C. change <u>seems</u> to <u>seem's</u>
- D. change <u>developer's</u> to <u>developers</u>

21. Which revision would improve the effectiveness of paragraph C?

- A. remove sentence 6
- B. move sentence 6 to follow sentence 7
- C. remove sentence 7
- D. move sentence 7 to follow sentence 8

22. Sentences 9 and 10: **Developers argue that the new jobs resulting from their development would boost the region's sagging economy. The influx of tourism would, too.**

The most effective combination of sentences 9 and 10 would include which group of words?

- A. their development, with an influx of jobs,
- B. new jobs and the influx of tourism resulting
- C. an influx of new jobs, say the developers, plus an influx of tourism,
- D. The region, to have an influx,

23. Sentence 13: **Come to a demonstration at 10 A.M. on Saturday, May 7, in front of the mayor's office, 34 Wilton road.**

Which correction should be made to sentence 13?

- A. insert a comma after <u>demonstration</u>
- B. remove the comma after <u>Saturday</u>
- C. change <u>mayor's</u> to <u>mayors</u>
- D. change <u>road</u> to <u>Road</u>

24. Sentence 15: **A strong turnout at this demonstration did send a message to developers.**

Which correction should be made to sentence 15?

- A. change <u>did</u> to <u>will</u>
- B. change <u>did</u> to <u>have</u>
- C. change <u>did</u> to <u>has</u>
- D. no change necessary

<u>Questions 25 through 31</u> refer to the following paragraphs.

Kites and Science

(A)

(1) Who doesn't enjoy flying a kite? (2) When you seen people in your community flying kites on a windy day, you might think that kites are just for fun. (3) Kites have been flown in countries around the world and for centuries, by young and old alike. (4) However, kite flying, it may surprise you to know, have been responsible for a number of scientific discoveries.

(B)

(5) In 1752, Benjamin Franklin used a kite to prove the presence of electricity in storm clouds. (6) He did it by flying a kite during a thunderstorm with a brass key attached to the end. (7) The story goes that when lightning struck the kite line and traveled down to the key, their was a spark of electricity.

(C)

(8) Kites also played a role in learning about the weather. (9) In 1749, Alexander Wilson of Scotland became the first scientist to send a thermometer aloft in a kite. (10) Starting in the 1890s, kites held meteorological instruments that also measured humidity and wind speed. (11) They measured barometric pressure, too.

(D)

(12) Kites were an early form of aircraft. (13) The Wright Brothers, inventors of the first plane, experimented with kites. (14) Alexander Graham Bell, the physicist and inventor, used kites to learn about problems of airplane construction.

(E)

(15) So the next time you see some neighborhood children flying kites, just think. (16) You may be watching budding young scientists.

25. Sentence 2: **When you <u>seen</u> people flying kites in your community on a windy day, you might think that kites are just for fun.**

Which is the best way to write the underlined portion of the sentence?

- A. might see
- B. saw
- C. see
- D. have seen

26. Sentence 3: **Kites have been flown in countries around the world and for centuries, by young and old alike.**

Which revision should be made to the placement of sentence 3?

- A. move sentence 3 to the beginning of paragraph A
- B. move sentence 3 to follow sentence 1
- C. remove sentence 3
- D. no revision is necessary

27. Sentence 4: **However, kite flying, it may surprise you to know, <u>have been</u> responsible for a number of scientific discoveries.**

Which is the best way to write the underlined portion of the sentence?

- A. would be
- B. has been
- C. were
- D. are

28. Sentence 6: **He did it by flying a kite during a thunderstorm with a brass key attached to the end.**

The most effective revision of sentence 6 would begin with which group of words?

- A. By flying a kite with a brass key
- B. The kite was flown during a thunderstorm
- C. A brass key was attached to the end
- D. During a thunderstorm, he flew a kite with

29. Sentence 7: **The story goes that when lightning struck the kite line and traveled down to the key, their was a spark of electricity.**

Which correction should be made to sentence 7?

- A. remove the comma after <u>key</u>
- B. replace <u>their</u> with <u>there</u>
- C. no correction is necessary
- D. insert a comma after <u>line</u>

30. Sentences 10 and 11: **Starting in the 1890s, kites held meteorological instruments that measured humidity and wind speed. They measured barometric pressure, too.**

The most effective combination of sentences 10 and 11 would include which group of words?

- A. one of the purposes was measuring wind
- B. humidity, wind speed, and barometric pressure
- C. barometric pressure was measured along with
- D. the measurement of barometric pressure

31. Sentence 14: **Alexander Graham <u>Bell the physicist and inventor used</u> kites to learn about problems of airplane construction.**

Which is the best way to write the underlined portion of the sentence?

- A. Bell, the physicist and inventor, used
- B. Bell the physicist and inventor, used
- C. Bell, the physicist and inventor used
- D. Bell, the physicist and inventor, he used

Questions 32 through 38 are based on the following passage.

What Is a Hybrid Car?

(A)

(1) A hybrid vehicle uses at least two different sources of power, you have probably seen examples of hybrid vehicles without realizing it. (2) Some types of trucks or buses, and some trains use a combination of diesel fuel and electric power. (3) The most common hybrid cars in use today combine gasoline and electric power.

(B)

(4) There are two primary types of hybrid engine designs: the parallel hybrid and the series hybrid. (5) In both kinds electric motors and gasoline-powered engines. (6) In the parallel-hybrid design, the electric motor and the gasoline engine can power the car together or independently. (7) In the series-hybrid design, the gasoline engine does not power the car directly. (8) Instead, it run a machine called a generator that charges the batteries or powers the electric motor. (9) The electric motor actually powers the car. (10) However, the car cannot move unless the gasoline engine is on. (11) One of the benefits of hybrid cars is their fuel efficiency.

(C)

(12) In some hybrid models, the gasoline engine is used only when the car will move faster than 15 miles per hour. (13) That reduces fuel consumption in heavy traffic. (14) The designers who have created the hybrid car have tried to increase its efficiency in every way they can think of. (15) Hybrids are made from lightweight materials. (16) It is designed to drive smoothly, without being slowed down by things like wind, and even the tires on hybrid cars are designed to make the car run as efficiently as possible.

32. Sentence 1: **A hybrid vehicle uses at least two different sources of power, you have probably seen examples of hybrid vehicles without realizing it.**

Which correction should be made to Sentence 1?

- A. change uses to will use
- B. change two different to two and different
- C. change power, you to power. You
- D. change realizing it to realizes it

33. Sentence 2: **Some types of trucks or buses, and some trains use a combination of diesel fuel and electric power.**

What is the best way to revise the underlined portion of the sentence?

- A. Some types of trucks, buses, some trains
- B. Some types of trucks or buses or trains
- C. Some types of trucks, buses, and trains
- D. Some types of trucks, buses, or trains

34. Sentence 5: **In both kinds electric motors and gasoline-powered engines.**

Which correction should be made to sentence 5?

- A. change both kinds to both kinds of
- B. change In both kinds to Both kinds have
- C. change motors and to motors, and
- D. change and to or

35. Sentence 8: **Instead, it run a machine called a generator that charges the batteries or powers the electric motor.**

Which correction should be made to sentence 8?

- A. remove the comma
- B. change it to those
- C. change run to runs
- D. change run to is running

36. Sentence 12: **In some hybrid models, the gasoline engine is used only when the car will move faster than 15 miles per hour.**

Which correction should be made to sentence 12?

- A. remove the comma
- B. change is used to is being used
- C. change will move to moves
- D. change faster to more

37. Sentence 16: **It is designed to drive smoothly, without being slowed down by things like wind, and even the tires on hybrid cars are designed to make the car run as efficiently as possible.**

Which correction should be made to sentence 16?

- A. change It is to They are
- B. change designed to design
- C. change wind, and to wind and
- D. change as efficiently to more efficiently

38. Which of the following would improve the effectiveness of the passage?

- A. delete sentence 4
- B. start a new paragraph with sentence 8
- C. move sentence 11 to the beginning of the next paragraph
- D. delete sentence 16

Questions 39 through 44 are based on the passage below.

Discounts for Student Skaters

To Whom It May Concern at Diego's Helmet Emporium:

(A)

(1) I am writing to you today to try and convince you to provide a discount for students wanting to buy one of your helmets. (2) A growing number of states across the country, including California and new Jersey, have passed laws that require people who use in-line skates and skateboards to wear a helmet. (3) Although some skaters are unhappy about these changes, these laws are based on common sense and logic. (4) I believe if the helmets could be purchased for less money, students would be more willing to buy them.

(B)

(5) Learning how to ride a skateboard or in-line skates are similar to learning how to ride a bicycle. (6) In the beginning, it can mean repeated stumbles and falls. (7) Knees and elbows are usually the first to get scraped up, they typically heal quickly. (8) Likewise, head injuries are more severe—they can even prove deadly. (9) Even a low-speed fall can do considerable damage, and the head has to be protected, and the right helmet—hopefully purchased from your store—can do just that if worn properly.

(C)

(10) Please consider providing a discount so that more students have the opportunity to be safe.

Best,
Kristin Zajchenko

39. Sentence 1: **I am writing to you today to <u>try and convince</u> you to provide a discount for students wanting to buy one of your helmets.**

What is the best revision of the underlined portion of sentence 1?

- A. try and hopefully convince
- B. try to convince
- C. trying to convince
- D. try, convince

40. Sentence 2: **A growing number of states across the country, including California and new Jersey, have passed laws that require people who use in-line skates and skateboards to wear a helmet.**

Which correction should be made to sentence 2?

- A. change <u>A growing number of states</u> to <u>A growing number, states</u>
- B. change <u>country, including</u> to <u>country including</u>
- C. change <u>California and new Jersey,</u> to <u>California and New Jersey,</u>
- D. change <u>people who use</u> to <u>people that use</u>

41. Sentence 5: **Learning how to ride a skateboard or in-line skates are similar to learning how to ride a bicycle.**

Which correction should be made to sentence 5?

- A. change <u>Learning how</u> to <u>To learn how</u>
- B. change <u>skateboard or</u> to <u>skateboard, or</u>
- C. change <u>are</u> to <u>is</u>
- D. change <u>similar to</u> to <u>a lot like</u>

42. Sentence 7: **Knees and elbows are usually the first to get scraped up, they typically heal quickly.**

An effective revision of sentence 7 would begin with which of the following phrases?

- A. Usually, knees
- B. Moreover, knees
- C. While knees
- D. Noting that knees

43. Sentence 8: **<u>Likewise, head injuries</u> are more severe—they can even prove deadly.**

What is the best way to revise the underlined portion of sentence 8?

- A. And additionally head injuries
- B. However, head injuries
- C. Similarly, head injuries
- D. Considering that head injuries

44. Sentence 9: **Even a low-speed fall can do considerable damage, and the head has to be protected, and the right helmet—hopefully purchased from your store—can do just that if worn properly.**

Which of the following would be the best way to revise Sentence 9?

- A. change the dashes to commas
- B. split it into two sentences
- C. change the commas to semicolons
- D. remove the first clause

<u>Questions 45 through 51</u> **are based on the following passage.**

Letter to the Editor

Dear Editor of *Western Weekly Digest*,

(1) In Major Cities all across the United States, a thick cloud of smoke hangs ominously on the horizon. (2) It's there in the morning when the sun rises and again at the end of the day. (3) The smog has become a normal part of our urban environments that weather forecasters all across the country issue daily reports about smog levels. (4) I am writing to urge you and all your readers for support of Proposition 278, in favor of stricter pollution guidelines for our city. (5) Clean air proposals have been a part of the environmental movement for decades. (6) In many gas stations around the world, cleaner gas that you can get at gas stations has become a mainstay. (7) Vehicle emission tests are now a mandatory part of any car's life. (8) Over the course of all those years, some progress has been made. (9) And yet for every gain made, thousands of new cars enter our already crowded streets, bringing us one step forward and two steps back. (10) This cannot continue. (11) According to the California Air Resources' Board, cars and trucks are the single largest source of air pollution in California. (12) In fact, almost they emit five times as many pollutants as the next greatest source of air pollution. (13) We must pass Proposition 278 in order to curb the growing menace of smog.

Best regards,
Ciara Wilson

45. Sentence 1: **In Major Cities all across the United States, a thick cloud of smoke hangs ominously on the horizon.**

Which correction should be made to sentence 1?

- A. change Major Cities to major cities
- B. change Cities all across to Cities, all across
- C. remove the comma
- D. change hangs ominously to ominously hangs

46. Sentence 3: **The smog has become a normal part of our urban environments that weather forecasters all across the country issue daily reports about smog levels.**

What is the best way to revise the underlined portion of sentence 3?

- A. The smog, having become a normal part
- B. The smog will have become a normal part
- C. The smog has become such a normal part
- D. The smog has not become a normal part

47. Sentence 4: **I am writing to urge you and all your readers for support of Proposition 278, in favor of stricter pollution guidelines for our city.**

What is the best way to revise the underlined portion of sentence 4?

- A. (No change)
- B. to urge all of you and your readers for support of
- C. to urge the support of you and all your readers for
- D. to urge you and all your readers to support

48. Sentence 6: **In many gas stations around the world, cleaner gas that you can get at gas stations has become a mainstay.**

Which of the following is the best revision of sentence 6?

- A. Gas is available to be purchased at gas stations worldwide.
- B. Cleaner gas is around the world.
- C. Cleaner gas has become a mainstay in many gas stations around the world.
- D. In many gas stations around the world, a mainstay has now become cleaner gas.

49. Sentence 11: **According to the California Air Resources' Board, cars and trucks are the single largest source of air pollution in California.**

Which correction should be made to sentence 11?

- A. insert a comma after According to
- B. change Air Resources' Board to air resources' board
- C. change Air Resources' Board to Air Resources Board
- D. remove the comma

50. Sentence 12: **In fact, almost they emit five times as many pollutants as the next greatest source of air pollution.**

What is the best way to revise the underlined portion of sentence 12?

- A. they almost emit five times
- B. they emit almost five times
- C. they emit five times almost
- D. almost they will emit five times

51. Which of the following revisions would improve the effectiveness of the passage?

- A. move sentence 1 to follow sentence 12
- B. remove sentence 4
- C. move sentence 8 to follow sentence 5
- D. move sentence 13 to follow sentence 7

You have completed Part One of the Language Arts: Writing Test.
You may take a 10-minute break before beginning Part Two.

PART II: ESSAY

Directions: Based on both passages on pages 694–695, write a response to the prompt below. This task may take up to 45 minutes to complete.

The following two passages give the two sides of a debate about whether schools in a certain community should continue to require physical education. Read both passages carefully, noting the strengths and weaknesses of each discussion. Then, write an essay in which you explain your own opinion on the issue. Be sure to use evidence from the passages provided as well as specific reasons and examples from your own experience and knowledge to support your position. Remember that every position exists within the context of a larger discussion of the issue, so your essay should, at minimum, acknowledge alternate and/or opposing ideas. When you have finished your essay, review your writing to check for correct spelling, punctuation, and grammar.

Your response will be scored based on:

- Development of a central position through explanation of supporting reasons, examples, and details from passages and personal experience
- Clear organization of ideas, including an introduction and conclusion, logical paragraphs, and effective transitions
- Language use, including varied word choice, varied sentence constructions, and appropriate voice
- Clarity and correctness of writing conventions

Passage A: Why Physical Education Should No Longer Be a Requirement for Graduation

This is the text of Councilwoman Juanita Sanchez's speech at last week's school board meeting.

The job market is increasingly competitive. Because of this, we must ensure that our students' education fully prepares them to succeed in the future. A limited budget and limited time during the school day force us to make difficult decisions concerning what we teach. We must be willing to make these decisions with the best interests of our students at heart. With these goals in mind, I support the proposal to eliminate physical education as a core requirement for high school graduation in our district.

Time spent completing physical education requirements is time away from more productive educational pursuits. While our state's standardized test scores have continued to rise in past years, we are still seeing results that are below average in both mathematics and reading. Added instructional time is necessary to see our test scores meet the standards set for us. This additional time spent on core subjects will also better prepare students for a pursuit of higher education after high school graduation.

No one is suggesting that physical education and fitness classes be completely eliminated from our curriculum. Physical education is a worthwhile pursuit and should be provided for those students who are interested. But it should be an elective, or optional, course in the same way that music, art, and theater classes are offered as electives. Thus, this outdated requirement will no longer get in the way of more academically important pursuits.

Passage B: Physical Education Is an Important Requirement for Students

Letter from concerned parent published in the City Journal *newspaper*

No one would disagree that preparing our students for a successful future is essential. Changes need to be made in order to help our children compete for college scholarships and career advancement. But as we make these changes, we have to be careful not to cause more harm than good. The current proposal places us in danger of damaging successful programs in our efforts to make improvements.

Having a healthy lifestyle is at least as important to a happy and successful future as mathematics and reading skills are. We currently are in the middle of an epidemic of health problems caused by lack of physical fitness among the children in our community. In our state, almost 20% of children between the ages of 12 and 18 are classified as obese. And obesity is linked to a number of life-threatening health problems including diabetes and heart disease. Thus, this is a trend that we must make every effort to reverse.

Programs to offer healthier lunch choices for students have already been introduced. It would be ridiculous to now eliminate requirements that teach our children about other aspects of healthy living. What good is longer time spent in so-called core classes if students aren't healthy enough to fully participate?

I understand that the School Board members have students' best interests at heart. And I agree that it is important to find ways to improve the math and reading scores of our students. Unfortunately, the current plan to eliminate physical education will do much more harm than good. There is a reason P.E. has been a part of our school curriculum for so many years!

STOP. You have completed the Language Arts: Writing Test.

Mathematics Practice Test

Mathematics Formula Sheet

This page displays formulas that you will be given when you take the HiSET exam. You can refer to this page as you work through the Mathematics Test.

Perimeter / Circumference

Rectangle

Perimeter = 2(*length*) + 2(*width*)

Circle

Circumference = 2π(*radius*)

Area

Circle

Area = π(*radius*)^2

Triangle

Area = $\frac{1}{2}$(*base*)(*height*)

Parallelogram

Area = (*base*)(*height*)

Trapezoid

Area = $\frac{1}{2}$($base_1$ + $base_2$)(*height*)

Volume

Prism/Cylinder

Volume = (*area of the base*)(*height*)

Pyramid/Cone

Volume = $\frac{1}{3}$(*area of the base*)(*height*)

Sphere

Volume = $\frac{4}{3}$π(*radius*)^3

Length

1 foot = 12 inches

1 yard = 3 feet

1 mile = 5,280 feet

1 meter = 1,000 millimeters

1 meter = 100 centimeters

1 kilometer = 1,000 meters

1 mile ≈ 1.6 kilometers

1 inch = 2.54 centimeters

1 foot ≈ 0.3 meter

Weight

1 pound = 16 ounces

1 ton = 2,000 pounds

1 gram = 1,000 milligrams

1 kilogram = 1,000 grams

1 kilogram ≈ 2.2 pounds

1 ounce ≈ 28.3 grams

Capacity / Volume

1 cup = 8 fluid ounces

1 pint = 2 cups

1 quart = 2 pints

1 gallon = 4 quarts

1 gallon = 231 cubic inches

1 liter = 1,000 milliliters

1 liter ≈ 0.264 gallon

PRACTICE QUESTIONS

Directions: Use 90 minutes to answer the following 50 questions. Refer to the formula sheet on pages 696–697 as needed.

1. Which of the following is equal to the expression below?

   $(3x + 2y)(5x - 6y)$

   - A. $8x - 4y$
   - B. $15x^2 - 12y^2$
   - C. $15x^2 + 10xy - 12y^2$
   - D. $15x^2 - 8xy - 12y^2$
   - E. $15x^2 + 8xy + 12y^2$

2. Bob has a basket with 3 bananas, 5 oranges, and 2 pears. If Bob selects a piece of fruit at random and then, without putting it back, selects a second piece of fruit at random, what is the probability that Bob will select 2 bananas?

   - A. $\frac{2}{3}$
   - B. $\frac{3}{5}$
   - C. $\frac{3}{10}$
   - D. $\frac{9}{100}$
   - E. $\frac{1}{15}$

3. What is the only positive solution of the equation $x^2 - 4x - 21 = 0$?

   - A. −7
   - B. −3
   - C. 3
   - D. 7
   - E. 21

4. What is the value of this expression?

   $$3 \times 5^2 + 2(4 - 18) + 3^3$$

   - A. −1,051
   - B. −324
   - C. 14
   - D. 56
   - E. 74

5. Simplify the following expression: $2x^2 - 2xy + 4xy$

   - A. $x(x + y)$
   - B. $x(x - y)$
   - C. $2x(x - y)$
   - D. $2x(x + y)$
   - E. $x(2x - y)$

6. If all the measurements are in meters, what is the area of the following figure, in meters squared?

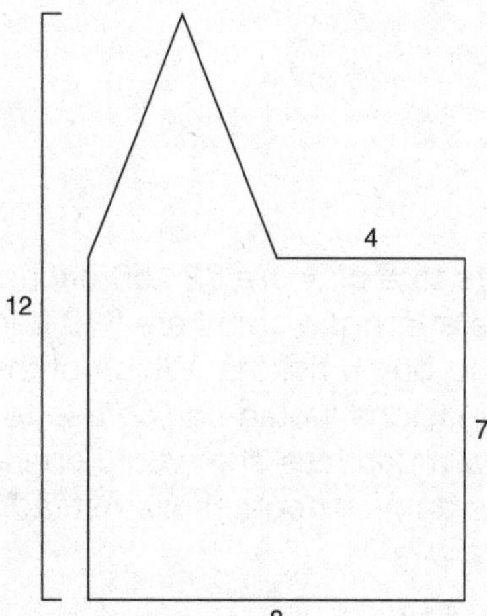

- A. 10
- B. 46
- C. 56
- D. 66
- E. 72

7. Simplify the following expression:
$x^2 + 2 + 7x + 3x^2 + 5x + 5$

- A. $3x^2 + 12x + 7$
- B. $4x^2 + 12x + 7$
- C. $4x^2 + 10x + 5$
- D. $3x^2 + 7x + 5$
- E. $5x^2 + 10x + 7$

8.

	A	***B***	***C***
1	–2	–4	1
2	8	4	3
3	5	2	–1

In the computer spreadsheet above, $-[A1 - (C2 - A3) + C2 * B1]$ is equal to which of the following? (Hint: on a spreadsheet, * means multiplication.)

- A. –22
- B. –12
- C. 12
- D. 22
- E. 32

9. Simplify the expression:
$(6x^4 + 7x + 5x^3) - (4x^4 - 2x^3 + 3x)$

- A. $10x^4 + 7x^3 + 18x$
- B. $2x^4 + 7x^3 + 4x$
- C. $2x^4 + 7x^3 + 18x$
- D. $10x^4 + 3x^3 + 12x$
- E. $10x^4 + 7x^3 + 12x$

10. The perimeter of the trapezoid below is 50. What is its area?

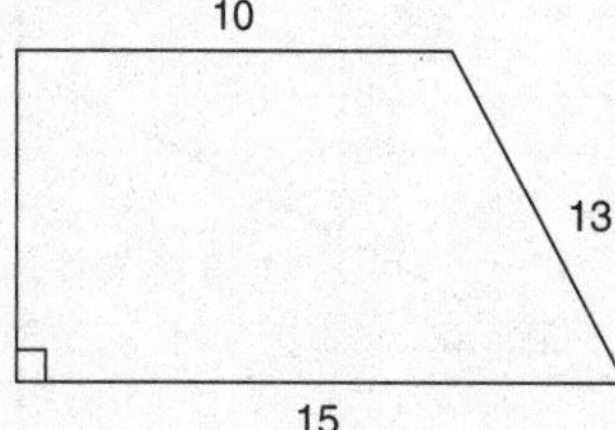

- A. 12
- B. 60
- C. 120
- D. 150
- E. 180

11. The graph of the equation $y = -\frac{3}{4}x + 1$ is a line that passes through points C and D on the coordinate plane. Which of the following points also lies on the graph of the equation?

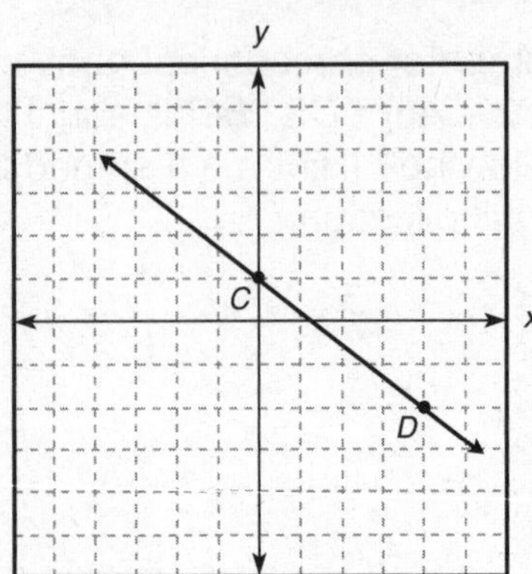

- A. (3, 1)
- B. (8, –5)
- C. (5, 3)
- D. (10, 6)
- E. (12, 7)

12. Which of the following equations correctly describes the line on the graph?

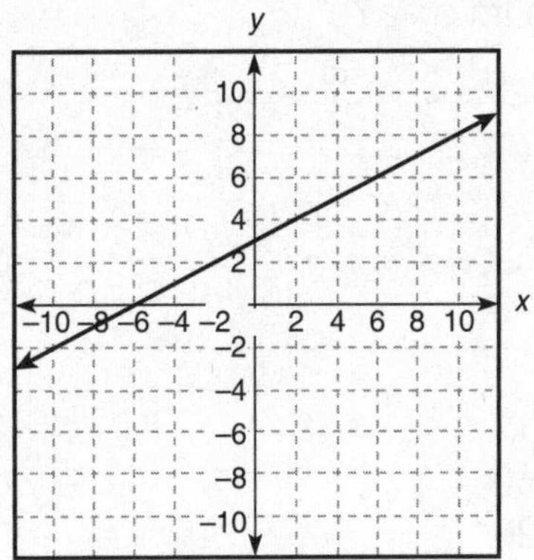

- A. $y = -\frac{1}{2}x - 6$
- B. $y = 2x + 3$
- C. $y = \frac{1}{2}x - 6$
- D. $y = \frac{1}{2}x + 3$
- E. $y = 2x - 6$

13. What is the 6th term in the sequence below?

1, 3, 7, 15, 31, __ , 127

- A. 62
- B. 63
- C. 68
- D. 77
- E. 85

14. Evening tickets to a play are $24.50 each. Tickets for the afternoon show are $19 each. Janice wants to buy 6 tickets. Which of the following expressions would Janice use to determine how much less she would spend if she chooses an afternoon show instead of an evening show?

- A. ($24.50 – $19) ÷ 6
- B. ($24.50 – $19) × 6
- C. ($24.50 + $19) × 6
- D. $24.50 × 6
- E. $24.50 ÷ 6

15. $(2x^3 - 4y)(3x^3 + 6y) =$

- A. $6x^9 + 24x^3y - 24y^2$
- B. $6x^9 - 24x^3y - 10y^2$
- C. $6x^6 + 12x^3y - 24y^2$
- D. $6x^6 - 12x^3y - 10y^2$
- E. $6x^6 - 24y^2$

16. What is the surface area of the cylinder below?

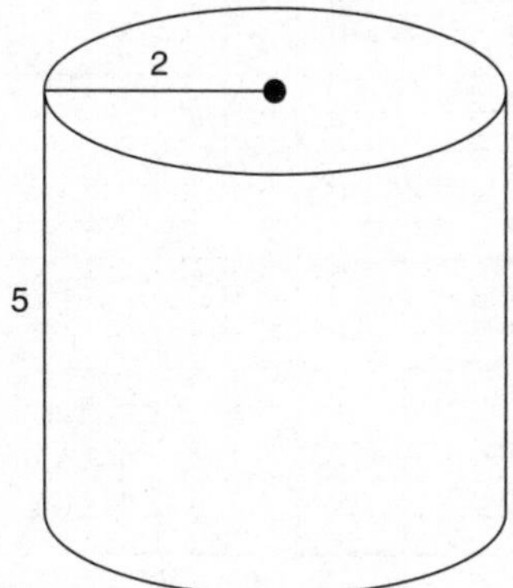

- A. 20π
- B. 28π
- C. 32π
- D. 50π
- E. 56π

17. $\dfrac{2x^2 - 6x - 36}{2x - 12} =$

- A. $x - 6$
- B. $x - 3$
- C. $x + 3$
- D. $x^2 + 3x + 18$
- E. $x^2 + 4x + 24$

18. Customers of Paul's Beauty Supply can make purchases online, from a catalog, or in the store.

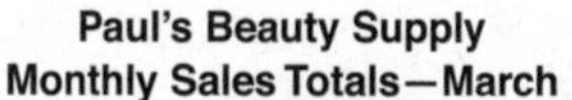

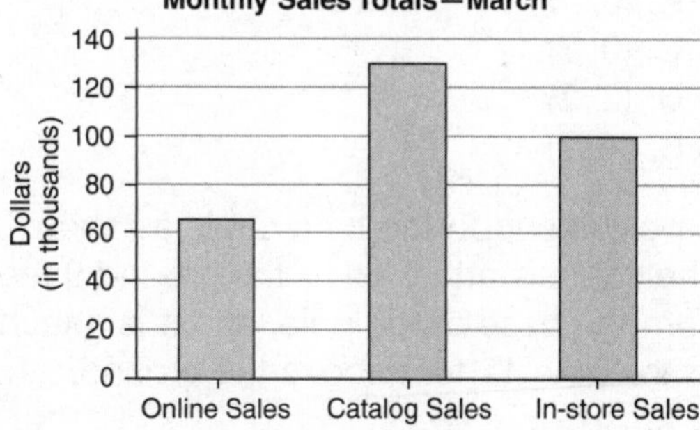

About how much more did the company make from catalog sales than from online sales in March?

- A. $35,000
- B. $65,000
- C. $130,000
- D. $195,000
- E. $215,000

19. Which of the following is a graph of the inequality $-2 \leq x < 4$?

A.
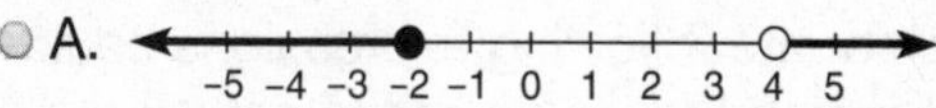

B. -5 -4 -3 -2 -1 0 1 2 3 4 5

C. -5 -4 -3 -2 -1 0 1 2 3 4 5

D. -5 -4 -3 -2 -1 0 1 2 3 4 5

E. -5 -4 -3 -2 -1 0 1 2 3 4 5

20. At what point does the line with the equation $y = 2x + 3$ intersect with the line with the equation $y = -\frac{1}{2}x - 7$?

- A. $(-4, -5)$
- B. $(0, -7)$
- C. $(0, 3)$
- D. $(2, 7)$
- E. $(4, 7)$

21. A pole is supported by a cable as shown. The cable is attached to the ground 9 feet from the base of the pole, and it is attached to the pole 12 feet above the ground.

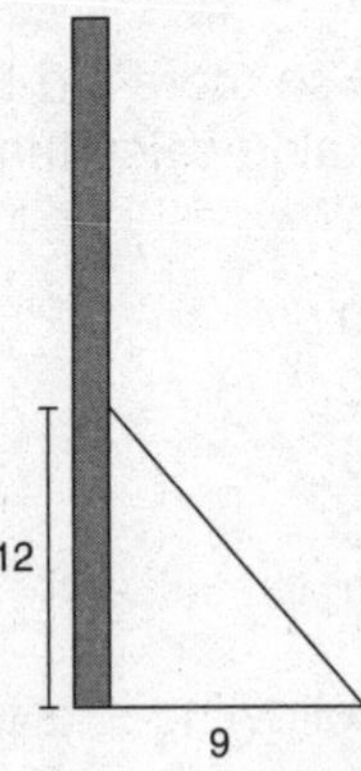

Which of the following expressions could be used to find the length of the cable?

- A. $9^2 + 12^2$
- B. $12^2 - 9^2$
- C. $\sqrt{9^2 + 12^2}$
- D. $\sqrt{12^2 - 9^2}$
- E. $12 + 9$

22. What is the slope of the line shown below?

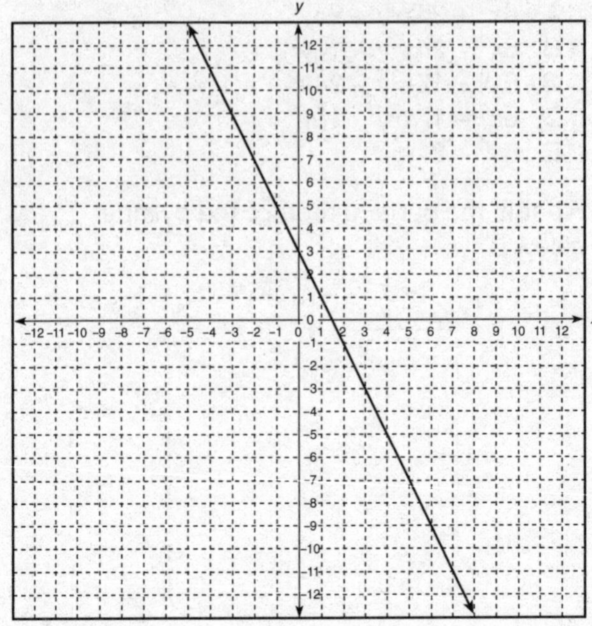

- A. -2
- B. $-\frac{1}{2}$
- C. $\frac{1}{2}$
- D. 2
- E. 4

23. One number is 12 more than 3 times another number. The sum of the two numbers is -20. What are the numbers?

- A. 8 and 12
- B. 8 and -12
- C. -2 and -18
- D. -8 and -12
- E. -2 and -12

24. Which of the following pairs of numbers is a solution to the equation $3x^2 - 54 = -21x$?

- A. –6 and 3
- B. –2 and 9
- C. –3 and 6
- D. –9 and 2
- E. –9 and –6

25. Jonas is a salesperson. He earns a base salary plus commissions on his sales. The following graph represents Jonas's annual earnings as a function of how much he sells.

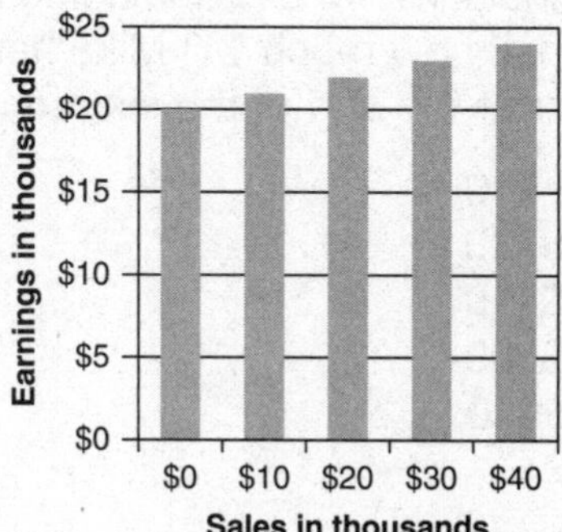

Which of the following equations represents Jonas's earnings, *e*, as a function of his sales, *s*?

- A. $e = 0.1s + 20{,}000$
- B. $e = 20{,}000s + 1{,}000$
- C. $e = 1{,}000s + 20{,}000$
- D. $e = 0.1s(1{,}000 + 20{,}000)$
- E. $e = s(1{,}000 + 20{,}000)$

26. A mountain resort charges for ski lessons as follows: each hour is $22.50 plus an initial $22.50 to reserve an instructor.

Which equation best describes the relationship between the total cost, *c*, and the number of hours of lessons, *h*?

- A. $c = 45h$
- B. $c = 45h - 22.5$
- C. $c = 22.5(h + 1)$
- D. $c = 22.5h + 45$
- E. $c = 45h + 22.5$

27. Clarissa has cylindrical jars that she would like to fill with colored water to use as decorations at a party. If the cylinders are 10 inches tall, and the bases have a radius of 4 inches, how many cubic inches of colored water will she need for each jar? Use 3.14 for pi, and round your answer to the nearest tenth.

- A. 50.2
- B. 160.0
- C. 502.4
- D. 1,004.8
- E. 1,024.6

28. Brad's average golf score after six rounds was 81. For the first five rounds his scores were 78, 86, 82, 81, and 82. What was his score on the sixth round?

- A. 81
- B. 80
- C. 79
- D. 78
- E. 77

29. A kayaker spends 2 hours paddling up a stream from point A to point B, quickly turns her kayak around, and immediately heads back downstream. It takes her only 1 hour to float back down the stream from point B to point A. If points A and B are 6 miles apart, what was the kayaker's average rate of speed in miles per hour?

- A. 12 mph
- B. 6 mph
- C. 4 mph
- D. 2 mph
- E. 1 mph

30. In the function $y = 3x + 10$, an input and output, respectively, could be

- A. 19 and 3
- B. 13 and 9
- C. 13 and 3
- D. 9 and 13
- E. 3 and 19

31. Risa wants to order business cards. A printing company determines the cost (C) to the customer using the following function, where b = the number of boxes of cards and n = the number of ink colors.

$$C = \$25.60b + \$14.00b(n - 1)$$

If Risa orders 4 boxes of cards printed in 3 colors, how much will the cards cost?

- A. $214.40
- B. $168.00
- C. $144.40
- D. $102.40
- E. $96.00

32. The Whitmans are trying to pay off their credit card debt, so they developed the following budget based on their monthly take-home pay.

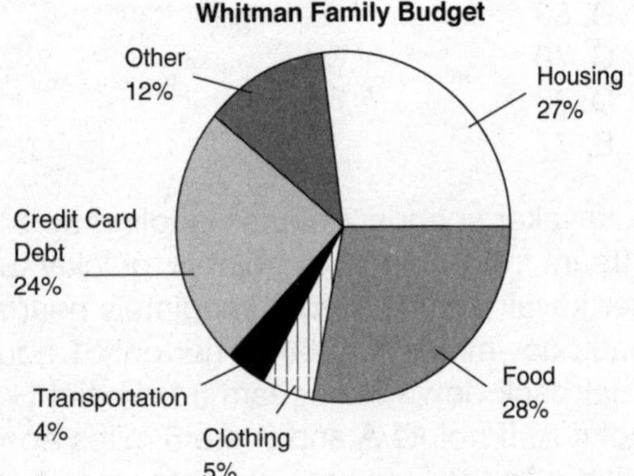

If the Whitmans's monthly take-home pay is $2500, about how much do they plan to pay each month on their credit card debt?

- A. $600
- B. $450
- C. $300
- D. $240
- E. $220

33. A market sells all varieties of pasta at a rate of 4 boxes for $5.00. Jennifer needs 3 boxes of ziti and 3 boxes of spaghetti. At this rate, how much will she spend for the pasta?

- A. $10.00
- B. $8.50
- C. $7.50
- D. $5.00
- E. $4.50

34. Mike borrowed $400 from his brother for six months. He agreed to pay simple interest at the annual rate of 5%. Including interest and principal, how much will Mike have paid his brother at the end of the six months?

- A. $10
- B. $120
- C. $410
- D. $500
- E. $530

35. Inge has been receiving a variety of advertisements in the mail. In order to figure out if the number of advertisements was increasing over time, she kept track of how many advertisements she received each week over an eight-week period. This is her record:

Week	Number of advertisements received
1st	3
2nd	4
3rd	6
4th	5
5th	4
6th	4
7th	7
8th	2

Which of the following dot plots accurately displays this data? Each dot represents a week, and the numbers on the dot plots represent the number of advertisements received.

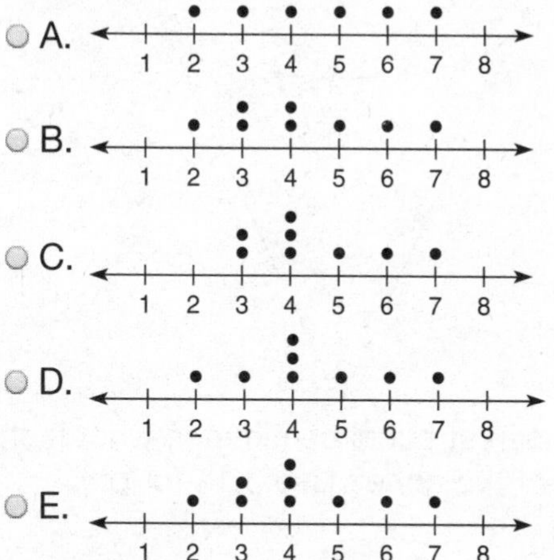

36. What is the value of the expression $3(2x - y) + (3 + x)^2$ when $x = 4$ and $y = 5$?

- A. 49
- B. 58
- C. 61
- D. 82
- E. 93

37. If the area of circle O is 36π, what is its diameter?

- A. 6
- B. 6π
- C. 12
- D. 18
- E. 18π

38. In 2011, Karen's base salary was \$52,500, and she earned an end-of-year bonus of \$6,250. In 2012, her base salary was raised to \$56,300 and her end-of-year bonus was \$4,100. What was the percent increase or decrease in her overall earnings from 2011 to 2012?

Round your answer to the nearest tenth of a percent.

- A. 0.3%
- B. 0.5%
- C. 1.4%
- D. 2.1%
- E. 2.8%

39. Each term in the second row is determined by the function $y = 5x + 4$.

x	1	2	3	4	...	15
y	9	14	19	24	...	

What number belongs in the shaded box?

- A. 29
- B. 36
- C. 47
- D. 65
- E. 79

40. Imtaez works as a server in a restaurant. On a certain night, the servers at his restaurant can earn a 50 cent bonus each time the dinner special is ordered. In order to qualify for the bonus, a server must submit at least 10 dinner special orders. Complete a linear equation that models the total bonus a server can expect to earn based on the number of dinner specials ordered, where *b* is the total bonus in dollars and *d* is the number of dinner specials ordered.

Which of the following equations could be used to find out how many dollars Imtaez will receive as a bonus if he sells at least 10 dinner specials?

- A. $b = 0.50d + 5$
- B. $b = 0.50d - 5$
- C. $b = d - 5(0.50)$
- D. $d = 0.50b + 5$
- E. $d = 0.50b - 5$

41. If $3x^2 + 4y = 12$ and $6x^2 + 6y = 18$, then $x =$

- A. 9
- B. 6
- C. 3
- D. 1
- E. 0

42. John needs to replace the boards on a 22-foot section of his fence. He plans to place the boards as shown below.
Note: Not drawn to scale.

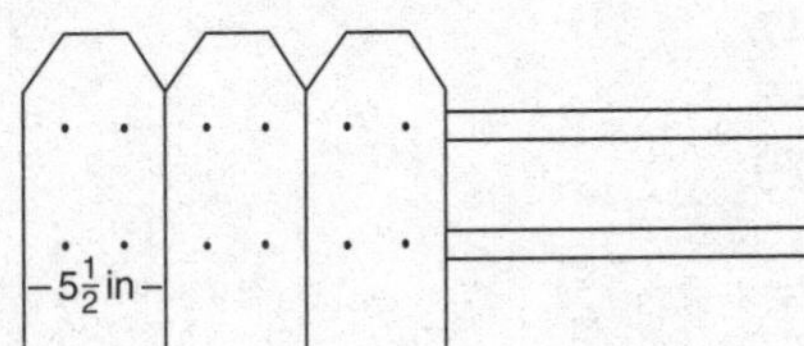

If the boards are $5\frac{1}{2}$ inches wide, how many boards should he buy to cover the distance?

- A. 4
- B. 12
- C. 48
- D. 121
- E. 133

43. Identify the solution to the following system of equations:

$y = x + 4$

$2y + 4x = 44$

- A. (6, 10)
- B. (10, 6)
- C. (6, 4)
- D. (4, 6)
- E. (4, 2)

44. A bag contains 12 red, 3 blue, 6 green, and 4 yellow marbles. If a marble is drawn from the bag at random, what is the probability that the marble will be either blue or yellow?

- A. 7%
- B. 12%
- C. 25%
- D. 28%
- E. 32%

45. The right cone shown below has a base with a radius of 6.4 cm.

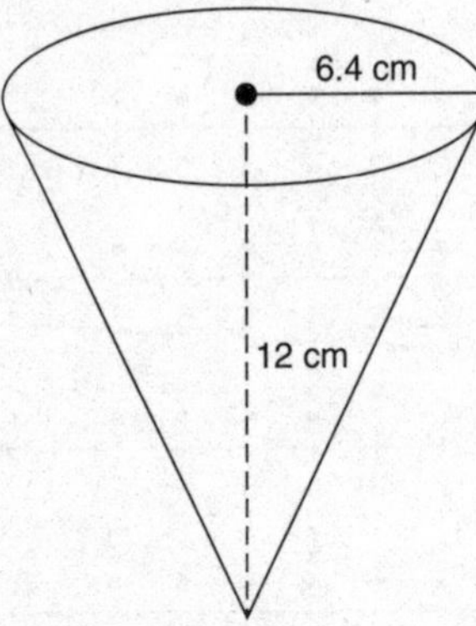

To the nearest cubic centimeter, what is the volume of the cone? Use 3.14 for pi.

- A. 40
- B. 81
- C. 129
- D. 514
- E. 722

46. Ten artists have entered an art show. There are three prizes to be awarded in the art show: first prize, second prize, and third prize. How many possible ways could those prizes be awarded among the ten artists?

- A. 128
- B. 256
- C. 480
- D. 640
- E. 720

47. At the end of baseball season, 5% of the children enrolled in a local youth baseball program will be chosen to play in the state tournament. If 12 children will be chosen to play in the tournament, how many children are enrolled in the program?

- A. 60
- B. 120
- C. 240
- D. 600
- E. 720

48. Fabio has his own computer repair business. He uses the following guidelines to estimate how long a project will take.

Install operating system: 1 hour
Replace motherboard: $1\frac{1}{2}$ hours
Reimage hard drive: 2 hours
Upgrade memory: 20 minutes
Install new hard drive: 45 minutes
Install sound card: 30 minutes
Install video card: 30 minutes

Fabio needs to install a new hard drive and an operating system for a customer. If Fabio charges $65 per hour, what will he charge the customer for his time?

- A. $94.25
- B. $105.00
- C. $113.75
- D. $146.25
- E. $152.50

49. There are approximately 1,335,000,000 cubic kilometers of water in Earth's oceans. Which of the following expresses that number in scientific notation?

- A. $1.335 \times 100 \times 100$
- B. 1.335×10^3
- C. 1.335×10^6
- D. 1.335×10^9
- E. 1.335×10^{10}

50. In the figure shown, opposite sides are parallel. What is the area of the following figure, in units squared?

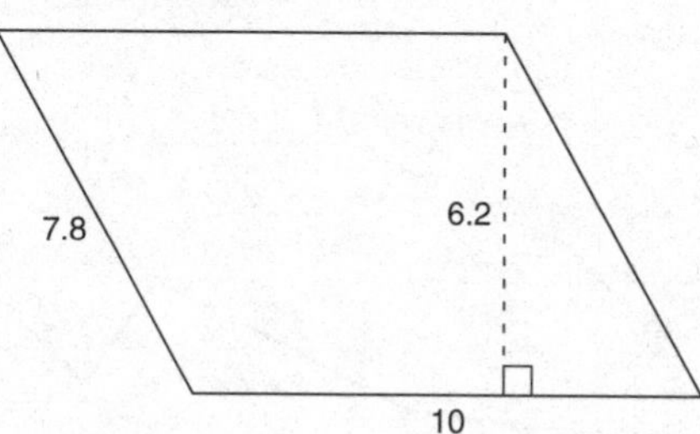

- A. 14
- B. 24
- C. 32
- D. 56
- E. 62

STOP. You have completed the Mathematics Practice Test.

Social Studies Practice Test

Directions: Use 70 minutes to answer the following 50 questions.

Questions 1 and 2 are based on the following paragraph and graph.

When the value of exported goods—those sold abroad—is greater than the value of imported goods—those bought from foreign nations—there is a favorable balance of trade. On the other hand, when imports are greater than exports, there is an unfavorable balance of trade.

Source: *Statistical Abstract of the United States*

1. Which of the following statements is supported by the paragraph and the graph?
   - A. Exports equaled imports at the start of the 2000s.
   - B. Exports exceeded imports throughout the 2000s.
   - C. The United States had a favorable balance of trade in merchandise during the 2000s.
   - D. The United States had an unfavorable balance of trade in merchandise during the 2000s.

2. Which of the following statements about 2009 is supported by the graph?
   - A. In 2009, a recession caused a significant drop in the value of imports.
   - B. In 2009, the value of imports fell by a greater amount than the value of exports did.
   - C. In 2009, the value of exports fell by a greater amount than the value of imports did.
   - D. In 2009, a drop in the value of imports caused a drop in the value of exports.

Question 3 is based on the following table.

In an opinion poll, people were asked, "In politics, as of today, do you consider yourself a Republican, a Democrat, or an independent?" The chart below represents the results, by month, for the first six months of 2013.

	Republicans %	Independents %	Democrats %
Jan 2013	27	38	33
Feb 2013	28	38	32
Mar 2013	27	36	35
Apr 2013	26	40	33
May 2013	28	39	32
Jun 2013	26	41	31

Source: Gallup

3. Which of the following statements about the first six months of 2013 is supported by the table?
   - A. Independents outnumbered Republicans in the ratio of 2:1.
   - B. There were roughly 10 percent more independents than Republicans.
   - C. Two percent of Americans surveyed belonged to a third party such as the Green Party.
   - D. More people identified as independents than as Democrats, and more identified as Democrats than as Republicans.

Questions 4 and 5 are based on the following information and graph.

What standard of living do people in other countries enjoy? There are different ways to answer that question. Many economists hold that one good way is to calculate *gross domestic product* (GDP) *per capita*. GDP per capita is found by adding up the value of all the goods produced and services performed in a given country in a year and then dividing that total (the GDP) by the number of people living in that country.

The map below shows GDP per capita for each country in the world in 2008. Some, but not all, of the countries are labeled with the name of the country.

Map of GDP Per Capita by Country

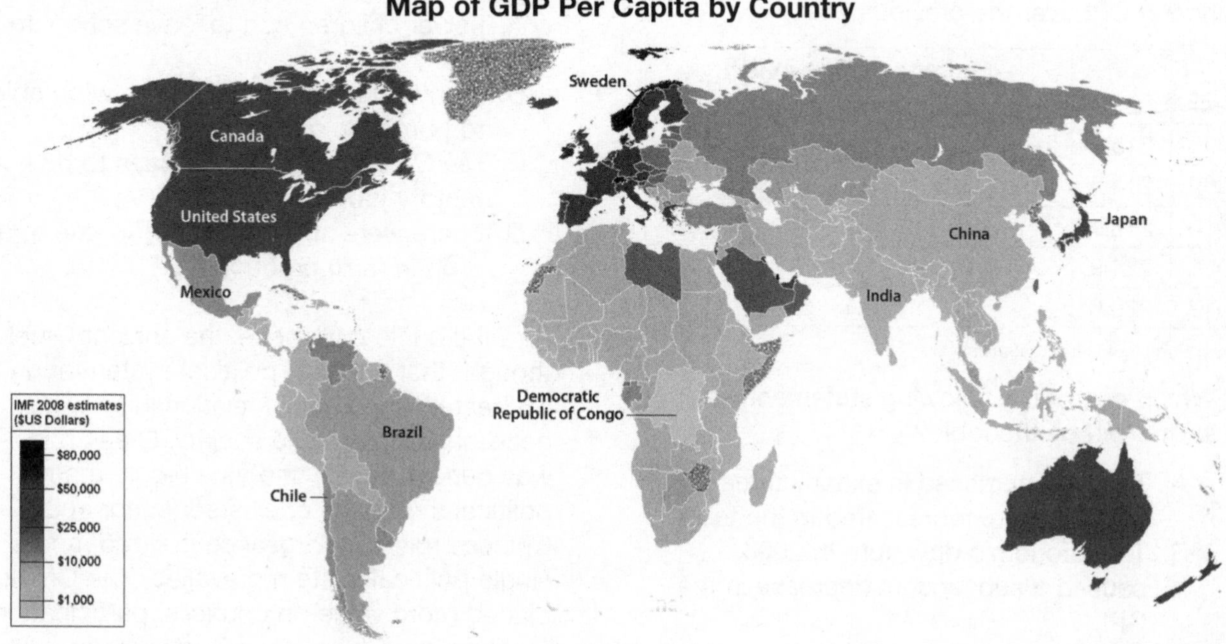

4. In 2008, which of the following continents had the highest percentage of countries with a GDP per capita of less than $10,000 per year?
   - A. Eurasia
   - B. North America
   - C. Africa
   - D. Australia

5. Which of the following statements about 2008 is supported by the map?
   - A. Differences in GDP per capita among African nations can be accounted for by oil and mineral deposits.
   - B. China had a higher GDP per capita than Japan because of its greater land area.
   - C. Having a long seacoast tended to have a positive effect on the GDP per capita of a nation.
   - D. European nations had, on average, higher GDP per capita than South American nations.

Question 6 refers to the following information and chart.

The Consumer Price Index (CPI) is a measure of the average prices paid by consumers for a typical assortment of goods and services, including housing, food, clothing, transportation, recreation, and medical care. A higher CPI indicates that prices have risen. The table below shows the CPI for several years, as well as the percent change in CPI over the previous year.

Year	CPI	Percent change in CPI over previous year
2008	215.3	3.8
2009	214.5	–0.4
2010	218.1	1.7
2011	224.9	3.1
2012	229.6	2.1

Source: Bureau of Labor Statistics

6. Which one of the following statements is supported by the table?
   - A. The CPI increased in exactly three of the five years represented in the table.
   - B. The economic downturn in 2008 caused a subsequent decrease in the CPI.
   - C. The CPI almost doubled between 2010 and 2011.
   - D. The CPI grew in all but one of the years represented in the table.

7. The period from the mid-1700s to the mid-1800s, during which manufacturers adopted new technologies such as steam engines and electrically powered machines, is referred to as the "Industrial Revolution." During this time, many people who were previously farmers began to work in factories.

   Which of the following was most likely a result of the Industrial Revolution?
   - A. Fewer children had to leave school to work.
   - B. Many lower-class individuals were able to purchase machinery.
   - C. Many people moved to cities to be near factory jobs.
   - D. There were shortages of food due to a drop in farm production.

8. Like the ancient Chinese, the ancient Greeks thought that a sound political system and well-established social relationships were necessary for a stable society. Greek rule was decentralized, and as a result, many political structures coexisted. In contrast, Chinese rule was largely centralized, and a single political system prevailed. The Greeks placed more value on councils, participation, and law; the Chinese, on bureaucracy, hierarchy, and rules.

   Based on the paragraph, what did the ancient Greeks and the ancient Chinese have in common in regard to politics and government?
   - A. Both governed through a hierarchical bureaucracy.
   - B. Both valued a stable political framework for society.
   - C. Both had centralized councils.
   - D. Both had decentralized political systems.

Question 9 refers to the following chart.

The Effect of World War II on Industry

Measure	1939	1940	1941
Index of manufacturing output (1939 = 100)	100	116	154
Corporate profits before taxes	$6.4 billion	$9.3 billion	$17 billion
Corporate profits after taxes	$5 billion	$6.5 billion	$9.4 billion

Source: Fute, Gilbert C., and Reese, Jim E. *An Economic History of the United States*

9. Which of the following best explains why the war had the effect on industry indicated by the chart?

   - A. Even before the United States entered the war, corporate profits had increased sharply.
   - B. Manufacturing output increased by over 50 percent in two years.
   - C. The war created a huge demand for military equipment and supplies.
   - D. With men gone to serve as soldiers, more women were employed in factories.

---

10. The U.S. president has a great deal of influence over foreign policy. In part, this is because international relations often require quick and decisive action, which is best undertaken by an individual. In times of foreign crisis, the public usually rallies to the support of the president, at least at first.

    Which of the following values probably underlies Americans' initial approval of a president's emergency foreign policy actions?

   - A. patriotism
   - B. imperialism
   - C. self-expression
   - D. self-sacrifice

11. To combat the anticompetitive nature of monopolies, or "trusts," such as US Steel, Standard Oil, and the American Tobacco Company, the US Congress passed the Sherman Antitrust Act in 1890. That act made it illegal for an individual to monopolize or conspire to monopolize an industry or to act with others to restrain trade or commerce among the States or abroad. While the Sherman Antitrust Act was, and remains, very influential, it was not sufficient to solve all of the problems raised by monopolies. Because of its broad language and its focus on the intent to create monopolies, courts interpreted the Sherman Antitrust Act differently and inconsistently in the many cases to which it was applied. As a result, Congress passed the Clayton Antitrust Act in 1914, which targeted specific actions—such as favorable price discrimination and exclusive dealings contracts—that were used to create monopolies.

    In the passage above, the writer's main point is that

   - A. courts struck down the Sherman Antitrust Act because its broad language made it unconstitutional.
   - B. problems with consistently enforcing the Sherman Antitrust Act led to further legislation to prevent monopolies.
   - C. monopolies like US Steel, Standard Oil, and the American Tobacco Company successfully avoided prosecution under the Sherman Antitrust Act.
   - D. the Sherman Antitrust Act ended monopolies like US Steel, Standard Oil, and the American Tobacco Company, but did not prevent new monopolies from arising.

Questions 12 through 13 are based on the following passage.

Environmental scientists have long been warning about the impact of unchecked carbon emissions into the atmosphere, a threat that many researchers conclude has already led to climate change. Of the many dangers of climate change, some of the most destructive involve lengthy droughts, diminishing fresh water supplies, and decreased world food production. Although some point to the potential benefits of the temperature changes, such as longer growing seasons and more temperate climates in some places, the hazards far outweigh any potential advantages. Since the United States has the second highest rate of carbon emissions per person, it must lead the way by dramatically cutting industrial emissions and finding alternate sources of fuel that do not release carbon dioxide as a by-product. Positive efforts are under way, particularly through the Environmental Protection Agency, which have fostered several international partnerships to limit the production of carbon dioxide.

12. With which one of the following would the author agree?
    - A. The United States has failed to take any action against carbon emissions.
    - B. The dangers of climate change are more significant than the possible benefits.
    - C. Wind energy is preferable to solar energy.
    - D. Climate change will not impact the world food supply.

13. Which of the following does the author give as a reason why the United States must lead the way in combating climate change?
    - A. Environmental scientists have long been warning about the dangers of climate change.
    - B. Climate change can lead to lengthy droughts and decreased food production.
    - C. Climate change may result in longer growing seasons.
    - D. The United States has the second highest rate of carbon emissions per person.

Questions 14 through 15 refer to the following map.

Forced Resettlement of Native Americans, 1830s

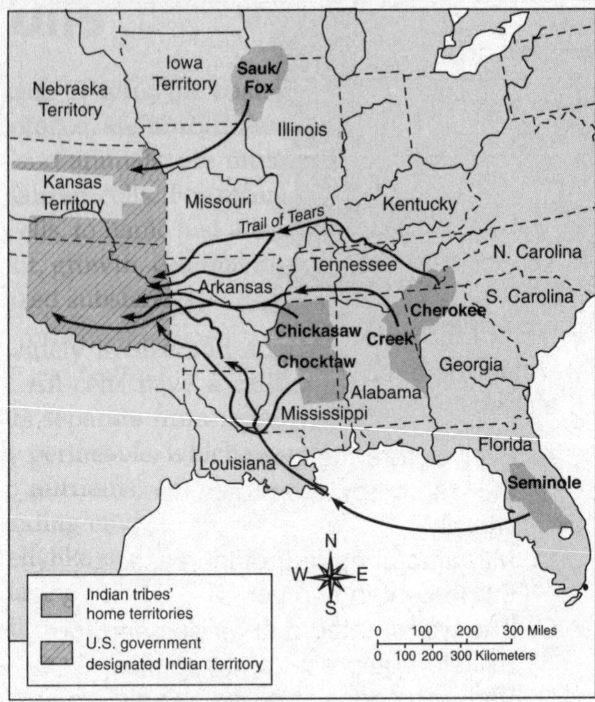

14. Which of the following is the most likely reason that Native American were forcibly relocated in the 1830s?
    - A. Whites wanted lands in the Kansas and Nebraska territory for settlement.
    - B. Whites wanted to take over Indian lands in the eastern states.
    - C. Indians of different tribes wanted to settle in a single Indian territory.
    - D. Indians in the eastern states wanted to look for gold in the West.

15. Which American Indian tribe was moved the farthest from its tribal lands?
    - A. the Sauk/Fox
    - B. the Cherokee
    - C. the Chocktaw
    - D. the Seminole

Question 16 refers to the following cartoon.

SENATOR ZILTCH
"I THOUGHT HE WAS A MEMBER OF A SPECIAL INTEREST GROUP... BUT I FOUND OUT HE'S ONLY A VOTER!"

16. With which of the following opinions would the cartoonist be most likely to agree?
    - A. People shouldn't have to stand around waiting to see their elected representatives.
    - B. Senators should pay attention to special interest groups as well as to voters.
    - C. Special interest groups are treated better than voters by members of Congress.
    - D. Senators are nicer to their constituents than are members of the House.

---

17. In the late 1800s, industrialization caused a large-scale migration from rural to urban areas in the United States. Parents who moved to cities with their children left behind the social support of their extended families. In addition, city families found that children, who were an asset on the farm because they could work at an early age, were more of an economic drawback in the city. As a consequence, the birthrate dropped during this period and average family size shrank.

    Which of the following is the best summary of this passage?
    - A. Industrialization led to increased urbanization in the late 1800s.
    - B. City families lost the social support of their extended families back on the farm.
    - C. Industrialization and urbanization caused many changes in family life in the late 1800s.
    - D. In the late 1800s, average family size shrank due to the fall in the birthrate.

Questions 18 and 19 refer to the following chart.

Acts of Parliament Directed at the American Colonies

Act	Description
Revenue Act of 1764 (Sugar Act)	Imposed duties (tariffs) on foreign sugar and luxuries to raise money for Great Britain
Quartering Act of 1765	Required colonists to provide food and shelter for British soldiers
Stamp Act of 1765	Required colonists to purchase revenue stamps for all important documents, including legal documents, newspapers, and ads
Declaratory Act of 1766	Asserted the right of Parliament to make laws for the colonies
Townshend Acts of 1767	Imposed new duties on the import of tea, glass, and paper

18. How did the Declaratory Act differ from all the other acts of Parliament shown in the chart?
    - A. It did not involve the quartering of British soldiers.
    - B. It related only to the import of luxury goods.
    - C. It did not impose direct economic costs on the colonists.
    - D. It was enacted long after the other acts of Parliament.

19. The information in this chart would have been most useful for the writing of which of the following documents?
    - A. The Declaration of Independence, which explained why the colonies broke away from Great Britain
    - B. The Articles of Confederation, which established a central government consisting of a congress
    - C. The U.S. Constitution, which established the structure of government for the newly independent nation
    - D. Washington's Farewell Address, in which he warned the new nation of policies and practices he thought unwise

Questions 20 and 21 are based on the following map.

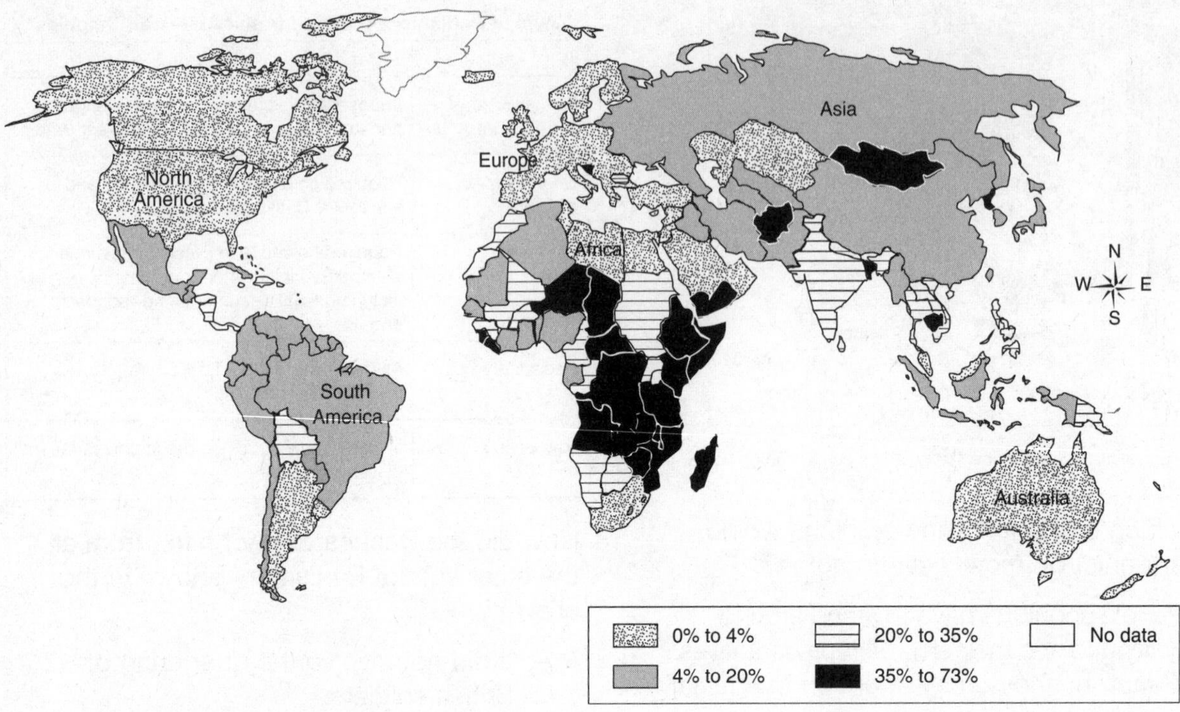

Source: The United Nations, World Food Program

20. According to the map, what is the percentage range of people in the United States who do not get enough food and nutrients?

   - A. 0% to 4%
   - B. 4% to 20%
   - C. 20% to 35%
   - D. 35% to 73%

21. Which of the following statements is supported by the information on the map?

   - A. All areas with more than 35% of the population undernourished are inland nations.
   - B. World hunger would disappear if food were distributed more fairly.
   - C. There are no areas of hunger in Europe or Australia.
   - D. Hunger is a major problem in many countries in Africa.

Questions 22 and 23 refer to the following chart.

Important Political Documents Preceding the Declaration of Independence and the U.S. Constitution

Year	Document	Description
1215	Magna Carta	Limited the power of the English king and granted rights to the nobles
1620	Mayflower Compact	Set rules by which the Pilgrims would govern themselves in Plymouth colony
1628	Petition of Right	Limited the English king's powers further
1636	Great Fundamentals	Established the first basic system of laws in the English colonies, in Massachusetts Bay Colony
1688	English Bill of Rights	Declared that the king rules with the consent of the people's representatives in Parliament; granted ordinary people certain rights

22. What do the Mayflower Compact and the Great Fundamentals have in common?

- A. Both limited the power of the king.
- B. Both granted rights to the nobles.
- C. Both established methods of self-government in English colonies.
- D. Both applied to the government in England.

23. One of the major grievances the American colonists had against the British was that the British taxed the colonists without granting them representation in the British Parliament. Part of the Declaration of Independence is a list of political and economic rights that American colonists complained that the British king had deprived them of.

By which of the following documents were the writers of the Declaration probably most influenced as they drafted their list?

- A. the Mayflower Compact
- B. the Petition of Right
- C. the Great Fundamentals
- D. the English Bill of Rights

24. The civil rights movement of the 1950s and 1960s inspired historians to reinterpret slavery's impact on U.S. society in general and on African Americans in particular. One interpretation that emerged was that slaves and owners were always in conflict and that slavery was destructive. The extent of slavery's destructiveness was debated. Some historians argued that slavery destroyed the culture and self-respect of the slaves and their descendants. Others thought that slaves overcame hardship by developing a unique African American culture that included, among many different things, strong religious and musical traditions.

Based on the paragraph, which of the following statements is an opinion rather than a fact?

- A. The civil rights movement took place during the middle of the twentieth century.
- B. The civil rights movement caused historians to take another look at slavery.
- C. Historians debated slavery's negative effects on slaves and their descendants.
- D. Slavery destroyed the culture of the slaves, diminishing their self-respect.

Questions 25 and 26 refer to the following paragraph and graph.

The market price of a product tends to change in a way that brings supply and demand into balance, a condition called equilibrium. This is illustrated in the graph below, which shows supply and demand for apples.

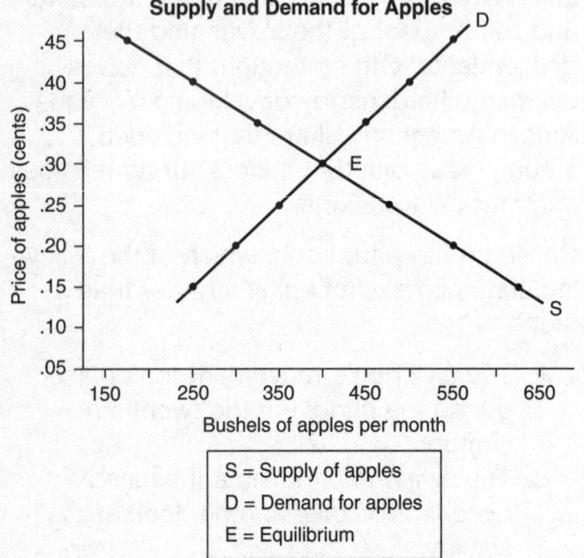

25. According to this graph, what is the market price of apples—also known as the price at equilibrium?
   - A. 45 cents
   - B. 30 cents
   - C. 20 cents
   - D. 15 cents

26. Which of the following would result if part of the apple crop were destroyed but demand remained the same?
   - A. Supply would increase.
   - B. The market price would remain the same.
   - C. The market price would go down.
   - D. The market price would go up.

Question 27 refers to the following paragraph and map.

The Battle of Fort Sumter was the first battle of the American Civil War. South Carolina had seceded from the Union and insisted that Union troops in South Carolina leave. A small band of Union soldiers was finally forced to evacuate Fort Sumter, on the South Carolina coast. After that, President Lincoln called for 75,000 volunteers to help put down the rebellion in the south. Following his call, four additional states seceded from the Union and joined the Confederacy. The progress of secession is shown here.

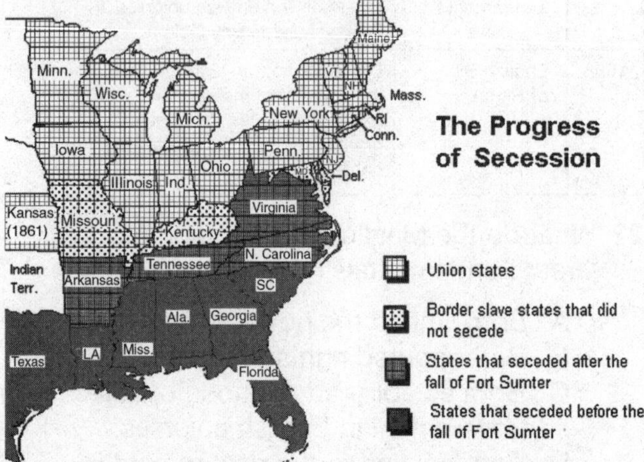

Reprinted from "The South Secedes," U.S. History Online Textbook, ushistory.org.

27. Which of the following states belonged to the Confederacy both before the battle of Fort Sumter and after the battle of Fort Sumter?
   - A. Iowa
   - B. North Carolina
   - C. Delaware
   - D. Alabama

Questions 28 through 30 refer to the following paragraph and diagram.

Most cases that arise under federal law are tried in the federal court system. The federal court system has several levels of courts and several routes by which cases may be appealed to a higher court.

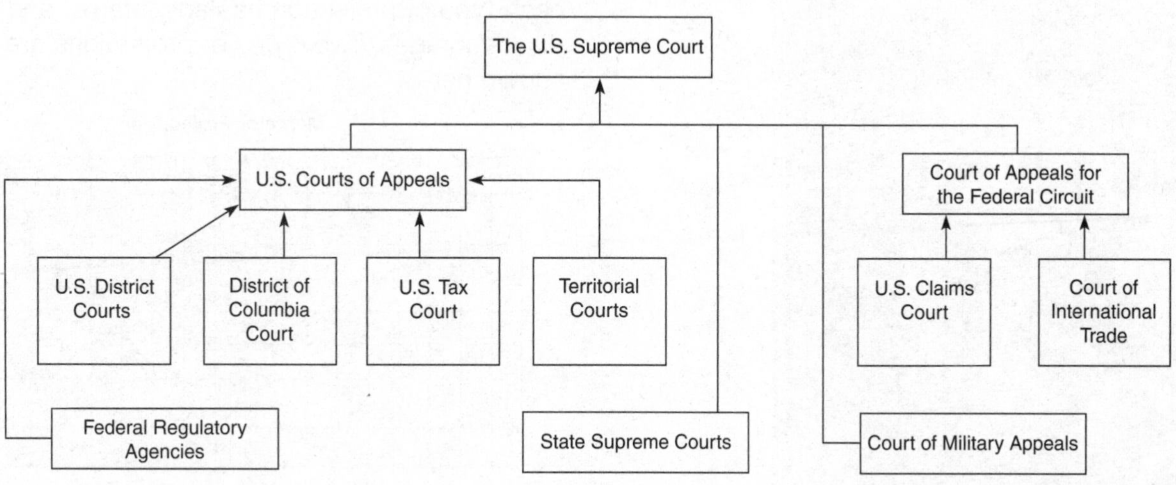

28. A U.S. import-export firm files a lawsuit against a foreign trading company. In which court is the suit most likely to be filed?

- A. the United States Claims Court
- B. the United States Court of Appeals
- C. the Court of International Trade
- D. the United States Tax Court

29. The U.S. Constitution established only the Supreme Court, but it gave Congress the power to create inferior (lower) federal courts.

Which of the following is the most likely reason that Congress established other federal courts?

- A. The justices of the U.S. Supreme Court were not well versed enough in the law to handle all federal cases.
- B. The volume and variety of federal cases were too great for a single court to handle.
- C. A system of inferior federal courts gave the United States prestige in the eyes of the rest of the world.
- D. The Supreme Court's power to interpret the Constitution was established in *Marbury v. Madison*.

30. If cases are not resolved in any of the lower federal courts, to which court may they eventually, finally be appealed?

- A. the Supreme Court of the United States
- B. the United States Courts of Appeals
- C. the Court of Appeals for the Federal Circuit
- D. the Court of Military Appeals

Question 31 refers to the following poster.

The poster below was published during World War I.

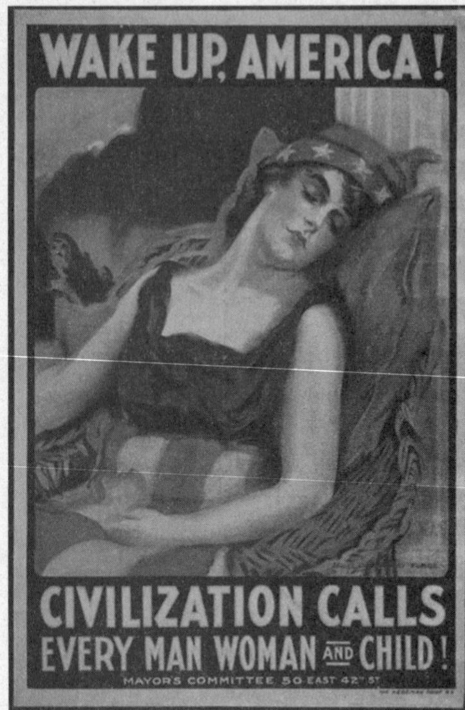

Source: Library of Congress. Poster by James Montgomery Flagg

31. Which of the following opinions is the artist attempting to propagate?

- A. Americans are not yet part of civilization.
- B. The war effort needs the help of everyone, including men, women, and children.
- C. Every man, woman, and child should rest in preparation for the war effort.
- D. Americans are part of a lazy civilization.

Questions 32 and 33 refer to the following paragraph and maps.

Mapmakers have devised many solutions to the problem of projecting the curved surface of Earth onto a flat piece of paper. However, all map projections involve some distortion, and each type of projection has advantages and disadvantages. Two types of projections are shown here.

Mercator Projection

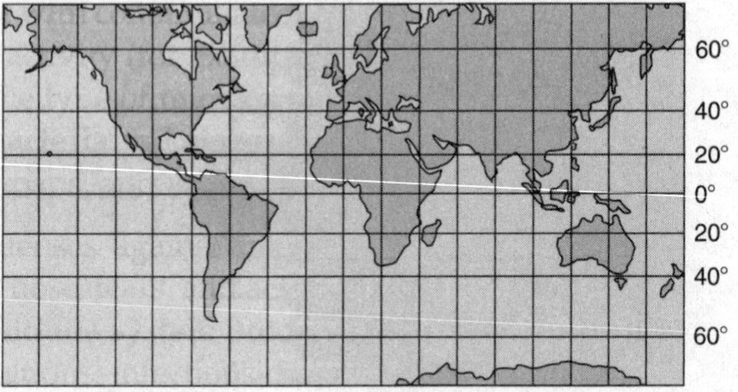

Interrupted Projection

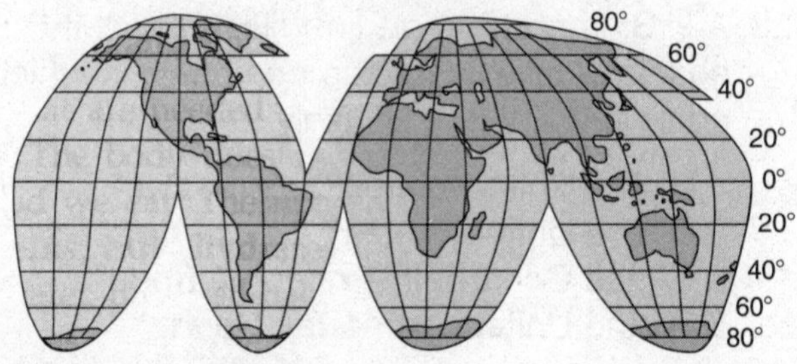

32. Approximately where is there the least distortion on these projections?

- A. at 60° north and south latitude
- B. at 40° north and south latitude
- C. at 20° north and south latitude
- D. at 0° latitude

33. A sailor who wanted to plan an around-the-world sailing trip decided to use the interrupted projection. What was wrong with his decision?

- A. The interrupted projection distorts distances across the continents at mid-latitudes.
- B. The interrupted projection distorts distances across the oceans.
- C. The interrupted projection distorts the shapes of mid-latitude land masses.
- D. The interrupted projection shows only a few of the world's oceans.

Question 34 refers to the following paragraph and map.

After the Roman Empire had reached its greatest extent in the 2nd century C.E., emperors consolidated its borders in various ways: where the frontiers were over land, they were seen as vulnerable, and so the emperors often built heavy fortifications, such as forts or walls to defend the borders; where there was a natural barrier like a river or a desert, light fortifications, such as watchtowers, were viewed as adequate; and where there were major barriers, such as the ocean, the emperors concluded that no defense was needed.

Northwestern Frontiers of the Roman Empire, 2nd Century CE

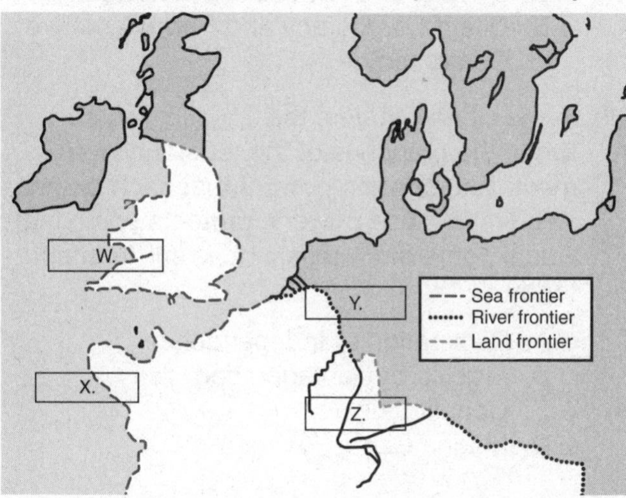

34. For which of the following frontiers would the Roman emperors have built no fortifications at all?

- A. W only
- B. W and X only
- C. W, X, and Y only
- D. W, Y, and Z only

35. Constitutional guarantees of fairness and equality under the law, our basic civil liberties, are called due process of law. The Fifth and Fourteenth Amendments state that government shall not deprive anyone of "life, liberty, or property, without due process of law." The Fifth Amendment protects people from actions of the federal government. The Fourteenth protects people specifically from actions of governments of the individual states.

What is a main difference between the Fifth and Fourteenth Amendments?

- A. The Fifth Amendment applies to adults, and the Fourteenth Amendment, to children.
- B. The Fifth Amendment applies to due process, and the Fourteenth Amendment, to freedom of speech.
- C. The Fifth Amendment applies to the federal government, and the Fourteenth Amendment, to state governments.
- D. The Fifth Amendment applies to life, and the Fourteenth Amendment, to liberty.

36. Haiti, which became a republic in 1804, is the second-oldest republic in the western hemisphere. Previously, it had been controlled by France and was important in the slave trade. Slaves in Haiti fought for independence for almost 10 years before finally breaking away from France. When the Republic of Haiti was established, it was the first independent nation in the Caribbean or Latin America. It would be several decades before another Caribbean nation would gain independence. Haiti was also the first democratic republic in the world to be led by African Americans. It is the only country in the western hemisphere where the dominant language is French.

    Which of the following is the best summary of this passage?

    - A. Several factors make Haiti unique among Caribbean nations.
    - B. Haiti became a republic in 1804, long before any other Caribbean nation.
    - C. Haiti has long been led by African Americans.
    - D. Haiti is a French-speaking republic in the Caribbean.

37. For many centuries, a set of important international trade routes, called the "Silk Road," brought traders from Europe into Asia and vice versa. Silk from China was being sold in Europe and Africa by the first century B.C.E. (if not before), and gold and other valuables from Europe and Africa flowed into the Far East in exchange. Over time, not only silk but also spices, minerals, and many other types of goods were carried along the Silk Road. As a by-product of this trade, ideas, religions, and even diseases were also carried back and forth between East and West.

    The city of Damascus was on one of the Silk Road routes. Which of the following was most likely true of Damascus?

    - A. Even its poorer citizens possessed silk clothing.
    - B. People in Damascus were aware of religions practiced elsewhere.
    - C. Some of the gold flowing into China was mined in Damascus.
    - D. People in Damascus never died from foreign diseases.

38. Review the table and answer the following question.

    Differences Between ______________

• Citizens vote on each issue or governmental action • The system of ancient Athens	• Citizens elect representatives who vote on issues or actions • The system of the United States national government

    Which of the following best completes the title of the table?

    - A. Democracy and Aristocracy
    - B. Democracy and Oligarchy
    - C. Direct Democracy and Referendum
    - D. Direct Democracy and Representative Democracy

39. In the United States, the _______ establishes the branches of the federal government, lists specific powers that each branch has, limits those powers, protects some individual rights of citizens, and is still in effect today.

    - A. Declaration of Independence
    - B. Articles of Confederation
    - C. Constitution
    - D. Magna Carta

Questions 40 and 41 are based on the following passage.

In 1096 C.E., peasants and soldiers from Europe invaded Jerusalem in the first of a long series of conflicts in the Middle East. The soldiers and their leaders were motivated by several factors. Some, who were influenced by the pope at the time, wanted to regain control of Christian holy sites. Some wanted to unite the Eastern and Western branches of the Christian church. Some were likely motivated by religious prejudice against Islam or Judaism. It is probable that some wanted to rob Middle Eastern cities of gold and other resources. Some may have been adventurers hoping to achieve personal glory. Regardless of why they happened, the resulting wars killed hundreds of thousands over a period of two centuries.

40. What historical event does the preceding passage describe?
    - A. the Crusades
    - B. the Wars of the Roses
    - C. the Palestinian Conflict
    - D. World War I

41. A famous historian described these wars as "the most signal and most durable monument of human folly that has yet appeared in any age or nation." Based on the passage, what did the historian most likely mean by the phrase "monument of human folly"?
    - A. a stone statue displaying the dates of the wars
    - B. a signal conveying the location of a monument
    - C. a reason to remember how foolish people can be
    - D. a structure erected in honor of those who died in the wars

42. Read the list contained in the box and answer the question.

    - Rising unemployment
    - Slowdown in consumer spending
    - Slowdown in business expansion
    - Businesses and consumers avoiding risk

    Which of the following does the preceding box describe?
    - A. inflation
    - B. recovery
    - C. saturation
    - D. recession

43. Which one of the following is most likely a consumer good rather than a producer good?
    - A. 16-by-10-foot sheets of aluminum
    - B. bricks of refined copper
    - C. 5-ounce tubes of oil paint
    - D. 1,000-foot bales of fiber-optic cable

44. James Madison, who helped draft the Constitution, wrote about it: "The powers delegated by the proposed Constitution to the federal government are few and defined. Those which are to remain in the State governments are numerous and indefinite. The former will be exercised principally on external objects, as war, peace, negotiation, and foreign commerce. . . . The powers reserved to the several states will extend to all the objects which, in the ordinary course of affairs, concern the lives, liberties, and properties of the people, and the internal order, improvement, and prosperity of the State."

What aspect of the United States government's structure was Madison describing?

- A. democracy
- B. federalism
- C. the Commerce Clause
- D. representation

45. The first three Articles of the Constitution of the United States define the powers of the legislative, executive, and judicial branches of the government. The following table gives brief summaries of the duties of those three branches:

Legislative	Executive	Judicial
• Makes laws • Declares war and raises armies • Establishes tariffs • Regulates commerce between the states	• Executes the laws • Establishes executive agencies to help execute laws	• Decides disputes between individuals or between branches of government and individuals

Which of the following functions is NOT performed by the Supreme Court of the United States?

- A. deciding whether state laws violate the Constitution
- B. deciding whether federal laws violate the Constitution
- C. hearing the final appeal in criminal cases
- D. outlawing behavior such as drug use or robbery

46. Much of the money spent on political campaigns is spent by individuals or companies who are not officially part of the campaign. For example, XYZ Corporation might pay for an expensive television ad supporting candidate Smith for election. Because some feel that this gives wealthy people or companies too much influence, the federal government restricted this type of spending in 2002. However, in 2010, the U.S. Supreme Court ruled that part of the 2002 law was unconstitutional because the law restricted the expression of political ideas.

Which of the following parts of the Constitution did the Supreme Court most likely base its decision on?

- A. the First Amendment, which protects the right of free speech
- B. the Commerce Clause, which gives Congress the power to regulate trade
- C. the Fifth Amendment, which prohibits government from taking property without legal process
- D. the Necessary and Proper Clause, which gives Congress the power to make laws

47. The National Labor Relations Act, passed by Congress in 1935, guarantees the right of workers to organize into unions, engage in collective bargaining, and strike if collective bargaining fails.

Which one of the following activities is most likely NOT protected by the National Labor Relations Act?

- A. George is offended by a joke made by a coworker and complains to his manager about it.
- B. Lupe tells her coworker that she thinks he should join a union and gives him a union pamphlet.
- C. Workers at the XYZ Company hold a vote about whether they want to be represented by a union.
- D. A union decides that negotiations with a company have failed and calls for a strike.

Questions 48 and 49 refer to the following form.

Fold and seal, or use an envelope

Instructions

Use this form to register to vote or update your current registration.

Print all information clearly using black or blue pen. Mail this completed form to your county elections office (address on back).

Deadline
This registration will be in effect for the next election if postmarked no later than the Monday four weeks before Election Day.

Voting
You will receive your ballot in the mail. Contact your county elections office for accessible voting options.

Public Information
Your name, address, gender, and date of birth will be public information.

Notice
Knowingly providing false information about yourself or your qualifications for voter registration is a class C felony punishable by imprisonment for up to 5 years, a fine of up to $10,000, or both.

Public Benefits Offices
If you received this form from a public benefits office, where you received the form will remain confidential and will be used for voter registration purposes only.

Registering or declining to register will not affect the assistance provided to you by any public benefits office. If you decline to register, your decision will remain confidential.

If you believe someone interfered with your right to register, or your right to privacy in deciding whether to register, you may file a complaint with the Washington State Elections Division.

Contact Information
If you would like help with this form, contact the Washington State Elections Division.

web www.vote.wa.gov
call (800) 448-4881
email elections@sos.wa.gov
mail PO Box 40229
Olympia, WA 98504-0229

For official use:

fold in half → ←

12 / 2014

Washington State Voter Registration Form

Register online at www.myvote.wa.gov.

1 Personal Information

last name first middle

date of birth (mm / dd / yyyy) ○ male ○ female

residential address in Washington apt #

city ZIP

mailing address, if different

city state and ZIP

phone number (optional) email address (optional)

2 Qualifications

If you answer *no*, do not complete this form.

○ yes ○ no **I am a citizen of the United States of America.**

○ yes ○ no **I will be at least 18 years old by the next election.**

3 Military / Overseas Status

○ yes ○ no **I am currently serving in the military.**
Includes National Guard and Reserves, and spouses or dependents away from home due to service.

○ yes ○ no **I live outside the United States.**

4 Identification — Washington Driver License, Permit, or ID

☐☐☐☐☐☐☐☐☐☐☐☐

If you do not have a Washington driver license, permit, or ID, you may use the last four digits of your Social Security number to register. x x x - x x - ☐☐☐☐

5 Change of Name or Address

This information will be used to update your current registration, if applicable.

former last name first middle

former residential address city state and ZIP

6 Declaration

I declare that the facts on this voter registration form are true. I am a citizen of the United States, I will have lived at this address in Washington for at least thirty days immediately before the next election at which I vote, I will be at least 18 years old when I vote, I am not disqualified from voting due to a court order, and I am not under Department of Corrections supervision for a Washington felony conviction.

sign here date here

48. What is the best way to get reliable information about voting in Washington State?

- A. Go to your congressional representative.
- B. Ask a neighbor who shares your voting precinct.
- C. Visit the www.vote.wa.gov website.
- D. Call 1-800-VOTEGOV.

49. Suppose the next election is to be held on Nov 7, 2017. It can be inferred that in order to vote you must

- A. have a valid Washington driver's license.
- B. be born on or before Nov 7, 1999.
- C. inform your county elections official of your intent to vote.
- D. remain in Washington State for 30 days prior to the election.

Question 50 refers to the following excerpt from Amendment XII to the Constitution.

The Electors shall meet in their respective states, and vote by ballot for President and Vice-President [. . .] The person having the greatest Number of votes for President, shall be the President, if such number be a majority of the whole number of Electors appointed; and if no person have such majority, then from the persons having the highest numbers not exceeding three on the list of those voted for as President, the House of Representatives shall choose immediately, by ballot, the President. But in choosing the President, the votes shall be taken by states, the representation from each state having one vote; a quorum for this purpose shall consist of a member or members from two-thirds of the states, and a majority of all the states shall be necessary to a choice.

50. It can be concluded that if no Presidential candidate receives a majority of the vote then

- A. a second election is held with only the top three candidates.
- B. the House of Representatives determines who becomes President.
- C. each state casts one vote for the President.
- D. a public quorum is held to debate who should be elected.

STOP. You have completed the Social Studies Practice Test.

Science Practice Test

Directions: Use 80 minutes to answer the following 50 questions.

Question 1 refers to the following paragraph and diagram.

Newton's third law of motion states that when one object exerts a force upon another object, the second object exerts an equal force on the first, in the opposite direction. An airplane in motion changes the speed and direction of the air, exerting a force on it. The opposing force of the air keeps the airplane aloft.

How an Airplane Flies

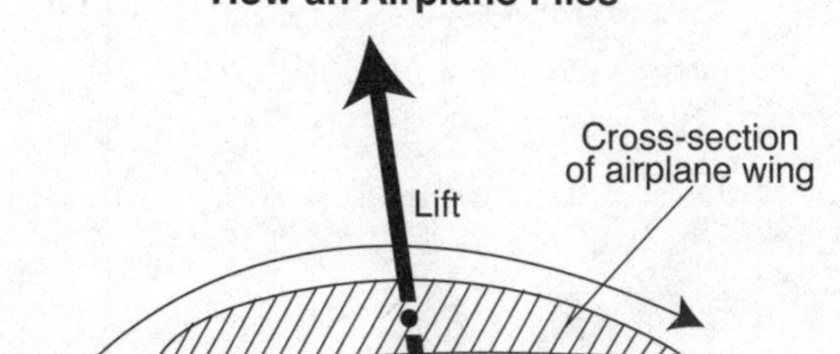

1. What vertical force holds the airplane up?

- A. lift
- B. Newton's third law
- C. weight
- D. air resistance

2. Sleep may have evolved in humans for several reasons. First, people were unable to hunt, gather food, or travel in the dark. Second, sleep provides an opportunity to repair our body's cells, especially those in the brain. Third, our body temperature is lower during sleep, which conserves energy. Fourth, during deep sleep the pituitary gland releases a growth hormone, so sleep may play a role in growth.

   Which of the following is the best title for this paragraph?

- A. "Sleep and Growth"
- B. "Our Brains During Sleep"
- C. "Why We Sleep"
- D. "The Role of Deep Sleep"

Questions 3 through 5 are based on the following information and graphic.

The processes that circulate nitrogen between the atmosphere, land, and organisms are called the nitrogen cycle.

The Nitrogen Cycle

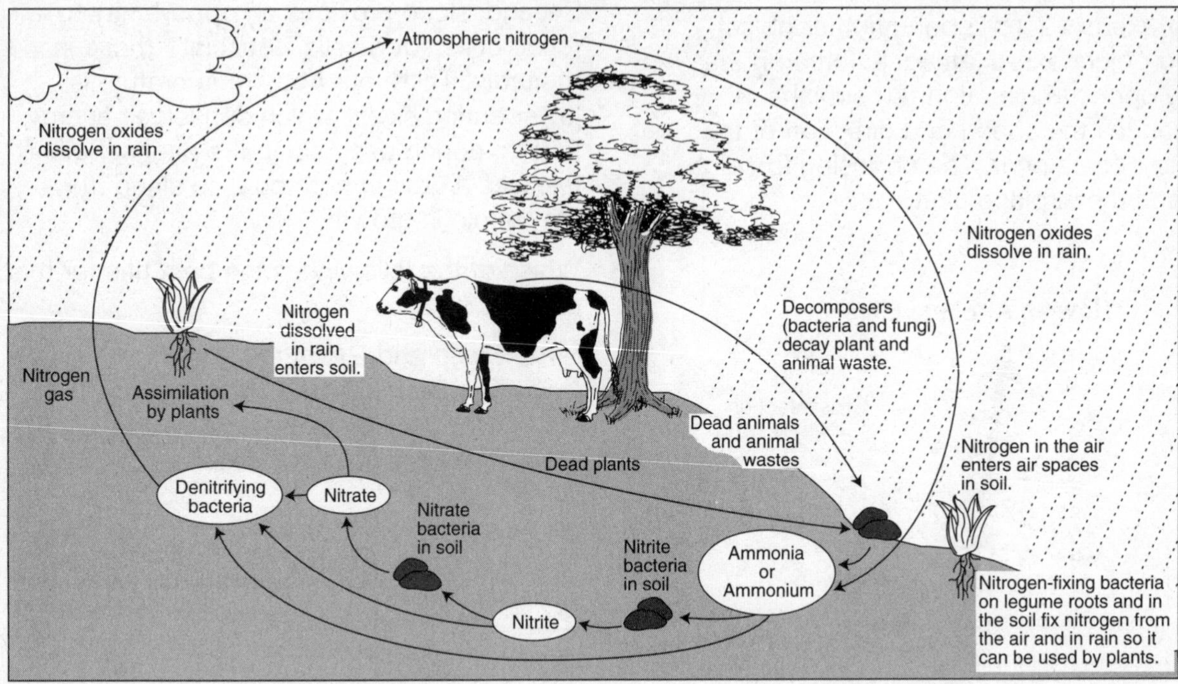

3. Nitrogen-fixing bacteria are found both in the soil and on the roots of legumes like peas and beans. From where do these bacteria get nitrogen?

- A. ammonia and ammonium
- B. the air and rainwater in the soil
- C. animals and animal wastes
- D. animal wastes and decaying plants

4. Which of the following statements is a conclusion about the nitrogen cycle rather than a detail in the diagram?

- A. Nitrogen oxides dissolve in rainwater.
- B. Nitrogen-fixing bacteria are found both in the soil and on the roots of legumes.
- C. The recycling of nitrogen through the biosphere involves many complex processes.
- D. Nitrite bacteria turn ammonia and ammonium into nitrites.

5. To increase the nitrogen content of the soil, many farmers spread synthetic fertilizers containing nitrogen compounds. What might an organic farmer who does not use synthetic fertilizers do to improve the fertility of the soil?

- A. switch to crops requiring more potassium
- B. compost with plant and animal wastes
- C. plant more non-leguminous plants
- D. switch to crops requiring more nitrogen

Question 6 refers to the following graph.

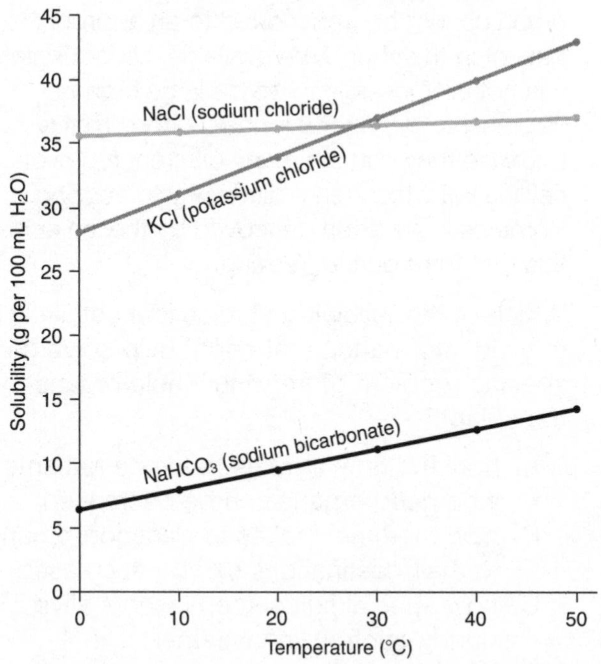

6. Which of the following statements is supported by the information in the graph?
   - A. About 15 grams of sodium bicarbonate will dissolve in 100 mL of water at 10°C.
   - B. About 30 grams of potassium chloride will dissolve in 100 mL of water at 30°C.
   - C. Sodium chloride shows the greatest increase in solubility with increase in temperature.
   - D. For the three compounds shown, solubility increases as temperature increases.

Questions 7 through 9 refer to the following paragraph.

Plants absorb nutrients and water through a system of roots comprised of living cells. A scientist wondered whether watering with different water temperatures would have an effect on house plants. He guessed that tepid water might be better for plants than cooler water. For six weeks, the scientist watered plants in Group A with 75°F water and watered plants in Group B with 50°F water. He recorded their growth during this period. At the end of six weeks, the plants in Group A were, on average, 1 inch taller than plants in Group B.

7. Which of the following statements from the passage describes the scientist's hypothesis?
   - A. A scientist wondered whether watering with different water temperatures would have an effect on house plants.
   - B. He guessed that tepid water might be better for plants than cooler water.
   - C. For six weeks, the scientist watered plants in Group A with 50°F water and watered plants in Group B with 75°F water.
   - D. He recorded their growth during this period.

8. Given the results of the experiment, which of the following conclusions is most valid?
   - A. Tepid water stimulated more plant growth than cooler water.
   - B. There is a direct correlation between water temperature and plant growth.
   - C. House plants need water in order to grow.
   - D. Houseplants should be watered with 75°F water.

9. Suppose the scientist wants to determine which temperature water will provide optimum growth for house plants. Based on the results of the scientist's original experiment, which temperature ranges should the scientist test next?
   - A. 20°F–60°F
   - B. 60°F–100°F
   - C. 100°F–140°F
   - D. 120°F–170°F

10. Atoms are composed of protons (positive charge), neutrons (no charge), and electrons (negative charge). Because an atom has an equal number of protons and electrons, it has a total charge of zero.

    What would happen if an atom lost an electron?

    - A. Its charge would become positive.
    - B. Its charge would become negative.
    - C. Its charge would remain neutral.
    - D. Its neutrons would gain a positive charge.

11. Weathering is the breaking down of rock by rain, frost, wind, and other elements. No transport is involved in weathering. The weathered rock remains in place. Weathering can be physical, involving abrasion—the wearing away of a surface—or changes in temperature; it can be chemical, involving chemical reactions; or it can be organic, involving the action of living things.

    Which of the following is an example of physical weathering?

    - A. the cracking of granite from the expansion of freezing water
    - B. the breakdown of calcite by reaction with acids in fertilizer
    - C. the transport of sand by the wind
    - D. the breakdown of crumbling rock in the soil by burrowing worms

12. When removed from the body, large organs live only a few hours or days under cold conditions. Therefore, organ transplants must be performed quickly. Many organs go to waste because the organ cannot be transported to an appropriate patient in the short time available. Unfortunately, it is not yet possible to freeze large organs to preserve them for a longer period. That's because they contain many different types of cells, all of which react differently to freezing. Some cells are even destroyed by the ice crystals that form during freezing.

    Which of the following studies is most likely to yield information that might help solve the specific problem of freezing whole organs for transplant?

    - A. how the time it takes to locate patients who need organs can be decreased
    - B. how the time it takes to transport organs to their destinations can be decreased
    - C. how special fluids keep insects alive during subfreezing weather
    - D. how radioactive isotopes can be used to diagnose the condition of donated organs

13. Most animals have bodies that exhibit either bilateral symmetry or radial symmetry. If you drew a straight line down the middle of an animal exhibiting bilateral symmetry, the two sides would be mirror images of one another. Such animals have a front end and a rear end. On the other hand, an animal exhibiting radial symmetry has a body consisting of similar parts arranged around a center.

    Which animal below displays a radially symmetrical body plan?

    - A. salt marsh greenhead fly

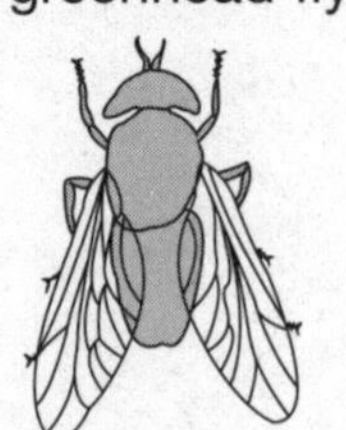

    - B. sea star

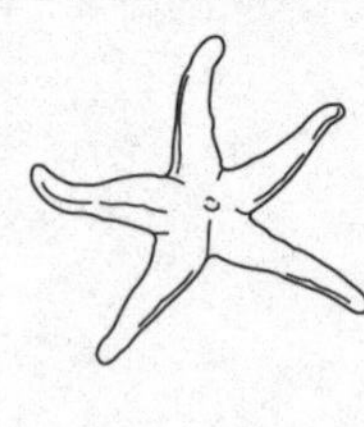

    - C. dogfish

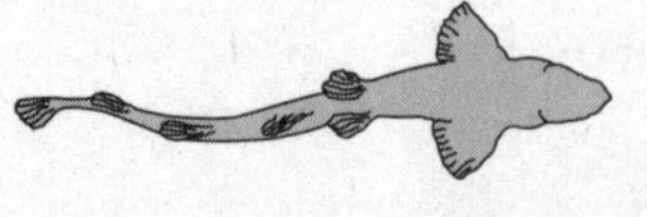

    - D. horseshoe crab

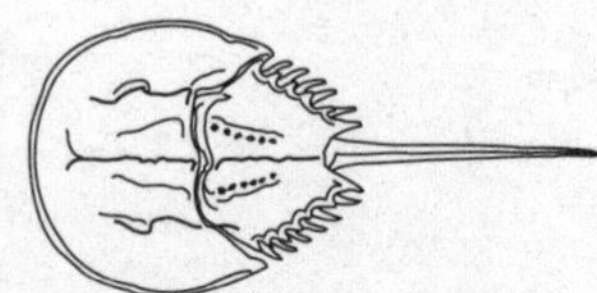

14. Hydrogen peroxide molecules are composed of two hydrogen atoms and two oxygen atoms. Water is also composed of hydrogen and oxygen, but water has one fewer oxygen atom than hydrogen peroxide does. Which of the following statements best describes the chemical reaction shown in the equation below?

$$2H_2O_2 \rightarrow 2H_2O + O_2$$

- A. Hydrogen peroxide is being made out of water and air.
- B. Hydrogen peroxide is decomposing into pure water.
- C. Hydrogen peroxide is decomposing into water and oxygen.
- D. Water and oxygen are combining to make hydrogen peroxide.

Question 15 refers to the following chart.

Melting and Boiling Points

Element	Melting Point, °F	Boiling Point, °F
Mercury	−38	675
Bromine	19	138
Iron	2,795	5,184
Carbon	6,420	8,720
Gold	1,945	5,379

15. Which of the following statements is supported by the information in the chart?

- A. Mercury and bromine are liquids at room temperature.
- B. Iron has a higher melting point than carbon.
- C. Iron has a higher boiling point than gold.
- D. Mercury, bromine, iron, carbon, and gold are all metals.

16. In 1969, the U.S. Surgeon General announced that infectious bacterial diseases would soon become a thing of the past because antibiotic drugs had become so effective against them. However, since that time, strains of disease-causing bacteria that are resistant to antibiotics have evolved. Some types of pneumonia and gastrointestinal infections are now untreatable by antibiotics. About 17 million people worldwide still die annually from infectious diseases.

Which of the following best explains why the U.S. Surgeon General's prediction was wrong?

- A. Antibiotic drugs are not effective against most disease-causing bacteria.
- B. Infectious diseases are also caused by viruses and parasites.
- C. Infectious diseases have remained a problem outside the United States.
- D. Bacteria quickly evolved resistance to antibiotic drugs.

17. A student did an experiment to see how far a ball would roll on different surfaces. He made five different ramps, each with a different surface: a plain pine board, a painted board, a board covered with sandpaper, a board covered with artificial turf, and a board covered with shag carpet. He set up his experiment on a smooth, level floor. To make the ramps, he raised one end of each board with a book. He collected four copies of the science textbook his class was using and set up four of the ramps with these books. He couldn't find a fifth copy of the book, so he used a thinner science study guide to set up the fifth ramp. He rolled a tennis ball down each ramp and measured how far the ball traveled each time. Then he compiled his data and drew conclusions.

Why was the student's experiment flawed?

- A. The student should have used a ball with a smooth surface rather than a tennis ball.
- B. The student should have used books of the same height for all of the ramps.
- C. The student should not have used sandpaper as one of the surfaces.
- D. For a control, the student should have rolled the ball across a piece of wood that was level.

Question 18 refers to the following paragraph and diagram.

Herbivores are animals that eat only plants; carnivores are animals that eat animals. Typical herbivore and carnivore teeth patterns are shown below.

Typical Teeth Patterns in Carnivores and Herbivores

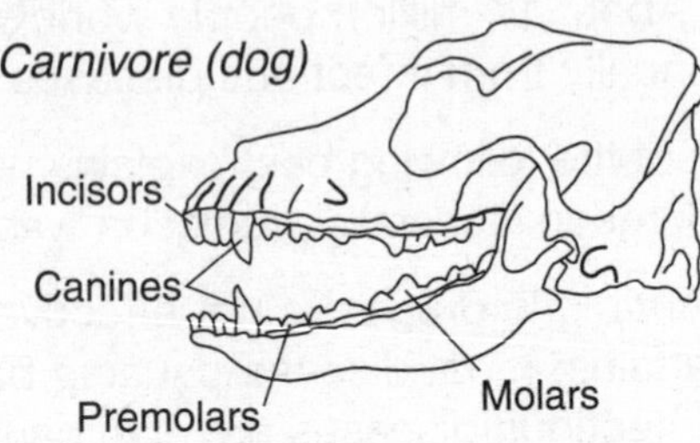

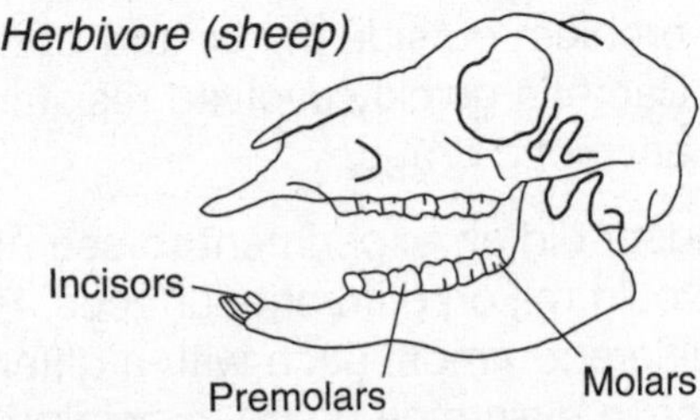

18. What is the most notable difference between the dog's teeth and the sheep's teeth?
   - A. The dog has fewer teeth than the sheep does.
   - B. The dog has molars and the sheep does not.
   - C. The dog has incisors and the sheep does not.
   - D. The dog has canines and the sheep does not.

Question 19 refers to the following chart.

The Five Largest Asteroids

Name	Average distance from sun (Earth = 1)	Time to orbit sun
Ceres	2.77	4.6 years
Pallas	2.77	4.6 years
Vesta	2.36	3.6 years
Hygeia	3.13	5.5 years
Interamnia	3.06	5.4 years

19. Which of the following statements is supported by the information in the chart?
   - A. Pallas is farther away from the sun than Hygeia is.
   - B. Of the five largest asteroids, Vesta has the longest orbital period.
   - C. The five largest asteroids are all farther from the sun than Earth is.
   - D. Of the five largest asteroids, only Interamnia takes more than five years to orbit the sun.

20. The American lobster, *Homerus americanus,* is typically bluish-green to brown in coloration. However, a rare genetic mutation, estimated to occur in 1 in 2 million lobsters, can result in a bright blue-colored shell. In 2011, 220 million pounds of lobsters, typically weighing 1–9 pounds each, were caught; two blue lobsters were reported in that time.

   In 2011, the experimental probability of catching a blue lobster was _______ the estimated probability of a lobster having the blue mutation.

   - A. greater than
   - B. approximately the same as
   - C. less than
   - D. dependent upon

Question 21 is based on the following diagram.

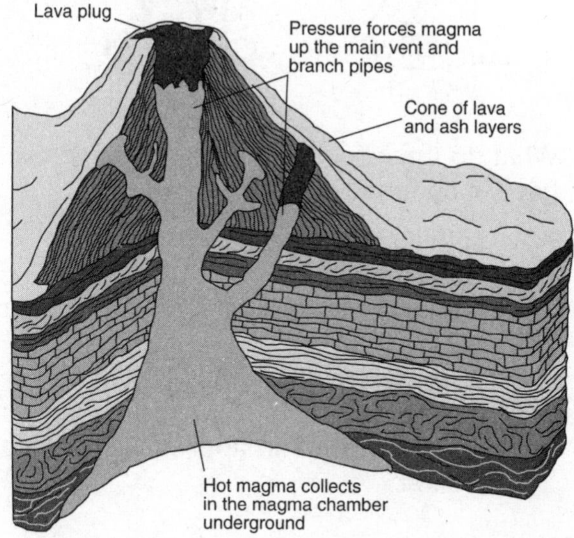

Structure of a Volcano
Lava plug
Pressure forces magma up the main vent and branch pipes
Cone of lava and ash layers
Hot magma collects in the magma chamber underground

21. Based on the diagram, what causes a volcano to erupt?

   - A. Pressure builds up inside the magma chamber and vent.
   - B. Magma flows down toward the underground chamber.
   - C. The lava plug at the top of the main vent wears away.
   - D. The lava plug at the top of the main vent collapses inward.

22. In a chemical reaction, the atoms of the reactants are rearranged to form products with different chemical and physical properties. A catalyst is a substance that speeds the rate at which a chemical reaction takes place. The catalyst itself is unchanged at the end of the reaction. In which of the following reactions is a catalyst at work?

   - A. when an acid is neutralized, as when hydrochloric acid is added to sodium hydroxide yielding sodium chloride and water
   - B. when food is digested, as when an enzyme in saliva called ptyalin breaks down starch into sugars without itself changing
   - C. when copper is oxidized by combining with nitric acid to yield copper nitrate, nitrogen dioxide, and water
   - D. when baking soda is heated, causing the sodium bicarbonate to break down, yielding carbon dioxide gas as a byproduct

23. For five years, researchers at the University of Wisconsin Medical School ran an experiment in which they evaluated the hearing of 3,753 people between the ages of 48 and 92. Of the group, 46 percent were nonsmokers, 30.3 percent were former smokers, and 14.7 percent still smoked. The scientists found that smokers were nearly 1.7 times as likely as nonsmokers to suffer hearing loss. The study suggests that age-related hearing loss might be preventable.

   Which of the following statements is most likely to have been the researchers' hypothesis?

   - A. Smoking has been shown to harm health in many different ways.
   - B. People can reduce their chances of developing age-related hearing loss by not smoking.
   - C. The University of Wisconsin study group consisted of 3,753 people between the ages of 48 and 92.
   - D. Smokers were nearly 1.7 times as likely as nonsmokers to suffer hearing loss.

Question 24 refers to the following graphs.

Elements in Humans and Bacteria

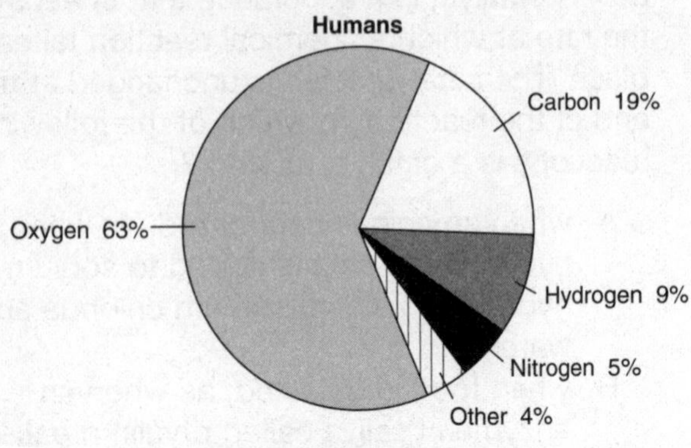

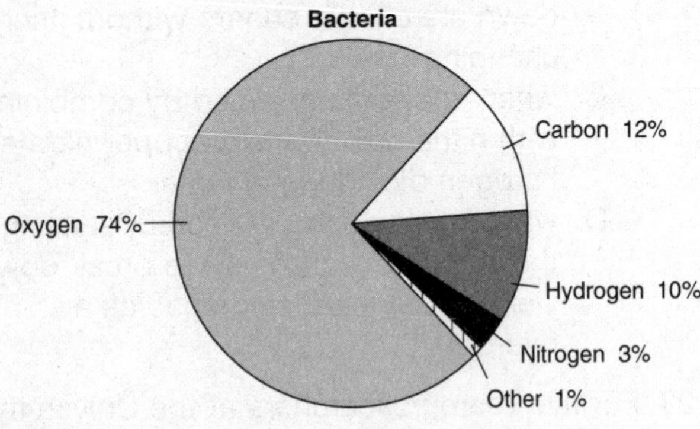

24. What is one of the main differences between the composition of humans and that of bacteria?

- A. Humans contain elements other than oxygen, carbon, nitrogen, and hydrogen and bacteria do not.
- B. Humans contain a higher percentage of oxygen than bacteria do.
- C. Humans contain a higher percentage of hydrogen than bacteria do.
- D. Humans contain a higher percentage of carbon than bacteria do.

Question 25 refers to the following diagrams.

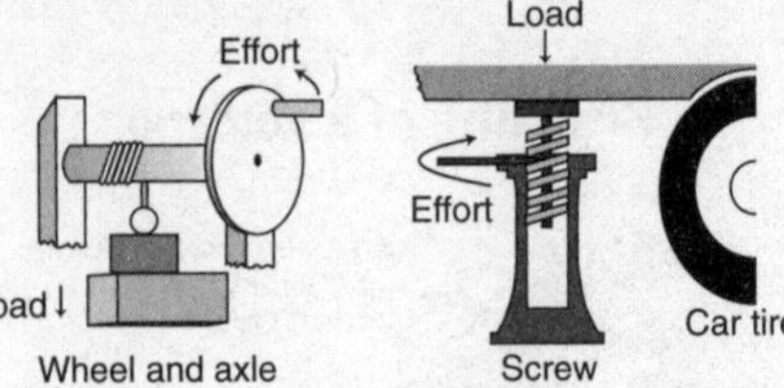

25. What do the wheel and axle and the screw have in common?

- A. Both increase the effort needed to move a load.
- B. Both involve effort applied with circular motion.
- C. Both involve effort applied with horizontal motion.
- D. Both involve effort applied with vertical motion.

---

26. During various periods in Earth's history, average global temperatures have dropped, resulting in ice ages. During an ice age, glaciers cover large regions of Earth. Scientists disagree about what causes ice ages. One hypothesis suggests that there have been long-term changes in Earth's orbit, causing the planet to periodically move farther from the sun. Another view proposes that a periodic increase in volcanic activity increases the dust in the atmosphere, blocking the sun's rays. Still another hypothesis suggests that changes in Earth's own radiant energy cause ice ages. And finally, other scientists propose that changes in the direction of ocean currents cause ice ages.

Which of the following statements is a fact and NOT an opinion or hypothesis?

- A. During an ice age, temperatures drop and ice covers vast areas of Earth.
- B. Changes in Earth's orbit cause temperature fluctuations and ice ages.
- C. Large amounts of volcanic dust blocking the sun's energy cause ice ages.
- D. Changes in Earth's own radiant energy cause ice ages.

Question 27 refers to the following diagram.

Ether (C_2H_6O)

```
    H     H
    |     |
H - C - O - C - H
    |     |
    H     H
```

Ethanol (C_2H_5OH)

```
    H   H
    |   |
H - C - C - OH
    |   |
    H   H
```

Key

C = Carbon

H = Hydrogen

O = Oxygen

27. What is the main difference between the hydrocarbons ether and ethanol?

- A. Ether has carbon, hydrogen, and oxygen atoms, and ethanol has only carbon and hydrogen atoms.
- B. Ether has three carbon atoms and ethanol has two carbon atoms.
- C. Ether has one oxygen atom and ethanol has two oxygen atoms.
- D. The arrangement of the carbon, hydrogen, and oxygen atoms in the two hydrocarbons is different.

---

28. The four types of processes that create minerals in Earth's crust are called *magmatic*, *hydrothermal*, *metamorphic*, and *surficial*. Magmatic processes involve the heating and cooling of magma deep inside the Earth's mantle to form crystals. Hydrothermal processes are caused by the movement of water within Earth's crust. Metamorphic processes involve combinations of heat, pressure, time, water, and various solutions to change existing mineral deposits and form new ones. Surficial processes are physical processes that affect rock at Earth's surface or in the loose material—soil and dust—that covers Earth's crust.

Fill in the blanks. Wind eroding away the softer components of sandstone is an example of a _________ process, while the movement of seawater through fractured rock underground is an example of a _________ process.

- A. magmatic; surficial
- B. hydrothermal; metamorphic
- C. surficial; hydrothermal
- D. metamorphic; hydrothermal

29. Earth's atmosphere has several distinct layers. The layer closest to Earth's surface, called the troposphere, is the densest. Most familiar weather phenomena, such as rain clouds and thunderstorms, occur exclusively in the troposphere. The layer above the troposphere is called the stratosphere. Blue jets, a type of upper-atmosphere lightning not typically seen from Earth's surface, occur in the stratosphere, generally several miles directly above a thunderstorm discharging ordinary lightning. However, phenomena occurring far above the stratosphere, such as meteor showers and auroras, may be visible from Earth's surface without a telescope.

Which of the following phenomena can occur in either the troposphere or the stratosphere?

- A. lightning
- B. meteor showers
- C. rain clouds
- D. blue jets

30. Brock's physics teacher has assigned everyone in his class the task of conducting an experiment. To write up their experiments, everyone must use the outline provided below.

Experiment Outline
Step 1. Formulate a question about a phenomenon.
Step 2. Form a hypothesis.
Step 3. Test the hypothesis through an experiment.
Step 4. Draw a conclusion.

The following choices represent the steps that Brock took, but they are not listed in order. Which one represents "Step 3. Test the hypothesis through an experiment"?

- A. Brock placed wooden cubes that weighed 1 cc, 10 cc, and 100 cc in water. He observed their buoyancy. Then he placed iron cubes of 1 cc, 10 cc, and 100 cc in water and observed their buoyancy.
- B. Brock said, "Since all the wooden cubes floated and all the iron cubes sank, it must be that size does not affect the buoyancy of an object in water."
- C. Brock asked, "Does size affect the buoyancy of an object in water?"
- D. Brock said, "For an object made of a given material, I predict that increasing the size of the object won't affect its buoyancy in water."

31. In 1993, after years of fluctuating water levels in their reservoir, the residents of Weyland County built a dam at one end of the reservoir to regulate and stabilize the water levels. Which point on the graph below most likely represents 1993?

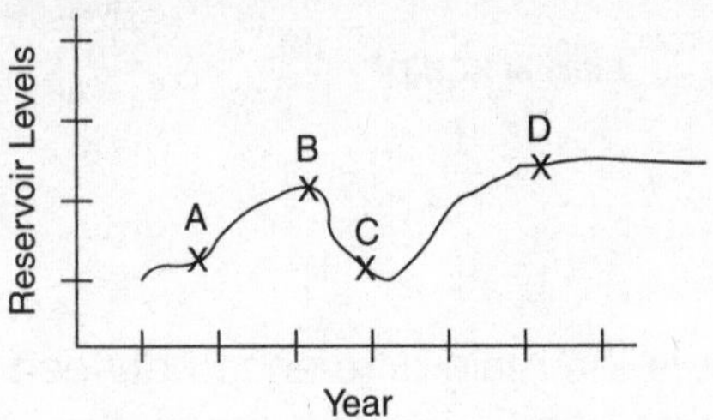

- A. A
- B. B
- C. C
- D. D

32. In the early 20th century, J. J. Thomson discovered the electron and proposed a theory of atomic structure that was dubbed the "plum pudding" model. At the time, plum pudding was a popular dessert and consisted of plum slices dispersed through creamy custard. Thomson suggested that the structure of an atom was similar to the structure of a plum pudding. That is, he believed that an atom was composed of individual electrons surrounded by a uniform cloud of positive charge. However, Ernest Rutherford later disproved this model. Rutherford proposed that atoms were composed of a dense, charged nucleus and electrons orbiting around this nucleus.

The subatomic particle that the plum in Thomson's model corresponds to is a(n)

- A. positron
- B. electron
- C. neutron
- D. proton

33. One property of a gas is that its molecules spread out to fill their container. Which of the following best illustrates this property of gases?

- A. A teacher's perfume can be detected at the back of the classroom.
- B. Rain puddles evaporate more quickly when the sun comes out.
- C. Water is produced when hydrogen gas is burned in oxygen gas.
- D. Liquid oxygen is denser than gaseous oxygen.

34. Photosynthesis is the process by which living plants take in carbon dioxide and water and turn those into nutrients and energy that the plant can use. The chemical equation for photosynthesis is:

$$6CO_2 + 6H_2O \rightarrow C_6H_{12}O_6 + 6O_2$$

Based on this equation, which of the following must be true?

- A. Plants do not need oxygen to survive.
- B. Oxygen is one of the products of photosynthesis.
- C. Plants produce oxygen out of pure energy.
- D. Photosynthesis destroys energy.

35. Air enters the human lungs through the left and right *bronchi*, which divide into smaller airways called *bronchioles*. The bronchioles end in sacs called *alveoli*, which are surrounded by tiny blood vessels called *capillaries*. Deoxygenated blood is pumped by the heart from the various parts of the body to the lungs. In the lungs, the blood takes on oxygen. This happens when oxygen moves from air in the alveoli to the blood in the surrounding capillaries. Oxygenated blood then leaves the lungs through the pulmonary veins and flows back to the various body parts.

The movement of oxygen from the alveoli into the surrounding capillaries is called *diffusion*. Which two bodily systems are involved in diffusion?

- A. urinary and respiratory
- B. circulatory and endocrine
- C. circulatory and respiratory
- D. respiratory and nervous

36. The Grand Canyon is one of the largest geological phenomena in the world. It is approximately 280 miles long and has a maximum depth of 6,000 feet. It was formed over the course of millions of years by the Colorado River. The movement of the river's water eroded, or carried away, layer after layer of rock to form the canyon. The walls of the canyon are composed of distinct rock layers and each layer corresponds to a different time period.

A geologist collects a rock sample from each layer of the canyon. What hypothesis could best be tested using the rock samples?

- A. Rock samples obtained from the bottom are older than rock samples obtained from the top.
- B. Flooding of the Colorado River is frequently due to heavy rainstorms.
- C. Rock layers tend to erode at the same rate no matter where in the world they are located.
- D. Winds have less force at the bottom of the Grand Canyon than at the top.

37. Hurricanes are circular storms with high wind speeds. These storms tend to form near the equator. The *Coriolis effect* causes hurricanes to rotate counterclockwise in the northern hemisphere and clockwise in the southern hemisphere. Initially, east-to-west trade winds tend to blow hurricanes westward. The Coriolis effect also causes hurricanes to move north or south toward one of the poles. When a hurricane moving toward one of the poles encounters the mid-latitude westerly winds, a hurricane turns eastward.

Global Wind Patterns

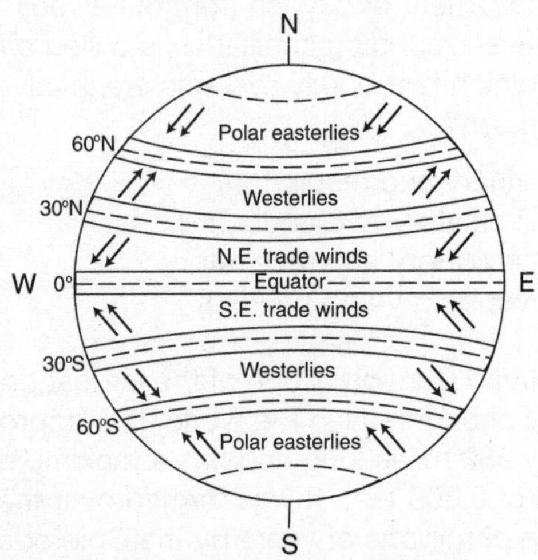

Which of the following most accurately describes the probable rotation and path of a hurricane in the northern hemisphere?

- A. It would rotate counterclockwise and move westward, then southward, and finally eastward.
- B. It would rotate clockwise and move eastward, then northward, and finally westward.
- C. It would rotate counterclockwise and move eastward, then northward, and finally westward.
- D. It would rotate counterclockwise and move westward, then northward, and finally eastward.

38. Newton's Law of Gravitation states that the force (represented by *F*) of gravitation (or attraction) between two objects is represented by the following equation:

$$F_g = \frac{Gm_1m_2}{r^2}$$

The equation shows that the force of gravitation is directly proportional to the product of the objects' masses (where each mass is represented by *m*) but inversely proportional to the square of the distance between them (where the distance between them is represented by *r*).

Consider two objects that both have the same mass. If the distance between these objects is increased, what will happen to the force of gravitation between them?

- A. The force will be increased.
- B. The force will be reduced.
- C. The force will not change.
- D. The force will change, but in a way that cannot be predicted.

39. Frogs living in temperate climates reproduce in the spring and summer months, when food is plentiful. They are often exposed to freezing temperatures during the winter. Frogs are amphibians—that is, creatures that live part of their lives on land and part of their lives in water.

Given this information, which of the following must be true?

- A. Frogs maintain a stable body temperature year-round, even in the winter.
- B. Frogs exposed to freezing temperatures during the winter invariably die.
- C. Frogs' bodies have a way to prevent their cells from freezing in cold temperatures.
- D. Frogs can find sufficient food in the winter to reproduce even in freezing temperatures.

40. In a healthy person, blood sugar levels in the bloodstream do not exceed a tightly controlled range. This metabolic control is called *homeostasis*. In a person with diabetes mellitus, homeostasis is interrupted, and blood sugar levels are higher than in a healthy individual. Diabetes mellitus can have a number of different causes. However, the most direct reason for high blood sugar is either the inability of the pancreas to produce sufficient insulin, or the inability of cells in the body tissues to respond to whatever insulin is produced.

    Which of the following might be an appropriate treatment for a person with diabetes mellitus?

    - A. bed rest
    - B. blood transfusions
    - C. insulin injections
    - D. medication to restore calcium homeostasis

41. The human liver performs a number of functions including protein synthesis and storage, turning carbohydrates into energy, and removing toxins from the body. The liver rids itself of toxins by producing bile, whose yellow color comes from a substance called *bilirubin*.

    Based on this information, which of the following symptoms is a primary indication of liver disease?

    - A. pain in the extremities due to neurological problems
    - B. hearing loss due to atherosclerosis
    - C. loss of night vision caused by vitamin A deficiency
    - D. jaundice, a yellow discoloration of the skin due to a systemic buildup of bilirubin

42. An old growth forest is a climax community and tends to be a fairly stable ecosystem. When the trees in an old growth forest burn or are cut down, they are replaced by a succession of other species, and the food web changes dramatically. Eventually, the forest returns to its climax state, but this process can take hundreds of years.

    Imagine a mature Adirondack hemlock forest in New York State shortly after all the trees were cut down sometime in the 19th century. Which of the following changes probably took place?

    - A. Shade-loving animal species, such as the red-backed salamander, were replaced by sun-loving species such as the northern black racer.
    - B. Sun-loving species, such as the northern black racer, were replaced by shade-loving species, such as the red-backed salamander.
    - C. The forest regenerated within a decade, and the climax community present before the forest was cut down became reestablished.
    - D. The forest was permanently replaced by grasslands.

43. The life cycle of many plants, including spore-producing plants such as ferns, takes place in two generations that alternate: the *gametophyte* generation and the *sporophyte* generation. In ferns, the gametophyte is a very small, heart-shaped structure. During the gametophyte generation, sex cells are produced, two of which fuse to produce a zygote. The zygote grows into the sporophyte. In ferns, the sporophyte is the familiar green plant with leaves, stems, and roots. During the sporophyte generation, gametes, which grow into the gametophyte, are produced.

Which of the following conclusions is supported by this information?

- A. Ferns are the only plants that have different forms in alternating generations.
- B. Most people would not recognize the gametophyte generation of a fern.
- C. Some animal life cycles consist of alternating generations with different forms.
- D. All plants that reproduce sexually have leaves, stems, roots, and flowers.

44. Light waves travel in a straight line, but when they strike most surfaces, they bounce off; this is known as reflection. When light is reflected off a smooth surface like a mirror, the incoming rays, called the incident rays, hit the surface at the same angle as the reflected rays bounce off it.

The Reflection of Light

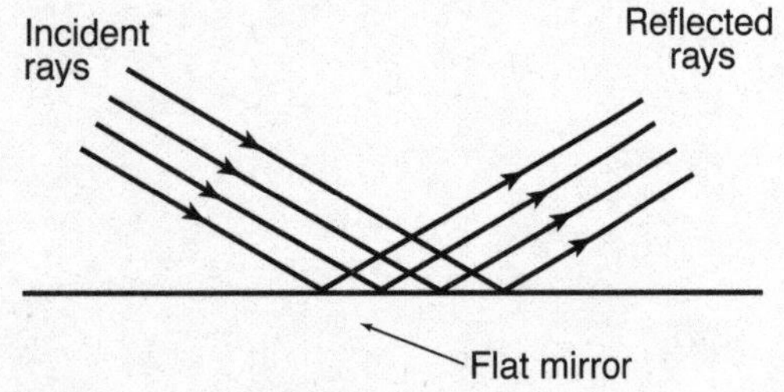

In the preceding diagram, all of the reflected light rays are parallel. Under which of the following circumstances would the reflected light rays travel in many different directions?

- A. if the source of light were distant
- B. if the surface were irregular or rough
- C. if the surface were perfectly flat
- D. if the incident rays were parallel

45. A student observes that a group of wildflowers located in the sunniest area of a field blooms earlier than other flowers in the same field, and hypothesizes that sunlight directly contributes to timing of the bloom cycle. How could this idea best be tested?

- A. Plant different varieties of flowers in the field and see which flower blooms first.
- B. Plant different varieties of flowers indoors in identical pots and outdoors in the field, and see which flower blooms first.
- C. Plant one type of flower indoors in identical pots and outdoors in the field, and see when each flower blooms.
- D. Plant one type of flower in identical pots, expose each pot to a different amount of sunlight, and see when each flower blooms.

Question 46 refers to the following diagram.

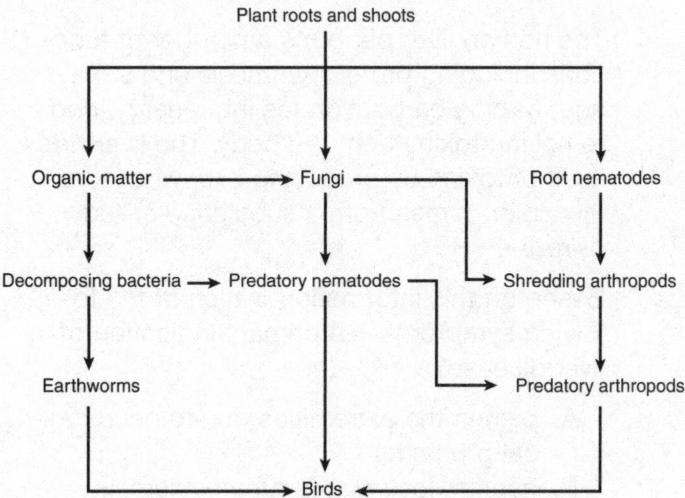

46. In the food web diagram above, the arrows point toward the organism that consumes the organism at the arrows' origin. Which of the following is most likely to occur first if the predatory nematode population decreases?

- A. Birds will no longer have a source of food.
- B. The amount of organic matter in the soil will increase.
- C. Shredding arthropods will have less competition for food.
- D. Decomposing bacteria will have more sources of food available.

Questions 47 through 50 refer to following paragraphs.

Dr. Morgan, a 20th century geneticist, breeds thousands of fruit flies and notices that one fruit fly has white eyes, even though fruit flies usually have red eyes. He investigates this phenomenon with two experiments.

Experiment I

Dr. Morgan breeds the white-eyed fruit fly with a red-eyed fruit fly in a vial filled with a food source. He removes them from the vial once eggs have been laid. Once the offspring are fully mature, he briefly renders them unconscious with ethanol and documents the sex and eye color of the new generation. He discovers that all offspring have red eyes.

Experiment 2

He conducts a second experiment, this time breeding a red-eyed male and female offspring from experiment 1 using the same procedure. He discovers that the white-eyed trait reappears, though only the males have white eyes.

Dr. Morgan replicates the experiment numerous times, each time getting the same results.

47. The independent variable in an experiment is the factor that is changed to determine its effect on other factors. What was the independent variable in experiment 1?
   - A. the sex of the adult fruit flies
   - B. the eye color of adult fruit flies
   - C. the sex of the offspring
   - D. the eye color of the offspring

48. Which the following is most likely the reason that Dr. Morgan used ethanol in experiments 1 and 2?
   - A. It is easier to observe the traits of unconscious fruit flies.
   - B. Ethanol changes the eye color of fruit flies.
   - C. Fruit flies require ethanol in order to mature into adults.
   - D. Fruit flies use ethanol as a source of food.

49. Which of the following best states the conclusions of experiments 1 and 2?
   - A. The trait for white eyes must be a mutation.
   - B. The eye color of offspring is random.
   - C. White-eyed fruit flies are inferior to red-eyed fruit flies.
   - D. The trait for white eyes is a recessive gene.

50. Suppose Dr. Morgan notices after numerous trials that white-eyed females can only be produced after breeding white-eyed males with red-eyed females from the second generation. Does Dr. Morgan have reliable evidence to support the hypothesis that the white-eyed gene is a sex-linked trait?
   - A. Yes, because his training as an embryologist makes him an expert on fruit fly genetics.
   - B. Yes, because his results were replicated and can be verified using a Punnett square.
   - C. No, because he didn't publish his findings in a respected journal.
   - D. No, because a Punnett square wouldn't predict white-eyed females of a sex-linked trait.

STOP. You have completed the Science Test.

Language Arts: Reading Practice Test Answers and Explanations

1. **A. Jumping from a roof before an audience** Cleo loves attention. Her bet that she can swing upside down from an oak tree would have resulted in her either winning her sisters' money or gaining attention because she got hurt. Jumping from a rooftop would provide Cleo with attention whether it went well or poorly.
2. **D. Pa's** In this paragraph, the author describes Pa's love for Cleo and why she has so much influence over him.
3. **C. Cleo says that she does not want a kiss but wants a copper instead.** The first paragraph begins with Pa giving each of the girls a copper. It then explains that, at some point in the past, Cleo urged her father to give them coppers instead of kisses for doing chores.
4. **C. Serena felt that she had no choice but to give Cleo her copper to stop Cleo from doing something unsafe.** Serena does not want to give Cleo her copper; rather, Cleo is "compelling unnecessary sacrifice." Cleo does so by threatening to do something dangerous.
5. **D. Pa could not really afford to give Cleo and her sisters money.** The quote explains that Pa did not really have enough money to give some to Cleo and her sisters for doing chores. The phrase "dig deep" suggests that it was a sacrifice for him to do without that money, although he wanted to be generous. The language in the quote is figurative rather than literal, so choice (B) is incorrect.
6. **B. Cleo's boldness and her family's love for her sometimes make them feel powerless to resist her.** This passage is chiefly concerned with Cleo's character, which is bold and daring, and with the fact that her family members clearly love her. Both in the case of Pa giving the girls coppers and in the case of the sisters giving theirs to Cleo, Cleo's family members sometimes feel that they cannot refuse her.
7. **A. A coin** You can infer that a "copper" is money from this quote: "Four coppers a day, six days a week was half a day's pay."
8. **D. Short-term profitability** The last sentence of paragraph 2 states that "these companies were too focused on their short-term profitability."
9. **A. Getting your product right the first time is more profitable than fixing mistakes later.** The correct answer comes from the first sentence of paragraph 4: "In the long run, the Detroit automakers learned the hard way that getting your product right the first time is less costly and more profitable than retrenching to play catch-up."
10. **C. They wanted to build quality cars with few repair problems.** The U.S. automakers produced cars with "far more problems than their foreign equivalents." This suggests that quality was a priority for the foreign automakers but not for domestic automakers looking to "keep their costs low and profits high."
11. **C. Emphasize U.S. automakers' preoccupation with keeping costs low and profits high in the short term, at the expense of their long-term outlook.** "Bean counter" is a derogatory term for an accountant or manager who is excessively concerned with keeping expenses low. The author uses this term to underscore the idea that the U.S. automakers failed to consider the "bigger picture"—that is, failed to consider their long-term outlook.
12. **A. Critical** The authors speak negatively of the cars produced by U.S. automakers in the 1970s and 1980s and include comments such as "to add insult to injury" and "weren't considering the bigger picture."
13. **A. U.S. automakers** The last paragraph states that U.S. automakers eventually "got their act together in the 1990s and have stopped the erosion of market share."
14. **D. is hoping her mother won't hear her asking for money.** The narrator misinterprets Marjie's actions. She thinks Marjie is asking for money for herself, not her mother. She therefore interprets Marjie's actions as trying to hide her request from her mother.
15. **C. Jennie is perplexed when the narrator blames Marjie.** When the narrator explains that she thought Marjie wanted the money for herself, "Jennie looked doubtful."
16. **B. Discuss it defensively** Jennie meets with the narrator directly to try to explain what happened and express concern. However, she misunderstands the narrator's explanation, apologizes for trying to borrow money, and reacts defensively when it is suggested that her daughter would ask for money on her own. Jennie would likely have this same defensive reaction if criticized by a boss.
17. **A. the narrator's thoughts.** The passage is written with a first person point of view from the narrator's perspective. This allows the reader access to the thoughts of the narrator as well as a description of the action that the narrator sees.
18. **C. They know each other but are not close.** The narrator is staying with Jennie and her family and obviously knows them, yet there is a formal tone to Jennie's explanation about borrowing money, and the narrator is unable to explain how she misunderstood Marjie and is left "floundering." Those aspects of their relationship help you infer they are not on close, intimate terms.
19. **C. Uncomfortable** Jennie feels she has to explain why she was going to borrow money from the narrator, and the narrator not only misinterprets Marjie's actions but has a difficult time explaining to Jennie "the whole of Marjie's act." Jennie appears to doubt her and states her children would never ask for money, leaving the narrator "floundering a bit." The entire situation ends with the narrator (and perhaps even the reader) feeling uncomfortable over the situation.

20. **C. Proud** Jennie's reaction in the last exchange with the narrator makes clear that she is proud and wants others to think well of her and her family.

21. **C. Shied away from** The narrator decides not to explain why she thought Marjie wanted the money for herself. That's because, as she says, "It isn't easy to give evidence against a child of five." Tattling on Marjie was something she shied away from, or "funked."

22. **C. There may be more people in poverty than the Census Bureau's official estimate suggests.** Overall, the passage conveys this main point. Choices (A) and (B) are details rather than main ideas, and choice (D) is not supported by the passage.

23. **C. The bar graph supports the claim that a different way to measure poverty would produce a different estimate of the rate of poverty.** The bar graph shows that the SPM would produce different estimates of how many people are poor, a claim that the author makes in paragraph 4.

24. **C. Higher rents can cause people to have less money for food.** Paragraph 3 explains that "higher rents may leave individuals with less money for food." Higher rents are the cause, and less money for food is the effect. Choices (B) and (D) are too extreme. Choice (A) distorts the passage: the poverty thresholds measure who is poor—they don't cause people to be poor.

25. **A. people over 65; people under 18** Use the graph to answer this question. The lighter gray bars represent the estimates of poverty using the SPM. That bar is higher than the dark gray bar for people over 65 and lower than the dark gray bar for people under 18.

26. **B. The student has overlooked the fact that other factors might impact how much money local governments receive from the federal government.** The student has read in the passage that government spending on poverty is affected by the estimated rate of poverty. But even if the estimated rate of poverty were higher, that does not necessarily mean that government (at any level) would automatically spend more on poverty. After all, many factors go into governmental decision-making.

27. **D. how best to spend public money.** Both writers discuss their thoughts about the best way to use funds to improve Glenwood.

28. **C. Improving them is a good use of funds right now.** While both writers agree that the parks are not in good repair, they disagree over whether improving them is the best way to use resources at the present time.

29. **D. Several restaurants downtown have survived the bad economy.** The business owner introduces her claim that the business district can attract new businesses in the second paragraph of the second passage. Choice (D) is one of the details used in that paragraph to support her claim.

30. **B. Investing in our community is important for the future of Glenwood.** Both writers are arguing that public resources should be invested in improving the community to help ensure its prosperity in the long term.

31. **B. Glenwood initially invested in building parks but then did not spend enough to maintain them.** You know from the passage that Glenwood has more than one public park, with paths, picnic areas, and shelters. So it must be the case that, at some point, Glenwood invested money to build these spaces. You also know that these spaces are not well maintained, so Glenwood must not have invested in their upkeep.

32. **C. To underscore the serious consequences his mother's death will have on the young Prince's future** The Emperor's younger son must be sent away from the palace. Now that his mother is no longer alive, the child's ties to the imperial court will weaken, and he will lose the Emperor's protection.

33. **B. News of the death of the Emperor's favorite concubine** The phrase "sad tidings" indicates that the Emperor has received a report from his messenger that his favorite concubine has died.

34. **D. Ironic** Irony is the name given to a state of affairs that is contrary to what one would expect. The meaning of the quoted proverb is that once someone has died (as the young Prince's mother has just done), that person is remembered with more affection than she received during her lifetime. The last paragraph explains that the people who disliked and resented the concubine during her lifetime began to like her after her death, and that is contrary to what one would expect.

35. **D. Public opinion is that the Emperor's older son, born to a woman with greater influence than the younger Prince's mother, should be the Emperor's heir.** The third paragraph states that an older Prince has a mother from a more influential family, and the public believes this Prince should be favored. In paragraph 4, the younger Prince is given a ceremony almost as lavish as one given to the older Prince, and the public disapproves.

36. **D. The family has experienced many disappointments and tragedies.** While all of the other answer choices are supported by pieces of text, none of them is a central idea of the passage. Choice (D) is supported by Mama's discussion of the house she once wanted in Morgan Park, the loss of the baby Claude, the frustration and disappointment experienced by Mr. Younger, and the refrain of the word "dreams" throughout the passage.

37. **C. His love for his children helped keep his dreams alive.** Mr. Younger's words explain that his love for his children helped him keep dreaming of a better life: "Seem like God didn't see fit to give the black man nothing but dreams, but He did give us children to make them dreams seem worthwhile." None of the other choices are supported by specific pieces of text.

38. **C. It suggests that the apartment is very run-down, and that the family feels trapped there.** While the family's apartment might actually have rats, the

phrase "rat trap" implies more than just that literal meaning (so choice (D) is incorrect). It suggests that the apartment is run-down and probably not worth the money the family spends on rent. The word "trap" also suggests that the family members themselves feel trapped. Choice (A) is incorrect because nothing suggests that the building attracts criminals. Choice (B) is unsupported by the passage because Ruth and Mama do not insult themselves in this way.

39. **A. The contrast between how hard it has been for the family to improve its situation and how much Mama would still like to try** Mr. Younger never gave up trying to improve his family's situation despite the fact that he got very discouraged about it from time to time. Mama still clings to the dream she and her husband once had of providing their family with a house. The quote ties together Walter Younger's experiences and Mama's current aspirations.

40. **C. It would suggest that Mama is lost in her own powerful memories.** If Mama turned away from Ruth, this scene would seem less like an ordinary conversation between the two women. It would suggest that Mama was so wrapped up in her own memories that she had almost forgotten that she was talking to Ruth.

Language Arts: Reading Practice Test Evaluation Chart

Questions 1–40

Circle the numbers of the questions that you got correct, and then total them in the last column of each row.

Content Area	Question Numbers	Number Correct/Total
Interpreting Informational Text Pages 70–95	8, 9, 10, 12, 13, 22, 24, 25, 31	____ /9
Analyzing Informational Text Pages 96–111	11, 23, 26, 27, 28, 29, 30	____ /7
Reading Literature Pages 112–127	1, 2, 3, 4, 5, 6, 7, 14, 15, 16, 17, 18, 19, 20, 21, 32, 33, 34, 35, 36, 37, 38, 39, 40	____ /24
TOTAL		____ **/40**

If you do not have time to review the entire Reading unit, you may want to review the sections that need the most work.

Language Arts: Writing Practice Test Answers and Explanations

Part I: Language Skills

1. **D. replace <u>hole</u> with <u>whole</u>** A hole is a place that is dug out of the ground; whole means "entire."
2. **D. change <u>add</u> to <u>adding</u>** The verb "add" should end with *-ing* to match "stripping" and "filling." All the verbs in a series should be in the same form.
3. **A. change <u>ceiling meet</u> to <u>ceiling meets</u>** "The ceiling" is a singular subject and requires a singular verb.
4. **C. is** The sentence should be in the present tense because the rest of the paragraph is in the present tense.
5. **C. remove the comma after <u>paint</u>** No comma is needed between the noun "paint" and the modifying phrase that follows it.
6. **A. missed, and go** Choice (A) corrects the comma splice with a logical conjunction.
7. **B. change <u>is</u> to <u>are</u>** The verb "are" agrees with the plural subject "gardens."
8. **B. insert a comma after <u>garden</u>** In a complex sentence, a comma should follow the dependent clause at the beginning of the sentence.
9. **B. insert a period after <u>sponsor</u> and capitalize <u>this</u>** Separating this sentence into two corrects the run-on.
10. **A. Next, choose a site for the garden.** Choice (A) is specific enough to be clear and general enough to cover all the details in the paragraph. It also includes a transition from the preceding paragraph.
11. **B. Start a new paragraph before sentence 3.** The first two sentences are about the benefits of community gardens. Sentence 3 begins a discussion of the steps involved in forming a community garden. Thus, a new paragraph is warranted.
12. **B. change <u>piece</u> to <u>peace</u>** A piece is a part of something; peace is a sense of calm and absence of conflict.
13. **C. replace <u>you're</u> with <u>your</u>** Because the workplace belongs to you, the possessive pronoun "your" is correct.
14. **A. disappear magically once you leave** What happens magically is that the symptoms disappear, not that you leave work. "Magically" should be placed closer to the part of the sentence that it modifies—symptoms disappearing.
15. **C. replace <u>we</u> with <u>you</u>** Because the rest of the passage uses the second-person pronoun "you,"this sentence should as well.
16. **A. change <u>older</u> to <u>older building</u>** A sentence needs both a subject and a verb. Here, the sentence was missing a noun to serve as its subject.
17. **D. the windows** The antecedent for the pronoun "they" was unclear; it did not appear until near the end of the sentence. Replacing "they" with "the windows" makes the meaning clear.
18. **A. delete the comma after <u>gas</u>** The phrase "deadly gas" is essential to the meaning of "carbon monoxide," so this comma is unnecessary.
19. **A. Tourism increases both air pollution and litter, which will** Choice (A) makes clear that tourists cause both pollution and litter.
20. **D. change <u>developer's</u> to <u>developers</u>** The word "developers" is plural—not possessive—so it should not have an apostrophe.
21. **C. remove sentence 7** The flyer focuses on the land on Compton Point. This sentence about other areas in the county is irrelevant and should be deleted.
22. **B. new jobs and the influx of tourism resulting** Choice (B) smoothly combines the two sentences into a single sentence with a compound subject.
23. **D. change <u>road</u> to <u>Road</u>** All parts of a proper noun must be capitalized.
24. **A. change <u>did</u> to <u>will</u>** The demonstration is in the future, so the message will be sent to developers in the future.
25. **C. see** The verb form "see" is required with the subject "you." "Seen" requires the helping verb "have," but the present perfect tense "have seen" is not needed in the sentence, just the simple present.
26. **B. move sentence 3 to follow sentence 1** With sentence 1, sentence 3 catches the reader's attention and gives background information about the topic of the whole article. Sentences 2 and 4 introduce the main idea of the article.
27. **B. has been** The verb needs to agree with the subject "kite flying," which is singular.
28. **D. During a thunderstorm, he flew a kite with** In the original sentence, it sounds as if the thunderstorm had a key attached to it.
29. **B. replace <u>their</u> with <u>there</u>** The word "their" is a possessive meaning "belonging to them." Its homonym, "there," is needed in this sentence.
30. **B. humidity, wind speed, and barometric pressure** Choice (B) combines two sentences that have related details.
31. **A. Bell, the physicist and inventor, used** The phrase "the physicist and inventor" is an appositive describing Bell, so that phrase should be set off with commas.
32. **C. change <u>power, you</u> to <u>power. You</u>** The sentence as written contains a comma splice. Answer choice (C) corrects the comma splice.
33. **C. Some types of trucks, buses, and trains** In the original, there are three items in a series: trucks, buses, and some train engines. So the three things should be separated with commas. But the three things should also display parallel construction: the phrase "some types of" should apply to all three of them.
34. **B. change <u>In both kinds</u> to <u>Both kinds have</u>** The sentence as written is missing a subject. Choice (B) corrects this.
35. **C. change <u>run</u> to <u>runs</u>** The subject of the sentence is singular ("it") and requires a singular verb ("runs").
36. **C. change <u>will move</u> to <u>moves</u>** The clause containing the verb "will move" modifies the main

clause, which is in the present tense ("is used"). Therefore, the modifying phrase should have the present tense as well.

37. **A. change It is to They are** The pronoun refers to "Hybrids" in the previous sentence and should be plural.
38. **C. move sentence 11 to the beginning of the next paragraph** Sentence 11 introduces a new idea which is discussed further in sentences 12 through 15. Thus, sentence 11 should be the topic sentence of the next paragraph.
39. **B. try to convince** "Try and convince" is not correct verb usage. "Try" should be followed by "to."
40. **C. change California and new Jersey to California and New Jersey** "New Jersey" is the name of a state and should be capitalized.
41. **C. change are to is** The subject of the sentence is "learning," which is singular and needs a singular verb.
42. **C. While knees** The sentence as written does not make clear the relationship between its first clause and its second. The writer is drawing a contrast between the frequency of injuries to knees and elbows and the low severity of those injuries.
43. **B. However, head injuries** The writer draws a contrast between head injuries, which can be severe, and the less serious knee and elbow injuries described in the previous sentence. Thus, a contrast word such as "However" is appropriate.
44. **B. split it into two sentences** As written, the sentence is overly long, with three independent clauses. Splitting it into two sentences would solve this problem.
45. **A. change Major Cities to major cities** The phrase "major cities" does not refer to any specific city and so should not be capitalized.
46. **C. The smog has become such a normal part** The phrase "that weather forecasters" later in the sentence refers back to this idea. Inserting the word "such" makes the phrase "that weather forecasters" follow logically.
47. **D. to urge you and all your readers to support** The correct idiom is "urge [someone] to [do something]."
48. **C. Cleaner gas has become a mainstay in many gas stations around the world.** The sentence as written is needlessly wordy. Choice (C) simplifies the original sentence without losing any of its meaning.
49. **C. change Air Resources' Board to Air Resources Board** The name of the board is the California Air Resources Board. In this case, "Resources" is a plural noun and not a possessive, so it does not take an apostrophe.
50. **B. they emit almost five times** The word "almost" should modify how much, so it should be placed before the phrase "five times."
51. **C. move sentence 8 to follow sentence 5** Sentence 8 introduces the idea that some progress has been made. Sentences 6 and 7 expand on that idea, so they should follow sentence 8.

Part II: Essay

Use the **Essay Scoring Guide on** pages 761–762 to evaluate your work.

Language Arts: Writing Practice Test Evaluation Charts

Questions 1–51

Circle the numbers of the questions that you got correct, and then total them in the last column of each row.

Content Area	Question Numbers	Number Correct/Total
Writing Effective Sentences Pages 136–157	2, 6, 9, 14, 32, 33	____ /6
Connecting Ideas Pages 158–169	10, 11, 21, 22, 30, 38, 43, 50	____ /8
Using Grammar Correctly Pages 170–187	3, 4, 7, 25, 26, 27, 35, 41	____ /8
Using Writing Mechanics Pages 188–203	1, 5, 8, 12, 13, 18, 20, 23, 29, 31, 40, 44, 45, 48, 51	____ /15
Polishing Your Writing Pages 230–255	15, 16, 17, 19, 24, 28, 34, 36, 37, 39, 42, 46, 47, 49	____ /14
TOTAL		____ **/51**

My essay score, based on the **Essay Scoring Guide** on pages 761–762, is _____.

If you do not have time to review the entire Writing unit, you may want to review the sections that need the most work.

MATHEMATICS PRACTICE TEST ANSWERS AND EXPLANATIONS

1. **D. $15x^2 - 8xy - 12y^2$** Use FOIL to distribute the terms in the expression:
$(3x)(5x) + (3x)(-6y) + (2y)(5x) + (2y)(-6y) = 15x^2 - 18xy + 10xy - 12y^2 = 15x^2 - 8xy - 12y^2$

2. **E. $\frac{1}{15}$** There are $3 + 5 + 2 = 10$ pieces of fruit in the basket, so the probability of Bob selecting one of the 3 bananas for the first trial is $\frac{3}{10}$. Because he is not putting the banana back, there are now 9 pieces of fruit remaining, 2 of which are bananas, so the probability of selecting a banana again is $\frac{2}{9}$. Therefore, the probability of selecting 2 bananas is $\frac{3}{10} \times \frac{2}{9} = \frac{6}{90} = \frac{1}{15}$.

3. **D. 7** First, factor to find the solutions to this quadratic equation: $x^2 - 4x - 21 = (x + 3)(x - 7)$. Then, set those factors equal to 0 to find the solutions to the quadratic equation: $x + 3 = 0$, $x = -3$ and $x - 7 = 0$, $x = 7$. The two solutions to the equation are –3 and 7. The question asks for the only positive solution, so the answer is 7.

4. **E. 74** Following the order of operations, first simplify anything in parentheses:
$(4 - 18)$ becomes -14.
Next, simplify any terms with exponents:
$5^2 = 25$ and $3^3 = 27$
Now you have:
$3 \times 25 + 2(-14) + 27$.
Next, do multiplication and division in the order in which they appear:
$3 \times 25 = 75$ and $2(-14) = -28$.
Last, add and subtract in the order in which they appear:
$75 + (-28) + 27 = 74$

5. **D. $2x(x + y)$** To simplify the polynomial, factor out any like terms: $2x(x - y + 2y)$. Then combine any like terms together: $2x(x + y)$

6. **D. 66** To find the area of the figure, break it into two distinct shapes, a rectangle and a triangle. The rectangle has dimensions of 7 m and 8 m. Plugging these in to the area formula for a rectangle yields: $A = lw = 8\text{ m} \times 7\text{ m} = 56\text{ m}^2$. The area for a triangle is $A = \frac{1}{2}bh$. In the triangle, the base is $8\text{ m} - 4\text{ m} = 4\text{ m}$ and the height is $12\text{ m} - 7\text{ m} = 5\text{ m}$. Plugging these values into the area formula for a triangle yields: $A = \frac{1}{2} \times b \times h = \frac{1}{2} \times 4\text{ m} \times 5\text{ m} = 10\text{ m}^2$. Lastly, add both of the areas for the combined area of the figure: $56\text{ m}^2 + 10\text{ m}^2 = 66\text{ m}^2$.

7. **B. $4x^2 + 12x + 7$** Combine like terms starting with the variable with the highest exponent, in this case: $x^2 + 3x^2 = 4x^2$. Next, combine the terms that contain a variable: $7x + 5x = 12x$. Lastly, combine the terms with no variables attached: $2 + 5 = 7$. Add these together: $4x^2 + 12x + 7$

8. **C. 12** Substitute appropriate values from the spreadsheet, then multiply, add, and subtract carefully, using order of operations:
$-[-2 - (3 - 5) + 3 \times (-4)] =$
$-[-2 - (-2) + (-12)] =$
$-[-2 + 2 - 12] =$
$-[-12] = 12$

9. **B. $2x^4 + 7x^3 + 4x$** Combine like terms from the exponent with the largest degree, which is 4: $6x^4 - 4x^4 = 2x^4$. Combine like terms from the exponent with the next largest degree, which is 3: $5x^3 + 2x^3 = 7x^3$. Finally, combine the terms from the exponent with the smallest degree: $7x - 3x = 4x$. The simplified polynomial is $2x^4 + 7x^3 + 4x$

10. **D. 150** The perimeter of the trapezoid is given as 50. Since the three sides shown add up to 38, the remaining side must be 12. The missing side is the height, so use the height and the two bases in the formula for the area of a trapezoid: $\frac{1}{2} \times 12(10 + 15) = 150$

11. **B. (8, –5)** Substitute the x and y values from each ordered pair into the equation. Only choice (B) makes the equation true.
$y = -\frac{3}{4}x + 1$
$-5 = -\frac{3}{4}(8) + 1$
$-5 = -6 + 1$
$-5 = -5$

12. **D. $y = \frac{1}{2}x + 3$** You can use the point-slope form to figure out the slope of the line first. Use (–6, 0) and (0, 3) as two points:
$0 - 3 = m(-6 - 0)$
$-3 = m(-6)$
$-3 = -6m$
$m = \frac{-3}{-6} = \frac{1}{2}$
Now that you have the slope of the line, use either of the points to plug into the equation for a line, $y = mx + b$. Using (0, 3):
$3 = \frac{1}{2}(0) + b$
$3 = 0 + b$
$b = 3$
The equation of the line is $y = \frac{1}{2}x + 3$

13. **B. 63** The pattern is that the next number is 1 more than double the previous number. To find the 6th term, use the 5th term, in this case 31: $31 \times 2 + 1 = 63$. To check your answer, confirm that 63 for the sixth term will yield 127 for the seventh term: $63 \times 2 + 1 = 127$.

14. **B. (\$24.50 – \$19) × 6** To determine how much Janice will save, she needs to determine the price difference between one evening and one afternoon ticket (\$24.50 – \$19) and then multiply that number by 6, the total number of tickets she intends to purchase. Thus, the equation that will supply her total savings is (\$24.50 – \$19) × 6.

15. **E. $6x^6 - 24y^2$** Use FOIL to distribute the terms in the expression: $(2x^3)(3x^3) + (2x^3)(6y) + (-4y)(3x^3) + (-4y)(6y) = 6x^6 + 12x^3y - 12x^3y - 24y^2 = 6x^6 - 24y^2$.

16. **B. 28π** Use the radius of 2 and the height of 5 in the formula for the surface area of a cylinder: $2\pi(2 \times 5) + 2\pi(2^2) = 20\pi + 8\pi = 28\pi$

17. **C. $x + 3$** Every term in the expression is divisible by two, so begin by simplifying: $\frac{2x^2 - 6x - 36}{2x - 12} = \frac{x^2 - 3x - 18}{x - 6}$.
Next, factor the numerator of the fraction and cancel:
$\frac{x^2 - 3x - 18}{x - 6} = \frac{(x - 6)(x + 3)}{x - 6} = x + 3$

18. **B. \$65,000** About \$130,000 was made from catalog sales. About \$65,000 was made from online sales. Subtract \$65,000 from \$130,000 to get \$65,000.

19. D. The ≤ symbol indicates "less than or equal to," which is indicated with a filled-in dot. The symbol < indicates "less than" (but not equal to), which is indicated with an open dot.

20. A. (–4, –5) Solve by graphing or by substitution. The point of intersection will be where the lines cross each other. The lines intersect at the point (–4, –5). To solve by substitution, use the first equation to substitute the value of y in the second equation:

$2x + 3 = -\frac{1}{2}x - 7$

$2\frac{1}{2}x = -10$

$x = \frac{-10}{2\frac{1}{2}} = -4$

Now use that value of x to find the value of y using the first equation:

$y = 2(-4) + 3 = -5$

The solution of the equation set is (–4, –5).

21. C. $\sqrt{9^2 + 12^2}$ The cable forms the hypotenuse of a triangle with side lengths of 9 feet and 12 feet. Use the Pythagorean theorem ($9^2 + 12^2 = c^2$) to determine the length of the hypotenuse c: $c = \sqrt{9^2 + 12^2}$.

22. A. –2 To find slope, calculate $\frac{\text{rise}}{\text{run}}$. In this case, the line moves up two units for each unit it moves to the left. Thus, the slope is negative: $\frac{2}{-1} = -2$

23. D. –8 and –12 To solve this system of linear equations, first write two equations with the information given. Call the numbers x and y. The first sentence tells you that $x = 12 + 3y$, and the second sentence tells you that $x + y = -20$. Rewrite the second equation so that x is isolated on one side of the equals sign: $x = -20 - y$. Now that each equation is written in terms of x, set the two expressions for x equal to each other: $12 + 3y = -20 - y$. Simplify this equation: $4y = -32$, so $y = -8$. Substitute this value for y back into the second equation: $x + (-8) = -20$, so x must equal –12.

24. D. –9 and 2 To find the solutions to this quadratic equation, start by setting it equal to 0. The equation then becomes $3x^2 + 21x - 54 = 0$. Then, divide each term by 3 to make the equation $x^2 + 7x - 18 = 0$. Now that the x^2 term has a coefficient of 1, factor the equation into two terms: $(x + 9)(x - 2)$. So $x + 9 = 0$, and $x - 2 = 0$. $x = -9$ and $x = 2$. The correct answer is (D).

25. A. $e = 0.1s + 20{,}000$ If Jonas sells nothing, he earns \$20,000 per year. Then, the graph shows that he earns 10%, or 0.1, of whatever he sells. (This is a linear equation: 20,000 is the y-intercept and 0.1 is the slope.)

26. C. $c = 22.5(h + 1)$ Because there is a charge of \$22.50 per hour, you need \$22.50h within the equation. Then, add the initial \$22.50 and the equation becomes $c = 22.50h + 22.50$. To simplify, factor out the \$22.50 from the right side of the equation: $c = 22.50(h + 1)$.

27. C. 502.4 This word problem is asking you for the volume of a cylinder. That formula is $V = \pi r^2 h$. Plug in the values you are given: $V = \pi \times 4^2 \times 10$. Substituting 3.14 for pi gives you $V = 3.14 \times 4^2 \times 10 = 502.4$

28. E. 77 Brad's average golf score would be found like this:

$\frac{\text{sum of scores}}{\text{number of scores}} = \text{average score}$

Plug the information you are given in the question into the formula and solve for the unknown:

$\frac{78 + 86 + 82 + 81 + 82 + x}{6} = 81$

$78 + 86 + 82 + 81 + 82 + x = 486$

$409 + x = 486$

$x = 77$

29. C. 4 mph The kayaker traveled for a total of 12 miles: 6 miles upstream and 6 miles downstream. This took her 3 hours (2 hours upstream + 1 hour downstream). Divide the distance by the time to find her average rate of speed per hour: $\frac{12\text{ miles}}{3\text{ hours}} = 4$ miles per hour.

30. E. 3 and 19 In the function, x is the input and y is the output. Plugging in each pair of numbers from the choices reveals that only (E) works as $19 = 3(3) + 10$.

31. A. \$214.40 Substitute 4 for b and 3 for n into the function. Then solve the equation:

$C = \$25.60(4) + \$14(4)(3 - 1)$

$= \$102.40 + \$112.00$

$= \$214.40$

32. A. \$600 Find 24% of \$2500. \$2500 × 0.24 = \$600. You could estimate this answer by thinking 24% is roughly $\frac{1}{4}$, and choice (A) is closest to one-fourth of the Whitmans' budget.

33. C. \$7.50 Six boxes of pasta will be purchased: 3 of ziti and 3 of spaghetti. Set up the proportion $\frac{4}{5} = \frac{6}{x}$ where x is the price of 6 boxes of pasta. Cross multiply and divide to solve for x: $5 \times 6 = 30$ and $30 \div 4 = 7.5$

34. C. \$410 Use the formula Simple interest = principal × rate × time. Note that time is expressed in terms of a year, so 6 months = $\frac{1}{2}$ year: $I = \$400 \times 0.05 \times \frac{1}{2}$, which equals \$10. This is the interest, so Mike will pay back the interest plus the \$400 principal for a total of \$410.

35. D.

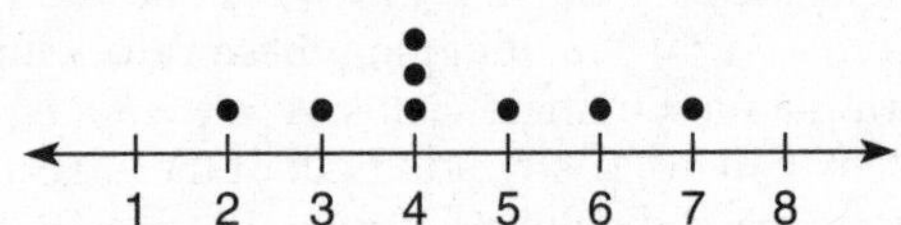

In three of the weeks, Inge received four advertisements, which are represented by the three dots above the number 4. In the remaining weeks, she received a different number of advertisements each week ranging in number from 2 to 7. Thus, there should be one dot above the numbers 2, 3, 5, 6, and 7.

36. B. 58 Plug in the values given for x and y and then follow the order of operations:

$3[2(4) - 5] + (3 + 4)^2 = 3(8 - 5) + 7^2 = 3(3) + 49 = 9 + 49 = 58$

37. C. 12 The formula for the area of a circle is $A = \pi r^2$, where r refers to the radius of the circle. The diameter of a circle (a straight line segment that goes from one edge of the circle to the other and passes through the center of the circle) is $2r$, or two times the length of the radius. The circle shown in this problem has an area of 36π. Plug that into the area formula and find the length of the circle's radius:

$36\pi = \pi r^2$
$\frac{36\pi}{\pi} = \frac{\pi r^2}{\pi}$
$36 = r^2$
$\sqrt{36} = \sqrt{r^2}$
$6 = r$

Now that you know the radius has a length of 6, multiply that length by 2 to get the diameter:
$6 \times 2 = 12$

38. **E. 2.8%** To calculate the percent increase or decrease from Karen's 2011 earnings to her 2012 earnings, first find exactly how much she earned in each year. In 2011, she earned \$52,500 + \$6,250, which equals \$58,750. In 2012, she earned \$56,300 + \$4,100, which equals \$60,400.
To calculate the percent change from 2011 to 2012, use the percent change formula: $\frac{\textit{amount of change}}{\textit{original value}}$
In this case, that gives you $\frac{60{,}400 - 58{,}750}{58{,}750} = \frac{1{,}650}{58{,}750}$, which equals .028, or 2.8%.

39. **E. 79** To get the answer, plug 15 into the equation for x: $y = 5(15) + 4 = 75 + 4 = 79$.

40. **B. $b = 0.50d - 5$** Imtaez would make 50 cents, or \$0.50, for each dinner, d, ordered. He will need to sell 10 dinner specials in order to start earning the bonus, so the bonus will be $10 \times \$0.50 = \$5$ less than $0.50d$, or $b = 0.50d - 5$.

41. **E. 0** To solve this system of equations, double the first equation, then subtract the second from the first:
$6x^2 + 8y = 24$
$\underline{6x^2 + 6y = 18}$
$2y = 6$
$y = 3$
Now plug $y = 3$ back into the first equation to solve for x:
$3x^2 + 4(3) = 12$
$3x^2 + 12 = 12$
$3x^2 = 0$
$x = 0$

42. **C. 48** First, convert the length of the section of fence into inches: 22×12 in $= 264$ in. Divide that number by the width of each board to find out how many boards will be required: $\frac{264}{5.5} = 48$.

43. **A. (6, 10)** You can solve either by graphing the lines or by substitution. To solve by substitution, use the first equation to substitute the value of y into the second equation:
$2(x + 4) + 4x = 44$
$2x + 8 + 4x = 44$
$6x + 8 = 44$
$6x = 36$
$x = 6$
Now use that value of x to find the value of y using the first equation:
$y = 6 + 4$
$y = 10$

44. **D. 28%** Probability is the ratio of the number of favorable outcomes to the number of possible outcomes. There are $12 + 3 + 6 + 4 = 25$ marbles in the bag. Therefore, 25 is the number of possible outcomes. 7 marbles are either blue or yellow. 7 is the number of favorable outcomes. $\frac{7}{25} \times \frac{4}{4} = \frac{28}{100}$, or 28%.

45. **D. 514** To find the volume of a cone, use the formula from the formula sheet: $V = \frac{1}{3}\pi r^2 h$. Plug in values from the question stem and the approximate value of pi:
$V = \frac{1}{3}\pi(6.4)^2(12)$
$V = \frac{1}{3}(3.14)(40.96)(12) \approx 514$.

46. **E. 720** This question asks how many orderings, or permutations, of three out of ten are possible. There are 10 possible winners of first place, 9 possible winners (since first place has now been named) of second place, and 8 possible winners of third place. Multiply: $10 \times 9 \times 8 = 720$.

47. **C. 240** Use the percent formula, $\% = \frac{\text{part}}{\text{whole}} \times 100\%$. You are given the part and the percent, and are solving for the whole:
$5\% = \frac{12}{x} \times 100\%$
$x = \frac{12 \times 100\%}{5\%}$
$x = 12 \times 20 = 240$

48. **C. \$113.75** It takes Fabio 45 minutes, or $\frac{3}{4}$ of an hour, to install a hard drive. It takes him exactly one hour to install an operating system. It will take him $1\frac{3}{4}$ hours to complete the job. Since he charges \$65 per hour, multiply $1\frac{3}{4}$ by \$65 to find the total charge:
$1\frac{3}{4} \times \$65 = \$113.75$

49. **D. 1.335×10^9** You move the decimal point 9 places to the left to get 1.335. Multiply this by 10^9 to get the scientific notation 1.335×10^9.

50. **E. 62** The area of a parallelogram is the base times the height: $A = b \times h = 10 \times 6.2 = 62$.

Mathematics Practice Test Evaluation Charts

Questions 1–50

Circle the numbers of the questions that you answered correctly, and then total them in the last column of each row.

Content Area	Question Numbers	Number Correct/Total
Number and Quantity I: Problem Solving Pages 260–285	29	____/1
Number and Quantity II: Decimals and Fractions Pages 286–309	42, 48	____/2
Number and Quantity III: Ratio, Proportion, and Percent Pages 310–329	33, 34, 38, 47	____/4
Statistics and Probability Pages 330–367	2, 18, 28, 32, 35, 44, 46	____/7
Algebraic Expressions Pages 368–401	1, 3, 4, 5, 7, 8, 9, 14, 15, 17, 36, 40, 49	____/13
Functions Pages 402–441	11, 12, 13, 19, 20, 22, 23, 24, 25, 26, 30, 31, 39, 41, 43	____/15
Geometry Pages 442–481	6, 10, 16, 21, 27, 37, 45, 50	____/8
TOTAL		**____/50**

If you do not have time to review the entire Mathematics unit, you may want to review the sections that need the most work.

Social Studies Practice Test Answers and Explanations

1. **D. The United States had an unfavorable balance of trade in merchandise during the 2000s.** According to the passage, the balance of trade is the difference between exports and imports. When imports are greater than exports, the balance of trade is unfavorable. Since the graph shows that imports consistently exceeded exports during the 2000s, you can conclude that the balance of trade in merchandise was unfavorable during the decade.
2. **B. In 2009, the value of imports fell by a greater amount than the value of exports did.** In 2009, the value of imports was about $600 million less than the previous year. In 2009, the value of exports was about $300 million less than the previous year. Therefore, choice (C) is the opposite of what the graph represents. Choices (A) and (D) are not supported, because the graph includes no information about what may have caused a fall in the value of imports and exports.
3. **D. More people identified as independents than as Democrats, and more identified as Democrats than as Republicans.** This statement was true for all months represented in the chart. Choice (A) overstates the numerical gap between independents and Republicans. Choice (B) might have looked tempting if you misread "10 percent more" as "10 percentage points more." Choice (C) is unsupported as well. While it's true that the three columns total to 98 percent for most months, you cannot draw an inference about the remaining 2 percent.
4. **C. Africa** Look for the continent with the highest percentage of countries colored light gray.
5. **D. European nations had, on average, higher GDP per capita than South American nations.** The darker gray shading in many European countries indicates a higher GDP per capita than that in South American nations. None of the other answer choices are supported because each one suggests a cause for differences in GDP per capita. The map conveys no information about what might cause differences in GDP per capita.
6. **D. The CPI grew in all but one of the years represented in the table.** Look at the second column, which lists the actual CPI. In each year except for 2009, the CPI was higher than the year before. Choice (A) is unsupported because the CPI grew in four of the five years (not three of them). Choice (B) is incorrect because the table contains no information about what caused changes in the CPI. Choice (C) might have looked tempting if you were looking at the third column of the table, but that third column represents not the CPI itself but the percent of change over the previous year.
7. **C. Many people moved to cities to be near factory jobs.** The passage states that many people left farms to work in factories. You can infer that many of them moved from rural areas, where farms are located, to urban areas, where factories are often located. The other choices are not supported by the facts given.
8. **B. Both valued a stable political framework for society.** The paragraph indicates that this was one thing the ancient Chinese and the ancient Greeks had in common.
9. **C. The war created a huge demand for military equipment and supplies.** The chart shows that there was a substantial increase in manufacturing output between 1939 (when World War II began in Europe) and 1941. Even though the United States did not enter the war until late 1941, industry had already geared up to sell equipment and supplies to the Allies in Europe.
10. **A. patriotism** The tendency of the American public to support a president's emergency foreign policy actions is sometimes called the "rally 'round the flag" effect.
11. **B. problems with consistently enforcing the Sherman Antitrust Act led to further legislation to prevent monopolies** In the passage, the author explains the intention behind the Sherman Antitrust Act: to make monopolies illegal. He goes on to outline the limitations of the act, arguing that its broad language rendered it insufficient to solve the problems created by monopolies. He concludes the paragraph by telling how Congress responded to the problems in the Sherman Antitrust Act by passing additional laws to control monopolistic practices.
12. **B. The dangers of climate change are more significant than the possible benefits.** The author states that climate change may lead to benefits such as longer growing seasons but that "the hazards far outweigh any potential advantages." Choices (A) and (D) are contradicted by the passage. The author does not address choice (C).
13. **D. The United States has the second highest rate of carbon emissions per person.** All of the choices are mentioned in the passage, but only choice (D) is directly related to the author's claim that the United States must lead the way in combating climate change.
14. **B. Whites wanted to take over Indian lands in the eastern states.** The graphic shows the Indians being moved away from eastern states to Kansas and Oklahoma. The question asks about "forcible" relocation, so the correct answer can't be about what Indians wanted.
15. **D. the Seminole** The Seminole tribe's home territory was in Florida, which was farthest from the new government-declared Indian Territory in the Midwest.
16. **C. Special interest groups are treated better than voters by members of Congress.** The cartoonist is using irony in the caption to indicate that he thinks members of Congress treat voters badly, but treat people who represent special interest groups well.
17. **C. Industrialization and urbanization caused many changes in family life in the late 1800s.** This covers the main points of the passage, which discusses the impact of industrialization and urbanization on the American family. The other choices are all supporting details.

18. **C. It did not impose direct economic costs on the colonists.** All of the other acts of Parliament shown in the chart cost the colonists money, whether by having to pay import taxes, buy revenue stamps, or use their own resources to shelter British soldiers.
19. **A. The Declaration of Independence, which explained why the colonies broke away from Great Britain** The acts of Parliament listed in the chart were grievances used to justify declaring independence.
20. **A. 0% to 4%** First find the United States on the map and see what shade it is colored. Then consult the map key to see the percentage of undernourished people that shade represents. The map indicates that the percentage range is 0% to 4%.
21. **D. Hunger is a major problem in many countries in Africa.** More than 20 nations in Africa have a very high percentage of undernourished people. The remaining options are not supported by the data on the map.
22. **C. Both established methods of self-government in the English colonies.** Both documents set forth rules and laws for the self-government of specific English colonies.
23. **D. the English Bill of Rights** The English Bill of Rights tied the king's right to rule to the consent of the people's representatives, and the colonists' major grievance was taxation without representation. The colonists felt they should be granted the same representation and rights as other British citizens, which were listed in the English Bill of Rights.
24. **D. Slavery destroyed the culture of the slaves, diminishing their self-respect.** According to the paragraph, this is an opinion, or belief, held by some historians. The other choices are all facts stated in the paragraph.
25. **B. 30 cents** According to the passage, market price is reached under equilibrium conditions—when supply equals demand. According to the graph, supply and demand cross each other—and so are equal—at 30 cents.
26. **D. The market price would go up.** When the supply decreases and demand stays the same, the market price increases. The same number of people want to buy fewer apples, so the people will generally be willing to pay more for the apples.
27. **D. Alabama** Iowa and Delaware never seceded, so they never belonged to the Confederacy. Alabama seceded before the Battle of Fort Sumter, so it belonged to the Confederacy both before and after the Battle of Fort Sumter. North Carolina also belonged to the Confederacy, but it didn't secede until after the Battle of Fort Sumter.
28. **C. the Court of International Trade** "International trade" is commerce with foreign companies, so the case would most likely be filed in the Court of International Trade.
29. **B. The volume and variety of federal cases were too great for a single court to handle.** It would be impractical to have just one court handling all cases; the workload would be too great.
30. **A. the Supreme Court of the United States** According to the passage, cases are appealed to higher level courts; according to the diagram, the Supreme Court is the highest court of appeal.
31. **B. The war effort needs the help of everyone, including men, women, and children.** The focus of the poster is to enlist the help of everyone in the country for the war effort. The sleeping woman represents an American population that needs to take action.
32. **D. at 0° latitude** On both of these projections, the distortions are greatest near the north and south poles. Along the equator (0° latitude), the maps look most alike and most similar to a globe; the distortions increase as you go north or south toward the poles.
33. **B. The interrupted projection distorts distances across the oceans.** The interrupted projection was a poor choice because ocean areas are cut apart on the map, making it very difficult to measure distances on an around-the-world voyage.
34. **B. W and X only** The passage states that the Roman emperors built no fortifications along sea frontiers. The map indicates that W and X were sea coasts. Y is a river frontier and so would have taken light fortifications. Z is a land barrier and so would probably have been heavily fortified.
35. **C. The Fifth Amendment applies to the federal government, and the Fourteenth Amendment, to state governments.** According to the passage, this is one of the main differences between the two amendments.
36. **A. Several factors make Haiti unique among Caribbean nations.** Most of the facts cited in the passage explain how Haiti differs from other nations. Choice (A) summarizes these facts. The other choices are details and fail to summarize the gist of the passage.
37. **B. People in Damascus were aware of religions practiced elsewhere.** If Damascus was on the Silk Road and traders from Europe, Africa, China, and other parts of the world passed through Damascus, then it is highly likely that the citizens of Damascus learned a little about those traders' cultures and religions. None of the other choices are supported by the facts given.
38. **D. Direct Democracy and Representative Democracy** The table's left column describes direct democracy, and its right column describes representative democracy. Thus, choice (D) is the best title for the table.
39. **C. Constitution** The sentence describes the U.S. Constitution. The Declaration of Independence (A) claimed that the colonies were no longer under English rule but did not establish the structure of government. The Articles of Confederation (B) established an older system of government and are no longer in effect. The Magna Carta (D) is an English document.
40. **A. the Crusades** The Crusades were a series of Medieval conflicts in which Europeans invaded Middle Eastern cities.
41. **C. a reason to remember how foolish people can be** The historian is using figurative language and is not describing a physical monument. "Folly" means

"foolishness or error." The historian is saying that people can look back to the Crusades as a reminder of how human error can have terrible consequences.

42. **D. recession** A recession is a general slowdown in economic activity; the list in the box describes the various facets of a recession.
43. **C. 5-ounce tubes of oil paint** Producer goods are goods sold to companies that manufacture products or provide services. Aluminum sheets, copper bricks, and large quantities of fiber optic cable would most likely be sold to such companies. Five ounces of oil paint is a small quantity, so would most likely be sold to an individual who enjoys painting.
44. **B. federalism** Madison's quote describes a division of powers between the national (or federal) government and the state governments. That division of powers is federalism.
45. **D. outlawing behavior such as drug use or robbery** Legislatures (such as Congress or state legislatures) write laws. Courts, such as the Supreme Court, may sometimes pass judgment about whether or not those laws are Constitutional, but courts do not write laws.
46. **A. the First Amendment, which protects the right of free speech** The last sentence of the passage states that the Court decided that the law restricted the expression of political ideas—in other words, that it restricted speech.
47. **A. George is offended by a joke made by a coworker and complains to his manager about it.** While many employers have policies prohibiting offensive jokes, the National Labor Relations Act does not cover that activity. It does cover employees discussing unions (B), joining unions (C), and striking (D).
48. **C. Visit the www.vote.wa.gov website.** The Washington State Vote Registration Form provides four ways to access further reliable information: web, call, email, or mail. The website matches answer choice (C). Neither a congressional representative (A) nor a neighbor (B) is an expert on voting rules and regulations. The phone number provided in choice (D) does not match the number provided by the form.
49. **B. be born on or before Nov 7, 1999.** According to the form, eligible voters must be "at least 18 years of age by the next election." While the form asks for a valid Washington driver's license (A), you may use an alternative form of ID such as a Social Security number. You only need to have claimed residence in Washington State for 30 days prior to the election, not physically remain in the state (D).
50. **B. the House of Representatives determines who becomes President.** The Amendment states that "if no person have the majority . . . the House of Representatives shall choose, by ballot, the President." The House of Representatives chooses from among the top three candidates, not a second election (A). Each state representative casts a vote, but the number of representatives for each state varies based upon population (C). There is no mention that the quorum be held in public for the purpose of debate (D).

Social Studies Practice Test Evaluation Charts

Questions 1–50

Circle the numbers of the questions that you got correct, and then total them in the last column of each row.

Content Area	Question Numbers	Number Correct/Total
U.S. History Pages 542–555	14, 15, 17, 18, 19, 22, 23, 24, 27, 31, 35	___ /11
Civics and Government Pages 556–569	3, 10, 16, 28, 29, 30, 38, 39, 44, 45, 46, 47, 48, 49, 50	___ /15
World History Pages 570–583	7, 8, 34, 36, 37, 40, 41	___ /7
Economics Online chapter	1, 2, 5, 6, 9, 11, 25, 26, 42, 43	___ /10
Geography Online chapter	4, 12, 13, 20, 21, 32, 33	___ /7
TOTAL		___ /50

Most of the Social Studies questions in this practice test also test one of the Social Studies skills discussed on pages 518–541. For the sake of simplicity and readability, those skills have been omitted from this chart. However, if you missed several questions on the Social Studies Practice Test, be sure to review not only the relevant content area, but also the relevant Social Studies skills.

If you do not have time to review the entire Social Studies unit, you may want to review the sections that need the most work.

Science Practice Test Answers and Explanations

1. **A. lift** As the diagram shows and the paragraph implies, the wing's weight and the opposing force of the air under it result in an upward force called *lift*.
2. **C. "Why We Sleep "** The topic of the paragraph is why sleep evolved in humans, and the paragraph cites several reasons for sleeping. The other options are too specific.
3. **B. the air and rainwater in the soil** According to the diagram, nitrogen-fixing bacteria take nitrogen from both the air and rain found in soil.
4. **C. The recycling of nitrogen through the biosphere involves many complex processes.** This is a general statement, or conclusion, that is supported by the various details in the diagram. The other statements are details from the diagram.
5. **B. compost with plant and animal wastes** According to the diagram, plant and animal waste contains nitrogen compounds that decomposers, including nitrite bacteria and nitrate bacteria, break down. In this way, composting with plant and animal wastes results in the addition of usable forms of nitrogen to the soil. So composting with organic waste (plant and animal materials) would be an alternative to synthetic fertilizers.
6. **D. For the three compounds shown, solubility increases as temperature increases.** The graph shows all three substances having increased solubility as the temperature rises from 0°C to 50°C. None of the other statements is supported by information in the graph.
7. **B. He guessed that tepid water might be better for plants than cooler water.** A hypothesis is a guess that a scientist intends to test through study or experiment. Choice (A) describes the question that the scientist is trying to answer, (C) describes the experiment, while (D) simply mentions what he recorded during the experiment.
8. **A. Tepid water stimulated more plant growth than cooler water.** The results show that plants watered with 75°F water grew more than plants watered with cooler 50°F water. A direct correlation (B) requires more than two data points in order to determine the trend. Choice (C) may be a true statement, but was not tested in this experiment. Choice (D) provides a recommendation based on the results.
9. **B. 60°F – 90°F** The initial results indicate that tepid water of 75°F produces more growth than cooler water at 50°F, therefore the scientist should test temperatures warmer and cooler than 75°F. Temperatures below 32°F would freeze the water, and the experiment has already shown that cooler water decreased plant growth compared to cooler temperatures (A). Temperatures greater than 100°F ((C) and (D)) should not be tested until warmer, non-tepid water can be tested.
10. **A. Its charge would become positive.** If an atom loses an electron, it has more protons than electrons, and thus it has a net positive charge. (Such an atom is called a positive ion.)
11. **A. the cracking of granite from the expansion of freezing water** This is an example of physical weathering because it involves changes of temperature causing physical effects on rock. Choice (C) is not an example of weathering because transport is involved.
12. **C. how special fluids keep insects alive during subfreezing weather** Understanding how insects can survive freezing may be a key to finding a way to freeze organs without destroying them.
13. **B. sea star** Of the four animals shown, only the sea star has a center section from which similar parts radiate. All the other animals are bilaterally symmetrical.
14. **C. Hydrogen peroxide is decomposing into water and oxygen.** The chemical reaction begins on the left-hand side of the equation, which represents two hydrogen peroxide molecules. Thus, it is incorrect to say that hydrogen peroxide is being made (as in choices (A) or (D)). Rather, hydrogen peroxide is decomposing, or breaking up, into two substances. What remains after the chemical reaction is written on the right-hand side of the equation. The question stem explains that water is composed of two hydrogen atoms and an oxygen atom, so the results of the reaction are water and O_2, which you can infer represents oxygen. Choice (B) is incomplete and (C) is correct.
15. **A. Mercury and bromine are liquids at room temperature.** Room temperature is about 70°F. The chart indicates that both mercury and bromine are liquids at that temperature: each has a melting point—the temperature at which it becomes a liquid—well below room temperature. Also, each has a boiling point—the temperature at which it goes from liquid to gas—well above room temperature.
16. **D. Bacteria quickly evolved resistance to antibiotic drugs.** In 1969, the Surgeon General did not anticipate that bacteria would evolve to be resistant to the antibiotics that had been so effective until that time.
17. **B. The student should have used books of the same height for all of the ramps.** The height of the ramp affects how far the ball rolls. So the height of the ramp should be a controlled variable in this experiment. By using one ramp that is not as high as the others, the student is introducing a second variable into the experiment, which makes his data invalid for the ramp that is lower than the others.
18. **D. The dog has canines and the sheep does not.** If you compare the two diagrams, you will see that the sheep does not have any canines; instead the sheep has a large gap where the canines would be.
19. **C. The five largest asteroids are all farther from the sun than Earth is.** According to the chart, Earth's distance from the sun is set at 1, so any value greater than 1 indicates that the asteroid is farther from the sun than Earth is. All the asteroids have distance values of 2 or greater, so they are all farther from the sun than Earth is.
20. **C. less than** If all the lobsters weighed the maximum of 9 lb, the 220 million pounds of lobster would still account for more than 20 million individual animals.

Two blue lobsters out of 20 million lobsters is substantially less likely than the estimated 1 in 2 million occurrence of the blue mutation.

21. **A. Pressure builds up inside the magma chamber and vent.** If you examine the diagram, you will see that hot magma wells up into the volcano's cone. You need to infer that when the pressure builds up sufficiently, the volcano explodes, or erupts. None of the other events described would cause a violent explosion from the inside of the volcano.
22. **B. when food is digested, as when an enzyme in saliva called ptyalin breaks down starch into sugars without itself changing** The catalyst is the enzyme ptyalin; you can identify ptyalin as the catalyst, because it aids the chemical reaction of digestion but itself remains unchanged after the reaction. None of the other reactions include a substance that remains unchanged.
23. **B. People can reduce their chances of developing age-related hearing loss by not smoking.** Of all the options, this is the only one that is a hypothesis that the researchers could have been testing with their experiment. (A) is too general to be a hypothesis for this experiment and is stated more like a conclusion than a hypothesis. The other options are facts relating to the study.
24. **D. Humans contain a higher percentage of carbon than bacteria do.** To find the correct answer, you must check each statement against the graphs to see whether the information in the graphs supports the statement. The graphs show that humans have a higher percentage of carbon than bacteria have.
25. **B. Both involve effort applied with circular motion.** The diagrams show that the effort applied to each of these machines is circular.
26. **A. During an ice age, temperatures drop and ice covers vast areas of Earth.** According to the passage, scientists aren't sure what causes ice ages. Choices (B), (C), and (D) each offer a different hypothesis for what causes an ice age. By contrast, choice (A) is an objective fact.
27. **D. The arrangement of the carbon, hydrogen, and oxygen atoms in the two hydrocarbons is different.** Although ether and ethanol both have the same number of carbon, hydrogen, and oxygen atoms, the different arrangements of atoms in each compound results in two substances with different properties.
28. **C. surficial; hydrothermal** The passage explains that surficial processes happen at the Earth's surface, so the action of wind would be one such process. Hydrothermal processes involve the movement of water underground, so the movement of seawater underground would be an example of a hydrothermal process.
29. **A. lightning** The passage states that thunderstorms, which often generate lightning, occur in the troposphere, and that blue jets, a special kind of lightning, occur in the stratosphere.
30. **A. Brock placed wooden cubes that weighed 1 cc, 10 cc, and 100 cc in water. He observed their buoyancy. Then he placed iron cubes of 1 cc, 10 cc, and 100 cc in water and observed their buoyancy.** This choice describes the experiment Brock conducted in order to test his hypothesis. Choice (B) describes "Step 4: Draw a conclusion." Choice (C) corresponds to "Step 1: Formulate a question about a phenomenon." Choice (D) was Brock's "Step 2: Form a hypothesis."
31. **D.**

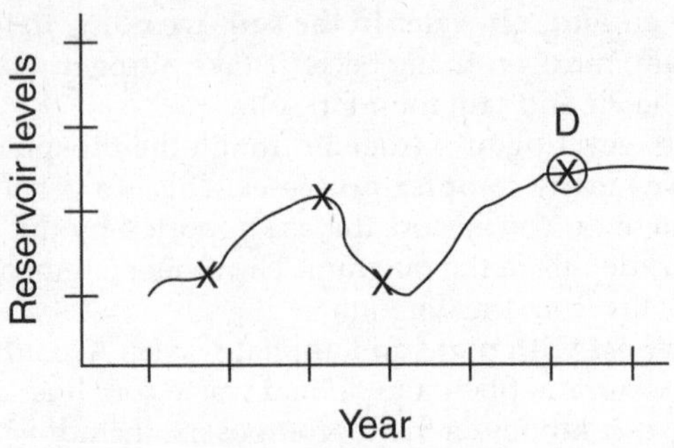

Since the dam was built to stop fluctuation, or change, in reservoir levels, 1993 must be the final year that reservoir levels changed.

32. **B. electron** In the model, the pudding is meant to represent the uniform cloud of positive charge and the plums are meant to represent the electrons.
33. **A. A teacher's perfume can be detected at the back of the classroom.** This is an example of diffusion, the spreading of gas molecules (perfume vapor) throughout a container (the classroom).
34. **B. Oxygen is one of the products of photosynthesis.** The products of the chemical reaction appear on the right-hand side of the arrow. One of those products is six atoms of O_2, which is oxygen.
35. **C. circulatory and respiratory** The passage describes how the heart and blood vessels, which are part of the circulatory system, work with the lungs, which are part of the respiratory system, to infuse blood with oxygen and carry it throughout the body.
36. **A. Rock samples obtained from the bottom are older than rock samples obtained from the top.** Multiple rock samples were obtained at corresponding depths and each depth corresponded to a different time period. The layers of rock samples could give the geologist information about when the layers were formed. They would be less likely to yield information about the causes of flooding or the speed of winds now. Choice (C) is incorrect because a geologist could not study rock layers worldwide using only samples from the Grand Canyon.
37. **D. It would rotate counterclockwise and move westward, then northward, and finally eastward.** The passage states that hurricanes tend to rotate counterclockwise in the Northern Hemisphere and that hurricanes initially move westward then toward the poles (which would be northward in the Northern Hemisphere), and finally eastward after encountering the mid-latitude westerly winds.
38. **B. The force will be reduced.** If the distance between the two objects were increased, the denominator of

the fraction shown in the equation would become bigger. Increasing the denominator of a fraction makes the value of the fraction smaller. So the force would be reduced.

39. **C. Frogs' bodies have a way to prevent their cells from freezing in cold temperatures.** All amphibians, frogs included, are ectothermic, or cold-blooded. Given the fact that frogs reproduce in the spring, if all the frogs of a given species died in the winter, the species would go extinct. So it must be that frogs have some physiological mechanism that prevents their cells from freezing when a frog's body temperature drops during the winter.
40. **C. insulin injections** Some cases of diabetes mellitus are caused by the inability of the pancreas to produce insulin. Individuals with this form of the disease can keep their blood sugar levels stable only by regular use of insulin.
41. **D. jaundice, a yellow discoloration of the skin due to a systemic buildup of bilirubin** The liver metabolizes bilirubin, so a buildup of this substance in the skin is strongly suggestive of liver disease.
42. **A. Shade-loving animal species, such as the red-backed salamander, were replaced by sun-loving species such as the northern black racer.** The immediate impact of cutting down an old growth forest is that species that favor a shaded forest habitat will be replaced by species favoring sunny, open spaces.
43. **B. Most people would not recognize the gametophyte generation of a fern.** This conclusion is supported by the fact that the gametophyte is a small, heart-shaped structure and that the sporophyte generation of the fern is the familiar plant, with roots, stems, and leaves.
44. **B. if the surface were irregular or rough** If a surface is rough, each light ray will hit the surface at a different angle. Therefore, light rays reflecting off of a rough surface travel in all different directions.
45. **D. Plant one type of flower in identical pots, expose each pot to a different amount of sunlight, and see when each flower blooms.** This experiment is testing the effect of sunlight on the bloom cycle, so only the amount of sunlight each plant is exposed to should change. Choice (C) changes the location of the plants without a clear measurement of sunlight while choices (A) and (B) also change the varieties of flowers.
46. **C. Shredding arthropods will have less competition for food.** Both predatory nematodes and shredding arthropods consume fungi, making them competitors for the same food source. Birds consume earthworms and predatory arthropods in addition to predatory nematodes, so they will have a source of food (A), and the amount of organic matter would eventually decrease as the populations of decomposing bacteria and fungi would have one fewer predator (B).
47. **B. the eye color of adult fruit flies** The research purposefully breeds a white-eyed fruit fly with a red-eyed fruit fly. The sex of the adult fruit-flies is not being measured; one male and one female fly are used for breeding purposes (A). Both the sex of the offspring (B) and the eye-color of the offspring (C) would be dependent variables, as those are traits being measured.
48. **A. It is easier to observe the traits of unconscious fruit flies.** The passage states that ethanol is used to briefly render the fruit flies unconscious so that Dr. Morgan can document their sex and eye color. It can be implied that unconscious fruit flies are easier to observe than fruit flies that are awake and moving. Choices (B), (C), and (D) are unsupported in the text.
49. **D. The trait for white eyes is a recessive gene.** When a white-eyed fly is bred with a red-eyed fly, all offspring are red-eyed. When those flies are bred with each other, the white-eyed trait reappears. This is consistent with the behavior of recessive genes, which would not be expressed in the first generation, but will reappear in the second. Because the results can be replicated, mutations (A) and lack of relationship (B) can be eliminated. While white-eyed fruit flies are less common, "Inferior" (C) is a value judgment that is not supported in the passage.
50. **B. Yes, because his results were replicated and can be verified using a Punnett square.** Dr. Morgan followed the scientific method and was able to replicate his results. His results can also be verified using a Punnett square of a recessive, sex-linked trait for white eyes on the X chromosome. When the white-eyed fly was bred with a red-eyed fly, all off-spring had red eyes. This is the expected outcome of the cross rr (white-eye fly) × RR (red-eye fly):

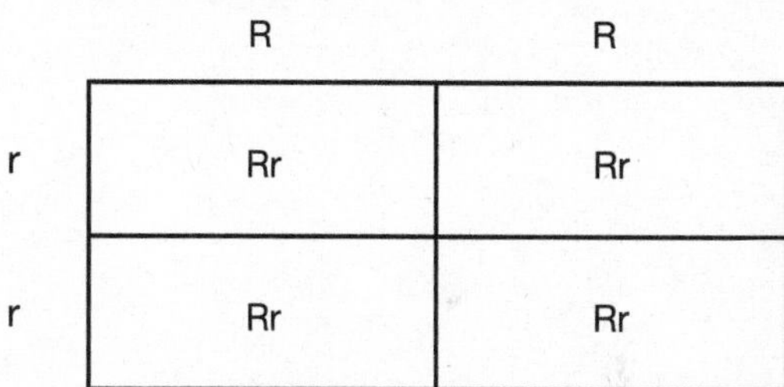

	R	R
r	Rr	Rr
r	Rr	Rr

Second generation females (X_RX_r) bred to white-eyed males (X_rY) is the only cross that will produce white-eyed females (X_rX_r).

	X_R	X_r
X_r	X_RX_r	X_rX_r
Y	X_RY	X_rY

Dr. Morgan's expertise in embryology may help him develop proper research questions in genetics, but it alone does not validate his hypothesis (A). While credible research is found within respected journals, the results of properly conducted research is still valid even if unpublished (C).

Science Practice Test Evaluation Charts

Questions 1–50

Circle the numbers of the questions that you got correct, and then total them in the last column of each row.

Content Area	Question Numbers	Number Correct/Total
Life Science Pages 616–635	2, 3, 4, 5, 7, 8, 9, 12, 13, 16, 18, 20, 23, 24, 35, 39, 40, 41, 43, 45, 46, 47, 48, 49, 50	____ /25
Physical Science Pages 636–651	1, 6, 10, 14, 15, 17, 22, 25, 27, 30, 32, 33, 34, 38, 44	____ /15
Earth and Space Science Online chapter	11, 19, 21, 26, 28, 29, 31, 36, 37, 42	____ /10
TOTAL		____ /50

Most of the Science questions in this practice test also test one of the Science skills discussed on pages 596–615. For the sake of simplicity and readability, those skills have been omitted from this chart. However, if you missed several questions on the Science Practice Test, be sure to review not only the relevant content area, but also the relevant Science skills.

If you do not have time to review the entire Science unit, you may want to review the sections that need the most work.

HiSET Exam Resources

Essay Scoring Guide

Writing Test: Essay Scoring Guide

1 Essays at this score point demonstrate weak command over writing an argument on a given substantive topic using valid reasoning and relevant and sufficient evidence.

- The response has little or no development of a central position or claim(s). No correct and/or understandable context of the topic is provided for the discussion. The writer's own position on the issue or claim(s) may not be clear. A few ideas may be provided but these lack explanation of ideas, only repeat ideas, or ideas are derived entirely from provided texts.
- The response lacks an introduction and/or conclusion, and fails to demonstrate any understanding of paragraphing. Transitions are not used or may be used incorrectly.
- Language control is minimal. Word choice and sentence structure are simple. The response lacks formal style and an objective tone.
- Minimal or no command of the conventions of standard English grammar and usage is demonstrated. Errors in capitalization, punctuation, and spelling frequently appear.

2 Essays at this score point demonstrate limited command over writing an argument on a given substantive topic using valid reasoning and relevant and sufficient evidence.

- The response demonstrates limited development of a central position or claim(s). A context of the topic that is only somewhat correct or understandable is provided for the discussion. The writer's own position on the issue or claim(s) may be somewhat unclear or confusing. A few ideas are provided but explanation is thin and/or superficial and parts of the explanation may be repetitious or derived too heavily from provided texts without interpretation.
- The introduction and conclusion are minimally developed. Some related ideas are grouped together though paragraphing may not be used. Few transitions are used.
- Beginning skill in language is demonstrated. Word choice is general and repetitive. The response has repetitive sentence structure and/or long, uncontrolled sentences. The response lacks formal style and/or an objective tone.
- Limited command of the conventions of standard English grammar and usage is demonstrated. Numerous errors in capitalization, punctuation, and spelling appear and may interfere with understanding.

3 Essays at this score point demonstrate partial command over writing an argument on a given substantive topic using valid reasoning and relevant and sufficient evidence.

- The response demonstrates partial development of a central position or claim(s). A brief context of the topic is provided for the discussion, including introduction of alternate claims and/or counterclaims. The writer's own position on the issue or claim(s) is evident. Several ideas with limited or uneven explanation are provided; few or only general examples and/or details support ideas. The response uses evidence drawn from provided texts but this is limited or overused, poorly chosen, or misrepresented.
- The response has an introduction and conclusion, though one or both of these may be underdeveloped. Ideas are grouped together in paragraphs, though the relationship among ideas may at times be unclear. Transitions are simple and used inconsistently.
- Some developing skill in language is demonstrated. Word choice is general and the response demonstrates a little variety in sentence structure, although a few long, uncontrolled sentences may be used. The response attempts to maintain formal style and an objective tone but may fail to sustain these throughout discussion.
- Partial command of the conventions of standard English grammar and usage is demonstrated. Errors in capitalization, punctuation, and spelling are regularly present throughout the response and may sometimes interfere with understanding.

4 Essays at this score point demonstrate adequate command over writing an argument on a given substantive topic using valid reasoning and relevant and sufficient evidence.

- The response demonstrates adequate development of a central position or claim(s). A context of the topic is provided for the discussion, including some discussion of alternate claims and/or counterclaims. The writer's own position on the issue or claim(s) is clear. Several ideas with adequate explanation are provided; some specific and relevant examples and/or details support ideas, including relevant evidence drawn selectively from provided texts and appropriately integrated.
- A clear, functional introduction and conclusion are provided. Relationships between ideas are clarified by organization: transitions are consistently used, though they may be simple, and some evidence of logical sequencing of ideas is demonstrated. The response uses appropriate paragraphing.
- Adequate skill in language use is demonstrated. Word choice is mostly specific and somewhat varied. The response demonstrates control of sentences with some variety in length and structure. A formal style is established and an objective tone maintained throughout the discussion.
- Adequate command of the conventions of standard English grammar and usage is demonstrated. Some errors in capitalization, punctuation, and spelling appear but do not interfere with understanding.

5 Essays at this score point demonstrate strong command over writing an argument on a given substantive topic using valid reasoning and relevant and sufficient evidence.

- The response demonstrates competent development of a central position or claim(s). A context of the topic is provided for the discussion, including balanced discussion of alternate claims and/or counterclaims. The writer's own position on the issue or claim(s) is clear and considered. Several ideas with complete explanation are provided; specific, relevant, and somewhat elaborated reasons, examples, and/or details support ideas, including clear and relevant evidence drawn from provided texts and skillfully integrated.
- The introduction and conclusion are clear and sufficient. Clear and appropriate paragraphing is used. Varied transitions and logical sequencing of ideas are used throughout to link major sections of text, create cohesion, and clarify relationships between ideas.
- The response demonstrates competent skill in language. Word choice is usually precise and varied. The response uses well-controlled sentences that are varied in length and complexity. A formal style is established and an objective tone maintained throughout. Counterclaims are discussed fairly, without bias.
- Able command of the conventions of standard English grammar and usage is demonstrated. Few errors in capitalization, punctuation, and spelling appear, and most are superficial.

6 Essays at this score point demonstrate superior command over writing an argument on a given substantive topic using valid reasoning and relevant and sufficient evidence.

- The response demonstrates expert development of a central position or claim(s). A context of the topic is provided for the discussion, including balanced discussion of the strengths and limitations of alternate claims and/or counterclaims. The writer's own position on the issue or claim(s) is clear, considered, and nuanced. Several ideas with effective and thorough explanation are provided; relevant and fully elaborated reasons, examples, and/or details support ideas, including compelling evidence drawn from provided texts and effectively integrated.
- The response has an effective introduction and conclusion. Clear and appropriate paragraphing is used, creating a coherent whole. Effective transitions and logical sequencing of ideas are used throughout to link major sections of text, create cohesion, and clarify the relationships between claims(s) and reasons, between reasons and evidence, and between claim(s) and counterclaims.
- The response demonstrates proficient skill in language. Word choice is precise, varied, and engaging. The response effectively varies sentence length and complexity. A formal style is established and an objective tone that enhances the effectiveness of the response maintained. Counterclaims are discussed fairly, without bias.
- Expert command of the conventions of standard English grammar and usage is demonstrated, and the response demonstrates sophisticated use of grammar, usage, and mechanics. Few or no errors in capitalization, punctuation, and spelling appear.

MATH MEMORY AIDS

Some questions require the use of formulas. While some will be provided to you on Test Day via a formula sheet, others (like those that follow) will NOT be provided. As such, you should know these prior to Test Day. You may tear this sheet out of your book to serve as a portable study resource.

Concept	Memory Aid
Order of operations: Parentheses, Exponents, Multiplication, Division, Addition, Subtraction, and work Left to Right	*Please excuse my dear Aunt Sally, Love Ron.*
Distance formula: $d = rt$	Remember this formula by creating a "dirt graph" as follows. ("Dirt" is a word play on "$d = rt$.") 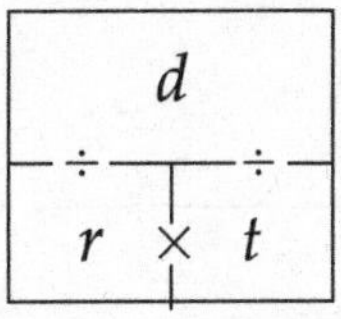 d ÷ ÷ $r \times t$ Cover the letter of the item you want to solve for, and what remains visible is the formula you need.

Concept	Memory Aid
Percent, part, and whole: base × rate = part	Use a similar box to remember how to calculate the relationship between percent, part, and whole. P ÷ ÷ B × R Cover the letter of the item you want to solve for, and what remains visible is the formula you need.
Multiplying binomials: $(x + a)(x + b)$ $= x^2 + bx + ax + ab$	FOIL: First, Outer, Inner, Last
Pythagorean theorem: $a^2 + b^2 = c^2$	Note that c is the longest side of the triangle; a and b are the other two sides of the triangle.
Quadratic formula	$x = \frac{-b \pm \sqrt{b^2 - 4ac}}{2a}$, where $ax^2 + bx + c = 0$ and $a \neq 0$

MATHEMATICS FORMULA SHEET

On the next two pages, you will find mathematical formulas that will be provided to you on Test Day. Please note that you should also know some formulas prior to testing. Some of these include Distance-Rate-Time, the Pythagorean theorem, and the quadratic formula. While these formulas will not be provided on your formula sheet on Test Day, they have been included as part of your Math Memory Aids resource on the previous pages.

Perimeter / Circumference

Rectangle

Perimeter = 2(*length*) + 2(*width*)

Circle

Circumference = 2π(*radius*)

Area

Circle

Area = π(*radius*)^2

Triangle

Area = $\frac{1}{2}$(*base*)(*height*)

Parallelogram

Area = (*base*)(*height*)

Trapezoid

Area = $\frac{1}{2}$(*base*$_1$ + *base*$_2$)(*height*)

Volume

Prism/Cylinder

Volume = (*area of the base*)(*height*)

Pyramid/Cone

Volume = $\frac{1}{3}$(*area of the base*)(*height*)

Sphere

Volume = $\frac{4}{3}$π(*radius*)^3

Length

1 foot = 12 inches

1 yard = 3 feet

1 mile = 5,280 feet

1 meter = 1,000 millimeters

1 meter = 100 centimeters

1 kilometer = 1,000 meters

1 mile ≈ 1.6 kilometers

1 inch = 2.54 centimeters

1 foot ≈ 0.3 meter

Capacity / Volume

1 cup = 8 fluid ounces

1 pint = 2 cups

1 quart = 2 pints

1 gallon = 4 quarts

1 gallon = 231 cubic inches

1 liter = 1,000 milliliters

1 liter ≈ 0.264 gallon

Weight

1 pound = 16 ounces

1 ton = 2,000 pounds

1 gram = 1,000 milligrams

1 kilogram = 1,000 grams

1 kilogram ≈ 2.2 pounds

1 ounce ≈ 28.3 grams

Breena Coates

CASES AND MATERIALS ON

FEMINIST JURISPRUDENCE

TAKING WOMEN SERIOUSLY

Second Edition

By

Mary Becker
Professor of Law
DePaul University College of Law

Cynthia Grant Bowman
Professor of Law
Northwestern University School of Law

Morrison Torrey
Professor of Law
DePaul University College of Law

AMERICAN CASEBOOK SERIES®

A THOMSON COMPANY

ST. PAUL, MINN., 2001

610 Opperman Drive
P.O. Box 64526
St. Paul, MN 55164–0526
1–800–328–9352

Printed in the United States of America

ISBN 0–314–24110–8

1st Reprint — 2003

To Joanne
To Ben, David and Michael
To Nancy B., Nancy G., Nancy L. and Nancy P.

*

Preface to the Second Edition

The first edition of this book was the product of the collaboration of three women who teach law and are committed to the participation of women as genuine equals in our society—in our educational, legal and political institutions, in the world of work, and in the family. We included a variety of materials, drawn both from standard legal sources, like cases and statutes, and from less typical sources from other disciplines, in order to raise central questions about the progress women have made toward these goals, the destinations that might be desirable, and the routes from here to there. Our goal was also to introduce the reader to the world of current feminist scholarship and activism. The presentation was thus grounded in feminism, although one pervasive theme was that there are many types of feminism, which may often lead to different conclusions on important issues. We also sought to include the perspectives of women of different races, classes, and sexual orientations, while knowing that our capacity to realize this goal was necessarily limited. We nonetheless endeavored to include readings from multiple perspectives and to raise questions from a variety of viewpoints.

Since publication of the first edition, there have been many new developments in the law concerning issues of vital importance to women. There has also been a flourishing of writing on feminism and feminist topics, including new work in areas such as critical race feminism, queer theory, and masculinities theory. This second edition continues the commitments of the original book but attempts to do much more. We continue to present a diversity of feminist perspectives on issues affecting women's lives—indeed, we broaden our presentation of those perspectives to take account of developments since publication of the first edition. As a result, this new edition is much more multi-cultural than its predecessor and presents international approaches to many issues as well. We have added a number of excerpts from new writings on masculinities, to include the developing perspectives of feminist men. Finally, we have chosen to pay more attention throughout the volume to issues affecting lesbians and gay men. As a result, an important new depth has been added to the many questions of gender and equality discussed throughout the book; viewing them from many differing perspectives, we gain opportunities for insights that were less accessible in the prior edition. Our goal remains the same: to invite controversy and discussion about all of the issues and perspectives included, and to lead us all to a more profound and inclusive understanding of the conditions of equality.

We are indebted to so many people for their assistance throughout the preparation of the first and second editions of this book—to the members of the Chicago Feminist Law Teachers Colloquium, where we met, discussed our ideas and received support, to the members of our respective faculties who helped us along the way, and to all the colleagues, students, and friends who supported us through the long journey. In particular, we thank Ben Altman, Pauline Bart, Mary Coombs, Charlotte Crane, Linda Kerber, Jane Larson, Sylvia Law, Beth Mertz, Martha Mahoney, Aviva Orenstein, Jane Rutherford, Marjorie B. Schaafsma, and Ilana Sultan for their generosity in reading and commenting on portions of this manuscript. We are also grateful to the many students who have read and reacted to most of these materials with us, including the feminist jurisprudence classes at DePaul, Northwestern, and the University of Chicago law schools and the gender, public policy and law classes in the Gender Studies Department at Northwestern. For research and other assistance, we thank Patricia Alcamo, Lawrence Arendt, Melissa Lee Benzon, Noelle Brennan, Linda Cecchin, Leslie M. Darling, Sabra Ebersole, Jennifer Figler, Connie Fleischer, Markus Funk, Myrna Galang, Mark Giangrande, Alison Gibbs, Dan Goldwin, Sarah Haiby, David Hirschman, Mary Hopp, Michele Knapp, Jennifer Laninga, Laura Lederer, Marcia Lehr, Tracy LeRoy, Raizel Liebler, Maggie Lyons, Justin Ma, Lisa Milam, Elizabeth Rosenblatt, Shawn Ryan, Lyn Schollett, William Schwesig, Sharon Seung, Heather Sloan, Joann Stetler, Kathleen Sullivan, Joshua Towle, Jannette Tucker, Karen Vitolins, Tara Waechter, Elizabeth Walker, Shanna Williams, and the Law Librarians at De Paul University College of Law and Northwestern University School of Law. Research support was provided to Mary Becker by the Dean's Faculty Research Fund of DePaul University College of Law during the summers of 1999 and 2000; to Cynthia Grant Bowman by the Stanford Clinton Sr. Research Fellowship during the 1992–1993 academic year, from the Stanford Clinton Sr. Faculty Fund during the summer of 1993, from the Julius Rosenthal Fund during the summers of 1998, 1999 and 2000, and to the Benjamin Mazur Research Professorship during the summer of 2000 and the 2000-2001 academic year; and to Morrison Torrey from the Dean's Faculty Research Fund of DePaul University College of Law during the summers of 1992, 1993, 1999, and 2000.

Finally, for purposes of clarity, the reader should know that citations, footnotes, concurring and dissenting opinions have been omitted from the cases and other materials included in this book without specifically noting that omissions have been made; footnotes remaining in excerpted materials retain their original numbers. Any footnotes added by the authors of this book are indicated by the use of small-case letters.

MARY BECKER
CYNTHIA GRANT BOWMAN
MORRISON TORREY

May 2001

Copyright Acknowledgements and Reprint Permissions

We gratefully acknowledge the authors and publishers who have allowed us to reprint excerpts from copyrighted materials, both those who are acknowledged here, in the order in which the excerpts appear in the book, and those who are acknowledged on the page where the specific reprinted materials appear.

Chapter 2:

Excerpts from "Conservative Free Speech and the Uneasy Case for Judicial Review," by Mary Becker in The University of Colorado Law Review, Vol, 64. Copyright © 1993 by Univ. of Colorado/Law Rev. Reproduced with permission of The University of Colorado/Law Rev.

Chapter 3:

Excerpts from "Consciousness Raising" by Catharine A. MacKinnon reprinted by permission from FEMINISM UNMODIFIED: DISCOURSES ON LIFE AND LAW by Catharine A. MacKinnon, Cambridge, Mass.: Harvard University Press, Copyright © 1987 by the President and Fellows of Harvard College.

Excerpts from IN A DIFFERENT VOICE by Carol Gilligan reprinted by permission of Harvard University Press from IN A DIFFERENT VOICE by Carol Gilligan, 25-29, Cambridge, Mass.: Harvard University Press. Copyright © 1982, 1993, by Carol Gilligan.

Excerpts from "The Problem of Marxism and Feminism" by Catharine A. MacKinnon reprinted by permission from TOWARD A FEMINIST THEORY OF THE STATE by Catharine A. MacKinnon, Cambridge, Mass.: Harvard University Press, Copyright © 1989 by the President and Fellows of Harvard College.

Excerpts from "Sexuality" by Catharine A. MacKinnon reprinted by permission from FEMINISM UNMODIFIED: DISCOURSES ON LIFE AND LAW by Catharine A. MacKinnon, Cambridge, Mass.: Harvard University Press, Copyright © 1987 by the President and Fellows of Harvard College.

Excerpts from "Difference and Dominance" by Catharine A. MacKinnon reprinted by permission from FEMINISM UNMODIFIED: DISCOURSES ON LIFE AND LAW by Catharine A. MacKinnon, Cambridge, Mass.: Harvard University Press, Copyright © 1987 by the President and Fellows of Harvard College.

Exerpts from "Sex Inequality" by Catharine A. MacKinnon reprinted by permission from SEXUAL HARASSMENT OF WORKING WOMEN by Catharine A. MacKinnon, New Haven, Conn.: Yale University Press, Copyright © 1979 by Yale University.

Excerpts from "Some Reflections on the Feminist Legal Thought of the 1970s" by Hon. Ruth Bader Ginsburg and Barbara Flagg in The University of Chicago Legal Forum, Vol. 1989. Copyright © 1989 by The Univ. of Chicago Law Sch/Studen. Reproduced with permission of The Univ. of Chicago Law Sch/Studen.

Excerpts from "The Difference in Women's Hedonic Lives: A Phenomenological Critique of Feminist Legal Theory" by Robin L. West in Wisconsin Women's Law Journal, Vol. 3. Copyright © 1987 by Wisconsin Women's Law Journal. Reproduced with permission of Wisconsin Women's Law Journal.

Excerpts from "Why Patriarchy?" in THE GENDER KNOT: UNRAVELING OUR PATRIARCHAL LEGACY by Allan G. Johnson. Reprinted permission of Temple University Press. © 1997 by Allan G. Johnson. All Rights Reserved.

Excerpts from "Towards a Substantive Feminism" by Mary Becker in University of Chicago Legal Forum, Vol. 1999. Copyright © 1999 by University of Chicago Law Sch/Studen. Reproduced with permission of University of Chicago Law Sch/Studen.

Excerpts from Margaret Jane Radin, "The Pragmatist and the Feminist," in Southern California Law Review, Vol. 63. Copyright © 1990 Southern California Law Review. Reprinted with the permission of Southern California Law Review.

Excerpts from Zillah Eisenstein, "Constructing a Theory of Capitalist Patriarchy and Socialist Feminism" from Critical Sociology, Volume 25, Number 2/3, pp. 196-217 (1999). Copyright Humanities Press, Inc. a wholly owned subsidiary of Brill Academic Publishers, Inc. Reprinted with permission of Brill Academic Publishers, Inc.

Exerpts from "Postmodernism and Gender Relations in Feminist Theory" by Jane Flax in Signs, Vol. 12. Copyright © 1987 by The University of Chicago. Reprinted with permission of Jane Flax and The University of Chicago Press, Chicago, Ill.

Excerpts from "The Quest for a Feminist Jurisprudence" by Carol Smart in FEMINISM AND THE POWER OF LAW by Carol Smart. Copyright © 1989 by Routledge. Reproduced with the permission of Taylor & Francis Books Ltd.

Excerpts from Jane Flax, "The End of Innocence" from FEMINISTS THEORIZE THE POLITICAL, edited by Judith Butler and Joan W. Scott. Copyright © 1992 by Routledge. Reproduced by permission of Routledge, Inc., part of The Taylor & Francis Group.

Excerpts from "Points Against Postmodernism," by Catharine A. MacKinnon reprinted by permission from Chicago-Kent Law Review, Vol. 75, SYMPOSIUM ON UNFINISHED FEMINIST BUSINESS, Chicago, Ill.: Chicago-Kent Law Review, Copyright © 2000 by Chicago-Kent College of Law.

Excerpts from "Race and Essentialism in Feminist Legal Theory" by Angela P. Harris in Stanford Law Review, Vol. 42. Copyright © 1990 by Stanford Law Rev. Reproduced with permission of Stanford Law Review.

Excerpts from "From Practice to Theory, or What Is a White Woman Anyway?," by Catharine A. MacKinnon reprinted by permission from Yale Journal of Law & Feminism, Vol. 4, New Haven, Mass.: Yale Journal of Law & Feminism, Copyright © 1991 by Yale University.

Excerpts from "Obscuring the Importance of Race: the Implications of Making Comparisons Between Racism and Sexism (or Other -Isms)" by Trina Grillo and Stephanie Wildman, in Duke Law Journal, Vol. 1991 and in PRIVILEGE REVEALED: HOW INVISIBLE PREFERENCES SHAPE AMERICA by Stephanie Wildman, Copyright © 1991 by Trina Grillo and Stephanie Wildman and Copyright © 1996 by New York University. Reprinted by permission of New York University Press and of Stephanie Wildman, for herself and for the Estate of Trina Grillo.

Excerpts from " Las Olvidadas—Gendered In Justice/Gendered Injustice: Latinas, Fronteras and The Law" by Berta Esperanza Hernandez-Truyol in Journal of Race & Justice, Vol. 1. Copyright © 1998 University of Iowa Law School Journal of Gender, Race, & Justice. Reprinted by permission of University of Iowa Law School Journal of Gender, Race, & Justice.

Excerpts from "We The People: Jurisprudence In Color" by Mari J. Matsuda in WHERE IS YOUR BODY? by Mari J. Matsuda. Copyright © 1996 by Mari J Matsuda. Reprinted by permission of Beacon Press, Boston.

Excerpts from "Critical Race Theory" by Mari J. Matsuda in WHERE IS YOUR BODY? by Mari J. Matsuda. Copyright © 1996 by Mari J Matsuda. Reprinted by permission of Beacon Press, Boston.

Excerpts from " Standing Beside My Sister, Facing The Enemy" by Mari J. Matsuda in WHERE IS YOUR BODY? by Mari J. Matsuda. Copyright © 1996 by Mari J. Matsuda. Reprinted by permission of Beacon Press, Boston.

Excerpts from " Feminist Jurisprudence: Grounding the Theories" by Patricia A. Cain in Berkeley Women's Law Journal, Vol. 4. Copyright 1989 by Univ. of Calif. Press (J). Reproduced with permission of Univ. of Calif. Press (J).

Excerpts from "Refashioning the Unfashionable: Claiming Lesbian Identities in the Legal Context" by Diana Majury in Canadian Journal of Women & Law, Vol. 7, North York, Ont. Copyright © 1994 University of Toronto Press Incorporated. Reprinted by permission of University of Toronto Press Incorporated.

Chapter 4:

Excerpts from "Pleasure under Patriarchy" by Catharine A. MacKinnon, from THEORIES OF HUMAN SEXUALITY, edited by James Geer and Will O'Donohue, reprinted with permission of the publishers,

Kluwen Academic/ Plenum Publishing Corp., New York, NY, Copyright © 1987 by Plenum Press, and with permission of the author.

Excerpts from "Occupation/Collaboration" from INTERCOURSE by Andrea Dworkin, reprinted with permission of the publishers, Free Press, a Division of Simon & Schuster, Inc., Copyright © 1987 by Andrea Dworkin, and with permission of the author.

Excerpts from "Feminism, Sexuality and Authenticity" by Ruth Colker reprinted with permission of the publisher, Boston University Law Review, from "Feminism, Sexuality and Self" by Ruth Colker, Copyright © 1988 by Trustees of Boston University, and with permission of the author.

Excerpts from "Ending Female Sexual Oppression" from FEMINIST THEORY: FROM MARGIN TO CENTER by bell hooks, reprinted with permission of the publisher, South End Press, Boston, MA. Copyright © 1984 by bell hooks.

Excerpts from "Social and Behavioral Construction of Female Sexuality" by Patricia Y. Miller and Martha R. Fowlkes, from SEX AND SCIENTIFIC INQUIRY, edited by Sandra Harding and Jean F. O'Barr, reprinted with permission of the publisher, The University of Chicago Press, Chicago, IL, Copyright © 1987 by the University of Chicago, and with permission of the authors.

Excerpts from "Organs and Orgasms" by Alix Shulman, from WOMAN IN SEXIST SOCIETY, edited by Vivian Gornick and Barbara K. Moran, reprinted with permission of the publisher, Basic Books, Inc., a member of Perseus Books, L.L.C., Copyright © 1971 by Basic Books, Inc.

Excerpts from "Lesbian Relationships: Implications for the Study of Sexuality and Gender" by Margaret Nichols, from HOMOSEXUALITY/HETEROSEXUALITY, edited by David P. McWhirter, Stephanie A. Sanders and June Machover Reinisch, reprinted with the permission of the publisher, Oxford University Press. Copyright © 1990 by The Kinsey Institute for Research in Sex, Gender and Reproduction.

Excerpts from "Lesbian 'Sex' (1987)" from WILLFUL VIRGIN: ESSAYS IN FEMINISM 1976-1992, by Marilyn Frye, reprinted with permission from the publisher, The Crossing Press, Freedom, California, Copyright © 1992.

Excerpts from "Hearts of Darkness" by Barbara Omolade, from POWERS OF DESIRE: THE POLITICS OF SEXUALITY, edited by Ann Snitow, Christine Stansell and Sharon Thompson, reprinted with permission of the publisher, Monthly Review Foundation, Copyright © 1983 by Snitow, Stansell and Thompson.

Chapter 5:

Excerpts from HARD BARGAINS by Linda Hirshman and Jane Larson, reprinted with permission of the publisher, Oxford University Press, Inc., Copyright © 1998 by Oxford University Press, Inc.

Excerpts from "Rape" by Susan Estrich, from The Yale Law Journal, Vol. 95, pp. 1087-1184, reprinted with permission of The Yale Law Journal Company and Fred B. Rothman & Company, Copyright © 1986 by Yale University, and with permission of the author.

Excerpts from "When Will We Be Believed? Rape Myths and the Idea of a Fair Trial in Rape Prosecutions" by Morrison Torrey, from 24 University of California-Davis Law Review, reprinted with permission of the publisher, University of California-Davis Law Review, Copyright © 1991 by the Regents of the University of California, and with permission of the author.

Excerpts from "Demarginalizing the Intersection of Race and Sex: A Black Feminist Critique of Antidiscrimination Doctrine, Feminist Theory and Antiracist Politics" by Kimberle Crenshaw, from 1989 University of Chicago Legal Forum, reprinted with permission of the publisher, Chicago Legal Forum, Copyright © 1989 by the University of Chicago.

Excerpts from LICENSE TO RAPE: SEXUAL ABUSE OF WIVES by David Finkelhor, Ph.D. and Kersti Yllo, Ph.D., Copyright © 1985 by David Finkelhor and Kersti Yllo, reprinted with permission of Henry Holt and Co., L.L.C.

Excerpts from RAPE IN MARRIAGE by Diana E.H. Russell, reprinted with permission of the publisher, Indiana University Press, Bloomington, Ind., Copyright © 1990 by Diana E.H. Russell, and with permission of the author.

Excerpts from "Medical and Legal Aspects of Rape and Resistance," by Mantese et al., from 12 Journal of Legal Medicine, reprinted with permission of the editor, authors, and publisher, Taylor and Francis, Copyright © 1991 by Taylor and Francis.

Excerpts from "The Cloak of Benevolence" by Susan Stefan, reprinted with permission of the author, Copyright © 1989 by Susan Stefan.

Excerpts from "The Confluence Model of Sexual Aggression" by Neil Malamuth, from SEX, POWER, CONFLICT: EVOLUTIONARY AND FEMINIST PERSPECTIVES, edited by David M. Buss and Neil M. Malamuth, reprinted with permission of the publisher Oxford University Press, Inc., Copyright © 1996 by Oxford University Press.

Excerpts from STOPPING RAPE: SUCCESSFUL SURVIVAL STRATEGIES by Pauline B. Bart and Patricia H. O'Brien, reprinted with permission of the publisher, Teachers College Press, Copyright © 1985 by Pergamon Press, and with permission of the authors.

Excerpts from "Sex Offender Legislation and the Antitherapeutic Effects on Victims" by Leonore M.J. Simon, from 41 Arizona Law Review, reprinted with permission of the Arizona Law Review, Copyright © 1999 by the Arizona Board of Regents, and with permission of the author.

Excerpts from FATHER-DAUGHTER INCEST by Judith Lewis Herman reprinted with permission of the publishers, Harvard University Press, Cambridge, Mass., Copyright © 1981 by the President and Fellows of Harvard College.

Excerpts from "Child Sexual Coercion" by Dean D. Knudson, from SEXUAL COERCION: A SOURCEBOOK ON ITS NATURE, CAUSES AND PREVENTION, edited by Elizabeth Grauerholz and Mary A. Koralewski, reprinted with permission of the publisher, Lexington Books, of the University Press of America, Copyright © 1991 by Lexington Books.

Excerpts from "The Manipulation of Legal Remedies to Deter Suits by Survivors of Childhood Sexual Abuse," by Cynthia Grant Bowman, from 92 Northwestern University Law Review, reprinted by permission of Northwestern University School of Law, Law Review, Copyright © 1998 by Northwestern University Law Review, and of the author.

Excerpts from "Reassessing Mother Blame in Incest" by Janet Liebman Jacobs, from 15 Signs, reprinted with permission of the publisher, The University of Chicago Press, Copyright ©1990 by the University of Chicago Press, and with permission of the author.

Excerpts from THE BATTERED WOMAN by Lenore E. Walker, Copyright © 1979 by Lenore E. Walker, reprinted with permission of Harper Collins Publishers, Inc.

Excerpts from BATTERED WOMEN AS SURVIVORS: AN ALTERNATIVE TO TREATING LEARNED HELPLESSNESS by Edward W. Gondolf with Ellen R. Fisher, Copyright © 1988 by Lexington Books, reprinted with permission of Rowman Littlefield Publishing Group.

Excerpts from WHEN MEN BATTER WOMEN: NEW INSIGHTS INTO ENDING ABUSIVE RELATIONSHIPS by Neil S. Jacobson and John M. Gottman, Copyright © 1998 by Simon & Schuster, reprinted with permission of Simon & Schuster.

Excerpts from "Domestic Violence: The Case for Aggressive Prosecution" by Donna Wills, reprinted with permission of the Regents of the University of California and of the author. Originally published in UCLA Women's Law Journal, Copyright © 1997, The Regents of the University of California. All Rights Reserved.

Excerpts from "Killing Her Softly: Intimate Abuse and the Violence of State Intervention" by Linda G. Mills, Copyright © 1999 by The Harvard Law Review Association, reprinted with permission of the Harvard Law Review Association and of the author.

Excerpts from JUSTIFIABLE HOMICIDE: BATTERED WOMEN, SELF-DEFENSE, AND THE LAW by Cynthia K. Gillespie, Copyright © 1987 by Ohio State University Press, reprinted with permission of Ohio State University Press.

Excerpts from "White Slavery: Myth or Reality" from THE LOST SISTERHOOD: PROSTITUTION IN AMERICA, 1900-1918 by Ruth Rosen, reprinted with permission of the publisher, Johns Hopkins University Press, Copyright © 1992 The Johns Hopkins University Press.

Excerpts from "Prostitution: A Contemporary Form of Slavery" by Dorchen Leidholdt, Co-Executive Director of the Coalition Against Trafficking in Women, United Nations Working Group on Contemporary

Forms of Slavery, Geneva, May 1998, Copyright © 1998 by Dorchen Leidholdt, reprinted with permission of the author.

Excerpts from THE IDEA OF PROSTITUTION by Sheila Jeffreys, reprinted with permission of the publisher, Spinifex Press, Copyright © 1997 Sheila Jeffreys.

Excerpts from "The Feminist Debate over Prostitution Reform: Prostitutes' Rights Groups, Radical Feminists and the (Im)possibility of Consent" by Jody Freeman, Professor of Law at University of California-Los Angeles, reprinted from 5 Berkeley Women's Law Journal pp. 75-109, reprinted with permission of the publisher, Copyright © 1990 by Berkeley Women's Law Journal, and with permission of the author.

Excerpts from "Pornography and Sexual Abuse of Women" by Mimi H. Silbert and Ayala M. Pines, from 10 Sex Roles, reprinted with permission of the publisher, Plenum Publishing Corp., and with permission of the authors.

Excerpts from "Model Antipornography Civil-Rights Ordinance" by Andrea Dworkin and Catharine A. MacKinnon, from PORNOGRAPHY & CIVIL RIGHTS: A NEW DAY FOR WOMEN'S EQUALITY, reprinted with permission of the authors, Copyright © 1988 by Andrea Dworkin and Catharine A. MacKinnon.

Excerpts from "Francis Biddle's Sister: Pornography, Civil Rights, and Speech" by Catharine A. MacKinnon reprinted by permission from FEMINISM UNMODIFIED: DISCOURSES ON LIFE AND LAW by Catharine A. MacKinnon, Cambridge, Mass.: Harvard University Press, Copyright © 1987 by the President and Fellows of Harvard College.

Excerpts from "Pornography and the Alienation of Male Sexuality" by Harry Brod, from 14 Social Theory and Practice 267 (Fall 1988), reprinted with permission of the publisher, Copyright © 1988 by Social Theory and Practice, and with permission of the author.

Chapter 6:

Excerpts from WOMAN'S BODY, WOMAN'S RIGHT: BIRTH CONTROL IN AMERICA (Revised Edition) by Linda Gordon, Copyright © 1976, 1990 by Linda Gordon, reprinted by permission of the Charlotte Sheedy Literary Agency and of the author.

Excerpts from ABORTION AND WOMAN'S CHOICE: THE STATE, SEXUALITY, AND REPRODUCTIVE FREEDOM (Revised Edition) by Rosalind Pollack Petchesky, Copyright 1984, 1990 by Rosalind Pollack Petchesky, reprinted with the permission of Northeastern University Press and of the author.

Excerpts from "Privacy v. Equality: Beyond *Roe v. Wade*" by Catharine A. MacKinnon reprinted by permission from FEMINISM UNMODIFIED: DISCOURSES ON LIFE AND LAW by Catharine A. MacKinnon, Cambridge, Mass.: Harvard University Press, Copyright © 1987 by the President and Fellows of Harvard College.

Excerpts from Thomson, Judith Jarvis; A DEFENSE OF ABORTION. Copyright © 1971 by Princeton University Press. Reprinted by permission of Princeton University Press.

Excerpts from FEMINISM WITHOUT ILLUSIONS: A CRITIQUE OF INDIVIDUALISM, by Elizabeth Fox-Genovese, Copyright © 1991 by The University of North Carolina Press, reprinted with permission of the publisher.

Excerpts from ABORTION AND THE POLITICS OF MOTHERHOOD, by Kristin Luker, Copyright © 1984 by the Regents of the University of California, reprinted with the permission of the Regents of the University of California, the University of California Press, and the author.

Excerpts from "The Creation of Fetal Rights: Conflicts with Women's Constitutional Rights to Liberty, Privacy, and Equal Protection" by Dawn E. Johnsen, reprinted by permission of The Yale Law Journal Company and Fred B. Rothman & Company from The Yale Law Journal, vol. 95, pages 599-625, and the author.

Excerpts from "Punishing Drug Addicts Who Have Babies: Women of Color, Equality, and the Right of Privacy" by Dorothy E. Roberts, Copyright © 1991 by the Harvard Law Review Association, reprinted by permission of the publisher and the author.

Exerpts from "Electronic Fetal Monitors: Marketing Forces and the Resulting Controversy" by Judith A. Kunisch, from HEALING TECHNOLOGY, Kathryn Ratcliff, ed., Copyright © 1989 by the University of Michigan Press, reprinted with permission of the publisher.

Chapter 7:

Excerpts from AMBITION AND ACCOMMODATION: HOW WOMEN VIEW GENDER RELATIONS by Roberta S. Sigel, Copyright © 1996 by the University of Chicago Press, reprinted by permission of the publisher and the author.

Excerpts from MARITAL EQUALITY: ITS RELATIONSHIP TO THE WELL-BEING OF HUSBANDS AND WIVES by Janice M. Steil, Copyright © 1997 by Sage Publications, reprinted by permission of Sage Publications, Inc.

Excerpts from "The Economic Costs of Marital Dissolution: Why Do Women Bear A Disproportionate Cost?" by Karen C. Holden and Pamela J. Smock, used with permission, from the Annual Review of Sociology, Volume 17, © 1991, by Annual Reviews http://www.AnnualReviews.org, and of the authors.

Excerpts from THE NEUTERED MOTHER, THE SEXUAL FAMILY AND OTHER TWENTIETH CENTURY TRAGEDIES by Martha Albertson Fineman, Copyright © 1995, reproduced by permission of Taylor & Francis, Inc./Routledge, Inc., http://www.routledge-ny.com, and of the author.

Chapter 8:

Excerpt from "Foreword," from OF WOMAN BORN: MOTHERHOOD AS EXPERIENCE AND INSTITUTION by Adrienne Rich. Copyright © 1986, 1976 by W.W. Norton & Company, Inc. Used by permission of W.W. Norton & Company, Inc.

Excerpt from THE REPRODUCTION OF MOTHERING: PSYCHOANALYSIS AND THE SOCIOLOGY OF GENDER by Nancy Chodorow, Copyright © 1978 by The Regents of the University of California, reprinted with permission of the Regents of the University of California and the University of California Press.

Excerpts from "Motherhood and Crime" by Dorothy E. Roberts, Copyright © 1993 by Dorothy Roberts, reprinted with permission of the Iowa Law Review and the author.

Excerpts from "Maternity Leave Policies: An International Survey," Copyright © 1988 by the President and Fellows of Harvard College and the Harvard Women's Law Journal, reprinted with the permission of the Harvard Women's Law Journal.

"Joey's Problem: Nancy and Evan Holt," from THE SECOND SHIFT by Arlie Hochschild and Ann Machung, copyright © 1989 by Arlie Hochschild. Used by permission of Viking Penguin, a division of Penguin Putnam Inc.

Excerpts from "Why Men Don't Rear Children: A Power Analysis" by M. Rivka Polatnick, Copyright © by M. Rivka Polatnick, reprinted with permission of the author.

Excerpts from WOMEN AND CHILDREN LAST by Ruth Sidel, Copyright © 1986 by Ruth Sidel. Used by permission of Viking Penguin, a division of Penguin Putnam Inc.

Excerpts from MAID IN THE U.S.A. by Mary Romero, Copyright © 1992 by Routledge, Inc. Reproduced by permission of Taylor & Francis, Inc./Routledge, Inc., http://www.routledge-ny.com, and of the author.

Excerpts from "The Value of Black Mothers' Work" by Dorothy E. Roberts, Copyright © 1994 by the Connecticut Law Review, reprinted with permission of the Connecticut Law Review and the author.

Excerpts from "Child Custody in the 21st Century: How the American Law Institute Proposes to Achieve Predictability and Still Protect the Individual Child's Best Interests" by Katharine T. Bartlett, Copyright © 1999 by Willamette Law Review, reprinted with permission of the Willamette Law Review and the author.

Excerpts from "Family Law and Gay and Lesbian Family Issues in the Twentieth Century" by David L. Chambers and Nancy D. Polikoff, Copyright © 2000 by the American Bar Association, reprinted with permission of the American Bar Association and the authors.

Excerpts from "The Economics of Divorce: Social and Economic Consequences of Property, Alimony, and Child Support Awards" by Lenore Weitzman, originally published in 28 UCLA L. Rev. 1181, Copyright ©

1981, The Regents of the University of California. All Rights Reserved. Reprinted with permission of the UCLA Law Review, William S. Hein & Co., Inc., and the author.

Chapter 9:

Excerpts from EDUCATED IN ROMANCE by Dorothy C. Holland and Margaret A. Eisenhart, reprinted with permission of the publisher, The University of Chicago Press, Copyright © 1990 by the University of Chicago, and with permission of the authors.

Excerpts from "Feminist Theory and Standardized Testing" by Phyllis Teitelbaum, from GENDER/BODY/KNOWLEDGE: FEMINIST RECONSTRUCTIONS OF BEING AND KNOWING, edited by Alison M. Jaggar and Susan R. Bordo, Copyright © 1989 by Rutgers, the State University, reprinted with permission of Rutgers University Press and of the author.

Excerpts from "The Future of Affirmative Action: Reclaiming the Innovative Ideal" by Susan Sturm and Lani Guinier, originally published in 84 California L. Review 953 (1996), reprinted with permission of the publisher California Law Review, Copyright © 1996 by California Law Review, and with permission of the authors.

Excerpts from POWER AT PLAY by Michael Messner, Copyright © 1992 by Michael A. Messner, reprinted by permission of Beacon Press, Boston.

Excerpts from "Public Response to Racist Speech: Considering the Victim's Story" by Mari J. Matsuda, from 87 Michigan Law Review, reprinted with permission of the publisher, Copyright © 1989 by Michigan Law Review Association, and with permission of the author; also appears in M. Matsuda, C. Lawrence, R. Delgado, K. Crenshaw, WORDS THAT WOUND: CRITICAL RACE THEORY, ASSAULTIVE SPEECH AND THE FIRST AMENDMENT, Westview Press (1993).

Excerpts from "If He Hollers Let Him Go: Regulating Racist Speech on Campus" by Charles R. Lawrence, III, from 1990 Duke Law Journal, reprinted with permission of the publisher, Duke Law Journal, Copyright © 1990 by Duke Law Journal.

Chapter 10:

Excerpts from "The Treaty of Amsterdam: The Next Step Towards Gender Equality" by Elizabeth F. Defeis in Boston College International & Comparative Law Review, Vol., 23. Copyright © 1999 by Boston College International & Comparative Law Review. Reprinted by permission of Boston College International & Comparative Law Review.

Excerpts from "The New Jurisprudence of Sexual Harassment" by Kathryn Abrams, reprinted from 83 Cornell Law Review 1169 (1998), with permission of the publisher, Cornell Law Review, Copyright © 1998 by Cornell Law Review, and with permission of the author.

Excerpts from "Treating Sexual Harassment with Respect" by Anita Bernstein, reprinted from 111 Harvard Law Review 445 (1997), with permission of the publisher, The Harvard Law Review Association, Copyright © 1997 by The Harvard Law Review Association, and with permission of the author.

Excerpts from "What's Wrong with Sexual Harassment?" by Katherine Franke, reprinted from 49 Stanford Law Review 691 (1997), with permission of the publisher, Stanford Law Review, Copyright © 1997 Stanford Law Review, and with permission of the author.

Excerpts from "Disaggregating Gender from Sex and Sexual Orientation: The Effeminate Man in the Law and Feminist Jurisprudence" by Mary Anne Case in Yale Law Journal, Vol. 105. Copyright © 1995 by Yale Law Journal Company Inc. Reproduced with permission of Yale Law Journal Company Inc.

Excerpts from "The Central Mistake of Sex Discrimination Law: The Disaggregation of Sex from Gender" by Katherine Franke in University of Pennsylvania Law Review, Vol. 144. Copyright 1995 by Univ. of Penn Law Rev. Reproduced with permission of Univ. of Penn Law Rev.

Excerpts from "The Proximate Causes of Employment Discrimination" by Barbara F. Reskin in Contemporary Sociology, Vol. 29, pp. 319, 320. Copyright © 2000 by American Sociological Association. Reprinted by permission of Barbara F. Reskin and the American Sociological Association.

Excerpts from "The Content of Our Categories: A Cognitive Bias Approach to Discrimination and Equal Employment Opportunity" by Linda Hamilton Krieger in Stanford Law Review, Vol. 47. Copyright © 1995 by Stanford Law Rev. Reproduced with permission of Stanford Law Rev.

Excerpts from "A Hair Piece: Perspectives on the Intersection of Race and Gender" by Paulette M. Caldwell, in Duke Law Journal, Vol. 1991. Copyright © 1991 by Paulette M. Caldwell. Reprinted with permission of Paulette M. Caldwell.

Excerpts from "Women's Work in Ontario: Pay Equity and the Wage Gap" by Elaine M. Todres in Ottawa L. Rev., Vol. 22. Copyright © 1990 by Elaine M. Todres. Reprinted with permission of Elaine M. Todres.

Chapter 11:

Excerpts from "The Legal Education of Twenty Women" by Catherine A. Weiss and Louise Melling, Copyright © 1988 by the Board of Trustees of the Leland Stanford Junior University, reprinted with the permission of the Stanford Law Review.

Excerpts from "Becoming Gentlemen: Women's Experiences at One Ivy League Law School" by Lani Guinier, Michelle Fine, and Jane Balin, with Ann Bartow and Deborah Lee Stachel, Copyright © 1994 by the Trustees of the University of Pennsylvania, reprinted with the permission of the University of Pennsylvania Law Review and William S. Hein & Company, Inc. and of Lani Guinier.

Excerpts from "Feminist Legal Theory, Feminist Lawmaking, and the Legal Profession" by Cynthia Grant Bowman and Elizabeth M. Schneider, Copyright © 1998 by Fordham Law Review, reprinted with the permission of the Fordham Law Review and the authors.

Excerpts from "Sex Discrimination or Gender Inequality?" by Leslie Bender, Copyright © 1989 by Leslie Bender and the Fordham Law Review, reprinted with the permission of the Fordham Law Review and the author.

Excerpts from "Portia in a Different Voice: Speculations on a Women's Lawyering Process" by Carrie Menkel-Meadow, Copyright © 1985 by Berkeley Women's Law Journal, reprinted from Berkeley Women's Law Journal Vol. 1, No. 1, pp. 39-63, by permission of the University of California Press and the author.

Excerpts from "The Mediation Alternative: Process Dangers for Women" by Trina Grillo, reprinted by permission of The Yale Law Journal Company and Fred B. Rothman & Company from The Yale Law Journal, Vol. 100, pages 1545-1610.

Excerpts from "Notes from the Field: A Reply to Professor Colker" by Sarah H. Burns, Copyright © 1990 by the President and Fellows of Harvard College and the Harvard Women's Law Journal, reprinted with the permission of the Harvard Women's Law Journal and the author.

Chapter 12:

Excerpts from Barbara R. Bergmann, SAVING OUR CHILDREN FROM POVERTY, © 1996 Russell Sage Foundation, New York, New York. Reprinted by permission of Russell Sage Foundation.

Summary of Contents

*

Table of Contents

Table of Cases

The principal cases are in bold type. Cases cited or discussed in the text are roman type. References are to pages. Cases cited in principal cases and within other quoted materials are not included.

*

CASES AND MATERIALS ON

FEMINIST JURISPRUDENCE

TAKING WOMEN SERIOUSLY

Second Edition

*

Chapter 1

THE HISTORICAL BACKGROUND OF FEMINIST LEGAL THEORY

The history of the women's movement in the United States is often described as two "waves." The "first wave" refers to the period from the Seneca Falls Convention in 1848 to passage of the Nineteenth Amendment granting women the right to vote in 1920; the "second wave" describes the developments from approximately 1960 to the present. It is sometimes assumed that the first wave consisted solely of the suffrage movement. In fact, however, feminists have inherited a rich history of struggles—intellectual, legal, and political—during which women repeatedly emphasized many themes in addition to political rights; these include the right to economic independence and equality, access to education, the right to control their own sexual and reproductive lives, rights to their children and property both within marriage and upon divorce, and the right to safety in the workplace, at home, and in public places. In this chapter we describe, in brief detail, the early years of the women's movement in the United States and show the broad-based and radical critique of gender and society that is a rich part of its legacy to modern feminists.

A. THE WOMAN MOVEMENT: 1840–1870

The seeds of the 19th–century "woman movement"[1] in the United States are said to have been planted at the 1840 Anti–Slavery Convention in London, during which Lucretia Mott and Elizabeth Cady Stanton were deprived of delegate status and consigned to the balcony, leading

1. Nineteenth-century women used the term "the woman movement" to refer both to the suffrage movement and to other struggles for social, legal and political reform; the use of the singular reflected the presumed unity of interests among women. The term "feminism" came into use in the 1910's, to denote a movement that was narrower in membership than the suffrage movement, yet broader in its intent to revolutionize many aspects of the relations between men and women. Nancy F. Cott, The Grounding of Modern Feminism 3 (1987).

them to launch a women's rights campaign when they returned home.[2] While this explanation is clearly oversimplified, it points to a number of important characteristics of the early woman movement. Many of its leaders, like Mott, Stanton, and the Grimké sisters, gained their initial political experience in the abolitionist movement, which offered them an egalitarian ideology and theory of social change.[3] Many of these women were among the first generation of women in the United States to receive a formal education, and they found a sense of purpose in abolitionism in a society where most forms of political and economic activity were closed to them. Because women were prohibited by custom from speaking in public to mixed assemblies of men and women, they quickly learned that in order to further the anti-slavery cause, they must press for their own rights as well.[4] Abolitionism gave these early feminists male allies like Frederick Douglass, Henry Blackwell (husband of Lucy Stone), and William Lloyd Garrison.

On July 19 and 20, 1848, the first Women's Rights Convention in the United States was held at Seneca Falls, New York, which is located between Syracuse and Rochester, close to the home of Elizabeth Cady Stanton. Approximately 250 women and 40 men attended in response to an advertisement placed in the local newspaper on July 14. The abolitionist leaders Lucretia Mott and Frederick Douglass were present. The Declaration of Sentiments and resolutions presented at the convention had been drafted by Stanton, Mott, Martha C. Wright, and Mary Ann McClintock and were modeled on the Declaration of Independence.[5] Elizabeth Cady Stanton argued strongly for the inclusion of a resolution demanding the right to vote; and it was the only resolution that did not pass unanimously, carrying only by a small margin.[6] Ironically, suffrage was to become almost the exclusive goal of one branch of the woman movement in the late 19th and early 20th centuries. Only one woman present at Seneca Falls lived to vote in the 1920 presidential election, the first following ratification of the Nineteenth Amendment.[7]

The Seneca Falls Declaration, which appears below, is the central document of this first period of activism by American women, when their efforts were concentrated primarily upon reform at the state level to improve the legal status of women. Note, however, that the list of grievances in the Declaration contains not only an attack on various discriminatory statutes but also a statement of fundamental feminist principles, attacking the "supremacy of man," the unequal allocation of

2. See Eleanor Flexner, Century of Struggle: The Woman's Rights Movement in the United States 71 (rev. ed. 1975; orig. pub. 1959).

3. See, e.g., Paula Giddings, When and Where I Enter: The Impact of Black Women on Race and Sex in America 55 (1984). Something similar happened in the 1960's, when white women joined the civil rights struggle and then formed their own groups in reaction to the unequal treatment they received within the Left. See, e.g., Sara Evans, Personal Politics: The Roots of Women's Liberation in the Civil Rights Movement and the New Left 23 (1979).

4. Flexner, above note 2, at 44–50.

5. Id. at 74–75.

6. Id. at 77.

7. Id.

power in family, state and church, and the different moral codes applied to men and women—an agenda shared by modern feminist theory.

THE DECLARATION OF SENTIMENTS

Seneca Falls, New York, July 19–20, 1848.

When, in the course of human events, it becomes necessary for one portion of the family of man to assume among the people of the earth a position different from that which they have hitherto occupied, but one to which the laws of nature and of nature's God entitle them, a decent respect to the opinions of mankind requires that they should declare the causes that impel them to such a course.

We hold these truths to be self-evident: that all men and women are created equal; they are endowed by their Creator with certain inalienable rights; that among these are life, liberty, and the pursuit of happiness; that to secure these rights governments are instituted, deriving their just powers from the consent of the governed. Whenever any form of government becomes destructive of these ends, it is the right of those who suffer from it to refuse allegiance to it, and to insist upon the institution of a new government, laying its foundation on such principles, and organizing its powers in such form, as to them shall seem most likely to effect their safety and happiness. Prudence, indeed, will dictate that governments long established should not be changed for light and transient causes; and accordingly all experience hath shown that mankind are more disposed to suffer, while evils are sufferable, than to right themselves by abolishing the forms to which they were accustomed. But when a long train of abuses and usurpations, pursuing invariably the same object evinces a design to reduce them under absolute despotism, it is their duty to throw off such government, and to provide new guards for their future security. Such has been the patient sufferance of the women under this government, and such is now the necessity which constrains them to demand the equal station to which they are entitled.

The history of mankind is a history of repeated injuries and usurpations on the part of man toward woman, having in direct object the establishment of an absolute tyranny over her. To prove this, let facts be submitted to a candid world.

He has never permitted her to exercise her inalienable right to the elective franchise.

He has compelled her to submit to laws, in the formation of which she had no voice.

He has withheld from her rights which are given to the most ignorant and degraded men—both natives and foreigners.

Having deprived her of this first right of a citizen, the elective franchise, thereby leaving her without representation in the halls of legislation, he has oppressed her on all sides.

He has made her, if married, in the eye of the law, civilly dead.

He has taken from her all right in property, even to the wages she earns.

He has made her, morally, an irresponsible being, as she can commit many crimes with impunity, provided they be done in the presence of her husband. In the covenant of marriage, she is compelled to promise obedience to her husband, he becoming, to all intents and purposes, her master—the law giving him power to deprive her of her liberty, and to administer chastisement.

He has so framed the laws of divorce, as to what shall be the proper causes, and in case of separation, to whom the guardianship of the children shall be given, as to be wholly regardless of the happiness of women—the law, in all cases, going upon a false supposition of the supremacy of man, and giving all power into his hands.

After depriving her of all rights as a married woman, if single, and the owner of property, he has taxed her to support a government which recognizes her only when her property can be made profitable to it.

He has monopolized nearly all the profitable employments, and from those she is permitted to follow, she receives but a scanty remuneration. He closes against her all the avenues to wealth and distinction which he considers most honorable to himself. As a teacher of theology, medicine, or law, she is not known.

He has denied her the facilities for obtaining a thorough education, all colleges being closed against her.

He allows her in Church, as well as State, but a subordinate position, claiming Apostolic authority for her exclusion from the ministry, and, with some exceptions, from any public participation in the affairs of the Church.

He has created a false public sentiment by giving to the world a different code of morals for men and women, by which moral delinquencies which exclude women from society, are not only tolerated, but deemed of little account in man.

He has usurped the prerogative of Jehovah himself, claiming it as his right to assign for her a sphere of action, when that belongs to her conscience and to her God.

He has endeavored, in every way that he could, to destroy her confidence in her own powers, to lessen her self-respect, and to make her willing to lead a dependent and abject life.

Now, in view of this entire disfranchisement of one-half the people of this country, their social and religious degradation—in view of the unjust laws above mentioned, and because women do feel themselves aggrieved, oppressed, and fraudulently deprived of their most sacred rights, we insist that they have immediate admission to all the rights and privileges which belong to them as citizens of the United States.

In entering upon the great work before us, we anticipate no small amount of misconception, misrepresentation, and ridicule; but we shall use every instrumentality within our power to effect our object. We shall employ agents, circulate tracts, petition the State and National legislatures, and endeavor to enlist the pulpit and the press in our behalf. We hope this Convention will be followed by a series of Conventions embracing every part of the country.

Resolutions

WHEREAS, The great precept of nature is conceded to be, that "man shall pursue his own true and substantial happiness." Blackstone in his Commentaries remarks, that this law of Nature being coeval with mankind, and dictated by God himself, is of course superior in obligation to any other. It is binding over all the globe, in all countries and at all times; no human laws are of any validity if contrary to this, and such of them as are valid, derive all their force, and all their validity, and all their authority, mediately and immediately, from this original; therefore,

Resolved, That such laws as conflict, in any way, with the true and substantial happiness of woman, are contrary to the great precept of nature and of no validity, for this is "superior in obligation to any other."

Resolved, That all laws which prevent woman from occupying such a station in society as her conscience shall dictate, or which place her in a position inferior to that of man, are contrary to the great precept of nature, and therefore of no force or authority.

Resolved, That woman is man's equal—was intended to be so by the Creator, and the highest good of the race demands that she should be recognized as such.

Resolved, That the women of this country ought to be enlightened in regard to the laws under which they live, that they may no longer publish their degradation by declaring themselves satisfied with their present position, nor their ignorance, by asserting that they have all the rights they want.

Resolved, That inasmuch as man, while claiming for himself intellectual superiority, does accord to woman moral superiority, it is preeminently his duty to encourage her to speak and teach, as she has an opportunity, in all religious assemblies.

Resolved, That the same amount of virtue, delicacy, and refinement of behavior that is required of woman in the social state, should also be required of man, and the same transgressions should be visited with equal severity on both man and woman.

Resolved, That the objection of indelicacy and impropriety, which is so often brought against woman when she addresses a public audience, comes with a very ill-grace from those who encourage, by their attendance, her appearance on the stage, in the concert, or in feats of the circus.

Resolved, That woman has too long rested satisfied in the circumscribed limits which corrupt citizens and a perverted application of the

Scriptures have marked out for her, and that it is time she should move in the enlarged sphere which her great Creator has assigned her.

Resolved, That it is the duty of the women of this country to secure to themselves their sacred right to the elective franchise.

Resolved, That the equality of human rights results necessarily from the fact of the identity of the race in capabilities and responsibilities.

Resolved, therefore, That, being invested by the Creator with the same capabilities, and the same consciousness of responsibility for their exercise, it is demonstrably the right and duty of woman, equally with man, to promote every righteous cause by every righteous means; and especially in regard to the great subjects of morals and religion, it is self-evidently her right to participate with her brother in teaching them, both in private and in public, by writing and by speaking, by any instrumentalities proper to be used, and in any assemblies proper to be held; and this being a self-evident truth growing out of the divinely implanted principles of human nature, any custom or authority adverse to it, whether modern or wearing the hoary sanction of antiquity, is to be regarded as a self-evident falsehood, and at war with mankind.

[At the last session Lucretia Mott offered and spoke to the following resolution:]

Resolved, That the speedy success of our cause depends upon the zealous and untiring efforts of both men and women, for the overthrow of the monopoly of the pulpit, and for the securing to woman an equal participation with men in the various trades, professions, and commerce.

As the Declaration of Sentiments so aptly puts it, married women were considered "civilly dead" in the first half of the 19th century, for the common law doctrine of coverture treated them as one being with their husbands, who exercised all rights on behalf of the unit. Thus married women were unable to own property in their own names, to enter into contracts, to hold title to the property they inherited or devise property, to hold property in their own earnings, or to gain guardianship or custody of their children in case of legal separation.[8] In the face of these laws, Lucy Stone and Henry Blackwell entered into marriage in 1855 "under protest," reading and signing at their wedding a document explicitly protesting against the legal rights given to the husband over his wife.[9]

At the time of the Seneca Falls Convention in 1848, the focus of the woman movement was upon these legal rights and on other social and economic issues, including the rights to divorce and to a more equal relationship within marriage, educational opportunity and employment,

8. See Norma Basch, In the Eyes of the Law: Women, Marriage, and Property in Nineteenth–Century New York 42–69 (1982).

9. For the text of the Stone–Blackwell protest, see Feminism: The Essential Historical Writings 103–05 (Miriam Schneir, ed. 1972).

and the concept of female inferiority enshrined in organized religion and politics. Married Women's Property Acts were ultimately passed in state after state in an effort to remedy the common law coverture restrictions. In some states, this was the result of determined political campaigns, during which women who had never been politically active went from door to door obtaining signatures on petitions for legislative change.[10] One of the first of these acts, passed in New York in 1848, appears below.

MARRIED WOMEN'S PROPERTY ACT

Laws of New York, ch. 200 (1848).

§ 1. The real and personal property of any female who may hereafter marry, and which she shall own at the time of marriage, and the rents, issues and profits thereof shall not be subject to the disposal of her husband, nor be liable for his debts, and shall continue her sole and separate property, as if she were a single female.

§ 2. The real and personal property, and the rents, issues and profits thereof of any female now married shall not be subject to the disposal of her husband; but shall be her sole and separate property as if she were a single female except so far as the same may be liable for the debts of her husband heretofore contracted.

§ 3. It shall be lawful for any married female to receive, by gift, grant, devise or bequest, from any person other than her husband and hold to her sole and separate use, as if she were a single female, real and personal property, and the rents, issues and profits thereof, and the same shall not be subject to the disposal of her husband, nor be liable for his debts.

§ 4. All contracts made between persons in contemplation of marriage shall remain in full force after such marriage takes place.

Although the Married Women's Property Acts were called for by women's rights advocates as a remedy for the "civil death" of women under coverture, the concern of many legislators (who were, of course, all male) was to insulate the estates of their married daughters from spendthrift sons-in-law and their creditors and to clarify the legal situation for those creditors in a time of economic upheaval.[11] In the South, the concern was often to protect the daughters' inheritance of slaves.[12] After the laws were passed, they were frequently interpreted so narrowly by the judiciary that the rights contemplated by statute were not extended to women in fact.[13] In New York, for example, another

10. Flexner, above note 2, at 86–89.

11. Basch, above note 8, at 124–26.

12. See Women's America: Refocusing the Past 532 (Linda K. Kerber and Jane Sherron De Hart, eds. 3d ed. 1991).

13. See Basch, above note 8, at 200–32.

Married Women's Property Act was passed in 1860. The 1860 statute was much broader in its protections than that passed in 1848, making mothers joint guardians of their children, equal in powers, rights, and duties with their husbands. The 1860 Act also, explicitly and in greater detail than the 1848 statute, gave women the right to own property, collect their own wages, sue in court, and have property rights upon their husbands' deaths. Again, the judicial interpretation of the 1860 statute was so narrow that it was necessary to pass yet another law in 1884, explicitly giving married women the right, among other things, to enter into contracts as if they were single persons, even though full contractual capacity was implied by the wording of the 1860 Act.[14] Thus, women's rights activists were compelled to return to the state legislatures repeatedly—or, believing that the inequity had been remedied, they turned their attention to other things, while each legislative advance was gutted by judicial interpretation.

In addition to legislative campaigns, after 1850 women's rights conventions and numerous local meetings were held on an annual basis in the Northern states. One of these women's rights conventions, which took place in Akron, Ohio in 1851, was the occasion for the famous "Ain't I A Woman?" speech by Sojourner Truth, an African American woman who was a former slave. The meeting, organized by white women, was being disrupted by hostile men when Truth took the podium to confront the anti-women's rights arguments.[15] Her powerful speech not only quieted the crowd but also presented a graphic reminder of the important issues of race and class that divided women at that time. The contents of her speech, emphasizing qualities of strength, starkly contrasted with the ideology of "true womanhood" in the 19th century—a pervasive stereotype in fiction and advice literature for women, encouraging them to cultivate the virtues of domesticity, purity, and submissiveness, and to remain in the private sphere of family while the world of work increasingly moved out of the home.[16]

Sojourner Truth's speech is included below to illustrate the dynamic interrelationship of the women's movement throughout its history with issues of race and class—through analogies, often-precarious alliances, and the continuing debate within feminist theory about the similarities and differences of interest between women of different races and classes.[17]

For the texts of the 1848 and 1860 New York Married Women's Property Acts, see id. at 233–35.

14. Id. at 224.

15. See Flexner, above note 2, at 90–91.

16. Barbara Welter, The Cult of True Womanhood: 1820–1860, 18 Am.Q. 151–52 (1966). It is not at all clear that this image of "true womanhood" ever corresponded to reality for most women. See, e.g., Jeanne Boydston, The Pastoralization of Housework, in Kerber and De Hart, above note 12, at 148 (the ideology of gender spheres in fact obscured the value of labor women performed in the household and marginalized working-class women who did not remain in the home).

17. For historically influential analogies between race and sex, see, e.g., Gunnar Myrdal, An American Dilemma: The Negro Problem and Modern Democracy 1073–78 (1962; orig. pub. 1944); Helen Mayer Hacker, Women as a Minority Group, 30 Social Forces 60 (1951). See also discussion of essentialism in Chapter 3, below.

SOJOURNER TRUTH, "AIN'T I A WOMAN?" (1851)

In Feminism: The Essential Historical Writings 94–95 (Miriam Schneir, ed. 1972).

Well, children, where there is so much racket there must be something out of kilter. I think that 'twixt the negroes of the South and the women at the North, all talking about rights, the white men will be in a fix pretty soon. But what's all this here talking about?

That man over there says that women need to be helped into carriages, and lifted over ditches, and to have the best place everywhere. Nobody ever helps me into carriages, or over mud-puddles, or gives me any best place! And ain't I a woman? Look at me! Look at my arm! I have ploughed and planted, and gathered into barns, and no man could head me! And ain't I a woman? I could work as much and eat as much as a man—when I could get it—and bear the lash as well! And ain't I a woman? I have borne thirteen children, and seen them most all sold off to slavery, and when I cried out with my mother's grief, none but Jesus heard me! And ain't I a woman?

Then they talk about this thing in the head; what's this they call it? [Intellect, someone whispers.] That's it, honey. What's that got to do with women's rights or negro's rights? If my cup won't hold but a pint, and yours holds a quart, wouldn't you be mean not to let me have my little half-measure full?

Then that little man in black there, he says women can't have as much rights as men, 'cause Christ wasn't a woman! Where did your Christ come from? Where did your Christ come from? From God and a woman! Man had nothing to do with Him.

If the first woman God ever made was strong enough to turn the world upside down all alone, these women together ought to be able to turn it back, and get it right side up again! And now they is asking to do it, the men better let them.

Obliged to you for hearing me, and now old Sojourner ain't got nothing more to say.

In 1860, the demand for women's rights was postponed in deference to the Civil War; but women activists also hoped that, after supporting the war effort, women would receive the vote along with the freed slaves.[18] Instead, the word "male" was introduced into the Constitution for the first time in the Fourteenth Amendment. Furthermore, efforts to include sex in the Fifteenth Amendment as one of the grounds upon which suffrage could not be abridged were not supported by women's former abolitionist allies, for fear that this would endanger extension of

18. Flexner, above note 2, at 81, 109.

the vote to Black males.[19] The debate over the Fifteenth Amendment and these bitter disappointments for women's rights activists led to the rupture of their alliance with the larger equal rights movement and to a split within the woman movement itself.

In 1869, women representatives to the American Equal Rights Association formed the National Woman Suffrage Association (NWSA), led by Elizabeth Cady Stanton and Susan B. Anthony, with the objective of securing the passage of a constitutional amendment to enfranchise women. This group, under Stanton's leadership, also continued the wide agenda embodied in the Declaration of Sentiments, including severe criticism of contemporary marriage and divorce law, a critique of religion, and a cultural critique of the many ways women were socialized to think of themselves as inferior.[20] Others, led by Lucy Stone and Henry Blackwell, split off to found the more cautious American Woman Suffrage Association (AWSA) and mounted campaigns for suffrage on a state-by-state basis. Unlike NWSA, AWSA avoided issues of divorce, religion, and the rights of working women, for fear of alienating other sections of the community from AWSA's single-minded quest for the vote.[21]

B. THE SUFFRAGE MOVEMENT: 1870–1920

Among its initial strategies, NWSA attempted a legal campaign to obtain the ballot. Susan B. Anthony registered to vote in 1872 in Rochester, New York, and she and 14 other women actually cast ballots. They were charged with violating a provision of the 1870 Civil Rights Act designed to prevent white men from canceling out Black male votes by casting more than one ballot.[22] Although Anthony was denied the right to testify on her own behalf in court, she made numerous public speeches before the trial in an attempt to influence prospective jurors; in these speeches she argued, among other things, that she was entitled to vote as one of the privileges and immunities guaranteed to citizens under the Fourteenth Amendment, that the condition of women was one of servitude, and that she was being denied a jury of her peers.[23] The case never made it to the jurors, however, as the judge directed a verdict of guilty on the criminal charges; but Anthony was not sentenced to jail and never paid the $100 fine.[24] At her sentencing, before the judge could silence her, Susan B. Anthony denounced the all-male legal system that had convicted her.[25]

19. Joan Hoff, Law, Gender, and Injustice: A Legal History of U.S. Women 146–49 (1991). Political self-interest was also a motivating factor, as the Northern-based Republicans did not want to endanger the political potential of attracting the Black male vote by introducing the woman question. Id. at 149.

20. Flexner, above note 2, at 155–56.

21. Id.

22. Hoff, above note 19, at 153.

23. Id. at 153–57.

24. Id. at 157–60.

25. For the text of Susan B. Anthony's speech in United States v. Susan B. Anthony, see Schneir, ed., above note 9, at 134–36.

Although other women also attempted to vote in the 1870's, only one case made it to the Supreme Court—that brought by Virginia Minor, who sued her local registrar of voting in Missouri.[26] Minor argued that the right to vote was one of the privileges and immunities of citizenship under the Fourteenth Amendment and that, if women were denied that right, the United States was not a republic but a despotism.[27] Rejecting this argument, the Court unanimously held that, although women were citizens, the Framers had never intended to enfranchise them.

After these failures, the suffrage movement essentially gave up on the courts and turned to the political arena. A suffrage amendment was introduced into Congress in 1868; and a later version referred to as the "Anthony Amendment" was introduced in 1878 and every subsequent year until 1896, when it disappeared from the congressional agenda until 1913.[28]

As the struggle for suffrage grew more protracted, the movement became increasingly focused upon that one goal. Demands concerning divorce, trade unionism, and prostitution were dropped, as were attacks upon organized religion and the earlier leaders' radical critique of marriage as an institution. Moreover, the demand for suffrage itself, originally based on natural law, was reformulated as an extension of women's traditional role as mothers and as critical to their ability to bring special insight and morality into political life.[29] Many proponents of the suffrage movement either emerged from or allied themselves with the temperance movement, aiming to protect women whose husbands' drinking dissipated their family income or resulted in domestic violence; but this alliance evoked opposition from brewing interests which proceeded to fund anti-suffrage campaigns.[30]

At the same time, the suffrage movement became increasingly and overtly racist and nativist. In the hope of attracting support from conservatives and Southerners, suffragists emphasized the value of granting the vote to women in order to counterbalance the votes of Black men and immigrants, and even suggested educational requirements to vote which would in effect have limited suffrage to middle-class white native-born citizens.[31] In the name of tactical expediency, the suffrage movement, reunited in 1890 into the National American Woman Suffrage Association (NAWSA), refused membership to the Black women's clubs, refused to support Black women's demands, and even segregated public functions of their own in deference to Southern "sensitivities."[32]

26. Minor v. Happersett, 88 U.S. (21 Wall.) 162, 22 L.Ed. 627 (1874).

27. Hoff, above note 19, at 171.

28. Flexner, above note 2, at 176–78.

29. See generally Aileen S. Kraditor, The Ideas of the Woman Suffrage Movement, 1890–1920 (1965).

30. See, e.g., Flexner, above note 2, at 185–89, 305.

31. Giddings, above note 3, at 124.

32. The African American women's federation of clubs was rejected for membership in NAWSA for fear it would lead to defeat of the suffrage amendment in the South, and in 1899 NAWSA refused to endorse a resolution brought by certain Black women against segregated accommodations in railroad carriages. Angela Y. Davis, Women, Race, and Class 144, 118 (1981).

In 1913, for example, the intrepid Black journalist, organizer, and international anti-lynching advocate Ida B. Wells was asked by the leaders of the Washington suffrage march to join the segregated section of the march rather than to walk with the Illinois delegation; Wells slipped out of the segregated group and asserted her place with the women from Illinois nonetheless.[33]

The Southern states opposed women's suffrage to the end,[34] so the suffragists' "expedient" racism turned out to be both tragic and fruitless; and it divided them from their natural allies. Black women consistently supported universal suffrage after the debate over the Civil War amendments; and at the end of Reconstruction they began to create organizations and institutions to assert equal rights, including suffrage, as well as to press their claims to education, entry into the professions, and other aspects of economic and social equality.[35] Educated and middle-class Black women also formed clubs which pressed for a variety of social reforms, such as child care and improvements in the status of working women.[36] Much of their attention, however, was focused upon the deprivation and violence visited upon Black men and women alike.

A stark example is the anti-lynching movement organized by Ida B. Wells in reaction to the rash of lynchings during this period.[37] It was only relatively late that women—Southern women in particular—began to see the fundamentally feminist nature of the anti-lynching movement. Lynching was almost invariably a response to allegations that a Black man had raped or sexually insulted a white woman in some fashion (often very minor).[38] Allegations of rape and the fear generated by the terrorism of barbaric public lynchings were clearly used as an excuse for subordinating Blacks. But it was only in the lynching epidemic of the 1920's that Southern white women began to confront the sexism implicit in the lynching mentality, to see chivalry as a means of control, and to link it to lynching.[39] As one historian put it, "pursuit of the black rapist represented a trade-off[;] * * * the right of the southern lady to protection presupposed her obligation to obey."[40]

Throughout this period, Black women were contending with sexual harassment by their employers and with an increase in domestic violence—problems they shared with white women.[41] Yet in other ways the experience of Black women differed from that of the white suffragists. Never considered the delicate flowers celebrated by the 19th-century cult of true womanhood,[42] Black women had worked in large numbers, as

33. Giddings, above note 3, at 127–28.

34. Flexner, above note 2, at 337.

35. Giddings, above note 3, at 75, 119.

36. Id. at 95–101.

37. See id. at 17–31, 89–92.

38. The irony of the lynching scenario, as Wells pointed out, was that while Black men were being falsely accused of raping white women, Black women were in fact raped by white men repeatedly with impunity, both during slavery and as domestic servants. Id. at 31.

39. Id. at 206–07.

40. Jacquelyn Dowd Hall, Revolt Against Chivalry: Jessie Daniel Ames and the Women's Campaign Against Lynching 151 (1979).

41. Giddings, above note 3, at 64, 101.

42. See note 16, above.

slaves and, after abolition, often as domestic servants, or, if they were fortunate enough to gain an education, teaching in African American schools.[43] Thus, when Black women organized into women's groups or clubs, their attention immediately turned to issues central to the welfare of working women and their children.[44] By contrast, the clubs formed by middle-class white women emphasized (although not exclusively) issues of more direct interest to them, such as establishing libraries and hospitals to benefit their communities and the provision of services to children.[45]

A substantial number of educated women also became involved in movements for social reform during the Progressive era. Some, like Jane Addams, Lillian Wald, and Florence Kelley, founded settlement houses, providing direct services to residents of lower-income and immigrant neighborhoods. These reformers also fought for political and economic reforms, such as safer conditions in factories and neighborhoods, and for minimum wage and maximum hour legislation, some of which applied only to women and children.[46] Others worked within the National Consumers League to support the needs of working class women, and working women and their allies struggled for better conditions through the Women's Trade Union League.[47]

At the end of the 19th century, there was still one issue upon which women's groups could all agree: extension of the suffrage to women. Although it took 50 years after passage of the Fifteenth Amendment, this goal was finally achieved in 1920, when the last state necessary ratified the Nineteenth Amendment. Some attribute this final victory to the importation of militant tactics from the British suffrage movement by Alice Paul and her Woman's Party.[48] The last years before suffrage were marked by mass marches, picketing, imprisonment of picketers, hunger strikes, and radical tactics not characteristic of the suffrage movement in the United States until that time. The long, slow process of lobbying on the national level continued as well, including several campaigns to target and defeat Senators who had voted against the suffrage amendment in 1918.[49] Perhaps most important, the numerous campaigns from 1890 to 1920 to win suffrage on the state level finally bore fruit on the national level: the number of votes for suffrage in Congress reflected the female suffrage that had been achieved in the states and thus the accountability of national representatives to an electorate that included women.[50] As a result of all these efforts, the

43. Giddings, above note 3, at 63, 77–78. Industrial opportunities were largely closed to Black women. Id. at 78.

44. Id. at 96–101.

45. Flexner, above note 2, at 182–84; Giddings, above note 3, at 97.

46. Flexner, above note 2, at 208–21.

47. William L. O'Neill, Everyone Was Brave: The Rise and Fall of Feminism in America 95–102 (1969).

48. Flexner, above note 2, at 259, 272–79. Women's suffrage was attained in Great Britain in 1918 for freeholders, wives of freeholders and women over 30, and extended to all women in 1928. Id. at 321, 390 n. 6.

49. Id. at 319–37.

50. See Anne F. Scott and Andrew M. Scott, One Half the People: The Fight for Woman Suffrage 161–62, 166–68 (1975).

Nineteenth Amendment finally became part of the United States Constitution on August 26, 1920.

C. FEMINISM AFTER THE NINETEENTH AMENDMENT

After the lengthy struggle for suffrage, the coalition that achieved it collapsed, some say of sheer exhaustion.[51] Others attribute this collapse to the suffragists' concentration upon one political goal, to the exclusion of social and economic issues; once that goal—the vote—did not turn out to be a panacea for the ills affecting women, interest in further activism was bound to wane.[52] A related explanation sees the conservatism and tactical expediency of the second and third generations of women's leaders as separating the movement from the earlier and broader critique of woman's place in marriage and the economy, thereby losing the grounding for a more long-lasting movement for change.[53]

It is clearly true that the suffragists had "oversold" the vote as an instrument through which newly enfranchised women would transform the values of the nation. Women did not turn out to vote in a massive and powerful bloc after 1920, and the differences of race and class that had been submerged in their unified demand for suffrage reemerged.[54] Moreover, NAWSA itself, after requiring decades of political activity, experience, and organizational skill of its supporters, designated as its successor organization the newly formed League of Women Voters (LWV), which determined to remain strictly non-partisan.[55]

The LWV also did not explicitly define itself as a feminist group, although its members pressed for many of the social programs supported by the women reformers of the Progressive era.[56] The National Woman's Party, on the other hand, defined itself as a feminist but single-issue group; its program was to strike a blow at the hundreds of discriminatory laws throughout the country by the passage of an Equal Rights Amendment (ERA) banning discrimination on the basis of sex.[57] The campaign for the ERA, described in more detail in Chapter Two, led to a serious split in the women's movement, as social reformers and trade union activists opposed the ERA for fear of its impact upon the sex-specific protective legislation they had worked so long to pass.

Though feminists were no longer unified in a mass movement after suffrage was achieved, in the 1920's women activists and social reformers continued their activity on a variety of issues critical to the welfare of women and children—federally supported infant and maternal health education, citizenship rights for wives of aliens, and child labor laws, for

51. See, e.g., Judith Hole and Ellen Levine, The Rebirth of Feminism 14 (1971).

52. William H. Chafe, The Paradox of Change: American Women in the 20th Century 32 (1991).

53. O'Neill, above note 47, at 273–74.

54. Chafe, above note 52, at 30.

55. Id. at 23–24.

56. Cott, above note 1, at 86.

57. Chafe, above note 52, at 48–49.

example.[58] Many of the women reformers involved in these struggles were instrumental in laying the groundwork for the New Deal and, indeed, performed important functions in the New Deal itself.[59] Eleanor Roosevelt played a central role in connecting the persons, programs, and ideas of the progressive social reformers with the Democratic Party during the 1920's and 30's.[60]

Most women who entered the workplace for the first time, as many did during the Depression and the labor shortage of the Second World War, were confronted with serious discrimination. They worked in sex-segregated jobs and were paid much less for their work than men. During the 1920's and 30's, over 40% of all women in manufacturing were in textiles, and more than 75% of women professionals were either teachers or nurses.[61] Many industries simply did not hire women—at least until their labor was required to replace the men who were drafted after the Japanese attack on Pearl Harbor; and when the veterans returned, women were ousted from their positions, though most remained in the workforce in other, but less well-paid, jobs.[62] Throughout this period, Black women were largely confined to the most marginal jobs.[63] Moreover, even during the years when women's labor was actively solicited for defense industries, the community services and child care that would have helped them combine their economic role with their roles within the family were largely unavailable.[64] Thus, the economic independence touted by earlier reformers as the result of employment outside the home turned out, for many women, to be a new form of exploitation.

For the mass of women, the interwar era was a confusing period. On the one hand, a revolution in dress and sexual mores produced the "flapper," the sexually liberated woman who drank and smoked and wore short dresses; on the other hand, this liberation from the customs of their mothers was accompanied by continuing fidelity to the goals of a traditional marriage, home, and family. More women married, and they married at a younger age; and for the first time, the number of women obtaining graduate degrees, entering professions, or aspiring to make use of their college degrees declined.[65] A new cult of domesticity, accompanied by psychoanalytic notions about the nature of women and media

58. Cott, above note 1, at 97–98.

59. Chafe, above note 52, at 34–41; J. Stanley Lemons, The Woman Citizen: Social Feminism in the 1920s 228, 243–44 (1973).

60. See, e.g., Blanche Wiesen Cook, Eleanor Roosevelt, Vol. I: 1884–1933 288–301, 319–79 (1992).

61. Chafe, above note 52, at 73.

62. Id. at 122–23, 159–60.

63. Giddings, above note 3, at 232–36.

64. See Chafe, above note 52, at 141–51. In wartime England, by contrast, "Central Kitchens" prepared meals for women factory workers to carry home to their families. Id. at 143. A few workplaces in the United States did provide federally subsidized child care during the war, notably the centers at the Kaiser shipbuilding plant in Portland, Oregon, which was open 24 hours a day and provided sick-child care, shopping services, and low-cost carry-out dinners. See Ruth Sidel, Women and Children Last 119–20 (1986).

65. Cott, above note 1, at 147; Chafe, above note 52, at 111–18.

promotion of consumption aimed at housewives, reinforced the traditional ideology of home and motherhood as woman's sphere.[66]

This "feminine mystique" was described by Betty Friedan in her 1963 book of that name, from which some date the beginning of the second wave of the women's movement in the United States.[67] There were, however, strong connections between the first and second waves of feminism in this country. While the second wave—the women's liberation movement of the 1960's—resulted in part from the mobilization of middle-class educated women by Friedan and from the politicization of younger radical women in the civil rights movement, it was also linked to earlier generations of women activists and social reformers through the involvement of older women like Eleanor Roosevelt, who was appointed to chair the President's Commission on the Status of Women in 1960.[68] The resurgent movement, described in the next chapter, renewed not only the critique of the social, legal, and economic status of women raised in the mid–19th century, but also the early reformers' cultural critique of women's lives.

66. Chafe, above note 52, at 104–116; Cott, above note 1, at 147–74.

67. Flexner, above note 2, at 344. The attribution is in the revised edition of Eleanor Flexner's classic, the original of which was published before Friedan's book.

68. See, e.g., Jane Sherron De Hart, The New Feminism and the Dynamics of Social Change, in Kerber and De Hart, eds., above note 12, at 502–12.

Chapter 2

CONSTITUTIONAL "EQUALITY"

A. HISTORICAL INTRODUCTION

After suffrage, Alice Paul and the Women's Party supported the first equal rights amendment for women (ERA). This version was first introduced into Congress in 1923:

> Men and women shall have equal rights throughout the United States and in every place subject to its jurisdiction. Congress shall have power to enforce this article by appropriate legislation.

Supporters argued that this amendment would eliminate the many distinctions between women and men in laws regulating employment, families, citizenship, competency, crimes, and sentences.[1]

A few examples from each area give a sense of the breadth of sex-specific regulation.[2] State laws often specified maximum hours or minimum wages for women workers in general or in certain industries, or banned women from bartending or working in factories at night. Family law was almost entirely sex-specific, with a preference for mothers as custodians of children of tender years after a divorce. The husband was head of the household with an obligation to support his wife and children and the right to determine the domicile of the family. His wife was obligated to provide homemaking and caretaking services. In many states married women were still denied full rights to contract and to own property, despite the passage of the Married Women's Property Acts described in Chapter 1.

Men were subject to the draft, and women could not serve as members of the armed forces prior to World War II, with the exception

1. Flora Davis, Moving the Mountain: The Women's Movement in America Since 1960 at 29, 33–34 (1991).

2. The discussion in text relies on the thorough descriptions of sex-specific laws in Leo Kanowitz, Women and the Law: The Unfinished Revolution (1969); Barbara A. Brown, Thomas I. Emerson, Gail Falk, and Ann E. Freedman, The Equal Rights Amendment: A Constitutional Basis for Equal Rights for Women, 80 Yale L.J. 871 (1971); John D. Johnston, Jr. and Charles L. Knapp, Sex Discrimination by Law: A Study in Judicial Perspective, 46 N.Y.U.L.Rev. 675 (1971).

of the Navy during World War I. Yet veterans often received powerful preferences for government employment as well as many other benefits under the G. I. Bill. Many states denied women the ability to serve on juries under the same rules as men. Age of majority tended to be lower for women than men, and women were allowed to marry at younger ages.

Criminal law routinely distinguished between women and men in statutes defining rape, statutory rape, and prostitution. Some statutes imposed harsher penalties on women than men. Laws governing places of public accommodation or entertainment often banned women from bars, wrestling matches, and other public events.

ERA supporters wanted to eradicate these and other discriminatory laws at a single blow. Throughout the 1920's and for decades to come, however, the vast majority of activists opposed the ERA. They worried about the consequences of eliminating all sex-specific family law as well as legislation "protecting" women workers because of their special needs and responsibilities. Although this position strikes some today as conservative, at the time the anti-ERA position was associated with progressives, and the ERA position was generally supported by economic conservatives opposed to all government regulation of employment. Indeed, Women's Party "[m]embers were conservative on most social issues."[3]

The progressive anti-ERA position had its roots in opposition to 19th century labor practices. Appalled by the sweat shop conditions under which many immigrants and other workers labored for low wages in American workplaces, reformers pushed for minimum wages, maximum hours, and other protections. Protectionist legislation varied from state to state and took many forms, including maximum hours, minimum wages, mandatory time off for lunch and breaks, and weight-lifting limits. These laws often applied only to women, and some statutes barred women from holding certain jobs at all, such as working at night in factories.[4]

Progressive reformers saw sex-specific legislation as important because—then as now—women working for wages often worked a second shift at home, and because some protections had as yet only been enacted for women. Some laws protected women from requirements beyond the strength of many women, such as lifting extremely heavy objects. In addition, ERA opponents feared that the ERA would indiscriminately wipe out sex-specific family laws, such as the husband's obligation to support his wife and children. More fundamentally, to progressives and socialists, the ERA was an individualistic approach

3. See Davis, above note 1, at 34; Katherine Pollak Ellickson, The President's Commission on the Status of Women: Its Formation, Functioning and Contribution 6 (1976); Judith Paterson, Be Somebody: A Biography of Marguerite Rawalt 140 (1986).

4. For a description of protectionist legislation, see Judith Baer, Chains of Protection (1978).

inconsistent with their basic frames of reference and their analysis of the social causes of inequalities.[5]

Protectionist legislation was not entirely and only bad for women, though much of it was. Laws banning women from certain kinds of employment—such as working in factories at night—doubtless hurt women, limiting them to lower paying jobs. And protectionist legislation reinforced stereotypes that women were weaker and therefore less desirable employees than men. But laws limiting women's hours in certain industries—such as maximum hours limits on women employed in laundries—probably helped women in situations in which employers nevertheless continued to employ women. Most women did work a second shift at home and were likely to be thankful for a law limiting wage work to twelve hours a day.

Between the passage of the suffrage amendment in 1920 and the beginning of the second wave of the women's movement in the early sixties, activist women remained divided into two camps, one supporting the early ERA and one opposed. Between 1923 and 1969, this ERA was introduced yearly in Congress. From 1940 on, the Republican party endorsed the ERA because it would eliminate protectionist legislation disliked by business. Democrats tended to oppose the ERA because the party was closely aligned with organized labor, a powerful advocate of protectionist legislation for workers. Throughout this period, the ERA was defeated by a coalition of social conservatives, who were opposed to change in the status of women, and Democrats and progressives, like Eleanor Roosevelt, who feared that the ERA would invalidate sex-specific protective legislation as well as sex-specific family support laws protecting women and children at divorce.[6]

The PCSW Compromise

In 1962, President Kennedy established the President's Commission on the Status of Women (PCSW) with Eleanor Roosevelt as its chair, just as the second-wave of the feminist movement was beginning to become visible. Women were living longer, and had greater control over reproduction. More women, whether married or single, were working for wages outside the home. Many younger women—like their foremothers in the 19th century—became involved in the struggle for racial and economic justice; many of these women objected to their subordinate and supportive positions within the civil rights, antiwar, and other "left" movements and were inspired by these movements to protest their mistreatment and subordination.[7]

5. Mary Becker, The Sixties Shift to Formal Equality and the Courts: An Argument for Pragmatism and Politics, 40 Wm. & Mary L. Rev. 209, 214 (1998).

6. See Ellickson, above note 3, at 6; Blanche Linden-Ward and Carol Hurd Green, American Women in the 1960s: Changing the Future 2–3 (1993); Jane Mansbridge, Why We Lost the ERA 8–9 (1986).

7. Jane Sherron De Hart, The New Feminism and the Dynamics of Social Change, in Women's America: Refocusing the Past 493 (Linda K. Kerber and Jane Sherron De Hart, eds., 3d ed. 1991).

Most, but not all, of the members of the PCSW were ERA opponents. Pauli Murray,[8] a member of the PCSW's Committee on Civil and Political Rights, suggested a compromise that broke the gridlock over the ERA which had divided the women's movement once suffrage was achieved. Murray was a longtime activist in the labor movement, the NAACP, and other civil rights organizations. She recommended that women seek equality through the courts under the Fourteenth Amendment, as civil rights activists had done in seeking equality for African Americans. Murray suggested that under such an approach, the courts could uphold sex-specific legislation that was good for women and strike sex-specific legislation that was bad for women. In its final report, the PCSW recommended going to the courts with the argument that the Equal Protection Clause banned discrimination against women and suggested that, if that failed, it *might* be appropriate to seek an ERA.

The PCSW compromise on the ERA was an important breakthrough. Virtually all activists committed to improving the status of women now agreed on a short-term strategy. Equally important, the PCSW brought together women leaders from all over the country and created forward momentum on women's issues just as the second wave of the feminist movement began. Betty Friedan's book, *The Feminine Mystique*, often seen as the start of the second wave, was also published in 1963. Suddenly, it was possible to talk about women's issues and even to use the word "feminist."[9] Many states had state commissions working on women's status, and soon every state would have such commissions.

Title VII and Support for a New ERA

In 1964, in the wake of the Kennedy assassination and in response to the civil rights movement which he was seen as having supported, Congress enacted the Civil Rights Act of 1964, which banned race discrimination in many settings including education (Title IX of the Act) and private employment (Title VII). Title VII eliminated one of the major barriers to an ERA.

The conventional wisdom is that "sex" was added as a floor amendment to Title VII in an attempt to derail the bill by adding an obviously ludicrous provision, but the story is far more complicated. In fact, many women and men worked for and supported the inclusion of "sex." The ban on sex discrimination was, however, added as a floor amendment in the House of Representatives by a conservative southerner who opposed Title VII's ban on race discrimination and hoped that the addition of "sex" would derail the bill. But on July 2, 1964, Title VII was enacted *with* the provision banning sex discrimination in private and public employment in the United States. By 1970, courts were interpreting Title VII as banning protective labor legislation. Thus, within a few

8. For information on Murray, see Pauli Murray, The Autobiography of a Black Activist, Feminist, Lawyer, Priest and Poet (1987).

9. Paterson, above note 3, at 152.

years of its passage, Title VII eliminated one of the strongest reasons for feminist and progressive opposition to the ERA.[10]

The drive for an ERA gained momentum throughout the 1960's as more and more mainstream women leaders became supporters. There was now new wording for the Amendment:

> Section 1. Equality of rights under the law shall not be denied or abridged by the United States or by any State on account of sex.
>
> Section 2. The Congress shall have the power to enforce, by appropriate legislation, the provisions of this article.

In May 1970, Senator Birch Bayh, a Democrat from Indiana and chairman of the Senate Judiciary Committee's Subcommittee on Constitutional Amendments, held hearings on the ERA—the first action in Congress in almost ten years. Later that year, the UAW became the first union to endorse the ERA. In May, 1971, the Senate Judiciary Committee held hearings, and testimony overwhelmingly ran in support of the amendment. In June of 1971 the Labor Department reversed its longstanding opposition and endorsed the ERA. In August, 1971, the ERA passed the House, and in February, 1972, the Senate. On that same day, the Hawaii legislature ratified the amendment and five more states adopted it within the next two days. By the end of 1973, 30 states had ratified the ERA. But opposition began building at this point, and only five more states ratified it for a total of 35, two short of the number needed. No state ratified it after 1977. By 1982 the period of ratification expired despite enormous efforts by feminists in heartbreaking campaigns in state after state.

Backlash

Opposition to the ERA mounted for two reasons, both connected to the Supreme Court. Most important was the Supreme Court's 1973 decision in Roe v. Wade, 410 U.S. 113, 93 S.Ct. 705, 35 L.Ed.2d 147 (1973), holding that women had a constitutional right to decide whether to have an abortion during the early stages of pregnancy. Abortion opponents immediately began to mobilize and tended generally to oppose changes in the status of women, including the ERA.[11]

The other difficulty was the success of Pauli Murray's idea: going to the courts for equality on the basis of sex under the Fourteenth Amendment to the Constitution. Murray had suggested litigation by a group focused on sex discrimination (patterned after the NAACP with its focus on race discrimination). The New York office of the American Civil Liberties Union organized a Women's Rights Project headed by Ruth Bader Ginsburg with precisely this goal. In 1971, the first of its cases was decided by the Supreme Court: Reed v. Reed, 404 U.S. 71, 92 S.Ct. 251, 30 L.Ed.2d 225 (1971). The Court held unconstitutional under the

10. For a more through discussion of the shift in opinion on an ERA in the sixties, see Becker, above note 5.

11. See Elizabeth Pleck, Failed Strategies, Renewed Hope, in Rights of Passage: The Past and Future of the ERA 106, 110 (Joan Hoff–Wilson ed., 1986).

Fourteenth Amendment a state statute preferring men over women as executors of the estates of deceased relatives. Another such case was decided in 1973, two more in 1974, four in 1975, and so on. As the Supreme Court expanded the reach of the Fourteenth Amendment, ERA opponents were increasingly successful in arguing that the ERA would make no difference apart from mandating women in combat and co-ed bathrooms, both of which were controversial.

Differences Among Second–Wave Activists

Both approaches widely accepted by feminists in the early seventies—fighting for the ERA and seeking sex equality under the Fourteenth Amendment—were liberal approaches. Both sought to maximize women's choices by giving women individual rights, rights to be treated like other individuals irrespective of sex. But not all feminists in the early years of the second wave were liberals. There were at least two other identifiable kinds of feminists: socialist feminists and radical feminists.

Liberal feminists regarded men as important allies who were also oppressed by rigid sex roles which denied them individual choice. Using a standard modeled on that developed in race cases made sense: government should treat all similarly situated individuals similarly regardless of sex (or race). Following the NAACP's example, these feminists worked within the system to achieve change by focusing on "gaining equal opportunity for women as individuals * * * consistent with the American creed."[12] Liberal feminists stressed the similarities, rather than the differences, between individual women and men, as well as the need to increase freedom for all people by eliminating sex-based roles and stereotypes. Liberal feminists focused at an early date on the legal system and on using the courts as instruments of change.

Socialist and radical feminists, with their backgrounds in the Left and civil rights movements, began what has become the preeminent feminist method: consciousness raising. The technique had originally been used to organize the poor by encouraging them to talk about their problems with each other in order to see the systemic social causes of their oppression and the need for political solutions. Women in the socialist movement, who were dissatisfied with their relegation to supportive positions as secretaries, typists, coffee makers, and lovers of movement men, began to use the consciousness raising technique themselves. Consciousness raising spread to all forms of feminism in the early years of the second wave. The point of consciousness raising is to realize that the personal is political. Women gathered in small groups to discuss personal problems. But by describing their experiences in a group of women, many of whom shared similar problems, women realized the systemic and political nature of the problems each faced.

12. William H. Chafe, The Paradox of Change: American Women in the 20th Century 237 (1991).

Socialist or Marxist feminists, in contrast to liberal feminists, located the sources of women's oppression in the structure of capitalism and regarded major structural changes as necessary. Feminists in this tradition stressed the needs, interests, and rights of groups more than those of individuals, and the connections between various forms of oppression, such as race and class. Socialist feminist groups focused upon uniting with other oppressed groups in fighting all forms of oppression, rather than organizing or struggling separately to advance the interests of women.

The third feminist grouping, radical feminists, identified men as the oppressors and did not consider sex discrimination as affecting women and men in similar ways. Like socialist feminists, they saw society as in need of major structural changes and were not especially interested in working for incremental change within the system, lest their energy be dissipated in easy but small victories. Radical feminists often staged public protests, such as picketing the 1968 Miss America contest and sit-ins at the offices of the *Ladies Home Journal* and *Newsweek* to protest "the ways in which the media's depiction of women perpetuated old stereotypes at the expense of new realities."[13]

Unlike socialist and liberal feminists, radical feminists stressed that women and men have conflicting interests. Radical feminists tended to favor separatism and emphasized the need to develop a women's culture, rather than building coalitions with men as liberal and socialist women did. To some extent, "radical" feminism came to mean feminists who were "woman-identified"[14] and who analyzed oppression primarily in terms of sex. In addition, the focus of radical analysis was typically on groups (e.g., capital versus labor), rather than the individuals central to liberal feminism (e.g., equal treatment of individual women and men).

Many radical feminists were lesbians, as were many women throughout the second wave. Within radical feminism, however, lesbian feminism became an identifiable intellectual approach as well as a political strategy. Some radical feminists regarded "heterosexuality as the cornerstone of male supremacy and lesbianism as the 'greatest threat' to its continued existence."[15] Some regarded lesbianism as essential for feminists, while others argued that sexual behavior was less important than being woman-identified. Building a women's culture free of the presence of men was especially important to many lesbian feminists.

There have been many bitter battles over homophobia within the second wave. During the first wave, "sexologists" and other "experts," who had recently discovered "female sexual inverts," warned that these "inverts" were responsible for demands for increased independence and freedom for women. Lesbian-baiting was thus used to frighten women away from the 19th century's woman movement. This pattern was repeated during the early years of the second wave, and many hetero-

13. De Hart, above note 7, at 512.

14. Chafe, above note 12, at 207.

15. De Hart, above note 7, at 512.

sexual feminists were hostile to lesbians, afraid that identification of themselves or of their organizations with lesbians would marginalize themselves, their groups and their cause. Many lesbians responded by becoming more, rather than less, visible and vocal, demanding recognition of the problems with heterosexuality and challenging women who assumed that they were heterosexual to analyze the connections between heterosexuality and their oppression.

Similarly, the relationship between black women and feminism has been complicated. Black feminist leaders have been important throughout the second wave,[16] and black women generally have been more supportive than white women of specific policy issues such as equal pay and government-supported child care. But many black women regard feminism in all its forms as a *white* women's movement. And, in fact, women in organized feminist groups, at both leadership and membership levels, have been disproportionately white. Many black women have been and are reluctant to give top priority to the elimination of sex discrimination abstracted from race discrimination, given the continuing strength of racism in America. In addition, white feminists' focus on sex renders invisible much of reality for black women, who experience a complicated combination of racism and sexism. Finally, the emphasis on liberal approaches to change through law has had the effect of doing the most for those women most like white men in power: elite white women. The feminist agenda has often consisted of issues of little interest to other women, such as the entrance of elite women into professions.[17]

Other women of color feel similar tensions. For many Latina women, problems caused by immigration rules and related social practices are far greater than, and often exacerbate, problems caused by sexism, with the result that solutions sought by the feminist movement have little relevance to their far greater needs. For example, effective police response to domestic violence is meaningless if one cannot call the police because of one's status as an illegal alien.

The Dominance of Liberal Feminism

Of these three strands of modern feminism—liberal, radical, and socialist feminism—one has dominated our understanding of sexual equality in law and throughout our culture: liberal feminism. As a result, we tend to think of sexual equality as the right of an individual not to be treated differently from another individual because of sex. It is a right that men as well as women can use to avoid being treated in terms of sex rather than as individuals. For liberals, equality is achieved when individuals face the same choices regardless of sex, thus enabling each individual to maximize her or his own self interest.

Liberal feminism became dominant within the women's movement in part because of the media's presentation of radical and socialist feminism as "ludicrous" and "beyond the pale" of acceptable discourse

16. For example, Pauli Murray, Shirley Chisholm, Barbara Jordan, and Eleanor Holmes Norton.

17. Jo Freeman, The Politics of Women's Liberation 38–43 (1975).

or protest.[18] Liberalism, with its use of widely accepted cultural norms, such as individualism and its commitment to incremental change within the existing order, has been less threatening and in some ways more effective than radical or socialist feminism. By the mid 1970's, radical feminism had "dissipated" as an identifiable branch of the women's movement,[19] and by 1977, socialist feminist groups had disintegrated as a result of disputes over whether sex or class analysis should take precedence. Both radical feminism and socialist feminism remain influential in the academy, however, as will be seen in the feminist theories discussed in Chapter 3.

B. THE DEVELOPMENT OF A CONSTITUTIONAL STANDARD FOR SEX EQUALITY

By 1971, when the Supreme Court handed down Reed v. Reed, 404 U.S. 71, 92 S.Ct. 251, 30 L.Ed.2d 225 (1971), a special constitutional standard for race discrimination was well established. In other cases and in general, the Court requires that legislation have only a rational basis, that is, that there be a plausible relationship between a statute and a legitimate governmental interest. Legislation scrutinized under this standard almost always stands. A different standard applies to legislation involving certain constitutional rights, such as the First Amendment guarantees of free speech and religious freedom or the Fourteenth Amendment guarantee of equal protection for certain "suspect" (vulnerable) groups.

The NAACP had argued successfully that government must not treat citizens differently on the basis of race in its challenge to Jim Crow segregation, the legally mandated separation of the races in the South in schools, seating on buses, restaurants, hotels and motels, washrooms, swimming pools, and even drinking fountains. When a statute classifies individuals on the basis of race, the most searching level of review is used—strict scrutiny, under which legislation survives judicial review only if the suspect classification is necessary to achieve some "legitimate overriding purpose independent of invidious racial discrimination." Loving v. Virginia, 388 U.S. 1, 11, 87 S.Ct. 1817, 1823, 18 L.Ed.2d 1010 (1967). Under this standard, all explicit racial classifications had fallen from 1945 through 1971, when the Supreme Court began to consider what standard might be appropriate in cases involving sex classifications. At that point, the racial classifications struck had always been harmful to racial minorities, the prototype being racial segregation; the first affirmative action case was decided only in 1978. Regents of the University of California v. Bakke, 438 U.S. 265, 98 S.Ct. 2733, 57 L.Ed.2d 750 (1978).

To this day, the standard for sex equality under the Constitution as well as in employment and education cases is a variation on the standard

18. Chafe, above note 12, at 235.

19. Alice Echols, Daring to Be Bad: Radical Feminism in America 1967–1975 287 (1989).

used in race cases. This approach remained unquestioned by almost all feminists from 1971 until the end of the seventies. We turn now to examine the development of that standard.

1. THE FIRST CASE

With the Supreme Court's decision in Reed v. Reed, 404 U.S. 71, 92 S.Ct. 251, 30 L.Ed.2d 225 (1971), all sex-specific laws became suspect. The Idaho statute at issue in *Reed* identified various categories of people who qualified for appointment as administrator of an estate. In the event there were two people of different sexes who were equally qualified in terms of their relationship to the decedent, the statute preferred the man as executor. Idaho justified the classification as a reasonable way to avoid a tie (without wasting state resources in a court hearing) by selecting the person more likely to have experience with business affairs.

The *Reed* case arose as a dispute between two separated adoptive parents. The mother had custody of their son. The boy, Skip, was reluctant to visit his father, a man described as "difficult" by his mother. When Skip was 16, his father requested a week-long visit. Skip did not want to go, and after two or three days, called his mother and asked if he could come home. His mother urged him to stay because "his father had visiting rights."[20] Skip committed suicide on Wednesday of that week, shooting himself with one of his father's guns, and both parents wanted to administer his estate.[21] The Idaho courts named the father as administrator, consistent with the terms of the Idaho statute. The mother was represented on appeal to the United States Supreme Court by the Women's Rights Project (WRP) of the ACLU. Ruth Bader Ginsburg and the other attorneys involved in this appeal argued that the strict scrutiny standard developed for racial classifications should also apply to classifications based on sex.

The Supreme Court recognized the legitimacy of the state's interest in minimizing courts' workloads. But the Court nevertheless regarded the preference as inconsistent with the Equal Protection Clause, stating its reason and describing the new standard in a single conclusory sentence:

> To give a mandatory preference to members of either sex over members of the other, merely to accomplish the elimination of hearings on the merits, is to make the very kind of arbitrary legislative choice forbidden by the Equal Protection Clause of the Fourteenth Amendment; and whatever may be said as to the positive values of avoiding intrafamily controversy, the choice in this context may not lawfully be mandated solely on the basis of sex.

On remand, the parents were named joint administrators of the estate of their deceased son.

20. Supreme Court Decisions and Women's Rights 40 (Claire Cushman, ed., 2001).

21. Id.

Notes on Reed

1. Is the standard for race discrimination, developed to deal with Jim Crow segregation, an appropriate model for sex discrimination? In what ways was or is sexual inequality different from Jim Crow? How are relationships between the races similar to relationships between the sexes, and in what ways are they different? Are laws explicitly classifying on the basis of sex as likely to hurt women as those explicitly discriminating on the basis of race? What sorts of laws and governmental practices will be perceived as sex discrimination under a standard banning classifications by sex? Will such an approach threaten desirable rules?

2. From the perspective of women of color, what are the problems with comparisons of race and sex discrimination? When we compare race and sex discrimination, do we miss the discrimination women of color face? Does the analogy of race discrimination to sex discrimination give white women the false sense that they understand the experiences of women of color? See Trina Grillo and Stephanie Wildman, Obscuring the Importance of Race: The Implication of Making Comparisons Between Racism and Sexism (or Other-Isms), in Stephanie Wildman, Privilege Revealed: How Invisible Preference Undermines America 85 (1996) (extract in Chapter 3).

3. Do you think that racial inequality is best addressed by a constitutional standard banning classifications based on race, particularly now that Jim Crow segregation has been dismantled and some race-specific rules (such as affirmative action) may actually benefit racial minorities? The Supreme Court has become increasingly hostile to race-based affirmative action in recent decades. Compare Regents of the University of California v. Bakke, 438 U.S. 265, 98 S.Ct. 2733, 57 L.Ed.2d 750 (1978) (upholding state university admission policy under which applicant's race was *one* factor to be taken into account and *not* a quota) with City of Richmond v. J.A. Croson Co., 488 U.S. 469, 109 S.Ct. 706, 102 L.Ed.2d 854 (1989) (striking city program setting aside 30% of city contracts for minority contractors in city with a 50% black population and a history of awarding only 99.33% of contracts to non minority businesses).

What other standards might be possible for racial discrimination? What are the causes of racial inequality? What government policies would best address these causes? Will progressive race-specific laws and governmental practices be needed to combat continuing racial inequality? Are courts too likely to hold progressive policies unconstitutional under a standard banning racial classifications?

2. FOUR VOTES FOR STRICT SCRUTINY

The ACLU WRP under Ruth Bader Ginsburg was amicus curiae in the next sex-discrimination case decided on Equal Protection grounds, Frontiero v. Richardson, 411 U.S. 677, 93 S.Ct. 1764, 36 L.Ed.2d 583 (1973), and succeeded in getting four votes for a strict scrutiny standard in sex cases. The plaintiff, a married woman who was an officer in the Air Force, argued that she was denied equal protection by laws automatically giving spousal benefits to married men but denying them to married women absent a showing that the wife provided more than half the husband's support.

Eight of the nine justices—all but Justice Rehnquist—agreed that the Air Force policy unconstitutionally discriminated on the basis of sex. But no five of the eight could agree on a standard. Justice Brennan, writing for four members of the Court, used strict scrutiny to strike the statute. He referred to our nation's "long and unfortunate history of sex discrimination," 411 U.S. at 684, 93 S.Ct. at 1769, and also noted that sex, like race, is an immutable but highly visible characteristic bearing no relation to ability to contribute to society, id. at 686, 93 S.Ct. at 1770. Finally, he explained that Congress had shown "an increasing sensitivity to sex-based classifications" over the previous decade by enacting the Equal Pay Act and Title VII and passing the ERA. Congressional concern was particularly relevant because of Congress' power to enforce the Equal Protection Clause under Section 5 of the Fourteenth Amendment. Once Justice Brennan had established strict scrutiny as the appropriate standard, it was easy to strike the statute in *Frontiero* since administrative convenience was the sole justification for differential treatment of women and men in the Air Force. The other four justices agreed that the Air Force policy at issue in *Frontiero* was unconstitutional, but applied the *Reed* standard rather than adopting strict scrutiny.

Notes on Frontiero

1. Once they realized that the Supreme Court would not extend strict scrutiny to sex, Ruth Bader Ginsburg and the WRP shifted their strategy, concentrating "on chipping away at sexual stereotyping through cases that demonstrated the inequities that may result to *males* from an unthinking application of generalizations about the sexes." Margaret A. Berger, Litigation on Behalf of Women: A Review for the Ford Foundation 18–19 (1980) (emphasis added). But they lost the first of these cases, Kahn v. Shevin, 416 U.S. 351, 94 S.Ct. 1734, 40 L.Ed.2d 189 (1974). The plaintiff was a widower challenging Florida's property tax exemption of $500 per year for widows. In a six-three decision (Brennan, Marshall, and White dissenting), the Court upheld the classification. The Court began by noting that women working full time tended to earn less than 60 cents for every dollar earned by men and that the death of a spouse would often force into this inhospitable market a widow who previously had depended on her spouse. In light of these realities, the Court upheld the classification as a reasonable measure "designed to further the state policy of cushioning the financial impact of spousal loss upon the sex for which that loss imposes a disproportionately heavy burden." Id. at 355, 94 S.Ct. at 1737. Would you have argued against the exemption for widows in *Kahn*? What are the strongest arguments for upholding the exemption? Is *Kahn* necessarily inconsistent with a liberal approach to sexual equality? Why?

2. The Women's Rights Project also lost the next case in which it filed an amicus brief, though it was brought by a woman and involved a particularly important issue: whether discrimination on the basis of pregnancy is

permissible. The case is reprinted below. How would you formulate an argument that pregnancy discrimination is sex discrimination?

3. PREGNANCY DISCRIMINATION

GEDULDIG v. AIELLO

Supreme Court of the United States, 1974.

417 U.S. 484, 94 S.Ct. 2485, 41 L.Ed.2d 256.

MR. JUSTICE STEWART delivered the opinion of the Court.

We cannot agree that the exclusion of this disability from coverage amounts to invidious discrimination under the Equal Protection Clause. * * * Although California has created a program to insure most risks of employment disability, it has not chosen to insure all such risks, and this decision is reflected in the level of annual contributions exacted from participating employees. This Court has held that, consistently with the Equal Protection Clause, a State "may take one step at a time, addressing itself to the phase of the problem which seems most acute to the legislative mind...." Particularly with respect to social welfare programs, so long as the line drawn by the State is rationally supportable, the courts will not interpose their judgment as to the appropriate stopping point. "(T)he Equal Protection Clause does not require that a State must choose between attacking every aspect of a problem or not attacking the problem at all."

* * *

The State has a legitimate interest in maintaining the self-supporting nature of its insurance program. Similarly, it has an interest in distributing the available resources in such a way as to keep benefit payments at an adequate level for disabilities that are covered, rather than to cover all disabilities inadequately. Finally, California has a legitimate concern in maintaining the contribution rate at a level that will not unduly burden participating employees, particularly low-income employees who may be most in need of the disability insurance.

These policies provide an objective and wholly noninvidious basis for the State's decision not to create a more comprehensive insurance program than it has. There is no evidence in the record that the selection of the risks insured by the program worked to discriminate against any definable group or class in terms of the aggregate risk protection derived by that group or class from the program.[20] There is no

20. The dissenting opinion to the contrary, this case is thus a far cry from cases involving discrimination based upon gender as such. The California insurance program does not exclude anyone from benefit eligibility because of gender but merely removes one physical condition—pregnancy—from the list of compensable disabilities. While it is true that only women can become pregnant it does not follow that every legislative classification concerning pregnancy is a sex-based classification * * *. Absent a showing that distinctions involving pregnancy are mere pretexts designed to effect an invidious discrimination against the members of one sex or the other, lawmakers are constitutionally free to include or exclude pregnancy from the coverage of legislation such risk from which men are protected and women are not. Likewise, there is no risk from which women are protected and men are not.[21]

The appellee simply contends that, although she has received insurance protection equivalent to that provided all other participating employees, she has suffered discrimination because she encountered a risk that was outside the program's protection. For the reasons we have stated, we hold that this contention is not a valid one under the Equal Protection Clause of the Fourteenth Amendment.

* * *

MR. JUSTICE BRENNAN, with whom MR. JUSTICE DOUGLAS and MR. JUSTICE MARSHALL join, dissenting.

* * *

California's disability insurance program was enacted to supplement the State's unemployment insurance and workmen's compensation programs by providing benefits to wage earners to cushion the economic effects of income loss and medical expenses resulting from sickness or injury. * * *

To achieve the Act's broad humanitarian goals, the legislature fashioned a pooled-risk disability fund covering all employees at the same rate of contribution, regardless of individual risk.[2] The only requirement that must be satisfied before an employee becomes eligible to receive disability benefits is that the employee must have contributed 1% of a minimum income of $300 during a one-year base period. * * * Benefits are payable for a maximum of 26 weeks, but may not exceed one-half of the employee's total base-period earnings. Finally, compensation is paid for virtually all disabling conditions without regard to cost, voluntariness, uniqueness, predictability, or "normalcy" of the disability. Thus, for example, workers are compensated for costly disabilities such as heart attacks, voluntary disabilities such as cosmetic surgery or sterilization, disabilities unique to sex or race such as prostatectomies or sickle-cell anemia, pre-existing conditions inevitably resulting in disability such as degenerative arthritis or cataracts, and "normal" disabilities such as removal of irritating wisdom teeth or other orthodontia.

as this on any reasonable basis, just as with respect to any other physical condition. The lack of identity between the excluded disability and gender as such under this insurance program becomes clear upon the most cursory analysis. The program divides potential recipients into two groups—pregnant women and nonpregnant persons. While the first group is exclusively female, the second includes members of both sexes. * * *

21. Indeed, the appellant submitted to the District Court data that indicated that both the annual claim rate and the annual claim cost are greater for women than for men. As the District Court acknowledged, "women contribute about 28% of the total disability insurance fund and receive back about 38% of the fund in benefits." Several amici curiae have represented to the Court that they have had a similar experience under private disability insurance programs.

2. California deliberately decided not to classify employees on the basis of actuarial data. Thus, the contribution rate for a particular group of employees is not tied to that group's predicted rate of disability claims.

Despite the Code's broad goals and scope of coverage, compensation is denied for disabilities suffered in connection with a "normal" pregnancy-disabilities suffered only by women. Disabilities caused by pregnancy, however, like other physically disabling conditions covered by the Code, require medical care, often include hospitalization, anesthesia and surgical procedures, and may involve genuine risk to life. Moreover, the economic effects caused by pregnancy-related disabilities are functionally indistinguishable from the effects caused by any other disability: wages are lost due to a physical inability to work, and medical expenses are incurred for the delivery of the child and for postpartum care.[5] In my view, by singling out for less favorable treatment a gender-linked disability peculiar to women, the State has created a double standard for disability compensation: a limitation is imposed upon the disabilities for which women workers may recover, while men receive full compensation for all disabilities suffered, including those that affect only or primarily their sex, such as prostatectomies, circumcision, hemophilia, and gout. In effect, one set of rules is applied to females and another to males. Such dissimilar treatment of men and women, on the basis of physical characteristics inextricably linked to one sex, inevitably constitutes sex discrimination.

* * *

California's legitimate interest in fiscal integrity could easily have been achieved through a variety of less drastic, sexually neutral means. As the District Court observed:

> Even using (the State's) estimate of the cost of expanding the program to include pregnancy-related disabilities, however, it is clear that including these disabilities would not destroy the program. The increased costs could be accommodated quite easily by making reasonable changes in the contribution rate, the maximum benefits allowable, and the other variables affecting the solvency of the program. For example, the entire cost increase estimated by defendant could be met by requiring workers to contribute an additional amount of approximately .364% of their salary and increasing the maximum annual contribution to about $119.

Text Note: Disparate Treatment and Disparate Impact

Title VII of the Civil Rights Act of 1964, whose passage is described earlier in this chapter, was enacted before the Supreme Court recognized the Equal Protection Clause of the Fourteenth Amendment as reaching any discrimination on the basis of sex. Courts recognize two kinds of employment discrimination claims under Title VII: disparate treatment and disparate impact.

A disparate treatment claim alleges that similarly-situated women and men have been treated differently. A disparate impact claim alleges that a

5. Nearly two-thirds of all women who work do so of necessity: either they are unmarried or their husbands earn less than $7,000 per year. * * * "[I]n 1972, a woman working full time had a median income which was only 57.9% of the median for males—a figure actually six points lower than had been achieved in 1955."

gender-neutral rule or policy has a disparate impact on women. For example, a requirement that employees be 5′ 10″ tall or taller and weigh at least 220 pounds has a disparate impact on women, who will disproportionately (relative to men) fail to meet this qualification. Here, there is a clear standard or baseline for comparison: the proportion of men who meet this standard (say 20%) can be compared with the proportion of women who meet this standard (say 3%). In light of this difference, the requirement obviously has a disparate impact on women.

Disparate treatment claims can be broken down further into two types: allegations of facial (open, overt) disparate treatment and allegations of subtle disparate treatment. Facial disparate treatment occurs when a rule or policy openly, on its face, by its very terms, treats women one way and men another. Thus, for example, a rule that excludes all women from night work in factories (as some protectionist legislation did) discriminates overtly—on its face—on the basis of sex. If a rule or policy explicitly discriminates on the basis of sex, there is no *additional* requirement of any particular intent. The intent to treat individuals differently because of their sex is demonstrated by the terms of the discriminatory policy itself. Nothing else is required. Since the passage of Title VII, overt discrimination has, of course, become increasingly rare.

The other form of disparate treatment is subtle and common even today. For example, a woman lawyer believes that her firm imposes a higher standard on women than men for promotion to partnership. The law firm has, of course, no policy *overtly* requiring women to be more productive workers, but there are no objective measures of productivity, nor any objective and reliable predictors of future value as a partner. If the woman lawyer sues, the ultimate question is whether in fact the employer treated men and women differently. The employer will argue that more men were promoted to partner than women, not because they were men, but because they were more valuable employees or displayed more of the traits which the firm associates with future success as a partner. Part of the plaintiff's case might be evidence that the employer routinely treats women in stereotypical ways as demonstrated, for example, by some partners routinely referring to some of the young women as "babes." Here, the intent of the employer—the intent to discriminate against women rather than merely select the most valuable partners—becomes a critical part of the plaintiff's demonstration that in fact women were treated differently from men.

Although disparate impact claims have been recognized under Title VII (subject to a defense of business necessity), such claims have never been recognized in constitutional cases. Disparate impact claims are not even recognized under the strict scrutiny standard applicable to constitutional cases involving racial discrimination. The Court's concern seems to be that disparate impact would not be workable as a constitutional standard because legislation routinely has all sorts of disparate impacts on all sorts of groups. For constitutional cases, disparate treatment must be shown, though unconstitutional disparate treatment can be either overt or subtle. If subtle, the plaintiff must establish an intent to discriminate on an impermissible basis.

Notes on Geduldig

1. As noted earlier, Reed v. Reed (1971) was the first case in which the Supreme Court held that the Equal Protection Clause of the Fourteenth Amendment banned some sex-based discrimination. *Reed* and the next two cases, Frontiero v. Richardson (1973) and Kahn v. Shevin (1974), all involved *facially* discriminatory rules treating all women one way and all men another. The *Reed* statute gave a preference to male over female relatives in selecting executors of estates. In *Frontiero,* the Air force automatically gave spousal benefits to wives of Air Force personnel, but gave such benefits to husbands only when an individual husband was dependent on his wife for more than half his support. In *Kahn,* a Florida statute gave a $500 property tax exemption to widows but not to widowers and was upheld as constitutional despite discrimination on the basis of sex as a reasonable measure to further a legitimate state policy, cushioning the loss of a spouse for the more economically vulnerable survivor.

Geduldig was the next case to reach the Court and the first in which the challenged rule arguably did not discriminate on its face between women and men. Women were in both categories: "pregnant women and nonpregnant persons" (to quote the language used by the Court in note 20). Because the classification was based not on "gender" but on pregnancy, the Court did not view it as overt discrimination on the basis of sex, i.e., as distinguishing on its face between women and men. Because there was no overt sex discrimination (according to the Court's analysis), the distinction is not disparate treatment on the basis of sex unless the employer adopted it in order to treat women one way and men another. Do you agree with the Court that the statute does not discriminate on its face on the basis of sex?

2. How would you frame a disparate treatment argument for the plaintiffs in *Geduldig* given the classification between "pregnant women and nonpregnant persons"? Does the fact that women received proportionately more in annual benefits than their share of contributions (see note 21 of the majority opinion) rebut your argument? In her brief for the plaintiffs, Wendy Williams (and co-counsel) argued:

> Classifications based upon physical characteristics unique to one sex are sex-based classifications. Sex unique characteristics, particularly the capacity to become pregnant, are what define a person as a man or a woman, and the legal benefits or burdens which are based on such characteristics are burdens or benefits conferred because of a person's gender-identity. * * * Whether differential treatment on the basis of pregnancy is justified must depend upon the purpose of legislation and whether the differences between that "unique" characteristic and other characteristics are relevant to that purpose.

Appellee's Brief in Geduldig v. Aiello, No. 73–640, at 24–25 (Oct. Term 1973). Why did the Court reject this approach? Can you think of other arguments that could be made to the Supreme Court? What features of the Court's approach made it easy to reject these arguments?

3. The discrimination standard developed by the Supreme Court is often described as "formal equality." Under this approach, similarly situated

individuals must be treated similarly regardless of sex (or race or other protected characteristics). The Court could have fashioned a formal equality standard (requiring that similarly situated individuals be treated similarly) that would encompass pregnancy discrimination as Wendy Williams argued in her brief. Wendy Williams has suggested that the Court reached its "cultural limits" on this issue, unable to move beyond the culture's definition of women as mothers to see that distinctions based thereon could be sex discrimination. Wendy W. Williams, The Equality Crisis: Some Reflections on Culture, Courts, and Feminism, 7 Women's Rts. L. Rep. 175 (1983). Do you agree? To the extent true, could you use this point to argue against a formal equality approach?

4. In an amicus brief filed by the Women's Rights Project, Ginsburg also argued that the California plan at issue in *Geduldig* was *overt* discrimination on the basis of sex:

> [T]he state applies a double standard. It allows men to recover for any condition which affects them, including conditions which affect only men. But it denies benefits to women disabled by pregnancy, a condition that affects only women. A policy of this kind is overt sex discrimination. * * *
>
> Pregnancy is a uniquely female condition. * * * The [lower court] noted at the outset that discrimination of this kind, since it is based on a sex-linked characteristic, is sex discrimination.

Amicus Brief of ACLU in Geduldig v. Aiello, No. 73–640, at 18–19 (Oct. Term 1973). Why did the Court reject Ginsburg's argument that the California statute discriminated *overtly* on the basis of sex?

5. Ginsburg also argued that California *intended* to discriminate on the basis of sex:

> Indeed, the conclusion that California's disability scheme discriminates on the basis of sex is inescapable, for appellant admits to a discriminatory motive. Throughout this litigation, California has contended that, in its view, women already receive a disproportionately high share of benefits because they contribute 28% to the funds and receive 38% of the benefits. Hence, the state legislature, to prevent an even greater distortion between male and female claimants, may exclude disabilities due to pregnancy. Appellant [the State of California] ignores the fact that women constitute 40% of the workforce. Their contribution of only 28% of the fund is reflective of the typically low wages received by women. Women in fact receive less in benefits than their percentage in the work force would lead one to expect. However, even if they did use the fund disproportionately, that would not justify an exclusion directed solely at women. One may wonder if disproportionate use of the fund by blacks or Catholics would be thought by appellant to be sufficient justification for limiting access of those groups to the fund. While appellant's argument is clearly without merit, the fact that it is pressed insistently leaves no doubt on the point considered here: exclusion from eligibility for benefits of women disabled due to pregnancy is expressly designed to discriminate against women as a class. The presence of a discriminatory motive should be taken into consideration by

> the Court in its analysis of whether the classification is constitutionally infirm.

Id. at 23–24. Why did this argument fail? How did the Court turn this point—Ginsburg's argument that California quite intentionally discriminated on the basis of sex when it decided to exclude pregnancy-related disabilities from coverage (because women would otherwise draw more than their share of benefits)—into an explanation that the plan did *not* discriminate on the basis of sex?

6. Recall that employees paid 1% of their wages (up to a certain specified amount) into the fund. See Brennan's dissent. Although women constituted 40% of the workforce, they contributed only 28% of the fund because of their lower pay. Why, as Ginsburg's brief asks, didn't the fund's designers check to see whether members of religious or racial minorities or other identifiable groups were drawing more than their share? Giving the contribution structure, low-wage workers in general were surely drawing more than their share of benefits. Why wasn't this seen as a problem and claims limited for all low-wage workers, not just women? Why did those in control of the plan only worry about *women* drawing more than their share? Do you think that women were drawing more than their share?

7. Can you specify the state's legitimate interest, the interest described by the majority in *Geduldig* as "distributing the available resources in such a way as to keep benefit payments at an adequate level for disabilities that are covered, rather than to cover all disabilities inadequately"? Why might a state reasonably decide to cover disability associated with elective surgery, including cosmetic surgery, but not disabilities associated with pregnancy, given the information included in footnote five of Justice Brennan's dissent? Even if the concern was that women were drawing more than their share of benefits, why not begin by cutting cosmetic and all other elective surgery for women to reduce women's draw? What assumptions about pregnant women could make rational a policy providing insurance for disabilities caused by cosmetic surgery or skiing accidents but denying it for pregnancy-related disabilities? In light of the assumptions about pregnant women that underlie the policy, do you agree with the Court that there is "an objective and wholly noninvidious basis [i.e., no discriminatory intent] for the State's decision" to cover all disabilities but those related to pregnancy?

8. Covering all of male workers' disabilities was an important goal of the fund. Why wasn't it equally important to cover all female workers' disabilities? If you think that there was sex discrimination in the design of the plan in *Geduldig*, how would you describe it? Was it based on animus, an intent to discriminate *against* women? Do you agree with the Court that there was no sex discrimination because California did not discriminate on the basis of sex *per se* (in and of itself) but rather on the basis of pregnancy in light of women's relative contributions and draw?

Does this analysis suggest that the formal equality standard applied in *Geduldig* is actually androcentric (male-centered) because it entitles women only to equal treatment under rules and practices developed by and for men? See Catharine A. MacKinnon, Feminism Unmodified 36–37 (1987). *Geduldig* seems to suggest that a woman must look and behave like a man to be protected by the constitutional sex equality standard because as soon as she is perceived as different (pregnant, for example), differential treatment is justified. Is this a problem? If so, could it be avoided by a different constitutional standard?

9. As described in the text note before these questions, disparate impact analysis looks to see whether a rule or policy has a disparate impact on certain groups relative to other groups. Did the California plan have a disparate impact on women? All men's disabilities were covered, but not all of women's. On the other hand, women drew more in benefits than men relative to their contributions (even without coverage of pregnancy-related disabilities). Is there a problem picking the appropriate baseline (i.e., a problem selecting the appropriate standard for comparison)? In considering whether the plan has a disparate impact on women, wouldn't one have to identify a single appropriate alternative for comparison so that one could consider whether the California plan at issue in *Geduldig* had a disparate impact on women relative to the alternative? Given that alternatives in this context could be structured many ways (some better, some worse for women), is this an insurmountable hurdle for the use of disparate impact in many constitutional cases? Why doesn't this problem occur in the employment context when, for example, a plaintiff challenges a height or weight requirement?

10. In an article written after *Geduldig* was decided, Wendy Williams argues "that laws and rules which do not overtly classify on the basis of sex, but which have a disproportionately negative effect upon one sex, warrant, under appropriate circumstances, placing a burden of justification upon the party defending the law or rule in court." Wendy W. Williams, Equality's Riddle: Pregnancy and the Equal Treatment–Special Treatment Debate, 13 N.Y.U.Rev.L. & Soc. Change 325, 330 (1984–1985). Can you fashion a workable disparate impact standard for constitutional cases? How would you define "appropriate circumstances"?

11. The same question—whether discrimination on the basis of pregnancy is sex discrimination—arises under Title VII. Although the meaning of discrimination under this statute is not always identical to its meaning under the Constitution (as described in the text note above on disparate treatment and disparate impact), the Supreme Court interpreted Title VII consistently with *Geduldig* in the context of pregnancy discrimination. In General Electric Co. v. Gilbert, 429 U.S. 125, 97 S.Ct. 401, 50 L.Ed.2d 343 (1976), the Supreme Court held that an employer did not discriminate on the basis of sex under Title VII when medical benefits did not include costs associated with pregnancy. As a result of pressure from women, Congress overturned *Gilbert* with the Pregnancy Discrimination Act of 1978 (PDA), 42 U.S.C.A. § 2000e(k). The PDA defines sex discrimination to include distinctions based on pregnancy, childbirth, or related medical conditions.

Geduldig's holding that discrimination on the basis of pregnancy is not overt sex discrimination under the Constitution was affirmed by the Court in Bray v. Alexandria Women's Health Clinic, 506 U.S. 263, 113 S.Ct. 753, 122 L.Ed.2d 34 (1993). The issue in *Bray* was whether one of the civil rights statutes (42 U.S.C. § 1985(c) (providing a private federal cause of action for private conspiracy to, among other things, deprive "any person or class of persons of the equal protection of the laws")) allowed the plaintiffs to sue protesters obstructing access to abortion clinics. The Court held that the cause of action was available against members of a private conspiracy only if the conspirators had discriminated against women as a class. But since discrimination on the basis of pregnancy (or its termination) was not discrimination on the basis of sex, under *Geduldig*, the § 1985(c) cause of action was unavailable.

4. SETTLING ON AN INTERMEDIATE STANDARD

CRAIG v. BOREN

Supreme Court of the United States, 1976.

429 U.S. 190, 97 S.Ct. 451, 50 L.Ed.2d 397.

MR. JUSTICE BRENNAN delivered the opinion of the Court.

The interaction of two sections of an Oklahoma statute prohibits the sale of "nonintoxicating" 3.2% beer to males under the age of 21 and to females under the age of 18. The question to be decided is whether such a gender-based differential constitutes a denial to males 18–20 years of age of the equal protection of the laws in violation of the Fourteenth Amendment.

* * *

Analysis may appropriately begin with the reminder that *Reed* emphasized that statutory classifications that distinguish between males and females are "subject to scrutiny under the Equal Protection Clause." To withstand constitutional challenge, previous cases establish that classifications by gender must serve important governmental objectives and must be substantially related to achievement of those objectives. * * *

We accept for purposes of discussion the District Court's identification of the objective underlying [the statute] as the enhancement of traffic safety. Clearly, the protection of public health and safety represents an important function of state and local governments. However, appellees' statistics in our view cannot support the conclusion that the gender-based distinction closely serves to achieve that objective and therefore the distinction cannot under Reed withstand equal protection challenge.

The appellees introduced a variety of statistical surveys. * * *

The most focused and relevant of the statistical surveys, arrests of 18–20-year-olds for alcohol-related driving offenses, exemplifies the ultimate unpersuasiveness of this evidentiary record. Viewed in terms of the correlation between sex and the actual activity that Oklahoma seeks to regulate—driving while under the influence of alcohol—the statistics broadly establish that .18% of females and 2% of males in that age group were arrested for that offense. While such a disparity is not trivial in a statistical sense, it hardly can form the basis for employment of a gender line as a classifying device. Certainly if maleness is to serve as a proxy for drinking and driving, a correlation of 2% must be considered an unduly tenuous "fit." Indeed, prior cases have consistently rejected the use of sex as a decisionmaking factor even though the statutes in question certainly rested on far more predictive empirical relationships than this.

* * *

[T]he showing offered by the appellees does not satisfy us that sex represents a legitimate, accurate proxy for the regulation of drinking and driving. In fact, when it is further recognized that Oklahoma's statute prohibits only the selling of 3.2% beer to young males and not their drinking the beverage once acquired (even after purchase by their 18–20–year-old female companions), the relationship between gender and traffic safety becomes far too tenuous to satisfy *Reed*'s requirement that the gender-based difference be substantially related to achievement of the statutory objective.

We hold, therefore, that under *Reed,* Oklahoma's 3.2% beer statute invidiously discriminates against males 18–20 years of age.

* * *

[Concurring opinions by Justices Powell, Blackmun and Stewart and a dissenting opinion by Chief Justice Burger have been omitted.]

MR. JUSTICE STEVENS, concurring.

* * *

In this case, the classification is not as obnoxious as some the Court has condemned, nor as inoffensive as some the Court has accepted. It is objectionable because it is based on an accident of birth, because it is a mere remnant of the now almost universally rejected tradition of discriminating against males in this age bracket, and because, to the extent it reflects any physical difference between males and females, it is actually perverse. The question then is whether the traffic safety justification put forward by the State is sufficient to make an otherwise offensive classification acceptable.

The classification is not totally irrational. For the evidence does indicate that there are more males than females in this age bracket who drive and also more who drink. Nevertheless, there are several reasons why I regard the justification as unacceptable. It is difficult to believe that the statute was actually intended to cope with the problem of traffic safety, since it has only a minimal effect on access to a not very intoxicating beverage and does not prohibit its consumption. Moreover, the empirical data submitted by the State accentuate the unfairness of treating all 18–21–year-old males as inferior to their female counterparts. The legislation imposes a restraint on 100% of the males in the class allegedly because about 2% of them have probably violated one or more laws relating to the consumption of alcoholic beverages. It is unlikely that this law will have a significant deterrent effect either on that 2% or on the law-abiding 98%. But even assuming some such slight benefit, it does not seem to me that an insult to all of the young men of the State can be justified by visiting the sins of the 2% on the 98%.

* * *

MR. JUSTICE REHNQUIST, dissenting.

The Court's disposition of this case is objectionable on two grounds. First is its conclusion that men challenging a gender-based statute which treats them less favorably than women may invoke a more stringent standard of judicial review than pertains to most other types of classifications. Second is the Court's enunciation of this standard, without citation to any source, as being that "classifications by gender must serve important governmental objectives and must be substantially related to achievement of those objectives." The only redeeming feature of the Court's opinion, to my mind, is that it apparently signals a retreat by those who joined the plurality opinion in Frontiero v. Richardson, from their view that sex is a "suspect" classification for purposes of equal protection analysis. I think the Oklahoma statute challenged here need pass only the "rational basis" equal protection analysis and I believe that it is constitutional under that analysis.

* * *

[T]he question [is] whether the incidence of drunk driving among young men is sufficiently greater than among young women to justify differential treatment. Notwithstanding the Court's critique of the statistical evidence, that evidence suggests clear differences between the drinking and driving habits of young men and women. Those differences are grounds enough for the State reasonably to conclude that young males pose by far the greater drunk-driving hazard, both in terms of sheer numbers and in terms of hazard on a per-driver basis. The gender-based difference in treatment in this case is therefore not irrational.

The Court's argument that a 2% correlation between maleness and drunk driving is constitutionally insufficient therefore does not pose an equal protection issue concerning discrimination between males and females. The clearest demonstration of this is the fact that the precise argument made by the Court would be equally applicable to a flat bar on such purchases by anyone, male or female, in the 18–20 age group; in fact it would apply a fortiori in that case given the even more "tenuous 'fit' " between drunk-driving arrests and femaleness. * * *

The Oklahoma Legislature could have believed that 18–20–year-old males drive substantially more, and tend more often to be intoxicated than their female counterparts; that they prefer beer and admit to drinking and driving at a higher rate than females; and that they suffer traffic injuries out of proportion to the part they make up of the population. * * * There being no violation of either equal protection or due process, the statute should accordingly be upheld.

Notes on Craig

1. Do you agree with Justice Stevens that the Oklahoma statute was objectionable because it was a "remnant of the now almost universally rejected tradition of discriminating against males in this age bracket"? Do you think the statute insults and discriminates against young men? What is the meaning of "discriminates *against*" to you? to the Court? Are rules against liquor sales to minors based on dislike of young people? What do you think were the real reasons for the differential treatment of young men and young women? What assumptions about young people and their relationships might explain this differential treatment? Could you argue that the Oklahoma statute actually discriminates against young women? How? Would you allow a man to challenge this discrimination? How important is the decision? Is discrimination with respect to the ability to buy alcohol an important aspect of the systemic subordination of women?

2. Which approach in *Craig*—Justice Brennan's, Justice Stevens,' or Justice Rehnquist's—do you prefer? Which has the potential to do the most for women in the short run? In the long run?

3. In a speech made while Reed v. Reed was pending before the Supreme Court but before the decision was handed down, Ruth Bader Ginsburg discussed whether there would be any need for the ERA if she was successful in Reed v. Reed. She stated that

> [I]t is at least arguable that the right of men to equal protection will be better secured by the equal rights laws guarantee [the ERA]. Supporters of the amendment maintain that it declares sex a prohibited classification, not merely a suspect classification. With few exceptions relating to personal privacy and physical characteristics unique to one sex, the constitutional mandate would be absolute if the amendment is adopted. Suspect classification, on the other hand, relates to the group that has borne the stigma of inferiority or second class treatment; it has not been used to shield the culture's dominant group from discrimination. Accordingly, the female sex could be aided by the suspect classification doctrine, while non-suspect status would be the lot of men. Thus laws discriminating against women might be subject to rigid scrutiny, while a disadvantage imposed by law on men would pass muster if supportable on any rational ground.

Ginsburg, Sex and Unequal Protection: Men and Women as Victims, 11 J. Family Law 347, 361–362 (1971). Was it a mistake to allow men to sue for sex discrimination (and whites to sue for race discrimination) under the Equal Protection Clause? What are the differences between a standard enforceable only by women and minorities and one enforceable by all? Which standard will better protect the interests of women and minorities? Why?

4. In a 1975 speech published in 1976, Ruth Bader Ginsburg suggested that the use of the word "sex" (as in "sex discrimination") might be evocative of sexuality, whereas gender "by contrast, has a neutral, clinical tone that may ward off distracting associations." She therefore recommended using "gender" instead of "sex." Ruth Bader Ginsburg, Gender and the Constitution, 44 Cincinnati L. Rev. 1, 1 (1976). At this time and, we

suspect, not coincidentally, the terminology used by the Supreme Court changed. Prior to *Craig*, decided in 1976, the Court occasionally used "gender" rather than "sex," but was more likely to use "sex." See, for example, the pre-*Craig* extracts in this chapter, in which "sex" is routinely used; "gender" is used only once by Justice Brennan in his dissent in *Geduldig*, where he refers to "a gender-linked disability peculiar to women." *Craig* marks a decided shift from "sex" to "gender." In *Craig*, the majority uses "gender" six times in the short extract above; in the extract of his dissent, Rehnquist uses "gender" three times.

What are the possible meanings of sex and gender? Are these two terms always interchangeable? Or is sex sometimes used to refer to physical sex (whether one was born a female or a male in terms of physical characteristics), while gender is sometimes used to refer to the cultural construct built on that physical reality (masculinity and femininity)? Are there other differences in the usage of these terms? Are there substantive consequences to assuming their equivalence for purposes of identifying discrimination? Do you see any differences between the meaning of sex discrimination and the meaning of gender discrimination?

5. Some feminists object to the sex-gender distinction on the following ground:

> sex, gender and sexuality are inextricably linked and cannot be disentangled from each other. This is the case both for those who see femininity and masculinity as culturally constructed and for those who assume that some essential difference exists prior to cultural influences. Feminists interested in asserting women's "difference" * * * often object to the sex-gender distinction because they see it as denying the specificity of women's bodily experience.

Stevi Jackson, Gender and Heterosexuality: A Materialist Feminist Analysis, in (Hetero)sexual Politics 11, 11 (Mary Maynard and June Purvis, eds. 1995). What is the point Jackson makes here about the use of "gender" being a denial of "women's bodily experiences"? Do you agree with Jackson?

6. Does physical "sex" have a "natural" reference, a meaning independent of culture and women's subordinate status? Postmodern feminists argue that our existing categories of women and men and even of sex are entirely the product of hierarchy, with no pre-hierarchical existence or meaning. For example, Monique Wittig, a French postmodern feminist, posits: " 'It is oppression that creates sex and not the contrary.' " Jackson, above note 5 at 16 (quoting Wittig, The Straight Mind and Other Essays 2 (1992)). Do you agree? What does it mean to say that sex has no pre-hierarchical existence or meaning? What term(s) do you think the Supreme Court should use?

7. *Craig* is widely understood as establishing an intermediate standard for review of legislation classifying by sex. Racial classifications are subject to the strictest of scrutiny, and therefore generally unconstitutional (because not necessary to the realization of a compelling governmental interest), unless seen as permissible affirmative action. But most legislative classifications are subject to the mildest of scrutiny, rational review, and are therefore generally constitutional (as long as there is a plausible and legitimate governmental interest bearing some—even weak—relationship to the classi-

fication). The standard for review established in *Craig* is between these two extremes: Sex-based classifications must "serve important governmental objectives and must be substantially related to the achievement of these objectives." Thus, the standard in cases involving sex discrimination is a weakened version of the standard for racial discrimination. Is this difference appropriate? Is it adequate in light of the problems with using race discrimination doctrine as a model for sex discrimination doctrine?

8. In 1979 the Supreme Court ruled for the husband in a divorce case involving a sex-specific alimony rule. Orr v. Orr, 440 U.S. 268, 99 S.Ct. 1102, 59 L.Ed.2d 306 (1979). The Court held that a statute authorizing judicial awards of alimony from men to women after divorce but not from women to men was unconstitutional because homemakers could be protected by gender-neutral rules that would not reinforce stereotypes of women as destined only for a dependent role. In fact, judges interpreting gender-neutral statutes have become less likely to give homemakers long-term awards; today even long-term homemakers receive in most cases only short-term "rehabilitative" awards for four years or so. For an early discussion of the dangers of a formal equality approach in family law, see Martha A. Fineman, Implementing Equality: Ideology, Contradiction and Social Change, 1983 Wis. L.Rev. 789. See also Patricia J. Williams, The Alchemy of Race and Rights 104–10 (1991) (criticizing formal equality under conditions of substantive inequality and likening the Court's equality standard to a machine that makes sausage no matter what you throw into it); Linda S. Greene, Race in the 21st Century: Equality Through Law?, 64 Tul.L.Rev. 1515 (1990) (discussing problems with formalism and equality).

C. THE STANDARD IN ACTION

1. THE MILITARY

PERSONNEL ADMINISTRATOR OF MASSACHUSETTS v. FEENEY

Supreme Court of the United States, 1979.

442 U.S. 256, 99 S.Ct. 2282, 60 L.Ed.2d 870.

MR. JUSTICE STEWART delivered the opinion of the Court.

This case presents a challenge to the constitutionality of the Massachusetts veterans' preference statute on the ground that it discriminates against women in violation of the Equal Protection Clause of the Fourteenth Amendment. * * * [A]ll veterans who qualify for state civil service positions must be considered for appointment ahead of any qualifying nonveterans. The preference operates overwhelmingly to the advantage of males.

The appellee Helen B. Feeney is not a veteran. She brought this action * * * alleging that the absolute preference formula * * * inevitably operates to exclude women from consideration for the best Massachusetts civil service jobs and thus unconstitutionally denies them the equal protection of the laws. * * *

The District Court found that the absolute preference afforded by Massachusetts to veterans has a devastating impact upon the employment opportunities of women. * * *

The Federal Government and virtually all of the States grant some sort of hiring preference to veterans. The Massachusetts preference, which is loosely termed an "absolute lifetime" preference, is among the most generous. * * *

The veterans' hiring preference in Massachusetts, as in other jurisdictions, has traditionally been justified as a measure designed to reward veterans for the sacrifice of military service, to ease the transition from military to civilian life, to encourage patriotic service, and to attract loyal and well-disciplined people to civil service occupations. * * * The Massachusetts law dates back to 1884, when the State, as part of its first civil service legislation, gave a statutory preference to civil service applicants who were Civil War veterans if their qualifications were equal to those of nonveterans. * * *

Notwithstanding the apparent attempts by Massachusetts to include as many military women as possible within the scope of the preference, the statute today benefits an overwhelmingly male class. This is attributable in some measure to the variety of federal statutes, regulations, and policies that have restricted the number of women who could enlist in the United States Armed Forces, and largely to the simple fact that women have never been subjected to a military draft.

When this litigation was commenced, then, over 98% of the veterans in Massachusetts were male; only 1.8% were female. And over one-quarter of the Massachusetts population were veterans. During the decade between 1963 and 1973 when the appellee was actively participating in the State's merit selection system, 47,005 new permanent appointments were made in the classified official service. 43% of those hired were women, and 57% were men. Of the women appointed, 1.8% were veterans, while 54% of the men had veteran status. A large unspecified percentage of the female appointees were serving in lower paying positions for which males traditionally had not applied.[22] * * *

The sole question for decision on this appeal is whether Massachusetts, in granting an absolute lifetime preference to veterans, has discriminated against women in violation of the Equal Protection Clause of the Fourteenth Amendment.

* * *

22. The former exemption for "women's requisitions," * * * may have operated in the 20th century to protect these types of jobs from the impact of the preference. However, the statutory history indicates that this was not its purpose. The provision dates back to the 1896 veterans' preference law and was retained in the law substantially unchanged until it was eliminated in 1971. * * * Since veterans in 1896 were a small but an exclusively male class, such a provision was apparently included to ensure that the statute would not be construed to outlaw a pre-existing practice of single-sex hiring explicitly authorized under the 1884 Civil Service statute. The veterans' preference statute at no point endorsed this practice. Historical materials indicate, however, that the early preference law may have operated to encourage the employment of women in positions from which they previously had been excluded.

When a statute gender-neutral on its face is challenged on the ground that its effects upon women are disproportionately adverse, a twofold inquiry is * * * appropriate. The first question is whether the statutory classification is indeed neutral in the sense that it is not gender-based. If the classification itself, covert or overt, is not based upon gender, the second question is whether the adverse effect reflects invidious gender-based discrimination. * * *

If the impact of this statute could not be plausibly explained on a neutral ground, impact itself would signal that the real classification made by the law was in fact not neutral. But there can be but one answer to the question whether this veteran preference excludes significant numbers of women from preferred state jobs because they are women or because they are nonveterans. Apart from the facts that the definition of "veterans" in the statute has always been neutral as to gender and that Massachusetts has consistently defined veteran status in a way that has been inclusive of women who have served in the military, this is not a law that can plausibly be explained only as a gender-based classification. Indeed, it is not a law that can rationally be explained on that ground. Veteran status is not uniquely male. Although few women benefit from the preference the nonveteran class is not substantially all female. To the contrary, significant numbers of nonveterans are men, and all nonveterans—male as well as female—are placed at a disadvantage. Too many men are affected by [the preference] to permit the inference that the statute is but a pretext for preferring men over women.

* * * The distinction made by [the preference] is, as it seems to be, quite simply between veterans and nonveterans, not between men and women.

The dispositive question, then, is whether the appellee has shown that a gender-based discriminatory purpose has, at least in some measure, shaped the Massachusetts veterans' preference legislation. * * * [S]he points to two basic factors. * * * The first is the nature of the preference, which is said to be demonstrably gender-biased in the sense that it favors a status reserved under federal military policy primarily to men. The second concerns the impact of the absolute lifetime preference upon the employment opportunities of women, an impact claimed to be too inevitable to have been unintended. The appellee contends that these factors, coupled with the fact that the preference itself has little if any relevance to actual job performance, more than suffice to prove the discriminatory intent required to establish a constitutional violation.

* * *

The appellee's ultimate argument rests upon the presumption, common to the criminal and civil law, that a person intends the natural and foreseeable consequences of his voluntary actions. Her position was well stated in the concurring opinion in the District Court: "Conceding ... that the goal here was to benefit the veteran, there is no reason to absolve the legislature from awareness that the means chosen to achieve this goal would freeze women out of all those state jobs actively sought by men. To be sure, the legislature did not wish to harm women. But the cutting-off of women's opportunities was an inevitable concomitant of the chosen scheme—as inevitable as the proposition that if tails is up, heads must be down. Where a law's consequences are that inevitable, can they meaningfully be described as unintended?"

* * *

"Discriminatory purpose," however, implies more than intent as volition or intent as awareness of consequences. It implies that the decisionmaker, in this case a state legislature, selected or reaffirmed a particular course of action at least in part "because of," not merely "in spite of," its adverse effects upon an identifiable group. Yet, nothing in the record demonstrates that this preference for veterans was originally devised or subsequently re-enacted because it would accomplish the collateral goal of keeping women in a stereotypic and predefined place in the Massachusetts Civil Service.

To the contrary, the statutory history shows that the benefit of the preference was consistently offered to "any person" who was a veteran. That benefit has been extended to women under a very broad statutory definition of the term veteran. The preference formula itself, which is the focal point of this challenge, was first adopted—so it appears from this record—out of a perceived need to help a small group of older Civil War veterans. It has since been reaffirmed and extended only to cover new veterans. When the totality of legislative actions establishing and extending the Massachusetts veterans' preference are considered, the law remains what it purports to be: a preference for veterans of either sex over nonveterans of either sex, not for men over women.

[The concurrence of Justices Stevens and White is omitted.]

MR. JUSTICE MARSHALL, with whom MR. JUSTICE BRENNAN joins, dissenting.

* * * In my judgment, Massachusetts' choice of an absolute veterans' preference system evinces purposeful gender-based discrimination. And because the statutory scheme bears no substantial relationship to a legitimate governmental objective, it cannot withstand scrutiny under the Equal Protection Clause.

* * *

That a legislature seeks to advantage one group does not, as a matter of logic or of common sense, exclude the possibility that it also intends to disadvantage another. Individuals in general and lawmakers in particular frequently act for a variety of reasons. As this Court [has] recognized, "[r]arely can it be said that a legislature or administrative body operating under a broad mandate made a decision motivated solely by a single concern." Absent an omniscience not commonly attributed to the judiciary, it will often be impossible to ascertain the sole or even dominant purpose of a given statute. Thus, the critical constitutional inquiry is not whether an illicit consideration was the primary or but-for cause of a decision, but rather whether it had an appreciable role in shaping a given legislative enactment. Where there is "proof that a discriminatory purpose has been a motivating factor in the decision, . . . judicial deference is no longer justified."

Moreover, since reliable evidence of subjective intentions is seldom obtainable, resort to inference based on objective factors is generally unavoidable. To discern the purposes underlying facially neutral policies, this Court has therefore considered the degree, inevitability, and foreseeability of any disproportionate impact as well as the alternatives reasonably available.

In the instant case, the impact of the Massachusetts statute on women is undisputed. Any veteran with a passing grade on the civil service exam must be placed ahead of a nonveteran, regardless of their respective scores. The District Court found that, as a practical matter, this preference supplants test results as the determinant of upper level civil service appointments. Because less than 2% of the women in Massachusetts are veterans, the absolute-preference formula has rendered desirable state civil service employment an almost exclusively male prerogative.

As the District Court recognized, this consequence follows foreseeably, indeed inexorably, from the long history of policies severely limiting women's participation in the military. Although neutral in form, the statute is anything but neutral in application. It inescapably reserves a major sector of public employment to "an already established class which, as a matter of historical fact, is 98% male." * * * Where the foreseeable impact of a facially neutral policy is so disproportionate, the burden should rest on the State to establish that sex-based considerations played no part in the choice of the particular legislative scheme.

Clearly, that burden was not sustained here. The legislative history of the statute reflects the Commonwealth's patent appreciation of the impact the preference system would have on women, and an equally evident desire to mitigate that impact only with respect to certain traditionally female occupations. Until 1971, the statute and implementing civil service regulations exempted from operation of the preference any job requisitions "especially calling for women." In practice, this exemption, coupled with the absolute preference for veterans, has created a gender-based civil service hierarchy, with women occupying low-grade clerical and secretarial jobs and men holding more responsible and remunerative positions.

[Justice Marshall concluded that the Massachusetts preference could not survive intermediate scrutiny under *Craig* once it was seen as a form of sex discrimination.]

Notes on Feeney

1. Do you agree that rules favoring soldiers and disfavoring motherhood, such as those at issue in *Feeney* and *Geduldig*, are not discrimination on the basis of sex? How does discrimination on the basis of sex operate? The Court in *Feeney* seems to assume that discrimination against women is motivated by some sort of conscious animus or ill will. Do you agree? Can you give examples from your own experience of sex discrimination or sexism that were entirely unconscious and inadvertent?

2. Why does the Supreme Court focus so much on the consciousness and motives of the discriminator in this case? How is *Feeney* different from earlier cases other than *Geduldig*? Why, in *Feeney*, as in *Geduldig*, is discriminatory intent necessary?

3. Is the requirement of intent in this kind of case both self-serving and self-centered, i.e., self-serving in that it is conservative and safe, rather than threatening, to the important sex-related privileges enjoyed by the men who adopted it, and self-centered in that it focuses not on the harm discrimination causes real women but on the mindset of powerful men? See Alan David Freeman, Legitimizing Racial Discrimination Through Antidiscrimination Law: A Critical Review of Supreme Court Doctrine, 62 Minn. L.Rev. 1049 (1978) (making similar points in the context of race discrimination).

4. If the Court were to adopt the standard suggested by David Strauss in his article, Discriminatory Intent and the Taming of *Brown*, 56 U.Chi. L.Rev. 935 (1989), the key question would be whether the legislature would have enacted the same statute were the groups reversed. This, Strauss argues, should be the key question: would the mostly male Massachusetts legislature have passed the veterans' preference statute had the vast majority of veterans been women? If not, then sex discrimination should be regarded as the but-for cause of the statute. Is this a workable alternative to the Court's standard?

How does the Court's standard differ from the reversing-the-groups standard? Which standard is more likely to capture discrimination on the basis of sex? What are the advantages or disadvantages of these two approaches? If you were to apply the reverse-the-groups test to the classification at issue in *Feeney*, would you conclude that the statute discriminated on the basis of sex?

5. In his article, David Strauss suggests that motherhood is much like military service: mothers, like soldiers, make important contributions to society, risking physical hazards and disruptions of careers, etc. Strauss, above note 4, at 1001. Christine Littleton made a similar point in an earlier article, Reconstructing Sexual Equality, 75 Calif.L.Rev. 1279, 1329–30 (1987), when she suggested that government should give soldiers and mothers the same benefits. Do you agree? Do you think that the failure of states to enact maternal preference statutes for state employment reveals sex discrimination? What problems do you see in attempting to improve the status of mothers by valuing mothering according to the value of soldiering? Are soldiering and mothering equally valuable?

6. Virtually all states as well as the federal government give preferences to veterans for government employment. Are these veterans' preferences in government employment equivalent to wages or other benefits for soldiers and veterans? Are there reasons to see this particular benefit as more problematic than other veterans' benefits? Should veterans' dominance in government be regarded as consistent with (a) a democracy? (b) the "Republican Form of Government" guaranteed by section four of Article IV of the United States Constitution? (c) sexual equality?

ROSTKER v. GOLDBERG

Supreme Court of the United States, 1981.

453 U.S. 57, 101 S.Ct. 2646, 69 L.Ed.2d 478.

JUSTICE REHNQUIST delivered the opinion of the Court.

The question presented is whether the Military Selective Service Act violates the Fifth Amendment to the United States Constitution in authorizing the President to require the registration of males and not females.

[Registration for the draft ended in 1975, but in 1980, in response to the Soviet invasion of Afghanistan, President Carter decided to reinstitute registration. In seeking funds for this purpose from Congress, he asked Congress to amend the Act to allow the registration and eventual conscription of women. Congress agreed to allocate the necessary funds but declined to amend the Act to include women. As a result, the statute at issue in this case, the Military Selective Service Act (MSSA), gave the President the power to register only men 18 to 26 years of age. The sole purpose of such registration was for use in a subsequent draft, though congressional action would be necessary to draft.

The case itself began in 1971 as part of the opposition to the Vietnam war. Eventually, one of the claims was that the Vietnam registration and draft of men was impermissible sex-based discrimination. After a number of years during which nothing happened, the District Court in 1980 found that the Act, recently given new vitality by President Carter, impermissibly discriminated on the basis of sex, in violation of the Due Process Clause of the Fifth Amendment (incorporating the Equal Protection Clause of the Fourteenth Amendment), which forbids such discrimination by the federal government under the standard articulated in Craig v. Boren, discussed above. The District Court concluded that no "important government interest" supported registration of only men. The court did not reach the issue of women in combat, since registration of women would not necessarily require their deployment in combat.]

* * *

This is not * * * merely a case involving the customary deference accorded congressional decisions. The case arises in the context of Congress' authority over national defense and military affairs, and perhaps in no other area has the Court accorded Congress greater deference. * * *

Not only is the scope of Congress' constitutional power in this area broad, but the lack of competence on the part of the courts is marked. * * *

This case is quite different from several of the gender-based discrimination cases we have considered in that, despite appellees' assertions, Congress did not act "unthinkingly" or "reflexively and not for any considered reason." The question of registering women for the draft not only received considerable national attention and was the subject of wide-ranging public debate, but also was extensively considered by Congress in hearings, floor debate, and in committee. Hearings held by both Houses of Congress in response to the President's request for authorization to register women adduced extensive testimony and evidence concerning the issue.

* * *

[T]he decision to exempt women from registration was not the " 'accidental by-product of a traditional way of thinking about females.' " In *Michael M.* [v. Sonoma County Superior Court, 450 U.S. 464 (1981) (extract in Chapter 5)] we rejected a similar argument because of action by the California Legislature considering and rejecting proposals to make a statute challenged on discrimination grounds gender-neutral. The cause for rejecting the argument is considerably stronger here. The issue was considered at great length, and Congress clearly expressed its purpose and intent.

* * *

Congress determined that any future draft, which would be facilitated by the registration scheme, would be characterized by a need for combat troops. The Senate Report explained, in a specific finding later adopted by both Houses, that "[i]f mobilization were to be ordered in a wartime scenario, the primary manpower need would be for combat replacements." * * *

Women as a group, however, unlike men as a group, are not eligible for combat. The restrictions on the participation of women in combat in the Navy and Air Force are statutory. * * * The Army and Marine Corps preclude the use of women in combat as a matter of established policy. Congress specifically recognized and endorsed the exclusion of women from combat in exempting women from registration. * * *

This is not a case of Congress arbitrarily choosing to burden one of two similarly situated groups, such as would be the case with an all-black or all-white, or an all-Catholic or all-Lutheran, or an all-Republican or all-Democratic registration. Men and women, because of the combat restrictions on women, are simply not similarly situated for purposes of a draft or registration for a draft.

Congress' decision to authorize the registration of only men, therefore, does not violate the Due Process Clause. The exemption of women from registration is not only sufficiently but also closely related to Congress' purpose in authorizing registration. The fact that Congress and the Executive have decided that women should not serve in combat fully justifies Congress in not authorizing their registration, since the purpose of registration is to develop a pool of potential combat troops. As was the case in *Schlesinger v. Ballard,* [419 U.S. 498 (1975) (holding that the navy can give women two extra years under up-or-out policy)], "the gender classification is not invidious, but rather realistically reflects the fact that the sexes are not similarly situated" in this case. The Constitution requires that Congress treat similarly situated persons similarly, not that it engage in gestures of superficial equality.

* * *

[A]ssuming that a small number of women could be drafted for noncombat roles, Congress simply did not consider it worth the added burdens of including women in draft and registration plans. * * *

Congress also concluded that whatever the need for women for noncombat roles during mobilization, whether 80,000 or less, it could be met by volunteers. * * *

Most significantly, Congress determined that staffing noncombat positions with women during a mobilization would be positively detrimental to the important goal of military flexibility. * * *

In light of the foregoing, we conclude that Congress acted well within its constitutional authority when it authorized the registration of men, and not women, under the Military Selective Service Act. The decision of the District Court holding otherwise is accordingly

Reversed.

JUSTICE WHITE, with whom JUSTICE BRENNAN joins, dissenting.

* * *

As I understand the record, * * * in order to secure the personnel it needs during mobilization, the Government cannot rely on volunteers and must register and draft not only to fill combat positions and those noncombat positions that must be filled by combat-trained men, but also to secure the personnel needed for jobs that can be performed by persons ineligible for combat without diminishing military effectiveness. The claim is that in providing for the latter category of positions, Congress is free to register and draft only men. I discern no adequate justification for this kind of discrimination between men and women. Accordingly, with all due respect, I dissent.

JUSTICE MARSHALL, with whom JUSTICE BRENNAN joins, dissenting.

The Court today places its imprimatur on one of the most potent remaining public expressions of "ancient canards about the proper role of women." It upholds a statute that requires males but not females to register for the draft, and which thereby categorically excludes women from a fundamental civic obligation. Because I believe the Court's decision is inconsistent with the Constitution's guarantee of equal protection of the laws, I dissent.

* * *

The Court * * * reasons that since women are not eligible for assignment to combat, Congress' decision to exclude them from registration is not unconstitutional discrimination inasmuch as "[m]en and women, because of the combat restrictions on women, are simply not similarly situated for purposes of a draft or registration for a draft." * * *

[A]lthough the Court purports to apply the *Craig v. Boren* test, the "similarly situated" analysis the Court employs is in fact significantly different from the *Craig v. Boren* approach. The Court essentially reasons that the gender classification employed by the MSSA is constitutionally permissible because nondiscrimination is not necessary to achieve the purpose of registration to prepare for a draft of combat troops. In other words, the majority concludes that women may be excluded from registration because they will not be needed in the event of a draft.

This analysis, however, focuses on the wrong question. The relevant inquiry under the *Craig v. Boren* test is not whether a *gender-neutral* classification would substantially advance important governmental interests. Rather, the question is whether the gender-based classification is itself substantially related to the achievement of the asserted governmental interest. Thus, the Government's task in this case is to demonstrate that excluding women from registration substantially furthers the goal of preparing for a draft of combat troops. Or to put it another way, the Government must show that registering women would substantially impede its efforts to prepare for such a draft. Under our precedents, the Government cannot meet this burden without showing that a gender-neutral statute would be a less effective means of attaining this end. As the Court explained in *Orr v. Orr,* 440 U.S. [268], 283 [(1979) (holding unconstitutional state divorce law providing for payment of spousal support only by men)]:

> Where, as here, the [Government's] ... purposes are as well served by a gender-neutral classification as one that gender classifies and therefore carries with it the baggage of sexual stereotypes, the [Government] cannot be permitted to classify on the basis of sex.

In this case, the Government makes no claim that preparing for a draft of combat troops cannot be accomplished just as effectively by *registering* both men and women but *drafting* only men if only men turn out to be needed. Nor can the Government argue that this alternative entails the additional cost and administrative inconvenience of registering women. This Court has repeatedly stated that the administrative convenience of employing a gender classification is not an adequate constitutional justification under the *Craig v. Boren* test.

* * *

Notes on Rostker

1. When is a statute distinguishing between women and men nevertheless constitutional under the standard articulated in the earlier cases? For example, what was the test articulated in Craig v. Boren? If a statute distinguishes between women and men (as the Oklahoma statute in that case did), it is constitutional if and only if . . . .? How would you come out if you were applying this standard to the male-only registration for military service at issue in *Rostker*? Who has the stronger analytical position on this question, the majority or Justice Marshall in dissent?

2. Do all the justices assume that it would be constitutional to send only men into combat? Wouldn't such a policy inevitably reinforce traditional sex roles? How would the Court justify upholding the constitutionality of such a policy despite this effect and its facial discrimination on the basis of sex?

3. The *Rostker* majority relies on the fact that the policy registering only women was adopted after Congress thought about the issue. The Court concludes that the policy was not therefore an " 'accidental by-product of a traditional way of thinking about females.' " Why does the Court ignore the possibility that it was the *deliberate* by-product of such thinking? Shouldn't the fact that the policy was adopted after deliberation count *against* it if based on traditional ways of thinking about women? As the Court itself viewed the matter, Congress decided not to register women because it was unwilling to draft women for combat. Isn't it possible, perhaps likely, that the no-combat policy was based in part on traditional sex roles and stereotypes?

4. Could you use the fact that combat soldiers bear arms to frame an argument that the Second Amendment bars the exclusion of women from combat? The Second Amendment provides that "A well regulated Militia, being necessary to the security of a free State, the right of the people to keep and bear Arms, shall not be infringed." Given the Second Amendment Congress could not pass a statute allowing only non-citizen mercenaries from other countries to bear arms in American military units. Why is it permissible to keep women, a majority of the citizenry, from carrying arms in the military? How do you think the Supreme Court would respond to an argument that under the Second Amendment, women cannot be deprived of the right to bear arms in the military? For a discussion of this argument, see Akhil Reed Amar, The Bill of Rights as a Constitution, 100 Yale L.J. 1131, 1202–03 (1991).

5. What are the reasons women might want to be included in the military, even in combat? Are there, for example, consequences in terms of women's power in politics and in the military? Think of a woman running against a veteran for public office, or applying for a job in Massachusetts state government. What are the chances of a woman with no combat

experience attaining high military rank, such as becoming Joint Chief of Staff? Why doesn't the Court even mention the *Feeney* problem in *Rostker*, i.e., that women are frozen out of many powerful political positions by the combination of differential participation rates of women and men in the modern military (differences required by Congress and based on women's ineligibility for combat) and veterans' preferences for state employment? Should it matter that different levels of government set these policies: the federal government limits women's military participation and state government then awards positions in state government to veterans?

6. In what other ways does the military, as currently structured, contribute to women's inequality? Consider, for example, the military's super-masculine culture, with its emphasis on training boys to be "real" men and the routine disparagement of girls and women during basic training. Or consider that the military teaches men to use violence. What are the likely results of such policies on the intimate relations of men and women and on their relative power in the private spheres? How might this difference affect domestic violence, stranger rape, date rape, marital rape, etc.? See Chapter 5 on prevalence of rape in the United States and on rape by military personnel.

7. Does the no-combat rule reflect and reinforce a taboo against women using violence in our culture? What is the relation between that taboo and the high levels of male-on-female violence, as described in Chapter 5?

8. Do you agree with the Court's assumption that the only-men-in-combat rule serves a significant governmental interest? What is that interest? How would you assess that interest? Are there alternative ways to serve that interest? Why isn't that interest weighed against women's interest in equality? How would the Court respond to the assertion that one of the interests served by the men-only combat rule is keeping women subordinate to men despite their majority status in a democracy? Why does this consideration—the political effects on women as citizens—disappear from the calculus in thinking about the issue under the Court's equal protection jurisprudence?

9. What are the strongest arguments that can be made *against* drafting women into the military or combat, given differences in the way girls and boys are socialized and macho military culture? If women are more pacifist than men, would that argue for or against their inclusion in the military in equal numbers? Can women's activities as pacifists ever be as effective as men's while they are excluded from the draft and combat? Think, for example, of women who opposed the Vietnam war and had no draft cards to burn. What are the strongest arguments for requiring women to serve in equal numbers and in equal capacities, despite the many differences in what such service would mean for women?

10. Would a supporter of equal military responsibilities for women necessarily believe that they should be sought in a Supreme Court case? What are the disadvantages, costs, and risks, of the sort of top-down change

the Supreme Court can force? What strategies might be preferable to integrate women into military power?

11. What is the relationship between sexism and homophobia in the military? For example, is there a connection between the no-women-in-combat rule and the military ban on "out" lesbians and gay men? In what ways does the military culture, with its glorification of "real" male warriors and denigration of the feminine, rest on the subordination of lesbians and gay men? Why are military women in nontraditional jobs especially likely to be accused of being lesbian? See Michelle M. Benecke and Kirstin S. Dodge, Military Women in Nontraditional Job Fields: Casualties of the Armed Forces' War on Homosexuals, 13 Harv. Women's L.J. 215 (1990).

12. Is there a relationship between the military's super-masculine culture, the exclusion of women from combat and widespread sexual harassment in the military? Women fear reporting or complaining about such harassment because the countercharge is often that the woman rejected the man's advances because she was a lesbian. See Lesbians, Long Overlooked, Are Central to Debate on Military Ban, N.Y.Times, May 4, 1993, at A23.

13. Are lesbians especially threatening to military norms and values? During 1999, 31% of "gay discharges" from the military were women, though women constitute only 14% of the military. Servicemembers Legal Defense Network, Conduct Unbecoming: Sixth Annual Report on "Don't Ask, Don't Tell" at 2 (2000) (available at www.sldn.org/reports/sixth.htm) (hereinafter "SLDN Report"). According to the SLDN Report, "[t]his is the highest percentage of women discharged since at least 1980." Id. Marital infidelity also seems more likely to be investigated when the adulterer is a female, not a male, soldier.

14. One of President Clinton's first actions after becoming president in 1993 was to attempt to end the military's ban on lesbian and gay soldiers. When that became politically impossible because of vehement opposition from many in the military and elsewhere, he compromised on a new policy of "don't ask, don't tell," which was supposed to be more accepting than the traditional ban. Under "don't ask, don't tell," soldiers were free to be gay or lesbian in their private lives; the military was not to ask about sexual orientation; and as long as gay and lesbian soldiers didn't tell people about their sexual orientation, they were free to serve in the military. But discharges of gay and lesbian soldiers have actually increased under the new policy. SLDN Report, above note 13, at 2 (although discharges were down slightly in fiscal 1999 from 1998, the discharge rate is still 73% higher than before "don't ask, don't tell"). Most service members "come out" because they face harassment, and those who report anti-gay harassment risk discharge. Id. For a pro-gay critique of much pro-gay scholarship and litigation in this area, see Diane H. Mazur, The Unknown Soldier: A Critique of "Gays in the Military" Scholarship and Litigation, 29 U.C. Davis L. Rev. 223 (1996).

15. Many countries have allowed gay and lesbian service members to serve openly for some time, including Australia, Austria, Belgium, Canada, Denmark, France, Finland, Germany, Iceland, Israel, Italy, Luxembourg, the Netherlands, Norway, Spain, Sweden, and Japan. Comment, U.S. and Great Britain: Restrictions on Homosexuals in the Military as a Barricade to

Effectiveness, 14 Dick. J. Int'l Law 613, 622 n.65 (1996). In 1999, the European Court of Human Rights unanimously ruled that Britain's ban on gays in the military "breached article 8 of the European convention, covering the right to respect for private life." Richard Norton–Taylor and Clare Dyer, Historic Ruling Ends Services Gay Ban, The Guardian, Sept. 28, 1999, at 3. Why is the United States so much more resistant than these other countries (including all of Europe) to allowing gay men and lesbians to serve openly in the military?

2. JURIES

In the federal judicial system and most state systems, statutes or rules allow litigants to exclude a certain number of jurors in both civil and criminal trials by the use of "peremptory challenges," challenges which need not specify a reason for eliminating the prospective juror. Jurors can also be challenged for cause, but such challenges must be supported by a reason for considering the individual juror likely to be biased in the case at bar. Peremptory and for-cause challenges are made after the jurors have filled out qualification forms giving a great deal of information about themselves and after voir dire, the questioning of the jurors about relevant experiences, attitudes, and possible biases by (depending on the specific rules in the jurisdiction) either the judge or lawyers for the litigants. The issue in the next case is whether the constitutional decisions banning race-based peremptory challenges should be extended to sex-based peremptory challenges.

J.E.B. v. ALABAMA

Supreme Court of the United States, 1994.

511 U.S. 127, 114 S.Ct. 1419, 128 L.Ed.2d 89.

JUSTICE BLACKMUN delivered the opinion of the Court.

* * *

On behalf of * * * T.B., the mother of a minor child, respondent State of Alabama filed a complaint for paternity and child support against petitioner J.E.B. * * * The trial court assembled a panel of 36 potential jurors, 12 males and 24 females. After the court excused three jurors for cause, only 10 of the remaining 33 jurors were male. The State then used 9 of its 10 peremptory strikes to remove male jurors; petitioner used all but one of his strikes to remove female jurors. As a result, all the selected jurors were female. [The jury found that the defendant was the father of the minor child after hearing scientific evidence demonstrating a 99.92% probability that he had fathered the child.]

* * *

We granted certiorari * * * to resolve * * * whether the Equal Protection Clause forbids peremptory challenges on the basis of gender as well as on the basis of race. Today we reaffirm what, by now, should be axiomatic: Intentional discrimination on the basis of gender by state actors violates the Equal Protection Clause, particularly where, as here, the discrimination serves to ratify and perpetuate invidious, archaic, and overbroad stereotypes about the relative abilities of men and women.

> [The common law traditionally excluded women from juries to shield women from ugliness in light of their fragility and innocence. In 1975, the Supreme Court held that women were constitutionally entitled to be on lists of potential jurors on the same terms as men. Taylor v. Louisiana, 419 U.S. 522 (1975). Thereafter, however, prosecutors and defendants remained free to strike jurors from a particular jury on the basis of their sex by the use of peremptory challenges, though race was held an impermissible basis for a peremptory strike in a criminal case in Batson v. Kentucky, 476 U.S. 79 (1986).]

* * *

[W]e do not weigh the value of peremptory challenges as an institution against our asserted commitment to eradicate invidious discrimination from the courtroom. Instead, we consider whether peremptory challenges based on gender stereotypes provide substantial aid to a litigant's effort to secure a fair and impartial jury. * * *

Far from proffering an exceptionally persuasive justification for its gender-based peremptory challenges, respondent maintains that its decision to strike virtually all the males from the jury in this case "may reasonably have been based upon the perception, supported by history, that men otherwise totally qualified to serve upon a jury might be more sympathetic and receptive to the arguments of a man alleged in a paternity action to be the father of an out-of-wedlock child, while women equally qualified to serve upon a jury might be more sympathetic and receptive to the arguments of the complaining witness who bore the child."[9]

We shall not accept as a defense to gender-based peremptory challenges "the very stereotype the law condemns." Respondent's rationale, not unlike those regularly expressed for gender-based strikes, is reminiscent of the arguments advanced to justify the total exclusion of women from juries. Respondent offers virtually no support for the conclusion that gender alone is an accurate predictor of juror's attitudes; yet it urges this Court to condone the same stereotypes that justified the wholesale exclusion of women from juries and the ballot box.[11] * * *

9. Respondent cites one study in support of its quasi-empirical claim that women and men may have different attitudes about certain issues justifying the use of gender as a proxy for bias. See R. Hastie, S. Penrod and N. Pennington, Inside the Jury 140 (1983). The authors conclude: "Neither student nor citizen judgments for typical criminal case material have revealed differences between male and female verdict preferences. ... The picture differs [only] for rape cases, where female jurors appear to be somewhat more conviction-prone than male jurors". The majority of studies suggest that gender plays no identifiable role in jurors' attitudes. * * *

11. Even if a measure of truth can be found in some of the gender stereotypes used to justify gender-based peremptory challenges, that fact alone cannot support discrimination on the basis of gender in jury selection. We have made abundantly

Discrimination in jury selection, whether based on race or on gender, causes harm to the litigants, the community, and the individual jurors who are wrongfully excluded from participation in the judicial process. The litigants are harmed by the risk that the prejudice which motivated the discriminatory selection of the jury will infect the entire proceedings. The community is harmed by the State's participation in the perpetuation of invidious group stereotypes and the inevitable loss of confidence in our judicial system that state-sanctioned discrimination in the courtroom engenders.

* * *

Our conclusion that litigants may not strike potential jurors solely on the basis of gender does not imply the elimination of all peremptory challenges. * * * Parties still may remove jurors whom they feel might be less acceptable than others on the panel; gender simply may not serve as a proxy for bias. * * * Even strikes based on characteristics that are disproportionately associated with one gender could be appropriate, absent a showing of pretext.[16]

If conducted properly, voir dire can inform litigants about potential jurors, making reliance upon stereotypical and pejorative notions about a particular gender or race both unnecessary and unwise. Voir dire provides a means of discovering actual or implied bias and a firmer basis upon which the parties may exercise their peremptory challenges intelligently.

* * *

Failing to provide jurors the same protection against gender discrimination as race discrimination could frustrate the purpose of *Batson* itself. Because gender and race are overlapping categories, gender can be used as a pretext for racial discrimination.[18] Allowing parties to remove racial minorities from the jury not because of their race, but because of

clear in past cases that gender classifications that rest on impermissible stereotypes violate the Equal Protection Clause, even when some statistical support can be conjured up for the generalization. * * * The generalization advanced by Alabama in support of its asserted right to discriminate on the basis of gender is, at the least, overbroad, and serves only to perpetuate the same "outmoded notions of the relative capabilities of men and women," * * * that we have invalidated in other contexts. * * * The Equal Protection Clause, as interpreted by decisions of this Court, acknowledges that a shred of truth may be contained in some stereotypes, but requires that state actors look beyond the surface before making judgments about people that are likely to stigmatize as well as to perpetuate historical patterns of discrimination.

16. For example, challenging all persons who have had military experience would disproportionately affect men at this time, while challenging all persons employed as nurses would disproportionately affect women. Without a showing of pretext, however, these challenges may well not be unconstitutional, since they are not gender-or race-based.

18. The temptation to use gender as a pretext for racial discrimination may explain why the majority of the lower court decisions extending Batson to gender involve the use of peremptory challenges to remove minority women. All four of the gender-based peremptory cases to reach the federal courts of appeals involved the striking of minority women.

their gender, contravenes well-established equal protection principles and could insulate effectively racial discrimination from judicial scrutiny.

Equal opportunity * * * reaffirms the promise of equality under the law—that all citizens, regardless of race, ethnicity, or gender, have the chance to take part directly in our democracy. * * * When persons are excluded from participation in our democratic processes solely because of race or gender, this promise of equality dims, and the integrity of our judicial system is jeopardized.

* * *

The judgment of the Court of Civil Appeals of Alabama is reversed and the case is remanded to that court for further proceedings not inconsistent with this opinion.

Chief Justice Rehnquist, dissenting.

I agree with the dissent of Justice Scalia, which I have joined. I add these words in support of its conclusion. Accepting Batson v. Kentucky, as correctly decided, there are sufficient differences between race and gender discrimination such that the principle of Batson should not be extended to peremptory challenges to potential jurors based on sex.

That race and sex discrimination are different is acknowledged by our equal protection jurisprudence, which accords different levels of protection to the two groups. Classifications based on race are inherently suspect, triggering "strict scrutiny," while gender-based classifications are judged under a heightened, but less searching, standard of review. Racial groups comprise numerical minorities in our society, warranting in some situations a greater need for protection, whereas the population is divided almost equally between men and women. Furthermore, while substantial discrimination against both groups still lingers in our society, racial equality has proved a more challenging goal to achieve on many fronts than gender equality.

* * * Batson is best understood as a recognition that race lies at the core of the commands of the Fourteenth Amendment. Not surprisingly, all of our post-Batson cases have dealt with the use of peremptory strikes to remove black or racially identified venirepersons, and all have described Batson as fashioning a rule aimed at preventing purposeful discrimination against a cognizable racial group. * * * Batson does not apply "[o]utside the uniquely sensitive area of race."

Under the Equal Protection Clause, these differences mean that the balance should tilt in favor of peremptory challenges when sex, not race, is the issue. Unlike the Court, I think the State has shown that jury strikes on the basis of gender "substantially further" the State's legitimate interest in achieving a fair and impartial trial through the venerable practice of peremptory challenges. The two sexes differ, both biologically and, to a diminishing extent, in experience. It is not merely "stereotyping" to say that these differences may produce a difference in outlook which is brought to the jury room. Accordingly, use of peremptory challenges on the basis of sex is generally not the sort of derogatory and invidious act which peremptory challenges directed at black jurors may be.

Justice O'Connor's concurring opinion recognizes several of the costs associated with extending Batson to gender-based peremptory challenges—lengthier trials, an increase in the number and complexity of appeals addressing jury selection, and a "diminished ... ability of litigants to act on sometimes accurate gender-based assumptions about juror attitudes." These costs are, in my view, needlessly imposed by the Court's opinion, because the Constitution simply does not require the result that it reaches.

JUSTICE SCALIA, with whom THE CHIEF JUSTICE and JUSTICE THOMAS join, dissenting.

Today's opinion is an inspiring demonstration of how thoroughly up-to-date and right-thinking we Justices are in matters pertaining to the sexes (or as the Court would have it, the genders), and how sternly we disapprove the male chauvinist attitudes of our predecessors. The price to be paid for this display—a modest price, surely—is that most of the opinion is quite irrelevant to the case at hand. The hasty reader will be surprised to learn, for example, that this lawsuit involves a complaint about the use of peremptory challenges to exclude *men* from a petit jury. To be sure, petitioner, a man, used all but one of *his* peremptory strikes to remove *women* from the jury (he used his last challenge to strike the sole remaining male from the pool), but the validity of *his* strikes is not before us. * * *

The Court also spends time establishing that the use of sex as a proxy for particular views or sympathies is unwise and perhaps irrational. The opinion stresses the lack of statistical evidence to support the widely held belief that, at least in certain types of cases, a juror's sex has some statistically significant predictive value as to how the juror will behave. This assertion seems to place the Court in opposition to its earlier Sixth Amendment "fair cross-section" cases. But times and trends do change, and unisex is unquestionably in fashion. Personally, I am less inclined to demand statistics, and more inclined to credit the perceptions of experienced litigators who have had money on the line. But it does not matter. * * * Even if sex was a remarkably good predictor in certain cases, the Court would find its use in peremptories unconstitutional.

Of course the relationship of sex to partiality *would have been* relevant if the Court had demanded in this case what it ordinarily demands: that the complaining party have suffered some injury. * * * But if men and women jurors are (as the Court thinks) fungible, then the only arguable injury from the prosecutor's "impermissible" use of male sex as the basis for his peremptories is injury to the stricken juror, not to the defendant. Indeed, far from having suffered harm, petitioner, a state actor under our precedents * * * has himself actually *inflicted* harm on female jurors. * * * Not only has petitioner, by implication of the Court's own reasoning, suffered no harm, but the scientific evidence presented at trial established petitioner's paternity with 99.92% accuracy. Insofar as petitioner is concerned, this is a case of harmless error if there ever was one; a retrial will do nothing but divert the State's judicial and prosecutorial resources, allowing either petitioner or some other malefactor to go free.

* * *

The irrationality of today's strike-by-strike approach to equal protection is evident from the consequences of extending it to its logical conclusion. If * * * sex-based [trial] stratagems do not survive heightened scrutiny—then the prosecutor presumably violates the Constitution when he selects a male or female police officer to testify because he believes one or the other sex might be more convincing in the context of the particular case, or because he believes one or the other might be more appealing to a predominantly male or female jury. A decision to stress one line of argument or present certain witnesses before a mostly female jury—for example, to stress that the defendant victimized women—becomes, under the Court's reasoning, intentional discrimination by a state actor on the basis of gender.

In order, it seems to me, not to eliminate any real denial of equal protection, but simply to pay conspicuous obeisance to the equality of the sexes, the Court imperils a practice that has been considered an essential part of fair jury trial since the dawn of the common law. The Constitution of the United States neither requires nor permits this vandalizing of our people's traditions.

For these reasons, I dissent.

Notes on J.E.B.

1. In *J.E.B.*, the Court describes the issue as "whether peremptory challenges based on gender stereotypes provide substantial aid to a litigant's effort to secure a fair and impartial jury." But isn't the whole peremptory-challenge jury-selection system bizarre if the goal is an impartial jury? Parties use their peremptory challenges to produce the jury most likely to be biased in their favor (and, when they can afford it, do so after very expensive consultants have tested for characteristics likely to associated with bias in favor of the person who has hired them). If one wanted an unbiased jury, is this the system one would design? Does this basic problem with peremptory challenges make the reasoning in *J.E.B.,* with its focus on producing a fair and impartial jury, somewhat surreal?

2. Is there a problem with the majority's assumption that if men and women react differently as jurors, a male juror would be as biased as a female juror (and vice versa)? The majority doubts that male and female jurors would react differently, but states in note 11 that even if there were a correlation between sex and juror attitudes, jurors could not be stricken on peremptory challenges because of their sex. But if men and women do have differing attitudes on some questions, should the legal system necessarily ignore those differences to ensure fair and impartial outcomes? Wouldn't

one's answer depend on whether one group was more likely to reach *accurate* conclusions? For example, if male jurors decide in favor of defendants in paternity actions when there is conclusive evidence of paternity (such as the evidence in this case, indicating with a 99.92% level of certainty that the defendant was the father), isn't there a serious problem of bias if any man is on the jury? Is ignoring the problem a solution?

According to Lorrie Luellig, there are a number of areas in which women may be less biased than men. She reports that "empirical studies illustrate that female jurors are more likely than male jurors to convict rape defendants." Luellig, Why *J.E.B. v. T.B.* Will Fail to Advance Equality: A Call for Discrimination in Jury Selection, 10 Wis. Women's L. J. 403, 421 (1995). Women are also *less* "influenced than their male counterparts by the rape victim's virginity, her social status, or society's myths about rape." Id. These male biases are exacerbated by the reality that rape law "has itself traditionally adopted a male viewpoint." Id. at 422. Luellig suggests that sexist attitudes, which generally are higher among men than among women, id. at 435–36, may also prejudice outcomes in other cases, such as those in which battered women have killed abusive partners. She concludes that "[I]n rape and battered women cases, the presence of women on a jury makes the jury less sexist—it makes the trial more impartial, not more biased." Id. at 428. Assuming that she is right about the empirical evidence, do you agree with her conclusion? How would you decide *J.E.B.* if you were a justice convinced of the accuracy of such evidence?

3. Luellig also points out that many studies show men are more likely to be chosen as the jury's foreperson and to be more influential than women jurors. Luellig, above note 2, at 431–32. Is this a problem? Would the Supreme Court see it as a problem? Solutions?

4. Between the 1994 decision of the Court in *J.E.B.* and the publication of Luellig's article in 1995, there were 68 appellate cases raising the issue of sex-based juror exclusion. Only three were civil. Luellig, above note 2, at 448–49. Of the 65 criminal appellate cases, 57 were brought by male criminal defendants seeking reversal of their convictions. Forty-seven percent of the men seeking reversals had been convicted of male-on-female crimes. In 91% of the 57 cases brought by men, men were objecting to the exclusion of men (i.e., the inclusion of women). Id. at 449–50. Should the Supreme Court have considered the interest of female victims of crime in a just verdict? Isn't there something odd about seeing the result in *J.E.B.* as important in terms of *women's* equality, given that its major effect seems to be giving male criminal defendants (almost half of whom have harmed a female victim) an argument for reversing convictions by juries with "too many" women, though the evidence suggests that women may be less biased than men in at least some of these cases?

5. In text and note 16, the *J.E.B.* majority states that peremptory challenges can be based on factors that result disproportionately in the exclusion of one sex or the other (such as being a veteran) as long as there is no showing of pretext, i.e., that the factor was really chosen *in order* to exclude women as such or men as such. Will it be easy or difficult for a lawyers to explain sex-based exclusions in neutral terms? How would you do so if you were a lawyer?

6. Is the majority inconsistent in asserting both that sex of jurors makes no difference and that the decision below should be reversed? How has the defendant been harmed, particularly in this case in which, as Justice Scalia points out, the DNA evidence indicates with a 99.92% level of confidence that the defendant is the father of the child?

7. Under *J.E.B.*, would the Constitution be violated by the prosecutor's choosing, as Justice Scalia suggests, a female police officer to testify (rather than a male police officer) before a predominantly female jury? Can you distinguish this hypo and *J.E.B.*? Is it unconstitutional for the state to use a female attorney to defend itself against a charge of sex discrimination in employment?

8. In his dissent, Chief Justice Rehnquist maintains that *J.E.B.* is wrongly decided because "[i]t is not merely 'stereotyping' to say that [women's and men's biological differences and, to a diminishing extent, differences in experience] may produce a difference in outlook which is brought to the jury room." Are differences in experiences of, for example, African American and white citizens such that they too might bring "a difference in outlook" to the jury room? Why does Rehnquist think that such differences in outlook would justify sex-based but not race-based peremptories?

9. In *J.E.B.*, the Supreme Court justifies its holding on the ground that the purpose of *Batson* (banning race-discrimination in peremptories) will be frustrated unless there is a parallel ban on "gender discrimination": "[B]ecause gender and race are overlapping categories, gender can [otherwise] be used as a pretext for racial discrimination." And in note 18, it indicates that most of the "lower court decisions extending *Batson* to gender involve the use of peremptory challenges to remove minority women." This is the Court's first use of intersectionality analysis, i.e., reasoning premised on the need to recognize that minority women experience intersecting forms of discrimination. Does the Court's substantive point—that the rule with respect to sex must parallel that with respect to race if minority women are to be protected—suggest that all solutions to discrimination must be parallel for sex and race? Do you agree?

10. Prior to *J.E.B.,* the Court considered a case in which the prosecutor used peremptory challenges to exclude two Latino jurors from a jury on the ground that they were bilingual and there was to be testimony in Spanish. (Because they were bilingual, their understanding of the testimony would not depend entirely on the official English translation, which is all that the judge and other jurors would understand.) Although a majority of Latinos are bilingual, the Court held that the exclusion on the basis of bilingualism (when the bilingual juror honestly states that she or he might not be able to disregard the original Spanish testimony) was not racial discrimination. Hernandez v. New York, 500 U.S. 352, 111 S.Ct. 1859, 114 L.Ed.2d 395 (1991). Juan Perea has pointed out that courts assume that all racism operates in the way white racism against African Americans has operated, i.e., in terms of a black-white paradigm. Minorities for whom discrimination operates in other ways are even less likely than African Americans to have their experiences of discrimination recognized as such by the courts. Juan F. Perea, Ethnicity and the Constitution: Beyond the Black

and White Binary Constitution, 36 Wm. & Mary L. Rev. 571, 594–603 (1995). Do you agree? How would you change the concept of race discrimination to avoid this problem?

11. How would a fair system for selecting an unbiased jury work? Should peremptory challenges be eliminated entirely? Just as sex can be used to exclude African American women from juries in the absence of a ban on sex-based peremptories, so too other factors can be used as pretexts for the exclusion of racial minorities and women from juries in a system that allows peremptories. Nancy Marder advocates the elimination of peremptories (and a slight-expansion of for-cause exclusions) in order to better serve the functions of the jury: to include a range of values and perspectives in public decisionmaking, to render accurate verdicts, and to ensure fairness. Nancy Marder, Beyond Gender: Peremptory Challenges and the Roles of the Jury, 73 Texas L. Rev. 1041 (1995).

D. BACK TOWARDS STRICT SCRUTINY?

UNITED STATES v. VIRGINIA

Supreme Court of the United States, 1996.

518 U.S. 515, 116 S.Ct. 2264, 135 L.Ed.2d 735.

[Justice Thomas took no part in the proceedings because his son was a student at the Citadel, which prior to 1995 was also a public all-male military college much like VMI.]

JUSTICE GINSBURG delivered the opinion of the Court.

Virginia's public institutions of higher learning include an incomparable military college, Virginia Military Institute (VMI). The United States maintains that the Constitution's equal protection guarantee precludes Virginia from reserving exclusively to men the unique educational opportunities VMI affords. We agree. * * *

VMI produces its "citizen-soldiers" through "an adversative, or doubting, model of education" which features "[p]hysical rigor, mental stress, absolute equality of treatment, absence of privacy, minute regulation of behavior, and indoctrination in desirable values." As one Commandant of Cadets described it, the adversative method "dissects the young student," and makes him aware of his "limits and capabilities," so that he knows "how far he can go with his anger, ... how much he can take under stress, ... exactly what he can do when he is physically exhausted."

VMI cadets live in spartan barracks where surveillance is constant and privacy nonexistent; they wear uniforms, eat together in the mess hall, and regularly participate in drills. Entering students are incessantly exposed to the rat line, "an extreme form of the adversative model," comparable in intensity to Marine Corps boot camp. Tormenting and punishing, the rat line bonds new cadets to their fellow sufferers and, when they have completed the 7-month experience, to their former tormentors.

VMI's "adversative model" is further characterized by a hierarchical "class system" of privileges and responsibilities, a "dyke system" for assigning a senior class mentor to each entering class "rat," and a stringently enforced "honor code," which prescribes that a cadet " 'does not lie, cheat, steal nor tolerate those who do.' " * * *

The District Court [ruled in favor of VMI, reasoning] that education in "a single-gender environment, be it male or female," yields substantial benefits. VMI's school for men brought diversity to an otherwise coeducational Virginia system, and that diversity was "enhanced by VMI's unique method of instruction." If single-gender education for males ranks as an important governmental objective, it becomes obvious, the District Court concluded, that the only means of achieving the objective "is to exclude women from the all-male institution—VMI." * * *

The [Court of Appeals for the Fourth Circuit] greeted with skepticism Virginia's assertion that it offers single-sex education at VMI as a facet of the State's overarching and undisputed policy to advance "autonomy and diversity." The court [explained that] "[a] policy of diversity which aims to provide an array of educational opportunities, including single-gender institutions, must do more than favor one gender." * * *

Remanding the case, the appeals court assigned to Virginia, in the first instance, responsibility for selecting a remedial course. * * * [T]he court suggested these options for the State: Admit women to VMI; establish parallel institutions or programs; or abandon state support, leaving VMI free to pursue its policies as a private institution. * * *

In response to the Fourth Circuit's ruling, Virginia proposed a parallel program for women: Virginia Women's Institute for Leadership (VWIL). The 4–year, state-sponsored undergraduate program would be located at Mary Baldwin College, a private liberal arts school for women, and would be open, initially, to about 25 to 30 students. Although VWIL would share VMI's mission—to produce "citizen-soldiers"—the VWIL program would differ, as does Mary Baldwin College, from VMI in academic offerings, methods of education, and financial resources.

* * *

Virginia returned to the District Court seeking approval of its proposed remedial plan, and the court decided the plan met the requirements of the Equal Protection Clause [as did a divided Court of Appeals for the Fourth Circuit.] * * *

The cross-petitions in this case present two ultimate issues. First, does Virginia's exclusion of women from the educational opportunities provided by VMI—extraordinary opportunities for military training and civilian leadership development—deny to women "capable of all of the individual activities required of VMI cadets," the equal protection of the laws guaranteed by the Fourteenth Amendment? Second, if VMI's "unique" situation as Virginia's sole single-sex public institution of higher education offends the Constitution's equal protection principle, what is the remedial requirement?

* * *

Without equating gender classifications, for all purposes, to classifications based on race or national origin,[6] the Court, in [decisions beginning with *Reed v. Reed* in 1971], has carefully inspected official action that closes a door or denies opportunity to women (or to men). * * * [T]he reviewing court must determine whether the proffered justification is "exceedingly persuasive." The burden of justification is demanding and it rests entirely on the State. The State must show "at least that the [challenged] classification serves 'important governmental objectives and that the discriminatory means employed' are 'substantially related to the achievement of those objectives.' " The justification must be genuine, not hypothesized or invented post hoc in response to litigation. And it must not rely on overbroad generalizations about the different talents, capacities, or preferences of males and females.

The heightened review standard our precedent establishes does not make sex a proscribed classification. Supposed "inherent differences" are no longer accepted as a ground for race or national origin classifications. Physical differences between men and women, however, are enduring: "[T]he two sexes are not fungible; a community made up exclusively of one [sex] is different from a community composed of both."

"Inherent differences" between men and women, we have come to appreciate, remain cause for celebration, but not for denigration of the members of either sex or for artificial constraints on an individual's opportunity. Sex classifications may be used to compensate women "for particular economic disabilities [they have] suffered," to "promot[e] equal employment opportunity, to advance full development of the talent and capacities of our Nation's people."[7] But such classifications may not be used, as they once were to create or perpetuate the legal, social, and economic inferiority of women. * * *

Virginia * * * asserts two justifications in defense of VMI's exclusion of women. First, * * * "single-sex education provides important educational benefits," and the option of single-sex education contributes to "diversity in educational approaches." Second, * * * "the unique VMI method of character development and leadership training," the school's

6. The Court has thus far reserved most stringent judicial scrutiny for classifications based on race or national origin, but last Term observed that strict scrutiny of such classifications is not inevitably "fatal in fact." Adarand Constructors, Inc. v. Pena, 515 U.S. 200, 237 (1995).

7. Several amici have urged that diversity in educational opportunities is an altogether appropriate governmental pursuit and that single-sex schools can contribute importantly to such diversity. Indeed, it is the mission of some single-sex schools "to dissipate, rather than perpetuate, traditional gender classifications." We do not question the State's prerogative evenhandedly to support diverse educational opportunities. We address specifically and only an educational opportunity recognized by the District Court and the Court of Appeals as "unique," an opportunity available only at Virginia's premier military institute, the State's sole single-sex public university or college.

adversative approach, would have to be modified were VMI to admit women. We consider these two justifications in turn.

Single-sex education affords pedagogical benefits to at least some students, Virginia emphasizes, and that reality is uncontested in this litigation.[8] Similarly, it is not disputed that diversity among public educational institutions can serve the public good. But Virginia has not shown that VMI was established, or has been maintained, with a view to diversifying, by its categorical exclusion of women, educational opportunities within the State. In cases of this genre, our precedent instructs that "benign" justifications proffered in defense of categorical exclusions will not be accepted automatically; a tenable justification must describe actual state purposes, not rationalizations for actions in fact differently grounded.

* * *

A purpose genuinely to advance an array of educational options, as the Court of Appeals recognized, is not served by VMI's historic and constant plan—a plan to "afford a unique educational benefit only to males." However "liberally" this plan serves the State's sons, it makes no provision whatever for her daughters. That is not equal protection.

Virginia next argues that VMI's adversative method of training provides educational benefits that cannot be made available, unmodified, to women. * * *

The District Court forecast from expert witness testimony, and the Court of Appeals accepted, that coeducation would materially affect "at least these three aspects of VMI's program—physical training, the absence of privacy, and the adversative approach." And it is uncontested that women's admission would require accommodations, primarily in arranging housing assignments and physical training programs for female cadets. It is also undisputed, however, that "the VMI methodology could be used to educate women." The District Court even allowed that some women may prefer it to the methodology a women's college might pursue. * * * The parties, furthermore, agree that "some women can meet the physical standards [VMI] now impose[s] on men." In sum, "neither the goal of producing citizen soldiers," VMI's raison d'etre, "nor VMI's implementing methodology is inherently unsuitable to women." * * *

8. On this point, the dissent sees fire where there is no flame. "Both men and women can benefit from a single-sex education," the District Court recognized, although "the beneficial effects" of such education, the court added, apparently "are stronger among women than among men." The United States does not challenge that recognition. Cf. C. Jencks and D. Riesman, The Academic Revolution 297–298 (1968):

> The pluralistic argument for preserving all-male colleges is uncomfortably similar to the pluralistic argument for preserving all-white colleges.... The all-male college would be relatively easy to defend if it emerged from a world in which women were established as fully equal to men. But it does not. It is therefore likely to be a witting or unwitting device for preserving tacit assumptions of male superiority—assumptions for which women must eventually pay.

It may be assumed, for purposes of this decision, that most women would not choose VMI's adversative method. [But] it is also probable that "many men would not want to be educated in such an environment." * * * [T]he question is whether the State can constitutionally deny to women who have the will and capacity, the training and attendant opportunities that VMI uniquely affords.

The notion that admission of women would downgrade VMI's stature, destroy the adversative system and, with it, even the school,[11] is a judgment hardly proved, a prediction hardly different from other "self-fulfilling prophec[ies]," once routinely used to deny rights or opportunities. When women first sought admission to the bar and access to legal education, concerns of the same order were expressed. * * *

Women's successful entry into the federal military academies, and their participation in the Nation's military forces, indicate that Virginia's fears for the future of VMI may not be solidly grounded.[15] * * *.

Virginia and VMI trained their argument on "means" rather than "end," and thus misperceived our precedent. Single-sex education at VMI serves an "important governmental objective," they maintained, and exclusion of women is not only "substantially related," it is essential to that objective. By this notably circular argument, the "straightforward" test *Mississippi Univ. for Women* described [excerpt in Chapter 9], was bent and bowed.

[Virginia's] misunderstanding and, in turn, the District Court's, is apparent from VMI's mission: to produce "citizen-soldiers," individuals " 'imbued with love of learning, confident in the functions and attitudes of leadership, possessing a high sense of public service, advocates of the American democracy and free enterprise system, and ready . . . to defend their country in time of national peril.' " Surely that goal is great enough to accommodate women, who today count as citizens in our American democracy equal in stature to men. Just as surely, the State's great goal is not substantially advanced by women's categorical exclusion, in total disregard of their individual merit, from the State's premier "citizen-soldier" corps. Virginia, in sum, "has fallen far short of establishing the 'exceedingly persuasive justification,' " that must be the solid base for any gender-defined classification.

* * *

[The Court turns to the second issue: the constitutionality of Virginia's remedy.] Virginia chose not to eliminate, but to leave untouched, VMI's exclusionary policy. For women only, however, Virginia proposed a separate program, different in kind from VMI and unequal in tangible

11. * * * Forecasts of the same kind were made regarding admission of women to the federal military academies.

15. Inclusion of women in settings where, traditionally, they were not wanted inevitably entails a period of adjustment. As one West Point cadet squad leader recounted: "[T]he classes of '78 and '79 see the women as women, but the classes of '80 and '81 see them as classmates." U.S. Military Academy, A. Vitters, Report of Admission of Women.

and intangible facilities. Having violated the Constitution's equal protection requirement, Virginia was obliged to show that its remedial proposal "directly address[ed] and relate[d] to" the violation, i.e., the equal protection denied to women ready, willing, and able to benefit from educational opportunities of the kind VMI offers. * * *

VWIL students participate in ROTC and a "largely ceremonial" Virginia Corps of Cadets, but Virginia deliberately did not make VWIL a military institute. The VWIL House is not a military-style residence and VWIL students need not live together throughout the 4–year program, eat meals together, or wear uniforms during the school day. VWIL students thus do not experience the "barracks" life "crucial to the VMI experience," the spartan living arrangements designed to foster an "egalitarian ethic." "[T]he most important aspects of the VMI educational experience occur in the barracks," the District Court found, yet Virginia deemed that core experience nonessential, indeed inappropriate, for training its female citizen-soldiers.

VWIL students receive their "leadership training" in seminars, externships, and speaker series, episodes and encounters lacking the "[p]hysical rigor, mental stress, ... minute regulation of behavior, and indoctrination in desirable values" made hallmarks of VMI's citizen-soldier training. Kept away from the pressures, hazards, and psychological bonding characteristic of VMI's adversative training, VWIL students will not know the "feeling of tremendous accomplishment" commonly experienced by VMI's successful cadets.

Virginia maintains that these methodological differences are "justified pedagogically," based on "important differences between men and women in learning and developmental needs," "psychological and sociological differences" Virginia describes as "real" and "not stereotypes." The Task Force charged with developing the leadership program for women, drawn from the staff and faculty at Mary Baldwin College, "determined that a military model and, especially VMI's adversative method, would be wholly inappropriate for educating and training most women." The Commonwealth embraced the Task Force view, as did expert witnesses who testified for Virginia.

As earlier stated, generalizations about "the way women are," estimates of what is appropriate for most women, no longer justify denying opportunity to women whose talent and capacity place them outside the average description. Notably, Virginia never asserted that VMI's method of education suits most men. It is also revealing that Virginia accounted for its failure to make the VWIL experience "the entirely militaristic experience of VMI" on the ground that VWIL "is planned for women who do not necessarily expect to pursue military careers." By that reasoning, VMI's "entirely militaristic" program would be inappropriate for men in general or as a group, for "[o]nly about 15% of VMI cadets enter career military service."

In contrast to the generalizations about women on which Virginia rests, we note again these dispositive realities: VMI's "implementing methodology'' is not ''inherently unsuitable to women,'' ''some women ... do well under [the] adversative model,'' ''some women, at least, would want to attend [VMI] if they had the opportunity,'' ''some women are capable of all of the individual activities required of VMI cadets,'' and ''can meet the physical standards [VMI] now impose[s] on men.'' It is on behalf of these women that the United States has instituted this suit, and it is for them that a remedy must be crafted,[19] a remedy that will end their exclusion from a state-supplied educational opportunity for which they are fit, a decree that will ''bar like discrimination in the future.''

In myriad respects other than military training, VWIL does not qualify as VMI's equal. VWIL's student body, faculty, course offerings, and facilities hardly match VMI's. Nor can the VWIL graduate anticipate the benefits associated with VMI's 157–year history, the school's prestige, and its influential alumni network. * * *

For the reasons stated, the initial judgment of the Court of Appeals is affirmed, the final judgment of the Court of Appeals is reversed, and the case is remanded for further proceedings consistent with this opinion.

CHIEF JUSTICE REHNQUIST, concurring in judgment.

[I agree with the outcome, but not the reasoning of the Court's decision, which suggests the possibility of a new constitutional standard in sex-discrimination cases.] * * *

In the end, the women's institution Virginia proposes, VWIL, fails as a remedy, because it is distinctly inferior to the existing men's institution and will continue to be for the foreseeable future. * * *

JUSTICE SCALIA, dissenting. * * *

[I]t is my view that, whatever abstract tests we may choose to devise, they cannot supersede—and indeed ought to be crafted *so as to reflect*—those constant and unbroken national traditions that embody the people's understanding of ambiguous constitutional texts. More specifically, it is my view that ''when a practice not expressly prohibited by the text of the Bill of Rights bears the endorsement of a long tradition of open, widespread, and unchallenged use that dates back to the beginning of the Republic, we have no proper basis for striking it down.''

The all-male constitution of VMI comes squarely within such a governing tradition. Founded by the Commonwealth of Virginia in 1839 and continuously maintained by it since, VMI has always admitted only men. And in that regard it has not been unusual. For almost all of VMI's more than a century and a half of existence, its single-sex status reflected the uniform practice for government-supported military colleges. * * * The people may decide to change the one tradition, like the other, through democratic processes; but the assertion that either tradi-

19. Admitting women to VMI would undoubtedly require alterations necessary to afford members of each sex privacy from the other sex in living arrangements, and to adjust aspects of the physical training programs. * * *

tion has been unconstitutional through the centuries is not law, but politics-smuggled-into-law.

And the same applies, more broadly, to single-sex education in general, which, as I shall discuss, is threatened by today's decision with the cut-off of all state and federal support. Government-run *non*military educational institutions for the two sexes have until very recently also been part of our national tradition. * * *

Although the Court in two places recites the test as stated in Hogan, which asks whether the State has demonstrated "that the classification serves important governmental objectives and that the discriminatory means employed are substantially related to the achievement of those objectives," the Court never answers the question presented in anything resembling that form. When it engages in analysis, the Court instead prefers the phrase "exceedingly persuasive justification" from *Hogan*. The Court's nine invocations of that phrase, and even its fanciful description of that imponderable as "the core instruction" of [earlier] Court's decisions would be unobjectionable if the Court acknowledged that whether a "justification" is "exceedingly persuasive" must be assessed by asking "[whether] the classification serves important governmental objectives and [whether] the discriminatory means employed are substantially related to the achievement of those objectives." Instead, however, the Court proceeds to interpret "exceedingly persuasive justification" in a fashion that contradicts the reasoning of *Hogan* and our other precedents.

* * *

Intermediate scrutiny has never required a least-restrictive-means analysis, but only a "substantial relation" between the classification and the state interests that it serves. Thus, in Califano v. Webster, 430 U.S. 313 (1977), we upheld a congressional statute that provided higher Social Security benefits for women than for men. We reasoned that "women . . . as such have been unfairly hindered from earning as much as men," but we did not require proof that each woman so benefited had suffered discrimination or that each disadvantaged man had not; it was sufficient that even under the former congressional scheme "women on the average received lower retirement benefits than men." The reasoning in our other intermediate-scrutiny cases has similarly required only a substantial relation between end and means, not a perfect fit. * * * There is simply no support in our cases for the notion that a sex-based classification is invalid unless it relates to characteristics that hold true in every instance.

Not content to execute a *de facto* abandonment of the intermediate scrutiny that has been our standard for sex-based classifications for some two decades, the Court purports to reserve the question whether, even in principle, a higher standard (i.e., strict scrutiny) should apply. * * * [This is] misleading, insofar as [it] suggests that we have not already categorically *held* strict scrutiny to be inapplicable to sex-based classifications. And [it is] * * * irresponsible, insofar as [it] destabilize[s] current law. Our task is to clarify the law—not to muddy the waters, and not to exact over-compliance by intimidation. * * *

The Court's intimations are particularly out of place because it is perfectly clear that, if the question of the applicable standard of review for sex-based classifications were to be regarded as an appropriate subject for reconsideration, the stronger argument would be not for elevating the standard to strict scrutiny, but for reducing it to rational-basis review. * * * [N]ormal, rational-basis review of sex-based classifications would be much more in accord with the genesis of heightened standards of judicial review, the famous footnote in United States v. Carolene Products Co., 304 U.S. 144 (1938), which said (intimatingly) that we did not have to inquire in the case at hand "whether prejudice against discrete and insular minorities may be a special condition, which tends seriously to curtail the operation of those political processes ordinarily to be relied upon to protect minorities, and which may call for a correspondingly more searching judicial inquiry." It is hard to consider women a "discrete and insular minority" unable to employ the "political processes ordinarily to be relied upon," when they constitute a majority of the electorate. And the suggestion that they are incapable of exerting that political power smacks of the same paternalism that the Court so roundly condemns. Moreover, a long list of legislation proves the proposition false.

* * *

The only hope for state-assisted single-sex private schools is that the Court will not apply in the future the principles of law it has applied today. That is a substantial hope, I am happy and ashamed to say. After all, did not the Court today abandon the principles of law it has applied in our earlier sex-classification cases? And does not the Court positively invite private colleges to rely upon our ad-hocery by assuring them this case is "unique"? * * *

In an odd sort of way, it is precisely VMI's attachment to such old-fashioned concepts as manly "honor" that has made it, and the system it represents, the target of those who today succeed in abolishing public single-sex education. The record contains a booklet that all first-year VMI students (the so-called "rats") were required to keep in their possession at all times. Near the end there appears the following period-piece, entitled "The Code of a Gentleman":

> Without a strict observance of the fundamental Code of Honor, no man, no matter how 'polished,' can be considered a gentleman. * * * He is the descendant of the knight, the crusader; he is the defender of the defenseless and the champion of justice . . . or he is not a Gentleman. [A gentleman] Does not lose his temper; nor exhibit anger, fear, hate, embarrassment, ardor or hilarity in public. Does not hail a lady from a club window. A gentleman never discusses the merits or demerits of a lady. Does not mention names exactly as he avoids the mention of what things cost. Does not borrow money from a friend, except in dire need. Money borrowed is

> a debt of honor, and must be repaid as promptly as possible. * * * . He treats people with courtesy, no matter what their social position may be. Does not slap strangers on the back nor so much as lay a finger on a lady. Does not "lick the boots of those above" nor "kick the face of those below him on the social ladder." Does not take advantage of another's helplessness or ignorance * * *.

I do not know whether the men of VMI lived by this Code; perhaps not. But it is powerfully impressive that a public institution of higher education still in existence sought to have them do so. I do not think any of us, women included, will be better off for its destruction.

Notes on VMI

1. Ginsburg, the justice who wrote the opinion in *VMI*, headed the Women's Rights Project in the early seventies and filed briefs in many of the early cases, as described earlier in this chapter. In *Frontiero*, Ginsburg argued unsuccessfully for a strict scrutiny standard in constitutional challenges based on sex discrimination. In *VMI,* does Ginsburg finally succeed in establishing strict scrutiny as the constitutional standard? What, if any, is the difference between the standard in *VMI* and that in Craig v. Boren ("classification by gender must serve important governmental objectives and must be substantially related to achievement of those objectives")? What difference does Scalia see?

2. Ginsburg states: " 'Inherent differences' between men and women, we have come to appreciate, remain cause for celebration but not for denigration of members of either sex or for artificial constraints on an individual's opportunity." Does this suggest that the Court recognizes all classifications based on inherent differences (such as pregnancy, physical size, upper-body strength, etc.) as sex discrimination, or does so at least when the classifications place "artificial constraints on an individual's opportunity"? If so, is that accurate in light of *Geduldig* and *Bray* (cases holding that pregnancy discrimination is not sex discrimination in constitutional cases)?

3. In a comparison of VMI and VWIL, Mary Anne Case reports: "Most cadets at VMI strive for excellence neither with respect to their shoes nor their grades. Rather, they learn what they can get away with, in matters military as well as academic." Case, Two Cheers for Cheerleading: The Noisy Integration of VMI and the Quiet Success of Virginia Women in Leadership, [1999] U. Chi. Legal Forum. 347, 371. They also learn to survive ritual humiliation, debasement, and as they become more senior in the Cadet corps, to humiliate and debase others. For example, "breakout" at VMI is the last event before the end of the probationary period for new cadets. As the final step of breakout, rats (first-year cadets) must climb to the top of a muddy hill despite the interference of upper classmen. Case describes breakout the first year after the admission of women:

> The final step of breakout began at the foot of a muddy field, artificially muddied by the hoses of the local fire department because, despite fears of hypothermia on an abnormally cold March day, the upperclassmen threatened not to participate unless there was "more water" to maxim-

> ize the rats' suffering. The rats had been up since before dawn and were exhausted; led in a semi-daze to the foot of the hill, they were then flung on their faces into the mud by upperclassmen, who mingled taunts with cautionary admonitions to shield their eyes from the mud. Some rats hurled themselves into the mud. Was the lesson they have learned to abase themselves rather than waiting to be abased? Surrounded by upperclassmen shouting abuse and impeding their path, the rats crawled on their faces across the field to the base of the hill. There, as they began to climb, apparently helpful upperclass hands reached down to pull them upwards. But, just as a rat reached the crest of the hill, the once helping hand let go, and worse, pushed him or her back down. Is the lesson here that you never knew whom to trust—although you may not refuse help, you can not rely on it either? Gradually, over the bodies of their classmates below, the rats pushed toward the summit. Is the lesson here that the only way to the top is to step on people? It was not, as I had expected, a lesson of conscious cooperative strategizing. The rats seemed lost in the isolated world of their own struggles, oblivious to those around them, grabbing each other's legs as if they were tree trunks—just something to hang onto.

Id. at 372–73. In contrast, at VWIL, the nULLS (first-year students, equivalent to "rats" at VMI) marked the end of the probationary period by working together cooperatively in solving logic problems and forming a human pyramid. After a 14–mile march they walk "through an arch of sabers held by upperclassmen to be welcomed into the corps." Id. at 372

Given these differences, are you surprised by the fact that VWIL cadets have outperformed VMI in ROTC and AMSC (American Association of Military Schools and Colleges) drill competitions? Id. at 377. Case suggests that this may be because many of the women at VWIL—including the woman who scored as top cadet in the competitions with VMI—have been cheerleaders, and cheerleading is the great preparation for military drill. Id. at 377. Is it a mistake to even mention this fact, because it reinforces stereotypes? Does Case's point about cheerleaders *only* reinforce stereotypes?

4. VWIL cadets have another advantage—besides the cheerleading backgrounds of many—over VMI cadets in drill competitions: the more supportive atmosphere of VWIL appears to be far more effective in training cadets in drill. Case reports that "[a]t the end of their first day training, the rats * * * at VMI were a sorry lot—terrified, sweating, shaking, and exhausted, they were unable to tell their left feet from their right. A day of drilling has many of them still tripping over their own feet and none of them smiling." Case, above note 3, at 378. In contrast, at the end of their first day, the women at VWIL "seemed to be having a good time" and had mastered an amazing amount of skill in military drill in one day. Case, above note 3, at 379.

Yet, reports Case, "the VWIL program, which arguably is the greater success of the two, has far less funding, far less attention and a far more uncertain future." Case, above note 3, at 350. What explains the greater likelihood of survival for VMI though VWIL may well be superior educationally (for men as well as women)? Why isn't this difference seen as an aspect of sex discrimination? Do you think that VMI was good for the men enrolled there? In addition to being less effective in drill competitions, how might the men at VMI have been harmed by the VMI culture?

5. The educational experts at the *VMI* trial testified that there is no evidence that VMI's adversative method is good for anyone. Case, above note 3, at 363–64. Case concludes that Virginia was "more interested in preserving a masculine standard at all costs than in training the best possible citizen-soldiers by the most suitable methods." Id. at 364. Despite the lack of evidence on the effectiveness of the "adversative method," does Ginsburg accept its superiority to the VWIL approach? See id. at 367 ("Kept away from the pressures, hazards, and psychological bonding characteristic of VMI's adversative training, VWIL students will not know the 'feeling of tremendous accomplishment' commonly experienced by VMI's successful cadets.")(quoting Ginsburg).

6. Is the preservation of an institution of super-masculine culture a legitimate governmental objective? Isn't it likely that admission of women to VMI *will* "destroy" the institution as it was prior to the Supreme Court's decision? Is the availability of diverse educational institutions (including single-sex educational institutions) a legitimate governmental objective? Does Ginsburg accept educational diversity (including single-sex institutions) as a legitimate governmental purpose (though she does not find it credible as Virginia's purpose in *VMI*)? Under what circumstances, if any, might she uphold a single-sex public educational institution?

7. The first women admitted to the Citadel, the only other all-male public military university, reported horrific levels of harassment and assault. The Citadel's policy was to treat the women the same as the men; the women were to look like men, act like men, and accept discipline like men. But during their first year, two of the four women reported being sprayed with flammable liquid and having their clothes set on fire, being harassed sexually, physically, and verbally, and forced to drink alcohol. Although these incidents were alleged to be part of the ritual hazing suffered by all new students, the women claimed that they were particular targets. Craig Whitlock, The Citadel under Siege, The News & Observer Raleigh, N.C., Jan. 26, 1977, at A1. Susan Faludi gives a fascinating description of the Citadel's dysfunctional super-masculine culture in Stiffed: The Betrayal of the American Man 114–121, 123–132, 136–140, 1433–151 (1999). In contrast, the women at VMI report being treated no worse than "the guys." Case, above note 3, at 375. See also Catherine S. Manegold, In Glory's Shadow: Shannon Faulkner, The Citadel, and a Changing America (2000); Laura Fairchild Brodie, Breaking Out: VMI and the Coming of Women (2000).

Would you consider attending VMI, the Citadel, or VWIL? Why or why not?

8. Does the manly code of honor quoted by Justice Scalia seem consistent with real life at VMI? Do upperclassmen treat rats with "courtesy" and refuse to " 'kick the face of those below * * * on the social ladder"? Are they defenders of the defenseless and the champions of justice? Are there parts of the code of honor that are troubling? What is wrong with showing feelings in public?

9. In his dissent, Scalia notes that most legislation is constitutional as long as it passes "rational-basis review." Heightened review for legislation

treating differently members of different groups—as in strict scrutiny for racial classifications—is justified by the need to protect "discrete and insular minorities" who cannot protect their own interests through ordinary politics. Women are actually a *majority* of the population. What arguments might justify heightened scrutiny for sex-based classifications despite women's majority status? Might heightened scrutiny pose problems for women? Might there be advantages for women in relying on legislative change *only*? Why does Ginsburg seem to want an even higher standard of review (strict scrutiny) rather than a return to rational basis?

10. What does Ginsburg see as the problem with *VMI* from the perspective of women and equality between the sexes? Can you see other problems with *VMI* from the perspective of women? Was sexism at VMI limited to the exclusion of women? What was the connection between VMI's exclusion of women and its glorification of super-masculinity? Why doesn't Ginsburg mention any of these other problems?

11. Whose standard is better for women, Ginsburg's or Scalia's? Which women would do better under Ginsburg's standard and which women would be hurt by her standard? Which women would do better under Scalia's standard and which women would be hurt by his standard?

E. TWENTIETH CENTURY EQUAL-PROTECTION SEX-DISCRIMINATION CASES 1971-2000[22]

CASE and TYPE (overt disparate treatment or disparate impact)	OUTCOME	RATIONALE	NOTES
1. Reed v. Reed, 404 U.S. 71 (1971). Overt disparate treatment.	Female pltf wins; Ct strikes statute creating preference for male estate executors.	This is the very sort of arbitrary classification forbidden by EPC; administrative expenses cannot justify sex-based preference.	Ginsburg litigates first successful sex-based equal protection challenge as part of the WRP.
2. Frontiero v. Richardson, 411 U.S. 677 (1973). Overt disparate treatment.	Female pltf wins; Ct strikes rule giving benefits to all spouses of men but only to economically dependent spouses of women in the Air Force.	Four votes for striking classification under strict scrutiny. Four for striking it under standard of *Reed*.	Ginsburg and the WRP argue for strict scrutiny in amicus brief.
3. Kahn v. Shevin, 416 U.S. 351 (1974). Overt disparate treatment.	Male pltf loses; Ct upholds property tax exemption of $500 a year for widows.	Reasonable measure to cushion effect of death of spouse for sex (women) "for which that loss imposes a disproportionately heavy burden."	Ginsburg and the WRP decide to bring cases with male pltfs after losing on strict scrutiny, hoping that the harm of stereotypes will be more visible.

22. This table summarizes all the Supreme Court cases interpreting sex discrimination under the Equal Protection Clause of the Fourteenth Amendment from the first case holding that the Equal Protection Clause prohibits discrimination on the basis of sex (Reed v. Reed) through the end of the twentieth century. In this chart, "pltf" is used for plaintiff, "deft" is used for defendant, "Ct" is used for Court, "EPC" is used for Equal Protection Clause, "WRP" is used for Women's Rights Project (of the ACLU), "SS" is used for Social Security, and "S & L" is used for Savings & Loan Association.

CASE and TYPE (overt disparate treatment or disparate impact)	OUTCOME	RATIONALE	NOTES
4. Geduldig v. Aiello, 417 U.S. 484 (1974). Ct sees neither disparate treatment nor disparate impact.	Female pltf loses; Ct upholds state disability plan covering all but pregnancy-related disabilities.	Ct explains that this is not sex discrimination but discrimination between "pregnant women and nonpregnant persons."	Ginsburg and WRP file amicus brief arguing that the state's plan is *overt* sex discrimination and that the state *intended* to treat women and men differently.
5. Schlesinger v. Ballard, 419 U.S. 498 (1975). Overt disparate treatment.	Male pltf loses; Ct upholds rule giving female officers two more years in rank under military up-or-out policy.	Distinction "reflects, not archaic and overbroad generalizations, but, instead, the demonstrable fact that male and female line officers in the Navy are not similarly situated with respect to opportunities for professional service."	
6. Taylor v. Louisiana, 419 U.S. 522 (1975). Overt disparate treatment.	Male deft in prosecution for kidnapping and rape wins challenge to exclusion of most women from juror rolls.	"Louisiana's special exemption for women operates to exclude them from petit juries, which in our view is contrary to the command of the Sixth and Fourteenth Amendments."	Overruling Hoyt v. Florida, 368 U.S. 57 (1961) (upholding Fla. rule excluding women from jury service in case in which wife was on trial for killing her abusive and unfaithful husband).
7. Weinberger v. Wiesenfeld, 420 U.S. 636 (1975). Overt disparate treatment.	Male pltf wins; Ct holds that widower must be given SS benefits available to widows.	The generalization "that men are more likely than women to be the primary supporters of their spouses and children is not entirely without empirical support. But such a gender-based generalization cannot suffice to justify the denigration of the efforts of women who do work and whose earnings contribute significantly to their families' support."	Main problem with SS from the perspective of women are distinctions between breadwinners and caretakers, not those between women and men.
8. Stanton v. Stanton, 421 U.S. 7 (1975). Overt disparate treatment.	Female pltf wins; Ct strikes statute creating different ages of majority for young women (18) and men (21) (and hence giving more years of parental support to young men).	"[W]e perceive nothing rational in" this legislation, "which, when related to the divorce decree, results in the appellee's liability for support for [a daughter] only to age 18 but for [a son] to age 21."	
9. Craig v. Boren, 429 U.S. 190 (1976). Overt disparate treatment.	Male pltf wins; Ct holds unconstitutional different rules on ability of young people to buy 3.2% beer.	Although females in this age group are less likely than males to drink and drive, a correlation of only 2% between being male and driving after drinking is too "tenuous a 'fit.'"	Ct shifts from "sex" to "gender" and settles on "intermediate" level of scrutiny: "classifications by gender must serve important governmental objectives and must be substantially related to achievement of those objectives."

CASE and TYPE (overt disparate treatment or disparate impact)	OUTCOME	RATIONALE	NOTES
10. Califano v. Goldfarb, 430 U.S. 199 (1977). Overt disparate treatment.	Male pltf wins; Ct strikes SS provision automatically giving benefits to widows by requiring that widowers show dependence on wife for at least 50% of support.	This statute "deprive[s] women of protection for their families which men receive as a result of their employment." It is unconstitutional "when supported by no more substantial justification than 'archaic and overbroad generalizations,' or 'old notions,' such as 'assumptions of dependency.' "	
11. Califano v. Webster, 430 U.S. 313 (1977). Overt disparate treatment.	Male pltf loses; Ct upholds temporary provision giving women advantage of being able to exclude two more low-earning years than men in calculating average monthly wage (resulting in higher SS draws after retirement).	"The more favorable treatment of the female wage earner enacted here was not the result of 'archaic and overbroad generalizations' about women." Rather, it "operated directly to compensate women for past economic discrimination."	In *Goldfarb* the differential SS provision "penalized women wage earners," whereas the one in *Webster* redresses " 'disparate treatment of women.' "
12. Fiallo v. Bell, 430 U.S. 787 (1977). Overt disparate treatment.	Male pltf loses; Ct upholds immigration rules giving mothers and their illegitimate children a more privileged status than fathers and their illegitimate children.	"Policies pertaining to the entry of aliens and their right to remain here are peculiarly concerned with the political conduct of government. * * * [T]he formulation of these policies is entrusted exclusively to Congress."	
13. Orr v. Orr, 440 U.S. 268 (1979). Overt disparate treatment.	Male pltf wins; Ct strikes alimony statute imposing obligation only on husbands to support wives.	Unnecessary for state to use sex as a proxy for need, since statute already provides for "individualized hearings at which the parties' relative financial circumstances are considered."	
14. Parham v. Hughes, 441 U.S. 347 (1979). Overt disparate treatment.	Male pltf loses; Ct upholds statute precluding father from suing for wrongful death of child if paternity had not been established prior to child's death.	State law need not afford unwed fathers all rights of unwed mothers because not similarly situated. Only paternity is uncertain at birth, and the father is less likely than the mother to establish a relationship with the child.	
15. Caban v. Mohammed, 441 U.S. 380 (1979). Overt disparate treatment.	Male pltf wins; Ct strikes state statute giving only unwed mothers right to consent to (or veto) adoption of child.	"In those cases where the father has never come forward to participate in the rearing of his child, nothing in the EPC precludes the State from withholding from him the privilege of vetoing the adoption of that child."	

CASE and TYPE (overt disparate treatment or disparate impact)	OUTCOME	RATIONALE	NOTES
16. Davis v. Passman, 442 U.S. 228 (1979). Overt disparate treatment.	Female pltf wins; Ct holds that Congressman who refuses to hire women for staff positions unconstitutionally discriminates on the basis of sex.	Plaintiff "has a federal constitutional right to be free of gender discrimination."	Focus of decision is on whether pltf has standing to bring an action for damages directly under the Constitution and without any statutory authorization.
17. Personnel Administrator of Massachusetts v. Feeney, 442 U.S. 256 (1979). Ct sees only disparate impact.	Female pltf loses; Ct holds preference for veterans in state employment is not sex discrimination, though under the preference 98% of state's civil servants at upper levels are male.	This statute reflects only "a preference for veterans." There is nothing suggesting that it was enacted to "accomplish the collateral goal of keeping women in a stereotypic and predefined place in the Massachusetts Civil Service."	Women were excluded from the military prior to WWII (except for WWI women in the Navy) and ever since then Congress has by statute authorized far fewer women than men in uniform.
18. Great American Federal S & L v. Novotny, 442 U.S. 366 (1979). Ct does not reach the merits of the discrimination claim.	Male pltf loses attempt to bring sex-discrimination claim—that he had been fired for supporting female co-workers—under § 1985(3), which redresses private conspiracies to deprive someone of their constitutional right to equal protection.	Court holds that rights enforceable by Title VII cannot be asserted under § 1985(3), a less-specific statute.	
19. Califano v. Westcott, 443 U.S. 76 (1979). Overt disparate treatment.	Female pltf wins; Ct strikes statute giving aid to low-income two-parent families when the father, but not the mother, was unemployed.	"For mothers who are primary providers for their families and who are unemployed, [the statute] is obviously gender based, for it deprives them and their families of benefits solely on the basis of sex."	
20. Wengler v. Druggists Mutual Insurance Company, 446 U.S. 142 (1980). Overt disparate treatment.	Male pltf wins; Ct strikes worker's compensation law requiring widower, but not widow, to show incapacitation or dependence in order to receive death benefits.	"The Missouri law indisputably mandates gender-based discrimination * * * against both men and women. The provision discriminates against a woman since, in the case of her death, benefits are payable to her spouse only if he is * * * dependent on her."	

CASE and TYPE (overt disparate treatment or disparate impact)	OUTCOME	RATIONALE	NOTES
21. Michael M. v. Superior Ct. of Sonoma County, 450 U.S. 464 (1981). Overt disparate treatment.	Male criminal deft loses. Ct upholds statutory rape law criminalizing "an act of sexual intercourse accomplished with a female not the wife of the perpetrator, where the female is under the age of 18 years."	Women and men are not similarly situated with respect to pregnancy and the "physical, emotional, and psychological consequences of sexual activity." The section protects "women from sexual intercourse at an age when those consequences are particularly severe."	The young woman was 16.5 years old, the young man 17.5 years. She told him to stop, but he hit her "back down on the bench." The latter facts are irrelevant to the Ct's analysis.
22. Kirchberg v. Feenstra, 450 U.S. 455 (1981). Overt disparate treatment.	Female pltf wins; Ct strikes down community property law giving husband unilateral control of jointly owned marital property.	"By granting the husband exclusive control over the disposition of community property, [the statute] clearly embodies the type of express gender-based discrimination that we have held unconstitutional."	
23. Rostker v. Goldberg, 453 U.S. 57 (1981). Overt disparate treatment.	Male pltf loses; Ct upholds selective service registration limited to males.	Since "[w]omen as a group" are not eligible for combat, they need not be registered.	Ct stresses that the decision to exempt women from registration for a possible draft was not an " 'accidental by-product of a traditional way of thinking about females,' " but made by Congress after hearings and debate on the issue.
24. Mississippi University for Women v. Hogan, 458 U.S. 718 (1982). Overt disparate treatment.	Male pltf wins; Ct holds that Mississippi cannot operate a nursing school for women only.	Ct rejects argument that this is affirmative action (compensation for discrimination) because there is no evidence women lack nursing opportunities; policy perpetuates stereotypes of nursing as women's work.	In her majority opinion, Sandra Day O'Connor uses the term "exceedingly persuasive" twice.
25. Heckler v. Mathews, 465 U.S. 728 (1984). Overt disparate treatment.	Male pltf loses; Ct upholds gender-based pension offset exception to SS survivor benefits as a temporary transitional measure to protect reliance on old rules in shift from system in which only widows were automatically entitled to survivors' benefits to gender-neutral system.	"Although the offset exception temporarily revives the gender-based eligibility requirement invalidated in *Goldfarb*, Congress's purpose" is not to provide for "females who are assumed to be economically dependent on the earnings of their spouses" (as was true in *Goldfarb*). Rather, this section was adopted "in order to protect the expectations of persons, both men and women, who had planned their retirements based on" law that pre-dated *Goldfarb*.	

CASE and TYPE (overt disparate treatment or disparate impact)	OUTCOME	RATIONALE	NOTES
26. Bray v. Alexandria, 506 U.S. 263 (1993). Ct sees only disparate impact.	Female pltf loses; Ct holds that obstruction of abortion facilities by protesters is not sex discrimination and not, therefore, actionable under § 1985(3), which allows suits against private actors who have conspired to deprive any one of equal protection of the laws.	Actions directed at women seeking abortions are not sex discrimination because not directed at "women by reason of their sex."	Ct affirms *Geduldig* in constitutional cases.
27. J.E.B. v. Alabama ex rel. T.B., 511 U.S. 127 (1994). Overt disparate treatment.	Male deft wins claim that the state discriminated on the basis of sex when it used preemptory challenges to exclude men from jury. (The deft used all but one of his challenges to strike women from the jury in this paternity action.)	This intentional discrimination by state actors ratifies and perpetuates invidious, archaic, and overbroad stereotypes about the relative abilities of women and men.	Blackmun, writing for majority, uses "exceedingly persuasive" twice, and O'Connor uses it twice in her concurrence.
28. U.S. v. Virginia, 518 U.S. 515 (1996). Overt disparate treatment.	Female pltf wins; Ct holds that Virginia Military Institute cannot admit only men.	"[N]o persuasive evidence that VMI's male-only admission policy 'is in furtherance of a state policy of 'diversity.' '" Ct holds that the notion that women would "destroy the adversative system was an unproven prediction, a self-fulfilling prophecy."	Ginsburg, who litigated *Reed* and argued for strict scrutiny in *Frontiero* writes the opinion of the Ct using "exceedingly persuasive" nine times. In note 6, Ginsburg states that "thus far" the Ct has reserved strict scrutiny for race cases.
29. Miller v. Albright, 523 U.S. 420 (1998). Overt disparate treatment.	Pltf is the daughter of a male citizen. Six justices uphold denial of citizenship although, had her mother been the U.S. citizen, she would have qualified for citizenship.	Of the six justices voting to dismiss, two held no standing, two held that the Ct lacked the power to grant relief, and two held discrimination permissible as serving important governmental interests.	

Sex and the Numbers: Who Sued, Who Won, Who Lost?

Women pltfs	won 7	lost 4	11 cases with women as pltfs
Men pltfs[23]	won 9	lost 9	18 cases with men as pltfs
TOTAL CASES	16 wins	12 losses	29 TOTAL CASES

Notes on Twentieth Century Equal Protection Cases 1971–2000

1. Should one be troubled by the fact that so many of the sex equality cases have been brought by men? Beginning with Reed v. Reed in 1971 through the end of 2000, the Court decided 29 constitutional sex discrimination cases. Men brought 18 of these cases, women 11. Of the 16 cases in which a sex-based equal protection argument won, the person making the argument was a man in most (9) cases. Are there any substantive consequences to these numbers? Would it have been better to limit the equal protection challenges to suits brought by women and members of minority groups? Recall Ginsburg's 1971 speech, quoted earlier in this chapter, in which she discussed what difference the ERA might make. She suggested that if the courts extended the Equal Protection Clause to sex discrimination, it would be doubtful that men could sue for discrimination absent an ERA. Should the Court have drawn the line suggested by Ginsburg in that speech and allowed only women (and racial minorities) to sue for sex discrimination under the Equal Protection Clause?

2. Are the cases in which the Supreme Court has found sex discrimination important or trivial relative to the sources of sexual inequality in our society? How important are they relative to *Geduldig*, *Feeney*, and *Rostker*, cases in which the Supreme Court was unable to see sex discrimination? If you conclude that women have "won" only the relatively unimportant cases, why do you think that has happened? Could this result have been avoided? How?

3. Has the Court's standard changed over time? If a legislative classification explicitly discriminates between women and men, is it likely to be sustained today (even though such a classification might have been upheld in the past)? For example, how do you think today's Supreme Court would come out in Kahn v. Shevin (1974)? The Court also upheld a sex-based classification that arguably favored women in Califano v. Webster (1977). In your opinion, would today's Court uphold the constitutionality of such

23. This category includes Miller v. Albright, case 29, in which the daughter of a male American citizen argues that the statute giving automatic citizenship to children of female American citizens (but not to the children of males) discriminates on the basis of sex.

provisions were they permanent? Would the Court be more or less likely to uphold such classifications under a strict scrutiny standard?

4. Would you support a constitutional standard of strict scrutiny for laws explicitly treating women one way and men another? Would an ERA require such a standard? What difference might such a standard make? Under typical formulations of strict scrutiny, a rule that discriminates on an impermissible basis such as race is constitutional only if it serves a "compelling governmental interest." Historically, race-based classifications have fallen unless the measure challenged was regarded as a form of affirmative action designed to redress past discrimination. Cf. Shelley v. Kraemer, 334 U.S. 1, 68 S.Ct. 836, 92 L.Ed. 1161 (1948) (holding unconstitutional racially restrictive covenants forbidding racial minorities from owning land) with Regents of the University of California v. Bakke, 438 U.S. 265, 98 S.Ct. 2733, 57 L.Ed.2d 750 (1978) (upholding affirmative action plan for educational program where race was one factor taken into account). In recent years, the Supreme Court has increasingly struck as unconstitutional race-based affirmative action plans. See, e.g., City of Richmond v. J.A. Croson Co., 488 U.S. 469, 109 S.Ct. 706, 102 L.Ed.2d 854 (1989) (holding unconstitutional a city's affirmative action plan to set aside a portion of city contracts for minority contractors); Adarand Constructors, Inc. v. Pena, 515 U.S. 200, 115 S.Ct. 2097, 132 L.Ed.2d 158 (1995) (holding unconstitutional Small Business Administration regulations creating a financial incentive for contractors to hire minority subcontractors).

In Craig v. Boren, the Court stated that under the intermediate standard for sex discrimination, a sex-based classification is permissible only if it serves important governmental objectives and is substantially related to achievement of those objectives. Can you think of any case that would come out differently before the same Court depending on whether the standard used was strict or intermediate? Would pregnancy discrimination be seen as an unconstitutional form of sex discrimination by today's Supreme Court under strict scrutiny but not under the intermediate standard?

5. Perhaps strict scrutiny would make the most difference in the cases in which the Court upheld as constitutional a classification explicitly treating women and men differently: Kahn v. Shevin; Schlesinger v. Ballard; Califano v. Webster; Fiallo v. Bell; Parham v. Hughes; Michael M. v. Superior Court of Sonoma County; Rostker v. Goldberg; and Heckler v. Mathews. Would any or all of these cases come out differently under strict scrutiny? Can you think of (other?) cases that might come out differently depending on which standard the Court uses? How do you think Ginsburg, Scalia, and the other members of today's Court would answer these questions?

6. As the chart above illustrates, the Court has *only* found sex discrimination in constitutional cases involving overt disparate treatment, i.e., rules or policies explicitly treating women one way and men another. As noted earlier in this chapter (in the text note on disparate treatment and disparate impact), under the Court's standard it is *possible* to find unconstitutional sex discrimination in cases without facial discrimination. Theoretically, a plaintiff can show that, though no formal rule or policy required differential treatment of women and men, women and men were in fact treated differently. Intent is a critical element in such cases, as illustrated by *Geduldig*

and *Feeney;* the plaintiff must show that, rather than discriminating on the basis of pregnancy or veteran status, the state actor *intended* to treat women and men differently. But, as illustrated by *Geduldig* and *Feeney*, no woman has ever won with such an argument in a constitutional case. It is now relatively rare for a state or state actor *explicitly* to discriminate between women and men. Is the difficulty of establishing a constitutional violation in the absence of an explicit sex-based classification a problem? Can you suggest any solutions?

7. Not surprisingly, the number of cases brought under the formal equality standard applicable in sex cases—which has thus far recognized sex discrimination only when overt—has declined over time. States and governmental entities no longer adopt policies and rules which discriminate facially on the basis of sex. Can you think of cases that might still be brought, instances in which governmental units do engage in overt sex discrimination? Write down three major factors contributing to women's inequality, factors as to which government has some influence. Would it be possible to bring a sex discrimination claim to challenge any of the items on your list? Even if it was a good idea to have the Supreme Court strike as unconstitutional statutes discriminating on the basis of sex in the past, is it a good idea for the future?

F. JUDICIAL REVIEW

MARY BECKER, CONSERVATIVE FREE SPEECH AND THE UNEASY CASE FOR JUDICIAL REVIEW

64 U. Colo. L. Rev. 975, 986–99, 1002–06, 1008–11 (1993).

In our democracy, the legislative and executive branches consist of, or are controlled by, people who are elected and accountable for their actions to the voters. Indeed, the legitimacy of our government is understood as based thereon. Yet federal judges limit the ability of the majority to govern. Federal judges are not elected, but appointed for life by the President with the advice and consent of the Senate. Their interpretations of the Constitution are final and binding on the other branches of government. Thus, a politically-insulated group often sets final and binding limits on what the other branches of government—and ultimately, "we the people"—can do. In so doing, binding judicial review degrades democratic deliberations. * * *

Judicial Bias

* * *

There are a number of ways in which judicial bias can be a problem for women. One obvious way is that the all-male Supreme Court which developed the discretionary intermediate standard for sex equality cases in the 1970s had an incentive to pick an approach that would maximize men's interests (in breaking rigid sex roles that sometimes hurt men) without requiring significant change in relationships between the sexes, since real change would often be detrimental to men. The current constitutional standard does, I believe, reflect and serve these needs and ends.

Judicial bias is often a very subtle, not easily perceived, problem. It need not be that judges hate women or even believe unconsciously that men are innately superior human beings to women. Bias will occur when judges look at the world from a perspective held by men more than women. The result of even so-subtle a bias will be legal rules better adapted to the needs of men than those of women. Consider, for example, the pregnancy discrimination cases in the 1970s, in which the Supreme Court (all men) held that sex discrimination (for both constitutional and Title VII purposes) does not include pregnancy discrimination: such discrimination is discrimination between pregnant and non-pregnant persons rather than discrimination on the basis of sex. * * *

An even more subtle form of judicial bias is the Court's primary commitment to its own legitimacy (or to the perception of its legitimacy). The Court's concern for its own legitimacy naturally results in decisions based on its own needs rather than on a commitment to equality between the sexes. I am fairly certain, for example, that the Court would be loath to require women to be treated exactly like men for all military purposes, including draft and combat, because its action would be seen as illegitimate by many Americans (though the Court's own approach to sex equality would seem to require such a result). Yet women can never be men's political equals while denied full military participation.

Given judicial interests conflicting with women's, it is not surprising that, in considering claims other than sex-discrimination, such as free speech or religion, the Justices have narrowed their consideration of what is relevant, excluding harms to women[47] rather than balancing the First Amendment's requirement of free speech against the Fourteenth Amendment's commitment to equality. In this fashion, negative rights that on their face have nothing to do with gender can serve to perpetuate the second class status of a majority of the population even if a commitment to equality between the sexes supposedly exists elsewhere in the Constitution. * * *

Although legislators are mostly male and many are no less biased than judges, they are subject to direct pressure from female constituents and do not operate within a system bounded by precedent. As women's political power continues to grow, this difference may become more important. Binding judicial review insulates decisions harmful to women—the commitment to formal equality, the refusal to consider harms to women in assessing free speech claims, the perception that sex discrimination and pregnancy discrimination are different things—from correction through women's participation in and pressure on the legislative process, where women can exercise significant power in light of their

47. American Booksellers Assoc. v. Hudnut, 771 F.2d 323 (7th Cir.1985); R.A.V. v. City of St. Paul, 112 S. Ct. 2538 (1992); Penelope Steator, Judicial Indifference to Pornography's Harm: American Booksellers v. Hudnut, 17 Golden Gate U. L. Rev. 297 (1987).

majority status. For example, the Title VII pregnancy discrimination case was overruled by Congress (so that sex discrimination in employment includes discrimination on the basis of pregnancy), though the Supreme Court recently affirmed the constitutional case. As this example also suggests, a top-down judicially-enforced approach to equality may also be inconsistent with the kind of experimentation necessary if we are ever to figure out either what equality between the sexes might look like or how to get there.

Experimentation

* * *

A pragmatist, like myself, considers it unlikely that human beings can divine the best solutions to complex issues in the abstract, using top-down theories, rather than through experimentation. A related problem is that not all approaches work as judicial standards. If the best approaches do not work as judicial standards, then binding judicial review will preclude them. * * *

The need for experimentation is particularly high in an area like equality between the sexes in which there is no consensus about what a world with sexual equality would look like let alone agreement on the means to get there. When the Court closes off certain approaches as unconstitutional, it may make exceedingly difficult or preclude the development of appropriate solutions. * * * There might also be more than one form of equality between the sexes, and the differences between various forms might be important. The Supreme Court, by taking the only approach it could apparently imagine in the 1970s, may rule out of bounds certain forms of equality superior to the one it picked. Perhaps also, different approaches may be appropriate at various times as well as in various contexts. * * * A decentralized approach would allow experimentation to see what sorts of rules work best, and work best at various times as well as various contexts, in seeking equality between the sexes.

* * *

Democratic Deliberations

There are a number of ways in which binding judicial review can interfere with political movements and impede quality in democratic deliberations. This point is especially important since women are a majority group; to the extent that binding judicial review is a barrier to women's successful use of their political power as a majority group, it is illegitimate. In the discussion that follows, I note three major problems: legitimizing the status quo; keeping important controversies off the agenda of ordinary politics while obscuring their difficulty; and interfering with political movements.

1. Legitimating the status quo.

An ineffective equality standard, such as that arguably adopted by the Court * * * legitimates and stabilizes the status quo, keeping men in control of what equality between the sexes means without effecting real change. If the Supreme Court requires equality between the sexes, what exists must be equality. If women complain thereafter, their whining cannot deserve serious consideration.

There exists a more insidious form of this problem. We revere our Constitution. To the extent that injuries to women are someone else's constitutional right (in the sense that effective remedies are unconstitutional), women are less likely even to see their injuries as such or as an appropriate point for political organization and protest. As Robin West has noted: "The tendency of all subordinated persons toward self-belittlement by trivializing the nature of their injuries is geometrically enhanced by the self-perception that their injuries do not exist because their infliction is constitutionally protected."[61] There can be no more effective way to deter effective political action by a majority group than to turn their injuries into the constitutional rights of others so effectively that the injuries become invisible as such, though not unfelt. Free speech often functions in this manner; take, for example, the question of regulation of pornography.

2. Keeping important controversies off the ordinary democratic agenda and obscuring their difficulty.

* * *

When constitutional issues are regarded as beyond the scope of ordinary politics, the public is deprived of the opportunity to learn through discussions about constitutional problems. Indeed, the language of our Supreme Court tends to mask, rather than illuminate, the complexity of constitutional questions, supporting its own legitimacy by making decisions seem inevitable. This tendency serves to hide the real issues and their complexity from the public.

* * *

Perhaps most troubling is the tendency of judicial review, by taking items off the ordinary political agenda and obscuring their difficulty, to impede or even preclude the development of a new consensus through the resolution of the issue in electoral politics. It seems quite likely that binding judicial review has made it difficult to work out any new consensus on * * * equality between the sexes. I discuss this point in more detail below.

* * *

3. Interference with political movements.

* * *

Binding judicial review can impede political movements even when the Supreme Court does not actually block success. The relegation of high matters, such as sexual equality, to the courts saps political move-

61. Robin West, Constitutional Skepticism, 72 B.U. L. Rev. 765 (1992).

ments of their strength, particularly after ineffective victories. At the same time, judicial review can mobilize the opposition, and the Court itself will be influenced by the resulting political climate, a climate it has helped create.

When ineffective judicial victories weaken a movement, there may be less grass-roots pressure for change. Yet, real change in the relationship between the sexes is unlikely without change at the grass-roots level. Decisions from on high are unlikely to transform intimate relationships.

Judicial victories protecting one or some outsider groups, but not all such groups, also interfere with the development of effective coalitions. This may be most harmful to the most [politically] vulnerable groups, such as lesbians, bisexuals, and gay men. Real or perceived judicial protection of less marginal groups, such as straight women or racial minorities, may mean that these groups are less likely to form effective coalitions with the more marginal groups. Judicial review is, therefore, a "divide and conquer" strategy.

In thinking about the effect of binding judicial review on outsiders' political movements, the appropriate baseline is how these movements would operate were there no such review. Had women focused all the time, energy, and money spent in the 1970s on a direct and single-minded focus on legislatures and legislative reform (including reform of abortion laws and of sex-specific legislation), rather than seeking binding judicial review in one form or another, women might well have ended the decade with more political experience and power. Women would have been different themselves and would have ended up in different places within important institutions. Women's consciousness would have been transformed by their experiences fighting for appropriate reforms. Instead, large amounts of time, energy, money, and commitment were spent on litigation campaigns and the drive for the ERA in the hope that male judges, operating within a tradition-bound system, would give women equality. Women are more likely to achieve real social equality as a result of a million and one piecemeal legislative changes than as a result of an abstract judicial standard.

The institution of binding judicial review has encouraged women, a majority group, to rely on mostly-male elite judges for equality rather than on their own political power, thus draining the strength from women's political movement for direct political power. This is dangerous for women. It becomes even more dangerous when one considers that it is futile to look to judges for much in the way of real social change * * *.

Notes on Judicial Review

1. Compare and contrast Becker's critique of binding judicial review in sex equality cases and the argument made by Justice Scalia in his dissent in *VMI* for an end to heightened scrutiny for sex-based classifications. What is similar? Different?

2. Becker states that "judicial review can impede political movements." In what ways did judicial review contribute to the defeat of the ERA drive?

3. Would there be political benefits to women were a legislature to enact a law explicitly treating women and men differently in a way harmful to women (in a system without judicial review of such legislation)? How might women react? Might they be likely to mobilize politically, push for more women in office, and make their voices heard in other ways? (Recall that the number of women in the Senate increased from three to six after the Senate confirmed Clarence Thomas's appointment to the Supreme Court despite Anita Hill's testimony about his sexual harassment of her. The Senate Judiciary Committee was all male and treated Hill in ways that angered many women, as did Thomas' confirmation.) How do you think women in your state would react if the state legislature passed a statute today banning (as some protectionist legislation did in the past) all women from night work in factories?

4. In a 1983 essay, Marilyn Frye states:

> [I]f one wants to determine whether a particular suffering, harm, or limitation is part of someone's being oppressed, one has to look at it *in context* in order to tell whether it is an element in an oppressive structure: one has to see if it is part of an enclosing structure of forces and barriers which tends to the immobilization and reduction of a group or category of people. * * * As soon as one looks at examples, it becomes obvious that not everything which frustrates or limits a person is oppressive, and not every harm or damage is due to or contributes to oppression.

Frye, Oppression in The Politics of Reality: Essays in Feminist Theory 10–11 (1983). Do you agree with Frye? Is judicial review of laws or policies for sex discrimination a problem in light of this point?

5. Becker's focus is on women, not racial minorities or other outsider groups. She suggests, however, that racial minorities might also be better off without binding judicial review:

> Binding judicial review of fundamental rights, such as speech, is likely to hurt minorities as well as women as it develops into a[n increasingly] conservative right. And, just as many feminists have been critical of the Court's approach to sexual inequality under the Fourteenth Amendment, many critical race scholars have been critical of the Court's decisions prohibiting racial classifications, as accomplishing too little while legitimating the status quo as "equality," thus weakening the political struggle for real social equality. Perhaps the Supreme Court's conservative approach to racial equality is becoming a barrier to further progress in a world without Jim Crow. The Court certainly seems eager to deny continuing problems in the relationship between the races as well as that between the sexes.

64 U. Colo. L. Rev. at 983. Do you think that binding judicial review is a valuable protection needed by members of vulnerable minority groups in a democracy? Or is it a conservative influence, tending to sap the strength of movements for social change while adopting a conservative notion of racial

equality? Apart from cases involving voting, the Court has also found race discrimination in constitutional cases *only* when it is overt. Overt discrimination on the basis of race is rare today outside the context of affirmative action. And increasingly the court holds race-based affirmative action unconstitutional. The case for judicial review of racial classifications is, therefore, becoming increasingly weak.

Another problem is that for many Asian and Latina/o Americans, ethnic identity involves a variable set of traits "including nationality, race, language, food, and cultural heritage and [physical] features, among other traits." Juan F. Perea, Ethnicity and the Constitution: Beyond the Black and White Binary Constitution, 36 Wm. & Mary L. Rev. 571 (1995). But even overt discrimination on the basis of these traits does not necessarily violate the Constitution. Hernandez v. New York, 500 U.S. 352, 111 S.Ct. 1859, 114 L.Ed.2d 395 (1991) (upholding exclusion of bilingual juror who honestly said he would not be able consider only the English translation of testimony in Spanish). In light of these problems, do you favor continued judicial review in race cases?

6. When imagining a world in which the races are equal, white Americans often seem to imagine one in which racial differences have disappeared because other races have been assimilated into white culture. But true racial equality might be more complicated. Indeed, more than one kind of racial equality might be possible. Imagine a world of racial equality in which there is respect for, and appreciation of, a diversity of cultures, ethnic groups, and races. Can you imagine other worlds of racial equality? Which one does the Supreme Court envision? Which one would you prefer? Does the Supreme Court's increasingly color-blind approach make some forms of racial equality more difficult to envision let alone achieve?

7. Why might binding judicial review be even more problematic for women than for racial minorities given women's majority status? Do women of all colors tend to deny conflicts of interest between women and men? Are members of other subordinate groups more likely to see the conflicts of interest between themselves and members of the dominant group? Why might this be so? Is it relevant that women and men live together in families? (Members of other subordinate groups are considerably less likely to live in family units with members of the dominant group.)

Do women of all colors tend to view their own personal experiences of inequality in their own homes and intimate relationships as personal rather than political? Are members of racial minorities more likely to see their experiences of race-linked problems as political? If women do tend to view the inequality they experience as personal, does it follow that anything tending to dampen women's political struggles is especially dangerous (particularly in light of women's majority status and the biases of mostly-male judges)?

8. Given that various forms of subordination overlap—African American women, for example, experience discrimination on the basis of race *and* discrimination on the basis of sex—it might seem impossible to have effective judicial review of racial classifications without also providing for judicial review of sex-based classifications. Cf. *J.E.B.* (with respect to discriminatory use of peremptory challenges to jurors, Supreme Court states that effective

ban on race-based preemptory challenges requires ban on sex-based preemptory challenges; otherwise minority women can be struck on the purported ground that they are women though actually they are struck because of their race). But with the exception of race cases involving voting procedures or district lines, the Court has recognized discrimination on the basis of race or sex *only* when a rule or policy *explicitly* discriminates on the prohibited basis. Given the very limited reach of judicial review, it would be possible to provide for such review only in race cases. If judicial review were available only for race-based legislation, it would nonetheless recognize as (and strike as unconstitutional) *overt* discrimination based on sex and race. For example, a statute banning African American women from certain desirable jobs would be unconstitutional because it discriminates on the basis of race. (It seems most unlikely that an intersectionality problem would arise in the context of voting procedures or district lines.)

9. When judges imagine a world in which the sexes are equal, what do they imagine? Do they imagine a world in which all differences between the sexes have disappeared? Or a world where there is equality because women are treated like men when they are like men? Might more be required for actual equality? When you imagine a world in which the sexes are equal, what do you imagine? Do the people in your class share a single vision of what a world in which women and men are equal would look like?

Chapter 3

FEMINIST THEORY

A. INTRODUCTION

During the 1970's, feminist scholars tended to assume that the liberal approach to sexual inequality—the approach adopted by the Supreme Court in the cases we looked at in Chapter 2—was the appropriate legal tactic. There was little "feminist theory" in the legal academy beyond the important insight that sex-specific laws perpetuate rigid sex roles.

Feminist theory exploded in the 1980's, not only in law but in other disciplines as well. In the legal literature, the first sign of this exciting development was the 1979 publication of Catharine A. MacKinnon's first book, Sexual Harassment of Working Women. This important work included a biting critique of liberal equality theory and argued that inequality could be better understood and redressed under MacKinnon's dominance theory. In subsequent work, she developed a sophisticated theory of how sex discrimination operates, and suggest an alternative approach to eliminating sexual inequality.

"Difference" became a major theme in feminist legal theory in the 1980's. Difference theory has at least two major strands, both rooted in earlier movement politics. One strand, with roots in the socialist and radical lesbian feminism of the seventies, considers differences among women of different races, classes, and sexual orientations. The other major strand discusses differences between women and men. Some radical feminists, often lesbian and uniformly critical of patriarchal culture, had argued for separatism and the development of an alternative woman's culture, which its proponents believed would be superior to male culture. In the academy, many women focused their attention on differences between women and men, some valorizing those attributes associated with women, as cultural feminists have in the past, and others arguing that any differences are the result of socialization and that their valorization is dangerous. Much of this debate focused on psychologist Carol Gilligan's influential book, In a Different Voice, published in 1982.

This chapter begins with a brief discussion of consciousness raising, *the* feminist method at the beginning of the second wave, when many women begin talking with other women in formal and informal all-women groups about their problems. We then turn to a set of readings on differences between women and men, including an extract from Gilligan's book. Next we present a variety of feminist theoretical approaches to inequality, beginning with MacKinnon's dominance theory but including feminist arguments for formal equality and many other strands of feminist theory as it developed in the final decades of the 20th century.

B. FEMINIST METHODOLOGY

CATHARINE A. MACKINNON, CONSCIOUSNESS RAISING

In Toward a Feminist Theory of the State 83, 86–88, 93–96, 101–05 (1989).

* * * What brings people to be conscious of their oppression as common rather than remaining on the level of bad feelings, to see their group identity as a systematic necessity that benefits another group, is the first question of organizing. The fact that consciousness-raising groups were there presupposes the discovery that they were there to make. But what may have begun as a working assumption becomes a working discovery: women are a group, in the sense that a shared reality of treatment exists sufficient to provide a basis for identification—at least enough to begin talking about it in a group of women. This often prearticulate consensus shapes a procedure, the purpose of which becomes to unpack the concrete moment-to-moment meaning of being a woman in a society that men dominate, by looking at how women see their everyday experience in it. Women's lives are discussed in all their momentous triviality, that is, as they are lived through. The technique explores the social world each woman inhabits through her speaking of it, through comparison with other women's experiences, and through women's experiences of each other in the group itself. Metaphors of hearing and speaking commonly evoke the transformation women experience from silence to voice. * * *

The fact that men were not physically present was usually considered necessary to the process. Although the ways of seeing that women have learned in relation to men were very much present or there would be little to discuss, men's temporary concrete absence helped women feel more free of the immediate imperative to compete for male attention and approval, to be passive or get intimidated, or to support men's version of reality. It made speech possible. With these constraints at some remove, women often found that the group confirmed awarenesses they had hidden, including from themselves. Subjects like sexuality, family, body, money, and power could be discussed more openly. The pain of women's roles and women's stake in them could be confronted critically, without the need every minute to reassure men that these changes were not threatening to them or to defend women's breaking of roles as desirable.

The all-woman context valued women to each other as sources of insight, advice, information, stimulation, and problems. By providing room for women to be close, these groups demonstrated how far women were separated and how that separation deprived women of access to the way their treatment is systematized. * * * The point of the process was not so much that hitherto-undisclosed facts were unearthed or that denied perceptions were corroborated or even that reality was tested, although all these happened. It was not only that silence was broken and that speech occurred. The point was, and is, that this process moved the reference point for truth and thereby the definition of reality as such. Consciousness raising alters the terms of validation by creating community through a process that redefines what counts as verification. This process gives both content and form to women's point of view.

Concretely, consciousness-raising groups often focused on specific incidents and internal dialogue: what happened today, how did it make you feel, why did you feel that way, how do you feel now? Extensive attention was paid to small situations and denigrated pursuits that made up the common life of women in terms of energy, time, intensity, and definition—prominently, housework and sexuality. * * *

Intercourse was interrogated: how and by whom it is initiated, its timing, woman's feelings during and after, its place in relationships, its meaning, its place in being a woman. Other subjects included interactions in routine situations like walking down the street, talking with bus drivers, interacting with cocktail waitresses. Women's stories—work and how they came to do it; children; sexual history, including history of sexual abuse—were explored. * * *

Perhaps the most pervasive realization of consciousness raising was that men as a group benefit from these same arrangements by which women are deprived. Women see that men derive many advantages from women's roles, including being served and kept in mind, supported and sustained, having their children cared for and their sexual needs catered to, and being kept from the necessity of doing jobs so menial they consider them beneath them unless there is no other job (or a woman) around. But the major advantage men derive, dubious though it may seem to some, is the process, the value, the mechanism by which their interest itself is enforced and perpetuated and sustained: power. Power in its socially male form. It is not only that men treat women badly, although often they do, but that it is their choice whether or not to do so. This understanding of power is one of the key comprehensions of feminism. The reality it points to, because it is everywhere and relatively invariant, appears to be nowhere separable from the whole, from the totality it defines.

* * *

These discussions explored the functioning of sex roles in even one's closest "personal" relations, where it was thought women were most "ourselves," hence most free. Indeed, the reverse often seemed to be the case. The measure of closeness often seemed to be the measure of the oppression. When shared with other women, one's most private events often came to look the most stereotypical, the most for the public. Each woman, in her own particular, even chosen, way reproduces in her most private relations a structure of dominance and submission which characterizes the entire public order. * * *

The analysis that the personal is the political came out of consciousness raising. It has four interconnected facets. First, women as a group are dominated by men as a group, and therefore as individuals. Second, women are subordinated in society, not by personal nature or by biology. Third, the gender division, which includes the sex division of labor which keeps women in high-heeled low-status jobs, pervades and determines even women's personal feelings in relationships. Fourth, since a woman's problems are not hers individually but those of women as a whole, they cannot be addressed except as a whole. In this analysis of gender as a nonnatural characteristic of a division of power in society, the personal becomes the political.

Pervasively implicit in these substantive insights is feminism's method of knowing about the world in its epistemological and political ramifications. Consciousness raising is a face-to-face social experience that strikes at the fabric of meaning of social relations between and among women and men by calling their givenness into question and reconstituting their meaning in a transformed and critical way. The most apparent quality of this method is its aim of grasping women's situation as it is lived through. The process identifies the problem of women's subordination as a problem that can be accessed through women's consciousness, or lived knowing, of her situation. This implicitly posits that women's social being is in part constituted or at least can be known through women's lived-out view of themselves. Consciousness raising attacks this problem by unraveling and reordering what every woman "knows" because she has lived it, and in so doing forms and reforms, recovers and changes, its meaning. This is accomplished through using the very instrument—women experiencing how they experience themselves—that is the product of the process to be understood. The apparent circularity of this as a theory of knowing about the world is not a barrier to analysis, but rather the core of the method, the way it breaks the circularity of that which it is attempting to understand in order to change. The seemingly self-enclosed character of feminist consciousness and the community it inhabits by creating it is, in reality, the opposite of solipsism: what it sees is that it is male reality that is self-enclosed. * * *

Consciousness raising discovered that one form of the social existence of male power is inside women. In this form, male power becomes self-enforcing. Women become "thingified in the head." Once incarnated, male superiority tends to be reaffirmed and reinforced in what can be seen as well as in what can be done. So male power both is and is not illusory. As it justifies itself, namely as natural, universal, unchangeable, given, and morally correct, it is illusory; but the fact that it is powerful is no illusion. Power is a social relation. * * *

* * *

As a way of knowing about social conditions, consciousness raising * * * shows women their situation in a way that affirms they can act to change it. Consciousness raising socializes women's knowing. It produces an analysis of woman's world which is not objective in the positivistic sense of being a perfect reflection of reality conceived as abstract object; it is certainly not distanced or aperspectival. It is collective and critical. * * *

Feminism locates the relation of woman's consciousness to her life situation in the relation of two moments: being shaped in the image of one's oppression, yet struggling against it. In so doing, women struggle against the world in themselves as well as toward a future. The real question, both for explanation and for organizing, is what is the relation between the first process, woman becoming her role, and the second, her rejection of it?

What is the feminist account of how women can come to reject the learning portrayed as so encompassing? The analysis of how one gets to be the way one is does not readily explain how some come to reject it, much less the view that one must and can change it into something specifically envisioned. What accounts for some women's turning upon their conditioning? In other words, what is the relationship between consciousness and material conditions for feminism? * * *

Feminism, through consciousness raising, has grasped the completeness of the incursion into who one really becomes through growing up female in a male-dominated society. This effect can be understood as a distortion of self. It is not only one's current self one is understanding, but the self that understands what one has become as a distortion. On one level, this is exactly right. On another level, it exposes a dilemma: understanding women's conditions leads to the conclusion that women are damaged. If the reality of this damage is accepted, women are in fact not full people in the sense that men are allowed to become. So on what basis can a demand for equal treatment be grounded? If women are what they are made, are determined, women must create new conditions, take control of their determinants. But how does one come to know this? On the other hand, if women go beyond the prescribed limitations on the basis (presumably) of something outside their conditions, such as being able to see the injustice or damage of inequality, what is the damage of inequality? * * *

Consciousness raising has revealed that male power is real. It is just not the only reality, as it claims to be. Male power is a myth that makes itself true. To raise consciousness is to confront male power in its duality: as at once total on one side and a delusion on the other. In consciousness raising, women learn they have learned that men are everything, women their negation, but the sexes are equal. The content of the message is revealed as true and false at the same time; in fact, each part reflects the other transvalued. If "Men are all, women their negation" is taken as social criticism rather than as simple description, it becomes clear for the first time that women are men's equals, everywhere in chains. The chains become visible, the civil inferiority—the inequality—the product of subjection and a mode of its enforcement. Reciprocally, the moment it is seen that this life as we know it is not equality, that the sexes are not socially equal, womanhood can no longer be defined in terms of lack of maleness, as negativity. For the first time, the question of what a woman is seeks its ground in and of a world understood as neither of its making nor in its own image, and finds, within a critical embrace of woman's fractured and alien image, the shadow world women have made and a vision of the possibility of equality. * * *

Notes on Consciousness Raising

1. If sexual inequality is socially constructed, how is it possible for women ever to come to see their oppression, even in consciousness raising groups? Are there limits on our ability to see inequality in our own society? Why, how, and when are any of us able to criticize our own culture?

2. How does MacKinnon deal with the tension between women's internalization of male power and women's ability to see male power? If male power is reality (indeed, the reality inside women's heads), how does MacKinnon think it ever becomes possible for any woman to see any of it?

3. MacKinnon states that "understanding women's conditions leads to the conclusion that women are damaged. If the reality of this damage is accepted, women are in fact not full people in the sense that men are allowed to become." Do you agree? Can you describe ways in which men as well as women are damaged by living in a culture in which women are to be feminine (supportive, nurturing, emotional, dependent) and men are to be masculine (powerful, fearless, successful, competitive, and, of course, non-emotional)? Are there ways in which women are hurt more than men and ways in which men are hurt more than women? Are there ways in which men are not full people in the sense that women are allowed to become? Why does MacKinnon only mention the ways women are damaged and less than full people?

4. MacKinnon states: "In consciousness raising, women learn they have learned that men are everything, women their negation, but the sexes are equal." Are girls and women bombarded with messages insisting both that (1) boys and men are superior to, more important than, girls and women; *and* (2) that women and men are equal? Can you give some examples of both sorts of messages? How did these conflicting messages make you feel as you were growing up? How do you respond now?

5. MacKinnon never uses the words "false consciousness," i.e., the notion that women sometimes act against their own self-interest because they have internalized—as part of their consciousness—male norms and standards. For example, one might regard a woman with perfectly normal breasts who chooses to have breast implants as doing so because of "false"

consciousness. Is a notion of something like false consciousness nevertheless implicit in MacKinnon's analysis of consciousness raising? If one's consciousness has been "raised," does it follow that one had a "false" or inadequate consciousness prior to its being raised?

C. DIFFERENCE IN THE EIGHTIES

This section presents two forms in which feminists in the 1980's faced the issue of difference. The first is an extract from Carol Gilligan's book, In a Different Voice, in which she discusses differences between a girl's and a boy's resolution of a moral dilemma. Gilligan is discussed in a number of subsequent readings, and some familiarity with her work has become necessary to follow feminist discussions in the 1990's. Next is a pair of extracts from briefs in a case that divided legal feminists in the 1980's over the question of how to accommodate differences. This case can be used as a concrete setting in which to apply the theoretical approaches presented in the readings in the remainder of this chapter.

CAROL GILLIGAN, IN A DIFFERENT VOICE

From In a Different Voice: Psychological Theory and Women's Development 25–29 (1982).

> [Psychologists had developed, prior to Gilligan's work, theoretical frameworks and scales for evaluating moral development. In this passage, Gilligan critiques Lawrence Kohlberg's scale as applied to two adolescents, one a girl and the other a boy, on the ground that Kohlberg rates as more mature the boy's approach because it is based on the "logic" of rules and hence superior to the more relational approach of the girl. The thesis of Gilligan's book is that psychologists have ignored or undervalued the relational caring voice when considering moral problems, preferring a voice that speaks of abstract rules.]

* * * While current theory brightly illuminates the line and the logic of the boy's thought, it casts scant light on that of the girl. The choice of a girl whose moral judgments elude existing categories of developmental assessment is meant to highlight the issue of interpretation rather than to exemplify sex differences per se. Adding a new line of interpretation, based on the imagery of the girl's thought, makes it possible not only to see development where previously development was not discerned but also to consider differences in the understanding of relationships without scaling these differences from better to worse.

The two children were in the same sixth-grade class at school and were participants in the rights and responsibilities study, designed to explore different conceptions of morality and self. The sample selected for this study was chosen to focus the variables of gender and age while maximizing developmental potential by holding constant, at a high level, the factors of intelligence, education, and social class that have been associated with moral development, at least as measured by existing scales. The two children in question, Amy and Jake, were both bright and articulate and, at least in their eleven-year-old aspirations, resisted easy categories of sex-role stereotyping, since Amy aspired to become a scientist while Jake preferred English to math. Yet their moral judgments seem initially to confirm familiar notions about differences between the sexes, suggesting that the edge girls have on moral development during the early school years gives way at puberty with the ascendance of formal logical thought in boys.

The dilemma that these eleven-year-olds were asked to resolve was one in the series devised by Kohlberg to measure moral development in adolescence by presenting a conflict between moral norms and exploring the logic of its resolution. In this particular dilemma, a man named Heinz considers whether or not to steal a drug which he cannot afford to buy in order to save the life of his wife. In the standard format of Kohlberg's interviewing procedure, the description of the dilemma itself—Heinz's predicament, the wife's disease, the druggist's refusal to lower his price—is followed by the question, "Should Heinz steal the drug?" The reasons for and against stealing are then explored through a series of questions that vary and extend the parameters of the dilemma in a way designed to reveal the underlying structure of moral thought.

Jake, at eleven, is clear from the outset that Heinz should steal the drug. Constructing the dilemma, as Kohlberg did, as a conflict between the values of property and life, he discerns the logical priority of life and uses that logic to justify his choice:

> For one thing, a human life is worth more than money, and if the druggist only makes $1,000, he is still going to live, but if Heinz doesn't steal the drug, his wife is going to die. (*Why is life worth more than money?*) Because the druggist can get a thousand dollars later from rich people with cancer, but Heinz can't get his wife again. (*Why not?*) Because people are all different and so you couldn't get Heinz's wife again.
>
> Asked whether Heinz should steal the drug if he does not love his wife, Jake replies that he should, saying that not only is there "a difference between hating and killing," but also, if Heinz were caught, "the judge would probably think it was the right thing to do." Asked about the fact that, in stealing, Heinz would be breaking the law, he says that "the laws have mistakes, and you can't go writing up a law for everything that you can imagine."

Thus, while taking the law into account and recognizing its function in maintaining social order (the judge, Jake says, "should give Heinz the lightest possible sentence"), he also sees the law as man-made and therefore subject to error and change. Yet his judgment that Heinz should steal the drug, like his view of the law as having mistakes, rests on the assumption of agreement, a societal consensus around moral values that allows one to know and expect others to recognize what is "the right thing to do."

Fascinated by the power of logic, this eleven-year-old boy locates truth in math, which, he says, is "the only thing that is totally logical." Considering the moral dilemma to be "sort of like a math problem with humans," he sets it up as an equation and proceeds to work out the solution. Since his solution is rationally derived, he assumes that anyone following reason would arrive at the same conclusion and thus that a judge would also consider stealing to be the right thing for Heinz to do. * * *

In contrast, Amy's response to the dilemma conveys a very different impression, an image of development stunted by a failure of logic, an inability to think for herself. Asked if Heinz should steal the drug, she replies in a way that seems evasive and unsure:

> Well, I don't think so. I think there might be other ways besides stealing it, like if he could borrow the money or make a loan or something, but he really shouldn't steal the drug—but his wife shouldn't die either.

Asked why he should not steal the drug, she considers neither property nor law but rather the effect that theft could have on the relationship between Heinz and his wife:

> If he stole the drug, he might save his wife then, but if he did, he might have to go to jail, and then his wife might get sicker again, and he couldn't get more of the drug, and it might not be good. So, they should really just talk it out and find some other way to make the money.

Seeing in the dilemma not a math problem with humans but a narrative of relationships that extends over time, Amy envisions the wife's continuing need for her husband and the husband's continuing concern for his wife and seeks to respond to the druggist's need in a way that would sustain rather than sever connection. Just as she ties the wife's survival to the preservation of relationships, so she considers the value of the wife's life in a context of relationships, saying that it would be wrong to let her die because, "if she died, it hurts a lot of people and it hurts her." Since Amy's moral judgment is grounded in the belief that, "if somebody has something that would keep somebody alive, then it's not right not to give it to them," she considers the problem in the dilemma to arise not from the druggist's assertion of rights but from his failure of response.

As the interviewer proceeds with the series of questions that follow from Kohlberg's construction of the dilemma, Amy's answers remain essentially unchanged, the various probes serving neither to elucidate nor to modify her initial response. Whether or not Heinz loves his wife, he still shouldn't steal or let her die; if it were a stranger dying instead, Amy says that "if the stranger didn't have anybody near or anyone she knew," then Heinz should try to save her life, but he should not steal the drug. But as the interviewer conveys through the repetition of questions that the answers she gave were not heard or not right, Amy's confidence begins to diminish, and her replies become more constrained and unsure. Asked again why Heinz should not steal the drug, she simply repeats, "Because it's not right." Asked again to explain why, she states again that theft would not be a good solution, adding lamely, "if he took it, he might not know how to give it to his wife, and so his wife might still die." Failing to see the dilemma as a self-contained problem in moral logic, she does not discern the internal structure of its resolution; as she constructs the problem differently herself, Kohlberg's conception completely evades her.

Instead, seeing a world comprised of relationships rather than of people standing alone, a world that coheres through human connection rather than through systems of rules, she finds the puzzle in the dilemma to lie in the failure of the druggist to respond to the wife. Saying that "it is not right for someone to die when their life could be saved," she assumes that if the druggist were to see the consequences of his refusal to lower his price, he would realize that "he should just give it to the wife and then have the husband pay back the money later." Thus she considers the solution to the dilemma to lie in making the wife's condition more salient to the druggist or, that failing, in appealing to others who are in a position to help.

Just as Jake is confident the judge would agree that stealing is the right thing for Heinz to do, so Amy is confident that, "if Heinz and the druggist had talked it out long enough, they could reach something besides stealing." As he considers the law to "have mistakes," so she sees this drama as a mistake, believing that "the world should just share things more and then people wouldn't have to steal." Both children thus recognize the need for agreement but see it as mediated in different ways—he impersonally through systems of logic and law, she personally through communication in relationship. Just as he relies on the conventions of logic to deduce the solution to this dilemma, assuming these conventions to be shared, so she relies on a process of communication, assuming connection and believing that her voice will be heard. Yet while his assumptions about agreement are confirmed by the convergence in logic between his answers and the questions posed, her assumptions are belied by the failure of communication, the interviewer's inability to understand her response.

Notes on Difference

1. There is some ambiguity in Gilligan's work with respect to whether the different voice she identifies, the relational caring voice, is *women's*. Do you think we can validly make such a generalization? Do you and your same-sex friends discuss as though obviously true ways in which women and men are different? Write down three ways in which, in your experience, women and men differ in interactions with others. When you refer to differences between women and men, do you mean that all men are one way and all women another?

2. Are Jake's responses devoid of attention to relationships and care? How would you respond to Heinz's dilemma? Is your response consistent

with Gilligan's findings? See generally Isabel Marcus, Paul J. Spiegelman, Ellen C. DuBois, Mary C. Dunlap, Carol J. Gilligan, Carrie J. Menkel–Meadow and Catharine A. MacKinnon, Feminist Discourse, Moral Values, and the Law—A Conversation, 34 Buff. L. Rev. 11 (1985).

3. There have been a number of criticisms of Gilligan's methods in general and of her analysis of the various interviews described in her book. See, e.g., Linda K. Kerber, Catherine G. Greeno, Eleanor E. Maccoby, Zella Luria, Carol B. Stack, and Carol Gilligan, On *In a Different Voice:* An Interdisciplinary Forum, 11 Signs 304 (1986); Judy Auerbach, Linda Blum, Vicki Smith, and Christine Williams, Commentary, On Gilligan's *In a Different Voice,* 11 Feminist Studies 149 (1985); Debra Nails, Social–Scientific Sexism: Gilligan's Mismeasure of Man, 50 Soc.Res. 643 (1983); John M. Broughton, Women's Rationality and Men's Virtues: A Critique of Gender Dualism in Gilligan's Theory of Moral Development, 50 Soc.Res. 597 (1983).

There have also been a number of experimental studies to determine whether women and men approach moral issues in different voices. Results have been mixed. Compare, e.g., William J. Friedman, Amy B. Robinson, and Britt L. Friedman, Sex Differences in Moral Judgments? A Test of Gilligan's Theory, 11 Psych. Women Q. 37 (1987) (finding no significant differences between women and men college students in responses to four hypothetical moral issues), with Mary K. Rothbart, Dean Hanley, and Marc Albert, Gender Differences in Moral Reasoning, 15 Sex Roles 645 (1986) (finding that, although both men and women college students used both moral orientations widely in response to hypothetical moral dilemmas, women were somewhat more likely to respond in terms of care and men in terms of rights); Maureen Rose Ford and Carol Rotter Lower, Gender Differences in Moral Reasoning: A Comparison of the Use of Justice and Care Orientations, 50 J. Personality and Soc. Psych. 777 (1986) (finding that the ethic of care was more likely to be used by more feminine males than by less feminine males). See also the discussion about moral reasoning in legal education in Chapter 11.

4. What sorts of implications might Amy's perspective have for various fields of law? For criminal law? For torts? For example, should tort law require individuals to act as Good Samaritans? See Leslie Bender, A Lawyer's Primer on Feminist Theory and Tort, 38 J. Legal Educ. 3 (1988). See also Lucinda M. Finley, A Break in the Silence: Including Women's Issues in a Torts Class, 1 Yale J. L. & Feminism 41 (1989).

5. Cultural feminism is often traced to In a Different Voice. Cultural feminists, like Gilligan, emphasize the value of traditional feminine values, qualities, and activities, such as caretaking and relationships. What are the dangers of this valorization of traditional femininity? Given current cultural values, what are the dangers of pushing *only* for equality without increasing our valuation of caretaking?

Text Note: California Federal Savings and Loan Association v. Guerra

479 U.S. 272, 107 S.Ct. 683, 93 L.Ed.2d 613 (1987).

In 1978, California enacted legislation requiring employers to provide unpaid leave for childbirth but not for other temporary disabilities.

The case arose when Lillian Garland, a single mother, sought to return to work as a receptionist after taking a two-month leave following the birth of her daughter. Her employer told her that her old job had been filled and that there were no similar positions available. Garland was unable to find another job immediately and, because of her unemployment, she lost her apartment and eventually custody of her daughter.

When Garland sought to enforce her right to maternity leave under the California statute, the legislation was challenged as inconsistent with the federal Pregnancy Discrimination Act (PDA), which mandates that pregnancy be treated the same as other temporary disabilities for all employment-related purposes. In this case, California Federal Savings and Loan v. Guerra (known as "Cal Fed"), the employer, argued that the California law was inconsistent with and preempted by the federal statute because the state legislation was sex-specific.

The *Cal Fed* case evoked substantial dispute among feminist activists, legal scholars, and lawyers. The American Civil Liberties Union and other groups filed an amicus brief, portions of which appear below, arguing that the California legislation was preempted by the PDA. The National Organization for Women (NOW), the NOW Legal Defense and Education Fund, and the National Women's Law Center, among others, filed an amicus brief arguing that the California statute should be upheld only if employers were required to provide unpaid disability leave to all employees. Professor Wendy Williams was of counsel to this group. A number of feminist law professors, labor unions, and other groups filed another amicus brief arguing that the California legislation should be upheld as enacted. Professors Christine Littleton and Judith Resnik served as counsel on this brief, portions of which appear below.

The *Cal Fed* case is presented as a case study to use in the discussions of various theoretical approaches in the rest of this chapter. Chapter 8 contains a fuller discussion of the issues for women and society raised by maternity or paternity leave policies.

AMICUS BRIEF OF THE ACLU, LEAGUE OF WOMEN VOTERS, ET AL. IN CALIFORNIA FEDERAL SAVINGS AND LOAN ASSOCIATION v. GUERRA

No. 85–494 (1985).

(arguing that the California statute is illegitimate sex discrimination).

Do women require, or are they entitled to, special pregnancy-related job benefits which men do not receive because they cannot become pregnant? Is pregnancy so different a disability as to negate the Congressionally-mandated right to legal equality between the sexes in the workplace? Does the fact that pregnancy is a unique physical condition, often of great personal consequence to the women and men involved, necessarily imply that it cannot be compared to other physical conditions that may similarly affect an employee's ability to work?

These questions have been answered unequivocally by Congress in the Pregnancy Discrimination Act ("PDA"), an amendment to Title VII.

The PDA embodies the legislative judgment that women will secure equality, equity and greater tangible benefits when legal distinctions based on sex and pregnancy are eliminated, and when the similarities in the rights and needs of both sexes are seen to override their differences. The PDA thus adopts the view that pregnancy is analogous to other temporary physical conditions that may affect an employee's ability to work.

Congress had ample reason to reject *all* pregnancy-based distinctions when it enacted the PDA. Historically, protective legislation like § 12945(b)(2), designed to compensate women for the burdens imposed by pregnancy and motherhood, reinforced the distinctions between male and female workers, with powerful adverse consequences for women workers. Protectionist laws reflect an ideology which values women most highly for their childbearing and nurturing roles. Such laws reinforce stereotypes about women's inclinations and abilities; they deter employers from hiring women of childbearing age or funnel them into less responsible positions; and they make women *appear* to be more expensive, less reliable employees. Recognizing this history and its legacy, Congress elected to make pregnancy comparable to other temporary physical conditions that may affect an employee's ability to work, so as to direct attention away from debilitating stereotypes about pregnant women and focus attention on workers' need for disability leave itself.

As Congress recognized, pregnancy is neither an appropriate nor rational proxy for the need for disability benefits. Overall disability data indicate that, even including pregnancy, women do not require significantly more disability leave than men, and that numerous factors other than pregnancy correlate better with work-related disability. Even if this were not the case, the provision of sex-specific benefits is still not justifiable, since the provision of benefits on a gender-neutral basis would serve the interests of pregnant women and the state equally well. For the same reason, the statute cannot be rationalized as affirmative action.

The task here is to recognize the real needs of pregnant workers without at the same time destroying their right to equality in the workplace and perpetuating stereotypes which have, for generations, cast women "into an apologetic place in relation to work." The provision of special benefits for pregnant workers places women perpetually outside the mainstream of the labor force, permanently marginalizing their role as workers, and is not the answer.

AMICUS BRIEF OF COALITION FOR REPRODUCTIVE EQUALITY IN THE WORKPLACE, ET AL. IN CALIFORNIA FEDERAL SAVINGS AND LOAN ASSOCIATION v. GUERRA

No. 85–494 (1985).

(arguing that the California statute is valid).

California law makes it an unfair employment practice for an employer to refuse to grant reasonable leave to female employees temporarily disabled by pregnancy, childbirth or related medical conditions. It thus remedies a form of sex discrimination not currently addressed by federal law—the discriminatory impact that inadequate leave policies have on working women's right of procreative choice.

Both men and women have a constitutional right to procreative choice, a fundamental right that includes the choice to become a parent. *Skinner v. Oklahoma,* 316 U.S. 535 (1942); *Cleveland Board of Education v. LaFleur,* 414 U.S. 632 (1974).

Leave policies that are inadequate to the needs of temporarily disabled workers may affect the *employment* interests of both sexes, but such policies additionally place a burden on working women's exercise of a fundamental *non*-employment right—the right of procreative choice—while having no impact whatsoever on the procreative rights of working men. A female employee subject to an inadequate leave policy is forced to choose between exercising her right to procreate and keeping her job—a choice her male co-workers never face.

California Government Code § 12945(b)(2) (West 1980) reduces the discriminatory impact of inadequate leave policies on women's procreative rights, while conferring no special benefit on any group of employees and imposing no special burden on others. It simply allows both male and female employees to exercise their procreative rights without jeopardizing their jobs.

In guaranteeing equal employment rights under Title VII, Congress could not have intended to prevent states from enabling equal exercise by working women and men of fundamental rights such as procreative choice. Absent a clear and manifest intent to preempt, states are free to enact labor legislation, especially legislation that prohibits discrimination. Title VII explicitly preserves state antidiscrimination laws that cover areas broader than those covered by Title VII, and encourages the states to take additional measures against sex discrimination.

Title VII preempts only those state laws that are unlawful under, or inconsistent with the purposes of, Title VII. The California statute is neither. It provides an additional remedy against sex discrimination. There is no inconsistency between Title VII's goal of removing artificial barriers to equal employment opportunity between the sexes and the California statute's effect of equalizing male and female employees' ability to exercise procreative choice without jeopardizing their jobs. The Pregnancy Discrimination Act ("PDA") does not alter this conclusion. The California statute must therefore be upheld.

Notes on Cal Fed

1. Which side do you think had the better argument over the impact of the California legislation? Did it eliminate entirely "the discriminatory impact that inadequate leave policies have on working women's right of

reproductive choice," as described in the Reproductive Equality in the Workplace brief? Even under the statute, leave was unpaid. Wouldn't even unpaid maternity leave have a disparate impact on the reproductive freedom of *most* women workers relative to men?

2. The Supreme Court held that the California legislation was not preempted by the PDA, because the PDA's legislative history indicated that Congress intended to prohibit discrimination *against* pregnancy, but not preferential treatment *for* pregnant workers. Because the California statute was not inconsistent with either the PDA or the purposes of Title VII, it was not preempted by federal law. California Fed. Sav. & Loan Ass'n v. Guerra, 479 U.S. 272, 107 S.Ct. 683, 93 L.Ed.2d 613 (1987).

3. Is the dispute over maternity leave, as the ACLU argues, just another episode in the long saga of feminists' struggle over protective legislation? If not, how is it different?

4. A study by the Families and Work Institute of state laws in Minnesota, Oregon, Rhode Island and Wisconsin indicates that laws mandating parental leave to care for a new child have been relatively easy for businesses to implement, cost little, and did not reduce other benefits to workers. Families and Work Institute, "Beyond the Parental Leave Debate: The Impact of Laws in Four States" (1991).

D. THEORETICAL APPROACHES TO (IN)EQUALITY

We now consider the work of a number of feminist legal theorists who have discussed various approaches to women's inequality. It would seem logical to begin with an analysis supporting formal equality, since formal equality was the initial approach of feminism in the 1960's and 1970's, the early years of the second wave. This is the approach described in Chapter 2. But during these early years, nothing very theoretical was written justifying this approach. Most early activists simply *assumed* that formal equality was appropriate. Doubts appeared in 1979 with the publication of Catharine MacKinnon's first book, Sexual Harassment of Working Women, which both criticized formal equality and proposed an alternative, dominance theory. After formal equality was attacked, supporters offered defenses. We begin, therefore, with Catharine MacKinnon's work on dominance theory, followed by a justification of formal equality written by Ruth Bader Ginsburg in the 1980's. These selections are followed by readings on relational feminism, pragmatic feminism, socialist feminism, postmodern feminism, critical race feminism, and lesbian feminism.

1. DOMINANCE THEORY

CATHARINE A. MACKINNON, THE PROBLEM OF MARXISM AND FEMINISM

In Toward a Feminist Theory of the State 3–4 (1989).

Sexuality is to feminism what work is to marxism: that which is most one's own, yet most taken away. Marxist theory argues that society is fundamentally constructed of the relations people form as they do and make things needed to survive humanly. Work is the social process of shaping and transforming the material and social worlds, creating people as social beings as they create value. It is that activity by which people become who they are. Class is its structure, production its consequence, capital a congealed form, and control its issue.

Implicit in feminist theory is a parallel argument: the molding, direction, and expression of sexuality organizes society into two sexes: women and men. This division underlies the totality of social relations. Sexuality is the social process through which social relations of gender are created, organized, expressed, and directed, creating the social beings we know as women and men, as their relations create society. As work is to marxism, sexuality to feminism is socially constructed yet constructing, universal as activity yet historically specific, jointly comprised of matter and mind. As the organized expropriation of the work of some for the benefit of others defines a class, workers, the organized expropriation of the sexuality of some for the use of others defines the sex, woman. Heterosexuality is its social structure, desire its internal dynamic, gender and family its congealed forms, sex roles its qualities generalized to social persona, reproduction a consequence, and control its issue.

Marxism and feminism provide accounts of the way social arrangements of patterned and cumulative disparity can be internally rational and systematic yet unjust. Both are theories of power, its social derivations and its maldistribution. Both are theories of social inequality. In unequal societies, gender and with it sexual desire and kinship structures, like value and with it acquisitiveness and the forms of property ownership, are considered presocial, part of the natural world, primordial or magical or aboriginal. As marxism exposes value as a social creation, feminism exposes desire as socially relational, internally necessary to unequal social orders but historically contingent.

CATHARINE A. MACKINNON, SEXUALITY

In Feminism Unmodified 5–8 (1987).

Since 1970, feminists have uncovered a vast amount of sexual abuse of women by men. Rape, battery, sexual harassment, sexual abuse of children, prostitution, and pornography, seen for the first time in their true scope and interconnectedness, form a distinctive pattern: the power of men over women in society. These abuses are as allowed de facto as they are prohibited de jure. Formal prohibition has done little to alter their frequency; it has helped make it hard to believe that they are so common. The reports that are believed are treated as if the events and their victims are statistically deviant, because the events they report have been branded as morally and legally deviant. In fact, it is the woman who has not been sexually abused who deviates.

The reason feminism uncovered this reality, its methodological secret, is that feminism is built on believing women's accounts of sexual use and abuse by men. The pervasiveness of male sexual violence against women is therefore not denied, minimized, trivialized, eroticized, or excepted as marginal or episodic or placed to one side while more important matters are discussed. The fact that only 7.8 percent of women in the United States have not been sexually assaulted or harassed in their lifetime is not considered inconsequential or isolated. The fact that sexual violation is a sexual practice is faced. A new paradigm begins here, one that fits the reality of the experience to be explained. All the ways in which women are suppressed and subjected—restricted, intruded on, violated, objectified—are recognized as what sex is for women and as the meaning and content of femininity.

If this is done, sexuality itself is no longer unimplicated in women's second-class status. Sexual violence can no longer be categorized away as violence not sex. Women do not thrive on violation, whether or not it is done through sex. But our rapists, serial murderers ("I killed my mother for the same reason I've killed all those other women. The reason was sex."), and child molesters ("It's as natural for me to have sex with children the way it's natural for some people to have sex with women.") enjoy their acts sexually and as men, to be redundant. It is sex *for them.* What is sex except that which is felt as sexual? When acts of dominance and submission, up to and including acts of violence, are experienced as sexually arousing, as sex itself, that is what they are. The mutual exclusivity of sex and violence is preserved in the face of this evidence by immunizing as "sex" whatever causes a sexual response and by stigmatizing questioning it as repressive, knowing that what is thereby exempted includes humiliation and brutality and molestation and murder as well as rape by any definition. Violence is sex when it is practiced as sex. If violation of the powerless is part of what is sexy about sex, as well as central in the meaning of male and female, the place of sexuality in gender and the place of gender in sexuality need to be looked at together.

When this is done, sexuality appears as the interactive dynamic of gender as an inequality. Stopped as an attribute of a person, sex inequality takes the form of gender; moving as a relation between people, it takes the form of sexuality. Gender emerges as the congealed form of the sexualization of inequality between men and women. So long as this is socially the case, the feelings or acts or desires of particular individuals notwithstanding, gender inequality will divide their society into two communities of interest. The male centrally features hierarchy of control. Aggression against those with less power is experienced as sexual pleasure, an entitlement of masculinity. For the female, subordination is sexualized, in the way that dominance is for the male, as pleasure as well as gender identity, as femininity. Dominance, principally by men, and submission, principally by women, will be the ruling code through which sexual pleasure is experienced. Sexism will be a political inequality that is sexually enjoyed, if unequally so.

Sexual abuse works as a form of terror in creating and maintaining this arrangement. It is a terror so perfectly motivated and systematically concerted that it never need be intentionally organized—an arrangement that, as long as it lasted, would seal the immortality of any totalitarianism. I have come to think that the unique effectiveness of terrorism, like that against Jews in Argentina, is that it is at once absolutely systematic and absolutely random: systematic because one group is its target and lives knowing it; random because there is no way of telling who is next on the list. Just to get through another day, women must spend an incredible amount of time, life, and energy cowed, fearful, and colonized, trying to figure out how not to be next on the list. Learning by osmosis what men want in a woman and trying to give it to them, women hope that being the wanted image will alter their odds. Paying attention to every detail of every incident of a woman's violation they can get their hands on, women attempt not to be her. The problem is, combining even a few circumstances, descriptions, conditions, and details of acts of sexual abuse reveals that no woman has a chance. To be about to be raped is to be gender female in the process of going about life as usual. Some things do increase the odds, like being Black. One cannot live one's life attempting not to be a Black woman. As Black women well know, one cannot save it that way, either.

Because the inequality of the sexes is socially defined as the enjoyment of sexuality itself, gender inequality appears consensual. This helps explain the peculiar durability of male supremacy as a system of hegemony as well as its imperviousness to change once it exists. It also helps explain some of the otherwise more bewildering modes of female collaboration. The belief that whatever is sexually arousing is, ipso facto, empowering for women is revealed as a strategy in male rule. It may be worth considering that heterosexuality, the predominant social arrangement that fuses this sexuality of abuse and objectification with gender in intercourse, with attendant trauma, torture, and dehumanization, organizes women's pleasure so as to give us a stake in our own subordination. It may even be that to be "anti-sex," to be against this sex that is sex, is to refuse to affirm loyalty to this political system of inequality whose dynamic is male control and use and access to women—which would account for the stigma of the epithet.

CATHARINE A. MACKINNON, DIFFERENCE AND DOMINANCE

In Feminism Unmodified 32–45 (1987).

What is a gender question a question of? What is an inequality question a question of? These two questions underlie applications of the equality principle to issues of gender, but they are seldom explicitly asked. I think it speaks to the way gender has structured thought and perception that mainstream legal and moral theory tacitly gives the same answer to them both: these are questions of sameness and difference. The mainstream doctrine of the law of sex discrimination that results is, in my view, largely responsible for the fact that sex equality law has been so utterly ineffective at getting women what we need and are socially prevented from having on the basis of a condition of birth: a chance at productive lives of reasonable physical security, self-expression, individuation, and minimal respect and dignity. Here I expose the sameness/difference theory of sex equality, briefly show how it dominates sex discrimination law and policy and underlies its discontents, and propose an alternative that might do something.

According to the approach to sex equality that has dominated politics, law, and social perception, equality is an equivalence, not a distinction, and sex is a distinction. The legal mandate of equal treatment—which is both a systemic norm and a specific legal doctrine—becomes a matter of treating likes alike and unlikes unlike; and the sexes are defined as such by their mutual unlikeness. Put another way, gender is socially constructed as difference epistemologically; sex discrimination law bounds gender equality by difference doctrinally. A built-in tension exists between this concept of equality, which presupposes sameness, and this concept of sex, which presupposes difference. Sex equality thus becomes a contradiction in terms, something of an oxymoron, which may suggest why we are having such a difficult time getting it.

Upon further scrutiny, two alternate paths to equality for women emerge within this dominant approach, paths that roughly follow the lines of this tension. The leading one is: be the same as men. This path is termed gender neutrality doctrinally and the single standard philosophically. It is testimony to how substance gets itself up as form in law that this rule is considered formal equality. Because this approach mirrors the ideology of the social world, it is considered abstract, meaning transparent of substance; also for this reason it is considered not only to be *the* standard, but *a* standard at all. It is so far the leading rule that the words "equal to" are code for, equivalent to, the words "the same as"—referent for both unspecified.

To women who want equality yet find that you are different, the doctrine provides an alternative route: be different from men. This equal recognition of difference is termed the special benefit rule or special protection rule legally, the double standard philosophically. It is in rather bad odor. Like pregnancy, which always calls it up, it is something of a doctrinal embarrassment. Considered an exception to true equality and not really a rule of law at all, this is the one place where the law of sex discrimination admits it is recognizing something substantive. * * *

The philosophy underlying the difference approach is that sex *is* a difference, a division, a distinction, beneath which lies a stratum of human commonality, sameness. The moral thrust of the sameness branch of the doctrine is to make normative rules conform to this empirical reality by granting women access to what men have access to: to the extent that women are no different from men, we deserve what they have. The differences branch, which is generally seen as patronizing but necessary to avoid absurdity, exists to value or compensate women for what we are or have become distinctively as women (by which is meant, unlike men) under existing conditions.

My concern is not with which of these paths to sex equality is preferable in the long run or more appropriate to any particular issue, although most discourse on sex discrimination revolves about these questions as if that were all there is. My point is logically prior: to treat issues of sex equality as issues of sameness and difference *is to take a particular approach.* I call this the difference approach because it is obsessed with the sex difference. The main theme in the fugue is "we're the same, we're the same, we're the same." The counterpoint theme (in a higher register) is "but we're different, but we're different, but we're different." Its underlying story is: on the first day, difference was; on the second day, a division was created upon it; on the third day, irrational instances of dominance arose. Division may be rational or irrational. Dominance either seems or is justified. Difference *is.*

There is a politics to this. Concealed is the substantive way in which man has become the measure of all things. Under the sameness standard, women are measured according to our correspondence with man, our equality judged by our proximity to his measure. Under the difference standard, we are measured according to our lack of correspondence with him, our womanhood judged by our distance from his measure. Gender neutrality is thus simply the male standard, and the special protection rule is simply the female standard, but do not be deceived: masculinity, or maleness, is the referent for both. Think about it like those anatomy models in medical school. A male body is the human body; all those extra things women have are studied in ob/gyn. It truly is a situation in which more is less. Approaching sex discrimination in this way—as if sex questions are difference questions and equality questions are sameness questions—provides two ways for the law to hold women to a male standard and call that sex equality.

Having been very hard on the difference answer to sex equality questions, I should say that it takes up a very important problem: how to get women access to everything we have been excluded from, while also valuing everything that women are or have been allowed to become or have developed as a consequence of our struggle either not to be excluded from most of life's pursuits or to be taken seriously under the terms that have been permitted to be our terms. It negotiates what we have managed in relation to men. Legally articulated as the need to conform normative standards to existing reality, the strongest doctrinal expression of its sameness idea would prohibit taking gender into account in any way.

Its guiding impulse is: we're as good as you. Anything you can do, we can do. Just get out of the way. I have to confess a sincere affection for this approach. It has gotten women some access to employment and education, the public pursuits, including academic, professional, and blue-collar work; the military; and more than nominal access to athletics.

It has moved to change the dead ends that were all we were seen as good for and has altered what passed for women's lack of physical training, which was really serious training in passivity and enforced weakness. * * *

Feminists have this nasty habit of counting bodies and refusing not to notice their gender. As applied, the sameness standard has mostly gotten men the benefit of those few things women have historically had—for all the good they did us. Almost every sex discrimination case that has been won at the Supreme Court level has been brought by a man. Under the rule of gender neutrality, the law of custody and divorce has been transformed, giving men an equal chance at custody of children and at alimony. Men often look like better "parents" under gender-neutral rules like level of income and presence of nuclear family, because men make more money and (as they say) initiate the building of family units. In effect, they get preferred because society advantages them before they get into court, and law is prohibited from taking that preference into account because that would mean taking gender into account. The group realities that make women more in need of alimony are not permitted to matter, because only individual factors, gender-neutrally considered, may matter. So the fact that women will live their lives, as individuals, as members of the group women, with women's chances in a sex-discriminatory society, may not count, or else it is sex discrimination. The equality principle in this guise mobilizes the idea that the way to get things for women is to get them for men. Men have gotten them. Have women? We still have not got equal pay, or equal work, far less equal pay for equal work, and we are close to losing separate enclaves like women's schools through this approach.

Here is why. In reality, which this approach is not long on because it is liberal idealism talking to itself, virtually every quality that distinguishes men from women is already affirmatively compensated in this society. Men's physiology defines most sports, their needs define auto and health insurance coverage, their socially designed biographies define workplace expectations and successful career patterns, their perspectives and concerns define quality in scholarship, their experiences and obsessions define merit, their objectification of life defines art, their military service defines citizenship, their presence defines family, their inability to get along with each other—their wars and rulerships—defines history, their image defines god, and their genitals define sex. For each of their differences from women, what amounts to an affirmative action plan is in effect, otherwise known as the structure and values of American society. But whenever women are, by this standard, "different" from men and insist on not having it held against us, whenever a difference is used to keep us second class and we refuse to smile about it, equality law has a paradigm trauma and it's crisis time for the doctrine.

What this doctrine has apparently meant by sex inequality is not what happens to us. The law of sex discrimination that has resulted seems to be looking only for those ways women are kept down that have *not* wrapped themselves up as a difference—whether original, imposed, or imagined. Start with original: what to do about the fact that women actually have an ability men still lack, gestating children in utero. Pregnancy therefore is a difference. Difference doctrine says it is sex discrimination to give women what we need, because only women need it. It is not sex discrimination not to give women what we need because then only women will not get what we need. Move into imposed: what to do about the fact that most women are segregated into low-paying jobs where there are no men. Suspecting that the structure of the marketplace will be entirely subverted if comparable worth is put into effect, difference doctrine says that because there is no man to set a standard from which women's treatment is a deviation, there is no sex discrimination here, only sex difference. Never mind that there is no man to compare with because no man would do that job if he had a choice, and of course he has because he is a man, so he won't.

Now move into the so-called subtle reaches of the imposed category, the de facto area. Most jobs in fact require that the person, gender neutral, who is qualified for them will be someone who is not the primary caretaker of a preschool child. Pointing out that this raises a concern of sex in a society in which women are expected to care for the children is taken as day one of taking gender into account in the structuring of jobs. To do that would violate the rule against not noticing situated differences based on gender, so it never emerges that day one of taking gender into account was the day the job was structured with the expectation that its occupant would have no child care responsibilities. Imaginary sex differences—such as between male and female applicants to administer estates or between males aging and dying and females aging and dying—I will concede, the doctrine can handle.

I will also concede that there are many differences between women and men. I mean, can you imagine elevating one half of a population and denigrating the other half and producing a population in which everyone is the same? What the sameness standard fails to notice is that men's differences from women are equal to women's differences from men. There is an *equality* there. Yet the sexes are not socially equal. The difference approach misses the fact that hierarchy of power produces real as well as fantasized differences, differences that are also inequalities. What is missing in the difference approach is what Aristotle missed in his empiricist notion that equality means treating likes alike and unlikes unlike, and nobody has questioned it since. Why should you have to be the same as a man to get what a man gets simply because he is one? Why does maleness provide an original entitlement, not questioned on the basis of *its* gender, so that is it women—women who want to make a case of unequal treatment in a world men have made in their image (this is really the part Aristotle missed)—who have to show in effect that they are men in every relevant respect, unfortunately mistaken for women on the basis of an accident of birth?

The women that gender neutrality benefits, and there are some, show the suppositions of this approach in highest relief. They are mostly women who have been able to construct a biography that somewhat approximates the male norm, at least on paper. They are the qualified, the least of sex discrimination's victims. When they are denied a man's chance, it looks the most like sex bias. The more unequal society gets, the fewer such women are permitted to exist. Therefore, the more unequal society gets, the *less* likely the difference doctrine is to be able to do anything about it, because unequal power creates both the appearance and the reality of sex differences along the same lines as it creates its sex inequalities.

The special benefits side of the difference approach has not compensated for the differential of being second class. The special benefits rule is the only place in mainstream equality doctrine where you get to identify as a woman and not have that mean giving up all claim to equal treatment—but it comes close. Under its double standard, women who stand to inherit something when their husbands die have gotten the exclusion of a small percentage of the inheritance tax, to the tune of Justice Douglas waxing eloquent about the difficulties of all women's economic situation.[22] If we're going to be stigmatized as different, it would be nice if the compensation would fit the disparity. * * *

The double standard of these rules doesn't give women the dignity of the single standard; it also does not (as the differences standard does) suppress the gender of its referent, which is, of course, the female gender. I must also confess some affection for this standard. The work of Carol Gilligan on gender differences in moral reasoning gives it a lot of dignity, more than it has ever had, more, frankly, than I thought it ever could have. But she achieves for moral reasoning what the special protection rule achieves in law: the affirmative rather than the negative valuation of that which has accurately distinguished women from men, by making it seem as though those attributes, with their consequences, really are somehow ours, rather than what male supremacy has attributed to us for its own use. For women to affirm difference, when difference means dominance, as it does with gender, means to affirm the qualities and characteristics of powerlessness.

* * *

I do not think that the way women reason morally is morality "in a different voice." I think it is morality in a higher register, in the feminine voice. Women value care because men have valued us according to the care we give them, and we could probably use some. Women think in relational terms because our existence is defined in relation to men. Further, when you are powerless, you don't just speak differently. A lot, you don't speak. Your speech is not just differently articulated, it is silenced. Eliminated, gone. You aren't just deprived of a language with which to articulate your distinctiveness, although you are; you are deprived of a life out of which articulation might come. Not being heard is not just a function of lack of recognition, not just that no one knows how to listen to you, although it is that; it is also silence of the deep

22. Kahn v. Shevin, 416 U.S. 351, 353 (1974).

kind, the silence of being prevented from having anything to say. Sometimes it is permanent. All I am saying is that the damage of sexism is real, and reifying that into differences is an insult to our possibilities.

So long as these issues are framed this way, demands for equality will always appear to be asking to have it both ways: the same when we are the same, different when we are different. But this is the way men have it: equal and different too. They have it the same as women when they are the same and want it, and different from women when they are different and want to be, which usually they do. Equal and different too would only be parity. But under male supremacy, while being told we get it both ways, both the specialness of the pedestal and an even chance at the race, the ability to be a woman and a person, too, few women get much benefit of either.

There is an alternative approach, one that threads its way through existing law and expresses, I think, the reason equality law exists in the first place. It provides a second answer, a dissident answer in law and philosophy, to both the equality question and the gender question. In this approach, an equality question is a question of the distribution of power. Gender is also a question of power, specifically of male supremacy and female subordination. The question of equality, from the standpoint of what it is going to take to get it, is at root a question of hierarchy, which—as power succeeds in constructing social perception and social reality—derivatively becomes a categorical distinction, a difference. Here, on the first day that matters, dominance was achieved, probably by force. By the second day, division along the same lines had to be relatively firmly in place. On the third day, if not sooner, differences were demarcated, together with social systems to exaggerate them in perception and in fact, *because* the systematically differential delivery of benefits and deprivations required making no mistake about who was who. Comparatively speaking, man has been resting ever since. Gender might not even code as difference, might not mean distinction epistemologically, were it not for its consequences for social power.

I call this the dominance approach, and it is the ground I have been standing on in criticizing mainstream law. The goal of this dissident approach is not to make legal categories trace and trap the way things are. It is not to make rules that fit reality. It is critical of reality. Its task is not to formulate abstract standards that will produce determinate outcomes in particular cases. Its project is more substantive, more jurisprudential than formulaic, which is why it is difficult for the mainstream discourse to dignify it as an approach to doctrine or to imagine it as a rule of law at all. It proposes to expose that which women have had little choice but to be confined to, in order to change it.

The dominance approach centers on the most sex-differential abuses of women as a gender, abuses that sex equality law in its difference garb could not confront. It is based on a reality about which little of a systematic nature was known before 1970, a reality that calls for a new conception of the problem of sex inequality. This new information includes not only the extent and intractability of sex segregation into poverty, which has been known before, but the range of issues termed violence against women, which has not been. It combines women's material desperation, through being relegated to categories of jobs that pay nil, with the massive amount of rape and attempted rape—44% of all women—about which virtually nothing is done; the sexual assault of children—38% of girls and 10% of boys—which is apparently endemic to the patriarchal family; the battery of women that is systematic in one quarter to one third of our homes; prostitution, women's fundamental economic condition, what we do when all else fails, and for many women in this country, all else fails often; and pornography, an industry that traffics in female flesh, making sex inequality into sex to the tune of eight billion dollars a year in profits largely to organized crime.

These experiences have been silenced out of the difference definition of sex equality largely because they happen almost exclusively to women. Understand: for this reason, they are considered *not* to raise sex equality issues. Because this treatment is done almost uniquely to women, it is implicitly treated as a difference, the sex difference, when in fact it is the socially situated subjection of women. The whole point of women's social relegation to inferiority as a gender is that for the most part these things aren't done to men. Men are not paid half of what women are paid for doing the same work on the basis of their equal difference. * * *

Looking at the difference approach and the dominance approach from each other's point of view clarifies some otherwise confusing tensions in sex equality debates. From the point of view of the dominance approach, it becomes clear that the difference approach adopts the point of view of male supremacy on the status of the sexes. Simply by treating the status quo as "the standard," it invisibly and uncritically accepts the arrangements under male supremacy. In this sense, the difference approach is masculinist, although it can be expressed in a female voice. The dominance approach, in that it sees the inequalities of the social world from the standpoint of the subordination of women to men, is feminist.

If you look through the lens of the difference approach at the world as the dominance approach imagines it—that is, if you try to see real inequality through a lens that has difficulty seeing an inequality as an inequality if it also appears as a difference—you see demands for change in the distribution of power as demands for special protection. This is because the only tools that the difference paradigm offers to comprehend disparity equate the recognition of a gender line with an admission of lack of entitlement to equality under law. Since equality questions are primarily confronted in this approach as matters of empirical fit—that is, as matters of accurately shaping legal rules (implicitly modeled on the standard men set) to the way the world is (also implicitly modeled on the standard men set)—any existing differences must be negated to merit equal treatment. For ethnicity as well as for gender, it is basic to mainstream discrimination doctrine to preclude any true diversity among equals or true equality within diversity.

* * *

I say, give women equal power in social life. Let what we say matter, then we will discourse on questions of morality. Take your foot off our necks, then we will hear in what tongue women speak. So long as sex equality is limited by sex difference, whether you like it or don't like it, whether you value it or seek to negate it, whether you stake it out as a grounds for feminism or occupy it as the terrain of misogyny, women will be born, degraded, and die. We would settle for that equal protection of the laws under which one would be born, live, and die, in a country where protection is not a dirty word and equality is not a special privilege.

CATHARINE A. MACKINNON, SEX INEQUALITY

In Sexual Harassment of Working Women 117–18 (1979).

A rule or practice is discriminatory, in the inequality approach, if it participates in the systemic social deprivation of one sex because of sex. The only question for litigation is whether the policy or practice in question integrally contributes to the maintenance of an underclass or a deprived position because of gender status. The disadvantage which constitutes the injury of discrimination is not the failure to be treated "without regard to" one's sex; that is the injury of arbitrary differentiation. The unfairness lies in being deprived *because* of being a woman or a man, a deprivation given meaning in the social context of the dominance or preference of one sex over the other. The social problem addressed is not the failure to ignore woman's essential sameness with man, but the recognition of womanhood to women's comparative disadvantage. In this approach, few reasons, not even biological ones, can justify the institutionalized disadvantage of women. Comparability of sex characteristics is not required because policies are proscribed which transform women's sex-based differences from men into social and economic deprivations. All that is required are comparatively unequal results.

Under the inequality approach, variables as to which women and men are not comparable, such as pregnancy or sexuality, would be among the *first* to trigger suspicion and scrutiny, rather than the last; they would not be exceptions to the rule. From the inequality perspective the question on the *Gilbert*[a] facts would be: is not the structure of the job market, which accommodates the physical needs, life cycle, and family expectations of men but not of women, integral to women's inferior

a. General Electric Co. v. Gilbert, 429 U.S. 125 (1976). The issue in *Gilbert* was whether Title VII's ban on sex discrimination in employment was violated by an employer's differential treatment of pregnancy-related expenses under a health insurance plan. The Court held that sex discrimination under Title VII did not include pregnancy discrimination. Congress subsequently amended Title VII and overruled *Gilbert*. The reasoning of *Gilbert* was much like that in *Geduldig,* the constitutional sex-equality pregnancy case included in Chapter 2.

employment status? What can then justify a policy that makes pregnancy, a condition unique and common to women as a gender, into a disadvantage in employment? The affirmative form of the argument is that the health needs of women workers should be accommodated equally with those of men.

Notes on Dominance Theory

1. What does MacKinnon mean when she says in Difference and Dominance, above, that the liberal standard adopted by the Supreme Court is not neutral, though it appears to be on its face, but rather a male standard, under which "man has become the measure of all things"? If government must treat women and men the same, under the same rules and standards, how is this approach "male"?

2. MacKinnon suggests that the women who have benefited most from the liberal difference standard are those whose biographies are most like men's. Do you agree? Is this a problem? How should we judge an equality standard? How would an agenda designed for the most vulnerable women differ from the agenda of feminist litigators pushing for formal equality in the 1970's?

3. How would MacKinnon assess whether we have reached equality? How does she measure inequality? According to MacKinnon, what should feminist activists strive for as the primary goal: if your eyes are on the prize, what are you looking at? Do you agree that this is the appropriate goal, short or long term?

4. How has power been defined in our culture? Who has defined it? Is there a sense in which MacKinnon's approach is androcentric (i.e., a male-centered standard)? Can you think of circumstances in which another goal might be more important for a woman or women as a group? Is power always your primary objective? If not, do you think it should always be the primary objective of the feminist movement?

5. According to Nancy Fraser, MacKinnon sees dominance and subordination in terms of individual relationships rather than in terms of groups and social structures. MacKinnon sees male dominance "as a dyadic power relation in which a male superordinate commands a female subordinate. It is a master/subject relation." Fraser, Justice Interruptus: Critical Reflections on the "Postsocialist" Condition 225 (1997) Is this an accurate description of MacKinnon's understanding of dominance and subordination? What would such an understanding of inequality miss?

6. Why is MacKinnon ambivalent about Gilligan's work and reluctant to identify the relational caring voice with women? Do you agree with her? If MacKinnon is right, and this is the voice of women because it is what men have valued women for, what follows? Are there reasons, apart from male insistence, why women might want to use this voice? What might be the advantages generally, and for women specifically, of valuing relationships and care in our society? How would MacKinnon respond?

7. If women are shaped by social circumstances and experiences in a male-dominated world, aren't men also shaped by social circumstances and

experiences? Does MacKinnon assume that men's voice is authentically male though she denies that women's voice is authentically female? Does she seem to suggest that men have an essential unchanging domineering nature?

8. There is a good deal of tension between trying to increase appreciation for work traditionally done by women, particularly caring for others, and changing women's status (and thus increasing women's power) by encouraging women to break out of traditional roles. How would MacKinnon resolve this conflict? How would you? How have you resolved this tension in your own life, and how do you plan to resolve it in the future? In your own life, have you gone single-mindedly after power and status?

9. How would MacKinnon analyze the issue in *VMI*, the last case excerpted in Chapter 2 involving the all-male military academy? What would she see as the core problem in that case? Compare MacKinnon's identification of the problem with that of Justice Ginsburg in her opinion in *VMI*. Which is more accurate in identifying the problem(s)?

10. Would MacKinnon support a law requiring employers to give employees unpaid maternity leave on the ground that such a policy would increase women's power by giving them the option of four months off at childbirth? Would she see such policies, perhaps even *paid* leave, as necessary for equality because otherwise the differences between women and men at and after childbirth are translated into advantages for men, who can easily continue working, and disadvantages for women, who cannot? Or would she regard such policies as unacceptable because such policies will (1) decrease women's power by reinforcing traditional stereotypes of women's and men's roles and (2) encourage women to be primary caretakers of children by giving mothers but not fathers time off for caretaking during infancy? Under dominance theory, should government officials be required to incorporate paid parental or maternal leave as part of unemployment compensation insurance systems, as many other North Atlantic nations have done? Can you think of other, perhaps better, remedies? How would a court select the appropriate one? See Mary E. Becker, Prince Charming: Abstract Equality, 1987 Sup.Ct.Rev. 201, 229–30.

11. According to the formal equality approach, inequality consists of treating similarly situated women and men differently. According to MacKinnon, most inequality results from treating differences differently, i.e., systematically valuing those traits, experiences, etc., associated with men and devaluing those associated with women. Which definition captures more sexual inequality? Which standard would work better in the hands of judges? Which judges? Might your answer depend on who the judges are?

12. Is a domination analysis the same across women of differing ages, races, classes, and sexual orientations? How might the power effects of various policies, such as that at issue in *Cal Fed*, vary across these groups? How should such differences be resolved in applying the dominance approach?

13. What is the relationship between formal equality and affirmative action as a contested issue? Would affirmative action be equally contested under MacKinnon's approach to inequality?

2. FORMAL EQUALITY

HON. RUTH BADER GINSBURG AND BARBARA FLAGG, SOME REFLECTIONS ON THE FEMINIST LEGAL THOUGHT OF THE 1970s

[1989] University of Chicago Legal Forum 9, 10–18.

* * *

I had the good fortune * * * to participate intensively in the sex equality litigation of the 1970s, and I would like to share with you some thoughts on what that litigation was about and how it bears on the jurisprudence of the 1980s.

* * *

I was lucky to be in the right place, at the right time. My post on a law faculty gave me the leeway to accomplish the work and the ACLU had the resources to start up, in 1971, a Women's Rights Project. (I note that the ACLU involvement meant men would be working alongside women in this effort, and that was important to me. I firmly believe that feminist endeavors, to realize their full potential, must deeply involve members of both sexes.)

The 1970s cases in which I participated under ACLU auspices all rested on the same fundamental premise: that the law's differential treatment of men and women, typically rationalized as reflecting "natural" differences between the sexes, historically had tended to contribute to women's subordination—their confined "place" in man's world—even when conceived as protective of the fairer, but weaker and dependent-prone sex. The arguments addressed to the courts were designed to reveal and to challenge the assumptions underpinning traditional sex-specific rules, and to move the Supreme Court in the direction of a constitutional principle that would provide for heightened, thoughtful review of gender classifications. * * *

The ACLU Women's Rights Project in the 1970s was hardly so bold or so prescient as to essay articulation of a comprehensive theoretical vision of a world in which men did not define women's place. The endeavor was less lofty, more immediately and practically oriented; it was, as I earlier stated, to pursue a series of cases that might illuminate the most common instances of gender distinctions in the law, and thereby provide a basis for the evolution of constitutional doctrine and attendant legislative change. I will mention three principal cases in which the Project participated to give you a sense of the effort: *Reed v. Reed, Frontiero v. Richardson*, and *Weinberger v. Wiesenfeld*.

Reed v. Reed was the turning point case. Decided in 1971, Sally Reed's case invalidated an Idaho statute that afforded men (in the particular case, Sally's estranged husband Cecil) an automatic preference over women for estate administration purposes. (The estate was that of

Sally's son Richard, who had committed suicide after the local court transferred him to his father's custody when he was no longer "of tender years.") Two years later, in *Frontieiro v. Richardson,* the Court held it unconstitutional to deny to female military officers housing and medical benefits covering their husbands on the same automatic basis as those family benefits were accorded to male military officers for their wives. Air Force Lieutenant Sharron Frontiero saw the measures as a denial of equal pay to her. In each instance, the statute in question presumed a wife's, but not a husband's, dependent status. *Reed* and *Frontiero* were ideal way pavers. Both presented gender distinctions rooted in sex-role stereotypes, distinctions defended solely on grounds of administrative convenience.

Legislation embodying the "separate spheres" mentality, but not susceptible of plausible compensatory rationalization, seemed in the 1970s the most promising focus of attention, and *Weinberger v. Wiesenfeld* fit that bill. When Paula Polatschek, a math teacher, died in childbirth in 1972, her husband, Stephen Wiesenfeld, applied for Social Security benefits for himself and their infant son, whom Stephen hoped to care for personally, he discovered that the Social Security Act awarded child-in-care benefits only to mothers, not to fathers. Stephen Wiesenfeld challenged this gender-based distinction, and ultimately won a unanimous judgment in the Supreme Court. The majority of Justices considered *Wiesenfeld*, like *Frontiero*, dominantly as an equal pay case: Paula's gainful employment netted the family less than a man's work. The Court also saw the law as discriminating against Stephen, who wanted to be a caring parent. Each of these views accurately described a fact of the case.

In *Reed*, *Frontiero*, and *Wiesenfeld* the Court took a closer look at the challenged classifications than would be expected under the rational basis test generally applicable at that time to group classifications not based on race. The initial strategy, pursued in *Reed* and *Frontiero*, was to argue for strict scrutiny of gender distinctions, in part by drawing an analogy between sex-and race-based classifications. That tack was modified in briefing *Wiesenfeld*. It was by then clear that one could not garner five votes for labeling sex a "suspect classification." But it was also apparent from the results in *Reed* and *Frontiero* that doctrinal specificity was not immediately necessary.

The driving force of the litigation was never a reflexive "me too," coattails-riding notion that if race classifications were suspect down the line, sex classifications should be too. Instead, the objective was to obtain thoughtful consideration of the assumptions underlying, and the purposes served by, sex-based classifications. In *Reed* the unanimous Court said very little, but commentators recognized that "some special sensitivity to sex as a classifying factor" was implicit in the Court's judgment. The *Frontiero* court divided on the appropriate rationale. A plurality of four ranked sex a suspect criterion, perhaps taking that stride too swiftly with only one building block—*Reed*—then in place. In *Wiesenfeld* and a number of cases thereafter, the High Court settled on a genuinely intermediate position, a standard tighter than the generally applicable minimum rationality test, but more supple than the strictest scrutiny.

In essence, the Court instructed Congress and state legislatures: rethink, reanalyze your position on these questions. Should you determine that compensatory legislation is in fact warranted, we have left you a corridor in which to move. But your classifications must be refined, tied to an income test, for example, and not grossly drawn solely by reference to sex. The Court's heightened mode of review persists, captured in equal protection jargon by the statement that, to survive court review, a classification must bear a substantial relationship to an important governmental objective.

Some observers have portrayed the 1970s litigation as assimilationist in outlook, insistent on formal equality, opening doors only to comfortably situated women willing to accept men's rules and be treated like men, even a misguided effort that harmed more women than it helped. These critics question the advocacy of strict scrutiny for gender classifications as in *Reed* and *Frontiero*, the representation furnished male plaintiffs as in *Wiesenfeld*, and the heavy focus on classifications that could be characterized as burdening both men and women.

Such comment seems to me not fair. The litigation of the 1970s helped unsettle previously accepted conceptions of men's and women's separate spheres, and thereby added impetus to efforts ongoing in the political arena to advance women's opportunities and stature. An appeal to courts at that time could not have been expected to do much more.

I repeat a key point that tends to be overlooked in some current analyses. The Supreme Court needed basic education before it was equipped to turn away from the precedents in place, decisions like *Goesaert v. Cleary* and *Hoyt v. Florida*. The Justices received relevant education as the 1970s wore on, publicly from the press and the briefs filed in court; privately, I suspect, from the aspirations of women, particularly the daughters, in their own families and communities. A teacher from outside the club, or the home crowd, seeking to open minds, however, knows she must keep it comprehensible and digestible, not too complex or intimidating, or risk losing her audience. That is all the more evident when her listeners have a long, heavy, and varied docket to manage; when they appreciate the value of consensus in collegial court statements about the law; and when they sense the limits of the judicial role in the republic the United States Constitution serves.

The logical progression from the 1970s litigation, it seems to me, is to another arena, not to the courts with their distinctly limited capacity, but to the legislature. Once the law books have been cleared of prescriptions of the kind Sally Reed, Sharon Frontiero, and Stephen Wiesenfeld challenged, what should one strive to enact instead? If women were dominant in our legislatures, what would their program be? Would they put through laws granting leave singularly to pregnant workers, with a guaranteed right to return to the job? Or would they press instead for legislation like the Family and Medical Leave Act, a measure that takes the woman at work as a model or motivator, but spreads out to shelter others: men and women who need time off not only to care for a newborn, but to attend to a seriously ill child, spouse, elderly parent or self? We do not yet have legislation of this sort but the very idea of it is no longer an impossible dream.

Notes on Formal Equality

1. How would Ginsburg respond to Gilligan? You might want to take a second look at Ginsburg's opinion in *VMI* (the final case in Chapter 2), where Virginia created a leadership school for women very much in the different-voice style. Would Ginsburg agree with MacKinnon's assessment of Gilligan?

2. Does the *Cal Fed* statute violate formal equality? Would Ginsburg strike the *Cal Fed* statute? Look especially at the last paragraph in Ginsburg's essay and her decision in *VMI,* the last case in Chapter 2.

3. Does Ginsburg see any downside to formal equality, or does she see it as simply the necessary first step, a step that has done no harm? Do you agree? Even if formal equality was a necessary first step, might it have advantaged some women more than others and hurt at least some women in some situations? Would there have been a downside to striking the California statute at issue in *Cal Fed* as the ACLU urged? What women would have been hurt the most? Who was the woman in *Cal Fed* itself? Does Ginsburg seem oblivious to any downside?

4. In the last paragraph of the above extract, Ginsburg states that formal equality under the courts is but the first stage in working towards equality and that the next stage will be in the legislative arena. But are some legislative solutions precluded by the current formal equality standard? Has going to the courts had other effects? Has it, in your view, actually interfered with political movements? Has the Supreme Court's narrow notion of equality come to dominate equality's meaning in the culture at large, making effective legislation less likely?

5. Feminists tend to agree that what we really need is *paid* parental leave, so that women in all classes as well as men can care for a newborn. What are the risks, especially for women who cannot afford unpaid leave, of settling for unpaid leave, as feminists did in supporting the Family and Medical Leave Act of 1993, discussed in Chapter 8? Why did feminists agree on settling for unpaid parental leave but split over settling for maternity leave?

3. RELATIONAL FEMINISM

ROBIN L. WEST, THE DIFFERENCE IN WOMEN'S HEDONIC LIVES: A PHENOMENOLOGICAL CRITIQUE OF FEMINIST LEGAL THEORY

3 Wis. Women's L.J. 81–83, 85–90, 93–94, 98, 101–02, 104, 111–18, 129, 139–42 (1987).

Women's subjective, hedonic lives are different from men's. The quality of our suffering is different from that of men's, as is the nature of our joy. Furthermore, and of more direct concern to feminist lawyers, the quantity of pain and pleasure enjoyed or suffered by the two genders is different: women suffer more than men. The two points are related. One reason that women suffer more than men is that women often find painful the same objective event or condition that men find pleasurable. The introduction of oxymorons in our vocabulary, wrought by feminist victories, evidences this difference in women's and men's hedonic lives. The phrases "date-rape," for example, and "sexual harassment" capture these different subjective experiences of shared social realities. * * *

Just as women's work is not recognized or compensated by the market culture, women's injuries are often not recognized or compensated *as injuries* by the legal culture. The dismissal of women's gender-specific suffering comes in various forms, but the outcome is always the same: women's suffering for one reason or another is outside the scope of legal redress. Thus, women's distinctive, gender-specific injuries are now or have in the recent past been variously dismissed as trivial (sexual harassment on the street); consensual (sexual harassment on the job); humorous (non-violent marital rape); participatory, subconsciously wanted, or self-induced (father/daughter incest); natural or biological, and therefore inevitable (childbirth); sporadic, and conceptually continuous with gender-neutral pain (rape, viewed as a crime of violence); deserved or private (domestic violence); non-existent (pornography); incomprehensible (unpleasant and unwanted consensual sex); or legally predetermined (marital rape, in states with the marital exemption).

It is not so clear, though, *why* women's suffering is so pervasively dismissed or trivialized by legal culture, or more importantly what to do about it. * * *

[I suggest that the] blanket dismissal of women's gender-specific suffering by the legal culture may be (partly) a reflection of the extent to which the pain women feel is *not understood,* and *that* it is not understood may be because it is itself different, and not just a product of our difference. Thus, it may be that women suffer more because we suffer differently. * * * If the pain women feel is different—not shared by men—then it is not surprising that men cannot readily emphathize with women who suffer, much less share in the effort to resist the source of their injuries. The strategic inference I draw is this: if we want to enlist the aid of the larger legal culture, the feel of our gender-specific pain must be described before we can ever hope to communicate its magnitude.

Focus on the "difference" of our hedonic lives also suggests a different way to address the related problem of "false consciousness." As feminists know all too well, it is not just the legal culture which trivializes women's suffering, women do so also. Again, if we focus on the distinctiveness of our pain, this becomes less surprising. An injury uniquely sustained by a disempowered group will lack a name, a history, and in general a linguistic reality. Consequently, the victim as well as the perpetrator will transform the pain into *something else,* such as, for example, punishment, or flattery, or transcendence, or unconscious pleasure. A victim's response to an injury which is perceived by the victim as deservedly punitive, consensual, natural, subconsciously desired, legally inevitable, or trivial will be very different from a response to an injury which is perceived as simply *painful.* We change our behavior in response to the threat of what we perceive as punishment; we diminish ourselves in response to injuries we perceive as trivial; we reconstruct our pasts in response to injuries we perceive as subconsciously desired; we negate our inner selves in response to injuries we perceive as consensual; and we constrain our potentiality in response to injuries we perceive as inevitable. We respond to pain, on the other hand, by resisting the source of the pain. The strategic inference should be clear: we must give voice to the hurting self, even when that hurting self sounds like a child rather than an adult; even when that hurting self voices "trivial" complaints; even when the hurting self is ambivalent toward the harm; and even when (especially when) the hurting self is talking a language not heard in public discourse. * * *

[I can think of four possible reasons for feminist legal theorists' failure to provide] rich descriptions of women's subjective, hedonic lives, particularly the pain in those lives * * *.

The first reason is linguistic. It is *hard* to talk about our pain and pleasure because they are different. Our language is inadequate to the task. * * * The second reason is psychological. Before we can convince others of the seriousness of the injuries we sustain, we must first convince ourselves, and so long as others are unconvinced, to some extent, we will be as well. * * * The third and underlying problem is political. The inadequacy of language and the problem of "false consciousness" are but reflections of what is surely the core obstacle to the development of feminist discourse on the nature of gender-specific pain, which is an unwilling and resisting audience. * * *

However, at least one reason—and perhaps the main reason—that feminist legal theorists have neglected the hedonic dimension of our difference * * * is * * * the emerging logic of feminist legal theory itself. By virtue of the models of legal criticism that feminist legal theorists have embraced, we've literally defined the subjective, hedonic aspect of our differences out of existence. * * *

[L]iberal-legal feminist theorists—true to their liberalism—want women to have more choices, and * * * *radical-legal* feminist theorists—true to their radicalism—want women to have more power. Both models direct our critical attention *outward*—liberalism to the number of choices we have, radicalism to the amount of power. * * * Neither model directs our critical attention *inward.* Consequently, and unsurprisingly, neither liberal nor radical feminist legal critics have committed themselves to the task of determining the measure of women's happiness or suffering.

Which is not to say that liberal and radical feminist legal theorists are unconcerned about women's subjective well-being. Rather, each group dismisses the normative significance of women's pain and suffering because of the essentially strategic choices made by the underlying (nonfeminist) politics embraced by that group, and the depictions of human nature those choices entail. That is, radicals, liberals, and feminists all have great concern for people's subjective happiness. But neither radical nor liberal legalism—nor their feminist derivatives—aim for happiness or well-being *directly.* * * * [L]iberal legalism assumes that, if free to do so, people will choose what will make them happy, and that therefore there exists a correlation between the objective act of consent and a subjective gain in happiness. On this assumption, liberal legalists seek to maximize not our subjective happiness, but our objective opportunities for choice. Radical legalism assumes that there exists a correlation between people's objective equality and subjective happiness, or well-being. On this assumption, radicals seek to maximize not our subjective happiness, but our objective equality. * * *

The cost *to women* of feminist legal theorists' endorsement of the anti-phenomenological methodology and anti-hedonic norms of the models they endorse is very high. It renders liberal and radical feminist legal theorists peculiarly uncritical—*as feminists*—of the visions of the human and thus of the normative assumptions of the models for legal criticism which they have respectively embraced. * * *

LIBERAL FEMINISM: CONSENT, AUTONOMY AND THE GIVING SELF

Perhaps the most widely held normative commitment of mainstream liberal legal theorists is that individuals should be free to choose their own style of life, and to exercise that freedom of choice in as many spheres as possible—economic, political and personal. * * *

I want to suggest * * * that many women, much of the time, consent to transactions, changes, or situations in the world so as to satisfy not their own desires or to maximize their own pleasure, as liberal legalism and liberal legal feminism both presume, but to maximize the pleasure and satiate the desires of others, and that they do so by virtue of conditions which only women experience. I will sometimes call the cluster of "other-regarding," other-pleasing motivations that rule these women's actions the "giving self," so as to distinguish it from the "liberal self": the cluster of self-regarding "rational" motivations presumed by liberal legalism. * * *

I believe that women become giving rather than liberal selves for a range of reasons—including our (biological) pregnability and our (social) training for our role as primary caretakers. * * * [In addition, a] fully justified fear of acquisitive and violent male sexuality * * * permeates many women's—perhaps all women's—sexual and emotional self-definition. Women respond to this fear by *re-constituting* themselves in a way that controls the danger and suppresses the fear. Thus: women define themselves as "giving selves" so as to obviate the threat, the danger, the pain, and the fear of being self-regarding selves from whom their sexuality is taken.

* * *

How do women respond to the total fear that accompanies the daily violence that characterizes an abusive domestic relationship? What does such fear *teach* you? A woman cannot live in a state of terror *every day* and what a battered woman learns in an abusive marriage is how to define herself in such a way that she can on occasion suppress the fear. Thus, what a violent intimate relationship taught me was to live *for the other.* * * * My purpose—my *only* reason for acting and my *only* motivation—was to serve *that* need of another. Fear taught me to view as literally incongruous the mere suggestion that I should expect to reap pleasure for myself from anything at all; surely not from sex, but nor from more ordinary sources, such as food, flowers, music, friendship or scenery. The notion that I would act—*or consent*—so as to further my own welfare or to create pleasure for myself was both inconceivable and unconceived: until circumstances and self-preservatory desperation inspired my exit, it never crossed my mind. * * * I did not have, much less act on, preferences. * * *

Many more women * * * know the fear and the threat of violence implicit in promiscuous heterosexuality. A "date" with a man who is utterly—aggressively—uninterested in your subjective well-being, and at the same time, utterly consumed by his expectation and his felt compulsion to *have you* is a frightening encounter. * * *

One way (there are others) that a young girl can respond to the "rising panic" she feels on a date is by defining herself as "giving." A straightforward, sensible, protective reaction to someone who is indifferent to your subjectivity, and at the same time must have you as an object, is to hide your subjective self and objectify and then give your sexual self for his pleasure and your safety. * * *

One way that (some) women respond to the pervasive, silent, unspoken and invisible fear of rape in their lives is by giving their (sexual) selves to a consensual, protective, and monogamous relationship. This is widely denied—but it may be widely denied because it is so widely presumed. It is, after all, precisely what we are supposed to do. * * *

Radical Feminism and the Ethical Primacy of Power and Equality

Radical feminist legal theory begins with a description of women which is diametrically opposed to that embraced by liberal feminists. Liberal feminists assume a definitional equality—a "sameness"—between the female and male experience of consensual choice, and then argue that the legal system should respect that fundamental, empirical equality. In sharp contrast, radical feminists assume a definitional inequality of women—women are definitionally the disempowered group—and urge the legal system to eradicate that disempowerment and thereby make women what they presently are not, and that is equal.

Radical feminism thus begins with a denial of the liberal feminist's starting assumption. Women and men are not equally autonomous individuals. Women, unlike men, live in a world with two sovereigns—the state and men—and this is true not just some of the time but all of the time. Women, unlike men, are definitionally submissive twice over; once vis-a-vis the state, and once vis-a-vis the superior power of men. A legal regime which ignores this central reality will simply perpetuate the fundamental, underlying inequality.

The cause of women's disempowerment, as well as its effect, is the expropriation of our sexuality. Women are the group, in Catharine MacKinnon's phrase, "from whom sexuality is expropriated," in the same sense that workers are, definitionally, the group from whom labor is expropriated. Women are the gender from whom sex is taken. Women as women suffer the threat of acquisitive and potentially violent male sexuality. The threat of male violence and violent sexuality both defines the class woman and causes her disempowerment and the expropriation of her sexuality, just as the threat of starvation and material deprivation both defines the worker, and causes his disempowerment and the expropriation of his labor.

This much, radical feminist legal theory shares with radical feminism, and with this much I am in full agreement. Where radical feminist legal theory has departed from radical feminism, I believe, is in the normative argument it draws from the insight that women are, definitionally, the group from whom sexuality is expropriated. The argument, I believe, owes more to radical legalism than to radical feminism. The argument has three steps.

First, radical feminist legal theory, like radical legalism, begins with a highly particularized although largely implicit description of the human being. People are, in short, assumed to be such that there exists a correlation between objectively equal distributions of power—including sexual power—and subjectively happy and good lives. Domination makes us evil and submission makes us miserable; substantive equality will make us both moral and happy; and both claims are true because of, and by reference to, this conception of our essential human nature. Radical legal theorists, including radical feminist legal theorists, are as committed to the equation of objective, substantive equality and subjective well being, and the view of our nature on which it rests, as the liberal legal theorist is committed to the equation of objective consent and subjective happiness.

Second, both radical legalism and radical feminist legalism draw from this depiction of the human being the normative inference that it is the imbalance of power which facilitates expropriation (of work for the radical legalist, of sex for the radical feminist legalist), rather than the expropriation itself, which is definitionally bad, and then the further inference that it is definitionally bad whether or not the expropriation it facilitates is experientially felt as painful. The strategic consequence immediately follows: radical legal reform should aim to eradicate hierarchy and thereby attain a substantively equal social world. Thus we should oppose not what makes us miserable—the violent expropriation of our work or our sexuality—but the hierarchy of power which facilitates it, for by doing so we will better target the true cause of our misery. We should support not what makes us happy, but what makes us substantively equal, because by doing so we will invariably further our true interest, even if not our felt pleasure. Thus, radical feminist legal theory shares with general radical legal thought a refusal to ground its opposition to expropriation (whether of sex or work) in the subjective suffering of the disempowered which such expropriation entails. Instead, for both groups expropriation must be opposed because it is symptomatic of the true cause of our misery—our material or sexual disempowerment, respectively—reflecting in turn our relative material or sexual inequality. The expropriation which the disempowered suffer is regarded by the radical as bad, but not because the expropriation has been shown to be painful, but instead because it is symptomatic of a larger violation of our essential nature, and hence of our inherent ideal.

Finally, radical feminist legal theorists share with radical legalists a methodological insistence that the correlation between objective equality and subjective well-being is foundational and definitional; it is therefore not something that can be discredited by counter-example. Both groups of theorists accordingly refuse to credit the phenomenological evidence that the essentially descriptive claims that underlie the normative commitment to substantive equality may be false. Thus, to radical legalists generally, and to radical feminist legalists in particular, the extent to which the disempowered desire anything other than their own empowerment, and anything at odds with an equalitarian idea, is the extent to which the disempowered are victims of false consciousness. Phenomenological reports by the disempowered of pleasure and desire that counter the radical correlation of equality and subjective well-being thus reinforce, rather than cast in doubt, the radical's definitional assumptions. They reflect the permeating influence of our objective condition, not the limit, imposed by subjective pleasure and desire, of the normative ideal.

The striking political contribution of radical *feminist* legal theory has been to extend the umbrella of the normative argument of radical legalism to include women as well as men, and thus to address hierarchies of gender as well as hierarchies dictated by class and race. * * *

Radical feminist legal theorists' failure to credit phenomenological reports of conflict between egalitarian ideals and women's subjective, hedonic, felt pleasures is generally benign, for one simple reason. The area of conflict is not great. Women want the fruits of substantive equality * * *. Over vast areas of our lives, there is no conflict between our desires, our felt pleasures, and radical feminist ideals.

In one area of our lives, however—namely our erotic lives—there has emerged a conflict between the radical feminist legal theorists' conception of an equalitarian ideal and women's subjective desire. The radical feminist's commitment to equality, and identification of the expropriation of our sexuality as the consequence of our relative disempowerment entails the normative conclusion that sexual inequality *itself* is what is politically undesirable. Thus, male dominance and female submission in sexuality *is* the evil: they express as well as *are* women's substantive inequality. But women report—with increasing frequency and as often as not in consciousness-raising sessions—that equality *in sexuality* is not what we find pleasurable or desirable. Rather, the experience of dominance and submission that go with the controlled, but fantastic, "expropriation" of our sexuality is precisely what *is* sexually desirable, exciting and pleasurable—in fantasy for many; in reality for some. This creates a conflict between theory and method as well as between stated ideal and felt pleasure: what should we *do* when the consciousness that is raised in consciousness-raising finds pleasure in what is definitionally regarded as substantively undesirable sexual submission, domination and erotic inequality? * * *

[Feminists on both sides of the pornography debate] definitionally exclude the very issue which should be of greatest concern to feminists, and that is the meaning and the value, to women, of the pleasure we take in our fantasies of eroticized submission. * * *

I believe that sexual submission has erotic *appeal* and *value* when it is an expression of *trust;* is damaging, injurious and painful when it is an expression of *fear;* and is *dangerous* because of its ambiguity: both others and we ourselves have difficulty in disentangling the two.

Conclusion: Women's Difference, and an Alternative Standard for a Feminist Critique of Law

Although liberal and radical legalism are typically contrasted, as I contrasted them in the bulk of this paper, I want briefly to suggest in this conclusion that it is by virtue of an assumption that liberalism and radicalism share that their respective chosen proxies for well-being—choice and power—are so at odds with women's subjective, hedonic lives. Both liberal and radical legalism share a vision of the human being—and therefore of our subjective well-being—as "autonomous." The liberal insists that choice is necessary for the "true" exercise of that autonomy—and thus is an adequate proxy for subjective well-being—while the radical insists the same for power. But this strategic difference should not blind us to their commonality. Both the liberal and the radical legalist have accepted the Kantian assumption that to be human is to be in some sense autonomous—meaning, minimally, to be differentiated, or individuated, from the rest of social life.

Underlying and underscoring the poor fit between the proxies for subjective well-being endorsed by liberals and radicals—choice and power—and women's subjective, hedonic lives is the simple fact that women's lives—because of our biological, reproductive role—are drastically at odds with this fundamental vision of human life. Women's lives are not autonomous, they are profoundly relational. This is at least the biological reflection, if not the biological cause, of virtually all aspects, hedonic and otherwise, of our "difference." Women, and only women, and most women, transcend physically the differentiation or individuation of biological self from the rest of human life trumpeted as the norm by the entire Kantian tradition. When a woman is pregnant her biological life embraces the embryonic life of another. When she later nurtures children, her needs will embrace their needs. The experience of being human, for women, differentially from men, includes the counter-autonomous experience of a shared physical identity between woman and fetus, as well as the counter-autonomous experience of the emotional and psychological bond between mother and infant.[89]

Our reproductive role renders us non-autonomous in a second, less obvious, but ultimately more far-reaching sense. Emotionally and morally women may benefit from the dependency of the fetus and the infant upon us. But materially we are more often burdened than enriched by that dependency. And because we are burdened, we differentially depend more heavily upon others, both for our own survival, and for the survival of the children who are part of us. Women, more than men, depend upon relationships with others, because the weakest of human beings—infants—depend upon us.

Thus, motherhood leaves us vulnerable: a woman giving birth is unable to defend herself against aggression; a woman nursing an infant is physically exposed; a woman nurturing and feeding the young is less able to feed herself. Motherhood leaves us unequal: because of her distinctive nurturing role, a mother is either stronger or weaker than those to whom she is closest. She is stronger than the infant, and because of her nurturing response to that fact she is weaker than her autonomous brother. Most assuredly, then, a mother is not autonomous; she is both depended upon and thereby dependent on others—she depends upon others who are stronger than she, as others who are weaker depend upon her. To the considerable degree that our potentiality for motherhood defines ourselves, women's lives are relational, not autonomous. As mothers we nurture the weak and we depend upon the strong. More than do men, we live in an interdependent and hierarchical natural web with others of varying degrees of strength.

The goals the liberal and radical seek—increased freedom and increased equality, respectively—are surely intended to benefit the subjective well-being of human beings. That is, they are intended to benefit the well-being of autonomous creatures. These goals will simply not serve women, if women are not "autonomous." If women's "difference" lies in the fact that our lives are relational rather than autonomous, and if autonomy is a necessary attribute of a human being, then women's difference rather abruptly implies that women are not human beings.

89. I am describing the way women's lives are, not the way they should be or have to be, and I therefore see no reason to distinguish biological from social causes of our counter-autonomous lives. If men became more nurturant of children, they too would become less "autonomous." My general point is that whatever subclass of adult human beings nurtures the young will be relatively less autonomous than the subclass that does not.

Politics that are designed to benefit human beings—including liberal and radical legalism—will leave women out in the cold.

This is not a novel insight: that women are not human as human is now conceived has in a sense always been the dominant problem for feminism. But the two characteristic ways in which modern feminist legal theorists have responded to this dilemma are both, I think, flawed. The liberal feminist's solution is to deny it. The fact that women become pregnant, give birth, and nurse infants is a difference that does not count. It does not make us any less "autonomous" than men. For reasons which by now should be familiar, this response does not work: if the last century has taught us anything at all, it is that this liberal strategy of denial is a disservice. If we embrace a false conception of our nature we can be sure of only one thing, and that is that legal reform based on such a conception will only occasionally—and then only incidentally—benefit real instead of hypothetical women.

The radical feminist's proposal is that we seek to become autonomous creatures. We are indeed not "autonomous," but what that reflects is our lack of power—our social, political and legal victimization—not our essential nature. To the extent that we become autonomous by gaining power, we will become the beneficiaries of the legal system designed to promote the well-being of just such people. This radical vision is at root deeply assimilationist—by gaining power, we become equal, as we become equal we become less "relational"—meaning less victimized—as we become less relational we become more autonomous, and as we become more autonomous we become more like "human beings—more like men. Radical assimilation, though, has costs no less weighty (and no less familiar) than liberal denial. There is no guarantee that women can become autonomous "human beings," no guarantee that women want to, and at heart, no persuasive argument that women should.

A very new and third response, which does not fit easily (or at all) within the liberal and radical models described above, and which I think has great promise, is that feminists should insist on women's humanity—and thus on our entitlements—and on the wrongness of the dominant conception of what it means to be a "human being." We should insist * * * [on] an equal "acceptance of our difference." This third course is surely more promising—it has truth and candor on its side—but without hedonistic criticism it is insufficient: which differences are to be accepted? The root of our difference may be that our lives are relational rather than autonomous, which is reflected in our needs and has its roots in our reproductive role. But even thus defined, our "difference" has many dimensions. If "difference" includes our differential suffering, or our differential vulnerability to sexual assault, or our differential endurance of pain, or our differentially negative self-esteem, then "acceptance" of those differences will backfire. We need more than just acceptance of our differences; we need a vocabulary in which to articulate and then evaluate them, as well as the power to reject or affirm them.

Notes on Women's Pleasures and Pains

1. Is West saying that all women are different from all men and that these differences are biologically based? Or is she saying that women today, as a group, tend to be different from men, as a group (though of course there will be overlap between women and men and variation among women and among men)? Is she saying that biology is the basis of whatever differences there are? Is it dangerous and essentialist (that is, equivalent to asserting that biology gives all women the same essential nature) to speak of women's unique physical experiences? Is it necessary? Does she see women's basic nature as determined by their reproductive role?

2. West says that "women are not human as human is now conceived." This is reminiscent of MacKinnon's statement in the first extract in this chapter, Consciousness Raising, that women are "damaged" and "are in fact not full people in the sense that men are allowed to become." What problem is West identifying? Is it the same problem MacKinnon is identifying? What solution is each suggesting? Do you agree with either or both?

3. What does West see as similar in liberal legalism and radical legalism? What does she see as different?

4. Do you agree with West that women feel less separate than men because of their experiences of pregnancy, heterosexual penetration, and breast feeding? Do you think that teenage girls who have not experienced pregnancy, heterosexual penetration, etc., are nevertheless (in general) more relational than teenage boys? What might explain such differences? Do girls and women have cultures that are different in relevant ways from those of boys and men? Might there be a connection between these cultural differences and women's nurture of the young, even though girls have yet to experience heterosexual penetration or motherhood?

5. Jennifer Nedelsky makes a somewhat similar point about the masculine bias in the liberal concept of human nature in Reconceiving Autonomy: Sources, Thoughts, and Possibilities, 1 Yale J. Law & Feminism 7 (1989). According to Nedelsky, the "autonomous individual" of liberalism is a being unconnected to others. Property is "the central symbol for this vision of autonomy, for it can both literally and figuratively provide the necessary walls. The most perfectly autonomous man is thus the most perfectly isolated." Id. at 12. Nedelsky points to the need to develop a more accurate concept of autonomy, one recognizing that:

> what actually enables people to be autonomous * * * is not isolation, but relationships—with parents, teachers, friends, loved ones—that provide the support and guidance necessary for the development and experience of autonomy. I think, therefore, that the most promising model, symbol, or metaphor for autonomy is not property, but child-rearing.

Id. Are women more likely to see people in terms of relationships—even when discussing autonomy—than men? Why might this be true even for lesbians who have not raised children? See also Jennifer Nedelsky, Law, Boundaries, and the Bounded Self, 30 Representations 162 (1990).

6. Is West's analysis heterocentric? What of a lesbian who has never been pregnant or experienced heterosexual intercourse (or experienced it only a few times); is she not essentially a woman? Would she be lacking the "essential" experiences and psychological feelings of women? Might this woman nevertheless see and feel herself as more connected to others and less individuated than men? Why?

7. Which view of what women need—liberal feminism's or radical feminism's or relational feminism's—do you think more accurate? Are there differences here for women in various classes and races? Which goal is strategically better for various groups of women?

8. Is it possible to talk about a material basis for differences between the sexes without thinking that all women and men are "essentially" and "biologically" different (and that all women are the same)? Is it likely that women's material experiences do tend to produce people somewhat different from those without such experiences? If we deny, for strategic reasons, the material bases for differences, are we devaluing—indeed erasing—pregnancy, nursing, etc., as significant human experiences?

9. Are there inherent dangers in focusing on women's pleasures and pains? West suggests that, apart from the erotic, there are few conflicts between women's pleasures and pains and substantive equality. Do you agree? Can you think of other conflicts? Might the *Cal Fed* issue be such a conflict? Why? Can you think of other similar conflicts posed by mothering and caretaking?

10. Might there be instances in which there are conflicts between women's emotions and equality, apart from children and the erotic? In a world of inequality, in which women are socialized differently from men, is success inherently uncomfortable for some women? There is some evidence that women regard success as inconsistent with femininity and that "the anticipation of success, especially in interpersonal competitive situations, can be regarded as a mixed blessing if not an outright threat." Martina S. Horner, Toward an Understanding of Achievement–Related Conflicts in Women, in The Psychology of Women: Ongoing Debates 169, 183 (Mary Roth Walsh, ed., 1987). Why might this be true? Is there a conflict between short-term comfort with a "feminine" role and long-term frustration with that role?

11. Is it true that women fear success? If you are a woman, do you? Do women in your law school class? Do men? There is little evidence that women's fear of success "has a substantial impact on women's lives and professional careers." Michele A. Paludi, Psychometric Properties and Underlying Assumptions of Four Objective Measures of Fear of Success, in Walsh, ed., above note 10, at 200. There is also disagreement about whether women and men differ in fear of success. Id.

12. What are the advantages and disadvantages of West's approach relative to liberal (or formal) equality and MacKinnon's dominance approach? Is there a sense in which West's approach is androcentric—perhaps because, as MacKinnon insists, the feminine voice is the voice created by male domination? Is there nevertheless a sense in which a relational approach is most consistent with feminist methodology? Should feminists

ignore women's subjective pains and pleasures? How would you resolve these tensions?

ALLAN JOHNSON, WHY PATRIARCHY?

In the Gender Knot: Unraveling Our Patriarchal Legacy 26, 31–41 (Temple University Press 1997).

More than anything else, patriarchy is based on control as a core principle around which entire societies are organized. What drives patriarchy as a system—what fuels competition, aggression, and oppression—is a dynamic relationship between control and fear. Patriarchy encourages men to seek security, status, and other rewards through control; to fear other men's ability to control and harm them; and to identify being in control as both their best defense against loss and humiliation and the surest route to what they need and desire.* * *

Patriarchy is grounded in a Great Lie that the answer to life's needs is disconnection and control rather than connection, sharing, and cooperation. The Great Lie separates men from what they need most by encouraging them to be autonomous and disconnected when in fact human existence is fundamentally relational. * * * Who are we if not our ties to other people—"I *am* ... a father, a husband, a worker, a friend, a son, a brother"? But patriarchal magic turns the truth inside out, and "self-made man" goes from oxymoron to cultural ideal. And somewhere between the need for human connection and the imperative to control, the two merge, and a sense of control becomes the closest many men ever come to feeling connected with anything, including themselves.

Patriarchy as Men's Problem

Patriarchy is usually portrayed as something that's primarily between women and men. At first blush this makes a lot of sense, given that "male" and "female" define each other and that women occupy an oppressed position in relation to men. Paradoxically, however, the cycle of control and fear that drives patriarchy has more to do with relations among men than with women, for it's men who control men's standing *as men*. With few exceptions, men look to other men to affirm their manhood, whether as coaches, friends, teammates, co-workers, sports figures, fathers, or mentors.

This contradicts the conventional wisdom that women hold the key to heterosexual men's sense of manhood. It's true that men often use women to show they measure up—especially by controlling women sexually—but the standards that are used are men's, not women's. Men also may try to impress women as "real men" in order to start and keep relationships with them, to control them, or to get sexual access and personal care. This doesn't prove they're real men, however. For affirmation they have to go to a larger male-identified world—from the local bar to sports to work—which is also where they're most vulnerable to other men. Whether in school locker rooms or in the heat of political campaigns, when a man is accused of being a "wimp" or of otherwise failing to measure up, it almost always comes from another man. And when a man suspects himself of being less than a real man, he judges *himself* through a patriarchal male gaze, not from a woman's perspective.

* * *

[There is a widespread belief] that macho displays of manhood are largely confined to lower-and working-class subcultures. The roots of men proving their manhood run deep in the upper classes, from the enthusiastic stampede of Britain's elite to the killing fields of World War I to Kennedy's sexually compulsive private behavior to the San Francisco Bohemian Grove retreats where captains of business and government gather to make deals, mock women in cross-dressing skits, and otherwise relax in the comfort of male privilege. Men, of course, aren't born to this; they must be trained and given ongoing incentives.

In the early 1960s, for example, I was a middle-class freshman at an all-male Ivy League college, a training ground for the sons of the elite. * * * In late fall, dorm residents who'd been accepted to fraternities prepared for "sink night," a time to celebrate their newfound "brotherhood" by getting very drunk. Before they went off, they warned freshmen not to lock our doors when we went to bed because they intended to pay us a visit later on and didn't expect to be stopped by a locked door. We didn't know what was coming, but there was no mistaking the dense familiar weight of men's potential for violence.

When they returned that night, screaming drunk, they went from door to door, rousting us from our beds and herding us into the hall. They lined us up and ordered us to drop our pants. Then one held a metal ruler and another a *Playboy* magazine opened to the centerfold picture, and the two went down the line, thrusting the picture in our faces, screaming "Get it up!" and resting our penises on the ruler. The others paced up and down the hall behind them, yelling, screaming, and laughing, thickening the air with a mixture of alcohol and the potential for violence. None of us protested, and of course none of us "measured up." We weren't supposed to (any man who'd managed an erection would have become a legend on the spot). That, after all, was the point: to submit to the humiliation, to mirror (like women) men's power to control and terrorize in what we later learned was a rite of passage called "the peter meter."

For them, perhaps, it was a passage to a fraternal bond forged in their shared power over the "others"; for us, it was a grant of immunity from having to submit again, at least in this place, to these men, in this way. But our lack of outrage and the general absence of talk about it afterward suggest we got something else as well. As outrageous as the peter meter was, it touched a core of patriarchal truth about men, power and violence that, as men, we found repellant yet ultimately acceptable. The truth is, we, too, got a piece of real-man standing that night, for by deadening and controlling ourselves in the face of an assault, we showed that we had the right stuff. Had anyone protested, he wouldn't have been seen as the more manly for his courage; more likely he'd have been called a sissy, a pussy, a little mama's boy who couldn't take it. And so we both lost and gained during our late-night dip in the patriarchal paradox of men competing and bonding at the same time.

What About Women?

In one sense, women, like all else in patriarchy, are something for men to control. The consequences of this are enormous because of the damage it does to women's lives, but controlling women is neither the point of patriarchy nor the engine that drives it. This means that women's place is more complicated than it might seem, especially in relation to competition among men.

This works in several ways. First, heterosexual men are encouraged to use women as badges of success to protect and enhance their standing in the eyes of other men. People routinely compliment a man married to a beautiful woman, for example, not because he had a hand in making her beautiful but because he has proprietary rights of access to her. In contrast, people are much less likely to compliment a man whose wife is financially successful—especially if she earns more than he does—because this threatens rather than enhances his status as a real man.

* * *

At the same time that men may compete with one another, they're also encouraged to bond around a common view of women as objects to be competed for, possessed, and used. When men tell sexist jokes, for example, or banter about women's bodies, they usually can count on other men to go along (if only in silence), for a man who objects risks becoming an outcast. Even if the joke is directed at his wife or lover, he's likely to choose his tie to men over loyalty to her by letting it pass with a shrug and perhaps a good-natured smile that leaves intact his standing as one of the guys. In this sense, the competitive dynamic of patriarchal heterosexuality brings men together and promotes feelings of solidarity by acting out the values of control and domination. This is partly why there is so much male violence against gay men: since gays don't use women in this way, their sexual orientation challenges not so much heterosexuality per se but male solidarity around the key role of control and domination in patriarchal heterosexuality. John Stoltenberg argues that violence against gays also protects male solidarity by protecting men from sexual aggression at the hands of other men:

> Imagine this country without homophobia: There would be a woman raped every three minutes and a man raped every three minutes. Homophobia keeps that statistic at a manageable level. The system is not fool-proof. It breaks down, for instance, in prison and in childhood—when men and boys are often subject to the same sexual terrorism that women live with almost all the time. But for the most part homophobia serves male supremacy by keeping males who act

like real men safe from sexual assault.[26]

A second part that women play in men's struggle for control is to support the idea that men and women are fundamentally different, because this gives men a clear and unambiguous turf—masculinity—on which to pursue control in competition with one another. Women do this primarily by supporting (or at least not challenging) femininity as a valid view of women and how they're supposed to be. The idea that male sexuality is inherently aggressive, predatory, and heterosexual, for example, defines a common ground for men in relation to both women and other men. To protect this, it's important that women not be sexually aggressive or predatory because this would challenge the idea of a unique male sexuality as a basis for male solidarity and competition.

When women challenge stereotypically feminine ways of acting, it makes it harder for men to see themselves clearly as men. This muddles men's relationships with men and their standing as real men under patriarchy. * * *

In a third sense, a woman's place is to support the key patriarchal illusion that men are independent and autonomous. An unemployed wife who sees herself as dependent, for example, props up images of male independence that mask men's considerable dependence on women for emotional support, physical comfort and a broad range of practical services. On the average, for example, married men are both mentally and physically healthier than single men and live longer, whereas for women just the opposite is true. Men also tend to have a much harder time adjusting to the loss of a spouse than women do, especially at older ages. And the standard model for a career still assumes a wife at home to perform support work, and any man (or woman) who doesn't have one is at a disadvantage.

* * *

You might think that such arrangements are a thing of the past, that with so many married women working outside the home, the breadwinner role is no longer male identified. But the superficial appearance of gender equity and balance masks a continuing imbalance that's revealed when we consider how men and women would be affected by leaving paid employment. If the woman in a two-earner household were to give up breadwinning, it might create hardships and negative feelings, but these probably wouldn't include making her feel less than a real woman. But for a man to give up the breadwinning role, he'd have to contend with far more serious threats to his sense of himself as a real man, and both women and men know it. This is why, when someone in a marriage has to leave paid employment—to take care of children or ailing relatives, for example—it is generally understood that it will be the woman, regardless of who earns more.

26. John Stoltenberg, "Pornography and Freedom," in *Men's Lives*, ed. Michael S. Kimmel and Michael A. Messner, (New York: Macmillan, 1989), 482–488.

A fourth aspect of women's place is to help contain men's resentment over being controlled *by other men* so that it doesn't overpower the male solidarity that's so essential to patriarchy. Most men are dominated by other men, especially at work, and yet judge their manhood by how much control they have in their own lives. It's a standard against which they're bound to fall short. If they rebel against other men—as in worker strikes—the risks are often huge and the gains short-lived. A safer alternative is to accept as compensation social support to control and feel superior to women. This provides both individual men and patriarchy with a safety valve for the frustration and rage that might otherwise be directed toward other men and at far greater risk to both individuals and the system as a whole. No matter what other men do to a man or how deeply they control his life, he can always feel culturally superior to women and take out his anger and frustration on them.

In this way, men are allowed to dominate women as a kind of compensation for their being subordinated to other men because of social class, race, or other forms of inequality. Ironically, however, their dominance of women supports the same principles of control that enable other men to subordinate them, a contradiction that is typical of oppressive systems. Man may buy into this so long as they can, in turn, enjoy the dominance that comes with applying those principles to women. The use of such compensation to stabilize systems also works with race and class inequality where one oppression is used to compensate for another.
* * *

Related to men's use of women as compensation is the expectation that women will take care of men who have been damaged by other men. When he comes home from work, he wants a woman there to greet and take care of him, whether or not she's been at work all day herself. On a deeper level, he wants her to make him feel whole again, to restore what he loses through his disconnected pursuit of control, to calm his fears—all, of course, without requiring him to face the very things about himself and patriarchy that produce the damage in the first place. When women fail to "make it better"—and they are bound to fail eventually—they are also there to accept the blame and receive men's disappointment, pain, and rage. Men who feel unloved, incomplete, disconnected, battered, humiliated, frightened, and anxious routinely blame women for not supporting or loving them enough. It's a responsibility women are encouraged to accept, which is one reason so many victims of domestic violence stay with the men who abuse them.

Misogyny

These days even the slightest criticism of men or male dominance can prompt accusations of "man hating" or "male bashing' " but only feminists seem to care about the cultural woman hating that's been around for millennia as part of everyday life under patriarchy. Men's hypersensitivity is typical of dominant groups such as whites who often react strongly when blacks refer to whites as "honkies" or merely express anger over continuing white resistance to dealing with the everyday reality of racism. But whites barely notice the racial hostility that pervades the lives of minorities, for part of white privilege is the subtle arrogance of not having to pay attention to how that privilege affects others. What men don't get about gender, white people don't get about race: whites don't have to go out of their way to *act* hatefully in order to participate in a society that produces hateful consequences for people of color. Simply flowing with the mainstream and going about business as usual is enough.

The cultural expression of misogyny—the hatred (*mis-*) of femaleness (*gyny*)—takes many forms. It's found in ancient and modern beliefs that women are inherently evil and a primary cause of human misery—products of what the Greek philosopher and mathematician Pythagoras called the "evil principle which created chaos, darkness, and woman." There is misogyny in the violent pornography that portrays women as willing victims of exploitation and abuse, in jokes about everything from mothers-in-law to the slapping around or "good fuck" that some women "need." Misogyny shaped the historical transformation of ancient wise-women healers into modern-day images of witches who roast and eat children; in the torture and murder of millions of women from the witch hunts of the Middle Ages to recent Serb terrorism in Bosnia; in the everyday reality of sexual coercion, abuse, violence, and harassment; in the mass media display of women's bodies as objects existing primarily to please men and satisfy the male gaze; in cultural ideals of slenderness that turn women against their own bodies and inspire self-hatred and denial; in the steady stream of sensationalized and sexualized mass media "entertainment" in which men terrorize, torture, rape, and murder women.

Not to be overlooked is the routine of insulting males with names that link them to females—sissy (sister), girl, pussy, son of a bitch, mama's boy. Notice, however, that the worst way to insult a woman isn't to call her a man or a "daddy's girl"; it's to call her a woman by another name by highlighting or maligning femaleness itself—bitch, whore, cunt. The use of such words as insults is made even worse by the fact that prior to patriarchy many had neutral or positive meanings for women. A "whore" was a lover of either sex; "bitch" was associated with the pre-Christian goddess of the hunt, Artemis–Diana; and "cunt" derives from several sources, including the goddesses of Cunti and Kunda, the universal sources of life.

It's difficult to accept the idea that in the midst of wanting, needing, and loving women—if only as sons in relation to mothers—men are involved in a system that makes misogynist feelings, thoughts, and behavior paths of least resistance. Most men would probably deny this affects them in any way; often the most sexist men are among the first to say how much they love women. But there's no escaping misogyny, because it isn't a personality flaw; it's a part of patriarchal culture. We're like fish swimming in a sea laced with it, and we can't breathe without passing it through our gills. Misogyny infuses into our cells and becomes part of who we are because by the time we know enough to reject it, it's too late. As with everything else in a culture, some people are exposed to more of it than others; but to suppose that anyone escapes untouched is both wishful and disempowering. It's wishful because it goes against what we know about socialization and the power of culture to shape reality; it's disempowering because if we believe that misogyny doesn't involve us, we won't feel compelled to do anything about it.

Misogyny plays a complex role in patriarchy. It fuels men's sense of superiority, justifies male aggression against women, and works to keep women on the defensive and in their place. Misogyny is especially powerful in encouraging women to hate their own femaleness, an example of internalized oppression. The more women internalize misogynist images and attitudes, the harder it is to challenge male privilege or patriarchy as a system. In fact, women won't tend to see patriarchy as even problematic since the essence of self-hatred is to focus on the self as the sole cause of misery, including the self-hatred.

In another sense, patriarchy promotes the hatred of women as a reaction to men's fear of women. Why should men fear women? Every oppressive system depends to some degree on subordinate groups being willing to go along with their own subordination. The other side of this, however, is the potential to undermine and rebel. This makes oppression inherently unstable and makes dominant groups vulnerable. Throughout the slave-holding South, for example, white people's fear of slave revolts was woven into the fabric of everyday life and caused many a restless night. And I suspect that much of the discomfort that whites feel around blacks today, especially black men, also reflects a fear that the potential for challenge and rebellion is never far from the surface. For men, the fear is that women will stop playing the complex role that allows patriarchy to continue, or may even go so far as to challenge male privilege directly. Women's potential to disrupt patriarchy and make men vulnerable is why it's so easy for women to make men feel foolish or emasculated through the mildest humor that focuses on maleness and hints at women's power to stop going along with the status quo. Making fun of men, however, is just the tip of the iceberg of what women can do to disturb the patriarchal order, and on some level most men know this and have reason to feel threatened by it.

In more subtle ways, misogyny arises out of a system that offers women to men as a form of compensation. Because patriarchy limits men's emotional and spiritual lives, and because men rarely risk being vulnerable with other men, they often look to women as a way to ease their sense of emptiness, meaninglessness, and disconnection. However, the patriarchal expectation that "real men" are autonomous and independent sets men up to both want and resent women at the same time. This is made all the worse by the fact that women can't possibly give men what they want. Caught in this bind, men could face the truth of the system that put them in it in the first place. They could look at patriarchy and how their position in it creates this dilemma. The path of least resistance, however, is to resent and blame women for what men lack, by accusing women of not being loving or sexual enough, of being manipulative, withholding, selfish bitches who deserve to be punished.

In a related sense, misogyny can reflect male envy of the human qualities patriarchy encourages men to devalue and deny in themselves as they avoid association with anything remotely female. Under patriarchy, women are viewed as trustees of all that makes a rich emotional life possible—of empathy and sympathy, vulnerability and openness to connection, caring and nurturing, sensitivity and compassion, emotional attention and expressiveness—all of which are driven out by the cycle of control and fear. On some level, men know the value of what they don't have and see women as privileged for being able to hold on to it. As a result, women live a double bind: the patriarchal ideology that supports women's oppression devalues the human qualities associated with being female, yet it also sets men up to envy and resent women for being able to weave those same qualities into their lives.

Finally, misogyny can be seen as a cultural result of men's potential to feel guilty about women's oppression. Rather than encourage men to feel guilty, patriarchal culture projects negative judgments about men onto women. When men do feel guilty, they can blame women for making them feel this way: "If you weren't there reminding me of how oppressed women are, then I wouldn't have to feel bad about myself as a member of the group that benefits from it." Anger and resentment play this kind of role in many oppressive systems. When middle-class people encounter the homeless on the street, for example, it's not uncommon for them to feel angry simply for being reminded of their privilege and their potential to feel guilty about it. It's easier to hate the messenger than it is to take some responsibility for doing something about the reality behind the message.

As a mainstay of patriarchal culture, misogyny embodies some of the most contradictory and disturbing aspects of gender oppression. When love and need are bound up with fear and envy, hate and resentment, the result is an explosive mixture that can twist our sense of ourselves and one another beyond recognition. If misogyny were merely a problem of bad personal attitudes, it would relatively easy to deal with. But its close connection to the cycle of control and fear that makes patriarchy work will make it part of human life as long as patriarchy exists.

Notes on Patriarchy

1. Do you agree with Johnson that patriarchy's driving force is *not* the desire to subordinate women? What does he see as the driving force of patriarchy? What exactly does he see as the relationship between patriarchy and women's subordination? Would MacKinnon agree with him? What would she see as the driving force of patriarchy? Which view is more accurate in your opinion?

2. Compare Johnson's focus on and analysis of power with MacKinnon's. Compare their attitudes towards men. (Look, for example, at the

fifth paragraph and the last paragraph of MacKinnon, Consciousness Raising, above.) How does Johnson explain men's subordination of women? How does MacKinnon? Which view is more accurate in your opinion?

3. In your view, based on heterosexual relationships you have observed first hand or been involved in, who is more dependent on their partner, the man or the woman? In what ways have you observed men depend on women? In what ways have you observed women depend on men? Why do we tend to think of only women as "dependent"?

4. Compare Johnson's discussion of patriarchy's "Great Lie" and West's critique of liberal and radical notions of what it means to be human (particularly for women). Do you think that the extract from Johnson belongs in this section on relational feminism? Why or why not?

5. Without stopping to think or censor yourself, write down 5 words you associate with masculinity and 5 words you associate with femininity. Compare your responses with those of other people in the course. If there is significant overlap, explain the source of your shared understanding of these words. How might these understandings of masculinity and femininity contribute to the subordination of women to men and harm men as well as women?

6. Do you agree with Johnson that there is a widespread belief "that macho displays of manhood are largely confined to lower-and working-class subcultures"? Do you agree with him that this belief is not true? Compare standards of masculinity for boys and men of various ages and classes. Do standards of masculinity also vary with culture? Can you describe some of the cultural variations of masculinity within the United States? How do standards of femininity vary for women of various classes or cultural backgrounds?

7. Can you identify some ways in which your fathers or brothers or other men you know have been hurt by the pressure to conform to narrow notions of masculinity?

8. Identify some ways in which whites routinely "participate in a society that produces hateful consequences for people of color," as described by Johnson. Identify some ways in which men routinely "participate in a society that produces hateful consequences" for women.

9. Do you agree with Johnson that men's superiority over women is a crucial component of male solidarity, operating as a reward (compensation) for the fact that most (all?) men are controlled by other men? If this is true, how would you expect male solidarity to manifest itself in ordinary politics? Do you see evidence of such effects?

10. What do you make of the story about the "peter meter"? What is the point of hazing rituals among young men, such as the rituals at VMI? Are such rituals more common among young men than young women? If so, why? Do you agree with Johnson's analysis of his peter-meter experience?

11. What does Johnson see as the links between homophobia and inequality between women and men? Do you agree? Do you see other links? Johnson mentions links between bias against gay men and inequality between the sexes. Can you see links between bias against lesbians and inequality between women and men?

12. Do you agree with Stoltenberg, quoted by Johnson above, that but for homophobia, as many men as women would be raped?

13. In the next to the last paragraph of the essay above, Johnson says that men do feel guilty about women's oppression, but misogyny helps men blame women for their guilt. Have you observed the phenomenon he describes in that paragraph? Have you seen men respond to the mere mention of proven facts (such as that many men rape women and that many husbands are violent) with rejoinders such as that the speaker is attacking men or hates men?

14. Does Johnson's explanation (in the last paragraph) of the complex mixture of emotions men feel towards women—love, need, fear, envy, hate, and resentment—help you understand male-on-female violence? What does explain why men sexually torture and violently rape women?

15. Most (all?) men do not feel on top of everything because they are not, particularly at work. And men suffer under patriarchy by, for example, distancing themselves from their emotions and denying their expression. Does it follow that men are oppressed as a group? Johnson says no.

> [A] group cannot oppress itself. A group can inflict injury on itself, and its members can suffer from their position in society. But if we say that a group can oppress or persecute *itself* we turn the concept of social oppression into a mere synonym for socially caused suffering, which it isn't. Oppression is a social phenomenon that happens between different groups in a society; it is a system of social inequality through which one group is positioned to dominate and benefit from the exploitation and subordination of another. This means not only that a group cannot oppress itself, but also that it cannot be oppressed *by society*. Oppression is a relation that exists *between groups,* not between groups and society as a whole.

Johnson, above, at 20; see also 20–23; 174–180. Would MacKinnon agree? Would Ginsburg? If Johnson is right, does it follow that formal equality is a fundamentally flawed approach to eliminating inequality between the sexes?

16. In a 1983 essay, Marilyn Frye describes oppression:

> The experience of oppressed people is that the living of one's life is confined and shaped by forces and barriers which are not accidental or occasional and hence avoidable, but are systematically related to each other in such a way as to catch one between and among them and restrict or penalize motion in any direction. It is the experience of being caged in: all avenues, in every direction, are blocked or booby trapped.
>
> Cages. Consider a bird cage. If you look very closely at just one wire in the cage, you cannot see the other wires.

Frye, Oppression in The Politics of Reality: Essays in Feminist Theory 1, 4 (1983). Frye points out that those on each side of a barrier face it, but they do not necessarily face similar barriers. Consider a prison wall. Would Frye agree with Johnson that men are not oppressed as men? Do you agree with either?

17. According to Johnson, women and men become invisible under different circumstances under patriarchy:

> In general, women are made invisible when they do something that might elevate their status, such as raising children into healthy adults or coming up with a brilliant idea in a business meeting. Men, however, are often made invisible when their behavior is socially undesirable and might raise questions about the appropriateness of male privilege. Although the vast majority of violent acts are perpetrated by men, for example, new accounts rarely call attention to the gender of those who rape, kill, beat, and torture others, while characteristics such as race, ethnicity, and age are routinely highlighted as socially significant.

Johnson, above at 156. Can you think of examples or counter-examples of each phenomenon?

MARY BECKER, TOWARDS A SUBSTANTIVE FEMINISM

[an earlier version of this essay appears in [1999] U. Chi. Legal Forum 21.]

Neither of the two dominant strands of feminism in the United States today can challenge patriarchy, with its glorification of masculinity defined in terms of power and control. Formal equality cannot do so because it is empty of values: it gives women only the right to what men are entitled to under the rules and values worked out by and for men. Dominance feminism, with its focus on power as it is defined in our society, does have a value (power), but it is a patriarchal value. And it is quite possible to give power to *some* women, women who share patriarchal values and attitudes (or who pretend they do), without threatening patriarchy as a social system. In this essay, I describe a Relational Feminism, with roots in cultural feminism, but building on the work of West and Johnson. Unlike formal equality and dominance feminism, relational feminism does have the potential to challenge patriarchy because it emphasizes values inconsistent with patriarchal values: caretaking and relationships.

RELATIONAL FEMINISM

Cultural feminism is often traced to Carol Gilligan's 1982 book, *In a Different Voice* (extract above). Cultural feminism generally means—across academic disciplines—a feminism celebrating the value of traditionally feminine qualities and activities, including in particular caring for others and valuing relationships. This valorization is sometimes described by critics as a claim that women are innately superior to men. And cultural feminism is routinely criticized for encouraging women to play their traditional roles, roles designed by and for men and inconsistent with any form of equality.

Robin West has developed the most thorough application of cultural feminism in legal contexts. In a recent book, Robin West argues that both justice (or some attribute of justice such as institutional consistency, personal integrity, or impartiality) and care are required for moral decisionmaking. In using the word "care," West begins with the nurture of individuals: "When we nurture, we nurture particular persons, not groups, nations, or species, and when we nurture a particular person, we seek to make that person as fulfilled as possible."[1] The "circle of care" can also extend to groups and be the basis of an egalitarian social order based on "a sense of brotherhood and sisterhood" rather than on "an abstract and bloodless zeal for consistency."[2]

Progressive social programs, such as "wealth redistribution, progressive taxation, welfare programs, or subsistence rights," can be based on empathy with those in need.[3] Empathy can be the basis for "a commitment to egalitarianism, albeit grounded in shared fellow feeling rather than in principle."[4] West concludes that "[o]f the two commitments" to egalitarianism, "one from principle" (an abstract commitment to equality for those similarly situated) and "one from fellow feeling" (an empathy-based commitment to help those in need), the commitment based on empathy may "prove to be the more enduring."[5]

West points out that a commitment to nurture based on needs, empathy, and feeling may also be less empty than a commitment to equality. An abstract commitment to equality, understood as treating similarly those similarly situated, will do little to help eliminate real social inequalities, since those who are unequal (the rich and the poor, the abled and the disabled, women who are caretakers as well as workers and men who are primarily workers) will not be similarly situated. On the other hand, a commitment to help those in need can translate into an obligation of those who are best off to help those in far-different circumstances because of "shared fellow feeling."[6] To the extent such empathy actually exists, there will be a commitment to doing something despite, indeed because of, differences.

The goal of relational feminism is a society in which all human beings, women as well as men, can find human fulfillment and happiness. We need, therefore to target *both* the cultural *over*valuation of masculine qualities and the cultural *under*valuation of feminine qualities; the cultural focus on men and their needs and the concomitant tendency to see women as less than fully human and their injuries or needs as the result of their own (unfortunate) choices. We must also target the cultural insistence that women and men are essentially different. In the ideal world of relational feminists, women and men would have access to the support and opportunities necessary for human fulfillment and happiness; valuable traits would be valued whether masculine or feminine and whether displayed by women or men. Relational feminism stresses the need to value community, relationships, and traditional feminine qualities because these valuable qualities have been so undervalued in our overly individualistic and masculinist culture.

Relational feminism does not reject as always inappropriate either the equal treatment of similarly-situated women and men (formal equality's focus) or more power as it is currently defined (dominance femi-

1. Robin West, Caring for Justice 69 (1997).

2. Id. at 72.

3. Id.

4. Id.

5. Id.

6. Id.

nism's focus). But relational equality has a different focus: working for human happiness and fulfillment for women (and men). Often, similar treatment of similarly-situated women and men will be appropriate from a relational feminist perspective. And often, giving more power, as it is currently described, to women will be appropriate. All else being equal, it is good (conducive to human happiness and fulfillment) for similar individuals to be treated similarly regardless of sex and good for women to have as much power, as it is currently described, as men. Sometimes, however, all is not otherwise equal, and other goods may be more important for women than either of these. More importantly, one's focus determines one's agenda and priorities. Relational feminism's focus will produce a quite different agenda with quite different priorities from either a formal equality or dominance focus.

VALUES AND PERSPECTIVES

1. *Commit to care and nurture others and to value the relationships and caretaking of others.* Allan Johnson characterizes our culture's insistence that people are separate and autonomous rather than fundamentally relational as patriarchy's "Great Lie." To counter this lie, we must insist on the value of just and caring relationships and of caretaking, with particular emphasis on the need to ensure the economic well-being of dependents' caretakers.

2. *Recognize that women and men sometimes have conflicting interests, and value policies serving women's needs when different from men's.* Because a patriarchal society is male-centered and male-identified, men's needs tend to dominate the agenda. In addition, patriarchy denies any conflicts of interest between women and men. An explicit focus on women's needs and how to meet them is necessary because a patriarchal culture's consideration of human needs will inevitably and even unintentionally focus on male needs and perspectives. A woman-centered focus will threaten patriarchy because it places women's needs at the center, an activity inconsistent with patriarchy's androcentrism.

3. *Value female sexual agency.* Patriarchy denies that women can be sexual agents making moral decisions in light of their own sexual desires. Patriarchy teaches that a woman should agree to sex with "her" man when he desires it regardless of whether she desires it or is likely to find it pleasurable. As beings with their own ends and purposes, women should be encouraged to develop as sexual agents, capable of saying "no" to sex they do not desire and of seeking their own sexual pleasures.

4. *Value qualities that are valuable regardless of whether they are displayed by a woman or a man.* Because patriarchy rests on the belief that women and men are essentially different, patriarchy values and rewards women and men for conforming to gender stereotypes. For example, in custody disputes, many courts consider economic stability as a reason for awarding custody to the father,

who has been the primary breadwinner throughout the marriage. In contrast, mothers who have worked for wages throughout the marriage, most of whom have also been primary caretakers of the children, often lose custody because they work outside the home. It is important to break the link between sex and valuation.

CONSTITUTIONAL STANDARDS AND COURT ENFORCEMENT

Patriarchy is far too malleable and flexible to be "caught" by any standard capable of being administered by courts. One could ask courts to determine whether a challenged rule or policy contributes to inequality between women and men under a relational feminist analysis, just as MacKinnon asks judges to determine whether a rule or policy contributes to the inequitable distribution of power between women and men. But neither standard would be judicially manageable. The problem is never one rule or practice in isolation, but how it works and what it means within its surrounding social structures. In addition, the answer depends on what alternative will ultimately replace the challenged rule, a matter beyond the control, and often beyond the knowledge, of courts.

Nor is any judicially-manageable standard consistent with the experimentation needed to discover what a world of equality between women and men might look like and what sorts of policies and approaches are appropriate in moving towards that world. We don't—and can't—know what is the ideal approach to inequality between all women and men in all variations of class, race, and culture in the United States.

Given the difficulty of figuring out the proper approach to a particular issue in this very complicated world, any approach to eliminating oppressions of race, class, sex, and sexual orientation must necessarily be experimental and tentative.

Notes on Feminism and Values

1. How would a relational feminist approach the issue in *Cal Fed*? What would be the key question? How would she begin thinking about the issue? What factors would she consider? How would she reach a conclusion? What sorts of results might make her rethink her position? Why might experimentation be desirable, even necessary?

2. What links can you see between cultural feminism, as exemplified in Gilligan's work, above, and relational feminism? What differences do you see?

3. Does relational feminism claim that women's values are superior to men's and that women are innately superior to men?

4. Does the relational feminism described above eliminate the problem with cultural feminism's valorization of traditionally feminine values? Can the problem be eliminated or is it inevitable given patriarchal culture's overvaluation of the masculine and undervaluation of the feminine? Do West, Johnson, and Becker successfully avoid valorizing women as morally superior beings? Does Becker's analysis encourage women to play traditional roles?

5. How would the focus of analysis and the agenda for change differ for a feminist committed to formal equality, dominance theory, and relational feminism? For formal equality, dominance feminism, and relational feminism, list the top 2–3 items you would include on the agenda. Are there links between the various agendas and the needs of women of varying classes and races?

6. In deciding whether a rule or policy contributes to inequality between the sexes under a relational feminist approach, what would you look at? How would you decide? In deciding whether a rule or policy contributes to inequality between the sexes under a dominance approach, what would you look at? How would you decide? What would be the difference between the two standards? Would either be judicially manageable?

7. Do you agree with Becker that "it is quite possible to give power to *some* women, women who share patriarchal values and attitudes (or who pretend they do), without threatening patriarchy as a social system"? Johnson also makes this point: "patriarchy can accommodate a limited number of powerful women so long as the society retains its essential patriarchal character, especially in being male identified." Johnson, above, at 7. Can you give examples from current world events or from your own experiences?

8. What kinds of policies would foster female sexual agency? What would female sexual agency look like? How would it differ from female sexuality in the United States today? In a world which recognized, respected, supported, and fostered female sexual agency, would women who did not want to become pregnant engage in uncontracepted heterosexual intercourse? Would women consent to unwanted sex? When would women engage in sexual activities? Might the meaning of "sex" change? How is "sex" defined in our culture (i.e., what would you count to answer the question: how many times did you have sex last month)?

9. Prepare a chart like the one that follows. Use it to identify and contrast some of the major differences among formal equality, dominance feminism, and relational feminism. In row 1, identify what a world of equality would look like under each theory. How would you know you had reached equality under each of the three approaches? In row 2, identify what each theory views as the major problem(s) associated with inequality. In row 3, describe what each theory views as the deep problem, root, or mainspring of inequality. In row 4, describe the ideal world each approach envisions. In row 5, list the values underlying each theory. In row 6, describe the method used by each approach. In rows 7 and 8, describe the strengths and weaknesses of each approach.

Theory	**Formal Equality** (Ginsburg, S.Ct.)	**Dominance Feminism** (MacKinnon)	**Relational Feminism** (Becker, West)
1. Equality Principle			
2. Targeted Inequalities			
3. Fundamental Problem			
4. Ideal World			

Theory	Formal Equality (Ginsburg, S.Ct.)	Dominance Feminism (MacKinnon)	Relational Feminism (Becker, West)
5. Values			
6. Method			
7. Strengths			
8. Weaknesses			

4. PRAGMATIC FEMINISM

MARGARET JANE RADIN, THE PRAGMATIST AND THE FEMINIST

63 S.Cal.L.Rev. 1699–1701, 1704, 1706–08 (1990).

I begin at the point it became clear to me that I was combining pragmatism and feminism. That point was in my thinking about the transition problem of the double bind in the context of contested commodification of sexuality and reproductive capacity. If the social regime permits buying and selling of sexual and reproductive activities, thereby treating them as fungible market commodities given the current capitalistic understandings of monetary exchange, there is a threat to the personhood of women, who are the "owners" of these "commodities." The threat to personhood from commodification arises because essential attributes are treated as severable fungible objects, and this denies the integrity and uniqueness of the self. But if the social regime prohibits this kind of commodification, it denies women the choice to market their sexual or reproductive services, and given the current feminization of poverty and lack of avenues for free choice for women, this also poses a threat to the personhood of women. The threat from enforced noncommodification arises because narrowing women's choices is a threat to liberation, and because their choices to market sexual or reproductive services, even if nonideal, may represent the best alternatives available to those who would choose them.

Thus the double bind: both commodification and noncommodification may be harmful. Harmful, that is, under our current social conditions. Neither one need be harmful in an ideal world. The fact that money changes hands need not necessarily contaminate human interactions of sharing, nor must the fact that a social order makes nonmonetary sharing its norm necessarily deprive or subordinate anyone. That commodification now tends toward fungibility of women and noncommodification now tends toward their domination and continued subordination are artifacts of the current social hierarchy. In other words, the fact of oppression is what gives rise to the double bind.

Thus, it appears that the solution to the double bind is not to solve but to dissolve it: remove the oppressive circumstances. But in the meantime, if we are practically limited to those two choices, which are we to choose? I think that the answer must be pragmatic. We must look carefully at the nonideal circumstances in each case and decide which horn of the dilemma is better (or less bad), and we must keep re-deciding as time goes on.

To generalize a bit, it seems that there are two ways to think about justice. One is to think about justice in an ideal world, the best world that we can now conceive. The other is to think about nonideal justice: given where we now find ourselves, what is the better decision? In making this decision, we think about what actions can bring us closer to ideal justice. For example, if we allow commodification, we may push further away any ideal of a less commodified future. But if we enforce noncommodification, we may push further away any ideal of a less dominated future. In making our decisions of nonideal justice, we must also realize that these decisions will help to reconstitute our ideals. For example, if we commodify all attributes of personhood, the ideal of personhood we now know will evolve into another one that does not conceive fungibility as bad. The double bind, then, is a problem involving nonideal justice, and I think its only solution can be pragmatic. There is no general solution; there are only piecemeal, temporary solutions.

I also think of the double bind as a problem of transition, because I think of nonideal justice as the process by which we try to make progress (effect a transition) toward our vision of the good world. I think we should recognize that all decisions about justice, as opposed to theories about it, are pragmatic decisions in the transition. At the same time we should also recognize that ideal theory is also necessary, because we need to know what we are trying to achieve. In other words, our visions and nonideal decisions, our theory and practice, paradoxically constitute each other.

Having discovered the double bind in true pragmatic fashion, by working on a specific problem, I now see it everywhere. The double bind is pervasive in the issues we have thought of as "women's issues." The reason it is pervasive is to be sought in the perspective of oppression. For a group subject to structures of domination, all roads thought to be progressive can pack a backlash. * * *

Perhaps it is obvious that the reason the double bind recurs throughout feminist struggles is that it is an artifact of the dominant social conception of the meaning of gender. The double bind is a series of two-pronged dilemmas in which both prongs are, or can be, losers for the oppressed. Once we realize this, we may say it is equally obvious that the way out of the double bind is to dissolve these dilemmas by changing the framework that creates them. That is, we must dissolve the prevalent conception of gender.

Calling for dissolution of the prevalent conception of gender is the visionary half of the problem: we must create a new vision of the meaning of male and female in order to change the dominant social conception of gender and change the double bind. In order to do that, however, we need the social empowerment that the dominant social conception of gender keeps us from achieving.

Then how can we make progress? The other half of the problem is the nonideal problem of transition from the present situation toward our ideal. Here is where the pragmatist feminist comes into her own. The pragmatist solution is to confront each dilemma separately and choose the alternative that will hinder empowerment the least and further it the most. The pragmatist feminist need not seek a general solution that will dictate how to resolve all double bind issues. Appropriate solutions may all differ, depending on the current stage of women's empowerment, and how the proposed solution might move the current social conception of gender and our vision of how gender should be reconceived for the future. Indeed, the "same" double bind may demand a different solution tomorrow from the one we find best today.

* * *

The pragmatists were famous for their theory of truth without the capital T—their theory that truth is inevitably plural, concrete, and provisional. John Dewey wrote, "Truth is a collection of truths; and these constituent truths are in the keeping of the best available methods of inquiry and testing as to matters-of-fact ." * * *

Pragmatism and feminism largely share, I think, the commitment to finding knowledge in the particulars of experience. It is a commitment against abstract idealism, transcendence, foundationalism, and atemporal universality; and in favor of immanence, historicity, concreteness, situatedness, contextuality, embeddedness, narrativity of meaning.

If feminists largely share the pragmatist commitment that truth is hammered out piecemeal in the crucible of life and our situatedness, they also share the pragmatist understanding that truth is provisional and everchanging. Too, they also share the pragmatist commitment to concrete particulars. Since the details of our life are connected with what we know, those details matter. Thus, the pragmatist and the feminist both arrive at an embodied perspectivist view of knowledge.

It is not surprising that pragmatists have stressed embodiment more than other philosophers, nor that feminists have stressed it even more. Once we understand that the details of our embodiment matter for what the world is for us (which in some pragmatist views is all the world is), then it must indeed be important that only one half of humans directly experience menstruation, pregnancy, birth, and lactation. So it is no wonder that feminists write about prostitution, contract motherhood, rape, child care, and the PMS defense. It is not just the fact that these are women's issues that makes these writings feminist—they are after all human issues—but specifically the instantiation of the perspective of female embodiment.

Another pragmatist commitment that is largely shared by feminists is the dissolution of traditional dichotomies. Pragmatists and feminists have rejected the dichotomy between thought and action, or between theory and practice. John Dewey especially made this his theme; and he also rejected the dichotomies of reason and feeling, mind and body, nature and nurture, connection and separation, and means and ends. In a commitment that is not, at least not yet, shared by modern pragmatists, feminists have also largely rejected the traditional dichotomy of public (man) and private (woman). For these feminists, the personal is political.

One more strong resonance between the pragmatist and the feminist is in concrete methodology. The feminist commitment to learning through consciousness raising in groups can be regarded as the culmination of the pragmatist understanding that, for consciousness to exist at all, there must be shared meaning arising out of shared interactions with the world. * * *

Notes on Pragmatic Feminism

1. Earlier writers discussed Radin's double bind using somewhat different terms. In a 1983 essay, Marilyn Frye defines oppression as being literally pressed in many directions:

> Something pressed is something caught between or among forces and barriers which are so related to each other that jointly they restrain, restrict or prevent the thing's motion or mobility. * * *
>
> One of the most characteristic and ubiquitous features of the world as experienced by oppressed people is the double bind—situations in which options are reduced to a very few and all of them expose one to penalty, censure or deprivation.

Frye, Oppression in The Politics of Reality: Essays in Feminist Theory 1, 2 (1983). As examples, Frye points to the pressures on young women to be, and to not be, sexually active and the pressures on all subordinated people to "smile and be cheerful," thus participating in the denial of their oppression, or face alternatives which are can be worse, such as loss of one's livelihood for being "mean, bitter, angry, or dangerous." Id. at 2–3. If you are a woman of any color or a member of a minority group, describe some of the double binds you face on a daily basis. Do you feel double binds within the law school? When interviewing with or working at law firms?

2. Christine A. Littleton called the double bind "the problem of transition." Littleton, Women's Experience and the Problem of Transition: Perspectives on Male Battering of Women, [1989] U. Chi. Legal F. 23. Littleton argued that in a world of inequality, there are no risk-free strategies for improving women's situation. Do you agree? Is the double bind always present or only usually or occasionally present when one considers how to resolve a legal issue?

3. Mari Matsuda has argued that pragmatism should be bent

> toward liberation in three ways: First, I would weight the pragmatic method to identify and give special credence to the perspective of the subordinated; second, I would add a first principle of anti-subordination; and third, I would claim that the use of pragmatic method with a normative first principle is not inconsistent.

Matsuda, Pragmatism Modified and The False Consciousness Problem, 63 S. Cal. L. Rev. 1763, 1764 (1990). Do you agree? What are the arguments for and against giving "special credence to the perspective of the subordinated"? How would a pragmatist approach the elimination of subordination?

4. At some level, each of the major feminist approaches described thus far is pragmatic. A dominance theorist would be pragmatic about how best to change the distribution of power between women and men. A formal equality feminist would be pragmatic about which gender-neutral rule to adopt, whether, for example, to adopt an unpaid parental leave policy as soon as it is politically feasible or hold out for paid parental leave. A relational feminist would be pragmatic about how best to improve the quality of women's lives. Are there nevertheless differences in how pragmatic these various approaches are? What are the advantages of pragmatism itself, that is, what are the advantages of adopting an approach that allows one to be pragmatic with respect to the end appropriate—which feminist approach to use—in particular circumstances?

5. Perhaps there are problems with any single approach. The three major approaches described so far might describe three competing goals, each of which is good, all else being equal: gender-neutral laws; increasing women's share of power; and increasing women's subjective pleasure and decreasing women's subjective pain. All else being equal, which it often is not, each of these goals is desirable. Rather than focus exclusively on any one goal, should we approach any particular issue by balancing all three in light of our analysis of that particular issue, with an eye towards doing what is best for women, particularly the most vulnerable women? Would this be relational feminism? What would be the advantages and disadvantages of such pragmatism?

6. How would a pragmatic feminist begin thinking about the issue in *Cal Fed?* How would she resolve the issue? How would you resolve it if you used a pragmatic analysis?

7. A pragmatic feminist would see experimentation as critically important, since as humans we are unable to imagine appropriate solutions to complex social problems using only abstract reason rather than trial and error. Do we need experimentation in approaching inequality between the sexes? What would a world of sexual equality look like? How would one get there from here? If we are unsure of either of these points, does that suggest the need for a pragmatic approach, one which permits experimentation with respect to ends and means?

8. Radin sees cultural feminism as problematic:

> Among feminist scholars, there is a critique of cultural feminism going on which starts from this question: If you were lucky enough to be a dominant group and wanted to dominate society, and you had the power to fashion the language in which people could construct their own identity and self-conception and ways in which they relate to other people, how would you construct a perfect subordinate group? Well, I think that you would make them cooperative, empathetic, nurturing of others, self-sacrificing, noncompetitive, and nonaggressive. The critique says that these characteristics that are attached to women may have been created under domination, and may need to be criticized rather

than ensconced as the essence of women and uncritically praised. Uncritical acceptance of cultural feminism may play into a form of backlash.

Margaret Radin, Please Be Careful with Cultural Feminism, 45 Stan. L. Rev. 1567, 1568 (1993). Would MacKinnon agree with Radin? See MacKinnon, Difference and Dominance, above. Does Becker's articulation of relational feminism avoid this problem? Why or why not? How would you resolve it?

9. What are the risks associated with *not* arguing for the need to place greater value on caretaking? Is it possible to argue that caretaking is undervalued without implying that only women should be caretakers and that women should only be caretakers? Does the need to increase our culture's valuation of (at least some) traditionally feminine traits and activities while working for equality create a double bind? If we increase the value associated with traditionally feminine roles and qualities, we encourage women to stay in such roles and, as a result, to stay subordinate since power in the current social system lies elsewhere. On the other hand, if we do not place greater value on caretaking, community, relationships, etc., but continue to push *only* for equality, we are likely to push women to compete more in the market on the terms created for workers without significant caretaking responsibilities. We may end up in a world with too little caretaking. Does Radin ignore the double bind with respect to valuation of traditionally feminine qualities and traits? Would you prefer to live in the world that exists today or in one in which women did no more caretaking than men and were as aggressive and competitive? What if women change and men do not? What if we end up in a world with too little caretaking? Would women be happier?

10. Add a column on pragmatic feminism to your theory chart (the chart describing and contrasting formal equality, dominance feminism, and relational feminism).

5. SOCIALIST FEMINISM

Text Note: Socialist Feminism

Many of the feminists who came out of the civil rights and antiwar movements in the 1960's were influenced by socialism. Greatly oversimplified, the socialist tradition emphasizes that historical change is determined by economic forces, on the one hand, and the accompanying mode of economic and social organization particular to that era, on the other. Each historical stage is characterized by a certain "mode" of production and accompanying "relations" of production. In the current period, a stage of capitalism, the means of production (factories, tools, capital) are privately owned and controlled by one class (the bourgeoisie); and labor is performed by another class (the working class or proletariat), who do not own the means of production (unlike, for example, peasant farmers in the past), but instead trade their labor to the owners of capital in return for a wage. Each historical period is also characterized by its dominant classes, and historical change is the result of class struggle. For example, the Industrial Revolution, during which work moved out of the home, where it had been under the ownership and control of the workers, and into factories, was accompanied by a political revolution—the liberal democratic revolution—to assure political control by the ascendant capitalist class.

Each economic revolution is thus accompanied by a political revolution, to establish the form of state which serves the economic purposes of the dominant class and maintains control by that class over other classes. For capitalism, the liberal democratic, or "nightwatchman," state, which assures order but guarantees a large measure of freedom in the "private" sphere, is said to perform these functions. History, according to socialist theory, is a dialectical process (that is, it proceeds by the confrontation of opposites which are then superseded by a new synthesis) of class struggle.

Within the socialist movement, women and some men had repeatedly asked what was known as "the woman question," pointing to the oppression of women during all historical periods; but the dominant presumption in socialist theory was that a revolution to overthrow capitalism and establish an economy owned and controlled by all would automatically result in the equality of women as well. Socialist feminists, starting from this theoretical and analytical framework, point out that throughout all historical stages the division of labor particular to that economic stage is *also* accompanied by patriarchy, that is, the dominance of men over women, and by a sexual division of labor in which women—as a group, regardless of their class—perform tasks that are less valued and paid less, and which benefit men as a class. Thus feminists within the socialist tradition began to ask whether another dialectic was at work, one based on gender, and to seek ways to combine this analysis with one based on class. The following excerpt is one example of such an attempt, referred to as "dual systems theory."

ZILLAH EISENSTEIN, CONSTRUCTING A THEORY OF CAPITALIST PATRIARCHY AND SOCIALIST FEMINISM

In Women, Class, and the Feminist Imagination 114–15, 129, 135–40.

(Karen V. Hansen and Ilene J. Philipson, eds. 1990).

Although there are socialist women who are committed to understanding and changing the system of capitalism, socialist feminists are committed to understanding the system of power deriving from capitalist patriarchy. I choose this phrase, capitalist patriarchy, to emphasize the existing mutual dependence of the capitalist class structure and male supremacy. Understanding the interdependence of patriarchy and capitalism is essential to the political analysis of socialist feminism. It becomes necessary to understand that patriarchy (as male supremacy) existed before capitalism and continues in postcapitalist societies. And yet to say that, within the present system of power, either patriarchy or capitalism causes the other is to fail to understand their present mutually reinforcing system and dialectical relationship, a relationship that must be understood if the structure of oppression is to be changed. Socialist feminism in this sense moves beyond singular Marxist analysis and isolated radical feminist theory. The capitalist class structure and the hierarchical sexual structuring of society are the problem.

Power is dealt with in a dichotomous way by socialist women and radical feminists. In these analyses, they see power as deriving from either one's sex or one's economic class position. The critique of power as it is rooted in the male/female distinction focuses most often on patriarchy. The critique of power as it is rooted in the bourgeoisie/proletariat distinction focuses on capitalism. One studies *either* the social relations of production *or* the social relations of reproduction, domestic *or* wage labor, the private *or* the public realms, the family *or* the economy, ideology *or* material conditions, the sexual division of labor *or* capitalist class relations, as oppressive. Even though almost all women are implicated in both sides of these activities, "woman" is dealt with as though she were not. Such a conceptual picture of woman hampers one's understanding of the complexity of her oppression. Dichotomy wins out over reality. * * *

Marxist analysis seeks a historical explanation of existing power relationships in terms of economic class relations, and radical feminism deals with the biological reality of power. Socialist feminism, on the other hand, analyzes power in terms of its class origins as well as its patriarchal roots. In such an analysis capitalism and patriarchy are not simply autonomous systems, but neither are they one and the same thing. They are, in present form, mutually dependent.

* * *

Although the sexual division of labor and society antedates capitalism, it has come to be further institutionalized and specifically defined through the nuclear family in terms of the needs of advanced capitalism. It now has much more form and structure than it did in precapitalist societies. In precapitalist society the home was defined as the producing economic unit. Men, women, and children worked together in the home or on the farm to produce the goods necessary for their lives. Women still were procreators and child raisers, but the necessities and organization of work *limited the impact* of the sexual role distinction. This is not to say that sexual equality existed but rather to point to the importance of understanding the specific structure and use of the sexual division of labor today.

With the rise of industrial capitalism, men were brought out of the home into the wage-labor economy, disrupting the earlier organization of labor. Women became relegated to the home, considered nonproductive, and viewed *solely* in terms of the previous loosely defined sex roles. Although women were "mothers" before industrial capitalism, this was not an exclusive role, whereas with industrial capitalism women became "housewives." "The housewife emerged, alongside the proletariat—the two characteristic laborers of developed capitalist society."[45] The work that women continued to perform in the home was not conceived of as work. Productive labor was now defined as wage labor, labor that produces surplus profit—capital. "In sheer quantity, household labor,

45. [See Eli] Zaretsky, "Capitalism, [the Family, and Personal Life]" [pts. 1–2, *Socialist Revolution* Nos. 13–14 (January–April 1973):] 114.

including child care, constitutes a huge amount of socially necessary production. Nevertheless, in a society based on commodity production, it is not usually considered 'real work' since it is outside of trade and the market place."[46]

* * *

All the processes involved in domestic work help in the perpetuation of the existing society. (1) Women stabilize patriarchal structures (the family, housewife, mother) by fulfilling these very roles. (2) Simultaneously, women are reproducing new workers, for both the paid and the unpaid labor force; they "care for" the men and children of the society. (3) They work in the labor force as well, for lesser wages. (4) They stabilize the economy through their role as consumers. And this role is perpetuated very specifically through patriarchal institutions and ideology. If the other side of production is consumption, the other side of capitalism is patriarchy.

It is important to note the discrepancy between patriarchal ideology and the material reality of women's lives [given the numbers of women working in the wage economy today.] * * * Because women are not defined as workers within the ruling ideology, however, they are not paid for their labor, or are paid less than men. The sexual definition of woman as mother keeps her in the home doing unpaid labor and/or enables her to be hired at a lower wage because of her sexual definition of inferiority. During periods of high unemployment women either do not find jobs or are paid at an even lower rate. The sexual division of labor and society remains intact even with women in the paid economy. Ideology adjusts to this by defining women as working mothers. And the two jobs get done for less than the price of one.

The bourgeoisie profits from the basic arrangement of women's work, as do all individual men who benefit from labor done for them in the home. All men, regardless of class, benefit, although differentially, from the system of privileges they acquire within patriarchal society. This system could not be organized as such if the ideology and structures of sex roles were not basic to the society. * * *

Once the sexual division of labor is challenged, particularly in terms of its connection to the capitalist order, one of the basic forms of the organization of work—especially affecting the home but with wide ramifications for the entire society—will be challenged. This challenge endangers a free labor pool (which infiltrates almost all aspects of living) and a cheap labor pool, and also endangers the fundamental social and political organization of the society, which is sexual hierarchy itself. The very order and control that derive from the arrangements of power implied in the sexual organization of society will be destroyed.

46. Margaret Benston, "The Political Economy of Women's Liberation," Free Press pamphlet, at 15.

If we realize that there are basically two kinds of work in capitalist society, wage labor and domestic labor, we realize that we must alter the way we think about workers. What is really needed at this point is further work on what class analysis specifically means for women. The assignment of class for a woman is often done in terms of her husband's class standing. That is, class categories are primarily male-defined categories; woman is not viewed as an autonomous being; the categories become confused. According to what criteria is a woman termed middle-class? * * *

What does it mean to say that a middle-class woman's life is different and easier than a working-class woman's life when her status as such is significantly different from that of her middle-class male "equivalent"? What of the woman who earns no money at all (as houseworker) and is termed middle class because her husband is? Does she have the same freedom, autonomy, or control over her life as the middle-class man who earns his own way? How does her position compare to that of a single woman with a poorly paid job?

* * *

A feminist class analysis must begin with distinctions drawn among women in terms of the work they do within the political economy as a whole (the family and the paid labor force). This would involve making distinctions among (1) working women outside the home, distinguishing professional from nonprofessional; (2) houseworkers, distinguishing housewives from wealthy women who do not work; (3) women who are houseworkers (housewives) and also work outside the home; (4) welfare women; and (5) unemployed women. Whether a woman is (a) married, (b) single, or (c) divorced is also important in analyzing how her work defines her class position. These class distinctions need to be further defined in terms of the issue of race.

We then need to study how women within these categories relate to the major activities of women in terms of the shared experience of women (rather than in terms of the class differentiations among them)—reproduction, child rearing, sexuality, consumption, maintenance of home. What we will discover in this exploratory feminist class analysis, then, is a complicated and varied pattern whose multigridded conceptualization mirrors the complexity of sex and class differentials in the reality of women's life and experience.

The model with which we would be working would direct attention to class differences within the context of the basic relationship between the sexual hierarchy of society and capitalism. Such an analysis of socialist feminism could continue to explore the relationships between these systems, which in essence are not separate systems and hence need to be dealt with in their internal web. Also, such an examination should serve one overriding objective of the liberation of woman. It should seek to realize her potential for living in social community rather than in isolated homes; her potential for creative work rather than alienating or mindless work; her potential for critical consciousness as opposed to false consciousness; and her potential for uninhibited sexuality arising from new conceptions of sexuality.

* * *

The importance of socialist feminist strategy, to the extent that it exists, is that it grows out of women's struggle with their daily existence—production, reproduction, children, consumption, jobs. The potential for revolutionary consciousness derives from the fact that women's lives under capitalist patriarchy are being squeezed, from the most intimate levels—such as how they feed their children—to the more public levels of their monotonous, tiring, low-skill, sex-defined, low-wage jobs. Women are working in the labor force, and for less, and they are maintaining the family system, having less to make do with. This is the base from which consciousness can develop. We need to try organizing political action and developing political consciousness about our oppression within the hierarchical sexual division of society and from an understanding of how this connects to the capitalist division of labor. * * *

Notes on Socialist Feminism

1. Do you think that women could be a revolutionary class? How do the interests of women differ according to the economic class of the woman and/or of her husband or father? What problems are caused by the fact that the interests of many women are so identified with those of the men with whom they share a household? Why might African American women or Hispanic women or other women of color be reluctant to use their energy and political power for a revolutionary class of *women*?

2. Does women's attainment of equality in the workplace require fundamental economic changes in the organization of work? What types of changes? Could domestic work be "socialized"? What might that mean? Would some forms of socialization be desirable and some undesirable?

3. Socialist feminists have done important work showing the many ways in which patriarchy supports the economic system in which we live, for example, by providing marginal workers, who can be drawn into the workforce as needed, who are paid less than men in the workplace, and who provide domestic labor for free. See, e.g., Heidi I. Hartmann, Capitalism, Patriarchy, and Job Segregation by Sex, in Women, Class, and the Feminist Imagination 146–48, 158, 168–70 (Karen V. Hansen and Ilene J. Philipson, eds. 1990). Can you think of other ways in which patriarchy serves capitalism?

4. What do you see as the strengths and weaknesses of socialist feminism? How might a socialist feminist approach the issue in *Cal Fed*? Add a column on socialist feminism to your theory chart.

5. With the possible exception of MacKinnon, feminist legal theorists tend not to display their debt to Marxism openly, although many advocate changes that could be characterized as socialist, such as paid parental leave, free quality education for all children, and universal health insurance. Why

do you think feminists are reluctant to identify themselves as socialists? What about for practicing lawyers? Can you think of arguments or strategies you might adopt as a lawyer that would be suggested by or influenced by socialist feminism?

6. What are some particular ways in which capitalism and patriarchy are mutually reinforcing? Can you give examples based on women's status as sexual objects for men and consumers for capitalists? What are the political effects of interaction in these areas?

7. Does Eisenstein discuss the interaction of race and class or sex, race, and class? Are there ways in which racism and capitalism are mutually reinforcing? Ways in which patriarchy, racism and capitalism are mutually reinforcing?

5. POSTMODERN FEMINISM

Some feminists regard themselves as postmodern theorists, and others are critical of postmodern feminism. Postmodernism is notoriously difficult to understand, in part because of the unfamiliar terminology. Postmodernism is also difficult to grasp substantively because it is so entirely *critical.* Postmodernism does not itself have an identifiable affirmative substantive agenda. Postmodernism *critiques* Western notions of objective reasoning and deconstructs (takes apart; demonstrates the inconsistencies inherent in) dichotomous terms like public and private, female and male, woman and man. We begin this section with a brief description of postmodernism by Jane Flax, an American political scientist. We then include an excerpt from Carol Smart, an English sociologist whose work has been translated into many languages and is quite influential in world feminism.

JANE FLAX, POSTMODERNISM AND GENDER RELATIONS IN FEMINIST THEORY

12 Signs 621, 624–26 (1987).

As a type of postmodern philosophy, feminist theory reveals and contributes to the growing uncertainty within Western intellectual circles about the appropriate grounding and methods for explaining and/or interpreting human experience. Contemporary feminists join other postmodern philosophers in raising important metatheoretical questions about the possible nature and status of theorizing itself. Given the increasingly fluid and confused status of Western self-understandings, it is not even clear what would constitute the basis for satisfactory answers to commonly agreed upon questions within feminist (or other forms of social) theory.

Postmodern discourses are all "deconstructive" in that they seek to distance us from and make us skeptical about beliefs concerning truth, knowledge, power, the self, and language that are often taken for granted within and serve as legitimation for contemporary Western culture.

Postmodern philosophers seek to throw into radical doubt beliefs still prevalent in (especially American) culture but derived from the Enlightenment, such as:

1. The existence of a stable, coherent self. Distinctive properties of this Enlightenment self include a form of reason capable of privileged insight into its own processes and into the "laws of nature."

2. Reason and its "science"—philosophy—can provide an objective, reliable, and universal foundation for knowledge.

3. The knowledge acquired from the right use of reason will be "True"—for example, such knowledge will represent something real and unchanging (universal) about our minds and/or the structure of the natural world.

4. Reason itself has transcendental and universal qualities. It exists independently of the self's contingent existence (e.g., bodily, historical, and social experiences do not affect reason's structure or its capacity to produce atemporal knowledge).

5. There are complex connections between reason, autonomy, and freedom. All claims to truth and rightful authority are to be submitted to the tribunal of reason. Freedom consists in obedience to laws that conform to the necessary results of the right use of reason. (The rules that are right for me as a rational being will necessarily be right for all other such beings.) In obeying such laws, I am obeying my own best transhistorical part (reason) and hence am exercising my own autonomy and ratifying my existence as a free being. In such acts, I escape a determined or merely contingent existence.

6. By grounding claims to authority in reason, the conflicts between truth, knowledge, and power can be overcome. Truth can serve power without distortion; in turn, by utilizing knowledge in the service of power both freedom and progress will be assured. Knowledge can be both neutral (e.g., grounded in universal reason, not particular "interests") and also socially beneficial.

7. Science, as the exemplar of the right use of reason, is also the paradigm for all true knowledge. Science is neutral in its methods and contents but socially beneficial in its results. Through its process of discovery we can utilize the "laws of nature" for the benefit of society. However, in order for science to progress, scientists must be free to follow the rules of reason rather than pander to the "interests" arising from outside rational discourse.

8. Language is in some sense transparent. Just as the right use of reason can result in knowledge that represents the real, so, too, language is merely the medium in and through which such representation occurs. There is a correspondence between "word" and "thing" (as between a correct truth claim and the real). Objects are not linguistically (or socially) constructed, they are merely *made present* to consciousness by naming and the right use of language.

The relation of feminist theorizing to the postmodern project of deconstruction is necessarily ambivalent. Enlightenment philosophers such as Kant did not intend to include women within the population of those capable of attaining freedom from traditional forms of authority. Nonetheless, it is not unreasonable for persons who have been defined as incapable of self-emancipation to insist that concepts such as the autonomy of reason, objective truth, and beneficial progress through scientific discovery ought to include and be applicable to the capacities and experiences of women as well as men. It is also appealing, for those who have been excluded, to believe that reason will triumph—that those who proclaim such ideas as objectivity will respond to rational arguments. If there is no objective basis for distinguishing between true and false beliefs, then it seems that power alone will determine the outcome of competing truth claims. This is a frightening prospect to those who lack (or are oppressed by) the power of others.

Nevertheless, despite an understandable attraction to the (apparently) logical, orderly world of the Enlightenment, feminist theory more properly belongs in the terrain of postmodern philosophy. Feminist notions of the self, knowledge, and truth are too contradictory to those of the Enlightenment to be contained within its categories. The way(s) to feminist future(s) cannot lie in reviving or appropriating Enlightenment concepts of the person or knowledge.

Feminist theorists enter into and echo postmodernist discourses as we have begun to deconstruct notions of reason, knowledge, or the self and to reveal the effects of the gender arrangements that lay beneath their "neutral" and universalizing facades. Some feminist theorists, for example, have begun to sense that the motto of the Enlightenment, "*sapere aude*—'Have courage to use your own reason,' "rests in part upon a deeply gender-rooted sense of self and self-deception. The notion that reason is divorced from "merely contingent" existence still predominates in contemporary Western thought and now appears to mask the embeddedness and dependence of the self upon social relations, as well as the partiality and historical specificity of this self's existence. What Kant's self calls its "own" reason and the methods by which reason's contents become present or "self-evident," it now appears, are no freer from empirical contingency than is the so-called phenomenal self.

In fact, feminists, like other postmodernists, have begun to suspect that all such transcendental claims reflect and reify the experience of a few persons—mostly white, Western males. These transhistoric claims seem plausible to us in part because they reflect important aspects of the experience of those who dominate our social world.

CAROL SMART, THE QUEST FOR A FEMINIST JURISPRUDENCE

In Feminism and the Power of Law 82–89 (1989).

EQUALITY v. DIFFERENCE

The search for a feminist jurisprudence has, to a large extent, been engendered by the equality/difference problem. These competing principles have dogged feminist politics since the nineteenth century, the basic question being whether women should be given special treatment by the state and the law on the basis of their uniquely female capacities and supposed characteristics, or whether justice would be better served by treating women as equal to men, with equal rights and responsibilities. * * *

* * *

Since the way forward for women in legal terms has been limited to one of two mutually exclusive avenues, it is little wonder that great angst has been created that, in making the wrong choice, we might jeopardize a major breakthrough for women. It should also be realized that this debate is linked to an operationalizable set of policy programs. We can actually envisage what needs to be done. For example, taking the equality approach we can construct new laws that extend considerably the scope of sex discrimination legislation. * * * Of course we have no guarantee that such extensions to the law would be any more effective than existing law. Nor do we have any guarantee that such legislation would not be used disproportionately by men to enhance their superordinate position.

We can also envisage the extension of the difference approach. For example, extending access to public welfare for women who are engaged in caring work; improving employment protection in relation to pregnancy and also in relation to child care. * * * These are all policies that are, or might quite easily be, envisaged on an agenda for legal and policy reform. Hence they are very attractive because they hold the promise of action and quantifiable "success" or "progress". If quantifying the amount of legislation passed to improve the position of women was the empirical reflection of a reduction in women's oppression, there would be no need for a feminist movement now. Indeed it has become fashionable to argue that we are now in a phase of post-feminism (using this term in its superficial meaning) either because so much has been achieved that no more is necessary, or because the inability of feminism to alter substantially the subordination of women has been revealed. The equality/difference debate nourishes both of these arguments.

Feminist work which challenges the epistemological neutrality of the legal system (especially if it does not have a blueprint for a feminist alternative) is necessarily less attractive to those who equate politics with institutional forms of change. The production of ideas is seen as a very inadequate substitute—even when we know that the old methods of law reform have been tried and failed. Yet we must escape from this interminable debate which has us going round in circles. Neither approach can guarantee that it will not ultimately be deleterious for women. The difference approach ultimately nourishes a crude sociobiology, the equality approach can be used as easily by men as by women and often to the detriment of women.

* * *

* * * [F]eminists should not be so anxious to turn to law * * *. Law not only represents itself as a solution, it also defines how we can think about women. For example, MacKinnon, who is most scathing about the futility of the equality/difference debate, none the less speaks constantly of women's inequality. This is a term which infests feminist consciousness to our detriment. If we talk of inequality we necessarily invoke two things. First the idea that we should be equal to *men*, and second that there are institutional means to achieve this. From that point we find we are back into the narrow confines of 'how do we achieve this equality, which laws need changing, how do we incorporate difference, and so on?' Unfortunately, the quest for a feminist jurisprudence when it appears in this narrow (and liberal) form prevents us from redefining the issues and the role that law may have in addressing these issues.

LAW AS A SITE OF POWER

* * * [Law] claims to speak truth with the power to disqualify alternative discourses and * * * law [is] a discursive field which disqualifies women's accounts and experiences. Both of these visions implicate law with masculinity. This is not a simple reductive statement akin to 'all law is man-made', rather it is intended to draw upon an understanding of how the constitution of law and the constitution of masculinity may overlap and share mutual resonances. * * *

Men as masculine subjects (not as biological entities) have a lot invested in many of the dominant discourses such as law and medicine, not simply because they may operate to serve their interests more than others' interests, but because masculinity is part of that world view. Little wonder then that law is so resistant to more radical forms of feminism but quite comfortable when it is presented in terms of equality, equal opportunity, or difference. The equality claim rests upon an assumption that individuals will be tested (by comparison with the male norm), and if found equal those few individuals will be allowed equality in some insignificant and discrete area of employment or training. Difference on the other hand simply confirms the difference (and dominance) of masculinity. The law has had little trouble with this concept in the past (only with the introduction of the principle of equality has it become troublesome). * * *

It is the work of feminism to deconstruct the naturalistic, gender-blind discourse of law by constantly revealing the context in which it has been constituted and drawing parallels with other areas of asocial life. Law is not a free-floating entity, it is grounded in patriarchy, as well as in class and ethnic divisions. I am uncertain that we should be searching for a feminist jurisprudence which we could substitute for this totality. Rather we should seek to shift the understanding of, for example, rape into a critical deconstruction of naturalist heterosexuality. Rape should not be isolated in 'law', it must be contextualized in the domain of sexuality. Equally, child abuse is not a problem of law, except inasmuch as both sexual abuse and law are exercises of power. But they are both exercised in the masculine mode, so that one is not the solution to the other. Finally women's low pay is not a matter of equality but of segregated labour markets, racism, the division of private and public, and the undervaluation of women's work. Law cannot resolve these structures of power, least of all when we recognize that its history, and the history of these divisions coincide.

Yet law remains a site of struggle. While it is the case that law does not hold the key to unlock patriarchy, it provides the forum for articulating alternative visions and accounts. Each case of rape, sexual abuse, domestic violence, equal pay, and so on provides the opportunity for an alternative account to emerge. This account may not emerge in court (indeed it would be silenced there), nor in the media, nor in the formulation of reformed legislation, but it can and does emerge in women's writing and feminist groups (e.g., Rape Crisis Groups, Incest Survivors Groups). This implies a different use of law than the strategy of law reform. * * * [T]he problem of attempting to construct a feminist jurisprudence is that it does not de-centre law. On the contrary, it may attempt to change its values and procedures, but it preserves law's place in the hierarchy of discourses which maintains that law has access to truth and justice. It encourages a 'turning to law' for solutions, it fetishizes law rather than deconstructing it. The search for a feminist jurisprudence is generated by a feminist challenge to the power of law as it is presently constituted, but it ends with a celebration of positivistic, scientific feminism which seeks to replace one hierarchy of truth with another.

Notes on Postmodern Feminism

1. What are Carol Smart's main points? Can you identify three you agree with and three you disagree with? Can you identify any postmodern intellectual approaches or insights, as described by Flax, in Smart's essay?

2. In her discussion of equality and difference, Smart advocates a politics based on feminist "challenges [to] the epistomological neutrality of the legal system" and seems to oppose a politics focused on "institutional forms of change." What does she see as the dangers of a politics which tries to change institutions?

3. Smart speaks of the need to deconstruct (e.g., "It is the work of feminism to deconstruct the naturalistic, gender-blind discourse of law by constantly revealing the context in which it has been constituted and drawing parallels with other areas of social life."). What exactly is she advocating here? Can you give an example of feminist deconstruction of a legal concept or term or doctrine?

4. What does Smart mean when she says that "child abuse is not a problem of law, except inasmuch as both sexual abuse and law are exercises of power. But they are both exercised in the masculine mode, so that one is

not the solution of the other." Is she saying that the legal system should ignore child abuse? That feminists should ignore the legal system's treatment of child abuse?

5. Smart sees the double bind facing women and concludes that neither the equality nor the difference approach "can guarantee that it will not ultimately be deleterious for women." But is there any guarantee that abandoning law reform "will not ultimately be deleterious for women"? Do you agree with Smart on the need to turn away from law reform as a feminist strategy?

6. Add a column on postmodern feminism to your theory chart (the chart describing and contrasting formal equality, dominance feminism, relational feminism, pragmatic feminism, and socialist feminism).

7. Do you think that postmodernism creates problems for feminist politics? What are these problems? Would, for example, Carol Smart be willing to support *any* political agenda or *any* law reform effort? Is postmodernism conservative in any sense?

Text Note: The Politics of Postmodernism

In a 1989 article, Kathleen Barry argued that postmodernism eliminates all meaningful analysis of women's subordination:

> There is, for the deconstructionist, no consciousness, no self, no identity except to the extent to which they are created to serve such false binary oppositions as masculine and feminine.
>
> This kind of relativism would be maddening in a world of equals but when it is used to decenter women as the subjects of feminist theory, it depoliticizes gender and serves the intellectual male hegemony of the academy.[7]

According to Barry, postmodern feminism "silence[s] feminism as a critique."[8] The appeal of postmodernism to women, including feminists, is that it is less threatening to men and relationships with men:

> At the core of women's use of deconstructionist theory is an attack against feminism not only to protect, or rationalize relationships with individual men, but to undermine and invalidate the radical feminist analysis of sexuality. But beyond that, by reducing class categories to differences among women, this analysis calls for a halt to feminist challenges of the most privatized and previously unspoken forms of domination. The deconstructionists' attraction to vagueness validates confusion as a permanent state of affairs. After 15 years of studying sexual domination and many more of experiencing it, I do not doubt permanent confusion is the easier route to choose.[9]

In a 1992 essay, Jane Flax responded to criticisms such as Barry's with the assertion that postmodernism is threatening to feminists because it

7. Kathleen Barry, Biography and the Search for Women's Subjectivity, 12 Women's Studies Int'l F. 561, 571 (1989).

8. Id. at 572.

9. Id. at 573.

challenges assumptions and understandings about the meaning of debates and the possibility of finding ideal ways to resolve them:

> Postmodernism calls into question the belief (or hope) that there is some form of innocent knowledge to be had. This hope recurs throughout the history of Western philosophy (including much of feminist theory). While many feminists have been critical of the content of such dreams, many have also been unable to abandon them.
>
> By innocent knowledge I mean the discovery of some sort of truth which can tell us how to act in the world in ways that benefit or are for the (at least ultimate) good of all. Those whose actions are grounded in or informed by such truth will also have *their* innocence guaranteed. They can only do good, not harm to others. They act as the servant of something higher and outside (or more than) themselves, their own desires and the effects of their particular histories or social locations. The discovery of such truth would enable political theorists and philosophers to solve a central philosophic and social problem: how to reconcile knowledge and power (or theory and practice).
>
> A central promise of Enlightenment and Western modernity is that conflicts between knowledge and power can be overcome by grounding claims to and the exercise of authority in reason. * * *
>
> Once we begin to make claims about gender injustice, we have irrevocably entered the realm of politics. We need to learn ways of making claims about and acting upon injustice without transcendental guarantees or illusions of innocence. * * *
>
> We need to learn to make claims on our own and others' behalf and to listen to those which differ from ours, knowing that ultimately there is nothing that justifies them beyond each person's own desire and need and the discursive practices in which these are developed, embedded, and legitimated.[10]

The disagreement between postmodern feminists and other feminists continues. In an article published in 2000, Catharine A. MacKinnon offers this criticism of the politics of postmodernism:

> I do know this: we cannot have this postmodernism and still have a meaningful practice of women's human rights, far less a women's movement. Ironically, and how postmodernism loves an irony, just as women have begun to become human, even as we have begun to transform the human so it is something more worth having and might apply to us, we are told by high theory that the human is inherently authoritarian, not worth having, untransformable, and may not even exist—and how hopelessly nineteenth-century of us to want it. * * *
>
> The reason postmodernism undermines a practice of human rights is not because it corrodes universality. Human rights in the real world are proving far less attached to their Enlightenment baggage than are the intellectuals who guard its theory. The reason is, the reality of violation is the only ground the violated have to stand on to end it. Power and its pretenders think they can dispense with ground because

10. Jane Flax, The End of Innocence, in Feminists Theorize the Political 445, 447, 459–60 (Judith Butler and Joan W. Scott, eds. 1992).

they are in no danger of losing theirs or the power that goes with it. Postmodernism vitiates human rights to the extent it erects itself on its *lack of* relation to the realities of the subordinated because it is only in social reality that human violation takes place, can be known, and can be stopped.

* * *

My feeling is, if the postmodernists took responsibility for changing even one real thing, they would learn more about theory than everything they have written to date put together. Instead, as practiced by postmodernists, the job of theory, as the blood sport of the academic cutting edge, is to observe and pass on and play with these big questions, out of touch with and unaccountable to the lives of the unequal. Their critically-minded students are taught that nothing is real, that disengagement is smart (not to mention career-promoting), that politics is pantomime and ventriloquism, that reality is a text (reading is safer than acting any day), that creative misreading is resistance (you feel so radical and comfortably marginal), that nothing can be changed (you can only amuse yourself). With power left standing, the feminism of this theory cannot be proven by any living woman. It is time to ask these people: what are you *doing*?[11]

Notes on Politics and Postmodernism

1. Do you agree with Barry and MacKinnon that postmodernism creates problems for feminist politics? What are these problems? Could you agree with both the Barry and Flax excerpts on the politics of postmodernism? Flax and MacKinnon? What would be on a postmodern feminist political agenda? What is on Smart's political agenda? MacKinnon's?

2. What does Flax mean when she says that there is no such thing as "innocent knowledge"? Do you agree with her on this point? If you would nevertheless advocate using the law to achieve (hopefully) social justice, how would you justify your position? How would MacKinnon respond to Flax's point?

3. Do you agree with Flax that "[w]e need to learn to make claims on our own and others' behalf and to listen to those which differ from ours, knowing that ultimately there is nothing that justifies them beyond each person's own desire and need and the discursive practices in which these are developed, embedded, and legitimated"? How would MacKinnon frame her objections?

4. What does MacKinnon mean when she states: "The reason postmodernism undermines a practice of human rights is not because it corrodes universality"? Does postmodernism corrode universality and therefore human rights?

5. What is the problem MacKinnon is pointing to when she explains that the problem postmodernism poses for progressive politics is that "the

11. Catharine A. MacKinnon, Symposium on Unfinished Feminist Business: Points Against Postmodernism, 75 Chi.-Kent L. Rev. 687, 710–712 (2000).

reality of violation is the only ground the violated have to stand on to end it"?

7. CRITICAL RACE FEMINISM

a. *Essentialist Critiques of Feminism*

Before beginning the readings in this section, write down two or three words describing who you are.

ANGELA P. HARRIS, RACE AND ESSENTIALISM IN FEMINIST LEGAL THEORY

42 Stan. L. Rev. 581, 585–86, 588–90, 598–615 (1990).

METHODOLOGY

* * *

In this article, I discuss some of the writings of feminist legal theorists Catharine MacKinnon and Robin West. I argue that their work, though powerful and brilliant in many ways, relies on what I call gender essentialism—the notion that a unitary, "essential" women's experience can be isolated and described independently of race, class, sexual orientation, and other realities of experience. The result of this tendency toward gender essentialism, I argue, is not only that some voices are silenced in order to privilege others (for this is an inevitable result of categorization, which is necessary both for human communication and political movement), but that the voices that are silenced turn out to be the same voices silenced by the mainstream legal voice of "We the People"—among them, the voices of black women.

This result troubles me for two reasons. First, the obvious one: As a black woman, in my opinion the experience of black women is too often ignored both in feminist theory and in legal theory, and gender essentialism in feminist legal theory does nothing to address this problem. A second and less obvious reason for my criticism of gender essentialism is that, in my view, contemporary legal theory needs less abstraction and not simply a different sort of abstraction. To be fully subversive, the methodology of feminist legal theory should challenge not only law's content but its tendency to privilege the abstract and unitary voice, and this gender essentialism also fails to do.

* * *

I do not mean in this article to suggest that * * * every experience is unique and no categories or generalizations exist at all. Even a jurisprudence based on multiple consciousness must categorize; without categorization each individual is * * * isolated * * * and there can be no moral responsibility or social change. My suggestion is only that we make our categories explicitly tentative, relational, and unstable, and that to do so is all the more important in a discipline like law, where abstraction and "frozen" categories are the norm. Avoiding gender essentialism need not mean that the Holocaust and a corncob are the same.

* * *

The notion that there is a monolithic "women's experience" that can be described independent of other facets of experience like race, class, and sexual orientation is one I refer to in this essay as "gender essentialism." A corollary to gender essentialism is "racial essentialism"—the belief that there is a monolithic "Black Experience," or "Chicano Experience." The source of gender and racial essentialism (and all other essentialisms, for the list of categories could be infinitely multiplied) is the * * * voice that claims to speak for all. The result of essentialism is to reduce the lives of people who experience multiple forms of oppression to addition problems: "racism + sexism = straight black women's experience," or "racism + sexism + homophobia = black lesbian experience." Thus, in an essentialist world, black women's experience will always be forcibly fragmented before being subjected to analysis, as those who are "only interested in race" and those who are "only interested in gender" take their separate slices of our lives.

Moreover, feminist essentialism paves the way for unconscious racism.* * * In a racist society like this one, the storytellers are usually white, and so "woman" turns out to be "white woman."

* * *

Modified Women and Unmodified Feminism: Black Women in Dominance Theory

MacKinnon sees sexuality as "a social sphere of male power of which forced sex is paradigmatic." * * * [B]lack women are victimized by rape just like white women, only more so: "Racism in the United States, by singling out Black men for allegations of rape of white women, has helped obscure the fact that it is men who rape women, disproportionately women of color." In this peculiar fashion MacKinnon simultaneously recognizes and shelves racism, finally reaffirming that the divide between men and women is more fundamental and that women of color are simply "women plus." MacKinnon goes on to develop a powerful analysis of rape as the subordination of women to men, with only one more mention of color: "[R]ape comes to mean a strange (read Black) man knowing a woman does not want sex and going ahead anyway."

This analysis, though rhetorically powerful, is an analysis of what rape means to white women masquerading as a general account; it has nothing to do with the experience of black women. For black women, rape is a far more complex experience, and an experience as deeply rooted in color as in gender.

For example, the paradigm experience of rape for black women has historically involved the white employer in the kitchen or bedroom as much as the strange black man in the bushes. During slavery, the sexual abuse of black women by white men was commonplace. Even after emancipation, the majority of working black women were domestic servants for white families, a job which made them uniquely vulnerable to sexual harassment and rape.

Moreover, as a legal matter, the experience of rape did not even exist for black women. During slavery, the rape of a black woman by any man, white or black, was simply not a crime. Even after the Civil War, rape laws were seldom used to protect black women against either white or black men, since black women were considered promiscuous by nature. * * *

Finally, for black people, male and female, "rape" signified the terrorism of black men by white men, aided and abetted, passively (by silence) or actively (by "crying rape"), by white women. Black women have recognized this aspect of rape since the nineteenth century. * * *

The rift between white and black women over the issue of rape is highlighted by the contemporary feminist analyses of rape that have explicitly relied on racist ideology to minimize white women's complicity in racial terrorism.

Thus, the experience of rape for black women includes not only a vulnerability to rape and a lack of legal protection radically different from that experienced by white women, but also a unique ambivalence. Black women have simultaneously acknowledged their own victimization and the victimization of black men by a system that has consistently ignored violence against women while perpetrating it against men. The complexity and depth of this experience is not captured, or even acknowledged, by MacKinnon's account.

MacKinnon's essentialist approach recreates the paradigmatic woman in the image of the white woman, in the name of "unmodified feminism." As in the dominant discourse, black women are relegated to the margins, ignored or extolled as "just like us, only more so." But "Black women are not white women with color." Moreover, feminist essentialism represents not just an insult to black women, but a broken promise—the promise to listen to women's stories, the promise of feminist method.

Robin West's "Essential Woman"

While MacKinnon's essentialism is pervasive but covert, Robin West expressly declares her essentialism. In the last section of *The Difference in Women's Hedonic Lives: A Phenomenological Critique of Feminist Legal Theory,* West argues:

> Both the liberal and the radical legalist have accepted the Kantian assumption that to be human is to be in some sense autonomous—meaning, minimally, to be differentiated, or individuated, from the rest of social life.

> Underlying and underscoring the poor fit between the proxies for subjective well-being endorsed by liberals and radicals—choice and power—and women's subjective, hedonic lives is the simple fact that women's lives—because of our biological, reproductive role—are drastically at odds with this fundamental vision of human life. Women's lives are not autonomous, they are profoundly relational.

In West's view, women are ontologically distinct from men, because "Women, and *only* women, and *most* women, transcend *physically* the differentiation or individuation of biological self from the rest of human life trumpeted as the norm by the entire Kantian tradition." That is, because only women can bear children, and because women have the social responsibility for raising children, our selves are profoundly different from male selves. "To the considerable degree that our potentiality for motherhood defines ourselves, women's lives are relational, not autonomous. As mothers we nurture the weak and we depend upon the strong. More than do men, we live in an interdependent and hierarchical natural web with others of varying degrees of strength."

This claim about women's essential connectedness to the world becomes the centerpiece of *Jurisprudence and Gender*. West begins the article with the question, "What is a human being?" She then asserts that "perhaps the central insight of feminist theory of the last decade has been that wom[e]n are 'essentially connected,' not 'essentially separate,' from the rest of human life, both materially, through pregnancy, intercourse, and breast-feeding, and existentially, through the moral and practical life." For West, this means that "all of our modern legal theory—by which I mean 'liberal legalism' and 'critical legal theory' collectively—is essentially and irretrievably masculine." This is so because modern legal theory relies on the "separation thesis," the claim that human beings are distinct individuals first and form relationships later.

Black women are entirely absent from West's work, in contrast to MacKinnon's; issues of race do not appear even in guilty footnotes. However, just as in MacKinnon's work, the bracketing of issues of race leads to the installation of white women on the throne of essential womanhood.

West's claims are clearly questionable on their face insofar as the experience of some women—"mothers"—is asserted to stand for the experience of all women. As with MacKinnon's theory, West's theory necessitates the stilling of some voices—namely, the voices of women who have rejected their "biological, reproductive role"—in order to privilege others. One might also question the degree to which motherhood, or our potential for it, defines us. For purposes of this article, however, I am more interested in the conception of self that underlies West's account of "women's experience."

West argues that the biological and social implications of motherhood shape the selfhood of all, or at least most, women. This claim involves at least two assumptions. First, West assumes (as does the liberal social theory she criticizes) that everyone has a deep, unitary "self" that is relatively stable and unchanging. Second, West assumes that this "self" differs significantly between men and women but is the same for all women and for all men despite differences of class, race, and sexual orientation: that is, that this self is deeply and primarily gendered. In a later part of the article, I will argue that black women can bring the experience of a multiple rather than a unitary self to feminist theory. Here I want to argue that the notion that the gender difference is primary to an individual's selfhood is one that privileges white women's experience over the experience of black women.

The essays and poems in This Bridge Called My Back[106] describe experiences of women of color that differ radically from one another. Some contributors are Lesbians; some are straight; some are class-privileged, and others are not. What links all the writings, however, is the sense that the self of a woman of color is not primarily a female self or a colored self, but a both-and self. * * *

A personal story may also help to illustrate the point. At a 1988 meeting of the West Coast "fem-crits," Pat Cain and Trina Grillo asked all the women present to pick out two or three words to describe who they were. None of the white women mentioned their race; all of the women of color did.

In this society, it is only white people who have the luxury of "having no color"; only white people have been able to imagine that sexism and racism are separate experiences. Far more for black women than for white women, the experience of self is precisely that of being unable to disentangle the web of race and gender—of being enmeshed always in multiple, often contradictory, discourses of sexuality and color. The challenge to black women has been the need to weave the fragments, our many selves, into an integral, though always changing and shifting, whole: a self that is neither "female" nor "black," but both-and. West's insistence that every self is deeply and primarily gendered, then, with its corollary that gender is more important to personal identity than race, is finally another example of white solipsism. By suggesting that gender is more deeply embedded in self than race, her theory privileges the experience of white people over all others, and thus serves to reproduce relations of domination in the larger culture. Like MacKinnon's essential woman, West's essential woman turns out to be white.

The Attractions of Gender Essentialism

* * *

If gender essentialism is such a terrible thing, why do two smart and politically committed feminists like Catharine MacKinnon and Robin

106. This Bridge Called My Back: Writings by Radical Women of Color (C. Moraga and G. Anzaldua 2d ed. 1983).

West rely on it? In this section I want to briefly sketch some of the attractions of essentialism.

First, as a matter of intellectual convenience, essentialism is easy. Particularly for white feminists—and most of the people doing academic feminist theory in this country at this time are white—essentialism means not having to do as much work, not having to try and learn about the lives of black women, with all the risks and discomfort that that effort entails. Essentialism is also intellectually easy because the dominant culture is essentialist—because it is difficult to find materials on the lives of black women, because there is as yet no academic infrastructure of work by and/or about black women or black feminist theory.

Second, and more important, essentialism represents emotional safety. Especially for women who have relinquished privilege or had it taken away from them in their struggle against gender oppression, the feminist movement comes to be an emotional and spiritual home, a place to feel safe, a place that must be kept harmonious and free of difference. * * *

Third, feminist essentialism offers women not only intellectual and emotional comfort, but the opportunity to play all-too-familiar power games * * *. White women stress women's commonality, which enables them to control the group's agenda; black women make reference to 200 years of slavery and argue that their needs should come first. Eventually, as the group seems ready to splinter into mutually suspicious and self-righteous factions, someone reminds the group that after all, women are women and we are all oppressed by men, and solidarity reappears through the threat of a common enemy. These are the strategies of zero-sum games; and feminist essentialism, by purveying the notion that there is only one "women's experience," perpetuates these games.

Finally, as Martha Minow has pointed out, "Cognitively, we need simplifying categories, and the unifying category of 'woman' helps to organize experience, even at the cost of denying some of it." Abandoning mental categories completely would leave us * * * autistic, * * * terrorized by the sheer weight and particularity of experience. No categories at all, moreover, would leave nothing of a women's movement, save perhaps a tepid kind of "I've got my oppression, you've got yours" approach. * * *

I want to talk about what black women can bring to feminist theory to help us move beyond essentialism and toward multiple consciousness as feminist and jurisprudential method. In my view, there are at least three major contributions that black women have to offer post-essentialist feminist theory: the recognition of a self that is multiplicious, not unitary; the recognition that differences are always relational rather than inherent; and the recognition that wholeness and commonality are acts of will and creativity, rather than passive discovery.

The Abandonment of Innocence

Black women experience not a single inner self (much less one that is essentially gendered), but many selves. This sense of a multiplicitous self is not unique to black women, but black women have expressed this sense in ways that are striking, poignant, and potentially useful to feminist theory. * * *

This experience of multiplicity is also a sense of self-contradiction, of containing the oppressor within oneself. In her article *On Being the Object of Property,* Patricia Williams writes about herself writing about her great-great-grandmother, "picking through the ruins for my roots." What she finds is a paradox: She must claim for herself "a heritage the weft of whose genesis is [her] own disinheritance." William's great-great-grandmother, Sophie, was a slave, and at the age of about eleven was impregnated by her owner, a white lawyer named Austin Miller. Their daughter Mary, Williams's great-grandmother, was taken away from Sophie and raised as a house servant.

When Williams went to law school, her mother told her, "The Millers were lawyers, so you have it in your blood." Williams analyzes this statement as asking her to acknowledge contradictory selves:

> [S]he meant that no one should make me feel inferior because someone else's father was a judge. She wanted me to reclaim that part of my heritage from which I had been disinherited, and she wanted me to use it as a source of strength and self-confidence. At the same time, she was asking me to claim a part of myself that was the dispossessor of another part of myself; she was asking me to deny that disenfranchised little black girl of myself that felt powerless, vulnerable and, moreover, rightly felt so.

The theory of black slavery, Williams notes, was based on the notion that black people are beings without will or personality, defined by "irrationality, lack of control, and ugliness." In contrast, "wisdom, control, and aesthetic beauty signify the whole white personality in slave law." In accepting her white self, her lawyer self, Williams must accept a legacy of not only a disinheritance but a negation of her black self: To the Millers, her forebears, the Williamses, her forebears, did not even have selves as such.

Williams's choice ultimately is not to deny either self, but to recognize them both, and in so doing to acknowledge guilt as well as innocence. * * *

This complex resolution rejects the easy innocence of supposing oneself to be an essential black self with a legacy of oppression by the guilty white Other. With such multilayered analyses, black women can bring to feminist theory stories of how it is to have multiple and contradictory selves, selves that contain the oppressor as well as the oppressed.

Strategic Identities and "Difference"

A post-essentialist feminism can benefit not only from the abandonment of the quest for a unitary self, but also from Martha Minow's realization that difference—and therefore identity—is always relational, not inherent. * * *.

[F]eminist theorizing about "women" must similarly be strategic and contingent, focusing on relationships, not essences. One result will be that men will cease to be a faceless Other and reappear as potential allies in political struggle. Another will be that women will be able to acknowledge their differences without threatening feminism itself. In the process, as feminists begin to attack racism and classism and homophobia, feminism will change from being only about "women as women" (modified women need not apply), to being about all kinds of oppression based on seemingly inherent and unalterable characteristics. We need not wait for a unified theory of oppression; that theory can be feminism.

Integrity as Will and Idea

* * *

Finally, black women can help the feminist movement move beyond its fascination with essentialism through the recognition that wholeness of the self and commonality with others are asserted (if never completely achieved) through creative action, not realized in shared victimization. Feminist theory at present, especially feminist legal theory, tends to focus on women as passive victims. For example, for MacKinnon, women have been so objectified by men that the miracle is how they are able to exist at all. Women are the victims, the acted-upon, the helpless, until by radical enlightenment they are somehow empowered to act for themselves. * * *

This story of woman as victim is meant to encourage solidarity by emphasizing women's shared oppression, thus denying or minimizing difference, and to further the notion of an essential woman—she who is victimized. But as bell hooks has succinctly noted, the notion that women's commonality lies in their shared victimization by men "directly reflects male supremacist thinking. Sexist ideology teaches women that to be female is to be a victim." Moreover, the story of woman as passive victim denies the ability of women to shape their own lives, whether for better or worse. It also may thwart their abilities. * * *

At the individual level, black women have had to learn to construct themselves in a society that denied them full selves. * * *

This insistence on the importance of will and creativity seems to threaten feminism at one level, because it gives strength back to the concept of autonomy, making possible the recognition of the element of consent in relations of domination, and attributes to women the power that makes culpable the many ways in which white women have actively used their race privilege against their sisters of color. * * *

However, at another level, the recognition of the role of creativity and will in shaping our lives is liberating, for it allows us to acknowledge and celebrate the creativity and joy with which many women have survived and turned existing relations of domination to their own ends.

Works of black literature like *Beloved, The Color Purple,* and *Song of Solomon,* among others, do not linger on black women's victimization and misery; though they recognize our pain, they ultimately celebrate our transcendence.

Finally, on a collective level this emphasis on will and creativity reminds us that bridges between women are built, not found. The discovery of shared suffering is a connection more illusory than real; what will truly bring and keep us together is the use of effort and imagination to root out and examine our differences, for only the recognition of women's differences can ultimately bring feminist movement to strength. This is hard work, and painful work; but it is also radical work, real work. * * *

Notes on Essentialism

1. Does Harris use postmodern notions or methods? Does she deconstruct any word(s) or concept(s)? Does Angela Harris think it is possible to continue to use the phrase "as a woman" or to analyze "gender injustice"? Does Harris believe feminist analysis is possible?

2. Is Harris saying that feminists cannot talk about women without committing the cognitive error of essentializing "women" or "woman"? Is it possible to make her points without using postmodern concepts?

3. Compare Harris' observation that essentialism allows white women to control the "women's" agenda and Flax's point about postmodernism as the end of innocence. Are they making the same point? Do you agree with either or both? See also Kimberlé Crenshaw, Demarginalizing the Intersection of Race and Sex: A Black Feminist Critique of Antidiscrimination Doctrine, Feminist Theory and Antiracist Politics, 1989 U.Chi.Legal F. 139, 154–57 (discussing "authoritative universal voice"). Compare Harris and Smart. Where do they agree and disagree?

4. Are many or even most differences between white and African American women based entirely on race, or are they associated also with class differences? Has the feminist agenda been skewed with respect to class as well as race? Would any of Angela Harris' points be relevant to an analysis of *Cal Fed*?

5. Are women in other subordinated groups likely to feel, as African American women often do, that they should keep quiet about gender inequities rather than go public in protest and undermine the solidarity of their group? How are such conflicts likely to be experienced by Latina American women? Asian American women? Women in other minority groups?

6. Derrick Bell discusses many ways in which racism has complicated relationships between black women and men. There is, for example, the shortage of young black men in the black community. In addition, Bell points to

> [t]he continuing powerlessness of black men[, which] affects black women as well, particularly strong black women. * * * Her strength makes her intolerant of weakness, particularly in those whose weakness

> threatens her survival. Thus, even though she may love a man, her contempt for weakness will come out. And if her man is black, you can believe that in this society there will be many opportunities for that weakness to be all too obvious—no matter how successful he is and how strong he tries to be. No matter how hard she tries to accept him as he is, her true estimate of his strength comes out in ways that her man reads as a lack of respect—and resents precisely because he knows damn well that because of this society's racism he can never earn the respect his woman wants to give, and cannot.

Derrick Bell, And We Are Not Saved: The Elusive Quest for Racial Justice 209–10 (1987). Bell describes how, for a black man, resisting racism and sexism at the same time is extraordinarily difficult. Is resistance to racism and sexism less complicated for white men? Other men of color?

7. Compare racism in feminism and sexism in the minority communities and within the civil rights movement. Are both obstacles to the advancement of black women and to the development of policies and laws meeting their needs? See Kimberlé Crenshaw, above note 3, at 139. How have the agendas of both the feminist and civil rights movements been skewed by sexism and racism, obscuring discrimination against black women and impeding needed reforms?

8. Harris concludes that if we focus on relationships, not essences, "men will cease to be a faceless Other and reappear as potential allies in political struggle." Why would this follow? Is Harris suggesting that men are only and always allies? West, Johnson, and Becker have all stressed that there are conflicts of interest between women and men and that we tend to deny such conflicts. See Mary Becker, Politics, Differences, and Economic Rights, [1989] U. Chi. Leg. F. 169; Allan Johnson, The Gender Knot: Unraveling Our Patriarchal Legacy 21 (1997); Robin West, Caring for Justice 133–38 (1997). Would Harris agree that (1) there are conflicts of interest between women and men; and (2) that it is important to recognize them? Do you agree? What are the risks associated with seeing men as (only?) allies?

9. According to Johnson, the criticism of feminism as "victim feminism

> works because it draws attention away from men as victimizers and focuses instead on women who are victimized. In one sense, critics are correct that focusing on women as victims is counterproductive, but not because we should instead ignore victimization altogether. The real reason to avoid an exclusive focus on women as victims is to free us to concentrate on the compelling fact that men are the ones who victimize, and such behavior and the patriarchal system that encourages it are the problem. Otherwise we might find ourselves concentrating on male victimization of women as something that *happens to* women without being *done by* men. The shift in focus can be as simple as the difference between saying "Each year 100,000 women are sexually assaulted" and "Each year men sexually assault 100,000 women."

Johnson, The Gender Knot, above note 8, at 110. Do you agree with Johnson's assessment of the appeal of the victim feminism critique? Would Harris agree with Johnson's assessment of the problem and the solution?

10. Do you agree with Harris that "the notion that women's commonality lies in their shared victimization by men 'directly reflects male supremacist thinking. Sexist ideology teaches women that to be female is to be a victim' "? Isn't the basic problem—the identification of women as victims—inherent in any critical analysis of women's social status, i.e., isn't it inherent in feminism? If this is true, why is this criticism leveled so consistently at MacKinnon? Is there something about MacKinnon's analysis that makes her particularly vulnerable to this criticism?

11. Do you agree with Harris that West's bracketing of issues of race leads "to the installation of white women on the throne of essential womanhood"? How does this happen? What are some of the consequences?

12. Other scholars of color have criticized African American writers for analyzing racism in terms of a black-white paradigm which "distorts history and contributes to the marginalization of non-Black peoples of color." Juan F. Perea, The Black/White Binary Paradigm of Race: The Normal Science of American Racial Thought, 85 Calif. L. Rev. 1213, 1213 (1997). Does Harris employ a black/white paradigm? Does she contribute to the "marginalization of non black peoples of color"? For responses to Perea's criticisms from African American scholars, see Leslie Espinoza and Angela P. Harris, Afterword: Embracing the Tar–Baby—LatCrit Theory and the Sticky Mess, 10 LaRaza L. J. 499 (1998); Athena D. Mutua, Shifting Bottoms and Rotating Centers: Reflections on LatCrit III and the Black/White Paradigm, 53 U. Miami L. Rev. 1177 (1999).

CATHARINE A. MACKINNON, FROM PRACTICE TO THEORY, OR WHAT IS A WHITE WOMAN ANYWAY?

4 Yale J.L. & Feminism 13, 18, 20–22 (1991).

In recent critiques of feminist work for failing to take account of race or class, it is worth noting that the fact that there is such a thing as race and class is assumed, although race and class are generally treated as abstractions to attack gender rather than as concrete realities, if indeed they are treated at all. * * * [R]ace and class are regarded as unproblematically real and not in need of justification or theoretical construction. Only gender is not real and needs to be justified. Although many women have demanded that discussions of race or class take gender into account, typically these demands do not take the form that, outside explicit recognition of gender, race or class do not exist. That there is a diversity to the experience of men and women of color, and of working class women and men regardless of race, is not said to mean that race or class are not meaningful concepts. I have heard no one say that there can be no meaningful discussion of "people of color" without gender specificity. * * *

In this connection, it has recently come to my attention that the white woman is the issue here, so I decided I better find out what one is. This creature is not poor, not battered, not raped (not really), not molested as a child, not pregnant as a teenager, not prostituted, not coerced into pornography, not a welfare mother, and not economically exploited. She doesn't work. She is either the white man's image of her—effete, pampered, privileged, protected, flighty, and self-indulgent—or the Black man's image of her—all that, plus the "pretty white girl" (meaning ugly as sin but regarded as the ultimate in beauty because she is white). She is Miss Anne of the kitchen, she puts Frederick Douglass to the lash, she cries rape when Emmett Till looks at her sideways, she manipulates white men's very real power with the lifting of her very well-manicured little finger. She makes an appearance in Baraka's "rape the white girl," as Cleaver's real thing after target practice on Black women, as Helmut Newton's glossy upscale hard-edged, distanced vamp, and as the Central Park Jogger, the classy white madonna who got herself raped and beaten nearly to death. She flings her hair, feels beautiful all the time, complains about the colored help, tips badly, can't do anything, doesn't do anything, doesn't know anything, and alternates fantasizing about fucking Black men with accusing them of raping her. As Ntozake Shange points out, all Western civilization depends on her. On top of all this, out of impudence, imitativeness, pique, and a simple lack of anything meaningful to do, she thinks she needs to be liberated. Her feminist incarnation is all of the above, and guilty about every single bit of it, having by dint of repetition refined saying "I'm sorry" to a high form of art. She can't even make up her own songs.

Beneath the trivialization of the white woman's subordination implicit in the dismissive sneer "straight white economically-privileged women" (a phrase which has become one word, the accuracy of some of its terms being rarely documented even in law journals) lies the notion that there is no such thing as the oppression of women as such. If white women's oppression is an illusion of privilege and a rip-off and reduction of the civil rights movement, we are being told that there is no such thing as discrimination on the basis of sex. What I am saying is, to argue that oppression "as a woman" negates rather than encompasses recognition of the oppression of women on other bases, is to say that there is no such thing as the practice of sex inequality.

Let's take this the other way around. [* * * [B]oth Mechelle Vinson [the plaintiff in an important sexual harassment case] and Lillian Garland [the woman who lost her job in *Cal Fed*] are African–American women. Wasn't Mechelle Vinson sexually harassed as a woman? Wasn't Lillian Garland pregnant as a woman? They thought so. The whole point of their cases was to get their injuries understood as "based on sex," that is, because they are women. The perpetrators, and the policies under which they were disadvantaged, saw them as women. What is being a woman if it does not include being oppressed as one? When the Reconstruction Amendments "gave Blacks the vote," and Black women still could not vote, weren't they kept from voting "as women"? When African–American women are raped two times as often as white women, aren't they raped as women? That does not mean their race is irrelevant and it does not mean that their injuries can be understood outside a racial context. Rather, it means that "sex" is made up of the reality of the experiences of all women, including theirs. It is a composite unit rather than a divided unitary whole, such that each woman, in her way, is all women. So, when white women are sexually harassed or lose their jobs because they are pregnant, aren't they women too?

* * *

In my view, the subtext to the critique of oppression "as a woman," the critique that holds that there is no such thing, is dis-identification with women. One of its consequences is the destruction of the basis for a jurisprudence of sex equality. An argument advanced in many critiques by women of color has been that theories of women must include all women, and when they do, theory will change. On one level, this is necessarily true. On another, it ignores the formative contributions of women of color to feminist theory since its inception. I also sense, though, that many women, not only women of color and not only academics, do not want to be "just women," not only because something important is left out, but also because that means being in a category with "her," the useless white woman whose first reaction when the going gets rough is to cry. I sense here that people feel more dignity in being part of any group that includes men than in being part of a group that includes that ultimate reduction of the notion of oppression, that instigator of lynch mobs, that ludicrous whiner, that equality coat-tails rider, the white woman. It seems that if your oppression is also done to a man, you are more likely to be recognized as oppressed, as opposed to inferior. Once a group is seen as putatively human, a process helped by including men in it, an oppressed man falls from a human standard. A woman is just a woman—the ontological victim—so not victimized at all.

Unlike other women, the white woman who is not poor or working class or lesbian or Jewish or disabled or old or young *does not share her oppression with any man.* That does not make her condition any more definitive of the meaning of "women" than the condition of any other woman is. But trivializing her oppression, because it is not even potentially racist or class-biased or heterosexist or anti-Semitic, does define the meaning of being "anti-woman" with a special clarity. How the white woman is imagined and constructed and treated becomes a particularly sensitive indicator of the degree to which women, as such, are despised.

Notes on Essentialism and Dominance Feminism

1. Does MacKinnon effectively rebut Harris' critique? Is she right in asserting that minority women prefer to associate with a group that includes men—and that the essentialist critique is based on that preference? Or are there good reasons why minority women often identify more with men of their class and race than with white women?

2. Do you agree with any of MacKinnon's points? Identify commonalities and differences between women across race and class. Why is it important sometimes to see the commonalities? How can it be dangerous?

3. How should conflicts of interest between and among women of various classes and races be resolved?

4. Martha Mahoney, in a reply to MacKinnon's article, criticizes MacKinnon's thoery as based on *harms* to women, ignoring what Marxsim ultimately was grounded on: a "positive claim about the dignity and potential of the oppressed." Arguing that feminism needs a positive vision of women's value, not just a "core *negative* claim" of sexual exploitation, Mahoney emphasizes exploring "ways to value the work women have done and the wisdom and love women have developed despite and because of conditions of oppression." Mahoney, Whiteness and Women, In Practice and Theory: A reply to Catharine MacKinnon, 5 Yale J.L. & Fem. 211, 224, 226–27 (1993). Illustrating this point, Mahoney states:

> motherhood is not easily incorporated into MacKinnon's vision because it is in some tension with her emphasis on what is done to women. *Pregnancy*, in contrast, is consistent with her emphasis on women as the objects of male domination, in part because it is a consequence of sexual intercourse with a man, and fits with a vision of women's-body-done-to-by-a-man. But raising children is both creative and oppressed. Understanding motherhood therefore requires a vision of women as actors in the world—shaping children's lives, struggling to meet the tasks society hands them with the resources available—as well as trapped with children in a system of male domination.

Id. at 238–239. Secondly, Mahoney uses housework to explore and uncover what she perceives to be the white privilege inherent in MacKinnon's analysis, concluding:

> That feminism must be concerned with struggle against racism, and that white feminists need an active agenda against racism (including white privilege), by recognizing that "women" will not be free until "women of color" experience freedom. We could reach the same conclusion by believing that racism is so deeply entwined and so profoundly implicated in all structures of gender oppression that it has harmed white women even as it has brought us privilege in many ways, so that we will never find freedom until we help transform all of these power relationships. Either way, white women need to work actively against white privilege.

Id. at 250. Do you think these points are a fair critique of MacKinnon? Could MacKinnon revise her theory to accommodate these criticisms? How? Would those revisions destroy (or undermine) her theory?

Do you agree with Mahoney that there is a relationship between MacKinnon's definition of women (those from whom sexuality is taken for the use of others) and her failure to incorporate mothering into her theory? What dangers does MacKinnon see in valuing positively the care and nurturing women provide? Are liberal feminists also likely to have trouble dealing with mothering? Why or why not? Relational feminists? Critical race feminists? How would pragmatic feminists approach such issues?

5. Mahoney posits that "MacKinnon's reductive method of identifying the oppression of women insistently reproduces a white norm: strip out all 'other' forms of oppression, identify the woman who is 'not poor or working

class or lesbian or Jewish or disabled or old or young,' and this white woman who 'does not share her oppression with any man' experiences oppression from men, which becomes a 'particularly sensitive indicator of the degree to which women, as such, are despised.' " Mahoney, above note 4, at 219 (quoting from MacKinnon, What is a White Woman Anyway?, above). Do you agree that MacKinnon sets up white women as the norm, white women's oppression as the measure of sex discrimination? What do you see as the problems with MacKinnon's approach?

6. What are the dangers of defining women as only innocent victims? Is it equally dangerous for all women? Is this definition likely both to miss many of the positive aspects of women's lives as well as the ways in which women oppress other women?

7. Are feminist theorists other than MacKinnon more likely to see women as agents with positive attributes and abilities? What are the differences between MacKinnon's approach, formal equality, relational feminism, and critical race feminism in terms of ability to see women in positive terms and as agents?

Text Note: Robin West Responds to Essentialist Critiques

Robin West, a relational feminist, is the second feminist criticized as essentialist by Harris. In her response, West identifies three possible essentialist criticisms of relational feminism: (1) all women are not identical and different from all men; (2) culture and socialization, not biology, create women and men; and (3) relational feminism is dangerous for women of color.[12]

On the first point, West agrees that "*nothing* true" can be said about women's essential nature (and whether "women have one") because the categories women and men will inevitably be overinclusive and underinclusive generalizations: "some men are caring, some women aren't; some men are subordinated, some women aren't."[13] Nevertheless West believes that there are *some* differences between the sexes:

> It truly would be extremely odd, as [Gilligan] argued, if it turned out that the vastly greater amount of child raising and housekeeping, the world over and throughout history, in which women engage—a fact apparently conceded by all—has *no impact whatsoever* on the moral orientations of the two sexes. Similarly, it really would be extremely odd if it turned out that our shared experience as infants and children under the protection and tutelage and love of *women*—our shared experiences derived from that fact that we are all *to woman* born—also has *no* differentiating effect or impact on the way the two sexes view relational ethics. It would be odd if it turned out that the experiences of pregnancy and childbirth, shared by the majority of all women everywhere, have no effect, and lend to women's perspectives no unifying and distinguishing threads.[14]

12. Robin West, Caring for Justice 11–21 (1997).

13. Id. at 18.

14. Id.

In response to the concern expressed by some feminists that acknowledging differences between the sexes will harm women since any mention of differences reinforces stereotypes, West states:

> There are at least two pragmatic reasons to resist—or at least remain uncommitted toward—the seductive [notion that there is] no "essence" that can inform either our political strategy or our moral discourse. The first is purely political: if one is concerned about furthering women's well-being, it won't do to deny the existence of women. The second, though, has less to do with the politics of women's equality and more to do with the quality of our public conversations. There is a real danger of cutting off fruitful inquiry if we cut off inquiry into sex and gender differences solely out of worries over stereotyping.[15]

Although West acknowledges that such contributions could be made without linking the ethic of care to differences between women and men, she gives two reasons why women should be linked to the ethic of care. First, if the ethic of care is a defensible moral position, "the experiences that inform it" are the source of its ethics and its value as a moral norm.[16] Further, if these experiences "are largely the experiences of women, then we need to know that: the experiences go to not only the 'value' but also the content of the ethic they ground."[17] Second, according to West, "if an ethic of care has been undervalued, we need to know" whether it has been "assigned a low value because it is of little value" or because the experiences informing it have been mostly women's, and women are undervalued. [18]

West believes that we should try to universalize the ethic of care (rather than limiting it to a concern of women only), but stresses that "[w]e will not understand either what such an ethic means or demands, or why this ethic has been so universally undervalued, without understanding its roots in women's' lives."[19]

The second criticism, nurture not nature, provokes West to wonder whether part of the essentialism concern is a covert fear on the part of feminists that there *are* nontrivial biological differences between women and men, and that any mention of such differences dooms all feminist projects; such differences will inevitably be used to justify "sexist *attitudes* and misogynist *practices*."[20] If *biology* is the problem—the source, for example, of the male inclination to rape—then arguably the problem is beyond our ability to rectify. Perhaps also the different moral voice, women's political subordination, and the perception of women's inferiority are also rooted in biology, a conclusion which evokes biology as destiny. West responds that injustice does not have to be the inevitable or justifiable result:

> It simply doesn't follow, [however,] from the existence of a biological difference between men and women, that a behavior associated with that difference or attribute is impervious to social or legal pressure. Rather, the existence of a biological root of an undesirable behavior counsels the *need*, indeed the imperative, for legal or social intervention; it hardly counsels the futility of it. Thomas Hobbes, to take an obvious

15. Id. at 19.

16. Id. at 20.

17. Id.

18. Id.

19. Id. at 20–21.

20. Id. at 13–14.

example, clearly believed that natural life was brutal, nasty, and short, but he concluded from that observation *not* that it could never therefore be otherwise, but rather that by constructing a legal leviathan it could quite dramatically and drastically be improved. * * * If there are demonstrable biological causes for [brutality against women], that strengthens rather than weakens the case for state intervention.[21]

Finally, in addressing the third criticism, of the racial implications of relational feminism, West acknowledges the challenge and complexity of the intersection of race and sex and agrees with Critical Race Feminists that African American women are "injured and subordinated in this culture in ways that simply *are not shared* by white women or black men."[22] Because the injuries to African American women are unique, West notes that their problems are likely to be "*exacerbated* rather than alleviated by a feminism or a civil rights movement that centralizes the norms and experiences of white women and black men, respectively."[23] The focus on "the subordination of *women as women*" may actually contribute to racism as well as to heterosexism:

> Black women * * * are subordinated in this culture not "as women" but as *black women,* and not "as blacks" but as black *women.* Lesbians are subordinated not just as women or as gays, but as *lesbians: as gay women.* A feminism that does not attend to the multiple, intersectional nature of the subordination of women of color, of lesbians, and of countless others runs the serious risk of underscoring, and feeding, the still rampant and still poisonous and unconscious racism and institutional heterosexism that continue [today]. Whatever gains may be had by furthering the shared interests of all women, if *that* is the cost, it may not be worth it: the flame of women's advancement, to switch metaphors, may simply not be worth the candle of progress of racial justice.[24]

West argues that the problem here is not essentialism, but racism (or homophobia). While recognizing the intersectionality of many women's subordination, she nonetheless argues that complexity does not negate the existence of any *one* of the axes of subordination. Just because black women and lesbian women may have experiences and interests different from white and heterosexual women does not mean "that *all* women don't share some experiences or interests."[25] For example, the fact that all women in society are more vulnerable to rape and domestic violence than men is not less true because black and white women experience these brutalities differently.[26]

Notes on Essentialism and Relational Feminism

1. Do you agree with Harris that West assumes "that everyone has a deep, unitary 'self' that is relatively stable and unchanging"? Look back at the extract from West's *Hedonic Lives* earlier in this chapter. Do you agree that West insists that every self is "deeply and primarily gendered" and that

21. Id.

22. Id. at 15.

23. Id.

24. Id. at 12.

25. Id. at 15–16.

26. Id.

this insistence implies that "gender is more important to personal identity than race"? Is there language in *Hedonic Lives* supporting Harris' claims?

2. Is West right in suggesting that to deny differences between women and men is to "deny the existence of women"? What does West mean by denying the existence of women?

3. On the first issue West discusses—whether all women are essentially the same—does she effectively rebut the essentialist critique? Is it possible to talk about differences between women and men if women do not share an essential nature? Is it important to do so? Do you and your peers talk about differences between women and men? If you do, is because you and your friends are essentialists?

4. Do you agree with West that talking about biological bases for differences between the sexes can lead not to acceptance of injustice, but to making a case for state intervention? What, if any, dangers do you see in mentioning biological differences?

5. Andrew Sullivan describes his own experiences with testosterone in an article in the New York Times Sunday Magazine. Sullivan takes testosterone shots every two weeks because of low testosterone levels associated with being H.I.V.-positive. He reports that testosterone results in a "deep surge of energy," "increased edginess and self-confidence," a shorter attention span for a few days, difficulty concentrating, a sharper wit, more impulsivity, a hunger-like need for sex, and that it functions as a very effective anti-depressant. Andrew Sullivan, The He Hormone, N.Y. Times Magazine, Apr. 2, 2000, 47, 48–49. When provoked within a few hours of an injection, Sullivan has exploded in anger. He believes that testosterone explains some of the persistent inequities between the sexes, especially in high-risk professions, such as "the military, contact sports, hazardous exploration, venture capitalism, politics, gambling." Id. at 69. Sullivan regards these results as unproblematic as long as women have equal access:

> We should do everything we can to ensure equal access, but it is foolish to insist that numerical inequality is always a function of bias rather than biology. This doesn't mean we shouldn't worry about individual cases of injustice; just that we shouldn't be shocked if gender inequality endures. And we should recognize that affirmative action for women (and men) in all arenas is an inherently utopian project.

Id. Sullivan's response to persistent inequities he sees as biologically based illustrates the reasons many feminists worry that any mention of biology or physical differences is dangerous. But perhaps testosterone does give men a significant edge in the most combative and competitive arenas, such as politics and trial work.

Assume for purposes of this paragraph that Sullivan is right. Should feminists continue to ignore biology? Can you think of ways, for example, to get more women into government despite men's higher levels of testosterone, ways we might not imagine were we unaware of the importance of the competitive edge testosterone gives men? After all, Sullivan does not claim "that women are not good at government. Those qualities associated with low testosterone—patience, risk aversion, empathy—can all lead to excellent governance. They are just lousy qualities in the crapshoot of electoral politics." Id. at 69. How might the electoral system be restructured to make it possible to elect people who do not have unusually high levels of testosterone? What about trial work? Do you think that there *might* be some significant differences between the sexes connected to hormonal levels or other physical differences?

Although men have far more testosterone today than women, it is not clear that this difference is entirely due to biological, rather than environmental, factors. Men have about 10–20 times as much testosterone as most women, but "[w]orking women have higher levels of testosterone than women who stay at home, and the daughters of working women have higher levels of testosterone than the daughters of housewives." Id. at 50. Trial lawyers have higher level of testosterone than other lawyers. It is impossible to distinguish between causes and effects of testosterone, since environment affects testosterone levels. Being in a macho position in a macho environment appears to increase one's testosterone level: midshipmen in the Navy "have higher levels of testosterone than plebes." Id. As Sullivan points out, "most of the studies of the psychological effects of testosterone take place in culturally saturated environments, so that the difference between cause and effect is often extremely hard to disentangle." Id.

6. For an article arguing that feminists should embrace biological differences as a strategic device "so that we may reveal the wholly inadequate job that the law has done in controlling nature's horrors," see Katharine K. Baker, Symposium on Unfinished Feminist Business: Biology for Feminists, 75 Chi.-Kent. L. Rev. 805, 806 (2000). For example, Baker posits:

> With regard to rape, the biological model suggests that the presence of physical violence is incidental—not central—to the crime of rape. Consent is the critical issue, as feminist law reformers have long recognized. For years, the law required physical signs of resistance as a way of proving nonconsent, but biology makes clear that consent and acquiescence are very different things. Many females acquiesce to sex only after being kidnapped, assaulted, or physically and emotionally harassed. Sex for a woman under these circumstances should be considered every bit as injurious as it is for the woman who is raped by the man who jumps out of the bushes with a knife. It is the victim's lack of consent that demarcates rape, and the biological account suggests that there are a myriad of situations in which women say yes to sex only because they have no meaningful choice.

Id. at 824. Do you agree with Baker's assessment of the positive potential of arguments based on biology? Can you think of other ways in which biological differences might be used to justify changes beneficial to women?

7. Is West's response to the third criticism, that relational feminism is dangerous for women of color, similar to MacKinnon's response to Harris? Are you convinced that both dominance and relational feminism are capable of recognizing and incorporating the different experiences and interests of women of different colors? Are both grounded on an assumption that women's experiences are universal? Take a specific experience of many women, such as motherhood, and compare it across race, sexual orientation, and class. In what ways is it the same? In what ways is it different? Does

relational feminism demand a commonality not to be found in the real world?

8. Can you offer similar criticisms of formal equality, i.e., that it is likely to do the most for those unusual women with resumes and life styles most like men's? Why or why not? Women of what classes and races are likely to benefit most from formal equality?

b. Toward a More Inclusive Feminism

TRINA GRILLO AND STEPHANIE WILDMAN, OBSCURING THE IMPORTANCE OF RACE: THE IMPLICATIONS OF MAKING COMPARISONS BETWEEN RACISM AND SEXISM (OR OTHER-ISMS)

In Stephanie Wildman, Privilege Revealed: How Invisible Preference Undermines America 85–102 (1996) (originally published in 1991).

While this Chapter was being written, Trina Grillo, who is of Afro–Cuban and Italian descent, was diagnosed as having Hodgkin's disease (a form of cancer) and underwent several courses of radiation therapy. In talking about this experience, she said that "cancer has become the first filter through which I see the world. It used to be race, but now it is cancer. My neighbor just became pregnant, and all I could think was "How could she get pregnant? What if she gets cancer?""

Stephanie Wildman, her coauthor, who is Jewish and white, heard this remark and thought, "I understand how she feels; I worry about getting cancer too. I probably worry about it more than most people, because I am such a worrier."

But Stephanie's worry is not the same as Trina's. Someone with cancer can think of nothing else. She cannot watch the World Series without wondering which players have had cancer or who in the players' families might have the disease. Having this worldview with cancer as a filter is different from just thinking or even worrying often about cancer. The worrier has the privilege of forgetting the worry sometimes, even much of the time. The worry can be turned off. The cancer patient does not have the privilege of forgetting about her cancer; even when it is not at the forefront of her thoughts, it remains in the background, coloring her world.

This dialogue about cancer illustrates a principal problem with comparing one's situation to another's. The "analogizer" often believes that her situation is the same as another's. Nothing in the comparison process challenges this belief, and the analogizer may think she understands the other's situation fully. The analogy makes the analogizer forget the difference and allows her to stay focused on her own situation without grappling with the other person's realities.

Yet analogies are necessary tools to teach and to explain, so that we can better understand each other's experiences and realities. We have no other way to understand others' lives, except by making analogies to our own experience. Thus the use of analogies provides both the key to greater comprehension and the danger of false understanding.

INTRODUCTION

Like cancer, racism/white supremacy is an illness. To people of color, who are the victims of racism/white supremacy, race is a filter through which they see the world. Whites do not look at the world through this filter of racial awareness, even though they also constitute a race. This privilege to ignore their race gives whites a societal advantage distinct from any received from the existence of discriminatory racism. Throughout this Chapter we use the term "racism/white supremacy" to emphasize the link between discriminatory racism and the privilege held by whites to ignore their own race.

Author bell hooks describes her realization of the connection between these two concepts: "The word racism ceased to be the term which best expressed for me exploitation of black people and other people of color in this society and ... I began to understand that the most useful term was white supremacy." She recounts how liberal whites do not see themselves as prejudiced or interested in domination through coercion, yet "they cannot recognize the ways their actions support and affirm the very structure of racist domination and oppression that they profess to wish to see eradicated." For these reasons, "white supremacy" is an important term, descriptive of American social reality.

This Chapter originated when the authors noticed that several identifiable phenomena occurred without fail in any racially mixed group whenever sex discrimination was analogized (implicitly or explicitly) to race discrimination. Repeatedly, at the annual meeting of the Association of American Law Schools (AALS), at meetings of feminist legal scholars, in classes on Sex Discrimination and the Law, and in law school women's caucus meetings, the pattern was the same. In each setting, although the analogy was made for the purpose of illumination, to explain sexism and sex discrimination, another unintended result ensued—the perpetuation of racism/white supremacy.

When a speaker compared sexism and racism, the significance of race was marginalized and obscured, and the different role that race plays in the lives of people of color and of whites was overlooked. The concerns of whites became the focus of discussion, even when the conversation supposedly had been centered on race discrimination. Essentialist presumptions became implicit in the discussion: it would be assumed, for example, that all women are white and all African Americans are men. Finally, people with little experience in thinking about racism/white supremacy, but who had a hard-won understanding of the allegedly analogous oppression, assumed that they comprehended the experience of people of color and thus had standing to speak on their behalf.

No matter how carefully a setting was structured to address the question of racism/white supremacy, these problems always arose. Each of the authors has unwittingly participated in creating these problems on many occasions, yet when we have tried to avoid them, we have found ourselves accused of making others uncomfortable. Even after we had identified these patterns, we found ourselves watching in amazement as they appeared again and again, and we were unable to keep ourselves from contributing to them.

We began to question why this pattern persisted. We concluded that these phenomena have much to do with the dangers inherent in what had previously seemed to us to be a creative and solidarity-producing process—analogizing sex discrimination to race discrimination. These dangers were obscured by the promise that to discuss and compare oppressions might lead to coalition building and understanding. On an individual psychological level, the way we empathize with and understand others is by comparing their situations with some aspects of our own. Yet comparing sexism to racism perpetuates patterns of racial domination by marginalizing and obscuring the different roles that race plays in the lives of people of color and of whites. The comparison minimizes the impact of racism, rendering it an insignificant phenomenon—one of a laundry list of isms or oppressions that society must suffer. This marginalization and obfuscation are evident in three recognizable patterns: (1) the taking back of center stage from people of color, even in discussions of racism, so that white issues remain or become central to the dialogue; (2) the fostering of essentialism, so that women and people of color are implicitly viewed as belonging to mutually exclusive categories, rendering women of color invisible; and (3) the appropriation of pain or the rejection of its existence that results when whites who have compared other oppressions to race discrimination believe they understand the experience of racism.

TAKING BACK THE CENTER

White supremacy creates in whites the expectation that issues of concern to them will be central in every discourse. Analogies serve to perpetuate this expectation of centrality. The center stage problem occurs because dominant group members are already accustomed to being center stage. They have been treated that way by society; it feels natural, comfortable, and in the order of things.

The harms of discrimination include not only the easily identified disadvantages of the victims (such as exclusion from housing and jobs) and the stigma imposed by the dominant culture, but also the advantages given to those who are not its victims. The white male heterosexual societal norm is privileged in such a way that its privilege is rendered invisible.

Because whiteness is the norm, it is easy to forget that it is not the only perspective. Thus, members of dominant groups assume that their perceptions are the pertinent ones, that their problems are the ones that need to be addressed, and that in discourse they should be the speaker rather than the listener. Part of being a member of a privileged group is being the center and the subject of all inquiry in which people of color or other nonprivileged groups are the objects.

So strong is this expectation of holding center stage that even when a time and place are specifically designated for members of a nonprivileged group to be central, members of the dominant group will often attempt to take back the pivotal focus. They are stealing the center—often with a complete lack of self-consciousness.

* * * At a[] gathering of law professors, issues of racism, sexism, and homophobia were the focus of the plenary session for the first time in the organization's history. * * * [F]ar fewer white males were present than would ordinarily attend such a session. After moving presentations by an African American woman, a Latino man, and a gay white man who each opened their hearts on these subjects, a question and dialogue period began.

The first speaker to rise was a white woman who, after saying that she did not mean to change the topic, said that she wanted to discuss another sort of oppression—that of law professors in the less elite schools. As professors from what is perceived by some as a less-than-elite school, we agree that the topic is important and it would have interested us at another time. But this questioner had succeeded in depriving the other issues of time devoted (after much struggle) specifically to them, and turned the spotlight once again onto her own concerns. She did this, we believe, not out of malice, but because she too had become a victim of analogical thinking.

The problem of taking back the center exists apart from the issue of analogies; it will be with us as long as any group expects, and is led to expect, to be constantly the center of attention. But the use of analogies exacerbates this problem, for once an analogy is taken to heart it seems to the center-stealer that she is not stealing the center, but rather is continuing the discussion on the same topic, and one that she knows well. So when the format of the program implicitly analogized gender and sexual preference to race, the center-stealer was encouraged to think, "Why not go further to another perceived oppression?"

When socially subordinated groups are lumped together, oppression begins to look like a uniform problem, and one may neglect the varying and complex contexts of the different groups being addressed. If oppression is all the same, then we are all equally able to discuss each oppression, and there is no felt need for us to listen to and learn from other socially subordinated groups.

FOSTERING ESSENTIALISM

* * *

To analogize gender to race, one must assume that each is a distinct category, the impact of which can be neatly separated, one from the other. The essentialist critique shows that this division is not possible. Whenever it is attempted, the experience of women of color, who are at the intersection of these categories and cannot divide themselves to compare their own experiences, is rendered invisible. Analogizing sex discrimination to race discrimination makes it seem that all the women are white and all the men African American. The experiential reality of women of color disappears.

THE APPROPRIATION OF PAIN OR THE REJECTION OF ITS EXISTENCE

Many whites think that people of color are obsessed with race and find it hard to understand the emotional and intellectual energy that people of color devote to the subject. But whites are privileged in that they do not have to think about race, even though they have one. White supremacy privileges whiteness as the normative model. Being the norm allows whites to ignore race, except when they perceive race (usually someone else's) as intruding on their lives.

Whites need to reject this privilege and to recognize and speak about their role in the racial hierarchy. Yet whites cannot speak validly for people of color, but only about their own experiences as whites. Comparing other oppressions to racial oppression gives whites a false sense that they fully understand the experience of people of color. Sometimes the profession of understanding by members of a privileged group may even be a guise for a rejection of the existence of the pain of the unprivileged. For people of color, listening to whites who profess to represent the experience of racism feels like an appropriation of the pain of living in a world of racism/white supremacy.

* * *

Not all people who learn about others' oppressions through analogy are blessed with an increased commitment to listening. White people who grasp an analogy between an oppression they have suffered and race discrimination may think they understand the phenomenon of racism/white supremacy in all its aspects. They may believe that their opinions and judgments about race are as fully informed and cogent as those of victims of racism. In this circumstance, something approximating a lack of standing to speak exists because the insight gained by personal experience cannot easily be duplicated, certainly not without careful study of the oppression under scrutiny. The power of comparisons undermines this lack of standing, because by emphasizing similarity and obscuring difference it permits the speaker implicitly to demonstrate authority about both forms of oppression. If we are members of the privileged halves of the social pairs, then what we say about the dichotomy will be listened to by the dominant culture. Thus, when we employ analogies to teach and to show oppression in a particular situation, we should be careful that in borrowing the acknowledged and clear oppression we do not neutralize it, or make it appear fungible with the oppression under discussion.

Given the problems that analogies create and perpetuate, should we ever use them? Analogies can be helpful. They are part of legal discourse as well as common conversation. Consciousness raising may be the beginning of knowledge. Starting with ourselves is important, and analogies may enable us to understand the oppression of another in a way we could not without making the comparison. It is important for whites to talk about white supremacy, rather than leaving all the work for people of color and without drawing false inferences of similarities from analogies. Questions remain regarding whether we can make analogies to race, particularly in legal argument, without reinforcing racism/white supremacy. There are no simple answers to this thorny problem. We will have to continue to struggle with it, and accept that our progress will be slow and tentative.

Notes on Comparing Race and Sex

1. In your classroom discussions of the similarities and differences between sex and race while you were reading Chapter 2, did the phenomena described by Grillo and Wildman occur? Did you notice it? Are there ways it could have been avoided or minimized?

2. What did you write down as the 2–3 words describing who you are? What did your classmates write down? Do you observe the phenomena that Grillo and Wildman observed when they tried this experiment? Did only members of racial minorities include race or ethnicity?

What about sex? Did all women tend to include "woman," "mother," or some other gendered term? Or were some women (particularly women in some? all? minority groups) less likely to include a gendered term than were white women? Did men of various groups include a gendered term? Were white men more likely to include a gendered term than a racial term?

3. If you are white, write down three ways in which you enjoy "white privilege." If you are straight, write down three ways in which you enjoy heterosexual privilege. If you are male, write down three ways in which you enjoy male privilege.

BERTA ESPERANZA HERNANDEZ–TRUYOL, LAS OLVIDADAS—GENDERED IN JUSTICE/GENDERED INJUSTICE: LATINAS, FRONTERAS AND THE LAW

1 J. Gender Race & Just. 354, 355–376, 378–385 (1998).

The dearth of information on Latinas, regardless of the fields one researches, ranging from law to psychology and from education to poverty, is evidence that Latinas are olvidadas [the forgotten ones, feminine]. The Latina consistently is lost in the statistical reporting maze. She either falls under the general category of Latino, the male-gendered ethnic descriptive, or in the catch-all of "minority" women where the Latina is undifferentiated from the Black, Asian, American Indian, and other women of color. Yet, as this piece will show, some aspects of Latinas' lives such as language, family and culture are not shared with all other women of color. These differences merit disaggregated consideration, evaluation, and reporting on Latinas to permit an understanding of Latinas' particular needs, conditions and positions.

Demographics: Las Olvidada—Quienes Somos

[The Fogotten One—Who We Are]

* * * Although Latinas/os share some aspects of culture and language, Latinas/os in the United States are a very diverse peoples of all colors and races, ethnicities, national origins, ancestries, religions, cultures and sexualities. Thus, despite the homogenizing effect of the single term Latina/o to describe a group, it is important to bear in mind the great heterogeneity of the individuals comprising the group. Indeed, Latinas'/os' panethnicity raises questions about the ability, viability or practicality of studying Latinas/os qua Latinas/os.

Latinas themselves are a heterogeneous group. Some are citizens, and some not; some are recent arrivals and some have been here for generations; some speak Spanish, some English, some both. Depending on the country of origin/ancestry, colloquialisms in the Spanish language differ. Yet notwithstanding these differences, their burdens are similar: Latinas face major obstacles in every road of life due to the experience of multi-layered discrimination. For Latinas, universal gender concerns are exacerbated and compounded by discrimination based on national origin, ethnicity, language, culture and race. In addition to the same challenges women face globally, Latinas also confront distinct issues, including an increased likelihood of raising children alone, rising poverty, poor educational status and a disproportionate threat from domestic violence and the AIDS virus. These multiple boundaries erect formidable obstacles to Latinas' attainment of justice.

Latinas are at the bottom of the pile regardless of what demographic factor one analyzes: education, work or income. Latinas/os are the least educated of all ethnic and racial groups in the United States. Significantly, the denial to Latinas of access to justice in education is particularly harmful as data suggests that the "biggest barrier for [Latinas' progress in society] is education."

In addition to the injustice confronted in the area of education, Latinas do not enjoy economic justice. Marginalized in the labor market, regardless of job distribution—whether we have glass-ceiling or sticky floor jobs—Latinas consistently are the lowest wage earners among all workers, including Non–Latina White Women (NLaW) and Black women. While in the 1980s the wages of women of color as a whole rose relative to the income of NLaW, Latinas' wages declined. Today, Latinas are twice as likely as NLaW to be in the lowest paying jobs.

Although the feminization of poverty phenomenon is global, it disproportionately affects women of color and, in particular, Latinas. Latinas, heads of households in 23% of families as compared with only 16% of non-Latina/o families, have the lowest median income of any group. Predictably, therefore, Latinas are also the least likely of all workers to have pension or health benefits. * * *

Even when employed outside of the home for pay, over a quarter of working Latinas are employed in the service industry. Of these jobs, one is prone to find Latinas working as maids, private household cleaners and servants, janitors, nursing aids and orderlies, cooks and child care takers—all very low paying jobs with little, if any, hope for advancement. Conversely, few Latinas hold managerial and professional positions. Moreover, data on Latina presence in management reveals that even these successful workers are concentrated in lower and middle management positions. Although disaggregated data for Latinas does not exist, it is logical to project that the combination of sex and ethnicity, each of which alone would effect invisibility in high ranks of management, results in the number of Latinas in senior management posts being infinitesimally small.

Sadly for Latinas, working full time does not ensure a "living wage" or even a non-poverty level wage. The latest figures available establish that a Latina earns $.54 for each dollar a NLaW earns. This 30–40% gap can be attributed to the multiple employment discriminations Latinas encounter as sex, race and ethnic "others." Adding insult to injury, a Latina with a college degree earns less than a NLaW with only a high school diploma.

Thus, as the previous discussion shows, regardless of classification, ranging from education to employment, from poverty to management, Latinas are truly mujeres marginadas—outsiders who define the margins. The following section explores structural bases of Latina marginalization.

Injustice—Fronteras/External Barriers: Social, Economic and Legal

Rights are meaningless to the population that cannot exercise them. Women's exclusion from participation in the public (indeed even the private) sphere is a direct result of their systematic exclusion, by custom and by law, from access to key elements of empowerment: education, physical and social freedom of movement, and mentorship by those already in power. It is evidence of structural inequality that cannot be addressed effectively by refinement of theoretical concepts or discourse on rights.

Structural inequality results in the perpetuation of injustice and ignorance despite all efforts to enact and enforce legal rights. The term "structural inequality" refers to the essential power imbalance between women and men, in which men have held most of the power to make decisions that affect women, families, and society. This imbalance results in fundamental injustice. Significantly, the same "imbalance" is true in this country on the basis of race/ethnicity. Latinas have a third degree of subordination because of their culture. This triple crown of gendered, racialized/ethnicized, and cultured injustice requires a total re/construction to integrate the faces of Latinas in justice.

That discrimination against Latinas exists in all aspects of life resulting in the marginalization of Latinas in public discourse is patent. One simply needs to point to the lack of data on Latinas to confirm that they have not been the objects or subjects of social scientific concern. Latinas' plight is compounded by their multiple differences from the normativo. One major factor for Latinas' invisibility lies in the nature of the system.

In general, external barriers to women's advancement include elements of "organizational culture" as well as factors of "organizational structure." * * *

FRONTERAS IN EDUCATION

Latinas/os face structural barriers in education. Indeed, some deeply troubling educational studies suggest bias might be at the root of Latina/o children's non-performance in school. For example, a report of the United States Commission on Civil Rights stated with respect to one study of Mexican–American educational attainment "that Anglo teachers tended to favor Anglo children over Mexican Americans in their praise, encouragement, attention and approval. Predictably, it was also found that Mexican American students participated in class less than Anglo students."[38] These teacher attitudes and interactions diminish the quality of the educational experience for Latina/o children, particularly when it becomes a reflection of teachers' lower academic expectations. Such inferior expectations consequently result in the lower self-esteem found in Latina/o students as compared with NLaW students. This data, considered together with studies that show similar classroom biases against girls, results in the erection of a doubly thick educational success barrier for Latinas.

Stories of lower expectations, as well as direction into less ambitious routes abound. One researcher "cites lower teacher expectations and a lack of socially and culturally relevant curricula as factors that discourage the overwhelming majority of Black and Puerto Rican students in New York City."[41]

* * *

That teachers have a great impact on the learning ability of students based upon the environment they create in the classroom is beyond peradventure. Thus, teachers who come to classes with attitudes of bias and stereotyping that prevent Latinas/os from achieving their full potential, effect and compound the daily educational injustices Latinas/os encounter. These educational complexities and difficulties are exacerbated for the poor and those who, because of linguistic barriers, are further perceived as "disadvantaged." As one report states:

38. U.S. Comm'n on Civil Rights, Puerto Ricans in the Continental United States: An Uncertain Future 103 (1976) [hereinafter Uncertain Future] (citing U.S. Comm'n on Civil Rights, Report V: Mexican American Education Study, Teachers and Students 43 (1973)).

41. [Clara E.] Rodriguez[, Puerto Ricans Born in the U.S.] 130–31 [(1989)].

> Despite their better judgment, people of another background often feel that disadvantaged children are by nature perverse, vulgar, or lazy. Children sense quickly the attitudes of school people toward them, and they retaliate against condescension or intolerance with hostility, absenteeism, and failure.[44]

* * *

Such reduced educational expectations of Latinas/os influence teachers in other ways. One researcher suggests that the net effect of race, class and/or gender bias may be a de facto "tracking" of Latina/o students into lower educational tracks,[47] thus creating compounded problems as the student navigates the educational system. This tracking data is disturbing if one adds the language problems to the mix. One psychologist noted a consistent underestimation of IQ by twenty points when Latina/o children were tested in English, a gap that was immediately overcome when the test was conducted in Spanish.[48]

Considering this information and adding the gender element to the mix, Latinas' underachievement in education is not surprising but predictable. Latina students suffering from the ethnic, cultural and racial biases imbued in the system also must manage the established gender biases that show that teachers systematically ignore girls in classrooms, fail to call on them, do not follow up with their answers and, overall, prefer to spend their time with and expend their efforts/energy on boy students. For the Latina student, young and older alike, absent systemic re/construction, the structural biases in the classroom will continue to rally against their success, indeed will be signposts for failure. Successful Latinas must overcome race, sex, ethnic and cultural barriers; yet * * * not even Latinas who have reached the hallowed halls of law school escape injustice.

Economic Fronteras

Structural barriers also account for Latinas' failure to enjoy economic justice. Researchers attribute the earning gap of Latinas to a variety of factors including: Latinas' low educational levels (limiting them to low-skill jobs); Latinas' concentration in low-wage service jobs; and employment discrimination, which affects both employment and pay levels. In addition, Latinas' opportunities may be hampered by their lack of English language fluency and literacy. Even when one accounts for

44. [U.S. Comm'n on Civil Rights, Puerto Ricans in the Continental United States:] Uncertain Future * * * at 103 [(1976)] (quoting National Education Association and American Association of School Administrators, Educational Policies Commission, Education and the Disadvantaged American 19 (as cited by Clarence Senior in Schreiber, The School Dropout 112)); see also Rodriguez, supra note [41], at 130.

47. Id. at 132 (noting that the de facto tracking is "indistinguishable from the systematic ordering of Hispanic students into nonacademic, nondemanding, or special educational tracks").

48. Uncertain Future, supra note 38, at 99 ("In my clinic, the average underestimation of IQ for a Puerto Rican kid is 20 points. We go through this again and again. When we test in Spanish, there's immediately a leap to 20 points higher than when he's tested in English.").

language, skill level and low educational attainment, Latinas' aggregated racial, ethnic and sex discriminations erect multiple barriers to Latinas' job opportunities and attainment of economic justice.

If one looks at working Latinas between the ages of eighteen and sixty-four, approximately half are immigrants, "a factor which has implications for education, language training, and overall socioeconomic status."[55] For undocumented Latinas, the available jobs are only in the low-skill, low-pay categories. Furthermore, due to their undocumented status, Latinas are often concentrated in the underground economy—housecleaning, child-care and the garment industry—where they lack even basic protections. While all domestic workers, particularly live-ins, suffer the plight of undefined roles and indeterminate hours, the vulnerability to abuse for undocumented workers is greater.

Undocumented workers report very high levels of sexual harassment and abuse, some labeling the employers' approach as a "lay down or layoff policy." Latinas do not report the prevalence of physical abuse because they fear being turned in to the authorities. This pattern of abuse remains true in instances where the violence is economic (even beyond the poverty wages they get paid). Many employers, taking advantage of the limited avenues for redress of undocumented workers, simply refuse to pay them for their work.

Fronteras in the Law

Legal Paradigms—The Conflation of Race, Ethnicity and Nationality

It is no surprise that in the justice system, structural barriers for Latinas exist, both in its theoretical foundation and in its practical, tangible manifestations. The normative legal paradigm in the United States presents an omnibus barrier for Latinas as many-layered others. For example, the system was created in the image of the founding fathers. Consequently, the system's image of what is normal is the white, Anglo/Western European, Judeo/Christian, English-speaking, educated, moneyed, propertied, heterosexual, physically and mentally able man—the quintessential "reasonable man." Pursuant to this structure, Latinas are a very different "other." Gender, race and ethnicity are three deviations from the norm all Latinas share. In addition, in light of the demographic information provided above, religion, class, language, culture, education and propertied status often add to the Latinas' differences from what has been constituted as normative.

In the United States, the dominant legal construct is ruled by a dichotomous black/white racial paradigm into which Latinas/os simply do not fit neatly. In this country, the rule of hypodescent, the so-called one-drop rule, defines as "Black" anyone who has one drop of Black blood, regardless of phenotype. Moreover, the construction of race in the United States conflates race with ethnicity. Indeed Latinas/os in this

55. [National Council of La Raza,] Untapped Potential[: A Look at Hispanic Women in the U.S.] 7 [(1996)].

country are considered not white and also not black because they are Latinas/os—regardless of phenotype or taxonomy. To be sure, this presents an absurd conflict as race and ethnicity are different categories.

This paradigm is in sharp contrast with Latinas/os' (at least caribenas/os') perspectives on race. While in the United States the one-drop rule operates to render Black anyone who has one drop of Black blood, the obverse is true in the Caribbean. There, the rule is blanqueamiento ("whitening") where one drop of white blood starts you en route to desirable whiteness. No doubt, both cultures (structures) favor the "white" (colonizer's) tez (complexion), but the approaches are dramatically different.

Thus, the result of the foundational black-white paradigm is to racialize ethnicity (and ethnicize race) with sometimes interesting, ironic, incoherent results. Existing race/ethnic categories of "white, not of Hispanic origin," "black, not of Hispanic origin," Hispanic, Asian, and American Indian are both under-and over-inclusive because, as they are race and ethnic categories, the de-racialization of ethnicity and the de-ethnicizing of race is wholly inappropriate. For example, an Afro–Cuban is both Black and Cuban, meaning s/he is both Black and of Hispanic origin, a dual classification that results in bias in both worlds. Interestingly, more recent categories' specific notations that Hispanics can be of any race still fail to recognize the realities and possibilities of the multiple discriminations to which Latinas/os are subjected on a daily basis.

These varied perspectives of race and the conflation/confusion of race and ethnicity, which also often become interchangeable and confused with national origin, stand in the way of Latinas' attaining justice and generate nativistic feelings. One manifestation is the rendering of all Latinas/os within the United States, regardless of citizenship, as "alien"—outsiders, others, different looking—a status that is compounded by the otherness effected by Spanish speaking and Spanish names.

The overarching racist/nativistic impetus behind recent immigration reform resulting from the confusion of the varied categories of race, ethnicity and nationality has even affected puertorriquenas/os who are U.S. citizens by birth. Data show that even though the Immigration Reform and Control Act of 1986 (IRCA) does not apply to native-born citizens, IRCA's employer sanction provisions have had a negative impact on puertorriquenas/os simply because they are perceived to be foreign because they "look" or "sound" different. One reported egregious rejection of a citizen's application (for an unskilled watch packer job) entailed a company's refusing the applicant's offer of a Puerto Rican birth certificate, social security card, and voter registration card as evidence of legal status and instead insisting on a "green card." The company lost the case, of course, and was chastised by the court for requesting from a citizen a document—the green card—that only foreigners can obtain. Nonetheless, this occurrence reveals the consequence of the dominant paradigm's conflation of race, ethnicity and nationality.

Thus, the philosophical underpinnings of the legal system, with the black-white paradigm as a foundation, and the othering of differences, which can render even citizens "alien," are wholly inadequate to examine the condition of Latinas in the United States. It is not surprising, then, that the system built on such an infrastructure—one that constructs and mandates analysis as a one-layered phenomenon—is deficient in addressing, accommodating and resolving the problems, needs and rights of this population—a population that by its characteristics is three layers removed from the most conventional of Latinas' sex, race and ethnic realities.

Fronteras in the Justice System

Beyond its theoretical underpinnings, other structural aspects of the justice system interfere with Latinas' attainment of justice. Latinas/os in the justice system who either provide or use services list the courts, police, social service agencies, governmental and welfare centers and the English-language media as discriminators.

> [In this section, Hernandez–Truyol describes the justice system experienced by Latinas in the United States, including crumbling, dirty facilities, language problems negotiating courthouses and courtrooms, and the under representation of Latinas/os on juries.]

* * *

Latina Gender Roles

Traditionally, in the cultura Latina the Latina's role is reproductive and domestic: child-raising and home-making. Latinas are taught by all—family, church and popular culture (majority and Latina/o alike)—that they are inferior to men. In addition, Latinas' identity is founded on a vision of the "ideal woman," fantasized in the image of the Virgin Mary. This ideal, "marianismo," "glorifie[s] [Latinas] as strong, long-suffering women who ha[ve] endured and kept Latino culture and the family intact."[101] Throughout history, and in the literature, Latinas are simultaneous and conflicting stereotypes: sentimental, gentle, passive, modest, docile, faithful, submissive, dependent, maternal and timid; at the same time they are pretty, seductive, flirtatious and impulsive.

* * *

To be sure, this mythical marianista model, in all its aspects, causes grave conflicts when girls are also expected to excel at, for example, math or law. As one writer has noted:

> [C]ultural values suggest [that] power is unfeminine and is viewed as a negative quality. The culture has socialized and trained Latinas to eliminate conflict instead of facing it. They learned early not to take risks, thereby placing a high value on security. They desire to create stability and do not understand the necessity for change in

101. [Gloria] Bonilla–Santiago, [Breaking Ground and Barriers: Hispanic Women Developing Effective Leadership] 11 [(1992)].

the corporate world. They often do not grasp the vision or mission of the organizations for which they work. They value loyalty and expect loyalty from their subordinates. They do not value the power of bargaining. If something does not feel right they back out instead of negotiating.[108]

Consider such statements in juxtaposition to the persona of a successful Latina litigator who must be firm, articulate, calm and strong. There is great dissonance.

Gender-role caricatures are myths so deeply embedded in culture and tradition that they have taken the stature of truths, reality. These myths, however, present great obstacles to the deconstruction of cultural gender roles that is needed to facilitate Latinas' progress in areas where they are now marginalized or fully excluded. In this context, any suggestion that "machismo" can include positive traits or that its "light side" is desirable is a tragic misapprehension. In any event, to deconstruct these chimerical truths it is imperative to understand the culture, race, class and gender underpinnings of the oppression.

THE ROLE OF LANGUAGE

One perpetrator of Latinas' marginalization at myriad dimensions is language. For example, the gendered nature of Spanish, where the male gender is the norm in both the spoken and written forms, renders Latinas non-existent, foreign, alien, non-belonging in their own tongue. This characteristic of Spanish-speak facilitates the male norm's obliteration of Latinas in their own ambiente—home, work and church—and is Latinas' ghost wherever they travel.

Similarly, Spanish-accented English speech, unlike most other accented versions, be it Midwestern, Southern or Northeastern, results in a qualitative judgment about the speaker. The Latina is unintelligent, uneducated and illiterate. Spanish-accented English becomes code for the negative, undesirable other and not for the exotic other that an Australian or French accent would invoke.

In addition, a Latina is affected by language if she does not speak English. Lack of English language skills immediately renders Latinas foreign, though we may be native-born citizens whose jurisdiction has Spanish as the native, official tongue. For example, anyone born in Puerto Rico is a native-born, Spanish-speaking citizen. Nothing in the Jones Act requires forsaking one's native tongue. Yet one's birthright citizenship is questioned because of speaking a language that is seen as a foreign tongue. All of these realities combine to marginalize, exclude and silence Latinas in virtually every aspect of their lives.

Notes on Las Olivadadas

1. Are the problems undocumented women face problems with which feminists, feminism, and the feminist movement should be concerned? Why

108. Id. at 7.

or why not? How would most NLaW women in the United States answer that question? Does this illustrate the problem Harris describes in the first selection in this section?

2. Immigration status causes many problems for immigrant women, particularly when their partners are violent and abusive. A woman who is here illegally will be extremely reluctant to call the police or use the legal system to protect herself and her children from harm. The immigration status of many immigrant women here legally depends on being married to a husband with legal status. The Violence Against Women Act ("VAWA") allows some women in abusive relationships to file for a waiver of this requirement. But many women who need the waiver cannot meet the many substantive requirements. In addition, applications for VAWA waivers require a great deal of documentation. Most immigrant women are unable to complete the complicated paperwork themselves. Also, much funding of lawyers for poor people comes from the federal government, and such funds cannot be used to support work on applications for VAWA waivers. For more thorough discussions of the many problems faced by immigrant women in abusive relationships, see Cecelia M. Espenoza, No Relief For The Weary: VAWA Relief Denied For Battered Immigrants Lost In The Intersections, 83 Marq. L. Rev. 163 (1999); Linda Kelly, Stories From The Front: Seeking Refuge For Battered Immigrants In The Violence Against Women Act, 92 NW. U.L. Rev. 665 (1998); Maurice Goldman, The Violence Against Women Act: Meeting Its Goals in Protecting Battered Immigrant Women?, 37 Fam. & Concil. Cts. Rev. 375 (1999); Lee J. Teran, Barriers To Protection At Home And Abroad: Mexican Victims Of Domestic Violence And The Violence Against Women Act, 17 B.U. Int'l L.J. 1 (1999).

3. What position should feminists take on immigration? Should feminists support open borders? Is any other position compatible with the needs of *all* women as women?

4. When you think about "race," do you automatically think "black/white"? How does discrimination against Latinas/os operate? How is it similar to and how is it different from discrimination against African Americans? Asian Americans?

5. The Supreme Court subjects classifications based on race and national origin to strict scrutiny. But distinctions based on language, culture, ethnicity, and immigration status are not subject to any scrutiny. For Latinas, can race and national origin be disentangled from language, culture, ethnicity, and immigration status? What are the consequences of the fact that, in reality, for many non-African American minority groups, discrimination on the basis of race and national origin (constitutionally suspect) is entangled with discrimination on the basis of language, culture, ethnicity, and immigration status (not constitutionally suspect)? Is the black-white paradigm in American culture and constitutional law part of the problem?

Are culture and language intertwined with race discrimination for many African Americans as well? Under the black/white paradigm, does the Constitution reach, for example, discrimination on the basis of linguistic or cultural differences even for African Americans?

6. Do you think it is possible to create a feminist theory that does not ignore or marginalize the very real differences among women of all colors?

MARI J. MATSUDA, WE THE PEOPLE: JURISPRUDENCE IN COLOR

In Where Is Your Body? 21–27 (1996).

What is the jurisprudential tradition that sets apart the emerging view of law developed by people of color? It encompasses several key elements: historical memory, duality, criticism, race consciousness, pragmatism, and utopianism. The methodology of this jurisprudence is grounded in the particulars of social reality and the experience of people of color. This method is consciously historical and revisionist, attempting to know history from the bottom—from the fear and namelessness of the slave, from the broken treaties of the indigenous Americans, and from the daily experience of racial hierarchy. Understanding history from the bottom has forced these scholars to sources often ignored: journals, poems, the records of practitioners, the rhetoric of intellectuals of color, oral histories, the writers' own experience of life in a hierarchically arranged world, and even to the dreams they dream at night in their sleep.

This methodology, which rejects presentist, eurocentric descriptions of social phenomena, offers a unique description of law. The description is realist. It accepts the standard teaching of street wisdom: law is essentially political. It accepts as well the pragmatic use of law as a tool for social change and the aspirational core of law as the human dream of peaceable existence. If these views seem contradictory, that is consistent with another component of outsider jurisprudence—it is jurisprudence recognizing, struggling within, and utilizing contradiction, dualism and ambiguity.

The world described by legal scholars of color is one infused with racism. This description ties law to racism, showing that law is both a product and a promoter of racism. Like the feminists who have shown that patriarchy has had its own march through history, related to but distinct from the march of class struggle, scholars of color have also shown how racism must be understood as a distinct phenomenon.

The hopeful part of the description offered by outsider theorists is the recognition of the vulnerability of racist structures. The few who have managed to subject the many to conditions of degradation have used a variety of devices, from genocide to liberal doublespeak, that reveal the deep contradictions and instability inherent in any racist organization of social life. All the sorrow songs of outsider jurisprudence are thus tempered by an underlying descriptive message of the possibility of human social progress.

This progress can lead to a just world free of existing conditions of domination. The prescriptive message of this jurisprudence offers signposts to guide our way there—the focus on effects. The need to attack the effects of racism in order to attack its deep, hidden, tangled roots characterizes outsider thinking about law. Outsiders thus search for

* * * legal tools that have a progressive effect, defying the habit of neutral principles to disappoint. They have proposed rachetlike measures—including affirmative action, reparations, and the criminalization of racist propaganda—to eliminate existing effects of oppression. These exciting doctrinal moves had their genesis in communities of people of color. Such measures are best implemented through formal rules, formal procedures, and formal concepts of rights because informality and oppression are frequent fellow travelers.

This identifies another tendency in jurisprudence by people of color: pragmatism and bottom-line instrumentalism in the use of law to achieve social change. Recall the litigants and lawyers of color bringing case after case challenging manifestations of racism throughout the history of this country. We have the famous cases—*Plessy, Brown, Korematsu, Lau,*[4]—and the unknown cases that pepper the reporters of every state in this nation: cases of ordinary people who suffered some racist affront—lying landlord, a surly theater usher, a biased employer—and chose to fight back. One of my fantasies is that someday we will put up bronze plaques in all the theaters, train stations, schools, factories, and offices where these people, with their lovely cacophony of African–American, Asian, Latino, and Native–American surnames, fought their legal fights.

Bringing these elements together offers a challenge to classical and critical jurisprudence and a vision of law unlike any other. The historical memory and consciousness of race allies us with realist, critical legal theorists, and legal historians of the instrumentalist and law-and-society schools. Frederick Douglass, as we know, was a legal realist before Oliver Wendell Holmes.

What sets the jurisprudence of color apart, however, from the various modernist and postmodernist schools is the pragmatism rooted in concrete political organizing. In this sense, the jurisprudence of color forms an uneasy alliance with neoformalists, liberal reformists, and civil libertarians in commitment to the use of the rule of law to fight racism and in an unwillingness to stand naked in the face of oppression without a sword, a shield, or at least a legal precedent in our hands. Scholars of color have attempted to articulate a theoretical basis for using law while remaining deeply critical of it.

As Jose Bracamonte pointed out in his foreword to the *Harvard Civil Rights—Civil Liberties* Minority Critique of Critical Legal Studies,[5]

4. *Plessy v. Ferguson,* 163 U.S. 537 (1896) (upholding a law requiring separate railway accommodations for whites and Blacks); *Brown v. Board of Education,* 347 U.S. 483 (1954) (holding that "[s]eparate educational facilities are inherently unequal" and that laws requiring or permitting racial segregation of schools violate equal protection); *Korematsu v. United States,* 323 U.S. 214 (1944) (upholding the internment of Japanese Americans during World War II on the ground of military necessity); and *Lau v. Nichols,* 414 U.S. 563 (1974) (holding that the school system's failure to provide English instruction to Chinese–American students with limited English proficiency violated equal protection).

5. Jose Bracamonte, Foreword, "Minority Critiques of the Critical Legal Studies

people of color cannot afford to indulge in deconstruction for its own sake. Our critique is goal oriented. The work produced by scholars of color ties pragmatic law reform to criticism and radical theory in a way no one on the jurisprudential scene, except for our feminist sisters, is doing.

Our alliance with feminism will be, I believe, most fruitful for us. Martha Minow's * * * foreword to the Supreme Court edition of the *Harvard Law Review*, * * * grapples with the ideas of difference, duality, and the tantalizing promise of law.[6] Out of the struggle to understand the ways in which mainstream legal consciousness is white, male, Christian, able-bodied, economically privileged, and heterosexual will come a legal theory more profound than any other we have seen emanating from Anglo–American law schools. I speak of nothing less than transcendence of the self-declared bankruptcy of modernist thought and of something as dear as peace, freedom, and justice—words our poets, organizers, and legal scholars have never been too shy to speak.

To close, let me offer a road map of the work we are doing and suggestions for what we need to do to develop the jurisprudence of color.

First, description tells the untold stories of experiences of people of color under law and documents the facts of both our contributions and our exclusion. Using lawyerly expertise in reading legal documents, we should mine the primary sources to describe the role of race in American legal history.

Next, doctrinal development and critique has a long history in the experience of people of color. This is the work that stretches and shapes legal categories and advocates particular legal results. We should resist the trap of downgrading descriptive and doctrinal work. This trap is particularly prevalent at elite law schools. Descriptive and doctrinal work is not second-class work. It is work that in itself presents a sophisticated theoretical position, namely, that a legal response to the immediate needs of oppressed communities is a valuable method for deriving a theory of law and justice.

That brings us to the final category: theory. As phase one of the theoretical project, we need to critique the texts of lawcases, casebooks, law review articles, and jurisprudence monographs—to show how mainstream writers fail to account for racism and the experience of outsiders. You no doubt have a favorite article in the critique genre, and I want to beg for more. Where are our critiques, for example, of the standard textbooks used in the law schools?

The second stage of our theoretical work—theory building—will follow from critique. From identifying what is missing from standard jurisprudence it follows that we have ideas about what to fill in. We are here in the particular physical sense of our personal genealogies because

Movement," *Harvard Civil Rights–Civil Liberties Law Review* 22 (1982): 297.

6. [Martha] Minow, "Justice Engendered," *Harvard Law Review* 101 (1987): 10.

we are the children of survivors, of people who judged correctly which fights to fight, when to lay low, and when to assert personhood. We are the children of generations before us who refused to accept the message of racial inferiority. Now I come dangerously close to privileging our experience in a way that is false. There are mistakes and villains in our histories. What I intend to suggest is only that there is something about life on this side of the color line that has theory-building potential. There is a reason that Justice Thurgood Marshall understands things not only about people of color but also about women, poor people, homosexuals, the physically disabled, and other outsiders that his colleagues in all their intelligence often fail to understand. It is not that being Black is a prerequisite to this understanding, as Justice Brennan demonstrates; rather, I want to identify and tap the source of Justice Marshall's vision that is related to his experience as a Black person.

Tapping that source is what jurisprudence is all about: the search for justice. The search for justice in the nuclear age carries an urgency previously unknown to humankind. As lawyers and theorists, let us go swiftly to our own histories and bring back to the law schools the truths we find there.

MARI J. MATSUDA, CRITICAL RACE THEORY: IN WHERE IS YOUR BODY?

53–54 (1996).

A jurisprudence includes a definition of justice. What is justice according to critical race theory?

It is antiracist.

It is substantive.

It is attainable.

Critical race theory, grounded as it is in a descriptive understanding of racism as a resilient, antiprogressive force in American history, suggests that an antiracist agenda is key to a conception of justice. Ending racism through law is an immediate prescriptive agenda, as is ending all forms of subordination.

A just world is one that heals the wounded among us, that brings back the lost and the wasted, that elevates all human beings to their highest potential. The only way to do this is through a substantive conception of rights. In addition to the language of process and equality familiar in liberal discourse, scholars of color add a language of entitlement and community.

Entitlement: each human being is entitled, in this rich nation of ours, to the material means to attain a decent life.

Community: the broader community has both special obligation to disadvantaged communities and affirmative duties to reverse longstanding patterns of exploitation and maldistribution. Only then can the entire community flourish.

Thus, these scholars call for nonneutral, asymmetrical concepts of law, such as affirmative action. Such prescriptions make sense only if one starts from a belief that subordination exists, that racism and other instruments of domination are widespread, and that advantage and disadvantage have little to do with merit and a lot to do with systemic, institutionalized oppression.

* * *

The prescription is an emotional one. Critical race theorists remind us that there are real human lives touched by law. They use the first person and speak of their parents, their children, their kin, and their daily lives. Their jurisprudence is also, in spite of a deeply critical stance, an optimistic one. Who but an optimist, after all, would see American racism and choose to write about it instead of conceding to its strength in preacknowledged defeat? That they write, enter theoretical debate, teach in law schools, speak to white audiences, and participate in community struggle is all a testimony of faith. The irony of their rejection as divisive, separatist, and impolitic is that if they were those things they would not be doing what they are doing.

MARI J. MATSUDA, STANDING BESIDE MY SISTER, FACING THE ENEMY: LEGAL THEORY OUT OF COALITION IN WHERE IS YOUR BODY?

63–64 (1996).

Looking at Subordination from Inside Coalition

When we work in coalition, we compare our struggles and challenge one another's assumptions. We learn a few tentative, starting truths—the building blocks of a theory of subordination.

We learn that all forms of oppression are not the same. We learn about our ignorances and of the gaps and absences in our knowledge. We learn that although all forms of oppression are not the same, certain predictable patterns emerge:

- All forms of oppression involve taking a trait, x, often with attached cultural meaning, and using x to make some group the other, reducing their entitlements and powers
- All forms of oppression benefit someone, and sometimes both sides of a relationship of domination have some stake in its maintenance.
- All forms of oppression have both material and ideological dimensions. Subordination leaves marks on the body. It is real. It is material; it is health, economy, and violence. Subordination is also ideology: language—including the language of science and law, rights, necessity, the market, neutrality, and objectivity—can serve to make domination seem natural and inevitable.
- In coalition we learn as well that there is a psychology to subordination, involving elements of sexual fear, need for control, self-hate, and other-hate.

- Finally, and most important, we learn in coalition that all forms of subordination are interlocking and mutually reinforcing, even as they are different and incommensurable.

Notes on Critical Race Feminism

1. According to Matsuda, Justice Thurgood Marshall understood "things not only about people of color but also about women, poor people, homosexuals, the physically disabled, and other outsiders that his colleagues in all their intelligence often fail to understand." She also notes that Justice Brennan's similar ability to understand indicates that "being Black is [not] a prerequisite to this understanding." But she nevertheless sees "Justice Marshall's vision [as] related to his experience as a Black person." For examples of Justices Marshall's and Brennan's insight into cases involving sex discrimination, see the three important cases in Chapter 2 in which the Court failed to see sex discrimination: *Geduldig* (Marshall joins Brennan's dissent), *Feeney* (Brennan joins Marshall's dissent); and *Rostker* (Brennan joins Marshall's dissent). Do you agree with Matsuda that there is a connection between Justice Marshall's experiences as a black person and his ability to see discrimination invisible to most of the Justices on the Court? If you answered yes, do you believe that this would be true of any black justice (such as Justice Thomas)? Is Matsuda making an essentialist claim? What exactly is the connection she sees?

2. Are female justices (Justices O'Connor and Ginsburg) more likely, because of their experiences as women, to see important aspects about the reality not just of women, but also of poor people, people of color, homosexuals, and the physically disabled?

3. In the last extract above, Matsuda describes five similarities in the ways in which various inequalities operate. Can you specify how these five aspects of inequality operate with respect to sex discrimination? (On her first point, for example, identify the trait on which sex discrimination is premised and describe its cultural meaning. How is it used to make women "the other"? How does it diminish women's entitlements and powers?) Do the same with various racial or ethnic groups. Does discrimination operate the same way with respect to African Americans and Latinas/Latinos? Does it operate in the same way with respect to women in other racial or ethnic groups? How does class complicate the analysis?

4. How would a critical race feminist agenda differ from a formal equality agenda? A dominance feminist agenda? A relational feminist agenda?

5. Add a column headed critical race feminism (as described by Matsuda and others in this section) to your theory chart (the chart describing and contrasting formal equality, dominance feminism, relational feminism, socialist feminism, and post-modern feminism). In terms of substantive goals and how to reach them, which feminist approach already on your chart is closest to Matsuda's vision?

8. LESBIAN FEMINISM

Text Note: Compulsory Heterosexuality

In a classic essay written in 1980, Adrienne Rich introduced the ideas of compulsory heterosexuality and the lesbian continuum. By *compulsory* heterosexuality, Rich refers to the fact that no woman can be said to have freely chosen heterosexuality today. In support, she cites the enormous amount of violence against women (why is it necessary?); the erasure of lesbian existence (because of men's fear of what might happen were there a visible alternative?); and the constant repetition in fairy tales, novels, movies, academic scholarship, etc., that women are "naturally" heterosexual (unnecessary if women truly are heterosexual by nature). Rich, Compulsory Heterosexuality and Lesbian Existence, 5 Signs 631 (1980).

Rich uses "lesbian continuum" to refer to the fact that all women depend on intimate connections with other women. Over the course of a life, every woman experiences close, intimate, relationships with other women as friends and allies against male tyranny. The first is with one's mother. But throughout their lives, girls and women depend on other girls and women for the richness of shared emotional lives. For all women, relationships with women are sources of energy, power, and strength. If we consider not just genital contact but the wide range of women's connections to other women, then we can see that every woman lives along a woman-connected-to-woman (or lesbian) continuum.

Notes on Compulsory Heterosexuality

1. Write down three sources of pressure on you in your own life to be heterosexual. Do you agree with Rich that it is difficult to know whether (hetero)sexuality is "chosen"? If heterosexuality is compulsory, why are so many heterosexual women so sure that they are "really" heterosexual?

2. What is the relationship between heterosexuality and women's subordination? Can you imagine a culture and legal system in which heterosexuality is not compulsory? In that world, what would be different about the stories we tell children? How would the legal system change? The media? Social interaction?

3. What are the advantages of thinking of women as identifying with women in various ways along Rich's lesbian continuum? What are the disadvantages? Does such an approach carry some risk of erasing lesbian existence and culture? See letters from Ann Snitow, Christine Stansell, and Sharon Thompson to Rich and her response, reprinted in Adrienne Rich, Blood, Bread, and Poetry 68–75 (1986).

4. Do you or the women you know find that woman-woman relationships or all-woman groups or projects are a source of energy? How and why? In your experience, have all-women projects or groups been controversial? Marilyn Frye suggests that such events are often controversial because

> [t]he woman-only meeting is a fundamental challenge to the structure of power. It is always the privilege of the master to enter the slave's hut.

> The slave who decides to exclude the master from her hut is declaring herself not a slave. The exclusion of men from the meeting not only deprives them of certain benefits (which they might survive without); it is a controlling of access, hence an assumption of power. It is not only mean, it is arrogant.

Frye, Oppression in The Politics of Reality: Essays in Feminist Theory 1, 2 (1983). Frye believes separatism is necessary for this very reason: "When those who control access have made you totally accessible, your first act of taking control must be denying access, or must have denial of access as one of its aspects." Id. Do you agree that some separatism is both necessary and controversial for that reason? Why were consciousness-raising groups only women? Was that a necessary condition for consciousness raising?

5. Define sexual orientation. What do you consider when identifying someone's sexual orientation?

6. Are you confident that you are innately heterosexual, homosexual, or bisexual? How do you know? Do you prefer chocolate or vanilla ice cream? Is your preference for chocolate or vanilla innate? How would you know whether your preference for chocolate or vanilla was innate? Do you think that we actually have access to such knowledge with respect to either ice cream flavors or sexual orientation?

7. Do you think that women's sexuality might be more fluid than men's? There is some evidence that this might be true. See Mary Becker, Women, Morality, and Sexual Orientation, 8 U.C.L.A. Women's L. J. 165, 211 (1998). How would you explain this possible difference between women and men?

8. Vera Whisman argues that "[I]n a non-heterosexist society, the question of whether homosexuality is a choice would command little attention." Whisman, Queer by Choice: Lesbians, Gay Men, and the Politics of Identity 3 (1996). Whisman sees personal accounts of whether one "chooses" to be lesbian or gay not as descriptions of actual experiences but as "devices which individuals select and use because of what they can do for one in the negotiation of a hostile world." Id. at 7. In her study, Whisman found that lesbians were more likely than gay men to believe they "choose" their sexuality. Id. at 121. Why is the question of "choice" so important in contemporary debates about homosexuality?

9. Mary Becker has suggested that many women do not have a sexual orientation:

> [S]exual orientation as normally understood—referring to whether the objects of one's desires have the physical sex of men or women—is simply not pointing at anything relevant for many women. For many women, whether a partner has the same or different physical sex is irrelevant to sexual pleasure, desire, and preferences. A partner's physical sex is simply not important independent of the relationship of care and connection in which it is encountered, in part because our sexuality is not organized around physical objects but around the quality of and emotional intimacy in a personal relationship.

* * *

It might seem that the category of bisexual includes people with no sexual orientation. But * * * "bisexual" refers not to someone who is indifferent to the physical sex of their lover(s)—someone without a sexual orientation—but to someone who craves lovers with male bodies and lovers with female bodies. Women with a fluid sexuality may not have "cravings" for people with particular kinds of genitals.

The assumption that a lover's physical sexual shape is of key importance is troubling not only because it does not reflect the reality of some women, but also because it camouflages sexual possibilities. * * * In our culture, a woman without a sexual orientation is likely to assume that she is a heterosexual * * *.

Becker, above note 7, at 208–10. Do you agree with Becker's definition of sexual orientation? Do you feel that you have a sexual orientation as that term is normally understood? Is your sexual orientation innate or chosen? Do you believe you have access to accurate information on these questions?

14. What are the risks—in personal, political, and legal settings—of talking about sexual orientation as something chosen? Imagine coming out to your parents or arguing for gay rights before a legislature or a court. What are the risks of mentioning choice in each of these settings? Might talk of "choice" be threatening to heterosexuals? Despite the downsides, might it be desirable to talk about choice in order to bring into the open some of the goodness of lesbian and gay relationships as well as some of the problems with heterosexual relationships, particularly for women? Do the advantages outweigh the disadvantages?

PATRICIA A. CAIN, FEMINIST JURISPRUDENCE: GROUNDING THE THEORIES

4 Berkeley Women's L.J. 191, 201–03, 205–07, 209, 210, 212–14 (1989).

[F]eminist legal theorists often ignore, or at best marginalize, lesbian experience. I call this the problem of the invisible lesbian. It is a problem that has serious consequences for the building of feminist legal theory.

* * *

One might expect cultural feminists and dominance theorists who engage in legal scholarship (such as Gilligan and MacKinnon, respectively) to acknowledge the relevance of lesbian experience in their writings. It is particularly surprising to discover the invisible lesbian problem in the work of cultural feminists. In disciplines other than law, feminist theorists working to reclaim women's culture and its values have often focused on lesbian community. But in legal scholarship, discussions of female value focus on "woman as mother."

* * *

Dominance theorists also tend to ignore lesbian experience. Catharine MacKinnon, for example, has argued that women are constantly and always subordinated to men. In MacKinnon's view, any special abilities for caring and connection come, not from the positive aspects of motherhood, but from the negative effects of subordination. Women build webs of connection to survive the subordination. "Women value care because men have valued us according to the care we give them.... "

To the claim that lesbian experience is different, that lesbians are not subordinate to men, that their care is not male-directed, MacKinnon appears to have two different responses. Her first response is that exceptions do not matter. MacKinnon's intent is to offer a critique of the structural condition of women as sexual subordinates and not to make existential claims about all women. It does not affect her theory that *all* women are not always subordinated to men. Thus, for MacKinnon, lesbian experience of non-subordination is simply irrelevant.

Her second response is more troubling. It goes beyond the assertion that lesbian experience is irrelevant; it denies the claim that lesbian experience is free from male domination.

> Some have argued that lesbian sexuality—meaning here simply women having sex with women, not with men—solves the problem of gender by eliminating men from women's voluntary sexual encounters. Yet women's sexuality remains constructed under conditions of male supremacy; women remain socially defined as women in relation to men; the definition of women as men's inferiors remains sexual even if not heterosexual, whether men are present at the time or not.

I find this passage objectionable for several reasons. My primary objection is that MacKinnon has defined lesbian sexuality to suit her purposes ("*simply* women having sex with women"—i.e., with nothing else changed except that a woman replaces a man). Although I do not dispute that lesbian couples can sometimes ape their heterosexual counterparts, I am infuriated by MacKinnon's silencing of the rest of lesbian experience. Where is MacKinnon's feminist method? To whom does she choose to listen? Would it not enrich her theory to recognize the reality of non-subordination that some lesbians claim as their experiential reality and ask about its relevance to her underlying theory? And yet, because her theory is premised on a single commonality among women, sexual subordination, MacKinnon fails to see the relevance of the lesbian claim to non-domination, even when it stands * * * in front of her.

* * *

I believe that current feminist legal theory is deficient and impoverished because it has not paid sufficient attention to the real life experiences of women who do not speak the "dominant discourse." Elsewhere I have urged that feminist law teaching ought to include "listening to difference" and "making connections." Here I urge the same for feminist legal scholarship.

* * *

I ask those of you in the audience who are heterosexual to focus on an important love relationship in your life. This could be a present relationship or a past one, or even the relationship you hope to have. I ask you: how would you feel about this relationship if it had to be kept utterly secret? Would you feel "at one with the world" if a slight mistake in language ("we" instead of "I") could lead to alienation from your friends and family, loss of your job? Would you feel at one with your lover if the only time you could touch or look into each other's eyes was in your own home—with the curtains drawn? What would such self-consciousness do to your relationship?

* * *

The invisibility of lesbian existence removes the lesbian possibility from view. If there are no lesbians, the only possibility is heterosexuality. Men will assume all women are equally available as sex partners. Women will choose men and never question that choice.

If the choice is never questioned, can it be an authentic choice? Do heterosexual women really choose men or are they victims of false consciousness? And if they are victims of false consciousness, then how do we know that most women are heterosexual? Might they not choose otherwise if they were truly free to choose?

Marilyn Frye offers a challenge to feminist academics and I want to echo her in repeating it here for feminist legal theorists:

> I want to ask heterosexual academic feminists to do some hard analytical and reflective work. To begin with, I want to say to them:
>
> I wish you would notice that you are heterosexual.
>
> I wish you would grow to the understanding that you choose heterosexuality.
>
> I would like you to rise each morning and know that you are heterosexual and that you choose to be heterosexual—that you are and choose to be a member of a privileged and dominant class, one of your privileges being not to notice.
>
> I wish you would stop and seriously consider, as a broad and longterm feminist political strategy, the conversion of women to a woman-identified and woman-directed sexuality. . . .[107]

Frye reports that a typical response by heterosexual women to such inquiries is that, although they may understand what she is saying, they cannot just up and decide to be lesbian. I, too, have women colleagues and friends who similarly respond, with a shake of the head, that they are hopelessly heterosexual, that they just are not sexually attracted to women.

107. Frye, *A Lesbian Perspective on Women's Studies* 194, 196 (M. Cruikshank, ed. 1982).

Frye says that she wants to ask such women (and so do I), "Why not? Why don't women turn you on? Why aren't you attracted to women?" These are serious questions. Frye encourages heterosexual women to consider the origins of their sexual orientation:

> The suppression of lesbian feeling, sensibility, and response has been so thorough and so brutal for such a long time, that if there were not a strong and widespread inclination to lesbianism, it would have been erased from human life. There is so much pressure on women to be heterosexual, and this pressure is both so pervasive and so completely denied, that I think heterosexuality cannot come naturally to many women; I think that widespread heterosexuality among women is a highly artificial product of the patriarchy.... I want heterosexual women to do intense and serious consciousness-raising and exploration of their own personal histories and to find out how and when in their own development the separation of women from the erotic came about for them. I would like heterosexual women to be as actively curious about how and why and when they became heterosexual as I have been about how and why and when I became lesbian.[110]

* * *

I, and other lesbians who live our private lives removed from the intimate presence of men, do indeed experience time free from male domination. When we leave the male-dominated public sphere, we come home to a woman-identified private sphere. That does not mean that the patriarchy as an institution does not exist for us or that the patriarchy does not exist during the time that we experience freedom from male domination. It means simply that we experience significant periods of nonsubordination, during which we, as women, are free to develop a sense of self that is our own and not a mere construct of the patriarchy.

* * *

The problem with current feminist theory is that the more abstract and universal it is, the more it fails to relate to the lived reality of many women. One problem with much feminist legal theory is that it has abstracted and universalized from the experience of heterosexual women. Consider again Marilyn Frye's challenge to heterosexual academic feminists: "I wish you would notice that you are heterosexual. I wish you would grow to the understanding that you choose heterosexuality ... that you are and choose to be a member of a privileged and dominant class, one of your privileges being not to notice."

* * *

My "lesbian standpoint" enables me to see two versions of reality. The dominant reality, which I experience as "theirs," includes the following: lesbians are not mothers, all women are dominated by men, male relationships are valuable and female relationships are not, lesbian

110. Id. at 196–97.

is a dirty word, lesbians are sick, women who live alone desire men, women who live together desire men, no one knows a lesbian, lesbians don't have families, all feminist legal theorists are heterosexual, all women in this room are heterosexual, lesbians are sex, most women are heterosexual and not lesbian.

By contrast, the reality that I live, the reality I call "mine," includes the following: some mothers are lesbian, many women are lesbian, many lesbian women are not dominated by men, many women do not desire men, lesbian is a beautiful word, lesbians are love, love is intimacy, the heterosexual/lesbian dichotomy is false, all lesbians are born into families, lesbians are family, some feminist legal theorists are lesbian, lesbians are brave.

Why is the lesbian so invisible in feminist legal theory? Why is "my reality" so different from "their reality?" And which reality is true? For the postmodernist, the last question is meaningless. But the first two are not.

Notes on Feminist Legal Theory and Lesbians

1. Women whose primary relationships are with other women cannot, of course, escape their culture's sexism and heterosexism. They may replicate some aspects of male-female relationships in their own woman-woman relationships, as MacKinnon points out when she discusses butch/femme roles, and are likely also to internalize some or much of their culture's negative attitude towards such relationships. Does it follow that women loving women can only escape the most superficial aspects of patriarchy? Why might it matter—both to the individuals and to the political struggle—that a woman invests her emotional, economic, and sexual energy and resources in another woman rather than a man? Is talking to a woman or a group of women different from talking to a man or to a group of men regardless of the sexual orientation of the women and regardless of whether they are butch or femme? Is helping to raise another woman's children different from raising a man's? Is supporting a woman economically and emotionally different from supporting a man, regardless of her sexual orientation and regardless of whether she is butch or femme? Are these differences trivial? What makes us label a woman as a butch? Does a woman who is butch have the social power or psychological make-up of a man, including a man's sense of entitlement?

2. Do you agree with Cain that feminists contribute to the suppression of lesbian existence? Think of the major items on the feminist agenda over the last thirty years or so and their relative importance for heterosexual and lesbian women. Even issues important to all women, such as domestic violence, often have in fact been addressed only in the context of the needs of heterosexual women. For example, many domestic violence statutes do not cover domestic violence when women are domestic partners. See discussion in Chapter 7.

3. Sarah Hoagland has argued that the feminist movement has been androcentric and heterocentric in that it has focused on ways to improve, and hence foster, women's relationships with men rather than on ways to

improve, and hence foster, women's relationships with each other. Hoagland, Lesbian Ethics 57–58 (1988) Feminist reform "forces women to prove that men's fears are unfounded—to prove that women, or 'real' women, are not lesbians or manhaters. It forces women to appear feminine and prove they are not threatening." Id. Do you agree? Do you feel such pressure, especially (perhaps) since you've been taking this course? What is the source of the pressure?

4. Hoagland also argues that "feminist reform makes the actual success of women's efforts depend on the intelligence, willingness, and benevolence of the men they're seeking to convince to enact reform." Hoagland, above note 3, at 57–58. And she maintains that "feminist reform sets up women to value change in men more highly than change in women," making any failure "a failure of effort on women's, not a refusal on men's part." Id. Do you agree? Is this inevitable?

DIANA MAJURY, REFASHIONING THE UNFASHIONABLE: CLAIMING LESBIAN IDENTITIES IN THE LEGAL CONTEXT

7 Canadian J. Women & Law 286, 306–17 (1994).

* * *

Lesbians have been subject to the sexism and male dominance of gay men within joint organizations and society at large. As a result, lesbians have been assumed to be the same as gay men; they have been subjected to, and judged by, the stereotypes of gay men; they have been assumed to have the same interest, goals and needs as gay men; they have been assumed to suffer from the same forms of discrimination, and in the same ways, as gay men.

As a female in this society, a lesbian's experience of inequality is very different from that of a gay man. She is likely to be in a worse economic situation than a gay man, in terms of current finances and economic opportunities; she is likely to have more limited and less remunerative job prospects than he; she is more likely to be trying to support children, with all of the attendant problems and expenses that child care presents in the context of the paid work force. Reproduction and child custody are issues of central concern to some lesbians, while, at best, they have been seen as peripheral to gay issues. While the use of psychiatry against lesbians and the pathologization of lesbians as mentally ill have been common practices historically, they have received little attention as gay concerns. The physical and sexual violence inflicted upon lesbians is different, in terms of where it takes place, the forms it takes, and its overall impact, from the violence to which gay men are subjected. The focus and import of issues of sex, sexuality, and sexual practice are different for lesbians than they are for gay men. Lesbians, particularly outspoken lesbian-identified lesbians, are being subjected to a vicious and virulent anti-lesbian, anti-woman backlash.

The term sexual orientation seems inappropriate and inadequate to ground the specific inequalities experienced by lesbians. There is no doubt that lesbians should support gay men as an oppressed group, as we should support any oppressed group. But the question is, given all the differences between lesbians and gay men, played out as they are in the context of the power imbalance of gender, is there enough in common to warrant treatment as a single group for anti-discrimination purposes? Are the discriminations experienced by lesbians and gays sufficiently similar to be lumped together under a single ground of discrimination? Are we looking for a new gender neutral term such as, for example, "sexual identity," that might more accurately capture the meaning of being a lesbian and that is capable of being defined in law and society as including lesbians in their realities, as well as gay men in theirs? Or is the hegemony of male dominance so overpowering, are the experiences and issues for lesbians and gays so different, as to necessitate that lesbians resist the identification of lesbian inequality with gay inequality and insist on the recognition of lesbians as a distinct group, experiencing discrimination, not under some umbrella term that includes gay men, but specific to lesbians? Or is lesbian discrimination an extreme form of discrimination against women; is sex discrimination the more appropriate umbrella under which to challenge lesbian discrimination?

Lesbian Inequality as Sex Inequality

* * *

The argument that discrimination against lesbians and gays is sex discrimination has generally been articulated, where it has been argued at all, as a formal equality argument. The argument, under the formal equality model, is that it is sex discrimination to deny women the rights that men have, or to restrict women in ways that men are not restricted in the exercise of their rights, including the right to have full and committed sexual relationships with women. The argument applies, in the converse, to support gay male rights. Thus, for example, the argument in support of the right to gay marriage is that to permit a man to marry a woman but at the same time to deny him the right to marry another man is to construct an unconstitutional classification "on account of sex." This is the classic formal equality, "but for sex" argument in which sex is put forward as the sole impediment to the right, privilege or benefit being sought. In the lesbian or gay context, the argument is that "but for" my gender, or alternatively "but for" the gender of my chosen partner, I would have access to the right being denied me. While the simplicity of this "but for sex" version of a sex equality argument may make it appear attractive, it is an argument that undermines, if not contradicts, an inequality-based approach. As with all formal equality arguments, the "but for sex" argument is premised on an assertion of compliance with the dominant standard. Lesbians and gays are put forward as the same as heterosexuals, gender being cast as an insignificant difference. To the extent that lesbians and gays are able and willing to "heterosexualize" themselves, they argue that they should have access to the privileges of heterosexuality. Thus lesbian mothers have been granted custody of their children as long as they appear to be heterosexual, that is, that they are not politically or sexually active as lesbians. A successful formal equality analysis in this context would mean that the least oppressed lesbians and gays, that is, those most like the dominant group, would be granted heterosexual status. As a corollary, the most oppressed lesbians and gays would be further marginalized and subject to more extreme forms of discrimination and subordination.

The fact that gays have by and large not been successful even under the formal equality model of sex discrimination is a reflection of the depth and resistance of the hatred and fear of lesbians and gays. Even when lesbians and gays present themselves as the same as heterosexuals, they are not accepted. If lesbians and gays were "just like" heterosexuals, then the only threat that we would pose would be to the strict gender differentiation imposed by heterosexuality. The rejection of even assimilated lesbians and gays is strong testament to the commitment to retain gender difference, that is to the preservation of gender inequality. This recognition that gender and sex inequality are the underpinnings of "sexual orientation" discrimination gives rise to the more complex, inequality-based analysis of lesbian discrimination as sex discrimination. Judicial rejection of the formal sex equality analysis of discrimination against lesbians and gays is premised on an asserted difference between lesbians and gays and their relationships on the one hand and heterosexuals and heterosexual relationships on the other. This "difference" is all about gender; it is described primarily in terms of sexual intercourse and reproduction, but also in terms of gender roles and ascribed gender qualities.

Lesbians are discriminated against because they challenge dominant understandings and meanings of gender in our society. And the more, and the more overtly, we challenge gender, the more, and the more overtly, we are discriminated against. Gender differentiation, premised on the subordination of women, is as essential to heterosexualism as it is to sexism. Lesbian inequalities are sex inequalities because they are rooted in a highly circumscribed definition of gender and gender roles, according to which women are seen only in relation to men. Women who define themselves, and who, in so doing, define themselves without any reference to men, are de-sexed; either they are seen as not women or their "sex", that is their lesbianism, is denied. Either way, this is sex discrimination at its most extreme.

Sexuality is one of the defining features of gender, in terms of both reproduction and presumed male sexual access to females. Gender stereotypes and the gender hierarchy are premised on heterosexuality. Heterosexuality and the gender stereotypes and hierarchy to which it gives rise have, in the past, been assumed to be biologically based, that is, seen as essential components of one's biological sex. In this heterosexual sexual context, the male is seen as aggressive, independent, dominant; the female is seen as passive, dependent, submissive. Male sexual violence against women is a reflection of, as well as a function of, the deeply rooted connections between gender inequality, sex and sexuality.

Heterosexuality becomes one of the demarcations and reinforcers of gender "difference" and of women's inequality. Heterosexuality is prescribed and promoted through law and other social institutions:

> History suggests that a primary purpose and effect of state enforcement of heterosexuality is to preserve gender differentiation and the relationships premised upon it. Thus, constitutional restraints against gender discrimination must also be applied to laws censuring homosexuality.[81]

Lesbian oppression functions to reinforce and perpetuate strict notions of gender differentiation. Lesbian inequality is the warning to girls and women not to challenge the prescribed meaning of being female in this society. Those girls and women who do start to assert their autonomy and to challenge their sexual subordination and the centrality/necessity of men in women's lives are often quickly and powerfully reminded that it could get worse. They are called "lesbian" or "dyke", not because they do, or are even thought to, have "sex" with women, but because the ostracism and increased inequality that the label "lesbian" represents are used to try to bring women back into gender line. Women and girls who do not focus their attention on men are called "man-haters", a term stereotypically understood as synonymous with lesbian, a term that is explicitly designed to re-focus attention back on men.

Discrimination against lesbians is sex discrimination, perhaps in its starkest and most overt form. It is important to argue lesbian discrimination as sex discrimination in legal fora as elsewhere, because this analysis challenges sex inequality in fundamental and radical ways. However, strategically, it is probably not advisable to leave lesbian inequalities to be addressed exclusively through the prohibition of sex discrimination. The lesbian discrimination as sex discrimination analysis requires a fairly sophisticated understanding of sex equality/inequality. As with any other uncharted equality territory, rejection of a sex equality analysis, at the first instance, is indicative neither of its validity as equality theory nor of its potential eventually to be integrated into our jurisprudence. It may take time for the lesbian sex discrimination analysis to be heard and understood in the courtroom, which is precisely why it is important to continue to speak it, develop it, argue its appropriateness and insist that it be heard and understood on our terms. Some of the equality arguments which now seem commonplace in our jurisprudence at first instance seemed incredibly risky and impossible to expect courts to understand.

It seems to me that there might, in most cases, be a substantial difference between arguing lesbian inequality as sex discrimination rather than as sexual orientation discrimination or even lesbian discrimination. Take, for instance, the "spousal" benefit cases. These cases have generally been presented in terms of heterosexual couples being given

81. [Sylvia] Law, [Homosexuality and the Social Meaning of Gender, [1988] Wis. L. Rev. 187,] at 230.

something that has not been given to so called "same-sex" couples. Lesbian and gay couples are seen as being denied these benefits because of their sexual orientation. A sex equality analysis of spousal benefits would more readily and clearly expose the gendered assumption of dependence, need, and obligation upon which most of these benefits are premised. Spousal benefits then perpetuate the gendered conditions which lend credence to these gendered assumptions. It is a self-perpetuating system of sexual inequality. A sex equality analysis would question the fundamental premise that benefits should necessarily or logically be disseminated through sexual relationships. A sex equality analysis would open up the larger question of why we as a society endorse such benefits and to whom, in the interests of fairness and equity, they should be allocated. If the issues are dependence, need, and obligation, why then are these not the criteria for distribution? Such an approach may provide the grounding for arguments for universalized benefits. It may be that not only the analysis, but the result, might be quite different from a sex equality perspective.

However, in the interim, as lesbian sex equality is being developed, lesbians need to be named specifically as a protected group in order to avoid lesbian claims being dismissed summarily, leaving lesbians without any legal protection against discrimination. While the sexual orientation umbrella, as it has been legally and socially constructed in the context of male supremacy, may be inappropriate, the sex umbrella, as it has been legally constructed, may, at least for the moment, be inadequate. The legal recognition of discrimination against lesbians as a prohibited ground of discrimination will provide the foot in the door that will enable the sex discrimination arguments to be made. Sex discrimination can be claimed and argued as a separate ground, in conjunction with the lesbian discrimination ground, as well as in conjunction with any other ground that may apply. While lesbian discrimination may be the ground which the court feels required to hear and consider in full, they will have to sit through, and at least give some thought to, the sex discrimination argument as well. In addition, the lesbian discrimination ground would be argued in terms of sex discrimination, that discrimination against lesbians is discrimination against women who are challenging the circumscribed meanings of gender. In Canada, sexual harassment had first to be included as a separate ground of discrimination before it was definitively recognized as a form of sex discrimination; lesbian discrimination may have to follow this same path.

Conclusion

* * *

While I feel myself on the verge of saying that discrimination against lesbians is fully understood and conceptualized as sex discrimination, I will always seem to pull back just short of that assertion. Is there something more that is discrimination against lesbians that is not captured by a sex discrimination analysis? While I have some persisting sense that there is something more and that I am missing a piece that makes lesbian inequality something separate from sex inequality, I do not know what that piece is.

Ruthann Robson argues that lesbian jurisprudence is not the same as feminist jurisprudence:

> Feminist jurisprudence is most often concerned with women *vis-à-vis* men; the difference/sameness debates on equality issues evince this preoccupation. The essential exercise is comparing women with men; the essential goal is equality with men.
>
> As I conceptualize lesbian jurisprudence, it has a different focus. If lesbians are women-identified women, then measurements are not relative to men; men's measurements are in some sense irrelevant.[90]

While I think (hope) that feminist jurisprudence is becoming less focused on women in relation to men and more on women in their own right, I would agree with Robson that lesbian jurisprudence cannot be collapsed into feminist jurisprudence. However, I do not think that the same argument applies to lesbian inequality as sex inequality. The sex inequality analysis is very much focused on lesbians as women, not in comparison to men, but in terms of challenging notions of gender. An inequality-based approach is directed toward redressing the inequalities experienced by lesbians, not to making the treatment of lesbians accord with the treatment of non-lesbians. However, Robson's rejection of attempts to collapse lesbianism into gender reinforces my concern that I am missing something unique about lesbian inequality.

* * *

This brings me back to the more fundamental question of whether all of these categories are irredeemably problematic because they are apparently mutually exclusive and negate the complexity and specificity of compound forms of discrimination. Perhaps this whole "boxed" human rights approach is so rigid and narrowly focused as to be incapable of expansion or flexibility. These same questions apply to the lesbian category, itself. But, in the face of the current very real life oppressions of lesbians, I think it politically unwise for lesbians and their supporters to abandon the category. To me this is tantamount to abandoning each other. Instead I claim with pride, joy, and fear—my lesbian identity.

Notes on Lesbians and Sex Equality

1. Is part of the challenge lesbians pose that lesbian couples are not identical to heterosexual couples? See, e.g., Lawrence A. Kurdek, The Allocation of Household Labor in Gay, Lesbian, and Heterosexual Married Couples, 49 J. Social Issues 127 (1993) (finding that household labor was more equitably divided in gay and lesbian couples than in heterosexual couples; in

90. [Ruthann] Robson, "Lesbian Jurisprudence?," [8 L. & Ineq. J. 443,] at 449 [(1989–90)].

heterosexual couples, the wife performs most of the tasks); Mary Becker, Women, Morality, and Sexual Orientation, 8 U.C.L.A. Women's L. J. 165 (1998) (discussing many differences between lesbian and heterosexual couples, including equitable division of household tasks, but stressing that both coerced and consensual unwanted sex appear to be far more common for women in heterosexual relationships than women in lesbian relationships). Which arguments for lesbian rights ignore such differences and which use such differences?

2. What does Majury see as the connection between discrimination against lesbians and sex discrimination? In the spousal-benefits case, discussed by Majury shortly before her conclusion, describe the argument for benefits for same-sex couples framed as an argument for nondiscrimination on the basis of sexual orientation. Describe the sex discrimination form of the argument. Which is more powerful? Which argument do you prefer analytically? Which is likely to be more threatening to listeners? Which would you use if arguing in a court and which would you use if arguing to a legislature?

3. Do you agree with Majury that the distribution of benefits to spouses (of employees or of workers covered by social security) is a form of sex discrimination? Explain. Could you make an argument that spousal benefits are sex discrimination using formal equality? Dominance feminism? Relational feminism? Critical race feminism? Which arguments are strongest?

4. Majury is troubled by conceptualizing discrimination against lesbians as *only* sex discrimination and finds herself "pull[ing] back just short" of asserting that "discrimination against lesbians is fully understood and conceptualized as sex discrimination." What differences might there be between discrimination against lesbians and sex discrimination? What dangers might there be for lesbians in understanding and conceptualizing discrimination against lesbians as (only) sex discrimination? If discrimination against lesbians is to some extent something other than or different from sex discrimination, what is the difference?

5. Majury believes that "lesbians" need to be explicitly included in anti-discrimination statutes at least "in the interim as lesbian sex equality is being developed." What does she mean by "lesbian sex equality"? Why should statutes specifically prohibit discrimination against "lesbians"? Why will the need for such specificity end with the development of lesbian sex equality?

6. Can sexism (i.e., bias against women as opposed to bias against lesbians) be eliminated by focusing on the needs of heterosexual women? Why might it be necessary to address the needs of lesbians in order to eliminate bias against straight women? Might the tendency of many heterosexual feminists to distance themselves from lesbians ultimately be self-defeating? Have you seen this tendency in groups you have been involved in? How have you responded?

Chapter 4

THE CONSTRUCTION OF FEMALE SEXUALITY

Introductory Note

Our sexuality is inextricably linked to how we view the world and how the world views us. The law is not neutral when it comes to sexuality; it institutionalizes our most intimate relationships, approving of and granting benefits to some (e.g., heterosexual marriage) and criminalizing others (e.g., homosexual sodomy). With whom, and under what circumstances, we choose to have a sexual relationship depends on how our sexuality is constructed—a complex blending of sex roles, biology, politics, coercion, pleasure, pain, power, and love.

This chapter begins with four very different feminist theories of sexuality. Catharine MacKinnon argues that sexuality is a construct of male power and is a dynamic of the inequality of the sexes. Andrea Dworkin posits that heterosexual intercourse is the expression of male contempt for women in its pure form and then addresses the role that women play in their own oppression. Alternatively, Ruth Colker urges a broader view of sexuality and suggests the possibility that male-female relationships and an environment of non-subordination may coexist. Finally, bell hooks urges us to reconsider the notion of sexual freedom and its current attachment to chosen norms; ultimately, she believes, ending sexual oppression will result in a decreased obsession with sexuality. Although all four approaches are conceptually abstract, they provide frameworks for considering the more concrete concerns addressed in the following section, on other difficulties negotiating pleasure under patriarchy.

A. SEXUALITY AND SUBORDINATION

CATHARINE A. MACKINNON, PLEASURE UNDER PATRIARCHY

In Theories of Human Sexuality

65–70, 75 (James Geer and William O'Donohue, eds. 1987).

Male dominance is sexual. Meaning: men in particular, if not men alone, sexualize hierarchy; gender is one. As much a sexual theory of gender as a gendered theory of sex, this is the theory of sexuality that will be advanced as feminist here. It is supported by recent work, both interpretive and empirical, on rape, battery, sexual harassment, the sexual abuse of children, prostitution, and pornography. These practices, taken together, express and actualize the distinctive power of men over women in society; their effective permissibility confirms and extends it. If you believe women's accounts of sexual use and abuse by men; if the pervasiveness of male sexual violence against women substantiated in these studies is not denied, minimized, or excepted as deviant or episodic; if the fact that only 7.8% of United States women are *not* sexually assaulted or harassed in their lifetimes is considered not ignorable, inconsequential, or isolated; if violation of women is understood as sexualized on some level—then sexuality itself can no longer be regarded as unimplicated. The meaning of practices of sexual violence cannot be categorized away as violence not sex, either. The male sexual role, these studies taken together suggest, centers on aggressive intrusion on those with less power. Such acts of dominance are experienced as sexually arousing, as sex itself. They therefore are. The evidence on the sexual violation of women by men thus frames an inquiry into the particular place of gender in sexuality as such.

A theory of sexuality that is feminist in my sense here locates sexuality within a theory of gender inequality; gender inequality is a critical term for the social hierarchy of men over women. To make a theory feminist, it is thus not enough that it be authored by a biological female. Nor that it describe female sexuality as different from (even if equal to) male sexuality, or as if sexuality in women ineluctably exists in some realm beyond, beneath, above, behind—in any event, fundamentally untouched and unmoved by—a sexist social order. For my purposes here, a theory of sexuality becomes feminist to the extent it treats sexuality as a construct of male power—defined by men, forced on women, and constitutive in the meaning of gender. Such an approach centers feminism on the perspective of the subordination of women to men as it identifies sex, that is, the sexuality of dominance and submission, as crucial, as a fundamental, as on some level definitive, in that process.[8]

* * *

8. It is unclear how varying the gender of the participants alters the politics of things sexual. For instance, some writers have argued that lesbian sexuality—here meaning simply women having sex with women rather than men—solves the sexuality problem by solving the gender problem in eliminating men from voluntary sexual encounters, e.g., Jill Johnston, *Lesbian nation* * * * (1974). It seems to me that this re-states sexuality's gender question rather than answers it. Women's sexuality remains constructed under conditions of male supremacy, women remain socially defined in relation to men as "women," and the definition of women remains sexual even if not heterosexual, whether men are there at the time or not. Unaddressed is whether sexuality is so gendermarked as to carry dominance and submission with it regardless of the gender of the immediate participants. I

A distinctively feminist theory, however provisionally advanced, would conceptualize social reality, including sexual reality, on its own terms. The question is, what are they? If women have been substantially deprived not only of our own experience but of terms of our own in which to view it, then a feminist theory of sexuality that seeks to understand women's situation in order to change it, must first identify and criticize the construct "sexuality" *as* a construct that has circumscribed and defined experience as well as theory. In feminist terms, then, the fact that male power *has power* means that the interests of male sexuality construct what sexuality as such means, including the standard way it is allowed and recognized to be felt and expressed and experienced, in a way that determines women's biographies, including our sexual ones. Existing theories, until they grasp this, will not only misattribute what they call female sexuality to women as such, as if it is not imposed on us daily; they will participate in enforcing the hegemony of this construct "sexuality," hence its construct "woman," on the world.

What is taken to be "sexuality," what sex means and what is meant by sex, when how and by whom and with what consequences to whom, is the issue. Such questions are almost never systematically confronted, even in discourses that purport feminist awareness. What sex *is*—how it comes to be attached and attributed to what it is, embodied and practiced as it is, contextualized in the ways it is, signifying and referring to what it does—is taken as given, except when explaining when it is thought to have gone wrong. It is as if "erotic," for example, can be taken as having an understood referent, although it is never defined, except to imply that it is universal yet individual, ultimately variable and plastic and essentially indefinable. But overwhelmingly positive. "Desire," the vicissitudes of which are endlessly extolled and philosophized in culture high and low, is not seen as fundamentally problematic or calling for explanation on the concrete, interpersonal operative level, unless (again) it is supposed to be there and isn't. To list and analyze what seem to be the essential elements for male sexual arousal, what has to be there for the penis to work, seems faintly blasphemous, like a pornographer doing market research. It is supposed to be both too individual and too universally transcendent for that. To suggest that the sexual might be continuous with something other than sex itself—something like culture, something like politics—is seldom done, is treated as detumescent, even by feminists. It is as if sexuality comes from the stork.

Sexuality, in the approach to be argued as feminist here, is not a discrete sphere of interaction or feeling or sensation or behavior in which preexisting social divisions may or may not be played out. It is a pervasive dimension throughout the whole of social life, a dimension along which gender pervasively occurs, at least in this culture. Dominance eroticized defines the imperatives of masculinity, submission erot-

tend to think so. This is not to say that women sexually choosing women can make no difference at all; and it *does* re-state the question.

icized defines femininity. So many of the distinctive features of women's status as second class—the restriction and constraint and contortion, the servility and the display, the self-mutilation and requisite presentation of self as a beautiful thing, the enforced passivity, the humiliation—are made into the content of sex for women. This is to identify not just a sexuality that is shaped under conditions of gender inequality, but this sexuality itself as the dynamic of the inequality of the sexes. This is to argue a sexual theory of the distribution of social power by gender, in which this sexuality that *is* sexuality is substantially what makes the gender division be what it is, which is male dominant, wherever it is, which is nearly everywhere. In this view, the feminist theory of sexuality is its theory of politics, its distinctive contribution to social and political explanation. * * *

In this approach, male power takes the social form of what men as a gender want sexually, which centers on power itself as socially defined. Masculinity is having it, femininity is not having it. Masculinity precedes male as femininity precedes female and male sexual desire defines both. Specifically, "woman" is defined by what male desire requires for arousal and satisfaction and is socially tautologous with "female sexuality" and "the female sex." In the permissible ways a woman can be treated, the ways that are socially considered not violations but appropriate to her nature, one finds the particulars of male *sexual* interests and requirements. In the concomitant sexual paradigm, the ruling norms of sexual attraction and expression are fused with gender identity formation and affirmation, such that sexuality equals heterosexuality equals the sexuality of (male) dominance and (female) submission.

* * *

To be clear: what is sexual is what gives a man an erection. Fear does; hostility does; hatred does; the helplessness of a child or a student or an infantilized or restrained or vulnerable woman does; revulsion does; death does. Whatever it takes to make a penis shudder and stiffen with the experience of its potency is what sexuality means culturally. Violation, conventionally through penetration and intercourse, defines the paradigmatic sexual encounter. Transgression, for which boundaries must first be created, then violated, is necessary for penetration to experience itself. All this suggests that what is called sexuality is the dynamic of control by which male dominance—in forms that range from intimate to institutional, from a look to a rape—eroticizes as man and woman, as identity and pleasure, that which maintains and defines male supremacy as a political system. Male sexual desire is thereby simultaneously created and serviced (but never satisfied once and for all) while male force is romanticized, even sacralized, by submersion in sex itself. Women embrace the standards of our place in this regime as "our own" to varying degrees and in varying voices—as our affirmation of identity and right to pleasure, in order to be loved and approved and paid, in order just to make it through another day.

Notes on MacKinnon's Pleasure Under Patriarchy

1. If MacKinnon is correct, and sexuality is a construct of male power, will it be possible for us ever to create our own authentic sexuality? Under what material and political conditions? Do you agree that sexuality is a pervasive dimension throughout our social lives? Provide some concrete examples. MacKinnon defines masculinity as dominance eroticized and femininity as submission eroticized. Can you articulate alternative definitions?

2. MacKinnon's article asks the question: "What do sexuality and gender inequality have to do with each other?" Does she adequately explain their relationship? Is she correct that hierarchy is sexy? That force is sex? That what is sexual is whatever results in an erect penis? Would she be more persuasive if she gave concrete examples? Can you think of some?

3. Ruth Colker suggests that MacKinnon's use of experiential discourse, or consciousness raising, is selective: she affirms women's descriptions of their lack of freedom but rejects their glimpses of freedom as inauthentic. Colker, Feminism, Sexuality and Authenticity, in At the Boundaries of Law 135, 141 (Martha A. Fineman and Nancy S. Thomadsen, eds. 1991). Colker states:

> For some women, intimate relationships with certain men may be an authentic and affirming expression of their sexuality. For other women, possibly the vast majority, such relationships may be one aspect (but not the "structure") of their oppression. A more contextual discussion of sexual relationships may illuminate those different experiences and give us a better understanding of how certain relationships can oppress women as well as how women can overcome that oppression. This may be more useful than making global statements about what forms of sexual expression are liberating or oppressive for all women.

Id. at 141. Do you agree? Would it be easier to understand MacKinnon's arguments if they were less abstract and were put into context? Colker also questions the primacy of sexuality in our lives and the corresponding primacy of confronting sexual issues through the law. Id. at 135. Is the law the proper, or most effective, place to confront sexual issues? If not, what is? Our personal lives?

4. Robin L. West also acknowledges the difficulty in dealing with our erotic lives, particularly the "conflict between the radical feminist legal theorists' conception of an equalitarian ideal and women's subjective desire." West, The Difference in Women's Hedonic Lives: A Phenomenological Critique of Feminist Legal Theory, 3 Wis. Women's L.J. 81, 116 (1987), excerpted in Chapter 3. She suggests that feminist legal theorists refuse to address this conflict between political ideal and subjective, erotic pleasure, and that this refusal threatens the survival of radical feminist theory. In her view, two strategies of avoidance have emerged:

> The first—advocated by Andrea Dworkin and Catharine MacKinnon—regards the undeniable reality of the pleasure many women find in the eroticization of controlled submission as simply an example—perhaps an example *par excellence*—of the false consciousness of the oppressed. The desires reflected in fantasies of erotic domination are false definitional-

> ly—they are false because the object of desire is submission, and submission is precisely what is definitionally *un*desirable. The second strategy—advocated by Sylvia Law and Nan Hunter—constitutes in essence a retreat to liberal principles. Fantasies are private and beyond political analysis; the role of law should be to expand, not shrink, the options available to women, including the option, if freely chosen, of masochistic desire, fantasy, practice and pleasure.

Id. at 117. What is an appropriate strategy to deal with this apparent conflict?

5. Sheila Jeffreys states that sexuality is important because "it is specifically through sexuality that the fundamental oppression, that of men over women, is maintained." Jeffreys, Anticlimax: A Feminist Perspective on the Sexual Revolution 291 (1991). She notes that other feminists have argued that heterosexuality is the "root of all other oppressions that exist under male supremacy" because it is based on and justified by the concepts of difference and hierarchy. Id. at 297. Thus, the aim of women's liberation must be the destruction of heterosexuality as a system. Id. at 299. Do you agree? How would the various feminist theorists discussed in Chapter 3 respond to this proposition?

Jeffreys believes the fight against male violence requires the reconstruction of male sexuality:

> Male sexuality must be reconstructed to sever the link between power and aggression and sexual pleasure. Only then can women be relieved of the restrictions placed upon their lives and opportunities by male sexual objectification and aggression. Men's pleasure in women's subordination is a powerful bulwark of their resistance to women's liberation. * * * It is not to be expected that men, gay or straight, will voluntarily choose to relinquish the pleasure and privilege they derive from the eroticised subordination of women.

Id. at 313. Because we cannot expect men to give up these privileges, to Jeffreys our hope lies only in other women creating experiences of sexual desire and practices which eroticize mutuality and equality. Id. What is your reaction to her suggestion? Do you think this is possible? Desirable?

6. Clyde W. Franklin, II, in his book, The Changing Definition of Masculinity (1984), claims that male sexuality is learned, not innate, and extends beyond women to relationships (or lack of them) with other men as well in our homophobic world. Dominance remains a strong theme in his analysis of Black male sexuality; however, Black men experience a double-bind. Black males are expected to exhibit "masculine" dominance among Blacks, but "feminine" submissiveness, passivity and cooperativeness in the larger white society. Id. at 52–62. How does this relate to expectations of Black women in a white patriarchal world?

7. Franklin also states that men equate having a penis and getting an erection with maleness and ego, so anything that causes an erection helps a man to keep hold on his identity. Franklin, above note 6, at 164. Is this consistent with MacKinnon's statement that whatever causes an erection is sexual? As long as male dominance in sexual matters persists, will male sexuality and female sexuality be unalterable? Franklin goes so far as to say

that dominance "is so firmly established in most heterosexual men's identities until it is nearly impossible for them to engage in sex unless the traditional sexual script characterizes the sexual-contact episode." Id. at 163. He believes this is the result of the socialization of American men to be dominant in order to be real men. Id. at 154–65. Would MacKinnon agree? Do you agree? Would the obverse be true for women?

ANDREA DWORKIN, OCCUPATION/COLLABORATION

In Intercourse 121, 122, 125–26, 133–35, 137–38, 140–43 (1987).

A human being has a body that is inviolate; and when it is violated, it is abused. A woman has a body that is penetrated in intercourse: permeable, its corporeal solidness a lie. The discourse of male truth—literature, science, philosophy, pornography—calls that penetration *violation*. This it does with some consistency and some confidence. *Violation* is a synonym for intercourse. At the same time, the penetration is taken to be a use, not an abuse; a normal use; it is appropriate to enter her, to push into ("violate") the boundaries of her body. She is human, of course, but by a standard that does not include physical privacy. She is, in fact, human by a standard that precludes physical privacy, since to keep a man out altogether and for a lifetime is deviant in the extreme, a psychopathology, a repudiation of the way in which she is expected to manifest her humanity.

* * *

Intercourse occurs in a context of a power relation that is pervasive and incontrovertible. The context in which the act takes place, whatever the meaning of the act in and of itself, is one in which men have social, economic, political, and physical power over women. Some men do not have all those kinds of power over all women; but all men have some kinds of power over all women; and most men have controlling power over what they call *their* women—the women they fuck. The power is predetermined by gender, by being male.

* * *

Physically, the woman in intercourse is a space inhabited, a literal territory occupied literally: occupied even if there has been no resistance, no force; even if the occupied person said yes please, yes hurry, yes more. Having a line at the point of entry into your body that cannot be crossed is different from not having any such line; and being occupied in your body is different from not being occupied in your body. It is human to experience these differences whether or not one cares to bring the consequences of them into consciousness. Humans, including women, construct meaning. That means that when something happens to us, when we have experiences, we try to find in them some reason for them, some significance they have to us or for us. * * * The measure of women's oppression is that we do not take intercourse—entry, penetration, occupation—and ask or say what it means: to us as a dominated group or to us as a potentially free and self-determining people. Instead, intercourse is a loyalty test; and we are not supposed to tell the truth unless it compliments and upholds the dominant male ethos on sex. * * * Anything men say on intercourse, any attitude they have, is valuable, knowledgeable, and deep, rooted in the cosmos and the forces of nature as it were: because they know; because fucking is knowing; because he knew her but she did not know him; because the God who does not exist framed not only sex but also knowledge that way. Women do not just lie about orgasm, faking it or saying it is not important. Women lie about life by not demanding to understand the meaning of entry, penetration, occupation, having boundaries crossed over, having lesser privacy: by avoiding the difficult, perhaps impossible (but how will we ever know?) questions of female freedom. We take oaths to truth all right, on the holy penis before entry. In so doing, we give up the most important dimension of what it means to be human: the search for the meaning of our real experience, including the sheer invention of that meaning—called creativity when men do it. If the questions make the holy penis unhappy, who could survive what the answers might do? Experience is chosen for us, then, imposed on us, especially in intercourse, *and so is its meaning*. We are allowed to have intercourse on the terms men determine, according to the rules men make. We do not have to have an orgasm; that terrible burden is on them. We are supposed to comply whether we want to or not. *Want* is active, not passive or lethargic. * * * Male sexual discourse on the meaning of intercourse becomes our language. It is not a second language even though it is not our native language; it is the only language we speak, however, with perfect fluency even though it does not say what we mean or what we think we might know if only we could find the right word and enough privacy in which to articulate it even just in our own minds. We know only this one language of these folks who enter and occupy us: they keep telling us that we are different from them; yet we speak only their language and have none, or none that we remember, of our own; and we do not dare, it seems, invent one, even in signs and gestures. Our bodies speak their language. Our minds think in it. The men are inside us through and through. We hear something, a dim whisper, barely audible, somewhere at the back of the brain; there is some other word, and we think, some of us, sometimes, that once it belonged to us.

There are female-supremacist models for intercourse that try to make us the masters of this language that we speak that is not ours. They evade some fundamental questions about the act itself and acknowledge others. They have in common a glorious ambition to see women self-determining, vigorous and free lovers who are never demeaned or diminished by force or subordination, not in society, not in sex. * * *

Male-dominant gender hierarchy, however, seems immune to reform by reasoned or visionary argument or by changes in sexual styles, either personal or social. This may be because intercourse itself is immune to reform. In it, female is bottom, stigmatized. Intercourse remains a means or the means of physiologically making a woman inferior: communicating to her cell by cell her own inferior status, impressing it on her, burning it into her by shoving it into her, over and over, pushing and thrusting until she gives up and gives in—which is called *surrender* in the male lexicon. In the experience of intercourse, she loses the capacity for integrity because her body—the basis of privacy and freedom in the material world for all human beings—is entered and occupied; the boundaries of her physical body are—neutrally speaking—violated. What is taken from her in that act is not recoverable, and she spends her life—wanting, after all, to have something—pretending that pleasure is in being reduced through intercourse to insignificance. She will not have an orgasm—maybe because she has human pride and she resents captivity; but also she will not or cannot rebel—not enough for it to matter, to end male dominance over her. She learns to eroticize powerlessness and self-annihilation. The very boundaries of her own body become meaningless to her, and even worse, useless to her. The transgression of those boundaries comes to signify a sexually charged degradation into which she throws herself, having been told, convinced, that identity, for a female, is there—somewhere beyond privacy and self-respect.

It is not that there is no way out if, for instance, one were to establish or believe that intercourse itself determines women's lower status. New reproductive technologies have changed and will continue to change the nature of the world. Intercourse is not necessary to existence anymore. Existence does not depend on female compliance, nor on the violation of female boundaries, nor on lesser female privacy, nor on the physical occupation of the female body. But the hatred of women is a source of sexual pleasure for men in its own right. Intercourse appears to be the expression of that contempt in pure form, in the form of a sexed hierarchy; it requires no passion or heart because it is power without invention articulating the arrogance of those who do the fucking. Intercourse is the pure, sterile, formal expression of men's contempt for women; but that contempt can turn gothic and express itself in many sexual and sadistic practices that eschew intercourse per se. Any violation of a woman's body can become sex for men; this is the essential truth of pornography. So freedom from intercourse, or a social structure that reflects the low value of intercourse in women's sexual pleasure, or intercourse becoming one sex act among many entered into by (hypothetical) equals as part of other, deeper, longer, perhaps more sensual lovemaking, or an end to women's inferior status because we need not be forced to reproduce (forced fucking frequently justified by some implicit biological necessity to reproduce): none of these are likely social developments because there is a hatred of women, unexplained, undiagnosed, mostly unacknowledged, that pervades sexual practice and sexual passion. * * *

Can intercourse exist without objectification and can objectification exist without female complicity in maintaining it as a perceived reality and a material reality too: can objectification exist without the woman herself turning herself into an object—becoming through effort and art a thing, less than human, so that he can be more than human, hard, sovereign, king? Can intercourse exist without the woman herself turning herself into a thing, which she must do because men cannot fuck equals and men must fuck: because one price of dominance is that one is impotent in the face of equality?

To become the object, she takes herself and transforms herself into a thing: all freedoms are diminished and she is caged, even in the cage docile, sometimes physically maimed, movement is limited: she physically becomes the thing he wants to fuck. It is especially in the acceptance of object status that her humanity is hurt: it is a metaphysical acceptance of lower status in sex and in society; an implicit acceptance of less freedom, less privacy, less integrity. In becoming an object so that he can objectify her so that he can fuck her, she begins a political collaboration with his dominance; and then when he enters her, he confirms for himself and for her what she is: that she is something, not someone; certainly not someone equal.

There is the initial complicity, the acts of self-mutilation, self-diminishing, self-reconstruction, until there is no self, only the diminished, mutilated reconstruction. It is all superficial and unimportant, except what it costs the human in her to do it: except for the fact that it is submissive, conforming, giving up an individuality that would withstand object status or defy it. * * * So the act goes beyond complicity to collaboration; but collaboration requires a preparing of the ground, an undermining of values and vision and dignity, a sense of alienation from the worth of other human beings—and this alienation is fundamental to females who are objectified because they do not experience themselves as human beings of worth except for their value on the market as objects. Knowing one's own human value is fundamental to being able to respect others: females are remade into objects, not human in any sense related to freedom or justice—and so what can females recognize in other females that is a human bond toward freedom? Is there anything in us to love if we do not love each other as the objects we have become? Who can love someone who is less than human unless love itself is domination per se? Alienation from human freedom is deep and destructive; it destroys whatever it is in us as humans that is creative, that causes us to want to find meaning in experiences, even hard experiences; it destroys in us that which wants freedom whatever the hardship of attaining it. * * * Being an object for a man means being alienated from other women—those like her in status, in inferiority, in sexual function. Collaboration by women with men to keep women civilly and sexually inferior has been one of the hallmarks of female subordination; we are ashamed when Freud notices it, but it is true. That collaboration, fully manifested when a woman values her lover * * * above any woman, anyone of her own kind or class or status, may have simple beginnings: the first act of complicity that destroys self-respect, the capacity for self-determination and freedom—readying the body for the fuck instead of for freedom. * * *

The brilliance of objectification as a strategy of dominance is that it gets the woman to take the initiative in her own degradation (having less freedom is degrading). The woman herself takes one kind of responsibility absolutely and thus commits herself to her own continuing inferiority: she polices her own body; she internalizes the demands of the dominant class and, in order to be fucked, she constructs her life around meeting those demands. It is the best system of colonialization on earth: she takes on the burden, the responsibility, of her own submission, her own objectification. In some systems in which turning the female into an object for sex requires actual terrorism and maiming—for instance, footbinding or removing the clitoris—the mother does it, having had it done to her by her mother. What men need done to women so that men can have intercourse with women is done to women so that men will have intercourse; no matter what the human cost; and it is a gross indignity to suggest that when her collaboration is complete—unselfconscious because there is no self and no consciousness left—she is free to have freedom in intercourse. When those who dominate you get you to take the initiative in your own human destruction, you have lost more than any oppressed people yet has ever gotten back. Whatever intercourse is, it is not freedom; and if it cannot exist without objectification, it never will be. Instead occupied women will be collaborators, more base in their collaboration than other collaborators have ever been: experiencing pleasure in their own inferiority; calling intercourse freedom. * * *

Notes on Dworkin's Concept of Collaboration

1. Many women disagree with Andrea Dworkin's statement that heterosexual intercourse is the expression of male contempt for women in its pure form. Instead, they believe that intercourse can represent mutual love and affection shared voluntarily. How would Dworkin respond? What do you think?

2. What is the importance of how we "name" certain events in our lives. Who has the power to name and enforce the use of words? For instance, is heterosexual intercourse "violation"? "penetration"? "occupation"? Should we take these common descriptions of intercourse literally? Why isn't intercourse described from the female perspective, i.e., "envelopment," "enclosure," "surrounding," and so forth? Is this itself indicative of hierarchy? Does it support Dworkin's position about the language of sexuality? Does it make a difference in our perception of events?

3. Can heterosexual intercourse be removed from a context of power relations in society? Can intercourse exist without the objectification of women? Would it be different if it could? Would it be compatible with women's equality, perhaps even an expression of it?

4. Do you agree that hatred of women is a source of sexual pleasure for men in its own right? How do you explain violent pornography and the apparent sexual entertainment and gratification men receive from it?

5. Do women have initial complicity in their objectification? How else do you explain what Dworkin calls acts of self-mutilation, self-diminishing, and self-reconstruction? Do women engage in self-mutilation to be sexually attractive to men? Why do we pierce our ears, have cosmetic surgery

(including dangerous breast implants and collagen injections), and hotwax or use electrolysis to eliminate unwanted body hair? Is it true that women do not experience themselves as human beings of worth except for their value on the market as objects, e.g., marriageability, attractiveness to men, etc.?

6. For 1,000 years Chinese mothers bound the feet of their daughters. See Andrea Dworkin, Woman Hating 111 (1974). Dworkin explains this horror as collaboration, meaning that women (mother to daughter) have taken the initiative in our own human destruction and objectification. Are there any other possible explanations?

Female circumcision continues to be practiced on millions of young girls in more than 20 African countries. Robyn Cerny Smith, Female Circumcision: Bringing Women's Perspectives into the International Debate, 65 S.Cal.L.Rev. 2449, 2450 (1992). Many of these operations are performed by women on girls between the ages of 10 and 12 (the year before puberty), and have physically and psychologically debilitating effects on females. See Clitoridectomy, in Women Against Violence Against Women 182–83 (dusty rhodes and Sandra McNeill, eds. 1985) (testimony of French women from Guinea presented at the International Tribunal on Crimes Against Women held in Brussels in 1976). Defenders of these tribal practices argue that they are "crucial to the continued survival of tribal groups as distinct cultural entities" and therefore should not be subjected to governmental intervention. Smith, above, at 2451. As Smith suggests, however, "this argument does not adequately take into consideration that gender hierarchy within each tribe, in which women are subordinate to men, is maintained by the practice of female circumcision." Id. What arguments can you make in support of the practice? Against it? Does the ritual of clitoridectomy support Dworkin's position that women collaborate "with men to keep women civilly and sexually inferior"?

7. Dworkin believes that the brilliance of objectification as a strategy of dominance is that it gets the woman to take the initiative in her own degradation. Can you think of examples to support this position? Examples to the contrary?

8. Another form of heterosexual activity is what Robin West calls "sexual altruism" in which women engage in consensual but unwanted sex with an intimate. According to West, this behavior is "often motivated neither by self-interest properly understood nor by an ethic of care but rather, and more simply, by *fear*—not, perhaps, of their partner, but more generally, of sexual violence from other men." West, Caring for Justice 114 (199_). This concept of sexual terrorism, what Susan Griffin called the "male protection racket" in her 1971 article, Rape: The All American Crime, in *Ramparts* 26, is discussed more fully in Chapter 5. However, Robin West also analyzes the relationship between pleasure and danger in sexuality for women:

> This profound existential fact—that the most primal source of pleasure, located in one's own body, is a source of danger and constitutes a risk to one's survival—is something all women must somehow learn to live with, *and* it is something only a very few men ever confront. The causal connections between pleasure, desire, and decision which I have suggested are central to liberalism are in a sense paradig-

> matically embodied, for a man, in his sexuality; his sexual pleasure uninterruptedly prompts desires, which in turn prompt decisions and actions. For a woman, there is no such paradigmatic connection. Between her own recognition of her sexuality as a source of pleasure and her decision to act on it, lies a hostile world in which that source of pleasure—her sexual body—is a source of profound danger. As the adolescent girl awakens to her adult sexuality, she awakens simultaneously, and necessarily, to her vulnerability to assault, rape, violence, and death. Rather than "learn" a connection between pleasure and action, she "learns" instead a connection between pleasure and violence; between pleasure and danger, between pleasure and fear.

West, above, at 114–115. What are the implications for female sexuality? Does West's analysis suggest even greater hurdles for women attempting to achieve sexual autonomy than either MacKinnon or Dworkin? In what ways?

9. Is there a way to save heterosexual intercourse? Is gender hierarchy immune to reform in sexual styles? How would the various feminist theorists identified in Chapter 3 respond to this problem?

RUTH COLKER, FEMINISM, SEXUALITY AND AUTHENTICITY

In At the Boundaries of the Law 135–38, 140, 144–46 (Martha A. Fineman and Nancy S. Thomadsen, eds. 1991), orig. pub., 68 B.U.L.Rev. 217 (1988).

As a radical feminist, I seek to discover and understand my authentic female sexuality as part of my authentic self. Radical feminist theory has assisted me considerably along that journey although I have also begun to question some of the assumptions within radical feminist theory concerning the primacy of sexuality in our lives and the corresponding primacy of confronting sexual issues through the law. Because radical feminist theory teaches us that our subjective perspective influences our politics, I need to place my critique within the context of my personal life to make my political perspective more clear.

I made the choice to pursue relationships with women in 1975 as a political choice—believing that relationships with men were difficult, if not impossible, to achieve under patriarchy and recognizing that I could make the deepest possible commitment to feminism through a woman-centered and woman-identified life. My sexual choice was embedded in my broader conception of how I wanted to lead my life politically. Nevertheless, I acknowledged that I was deeply attracted to some men and occasionally found myself in intimate relationships with a man. When I was in an intimate relationship with a woman, however, I found that my personal and political life were in harmony in a way that they never were when I was in a relationship with a man.

In 1986, I ended a seven-year intimate relationship with a woman and began an intimate relationship with a man. In 1989, as I write these words, I am involved intimately with a man. I have begun to question whether my previous decision to seek intimate relationships only with women was too sex-specific and inconsistent with my authentic self. I have also begun to wonder whether I have placed too much emphasis on my sexual self as part of my authentic self. At this point in my life, the satisfaction and authenticity that I find in my life seems more dependent than ever on the political/legal work that I do on behalf of women, gays and lesbians rather than on the sex of my sexual partner. Sadly, however, I find that other radical feminists often "judge" my feminist politics by my choice of sexual partner rather than by my political/legal activities in the community.

* * *

Thus, I find myself wanting to determine whether I can choose relationships with men and continue on my journey towards authenticity. Many radical feminists have told me that my concept of authenticity is inconsistent with feminist theory, unhelpful, and more generally, is simply wrong-headed. I believe that we have an authentic self because assuming that we do *not* have an authentic self makes no sense to me. For example, through our feminist work, we try to peel away social influences that limit our authenticity or freedom. If we are successful in our attempts to peel away those influences, what would be left? It only makes sense for me to assume that what would be left would be our authentic selves. Moreover, that authentic self must embody both a state of being as well as an ideal self. Otherwise, there is little point in trying to peel away those influences. Similarly, I consider the source of our feminist visions. They must come from some intuitive sense of each of our human possibilities. We need some measuring rod through which we can construct a critique and be confident that we can be more fully human than we are now, or, again our feminist struggles would make no sense. Therefore, I believe that our perception of and faith in our authentic self is fundamental to our continued passion to discover and experience our freedom or authentic self.

We must expend considerable energy trying to discover and experience our authentic sexuality because forces such as patriarchy have limited our sexuality. Women's struggles to discover their authentic sexuality have two major components. The first component encompasses trying to determine our sexual preference within a homophobic and heterosexist society. * * *

The second component of women's journey to discover their authentic sexuality is the struggle against a narrow and strongly normative conception of "good" sex within a particular form of sexuality. * * *

Radical feminist theory, as exemplified by MacKinnon, raises, but does not resolve, several fundamental dilemmas within radical feminist theory: how important women's authentic sexuality *should* be to their authentic self, how women can *know* when they have discovered their authentic sexuality, and how women can construct their sexuality politically while retaining their authenticity. * * *

The fact that women are not presently experiencing their authentic sexuality does not mean that women should necessarily place a priority on trying to discover their authentic sexuality. An emphasis on sexuality within a woman's life may be feminine but not feminist. Patriarchy has made sexuality a crucial component of women's lives by making it central to women's oppression and subordination. Because women have never had the freedom to experience their authentic sexuality, it is impossible to know whether expressions of sexuality would be central to a woman's free and authentic life. In a transformed society, the importance of sexuality in a woman's life might dissipate or disappear. In existing society, the energy that women expend on developing sexual connectedness, love, compassion, etc., may be evidence of their brokenness and subordination rather than their authenticity.

* * *

Feminists often argue that society has overemphasized the importance of the physically intimate and procreative aspects of sexuality. They suggest that women might define sexuality quite differently if they could define it from their own perspective. By thinking of love broadly, removed from the arena of physical intimacy and procreation, women might be able to begin to consider the positive life-building potential of love within their lives removed from the subordinating sexuality that they have often experienced under patriarchy. This spiritual conception of love would seem to be able to guide women in determining how to relate to themselves as well as others. This conception of the role of love and sexuality in women's lives could make the radical feminist maxim that the "personal is political" a more meaningful statement because it would expose the full range and importance of the love and compassion that women create in their lives.

* * *

If radical feminists are correct that women are unlikely to experience intimate relationships with men authentically under patriarchy, they raise a troubling problem about expressions of authenticity. Is a woman who glimpses that her authentic sexuality can include relationships with men destined not to be able to experience that aspect of herself? And, if women are going to interact intimately with men anyway, how can those interactions best move them toward discovering and experiencing their authentic sexuality? Formulated in this way, I do not question the authenticity of some women not experiencing intimate relationships with men when they perceive that such relationships would not be consistent with their authentic sexuality.

I am not as skeptical as many radical feminists of the possibility of movement toward freedom or authenticity within a woman's intimate relationship with a man. Although society tries to define sexual expressiveness narrowly, women may be able to work to overcome those forces in their internal lives.

* * *

This brings me to the basic question of what are the preconditions of intimacy. If non-subordination is a precondition for intimacy and true non-subordination must exist on both an internal and external level, the task for women is to create an environment of non-subordination. Is there any way that external subordination can *not* impinge on a male-female relationship?

For example, I feel the pull of compulsory heterosexuality and know that even if I choose to pursue intimacy with a man *despite* rather than *because* of compulsory heterosexuality, that choice will nevertheless reinforce that institution in the minds of others.

* * *

Although a feminist may be able to discover her authentic desire to pursue a relationship with a particular man, she must be able to sustain the expression of her desire within an externally constraining environment. A relationship with a man could become an inauthentic expression of a woman's sexuality because of her inability to fit that expression freely into her external environment. For a politically conscious feminist, the external forces of compulsory heterosexuality may make certain expressions of her authentic sexuality difficult, if not impossible, because those external forces would make a choice of heterosexuality feel subordinating. Thus, it is crucial that we develop legal-political strategies to limit, and eventually eliminate, the effects of compulsory heterosexuality.

Notes on Colker's Theory of Sexuality and Authenticity

1. Colker states that some radical feminists judge her feminist politics by her choice of sexual partner rather than by her political/legal activities in the community. Is this fair? Is it necessary to be either lesbian or celibate in order to realize sexual equality? Is sexuality separable from love and compassion and intimacy?

2. How important do you think sexuality would be under conditions of equality? Colker believes it is impossible to know under current patriarchal conditions. Do you think that "the energy that women expend on developing sexual connectedness, love, compassion, etc., may be evidence of their brokenness and subordination rather than their authenticity"? What feminist theories in Chapter 3, above, are most compatible with Colker's position?

3. Is there too much emphasis on the physical, as opposed to the spiritual, aspects of love? How is this manifested?

4. In her conclusion to Feminism, Sexuality and Authenticity, Colker asks:

> What is the relationship between authentic expressions of sexuality and authentic self? What is authentic sexuality? Can we even begin to understand authentic sexuality until we better understand love and compassion generally? How can we best conduct the journey toward authenticity?

Id. at 147. How would you answer these questions? Do you agree with Colker that if we "peel away social influences that limit our authenticity," what would be left is our "authentic selves"? How can we know when we have discovered our "authentic sexuality"?

5. Is there any solution to Colker's concern that, assuming her heterosexual relationship is her "authentic" sexuality, the external force of compulsory heterosexuality makes her choice "feel subordinating"? Do you agree with her that a "free" heterosexuality is possible only if compulsory heterosexuality is ended?

6. Many women regard the choice to avoid heterosexual relationships as a political choice. See, e.g., Sarah Lucia Hoagland, Lesbian Ethics: Toward New Value 67 (1988) ("heterosexualism * * * de-skills a woman, makes her emotionally, socially, and economically dependent, and allows another to dominate her 'for her own good' all in the name of 'love' "). In what ways do intimate relationships with men either advance or hinder women's struggle for equality? Do you think that emotional investment in a heterosexual relationship (or the hope of such an investment in the future) creates a need to deny conflicting interests between the sexes? Do such relationships divide women into subgroups with conflicting interests (those who expect to be economically linked with men and those who do not)? Do such relationships limit women's rise in elites, including political elites, because of expectations that *she* will be primarily responsible for domestic work and caretaking? See Mary E. Becker, Politics, Differences and Economic Rights, 1989 U.Chi. L.Rev. 169, 183–88.

7. Should heterosexuals feel ethically compelled to avoid heterosexual privileges until same-sex marriage is recognized? Or marriage is abolished? What costs would a heterosexual couple (and their children) face in adopting this strategy? See Ruth Colker, Marriage, 3 Yale J.L. & Feminism 321 (1991). Colker was committed to disavowing heterosexual privilege by not marrying, but found the costs impossibly high when she met a Canadian man; they wanted to be able to work in the same country and raise a child. Are there other ways in which heterosexuals can decline heterosexual privilege?

8. Does Colker leave you more optimistic about the possibility of non-subordinating heterosexuality? Is it possible for heterosexuality not to be subordinating to women? Is it necessary to say who is right—MacKinnon, Dworkin or Colker? Are they all correct in their analyses of sexuality?

9. Do you think the law is the correct vehicle to confront sexual issues? Does it depend on the specific sexual issue, for example, whether to define it as a "crime," such as rape or incest? Can the law help to eliminate compulsory heterosexuality? How? For example, what effect would the repeal of marriage laws have on compulsory heterosexuality?

BELL HOOKS, ENDING FEMALE SEXUAL OPPRESSION

In Feminist Theory: From margin to center 148–50, 152–56 (1984).

It has been a simple task for women to describe and criticize negative aspects of sexuality as it has been socially constructed in sexist society, to expose male objectification and dehumanization of women, to denounce rape, pornography, sexualized violence, incest, etc. It has been a far more difficult task for women to envision new sexual paradigms, to change the norms of sexuality. The inspiration for such work can only emerge in an environment where sexual well-being is valued. Ironically, some feminists have tended to dismiss issues of sexual pleasure, well-being, and contentedness as irrelevant. Contemporary emphasis on sexual revolution or anything-goes-sexual-expression has led many women and men to assume that sexual freedom already exists and is even overvalued in our society. However, this is *not* a culture that affirms real sexual freedom.

* * *

Sexual freedom can exist only when individuals are no longer oppressed by a socially constructed sexuality based on biologically determined definitions of sexuality: repression, guilt, shame, dominance, conquest, and exploitation. To set the stage for the development of that sexual freedom, the feminist movement must continue to focus on ending female sexual oppression.

The focus on "sexual liberation" has always carried with it the assumption that the goal of such effort is to make it possible for individuals to engage in more and/or better sexual activity. Yet one aspect of sexual norms that many people find oppressive is the assumption that one "should" be engaged in sexual activity. This "should" is one expression of sexual coercion. Advocates of sexual liberation often imply that any individual who is not concerned about the quality of their experience or exercising greater sexual freedom is mentally disturbed or sexually repressed. When primary emphasis is placed on ending sexual oppression rather than on sexual liberation it is possible to envision a society in which it is as much an expression of sexual freedom to choose not to participate in sexual activity as it is to choose to participate.

* * *

It is important for women, especially those who are heterosexual, to know that they can make a radical political commitment to feminist struggle even though they are sexually involved with men (many of us know from experience that political choice will undoubtedly alter the nature of individual relationships). All women need to know that they can be politically committed to feminism regardless of their sexual preference. They need to know that the goal of feminist movement is not to establish codes for a "politically correct" sexuality. Politically, feminist activists committed to ending sexual oppression must work to eliminate the oppression of lesbians and gay men as part of an overall movement to enable all women (and men) to freely choose sexual partners.

Feminist activists must take care that our legitimate critiques of heterosexism are not attacks on heterosexual *practice*. As feminists, we must confront those women who do in fact believe that women with heterosexual preferences are either traitors or likely to be anti-lesbian.

Condemnation of heterosexual practice has led women who desire sexual relationships with men to feel they cannot participate in feminist movement. They have gotten the message that to be "truly" feminist is not to be heterosexual. It is easy to confuse support for non-oppressive heterosexual practice with the belief in heterosexism. * * *

There are some feminists (and I am one) who believe that feminist movement to end sexual oppression will not change destructive sexual norms if individuals are taught that they must choose between competing sexualities (the most obvious being heterosexuality and homosexuality) and conform to the expectations of the chosen norm. Sexual desire has varied and multiple dimensions and is rarely as "exclusive" as any norm would suggest. A liberatory sexuality would not teach women to see their bodies as accessible to all men, or to all women for that matter. It would favor instead a sexuality that is open or closed based on the nature of individual interaction. Implicit in the idea of sexual preference is the assumption that anyone of the preferred sex can seek access to one's body. This is a concept that promotes objectification. In a heterosexual context it makes everyone, especially women, into sex objects. Given the power differential created by sexist politics, women are likely to be approached by any man since all men are taught to assume they should have access to the bodies of all women. Sexuality would be transformed if the codes and labels that strip sexual desire of its specificity and particularity were abandoned. * * *

A shift that will undoubtedly emerge as the struggle to end sexual oppression progresses will be decreased obsession with sexuality. This does not necessarily mean that there will be decreased sexual activity. It means that sexuality will no longer have the importance attributed to it in a society that [uses] sexuality for the express purposes of maintaining gender inequality, male domination, consumerism, and the sexual frustration and unhappiness that deflects attention away from the need to make social revolution. * * * Feminist efforts to develop a political theory of sexuality must continue if sexist oppression is to be eliminated. Yet we must keep in mind that the struggle to end sexual oppression is only one component of a larger struggle to transform society and establish a new social order.

Notes on hooks' Proposal to End Female Sexual Oppression

1. Do you agree that it is difficult for women to envision positive sexual paradigms? Do you think it is a mistake for some feminists to have dismissed issues of sexual pleasure as irrelevant? Do you think feminists emphasize sexuality too much?

2. How is celibacy viewed in our society? Is it a legitimate expression of sexual liberation? Are we obsessed with sexuality? Is sexuality central to feminist theory? To oppression of women?

3. Is bell hooks correct in asserting that ours is not a culture which affirms true sexual freedom, including abstention? In what ways do you

think young people and adults are pressured or coerced into certain forms of sexual behavior? Given the absence of safe and reliable birth control, together with the fact that coitus frequently does not achieve female orgasm, would heterosexual practices differ in a society in which women had more power and real sexual agency? Would one expect teenage girls to risk pregnancy through unprotected heterosexual intercourse? Why do teens have unprotected sex? Do male and female teens have differing reasons for engaging in unprotected sex?

4. Are there any points upon which all four writers—MacKinnon, Dworkin, Colker and hooks—agree? What are they?

5. What role does the possibility of pregnancy play in negotiating pleasure in a heterosexual relationship? Clearly, the burdens of pregnancy and childrearing have never been equal between men and women. However, the advent of available, relatively effective birth control 30 years ago is said to have liberated women and created a sexual revolution. See Deirdre English, The Fear That Feminism Will Free Men First, in Powers of Desire: The Politics of Sexuality 477 (Ann Snitow, Christine Stansell and Sharon Thompson, eds. 1983). Was it possible for women to discover their own sexuality before they had the ability to separate intercourse from reproduction? What have been the results of the sexual revolution? Are they positive for women? Did the sexual revolution "liberate" women? Is bell hooks correct that the sexual revolution simply encouraged more sex, rather than better sex?

Even today, no birth control method is totally effective. Most women still start their sexual lives worried about pregnancy. How does this affect their experience of sexuality and their ability to derive pleasure from it? Why, other than that they lack the power to be sexual agents, would women "agree" to risk pregnancy through imperfectly protected heterosexual intercourse, given their ability to enjoy other sexual activities *more* (at least as measured by orgasms)?

B. OTHER DIFFICULTIES NEGOTIATING PLEASURE UNDER PATRIARCHY

PATRICIA Y. MILLER AND MARTHA R. FOWLKES, SOCIAL AND BEHAVIORAL CONSTRUCTIONS OF FEMALE SEXUALITY

In Sex and Scientific Inquiry 147, 149–53 (Sandra Harding and Jean F. O'Barr, eds. 1987).

The most comprehensive and, in their day, controversial studies are Kinsey's of male and female sexual behavior,[3] which broke new ground in depicting the norms of sexual activity, not in terms of what people should do, but in terms of what they, in fact, do. The overriding argument of Kinsey's work is that ideas of what should be ought to be

3. A.C. Kinsey, W.B. Pomeroy, and C.E. Martin, Sexual Behavior in the Human Male (* * * 1948); A.C. Kinsey et al., Sexual Behavior in the Human Female (* * * 1953).

refashioned to be consonant with what people actually—and naturally—do. Yet insofar as what people actually do represents a departure from the expected conventions and mores of social behavior, Kinsey rests his case for tolerance of those departures on the grounds that they are in the service of socially desired norms, particularly those of heterosexual marriage. Thus, for men and women alike, all premarital erotic and sexual activity is seen as facilitating adjustment to marriage. Kinsey is critical of the double standard of male and female sexual behavior that works disproportionately to inhibit women's sexual activity outside of marriage.

However, Kinsey's support for increased female sexual autonomy is rendered suspect by his own double standard. Although Kinsey is concerned that women are able to experience sexual satisfaction as it is manifest in orgasmic outlet, his advocacy of women's premarital sexual activity is prompted as much by his commitment to the satisfaction of male sexual needs and desires as to that of women's. Premarital sexual activity is seen as a useful socializing agent for women in their relationships with men, as it enables women to learn to adjust emotionally to various types of men. Since Kinsey's own data show that coitus (both marital and premarital) is far less frequently a source of orgasmic release for women than for men, he is essentially encouraging women to seek premarital coitus in the service of male physiological release.

A similar bias is revealed in Kinsey's interpretation of his finding that female sexual unresponsiveness is a major factor in women's premarital coital reluctance. A man, of course, may reach orgasm through coitus without doing much at all to arouse or stimulate response in his female partner. Rather than portraying men as the victims of women's unresponsiveness, it would be fairer to suggest that women may be victimized by men's self-interest and failure to show the consideration necessary to incorporate female orgasm into the coital experience.

The female orgasm itself is emphasized by Kinsey as a source of satisfaction and reassurance to the male. He states that "orgasm cannot be taken as the sole criterion for determining the degree of satisfaction which a female may derive from sexual activity ... Whether or not she herself reaches orgasm, many a female finds satisfaction in knowing that her husband or other sexual partner has enjoyed the contact, and in realizing that she has contributed to the male's pleasure." The assumption that women can do quite nicely without an orgasmic accompaniment to coitus may be correct. But it is supported by no data from the females themselves about the place and meaning of sexual satisfaction in their marriage relationships.

Overall, when compared to males, Kinsey's females show a greater uniformity in their sexual behavior with respect to the impact of selected social variables, and they also exhibit consistently less sexual responsiveness and lower frequencies of orgasm than men. The differences between the sexual responsiveness of men and women are attributed to the greater "psychologic conditionability" or flexibility of men. Although

Kinsey does acknowledge the essential likeness of the physiological experience of sexual arousal and orgasm for men and women (in anticipation of the work of Masters and Johnson a decade later), he also views women as having less well-developed sexual interests than men and as more willing than men to subordinate those interests to an overriding commitment to home and family.

What Kinsey overlooked, of course, was the powerful influence of sex role itself as a variable in conditioning sexual response and behavior. Men are expected and socialized to be autonomous in their activities, including their sexual activities. Whereas males are encouraged to give full expression to their sexuality as an indication and demonstration of their masculinity, female sexual response has traditionally been thought to be appropriately derived from relationships with men and their needs. It is unquestionably true that women's sexuality is affected by socialization into the female sex role and the subordinate status attached to it in common ways that both supersede and preclude the potential effect of other social variables (at least, the social variables selected by Kinsey).

Kinsey's determination that women are generally less capable of sexual autonomy by virtue of being less psychologically conditionable itself reinforces a double standard for male and female sexual behavior. It also constitutes a license for the perpetuation of predatory male sexual activity. It is precisely this predatory context which renders a derivative, rather than an autonomous, female sexuality functional. If women are to be sexually autonomous in a fashion similar to men, they must also participate in the social, political, and economic autonomy that has been granted to men. To suggest otherwise is to suggest that women should simply become more readily available to men for sex on the terms that men determine as a consequence of their dominant social roles. This would have the effect, on the one hand, of enhancing women's vulnerability to exploitation by men as sex objects and, on the other, of removing their sexuality from marriage (or potential marriage), thereby weakening the major institutional source of security and social approval accessible to them in a patriarchal society.

In contrast to Kinsey, Masters and Johnson in *Human Sexual Response* addressed the question of women's sexual autonomy solely and specifically in terms of physiological functioning.[8] Their documentation of a specifically orgasmic physiology for the female, including her multiple orgasmic potential, is both testimony and tribute to women's innate sexual capacities. In what we can only hope is a final debunking of the Freudian distinction between the vaginal and clitoral orgasm, Masters and Johnson use the evidence of their laboratory observations to recognize the clitoris: "The clitoris is a unique organ in the total of human anatomy. Its express purpose is to serve both as a receptor and transformer of sensual stimuli. Thus the female has an organ system which is totally limited in physiologic function to initiating or elevating levels of

8. W.H. Masters and V.E. Johnson, Human Sexual Response (* * * 1966).

sexual tension. No such organ exists within the anatomic structure of the human male."

Thus Masters and Johnson established unequivocally the physiological ability of women to achieve orgasm and dispelled any doubts that females might in any way be possessed of a lesser sexuality than males. Their findings indicate that women's orgasmic capacities are a given, and that the key variable in the achievement of successful orgasmic outcome for women is the quality of sexual attention they receive. Gone are both Kinsey's nonresponsive woman and the woman who develops her sexual responses in order to be able to fulfill male needs. Ironically, however, Masters and Johnson's own data show clearly that the sexual autonomy of women is manifest not only in their physiological functioning but in the nature of their response to sexual stimulation as well. For women "the maximum physiologic intensity of orgasmic response subjectively reported or objectively recorded has been achieved by self-regulated mechanical or automanipulative techniques. The next highest level of erotic intensity has resulted from partner manipulation, again with established or self-regulated methods, and the lowest intensity of target-organ response was achieved during coition."

It is not difficult to read this statement as the ultimate testimony to the autonomy of female sexuality. The female orgasmic response is demonstrably not correlated with—or, more accurately, is negatively correlated with—conventional heterosexual coitus. However, if the clitoris is no respecter of heterosexual intercourse, Masters and Johnson find that the vagina is. While the clitoris behaves like a wanton child, female vaginal response and activity are portrayed by Masters and Johnson as staunch defenders of the wisdom of copulation and, therefore, presumably, of the conventional heterosexual relationship:

> The vaginal barrel performs a dual role, providing the primary physical means of heterosexual expression for the human female and serving simultaneously as an integral part of her conceptive mechanism ... *To appreciate vaginal anatomy and physiology is to comprehend the fundamentals of the human female's primary means of sexual expression* [emphasis added]. In essence, the vaginal barrel responds to effective sexual stimulation for penile penetration. Just as a penile erection is a direct physiologic expression of a psychologic demand to mount, so expansion and lubrication of the vaginal barrel provides direct physiologic indication of an obvious mounting invitation.

Masters and Johnson's conceptualization of the vagina—preparing for and accommodating to copulation and facilitating in multiple and essential ways the conceptive process—is a powerful corrective to the autonomous functioning and responsiveness of the clitoris. Their discussion of the vagina must be read basically as a statement of women's intrinsic heterosexuality and as a rejection of sexual activity that does not involve the vagina. Women's sexuality has again been reined in to conform to traditional heterosexual expectations. To be sure, an autonomous female sexuality is ultimately a social construction rather than simply a physiological reality. However, Masters and Johnson must be faulted for overriding their physiological data in a way that maintains rather than challenges traditional social constructions of women's sexuality.

For all that the majority of women themselves may sympathize with Masters and Johnson's sympathies for the heterosexual alliance, their research tells us much more about how people do sex than about sexual relationships as such. While it is helpful to know something of the sexual techniques that are the precondition for bringing women to orgasm, it seems more salient to have some understanding of the kinds of relationships and communications between partners that predispose them to knowing or wanting to know those techniques. The major variable influencing the achievement of sexual fulfillment for women as well as men is, undoubtedly, not merely technique but the quality of the relationship itself. Masters and Johnson offer no recognition that effective and meaningful sexual activity is not defined solely by the achievement of orgasm, but may involve a wide range of behaviors and contacts that are expressive of caring and commitment between partners. Masters and Johnson have followed Kinsey's behaviorist lead to its logical conclusion. They have earned for women the right to have equal time and space with men on the sexual production line.

ALIX SHULMAN, ORGANS AND ORGASMS

In Woman in Sexist Society: Studies in Power and Powerlessness 292, 293–96 (Vivian Gornick and Barbara K. Moran, eds. 1971).

Organs

It has long been known that the clitoris is endlessly more sensitive than the vagina, more sensitive than the penis too, if one judges by the number of nerve endings in the organs. In fact, anatomically, the clitoris and the penis have many similarities since they develop from the same cells in the female or male fetus. Yet, as Ruth Herschberger pointed out in her brilliant 1948 book on female sexuality, *Adam's Rib,* society refuses to acknowledge it: "It was quite a feat of nature to grant the small clitoris the same number of nerves as the penis. It was an even more incredible feat that society should actually have convinced the possessors of this organ that it was sexually inferior to the penis." The vagina, on the other hand, is for the most part so little sensitive that women commonly wear a diaphragm or tampon in it, and even undergo surgery on it, without feeling any sensation at all.

Despite the known anatomical facts and the experiences of many, many women, men usually insist that the vagina *is* the organ of female pleasure. Most of them insist, and probably believe, that women, like men, achieve orgasm by means of the movement of the penis back and forth into the vagina. While perpetuating this myth of vaginal primacy, from which they so readily benefit, the male "experts" make a small concession to the puzzling discrepancies in the "facts." Taking their cue from Freud, they claim that there are *two* kinds of orgasm: vaginal and clitoral. But of the two, they argue, only the vaginal kind, which is adapted to the male anatomy and suits male pleasure, is necessary, is valuable; the clitoral kind is not. Here is Freud himself:

> In the phallic phase of the girl, the clitoris is the dominant erotogenic zone. But it is not destined to remain so; with the change to femininity, the clitoris must give up to the vagina its sensitivity, and, with it, its importance, either wholly or in part. This is one of the two tasks which have to be performed in the course of the woman's development; the more fortunate man has only to continue at the time of his sexual maturity what he has already practiced during the period of early sexual expansion.[2]

A woman who fails to transfer her sexual sensitivity from the clitoris to the vagina at puberty is, according to Freud, regressive, infantile, neurotic, hysteric, and frigid. The vaginal orgasm is supposedly mature, beautiful and good, while the clitoral orgasm is infantile, perverse, bad. A woman is frigid according to many of Freud's followers even today, if she does not have vaginal orgasms even though she may have frequent clitoral orgasms.

In their jokes and in their pornography, in their theories and in their marriage manuals, men treat the clitoris as simply one more erogenous zone like the breasts, underarms, or ears, to be used to arouse a woman sexually so that she will permit intercourse. They may remember the clitoris in foreplay, but for real sex, back to the vagina! The true center of female sexuality, the clitoris, is never identified for little girls who, when they accidentally discover they have one, often think themselves freaks to have on their bodies such a sensitive, unnamed thing. Most girls are not even told about the clitoris at puberty, when they may be instructed in the rites of feminine hygiene and intercourse. The diagrams of female genital anatomy that accompany most tampons and birth control devices usually illustrate the urinary bladder and the ovaries, but hardly ever the clitoris.

Orgasms

Women know from personal experience that there is only one kind of orgasm, no matter what name it is given, vaginal, clitoral, psychological. It is a sexual orgasm. Women know there is only one set of responses, one group of things that happen in their bodies during orgasm. It may vary in intensity from one experience to another, but for any woman who has ever masturbated, orgasm is unmistakable and certainly cannot be confused with anything else. No woman masturbating ever wonders whether or not orgasm has occurred. She has no doubts about that. When it happens, she knows it.

2. Sigmund Freud, *New Introductory Lectures on Psycho-Analysis* (* * * 1946), pp. 151–152.

The recent laboratory research on female sexuality conducted by Virginia Johnson and William E. Masters confirms clinically what women know to be true from their own experience. If a woman experiences orgasm during intercourse, it is not a special kind of orgasm with a special set of physiological responses; it is like any other orgasm. Without exception, the Masters–Johnson data show that all orgasms, *no matter what kind of stimulation produces them,* result in almost identical bodily changes for all women—vaginal contractions, increase in body temperature, increase in pulse and respiration rate, and so forth. Though it is produced through the clitoris, the orgasm occurs as well in the vagina, the anus, the heart, the lungs, the skin, the head.

Given this clarity about what an orgasm feels like, why then does a woman occasionally confess she "doesn't know" whether or not she has had orgasm during intercourse? If orgasm had occurred, she would know it. Since she does not know it, it cannot have occurred. Nevertheless, since she has been taught to expect some special kind of orgasm called vaginal orgasm which can occur only during intercourse, she wonders. She can not know what such an orgasm is supposed to feel like because *there is no such thing.* The sensations of a penis in a vagina are indeed different from other sensations; accompanied by the right emotions they may be so pleasurable as to tempt a woman to hope that they can somehow qualify for that mysterious, desirable thing that has been touted as vaginal orgasm, even though they may not at all resemble the sensations she knows as orgasm. If she does not take advantage of the mystery and confusion surrounding the term to believe that perhaps she has indeed had a vaginal orgasm, she may feel compelled at least to pretend that she has. If not, she must submit to being called frigid or infantile by professional name-calling psychologists, doctors, and all who listen to them, and she must risk the displeasure and reprisal of her mate.

Notes on Female Orgasms

1. The importance of perspective is illustrated by Kinsey's interpretation of female sexual unresponsiveness as a major factor in women's premarital coital reluctance. He concludes that men are victimized by female unresponsiveness (colloquially known as "frigidity"). Miller and Fowlkes suggest instead that women are victimized by men's self-interest and failure to show the consideration necessary to incorporate female orgasm into the coital experience. These are two opposite views derived from the identical result, i.e., female sexual unresponsiveness. Why do you think that Kinsey and later researchers drew opposite conclusions from the same "data"?

All sex surveys are subject to a variety of criticisms: researchers often have an agenda, samples are not representative (e.g., lack of racial, class, geographic, age and educational level diversity), and people lie (or are inaccurate) when they speak of their sexual activities. It is alleged that Kinsey, a homosexual and masochist, was biased and determined to remove guilt and repression from human sexuality. See Sarah Boxer, Truth or Lies?

In Sex Surveys, You Never Know, New York Times, § B, pg. 7, col. 4, July 22, 2000. In 1994 the results of the National Health and Social Life Survey were published in *The Social Organization of Sexuality* by Edward O. Lauman and John H. Gagnon. That survey, based on interviews with a random sample of over 3400 people between 18 and 59, revealed:

> low rates of homosexuality and promiscuity, high rates of marital fidelity and connubial bliss. It showed that in a given year most Americans have only one sex partner; that the median lifetime number of partners for women is two and for men is six; that most people have sex less than twice a week and it's over quickly; that most Americans are happy with their sex lives and partners. It also showed that people most often have sex with members of their own class.

Id. Thus it seems that there is a great deal of inconsistent results among sex surveys. How do you explain this?

2. Kinsey also stated that whether or not the woman reaches orgasm, many females derive satisfaction in knowing that her sexual partner has enjoyed the contact and that she has contributed to his pleasure. Does this support Dworkin's assertion that women have learned to suppress their authentic sexuality in order to survive in a world dominated by men? What would Ruth Colker say? Is it possible to take pleasure empathetically from the pleasure of another? Is it pleasurable to give pleasure? How, if at all, would this differ in lesbian relationships?

3. After Kinsey, it took almost two decades for Masters and Johnson to report that the problem was not frigid women but that men failed to provide quality sexual attention. Ironically, they found that women's maximum physiologic intensity of orgasmic response was achieved by automanipulative techniques; the lowest intensity was achieved during coition. Thus, the female orgasmic response is not correlated with intercourse (or is negatively correlated). How, then, can we explain the dominance of intercourse in heterosexual relationships? Does this support Dworkin's position?

4. Miller and Fowlkes state that "if women are to be sexually autonomous * * *, they must also participate in the social, political, and economic autonomy that has been granted to men." What would be the social, political, and economic prerequisites to achieve full female sexual agency? Would there still be reasons why young women might risk unprotected heterosexual intercourse in such a world? Do young elite women (such as most women in your law school class) feel that they are free sexual agents? Are they? Are you?

5. Alix Shulman's article, Organs and Orgasms, was written in 1971. How much has changed since then? Do instructions accompanying tampons now contain the clitoris in illustrations? Are girls told about the clitoris during puberty? Are boys? Are we told more about the male sex organ than about our own? Does this contribute further support for Dworkin?

What, if anything, were you taught about sexual pleasure in sex education classes in grade school and after? Did the material necessarily convey some basic information about male sexual pleasure, since it is closely connected to pregnancy? Are boys more likely to discuss masturbation in their sex education class while the girls' class is more likely to focus on prevention of pregnancy? Why? Why is masturbation not presented as an alternative to heterosexual intercourse in order to prevent pregnancy? What should be taught if students are to learn about female sexual pleasure? What are the likely obstacles to inclusion of such material in grade school, high school, and college curricula?

Sweden introduced sex education to public schools in 1942, and ten years later made it mandatory beginning with first grade. See Elissa Germaine, Adolescent Girls, Sexuality & (Lack of) Sex Education 36 (2000) (unpublished paper). The sex education program dictated by the government includes:

> teaching that sex need not take place in marriage; providing specific information about contraception at an early age; thoroughly discussing abortion and homosexuality; characterizing interpersonal relationships "by responsibility, consideration and concern for a fellow human being;" and making clear that forced sex, casual sex, sexual promiscuity, and different standards for the sexuality of males and females are wrong.

Id. at 36–37. Do you think the Swedish system could serve as a model for the United States? Why or why not?

6. Do the readings suggest that simultaneous orgasms for a man and woman having conventional heterosexual intercourse are unlikely? Is that the impression one gets from the media, especially movies? What are the effects of creating an expectation that if sex is "good," orgasms are simultaneous? Do men continue to expect orgasms to be simultaneous, though we know that result is rare? If so, why? Are they unfamiliar with the basic facts of female pleasure? Are there other reasons? Would you support legislation requiring major movie production companies to show simultaneous orgasms in only a realistic proportion of sex scenes? What justifications could one advance for such regulation? Would such regulation result in increased female sexual pleasure?

Do you think the male expectation of simultaneous orgasms results in women faking orgasms? In the movie "Harry Met Sally," the female lead demonstrates in a restaurant how women fake orgasms when the male lead says he "would know" if any woman he had sex with had faked her orgasm. Have you ever "faked" an orgasm? Do you think women fake orgasm more than men do? How do you explain the faked orgasm phenomenon, which apparently is quite common?

7. Does dominance by one partner in sex translate into dominance in other aspects of a relationship? Does equality in non-sexual aspects of a relationship translate into non-dominant sexual behavior?

MARGARET NICHOLS, LESBIAN RELATIONSHIPS: IMPLICATIONS FOR THE STUDY OF SEXUALITY AND GENDER

In Homosexuality/Heterosexuality 350, 351–59 (David P. McWhirter, Stephanie A. Sanders, and June Machover Reinisch, eds. 1990).

Lesbianism has always been less understood than male homosexuality. In part because of simple sexism, in part because most research has found the incidence of lesbianism to be lower than rates of male homosexuality, women who love other women are less frequently studied. And yet ample evidence exists to suggest that lesbians are not simply female reproductions of gay men. In fact, because lesbians seem so different from gay men at times, contrasting gay male relationships with lesbian relationships with heterosexual relationships, as Blumstein and Schwartz did in their highly creative work, gives us exciting opportunities to observe the interaction of gender, sex, and relationships. Such study yields important knowledge about the social construction of our sex roles, our sexuality, and our loves.

To emphasize what we can learn about socialization does not exclude the possible contribution that biology, including genetic and prenatal influence, plays in the development of sexuality. Yet certain social forces seem undeniable. To anyone studying lesbianism in any depth, the role of sex role socialization and cultural attitudes toward women seems unmistakable. * * *

Indeed, even the lower incidence of homosexuality in women may be in part a reflection of the socialization of women. For example, it has been amply documented that lesbian women, when compared to gay men, tend to recognize and act upon their same-sex attractions at a later age. Higher percentages of lesbians have had heterosexual sex and a higher percentage marry heterosexually. However, married gay men stay married longer and report being happier in their marriages, prompting Bell and Weinberg to say:

> Women were less likely to behave sexually in accordance with their true interests ... It is possible that lesbians' greater heterosexuality simply reflects a history of accommodation to males in a sexual context or of conformity to social expectations.

In other words, the relative ratio of gay men to lesbians may reflect men's relatively higher rates of *all* kinds of sexual activity coupled with women's relative lack of personal freedom to live their lives as they choose. Women in this culture have generally fewer life options than men, including the option to openly live out one's homosexuality.

* * *

A Brief Historical Overview of Lesbian Relationships

When one takes even a cursory look at historical and anthropological evidence, it becomes clear that the "essentialist" view of sexual orientation, which regards orientation as an almost immutable trait like skin color or height, cannot encompass all the variations of same-sex behavior that we know to exist and to have existed in the past. Three illustrations of the forms that lesbian relationships have taken in this country in the last century and a half will clarify this point. For example, Lillian Faderman's fascinating book *Surpassing the Love of Men* describes the "romantic friendships" common among upper-middle-class women of the previous two centuries. During these years, a number of single, childless women lived in lifelong companionships with other women that often enabled them to live more career-oriented or at least intellectually oriented lives than would have been possible in traditional wife/mother roles. From accounts that some of these women have left behind (diaries, letters, and so on), Faderman concludes that many "Boston marriages," as they were often called, were emotionally passionate, intimate relationships comparable to heterosexual marriage but often probably without a genital sexual component. The women involved in these companionships did not consider themselves "lesbians;" indeed, for much of this time period neither the word nor the concept for lesbianism existed. Nevertheless, Faderman, who has since drawn parallels between these women and today's radical lesbian feminists, argues that they be considered "gay" relationships on the basis of their romantic/emotional component and their structural similarities to heterosexual marriage. Faderman's analysis raises interesting questions about how one defines sexual orientation (Is a relationship lesbian if genital sexual contact is absent?), but also highlights the interaction of sexual orientation/sexual identity with the sociopolitical functions served by the homosexual role. It is extremely important to recognize that women in romantic friendships were, by virtue of their "lesbianism," able to be free of many of the social constraints experienced by heterosexually married women. Thus, seen in this context, sexual orientation means far more than the seemingly neutral choice of gender of the romantic or sexual partner. When cultures use gender as a primary organizing principle for the structuring of nearly every aspect of an individual's life, then the choice of gender of partner must of necessity be laden with social meaning and implication. As we will see in the next section, there is increasing evidence that at least for some people, sexual attraction is not immutably determined from birth. Given this, it is almost irresistible to conclude that the social meanings, roles, and functions attached to gender must in some way influence the development and expression of sexual orientation.

Looking at history shows us that the theme enunciated by "romantic friendships"—that of escaping the traditional roles culturally assigned to women—repeats itself over and over again in lesbian relationships. Jonathan Katz documents the phenomenon of "passing women" in America around the turn of the century. During this era, a number of women dressed as men and used male names, taking on male identities and roles and often "marrying" women. They disguised themselves in this way and often assumed a male persona for their entire adult lives, unknown as women to their closest associates, and sometimes even to their "wives." Some achieved great prominence in business and politics, holding elected office as men, and they were not discovered to be female until after death, upon autopsy or preparation of the body for burial. What we know of these individuals comes largely from newspaper accounts after death revealed their true identities, less frequently from personal diaries. The few accounts they left behind in their own words strongly suggest that "passing women" were motivated at least as much by their desire to escape the limited social roles available to women as they were to actualize their same-sex erotic attractions. Again, the social meanings attached to gender appear to interact with sexual orientation.

The third piece of historical data we can consider is the growth of lesbian-feminist culture in the 1970s. During this decade, many women seemed to come to a recognition of their same-sex attractions through the vehicle of the women's movement. Typically, the lesbian who "came out" in this way was largely unaware of her same-sex impulses until adulthood. Often she had married heterosexually and was dissatisfied with her relationships with men for a variety of reasons that found articulation through the political philosophy of feminism. Many such women began actively pursuing a lesbian life-style only after a personal political transformation and after seeing lesbianism validated by women's groups and organizations. They often consider their lesbianism a "choice" and rationalize their new life-style with the rhetoric of feminism:

> Women who came to lesbianism reject the notion that lesbianism is a sexual identity. This is not to say that sexual expression is usually absent in the new gay women's lives; rather, sexual activity is for them generally only one aspect and perhaps a relatively unimportant aspect of their commitment to a lesbian lifestyle. Lesbianism in this context, or, more precisely, lesbian-feminism, is defined as a political choice more than a sexual preference ... less a personal choice about who to sleep with than a uniting of women against patriarchal power. Lesbian feminists deny that the choice to be lesbian arises from sexual interest or sexual proclivity.... Instead, lesbian feminists define lesbianism in much more inclusive terms: a lesbian's entire sense of self centers on women.

In some ways, lesbian feminists have articulated in defiantly political terms what "passing women" articulated in an individualistic framework and what remained without voice for women in romantic friendships.

It is not suggested here that sexism is the sole determinant of lesbian relationships. In addition to personal, interpersonal, and family dynamics, biologic or innate predisposition is quite likely to play a role in the unfolding of sexual orientation. For some individuals, the cultural loading of gender may have little or nothing to do with their expression of sexual identity. Moreover, it is just as likely that for many people the social functions assigned to gender may shape the manifestation of sexual orientation but not the initial formation of erotic attractions. For example, lesbians in the 1950s often assumed rigid "butch-femme" roles in their couple relationships, and the butch-femme phenomenon seems more related to an imitation of existing heterosexual models of relationships than to the formation of erotic attraction. As we shall see in the section on lesbian couples, sex role socialization may influence the dynamics of female-female pairings in a way independent of the origins of same-sex erotic pull. Nevertheless, the study of the differentiation of sexual orientation can be greatly enhanced by considering the various functions, roles, and meanings that directly or indirectly accrue to a homosexual versus heterosexual life-style. Same-sex erotic attraction is probably a necessary but not sufficient condition for homosexual behavior or identity. For some lesbians, the cultural roles assigned to women seem to influence the expression of attraction.

Bisexuality in Women and Its Relationship to Lesbianism

Additional insight about sexual orientation in women can be achieved by reviewing some of the newer research on bisexuality in women. The study of bisexuality is made more difficult by lack of a precise definition. Do we use as our criterion fantasy, attraction, or behavior, and do we attend to quantity or quality of contact, sexual versus relationship aspects, history over a life span or recent behavior? Masters and Johnson, for example, found what they termed "cross-preference encounter" sexual fantasies to be quite common for all their subjects. Lesbian sexual fantasies were the fifth most common fantasy among women who identify as heterosexual, and heterosexual fantasies ranked third for self-identified lesbians. Bell and Weinberg reported that only half of lesbian women rate their feelings and attractions as exclusively gay. Hyde, in interpreting data from both the Kinsey surveys and the Hune survey of the 1970s, estimated that on the basis of same-and opposite-sex behavior in adulthood, approximately 15% of women are bisexual and less than 1% exclusively homosexual. Bell and Weinberg additionally estimated that more than one third of their lesbian sample exhibited what they called a "partial bisexual style," that is, some current pleasurable heterosexual activity and attractions despite a predominantly gay life-style and lesbian identity. Moreover, even among their "heterosexual control group," 10% of women were behaviorally bisexual. These statistics suggest that (1) far more women *behave* bisexually and/or experience bisexual fantasies and attractions than are self-labeled as bisexual; (2) lesbianism is something of a residual category in this culture, that is, large percentages of women who self-label as gay are in fact both erotically and behaviorally bisexual, not just in terms of life history but also with regard to their current behavior and feelings. Lesbian means "not exclusively heterosexual" as much as it means "exclusively homosexual." In a sense, these data make lesbianism an even more interesting phenomenon. Clearly, lesbianism is not merely a matter of an overwhelming, single-focus sexual attraction. These facts about bisexuality make the nonbiologic factors operative in lesbianism even more relevant and give insight into the claim of some gay women that they "chose" their sexual orientation.

* * * From a cursory examination of bisexuality in women, we see that female sexual orientation, at least for some, can be fluid and dynamic and that by implication lesbianism is a multifactored life-style, not merely the expression of a biological imperative or of some intransigent orientation fixed early in childhood.

LESBIAN COUPLES: IMPLICATIONS FOR THE STUDY OF RELATIONSHIPS

* * *

The most striking differences between lesbian couples and other kinds of couples have to do with sexuality and sexual frequency. *Single* lesbians have less frequent sex and fewer different partners than do gay men. This is not surprising because at least until the advent of AIDS, gay men were probably more sexually active than anyone else in the culture. And some research suggests that, overall, lesbians may be more sexually responsive and more satisfied with the sex they do have than are heterosexual women. Masters and Johnson speculate that the sexual techniques of lesbians, which tend to be sensuous, less genitally and orgasm focused, and less oriented to vaginal penetration, are generally more suited to the sexual needs of women than is heterosexual sexual activity.

Lesbians do not seem to have pervasive sexual problems. Clinical reports do not suggest, for example, that gay women have significant rates of orgasmic dysfunction * * *. But lesbians do seem to have strikingly low rates of sex *within long-term committed relationships.*

Most clinicians and sex therapists working with lesbian couples have noted the high prevalence of sexual desire disorders among such couples. Sociologists Blumstein and Schwartz, comparing heterosexual married and unmarried couples, gay male, and lesbian couples, have given us the most comprehensive data we have on this topic. They found that lesbian couples in long-term relationships have sex far less frequently than any other type of couple studied. Only about one third of lesbians in relationships of 2 years or more had sex once a week or more. Forty-seven percent of lesbians in relationships of over 5 years had sex once a month or less. This is in striking contrast, for example, to heterosexual married couples: two thirds of these couples together more than 5 years had sex once a week or more, and only 15% had sex once a month or less.

That this dynamic is related to lesbians' status as women rather than to the homosexual nature of the coupling is evident from the Blumstein and Schwartz data on gay male couples. Gay men have slightly less sex in their primary relationships than do heterosexual couples; on the other hand, gay males have the highest rates of extra-marital sex. This means that lesbians in couple relationships are less sexual both within and outside the relationship than any other group, just as uncoupled lesbians have less frequent sex and fewer partners than do gay men.

Moreover, Blumstein and Schwartz's findings indicate other differences as well. Their lesbian subjects preferred hugging, cuddling, and other nongenital physical contact to genital sex, reminiscent of reports from heterosexual women in such surveys as the *Hite Report.* Similarly, * * * [other researchers] found lesbians to be more constricted in their range of sexual techniques than other couples. For example, 61% of lesbian couples have oral sex "infrequently or not at all," leaving the repertoire of the majority of couples limited to manual stimulation and tribadism [lesbian practice simulating heterosexual intercourse]. Lesbians have about the same rates of nonmonogamy as do heterosexuals (28% report at least one extramarital episode), although they have far less "outside" sex than gay men, for whom nonmonogamy is the norm rather than the exception. Moreover, both lesbians and gay men tend to have sex in the context of an "open" relationship in contrast to the secretive "infidelities" common among heterosexuals. But lesbians, like heterosexual women and unlike both gay and straight men, are likely to have "affairs" rather than just sexual encounters. Finally, Blumstein and Schwartz reported that one half of lesbians in couples with a low frequency of genital contact said that they were dissatisfied with their sexuality. And in an 18–month follow-up of all couples, lesbian couples had the highest rates of dissolution of any couple type. The pattern of breakup was significant: one partner had an outside affair and subsequently left the primary relationship for the new lover.

How are we to explain these findings? They fly in the face of not only the belief that women culturally form the "glue" that holds relationships together but also findings showing the high value lesbians place on relationships, the high percentages of lesbians that are members of committed couples at any given time, and the general level of satisfaction lesbians report about the sexual encounters they do have. It seems clear, given the dissimilarities between gay male and lesbian couples, that we must interpret these findings as dynamics of woman-to-woman pairings, the effects of female socialization multiplied rather than concomitants of homosexuality. Given that, what sense can be made of the data on lesbian couples to shed light upon femininity as expressed in this culture?

It appears, first, that the recognizably feminine values of relationship orientation and egalitarianism may influence the tendency to *be* coupled but not necessarily the ability to make a relationship last. On this point, it is important to stress that we have only one study * * * that gives us hard data on longevity of lesbian couples. Moreover, Blumstein and Schwartz themselves are quick to remind us that the variable of *social sanction* seems to be the predominant factor correlated with relationship longevity. That is, heterosexual married couples stay together longer than any type of unmarried couple, be it heterosexual, gay male, or lesbian, and the differences between longevity of married versus unmarried couples are far greater than differences among any type of unmarried couple. Nevertheless, it is safe to assume at this juncture that lesbian couples do *not* experience more longevity than other types of couples, which is what one would assume from the stereotype that women provide the "glue" of relationships. Further, although lesbian sex may be more pleasurable and intrinsically/biologically "right" for women than more genitally/orgasmically focused sex, this does not seem to contribute to frequency of sexual encounters within a long-term relationship.

To an extent, the data on frequency of sex within lesbian relationships forces us to examine our beliefs about the significance of sexual interaction within any committed relationship. Just as Faderman argued, in her work on "romantic friendships," for a definition of lesbianism that did not necessarily include genital sex, so it is probably true that some lesbians are not disturbed by the infrequency or even total absence of genital sex in their relationships. * * * Some lesbians simply do not place a high priority on sex, and in this regard they resemble some heterosexual women. Schreiner–Engel, for example, reported that even among heterosexual subjects who define themselves as suffering from problems of low sexual desire, men and women differ markedly, with men reporting situational or secondary desire disorders and women reporting primary problems: half of these women report *never* experiencing sexual desire. And all surveys of sexual behavior show women, overall, to be less sexually active than men. To an extent lesbian couples may simply enact the sexual desires of women in general. While it may not be true that women provide the "glue" in relationships, it is possible that men tend to provide the major push for frequent sex in long-term relationships.

Thus, one interpretation of the data on sexuality in lesbian relationships is that the low frequency of genital sex coupled with a relatively constricted sexual repertoire and high frequency of nongenital physical expression of affection represents a "true" expression of female sexuality. For some lesbians this is undoubtedly the case. However, just as some women have high sexual needs and desires for a broad range of sexual/genital activities, some lesbians clearly are dissatisfied with the sexual patterns that predominate in their long-term relationships. Some evidence for this is direct: many lesbians *report* dissatisfaction, and low sexual frequency is often noted as a complaint of lesbians seeking couple counseling. Other evidence is indirect: we can infer that the relatively higher dissolution rate for lesbian relationships found by Blumstein and Schwartz may be related to low rates of sexual contact. In fact, the pattern found in the Blumstein and Schwartz study is one frequently noted by clinicians working with lesbian couples. That pattern consists of a sharp decrease or even absence of sex in the couple after a few years, followed by one member's seeking an outside lover and eventually leaving her partner for that lover.

This evidence suggests that we need to consider the low rates of sexual expression found in long-term lesbian relationships as a problem for at least some gay women rather than simply an expression of female sexuality in its "natural" form (i.e., not influenced by a male presence).

MARILYN FRYE, LESBIAN "SEX" (1987)

In Willful Virgin: Essays in Feminism 1976–1992, 109–113 (1992).

Recent discussions of lesbian "sex" frequently cite the findings of a study on couples by Blumstein and Schwartz[3] which is perceived by most of those who discuss it as having been done well, with a good sample of couples—lesbian, male homosexual, heterosexual nonmarried and heterosexual married couples. These people apparently found that lesbian couples "have sex" far less frequently than any other type of couple, that lesbians couples are less "sexual" as couples and as individuals than anyone else. In their sample, only about one third of lesbians in relationships of two years or longer "had sex" once a week or more; 47% of lesbians in long term relationships "had sex" once a month or less, while among heterosexual married couples only 15% had sex once a month or less. And they report that lesbians seem to be more limited in the range of their "sexual" techniques than are other couples.

When this sort of information first came into my circle of lesbian friends, we tended to see it as conforming to what we know from our own experience. We were not surprised to hear that we "had" less "sex" than anyone else or that in our long-term relationships we "had sex" a great deal less frequently than other sorts of couples. This seemed to pretty much fit our knowledge of ourselves and of each other. But on more reflection, and looking again at what has been going on with us in our long-term relationships, the nice fit between this report and our experience seemed not so perfect after all.

It was brought to our attention during our ruminations on this that what 85% of long-term heterosexual married couples do more than once a month takes on the average 8 minutes to do.

Although in my experience lesbians discuss their "sex" lives with each other relatively little (a point to which I will return), I know from my own experience and from the reports of a few other lesbians in long-term relationships, that what we do that, on average, we do considerably less frequently, takes on the average, considerably more than 8 minutes to do. Maybe about 30 minutes at the least. Sometimes maybe about an hour. And it is not uncommon that among these relatively uncommon occurrences, an entire afternoon or evening is given over to activities organized around doing it. The suspicion arises that what 85% of heterosexual married couples are doing more than once a month and what 47% of lesbians couples are doing less than once a month is not the same thing. And if they are not doing the same thing, how was this research done that would line these different things up against each other to compare how many times they were done?

I remember that one of my first delicious tastes of old gay lesbian culture occurred in a bar where I was chatting with some other lesbians I was just getting acquainted with. One was talking about being busted out of the Marines for being gay. She had been put under suspicion somehow, and was sent off to the base psychiatrist to be questioned, her perverted tendencies to be assessed. He wanted to convince her she had

3. Philip Blumstein and Pepper Schwartz, *American Couples* (NY: William Morrow and Company, 1983).

only been engaged in a little youthful experimentation and wasn't really gay. To this end, he questioned her about the extent of her experience. What he asked was, "How many times have you had sex with a woman?" At this, we all laughed and giggled: what an ignorant fool he was! What does he think he means by "times"? What will we count? What's to *count*?

Another of my friends years later, discussing the same conundrum, said that she thought maybe every time you got up to go to the bathroom, that marked a "time." The joke about "how many times" is still good for a chuckle from time to time in my life with my lover. I have no memory of any such topic providing any such merriment in my years of sexual encounters and relationships with men. It would have been very rare indeed that we would not have known how to answer the question "How many times did you do it?"

If what heterosexual married couples do that the individuals report under the rubric "sex" or "have sex" is something that in most instances can easily be individuated into countable instances, this is more evidence that it is not what long-term lesbian couples do . . . or, for that matter, what short-term lesbian couples do.

What violence did the lesbians do their experience by answering the same question the heterosexuals answered, as though it had the same meaning for them? How did the lesbians figure out how to answer the questions "How frequently?" or "How many times?" My guess is, for starters, that different individuals figured it out differently, to some degree. Some might have counted a two or three-cycle evening as one "time" they "had sex"; some might have counted that as two or three "times." Some may have counted as "times" only the times both partners had orgasms; some may have counted as "times" occasions on which at least one had an orgasm; some may not have orgasms or have them rarely and may not have figured orgasms into the calculations; perhaps they counted as a "time" every episode in which both touched the other's vulva more than fleetingly and not for something like a health examination. For some, to count every reciprocal touch of the vulva would have made them count as "having sex" more than most people with work to do would dream of having time for; how do we suppose those individuals counted "times"? Is there any good reason why they should not count all those as "times"? Does it depend on how fulfilling it was? (Was anybody else counting by occasions of fulfillment?)

We have no idea how individual lesbians individuated their so-called "sexual acts" or encounters; we have no idea what it means when they said they did it less than once a month. But this raises questions for how the heterosexuals individuated and counted their sexual acts or encounters. I think many lesbians, when pressed to answer a question like "How many times a month do you have sex?" count times both partners had orgasms. That seems to them definitive enough. Did the heterosexuals who responded to these questions count only the times both parties had orgasms? Did the men count all the times they had orgasms, and the women count all the times they had orgasms? If so, one would expect the authors of the study to have noted a considerable difference between the reports of the women and of the men in the samples of heterosexual couples. In my experience, and by my reading of the predominant culture generally heterosexual pairs count as having had sex whether the woman had an orgasm or not. And in my experience and by my reading of the culture at large, heterosexual pairs might not count themselves as having had sex if all that was done was the man digitally stimulated the woman's clitoris until she had an orgasm. I think that if the heterosexual women counted "times" according to the standard meaning of "have sex" in English, they counted not according to their own experience of orgasm or even arousal, but according to their partners' orgasms and ejaculations. One wonders how heterosexual women would have individuated and counted the incidents of "having sex" in their relationships if they had not counted according to their partners' orgasms and ejaculations, or how they did count "times" if they did not count them this way. If the havings of sex by heterosexual married couples did take on the average 8 minutes, my guess is that in a large number of those cases the women did not experience orgasms. My guess is that neither the women's pleasure nor the women's orgasms were pertinent in most of the individuals' counting and reporting the frequency with which they "had sex."

So, do lesbian couples really "have sex" any less frequently than heterosexual couples? My own view is that lesbian couples "have sex" a great deal less frequently than heterosexual couples: I think, in fact, we don't "have sex" at all. By the criteria that I'm betting most of the heterosexual people used in reporting the frequency with which they have sex, lesbians don't have sex. There is no male partner whose orgasm and ejaculation can be the criterion for counting "times." (I'm willing to draw the conclusion that heterosexual women don't have sex either, that what they report is the frequency with which their partners had sex.)

Notes on Sexuality and Lesbian Relationships

1. Do you think that the study of lesbian relationships yields information relevant to all women? Why? Are lesbians less subject to male control? What aspects of lesbian relationships might be particularly relevant and important? What can the study of gay relationships tell us about men?

2. What are the positive aspects of relating romantically only to women? Do you think that women who choose lesbianism as a political choice are opting out of the struggle to change the societal subordination of women? Is separatism a viable option?

Can you be a feminist without being a lesbian? Marilyn Frye believes that:

> [f]emale heterosexuality is not a biological drive or an individual woman's erotic attraction or attachment to another human animal which happens to be male. Female heterosexuality is a set of social

institutions and practices defined and regulated by patriarchal kinship systems, by both civil and religious law, and by strenuously enforced mores and deeply entrenched values and taboos. Those definitions, regulations, values and taboos are about male fraternity and the oppression and exploitation of women.

Frye, Willful Virgin or Do You Have to Be a Lesbian to Be a Feminist? 1990 124, 132, in Willful Virgin: Essays in Feminism 1976–1992 (1992). She therefore concludes that "feminism, which is thoroughly anti-patriarchal, is not compatible with female heterosexuality, which is thoroughly patriarchal." Id. What do you think? Do you agree with her view of female heterosexuality? Ironically, Frye also notes that the linking of feminism and lesbianism, in a world of women's homophobia and lesbian-hating, serves to restrain radical feminism. Id. at 128.

3. Do you agree with Lillian Faderman that partners in Boston marriages in which there was no genital contact were nonetheless lesbians? How do you define lesbianism? How does Nichols define it? How do these definitions compare to Adrienne Rich's "lesbian continuum" discussed in Chapter 3, above?

4. Were you familiar with the phenomenon of women passing as men? Does such conduct demonstrate how difficult it must have been to avoid the social roles assigned to women? See Marjorie Garber, Vested Interests: Cross–Dressing and Cultural Anxiety (1997). Can you draw parallels between women passing as men and light-skinned Blacks passing as whites? See generally, Kathy Russell, Midge Wilson, and Ronald Hall, The Color Complex: The Politics of Skin Color Among African Americans (1992).

5. What do you conclude from the dissimilarities described in the data between gay male relationships and those of lesbians? For instance, according to Nichols, above, (1) gay males have the highest amount of extramarital sexual relationships; (2) lesbians are less sexual both within and outside their relationships; (3) lesbians prefer nongenital physical contact to genital contact; (4) lesbians are more likely to have "affairs" than sexual encounters; and (5) lesbian couples have the highest rates of dissolution, with a pattern of one partner leaving the primary relationship for a new lover. What do you think accounts for each of these differences? What conclusions do you draw from them? Nichols focuses primarily on the longevity of these relationships and the quality and quantity of sexual activity. What else would you investigate?

6. After reading the Frye excerpt, what do you think of the Blumstein and Schwartz study cited and relied upon by Nichols? Is the study flawed in basic ways? Does "sex" have to be more specifically defined? Does the study compare apples and oranges, i.e., heterosexuals and lesbians? How do *you* define "sex"? Before reading the Frye excerpt, did you have the same concerns she expresses about the Blumstein and Schwartz study? How would you design a sexuality study of heterosexuals and homosexuals?

7. Does it surprise you that a majority of lesbians rate a committed relationship as the most important value in their lives? Nichols suggests that it is a result of being socialized to value relationships more highly than careers or other life goals. Do you agree? Or do you think it is an expression of women's authentic nature? Is this value system exploited by men? Even

though women value relationships highly, Nichols' interpretation of the data "that lesbian couples do *not* experience more longevity than other types of couples" is that women do not provide the "glue" of relationships. Do you agree? Or is serial monogamy the "true" human condition?

8. How easy is it to change what we have been taught about sexual relations? For instance, Margaret Nichols notes that "[a]s women, we are not only taught to wait for our partner to ask for sex although we may want it; but we are also taught not even to pay attention to our own sexual desires unless or until we are approached by our partner." Nichols, Lesbian Sexuality: Issues and Developing Theory, in Lesbian Psychologies 103 (Boston Lesbian Psychologies Collective, eds. 1987). As a result, she suggests that "we are less likely to pressure a reluctant partner to have sex," and, in fact, probably view such pressure as "male" behavior and thus abusive. Id. As adults, how easy do you think it is to change these sexual responses and attitudes?

9. In other sexuality studies, heterosexual men report more physical and emotional satisfaction with partnered sex than do heterosexual women, including married as well as single persons. See Paul England, Marriage, the Costs of Children, and Gender Inequality 320, 336, in Linda J. Waite, ed., The Ties That Bind: Perspectives on Marriage and Cohabitation (2000), citing the National Health and Social Life Survey presented by Waite in 1995 and Waite and Gallagher in 2000. What conclusions can you draw from this finding? Does it surprise you? How do you explain it?

BARBARA OMOLADE, HEARTS OF DARKNESS

In Powers of Desire: The Politics of Sexuality 350, 351–52, 354–55, 357–58, 363–65 (Ann Snitow, Christine Stansell and Sharon Thompson, eds. 1983).

The sexual history of the United States became fused with contradiction and duality, with myth and distortion, with the white man's hate and desire for the black woman, with competition and jealousy between white and black women for white men, with love and struggle between black men and black women. American sexual history reflects the development of patriarchal control stretched to its maximum extent by European men operating within a racial caste system supported by state power in which white maleness becomes the only definition of being. Simultaneously, the extremes of American patriarchy, particularly under slavery, pushed black women outside traditional patriarchal protection, thereby transforming all previous definitions of womanhood, particularly the idea that woman requires male protection because of her innate weakness and inferiority. Black women were oppressed and exploited labor and as such were forced to redefine themselves as women outside of and antagonistic to the racial patriarch who denied their being. Most black women refused to accept the traditional notions of subordination of woman to man. The black woman resisted racial patriarchy by escaping, stealing, killing, outsmarting, and bargaining with her white master while she had sex with him, had babies by him, ministered to his needs growing "to know all there was to know about him." At the same time, most black women accepted traditional notions of patriarchy from black men because they viewed the Afro–Christian tradition of woman as mother and wife as personally desirable and politically necessary for black people's survival.

The racial patriarchy of the white man enabled him to enact his culture's separation between the goodness, purity, innocence, and fraility [sic] of woman with the sinful, evil strength, and carnal knowledge of woman by having sex with white women who came to embody the former and black women who came to embody the latter. The white man's division of the sexual attributes of women based on race meant that he alone could claim to be sexually free: he was free to be sexually active within a society that upheld the chastity and modesty of white women as the "repositories of white civilization." He was free to be irresponsible about the consequences of his sexual behavior with black women within a culture that placed a great value on the family as a sacred institution protecting women, their progeny and his property. He was free to use violence to eliminate his competition with black men for black or white women, thus breaking the customary allegiance among all patriarchs. He was also free to maintain his public hatred of racial mixing while privately expressing his desire for black women's bodies. Ultimately, white men were politically empowered to dominate all women and all black men and women; this was their sexual freedom.

* * *

But though it was beyond *her* concept of enslavement, it was not beyond her master's, for every part of the black woman was used by him. To him she was a fragmented commodity whose feelings and choices were rarely considered: her head and her heart were separated from her back and her hands and divided from her womb and vagina. Her back and muscle were pressed into field labor where she was forced to work with men and work like men. Her hands were demanded to nurse and nurture the white man and his family as domestic servant whether she was technically enslaved or legally free. Her vagina, used for his sexual pleasure, was the gateway to the womb, which was his place of capital investment—the capital investment being the sex act and the resulting child the accumulated surplus, worth money on the slave market.

The totalitarian system of slavery extended itself into the very place that was inviolable and sacred to both African and European societies—the sanctity of the woman's body and motherhood within the institution of marriage. Although all women were slaves under patriarchy, the particular enslavement of black women was also an attack on all black people. All sexual intercourse between a white man and a black woman irrespective of her conscious consent became rape, because the social arrangement assumed the black woman to be without any human right to control her own body. And the body could not be separated from its color.

Racial oppression tends to flow from the external to the internal: from political institutions, social structures, the economic system and military conquest, into the psyche and consciousness and culture of the oppressed and the oppressor. In contrast, sexual oppression tends to direct itself directly to the internal, the feeling and emotional center, the private and intimate self, existing within the external context of power and social control. Black women fused both racial and sexual oppression in their beings and movements in both black and white worlds.

* * *

Though she had no privacy, away from the view of all, could the black woman have ever desired and loved her master/lover? Could she have separated the hands that whipped her body from the hands that gripped her body in lovemaking? After all, the master/lover was only a man, who desired the slave woman and had the power to take her as a woman. Patriarchal society would define the perfect man as the perfect master, and it was the submissiveness of the slave woman that made her the perfect slave and the perfect woman. After all, a man's power over a woman was like the master's power over a slave. It came from "innate superiority." But the intimate place of desire and fulfillment of the submissive and perfected woman was in violent conflict with the rage and humiliation and forced labor of being a slave woman forced to lie in the arms of the enslaver, the enemy ultimately responsible for her humiliation and her suffering. * * *

History, traditionally written as a record of public events, has obscured and omitted the relationship between public events and private acts. Therefore, sex has always been in the closet of American history hidden away from and kept outside the public realm of political and economic events. White men used their power in the public sphere to construct a private sphere that would meet their needs and their desire for black women, which if publically [sic] admitted would have undermined the false construct of race they needed to maintain public power. Therefore, the history of black women in America reflects the juncture where the private and public spheres and personal and political oppression meet.

The master/lover ruled over the world; he divided it up and called everyone out of their name. During the day, he would call her "wench," "negress," "Sable Venus," "dusky Sal," and "Auntie." He described and wrote about her endurance, ate her biscuits, and suckled her breasts. At night he would chant false endearments and would feel engulfed within her darkness. He would accuse her of raping herself, naming his lesser brothers as the fathers of his and her children. He would record every battle, keep every letter, document each law, building monuments to himself, but he would never tell the true story, the complete story of how he used to rape to make the profit, of how he used the bodies of women to satisfy his needs. He would never tell how he built a society with the aid of dark-skinned women, while telling the world he did it alone.

He would cover the tracks between his house and hers, he would deny the semen-stained sheets she was forced to wash. History would become all that men did during the day, but nothing of what they did during the night. He would forget her children. He would deny his love or lust for her. He would deny his failure to obey his own laws. He refused to listen to the logical extension of his argument for the massacres, the slave raids, the genocide, the lynch mobs, the Ku Klux Klan. He could not live up to his own fears and arguments against mongrelization of the race, the separation of black from white. He built an exterior world that reflected his fragmented insides.

But the woman learned to face him, the rapist who hated and loved her with such passion. She learned to use her darkness to create light. She would make the divided, white and black, external and internal world into wholeness. She would "lean on Jesus," reaching out to help and for help, and would gather around her children and kin to help them make the world whole and livable. She would mother all the children—black and white—and serve both men—conqueror and conquered—knowing "all there was to know," for she could not separate the color from the woman.

Only a few daring men, mostly black ones, would recognize that only she understood what it had taken for white men to dominate the world and what it would mean, finally, to be free. But some black women who voiced what they knew did not survive:

> A slave woman ain't allowed to respect herself, if she would. I had a pretty sister, she was whiter than I am, for she took more after her father. When she was 16 years old, her master sent for her. When he sent for her again, she cried and didn't want to go. She told mother her troubles, and she tried to encourage her to be decent and hold up her head above such things if she could. Her master was so mad, to think she had complained to her mother, that he sold her right off to Louisiana, and we heard afterward that she died there of hard usage.[68]

But others sold down river survived and remembered their mothers and fathers, remembered the white master/lover, the black master/lover, and the black brother/lover. They, in their turn, gave their daughters and sons the gifts of determination and freedom, the will to love and the strength to have faith. Some would accept these gifts, some would reject them. History, however, would obliterate the entire story, occasionally giving it only a false footnote. But deep within the daughters' hearts and minds it would be remembered and this memory would become the historical record everything had to be measured by.

Notes on Sexuality and Slavery

1. Does Barbara Omolade's description of the slave woman forced to lie in the arms of the enslaver offer a paradigm for all sexual oppression? Does a woman have free choice to desire and love a man under conditions of social, economic and political inequality?

68. John Blassingame, ed., Slave Testimony: Two Centuries of Letters, Speeches, Interviews and Autobiographies 256 (1977).

2. Did white women suffer any consequences as a result of their husbands' sexual abuse of Black women? Were their lives made better or worse by the rape of African American women? Do you think white women perceived these consequences at the time? Why do you think white women did not align themselves with Black women?

3. Is it possible to separate race from sex? Did white men rape Black women because they were Black or because they were women? Are there other reasons as well? Is Omolade correct in contrasting racial oppression (flowing from external to internal) to sexual oppression (directly to the internal)? What are the practical differences?

4. Why do you think Black women "resisted racial patriarchy" but "accepted traditional notions of patriarchy from black men"? How do you interpret these different forms of patriarchy? Barbara Omolade suggests they subordinated themselves in order to assure the survival of Black people. Is this still true today? See generally Kimberle Crenshaw, Mapping the Margins: Intersectionality, Identity Politics, and Violence Against Women of Color, 43 Stan. L. Rev. 1241, 1253–65 (1993) (criticizing Shahrazad Ali who proposes that "patriarchy is beneficial for the Black community, and that it must be strengthened through coercive means if necessary"); Adrienne D. Davis, The Private Law of Race and Sex: An Antebellum Perspective, 51 Stan. L.Rev. 221 (1999).

5. What lessons can all women learn from the African American woman's experiences and survival strategies?

Chapter 5

VIOLENCE AGAINST WOMEN

A. INTRODUCTION

The amount of violence against women and children in America is staggering: one out of every two married women will be beaten on at least one occasion by her husband;[1] almost one out of every three girls will be sexually assaulted before age 18;[2] and almost one out of every two women is raped or survives an attempted rape,[3] of which over two-thirds

1. Joan Zorza, The Criminal Law of Misdemeanor Domestic Violence, 1970–1990, 83 J.Crim.L. & Criminology 46, 46 (1992). Pregnancy is a high risk time for women—one out of every six pregnant women is abused physically and/or sexually during pregnancy. Judith McFarlane, Barbara Parker, Karen Socken, and Linda Bullock, Assessing for Abuse During Pregnancy: Severity and Frequency of Injuries and Associated Entry Into Prenatal Care, 267 J.A.M.A. 3176, 3177 (1992).

2. Diana E.H. Russell, The Secret Trauma: Incest in the Lives of Girls and Women 74 (1986). Sexual abuse of young children has become common: 14% of boys and 27% of girls are victims, with most instances involving family members. Leonore M.J. Simon, Offender Legislation and the Antitherapeutic Effects on Victims, 41 Ariz. L. Rev. 485, 491 (1999). In fact, less than 10% of all child molestations are committed by strangers; fathers are responsible for 20%, stepfathers 29%, other relatives 11%, and acquaintances of the family 30%. Id. at 490–91. This data must be considered cautiously, however, since it is estimated that only 3% of child sex abuse is reported to the authorities. Id. at 491, n. 24. Moreover, according to the Department of Justice, teen females aged 16 to 19 are 3.5 times more likely than the general population to be victims of rape, attempted rape, or sexual assault. See National Crime Victimization Survey, Bureau of Justice Statistics, U.S. D.O.J. (1996). In a survey of college students, 53.7% of the responding females had been forced into some type of sexual act since the age of 14. Mary P. Koss, Hidden Rape: Sexual Aggression and Victimization in a National Sample of Students in Higher Education, in Rape and Sexual Assault II 3, 10 (Ann Wolbert Burgess ed., 1988). Five out of six victims knew their assailant; almost three out of five were dates. Over 40% of the victims had sex again with the offender at a later time. Id.

3. Diana E.H. Russell, Sexual Exploitation: Rape, Child Sexual Abuse, and Workplace Harassment 35 (1984) (in a study conducted in San Francisco, Russell found that when categories of rape and attempted rape were combined, 44% of women responded affirmatively). Official rape report statistics can be unreliable:

> In 1994, there were 102,096 reported rapes and attempted rapes resulting in 36,610 arrests for forcible rape. Such official statistics that base the number of rapes on the number reported to the police are a far cry from the estimated 500,000 women victims who report rapes in victim surveys.

Simon, note 2 above, at 500.

are committed by someone she knows or loves.[4] While there are no official statistics about the number of women who have been harassed on the street, received obscene phone calls,[5] or been subjected to a man exposing his genitals to her in public, it is difficult to find any woman who has not experienced these assaults. Women are targeted for this violence because they are women.[6] Rape overwhelmingly involves male perpetrators and female victims.[7]

What is the practical effect of violence and the threat of violence against women? Sandra McNeill, in her study of flashing (men publicly exposing their genitals), states:

> While there are no laws explicitly denying women free access to public places at all times, in practice their freedom is curtailed by men who attack them, men who threaten to attack them, insuffi-

4. According to the Department of Justice, 28% were raped by a husband or boyfriend; 35% by acquaintances; and 55% by relatives other than husbands. Violence Against Women, Bureau of Justice Statistics, U.S. D.O.J. (1994). Additionally, 68% of rapes occur between 6 p.m. and 6 a.m., and over 45% of rapists were reported to have been under the influence of alcohol or drugs. Id. Almost six out of ten sexual assaults occur in the victim's home or in the home of a family member or friend. Sex Offenses and Offenders: An Analysis of Data on Rape and Sexual Assault, Bureau of Justice Statistics, U.S. D.O.J. (1996). It is interesting to note that the military culture appears to encourage rape: "the ratio of military rape rates to civilian rape rates is substantially larger than the ratio of military rates to civilian rates of other violent crime." Madeline Morris, By Force of Arms: Rape, War, and Military Culture, 45 Duke L.J. 651, 653 (1996).

5. A small study of women (58 self-selected respondents) found that more than 90% reported receiving several to many obscene phone calls. Carole J. Sheffield, The Invisible Intruder: Women's Experiences of Obscene Phone Calls, in Violence Against Women: The Bloody Footprints at 73–75 (Pauline B. Bart and Eileen Geil Moran, eds. 1993).

6. Kathleen Barry defines crimes against women "as those acts of violence which are directed at women because of their female sexual definition. In committing a crime against a woman, sexual satisfaction, usually in the form of orgasm, is one of the intended outcomes of sexual violence for the aggressor who unites sex and violence to subdue, humiliate, degrade and terrorize his female victim." Barry, Social Etiology of Crimes Against Women, 10 Victimology 164 (1985).

In fact, the situation of women worldwide is one of deprivation and violence. In no country is women's quality of life equal to that of men. Martha C. Nussbaum, Sex & Social Justice 31 (1999). Nussbaum points to the "missing women" quotient developed by Nobel Prize winners Jean Dreze and Amartya Sen in which sub-Saharan Africa, "where there is great poverty but little evidence of gender discrimination in basic nutrition and health," becomes a baseline to compare female/male ratios when asking the question, "How many more women than are now in Country C would be there if its sex ratio were the same as that of sub-Saharan Africa?" According to those figures,

> the number of missing women in Southeast Asia is 2.4 million; in Latin America, 4.4; in North Africa, 2.4; in Iran, 1.4; in China, 44.0; in Bangladesh, 3.7; in India, 36.7; in Pakistan, 5.2; in West Asia, 4.3.

Id. at 32. In a study released in December of 1999, it was reported that"[a]round the world at least one woman in every three has been beaten, coerced into sex, or otherwise abused in her lifetime. Most often the abuser is a member of her own family." Population Reports, Series L, No. 11 at 1, Population Information Program, Center for Communication Programs, The Johns Hopkins University School of Public Health in collaboration with The Center for Health and Gender Equity, http://www.genderhealth.org. (Dec. 1999).

7. Deborah W. Denno, Introduction: Why Rape is Different, 63 Fordham L. Rev. 125, 127, n. 9 (less than one percent of men in non-prison populations report being raped). Nonetheless, it appears that men, as a result of sexual assault, suffer as much psychological and physical harm as women who are raped. Id., n. 10. The number of men in prison who are raped is estimated to be between 19 and 45%. Id., n. 11.

> cient law enforcement against these men, and a tendency for the media to trivialize all incidents except the most serious ones—and these they sensationalise.[8]

McNeill's study, while addressing what is considered one of the least "dangerous" forms of violence against women, suggests how all forms of violence, no matter how "trivial," create a system of constant reminders to women that we are vulnerable and targets *solely* by virtue of our gender.[9] The dynamics of this violence do not require that every woman be a victim, nor that every victim suffer all possible consequences. The knowledge that such things can and do happen serves to keep all women in the psychological condition of being aware that they are potential victims.[10]

Carole Sheffield argues that violence and the threat of violence against women is a form of terrorism which pervades women's lives:

> No aspect of well-being is more fundamental than freedom from personal harm motivated by hatred or fear of one's ascribed characteristics, that is, freedom from ideologically justified violence against one's person. Without such freedom it is impossible to implement other choices. * * *
>
> *Sexual terrorism* is the system by which males frighten, and by frightening, dominate and control females. It is manifested through actual and implied violence. All females are potential victims—at any age, any time, or any place, and through a variety of means: rape, battery, incest, sexual abuse of children, sexual harassment, prostitution, and sexual slavery. The subordination of women in all other spheres of the society rests on the power of men to intimidate and to punish women sexually.
>
> * * *
>
> Among the major goals of any system of terror are the erosion of public support for victims and acquisition of respectability for one's own cause. The effectiveness of all the other elements of terrorism can be judged by an examination of societal responses. With regard to sexual terrorism, the evidence is that such acts are the least reported of crimes and that when reported are least likely to be brought to trial or to result in conviction.[11]

8. Sandra McNeill, Flashing: Its Effect on Women, in Women, Violence and Social Control 93 (Jalna Hanmer and Mary Maynard, eds. 1987). For an excellent analysis of how the press covers sex crimes, see Helen Benedict, Virgin or Vamp (1992).

9. An FBI study on serial rapists found that so called "nuisance offenses," i.e., voyeurism, obscene phone calls and flashing, are often precursors to more violent crimes. Robert R. Hazelwood and Janet Warren, The Serial Rapist: His Characteristics and Victims, FBI Law Enforcement Bulletin 18, 21 (Feb. 1989). See also Cynthia Grant Bowman, Street Harassment and the Informal Ghettoization of Women, 106 Harv. L.Rev. 517, 536 (1993) (rapists frequently harass women on the street as a form of "rape-testing" to determine who is a potential vulnerable, passive victim).

10. See Sandra S. Tangri, Martha R. Burt, and Leanor B. Johnson, Sexual Harassment at Work: Three Explanatory Models, 38 J.Soc.Issues 33, 48 (1982); Margaret T. Gordon and Stephanie Riger, The Female Fear (1989).

11. Carole J. Sheffield, Sexual Terrorism: The Social Control of Women, in Ana-

This is a strong indictment of a legal system which does little to stop this social control of women. In fact, it is widely accepted as inevitable that women should live under the threat of male violence, or even that women "deserve" or "want" the abuse they receive.

Another aspect of violence against women is the way society views women who fight back.[12] Women, unlike men, typically do not kill strangers or even casual acquaintances, except in very rare cases of self-defense.[13] Men commit 85% of all homicides; and when women do kill, the majority murder spouses or boyfriends who have battered them for years.[14] However, the legal system has failed to respond by revisioning traditional self-defense concepts, leaving governors to grant clemency on an arbitrary basis.[15]

Although we have included numerous manifestations of violence against women—from child sex abuse to the way the mental health industry treats women—in this single chapter, it would be a mistake to think we can isolate violence from any other aspect of our lives, including mothering, marriage, reproduction, work, education, and sexuality. As you read the following materials, think about how the many forms of violence against women are integrated into a single, pervasive system and the impact of that system on our lives.

Note: Some of the material in this chapter may be disturbing to readers. Also, while we recognize the distinction between "victim" and "survivor," we have used those terms interchangeably in this chapter without intending to imply a negative meaning to "victim."

lyzing Gender 171, 183 (Beth B. Hess and Myra Marx Ferree, eds. 1987).

12. See generally Phyllis Chesler, A Double Standard for Murder?, N.Y. Times, Jan. 8, 1992, § A, at 19; Marianne Wesson, Myths of Violence and Self-Defense: Myths for Men, Cautionary Tales for Women, 1 Tex. J. Women & Law 1 (1992).

13. Alison Bass, Prostitute a Rarity Among Mostly Male Serial Killers, Houston Chronicle, Mar. 25, 1992, § Houston, at 4. A 1996 review of British, European, and American data indicates that women's share of violent offenses has remained relatively stable for several years at about 11 percent. Gerda Siann, "Come out and fight like a woman": Gender Differences in Violent Behavior, in Gender Perceptions and the Law 49, 50 (Christine R. Barker, Elizabeth A. Kirk and Monica Sah, eds. 1997).

14. Guns May Not Keep Women Safe, Chi. Trib., July 19, 1992, News § , at 19 (citing 12–year study by Arthur Kellermann and James Mercy, based on FBI Uniform Crime Reports, finding that 14.7% of homicides were committed by women; 60% of those murder victims were spouses or boyfriends).

15. See, e.g., Joan H. Krause, Of Merciful Justice and Justified Mercy: Commuting the Sentences of Battered Women Who Kill, 46 Fla. L. Rev. 699 (1994); Linda L. Ammons, Discretionary Justice: A Legal and Policy Analysis of a Governor's Use of the Clemency Power in the Cases of Incarcerated Battered Women, 3 J. L. & Pol'y 1 (1994); Alison Madden, Clemency for Battered Women Who Kill Their Abusers: Finding a Just Forum, 4 Hastings Women's L.J. 1 (1993); Mithra Merryman, A Survey of Domestic Violence Programs in Legal Education, 28 N. Eng. L. Rev. 383 (1993).

B. RAPE

1. CONSENT TO SEXUAL ACTIVITY

LINDA R. HIRSHMAN AND JANE E. LARSON, Rape: The Baseline in Hard Bargains: The -Politics of Sex

268–72 (1998).

Forcible rape is the direct use of superior power to bypass consent and gain sexual access. When men and women come together to negotiate the exchange of sexual access, the law against rape is a key determinant of the initial distribution of their sexual bargaining power. In his economic analysis of sexual regulation, Sex and Reason, Judge Richard Posner suggests that men will rape more when the bride price is high. Conversely, men should marry more if the cost of rape is high.

Direct historical evidence of the struggles between individual men and women that ended in rape is scarce. But history does offer plentiful proof that rape law establishes the relative power of men and women in bargaining for consensual sex. Ancient societies treated rape as an injury to the victim's father, guardian, or husband, and provided him strong redress, including rights of private violence. Wives, daughters and female slaves in elite households thus enjoyed strong, albeit secondhand, bargaining power in their sexual dealings with predatory males. This power was not an extension of the females' sexual will; to the contrary, patriarchs often used rape law to separate their women from desired sexual partners. But a woman under such a regime could at least deny sex to some men, even if she lacked the autonomy to grant access to others. This describes, for example, the white woman in the antebellum South, whose sexual position was more secure and dignified than that of an enslaved woman explicitly denied the protections of rape law, or even of a free black woman, who was regarded by social custom as simply "unrapeable."

Beginning in the late middle ages, European law reconceived rape as a protection of female bodily integrity, placing the right to invoke the law in the hands of the victim. Perhaps because this law redistributed power from men to women (instead of from man to man, as the ancient law did), the law was weakly enforced. With women given some power to act in their own sexual interests, the fear arose that victims would manipulate this power by lying to protect reputation, wreak revenge, or blackmail innocent men. Nowhere other than in the law of rape is the redistributive agenda of strengthening the weaker player in male-female sex more visible.

The political struggles in the nineteenth and twentieth centuries, first to strengthen, then to weaken, and again to strengthen rape law likewise track gender politics. In our own era, male-female sexual bargaining takes place against the backdrop of libertine deregulation in which the mutuality of consent has replaced the formality of marriage as the baseline for sexual access. By replacing marital status with free sexual contract, libertinism freed people to negotiate endlessly varied, one-on-one sexual bargains. In this free market regime, rape law is the only broad legal constraint on heterosexual sex.

Free market systems ordinarily offer strong limits on access (e.g., private property) as a precondition for secure dealing. Thus a strong rape law should be the foundation of the libertine regime. But one reason people are willing to accept strong protection for private property is that they can expect to be a buyer or a seller at different times. As we have seen, men and women are not similarly situated with respect to the law of rape; even if victims may be of either sex, offenders are almost invariably males.

If the stronger player cannot just take sex but must get consent, and the mere possibility of mutual pleasure is not enough to justify the sex in every instance, the stronger player must concede that the partner he wants may have a different sexual agenda. (This analysis does not change if males and females always seek different sexual ends, or do so only sometimes.) He will have to go some distance toward satisfying her ends if he wants her agreement to cooperate. (The desiring weaker player must also do so, but she never has the option of using superior force.) Bargaining for consent thus begins. Perhaps he must make himself a more agreeable companion, or promise her more mutuality of pleasure, or agree to forego sex with others, or use a condom.

Attaching legal consequences to particular forms of sexual access thus functions as a price increase. This insight illuminates the stakes in ongoing debates over sex policy such as whether silence should be treated as consent or not. Those favoring a requirement of explicit and affirmative consent seek to raise the price of sexual access; those opposing, to lower it.

In sum, rape law is the baseline: It establishes a level of permissible sexual conduct below which no private agreement can fall, no matter how superior the bargaining position of the stronger player. We propose to raise the baseline price of sexual consent by requiring an affirmative "yes" as the condition for intimate access between adults. In order to bar the use of the natural social advantage of age in sexual bargaining, we propose to constrain older men and women from seeking sex (consensual or not) with girls and boys. But we also would remove some conduct that involves no categorical abuse of authority, but is nonetheless prohibited as "statutory rape," from the reach of the law altogether.

To the degree that past rape reforms have begun from or continued the common law understanding of rape as forcible sexual imposition, they do not correspond to modern understandings of what is right and wrong about heterosexual conduct. Violence is bad, but force and threat are just one manifestation of a larger category of bad behavior-refusal to respect another's autonomy. Legal scholar Stephen Schulhofer [Taking Sexual Autonomy Seriously, 11 Law & Phil. 35 (1992)] argues for reconceiving the range of punishable sexual impositions that current law typically tries to shoehorn into the category of rape as a more nuanced range of offenses against autonomy. His alternative places consent rather than force at the center of criminal sex law.

Sexual line-drawing balances the risk of deterring wanted contacts against the risk of encouraging unwanted contacts. Where the conduct interferes minimally with the victim's bodily integrity and decisional autonomy, we conclude the risk should fall on the side of encouraging more sexual contacts, even at the risk of allowing some undesired intrusions. So, for example, a person may not want a business acquaintance to hold her hand and look meaningfully into her eyes when she offers a handshake, but if he does this, even without her consent, the interference with her control over her sexuality is relatively minor, albeit annoying. (As a technical matter, any unconsented touching is a civil battery and, depending on the circumstances, may also amount to sexual harassment.)

Schulhofer argues that a focus on autonomy suggests different rules about what constitutes consent with respect to minor as opposed to significant intrusions on the body. For minor intrusions on the body, such as an unwanted kiss or hug, consent should be presumed and a clear "no" required to prove criminal interference with sexual autonomy.

If, however, what is at stake is intimate access to the body—the genitals and other sexualized parts of the body, such as breasts, buttocks, and crotch—any mistake is far more consequential. If a person is touched or penetrated in these places without consent, her interest in controlling access to her sexuality is profoundly impaired. Where the unwanted intrusion is significant and/or directed at the sexual body, such as penetration of the vagina, anus, or mouth, or grabbing of the breasts, buttocks, or crotch, only positive and clear agreement to such contact should suffice. Silence and ambiguity would be construed against the intruder.

Note that Schulhofer's theory includes sexual contact that is not forced or threatened, but still may not be consensual. Such cases involve what is perhaps the ordinary instance of acquaintance rape where a woman remains silent or is ambiguous about her unwillingness, or where her consent is equivocal and a man simply proceeds on the theory that "she didn't say yes, but she didn't say no, either." The libertine position is that adults should bear the burden of explicit rejection in all cases. Schulhofer suggests to the contrary that where sex is taken peaceably but without unequivocal consent, the sexual imposition is still a crime, although a lesser wrong than forced sex. We agree.

Sexual contact obtained by force or its threat, or without clear and affirmative consent, violates the victim's right to bargain for the conditions of sexual access. Yet the character of injury in forced sex is both different and greater than in nonconsensual sex. In forced sex, the violent party extracts more benefit from the sexual transaction than the party who acts simply without consent. The violent party gets the conscious participation of the disempowered partner or the sick thrill of forcing the victim to witness her own domination. Because this violence not only violates sexual autonomy, but also threatens public order and social norms of peaceability and respect for the physical boundaries of the body, the strongest criminal sanctions should apply. Force and threat most strongly restrain the human freedom to bargain and should be prohibited in all instances.

The lines drawn by this allocation of the burdens of consent, ambiguity, and silence are clear and intuitive and present no fairness problems. The rules follow conventional understandings of the zones of the body as well as commonsense rules of respectful conduct, and thus are comprehensible to the lay person. By forcing the stronger player to bargain with the weaker for an explicit consent, we begin to ensure mutuality as a condition for all adult sexual exchanges. Each party will get a fair and reliable chance to ask for something of what he or she wants from the sex, even if we cannot assure that the benefits of cooperation will always (or even usually) be divided equally. Under our proposed rules the weaker player can extract a higher price for sexual consent than under a narrower definition of rape as a prohibition on force, or even coercion. At the same time, our proposed rules allow for a lively and diverse range of sexual bargains, not imposing any single vision of "good" sex between adult men and women.

Notes on Sexual Bargains

1. What do you think about analyzing sexuality in terms of economics and bargaining power? Do you think that rape laws were intended to redistribute bargaining power from men to women? Do you agree that rape law is the only "broad legal constraint on heterosexual acts"? Do you think it is effective to analyze sex as an economic transaction? What might be lost in such an analysis?

2. Donald Dripps believes that heterosexual sexual experiences do not necessarily offer the same erotic pleasure for men and women:

> Whatever we give and take when we make heterosexual sexual love, we are giving and taking different experiences depending on our gender. If that is so, there seems to be no principled distinction between exchanging female erotic pleasure for male erotic pleasure on the one hand, and exchanging male erotic pleasure for financial security, for status, or what have you on the other.

Dripps, Panel Discussion: Men, Women and Rape, 63 Fordham L. Rev. 125, 143 (1994). Do you agree with his analysis?

Robin West responded to his position:

> to the considerable extent to which men and women do trade sexual pleasure for something else—money, status, a promise not to be beaten up, a promise not to have the children beaten up—those trades may well be unjustified, even if consensual, where they cause more harm on balance than pleasure. I think that many such trades do. Suffering unwanted, undesired, unpleasurable, painful penetration of one's body in exchange for food, shelter, money, a promise not be physically assaulted, or perhaps most commonly, protection against other men's sexual aggressiveness, and suffering these penetrations over an extended

period of time repeatedly causes damage—damage to a woman's sense of autonomy, damage to her integrity and damage to her sense of self-worth.

West, Panel Discussion: Men, Women and Rape, 63 Fordham L. Rev. 125, 155 (1994). With which of these two positions do you agree? Does this debate give a different perspective on sex as an economic transaction?

3. Do you prefer Schulhofer's analysis based on autonomy? Should consent, and not force, be at the center of criminal sex law? Do you think it is dangerous to presume that there is consent for "minor intrusions on the body"? Can you give examples of problems that may arise? Does it make sense to draw a line between "minor intrusions" and the more consequential "intimate access?" Do you agree that "where sex is taken peaceably but without unequivocal consent" it is still a crime but a lesser one than forced sex? How should silence or ambiguity be construed? As presumed consent? Why or why not?

4. Hirshman and Larson state that "[b]y forcing the stronger player to bargain with the weaker for an explicit consent, we begin to ensure mutuality as a condition for all adult sexual exchanges." Do you agree? Even though the authors acknowledge that benefits will most likely not be divided equally, they believe the weaker party can extract a higher price under their proposal to require express consent for intimate access. Does rape law only change the gender power dynamics if prosecutors actually charge and prosecute the "lesser" rapes, e.g., date rape and marital rape? In what other ways might women increase their sexual bargaining power?

GOLDBERG v. MARYLAND

Court of Special Appeals of Maryland, 1979.

41 Md.App. 58, 395 A.2d 1213.

On October 18, 1977, Randy Jay Goldberg, the appellant, was found guilty by a jury in the Circuit Court for Baltimore County, of rape in the second degree. The appellant was sentenced to a five year term, of which the first two years were to be served in a work release program at the jail and the remaining three years on probation.

* * *

The eighteen year old prosecuting witness was a high school senior who worked part-time as a sales clerk in the Merry–Go–Round clothing store at Towson Plaza. Around 1:00 P.M., on August 10, 1977, she was at work when the appellant, aged twenty-five, entered the store. The prosecuting witness started out trying to sell the appellant clothing but ended up being sold a story by the appellant that he was a free-lance agent and thought she was an excellent prospect to become a successful model. They arranged to meet at 5 o'clock when she got off from work.

When the appellant returned for her at 5:00 P.M., she asked him for "any ID to show me if you are who you say you are". He showed her his driving license with his picture on it. This satisfied her: "Well, I figured that he wouldn't ... if he was planning to harm me in any way ...

wouldn't give his name like that, and I figured that, you know, he was who he said he was. I believed him''. Despite some cautioning from her employer she drove off with the appellant at 5:10 P.M. in a silver-grey Cadillac Eldorado. The appellant was actually a student at Catonsville Community College and the car belonged to his mother. Appellant told her he was taking her to ''a temporary studio'' in the Pikesville area. When the ''studio'' was found to be closed, they drove to a condominium building on Slade Avenue. Upon arrival there she stayed in the car while appellant went inside. Shortly, he returned to the car and told her he had contacted a friend who said they could use his house for his ''studio''. When they arrived at the friend's house, she helped appellant find a door that was open. The door led to the kitchen which she described as ''very dirty'' and she ''didn't, you know, understand why we were coming here''. From the kitchen they walked into the bedroom which by contrast she described as being ''really made up really nice'' with ''a queen sized bed, real big bed, with a red velvet bedspread, and a big backboard on the back.'' She was ''pretty impressed by the room''.

Soon after they entered the bedroom, appellant ''motioned'' her to sit beside him on the bed. Instead, she sat on a chair at the foot of the bed. Appellant then said it was hot in the room and took his shirt off. When asked her reaction to appellant's removing his shirt she responded: ''He told me he was hot, so I figured—so I figured he was hot''. She then stood up and appellant ''came over to me and he started unbuttoning my blouse. He said this is what I want you to do''. She pulled her blouse together and said ''no''. Asked to describe what happened next she said:

> ''He just kept on smooth-talking me and saying I won't hurt you. This is what I do to all the models that I interview. And he, you know, started motioning me to take my blouse off and everything, and then I went through the same thing with every piece of clothing. It was like, you know, he kept on trying to tell me to take it off, and I didn't want to. And he kept on trying to convince me that—he was still trying to convince me that this was this modeling job, and I knew that it wasn't any more.''

She said she removed her clothes because she ''was really scared of him''. ''There was nothing I could do''. When asked what caused her fright she said: ''Because he was—he was so much bigger than I was, and, you know, I was in a room alone with him, and there was nothing, no buildings around us, or anything * * *. It was like being trapped or something''. On cross-examination she said she was ''afraid'' she was ''going to be killed''.

After her clothes were removed, the appellant ''pushed'' her down on the bed and tried ''to move [her legs] in different ways, and [she] kept pulling them together, and telling him that [she] didn't want to do it, and just wanted to go home''. He kept telling her that he wouldn't hurt her ''and just to relax''. But she was ''just really scared'' and she was ''shaking and my voice was really shaking'' and she ''kept on telling him

[she] wanted to go home", and that "[she] didn't want to do this"; that she "didn't want to be a model, and [she] didn't want to do it any more. Just to let [her] alone". When asked, "And what was his reaction?", she testified as follows:

"A. He was just—he was just really cool about the whole thing, telling me not to worry, and he wouldn't hurt me, and to relax.

Q. All right. Now, after you were on the bed, and he was moving your legs around, what, if anything, occurred next?

A. Well, he kept on trying to make me get in different positions, and kept on telling me to look sexual or something like that. I don't know what the word was.

Q. All right. And what, if anything, occurred after he said that?

A. He laid me down and placed his hands on my vagina and told me he was doing that to make me relax. I told him that it didn't make me relax.

Q. All right. Then what happened after he placed his hands on your vagina?

A. He went into the other room, and I couldn't see him. He wasn't facing me, and had his back to me, and his hands down by his belt buckle. And I realized what he was doing, and I jumped up and grabbed my clothes and started putting them on. Then he came in and pulled them away from me and said no.

Q. What did he say?

A. He said don't worry. What are you doing that for? I am not going to hurt you, and he kept telling me just to relax, and not to be nervous. And he laid me down on the bed and tried to get me to do that stuff again, and I told him I didn't want to do that.

Q. What happened then?

A. And then he put his arms up on my stomach and his torso was in between my legs. He said just take your time; take a deep breath. And then he moved up on me and placed his penis in my vagina.

Q. What were you doing when this occurred?

A. I squeezed my legs together and got really tense, and I just started crying real hard. And I told him not to do that to me.

Q. And what was his response?

A. He didn't say anything. Just stayed there. And then I felt him move.

Q. How long was he on top of you?

A. Not very long.

Q. How long was he moving?

A. I guess for about two minutes, and then I felt him. Just for about two minutes.

Q. Did the Defendant ejaculate to your knowledge?

A. Yes, I think he did.

Q. Now, what, if anything, occurred after the Defendant ejaculated?

A. He got up and he said that if I can't enjoy it, then he can't enjoy it."

The appellant then asked her to go to dinner with him but she declined and he drove her to her home where she lived with her parents. On the way home, the appellant gave her his telephone number which she wrote down on a piece of paper. At his request she gave him her telephone number by writing it on a piece of paper with her lipstick. Although she told him she "would never see him again", she said she gave him her correct telephone number because she "didn't want to get him suspicious of me". They had a "general conversation about sex" in which he told her that "girls act like they don't want to, but they really do". She told him that he "had the wrong impression of [her]"; that she "didn't want him to do that". She further testified, somewhat inconsistently as follows:

> "I told him I didn't want that. I told him I didn't like him doing that to me, and didn't let him. I didn't make him think that I enjoyed all of it, and that I ever wanted to do it again, because I know I would never do it again. Never. I know I would never get near him again."

The appellant let her off at her home at 6:25 P.M., 1¼ hours after she left her place of employment with him at 5:10 P.M. Before the appellant drove off she told him to "drive home safely . . . I guess I was being more sarcastic than anything". She estimated that they had been at the house where the alleged rape took place for 30 minutes.

When she arrived inside her house she "walked straight past my parents" to her upstairs room. She said nothing to them because she was "just scared, nervous, just you know, I wanted to go upstairs and just clean myself up and just forget, you know, about it. Just think". After cleaning herself and using a contraceptive, she called her boyfriend on the telephone and talked to him for "about three minutes". She did not tell him "what happened" because she "didn't know how he would take it". She then called her girlfriend and told her that she "had a problem, and that I was raped today. . . ." She did not relate the details of the "rape". She told her girlfriend not to tell anybody and not to tell her girlfriend's boyfriend, "but she told him anyways". She contemplated calling the police but said she "didn't know who to call", so she called her girlfriend back and asked what she should do. Shortly thereafter the girlfriend and the girlfriend's boyfriend came to her house and after picking up her own boyfriend the four young people eventually went to the police station where the "rape" was reported at approximately 9:00 P.M. According to the girlfriend, the prosecuting witness did not want to report the matter but "[w]e convinced her into going to the police".

After reporting the incident the prosecuting witness was taken to the Greater Baltimore Medical Center for a physical examination. The examining physician's "Impression" was "Recent sexual intercourse", but he found "no evidence of recent trauma" to any part of her body, including the "perineal and genital" areas.

Testifying in his own behalf, the appellant admitted having sexual relations with the prosecuting witness at the time and place alleged, but maintained that it was mutually consensual and that the prosecuting witness did not appear to be frightened at any time.

Prior to 1976, the Maryland rape statute was primarily a sentencing law, fixing the penalties without actually defining the crime. The common law definition of rape that has been applied in Maryland is: "the act of a man having unlawful carnal knowledge of a female over the age of ten years by force without the consent and against the will of the victim".

By Chapter 573 of the Laws of 1976, effective July 1, 1976, the Legislature * * * [has provided that:]

> "A person is guilty of rape in the second degree if the person engages in vaginal intercourse with another person: (1) By force or threat of force against the will and without the consent of the other person. . . ."

* * *

The terms "force," "threat of force," "against the will" and "without the consent" are not defined by the 1976 Act. We therefore look to the "judicially determined meaning" of these elements of the common law crime of rape. In doing so, we conclude that the evidence was legally insufficient to sustain the conviction and the judgment will be reversed. We reach this conclusion because on the record before us, viewing the evidence in the light most favorable to the State, we find legally insufficient evidence of the requisite element of "force or threat of force".

There was certainly no "threat of force". On the contrary, the prosecuting witness on numerous occasions in her testimony negated that element. As to actual force, the only arguable evidence is the prosecuting witness' testimony that after she herself had removed all her clothes, the appellant put his hands on her shoulders and "pushed" her down on the bed. This is negated, however, by her further testimony on cross-examination that "he didn't push but guided [her] on the bed". She admitted that she was not "injured or anything" by the encounter. This, of course, is consistent with the findings of the physician who subsequently examined her. Those findings so far as they relate to the use of any actual force were completely negative. But *actual physical* force is not an indispensable element of the crime of rape.

As said by the Court of Appeals:

> "Force is an essential element of the crime and to justify a conviction, the evidence must warrant a conclusion either that the victim resisted and her resistance was overcome by force *or that she was prevented from resisting by threats to her safety.* But no particular amount of force, either actual or constructive, is required to constitute rape. Necessarily that fact must depend upon the prevailing circumstances.... [F]orce may exist without violence. If the acts and threats of the defendant were reasonably calculated to create in the mind of the victim—having regard to the circumstances in which she was placed—a real apprehension, due to fear, of imminent bodily harm, serious enough to impair or overcome her will to resist, then such acts and threats are the equivalent of force." * * *

Since resistance is necessarily relative, the presence or absence of it must depend on the facts and circumstances in each case. But the real test, which must be recognized in all cases, is whether the assault was committed without the consent and against the will of the prosecuting witness.

> "The kind of fear which would render resistance by a woman unnecessary to support a conviction of rape includes, but is not necessarily limited to, a fear of death or serious bodily harm, or a fear so extreme as to preclude resistance or a fear which would well nigh render her mind incapable of continuing to resist, or a fear that so overpowers her that she does not dare resist."

Applying these principles to the present case, we hold that the evidence is legally insufficient to warrant a finding by the jury that the prosecutrix exerted the necessary degree of resistance that was overcome by force or that she was prevented from resisting by fear based upon reasonable apprehension of bodily harm.

The State argues that the "totality of [the] circumstances" caused the prosecutrix's fear of being killed and that the fear was a reasonable fear, thus rendering more resistance than that exerted by her unnecessary. First of all, we find nothing in the record evidencing any real resistance by the prosecutrix to anything the appellant said or did. It is true that she *told* the appellant she "didn't want to do that [stuff]". But the resistance that must be shown involves not merely verbal but *physical* resistance "to the extent of her ability at the time". The State points to her testimony that when penetration occurred she "squeezed [her] legs together and got really tense". Assuming that this was evidence of her reluctance, even unwillingness, to engage in vaginal intercourse, it was not evidence that she resisted "to the extent of her ability" *before* the intercourse occurred.

We are left therefore with the question of whether the prosecutrix's lack of resistance was caused by fear based upon reasonable apprehension of physical harm. We find no legally sufficient evidence warranting an affirmative answer to that question. As we said [in an earlier case]: "... [W]here the victim's story could not be corroborated by wounds, bruises or disordered clothing, the lack of consent could be shown by fear based upon reasonable apprehension." * * *

On the record before us, we find the evidence legally insufficient to warrant a conclusion that the appellant's words or actions "were reasonably calculated to create in the mind of the victim" a reasonable fear that if she had resisted he would have harmed her, or that, faced with such resistance, he would have used force to overcome it. The prosecutrix swore that the reasons for her fear of being killed if she did not accede to appellant's advances were two-fold: 1) she was alone with the appellant in a house with no buildings close by and no one to help her if she resisted, and 2) the appellant was much larger than she was. In the complete absence of any threatening words or actions by the appellant, these two factors, as a matter of law, are simply not enough to have created a reasonable fear of harm so as to preclude resistance and be "the equivalent of force". Without proof of force, actual or constructive, evidenced by words or conduct of the defendant or those acting in consort with him, sexual intercourse is not rape. This is so even though the intercourse may have occurred without the actual consent and against the actual will of the alleged victim. Thus it is that [in] the absence of actual force, unreasonable subjective fear of resisting cannot convert the conduct of the defendant from that which is non-criminal to that which is criminal.

SUSAN ESTRICH, RAPE

95 Yale L.J. 1087, 1092–93, 1107–08, 1118–22, 1125–32 (1986).

At one end of the spectrum is the "real" rape, what I will call the traditional rape: A stranger puts a gun to the head of his victim, threatens to kill her or beats her, and then engages in intercourse. In that case, the law—judges, statutes, prosecutors and all—generally acknowledge that a serious crime has been committed. But most cases deviate in one or many respects from this clear picture, making interpretation far more complex. Where less force is used or no other physical injury is inflicted, where threats are inarticulate, where the two know each other, where the setting is not an alley but a bedroom, where the initial contact was not a kidnapping but a date, where the woman says no but does not fight, the understanding is different. In such cases, the law, as reflected in the opinions of the courts, the interpretation, if not the words, of the statutes, and the decisions of those within the criminal justice system, often tell us that no crime has taken place and that fault, if any is to be recognized, belongs with the woman. In concluding that such acts—what I call, for lack of a better title, "non-traditional" rapes—are not criminal, and worse, that the woman must bear any guilt, the law has reflected, legitimized, and enforced a view of sex and women which celebrates male aggressiveness and punishes female passivity. And that vision, while under attack in recent years, continues to be a dominant force in our society and in the law of rape.

* * * [T]he answer is not to write the perfect statute. While some statutes invite a more restrictive application than others, there is no "model statute" solution to rape law, because the problem has never been the words of the statutes as much as our interpretation of them. A typical statute of the 1890's—punishing a man who engages in sexual intercourse "by force" and "against the will and without the consent" of the woman—may not be all that different from the "model" statute we will enforce in the 1990's. The difference must come in our understanding of "consent" and "will" and "force."

* * *

The requirement of force is not unique to the law of rape. But rape is different in two critical respects. First, unlike theft, if "force" is not inherent in noncriminal sex, at least physical contact is. Certainly, if a person stripped his victim, flattened that victim on the floor, lay down on top, and took the other person's wallet or jewelry, few would pause before the conclusion of a forcible robbery. Second, rape does not involve "one person" and "another person." It involves, in practice if not everywhere by definition, a male person using "force" against a female person. The question of whose definition of "force" should apply, whose understanding should govern, is therefore critical.

The distinction between the "force" incidental to the act of intercourse and the "force" required to convict a man of rape is one commonly drawn by courts. Once drawn, however, the distinction would seem to require the courts to define what additional acts are needed to constitute prohibited rather than incidental force. This is where the problems arise. For many courts and jurisdictions, "force" triggers an inquiry identical to that which informs the understanding of consent. Both serve as substitutes for a *mens rea* requirement. Force is required to constitute rape, but force—even force that goes far beyond the physical contact necessary to accomplish penetration—is not itself prohibited. Rather, what is required, and prohibited, is force used to overcome female nonconsent. The prohibition is defined in terms of a woman's resistance. Thus, "forcible compulsion" becomes the force necessary to overcome reasonable resistance. When the woman does not physically resist, the question becomes then whether the force was sufficient to overcome a reasonable woman's will to resist. Prohibited force turns on the judge's evaluation of a reasonable woman's response.

* * *

[After describing *Goldberg* and similar cases, Estrich describes the approach taken by these decisions. This approach] judges the woman, not the man. It asks—as did the court in each of these cases—whether the will of the reasonable woman would have been overcome given the circumstances. The focus is on women generally, and on the victim as she compares (poorly) to the court's assessment of the reasonable woman. The court then proceeds to conclude that a reasonable woman's will would not have been overcome in those circumstances, because there is no "force" as men understand it.

Such an approach accomplishes two things. First, it ensures broad male freedom to "seduce" women who feel powerless, vulnerable, and afraid; the force standard guarantees men freedom to intimidate women and exploit their weaknesses, as long as they don't "fight" with them. Second, it makes clear that the responsibility and blame for such seductions belong with the woman. Because the will of a reasonable woman by definition would not have been overcome, a particular woman's submission can only mean that she is sub-par as women go or that she was complicitous in the intercourse.

It is one thing to argue that none of the men in these cases should be considered in the same category (in terms of their blameworthiness, their dangerousness, or the harm caused by their actions), as the man who puts a gun to his victim's head and threatens to kill her if she refuses to have sex. It is quite another to argue that these men have committed no crime.

Most striking about these cases is the fact that had these men been seeking money instead of sex, their actions would plainly violate traditional state criminal prohibitions. Had Mr. Goldberg used his modeling agent story to secure money rather than sex, his would be a case of theft by deception or false pretenses. * * *

Lying to secure money is unlawful theft by deception or false pretenses, a lesser crime than robbery, but a crime nonetheless. Yet lying to secure sex is old-fashioned seduction—not first-degree rape, not even third-degree rape. A threat to expose sexual information has long been considered a classic case of extortion, if not robbery itself. But securing sex itself by means of a threat short of force has, in many jurisdictions, been considered no crime at all.

To the argument that it is either impossible or unwise for the law to regulate sexual "bargains" short of physical force, the law of extortion stands as a sharp rebuke: It has long listed prohibited threats in fairly inclusive terms. While extortion may be a lesser offense than robbery, it is nonetheless prohibited.

It is almost certainly impossible to expect that the law could address all of the techniques of power and coercion which men use against women in sexual relations. I am not suggesting that we try. Rather, I am suggesting that we do something that is actually quite easy—prohibit fraud to secure sex to the same extent we prohibit fraud to secure money, and prohibit extortion to secure sex to the same extent we prohibit extortion to secure money. Many states already have criminal coercion or fraud provisions that are worded with sufficient breadth (e.g., "engage in conduct") to be applied to prohibit such coerced sex. But cases enforcing such prohibitions are relatively rare, and the results have been divided. The broad reach of such statutes not only invites overbreadth challenges and claims of lack of warning, but fails to make clear that loss of bodily integrity is a different and greater injury than loss of money and thus merits greater punishment. Criminal coercion statutes are, at best, poor substitutes for an expanded understanding of the "force" that makes sex rape.

* * *

Rape is [also] unique * * * in the definition which has been accorded to consent. That definition makes all too plain that the purpose of the consent rule is not to protect female autonomy and freedom of choice, but to assure men the broadest sexual access to women. In matters of sex, the common law tradition views women ambivalently at best: Even when not intentionally dishonest, they simply cannot be trusted to know what they want or to mean what they say. While the cases that engendered this tradition date from the 1870's and 1880's, the law reviews of the 1950's and 1960's, and the appellate cases of the 1970's and 1980's, have perpetuated it.

The justification for the central role of consent in the law of rape is that it protects women's choice and women's autonomy in sexual relations. Or, as one leading commentator put it: "In all cases the law of rape protects the woman's discretion by proscribing coitus contrary to her wishes." Not exactly. * * * [T]he law does not protect the woman from "coitus contrary to her wishes" when there is no "force." Secondly, the definition of nonconsent requires victims of rape, unlike victims of any other crime, to demonstrate their "wishes" through physical resistance.

* * *

In *Goldberg v. State,* * * * the court drew a bright line between verbal and physical resistance: "It is true that she *told* the appellant she 'didn't want to do that [stuff].' But the resistance that must be shown involves not merely verbal but *physical* resistance 'to the extent of her ability at the time.' "

No similar effort is required of victims of other crimes for which consent is a defense. In trespass, for example, the posting of a sign or the offering of verbal warnings generally suffices to meet the victim's burden of nonconsent; indeed, under the Model Penal Code, the offense of trespass is aggravated where a defendant is verbally warned to desist and fails to do so. A defendant's claim that the signs and the warnings were not meant to exclude him normally goes to his *mens rea* in committing the act, not to the existence of consent.

In robbery, claims that the victim cooperated with the taking of the money or eased the way, and thus consented, have generally been unsuccessful. Only where the owner of the property actively participates in planning and committing the theft will consent be found. Mere "passive submission" or "passive assent" does not amount to consent—except in the law of rape.

That the law puts a special burden on the rape victim to prove through her actions her nonconsent (or at least to account for why her actions did not demonstrate "nonconsent"), while imposing no similar burden on the victim of trespass, battery, or robbery, cannot be explained by the oft-observed fact that consensual sex is part of everyday life. Visiting (trespass with consent) is equally everyday, as is philanthropy (robbery with consent), and surgery (battery with consent). Instinctively, we may think it is easier in those cases to tell the difference between consent and nonconsent. But if so, it is only because we are willing to presume that men are entitled to access to women's bodies (as opposed to their houses or their wallets), at least if they know them, and to accept male force in potentially "consensual" sexual relations.

Were the purpose of the consent requirement really to afford autonomy to women, there is no reason why a simple but clearly stated "no" would not suffice to signify nonconsent. Viewing women as autonomous human beings would mean treating them as persons who know what they want and mean what they say. A woman who wanted sex would say yes; a woman who did not would say no, and those verbal signals would be respected.

From a woman's point of view, the danger in this position is that many women who say "yes" are not in fact choosing freely, but are submitting because they feel a lack of power to say "no." From some men's point of view, the problem is that some women who say "no" would be willing to say "yes," or at least to "go along," if properly pressured. The "no means yes" philosophy, from this perspective, affords sexual enjoyment to those women who desire it but will not say so—at the cost of violating the integrity of all those women who say "no" and mean it.

A system of law that has traditionally celebrated female chastity and frowned upon sex outside of marriage might be expected to err on the side of less sex and to presume nonconsent in the absence of evidence to the contrary. But if ours has now become a society in which women have been "liberated" to say yes that provides all the more reason—if more were needed—to respect a no. If the stigma attached to saying yes has been eliminated, then so have the grounds for claiming that no means yes. That we treat women in sexual encounters more like spectators at sporting events (where consent is presumed) than like owners of property (who are merely required to post a sign or verbally communicate nonassent) is only partly explained by the fact that rape is a more serious offense than trespass. It also reflects a view of women as lacking in autonomy, if not integrity, and secures the priority of men's sexual satisfaction.

In the 1950's and 1960's, the leading law journals in this country provided detailed explanations of why women could not be relied upon to know what they wanted or mean what they said; how it was that many women enjoyed physical struggle as a sexual stimulation; and how unfair it would be to punish men who realized that "no" means "yes," only to have their ambivalent partners lie after the fact. * * *

Perhaps the most influential of all such commentary was the often and still-cited *Yale Law Journal* Note[a] on what women want. Relying on Freud, the author pointed out that it is not simply that women lie, although there is an "unusual inducement to malicious or psychopathic accusation inherent in the sexual nature of the crime." Even the "normal girl" is a confused and ambivalent character when it comes to sex. Her behavior is not always an accurate guide to her true desires; it may suggest resistance when in fact the woman is enjoying the physical struggle * * *.

And if women are ambivalent toward sex, it follows that it would be unfair to punish the man who was not acting entirely against her wishes * * *.

In short, the problem is not only that some women lie, but that many women do not in fact know what they want, or mean what they say—at least when they say no. And the presence of force does not even prove rape, because many women enjoy and depend on force. According to this view, insisting that women do more than simply say no to sex is an essential means of protecting the man who exercises his judgment to ignore a woman's words of protestation.

Nonconsent, defined as physical resistance, serves this notice function in two ways. First, resistance defines the limits of force. The law avoids the task of inquiring into how much force in sex is too much by defining proscribed force according to victim resistance. Second, physical resistance means that this woman in fact means what she says; men are free to ignore words, but resistance signifies that no, in this case, means no. Resistance thus serves to give notice that sex is indeed unwelcome, that force is just that, and that the man has crossed the line.

* * *

[In parts of her Article not included in this excerpt, Estrich describes the "utmost resistance" requirement of the 19th century and early 20th century.]

Eventually, the "utmost resistance" standard came to be replaced by a "reasonable resistance" standard: Chastity may be valuable, but judges came to realize that it may not be more valuable than life itself. The reasonable resistance standard spares the woman the choice of risking her life or serious injury to prevent unwanted sex, instead asking whether she had offered "reasonable" resistance. But for many courts, saying "no"—passive resistance—does not count as resistance. In those courts, the understanding of the law review authors of the 1950's and 1960's, that "no means yes," continues to have the force of law.

The consent standard, like the force standard, thus emerges as another means to protect men against unfair convictions by giving them full and fair warning that their (forceful) advances constitute an unwelcome rape rather than a welcome, or at least accepted, seduction. An

a. Note, Forcible and Statutory Rape: An Exploration of the Operation and Objectives of the Consent Standard, 62 Yale L.J. 55 (1952).

alternative approach to this fair warning problem would be to spell out the crime or crimes of "rape" in detail, without regard to the response of the woman. In fact, most courts recognize the use of deadly weapons or a threat of imminent death as criminal without the need for too much reliance on the woman's response, at least most of the time. But to go further and prohibit all forms of physical force would inject the criminal law into what many conceive as private and appropriate choices: It is one thing to ban guns and deadly weapons, or even fraud and extortion, but quite another to say that "love bites" or vigorous thrashing or pushing is criminal regardless of consent.

Our inability or unwillingness to detail the sexual practices that we as a society will not tolerate, regardless of consent, creates the law's heavy reliance on the behavior of the woman. Because the law has provided that if the woman "consents"—regardless of the amount of force used—intercourse is not rape, men have a right to fair warning as to consent. But the consent standard does not necessarily lead to the denial of autonomy to women, or to the "no means yes" philosophy. Quite the contrary, the consent standard could be viewed as a means to afford women their deserved freedom to engage in sex however they choose—whether that is sex with women or sex with forcible penetration. The harm of rape, or part of it, is the denial of that freedom. Indeed, a consent standard that allowed the individual woman to say "yes" as well as "no," to define all of the limits of permissible sex for herself and then to have that definition incorporated and respected in law, would be a means of empowering women. It could also expand liability for criminal sex to any man who refuses to respect those limits.

Many feminists would argue that as long as women are powerless relative to men, viewing a "yes" as a sign of true consent is misguided. Yet if a "yes" might really mean "no," we might at least agree to respect the courage of a woman who dared to say "no." The insistence that men are entitled not only to presume consent from silence but actually to ignore a woman's explicit words makes all too clear the law's absolute determination not to empower women at all. The fear that women, acting from shame or spite or vengeance, will abuse any power they are afforded in sexual relations at the expense of "innocent" men is the most pervasive theme in the legal commentary on rape. A consent standard that further empowered women and potentially eased the burden of proving rape—limited sexual access—has been plainly unacceptable.

The refusal of the law (and the society it reflects) either to limit the scope of seduction regardless of consent or to empower women through the consent standard creates the fair warning problem that demands a resistance standard as its answer. We could seek to prohibit certain forms of seduction. We could seek to empower women, at least when they say no. Both alternatives would mean less freedom for men to coerce submission and secure sexual access. Both would eliminate the need for women to resist physically. Having chosen neither, we have created a fair warning problem whose only solution, at least to many courts and commentators, is to interpret force and consent in ways that punish women for "complicity" in sex, making their conduct the determinant of liability and the subject of our verdicts. There is nothing inevitable about either the problem or the solution.

Notes on Consent

1. Even though the jury convicted the defendant in *Goldberg,* the appellate court failed to find that he used any "force" or "threat of force" in obtaining sex with the prosecuting witness. Did you find any evidence of force or threat of force in the testimony? What? From whose perspective is force, or threat of force, defined? Could you write an appellate decision in which the conviction under the Maryland law would be affirmed? How would it differ from the opinion in *Goldberg?*

2. Do women, especially young women, still sometimes say "no" when they mean "yes"? Why? Does this mean that "no" should not mean "no"? Do women sometimes give men "mixed signals" about whether they want sex or not? Would it be practical to expect the sexual initiator to *ask* his partner whether she wants to have heterosexual intercourse? To sign a consent form? Would either requirement be consistent with social norms for heterosexuals?

To address these kinds of issues, Antioch College promulgated a Sexual Offense Policy stipulating that "if one person wants to initiate moving to a higher level of sexual intimacy in an interaction, that person is responsible for getting the verbal consent of the other person(s) involved before moving to that level." See Phil McCombs, Taking a Look at Love, Wash. Post, Feb. 16, 1996, at F5. While this policy was subjected to a great deal of criticism in the media (and even a Saturday Night Live skit), there is no evidence that the Policy has inhibited sexual relations at Antioch. See Jason Vest, The School That's Put Sex to the Test; At Antioch, A Passionate Reaction to Consent Code, Wash. Post, Dec. 3, 1993, at G1. It appears that the policy is not stopping sex but rather forcing students to talk about it. Do you think the policy is a good idea? What kinds of reactions would you anticipate if your school adopted a similar policy?

3. Mary I. Coombs acknowledges the difficulty and dangers of exploring, through telling our stories honestly, what we consider sexual violation as opposed to sexual pleasure:

> As part of the long-term struggle for understanding and transformation, we need to examine our own experiences of sexuality and the social and psychological dynamics of those experiences. The world is not divided neatly into good sex, on the one hand, and rape and violation on the other. There are situations that fit into neither category: endured sex; "bad" sex; degrading, unpleasant, and offensive encounters; sex when one participant wants to please the other or is willing to tolerate sex for the partner's good qualities. Women need to explore the full range of arguably sexual activities and their reactions to them. For instance, a woman may say "no," but mean, "not yet; I'm not sure; let's keep talking." When sex then occurs, it is still desired despite the initial "no." Conversely, a woman may say "yes" to please a man or avoid an

> anticipated argument, though she did not want sex. The last category of stories in which "no" sometimes does not mean "no" can be misused or misunderstood. Although we may want to be careful where and to whom we tell these stories, we must find a place for these conversations in which we can examine our understandings of the boundaries of pleasure and danger.

Coombs, Telling the Victim's Story, 2 Tex.J.Women & L. 277, 311–12 (1993). Is it safe for women to do what Coombs suggests? Is it possible to establish one standard (no may mean yes) socially and impose a different standard (no means no) legally?

4. Do you think most people believe that no means no? Or, consistent with the range of sexual experiences Mary Coombs discusses, would most people think no sometimes means yes? Or that a woman's behavior implies a "yes"? How do you think most young people view this issue? Almost one-third of college students surveyed in 1991 said that if a woman says "no" to sex, she really means "maybe" or even "yes" and that women desire and enjoy rape. Andrew E. Taslitz, Patriarchal Stories I: Cultural Rape Narratives in the Courtroom, 5 Rev. L. & Women's Studies 389, 468 (1996). The same study revealed that "almost one-quarter of the students agreed that women frequently cry rape falsely, that rape is often provoked by the victim, and that any woman can prevent rape if she really wants to do so." Id. Taslitz believes these numbers are low "because university students are more likely to hold progressive views about rape than are the less educated, suggesting that an even larger percentage of the populace * * * is likely to admit to patriarchal views." Id.

5. In a survey of 1700 Rhode Island adolescents, 24% of the boys and 16% of the girls said it is acceptable for a man to force a woman to have sex with him if he has spent money on her; 65% of the boys and 47% of the girls said it is acceptable for a man to force sex with a woman if he has been dating her for more than six months; 87% of the boys and 79% of the girls said rape is acceptable if a couple is married; and 31% of the boys and 32% of the girls believed it would not be improper to rape a woman who was sexually active. Jacqueline Jackson Kikuchi, Rhode Island Develops Successful Intervention Program for Adolescents, National Coalition Against Sexual Assault News, Fall 1988, at 26–27. What are the implications of this study? Does it suggest that what a woman says should be irrelevant or, alternatively, that her no should mean no?

6. Catharine A. MacKinnon identifies how the law applies a type of sliding scale of consent, depending upon the woman's relationship to the alleged rapist:

> The law of rape divides women into spheres of consent according to indices of relationship to men. Which category of presumed consent a woman is in depends upon who she is relative to a man who wants her, not what she says or does. These categories tell men whom they can legally fuck, who is open season and who is off limits, not how to listen to women. The paradigm categories are the virginal daughter and other young girls, with whom all sex is proscribed, and the whorelike wives and prostitutes, with whom no sex is proscribed. Daughters may not consent; wives and prostitutes are assumed to, and cannot but. Actual

consent or nonconsent, far less actual desire, is comparatively irrelevant. If rape laws existed to enforce women's control over access to their sexuality, as the consent defense implies, no would mean no, marital rape would not be a widespread exception, and it would not be effectively legal to rape a prostitute.

MacKinnon, Rape: On Coercion and Consent, in Toward a Feminist Theory of the State 171, 175 (1989). Does MacKinnon's position preclude the type of exploration urged by Mary Coombs? Does MacKinnon argue that yes often means no? Under what conditions would MacKinnon find "consent"?

7. MacKinnon states in above note 6 that prostitutes are assumed to consent. Consider the case in which two defendants were convicted of rape and false imprisonment and one of them of forcible oral copulation; the defendants offered evidence that the alleged victim had pled guilty to prostitution in the past. Is it an abuse of the trial judge's discretion *not* to admit that evidence? What if there were additional evidence that she solicited in the very area where the alleged crime occurred and that her specialty was oral copulation? See People v. Varona, 143 Cal.App.3d 566, 192 Cal.Rptr. 44 (1983)(reversing conviction). Do prior convictions for prostitution suggest consent in general? Why or why not? See New York v. Doe, 170 Misc.2d 762, 651 N.Y.S.2d 1012 (1996)(holding complainant's alleged prior acts of prostitution relevant because it is the identical type of conduct the defendants assert here).

Defendants often argue that sex with a prostitute was consensual, but she cried "rape" when she was not paid, thus establishing a motive for her fabricated testimony. See New Mexico v. Johnson, 121 N.M. 77, 908 P.2d 770 (N.M.App.1995); People v. Casas, 181 Cal.App.3d 889, 226 Cal.Rptr. 285 (Cal. App.1986) (dissenting judge stating that the jury had to determine if the defendant had "purchased consent" and if the complaining witness was "in the business of consenting"). In a 1986 case, a California judge dismissed a rape charge saying that a working prostitute could not be raped. Metro Digest, L.A. Times, Jan. 10, 1991, § B, at 2. Judge Alson called the case a "breach of contract between a whore and trick." Id. To these judges, is rape of a prostitute really "theft"? The dissent in the *Casas* case, above, also stated that when consent is involved, "there is an enormous difference * * * between a sexually active woman and a prostitute." People v. Casas, 181 Cal.App.3d 889, 898, 226 Cal.Rptr. 285, 291 (Cal. App.1986). Should there be different rules for alleged rape in the "commercial sex activity" context? Why or why not?

Sexual violence against prostitutes is common. Mimi H. Silbert and Ayala M. Pines, Victimization of Street Prostitutes, 7 Victimology 122 (1983). The Silbert and Pines study found that 70% of the prostitutes in their study (aged 10 to 46, with 70% under age 21) have been victimized since becoming prostitutes by either customer rape or clients going beyond the work contract an average of 31.3 times. Approximately 65% of the prostitutes reported being physically abused or beaten by a customer an average of 4.3 times. Id. at 127. An astounding number, 73%, experienced rapes totally unrelated to their work as prostitutes (148 women in 193 rapes). Id. at 128. If, as seems to be the case, prostitutes are raped *more often* than other women, why is it virtually impossible to convict their rapists?

8. Reliability of prostitutes as witnesses is frequently an issue in rape cases. See Tracy Wilkinson, Victim of Alleged Rape May Have Fled Because of History as Prostitute, L.A. Times, Nov. 17, 1990, § B, at 3. Why are prostitutes considered less believable than other women?

9. Similarly, women in prison are raped with impunity. According to Human Rights Watch, sexual abuse of women prisoners is rampant:

> Our findings indicate that being a woman prisoner in U.S. state prisons can be a terrifying experience. If you are sexually abused, you cannot escape from your abuser. Grievance or investigatory procedures, where they exist, are often ineffectual, and correctional employees continue to engage in abuse because they believe they will rarely be held accountable, administratively or criminally. Few people outside the prison walls know what is going on or care if they do know. Fewer still do anything to address the problem.
>
> * * *
>
> We found that male correctional employees have vaginally, anally, and orally raped female prisoners and sexually assaulted and abused them. We found that in the course of committing such gross misconduct, male officers have not only used actual or threatened physical force, but have also used their near total authority to provide or deny goods and privileges to female prisoners to compel them to have sex or, in other cases, to reward them for having done so. In other cases, male officers have violated their most basic professional duty and engaged in sexual contact with female prisoners absent the use or threat of force or any material exchange. In addition to engaging in sexual relations with prisoners, male officers have used mandatory pat-frisks or room searches to grope women's breasts, buttocks, and vaginal areas and to view them inappropriately while in a state of undress in the housing or bathroom areas. Male correctional officers and staff have also engaged in regular verbal degradation and harassment of female prisoners, thus contributing to a custodial environment in these state prisons for women which is often highly sexualized and excessively hostile.

Human Rights Watch, All Too Familiar: Sexual Abuse of Women in U.S. State Prisons, http://www.hrw.org/hrw/summaries/s.us96d.html. See also Ashley E. Day, Cruel and Unusual Punishment of Female Inmates: The Need for Redress Under 42 U.S.C. § 1983, 38 Santa Clara L. Rev. 555, n. 11 (1998) (estimating that in Hawaii's Prison for Women, half the guards participated in a coercive "sex ring" involving as many as 25% of the female inmates).

The dilemma for women prisoners is becoming even greater. With the era of the prison industrial complex, "the rate of increase in the numbers of women prisoners has surpassed that of men." Angela Y. Davis, Public Imprisonment and Private Violences: Reflection on the Hidden Punishment of Women, 24 New Eng. J. Crim. & Civ. Confinement 339, 347 (1998). According to criminologist Elliot Currie,

> [f]or most of the period after World War II, the female incarceration rate hovered at around 8 per 100,000; it did not reach double digits until 1977. Today it is 51 per 100,000.... At current rates of increase, there

> will be more women in American Prisons in the year 2010 than there were inmates of both sexes in 1970. When we combine the effects of race and gender, the nature of these shifts in the prison population is even clearer. The prison incarceration rate for black women today exceeds that for white men as recently as 1980.

Id. at 347, citing Elliot Currie, Crime and Punishment in America 14 (1998). Who are the women prisoners today? According to Day, "in the United States, the average female inmate is thirty-six years old, Caucasian, has dependent children, and is incarcerated for a drug related offense. Typically, female inmates have a history of physical and/or sexual abuse before they are incarcerated, which makes them even more susceptible to abuse by male guards of officials." Day at 555.

What kind of sexual bargaining power do women prisoners have under the Hirshman and Larson analysis? Does the criminal rape law only redistribute sexual power for a select, few, "good" women?

10. Given liberalism's traditional stress on both choice without coercion and privacy (i.e., freedom from state intrusion) in intimate matters, how would a liberal feminist view the issue of consent in the context of rape?

11. Susan Estrich is skeptical that statutory reform will make a difference unless judges interpret the law in a way that empowers women. Nonetheless, many feminists, beginning in the 1970's, focused on legislation to improve women's ability to establish that a rape occurred. Martha Chamallas summarizes some of these changes:

> Landmark reform legislation in Michigan eliminated the consent issue altogether and framed the crime of rape solely in terms of the type and amount of force used by the defendant. Underlying the Michigan approach is a presumption that certain types of coercive behavior (for example, where a weapon is displayed) are per se unlawful. In such cases, there is no need to address the question of the subjective consent of the victim.
>
> Other states have taken a different approach and have tried to rehabilitate the concept of consent by defining consent from the victim's standpoint. Wisconsin, for example, has narrowed the definition of consent to include only those overt acts or words of the victim indicating freely given consent. Under such a standard, a man is subject to criminal prosecution if he has sexual intercourse with a passive woman without first securing her express consent. Additionally, Illinois has demonstrated more trust in the credibility and reliability of rape complainants by shifting the burden of production to the defendant to present some evidence of consent before the issue is interjected into the criminal prosecution. This represents an important change from the traditional allocation which assigns the victim's lack of consent as an element of the state's case.

Chamallas, Consent, Equality and the Legal Control of Sexual Conduct, 61 S.Cal.L.Rev. 777, 799–800 (1988). Do you perceive any benefits in these changes? Are they likely, absent changes in attitudes, to solve any of the problems Estrich identifies? Which state's approach do you consider to be best for women—Michigan, Illinois or Wisconsin? Can you draft an even better statute?

12. Susan Estrich compares rape to other crimes, such as robbery, extortion, trespass and fraud. Should there be a tort of sexual fraud? Would the defendant in *Goldberg* be liable, regardless of the victim's resistance, if there were a crime of sexual fraud, i.e., lying to secure sex, as described by Estrich, above? What would be the advantages and disadvantages of such a crime? How would the various feminist theorists described in Chapter 3 approach this question? See Patricia J. Falk, Rape by Fraud and Rape by Coercion, 64 Brooklyn L. Rev. 39 (1998); Jane E. Larson, "Women Understand So Little, They Call My Good Nature 'Deceit' ": A Feminist Rethinking of Seduction, 93 Colum.L.Rev. 374 (1993).

13. Before we ascribe the results in *Goldberg* to an out-of-date court (1979) and a naive victim (did she "ask" for it by being so foolish?), in 1994 another court reversed a rape conviction because the defendant there did not use "forcible compulsion" either. Commonwealth v. Berkowitz, 537 Pa. 143, 641 A.2d 1161 (Pa. 1994). In that case a college student, after class, went to her dormitory where she had an alcoholic drink and then waited for her boyfriend. When he failed to appear, she went to a friend's room. After knocking, she opened the unlocked door and found her friend's roommate, Robert Berkowitz, sleeping on the bed. He asked her to stay for a while, and she agreed. He asked for a back-rub; she declined. He suggested she sit on the bed; she declined and sat on the floor. Berkowitz

> then moved to the floor beside her, lifted up her shirt and bra and massaged her breasts. He then unfastened his pants and unsuccessfully attempted to put his penis in her mouth. They both stood up, and he locked the door. He returned to push her onto the bed, and removed her undergarments from one leg. He then penetrated her vagina with his penis. After withdrawing and ejaculating on her stomach, he stated, "wow, I guess we just got carried away," to which she responded, "No, we didn't get carried away, you got carried away."

Id. at 1163. According to the court, the victim provided no testimony which "clearly or adequately describes the use of force or the threat of force against her." Id. at 1164. She agreed that Berkowitz did not use his hands to restrain her during penetration and that his body weight on top of her was the only force he applied. Additionally, Berkowitz did not verbally threaten her. Although she testified that she sought to leave the room, the record demonstrated that the door easily could be unlocked and that the victim was aware of that fact, but that she never attempted to go to the door and unlock it. However, she testified that she said "no" throughout the encounter.

The court found that saying "no" continuously was relevant only to the issue of consent, not to the issue of force. Pennsylvania defines rape as follows: "A person commits a felony of the first degree when he engages in sexual intercourse with a complainant: (1) by forcible compulsion; (2) by threat of forcible compulsion that would prevent resistance by a person or reasonable resolution * * *." 18 Pa. C.S. § 3121. On the other hand, indecent assault is "indecent contact with another ... without the consent of the other person." 18 Pa. C.S. § 3126. After considering legislative history, the court determined that penal statutes must be strictly construed and that the crime of rape required "forcible compulsion." Since it did not require lack of consent in the rape statute, the court decided that "forcible compulsion" must be interpreted as something more than a lack of consent. Since there was no testimony to establish force, the jury could not have found Berkowitz guilty of rape.

Do you agree with the court's finding of lack of force? Do you think that men and women perceive "force" differently? Do you think that there should be a distinction between "lack of consent" and "force" to establish the crime of rape? See generally Daphne Edwards, Acquaintance Rape & the "Force" Element: When "No" Is Not Enough, 26 Golden Gate U.L. Rev. 241 (1996).

2. RAPE MYTHS

MORRISON TORREY, WHEN WILL WE BE BELIEVED? RAPE MYTHS AND THE IDEA OF A FAIR TRIAL IN RAPE PROSECUTIONS

24 U.C.Davis L.Rev. 1013, 1025–31, 1022–24 (1991).

MYTHS ABOUT RAPE VICTIMS

The classic rape myths can be summarized into four categories: (1) only women with "bad" reputations are raped; (2) women are prone to sexual fantasies; (3) women precipitate rape by their appearance and behavior; and—by far the most potent myth—(4) women, motivated by revenge, blackmail, jealousy, guilt, or embarrassment falsely claim rape after consenting to sexual relations. None of these myths survives scrutiny.

First, although the myth is that mainly "bad girls" are raped, behavioral science has demonstrated a contrary reality. A study of rape done in the District of Columbia found that in 82 percent of the rapes studied, the rape victim had a "good reputation." Moreover, the statistics concerning the number of rape victims who are attacked by men they know well further undermine this myth: a national crime survey found that over half of the women raped knew their attacker or were married to him.

Second, dubious psychoanalytic theory has profoundly imprinted the notion that false charges are rooted in women's fantasies of rape. Susan Estrich describes this phenomenon as primarily a male invention:

> Men have written for decades about women's rape fantasies—about our supposed desire to be forcibly ravished, to "enjoy" sex without taking responsibility for it, to be passive participants in sexual ecstasy which, when we are spurned in the relationship or caught in the act and forced to explain, we then call "rape."[58]

Even though some psychoanalysts once believed that women's rape fantasies were prevalent, if not universal, that belief has been widely discredited.[59] Nonetheless, this myth continues to thrive in our patri-

58. Susan Estrich, Real Rape 5 (1987).

59. * * * Jeffrey Masson, The Assault on Truth: Freud's Suppression of the Seduction Theory 107–19 (1984). * * *

archy,[60] sometimes with a new wrinkle.

Third, most rapes are not provoked by women. According to the National Commission on Crimes of Violence, only four percent of reported rapes involve any precipitative behavior by the victim, consisting of as little as a gesture. A 1987 study concluded that the impetus for sexual assault lies in the attacker and not in the appearance and behavior of the victim, further persuasive evidence refuting this myth. The fact that 82 percent of rapes are planned or partly planned in advance, and not spontaneous, is even more convincing. These rapists choose their victims based on accessibility and vulnerability, not attractiveness.

* * * [Fourth,] there is the particularly vicious myth of false claims—a myth that underlies many of the evidentiary rules and jury instructions used in rape trials. Perhaps the first official judicial recognition of this mythical moral flaw in women is the oft-quoted, classic statement of the 17th century English jurist, Sir Matthew Hale. Hale asserted that rape charges are "easily to be made and hard to be proved, and harder to be defended by the party accused, tho' never so innocent." Three centuries later, this statement of deep distrust of female rape complainants is still being cited as legal authority.

In fact, there is no empirical data to prove that there are more false charges of rape than of any other violent crime. Estimates indicate that only two percent of all rape reports prove to be false, a rate comparable to the false report rate for other crimes. Unfortunately, reports of a high proportion of "unfounded" rape complaints may have contributed to this myth that women falsely cry rape.

Many valid rape complaints go through an "unfounding" process, in which "the police establish that no forcible rape offense or attempt occurred." For instance, in 1968 police reported that one-fifth of received rape complaints were "unfounded." However, the term "unfounded" is technical and does not indicate whether the rape report is false; rather, it means that for one reason or another, the police decided not to pursue the complaint. Most of the complaints deemed "unfounded" by police involve at least one of the following factors: (1) evidence that the victim was intoxicated; (2) the victim's delay in reporting; (3) lack of physical conditions supporting the allegation; (4) the victim's refusal to submit to a medical examination; (5) existence of a previous relationship between the victim and the offender; (6) the use of a weapon without accompanying battery; (7) the victim's failure to preserve the necessary physical evidence; or (8) the victim's refusal to cooperate fully with the police. In other words, an unfounded complaint is one in which, although a rape

60. Results from the San Antonio survey revealed the following rates of agreement with the statement that "even though women are terrified of being raped, somewhere in the back of their minds there is a curiosity and excitement about rape": Anglo men, 27%; Anglo women, 17%; Black men, 84%; Black women, 7%; Mexican American men, 24%; and Mexican American women, 32%. * * * [Joyce E. Williams & Karen A. Holmes, The Second Assault: Rape and Public Attitudes * * * (1981) (reporting on first cross-cultural study of public attitudes about rape, conducted in San Antonio, Texas).] at 135 table 17.

may have occurred, the police have determined that barriers exist to obtaining a conviction in court. Many of these barriers rest on rape myths.

Ironically, empirical research indicates that the exact opposite of the false claim myth is true: most victims never report the crime of rape. Victims have good reasons for not doing so. Shame and fear are primary considerations for many women. Additionally, women know that even if the police believe them, the experience of a trial is grueling and frequently provokes responses in the victim similar to those caused by the actual rape. Other emotional and psychological factors inhibit the reporting of rape: "rape victims who admit they were raped often suffer in their personal relationships because acquaintances, friends, and lovers sometimes withdraw, deny the incident, blame or disbelieve the victim, or even abandon the victim out of ignorance, anger, fear or hurt."[78] The myth is false claims of rape; the reality is severe underreporting of rape.

In short, the empirical data refute each and every one of the classic rape myths relating to victim behavior. The inevitable question, then, is why these myths are so ingrained and accepted in our society. * * *

The Normality of Men Who Rape

The traditional psychiatric view of rape as a mental aberration has been challenged persuasively by several feminist theorists who argue that rapists and "normal" men are essentially similar.[39] Multiple studies have verified this view. Instead of finding a relationship between sexual aggressivity and scores on the psychopathic deviant scale in the most widely used personality assessment test, researchers have discovered a link between sexual aggressivity and socially acquired attitudes about rape, women, and sexual relations.

The results of a study of junior college students further support the position that rapists are "normal." The students in the study showed a generally callous attitude about rape that was strikingly similar to the attitudes of many convicted rapists. James Check and Neil Malamuth concluded from the results of this study that "many rape-related attitudes, as well as much rape-related behavior, are the products of our sex-role socialization" and not abnormal behavior. Unfortunately, this data is not widely known, and the public strongly embraces the myth that rapists are "sick, emotionally disturbed" men.[46]

78. [Toni M.] Massaro, [Experts, Psychology, Credibility, and Rape: The Rape Trauma Syndrome Issue and Its Implications for Expert Psychological Testimony, 69 Minn.L.Rev. 395] * * * at 422–23 [(1985)]. Unfortunately, victims may accept these reactions and blame themselves for the incident. * * *

39. * * * Susan Brownmiller, Against Our Will: Men, Women and Rape (1975).

46. * * * [Williams & Holmes, at 136, table 18]. The * * * study * * * showed the following rates of belief among the people surveyed in the myth that rapists are "sick, emotionally disturbed men": 91% of Anglo men and 92% of Anglo women; 83% of Black men and 98% of Black women; and 87% of Mexican American men and 63% of Mexican American women. * * *

Another indication that rapists are what psychologists call "normal" men is the number of men who rape or who indicate they would be likely to rape if there were no possibility of sanctions. In one study college male subjects believed that close to half of the male population would rape if they were assured that they would not be caught and punished. With respect to their own potential involvement, over half did not rule out the possibility that they would act in the same fashion as the man portrayed in a fictional rape account if they could be certain they would not be caught and punished. Ironically, a large portion of the public believes that men can commit rape and get away with it. And, unfortunately, this is *not* a myth: conviction rates for rape are estimated to be as low as one to four percent.

In a study of high school males, 50 percent of those interviewed "believed it acceptable 'for a guy to hold a girl down and force her to have sexual intercourse' in various situations, such as when 'she gets him sexually excited' or 'she says she's going to have sex with him and then changes her mind.' "Research with men from the general community yielded very similar data. With half of the male population responding in such a fashion, the rapist profile closely resembles an everyday man for whom rape is an extension of normal sexual behavior and socialization rather than the product of a sick and aberrant mind.

KIMBERLE CRENSHAW, DEMARGINALIZING THE INTERSECTION OF RACE AND SEX: A BLACK FEMINIST CRITIQUE OF ANTIDISCRIMINATION DOCTRINE, FEMINIST THEORY AND ANTIRACIST POLITICS

1989 U.Chi.Legal F. 139, 157–60.

A central political issue on the feminist agenda has been the pervasive problem of rape. Part of the intellectual and political effort to mobilize around this issue has involved the development of a historical critique of the role that law has played in establishing the bounds of normative sexuality and in regulating female sexual behavior. Early carnal knowledge statutes and rape laws are understood within this discourse to illustrate that the objective of rape statutes traditionally has not been to protect women from coercive intimacy but to protect and maintain a property-like interest in female chastity. Although feminists quite rightly criticize these objectives, to characterize rape law as reflecting male control over female sexuality is for Black women an oversimplified account and an ultimately inadequate account.

Rape statutes generally do not reflect *male* control over *female* sexuality, but *white* male regulation of *white* female sexuality. Historically, there has been absolutely no institutional effort to regulate Black female chastity. Courts in some states had gone so far as to instruct juries that, unlike white women, Black women were not presumed to be chaste. Also, while it was true that the attempt to regulate the sexuality of white women placed unchaste women outside the law's protection, racism restored a fallen white woman's chastity where the alleged assailant was a Black man. No such restoration was available to Black women.

The singular focus on rape as a manifestation of male power over female sexuality tends to eclipse the use of rape as a weapon of racial terror. When Black women were raped by white males, they were being raped not as women generally, but as Black women specifically: Their femaleness made them sexually vulnerable to racist domination, while their Blackness effectively denied them any protection. This white male power was reinforced by a judicial system in which the successful conviction of a white man for raping a Black woman was virtually unthinkable.

In sum, sexist expectations of chastity and racist assumptions of sexual promiscuity combined to create a distinct set of issues confronting Black women. These issues have seldom been explored in feminist literature nor are they prominent in antiracist politics. The lynching of Black males, the institutional practice that was legitimized by the regulation of white women's sexuality, has historically and contemporaneously occupied the Black agenda on sexuality and violence. Consequently, Black women are caught between a Black community that, perhaps understandably, views with suspicion attempts to litigate questions of sexual violence, and a feminist community that reinforces those suspicions by focusing on white female sexuality. The suspicion is compounded by the historical fact that the protection of white female sexuality was often the pretext for terrorizing the Black community. Even today some fear that antirape agendas may undermine antiracist objectives. This is the paradigmatic political and theoretical dilemma created by the intersection of race and gender: Black women are caught between ideological and political currents that combine first to create and then to bury Black women's experiences.

Notes on Rape Myths

1. One of the rape myths is that women fantasize about being raped. Several studies show that some females do fantasize about being rape victims, but that those are *negative* fantasy experiences. Positive fantasies do include seduction, but not *real* rapes. See, e.g., Eugene J. Kanin, Female Rape Fantasies: A Victimization Study, 7 Victimology 114 (1982) (importance of distinguishing between seduction and rape fantasies); Susan B. Bond and Donald L. Mosher, Guided Imagery of Rape: Fantasy, Reality, and the Willing Victim Myth, 22 J.Sex Res. 162, 177 (1986) ("Neither the crime of rape nor the imagining of a realistic rape generate sexual arousal, enjoyment, or pleasure."). What is the difference between seduction and rape? Can you articulate a satisfactory legal definition? Does "seduction" imply that "no" does not always mean "no"?

2. The myth is that Black men rape white women; the reality is that most rape is intraracial. Irene Sege, Race, Violence Make Complex Picture, Boston Globe, Jan. 31, 1990, National/Foreign § , at 1 ("Seventy percent of

black rape victims were raped by blacks, and 78 percent of white rape victims were raped by whites."). How does this myth affect both white women (who are raped primarily by white men) and Black women (who live in a community in which accusations of rape have been used against Black men as a form of terrorism)? Jennifer Wriggins addresses the implications of the legal system's failure to address this myth of Black on white rape:

> The legal system's treatment of rape both has furthered racism and has denied the reality of women's sexual subordination. It has disproportionately targeted Black men for punishment and made Black women both particularly vulnerable and particularly without redress. It has denied the reality of women's sexual subordination by creating a social meaning of rape which implies that the only type of sexual abuse is illegal rape and the only form of illegal rape is Black offender/white victim. Because of the interconnectedness of rape and racism, successful work against rape and other sexual coercion must deal with racism. Struggles against rape must acknowledge the differences among women and the different ways that groups other than women are disempowered. * * *

Wriggins, Rape, Racism and the Law, 6 Harv.Women's L.J. 103, 140–41 (1983). See also Lisa A. Crooms, Speaking Partial Truths and Preserving Power: Deconstructing White Supremacy, Patriarchy, and the Rape Corroboration Rule in the Interest of Black Liberation, 40 How. L.J. 459 (1997); Elisabeth M. Iglesias, Rape, Race, and Representation: The Power of Discourse, Discourses of Power, and the Reconstruction of Heterosexuality, 49 Vand. L. Rev. 868 (1996); Darci E. Burrell, Comment, Myth, Stereotype, and the Rape of Black Women, 4 U.C.L.A. Women's L.J. 87 (1993). How can the law best respond to these concerns? How can feminists effectively deal with these differences?

3. In a study conducted by Democratic staff members of the Senate Judiciary Committee in conjunction with consideration of the Violence Against Women Act, discussed in greater detail in a text note below, it was found that only two percent of rapists serve prison time. Michael Tackett, Study Details Rape Victims' Obstacles, Chi.Trib., May 28, 1993, § 1, at 3. The study further discovered that:

> More than half of all rape prosecutions are dismissed before trial or result in acquittal. A rape case is twice as likely to be dismissed as a murder case.
>
> Nearly a quarter of convicted rapists never serve time in prison, and almost half of convicted rapists serve a year or less behind bars.
>
> A robber is 30 percent more likely to be convicted than a rapist.
>
> * * *
>
> [T]he study estimated that at least 84 percent of all rapes are not reported; of those reported, no attacker was arrested 62 percent of the time; and when someone was arrested, the case was dismissed 48 percent of the time.

Id. What, if anything, does this empirical data tell you about the rape myths? As a rape victim, knowing these statistics, would you want to go through a criminal trial? Why do you think robbers are 30% more likely to be convicted than a rapist? Does this statistic support Susan Estrich's comparison of property crimes and rape? Are you surprised that 75% of convicted rapists serve a year or less behind bars?

4. In a rape prosecution in October of 1989 in Florida, a woman who had worn a lace miniskirt with no underwear was slashed with a knife, hit with a rock, and raped twice. A jury of three men and three women, however, acquitted the defendant on kidnapping and rape charges. In explaining the verdict, the jury foreman said: "We felt she (the woman) asked for it the way she was dressed. The way she was dressed with that skirt, you could see everything she had. She was advertising for sex." AP, Jury: Woman in Rape Case "asked for it," Chi.Trib., Oct. 6, 1989, News § , at 11. Is this consistent with the rape myths described above? Is there any way this bias can be remedied? The Florida Legislature acted to expand its rape shield statute to exclude "evidence presented for the purpose of showing that manner of dress of the victim at the time of the offense incited the sexual battery." West's Fla.Stat.Ann. § 794.022(3) (Supp.1991). Will this solve the problem? Does it address the fundamental problem of rape myths? The jury in the William Kennedy Smith rape trial was allowed to hold and examine the victim's undergarments after being told some items were purchased from Victoria's Secret. How was this information relevant? Was it prejudicial?

In the spring of 1999, Italy's highest appeals court overturned a rape conviction because the victim was wearing jeans at the time the alleged rape took place. The court stated that "it is common knowledge that it is nearly impossible to even partially remove jeans from a person without their cooperation ..." The five judges who wrote the opinion were all male. Italian women, protesting the decision, wore denim to demonstrate solidarity with the victim. In fact, 60% of Italians polled about the ruling criticized it, indicating that sexual violence was a national emergency. It was predicted that the court's unpopular decision may do more than any legislation to change Italian attitudes toward sexual violence. See Greg Burke, Judged by Her Jeans: Italian women are up in arms after a court declares that a woman who is wearing jeans can't be raped, Time International, Mar. 1, 1999. What do you think is more effective: legislative change or public protest? How would you mobilize public protest around this issue?

5. An FBI study of serial rapists also dispels many myths about rapists. Robert R. Hazelwood and Janet Warren, The Serial Rapist: His Characteristics and Victims (Part 1), 58 FBI Law Enforcement Bulletin 10 (Jan. 1989) and (Conclusion), 58 FBI Law Enforcement Bulletin 18 (Feb. 1989). "Of the 41 serial rapists interviewed, 54% had generally stable employment"; "71% had been married at least once"; "51% had served in the Armed Forces"; "52% scored above average on intelligence tests"; "54% were raised in average or above-average socioeconomic environments"; "76% had been sexually abused as children"; and "36% collected pornography." Id., Jan. 1989 at 14. The authors noted that their "findings ... contradict popular stereotypes which characterize the serial rapist as a lonely, isolated person who lives alone and has little or no contact with his family" and that the rapists "tended to meet people easily, [and] eventually attempted to dominate the relationship." Id. at 16, 17. When asked what factors influenced

their selection of victims, 98% reported they chose victims based on availability and 95% on gender; only 39% depended on physical characteristics and 15% on the victim's clothing. Id., Feb. 1989 at 23. What is the implication of this data for the myths described earlier?

6. Another issue in many cases is whether the victim made a "prompt complaint" to the police or other third party. Why is this relevant? Many courts require evidence of a prompt complaint in order to negate the inference of a recent fabrication. See, e.g., People v. Brown, 170 Ill.App.3d 273, 281, 120 Ill.Dec. 712, 524 N.E.2d 742, 747 (1988) ("[E]vidence of the victim's prompt complaint should be admissible to overcome the adverse inference which would otherwise arise from her silence."). In fact, as a result of the stigmatization of rape and fear of reprisal, many rape victims do not report sexual assaults promptly to their family or friends, much less to a stranger. See Mary P. Koss, Hidden Rape: Sexual Aggression and Victimization in a National Sample of Students in Higher Education, in Rape and Sexual Assault 3, 3 (Ann Burgess, ed. 1988). The National Women's Study found that 25% of the rapes reported to police were over 24 hours old. National Victim Center and Crime Victim Research Center, Rape in America: A Report to the Nation 5 (1992). Is a rape myth at the bottom of the prompt complaint doctrine?

7. One proposal that Morrison Torrey offers to address the prejudice created by rape myths is to require all fact-finders to be "de-briefed" by expert witnesses in order to counter their belief in rape myths. Torrey, 24 U.C.Davis L.Rev. at 1066–71. Is that a practical solution? Can you think of any other ways to deal with the effects of judges and juries believing in rape myths?

8. In the above excerpt about rape myths, the problem of police "unfounding" is discussed. In an early study, police were shown to approach rape cases with the expectation that three of every five complainants are either untruthful or mistaken. Shirley Feldman–Summers & Gayle C. Palmer, Rape as Viewed by Judges, Prosecutors, and Police Officers, 7 Crim. Just. & Behav. 19, 36 (1980). This problem has been confirmed in more recent studies. Police continue to consider the following factors in decision-making: victim resistance, relationship between victim and offender, credibility and personality of the victim (presumed victim precipitation of the assault, prior sexual history, having willingly met with the assailant, intoxication or a history of drug/alcohol use), prior rape complaints that were dismissed, delay in reporting the assault, lack of victim willingness to cooperate with prosecution, lack of a weapon or physical injury, and lack of corroboration. Kimberly A. Lonsway, Police and Sexual Assault Response: A Review, ABF Working Paper #9604 at 7 (1998). Rape myth acceptance is widespread and continues to be a part of police ideology. Id. at 5. In fact, "the prior relationship between the rape victim and offender has been described as a primary determinant of police attitudes." Id. at 7. Rape victims appear to be aware of this, since "of all the factors which influence a victim's decision to report, the relationship between the victim and the rapist appears to be the most important." Id. at 17. Ironically, we know that approximately 2/3 of all rapes are committed by someone the victim knows. While some police departments are attempting to improve their responses to sexual assault complaints, very few training programs have been evaluated for effectiveness. However, one

program created "to sensitize individuals to the trauma caused by rape and to provide information to prevent this crime from occurring" which included a "rape victim specialist" as a liaison among police, victim and the courts, appears to offer a possible solution. Police rates of arrest improved from 28% to 80%; conviction rates increased from 18% to 80%. Id. at 24. This seems to be dramatic. Do you think that better police training might improve the picture for rape victims?

9. There is a popular belief that if men knew someone who was raped, their attitudes about rape would change and their endorsement of rape myths would decrease. A study published in 1992 found that while actual acquaintance with a rape survivor resulted in greater rejection of rape myths than by those who did not claim an acquaintance, "contemplating exposure [imagining that the subject knows a victim] increased rejection of rape myths for women but slightly increased men's endorsements [of rape myths]." Alan L. Ellis, Chris S. O'Sullivan and Bruce A. Sowards, The Impact of Contemplated Exposure to a Survivor of Rape on Attitudes toward Rape, 22 J. App. Soc. Psych. 889 (1992). These results suggest how difficult it is to prepare appropriate rape education materials; utilizing a component in which men "imagine" knowing someone who was raped might achieve negative results. Why do you think this is so?

10. Two popular books, Katie Roiphe's *The Morning After: Sex, Fear, and Feminism* (1994) and Naomi Wolf's *Fire With Fire: The New Female Power and How to Use It* (1994), are highly critical of feminist work on date rape (as well as sexual harassment and pornography), claiming that feminists have turned women into victims. Instead, according to these authors, feminists should be concentrating on women's individual agency, choice, and exercise of responsibility—or so-called "power feminism." By focusing on women's victimization, these authors believe that feminists have reinforced stereotypical views of women as fragile and passive. In response, Elizabeth Schneider states that

> their complaint of "victim feminism" and solution of "power feminism" are simplistic in failing to grapple with the systematic nature of women's subordination and women's active efforts to resist such subordination. Regretfully, they also demonstrate a lack of compassion for women, particularly women who are not in situations where they can assert "power feminism." Both books underscore the fundamental inadequacy of focusing on *either* victimization *or* agency (reconceived as "victim feminism" or "power feminism") to capture the complexity of struggle in women's lives and highlight the way this false dichotomy leads to problematic extremes.

Schneider, Feminism and the False Dichotomy of Victimization and Agency, 38 N.Y.L. Sch. L. Rev. 387, 394 (1993). With which of these views do you agree? In chapter three, above, Angela Harris also criticized MacKinnon for portraying women as victims without any agency. Is there any way to reconcile these views?

3. RAPE SHIELD RULES

FEDERAL RULE OF EVIDENCE 412

Sex Offense Cases; Relevance of Alleged Victim's Past Sexual Behavior or Alleged Sexual Predisposition.

(a) Evidence generally inadmissible.—The following evidence is not admissible in any civil or criminal proceeding involving alleged sexual misconduct except as provided in subdivisions (b) and (c):

(1) Evidence offered to prove that any alleged victim engaged in other sexual behavior.

(2) Evidence offered to prove any alleged victim's sexual predisposition.

(b) Exceptions.—

(1) In a criminal case, the following evidence is admissible, if otherwise admissible under these rules:

(A) evidence of specific instances of sexual behavior by the alleged victim offered to prove that a person other than the accused was the source of semen, injury or other physical evidence;

(B) evidence of specific instances of sexual behavior by the alleged victim with respect to the person accused of the sexual misconduct offered by the accused to prove consent or by the prosecution; and

(C) evidence the exclusion of which would violate the constitutional rights of the defendant.

(2) In a civil case, evidence offered to prove the sexual behavior or sexual predisposition of any alleged victim is admissible if it is otherwise admissible under these rules and its probative value substantially outweighs the danger of harm to any victim and of unfair prejudice to any party. Evidence of an alleged victim's reputation is admissible only if it has been placed in controversy by the alleged victim.

[Rule then outlines the procedure to determine admissibility.]

NEW HAMPSHIRE v. COLBATH

Supreme Court of New Hampshire, 1988.

130 N.H. 316, 540 A.2d 1212.

SOUTER, JUSTICE.

In this appeal from his conviction on a charge of aggravated felonious sexual assault, the defendant * * * assigns * * * error to rulings that barred the jury from considering evidence of the complainant's public behavior with men other than the defendant in the hours preceding the incident, as bearing on the defense of consent. * * * [W]e reverse and remand for a new trial.

During the noon hour of June 28, 1985, the defendant, Richard Colbath, went with some companions to the Smokey Lantern tavern in Farmington, where he became acquainted with the female complainant. There was evidence that she directed sexually provocative attention toward several men in the bar, with whom she associated during the ensuing afternoon, the defendant among them. He testified that he had engaged in "feeling [the complainant's] breasts [and] bottom [and that she had been] rubbing his crotch" before the two of them eventually left the tavern and went to the defendant's trailer. It is undisputed that sexual intercourse followed; forcible according to the complainant, consensual according to the defendant. In any case, before they left the trailer the two of them were joined unexpectedly by a young woman who lived with the defendant, who came home at an unusual hour suspecting that the defendant was indulging in faithless behavior. With her suspicion confirmed, she became enraged, kicked the trailer door open and went for the complainant, whom she assaulted violently and dragged outside by the hair. It took the intervention of the defendant and a third woman to bring the melee to an end.

As soon as the complainant returned to town she accused the defendant of rape, and the police promptly arrested and charged him accordingly. * * *

[W]e reach the principal and meritorious issue in this appeal, raised by the defendant's objection to the jury instruction that evidence of the complainant's behavior with men other than the defendant in the hours preceding the incident was immaterial, or irrelevant, to the question of the defendant's guilt or innocence. * * *

The trial judge first allowed the defense to elicit testimony from the complainant that at one point during the afternoon she had been sitting in the lap of one of the defendant's companions named Gillis. Shortly after that testimony, and before the defendant had called any witnesses, the State moved for a ruling *in limine* to prohibit defense witnesses from testifying about the complainant's behavior in the tavern with any other men than the defendant. * * * [After argument to the judge on this issue, he granted] the prosecution's motion, for the stated reason that the complainant's "conduct with others is not material on the issue of whether or not she consented to have sexual intercourse with" the defendant. The court later supplemented this reason with the alternative grounds that the testimony in question was inadmissible as evidence of character, and inadmissible as well under the rape shield law, which bars evidence of "[p]rior consensual sexual activity between the victim and any person other than" the defendant, when offered to prove an offense under [the rape statute].

This ruling did not end the matter, however. Although the court had ordered defense counsel not to ask his own witnesses about the complainant's behavior with third parties, further evidence of such activity did come in through the State's next witness, Candice Lepene. She testified on direct examination that the complainant had left the tavern in the company of various men several times during the afternoon, and the court admitted her statement to the police, quoted above, that she had seen "a girl with dark hair hanging all over everyone and making out with Richard Colbath and a few others." On cross-examination Lepene was permitted to testify further about her earlier statement.

When it came time for jury instructions, however, the court's charge reflected its earlier ruling on the motion *in limine*. First, the judge reminded the jurors that he had received evidence of the complainant's public activities with various men on the afternoon of the 28th, including her own admission that she had engaged in close physical contact with at least one man besides the defendant. Then the judge explained that he had allowed the jury to hear this testimony only to provide background information, and he went on to instruct the jurors plainly that the complainant's "conduct with other individuals is not relevant on the issue of whether or not she gave consent to sexual intercourse."

That part of the charge was tantamount to an instruction that the jury could not consider the evidence in question as bearing on guilt or innocence, and we therefore treat it as equivalent to an order striking the testimony about the complainant's openly observed behavior with other men during the course of the afternoon. * * *

Despite the absolute terms of the shield law's prohibition, our cases have consistently reflected the common recognition that such a statute's reach has to be limited by a defendant's State and national constitutional rights to confront the witnesses against him and to present his own exculpatory evidence. Thus, this court has held that a rape defendant must be given an opportunity to demonstrate that the "probative value [of the statutorily inadmissible evidence] in the context of that particular case outweighs its prejudicial effect on the prosecutrix."

* * *

As soon as we address this process of assigning relative weight to prejudicial and probative force, it becomes apparent that the public character of the complainant's behavior is significant. On the one hand, describing a complainant's open, sexually suggestive conduct in the presence of patrons of a public bar obviously has far less potential for damaging the sensibilities than revealing what the same person may have done in the company of another behind a closed door. On the other hand, evidence of public displays of general interest in sexual activity can be taken to indicate a contemporaneous receptiveness to sexual advances that cannot be inferred from evidence of private behavior with chosen sex partners.

In this case, for example, the jury could have taken evidence of the complainant's openly sexually provocative behavior toward a group of men as evidence of her probable attitude toward an individual within the group. Evidence that the publicly inviting acts occurred closely in time to the alleged sexual assault by one such man could have been viewed as indicating the complainant's likely attitude at the time of the sexual activity in question. It would, in fact, understate the importance of such evidence in this case to speak of it merely as relevant. We should recall that the fact of intercourse was not denied, and that the evidence of assault was subject to the explanation that the defendant's jealous living companion had inflicted the visible injuries. The companion's furious behavior had a further bearing on the case, as well, for the jury could have regarded her attack as a reason for the complainant to regret a voluntary liaison with the defendant, and as a motive for the complainant to allege rape as a way to explain her injuries and excuse her undignified predicament. With the sex act thus admitted, with the evidence of violence subject to exculpatory explanation, and with a motive for the complainant to make a false accusation, the outcome of the prosecution could well have turned on a very close judgment about the complainant's attitude of resistance or consent.

Because little significance can be assigned here either to the privacy interest or to a fear of misleading the jury, the trial court was bound to recognize the defendant's interest in presenting probably crucial evidence of the complainant's behavior closely preceding the alleged rape. Thus, the facts of this case well illustrate the court's previous observation that the sexual activities of a complainant immediately prior to an alleged rape may well be subject to a defendant's constitutional right to present evidence. The demand of the Constitution is all the clearer when those activities were carried on in a public setting. Because the jury instruction effectively excluded the evidence in question, the conviction must be reversed and the case remanded for a new trial.

Notes on Rape Shield Statutes

1. Do you think that the complainant in *Colbath* was raped? If not, why not? Even if you think she might not have been raped, do you agree with the outcome in the appellate decision reversing the conviction? How relevant do you consider evidence that a complaining witness has been sexually provocative with a group of men in a bar when she charges rape after leaving the bar with the alleged rapist? Do you agree with Justice Souter that "public displays of a general interest in sexual activity can be taken to indicate a contemporaneous receptiveness to sexual advances that cannot be inferred from evidence of private behavior with chosen sex partners"? Do you understand why he might say this? Have you ever flirted in a "public" place or otherwise behaved, or dressed, in a sexually provocative manner in a public place? If so, what message did you mean to communicate? Might a woman engage in sexually provocative behavior in "public" and still not want to engage in intercourse? What risks are associated with allowing the jury to hear the evidence? With excluding the evidence? If you were the judge, would you admit this evidence? See, e.g., Kit Kinports, Evidence Engendered, 1991 U.Ill.L.Rev. 413, 430–34.

2. Justice Souter suggests that one reason for rape shield statutes is that otherwise evidence with "potential for damaging the sensibilities" might be admitted. What does he mean? Whose sensibilities? Later, he refers to "privacy interest[s]" and "misleading the jury" as the concerns behind

the enactment of rape shield statutes. Are there other reasons for rape shield statutes? Do you agree with him that neither privacy nor concern about misleading the jury are of any "significance" in this case? What assumptions could explain his assumption that neither interest is of significance in this case?

3. In *Colbath,* the trial court did admit evidence of the alleged victim's "public" conduct with the defendant and other men, but instructed the jury that they could not consider that evidence in deciding if the defendant was guilty because her "conduct with other individuals is not relevant on the issue of whether or not she gave consent to sexual intercourse." Could you also argue that this evidence might be more prejudicial than probative? Is this a stronger rationale for excluding the evidence from the jury's consideration than the trial court's assertion that it was not relevant? Why or why not?

4. The usual exception to the rape shield rule is to allow introduction of evidence regarding the victim's prior sexual conduct only with the defendant and only if consent is at issue. What assumptions underlie this exception? Are they well founded? How relevant is the fact that you consented in the past with a particular man to whether you subsequently consented and then complained of rape? What assumptions would make your prior consent determinative?

5. Another exception to the rape shield statute is for evidence about the victim's prior sexual conduct with third persons for purposes other than to prove consent or lack of credibility, such as to establish the source of semen or the source of the victim's physical injury. With the current technology of DNA identification, is evidence about sexual activity ever necessary today to determining the source of semen? Shouldn't the prosecution automatically run a DNA test? The semen will either match the defendant's DNA or it will not.

6. Should the prosecutor be able to admit evidence that the complaining witness was a virgin before the alleged rape? Or is that also barred by the rape shield rule? See People v. Johnson, 671 P.2d 1017 (Colo.App.1983) (not error for physician and victim to testify that the victim was a virgin); Forrester v. State, 440 N.E.2d 475 (Ind.1982) (physician's testimony that victim's hymen was recently torn was proper since rape shield statute designed to protect the victim, not the accused); State v. Singleton, 102 N.M. 66, 691 P.2d 67 (N.M.App.1984) (testimony by the victim that she pleaded with the defendant not to rape her because she was a virgin was relevant and outweighed any prejudicial effect). Is testimony about the absence of past sexual experience different from testimony about past sexual experience? Why or why not?

7. The Supreme Court has ruled on whether evidence of the victim's current living arrangements is admissible. Olden v. Kentucky, 488 U.S. 227, 109 S.Ct. 480, 102 L.Ed.2d 513 (1988). The defendant in *Olden* wanted to introduce evidence that Matthews, the alleged victim, was cohabiting with a third party, a male named Russell. The Kentucky court, acknowledging the relevance of the testimony to the defendant's theory of the case, nonetheless held that even though evidence of the cohabitation was not barred by the State's rape shield law, it was properly excluded because of its highly

prejudicial impact, given that Matthews was white and Russell was Black. The Kentucky court believed this evidence would create extreme prejudice against the prosecutrix. The Supreme Court reversed, finding that the state court failed to give adequate weight to the defendant's Sixth Amendment rights of confrontation and cross-examination. Should this evidence be excluded under a rape shield statute? When should the Sixth Amendment require evidence of prior or contemporaneous sexual activity by a complaining witness in a rape case to be admitted?

8. Comments to F.R.E. 412 indicate that "past sexual behavior" encompasses all activities that involve actual physical conduct. See, e.g., United States v. Galloway, 937 F.2d 542 (10th Cir.1991), cert. denied, 506 U.S. 957, 113 S.Ct. 418, 121 L.Ed.2d 341 (1992) (use of contraceptives inadmissible since use implies sexual activity); United States v. One Feather, 702 F.2d 736 (8th Cir.1983) (birth of an illegitimate child inadmissible); State v. Carmichael, 240 Kan. 149, 727 P.2d 918, 925 (Kan. 1986) (evidence of venereal disease inadmissible). The notes further explain that the word "behavior" should be construed to include activities of the mind, such as fantasies or dreams. The rule has been amended to extend protection, i.e., inadmissibility, of evidence that is offered to prove the victim's sexual predisposition, covering evidence that may have a sexual connotation for the factfinder, including such things as the victim's mode of dress, speech, or lifestyle. Interestingly, Rule 412 applies to civil "sexual misconduct," which means both sexual battery and sexual harassment.

Would F.R.E. 412 have made a difference in any of the cases discussed previously in this chapter? Note that F.R.E. 412 only goes to admissibility of evidence; it does not affect discovery. Does the applicability of 412 to civil cases affect the way you would advise a rape survivor client?

Jane Harris Aiken, in writing about these changes, stated:

> If courts follow the rules and the Advisory Committee Notes interpreting Rules 412 and 415 [admissibility of defendant's prior commission of sexual offenses in a civil case], a plaintiff's sexual misconduct case today will look very different than it would have just three years ago. Instead of voluminous testimony regarding the plaintiff's dress and personal fantasies, the record might include testimony about the defendant's prior misconduct. Instead of broad discovery into the plaintiff's sex life, discovery might be directed toward prior sexual misconduct by the defendant.

Aiken, Sexual Character Evidence in Civil Actions: Refining the Propensity Rule, 1997 Wis. L. Rev. 1221, 1223. However, Aiken has found that "judges simply are not admitting sexual character evidence offered to show general propensity. When they encounter such evidence in civil cases, courts invoke discretionary authority to exclude it." Id. at 1225. According to her research, in every reported case (other than stranger rape or child molestation), courts have sustained Rule 403 objections to Rule 415 evidence. Id. Is this consistent with how judges rule on the admissibility of evidence under the criminal rape shield statute? Once again, does it matter what legislative reform occurs if factfinders continue to apply myths and stereotypes?

4. VIOLENCE AGAINST WOMEN ACT

Text Note: Violence Against Women Act

Women's groups lobbied hard to get Congress to pass a law creating "federal protections for women on the grounds that states were not vigorously pursuing cases involving violence against women."[16] According to D.C. Representative Eleanor Holmes Norton, "VAWA gives women what blacks have had since the Civil War—civil protection. There is still plenty of racial violence in this country, but there is less because those laws are on the books and are invoked."[17] President Clinton signed into law the Violence Against Women Act ("VAWA") as part of an omnibus crime bill, the Violent Crime Control Act of 1994, 108 Stat. 1796, Pub. L. 103–322. An essential part of VAWA is the establishment of a private cause of action for victims to recover damages for violent crimes, § 13981:

> (a) Purpose
>
> * * * [I]t is the purpose of this part to protect the civil rights of victims of gender motivated violence and to promote public safety, health, and activities affecting interstate commerce by establishing a Federal civil rights cause of action for victims of crimes of violence motivated by gender.
>
> * * *
>
> (c) Cause of action
>
> A person * * * who commits a crime of violence motivated by gender * * * shall be liable to the party injured, in an action for the recovery of compensatory and punitive damages, injunctive and declaratory relief, and such other relief as a court may deem appropriate.
>
> * * *
>
> (d) Definitions
>
> * * *
>
> (2) the term "crime of violence" means—* * *
>
> > (b) includes an act or series of acts that would constitute a felony * * * but for the relationship between the person who takes such action and the individual against whom such action is taken [i.e., applies to cases of marital rape and domestic violence which would be excluded under state laws providing for some variation of a marital rape exemption or interspousal tort immunity].
>
> * * *
>
> (e) Limitation and procedures
>
> > (1) Limitation
> >
> > Nothing in this section entitles a person to a cause of action under subsection (c) of this section for random acts of violence unrelated

16. Editors, Christy's Crusade, Ms. Magazine 53, 54 (Ap/May 2000).

17. Id. at 61.

to gender or for acts that cannot be demonstrated, by a preponderance of the evidence, to be motivated by gender * * *.

(2) No prior criminal action

Nothing in this section requires a prior criminal complaint, prosecution, or conviction to establish the elements of a cause of action under subsection (c) of this section.

* * *

In addition to providing a federal civil rights claim for crimes of violence motivated by gender, VAWA also has provisions intended to improve the responses of police, prosecutors and judges to domestic violence and sex crimes. Several provisions specifically address domestic violence concerns.

However, in resolving a conflict among the circuits, the Supreme Court decided in the spring of 2000 that § 13981 is unconstitutional on two grounds: (1) relying on *United States v. Lopez*, 514 U.S. 549, 115 S.Ct. 1624, 131 L.Ed.2d 626 (1995) (finding an insufficient nexus between interstate commerce and the Gun–Free School Zone Act of 1990), the federal civil cause of action did not have a sufficient nexus to interstate commerce under the Commerce Clause; and (2) the state action requirement under § 5 of the Fourteenth Amendment was not satisfied. U.S. v. Morrison, 529 U.S. 598, 120 S.Ct. 1740, 146 L.Ed.2d 658 (2000).

Another section of VAWA, not at issue in *Morrison*, includes amendments to the federal rules of evidence. Contrary to generally accepted and traditional evidentiary rules, VAWA provides that:

(1) In a criminal case in which the defendant is accused of an offense of sexual assault, evidence of the defendant's commission of another offense or offenses of sexual assault is admissible, and may be considered for its bearing on any matter to which it is relevant (F.R.E. 413);

(2) In a criminal case in which the defendant is accused of an offense of child molestation, evidence of the defendant's commission of another offense or offenses of child molestation is admissible, and may be considered for its bearing on any matter to which it is relevant (F.R.E. 414); and

(3) In a civil case in which a claim for damages or other relief is predicated on a party's alleged commission of conduct constituting an offense of sexual assault or child molestation, evidence of that party's commission of another offense or offenses of sexual assault or child molestation is admissible and may be considered as provided in Rule 413 and Rule 414 of these rules (F.R.E. 415).

Additionally, the "rape shield" rule, F.R.E. 412, discussed above, was extended to apply to civil as well as criminal actions.

Notes on VAWA

1. Note that VAWA addressed violence motivated by *gender* rather than violence based on *sex* discrimination. Of course, "violence on the basis of sex" sounds bizarre in the context of rape. But recall from Chapter 2 that since *Craig v. Boren* (1976), the Supreme Court Justices (other than Scalia)

have consistently referred to "gender" rather than "sex" discrimination in applying constitutional and other anti-discrimination laws. This shift probably stems from Ruth Bader Ginsburg's proposal, discussed in Chapter 2, to use gender (which has a "neutral, clinical tone") rather than sex (which is evocative of sexuality). Is rape a crime of sex discrimination or a crime of gender discrimination? What is the difference?

How would you prove that a rape was a form of sex discrimination? How would you prove that a rape was a form of gender discrimination? Are sex and gender discrimination necessarily synonymous in the context of rape? Which is more accurate? What does each leave out?

2. What were the benefits of having a private cause of action under VAWA? The drawbacks? Prior to the Supreme Court declaring § 13981 unconstitutional in *U.S. v. Morrison*, would you have advised a client to file suit under that provision? Would you have filed such a claim as plaintiff? Why or why not? What factors would you consider in reaching a decision? Would you recommend that rape victims sue their rapists for civil damages under a state tort action, if there is a criminal conviction for sexual assault? Why or why not? In the absence of a criminal conviction? Why might a civil suit be preferable to a criminal prosecution? Who controls the suit, the victim or the prosecutor? What is the burden of proof for a civil versus criminal suit? What costs or disadvantages might be associated with bringing a civil suit? For example, might some decisionmakers be even more reluctant to believe a woman seeking money?

Would the *Berkowitz* case, above note 13, at * * *, have been a good candidate for a civil suit under VAWA or a state tort action? Why or why not? Would you have advised the victim not to file a criminal complaint but rather pursue a civil suit? What factors would enter into that judgment? Burdens of proof? Constitutional protections afforded defendants? How deep the defendant's pocket is? How difficult do you think it might be to prove that the assault was "motivated by gender?" In commenting about VAWA, Representative Eleanor Holmes Norton noted that in order to prevail, "a woman has to prove more than a crime itself. She has to show that words said or actions taken prove a special animus was directed toward her because she's a woman. That's a very high burden to meet." Editors, Christy's Crusade, Ms. Magazine 53, 61 (Ap/May 2000). Note that in Bray v. Alexandria Women's Health Clinic, 506 U.S. 263, 113 S.Ct. 753, 122 L.Ed.2d 34 (1993), the Supreme Court held that acts opposing abortion could not be considered motivated by "invidiously discriminatory animus" directed at women as a class because there were alternative explanations for the opposition to abortion. Applying the *Bray* standard, rape probably cannot be viewed as implicitly motivated by gender animus so long as alternative explanations for an individual rape (e.g., not hate but desire?) exist. See generally Jennifer Gaffney, Amending the Violence Against Women Act: Creating a Rebuttable Presumption of Gender Animus in Rape Cases, 6 J. L. & Pol'y 247 (1997). How would you go about proving gender animus?

In attempting to define animus, is the language and interpretation of Title VII helpful? See Liu v. Striuli, 36 F.Supp.2d 452 (D.R.I.1999) (holding that requisite amount of animus can be analyzed in Title VII framework; if it satisfies Title VII, it will be satisfied in state Gender Motivated Violence Act).

3. Why do you think Congress passed the VAWA? Does the law represent a recognition that the criminal law system is unable to respond appropriately to crimes of violence against women? What are the failures of criminal justice with regards to violence against women? Should we be attempting to reform the criminal system rather than resorting to civil suits? Which is likely to be more successful from an institutional perspective? An individual perspective? Now that § 13981 has been declared unconstitutional, what legislative strategy should be developed? Even after *U.S. v. Morrison*, can a rape survivor file a civil suit under state tort law?

4. Illinois, like many other states, has enacted a Hate Crime Statute, Ill.–S.H.A. 720 ILCS 5/12–7.1 (1993). The law provides that:

> A person commits a hate crime when, by reason of the race, color, creed, religion, ancestry, gender, sexual orientation, physical or mental disability, or national origin of another individual or group of individuals, he commits assault, battery, aggravated assault, misdemeanor theft, criminal trespass to residence, misdemeanor criminal damage to property, criminal trespass to vehicle, criminal trespass to real property, mob action or disorderly conduct * * *.

Id. at 7.1(a). To provide additional strength, the statute also creates a civil cause of action for anyone who is injured, or whose property is damaged, by a hate crime. Courts may award compensatory and punitive damages, as well as attorney's fees. Id. at 7.1(c).

Does this law apply to rape? Could you persuade a court that rape constitutes a "hate crime"? What arguments would you make? What kinds of evidence would you use to establish your claim? Does the Violence Against Women Act in effect create a hate crime for sexual assault? To date, no one has been charged under the Illinois law with a gender-based hate crime, though charges are routinely filed for hate crimes based on race and sexual orientation. What might explain this? Do you think gender-based hate crimes occur less often?

5. Women may have yet another course of action in combating rapes by public officials. The Supreme Court has held that a Reconstruction-era criminal statute, 18 U.S.C. § 242 [the 1874 statute which makes it a crime for government officials to use their official authority to willfully deprive someone of rights "protected by the Constitution"], may be used to prosecute government personnel who use their official powers to commit sexual assault or rape. United States v. Lanier, 520 U.S. 259, 117 S.Ct. 1219, 137 L.Ed.2d 432 (1997). In a unanimous opinion, the Court directed the Sixth Circuit to consider reinstating the conviction of Tennessee judge David W. Lanier, who was accused of violating the constitutional rights of five women employees by assaulting them sexually while he served as a state judge. Justice Souter stated that the proper standard under § 242 is whether past decisions give reasonable warning that the conduct at issue violated constitutional rights. Liability may be imposed only if the unlawfulness of the defendant's conduct is apparent in light of pre-existing law. Lanier was convicted in 1992 on seven counts relating to willfully depriving a person of rights and privileges guaranteed by the Constitution and was sentenced to

25 years in prison. According to the Justice Department, the government has used the law to prosecute some 30 sexual assault cases since 1981. The cases typically involved women in custody who were assaulted by a jailer (three cases), police officer (seven cases), border patrol agent or INS agent (two cases), or school board officials (six cases). The 1874 law was also used in federal prosecutions of the Los Angeles police officers involved in the videotaped beating of motorist Rodney King.

5. MARITAL RAPE

DAVID FINKELHOR AND KERSTI YLLO, LICENSE TO RAPE: SEXUAL ABUSE OF WIVES

86–89 (1985).

* * * Women can be coerced, tricked, pressured, and bullied into having sex in a variety of ways, all of which are unpleasant and demeaning. These different kinds of coercion can be categorized into four basic types: social coercion; interpersonal coercion; threatened physical coercion; and physical coercion.

Social coercion is the pressure women feel as a result of social expectations or conventions. Many women believe they must have sex with their husbands because it is their duty, part of their role as wives. * * *

Interpersonal coercion occurs when a woman has sex with her husband in the face of threats that are *not* violent in nature. If she does not have sex with him, she feels that her husband will be angry with her, or she believes her husband will deprive her of money or help she needs. For example, some husbands have threatened to leave or to have affairs with other women if the wives don't comply. * * * They have sex to avoid the implied threat of unpleasantness or conflict with their husbands.

* * *

Interpersonal coercion can be devastating and traumatic, even though no physical force is involved. Much depends on the nature of the threat. A woman who believes that she will not be able to survive if her husband leaves may suffer greatly from the anxiety. The interpersonal threats that a husband uses to force his wife may also be overwhelming because of their persistence and their abusiveness. She may find them humiliating, psychologically debilitating, and shattering to her sense of self-confidence and self-esteem.

Moreover, even when threats are relatively minor and merely concern having to face a husband's anger or having to get some special favor, it is intrinsically unfair and demeaning to have to perform sexually in exchange for ordinary decent and respectful behavior. That many women are obliged to accept this bargain is a testimony to the small amount of power and resources they control in their marriages.

Threatened physical coercion can range from an explicit threat to kill a woman if she doesn't comply, to the implied threat that she could get hurt if she doesn't cooperate.

* * *

The fourth category, *physical* coercion, involves a man physically subduing his wife or striking her to get her to comply. This is the kind of force most people think of when they hear the term "rape."

* * *

Coercion other than physical is often difficult to diagnose. For example, some women live under extremely unequal and oppressive conditions, but they do not report feeling forced to have sex. Perhaps their sense of duty is so internalized that they are not at all in touch with any sense of unpleasantness connected to it. Though there may be coercion present here, without their awareness of it, it is difficult to tell. Does this constitute marital rape?

DIANA E.H. RUSSELL, HUSBANDS WHO RAPE THEIR WIVES

In Rape in Marriage 119, 128–131 (1990).

[Diana Russell, a sociologist, has done a great deal of research about violence in women's lives. In Rape in Marriage, she discusses a 1978 survey of 930 San Francisco women 18 years of age and older. She discovered that 87 women in the study were the victims of at least one completed or attempted rape by their husbands or ex-husbands, or 14% of the 644 women who had ever been married. Thus, approximately one in every seven women who had ever been married was willing to disclose an experience of sexual assault by their husbands.]

Social Characteristics of Husbands-Rapists

Data showing that violent crimes are generally more prevalent in the lower class, and consequently among Black people, while well documented by official statistics, are nevertheless a sensitive subject for some people. Whatever one believes about this, it would be wrong to presume that these statistics can be applied to violence and sexual abuse within the family, since such acts are even less likely to be reported than violence and sexual abuse outside of the family. We'll examine this controversial question as it relates to wife rape.

Education

* * *

With regard to the education of the husband-rapists who were twenty-five years and older in our survey, 20 percent were reported by their wives to have had some high school or less, 24 percent were high school graduates, 22 percent had had some college education, 20 percent were college graduates, and 14 percent had at least some postgraduate education. On the face of it, it seems then that there may be little relationship between wife rape and a man's education. * * *

Occupation

Our findings on the occupations of husband-rapists are quite contrary to the findings reported in studies of wife beaters.[b] Almost one-third of husband-rapists (32 percent) had lower-class occupations (operatives, laborers, and service and transportation workers), as compared with the exact same percentage who had middle-class occupations (sales, clerical, crafts), and just over one-third (36 percent) who had upper-middle-class occupations (professional, technical, managerial).

* * *

Income

Raped wives were asked what their total household income was at the time their husband first raped them. * * * Taking into account the number of people that were dependent on this income, 20 percent of husband-rapists and their wives were living below the poverty line at the time. This is a much lower percentage than would be anticipated on the basis of available data on the victims of extramarital rape. For example, the National Commission on Causes and Prevention of Violence found that females with a family income of under $6,000 in 1967 (the equivalent of $10,890 in 1978) reported being raped 3–5 times more frequently than those with family incomes over $6,000. In our survey the family income of approximately 41 percent of wife rape victims was below $10,890 while 59 percent had family incomes above this figure.

Race or Ethnic Identification

* * *

In our study, while husband-rapists are found in all racial or ethnic groups, the frequency between the groups varies considerably. While 68 percent of the respondents were white women, 73 percent of the husband-rapists were white. The percentage of Latino husband-rapists (10 percent) was also slightly larger than the percentage of respondents who were Latinas (7 percent). On the other hand, 10 percent of the husband-rapists were Black, exactly the same percentage as Black women respondents. The biggest discrepancy of all was in the Asian group; while they constituted 12 percent of the wives interviewed, only 4 percent of the husband-rapists were Asian.

* * *

b. Murray Straus, Richard Gelles, and Suzanne Steinmetz have reported that "the rate of violence between husbands and wives was twice as high in the families of blue collar workers (men and women) than for white collar workers" (*Behind Closed Doors,* p. 149). Other studies, not based on random samples, have reported the same finding. * * *

AGE

Many different studies report that the extramarital rapist is primarily a young man between the ages of fifteen and twenty-four. In our study, just over one-third (37 percent) of the husband-rapists were twenty-five years or younger; only 9 percent were twenty years or younger whereas 57 percent were between twenty-one and thirty years of age, 25 percent between thirty-one and forty, and only 9 percent were forty-one years and older. It seems then that husband-rapists are an older group of men than what Susan Brownmiller [author of *Against Our Will: Men, Women and Rape* (1975)] refers to as "the police blotter rapist"—that is, rapists who are recorded in the police statistics. Since the age of the husband-rapists was gauged by their age the first time they raped their wives, the difference between marital and extramarital rapists is even greater than indicated by these figures. The reason may be simply that a large proportion of fifteen-to twenty-four-year-old men are not married.

In general, then, while our survey is not definitive on these matters, it seems that husband-rapists are almost equally likely to come from the upper middle, middle, and lower social classes. In addition, husband-rapists are disproportionately white and Latin (to a very slight degree), while Asian men are very under-represented. The percentage of Black men who are husband-rapists is exactly the same as the percentage of Black women who were raped wives. This in itself tends to confirm the lack of relationship between social class and wife rape; because of racism, Black people are disproportionately situated in the lower class. Our data on household income, while suggesting that wife rape more commonly occurs in lower income groups, also show that it occurs frequently in higher income groups. It appears, then, that the social characteristics of husband-rapists may differ greatly from men who rape women other than their wives.

Text Note: Repeal of Marital Rape Exemptions

Traditionally, wives were presumed to consent; husbands had an absolute right to intercourse with their wives. The philosophical underpinning of the marital rape exemption has been traced to the apostle Paul:

> The husband must give his wife what she has the right to expect, and so too the wife to the husband. The wife has no rights over her own body; it is the husband who has them. In the same way, the husband has no rights over his body; the wife has them. Do not refuse each other except by mutual consent, and then only for an agreed time, to leave yourselves free for prayer; then come together again in case Satan should take advantage of your weakness to tempt you.[18]

18. 1 Cor. 7: 2–6. Interestingly, most legal commentators attribute the marital rape exemption to seventeenth-century jurist Lord Chief Justice Hale who opined that "the husband cannot be guilty of a rape committed by himself upon his lawful wife for by their mutual matrimonial consent and contract the wife hath given up herself in this kind unto her husband, which she cannot retract." Matthew Hale,

An understanding that this passage made marital rape morally impossible eventually found its way into Medieval Roman Catholic Canon Law. From Canon Law, the marital exemption, like most canonical regulation of sex and marriage, made its way into early English common law and, eventually, our law.[19] The common law, at least by the 19th century, gave a different reason for the exemption. The "Christian" reason for the exemption was the marital debt the spouses owed each other: each had all the rights to the others' body. The American version was that the wife was the husband's property; the two were one, and that one was him.

By defining rape as intercourse with a woman "not his wife," a majority of states immunized husbands from prosecution by statute as late as 1977; other states simply relied on the common law exemption.[20] However, the extensive reforms in rape laws that began in the 1970s extended to the repeal of the marital rape exemption.

According to the National Clearinghouse on Marital and Date Rape, all 50 states have now removed the absolute marital exemption to rape laws.[21] Even though many states have eliminated the absolute exemption, they still treat marital rape differently from non-spousal rape. For example, some states accord a lower level of criminality to marital rapes; others require serious bodily harm.[22] Some states even include cohabitants and former spouses within these "partial" exemptions.[23] Even when marital rape is recognized as a crime, husbands are rarely prosecuted and convicted.

For example, when South Carolina removed its marital exemption in 1991, one of the first rape cases prosecuted, State v. Crawford, illustrated the difficulty of convincing a jury that a husband can rape his wife.[24] At trial, the wife testified that her husband dragged her by the throat into a bedroom, tied her hands and legs with rope and a belt, put duct tape on her

The History of the Pleas of the Crown (1971), ch. LVIII, at 629.

19. Mary Becker, Family Law in the Secular State: Two Are Better than One, [2001] U. Ill. L. Rev. ___, ___ (forthcoming).

20. Susan Estrich, Real Rape 73 (1987).

21. National Clearinghouse on Marital and ___ Date ___ Rape (http://members.aol.com.ncmdr/index.html). Only 17 states and the District of Columbia have completely abolished the exemption. Id.

22. For example, Arkansas exempts a spouse from prosecution for raping a spouse who is mentally defective or mentally incapable; Illinois requires the victim spouse to report the offense within 30 days (ten days for Virginia); Maryland exempts spouses from certain sexual offenses unless the parties live separate and apart without cohabitation and without interruption either pursuant to a written separation agreement, a decree of limited divorce, or for six months prior to the offense; Texas requires a showing of bodily injury or a threat of bodily injury; and West Virginia mandates that lack of consent must be established from forcible compulsion, the infliction of serious bodily injury, or the use of a deadly weapon during the commission of the offense. See Richard A. Posner and Katherine B. Silbaugh, A Guide to America's Sex Laws 35–43 (1996).

23. The marital privilege has been extended to cohabitants in five states and to dates in one state (Delaware). Id. See Robin West, Equality Theory, Marital Rape, and the Promise of the Fourteenth Amendment, 42 Fla.L.Rev. 45, 46, 48 (1990).

24. Facts about the *Crawford* case are compiled from: NBC Dateline, June 2, 1992 (separate interviews of Mr. and Mrs. Crawford); Larry King Live, A Controversy Over Marital Rape, CNN, May 15, 1992, Tr. #562–1 (interview with Mr. Crawford and his defense attorney); Sonya Live, Spousal Rape Laws, CNN, July 31, 1992, Tr. #105 (interview with Mrs. Crawford); Linda Goldston, California Moves to Strengthen Law for Prosecuting Spouse Rape, Houston Chronicle, Aug. 2, 1992, § A, at 13; Carolyn Pesce, Marital Rape: Verdict, USA Today, Apr. 21, 1992, News § , at 3A.

eyes and mouth, and dressed her in stockings and a garter belt. He then had intercourse with her, sexually assaulted her with foreign objects, and threatened her with a knife which he ran around her breast and her stomach. The jury saw this transpire because the husband made a 30–minute videotape of the event. Her muffled screams could hardly be heard through the duct tape. At trial, the wife claimed that her cries were of pain, and that none of these activities were consensual.

When the husband testified, he claimed her cries were of pleasure during the rough sex. His defense was that when his wife said no to sex, he did not think she was serious; he knew she meant yes. He explained that they had engaged in similar sex games in the past, which he had also videotaped. The judge permitted the wife's former husband to testify that she had allowed him to tie her up many times and that she enjoyed violent, abusive treatment (under the marital rape law in South Carolina, the woman's past sexual history could be admitted in court). However, the judge excluded testimony from the accused's former wife that he had assaulted and raped her, too, during their marriage (the defendant's prior sexual activity was inadmissible).

Additional facts were ascertained at trial: (1) when the police arrested the defendant, they found him driving in his neighborhood with his vehicle's lights off; (2) before trial the defendant wrote his wife apologetic letters from prison; (3) the couple had planned to separate the night of the alleged rape; and (4) the defendant did not untie his wife when he left the house so that she had to struggle to get loose before she ran naked to a neighbor's house for help.

It took the eight-woman and four-man jury less than an hour to find the husband not guilty after a two-day trial. Jurors said there was not enough evidence to convict. The victim's response to the verdict was: "If it had been a stranger doing that to me, the whole community would have been in an uproar, a lynching party. But because it was my husband, it was OK."

Notes on Marital Rape

1. Do you think that all of the types of coercion identified by Finkelhor and Yllo should be recognized by the law as coercion? When a wife submits to sex because her husband threatens to leave her unless she does, is that rape? Why or why not? Is there a difference between rape and sex that a woman has, even though she would prefer not to, because she feels it is her duty or because she wants her partner to be happy? Even if it is not rape, is there any reason to be concerned when women agree to unwanted sex to preserve the peace?

2. Finkelhor and Yllo state that the interpersonal coercion husbands apply to their wives in order to obtain sex can be "humiliating, psychologically debilitating, and shattering to her sense of self-confidence and self-esteem." Thus, in addition to the physical invasion, wives suffer in many more ways when raped by their husbands than if they were raped by a stranger. Because of these additional injuries, should marital rape be treated more or less harshly than stranger rape? How do you explain the fact that marital rape is not only treated less harshly, but until relatively recently was not even considered a crime?

3. Finkelhor and Yllo also conclude that because some married women live under such extreme oppression, they do not even recognize the coercion their husbands apply to obtain sex. Can the law remedy this situation? See Chapter 7, discussing power between husband and wife in marriage. If women, as caretakers, had strong economic rights at divorce, would they be able to say "no" more often in marriage? Would this be a good thing? Can you think of other ways to alter the power balance in bargaining about sex in marriage? What would Hirshman and Larson say?

4. From the results of her survey, Russell concludes that "the social characteristics of husband-rapists may differ greatly from men who rape women other than their wives." What could explain this difference? What is it about marriage that encourages men who would not otherwise rape to rape their wives? Do you think the passage from Paul, quoted in the text note above, continues to affect the attitudes of those who believe a man cannot rape his wife?

5. Why do you think the jury acquitted the husband in the *Crawford* case? Do you think showing the jury the videotape in the South Carolina case might actually have hurt the prosecution? Why? What do we think of women when we see pictures of them naked, exposed, and being sexually used by a man? What are the differences between this videotape and the videotape of Rodney King, an African American man, being beaten by police? (The defense in that case argued that the force used in subduing Mr. King was justified.)

6. Why would eight women vote to acquit? Do you think a jury with eight African Americans would vote to acquit the police defendants in the Rodney King trial? Why didn't women take to the streets and riot after the South Carolina acquittal? What is the difference between race and sex that would explain these results? Would further changes in the South Carolina rape law help? If not, what would change the outcome in this case?

7. The judge allowed the defense in *Crawford* to introduce evidence of past "sex games" between the husband and wife. Why are such events relevant to the consent issue? If she had consented in the past without alleging rape, why doesn't that support her claim now that she *was* raped? Can you make any argument that this evidence is relevant to the defendant's case? Would the new F.R.E. 412 exclude this evidence?

8. Many women feel pressured by their partners to play such "sex games." Does past practice within marriage indicate real "consent"? Why do you think that admitting such evidence would be important to the defendant, given its marginal relevance? As judge, would you admit it?

9. Would you have admitted the evidence offered by the defendant's prior wife that he had also assaulted and raped her? Is it now admissible under F.R.E. 413? Is that evidence relevant? Does its probative value outweigh possible prejudicial effects against the defendant? What are the strongest arguments you could make in support of admitting such evidence? Does it seem fair to admit evidence about the wife's prior sexual activities but not the husband's?

10. After traditional common law justifications for the marital rape exemption were rejected, new arguments sprouted up to protect husbands

from criminal liability for raping their wives. For instance, the appellate court in *M.D.*, in which a husband was convicted of criminal sexual assault after ramming his fist with an egg into his wife's vagina, considered arguments that the government should not intrude into marital privacy and should promote reconciliation between spouses. People v. M.D., 231 Ill. App.3d 176, 172 Ill.Dec. 341, 595 N.E.2d 702 (Ill.App.1992). Citing Griswold v. Connecticut, 381 U.S. 479, 85 S.Ct. 1678, 14 L.Ed.2d 510 (1965), the Illinois court, while acknowledging rights of married persons, nonetheless refused to extend the marital privacy right to nonconsensual marital relations. In doing so, the court stated that "a sexual assault perpetrated by one spouse upon the other also has a maximum destructive impact upon the marital relationship." 595 N.E.2d at 711. Can you envision other ways that the right of privacy might be used to insulate men from criminal liability for acts of violence in the family?

6. PHYSICAL AND PSYCHOLOGICAL EFFECTS OF SEXUAL ASSAULT

GERARD MANTESE, VITO MANTESE, THERESAMARIE MANTESE, JOSEPH MANTESE, MARY L. MANTESE, AND CHRISTINE ESSIQUE, MEDICAL AND LEGAL ASPECTS OF RAPE AND RESISTANCE

12 J. Legal Med. 59, 61–64 (1991).

PSYCHOLOGICAL INJURY TO RAPE VICTIMS

* * *

The low incidence of reporting [rape] sometimes has been interpreted to mean that victims experience little psychological trauma from the attack. In fact, immediately after the assault, some victims appear unaffected and highly controlled. In actuality, this response may be a defense mechanism by which victims cope with the psychological trauma of the attack, subsequent societal attacks on their integrity, disruption of personal relationships, and the recurrence of unresolved conflicts.

As a result of the rape, the victim often experiences intense attacks on her psychic equilibrium, requiring the activation of defense mechanisms. These defense mechanisms generally function adequately, and with counseling, 80%–90% of victims will return to normal functioning within four to six months after the rape. However, many victims often continue to suffer severe psychological trauma from the assault. Intensive psychotherapy is sometimes required for the victim to deal effectively with the impact of the assault.

Post-rape trauma is categorized as a posttraumatic stress disorder in the *Diagnostic and Statistical Manual of Mental Disorders III–R*. Prominent symptoms of this disorder include intrusive thoughts, nightmares, fear/anxiety reactions, impaired interpersonal relationships, depression, and sexual dysfunction. Other symptoms may include somatic disturbances, self-blame, anger, revenge, or denial.

The reaction to rape-induced trauma can be acute (immediate onset lasting for six months), chronic (lasting more than six months), or delayed (a pseudo-adjustment period followed by reemergence of symptoms months after the assault). There is, in fact, an initial acute reaction appearing in nearly all rape victims. This reaction includes feelings of terror, mistrust, depression, rage, and guilt. Anger and guilt usually predominate. The victim also may feel shame and self-disgust. Rape also may destroy the victim's sense of autonomy over her body.

Moreover, victims may experience sexual arousal during a rape, and this may engender subsequent feelings of guilt, shame, and panic about sexual identity. It is perhaps for this reason that sexual arousal is rarely reported by the victim. The arousal, which is usually caused by the assailant's deliberate attempt to physically stimulate the victim, can cause the victim to believe that she enjoyed the sexual assault and even wished for it to occur. This, in turn, can lead to self-blame and disgust and intense feelings of guilt. These emotions are not easily resolved and can lead to long-term problems with sexual identity and sexuality.

In addition to sexual dysfunction, victims may experience intense depression, anxiety, and vulnerability. The victim often will institute considerable changes in her lifestyle to overcome these feelings. For example, the victim may change jobs, purchase security devices, live with others rather than alone, and relocate her residence, even to a new geographic area. Rape victims also may make career and lifestyle decisions that lessen their contact with people, particularly men and unfamiliar persons. This activity response has been noted years following the rape. Further, significant problems with sleeping and eating may follow immediately.

Chronic forms of posttraumatic stress disorder may be manifested by the same behavior that is present in the acute form. Such disorders may be present for as long as 50 years after the attack. In addition, phobias may develop and persist.

Thus, the effects of the rape are far-reaching. Moreover, husbands and family can be adversely affected by the assault. Mistrust, anger, and sexual dysfunction may develop in a husband. This may require post-rape counseling for the husband and family members if these problems are to be resolved.

Physical Injury and Pregnancy From Rape

There is a high likelihood that a rape victim will be severely injured both physically and psychologically during the attack. A victim may also experience anxiety over the risk of contracting an infectious disease or becoming pregnant as a result of the rape. This additional anxiety in women increases the psychological impact of the rape and makes resolution of the injury more difficult and prolonged.

The likelihood of a pregnancy following rape is unknown. It is estimated to be between two percent to four percent, the same probability of pregnancy from any one unprotected coital act. By contrast, the risk of contracting a sexually transmitted disease following a rape appears to be significant, estimated by some commentators to be as high as 30%. Post-rape infections have been shown to include gonorrhea, chlamydial infections, trichomoniasis, and bacterial vaginosis. While it is not entirely clear whether the infections reported in this study were present prior to the attacks, this information is disturbing and supports the fear that victims are at significant risk of developing sexually transmitted diseases. In addition, because the Human Immunodeficiency Virus (HIV) is rapidly becoming more prevalent in the heterosexual population, all rape victims must be considered at risk for developing Acquired Immune Deficiency Syndrome (AIDS), a fatal and as yet incurable disease. Furthermore, rapes are becoming more violent and often include such acts as anal and oral penetration. These acts increase the likelihood of passing the HIV from attacker to victim.

It may take up to six months to obtain seroconversion results to determine if the victim is HIV antibody positive. If the results are positive, the patient is then at risk for developing and dying from AIDS for the next 10 years. Thus, the fear of death may remain with the victim for a considerable time following a rape. The risk of transmitting AIDS to other sexual partners and to children will heighten the trauma to the victim and infringe on her personal relationships.

SUSAN STEFAN, THE CLOAK OF BENEVOLENCE

Paper presented at the Center for Advanced Feminist Studies (Oct. 1989).

* * *

Until very recently no one thought to make the connection between the fact of living in fear of rape and assault at home and the mental health of women in that situation. Women by the thousands were admitted to psychiatric hospitals, treated and discharged without a single inquiry as to a history of sexual abuse or violence. Then researchers (almost all women) began asking patients these questions. And what they found was this:

* * A recent survey of female psychiatric inpatients in the *American Journal of Psychiatry* revealed that 72% reported a history of physical or sexual abuse; 54% were sexually abused, of these, almost half (44%) reported sexual abuse before the age of 16. Most of this childhood sexual abuse was perpetrated by fathers and brothers.[7]

* * Another study in *The American Journal of Psychiatry* found that of the female patients on a state hospital unit who were chronically institutionalized and actively psychotic, 46% reported histories of childhood incest. The study discussed the implications of a possible relationship between incest and severe, intractable psychotic disorder.[8]

7. Bryer, Nelson, Miller and Krol, "Childhood Sexual and Physical Abuse as Factors in Adult Psychiatric Illness," 144 *American Journal of Psychiatry* 1426 (1987).

8. Beck and Van der Kolk, "Reports of Childhood Incest and Current Behavior of

* * Compared to nonbattered women, battered women are 5 times more likely to attempt suicide and 3 times more likely to be diagnosed with a mental disorder. 38% of battered women are diagnosed as depressed or having another disorder and 10% become psychotic.[9]

This means one of two things. Either 72% of women in our society are abused, and half are victims of incest, so that these women in institutions just represent a statistical sample of women in society, or else men's violence is a very powerful determinant in driving women into institutions, driving them crazy, driving them into the arms of psychiatry.

Now, let's look at the response of psychiatrists and, to a lesser extent, psychologists, when these women come to their attention. The first, vast reaction is to ignore entirely the matter of prior physical or sexual abuse. This information is rarely sought when a woman is hospitalized. It is important to remember in this context that the psychiatric profession, by controlling what they consider to be important enough to ask about, control the development of knowledge and thus shape the picture of what is perceived to be happening when a woman is admitted for treatment. And that control and that picture in turn has political consequences. Psychiatric knowledge and assumptions, like all assumptions, have a social, historical and political context. They do not exist free of culture or ideology. The context in which psychiatric knowledge develops and is used shapes how people are treated and how they are perceived. So the first point is that the unasked questions are important—what is not considered relevant is relevant.

If, as rarely happens, women insist on answering questions that have not been asked and try to tell about the abuse, they are still ignored. Kurz and Stark in 1987 learned that while 75% of battered women volunteered the information that they had been abused, the problem was acknowledged by doctors in only 5% of the cases. When there is a response, it is often inappropriate—battered, raped, abused women are given medication, or shock treatment, or blamed for not leaving the men who abuse them. One study of how abused women were treated at general hospitals, not psychiatric hospitals, found that

> [i]nterestingly, however, although abuse is not officially acknowledged, abused women are treated differently from other women. What we call an "implicit diagnosis" starts with denial of care or the prescription of inappropriate pain medication, progresses through the frequent use of tranquilizers and often ends with frankly punitive referrals to state institutions.

Finally, when it became apparent that violence against women was epidemic and its casualties could no longer be ignored, silenced or

Chronically Hospitalized Psychotic Women," 144 *American Journal of Psychiatry* 1474 (November 1987).

9. Stark and Flitcraft, "Personal Power and Institutional Victimization: Treating the Dual Trauma of Woman Battering," in *Post-Traumatic Therapy and Victims of Violence,* Brunner-Mazel, p. 120.

medicated, "syndromes" were created to categorize those who suffered from violence: rape trauma syndrome, battered woman's syndrome, incest survivor's syndrome, self-defeating personality disorder. Women who experience violence are labeled sick and must be treated.

* * * I am deeply suspicious of turning social experiences into psychiatric categories, for the following two reasons:

1. If a certain reaction to incest or rape or battering is labeled as a syndrome or disorder, the assumption is that there is a right and wrong way to react to these events, or at least a healthy and unhealthy way to react. Psychiatric categories inherently describe abnormal or pathological symptoms or reactions. I think to do this delegitimizes the spectrum of personal reactions in these cases and makes the victim the sick one rather than the attacker. To be more specific, I would like to see the law recognize that a woman who killed after being beaten severely over a long period of time and was under constant threat of death and could not, for very understandable reasons, such as economic reasons, leave the situation, acted in self-defense, and not that her action was abnormal but excusable because it was the product of pathology requiring treatment. * * *

2. By labeling a reaction to rape or battering or incest as a medical condition to be treated, it is more likely to be removed from the political sphere—seen as an individual's medical condition and not a focal point for political action. The sufferers are sick and not the society.

* * *

Women are told that it is they that must be cured, their version of reality labeled hallucinations and delusions that must be obliterated, their stories disbelieved and discredited. * * * This is a society where people who are the victims of violence are labeled as sick and the perpetrators of violence are for the most part less stigmatized and labeled. * * *

At this stage, you may say (or think) that a critique of the etiology of mental illness is no reason to attack the act of treatment * * *. So now I want to get to what happens to the institutionalized woman in the name of treatment of her problems, to pierce this veil of benevolence and treatment. * * * [T]he institution is not a treatment setting so much as the town dump in America's City on a Hill, the place for the wreckage of a violent patriarchal society with no mercy on its poor. It is at the same time a painfully accurate and even intensified mirror of that society, so that those who have been injured in the process of getting there are hurt even more once they are there.

* * *

One study showed that 73% of psychotropic [affecting mental activity] drug prescriptions written by doctors are written for women, and 27% are written for men. Another noted that, although women made up 58% of all outpatient doctor visits, they received 78% of all psychotropic drug prescriptions. We also get the majority of electric shock treatments. In California, in the last quarter of 1977, 74% of the persons who received shock treatment were female. At least one textbook recommends a higher voltage for women, and women tend to get shock many more times in the course of treatment than men. If you ask a psychiatrist about this, he will say—and I use the word "he" on purpose—that more women get shock because it is traditionally used for depression and many more women are depressed than men. This may well be true, but to me it leaves a major question unanswered, namely, why are so many more women than men depressed? It is difficult for me to believe that the answer lies solely in the distribution of certain chemicals in the brain.

Second, not only do women get most of the medications, they often receive them as the result of a doctor or psychiatrist misdiagnosing a physical condition as a mental problem. Women have a tremendous credibility problem in this society, trying to get believed, and it carries over to their interaction with doctors.

Finally, the prescription of medication both reinforces a woman's perception that something is the matter with her, rather than her situation, and it may obscure a solution to the underlying problem that makes her anxious or depressed in the first place. With medication, the woman is placed in the all-too-familiar "sick role" and the goal of treatment is to reduce symptoms of anxiety or depression and help the woman cope in the situation she finds herself in rather than changing it. Use of medication may promote a passive stance. To summarize, in the words of one commentator, medication has

> been used frequently to silence the distress of women and to diminish the conscious pain they are suffering. If you believe anxiety and depression are signs of a problem that needs to be addressed, a diminution of such symptoms is not only not helpful but perhaps harmful. It is therefore important in the case of women and medications to look at when and why they are prescribed and whether they are being used to silence rightful complaints or anger about husband, job or family which others prefer not to hear.[23]

Notes on the Effects of Violence Against Women

1. A growing number of courts and legislatures have recognized that not all victims react to rape in ways that a jury biased with firmly held beliefs about rape can understand. Acknowledging that actual victim responses contradict many of the commonly held misconceptions about rape, these jurisdictions allow introduction of expert testimony about Rape Trauma Syndrome (RTS). The term RTS comes from a study of 92 adult, heterogeneous female rape victims conducted by Ann Wolbert Burgess and Lynda Lytle Holmstrom. Burgess and Holmstrom, Rape Trauma Syndrome,

23. Bernardez, "Sex Differences in Women's Mental Health Problems and Their Causes," in *Women and Mental Health* at 23.

131 Am.J. Psychiatry 981 (1974). They found that the rape victims they studied had a two-stage reaction to the sexual assault, with behavioral, somatic, and psychological responses at each stage. Id. at 982. As originally intended, expert testimony on RTS states that the victim reacted in ways similar to other women who have been raped, hence reinforcing the victim's credibility. See Karla Fischer, Defining the Boundaries of Admissible Expert Psychological Testimony on Rape Trauma Syndrome, 1989 U.Ill.L.Rev. 691.

Susan Stefan is critical of the general concept of RTS for two reasons: (a) it suggests that there is a right and wrong way to react to rape, thus delegitimizing personal reactions and resulting in labeling the victims "sick," not the perpetrators; and (b) it removes the issue of rape from the political sphere, suggesting that the sufferers are sick, not society. Unfortunately, Stefan's critique has proven true in another way, as defense attorneys are beginning to appropriate RTS expert testimony to show that the victim's behavior is *inconsistent* with that of a rape victim suffering from RTS. See Henson v. State, 535 N.E.2d 1189, 1192–93 (Ind.1989). Can you anticipate other problems that may arise from the admission of expert testimony on RTS? Should a defendant be entitled to have his psychiatric expert examine the complaining witness if the prosecutor intends to present evidence from an *examining* expert that the victim of a sexual assault suffers from RTS? See People v. Wheeler, 151 Ill.2d 298, 176 Ill.Dec. 880, 602 N.E.2d 826, 833 (Ill. 1992) ("where victim exercises his or her right to refuse an examination, the State may not introduce evidence of rape trauma syndrome through the testimony of an examining expert").

2. The National Institute of Mental Health has recognized that "[v]iolence poses a particular threat for women and significantly contributes to serious negative mental health consequences." Women's Mental Health: Agenda for Research 11 (Anita Eichler and Delores L. Paron, eds. 1987). The consequences of both physical and sexual abuse include depression, anxiety, impaired self-esteem, post-traumatic stress disorder, and substance abuse. Does the law take this into account in the prosecution of sexual assault? Could evidentiary and other rules be developed to ameliorate these effects in the courtroom?

3. Diane Hudson was shocked to discover that twice as many women as men receive leucotomies (a type of psychosurgery previously known as lobotomies). Hudson, You Can't Commit Violence Against an Object: Women, Psychiatry and Psychosurgery, in Women, Violence and Social Control 110, 120 (Jalna Hanmer and Mary Maynard, eds. 1987). She regards psychosurgery as:

> directed predominantly at women in order to modify behaviour felt by the women's relatives, husbands, psychiatrists, and often by the women themselves to be undesirable. * * *
>
> All the women in the case studies experienced the "threat of violence", * * * which forced them to comply with a code of behaviour felt to be desirable by others. This threat of violence is seen at its clearest in the stance taken by the psychiatric profession towards the women in their care. The threats included long-term psychiatric hospitalisation, electro-convulsive therapy, and, at the extreme end of the spectrum, leucotomy. * * * When women receive a psychiatric label,

> their definitions of reality are dismissed as skewed or invalid. This enables the men in their lives, husbands, fathers or psychiatrists, to define reality for them. Controlling the woman's behaviour in this way is possible due to the subliminal fear of violence that all women experience and which confines their behaviour into channels acceptable by men. This can be experienced as unease, a concern to behave properly in case one is laughed at or ridiculed. Fear can be activated by actual violence to the woman, or by her knowledge that violence can occur in particular situations. * * *

Id. at 110–11. Is this another effect of rape, the fear that any woman can be raped at any given time? How does this affect the way that women live their lives?

4. In the Mantese et al. excerpt, the spread of AIDS to heterosexuals and the danger this poses for rape victims is discussed. In a survey of rape crisis counselors the fear of getting HIV was identified as the fastest growing concern among rape victims. Michael Matza, AIDS Conundrum, Chi. Trib., Womanews at 4 (Nov. 15, 1992). Should an alleged victim be able to require an alleged rapist to be tested for HIV? Would it be constitutional to require a sexual assault defendant, prior to conviction, to undergo an HIV test? Some states have passed laws compelling HIV testing of rape suspects. See Royce Richard Bedward, AIDS Testing of Rape Suspects: Have the Rights of the Accused Met Their Match?, 1990 U.Ill.L.Rev. 347; Bernadette Pratt Sadler, When Rape Victims' Rights Meet Privacy Rights: Mandatory HIV Testing, Striking the Fourth Amendment Balance, 67 Wash. L. Rev. 195 (1992) (arguing that mandatory HIV testing violates the Fourth Amendment's prohibition against unreasonable searches and seizures and that the victims' interests are not furthered by such testing); Barbara Danko, The Fourth Amendment's Challenge to Mandatory AIDS Testing of Convicted Sexual Offenders: Has the AIDS Virus Attacked Our Constitutional Right to Privacy?, 4 Seton Hall Const. L.J. 279 (1993) (arguing that Washington's mandatory HIV testing statute violates the Fourth Amendment because there is no valid state interest which justifies negating the probable cause requirement).

7. WHY MEN RAPE

Text Note: Is Rape Sex or Violence?

Many feminists believe that rape is about power and domination through violence. Other feminists, most notably Catharine MacKinnon, theorize that rape is "sexualized violence" and that the debate over whether it is sex or violence creates a false dichotomy. Recent entrants into the debate about why men rape are evolutionary biologists and psychologists. According to the evolutionists,

> Evolutionary explanations of rape focus on the evolved differences in male and female *sexuality*. More specifically, modern evolutionary theory assumes that humans, like all living organisms, are bundles of adaptations and the by-products of those adaptations. These adaptations include proximate mechanisms such as emotions, desires, and other physiological responses to environmental stimuli. * * * However, the

> mechanisms motivating the actual rape behavior are those involved in male sexual arousal. These mechanisms include beauty detection, desire for impersonal sex, desire for partner variety, visual arousal patterns, and perhaps mechanisms designed to adjust these sexual responses to the specific act of rape. The evolutionary approach to rape sits upon the bedrock theories of sexual selection and parental involvement. These theories explain why human males have this specific set of sexual desires and arousal patterns, and not others, and why these desires and patterns often differ so profoundly from the evolved sexual desires and arousal patterns of human females.[25]

This position has sometimes been interpreted as biologically deterministic, impervious to cultural, social, or individual influences. As a result, many feminists have been concerned that the evolutionary explanation will offer a defense to rapists. Evolutionists respond that:

> The debate over sexual motivation for rape concerns how the world is; it does not imply anything about how people should behave. However, once one takes the position that rape should be prevented, the debate over the role of sexual motivation also has tremendous practical implications. Realizing that sexual motivation is necessary for rape to occur is crucial because it implies that without sexual motivation rape will not occur. Further, even though desire for power, violence, domination, or control may be involved in some rapes, they are not necessary for a rape to occur, and eliminating these desires will not necessarily prevent rape.[26]

In the search for answers about why men rape, all explanations should at least be considered. Sophisticated and ethical evolutionary biologists/psychologists offer a nuanced and complex explanation as demonstrated by the following excerpt.

NEIL M. MALAMUTH, THE CONFLUENCE MODEL OF SEXUAL AGGRESSION: FEMINIST AND EVOLUTIONARY PERSPECTIVES

In Sex, Power, Conflict: Evolutionary and Feminist Perspectives at 269, 271–80.

(David M. Buss and Neil M. Malamuth, eds. 1996).

[The author, a psychologist who has conducted numerous empirical studies involving male sexual aggression against women, begins this article by explaining the source of his interest in evolutionarily-based explanations of male sexual aggression. Feminist colleagues had asked him to critique the new wave of evolutionary theories explaining rape which, in their view, were "biologically deterministic." After reviewing evolutionary analyses of rape, the author was surprised at their cogency and convincing explanations which he did not consider to be "biologically

25. Craig T. Palmer, David N. DiBari, and Scott A. Wright, "Is It Sex Yet?" Theoretical and Practical Implications of the Debate Over Rapists' Motives, 39 Jurimetrics J. 271, 272–73 (1999).

26. Id. at 273. See also Randy Thornhill and Craig Palmer, Why Men Rape, Why Women Suffer: Rape, Evolution, and the Social Sciences (1999).

deterministic." These new analyses do challenge a feminist view of coercive sex as motivated by power and not sex. However, they also offer an explanation for why women, unlike men, have not created a culture of female dominance over men; the author does not believe that an explanation which relies solely on greater male physical strength or the mothering role of females is sufficient. Nonetheless, Malamuth emphasizes that the evolutionary theories do not suggest that male dominance is inevitable or natural.]

The basic underlying "force" that designed the human mind is natural selection, that is, reproductive success or "fitness." According to evolutionary psychology, to understand the human mind today it is essential to analyze the psychological mechanisms (i.e., information-processing algorithms or decision rules) that evolved in ancestral environments. These mechanisms continue to guide our reactions (i.e., emotions, thoughts, behaviors) in contemporary environments. * * * Although under ancestral environments these mechanisms contributed to reproductive success and were therefore transmitted to subsequent generations, in current environments they may or may not contribute to any type of "success." While the mind was designed by natural selection processes operating in ancestral environments to promote fitness, people are not presumed to strive consciously to achieve the goal of fitness. In other words, people do not consciously "choose" their actions in order to promote fitness, but the types of mind mechanisms that evolved in ancestral environments and that can be "activated" in current environments were naturally selected because in those earlier environments they had fitness-favoring consequences.

Adaptations are responses that were naturally selected (i.e., increased reproductive success) in the evolutionary history of our species. Human responses may be adaptations, by-products of adaptations, or *noise* (e.g., mutations, genetic drift, etc.). Much effort is directed within this approach, by formulating testable hypotheses, to understanding which of these three possibilities particular behaviors represent. Because a behavior may have been adaptive in evolutionary environments, and therefore contributed to the current structure of the mind, does not mean that such a behavior is desirable, moral, or inevitable.

Some people fail to understand properly the implications of this approach. They falsely believe that it suggests that humans are *hard wired* or do not make choices. On the contrary, evolutionary approaches focus on the interaction between organisms and their environments and how organisms change their behavior in different environments. In humans, behavior is viewed as highly flexible in that the mind is very much attuned to situational information and can take a variety of forms precisely because we have complex, situation-contingent psychological mechanisms. In our species, social interactions are a very crucial part of the environment. Cultures that humans create reflect characteristics of the human mind and also shape the behaviors elicited in social environments.

* * *

Individual Differences

With respect to individual differences, evolutionary psychology often focuses on the developmental learning environments experienced by each person (the ontogenetic histories of humans are not uniform), although there is also recognition of inherited differences that may affect interactions with the environment. It is important to note that evolutionary selective pressures have been essentially the same for all humans in most domains in which problem-solving adaptations (e.g., how to regulate heat, how to detect cheaters, etc.) occurred. Therefore, psychological mechanisms are generally universal for all humans (i.e., species typical). However, their behavioral manifestations are not invariant or *fixed.* Such mechanisms process environmental information (e.g., the likely consequences of various behaviors). Their expression (in behavior) is expected to vary, both developmentally and contemporarily, with the nature of the environment. To understand the role of experience, however, it is essential to understand the learning mechanisms pertaining to differing domains (e.g., the role of experience may have different effects in areas such as deception detecting, mate selection, anger control, etc.). These mechanisms evolved in human minds within ancestral environments. * * *

Individuals' long-term "occupancy" of differing roles or situations can also be important. For example, a man who is married to a woman who gets a great deal of attention from other men may frequently show jealousy as compared to a man whose wife seldom receives much attention. Both, however, may have the same underlying jealousy mechanisms. Or, a man who is frequently rejected by women may appear to be habitually "feeling rejected" as compared to one who is relatively seldom rejected. Individual differences in feeling rejected here are not necessarily due to inherited or developmental differences (although these can directly or indirectly be contributors as well), but to being frequently in recurring environmental conditions that activate the relevant mechanisms. However, the threshold for activation of the mechanisms may become adjusted or recalibrated. In the example above, the man may become relatively prone to perceiving rejection or being suspicious of women's intentions so that he indeed feels rejected in circumstances that would not elicit that reaction in other men.

Gender Differences

In terms of gender similarities and differences, males and females are expected to have the same psychological mechanisms in those domains in which natural selection processes favored the same "solutions" to adaptive problems regardless of the solver's gender. Correspondingly, mechanisms are expected to differ in domains for which differing solutions or strategies have been more successful in evolutionary history for the different sexes. One of these areas is sexuality, for which the natural selection processes differed somewhat for males and females, resulting in sexual dimorphism in relevant psychological mechanisms.

* * *

Mechanisms Underlying Sexuality

The psychological mechanisms governing male sexuality are not the same as those guiding female sexuality; this is due to the different reproductive consequences for the two genders in ancestral environments of sexual behavior. These created differences in the type of "mating strategies" most adaptive for each gender.

Differences in mating strategies can be traced to the minimum "parental investment" required to produce an offspring. In our species, the parental investment required to produce offspring is much greater for females (i.e., nine months for females vs. minutes for males). Given that females can only produce a maximum of 20 offspring in a lifetime, having sex with a relatively large number of males is unlikely to have adaptive advantages. It is generally far better to invest more in each offspring by carefully selecting a mate with good genes who will participate in the raising of the offspring. For males, having intercourse with a larger number of fertile females was likely to be correlated with reproductive success since in ancestral environments contraceptive devices were not available, and the upper limit for siring offspring has been much higher than for females. Even totally "uninvested" sex may therefore have had favorable reproductive consequences.

In light of these differences, men and women differ considerably in their orientation to *impersonal sexuality,* that is, sex not associated with affection and bonding that typically characterize long-term relationships. Although males are capable of "personal sex" involving bonding emotions such as love, the psychological mechanisms underlying their sexual behavior also foster impersonal sex to a greater degree than females. Similarly, although females are capable of impersonal sexuality, their psychological mechanisms are relatively more consonant with personal sex. * * *

If male sexuality were unconstrained by real-life exigencies such as competition and threats from other men, rejection by females, and limited resources, the mechanisms governing this domain would result in sex with many fertile women. Such desires are indeed revealed in the sexual fantasies of men. * * *

Sexuality Mechanisms and Sexual Coercion

It may be said that the sexuality mechanisms in the minds of men set the stage for the occurrence of coercive sexuality. Because of their greater capacity for impersonal sex, men can be fully sexually functional in the face of an unwilling sexual partner who has no emotional desire for or bonds with the male. The progeny of such sex would be likely to contribute to the man's reproductive success even if the man is also having intercourse with willing partners.

The male potential for coercive sex is not simply a function of body differences such as physical strength or anatomical ability to "penetrate," as emphasized by some feminists. It is just as feasible for a woman to coerce a man to engage in oral sex by threatening him with a gun as for a man to similarly coerce a woman. There is also a crucial difference of minds. Even in situations in which the potential for females to coerce males is as high as for males to coerce females, it is expected that gender differences will occur even if males and females were raised in the identical environments. This is particularly true when environmental conditions are conducive to coercive sex. Wartime is a good example. For instance, in the recent conflict in Bosnia, many men raped women, but it is doubtful that many women coerced men. These men were, in most cases, probably unlikely to commit such atrocities under peacetime conditions. Similarly, in Japan, a country where the known rate of rape is very low under peacetime conditions, during World War II very large numbers of men had coercive sex with Korean women.

Overall, the evolutionary approach suggests that the highly controversial assertion made by some feminists that "all men are real or potential rapists" has some validity, but only if their developmental and current environments do not strongly discourage such acts. In the identical environmental conditions that prompt many men to commit coercive sex, it is expected that the minds of women would not prompt them to coercion.

Individual differences among men in their proneness to impersonal sexuality may help predict their likelihood of engaging in coercion, particularly in the context of an environment that discourages such acts. In such an environment, the role of other mechanisms that interact with the sexuality mechanisms may be particularly important.

Mechanisms Underlying Hostility/Dominance

Conflict often occurs in the context of human interactions. From the perspective of evolutionary psychology, conflict between individuals is related to the degree to which their reproductive interests are at odds. Coercion is one of the tactics that may be used to deal with conflict. Coercion typically involves using force to attain one's interests at the expense of others. The human system appears to contain an interrelated "network" of responses, including emotions (e.g., anger, hostility, jealousy, etc.), attitudes (e.g., acceptance of the use of violence), and motor tendencies (e.g., impulsivity) that may be "mobilized" to activate behavioral tactics that serve coercive goals.

* * *

Within the evolutionary framework, one important source of potential conflict between male and female interests stems from male uncertainty of parenthood. Since only females give birth to children, a male may be uncertain that a child being born was conceived by him, whereas the woman can be certain that the child to which she is giving birth was conceived by her. Consequently, natural selection operated on those male characteristics that served to increase the likelihood that the men are investing in their own offspring. If a man had intercourse with more than one woman prior to each woman becoming pregnant, it did not affect the maternity certainty of each woman. However, if a woman had intercourse with more than one man prior to her becoming pregnant, it reduced the paternal certainty of each of the men. This resulted in the evolution within the male mind of a psychology with greater proprietary feelings. Men are predicted to be more likely to dominate, monopolize, and control the sexuality of women. The extent to which men try to accomplish this and the methods they use differ, depending on social conditions, but the underlying psychological mechanisms are universal in male minds.

* * *

COMPARING AND INTEGRATING THE FEMINIST AND EVOLUTIONARY APPROACHES

* * * While feminists have emphasized the role of men's desire to dominate women as the basic underlying factor causing rape and other forms of violence against women (a form of group domination), evolutionary psychology provides a model of the design of mind differences between the genders that helps explain the origin of such an orientation to dominance.

According to evolutionists, as noted above, the basic underlying "force" that designed the human mind is natural selection, that is, reproductive success within ancestral environments. Many feminists have argued that rape is essentially one of many forms of male assertion of power over women and have emphasized that it is not a "sexual" act. In contrast, evolutionary theorists have emphasized that mechanisms governing sexuality in the male mind play an important role in motivating rape. It is important to recognize that this view differs from the traditional psychiatric view of rape as a product of aberrant or "pent up" sexuality. Rather, the evolutionary approach emphasizes that the male mind generally possesses characteristics that enable coercive sex to occur in various circumstances. This view is similar to that of many feminists who have argued that rapists and "normal" men differ in degree of coercion, but not in kind. Whereas feminists have explained the origin of such male motivation and behavior in cultural socialization terms, evolutionists contend that even with the identical socialization experiences men and women would differ considerably in this domain. Although the occurrence of coercive sex is certainly not viewed as inevitable, the existence of underlying mechanisms that contribute to such acts differs in the minds of males and females.

Consequently, the role of learning can only be properly understood in the framework of the mind that translates environmental input into behavior, both throughout the lifespan and in the immediate situation. Women are targeted by men for domination not only because they bear the "commodity" of new life and are physically weaker, but because sexual desire is one of the proximate mechanisms motivating rape. In ancestral environments, such coercive sex may have increased men's reproductive success under some circumstances since having intercourse was highly correlated with pregnancy prior to the advent of contraceptive devices. Both the feminist and evolutionary approaches view coercive sex not as "crazy behavior," but as fulfilling certain functions for the aggressors. Feminists have considered one set of interrelated socio-political and psychological mechanisms (i.e., asserting dominance, feeling superior, etc.), while evolutionists have emphasized how the fitness consequences in ancestral environments formed such proximate feelings and other reactions. In general, then, the feminist approach largely views rape as a by-product of men's desire to dominate women, while the evolutionary approach sees mechanisms underlying male sexuality as being fundamental to rape specifically and to men's motivation for control or domination generally.

Notes on Why Men Rape

1. Do you find Malamuth's explanation of evolutionary psychology compelling in explaining male motivation to rape? Does it offer a reasonable explanation for male dominance as well as coercive sexuality? Does it explain why women do not, generally, sexually coerce men? Does Malamuth support the conclusion that rape is committed by "normal," and not "crazy," men? Do you think Malamuth is successful in showing how feminist and evolutionary theories can be compatible? What does Malamuth's approach suggest about the possibility of stopping rape?

How would Malamuth explain the use of rape during war? See generally Deborah Blatt, Recognizing Rape as a Method of Torture, 19 N.Y.U. Rev. L. & Soc. Change 821 (1992); Yolanda S. Wu, Note, Genocidal Rape in Bosnia: Redress in United States Courts Under the Alien Tort Claims Act, 4 UCLA Women's L.J. 101 (1993).

2. Why do you think some feminists are concerned about the evolutionary analysis of coercive sexuality? Do you think Malamuth adequately defuses this concern? What do you think is the appropriate response when "science" offers a conflicting, or alternative, explanation for social behavior? Surely Thornhill and Palmer are correct in their belief that understanding the motivation of rapists is essential if we are ever going to have an ability to eliminate rape. Are the rape as "violence" and rape as "sex" sides of the debate incompatible? How would you resolve this issue? What are the implications for stopping rape? See also Randy Thornhill and Nancy Wilmsen Thornhill, The Evolutionary Psychology of Men's Coercive Sexuality, 15 Behav. & Brain Sci. 363, 372 (1992) (aggressive domination has been documented to facilitate the sexual arousal of men).

3. Owen Jones states that "[e]xisting theories of human rape that do not include at least some measure of life science perspectives * * * leave at least the following important questions unanswered:

> 1. Why is rape overwhelmingly a male rather than female behavior in all species in which it is observed? * * *
>
> 2. Why does rape so rarely result in serious physical injury or death, across all populations of species in which it is observed, and across all the world's many human cultures? * * *
>
> 3. Why are reproductive-aged victims of rape, in other species as well as our own, and across all human cultures, so overrepresented, compared to the population of all possible victims of rape? * * *

> 4. Considering all the different kinds of sexual assaults on females of all ages, why are rapists more likely to rape reproductive-aged females penile-vaginally than they are to rape non-reproductive-aged females penile-vaginally? * * *
>
> 5. Why do reproductive-aged victims of penile-vaginal rape appear to be more traumatized, on average, than similar victims who are older or younger? * * *
>
> 6. From among all sexual assaults, why is vaginal rape, on average, apparently more traumatizing than oral or anal rape? * * *
>
> 7. Why does the mean age of rapists remain at about twenty-five over time, when most rapists are never caught or punished? * * *
>
> 8. Why does the age distribution for raped women differ so markedly from the age distribution of robbed women? * * *
>
> 9. Why does the age distribution for raped women differ so markedly from the age distribution of murdered women? * * *

Owen D. Jones, Sex, Culture, and the Biology of Rape: Toward Explanation and Prevention, 87 Cal. L. Rev. 827, 897–99 (1999). Which of these questions do you find compelling and which not? Can you answer his questions without referring to evolutionary concepts? Does it suggest that we should be looking at different things when exploring ways to stop rape of reproductive-aged women and other women?

4. Cheryl Hanna raises some interesting questions about the "girl power" movement, which is premised upon empowerment, encouraging girls to be aggressive and self-assertive. Hanna, Sometimes Sex Matters: Reflections on Biology, Sexual Aggression, and Its Implications for the Law, 39 Jurimetrics 261, 264 (1999). After learning more about biology and sexual aggression, she

> began to see that one of the dangers of the "girl power" movement is that it fails to explicitly teach young women that their sexual motivations may not be the same as their male counterparts. Even though girls may try to emulate male aggressiveness, they are not trying to be like boys; rather, they are trying to attract them. Because of their new-found sexual freedom, however, girls may be putting themselves in situations where they are more, rather than less, vulnerable to male aggression. The "girl power" movement can be understood biologically as part of a female counter-strategy to reduce male violence by refusing to be sexually passive. Yet, paradoxically, rather than decrease male sexual coercion, the culture of "girl power" may simply be shifting the variables upon which females compete for males. If being powerfully "in your face" becomes attractive to men, then by buying into "girl power," young women may be getting more than they bargained for.

Id. How would you assess the success of "girl power" in combating male sexual aggression?

5. During 1980 and 1981, Diana Scully and Joseph Marolla interviewed 114 men incarcerated in Virginia who were convicted of raping adult women. Scully and Marolla, "Riding the Bull at Gilley's": Convicted Rapists Describe the Rewards of Rape, in Violence Against Women: The Bloody Footprints 26,

31 (Pauline B. Bart and Eileen Geil Moran, eds. 1993). They made the following conclusions about "how these men viewed sexual violence and what they gained from their behavior":

> We found that rape was frequently a means of revenge and punishment. Implicit in revenge rapes was the notion that women were collectively liable for the rapists' problems. In some cases, victims were substitutes for significant women against whom the men desired to take revenge. In other cases, victims were thought to represent all women, and rape was used to punish, humiliate, and "put them in their place." In both cases women were seen as a class, a category, not as individuals. For some men, rape was almost an afterthought, a bonus added to burglary or robbery. Other men gained access to sexually unavailable or unwilling women through rape. For this group of men, rape was a fantasy come true, a particularly exciting form of impersonal sex that enabled them to dominate and control women by exercising a singularly male form of power. These rapists talked of the pleasures of raping—how for them it was a challenge, an adventure, a dangerous and "ultimate" experience. Rape made them feel good, and in some cases, even elevated their self-image.
>
> * * *
>
> Our data demonstrate that some men rape because they have learned that in this culture sexual violence is rewarding. Significantly, the overwhelming majority of these rapists indicated they never thought they would go to prison for what they did. Some did not fear imprisonment because they did not define their behavior as rape. Others knew that women frequently do not report rape and that in those cases that are reported conviction rates are low, and therefore they felt secure. These men perceived rape as a rewarding, low-risk act. Understanding that otherwise normal men can and do rape is critical to the development of strategies for prevention.

Id. at 42–43. Does this information suggest any additional strategies for stopping rape? What about mandatory education programs to demythologize the rape myths? Increased sentences for convicted rapists? Or will that only make juries less likely to convict? Does the Scully and Marolla study conflict with Malamuth's conclusions? Can you integrate the two studies?

6. David Lisak and Susan Roth evaluated 15 unreported rapists and 15 control subjects, all male college students. Lisak, Sexual Aggression, Masculinity, and Fathers, 16 Signs 238 (1991). They found that, while there were no apparent differences between the two groups in the fathers' occupations (typically white collar and high paying), there were some differences in the occupational status of the subjects' mothers. They discovered that 9 out of 15 of the rapists' mothers did not work outside the home. In contrast, only four of the control subjects' mothers did not work outside the home. Other findings:

> (1) "rapists scored significantly higher than control subjects on standardized measures of hostility toward women, underlying anger motivations, dominance as a motive for sexual interactions, underlying power motivations, and on two indices of hypermasculinity"; (2) "rapists made

> significantly more negative statements and significantly fewer positive statements about their fathers"; (3) rapists "made significantly more negative statements about their mothers, but not fewer positive statements"; (4) "the worse the subject's relationship with his father, the more did he express hostility toward women, dominance over women, underlying power motivations, and hypermasculine attitudes"; (5) "subjects' relationships with their mothers did not correlate with any of these measures."

Id. at 248–49. The experimenters concluded that "the basic conflict with mothers centered on their involvement with their sons, while the conflict with fathers centered on their noninvolvement." Id. at 255. Lisak suggests that inadequate fathering, in the context of the nuclear family, "can result in an array of adverse consequences, from various forms of psychopathology to low self-esteem, poor cognitive development, antisocial behavior, and hypermasculine behavior." Id. at 257. Is this a new perspective? If inadequate mothering is not the root of misogyny, but rather inadequate fathering, is this any solace? What is the solution? Does this study necessarily conflict with the Malamuth excerpt?

8. STOPPING RAPE: INDIVIDUAL AND LEGAL RESPONSES

PAULINE B. BART AND PATRICIA H. O'BRIEN, STOPPING RAPE: SUCCESSFUL SURVIVAL STRATEGIES

32–34, 105–07 (1985).

> [Dr. Bart, a leading voice in the women's movement since the 1960's, is a sociologist; she and Dr. O'Brien have extensive clinical experience working with raped and battered women. This book is based on an analysis of 94 interviews with women 18 or older who had been attacked and avoided being raped (51) or had been raped (43) in the two years prior to the interview.]

Women are in a double bind. On the one hand, we are told that fighting back will only excite a rapist or make him angry. This assumes he is not already angry and that fighting back immediately is the most dangerous strategy. We are also warned that resistance will result in serious injury if not mutilation and death, with parts of our bodies turning up in garbage cans and under park benches.

On the other hand, rape has traditionally been legally defined as carnal knowledge of a woman not his wife by a man over 14 *by force and against her will.* * * * Therefore, in order to legally prove rape, the woman has to prove it was against her will, and the best way to prove that she is not willing is *not* by saying "please don't," or "I have my period." The best way to prove that the sexual act is not consensual is by physical resistance.

* * *

When the women described their assaults, distinct types of defense techniques emerged:

1. Fleeing or trying to flee from the attacker(s)
2. Screaming, yelling or talking loudly, usually in an effort to attract attention

3. Using "affective verbal" techniques, including begging and pleading with the assailant, trying to gain his sympathy
4. Using "cognitive verbal" techniques, including attempting to reason with the assailant, conning him, making him "see her as a person," stalling, etc.
5. Experiencing environmental intervention: someone or something in the surroundings that intruded on the scene and either caused the assailant to stop the assault and/or gave the woman an opportunity to escape
6. Using physical force, ranging from the woman pushing back the assailant to self-defense techniques.

In addition to using more different *kinds* of strategies, women who stopped their rapes were most likely to yell, scream, or use physical force. There was also more likely to be environmental intervention (i.e., other people such as the police intruding).

Women who were raped were more likely to plead or cry. About four fifths of the women in our study tried to talk their way out of the rape. This was rarely effective by itself, but no more characteristic of raped women than of women who were not raped. The most effective combination of strategies was physical force and yelling. * * *

Two warnings, however, must be noted. First, the group of women who spoke to us were obviously those who had survived attacks, and were not permanently, totally, or nearly totally incapacitated. The women whose horrible deaths are reported with relish in lurid media accounts are not in our sample.

* * *

One of the most important findings was that when a woman used physical force as a defense technique together with another technique, her chances of avoiding [rape] increased (no women in our study used physical force alone). In fact, the more additional strategies she used, the greater her chances. Of the 13 women who used physical force plus one additional strategy, 6 avoided rape and 7 were raped. Nine women who used physical force and two additional strategies avoided rape. None of the 13 women who used three or four strategies in addition to physical force was raped.

* * *

When we looked at socioeconomic and demographic factors to see if they resulted in rape or rape avoidance, rape avoiders were more likely to be taller and heavier than raped women. Two thirds of the women who avoided rape had never been married, while women who had been married more than once or who were divorced were least likely to avoid rape. Oldest (but not only children) daughters were more likely to avoid rape, particularly if they had a major responsibility for housework and care of siblings; 69 percent of oldest daughters avoided rape when attacked. Although mothers of women who avoided rape had more college and post-graduate education than women who were raped, the occupation of mothers was not associated with avoidance, nor was the subject's holding a nontraditional job (e.g., electrician).

There are three childhood socialization variables that were associated with stopping sexual assaults: parental response to childhood aggression, childhood idea of what she thought her life would be like when she grew up, and childhood sports. Although it made no difference for rape avoidance whether the subjects fought physically with other children, or even if they won or lost those childhood battles, the parents of women who were raped were more likely to both have intervened in such fights and to have punished the use of violence. Moreover, the parents of women who were raped were less likely to have counseled their daughters to fight back in quarrels with their peers. It follows that women whose parents knew about the fights but did not intervene learned that they had to take care of themselves and had experience in doing so.

Women who avoided rape were more likely to have played football, a contact sport, than raped women. Football teaches women that physical contact—being knocked down, even hurt—is not the end of the world, something that most boys but few girls learn. It seems logical that such experience is helpful when a woman is attacked in less benign contexts.

Not only were the rape avoiders more likely to engage in contact sports and have had parents who allowed them to fight their own battles, but they were less likely to have mentioned marriage and children and more likely to mention paid employment when asked what they thought their lives would be like when they grew up.

* * *

When the women's adult socialization experiences were analyzed, the women who avoided rape were more competent in managing stress and/or emergencies and possessed skills enabling them to be independent.

As Henley [Nancy Henley, a psychologist] pointed out:

> An attitude study in 1959 documented the psychological connection between chivalry and misogyny: attitudes favoring chivalry went hand-in-hand with those favoring the open subordination of women—and both were positively correlated with antidemocratic attitudes.

The practice of keeping women passive, doing things for them in the physical world such as opening doors and moving heavy furniture, not only gives women a feeling of inability to cope, but it alienates them from the physical world. * * *

Additionally, women who avoided being raped were more likely than raped women to mention a woman they knew personally rather than a woman in public life when asked which woman in public or private life they admired and why. Raped women were more likely to mention role models in public life. While the number of cases were small, it was only raped women who said that they admired women who were successfully able to combine an occupation with their *role as a woman*. Mothers of raped women were more likely to want their daughters to combine marriage with a traditional occupation, while mothers of women who avoided rape wanted them to have marriage and a career, although the career was not specified. Both groups of women described their mothers as strong, and they were similar in the ratio of positive-to-negative adjectives they applied to their mothers.

Notes on Resisting and Stopping Rape

1. Bart and O'Brien identify a doublebind for women who are sexually assaulted: we are told that if we resist a rapist we may anger him and escalate the violence, but if we do not physically resist we will have a difficult time legally proving it was rape and not consensual sex, as illustrated by the *Goldberg* case, above. If you were prosecuting Mr. Goldberg, could you use this doublebind to your advantage? How?

2. Bart and O'Brien also report that "[t]wo thirds of the women who avoided rape had never been married, while women who had been married more than once or who were divorced were least likely to avoid rape." How does this finding relate to the materials on marital rape? Does marriage condition women not to fight back? What role does the law play in reinforcing the vulnerability of women in marriage?

3. As an attempt at self-help when university officials were unresponsive to complaints about sexual assault on campus, women students at Brown University wrote names of alleged rapists on the women's bathroom walls at the school's library. Students said the list was meant to warn other women, not to publicize the names. Male students were angered and complained to university officials. Was this an appropriate action by the women students? Was it fair to the men whose name appeared on the wall without any hearing on the charges? Why or why not? Can you think of other types of "self-help" that women could use?

4. Several studies have recently attempted to assess the effectiveness of college rape education. In reviewing the two-hour mandatory rape education workshop for freshmen at the University of Illinois, two researchers found, among other results, that (1) as expected, attitudinal rebounding occurred, with the immediate positive change eroding after seven weeks although sexual assault knowledge appeared to continue, and (2) students who participated in multiple rape educational programs demonstrated superior outcomes, including greater rejection of cultural rape myths. Kimberly A. Lonsway and Chevon Kothari, First Year Campus Acquaintance Rape Education (FYCARE): Evaluating the Impact on Knowledge, Ideology, and Behavior, ABF Working Paper #9720, 25–28 (1998). Other researchers, in assessing a sexual assault prevention program for college women, discovered that, although the program did not appear to decrease the incidence of sexual assault for women with a sexual assault history, it was effective for

women without previous sexual assaults. Kimberly A. Hanson and Christine A. Gidycz, Evaluation of a Sexual Assault Prevention Program, 61 J. Counseling & Clinical Psych. 1046 (1993). See also Mary Margaret Fonow, Laurel Richardson and Virginia A. Wemmerus, Feminist Rape Education: Does It Work?, 6 Gender & Soc. 108 (1992) (finding "significant gender differences in students' attitudes on all the scales, with women being more knowledgeable about rape, less likely to blame the victim, and less accepting of adversarial sexual beliefs and gender-role conservatism" and that "rape education intervention works in changing some attitudes about rape for both men and women students."). In light of these findings, do colleges have an obligation to their students to provide such programs? Why or why not?

5. There appear to be substantial data that education can change male attitudes about rape and rape myths. See Barbara J. Gilbert, Martin Heesacker and Linda J. Gannon, Changing the Sexual Aggression–Supportive Attitudes of Men: A Psychoeducational Intervention, 38 J. Counseling Psych. 197 (1991); Gloria J. Fischer, College Student Attitudes Toward Forcible Date Rape: Changes After Taking a Human Sexuality Course, 12 J. Sex Ed. & Therapy 42 (1986). An article published in 1991 reported that:

> College men in this study were found to have substantially greater tendencies to blame the victims for occurrences of date and acquaintance rape than were women. Additionally, men, as compared with women, believed many more factual misconceptions surrounding issues of date and acquaintance rape. Many men lacked information about the seriousness of the issue, had little understanding of women's perceptions of rape and behaviors surrounding it, and had never analyzed the social mores and their own perspectives on sexual aggression. These misconceptions led to a lack of understanding, especially by men, of the seriousness of the problem, underestimation of the extent of sexual aggression on college campuses, and a moral code that perpetuates violence against women which is unacceptable.
>
> In addition to supporting previous findings about students' misconceptions about rape, this study also demonstrated that these misconceptions can be changed through mediated instruction and facilitated discussion. This approach provides facts about rape; enables students to explore their own beliefs, values, and feelings; and creates an opportunity for male and female students to share openly their perspectives leading to a reduction in the myths that surround a serious social problem. The changes that occurred as a result of the approach that was used in this study suggest that mediated rape awareness programs can be a potent factor in increasing students' understanding of the issues, changing attitudes, and ultimately changing the behaviors of both sexes that contribute to rape and other forms of sexual aggression.

Patrick J. Harrison, Jeannette Downes and Michael D. Williams, Date and Acquaintance Rape: Perceptions and Attitude Change Strategies, 32 J. College Student Dev. 131, 138 (1991). Do these results suggest that tax dollars might be better spent on educational programs about rape? How could such programs be implemented?

6. According to a 1992 study involving a survey of 370 agencies that provide crisis counseling to rape victims, victims would be more willing to report rapes if there were:

—Public education about acquaintance rape	99%
—Laws protecting the confidentiality of rape victims and prohibiting news media from disclosing their names and addresses	97%
—Expansion of counseling of advocacy services for victims and their families	97%
—Mandatory HIV testing of individuals who become indicted on sexual assault charges	80%
—Free abortions and pregnancy counseling for rape victims who become pregnant	77%
—Confidential free testing for possible transmission of HIV/AIDS or other sexually transmitted diseases to victims	57%

National Victim Center and Crime Victims Research and Treatment Center, Rape in America: A Report to the Nation 11 (Apr. 23, 1992). How would one go about making public policy based on these responses? Taking political action to bring about these changes?

LEONORE M.J. SIMON, SEX OFFENDER LEGISLATION AND THE ANTITHERAPEUTIC EFFECTS ON VICTIMS

141 Ariz. L. Rev. 485, 516–23 (1999).

When the legal system places so much emphasis on the rare stranger sex offender, it undermines the ability of society to vindicate current victims of nonstranger assaults and protect prospective victims from future sex crimes. Focusing on the stranger offender is antitherapeutic in that policy makers are reacting to the sensational stranger sex crime while neglecting the daily reality of rape and sexual assault in the lives of women and children who are assaulted by nonstrangers. Taking precautions against the stranger sex offender lulls society and prospective rape victims into a false sense of security. * * * There are several other ways in which the exclusive focus on the stranger sex offender has iatrogenic effects for current and prospective victims of rape and sexual assault.

A. Current Victims

Current victims, the majority of whom have been victimized by a nonstranger, are likely to suffer in several ways. First, they are unlikely to define their victimization as a crime. This occurs because most individuals in society think of crime as a phenomenon that is perpetrated by strangers, and they tend to fear the stranger criminal. When they are victimized by someone they know, particularly in a sexual manner, victims often are confused about what happened to them. I think the Kathleen Willey case in the U.S. exemplifies the confusion and reaction by a victim when a man she knows and admires (here President Clinton) gropes and fondles her unexpectedly. Assuming events occurred as Ms.

Willey recounted them, she was probably both embarrassed and shocked. It also may explain why she continued to write him letters seeking a job, as though nothing untoward had occurred. She was in denial and needed a job desperately. Like the Willey case, it is not uncommon for a woman who has been raped or sexually assaulted by a man she knows to continue to see him after the assault. The confusion is more extreme in the case of children who are sexually abused by a family member or acquaintance. They have been admonished not to talk with strangers but generally have not been schooled in refusing their fathers' sexual advances. For example, assume a 11–year-old girl whose father has warned her to stay away from a strange man (e.g., pedophile) living down the block. One day when father and daughter are alone, the father fondles her breasts. The 11–year-old girl is made uncomfortable by this event but may not define the act as a sexual assault. In most cases, if the acts are not defined by the victim as a crime, they will not be reported, and there remains an increased likelihood of continuing and escalating risk of sexual assault by the perpetrator. In fact, in many of these cases, the perpetrator himself does not define his conduct as a crime by engaging in cognitive distortions that minimize or rationalize his behavior or that blame the victim. Thus, by focusing attention on the stranger sex offender, current victims of nonstranger offenders remain at increased risk of revictimization of either the same offender or a different offender. Not defining an act or acts as sexual abuse may be one of the reasons that victims of childhood adolescent sexual abuse are at increased risk to experience later victimization in adulthood.

A second way current victims of sex crimes are adversely affected by sex offender legislation occurs after a sex offense is reported. Police and prosecutors generally are more interested in going after the stranger offender because legal actors often do not define sex cases involving acquaintances or family members as crimes. A woman who reports that she has been raped by her boyfriend or ex-boyfriend raises legal eyebrows. * * * If the victim resumes her relationship with the offender after the sexual assault (not an uncommon occurrence), law enforcement and prosecutors may further doubt the victim's credibility. The same logic is not applied by police to the majority of aggravated assaults or attempted murders between males who resume their relationship with each other after the incident. The credibility of these male victims is not an issue. Such legal policies and double standards hinder the ability of current rape and assault victims (particularly females) to receive satisfaction from the legal system. In addition, the victim's experience with legal actors in nonstranger rapes and sexual assaults results in further trauma because of the implicit and explicit victim-blaming that occurs. In fact, the legal and social response to women who are raped by nonstrangers can be so traumatic that psychological symptoms thought to be associated with the sexual assault may actually be a result of the lack of support a victim feels from others. For example, acquaintances and family members of the victim may engage in unsupportive victim-blaming behavior. Consequently, to be a rape victim of a nonstranger usually results in a second trauma since the social and legal response to her victimization and impedes her ability to heal.

A third way in which current victims are adversely affected by the legal polity is the availability of more lenient treatment of nonstranger perpetrators by the legal system. Nowhere is this more true than in the realm of child molestation cases within families. In Washington, as in many states, sex criminals are afforded treatment as a sentencing alternative. This treatment, I may add, is of unproven effectiveness. This legal policy presupposes that the crime was the result of a mental illness and can be treated with therapy. Evaluations of sex offender treatments find that treated and untreated sex offenders are equally likely to be convicted of a new offense. The availability of treatment to offenders who commit sex crimes at a time when general criminal offenders do not have the option for treatment further reinforces everyone's perception that what occurred was not a real crime. Even if the offender goes to prison and treatment is available there, there is a preference among treatment providers for incest offenders who are believed to be more amenable to treatment. Consequently, the victim is left with the impression that here victimization was not as serious as it would have been if it were committed by a "non-mentally ill" stranger. In addition, the family is likely to be lulled into a sense of security when the offender is in treatment, which is dangerous if the treatment is not effective.

A fourth way in which the current victims of sexual assault are underserved by legal policies is the focus on specialization. By this I mean the tendency, when investigating a rape, for example, of police to round up the registered sex offenders. I have seen this occur and backfire repeatedly in various jurisdictions. Many times, the perpetrator is never apprehended. In cases where the rapist is arrested, it is often the case that he has no prior convictions for any sex crime but has a varied criminal history. * * * Although there is a public and police misconception that offenders who commit sex crimes specialize in sex crimes, empirical evidence indicates that, like other types of offenders, sex offenders commit a wide variety of crimes. When investigating a sex crime, restricting the focus to registered sex offenders is likely to miss suspects with no known criminal record for sex crimes. * * *

Current victims of sexual offenses are neglected by current policies in yet another way. Efforts to reach out to individuals in high-risk situations in order to terminate what may be ongoing victimization are limited. In the area of child sexual abuse, the 1980s saw the growth of sexual abuse prevention education programs for children. The availability of such programs has been reduced since then due to cost-cutting measures affecting schools and community groups. Although studies of the efficacy of child education prevention programs have been conducted, very few evaluations examine the number of children who were being molested who used such outreach efforts to terminate their abuse by reporting it. In fact, many who question the effectiveness of the child education programs in preventing future victimization recognize the potential ability of these programs to elicit early disclosure of abuse, thereby preventing continued abuse. Although the literature in the area has not addressed the issue, arguably programs that educate parents about the prevalence and incidence of child sexual abuse may lead parents to question their own parenting practices, as in the case of a mother who has acceded to her husband's demands to interact in inappropriate ways with her daughters from a previous marriage. For parents who themselves were sexually abused or raised in troubled families, such training could help them distinguish among appropriate, potentially troublesome, and inappropriate sexual interests or behaviors, leading them to better monitor their children's behaviors and activities.

B. Prospective Victims

Current laws and policies toward sex offenders have antitherapeutic effects on prospective victims of nonstrangers. This is because as long as the public focus is on the stranger sex criminal, prevention of the majority of sex offense cases is probably not undertaken. As long as parents are worried exclusively about the stranger child molester lurking in dark alleys, they are not as likely to be in a position to protect their children from the nonstranger. This is presumably because most parents do not know that their children are at substantially higher risk of being sexually victimized by a family member or acquaintance. It is not uncommon, then, for a mother whose child tells her about the sexual abuse perpetrated by her husband to react in denial. This may be because her home is the last place she has been socialized to expect predatory behavior (or because if she admitted to herself that it did happen in her home, she would also have to admit that she failed to protect her child).

There are several ways in which prevention opportunities are missed that would benefit prospective victims of nonstranger sex offenses. First, most people do not have accurate information on which to base their behavior. Without educating the public about the prevalence and incidence of sex crimes committed by nonstrangers, arguably the community is not in a position to prevent victimization from offenders they know. In child sexual abuse cases, most parents may not know that the danger from nonstrangers greatly exceeds the danger from stranger sex crimes. Since many nonstranger child sex abuse cases continue for a long period of time before they are reported (if they are reported), the lack of a parent's vigilance not only fails to protect the child from the first abusive incident, but also from each subsequent incident. In addition, sexual abuse as a child is a risk factor for further victimization by another perpetrator in childhood or adulthood. Consequently, failure to protect a child from sexual abuse can doom that child to a lifetime of repeat victimization. Since a substantial proportion of molestation crimes are committed by fathers, stepfathers, and brothers, it is not clear how educating the parents or the mothers can have preventive effects. Theoretically, parent education efforts can strengthen parents' protective instincts and capacities so that they do not negligently or knowingly allow spouses or others to abuse their children. Evaluations of existing parenting workshops have not been promising, largely because few parents attend these sessions, and those who do often have a prior interest or familiarity with the topic. In addition to educating parents about inappropriate and appropriate sexual interests and behaviors, broader parenting issues can be addressed. Parent education programs can emphasize communication skills to create a context in which secrets or manipulation by another adult becomes more difficult.

* * *

The public generally has very little information on the prevalence of forcible rape by nonstrangers. Parents do not educate their daughters (and sons) about the dangers of dating relationships or avoiding high risk situations such as alcohol with males who are known to them. Parents probably do not educate their daughters about not finding themselves alone with a man in a place where no one can intervene. Parents presumably may not educate their daughters about casual acquaintances or friends of the family who might look for an opportunity to victimize the daughters. Parents arguably also fail to educate their daughters about how to resist the pressure to have unwanted sex. Because sex is such an uncomfortable topic between parents and teenagers, if a rape occurs, the victim may be unable to tell her parents. Victims also may not tell their parents for fear of being blamed. All this is unfortunate because teenage girls have the highest rape victimization rate of any age group.

Notes on Legal Attempts to Stop Rape

1. Unfortunately, as Susan Estrich predicted in her excerpt above, statutory reform focusing on consent and resistance has made little or no difference in stopping rape. Empirical studies of rape reforms in Michigan, Washington, California, Canada, and six urban environments were remarkably identical in their findings that there was little or no instrumental effect, i.e., no increase in complaints, arrests, prosecutions, and convictions. See Morrison Torrey, Feminist Legal Scholarship on Rape: A Maturing Look at One Form of Violence Against Women, 2 Wm. & Mary J. Women & Law 35, 45–46 (1995). Nonetheless, after Cassia Spohn and Julia Horney hypothesized that the reforms may have a more subtle impact, they investigated to determine if the justice system took more seriously "simple" rapes, those incidents not involving extrinsic violence, multiple assailants, or no prior relationship between the victim and offender. They concluded:

> our findings provide mixed evidence concerning the impact of rape law reform. The fact that the strong and comprehensive Michigan reforms not only did not produce the dramatic instrumental results envisioned by reformers, but did not even produce the more subtle effects investigated here, provides additional evidence that reformers had unrealistic expectations for the rape law reforms. On the other hand, the fact that the proportion of simple rape cases bound over for trial increased significantly in the post-reform period suggests that more borderline cases are being reported by victims, and accepted by police and prosecu-

tors. It suggests that the rape law reforms have produced a climate more conducive to the full prosecution of cases of simple rape.

Spohn and Horney, The Impact of Rape Law Reform on the Processing of Simple and Aggravated Rape Cases, 86 J. Crim. L. & Criminology 861, 994 (1996). See generally Spohn and Horney, Rape Law Reform: A Grassroots Revolution and Its Impact (1992). If legislative reform focusing on the elements necessary to prove rape is not the answer, what *is* the solution?

This failure of legislative rape reform appears consistent with empirical data suggesting that law reform that precedes changes in social attitudes is doomed to failure. See Gerald N. Rosenberg, The Hollow Hope: Can Courts Bring About Social Change? (1991). Can you think of any legal reform that preceded changed social attitudes that was successful?

2. Many states have attempted to deal with repeat sexual offenders through probation, parole, and sentencing schedules. For example, Washington responded to the high rate of recidivism of sex offenders by extending their imprisonment through its "Sexually Violent Predators Act." West's Rev.Code Wash.Ann. 71.09 (1990). The Act provides for post-sentence indefinite civil commitment for sexually violent predators, individuals convicted of, or charged with (but not tried because of incompetency) a crime of sexual violence and suffering from a mental abnormality or personality disorder which makes them likely to engage in predatory acts of sexual violence. See Lisa Taeko Greenlees, Washington State's Sexually Violent Predators Act: Model or Mistake, 29 Am.Crim.L.Rev. 107 (1991). Can you anticipate any constitutional problems with such a law? Is this law simply a variation on general civil commitment statutes, in which anyone who is a danger to himself or others may be involuntarily committed?

In 1997, the Supreme Court upheld one of these sexually violent predator acts in Kansas v. Hendricks, 521 U.S. 346, 117 S.Ct. 2072, 138 L.Ed.2d 501. Justice Thomas, writing for the majority, stated:

> To the extent that the civil commitment statutes we have considered set forth criteria relating to an individual's inability to control his dangerousness, the Kansas Act sets forth comparable criteria and Hendricks' condition doubtless satisfies those criteria. The mental health professionals who evaluated Hendricks diagnosed him as suffering from pedophilia, a condition the psychiatric profession itself classifies as a serious mental disorder. Hendricks even conceded that, when he becomes "stressed out," he cannot "control the urge" to molest children. This admitted lack of volitional control, coupled with a prediction of future dangerousness, adequately distinguishes Hendricks from other dangerous persons who are perhaps more properly dealt with exclusively through criminal proceedings. Hendricks' diagnosis as a pedophile, which qualifies as a "mental abnormality" under the Act, thus plainly suffices for due process purposes.

Id. at 360. A state's "three strikes and you're out" law [providing for extended incarceration after a violent third offense] can also prolong incarceration for repeat offenders. Would you support a sexual predator statute similar to Washington's? Why or why not?

3. Another experiment has been to require convicted sex offenders to register with the local authorities upon their release from prison. In fact, the 1994 Federal Crime Bill requires all states to institute a registry of convicted sex offenders or lose federal funding. See generally Robert E. Freeman–Longo, Reducing Sexual Abuse in America: Legislating Tougher Laws or Public Education and Prevention, 23 New Eng. J. Crim. & Civ. Confinement 303 (1997). Similar public notice laws, such as "Megan's Law" (named for Megan Kanka after she was sexually assaulted and murdered by a released sex offender in her New Jersey neighborhood), require law enforcement agencies to notify the public when a registered sex offender moves into the community. Do you think this is a good policy? How do you think it will affect released sex offenders? Do you think the community has a right to know if a convicted sex offender moves in? What about the rights of a criminal defendant who has served his punishment and wants to start anew? How would you balance the conflicting interests?

4. At least six states have passed laws allowing, and in some cases requiring, chemical treatments of certain sex offenders, including rapists, as a condition of parole. Many other states are considering such legislation. Commonly referred to as "chemical castration," the treatment involves regular chemical injections of drugs such as Depo–Provera, which shrinks the testicles, inhibits the release of testosterone and other hormones that affect the brain's tendency to sexually fantasize, and reduces sex drive in men. These effects are reversible if treatments stop. As of yet, there is little empirical data to suggest that this treatment affects recidivism. See generally Lisa Keesling, Practicing Medicine Without a License: Legislative Attempts to Mandate Chemical Castration for Repeat Sex Offenders, 32 John Marshall L. Rev. 381, 384 (1999). These laws appear to be vulnerable to constitutional challenges on the basis of the First, Eighth, and Fourteenth Amendments. Id. Some courts have even attempted to require surgical castration, an out-patient procedure in which the testicles are removed and permanent sterilization results. Id. at 390. If rape is violence, and not sex, should these treatments be effective? Should they only apply to rapists of a certain age? See Owen D. Jones, Sex, Culture, and the Biology of Rape: Toward Explanation and Prevention, 87 Cal. L. Rev. 827, 912–30 (1999).

5. Yet another possible institutional response to rape has been suggested by Katharine K. Baker—shaming date rapists. She notes that:

> The disregard for the question of consent on the part of men has led to a massive victimization of women. Criminally punishing nonconsensual sex has proved difficult, however, precisely because the legal proscription on nonconsensual sex competes with the masculinity norm, biological theory and popular belief, all of which re-enforce and legitimate the notion that men crave sex regardless of consent. Given this tension between the law and other well-established norms, it should come as little surprise that a sizable number of men have yet to internalize the moral wrong of nonconsensual sex. And even those men who have internalized the abstract wrong of non-consensual sex can have difficulty concretely identifying what nonconsensual sex is. This difficulty stems both from well established sexual behavior roles that shun explicit communication and from our continuing reluctance to explicitly discuss, both societally and individually, what consent is. Finally, the constitu-

tional protections afforded defendants make convictions particularly difficult to secure in cases, like date rape, in which consent is the only issue.

Baker, Sex, Rape and Shame, 79 B.U. L. Rev. 663, 693–94 (1999). The alternative Baker proposes lies in her suggested sanction: in a closed community, such as a college, shaming the offenders. She argues that shame sanctions can subvert the linking between masculinity and sexual activity in addition to affording the victim a sense of vindication. Rather than expelling students found guilty, shaming sanctions could include being required to wear a bright orange armband; publishing the rapist's picture with the armband in the school newspaper; banning the rapist from extracurricular activities through which esteem is achieved; and listing his affiliations (such as fraternity, sports teams, etc.) so that they share his shame. Id. at 698. How do you assess the likelihood of shaming to be successful in eliminating college date rape? Can you think of other possible sanctions? What are the goals of fashioning alternative sanctions?

Note that universities, in order to be eligible for federal funds, must now collect data on campus rape and maintain sexual assault policies which provide for disciplinary procedures, usually less formal than criminal proceedings, e.g., relaxed evidentiary rules, non-unanimous convictions, less rigid standards of proof. See Higher Education Amendments of 1991 § 486(c)(1)-(2), 20 U.S.C. §§ 1092(f)(1)(F)(1994); § 1092(f)(7)(B)(i)-(B)(iii).

7. Would you favor a law that prohibits the media from disclosing the names of rape victims? According to the National Women's Study, 78% of rape victims and 76% of all American women surveyed favored such legislation. National Victim Center and Crime Victims Research and Treatment Center, Rape in America: A Report to the Nation 9 (Apr. 23, 1992). Over 90% of rape crisis agencies favored such laws. Id. at 11. See Deborah W. Denno, Perspectives on Disclosing Rape Victims' Names, 61 Fordham L. Rev. 1113 (1993). Would you be more likely to report a rape if you knew your name would not be published in the paper?

8. Occasionally male defendants attempt to introduce cultural evidence to rebut the prosecution's proof of mens rea or criminal intent in crimes of violence against women. Many feminists have vigorously opposed the use of the "cultural" defense as condoning the violence against women. According to Holly Maguigan, this has created a "tension between multiculturalist and feminist values [which] is presented most clearly in cases such as *Chen* [in which a Chinese immigrant did not deny killing his wife, but offered evidence that he murdered her after learning of her infidelity] and *Rhines* [in which an African American male did not deny intercourse with an African American complainant, but contended that he made a reasonable mistake about her consent because Black people speak to each other very loudly], in which outsider men are charged with family or anti-woman violence and seek to use cultural information in their defense." Maguigan, Cultural Evidence and Male Violence: Are Feminist and Multiculturalist Reformers on a Collision Course in Criminal Courts?, 70 N.Y.U. L. Rev. 36 (1995). How would you resolve this issue? The author suggests that there is a middleground; she would allow "offers of proof by defense counsel that make clear that cultural evidence is intended to prove the defendant's state

of mind, not to support the assertion of a separate 'cultural defense.' " Id. at 42. Do you find this proposal an acceptable compromise? What are the dangers of allowing evidence about male-dominated cultures in criminal prosecutions? What are the dangers of excluding it?

9. STATUTORY RAPE

MICHAEL M. v. SUPERIOR COURT OF SONOMA COUNTY

Supreme Court of the United States, 1981.

450 U.S. 464, 101 S.Ct. 1200, 67 L.Ed.2d 437.

JUSTICE REHNQUIST announced the judgment of the Court and delivered an opinion, in which THE CHIEF JUSTICE, JUSTICE STEWART, and JUSTICE POWELL joined.

The question presented in this case is whether California's "statutory rape" law, § 261.5 of the [California Code] violates the Equal Protection Clause of the Fourteenth Amendment. Section 261.5 defines unlawful sexual intercourse as "an act of sexual intercourse accomplished with a female not the wife of the perpetrator, where the female is under the age of 18 years." The statute thus makes men alone criminally liable for the act of sexual intercourse.

In July 1978, a complaint was filed in the Municipal Court of Sonoma County, Cal., alleging that petitioner, then a 17½–year–old male, had had unlawful sexual intercourse with a female under the age of 18, in violation of § 261.5. The evidence adduced at a preliminary hearing showed that at approximately midnight on June 3, 1978, petitioner and two friends approached Sharon, a 16½–year–old female, and her sister as they waited at a bus stop. Petitioner and Sharon, who had already been drinking, moved away from the others and began to kiss. After being struck in the face for rebuffing petitioner's initial advances, Sharon submitted to sexual intercourse with petitioner. Prior to trial, petitioner sought to set aside the information on both state and federal constitutional grounds, asserting that § 261.5 unlawfully discriminated on the basis of gender. The trial court and the California Court of Appeal denied petitioner's request for relief and [the Supreme Court of California affirmed the denial].

* * *

Our cases have held * * * that the traditional minimum rationality test takes on a somewhat "sharper focus" when gender-based classifications are challenged. * * *

Underlying these decisions is the principle that a legislature may not "make overbroad generalizations based on sex which are entirely unrelated to any differences between men and women or which demean the ability or social status of the affected class." * * * But * * * this Court has consistently upheld statutes where the gender classification is not invidious, but rather realistically reflects the fact that the sexes are not similarly situated in certain circumstances. * * *

Applying those principles to this case, the fact that the California Legislature criminalized the act of illicit sexual intercourse with a minor female is a sure indication of its intent or purpose to discourage that conduct. Precisely why the legislature desired that result is of course somewhat less clear. This Court has long recognized that "[i]nquiries into congressional motives or purposes are a hazardous matter," and the search for the "actual" or "primary" purpose of a statute is likely to be elusive. * * *

The justification for the statute offered by the State * * * is that the legislature sought to prevent illegitimate teenage pregnancies. * * *

We need not be medical doctors to discern that young men and young women are not similarly situated with respect to the problems and the risks of sexual intercourse. Only women may become pregnant, and they suffer disproportionately the profound physical, emotional, and psychological consequences of sexual activity. The statute at issue here protects women from sexual intercourse at an age when those consequences are particularly severe.

The question thus boils down to whether a State may attack the problem of sexual intercourse and teenage pregnancy directly by prohibiting a male from having sexual intercourse with a minor female. We hold that such a statute is sufficiently related to the State's objectives to pass constitutional muster.

Because virtually all of the significant harmful and inescapably identifiable consequences of teenage pregnancy fall on the young female, a legislature acts well within its authority when it elects to punish only the participant who, by nature, suffers few of the consequences of his conduct. It is hardly unreasonable for a legislature acting to protect minor females to exclude them from punishment. Moreover, the risk of pregnancy itself constitutes a substantial deterrence to young females. No similar natural sanctions deter males. A criminal sanction imposed solely on males thus serves to roughly "equalize" the deterrents on the sexes.

We are unable to accept petitioner's contention that the statute is impermissibly underinclusive and must, in order to pass judicial scrutiny, be broadened so as to hold the female as criminally liable as the male. It is argued that this statute is not *necessary* to deter teenage pregnancy because a gender-neutral statute, where both male and female would be subject to prosecution, would serve that goal equally well. The relevant inquiry, however, is not whether the statute is drawn as precisely as it might have been, but whether the line chosen by the California Legislature is within constitutional limitations.

In any event, we cannot say that a gender-neutral statute would be as effective as the statute California has chosen to enact. The State persuasively contends that a gender-neutral statute would frustrate its interest in effective enforcement. Its view is that a female is surely less likely to report violations of the statute if she herself would be subject to criminal prosecution. In an area already fraught with prosecutorial difficulties, we decline to hold that the Equal Protection Clause requires a legislature to enact a statute so broad that it may well be incapable of enforcement.

* * *

In upholding the California statute we also recognize that this is not a case where a statute is being challenged on the grounds that it "invidiously discriminates" against females. To the contrary, the statute places a burden on males which is not shared by females. But we find nothing to suggest that men, because of past discrimination or peculiar disadvantages, are in need of the special solicitude of the courts. * * * As we have held, the statute instead reasonably reflects the fact that the consequences of sexual intercourse and pregnancy fall more heavily on the female than on the male.

Accordingly the judgment of the California Supreme Court is *Affirmed.*

* * *

JUSTICE BLACKMUN, concurring in the judgment.

It is gratifying that the plurality recognizes that "[a]t the risk of stating the obvious, teenage pregnancies ... have increased dramatically over the last two decades" and "have significant social, medical, and economic consequences for both the mother and her child, and the State." There have been times when I have wondered whether the Court was capable of this perception, particularly when it has struggled with the different but not unrelated problems that attend abortion issues.

* * *

I think, too, that it is only fair, with respect to this particular petitioner, to point out that his partner, Sharon, appears not to have been an unwilling participant in at least the initial stages of the intimacies that took place the night of June 3, 1978.* Petitioner's and

* Sharon at the preliminary hearing testified as follows:

"Q. [by the Deputy District Attorney]. * * * Would you briefly describe what happened that night? Did you see the defendant that night in Rohnert Park? 'A. Yes.' 'Q. Where did you first meet him?' 'A. At a bus stop.' 'Q. Was anyone with you?' 'A. My sister.' 'Q. Was anyone with the defendant?' 'A. Yes.' 'Q. How many people were with the defendant?' 'A. Two.' 'Q. Now, after you met the defendant, what happened?' 'A. We walked down to the railroad tracks.' 'Q. What happened at the railroad tracks?' 'A. We were drinking at the railroad tracks and we walked over to this bush and he started kissing me and stuff, and I was kissing him back, too, at first. Then, I was telling him to stop—'Q. Yes.' 'A.—and I was telling him to slow down and stop.' He said, 'Okay, okay.' But then he just kept doing it. He just kept doing it * * *. We was laying there and we were kissing each other, and then he asked me if I wanted to walk him over to the park; so we walked over to the park and we sat down on a bench and then he started kissing me again and we were laying on the bench. And he told me to take my pants off. I said, 'No,' and I was trying to

Sharon's nonacquaintance with each other before the incident; their drinking; their withdrawal from the others of the group; their foreplay, in which she willingly participated and seems to have encouraged; and the closeness of their ages (a difference of only one year and 18 days) are factors that should make this case an unattractive one to prosecute at all, and especially to prosecute as a felony, rather than as a misdemeanor chargeable under § 261.5. But the State has chosen to prosecute in that manner, and the facts, I reluctantly conclude, may fit the crime.

JUSTICE BRENNAN, with whom JUSTICES WHITE and MARSHALL join, dissenting.

* * *

Until very recently, no California court or commentator had suggested that the purpose of California's statutory rape law was to protect young women from the risk of pregnancy. Indeed, the historical development of § 261.5 demonstrates that the law was initially enacted on the premise that young women, in contrast to young men, were to be deemed legally incapable of consenting to an act of sexual intercourse. Because their chastity was considered particularly precious, those young women were felt to be uniquely in need of the State's protection. In contrast, young men were assumed to be capable of making such decisions for themselves; the law therefore did not offer them any special protection.

* * *

JUSTICE STEVENS, dissenting.

* * *

In this case, the fact that a female confronts a greater risk of harm than a male is a reason for applying the prohibition to her—not a reason for granting her a license to use her own judgment on whether or not to assume the risk. * * * And, if we view the government's interest as that of a *parens patriae* seeking to protect its subjects from harming themselves, the discrimination is actually perverse. Would a rational parent making rules for the conduct of twin children of opposite sex simultaneously forbid the son and authorize the daughter to engage in conduct

get up and he hit me back down on the bench and then I just said to myself, 'Forget it,' and I let him do what he wanted to do and he took my pants off and he was telling me to put my legs around him and stuff—"

* * *

"Q. Did you have sexual intercourse with the defendant?" "A. Yeah." "Q. He did put his penis into your vagina?" "A. Yes." "Q. You said that he hit you?" "A. Yeah." "Q. How did he hit you?" "A. He slugged me in the face." "Q. With what did he slug you?" "A. His fist." "Q. Where abouts in the face?" "A. On my chin." "Q. As a result of that, did you have any bruises or any kind of an injury?" "A. Yeah." "Q. What happened?" "A. I had bruises." "The Court: Did he hit you one time or did he hit you more than once?" "The Witness: He hit me about two or three times." * * *

"Q. Now, you said you had been drinking, is that correct?" "A. Yes." "Q. Would you describe your condition as a result of the drinking?" "A. I was a little drunk."

* * *

that is especially harmful to the daughter? That is the effect of this statutory classification.

* * *

The fact that the California Legislature has decided to apply its prohibition only to the male may reflect a legislative judgment that in the typical case the male is actually the more guilty party. Any such judgment must, in turn, assume that the decision to engage in the risk-creating conduct is always—or at least typically—a male decision. If that assumption is valid, the statutory classification should also be valid. But what is the support for the assumption? It is not contained in the record of this case or in any legislative history or scholarly study that has been called to our attention. I think it is supported to some extent by traditional attitudes toward male-female relationships. But the possibility that such a habitual attitude may reflect nothing more than an irrational prejudice makes it an insufficient justification for discriminatory treatment that is otherwise blatantly unfair.

Notes on Statutory Rape

1. Why does Justice Blackmun regard this case as an unattractive one for prosecution? Do you agree with his statement that Michael's "partner" Sharon was *not* an "unwilling participant"? What would make the case more attractive to Justice Blackmun? Frances Olsen has suggested that the "explanation for Blackmun's distaste for the prosecution seems to be that Sharon did not fit the 'chaste and naive' image associated with statutory rape victims. In other words, Blackmun endorsed the double standard of sexual morality, under which men may aggress sexually against one class of females, but must leave the 'higher' class chaste." Olsen, Statutory Rape: A Feminist Critique of Rights Analysis, 63 Tex.L.Rev. 387, 417 (1984). Do you agree with this assessment? Why do you think Sharon did not fight back; why did she just lie there?

2. Is California correct that men are more willing to risk pregnancy during sexual intercourse? Do you need social science data to support this assumption? Is it appropriate to take judicial notice of this fact?

3. The defense in *Michael M.* contended that the statute at issue should be gender neutral, i.e., hold the female criminally liable also. However, the Court was persuaded by the State's argument that under a gender-neutral statute females would be less likely to report violations because they, too, would be subject to criminal prosecution. Are there benefits of a gender-neutral statutory rape law? What are they?

4. Catharine MacKinnon notes that sex is proscribed with the "virginal daughter and other young girls." MacKinnon, Toward a Feminist Theory of the State 175–76 (1989). Is that what statutory rape laws are all about? Does it make sense that the day before she turns 18 a young girl cannot say yes, and the next day she can? Is MacKinnon correct when she states that the legal age of consent "defines those above the age line as powerful whether they actually have power to consent or not. The vulnerability girls share

with boys—age—dissipates with time. The vulnerability girls share with women—gender—does not." Id.

5. In light of the historical reasons for enacting sex-specific statutory rape laws, described by Justice Blackmun in his concurrence, what are the strongest arguments for striking a sex-specific statutory rape law? Do you agree with the majority that California's statute does not invidiously discriminate against females? What are the strongest arguments for upholding a statutory rape law like California's?

6. Why was this case prosecuted? Why didn't the prosecution charge Michael M. with rape? Was this rape? Would it be rape if no meant no? Would this be an easy case for the prosecution to win under a no-means-no standard? What problems would remain?

7. Does the question posed in *Michael M.,* whether to strike a sex-specific statutory rape law, present a "double bind?" (A double bind is created when both solutions, e.g., legalizing prostitution or eliminating prostitution, result in adverse effects for the oppressed group.) See also Olsen, above note 1 (discussing advantages and disadvantages of sex-specific statutory rape laws).

8. Most states that have eliminated sex-specific legislation like that at issue in *Michael M.* now have sex-neutral rules which require an age gap of two to five years for statutory rape as well as a "victim" under 15 or 16 or 17, e.g., it would be unlawful for a 20-year-old person to have sex with a 15-year-old person. What are the advantages and disadvantages of these two alternatives, i.e., the statutory rape law in California in *Michael M.,* or a neutral rule requiring an age gap? Would the neutral rule have "protected" Sharon? What sorts of girls might tend to need the sex-specific rule most, "good" girls or "bad" girls? How might class and race be relevant to this question? None of the opinions in *Michael M.* seem to illuminate this very real conflict; rather, the majority and dissenters all ignore it. Why?

According to the Alan Guttmacher Institute, almost 40% of girls aged 15 to 17 have had sex at least once, and 64% of sexually active girls in this age group had partners within two years of their age; 29% had sex with partners three to five years older. Laura Mecker, Study: Girls plus older men equal babies, Associated Press, Herald–Palladium, Aug. 13, 1999 at 10A. However, the 7% having intercourse with men over five years older account for almost 20% of teen pregnancies. Id. Why do you think this is? Do these statistics affect your response to the sex-neutral law? How?

9. According to Heidi Kitrosser, "per se age restrictions are well out of step with public, legislative, and judicial thinking." Kitrosser, Meaningful Consent: Toward a New Generation of Statutory Rape Laws, 4 Va. J. Soc. Pol'y & Law 287, 327 (1997). She proposes a new approach which would include: (1) abolishing the force requirement; (2) defining consent progressively, i.e., to be proven as either an affirmative defense or as an element of the crime, it must have some manifestation in either words or actions indicating freely-given agreement to engage in sex; (3) a combination of status and age provisions that make sexual relations between minors below a certain age and adults in particular positions of authority, trust, or supervision over them criminal as a matter of law; (4) gender neutrality; and (5) abrogating chastity and promiscuity provisions. Id. at 328–337. Kitrosser

believes her proposal "more closely fits the notion of adolescent sexual autonomy, with a focus on meaningful consent as opposed to coerced submission or acquiescence." Id. at 321. Can you identify other possible reforms which will provide protection to minors while acknowledging their sexual autonomy? See also Michelle Oberman, Turning Girls into Women: Re–Evaluating Modern Statutory Rape Law, 85 J. Crim. L. & Criminology 15 (1994).

10. Would protections for young women or men under age 18 be needed in a world in which there was real equality between the sexes? Might different rules be appropriate in a world in which women and men are not equal?

11. In State of Florida v. Rodriguez, No. 92–47–CF–JL (July 21, 1992), a circuit court struck the Florida statutory rape statute criminalizing sexual relations between someone over 18 and someone under 16, as a violation of the 14–year–old girl's right to privacy. The minor's mother appears to have been the complaining witness who convinced the prosecutor to bring criminal charges against her pregnant daughter's 19–year–old boyfriend. The judge did not discuss why the Florida statute might be desirable policy. Instead, he explained that he was "inescapably compelled" by the "logic" of the Florida constitution's privacy provision and an earlier Florida case in a very different context (parental notification of abortion statute struck down as a violation of a minor's privacy right). What, if any, are the dangers of this approach? How can minors be protected from sexual abuse if they have a privacy interest in sexual relations with older people? Can you suggest a statutory solution?

12. How would the various feminist theorists discussed in Chapter 3 respond to the question of whether statutory rape laws are discriminatory against (a) men or (b) women?

C. CHILD SEX ABUSE

1. INCEST AND CHILD SEX ABUSE

JUDITH LEWIS HERMAN, FATHER–DAUGHTER INCEST

9–12, 18, 129, 131–32, 163–65, 202 (1981).

[Judith Herman is a psychiatrist who, after becoming alarmed by the number of her patients with a history of incest, found the literature discussing overt incest was "so contaminated by sexist bias as to be essentially useless." As a result, she decided to write about it herself.]

The patriarch of modern psychology stumbled across the incest secret in the early and formative years of his career. It was Freud's ambition to discover the cause of hysteria, the archetypal female neurosis of his time. In his early investigations, he gained the trust and confidence of many women, * * * [women] from prosperous, conventional families, unburdened painful memories of childhood sexual encounters with men they had trusted: family friends, relatives, and fathers. Freud initially believed his patients and recognized the significance of their confessions. In 1896, with the publication of two works, *The Aetiology of Hysteria* and *Studies on Hysteria,* he announced that he had solved the mystery of the female neurosis. At the origin of every case of hysteria, Freud asserted, was a childhood sexual trauma.

But Freud was never comfortable with this discovery, because of what it implied about the behavior of respectable family men. If his patients' reports were true, incest was not a rare abuse, confined to the poor and the mentally defective, but was endemic to the patriarchal family. Recognizing the implicit challenge to patriarchal values, Freud refused to identify fathers publicly as sexual aggressors.[c] * * *

For years after Freud disavowed the seduction theory, clinicians maintained a dignified silence on the subject of incest. Helene Deutsch's massive *Psychology of Women,* published in 1944, makes no mention of it whatsoever. As recently as 1975, a basic American psychiatry textbook estimated the frequency of all forms of incest as one case per million.

The legacy of Freud's inquiry into the subject of incest was a tenacious prejudice, still shared by professionals and laymen alike, that children lie about sexual abuse. This belief is by now so deeply ingrained in the culture that children who dare to report sexual assaults are more than likely to have their complaints dismissed as fantasy. Within the medical profession, denial persists even in the presence of incontrovertible physical evidence, such as venereal disease in children. Rather than acknowledge the possibility of sexual abuse, physicians have been known to assert that children can contract venereal disease from clothing, towels, or toilet seats, an idea that transcends the limits of biological possibility and which would be considered laughable if applied to adults.

Prejudice against the child victim within the medical profession bolsters a similar prejudice within the legal profession. The most famous legal text ever published in this country, John Henry Wigmore's *Treatise on Evidence* (1934), set forth a doctrine impeaching the credibility of any female, especially a child, who complained of a sex offense. Wigmore warned that women and girls were predisposed to bring false accusations against men of good character, and that these accusations might convince unsuspecting judges and juries. He therefore recommended that any female complainant, but especially a girl who accused her father of incest, should be examined by a psychiatrist to determine her credibility.

* * *

c. Rejecting women's accounts of incestuous abuse by their fathers because of his own inability to believe that this problem could be so widespread, Freud posited that all children have incestuous fantasies about the parent of the opposite sex and constructed much of his theory around this assumption about childhood sexuality. Thus, Freud concluded that little girls desired their fathers and fantasized about interacting with them sexually, rather than accepting the apparent reality of widespread incest reported to him by women who came to him for assistance overcoming "hysteria" or other neurotic symptoms.

A half-century after Freud repudiated his seduction theory, incest was "discovered" for a second time. New information was unearthed not by clinicians, who had willfully blinded themselves to the reality, but by social scientists, who were relatively uninfluenced by psychoanalytic tradition. * * *

The results [of the social scientists' surveys] were remarkably consistent. One fifth to one third of all women reported that they had had some sort of childhood sexual encounter with an adult male. Between four and twelve percent of all women reported a sexual experience with a relative, and one woman in one hundred reported a sexual experience with her father or stepfather.

* * *

Incest was rediscovered for a third time in the 1970s by the women's liberation movement. As feminists brought the reality of sexual oppression to public consciousness, many previously forbidden or ignored subjects, such as rape, wife-beating, and sexual abuse of children, became legitimate topics for serious research. And this time, the information could not be suppressed once it was uncovered, for it began to reach the awareness of those who stood in the greatest need of knowledge, namely, the victims themselves.

* * *

Most incest victims both long and fear to reveal their secret. In childhood, fear usually overcomes any hope of relief; most girls dread discovery of the incest secret and do not reveal it to anyone outside the family. They believe that no recourse is available to them and that disclosure of the secret would lead to disaster. But as the daughters grow up, the burden of secrecy becomes increasingly difficult to endure. The child who has remained silent for many years may finally be driven to seek outside help.

Unfortunately, given the current state of law enforcement, child protective services, and the mental health professions, the child victim has good reason to fear exposure. Too often, because of bias and ignorance within the helping professions and the criminal justice system, the intervention of outsiders is destructive to both parents and child. The victim who reveals her secret implicitly challenges a traditional and cherished social value, the right of a man to do as he pleases in his own home. And in effect, if not by intention, society punishes the child who has the temerity to accuse her father. * * *

The precipitant for disclosure is often a change in the terms of the incestuous relationship which makes it impossible for the daughter to endure it any longer. When the daughter reaches puberty, the father may attempt to initiate intercourse. This new intrusion, and the risk of pregnancy which it entails, may drive the daughter to attempt to end the relationship at any cost. Another common precipitant for the breaking of secrecy is the father's attempt to seclude his adolescent daughter and restrict her social life. As the father's jealous demands become more and more outrageous, she may at last decide to risk the retribution which has been so often threatened rather than submit. Finally, the daughter may decide to break secrecy in order to protect younger siblings even more helpless than herself:

> *Rita:* My younger sisters were growing up, and I was afraid he might start on them. I couldn't see that. I could put up with it for myself, I was willing to tolerate it, but I couldn't see him starting up with my sisters. That's when I went to the authorities.

* * *

On the books, the punishments for sexual relations with children often appear to be extremely harsh. In seventeen states, a man could theoretically receive a life sentence for intercourse with his prepubertal child, and in three states (Florida, Mississippi, and Oklahoma), it would be theoretically possible for him to receive the death penalty. In practice, however, these crimes are rarely prosecuted and even more rarely punished. The obstacles to enforcement of the laws against sexual abuse are numerous. The victim is usually afraid to complain. If she does complain, however, she puts herself at the mercy of a male-dominated criminal justice system which offers more comfort and protection to the male sex offender than to the female victim.

Females who press charges of sexual assault are often portrayed as spiteful and vindictive. In fact, most incest victims will endure almost any amount of abuse rather than subject their fathers to the punishments prescribed by law. The threat of severe penalties for sexual crimes does little to deter fathers from molesting their children; it does a great deal, however, to reinforce the secrecy of the forbidden relationship. Incestuous fathers are usually keenly aware that they are breaking the law, and often they enjoin their daughters to silence by portraying the terrifying punishments which will befall them if the secret is disclosed. No matter how miserable a daughter may be, she is likely to remain silent as long as she fears that a word from her will loose the full vengeance of the law upon her father, her family, and herself:

> *Rita:* Although he was a no-good bastard, he did try to keep us together, which I knew was my mother's wish. And all I could do was picture my father in prison for years to come, without his kids, with nobody. All I could visualize was him sitting in a cell by himself, just thinking, you know. That hurt. I could picture my father going home from work, walking up the stairs to our apartment, opening the door expecting to find us kids running around, and there'd be nobody there. Then he'd turn around and there'd be two detectives waiting to take him to the police station. And I didn't like that picture. It seemed so cold, unfeeling, hard, something like that. That wasn't the type of person I was.

The daughter does not want to see her father punished. She wants him to stop abusing her, to start behaving like a trustworthy parent, and to make amends for his past mistreatment. If she is very alienated from her father or has despaired of his ability to reform, she may want him to leave the family; rarely does she want to see him in prison. She turns to the law only in desperation, when the incestuous relationship has become so unbearable that she is willing to take any risk in order to put an end to it.

It is difficult to estimate the percentage of incest cases which reach the state of a formal complaint. In our study, three out of the forty victims (7.5 percent) filed charges with the police. In a similar study of clinic patients in California, seven out of thirty-eight cases (17 percent) reached the preliminary stages of court involvement. Estimates that derive from general surveys rather than from clinical literature are even lower. In one study, only six percent of over three hundred women who had had sexual experiences with adults before the age of thirteen recalled that the incident had been reported to the police. And in the state of Illinois, the Child Advocate Association of Chicago estimated that only about three percent of the approximately 22,000 cases of intrafamily sexual abuse are reported to the police each year.

Even when legal proceedings are begun, the chances that an incestuous father will be convicted and imprisoned are remote. As a defendant charged with a sexual offense, he has vastly greater legal protection than the child who accuses him. First, he has the constitutional rights, guaranteed to all criminal defendants, to be considered innocent until proven guilty, to confront his accuser in a public trial, and to cross-examine any witness against him. These safeguards, designed for adversary proceedings between adults, give an enormous advantage to the defendant, where the only witness for the prosecution is a child, dependent on his care and habitually obedient to his authority. In addition, many states require corroboration of the victim's testimony against any person accused of sex offenses. Since the incestuous relationship almost always occurs in secrecy, this requirement makes conviction of the father virtually impossible.

* * *

Prosecution of a case of incest usually takes from four months to over a year. From the time of the initial complaint until final disposition of the case, the father is at liberty and, unless specifically restricted by the court, has free access to his wife and daughters. In no other criminal situation does the defendant have such power over the complainant. Though some fathers confess after the charge is made, many steadfastly deny the daughter's accusations and relentlessly pressure their daughters to retract the charges. Many mothers rally to the fathers' side. Even if they believe their daughters, they plead with them to drop the charges. If the daughter persists against her parents' will, she may be vilified, ostracized, and threatened with expulsion from the family. Few girls are strong enough to withstand this kind of pressure without wavering. A twelve-year-old girl, who recanted on the witness stand, explained her reasons: "We went to court and my mother told me to lie. I told her I'm not gonna tell no lie. But she said you better. I didn't know what she was gonna do, so I went ahead and told them it wasn't true. Then after that I had to go see a detective. He said he believed me, he knew my story was true. I cried about it because I couldn't change what I had done. Then my father came around and asked me to have sex with him again."

* * *

The sexual abuse of children is as old as patriarchy itself. Fathers have had sexual relations with their children from time immemorial, and they are likely to continue to do so for a long time to come. As long as fathers dominate their families, they will have the power to make sexual use of their children. Most fathers will choose not to exercise this power; but as long as the prerogative is implicitly granted to all men, some men will use it.

If incestuous abuse is indeed an inevitable result of patriarchal family structure, then preventing sexual abuse will ultimately require a radical transformation of the family. The rule of the father will have to yield to the cooperative rule of both parents, and the sexual division of labor will have to be altered so that fathers and mothers share equally in the care of children. These ambitious, even visionary changes will not be the work of one lifetime.

DEAN D. KNUDSEN, CHILD SEXUAL COERCION

In Sexual Coercion 17–18, 21–22 (Elizabeth Grauerholz and Mary A. Koralewski, eds. 1991).

Throughout history, adults have used young boys and girls for sexual pleasure. It was not until the sixteenth century that laws were passed in England to protect boys from sodomy and girls under the age of 10 from rape. The concept of age of consent, which emerged after the exposure of international prostitution rings, developed only in the nineteenth century and set the age at which a girl could consent to sexual activities at 10, then 12, and finally, in 1885, at 16.

Similar developments in the United States resulted in a gradual increase in the age of consent. In 1886, this age was 10 in most states but ranged from 7 in Delaware to 12 in four states; by 1897 most states had raised the age to 14, but three states had the low age of 10 and five had the age of 18 for girls. Most states now have established 14 or 15 as the age of consent, defining children under that age as incapable of giving consent to sexual activities.

* * *

The concepts of age and coercion are intrinsic to definitions of child sexual abuse. Coercion may take many forms: force or the threat of force, deception, trickery, or other actions the child cannot resist because of his or her ignorance, immaturity, or mental condition. The two basic conditions for consent—knowledge about the social meanings, acceptability, and consequences or risk associated with the behavior and the right to say yes or no—do not apply to child sexual activities with adults because "children, by their nature, are incapable of truly consenting to sex with adults". * * *

Child victims of sexual coercion are more likely to be girls than boys at all age levels. Reports from hospital and clinical samples indicate that female victims outnumber males by a ratio of four to one. * * * However, several studies of male victims indicate that fewer of such cases may be reported officially or defined as abuse by boys or their caretakers.

Based on official reports and various samples, boys appear more likely than girls to be assaulted in public places, to be victimized by nonfamily or strangers, and to experience threats, force, and injuries during the incident. * * *

Most sexual coercion directed toward children appears to be fondling, for both boys and girls at all ages. However, at least two hospital studies found that most sexually abused children experienced oral, anal, or vaginal penetration. Such discrepancies probably reflect sample differences, with severe cases especially where physical trauma occurred more likely to be included in hospital populations.

Most sexually abused children—perhaps two-thirds—are victimized only once. However, forced sexual intercourse that is perpetrated by family members or friends rather than strangers is more likely to involve multiple contacts over an extended period. Actions over an extended period of time may take the form of a courting process during which the victim is groomed for further, and more intrusive, experiences. Thus, the duration of the abuse is associated with the type and perpetrator of sexual coercion.

For female victims of all ages, men are the perpetrators in 95 percent or more of the cases. When both boy and girl victims are included in the analyses, more women are likely to be involved as perpetrators.

Notes on Child Sex Abuse

1. Why do you think laws against incest evolved? To protect children or out of concern about genetic inbreeding? See Leigh B. Bienen, Defining Incest, 92 Nw. Univ. L. Rev. 1501 (1998) (extensive discussion of U.S. legal treatment of incest).

2. Do you think adults believe children who say they have been abused? Do you think that Freud's suppression of his discovery of childhood sexual abuse is related to the contemporary disbelief of children's accounts of sex abuse? Or of the life experiences recounted by adult female patients? See Jeffrey M. Masson, The Assault on Truth: Freud's Suppression of the Seduction Theory 107–44 (1992) (describing intense social pressure by friends and peers upon Freud to recant his initial theory about child sex abuse). What about the lingering effects of Wigmore's pronouncement that women and girls were predisposed to bring false accusations against men of good character? Do you perceive continuing effects of this in contemporary evidentiary rules and presumptions? Keep this in mind when you read the cases that follow.

3. Does the potential harshness of penalties for conviction of child sex abuse help or hurt prosecutions of those crimes? Is incarceration the best answer for child molesters? What alternatives are there? What frequently occurs now is that the abused child is removed from the home and placed in foster care, thus separating the victim from her usual sources of security and love. Is this an appropriate response? As a child victim of incest, wouldn't you perceive this as a punishment for speaking out?

4. What do you think causes incest? Is Herman correct that incestuous abuse is an inevitable result of the sexual division of labor in most families, with women primarily responsible for child care? How and why might that be so? In fact, one study discovered that one of the most common characteristics of incestuous fathers is their virtual or complete absence from the home and child care responsibilities during the child's early years. Hilda Parker and Seymour Parker, Father–Daughter Sex Abuse: An Emerging Perspective, 56 Am. J. Orthopsychiatry 531, 541 (1986).

A traditional, patriarchal family structure, in which the father has complete control and the children are viewed as subordinate to adults and females are considered both subordinate and subservient, is one of the more common traits in incestuous families. Lynne Olman Lourim, Parents and the State: Joining Forces to Report Incest and Support Its Victims, 28 U. Mich. J.L. Ref. 715, 720 (1995); see also Pamela C. Alexander and Shirley L. Lupfer, Family Characteristics and Long Term Consequences Associated with Sexual Abuse, 16 Archives of Sex. Behav. 235, 244 (1987). Recall the socialist feminist critique of the nuclear, patriarchal family in Chapter 3, above. What is the solution? Can, or should, the law play a part in regulating family structures?

5. Two researchers interviewed 14 male perpetrators of child sex abuse recruited from prison and community-based treatment programs. Their victims, ranging in age from four months to 14 years, included both sexes, related and not to the offenders. The study found that "[p]erpetrators' accounts suggest that sexual abuse of children feels good to them and that, during the sexual act, perpetrators view the child victim as an object." Jane F. Gilgun and Teresa M. Connor, How Perpetrators View Child Sexual Abuse, Social Work 249 (May 1989). In fact, the offenders "were so focused on their own needs that they were unable to see their victims as anything other than sources of pleasure." Id. at 250. How does this relate to Catharine MacKinnon's view, in Chapter 4, above, that women must be objectified in order for men to be able to perform sexually? The more child care responsibilities a father has during the child's early years, the less likely he is to sexually abuse the child. See Lourim, above note 4, at 722. Do you think that is because the more care a father gives to a child, the more likely he is to view the child as a person and not an object (or "his property")?

Russell states that approximately one in six women are abused by family members before the age of 18 and one in approximately eight are so abused before the age of 14. When non-family abuse is included, over one quarter of girls have experienced sexual abuse before the age of 14, and over one third by the age of 18 years. Diana E.H. Russell, The Secret Trauma: Incest in the Lives of Girls and Women 74 (1986). In one study, fathers committed the abuse in 30% and step-fathers in 41% of the cases. Lourim, above, at 718.

Knowing these statistics, do you think fathers should have a greater role in rearing daughters? Should they be awarded sole custody of daughters?

6. Does it surprise you that girls are four times more likely to be sexually abused than boys? How do you explain this?

7. Current evidence suggests about 5% of abused girls and 20% of abused boys are victimized by females. Russell, above note 5, at 312. Does this surprise you? Do you think that women sexually abuse children for the same reasons that men do? Some evidence suggests that, rather than becoming child molesters themselves, women who are molested as children continue a pattern of victimization as adults. See Herman, above, at 29.

8. Can incest be non-abusive? Diana Russell contends that when brothers and sisters or cousins who are peers engage in mutually desired sex play, it is not abusive. Russell, above note 5, at 39. Do you agree? Can sexual relationships between parents and children be non-abusive? Why or why not?

9. Is creating a statutory age of consent appropriate, or should there be a case by case determination of whether a specific person is competent to consent? How does this relate to the issues in the *Michael M.* case above? The North American Man–Boy Love Association (NAMBLA) wants to remove any legal age of consent. What arguments can you make in support of NAMBLA's position? In opposition? How would a proponent of the feminist theories discussed in Chapter 3 respond to NAMBLA?

2. CRIMINAL PROSECUTION OF CHILD SEX ABUSE

PEOPLE v. TINSLEY

Court of Appeals of California, 1992.

8 Cal.Rptr.2d 745.

[In denying review, the California Supreme Court ordered that the opinion be not officially published.]

Dwaine Beverly Tinsley appeals his convictions for 5 counts of child molestation. A primary issue for resolution is whether pornographic visual material repeatedly shown to a minor victim of alleged sex crimes by the perpetrator is relevant solely because it may have subjected the child to an atmosphere of sexual permissiveness. We conclude that such evidence is irrelevant and highly prejudicial where the prosecution has failed to establish any evidentiary link between exhibition of the pornographic material and commission of the alleged offenses. On this basis we reverse the convictions and order that defendant be afforded a new trial.

* * *

At the time of the alleged offenses, appellant was a cartoonist for Hustler Magazine, a publication which he states specializes in sexual/social outrage. Appellant's cartoons were drawn in his studio at his residence. They concerned sexually explicit subjects, as well as political, ethical, racial, religious and other topics. He concedes the cartoons were intended to offend the public. A cartoon character appellant created was "Chester the Molester," who he depicted as molesting young girls. The trial court allowed the prosecution to introduce into evidence some 3,200 cartoons, including sexual and non-sexual topics, which were contained in published anthologies or collections of Hustler cartoons. Not all of the cartoons were drawn by appellant.

The alleged victim in this case is appellant's daughter, A. A. was born in 1970 to appellant and B. Until she was 13 years old, A. lived with her mother. B. was physically abusive to A. A. went to live with appellant after he obtained custody of her. Appellant was married to "Mama S." and they had a daughter, S.

A. testified to having a long-term sexual relationship with appellant. According to her testimony, the alleged crimes started when she was 11 years old while visiting appellant. He allegedly put his fingers into her vagina. She stated that several other similar incidents occurred over the following several years.

A. testified that she and appellant began having sexual intercourse several months after she moved into his home. These episodes were fairly routine. Mama S. and daughter S. would be out of the house. Appellant would ask A. if she wanted to lie down. A. and appellant would go into the master bedroom and undress. A. would orally copulate appellant until he achieved an erection. They would then have vaginal intercourse. Appellant would ejaculate outside A. unless she was menstruating. Appellant would on occasion orally copulate A.

At trial, A. recalled about seven specific instances when she and appellant had sexual intercourse. These episodes allegedly occurred during a four-year period up to the time A. was a senior in high school.

A. testified that she knew what her father did for employment even before living with him. She had access to appellant's study and to his cartoons without restriction. She liked to be in her father's study with him, and used to watch him draw. She was familiar with the anthologies of cartoons admitted into evidence and with the character Chester the Molester. Appellant had on several occasions given her autographed copies of the anthologies to give to her friends at school.

Besides making his drawings available to A., A. testified that appellant also showed her his monthly work product of about 40 cartoons. There was no discussion of the cartoons; appellant would simply show them to her. On occasion, appellant would show A. a specific cartoon. A. testified that some of these reminded her of the sex she had with appellant. One she remembered showed a woman lying on the bed with a man after sex and the caption read: " 'Phew, that was the best 20 seconds of my life.' " Another showed a man pleading with a woman for sex.

In addition, A. testified that appellant would sometimes show her a cartoon and ask her if it looked familiar. A. testified that these drawings were usually about sex.

Once A. heard appellant say in a telephone conversation words to the effect that one had to experience things to write about them. She testified that she once asked appellant if he got any ideas from her, and he said yes, stating he also got ideas from Mama S. and daughter S. Appellant told A. that she was the inspiration for one cartoon showing a teenager hitchhiking with a sign which read: " 'Alienated teenager. Please give me a free ride to adulthood.' "

A. recognized one cartoon shown to her by the prosecutor which portrayed a girl talking on the telephone and a man was about to put his hand into her pants. The caption read: " 'Gee, I'd love to go to the drive-in, Tommy, but my dad has some, oh, extra household chores for me to do tonight.' "

A. also was familiar with several other cartoons shown to her by the prosecutor which featured Chester the Molester. One showed Chester surrounded by three naked little girls. The caption read: " 'It's 11:00. Do you know where your children are?' " The other depicted Chester at a playground lying at the bottom of a slide with his tongue hanging out and a girl going down the slide with her legs open. A third cartoon showed Chester sitting with his pants down and a puppet on his penis. A young girl is looking at him, smiling. The caption read: " 'Come on, sugar, give widdo Rodney a kiss kiss.' " A. further testified that she was familiar with a cartoon showing three little boys watching their father masturbate as he read a girlie magazine while their mother looked on. The caption stated: " 'Honestly, Newton, do you really think this is the time and place to show the boys how to masturbate?' "

A. never told anyone about the sexual relationship she had with appellant while she was living with him. Before moving into appellant's home, she told a girlfriend about the initial incident with appellant when he put his fingers in her vagina. However, when A. saw her friend did not believe her, she told the friend the incident never happened.

A. used marijuana while living with appellant. In high school, she started using cocaine. As her use increased, she became more rebellious at home. Her relationship with appellant broke down. Appellant and Mama S. sent A. to a therapist. The therapist testified that while counseling A. she never learned of A.'s alleged sexual relationship with appellant.

A. eventually moved out of appellant's home into a residence she shared with her boyfriend Mike Cohen. A. did not tell Cohen about her alleged sexual relationship with appellant. One day, Cohen overheard A. talking to her father on the telephone. A. had called him to ask for money and he had refused. A. threatened to expose the secret she had with him. After A. hung up the telephone, Cohen called appellant and confronted him with molesting A. Appellant denied it.

Several weeks later, A. told her boss at work about her relationship with appellant. Her boss, a former police officer, contacted the police. The police arranged for a "cool call," that is, for A. to call appellant and confront him with their relationship while being tape recorded. During the call, appellant refused to discuss A.'s allegations concerning their sexual relationship; however, he did not deny its existence.

Appellant testified, denying any sexual contact with A. His defense also was aimed at discrediting A. with evidence of her drug addiction, personality disorders, reputation for dishonesty, and sexual activity outside the home.

Appellant argues the cartoons admitted into evidence did not tend to prove any issue in the case. He further argues the cartoons were introduced by the prosecution for an improper motive—to use them as evidence of his alleged predisposition to commit the charged offenses. His arguments have merit.

* * *

As below, the People theorize on appeal that the cartoons were admissible on the issue of appellant's intent or state of mind. Respondent explains that appellant used the cartoons to perpetuate the crimes against his daughter by showing them to her on a monthly basis, by giving her unlimited access to the cartoons, by giving her cartoons to take to her friends, and by asking her if some of the cartoons looked familiar. Respondent asserts that these acts were intended by appellant to persuade or indoctrinate the child on the acceptability of sex between older men and young girls, thereby facilitating his sex with her.

We disagree. The People failed to present any specific facts showing appellant actually used the cartoons to "indoctrinate" A. Since there is no evidence to support such use, the inference respondent seeks from the cartoons, that they were an aid in accomplishing sex with the child, is speculative.

No evidence is admissible except relevant evidence. Relevant evidence is evidence having any tendency in reason to prove or disprove any disputed fact. The trial court is vested with wide discretion in determining the relevance of evidence. However, the court has no discretion to admit irrelevant evidence. Evidence providing only speculative inferences is irrelevant.

The trial court admitted the cartoon evidence on the condition that A. would testify they were shown or made available to her on an ongoing basis. Yet, that on numerous occasions she looked at appellant's cartoons does not by itself have any tendency in reason to prove appellant intended thereby to induce her into having sex with him. The drawings were appellant's employment product and he performed this work at home.

There is no evidence that the cartoons had any influence on or reflected appellant's state of mind at the time of the alleged crimes. No testimony establishes that appellant said or did anything directly to A. from which the jury could infer the cartoons were used for the purpose of accomplishing sexual gratification. The record does not even reflect what specific cartoons appellant showed A. from his monthly work product. In addition, the theory that appellant needed an aid to induce

A. into having sex is inconsistent with the evidence, which indicates she compliantly went into the bedroom with appellant whenever he asked her if she wanted to lie down.

The only information in A.'s testimony which might have had a tendency to show a connection between the cartoons and the alleged crimes was her statement that she overheard appellant say one had to experience life to write about it. On the other hand, this evidence is insufficient since the record does not establish the cartoons were part of any scheme by appellant to seduce A. She did not testify that appellant showed her the cartoons prior to them engaging in sex. Nor, according to A.'s testimony, was there any discussion accompanying the exhibition of appellant's monthly work product. From all indications in the record, A.'s viewing of the cartoons and her alleged sexual conduct with appellant were entirely separate and distinct occurrences. Respondent's assertion that they were related to each other is merely theoretical.

That appellant might have asked A. if some cartoons "looked familiar" also is insignificant. Assuming appellant had asked this question, A. failed to testify that this question related to any specific cartoon[s]. Indeed, out of the 3,200 cartoons exhibited to the jury, only one involving incest was shown to A. by the prosecutor. As to this one cartoon, there was no testimony by A. that appellant had specifically asked her to look at it or had discussed it with her in any manner.

Standing alone and without any logical tendency to prove any criminal act by appellant, the cartoons merely provided evidence of his admittedly distorted world view, clearly not an issue.

Assuming solely for argument's sake the disgusting cartoons had some relevance, their prejudice far outweighed their probative value. All of the cartoons, in appellant's words, were designed to denigrate every segment of the population. Many were about extremely offensive non-sexual subjects.

* * *

In State v. Nolan, 717 S.W.2d 573 (Mo.App.1986), the defendant was convicted of molesting a minor girl, the daughter of his live-in girlfriend. At issue was the relevance of a "Show Me" book, purportedly a teaching aid for sex education which contained sexually explicit photographs of nude children. The reviewing court held the evidence was relevant to demonstrate defendant showed the book to the victim to make her more receptive by persuading her that sexual contacts gave pleasure and were not wrong. Defendant kept the book in a drawer, easily accessible to all the children in the household. As such, the court held, the book "would tend to create an atmosphere of sex consciousness, ... The jury could reasonably find that defendant's display of the book to young girls of very short acquaintance and outside his family was inappropriate conduct indicating his preoccupation with sex, making it reasonable to believe that he took advantage of the victim."

We disagree with the reasoning of Nolan, which basically comprises the People's theory for justifying the admission of the cartoons in this case, i.e., that they created a sexually permissive "atmosphere" intended to make the victim more willing to engage in sexual activities. As in our case, there was no evidence in Nolan that the sexually explicit material was an inexorable part of the defendant's criminal acts. Nolan merely admitted he had been aroused by the book. The appellate court's theory, that the evidence was relevant because it "created an atmosphere of sex consciousness," dangerously leaves the door open to the admission of highly prejudicial evidence in child abuse cases grounded on speculative inferences about an accused's ownership of sexually explicit material.

* * *

Respondent advances several alternative theories for its position that the obscene cartoons were properly admitted.

First, its claim, that the cartoons had "inherent" relevancy by demonstrating the prevalence of sexually oriented literature in appellant's home, seriously misconstrues the law. We have found no authority for its proposition that some types of evidence are admissible based solely on some sort of innate relevance. The relevance of proffered evidence in every criminal case is determined by whether it has any probative connection to the alleged criminal acts. A piece of evidence which has no probative value in establishing a disputed issue is irrelevant and must not be admitted.

Also without merit is respondent's theory that "exploitation" of an alleged victim may be implied from defendant's conduct, in this case, appellant's showing of the cartoons to the victim. Respondent bases this theory on inapposite authority involving whether a defendant's acts upon another person were accomplished by force or fear. In this case, there is no evidence that appellant used force or fear to allegedly accomplish sex with A.

Next, respondent's attempt to characterize the cartoon evidence as probative of appellant's intent is disingenuous. Absent any evidentiary link between the cartoons and the alleged crimes, no criminal intent could be inferred from appellant merely showing his work to his daughter or permitting her unsupervised access to the material.

* * *

Implicit in the prosecutor's statements about appellant's lifestyle was the notion that if appellant was depraved enough to create Chester the Molester, he must have transferred this sick attitude to the relationship with his own daughter, thereby making it probable that he molested her. The prosecution seems to have been more preoccupied with the fact appellant drew the cartoons than its concern that the cartoons were shown A. Its correlation between lifestyle and criminal act constituted no more than an impermissible use of the cartoons as character evidence. Evidence about a defendant's character which attempts to establish an inference of his predisposition to commit crime is prohibited.

Does the erroneous admission of the cartoons and their subsequent utilization by the prosecution as prohibited character evidence require the reversal of appellant's convictions? Yes.

Notes on Criminal Prosecution of Child Sexual Abuse

1. Rules of evidence generally prohibit character evidence as more prejudicial than probative. See, e.g., Federal Rule of Evidence 404. The comments to F.R.E. 404 explain that evidence of a violent disposition should not be admissible to show that the defendant acted violently in this instance. There are a number of dangers to a criminal defendant contemplated by the rule, particularly the danger that the jury will conclude (regardless of the strength of other evidence) that the defendant, if violent, committed this violent crime or deserves punishment for being so violent regardless of whether he actually committed this crime. There are, however, a number of exceptions to this rule. Evidence of character (or prior bad acts) is admissible to show motive, opportunity, intent, preparation, plan, knowledge, or identity (modus operandi or "signature," e.g., the killer always wore a red ski mask), or weapon (where weapon is unusual enough to identify defendant). Should any of these exceptions be used as the basis for admitting some or all of the cartoons in *Tinsley?* Why might it be especially important that such evidence be available in incest cases? Note that in deciding whether an exception allows admission of character evidence, courts do consider availability of other credible evidence. See, e.g., Morgan v. Foretich, 846 F.2d 941, 944 (4th Cir.1988) (holding that in tort action for damages from child abuse, in light of the lack of other corroborative evidence, evidence that defendant had abused older sister was admissible to show identity, since only defendant had access to both girls); see also Katharine K. Baker, Once a Rapist? Motivational Evidence and Relevancy in Rape Law, 100 Harv. L. Rev. 563 (1997).

How would the California court have responded, do you think, to an argument that at least some of the cartoons were admissible under one of the general exceptions to the ban on character evidence?

2. In *Tinsley,* the defendant introduced evidence that the alleged victim was promiscuous. Should that evidence have been excluded under a rape shield statute? What does her promiscuity establish? Does it, in fact, corroborate her story rather than suggest a defense for her father? Why did the father think this evidence would help him rather than hurt him?

Incest victims have a high rate of suicide attempts; 38% of incest victims have attempted suicide at least once. Lynne Olman Lourim, Parents and the State: Joining Forces to Report Incest and Support Its Victims, 28 U. Mich. J.L. Ref. 715, 716 (1995). Additionally, approximately 41% of female illegal drug users are victims of incest. Jean Renvoize, Incest: A Family Pattern 160 (1982). As a prosecutor, could you use such information to explain behavioral patterns of alleged victims?

3. Should a father who makes his living by creating cartoons about child molestation have custody of his daughter? Do you agree with the court in *Tinsley* that pornographic visual material repeatedly shown to a minor

victim of alleged sex crimes by the perpetrator is irrelevant to the molester's prosecution? What arguments can you make for its relevancy?

4. Pornography is frequently used in child sexual abuse, either to encourage the child to participate (showing the child that the sexual activity is socially acceptable because others do it) or to record the sexual activity (for blackmail, profit, or later viewing by the abuser). For instance, Donald Mobbs photographed and videotaped sexual acts of his stepdaughter. See Mobbs v. Arkansas, 307 Ark. 505, 821 S.W.2d 769 (1991); see also Missouri v. Hassler, 690 S.W.2d 178 (Mo.App.1985) (after intercourse with his 11–year–old sister-in-law, the defendant took nude photographs of the victim). How do you perceive the relationship between child sex abuse and pornography? See also New York v. Ferber, 458 U.S. 747, 102 S.Ct. 3348, 73 L.Ed.2d 1113 (1982) (upholding constitutionality of law criminalizing child pornography because the welfare of the children engaged in the production of pornography outweighed the value of the child pornography). Diana Russell reports that in a study of non-incarcerated child molesters, 42% implicated pornography in the commission of their offenses. Russell, Pornography and Rape: A Causal Model, 9 Pol.Psych. 41, 68 (1988). Do you think this empirical and anecdotal data is sufficient to draw a connection between pornography and child sex abuse? Does this evidence prove that pornography "causes" child sex abuse? Is the relationship between pornography and child sex abuse sufficient for a state to ban or criminalize child pornography?

5. Priscilla Alexander estimates that the 500,000 adolescents working as prostitutes in America see an average of 300 customers a year (less than the 1500 that the average adult street prostitute sees). Alexander, Prostitution: A Difficult Issue for Feminists, in Sex Work: Writings by Women in the Sex Industry 184, 205 (Frederique Delacoste and Alexander, eds. 1987). As a result, there are about 150,000,000 cases of sexual abuse of juveniles that are not prosecuted. Id. Yet current laws focus on the juvenile prostitute as the criminal. Is this consistent with child sex abuse laws? Is there any legitimate reason for distinguishing juvenile prostitutes from other juveniles who engage in sexual activity with adults? Does this distinction in criminal prosecutions imply that juveniles can "consent" to sexual activity?

6. Herman states that incest laws are rarely enforced, the threat of punishment does little to inhibit incestuous fathers, and the possibility of punishment does nothing to rehabilitate them. In fact, many observers argue that legal intervention in incestuous families inevitably does more harm than good. Do you agree? Does legal intervention have to be destructive to children? How can this be avoided? What remedies would you suggest?

7. Herman also notes that incest victims do not want to punish their violators; they only want them to stop abusing them. For instance, in one case the victim told a close friend and her younger sister that the defendant had been abusing her. People v. Manuel M., (unpublished opinion, Cal.App. 1991). However, the victim refused to testify at the defendant's preliminary hearing, even when the magistrate threatened to fine her and warned her that if she didn't testify her father would not be prosecuted and he would be free to continue to abuse her or her younger siblings. Even after appeals to her self-esteem, the victim reiterated that she would refuse to testify because she still loved her father and did not want to see him in jail. Is the

daughter's refusal to testify in *Manuel M.* consistent with Herman's conclusions? Does this problem illustrate the ineffectiveness of using criminal laws to deal with incest? Is there any better way?

8. Some courts have become more sensitive to abused children who take the witness stand. While they are generally not concerned with the intimidation of the children by the courtroom atmosphere, they are concerned with the fear and other intense emotions the children feel when they are face to face with the defendant in the courtroom. In an attempt to lessen such feelings, while still protecting the defendant's Sixth Amendment right to confrontation, some courts have used either closed circuit television to transmit testimony to the courtroom or screens to shield the child in the courtroom. However, in Coy v. Iowa, Justice Scalia found that the use of a screen violated the constitutional rights of a defendant accused of sexually abusing two 13–year–old girls and stated that a screen could be used "only when necessary to further an important public policy." 487 U.S. 1012, 1021, 108 S.Ct. 2798, 2803, 101 L.Ed.2d 857, 867 (1988). However, in 1990, Justice O'Connor found constitutional a Maryland law permitting the use of closed circuit television testimony by child victims of sexual abuse. Maryland v. Craig, 497 U.S. 836, 110 S.Ct. 3157, 111 L.Ed.2d 666 (1990). She articulated a three-part test: (1) the court must make a case-by-case determination to decide if one-way closed circuit television is necessary to protect the welfare of the child; (2) the court must determine if the child would be traumatized not by the courtroom but by the presence of the defendant; and (3) the emotional distress of the child must be more than *de minimis.* Justice Scalia dissented, stating that the Sixth Amendment did not allow a balancing test concerning the victim's interests. Should the constitutional rights of a defendant accused of child sexual abuse be more important than possible further traumatization of the victim? Is the interpretation of the Sixth Amendment based on the model of an adult-to-adult confrontation? Should this make a difference? Can you think of additional adjustments to courtroom procedures to protect abused children?

9. Are the victims of child sexual abuse less credible than other victims of crimes? Why? In a case involving the alleged molestation of a nine-year-old girl by her stepfather, the defendant denied any sexual activity and asserted that the girl was lying. Arizona v. Crane, 166 Ariz. 3, 799 P.2d 1380 (App.1990). However, the court was convinced of the child's veracity because she was able to describe semen, which the court found highly unusual for a child of her age. Additionally, the court found that "the victim's testimony of the one incident where defendant told her to close her legs, taken in connection with the wife's testimony that defendant told her to do the same thing when they had sex, considering that the victim has never seen them do this, or been told that they did this, gives strong credibility to the victim's story." 166 Ariz. at 7, 799 P.2d at 1384. Does the *Crane* case suggest the kinds of corroboration that courts will require for convictions? How often do you think there will be a corroborating witness to the events? Like rape, doesn't child abuse most often occur in private with no witnesses? Under what circumstances is a mother likely to testify against the child's father? In a credibility contest with no corroboration, who is more likely to be believed, the father or the daughter?

3. CIVIL SUITS FOR CHILD SEX ABUSE

CYNTHIA GRANT BOWMAN, THE MANIPULATION OF LEGAL REMEDIES TO DETER SUITS BY SURVIVORS OF CHILDHOOD SEXUAL ABUSE

92 Nw. U.L. Rev. 1481, 1481–86, 1498–99 (1998).

In the past decade, adult survivors of childhood sexual abuse have begun to confront their abusers in court and to demand civil damages for the injuries resulting from that abuse. Because of changes in the statutes of limitations applied to civil sexual abuse cases, these lawsuits can now be brought long after the events transpired, and even in circumstances where the memories of abuse have not been continuous. Thus, for example, children who were subjected to abuse by family members, priests, or teachers, and who for a complex variety of reasons, including repression or dissociative amnesia, did not speak out at the time of the abuse, are now able to hold their abusers accountable. Given the traditional silence about sexual abuse and children's widely held fear that they would not be believed or would be punished if they "told," this marks a substantial turning of the tables.

Civil damage suits not only allow survivors to tell their stories; they also enable them to obtain compensation for continuing injuries, including funds to cover therapy and the other assistance survivors need to recover from the psychological damage inflicted. From the point of view of the community, these lawsuits can expose those who have long escaped accountability, punishing past abusers and hopefully preventing those individuals from perpetrating further abuse. These lawsuits put all abusers on notice that they may be called to account for their actions, thus presumably resulting in more general deterrence. Finally, the publicity generated by many of these lawsuits educates the public, helping to dispel the myths that child abuse is either rare or confined to marginal groups in the population. Hopefully, heightened public awareness of child sexual abuse will encourage greater vigilance and increase protective measures against such abuse.

I. Social and Legal Backlash

The "discovery" of childhood sexual abuse in recent decades has led both to the increased enforcement of child welfare laws and to the development of legal claims for adult survivors. Because most personal injury lawsuits are subject to a two-year statute of limitations, however, the viability of survivor suits depended upon the judicial application of a "discovery rule" to this category of cases, tolling the limitations period until the plaintiff discovered her injury. "Discovery" in the sexual abuse context can occur in one of two ways, depending upon whether the plaintiff's memory of the abuse was continuous or recovered. Courts and commentators have styled these "Type I" and "Type II" situations: in Type I cases, the victim never forgot the sexual abuse, but either failed to understand the connection between the abuse and her injuries or was not psychologically able to sue until much later; in Type II cases, on the other hand, the victim's memory of the abuse was repressed and then later recovered. In both of these situations, most victims of abuse had no legal remedy in the past, and consequently most perpetrators were never held accountable for their actions unless they were caught and criminally prosecuted at the time of the abuse—a vast minority of all cases.

Reacting to this perceived injustice, the majority of states now provide by statute some form of delayed discovery rule for victims of childhood sexual abuse.[3] As a result, numerous suits have entered the legal system that previously would have been barred by the statute of limitations. This represents a substantial legal and social change; for the first time, large numbers of perpetrators of child sexual abuse may now be held accountable for their past conduct. At the same time, or perhaps in a complex relation of cause and effect, a great deal of publicity has suddenly focused upon survivors' claims—popular and scholarly articles and books, appearances on talk shows, movies, and the like. Organizations to assist survivors have also formed, and the therapeutic community now pays far greater attention to treating survivors' injuries.

"Type II" cases, based upon recovered or delayed-recall memories, have been particularly controversial. There is substantial debate within both the scientific and legal communities as to the existence and reliability of delayed-recall memories. * * * [However,] there is solid evidence to support the reliability of recovered memories of childhood sexual abuse. A recent review of the scientific literature reveals that there are more than thirty studies documenting repression (or "dissociative amnesia").[5] There are also verified accounts of accurate and multiply corroborated repressed and recovered memories, such as that involving Father Porter, who molested a number of children during the 1960s.[6] Longitudinal studies have also tracked women whose histories of sexual abuse in childhood were documented in court and hospital records, and found that substantial numbers "forgot" the abuse during some period.[7] More-

3. At least 25 states provide by statute for some type of delayed accrual of a sexual abuse action, of which 16 permit Type I discovery. * * * Other states provide an extended period of time to sue with no delayed accrual. See Conn. Gen. Stat. Ann. § 52–577d (West 1991); Ga. Code Ann. § 9–3–33.1 (Michie Supp. 1995); Idaho Code § 6–1701–1705 (1990); La. Rev. Stat. Ann. § 2800.9 (West Supp. 1997); Tex Civ. Prac. & Rem. Code Ann. § 16.0045 (West 1997).

5. See Daniel Brown et al., Memory, Trauma Treatment And Law 154–211 (1997).

6. When one of Father Porter's victims began to remember the abuse in 1989, he was able to obtain confirmation not only from the perpetrator himself but also from other victims who came forward after the case received media attention. See Elinor Burkett & Frank Bruni, A Gospel of Shame: Children, Sexual Abuse, and the Catholic Church 3–9, 11–21 (1993). A similar case involved Brown University Professor Ross Cheit and other victims of abuse by a boys' choir camp director, of which multiple corroboration was obtained 25 years after Cheit remembered the events. See Miriam Horn, Memories Lost and Found, U.S. News & World Rep., Nov. 29, 1993, at 52.

7. A total of 75 of the 129 women in one study recalled the details of the abuse during follow-up interviews 17 years after it had occurred, and of those 75, 16% reported a significant period of time during which they had forgotten the abuse and then later recovered the memory. See Linda Meyer Williams, Recall of Childhood Trauma: A

over, recent research shows that recovered memories of abuse can be as accurate as continuous memories in some instances. In short, it is clear that memories of childhood sexual abuse may be either continuous or recovered. It is also clear that both accurate and inaccurate memories of abuse are possible, a fact that the legal system, having changed the rules to allow these memories into court, must confront—as it is required to deal with the credibility and validity of memories in all types of cases.

One result of these legal developments has been to help break adult women's silence about the sexual abuse that they suffered as children and to challenge the accepted social order with regard to men's treatment of women. What has been the reaction to this major departure from the status quo? Commentators have described the social backlash resulting from the assertion of women's rights during the last few decades. Parts II through IV of this Essay describe a subcase of this larger backlash: the retaliatory development of legal claims designed to eviscerate newly created legal remedies for abuse survivors.

This legal backlash is a typical strategy of those who are threatened by legal and social change in our society, and has been especially apparent in the area of race discrimination. Just as the analogy between race and sex dominated the development of antidiscrimination standards, analogous legal strategies developed to counter and prevent litigation designed to assert each group's newly won rights. The massive resistance to *Brown v. Board of Education* took the form not only of social reaction and civil disobedience (George Wallace in the schoolhouse door) but also of well-organized legal campaigns designed to deter the exercise of the newly interpreted right to equality in education (then defined as desegregation). Since most of the desegregation cases were brought by a single organization, the National Association for the Advancement of Colored People ("NAACP"), a central offensive tactic was to prevent the NAACP from instituting lawsuits. In Mississippi, for example, the legislature enacted a statute making it a crime for an organization to file a desegregation suit in state court. Virtually all the Southern states passed legislation attacking the NAACP in a variety of ways and seeking to prevent it from filing desegregation suits in their jurisdictions. State attorneys general also filed legal actions seeking to enjoin the NAACP, as a foreign corporation, from any activities in their states. Perhaps because this backlash involved race rather than sex, or perhaps because we are temporally removed from it, we have no trouble seeing the anti-*Brown* legal campaign as a way to continue historic racial oppression by preventing formerly oppressed groups from exercising legal rights intended to redress that oppression. Today, an analogous campaign is at work to impede the exercise of legal rights by survivors of childhood sexual abuse.

Prospective Study of Women's Memories of Child Sexual Abuse, 62 J. Consulting & Clinical Psychol. 1167 (1994).

The organizational fulcrum of this campaign is the False Memory Syndrome Foundation of Philadelphia, a group founded in 1992 by parents accused by their children of sexual abuse.[13] Among its numerous activities, which include local support groups, national lobbying campaigns, and promotion of research, the FMSF coordinates an organized, proactive litigation campaign in this area. Its monthly newsletter publicizes litigation strategies to counter survivor claims and advertises pleading and brief banks that are available for a modest fee, presumably to encourage the filing of lawsuits in other states based upon these models. Moreover, in various states the FMSF has filed lengthy amicus curiae briefs that attack the existence and reliability of recovered memories, aligning itself with the accused perpetrators of childhood sexual abuse in cases concerning, for example, the applicable statutes of limitations, third-party liability of therapists, and the admissibility into evidence of testimony based upon recovered memory. In short, the FMSF legal activity is directed not only at defending suits against alleged abusers, but also at preventing and deterring claims of childhood sexual abuse from ever receiving a hearing on the merits in court.

Among the weapons developed in this campaign are several tort actions essentially designed to punish those who confront perpetrators of sexual abuse that has been remembered belatedly, to deter abuse survivors from filing lawsuits for damages, and to warn off both the therapists and attorneys who might help abuse survivors by exposing both groups to liability based upon novel legal theories [including] malpractice suits by accused parents against their child's therapist [for malpractice, intentional or negligent infliction of emotional distress, defamation, and the like],[d] the use of loss of consortium (or loss of society of child) claims by an accused parent against his child's therapist,[e] and lawsuits brought by accused parents against lawyers who file civil actions for sexual abuse on behalf of their children.[f] * * *

[In Parts II–IV, the author evaluates each of these three causes of action on grounds both of law and of policy, concluding that:

1. Tort suits by a third party (usually the alleged abuser) against a patient's therapist, among other things, violate ordinary legal rules prohibiting most third party actions, contravene professional norms about therapist-patient confidentiality and conflicts of interest, and rob the abuse survivor of agency, accountability and

13. On the history of the FMSF and its founding members, see Moira Johnston, Spectral Evidence: The Ramona Case: Incest, Memory and Truth on Trial in Napa Valley 200 (1997).

d. For an extended treatment of a third-party claim against the therapist treating an adult survivor of child sex abuse, see Cynthia Grant Bowman and Elizabeth Mertz, A Dangerous Direction: Legal Intervention in Sexual Abuse Survivor Therapy, 109 Harv. L. Rev. 549 (1996).

e. See, e.g., Doe v. McKay, 183 Ill.2d 272, 700 N.E.2d 1018 (1998).

f. For analysis of one such claim, see Cynthia Grant Bowman and Elizabeth Mertz, Attorneys as Gatekeepers to the Court: The Potential Liability of Attorneys Bringing Suits Based on Recovered Memories of Childhood Sexual Abuse, 27 Hofstra L. Rev. 223 (1998).

voice by treating her as a puppet of a manipulative therapist rather than suing her directly for her actions.

2. In addition to these general considerations, loss of consortium actions against an abuse survivor's therapist for alienation inappropriately extend this common law cause of action for loss of services to a situation in which the loss is not the result of physical injury, does not result in death, and is the consequence of a conscious choice by a competent adult child.

3. Claims brought by accused abusers against the attorney pursuing an action by the adult survivor against them contradict established principles of attorney liability and third-party malpractice law, on the one hand, and of malicious prosecution or abuse of civil proceedings cases, on the other; they also raise serious problems of potential conflict of interest between the attorney and his or her client.]

V. Conclusion

In sum, each of the three actions described above—third-party suits against therapists, actions for loss of society of a child, and malpractice or malicious prosecution proceedings against attorneys—are unprecedented and inappropriate extensions of the common law. When evaluated in individual instances, they may be seen simply as creative lawyering—arguments for a good-faith extension of the law to protect a client (the defendant accused of abuse). If we evaluate this question in a societal rather than individual context, however, it appears in a new guise: that of a legal community reaching for any far-fetched solution to recap the bottle out of which women's allegations of abuse, long overdue, have escaped. * * * [E]ach of these unprecedented actions should be rejected on a variety of public policy grounds. Some of these policy grounds may vary with the context, be it an action against therapist or attorney, but they share a concern for protecting the voices of those who come forward with claims of abuse.

Finally, preemptive suits against therapists treating survivors and retaliatory suits against attorneys representing them are among the battery of legal maneuvers aimed at keeping childhood sexual abuse claims out of court. Each of these actions should be rejected because they are part of a concerted campaign to close the courts to a particular variety of cases, ones that involve allegations of abuse and noncontinuous memory. Given the fact of widespread abuse, on the one hand, and the vagaries of memory, on the other, some of these claims may prove to be "true" in a legal sense and others not; but broad generalizations about a category of cases will not sort out the differences between true and false claims of abuse. Instead, like other personal tort claims, they should be submitted to judicial scrutiny in all their fact-contingency.

Notes on Civil Suits for Child Sex Abuse

1. What are the benefits of civil actions to remedy child sex abuse? What are the potential disadvantages? How might discovery and the trial itself be problematic? What would you advise a survivor of childhood sexual abuse to consider in deciding whether or not to confront her abuser in a civil courtroom?

2. What are the purposes of statutes of limitations in general? How are those purposes served or disserved in the instance of incest? Can you give examples of other situations in which the underlying harm or injury is not discovered for years and the statute of limitations is extended?

How is the balance between justice for the victim and fairness to the defendant to be struck? How might that balance be different in civil versus criminal cases?

3. In Marsha V. v. Gardner, 231 Cal.App.3d 265, 281 Cal.Rptr. 473 (1991), the court found the pragmatic concerns about stale claims to outweigh the right of a survivor of incest to bring a civil suit against her abuser when she discovered, as a result of intensive psychotherapy, "the relationship of the physical and mental distress she was suffering to the acts of sexual molestation" by her stepfather. 231 Cal. App. 3d at 269, 281 Cal. Rptr. at 474. Why do you think the court balanced the competing interests in the way it did? Does this case demonstrate the need for the law to reevaluate its rules in light of women's experiences of the world? Consider that the victim's natural reaction to sexual abuse may result in disassociation and repression of memories that aid the abuser in escaping civil responsibility for his actions.

4. Would you be more likely to extend the statute of limitations in a Type I case, in which the victim remembered the abuse but did not connect it with her injuries until some later date (for example, as a result of psychotherapy), or in a Type II case, in which the victim suffered from traumatic repression and did not recover memories of the abuse until later in life? Why?

5. What explains the apparent backlash against the assertion of claims by survivors of childhood sexual abuse described above?

4. MOTHER BLAMING

JANET LIEBMAN JACOBS, REASSESSING MOTHER BLAME IN INCEST

15 Signs 500–02, 514 (1990).

The most important studies of incest to date reveal the extent to which the mother becomes the focus for feelings of anger, hatred, and betrayal on the part of daughters who were abused by their fathers. In this regard, Judith Herman reports that "whatever anger these women did feel was most commonly directed at women rather than men. With the exception of those who had become conscious feminists, most of the incest victims seemed to regard all women, including themselves, with contempt. . . .They identified with the mothers they despised and included themselves among the ranks of fallen and worthless women." Similarly, Karen Meiselman found in her study of incest victims that 40 percent of the women expressed strong negative feelings toward their fathers while 60 percent were forgiving, with the reverse percentages being true for their attitudes toward their mothers. Thus, she concludes, as does Herman, that negative relationships with the mother prevail.

These findings are supported by clinical data from an incest support group project that treated twelve girls, ages thirteen to nineteen, who had been victims of sexual abuse. Treatment of these young women through support group therapy reveals that they, too, possess deep feelings of rage toward their mothers. For instance, Janie had been sexually abused by her father since the age of ten. She repeatedly spoke to the group about her hatred for her mother: "I hate my mother. I have no use for her. The social worker wanted me to see her but I said, no way. Fuck you and fuck her. I never want to see her again for the rest of my life." As Janie's attitude clearly expresses, the apparent effect of sexual abuse on the child-victim is to destroy the mother-daughter bond in such a way that it is the mother who is thought culpable and responsible for the violation and betrayal that are experienced as a result of the incest.

Theories of Mother Blame and the Dysfunctional Family

The prevalence of mother blame among incest survivors is a troubling phenomenon, particularly as existing theories of sexual abuse and family pathology incorporate both subtly and explicitly a strong bias toward mother blame. A review of the literature on incest reveals a family dysfunction approach that casts the mother in the role of the parent who is somehow impaired: she is unable or unwilling to carry out her functions as caretaker for her children and sexual provider for her husband, and so becomes a collaborator in the incestuous relationship. The family dysfunction approach thus supports the notion that the mother is in some way responsible for the acts of the father, a view that is consistent with cultural norms that justify male violence by blaming the female victim for the actions of the aggressor.

Theories about the role of the mother in the incestuous family can be classified into the following categories: the mother as colluder; the mother as helpless dependent; and the mother as victim herself. As collusionary participant in the incest relationship, the mother is the parent who, either intentionally or inadvertently, sacrifices her daughter in the service of her own needs. * * *

The subjective reality of the child, as it is constructed through the process of primary maternal bonding and perpetuated through cultural ideology, includes an idealized and omnipotent mother figure around which the child's expectations of safety and security develop. Feminist interpretations of patriarchal power need to take full account of the reality of the child's subjective experience of her mother as the most powerful figure in the child's emotional life if we are to understand fully the processes by which patriarchy is sustained. In turn, analysis of family violence and its effect on the child must take into account the significance of maternal control and influence if we are to offer effective therapeutic support. It must be pointed out, however, that in stressing the significance of the mother in the emotional life of the daughter who has experienced incest, the intent is not to perpetuate the misogynistic tradition of mother blame. Rather, in recognizing and addressing the child's perspective on power relations within the family, it becomes painfully clear that as long as children are exclusively nurtured by women, the victimizers will not be held accountable for their actions.

Notes on Mother Blaming

1. Louise Armstrong, in her 1978 book, Kiss Daddy Goodnight, was one of the first women to speak out publicly against incest. She has since written a devastating critique of how society has responded:

> In these ten years things have become unimaginably worse—for child victims, now, and for the women, their mothers, who try to protect those children. And for survivors, who now find the very stuff of their trauma, their degradation, their violation as children, the common currency of talk show guest "experts" and "professionals"; find their courageous speaking-out transformed into no more than a new plot option for ongoing dramatic series.
>
> * * *
>
> And, of course, we have that immense backlash from fathers' rights groups, which now threatens to re-entomb children and women in silence—in fear for their very safety once again.
>
> This society has now devised systematic torments for children who tell of abuse. We label these torments "help." We now tell children in schools to tell. And when they do tell, we either disbelieve them, or we encourage the empowered intervention system to yank them from their mothers into foster care.
>
> * * *
>
> When a mother now attempts to protect her child by divorcing the abuser, or when she discovers the abuse after divorce, on visitation, there is a near certainty that she will be disbelieved: perceived as a "vengeful" woman in an "acrimonious" divorce dispute. * * *

Armstrong, Making an Issue of Incest, in The Sexual Liberals and the Attack on Feminism 43–44 (Dorchen Leidholdt and Janice G. Raymond, eds. 1990). In fact, many mothers have lost not only custody but also visitation with children they are trying to protect from abusing fathers. As a result, many mothers turn to an "underground railroad" to keep children away from fathers courts have granted custody and/or unsupervised visitation. Dr. Elizabeth Morgan spent 25 months in jail for contempt of court when she refused to divulge the whereabouts of her daughter Hilary, who allegedly had been sexually abused by her father, Dr. Eric Foretich. AP, Girl Wins Damages Over Program, N.Y. Times, Mar. 24, 1992, § A, at 12. Is Armstrong correct that there is a bias against mothers who attempt to keep children safe from abusing fathers? Why might the father seem more credible?

2. In June of 1992 Joel Steinberg lost his final appeal of his conviction for first-degree manslaughter as a result of the death of his six-year-old illegally adopted daughter, Lisa. Robin Topping, Steinberg Loses Appeal, Newsday, June 12, 1992, News §, at 6. At his trial, Steinberg's live-in lover, Hedda Nussbaum, received immunity for her testimony about Steinberg's frequent physical brutality and abuse of Lisa. Nussbaum claimed that she suffered from a mental disability as a result of Steinberg's torture of her over the several years of their relationship. Emily Sachar, Nussbaum Says Joel Drove Her Insane, Newsday, Sept. 7, 1990, News §, at 27. Nussbaum alleged that Steinberg burned her body with a torch, urinated on her, thrashed her genitals with a stick, and psychologically tortured her. Many people, including several feminists, blamed Nussbaum for allowing Steinberg to abuse Lisa. Is this just another form of "mother-blaming," or is it a legitimate criticism? After all, Nussbaum was aware of Steinberg's abuse of Lisa.

3. Mothers of incest victims typically have low self-esteem and are dependent on their spouses both financially and emotionally, making the women less likely to report or try to stop the abuse. Cynthia A. Solin, Displacement of Affect on Families Following Incest Disclosure, 56 Am. J. Orthopsychiatry 570, 571 (1986). Additionally, incest families tend to be "less cohesive and adaptable" than non-incest families, and there may be an "emotional distance" between family members that promotes parental "apathy towards their children" and makes it difficult for children to disclose the abuse to the other parent. Lynne Olman Lourim, Parents and the State: Joining Forces to Report Incest and Support Its Victims, 28 U. Mich. J.L. Ref. 715, 720 (1995). What does this information suggest about the culpability of mothers? Almost 25% of mothers of victims side with the offender upon disclosure, although mothers no longer involved with the offender are more likely to act to protect the child. Id. at 726. Are you surprised by the large number of mothers who either deny the abuse or blame the child?

In one study, approximately one in four incest offenders reported that they did not have satisfactory sexual relations with their wives prior to molesting their children. Id. at 720. Is this yet another way to shift blame to mothers?

4. The question of a mother's criminal liability for physical abuse of children by the mothers' boyfriends was the issue in two cases consolidated on appeal in Illinois. People v. Stanciel and People v. Peters, 153 Ill.2d 218, 180 Ill.Dec. 124, 606 N.E.2d 1201 (1992). Violetta Burgos lost custody of her daughter, Electicia, after her boyfriend, Elijah Stanciel, broke the child's leg. As a condition of regaining custody, Burgos agreed not to have any further contact with Stanciel. Nonetheless, Burgos surreptitiously continued her relationship with Stanciel, letting him assume the role of disciplinarian over Electicia. In 1986 three-year-old Electicia was beaten to death by Stanciel. The Illinois Supreme Court affirmed Burgos' conviction for murder under an accountability statute: "Either before or during the commission of an offense * * * he solicits, aids, abets, * * * such other person in the * * * commis-

sion of the offense." 720 ILCS 5/5–2 (1999). The court found that because the offense committed, i.e., murder, is a general intent crime, the accessory law does not require specific intent. The inference of a common criminal design was based upon the facts that Burgos not only disobeyed her custody agreement but also authorized a known abuser to discipline her daughter. Furthermore, because of the extent of Electicia's injuries, the court believed that Burgos could not have been unaware of the abuse.

In the *Peters* case, the mother's boyfriend, Kenneth Jacobsen, beat to death her son Bobby while she was absent. Peters would routinely leave Bobby in Jacobsen's care while she worked. She accepted Jacobsen's explanations for the bruises and burns she discovered on her son's body over a six-month period. She testified at trial that she never saw Jacobsen abuse Bobby. However, based upon the testimony of other witnesses and Peters' statement at the hospital ("I told you this would happen"), the trial court inferred that Peters had knowledge of Jacobsen's abusive behavior and still allowed him to continue to care for Bobby.

The Illinois Supreme Court held that the parent-child relationship creates an affirmative duty to protect children from threats of third parties. The evidence was sufficient to establish that both mothers either knew or should have known of the serious nature of the injuries their children were suffering. Although neither Burgos nor Peters themselves abused their children, they ignored the danger posed by their boyfriends and, in doing so, aided in the murders of the children.

How would you decide these cases? What if the abusers were not boyfriends but husbands? Would the mothers have the same duty to protect their children from their fathers? If so, would Dr. Morgan, in the case described, above note 1, be criminally liable if she allowed her ex-husband visitation with the daughter he allegedly had sexually abused? Would a court order requiring visitation be a defense in a criminal suit against her? See also V. Pualani Enos, Recent Development: Prosecuting Battered Mothers: State Laws' Failure to Protect Battered Women and Abused Children, 19 Harv. Women's L.J. 229 (1996); Mary E. Becker, Symposium: Domestic Violence, Child Abuse, and the Law: Double Binds Facing Mothers in Abusive Families: Social Support Systems, Custody Outcomes, and Liability for Acts of Others, 2 U. Chi. L. Sch. Roundtable 13 (1995).

5. In two tort cases mothers were found civilly liable for sexual abuse by fathers. See Mark Hansen, Liability for Spouse's Abuse: New Theory Holds Mothers Accountable for Failing to Protect Children, A.B.A.J., Feb. 1993, at 16. Denise Richie, who was molested by her father on a weekly basis from age 12 to 17, when she ran away, accused her mother of ignoring the abuse. The daughter said she was angrier at her mother than her father. The Minnesota jury found her mother jointly liable for part of a $2.4 million award. In a Texas bench trial, the judge awarded two sisters, then aged 16 and 18, $3.4 million in damages against their mother (assessed 50% of the liability) and stepfather. The daughters had told their mother about the abuse, but, when their stepfather denied it, she did not take any action. What exactly is a mother's obligation when a daughter complains of abuse? To report the husband to the police? Should mothers be (a) morally, (b)

civilly, or (c) criminally responsible for stopping abuse by men? What are the strongest arguments on both sides of these issues?

D. DOMESTIC VIOLENCE

In 1998 about one million violent crimes were committed against intimate partners, 85% of these against women.[27] According to the Surgeon General, battering by husbands, ex-husbands, or boyfriends is the single largest cause of injury to women and accounts for one fifth of all emergency room cases; it is estimated that 50% of all married women will be beaten on at least one occasion by their husbands.[28] About one-third of all female homicide victims since 1976 were killed by their intimate partners.[29] In short, domestic violence, or intimate abuse, is a major form of violence perpetrated against women, and remedies for this problem are essential to the security and well-being of women in our society.

Domestic violence was not consistently recognized as a serious social problem until attention was focused upon it in the 1970's as a result of the Second Wave of the women's movement. Beating one's wife, known as the right of chastisement, was long condoned by the common law; the right was not formally repudiated in the United States until the latter part of the 19th century. Yet when the common law right of chastisement was abolished, the case law developed doctrines that continued effectively to shield domestic violence from public intervention—the doctrines of marital privacy and of inter-spousal tort immunity.[30] As a result, although domestic violence was no longer legally approved, its victims had no effective civil or criminal remedies.

The extent of domestic violence in the United States and the plight of the abused woman were widely studied and publicized during the 1970's.[31] The publicity was accompanied by efforts at legal reform, aimed at providing more effective and easily accessible legal remedies for abused women, including orders of protection that can be obtained ex parte (without notice) and grant broad relief, such as child custody, support, and exclusive possession of the marital residence, in addition to an injunction against harassment or even contact with the petitioner.[32]

27. U.S. Dep't of Justice, Bureau of Justice Statistics, Special Report: Intimate Partner Violence 1 (2000) ("Special Report"). Intimate partner violence made up 22% of violent crime against women between 1993 and 1998, and 3% of the violence against men.

28. See Joan Zorza, The Criminal Law of Misdemeanor Domestic Violence, 1970–1990, 83 J.Crim.L. & Criminology 46, 46 (1992).

29. Special Report, above note 27, at 1, 3.

30. See Reva B. Siegel, "The Rule of Love": Wife Beating as Prerogative and Privacy, 105 Yale L.J. 2117, 2150–70 (1996).

31. See, e.g., Lenore Walker, The Battered Woman (1979); Terry Davidson, Conjugal Crime: Understanding and Changing the Wifebeating Pattern (1978); Del Martin, Battered Wives (1976); Murray A. Straus, Richard J. Gelles and Suzanne K. Steinmetz, Behind Closed Doors: Violence in the American Family (1980).

32. See, e.g., 750 ILCS 60/101 et seq. (originally passed in 1982).

Today, all 50 states have some form of civil domestic violence code.[33]

Statutory reform is not effective without cooperation from law enforcement personnel, however. Traditionally, domestic violence calls were either ignored by the police or treated differently from other crimes; often the police would just try to calm the batterer down and then leave without making an arrest; and sometimes they did nothing at all. In 1976, major class action lawsuits were filed on behalf of victims of domestic violence in Oakland, California and New York City. These suits resulted in settlements or consent judgments incorporating new policies on the part of police departments responding to domestic violence calls, including, among other things, pro-arrest policies and informing victims of their right to obtain a protective order and of other available services.[34] Many more police departments reexamined their policies after a federal jury awarded one plaintiff $2.3 million in 1984 for police failure to protect her against an abusive husband.[35]

More recently, domestic violence has been defined as a subject for serious societal concern and study. Under pressure from activists, police departments have become more sensitive to the dynamics of domestic violence, and, as we describe below, have experimented with mandatory arrest policies. Local prosecutors have added special domestic violence units, and some now pursue no-drop or mandatory prosecution policies. Additional resources also became available for law enforcement, training, and shelters under the Violence Against Women Act in 1994.[36] The Act authorized expenditures to the states for domestic violence prevention and prosecution, but conditioned the funds upon the recipient states giving full faith and credit to orders of protection issued by other states, providing government assistance with service of process, criminalizing violations of protective orders, and encouraging, by law or policy, the arrest of domestic violence offenders who violate the terms of a protective order.[37] VAWA also made it a federal crime to cross state lines for the purpose of abusing a domestic partner.[38] In addition, federal funding for shelters was doubled, and new grants were given to train police and prosecutors, set up special units and track incidents.[39]

Some progress appears to have been made, as Department of Justice statistics released in 2000 show that the rate of intimate partner violence against women decreased 21% from 1993 to 1998; and murders attributable to intimate partners decreased from 3,000 in 1976 to about 1,830 in 1998.[40] At the same time, substantial problems remain, and

33. See Catherine F. Klein and Leslye E. Orloff, Providing Legal Protection for Battered Women: An Analysis of State Statutes and Case Law, 21 Hofstra L. Rev. 801 (1993) (providing an in-depth analysis of state civil protection order statutes).

34. See, e.g., Zorza, above note 28, at 54–59.

35. Thurman v. City of Torrington, 595 F.Supp. 1521 (D.Conn.1984).

36. Title IV of the Violent Crime Control Act of 1994, 108 Stat. 1796, Pub. L. 103–322.

37. See 18 U.S.C. §§ 2265 (2000); 3796hh(c) (2000).

38. 18 U.S.C. § 2261 (2000).

39. 42 U.S.C. § 10410 (2000).

40. Special Report, above note 27, at 1, 2–3.

many of the remedies and experiments generate their own problems or exacerbate others. For example, even when an offender is arrested, he is rarely detained for more than a few hours; and the consequences of conviction are typically mild—all of which may leave the woman who signed the complaint a sitting target for further, retaliatory violence. Moreover, the moment when the woman in fact leaves, or attempts to leave, is the most dangerous time; more than half the men who kill their spouses do so after they have separated.[41]

In this section, we examine a number of major issues that arise in a feminist examination of the problem of domestic violence and appropriate remedies for it. We first discuss conflicting views of the battered woman herself, as victim or survivor, supplementing this discussion with perspectives concerning domestic violence by women of color and gay and lesbian people. Second, we examine theories about why intimate abuse occurs—why men batter their intimate partners and whether there are effective legal and/or therapeutic interventions in the individual case. Third, we turn to more general questions involved in society's use of the law to intervene in situations of domestic violence, including the response by police and the debate over mandatory prosecution. Finally, we examine the legal system's treatment of battered women who kill their abusers.

1. THE BATTERED WOMAN

LENORE E. WALKER, THE BATTERED WOMAN

45–54 (1979).

[Lenore Walker, a psychologist, based this influential study upon interviews with hundreds of battered women.]

Learned Helplessness

The area of research concerned with early-response reinforcement and subsequent passive behavior is called learned helplessness. Experimental psychologist Martin Seligman hypothesized that dogs subjected to noncontingent negative reinforcement could learn that their voluntary behavior had no effect on controlling what happened to them. If such an aversive stimulus was repeated, the dog's motivation to respond would be lessened.

Seligman and his researchers placed dogs in cages and administered electrical shocks at random and varied intervals. These dogs quickly learned that no matter what response they made, they could not control the shock. At first, the dogs attempted to escape through various voluntary movements. When nothing they did stopped the shocks, the dogs ceased any further voluntary activity and became compliant, passive, and submissive. When the researchers attempted to change this procedure and teach the dogs that they could escape by crossing to the

41. Martha R. Mahoney, Legal Images of Battered Women: Redefining the Issue of Separation, 90 Mich. L. Rev. 1, 64–65 (1991).

other side of the cage, the dogs still would not respond. In fact, even when the door was left open and the dogs were shown the way out, they remained passive, refused to leave, and did not avoid the shock. It took repeated dragging of the dogs to the exit to teach them how to respond voluntarily again. The earlier in life that the dogs received such treatment, the longer it took to overcome the effects of this so-called learned helplessness. However, once they did learn that they could make the voluntary response, their helplessness disappeared.

* * *

Once we believe we cannot control what happens to us, it is difficult to believe we can ever influence it, even if later we experience a favorable outcome. This concept is important for understanding why battered women do not attempt to free themselves from a battering relationship. Once the women are operating from a belief of helplessness, the perception becomes reality and they become passive, submissive, "helpless." They allow things that appear to them to be out of their control actually to get out of their control. When one listens to descriptions of battering incidents from battered women, it often seems as if these women were not actually as helpless as they perceived themselves to be. However, their behavior was determined by their negative cognitive set, or their perceptions of what they could or could not do, not by what actually existed. The battered women's behavior appears similar to Seligman's dogs, rats, and people.

* * *

Thus, in applying the learned helplessness concept to battered women, the process of how the battered woman becomes victimized grows clearer. Repeated batterings, like electrical shocks, diminish the woman's motivation to respond. She becomes passive. Secondly, her cognitive ability to perceive success is changed. She does not believe her response will result in a favorable outcome, whether or not it might. Next, having generalized her helplessness, the battered woman does not believe anything she does will alter any outcome, not just the specific situation that has occurred. She says, "No matter what I do, I have no influence." She cannot think of alternatives. She says, "I am incapable and too stupid to learn how to change things." Finally, her sense of emotional well-being becomes precarious. She is more prone to depression and anxiety.

* * *

Another point we observed relative to depression concerned anxiety levels of battered women. When these women discussed living under the threat and fear of battering, there was less anxiety than we expected. In fact, in many cases it seemed that living with the batterer produced less anxiety than living apart from him. Why? She often feels that she has the hope of some control if she is with him. Another explanation is that a fear response motivates a search for alternate ways of responding that will avoid or control the threat. Anxiety is, in essence, a call to danger.

Physiologically the autonomic nervous system sends out hormones that are designed to cope with the immediate stress. Once this stress is under control, anxiety returns to a normal level. Or higher levels of hormones are constantly emitted in order to live under such pervasive stress. This reaction will also occur when certain threats are considered uncontrollable. What also happens in this situation is that anxiety does not return to a normal level; rather, it decreases and depression takes over.

How Battered Women Become Victimized

There seems to be little doubt that feelings of powerlessness by both men and women contribute to the cause and maintenance of violent behavior. However, although many men do indeed feel powerless in relation to their control over their lives, it is my contention that the very fact of being a woman, more specifically a married woman, automatically creates a situation of powerlessness. This is one of the detrimental effects of sex-role stereotyping.

Women are systemically taught that their personal worth, survival, and autonomy do not depend on effective and creative responses to life situations, but rather on their physical beauty and appeal to men. They learn that they have no direct control over the circumstances of their lives. * * *

Cultural conditions, marriage laws, economic realities, physical inferiority—all these teach women that they have no direct control over the circumstances of their lives. Although they are not subjected to electrical shocks as the dogs in the experiments were, they are subjected to both parental and institutional conditioning that restricts their alternatives and shelters them from the consequences of any disapproved alternatives. Perhaps battered women, like the dogs who learn that their behavior is unrelated to their subsequent welfare, have lost their ability to respond effectively.

* * *

If battering behavior is maintained by perceptions of helplessness, can this syndrome be stopped? Turning back to the animal studies, we see that the dogs could only be taught to overcome their passivity by being dragged repeatedly out of the punishing situation and shown how to avoid the shock. Just as the dogs have helped us understand why battered women do not leave their violent situations voluntarily, perhaps they can also suggest ways the women can reverse being battered. A first step would seem to be to persuade the battered woman to leave the battering relationship or persuade the batterer to leave. This "dragging" may require help from outside, such as the dogs received from the researchers. The safe houses for battered women are very effective here. Secondly, battered women need to be taught to change their failure expectancy to reverse a negative cognitive set. They need to understand what success is, to raise their motivation and aspiration levels, to be able to initiate new and more effective responses, so they can learn to control their own lives. Self-esteem and feelings of competence are extremely important in protecting against feelings of helplessness and depression. Women must be able to believe that their behavior will affect what happens to them. Counseling or psychotherapy can teach women to control their own lives and to be able to erase that kind of victim potential.

EDWARD W. GONDOLF WITH ELLEN R. FISHER, BATTERED WOMEN AS SURVIVORS: AN ALTERNATIVE TO TREATING LEARNED HELPLESSNESS

11–12, 17–22, 24–25 (1988).

Our assertion that battered women are active survivors raises a fundamental theoretical issue. It appears to contradict the prevailing characterization that battered women suffer from learned helplessness. According to learned helplessness, battered women tend to "give up" in the course of being abused; they suffer psychological paralysis and an underlying masochism that needs to be treated by specialized therapy. Our survivor hypothesis, on the other hand, suggests that women respond to abuse with helpseeking efforts that are largely unmet. What the women most need are the resources and social support that would enable them to become more independent and leave the batterer. (See table 2–1).

* * *

Table 2–1

Comparison of Learned Helplessness and Survivor Hypothesis

Learned Helplessness

1. Severe abuse fosters a sense of helplessness in the victim. Abuse as a child and the neglect of help sources intensifies [sic] this helplessness. The battered woman is consequently severely victimized.
2. The victim experiences low self-esteem, self-blame, guilt, and depression. The only way to feel some sense of control over what is otherwise an unpredictable environment is to think that "if I change my ways, things will get better." But the abuse continues.
3. The victim eventually becomes psychologically paralyzed. She fails to seek help for herself and may even appear passive before the beatings. When she does contact a help source, she is very tentative about receiving help and is likely to return to the batterer despite advice or opportunity to leave.
4. This vulnerability and indecisiveness prolongs the violence and may contribute to its intensification. Some observers argue that this tendency may reflect an underlying masochism in the battered women. The woman may feel that she deserves to be beaten and accepts it as a fulfillment of her expectation.

5. Battered women as victims need primarily psychological counseling to treat their low self-esteem, depression, and masochism. Cognitive therapy that addresses attributions of blame for the abuse may also be particularly effective in motivating the victim.

Survivor Hypothesis

1. Severe abuse prompts innovative coping strategies from battered women and efforts to seek help. Previous abuse and neglect by help sources lead women to try other help sources and strategies to lessen the abuse. The battered woman, in this light, is a "survivor."
2. The survivor may experience anxiety or uncertainty over the prospects of leaving the batterer. The lack of options, know-how, and finances raise fears about trying to escape the batterer. The battered woman may therefore attempt to change the batterer instead of attempting to leave.
3. The survivor actively seeks help from a variety of informal and formal help sources. There is most often inadequate or piecemeal helpgiving that leaves the woman little alternative but to return to the batterer. The helpseeking continues, however.
4. The failure of help sources to intervene in a comprehensive and decisive fashion allows abuse to continue and escalate. The inadequacy of help sources may be attributed to a kind of learned helplessness experienced in many community services. Service providers feel too overwhelmed and limited in their resources to be effective and therefore do not try as hard as they might.
5. Battered women as survivors of abuse need, most of all, access to resources that would enable them to escape the batterer. Community services need to be coordinated to assure the needed allocation of resources and integrated to assure long-term comprehensive intervention.

---

* * *

[The authors describe Lenore Walker's theory of learned helplessness and other authors' theories of female masochism.]

Toward a Survivor Theory

The Survivor Hypothesis

The alternative characterization of battered women is that they are active survivors rather than helpless victims. As suggested above, battered women remain in abusive situations not because they have been passive but because they have tried to escape with no avail. We offer, therefore, a survivor hypothesis that contradicts the assumptions of learned helplessness: Battered women increase their helpseeking in the face of increased violence, rather than decrease helpseeking as learned helplessness would suggest. More specifically, we contend that helpseeking is likely to increase as wife abuse, child abuse, and the batterer's antisocial behavior (substance abuse, general violence, and arrests) increase. This helpseeking may be mediated, as current research suggests, by the resources available to the woman, her commitment to the relationship, the number of children she has, and the kinds of abuse she may have experienced as a child.

The fundamental assumption is, however, that woman [sic] seek assistance in proportion to the realization that they and their children are more and more in danger. They are attempting, in a very logical fashion, to assure themselves and their children protection and therefore survival. Their effort to survive transcends even fearsome danger, depression or guilt, and economic constraints. It supersedes the "giving up and giving in" which occurs according to learned helplessness. In this effort to survive, battered women are, in fact, heroically assertive and persistent.

* * *

The Myth of Masochism

The implications of female masochism raised with learned helplessness have been similarly challenged. As the empirical studies suggest, battered women do not appear to be "victim prone." Women contribute to the violence only in the fact that they are female. As Paula Caplan (1985) in The Myth of Female Masochism forcefully argues, too often the feminine qualities of self-denial, trustfulness, nurturing, and friendliness are reinterpreted as naivete and vulnerability.

Furthermore, it is highly debatable that assertiveness and carefulness in themselves can lessen one's vulnerability. Numerous studies have shown that male violence is for the most part indiscriminate and unpredictable. Gloria Steinem (1983) poignantly alludes to this in reevaluating the severely abused porno star, Linda Lovelace. She likens looking for some predisposition or inclination for abuse to asking, "What in your background led you to a concentration camp?"

* * *

Even in the midst of severe psychological impairment, such as depression, many battered women seek help, adapt, and push on. This is not to say that we should expect battered women, or other survivors of misfortune, to bounce back on their own. Rather, by receiving the proper supports, one's inner strength can be realized, resiliency demonstrated, and a new life made.

This process is one that must be supported by helpers rather than invoked by them. This is accomplished by what some call a reflexive approach; that is, helpers accentuate the potential for self-transcendence in others by displaying it in themselves. The challenge is, therefore, for helpers to express resiliency, determination, and optimism, rather than succumb to the learned helplessness of so many bureaucratized help sources. As a result, so-called clients are more likely to discover and express their own resiliency. This approach is not some pollyanna or positive thinking. It is a matter of community building—that is, creating a place where positive role models promote mutual support.

Shelters have afforded one of the most promising experiments in this regard. Women and children, by virtue of their circumstances, are joined in a kind of intentional community where not only emotions and experience are shared but also the common tasks of daily life. The "muddling with the mundane" in the communal living arrangements of shelters—the negotiating and even haggling over food, shelter, and children—potentially teaches much in itself. If managed effectively, shelter life may encourage women to assert themselves in new ways, clarify issues and fears, and collaborate with other women in need. In the process, the intimidating isolation that so many battered women experience is broken and an internal fortitude released.

Redefining the Symptoms

* * *

The so-called symptoms of learned helplessness may in fact be part of the adjustment to active helpseeking. They may represent traumatic shock from the abuse, a sense of commitment to the batterer, or separation anxiety amidst an unresponsive community. All of these are quite natural and healthy responses but not entirely acceptable ones in a patriarchal (or male-dominated) society that values cool detachment. Not to respond with some doubts, anxiety, or depression would suggest emotional superficiality and denial of the real difficulties faced in help-seeking.

First, the symptoms of learned helplessness may be a temporary manifestation of traumatic shock. Many of the women arriving at shelters have suffered severe physical abuse equivalent to what one might experience in a severe auto accident. What appears as physical unresponsiveness or psychological depression may therefore be more an effort of the body and mind to heal themselves. The women, rather than being passive and withdrawn personalities, are going through a necessary healing process. They need not so much psychotherapy as time and space to recuperate.

Second, the symptoms may reflect an effort by battered women to save the relationship. Seeking help represents, in some sense, an admission of failure to fulfill the traditional female role of nurturing and domesticity. It appears to some women, too, as a breach of the marriage vow to love and honor one's spouse. As several of the interview studies show, battered women do initially blame themselves for not being nurturing, supportive, or loving enough to make the marriage work. It is important, however, to distinguish this initial sense of failure from the sense of an uncontrollable universe which underlies learned helplessness.

Third, the depression and guilt in some shelter women may be an expression of separation anxiety that understandably accompanies leaving the batterer. The women face tremendous uncertainty in separating even temporarily from the batterer. They fear reprisals for leaving, loss of custody of the children, and losing their home and financial support. The unknown of trying to survive on one's own can be as frightening as returning to a violent man. The prospects of obtaining employment sufficient to support oneself and children are minimal for most shelter women, especially considering their lack of previous experience and education. This coupled with the feminization of poverty in contemporary America makes a return to the batterer the lesser of the two evils. At least there is a faint hope that the batterer will change, whereas the prospects for change in the larger community seem less favorable.

* * *

Addressing Patriarchal Assumptions

There is a temptation to leave the survivor critique of community services at this practical level. That is, there are deficiencies in our help sources that need to be remediated to better support the helpseeking efforts of battered women. But this critique fails to expose the underlying assumptions that contribute to the preoccupation with learned helplessness in the first place and to the breakdown of help sources in the second.

According to feminist analysis, patriarchy—a system of male dominance—underlies much of the tendency to characterize women as deficient and to respond insufficiently. But it emerges in the helpseeking of battered women not so much as a conscious conspiracy of males against females but as a style of thought and interaction that is "masculine" in its deference to hierarchy, expertise, technique, and individualism. This approach has emphasized a pathological analysis of problems, a medical model of treatment, and privitization [sic] of family life.

The first patriarchal assumption rooted deep in our society is that problems are caused by some individual pathology. Our social policies tend to address deviance and dysfunction in individuals or families rather than in the structures of society as a whole. In fact, social policy is more often used to preserve that social structure rather than change it. The result is that individuals are to be restrained or managed for the social well-being. Our social science must therefore identify what is "wrong" with individuals and find ways to "fix" them or bring them back to the norm. Allocating resources to women in a way that would increase their social status or power is therefore resisted.

A second patriarchal assumption is that the medical model of professional expertise is the most appropriate form of treatment. The medical model has loosely been characterized as experts treating the problem "within" the person. That is, there is some dysfunction in the body or mind that is responsible for socially deviant acts. This orientation has given rise to an abundance of clinical psychologies that look for the root of our problems in the dysfunction of our thought processes and seek to right them through expert persuasion. Most of these "treatments" are technique-based; they impersonalize the helping process by slighting the emotional nurturing, mutual self-disclosure, and long-term commitment that are so fundamental to the feminine perspective.

A third patriarchal assumption at odds with the survivor notion is the continued privatization of family life. At a time of tremendous social transition and dislocation, there is a tendency to allow and expect families to fend for themselves in the name of autonomy. While families or individual family members may receive "treatment," it is increasingly difficult to obtain adequate housing, child care, income assistance, and meaningful employment. * * *

The point is this: In order to more substantially and realistically address social problems on the order of wife abuse, we ultimately need to relax our underlying masculine assumptions about "the way it spozed to be." We must dare to confront the demands of social reform from a more feminine point of view.

Notes on Battered Women

1. What are the implications of the different paradigms proposed by Walker and by Gondolf? Do they dictate different legal treatment of domestic violence? What if some women respond as Walker describes and others as Gondolf and Fisher posit?

2. Walker mentions marriage as a factor in the occurrence of domestic violence. Yet violence is a serious problem in both heterosexual cohabiting relationships and in gay and lesbian relationships as well. Are we forced to conclude that domestic violence is inherent in sexually intimate relationships in general today? To the extent the institution of marriage is implicated, are there any reforms that you think would decrease the violence? If marriage were not conceived of by our legal system as an irretrievably private institution, would this diminish the amount of violence? How would this impact upon other types of rights for women, especially reproductive rights?

3. How would a radical feminist analyze the problem of domestic violence? Would her analysis be different from that by a socialist feminist? How would a relational feminist view this problem? Would they be likely to reach different conclusions about solutions to recommend? What would a pragmatic feminist say?

4. To what extent is spousal abuse a problem of male-female relations, and to what extent is it a problem of a more generalized relationship between love and violence, sexuality and power?

5. Domestic violence is a substantial problem for African American women; in 1998 they were the victims of intimate partner violence at a rate of 11.1% per 1,000, as compared with 8.2% per 1,000 European American women, and were the victims of murders by intimate partners at a rate of 4.5 per 100,000, versus 1.75 per 100,000 European American women. U.S. Dep't of Justice, Bureau of Justice Statistics, Special Report: Intimate Partner Violence 4, 10, App. Table 3 (2000); Fox Butterfield, Study Shows a Racial Divide in Domestic Violence Cases, N.Y. Times, May 18, 2000, at A16. African American feminists sometimes attribute this violence to the legacy of

slavery and racism, as well as to Eurocentric gender ideology and its notions of both Black and white masculinity: "Those Black men who wish to become 'master' by fulfilling traditional definitions of masculinity—both Eurocentric and white-defined for African–Americans—and who are blocked from doing so can become dangerous to those closest to them." Patricia Hill Collins, Black Feminist Thought: Knowledge, Consciousness, and the Politics of Empowerment 186 (1990). See also Beth Richie, Battered Black Women: A Challenge for the Black Community, The Black Scholar, Mar./Apr. 1985, at 41–42. Yet African American women may be reluctant to break silence about this problem within the Black community, lest they appear disloyal to Black men, and reluctant to enlist the help of the police for protection, when the criminal system has historically treated Black males so discriminatorily. See, e.g., Kimberlé Crenshaw, Mapping the Margins: Intersectionality, Identity Politics, and Violence Against Women of Color, 43 Stan. L. Rev. 1241, 1253–65 (1993). Patricia Hill Collins, among others, suggests that an Afrocentric analysis of domestic violence nonetheless "must avoid excusing abuse as an inevitable consequence of the racism Black men experience. Instead, we need a holistic analysis of how race, gender, and class oppression frame the gender ideology internalized by both African–American women and men." Collins, above, at 188. Can you think of ways in which such an analysis would contribute to the creation of effective remedies for domestic violence in communities of color? What are they?

How is the experience of domestic violence different for women of color and for European American women? Are the ways in which this violence may be experienced differently by the two groups relevant to the question of what should be done to stop it? To the legal response? How or how not? Are the conditions of safety different for the two groups? See, e.g., Soraya M. Coley and Joyce O. Beckett, Black Battered Women: Practice Issues, Social Casework, Oct. 1988, at 483–90 (describing ways to make shelters culturally sensitive to African–American battered women).

6. Women in the Latino community are also vulnerable to domestic violence, a vulnerability that is exacerbated by their overrepresentation in low-paying jobs, frequently limited English, and lower levels of educational attainment. Jenny Rivera, Domestic Violence Against Latinas by Latino Males: An Analysis of Race, National Origin, and Gender Differentials, 14 B.C. Third World L.J. 231, 237–39 (1994). Cultural norms and stereotypes, as well as patriarchal family structures, may also restrict Latinas' social and educational mobility. Id. at 241. Like African American women, they are suspicious of police, prosecutors and judges, who may be culturally distant from the Latino community and have acted repressively toward it in the past. Id. at 246–50. Particularly difficult problems are experienced by women who are either undocumented or immigrants with conditional status, whose rights to remain in the country depend upon remaining married to the abusive husband. See Michelle J. Anderson, A License To Abuse: The Impact of Conditional Status on Female Immigrants, 102 Yale L.J. 1401 (1993). Moreover, Latinas are less likely to seek help when they are abused, and shelters and other social service agencies are often ill-equipped to deal with their needs. Rivera, above, at 251–55. What, if any, legal changes can address these problems? Are there extra-legal programs that might be more effective in increasing the safety of Latina women?

7. In addition to problems with language, immigration status, and mistrust of the police, Asian American women seeking remedies for domestic violence experience problems unique to their culture and community. Asian American communities are overwhelmingly immigrant and often speak a variety of languages (e.g., Lao, Hmong, languages from the Indian subcontinent) for which specialized services—police investigatory resources, counselors, and battered women's shelters, for example—are not available. Karin Wang, Battered Asian American Women: Community Responses from the Battered Women's' Movement and the Asian American Community, 3 Asian L.J. 151, 162–67 (1996). Moreover, female immigrants may have come to this country specifically for the purpose of arranged marriages and are especially vulnerable. Id. at 166–68. Traditional Asian American communities typically emphasize family unity and "keeping face" more than the rights of the individual within the family; and the role of women is subordinate to that of men. Id. at 168–71. Yet, while women are expected to stay in the home, the poverty in which many recent immigrant families find themselves requires many to find work in the paid labor market, thus transforming traditional gender roles and creating a source of threat to many men. Id. at 170–71. Asian American civil rights groups, however, have tended to ignore the problems of women; and European American domestic violence groups have tended to ignore the special needs of Asian American women. Id. at 178–81. The plight of battered women in this community has been exacerbated by the well-publicized cases in which Asian American men have raised a "cultural defense" in trials for murdering their wives, arguing that traditional values about adultery and the role of women should provide either an excuse or mitigation for their crimes. In one such case, a recent Chinese immigrant who killed his wife by bludgeoning her with a claw hammer, was sentenced to manslaughter rather than murder and placed on probation after he introduced evidence that his violent response to her adultery was normal in his culture of origin. See Holly Maguigan, Cultural Evidence and Male Violence: Are Feminist and Multiculturalist Reformers on a Collision Course in Criminal Courts?, 70 N.Y.U. L. Rev. 36 (1995); Leti Volpp, (Mis)identifying Culture: Asian Women and the "Cultural Defense," 17 Harv. Women's L.J. 57 (1994). (In fact, the cultural evidence introduced in this trial was highly questionable. See Volpp, above, at 70.) When, if ever, should the cultural traditions of the couple involved in a violent relationship be considered by the legal system?

8. Domestic violence can also be a problem for Native American women, especially as a result of the destruction of traditional culture. For example, Navajo culture was not only gender egalitarian but also matrilocal, that is, a married couple would live with or near the wife's family, who would protect her from any abuse. See James W. Zion and Elsie B. Zion, Hozho' Sokee'—Stay Together Nicely: Domestic Violence Under Navajo Common Law, 25 Ariz. St. L.J. 407, 412–15 (1993). Forced relocation, forced livestock reduction, and the assignment of title to land, however, reduced the power of women, as men were forced into the wage economy and generally assigned the title to land and livestock; divorce, freely available under traditional law, was also prohibited. Id. at 419–20; see also Donna Coker, Enhancing Autonomy for Battered Women: Lessons from Navajo Peacemaking, 47 UCLA L. Rev. 1, 16–22 (1999). After the deaths of two women from

domestic violence, in 1991 the Navajo Nation Council passed a Domestic Abuse Protection Act, which authorized tribal courts to issue protective orders but also encouraged use of the Peacemaker Courts, which were modeled upon institutions of Navajo common law. Zion and Zion, above, at 407–08; Coker, above, at 32. The Peacemaker Courts use a blend of mediation, restorative justice, therapeutic intervention, family counseling, and Navajo religious teaching and offer a broad range of remedies, including reparations in the form of money, goods, or personal services and referrals to a variety of support systems, including referring the abuser to traditional healing ceremonies. Coker, above, at 35–36, 42–46. Could similar institutions be of help in other communities? What, if any, problems do you see with them? (See Grillo excerpt in Chapter 11 on pitfalls of mediation in domestic violence cases.)

9. Recent attention has been given to the problem of battering in the lesbian community as well. See, e.g., Ruthann Robson, Lavender Bruises: Intra–Lesbian Violence, Law and Lesbian Legal Theory, 20 Golden Gate U.L. Rev. 567 (1990). The legal problem is complicated in the lesbian situation by the failure in some instances of domestic violence statutes to cover lesbians in battering relationships and by the reluctance of many in the lesbian community to seek help either from the police or from a legal system that is seen as patriarchal and oppressive. Id. at 577, 581–91. How is the lesbian battering situation similar to, and/or different from, domestic violence between heterosexual couples? What remedies are appropriate in the case of intra-lesbian violence?

10. Much current analysis, especially feminist analysis, of domestic violence does not capture the phenomenon of battering in the gay community and, indeed, makes it invisible by focusing on female victims, marriage, and male-female sex role socialization. See Patrick Letellier, Gay and Bisexual Male Domestic Violence Victimization: Challenges to Feminist Theory and Responses to Violence, 9 Violence and Victims 95, 95–97 (1994). According to Letellier, based upon his own personal experience and clinical experience in the San Francisco District Attorney's Domestic Violence Project, gay and bisexual men are unable to see themselves as victims, in part because this role is inconsistent with a male social role, in part because they are more likely to fight back, and in part because of their own internalization of our society's widespread homophobia and resulting belief that they are somehow being rightfully punished. Id. at 98–102. As a result, male battery victims are unlikely to seek help; and, even if they do, there are virtually no resources (no shelters, few organizations) available to assist them. Id. at 102. What, if any, legal changes can you think of to address this problem? Changes outside the legal system? How can the experience of gay and bisexual males inform feminist theory about domestic violence and make it more inclusive?

11. The presence of domestic violence can play a role in decisions about custody for children, making women reluctant to leave lest they lose custody. Since the advent of the "best interest of the child" standard for custody, many courts are uncomfortable terminating parental rights because of abuse, even when the abuser has killed or seriously injured the mother. See Naomi R. Cahn, Civil Images of Battered Women: The Impact of Domestic Violence on Child Custody Decisions, 44 Vand. L. Rev. 1041, 1072 (1991). In most cases, courts regard domestic violence as irrelevant to custody decisions

or do not take it seriously, unless the victim proves that the parental violence had a direct impact on the child. Id. at 1044, 1072–82. Moreover, in cases where the woman kills or injures her abuser, the images of learned helplessness and dysfunctionality that may be used to explain why she did not leave are directly counter to the appearance of competence and strength the mother needs to present in order to obtain custody. Martha R. Mahoney, Legal Images of Battered Women: Redefining the Issue of Separation, 90 Mich. L. Rev. 1, 49 (1991). How is the courts' reluctance to take parental violence into account more generally in custody decisions likely to influence the actions of the mother? Of the abuser? What impact is it likely to have on the child?

2. THE BATTERER

NEIL S. JACOBSON AND JOHN M. GOTTMAN, WHEN MEN BATTER WOMEN: NEW INSIGHTS INTO ENDING ABUSIVE RELATIONSHIPS

36–39, 43–46, 93–97 (1998).

[Psychologists Jacobson and Gottman used both structured interviews and laboratory observation to study a total of 201 couples, 63 of whom were in battering relationships.]

Although there is still a tendency for professionals to talk about batterers as if they were all alike, there is growing recognition that there are different types of batterers. There are at least two distinguishable types that have practical consequences for battered women, and perhaps more. Each type seems to have its unique characteristics, its own family history, and perhaps different outcomes when punished by the courts or educated by groups for batterers. * * * [W]e think a compelling case can be made for at least two subtypes, roughly corresponding to our distinction between the Cobras and the Pit Bulls.

Cobras

Cobras appear to be criminal types who have engaged in anti-social behavior since adolescence. They are hedonistic and impulsive. They beat their wives and abuse them emotionally, to stop them from interfering with the Cobras' need to get what they want when they want it. Although they may say that they are sorry after a beating, and beg their wives' forgiveness, they are usually not sorry. They feel entitled to whatever they want whenever they want it, and try to get it by whatever means necessary. Some of them are "psychopaths," which means they lack a conscience and are incapable of feeling remorse. In fact, true psychopaths have diminished capacity for experiencing a wide range of emotions and an inability to understand the emotions of others: they lack the ability to sympathize with the plight of others, they do not experience empathy, and even apparent acts of altruism are actually thinly veiled attempts at selfishness. They do not experience soft emotions such as sadness, and rarely experience fear unless it has to do with the perception that something bad is about to happen to *them*.

But not all Cobras are psychopaths. Whether psychopathic or merely antisocial, they are incapable of forming truly intimate relationships with others, and to the extent that they marry, they do so on their terms. Their wives are convenient stepping-stones to gratification: sex, social status, economic benefits, for example. But their commitments are superficial, and their stance in the relationship is a "withdrawing" one. They attempt to keep intimacy to a minimum, and are most likely to be dangerous when their wives attempt to get more from them. They do not fear abandonment, but they will not be controlled. Their own family histories are often chaotic, with neither parent providing love or security, and they were often abused themselves as children.

As adults, they can be recognized by their history of antisocial behavior, their high likelihood of drug *and* alcohol abuse, and the severity of their physical and emotional abuse. Their wives fear them, and are often quite depressed. But fear and depression do not completely explain why the women are unlikely to leave the relationship. Nor is it simply that they lack economic and other resources: indeed, Cobras are often economically dependent on their wives. Despite the fact that they are being severely abused, it is often the women rather than the men who continue to fight for the continuance of the relationship. It is these couples where the men exude macabre charisma.

Pit Bulls

The Pit Bulls are more likely to confine their violence to family members, especially their wives. Their fathers were likely to have battered their mothers, and they have learned that battering is an acceptable way to treat women. But they are not as likely as the Cobras to have criminal records, or to have been delinquent adolescents. Moreover, even though they batter their wives and abuse them emotionally, unlike the Cobras the Pit Bulls are emotionally dependent on their wives. What they fear most is abandonment. Their fear of abandonment and the desperate need they have *not* to be abandoned produce jealous rages and attempts to deprive their partners of an independent life. They can be jealous to the point of paranoia, imagining that their wives are having affairs based on clues that most of us would find ridiculous.

The Pit Bulls dominate their wives in any way they can, and need control as much as the Cobras do, but for different reasons. The Pit Bulls are motivated by fear of being left, while the Cobras are motivated by a desire to get as much immediate gratification as possible. The Pit Bulls, although somewhat less violent in general than the Cobras, are also capable of severe assault and murder, just as the Cobras are. Although one is safer trying to leave a Pit Bull in the short run, Pit Bulls may actually be more dangerous to leave in the long run. Cobras strike swiftly and with great lethality when they feel threatened, but they are also easily distracted after those initial strikes and move on to other targets. In contrast, Pit Bulls sink their teeth into their targets; once they sink their teeth into you, it is hard to get them to let go!

It is not clear how Cobras and Pit Bulls are apportioned within the battering population. In our sample, 20 percent of the batterers were Cobras. Interestingly, Dr. Robert Hare, an internationally renowned expert on psychopaths, estimates that 20 percent of batterers are psychopaths. This correspondence is provocative. However, our guess is that Cobras constitute a larger percentage of the clinical or criminal population of batterers than the 20 percent found in our study. The Cobras fit the profile of the type of batterer who comes into contact with the criminal justice system much more than the Pit Bulls do. The profile of the Cobra also describes those referred by judges to treatment groups much better than the profile of the Pit Bull.

* * *

[B]attering seldom stops on its own. We found in our research that while many men decrease their level of violence over time, few of them stop completely. And when they do stop, the emotional abuse usually continues.

This is quite important, because most research considers only physical abuse. But emotional abuse can be at least as effective a method of maintaining control, if the physical violence was once there. Once a batterer has achieved dominance through violence and the threat of more violence, emotional abuse often keeps the battered woman in a state of subjugation without the batterer having to use physical force. Since the violence is used in order to obtain control, it is more convenient for the batterer to restrict himself to emotional abuse. That abuse reminds her that the threat of violence is always present, and this threat is often sufficient to retain control. Any intervention which defines success without taking emotional abuse into account will inflate its effectiveness. In our sample, although many batterers *decreased* the frequency and severity of their violence over time, almost none of them stopped completely *and* also ended the emotional abuse.

* * *

[B]ecause psychotherapy is available for batterers, judges often find some referrals for court-mandated treatment irresistible as alternatives to imprisonment, especially since domestic assault charges are often misdemeanors rather than felonies.

Unfortunately, what appears at first glance to be an enlightened alternative to imprisonment is often a mistake. There is very little evidence that currently existing treatment programs for batterers are effective, and much reason to be concerned that in their present form, they are unlikely to stop the violence and even less likely to end the emotional abuse. Yet people in our culture believe in psychotherapy, and battered women are no exception. Therefore, when their husbands are "sentenced" to psychotherapy they may be lulled into a false sense of security, thus leading them to return home from a shelter falsely convinced that they are now safe.

* * *

Violent criminals who assault strangers are seldom offered psychotherapy as an alternative to prison, in contrast to perpetrators of wife battering. What does this tell us about the criminal justice system and how it views "family violence?" Family violence is still regarded as less serious than violence against strangers, even though most women who are murdered are not killed by strangers but by boyfriends, husbands, ex-husbands, and ex-boyfriends. But accountability is a prerequisite to decreased violence. We believe that referrals to psychotherapy, in the absence of legal sanctions, send the wrong message to batterers: they have gotten away with a violent crime with nothing but a slap on the wrist. * * *

We have no illusions about the rehabilitative power of prison, but at least prison stops the violence temporarily and gives the battered woman time to make plans. It also sends a powerful message to the batterer.

* * *

Cobras and Pit Bulls Are Different

We discovered a number of very interesting and important factors that distinguished Cobras from Pit Bulls.

Cobra Violence is More Severe. Even though the violence was as common among the Pit Bulls as it was among the Cobras, the severity of violence was much greater among the Cobras. For example, 38 percent of the Cobras had threatened their wives with a knife or a gun, compared to only 4 percent of the Pit Bulls. Whereas none of the Pit Bulls had actually used a knife or gun in a violent episode, 9 percent of the Cobras had either stabbed or shot their wives. Almost all of the Cobras had beaten up their wives with closed fists, often including choking (91 percent), whereas the percentage was significantly smaller (though still large) in the Pit Bulls (62 percent). * * * However, it is important to note that Cobras hold no monopoly on beatings, since the majority of Pit Bulls had also severely beaten their wives.

Cobras Commit More Emotional Abuse. The Cobras were more emotionally abusive than the Pit Bulls, as evidenced by their significantly higher rates of belligerence and contempt, particularly at the very start of the laboratory interaction. * * * Pit Bulls became more emotionally abusive over the course of the conflict discussion, a kind of slow burn in which they became increasingly heated and began to lose control. In contrast, Cobras always stayed in control.

Cobras Have More Chaotic, Traumatic Childhoods. In many ways we were left with the impression that Cobras had come from backgrounds that more seriously crushed something very fragile that every child begins life with, a kind of implicit trust that despite all their limitations, parents have the child's best interest at heart. Our image was that this horrible childhood background had somehow led the Cobras to vow to themselves that no one would ever control them again. * * *

Cobras came from more chaotic family backgrounds than Pit Bulls, although the Pit Bulls were more likely to have had batterers as fathers. Specifically, 78 percent of the Cobras in our study came from families where there was some kind of violence in the home when they were children, compared to 51 percent of the Pit Bulls. Even this 51 percent figure is high, since in the population at large (a still alarmingly high) 20 to 25 percent of children grow up in violent homes. So both types of batterers are more likely than members of the general population to have grown up in violent homes.

Twenty-three percent of the Pit Bulls came from families in which their fathers beat up their mothers and the violence went only one way. The Cobras almost invariably came from childhoods that were quite traumatic, with violence manifesting itself in a variety of ways, including having very violent mothers who abused them. * * *

* * *

Cobras and Their Wives Do Not Easily Separate or Divorce. The marriages of the Cobras were less likely to end in separation or divorce, at least over the two-year follow-up period of our study, than the marriages of the Pit Bulls. In fact, at the two-year follow-up not a single couple in the Cobra group had separated, and the one divorced couple (Roy and Helen) were still living together! In contrast, almost half of the couples married to Pit Bulls were separated or divorced at the end of two years.

We think that the relative "stability" of Cobra marriages stems in large part from the terrible fear that these wives have of leaving their husbands. However, based on our final interviews with the women between 1995 and 1996, and our informal observations of the laboratory interactions, these couples also seemed more attached than the Pit Bull couples. * * * [T]he typical pattern among the Cobra couples was for the wives to be quite committed to the marriages, despite the violence, while the husbands avoided intimacy, demonstrated ambivalence about commitment to the relationship, and engaged in a great deal of provocative, destructive behavior beyond the violence.

Cobras Are More Violent Outside as Well as Inside the Marriage. Cobras were much more likely to have a history of violence outside the marriage than Pit Bulls. While 44 percent of the Cobras had histories of violence outside the marriage, only 3 percent of the Pit Bulls had such histories. Virtually all of the Cobras who had been violent outside the marriage were violent with a wide variety of people, including people at work and other family members and acquaintances; most of them had gotten into at least occasional violent altercations with strangers. In contrast, the Pit Bulls were almost never violent toward friends or other family members, and none of those in our sample reported violence directed toward strangers.

Cobras Had More Mental Illness. Cobras were much more likely than the Pit Bulls to qualify for a diagnosis of "personality disorder," specifically "antisocial personality disorder." People with antisocial personality disorders have long histories of impulsive, criminal-like behavior, including but not limited to violence. Typically these disorders go all the way back to adolescence. * * * While some of the Pit Bulls (about 33 percent) qualified as antisocial, fully 90 percent of the Cobras met the criteria for this classification. Also, even though the two groups of batterers did not differ in their likelihood of abusing alcohol (both abused alcohol at high rates), the Cobras were more likely to be dependent on illegal drugs such as cocaine and heroin, and pharmaceutical addictive drugs.

Notes on Why Men Batter

1. What are the implications of Jacobson and Gottman's study of male batterers for the legal and societal response to battering? Should there be different legal responses to Cobras and Pit Bulls? Is that possible? Is psychological treatment ever an appropriate disposition for a domestic violence case that has been brought to court? What implications does the Jacobson and Gottman study have, if any, for safety planning for victims of domestic violence?

2. All of the authors excerpted in this section have pointed to the importance of psychological and emotional abuse and its integral relation to physical violence. Is there any way the legal system can address abuse that does not result in physical contact? If so, how?

3. The authors excerpted in this section also agree on the correlation between domestic abuse and abuse in the batterer's family of origin, either as a direct victim or a child spectator to abuse of the mother. How can we attempt to interrupt this intergenerational transmission of violence? What implications does it have for the treatment of domestic abuse by the legal system?

4. Another very prominent expert on batterers is Donald Dutton, a psychology professor who directs the Assaultive Husbands Program in Vancouver, British Columbia. Dutton's research focuses on batterers who fit the profile he calls the "abusive personality," about 30% of all repeat batterers; these offenders' conduct is cyclical and directed primarily at their intimates, functioning to control them and relieve the batterer's own fears of abandonment. See Donald G. Dutton, The Abusive Personality: Violence and Control in Intimate Relationships 53–68 (1998). As study of and knowledge about male batterers have been growing, others present slightly varying typologies and profiles of batterer characteristics. See, e.g., Richard M. Tolman and Larry W. Bennett, A Review of Quantitative Research on Men Who Batter, 5 J. Interpersonal Violence 87, 98–100 (1990); Donald G. Dutton, The Domestic Assault of Women: Psychological and Criminal Justice Perspectives 120–31 (rev'd ed. 1995) (describing typologies by others); Edward W. Gondolf, Male Batterers, in Family Violence: Prevention and Treatment 230, 232–36 (Robert L. Hampton et al., eds. 1993). This expertise could be useful in court, both to prosecute batterers (especially in homicide cases, where the victim cannot testify) and to defend battered women who kill their abusers. Expert testimony could, for example, set the violence in context and explain

to factfinders evidence that might otherwise seem confusing, such as the apparent charm of many domestic violence defendants and their lack of any criminal record. See Myrna S. Raeder, The Better Way: The Role of Batterers' Profiles and Expert "Social Framework" Background in Cases Implicating Domestic Violence, 68 U. Colo. L. Rev. 147, 182–84 (1979). Yet profile evidence is generally found inadmissible in the prosecution's case because of the ban on character and prior bad acts evidence. Id. at 160–67; see Fed. R. Evid. 404. Do you think these rules of evidence should be changed in cases involving this type of repeated, cyclical offense? If so, how would you change them? Are there other ways in which such evidence could be admitted, so long as the expert did not testify that the defendant conformed to the profile?

5. The causes of battering appear to be sociological, political, and psychological. If so, what possible solutions are there for the problem of spousal abuse in the individual case? In the aggregate? Would in-depth psychotherapy with each offender (or potential offender?) be necessary?

6. Wayne Ewing argues that male abusiveness is not simply tolerated in our society, but that "[v]iolence is taught as the normal, appropriate and necessary behavior of power and control," and can only be understood in the context of what he calls "the civic advocacy of violence":

> The teaching of violence is so pervasive, so totally a part of male experience, that I think it best to acknowledge this teaching as a *civic,* rather than as a cultural or as a social phenomenon. * * *
>
> Analyses which interweave the advocacy of male violence with "Super-Bowl Culture" have never been refuted. It is too obvious. Civic expectations—translated into professionalism, financial commitments, city planning for recreational space, the raising of male children for competitive sport, * * *—all result in the monument of the National Football League, symbol and reality at once of the advocacy of violence.

Ewing, The Civic Advocacy of Violence, in Men's Lives 301, 304–05 (Michael S. Kimmel and Michael A. Messner, eds. 1995). What do you think of this argument? If you agree, what does this say about the possibility of solving the problem of domestic violence in our society as a whole? If the attributes of batterers are simply those of "Everyman," what is to be done? How can one explain the fact that some men do *not* batter their spouses and girlfriends? Moreover, even if violence is general, why are women its target?

7. Jeffrey Fagan, who has studied desistance from domestic violence and compared it with desistance from other types of criminal behavior, reports that early legal intervention yields better prospects for desistance than intervention later in a protracted battering relationship. Jeffrey Fagan, Cessation of Family Violence: Deterrence and Dissuasion, in Family Violence 377, 415 (Lloyd Ohlin and Michael Tonry, eds. 1989). He argues for combining aversive experiences for the batterer with economic and social supports for victims to correct the power imbalance between victims and their batterers:

> * * * Aversive experiences play an important role in forming the resolve to desist, as does the decline of gratification associated with it. Extraction from the social systems that support and validate wife

> battery, the substitution of new social networks for batterers with different normative values, balancing marital power (through help sources for victims), and identity transformations that embed batterers within new networks are critical elements of desistance. The maintenance of external restraints, both by significant relationships and others, reinforces the new behavioral norms and restrains the old ones. * * *
>
> Shelters are important in balancing the power of victims with batterers and allowing victims to establish internal sanctions absent fears of physical reprisal. Other help sources help victims avoid economic reprisals and provide social supports for demanding an end to violence. They directly allow victims to raise the personal "costs" of continuing violence. Criminal sanctions also restrain battering by raising its social costs. Massive public education can erode the cultural supports for violence by bringing to public debate the consequences of traditional sex roles. In other words, policy must attend to the postcessation environment to provide *cultural* supports for the changing status of women.

Id. at 413, 415. If you were a policymaking official in a major metropolitan area, what specific programs would you recommend to effectuate the ambitious goals outlined in this excerpt? How would they be financed? What administrative agencies would run them? Would you rely primarily upon public programs, or would some of them be privately run? Be specific.

Why should women have to leave home and go to a shelter? Why not remove the batterer from the home? How could that be accomplished?

8. Several authors have noted how the defense of provocation, or heat-of-passion homicide (at least as it has been developed in recent American case law), in fact resembles the justifications batterers give for their conduct; it is often used to reduce the charge of murder to manslaughter in cases where men kill their intimate partners—or, more frequently, their ex-partners—because of real or imagined infidelity and the woman's attempts to leave the relationship. See Donna K. Coker, Heat of Passion and Wife Killing: Men Who Batter/Men Who Kill, 2 S. Cal. Rev. L. & Women's Stud. 71, 106–11 (1992); Victoria Nourse, Passion's Progress: Modern Law Reform and the Provocation Defense, 106 Yale L.J. 1331, 1351–66 (1997). Victoria Nourse's extensive study of intimate homicide cases from 1980 to 1995 shows that in 2/3 of the cases, juries were allowed to return a verdict of manslaughter based on provocation where the couple was separated, divorced, or estranged, or in which the victim sought to leave. Nourse, above, at 1345–47. Indeed, most spousal murder cases resulting in conviction result in a manslaughter rather than a murder disposition. Id. at 1348 (citing Department of Justice statistics). Should the heat-of-passion defense be abolished for this reason? What would be the impact upon the defense of battered women who kill their abusers? Can you think of ways to reform the defense without abolishing it? See Nourse, above, at 1389–99 (proposing a theory of "warranted excuse").

3. POLICE RESPONSE TO DOMESTIC VIOLENCE

HYNSON v. CITY OF CHESTER

United States Court of Appeals, Third Circuit, 1988.

864 F.2d 1026.

Shortly after midnight on October 15, 1984, Alesia Hynson was shot and killed by her former boyfriend, Jamil Gandy, the father of one of her two children. Prior to her death, Hynson had sought and obtained a temporary protection from abuse order, which had expired. Under Pennsylvania law, a defendant who violates a valid protection from abuse order can be arrested without a warrant and held in indirect criminal contempt.

On October 14, 1984, Ms. Hynson accompanied her sister and her cousin to an "after hours club" in the City of Chester, leaving her children with a babysitter. While at the club Hynson was approached and threatened by Gandy. After Gandy left the club, he went to Hynson's residence and broke a window, attempting to gain entry. Frightened, the babysitter called the police, but no one responded. (The photocopy of a page in the police log book indicates the presence of an incorrect address.) When the women returned from the club and heard of Gandy's attempted entry, Hynson's sister called the police.

Three officers responded to the call * * *. The women explained that Gandy had attempted to enter the apartment and had threatened Ms. Hynson at the club. When Hynson mentioned the protection from abuse orders but could not produce a valid order, one of the officers radioed the police department to verify if one had been issued. There is a factual dispute concerning what happened next. The police officers aver that they, learning that there was no current order, asked Ms. Hynson if she wished to accompany them to the club to identify Gandy and that she refused and expressed a desire to leave with her children. The plaintiffs aver that the police officers never made this request and if so, it would have been foolhardy and dangerous for her to have accompanied them. The police remained until she had departed for her mother's residence. Approximately twenty hours later, Gandy went to Ms. Hynson's place of employment where he shot and killed her.

The plaintiffs, the decedent's mother and children, brought this § 1983 claim seeking money damages against the City of Chester, the police department, individual officers and numerous other defendants not involved here, alleging that the defendants violated Hynson's rights to * * * equal protection of the laws.

* * *

The seminal case dealing with the discriminatory application of a facially neutral law is Yick Wo v. Hopkins, 118 U.S. 356, 6 S.Ct. 1064, 30 L.Ed. 220 (1886), in which the Supreme Court invalidated a San Francisco ordinance banning the operation of laundries in wooden buildings without first obtaining a license from the board of supervisors. When it was demonstrated to the Court that all Chinese petitioners were denied a license while all but one non-Chinese petitioners were granted a license, the Court invalidated the ordinance because it was "applied and administered by public authority with an evil eye and an unequal hand...."

The case presently before us involves a claim that the City of Chester police officers engage in a custom, policy and practice of failing to respond to complaints made by females against males known to them. In other words, Hynson argues that the police officers treat domestic abuse cases differently than non-domestic abuse cases. By failing to consider Alesia Hynson's complaint against her former boyfriend as seriously as they would consider the complaint of a female against an unknown assailant, Hynson contends, the police officers denied her the equal protection of the law which ultimately resulted in her tragic death.

* * * The police policy towards battered women can take a variety of forms, from an outright refusal to arrest batterers and to recognize domestic violence as a criminal matter, to a practice of giving domestic violence calls lower priority than non-domestic disputes. Sometimes police policy is explained in written manuals. Often it is not in writing, but is demonstrated by a pattern of police behavior that treats assaults by men against their wives less seriously than assaults by strangers.... The police non-arrest policy is most commonly justified by a belief in "family privacy", a doctrine dictating that the state should not intervene in domestic matters. It is obvious that lawsuits requesting injunctions and monetary awards for damages resulting from such policies will cause municipal and metropolitan police agencies to reconsider their policies toward domestic violence.

The Court of Appeals for the Tenth Circuit recently decided Watson v. Kansas City, 857 F.2d 690 (10th Cir.1988), where the plaintiff—a police officer's wife—produced evidence of numerous instances of abuse which were known to her husband's superiors who took no disciplinary action against him. Neither was he arrested when she pressed charges against him. The court considered the statistical evidence produced by the plaintiff in support of her allegation that nondomestic assault cases were more likely to lead to an arrest than domestic assault cases[42] and concluded that the statistical evidence, coupled with evidence that the officers received training in defusing domestic violence situations, was sufficient to demonstrate that a pattern of deliberate indifference might exist on the part of the police department. * * * [The appellate court in *Watson* reversed a grant of summary judgment for the defendants on Mrs. Watson's first claim, concerning the police policy of affording less protection to victims of domestic violence than to victims of non-domestic attacks.]

42. The plaintiff presented evidence that of 608 nondomestic assault cases in Kansas City during the period of January 1, 1983 to September 8, 1983 there were 186 arrests (31%). Of 369 domestic assaults there were 69 arrests (16%).

Along with her allegation of discrimination on the basis of her membership in the class of victims of domestic abuse, Watson also contended that she was denied police protection because of her sex. The court of appeals affirmed the district court's summary judgment against Watson because she failed to demonstrate that a policy discriminating against victims of domestic violence necessarily adversely affected women.

* * *

We agree with the *Watson* court that if the categories used by the police in administering the law are domestic violence and nondomestic violence, this is not sufficient to raise a claim for gender-based discrimination absent a showing of an intent, purpose or effect of discriminating against women. In order to survive summary judgment, a plaintiff must proffer sufficient evidence that would allow a reasonable jury to infer that it is the policy or custom of the police to provide less protection to victims of domestic violence than to other victims of violence, that discrimination against women was a motivating factor, and that the plaintiff was injured by the policy or custom. This is the essence of the constitutional right which the plaintiffs must show was clearly established at the time of the alleged violation in order to negate the police officers' qualified immunity.

[Under Harlow v. Fitzgerald, 457 U.S. 800, 102 S.Ct. 2727, 73 L.Ed.2d 396 (1982), municipal officers are immune from suit if the right allegedly violated was not "clearly established" at the time of their action.]

BROWN v. GRABOWSKI

United States Court of Appeals for the Third Circuit, 1990.

922 F.2d 1097.

Deborah Evans was found frozen to death in the trunk of her car in February of 1985 in a motel parking lot in Iselin, New Jersey. Clifton McKenzie, Evans' former live-in boyfriend, had abducted her and imprisoned her there. In a separate episode, which occurred shortly before this fatal abduction, McKenzie had held Evans hostage for a period of three days, during which he repeatedly threatened and sexually assaulted her. During the weekend following this preliminary reign of terror, members of Evans' family and Evans herself related these events to Patrolman William Schwartz and Detective Felix Grabowski of the Police Department of Roselle Borough, where Evans lived and where most of the events took place. Despite the entreaties of Evans and her family, however, no criminal charges against McKenzie were filed.

* * *

This incident constituted one of the factors that prompted an investigation of the Roselle Police Department's Detective Bureau by the Union County Prosecutor's Office. * * * The Prosecutor's investigation also produced evidence of a long-standing failure to follow up on reports of domestic violence. Indeed, the Department had no records whatsoever of crimes involving domestic violence. Grabowski later stated that he never had filed a domestic violence report and could not recall informing specific victims of domestic violence of their rights under the Domestic Violence Act.

* * *

Plaintiff maintains that Grabowski and Schwartz denied Evans her constitutional right of access to the civil courts by failing to inform her adequately of her rights under New Jersey law. * * *

The due process clause of the fourteenth amendment imposes upon state actors an obligation to refrain from preventing individuals from obtaining access to the civil courts. But only when the state has custody of an individual must its actors, to ensure that the individual receives due process, provide assistance in gaining access to the courts. See Bounds v. Smith, 430 U.S. 817, 97 S.Ct. 1491, 52 L.Ed.2d 72 (1977) (fundamental right of access to the courts requires prison authorities to assist inmates in preparation and filing of meaningful legal papers). Evans' constitutional right of access to the civil courts, therefore, does not appear expansive enough to encompass the right to receive assistance in gaining court access accorded to her by New Jersey's Domestic Violence Act.

Plaintiff's combined statutory and constitutional claim is, at core, coterminous with her claim that Grabowski and Schwartz violated Evans' due process right to police protection, on which the district court granted summary judgment for the defendants. Each claim ultimately is governed by the Supreme Court's decision in *DeShaney* [v. Winnebago County Dep't of Social Service, 489 U.S. 189, 109 S.Ct. 998, 103 L.Ed.2d 249 (1989)] * * *. *DeShaney* establishes a line, conceptually distinct, although sometimes difficult to draw, between a state's obligation to refrain from depriving its citizens of life, liberty, or property without due process of law, and a state's affirmative obligation to protect its citizens from such deprivations at the hands of private actors. *DeShaney* held that in the absence of an affirmative exercise of state power that "so restrains an individual's liberty that it renders him unable to care for himself," a state has no positive duty to ensure that the individual's life, liberty, or property "do not come to harm through other [than state] means." Id. at 1005, 1003.[11] * * *

11. In *DeShaney,* a mother, on behalf of her infant son, brought a section 1983 action alleging that the Winnebago Department of Social Services had deprived the son of his liberty interest in bodily integrity in violation of his substantive due process rights under the fourteenth amendment. For more than a year, the Department of Social Services had received, from hospital personnel and those who knew the child, information strongly suggesting that his father was abusing him. Due to his father's continual beatings, the child sustained brain damage so severe that he fell into a life-threatening coma and is now profoundly retarded. The child's mother contended that the Department, because it should have been or actually was aware of the danger to her child, had a constitutional obligation to intervene to protect him from his father. The Supreme Court, however,

[U]nder *DeShaney* * * *, the Domestic Violence Act cannot be construed as creating either a quasi-custodial relationship between defendants and Evans or any concomitant constitutional duty on their part to assist Evans in seeking protection from her assailant in the civil courts. * * *

[The court then holds that plaintiff's equal protection claims are barred by the doctrine of qualified immunity, because the crime took place in 1985, when there was only one reported case and several law review articles about the problem of police non-response to domestic violence cases. Thus, the court concludes, plaintiff's right was not clearly established for purposes of immunity analysis at that time. Claims against the police chief for failure to train and supervise his officers fail on the same grounds.]

Notes on Police Response to Domestic Violence

1. Does a police policy to provide less protection to victims of domestic violence than to other victims of violence constitute discrimination on the basis of sex? Why or why not? How would a plaintiff show, as the *Hynson* court says she must in order to survive summary judgment, that discrimination against women was the motivating factor in such a policy or practice? What types of evidence would she need to put on, given that the statistical evidence set forth in the *Watson* case (described in *Hynson*) was not adequate? Would it make a difference if sex discrimination claims were subject to strict scrutiny? Or are domestic violence victims deprived of a remedy by the *Feeney* case (in Chapter 2)?

2. What factors do you think account for the well-documented reluctance of police to pursue domestic violence claims? (Note that the abuser in *Watson* was himself a policeman.) Is the traditional split between the public and private spheres the culprit here?

3. *Should* people be able to sue the police for non-protection? Under what circumstances? In general? Is it true that the rights at issue here—in essence, for police protection against assault, battery, and murder—were not "clearly established" in 1985?

4. *DeShaney* and *Grabowski* both rely on the assumption that the state has no affirmative duty to protect individuals who are not in state custody. Each court is hard pressed to outline the difference between what is often referred to as "negative freedom" (not preventing the individual from exercising her rights) and "positive freedom" (state action to enable the individual to exercise her rights). Where the state fails to protect its citizens from violence perpetrated against them by other citizens in the face of requests for protection, is the *DeShaney* approach in fact consistent with the basic premises of liberal democratic government? See Susan Bandes, The Negative Constitution: A Critique, 88 Mich.L.Rev. 2271 (1990). Isn't police protection under these circumstances at the core of the theoretical justification for entry into civil government, that is, the establishment of a central

emphasized that the father—not the Department of Social Services—had harmed the child and held that the Department's failure to provide the child with adequate protection did not amount to a deprivation of his due process rights.

authority as a means of protecting individuals from the war of all against all? See Thomas Hobbes, Leviathan pt. I, ch. 13 (1651).

5. A number of experiments have attempted to document the connection between various responses by the police to domestic violence calls and the potential for recidivism, measured by repeat violence within a given number of months. In the Minneapolis experiment, arresting the offender was found to substantially reduce repeat violence, as compared to attempting to counsel the parties or sending the assailant away from home for several hours. Lawrence W. Sherman and Richard A. Berk, The Specific Deterrent Effects of Arrest For Domestic Assault, 49 Am. Soc. Rev. 261, 261 (1984). Other studies have had mixed results, with some showing that arrest may deter further violence by certain types of offenders—those who are employed, middle-class and white—but potentially be harmful for women who are Black and poor, by causing repeat violence in retaliation for the arrest. Lawrence W. Sherman et al., The Variable Effects of Arrest on Criminal Careers: The Milwaukee Domestic Violence Experiment, 83 J. Crim. L. & Criminology 137, 158–63 (1992). (In the Milwaukee experiment, the alternate dispositions were standard arrest (usually overnight), short arrest (release within two hours), and warning; other experiments also included counseling.) If the effects of arrest are variable according to class, race and employment status, as Sherman et al. state, what do you think might account for this variance? In light of the variance, what policies should be followed by police departments answering domestic violence calls?

6. As discussed in Section 1, above (at notes 6–7), problems with involving the police in domestic violence are exacerbated in communities of color, where the police are regarded with deep-seated and historically realistic suspicion and an arrest may lead to retaliation against the victim or even deportation both for the batterer and his victim. However, midst an overall trend of increased reporting of domestic violence to the police, African American women now report their victimization at significantly higher rates than other groups (67% versus 50% for white women), as do Hispanic females (65% versus 52% for non-Hispanic females). Dep't of Justice, Bureau of Justice Statistics, Special Report: Intimate Partner Violence 7 (2000). How would you explain these recent trends?

7. Victims of gay and bisexual male domestic violence are extremely reluctant to call the police because of well-documented homophobia among the police themselves, who rarely arrest the batterer unless the victim has sustained extremely serious injuries or, if they do, arrest the victim as well, and often submit both to degrading treatment. Patrick Letellier, Gay and Bisexual Male Domestic Violence Victimization: Challenges to Feminist Theory and Responses to Violence, 9 Violence and Victims 95, 102–03 (1994). "Mutual combat" arrests are more common because male victims, unlike females, are socially conditioned to strike back when physically attacked; their more equal physical strength also makes them more capable of self-defense and less susceptible to serious injury, although this does not, of course, lessen the culpability of the aggressor. Id. at 100–02. Moreover, reporting an attack and thus publicizing the problem will likely result in requiring the victim to reveal his sexual orientation and perhaps suffer severe consequences from the community, his employer, and health insurers. Id. at 103. What can be done to encourage the law enforcement community

to respond effectively to gay and bisexual battering, in a manner that is sensitive to these substantial problems? Would legal change help, or is this simply a social and/or political issue?

4. THE DEBATE OVER MANDATORY PROSECUTION

DONNA WILLS, DOMESTIC VIOLENCE: THE CASE FOR AGGRESSIVE PROSECUTION

7 UCLA Women's L.J. 173, 173–176, 179–82 (1997).

[Donna Wills is the Head Deputy in the Family Violence Division of the Los Angeles County District Attorney's Office.]

Prosecutors throughout the country, and especially in the State of California, have begun taking a more aggressive stance towards domestic violence prosecutions by instituting a "no drop" or "no dismissal" policy. Based on my experience as a veteran prosecutor who specializes in these cases, I firmly believe that this policy is the enlightened approach to domestic violence prosecutions. Fundamentally, a "no drop" policy takes the decision of whether or not to prosecute the batterer off the victim's shoulders and puts it where it belongs: in the discretion of the prosecutors whose job it is to enforce society's criminal laws and hold offenders accountable for their crimes. The prosecutor's client is the State, not the victim. Accordingly, prosecutorial agencies that have opted for aggressive prosecution have concluded that their client's interest in protecting the safety and well-being of all of its citizens overrides the individual victim's desire to dictate whether and when criminal charges are filed.

Aggressive prosecution is the appropriate response to domestic violence cases for several reasons. First, domestic violence affects more than just the individual victim; it is a public safety issue that affects all of society. Second, prosecutors cannot rely upon domestic violence victims to appropriately vindicate the State's interests in holding batterers responsible for the crimes they commit because victims often decline to press charges. Third, prosecutors must intervene to protect victims and their children and to prevent batterers from further intimidating their victims and manipulating the justice system.

II. Domestic Violence is a Public Safety Issue

Domestic violence is a societal, not merely an individual, problem; it is not just about two people in a private relationship working out their "family problems." The harm caused by this violence refuses to be neatly confined between the abuser and the victim. Rather, domestic violence impacts everyone: children, neighbors, extended family, the workplace, hospital emergency rooms, good samaritans who are killed while trying to intervene, and the death row inmates who cite it as a reason not to be killed. The State has a legitimate interest in maintaining public safety, especially by ensuring that domestic violence offenders are not allowed to flourish unabated.

Domestic violence advocates were correct in supporting laws that codified domestic violence as both a crime against the individual *and* a crime against the State. When prosecutors file charges, we enforce these laws and reinforce the fact that domestic violence is criminal conduct. In California, the Penal Code explains why special attention should be devoted to the prosecution of batterers: "The Legislature hereby finds that spousal abusers present a clear and present danger to the mental and physical well-being of the *citizens* of the State of California."[4] Besides being "an unacknowledged epidemic in our society," domestic violence is the leading cause of injury to women, a major factor in female homicide, a contributing factor to female suicide, a major risk for child abuse, and a major precursor for future batterers and violent youth offenders. The State cannot ignore the human tragedies that are caused by domestic violence.

The primary duty of government is to protect its citizens from assault as vigorously in the home as on the streets. The victims subject to domestic abuse are often not the only people who suffer. Most notably, children are secondary victims of violence in the home. The link between domestic violence and child abuse, both emotional and physical, cannot be ignored. Each year, between three and ten million children are forced to witness the emotional devastation of one parent abusing or killing the other. Many are injured in the "crossfire" while trying to protect the assaulted parent, or are used as pawns or shields and are harmed by blows intended for someone else. Some are born with birth defects because their mothers were battered during pregnancy. Children of domestic violence are silent victims who suffer without the options available to adults. Thus, aggressive prosecution furthers the State's goal of protecting not only the victim, but also the children in homes where domestic violence occurs.

Researchers have yet to determine the extent to which aggressive prosecution actually combats the problem of domestic violence. Although some recent studies have questioned whether mandatory arrest of batterers is beneficial in deterring domestic violence, such studies are misleading. No studies have focused on the incremental effects that aggressive prosecution has had on controlling, if not eliminating, recidivism. Nor has current research addressed the role of aggressive prosecution in decreasing the public's tolerance of domestic violence. Prosecutors realize all too well that criminal intervention alone may not be the ultimate "cure" for domestic violence any more than it is a complete solution to gang violence, carjackings, sexual assaults, child abuse, or any other kind of anti-social violence perpetrated by one human being against another. Indeed, criminal intervention does not guarantee that a batterer will forever refrain from further violence. However, failure to try to achieve this goal is not an acceptable alternative. Research notwithstanding, aggressive prosecution of batterers is a criminal justice decision predicated on what is best for the common good, not a scienti-

4. Cal. Penal Code § 273.8 (West 1988) (amended 1994) (emphasis added).

fically formulated antidote guaranteed to transform batterers into peaceful spouses or model partners.

* * *

IV. Batterers Must Not Be Allowed to Control Justice

Batterers are "master manipulators." They will do anything to convince their victims to get the prosecution to drop the charges. They call from jail threatening retaliation. They cajole their victim with promises of reform. They remind her that they may lose their jobs and, hence, the family income. They send love letters, pledging future bliss and happiness. They have their family members turn off the victim's electricity and threaten to kick the victim and her children out into the street. They pay for the victim to leave town so that she will not be subpoenaed. They use community property to pay for an expensive lawyer to try to convince the jury that the whole thing was the victim's fault and that she attacked him. They prey on the victim's personal weaknesses, especially drug and alcohol abuse, physical and mental disabilities, and her love for their children. They negotiate financial and property incentives that cause acute memories of terror and pain to fade dramatically. Prosecutors watch with practiced patience as these vulnerable victims succumb to their batterers' intimidation and manipulation. Then, "no drop" prosecutors try to hold the batterers responsible regardless of the victims' lack of cooperation by using creative legal maneuvering.

Supporters of "no drop" domestic violence policies realize that empowering victims by giving them the discretion to prosecute, or even to threaten to prosecute, in actuality only empowers batterers to further manipulate and endanger their victims' lives, the children's lives, and the safety and well-being of the entire community. By proceeding with the prosecution with or without victim cooperation, the prosecutor minimizes the victim's value to the batterer as an ally to defeat criminal prosecution. A "no drop" policy means prosecutors will not allow batterers to control the system of justice through their victims.

* * *

When the 911 call is made to law enforcement, the criminal justice system is triggered. When the report of violence is made, that moment signifies that the victim is *without the power to get the batterer to stop the violence*. However, the criminal justice system is not without power to encourage the batterer to cease and desist. Arrest and prosecution, however temporary, serve notice on the batterer that what he did was wrong and warrants his immediate removal from the community. It also gives the victim a breather—time and opportunity to access counseling services, to investigate alternatives to life with a violent partner, to form a plan for safety, and to have authority focused on the batterer to stop the violence.

Prosecutors are aware of complaints that "no drop" policies make battered women feel "powerless" to keep the government, specifically the courts, from "interfering" in their lives. Some object to the court "dictating" what will happen to the case and the abuser in the aftermath of reporting the abuse. However, prosecutors must seize the "window of opportunity" given to us by the report of violence to get the batterer's attention. Working closely with victim advocates, prosecutors try to convince battered women to see the wisdom of criminal justice intervention. We tell the victims that we proceed with the prosecution because we cannot allow the batterer to believe that physical abuse is acceptable. We tell them that left without intervention, the violence may increase both in frequency of occurrence and severity of injury, often leading to the tragic scenario where he kills her or she kills him while defending herself against his aggression. We tell victims that the children suffer when they see their mother hurt and that the children need their mother to stay alive and well. We try to help them form a safety plan and deal with their fear, financial concerns, and future uncertainties, *with or without the batterer*.

* * *

No humane society can allow any citizen, battered woman or otherwise, to be beaten and terrorized while being held emotionally hostage to love and fear or blackmailed by financial dependence and cultural mores. As guardians of public safety, prosecutors must proceed against domestic violence offenders *with or without victim cooperation* as long as there is legally sufficient evidence. This policy of aggressive prosecution adopts the wisdom that "[t]here is no excuse for domestic violence." * * *

LINDA G. MILLS, KILLING HER SOFTLY: INTIMATE ABUSE AND THE VIOLENCE OF STATE INTERVENTION

113 Harv. L. Rev. 550, 567–68, 576–77, 582–85, 595–97, 609–11 (1999).

[I. MANDATORY POLICIES]

* * * Very few studies have tested the effectiveness of mandatory prosecution policies in eliminating violence in battered women's lives. Indeed, the one randomized study specific to the topic, conducted by David Ford and Jean Regoli in 1986, suggested mixed results at best.[81] Ford and Regoli assigned batterers to one of three tracks: pre-trial diversion, prosecution and rehabilitation, or prosecution and other sanctions (such as jail time). The study found that if a battered woman files charges in a jurisdiction that permits her to drop the case and she refuses to drop it, she is at lower risk of subsequent abuse than if she had been in a jurisdiction that made that decision for her through a mandatory prosecution policy. Ford and Regoli surmised that prevention

81. *See* David A. Ford & Mary Jean Regoli, *The Criminal Prosecution of Wife Assaulters: Process, Problems, and Effects*, *in* LEGAL RESPONSES TO WIFE ASSAULT: CURRENT TRENDS AND EVALUATION 127, 151–57 (N. Zoe Hilton ed., 1993).

of future incidents of violence was related to the victim's "power" to drop the charges.

A recent study on the effects of prosecution on recidivism presented striking results.[85] After reviewing a large sample of domestic violence misdemeanor cases (1133), the researchers found that prosecution had no effect on the likelihood of re-arrest of the batterer within a six-month period. More specifically, Robert Davis and his co-authors determined that recidivism was unaffected by whether a case was dropped, dismissed, or prosecuted. While the authors warned that their findings were tentative, they nevertheless concluded that "there is little support for the idea that law enforcement responses to domestic violence misdemeanors reduce or eliminate violence." Given these study findings, the advantages of mandatory interventions do not clearly outweigh the disadvantages, especially if these interventions protect the safety of white women at the expense of African–American women.

* * *

[II. CLINICAL CONCERNS]

[Mills next discusses the clinical literature on treatment of survivors of traumatic events.]

B. The Healing Process

* * *

Certain clinical rules govern a healing relationship. For example, the empowerment of the survivor is the most important goal. Empowerment provides a space for the battered woman to decide how to proceed in the healing process. This kind of empowerment does not imply that she is obligated to choose among options; rather, it suggests the need for those involved in the healing process to present options and relevant data, encouraging the survivor to choose the path with which she is most comfortable. In Herman's terms:

> [The survivor] must be the author and arbiter of her own recovery. Others may offer advice, support, assistance, affection, and care, but not cure. Many benevolent and well-intentioned attempts to assist the survivor founder because this fundamental principle of empowerment is not observed. No intervention that takes power away from the survivor can possibly foster her recovery, no matter how much it appears to be in her immediate best interest.[138]

Hence, helping victims restore power and control and diminishing their helplessness by increasing their choices can contribute significantly to reversing the negative dynamics that dominate the abusive relationship.

85. *See* [Robert C. Davis, Barbara E. Smith & Laura B. Nickles, The Deterrent Effect of Prosecuting Domestic Violence Misdemeanors, 44 Crime & Delinq. 434 (1998)], at 441.

138. [Judith Lewis Herman, Trauma and Recovery 133 (1997)].

This reversal, in turn, fosters the victim's capacity to engage in a healthy and affirming relationship. * * *

* * *

C. *Clinical Explanations for State Actors' Violence*

* * *

The view that state responsibility in domestic violence cases should be limited to the goal of protection is conceptually narrow and clinically inappropriate. This position neglects the state's collective obligation to its victimized citizenry to respond to intimate abuse in ways that reliably interrupt patterns of violence and that begin to eradicate the underlying dynamics that cause violent ruptures in the first place. * * *

Mandatory interventions, such as arrest, prosecution, and reporting, treat battered women as fragile, uncooperative, mentally ill, and/or indecisive. These reactions may, in their simplest form, be manifestations of state actors' unexpressed desire to silence or to mask their feelings of guilt, rage, and shame, which their interactions with victims of abuse so easily generate. These unexpressed feelings and countertransference reactions are not without consequences; they infect the state's relationships with battered women and reduce the possibility of developing a healing dynamic that may actually result in transformation.

That state actors are likely to feel overwhelmed and helpless in the face of their interactions with survivors of intimate abuse is understandable. Battered women's stories are painful for anyone to hear. For state actors, who are not trained to anticipate their own reactions, victims' abuse histories can be threatening, even unbearable. I fear that, instead of working through their feelings in ways that facilitate their relationships with the battered women, state actors become infected by the violence they witness and inadvertently reproduce its most destructive forms.

* * *

[III. Schematic of State Violence]

* * *

B. *State Officials as Abusers*

From the accumulated evidence, a dynamic between the state and the battered woman emerges that distinctly mimics the violent dynamic in the battering relationship. Three correlative themes are the most problematic. First, mandatory interventions reinforce the battered woman's psychic injury and encourage feelings of guilt, low self-esteem, and dependency. Mandatory interventions are predicated on the assumption that state actors are incapable of distinguishing between battered women who are truly suffering from "learned helplessness" and battered women who are capable of making reasoned decisions about which healing strategies to pursue. * * *

Second, mandatory interventions may have the ironic effect of realigning the battered woman with the batterer. Some studies suggest and numerous authors have surmised that when the battered woman has a negative interaction with the state, she is less likely to rely on governmental assistance in the future. Indeed, some have argued, as I am arguing, that if a battered woman is given the choice between abuse by the batterer, which is familiar, and abuse by state actors, which is unfamiliar, she is likely to choose the abuse she knows best.

Finally, mandatory interventions deny the battered woman an important opportunity to partner with the state to help ensure her future safety. The Ford and Regoli study, along with the clinical literature discussed in Part II, clearly indicates the importance of developing new methods for encouraging battered women to engage with state actors in the development of tailored and strategic responses to the women's situations that reflect their and their children's best interests. * * *

IV. SURVIVOR-CENTERED MODEL

* * *

A. *Elements of a Survivor–Centered Model*

To counteract the destructive dynamics of the current relationship between the state and battered women described in sections II and III, I have developed a Survivor–Centered Model of state response to domestic violence. This approach assumes that the victim of domestic violence is searching for a path toward healing, that state actors should help facilitate her psychological health as well as her physical safety, and that the victim of domestic violence is in the best position to dictate the terms of her healing. In opposition to the current destructive dynamics of the state's relationship with the battered woman, I present a framework for reversing the destructive typologies of emotional abuse described earlier. I describe eight subcategories of the Survivor–Centered Model and analyze how each element can encourage state actors to relate in healthier ways toward battered women. * * *

[Here Mills describes the eight elements of her approach: acceptance, respect, reassurance, engagement, resocialization, empowerment, emotional responsiveness, and liberation.]

* * *

B. *A New State Dynamic in Intimate Abuse Cases*

In light of the importance of adopting a new state dynamic in intimate abuse cases, state actors should heed the clinical call to action. To engage constructively in dialogue with battered women, state actors must be more sensitive to the psychological state of the battered woman. State actors should expect that battered women will appear anxious, overwhelmed, confused, and angry, or helpless, docile, or detached. State actors should expect these distinct emotional reactions from survivors of violence, and they should identify these reactions as unique opportunities for and possible indications of healing. That agents currently view these emotions as deviant, inappropriate, or "uncooperative," rather than as indicative of the trauma that the state seeks to address, is one of the primary impediments to effective interaction with survivors of intimate abuse.

Battered women who seek the state's assistance require, first and foremost, reconnection and relationship. The few studies that have explored these issues have found that battered women feel most satisfied with state interactions when they feel heard. Even in her confusion, the battered woman is conscious and wants a response that she can control. This response may involve the survivor's need for a savior or protector, someone she initially idealizes, as she attempts to work through her trauma history. Under these circumstances, state officials can function as partners in helping her come to terms with her sense of vulnerability and helplessness. Having her story heard and her individual situation recognized may be the first step on the battered woman's path to healing and change.

Knowing that the "omnipotent savior" dynamic is likely to emerge in their relationship with the battered woman, and that the fragile reconnection the survivor seeks is likely to fail if she perceives a replication of the original abuse in the criminal justice process, state actors need to honor the long-term healing connection over a short-term solution of arresting and prosecuting the batterer. Given the scant evidence that mandatory interventions reduce violence, and the obvious fact that a battered woman's resolution to terminate the abusive relationship is the most enduring hope for her long-term safety, state actors should turn their attention toward the healing strategies that are most likely to alter permanently patterns of violence.

Acceptance, respect, reassurance, engagement, resocialization, empowerment, emotional responsiveness, and liberation represent the antithesis to abuse. Reorienting the relationship between battered women and state actors using a Survivor–Centered Model of interaction provides a critical opportunity for healing through state intervention. If the survivor desired to arrest and prosecute, especially after advocates had an opportunity to inform her of the effectiveness of these actions, then prosecutors could proceed with legal measures. If, on the other hand, the battered woman sought alternative responses, including counseling for herself or the batterer, state actors would respect those desires instead.

Karla Fischer and Mary Rose studied factors that encourage battered women to leave their abusive relationships.[264] Their provocative study tried to determine the point at which battered women decide "enough is enough." State actors can help survivors make their way toward "enough is enough" by listening closely to the battered woman's

264. *See* [Karla Fischer and Mary Rose, When "Enough Is Enough": Battered Women's Decision Making Around Court Orders of Protection, 41 Crime & Delinq. 414 (1995)] at 414.

narrative and by responding in ways that reinforce healthy interaction. Forming a healthy relationship with the battered woman might be just the impetus she needs to understand that she is entitled to a different kind of love. This realization may or may not result in leaving the abusive relationship. As I discussed earlier, leaving may not be an option for cultural, financial, or religious reasons. Consistent with the clinical literature, a Survivor–Centered Approach would help a battered woman take steps toward her own recovery, in or out of the abusive relationship, while she pursued more direct methods of treatment through therapy.

Notes on Mandatory Prosecution

1. Do you think that policies like "no-drop" or mandatory prosecution, which take the decision to prosecute her abuser out of the abused woman's hands, are a good idea? What are the pro's and con's of such a policy? How are we to balance the woman's interest against that of her children and the public interest in interrupting the intergenerational transmission of violence? Is failure to prosecute in effect rewarding batterers' ability to manipulate and giving them a "green light" for further abuse?

2. Does Mills' proposal for a survivor-centered model for prosecutors in effect require law enforcement officials to act as therapists? Is this appropriate?

3. How would the different theorists discussed in Chapter 3 analyze the issue of mandatory prosecution? What would each recommend?

4. Pro-prosecution policies in fact vary from "hard" to "soft" no-drop. The first is typified by San Diego, where every felony case is pursued, despite the victim's wishes. In jurisdictions that thus mandate victim participation, the woman may be required to sign statements, be photographed, be interviewed, provide the state with other evidence, produce her children, and appear throughout the proceedings. Cheryl Hanna, No Right To Choose: Mandated Victim Participation in Domestic Violence Prosecutions, 109 Harv. L. Rev. 1850, 1867 (1996). In some instances, domestic violence victims have even been imprisoned for failure to testify. Id. at 1894. After implementing a hard no-drop policy, homicides related to domestic violence fell in San Diego from 30 in 1985 to seven in 1994. Id. at 1862–64. Soft no-drop policies do not force victims to participate but provide them with support services and strongly encourage them to pursue the case. Id. at 1863. Studies show that assigning a domestic violence advocate to shelter clients or simply the availability of social support from family and friends can in fact substantially decrease repeat violence and increase the woman's effectiveness in ending the relationship; one study showed that victims with interpersonal support were twice as likely voluntarily to cooperate with the prosecution. See Deborah Epstein, Effective Intervention in Domestic Violence Cases: Rethinking the Roles of Prosecutors, Judges, and the Court System, 11 Yale J. Law & Feminism 3, 19–20 (1999). How should these various statistics and studies be weighed? What if the groups who are especially resistant to reporting and prosecuting domestic abuse are women of color?

5. Cheryl Hanna, a former prosecutor in the Baltimore Domestic Violence Unit, believes that mandatory prosecution is a better policy choice

than dismissing cases when women refuse to participate, even though the solution is imperfect and entails risks to the victim's sense of autonomy. Hanna, above note 4, at 1856. She reaches this conclusion through application of the pragmatic feminist approach described in Chapter 3, concluding that "At this point in history * * * the long-term benefits of mandated participation outweigh the short-term costs * * * [and] we need to examine the influence that mandated participation has on the effectiveness of the criminal justice system as well as the impact of such a policy on individual women." Id. at 1888. What are the short- and long-term costs and benefits of mandatory prosecution in your opinion? How do you assess them? How would Linda Mills, in the excerpt above?

6. In 1996, the District of Columbia adopted a no-drop policy that led to an enormous increase in domestic violence cases—from 40 misdemeanor cases out of 19,000 emergency domestic violence calls in 1989 to 8,000 by 1997–98—and has resulted in a 69% conviction rate, which approximates that in other misdemeanor bench trials. Epstein, above note 4, at 16. However, the prosecutors rely heavily on evidence other than victim testimony, introducing photographs, tapes of calls to the "911" emergency number, hospital records, and police testimony in every case where it is available. In fact, the state relies *exclusively* upon this type of evidence half the time, when the victim refuses to testify; yet the conviction rate in both types of cases is identical. Id. at 18. To what would you attribute this result? What policy implications would you draw from it? (The D.C. changes were part of a larger reform of the domestic violence system, including the establishment of integrated domestic violence courts that handle both civil and criminal cases arising out of domestic violence, coordinate information about various incidents and claims, and offer a broad range of civil and criminal, short- and long-term remedies. See id. at 21–38.)

7. Even in jurisdictions with mandatory arrest and/or no-drop policies, the chances that an arrest will lead to a conviction are low and that a prosecution will result in prison time are exceedingly slim. An American Lawyer study of all domestic violence arrests in 11 jurisdictions across the country on a randomly selected day, June 18, 1995, revealed that jail or prison sentences were rare, even in jurisdictions with aggressive prosecutorial policies, such as San Diego, Dade County, and the Bronx. A total of 95 of the 140 June 18 arrests were dismissed, almost invariably because the victim refused to testify. Only 16 of the 44 defendants who were convicted or pled no contest served any time at all; most were either released on probation, received suspended sentences or were diverted into treatment programs for batterers, despite the extremely serious injuries many had inflicted upon their victims. Of the June 18 defendants who were convicted, only one was actually sentenced to a year in jail, and that only because he had two prior felony convictions; two other one-year sentences were handed out, but one was suspended and the other reduced to 60 days. Alison Frankel, Domestic Disaster, Am. Lawyer, June 1996, at 55–73. See also Eve S. Buzawa and Carl G. Buzawa, Domestic Violence: The Criminal Justice Response (2d ed. 1996) (reporting that of 1,408 cases in Ohio during 1980, after passage of a new domestic violence statute, 1,142 were dismissed, and only 166 guilty pleas or verdicts resulted; only 60 convicted defendants spent any time in jail, and only 1/3 of those spent more than 20 days). How would you account for the

very low rate of conviction and minimal sentences served in domestic violence cases? What, if anything, do you believe should be done about this problem?

8. What do you think explains the courts' (and often victims' and prosecutors') preference for treatment over incarceration, despite evidence that treatment may have little effect? See Cheryl Hanna, The Paradox of Hope: The Crime and Punishment of Domestic Violence, 39 Wm. & Mary L. Rev. 1505, 1533 (1998) (reporting on studies finding that men arrested and treated resume their violent behavior at the same rate as men arrested and not treated and other studies finding no significant difference in recidivism rates between those who complete treatment programs and those who drop out).

5. WOMEN WHO KILL THEIR BATTERERS

STATE v. KELLY

Supreme Court of New Jersey, 1984.

97 N.J. 178, 478 A.2d 364.

I.

On May 24, 1980, defendant, Gladys Kelly, stabbed her husband, Ernest, with a pair of scissors. He died shortly thereafter at a nearby hospital. The couple had been married for seven years, during which time Ernest had periodically attacked Gladys. According to Ms. Kelly, he assaulted her that afternoon, and she stabbed him in self-defense, fearing that he would kill her if she did not act.

Ms. Kelly was indicted for murder. At trial, she did not deny stabbing her husband, but asserted that her action was in self-defense. * * *

II.

The day after the[ir] marriage, Mr. Kelly got drunk and knocked Ms. Kelly down. Although a period of calm followed the initial attack, the next seven years were accompanied by periodic and frequent beatings, sometimes as often as once a week. During the attacks, which generally occurred when Mr. Kelly was drunk, he threatened to kill Ms. Kelly and to cut off parts of her body if she tried to leave him. Mr. Kelly often moved out of the house after an attack, later returning with a promise that he would change his ways. Until the day of the homicide, only one of the attacks had taken place in public.

The day before the stabbing, Gladys and Ernest went shopping. They did not have enough money to buy food for the entire week, so Ernest said he would give his wife more money the next day.

The following morning he left for work. Ms. Kelly next saw her husband late that afternoon at a friend's house. She had gone there with her daughter, Annette, to ask Ernest for money to buy food. He told her to wait until they got home, and shortly thereafter the Kellys left. After walking past several houses, Mr. Kelly, who was drunk, angrily asked "What the hell did you come around here for?" He then grabbed the collar of her dress, and the two fell to the ground. He choked her by pushing his fingers against her throat, punched or hit her face, and bit her leg.

A crowd gathered on the street. Two men from the crowd separated them, just as Gladys felt that she was "passing out" from being choked. Fearing that Annette had been pushed around in the crowd, Gladys then left to look for her. * * *

After finding her daughter, Ms. Kelly then observed Mr. Kelly running toward her with his hands raised. Within seconds he was right next to her. Unsure of whether he had armed himself while she was looking for their daughter, and thinking that he had come back to kill her, she grabbed a pair of scissors from her pocketbook. She tried to scare him away, but instead stabbed him.

[Ms. Kelly was convicted of reckless manslaughter.]

III.

The central question in this case is whether the trial court erred in its exclusion of expert testimony on the battered-woman's syndrome. * * *

* * *

As the problem of battered women has begun to receive more attention, sociologists and psychologists have begun to focus on the effects a sustained pattern of physical and psychological abuse can have on a woman. The effects of such abuse are what some scientific observers have termed "the battered-woman's syndrome," a series of common characteristics that appear in women who are abused physically and psychologically over an extended period of time by the dominant male figure in their lives. Dr. Lenore Walker, a prominent writer on the battered-woman's syndrome, defines the battered woman as one who is repeatedly subjected to any forceful physical or psychological behavior by a man in order to coerce her to do something he wants her to do without concern for her rights. Battered women include wives or women in any form of intimate relationships with men. Furthermore, in order to be classified as a battered woman, the couple must go through the battering cycle at least twice. Any woman may find herself in an abusive relationship with a man once. If it occurs a second time, and she remains in the situation, she is defined as a battered woman.

According to Dr. Walker, relationships characterized by physical abuse tend to develop battering cycles. Violent behavior directed at the woman occurs in three distinct and repetitive stages that vary both in duration and intensity depending on the individuals involved.

Phase one of the battering cycle is referred to as the "tension-building stage," during which the battering male engages in minor battering incidents and verbal abuse while the woman, beset by fear and tension, attempts to be as placating and passive as possible in order to stave off more serious violence.

Phase two of the battering cycle is the "acute battering incident." At some point during phase one, the tension between the battered woman and the batterer becomes intolerable and more serious violence inevitable. The triggering event that initiates phase two is most often an internal or external event in the life of the battering male, but provocation for more severe violence is sometimes provided by the woman who can no longer tolerate or control her phase-one anger and anxiety.

Phase three of the battering cycle is characterized by extreme contrition and loving behavior on the part of the battering male. During this period the man will often mix his pleas for forgiveness and protestations of devotion with promises to seek professional help, to stop drinking, and to refrain from further violence. For some couples, this period of relative calm may last as long as several months, but in a battering relationship the affection and contrition of the man will eventually fade and phase one of the cycle will start anew.

The cyclical nature of battering behavior helps explain why more women simply do not leave their abusers. The loving behavior demonstrated by the batterer during phase three reinforces whatever hopes these women might have for their mate's reform and keeps them bound to the relationship.

Some women may even perceive the battering cycle as normal, especially if they grew up in a violent household. Or they may simply not wish to acknowledge the reality of their situation.

Other women, however, become so demoralized and degraded by the fact that they cannot predict or control the violence that they sink into a state of psychological paralysis and become unable to take any action at all to improve or alter the situation. There is a tendency in battered women to believe in the omnipotence or strength of their battering husbands and thus to feel that any attempt to resist them is hopeless.

In addition to these psychological impacts, external social and economic factors often make it difficult for some women to extricate themselves from battering relationships. A woman without independent financial resources who wishes to leave her husband often finds it difficult to do so because of a lack of material and social resources.

Even with the progress of the last decade, women typically make less money and hold less prestigious jobs than men, and are more responsible for child care. Thus, in a violent confrontation where the first reaction might be to flee, women realize soon that there may be no place to go. Moreover, the stigma that attaches to a woman who leaves the family unit without her children undoubtedly acts as a further deterrent to moving out.

In addition, battered women, when they want to leave the relationship, are typically unwilling to reach out and confide in their friends, family, or the police, either out of shame and humiliation, fear of reprisal by their husband, or the feeling they will not be believed.

* * *

Finally, battered women are often hesitant to leave a battering relationship because, in addition to their hope of reform on the part of their spouse, they harbor a deep concern about the possible response leaving might provoke in their mates. They literally become trapped by their own fear. Case histories are replete with instances in which a battered wife left her husband only to have him pursue her and subject her to an even more brutal attack.

The combination of all these symptoms—resulting from sustained psychological and physical trauma compounded by aggravating social and economic factors—constitutes the battered-woman's syndrome. Only by understanding these unique pressures that force battered women to remain with their mates, despite their long-standing and reasonable fear of severe bodily harm and the isolation that being a battered woman creates, can a battered woman's state of mind be accurately and fairly understood.

The voir dire testimony of Dr. Veronen, sought to be introduced by defendant Gladys Kelly, conformed essentially to this outline of the battered-woman's syndrome. * * * Dr. Veronen concluded that defendant was a battered woman and subject to the battered-woman's syndrome.

In addition, Dr. Veronen was prepared to testify as to how, as a battered woman, Gladys Kelly perceived her situation at the time of the stabbing, and why, in her opinion, defendant did not leave her husband despite the constant beatings she endured.

IV.

Whether expert testimony on the battered-woman's syndrome should be admitted in this case depends on whether it is relevant to defendant's claim of self-defense * * *.

Self-defense exonerates a person who kills in the reasonable belief that such action was necessary to prevent his or her death or serious injury, even though this belief was later proven mistaken. "Detached reflection cannot be demanded in the presence of an uplifted knife," Justice Holmes aptly said, Brown v. United States, 256 U.S. 335, 343, 41 S.Ct. 501, 502, 65 L.Ed. 961, 963 (1921); and the law accordingly requires only a reasonable, not necessarily a correct, judgment.

* * *

V.

Gladys Kelly claims that she stabbed her husband in self-defense, believing he was about to kill her. The gist of the State's case was that

Gladys Kelly was the aggressor, that she consciously intended to kill her husband, and that she certainly was not acting in self-defense.

The credibility of Gladys Kelly is a critical issue in this case. * * * The expert testimony offered was directly relevant to one of the critical elements of that account, namely, what Gladys Kelly believed at the time of the stabbing, and was thus material to establish the honesty of her stated belief that she was in imminent danger of death.

* * *

We also find the expert testimony relevant to the reasonableness of defendant's belief that she was in imminent danger of death or serious injury. We do not mean that the expert's testimony could be used to show that it was understandable that a battered woman might believe that her life was in danger when indeed it was not and when a reasonable person would not have so believed * * *. Rather, our conclusion is that the expert's testimony, if accepted by the jury, would have aided it in determining whether, under the circumstances, a reasonable person would have believed there was imminent danger to her life.

At the heart of the claim of self-defense was defendant's story that she had been repeatedly subjected to "beatings" over the course of her marriage. While defendant's testimony was somewhat lacking in detail, a juror could infer from the use of the word "beatings," as well as the detail given concerning some of these events (the choking, the biting, the use of fists), that these physical assaults posed a risk of serious injury or death. When that regular pattern of serious physical abuse is combined with defendant's claim that the decedent sometimes threatened to kill her, defendant's statement that on this occasion she thought she might be killed when she saw Mr. Kelly running toward her could be found to reflect a reasonable fear * * *.

The crucial issue of fact on which this expert's testimony would bear is why, given such allegedly severe and constant beatings, combined with threats to kill, defendant had not long ago left decedent. Whether raised by the prosecutor as a factual issue or not, our own common knowledge tells us that most of us, including the ordinary juror, would ask himself or herself just such a question. * * * To some, this misconception is followed by the observation that the battered wife is masochistic, proven by her refusal to leave despite the severe beatings; to others, however, the fact that the battered wife stays on unquestionably suggests that the "beatings" could not have been too bad for if they had been, she certainly would have left. The expert could clear up these myths, by explaining that one of the common characteristics of a battered wife is her inability to leave despite such constant beatings; her "learned helplessness"; her lack of anywhere to go; her feeling that if she tried to leave, she would be subjected to even more merciless treatment; her belief in the omnipotence of her battering husband; and sometimes her hope that her husband will change his ways.

* * *

Depending on its content, the expert's testimony might also enable the jury to find that the battered wife, because of the prior beatings, numerous beatings, as often as once a week, for seven years, from the day they were married to the day he died, is particularly able to predict accurately the likely extent of violence in any attack on her. That conclusion could significantly affect the jury's evaluation of the reasonableness of defendant's fear for her life.

[Reversed and remanded for a new trial.]

CYNTHIA K. GILLESPIE, JUSTIFIABLE HOMICIDE: BATTERED WOMEN, SELF-DEFENSE, AND THE LAW

179–81 (1989).

As the use of battered woman syndrome testimony in women's self-defense trials has become more widespread, some feminist commentators have begun to express uneasiness with the direction that it is taking. Their concern is with both the content of the testimony and the way that some appellate courts seem to be interpreting what the experts say. Professor Elizabeth Schneider argues that testimony that focuses on the helplessness and passivity of battered women tends to reinforce some of the very stereotypes about women that expert testimony about the battered woman syndrome was originally intended to counter.[g] The legal system's traditional expectation that a woman who kills a man will rely on an insanity or impaired mental capacity defense (if she does not simply plead guilty to murder or manslaughter), reflects a stereotype of women as irrational and emotional—incapable of behaving as reasonable men would. This stereotype is perpetuated in another form when attorneys and their experts frame battered woman syndrome testimony primarily or exclusively to explain why a battered woman did not leave or seek help. Rather than underscoring the reasonableness and need for her violent act, such testimony instead sometimes paints the battered woman as so damaged or emotionally disabled by the violence that her perception of reality is distorted; thus, her ability to act reasonably, or to act at all, is impaired. While it is important to explain to the jury why the woman stayed and tolerated the violence, testimony that overemphasizes that issue and neglects the far more essential one of reasonableness may well leave the jury without an explanation of how a woman who was rendered so helpless by her situation could ever have committed an act as aggressive as killing.

Even where expert testimony is not framed solely in terms of passivity and helplessness, judges and appellate courts frequently seem to hear it that way anyway. The language that a number of appellate courts have used in permitting the testimony suggests that battered woman syndrome is being understood not as probative of the woman's

g. Elizabeth M. Schneider, Describing and Changing: Women's Self-Defense Work and the Problem of Expert Testimony on Battering, 9 Women's Rts. L. Rep. 195 (1986).

reasonableness but, quite the opposite, as a new and excusable form of female irrationality, not quite insanity but something close to it. As Professor Schneider has observed:

> ... "[B]attered woman syndrome" carries with it stereotypes of individual incapacity and inferiority which lawyers and judges may respond to precisely because they correspond to stereotypes of women which the lawyers and judges already hold. Battered woman syndrome does not mean, but can be heard as reinforcing stereotypes of women as passive, sick, powerless and victimized. Although it was developed to merely *describe* the common psychological characteristics which battered women share, and it is undoubtedly an accurate description of these characteristics, battered woman syndrome can be misused and misheard to enshrine the old stereotypes in a new form. This repeats an historic theme of treatment of women by the criminal law—women who are criminals are viewed as crazy or helpless or both.

Phyllis Crocker has pointed out that the courts are allowing battered woman syndrome testimony to establish a new stereotype, that of the *bona fide* battered woman.[h] Some expert testimony appears to have given the courts the impression that all battered women are exactly the same and react to their situation in identical ways. If a woman does not fit this preconceived pattern she may not be regarded as a battered woman, whatever the reality of her experience. There have already been a number of court opinions that have relied on deviations from this battered-woman stereotype—that a woman was not absolutely passive but fought back in the past, that she was not economically dependent but held a good job, that she owned or knew how to use a pistol, that her husband left her rather than her being unable to leave her husband, or that she was hit only once before the final assault—to uphold trial judges' exclusion of expert testimony about battering. Crocker points out that women defendants are getting caught between two sets of stereotypes. Prosecutors argue that because she didn't leave or get help or fight back, the violence a woman experienced must not have been so bad; therefore, her fear was unreasonable. Appellate courts, on the other hand, rule that if she did leave, get help or fight back, she wasn't really a battered woman.

In this connection, Professor Schneider has also raised the difficult question of whether the current battered woman syndrome model may be based too much on the experiences of middle- and upper-income white women whose passive responses to spousal violence may be different from those of women from other economic or ethnic backgrounds. Some battered woman defendants may not only be penalized for not acting like reasonable men, they may be penalized for not acting like middle-class white women as well.

h. Phyllis L. Crocker, The Meaning of Equality for Battered Women Who Kill Men in Self-Defense, 8 Harv. Women's L.J. 121 (1985).

Phyllis Crocker also expresses concern that a "reasonable battered woman" standard is developing to replace the reasonable-man standard in battered women cases, leaving the reasonable-man standard untouched in all other kinds of self-defense cases. A woman defendant's conviction or acquittal consequently may turn on whether she can prove she was a genuine battered woman rather than whether she acted in reasonable and necessary self-defense. In addition, Crocker sees an assumption developing that a woman's right to defend herself, and to present evidence supporting the reasonableness of her action, only applies to battered women and not women who defend themselves against rapists and other attackers who are not their domestic partners. * * *

Notes on Battered Women Who Kill Their Abusers

1. According to Department of Justice statistics, 33% of the women slain in 1998 were murdered by their intimate partners, while only 4% of the men murdered in the same year were killed by their intimate partners. U.S. Dep't of Justice, Bureau of Justice Statistics, Special Report: Intimate Partner Violence 2 (2000) ("Special Report"). In absolute terms, approximately 1,373 women were killed by intimate partners in 1998, compared with 457 men. Id. at 1. When a woman does kill her abuser, the circumstances may not quite "fit" the traditional law of self-defense, which requires, among other things, that the woman reasonably believe that she was in imminent danger of death or serious bodily harm at the time of the killing, that the force used be proportionate to the force threatened or used against her (e.g., not a gun against a fist), and sometimes that the person killing in self-defense retreat from the situation, if possible. See Kit Kinports, Defending Battered Women's Self–Defense Claims, 67 Or. L. Rev. 393, 408, 437 (1988). Commentators have pointed out that these requirements developed in the common law from a self-defense scenario based upon archetypically male situations, such as bar room brawls, involving a confrontation between two persons of roughly equal strength. See, e.g., Cynthia K. Gillespie, Justifiable Homicide: Battered Women, Self–Defense, and the Law 31–49 (1989). Women who kill their abusers may have trouble, for example, if they used deadly force to equalize the strength difference between themselves and their abusers, or killed after a long history of abuse but not in the middle of an attack; moreover, the "duty to retreat" makes little sense if one is being attacked in one's own home.

In thinking about women who kill their abusers, many people think of the situation presented in the "Burning Bed" movie, based on the true story of how Francine Hughes killed her husband by pouring gasoline on him and setting him afire while he was sleeping, after years of abuse and unsuccessful attempts to escape the marriage; she was ultimately acquitted on grounds of temporary insanity. Martha R. Mahoney, Legal Images of Battered Women: Redefining the Issue of Separation, 90 Mich. L. Rev. 1, 35 (1991). Does the killing in State v. Kelly present similar problems under the typical self-defense standard? Might a man who stabbed his neighbor after a history of violent attacks by the victim have been acquitted on these same facts?

2. Should the fact that a woman has been battered in the past constitute an excuse (i.e., the act was wrong but the actor is not considered morally blameworthy) or a justification (i.e., the act itself is considered morally justified because it avoids a greater harm)? See Cathryn Jo Rosen, The Excuse of Self–Defense: Correcting a Historical Accident on Behalf of Battered Women Who Kill, 36 Am. U.L. Rev. 11 (1986). What are the implications of choosing one or the other? The dangers? What other alternatives are there for defending the abused woman who kills under current self-defense law?

3. Could the situation in State v. Kelly be treated as manslaughter, or second degree murder, under the laws of your state? What about the Burning Bed case? In Illinois, second degree murder, which is still a Class 1 felony (punishable with a minimum 4–year and maximum 15–year sentence), requires that:

> At the time of the killing he [sic] is acting under a sudden and intense passion resulting from serious provocation by the individual killed * * *. Serious provocation is conduct sufficient to excite an intense passion in a reasonable person.

720 ILCS 5/9–2 (2000). Can the facts of a battering relationship fit "heat of passion" manslaughter?

4. How would (1) Mrs. Kelly, in the case above, and (2) Francine Hughes, in *The Burning Bed,* have fared under the following alternatives to the current self-defense standard: (a) self-defense with no requirement of imminence or duty to retreat, or (b) battered woman manslaughter?

5. Holly Maguigan concludes, based on an exhaustive survey of the appellate cases, that the typical killing by a battered woman of her abuser in fact takes place in the context of an attack upon her. Maguigan, Battered Women and Self–Defense: Myths and Misconceptions in Current Reform Proposals, 140 U. Pa. L. Rev. 379, 397 (1991) (finding that 75% of the incidents involved confrontations, and only 20% fell into the category of contract killing, sleeping man, or defendant as initial aggressor during a lull in the violence). If this is so, Maguigan concludes, there is no need to change the substantive law of self-defense specifically to accommodate the defense of these women, and to do so may be dangerous to women's interests in general. Id. at 442–50. Nonetheless, battered women who kill are repeatedly convicted, although many of their convictions are subsequently reversed on appeal, at much higher rates than in other homicide and felony appeals. Id. at 432–33. The reason they fail to receive a fair trial, Maguigan concludes, is not the inadequacy of the law, but its application by trial judges who are biased. Id. at 383. Is this an easier or a harder problem to attack? How can it be addressed?

6. Testimony about the battered woman syndrome is obviously a two-edged sword: it paints women as helpless victims and results in courts finding women who deviate from this new stereotype not to be justified in their actions, yet it explains the situation of the woman who fails to leave an abusive situation to a jury who may not otherwise find this behavior explicable. See, e.g., Elizabeth M. Schneider, Equal Rights to Trial for Women: Sex Bias in the Law of Self–Defense, 15 Harv.C.R.–C.L.L.Rev. 623 (1980); Phyllis L. Crocker, The Meaning of Equality for Battered Women

Who Kill Men in Self–Defense, 8 Harv.Women's L.J. 121 (1985). On balance, do you think that the use of battered woman testimony helps or harms women? Why or why not? Who is the "reasonable" battered woman? How does she act? For difficulties in ascertaining "reasonableness," see discussion of the reasonable woman standard in sexual harassment cases in Chapter 10.

7. Martha Mahoney points out that in many, if not most, cases domestic violence victims in fact did attempt to leave but that their attempts at separation were greeted with further and often more intense violence, as well as violent attempts to get them back if they succeed in leaving—a phenomenon she has aptly named "separation assault." Mahoney, above note 1, at 61–68. In fact, more than half the men who kill their spouses do so after they have separated, while less than 10% of women who kill their abusers do so when they are separated. Id. at 64–65. Mahoney argues, persuasively, that feminist lawyers should endeavor to replace the perennial question "Why didn't she leave?" with the concept of separation assault, to show the essential relationship of power and control that prevents the woman from leaving, even if she tries. Id. at 82, 94. How will this evidence come in at trial?

8. Justice Department statistics show a sharp decline (23%) in domestic killings between 1993 and 1998. However, much of this decrease is explained by the enormous decline in the number of men murdered by an intimate partner (most presumably in self-defense), which fell by 60% since 1976; white females are the only group for whom intimate homicide has not decreased since 1976. (The number of African American females killed by intimates dropped 45%.) Special Report, above note 1, at 3. How would you explain these seemingly anomalous statistics?

E. PROSTITUTION

1. WHITE SLAVE TRAFFIC

RUTH ROSEN, WHITE SLAVERY: MYTH OR REALITY

In The Lost Sisterhood: Prostitution in America, 1900–1918 112, 121–22 (1982).

Of all the foreign girls and women imported into the United States, Chinese and Japanese women probably suffered the cruelest treatment and enslavement. In part, this resulted from the strong antagonism against Asians prevalent on the West Coast. It is also true that Asian women made extremely inexpensive and easy targets within their own country. The first traffic in Chinese women apparently began during the middle of the nineteenth century. Around 1854, six hundred women were imported from China by the Hip–Yee Tong. Finding Chinese women for importation was not a difficult task. The extreme impoverishment and destitution among most families made daughters a serious liability in prerevolutionary China. Just as some parents actually broke their children's limbs to seek charity, certain families welcomed promises of marriage and payment for their daughters, even when they suspected that the girls might be sold as concubines within China.

The number of Chinese prostitutes on the West Coast apparently so offended Californians that the importation of Chinese women for "immoral purposes" was outlawed in California in 1870. After the Chinese Exclusion Act of 1882, white slavers had to devise new means of importing Chinese women into the United States for prostitution. Bribing or blackmailing immigration officials were some of the "business methods" commonly used. Due to the difficulty of securing passage for such women, the prices of Chinese white slaves skyrocketed.

In most recorded cases, Chinese girls continued to be purchased from their families. One Chinese man, for example, paid a family $140 for their daughter by promising to send her to school in America. Given the feudal and patriarchal attitudes toward women at the time, the daughter had little choice but to obey her parents. Passing the customs officers as father and daughter, or using a forged certificate of citizenship, the procurer then forced the young girl into prostitution in Boston. Soon after, he made a handsome profit by selling her to a Chinese woman for three thousand dollars.

In another documented case, a Chinese mother made arrangements for her daughter to be married in a distant city. Instead, the procurer transported the bride-to-be to the United States. "One thousand five hundred and thirty dollars were paid for me," the girl later recalled. "I saw the money paid and I . . . was placed in her den. They forced me to do their bidding, but I cried and resisted. I did not want to live this life. They starved me for days, tying me where food was almost in reach of me . . . then they beat me time after time and threatened to kill me if I did not behave right."

Stories such as these were told to missionaries who received runaway slaves at rescue homes in San Francisco and Berkeley. In addition, such rescue workers and missionaries learned that false promises of marriage and outright kidnapping were indeed the most common methods of importing Chinese women into "yellow" slavery. In many cases, the procurers had made contracts with parents which had no legal status in the United States; nevertheless, Chinese tongs, or organized Chinese political societies in the United States, attempted to enforce these contracts between procurers and Chinese families.

A white slave market soon grew around Dupont Street in San Francisco. There, Chinese white slaves were directly brought from ships to endure a humiliating physical examination by potential buyers. In an apartment called the "Queen's Room," young girls were subjected to the kind of dehumanizing objectification that Africans had experienced upon landing in the hands of southern auctioneers. Many of these girls, often as young as eleven and twelve, ended up as slaves of the infamous crib system—viewed by one reformer as the worst form of American sexual slavery. He described the cribs as "small rooms opening into inner passages by means of a barred window and door, which is kept locked by the manager, the key being given to men as they apply to him. Within these little cells, scantily furnished, are kept young girls, most of them Chinese and Japanese, but some of them European and American. They have little light or air, are rarely allowed to leave their rooms, and the manager receives the money."

Occasionally, when these girls managed to escape, members of tongs, or of the white slave trade, spread throughout northern California, searching for runaway slaves and returning them to their "owners." Thus, in many respects, Chinese white slaves became virtual chattel. Sometimes they did not even understand that they were "owned" by someone else until they found a rescue home or missionary that helped them escape their pursuers. Such women, as the Immigration Commission recognized in their report, had "become real slaves ... and unless some man ... is ready to marry them, their position is practically that of permanent slavery." In other words, unless a woman, like a black slave in the nineteenth century, could buy her freedom—and legend has it that some did—she remained the property of her procurers.

PROSTITUTION: A CONTEMPORARY FORM OF SLAVERY DORCHEN LEIDHOLDT, CO-EXECUTIVE DIRECTOR, COALITION AGAINST TRAFFICKING IN WOMEN, UNITED NATIONS WORKING GROUP ON CONTEMPORARY FORMS OF SLAVERY

Geneva, May 1998.

http://www.uri.edu/artsci/wms/hughes

The Coalition is an international non-governmental organization with regional headquarters and networks in Asia, Latin America, North America, Europe, Africa, and Australia. The Coalition works against all practices of sexual violence and exploitation, including but not limited to rape, incest, intimate violence, prostitution, sex trafficking, sex tourism, mail order bride markets, sexual harassment, pornography, involuntary sterilization and childbearing, female genital mutilation, and temporary marriage or marriage of convenience for the purpose of sexual exploitation.

The focus of our work is on sexual exploitation, which we define as the sexual violation of a person's human dignity, equality, and physical or mental integrity and as a practice by which some people (primarily men) achieve power and domination over others (primarily women and children) for the purpose of sexual gratification, financial gain, and/or advancement. The Coalition recognizes that, in order to carry out their practices and achieve their goals, sexual exploiters are facilitated by and make use of long-standing social hierarchies, especially the domination of men over women, of adults over children, of rich over poor, of racial and ethnic majorities over racial and ethnic minorities, and of so-called "First World" over so-called "Third World" countries.

We believe that all of the practices I have just described are proper areas of inquiry for the Working Group on Contemporary Forms of Slavery. We define slavery as the domination and control by an individual or group over other individuals or groups through violence, the threat of violence, or a history of violence. Slavers are motivated by a desire for sexual gratification, economic gain, or power and domination, or a combination of these factors. We reference the definition of slavery in the Convention on Slavery, Forced Labor, and Similar Institutions and Practices: "Slavery is the status or condition of a person over whom any or all of the powers attaching to the right of ownership are exercised." All of the practices addressed by the Coalition emerge from the historical reality of the chattel status of women and children and represent an attempt to revive and maintain it. Moreover, * * * unlike traditional forms of slave ownership in which the person enslaved was regarded as a capital investment, to be maintained and guarded over a long period of time, contemporary forms of slavery often reflect a valuation of the enslaved as a temporary, disposable commodity, to be consumed and discarded.

For example, prostitution, in the vast majority of cases, represents the ownership of women and children by pimps, brothel owners, and sometimes even customers for the purpose of financial gain, sexual gratification, and/or power and domination. Of those women who appear to work in prostitution voluntarily, many if not most endured situations of enslavement as children, in thrall to sexually abusive adults, or as adolescents or young women subjected to the violent subjugation of abusive husbands or boyfriends. That subjugation is continued in prostitution, whether over the long term by the pimp, who controls her every movement and confiscates her earnings, or, for a shorter duration by the customer, who buys her body for a night or week and requires total compliance with his sexual demands. Female genital mutilation, though not a form of slavery in itself, is closely tied to slavery-like practices: it is a method by which a male dominated society ensures the subordination of women and girls to their fathers and husbands; it is a strategy to destroy a woman's experience of her sexuality and thus the ownership of her body.

The Coalition urges the Working Group on Contemporary Forms of Slavery to encourage research and study on the way these different practices work together, albeit differently in different cultures, to perpetuate the chattel status of women and children. The Coalition also urges the Working Group to continue to address slavery and slavery-like practices that affect primarily women and children. The Coalition notes that the practices of slavery affecting these groups may be characterized by different forms, dynamics, and motivations from the practices of slavery directly primarily against men for purposes of forced labor. Any definition of slavery that excludes those practices directed against women and children is overly narrow and is a product of gender bias.

The subject of my remarks concerns the context into which we place and understand the trafficking of women and girls for the purposes of sexual exploitation. Over the last five years, many organizations have addressed the issue of trafficking in women but ignored its relationship to other practices of sexual violence and exploitation, specifically sex tourism, military prostitution, sexual exploitation on the internet, and organized prostitution. Similar distinctions have been made between adult and child sexual exploitation and between so-called forced and so-called voluntary prostitution. Although there are many motivations for making these distinctions, the cumulative effect is organizing efforts and analyses that address only the most severe and obvious abuses while ignoring the institutionalized sexual exploitation and abuse that is the economic foundation of the sex industry. Although these distinctions are sometimes made in the name of the victim, in fact they serve to protect the industry and its customers at the expense of the victim.

The first distinction that is made is that between sex trafficking and other practices of sexual exploitation, most notably organized prostitution. This is a distinction that the drafters of the 1949 Convention [for the Suppression of the Traffic in Persons and of the Exploitation of the Prostitution of Others] considered and rejected, uniting in both title and text the trafficking in persons with the exploitation of the prostitution of others. The connections between trafficking and organized prostitution, evident in 1949, are even more pronounced in the global sex industry of 1998. The fact is that organized prostitution is the economic and structural foundation of sex trafficking. Although it is not often recognized, many of the women and girls who are trafficked start out being prostituted to local men by local pimps and brothel owners. Often when they are deported back to their countries of origin, they are prostituted again, locally. Coalition representatives have met with many such women during site visits to the Philippines and Thailand. The survivor of sex trafficking who testified before the United Nations General Assembly in 1996 started out in child prostitution in Puerto Rico before being trafficked through Honduras, only to end up back in prostitution in the United States. Sex tourism, a form of prostitution controlled by local or global economic interests, is often the launching pad for sex trafficking, but is not considered such as it involves sexual exploitation of local women in their country of origin.

The fact is that sex trafficking and organized prostitution are inextricably connected and share fundamental characteristics. The victims who are targeted are the same—poor, minority, or so-called Third World women and children, frequently with histories of physical and sexual abuse. The customers are the same—men with disposable income who achieve sexual gratification by purchasing and invading the body of a woman or child. The dynamics of power and control employed by the sex industry profiteers are the same, whether they take the form of violence and threats of violence, debt bondage, torture, imprisonment, and/or brainwashing. The harm to the victims is the same—trauma, sexually transmitted diseases, drug and alcohol addiction, the physical toll of repeated beatings by customers and pimps, the psychological and physical toll of repeated and unwanted sex, and the destruction of the sense of self, identity, and sexuality. The harm to society is the same—the reification of sex- and race-based hierarchies. Whether they purchase women who are trafficked or those who are otherwise prostituted, sex industry consumers move from the brothel into the world, that experience coloring their relations to women and girls in the rest of society. Some American men stationed in South East Asia during the Vietnam War have talked about how their immersion in military prostitution profoundly damaged their ability to relate to women and girls back home. A few former sex industry consumers, who have become leaders in the movement against sexual exploitation, have discussed similar effects of participating as customers of the sex trade. Certainly, the injuries to their sense of self and sexuality are mild compared to those of the young women who are reduced to sexual merchandise by the industry. Nevertheless, we must acknowledge that the sex industry also harms men, impairing their ability to experience sexual relations that are premised on mutual respect and equality.

The second distinction that is frequently made, to the detriment of victims and the benefit of the sex industry, is that between the sexual exploitation of children and of adults. The problem with this position is that by failing to criticize the sexual exploitation of adults, it legitimizes it. For example, to decry the prostitution of a fifteen-year-old girl but to fail to speak out against the prostitution of her seventeen-year-old sister is to tacitly sanction the sexual exploitation of the older girl. Many organizations have organized to end the sexual exploitation of children, a laudable goal, but have failed to see that the sexual exploitation of children is inextricably connected to that of adults. Studies show that in the West, at least 70 percent of the adults exploited by the sex industry were sexually abused as children. They also show that the average age of entry into prostitution is 16 or younger. It is clear that the sexually exploited children of today are the prostituted adults of tomorrow, and, as the French abolitionist organization, Le Nid, declares, "In every whore, there is a little girl murdered." Although some sex industry consumers are fixated on sex with young children, many sexually exploit young girls and young women interchangeably. We will not be able to end the sexual exploitation of children until we take a stand and develop strategies against sexual exploitation of all human beings.

The third and most problematic distinction that has recently emerged is that between so-called forced and so-called voluntary prostitution. By limiting the pool of people who can be identified as victims while simultaneously protecting large segments of the sex industry, this is the best gift that pimps and traffickers could have received. This distinction creates a vision of prostitution that is freely chosen; a vision that can be maintained only by ignoring all of the social conditions that force women and girls into conditions of sexual exploitation. The proponents of this distinction are sending the following message: "Don't pay attention to the poverty, the familial pressure, the incest she survived, the battering by her boyfriend, the lack of employment options available to her. Just ask whether there is a gun pointed at her head or whether she is being overtly deceived. No gun, no deceit; then no problem; not only is she voluntarily in the sex industry, she is a 'sex worker.' " Under this analysis, the pimp who recruited her, the brothel owner who reaps profits by selling her to sex tourists, and the trafficker who sends her abroad are rehabilitated as so-called "third-party managers."

What are the consequences of conceptualizing prostitution as free or forced, and the legitimization of prostitution as "sex work" that inevitably follows? There are many. First, governments, especially those of poor countries, realize that they can reduce their unemployment rate and increase their gross national product by moving unemployed women and girls into organized prostitution. This is most likely to happen in countries with strong internal sex industries fueled by the profits of sex tourists. In Belize, for example, the government touts prostitution as work for poor women. Not only does it feel no shame at doing so, but proudly reports on this approach in its 1996 report to CEDAW, stating, "Recognized prostitution in Belize is a gender-specific form of migrant labor that serves the same economic function for women as agricultural work offers to men and often for better pay." When governments recognize prostitution as sex work for poor women, organized prostitution, sex tourism and sex trafficking increase.

Second, when prostitution is accepted by a society as sex work, it becomes even more difficult for poor women and girls, socialized into an ethos of self-sacrifice, to resist economic and familial pressures to enter prostitution. As the numbers of prostituted women and girls expand, growing numbers become infected with HIV and die of AIDS while a smaller but still significant percentage are murdered by pimps or customers. Those women fortunate enough to survive sexual exploitation emerge, usually in their 30's, when they are no longer marketable commodities, with no job skills, traumatized from years of enduring unwanted sex and violence, and physically debilitated from sexually transmitted diseases and the substance abuse necessary to endure the sex of prostitution. What is available to these women? Destitution or a career as a madam or mama san, helping the pimps control the younger women who are marketable commodities.

Third, when prostitution is recognized as "sex work," legalization follows; pimps, sex industry cartels, and sex businesses openly flourish, regulated only by the demands of the marketplace. Fourth, when prostitution is legitimized as sex work, men and boys are sent the message that purchasing the body of a woman or girl for sex is no different from buying a pack of cigarettes. With no social stigma attached to buying prostitutes, the demand for prostitution escalates. At the same time, women and girls internalize the message that the female body is a marketable commodity. Girls begin to see prostitution as a career option, unaware that sex work is a trap that will deprive them of control over their lives. Fifth, when prostitution is legitimized as sex work, the values and dynamics of prostitution spill over into other areas of society, influencing the valuation and treatment of women and girls and lowering their status.

Some have argued that since criminal sanctions have clearly not slowed the growth of the sex industry or lessened the exploitation of victims, the only recourse is to recognize prostitution as sex work and legalize the sex industry. Criminal sanctions have not worked it is true, but that is because in most instances they have been directed against the victims. Few countries invest law enforcement resources in the investigation and prosecution of sex industry profiteers and fewer still address criminal sanctions against the customers, who fuel the demand side of the industry. And while some countries have conducted effective and well funded campaigns against domestic violence and rape, building networks of shelters for victims and offering counseling and legal services, women and girls in conditions of sexual exploitation have been deprived of the support systems and advocacy provided other victims of male violence.

To begin to address the enslavement of women and girls by local and global sex industries, we must take the following steps:

Recognize that sex trafficking, sex tourism, military prostitution, sexual exploitation on the internet, and organized prostitution are interrelated practices of gender-based domination and control that constitute contemporary forms of slavery.

Commission a preparatory group to address the need for an optional protocol to strengthen the application of the 1949 Convention and explore the need for a new Convention Against All Forms of Sexual Exploitation.

Call for local, national, regional, and international law enforcement strategies that depenalize the victims of sexual exploitation while penalizing sex industry profiteers and customers.

Urge countries to expand and develop shelters and counseling services, medical care providers, and legal services for all victims of male violence against women, including sex industry victims and survivors.

Notes on White Slave Traffic

1. One of the earliest attempts to regulate prostitution in the United States was the Alien Prostitution Importation Act of 1875. The Act made it illegal to import women from other countries for the purpose of prostitution. By the early part of 1900 public concern about prostitution began to grow and Congress held hearings to determine how to curb it. On June 25, 1910, Congress passed the White Slave Traffic Act, more commonly known as the Mann Act. 18 U.S.C.A. §§ 2421–2424 (1982). The Act prohibited transportation across state lines of "any woman or girl for the purpose of prostitution or debauchery, or for any other immoral purpose." For over 50 years, it was the only federal legislation which dealt with prostitution. Today, the Act is still utilized where minors are transported across state lines. See generally Marlene D. Beckman, The White Slave Traffic Act: The Historical Impact of a Criminal Law Policy on Women, 72 Geo. L. J. 111 (1984).

The scope of liability under the Mann Act was one of the most hotly debated issues during its passage. Clearly, the statutory meaning of "immoral purpose" was subject to broad interpretation by the courts. Does "immoral purpose" include bringing a mistress to the United States from England? See United States v. Bitty, 208 U.S. 393, 28 S.Ct. 396, 52 L.Ed. 543 (1908) (includes the importation of a woman to live as a concubine with the person importing her). Does it include the polygamous practices of Mormons? See Cleveland v. United States, 329 U.S. 14, 67 S.Ct. 13, 91 L.Ed. 12 (1946) (yes, multiple marriages are immoral). What if the purpose of the transportation across state lines was the filming of a pornographic movie? See United States v. Roeder, 526 F.2d 736 (10th Cir.1975) (yes). Is rape an "immoral purpose" under the Mann Act? See United States v. Mitchell, 778 F.2d 1271 (7th Cir.1985) (yes).

2. While the Mann Act allows prosecutors to bring a *criminal* action against a person who intends to prostitute a female, it requires that prostitution be the "dominant motive" for transporting a woman across state lines. Recently some women have suggested that the Racketeer Influenced and Corrupt Organizations Act ("RICO"), 18 U.S.C.A. §§ 1961–1968, could be used to bring a *civil* cause of action by anyone who is injured by a prostitution ring. RICO provides a private cause of action for anyone injured by the investment in, acquisition or operation of an "enterprise" that affects interstate commerce through a "pattern of racketeering activity"; according to the law, racketeering includes trafficking in women. To encourage private suits, Congress provided for triple damages, court costs, and attorney's fees. The argument for its use is that prostitution has grown and changed over the last century, and the nature and organization of prostitution rings fits the pattern of racketeering RICO was meant to control. See Lan Cao, Illegal Traffic in Women: A Civil RICO Proposal, 96 Yale L.J. 1297 (1987). Does a civil RICO approach make better sense than the criminal approach? Why? Who has the power to decide to sue? To control the suit? In general, do you think civil or criminal actions are better for women? Why?

3. As demonstrated by the Leidholdt excerpt, the international human rights community has recently become more concerned about the trafficking in women and children, questioning the effectiveness of the 1949 Convention for the Suppression of the Traffic in Persons and of the Exploitation of the Prostitution of Others. That original Convention was signed and ratified only by a small number of countries (67 countries compared with 126 countries for the International Convention on Social, Economic and Cultural Rights and 125 countries for the International Convention on Civil and Political Rights). Several countries (such as Australia, Sweden, the Netherlands, and Britain) which historically have supported international women's rights did not sign. Parties to the Convention agree to punish any persons who procure women for the purposes of prostitution or make a profit from prostituting others, outlawing such actions even when the prostituted persons are "consenting," i.e., there is no distinction between "forced" and "free" prostitution. Persons who keep or manage brothels, or let or rent buildings "for the purpose of the prostitution of others," are also to be punished. Sheila Jeffreys comments upon more recent occurrences:

> Until the late 1980s it does not seem to have been the case that the international human rights community considered prostitution inconsistent with certain basic human rights, such as the right to dignity and integrity of the person, though they may not have been in favour of establishing this understanding in a convention. The report of the UN

Rapporteur, J. Fernand–Laurent, in 1983 stated that prostitution was a form of slavery, and recommended that national authorities seek co-operation with social organisations, including organisations of prostituted women, "but only when they do not call for prostitution to be recognised as a profession." * * *

The International Meeting of Experts on Sexual Exploitation, Violence, and Prostitution in 1991, organised through the Coalition Against Trafficking in Women and UNESCO, was called to draft a new convention. It is entitled the *Convention Against Sexual Exploitation*. This Convention answers the need, which feminist human rights theorists have been demonstrating, for a convention specifically penalising violence against women. But whereas other discussions of how to proceed have excluded prostitution, this proposal has both trafficking and prostitution as central to its concerns. Sexual exploitation is defined as:

> a practice by which person(s) achieve sexual gratification or financial gain or advancement through the abuse of a person's sexuality by abrogating that person's human right to dignity, equality, autonomy, and physical and mental well-being.

It is defined as including, but not being limited to, female infanticide, wife and widow murder, battering, pornography, prostitution, genital mutilation, female seclusion, dowry and bride price, forced sterilisation and forced child-bearing, sexual harassment, rape, incest, sexual abuse and trafficking, temporary marriage, and sex predetermination.

Jeffreys, The Idea of Prostitution 325, 333–35 (1997). Do you agree that prostitution is a form of slavery? Why or why not? Many women who decide to enter into prostitution believe it is their best economic option; what impact will a Convention prohibiting prostitution have on them? Is there a better way to address the problems of prostitution? Do you think the international community can have an effect on prostitution? Why or why not? Do you think Leidholdt's recommendations will work? Are they likely to be enacted?

4. According to the Coalition Against Trafficking in Women's ("CATW") Factbook on Global Sexual Exploitation, the largest sex industry market for Asian women is Japan, where over 150,000 non-Japanese women are in prostitution, more than half Filipina. The money earned in the sex industry in Japan is equivalent to its defense budget. Donna M. Hughes, Laura Joy Sporcic, and Nadine Z. Mendelsohn, The Factbook on Global Sexual Exploitation, http://www.uri.edu.artsci.wms.hughes. However, trafficking is a problem not only in foreign countries but also in the United States. For example, according to the Factbook 5,000 Filipina mail order brides have entered the U.S. every year since 1986; the American mail-order bride industry is a multi-million dollar business. Why do you think American men "order" brides from the Asia Pacific? What would you propose as a solution to this importation of foreign women for sexual services?

In April, 2000, Senator Paul Wellstone introduced comprehensive legislation, the Trafficking Victims Protection Act of 2000, that aims to prevent trafficking in persons, provide protection and assistance to those who have been trafficked, and severe punishment for those responsible for trafficking. According to Wellstone, as many as 50,000 women and children are brought into the U.S. each year and forced to work as prostitutes, forced laborers, or servants. Worldwide, trafficking is estimated to affect up to 2 million persons.

5. Sex tourism, when people (primarily men) travel to other countries specifically to buy sex, appears to be on the rise. Julia O'Connell Davidson addresses this phenomenon:

> The term "sex tourism" is widely associated with organized sex tours, often conjuring up images of groups of middle-aged businessmen being shepherded into state-sanctioned brothels in South Korea or Go Go bars in the Philippines and Thailand. But if sex tourism is defined as consisting of people from economically developed nations traveling to underdeveloped countries "specifically to purchase the sexual services of local women [and men]", it embraces a far broader range of people, activities and locations. Male sex tourists of all ages travel to Brazil and some African and Caribbean countries as well as to South East Asia; Bali, the Gambia and the Caribbean are popular destinations for female sex tourists. The nature and terms of the exchanges between sex tourists and local people vary enormously, as does the degree to which any third party, including the state, is involved. * * *
>
> An analysis of sex tourism which fails to consider its economics is doomed to provide only a partial explanation of the phenomenon, for without the obscene disparity in average per capita incomes between the countries which host sex tourists and those which supply them, sex tourism would be a marginal activity of a very different character. * * * In Thailand, a prostitute can be rented for almost twenty-four hours for as little as 500 Baht (around 18 pounds) [approximately $34], a sum of money that would barely secure a man a ten-minute blow job in Britain.

Davidson, British Sex Tourists in Thailand, in (Hetero)sexual Politics 42–3, 45 (Mary Maynard and June Purvis, eds. 1995). Hence, the flow of sex tourists is generally from the economically developed countries to poorer countries of South East Asia, Africa, Latin America and the Caribbean. Eastern Europe is quickly developing as a destination to attract sex tourists and export child prostitution. What is the responsibility of economically developed countries to address this problem? What recommendations would you make?

6. The use of children in sex tourism is growing. In 1996, representatives from over 120 countries met in Sweden at the first World Congress Against Commercial Sexual Exploitation of Children. In the words of the General Rapporteur, Professor Vitit Muntarbhorn of Thailand, "there can be no more delusions; no-one can deny that the problem of children being sold for sex exists, here and now, in almost every country in the world." See Tourism and Children in Prostitution, World Congress Against Commercial Sexual Exploitation of Children, www.childhub.ch/webpub/csechome. One organization, End Child Prostitution in Asian Tourism (ECPAT), claims success in promoting transnational governmental cooperation, extraterritorial legislation allowing governments to bring their nationals to trial for crimes committed in other countries, and in drawing public attention to the arrest, detention, and conviction of paedophiles engaged in sex tourism. See www.ecpat.org. ECPAT, in its 1994 Development Manual, states that Brazil

has over 500,000 children available for tourists; there are 400,000 in India; between 200,000 and 850,000 in Thailand; and 100,000 in Taiwan. Id. at 21, 28–9, 37. It estimates that child sex tourism generated from $20–23 billion in the 1993–95 period. Id. at 29. In an attempt to address this problem, Australia passed a law, the Child Sex Tourism Amendment Act, in 1994. This Act makes sexual activity with a child under 16 years committed in an overseas country by an Australian citizen or resident a criminal offense in Australia. The laws apply to individuals, companies or corporations and provide for a term of imprisonment of up to 17 years and fines of up to $500,000. It is also an offence to encourage, benefit or profit from any activity that promotes sexual activity with children. Do you think this law will make any difference? Do the economic incentives to trading in children's sexuality seem impossible to overcome? What kinds of other strategies do you think could work?

2. PROSTITUTES AND THE LAW

KATHLEEN BARRY, THROWAWAY WOMEN

In Female Sexual Slavery 121 (1979).

All kinds of women are vulnerable to slave procurers. The assumption that only women of a particular class, race, or age group are potential victims of female sexual slavery has followed from the inability to recognize sexual domination as it underpins all other forms of oppression. It is true that some procuring methods are adapted to particular groups of women and the strategy that works in rural poverty may not work in an urban bus station. But it is primarily procurers and their interests and only secondarily women's age, race or economic class that determine who will end up forced into prostitution.

The other major cause of sex slavery is the social-sexual objectification of women that permeates every patriarchal society in the world. Identifying women first as sexual beings who are responsible for the sexual services of men is the social base for gender-specific sexual slavery. As most women know, being sexually harassed while walking alone down a street, or sitting in a bar or restaurant without a man, is a poignant reminder of our definition as sexual objects. Spurning those advances and reacting against them are likely to draw indignant wrath from the perpetrator, suggesting the extent to which many men assume the sexual objectification of *any* woman as their right. Under such conditions, sexual slavery lurks at the corners of every woman's life.

Increasingly, stereotyped female-gender characteristics are becoming the means of identifying prostitutes. In 1975 a Danish court ruled on a prostitution case that had ramifications for all women when it agreed that a policeman could identify a woman as a prostitute *from the way she walked.* The court fined the woman for soliciting based only on the testimony of a policeman who said, "I took action only when she was obviously soliciting, and that was easily determined from the way she walked."

CITY OF PORTLAND v. MILLER

Oregon Court of Appeals, 1983.

62 Or.App. 145, 659 P.2d 980.

Defendant appeals her conviction for loitering to solicit prostitution, in violation of Portland city ordinance 14.24.050. She contends that the ordinance is unconstitutionally vague and overbroad and that there was insufficient evidence to convict. Because we reverse for insufficient evidence, we do not reach the constitutional issues.

The ordinance provides, in pertinent part:

"As used in this section, 'prostitution' means an act of sexual intercourse or sodomy between two persons, not married to each other, in return for the payment of money or other valuable consideration by one of them.

"* * *

"(b) It is unlawful for any person to loiter in or near any street or public place in a manner and under circumstances manifesting the purpose of inducing, enticing, soliciting or procuring another to commit an act of prostitution. Among the circumstances which may be considered in determining whether such purpose is manifested are that the person repeatedly beckons to, stops or attempts to stop motor vehicle operators by hailing them or gesturing to them. * * *"

The state's evidence at that point was that on a cold November night, two vice officers, Wong and Roberts, were investigating prostitution and drug activity in downtown Portland. They were stationed on the third or fourth floor of a parking structure across the street from Dinty Moore's Tavern and the Lotus Cardroom. They watched the pedestrian traffic in front of those establishments. About 7:10 p.m., they saw defendant alight from a white Cadillac that had pulled up in front of Dinty Moore's. She was wearing tight, white cotton pants, tucked in her boots, and a brown, waist-length fur jacket. Neither officer knew who she was. Wong watched her for 30 to 40 minutes. Roberts was with him for the first 15 minutes. During that time, they saw defendant wave at passing vehicles and approach a man on the sidewalk and engage him in conversation. He finally walked around her, shaking his head as if to say "no." Defendant then went into Dinty Moore's for a few minutes, came back out and walked over to the front of the Lotus Cardroom where she again waved and smiled as cars drove by. Meanwhile, Roberts drove around the block in his unmarked car, intending to "contact" her. She did not wave or pay any attention to him as he drove by. Roberts had been "in vice" only about three months and had no reason to believe defendant was familiar with him.

While defendant stood near the corner smiling at passing cars, several cars slowed but none stopped, and defendant did not talk to any of the drivers. About 7:40 p.m., she walked back to and entered Dinty

Moore's. Roberts had rejoined Wong, and at 8 p.m. they descended from their viewpoint and entered Dinty Moore's. They found defendant sitting at the bar having a hard-boiled egg and a drink. They identified themselves and asked defendant to step outside, where they asked her what she had been doing in the area for the past 40 minutes. Roberts did not remember any particular statements by defendant. Wong, however, recalled that she said she had not been outside at all and had just been let off by a friend.

The state argues that the evidence was sufficient to permit a rational trier of fact to draw the inference that defendant had intended to solicit prostitution. We disagree. It may have been sufficient to give a reasonable police officer reasonable suspicion to stop and question defendant, but we cannot say it was enough to prove beyond a reasonable doubt the requisite intent to solicit a prohibited act for consideration.

* * *

This offense, like any other, consists of certain essential elements, each of which requires proof beyond a reasonable doubt. * * * The necessary element of defendant's specific intent is lacking here. * * * Defendant's activity may have been "in the manner of," but evidence that defendant "hung around" in the manner of working prostitutes does not, without more, establish the requisite intent. Simply stated, it is not a violation of the law merely to look like a prostitute might. The ordinance demands more than that.

Reversed.

Notes on the Legal Treatment of Prostitution

1. Does *Portland v. Miller* support Barry's argument that any woman may be considered a prostitute as a result of stereotyped female-gender characteristics? If you dress like a prostitute, look like one, walk like one, stand on a street corner and wave at strangers in cars, are you one? Is this a way to control women who do not conform to social expectations for gender roles? Is it a successful way to divide women into two groups: good girls and bad girls (prostitutes)? How does this harm women?

2. Margaret A. Baldwin, a law professor and anti-prostitution activist, addresses the issue of women "distancing" themselves from prostitutes in her article, Split at the Root: Prostitution and Feminist Discourses of Law Reform, 5 Yale J. Law & Feminism 47, 48 (1992):

> In the design of existing law, in the behavior of individual men, and in the leading strategies of feminist law reform, the relationship is cast in oppositional terms: whoever a "prostitute" is, "other women" are not. In substance, the distinction provides a handy means of identifying appropriate female objects of punishment and contempt. To be deemed a "prostitute," whether by the state, by a john, or by any other man for that matter, immediately targets a girl or woman for arrest, for sexual assault, for murder, or, at the very least, dismissive scorn. Victims of rape, of incest, of domestic battery, of sexual harassment, are quite

> familiar with this difficulty. Declared to be "whores" and "sluts" by the men who abuse them, women then confront a legal system which puts the same issue in the form of a question: was she in fact a "slut" who deserved it, as the perpetrator claims, or not-a-slut, deserving of some redress?

Id. at 48. What do women get out of distancing themselves from prostitutes? Do women have any choice? Are women in a double bind? If you were the defense attorney in a rape prosecution, would you argue that the complaining witness was a prostitute? If so, are you inevitably contributing to the "rapeability" of prostitutes?

3. A typical pandering law states that a person is guilty "who knowingly . . . compels, induces or encourages any person to lead a life of prostitution." Ariz.Rev.Stat. § 13–3209(4) (1999). Thus, because a defendant may be convicted of the "criminal activity exclusively through words, the statements are the whole of the crime." Arizona v. Daugherty, 173 Ariz. 548, 845 P.2d 474 (App.1992) (conviction of defendant who ran a "modeling and companionship" service after an undercover policewoman, under pretense of seeking employment, was told about prostitution acts she would be expected to perform as a "model" for the company). What is the public policy behind pandering laws? Are there First Amendment concerns with pandering laws?

Margaret A. Baldwin drafted a law providing for a private cause of action for those coerced into prostitution to sue their pimps for compensatory and punitive damages, and the Florida legislature passed the legislation in 1992. Fla. Stat. ch. 769.09 (1992). See Baldwin, Strategies of Connection: Prostitution and Feminist Politics, 1 Mich. J. Gender & L. 65, 70–71 (1993). In grappling with a statutory definition of "coercion," Baldwin attempted to identify the conditions under which females are induced to prostitution:

> (k) Restraint of speech or communication with others.
>
> (*l*) Exploitation of a condition of developmental disability, cognitive limitation, affective disorder, or substance dependency.
>
> (m) Exploitation of victimization by sexual abuse.
>
> (n) Exploitation of pornographic performance.
>
> (*o*) Exploitation of human needs for food, shelter, safety, or affection.

Id. at 72. Thus, according to Baldwin, "[t]hese provisions affirm simply that women and girls are not available for prostitution, and do not consent to it, but the fact of being human, with real needs, real vulnerabilities, and real wounds." Id. See also Beverly Balos and Mary Louise Fellows, A Matter of Prostitution: Becoming Respectable, 74 N.Y.U. L. Rev. 1220 (1999).

Does this offer a better option for prostitutes? What do you think of the trend of women utilizing civil suits to redress violence rather than the criminal justice system? See also Catharine A. MacKinnon, Prostitution and Civil Rights, 1 Mich. J. Gender & L. 13 (1993).

4. In another case, a defendant successfully appealed his conviction for "procuring for prostitution a person," arguing that he offered money to a 12–year-old girl to have sex with him and, therefore, he was only guilty of solicitation. The procuring statute states: "A person who procures for prostitution, or causes to be prostituted, any person * * * commits a felony

* * *." Prostitution is "the giving or receiving of the body for sexual activity for hire but excludes sexual activity between spouses" and "involves a financial element." Furthermore, it is unlawful "[t]o solicit, induce, entice, or procure another to commit prostitution, lewdness, or assignation." * * * Register v. Florida, 715 So.2d 274 (Fla.App., 1998). Why aren't movie producers who pay actors to engage in sexual activity prosecuted and convicted under these types of statutes?

5. A study in New York found that only one percent of those arrested for prostitution were johns. JoAnn L. Miller, Prostitution in Contemporary American Society, in Sexual Coercion 45, 53 (Elizabeth Grauerholz and Mary A. Koralweski, eds. 1991). Because of this gross disparity in arrest rates between prostitutes and customers, women frequently have made a formal equality anti-discrimination argument in defending against prostitution charges: the state's selective prosecution of only the women (prostitutes) is in violation of the 14th Amendment's Equal Protection Clause. This strategy has been minimally effective. See, e.g., State v. Wilbur, 110 Wash.2d 16, 749 P.2d 1295 (1988) (dismissing equal protection challenge); People v. Superior Court, 19 Cal.3d 338, 138 Cal.Rptr. 66, 562 P.2d 1315 (1977). But see Wisconsin v. McCollum, 159 Wis.2d 184, 464 N.W.2d 44 (App.1990) (upholding equal protection challenge when only women arrested in raid of bar where female performers exchanged sexual fondling for tips). Why do you think police arrest sellers (prostitutes) and not buyers (johns)? Courts often justify such differential treatment by comparing them to drug enforcement policies: it is best to go after those making money on the transaction. Is this analogy appropriate? With drugs, prosecutors often go up the "food chain," offering immunity to low level street sellers to reach drug kingpins. If drugs and prostitution are analogous, why don't prosecutors offer prostitutes immunity in order to obtain evidence against pimps? Can police believe that arresting street prostitutes will eliminate prostitution? Why do police arrest street prostitutes? Is it to keep them from working in the "wrong" neighborhoods? What other motives could police have? Does it force street prostitutes to "buy" protection from police harassment?

6. The Mann Act and RICO, discussed above, are two examples of federal legislation that can be used to control prostitution, but most such regulation occurs at the state and local level. States and cities have used a variety of approaches to deal with prostitution, some more effective than others. But, until recently, almost all the regulations were aimed at the prostitutes themselves. For example, solicitation statutes and loitering ordinances have been two of the most popular methods of controlling prostitution. It was not until the late 1970's that women's organizations began to target the role of clients and pimps in prostitution. In response, some states and cities drafted laws which made pimping and pandering illegal. Others experimented with ordinances focusing more attention on the customer, such as laws which allow the police to print in the local paper the names of men arrested for soliciting. See UPI, Letter May Hit Home in Prostitution Drive, N.Y. Times, June 30, 1985, § 1, at 22 (Portland, Oregon police chief says four local papers agree to publish names of men cited for soliciting prostitutes). Other examples of a customer-based approach are forfeiture ordinances which allow police to permanently confiscate any car used to solicit a prostitute. See Commentary, No Hookers on Wheels, Washington

Times, Aug. 12, 1992, at G2 (D.C. City Council enacts the "Safe Streets Forfeiture Emergency Amendment Act of 1992," under which the cars in which people solicit prostitutes, the money with which they solicit and any other property in the car at the time is confiscated). Other experiments have included testing customers for sexually transmitted diseases with the results released to the spouse of a married person convicted of pandering; losing driving privileges for a year; listing names and photos of those arrested for solicitation on police internet pages; showing men arrested for solicitation on the city cable show ("John TV"); and mandatory "John School" during which those convicted of solicitation are taught about prostitution. One such John School is conducted in San Francisco and is available to first offenders for $500; if they complete the class, their record is expunged. Modeled after traffic schools for bad drivers, key topics include: discussions of legal and practical consequences of solicitation; medical information about sexually transmitted diseases; former prostitutes talking about their lives of violence and drugs; and how pimps recruit women and girls. See For Patrons of Prostitutes, Remedial Instruction, N.Y. Times, Mar. 18, 1999, at § A, pg. 1. Can you think of other ways to target customers and/or pimps?

7. In a survey conducted in conjunction with a psychoeducational program developed to treat men charged with solicitation of female prostitutes, it was discovered that "men may solicit prostitutes with mixed motivations and internal conflict," suggesting that these kinds of programs may hold great potential for success. Steven Sawyer, B.R. Simon Rosser, and Audrey Schroeder, A Brief Psychoeducational Program for Men Who Patronize Prostitutes, 26 J. of Offender Rehab. 111, 123 (1998). In the small, relatively homogeneous group, there were some interesting responses: 54% described oral sex as the "ideal sex act with a prostitute"; 63% disagreed that "there is nothing wrong with prostitution"; only 6% agreed that "it would be OK if my daughter grew up to be a prostitute"; 61% disagreed that women choose to be prostitutes because they want to be; 69% disagreed that "prostitutes enjoy their work"; and 69% said it would not "be OK if my son went to prostitutes." Id. at 119, 121. Is this information helpful in formulating strategies to discourage men from using prostitutes?

3. SEX WORK OR EXPLOITATION OF WOMEN?

JODY FREEMAN, THE FEMINIST DEBATE OVER PROSTITUTION REFORM: PROSTITUTES' RIGHTS GROUPS, RADICAL FEMINISTS AND THE (IM)POSSIBILITY OF CONSENT

5 Berkeley Women's L.J. 75–79, 81–88, 90, 92–94, 102, 105–08 (1989–90).

* * *

Throughout the article, I treat prostitutes' rights groups as having the same ideological base as those we might call liberal feminists. They see sex-trade workers as respectable women doing dignified work. Radical feminists, in contrast, assume that prostitutes are victims of coercion in a society that services men by objectifying and subordinating women. Because their visions of the work are incompatible, it is hard to imagine both groups on the same side of the prostitution debate. * * *

Despite their differences, both prostitutes' rights groups and radical feminists can be distinguished from anti-feminists in the sense that neither claims that prostitution is obscene, immoral, or offensive in isolation from its context. Neither group seeks to criminalize prostitution because it is an affront to heterosexual monogamy and, therefore, dangerous to traditional morality. This latter perspective is more properly attributable to anti-feminist groups. Analyzing the reasons behind the prostitutes' rights groups' and radical feminist approaches to prostitution makes it possible to highlight how they differ from anti-feminists with whom neither wants to be associated. It is an obvious irony that radical feminists and conservative anti-feminist groups are both anti-pornography and anti-prostitution, despite their completely different world views.

I am more sympathetic to the long-term view of radical feminists that prostitution should be eradicated, than to what I perceive to be the liberal (and only reluctantly feminist) position of prostitutes' rights groups. I do not claim, therefore, that decriminalization alone is the answer to the problem of prostitution. Only broad social and economic reforms, coupled with profound changes in our most deeply entrenched cultural norms, would eliminate the causes of prostitution. Because that amount of structural change is an unrealistic immediate goal, I think it is important to support decriminalization as an interim measure, without abandoning the purpose or eradicating prostitution.

The challenge of reforming prostitution laws poses an inescapable dilemma: to resist the commodification of women's sexuality, which requires circumscribing choices that some women themselves insist are voluntary, or to support the right of women to do the work they say they want to do, at the cost of reinforcing male dominance. The first approach is interventionist: it can be condescending, patronizing, and insensitive. The second is permissive: it appears to endorse the objectification of women and is, therefore, counterproductive if one is interested in dismantling gender hierarchy. This dilemma seems to recur whenever feminists try to remedy social inequality and empower women as a class, without punishing individual women in the process. It is a problem of transition from an unequal to an equal world.

* * *

In North America, there are three prevalent models for regulating prostitution. The first is criminalizing prostitution per se, as well as all the activities surrounding it, such as procuring, living off the avails, and keeping a bawdy-house. The second is legalization, which requires a licensing scheme that could entail fingerprinting, registration, and mandatory health checks. The final option involves criminalizing virtually every activity surrounding prostitution, but not prostitution per se.

* * *

Women who have been, or are presently, in the sex trade disagree over many contentious issues: whether their work is chosen, whether they participate in their own oppression, and whether their economic self-interest should outweigh the concern that prostitution contributes to women's subordination. Prostitutes' rights groups, such as Cast Off Your Old Tired Ethics (COYOTE) and the Canadian Organization for the Rights of Prostitutes (CORP), demand that prostitution be decriminalized because it is dignified, respectable work. CORP's leadership says prostitutes should be entitled to organize, advertise, pay taxes, and receive unemployment insurance. * * *

CORP actually views prostitution as superior to many other jobs since it has distinct advantages: women set their hours and wages, work where they want to, and service only customers they choose. Prostitutes' rights groups say prostitution empowers women because it enables them to earn a living in an environment they control, or would control but for state interference. Margo St. James [who has never worked as a prostitute], of COYOTE, objects to the double standard inherent in the criminalization of prostitution: "The state's idea is that these are deviant women and normal men. But they are doing the same thing; they're engaging in the same act." CORP's spokesperson, Valerie Scott, makes prostitution sound as mundane as anything else: "Ever since I was five, I dreamed of getting into the sex industry."

The National Task Force on Prostitution (NTFP), an American organization promoting prostitutes' rights, argues that despite some exceptions, prostitution amounts to a voluntary exchange of sexual services for money. The NTFP seeks to empower prostitutes to bargain with employers and improve their working conditions. The NTFP is similar to COYOTE and CORP in support of prostitution as legitimate work, as is the English Collective of Prostitutes, which argues that "for some women to get paid for what all women are expected to do for free is a source of power for all women to refuse *any* free sex."

* * *

Delores French, another outspoken representative of prostitutes' rights, says that she loves being a prostitute and that "[i]t's the most honest, rewarding work I've ever done." She recounts how she became a prostitute shortly after a life-threatening experience made her regret "all the things I hadn't done." She decided to "grab every appealing opportunity that came along and to experience as much about living as possible." Her husband, the vice-president of the Georgia Civil Liberties Union, understands her job. He says, "[O]ur jobs are quite similar: We both free-lance, we both get paid in advance, we both try to get our clients off." * * *

Before accepting the CORP * * * position as the definitive word on what prostitutes think, one should consider that women in the industry have not yet reached a consensus on whether prostitution is empowering for women. Some align themselves with * * * French: the money is attractive and their husbands support their decision to work as prostitutes. * * *

However, others testify to the harmful aspects of the trade. They recall emerging from years of denial or guilt and finally realizing that they had been oppressed by prostitution. For example, Judy Helfand says that she used to think turning men on sexually was an affirmation of her sexual power, but later changed her mind:

> What I never saw was that in basing my self worth on men's desire I was far from developing a true sense of worth based on self love.
>
> I see this false sense of power as one way internalized oppression keeps us down.... I see that wanting men to want you sexually is what men want.

In an exchange at a conference on prostitution and pornography, one participant asked, "What's so terrible about fucking for a living? I like it, I can live out my fantasies." Another replied,

> I don't know how you can possibly say, as busy as you are as a lady of the evening, that you like every sexual act, that you work out your fantasies! Come on, get serious! ... Can you count how many tricks you've had? You mean you have that many fantasies? Isn't is about having money to survive? ... Can't we teach women some skills so they can survive? I know that's your opinion, you like it, but prostitution to me was degrading. I grew to hate it. If I had had to fuck one more of them—boy, I would have killed him!

There are also organizations that work in direct opposition to CORP, COYOTE and the NTPF. Sarah Wynter, founder and editor of Women Hurt in Systems of Prostitution Engaged in Revolt (WHISPER), argues,

> There has been a deliberate attempt to validate men's perceived need, and self-proclaimed right, to buy and sell women's bodies for sexual use. This has been accomplished, in part, by euphemizing prostitution as an occupation. Men have promoted the cultural myth that women actively seek out prostitution as a pleasurable economic alternative to low-paying, low-skilled, monotonous labor, conveniently ignoring the conditions that insure women's inequality and the preconditions which make women vulnerable to prostitution.

Wynter maintains that prostitution is not a "valid," freely chosen occupation. She wants us "to stop defining prostitution as a victimless crime, and acknowledge it for what it is—a crime committed against women by men."

Despite their disagreement over whether prostitution is a legitimate occupation, virtually all those with experience inside the industry agree that the current conditions under which prostitutes must work are intolerable.

* * *

The assumptions about consent and coercion that inform the prostitutes' rights groups' position can be traced to traditional liberal theory, which is committed to autonomy, individualism, and minimal state interference in private choice. Liberal theory is premised on an assumption that individuals are atomistic, pre-social beings who exist independent of their community. The justification for state power in the liberal paradigm is the notion of implied consent: individuals surrender a certain amount of authority to the state in order to protect the autonomy of everyone.

Feminist and critical legal studies have attempted to expose the inability of liberal theory to account for our connections to others, or our "social constitutiveness." The central features of liberalism—the public/private distinction, a highly individualistic conception of rights—are commonly attacked as inappropriate for, and unresponsive to, feminist demands for equality and freedom.

To the extent that liberal feminism is traceable to liberalism, it too accepts the notion of a pre-social autonomous individual capable of consent and choice. * * * In my view, members of CORP and COYOTE and those feminists that support their position are essentially liberal and only reluctantly feminist. Their vision is one of equal access to an equality defined and perpetuated by men; it is not concerned with the sexual subordination of women as a "class" and the need for structural change.

* * *

Because it [liberal feminism] assumes that people are autonomous, self-interested actors, I understand liberal feminist analysis to begin with a presumption of consent. That is, in the absence of clear evidence to the contrary, a woman who says "yes" consents, regardless of the social context, the woman's past experience, or the constraints of ascribing meaning to language. Because the liberal feminist is committed to maximizing autonomy and individual choice, she presumptively sees individual expressions of sexuality as implicitly consensual, liberating, and empowering. Commercializing sex per se does not bother her; it is up to the individual woman to decide if she wants to use her body in a way that brings her money and satisfaction, even if that means trading in sex.

* * *

CORP and COYOTE's essentially liberal argument is that women and men should be permitted to use their bodies and express their sexuality as they see fit. Underlying this position is an assumption that choice is possible and that prostitutes are entitled to determine for themselves whether selling sex is harmful. They encourage prostitution as sexual expression, even if it is considered "deviant," because it is private, freely chosen, and harmless to those not involved in the transaction. Harm is defined restrictively so that contributing to the subordination of women as a class does not count.

* * *

CORP does not seem concerned with the extent to which authentic choice depends on the context in which it is exercised. CORP's leadership argues that decriminalizing and legitimizing prostitution promotes autonomy and is also the only effective way of minimizing the coercion present in "exceptional" cases. If prostitutes are permitted to organize, form support groups, and run self-help networks, they will then be able to exert some control over the coercive elements of the sex-trade. Putting power into the hands of the women in the industry will enable them to prevent the worst abuses of the system. Obviously, the "consent is possible" approach is fuelled by the claim that prostitutes make free choices. Many feminists have challenged that claim by questioning the accuracy of the liberal version of freedom. Radical feminists have directed their attention, instead, to coercion.

* * *

Contrary to liberal feminism, radical feminism focuses on sexuality as the mechanism of women's oppression. * * * Radical feminists reject the notion that women are empowered by fulfilling male desire, and they see the desire for prostitution as male.* * * Radical feminists say that prostitution is not a harmless, "private" transaction but a powerful means of creating, reinforcing, and perpetuating the objectification of women through sexuality. They do not take the criminalization of prostitution to mean that society is committed to undoing the subordination of women. Rather, it serves as proof that female sexuality is not only manufactured by men, but also legally controlled through the exercise of authority in order to keep women isolated and powerless. Society's acceptance of the persistent male demand for prostitutes only reminds us that all women are thought to be accessible (for a price) and that their commodification is natural.

* * *

Radical feminism understands prostitution to be a microcosm of gender hierarchy. It not only encapsulates but reinforces the objectification of women. Even an argument that prostitution has "therapeutic" potential for providing sex to those who are socially or sexually dysfunctional cannot, to the radical feminist, redeem an institution that is so central to male dominance. * * *

The liberal would criticize the radical feminist approach as patronizing. It tells women who hold a positive view of prostituting themselves that they are deluded. It denies the reality and validity of their experience. The radical approach to the prostitution debate, with its condemnation of the subordination inherent in prostitution and its emphasis on power relations at a macro level, is not helpful for prostitutes who feel that state regulation, not male-defined sexuality, is responsible for the lack of control over their lives.

* * *

Ideally, we think of sexuality as something we experience consensually, mutually, and equally. Conceiving of sexuality in market terms dehumanizes how we think and act about something extremely important to our conception of self. It would reduce sexuality to just another fungible good because commodification leads to "the domino effect"—the tendency in our society to completely commodify in all respects and for all purposes that which is commodified at all. The existence of some commodified sexual interactions threatens to contaminate everyone's sexuality. Under ideal conditions, to avoid the domino effect, we must reject prostitution as a valid occupation. Its effect on human flourishing is devastating because it objectifies women as a class and encourages a view of sexuality as a severable, tradeable good.

* * *

Disagreement over what is acceptable sexuality—the fact that what one feminist [Kathleen Barry] calls "valueless individualism" and another calls freedom—stems from incompatible understandings of consent. However, since we do not know whether consent is possible, I am partial to the radical feminist presumption of coercion and the implications that flow from it. * * * Given the overwhelming abuse of women by men and the extent to which sexuality is used to keep women subservient, a presumption of coercion appears not only logical but healthy. * * *

I am also convinced that feminists must look beyond their individual experience. This approach does not require women to negate their individual experience. This approach does not require women to negate their individuality; it simply means having a sex-class orientation and a broad, flexible notion of harm. * * *

If equal opportunity were a reality, if women were not excluded from or ghettoized in the employment market, if they were not sexually harassed on the job, and if they were not socialized to be dependent and submissive, then arguably prostitution would not embody male dominance and female submission. However, I find it difficult to imagine a society of equality in which commercial sex were still sought after; commercial sex seems inextricably linked to gender hierarchy. * * *

Criminalization only makes life more difficult for prostitutes, minimizing their chances of leaving the trade. The way to empower women is not to punish them for being powerless. Anything that pushes prostitution further underground and makes it more dangerous also makes it more profitable to pimps. If prostitution were decriminalized it would not necessarily be unregulated. Prostitutes would still be subject to sections of the relevant criminal code pertaining to nuisance, indecency, and causing a public disturbance. They would also have to abide by municipal zoning laws.

Even though I am sympathetic to the radical presumption of coercion, CORP's argument should be given some weight not because prostitution is legitimate and fully consensual, but rather because everyone's choices are limited in this world, and prostitutes should be entitled to make the best of a bad situation. However, not all aspects of the trade should be decriminalized * * *, procuring and living off the avails of prostitution should still be criminal where this is effected through threats and coercion.

The best short-term approach to reform entails removing prostitution from the criminal realm (subject to exceptions for pimping through coercion) so that it becomes an issue of gender equality and, at the same time, taking affirmative steps to destroy the conditions that create male consumption and drive women to the trade. We should decriminalize prostitution per se, permit small groups to operate out of their own homes, provide education and information programs for those trying to leave the trade, and devote the money presently used for criminal law enforcement to prostitute self-help networks, havens, and halfway houses.

Reform should also include provisions for vigorously prosecuting pimps who coerce women, particularly juveniles, into the trade. We should initiate training programs for women with little or no education, increase the minimum wage, finance businesses run by and for women, and design cooperative living and working arrangements for runaways and those with no place to go. Special police task forces should be devoted to prosecuting pimps but should be trained to treat prostitutes humanely. Public funds should be spent on the street and in the schools to raise awareness about equality, sexual abuse, and incest, as well as sexuality in general.

Notes on the Analysis of Prostitution

1. Who has the better argument in the debate over prostitution, liberal or radical feminists? Should women be able to decide for themselves if they want to "sell" their bodies? Can sex work be defined as simply the exchange of money for sex acts and services of various kinds? Is the liberals' argument for individual choice without coercion persuasive to you? Identify specific values underlying both sides of this debate. Can you make a feminist argument for continuing to make prostitution illegal for prostitutes? How would the various feminist theories described in Chapter 3 view prostitution? What legal changes would each advocate?

2. In 1998, the International Labor Organization (ILO), the official labor agency of the UN, called for the economic recognition of the sex industry. According to the ILO, this would include extending labor rights and benefits to sex workers, improving working conditions, and taxing its monetary exchanges. Lin Lean Lim, The Sex Sector: the Economic and Social Bases of Prostitution in Southeast Asia 212–13 (1998). Janice Raymond issued a spirited response, arguing that "contrary to the benign picture of prostitution painted by the ILO report, the violence that prostituted women endure is more acute and much more frequent than that experienced by other women." Raymond, Legitimating Prostitution as Sex Work: UN Labor Organization (ILO) Calls for Recognition of the Sex Industry (1998), http://www.uri.edu/artsci/wms/hughes/catw/legit.htm. Is this a reason *not* to legitimize prostitution? Or is the violence against prostituted women a

reason to legalize prostitution? See also Sylvia Law, Commercial Sex: Beyond Decriminalization, 73 S. Cal. L. Rev. 523 (2000); Alexandra Bongard Stremler, Sex for Money and the Morning After: Listening to Women and the Feminist Voice in Prostitution Discourse, 7 Univ. Fla. J. Law & Pub. Pol'y 189 (1994–95).

3. An additional problem in this debate is the diametrically opposed descriptions of their work that prostituted women provide. See, e.g., Sex Work: Writings by Women in the Sex Industry (Priscilla Alexander and Frederique Delacoste, eds. 1987). What explains this phenomenon? Is this a kind of "false consciousness?" Whom do you believe? Is it important to decide which description is reality for women? How would a post-modern feminist respond? When prostituted women themselves celebrate prostitution, Sheila Jeffreys believes they are engaging in what deviancy sociologists call "neutralising techniques":

> Sociologists use the term to describe the way in which socially despised and marginalized groups create rationalisations which enable them to survive their marginal condition. Such techniques may be employed because the only alternative available may be the painful one of self-contempt. The idea that prostitution is freely chosen is such a technique.

Jeffreys, The Idea of Prostitution 137 (1997). Do you think "neutralising techniques" explain the conflicting reports of the experiences of prostituted women? If not, how do you explain the vast discrepancies?

4. JoAnn L. Miller asks: "Is prostitution the prototype of sexual liberation or the embodiment of sexual oppression?" Miller, Prostitution in Contemporary American Society, in Sexual Coercion 45, 47 (Elizabeth Grauerholz and Mary A. Koralewski, eds. 1991). She concludes that "[b]ecause members of the less powerful group are compelled or forced, physically or psychologically, to engage in a sexual act, prostitution is fundamentally coercive and exploitative." Id. Do you agree? Or is this paternalistic?

5. Researchers affirm that women who are prostituted tend to have had early sexual experiences, usually under conditions of physical coercion. Miller, above note 4, at 51. "They tend to manifest poor self-images, perceptions of stigmatization, and manifestations of depression, anxiety, cynicism, and alienation." Id. According to Evelina Giobbe, when WHISPER conducted interviews for its Oral History Project, 90 per cent of the women who participated had been subjected to physical and sexual abuse during childhood (approximately 90 percent had been battered in their families; 74 percent had been sexually abused between the ages of 3 and 14, 93 percent by a family member). Jeffreys, above note 3, at 257; see also Mimi H. Silbert and Ayala M. Pines, Pornography and Sexual Abuse of Women, 10 Sex Roles 857 (1984) (study of prostitutes documenting "stunning amounts" of sexual abuse in their childhood). Do these findings suggest any conclusions about how "voluntary" prostitution work is?

6. Mimi H. Silbert and Ayala M. Pines discovered extremely high levels of violence against prostitutes, both on and off the job. Silbert and Pines, Occupational Hazards of Street Prostitutes, 8 Crim.Just. & Behavior 395, 397–98 (1981). Which side of the debate does this empirical research sup-

port? Would it increase or decrease if prostitution were decriminalized? In what ways?

7. The health implications of sex work are often ignored. In addition to serious injuries, ranging from 8 to 23% according to various studies, the emotional and psychological effects have been documented. See Vednita Carter and Evelina Giobbe, Duet: Prostitution, Racism and Feminist Discourse, 10 Hastings Women's L.J. 37, 47–49 (1999). In one study, prostitutes "reported an average of six stress-related disorders, most frequently depression, insomnia, flashbacks and sexual dysfunction." Id. at 48. Another study found that 68 percent of working prostitutes suffered from posttraumatic stress disorder. Id. Between 75 to 95 percent were chemically dependent; in fact one study found that 55 percent of the sample "reported always being high when turning a trick." Id. at 49. What do these health implications say about the "job" of prostitution?

8. Under capitalism, don't the majority of adult human beings "sell" their labor, whether it be as a secretary, lawyer, teacher or prostitute? How does sex work differ from other forms of labor? Christine Overall suggests that there are important differences between sex work and other work performed mostly by women:

> The fact that it is men and not women who buy prostitutes' services is not, surely, just for women's lack of equal opportunity to do so. Unlike other forms of labor mostly performed by women, prostitution is dependent both for its value and for its very existence upon the cultural construction of gender roles in terms of dominance and submission. While women are taught to render sexual services for recompense and often to regard that rendering as part of what it means to be a woman, men are encouraged to seek and expect sexual services and, indeed, to regard the acquisition of sexual services as part of what it means to be a man.

Overall, What's Wrong with Prostitution? Evaluating Sex Work, 17 Signs 705, 719 (1992). Do you agree? Compare, on an ethical level, working as a prostitute and as a hired gun (a lawyer or expert witness working for the tobacco industry in litigation, for example). Which form of employment is more unethical? Which is generally regarded as raising greater moral concerns? Why? Why might you regard working as a hired gun for the tobacco industry as more unethical, but still prefer your daughter to do that sort of work rather than earn her living as a prostitute?

9. Jackie MacMillan believes that the institution of prostitution affects all women:

> Prostitution is an important issue for feminists because prostitutes most clearly express the cultural valuation and image of women as primarily sexual beings. Their behavior and dress simply make explicit the expected female behavior. They are explicitly marketing a sexual product/service. Prostitutes approach their work in a calculated, sexually detached way. Only in male fantasies are prostitutes motivated by sexual drives. For women, genital activity is not necessarily sexual activity.

> While many women will never turn a trick, the institution of prostitution affects all women. The illegality of prostitution is used to control both prostitutes and "straight" women, and to pit them against each other.
>
> Prostitution makes clear women's status as property or commodity. Most women become private property through marriage. * * *
>
> Prostitutes, like wives, are treated like commodities. But in contrast to wives, prostitutes are regarded as public property. * * *

MacMillan, Prostitution as Sexual Politics, 4 Quest 41–43 (1977). Do you agree with this analysis? In what ways are marriage and prostitution similar? How are they different? In what ways are husbands and wives, johns and prostitutes similar? Different?

10. Does the availability of prostitutes result in fewer rapes of non-prostituted women? That is, is the prostitute supply and rape rate inversely correlated? Owen Jones had difficulty testing this hypothesis, but points to evidence from Australia "that the conviction rate for rape and attempted rape in the seven-year period following the closure of brothels in the territory of Queensland was triple the rate for the seven-year period prior to the closures" and that "the socio-economic and demographic characteristics of those convicted correlated positively with those of the men who had most frequented brothels during more permissive times." Jones, Sex, Culture, and the Biology of Rape, 87 Cal. L. Rev. 827, 928 (1999). While noting that this data is not dispositive, Jones states: "to the extent that patterns of rape reflect male psychological predispositions toward sexual behavior generally, prostitution rates and rape rates may trade against each other." Id. at 929. Is this another reason to argue in support of legalizing prostitution—to minimize the rape of non-prostituted women? Jones concludes that "biobehavioral theory suggests that legalizing prostitution might therefore cause the overall rape rate to decline." Id. What do you think of this justification to decriminalize prostitution? Does it concretize the schism between prostituted and non-prostituted women?

11. Does the fact that African American women were bought and sold in slavery for over two hundred years in this country have any bearing on the large number of African American women who are involved in prostitution today? See Vednita Carter and Evelina Giobbe, Duet: Prostitution, Racism and Feminist Discourse, 10 Hastings Women's L.J. 37 (1999). What part does racism play in perpetuating prostitution? What other factors might contribute to the trafficking of women of color?

Carter and Giobbe criticize the international prostitutes' rights movement as being racist and classist:

> The overwhelmingly white leadership of this well-funded movement is comprised of academics [Priscilla Alexander, Gail Petersen] and attorneys [ACLU] who *don't have to do* sex work, and middle-aged former sex workers who *no longer do sex work*. These individuals exploit third world women of color who have *few viable alternatives to sex work* and promote the prostitution of American women who are trapped in a cycle of poverty and despair. * * * Summarized briefly, their position holds that prostitution is a job. * * * This view ignores the social context in

which prostitution occurs, especially the race/class power differential that exists between prostitutes and their customers.

Id. at 49–50. Before taking a position, do you want to know the racial and class implications? How do you go about doing that? Is looking at the leaders of the movement revealing?

12. Historian Ruth Rosen's analysis of the Victorian attitude about prostitution and its relation to class, gender and racial systems is particularly insightful:

> Although prostitutes were prevailingly characterized as outcasts with no place in society, in actuality they held an important place and served vital social functions. Economically, prostitution was a source of income to the police, to procurers, madams, doctors, politicians, and liquor interests. Politically, it upheld gender and class divisions. The singling out of a caste of degraded women served as an object lesson and a threat to other women. The specter of the whore was always before them as a reminder of what they might become or how they might be treated if they failed to live up to the angel image or lived outside of male protection. For men, prostitution upheld the double standard, the polarized images of women as angelic or monstrous, but in neither case fully human, and the ideology that women existed to serve men. The association of prostitution with lower-class, immigrant, and nonwhite populations served to divide women from one another. It also justified the low ranking of these populations in the social hierarchy.

Rosen, The Lost Sisterhood 6–7 (1982). To what extent does her analysis apply today?

13. Mary E. Hawkesworth notes that the sexologist, Havelock Ellis, "characterized prostitution as a 'distraction from the dull and respectable monotony of marriage' and hinted that prostitution could actually be seen as a contributor to the stability of marriage. By providing sexual services as an outlet for the pent-up energies of the highly sexed male who has been mismatched with a woman disinterested in sex, the prostitute can save the companionate marriage through the elimination of male sexual frustration." Hawkesworth, Brothels and Betrayal: On the Functions of Prostitution, 7 Int'l J. Women's Stud. 81, 83 (1984). Is this a legitimate social function of prostitution? Is it a critique of prostitution or of marriage? Does it suggest that our evaluation of prostitution, or of marriage, should change?

Sheila Jeffreys contributes another perspective on how prostitution and marriage interact:

> Oral sex was a practice that wives seemed unwilling to provide for their husbands, so they used prostituted women for access to their mouths and for the performance of other practices that they wanted and their wives did not. Thus the existence of prostitution enforced in these men the idea that the sex of prostitution was what sex was, and what they had the right to demand, either from wives or prostitutes. The ability to use prostituted women enabled men to avoid having to have an egalitarian sexual relationship in which sexual practices needed to be negotiated and pleasing to both parties. As one john put it, prostitution gave him "the freedom of not having to do things the way your wife wants you to

> do them." * * * In regard to men's demand for oral sex, * * * wives will eventually be persuaded to provide it. Wives will eventually provide all the services that men presently visit prostitutes for, and men will change their demands of prostitutes over time.

Jeffreys, above note 3, at 238–9. How does this affect your analysis? Should wives encourage their husbands to use prostitutes?

14. Sheila Jeffreys believes that the ideology of sexual liberalism created by the sexual revolution resulted in a "view of sex as the masculine need for sexual aggression which must be met by women's desire to submit and service men." Jeffreys, above note 3, at 36. In fact, she suggests "that the theorists and publicists of the sexual revolution—sexologists such as Masters and Johnson and sex advice doctors such as Alex Comfort [author of The Joy of Sex]—constructed a theory of practice of sexuality based on prostitution. Prostitution formed the model for effective sexual functioning, men's sexual practice modeled on the johns and women's on the prostituted women." Id. Does this suggest another "harm" of prostitution?

15. Beverly Balos and Mary Louise Fellows believe that

> prostitution, through the consent/coercion and private/public dualities, enforces and reinforces social, economic, and political hierarchical differences. As a way to understand prostitution's role in maintaining subordinated social categories, * * * [they] focus on the distinction between unworthy/degenerate and worthy/respectable women and the two ways prostitution functions to maintain this distinction. First, prostitution functions as a paradigm for degeneracy that supports social inequalities based on class, disability, gender, race and sexuality. Second, it functions as a practice of inequality.

Balos and Fellows, A Matter of Prostitution: Becoming Respectable, 74 N.Y.U. L. Rev. 1220, 1227 (1999). Under their analysis, should prostitution be an option for individual women? Should individual choices (such as the decision to become a prostitute under the liberal feminist perspective) which contribute to the maintenance of social subordination of groups be encouraged? Permitted? How does one go about deciding this question?

F. PORNOGRAPHY

1. PORNOGRAPHY AND VIOLENCE AGAINST WOMEN

MINNESOTA v. HERBERG

Supreme Court of Minnesota, 1982.

324 N.W.2d 346.

* * *

Defendant, who is now 39, is a compulsive sex offender who was first convicted in 1973 in Douglas County of attempted aggravated rape of a 15-year-old female. After failing in treatment, defendant was sentenced to prison, where he remained until 1977, when he was paroled.

We are concerned primarily with the conduct of defendant that occurred on the afternoon of July 17, 1981. On that day defendant was driving north of Sauk Centre, which is in Stearns County, when he spotted a 14–year–old girl on her bicycle. Defendant stopped and, using a knife, forced the girl into his car, tied her hands with his belt, pushed her on the floor and covered her with a blanket.

He then drove a short way into Todd County and turned onto a gravel road, where he stopped. There he used his knife to cut off her clothes. He then inserted some of his fingers into her vagina. He also cut her vagina with the knife.

Feeling perhaps that they were in an area where they might be observed, defendant had the victim dress herself and he then drove to a gravel pit in a nearby Todd County township. There he ordered her to remove her clothes again and forced her to remove his also. He then made her stick a safety pin into the nipple of her left breast. He then forced her to ask him to hit her. After hitting her, he forced her to commit fellatio and to submit to anal penetration. He made her use a cigarette to burn herself on a breast and near the pubic area. He then defecated and urinated on her face, forcing her to ingest some of the excrement and urine. He then made her urinate into a cup and drink it. He then took a string from her blouse and choked her to the point of unconsciousness, leaving burn marks on her neck. Then, after cutting her with his knife in a couple places, he drove her back to the area from which he had abducted her and released her.

It appears that in committing these various acts, defendant was giving life to some stories he had read in various pornographic books. These books, which were seized from defendant following his arrest, bear titles such as *Violent Stories of Kinky Humiliation, Violent Stories of Dominance and Submission, Bizarre Sex Crimes: Shamed Victims,* and *Watersports Fetish: Enemas and Golden Showers.*

MIMI H. SILBERT AND AYALA M. PINES, PORNOGRAPHY AND SEXUAL ABUSE OF WOMEN

10 Sex Roles 857, 863–66 (1984).

> [This study involved 200 juvenile and adult, current and former, women street prostitutes in the San Francisco area, and was aimed at studying sexual abuse of street prostitutes both prior to and following entrance into prostitution. The youngest subject was 10 and the oldest was 46; almost 60% of the current prostitutes were under 16 years of age. The racial make-up of the group was 69% white, 18% Black, 11% Hispanic, 2% American Indian, and 1% Asian.]

The study generated an enormous amount of data, quantitative as well as qualitative, documenting stunning amounts of sexual abuse of street prostitutes as part of their job, outside of their work environment, and in their childhood prior to entering prostitution. Many of the open descriptions of these sexual assaults made reference to the role played by pornography. These references were unsolicited by the interviewers.

Since the relationship between sexual abuse and pornography was unexpected, no questions addressed it directly. Only after the data collection was completed, was the content from 193 cases of rape (reported by 73% of the women), and from 178 cases of juvenile sexual abuse (reported by 60% of the women), analyzed for any mentioned relationship between these incidents and pornography. * * *

Out of 193 cases of rape, 24% mentioned allusions to pornographic material on the part of the rapist. This figure is even more significant when it is understood that these comments were made by respondents without any solicitation, or reference to the issues of pornography by the interviewer. The comments followed the same pattern: the assailant referred to pornographic materials he had seen or read and then insisted that the victims not only enjoyed the rape but also the extreme violence. For example, the following is a typical comment reported by victims as one in which the assailant made reference to his prior use of pornography. "I know all about you bitches, you're no different; you're like all of them. I seen it in all the movies. You love being beaten" (He then began punching the victim violently). "I just seen it again in that flick. He beat the shit out of her while he raped her and she told him she loved it; you know you love it; tell me you love it." The assailant continued to beat and slap the woman while raping her, repeating his demand that she say that she loved it, just like the woman he saw in the movies. In the majority of cases, there were no distinctive features about the victims, their situations, or the factors of the rape, which could account for the assailants' mentioning their involvement with pornography. In 12% of the 193 cases of rape, the assailant mentioned his involvement with pornography as a response to the victim's telling the assailant she was a prostitute.

In 19% of the rape cases, the victims tried to stop the violence of the rape by telling the assailant that they were prostitutes. For example, "Calm down. I'm a hooker. Relax, and I'll turn you a free trick without all this fighting." Rather than assuage the violence, this assertion only exacerbated the problem; the assailants *increased* the amount of violence in every single case. They became furious at hearing the woman say she was a prostitute. Most started screaming, demanding that she take back what she had said, insisting on taking her by force. In order to reassert their own control, assailants then became extremely violent. In all 19% of the cases in which the victim told the rapist she was a prostitute, the victim sustained even more serious injuries than those prostitutes who did not disclose their prostitution status. * * *

In 12% of the 193 cases, the victims who told the rapists that they were prostitutes not only received more violent abuse than those who didn't tell, but also elicited overt comments from the assailants related to pornography. (In most of the other cases in which victims told the rapists they were prostitutes, indirect references were made to pornography.) An analysis of the 12% of the cases in which victims disclosed they were prostitutes reveals that there is a pattern of response among the assailants to the disclosure. In hearing that their victims were prostitutes, the assailants responded in a manner characterized by the following four elements: (1) their language became more abusive, (2) they became significantly more violent, beating and punching the women excessively, often using weapons they had shown the women, (3) they mentioned having seen prostitutes in pornographic films, the majority of them mentioning specific pornographic literature, and (4) after completing the forced vaginal penetration, they continued to assault the women sexually in ways they claimed they had seen prostitutes enjoy in the pornographic literature they cited. For example, "After I told him I'd turn him a free trick if only he'd calm down and stop hurting me, then he just really blew his mind. He started calling me all kinds of names, and then started screaming and shrieking like nothing I'd ever heard. He sounded like a wailing animal. Instead of just slapping me to keep me quiet, he really went crazy and began punching me all over. Then he told me he had seen whores just like me in (three pornographic films mentioned by name), and told me he knew how to do it to whores like me. He knew what whores like me wanted ... After he finished raping me, he started beating me with his gun all over. Then he said, 'You were in that movie. You were in that movie. You know you wanted to die after you were raped. That's what you want; you want me to kill you after this rape just like (specific pornography film) did.' " This particular woman suffered, in addition to forced vaginal penetration, forced anal penetration with a gun, excessive bodily injuries, including several broken bones; and a period of time in which the rapist held a loaded pistol at her vagina, threatening to shoot, insisting this was the way she had died in the film he had seen. He did not, in fact, shoot after all.

Similar results were found in regard to the subjects' experiences of juvenile sexual exploitation. Ten percent of the 200 respondents noted that they had been used as children in pornographic films and magazines. It is significant to note that these comments were made simply in open-ended descriptions of their lives; unfortunately, there were no specific questions on the survey instrument designed to elicit information about the juveniles' relationship to pornography. Therefore, it is assumed that the actual response to this question would be notably higher. All of the respondents who described being used in pornographic films and magazines were under the age of 13 when they were victimized in this way.

Again, in unsolicited comments, 22% of the 178 cases of juvenile sexual exploitation mentioned the use of pornographic materials by the adult prior to the sexual act. The particular manner in which the adult used the pornographic materials varied. For a few, they used the materials to try to persuade the children with comments such as, "Now doesn't that look like something that you and I would have a good time doing together? Come on look at that. Doesn't that make you want to come with me?" Others used pornographic materials to attempt to legitimize their actions. Several victims report that the abuser showed them pictures depicting children involved in sexual acts with adults to convince them that it was acceptable behavior and that it was something they wanted to do. These abusers stated, for example, "See the expression on her face; that's exactly how you look at me." Others used the pornographic materials to arouse themselves prior to abusing the child. For example, one of the subjects in the study described a primitive movie projector her father had set up in the garage. He used to show himself and his friends pornographic movies to get them sexually aroused before they would rape her. (She was 9 at the time.) Her brother would also watch the movies when the father was gone; then he also abused her sexually.

Thirty-eight percent of the 200 women prostitutes interviewed reported that they had been involved in the taking of sexually explicit photographs of themselves when they were children for commercial purposes, and/or the personal gratification of the photographer. The subjects were under the age of 16 years old. It should be noted that while many of the descriptions were open-ended comments included in their stories, some were responses given to questions of how they earned a living once they ran away from home and before they began prostituting.

It is likely, given the numbers who spontaneously described their involvement with pornography, that the cases of pornographic abuse of children would be significantly higher among the prostitute population if studied overtly.

Text Note: Research About Pornography and Violence Against Women

The relationship between pornography and violence against women has been the subject of hundreds of behavioral science studies. Obviously, while one cannot expose subjects to pornography and then follow them to see if they aggress against women, some studies have exposed male subjects to pornography and then (1) solicited self-reported responses about subsequent actual aggression against women or (2) watched subjects deliver what they believed to be electric shocks to women.[42] Meta-analyses have found "that consumption of material depicting nonviolent sexual activity increases aggressive behavior, and that media depictions of violent sexual activity generates more aggression than those of nonviolent sexual activity"[43] and that "exposure to pornography, at least in experimental settings, increases the acceptance of rape myths."[44]

In laboratory studies, researchers rely on "attitudes, arousal patterns, and aggressive behavior in the laboratory."[45] Attitudes are usually assessed

42. See generally Diana E.H. Russell, Against Pornography: The Evidence of Harm 142–48 (1993).

43. Mike Allen, Dave D'Alessio and Keri Brezgel, A Meta-Analysis Summarizing the Effects of Pornography II: Aggression After Exposure, 22 Human Communication Research 258 (1995).

44. Mike Allen, Tara Emmers, Lisa Gebhardt, and Mary A. Giery, Exposure to Pornography and Acceptance of Rape Myths, 45 J. of Communication 5, 19 (1995).

45. Edward Donnerstein, Pornography: Its Effect on Violence Against Women, in Pornography and Sexual Aggression 53 (Neil M. Malamuth and Donnerstein, eds. 1984).

by various instruments, or scales, which have been developed and tested for significant relationships with the criterion measures.[46] These results are often criticized as being merely "attitudinal," and not indicative of what the subjects would actually do in the real world. But scientists have also developed tests to measure physiological responses as well as attitudes. For instance, studies have compared subjects' self-reported likelihood of raping to see if it is correlated with an erection: it is.[47] Additionally, several studies reveal a connection between attitudes and actual sexual aggressiveness reported by the subjects.[48]

Laboratory experiments themselves are often criticized as artificial and vulnerable to demand characteristics, i.e., subjects want to please the researchers and give the answer they think the researcher wants. Avoiding this concern, Neil Malamuth and James Check created a *field* experiment to determine the effects of mass media exposure on acceptance of violence against women; they discovered that exposure to films (outside the laboratory) showing violent sexuality increased male subjects' acceptance of interpersonal violence against women and their acceptance of rape myths.[49]

Moreover, evidence gathered from the real world—anecdotal,[50] sworn testimony in public hearings,[51] police reports,[52] studies of perpetrators of sexual violence,[53] and data gathered from the lives of women[54]—is available

46. Neil M. Malamuth, The Attraction to Sexual Aggression Scale: Part One, 26 J. Sex Res. 26 (1989); Malamuth, The Attraction to Sexual Aggression Scale: Part Two, 26 J. Sex Res. 324 (1989). For instance, when asking men if they would rape if they could be assured they would not be caught, researchers can use either a single item to assess likelihood of rape (LR), an additional item to assess likelihood of forced sex (LF), or a three-level hierarchy based on these two items (LFR). The need to use both LR and LF is because subjects may not consider forcible intercourse "rape"; therefore, both definitions are necessary to capture valid data.

47. Neil M. Malamuth and James V.P. Check, Penile Tumescence and Perceptual Responses to Rape As a Function of Victim's Perceived Reactions, 10 J. Applied Soc. Psych. 528 (1980).

48. Neil M. Malamuth, Sexually Violent Media, Thought Patterns, and Antisocial Behavior, 2 Pub.Comm. & Behav. 159, 190 (1989).

49. Malamuth and Check, The Effects of Mass Media Exposure on Acceptance of Violence Against Women: A Field Experiment, 15 J.Res. Personality 436, 437–38 (1981).

50. See, e.g., Laura Lederer, Then and Now: An Interview with a Former Pornography Model, in Take Back the Night 57 (Lederer, ed. 1980); Kathleen Barry, Female Sexual Slavery (1979).

51. Catharine A. MacKinnon and Andrea Dworkin, eds., In Harm's Way: The Pornography Civil Rights Hearings (1997)(transcripts of the Minneapolis, Indianapolis, Los Angeles, and Massachusetts hearings on pornography and civil rights).

52. For example, in a study of more than 40 child sex abuse cases investigated by the L.A. Police Department between October 1976 and March 1977, pornographic photos were found to be present in every case. Haven Bradford Gow, The Bitter Harvest of Pornography, N.Y. Times, Apr. 23, 1986, § A, at 22. Also, a 1988 FBI study of 36 sex serial killers found that 81% ranked pornography highest of many sexual interests. Catherine Foster, "Porno," Violence in Media Targeted, Christian Science Monitor, Dec. 4, 1990, U.S. § , at 4.

53. For example, William Marshall found that ten of 18 Canadian incarcerated rapists that he interviewed confessed that pornography influenced them to force females to have sex. Gow, above note 52. Because of concerns that incarcerated offenders may be currying favor, a group of behavioral scientists evaluated the use of pornography by 256 non-incarcerated perpetrators of sexual offenses and discovered that 56% of the rapists and 42% of the child molesters "implicated pornography in the commission of their offenses." Diana E.H. Russell, Pornography and Rape: A Causal Model, 9 Pol.Psych. 41, 68 (1988).

54. Evelyn Sommers and James Check analyzed the presence of pornography and in great quantities. This evidence is consistent in revealing the links between pornography and multiple forms of male aggression against women.

In 1984 two of the major researchers in this area of pornography and violence against women, Neil Malamuth and Edward Donnerstein, reviewed the findings of hundreds of studies. Malamuth concluded that the studies demonstrated several consistent results: men who viewed pornography (1) became desensitized to women, (2) had an increased likelihood of raping when they had no fear of being caught, (3) were less likely to believe a woman who claims to have been raped, (4) were less likely to impose stiff penalties on rapists, and (5) exhibited increased aggression toward women.[55] Donnerstein summarized the findings: "there is a direct causal relationship between exposure to aggressive pornography and violence against women."[56] In fact, Donnerstein felt so strongly about the connection between pornography and violence against women that he testified in support of the Minneapolis Anti–Pornography Ordinance during public hearings[57] and as an expert for the defense in a case in which the defendant brutally raped and murdered his victim, Schiro v. Clark.[58] In *Schiro*, Donnerstein testified that:

> after a short exposure to aggressive pornography "non-rapist populations * * * begin to endorse myths about rape." ... "They begin to say that women enjoy being raped and they begin to say that using force in sexual encounters is okay. Sixty percent of the subjects will also indicate that if not caught they would commit the rape themselves."[59]

both sexual and nonsexual violence in the lives of a group of battered women drawn from shelters and counseling groups and a comparison group of women from a mature university population. They discovered that the partners of the battered women read or viewed significantly greater amounts of pornographic materials than did the partners of the comparison group. Sommers and Check, An Empirical Investigation of the Role of Pornography in the Verbal and Physical Abuse of Women, 2 Violence and Victims 189 (1987).

55. Malamuth, Aggression Against Women: Cultural and Individual Causes, in Pornography and Sexual Aggression 27–28; Donnerstein, above note 45, at 36–38. See also, Donnerstein, Pornography: Its Effect on Violence Against Women, in Pornography and Sexual Aggression 53–81 (both aggressive and nonaggressive pornography create attitudes that can directly influence aggressive behavior against women).

56. Id. at 78.

57. MacKinnon and Dworkin, above note 51, at 44–60. See also id. at 60; 75; 80–81; 99; 222; 283; 290–310.

58. 963 F.2d 962 (7th Cir.1992), aff'd, 508 U.S. 905, 113 S.Ct. 2330, 124 L.Ed.2d 243 (1993)(arguing that pornography, not the defendant, was responsible for the brutal crime).

59. 963 F.2d at 972 (citations to transcript omitted). Another defense expert in *Schiro*, Dr. Frank Osanka, "testified that Schiro viewed pornographic films from age six, and throughout his childhood and his adulthood, that led him to be aroused by women's pain and taught him techniques of rape." Id. As the Seventh Circuit noted, the autobiographical statement of the defendant himself also addressed the role of pornography in his acts of aggression against women: "I can remember when I get horny from looking at girly books and watching girly shows that I would want to go rape somebody. Every time I would jack off before I come I would be thinking of rape and the women I had raped and remembering how exciting it was. The pain on their faces. The thrill, the excitement." Id.

However, in 1987 Donnerstein and two other colleagues published an additional survey of the continuing research about the effects of pornography. In this book, The Question of Pornography, the authors stated:

> our discussion of the research * * * will emphasize that, for the most part * * *, sexually explicit images, per se, do not in the short run facilitate aggressive behavior against women, change attitudes about rape, or influence other forms of antisocial behavior. Instead, the research

Other researchers have discovered various effects of prolonged consumption of common pornography, including the trivialization of both rape and child sex abuse as criminal offenses. Prolonged consumption of nonviolent and violent pornography: (1) "promotes insensitivity toward victims of sexual violence"; (2) "promotes men's belief of having the propensity for forcing particular sexual acts on reluctant female partners"; and (3) "promotes men's belief of being capable of committing rape."[60]

Notes on Pornography and Violence Against Women

1. How are pornography and erotica generally defined in our culture? How would you define them? Are these distinct categories? Can you distinguish between pornography and erotica? Gloria Steinem explains erotica as follows:

> Look at or imagine images of people making love; really making love. Those images may be very diverse, but there is likely to be a mutual pleasure and touch and warmth, an empathy for each other's bodies and nerve endings, a shared sensuality and a spontaneous sense of two people who are there because they *want* to be.

Steinem, Erotica vs. Pornography, Outrageous Acts and Everyday Rebellions 247 (1983). She contrasts erotica with pornography:

> Now look at or imagine images of sex in which there is force, violence, or symbols of unequal power. They may be very blatant: whips and chains of bondage, even torture and murder presented as sexually titillating, the clear evidence of wounds and bruises, or an adult's power being used sexually over a child. They may be more subtle: the use of class, race, authority, or just body poses to convey conqueror and victim; unequal nudity, with one person's body exposed and vulnerable while the other is armored with clothes; or even a woman by herself, exposed for an unseen but powerful viewer whom she clearly is trying to please. (It's interesting that, even when only the woman is seen, we often know whether she is there for her own pleasure or being displayed for someone else's.) But blatant or subtle, there is no equal power or mutuality. In fact, much of the tension and drama comes from the clear idea that one person is dominating another.

Id. Do you agree with the distinctions she makes? Steinem herself indicates that it is a problem "untangling sex from aggression and violence or the threat of it" primarily because there is so little erotica to compare to

> indicates that it is the violent images fused with sexual images in some forms of pornography, or even the violent images alone, that account for many of the antisocial effects reported by social science researchers.

Donnerstein, Daniel Linz, and Steven Penrod, The Question of Pornography: Research Findings and Policy Implications 2 (1987). Nonetheless, their book describes "studies that have found that individuals exposed to certain types of materials respond with blunted sensitivity to violence against women, calloused attitudes about rape, and sexual arousal to rape depictions and laboratory simulations of aggression against women, among other antisocial effects." Id. at 5. This book ignores work by Dolf Zillman, below note 60, which is squarely and solidly to the contrary.

60. Dolf Zillman, Effects of Prolonged Consumption of Pornography, in Pornography: Research Advances and Policy Considerations 127, 154–55 (Zillman and Jennings Bryant, eds. 1989).

pornography. Can you give examples of what you consider erotica? Why do you think there is so little erotica? What explanation would MacKinnon give? Is it because of a heterosexuality premised upon male domination and female objectification?

2. Diana E.H. Russell, in Pornography and Rape: A Causal Model, 9 Professor of Law. Psych. 41 (1988), has suggested that pornography might be causally related to violence and abuse in a number of ways:

> In order for rape to occur, a man must not only be predisposed to rape, but his internal and social inhibitions against acting out rape desires must be undermined. My theory in a nutshell is that pornography (1) predisposes some men to want to rape women or intensifies the predisposition in other men already so predisposed; (2) undermines some men's internal inhibitions against acting out their rape desires; and (3) undermines some men's social inhibitions against the acting out.

Id. at 41. Are there other ways in which pornography might be causally related to violence and abuse?

3. Police tend to believe there is a link between sexual violence and pornography because so many defendants, as in *Herberg,* have stashes of violent pornography. Why might a social scientist criticize the assumption of a link on the basis of what the police find in defendants' possession? How would you assess the value of the evidence the police find in light of the problems a social scientist would see? What evidence would you require to "prove" the link?

Under what circumstances would you regard pornography as "causing" violence against women? In *Herberg,* might the pornography have "caused" the violence in some sense? On the other hand, might the violence have occurred even if the defendant had not consumed pornography? Is there any way to be sure whether this (or equivalent) violence and abuse would have occurred in the absence of any pornography? At what level of certainty would the balance tip in favor of preventing possible violence and against the First Amendment rights of publishers of pornography?

4. Diana Russell conducted a survey in 1978 of 930 randomly selected adult female residents of San Francisco to ascertain the respondents' experiences with rape. Diana E.H. Russell, Sexual Exploitation: Rape, Child Sexual Abuse, and Workplace Harassment 34–41 (1984). The women in her sample were asked: "Have you ever been upset by anyone trying to get you to do what they'd seen in pornographic pictures, movies, or books?" The results were as follows:

> Twenty-one of the victims of wife rape (24 percent) answered yes, a considerably higher percentage than that reported by women drawn in the sample as a whole (10 percent). Those who answered yes were then asked to briefly describe the experience that upset them the most. Although women were not specifically asked what their relationship was to the person with whom they had this upsetting experience, in eight instances victims of wife rape volunteered that the person involved was a husband. This means that well over one-third (38 percent) of these unwanted experiences, which the women believed were inspired by pornography, involved husbands. While nothing can be proven by this

> high percentage, particularly since only eight cases are involved, the fact that 9 percent of the victims of wife rape spontaneously mentioned that their husbands were influenced by pornography raises the question of whether there is a causative relationship between the husband's use of pornography and their sexual abuse of their wives.

Id. at 84. Do these statistics suggest a link between violence and pornography? Or do they suggest that people who enjoy violent sex are likely to enjoy visual images of such sex?

5. Why do men who consume violent pornography want women to want to be hurt by men (at least in fantasy)? Why would that be a pleasurable notion? As Catharine MacKinnon has put it, in the pornographic model, or under conditions of male dominance, "men desperately want women to desperately want possession and cruelty and dehumanization." MacKinnon, A Feminist/Political Approach: Pleasure under Patriarchy, in Theories of Human Sexuality 65, 76 (James Geer and William O'Donohue, eds. 1987). Consider this question both in the context of (a) soft bondage and (b) the gruesome scenarios described in the Silbert and Pines study.

6. In some cultures pornography is banned, but nonetheless violence against women occurs. The United States has the highest reported rape rate in the world, though it is by no means the only culture in which violent pornography is readily available. Marney Keenan, The Female Fear, Chi. Trib., Apr. 16, 1989, § 6, at 1. Would you conclude that there is no link between pornography and violence against women? What conclusions can be drawn from these statistics?

2. ANTI-PORNOGRAPHY CIVIL RIGHTS ORDINANCE

MODEL ANTIPORNOGRAPHY CIVIL-RIGHTS ORDINANCE

Andrea Dworkin and Catharine A. MacKinnon, Pornography & Civil Rights: A New Day for Women's Equality, Appendix D (1988).

> [In 1983, Minneapolis was the first city to consider a form of the Model Antipornography Civil-Rights Ordinance, drafted by Andrea Dworkin and Catharine MacKinnon. After two days of public hearings, the Minneapolis City Council found that pornography violated women's civil rights and adopted a version of the Ordinance as law on December 30, 1983. After the mayor vetoed the law on January 5, 1984, it was reenacted in amended form on July 13, 1984, and vetoed once again by the mayor on the same day. Subsequently, a similar Ordinance was enacted by the Indianapolis City Council in 1984, but later was declared unconstitutional in American Booksellers Association, Inc. v. Hudnut, which is excerpted below. On November 8, 1988, 62% of the voters in Bellingham, Washington, affirmed a referendum adopting a similar antipornography law. This Ordinance later was declared unconstitutional in Village Books v. City of Bellingham, No. 88-1470 (W.D.Wash. Feb. 9, 1989). The Ordinance has been considered for adoption in Cambridge, Massachusetts; Los Angeles, California; Madison, Wisconsin; the Common-

wealth of Massachusetts; Sweden; Germany; New Zealand; and the Philippines.[i]]

Section 2. DEFINITIONS

1. "Pornography" means the graphic sexually explicit subordination of women through pictures and/or words that also includes one or more of the following:

a. women are presented dehumanized as sexual objects, things or commodities; or

b. women are presented as sexual objects who enjoy humiliation or pain; or

c. women are presented as sexual objects experiencing sexual pleasure in rape, incest, or other sexual assault; or

d. women are presented as sexual objects tied up or cut up or mutilated or bruised or physically hurt; or

e. women are presented in postures or positions of sexual submission, servility, or display; or

f. women's body parts—including but not limited to vaginas, breasts, or buttocks—are exhibited such that women are reduced to those parts; or

g. women are presented being penetrated by objects or animals; or

h. women are presented in scenarios of degradation, humiliation, injury, torture, shown as filthy or inferior, bleeding, bruised or hurt in a context that makes these conditions sexual.

2. The use of men, children, or transsexuals in the place of women in (1) of this definition is also pornography for purposes of this law.

* * *

Section 3. CAUSES OF ACTION

1. *Coercion into pornography.* It is sex discrimination to coerce, intimidate, or fraudulently induce (hereafter, "coerce") any person into performing for pornography, which injury may date from any appearance or sale of any product(s) of such performance(s). The maker(s), seller(s), exhibitor(s) and/or distributor(s) of said pornography may be sued for damages and for an injunction, including to eliminate the product(s) of the performance(s) from the public view.

Proof of one or more of the following facts or conditions shall not, without more, preclude a finding of coercion:

i. See generally, Margaret A. Baldwin, Pornography and the Traffic in Women: Brief on Behalf of Trudee Able–Peterson, et al., Amici Curiae in Support of Defendant and Intervenor–Defendants, *Village Books v. City of Bellingham,* 1 Yale J.L. & Feminism 111 (1989); James Lindgren, Defining Pornography, 141 U.Pa.L.Rev. 1153, 1157 (1993).

a. that the person is a woman; or

b. that the person is or has been a prostitute; or

c. that the person has attained the age of majority; or

d. that the person is connected by blood or marriage to anyone involved in or related to the making of the pornography; or

e. that the person has previously had, or been thought to have had, sexual relations with anyone, including anyone involved in or related to the making of the pornography; or

f. that the person has previously posed for sexually explicit pictures with or for anyone, including anyone involved in or related to the making of the pornography; or

g. that anyone else, including a spouse or other relative, has given permission on the person's behalf; or

h. that the person actually consented to a use of a performance that is then changed into pornography; or

i. that the person knew that the purpose of the acts or events in question was to make pornography; or

j. that the person showed no resistance or appeared to cooperate actively in the photographic sessions or events that produced the pornography; or

k. that the person signed a contract, or made statements affirming a willingness to cooperate in the production of the pornography; or

l. that no physical force, threats, or weapons were used in the making of the pornography; or

m. that the person was paid or otherwise compensated.

2. *Forcing pornography on a person.* It is sex discrimination to force pornography on a person in any place of employment, education, home, or any public place. Complaints may be brought only against the perpetrator of the force and/or the entity or institution responsible for the force.

3. *Assault or physical attack due to pornography.* It is sex discrimination to assault, physically attack, or injure any person in a way that is directly caused by specific pornography. Complaints may be brought against the perpetrator of the assault or attack, and/or against the maker(s), distributor(s), seller(s), and/or exhibitor(s) of the specific pornography.

4. *Defamation through pornography.* It is sex discrimination to defame any person through the unauthorized use in pornography of their proper name, image, and/or recognizable personal likeness. For purposes of this section, public figures shall be treated as private persons. Authorization once given can be revoked in writing any time prior to any publication.

5. *Trafficking in pornography.* It is sex discrimination to produce, sell, exhibit, or distribute pornography, including through private clubs.

a. Municipal, state, and federally funded public libraries or private and public university and college libraries in which pornography is available for study, including on open shelves but excluding special display presentations, shall not be construed to be trafficking in pornography.

b. Isolated passages or isolated parts shall not be the sole basis for complaints under this section.

c. Any woman may bring a complaint hereunder as a woman acting against the subordination of women. Any man, child, or transsexual who alleges injury by pornography in the way women are injured by it may also complain.

* * *

Section 5. ENFORCEMENT

1. *Civil Action.* Any person who has a cause of action under this law may complain directly to a court of competent jurisdiction for relief.

2. *Damages.*

a. Any person who has a cause of action under this law, or their estate, may seek nominal, compensatory, and/or punitive damages without limitation, including for loss, pain, suffering, reduced enjoyment of life, and special damages, as well as for reasonable costs, including attorneys' fees and costs of investigation.

b. In claims under Sec. 3(5), or other than against the perpetrator of the assault or attack under Sec. 3(3), no damages or compensation for losses shall be recoverable against maker(s) for pornography made, against distributor(s) for pornography distributed, against seller(s) for pornography sold, or against exhibitor(s) for pornography exhibited, prior to the effective date of this law.

3. *Injunctions.* Any person who violates this law may be enjoined except that:

a. In actions under Sec. 3(5), and other than against the perpetrator of the assault or attack under Sec. 3(3), no temporary or permanent injunction shall issue prior to a final judicial determination that the challenged activities constitute a violation of this law.

b. No temporary or permanent injunction shall extend beyond such pornography that, having been described with reasonable specificity by said order(s), is determined to be validly proscribed under this law.

CATHARINE A. MACKINNON, FRANCIS BIDDLE'S SISTER: PORNOGRAPHY, CIVIL RIGHTS, AND SPEECH

In Feminism Unmodified: Discourses on Life and Law
163, 171–79, 181–83, 186–87, 193–94 (1987).

In pornography, there it is, in one place, all of the abuses that women had to struggle so long even to begin to articulate, all the *unspeakable* abuse: the rape, the battery, the sexual harassment, the prostitution, and the sexual abuse of children. Only in the pornography it is called something else: sex, sex, sex, sex, and sex, respectively. Pornography sexualizes rape, battery, sexual harassment, prostitution, and child sexual abuse; it thereby celebrates, promotes, authorizes, and legitimizes them. More generally, it eroticizes the dominance and submission that is the dynamic common to them all. It makes hierarchy sexy and calls that "the truth about sex" or just a mirror of reality. Through this process pornography constructs what a woman is as what men want from sex. This is what the pornography means.

Pornography constructs what a woman is in terms of its view of what men want sexually, such that acts of rape, battery, sexual harassment, prostitution, and sexual abuse of children become acts of sexual equality. Pornography's world of equality is a harmonious and balanced place. Men and women are perfectly complementary and perfectly bipolar. Women's desire to be fucked by men is equal to men's desire to fuck women. All the ways men love to take and violate women, women love to be taken and violated. The women who most love this are most men's equals, the most liberated; the most participatory child is the most grown-up, the most equal to an adult. Their consent merely expresses or ratifies these preexisting facts.

The content of pornography is one thing. There, women substantively desire dispossession and cruelty. We desperately want to be bound, battered, tortured, humiliated, and killed. Or, to be fair to the soft core, merely taken and used. This is erotic to the male point of view. Subjection itself, with self-determination ecstatically relinquished, is the content of women's sexual desire and desirability. * * *

What pornography *does* goes beyond its content: it eroticizes hierarchy, it sexualizes inequality. It makes dominance and submission into sex. Inequality is its central dynamic; the illusion of freedom coming together with the reality of force is central to its working. Perhaps because this is a bourgeois culture, the victim must look free, appear to be freely acting. Choice is how she got there. Willing is what she is when she is being equal. It seems equally important that then and there she actually be forced and that forcing be communicated on some level, even if only through still photos of her in postures of receptivity and access, available for penetration. Pornography in this view is a form of forced sex, a practice of sexual politics, an institution of gender inequality.

* * *

In Andrea Dworkin's definitive work, *Pornography: Men Possessing Women,* sexuality itself is a social construct gendered to the ground. Male dominance here is not an artificial overlay upon an underlying inalterable substratum of uncorrupted essential sexual being. Dworkin presents a sexual theory of gender inequality of which pornography is a constitutive practice. The way pornography produces its meaning constructs and defines men and women as such. Gender has no basis in anything other than the social reality its hegemony constructs. Gender is what gender means. The process that gives sexuality its male supremacist meaning is the same process through which gender inequality becomes socially real.

In this approach, the experience of the (overwhelmingly) male audiences who consume pornography is therefore not fantasy or simulation or catharsis but sexual reality, the level of reality on which sex itself largely operates. Understanding this dimension of the problem does not require noticing that pornography models are real women to whom, in most cases, something real is being done; nor does it even require inquiring into the systematic infliction of pornography and its sexuality upon women, although it helps. What matters is the way in which the pornography itself provides what those who consume it want. Pornography *participates* in its audience's eroticism through creating an accessible sexual object, the possession and consumption of which *is* male sexuality, as socially constructed; to be consumed and possessed as which, *is* female sexuality, as socially constructed; pornography is a process that constructs it that way.

The object world is constructed according to how it looks with respect to its possible uses. Pornography defines women by how we look according to how we can be sexually used. Pornography codes how to look at women, so you know what you can do with one when you see one. Gender is an assignment made visually, both originally and in everyday life. A sex object is defined on the basis of its looks, in terms of its usability for sexual pleasure, such that both the looking—the quality of the gaze, including its point of view—and the definition according to use become eroticized as part of the sex itself. This is what the feminist concept "sex object" means. In this sense, sex in life is no less mediated than it is in art. Men have sex with their image of a woman. It is not that life and art imitate each other; in this sexuality, they *are* each other.

* * *

Obscenity law provides a very different analysis and conception of the problem of pornography. In 1973 the legal definition of obscenity became that which the average person, applying contemporary community standards, would find that, taken as a whole, appeals to the prurient interest; that which depicts or describes in a patently offensive way—you feel like you're a cop reading someone's *Miranda* rights—sexual conduct specifically defined by the applicable state law; and that which, taken as a whole, lacks serious literary, artistic, political or scientific value.[36] Feminism doubts whether the average person gender-neutral exists; has more questions about the content and process of defining what community standards are than it does about deviations from them; wonders why prurience counts but powerlessness does not and why sensibilities

36. Miller v. California, 413 U.S. 15, 24 (1973).

are better protected from offense than women are from exploitation; defines sexuality, and thus its violation and expropriation, more broadly than does state law; and questions why a body of law that has not in practice been able to tell rape from intercourse should, without further guidance, be entrusted with telling pornography from anything less. Taking the work "as a whole" ignores that which the victims of pornography have long known: legitimate settings diminish the perception of injury done to those whose trivialization and objectification they contextualize. Besides, and this is a heavy one, if a woman is subjected, why should it matter that the work has other value? Maybe what redeems the work's value is what enhances its injury to women, not to mention that existing standards of literature, art, science, and politics, examined in a feminist light, are remarkably consonant with pornography's mode, meaning, and message. And finally—first and foremost, actually—although the subject of these materials is overwhelmingly women, their contents almost entirely made up of women's bodies, our invisibility has been such, our equation as a sex *with* sex has been such, that the law of obscenity has never even considered pornography a women's issue.

Obscenity, in this light, is a moral idea, an idea about judgments of good and bad. Pornography, by contrast, is a political practice, a practice of power and powerlessness. Obscenity is ideational and abstract; pornography is concrete and substantive. The two concepts represent two entirely different things. Nudity, excess of candor, arousal or excitement, prurient appeal, illegality of the acts depicted, and unnaturalness or perversion are all qualities that bother obscenity law when sex is depicted or portrayed. Sex forced on real women so that it can be sold at a profit and forced on other real women; women's bodies trussed and maimed and raped and made into things to be hurt and obtained and accessed, and this presented as the nature of women in a way that is acted on and acted out, over and over; the coercion that is visible and the coercion that has become invisible—this and more bothers feminists about pornography. Obscenity as such probably does little harm. Pornography is integral to attitudes and behaviors of violence and discrimination that define the treatment and status of half the population.

* * *

To define pornography as a practice of sex discrimination combines a mode of portrayal that has a legal history—the sexually explicit—with an active term that is central to the inequality of the sexes—subordination. Among other things, subordination means to be in a position of inferiority or loss of power, or to be demeaned or denigrated. To be someone's subordinate is the opposite of being their equal. The definition does not include all sexually explicit depictions *of* the subordination of women. That is not what it says. It says, this which *does* that: the sexually explicit that subordinates women. To these active terms to capture what the pornography *does*, the definition adds a list of what it must also contain. This list, from our analysis, is an exhaustive description of what must be in the pornography for it to do what it does behaviorally. Each item in the definition is supported by experimental, testimonial, social, and clinical evidence. We made a legislative choice to be exhaustive and specific and concrete rather than conceptual and general, to minimize problems of chilling effect, making it hard to guess wrong, thus making self-censorship less likely, but encouraging (to use a phrase from discrimination law) voluntary compliance, knowing that if something turns up that is not on the list, the law will not be expansively interpreted.

The list in the definition, by itself, would be a content regulation. But together with the first part, the definition is not simply a content regulation. It is a medium-message combination that resembles many other such exceptions to First Amendment guarantees.

To focus what our law is, I will say what it is not. It is not a prior restraint. It does not go to possession. It does not turn on offensiveness. It is not a ban, unless relief for a proven injury is a "ban" on doing that injury again. Its principal enforcement mechanism is the civil rights commission, although it contains an option for direct access to court as well as de novo judicial review of administrative determinations, to ensure that no case will escape full judicial scrutiny and full due process. I will also not discuss various threshold issues, such as the sources of municipal authority, preemption, or abstention, or even issues of overbreadth or vagueness, nor will I defend the ordinance from views that never have been law, such as First Amendment absolutism. I will discuss the merits: how pornography by this definition is a harm, specifically how it is a harm of gender inequality, and how that harm outweighs any social interest in its protection by recognized First Amendment standards.

This law aspires to guarantee women's rights consistent with the First Amendment by making visible a conflict of rights between the equality guaranteed to all women and what, in some legal sense, is now the freedom of the pornographers to make and sell, and their consumers to have access to, the materials this ordinance defines. Judicial resolution of this conflict, if the judges do for women what they have done for others, is likely to entail a balancing of the rights of women arguing that our lives and opportunities, including our freedom of speech and action, are constrained by—and in many cases flatly precluded by, in, and through—pornography, against those who argue that the pornography is harmless, or harmful only in part but not in the whole of the definition; or that it is more important to preserve the pornography than it is to prevent or remedy whatever harm it does.

* * * This ordinance enunciates a new form of the previously recognized governmental interest in sex equality. Many laws make sex equality a governmental interest. Our law is designed to further the equality of the sexes, to help make sex equality real. Pornography is a practice of discrimination on the basis of sex, on one level because of its role in creating and maintaining sex as a basis for discrimination. It

harms many women one at a time and helps keep all women in an inferior status by defining our subordination as our sexuality and equating that with our gender. It is also sex discrimination because its victims, including men, are selected for victimization on the basis of their gender. But for their sex, they would not be so treated.

* * *

Its particularity to one side, the *approach* to the injury is supported by a whole array of prior decisions that have justified exceptions to First Amendment guarantees when something that matters is seen to be directly at stake. What unites many cases in which speech interests are raised and implicated but not, on balance, protected, is harm, harm that counts. In some existing exceptions, the definitions are much more open-ended than ours. In some the sanctions are more severe, or potentially more so. For instance, ours is a civil law; most others, although not all, are criminal. Almost no other exceptions show as many people directly affected. Evidence of harm in other cases tends to be vastly less concrete and more conjectural, which is not to say that there is necessarily less of it. None of the previous cases addresses a problem of this scope or magnitude—for instance, an eight-billion-dollar-a-year industry. Nor do other cases address an abuse that has such widespread legitimacy. Courts have seen harm in other cases. The question is, will they see it here, especially given that the pornographers got there first. I will confine myself here to arguing from cases on harm to people, on the supposition that, the pornographers notwithstanding, women are not flags.

* * *

Pornography defines what a woman is through conditioning the male sexual response to that definition, to the unilateral sexuality pornography is part of and provides. Its power can be illustrated by considering the credibility problems Linda Marchiano encounters when she says that the presentation of her in *Deep Throat* is not true, in the sense that she does not and did not feel or enjoy what the character she was forced to portray felt and enjoyed. Most concretely, before "Linda Lovelace" was seen performing deep throat, no one had ever seen it being done in that way, largely because it cannot be done without hypnosis to repress the natural gag response. *Yet it was believed.* Men proceeded to demand it of women, causing the distress of many and the death of some. Yet when Linda Marchiano now tells that it took kidnapping and death threats and hypnosis to put her there, that is found *difficult to believe.*

The point is not only that when women can be coerced with impunity the results, when mass-produced, set standards that are devastating and dangerous for all women. The point is also that the assumptions the law of the First Amendment makes about adults—that adults are autonomous, self-defining, freely acting, *equal* individuals—are exactly those qualities that pornography systematically denies and undermines for women. Some of the same reasons children are granted some specific legal avenues for redress—relative lack of power, inability to command respect for their consent and self-determination, in some cases less physical strength or lowered legitimacy in using it, specific credibility problems, and lack of access to resources for meaningful self-expression—also hold true for the social position of women compared to men. It is therefore vicious to suggest, as many have, that women like Linda Marchiano should remedy their situations through the exercise of more speech. Pornography makes their speech impossible, and where possible, worthless. Pornography makes women into objects. Objects do not speak. When they do, they are by then regarded as objects, not as humans, which is what it means to have no credibility. Besides, it is unclear how Ms. Marchiano's speech is supposed to redress her injury, except by producing this legal remedy, since no amount of saying anything remedies what is being *done* to her in theaters and on home videos all over the world, where she is repeatedly raped for public entertainment and private profit.

* * *

As part of the relief for people who can prove this was done to them, our law provides an injunction to remove these materials from public view. The best authority we have for this is the *Ferber* case, which permits criminal prohibitions on child pornography. That case recognized that child pornography need not be obscene to be child abuse. The Court found such pornography harmful in part because it constituted "a permanent record of children's participation and the harm to the child is exacerbated by circulation." This was a film, by the way, largely of two boys masturbating. The sensitivities of obscenity law, the Court noted, were inapt because "a work which, taken on the whole, contains value may nevertheless embody the hardest core of child pornography." Whether a work appeals to the prurient interest is not the same as whether a child is physically or psychologically harmed to make it.

Both of these reasons apply to coerced women. Women are not children, but coerced women are effectively deprived of power over the expressive products of their coercion. Coerced pornography should meet the test that "the evil to be restricted . . . overwhelmingly outweighs the expressive interests, if any, at stake." Unless one wishes to retain the incentive structure that has introduced a profit motive into rape, pornography made this way should be able to be eliminated.

* * *

To reach the magnitude of this problem on the scale it exists, our law makes trafficking in pornography—production, sale, exhibition, or distribution—actionable. Under the obscenity rubric, much legal and psychological scholarship has centered on a search for the elusive link between harm and pornography defined as obscenity. Although they were not very clear on what obscenity was, it was its harm they truly could not find. They looked high and low—in the mind of the male consumer, in society or in its "moral fabric," in correlations between variations in levels of antisocial acts and liberalization of obscenity laws. The only harm they have found has been harm to "the social interest in order and morality." Until recently, no one looked very persistently for harm to women, particularly harm to women through men. The rather obvious fact that the sexes *relate* has been overlooked in the inquiry into the male consumer and his mind. The pornography doesn't just drop out of the sky, go into his head, and stop there. Specifically, men rape, batter, prostitute, molest, and sexually harass women. Under conditions of inequality, they also hire, fire, promote, and grade women, decide how much or whether we are worth paying and for what, define and approve and disapprove of women in ways that count, that determine our lives.

If women are not just born to be sexually used, the fact that we are seen and treated as though that is what we are born for becomes something in need of explanation. If we see that men relate to women in a pattern of who they see women as being, and that forms a pattern of inequality, it becomes important to ask where that view came from or, minimally, how it is perpetuated or escalated. Asking this requires asking different questions about pornography than the ones obscenity law made salient.

* * *

For those of you who still think pornography is only an idea, consider the possibility that obscenity law got one thing right. Pornography is more actlike than thoughtlike. The fact that pornography, in a feminist view, furthers the idea of the sexual inferiority of women, which is a political idea, doesn't make the pornography itself into a political idea. One can express the idea a practice embodies. That does not make that practice into an idea. Segregation expresses the idea of the inferiority of one group to another on the basis of race. That does not make segregation an idea. A sign that says "Whites Only" is only words. Is it therefore protected by the First Amendment? Is it not an act, a practice, of segregation because what it means is inseparable from what it does? *Law* is only words.

Text Note: Feminist Opposition to the Ordinance

Not all feminists have supported the civil rights approach to creating a cause of action for women harmed by pornography.[61] In a 1993 article, Lisa Duggan, Nan D. Hunter and Carole S. Vance opposed the Anti-pornography Ordinance for the following reasons:

61. Lisa Duggan, Nan D. Hunter, and Carole S. Vance, False Promises: Feminist Anti–Pornography Legislation, 38 N.Y.L. School L. Rev. 133 (1993). See also Nan D. Hunter and Sylvia A. Law, Brief Amici Curiae of Feminist Anti–Censorship Taskforce, et al., in American Booksellers Association, Inc. v. Hudnut, 21 U. Mich. J.L. Ref. 69 (1987–88); Thomas I. Emerson, Pornography and the First Amendment: A Reply to Professor MacKinnon, 3 Yale L. & Policy Rev. 130 (1984) (article written in response to an earlier article by Catharine MacKinnon, Not a Moral Issue, 2 Yale L. & Policy Rev. 321 (1984).

(1) Even though they acknowledge that the Ordinance is civil, not criminal, they believe that the "censoring impact would be substantially as severe as criminal obscenity laws" and that "[m]aterials could be removed from public availability by court injunction, and publishers and booksellers could be subject to potentially endless legal harassment."[62] The "trafficking" section, believed by the authors to be the "heart" of the Ordinance, "would allow almost anyone to seek the removal of any materials falling within the law's definition of pornography."[63] They believe that "the prospect of having to defend a potentially infinite number of privately filed complaints creates at least as much of a chilling effect against pornographic or sexual speech as does a criminal law. And as long as representatives of the state—in this case, judges—have ultimate say over the interpretation, the distinction between this Ordinance and 'real' censorship will not hold."[64]

(2) The definition of pornography is too vague, leaving the interpretation of critical phrases to plaintiffs and judges. They particularly point to the term "subordination" as being problematic: "[t]o some, *any* graphic sexual act violates women's dignity and therefore subordinates them. To others, consensual heterosexual lovemaking within the boundaries of procreation and marriage is acceptable, but heterosexual acts that do not have reproduction as their aim lower women's status and hence subordinate them. Still others accept a wide range of non-procreative, perhaps even nonmarital, heterosexuality but draw the line at lesbian sex, which they view as degrading."[65]

(3) The Ordinance is over-inclusive in that it is not limited to portrayals of violence against women: "only four [of the nine criteria listed in the Ordinance] involve the intersection of violence, sexual explicitness, and sexism, and then only arguably." Moreover, they question whether "images with all three characteristics do in fact cause violence against women."[66]

(4) The Ordinance is under-inclusive in that it "targets material that is sexually explicit and sexist, but ignores material that is violent and sexist, violent and sexually explicit, only violent, or only sexist." They argue that "[f]or proponents to exempt violent and sexist images, or even sexist images, from regulation is inconsistent, especially since they are so pervasive."[67]

(5) The Ordinance legislates a type of sexual norm, exploiting "everyone's relative ignorance and anxious ambivalence about sex, distorting and oversimplifying what confronts us in building a sexual politics." They argue that "in sex, as in few other areas of human behavior, unexamined and unjustifiable prejudice passes itself off as considered opinion about what is desirable and normal."[68]

(6) The Ordinance reinforces the traditional view of sex as "degrading to women."[69]

62. Duggan, Hunter and Vance, above note 61, at 135.

63. Id. at 153.

64. Id. at 154.

65. Id. at 149–50.

66. Id. at 144.

67. Id. at 149.

68. Id. at 151.

69. Id. at 152.

(7) The Ordinance embodies "a political view that holds pornography to be a central force in 'creating and maintaining' the oppression of women."[70] Duggan, Hunter and Vance argue that "the studies cited by Ordinance supporters do not support the theory that pornography causes violence against women." Moreover, history contradicts this view since women were oppressed (e.g., witches were burned, women were considered chattel, husbands beat and raped wives) long before the advent of generally available pornography. (If there is any "communication medium" for woman-hating, according to the authors, it is religion.) Instead, they argue that "fundamental social and economic structures of society" cause women's oppression.[71]

(8) Pornography is not necessarily a lie about women and their sexual pleasure: "[w]hen mutually desired sexual experiences are depicted, pornography is not 'libelous.' " In other words, some women are sexual masochists, and to declare that "sadomasochism is a 'lie' about sexuality reflects an arrogance and moralism that feminists should combat, not engage in."[72]

(9) Pornography can benefit women. Pornography "magnifies the misogyny present in the culture and exaggerates the fantasy of male power;" it has "served to flout conventional sexual mores, to ridicule sexual hypocrisy, and to underscore the importance of sexual needs." According to these authors,

> Pornography carries many messages other than woman-hating; it advocates sexual adventure, sex outside of marriage, sex for no reason other than pleasure, casual sex, anonymous sex, group sex, voyeuristic sex, illegal sex, public sex. Some of these ideas appeal to women reading or seeing pornography, who may interpret some images as legitimating their own sense of sexual urgency or desire to be sexually aggressive. Women's experience of pornography is not as universally victimizing as the Ordinance would have it.[73]

(10) The Ordinance plays into the hands of the far right, contributing to the "further narrow[ing] of the public realm of sexual speech" which "coincides all too well with the privatization of sexual, reproductive and family issues." Additionally, the Ordinance could be used to achieve homophobic goals by providing legal recourse for plaintiffs who perceive lesbianism as "a 'degrading' form of 'subordination.' "[74]

(11) Finally, the Ordinance diverts energy from movements to "enact other, less popular laws that would genuinely empower women—comparable worth legislation, for example, or affirmative action requirements, or fairer property and support principles in divorce laws."[75]

In sum, these authors believe that "the sexual images in question do not cause more harm than other aspects of misogynist culture;" "sexually explicit speech, even in male-dominated society, serves positive social functions for women;" and "the passage and enforcement of anti-pornography

70. Id. at 153.
71. Id. at 155.
72. Id. at 156.
73. Id.
74. Id. at 158.
75. Id.

laws such as those supported in Minneapolis and Indianapolis are more likely to impede, rather than advance, feminist goals."[76]

Notes on the Model Ordinance

1. Duggan et al. spend little time addressing the "harms" of pornography, yet they conclude that pornography does not cause harm. As noted above, there is a substantial amount of evidence of the harms, including the testimony of women who have been harmed in specific ways by pornography. Since the Ordinance only provides a remedy if a plaintiff can *prove* a harm, is this critique of the Ordinance legitimate? If there is a possibility that pornography does harm women, should they be precluded from a remedy if they can prove the harm?

2. Some critics of the Ordinance, including Duggan et al., are concerned that it is not limited to violence or coercion. Does the Ordinance provide a cause of action for freely chosen sexual activity? Sexual materials that do not show physical aggression often objectify women, reinforcing gender-based stereotypes. Moreover, materials that do not show physical aggression may nonetheless require physical aggression in their production, such as those in which women are forced to act as if they are enjoying themselves (for example, Linda Marchiano in Deep Throat) and may also result in their viewers' physical aggression against other women (for example, the results of the experiments described above). How much evidence of harm—and what kind of harm—would you require before including what Duggan et al. call "nonviolent" pornography within the Ordinance?

3. Should government provide a cause of action for any woman harmed as a result of sexist speech, including all sexist advertising, movies, and other media speech? Duggan et al. suggest that the Ordinance is inconsistent because it does not provide such an action. Would you support this broad remedy? Does the Ordinance fail because it does not address *every* possible form of sexism?

4. Duggan et al. point to the Ordinance's definition of pornography as too vague and vulnerable to potential misuse. They are particularly concerned that "subordination" is not defined in the Ordinance. How does MacKinnon define subordination? Do you think courts and juries can apply the definition of pornography in the Ordinance? Can you define "pornography" in more concrete terms? Do the specific contexts listed in the Ordinance's definition help? In a study measuring law students' ability to use the definition of pornography in the Ordinance and the *Miller* test for obscenity, James Lindgren concluded that the students were best able to apply consistently the definition in the Ordinance. Lindgren, Defining Pornography, 141 U.Pa.L.Rev. 1153, 1214–15 (1993). Lindgren found that the "crucial element in the MacKinnon–Dworkin test [that makes it easier to apply] was subordination." Id. at 1215. Do other statutes provide definitions more concrete than those in the Ordinance? For example, do you know of any statutes that define terms such as "reasonable" and "discrimination"? Does that make them too "vague" to withstand judicial scrutiny?

76. Id. at 154.

5. Does the definition of pornography include sexual material that may appeal to some women? If so, is it wise or good policy to subject to civil liability materials that some women perceive as helpful in discovering their sexuality? How does Catharine MacKinnon address this point? Robin West? See West, Hedonic Lives, in Chapter 3. Are there other ways that the Ordinance might hurt women seeking to explore their own sexuality? Are there ways that the Ordinance might help women seeking to create and explore a sexuality that is their own? What special problems does the Ordinance pose for lesbians and gay men? Dworkin and MacKinnon, in response to the question "under the Ordinance, won't gay and lesbian materials be the first to go?", respond that:

> In some places, under obscenity laws, graphic sexually explicit materials presenting homosexual sex acts are made illegal *per se*. The Ordinance does not do this. The Ordinance requires proof of actual harm before any materials can be found illegal. The harm cannot be a moral one—say, that someone is offended by the materials or believes they are not proper family entertainment or finds that they violate their religious beliefs. The harm proven must be a harm of coercion, assault, defamation, or trafficking in sex-based subordination. The fact that the participants in the sex acts shown are of the same sex is not itself a form of sex-based subordination. Only materials that can be *proven harmful* can be reached, and only by their victims, not by the government. The particular question of lesbian and gay materials under the Ordinance then becomes: if any lesbian or gay material can be proven to do harm to direct victims, is there a good reason that it ought to be exempt under the Ordinance simply *because* the materials show gay or lesbian sex?

Andrea Dworkin and Catharine A. MacKinnon, Pornography & Civil Rights: A New Day for Women's Equality 85–86 (1988). In fact, Dworkin and MacKinnon believe that the Ordinance is part of gay and lesbian liberation since "[a]ll lesbians have necessarily suffered from the pornographers' definition of lesbian that is so central to the violence, hatred, contempt and discrimination directed against lesbians in society." Id. at 87.

6. Duggan et al. argue that pornography does not cause women's oppression, citing a long history of misogyny preceding the extensive availability of pornography; they argue that "fundamental social and economic structures of society" cause women's oppression. How would you respond to this criticism? Dworkin and MacKinnon reply to this issue by stating "[i]f pornography hurts women now, doesn't something need to be done about it?" Also, they note that lower pay subordinates women, but it is a "result," not a "cause" of misogyny, yet "[n]o one would suggest that feminists abandon the fight, including the legal fight, for equal pay because it is 'only a symptom,' not a cause, of patriarchy itself." Dworkin and MacKinnon, above note 5, at 72–73. Do you agree with the distinction between a symptom and the cause of women's oppression? Do all the symptoms, as well as the cause, need to be attacked? Is rape a symptom or a cause?

7. The Feminist Anti–Censorship Taskforce ("FACT"), a group of feminists who opposed the Ordinance, urged the Seventh Circuit to find the Indianapolis Ordinance unconstitutional in the *Hudnut* case, below. See Nan D. Hunter and Sylvia A. Law, Brief Amici Curiae of Feminist Anti–Censor-

ship Taskforce, et al., in American Booksellers Association, Inc. v. Hudnut, 21 U. Mich. J.L. Ref. 69 (1987–88). Many of the feminists who signed the FACT Brief were academics, writers, and artists. The Brief states that "experimentations in feminist art which deal openly and explicitly with sexual themes will be easily targeted for suppression * * *." Do Duggan et al. share this concern? How would MacKinnon and Dworkin respond? If feminist art falls within the definition of pornography, and a plaintiff can prove actual injury as a result of the art, should the artist be immune from damages?

8. Some people believe pornography has a cathartic effect on men who would otherwise act out their fantasies. See C. Crepault and M. Couture, Men's Erotic Fantasies, 9 Archives Sex. Behav. 565, 566 (1980) (viewing pornography "may allow partial relief of unfulfilled or unrealizable desires"). In other words, the explicit image or the fantasy provoked by it serves as a substitute for socially unacceptable behavior. What kind of evidence would you require to establish that pornography might sometimes avoid actual harm to women? To date, there are no data to support such a hypothesis.

9. Researchers studying pornography generally "debrief" subjects in order to comply with ethical considerations (i.e., you cannot expose a subject to material that you believe will make that individual more aggressive or hostile to women without ameliorating the effects). Scientists claim they have had some success (at least short-term) in reversing the effects of pornography on subjects by providing information that contradicts the messages of pornography. Neil M. Malamuth and James V. P. Check, Debriefing Effectiveness Following Exposure to Pornographic Rape Depictions, 20 J. Sex Res. 1 (1984). Is their claim susceptible to scientific proof? Does this suggest that more speech is the solution to the possible harm of pornography? Might there be market failure in the "marketplace of ideas" in debriefing pornography consumers? Could government regulation, such as mandating safety labeling, cure this problem? Why or why not? There is a movement away from behavioral science studies on the relationship between pornography and aggression against women because of "an increasing concern with the rights of human subjects," i.e., the ethical problems about the likelihood that people would be harmed as a result of the subjects' exposure to pornography. Mike Allen, Dave D'Alessio and Keri Brezgel, A Meta–Analysis Summarizing the Effects of Pornography II: Aggression After Exposure, 22 Human Communication Research 258, 276 (1995).

10. Is it likely that anti-pornography legislation, such as the Ordinance, would help some women at some times in some circumstances and hurt some women at some times in some circumstances? For example, under the Ordinance, perhaps the *Herberg* rape would have been less likely, or, had it occurred, the survivor might have been more likely to have a damage action against a deep-pocket pornographer. On the other hand, under the Ordinance, some sexual material some women find subjectively pleasurable might be less available. How would you resolve these conflicting interests? Is it as simple as balancing some people's sexual pleasure from pornography against actual harm to others?

11. Under the Ordinance, certain circumstances, such as a signed contract, will not bar the plaintiff from proving she was coerced into making pornography. Is this contrary to current contract law? Does the Ordinance state that women cannot *voluntarily* participate in the production of pornography? Is this equivalent to the 19th century rule that married women could not contract? How would you distinguish the two?

12. Duggan et al. argue that even though the Ordinance is civil, its "censoring impact" would be similar to criminal obscenity laws. What role does the government play in the enforcement of the Ordinance? Is any material "banned" under the Ordinance? (Note that an injunction addressing specific material is enforceable only after the court of last appeal rules.) Is simple possession of pornography illegal under the Ordinance?

13. Duggan et al. argue that the Ordinance is based on a view that "sex is degrading to women, but not to men." Do you agree? Doesn't the Ordinance provide only that graphic sexually explicit subordination of women through pictures or words violates their civil rights? Do Duggan et al. go too far in suggesting that the Ordinance condemns all sexual activity?

14. What legal or social changes might be more effective than the Ordinance in lowering violence against women and increasing women's sexual agency? Is there a double bind for women with respect to regulation of pornography? Might there be more speech, and more diverse communities with varying speech, if local governments were allowed to experiment with various approaches to pornography, such as the Ordinance?

HARRY BROD, PORNOGRAPHY AND THE ALIENATION OF MALE SEXUALITY IN RETHINKING MASCULINITY: PHILOSOPHICAL EXPLORATIONS IN LIGHT OF FEMINISM

(Larry May & Robert A. Strikwerda, eds.) 149, 151–54, 158–59, 160–62 (1992).

I shall be claiming that pornography has a negative impact on men's own sexuality. This is a claim that an aspect of an oppressive system, patriarchy, operates, at least in part, to the disadvantage of the group it privileges, men. This claim does not deny that the overall effect of the system is to operate in men's advantage, nor does it deny that the same aspect of the system under consideration, that is, male sexuality and pornography under patriarchy, might not also contribute to the expansion and maintenance of male power even as it also works to men's disadvantage. * * * I view raising consciousness of the prices of male power as part of a strategy through which we could at least potentially mobilize men against pornography's destructive effects on both women and men.

* * *

In terms of both its manifest image of and its effects on male sexuality, that is, in both intrinsic and consequentialist terms, pornography restricts male sensuality in favor of a genital, performance oriented male sexuality. Men become sexual acrobats endowed with oversized and overused organs * * *. To speak non-euphemistically, using penile performance as an index of male strength and potency directly contradicts biological facts. There is no muscle tissue in the penis. Its erection when aroused results simply from increased blood flow to the area. All social mythology aside, the male erection is physiologically nothing more than localized high blood pressure. Yet this particular form of hypertension has attained mythic significance. Not only does this focusing of sexual attention on one organ increase male performance anxieties, but it also desensitizes other areas of the body from becoming what might otherwise be sources of pleasure. A colleague once told me that her favorite line in a lecture on male sexuality I used to give in a course I regularly taught was my declaration that the basic male sex organ is not the penis, but the skin.

The predominant image of women in pornography presents women as always sexually ready, willing, able, and eager. The necessary corollary to pornography's myth of female perpetual availability is its myth of male perpetual readiness. Just as the former fuels male misogyny when real-life women fail to perform to pornographic standards, so do men's failures to similarly perform fuel male insecurities. Furthermore, I would argue that this diminishes pleasure. Relating to one's body as a performance machine produces a split consciousness wherein part of one's attention is watching the machine, looking for flaws in its performance, even while one is supposedly immersed in the midst of sensual pleasure. This produces a self-distancing self-consciousness which mechanizes sex and reduces pleasure. (This is a problem perpetuated by numerous sexual self-help manuals, which treat sex as a matter of individual technique for fine-tuning the machine rather than as human interaction. I would add that men's sexual partners are also affected by this, as they can often intuit when they are being subjected to rote manipulation.)

* * *

In terms of the discourse of what it understands to be "free" sex, pornographic sex comes "free" of the demands of emotional intimacy or commitment. It is commonly said as a generalization that women tend to connect sex with emotional intimacy more than men do. Without romantically blurring female sexuality into soft focus, if what is meant is how each gender consciously thinks or speaks of sex, I think this view is fair enough. But I find it takes what men say about sex, that it doesn't mean as much or the same thing to them, too much at face value. I would argue that men do feel similar needs for intimacy, but are trained to deny them, and are encouraged further to see physical affection and intimacy primarily if not exclusively in sexual terms. This leads to the familiar syndrome wherein, as one man put it:

> Although what most men want is physical affection, what they end up thinking they want is to be laid by a Playboy bunny.

This puts a strain on male sexuality. Looking to sex to fulfill what are really non-sexual needs, men end up disappointed and frustrated. Sometimes they feel an unfilled void, and blame it on their or their partner's inadequate sexual performance. * * * A confession that sex is vastly overrated often lies beneath male sexual bravado. I would argue that sex seems overrated because men look to sex for the fulfillment of nonsexual emotional needs, a quest doomed to failure. Part of the reason for this failure is the priority of quantity over quality of sex which comes with sexuality's commodification. As human needs become subservient to market desires, the ground is laid for an increasing multiplication of desires to be exploited and filled by marketable commodities.

For the most part the female in pornography is not one the man has yet to "conquer," but one already presented to him for the "taking." The female is primarily there as sex object, not sexual subject. Or, if she is not completely objectified, since men do want to be desired themselves, hers is at least a subjugated subjectivity. But one needs another independent subject, not an object or a captured subjectivity, if one either wants one's own prowess validated, or if one simply desires human interaction. Men functioning in the pornographic mode of male sexuality, in which men dominate women, are denied satisfaction of these human desires. Denied recognition in the sexual interaction itself, they look to gain this recognition in wider social recognition of their "conquest."

To the pornographic mind, then, women become trophies awarded to the victor. For women to serve this purpose of achieving male social validation, a woman "conquered" by one must be a woman deemed desirable by others. Hence pornography both produces and reproduces uniform standards of female beauty. Male desires and tastes must be channeled into a single mode, with allowance for minor variations which obscure the fundamentally monolithic nature of the mold. Men's own subjectivity becomes masked to them, as historically and culturally specific and varying standards of beauty are made to appear natural and given. The ease with which men reach quick agreement on what makes a woman "attractive," evidenced in such things as the "1–10" rating scale of male banter and the reports of a computer program's success in predicting which of the contestants would be crowned "Miss America," demonstrates how deeply such standards have been internalized, and consequently the extent to which men are dominated by desires not authentically their own.

* * *

[T]he debate over whether pornography reflects men's power or powerlessness, as taken up recently by Alan Soble in his book *Pornography: Marxism, Feminism, and the Future of Sexuality*, can be resolved if one makes a distinction such as I have proposed between personal and institutional male power. Soble cites men's use of pornographic fantasy as compensation for their powerlessness in the real world to argue that "pornography is therefore not so much an expression of male power as it is an expression of their lack of power." In contrast, I would argue that by differentiating levels of power one should more accurately say that pornography is both an expression of men's public power and an expression of their lack of personal power. The argument of this paper is that pornography's image of male sexuality works to the detriment of men personally even as its image of female sexuality enhances the powers of patriarchy. It expresses the power of alienated sexuality, or, as one could equally well say, the alienated power of sexuality.

With this understanding, one can reconcile the two dominant but otherwise irreconcilable images of the straight male consumer of pornography: on the one hand the powerful rapist, using pornography to consummate his sexual violence, and on the other hand the shy recluse, using it to consummate his masturbatory fantasies. Both images have their degree of validity, and I believe it is a distinctive virtue of the analysis presented here that one can understand not only the merits of each depiction, but their interconnection.

* * *

I have argued throughout this paper that pornography is a vehicle for the imposition of socially constructed sexuality, not a means for the expression of autonomously self-determined sexuality. (I would add that in contrasting imposed and authentic sexualities I am not endorsing a sexual essentialism, but simply carving out a space for more personal freedom.) Pornography is inherently about commercialized sex, about the eroticization of power and the power of eroticization. * * * Any distinction between pornography and erotica remains problematic, and cannot be drawn with absolute precision. Yet I believe some such distinction can and must be made. I would place the two terms not in absolute opposition, but at two ends of a continuum, with gray areas of necessity remaining between them. The gradations along the continuum are marked not by the explicitness of the portrayal of sexuality or the body, nor by the assertiveness, passivity of persons, nor by any categorization of sexual acts or activities, but by the extent to which autonomous personhood is attributed to the person or persons portrayed. Erotica portrays sexual subjects manifesting their personhood in and through their bodies. Pornography depicts sex objects, persons reduced to their bodies. While the erotic nude presents the more pristine sexual body before the social persona is adopted through donning one's clothing, the pornographic nude portrays a body whose clothing has been more or less forcibly removed, where the absence of clothing remains the most forceful presence in the image. Society's objectification remains present, indeed emphasized, in pornography, in a way in which it does not in erotica. Erotica, as sexual art, expresses a self, whereas pornography, as sexual commodity, markets one. The latter "works" because the operation it performs on women's bodies resonates with the "pornographizing" the male gaze does to women in other areas of society. These distinctions remain problematic, to say the least, in their application, and disagreement in particular cases will no doubt remain. Much more work needs to be done before one would with any reasonable confidence distinguish authentic from imposed, personal from commercial, sexuality. Yet I believe this is the crucial question, and I believe these concepts correctly indicate the proper categories of analysis. Assuming a full definition of freedom as including autonomy and self-determination, pornography is therefore incompatible with real freedom.

* * *

I would like to conclude with some remarks on the practical import of this analysis. First of all, if the analysis of the relationship between pornography and consumerism and the argument about pornography leading to violence are correct, then a different conceptualization of the debate over the ethics of the feminist anti-pornography movement emerges. If one accepts, as I do, the idea that this movement is not against sex, but against sexual abuse, then the campaign against pornography is essentially not a call for censorship but a consumer campaign for product safety. The proper context for the debate over its practices is then not issues of free speech or civil liberties, but issues of business ethics. Or rather, this is the conclusion I reach remaining focused on pornography and male sexuality. But we should remember the broader context I alluded to at the beginning of this paper, the question of pornography's effects on women. In that context, women are not the consumers of pornography, but the consumed. Rather than invoking the consumer movement, perhaps we should then look to environmental protection as a model. Following this line of reasoning, one could in principle then perhaps develop under the tort law of product liability an argument to accomplish much of the regulation of sexually explicit material some are now trying to achieve through legislative means, perhaps developing a new definition of "safe" sexual material.

Notes on Men and Pornography

1. Pornography *is* sex education for many adolescent boys. In a study of middle-class adolescents (average age of 14) in Canada, James Check found that a third of the boys (but only two percent of girls) watch video pornography at least once a month. Check, Teenage Training: The Effects of Pornography on Adolescent Males in The Price We Pay: The Case Against Racist Speech, Hate Propaganda and Pornography 89, 89–90 (Laura Lederer and Richard Delgado, eds. 1995). Check reports: "Twenty-nine percent of the boys ... said that pornography was *the most significant source* [of information] among those listed [teachers, peers, parents, books, schools, magazines, and pornography]." Id. at 90. The girls in the study were not regular consumers of pornography and "did not [therefore] find pornography the most significant source of sex information in their lives." Id. Check also found that 43% of the boys (and 16% of the girls) thought it "definitely okay," "maybe okay," or weren't sure about whether it was okay for a boy to hold a girl down and force her "to have intercourse if the boy has been sexually excited." Id. at 90–91. Check reported that "only 71 percent of the girls and 35 percent of the boys said it's "*definitely not* okay." Id. at 91. According to Check, studies in California and Rhode Island have replicated these data. Id. The boys who said it was OK watched pornography regularly and regarded it as their best source of sex information. Id. at 90–91. Does this change your views on the harms of pornography? Why do you think boys rely so much on pornography for their sex education?

2. How precisely does Brod see pornography as harming men? Is the Check study, discussed in note 1 above, consistent or inconsistent with Brod's analysis? If, in fact, a third of adolescent males learn about sex primarily from pornography, and those young men are more likely (than other young men) to rape women (because they do not see coerced sex as definitely wrong), are the pornography-educated young men harmed? How? What would Brod say about the role of pornography in exploring personal sexual autonomy and self-determination?

3. Why have we heard so little about pornography's harms to men in the ongoing discussion about its regulation? For a description of harm to male porn stars, see Susan Faludi, Stiffed: The Betrayal of the American Male 530–74 (1999).

4. Do you agree with Brod that pornography harms men even as it reinforces patriarchy? How can pornography do both?

5. Brod's analysis of pornography's harm to men is most consistent with which feminist theoretical approach described in Chapter 3? Is this a strength or a weakness of that approach?

6. What about other pornographic material available to children in the technological age? During the year ending February 28, 1984, 180 million calls were made to a single Dial–A–Porn service. From calls to one California Dial–A–Porn line during an 11 month period ending in 1988, AT & T collected $5.5 million in revenues, of which $650,000 went to the porn service. Dan Brown and Jennings Bryant, The Manifest Content of Pornography in Pornography: Research Advances and Policy Considerations 3, 19–20 (Dolf Zillman and Jennings Bryant, eds. 1989). Typical "call content includes verbal descriptions of sex acts, sometimes in an imaginary participatory format. Examples are lesbian activity, sodomy, rape, incest, excretory functions, bestiality, sadomasochistic abuse, and sex acts with children." Id. After several attempts to regulate the industry to prevent children from gaining access to the call content, the Federal Communications Commission finally imposed a blanket prohibition on indecent as well as obscene interstate commercial telephone messages. However, when a "Dial–A–Porn" service brought an action to prevent enforcement, the Supreme Court held that: (1) prohibition of obscene telephone messages was constitutional, and (2) denial of adult access to telephone messages which were indecent but not obscene far exceeded that which was necessary to limit access of minors to such messages and did not survive constitutional scrutiny. Sable Communications of California, Inc. v. FCC, 492 U.S. 115, 109 S.Ct. 2829, 106 L.Ed.2d 93 (1989). Can you think of any constitutional ways to limit children's access to pornography? See also Denver Area Educ. Telecomm. Consortium, Inc. v. FCC, 518 U.S. 727, 116 S.Ct. 2374, 135 L.Ed.2d 888 (1996) (finding portions of the Cable Television Consumer Protection and Competition Act of 1992 unconstitutional); Reno v. ACLU, 521 U.S. 844, 117 S.Ct. 2329, 138 L.Ed.2d 874 (1997) (declaring portions of the Communications Decency Act of 1996 unconstitutional).

7. What is the effect of the now-widespread availability of pornography on the Internet upon the possibility of regulating distribution of these materials to minors? Is there any way to restrict what children view on the Web? Legally? Would such regulation be constitutional? What other ways

can you think of to deal with this problem? Would the Anti–Pornography Ordinance apply to the Internet?

AMERICAN BOOKSELLERS ASSOCIATION, INC. v. HUDNUT

United States Court of Appeals, Seventh Circuit, 1985.

771 F.2d 323, affirmed mem., 475 U.S. 1001, 106 S.Ct. 1172, 89 L.Ed.2d 291 (1986).

[The statutory material at issue in *Hudnut* were sections of Chapter 16 of the Code of Indianapolis and Marion County that addressed pornography as sex discrimination. Those provisions varied in several ways from the Model Ordinance, including limiting the trafficking cause of action to pornography that shows violence.]

Indianapolis enacted an ordinance defining "pornography" as a practice that discriminates against women. "Pornography" is to be redressed through the administrative and judicial methods used for other discrimination. The City's definition of "pornography" is considerably different from "obscenity," which the Supreme Court has held is not protected by the First Amendment.

To be "obscene" under *Miller v. California,* 413 U.S. 15 (1973), "a publication must, taken as a whole, appeal to the prurient interest, must contain patently offensive depictions or descriptions of specified sexual conduct, and on the whole have no serious literary, artistic, political, or scientific value."

Offensiveness must be assessed under the standards of the community. Both offensiveness and an appeal to something other than "normal, healthy sexual desires" are essential elements of "obscenity."

* * *

The Indianapolis ordinance does not refer to the prurient interest, to offensiveness, or to the standards of the community. It demands attention to particular depictions, not to the work judged as a whole. It is irrelevant under the ordinance whether the work has literary, artistic, political, or scientific value. The City and many amici point to these omissions as virtues. They maintain that pornography influences attitudes, and the statute is a way to alter the socialization of men and women rather than to vindicate community standards of offensiveness. And as one of the principal drafters of the ordinance has asserted, "if a woman is subjected, why should it matter that the work has other value?" Catharine A. MacKinnon, *Pornography, Civil Rights, and Speech,* 20 Harv.Civ.Rts.—Civ.Lib.L.Rev. 1, 21 (1985).

Civil rights groups and feminists have entered this case as amici on both sides. Those supporting the ordinance say that it will play an important role in reducing the tendency of men to view women as sexual objects, a tendency that leads to both unacceptable attitudes and discrimination in the workplace and violence away from it. Those opposing the ordinance point out that much radical feminist literature is explicit and depicts women in ways forbidden by the ordinance and that the ordinance would reopen old battles. It is unclear how Indianapolis would treat works from James Joyce's *Ulysses* to Homer's *Iliad;* both depict women as submissive objects for conquest and domination.

We do not try to balance the arguments for and against an ordinance such as this. The ordinance discriminates on the ground of the content of the speech. Speech treating women in the approved way—in sexual encounters "premised on equality"—is lawful no matter how sexually explicit. Speech treating women in the disapproved way—as submissive in matters sexual or as enjoying humiliation—is unlawful no matter how significant the literary, artistic, or political qualities of the work taken as a whole. The state may not ordain preferred viewpoints in this way. The Constitution forbids the state to declare one perspective right and silence opponents.

* * *

"If there is any fixed star in our constitutional constellation, it is that no official, high or petty, can prescribe what shall be orthodox in politics, nationalism, religion, or other matters of opinion or force citizens to confess by word or act their faith therein." West Virginia State Board of Education v. Barnette, 319 U.S. 624, 642 (1943). Under the First Amendment the government must leave to the people the evaluation of ideas. Bald or subtle, an idea is as powerful as the audience allows it to be. A belief may be pernicious—the beliefs of Nazis led to the death of millions, those of the Klan to the repression of millions. A pernicious belief may prevail. Totalitarian governments today rule much of the planet, practicing suppression of billions and spreading dogma that may enslave others. One of the things that separates our society from theirs is our absolute right to propagate opinions that the government finds wrong or even hateful.

* * *

Under the ordinance graphic sexually explicit speech is "pornography" or not depending on the perspective the author adopts. Speech that "subordinates" women and also, for example, presents women as enjoying pain, humiliation, or rape, or even simply presents women in "positions of servility or submission or display" is forbidden, no matter how great the literary or political value of the work taken as a whole. Speech that portrays women in positions of equality is lawful, no matter how graphic the sexual content. This is thought control. It establishes an "approved" view of women, of how they may react to sexual encounters, of how the sexes may relate to each other. Those who espouse the approved view may use sexual images; those who do not, may not.

Indianapolis justifies the ordinance on the ground that pornography affects thoughts. Men who see women depicted as subordinate are more likely to treat them so. Pornography is an aspect of dominance. It does not persuade people so much as change them. It works by socializing, by establishing the expected and the permissible. In this view pornography is not an idea; pornography is the injury.

There is much to this perspective. Beliefs are also facts. People often act in accordance with the images and patterns they find around them. People raised in a religion tend to accept the tenets of that religion, often without independent examination. People taught from birth that black people are fit only for slavery rarely rebelled against that creed; beliefs coupled with the self-interest of the masters established a social structure that inflicted great harm while enduring for centuries. Words and images act at the level of the subconscious before they persuade at the level of the conscious. Even the truth has little chance unless a statement fits within the framework of beliefs that may never have been subjected to rational study.

Therefore we accept the premises of this legislation. Depictions of subordination tend to perpetuate subordination. The subordinate status of women in turn leads to affront and lower pay at work, insult and injury at home, battery and rape on the streets. In the language of the legislature, "[p]ornography is central in creating and maintaining sex as a basis of discrimination. Pornography is a systematic practice of exploitation and subordination based on sex which differentially harms women. The bigotry and contempt it produces, with the acts of aggression it fosters, harm women's opportunities for equality and rights [of all kinds]."

Yet this simply demonstrates the power of pornography as speech. All of these unhappy effects depend on mental intermediation. Pornography affects how people see the world, their fellows, and social relations. If pornography is what pornography does, so is other speech. * * * Seditious libel is protected speech unless the danger is not only grave but also imminent.

Racial bigotry, anti-semitism, violence on television, reporters' biases—these and many more influence the culture and shape our socialization. None is directly answerable by more speech, unless that speech too finds its place in the popular culture. Yet all is protected as speech, however insidious. Any other answer leaves the government in control of all of the institutions of culture, the great censor and director of which thoughts are good for us.

Sexual responses often are unthinking responses, and the association of sexual arousal with the subordination of women therefore may have a substantial effect. But almost all cultural stimuli provoke unconscious responses. Religious ceremonies condition their participants. Teachers convey messages by selecting what not to cover; the implicit message about what is off limits or unthinkable may be more powerful than the messages for which they present rational argument. Television scripts contain unarticulated assumptions. People may be conditioned in subtle ways. If the fact that speech plays a role in a process of conditioning were enough to permit governmental regulation, that would be the end of freedom of speech.

It is possible to interpret the claim that pornography is the harm in a different way. Indianapolis emphasizes the injury that models in pornographic films and pictures may suffer. The record contains materials depicting sexual torture, penetration of women by red-hot irons and the like. These concerns have nothing to do with written materials subject to the statute, and physical injury can occur with or without the "subordination" of women. As we discuss * * *, a state may make injury in the course of producing a film unlawful independent of the viewpoint expressed in the film.

The more immediate point, however, is that the image of pain is not necessarily pain. In Body Double, a suspense film directed by Brian DePalma, a woman who has disrobed and presented a sexually explicit display is murdered by an intruder with a drill. The drill runs through the woman's body. The film is sexually explicit and a murder occurs—yet no one believes that the actress suffered pain or died. * * * Depictions may affect slavery, war, or sexual roles, but a book about slavery is not itself slavery, or a book about death by poison a murder.

Much of Indianapolis's argument rests on the belief that when speech is "unanswerable," and the metaphor that there is a "marketplace of ideas" does not apply, the First Amendment does not apply either. The metaphor is honored; Milton's *Aeropagitica* and John Stewart Mill's *On Liberty* defend freedom of speech on the ground that the truth will prevail, and many of the most important cases under the First Amendment recite this position. The Framers undoubtedly believed it. As a general matter it is true. But the Constitution does not make the dominance of truth a necessary condition of freedom of speech. To say that it does would be to confuse an outcome of free speech with a necessary condition for the application of the amendment.

* * *

We come, finally, to the argument that pornography is "low value" speech, that it is enough like obscenity that Indianapolis may prohibit it. Some cases hold that speech far removed from politics and other subjects at the core of the Framers' concerns may be subjected to special regulation. These cases do not sustain statutes that select among viewpoints, however. * * *

At all events, "pornography" is not low value speech within the meaning of these cases. Indianapolis seeks to prohibit certain speech because it believes this speech influences social relations and politics on a grand scale, that it controls attitudes at home and in the legislature. This precludes a characterization of the speech as low value. True, pornography and obscenity have sex in common. But Indianapolis left out of its definition any reference to literary, artistic, political, or scientific value. The ordinance applies to graphic sexually explicit subordination in works great and small. The Court sometimes balances the value of speech against the costs of its restriction, but it does this by category of speech and not by the content of particular works. Indianapolis has created an approved point of view and so loses the support of these cases.

Any rationale we could imagine in support of this ordinance could not be limited to sex discrimination. Free speech has been on balance an ally of those seeking change. Governments that want stasis start by restricting speech. Culture is a powerful force of continuity; Indianapolis paints pornography as part of the culture of power. Change in any complex system ultimately depends on the ability of outsiders to challenge accepted views and the reigning institutions. Without a strong guarantee of freedom of speech, there is no effective right to challenge what is.

The definition of "pornography" is unconstitutional. No construction or excision of particular terms could save it. The offense of trafficking in pornography necessarily falls with the definition. * * *

The offense of coercion to engage in a pornographic performance, for example, has elements that might be constitutional. Without question a state may prohibit fraud, trickery, or the use of force to induce people to perform—in pornographic films or in any other films. Such a statute may be written without regard to the viewpoint depicted in the work. * * * We suppose that if someone forced a prominent political figure, at gunpoint, to endorse a candidate for office, a state could forbid the commercial sale of the film containing that coerced endorsement. The same principle allows a court to enjoin the publication of stolen trade secrets and award damages for the publication of copyrighted matter without permission.

* * *

The offense of forcing pornography on unwilling recipients is harder to assess. Many kinds of forcing (such as giving texts to students for translation) may themselves be protected speech. * * *

The section creating remedies for injuries and assaults attributable to pornography also is salvageable in principle, although not by us. The First Amendment does not prohibit redress of all injuries caused by speech. Injury to reputation is redressed through the law of libel, which is constitutional subject to strict limitations. Cases such as *Brandenburg v. Ohio* and *NAACP v. Claiborne Hardware* hold that a state may not penalize speech that does not cause immediate injury. But we do not doubt that if, immediately after the Klan's rally in *Brandenburg,* a mob had burned to the ground the house of a nearby black person, that person could have recovered damages from the speaker who whipped the crowd into a frenzy. All of the Justices assumed in *Claiborne Hardware* that if the threats in Charles Evers's incendiary speech had been a little less veiled and had led directly to an assault against a person shopping in a store owned by a white merchant, the victim of the assault and even the merchant could have recovered damages from the speaker.

* * *

Much speech is dangerous. Chemists whose work might help someone build a bomb, political theorists whose papers might start political movements that lead to riots, speakers whose ideas attract violent protesters, all these and more leave loss in their wake. Unless the remedy is very closely confined, it could be more dangerous to speech than all the libel judgments in history. The constitutional requirements for a valid recovery for assault caused by speech might turn out to be too rigorous for any plaintiff to meet. But the Indianapolis ordinance requires the complainant to show that the attack was "directly caused by specific pornography", and it is not beyond the realm of possibility that a state court could construe this limitation in a way that would make the statute constitutional. We are not authorized to prevent the state from trying.

Again, however, the assault statute is tied to "pornography," and we cannot find a sensible way to repair the defect without seizing power that belongs elsewhere. * * *

No amount of struggle with particular words and phrases in this ordinance can leave anything in effect. The district court came to the same conclusion. Its judgment is therefore AFFIRMED.

Notes on Hudnut

1. Even though the *Hudnut* court accepts the premises of the Ordinance, i.e., that depictions of subordination lead to employment discrimination, battery, rape and "harm women's opportunities for equality," it nonetheless finds the First Amendment superior to the Ordinance's attempt to obtain equality for women. Do you agree with the court that the Fourteenth Amendment's promise of equality must give way to the First Amendment's protection of speech? For discussions of other ways to read these amendments, see, e.g., Akhil Reed Amar, The Supreme Court, 1991 Term; The Case of the Missing Amendments: *R.A.V. v. City of St. Paul,* 106 Harv.L.Rev. 124 (1992); Akhil Reed Amar, The Bill of Rights and the Fourteenth Amendment, 101 Yale L.J. 1193 (1992); Morrison Torrey, Thoughts About Why the First Amendment Operates to Stifle the Freedom and Equality of a Subordinated Majority, 21 Women's Rts. Rep. 25 (1999).

2. Are all content-based laws unconstitutional? For instance, bribes, threats, fighting words, defamation, misleading commercial speech, TV and radio advertisements for cigarettes and casinos, advocating the violent overthrow of the government, obscenity, child pornography and certain forms of labor speech are all subjected to some form of government regulation. See Cass R. Sunstein, Pornography and the First Amendment, 4 Duke L.J. 589, 613–15 (1986). In addition, employment discrimination law prohibits speech that is part of a harassing environment. How can you distinguish those restrictions from the civil action proposed in the Ordinance? How would Judge Easterbrook?

3. Was the First Amendment ever intended to protect *all* speech? The Comstock Law, enacted by Congress in 1873, banned the use of the mail to distribute obscenity and specified that information about birth control was

obscene. Handbook of American Women's History 125 (Angela Howard Zophy and Frances M. Kavenic, eds. 1990) (entry for Comstock Law). The Comstock Law was upheld by the U.S. Supreme Court. Id. at 480 (entry for pornography). In 1914, Margaret Sanger was indicted, under this law, for publishing birth control information. Id. at 529 (entry for Margaret Sanger). If the framers actually intended to protect all speech, why didn't the Supreme Court protect the dissemination of information about birth control during the late 19th and early 20th Centuries?

Even if the Founding Fathers intended to protect *all* speech in enacting the First Amendment, should their intent be controlling today? As Mary Becker notes, women not only were excluded from drafting both the Constitution and the Bill of Rights but also, as a matter of social policy, were not permitted to even speak in public at that time. Becker, Conservative Free Speech and the Uneasy Case for Judicial Review, 64 U.Colo.L.Rev. 975, 976 (1993). Should women be bound by an interpretation of a document written when they had no rights of citizenship?

Even if original intent is an appropriate standard to apply in interpreting the First Amendment, could the Founding Fathers possibly have anticipated (1) the scope of modern judicial review (the first case striking a state law on First Amendment grounds was not decided until 1931) or (2) the power of the mass media to produce and distribute pornography? Would the Founding Fathers have likely imagined that modern pornographic material would be considered protected from government regulation by the First Amendment?

4. Does the court give appropriate weight to the fact that pornography is more likely to cause sexual arousal than is racist or anti-semitic speech, i.e., orgasm is a powerful reinforcement? Are there other ways to distinguish the examples of "speech" in above note 2, from pornography?

5. The *Hudnut* court states that the "image of pain is not necessarily pain." But in much pornography, the image of pain *is* pain for the woman used in making the pornography. How would Judge Easterbrook respond to this point?

6. The *Hudnut* opinion states that "[i]t is unclear how Indianapolis would treat works from James Joyce's *Ulysses* to Homer's *Iliad;* both depict women as submissive objects for conquest and domination." Do *Ulysses* and the *Iliad* meet the definition of pornography contained in the Ordinance? Under what circumstances would someone be able to sue the publisher of these works? Is pornography *itself* illegal under the Ordinance?

7. Is it true that the government has not declared a sexual orthodoxy, as Judge Easterbrook's opinion in *Hudnut* suggests, i.e., that the state has not "declare[d] one [sexual] perspective right and silence[d] opponents"? What about lesbian and gay sexuality? Why are most lesbians and gay men closeted (silenced) if the state may not ordain an orthodox sexuality? What makes the relevant state regulations, such as prohibiting same-sex marriages, imposing criminal penalties on homosexual "sodomy," etc., look like something other than the regulation of speech?

8. It is possible to criminalize child pornography. In *Ferber,* the Supreme Court found that the "prevention of sexual exploitation and abuse of

children constitutes a government objective of surpassing importance." New York v. Ferber, 458 U.S. 747, 757, 102 S.Ct. 3348, 73 L.Ed.2d 1113 (1982). Is the main distinction between children and adult women the possibility of "consent?" If so, should the coercion cause of action in the Ordinance be constitutional if a plaintiff can prove she did not consent to being used in the production of pornography? Do the reasons for banning child pornography in *Ferber* extend to women as well? Is it demeaning to analogize women to children in this context?

9. Have you ever seen pornography that is beyond anything you could imagine enjoying, even as fantasy? If you have not seen such pornography, consider how you would feel on viewing the pornography described in *Herberg* and the Silbert and Pines study. Or look at the examples of pornography in Against Pornography: The Evidence of Harm (1993) by Diana E.H. Russell. What is the message you receive? Is it possible for women simply to respond with more speech? Or does the pornography "chill" or silence the speech of women? Does a culture with high levels of pornography create problems for women in terms both of speech and of exploring their own sexuality?

10. American free speech advocates often assert that tolerance of racist and sexist speech is necessary for tolerance of both outsider groups and unpopular speech, particularly unpopular political speech. During the McCarthy era, however, there was widespread tolerance of racist speech and intolerance of political speech, e.g., Communist speech. In Weimar Germany, there was tolerance of racist Nazi hate speech, followed by the Holocaust. In Germany today, there are state-imposed limits on racist hate speech, even in art (e.g., pop music). In America, such limits would probably be found to violate the First Amendment. What are the advantages and disadvantages of these two approaches?

11. Does the *Hudnut* opinion suggest that some aspects of the Ordinance might pass constitutional muster? Which ones? Could you revise the Ordinance to satisfy the court?

12. Could or should the feminist critique of pornography be used to lessen the responsibility of individual men for violence against women? In Schiro v. Clark, 963 F.2d 962 (7th Cir.1992), aff'd, 508 U.S. 905, 113 S.Ct. 2330, 124 L.Ed.2d 243 (1993), the defendant argued that he was a sexual sadist and that his extensive viewing of rape pornography and snuff films left him unable to distinguish between right and wrong. To support his claim of mitigating circumstances in his trial for rape and murder (and to avoid the death penalty), Schiro offered the testimony of expert Edward Donnerstein who stated that "pornography generally encourages men to commit acts of violence against women." While acknowledging its finding in *Hudnut* that "pornographic depictions of the subordination of women perpetuate the subordination of women and violence against women," the Seventh Circuit refused to excuse Schiro by reason of insanity. The court noted that it:

> held that under the First Amendment pornography may not be banned because its harmful effects depend on mental intermediation. It would be impossible to hold both that pornography does not directly cause violence but criminal actors do, and that criminal actors do not cause violence, pornography does. * * * The recognition in *Hudnut* that

> pornography leads to violence against women does not require Indiana to establish a defense of insanity by pornography. In *Hudnut* we said that pornographers may be liable for rape just as the instigator of a riot could be held liable for inciting that riot. *Hudnut* does not suggest that the rioter or the rapist is not also culpable for his own conduct.

963 F.2d at 972. If Schiro identified the specific pornography that incited him to commit the rape and murder, could Indiana bring criminal charges against the producer of that pornography? What solution does the Ordinance offer? See Catharine A. MacKinnon, Only Words 95–97 (1993). Did Indianapolis attempt to "ban" pornography through the Ordinance? Why does the court use that language?

13. Many states have enacted pandering laws to prevent profiteering in prostitution. Could pandering laws also be used to prosecute pornographers? The California Supreme Court reversed the pandering conviction of a film producer who paid actors to copulate on screen in People v. Freeman, 46 Cal.3d 419, 250 Cal.Rptr. 598, 758 P.2d 1128 (1988), cert. denied, 489 U.S. 1017, 109 S.Ct. 1133, 103 L.Ed.2d 194 (1989). The *Freeman* court criticized an earlier decision, People v. Fixler, 56 Cal.App.3d 321, 128 Cal.Rptr. 363 (1976), in which the accused panderers were photographers who procured "models" for engaging in several types of sexual activity while being photographed. In that case, the court held:

> It seems self-evident that if A pays B to engage in sexual intercourse with C, then B is engaging in prostitution and that situation is not changed by the fact that A may stand by to observe the act or photograph it. A criminal act is not made any the less criminal by pictorial recordation of the act.

56 Cal.App.3d at 325, 128 Cal.Rptr. at 365. Are actors in pornographic films engaging in prostitution? Could prostitution laws be used to regulate pornography?

14. Can prostitutes insulate themselves from criminal charges by asserting First Amendment rights when their sexual activity is arguably also "theater"? Is there a difference between "dancing" in adult bookstore booths and "acting" in pornographic films when the conduct involved in both falls within statutory definitions of prostitution? The court in Arizona v. Taylor upheld a prostitution conviction, rejecting the defendant's argument that the state had to prove that the performance by women of sexual acts upon each other for the gratification of customers who pay to watch was "obscene" in order for their conduct not to be protected by the First Amendment. 167 Ariz. 429, 808 P.2d 314 (App.1990).

15. Is nude dancing protected by the First Amendment? See Barnes v. Glen Theatre, Inc., 501 U.S. 560, 111 S.Ct. 2456, 115 L.Ed.2d 504 (1991) (holding that while nude dancing is marginally expressive conduct under the First Amendment, enforcement of Indiana's public indecency law to prevent totally nude dancing is not unconstitutional). Can a city regulate sexually oriented businesses through zoning, licensing and inspections? See Paris Adult Bookstore II v. City of Dallas, 493 U.S. 215, 110 S.Ct. 596, 107 L.Ed.2d 603 (1990) (holding that licensing scheme without adequate procedural safeguards violated the First Amendment); Young v. American Mini Theatres, Inc., 427 U.S. 50, 96 S.Ct. 2440, 49 L.Ed.2d 310 (1976) (holding that

zoning regulations applied to motion picture theaters are not unconstitutional).

16. In 1992 the Canadian Supreme Court unanimously upheld the Canadian criminal obscenity law ("any publication a dominant character of which is the undue exploitation of sex, or of sex and any one or more of the following subjects, namely, crime, horror, cruelty and violence, shall be deemed to be obscene") in *Butler v. Regina,* [1992] 1 S.C.R. 452. Mr. Justice Sopinka wrote:

> [I]f true equality between male and female persons is to be achieved, we cannot ignore the threat to equality resulting from exposure to audiences of certain types of violent and degrading material. Materials portraying women as a class as objects for sexual exploitation and abuse have a negative impact on "the individual's sense of self-worth and acceptance."

Sopinka further clarified the law by stressing that sexually explicit erotica without violence that is not degrading or dehumanizing would not be prohibited under the law; neither would sexually explicit material which has scientific, artistic or literary merit. In its opinion, the court recognized that the obscenity law limits freedom of expression but found this limitation justified because prevention of the harms associated with the dissemination of pornography was a pressing and substantial concern warranting such a restriction.

Thus, the Canadian Supreme Court interpreted "obscenity" in a way more consistent with the definition of pornography under the Model Ordinance. Do you think such a reconsideration of how we define "obscenity" under constitutional law is possible in the United States? Why or why not? Which would you prefer, pornography being criminalized under a new definition of obscenity (with enforcement by the government), or subject to civil liability under the Ordinance?

17. In Illinois, individuals who are victims of sex crimes now have the ability to sue pornographers (manufacturers, producers or wholesale distributors) whose "obscene" materials were possessed or viewed by the perpetrator of the sex crime, providing the offender is convicted under specified criminal statutes and that the pornographer knew, or had reason to know, that the material was likely to cause one of the specified crimes. 720 ILCS 5/12–18.1 (1999). While there has yet to be a case brought under this statute, the facts of a 1990 criminal conviction for aggravated criminal sexual assault illustrate the problems and potential of the Illinois law. See Illinois v. M.D., 231 Ill.App.3d 176, 172 Ill.Dec. 341, 595 N.E.2d 702 (1992). In that case the husband rammed his fist, holding a raw egg in its shell, several inches into his wife's vagina. At trial the husband denied that he used his fist to sexually assault his wife. He claimed that the injuries occurred accidentally during a form of sex play *which he had copied from a pornographic movie.* Although he described one of the movies he had viewed earlier in the day as using an egg as part of foreplay, he did not provide the title of the movie. The jury convicted him on one count of aggravated criminal sexual assault and battery. Although several parties have informed the wife about the existence of the civil liability statute, she did not file a claim. In addition to identifica-

tion of the movie, what other problems would she face in suing the producer of the pornography?

18. In 1997, the Fourth Circuit reversed the lower court's dismissal of a wrongful death action against the internet publisher of a handbook for contract killers which was relied upon in the executions of the plaintiff's sister and eight-year-old paraplegic nephew. The sister's ex-husband hired the hitman in order to inherit his son's trust fund. Rice v. Paladin Enterprises, Inc., 128 F.3d 233 (4th Cir.1997), cert. denied, 523 U.S. 1074, 118 S.Ct. 1515, 140 L.Ed.2d 668 (1998). The Fourth Circuit did not find First Amendment arguments ("abstract advocacy") persuasive as a defense and, because state law recognizes civil liability for acting with the purpose of aiding and abetting murder, the case was remanded to determine if the publisher had the requisite intent. The court noted at least four theories that would support a jury finding of the requisite intent: (1) "the declared purpose of *Hit Man* [the book] itself is to facilitate murder"; (2) the book's "extensive, decided and pointed promotion of murder is highly probative" of intent; (3) Paladin's marketing strategy was meant to attract criminals; and (4) the book's only genuine use was to facilitate murder. Id. at 253–55. After the Supreme Court denied certiorari, Paladin Enterprises agreed to a multimillion dollar settlement and removed the book from circulation. See Boulder Publisher Ends "Hit" Manual Suit, Costs Paladin Millions to Settle, Denver Post, May 22, 1999, at B–01. Does this precedent have relevance to recovering from pornographers for the harms of their product?

19. Considering all of these alternatives, which one do you think best: the Model Ordinance; adopting the Canadian definition of obscenity; creating a private cause of action available only after one or more criminal convictions (as in Illinois); or no regulation of pornography at all (the status quo)? Can you create a better solution to the problem?

Chapter 6

WOMEN AND REPRODUCTION

A. INTRODUCTION

Women's capacity to control reproduction is central to their lives. The ability to plan whether to have children, how many, and when, is critical to equality in the workplace, educational plans, political participation—indeed, to control over the way in which our lives are spent in general. For these reasons, the availability, effectiveness, and accessibility of birth control has played an important role in the history of the women's movement, culminating in the struggle over abortion that has dominated the debate for the recent decades. This history forms the subject of the first part of this chapter, along with the analysis of feminist scholars and lawyers who have played a part in the movement for reproductive rights.

Women's relationship to their reproductive capacity presents some of the most difficult problems for the law to resolve—or even to conceptualize adequately. The entity represented by the symbiotic unity of a woman and her fetus is envisaged repeatedly as a relationship between two separate persons with conflicting rights. Hence the legal system has attempted to "save" babies from their mothers, by means such as imprisoning pregnant women who take cocaine, compelling women to submit to caesarean sections against their will, and controlling the conditions of childbirth, in ways having profound race and class implications. Feminist lawyers and legal scholars have become involved in all of these debates and have played central roles in litigation and legislation that have proved essential to protecting women's autonomy and bodily integrity.

Further, while new technology may bear hope for increasing women's control over their bodies, it also has presented serious dangers of use for controlling women instead. Whether new forms of reproductive technology will be used against women or can be used by them, and whether and to what extent women should be free to choose what to do with their own bodies, including offering them to bear children as surrogates for others, have provoked a substantial amount of debate in the feminist community. The final sections of this chapter present portions of that debate, in a form which invites us to draw connections between the issues involved in that debate and the larger struggle over a feminist vision of humanity and equality.

B. BIRTH CONTROL AND STERILIZATION

LINDA GORDON, WOMAN'S BODY, WOMAN'S RIGHT: BIRTH CONTROL IN AMERICA

28–29, xix–xx, 397–400, 419–21 (rev. ed. 1990; orig. pub. 1976).

Because of the different interest of men and women in the practice of birth control, differences in birth-control techniques have social significance. Some techniques are more amenable than others to being used independently and even secretly by women; some give full control to men; others are more likely to be used cooperatively. Thus it is important to be specific when considering birth control. For example, a list of the types of birth control might look like this: infanticide; abortion; sterilizing surgery; withdrawal by the male (*coitus interruptus*); melting suppositories designed to form an inpenetrable coating over the cervix; diaphragms, caps, or other devices which are inserted into the vagina over the cervix and withdrawn after intercourse; intrauterine devices; internal medicines—potions or pills; douching and other forms of action after intercourse designed to kill or drive out the sperm; condoms; and varieties of the rhythm methods, based on calculating the woman's fertile period and abstaining from intercourse during it. All these techniques were practiced in the ancient world and in modern preindustrial societies. Indeed, until the modern hormone-suppressing pill there were no essentially new birth-control devices, only improvements of the old. (The historical trend, on the contrary, has been toward the elimination of certain methods as they have come to seem to us dangerous or in violation of our moral sensibilities.)

The basic principles of birth control—contraception and abortion—are simple. People have been designing homemade contraceptive formulas and performing homemade abortions for years, and many of them produced significant results. These techniques cannot compete with the pill or with today's legal abortions for effectiveness and safety, but when they were developed they were extraordinary achievements. On a societal level, even a small percentage of effectiveness makes a great impact on the birth rate. Today women want to have 100 per cent certainty that their pregnancies will be voluntary, a reasonable and practicable desire. But the development of that desire was itself produced by its historic possibility. Lacking that kind of effective contraception, women in preindustrial societies did not form such high expectations.

* * *

The birth-control movement passed through three distinct stages. Each stage was identified with a different term for reproductive control.

The first was "voluntary motherhood," a slogan advanced by feminists in the second half of the nineteenth century. It expressed very exactly the emphasis on choice, freedom, and autonomy for women around which the "woman movement" was unified. Voluntary motherhood was a basic plank in the feminist platform, much more universally endorsed than woman suffrage and reaching further to describe and change the total plight of women than any other single issue. Stage two, approximately 1910–1920, produced the term "birth control." It represented not only a new concept but a new organizational phase, with separate birth-control leagues created mainly by feminists in the large socialist movement. It stood not only for women's autonomy but for a revolutionizing of the society and the empowering of the powerless—the working class and the female sex primarily. (* * * [A]lthough "birth control" was originally associated with this specific, radical movement, it has since become the accepted generic term for reproductive control.) * * * From 1920 on, the movement evolved away from the radicalism of its second stage into a liberal reform movement. This stage three finally produced a new slogan, "planned parenthood," in the 1940s, though the new content had been developed in the 1930s.

From one perspective, these three stages were part of a continuous process away from a solely woman-centered, feminist use of birth control. From another point of view, however, the three stages delineated the rise and fall of a broad social analysis of the contribution that reproductive self-determination could make to over-all human liberation. The second phase included men among the beneficiaries of birth control because it was concerned with the over-all power structure in the society. Birth controllers of the 1910–1920 period considered men as well as women damaged by the subjection of women, and especially lamented the weakening of the whole working class by the inequalities within it. They wished to use birth control not just to help women win equality with the men of their own class, but to strengthen the whole working class for the struggle to democratize the whole society. Planned parenthood, in the 1940s, had shed not only a feminist orientation but also eschewed any organizational interest in restructuring power in the society.

* * *

The renewal of feminism in the late 1960s gave birth to a fourth birth-control movement, more complex than any previous because it focused not only on contraception but also abortion and sterilization, and because it was more widespread than ever before. So complex was this fourth wave of the reproduction-control movement that it had no single slogan, but the best generic name for its goal was "reproductive rights."

Reproductive-rights struggles occupied a bigger proportion of the energies of the women's movement than voluntary motherhood had in the 1870s or birth control in 1910–20; they also influenced the entire U.S. political context more than previously. Never before in the history of the birth-control movement—not in its free-love associations, not in the "race suicide" debates, not in the civil disobedience of the early twentieth-century campaign for the legalization of contraception—had birth control ever been so controversial. The major reason for the heightened passion about reproduction issues is precisely that they seemed to express the core aims of the women's liberation movement, and for this reason became the major focus of the backlash against feminism. Recent birth-control politics has also become an arena for conflict between liberal and new conservative ideas about personal freedom, sexual morality, and social welfare.

* * *

First, the demand for women's autonomous control of their reproduction, signaled by the slogan "control over our own bodies," once again identified a claim for reproductive rights that rested on a critique of male domination and a demand for women's liberation, and once again differentiated this claim from population control or eugenic motives. This wave of birth-control agitation rested on a more advanced feminist program than had the previous wave: a program that invented a new word—"sexism"—condemning practices once not even reprehensible, and an analysis that for the first time challenged not only inequality but gender itself, including the view that motherhood had to be women's primary identity.

Second, a conservative response identified abortion and unlimited access to contraception with sexual permissiveness and subversion of "tradition," the family, and "morality." Conservatives attacked women's new aspirations by redefining abortion as murder. Like previous antifeminist reactions, this one was by no means simply a men's movement, but gained support from women who did not see their own interests in the dominant feminist imagery, including some who saw feminism as antagonistic to women's interests. In the 1970s a new conservatism, self-titled the "New Right," focused far more on these social/sexual issues and less on economic ones than had earlier conservative responses, and thus made birth-control issues, particularly abortion, far more prominent in the conservative political agenda than previously.

Third, in response to the conservative attacks and the weakening of the women's liberation movement, the campaign for reproductive rights once again tended to lose its exclusively feminist identity. Destabilized by the attack on aborting women as selfish, frivolous, immoral, and murderous, birth controllers retreated from a key slogan of the previous decade—"abortion on demand." Defenders of abortion rights relied largely on arguments for individual women's right to choice rather than defining abortion rights as a *social* need that benefits everyone in the long run. The individual-rights defense of abortion rights encouraged a convergence between women's liberation and mainstream birth-control and population-control organizations, solidified in response to threats from the New Right. This convergence, as distinct from that in the 1920–60 period, was based on a more feminist common denominator than had prevailed earlier. There was less defense of birth control in terms of promoting better motherhood, more recognition of women's rights to sexual freedom and equality in the public sphere.

* * *

The range of contraceptive choices is no greater now than it was twenty years ago. When this disappointment first became evident there were a variety of responses. Some blamed feminists, accusing them of overreacting and causing panic about the dangers of the most "effective" contraceptives. In fact, the only case which might qualify as an example of overreaction to the fear of health hazard—the withdrawal of IUDs from the market * * *—was not a product of feminist pressure but of other market and legal forces. Others blamed government overregulation, still others, inadequate research funds.

The first feminist critiques blamed a rather simply conceived sexism, expressed in research priorities: Why weren't the experts developing a male contraceptive? Why wasn't there adequate safety testing? These disturbing questions are not, of course, specific to birth control but to the research priorities in many public-health issues. Physician-anthropologist Melvin Konner raised the question regarding breast cancer: "I wonder," he wrote, "what would happen if more than 100,000 men a year got [testicular cancer] and if a third of them, after agonizing treatments, eventually died.... * Something tells me that ... we would by now have seen an unprecedented commitment of resources to its cure."

* * *

[T]he right motivation makes people good contraceptors even with imperfect tools. Like legal rights, contraception works only on the basis of preconditions that include not only motivation and access, but also an expectation of being able to control one's destiny and to reap rewards from that control. Recent patterns of contraceptive development have in some respects actually discouraged this taking of personal responsibility. The orientation to a technological solution, first, deemphasized the reforms needed to spread the economic and social preconditions for contraceptive use, reforms designed to ameliorate poverty, reduce power differentials between men and women, provide women with more educational and work opportunities, and lessen sexual shame. Second, in recreating contraception not as a human action but as a commodity, the "magic bullet" approach discouraged personal responsibility and led contraceptive users to think of themselves as consumers waiting for the perfect product. The mid-twentieth-century gangbusters approach to technological development, driven in the case of drugs by the scramble of multinational pharmaceutical corporations for the huge markets that made their expensive labs profitable, provided no incentive to consider

* The figures for breast cancer are 130,000 new malignancies per year, one-third of them fatal. [Approximately 214,900 new cases of breast cancer were diagnosed in 1999. American Cancer Society, Breast Cancer Facts & Figures 1999–2000 1 (2000).]

the long-term health consequences and/or discomforts of new chemicals and "devices," and these dangers in turn further discouraged active contracepting. Finally, the female-only focus of high-tech contraception reinforces the view of birth control as women's responsibility and avoids the discussion and sharing of sexual as well as birth-control planning that barrier methods encourage.

But just as the feminist critique of contraceptive development grew broader and more complex, it was forced to divide into numerous particular campaigns, particularly about the safety of specific contraceptives. Feminists became leaders of what was in effect a consumer-protection movement. * * *

Notes on Birth Control

1. As Linda Gordon points out in the passage above, the relationship among research, technology, and politics in the area of birth control is very complex. The lack of research into barrier methods (such as diaphragms and condoms) and male contraceptives is only one example. A World Health Organization study reported in 1996 that injections of testosterone reduced sperm in semen to very low levels, resulting in a 97% effectiveness rate, yet widespread research on male contraceptives is being carried out only in China and, if successful, would not be exported for use in the U.S. Kimberly Mills, Revolutionizing Birth Control; Research Tests Testosterone as Male Birth Control Method, Seattle Post–Intelligencer, May 5, 1996, at E1. Research has concentrated not only on methods to be used by women, but also on methods that do not require action at the time of intercourse, such as the contraceptive pill and hormonal implants, like Norplant. Kim Yanoshik and Judy Norsigian, Contraception, Control and Choice: International Perspectives, in Healing Technology 70 (Kathryn Strother Ratcliff, ed. 1989). Why do you think this is so? Whom does this burden?

The lack of funding of contraception research is one aspect of a more general lack of attention to research on women's health issues and the underlying male model of health and the body. In recent years the disparity in research on women's health has received more attention, leading to revelations that no female subjects were used in a variety of major longitudinal studies. Research on the protective qualities of aspirin against heart attacks, for example, was performed on 22,071 men and no women. See Michelle Oberman and Margie Schaps, Women's Health and Managed Care, 65 Tenn. L. Rev. 555, 578 (1998); Leonard Abramson, Uncaring Women's Health Care, N.Y. Times, May 14, 1990, at A17. To redress these disparities, several Congresswomen introduced a bill to require gender equity in funding medical research, which resulted in the creation of an Office of Research on Women's Health within the National Institutes of Health and the funding of the Women's Health Initiative, a $625 million study of more than 100,000 women, on the causes and treatment of diseases such as breast cancer, heart disease, and osteoporosis. Nancy McVicar, Women's Health Quest for Better Medicine in Many Ways, Women Are Second–Class Citizens in Matters of Health Care, Ft. Lauderdale Sun–Sentinel, Mar. 21, 1999, at 1G.

2. The long unavailability of RU 486, the "abortion pill," in the United States is another case study in the interaction between politics and technology. RU 486 was developed in 1980 and is used extensively in France, Britain, Sweden, and China as a method of inducing abortion as early as the second week after conception without surgery, thus allowing women to avoid the clinics that have become the target of protests and violence. Aaron Zitner, The Boston Globe, Sunday Magazine, Nov. 23, 1997, at 18. After protests and boycott threats by "right-to-life" groups, the initial manufacturer dropped the drug, but was subsequently ordered to market it by the French government, which declared that RU 486 was the "moral property of women, not just the drug company." Etienne–Emile Baulieu, The "Abortion Pill" 49 (1991) (written by scientist-developer of the drug). The combination of anti-abortion protests, which played a role in the Food and Drug Administration's barring importation of the drug, and the drug company's fear of a boycott of its other products prevented the introduction of RU 486 into the United States, even as a treatment for other medical conditions. See, e.g., Lawrence Lader, RU 486 106–08 (1991). Although the Clinton Administration lobbied to have the drug marketed in the U.S., the European company then producing RU 486 ceased production and marketing, and other pharmaceutical firms did not undertake to do so, as a result of fears of boycott, liability concerns arising from litigation involving other methods of contraception, and other cost concerns. Margaret Talbot, The Little White Bombshell, N.Y. Times Magazine, July 11, 1999, at 39. The patent and rights to RU 486 in the U.S. now belong to a non-profit organization. Id. Although the FDA found in September 1996, after clinical trials, that RU 486 was both safe and effective, it was not finally approved for marketing until September 28, 2000. Gina Kolata, U.S. Approves Abortion Pill, N.Y. Times, Sept. 29, 2000, at A1. Its use is limited to the first seven weeks of pregnancy. Id.

3. Historically, African Americans have been suspicious about birth control as a form of "genocide," both because of the movement's early ties to eugenics and because the call to control population growth has typically focused upon controlling the birth rates of non-white women. See, e.g., Dorothy Roberts, Killing The Black Body 56–103 (1997); Angela Y. Davis, Women Race & Class 202–15 (1981). A recent debate involves Norplant, a hormonal contraceptive that is implanted under the skin in a woman's upper arm and effectively prevents pregnancy for up to five years, yet is entirely reversible when removed. There are also potential side effects, especially for women who have heart problems, high blood pressure, or diabetes, as many African American women do; and while Medicaid covers the cost of implanting Norplant, women experience difficulty getting it removed. Roberts, above, at 108, 122–33. Yet bills were introduced in several states mandating insertion of Norplant in cases where a woman has been convicted of child abuse; judges have made insertion of Norplant a condition of probation in child abuse cases; and other proposals have offered incentives to women on welfare to use Norplant. See, e.g., Stacey L. Arthur, The Norplant Prescription: Birth Control, Woman Control, or Crime Control?, 40 U.C.L.A. L.Rev. 1 (1992); Roberts, above, at 109–10; see also Catherine Albiston, The Social Meaning of the Norplant Condition: Constitutional Considerations of Race, Class, and Gender, 9 Berkeley Women's L.J. 9 (1994) (examining the constitutionality of conditioning probation upon implantation of Norplant).

Yet no one has proposed either ordering or bribing men on welfare, or the fathers of children on welfare, or men convicted of physical abuse of children to undergo a vasectomy (or, more analogously, chemical castration), causing one journalist to ask "Why are women the sole target of attempts to punish and control reproduction?". Stephanie Denmark, Birth Control Tyranny, N.Y. Times, Oct. 19, 1991, at A23. How would you answer this question?

Problems with Norplant have led to a decline in its use in the U.S. and a focus upon injectable contraceptives such as Depo–Provera, which prevents pregnancy for three months. Dorothy Roberts points out that both injections and Norplant are long-acting and not controlled by the user after the initial decision, reflecting an assumption that poor Black women and women in Third World countries (where both Norplant and injections are pushed by drug companies and "population control" groups) are incapable of taking responsibility for their own sexuality and reproduction. Roberts, above, at 136–48.

4. Another form of contraception widely used in other parts of the world is the intrauterine device, or IUD. An early IUD, the Dalkon Shield, caused infections, miscarriages and some deaths, leading to widespread products liability litigation, and was banned in 1975. A new generation of IUD's which are being used safely and with apparent satisfaction by women in Europe is not available in the U.S., largely as a result of the Dalkon Shield experience and fears of lawsuits. How should we balance the right to compensate those harmed by contraceptives against the disincentives to development and marketing of newer and more varied forms of contraception in the U.S.? See Sylvia A. Law, Tort Liability and the Availability of Contraceptive Drugs and Devices in the United States, 23 N.Y.U. Rev. L. & Soc. Change 339, 365–68 (1997) (arguing that the Dalkon Shield litigation, which led to the bankruptcy of A.H. Robins Company, should not deter manufacturers of other contraceptives, because liability in the Dalkon Shield case rested upon the company's fraudulent concealment of known risks).

5. The failure of medical insurers to cover the costs of most forms of reversible contraception, including birth control pills, despite the fact that the costs of unintended pregnancy and/or abortion are far higher, raises issues of sex discrimination under the Pregnancy Discrimination Act. See Sylvia A. Law, Sex Discrimination and Insurance for Contraception, 73 Wash. L. Rev. 363 (1998). This fact was placed in relief by the rush to subsidize the costs of the new male impotence drug, Viagra, causing a number of states to introduce "contraceptive equity" bills. Carey Goldberg, Insurance for Viagra Spurs Coverage for Birth Control, N.Y. Times, June 30, 1999, at A1. In Japan, the government approval process for Viagra took less than six months, while low-dose oral contraceptives for women were not approved by the government until June 2, 1999. Sheryl WuDunn, Japan's Tale of Two Pills: Viagra and Birth Control, N.Y. Times, Apr. 27, 1999, at F1; Sonni Efron, Japan OK's Birth Control Pill After Decades of Delay, L.A. Times, June 3, 1999, at A1. While some Japanese expressed concern that introduction of the pill would increase promiscuity and also decrease use of condoms, which protect against AIDS and other sexually-transmitted diseases, others voiced the hope that the availability of birth control pills would

reduce the rate of abortions, which terminate approximately one in every four pregnancies in Japan. Id.

6. The United States has the highest rate of teenage pregnancy and childbearing in the industrialized world. Kristen Luker, Dubious Conceptions: The Politics of Teenage Pregnancy 169 (1996). In 1996, about 880,000 pregnancies occurred among women aged 15 to 19 (about 1/3 are aborted), although 62% of those were to 18– and 19–year-olds, who would be legal adults in many areas. Alan Guttmacher Institute, Teenage Pregnancy: Overall Trends and State-by-State Information, Apr. 1999, Tables 3–4. American women have traditionally had babies at an early age, with the recent tendency of middle-class educated women and double-income couples to delay having children marking a deviation from that pattern. Luker, above, at 9, 102–05, 169. The birth rate for 15– to 19–year-old girls in fact declined from a peak in 1991 to a low of 483,220 babies born to mothers 19 or younger in 1997, with about 80% of this decrease attributed to more effective contraception. Judith Havemann, Birth Rate of Teens Is Down, Contraceptive Use Rises, Experts Say, Wash. Post, Apr. 29, 1999, at A3. In 1998, girls 15 to 17 had the lowest birth rate in 40 years, with African Americans recording the lowest rate since data were first gathered in 1960. Marc Lacey, Teen–Age Birth Rate in U.S. Falls Again, N.Y. Times, Oct. 27, 1999, at A14. Although proportionally more of these births are to African American and Hispanic teenagers, patterns of sexual activity are in fact converging among teenagers of all races. Luker, above, at 91. One student of the phenomenon notes that characterizing the "problem" as one of teen pregnancy—not of abortion or premarital sex or out-of-wedlock births (2/3 of which are to women aged 20 and older)—blends two types of public concerns: the *reproductive* behavior of poor and African American teenagers and the *sexual* behavior of affluent white girls. Constance Nathanson, Dangerous Passage: The Social Control of Sexuality in Women's Adolescence 32–36, 45 (1991). The problems of poor teenaged mothers, such as medical problems during pregnancy, low-birthweight babies, and school drop-out rates, appear to have much more to do with their poverty than with their pregnancy; in other words, they result from a societal condition rather than a personal choice. Luker, above, at 109–28.

Several studies have suggested that adolescent girls who become pregnant are more likely than their sexually active peers to be traditional in sex-role orientation, while teenagers using birth control are less likely to hold traditional gender-based views of self and more likely to exhibit a sense of self-determination. AAUW Report: How Schools Shortchange Girls 65 (1992). How can this problem be addressed? Is sex education and the availability of birth control in schools the answer? What do you think should be included in the education schools give adolescent girls on this subject? Most sex education concentrates solely on the dangers of sex—AIDS, sexually-transmitted diseases, pregnancy—and fails to acknowledge and discuss sexual pleasure, especially female sexual pleasure. However, research shows a correlation between negative attitudes toward sex and non-use of contraceptives by teenagers, perhaps because teenagers with sex-negative attitudes feel guilty and thus fail to seek contraceptive information or are ashamed to be seen as "prepared." See, e.g., Andrew M. Boxer, Adolescent Pregnancy and Parenthood in the Transition to Adulthood, in Early Parenthood and

Coming of Age in the 1990s 46, 47–50 (Margaret K. Rosenheim and Mark F. Testa, eds. 1992). Might there be reasons teenage girls get pregnant, other than lack of education about birth control or unwillingness to use it, such as simply wanting to have a child to love and to give them a sense of purpose and identity? See, e.g., Constance Willard Williams, Black Teenage Mothers: Pregnancy and Child Rearing from Their Perspective (1991). Finally, few social programs aimed at teen pregnancy take into account the fact that 30% of pregnancies in mothers 15 and younger are the result of sexual activity with a male six or more years older and thus the product of statutory rape, child sexual abuse, and/or involuntary or coerced sexual activity. See Luker, above, at 119, 148.

ROSALIND POLLACK PETCHESKY, ABORTION AND WOMAN'S CHOICE: THE STATE, SEXUALITY, & REPRODUCTIVE FREEDOM

178–82 (rev. ed. 1990; orig. pub. 1984).

By the late 1970s in the United States, surgical sterilization had become the most prevalent form of contraception among women over the age of twenty-five.[a] * * * Its virtual irreversibility puts sterilization into a different category of fertility control from abortion or nonpermanent contraception. The great majority of women getting sterilized for contraceptive purposes are different from most women getting abortions. Women who seek sterilization are married at the time of being sterilized (87 percent), and their peak ages are around 30–34 (as opposed to 18–19 among women getting abortions). They do not want or expect to have any more children (unless they have been sterilized involuntarily or have not been informed that the operation is irreversible). Since most of the women who get abortions are unmarried, have had no children, and are under twenty-five, one would assume that for them, sterilization is not an acceptable alternative to abortion.

* * *

Moreover, while sterilization and abortion rates rose along a similar curve during the 1970s, and reflect a similarly complex weave of economic, medical, and social conditions, they are nonetheless clearly distinct phenomena. For one thing, the medical histories of sterilization and abortion are extremely different. Sterilization was always an alternative initiated through institutionalized medical means. Today it is an increasingly technical and complicated procedure, administered necessarily in a medical setting and requiring specialized surgical skill. Abortion was traditionally a procedure that remained in women's and lay practitioners' hands and only belatedly was incorporated—and then halfhearted-

a. After dramatic increases between 1965 and 1982 (from 16% to 42%), the prevalence of surgical sterilization of either husband or wife reported by women between 15 and 44 years old stabilized at approximately 40% of women who were or ever had been married; in 1995, 24% of married women reported a tubal ligation, and 15% that their husbands had had a vasectomy. Nat'l Center for Health Statistics, Dep't of Health and Human Services, Surgical Sterilization in the United States: Prevalence and Characteristics, 1965–95 1, 10–11 (1998).

ly—into regular medical practice. Although technically defined as surgery, abortion in the early stages of pregnancy is a relatively simple procedure that could be performed adequately by trained nurse-midwives working under sanitary conditions with good hospital backup in case of complications. * * * The shift in sterilization trends and policies, however—from a cautious, restrictive policy twenty years ago to one of strong advocacy beginning in 1970—was largely *initiated* by physicians and family planners. This shift directly reflects adverse reports and women's own fears about the health hazards of the pill, particularly for older women, and the search by clinicians for a medically controlled substitute. Thus, while they represent parallel trends, the recent increases in sterilization and abortion really grow out of different dynamics in the political dialectic of reproductive control.

An important part of the history of sterilization that sets it apart from abortion is the incidence of coercive sterilization and sterilization abuse among mainly poor, immigrant, and minority women in the United States. While instances of coercion or pressure on women to get an abortion surely occur, they have nothing of the systematic, state-sanctioned character of involuntary sterilization, as a look at public policy immediately makes clear. Legislative proposals to allow the involuntary sterilization of certain groups on eugenic grounds have a long history, linked to private upper-class organizations promoting "racial betterment and WASP purity." Today sterilization programs are more subtle but nonetheless motivated by population control objectives aimed at particular groups—the "surplus" poor. A deliberate policy of manipulation if not coercion is involved when medical associations and family planning agencies advocate sterilization as a preferred form of birth control, particularly to low-income women and women of color, while withholding or minimizing information about other methods of fertility control. Such a policy is evident in the continued reimbursement by Medicaid, along with most commercial and employment-related health insurance, of 90 percent of the costs of contraceptive sterilization, while funds for abortion are cut off in most states. Practices such as the failure to inform patients adequately, in their own language, that sterilization is irreversible; the failure to provide full information about nonpermanent alternatives (including abortion); the threat of withholding welfare or Medicaid benefits to a woman or her children if she refuses "consent" in sterilization; making permanent sterilization the condition of a voluntarily sought abortion (the notorious "package deal"); using hysterectomy—with its enormously increased risks and drastic consequences—as a form of sterilization; or sterilizing minors or the mentally incompetent are all forms of sterilization abuse prohibited by the 1978 Federal Sterilization Regulations. Yet auditors' reports on federally funded sterilizations in a number of states suggest that such abuses continue in many hospitals that service the poor, largely because of the lack of effective government enforcement machinery.

Nearly all of the documented or court-adjudicated instances of sterilization abuse during the 1970s involved women who were poor and either black, Mexican–American, Puerto Rican, or Native American, or women who were incarcerated or mentally incompetent. Neo-eugenic policies and abusive practices may have played a part in effecting class and race differences in sterilization rates. National survey data from 1975–76 indicate that low-income women and women with little education (high school or lower) have significantly higher rates of sterilization than their middle-class counterparts. Moreover, among low-income, black, and Hispanic groups, it is much more likely to be women rather than men who become sterilized, for reasons that have to do with ethnic culture and history as well as clinical practices; vasectomies occur primarily among white middle-class married men. A recent report by researchers with the federal Health Care Financing Administration shows that female Medicaid recipients are between *two and four times more likely* (depending on geographical region) to be sterilized than are women not dependent on Medicaid; and nearly all Medicaid sterilizations are performed on women.

Abortion rates too tend to be higher among Medicaid-dependent and minority women than among white middle-class women. How, then, can we argue that these differentials indicate women's self-determination in the one case and abuse or nonchoice in the other? Surely the higher rates of sterilization among poor women reflect some of the same social and economic constraints and class divisions within the medical care system that structure the abortion decision among poor women (who are disproportionately women of color). In both cases, the decision is more often than not the product of a conscious, rational determination by poor women to deal with the situation at hand, rather than of manipulations or lies by doctors. In some cases sterilization may be viewed by a woman as a definite relief, a solution to her birth control problems that eliminates fear of pregnancy and hassles with men.

Generally speaking, it is not the technology of a birth control method that makes it abusive or malevolent, but the social arrangements in which that technique is embedded—the degree to which those arrangements allow for the user's conscious participation and control and respond to her personal and biological needs. Sterilization or even hysterectomy may satisfy these criteria in particular cases, depending on the situation. The same may be said for abortion. Yet, recognizing this, we also have to recognize that sterilization has been and remains distinct from abortion both in its historical uses and its practical consequences for women. In the case of sterilization, it is possible to imagine, as some demographers do, that logically, because the method is permanent, its use *always* connotes voluntary choice to terminate childbearing. In reality, we have to deal with a well-documented history in which surgical sterilization has been imposed on women without their knowledge or consent, or without their understanding that the procedure was permanent. This has not occurred with abortion, at least not in the United States or Western Europe. Involuntary sterilization, not involuntary abortion, has been the nucleus of state-sponsored eugenic and neo-eugenic population control policies precisely because it is medically controlled and is permanent. It eliminates a potential "breeder," not just a potential child; and it does not have a long-standing tradition of popular practice behind it. From the point of view of a neo-eugenicist public policy the coincidence of antiabortion and prosterilization programs is not contradictory but rather class and race specific.

Given recurrent patterns of abuse and worsening economic conditions for poor women in the United States, it seems reasonable to expect that denial of abortion funding and further restriction of legal abortions will result in higher rates of sterilization among poor women; abortion cutbacks and sterilization abuse are in this sense "opposite sides of a coin." Yet, * * * Medicaid-dependent women denied abortion funds do not seem to have turned to sterilization as an alternative. Rather, they continue to seek abortions using any means they can. This indicates that sterilization is not an adequate substitute for abortion for most women, in most circumstances; its irreversibility entirely transforms the meaning of "costs" and "risks," putting not a pregnancy but a woman's whole reproductive capacity on the line. It also indicates that political struggles over sterilization abuse by feminists and Third World groups apparently have had an impact on women's consciousness.

Notes on Sterilization and Sterilization Abuse

1. All of the abuses described in the Petchesky excerpt above actually happened to large numbers of women and were stopped only after lawsuits and political outcry, confirming the fears of women of color about genocide. One suit, Madrigal v. Quilligan, was an unsuccessful class action concerning sterilizations performed upon numerous poor and Latina women at the Los Angeles County Hospital during the 1970's without their informed consent, and sometimes even without their knowledge, when they went to the hospital to give birth. See Claudia Dreifus, Sterilizing the Poor, in Feminist Frameworks: Alternative Theoretical Accounts of the Relations Between Women and Men 58–66 (2d ed., Alison M. Jaggar and Paula S. Rothenberg, eds. 1984); Madrigal v. Quilligan, No. CV75–2057 JWC, slip op. (unpublished) (C.D. Cal. June 30, 1978), aff'd, 639 F.2d 789 (9th Cir.1981). In another case, the Relf sisters, aged 12 and 14, were sterilized after welfare officials asked their mother to take them to the hospital for shots and then had her sign a consent form for sterilization, although she was illiterate and they did not explain to her what she was signing. Relf v. Weinberger, 372 F.Supp. 1196 (D.D.C.1974). Compulsory sterilization was particularly widespread in U.S. teaching hospitals and was often required as a condition of obtaining an abortion in them. Thomas Shapiro, Sterilization Abuse and Patterns of Female Sterilization, in Population Control Politics 87, 92 (1985). Publicity about these and other cases, as well as substantial pressure and input from feminists involved in the reproductive rights movement, ultimately resulted in the issuance of guidelines by the Department of Health, Education and Welfare to assure informed consent. See, e.g., Linda Gordon, Woman's Body, Woman's Right 433–34 (rev'd ed. 1990). Although there is general agreement that the regulations are not typically observed, the problem of coerced sterilization also appears to have diminished since

that time. Id. at 435–36; see also Shapiro, above, at 93–94. What does this say about whether the law is an effective instrument of social change for women? Might the class action suits be seen as simply another form of publicity and political pressure?

2. The United States is not the only country in which forced sterilizations took place as a result of the eugenics movement. Compulsory sterilization of those considered unfit to parent, by reason of mental illiness, retardation, physical disease, hereditary defects, or anti-social tendencies, were carried out in Sweden under a law that went into effect in 1935 and was not repealed until 1976. Approximately 63,000 people were sterilized in Sweden, compared with some 61,540 eugenic sterilizations in the United States. See Stephanie Hyatt, A Shared History of Shame: Sweden's Four-Decade Policy of Forced Sterilization and the Eugenics Movement in the United States, 8 Ind. Int'l & Comp. L. Rev. 475 (1998).

3. For descriptions of the types of lawsuits that may be brought to challenge coercive sterilization practices, see Dick Grosboll, Sterilization Abuse: Current State of the Law and Remedies for Abuse, 10 Golden Gate U.L. Rev. 1147, 1163–87 (1980). These include federal civil rights suits and state law claims based on negligence or battery. Can you think of others (apart from the informed consent litigation described in note 1, above)?

4. What do you think of Petchesky's conclusion that methods of birth control are not driven by technology but by the social relations in which the technology is embedded? Can you think of other examples of technology being driven by social relations? The Petchesky excerpt is a good illustration of socialist feminist analysis. What would a radical feminist be likely to say about the relationship between technology and the availability of different methods of birth control?

5. Draft a consent form a woman who was unrepresented by counsel could sign to indicate her informed consent to sterilization. Are there additional rules you would want to impose about the conditions under which it could be executed? What are they?

6. What do you see as similarities and differences between forced sterilization and compelled implantation of Norplant?

7. Women who report a sterilizing operation for themselves or their husbands or partners are more likely to be married and to be between the ages of 35 and 44 years old. Nat'l Center for Health Statistics, Dep't of Health and Human Services, Surgical Sterilization in the United States: Prevalence and Characteristics, 1965–1995 7, 10 (1998). The most common reason women reported for having a tubal ligation was that the woman did not want more children (71 percent). Id. at 8. In 1995, 24% of married women reported having had a tubal ligation, while only 15% reported that their husbands had had a vasectomy. Id. at 1. Yet tubal ligation is ten times more expensive than vasectomy and requires general anesthesia, with its attendant risks. Abe Amidor, Getting Fixed, Indianapolis Star, Mar. 21, 1999, at J1. Why do you think so many more women are sterilized than men, given the comparative ease of vasectomy versus the invasive, costly, and riskier nature of the procedure required to sterilize a woman?

8. Women who desire sterilization may have a difficult time obtaining it. Sterilization services, like abortions, are not provided at any Roman Catholic health facilities, despite the fact that they may be the only hospitals in an area; in Illinois, 30% of the state's community hospitals are Catholic-owned. Bruce Japsen, Cardinal Fights AMA Measure: At Issue: Providing Sterilization Services, Chi. Tribune, June 13, 2000, § 3, at 1, 4.

GRISWOLD v. CONNECTICUT

Supreme Court of the United States, 1965.

381 U.S. 479, 85 S.Ct. 1678, 14 L.Ed.2d 510.

MR. JUSTICE DOUGLAS delivered the opinion of the Court.

Appellant Griswold is Executive Director of the Planned Parenthood League of Connecticut. Appellant Buxton is a licensed physician and a professor at the Yale Medical School who served as Medical Director for the League at its Center in New Haven—a center open and operating from November 1 to November 10, 1961, when appellants were arrested.

They gave information, instruction, and medical advice to married persons as to the means of preventing conception. They examined the wife and prescribed the best contraceptive device or material for her use. Fees were usually charged, although some couples were serviced free.

The statutes whose constitutionality is involved in this appeal are §§ 53–32 and 54–196 of the General Statutes of Connecticut (1958 rev.). The former provides: "Any person who uses any drug, medicinal article or instrument for the purpose of preventing conception shall be fined not less than fifty dollars or imprisoned not less than sixty days nor more than one year or be both fined and imprisoned."

Section 54–196 provides: "Any person who assists, abets, counsels, causes, hires or commands another to commit any offense may be prosecuted and punished as if he were the principal offender."

The appellants were found guilty as accessories and fined $100 each * * *.

[S]pecific guarantees in the Bill of Rights have penumbras, formed by emanations from those guarantees that help give them life and substance. Various guarantees create zones of privacy. The right of association contained in the penumbra of the First Amendment is one * * *. The Third Amendment in its prohibition against the quartering of soldiers "in any house" in time of peace without the consent of the owner is another facet of that privacy. The Fourth Amendment explicitly affirms the "right of the people to be secure in their persons, houses, papers, and effects, against unreasonable searches and seizures." The Fifth Amendment in its Self-Incrimination Clause enables the citizen to create a zone of privacy which government may not force him to surrender to his detriment. The Ninth Amendment provides: "The enumeration in the Constitution, of certain rights, shall not be construed to deny or disparage others retained by the people."

* * *

The present case, then, concerns a relationship lying within the zone of privacy created by several fundamental constitutional guarantees. And it concerns a law which, in forbidding the use of contraceptives rather than regulating their manufacture or sale, seeks to achieve its goals by means having a maximum destructive impact upon that relationship. * * * Would we allow the police to search the sacred precincts of marital bedrooms for telltale signs of the use of contraceptives? The very idea is repulsive to the notions of privacy surrounding the marriage relationship.

We deal with a right of privacy older than the Bill of Rights—older than our political parties, older than our school system. Marriage is a coming together for better or for worse, hopefully enduring, and intimate to the degree of being sacred. It is an association that promotes a way of life, not causes; a harmony in living, not political faiths; a bilateral loyalty, not commercial or social projects. Yet it is an association for as noble a purpose as any involved in our prior decisions.

Reversed.

MR. JUSTICE GOLDBERG, whom THE CHIEF JUSTICE and MR. JUSTICE BRENNAN join, concurring.

* * *

The language and history of the Ninth Amendment reveal that the Framers of the Constitution believed that there are additional fundamental rights, protected from governmental infringement, which exist alongside those fundamental rights specifically mentioned in the first eight constitutional amendments.

* * *

To hold that a right so basic and fundamental and so deep-rooted in our society as the right of privacy in marriage may be infringed because that right is not guaranteed in so many words by the first eight amendments to the Constitution is to ignore the Ninth Amendment and to give it no effect whatsoever. Moreover, a judicial construction that this fundamental right is not protected by the Constitution because it is not mentioned in explicit terms by one of the first eight amendments or elsewhere in the Constitution would violate the Ninth Amendment, which specifically states that "(t)he enumeration in the Constitution, of certain rights shall not be construed to deny or disparage others retained by the people."

* * *

I agree with Mr. Justice Harlan's statement in his dissenting opinion in Poe v. Ullman, 367 U.S. 497, 551–552, 81 S.Ct. 1752, 1781: "Certainly the safeguarding of the home does not follow merely from the sanctity of property rights. The home derives its pre-eminence as the seat of family life. And the integrity of that life is something so fundamental that it has been found to draw to its protection the principles of more than one explicitly granted Constitutional right. * * * Of this whole 'private realm of family life' it is difficult to imagine what is more private or more intimate than a husband and wife's marital relations."

The entire fabric of the Constitution and the purposes that clearly underlie its specific guarantees demonstrate that the rights to marital privacy and to marry and raise a family are of similar order and magnitude as the fundamental rights specifically protected.

* * *

Surely the Government, absent a showing of a compelling subordinating state interest, could not decree that all husbands and wives must be sterilized after two children have been born to them. Yet by their reasoning such an invasion of marital privacy would not be subject to constitutional challenge because, while it might be "silly," no provision of the Constitution specifically prevents the Government from curtailing the marital right to bear children and raise a family. * * * [I]f upon a showing of a slender basis of rationality, a law outlawing voluntary birth control by married persons is valid, then, by the same reasoning, a law requiring compulsory birth control also would seem to be valid. In my view, however, both types of law would unjustifiably intrude upon rights of marital privacy which are constitutionally protected.

* * *

Finally, it should be said of the Court's holding today that it in no way interferes with a State's proper regulation of sexual promiscuity or misconduct. As my Brother Harlan so well stated in his dissenting opinion in Poe v. Ullman, supra, 367 U.S. at 553, 81 S.Ct. at 1782:

> "Adultery, homosexuality and the like are sexual intimacies which the State forbids * * * but the intimacy of husband and wife is necessarily an essential and accepted feature of the institution of marriage, an institution which the State not only must allow, but which always and in every age it has fostered and protected. It is one thing when the State exerts its power either to forbid extra-marital sexuality * * * or to say who may marry, but it is quite another when, having acknowledged a marriage and the intimacies inherent in it, it undertakes to regulate by means of the criminal law the details of that intimacy."

Notes on **Griswold**

1. Both Justice Douglas and Justice Goldberg had to reach behind the language and history of the Constitution in order to find a right of privacy that included the right to contraception, which they located, respectively, in "penumbras, formed by emanations" from the Bill of Rights, and in the "forgotten" Ninth Amendment. Does the result they reached strike you as appropriate as a matter of constitutional interpretation? Which route do you prefer? Is there a better route, in your opinion? What are the pro's and con's of having located the right of reproductive control in the individual right to privacy? Does this further insulate "family" matters from state review and

intervention? Can you think of alternative arguments that might have been effective in striking down the Connecticut law prohibiting use of contraceptives? Would arguments based on equal protection or liberty be more useful? Can you make an argument under the Fourteenth Amendment? How? How would adherents of the differing feminist perspectives described in Chapter 3 articulate a constitutional basis for reproductive autonomy?

2. Although both the opinion of the Court in *Griswold* and the concurrence emphasized the connection between the right of reproductive privacy and the marital relationship, the Court subsequently held, on equal protection grounds, that this right extended to single persons as well, stating that "the marital couple is not an independent entity with a mind and heart of its own, but an association of two individuals each with a separate intellectual and emotional makeup. If the right of privacy means anything, it is the right of the *individual,* married or single, to be free from unwarranted governmental intrusion into matters so fundamentally affecting a person as the decision whether to bear or beget a child." Eisenstadt v. Baird, 405 U.S. 438, 453, 92 S.Ct. 1029, 1038, 31 L.Ed.2d 349, 362 (1972) (emphasis in original). Can you articulate any other bases for extending this constitutional right to individuals? (In 1977, the Court held that even unmarried minors could not be denied over-the-counter contraceptives. Carey v. Population Services Int'l, 431 U.S. 678, 97 S.Ct. 2010, 52 L.Ed.2d 675 (1977). Does *Eisenstadt* support a woman's right to abortion? What argument would you make in this respect?

3. Is the result in Bowers v. Hardwick, 478 U.S. 186, 106 S.Ct. 2841, 92 L.Ed.2d 140 (1986), upholding a state law criminalizing homosexual sodomy between two consenting adults in the privacy of their home, implicit in *Griswold* ? How or how not? Who is likely to be protected by a notion of privacy grounded in "tradition"? All citizens? Or only those involved in relationships that have traditionally been accepted, or engaged in, by the majority? Is such a standard likely to pose problems for women in general as well as for lesbians and gay men? Would it have been better had *Griswold* come out the other way? What would the likely consequences of such a decision have been—that states would continue to ban birth control? Or would changing social mores have led to the repeal or nonenforcement of restrictions in any case?

C. ABORTION

A note about sources: To a large extent, the sources in this section have been drawn from materials created in the course of actual litigation. We have chosen to do so, despite the obvious dangers of bias introduced by using documents designed for advocacy, in order to show how feminist theories have been used in this area and how theories developed by feminist lawyers and law professors have in fact influenced the law on this issue, as well as to give the reader a lively sense of the passion involved in the debate over abortion in the United States. For law student readers, our intent is also to show how theory may inform and, in fact, transform practice.

1. ABORTION AND AMERICAN HISTORY

AMICUS BRIEF OF 250 AMERICAN HISTORIANS IN *PLANNED PARENTHOOD OF SOUTHEASTERN PENNSYLVANIA v. CASEY*

Nos. 91–744 and 91–902 (1992).

[This amicus brief was written by law professors Sylvia Law, Jane E. Larson, and Clyde Spillenger. The issues litigated in *Casey* are summarized in Section C2, below.]

II. At the Time the Federal Constitution Was Adopted, Abortion Was Known and Not Illegal.

* * * Through the nineteenth century, American common law decisions uniformly reaffirmed that women committed no offense in seeking abortions. Both common law and popular American understanding drew distinctions depending upon whether the fetus was "quick," i.e. whether the woman perceived signs of independent life. There was some dispute whether a common law misdemeanor occurred when a third party destroyed a fetus, after quickening, without the woman's consent. But early common law recognition of this crime against a pregnant woman did not diminish the woman's liberty to end a pregnancy herself in its early stages.

Abortion was not a pressing social issue in colonial America, but as a social practice, it was far from unknown. Herbal abortifacients were widely known, and cookbooks and women's diaries of the era contained recipes for such medicines. Recent studies of the work of midwives in the 1700s report cases in which the midwives appeared to have provided women abortifacient compounds. Such treatments do not appear to have been regarded as extraordinary or illicit by those administering them.

* * *

In the late eighteenth century, strictures on sexual behavior loosened considerably. The incidence of premarital pregnancy rose sharply; by the late eighteenth century, one third of all New England brides were pregnant when they married, compared to less than ten percent in the seventeenth century. Falling birth rates in the 1780s suggest that, at the time of the drafting of the Constitution, the use of birth control and abortion was increasing.

III. Through the Nineteenth Century, Abortion Became Even More Widely Accepted and Highly Visible.

Through the nineteenth century and well into the twentieth, abortion remained a widely accepted practice, despite growing efforts after 1860 to prohibit it. * * *

Urban couples limited family size for economic reasons: working-class married women, faced with the material difficulty of managing a family budget on a single male wage, resorted to abortion as the most effective available means of "conscious fertility control."

* * * The most common methods of abortion in the nineteenth century involved self administered herbs and devices available from pharmacists. Nonetheless, women also relied on professional abortionists: in 1871, New York City, with a population of less than one million, supported two hundred full-time abortionists, not including doctors who also sometimes performed abortions.

For most of the nineteenth century, abortion was a visible as well as common practice. "Beginning in the early 1840s abortion became, for all intents and purposes, a business, a service openly traded in the free market.... [Pervasive advertising told Americans] not only that many practitioners would provide abortion services, but that some practitioners had made the abortion business their chief livelihood. Indeed, abortions became one of the first specialties in American medical history."[26]

IV. Nineteenth-Century Abortion Restrictions Sought to Promote Objectives That Are Today Either Plainly Inapplicable or Constitutionally Impermissible.

[B]etween 1850 and 1880, the newly formed American Medical Association, through some of its active members, became the "single most important factor in altering the legal policies toward abortion in this country."[27]

The doctors found an audience for their effort to restrict abortion because they appealed to specific social concerns and anxieties: maternal health, consumer protection, discriminatory ideas about the properly subordinate status of women, and racist/nativist fears generated by the fact that elite Protestant women often sought abortions. Some of those doctors also sought to attribute moral status to the fetus.

A. From 1820–1860, Abortion Regulation in the States Rejected Broader English Restrictions and Sought to Protect Women From Particularly Dangerous Forms of Abortion.

In 1803, English law made all forms of abortion criminal. Despite this model, for two decades, no American state restricted access to abortion. In 1821, when one state, Connecticut, acted, it prohibited only the administration of a "deadly poison, or other noxious and destructive substance" as a means of bringing about an abortion. Moreover, the act applied only after quickening, and punished only the person who administered the poison, not the woman who consumed it. * * *

In 1830, Connecticut became the first state to punish abortion after quickening. In the same year, New York, also animated by a concern for

26. J. Mohr, Abortion in America: The Origins and Evolution of National Policy 47 (1978).

27. J. Mohr, supra, at 157.

patient safety, considered a law to prohibit any surgery, unless two physicians approved it as essential. Before scientific understanding of germ theory and antisepsis, any surgical intervention was likely to be fatal. The New York act finally adopted applied only to surgical abortion and included the first "therapeutic" exception, approving abortion where two physicians agreed that it was "necessary." As the Court recognized in Roe v. Wade, until the twentieth century, abortion, particularly when done through surgical intervention, remained significantly more dangerous to the woman than childbirth. Because these early abortion laws were drafted and justified to protect women, they did not punish women as parties to an abortion.

None of these early laws, restricting forms of abortion thought to be particularly unsafe, were enforced. That absence itself speaks powerfully, particularly because abortion was a prevalent practice in this era. Despite legislative action and medical opposition, the common and openly tolerated practice suggests that many Americans did not perceive abortion as morally wrong.

B. A Central Purpose of Abortion Regulation in the Nineteenth Century Was to Define Who Should Be Allowed to Control Medical Practice.

Physicians were the principal nineteenth-century proponents of laws to restrict abortion. A core purpose of the nineteenth-century laws, and of doctors in supporting them, was to control medical practice in the interest of public safety. * * *

The nineteenth century movement to regulate abortions was one chapter in a campaign by doctors that reflected a professional conflict between "regulars" (those who ultimately became the practitioners and proponents of scientific medicine) and "irregulars." As James Mohr explains:

> If a regular doctor refused to perform an abortion he knew the woman could go to one of several types of irregulars and probably receive one.... As more and more irregulars began to advertise abortion services openly, especially after 1840, regular physicians grew more and more nervous about losing their practices to healers who would provide a service that more and more American women after 1840 began to want. * * * The best way out of these dilemmas was to persuade state legislators to make abortion a criminal offense. Anti-abortion laws would weaken the appeal of the competition and take the pressure off the more marginal members of the regulars' own sect.[42]

* * *

42. J. Mohr, supra, at 37. [The doctors were scornful of the midwives' "folklore" about the importance of quickening as well, maintaining the superiority of their own "scientific" knowledge as to when life began. Presumably their desire to put the midwives out of practice took precedence over an obvious competing motivation—simply to perform the abortion and collect the fee themselves.]

C. Enforcement of Sharply Differentiated Concepts of the Roles and Choices of Men and Women Underlay Regulation of Abortion and Contraception in the Nineteenth Century.

* * * In addition, physicians persuaded political leaders (who were, of course, uniformly male) that "abortion constituted a threat to social order and to male authority."[44] Since the 1840s, a growing movement for women's suffrage and equality had generated popular fears that women were departing from a purely maternal role—fears fueled by the decline in family size during the nineteenth century. A central rhetorical focus of the woman's movement was framed by a new perception of women as the rightful possessors of their own bodies.

In 1871, the American Medical Association's Committee on Criminal Abortion described the woman who sought an abortion:

> She becomes unmindful of the course marked out for her by Providence, she overlooks the duties imposed on her by the marriage contract. She yields to the pleasures—but shrinks from the pains and responsibilities of maternity; and, destitute of all delicacy and refinements, resigns herself, body and soul, into the hands of unscrupulous and wicked men.[47]

* * *

Against what they saw as an inequitable vision of gender relations, the women's movement of the nineteenth century affirmed that women—even married women—should have basic rights of self-governance, including the right to decide whether to bear a child. Early feminists sought to enhance women's control of reproduction through a campaign for "voluntary motherhood," ideally to be achieved through periodic abstinence from sexual relations. They attempted, with limited success, to analogize women's control over reproduction to the structure of rights that had overturned chattel slavery. * * *

Opposition to abortion and contraception were closely linked, and can only be understood as a reaction to the uncertainties generated by changes in family function and anxieties created by women's challenges to their historic roles of silence and subservience. These challenges were critical factors motivating the all-male state legislatures that adopted restraints on women, including restrictions on abortion. In opposition to the feminist demand for control of reproduction, the federal government in 1873 took the lead in banning access to information about both contraception and abortion [with the Comstock Act]. * * *

D. Nineteenth–Century Contraception and Abortion Regulation Also Reflected Ethnocentric Fears About the Relative Birthrates of Immigrants and White Protestants.

* * *

44. C. Smith–Rosenberg, Disorderly Conduct 235 (1985).

47. Atlee & O'Donnell, Report of the Committee on Criminal Abortion, 22 Transactions of the American Medical Association 241 (1871), quoted in C. Smith–Rosenberg, supra, at 236–37.

Beginning in the 1890s, and continuing through the first decades of the twentieth century, * * * nativist fears coalesced into a drive against what was then called "race suicide." The "race suicide" alarmists worried that women of "good stock"—prosperous, white, and Protestant—were not having enough children to maintain the political and social supremacy of their group. Anxiety over the falling birth rates of Protestant whites in comparison with other groups helped shape policy governing both birth control and abortion. As James Mohr points out, "The doctors both used and were influenced by blatant nativism.... There can be little doubt that Protestants' fears about not keeping up with the reproductive rates of Catholic immigrants played a greater role in the drive for anti-abortion laws in nineteenth-century America than Catholic opposition to abortion did."[64]

V. Enforcement of Abortion Restrictions in the First Half of the Twentieth Century Followed Entrenched Ethnic and Class Differentiations, Affirmed Traditional Concerns About Enforcing Gender Roles, and Imposed Enormous Costs Upon Women.

The statutory restrictions on abortion remained virtually unchanged from the early twentieth century until the 1960s. Physicians were allowed to perform abortions only "to preserve the mother's life." Nonetheless, the incidence of abortion remained high, ranging from one pregnancy in seven at the turn of the century, to one in three in 1936. Most abortions were performed illegally. Legal restrictions did not stop abortion, but made it humiliating and dangerous.

AMICUS BRIEF OF FEMINISTS FOR LIFE IN *BRAY v. ALEXANDRIA WOMEN'S HEALTH CLINIC*

No. 90–985 (1991).

[This amicus brief was written by Mary Krane Derr, a graduate student at the University of Chicago. The *Bray* case was an unsuccessful attempt to establish that anti-abortion protesters blocking access to abortion clinics were violating the civil rights of women seeking abortions.]

A. The Early Feminists, Although Critical of Prevailing Cultural Attitudes Regarding Sexuality and the Role of Women in Marriage, Were Resolutely Opposed to Abortion.

* * * Contrary to prevailing assumptions, * * * feminists have not traditionally argued for the moral and legal acceptability of abortion. The nineteenth century founding mothers of the women's movement did not view legalized abortion as a solution to, but rather, as an abhorrent consequence of, the oppressions and disenfranchisement of women.

64. See J. Mohr, supra note 2, at 167. Horatio Robinson Storer, who spearheaded the American Medical Association's mid-nineteenth century antiabortion campaign, frequently referred to racial themes. Id. at 180–90; H. Storer, Why Not? A Book for Every Woman 85 (1866) ("[S]hall the great territories of the Far West be filled by our children or by those of aliens?").

The testimony of these women—including Elizabeth Cady Stanton, Victoria Woodhull, and Matilda Gage—reveal a radical stance against the mistreatment of women inside and outside of marriage, a frank understanding and acceptance of female sexuality, and an uncompromising view that abortion is "ante-natal murder," "child-murder," or "ante-natal infanticide." The early feminists did not oppose abortion out of adherence to social norms. As will be seen below, they were not timid in challenging prevailing and fundamental notions of the marriage relationship, some of which prevail to this day.

* * *

Early feminist opposition to abortion was deep-seated, and addressed the causes of abortion, not just the practice. In this way, it was distinguished from other anti-abortion efforts including those of the American Medical Association. Feminists documented that abortion was caused by, among other things, culturally enforced ignorance about sexual and reproductive physiology, especially family planning and fetal development; cultural construction of pregnancy as a pathological condition; a sexual double standard which permitted men to be sexually and parentally irresponsible; the social valuing of "legitimacy" over children's lives and women's well-being; and lack of social and economic support for mothers, especially single ones. Two overriding principles emerge from this early feminist literature: a condemnation of abortion as the murder of children; and the conviction that marital, social, and economic liberation of women would bolster, and not undermine, protection for the unborn.

* * *

D. *Early Feminist Opposition to Abortion Was Joined to Condemnation of Male Sexual Irresponsibility and Coercion, and the Lack of Economic and Social Support for Pregnant Women Abandoned by the Fathers of Their Children.*

1. The early feminists called for prevention of the circumstances giving rise to abortion. Their concern for the lives of unborn children did not preclude, but was interwoven with, a broader concern for women with crisis pregnancies, children already born, and their mothers. * * *

2. The early feminists condemned social attitudes, especially sexual double standards, which contributed to an increasing incidence of abortion. General social attitudes likewise played a role in the promotion and tolerance of abortion. Sarah F. Norton, itinerant lecturer and author, noted that "[s]ociety has come to believe it an impertinence in children to be born at all ... [T]he single fact that child murderers practice their profession without let or hindrance, and open infant butcheries unquestioned, establishing themselves with an impunity that is not allowed to the slaughterers of cattle is, of itself, sufficient to prove that society makes a demand which they alone can supply." Tragedy, Social and Domestic, Woodhull & Claflin's Weekly, Nov. 19, 1870.

At the root of this demand were social attitudes regarding sexual behavior, illegitimacy, and the nature of pregnancy itself. The sexual "double standard"—which permitted men to behave in an irresponsible fashion, but punished the women being victimized—was universally condemned. * * *

3. The early feminists believed that the liberation of women from positions of social inequality and sexual dominance would lead to increased protection for the unborn. Since the early feminists viewed abortion as a byproduct of sexual domination by men, and the unequal position of women in society, it is not surprising that they saw equality between the sexes as a necessary prerequisite to the eradication of abortion, and an end to sexual double standards, as addressing the root cause of abortion, and eradicating it.

Notes on the Uses of History in Abortion Litigation

1. The history of abortion in the United States has been an important source of constitutional interpretation on this issue. Why should what has been done in the past be such an important source? Whose actions should we look to? The "new history" would look to those of ordinary people (for example, the abortifacient recipes in women's cookbooks described in the Historians' Brief, above), rather than to the pronouncements of legislators and doctors. If abortion was in fact a misdemeanor, but laws against it were not enforced, what conclusions should we draw? On the other hand, if one believes that abortion is morally wrong, like slavery was, why should the history of its practice offer us guidance for the future?

2. Do the Historians' Brief and the Feminists for Life Brief meet head on? Are their versions of history consistent? How or how not?

3. The excerpt from the AMA's 1871 committee report included above gives some flavor of the extent to which the historical debate over abortion has been a debate about woman's proper role; the report reflects the image of an aborting woman as selfish and therefore immoral. One modern commentator believes that the rhetoric of choice in the continuing debate over the right of abortion, which emphasizes autonomous individuals with rights, making choices in pursuit of their own self-interest, exacerbates the fears of anti-abortion advocates by awakening fears of selfish mothers; moreover, this model of individual choice does not accurately describe how women make decisions about abortion and, indeed, about their lives in general. Joan Williams, Gender Wars: Selfless Women in the Republic of Choice, 66 N.Y.U. L. Rev. 1559 (1991). How do you think this rhetoric of individual freedom and choice could, or should, be altered? Would the rhetoric you envisage fit into legal theories upon which the abortion right could be defended? How?

4. The Historians' Brief describes the connection between abortion regulation and racism in the past. Do racism and anti-immigrant feelings continue to play into the abortion debate today? Is it possible that some of the opinions that make up the pro-choice majority are actually expressing hostility to women of color and their children and see abortion as a form of eugenics? Might the history of racism, eugenics, and sterilization abuse

cause African American women to have more complicated attitudes toward abortion than women who do not share this history of abuse? See, e.g., Angela Y. Davis, Women Race & Class 202–15 (1981).

5. It is important to set the opposition of 19th-century feminists to abortion in the context of their opposition to birth control as well. Linda Gordon points out that this opposition was grounded in attitudes central to the welfare of women: fear that the sexual freedom and promiscuity that contraception made possible would lead to greater infidelity by husbands and economic instability for wives as marriages broke up, on the one hand, and a preference for more natural methods of birth control, including abstinence and the right of a wife unilaterally to refuse her husband, on the other. The latter was important to 19th-century women, not only because they had been socialized to regard sex as simply their "wifely duty," but also out of realistic fears of the physical dangers—pregnancy, childbirth, and venereal diseases—potentially resulting from intercourse. Moreover, by joining their call for voluntary motherhood with a demand for the right to unilateral abstinence, many women directly expressed their understandable hostility to the traditional form of intercourse, defined by male desires with little regard to women's sexual pleasure. Gordon, Woman's Body, Woman's Right: Birth Control in America 95–108 (rev. ed. 1990).

2. FROM ROE v. WADE TO *CASEY*

ROE v. WADE

Supreme Court of the United States, 1973.

410 U.S. 113, 93 S.Ct. 705, 35 L.Ed.2d 147.

MR. JUSTICE BLACKMUN delivered the opinion of the Court.

* * *

Jane Roe, a single woman who was residing in Dallas County, Texas, instituted this federal action in March 1970 against the District Attorney of the county. She sought a declaratory judgment that the Texas criminal abortion statutes were unconstitutional on their face, and an injunction restraining the defendant from enforcing the statutes.

Roe alleged that she was unmarried and pregnant; that she wished to terminate her pregnancy by an abortion "performed by a competent, licensed physician, under safe, clinical conditions"; that she was unable to get a "legal" abortion in Texas because her life did not appear to be threatened by the continuation of her pregnancy; and that she could not afford to travel to another jurisdiction in order to secure a legal abortion under safe conditions. * * *

It perhaps is not generally appreciated that the restrictive criminal abortion laws in effect in a majority of States today are of relatively recent vintage. Those laws, generally proscribing abortion or its attempt at any time during pregnancy except when necessary to preserve the pregnant woman's life, are not of ancient or even of common-law origin.

Instead, they derive from statutory changes effected, for the most part, in the latter half of the 19th century.

* * *

The common law. It is undisputed that at common law, abortion performed before "quickening"—the first recognizable movement of the fetus in utero, appearing usually from the 16th to the 18th week of pregnancy—was not an indictable offense. The absence of a common-law crime for pre-quickening abortion appears to have developed from a confluence of earlier philosophical, theological, and civil and canon law concepts of when life begins. These disciplines variously approached the question in terms of the point at which the embryo or fetus became "formed" or recognizably human, or in terms of when a "person" came into being, that is, infused with a "soul" or "animated." A loose consensus evolved in early English law that these events occurred at some point between conception and live birth. This was "mediate animation." Although Christian theology and the canon law came to fix the point of animation at 40 days for a male and 80 days for a female, a view that persisted until the 19th century, there was otherwise little agreement about the precise time of formation or animation. There was agreement, however, that prior to this point the fetus was to be regarded as part of the mother, and its destruction, therefore, was not homicide. * * *

Whether abortion of a quick fetus was a felony at common law, or even a lesser crime, is still disputed. * * * [M]ost American courts ruled, in holding or dictum, that abortion of an unquickened fetus was not criminal under their received common law, others followed Coke in stating that abortion of a quick fetus was a "misprision," a term they translated to mean "misdemeanor." * * * In 1828, New York enacted legislation that, in two respects, was to serve as a model for early anti-abortion statutes. First, while barring destruction of an unquickened fetus as well as a quick fetus, it made the former only a misdemeanor, but the latter second-degree manslaughter. Second, it incorporated a concept of therapeutic abortion by providing that an abortion was excused if it "shall have been necessary to preserve the life of such mother, or shall have been advised by two physicians to be necessary for such purpose." By 1840, when Texas had received the common law, only eight American States had statutes dealing with abortion. It was not until after the War Between the States that legislation began generally to replace the common law. Most of these initial statutes dealt severely with abortion after quickening but were lenient with it before quickening. * * *

Gradually, in the middle and late 19th century the quickening distinction disappeared from the statutory law of most States and the degree of the offense and the penalties were increased. By the end of the 1950's a large majority of the jurisdictions banned abortion, however and whenever performed, unless done to save or preserve the life of the mother. * * * In the past several years, however, a trend toward liberalization of abortion statutes has resulted in adoption, by about one-third of the States, of less stringent laws * * *.

It is thus apparent that at common law, at the time of the adoption of our Constitution, and throughout the major portion of the 19th century, abortion was viewed with less disfavor than under most American statutes currently in effect. Phrasing it another way, a woman enjoyed a substantially broader right to terminate a pregnancy than she does in most States today. At least with respect to the early stage of pregnancy, and very possibly without such a limitation, the opportunity to make this choice was present in this country well into the 19th century. Even later, the law continued for some time to treat less punitively an abortion procured in early pregnancy.

* * *

Th[e] right of privacy, whether it be founded in the Fourteenth Amendment's concept of personal liberty and restrictions upon state action, as we feel it is, or, as the District Court determined, in the Ninth Amendment's reservation of rights to the people, is broad enough to encompass a woman's decision whether or not to terminate her pregnancy. The detriment that the State would impose upon the pregnant woman by denying this choice altogether is apparent. Specific and direct harm medically diagnosable even in early pregnancy may be involved. Maternity, or additional offspring, may force upon the woman a distressful life and future. Psychological harm may be imminent. Mental and physical health may be taxed by child care. There is also the distress, for all concerned, associated with the unwanted child, and there is the problem of bringing a child into a family already unable, psychologically and otherwise, to care for it. In other cases, as in this one, the additional difficulties and continuing stigma of unwed motherhood may be involved. All these are factors the woman and her responsible physician necessarily will consider in consultation.

* * *

The Constitution does not define "person" in so many words. Section 1 of the Fourteenth Amendment contains three references to "person." The first, in defining "citizens," speaks of "persons born or naturalized in the United States." The word also appears both in the Due Process Clause and in the Equal Protection Clause. "Person" is used in other places in the Constitution * * *. But in nearly all these instances, the use of the word is such that it has application only postnatally. None indicates, with any assurance, that it has any possible prenatal application.

All this, together with our observation that throughout the major portion of the 19th century prevailing legal abortion practices were far freer than they are today, persuades us that the word "person," as used in the Fourteenth Amendment, does not include the unborn. * * *

The pregnant woman cannot be isolated in her privacy. She carries an embryo and, later, a fetus, if one accepts the medical definitions of the developing young in the human uterus. The situation therefore is inherently different from marital intimacy, or bedroom possession of obscene material, or marriage, or procreation, or education * * *.

We need not resolve the difficult question of when life begins. When those trained in the respective disciplines of medicine, philosophy, and theology are unable to arrive at any consensus, the judiciary, at this point in the development of man's knowledge, is not in a position to speculate as to the answer.

It should be sufficient to note briefly the wide divergence of thinking on this most sensitive and difficult question. There has always been strong support for the view that life does not begin until live birth. This was the belief of the Stoics. It appears to be the predominant, though not the unanimous, attitude of the Jewish faith. It may be taken to represent also the position of a large segment of the Protestant community, insofar as that can be ascertained; organized groups that have taken a formal position on the abortion issue have generally regarded abortion as a matter for the conscience of the individual and her family. As we have noted, the common law found greater significance in quickening. Physicians and their scientific colleagues have regarded that event with less interest and have tended to focus either upon conception, upon live birth, or upon the interim point at which the fetus becomes "viable," that is, potentially able to live outside the mother's womb, albeit with artificial aid. Viability is usually placed at about seven months (28 weeks) but may occur earlier, even at 24 weeks. The Aristotelian theory of "mediate animation," that held sway throughout the Middle Ages and the Renaissance in Europe, continued to be official Roman Catholic dogma until the 19th century, despite opposition to this "ensoulment" theory from those in the Church who would recognize the existence of life from the moment of conception. The latter is now, of course, the official belief of the Catholic Church. * * * Substantial problems for precise definition of this view are posed, however, by new embryological data that purport to indicate that conception is a "process" over time, rather than an event, and by new medical techniques such as menstrual extraction, the "morning-after" pill, implantation of embryos, artificial insemination, and even artificial wombs.

In areas other than criminal abortion, the law has been reluctant to endorse any theory that life, as we recognize it, begins before live birth or to accord legal rights to the unborn except in narrowly defined situations and except when the rights are contingent upon live birth. * * * In short, the unborn have never been recognized in the law as persons in the whole sense.

In view of all this, we do not agree that, by adopting one theory of life, Texas may override the rights of the pregnant woman that are at stake. We repeat, however, that the State does have an important and legitimate interest in preserving and protecting the health of the pregnant woman, whether she be a resident of the State or a non-resident who seeks medical consultation and treatment there, and that it has still another important and legitimate interest in protecting the potentiality of human life. These interests are separate and distinct. Each grows in substantiality as the woman approaches term and, at a point during pregnancy, each becomes "compelling."

With respect to the State's important and legitimate interest in the health of the mother, the "compelling" point, in the light of present medical knowledge, is at approximately the end of the first trimester. This is so because of the now-established medical fact * * * that until the end of the first trimester mortality in abortion may be less than mortality in normal childbirth. It follows that, from and after this point, a State may regulate the abortion procedure to the extent that the regulation reasonably relates to the preservation and protection of maternal health. Examples of permissible state regulation in this area are requirements as to the qualifications of the person who is to perform the abortion; as to the licensure of that person; as to the facility in which the procedure is to be performed, that is, whether it must be a hospital or may be a clinic or some other place of less-than-hospital status; as to the licensing of the facility; and the like.

This means, on the other hand, that, for the period of pregnancy prior to this "compelling" point, the attending physician, in consultation with his patient, is free to determine, without regulation by the State, that, in his medical judgment, the patient's pregnancy should be terminated. If that decision is reached, the judgment may be effectuated by an abortion free of interference by the State.

With respect to the State's important and legitimate interest in potential life, the "compelling" point is at viability. This is so because the fetus then presumably has the capability of meaningful life outside the mother's womb. State regulation protective of fetal life after viability thus has both logical and biological justifications. If the State is interested in protecting fetal life after viability, it may go so far as to proscribe abortion during that period, except when it is necessary to preserve the life or health of the mother.

HARRIS v. McRAE

Supreme Court of the United States, 1980.

448 U.S. 297, 100 S.Ct. 2671, 65 L.Ed.2d 784.

Mr. Justice Stewart delivered the opinion of the Court.

This case presents statutory and constitutional questions concerning the public funding of abortions under Title XIX of the Social Security Act, commonly known as the "Medicaid" Act, and recent annual Appropriations Acts containing the so-called "Hyde Amendment." * * * The constitutional question * * * is whether the Hyde Amendment, by denying public funding for certain medically necessary abortions, contravenes the liberty or equal protection guarantees of the Due Process Clause of the Fifth Amendment, or either of the Religion Clauses of the First Amendment.

* * *

In Maher v. Roe, 432 U.S. 464, 97 S.Ct. 2376, 53 L.Ed.2d 484 [1977], the Court was presented with the question whether the scope of personal constitutional freedom recognized in Roe v. Wade included an entitlement to Medicaid payments for abortions that are not medically necessary. At issue in *Maher* was a Connecticut welfare regulation under which Medicaid recipients received payments for medical services incident to childbirth, but not for medical services incident to nontherapeutic abortions.

It was the view of this Court that "the District Court misconceived the nature and scope of the fundamental right recognized in *Roe*." The doctrine of Roe v. Wade, the Court held in *Maher*, "protects the woman from unduly burdensome interference with her freedom to decide whether to terminate her pregnancy," such as the severe criminal sanctions at issue in Roe v. Wade, or the absolute requirement of spousal consent for an abortion challenged in Planned Parenthood of Central Missouri v. Danforth, 428 U.S. 52, 96 S.Ct. 2831, 49 L.Ed.2d 788 [1976].

But the constitutional freedom recognized in *Wade* and its progeny, the *Maher* Court explained, did not prevent Connecticut from making "a value judgment favoring childbirth over abortion, and ... implement[ing] that judgment by the allocation of public funds."

* * *

The Hyde Amendment, like the Connecticut welfare regulation at issue in *Maher*, places no governmental obstacle in the path of a woman who chooses to terminate her pregnancy, but rather, by means of unequal subsidization of abortion and other medical services, encourages alternative activity deemed in the public interest. The present case does differ factually from *Maher* insofar as that case involved a failure to fund nontherapeutic abortions, whereas the Hyde Amendment withholds funding of certain medically necessary abortions.

* * * [A]lthough government may not place obstacles in the path of a woman's exercise of her freedom of choice, it need not remove those not of its own creation. Indigency falls in the latter category. The financial constraints that restrict an indigent woman's ability to enjoy the full range of constitutionally protected freedom of choice are the product not of governmental restrictions on access to abortions, but rather of her indigency. Although Congress has opted to subsidize medically necessary services generally, but not certain medically necessary abortions, the fact remains that the Hyde Amendment leaves an indigent woman with at least the same range of choice in deciding whether to obtain a medically necessary abortion as she would have had if Congress had chosen to subsidize no health care costs at all. We are thus not persuaded that the Hyde Amendment impinges on the constitutionally protected freedom of choice recognized in *Wade*.

Notes on Roe and Harris

1. The opinion in Roe v. Wade agrees with the Historians' Brief's conclusions about abortion in American history, yet the story ends different-

ly: the Historians' Brief with the tragedy of dangerous and illegal abortions, and the *Roe* Court's account with the trend toward liberalization of abortion laws in the late 1960's. Would it have been better to have allowed this process of state-by-state liberalization to run its course? What factors would you take into account in making your counter-historical assessment on this question? Mary Ann Glendon points out that most Western European nations eased access to abortion in the 1970's and that abortion is much less controversial in those countries than it is in the United States today; she argues that the debate here has been so passionate and divisive at least in part because it has been carried out in the language of individual rights, rather than of communal responsibilities and relationships, a fact which may be attributable to the judicial forum. Glendon, Abortion and Divorce in Western Law 10–62 (1987). Gerald N. Rosenberg also notes that limits on Medicaid funding and the violent and harassing tactics used by anti-abortion protesters at abortion clinics arose only after Roe v. Wade, although the right to abortion was becoming established in most states prior to the *Roe* decision. Rosenberg, The Hollow Hope: Can Courts Bring About Social Change? 185–89 (1991). Is it possible that women would have been better off as a class and the right to abortion safer today if it had been won in legislatures rather than in the courts?

2. The woman and her life are almost absent from the discussion of abortion in Roe v. Wade, which becomes instead the story of the fetus and the doctor. Reva Siegel sees this as resulting from the fact that the Court typically reasons about reproductive regulation in physiological paradigms, seeing regulation as state action that concerns women's bodies rather than women's roles, despite the fact that the social role of women was clearly the central concern in the historical debate about abortion. Siegel, Reasoning from the Body: A Historical Perspective on Abortion Regulation and Questions of Equal Protection, 44 Stan.L.Rev. 261 (1992). Is this a necessary result of grounding the right to abortion on the right to privacy? What other theories can you think of which might have been used to argue Roe v. Wade? Were they available when it was argued? Later sections of this chapter present a number of alternative theories upon which the abortion right might be grounded. For an account by the attorney who litigated on behalf of Jane Roe, see Sarah Weddington, A Question of Choice (1992).

3. What is the importance of the many references in *Roe* to religious beliefs about abortion and the beginning of life? Do they raise any First Amendment concerns? In the *Webster* case, below, a large number of religious groups submitted an amicus brief arguing that restrictions on the right of procreative freedom invade the religious freedoms protected by the Free Exercise Clause of the First Amendment. Because of the diversity of views on abortion among religious groups, they argued, state regulation of this area will necessarily clash with the strongly-held religious beliefs of some groups and individuals, dictating that the issue should be left to the private sphere. Brief Amicus Curiae for American Jewish Congress, et al., in Webster v. Reproductive Health Services, No. 88–605 (1989) (written by law professors Martha Minow and Aviam Soifer). What do you think of this argument? What if state regulation is *essential* to the religious beliefs of some groups, because they believe abortion is murder and thus cannot be

permitted by our society? Can you think of other areas in which constitutional decisions have been founded upon religion?

4. After *Harris,* the ability of an indigent woman to obtain an abortion was severely restricted. Even if the abortion is deemed medically necessary, states are not required to pay for it under the Medicaid program, although Medicaid does pay for other types of health services for indigent women. Is it constitutional for the federal government to treat pregnancy differently from other types of medical conditions? See discussion of *Geduldig* case in Chapter 3, above. Do rules developed in other contexts logically extend to abortion? Why or why not? Is it possible to attack the holding in *Harris* solely on the basis of formal equality? How? Does it make any difference that Medicaid does pay for sterilization as well as for childbirth, and that women on welfare have at times been *encouraged* to seek sterilization?

5. The Supreme Court cases, with their narrow focus on the right to be left alone by government (i.e., we are all equally free to have *and* to pay for an abortion), seem to protect relatively well-off adult white women the most and ignore the primary reproductive issues for poor women, especially poor women of color. For these women, the top priority may not be the ability to *avoid* having children but rather the ability to have them under conditions of reasonable economic, physical, and emotional security. Can these types of reproductive issues be addressed by the courts? How or how not?

WEBSTER v. REPRODUCTIVE HEALTH SERVICES

Supreme Court of the United States, 1989.

492 U.S. 490, 109 S.Ct. 3040, 106 L.Ed.2d 410.

[Appellees, state-employed health professionals and private nonprofit corporations providing abortion services, brought suit for declaratory and injunctive relief challenging the constitutionality of a Missouri statute which (1) set forth "findings" in its preamble that "[t]he life of each human being begins at conception," (2) specified that a physician, prior to performing an abortion on any woman whom he has reason to believe is 20 or more weeks pregnant, must ascertain whether the fetus is "viable," (3) prohibited the use of public employees and facilities to perform or assist abortions not necessary to save the mother's life, and (4) made it unlawful to use public funds, employees, or facilities for the purpose of "encouraging or counseling" a woman to have an abortion not necessary to save her life.

The Court declined to rule on the constitutionality of the preamble because, though it expressed the State's preference for childbirth over abortion, it did not regulate abortions. A majority of the Court upheld the viability-testing requirement, though the Justices were split on the rationale for doing so. Relying on Harris v. McRae, above, the Court also upheld the statute's ban on the use of public facilities and employees to perform abortions not necessary to save the life of the mother, on the ground that the government has no affirmative duty to provide assistance to women wishing to terminate their pregnancies. The Court held that the constitutionality of the provision prohibiting the use of public funds to counsel women to have nontherapeutic abortions was moot because the provision was aimed at state officers responsible for allocating public funds, not at physicians or health care providers.

The *Webster* opinion is notable for the deep divisions among the Justices represented in the five separate opinions filed, and the willingness of at least four members of the Court to overrule Roe v. Wade.]

Chief Justice Rehnquist announced the judgment of the Court and delivered the opinion of the Court with respect to Parts I, II–A, II–B, and II–C, and an opinion with respect to Parts II–D and III, in which Justice White and Justice Kennedy join.

* * *

Stare decisis is a cornerstone of our legal system, but it has less power in constitutional cases, where, save for constitutional amendments, this Court is the only body able to make needed changes. We have not refrained from reconsideration of a prior construction of the Constitution that has proved "unsound in principle and unworkable in practice." We think the *Roe* trimester framework falls into that category.

In the first place, the rigid *Roe* framework is hardly consistent with the notion of a Constitution cast in general terms, as ours is, and usually speaking in general principles, as ours does. The key elements of the Roe framework—trimesters and viability—are not found in the text of the Constitution or in any place else one would expect to find a constitutional principle. * * *

In the second place, we do not see why the State's interest in protecting potential human life should come into existence only at the point of viability, and that there should therefore be a rigid line allowing state regulation after viability but prohibiting it before viability. * * *

Justice O'Connor, concurring in part and in the judgment.

* * *

[T]here is no necessity to accept the State's invitation to reexamine the constitutional validity of Roe v. Wade. * * * Quite simply, "[i]t is not the habit of the court to decide questions of a constitutional nature unless absolutely necessary to a decision of the case." The Court today has accepted the State's every interpretation of its abortion statute and has upheld, under our existing precedents, every provision of that statute which is properly before us. * * * When the constitutional invalidity of a State's abortion statute actually turns on the constitutional validity of Roe v. Wade, there will be time enough to reexamine *Roe.* And to do so carefully.

* * *

Justice Scalia, concurring in part and concurring in the judgment.

* * * I join Parts I, II–A, II–B, and II–C of the opinion of the Court. As to Part II–D, I share Justice Blackmun's view that it effectively would overrule Roe v. Wade. I think that should be done, but would do it more explicitly. * * *

JUSTICE BLACKMUN, with whom JUSTICE BRENNAN and JUSTICE MARSHALL join, concurring in part and dissenting in part.

Today, Roe v. Wade, and the fundamental constitutional right of women to decide whether to terminate a pregnancy, survive but are not secure. Although the Court extricates itself from this case without making a single, even incremental, change in the law of abortion, the plurality and JUSTICE SCALIA would overrule *Roe* (the first silently, the other explicitly) and would return to the States virtually unfettered authority to control the quintessentially intimate, personal, and life-directing decision whether to carry a fetus to term. Although today, no less than yesterday, the Constitution and the decisions of this Court prohibit a State from enacting laws that inhibit women from the meaningful exercise of that right, a plurality of this Court implicitly invites every state legislature to enact more and more restrictive abortion regulations in order to provoke more and more test cases, in the hope that sometime down the line the Court will return the law of procreative freedom to the severe limitations that generally prevailed in this country before January 22, 1973. * * *

I fear for the future. I fear for the liberty and equality of the millions of women who have lived and come of age in the 16 years since *Roe* was decided. I fear for the integrity of, and public esteem for, this Court.

I dissent.

PLANNED PARENTHOOD OF SOUTHEASTERN PENNSYLVANIA v. CASEY

Supreme Court of the United States, 1992.

505 U.S. 833, 112 S.Ct. 2791, 120 L.Ed.2d 674.

[At issue in this case were the provisions of the Pennsylvania Abortion Control Act of 1982 (1) requiring informed consent before an abortion and specifying that certain information must be provided at least 24 hours before the abortion; (2) requiring consent of one of the parents of a minor seeking an abortion with the option of judicial bypass in certain circumstances; (3) requiring spousal notification by married women seeking abortions; (4) defining "medical emergency" as a condition that necessitates an abortion to avoid death or serious, irreversible harm to the mother and exempting women in that condition from the above requirements; and (5) imposing various reporting requirements for facilities that perform abortions.

Justices O'Connor, Kennedy, and Souter, writing for the majority, reaffirmed the essential holding of Roe v. Wade—a woman's right to an abortion before fetal viability—but rejected its trimester framework. The medical emergency definition and exemption, informed consent requirement, parental consent requirement (with judicial bypass), and record-keeping provisions were upheld using an "undue burden" standard, described in the excerpt below. The spousal notification requirement was held unconstitutional, because it imposed an undue burden on women who fear abuse from their husbands, as were the reporting requirements pertaining to it.]

JUSTICES O'CONNOR, KENNEDY, and SOUTER announced the judgment of the Court.

* * *

After considering the fundamental constitutional questions resolved by *Roe,* principles of institutional integrity, and the rule of stare decisis, we are led to conclude this: the essential holding of Roe v. Wade should be retained and once again reaffirmed.

* * *

[I]n this case we may inquire whether *Roe*'s central rule has been found unworkable; whether the rule's limitation on state power could be removed without serious inequity to those who have relied upon it or significant damage to the stability of the society governed by the rule in question; whether the law's growth in the intervening years has left *Roe*'s central rule a doctrinal anachronism discounted by society; and whether *Roe*'s premises of fact have so far changed in the ensuing two decades as to render its central holding somehow irrelevant or unjustifiable in dealing with the issue it addressed.

* * *

The inquiry into reliance counts the cost of a rule's repudiation as it would fall on those who have relied reasonably on the rule's continued application. * * *

Abortion is customarily chosen as an unplanned response to the consequence of unplanned activity or to the failure of conventional birth control, and except on the assumption that no intercourse would have occurred but for *Roe*'s holding, such behavior may appear to justify no reliance claim. Even if reliance could be claimed on that unrealistic assumption, the argument might run, any reliance interest would be de minimis. * * *

To eliminate the issue of reliance that easily, however, one would need to limit cognizable reliance to specific instances of sexual activity. But to do this would be simply to refuse to face the fact that for two decades of economic and social developments, people have organized intimate relationships and made choices that define their views of themselves and their places in society, in reliance on the availability of abortion in the event that contraception should fail. The ability of women to participate equally in the economic and social life of the Nation has been facilitated by their ability to control their reproductive lives. See, e.g., R. Petchesky, Abortion and Woman's Choice 109, 133, n. 7 (rev. ed. 1990). The Constitution serves human values, and while the effect of reliance on *Roe* cannot be exactly measured, neither can the certain cost of overruling *Roe* for people who have ordered their thinking and living around that case be dismissed.

* * *

We conclude that the basic decision in *Roe* was based on a constitutional analysis which we cannot now repudiate. The woman's liberty is not so unlimited, however, that from the outset the State cannot show its concern for the life of the unborn, and at a later point in fetal development the State's interest in life has sufficient force so that the right of the woman to terminate the pregnancy can be restricted.

That brings us, of course, to the point where much criticism has been directed at *Roe,* a criticism that always inheres when the Court draws a specific rule from what in the Constitution is but a general standard. We conclude, however, that the urgent claims of the woman to retain the ultimate control over her destiny and her body, claims implicit in the meaning of liberty, require us to perform that function. Liberty must not be extinguished for want of a line that is clear. And it falls to us to give some real substance to the woman's liberty to determine whether to carry her pregnancy to full term.

We conclude the line should be drawn at viability, so that before that time the woman has a right to choose to terminate her pregnancy. * * *

We reject the trimester framework, which we do not consider to be part of the essential holding of *Roe.* * * * A logical reading of the central holding in *Roe* itself, and a necessary reconciliation of the liberty of the woman and the interest of the State in promoting prenatal life, require, in our view, that we abandon the trimester framework as a rigid prohibition on all previability regulation aimed at the protection of fetal life. * * *

* * * The fact that a law which serves a valid purpose, one not designed to strike at the right itself, has the incidental effect of making it more difficult or more expensive to procure an abortion cannot be enough to invalidate it. Only where state regulation imposes an undue burden on a woman's ability to make this decision does the power of the State reach into the heart of the liberty protected by the Due Process Clause.

* * *

A finding of an undue burden is a shorthand for the conclusion that a state regulation has the purpose or effect of placing a substantial obstacle in the path of a woman seeking an abortion of a nonviable fetus. A statute with this purpose is invalid because the means chosen by the State to further the interest in potential life must be calculated to inform the woman's free choice, not hinder it. And a statute which, while furthering the interest in potential life or some other valid state interest, has the effect of placing a substantial obstacle in the path of a woman's choice cannot be considered a permissible means of serving its legitimate ends. * * *

[The Court held that the statute's definition of "medical emergency" and requirement of informed consent did not place an undue burden on the abortion right.]

[*Spousal notification*]

Section 3209 of Pennsylvania's abortion law provides, except in cases of medical emergency, that no physician shall perform an abortion on a married woman without receiving a signed statement from the woman that she has notified her spouse that she is about to undergo an abortion. * * *

The District Court heard the testimony of numerous expert witnesses, and made detailed findings of fact regarding the effect of this statute. * * *

These findings are supported by studies of domestic violence. The American Medical Association (AMA) has published a summary of the recent research in this field, which indicates that in an average 12–month period in this country, approximately two million women are the victims of severe assaults by their male partners. In a 1985 survey, women reported that nearly one of every eight husbands had assaulted their wives during the past year. The AMA views these figures as "marked underestimates," because the nature of these incidents discourages women from reporting them, and because surveys typically exclude the very poor, those who do not speak English well, and women who are homeless or in institutions or hospitals when the survey is conducted. * * *

Other studies fill in the rest of this troubling picture. Physical violence is only the most visible form of abuse. Psychological abuse, particularly forced social and economic isolation of women, is also common. L. Walker, The Battered Woman Syndrome 27–28 (1984). Many victims of domestic violence remain with their abusers, perhaps because they perceive no superior alternative. Many abused women who find temporary refuge in shelters return to their husbands, in large part because they have no other source of income. Returning to one's abuser can be dangerous. Recent Federal Bureau of Investigation statistics disclose that 8.8% of all homicide victims in the United States are killed by their spouse. Thirty percent of female homicide victims are killed by their male partners.

* * * In well-functioning marriages, spouses discuss important intimate decisions such as whether to bear a child. But there are millions of women in this country who are the victims of regular physical and psychological abuse at the hands of their husbands. Should these women become pregnant, they may have very good reasons for not wishing to inform their husbands of their decision to obtain an abortion. Many may

have justifiable fears of physical abuse, but may be no less fearful of the consequences of reporting prior abuse to the Commonwealth of Pennsylvania. Many may have a reasonable fear that notifying their husbands will provoke further instances of child abuse * * *. Many may fear devastating forms of psychological abuse from their husbands, including verbal harassment, threats of future violence, the destruction of possessions, physical confinement to the home, the withdrawal of financial support, or the disclosure of the abortion to family and friends. These methods of psychological abuse may act as even more of a deterrent to notification than the possibility of physical violence * * *. And many women who are pregnant as a result of sexual assaults by their husbands will be unable to avail themselves of the exception for spousal sexual assault, because the exception requires that the woman have notified law enforcement authorities within 90 days of the assault, and her husband will be notified of her report once an investigation begins. * * *

The spousal notification requirement is thus likely to prevent a significant number of women from obtaining an abortion. It does not merely make abortions a little more difficult or expensive to obtain; for many women, it will impose a substantial obstacle. We must not blind ourselves to the fact that the significant number of women who fear for their safety and the safety of their children are likely to be deterred from procuring an abortion as surely as if the Commonwealth had outlawed abortion in all cases.

* * *

If this case concerned a State's ability to require the mother to notify the father before taking some action with respect to a living child raised by both, therefore, it would be reasonable to conclude as a general matter that the father's interest in the welfare of the child and the mother's interest are equal.

Before birth, however, the issue takes on a very different cast. It is an inescapable biological fact that state regulation with respect to the child a woman is carrying will have a far greater impact on the mother's liberty than on the father's. The effect of state regulation on a woman's protected liberty is doubly deserving of scrutiny in such a case, as the State has touched not only upon the private sphere of the family but upon the very bodily integrity of the pregnant woman. * * *

Section 3209 embodies a view of marriage consonant with the common-law status of married women but repugnant to our present understanding of marriage and of the nature of the rights secured by the Constitution. Women do not lose their constitutionally protected liberty when they marry. * * *

* * *

[Justice Stevens agreed with the majority, but would have retained the trimester framework and have struck down the informed consent requirement as imposing an undue burden on a woman seeking an abortion. Justice Blackmun dissented from much of the majority opinion, in favor of retaining the trimester framework and fundamental interest standard of Roe v. Wade; he would have also invalidated the counseling and 24-hour delay, parental consent, and reporting requirements.]

CHIEF JUSTICE REHNQUIST, with whom JUSTICE WHITE, JUSTICE SCALIA, and JUSTICE THOMAS join, concurring in the judgment in part and dissenting in part.

* * *

The joint opinion * * * points to the reliance interests involved in this context in its effort to explain why precedent must be followed for precedent's sake. Certainly it is true that where reliance is truly at issue, as in the case of judicial decisions that have formed the basis for private decisions, "[c]onsiderations in favor of stare decisis are at their acme." But * * * any traditional notion of reliance is not applicable here. The Court today cuts back on the protection afforded by *Roe,* and no one claims that this action defeats any reliance interest in the disavowed trimester framework. Similarly, reliance interests would not be diminished were the Court to go further and acknowledge the full error of *Roe,* as "reproductive planning could take virtually immediate account of" this action.

The joint opinion thus turns to what can only be described as an unconventional—and unconvincing—notion of reliance, a view based on the surmise that the availability of abortion since *Roe* has led to "two decades of economic and social developments" that would be undercut if the error of *Roe* were recognized. The joint opinion's assertion of this fact is undeveloped and totally conclusory. In fact, one can not be sure to what economic and social developments the opinion is referring. Surely it is dubious to suggest that women have reached their "places in society" in reliance upon *Roe,* rather than as a result of their determination to obtain higher education and compete with men in the job market, and of society's increasing recognition of their ability to fill positions that were previously thought to be reserved only for men.

In the end, having failed to put forth any evidence to prove any true reliance, the joint opinion's argument is based solely on generalized assertions about the national psyche, on a belief that the people of this country have grown accustomed to the *Roe* decision over the last 19 years and have "ordered their thinking and living around" it. As an initial matter, one might inquire how the joint opinion can view the "central holding" of *Roe* as so deeply rooted in our constitutional culture, when it so casually uproots and disposes of that same decision's trimester framework. Furthermore, at various points in the past, the same could have been said about this Court's erroneous decisions that the Constitution allowed "separate but equal" treatment of minorities, see Plessy v. Ferguson, 163 U.S. 537, 16 S.Ct. 1138, 41 L.Ed. 256 (1896) * * *. The "separate but equal" doctrine lasted 58 years after *Plessy* * * *. However, the simple fact that a generation or more had grown used to these major decisions did not prevent the Court from correcting its errors in those cases, nor should it prevent us from correctly interpreting the Constitution here.

[Justices Rehnquist, White, Scalia, and Thomas concurred in most of the majority opinion but would have overruled Roe v. Wade and thus would have upheld even the spousal notification requirement using a rational relationship standard, rather than the undue burden test.]

Notes on Webster and Casey

1. After *Webster,* when only the vote of Justice O'Connor prevented Roe v. Wade from being overruled, proponents of the right to abortion feared the worst. Instead, the *Casey* Court not only refused to overturn *Roe,* but also included new feminist arguments and research in its analysis. The woman's presence, her life and her concerns, move to center stage in sections of the joint opinion. How would you explain this change?

2. Who has the better of the argument over reliance: the joint opinion or the dissent? Is the discussion of reliance in *Casey* just the standard way a court considers whether to overrule its own prior opinions? Or does the joint opinion mean something more by its discussion of reliance? Have you or women in your generation relied on the right to abortion? How? Would this reliance disappear if women were simply given a 90–day warning that the right was to be taken away?

How convincing is the reliance argument? Is it typically one that women can employ in litigation? A reliance argument is most effectively used by defenders of the status quo. Could an argument be made against the regulation of pornography on these grounds? Many people (especially men) have constructed their sexuality based on notions of dominance and violence in reliance on the continuing availability of violent pornography. Thus, it could be considered unfair to change the rules on them now, as they may not be able to construct a new sexuality easily as adults. How would you distinguish these two situations? Can you distinguish reliance on Roe v. Wade from reliance on the "separate but equal" doctrine, an analogy suggested in the excerpt above?

There is another kind of reliance the Court does not mention in *Casey*—that of pro-choice activists, who did not continue to press for legislative liberalization on abortion in the 1970's, in reliance on Roe v. Wade. Why doesn't the majority mention this kind of reliance? Should this type of reliance be protected more, or less, than the reliance of women as individuals in making choices and forming goals, values, and self images? What differences are there between the Court's reliance argument and women's political reliance on the availability of abortion rights? Could some of the points in the reliance discussion be made without reference to reliance as such?

3. In situations not involving domestic violence, what, if any, rights do you think fathers should have in relation to the decision to abort? Compare the discussion of this issue in *Casey* with that in Planned Parenthood of Central Missouri v. Danforth, 428 U.S. 52, 67–71, 96 S.Ct. 2831, 2840–42, 49 L.Ed.2d 788 (1976). See also Andrea M. Sharrin, Potential Fathers and Abortion: A Woman's Womb Is Not A Man's Castle, 55 Brook. L.Rev. 1359

(1990). Does it make any difference that men are still obligated to support children they would have preferred to abort?

4. Another main issue in *Casey* was the requirement of parental notification and consent prior to a minor's obtaining an abortion. The Pennsylvania statute provided that an unemancipated young woman under 18 could not obtain an abortion without the consent of one of her parents or guardian, except in an emergency; if no parental consent were given, however, a court could nonetheless authorize the abortion if it determined that she was mature enough to give informed consent or that an abortion was in her best interest ("judicial bypass"). *Casey,* 505 U.S. at 899, 112 S.Ct. at 2832, 120 L.Ed.2d at 728–29. The *Casey* Court upheld the one-parent consent requirement, provided that there was an adequate procedure for judicial bypass. One author argues that "despite consistent judicial language to the contrary, parental involvement laws have more to do with limiting abortion rights than with promoting family communication and prudent teenage decision-making." J. Shoshanna Ehrlich, Journey Through the Courts: Minors, Abortion and the Quest for Reproductive Fairness, 10 Yale J. Law and Feminism 1, 2 (1998).

Studies of minors who are unwilling to notify their parents show that this decision is only partly associated with fear of parental disagreement about the choice of abortion; other reasons for not notifying parents include multiple concurrent family stresses, an absent father (in states requiring two-parent consent), family violence, parental substance abuse, and a feeling of having "betrayed" the family by becoming pregnant. See Robert W. Blum, Michael D. Resnick, and Trisha Stark, Factors Associated with the Use of Court Bypass by Minors to Obtain Abortions, 22 Family Planning Perspectives 158, 160 (July–Aug. 1990). What are the pro's and con's of the different possible approaches to minors' obtaining abortions? Should they be able to do so without parental consent? At what age? Under what conditions? Could they obtain other types of medical treatment or surgery without parental consent? Can they obtain oral contraceptives? Do you think a judge should be involved in this decision? Are judges (who are still primarily male) satisfactory substitutes for parents? Do you think most teenagers are capable of making this decision on their own? Of approaching a court on their own? If teenage girls are deterred from seeking a legal abortion, what is the likely consequence? Is a girl not mature enough to make the abortion decision mature enough to bear a child? Should there be an exception to parental notice requirements for victims of incest?

5. Will cases regarding the right to abortion be argued differently after *Casey?* How? What would you emphasize if you were writing a brief concerning whether a given state regulation placed an "undue burden" on the woman's right to choose? Who should decide what is "undue," and how?

6. The Supreme Court has only decided one case since *Casey* in which it indicated how the undue burden standard would be applied. This case involved a state law forbidding what it termed "partial birth abortion," a method of abortion sometimes used in pregnancies of 12 to 24 weeks duration (about 90% of all abortions performed in the U.S. take place before 12 weeks). Stenberg v. Carhart, 530 U.S. 914, 120 S.Ct. 2597, 147 L.Ed.2d 743 (2000). Because the statute did not contain an

exception for maternal health, while a substantial number of doctors believe that the challenged method was less risky for the woman, and could be interpreted to cover other procedures commonly performed in the first trimester as well, the Court found, by a 5–to–4 vote, that it placed a substantial obstacle in the path of a woman seeking to abort a nonviable fetus and thus was an undue burden upon the right to an abortion. Why do you think anti-abortion groups challenge procedures that are used in such a small percentage of all abortions? How would you rewrite the Nebraska statute so as to make it constitutional? Is it possible to do so?

3. THE BATTLE OVER ABORTION SINCE *CASEY*

Text Note

After Roe v. Wade, the battle over abortion took place in the streets as well. Anti-abortion forces were initially led by Catholics, many of whom had emerged from the anti-war and civil rights movement and coalesced into the Pro–Life Action Network led by Joseph Scheidler. By the late 1980's, however, a younger, fundamentalist Protestant leadership had come to the fore, organized into Operation Rescue, whose tactics became increasingly extreme. See James Risen and Judy L. Thomas, Wrath of Angels: The American Abortion War (1998). Street protests became efforts to block access to clinics where abortions were performed. In response, feminist groups filed suits to enjoin or restrain such conduct, for example, by imposing buffer zones to prevent Operation Rescue's supporters from harassing patients walking to and from abortion clinics. Three of these cases ultimately reached the Supreme Court. In one, the Court upheld the establishment of a 36–foot buffer zone protecting entrances to a clinic and its parking lot. Madsen v. Women's Health Center, Inc., 512 U.S. 753, 114 S.Ct. 2516, 129 L.Ed.2d 593 (1994). In another case, while upholding a 15–foot fixed buffer zone around clinic doorways, driveways, and parking lot entrances, the Court struck down a 15–foot "floating" buffer that prohibited demonstrating within 15 feet of any person entering or leaving the clinic, on the ground that it burdened more speech than necessary to serve the government interests in public safety, protection of property rights, and protection of a woman's freedom to seek pregnancy-related services. Schenck v. Pro–Choice Network of Western New York, 519 U.S. 357, 117 S.Ct. 855, 137 L.Ed.2d 1 (1997). Yet the Court subsequently upheld against First Amendment challenge an 8–foot floating buffer zone that was more narrowly tailored—a Colorado criminal statute prohibiting protesters from knowingly approaching within eight feet of an individual who is within 100 feet of a health care facility entrance without that individual's consent. Hill v. Colorado, 530 U.S. 703, 120 S.Ct. 2480, 147 L.Ed.2d 597 (2000).

More violent anti-abortion protests erupted in the 1990's, including arson and bombing of clinics as well as the murder of doctors who performed abortions. See Risen and Thomas, above; Karen O'Connor, No Neutral Ground? Abortion Politics in an Age of Absolutes (1996). In 1995, a breakaway group from Operation Rescue produced a "Deadly Dozen" list containing the names of abortion providers, which was subsequently published on the Internet; by January 1996 five of those on the list had been shot or subjected to other forms of violence. O'Connor, above, at 172. One doctor, David Gunn, and the doctor who replaced him, along with an escort, were murdered at a clinic in Pensacola, Florida in 1993 and 1994. Risen and Thomas, above, at 339–49, 361–65. Another abortion opponent entered two abortion clinics in Boston in 1994, shooting and killing two receptionists and injuring others. Id. at 367–68. And in October 1998, Dr. Barnett Slepian, an abortion provider in Buffalo, where the *Schenck* case had arisen, was murdered by a gunman shooting through a window of Dr. Slepian's home. Jim Yardley and David Rohde, Abortion Doctor in Buffalo Slain; Sniper Attack Fits Violent Pattern, N.Y.Times, Oct. 25, 1998, at A1. The first shootings were followed by passage of the Freedom of Access to Clinic Entrances Act (FACE) in May 1994, which made it a federal crime to block access to clinics or to commit acts aimed at denying a woman access to an abortion. 18 U.S.C.A. § 248 (West 1999). A federal court also issued a permanent injunction under FACE against groups' disseminating the "Deadly Dozen" list and poster and a list of names and information about abortion providers (known as the "Nuremberg Files") on the Internet, which was subsequently overturned on First Amendment grounds. Planned Parenthood of the Columbia/Willamette, Inc. v. American Coalition of Life Activists, 41 F. Supp. 2d 1130 (D.Or.1999), vacated, 2001 WL 293260 (9th Cir. Mar. 28, 2001).

Pro-choice lawyers also sought damage remedies against the groups seeking to blockade abortion clinics. One suit challenged Operation Rescue's blockades as a violation of the Ku Klux Klan Act, alleging that they formed part of a conspiracy to deprive women of rights protected by the equal protection clause; this suit failed, as the Supreme Court held that the act did not apply to abortion protesters because their activities were not designed to discriminate against women as a class. Bray v. Alexandria Women's Health Clinic, 506 U.S. 263, 113 S.Ct. 753, 122 L.Ed.2d 34 (1993). Another action, based upon the Racketeer Influenced and Corrupt Organizations Act (RICO), maintained that Joseph Scheidler's PLAN, Operation Rescue, and other militant anti-abortion groups were engaged in a conspiracy to drive abortion clinics out of business through violence or threats of violence. After 12 years of pre-trial proceedings, including an appeal to the Supreme Court (which held that RICO did not require an economic motive), the case resulted in a jury verdict and a large damage award in favor of the National Organization for Women, litigating on behalf of several abortion clinics. See NOW v. Scheidler, 510 U.S. 249, 114 S.Ct. 798, 127 L.Ed.2d 99 (1994); 897 F.Supp. 1047 (N.D.Ill.1995); No. 86 C 7888 (N.D. Ill. Sept. 19, 1997); 1997 WL 610782 (N.D.Ill.1997). Defendant was ultimately held liable for $54,471.28 to the Summit Women's Health Organization and for $31,455.64 to the Delaware Women's Health Organization, trebled under 18 U.S.C. § 1964(c) to $163,413.84 and $94,366.92, respectively. 1999 WL 571010 (N.D.Ill.1999). See also Fay Clayton and Sara N. Love, *NOW v. Scheidler*: Protecting Women's Access to Reproductive Health Services, 62 Albany L. Rev. 967 (1999) (written by counsel for plaintiffs). The accumulating damages from the RICO case, as well as for repeatedly violating court injunctions, took a severe toll on the major anti-abortion groups, which were also split by interpersonal quarrels and disagreements over the use of violence. See Risen and Thomas, above, at 295–314.

Abortion also became a central issue in national elections and contributed to the developing "gender gap" in voting patterns for President and in Congressional races. See O'Connor, above, at 115–53. The extreme division of public opinion on the issue, however, made it difficult to make abortion policy in the legislative arena, leaving the resolution of most issues to the courts (who were, as we have seen in *Casey*, often severely divided as well). When Bill Clinton was elected President in 1992, owing a good deal to support from pro-choice women, he immediately issued a number of executive orders reversing the "gag" rule on abortion counseling, the ban on fetal tissue research by federally funded researchers, directing the Secretary of Health and Human Services to review the ban on importation of RU 486, and lifting the ban on abortions in military hospitals overseas, as well as on the granting of U.S. aid to international programs that included abortion counseling. Id. at 151.

Notes on Abortion Since Casey

1. While pro-choice forces have enjoyed a good measure of success in the legal sphere, the increasingly violent responses of anti-abortion militants have played a role in decreasing the numbers of doctors willing to perform abortions, and medical residency programs providing routine training in first-semester abortions also declined from 23% in 1985 to 12% in 1991. Risen and Thomas, above, at 376. By 1994, two decades after Roe v. Wade, abortions were unavailable in 85% of U.S. counties, in part because of the refusal of Catholic hospitals to allow abortions to be performed. O'Connor, above, at 172–73. The availability of abortion may also be restricted for those relying upon public hospitals. One 26–year-old mother of two was denied an abortion at a Louisiana public institution, despite the fact that she was on the list for a heart transplant when she became pregnant. Her heart condition qualified her for disability benefits, including Medicaid; but the abortion was denied under Louisiana law, which allows abortions in public institutions only when the mother's life is endangered or in cases of rape or incest. When a panel of doctors concluded that her chance of dying was 50% or less, the state university medical center refused the abortion, which was subsequently performed in Texas after abortion rights organizations mobilized to pay for the procedure. Ruth Sorelle, Louisiana Woman Gets Abortion Here; Heart Defect Spurs Procedure in Texas, Houston Chronicle, Oct. 21, 1998, at 29. In short, although the right to abortion may exist, its availability may be extremely limited for a variety of reasons. What lessons do you think can be drawn about the relationship of law to social change in an area where public opinion is sharply divided?

2. The First Amendment has played an important role in much of the abortion-related litigation in the 1990's. It was raised on behalf of the anti-abortion protesters in *Schenck* and *Madsen*, the clinic access cases described above, with some success in relation to floating buffer zones. In 1991, the Supreme Court upheld the so-called "gag rule," which prohibited doctors and clinics receiving federal funds from counseling about abortion or providing referrals for that purpose, on the grounds that the government was simply choosing, as in Harris v. McRae, excerpted above, to subsidize family planning services that lead to conception and childbirth and declining to

promote abortion. Rust v. Sullivan, 500 U.S. 173, 111 S.Ct. 1759, 114 L.Ed.2d 233 (1991). The dissent pointed out that the Court was thereby upholding viewpoint-based suppression of speech for the first time. Dorothy Roberts adds that the decision did particular violence to women of color, because it "upheld regulations that deliberately withheld from women in these communities knowledge critical to their reproductive health and autonomy." Roberts, *Rust v. Sullivan* and the Control of Knowledge, 61 Geo. Wash. L. Rev. 587, 590 (1993). More recently, a federal court overturned, as violating the First Amendment, a judgment against abortion opponents who had published on the Internet a "hit list" of abortion doctors (with lines drawn through the names of those who had already been murdered). Planned Parenthood v. American Coalition of Life Activists, 2001 WL 193260 (9th Cir. Mar. 28, 2001). Can you reconcile the decisions in these cases?

3. How do you think the struggle over abortion will be affected by the final approval of RU 486 for use in the United States, which occurred in September 2000?

4. ALTERNATIVE THEORIES SUPPORTING THE RIGHT TO ABORTION

As should be obvious from the amicus briefs in the previous section, feminist lawyers and law professors have played a central role in the struggle over legal regulation of abortion. In this section we present another way in which academics have attempted to further this debate, by developing alternative theories upon which the right to abortion might be based, instead of upon the right to privacy embraced in Roe v. Wade. The excerpts and notes below present examples of arguments based upon women's experiences of abortion, a variety of arguments based upon self-defense, an approach grounded in equal protection, and a relational perspective based on caring.

CATHARINE A. MACKINNON, PRIVACY v. EQUALITY: BEYOND ROE v. WADE (1983)

In Feminism Unmodified 93, 94–96, 99 (1987).

Roe v. Wade guaranteed the right to choose abortion, subject to some countervailing considerations, by conceiving it as a private choice, included in the constitutional right to privacy. In this critique of that decision, I first situate abortion and the abortion right in the experience of women. The argument is that abortion is inextricable from sexuality. * * *

Most women who seek abortions became pregnant while having sexual intercourse with men. Most did not mean or wish to conceive. In contrast to this fact of women's experience, which converges sexuality with reproduction with gender, the abortion debate has centered on separating control over sexuality from control over reproduction, and on separating both from gender and the life options of the sexes. Liberals have supported the availability of the abortion choice as if the woman just happened on the fetus. The political right, imagining that the intercourse preceding conception is usually voluntary, urges abstinence, as if sex were up to women, while defending male authority, specifically including a wife's duty to submit to sex. Continuing with this logic, many opponents of state funding of abortions, such as supporters of some versions of the Hyde Amendment, would permit funding of abortions when pregnancy results from rape or incest. They make *exceptions* for those special occasions during which they presume women did *not* control sex. From all this I deduce that abortion's proponents and opponents share a tacit assumption that women significantly do control sex.

Feminist investigations suggest otherwise. Sexual intercourse, still the most common cause of pregnancy, cannot simply be presumed coequally determined. Feminism has found that women feel compelled to preserve the appearance—which, acted upon, becomes the reality—of male direction of sexual expression, as if male initiative itself were what we want, as if it were that which turns us on. Men enforce this. It is much of what men want in a woman. It is what pornography eroticizes and prostitutes provide. Rape—that is, intercourse with force that is recognized as force—is adjudicated not according to the power or force that the man wields, but according to indices of intimacy between the parties. The more intimate you are with your accused rapist, the less likely a court is to find that what happened to you was rape. Often indices of intimacy include intercourse itself. If "no" can be taken as "yes", how free can "yes" be?

Under these conditions, women often do not use birth control because of its social meaning, a meaning we did not create. Using contraception means acknowledging and planning the possibility of intercourse, accepting one's sexual availability, and appearing nonspontaneous. It means appearing available to male incursions. A good user of contraception can be presumed sexually available and, among other consequences, raped with relative impunity. (If you think this isn't true, you should consider rape cases in which the fact that a woman had a diaphragm in is taken as an indication that what happened to her was intercourse, not rape. "Why did you have your diaphragm in?") From studies of abortion clinics, women who repeatedly seek abortions (and now I'm looking at the repeat offenders high on the list of the right's villains, their best case for opposing abortion as female irresponsibility), when asked why, say something like, "The sex just happened." Like every night for two and a half years. I wonder if a woman can be presumed to control access to her sexuality if she feels unable to interrupt intercourse to insert a diaphragm; or worse, cannot even want to, aware that she risks a pregnancy she knows she does not want. Do you think she would stop the man for any other reason, such as, for instance, the real taboo—lack of desire? If she would not, how is sex, hence its consequences, meaningfully voluntary for women? Norms of sexual rhythm and romance that are felt interrupted by women's needs are constructed against women's interests. Sex doesn't look a whole lot like freedom when it appears normatively less costly for women to risk an undesired, often painful, traumatic, dangerous, sometimes illegal, and potentially life-threatening procedure than to protect themselves in advance. Yet abortion policy has never been explicitly approached in the context of how women get pregnant, that is, as a consequence of intercourse under conditions of gender inequality; that is, as an issue of forced sex.

* * *

In the context of a sexual critique of gender inequality, abortion promises to women sex with men on the same reproductive terms as men have sex with women. So long as women do not control access to our sexuality, abortion facilitates women's heterosexual availability. In other words, under conditions of gender inequality, sexual liberation in this sense does not free women; it frees male sexual aggression. The availability of abortion removes the one remaining legitimized reason that women have had for refusing sex besides the headache. * * *

BRIEF FOR THE AMICI CURIAE WOMEN WHO HAVE HAD ABORTIONS, IN *WEBSTER v. REPRODUCTIVE HEALTH SERVICES*

No. 88–605 (1989).

[This brief, known as the "Voices Brief," relies upon letters from some 2,887 women who have had abortions and 627 friends of women who have had abortions, describing their abortion decisions and their experiences both before and after Roe v. Wade.]

* * *

The conditions under which illegal abortions were performed were bad. It was estimated that "as many as 5,000 American women die[d] each year as a direct result of criminal abortion. The figure of 5,000 may be a minimum estimate, inasmuch as such deaths are mislabeled or unreported." R. Schwarz, Septic Abortion 7 (1968). * * *

A large number of illegal abortions were self-induced or performed by unskilled and untrained personnel working under dangerous septic conditions, unaccountable to professional guidelines and safeguards and unreached by ordinary government licensing procedures or other safeguards. Medical procedures, record-keeping and referral techniques were guided by concerns about detection, not best medical judgment.

The women received treatment which was often delayed under conditions of severe physical and emotional stress. The process was degrading. Follow up care was entirely lacking or inadequate. These dangerous and humiliating conditions existed precisely because abortions were illegal; they are graphically described by some amici:

* * *

> I am a 60 year old woman deeply troubled by the possibility that women's constitutional right to determine their own reproductive rights is being threatened and may be taken away....
>
> When I was in my twenties I had an illegal abortion. There were no other options that I saw at that time. Because of the illegality, it was extremely difficult to find someone who would discuss how to find someone to help me. People were afraid. As a consequence, when I finally found a source I had gone beyond the time of a safe procedure. I lied to the "doctor" because I knew he wouldn't do it if I told him how far along I was.... He insisted I come by myself which I did. Is there any way I can describe my fear. He was unclean, he joked a lot, his hands were rough, his breath was bad. He forcefully approached me to have sex with him because "what harm would there be under the circumstance?" That, of course, explained his reason for insisting that I come alone. So, on top of the fear for my physical safety in that situation, the agony of decision about what I was doing, the need to keep this secret away from everyone I knew and face it alone, there was the disgust, repulsion and deep fear that if I didn't do what he wanted he would send me away....
>
> I never want another woman to have to experience what I went through. My plea is that simple.

* * *

In deciding whether to bear a child or have an abortion, a woman thoughtfully considers the realities of motherhood, her obligations to herself and her family, and the social and economic injustices which she (and her offspring) must face. Her assessment is highly contextual and personal. Furthermore, it is moral—deriving from her diverse duties and her ability to fulfill them, which only she can evaluate.

* * *

Women express a variety of concerns in assessing their responsibilities including competing demands within the family, lack of adequate financial resources, and existing health problems incompatible with pregnancy and childbirth. Usually more than one factor is important.

Women weigh these concerns, as well as the highly demanding responsibilities that accompany motherhood. Most of the women who have abortions choose at some time to become mothers, but they choose to do so at times when they are financially, physically and emotionally prepared properly to care for a child. * * *

* * *

> I have personally had an abortion.... I was twenty-five years old at the time, divorced with two small children, ages five and seven, and a senior in college.... I was putting myself through college with the help of my family, raising my children as a single parent with very little emotional or financial support from my

extremely immature ex-husband; I was making grades good enough to consistently keep me on the dean's honor roll and contemplating going to graduate school.

When I became pregnant I was terrified at the prospect of bringing another child into the world, knowing that I was already strained to the limit, both financially and emotionally with the two children I had. I felt certain that bearing this child would be a disaster for me, my educational plans, my children and possibly for the relationship with the father. After an incredible amount of soul-searching discussions with the father and with doctors and counselors . . . I decided to have an abortion.

* * *

I am a divorced professional woman, who is raising three children alone. I barely make it from paycheck to paycheck. My children are very healthy, happy and loved. . . .

I have yet to receive any assistance of any kind in raising my children.

Most times, I feel like I am at the end of the ropes, juggling a career (I am forced to work 2 jobs to support my children, but one of them is a career), finances which are barely met, childraising alone. . . .

I chose abortion. I chose to limit myself to dealing with the too much responsibility I have now. All women should have the right to choose how much responsibility they feel they are able to handle. Especially since she is the only one she knows she can count on.

* * *

Some women facing unplanned pregnancies are already dealing with troubled families, abusive spouses and extreme emotional distress. Some of these women decide that they should not bring a child (or another child) into such an environment:

In 1984 I became pregnant by accident. I was married to a man who had become a physically abusive alcoholic. We had one child, age 3, at the time. I didn't see any way out of the relationship for myself. . . . My husband was not then working. . . . I was the sole support for my family at this time and had virtually no help from my husband in any area of responsibility. I was emotionally distraught much of the time because I felt I was not providing the material or emotional environment that my child deserved, and because of the constant pressures of physical and emotional abuse. . . . I knew I could not add the work of caring for another child to my burden, it would have broken me. . . . With no joy in my heart but with the knowledge that I was certainly making the right choice I had an abortion.

* * *

Some women are struggling with alcohol or drug abuse that they are unable to overcome at the time of pregnancy.

> I was 38 years old, married with two children. We were and are still a typical suburban family—as far as the outside world can see. But life was not ordinary for us in 1982. I was (I am) chemically addicted to the drug alcohol. Beginning in October, 1981 I made my first feeble attempts at recovery from alcoholism.... I wandered in and out of AA meetings....
>
> In the midst of this rollercoaster ride of addiction—in February, 1982, I realized I could be pregnant.... I was frantic, frightened, drained physically, emotionally, spiritually from my alcoholism. I could not manage my own life. The prospect of a baby was overwhelming!.... I chose to have an abortion....
>
> I continued efforts toward recovery, and with the help of support of AA, I have not had a drink since April 13, 1982.

* * *

Many women have faced the revelation that the fetus may be born with serious disabilities. Here again, the woman must decide, ideally with the best available and least biased information and support, whether she can meet existing responsibilities and provide for the expected new responsibility. In addition, some women decide that they cannot give birth to a child who they know would live a lifetime of tragic pain.

> I would never, never, never, in a million years, deliberately and knowingly bring another Tay–Sachs child into the world. The knowledge that I have the ability to spare another child the degradation that my cherished daughter is going through means everything to me. It would be a crime to put another child through the humiliation and pain that this cruel disease inflicts.
>
> At the same time, the hope of someday having a healthy child, and the knowledge that it can happen if we will only have the strength to keep trying, is one of the few things that is helping to keep me sane through the anguish of watching my child slowly die. If abortion were to be made illegal, I would have to give up that hope, as I would never take the risk of conceiving and having to bear another child with Tay–Sachs.[37]

AMICUS BRIEF OF THE NATIONAL COUNCIL OF NEGRO WOMEN, ET AL., IN *WEBSTER v. REPRODUCTIVE HEALTH SERVICES*

No. 88–605 (1989).

[This brief was filed on behalf of a number of organizations repre-

37. Tay–Sachs is a genetic disease occurring in infants and children. Children afflicted with Tay–Sachs disease, or one of the similar allied diseases, suffer slow degeneration, severe mental and physical impairment, resulting in their deaths in infancy or very early childhood.

senting African American, Asian American, Latina and Native American women.]

While Roe v. Wade benefited women of all classes, races and ages, its effect on the health and mortality of poor women, particularly women of color, was, and still is, especially significant. * * *

Laws restricting access to abortion * * * did not prevent women from seeking abortions. While a small number of upper and middle class women had access to safe, sanitary abortions in private hospitals and doctors' offices, and some others were able to afford travel to safer illegal providers, poor women, unable to afford the cost of either long distant trips or private doctors, were forced to resort to illegal abortions under the most frightening, unhygienic and often life-threatening conditions. Permanent loss of reproductive capacity or death were not uncommon. Because of the generally poor quality of health care available in their communities, women of color were disproportionately represented among those who died or were left sterile by illegal abortions. One study estimated that mishandled criminal abortions were the principal cause of maternal death in the United States, in the 1960's, killing 5,000 women a year. However, women of color risked their lives at much higher rates than did white women if they chose not to continue their pregnancy.

In 1965, in New York, for example, although there were 4 abortion deaths for every 100,000 live births for white women; for non-white women there were 56 abortion deaths per 100,000; for Puerto Rican women, there were 61.

* * *

Between 1967–1969 when abortions were not legal in New York, and 1970–1972 when they were legal, the average annual rate of abortion-related death fell by 51% in New York State. In the 19 comparative states the decline was substantially less—29%.

After legalization [nation-wide, by Roe v. Wade], the change nationally was similar. Despite the drop in the overall number of maternal deaths after *Roe,* however, a greater percentage of women of color than white women continued to die from illegal abortions. Between 1975 and 1979, several years after abortion was legalized, 82% of the women who died after illegal abortions were African–American and Latina.

[The authors then discuss the impact upon women of color of the regulations and restrictions challenged in *Webster.*]

* * *

1. Laws Requiring That All Abortions Be Performed in Hospitals Would Effectively Preclude Abortions for Poor Women and Women of Color.

* * *

To require that abortions be performed in hospitals will place an added burden on the already inadequate delivery of health care to the poor. For general health care, poor families are dependent on public hospitals which are severely overcrowded and understaffed.

Even though hospitals are the ordinary source of medical care for the poor, access to abortions in hospitals is limited and in most communities unavailable. In 1979–1980 only 17% of all public hospitals in the United States reported doing at least one abortion and only 22% of all abortions took place in hospitals, with a mere 32% of those hospitals providing abortions after 14 weeks of pregnancy. For Native American women who live on reservations,[35] and African–American women in the rural South, there has been even less access. To require that all abortions be performed at hospitals would severely restrict the numbers of abortion providers. Additionally, it would render abortion inaccessible to women in most communities in the country.

* * *

If states are permitted to require hospitalization for abortion throughout pregnancy, the cost of an abortion will increase artificially. The cost of abortions in hospitals is at least five times greater than the cost of clinic abortions. Although a first-trimester abortion in a clinic costs $200–300, the same abortion in a hospital costs $1200–1300. The cost for women who require second-trimester hospital abortions is even greater.

The cost of an in-hospital first-trimester abortion would be almost four times the average monthly AFDC payment ($375) for a family of three. Medicaid-eligible women who receive an average of $375 per month for themselves and their children cannot afford $200–$300 for a first-trimester clinic abortion. Yet many women, living in states which do not fund abortions, have managed to pay this sum by using all or part of their meager grants for daily living expenses. Increasing the cost to $1200 or $1300 will foreclose that option, making illegal abortion, once again, the only choice for poor women.

* * *

The increased cost of abortion is only part of the financial burden created by a hospitalization requirement. The cost of travel, of overnight stays, of childcare and of lost time from employment need to be factored in. The impact of a hospitalization requirement would fall especially heavily upon teenagers from poor families or those with no independent access to resources.

35. Almost half a million Native Americans live on reservations and in historic trust areas. Yet no Indian Health Service clinic or hospital were [sic] permitted to perform abortions even when there was private payment until 1982. Then federal regulations permitted abortions at Indian Health Service facilities, but only when the woman's life is endangered.

Notes on Women's Experience of Abortion

1. Does the opinion for the *Casey* plurality appreciate the importance of the conditions under which women have sex, which are emphasized by MacKinnon in the excerpt above? What would you have added to the discussion? How important is the fact that "[w]omen are highly and positively rewarded for being available to men, for desiring to please men, and for identifying their self-esteem and well-being with male sexual desire and approval"? Jane E. Larson, "Women Understand So Little, They Call My Good Nature 'Deceit' ": A Feminist Rethinking of Seduction, 93 Colum.L.Rev. 374, 427 (1993). For a description, based on interviews with women in abortion clinics, of the variety of reasons women have sex without contraception even when they do not want to become pregnant, see Kristin Luker, Taking Chances: Abortion and the Decision Not to Contracept (1991 ed.; orig. pub. 1975). Those reasons include the contradictory images in our culture of female sexuality, so that women, although expected to be accessible and responsive to men, are regarded as somehow vulgar if they prepare for sex in advance. Id. at 46–47.

2. In another article, Professor MacKinnon also asks whether women would still need abortions if sex equality were achieved, so that all sex were genuinely voluntary, and safe and effective contraception were available. At that point, MacKinnon professes, an approach based on privacy might make sense and the father's point of view be taken into account as well. Catharine A. MacKinnon, Reflections on Sex Equality Under Law, 100 Yale L.J. 1281, 1327 (1991). What do you think? If there truly were completely safe and effective methods of contraception and women were able to be sexual or not without regard for economic security or social approval, would that change your views on the right to abortion? Why or why not?

3. In a 1985 law review article, Ruth Bader Ginsburg indicated that she believed that Roe v. Wade would not have occasioned such violent opposition if it had been couched in terms of a sex equality rationale rather than as an issue of patient-physician autonomy, and that this approach might have changed the treatment of public funding cases as well. Ginsburg, Some Thoughts on Autonomy and Equality in Relation to *Roe v. Wade*, 63 N.C.L. Rev. 375, 382, 386 (1985). How would the approach Justice Ginsburg suggested in her 1985 article differ from MacKinnon's? Although this approach has not yet emerged in any of the abortion cases in which now-Justice Ginsburg has participated on the Supreme Court, how might her presence there affect consideration of the issues presented in this jurisprudence?

4. The Voices Briefs represent a very different type of legal document, emerging from the stories women told of their own life experience, recounted in their own terms and not in the language of abstract legal doctrine. What do you think of breaking the bounds of accepted legal discourse in this fashion? Under what circumstances do you think it is or is not a good idea? One feminist legal scholar has argued that the only genuinely authentic form of feminist litigation is a dialogue based upon an understanding of the impact of abortion regulation upon women's well-being and of the interests at stake on each side of the issue. Ruth Colker, Feminist Litigation: An Oxymoron?—A Study of the Briefs Filed in *William L. Webster v. Reproduc-*

tive Health Services, 13 Harv.Women's L.J. 137 (1990). Could one effectively brief a case based on such a dialogue? How?

5. The Women of Color Brief also juxtaposes "real world" experience to abstract discussion of legal doctrine—in this case to the doctrine of "undue burden." This type of argument, demonstrating that a regulation like the requirement that abortions take place in the hospital, which may not seem burdensome unless viewed in context (real lack of access to hospitals by women living in rural areas or on Indian reservations), is a much more familiar type of legal argumentation, in the style of a "Brandeis brief" (so called after the brief filed by Brandeis in Muller v. Oregon, 208 U.S. 412, 28 S.Ct. 324, 52 L.Ed. 551 (1908), using statistical and sociological data to support upholding legislation limiting hours of women working in laundries by detailing the effects of working long hours on women and their families). Is this type of argument, about actual access to abortion services, likely to succeed in light of Harris v. McRae?

6. Is making abortion a top priority item on the feminist agenda a form of heterosexism?

7. Andrea Dworkin has said that birth control and abortion are another way of ensuring men access to women's sexuality. See Andrea Dworkin, Right–Wing Women 93–100 (1978). If male support for birth control and abortion is based on men's desire for heterosexual intercourse without any consequences, does it follow that women would be better off without birth control and abortion?

JUDITH JARVIS THOMSON, A DEFENSE OF ABORTION

1 Phil. & Pub. Aff. 48–49, 52–53, 59–62, 65–66 (1971).

I propose, then, that we grant that the fetus is a person from the moment of conception. How does the argument go from here? Something like this, I take it. Every person has a right to life. So the fetus has a right to life. No doubt the mother has a right to decide what shall happen in and to her body; everyone would grant that. But surely a person's right to life is stronger and more stringent than the mother's right to decide what happens in and to her body, and so outweighs it. So the fetus may not be killed; an abortion may not be performed.

It sounds plausible. But now let me ask you to imagine this. You wake up in the morning and find yourself back to back in bed with an unconscious violinist. A famous unconscious violinist. He has been found to have a fatal kidney ailment, and the Society of Music Lovers has canvassed all the available medical records and found that you alone have the right blood type to help. They have therefore kidnapped you, and last night the violinist's circulatory system was plugged into yours, so that your kidneys can be used to extract poisons from his blood as well as your own. The director of the hospital now tells you, "Look, we're sorry the Society of Music Lovers did this to you—we would never have permitted it if we had known. But still, they did it, and the violinist now is plugged into you. To unplug you would be to kill him. But never mind, it's only for nine months. By then he will have recovered from his ailment, and can safely be unplugged from you." Is it morally incumbent on you to accede to this situation? No doubt it would be very nice of you if you did, a great kindness. But do you *have* to accede to it? What if it were not nine months, but nine years? Or longer still? What if the director of the hospital says, "Tough luck, I agree, but you've now got to stay in bed, with the violinist plugged into you, for the rest of your life. Because remember this. All persons have a right to life, and violinists are persons. Granted you have a right to decide what happens in and to your body, but a person's right to life outweighs your right to decide what happens in and to your body. So you cannot ever be unplugged from him." I imagine you would regard this as outrageous, which suggests that something really is wrong with that plausible-sounding argument I mentioned a moment ago.

In this case, of course, you were kidnapped; you didn't volunteer for the operation that plugged the violinist into your kidneys. Can those who oppose abortion on the ground I mentioned make an exception for a pregnancy due to rape? Certainly. They can say that persons have a right to life only if they didn't come into existence because of rape; or they can say that all persons have a right to life, but that some have less of a right to life than others, in particular, that those who came into existence because of rape have less. But these statements have a rather unpleasant sound. Surely the question of whether you have a right to life at all, or how much of it you have, shouldn't turn on the question of whether or not you are the product of a rape. And in fact the people who oppose abortion on the ground I mentioned do not make this distinction, and hence do not make an exception in case of rape.

* * *

The main focus of attention in writings on abortion has been on what a third party may or may not do in answer to a request from a woman for an abortion. This is in a way understandable. Things being as they are, there isn't much a woman can safely do to abort herself. So the question asked is what a third party may do, and what the mother may do, if it is mentioned at all, is deduced, almost as an afterthought, from what it is concluded that third parties may do. But it seems to me that to treat the matter in this way is to refuse to grant to the mother that very status of person which is so firmly insisted on for the fetus. For we cannot simply read off what a person may do from what a third party may do. Suppose you find yourself trapped in a tiny house with a growing child. I mean a very tiny house, and a rapidly growing child—you are already up against the wall of the house and in a few minutes you'll be crushed to death. The child on the other hand won't be crushed to death; if nothing is done to stop him from growing he'll be hurt, but in the end he'll simply burst open the house and walk out a free man. Now I could well understand it if a bystander were to say, "There's nothing we can do for you. We cannot choose between your life and his, we cannot be the ones to decide who is to live, we cannot intervene." But it cannot be concluded that you too can do nothing, that you cannot attack it to save your life. However innocent the child may be, you do not have to wait passively while it crushes you to death. Perhaps a pregnant woman is vaguely felt to have the status of house, to which we don't allow the right of self-defense. But if the woman houses the child, it should be remembered that she is a person who houses it.

* * *

In sum, a woman surely can defend her life against the threat to it posed by the unborn child, even if doing so involves its death. * * *

* * *

There is room for yet another argument here, however. We surely must all grant that there may be cases in which it would be morally indecent to detach a person from your body at the cost of his life. Suppose you learn that what the violinist needs is not nine years of your life, but only one hour: all you need do to save his life is to spend one hour in that bed with him. Suppose also that letting him use your kidneys for that one hour would not affect your health in the slightest. Admittedly you were kidnapped. Admittedly you did not give anyone permission to plug him into you. Nevertheless it seems to me plain you *ought* to allow him to use your kidneys for that hour—it would be indecent to refuse.

Again, suppose pregnancy lasted only an hour, and constituted no threat to life or health. And suppose that a woman becomes pregnant as a result of rape. Admittedly she did not voluntarily do anything to bring about the existence of a child. Admittedly she did nothing at all which would give the unborn person a right to the use of her body. All the same it might well be said, as in the newly emended violinist story, that she *ought* to allow it to remain for that hour—that it would be indecent in her to refuse.

* * *

So my own view is that even though you ought to let the violinist use your kidneys for the one hour he needs, we should not conclude that he has a right to do so—we should say that if you refuse, you are, like the boy who owns all the chocolates and will give none away, self-centered and callous, indecent in fact, but not unjust. And similarly, that even supposing a case in which a woman pregnant due to rape ought to allow the unborn person to use her body for the hour he needs, we should not conclude that he has a right to do so; we should conclude that she is self-centered, callous, indecent, but not unjust, if she refuses. The complaints are no less grave; they are just different. However, there is no need to insist on this point. If anyone does wish to deduce "he has a right" from "you ought," then all the same he must surely grant that there are cases in which it is not morally required of you that you allow that violinist to use your kidneys, and in which he does not have a right to use them, and in which you do not do him an injustice if you refuse. And so also for mother and unborn child. Except in such cases as the unborn person has a right to demand it—and we were leaving open the possibility that there may be such cases—nobody is morally *required* to make large sacrifices, of health, of all other interests and concerns, of all other duties and commitments, for nine years, or even for nine months, in order to keep another person alive.

* * *

My argument will be found unsatisfactory on two counts by many of those who want to regard abortion as morally permissible. First, while I do argue that abortion is not impermissible, I do not argue that it is always permissible. There may well be cases in which carrying the child to term requires only Minimally Decent Samaritanism of the mother, and this is a standard we must not fall below. I am inclined to think it a merit of my account precisely that it does *not* give a general yes or a general no. It allows for and supports our sense that, for example, a sick and desperately frightened fourteen-year-old schoolgirl, pregnant due to rape, may *of course* choose abortion, and that any law which rules this out is an insane law. And it also allows for and supports our sense that in other cases resort to abortion is even positively indecent. It would be indecent in the woman to request an abortion, and indecent in a doctor to perform it, if she is in her seventh month, and wants the abortion just to avoid the nuisance of postponing a trip abroad. The very fact that the arguments I have been drawing attention to treat all cases of abortion, or even all cases of abortion in which the mother's life is not at stake, as morally on a par ought to have made them suspect at the outset.

Notes on Abortion and Self-Defense

1. What do you think of Thomson's argument about the morality of abortion and, in particular, the circumstances when it is not morally acceptable? (Note that the "famous violinist" article was written before Roe v. Wade.) Are there limits, based upon your own moral standards, that you would place on the times and/or reasons a woman should exercise this right? What are they? To what extent do you think that those limits should be embodied in the law? If those limits—and your underlying moral standards—are based upon religious beliefs, does this pose any problems under the First Amendment?

2. Ellen Willis makes a more straightforward argument for abortion based on self-defense:

> * * * Most people would agree * * * that killing in defense of one's life or safety is not murder. And most would accept a concept of self-defense that includes the right to fight a defensive war or revolution in behalf of one's independence or freedom from oppression. * * * The point is that it's impossible to judge whether an act is murder simply by looking at the act, without considering its context. Which is to say that it makes no sense to discuss whether abortion is murder without considering why women have abortions and what it means to force women to bear children they don't want.

> We live in a society that defines childrearing as the mother's job; a society in which most women are denied access to work that pays enough to support a family, childcare facilities they can afford, or any relief from the constant, daily burdens of motherhood; a society that forces mothers into dependence on marriage or welfare and often into permanent poverty * * *. Under these conditions the unwillingly pregnant woman faces a terrifying loss of control over her fate. * * * However gratifying pregnancy may be to a woman who desires it, for the unwilling it is literally an invasion * * *. Clearly, abortion is by normal standards an act of self-defense.

Ellen Willis, Abortion: Is a Woman a Person?, in Powers of Desire: The Politics of Sexuality 471, 473 (Ann Snitow, Christine Stansell, and Sharon Thompson, eds. 1983). What are the elements of the law of self-defense? Do they "fit" the abortion situation? Even if self-defense does fit it, Sylvia Law asks whether the analogy can realistically be extended beyond "the limited circumstances in which the mother reasonably believes that she will suffer death or great bodily harm. Further, even if it is legally justifiable to kill an innocent person who threatens our life or well-being, the morality of such killing seems dubious." Sylvia A. Law, Rethinking Sex and the Constitution, 132 U. Pa. L. Rev. 955, 1022 (1984). Law thus questions the usefulness of self-defense as a basis upon which to defend the right to abortion, while supporting it on other grounds. For other situations in which women have sought to use the law of self-defense and sometimes encountered difficulty, see the discussion of women who kill their abusers in Chapter 5.

3. Eileen McDonagh claims that introducing the notion of consent to pregnancy, and distinguishing it from consent to intercourse, may provide a route out of the irreconcilable arguments in the abortion debate. McDonagh, Breaking the Abortion Deadlock: From Choice To Consent (1996). She argues for a theory of the right to abortion based not upon choice and privacy but instead upon consent to pregnancy, analogizing the intrusion of the fetus to other bodily intrusions, such as rape, which justify a right to self-defense. Thus McDonagh accepts the anti-abortion movement's argument that the fetus is a form of human life but argues that its implanting itself is the direct cause of pregnancy; "if it makes a woman pregnant without her consent, it severely violates her bodily integrity and liberty." Id. at 6. The fetus, in short, is analogized to an assailant, and the right to abortion becomes simply a variant of the right under liberal theory to defend oneself against nonconsenual invasion. The woman may choose to be altruistic and nurture the fetus for nine months, or she may defend herself against the massive bodily changes, risks, and intrusions of pregnancy by using deadly force against it. This changes the terms of the debate away from an emphasis upon negative freedom from the state (privacy doctrine) to "a woman's right to the assistance of the state to stop the fetus as a private party from intruding on her bodily integrity and liberty without consent," thus mandating public funding of abortion as well. Id. How do you react to this argument? Does it offer hope, as McDonagh claims, of breaking the impasse between the absolutist positions in the abortion debate? See Robin West, Liberalism and Abortion, 87 Geo. L.J. 2117 (1999) (reviewing McDonagh's arguments and describing the limitations of both analogical thinking and of liberal constitutionalism in relation to abortion).

4. What is the rationale underlying the exception for abortions in the case of rape or incest? Does non-consent capture the whole story? Is the story then a consistent one? Reva Siegel suggests that popular support for rape and incest exceptions from abortion statutes rests on normative judgments that ordinarily pregnancy is the "sexual fault" of the woman. Siegel, Reasoning from the Body: A Historical Perspective on Abortion Regulation and Questions of Equal Protection, 44 Stan. L. Rev. 261, 361 (1992). For those who consider abortion to be murder, isn't it inconsistent to permit it under any circumstances?

5. Reva Siegel describes abortion-restrictive regulation as the use of public power to force women to bear children. Siegel, note 4 above, at 277. Can you think how one might develop legal arguments based on the idea that prohibiting abortion is compelling childbirth? Andrew Koppelman suggests that the Thirteenth Amendment, which prohibits slavery, might be used for this purpose. Andrew Koppelman, Forced Labor: A Thirteenth Amendment Defense of Abortion, 84 Nw. U.L. Rev. 480 (1990). What do you think of this suggestion?

AMICUS BRIEF OF 274 ORGANIZATIONS IN SUPPORT OF *ROE v. WADE,* IN *TURNOCK v. RAGSDALE*

Nos. 88–790 and 88–805 (1989).

[This amicus brief was written by law professors Kathleen M. Sullivan and Susan R. Estrich in a case challenging regulations restricting abortion; the case was ultimately settled before argument in the Supreme Court.]

* * *

Because abortion restrictions both discriminate uniquely against women, and do so in a way that intrudes on women's basic interests in bodily integrity, procreation, and health, such laws should trigger strict scrutiny.

A. Sex Classifications That Interfere With Bodily Integrity and Procreation Are Impermissible in the Absence of Compelling Justification.

This Court has held that measures classifying on the basis of gender are unconstitutional unless the party supporting the measure can "carry the burden of showing an 'exceedingly persuasive justification' for the classification." Mississippi University for Women v. Hogan, 458 U.S. 718, 724 (1982). A "searching analysis" is required because gender-based measures often reflect the "mechanical application," of " 'old notions' and 'archaic and overbroad' generalizations," and operate to "put women not on a pedestal, but in a cage." Thus, this Court has repeatedly struck down legislation that restricted the exercise by both men and women of liberty in social roles, recognizing that "[n]o longer is the female destined solely for the home and the rearing of family, and only the male for the marketplace and the world of ideas."

Exacting as it is, this scrutiny escalates to the highest level where, as here, legislation that discriminates on the basis of gender also intrudes on basic interests in bodily integrity, procreation, health, family, and sometimes life itself. The "fundamental rights" branch of equal protection jurisprudence makes clear that, where legislation classifies with respect to such basic interests, any deference that would otherwise be given the legislature attenuates. Rather, such legislation may be upheld only if it survives the strictest and most searching kind of review. Thus, in Skinner v. Oklahoma, 316 U.S. 535, this Court applied strict scrutiny under the Equal Protection Clause to a compulsory sterilization law that discriminated among categories of thieves—a kind of line-drawing that otherwise would not have been suspect. * * * If cases such as Skinner * * * treat impact on the fundamental rights to procreate and to marry as escalating the standard of review from minimal to strict, then surely the impingement of abortion laws on procreation, health, marriage, and family interests should escalate judicial scrutiny the lesser distance from heightened to strict review. Thus, the gender-based discrimination worked by restrictive abortion laws should be reviewed strictly.

B. RESTRICTIVE ABORTION LAWS CLASSIFY ON THE BASIS OF SEX.

The direct impact of abortion restrictions falls, exclusively, on a class of people that consists only of women. Only women get pregnant; only women have abortions; only women will be forced to endure unwanted pregnancies and adverse health consequences if abortions are restricted; only women are injured by dangerous, illegal abortions where legal ones are unavailable; and only women will bear children if abortions are unavailable.

The fact that the laws do not mention "women" is irrelevant. A law restricting "all abortions" is the precise equivalent of a law restricting "all abortions sought by women." A classification based on pregnancy is, by biological definition, a classification based on gender.

* * *

Moreover, abortion restrictions, like the most classic gender-based restrictions on women seeking to participate in the worlds of work and ideas, have historically rested on archaic stereotypes of women as persons whose "paramount destiny and mission ... [is] to fulfill the noble and benign office of wife and mother." Bradwell v. Illinois, 16 Wall. 130, 142 (1873) (Bradley, J., concurring). Legislation prohibiting abortion, largely a product of the years between 1860 and 1880, reflected precisely the same ideas about the natural and proper role of women as did the legislation of the same period—long-since discredited—that prohibited women from serving on juries or participating in the professions, including the practice of law.

Perhaps not surprisingly, modern studies have found that support for laws banning abortion continues to be an outgrowth of the same sort of stereotypical notions that women's only appropriate roles are those of mother and housewife; in many cases, such laws have emerged as a direct reaction to the increasing number of women who work outside the home. See generally K. Luker, Abortion and the Politics of Motherhood 192–215 (1984). It is, of course, precisely such stereotypes, as they are reflected in legislation, that have over and over again been the focus of this Court's modern equal protection cases.

C. The Political Process Is Inadequate to Protect Access to Abortion for All Women.

* * * This Court has long interpreted the Equal Protection Clause to require even-handedness in legislation, lest the powerful few too casually trade away for others key liberties that they are careful to reserve for themselves. For example, the Court once struck down under the Equal Protection Clause a law permitting castration of recidivist chicken thieves but sparing white-collar embezzlers the knife. Skinner v. Oklahoma, 316 U.S. 535. The implication of Skinner was that, put to an all-or-nothing choice, legislators would rather sterilize no one than jeopardize people like themselves. Thus equality serves as a backstop to liberty.

Every restrictive abortion law has been passed by a legislature in which men constitute a numerical majority. And every restrictive abortion law, by definition, contains an unwritten clause exempting all men from its strictures. To rely on state legislatures to protect women against "abortion regulation reminiscent of the dark ages," Webster, 109 S.Ct. at 3058, ignores the fact that the overwhelming majority of "those who serve in such bodies," like the Oklahoma legislators who supported sterilization for workingmen's crimes, are not directly affected at all by the penalties they are imposing. It is precisely in such cases that strict scrutiny is required, to protect against the very real danger that those in power will too casually impose burdens on others, in this case on women, that they would not have imposed upon themselves.

That is particularly so where, as here, the women most likely to be affected are those whom the political process protects least well. A world without Roe will not be a world without abortion, but a world in which abortion is accessible according to one's constitutional caste. While affluent women will travel to jurisdictions where safe and legal abortion is available, paying whatever is required, restrictive abortion laws—and, with them, the life-threatening prospect of the back-alley abortion—will disproportionately descend upon "those without . . . adequate resources" to avoid them. Griswold, 381 U.S. at 503 (White, J., concurring). Those for whom the burdens of an unwanted pregnancy may be the most crushing—the young, the poor, women whose color already renders them victims of discrimination—will be the ones least able to secure a safe abortion.

In the years prior to Roe, "[p]oor and minority women were virtually precluded from obtaining safe, legal procedures, the overwhelming majority of which were obtained by white women in the private hospital services on psychiatric indications."[28] Women denied access to safe and legal abortions often had dangerous and illegal ones. Mishandled criminal abortions were, one detailed study found, the principal cause of maternal deaths in the 1960's, and mortality rates for African–American women were as much as nine times higher than for white women. In 1972, women of color accounted for sixty-four percent of the deaths associated with illegal abortions in this country.

To trust the political process to protect these women is to ignore completely the lessons of history. Time and again, this Court has recognized its special duties to protect minorities whose rights can too easily be trampled by legislative majorities. For in such cases, there are no political checks: legislators can, without difficulty, "escape the political retribution that might be visited upon them if larger numbers were affected." Railway Express Agency v. New York, 336 U.S. 106, 112–13 (1949) (Jackson, J., concurring). Or, if people like them were affected.

Notes on Equal Protection

1. As we have seen above, the Court in Roe v. Wade rested the right to abortion upon a fundamental right to privacy; and some of its defenders, notably the American Civil Liberties Union's Reproductive Rights Project, insist upon defending it on privacy grounds alone. Many feminists think that is a mistake, both because the foundation of privacy has turned out to be somewhat shaky and because it reinforces the public/private distinction which has not served women well. See, e.g., Catharine A. MacKinnon, Privacy v. Equality, excerpted above, in Feminism Unmodified, at 93–102. The brief above is an attempt to defend the right to abortion while resting it upon grounds of equality instead. What are the advantages and disadvantages of basing legal arguments for abortion on equal protection rather than upon privacy? Are they likely to succeed, given the current state of equal protection law as applied to women? See Chapter 2. What are the differences between abortion and sterilization in this respect? Does it help or hurt the argument for abortion to link the two issues, as done in the brief above?

2. Other commentators suggest that it is necessary to revision equal protection law before it will work for women in this context. Reva Siegel suggests, for example, that abortion-restrictive regulation must be seen as caste legislation, a mode of regulating women's conduct to compel them to perform the work that has traditionally defined their subordinate social role and status, both within the home and in the workplace. Siegel, Reasoning from the Body: A Historical Perspective on Abortion Regulation and Questions of Equal Protection, 44 Stan. L. Rev. 261, 351 (1992). How is the rape exception an example of a legislative determination based on one of these assumptions?

3. In this chapter, we have examined at least four different approaches to abortion, based on (1) a constitutional right to privacy (Roe v. Wade and its progeny), (2) the real world, "felt" experiences of women, (3) self-defense,

28. Polgar & Fried, The Bad Old Days: Clandestine Abortions Among the Poor in New York City Before Liberalization of the Abortion Law, 8 Fam.Plan.Persp. 125 (1976). * * *

and (4) equal protection. In addition, Robin West argues for a right to reproductive freedom and abortion based upon an ethic of care:

> [R]eproductive freedom, and the abortion rights that at least in the short term must be a part of that freedom, particularly given the continuing climate of hostility toward children and their caretakers that exists in this culture, is a necessary prerequisite for nurturant relationships between the pregnant woman and the fetus, as well as between the mother and child, which an ethic of care seeks to encourage. Without that freedom, the "relationship" is one of nonconsensual servitude, not nurturant, interdependent care. Reproductive freedom is as necessary to nurturance, in other words, as it is to an abstract consistency between the choice of men and women in this culture.
>
> If this is right, then two consequences follow for our constitutional jurisprudence. First, the case for reproductive freedom ought to be cast as precisely that—the case for reproductive *freedom*. As numerous feminists have now pointed out, it should not be cast as an argument for abortion "rights" grounded in an abstract concern for sexual "privacy"—an argument which almost blithely, and indeed almost cruelly, ignores the degree to which sexual privacy has meant, for women, only that their sexual violation is shielded from public scrutiny and legal compensation by a wall of secrecy and privilege. But nor should it be grounded in an equally abstract concern for formal gender equality—which *also* blithely ignores the degree to which women's reproductive nurturant practices, including the practice of nurturing fetal life—is constitutive of the ethic of care.
>
> * * * [R]eproductive freedom might better be viewed, consistently with the nurturant practices at the heart of the ethic of care, as a necessary *positive* liberty to secure women's and children's well-being, and the nurturant practices and values that secure them. If we want nurturant relationships between parents and children to be a part of our social world, and hence a part of the positive liberty each individual is entitled to possess in order to participate in that social world, then we must allow women the freedom to choose to terminate or carry a pregnancy to term. The justification for this freedom, in other words, does not stem from a right to violate or abandon fetal life consistently with men's apparent inclination to do so. It must stem, rather, from a right to create materially secure, consensual, and safe nurturant relationships.

West, Caring for Justice 72–74 (1997). How is West's argument different from arguments based on privacy, self-defense, or equality?

4. West's position includes the argument that children will be best cared for by mothers who can control when their children are born. In fact, the availability of abortion appears to affect not the decision whether to have children so much as the timing of their births. A 1994–1995 national survey of 9,985 abortion patients shows that women who have had a child are more likely to have an abortion than those who have never had a child and that 66% of women who have had an abortion intend to have more children. Stanley K. Henshaw and Kathryn Kost, Abortion Patients in 1994–1995: Characteristics and Contraceptive Use, 28 Family Planning Perspectives 140,

142–44 (1996). (Interestingly, Catholics are as likely as other women in the general population to have an abortion. Id.) Several studies also show that the availability of abortion in a nation or U.S. state correlates positively with that nation's or state's generous social provisions for children. The nations with the most liberal abortion laws include those with the most extensive provisions for child welfare as well. Katha Pollitt, Anti–Choice, Anti–Child, The Nation, Nov. 15, 1999, at 10. Similarly, a 50–state study shows that the U.S. states with the most restrictive abortion laws are also the least likely to provide support for services to children. Jean Reith Schroedel, Is the Fetus a Person?: A Comparison of Policies Across the Fifty States 153–56 (2000). What do you think explains this seeming anomaly?

5. How do the different approaches summarized in note 3 above compare with, or rely upon, the differing feminist theories presented in Chapter 3? For example, is the Voices Brief an example of relational feminism? Where do MacKinnon's views about abortion fit into these categories? Is Judith Jarvis Thomson a formal equality theorist? What about Estrich and Sullivan, in the excerpt above? What would be the approach of a pragmatic feminist? A socialist feminist?

5. FEMINISM AND OPPOSITION TO ABORTION

ELIZABETH FOX–GENOVESE, FEMINISM WITHOUT ILLUSIONS: A CRITIQUE OF INDIVIDUALISM

83–85 (1991).

It is not easy to reconcile the feminist metaphors of motherhood and community with the feminist defense of abortion on the grounds of absolute individual right. Surely, the special sense of human connection and nurture that so many feminists attribute to women derives primarily from women's special roles as the bearers and rearers of children. Jennifer Nedelsky has thus recently proposed that feminists reconceptualize the ideal of autonomy to ground it in child rearing.[87] Sara Ruddick has suggested that all women differ from men in their propensity to "maternal thinking."[88] Either abortion entails the killing of babies or it does not. If it does, then there are no legitimate grounds for allowing it, not even rape or incest. If it does not, then there are only the narrowest of pragmatic grounds for preventing it. The problem remains: Are we dealing with two lives or one? No precedent in individualist theory helps us to understand the issue, for the men upon whom individualism was predicated do not bear children.

It is not easy to reconcile the defense of women's rights to abortion on the grounds of privacy with sustained attempts on the part of the women's movement to break down other aspects of what was traditionally viewed as the privacy of the family. Most of us applaud the state's growing willingness to help to protect women and children against sexual or physical abuse by husbands and fathers. But only very recently

87. Nedelsky, "Reconceiving Autonomy."

88. Ruddick, "Maternal Thinking."

would all interference between a man and a wife have been viewed as an invasion of privacy. In effect, the defense of a woman's right to abortion as a matter of privacy represents a decisive reinforcement of the extreme individualistic view of society as composed of atomized individuals. More frighteningly, by implicitly identifying reproduction as a woman's individual right, it dismisses men's claims and dissolves their responsibilities to the next generation.

Abortion challenges feminists to come to terms with the contradictions in their own thought, notably the contradiction between the commitment to community and nurture and the commitment to individual right. Without doubt, the easiest way would be to reach some determination about our collective definition of life. Most Americans would probably accept a definition of life linked to the notion of viability and accept abortion on demand up to the twentieth week of pregnancy. Without some such agreement on the definition of life, the right to abortion opens the specter of any individual's right to kill those who depend upon her and drain her resources—elderly parents, terminally ill or handicapped children. Without some such agreement, the right to abortion—the woman's rights to sexual self-determination—can logically lead to the right to murder with impunity. How are we to link women as the embodiments of "maternal thinking" with such a position?

* * *

Abortion confronts us with a collective social, economic, political, and moral problem that we can only solve collectively and in frank acknowledgment that no solution will escape intellectual inconsistencies and some unresolved moral tensions. Abortion forces us to recognize provision for children as a collective responsibility. Increasingly, the responsibility for children penalizes women by curtailing their social and economic opportunities. By forcing women to bear and rear children they do not want and for whom they cannot adequately provide, society is pitting women's lives against children's and consigning women to social and economic marginality. But the difficulty and sacrifice do not constitute a moral, or even a political, justification for abortion. They constitute a justification for enhanced medical and educational programs for all children and hence for the acceptance of collective principles.

AMICUS BRIEF OF FEMINISTS FOR LIFE, IN *BRAY v. ALEXANDRIA WOMEN'S HEALTH CLINIC*

No. 90–985 (1991).

* * *

One reason for the continuing controversy concerning abortion on demand is that a majority of American women do not agree with respondents' underlying assumption that equal protection under the Fourteenth Amendment requires unlimited abortion on demand. A recent poll conducted by the Gallup Organization revealed that there is no "gender gap" on abortion: indeed, women are as likely, and in some cases, more likely than men to oppose abortion. For example, only 17 percent of women and 20 percent of men believe that an abortion is acceptable, even during the first trimester, if the pregnancy was unplanned and would interrupt a woman's career. A mere 7 percent of women and 11 percent of men believe a first trimester abortion is acceptable as a means of birth control. Only 26 percent of women and 30 percent of men believe first trimester abortion is acceptable if continuing the pregnancy would require a teenager to drop out of school, and 20 percent of women and 30 percent of men approve of abortion where the birth of a child would create a financial burden. And 53 percent of women and 47 percent of men believe the unborn child's "right to be born" outweighs, at the moment of conception, the woman's "right to choose" whether she wants to have a child.

* * *

The broader dispute over abortion is manifested by a division in feminist theory over whether "women can [ ] ever achieve the fulfillment of feminist goals in a society permissive toward abortion." Callahan, Abortion & the Sexual Agenda, Commonweal 232, 232 (April 25, 1986). Respondent N.O.W. holds that abortion is essential to their notion of the feminist agenda. Many others, including, in fact, a majority of American women, hold that a more encompassing and truly feminist vision of justice demands protection for the unborn child. Id. at 234. A contrast is sometimes drawn in feminist theory between "cultural" feminists, who emphasize the importance of women in the creation and nurturing of human life, and "radical" feminists, who identify this very role as the source of oppression of women.[26] These contrary views of feminism offer different conclusions on whether abortion is necessary for the social and political emancipation of women, and whether opposition to abortion is, per se, discrimination against women. Bayles, Feminism and Abortion, The Atlantic Monthly 83, 85 (April 1990).

KRISTIN LUKER, ABORTION AND THE POLITICS OF MOTHERHOOD

193, 199–200, 206–07, 209–10 (1984).

* * * [T]he abortion debate has become a debate about women's contrasting obligations to themselves and others. New technologies and the changing nature of work have opened up possibilities for women outside of the home undreamed of in the nineteenth century; together, these changes give women—for the first time in history—the option of deciding exactly how and when their family roles will fit into the larger context of their lives. In essence, therefore, this round of the abortion debate is so passionate and hard-fought *because it is a referendum on the place and meaning of motherhood.*

* * *

26. See West, Jurisprudence and Gender, 55 U.Chi.L.Rev. 1, 13 (1989); MacKinnon, Feminism, Marxism, Method, and the State: Toward Feminist Jurisprudence, 8 Signs: Journal of Women in Culture and Society 635, 636, n. 4 (1983).

For example, pro-life women have *always* valued family roles very highly and have arranged their lives accordingly. They did not acquire high-level educational and occupational skills, for example, because they married, and they married because their values suggested that this would be the most satisfying life open to them. Similarly, pro-choice women postponed (or avoided) marriage and family roles because they chose to acquire the skills they needed to be successful in the larger world, having concluded that the role of wife and mother was too limited for them. Thus, activists on both sides of the issue are women who have a given set of values about what are the most satisfying and appropriate roles for women, and they have made *life commitments that now limit their ability to change their minds.* Women who have many children and little education, for example, are seriously handicapped in attempting to become doctors or lawyers; women who have reached their late forties with few children or none are limited in their ability to build (or rebuild) a family. For most of these activists, therefore, their position on abortion is the "tip of the iceberg," a shorthand way of supporting and proclaiming not only a complex set of values but a given set of social resources as well.

* * *

It is stating the obvious to point out that the more limited the educational credentials a woman has, the more limited the job opportunities are for her, and the more limited the job opportunities, the more attractive motherhood is as a full-time occupation. In motherhood, one can control the content and pace of one's own work, and the job is *intrinsically meaningful.* Compared with a job clerking in a supermarket (a realistic alternative for women with limited educational credentials) where the work is poorly compensated and often demeaning, motherhood can have compensations that far transcend the monetary ones. As one woman described mothering: "You have this little, rough uncut diamond, and you're the artist shaping and cutting that diamond, and bringing out the lights . . . that's a great challenge."

All the circumstances of her existence will therefore encourage a pro-life woman to highlight the kinds of values and experiences that support childbearing and childrearing and to discount the attraction (such as it is) of paid employment. Her circumstances encourage her to resent the pro-choice view that women's most meaningful and prestigious activities are in the "man's world."

Abortion also has a symbolic dimension that separates the needs and interests of homemakers and workers in the paid labor force. Insofar as abortion allows a woman to get a job, to get training for a job, or to advance in a job, it does more than provide social support for working women over homemakers; it also seems to support the value of economic considerations over moral ones. Many pro-life people interviewed said that although their commitment to traditional family roles meant very real material deprivations to themselves and their families, the moral benefits of such a choice more than made up for it.

* * *

Pro-life people and pro-life women in particular have very real reasons to fear such a state of affairs. Not only do they see an achievement-based world as harsh, superficial, and ultimately ruthless; they are relatively less well-equipped to operate in that world. A considerable amount of social science research has suggested, at least in the realm of medical treatment, that there is an increasing tendency to judge people by their official (achieved) worth. Pro-life people have relatively fewer official achievements in part because they have been doing what they see as a moral task, namely, raising children and making a home; and they see themselves as becoming handicapped in a world that discounts not only their social contributions but their personal lives as well.

* * *

But pro-life women, like all women, are facing a devaluation of these resources. As American society increasingly becomes a service economy, men can buy the services that a wife traditionally offers. Cooking, cleaning, decorating, and the like can easily be purchased on the open market in a cash transaction. And as sex becomes more open, more casual, and more "amative," it removes one more resource that could previously be obtained only through marriage.

Pro-life women, as we have seen, have both the value orientations and social characteristics that make marriage very important. Their alternatives in the public world of work are, on the whole, less attractive. Furthermore, women who stay home full-time and keep house are becoming a financial luxury. Only very wealthy families *or families whose values allow them to place the nontangible benefits of a full-time wife over the tangible benefits of a working wife* can afford to keep one of its earners off the labor market. To pro-life people, the nontangible benefit of having children—and therefore the value of procreative sex—is very important. Thus, a social ethic that promotes more freely available sex undercuts pro-life women two ways: it limits their abilities to get into a marriage in the first place, and it undermines the social value placed on their presence once within a marriage.

For pro-choice women, the situation is reversed. Because they have access to "male" resources such as education and income, they have far less reason to believe that the basic reason for sexuality is to produce children. They plan to have small families anyway, and they and their husbands come from and have married into a social class in which small families are the norm. For a number of overlapping reasons, therefore, pro-choice women believe that the value of sex is not primarily procreative: pro-choice women value the ability of sex to promote human intimacy more (or at least more frequently) than they value the ability of sex to produce babies. But they hold this view because they can afford to. When they bargain for marriage, they use the same resources that they use in the labor market: upper-class status, an education very similar to a man's, side-by-side participation in the man's world, and, not least, a salary that substantially increases a family's standard of living.

It is true, therefore, that pro-life people are "anti-sex." They value sex, of course, but they value it for its traditional benefits (babies) rather than for the benefits that pro-choice people associate with it (intimacy). Pro-life people really do want to see "less" sexuality—or at least less open and socially unregulated sexuality—because they think it is morally wrong, they think it distorts the meaning of sex, and they feel that it *threatens the basis on which their own marital bargains are built.*

Notes on Feminist Opposition to Abortion

1. Does changing the terms of the abortion argument to emphasize abortion as a right flowing from the Equal Protection Clause rather than from the right of privacy address any of the issues raised by Elizabeth Fox–Genovese in the excerpt above? To what extent? What about grounding abortion rights in an ethic of care, as suggested by Robin West in the excerpt included in the notes to the previous section?

2. Is the right to abortion, as Fox–Genovese argues, a slippery slope leading to euthanasia for elderly and handicapped persons? Why or why not? If not, how can you be sure? Does this trouble you?

3. Based upon your reading in this course, do you think it is fair to say that radical feminists see motherhood as a source of oppression, while relational feminists see it as a source of strength? What do you think? Does it depend at all upon the social and political conditions surrounding childbirth and childrearing? In what ways?

4. Elizabeth Fox–Genovese suggests in the excerpt above that a pro-choice stance is inconsistent with the tenets of relational feminism. Linda C. McClain points out, however, that Carol Gilligan and Robin West strongly support the right to abortion, while the more striking convergence of themes—abortion as supportive of irresponsible men's sexual access to women and as necessitated by a society that does not accommodate the needs of pregnant women and mothers—is between Feminists for Life arguments and those of radical feminists like MacKinnon and Dworkin. McClain, Equality, Oppression, and Abortion: Women Who Oppose Abortion Rights in the Name of Feminism, in Feminist Nightmares: Women At Odds: Feminism and the Problem of Sisterhood 165 (Susan Ostrov Weisser and Jennifer Fleischner, eds. 1994). With which do you agree? Is the Feminists for Life position more in tune with the theoretical foundations of relational feminism or of radical feminism? Is there any common ground based upon these similarities?

5. One difference between the anti-abortion movement in the 19th century and now is that the modern anti-abortion movement consists primarily of women. See Luker, excerpt above, at 194. How do you explain the fact that so many women oppose abortion? Yet the leaders of the anti-abortion movement are predominantly male. See James Risen and Judy L.

Thomas, Wrath of Angels: The American Abortion War 120, 219, 296 (1998). Why? Marilyn Frye suggests that abortion is particularly threatening to men, and thus to male-identified women (whom she calls "patriarchal loyalists"), because it is an example of a woman's willingness to separate from a being that is dependent on her:

> The woman who is free to see the fetus as a parasite might be free to see the man as a parasite. * * * The woman who is capable (legally, psychologically, physically) of decisively, self-interestedly, independently rejecting the one parasite, is capable of rejecting, with the same decisiveness and independence, the like burden of the other parasite. In the eyes of the other parasite, the image of the wholly self-determined abortion, involving not even a ritual submission to male veto power, is the mirror image of death.

Frye, The Politics of Reality: Essays in Feminist Theory 100–01 (1983). Is there any truth to this argument? On what do you base your conclusions about its cogency?

6. Some feminists might say that an anti-abortion feminist is an oxymoron. What do you think?

7. Kristin Luker's research shows that activists on both sides of the abortion question are in effect representing their own self-interest: pro-choice activists are drawn primarily from upper-income, educated women who are employed, many of them as professionals, while anti-abortion activists tend to be lower-income women with less formal education, who are homemakers. Luker, excerpt above, at 194–97. If so, is there any common ground upon which the two groups can meet? Do the facts about the differing class and cultural backgrounds of the two groups suggest any ways in which the debate might be changed in order to make it more fruitful and less divisive? For a variety of perspectives on the nature of the abortion debate in this country, see, e.g., Faye D. Ginsburg, Contested Lives: The Abortion Debate in an American Community (1989) (viewing the debate as over the meaning of women's lives and the role of nurturance and arguing that the opposing sides have a common interest in helping women with unplanned pregnancies); Laurence H. Tribe, Abortion: The Clash of Absolutes (1990) (arguing that the debate's current focus on "absolutes"—women's right to liberty versus the fetus' right to life—is oversimplified and counterproductive and suggesting that both sides should work toward a world of only wanted pregnancies); Ruth Colker, Abortion & Dialogue: Pro–Choice, Pro–Life, and American Law (1992) (calling for a reshaping of the conversation toward a focus on both sides' interest in love and life and the creation of social conditions which allow women both a meaningful choice and life); Eileen L. McDonagh, Breaking the Abortion Deadlock: From Choice to Consent (1996) (arguing that deadlock can be broken by viewing fetus as the cause of pregnancy and thus changing the terms of the debate from privacy and choice to focus upon the woman's consent to pregnancy and a related right to self-defense).

D. "COCAINE BABIES" AND THE "PREGNANCY POLICE"

DAWN E. JOHNSEN, NOTE, THE CREATION OF FETAL RIGHTS: CONFLICTS WITH WOMEN'S CONSTITUTIONAL RIGHTS TO LIBERTY, PRIVACY, AND EQUAL PROTECTION

95 Yale L.J. 599, 604–09, 613, 615–17, 620, 624–25 (1986).

[When she wrote this article, Dawn Johnsen was the Legal Director of the National Abortion Rights Action League.]

* * *

Conceptualizing the fetus as an entity with legal rights independent of the pregnant woman has made possible the future creation of fetal rights that could be used against the pregnant woman. In some instances, this potential has already been realized.

* * *

In one such case, a Michigan court held that a child could sue his mother for taking tetracycline during her pregnancy, allegedly resulting in the discoloration of the child's teeth.[18] The court stated that the appropriate standard for liability was that of the "reasonable" pregnant woman. Another court has suggested that a woman may be sued by her child for not preventing its birth if she had prior knowledge of the probability of its being born "defective."[20] In some states, a woman can be deprived of custody of her child even before its birth if the state feels that her actions during pregnancy endanger the fetus. In Michigan, a state whose laws do not expressly extend to "prenatal abuse," a court held that evidence of a woman's prenatal "abuse" or "neglect" could be considered during proceedings instituted by the state to deprive her of custody of her newborn child.[22] The court further held that this evidence could be obtained by reviewing the woman's medical records without her consent, records whose confidentiality was protected by both federal and state statutes. * * * Perhaps most alarmingly, states have taken direct injunctive action against pregnant women. Courts have seized custody of fetuses (i.e., of pregnant women) in order to enjoin women from taking drugs that are potentially harmful to fetuses. * * *

[A]bsent an increased awareness of the costs to women's autonomy, these rights will almost certainly continue to expand. Given the fetus's complete physical dependence on and interrelatedness with the body of the woman, virtually every act of the pregnant woman has some effect on the fetus. A woman could be held civilly or criminally liable for fetal

18. Grodin v. Grodin, 102 Mich.App. 396, 301 N.W.2d 869 (1980).

20. * * * Curlender v. Bio–Science Laboratories, 106 Cal.App.3d 811, 829, 165 Cal. Rptr. 477, 488 (1980) (dictum).

22. In re Baby X, 97 Mich.App. 111, 293 N.W.2d 736 (1980) (within twenty-four hours of birth, child began exhibiting signs of drug withdrawal).

injuries caused by accidents resulting from maternal negligence, such as automobile or household accidents. She could also be held liable for any behavior during her pregnancy having potentially adverse effects on her fetus, including failing to eat properly, using prescription, nonprescription and illegal drugs, smoking, drinking alcohol, exposing herself to infectious disease or to workplace hazards, engaging in immoderate exercise or sexual intercourse, residing at high altitudes for prolonged periods, or using a general anesthetic or drugs to induce rapid labor during delivery. * * *

In addition to advocating expansion of criminal penalties and tort recovery, commentators have advocated a wide range of new forms of state regulation of pregnant women's behavior. One such suggestion is that public benefits be withheld from pregnant women who refuse to submit to physical examinations or to abstain from drugs or alcohol. "High risk" parents could be required to undergo genetic or post-conception screening. Pregnant women could be prohibited from drinking alcohol and required to submit to breathalyzer tests to ensure compliance. One commentator has even proposed allowing punitive damages against women who intentionally harm their fetuses.

Perhaps the most foreboding aspect of allowing increased state involvement in pregnant women's lives in the name of the fetus is that the state may impose direct injunctive regulation of women's actions. When expanded to cover fetuses, child custody provisions may be used as a basis for seizing custody of the fetus [in utero] to control the woman's behavior. * * * Nevertheless, advocates of fetal rights have proposed that the state increasingly take custody of fetuses and, in some cases, civilly commit pregnant women to "protect" their fetuses.

This threat appears particularly immediate in the area of coerced medical treatment of pregnant women. * * * This phenomenon, troubling in its own right, is susceptible to even more dangerous expansion given new procedures in fetal therapy and fetal surgery. When fully developed, these procedures, which had promised to enhance women's reproductive freedom, may be used to restrict it. Some in the medical profession advocate compulsory medical treatment, including forced surgery, where it is determined by medical professionals to be in the interest of the fetus. * * *

* * *

Allowing the state to control women's actions in the name of fetal rights, however, reflects a view of the fetus as an entity separate from the pregnant woman, with interests that are hostile to her interests. In fact, by granting rights to the fetus assertable against the pregnant woman, and thus depriving the woman of decisionmaking autonomy, the state affirmatively acts to create an adversarial relationship between the woman and the fetus. By separating the interests of the fetus from those of the pregnant woman, and then examining, often post hoc, the effect on the fetus of isolated decisions made by the woman on a daily basis during pregnancy, the state is likely to exaggerate the potential risks to the fetus and undervalue the costs of the loss of autonomy suffered by the woman.

Where the woman has chosen not to exercise her right to abort her fetus, she is likely to care deeply about the well-being of the child she will bear. It is therefore more rational to assume that women will consider potentially harmful effects to their children resulting from their actions during pregnancy than to subject all women to state regulation of their actions during pregnancy. Furthermore, because the decisions a woman makes throughout her pregnancy depend on her individual values and preferences, complicated sets of life circumstances, and uncertain probabilities of daily risk, the woman herself is best situated to make these complex evaluations.

* * *

There have been few attempts at state intrusion of the magnitude and sweeping nature involved in state regulation of pregnant women's actions. Courts have held unconstitutional even isolated instances of the type of intrusions to which pregnant women would be continually subjected. For example, the Supreme Court has held that the state may not compel criminal suspects to undergo certain medical procedures,[69] and a federal circuit court has recognized the right of even involuntarily committed mental patients to refuse medical treatment.[70] The fact that these prohibited attempts at intrusions have involved those over whom the state traditionally exerts a great deal of authority—criminal defendants and mental patients—suggests the radical nature of the fetal rights trend and its incompatibility with our heritage of civil liberties. * * *

Existing liberty and privacy doctrine recognizes the threat to pregnant women's autonomy posed by fetal rights laws. Yet existing doctrine does not describe the full extent of the injury involved, for it does not identify the sex-specific nature of that injury. Only women can suffer the great intrusions of such laws, for only women have the ability to bear children. Fetal rights laws would not only infringe on constitutionally protected liberty and privacy rights of individual women, they would also serve to disadvantage women as women by further stigmatizing and penalizing them on the basis of the very characteristic that historically has been used to perpetuate a system of sex inequality.

* * *

69. For example, in Rochin v. California, the Court held that the forcible pumping of a criminal suspect's stomach violated the individual's Fourteenth Amendment due process rights, and was "conduct that shocks the conscience." 342 U.S. 165, 172 (1952). * * *

In Winston v. Lee, the Court held that to remove surgically a bullet from a suspect's body against his will for use as evidence against him would violate his constitutional rights. 105 S.Ct. 1611 (1985). * * *

70. * * * Rennie v. Klein, 653 F.2d 836 (3d Cir.1981), vacated on other grounds, 458 U.S. 1119 (1982), on remand, 720 F.2d 266 (3d Cir.1983) (reaffirming constitutional right to refuse drugs). * * *

Granting rights to fetuses in a manner that conflicts with women's autonomy reinforces the tradition of disadvantaging women on the basis of their reproductive capability. By subjecting women's decisions and actions during pregnancy to judicial review, the state simultaneously questions women's abilities and seizes women's rights to make decisions essential to their very personhood. The rationale behind using fetal rights laws to control the actions of women during pregnancy is strikingly similar to that used in the past to exclude women from the paid labor force and to confine them to the "private" sphere. Fetal rights could be used to restrict pregnant women's autonomy in both their personal and professional lives, in decisions ranging from nutrition to employment, in ways far surpassing any regulation of the actions of competent adult men. The state would thus define women in terms of their childbearing capacity, valuing the reproductive difference between women and men in such a way as to render it impossible for women to participate as full members of society. In light of the great threat to women's right to equality posed by legal recognition of the fetus, the state should bear the burden of ensuring that any law granting fetal rights does not disadvantage women or in any way infringe on the autonomy of pregnant women.

DOROTHY E. ROBERTS, PUNISHING DRUG ADDICTS WHO HAVE BABIES: WOMEN OF COLOR, EQUALITY, AND THE RIGHT OF PRIVACY

104 Harv.L.Rev. 1419, 1420–21, 1428–30, 1432–36, 1440–41, 1445–49, 1481 (1991).

A growing number of women across the country have been charged with criminal offenses after giving birth to babies who test positive for drugs. The majority of these women * * * are poor and Black. Most are addicted to crack cocaine. * * *

Crack cocaine appeared in America in the early 1980s, and its abuse has grown to epidemic proportions. Crack is especially popular among inner-city women. Indeed, evidence shows that, in several urban areas in the United States, more women than men now smoke crack. Most crack-addicted women are of childbearing age, and many are pregnant. This phenomenon has contributed to an explosion in the number of newborns affected by maternal drug use. Some experts estimate that as many as 375,000 drug-exposed infants are born every year. * * *

Babies born to drug-addicted mothers may suffer a variety of medical, developmental, and behavioral problems, depending on the nature of their mother's substance abuse. Immediate effects of cocaine exposure can include premature birth, low birth weight, and withdrawal symptoms. Cocaine-exposed children have also exhibited neurobehavioral problems such as mood dysfunction, organizational deficits, poor attention, and impaired human interaction, although it has not been determined whether these conditions are permanent. Congenital disorders and deformities have also been associated with cocaine use during pregnancy. According to NAPARE [National Association for Perinatal

Addiction Research and Education], babies exposed to cocaine have a tenfold greater risk of suffering sudden infant death syndrome (SIDS).

* * *

The response of state prosecutors, legislators, and judges to the problem of drug-exposed babies has been punitive. They have punished women who use drugs during pregnancy by depriving these mothers of custody of their children, by jailing them during their pregnancy, and by prosecuting them after their babies are born.

* * *

Poor Black women bear the brunt of prosecutors' punitive approach. These women are the primary targets of prosecutors, not because they are more likely to be guilty of fetal abuse, but because they are Black and poor. Poor women, who are disproportionately Black, are in closer contact with government agencies, and their drug use is therefore more likely to be detected. Black women are also more likely to be reported to government authorities, in part because of the racist attitudes of health care professionals. Finally, their failure to meet society's image of the ideal mother makes their prosecution more acceptable.

To charge drug-addicted mothers with crimes, the state must be able to identify those who use drugs during pregnancy. Because poor women are generally under greater government supervision—through their associations with public hospitals, welfare agencies, and probation officers—their drug use is more likely to be detected and reported. * * * The government's main source of information about prenatal drug use is hospitals' reporting of positive infant toxicologies to child welfare authorities. Hospitals serving poor minority communities implement this testing almost exclusively. Private physicians who serve more affluent women perform less of this screening both because they have a financial stake both in retaining their patients' business and securing referrals from them and because they are socially more like their patients.

* * *

Health care professionals are much more likely to report Black women's drug use to government authorities than they are similar drug use by their wealthy white patients. A study recently reported in The New England Journal of Medicine demonstrated this racial bias in the reporting of maternal drug use.[71] Researchers studied the results of toxicologic tests of pregnant women who received prenatal care in public health clinics and in private obstetrical offices in Pinellas County, Florida. Little difference existed in the prevalence of substance abuse by pregnant women along either racial or economic lines, nor was there any significant difference between public clinics and private offices. Despite similar rates of substance abuse, however, Black women were *ten times*

71. Chasnoff, Landress & Barrett, The Prevalence of Illicit-Drug or Alcohol Use During Pregnancy and Discrepancies in Mandatory Reporting in Pinellas County, Florida, 322 NEW ENG.J.MED. 1202, 1205 (table 3) (1990).

more likely than whites to be reported to public health authorities for substance abuse during pregnancy. * * *

It is also significant that, out of the universe of maternal conduct that can injure a fetus, prosecutors have focused on crack use. The selection of crack addiction for punishment can be justified neither by the number of addicts nor the extent of the harm to the fetus. Excessive alcohol consumption during pregnancy, for example, can cause severe fetal injury, and marijuana use may also adversely affect the unborn. The incidence of both these types of substance abuse is high as well. * * * Therefore, selecting crack abuse as the primary fetal harm to be punished has a discriminatory impact that cannot be medically justified.

* * *

The systematic, institutionalized denial of reproductive freedom has uniquely marked Black women's history in America. An important part of this denial has been the devaluation of Black women as mothers. A popular mythology that degrades Black women and portrays them as less deserving of motherhood reinforces this subordination. * * *

[Here Professor Roberts discusses the brutal denial of Black women's autonomy and reproductive control under slavery.]

The disproportionate number of Black mothers who lose custody of their children through the child welfare system is a contemporary manifestation of the devaluation of Black motherhood. This disparate impact of state intervention results in part from Black families' higher rate of reliance on government welfare. Because welfare families are subject to supervision by social workers, instances of perceived neglect are more likely to be reported to governmental authorities than neglect on the part of more affluent parents. Black children are also removed from their homes in part because of the child welfare system's cultural bias and application of the nuclear family pattern to Black families. Black childrearing patterns that diverge from the norm of the nuclear family have been misinterpreted by government bureaucrats as child neglect. For example, child welfare workers have often failed to respect the longstanding cultural tradition in the Black community of shared parenting responsibility among blood-related and non-blood kin. The state has thus been more willing to intrude upon the autonomy of poor Black families, and in particular of Black mothers, while protecting the integrity of white, middle-class homes.

This devaluation of Black motherhood has been reinforced by stereotypes that blame Black mothers for the problems of the Black family. * * *

Informed by the historical and present devaluation of Black motherhood, we can better understand prosecutors' reasons for punishing drug-addicted mothers. * * *

It is important to recognize at the outset that the prosecutions are based in part on a woman's pregnancy and not on her illegal drug use alone. Prosecutors charge these defendants not with drug use, but with child abuse or drug distribution—crimes that relate to their pregnancy. * * *

When a drug-addicted woman becomes pregnant, she has only one realistic avenue to escape criminal charges: abortion. Thus, she is penalized for choosing to have the baby rather than having an abortion. * * * Thus, it is the *choice of carrying a pregnancy to term* that is being penalized.

* * *

The history of overwhelming state neglect of Black children casts further doubt on its professed concern for the welfare of the fetus. When a society has always closed its eyes to the inadequacy of prenatal care available to poor Black women, its current expression of interest in the health of unborn Black children must be viewed with suspicion. The most telling evidence of the state's disregard of Black children is the high rate of infant death in the Black community. In 1987, the mortality rate for Black infants in the United States was 17.9 deaths per thousand births—more than twice that for white infants (8.6). * * *

The main reason for these high mortality rates is inadequate prenatal care. Most poor Black women face financial and other barriers to receiving proper care during pregnancy. In 1986, only half of all pregnant Black women in America received adequate prenatal care. * * *

The cruelty of this punitive response is heightened by the lack of available drug treatment services for pregnant drug addicts. Protecting the welfare of drug addicts' children requires, among other things, adequate facilities for the mother's drug treatment. Yet a drug addict's pregnancy serves as an obstacle to obtaining this treatment. Treatment centers either refuse to treat pregnant women or are effectively closed to them because the centers are ill-equipped to meet the needs of pregnant addicts. Most hospitals and programs that treat addiction exclude pregnant women because their babies are more likely to be born with health problems requiring expensive care. * * *

Finally, and perhaps most importantly, ample evidence reveals that prosecuting addicted mothers may not achieve the government's asserted goal of healthier pregnancies; indeed, such prosecutions will probably lead to the opposite result. Pregnant addicts who seek help from public hospitals and clinics are the ones most often reported to government authorities. The threat of prosecution based on this reporting forces women to remain anonymous and thus has the perverse effect of deterring pregnant drug addicts from seeking treatment. For this reason, the government's decision to punish drug-addicted mothers is irreconcilable with the goal of helping them.

* * *

A policy that attempts to protect fetuses by denying the humanity of their mothers will inevitably fail. We must question such a policy's true concern for the dignity of the fetus, just as we question the motives of the slave owner who protected the unborn slave child while whipping his pregnant mother. Although the master attempted to separate the mother and fetus for his commercial ends [because the child would become his property], their fates were inextricably intertwined. The tragedy of crack babies is initially a tragedy of crack-addicted mothers. Both are part of a larger tragedy of a community that is suffering a host of indignities, including, significantly, the denial of equal respect for its women's reproductive decisions.

Notes on "Fetal Protection"

1. Many of the things predicted in Dawn Johnsen's 1986 article have already happened. Pamela Rae Stewart was charged in California with taking drugs while pregnant, with failing to seek prompt medical attention when she experienced vaginal bleeding, and with failing to follow her doctor's orders to refrain from sexual intercourse during pregnancy, although the charges were ultimately dismissed. People v. Pamela Rae Stewart, No. M508197 (San Diego Mun. Ct. 1987). Another pregnant woman, Brenda Vaughan, was arrested for theft; when she tested positive for cocaine, the judge sentenced her to 180 days in prison because, as he stated, he would "be darned if I'm going to have a baby born that way." Victoria Churchville, D.C. Judge Jails Woman as Protection for Fetus, Wash. Post, July 23, 1988, at A1. Waiters have even refused to serve alcohol to pregnant women customers in restaurants and taverns, leading to the epithet "pregnancy police." Robb London, Two Waiters Lose Jobs for Liquor Warning to Woman, N.Y. Times, Mar. 30, 1991, at A7. The most common legal action against drug-addicted mothers is one for child abuse, resulting in removal of the children from their mother's custody soon after birth. See, e.g., Michelle Oberman, Sex, Drugs, Pregnancy, and the Law: Rethinking the Problems of Pregnant Women Who Use Drugs, 43 Hastings L.J. 505, 519–25 (1992).

One particularly egregious criminal case was ultimately overturned with the assistance of national reproductive rights groups. Jennifer Johnson was convicted in Florida for "delivery" of drugs to her unborn child under a drug trafficking statute and sentenced to one year in a drug rehabilitation center and *fifteen* years of probation, during which she was ordered, among other things, to remain drug and alcohol free, submit to random drug testing, and keep her probation officer apprised of any future pregnancies, so that they could be supervised by the court. Her conviction was upheld by the Florida appellate court, but reversed by the Florida Supreme Court. Johnson v. Florida, 602 So.2d 1288 (Fla.1992).

On what legal theories can punitive treatment of drug-addicted mothers be challenged? Can you construct an argument based on equal protection? See Oberman, above, at 526–45. What arguments might you raise based on the right of privacy? See Note, Maternal Rights and Fetal Wrongs: The Case against the Criminalization of "Fetal Abuse," 101 Harv. L. Rev. 994 (1988). Do you see any due process problems? See Doretta Massardo McGinnis, Prosecution of Mothers of Drug–Exposed Babies: Constitutional and Criminal Theory, 139 U. Pa. L. Rev. 505, 508–16 (1990). Does it violate the cruel and unusual punishment clause of the Eighth Amendment? See Dawn Marie Korver, The Constitutionality of Punishing Pregnant Substance Abusers under Drug Trafficking Laws: The Criminalization of a Bodily Function, 32 B.C.L.Rev. 629, 656–60 (1991).

2. For an interesting study of the process by which drug use in pregnancy was discovered by the media as a social problem and then institutionalized both in the legislatures and prosecutors' offices, see Laura E. Gomez, Misconceiving Mothers: Legislators, Prosecutors, and the Politics of Prenatal Drug Exposure (1997). Gomez describes the Pamela Rae Stewart prosecution, described in note 1, above, as having ignited a movement among feminists and their allies to defeat the initial very punitive reaction to this social problem. Id. at 42–62. The problem was initially portrayed as particular to poor women of color and connected to other social problems associated by many with this group, as well as to the fetal rights philosophy of the anti-abortion movement. Id. at 117–20. When feminist and reproductive rights groups portrayed it instead as a public health problem deserving of medical rather than criminal treatment, they were successful, according to Gomez, because they were able to define the problem as affecting the reproductive freedom of all women:

> [W]omen's problems are not universally medicalized, and problems linked to white, middle-class women are substantially more likely to be so categorized than those associated with poor or racial-minority women. Part of the strategy to medicalize rather than criminalize prenatal drug exposure, then, depended on recasting it as a more generic women's problem rather than as one limited to a subset of women presumably more apt to be viewed as having criminal propensities.

Id. at 122. How could this strategy be adapted to abortion? Is this a good idea?

3. Wisconsin and South Dakota have recently amended their statutes to provide for taking women into custody if they are pregnant and abusing alcohol. S.D. Codified Laws § 34–20A–63 (1998); Wis. Stat. § 48.193 (1999). Are there any reasons to distinguish between the legal treatment of drugs and alcohol?

4. Professor John A. Robertson argues that once a woman conceives and then makes the decision not to have an abortion, she loses the liberty to act in ways that would harm the fetus:

> The mother has, if she conceives and chooses not to abort, a legal and moral duty to bring the child into the world as healthy as is reasonably possible. She has a duty to avoid actions or omissions that will damage the fetus and child, just as she has a duty to protect the child's welfare once it is born until she transfers this duty to another.

Robertson, Procreative Liberty and the Control of Conception, Pregnancy, and Childbirth, 69 Va. L. Rev. 405, 438 (1983). What do you think of this argument? If a mother intentionally causes brain damage to her infant after birth, there is no question that she may be prosecuted for child abuse. What, if any, duties do you believe a pregnant woman has to the fetus she is carrying? Fetal surgery is now available to repair many potentially fatal conditions in utero. See Monica J. Casper, The Making of the Unborn Patient: A Social Anatomy of Fetal Surgery (1998) (describing the history, practice, conflicts, and ethical issues involved in fetal surgery). Could women be compelled to consent to prenatal surgery to save the life of a fetus?

5. Does the state have any obligations to the fetus of a drug-addicted mother? If so, is there any inconsistency with DeShaney v. Winnebago County Dep't of Social Services, 489 U.S. 189, 109 S.Ct. 998, 103 L.Ed.2d 249 (1989) (holding that the state has no obligation to intervene to protect a child from abuse, even abuse of which it is aware)? If the state has no obligation under *DeShaney* even *after* the child is born, why are we willing to impose so much on the mother even before the child is born?

6. The problem of drug use by women is clearly a serious one. To address it, it is obviously relevant to ask why women use drugs in the first place. Drug-addicted women tend to suffer from low self-esteem and severe depression. See Amin N. Daghestani, Psychosocial Characteristics of Pregnant Women Addicts in Treatment, in Drugs, Alcohol, Pregnancy and Parenting 7, 8, 11 (Ira J. Chasnoff, ed. 1988). Moreover, researchers estimate that 70% to 100% of all women drug abusers are victims of incest or sexual violence. Oberman, above note 1, at 512 n. 31. To recover from their addiction requires facing the painful memories of this abuse, as well as the reality of racism, sexism, and poverty. While addictive substances are readily accessible to mask this pain, drug rehabilitation is not as available. Moreover, addicts run a high risk of pregnancy. Low self-esteem, coupled with the fact that her partner may be abusive, renders the addicted woman less able to control the circumstances of intercourse, and many contraceptive methods are not well suited to the needs of addicted women. Id. at 512–13. Are any of these facts legally relevant to defending an addicted mother against criminal charges? How might you raise them in her defense?

7. As Dawn Johnsen describes above, the punitive approach is based on an adversarial model of the mother-child relationship, in which the mother and fetus are viewed as two distinct entities with separate and conflicting interests and rights. Catharine MacKinnon has suggested that the law has never adequately conceptualized either the woman's relationship to her fetus or the fetus itself, because they have been understood from a male perspective, "from the observing outsider." MacKinnon, Reflections on Sex Equality Under Law, 100 Yale L.J. 1281, 1309 (1991). What do you think is an appropriate conceptualization of the entity represented by the pregnant woman? Are there any analogies or metaphors one could borrow from other fields of law? For a collection of feminist essays analyzing the construction of the fetus as a subject, see Fetal Subjects, Feminist Positions (Lynn M. Morgan and Meredith W. Michaels, eds. 1999).

8. Some experiments indicate that cocaine may in fact attach itself to the sperm of men who use the drug and enter an egg at the moment of conception, thus damaging the fetus. Ricardo Yazigi, et al., Demonstrations of Specific Binding of Cocaine to Human Spermatozoa, 266 J.A.M.A. 1956 (Oct. 9, 1991). Why do you think people in general, and the law in particular, have assumed that the woman is the one to be held responsible for genetic damage to the fetus?

What about people who smoke tobacco around pregnant women, now that it is clear that passive smoking can have negative effects on the fetus: should they be held liable for potential damage? Why or why not? What about a father who smokes around a pregnant woman? A child with asthma? Should the state prosecute him?

9. Treatment programs generally don't accept pregnant women because they see the pregnancy as "too complicating" a factor in the treatment and especially for their research programs. See Oberman, above note 1, at 517–18. Can you construct an argument based on equal protection against refusal to accept a pregnant addict into a program that is heavily reliant upon federal research funds?

10. Which of the feminist theories discussed in Chapter 3 is most helpful in analyzing the issues involved in society's treatment of drug-addicted mothers? Which is most helpful in making arguments to a court imposing sanctions upon an addicted mother? Which is, or are, most helpful in making arguments to the legislature?

11. Should children be able to sue their mothers for harm caused to them in utero? Can you distinguish this situation from suits against third parties who have injured the fetus, for example, by intentionally assaulting the pregnant woman? On what grounds?

12. Twenty-three percent of women seeking prenatal care are battered women. American Medical Association, Diagnostic and Treatment Guidelines on Domestic Violence 6 (1992). Should fathers who beat pregnant women be jailed for the duration of the pregnancy? By analogy to drug-addicted mothers, should fathers guilty of abusing the mother automatically have their custody rights terminated?

E. WHO CONTROLS CHILDBIRTH?

1. THE MEDICALIZATION OF CHILDBIRTH

JUDITH R. KUNISCH, ELECTRONIC FETAL MONITORS: MARKETING FORCES AND THE RESULTING CONTROVERSY

In Healing Technology 41, 43–44, 48–49, 53–54, 58 (Kathryn Ratcliff, ed. 1989).

Contemporary childbirth is defined as an acute event requiring aggressive medical management with frequent pharmacological and surgical interventions. For most women, childbirth has lost its personal and familial character. The childbearing mother has become a passive patient directed through the birth experience by an assortment of medical professionals. These health care professionals take control of the pregnancy away from the birthing woman, asserting that medical management is superior to the natural biology of the event.

* * *

An electronic fetal monitor is a machine that evaluates the status of the fetus during labor. It is used to identify cases of fetal distress. Proponents of this technology see labor as a time of stress to the fetus due primarily to the rigors of uterine contractions. The stress of labor may produce adverse consequences to the infant from a lack of oxygen to the fetal brain, including brain damage, tissue damage, and even death. Others agree stress is present but see it as a normal part of birth. Monitoring is conducted either externally, through the mother's abdomen, or from inside the uterus itself. Two measurements are usually obtained: the fetal heart rate, and the strength of maternal uterine contractions. External monitoring is accomplished by placing two belts across the lower abdomen of the laboring woman. * * * Internal monitoring is utilized after rupture of the amniotic membrane. In this case, electrodes are passed through the vaginal canal and cervical opening into the uterus. One electrode measures the force of uterine contractions. The other, a small device which is screwed or clipped to the fetal scalp, obtains fetal electrocardiogram readings. Internal monitoring is the more precise of the two methods.

Prior to development of EFM technology, fetal status during labor was monitored by periodic auscultation (i.e., listening to the fetal heartbeat using a fetoscope, similar to a stethoscope). Uterine contractions were measured for duration, frequency, and intensity by a labor attendant using manual palpitation. This technique required professional attendance at the bedside of the laboring woman and consistency in recording maternal and fetal response to labor.

* * *

The advantages of EFM are its ability to provide continuous readout of data, and avoidance of human error in counting fetal heart beats and evaluating uterine contraction strength. It reduces personnel needs for each laboring woman. The EFM paper tracing record also provides reference to ascertain patterns of heart rate and uterine contractions as labor progresses, and creates a "paper trail" for insurors of both doctors and patients.

The disadvantages of EFM include limited movement for the woman attached to a monitor. Most women are monitored throughout their labor, and this requires the woman to remain in bed, unable to move about or change position, for this will disturb the belts across her abdomen. Forced immobility and unnatural position in bed lead to discomfort and lack of control over labor management by women, and may actually cause problems in labor. An additional disadvantage with use of EFM is that professional attention is directed to readout data supplied by the machine and there is less "laying on of hands" by labor attendants. * * *

The physician was able to enter a labor room and read the complete record of everything that had happened while he/she was gone. Since labor may take many hours, observation by machine was viewed as quite practical and helpful. Indeed, the machine came to be perceived as providing more reliable information than nursing attendants in monitoring maternal and fetal status. This preference may in part be due to a physician bias concerning nurses and their professional abilities. Or it may represent a false confidence that machines protect us against human error. But in this way, of course, technology was placed ahead of biology, and obstetrics came to rely even more on a male definition of machine-oriented manipulation of biological events.

At the same time, other influences on birthing practice emerged. * * *

The introduction of awake and aware childbirth in this country by such pioneers as Marjorie Karmel and Elizabeth Bing brought to labor rooms a new definition of practice. Women began to learn about the physiology of birth, to participate actively, and to control events surrounding the birth itself. Consumer groups sprang up around the country and couples began taking classes to prepare themselves mentally and physically for the rigors of birthing. Women became active consumers of health care and were no longer content to settle for passivity in receiving care. * * *

For many physicians, this change in attitude, together with renewed popularity of home birth and midwives, was highly threatening. Obstetricians resented having alert patients who asked questions and requested information. Many were highly indignant that women no longer were intimidated by the medical training required for obstetrical specialties. These women viewed birthing as a natural event requiring little or no intervention. To make matters worse, husbands and boyfriends were accompanying women into labor and delivery. The physician was no longer the central figure. Everyone's attention was directed to the birthing couple. What better way to regain control than by bringing in a machine that only a sophisticated physician could read and interpret. Once again, the obstetrician was indispensable, his/her word was authority, and woman was reduced to passive object.

* * *

A chronological time line of events surrounding introduction and use of EFM shows 1976 as a key year. By this time EFM was firmly established as a standard of care in obstetrics. * * * In 1976, however, a major controversy emerged regarding use of the machine. It was reported that caesarean birthrates in the United States had tripled between 1968 and 1976. * * *

The large increase in caesarean births caused health care professionals and consumers to examine what had changed in childbirth experience to cause such a drastic rise in surgical delivery. What stood out was the rapid introduction and diffusion of EFM into the labor experience. Health care professionals and consumers asked the same question: "Was there a sudden rise in infant distress in labor, or might the monitor be pointing out signs of fetal reaction to labor that, although they look abnormal, in fact occur routinely during the course of the labor experience?" * * *

One cannot deny the important contribution of electronic fetal monitoring to management of high-risk cases. The information gained from the monitor on the high-risk fetus's response to the rigors of labor has contributed significantly to reduction of morbidity and mortality in the labor and delivery experiences of thousands of women. For those women whose pregnancies are complicated by illness and jeopardized fetal well being, the electronic fetal monitor has been but one of many technological advances helping them to secure the safest birth possible. * * *

Notes on the Medicalization of Childbirth

1. What do you think motivates the medicalization of childbirth? What role do lawyers play in this process?

2. Is it possible to take advantage of the benefits of new technology like electronic fetal monitoring without being taken over by it? How?

3. The "natural childbirth" movement educated women about childbirth and the dangers of anesthesia yet failed to recapture the process of birth from the "experts." What lessons can be drawn from this movement?

4. In 1900, over 50% of births in this country were attended by midwives, and most took place at home. Debra Evenson, Midwives: Survival of an Ancient Profession, 7 Women's Rts. L. Rep. 313, 315 (1982). By 1973, less than one percent of babies in the United States were delivered by midwives, who had been displaced by the medical profession and hospital birth, although midwives delivered 80% of babies in the rest of the world, including in every major industrial nation except the United States and Canada. Gena Corea, The Hidden Malpractice: How American Medicine Mistreats Women 257, 259 (1985). At the same time, the United States ranked fourteenth in infant mortality and tenth in maternal mortality. Id. at 259. Today, many states license nurse-midwives, who practice in hospitals and under the supervision of doctors; but only a few license lay-midwives, who typically deliver at home with medical backup in cases of emergency. See Donna M. Peizer, A Social and Legal Analysis of the Independent Practice of Midwifery: Vicarious Liability of the Collaborating Physician and Judicial Means of Addressing Denial of Hospital Privileges, 2 Berkeley Women's L.J. 139, 141–43 (1986); Charles Wolfson, Midwives and Home Birth: Social, Medical, and Legal Perspectives, 37 Hastings L.J. 909, 958–60 (1986). The practice of midwifery is seriously hampered by denial of hospital privileges to midwives and by physicians' fear of vicarious liability if they serve as "backup." Peizer, above, at 161–65, 199–201. What legal arguments might be used to overcome either of these obstacles? See id. at 174–87 (independent contractor status), 204–39 (constitutional, common law, and antitrust remedies for denial of hospital privileges). Midwives are also being actively prosecuted in some states as a result of physician pressure on the legislatures. See, e.g., Raymond G. DeVries, Regulating Birth: Midwives, Medicine, & the Law 55, 131 (1985).

5. Barbara Katz Rothman states that:

> The medical model sees a vulnerable fetus caught in a woman's body (the child of man held by women) and a woman, although stronger than the fetus, also made vulnerable by its intrusion (weakened by what the man has "done to her," what he has growing in her). The job of the obstetrician is to help effect the separation of the two, so they can "recover," so that the woman can "return to normal," and the baby can

be "managed" separately. The ideologies of technology and patriarchy focus the vision and the work of obstetrics.

Rothman, Midwifery as Feminist Praxis, in Recreating Motherhood: Ideology and Technology in a Patriarchal Society 171 (1989). By contrast, Rothman describes midwifery as "feminist praxis," intended "to transform, to create, the birth experience to meet the needs of women. It is a social, political activity, dialectically linking biology and society, the physical and the social experience of motherhood. The very word *midwife* means *with the woman.* That is more than a physical location: it is an ideological and political stance. Midwifery represents a rejection of the artificial dualisms of patriarchal and technological ideologies." Id. at 170. What does Rothman mean by her statement that "What midwifery offers us is . . . a reconceptualization of the 'facts' of procreation"? See id. at 172. How might a midwife reconceptualize the "facts" of fetal distress indicated on an electronic fetal monitor? Rothman says the medical model sees the fetus as "caught in a woman's body," with both waiting to be set free of one another. Id. at 171. How does this image compare with those of the woman-fetus relationship we have encountered in the abortion section, above? With Dawn Johnsen's? See excerpt in Section D, above. With Eileen McDonagh's? See note 3 in Notes on Abortion and Self-defense, in Section C4, above.

2. FORCED CAESAREANS

JESSIE MAE JEFFERSON v. GRIFFIN SPALDING COUNTY HOSPITAL

Supreme Court of Georgia, 1981.

247 Ga. 86, 274 S.E.2d 457.

On Thursday, January 22, 1981, the Griffin Spalding County Hospital Authority petitioned the Superior Court of Butts County * * * for an order authorizing it to perform a caesarean section and any necessary blood transfusions upon the defendant, an out-patient resident of Butts County, in the event she presented herself to the hospital for delivery of her unborn child, which was due on or about Monday, January 26. * * *

On Friday, January 23, the Georgia Department of Human Resources, acting through the Butts County Department of Family and Children Services, petitioned the Juvenile Court of Butts County for temporary custody of the unborn child, alleging that the child was a deprived child without proper parental care necessary for his or her physical health, and praying for an order requiring the mother to submit to a caesarean section. After appointing counsel for the parents and for the child, the court conducted a joint hearing in both the superior court and juvenile court cases and entered the following order on the afternoon of January 23:

* * *

"Based on the evidence presented, the Court finds that Jessie Mae Jefferson is due to begin labor at any moment. There is a 99 to 100 percent certainty that the unborn child will die if she attempts to have the child by vaginal delivery. There is a 99 to 100 percent chance that the child will live if the baby is delivered by Caesarean section prior to the beginning of labor. There is a 50 percent chance that Mrs. Jefferson herself will die if vaginal delivery is attempted. There is an almost 100 percent chance that Mrs. Jefferson will survive if a delivery by Caesarean section is done prior to the beginning of labor. The Court finds that as a matter of fact the child is a human being fully capable of sustaining life independent of the mother.

"Mrs. Jefferson and her husband have refused and continue to refuse to give consent to a Caesarean section. This refusal is based entirely on the religious beliefs of Mr. and Mrs. Jefferson. * * *

"Based on these findings, the Court concludes and finds as a matter of law that this child is a viable human being and entitled to the protection of the Juvenile Court Code of Georgia. The Court concludes that this child is without the proper parental care and subsistence necessary for his or her physical life and health.

"Temporary custody of the unborn child is hereby granted to the State of Georgia Department of Human Resources and the Butts County Department of Family and Children Services. The Department shall have full authority to make all decisions, including giving consent to the surgical delivery appertaining to the birth of this child. The temporary custody of the Department shall terminate when the child has been successfully brought from its mother's body into the world or until the child dies, whichever shall happen."

IN RE A.C.

District of Columbia Court of Appeals, 1987.

533 A.2d 611.

A.C. was diagnosed with leukemia when she was thirteen years old. As part of her treatment, she underwent a number of major surgical procedures, therapy, and chemotherapy. When she was twenty-seven years old, after her cancer had been in remission for three years, A.C. married. At the time she became pregnant, she had not undergone chemotherapy for more than a year. In her fifteenth week of pregnancy, she was referred to the hospital's high-risk pregnancy clinic.

When A.C. was approximately twenty-five weeks pregnant, she went to her regularly scheduled prenatal visit complaining of shortness of breath and some pain in her back. Her physicians subsequently discovered that she had a tumor mass in her lung which was most likely a metastatic oxygenic carcinoma. She was admitted to the hospital on June 11 and her prognosis was terminal.

On June 15, during A.C.'s twenty-sixth week of pregnancy, A.C., her physicians, her mother, and her husband discussed the possibility of providing A.C. with radiation therapy or chemotherapy to relieve her pain and to continue her pregnancy. Her physicians believed that her unborn child's chances of viability would be greatly increased if it were delivered when it had reached twenty-eight weeks gestational age. By June 16, the date on which the hospital sought the declaratory order in the Superior Court, A.C. had been heavily sedated so that she could continue to breathe. Her condition was declining, and the attending medical staff concluded that passive treatment was appropriate because the mother would not survive and the child's chances of survival were grim. The hospital administration then decided to test this decision in the Superior Court.

The trial court appointed counsel for A.C. and the fetus, respectively. The District of Columbia was permitted to intervene for the fetus as parens patriae. A hearing was held at the hospital and was transcribed.

There was some dispute about whether A.C. would have chosen to have a Caesarean section on June 16. Before she was sedated, A.C. indicated that she would choose to relinquish her life so that the fetus could survive should such a choice present itself at the fetus' gestational age of twenty-eight weeks. Her physicians never discussed with her what her choice would be if such a choice had to be made before the fetus reached the twenty-eight-week point. The fetus was suffering oxygen starvation and resultant rapid heart rate. There was at that point less than 20 percent chance that it would be afflicted with cerebral palsy, neurological defects, deafness and blindness. There was not a clear medical consensus on the course of A.C.'s treatment. Those physicians who objected to the proposed surgery did so because A.C. refused her consent to the procedure, not because the surgery was medically objectionable. One physician testified that he believed that A.C. would not have wanted to deliver a baby that might have to undergo the pain of having handicaps that are associated with premature delivery. Another physician believed that A.C. would not have refused permission for the Caesarean section to be performed. During the course of her pregnancy, however, A.C. was aware that a number of medications she was taking might harm the fetus. Nevertheless, she expressed a desire to her physicians to be kept as comfortable as possible throughout her pregnancy and to maintain the quality of her life.

The trial court determined that the fetus was viable and that the District of Columbia had an interest in protecting the potential life of the fetus. See Roe v. Wade, 410 U.S. 113, 93 S.Ct. 705, 35 L.Ed.2d 147 (1973). * * *

Shortly after the trial judge made his decision, A.C. was informed of it. She stated, during a period of lucidity, that she would agree to the surgery although she might not survive it. When another physician went to A.C. to verify her decision, she apparently changed her mind, mouthing the words, "I don't want it done." There was no explanation for either decision.

After our Clerk was advised of the desire to appeal, a telephonic hearing was had before a hastily assembled division of the court. The trial judge's findings were read to us, and we heard from counsel and an attending physician. The latter answered questions respecting the relative chances of survival of both A.C. and the fetus with and without the surgery. He also informed us of the rapid decline of A.C. and the need to proceed promptly with the surgery, if it was decided to do so. There was no time to have the transcript read or to do effective research. The atypical nature of the appellate hearing included our hearing directly from one of the physicians.

The court based its decision to deny a stay on the medical judgment that A.C. would not survive for a significant time after the surgery and that the fetus had a better, though slim, chance if taken before A.C.'s imminent death. If A.C. died before delivery, the fetus would die as well. Though A.C. might have lived twenty-four to forty-eight hours, the surgery might have hastened her death. The ordinary question of likelihood of ultimate success on the merits was deemed subsumed in the immediate necessity to balance the delicate interests of fetus survival with the mother's condition and options on her behalf.

[The operation was performed; both mother and child died soon thereafter.]

* * *

It is appropriate here to state that this case is not about abortion. * * * [A]s a matter of law, the right of a woman to an abortion is different and distinct from her obligations to the fetus once she has decided not to timely terminate her pregnancy. With a viable fetus, a balancing of interests must replace the single interest of the mother, and as in this case, time can be a critical factor.

We next view this case within the context of its closest legal analogues: the right of an adult to refuse medical treatment and the right of a parent to refuse medical treatment on behalf of offspring.

* * *

The fundamental right to bodily integrity encompasses an adult's right to refuse medical treatment, even if the refusal will result in death. * * *

The state's interest in preserving life usually will not override an adult's right to refuse medical treatment. In most cases where a court orders an adult to receive medical treatment against his consent, it will be to protect innocent third parties who would be harmed by the adult's decision.

* * *

Courts have used this reasoning to hold that parents may not withhold life-saving treatment from their children because of the parents' religious beliefs. The state may intervene even when a parent's refusal of medical treatment for his or her child does not place the child in danger of imminent death.

* * *

There is a significant difference, however, between a court authorizing medical treatment for a child already born and a child who is yet unborn, although the state has compelling interests in protecting the life and health of both children and viable unborn children. Where birth has occurred, the medical treatment does not infringe on the mother's right to bodily integrity. With an unborn child, the state's interest in preserving the health of the child may run squarely against the mother's interest in her bodily integrity.

It can be argued that the state may not infringe upon the mother's right to bodily integrity to protect the life or health of her unborn child unless to do so will not significantly affect the health of the mother and unless the child has a significant chance of being born alive. Performing Caesarean sections will, in most instances, have an effect on the condition of the mother. That effect may be temporary in otherwise normal patients. The surgery presents a number of common complications, including infection, hemorrhage, gastric aspiration of the stomach contents, and postoperative embolism. It also produces considerable discomfort. In some cases, the surgery will result in the mother's death.

Even though we recognize these considerations, we think they should not have been dispositive here. The Caesarean section would not significantly affect A.C.'s condition because she had, at best, two days left of sedated life; the complications arising from the surgery would not significantly alter that prognosis. The child, on the other hand, had a chance of surviving delivery, despite the possibility that it would be born handicapped. Accordingly, we concluded that the trial judge did not err in subordinating A.C.'s right against bodily intrusion to the interests of the unborn child and the state, and hence we denied the motion for stay.

IN RE A.C.

District of Columbia Court of Appeals, 1990 (en banc).

573 A.2d 1235.

We are confronted here with two profoundly difficult and complex issues. First, we must determine who has the right to decide the course of medical treatment for a patient who, although near death, is pregnant with a viable fetus. Second, we must establish how that decision should be made if the patient cannot make it for herself—more specifically, how a court should proceed when faced with a pregnant patient, in extremis, who is apparently incapable of making an informed decision regarding medical care for herself and her fetus. * * *

There was no evidence before the court showing that A.C. consented to, or even contemplated, a caesarean section before her twenty-eighth week of pregnancy. There was, in fact, considerable dispute as to whether she would have consented to an immediate caesarean delivery at the time the hearing was held. * * *

> [The court found the case not to be moot, even though A.C. and her baby were dead, because the hospital treated high-risk pregnancy and was likely to face a similar situation again.]

[O]ur analysis of this case begins with the tenet common to all medical treatment cases: that any person has the right to make an informed choice, if competent to do so, to accept or forego medical treatment. * * *

In the same vein, courts do not compel one person to permit a significant intrusion upon his or her bodily integrity for the benefit of another person's health. McFall v. Shimp, 10 Pa.D. & C.3d 90 (Allegheny County Ct.1978). In McFall the court refused to order Shimp to donate bone marrow which was necessary to save the life of his cousin, McFall. * * * Even though Shimp's refusal would mean death for McFall, the court would not order Shimp to allow his body to be invaded. It has been suggested that fetal cases are different because a woman who "has chosen to lend her body to bring [a] child into the world" has an enhanced duty to assure the welfare of the fetus, sufficient even to require her to undergo caesarean surgery. Surely, however, a fetus cannot have rights in this respect superior to those of a person who has already been born.[8]

* * *

What we distill from the cases * * * is that every person has the right, under the common law and the Constitution, to accept or refuse medical treatment. This right of bodily integrity belongs equally to persons who are competent and persons who are not. Further, it matters not what the quality of a patient's life may be; the right of bodily integrity is not extinguished simply because someone is ill, or even at death's door. To protect that right against intrusion by others—family members, doctors, hospitals, or anyone else, however well-intentioned—we hold that a court must determine the patient's wishes by any means available, and must abide by those wishes unless there are truly extraordinary or compelling reasons to override them. When the patient is incompetent, or when the court is unable to determine competency, the substituted judgment procedure must be followed.

> [Under the doctrine of substituted judgment, the court attempts to determine what choice the individual would make, if competent, based upon her previously expressed opinions; typically, family members testify about the patient's opinions, predispositions and values.]

* * * The trial court never made any finding about A.C.'s competency to decide. Undoubtedly, during most of the proceedings below, A.C. was incompetent to make a treatment decision; that is, she was unable

8. There are also practical consequences to consider. What if A.C. had refused to comply with a court order that she submit to a caesarean? Under the circumstances, she obviously could not have been held in civil contempt and imprisoned or required to pay a daily fine until compliance. Enforcement could be accomplished only through physical force or its equivalent. A.C. would have to be fastened with restraints to the operating table, or perhaps involuntarily rendered unconscious by forcibly injecting her with an anesthetic, and then subjected to unwanted major surgery. Such actions would surely give one pause in a civilized society, especially when A.C. had done no wrong.

to give an informed consent based on her assessment of the risks and benefits of the contemplated surgery. The court knew from the evidence that A.C. was sedated and unconscious, and thus it could reasonably have found her incompetent to render an informed consent; however, it made no such finding. On the other hand, there was no clear evidence that A.C. was competent to render an informed consent after the trial court's initial order was communicated to her.

We think it is incumbent on any trial judge in a case like this, unless it is impossible to do so, to ascertain whether a patient is competent to make her own medical decisions. Whenever possible, the judge should personally attempt to speak with the patient and ascertain her wishes directly, rather than relying exclusively on hearsay evidence, even from doctors. It is improper to presume that a patient is incompetent. We have no reason to believe that, if competent, A.C. would or would not have refused consent to a caesarean. We hold, however, that without a competent refusal from A.C. to go forward with the surgery, and without a finding through substituted judgment that A.C. would not have consented to the surgery, it was error for the trial court to proceed to a balancing analysis, weighing the rights of A.C. against the interests of the state.

* * * An even more serious consequence of court-ordered intervention is that it drives women at high risk of complications during pregnancy and childbirth out of the health care system to avoid coerced treatment. Second, and even more compellingly, any judicial proceeding in a case such as this will ordinarily take place—like the one before us here—under time constraints so pressing that it is difficult or impossible for the mother to communicate adequately with counsel, or for counsel to organize an effective factual and legal presentation in defense of her liberty and privacy interests and bodily integrity. * * *

In this case A.C.'s court-appointed attorney was unable even to meet with his client before the hearing. By the time the case was heard, A.C.'s condition did not allow her to be present, nor was it reasonably possible for the judge to hear from her directly. The factual record, moreover, was significantly flawed because A.C.'s medical records were not before the court and because Dr. Jeffrey Moscow, the physician who had been treating A.C. for many years, was not even contacted and hence did not testify. Finally, the time for legal preparation was so minimal that neither the court nor counsel mentioned the doctrine of substituted judgment, which—with benefit of briefs, oral arguments, and above all, time—we now deem critical to the outcome of this case. * * *

Notes on Forced Caesareans

1. The medical condition preventing Jessie Mae Jefferson from natural delivery was placenta previa, that is, the placenta had moved down near the cervix. After the court order, Ms. Jefferson did not return to the hospital, but the placenta shifted and a healthy baby was delivered naturally. Kenneth Jost, Mother versus Child, A.B.A. J. 84, 86 (Apr. 1989). What if the

placenta had not moved? Do you think that legal intervention is appropriate, for example, when a full-term baby is in the birth canal, the cord is wrapped around her neck, and the parents are opposed to any surgical intervention? Is there any scenario in which you think compelled caesarean section is appropriate? Does it make any difference if the parents' opposition is based upon religious or other grounds? What if the medical crisis in A.C. had taken place 10 to 12 days later in her pregnancy? Would this affect your assessment of the rights of the fetus in that case? Do you think there are any circumstances where the courts should be involved in decisions concerning childbirth? What are they? If there are some circumstances when compelled caesareans might be appropriate, what procedures would take into account the interests of all parties involved?

2. One of the interesting aspects of the treatment of the Angela Carder (A.C.) case is the stark difference between the interests taken into account by the different levels of court. At the trial level and in the expedited appeal, the testimony was primarily from doctors, and the court turned to Roe v. Wade's trimester analysis for precedent (as did the *Jefferson* court, along with the law of child neglect). By contrast, the en banc appeals court, with more time for briefing and consideration of the issues, considered the woman's rights and turned to an entirely different case law, that of informed consent. Indeed, it reenvisioned the pregnant woman as an autonomous decision-maker. What, if anything, does this say about (1) the treatment women can typically expect from trial level courts, and (2) the importance of litigating precedents concerning issues like this? What other reasons might there be for the difference between the different courts' judgments in this case?

3. Angela Carder's family also filed civil claims against the hospital for deprivation of human rights, discrimination, wrongful death, malpractice, and other claims arising out of the treatment of Ms. Carder; the suit was settled with a monetary award and the development of new policies by the hospital to affirm the autonomy of pregnant patients, announcing its intention to make similar decisions in the future within the doctor-patient relationship and not by involving the courts. ACLU, Reproductive Rights Update, Dec. 7, 1990, at 1–2. Can you think of other legal theories upon which to defend women's autonomy in relation to decisions about pregnancy and childbirth? See, e.g., Michelle Oberman, Mothers and Doctors' Orders: Unmasking the Doctor's Fiduciary Role in Maternal–Fetal Conflicts, 94 Nw. U. L. Rev. 451 (2000) (arguing that the typical conflict arises not between mother and fetus but between mother and doctor, in breach of the doctor's fiduciary duty to his patient, and suggesting lawsuits for breach of fiduciary duty as a potential remedy).

4. Most of the cases in which court orders have been sought to compel caesareans involved women who were African American, Asian, or Hispanic, and most of the women were being treated in a teaching hospital clinic or were receiving public aid. Veronika E.B. Kolder et al., Court–Ordered Obstetrical Interventions, 316 New Eng. J. Med. 1192, 1193 (1987). Why are non-white and poor women at a significantly greater risk of this type of compelled medical treatment? See Lisa C. Ikemoto, Furthering the Inquiry: Race, Class, and Culture in the Forced

Medical Treatment of Pregnant Women, 59 Tenn. L. Rev. 487, 510–16 (1992) (pointing to the authoritarian nature of medical institutions, the imposition of notions of "good" and "bad" mothers, and the failure to attend to the voice of the woman or to the cultural context of birth).

5. To what extent have the problems presented by forced caesareans been caused by the interaction of new technology and the interrelated issues of the standard of care in medical malpractice cases? Just because a certain technology is available, does a doctor have to use it? See, e.g., Nancy K. Rhoden, The Judge in the Delivery Room: The Emergence of Court–Ordered Caesareans, 74 Calif. L. Rev. 1951, 2010–23 (1986).

6. This chapter has discussed a large number of attempts to control women in relation to the conception, gestation, and birth of children—restrictions on abortion, compelled contraception (e.g., court-ordered implantation of Norplant), sterilization abuse, a wide variety of "fetal protection" measures, punitive measures taken against drug-addicted mothers, and forced caesareans. Lisa Ikemoto argues that the ideology of motherhood, combined with a tendency to defer to those with "scientific" knowledge, is being transformed by these measures into a "Code of Perfect Pregnancy," institutionalized as legal duties. Ikemoto, The Code of Perfect Pregnancy: At the Intersection of the Ideology of Motherhood, the Practice of Defaulting to Science, and the Interventionist Mindset of Law, 53 Ohio State L.J. 1205 (1992). The resulting model of the Good Mother, moreover, looks very like the image of a white, middle-class mother and measures "outgroup women" against this standard. Id. at 1305. To the extent that you agree with this description, what explains this phenomenon?

F. "SURROGATE" MOTHERHOOD

IN THE MATTER OF BABY M

Supreme Court of New Jersey, 1988.

109 N.J. 396, 537 A.2d 1227.

In February 1985, William Stern and Mary Beth Whitehead entered into a surrogacy contract. It recited that Stern's wife, Elizabeth, was infertile, that they wanted a child, and that Mrs. Whitehead was willing to provide that child as the mother with Mr. Stern as the father.

The contract provided that through artificial insemination using Mr. Stern's sperm, Mrs. Whitehead would become pregnant, carry the child to term, bear it, deliver it to the Sterns, and thereafter do whatever was necessary to terminate her maternal rights so that Mrs. Stern could thereafter adopt the child. * * * Although Mrs. Stern was not a party to the surrogacy agreement, the contract gave her sole custody of the child in the event of Mr. Stern's death. * * *

Mr. Stern, on his part, agreed to attempt the artificial insemination and to pay Mrs. Whitehead $10,000 after the child's birth, on its delivery to him. * * *

William and Elizabeth Stern were married in July 1974, having met at the University of Michigan, where both were Ph.D. candidates. Due to financial considerations and Mrs. Stern's pursuit of a medical degree and residency, they decided to defer starting a family until 1981. Before then, however, Mrs. Stern learned that she might have multiple sclerosis and that the disease in some cases renders pregnancy a serious health risk. Her anxiety appears to have exceeded the actual risk, which current medical authorities assess as minimal. Nonetheless that anxiety was evidently quite real, Mrs. Stern fearing that pregnancy might precipitate blindness, paraplegia, or other forms of debilitation. Based on the perceived risk, the Sterns decided to forego having their own children. The decision had special significance for Mr. Stern. Most of his family had been destroyed in the Holocaust. As the family's only survivor, he very much wanted to continue his bloodline.

* * *

Mrs. Whitehead's response apparently resulted from her sympathy with family members and others who could have no children (she stated that she wanted to give another couple the "gift of life"); she also wanted the $10,000 to help her family.

* * *

Mrs. Whitehead realized, almost from the moment of birth, that she could not part with this child. She had felt a bond with it even during pregnancy. Some indication of the attachment was conveyed to the Sterns at the hospital when they told Mrs. Whitehead what they were going to name the baby. She apparently broke into tears and indicated that she did not know if she could give up the child. She talked about how the baby looked like her other daughter, and made it clear that she was experiencing great difficulty with the decision.

Nonetheless, Mrs. Whitehead was, for the moment, true to her word. Despite powerful inclinations to the contrary, she turned her child over to the Sterns on March 30 [1986] at the Whiteheads' home.

* * *

Later in the evening of March 30, Mrs. Whitehead became deeply disturbed, disconsolate, stricken with unbearable sadness. She had to have her child. She could not eat, sleep, or concentrate on anything other than her need for her baby. The next day she went to the Sterns' home and told them how much she was suffering.

The depth of Mrs. Whitehead's despair surprised and frightened the Sterns. She told them that she could not live without her baby, that she must have her, even if only for one week, that thereafter she would surrender her child. The Sterns, concerned that Mrs. Whitehead might indeed commit suicide, not wanting under any circumstances to risk that, and in any event believing that Mrs. Whitehead would keep her word, turned the child over to her. * * *

[When the child was not returned, Mr. Stern filed suit to enforce the surrogacy contract, and the Whiteheads fled to Florida with Baby M; the Sterns traced the baby to her grandparents' home in Florida, filed supplementary proceedings, and forcibly removed the child, who was returned to New Jersey and turned over to the Sterns.]

Soon after the conclusion of the [two-month] trial, the trial court * * * held that the surrogacy contract was valid; ordered that Mrs. Whitehead's parental rights be terminated and that sole custody of the child be granted to Mr. Stern; and, after hearing brief testimony from Mrs. Stern, immediately entered an order allowing the adoption of Melissa by Mrs. Stern, all in accordance with the surrogacy contract. * * *

II. Invalidity and Unenforceability of Surrogacy Contract

* * *

The surrogacy contract conflicts with: (1) laws prohibiting the use of money in connection with adoptions; (2) laws requiring proof of parental unfitness or abandonment before termination of parental rights is ordered or an adoption is granted; and (3) laws that make surrender of custody and consent to adoption revocable in private placement adoptions.

* * *

[First,] Mr. Stern knew he was paying for the adoption of a child; Mrs. Whitehead knew she was accepting money so that a child might be adopted; the Infertility Center knew that it was being paid for assisting in the adoption of a child. * * * It strains credulity to claim that these arrangements, touted by those in the surrogacy business as an attractive alternative to the usual route leading to an adoption, really amount to something other than a private placement adoption for money.

* * *

[Second,] where there has been no written surrender to an approved agency * * *, termination of parental rights will not be granted in this state absent a very strong showing of abandonment or neglect. That showing is required in every context in which termination of parental rights is sought, * * * even where the petitioning adoptive parent is, as here, a stepparent. * * *

[Third,] [t]he provision in the surrogacy contract whereby the mother irrevocably agrees to surrender custody of her child and to terminate her parental rights * * * is one more indication of the essential nature of this transaction: the creation of a contractual system of termination and adoption designed to circumvent our statutes.

* * *

The surrogacy contract's invalidity * * * is further underlined when its goals and means are measured against New Jersey's public policy. The contract's basic premise, that the natural parents can decide in advance of birth which one is to have custody of the child, bears no relationship to the settled law that the child's best interests shall determine custody. * * *

The surrogacy contract guarantees permanent separation of the child from one of its natural parents. Our policy, however, has long been that to the extent possible, children should remain with and be brought up by both of their natural parents. * * *

The surrogacy contract violates the policy of this State that the rights of natural parents are equal concerning their child, the father's right no greater than the mother's. * * * The whole purpose and effect of the surrogacy contract was to give the father the exclusive right to the child by destroying the rights of the mother.

* * *

Under the contract, the natural mother is irrevocably committed before she knows the strength of her bond with her child. She never makes a totally voluntary, informed decision, for quite clearly any decision prior to the baby's birth is, in the most important sense, uninformed, and any decision after that, compelled by a pre-existing contractual commitment, the threat of a lawsuit, and the inducement of a $10,000 payment, is less than totally voluntary. Her interests are of little concern to those who controlled this transaction.

* * *

Worst of all, however, is the contract's total disregard of the best interests of the child. There is not the slightest suggestion that any inquiry will be made at any time to determine the fitness of the Sterns as custodial parents, of Mrs. Stern as an adoptive parent, their superiority to Mrs. Whitehead, or the effect on the child of not living with her natural mother.

This is the sale of a child, or, at the very least, the sale of a mother's right to her child, the only mitigating factor being that one of the purchasers is the father. Almost every evil that prompted the prohibition on the payment of money in connection with adoptions exists here.

* * *

Intimated, but disputed, is the assertion that surrogacy will be used for the benefit of the rich at the expense of the poor. In response it is noted that the Sterns are not rich and the Whiteheads not poor. Nevertheless, it is clear to us that it is unlikely that surrogate mothers will be as proportionately numerous among those women in the top twenty percent income bracket as among those in the bottom twenty percent. Put differently, we doubt that infertile couples in the low-income bracket will find upper income surrogates.

In any event, even in this case one should not pretend that disparate wealth does not play a part simply because the contrast is not the dramatic "rich versus poor." At the time of trial, the Whiteheads' net assets were probably negative—Mrs. Whitehead's own sister was foreclosing on a second mortgage. Their income derived from Mr. Whitehead's labors. Mrs. Whitehead is a homemaker, having previously held part-time jobs. The Sterns are both professionals, she a medical doctor, he a biochemist. Their combined income when both were working was about $89,500 a year and their assets sufficient to pay for the surrogacy contract arrangements.

The point is made that Mrs. Whitehead agreed to the surrogacy arrangement, supposedly fully understanding the consequences. Putting aside the issue of how compelling her need for money may have been, and how significant her understanding of the consequences, we suggest that her consent is irrelevant. There are, in a civilized society, some things that money cannot buy. * * *

[The surrogacy contract was thus found to be unenforceable as against public policy.]

* * *

V. Custody

* * * With the surrogacy contract disposed of [having been found unenforceable], the legal framework becomes a dispute between two couples over the custody of a child produced by the artificial insemination of one couple's wife by the other's husband. Under the Parentage Act the claims of the natural father and the natural mother are entitled to equal weight * * *. The applicable rule given these circumstances is clear: the child's best interests determine custody.

* * *

Our custody conclusion is based on strongly persuasive testimony contrasting both the family life of the Whiteheads and the Sterns and the personalities and characters of the individuals. The stability of the Whitehead family life was doubtful at the time of trial. Their finances were in serious trouble (foreclosure by Mrs. Whitehead's sister on a second mortgage was in process). Mr. Whitehead's employment, though relatively steady, was always at risk because of his alcoholism, a condition that he seems not to have been able to confront effectively. Mrs. Whitehead had not worked for quite some time, her last two employments having been part-time. One of the Whiteheads' positive attributes was their ability to bring up two children, and apparently well, even in so vulnerable a household. Yet substantial question was raised even about that aspect of their home life. The expert testimony contained criticism of Mrs. Whitehead's handling of her son's educational difficulties. Certain of the experts noted that Mrs. Whitehead perceived herself as omnipotent and omniscient concerning her children. She knew what they were thinking, what they wanted, and she spoke for them. As to Melissa, Mrs. Whitehead expressed the view that she alone knew what that child's cries and sounds meant. Her inconsistent stories about various things engendered grave doubts about her ability to explain honestly and sensitively to Baby M—and at the right time—the nature of her origin. Although faith in professional counseling is not a sine qua non of parenting, several experts believed that Mrs. Whitehead's contempt for professional help, especially professional psychological help, coincided with her feelings of omnipotence in a way that could be devastating to a child who most likely will need such help. In short, while love and affection there would be, Baby M's life with the Whiteheads promised to be too closely controlled by Mrs. Whitehead. The prospects for wholesome, independent psychological growth and development would be at serious risk.

The Sterns have no other children, but all indications are that their household and their personalities promise a much more likely foundation for Melissa to grow and thrive. There is a track record of sorts—during the one-and-a-half years of custody Baby M has done very well, and the relationship between both Mr. and Mrs. Stern and the baby has become very strong. The household is stable, and likely to remain so. Their finances are more than adequate, their circle of friends supportive, and their marriage happy. Most important, they are loving, giving, nurturing, and open-minded people. They have demonstrated the wish and ability to nurture and protect Melissa, yet at the same time to encourage her independence. Their lack of experience is more than made up for by a willingness to learn and to listen, a willingness that is enhanced by their professional training, especially Mrs. Stern's experience as a pediatrician. They are honest; they can recognize error, deal with it, and learn from it. They will try to determine rationally the best way to cope with problems in their relationship with Melissa. When the time comes to tell her about her origins, they will probably have found a means of doing so that accords with the best interests of Baby M. All in all, Melissa's future appears solid, happy, and promising with them.

[The court awarded custody to the Sterns but held that Mrs. Whitehead was entitled to visitation at some point, to be determined by the trial court.[b]]

Notes on Baby M

1. What are the similarities and differences between a surrogacy arrangement and an adoption? See Margaret Jane Radin, Market–Inalienability, 100 Harv. L. Rev. 1849, 1928–29 (1987). Isn't adoption frequently motivated by economic reasons as well?

2. The trial court in *Baby M* had decided the case as one of contract law. After finding that the agreement was not unconscionable or voidable for fraud, it held that Mary Beth Whitehead had breached the contract and, finding that to do so was in the child's best interest, ordered specific performance, terminating Mrs. Whitehead's parental rights. In the Matter of Baby M, 217 N.J.Super. 313, 525 A.2d 1128 (1987). Thus, in both the *Baby M* case and the *A.C.* case, excerpted in Section E2 above, the trial level court appears to have ignored basic principles of law: in *Baby M,* principles governing custody, adoption, and termination of parental rights, and in *A.C.*, the doctrine of informed consent. Why do you think this was so? Is it

b. The court ordered that Whitehead should have visitation two days a week, every other weekend, and two weeks each summer. See Susan Squire, Whatever Happened to Baby M?, Redbook, Jan. 1994, at 60, 64.

because the rights of a woman were at stake? Or those of a child? (The time constraints that applied in *A.C.* cannot explain *Baby M,* for the two-month trial attracted a great deal of attention and legal discussion; Mary Beth Whitehead's interests were vigorously pressed at every stage, and many feminists became involved as amici curiae in the New Jersey Supreme Court.)

3. How did considerations of class affect the court's conclusion in *Baby M?* Do you agree with the assumption that low-income infertile women are unlikely to find upper-income surrogates? If so, what conclusions can be drawn from this fact? Was the income differential between the two parties here used differently by the court when it determined the validity of the contract, on the one hand, and when it decided the custody question, on the other? Is the court's treatment of the disparity consistent with usual principles of contract law (which typically do not take the economic positions of the contractors into account) and of family law (where custody determinations are not supposed to rest on wealth)? How or how not? Did class considerations determine the outcome in *Baby M?*

4. Did Mary Beth Whitehead win this case or lose it? What, if any, problems stem from the Parentage Act's provision that the rights of the natural mother and the natural father are to be given equal weight? Should that principle apply differently in the surrogacy situation? Or is it inapt in other situations as well?

5. How was the Court's decision to award custody to the Sterns affected, or not affected, by each of the following factors: class bias, cultural bias, bias in favor of a particular parenting style, bias in favor of professionals, especially doctors and psychiatrists, and bias created by the length of the appellate period?

6. How should the fact that Mr. Stern's family perished in the Holocaust count in a court's decision of this case? Do you think it influenced the decision here? What about Mrs. Stern's unwillingness to be pregnant, which appears to have been based upon unfounded fears?

Text Note: Feminism and Surrogacy

Like Mary Beth Whitehead, the first legal surrogate mother, Elizabeth Kane, regretted her decision, apparently went into a major depression touched off by giving up the child, and believed that her decision had a severely negative impact on her other children. See Elizabeth Kane, Birth Mother: The Story of America's First Legal Surrogate Mother 274–83 (1988). Surrogacy, she wrote, "is nothing more than the transference of pain from one woman to another. One woman is in anguish because she cannot become a mother, and another woman may suffer for the rest of her life because she cannot know the child she bore for someone else." Id. at 275. Others point out that this situation is no different from adoption and allege that fewer surrogate mothers regret their decision than mothers who give up children for adoption. Lori B. Andrews, Surrogate Motherhood: The Challenge for Feminists, in Surrogate Motherhood 167, 171 (Larry Gostin, ed. 1990) (alleging, without supporting citations, that only 1% of surrogate mothers regret their decision). Lori Andrews also argues that prohibiting women from entering into prenatal surrogacy contracts is similar to 19th-century views of women as incompetent to enter into contracts and to make important decisions for themselves and reflects stereotypes of women as emotional and driven by hormonally caused irrationality. Id. at 172–73. By contrast, sperm donors are regularly held to the pre-conception sale of their parental rights. Id. at 170.

Other feminists have expressed concerns that poor women and women of color will be exploited as "breeders." See, e.g., Gena Corea, The Mother Machine 213–49, 272–82 (1988). Those seeking to obtain genetic children through surrogacy arrangements are almost entirely white married couples in their late thirties or early forties, generally well-off and well-educated. R. Alta Charo, Legislative Approaches to Surrogate Motherhood, in Surrogate Motherhood 88, 88–89 (Larry Gostin, ed. 1990). By contrast, Carmel Shalev argues that "A free market [in surrogacy] would allow a new source of productive activity for women who presently have limited income-earning opportunities, with two positive distributive effects: a shift of wealth from the childless consumers to the presumably less advantaged reproducers, and a reallocation of economic returns away from the exploiting intermediaries to the birth mothers." Shalev, Birth Power: The Case for Surrogacy 158 (1989). Other feminists (and the New Jersey Supreme Court in *Baby M)* raise the question whether there are some things that money should not be able to buy. See Margaret Jane Radin, Market–Inalienability, 100 Harv. L. Rev. 1849 (1987).

There are a wide variety of approaches states may choose in deciding how to treat surrogacy—for example, making surrogacy contracts enforceable, making them voidable but requiring the payment of damages for breach, making all such contracts void, or criminalizing surrogacy arrangements. To address concerns about exploitation, especially of gestational mothers (where a woman essentially serves as the "incubator" for the fertilized egg of another couple), and about the negative impact of surrogacy upon adoption, Martha Field suggests the following approach: Surrogacy contracts should be permitted but non-enforceable. The birth mother could change her mind during pregnancy or shortly after, yet the genetic father would be liable for child support, thus creating a disincentive for surrogacy arrangements. Martha A. Field, Surrogacy Contracts: Gestational and Traditional: The Argument for Nonenforcement, 31 Washburn L.J. 1, 5–13 (1991). Moreover, rather than beginning a child's life with a custody struggle, a bright-line rule would dictate that custody of newborns be given to the birth mother. In this way, surrogacy would remain an option for some, yet society would not encourage an arrangement that has no net social benefit, especially in light of the need for adoptive parents. See also Martha Field, Surrogate Motherhood (1988).

Notes on Surrogacy

1. Mary Beth Whitehead obviously suffered an intense depression touched off by the loss of giving up her birth child, yet Lori Andrews alleges that few surrogate mothers regret their decision—many fewer than experience major grief over giving up children for adoption. Does it matter how few, if the loss is extreme for some women? Might this perhaps support

having nonenforceable contracts, as Martha Field suggests, since most women would go through with the arrangement anyway? On the other hand, should some women's difficulty handling the loss result in prohibiting the arrangement for all women? How do you distinguish this situation from abortion, which many women also experience as a loss and occasion for mourning? Is this a problem that could be dealt with simply by psychological screening of potential surrogate mothers?

2. Should sperm donorship and surrogate motherhood be treated similarly, as Lori Andrews argues, or differently, as the *Baby M* court concluded, based upon the different amounts of time invested by the sperm donor and surrogate mother? Do you find the court's analysis of this distinction an adequate one? Does it make a difference if your view of the parent-child relationship is based on biology, genetics, or property notions? What if your theory of property is based upon a labor theory of value (basing the value of a commodity upon the labor mixed with it)? See, e.g., John Locke, Second Treatise on Civil Government, ch. 5, § 27 (1690). How does it change things if you subscribe instead to an exchange theory of value, whereby the value of a commodity is determined by the law of supply and demand? What about property rights conceived as relational? See Margaret Jane Radin, Property and Personhood, 34 Stan. L. Rev. 957 (1982). How, if at all, does the application of these theories change if the surrogacy is gestational rather than genetic?

3. Surrogacy has been analogized, variously, to babyselling (because money is exchanged in the transaction), slavery (because of the surrogate mother's position as a "breeder" for another couple), and prostitution (because of the payment for use of the surrogate's body). Should one be able to sell any of these things—a baby, one's body, a body part? How does surrogacy compare to, and contrast with, prostitution?

4. What is likely to happen if we prohibit surrogacy? Would it continue to exist nonetheless? Would it be harder or easier to protect the most vulnerable potential surrogates if surrogacy is not criminalized and thus can be regulated? What regulations would you suggest? How much should the woman be paid and when? What other regulations are necessary to prevent exploitation? Should the children born of surrogacy be permitted to trace their birth mothers, and vice versa? How about the children of sperm donors?

5. What do you think of Martha Field's argument that surrogacy contracts should be permitted but nonenforceable? Does this compromise adequately balance the interests of all the parties involved? Do you think it appropriate to expand the interests considered beyond the immediate parties to consider the interests, for example, of children who might otherwise be adopted?

6. How would the course of the *Baby M* case have been changed if the principles Martha Field suggests had been in effect? Would there have been any case at all? How would the actions of the parties have been influenced, do you think?

7. How would proponents of the various feminist theories presented in Chapter 3 approach the surrogacy issue?

8. Is it fair to make a father who is party to a surrogacy arrangement that falls through pay child support? Why or why not? What rules should govern a surrogacy contract if the child born pursuant to it is born with a handicap or deformity? See Angela R. Holder, Surrogate Motherhood and the Best Interests of Children, in Surrogate Motherhood 79–80 (Larry Gostin, ed. 1990).

JOHNSON v. CALVERT

Supreme Court of California, In Bank, 1993.

5 Cal.4th 84, 851 P.2d 776, 19 Cal.Rptr.2d 494

* * *

Mark and Crispina Calvert are a married couple who desired to have a child. Crispina was forced to undergo a hysterectomy in 1984. Her ovaries remained capable of producing eggs, however, and the couple eventually considered surrogacy. In 1989 Anna Johnson heard about Crispina's plight from a coworker and offered to serve as a surrogate for the Calverts.

On January 15, 1990, Mark, Crispina, and Anna signed a contract providing that an embryo created by the sperm of Mark and the egg of Crispina would be implanted in Anna and the child born would be taken into Mark and Crispina's home "as their child." Anna agreed she would relinquish "all parental rights" to the child in favor of Mark and Crispina. In return, Mark and Crispina would pay Anna $10,000 in a series of installments, the last to be paid six weeks after the child's birth. Mark and Crispina were also to pay for a $200,000 life insurance policy on Anna's life.

The zygote was implanted on January 19, 1990. Less than a month later, an ultrasound test confirmed Anna was pregnant.

Unfortunately, relations deteriorated between the two sides. Mark learned that Anna had not disclosed she had suffered several stillbirths and miscarriages. Anna felt Mark and Crispina did not do enough to obtain the required insurance policy. She also felt abandoned during an onset of premature labor in June.

In July 1990, Anna sent Mark and Crispina a letter demanding the balance of the payments due her or else she would refuse to give up the child. The following month, Mark and Crispina responded with a lawsuit, seeking a declaration they were the legal parents of the unborn child. Anna filed her own action to be declared the mother of the child, and the two cases were eventually consolidated. The parties agreed to an independent guardian ad litem for the purposes of the suit.

The child was born on September 19, 1990 * * *. The parties agreed to a court order providing that the child would remain with Mark and Crispina on a temporary basis with visits by Anna.

[The court first discussed determination of parentage under the standards of the Uniform Parentage Act, concluding that both Anna and Crispina had adduced evidence of a mother-child relationship under the Act but that California law recognizes only one natural mother.]

* * *

Because two women each have presented acceptable proof of maternity, we do not believe this case can be decided without enquiring into the parties' intentions as manifested in the surrogacy agreement. Mark and Crispina are a couple who desired to have a child of their own genetic stock but are physically unable to do so without the help of reproductive technology. They affirmatively intended the birth of the child, and took the steps necessary to effect in vitro fertilization. But for their acted-on intention, the child would not exist. Anna agreed to facilitate the procreation of Mark's and Crispina's child. The parties' aim was to bring Mark's and Crispina's child into the world, not for Mark and Crispina to donate a zygote to Anna. Crispina from the outset intended to be the child's mother. Although the gestative function Anna performed was necessary to bring about the child's birth, it is safe to say that Anna would not have been given the opportunity to gestate or deliver the child had she, prior to implantation of the zygote, manifested her own intent to be the child's mother. No reason appears why Anna's later change of heart should vitiate the determination that Crispina is the child's natural mother.

We conclude that although the Act recognizes both genetic consanguinity and giving birth as means of establishing a mother and child relationship, when the two means do not coincide in one woman, she who intended to procreate the child—that is, she who intended to bring about the birth of a child that she intended to raise as her own—is the natural mother under California law.

* * *

The argument that a woman cannot knowingly and intelligently agree to gestate and deliver a baby for intending parents carries overtones of the reasoning that for centuries prevented women from attaining equal economic rights and professional status under the law. To resurrect this view is both to foreclose a personal and economic choice on the part of the surrogate mother, and to deny intending parents what may be their only means of procreating a child of their own genetic stock. Certainly in the present case it cannot seriously be argued that Anna, a licensed vocational nurse who had done well in school and who had previously borne a child, lacked the intellectual wherewithal or life experience necessary to make an informed decision to enter into the surrogacy contract.

* * *

KENNARD, JUSTICE, dissenting.

* * * In my view, the woman who provided the fertilized ovum and the woman who gave birth to the child both have substantial claims to

legal motherhood. Pregnancy entails a unique commitment, both psychological and emotional, to an unborn child. No less substantial, however, is the contribution of the woman from whose egg the child developed and without whose desire the child would not exist.

* * *

The proposition that a woman who gives birth to a child after carrying it for nine months is a "substantial factor" in the child's birth cannot reasonably be debated. Nor can it reasonably be questioned that "but for" the gestational mother, there would not be a child. Thus, the majority's reliance on principles of causation is misplaced. Neither the "but for" nor the "substantial factor" test of causation provides any basis for preferring the genetic mother's intent as the determinative factor in gestational surrogacy cases: Both the genetic and the gestational mothers are indispensable to the birth of a child in a gestational surrogacy arrangement.

* * *

The majority's approach entirely devalues the substantial claims of motherhood by a gestational mother such as Anna. True, a woman who enters into a surrogacy arrangement intending to raise the child has by her intent manifested an assumption of parental responsibility in addition to her biological contribution of providing the genetic material. But the gestational mother's biological contribution of carrying a child for nine months and giving birth is likewise an assumption of parental responsibility. A pregnant woman's commitment to the unborn child she carries is not just physical; it is psychological and emotional as well. * * * A pregnant woman intending to bring a child into the world is more than a mere container or breeding animal; she is a conscious agent of creation no less than the genetic mother, and her humanity is implicated on a deep level. Her role should not be devalued.

Notes on Johnson v. Calvert

1. The text of the letter sent by Anna Johnson to the Calverts during her pregnancy, included in a footnote to the appellate court opinion, explains more about the dispute that arose between the two parties to the surrogacy contract:

> I am writing you this letter to inquire if an early payment can be made of what is left to be paid of me. [Anna was to be paid a total of $10,000, but in installments spread out over the pregnancy.] I would not ask if it weren't important and I feel that this is important because it deals with the well-being of the baby. The lady that owns the house in which I reside is selling it, so I must be out by the 10th of August. Since I am to be hospitalized for three weeks due to the pyleonephritis [sic] & premature contractions I need to find another place to live prior to this! Due to the complications of this pregnancy, I am unable to return to work until the delivery of this baby so my income is limited. I do not get enough from disability to make a two month rent deposit plus, the

> security deposit & have the telephone reconnected. I don't think you'd want your child jeopardized by living out on the street. I have looked out for this child's well being thus far, is it asking too much to look after ours?
>
> I'm imploring nicely and trying not to be an ogre about this. But you must admit, you have not been very supportive mentally the entire pregnancy & you've showed a lack of interest unless it came to an ultrasound. I am asking you for help in paying off the final five thousand. There's only two months left & once this baby is born, my hands are free of this deal. But see, this situation can go two ways. One, you can pay me the entire sum early so I won't have to live in the streets, or two you can forget about helping me but, calling it a breach of contract & not get the baby.! I don't want it to get this nasty, not coming this far, but you'd want some help too, if you had no where to go & have to worry about not only yourself but your own child & the child of someone else!!! Help me find another place & get settled in before your baby's born.

Anna J. v. Mark C., 286 Cal.Rptr. 369, 373 n. 11 (Cal.App.1991). Does this letter change your assessment of the rights and obligations of the parties to this case? Could these issues be addressed in the context of surrogacy law? How?

2. Does it make any difference to your analysis of the decision in Johnson v. Calvert to know that the couple desiring the baby via the surrogacy arrangement was a white man and a Filipina woman, and that the woman giving birth to the baby was African American? See Dorothy Roberts, Killing the Black Body: Race, Reproduction, and the Meaning of Liberty 280 (1997).

3. Justice Kennard, the dissenting judge, argued that the Uniform Status of Children of Assisted Conception Act provides appropriate safeguards in a situation like that in Johnson v. Calvert. The Act provides that "a woman who gives birth to a child is the child's mother" (§ 2) unless a court has approved a surrogacy agreement before conception. In the absence of such court approval, any surrogacy agreement would be void. U.L.A., Uniform Status of Children of Assisted Conception Act § 5(b)(1999). If, however, the arrangement for gestational surrogacy has court approval, "the intended parents are the parents of the child." Id., § 8(a)(1). The model legislation provides for the court to appoint a guardian ad litem for the intended child and legal counsel for the surrogate mother. Before approving a surrogacy arrangement, the trial court must conduct a hearing and enter detailed findings, including, among other things, that medical evidence shows the intended mother's inability to bear a child or that for her to do so poses an unreasonable risk to the unborn child or to the physical or mental health of the intended mother and that all parties have received professional mental health counseling pertaining to the effect of the surrogacy arrangement. Id., § 6(b). These provisions, according to Justice Kennard, serve to minimize the potential for overreaching and to ensure that all parties to a surrogacy arrangement understand their respective roles and obligations. Johnson v. Calvert, 5 Cal. 4th at 111, 851 P.2d at 794, 19 Cal. Rptr. 2d at 512 (Kennard, J., dissenting). "Moreover, by requiring judicial approval, the

model act would significantly discourage the rapid expansion of commercial surrogacy brokerage and the resulting commodification of the products of pregnancy." Id. at 117, 851 P.2d at 798, 19 Cal. Rptr. 2d at 516. Do you think the legislation will take care of all these problems? Is it necessary? Should a couple be required to obtain court approval that the surrogacy is a matter of medical necessity? Why or why not?

The Uniform Act has been adopted by two states. N.D. Cent. Code §§ 14–18–01 to 14–18–07 (1997); Va. Code Ann. §§ 20–156 to 20–165 (Michie Supp. 1999). Almost half the states have passed some legislation concerning surrogacy, some of it quite restrictive. Michigan criminalizes surrogacy; Arizona, New York, North Dakota and Utah deem all surrogacy contracts void and unenforceable; Kentucky, Louisiana, Nebraska, and Washington legislation voids surrogacy for compensation; and Florida, New Hampshire, and Virginia make unpaid surrogacy contracts enforceable but surround them with a variety of regulations. See Lisa L. Behm, Legal, Moral & International Perspectives on Surrogate Motherhood: The Call for a Uniform Regulatory Scheme in the United States, 2 DePaul J. Health Care L. 557, 581–85 (1999). See, e.g., Ariz. Rev. Stat. Ann. § 25–218 (West 1998); Fla. Stat. Ann. § 742.15–742.16 (West 1998); Ky. Rev. Stat. Ann. §§ 199.950(2), 199.590(4), 199.990 (Michie/Bobbs–Merrill 1995); La. Rev. Stat. Ann. § 9:2713 (West 1998); Mich. Comp. Laws Ann. §§ 722.851–722.863 (West 1998); Neb. Rev. Stat. § 25–21,200 (1998); N.H. Stat. Ann. §§ 168–B:1–168–B:28 (West Supp. 1999); N.Y. Domestic Relations Law § 122 (McKinney 1998); Utah Code § 76–7–204 (1998); Va. Code Ann. §§ 20–156 to 20–165 (Michie Supp. 1998); Wash. Rev. Code Ann. §§ 26.26.210 to 26.26.260 (West 1998). What is the law in your state regarding surrogacy? Whose interests does the law protect? Whose does it hurt?

4. In contrast to Johnson v. Calvert, where the baby arguably had two mothers, in another California case the trial court found that a child born from a surrogacy arrangement had *no* lawful parents! This case, involving a divorcing couple who had caused an embryo, genetically unrelated to either of them, to be implanted in a surrogate mother who carried and gave birth to the child, arose because the husband in the couple argued that he was not liable for child support. Justice Sills, author of the opinion in Johnson v. Calvert, overturned the trial court's finding on appeal based on *Johnson*'s intent test, well-established law that a husband who consents to the artificial insemination of his wife has a duty to support the resulting child, and the state's compelling interest in establishing parentage for all children. In re Marriage of Buzzanca, 61 Cal.App.4th 1410, 72 Cal.Rptr.2d 280 (Cal.App. 1998). In *Buzzanca*, the woman who actually gave birth to the child was not genetically related to it and did not make any claim to parenthood or custody herself. What if either or both of these circumstances were different? Would it affect the court's decision? Would it affect your own evaluation of a just resolution of the case? How and why? What exactly is the state's compelling interest here? Why can't a child have two mothers?

G. REPRODUCTIVE TECHNOLOGY: BOON OR BANE FOR WOMEN?

DAVIS v. DAVIS

Supreme Court of Tennessee, 1992.

842 S.W.2d 588, *cert. denied,* 507 U.S. 911, 113 S.Ct. 1259, 122 L.Ed.2d 657 (1993).

This appeal presents a question of first impression, involving the disposition of the cryogenically-preserved product of in vitro fertilization (IVF), commonly referred to in the popular press and the legal journals as "frozen embryos." The case began as a divorce action, filed by the appellee, Junior Lewis Davis, against his then wife, appellant Mary Sue Davis. The parties were able to agree upon all terms of dissolution, except one: who was to have "custody" of the seven "frozen embryos" stored in a Knoxville fertility clinic that had attempted to assist the Davises in achieving a much-wanted pregnancy during a happier period in their relationship.

I. Introduction

Mary Sue Davis originally asked for control of the "frozen embryos" with the intent to have them transferred to her own uterus, in a post-divorce effort to become pregnant. Junior Davis objected, saying that he preferred to leave the embryos in their frozen state until he decided whether or not he wanted to become a parent outside the bounds of marriage.

* * *

We note, in this latter regard, that their positions have already shifted: both have remarried and Mary Sue Davis (now Mary Sue Stowe) has moved out of state. She no longer wishes to utilize the "frozen embryos" herself, but wants authority to donate them to a childless couple. Junior Davis is adamantly opposed to such donation and would prefer to see the "frozen embryos" discarded. * * *

IVF involves the aspiration of ova from the follicles of a woman's ovaries, fertilization of these ova in a petri dish using the sperm provided by a man, and the transfer of the product of this procedure into the uterus of the woman from whom the ova were taken. Implantation may then occur, resulting in a pregnancy and, it is hoped, the birth of a child.

Beginning in 1985, the Davises went through six attempts at IVF, at a total cost of $35,000, but the hoped-for pregnancy never occurred. Despite her fear of needles, at each IVF attempt Mary Sue underwent the month of subcutaneous injections necessary to shut down her pituitary gland and the eight days of intermuscular injections necessary to stimulate her ovaries to produce ova. She was anesthetized five times for the aspiration procedure to be performed. Forty-eight to 72 hours after each aspiration, she returned for transfer back to her uterus, only to receive a negative pregnancy test result each time.

The Davises then opted to postpone another round of IVF until after the clinic with which they were working was prepared to offer them cryogenic preservation, scheduled for November 1988. Using this process, if more ova are aspirated and fertilized than needed, the conceptive product may be cryogenically preserved (frozen in nitrogen and stored at sub-zero temperatures) for later transfer if the transfer performed immediately does not result in a pregnancy. * * * [O]n their last attempt, on December 8, 1988, the gynecologist who performed the procedure was able to retrieve nine ova for fertilization. The resulting one-celled entities, referred to before division as zygotes, were then allowed to develop in petri dishes in the laboratory until they reached the four-to eight-cell stage.

* * *

After fertilization was completed, a transfer was performed as usual on December 10, 1988; the rest of the four to eight-cell entities were cryogenically preserved. Unfortunately, a pregnancy did not result from the December 1988 transfer, and before another transfer could be attempted, Junior Davis filed for divorce—in February 1989. * * *

* * *

V. The Enforceability of Contract

* * *

We believe, as a starting point, that an agreement regarding disposition of any untransferred preembryos in the event of contingencies (such as the death of one or more of the parties, divorce, financial reversals, or abandonment of the program) should be presumed valid and should be enforced as between the progenitors. This conclusion is in keeping with the proposition that the progenitors, having provided the gametic material giving rise to the preembryos, retain decision-making authority as to their disposition.

* * *

It might be argued in this case that the parties had an implied contract to reproduce using in vitro fertilization * * *. The problem with such an analysis is that there is no indication in the record that disposition in the event of contingencies other than Mary Sue Davis's pregnancy was ever considered by the parties, or that Junior Davis intended to pursue reproduction outside the confines of a continuing marital relationship with Mary Sue. We therefore decline to decide this case on the basis of implied contract or the reliance doctrine.[21]

* * *

21. We also point out that if the roles were reversed in this case, it is highly unlikely that Junior Davis could force transfer of the preembryos to Mary Sue over her objection. Because she has an absolute right to seek termination of any resulting pregnancy, at least within the first trimester, ordering her to undergo a uterine transfer

VI. THE RIGHT OF PROCREATIONAL AUTONOMY

* * * We conclude that the answer to this dilemma turns on the parties' exercise of their constitutional right to privacy.

* * *

[T]he right of procreational autonomy is composed of two rights of equal significance—the right to procreate and the right to avoid procreation. Undoubtedly, both are subject to protections and limitations.

The equivalence of and inherent tension between these two interests are nowhere more evident than in the context of in vitro fertilization. None of the concerns about a woman's bodily integrity that have previously precluded men from controlling abortion decisions is applicable here. We are not unmindful of the fact that the trauma (including both emotional stress and physical discomfort) to which women are subjected in the IVF process is more severe than is the impact of the procedure on men. In this sense, it is fair to say that women contribute more to the IVF process than men. Their experience, however, must be viewed in light of the joys of parenthood that is desired or the relative anguish of a lifetime of unwanted parenthood. As they stand on the brink of potential parenthood, Mary Sue Davis and Junior Lewis Davis must be seen as entirely equivalent gamete-providers.

* * *

* * * In this case, the Court must deal with the question of genetic [separated from gestational] parenthood. We conclude, moreover, that an interest in avoiding genetic parenthood can be significant enough to trigger the protections afforded to all other aspects of parenthood. The technological fact that someone unknown to these parties could gestate these preembryos does not alter the fact that these parties, the gamete-providers, would become parents in that event, at least in the genetic sense. The profound impact this would have on them supports their right to sole decisional authority as to whether the process of attempting to gestate these preembryos should continue. This brings us directly to the question of how to resolve the dispute that arises when one party wishes to continue the IVF process and the other does not.

VII. BALANCING THE PARTIES' INTERESTS

* * * One way of resolving these disputes is to consider the positions of the parties, the significance of their interests, and the relative burdens that will be imposed by differing resolutions. * * *

Beginning with the burden imposed on Junior Davis, we note that the consequences are obvious. Any disposition which results in the gestation of the preembryos would impose unwanted parenthood on him, with all of its possible financial and psychological consequences. The

would be a futility. Ordering donation over objection would raise the other constitutional problems discussed in Section VI.

impact that this unwanted parenthood would have on Junior Davis can only be understood by considering his particular circumstances, as revealed in the record.

Junior Davis testified that he was the fifth youngest of six children. When he was five years old, his parents divorced, his mother had a nervous break-down, and he and three of his brothers went to live at a home for boys run by the Lutheran Church. Another brother was taken in by an aunt, and his sister stayed with their mother. From that day forward, he had monthly visits with his mother but saw his father only three more times before he died in 1976. Junior Davis testified that, as a boy, he had severe problems caused by separation from his parents. He said that it was especially hard to leave his mother after each monthly visit. He clearly feels that he has suffered because of his lack of opportunity to establish a relationship with his parents and particularly because of the absence of his father.

In light of his boyhood experiences, Junior Davis is vehemently opposed to fathering a child that would not live with both parents. Regardless of whether he or Mary Sue had custody, he feels that the child's bond with the non-custodial parent would not be satisfactory. He testified very clearly that his concern was for the psychological obstacles a child in such a situation would face, as well as the burdens it would impose on him. Likewise, he is opposed to donation because the recipient couple might divorce, leaving the child (which he definitely would consider his own) in a single-parent setting.

Balanced against Junior Davis's interest in avoiding parenthood is Mary Sue Davis's interest in donating the preembryos to another couple for implantation. Refusal to permit donation of the preembryos would impose on her the burden of knowing that the lengthy IVF procedures she underwent were futile, and that the preembryos to which she contributed genetic material would never become children. While this is not an insubstantial emotional burden, we can only conclude that Mary Sue Davis's interest in donation is not as significant as the interest Junior Davis has in avoiding parenthood. If she were allowed to donate these preembryos, he would face a lifetime of either wondering about his parental status or knowing about his parental status but having no control over it. He testified quite clearly that if these preembryos were brought to term he would fight for custody of his child or children. Donation, if a child came of it, would rob him twice—his procreational autonomy would be defeated and his relationship with his offspring would be prohibited.

The case would be closer if Mary Sue Davis were seeking to use the preembryos herself, but only if she could not achieve parenthood by any other reasonable means. We recognize the trauma that Mary Sue has already experienced and the additional discomfort to which she would be subjected if she opts to attempt IVF again. Still, she would have a reasonable opportunity, through IVF, to try once again to achieve parenthood in all its aspects—genetic, gestational, bearing, and rearing.

Further, we note that if Mary Sue Davis were unable to undergo another round of IVF, or opted not to try, she could still achieve the child-rearing aspects of parenthood through adoption. The fact that she and Junior Davis pursued adoption indicates that, at least at one time, she was willing to forego genetic parenthood and would have been satisfied by the child-rearing aspects of parenthood alone.

Notes on Reproductive Technology

1. Is Davis v. Davis rightly decided? Why? If Mrs. Davis intended to have the embryo implanted in her own body, should it have come out differently? Why or why not? In a similar Israeli case, the mother wanted to implant the frozen embryos in a gestational surrogate (her own womb having been removed), as the divorcing couple had planned, and raise the child herself. See Daphne Barak-Erez and Ron Shapira, The Delusion of Symmetric Rights, 19 Oxford J. Legal Stud. 297, 300 (1999) (discussing the *Nachmani* case). The Israeli Supreme Court ultimately decided in favor of the mother, primarily on the basis that the right to become a parent is more important than the right to avoid parenthood. Id. at 303. Is balancing the relative benefits and burdens the appropriate test? What, if any, concerns would you have with that approach? Is it better than a contract approach?

2. Do you agree with the *Davis* court that if the parties had entered into a contract at the time of the freezing of the embryos, their intentions expressed in it should govern the situation upon divorce? If so, should IVF (in vitro fertilization) clinics be regulated so as to require entry into such a contract as a condition of treatment? Is it possible to argue consistently that such a contract should be enforced, but that surrogacy contracts should not be? If the contract provided that the embryo would be implanted, even if they divorced, could it ever be enforceable?

States have differed in their answers to these questions. The New York Court of Appeals enforced an agreement in a divorce case that provided that the couple's frozen embryos be donated to the IVF clinic. Kass v. Kass, 91 N.Y.2d 554, 567–69, 673 N.Y.S.2d 350, 696 N.E.2d 174, 181–82 (1998). By contrast, the Supreme Judicial Court of Massachusetts held that a prior agreement regarding the disposition of frozen preembryos was unenforceable if it compelled one of the parties to become a parent against his or her will. A.Z. v. B.Z., 431 Mass. 150, 159–60, 725 N.E.2d 1051, 1057–58 (2000). A number of states have enacted statutes on the issue. See Fla. Stat. Ann. § 742.17 (West 2000) (requiring couples to execute written agreement for disposition in event of death, divorce, or other unforeseen circumstances); N.H. Rev. Stat. Ann. §§ 168–B:13—168–B:15, 168–B:18 (2000) (requiring couples to undergo counseling and setting 14–day limit for maintenance of ex utero prezygotes); La. Rev. Stat. Ann. §§ 9:121–9:133 (2000) (providing that prezygote is to be considered a "juridical person" that must be implanted). Which of these approaches do you think is the best?

3. The new reproductive technologies have led to mix-ups and concomitant legal and ethical problems. One white woman, for example, brought suit against a fertility clinic for having inseminated her with a Black man's sperm, instead of her husband's. See Dorothy Roberts, Killing the Black

Body: Race, Reproduction, and the Meaning of Liberty 251 (1997). In another case, a fertility doctor mistakenly implanted fertilized eggs from two different women—one white and one black—into one of the two during an in vitro procedure. Five months after the babies' birth, the couples agreed to hand the black baby over to the black couple, although they subsequently went to court over visitation; the decision resulted in the twins being separated from one another almost half a year after birth. Jim Yardley, Joseph's Mother Donna vs. His Mother Deborah, N.Y. Times, June 30, 1999, at A23. What sorts of remedies should be available in these and similar cases?

4. The EEOC found in April 1999 that an employer had violated federal disability laws and the Civil Rights Act when it denied medical insurance coverage for a woman's infertility treatments and the care necessitated by her resulting miscarriage. Randy Kennedy, U.S. Agency Says Employer Should Pay for a Woman's Infertility Treatments, N.Y. Times, Apr. 29, 1999, at B5. It based its ruling on a Supreme Court case including HIV within the ADA and finding that reproduction was "a major life activity" in the context of the disabilities act. Bragdon v. Abbott, 524 U.S. 624, 118 S.Ct. 2196, 141 L.Ed.2d 540 (1998); see also Note, Reproduction Constitutes a "Major Life Activity" Under the ADA: Implications of the Supreme Court's Decision in *Bragdon v. Abbott*, 32 Creighton L. Rev. 1357 (1999) (arguing against inclusion of reproduction under the ADA). What do you think of this ruling? Should infertility be recognized as a disability and covered by prohibitions against discrimination on that basis? Dorothy Roberts suggests that the enormous resources directed into reproductive technology by insurance coverage might better be spent on research on and improvement of the conditions that lead to infertility. Roberts, above note 3, at 290–92. What, if any, legal challenges can be made to legislation that requires insurance companies to pay for IVF but not for abortions?

5. Professor Elizabeth Bartholet argues, based on her own unsuccessful experience with IVF, that this form of technology reinforces and exploits women's conditioning that fertility, pregnancy, childbirth, and mothering are critical to their identities. Bartholet, Family Bonds: Adoption & the Politics of Parenting 29–30, 187–98 (1993). See also Sarah Franklin, Embodied Progress: A Cultural Account of Assisted Conception 101–97 (1997) (describing women's experience of IVF); Silvia Tubert, How IVF Exploits the Wish to Be a Mother: A Psychoanalyst's Account, 14 Genders 33 (1992). In the early 1980's, when Bartholet was attempting IVF, it cost $5,000 for a full treatment cycle, and the chance of a successful pregnancy resulting was about 5%; Bartholet herself went through eight unsuccessful cycles, accompanied by a considerable amount of physical and emotional pain, over a ten-year period. Bartholet, above, at 28, 192–98. Bartholet argues for substantial regulation of IVF, including mandating research and full disclosure of information about the realistic possibilities for success through the process, and against coverage of IVF by medical insurance; she also believes that the legal system as a whole is massively biased in favor of reproduction and biological parenthood and against adoptive parenthood, which is made extremely onerous. Bartholet, above, at 62–85, 201–17. What do you think of these suggestions? What regulations would you suggest?

6. Women of color and poor women have substantial infertility problems yet are unlikely to have access to the high-tech treatments now available; in fact, the majority population fails to see this as an issue, based on the perception that poor women are already "too fertile." Yet fertility and genetic parenthood may be even more heavily charged issues within many minority communities and cultures. Motherhood may be central to a woman's status, for example, and masculinity defined at least in part by the ability to father children. In addition, adoption agencies may impose many barriers upon adoptions by people of color or persons from lower socioeconomic groups. See Laurie Nsiah–Jefferson and Elaine J. Hall, Reproductive Technology: Perspectives and Implications for Low–Income Women and Women of Color, in Healing Technology 108–11 (Kathryn Strother Ratcliff, ed. 1989). Moreover, whereas infertile white couples have a relatively easy time finding donors, African Americans and other people of color find that their options are extremely limited because of a severe lack of Black and racial minority donors of eggs or sperm. Paul Shepard, Infertile Minority Couples Find Few Willing Donors, Charlotte Observer, July 4, 1999, at 12A. How, if at all, can these problems be addressed? See also Roberts, above note 3, at 250–54 (noting economic barriers for African Americans as well).

7. Radical feminists are heavily critical of, and largely opposed to, the new reproductive technologies, pointing to the dangers, for example, of "reproductive brothels" for eugenic breeding and the rise of an international traffic in reproduction, based upon exploitation of third-world women. See, e.g., Gena Corea, The Reproductive Brothel, in Man–Made Women: How New Reproductive Technologies Affect Women 38, 43–44 (Corea et al., eds. 1985) (the term "reproductive brothel" is Andrea Dworkin's). See also Corea, The Mother Machine 213–15, 245 (1985). Socialist feminists, on the other hand, have criticized the radical stance on this issue as based upon an image of women as passive victims, of patriarchy as simply a male plot, and of technology as having a force of its own, separate from the social conditions of its control. See, e.g., Rosalind Pollack Petchesky, Fetal Images: The Power of Visual Culture in the Politics of Reproduction, 13 Feminist Studies 263, 278–80 (1987). The solution, from this perspective, is to alter the conditions under which technology is used and to employ it in the interests of women. For a description of this debate among feminists from the admittedly biased perspective of a radical feminist, see Janice G. Raymond, Reproductive Technologies, Radical Feminism, and Socialist Liberalism, 2 Reproductive & Genetic Engineering 133 (1989). How would liberal feminists come down on this question? A pragmatic feminist?

What do you think? Are the problems envisaged by many feminists in connection with the new reproductive technologies ones that can be solved only by pushing the genie back into the bottle? Are some of them produced by the law's inability to handle the problems of the new technology? Will they be adequately addressed after the legal categories adapt to the new technology, as the common law has done in numerous historical instances? Or would other changes be necessary as well? What are they?

The possibilities and potential drawbacks of repro-tech have been the subject of a good deal of interdisciplinary literature in the late 1990's. See, e.g., Cyborg Babies: From Techno–Sex to Techno–Tots (Robbie Davis–Floyd and Joseph Dumit, eds. 1998) (including cultural anthropologists' arguments that the "cyborgification" of modern life has fundamentally changed reproduction and child-rearing, requiring our society to face new ethical and moral problems); Valerie Hartouni, Cultural Conceptions: On Reproductive Technologies and the Remaking of Life (1997) (describing ways in which cultural "shaping" affects contemporary debates over reproductive practices and processes).

Chapter 7

LAW, WOMEN, AND INTIMATE RELATIONSHIPS

A. INTRODUCTION

How would intimate relationships be structured in a just society? Would marriage exist at all? Western political philosophy has tended either to ignore these questions or to presume that the patriarchal family is the basis of any society. By contrast, Susan Moller Okin suggests that in the just society, which both ensured justice for women and raised fair-minded citizens in a just environment, families might look quite different:

> In a just society, the structure and practices of families must give women the same opportunities as men to develop their capacities, to participate in political power and influence social choices, and to be economically secure. But in addition to this, families must be just because of the vast influence that they have on the moral development of children. The family is the primary institution of formative moral development. And the structure and practices of the family must parallel those of the larger society if the sense of justice is to be fostered and maintained. While many theorists of justice, both past and present, appear to have denied the importance of at least one of these factors, my own view is that both are absolutely crucial. A society that is committed to equal respect for all of its members, and to justice in social distributions of benefits and responsibilities, can neither neglect the family nor accept family structures and practices that violate these norms, as do current gender-based structures and practices. It is essential that children who are to develop into adults with a strong sense of justice and commitment to just institutions spend their earliest and most formative years in an environment in which they are loved and nurtured, *and* in which principles of justice are abided by and respected. What is a child of either sex to learn about fairness in the average household with two full-time working parents, where the mother does, at the very least, twice as much family work as the father?

> What is a child to learn about the value of nurturing and domestic work in a home with a traditional division of labor in which the father either subtly or not so subtly uses the fact that he is the wage earner to "pull rank" on or to abuse his wife? What is a child to learn about responsibility for others in a family in which, after many years of arranging her life around the needs of her husband and children, a woman is faced with having to provide for herself and her children but is totally ill-equipped for the task by the life she agreed to lead, has led, and expected to go on leading?[1]

This chapter addresses Okin's questions in a number of contexts. We begin with an evaluation of traditional marriage and of its impact upon the happiness and welfare of women. After a general exploration of the distribution of power and well-being in marriage, including the division of household labor and the economic impact of divorce, we consider a variety of suggestions for change in the institution, from substantial "tinkering" with post-divorce remedies based on contract, partnership or commercial law, to major changes in the legal treatment, including taxation, of housework, to the total abolition of all legal privileges accorded to marriage. In the final sections, we consider whether cohabitants should be treated as though they were married and examine the issues involved in the debate over same-sex marriage.

B. MARRIAGE, POWER AND WELL BEING

ROBERTA S. SIGEL, AMBITION & ACCOMMODATION: HOW WOMEN VIEW GENDER RELATIONS

96–98, 167–68 (1996).

[Sigel's study is based on a telephone survey of 600 New Jersey residents, both male and female, and focus groups involving 50 others, in six all-male or all-female groups, concerning their perceptions of the past and present status of gender relations. The first excerpt below is about women's responses; the second about men's.]

The political or apolitical nature of these women's responses to what most of them perceived as an unjust situation becomes more comprehensible when one becomes acquainted with the areas which most seem to trouble them. In analyzing the focus group transcripts, I have focused on the topics cited with the greatest regularity. One topic, housework, commanded an extraordinary amount of their attention. Much of the women's groups' two hours together was devoted to complaining about the unfair division of labor at home, especially the lack of cooperation they receive from their partners. My first inclination had been to bypass those conversations rather than to include them in a chapter on political involvement. I abandoned that idea when I realized what a central role these everyday activities played in the formation of their gendered perspectives.

1. Susan Moller Okin, Justice, Gender, and the Family 22–23 (1989).

The household division of labor may well have been the occasion that first made some of these women conscious of their inferior status in the constellation of things, so that they began to consider the situation at home as symptomatic of women's inferior status in society at large. So long as they stayed home while the spouses went out to work, the structure of inequality may not have been apparent to them. But once they too went into the labor market and still were expected to shoulder the main burden of the household, the discrepancy between male and female statuses became obvious and may have provided the spark that ignited their sense of second-class citizenship.

That employed women carry a much heavier burden of domestic responsibilities than their male partners is by now hardly news * * *. Still I was surprised that the issue of the "second shift" dominated the focus group discussions to the extent that it did and to the exclusion of other social problems and their political implications. * * *

All of their complaints about the heavy burden of their many and varied domestic responsibilities notwithstanding, only a few of the participants reported having attempted to create a more equitable division of labor at home. Ironically, the one woman who did notice a dramatic change in her blue-collar husband, who "never helped me when the children were small, and I needed it most," and who now helps her "quite a bit, now we are doing pretty good," was a woman in her fifties of a traditional immigrant background. Her tale provoked considerable astonishment in the group, leading one woman to inquire in wonderment: "how did you bring him around?" The storyteller paused briefly and then conceded that it was not she who was able to accomplish this result but her children: "It's just through time because the world changes; the kids changed, the generation and everything changed." She gave major credit to her daughter and then added: "They [the men] see it on TV. They listen to other people. My son grows up, he brings girls, they talk, he listens. And that is how you learn." She did mention, however, that the change came about very gradually. "You can't do it overnight, otherwise you wind up [divorced.]" Others reported that their attempts to have husbands share in running the house usually had not met with similar success, and a few did not even make the attempt. In a typical instance, a full-time clerical worker in her early forties felt particularly put upon and complained that she can expect no help with childcare (she has four children) or housework beyond an occasional lawn-mowing. When the moderator asked: "Have you ever chatted about dividing up responsibilities or anything like that?" The woman replied: "Well, he would not even listen to that. He feels like he works hard enough doing his things. So, whatever I do is, you know, you are supposed to do."

Many women of all ages in these groups are dissatisfied with their current domestic arrangements. Younger women especially tend to view the "second shift" as a forceful indication that women have not yet achieved true equality. A recently married college graduate, for example, "would not say we have an equal partnership" because her husband, though he helps a good deal, shrinks from certain chores, such as cleaning the bathroom. To her, equality between the genders requires sharing chores equally. Listening to this tale, a woman in her fifties retorted that the young woman really has nothing to complain about. "When I was young and had to go out to work and had children, I got no help. Either you're a mother or you get a divorce. So I said to myself: Hang in there, Mary." Others quickly added that even today things haven't changed all that much for most women. One member summarized it for almost all: "Men want to be treated like a prince, that is the attitude that a lot of men have right now, and they feel entitled to it because their mothers raised them that way, and now it is little wife who takes care of the house and cleans, puts the clean underwear in the drawer and makes sure that he has clean shirts." What most annoyed these handmaidens to princes was that their work is taken for granted and that so little consideration is shown to them at home. Their feelings were very much in keeping with the finding * * * that in the domestic realm women are most likely to feel relatively deprived when they are not accorded the consideration they feel they deserve, whereas in the workplace perceptions of monetary discrimination are those most likely to cause feelings of relative deprivation.

Listening to these conversations about the domestic scene, the observers gathered behind the one-way mirror of the recording studio had the collective impression that the women they observed were both hurt and angry but simultaneously resigned to the realization that drastic change in domestic arrangements was not to occur in the immediate future. Some in the focus group apparently share this perspective. One member put this impression succinctly when she suddenly exclaimed: "See how resigned everyone sounds. We all have a note of resignation." Her comments and those of others suggest that for these women "the gender roles implicit in the marriage relationship basically remained unaltered."

* * *

[The following excerpt is from the chapter on "The Male Perspective."]

The inequitable division of labor in the household was one of the major sources for women's complaints. Listening to the focus group men discuss the topic, one suspects that women's complaints have merit. The men we observed were not particularly empathic with the dual responsibility thrust upon wives as they are working two shifts, one at home and one at work. When the male telephone respondents were asked if "too much is demanded of today's young women because they are expected to be good workers as well as good homemakers and parents," 51 percent rejected the notion that too much is demanded while 60 percent of the women believed that the demands are excessive. In the focus groups, men simply ignored the subject, as though it were quite natural to expect women to work two shifts, perhaps assuming that they could do it with as much ease as they might add a weekly aerobics class. If they mentioned it at all—as a few blue-collar men did—they did so to complain about demands their working wives are beginning to make on them, especially with respect to help in the house. Our maintenance worker expressed this complaint in his usual colorful way: "My wife works in a bank. She's in air-conditioning all day. I work in a factory. I'm in the heat all day. I come home, and she gets pissed off because I don't have dinner ready." The college student who declared, "It is hard out there. Hard even for girls. It is easier to get married and have a husband who works real hard" is a distinct exception; for most group members the second shift is a nonproblem. In the female focus groups, as we saw earlier, men's lack of cooperation in the domestic sphere carried at least as much, if not more, emotional baggage as any other gender-based inequity about which they complained. Because women related that the uneven division-of-labor was becoming a source of conflict between men and women, I was surprised at the male focus groups' failure to discuss the topic at even a moderate length. Apparently, they either do not notice the uneven division of labor as such, or believe it poses no problem, and it only becomes a problem for them when their wives or partners want to alter the division, that is, when it interferes with men's personal comfort or preferences, as when weekends are taken up by chores instead of relaxation, or when they are called upon to help with housework. Male telephone respondents again voiced more egalitarian sentiments than did the focus group participants. Asked how labor should be divided in the household when both partners are employed, over two-thirds believed it should be divided evenly (an opinion held by 90 percent of the women), and virtually no man believed that men should be exempt from domestic responsibilities. * * * [A] national survey [was] conducted in 1978 in which 67 percent of the men expressed the same sentiments. Apparently not much has changed since; good intentions there were aplenty then and still are. However, only a small segment of the males in our study (14 percent) believed that equal sharing actually takes place. Nor do either men or women doubt that the customary arrangement is unfair (68:73 percent respectively). The telephone respondents' expressions of concern, in contrast to the focus group's relative silence on the topic, can probably be explained because interviewees were required to deal with the issue, so they gave the socially desirable response that the current arrangement was not fair. But in the focus groups, where no such stimulus was provided, men rarely raised the issue because for them it was not an issue of any consequence. The middle-class group all but ignored it, whereas in the blue-collar group some fleeting comments are made to the effect that the wife may complain that "I don't uphold my end," as one man puts it, and they may even concede that the complaint is justified. But it is stated matter-of-factly without any discussion that maybe something could be done about it. That the men in the focus groups never addressed the issue seriously may support Jessie Bernard's [The Future of Marriage] (1972) argument, namely, that men and women operate under two different marriage contracts. It would seem that in many families even today the husband's contract ("the husband's marriage" as she called it) requires little change in his lifestyle and work responsibilities, whereas "the wife's marriage" requires taking on the additional obligation of functioning as a housewife.

JANICE M. STEIL, MARITAL EQUALITY: ITS RELATIONSHIP TO THE WELL-BEING OF HUSBANDS AND WIVES

24, 29–30, 32–35, 39–42 (1997).

The Relationship Between Marital Power and Partners' Well-Being

[After surveying the voluminous social science literature on power and well-being in marriage, Steil and her colleagues tested this relationship by sampling 815 primarily white dual-career couples who had participated in a national survey on paid employment and family work. Beginning with a definition of power as "the ability to influence important decisions and to get others to do what they otherwise wouldn't," respondents were asked to indicate how the responsibility for making major decisions and the performance of a number of household and child-care tasks were allocated.]

* * *

Predictors of Decision-Making Say and Domestic Task Sharing

* * * *Resources* have been defined as anything one partner brings to a relationship that helps the other partner satisfy needs or achieve goals. Yet economic resources, such as income and job prestige, seem to play a disproportionate role in determining marital influence. Husbands, who have traditionally earned more and held more prestigious jobs than wives, have had more financial and status resources to bring to the relationship and, according to some, these have been exchanged for greater authority and less work at home. To test this idea, we looked at the effect of husbands' and wives' absolute earnings, their earnings relative to their spouses' earnings, and age, education, and perceived job importance as predictors of decision-making say and responsibility sharing.

Analyses showed no effect for partners' absolute earnings. Thus, how much one earned was unrelated to the amount of influence one had. One's earnings relative to one's spouse was an important predictor of marital power for women without children but was unrelated to the power of mothers. The more a woman without children earned relative to her husband, the less responsibility she had for the house and the greater her say in marital decisions. For women who were mothers, however, earnings relative to their spouses' earnings were unrelated to any of the responsibility or influence variables. Thus, it seemed that earning power relative to one's spouse did not work the same way for women with children as it did for women without children.

When we looked at the effects of all the factors, we found that the single most important predictor overall was not any of the income variables but rather perceived career importance. For husbands and wives without children, the more important they perceived their own jobs to be, relative to their spouses' jobs, the more responsibility they had for decision making. Also, for mothers, the more they valued their own jobs relative to their husbands' jobs, the greater their say in decision making and the less responsibility they had for household tasks.

But child care was a different story. Neither perceived job importance nor earnings relative to her spouse were related to a mother's responsibility for child care. Thus, for mothers, no matter how much they earned, either in absolute terms or in relation to their spouses' earnings, and no matter how important they perceived their own job to be relative to their husbands' job, they still retained the major responsibility for the children.

* * *

Domestic Task Sharing and Psychological Well–Being

We then turned to the primary question of the study: To what extent did say in decision making and responsibility for domestic work predict the frequency of husbands' and wives' self-reported symptoms after marital and career satisfaction were considered? For those with the most power, that is, husbands and wives without children, there was little relationship between the measures of marital influence and well-being. Indeed, the only relationship to reach significance was contrary to our hypotheses. For husbands without children, the more they shared in the work of the home, the *less* dysphoric symptomatology [e.g., feeling worthless, lonely, sad, irritable, having trouble concentrating, or being bothered by irrational fears] they reported.

When we considered the relationships between responsibility, influence and well-being among those with the least influence, that is, the employed mothers, we found quite a different picture. Here, the relationships were quite strong. The more equal a mother's say in decision making and the more her husband shared in the responsibilities of child care, the less dysphoria she reported. She was less likely to report feeling lonely, sad, irritable, worried, tense, weepy, fearful, worthless, and disinterested in sex. For mothers, then, greater husband involvement in child care and equal say in decision making were both associated with greater well-being. Contrary to expectation, however, increased husband responsibility for household tasks was associated with higher, rather than lower, levels of dysphoric symptoms for the mother in this sample.

Why should greater husband involvement in household tasks be associated with greater distress for their partners? * * *

* * * Blumstein and Schwartz (1983) found that the more housework husbands did, the more couples fought about it. Do husbands who help resent it and extract a cost for their labors? * * *

* * *

[I]t was not the presence of children, per se, that was associated with reductions in well-being. Rather, the arrival of children seemed to undermine the relative equality of the relationships by reactivating traditional gender roles, and it was this relative inequality that was associated with increases in psychological symptomatology. * * *

The findings, however, also raise a number of questions. Why do employed wives with children suffer a decline in influence compared to wives without children? Do they step back from their careers after the birth of their children and begin to de-emphasize the importance of their own jobs compared to their husbands'? There was no evidence of career de-emphasis on the part of the mothers in this sample. Mothers did not rate their careers as being less important. Furthermore, for this sample, the mothers actually reported somewhat higher earnings than their childless counterparts.

* * * But what is perceived job importance really measuring? Is it measuring partners' self-esteem? Is it measuring their sense of entitlement to pursue their careers? Is it measuring a sense of entitlement to more equal sharing so that they *can* pursue their careers?

* * *

Overall, the general pattern of findings seems to support the notion that the ways in which domestic responsibilities and say in decision making are shared are related to partners' marital satisfaction and wives' psychological well-being. The findings of the studies of decision-making say are the most consistent and therefore easiest to interpret. These studies show that a wife's dominance in decision making, which is relatively rare, is associated with the lowest levels of marital satisfaction for both partners. A husband's dominance in decision-making say may be more frequently associated with satisfaction for husbands than for wives, whereas equal sharing may be associated with the highest levels of satisfaction for wives. When we considered other measures in addition to marital satisfaction, the findings suggest that relatively equal say is most beneficial for relationships. Relatively equal relationships were characterized by more mutually supportive communication, less manipulative forms of influence, and greater sexual and marital satisfaction for both partners than were relationships in which either one of the partners was dominant.

* * *

[S]ome of the patterns seem consistent. First of all, there is no evidence that husbands are impaired through increased participation in domestic work. Although it is true that husbands did less than wives, the fact that husbands' participation in housework did not cause reductions in well-being for men supports the notion that it is not just the nature of domestic work that impairs well-being. * * * Thus, the more a husband shares in the work of the home, the less it may seem that a person of lower status is doing menial work for a person of higher status, and the invidious message of a status difference is replaced by a sense of mutual cooperation and sharing.

* * * [E]arnings relative to one's spouse and one's perceived career importance predicted husbands' involvement in housework but not child care. Consistent with subsequent studies' findings, husbands' involvement in child care and domestic work were not associated in the same ways with wives' well-being. Once again, it seems that it is important to consider not only how much husbands and wives do but how what they do is perceived. * * * To what extent is a wife's identity defined by her role of homemaker and mother? To what extent is a husband's identity defined by his ability to provide? Do these gender identities determine the ways in which men's domestic work is perceived—as willing participation in shared responsibilities? Or as threatening to husbands and wives alike? * * *

The inconsistencies are exacerbated when we look at the limited number of studies among Hispanics. Yet there are no studies that systematically compare the relationship between partner well-being and partner involvement in child care and household work across ethnic groups and no studies of these relationships among blacks.

In short, the findings of the studies are consistent with the hypothesis that gender differences in emotional well-being and mental health are associated with gender differences in power and status. Yet they do not seem to tell the whole story, and they do not preclude other possible explanations. They do not examine the psychological meanings of housework, child care, or equal sharing for men or for women or across race and class. Thus, in some ways, they raise as many questions as they answer. Would the well-being differences be eliminated if relationships were in fact equal? Is it really equality of power that matters? Or is it something else? Partners' perceptions of their social roles? A sense of fairness? Perceptions of support? And if equality is important, how should it be defined? How should it be measured? Why does it matter? * * *

Notes on Power and Well–Being in Marriage

1. How would you answer the questions posed in the last paragraph of the Steil excerpt, immediately above? Why do you think a wife's earning power vis à vis her spouse is unrelated to her power once she has children?

2. If you received a grant to study the issue of power within marriage and emotional well-being in marriage among Hispanic and/or African American groups, what questions would you want to ask? Would your focus be any different from that in the Steil study? Do you have any hypotheses about how the results might be different from or similar to those in the excerpt above?

3. How would the following factors be likely to influence power in marriage, and which partner would each factor empower in most marriages? Consider: emotional dependence; commitment to the marriage; options at

divorce; economic dependence (especially in light of divorce options); age; membership in socially dominant group (such as men, whites, upper class, Harvard graduates, Ph.D.'s, etc.); children who need care; appearance; the need to be socially accepted as a "couple."

4. Are women afraid to exercise power because they fear being selfish and destructive and perceive their exercise of power as hazardous to their intimate relationships? See Jean Baker Miller, Women and Power, in Women, Power, and Therapy: Issues for Women 1 (Marjorie Braude, ed. 1988) (defining power as the capacity to effect change, to move something from one state or point to another, and suggesting that women are afraid to exercise power because women are conditioned to live for others).

5. Think of all the ways in which sexuality might affect or reveal power in marriage. A study of couples in the Netherlands by Aafke Komter focused on how women and men would change their sex lives, indicating that sex is something women tend to regard as a duty they owe men, i.e., it is men who desire sex and women who supply it. Komter, Hidden Power in Marriage, 3 Gender & Soc'y 187, 200–201 (1989). Does this give women power over men (being able to say no), or does it reveal women's lack of power (they feel unable to say no)? Should the more desired partner have more power? Why doesn't men's supposedly greater sexual desire translate into power for women?

Think of the relationship between power, on the one hand, and the correlation between sexual norms in one's culture and one's own sexual pleasures, on the other. For example, what is the effect on women's power of living in a culture in which heterosexual sex is defined as heterosexual intercourse, though many women appear to enjoy other pleasures more? What is the effect of this cultural definition on power in marriage? If only one partner were regarded by the couple's culture as having a sexuality unstoppable once aroused, how would that perception affect power in marriage?

6. How do relationships with children affect power in marriage? If one parent is less sensitive to the needs of children or violent to them, what is the effect on power between the spouses? Does satisfaction of children's needs count, in some marriages, as satisfaction of the needs of one parent only? Which parent would that tend to be? How might custody standards at divorce affect power during marriage? How might concern about the economic well-being of children after divorce affect power during marriage? How might concern about one's own economic status after divorce affect power in marriage? See, e.g., Penelope Eileen Bryan, The Coercion of Women in Divorce Settlement Negotiations, 74 Denver U.L. Rev. 931, 931–35 (1997) (describing how a variety of unfair background conditions, including custody standards, concern for children, and unequal economic power affect divorce negotiations and settlements). See also Bryan, Women's Freedom to Contract at Divorce: A Mask for Contextual Coercion, 47 Buffalo L. Rev. 1153 (1999).

7. Should we measure power in marriage by comparing hours spent on tedious household chores (the more hours, the less the power) or by comparing hours of leisure (the more leisure, the more power)? As the studies above show, although women's hours working outside the home have

risen dramatically over the last 30 years, there has been no dramatic change in men's domestic labor. Why haven't women insisted on a more just distribution of labor? What does this suggest about the relative distribution of power in marriage?

8. As Steil notes, there is considerable evidence that men's higher wages support their greater power in marriage. In a study of lesbian, gay, and heterosexual couples, where power was measured in terms of partners' ratings of their relative power, the authors found a correlation between power and wages except for lesbian couples. Philip Blumstein and Pepper Schwartz, American Couples: Money, Work, Sex 53–77 (1983). This study suggests that higher wages tend to give the higher-earning partner, whether husband or wife or gay male (but not lesbian partner), more power in terms both of monetary decisions and self-ratings of relative power.

In contrast, Arlie Hochschild found no correlation between the wage gap and the leisure gap (the fact that working mothers have less leisure time than working fathers in most marriages): higher-earning men were not less likely to share domestic burdens; however, men who earned less than their wives *were* less likely to share. Hochschild, The Second Shift 221 (1989). Can this finding be reconciled with the Pepper–Schwartz findings? Why might higher wages actually increase a woman's domestic responsibilities?

9. What is the effect on relative power in marriage of being the spouse society regards as the breadwinner versus the spouse society regards as the primary caretaker (the person called by the school or day care center when there is a problem or the child is sick)? See Blumstein and Schwartz, above note 8, at 56–59 (belief of either spouse in male provider role increases husband's power in marriage, even if the wife earns more).

10. Beginning in adolescence, there is a self-esteem gap. Women are likely to have lower self-esteem than men and are likely to attribute success to luck and failure to their own incompetence, whereas men are likely to attribute failure to luck and success to their own competence. See, e.g., Pamela Robison–Awana, Thomas J. Kehle, and William R. Jenson, But What About Smart Girls? Adolescent Self–Esteem and Sex Role Perceptions as a Function of Academic Achievement, 78 J. Educ. Psych. 179 (1986) (showing 7th–grade boys had higher self-esteem than 7th–grade girls); Pauline Rose Clance and Maureen Ann O'Toole, The Imposter Phenomenon: An Internal Barrier to Empowerment and Achievement, 6 Women & Therapy 51 (1987) (discussing high-achieving women's tendency to feel like imposters). See also Mary Pipher, Reviving Ophelia: Saving the Selves of Adolescent Girls (1994). What does this self-esteem gap suggest about the distribution of power in marriage?

11. Despite (or because of?) the racism they face, African American women tend to have high self-esteem. See, e.g., Janice E. Hale–Benson, Black Children: Their Roots, Culture, and Learning Styles (1986). Why is there this difference between African American and white women? Do their different expectations of marriage account for it, at least in part? Are African American girls expected to grow into women who are more independent than the women white girls are expected to become? Are white girls, perhaps, expected to suppress themselves more in order to find Prince Charming, who will thereafter be primarily responsible for their economic needs? Although

Black women tend to have high self-esteem and are sometimes eager for the luxury of being able to stay home with their children, one study of professional Black women found higher self-esteem among those pursuing careers than among those who had become homemakers. Pamela Hayling Hoffman and Janice Hale–Benson, Self–Esteem of Black Middle–Class Women Who Choose To Work Inside or Outside the Home, 15 J. Multicultural Counseling & Development 71, 76–78 (1987).

12. With respect to physical health, both married women and married men tend to be healthier than single people, though marriage seems to give men a somewhat greater physical health advantage than women. See, e.g., Robert H. Coombs, Marital Status and Personal Well–Being: A Literature Review, 40 Family Relations 97 (1991) (inverse relationship, especially for men, between marriage and alcoholism, suicide, morbidity and wide range of psychiatric disorders); Lee A. Lillard and Linda J. Waite, 'Til Death Do Us Part: Marital Disruption and Mortality, 100 Am. J. Sociol. 1131 (1995) (opining that marriage improves health and mortality of men perhaps due to household management skills and labor of wife and improves women's health and mortality through improved financial well-being). It is generally thought that women are more anxious to marry than men are. Is this true, in your experience? Why, in light of the fact that marriage seems to give men more advantages in terms of mental and physical health?

For discussions of how the media fosters women's anxiety about their chances of marriage, see Jennifer Jaff, Wedding Bell Blues: The Position of Unmarried People in American Law, 30 Ariz.L.Rev. 207, 213–14 (1988); Susan Faludi, Backlash: The Undeclared War Against American Women 99–104 (1991).

13. Marriage appears to correlate with mental as well as physical health for both men and women. A review of the literature and a 17–nation (all Western industrial nations) study show a positive relation between marriage and happiness, in part because of health and economic benefits and in part attributable to emotional support. See Steven Stack and J. Ross Eshleman, Marital Status and Happiness: A 17–Nation Study, 60 J. Marriage & Family 527, 534 (1998) (based on data on 18,000 adults in 17 nations collected during 1981–1983). Although some have hypothesized that the relationship between marriage and mental health may diminish as there is more economic, social, and normative support for remaining single, recent longitudinal studies of younger people show that, in general, being married is still associated with positive mental health. See, e.g., Allan V. Horwitz, Helene Raskin White, and Sandra Howell–White, Becoming Married and Mental Health: A Longitudinal Study of a Cohort of Young Adults, 58 J. Marriage & Family 895 (1996). Married women are, in general, happier than single women, including cohabiting single women; researchers explain this "marriage bonus" by the greater commitment and personal support, as well as financial advantages of marriage. Stack and Eshleman, above, at 534.

One possible hypothesis for the inverse relationship between marriage and depression is that psychologically healthier people get married and those with poor mental health are less likely both to get married and to stay married. This so-called "self-selection hypothesis" appears to have been disproved by recent studies, however. See, e.g., Coombs, above note 12;

Nadine F. Marks, Flying Solo at Midlife: Gender, Marital Status, and Psychological Well-being, 58 J. Marriage & Family 917, 930 (1996) (finding that single women are generally superior in mental ability and personality compared with married women, contrary to the negative selection hypothesis). Most recent studies point to the beneficial effect upon psychological well-being of having a confidant who offers intimate emotional support and the opportunity for self-disclosure, which are often available from a spouse in modern companionate marriage. See, e.g., Marks, above; Catherine E. Ross, Reconceptualizing Marital Status As a Continuum of Social Attachment, 57 J. Marriage & Family 129 (1995).

Much depends, however, on the quality of the marital relationship; being in a bad relationship produces higher distress levels than being alone. Id. This connection appears to be stronger for women than for men. One study suggests that unhappily married women are more likely to be depressed than their husbands because the quality of their relationships is more integral to feelings of self-esteem for women than for men. Laurie N. Culp and Steven R.H. Beach, Marriage and Depressive Symptoms: The Role and Bases of Self–Esteem Differ by Gender, 22 Psychology of Women Q. 647 (1998).

14. In an essay on the "sociology of superordinates," William J. Goode makes the following points:

> 1. The observations made by either men or women about members of the other sex are limited and somewhat biased by what they are most interested in and by their lack of opportunity to observe behind the scenes of each others' lives. However, far less of what men do is determined by women; what men do affects women much more. As a consequence, men are often simply less motivated to observe carefully many aspects of women's behavior and activity because women's behavior does not usually affect what men propose to do. By contrast, almost everything men do will affect what women *have* to do, and thus women are motivated to observe men's behavior as keenly as they can.
>
> 2. Since any given cohort of men know they did not create the system that gives them their advantages, they reject any charges that they conspired to dominate women.
>
> 3. Since men, like other dominants or superordinates, take for granted the system that gives them their status, they are not aware of how much the social structure, from attitude patterns to law, pervasively yields small, cumulative, and eventually large advantages in most competitions. As a consequence, they assume that their greater accomplishments are actually the result of inborn superiority.
>
> 4. As a corollary to this male view, when men weigh their situation, they are more aware of the burdens and responsibilities they bear than of their unearned advantages.
>
> 5. Superiors, and thus men, do not easily notice the talents or accomplishments of subordinates, and men have not in the past seen much wisdom in giving women more opportunities for growth, for women are not capable of much anyway, especially in the areas of men's special skills. Thus, in the past, few women have embarrassed men by

becoming superior in those areas. When they did, their superiority was seen, and is often still seen, as an odd exception. As a consequence, men see their superior position as a just one.

6. Men view even small losses of deference, advantages, or opportunities as large threats. Their own gains, or their maintenance of old advantages, are not noticed as much.

Goode, Why Men Resist, in Rethinking the Family: Some Feminist Questions 287, 294–95 (Barrie Thorne and Marilyn Yalom, eds. 1992). With which of these points do you agree? With which do you disagree? To the extent true, what is the effect of these factors on power and potential for change within marriage?

15. Do you agree that through marriage "women especially come to have a vested interest in the social unit that at the same time imposes inequalities on them"? Goode, above note 14, at 296. See also Mary E. Becker, Politics, Differences, and Economic Rights, 1989 U. Chi. Legal F. 169, 183–86. Why does this occur? Is this vested interest real or illusory?

16. If, as Sigel's study seems to illustrate, men don't see the problem of their wives' double burden in the family, how can these men see a problem with their female co-worker's struggles to balance home and work?

C. THE ECONOMIC CONSEQUENCES OF DISSOLVING AN INTIMATE RELATIONSHIP

KAREN C. HOLDEN AND PAMELA J. SMOCK, THE ECONOMIC COSTS OF MARITAL DISSOLUTION: WHY DO WOMEN BEAR A DISPROPORTIONATE COST?

17 Ann. Rev. Soc. 52–53, 57–63, 68–70, 72–74 (1991).

There is little dispute that women without husbands are worse off economically than their married peers or than they themselves were when still married. Households headed by women, whether by young mothers or elderly women (typically without children), are more likely to be poor than households headed by men of similar age. * * *

It is important to start the discussion by recognizing that the standard measures of well-being treat all family members who live together in one household as an economic unit within which resources are assumed to be equally shared. By these assumptions wives cannot be worse off than their husbands—unequal market earnings (or other income receipts) are assumed to convert into equally accessible income in the family unit. Similarly, children cannot be worse off than the parents with whom they reside.

When marriages dissolve through divorce any inequality in the sharing of resources can be directly observed. Following divorce, it is assumed that no sharing occurs between separated parents or between noncustodial parents and their children unless income transfers (or expenditure payments) are explicitly reported. Divorced status *defines* separate consumption units.

Marital dissolution through death, on the other hand, leaves only one consumption unit. In widowhood, sharing of income can extend beyond marriage only through a transfer to the survivor—through insurance or inheritance—of resources previously paid solely to the deceased spouse. In the absence of such transfers, the economic status of the widow is substantially lowered.

The "story" that the marital dissolution literature seeks to explain is why equal sharing between marriage partners ceases upon marital dissolution. One may conclude that in divorce sharing ceases when "caring" does and that the spouse with the larger income attempts to retain a disproportionate share of the former household's total resources. Emotional alienation leads to sharp economic division.

A similarly facile explanation is not available, however, in the case of widowhood. Husbands are presumed to care for their wives, and, in contrast to the situation in divorce, an active insurance market has developed to enable husbands to ensure the continued well-being of the widow. Yet, as we show here, the widowhood literature finds declines in economic well-being for newly widowed women similar in magnitude to those for women who become divorced.

What are the common threads that bind these women to a common experience as their marriages dissolve? * * *

Effects of Separation and Divorce on Women's Economic Well-Being

Numerous longitudinal studies concur that separation and divorce have detrimental economic consequences for women. These studies track economic well-being through time, comparing predivorce to postdivorce economic status. Three central themes emerge from this literature. First, despite a wide range of estimates across studies and subgroups of women, there is remarkable consensus that divorce is associated with economic decline for women. Second, gender differentials are marked, with men generally better off following separation and divorce, relative both to women and to their predisruption standard of living. Third, unless women remarry, the economic deterioration they experience is likely to be prolonged.

Short–Term Effects

* * *

Estimates of declines in income-to-needs experienced by women following separation or divorce range from a low of −6.7% to a high of −73%. Corcoran (1979)[a] and Stirling (1989)[b] report declines in income-

a. M. Corcoran, The Economic Consequences of Marital Dissolution for Women in the Middle Years, 5 Sex Roles 343 (1979).

b. K.J. Stirling, Women Who Remain Divorced: The Long-term Economic Consequences, 70 Soc. Sci. Q. 549 (1989).

to-needs of approximately 20 to 30%. While Duncan & Hoffman[c] report an overall decrease of only 13%, they show considerable variance among women, with both black women and white women who were relatively well-off during marriage experiencing a decline in income-to-needs of 20 to 30%.

Evidence of Gender Differentials: The Unequal Costs of Divorce

There is no simple answer to the question of how much decline in economic status women will experience following separation and divorce. Some decline in economic well-being is expected when one household becomes two simply due to losses in economies of scale. What is problematic is the overwhelming evidence, which we review below, that men—unlike women—experience an increase in economic well-being upon divorce. In theory, a disparity in outcomes between divorced men and women could be explained merely by gender inequalities in earning power. However, to the extent that children are involved in a separation and divorce, it is more difficult to explain this disparity. In the case of divorce, children have two living parents that presumably care about their economic welfare. We might therefore expect that the standard of living in postdivorce households with children would more often reflect that of the nonresidential parent, who is generally the father.

* * *

Available evidence indicates that, unlike women's, men's standard of living improves following separation or divorce. Hoffman (1977)[d] estimates that the income-to-needs ratio of separated and divorced men increases by 16.5%, even after deductions for alimony and child support payments. Duncan & Hoffman (1985) report an increase of 13% in income-to-needs between the year before marital disruption and the year after disruption, with all subgroups of men in their sample experiencing an improvement. By the second year after disruption, men's average income-to-needs rise to 24% above predivorce levels. Weitzman's (1985)[e] data suggest that, even after deductions for child support and alimony awards, men experience a 42% improvement in income-to-needs.

How can this evidence be reconciled with the economic hardship that women experience after divorce? Rather than promoting equality in the postdivorce standard of living between men and women, children appear key to this inequality; more precisely, the differential responsibility for children undertaken by men and women is crucial. First, few men assume physical custody of their children following separation or divorce. This translates into a substantial decrease in "needs" for fathers.

c. G.J. Duncan & S.D. Hoffman, Economic Consequences of Marital Instability, in Horizontal Equity, Uncertainty, and Economic Well–Being 427 (M. David & T. Smeeding, eds., 1985).

d. S. Hoffman, Marital Instability and the Economic Status of Women, 14 Demography 67 (1977).

e. L.J. Weitzman, The Divorce Revolution: The Unexpected Social and Economic Consequences for Women and Children in America (1985).

Second, only a minority of men fully comply with child support awards, and, even when they do, payments are meager. Third, husbands tend to earn more than wives, which is related to gender inequities in nonmarket work and childcare both during marriage and after divorce. The upshot is that men retain a larger share of the family's income, while their economic needs decrease more than their income.

Longer–Term Effects of Divorce: Do Women Recover?

* * *

Most longitudinal studies indicate that women's economic vulnerability is prolonged for at least five years, unless remarriage occurs, and despite dramatic increase in labor force participation and hours worked upon separation and divorce. Earnings constitute the primary source of income for most separated and divorced women; while some subgroups of women manage to increase their incomes slightly over time, this does not bring them near predisruption income-to-needs levels. * * *

Studies agree that remarriage is the most likely route to economic recovery. * * *

EFFECTS OF WIDOWHOOD ON WOMEN'S ECONOMIC WELL–BEING

Despite changes over the past two decades in pension and social security policy that have sought specifically to improve the economic security of widows, longitudinal studies show that the economic consequences of widowhood are no less detrimental to women than are those of divorce and separation. * * *

Short–Term Effects

Measures of economic change when women are widowed typically compare poverty status or income-to-needs during a year early in widowhood to that in the last year the husband was alive. The "short-term" period depends upon the inter-survey period for the panel, which is two years in the Retirement History Study (RHS) * * *.

Using selected years of data from the RHS, Hurd & Wise (1989)[f] report an increase in poverty rates from 9 to 42% as women are widowed. * * *

A substantial fall in income is a hazard faced not only by the poor. Examining that risk across income groups shows that greater pre-widowed income protects against poverty (which can be entered only with a large absolute income decline), but that higher income women are more likely to suffer a substantial decline in income-to-needs when widowed. * * *

f. M. Hurd & D.A. Wise, The Wealth and Poverty of Widows: Assets Before and After the Husband's Death, in The Economics of Aging (D. Wise, ed. 1989).

The Unequal Costs of Widowhood: Evidence of Gender Differentials

* * *

Studies that compare the experience of widows and widowers show that the economic experience of the widowers differs from that of widows. * * * [W]hile the needs-adjusted income of women falls sharply when their husbands die, men's incomes remain stable upon the deaths of their wives.

Women suffer a large fall in income when their husbands die for largely the same reasons women suffer upon divorce. Similarly, the disparate effect on women and men of divorce and widowhood have [sic] like explanations. * * *

The relative well-being of divorced wives and husbands or of widows and widowers is closely linked to economic independence of the individual spouses and the mechanisms developed by society to facilitate or compel the sharing of resources beyond the married state. As is true of divorced women, widows lose direct access (previously obtained through shared living) to any income that was previously (and, in divorce, continues to be) paid solely to the husband. Consider, for example, two couples with identical earnings contributed by the husband. At the time one couple separates into two houses and the husband of the other dies, the female-headed households *by definition* no longer have direct access to the (ex- or deceased) husband's earnings.

The divorced wife may be able to negotiate some sharing (perhaps by court order) in her ex-husband's earnings, while for the widowed woman no such initiative *after* marital dissolution is possible. On the other hand, the widow may be shielded by private or social insurance against the income consequences of her husband's death; the absence of equivalent "divorce" insurance removes that source of *predissolution*-determined security for the divorced woman. If eventually divorced or widowed couples are no different with respect to the control of income when married, and if husbands fail to protect their wives against the risk of marital dissolution, observed effects of widowhood and divorce will be similar.

In the United States, social security provides almost universal insurance against the economic consequences of widowhood. Survivor benefits are paid either if the widow has a child under the age of 16, or is 60 or older (50 if disabled). Younger widows without young children receive no protection. A second leg of protection for widows is the pensions in which their husbands may have been vested. Since the passage of the 1974 Employee Retirement Income Security Act, pensions must offer a joint and survivor benefit (that is, a pension some share of which continues to the survivor) as the default form. Nevertheless, pension income may not continue to the widow—husbands may choose a single life pension (although under the 1984 Retirement Equity Act the wife must concur), pension plans may offer lump sum payments as the primary payment form (thereby by-passing the ERISA requirement), and pensions may deny payment of survivor benefits to the widow until that time the deceased husband *would have* reached age of eligibility for retirement benefits. * * *

CONTRIBUTING FACTORS

* * *

A * * * [key] factor is the preexisting economic vulnerability of women in general relative to men, owing to the disadvantages women face in the labor market *regardless of marital status.* * * * The crucial point is that whatever is the source of their lower earnings potential, when thrust into the role of primary earner, formerly married women are unlikely to match the earnings of the deceased or former husbands.

The ability to successfully combine continued market work with marriage and parenthood is a strong predictor of a formerly married woman's chance of maintaining her economic well-being beyond marriage. * * *

How does being married and a parent (versus general social or market forces affecting all women) influence earnings potential? That they do is shown by the advantaged earnings and attainment positions of never-married, childless women. While it is difficult to disentangle the effects on earnings of parenthood from those of marriage—since the majority of married couples have had or anticipate having children—there is a large literature suggesting some central mechanisms. First, marriage itself may limit women's job options and earnings, as evidenced by the cost of family migration for wives both in terms of earnings and future earnings-based retirement benefits from social security and pensions. Second, marriage and parenthood are characterized by gender inequality in the division of home work. As mothers of minor children, women tend to be the primary parent and to do the larger share of nonmarket work even if they also work outside the home. Estimates of the division of household labor indicate that women spend twice as much time as men per day doing housework and caring for children. Third, when family responsibilities are associated with reductions in market work, this usually falls to women. Many women withdraw from the labor force in the time surrounding childbirth. * * *

If upon divorce women received large property settlements and if husbands left large estates to widows, income-based measures would underestimate the actual level of economic well-being of women following marital disruption. It is broadly accepted that full measures of economic well-being—both of married couples and unmarried men and women—should include the value of property and financial wealth. The issue is whether the share of the married household's assets given to the wife following divorce or husband's death compensates for the disproportionate income outcomes for the wife.

* * *

In view of this, in divorce cases an expanded definition of "divisible" marital property to include spouse's potential earnings and pensions would partially compensate women for the loss not just of their husband's current income, but of the future security jointly built through the work efforts of the earner(s), the indirect contributions of each spouse, and investments in the family during marriage. Current definitions of marital property as tangible assets contribute to women bearing a disproportionate economic cost of divorce.

Finally, US social policy alleviates economic hardship following divorce and widowhood only for a small group of women. Unlike other industrialized countries, the United States fails to provide universal child allowances, subsidized childcare, national health insurance, or guaranteed minimum child support benefits that might otherwise smooth the income effects of marital dissolution. * * *

Taken together, it is difficult to escape the conclusion that much of the association between marital dissolution and women's economic insecurity lies in the fact that parenthood's costs are disproportionately borne by women even long after the children leave home. This division of responsibility may be functional within marriage if, as some theorists argue, women have a comparative advantage in home labor owing either to their biological commitment to childbearing or to role socialization processes and labor market discrimination. In marriage, husbands' earnings and pensions "insure" their wives against lower earnings potential. Once outside the marriage the economic shortfall exacts a high toll on the life chances of children and single mothers. Continued sharing after marriage must come in the form of explicit transfers from husband to wife, either through the division of assets, child support payments, or insurance against death. The absence of such transfers is compounded by women's disproportionate financial and time responsibility for children after divorce (and sole responsibility after widowhood), the incompatibility of primary parenting and full-time work, and the lack of affordable child care. It is not surprising that approximately one in two female-headed families with children lives in poverty and that over one quarter of elderly women alone are poor.

Notes on the Economic Consequences of Marital Dissolution

1. According to a 1992 census report on the elderly, only 4.9% of elderly white married women are poor, whereas 23.8% of elderly white women living alone are below the poverty level. Of African American women, 18.4% of older married women are poor, whereas 57.5% of older Black women living alone are below the poverty level. United States Bureau of the Census, 65+ in the United States 8–14, 8–16 (Table 8–3) (1996). Part of the problem for elderly women is that women are less likely than men to be firmly attached to the labor market throughout their adult lives and, even when working, are less likely to hold jobs in sectors with good pensions; they are also likely to earn less during life, and pension benefits tend to be tied to lifetime earnings. See, e.g., Angela O'Rand and John C. Henretta, Midlife Work History and Retirement Income, in Women's Retirement: Policy Implications of Recent Research 25 (Maximiliane Szinovacz, ed. 1982). These factors cannot, however, explain the economic similarities between widows and divorcees, since husbands might be expected to ensure the well-being of widows. Why aren't widows better protected by (1) their husbands or (2) welfare safety nets?

2. In most divorces, the husband walks away with significantly better Social Security protection than the wife, though it would be easy enough to divide Social Security entitlements equally as they are earned during marriage. In a traditional marriage, with a breadwinner husband and homemaker wife, only the husband walks away from a marriage lasting less than ten years (the average marriage lasts only seven years) with a Social Security claim for the contributions made to the fund during the marriage. Even if the marriage lasts ten years, the ex-wife walks away with 50% of his claim; and his increases to 150% if he remarries, whereas hers is likely to end at her remarriage. At retirement, a woman must choose between filing a claim based on her own earnings record and on her status as ex-wife. Because of this provision, women often receive no increase in their Social Security benefit from combining years in the wage labor market with years of homemaking, though most women combine years of homemaking (with perhaps part-time wage work) with years of full-time wage work. If a couple stays married until death (usually of the husband), the widow's draw after his death will be only two-thirds of their joint draw, though for one person to live on the same level as a couple, that person needs 80% of the couple's income. Given women's lower pay and weaker attachment to the wage-labor market because of their caretaking responsibilities, combined with the structure of Social Security, it is not surprising that 13% of elderly women live in poverty, whereas only 7% of elderly men do. See Mary E. Becker, Obscuring the Struggle: Sex Discrimination, Social Security, and Stone, Seidman, Sunstein, & Tushnet's *Constitutional Law*, 89 Colum. L. Rev. 264, 286–87 (1989); Susan B. Garland, Making Social Security More Women Friendly, Business Week, May 22, 2000, at 103–04; Karen C. Burke and Grayson M.P. McCouch, 16 N.Y.L. Sch. J. Hum. Rts. 375, 375–87 (1999). Current reform proposals may well make the system even more inadequate for women. See Burke and McCouch, above, at 386–402.

3. A study by Pamela Smock found that divorce is as costly for those young women who separated or divorced in the 1980's as it was for those who experienced these events in the late 1960's through the mid 1970's. Gender inequality after divorce is not decreasing over time, despite married women's and mothers' increased labor force attachment. Smock found no differences between the cohorts in terms of socioeconomic prospects. Smock concludes:

> The process influencing postdisruption outcomes has remained relatively constant. Relatedly, it is important to emphasize that women's average earnings are quite low in both cohorts, roughly $9,000 to $11,000 per year. It is likely that without (1) marked change in the wages available to most women, (2) public policies that support child-rearing activities, and (3) affordable child care, economic prospects outside of marriage for many women will remain poor. However "prepared" women may increasingly be for marital disruption, it is not in ways sufficient to cushion its economic costs.

Smock, The Economic Costs of Marital Disruption for Young Women in the United States: Have They Declined over the Past Two Decades?, Institute for Research on Poverty, University of Wisconsin–Madison, Discussion Paper No. 984–92 (Sept. 1992); see also Smock, Gender and the Short–Run Economic Consequences of Marital Disruption, 73 Social Forces 243 (1994).

Given these findings, and those described in Holden and Smock, above, what advice would you give a girl on the threshold of adulthood today?

4. Given the economic problems women face at divorce, why don't women bargain for greater economic protection before they marry or agree to be caretakers? Would it be a good idea to return this whole area to private contracting? Why or why not? Why is it that pre-marital contracts are overwhelmingly documents in which women *waive* their rights at the death of the man or at divorce? See Katharine B. Silbaugh, Marriage Contracts and the Family Economy, 93 Nw. U. L. Rev. 65, 134 (1998) (premarital contracts are overwhelmingly drafted in practice to benefit the person with the money in the relationship). The courts' willingness to enforce contracts having to do with monetary benefits and refusal to enforce provisions concerning non-monetary exchanges may have something to do with this. See id., passim.

In a survey of marriage license applicants in a major Virginia city, participants were asked to estimate the chances of a future divorce. Over 50% reported that the probability of their marriage ending in divorce was 0 percent! Ninety-five percent of women who expected to have children expected primary custody at divorce, while 40% of similar men expected to get primary custody at divorce. Moreover, although only about half of child support payments ordered at divorce are actually made, 98% of respondents who expected to receive child support in the event of a divorce believed that *their* spouse would comply fully and make all payments. Only 1.5% of respondents expressed any interest in a prenuptial agreement on the economic consequences of divorce. None were interested in a pre-marital agreement on custody. Lynn A. Baker and Robert E. Emery, When Every Relationship Is Above Average: Perceptions and Expectations of Divorce at the Time of Marriage, 17 L. & Hum. Behav. 439 (1993). Do these results suggest problems with contracts formed by people marrying?

Why don't women bargain for better rights at divorce today? How would bargaining work? Which of the following factors would give one party a stronger bargaining position with respect to child custody, property division, and economic support at divorce: age; wealth (present and future); being the person more emotionally committed to the marriage (more in love); being the more aggressive person; being the more violent person; having superior options in terms of alternative relationships; being from a socially dominant group; being more committed to having children?

5. Many women choose to be mothers with weaker ties to the labor market than their children's fathers. This weaker connection contributes to the higher poverty rates of divorced and widowed women, as discussed in the excerpt above. Does women's "choice" mean we need not be concerned about the economic consequences of divorce and widowhood for women?

6. There are several key components to women's post-divorce poverty as described by Holden and Smock, including the facts that (1) almost no ex-wives get alimony, and even the lucky few who do get it receive only short-term "rehabilitative" alimony; (2) women get at most half the couple's accumulated property at divorce, which tends to be little in most families; (3) the husband usually walks away with the family largest asset, his future income stream; and (4) fathers extract economic concessions by threatening custody challenges. A fifth component is that child support awards are low

and poorly enforced. See Chapter 8, Section G, below. A sixth problem, as noted in note 2 above, is that in most families, the husband walks away with better Social Security protection than the wife. Additional problems are presented by the "gap" between male and female wages in the labor market and the limitations imposed on women's labor market participation by their child care responsibilities as (in most instances) single custodial parents. The absence of child care priced at levels affordable at women's wages obviously exacerbates this problem. See note 9 at 718–19, below. What kinds of changes would you propose to address any or all of these problems? How many of them can be brought about through litigation? How many through legislation?

D. SUGGESTIONS FOR CHANGE IN THE LEGAL TREATMENT OF INTIMATE RELATIONSHIPS

MARTHA ALBERTSON FINEMAN, THE NEUTERED MOTHER, THE SEXUAL FAMILY AND OTHER TWENTIETH CENTURY TRAGEDIES

228–35 (1995).

Concurrently (and complementarily), the legal roles of Husband–Father, Wife–Mother, and Child–Adult are formulated in the context of the relationship that resides in the contrived institution of the official family, which is entitled to privacy and protection from intervention, regulation, and the state. Dependency is naturally assigned to this private family by the state. Within the family, this dependency is further directed by continued gendered role division.

Because we are concerned with this institution from a functional perspective, as a complement to the state designated to care for dependencies, we must consider the natural family a failure. In its historic form it is not adequate to handle both the demands for equality and the contemporary manifestations of inevitable and derivative dependency.[g] It is essential that we begin to reconceptualize the relationship between law and the family in regard to these dependencies. In doing so, we should keep a few basic principles in mind. First, we must abandon the pretense that we can achieve gender equality through family-law reform. The egalitarian family myth remains largely unassisted by other ideological and structural changes in the larger society and is belied by the statistics reflecting the ways women and men live.

We also should recognize that family policy is a form of state regulation. We must therefore, be explicit about the norms and values motivating public and legal decisions about what should be protected or encouraged through social and economic subsidies. Furthermore, family policy must be secular, not based on a religious model. It should

g. By "inevitable and derivative dependencies" Fineman means the dependency of the human infant and child, the elderly, and the sick or handicapped, on the one hand, and the dependency of the person who is the caretaker of other dependents, on the other hand.

reference the functional aspirations we have for families in our society and be supportive of those aspirations. I, therefore, propose two recommendations for legal reform: the abolition of the legal supports for the sexual family and the construction of protections for the nurturing unit of caretaker and dependant exemplified by the Mother/Child dyad. These proposals are intended to direct policy discussions toward support for caretaking.

A. Ending Marriage as a Legal Category

Consistent with the first goal, we should abolish marriage as a legal category and with it any privilege based on sexual affiliation. I want to emphasize I am addressing only the legal significance of marriage. There would be no special legal rules governing the relationships between husband and wife or defining the consequences of the status of marriage as now exist in family law. In fact, these categories would no longer have any legal meaning at all. Instead, the interactions of female and male sexual affiliates would be governed by the same rules that regulate other interactions in our society—specifically those of contract and property, as well as tort and criminal law. The illusive equality between adults in sexual and all other areas would thus be asserted and assumed, a result that to many will be symbolically appealing. Women and men would operate outside of the confines of marriage, transacting and interacting without the fetters of legalities they did not voluntarily choose. Of course, people would be free to engage in "ceremonious" marriage; such an event would, however, have no legal (enforceable in court) consequences. If they didn't execute a separate contract, there would be no imposed terms as now operate in the context of marriage. Any legal consequences would have to be the result of a separate negotiation. Mere agreement to form a live-in sexual relationship would not suffice.

This proposal is actually not very farfetched. We already encourage antenuptual [sic] agreements that are contractual deviations from state-imposed marriage consequences. No-fault divorce makes marriage a "tenuous" relationship. Opportunities for individual bargaining about economic and other aspects of sexual relations typically now occur at the termination of the relationship. Separation agreements (contracts) are the norm, not judicial decrees. My proposal would merely mandate that such bargaining occur prior to the termination of the relationship, ideally before the couple becomes too "serious." This is what occurs in some nonmarital cohabitation cases. Many states have begun to recognize such contractual commitments (promises) about sharing assets or providing compensation for "services" in marriage-like arrangements. Even if promises are not explicit, equity sometimes intervenes to protect "expectations" or to reimburse and compensate contributions to the accumulation of property.

One benefit of abolishing marriage as a legal category (upon which a whole system of public and private subsidies and protections is based) is that the state interest in bolstering the institution would dissolve. Adult, voluntary sexual interactions would be of no concern to the state since there would no longer be a state-preferred model of family intimacy to protect and support. Therefore, all such sexual relationships would be permitted—nothing prohibited, nothing privileged. Of course, children would continue to be protected by incest and other laws, and rape would continue to be subject to criminal sanctions. Voluntary sexual relationships between adults would be unregulated, however.

* * *

This proposal to abolish marriage as a legal category, which I realize may be viewed as quite radical, is necessary given the ideological position of the sexual family and its role in maintaining inequality. This very position, however, forces the conclusion that the institution is incapable of reform. As long as it exists, it will continue to occupy a privileged status and be posited as the ideal, defining other intimate entities as deviant. Instead of seeking to eliminate this stigma by analogizing more and more relationships to marriage, why not just abolish the category as a legal status and, in that way, render all sexual relationships equal with each other and all relationships equal with the sexual?

B. Mother/Child Dyad

The second objective—securing protections for the nurturing units—reflects concern for the "weaker" members of society, the dependents who need protection. If marriage has no legal significance and the traditional family is not state subsidized and supported, these dependencies will be more visible. Hopefully, they will also become the object of generalized societal concern. One solution to inevitable dependencies unanchored by the private family would be the direct assumption of responsibility by the state through public institutions. I am uncomfortable with such unmediated state power, and would therefore want to maintain the concept of family privacy, merely drawing the line around a non-traditional configuration of family. * * * In my newly redefined legal category of family, I would place inevitable dependents along with their caregivers. The caregiving family would be a protected space, entitled to special, preferred treatment by the state.

The new family line, drawn around dependency, would mark the boundaries of the concept of family privacy. The unit would also have legitimate claims on the resources of society. Specifically, I envision a redistribution or reallocation of social and economic subsidies now given to the natural family that allow it to function "independently" within society. Family and welfare law would be reconceived so as to support caretaking as the family intimacy norm.

This re-envisioning reflects current empirical and social reality as to evolving family form. Instead of being a society where our ideals and our ideology (the private, natural family) are out of sync with the real lives of many of our citizens, we would become a society that recognized and accepted the inevitability of dependency. We would face, value, and therefore subsidize, caretaking and caretakers.

* * *

C. Mother and Metaphor

As a concluding matter, I want to explicitly address my device of the Mother/Child metaphor. Abandoning myself to ideological utopianism, I have concluded that what is necessary in order to confront the hegemony of the sexual-natural family is an equally powerful cultural symbol. The most vivid and shared image of connection is the Mother/Child dyad. This is the prototypical nurturing unit, a fitting substitute for the Husband/Wife dyad that forms the basic unit of the sexual family. I propose Mother/Child as the substitute core of the basic family paradigm. Our laws and policies would be compelled to focus on the needs of this unit. Mother/Child would provide the structural and ideological basis for the transfer of current societal subsidies (both material and ideological) away from the sexual family to nurturing units.

The need for a positive societal vision is the reason the Mother/Child metaphor is appropriate. In excavating the image, I want to pull in the powerful resonances it has across a variety of discourses. Sara Ruddick combines positive images of Mother in arguing for "peace politics" based on maternal practices: "Preservative love, singularity in connection, the promise of birth and the resilience of hope, the irreplaceable treasure of vulnerable bodily being—these cliches of maternal work are enacted in public, by women." Mother is an embodied concept with biological, anthropological, theological, and social implications that give it strength in the public sphere. It is also a concept that embodies the dependency that is inevitable in the form of the Child. The Child is part of the Mother—the embodiment of the idea of derivative dependency now hidden in the private family. Mother is a metaphor with power to make the private visible.

I have deliberately (even defiantly) chosen not to make my alternative vision gender neutral by substituting terms such as "caretaker" and "dependent" for "Mother" and "Child," although that is the interrelationship in all its forms that I seek to address. Historically, and in terms of its cultural cachet, mothering is a gendered concept and, partly for that reason, is qualitatively different from terms currently (incorrectly) substituted for it such as "caretaker."

I realize that affirmatively introducing Mother into a feminist debate will be considered by many to be too dangerous, but I believe it is essential that we reclaim the term. Motherhood has unrealized power—the power to challenge the hold of sexuality on our thinking about intimacy; the power to redefine our concept of the family, which may be why men have tried for so long to control its meaning. The Mother/Child metaphor represents a specific practice of social and emotional responsibility. The strength of the image is in its redistributive potential, grounded on empirical evidence ("reality") about the need for and the assumption of caretaking.

* * *

Two additional theoretical caveats are necessary. First, I believe that men can and should be Mothers. In fact, if men are interested in acquiring legal rights of access to children (or other dependents), I argue they must be Mothers in the stereotypical nurturing sense of that term—that is, engaged in caretaking. Second, the Child in my dyad stands for all forms of inevitable dependency—the dependency of the ill, the elderly, the disabled, as well as actual children. The child is an embodied concept, exemplifying the need for physical caretaking.

Notes on Ideas for Legal Change

1. Fineman suggests restructuring our treatment of the family around the mother/child dyad rather than the sexual couple, positing that such a radical move would either (or both?) force individuals into private contractual ordering of their relationships and/or the society to subsidize the caretaking of dependents of all sorts. What do you think of this suggestion? Does its lack of short-term practicality detract fatally from its power as an aspirational symbol? Or do we, as Fineman suggests, need new and powerful symbols (like the mother/child metaphor) to change the ways in which we order our relationships by law? Should we re-focus our attention upon relationships of dependency?

2. Despite its increased prevalence, there are indications that non-marital cohabitation may have negative impacts upon individual happiness, especially for women. The 1999 report of the National Marriage Project at Rutgers University concluded that persons who cohabit rather than marry are significantly more depressed; their unions are more likely to dissolve; and children living in their households are more likely to be sexually or physically abused. David Popenoe and Barbara Dafoe Whitehead, Should We Live Together? What Young Adults Need to Know about Cohabitation before Marriage: A Comprehensive Review of Recent Research (National Marriage Project, Rutgers, 1999). Moreover, the 17–nation study discussed above shows that married persons were happier than those who cohabited, a correlation that held for every nation except Northern Ireland. Steven Stack and J. Ross Eshleman, Marital Status and Happiness: A 17–Nation Study, 60 J. Marriage & Family 527, 533–34 (1998). (However, in countries with low divorce rates, married persons were comparatively less happy, indicating that ease of exit may be a requirement for marital happiness. Id. at 527.) There is also evidence that single mothers are less happy than married mothers (although the well-being of both single and married mothers relates most directly to their children's well-being and their relationships with their children). David H. Demo and Alan C. Acock, Singlehood, Marriage, and Remarriage: The Effects of Family Structure and Family Relationships on Mothers' Well–Being, 17 J. Family Issues 388, 389, 403–05 (1996) (finding single mothers have lower well-being, are more depressed, and have lower self-esteem than married mothers, perhaps because of the chronic stress of solo work and parenting).

What, if any, implications do these studies have for Fineman's proposal that we abolish marriage as a legal category?

3. There has been a good deal of writing by feminists about the idea of reducing family law relationships to private contractual ordering. See, e.g., Marjorie M. Shultz, Contractual Ordering of Marriage: A New Model for State Policy, 70 Cal. L. Rev. 207, 253 (1982) (arguing that contract offers an approach to individual fulfillment through negotiation between equal parties); Margaret Brinig and June Carbone, The Reliance Interest in Marriage and Divorce, 62 Tulane L. Rev. 855 (1988) (evaluating remedies available upon divorce under reliance theory of contract damages); Jana B. Singer, The Privatization of Family Law, 1992 Wis. L. Rev. 1443 (tracing and critiquing the increasing privatization of family law in a variety of areas, including court approval of both premarital contracts and contracts between cohabitants); Katharine B. Silbaugh, Marriage Contracts and the Family Economy, 93 Nw. U. L. Rev. 65 (1998) (arguing that monetary contracts should not be enforced if nonmonetary contracts are not). However, there are substantial problems with contractual ordering, stemming both from power differentials between the parties and from couples' refusal to recognize the statistical risks of divorce at the time of entry into marriage. Jana Singer suggests that privatization contains further problems, including its potential to divert attention from attempts to reform family law doctrine and "to imagine alternative forms of public ordering," including advocacy of sharing principles in both marriage and divorce. Singer, above, at 1556–60. Privatization also reinforces the notion of the public/private split, which has harmed women in many ways by isolating women within families and supporting the position that the public has little interest in what goes on within the hearth. Id. at 1560–64.

If the protections of current family law were unavailable, would women bargain for adequate safeguards, in your opinion, and avoid entry into relationships of dependency if they could not obtain them?

4. Another model that has been suggested for the private-law ordering of family relationships is to analogize them to business partnerships. Thus, for example, Cynthia Starnes advocates treating the dissolution of marriage like the dissolution of a partnership prior to expiration of its "term." Under this model, the dissociated spouse would receive the right to a buyout of her interest in any income-generating marital enterprise that continues after dissociation as a result of the human capital of her spouse, capital enhanced during the marriage by education or labor force participation. Starnes also proposes a mathematical model for calculating enhanced earnings and a sliding scale basing the buyout price on the length of the marriage. See Starnes, Divorce and the Displaced Homemaker: A Discourse on Playing with Dolls, Partnership Buyouts and Dissociation Under No–Fault, 60 U.Chi. L.Rev. 67, 131–37 (1993). Do you think this remedy is appropriate? Does a spouse have an "ownership" interest in the education, training, and skills of the other spouse? Does it make a difference if the couple does or does not have children?

5. Other feminists have turned to commercial law in the search for remedies for caretaker-spouses. For example, Martha Ertman suggests the use of security agreements to protect the primary homemaker's interest in her "loan" to the primary wage-earning spouse. These "Premarital Security Agreements" would grant the creditor homemaker a security interest in post-divorce income as well as in marital property, on the ground that this

income includes the extension of credit from the primary homemaker by her specialization in domestic labor—a debt that will go unpaid if the marriage does not last. Martha M. Ertman, Commercializing Marriage: A Proposal For Valuing Women's Work Through Premarital Security Agreements, 77 Tex. L. Rev. 17 (1998). Although Ertman's formula and collection mechanism are perhaps the most elaborately described, a variety of proposals for post-divorce income sharing have gained the support of feminist scholars. See, e.g., June Carbone, Income Sharing: Redefining the Family in Terms of Community, 31 Houston L. Rev. 359 (1994); Jane Rutherford, Duty in Divorce: Shared Income As a Path to Equality, 58 Fordham L. Rev. 539 (1990); Jana Singer, Divorce Reform and Gender Justice, 67 N.C. L. Rev. 1103 (1989). What do you think the impact of a commercial arrangement like Ertman's would be upon intimate relationships? Do you find it a promising avenue to protect the interests of the more vulnerable spouse?

6. All of the remedies discussed above—contract, partnership, and commercial law—essentially return the regulation of intimate relationships to the private sphere. Fineman's preferred solution, however, is to make many of the responsibilities involved in dependency relationships into public obligations, ones the society would subsidize. This approach to family support is consonant with that taken by most European countries. See, e.g., Barbara A. Bergmann, Saving Our Children From Poverty: What the United States Can Learn From France (1996) (contrasting French government child care programs, direct payments to raise children's living standards, and provision of free medical services to children with the lack of such programs in the U.S.). Do you think a similar approach could work in the United States? Why or why not?

7. Other feminists envisage the problems attendant upon dependency as a subcase of our legal system's treatment of unpaid domestic labor not as work, but simply a gift of love. See, e.g., Katherine Silbaugh, Turning Labor into Love: Housework and the Law, 91 Nw. U. L. Rev. 1 (1996). Unlike the fields of sociology and of economics, which have in recent years turned their attention to the wealth produced by housework (economists estimate the value of housework at from 24% to 60% of the Gross Domestic Product, id. at 17), the law continues to ignore the value of domestic labor across the board—not only in property distribution and maintenance at divorce, but also as consideration for premarital contracts, in bankruptcy and estates, in the structure of Social Security payments, in actions for loss of consortium, in taxation, in labor law, and in the bases for welfare reform, which assume that a poor woman's caring for her children does not constitute productive labor. Id. at 8–21, 27–79. One, albeit drastic, way to address this problem is suggested by Nancy Staudt, who proposes that houseworkers' labor be recognized by imputing it as income to the couple and subjecting it to taxation. Staudt, Taxing Housework, 84 Geo. L.J. 1571 (1996). This would result in ensuring women independent social welfare benefits, such as Social Security accounts, based on the economic value of their own labor rather than their spouses'. Id. at 1574, 1598–99.

Staudt's proposal is different from much of the previous literature on the gendered basis of the Tax Code, which focused instead on how the tax structure creates disincentives for women to enter the labor force and thus encourages them to be economically dependent upon men. See, e.g, Grace

Blumberg, Sexism in the Code: A Comparative Study of Income Taxation of Working Wives and Mothers, 21 Buff. L. Rev. 49 (1972); Edward J. McCaffery, Slouching Toward Equality: Gender Discrimination, Market Efficiency, and Social Change, 103 Yale L. J. 595 (1993); McCaffery, Taxation and the Family: A Fresh Look at Behavioral Gender Biases in the Code, 40 U.C.L.A. L. Rev. 983 (1993). Commentators like Blumberg and McCaffery advocate tax reform that encourages women to enter the workforce, while Staudt argues that women's workforce participation does not in fact respond in a major way to tax incentives. Women, especially poor women and women of color, work because they have to. Perhaps paradoxically, African American women also appreciate the work involved in household labor and its value. See Staudt, above, at 1586–92. In your opinion, who has the better of this debate? Should the tax structure encourage women's entry into the paid labor force or assign value to household labor as an independent economic enterprise, even at the price of requiring the payment of taxes on it?

E. THE LEGAL TREATMENT OF COHABITATION

HEWITT v. HEWITT

Supreme Court of Illinois, 1979.

77 Ill.2d 49, 31 Ill.Dec. 827, 394 N.E.2d 1204.

The issue in this case is whether plaintiff Victoria Hewitt, whose complaint alleges she lived with defendant Robert Hewitt from 1960 to 1975 in an unmarried, family-like relationship to which three children have been born, may recover from him "an equal share of the profits and properties accumulated by the parties" during that period.

* * *

The factual background alleged or testified to is that in June 1960, when she and defendant were students at Grinnell College in Iowa, plaintiff became pregnant; that defendant thereafter told her that they were husband and wife and would live as such, no formal ceremony being necessary, and that he would "share his life, his future, his earnings and his property" with her; that the parties immediately announced to their respective parents that they were married and thereafter held themselves out as husband and wife; that in reliance on defendant's promises she devoted her efforts to his professional education and his establishment in the practice of pedodontia, obtaining financial assistance from her parents for this purpose; that she assisted defendant in his career with her own special skills and although she was given payroll checks for these services she placed them in a common fund; that defendant, who was without funds at the time of the marriage, as a result of her efforts now earns over $80,000 a year and has accumulated large amounts of property, owned either jointly with her or separately; that she has given him every assistance a wife and mother could give, including social activities designed to enhance his social and professional reputation.

* * *

In finding that plaintiff's complaint stated a cause of action on an express oral contract, the appellate court adopted the reasoning of the California Supreme Court in the widely publicized case of Marvin v. Marvin (1976), 18 Cal.3d 660, 134 Cal.Rptr. 815, 557 P.2d 106. * * *

The issue of whether property rights accrue to unmarried cohabitants can not, however, be regarded realistically as merely a problem in the law of express contracts. Plaintiff argues that because her action is founded on an express contract, her recovery would in no way imply that unmarried cohabitants acquire property rights merely by cohabitation and subsequent separation. However, * * * if common law principles of express contract govern express agreements between unmarried cohabitants, common law principles of implied contract, equitable relief and constructive trust must govern the parties' relations in the absence of such an agreement. In all probability the latter case will be much the more common, since it is unlikely that most couples who live together will enter into express agreements regulating their property rights. The increasing incidence of nonmarital cohabitation referred to in *Marvin* and the variety of legal remedies therein sanctioned seem certain to result in substantial amounts of litigation, in which, whatever the allegations regarding an oral contract, the proof will necessarily involve details of the parties' living arrangements.

* * * There are major public policy questions involved in determining whether, under what circumstances, and to what extent it is desirable to accord some type of legal status to claims arising from such relationships. Of substantially greater importance than the rights of the immediate parties is the impact of such recognition upon our society and the institution of marriage. Will the fact that legal rights closely resembling those arising from conventional marriages can be acquired by those who deliberately choose to enter into what have heretofore been commonly referred to as "illicit" or "meretricious" relationships encourage formation of such relationships and weaken marriage as the foundation of our family-based society? In the event of death shall the survivor have the status of a surviving spouse for purposes of inheritance, wrongful death actions, workmen's compensation, etc.? And still more importantly: what of the children born of such relationships? What are their support and inheritance rights and by what standards are custody questions resolved? What of the sociological and psychological effects upon them of that type of environment? Does not the recognition of legally enforceable property and custody rights emanating from nonmarital cohabitation in practical effect equate with the legalization of common law marriage at least in the circumstances of this case? And, in summary, have the increasing numbers of unmarried cohabitants and changing mores of our society reached the point at which the general welfare of the citizens of this State is best served by a return to something resembling the judicially created common law marriage our legislature outlawed in 1905?

* * *

The issue, realistically, is whether it is appropriate for this court to grant a legal status to a private arrangement substituting for the institution of marriage sanctioned by the State. The question whether change is needed in the law governing the rights of parties in this delicate area of marriage-like relationships involves evaluations of sociological data and alternatives we believe best suited to the superior investigative and fact-finding facilities of the legislative branch in the exercise of its traditional authority to declare public policy in the domestic relations field. * * *

We cannot confidently say that judicial recognition of property rights between unmarried cohabitants will not make that alternative to marriage more attractive by allowing the parties to engage in such relationships with greater security. * * * In thus potentially enhancing the attractiveness of a private arrangement over marriage, we believe that the appellate court decision in this case contravenes the Act's policy of strengthening and preserving the integrity of marriage.

* * *

Plaintiff's allegations disclose a relationship that clearly would have constituted a valid common law marriage in this State prior to 1905. The parties expressly manifested their present intent to be husband and wife; immediately thereafter they assumed the marital status; and for many years they consistently held themselves out to their relatives and the public at large as husband and wife. * * * Further, in enacting the Illinois Marriage and Dissolution of Marriage Act, our legislature considered and rejected the "no-fault" divorce concept that has been adopted in many other jurisdictions, including California. Illinois appears to be one of three States retaining fault grounds for dissolution of marriage. Certainly a significantly stronger promarriage policy is manifest in that action, which appears to us to reaffirm the traditional doctrine that marriage is a civil contract between three parties—the husband, the wife and the State. The policy of the Act gives the State a strong continuing interest in the institution of marriage and prevents the marriage relation from becoming in effect a private contract terminable at will. This seems to us another indication that public policy disfavors private contractual alternatives to marriage.

* * *

Appellate court reversed; circuit court affirmed.

Notes on Cohabitation

1. Do you agree with the result in *Hewitt?* Would you find a contractual basis for recovery in this situation? Why should a long-term homemaker wife be entitled to a division of the marital property, rehabilitative maintenance and/or other remedies, but not Mrs. Hewitt?

2. What would Martha Fineman, whose work is excerpted in the previous section, think of the result reached by the *Hewitt* court? Would she believe that Mrs. Hewitt should be treated as though the couple had been

married? Or that, as the court questions, "the increasing numbers of unmarried cohabitants and changing mores of our society [have] reached the point at which the general welfare of the citizens of this State is best served by a return to something resembling the judicially created common law marriage our legislature outlawed in 1905?" What would Fineman's remedy for the *Hewitt* situation be?

3. Illinois now has a modified version of no-fault divorce. 750 ILCS 5/401(a)(2) (adding "irreconcilable differences" as grounds for divorce, provided parties have lived separate and apart for two years or sign a waiver of the two-year period after having lived separate and apart for six months). Would this change the outcome in *Hewitt?*

4. Do you agree with the *Hewitt* court's statement that "the law governing the rights of parties in this delicate area of marriage-like relationships involves evaluations of sociological data and alternatives we believe best suited to the superior investigative and fact-finding facilities of the legislative branch"? Why or why not? What are the relevant "facts" the court has in mind? How would the Illinois Senate and General Assembly go about investigating and "finding" these facts? (In fact, the Illinois legislature has not changed the law prohibiting common law marriage.) Does the prohibition on common law marriage necessarily mean that the consequences of termination are the absence of any property rights whatsoever? Are persons who live together therefore "on notice" of this fact and thus assumed to know that they should make contractual provisions for their property? Can they do so under *Hewitt?* Do you think this is a realistic assumption in most instances?

5. Marvin v. Marvin, 18 Cal.3d 660, 134 Cal.Rptr. 815, 557 P.2d 106 (1976), was the first high-profile "palimony" case, i.e., a lawsuit by an unmarried cohabitant for economic rights at separation analogous to those given in divorce. Although the California appellate court initially indicated that recovery could be based either on an explicit or implicit contract or on equitable principles, Michelle Marvin received nothing in the end. The trial judge found no contract because actor Lee Marvin intended to avoid the economic consequences of marriage by avoiding marriage, but did award $104,000 to Michelle Marvin for her economic "rehabilitation." The California appellate court reversed this award, however, on the ground that there was no contract and that Michelle Marvin was not injured by the relationship, but rather benefited from it. Do you agree with this result? What if Michelle and Lee had had children and Michelle had spent her time caring for them as well as serving as Lee's companion and hostess?

6. What if Mrs. Hewitt or Michelle Marvin had made economic rather than domestic contributions to their relationships, but the property ended up titled in the names of Mr. Hewitt and Mr. Marvin? Would you allow recovery in this situation? Would your analysis turn on contract notions? All courts give recovery when the non-title-holding partner has contributed cash. But recovery is uncertain or denied in many jurisdictions when the contributions are domestic, i.e., women's traditional work in the home. What might explain the traditional presumption that "services performed in the context of a 'family or marriage relationship' were presumed gratuitous"?

Watts v. Watts, 137 Wis.2d 506, 405 N.W.2d 303, 312 n. 19 (1987). Conversely, should an opposite presumption apply in the absence of marriage?

7. Census data show that the numbers of cohabiting couples grew from 1.1 million in 1977 to 4.9 million in 1997, from 1.5% to 4.8% of all households. Lynne M. Casper, Philip N. Cohen, and Tavia Simmons, How Does POSSLQ Measure Up? Historical Estimates of Cohabitation, U.S. Bureau of the Census, Population Division Working Paper No. 36 (1999). (POSSLQ is an abbreviation for Persons of the Opposite Sex Sharing Living Quarters.) Two groups—children whose parents divorced and divorced persons themselves—are more likely to cohabit than to marry. The rate of marriage in the U.S. in 1998 was the lowest since 1958, 8.3 per 1,000 people. See Eric Nagourney, Study Finds Families Bypassing Marriage, N.Y. Times, Feb. 15, 2000, at D8. Indeed, the second-year report of the Rutgers Marriage Project found that young men and women today may not focus upon finding marriage partners when they date, but are instead more concerned with having fun and making money than with forming lasting relationships. The State of Our Unions 2000: The Social Health of Marriage in America 8–9 (National Marriage Project, Rutgers, 2000). They are pessimistic (or realistic?) about the possibility of forming a lasting relationship, see divorce as a potential economic liability, and may have developed somewhat mercenary mating habits as a form of self-protection, according to the authors of the study. See id. at 15–17.

Yet studies in the U.S. and other industrialized nations show that married persons are happier than those who cohabit. See, e.g., Steven Stack and J. Ross Eshleman, Marital Status and Happiness: A 17–Nation Study, 60 J. Marriage & Family 527, 534 (1998). What factors do you think account for these differences between married and cohabiting couples? What, if anything, do they say about marriage as an institution? About the aspirations of the young people described in the Rutgers study?

8. If married people are happier than cohabitants, does this fact support the result in *Hewitt*? What is the likely result of the court's decision? If men (or the economically stronger partner) avoid marriage in order to avoid the economic consequences upon its dissolution, is the *Hewitt* result likely to increase or decrease cohabitation? If, by contrast, cohabitants are treated as though they were married for purposes of property distribution and spousal support, will this increase cohabitation relative to marriage, as the *Hewitt* court assumes, or decrease it? How are we to evaluate the human costs involved?

9. What are the problems with contract (whether explicit or implicit) as *the* solution for non-married cohabitants? Consider the problems, discussed above, of using pre-marital contracts to address the economic problems of divorcing women. Are there fewer or more problems with expecting contract law to resolve how the courts should decide disputes upon separation of people who do not marry? Do you agree with the *Hewitt* court that denying Mrs. Hewitt a recovery will encourage marriage? Doesn't this result give breadwinners, like Mr. Hewitt, an incentive *not* to marry? In general, do you think men or women are more in need of an incentive to marry?

10. The Hewitts were married in Iowa and should have been eligible for treatment as a common law marriage, based upon the allegations

concerning their intentions and continuous "holding out" as a married couple. Common law marriage is still recognized in 12 U.S. jurisdictions. Cynthia Grant Bowman has suggested that the non-recognition or abolition of common law marriage has had harmful effects on women, and especially upon poor women and women of color. Bowman, A Feminist Proposal to Bring Back Common Law Marriage, 75 Or. L. Rev. 709 (1996). The common law marriage doctrine protected women in Mrs. Hewitt's position—that is, women who had invested heavily in a relationship recognized by the community as a marriage—by granting them not only remedies upon divorce but also inheritance rights, Social Security, and workers' compensation benefits, among other things. Id. at 754–70.

As a normative matter, do you believe we should treat cohabitants as though they were married? If we did so, would it improve the power of women (even in marriage)?

11. Many Western European countries have for some time provided a variety of benefits for cohabitants. See Mary Ann Glendon, The Transformation of Family Law: State, Law, and Family in the United States and Western Europe 255–77 (1989). Moreover, in late 1999, France passed a law providing for entry into a "civil solidarity pact," a union open to couples of any kind, including same-sex couples. Suzanne Daley, French Couples Take Plunge That Falls Short of Marriage, N.Y. Times, Apr. 8, 2000, at A1. Couples who enter such a union undertake financial responsibility for one another, own any purchases or debts jointly, are eligible for one another's employment benefits, and after three years may file a joint income tax return; the pact can be dissolved unilaterally with three months' notice. Id. at A4. In the four months after the law went into effect, almost 14,000 couples entered into such unions, about 40% of them heterosexual. Id. at A1. If a similar law were passed in this country, do you think heterosexual couples would take advantage of it? Why or why not? Would you advise a female client to enter into such a pact or to elect traditional marriage instead? Why?

F. SAME-SEX MARRIAGE

For many people, marriage is the intimate union of a man and a woman. Only that combination can generate children genetically linked to both partners. But beginning with a case decided in 1971, gay and lesbian couples began to challenge their inability to receive a marriage license.[2] The second case was decided two years later,[3] and, after a hiatus of twenty years, four cases were decided in the 1990's.[4]

2. Baker v. Nelson, 291 Minn. 310, 191 N.W.2d 185 (1971) (interpreting statute as allowing issuance of marriage licenses only to heterosexual couples and upholding the constitutionality of the statute).

3. Jones v. Hallahan, 501 S.W.2d 588, 589 (Ky. App. 1973) (interpreting statute as allowing marriage only of heterosexual couples though no language in state marriage statutes suggested such a limitation).

4. See Dean v. District of Columbia, 653 A.2d 307 (1995) (rejecting equal protection challenge to limitation of marriage to heterosexual couples); Baehr v. Lewin, 74 Haw. 645, 852 P.2d 44 (1993) (described later in text in this section); Brause v. Bureau of Vital Statistics, 1998 WL 88743 (Alaska Super.1998) (described later in text in this section)); Baker v. Vermont, 170 Vt. 194, 744 A.2d 864 (Vt.1999) (extract appears later in text in this section).

Although no new cases were decided during the 1980's, gay and lesbian activists and intellectuals spent a fair amount of energy debating whether they should seek marriage rights during the late eighties and into the nineties. Advocates in favor of working for marriage rights argued that gay and lesbian couples should be eligible to receive the many palpable benefits that come with marriage and that their relationships needed and deserved the support marriage afforded heterosexual couples as well as the protections of divorce law. They noted that marriage rights were the ultimate test of the willingness of the (heterosexual) majority to grant gay men and lesbians fully equal rights, arguing that until marriage is available to lesbian and gay couples, all lesbians and gay men will continue to face inequality and second-class status.[5]

Opponents made arguments much like those made by Martha Fineman in her proposal to abolish marriage, included earlier in this chapter. Opponents argued that marriage is an inherently patriarchal institution, one that people committed to liberation, particularly women, should avoid. Marriage rights will help most those who are best off and will do least for those who are worst off; for example, couples in which at least one partner has a job with benefits will get more out of marriage than couples in which neither partner has health insurance. Universal health insurance would be a better solution to the problem of health benefits for covered workers. Further, marriage will divide lesbians and gay men into good gays (monogamous married folk) and bad gays (others), hardly a goal of a movement committed to sexual liberation. In this view, domestic partnerships and other novel approaches are preferable to marriage given its baggage.[6]

Although lesbian and gay leaders and activists were divided on whether to seek same-sex marriage, ordinary lesbians and gay men strongly supported seeking marriage rights. And, of course, it was impossible for the leaders and intellectuals of the movement to control the docket of courts. Cases brought by lesbian and gay couples themselves during the 1990's made the right to marry a highly visible and controversial issue.

Plaintiffs in these cases have made one or both of two arguments, one statutory and the other constitutional. Courts facing a statutory challenge—an argument that plaintiffs are entitled to a marriage license under the relevant state marriage statutes—have relied on the ordinary understanding of marriage to dismiss the plaintiffs' claims, even when the relevant statutes contain no language suggesting a requirement that couples be of opposite sex to marry.[7]

5. See Thomas Stoddard, Why Gay People Should Seek the Right to Marry, OUT/LOOK, Nat'l Gay & Lesbian Q., Fall 1989, at 9, reprinted in Lesbian and Gay Marriage: Private Commitments, Public Ceremonies 13 (Suzanne Sherman, ed. 1992).

6. See, e.g., Nancy D. Polikoff, We Will Get What We Ask For: Why Legalizing Gay and Lesbian Marriage Will Not "Dismantle the Legal Structure of Gender in Every Marriage," 79 Va. L. Rev. 1535 (1993).

7. See, e.g., Jones v. Hallahan, 501 S.W.2d 588 (Ky.App.1973).

Some challengers have argued that the state's refusal to grant them a marriage license unconstitutionally discriminates on the basis of sex in violation of state or federal constitutions, citing Loving v. Virginia.[8] In that 1967 case, the Supreme Court held that Virginia's criminal law against marriages between members of the "white race" and of "other races" was a denial of the fundamental right to marry and discriminated unconstitutionally on the basis of race.[9] The state of Virginia argued that because anti-miscegenation "statutes punish equally both the white and the Negro participants in an interracial marriage, these statutes, despite their reliance on racial classifications do not constitute an invidious discrimination based upon race."[10] The Court rejected this argument:

> There can be no question but that Virginia's miscegenation statutes rest solely upon distinctions drawn according to race. The statutes proscribe generally accepted conduct if engaged in by members of different races. * * * At the very least, the Equal Protection Clause demands that racial classifications, especially suspect in criminal statutes, be subjected to the "most rigid scrutiny," and, if they are ever to be upheld, they must be shown to be necessary to the accomplishment of some permissible state objective, independent of the racial discrimination which it was the object of the Fourteenth Amendment to eliminate. * * *
>
> There is patently no legitimate overriding purpose independent of invidious racial discrimination which justifies this classification. The fact that Virginia prohibits only interracial marriages involving white persons demonstrates that the racial classifications must stand on their own justification, as measures designed to maintain White Supremacy.[11]

By analogy, gay and lesbian challengers have argued that if race-based restrictions on who can marry whom discriminate on the basis of race, then sex-based restrictions on who can marry whom discriminate on the basis of sex.[12] Most courts also rejected this argument.

In three of the cases brought in the 1990's, however, judges in Hawaii, Alaska, and Vermont ruled in favor of same-sex couples on various constitutional claims. In Alaska, a lower court held that the denial of a marriage license to a gay couple constituted the denial of the fundamental right to marry under the Alaskan Constitution and was constitutional only if the state could show a "compelling interest."[13] But a referendum amended the Alaska Constitution specifically to provide for the constitutionality of marriage limited to heterosexual couples, thereby mooting the case prior to the hearing on Alaska's compelling governmental interest.

8. See, e.g., Baker v. Nelson, 191 N.W.2d at 187 (citing Loving v. Virginia, 388 U.S. 1, 87 S.Ct. 1817, 18 L.Ed.2d 1010 (1967)).

9. See *Loving*, 388 U.S. at 2.

10. Id. at 8.

11. Id. at 11.

12. See, e.g., Baker v. Nelson, 191 N.W. 2d at 187.

13. Brause v. Bureau of Vital Statistics, 1998 WL 88743 (Alaska Super.1998).

In Baehr v. Lewin,[14] the Supreme Court of Hawaii held that the denial of a marriage license to a lesbian and gay couple was a violation of the Equal Rights Amendment to the Hawaiian Constitution. The court reasoned that if a statute banning interracial marriage discriminated on the basis of race, as the United States Supreme Court had held in Loving v. Virginia, then a statute banning same-sex marriage discriminated on the basis of sex in violation of the provision against sex discrimination in the Hawaiian Constitution. The Hawaiian Supreme Court remanded to give the state an opportunity to justify the sex-based classification as serving compelling governmental purposes. At trial, Hawaii failed to bear this burden, and the ban on same-sex marriage in Hawaii was held unconstitutional.[15] While this decision was on appeal, however, a referendum amended the Hawaiian Constitution to provide that the legislature could limit marriage to heterosexual couples, thus mooting the Hawaiian case.

The Vermont case went all the way to a final judgment holding the challenged marriage law unconstitutional. An extract of this decision appears below.

BAKER v. VERMONT

Supreme Court of Vermont, 1999.

170 Vt. 194, 744 A.2d 864.

* * *

Plaintiffs are three same-sex couples who have lived together in committed relationships for periods ranging from four to twenty-five years. Two of the couples have raised children together. Each couple applied for a marriage license from their respective town clerk, and each was refused a license as ineligible under the applicable state marriage laws. Plaintiffs thereupon filed this lawsuit * * * seeking a declaratory judgment that the refusal to issue them a license violated the marriage statutes and the Vermont Constitution.

* * * The trial court * * * dismissed the complaint. * * * This appeal followed.

I. The Statutory Claim

Plaintiffs initially contend the trial court erred in concluding that the marriage statutes render them ineligible for a marriage license [because the statutes do not explicitly define marriage as requiring a man and a woman]. * * *

* * * [T]he plain and ordinary meaning of "marriage" is the union of one man and one woman as husband and wife. [After quoting dictionary definitions of marriage as heterosexual, the court discusses various Vermont statutory provisions and caselaw suggesting that mar-

14. 74 Haw. 645, 852 P.2d 44 (1993).

15. Baehr v. Miike, 80 Haw. 341, 345, 910 P.2d 112 (1996).

riage requires a man and a woman–such as the references to "bride" and "groom" in the statute authorizing the issuance of licenses and cases granting an annulment if the husband is impotent. The court concludes that under Vermont statutes, marriage consists of a man and a woman.]

* * *

II. The Constitutional Claim

* * * One of the fundamental rights included in Chapter I of the Vermont Constitution of 1777, entitled "A Declaration of Rights of the Inhabitants of the State of Vermont," the Common Benefits Clause as originally written provided:

> That government is, or ought to be, instituted for the common benefit, protection, and security of the people, nation or community; and not for the particular emolument or advantage of any single man, family or set of men, who are a part only of that community * * * .

Vt. Const. of 1777, ch. I, art. VI.[6]

* * * The concept of equality at the core of the Common Benefits Clause was not the eradication of racial or class distinctions, but rather the elimination of artificial governmental preferments and advantages. * * *

The language and history of the Common Benefits Clause * * * [indicate] that a relatively uniform standard, reflective of the inclusionary principle at its core, must govern our analysis of laws challenged under the Clause * * * rather than the rigid, multi-tiered analysis evolved by the federal courts under the Fourteenth Amendment * * * .

* * * The first step in our analysis is to identify the nature of the statutory classification. As noted, the marriage statutes apply expressly to opposite-sex couples. Thus, the statutes exclude anyone who wishes to marry someone of the same sex.[13]

6. The current version differs from the original only in that the gender-neutral terms "person" and "persons" have been substituted for "man" and "men." See Vt. Const., Ch. II § 76. This revision was not intended to "alter the sense, meaning or effect of the" provision. Id.

13. Relying largely on federal precedents, our colleague [Justice Johnson] in her concurring and dissenting opinion suggests that the statutory exclusion of same-sex couples from the benefits and protections of marriage should be subject to heightened scrutiny as a "suspect" or "quasi-suspect" classification based on sex. All of the seminal sex-discrimination decisions, however, have invalidated statutes that single out men or women as a discrete class for unequal treatment.

* * * [T]he marriage laws are facially neutral; they do not single out men or women as a class for disparate treatment, but rather prohibit men and women equally from marrying a person of the same sex. "In order to trigger equal protection analysis at all . . . a defendant must show that he was treated differently as a member of one class from treatment of members of another class similarly situated." Here, there is no discrete class subject to differential treatment solely on the basis of sex; each sex is equally prohibited from precisely the same conduct.

Indeed, most appellate courts that have addressed the issue have rejected the claim that defining marriage as the union of one man and one woman discriminates on the basis of sex.

Next, we must identify the governmental purpose or purposes to be served by the statutory classification. The principal purpose the State advances in support of excluding same-sex couples from the legal benefits of marriage is the government's interest in "furthering the link between procreation and child rearing." * * *

[T]he State has a legitimate and long-standing interest in promoting a permanent commitment between couples for the security of their children. It is equally undeniable that the State's interest has been advanced by extending formal public sanction and protection to the union, or marriage, of those couples considered capable of having children, i.e., men and women. And there is no doubt that the overwhelming majority of births today continue to result from natural conception between one man and one woman.

It is equally undisputed that many opposite-sex couples marry for reasons unrelated to procreation, that some of these couples never intend to have children, and that others are incapable of having children. Therefore, if the purpose of the statutory exclusion of same-sex couples is to "further[ ] the link between procreation and child rearing," it is significantly under-inclusive. The law extends the benefits and protections of marriage to many persons with no logical connection to the stated governmental goal.

Furthermore, * * * a significant number of children today are actually being raised by same-sex parents, and * * * increasing numbers of children are being conceived by such parents through a variety of assisted-reproductive techniques. * * *.

* * * The Vermont Legislature has not only recognized this reality, but has acted affirmatively to remove legal barriers so that same-sex couples may legally adopt and rear the children conceived through such efforts.

Therefore, to the extent that the State's purpose in licensing civil marriage was, and is, to legitimize children and provide for their securi-

Although the concurring and dissenting opinion [of Justice Johnson] invokes the United States Supreme Court decision in Loving v. Virginia, 388 U.S. 1 (1967), the reliance is misplaced. There the high court had little difficulty in looking behind the superficial neutrality of Virginia's anti-miscegenation statute to hold that its real purpose was to maintain the pernicious doctrine of white supremacy. Our colleague argues, by analogy, that the effect, if not the purpose, of the exclusion of same-sex partners from the marriage laws is to maintain certain male and female stereotypes to the detriment of both. To support the claim, she cites a number of antiquated statutes that denied married women a variety of freedoms, including the right to enter into contracts and hold property.

The test to evaluate whether a facially gender-neutral statute discriminates on the basis of sex is whether the law "can be traced to a discriminatory purpose." Personnel Administrator v. Feeney, 442 U.S. 256, 272 (1979). The evidence does not demonstrate such a purpose. It is one thing to show that long-repealed marriage statutes subordinated women to men within the marital relation. It is quite another to demonstrate that the authors of the marriage laws excluded same-sex couples because of incorrect and discriminatory assumptions about gender roles or anxiety about gender-role confusion. That evidence is not before us. Accordingly, we are not persuaded that sex discrimination offers a useful analytic framework for determining plaintiffs' rights under the Common Benefits Clause.

ty, the statutes plainly exclude many same-sex couples who are no different from opposite-sex couples with respect to these objectives. If anything, the exclusion of same-sex couples from the legal protections incident to marriage exposes their children to the precise risks that the State argues the marriage laws are designed to secure against. In short, the marital exclusion treats persons who are similarly situated for purposes of the law, differently.

The State also argues that because same-sex couples cannot conceive a child on their own, their exclusion promotes a "perception of the link between procreation and child rearing," and that to discard it would "advance the notion that mothers and fathers ... are mere surplusage to the functions of procreation and child rearing." Apart from the bare assertion, the State offers no persuasive reasoning to support these claims. Indeed, it is undisputed that most of those who utilize non-traditional means of conception are infertile married couples and that many assisted reproductive techniques involve only one of the married partner's genetic material, the other being supplied by a third party through sperm, egg, or embryo donation. The State does not suggest that the use of these technologies undermines a married couple's sense of parental responsibility, or fosters the perception that they are "mere surplusage" to the conception and parenting of the child so conceived. Nor does it even remotely suggest that access to such techniques ought to be restricted as a matter of public policy to "send a public message that procreation and child rearing are intertwined." Accordingly, there is no reasonable basis to conclude that a same-sex couple's use of the same technologies would undermine the bonds of parenthood, or society's perception of parenthood.

* * * We [now] turn * * * from the principal justifications advanced by the State to the interests asserted by plaintiffs.

* * * [T]he benefits and protections incident to a marriage license * * * include, for example, the right to receive a portion of the estate of a spouse who dies intestate and protection against disinheritance through elective share provisions; preference in being appointed as the personal representative of a spouse who dies intestate; the right to bring a lawsuit for the wrongful death of a spouse; the right to bring an action for loss of consortium; the right to workers' compensation survivor benefits; the right to spousal benefits statutorily guaranteed to public employees, including health, life, disability, and accident insurance; the opportunity to be covered as a spouse under group life insurance policies issued to an employee; the opportunity to be covered as the insured's spouse under an individual health insurance policy; the right to claim an evidentiary privilege for marital communications; homestead rights and protections; the presumption of joint ownership of property and the concomitant right of survivorship; hospital visitation and other rights incident to the medical treatment of a family member; and the right to receive, and the obligation to provide, spousal support, maintenance, and property division in the event of separation or divorce. * * *

* * * The legal benefits and protections flowing from a marriage license are of such significance that any statutory exclusion must necessarily be grounded on public concerns of sufficient weight, cogency, and authority that the justice of the deprivation cannot seriously be questioned. Considered in light of the extreme logical disjunction between the classification and the stated purposes of the law—protecting children and "furthering the link between procreation and child rearing"—the exclusion falls substantially short of this standard. The laudable governmental goal of promoting a commitment between married couples to promote the security of their children and the community as a whole provides no reasonable basis for denying the legal benefits and protections of marriage to same-sex couples, who are no differently situated with respect to this goal than their opposite-sex counterparts. Promoting a link between procreation and childrearing similarly fails to support the exclusion. We turn, accordingly, to the remaining interests identified by the State in support of the statutory exclusion.

The State asserts that a number of additional rationales could support a legislative decision to exclude same-sex partners from the statutory benefits and protections of marriage. Among these are the State's purported interests in "promoting child rearing in a setting that provides both male and female role models * * *." It is conceivable that the Legislature could conclude that opposite-sex partners offer advantages in this area, although we note that child-development experts disagree and the answer is decidedly uncertain. * * * [But i]n 1996, the Vermont General Assembly enacted, and the Governor signed, a law removing all prior legal barriers to the adoption of children by same-sex couples. At the same time, the Legislature provided additional legal protections in the form of court-ordered child support and parent-child contact in the event that same-sex parents dissolved their "domestic relationship." In light of these express policy choices, the State's arguments that Vermont public policy favors opposite-sex over same-sex parents or disfavors the use of artificial reproductive technologies, are patently without substance.

Similarly, the State's argument that Vermont's marriage laws serve a substantial governmental interest in maintaining uniformity with other jurisdictions cannot be reconciled with Vermont's recognition of unions, such as first-cousin marriages, not uniformly sanctioned in other states. * * *

The State's remaining claims (e.g., recognition of same-sex unions might foster marriages of convenience or otherwise affect the institution in "unpredictable" ways) may be plausible forecasts as to what the future may hold, but cannot reasonably be construed to provide a reasonable and just basis for the statutory exclusion. The State's conjectures are not, in any event, susceptible to empirical proof before they occur.

[The Remedy]

* * * Although plaintiffs sought injunctive and declaratory relief designed to secure a marriage license, their claims and arguments here

have focused primarily upon the consequences of official exclusion from the statutory benefits, protections, and security incident to marriage under Vermont law. While some future case may attempt to establish that—notwithstanding equal benefits and protections under Vermont law—the denial of a marriage license operates per se to deny constitutionally protected rights, that is not the claim we address today.

We hold only that plaintiffs are entitled under Chapter I, Article 7, of the Vermont Constitution to obtain the same benefits and protections afforded by Vermont law to married opposite-sex couples. We do not purport to infringe upon the prerogatives of the Legislature to craft an appropriate means of addressing this constitutional mandate, other than to note that the record here refers to a number of potentially constitutional statutory schemes from other jurisdictions. These include what are typically referred to as "domestic partnership" or "registered partnership" acts, which generally establish an alternative legal status to marriage for same-sex couples, impose similar formal requirements and limitations, create a parallel licensing or registration scheme, and extend all or most of the same rights and obligations provided by the law to married partners.

* * * A sudden change in the marriage laws or the statutory benefits traditionally incidental to marriage may have disruptive and unforeseen consequences. Absent legislative guidelines defining the status and rights of same-sex couples, consistent with constitutional requirements, uncertainty and confusion could result. Therefore, we hold that the current statutory scheme shall remain in effect for a reasonable period of time to enable the Legislature to consider and enact implementing legislation in an orderly and expeditious fashion.

Dooley, J., concurring.

I concur in [all but the majority's reasoning on the constitutional claim]. * * *

The marriage statutes do not facially discriminate on the basis of sexual orientation. There is, however, no doubt that the requirement that civil marriage be a union of one man and one woman has the effect of discriminating against lesbian and gay couples, like the plaintiffs in this case, who are unable to marry the life partners of their choice. [Justice Dooley regards Vermont's refusal to grant the benefits of marriage to same-sex couples as discrimination against a suspect class and, for that reason, a violation of the Vermont Constitution.] * * *

Johnson, J., concurring in part and dissenting in part.

* * * I concur with the majority's holding, but I respectfully dissent from its novel and truncated remedy, which in my view abdicates this Court's constitutional duty to redress violations of constitutional rights. I would grant the requested relief and enjoin defendants from denying plaintiffs a marriage license based solely on the sex of the applicants.

* * *

[The State's Limited Interest in Regulating Marriage]

My dissent from the majority's mandate is grounded on the government's limited interest in dictating public morals outside the scope of its police power, and the differing roles of the judicial and legislative branches in our tripartite system of government.* * *

This case concerns the secular licensing of marriage. The State's interest in licensing marriages is regulatory in nature. The regulatory purpose of the licensing scheme is to create public records for the orderly allocation of benefits, imposition of obligations, and distribution of property through inheritance. Thus, a marriage license merely acts as a trigger for state-conferred benefits. In granting a marriage license, the State is not espousing certain morals, lifestyles, or relationships, but only identifying those persons entitled to the benefits of the marital status.

Apart from establishing restrictions on age and consanguinity related to public health and safety, the statutory scheme at issue here makes no qualitative judgment about which persons may obtain a marriage license. Hence, the State's interest concerning the challenged licensing statute is a narrow one, and plaintiffs have prevailed on their constitutional claim because the State has failed to raise any legitimate reasons related to public health or safety for denying marital benefits to same-sex couples. * * *

* * *

[Analysis of Denial of Marriage to Same–Sex Couples as Sex Discrimination]

* * * This is a straightforward case of sex discrimination.

* * * A woman is denied the right to marry another woman because her would-be partner is a woman, not because one or both are lesbians. Similarly, a man is denied the right to marry another man because his would-be partner is a man, not because one or both are gay. Thus, an individual's right to marry a person of the same sex is prohibited solely on the basis of sex, not on the basis of sexual orientation. Indeed, sexual orientation does not appear as a qualification for marriage under the marriage statutes. The State makes no inquiry into the sexual practices or identities of a couple seeking a license.

The State advances two arguments in support of its position that Vermont's marriage laws do not establish a sex-based classification. The State first contends that the marriage statutes merely acknowledge that marriage, by its very nature, cannot be comprised of two persons of the same sex. Thus, in the State's view, it is the definition of marriage, not the statutes, that restricts marriage to two people of the opposite sex. This argument is circular. It is the State that defines civil marriage under its statute. * * *

The State's second argument * * * is that the marriage statutes do not discriminate on the basis of sex because they treat similarly situated males the same as similarly situated females. Under this argument, there can be no sex discrimination here because "[i]f a man wants to marry a man, he is barred; a woman seeking to marry a woman is barred in precisely the same way. For this reason, women and men are not treated differently." But consider the following example. Dr. A and Dr. B both want to marry Ms. C, an X-ray technician. Dr. A may do so because Dr. A is a man. Dr. B may not because Dr. B is a woman. Dr. A and Dr. B are people of opposite sexes who are similarly situated in the sense that they both want to marry a person of their choice. The statute disqualifies Dr. B from marriage solely on the basis of her sex and treats her differently from Dr. A, a man. This is sex discrimination.

I recognize, of course, that although the classification here is sex-based on its face, its most direct impact is on lesbians and gay men, the class of individuals most likely to seek same-sex marriage. Viewing the discrimination as sex-based, however, is important. Although the original purpose of the marriage statutes was not to exclude same-sex couples, for the simple reason that same-sex marriage was very likely not on the minds of the Legislature when it passed the licensing statute, the preservation of the sex-based classification deprives lesbians and gay men of the right to marry the life partner of their choice. If, as I argue below, the sex-based classification contained in the marriage laws is unrelated to any valid purpose, but rather is a vestige of sex-role stereotyping that applies to both men and women, the classification is still unlawful sex discrimination even if it applies equally to men and women.

Although Vermont has not had occasion to consider the question, most, if not all, courts have held that the denial of rights or benefits on the basis of sex subject the state's action to some level of heightened scrutiny. This is so because the sex of an individual "frequently bears no relation to ability to perform or contribute to society." Moreover, in some cases, such as here, sex-based classifications "very likely reflect outmoded notions of the relative capabilities of men and women."

I do not believe that it is necessary to reach the question in this case, however, because in my view, the justifications asserted by the State do not satisfy even our rational-basis standard under the Common Benefits Clause, which requires that the classification be "reasonably related to the promotion of a valid public purpose." * * *

Before applying the rational-basis standard to the State's justifications, it is helpful to examine the history of the marriage laws in Vermont. There is no doubt that, historically, the marriage laws imposed sex-based roles for the partners to a marriage—male provider and female dependent—that bore no relation to their inherent abilities to contribute to society. Under the common law, husband and wife were one person. The legal existence of a woman was suspended by marriage; she merged with her husband and held no separate rights to enter into a contract or execute a deed. * * *

Starting in the late nineteenth century, Vermont, like other states, began to enact statutes, such as the Rights of Married Women Act to grant married women property and contractual rights independent of their husbands. * * *

Today, the partners to a marriage are equal before the law. A married woman may now enter contracts, sue and be sued without joining her husband, purchase and convey property separate from her husband, own property, and collect rents and profits from it. As the Legislature enacted statutes to confer rights upon married women, this Court abolished common-law doctrines arising from the common law theory that husband and wife were one person and that the wife had no independent legal existence

The question now is whether the sex-based classification in the marriage law is simply a vestige of the common-law unequal marriage relationship or whether there is some valid governmental purpose for the classification today. In support of the marriage statutes, the State advances public purposes that fall into three general categories.

In the first category, the State asserts public purposes—uniting men and women to celebrate the "complementarity" (sic) of the sexes and providing male and female role models for children—based on broad and vague generalizations about the roles of men and women that reflect outdated sex-role stereotyping. The State contends that (1) marriage unites the rich physical and psychological differences between the sexes; (2) sex differences strengthen and stabilize a marriage; (3) each sex contributes differently to a family unit and to society; and (4) uniting the different male and female qualities and contributions in the same institution instructs the young of the value of such a union. The State relies on social science literature, such as Carol Gilligan's In a Different Voice: Psychological Theory and Women's Development (1982), to support its contention that there are sex differences that justify the State requiring two people to be of opposite sex to marry.

The State attempts to analogize this case to the changes in law brought about by women's participation in the legal profession starting in the 1970s, arguing that women have brought a different voice to legal theory and practice. The State also points to United States v. Virginia, 518 U.S. 515, 533 (1996) (hereinafter VMI), arguing that an institution or community made up exclusively of one sex is different from a community composed of both. The goal of diversity has been recognized to justify affirmative action programs in public broadcasting and education. Similarly, the recognition that women may contribute differently from men is a valid argument for women's full participation in all aspects of public life. The goal of community diversity has no place, however, as a requirement of marriage.

To begin with, carried to its logical conclusion, the State's rationale could require all marriages to be between people, not just of the opposite sex, but of different races, religions, national origin, and so forth, to promote diversity. Moreover, while it may be true that the female voice or point of view is sometimes different from the male, such differences are not necessarily found in comparing any given man and any given woman. The State's implicit assertion otherwise is sex stereotyping of the most retrograde sort. Nor could the State show that the undoubted differences between any given man and woman who wish to marry are more related to their sex than to other characteristics and life experiences. In short, the "diversity" argument is based on illogical conclusions from stereotypical imaginings that would be condemned by the very case cited for its support. See VMI, 518 U.S. at 533 (justifications for sex-based classifications "must not rely on overbroad generalizations about different talents, capabilities, or preferences of males and females."). * * *

None of the State's justifications meets the rational-basis test under the Common Benefits Clause. Finding no legally valid justification for the sex-based classification, I conclude that the classification is a vestige of the historical unequal marriage relationship that more recent legislative enactments and our own jurisprudence have unequivocally rejected. The protections conferred on Vermonters by the Common Benefits Clause cannot be restricted by the outmoded conception that marriage requires one man and one woman, creating one person—the husband.

Notes on **Baker v. Vermont**

1. What do you think of the Baker v. Vermont court's reasoning on the statutory claim? Should a marriage statute which does not *explicitly* define marriage as the union of a man and a woman be interpreted as so limited? What if–as is true of some state marriage laws–there are no words anywhere in the marriage statutes even suggesting a man and a woman? Why do most people in the United States today regard marriage as necessarily the union of a man and a woman? How would Justice Johnson answer this question? Do you agree with her?

Why have western cultures traditionally limited marriage to heterosexual unions? What was the purpose of marriage in the societies from which we inherited our notion of marriage? Mary Becker suggests that the ancient pre-Christian cultures of Israel, Greece, Rome and Germany viewed marriage as necessarily the union of a man and a woman because its purpose was to ensure the man that the woman's children were his children, to assure her family that her children would be his legitimate heirs, and to give her the status of wife (rather than the lower status of concubine). Christianity has been even more influential on our notions of marriage than these ancient cultures. Medieval canon law is the basis for our legal regulation of marriage and sexuality. Christianity valued virginity highly and regarded all sex as inferior to virginity; the only sex that was not sin was uncontracepted sex in marriage. Thus, for Christians, marriage was the one place for licit sex, and since the only licit sex was procreative, marriage was necessarily limited to heterosexual couples. See Mary Becker, Family Law in the Secular State and Restrictions on Same–Sex Marriage: Two Are Better Than One, 2001 U. Ill. L. Rev. 1, 17–27. Are these the goals of marriage today? What should be the purposes of marriage regulation today?

2. Is a requirement that men marry women and that women marry men a form of overt, facial sex discrimination? Compare the views of the writers of the various opinions in Baker v. Vermont. Which justice offers the best analysis of this question? Is the majority right in claiming in footnote 13 that "[a]ll of the seminal sex-discrimination decisions * * * have invalidated statutes that single out men or women as a discrete class for unequal treatment"? How does Justice Johnson respond to this point? Would the Supreme Court regard a statute requiring all girls to go to girls' schools and all boys to boys' schools as something other than sex discrimination? What of a statute that required employers to have separate departments for female and male employees? Would these statutes discriminate on the basis of sex–or would they simply apply the same treatment to women and to men?

3. What do you think of the strength of the analogy between the race discrimination argument in Loving v. Virginia, the miscegenation case described above, and the sex discrimination argument in same-sex marriage cases? In Baker v. Nelson, 291 Minn. 310, 191 N.W.2d 185 (1971), the first case in which a gay couple raised *Loving* in the context of a sex-discrimination challenge to the denial of a marriage license, the court regarded *Loving* as totally irrelevant:

> Virginia's antimiscegenation statute, prohibiting interracial marriages, was invalidated solely on the grounds of its patent racial discrimination. * * *
>
> *Loving* does indicate that not all state restrictions upon the right to marry are beyond reach of the Fourteenth Amendment. But in commonsense and in a constitutional sense, there is a clear distinction between a marital restriction based merely upon race and one based upon the fundamental difference in sex.

291 Minn. at 315, 191 N.W. at 187. See also Dean v. District of Columbia, 653 A.2d 307 (1995) (similar). Can you articulate the commonsense (and constitutional?) difference the court refers to here? Do you find this convincing? Do you think that bans on same-sex marriage (or laws against consensual sodomy) are equivalent to anti-miscegenation statutes? See Carrie G. Costello, Legitimate Bonds and Unnatural Unions: Race, Sexual Orientation, and Control of the American Family, 15 Harv. Women's L.J. 79, 171 (1992):

> The process of defining legitimate bonds and unnatural unions fortified a system of racial caste, and both the caste system and the definitional process long outlived racial bondage. The tactics employed in the control of racial Others remain effective today. These tactics are currently being utilized in the control of other groups, including queer people; the Order destabilizes the Other through the denial of familial rights. Spurred on in the struggle to secure these familial rights, lesbians and gay men, among others, provide the threat of subversion against which the hegemonic Order needs to unite itself. Control of the definition of the family is a powerful tool, and the Order will continue to seek to employ it to constitute itself and control its Others far into the future.

Why is same-sex marriage seen as such a threat to heterosexual marriage? Is the institution of heterosexual marriage so fragile? What are the causes of the fragility of heterosexual marriages today?

4. One possible distinction is that in *Loving,* the Court saw the link between anti-miscegenation laws and "White Supremacy." 388 U.S. at 7, 82 S.Ct. at 1821, 18 L.Ed.2d at 1015. Is there a link between the ban on same-sex marriages and "Male Supremacy"? How might this link work? John Stoltenberg suggests:

> The system of male supremacy requires gender polarity, with real men as different from real women as they can be, and with men's social superiority to women expressed in public and private in every way imaginable. Homophobia is, in part, how the system punishes those who deviate and seem to dissent from it.

Stoltenberg, You Can't Fight Homophobia and Protect the Pornographers at the Same Time—An Analysis of What Went Wrong in *Hardwick,* in The Sexual Liberals and the Attack on Feminism 184, 184–85 (Dorchen Leidholdt and Janice G. Raymond, eds. 1990). Do you think homophobia "is a reaction to violation of gender norms, rather than simply scorn for the violation of norms of sexual behavior"? Sylvia A. Law, Homosexuality and the Social Meaning of Gender, 1988 Wis.L.Rev. 187, 187. Is the purpose of limiting marriage to heterosexuals to regulate sexual behavior or to enforce gender norms? Is it both?

5. What does Justice Johnson see as the substantive connection between sex discrimination and the ban on same-sex marriage? What does the majority think of this analysis? What connections do you see between the social inequality of women and men and bans on same-sex marriage? Are there connections other than the historical origins of marriage as a patriarchal institution? Does Vermont's justification—that marriage should be limited to heterosexuals so that children have "both male and female role models"—suggest another connection? What of the fact that women are more likely to find equality with respect to domestic responsibilities and caretaking in lesbian than in heterosexual couples? See Mary Becker, Women, Morality, and Sexual Orientation, 8 U.C.L.A. Women's L. J. 165, 206 (1998) (suggesting that many women have a fluid sexuality and discussing advantages for women in lesbian relationships, such as a more equitable division of housework and caretaking labor). If, as Becker suggests, many women have a fluid sexuality, whose interest is served by keeping same-sex unions socially unacceptable?

6. Is there an important difference between the ban on same-sex marriage and anti-miscegenation statutes? Why did anti-miscegenation laws *require* intra-group marriages, whereas the traditional ban on same-sex marriage does exactly the opposite, banning intra-group unions? Does this difference have political consequences? What are they?

7. What do you think of the state's use of the following argument described in Justice Johnson's opinion?

> The State attempts to analogize this case to the changes in law brought about by women's participation in the legal profession starting in the 1970s, arguing that women have brought a different voice to legal theory and practice. The State also points to United States v. Virginia [the VMI case in Chapter 2, above], arguing that an institution or community made up exclusively of one sex is different from a community composed of both.

Do you agree that *VMI* supports the state's position in Baker v. Vermont? The state also used Carol Gilligan's work to argue "that there are sex differences that justify the State requiring two people to be of opposite sex to marry." Is this a fair use of Gilligan? Would you oppose extension of marriage to same-sex couples for this reason?

8. Are bans on same-sex marriage a form of overt discrimination on the basis of sexual orientation? If not, do they discriminate in effect against gay men and lesbians? Compare the views of the writers of the various opinions in Baker v. Vermont. Which justice offers the most convincing analysis of these questions?

9. Should gay men and lesbians be regarded as a suspect class for purposes of constitutional analysis? The Supreme Court has often discussed immutability as an important factor in finding that classifications based on sex and race are subject to heightened scrutiny. Is–or should it be–a *necessary* factor for heightened scrutiny? See Janet E. Halley, Sexual Orientation and the Politics of Biology: A Critique of the Argument From Immutability, 46 Stan. L. Rev. 503, 507–16 (1994) (arguing that the Supreme Court has never stated it is a *necessary* finding and noting its absence in religion and alienage cases). Why is immutability—or a genetic basis for homosexuality—so important in the national debate? Should it be? If some women do have a fluid sexuality, should the fact that they choose a relationship with another woman—because they find it more emotionally satisfying or more equal in terms of domestic responsibilities–mean that their partnership should be forbidden?

10. Recall that the Court in Loving v. Virginia struck the Virginia anti-miscegenation law on the ground that it interfered with the fundamental right to marry (as well as on the ground that it violated the equal protection clause because it discriminated on the basis of race). In Turner v. Safley, 482 U.S. 78, 107 S.Ct. 2254, 96 L.Ed.2d 64 (1987), the Supreme Court recognized (and constitutionally protected) the non-procreative purposes of marriage, holding that the fundamental right to marry extends to prisoners even though inmates have no constitutional right to conjugal visits. After noting that the right to marry "is subject to substantial restrictions as a result of incarceration," the Court noted that "[m]any important attributes of marriage remain." Id. at 79. The court listed three: (1) marriage is "an expression of emotional support and public commitment"; (2) marriage has spiritual significance to many people and "the commitment of marriage may be an exercise of religious faith as well as an expression of personal dedication"; and (3) marriage is often "a precondition to government benefits (e.g., Social Security benefits), property rights (e.g., tenancy by the entirety, inheritance rights), and other, less tangible benefits." Id. at 95–96. The Court concluded that "[t]hese incidents of marriage, like the religious and personal aspects of the marriage commitment, are unaffected by the fact of confinement or the pursuit of legitimate corrections goals." Id. at 96. With respect to a claim based on the fundamental right to marry, can you distinguish same-sex marriage claims and those in Loving v. Virginia or Turner v. Safley?

It is nevertheless clear that the Supreme Court, at least as constituted in 1986, would have affirmed a ban on same-sex marriage. Cf. Bowers v.

Hardwick, 478 U.S. 186, 106 S.Ct. 2841, 92 L.Ed.2d 140 (1986) (upholding state sodomy law applied to consensual behavior in private between two men). Although the same-sex marriage case could raise a claim based on the equal protection clause or denial of the fundamental right to marry, whereas *Bowers* involved a privacy claim, *Bowers* leaves no room for doubt on how the 1986 Court would have ruled in a same-sex marriage case.

How do you think today's Court would rule, given Romer v. Evans, 517 U.S. 620, 116 S.Ct. 1620, 134 L.Ed.2d 855 (1996) (holding unconstitutional Colorado constitutional amendment prohibiting the state and all its subdivisions from prohibiting discrimination on the basis of "homosexual, lesbian or bisexual orientation, conduct, practices or relationships")? The *Evans* Court regarded Amendment 2 as unprecedented in the breadth with which it "denied protection across the board" to a group defined by a single trait. Id. at 633. The Court was unable to see any explanation for the statute other than "animosity toward the class of persons affected." Id. at 634.

> We must conclude that Amendment 2 classifies homosexuals not to further a proper legislative end but to make them unequal to everyone else. This Colorado cannot do. A State cannot so deem a class of persons a stranger to its laws.

Id. at 635. The *Evans* Court did not mention Bowers v. Hardwick. It is, therefore, not at all clear how far Romer v. Evans might reach in protecting lesbians and gay men from legislative classifications singling them out for disfavored treatment. What distinctions might be made between Amendment 2 and denial of marriage to same-sex couples? Does Romer v. Evans suggest that the Court might regard denial of marriage to same-sex couples as unconstitutional?

Which argument do you think would have greater chance of success: that denial of same-sex marriage rights (a) discriminates on the basis of sex; (b) discriminates impermissibly against homosexuals; or (c) interferes with the fundamental right to marry?

11. Assuming a constitutional violation, what is your view on the appropriate remedy? Why didn't the majority simply order the state to issue marriage licenses to lesbian and gay couples? Are there advantages to the majority's approach in terms of selecting a path less likely to lead to a backlash and constitutional repeal of marriage rights? What would Justice Johnson say on this point?

12. What are the strongest policy arguments for the ban on same-sex marriages? If you were a lawyer for Vermont, what arguments would you have used to defend the ban? Opponents of same-sex marriage often regard extension of marriage to gay men and lesbians as "uniquely destructive of an institution, traditional heterosexual marriage, which itself is the keystone of the existing social order." Hannah Schwarzschild, Same–Sex Marriage and Constitutional Privacy: Moral Threat and Legal Anomaly, 4 Berkeley Women's L.J. 94, 122 (1988–89) (describing opponents' views). Do you think this is the basis for the opposition to same-sex marriage? Here is an argument raised in a 1977 law review article:

> * * * The most threatening aspect of homosexuality is its potential to become a viable alternative to heterosexual intimacy. This argument

is premised upon the belief that the practice of an alternative mode of sexual relations will inimically affect the predominant mode. Thus, any recognition of a constitutional right to practice homosexuality would undermine the value of heterosexuality and the institutions and practices—conventional marriage and childrearing—associated with it.

This state concern, in our view, should not be minimized. The nuclear, heterosexual family is charged with several of society's most essential functions. It has served as an important means of educating the young; it has often provided economic support and psychological comfort to family members; and it has operated as the unit upon which basic governmental policies in such matters as taxation, conscription, and inheritance have been based. Family life has been a central unifying experience throughout American society. Preserving the strength of this basic, organic unit is a central and legitimate end of the police power. The state ought to be concerned that if allegiance to traditional family arrangements declines, society as a whole may well suffer.

* * *

In seeking to regulate homosexuality, the state takes as a basic premise that social and legal attitudes play an important and interdependent role in the individual's formation of his or her sexual destiny. A shift on the part of the law from opposition to neutrality arguably makes homosexuality appear a more acceptable sexual lifestyle, particularly to younger persons whose sexual preferences are as yet unformed. Young people form their sexual identity partly on the basis of models they see in society. If homosexual behavior is legalized, and thus partly legitimized, an adolescent may question whether he or she should "choose" heterosexuality. At the time their sexual feelings begin to develop, many young people have more interests in common with members of their own sex; sexual attraction rather than genuine interest often first draws adolescents to members of the opposite sex. If society accorded more legitimacy to expressions of homosexual attraction, attachment to the opposite sex might be postponed or diverted for some time, perhaps until after the establishment of sexual patterns that would hamper development of traditional heterosexual family relationships. For those persons who eventually choose the heterosexual model, the existence of conflicting models might provide further sexual tension destructive to the traditional marital unit.

J. Harvie Wilkinson III and G. Edward White, Constitutional Protection for Personal Lifestyles, 62 Cornell L.Rev. 563, 595–96 (1977). Do the reasons Wilkinson and White proffer for discouraging same-sex relationships constitute compelling state interests? Were such arguments made in Baker v. Vermont? If marriage is so essential to a stable social structure, shouldn't it be available to all couples?

13. Many opponents of same-sex marriage believe such intimate relationships are sinful. Other religious people strongly support same-sex marriage. Is the sinfulness of homosexuality (in the view of some) a legitimate reason for a secular state to proscribe same-sex marriage? Is there any way to put this point in secular terms? Would putting it in secular terms make it less objectionable? For a discussion of the "long influence of the Christian

Church on legalized homophobia," see Rev. Ellen M. Barrett, Legal Homophobia and the Christian Church, 30 Hastings L.J. 1019 (1979).

14. Can the view that heterosexual marriage provides the most beneficial family structure for children be formulated as a legitimate governmental interest justifying the limitation of marriage to heterosexual couples? Is it possible for a state to make a convincing argument on this basis if it (a) has statutes providing that when a married woman has a child by artificial insemination with her husband's agreement, the child is the child of both of them; or (b) allows, either through statutes or case law, a lesbian or gay-male couple to adopt? Even without such laws, are there problems with this argument from the perspective of children?

15. What do you see as the role of the state in regulating marriage, i.e., what are the legitimate ends of the secular state in regulating marriage in a diverse society in the 21st century? Compare your view with Justice Johnson's: what does she see as the legitimate purposes of the state in regulating marriage? Can you argue for a broader role for the state than Justice Johnson would and yet argue for the extension of marriage to gay and lesbian couples? Look over the earlier readings in this chapter. Do they–especially the readings on the benefits of marriage and the need of children and their caretakers for economic security at divorce–suggest an answer to these questions?

Given your view of the state's legitimate role in regulating marriage, do you think that as a matter of sound family law policy marriage itself should be extended to same-sex couples? Should some alternative form of union (perhaps "civil unions" carrying all the rights of marriage) be extended instead of marriage? Should neither be extended in order to protect and preserve the institution of marriage?

16. What harms are caused by failing to recognize same-sex marriage? In what ways are lesbian and gay relationships made more difficult and more costly as a result? How are children in households headed by same-sex partners affected by the inability of the adults who are parenting them to marry? Lesbians are nearly as likely as other women to be in households with children, and gay men are half as likely as heterosexual men to live in such households. See Lee Badge, Income Inflation: The Myth of Affluence Among Gay, Lesbian, and Bisexual Americans 18 (1998) (32% of lesbians and 36% of heterosexual women have children under 18 at home; 15% of gay men and 28% of heterosexual men have children at home). Do you agree with the Baker v. Vermont court that children living in gay and lesbian households would be better off if the adults they are living with married? How would you balance these costs against the claims of opponents of same-sex marriage that same-sex relationships are sinful, that same-sex marriage threatens the institution of heterosexual marriage, and that recognition of same-sex marriages will decrease the probability that in the future children will live in households with two adults to whom they are biologically related? If heterosexual marriage is failing, should the state come to its rescue? What measures would most strengthen heterosexual marriage? Would you support them?

17. What problems arise when gay and lesbian couples split up and divorce is not available because marriage was not available? How are these

problems different from the problems faced by heterosexual cohabiting couples who split up?

18. What do you make of the intra-community debate in the 1980's and early 1990's, described above, about whether to push for marriage rights or for a more universal progressive agenda? Researchers report that married people (women as well as men) enjoy a marriage bonus: they are healthier, happier, and better off financially than those who are single or cohabiting. See Linda J. Waite and Maggie Gallagher, The Case for Marriage (2000). Does the marriage bonus suggest that alternatives such as universal health care and domestic partnership might not be sufficient? Do you think that feminists and gay-rights activists should be working for the abolition of marriage rather than its extension to lesbian and gay couples?

Text Note: Choice of Law Questions and Legislative Responses at Home and Abroad

If same-sex marriages were recognized in one state, say the state of Hawaii—which looked likely between 1993 and 1998—what would happen if a couple from another state went to Hawaii for a combined wedding and honeymoon? Would they be married in their home state when they returned? Activists on both sides—at least those who spoke to the issue in the national media—agreed that couples would be married in their home states when they returned from their Hawaiian wedding and honeymoon. Advocates for same-sex marriage in the Hawaii case argued that Article IV of the United States Constitution, requiring each state to give "Full Faith and Credit * * * to the public Acts, Records, and judicial proceedings of every other State," would require other states to recognize their residents' Hawaiian marriages. Opponents argued that legislation "protecting" marriage was therefore desperately needed. They proposed DOMA's (Defense of Marriage Acts) in each state expressly providing that the state would not recognize same-sex marriages when their residents travelled to Hawaii (or elsewhere) to marry. At least 33 states have enacted such legislation.[16] Congress also passed a national DOMA, which provides that no state need recognize a same-sex marriage from another state and defines marriage for purposes of federal regulations and benefits as limited to heterosexuals.[17]

Although advocates and opponents of same-sex marriage tended to agree that, unless states passed DOMA legislation, they would be bound to recognize the same-sex marriages of their residents who went to Hawaii for their weddings, the law was uniformly to the contrary. The general (common law, not constitutional law) choice of law rule is that a marriage valid where performed is valid everywhere. But there is a public policy exception: if a state considers its restrictions on marriage a serious enough concern (e.g., incest prohibitions), it need not give full faith and credit to a marriage performed in another state and legal there but violating the local state's marriage statute.[18] A marriage is more vulnerable to challenge under this

16. David Goodman, A More Civil Union: Vermont's legal recognition of same-sex couples has brought the latest struggle for gay rights out of the closet—and onto the stage of national politics, Mother Jones, 48, 78 (July/August 2000).

17. 1 U.S.C. § 7 (1997).

18. Homer H. Clark, The Law of Domestic Relations in the United States 85 (2d ed. 1988).

public-policy exception if it involves residents who went to another state for their wedding ceremony in order to evade restrictions in their home state (rather than residents of another state who had moved to the home state after a marriage valid in the state in which they were residing at the time). This public-policy exception has not been seen as unconstitutional under the full faith and credit clause.[19] The full faith and credit clause "as it is now interpreted by the Supreme Court, is not much of a constraint on states' power to fashion choice of law rules."[20] (Note also that a marriage license—unlike a divorce, to which full faith and credit does apply—is not a judicial judgment.)

Thus, under established law, there was no need for a federal DOMA to give states authority to refuse to recognize a same-sex marriage performed elsewhere. The states already had that power.[21] Prior to Baehr v. Lewin, the Hawaiian case, some states had statutes explicitly providing that a marriage valid where performed was valid in the home state. Others had statutes explicitly providing the opposite: that a marriage invalid in the home state was invalid if performed elsewhere involving residents who had travelled out of state. Many courts decided on a case-by-case basis under common law principles whether their state's interest in the policy at issue was strong enough to warrant refusal to recognize a marriage valid where performed. Some state DOMA's did, however, change existing law. In states, such as California, where a statute provided that a marriage valid where performed was valid in California, the state DOMA changed the law with respect to potential same-sex marriages from other states. And in states in which the public policy exception was applied by courts using common law principles, state DOMA's ensured that courts will hold such marriages invalid. But state DOMA's were also enacted in states like Illinois, in which there was no need to prevent the residents-go-to-Hawaii-for-wedding-and-honeymoon scheme, since Illinois law already provided that residents who married elsewhere to evade Illinois restrictions are not validly married in Illinois.[22]

Despite state DOMA's, it is difficult to imagine that if marriage is ever recognized in one state, say the state of Bliss, all marriages of residents who live in Bliss at the time of the marriage will be wholly ignored when they subsequently move to another state. Imagine, for example, a married lesbian

19. See Larry Kramer, Same-Sex Marriage, Conflict of Laws, and the Unconstitutional Public Policy Exception, 106 Yale L.J. 1965, 1975–1976 (1997) ("With or without explicit authorization from Congress or state legislatures, courts are relatively free to make an exception to the place of celebration rule for same-sex marriages. They are most likely to do so, moreover, in cases * * * in which a couple travels to Hawaii to get married with no intention of changing domiciles. If applied, the exception almost certainly will lead to a declaration that such marriages are invalid."). Kramer argues that the public policy exception to the general rule of recognition (a marriage valid where performed is valid everywhere) should be regarded as unconstitutional under the full faith and credit clause. But this is a novel argument that the "public policy doctrine ought to be deemed unconstitutional," not that it has ever been held to be unconstitutional. Id. at 1966.

20. Andrew Koppelman, Dumb and DOMA: Why the Defense of Marriage Act Is Unconstitutional, 83 Iowa L. Rev. 1, 10 (1997).

21. The federal DOMA, however, disallows federal benefits to married same-sex couples, as discussed below. For an argument that both provisions in the federal DOMA are unconstitutional under Romer v. Evans (517 U.S. 620, 636, 116 S.Ct. 1620, 1623, 134 L.Ed.2d 855 (1996)), see Koppelman, above note 20.

22. 750 ILCS 5/216 (2000).

couple with three children who move from Bliss to Illinois. One partner has been a full-time homemaker. Under the law of Bliss, both are legally parents of the children (though the children are biologically related only to the stay-at-home parent) under the Bliss statute providing that when a married couple has a child as a result of artificial insemination, the child is legally related to the biological parent's spouse. All the assets are titled in the breadwinning partner's name. It seems unlikely that every judge in Illinois would actually be willing to hold that the breadwinning partner has no link to the children, no right to argue for custody or visitation, and no obligation to support them, or to hold that the stay-at-home partner has no claim to the assets titled in the breadwinning partner's name or to spousal support (if appropriate) when they split up.[23]

The Vermont Act Relating to Civil Unions

In April of 2000, the Vermont legislature responded to *Baker* by enacting An Act Relating to Civil Unions. Under this statute, same-sex couples (and only same-sex couples) can enter into a "civil union" with requirements, rights, and obligations which precisely parallel those applicable to married couples. Like a marriage, a civil union begins with a license and a ceremony presided over by a judge, justice of the peace, or member of the clergy. Partners to a civil union have all the "benefits, protections and responsibilities under law, whether they derive from statute, administrative or court rule, policy, common law or any other source of civil law, as granted to spouses in a marriage." For example, partners to a civil union enjoy rights to children and to employment-related insurance benefits which parallel those of married couples. Like a marriage, a civil union terminates only on death or divorce, and all the laws of divorce apply to the dissolution of civil unions. A married person cannot enter into a civil union, and a person in a civil union cannot marry.[24]

The Act does not, of course, entitle those united in a civil union to federal benefits. Under the Defense of Marriage Act enacted by Congress in 1996, "marriage" for purposes of federal law "means only a legal union between one man and one woman as husband and wife and the word 'spouse' refers only to a person of the opposite sex who is a husband or wife."[25] Because of this provision, Vermont couples united in a civil union are nevertheless excluded from Social Security coverage, marital status for federal tax purposes, and a host of other federal benefits which DOMA limits explicitly to heterosexual marriage.

23. These results would, however, be mandated by current Illinois law, given the Illinois DOMA, 750 ILCS 5/213.1 (1996), and Hewitt v. Hewitt (excerpt in text above).

24. Public Act 91, H. 847, Vermont 2000 Session Laws (65th Biennial Session (2000)), at scattered cites in 8, 14, & 15 V.S. See 14 V.S. §§ 1202(2) & 1202(3) (same-sex couples can enter into a "civil union"); 18 V.S. §§ 5160(a)(clerk is to issue a civil union license), 5161(a)(same), 5161(a)(ministers, priests, etc. are authorized to certify civil unions); 15 V.S. § 1204(f)("The rights of parties to a civil union, with respect to a child of whom either becomes the natural parent during the term of the civil union, shall be the same as those of a married couple."); 15 V.S. § 1204(d)("The law of domestic relations, including annulment, separation and divorce, child custody and support, and property division and maintenance shall apply to parties to a civil union.").

25. 1 U.S.C. § 7.

As of today, Vermont has gone further than any other state in extending marriage-like rights to same-sex couples, though ironically the Vermont Civil Union Act also amends the Vermont marriage statute so that "civil marriage" is now explicitly defined as "a union between a man and a woman."[26] Vermont law now explicitly denies the status of marriage to same-sex couples: the legislative findings include that a civil union "does not bestow the status of civil marriage."[27] Thus, even in Vermont, marriage continues to be limited to the intimate union of a man and a woman.

Domestic Partnerships

Although no state other than Vermont has state-wide legislation giving same-sex partners who follow the appropriate registration requirements all the benefits of marriage the state is able to give, many counties and municipalities[28] have domestic partnership registries giving residents who register as domestic partners as much as the county or municipality can give (employees of the local entity are entitled to fringe benefits for their partners when they register, but non-employees typically do not receive much other than the symbol of registration). Also, a number of universities and corporations give health and other benefits to the partner of an employee who has registered their partnership.[29] Some of these registry programs are open to heterosexual as well as same-sex unmarried couples. Others are open only to same-sex couples, as with Vermont civil unions. Typically, registration requires that both partners sign and submit an affidavit indicating that they do some combination of the sharing activities typically seen in traditional married couples, such as sharing a household and household expenses, having joint bank accounts, having wills leaving a significant portion of each estate to the other, or being economically responsible for each other.

Abroad

According same-sex couples some sort of second-tier recognition–such as Vermont's civil unions–and slowly inching towards marriage is a general trend in western democracies. The Netherlands has had a form of second-tier recognition for same-sex couples for some time, and recently became the first country to offer full marriage rights, including the word "marriage," to same-sex couples. In the Scandinavian countries, same-sex couples can enter into "registered partnerships," with most of the benefits and responsibilities of marriage (and called "gay marriage" by most citizens).[30] In 1999, France adopted a law allowing any couple who shares a home (including a brother and sister or a priest and housekeeper) to enter into a "civil solidarity pact"

26. 18 V. S. § 5131. See also 15 V.S. § 1201(4) ("marriage" means the legally recognized union of "one man and one woman.").

27. Public Act 91, H. 847, Vermont 2000 Session Laws (65th Biennial Session § 1(10) (2000)).

28. For example, Madison, Wisconsin, San Francisco, Chicago, Cook County, and Oak Park, Illinois, all have such registries.

29. For example, the major U.S. auto companies, Disney, American Airlines, Northwestern University and the University of Chicago have such policies.

30. E.J. Graff, Same–Sex Spouses in Canada, The Nation, July 12, 1999, at 23.

(known as PACS in France, an acronym).[31] The law does not, however, grant any rights with respect to children to registered partners. In general, European countries have been slower than some states in the United States to allow stranger adoption by lesbian and gay couples, apparently because of fear that such a policy might make some third-world countries unwilling to allow their children to be sent for adoption to a country with such a policy.

In 1999, the Supreme Court of Canada held that denying same-sex partners the rights and responsibilities enjoyed by heterosexual couples in common law marriages was unconstitutional.[32] Like the Vermont court in Baker v. Vermont, the Canadian Court left the question of remedy to the provincial legislatures. They could either do nothing, in which case in six months heterosexual common law couples (couples who have lived together for three years or who have lived in a relationship of some permanence and have a child, whether natural or adopted) would lose rights to support when they split up. Or they could extend full marriage and common law rights to same-sex couples. Or they could give same-sex cohabiting couples common law marriage status when they meet the requirements of common law status. As of June, 1999, every province but Alberta had indicated its intention to take the third of these three alternatives.[33]

Notes on Choice of Law and Legislative Responses

1. Why do you think the Vermont legislature created civil unions for same-sex couples and limited marriage to heterosexual couples? If these two forms of intimate relationships have different status, what is the difference? Is one of higher status than the other? Which? Is there any justification for the distinction other than a commitment to reserving the (higher?) status of marriage for the heterosexual majority? Is a deliberately created status differential based on sexual orientation constitutional under Romer v. Evans, 517 U.S. 620, 116 S.Ct. 1620, 134 L.Ed.2d 855 (1996)? See Jane S. Schachter, *Romer v. Evans* and Democracy's Domain, 50 Vand. L. Rev. 361, 381 (1997) ("The [*Romer*] opinion also raises, but does not answer clearly, the critical question whether intolerance of homosexuality framed in terms of traditional values is the same thing as anti-gay animus.").

2. Will Vermont civil unions afford families headed by gay and lesbian couples the advantages enjoyed by families headed by heterosexual couples as described in the earlier material in this chapter on the marriage bonus? Do you think that there will be (in the real world, not just the statute books) any status or other difference between marriages and civil unions? Or, as in the Scandinavian countries, will people refer to civil unions as gay marriage? Are civil unions and other second-tier approaches necessary steps on the road to full marriage rights?

3. The Roman Catholic church regards contraception, abortion, and homosexuality as sinful (indeed, each is a "mortal" sin, i.e., a sin which, if

31. Suzanne Daley, France Gives Legal Status to Unmarried Couples, N.Y. Times, Apr. 18, 2000, at A3.

32. M. v. H., File No. 25838, Supreme Court of Canada, 1999 Can. Sup. Ct. LEXIS 298.

33. Alan Silverstein, How Will Supreme Court's Same–Sex Ruling Affect Property Rights?, Toronto Star, June 19, 1999.

not forgiven before death, dooms the perpetrator to eternal damnation). The Catholic church today does whatever it can—including filing amicus briefs and exerting pressure on legislatures—to make abortions illegal and to keep marriage limited to heterosexuals. But it no longer uses its political influence to oppose all forms of contraception. Both the Roman Catholic and Mormon churches have been very active in opposing gay rights, particularly the right to marry or the right to marriage-like status, such as civil unions in Vermont.

What should legislators who belong to religious institutions with positions such as that of the Catholic and Mormon churches do when faced with legislation authorizing civil unions or even marriages between same-sex couples? In a society with many religions taking different positions on many issues, under what circumstances is it appropriate for a religious organization to try to use the political system to make its religious rule the law of the land?

4. Recall the debate among lesbian and gay intellectuals and activists in the late 1980's and into the 1990's about whether to seek marriage. Given the specificity of many domestic partnership registration requirements (requiring, e.g., joint bank accounts or joint ownership of a home), are such schemes that distinguishable from traditional marriage? Do you think that it has been a mistake to focus so much energy in the 1990's on the marriage issue?

Chapter 8

WOMEN AND CHILDREN

A. INTRODUCTION

The fact of motherhood affects women's daily lives in numerous ways, from pregnancy, to the needs for maternity leave and child care for women who work outside the home, to the rigors of the "second shift" of housework at the end of the working day. Numerous issues of law and policy arise in connection with caretaking and women's relationship to children and child care. We deal with those issues in this chapter under three broad rubrics: (1) mothering, (2) maternity leave and child care, (3) custody and support of children after divorce.

Most children are nurtured by women, and this fact has a profound effect upon those children as adults and, through them, upon gender relations in society. To what extent does this impact arise inexorably from the simple reality that women give birth and that human offspring require a long period of care before maturity? Feminists question whether it is inevitable, or even desirable, that the nurture of children be performed primarily by women in an ideal society, or that motherhood have the kinds of consequences it traditionally has in our culture. For a genuine emancipation of women, including their effective integration into the world of work, it may prove necessary to contemplate alternatives to the traditional concept of family as a unit within which almost exclusively women tend to the emotional and physical needs of its members.

It is increasingly obvious that the work of childrearing requires support from the society as a whole if women are to be equal participants in the world of work and public affairs. We consider a number of legal and policy issues that arise in connection with the birth and care of children, including, for example, whether and under what conditions maternity leave should be provided to female workers, an issue that provoked the debate among feminists described in Chapter 3. Important questions of social policy are also raised by legislation that ensures family or parental leave or gives favorable tax treatment to expenses for the care of children. In all of these debates over law and policy, one theme reappears: the legal, economic and social devaluation of the work of raising children—either because the care of children has traditionally been "women's work" or because child care is undervalued in its own right and has therefore become women's work.

By contrast, women themselves value their relationship to their children with an intensity the economic system does not share. In most instances, women are children's primary caretakers within marriage and their custodians, either as single parents or as custodial parents after divorce.[1] When those children are not the product of a traditional nuclear family, or when marriage dissolves, the relationship between women and children is translated into the various standards governing custody. Moreover, since women most commonly have custody, standards governing the provision of child support present legal and economic issues of particular import to women, and the enforcement (or non-enforcement) of child support laws is critical to their welfare.

For all of these reasons, legal issues concerning women and children have been of special interest to feminist legal scholars. The panoply of issues raised by feminists concerning women in their role as mothers is the subject of this chapter.

B. MOTHERING

ADRIENNE RICH, OF WOMAN BORN: MOTHERHOOD AS EXPERIENCE AND INSTITUTION

11–13 (1986; Orig. Pub. 1976).

All human life on the planet is born of woman. The one unifying, incontrovertible experience shared by all women and men is that months-long period we spent unfolding inside a woman's body. Because young humans remain dependent upon nurture for a much longer period than other mammals, and because of the division of labor long established in human groups, where women not only bear and suckle but are assigned almost total responsibility for children, most of us first know both love and disappointment, power and tenderness, in the person of a woman.

We carry the imprint of this experience for life, even into our dying. Yet there has been a strange lack of material to help us understand and use it. We know more about the air we breathe, the seas we travel, than about the nature and meaning of motherhood. In the division of labor according to gender, the makers and sayers of culture, the namers, have been the sons of the mothers. There is much to suggest that the male mind has always been haunted by the force of the idea of *dependence on a woman for life itself*, the son's constant effort to assimilate, compensate for, or deny the fact that he is "of woman born."

1. In 1995, 85% of custodial parents were women. Census Bureau, Current Population Reports, Mar. 1999, Child Support for Custodial Mothers and Fathers: 1995, at 1.

Women are also born of women. But we know little about the effect on culture of that fact, because women have not been makers and sayers of patriarchal culture. Women's status as childbearer has been made into a major fact of her life. Terms like "barren" or "childless" have been used to negate any further identity. The term "nonfather" does not exist in any realm of social categories.

Because the fact of physical motherhood is so visible and dramatic, men recognized only after some time that they, too, had a part in generation. The meaning of "fatherhood" remains tangential, elusive. To "father" a child suggests above all to beget, to provide the sperm which fertilizes the ovum. To "mother" a child implies a continuing presence, lasting at least nine months, more often for years. Motherhood is earned, first through an intense physical and psychic rite of passage—pregnancy and childbirth—then through learning to nurture, which does not come by instinct.

A man may beget a child in passion or by rape, and then disappear; he need never see or consider child or mother again. Under such circumstances, the mother faces a range of painful, socially weighted choices: abortion, suicide, abandonment of the child, infanticide, the rearing of a child branded "illegitimate," usually in poverty, always outside the law. In some cultures she faces murder by her kinsmen. Whatever her choice, her body has undergone irreversible changes, her mind will never be the same, her future as a woman has been shaped by the event.

Most of us were raised by our mothers, or by women who for love, necessity, or money took the place of our biological mothers. Throughout history women have helped birth and nurture each others' children. Most women have been mothers in the sense of tenders and carers for the young, whether as sisters, aunts, nurses, teachers, foster-mothers, stepmothers. Tribal life, the village, the extended family, the female networks of some cultures, have included the very young, very old, unmarried, and infertile women in the process of "mothering." Even those of us whose fathers played an important part in our early childhood rarely remember them for their patient attendance when we were ill, their doing the humble tasks of feeding and cleaning us; we remember scenes, expeditions, punishments, special occasions. For most of us a woman provided the continuity and stability—but also the rejections and refusals—of our early lives, and it is with a woman's hands, eyes, body, voice, that we associate our primal sensations, our earliest social experience.

* * * I try to distinguish between two meanings of motherhood, one superimposed on the other: the potential relationship of any woman to her powers of reproduction and to children; and the institution, which aims at ensuring that potential—and all women—shall remain under male control. This institution has been a keystone of the most diverse social and political systems. It has withheld over one-half the human species from the decisions affecting their lives; it exonerates men from

fatherhood in any authentic sense; it creates the dangerous schism between "private" and "public" life; it calcifies human choices and potentialities. In the most fundamental and bewildering of contradictions, it has alienated women from our bodies by incarcerating us in them. At certain points in history, and in certain cultures, the idea of woman-as-mother has worked to endow all women with respect, even with awe, and to give women some say in the life of a people or a clan. But for most of what we know as the "mainstream" of recorded history, motherhood as institution has ghettoized and degraded female potentialities.

The power of the mother has two aspects: the biological potential or capacity to bear and nourish human life, and the magical power invested in women by men, whether in the form of Goddess-worship or the fear of being controlled and overwhelmed by women. We do not actually know much about what power may have meant in the hands of strong, prepatriarchal women. We do have guesses, longing, myths, fantasies, analogues. We know far more about how, under patriarchy, female possibility has been literally massacred on the site of motherhood. Most women in history have become mothers without choice, and an even greater number have lost their lives bringing life into the world.

Women are controlled by lashing us to our bodies. * * *

NANCY CHODOROW, THE REPRODUCTION OF MOTHERING: PSYCHOANALYSIS AND THE SOCIOLOGY OF GENDER

173–74, 176, 182–83, 185, 204, 206, 208 (1978).

[According to Freudian psychoanalytic theory, children go through a series of psychosexual stages in early childhood, culminating in the oedipal complex, so called after Sophocles' Oedipus, who unknowingly killed his father and married his mother. In the oedipal stage, the child is attracted to the parent of the opposite sex. The boy, supposedly fearful that he will be castrated (the fate he assumes befell his female relatives), resolves his fears by repressing his attraction for the mother, identifying with his father, and internalizing the father's authority in the form of a "super-ego," or conscience. The psychosexual development of the girl is more complex. In this excerpt, Chodorow draws upon psychoanalytic theory to attempt to explain the ambivalent, often hostile, attitudes boys and the men they become develop toward women, as well as the "reproduction" of mothering in the women into whom girl children develop.]

Girls and boys develop different relational capacities and senses of self as a result of growing up in a family in which women mother. These gender personalities are reinforced by differences in the identification processes of boys and girls that also result from women's mothering. Differing relational capacities and forms of identification prepare women and men to assume the adult gender roles which situate women primarily within the sphere of reproduction in a sexually unequal society.

GENDER IDENTIFICATION AND GENDER ROLE LEARNING

All social scientists who have examined processes of gender role learning and the development of a sense of identification in boys and girls have argued that the asymmetrical organization of parenting in which women mother is the basic cause of significant contrasts between feminine and masculine identification processes. Their discussions range from concern with the learning of appropriate gender role behavior—through imitation, explicit training and admonitions, and cognitive learning processes—to concern with the development of basic gender identity. The processes these people discuss seem to be universal, to the extent that all societies are constituted around a structural split, growing out of women's mothering, between the private, domestic world of women and the public, social world of men. Because the first identification for children of both genders has always been with their mother, they argue, and because children are first around women, women's family roles and being feminine are more available and often more intelligible to growing children than masculine roles and being masculine. Hence, male development is more complicated than female because of the difficult shifts of identification which a boy must make to attain his expected gender identification and gender role assumption. Their view contrasts sharply to the psychoanalytic stress on the difficulties inherent in feminine development as girls make their convoluted way to heterosexual object choice.

Because all children identify first with their mother, a girl's gender and gender role identification processes are continuous with her earliest identifications and a boy's are not. A girl's oedipal identification with her mother, for instance, is continuous with her earliest primary identification (and also in the context of her early dependence and attachment). The boy's oedipal crisis, however, is supposed to enable him to shift in favor of an identification with his father. He gives up, in addition to his oedipal and preoedipal attachment to his mother, his primary identification with her.

What is true specifically for oedipal identification is equally true for more general gender identification and gender role learning. A boy, in order to feel himself adequately masculine, must distinguish and differentiate himself from others in a way that a girl need not—must categorize himself as someone apart. Moreover, he defines masculinity negatively as that which is not feminine and/or connected to women, rather than positively. This is another way boys come to deny and repress relation and connection in the process of growing up.

* * *

Girls' identification processes, then, are more continuously embedded in and mediated by their ongoing relationship with their mother. They develop through and stress particularistic and affective relationships to others. A boy's identification processes are not likely to be so embedded in or mediated by a real affective relation to his father. At the same time, he tends to deny identification with and relationship to his mother and reject what he takes to be the feminine world; masculinity is defined as much negatively as positively. Masculine identification processes stress differentiation from others, the denial of affective relation, and categorical universalistic components of the masculine role. Feminine identification processes are relational, whereas masculine identification processes tend to deny relationship.

* * *

Both sexes learn to feel negatively toward their mother during the oedipal period. A girl's negative feelings, however, are not so much contempt and devaluation as fear and hostility: "The little girl, incapable of such contempt because of her own identical nature, frees herself from the mother with a degree of hostility far greater than any comparable hostility in the boy."[16] A boy's contempt serves to free him not only from his mother but also from the femininity within himself. It therefore becomes entangled with the issue of masculinity and is generalized to all women. A girl's hostility remains tied more to her relationship to her mother (and/or becomes involved in self-depreciation).

A boy's oedipus complex is directly tied to issues of masculinity, and the devaluation of women is its "normal" outcome. A girl's devaluation of or hostility toward her mother may be a part of the process, but its "normal" outcome, by contrast, entails acceptance of her own femininity and identification with her mother. Whatever the individual resolution of the feminine oedipus complex, however, it does not become institutionalized in the same way.

Freud "explains" the development of boys' contempt for mothers as coming from their perception of genital differences, particularly their mother's "castration." He takes this perception to be unmediated by social experience, and not in need of explanation. As many commentators have pointed out, it did not occur to Freud that such differential valuation and ensuing contempt were not in the natural order of things. However, the analysis of "Little Hans," which provides the most direct (reported) evidence that Freud had for such an assumption, shows that in fact Hans's father perpetuated and created such beliefs in his son—beliefs about the inferiority of female genitalia, denial of the feminine role in gestation and parturition, views that men have something and women have nothing, rather than having something different.[17]

Karen Horney, unlike Freud, does take masculine contempt for and devaluation of women as in need of interactive and developmental explanation.[18] According to her, these phenomena are manifestations of a

16. Brunswick, 1940, "The Preoedipal Phase," p. 246.

17. Freud, 1909, "Analysis of a Phobia."

18. Horney, 1932, "The Dread of Women."

deeper "dread of women"—a masculine fear and terror of maternal omnipotence that arises as one major consequence of their early caretaking and socialization by women. Psychoanalysts previously had stressed boys' fears of their fathers. Horney argues that these fears are less severe and therefore less in need of being repressed. Unlike their fears of a mother, boys do not react to a father's total and incomprehensible control over his child's life at a time when the child has no reflective capacities for understanding: "Dread of the father is more actual and tangible, less uncanny in quality." Moreover, since their father is male like them, boys' fears of men do not entail admission of feminine weakness or dependency on women: "Masculine self-regard suffers less in this way."

Dread of the mother is ambivalent, however. Although a boy fears her, he also finds her seductive and attractive. He cannot simply dismiss and ignore her. Boys and men develop psychological and cultural/ideological mechanisms to cope with their fears without giving up women altogether. They create folk legends, beliefs, and poems that ward off the dread by externalizing and objectifying women: "It is not ... that I dread her; it is that she herself is malignant, capable of any crime, a beast of prey, a vampire, a witch, insatiable in her desires ... the very personification of what is sinister." They deny dread at the expense of realistic views of women. On the one hand, they glorify and adore: "There is no need for me to dread a being so wonderful, so beautiful, nay, so saintly." On the other, they disparage: "It would be too ridiculous to dread a creature who, if you take her all round, is such a poor thing."

* * *

Too much of mother results from the relative absence of the father and nearly exclusive maternal care provided by a woman isolated in a nuclear household. It creates men's resentment and dread of women, and their search for nonthreatening, undemanding, dependent, even infantile women—women who are "simple, and thus safe and warm." Through these same processes men come to reject, devalue, and even ridicule women and things feminine.

Women's mothering produces a psychological and ideological complex in men concerning women's secondary valuation and sexual inequality. Because women are responsible for early child care and for most later socialization as well, because fathers are more absent from the home, and because men's activities generally have been removed from the home while women's have remained within it, boys have difficulty in attaining a stable masculine gender role identification. Boys fantasize about and idealize the masculine role and their fathers, and society defines it as desirable.

Given that men control not only major social institutions but the very definition and constitution of society and culture, they have the power and ideological means to enforce these perceptions as more general norms, and to hold each other accountable for their enforcement.

(This is not solely a matter of force. Since these norms define men as superior, men gain something by maintaining them.) The structure of parenting creates ideological and psychological modes which reproduce orientations to and structures of male dominance in individual men, and builds an assertion of male superiority into the definition of masculinity itself.

* * *

As they develop these wants and needs, women also develop the capacities for participating in parent-child relationships. They develop capacities for mothering. Because of the structural situation of parenting, women remain in a primary, preoedipal relationship with their mother longer than men. They do not feel the need to repress or cut off the capacity for experiencing the primary identification and primary love which are the basis of parental empathy. Also, their development and oedipal resolution do not require the ego defense against either regression or relation which characterizes masculine development. Women also tend to remain bound up in preoedipal issues in relation to their own mother, so that they in fact have some unconscious investment in reactivating them. When they have a child, they are more liable than a man to do so. In each critical period of their child's development, the parent's own development conflicts and experiences of that period affect their attitudes and behavior. The preoedipal relational stance, latent in women's normal relationship to the world and experience of self, is activated in their coming to care for an infant, encouraging their empathic identification with this infant which is the basis of maternal care.

* * *

Women's mothering includes the capacities for its own reproduction. This reproduction consists in the production of women with, and men without, the particular psychological capacities and stance which go into primary parenting. * * *

Women's mothering, then, produces psychological self-definition and capacities appropriate to mothering in women, and curtails and inhibits these capacities and this self-definition in men. The early experience of being cared for by a woman produces a fundamental structure of expectations in women and men concerning mothers' lack of separate interests from their infants and total concern for their infants' welfare. Daughters grow up identifying with these mothers, about whom they have such expectations. This set of expectations is generalized to the assumption that women naturally take care of children of all ages and the belief that women's "maternal" qualities can and should be extended to the nonmothering work that they do. All these results of women's mothering have ensured that women will mother infants and will take continuing responsibility for children.

DOROTHY E. ROBERTS, MOTHERHOOD AND CRIME

79 Iowa L. Rev. 95, 130–34 (1993).

C. Black Mothers' Insight: Families as Locations of Oppression and Resistance

The experience of black mothers suggests a more complex political interpretation of motherhood because history indicates that they have viewed their homes as complicated locations of both oppression and resistance. Black mothers contradict the separate spheres ideology expressed both in the traditional division of male work and female domesticity, and in the feminist conception of the private realm as the locus of women's subordination.

First, the dominant societal conception of family life that opposes motherhood versus wage labor has never described Black women's lives. Separate spheres ideology dictates that men sustain the family economically and represent it in the public sphere, while women care for the private realm of children and the home. Black women, however, traditionally have mothered while working. Black women raised their children when they worked in the field during slavery and, after emancipation, many continued to raise their children while earning a living outside the home. Patricia Hill Collins believes that this aspect of Black motherhood is as much a product of self-definition as racial oppression.[179] She argues that West African tradition explains many of the features of Black mothering that confound the Eurocentric ideal of mother.

Second, black women's history of working in a racist world also complicates the feminist interpretation of the family as an institution of violence and subordination. Historically, Black women have viewed work outside the home as an aspect of racial subordination and the family as a site of solace and resistance against white oppression. Black women's attention to domestic duties within their own home has defied the expectation of total service to whites. Black women's housework and care for family members directly benefited Black people, rather than white masters and employers. Angela Davis observed that "slavewomen perform[ed] the only labor of the slave community which could not be directly and immediately claimed by the oppressor."[184]

Moreover, the immediate concern of many Black mothers is just as likely to be state encroachments on their autonomy as domestic abuse of power. State-coerced sterilization and the prosecution of women who use drugs during pregnancy are examples of state intervention that pose a much greater threat for Black women than for white women. With regard to child custody, the primary concern of white middle-class women is private custody battles upon divorce. For most women of color,

179. Collins [The Meaning of Motherhood in Black Culture and Black Mother/Daughter Relationships, 4 Sage 3 (1987)] at 4* * *.

184. Angela Davis, The Black Woman's Role in the Community of Slaves, 3 Black Scholar 2, 7 (1972)* * *.

the dominant threat is the state's termination of their parental rights. The emancipatory meaning of Black domesticity does not minimize the exploitative aspects of Black women's labor in their homes or negate the existence of domestic violence against Black women and children. It suggests, however, a political interpretation of the home that espouses the possibility of a liberated motherhood.

Black women's tradition of recognizing motherhood as a potentially radical vocation bears closer examination. First, Black women historically have experienced motherhood as an empowering denial of the dominant society's denigration of their humanity. Bearing and nurturing Black children ensure the life of the Black community. Bearing and nurturing Black children counteract a racist society's power to kill Black children through poverty, malnutrition, inadequate health care, and unsafe housing. Bearing and nurturing black children defy the dehumanizing message that Black people do not deserve to procreate.

Second, Black women historically have practiced mothering in a way that overcomes some of the burdens of motherhood and holds the potential for the collective transformative action of mothers. Historically, Black women have not mothered their children in isolation, nor does the Black community confine the act of mothering to birth mothers. Black women share a rich tradition of women-centered, communal child care. These cooperative networks include members of the extended family (grandmothers, sisters, aunts, and cousins) as well as nonblood kin and neighbors. Patricia Hill Collins uses the term "othermothers" to describe the women who help biological mothers by sharing mothering responsibilities. The relationship between othermothers and children ranges from daily assistance to long-term care or informal adoption. Relying on other women to share the burdens of motherhood is a potentially radical alternative to the harmful responses of child abuse and self-isolation.

Third, Black women have recognized that children can give women the motivation, courage, and insight to resist oppression. Concern for children has often served as the foundation for formal collective struggles among Black women, such as the Sisterhood of Black Single Mothers in Brooklyn and the Welfare Mothers' Movement. It may be that the experience of communal mothering leads some Black women to become community activists in order to make a better life for the entire community's children.

Black women often mother for political ends. Karen Brodkin Sacks, for example, found that the Black women involved in a union organizing drive at a local medical center brought family events into the workplace to create unity among workers. These women used familistic skills and shared a family idiom to conceptualize relationships with their co-workers.[198] The Black women at the medical facility were able to take on key organizing roles because of the skills they acquired in playing a

198. Sacks, [Gender and Grassroots Leadership, in Women and the Politics of Empowerment 77 (Ann Bookman & Sandra Morgen eds., 1988)] at 80–87.

central role in their families—"keeping people together, ensuring that obligations are fulfilled, and acting to express the group consensus."[199] The political activism of Black mothers invites a feminist revision of the relationship between work, family, and political action. Motherhood for many Black women, far from hindering Black women's political activism, has actually fostered their political activism.

Notes on Mothering

1. What does Adrienne Rich mean when she describes mothering as an institution? What are the rules of this institution insofar as you have been able to infer them from the experience of your own life? Who legislates those rules? Are the rules a product of your race and class as well as gender? How? How do these rules affect your life as a student and/or lawyer? How would this question be answered differently by a man than by a woman? Is it possible to escape the "institution" of motherhood in our culture, that is, can one "mother" without being controlled by its rules?

2. Rich points to the very different meanings attached to the verbs "to mother" and "to father." Given this difference, what do we mean when we use the term "to parent" (as in "parental leave")? Some feminists object to the use of the term "parenting" or "caretaking," opting instead to speak of "mothering," whether performed by a woman or a man, to underscore the different meanings of these terms, as well as the reality that most nurturing is still performed by women, and to emphasize the central importance of the functions described by "mothering." See, e.g., Martha Albertson Fineman, The Neutered Mother, The Sexual Family and Other Twentieth Century Tragedies 233–35 (1995). "Parenting," on the other hand, points to a future where both men and women share the nurturing of children. Which terminology do you prefer and why?

3. Does Chodorow's theory adequately explain why women are the primary caretakers and nurturers of children? What other explanations can you think of for this near universal phenomenon? Do the different "schools" of feminist theory discussed in Chapter 3 suggest any different explanations?

4. Does Chodorow adequately explain misogyny? What do you think of her explanation? Does Chodorow's theory of gender differentiation account for male domination in society in general? How can we explain change between historical periods and differences among cultures? See Iris Marion Young, Is Male Gender Identity the Cause of Male Domination?, in Throwing Like a Girl and Other Essays in Feminist Philosophy and Social Theory 36–61 (1990). What other explanations can you offer for the persistence of these almost universal institutions?

5. Chodorow seems to suggest that men are the solution and that women cannot be adequate caretakers for a nonsexist next generation. Her solution is to bring men more fully into the "mothering" process and thus create a system of dual or more egalitarian parenting. How well do you think this will work, given the characteristics of adult males and females described by Chodorow? Do we have any reason to believe that men, as a group, can be

199. Id. at 90.* * *

good "mothers," given that men today aren't very interested in caretaking? How might this change? Would changes in the nature and organization of work be necessary? In the attitude of the two genders toward work?

6. Adrienne Rich states that "large numbers of men could, in fact, undertake child care on a large scale without radically altering the balance of male power in a male-identified society." Rich, Compulsory Heterosexuality and Lesbian Existence, in Blood, Bread and Poetry: Selected Prose 1979–1985 36 (1986). Do you think Chodorow is right on this point, or Rich? Would having men mother make that much difference in a world in which whatever men do is valued more than what women do? In other words, is women's mothering the cause of social inequality, or is inequality simply replicated by women's mothering under conditions of inequality between mothers and fathers? Which is the cart and which is the horse?

7. In what senses is Chodorow's analysis, and her solution, heterosexist (or homophobic)? How does her analysis apply to lesbian parents?

8. The Roberts excerpt is a good example of anti-essentialist analysis, adding to our understanding of motherhood by forcing us to include the perspective of African American women and breaking down easy dichotomies between the public and private spheres. What are the implications of Roberts' description of motherhood as a liberatory—even a political—experience? Do these implications pertain only to women of color? In what ways might the interests and attitudes of white and Black, professional, middle-class, and working-class mothers, and mothers receiving public assistance differ about the role of motherhood in a woman's life? Can you think of ways in which their interests are congruent?

9. What lessons might our society draw from the more collective/communal childrearing practices of the African American community described by Roberts?

10. One African American writer, bell hooks, has criticized white middle-class feminists for having alienated poor and non-white women by attacking motherhood in the early years of the current women's movement and then for romanticizing motherhood in a new version of the 19th-century cult of domesticity. hooks, Revolutionary Parenting, in Feminist theory from margin to center 133–36 (1984). This romanticization is dangerous, in hooks' opinion, both because it "reenforce[s] central tenets of male supremacist ideology" and because it undermines women's involvement in other types of work at a time when many teenagers are bearing children rather than developing a connection to the world of work. Why do you think contemporary feminists may have "flip-flopped" in their views of mothering? Is what hooks describes as a new cult of domesticity the same as the 19th-century variety (which exalted the role of the woman—at least the middle-class white woman—within the home, at the price of disqualifying her from playing any role in the public world), given that the new domesticity takes place in a context where most women have entered the paid labor force?

11. Several authors have suggested that mothering can offer a fruitful model for political and legal relationships. Sara Ruddick, for example, argues that the injection into public life of a mother's interests in preserving life, fostering growth, and attentive love could transform society. Sara Ruddick, Maternal Thinking (1989). Is this simply a new version of the suffragists'

argument that giving the vote to women would lead to a new morality in public life? How is it different? Virginia Held points to the revolutionary potential of replacing the contractual paradigm underlying much of Western social and political thought (e.g., the foundation of the state through an original social contract hypothesized by philosophers such as Hobbes, Locke and Rousseau, whereby rational individuals decided to trade the unlimited freedom of the state of nature for the security of the civil state) with a paradigm of the mother-child relationship as the primary social relationship—one which involves dependence, vulnerability, caring, and responsibility, rather than autonomy, self-interest, privacy, and the exercise of power. Virginia Held, Mothering versus Contract, in Beyond Self–Interest 287–304 (Jane J. Mansbridge, ed. 1990). What might the social contract look like if it had been designed by women? Or by individuals who do not yet know what gender role they will be assigned to play in society? What would a formal equality theorist say? How about a socialist feminist? A relational feminist? a dominance/inequality theorist? Would these theorists suggest different strategies for women now?

C. MATERNITY LEAVE: GOOD OR BAD FOR WOMEN?

The issues involved in provision of maternity leave have provoked substantial debate among feminists. We have already encountered this debate in Chapter 3, in connection with the disagreement among feminist lawyers over whether to support legislation requiring employers to provide their employees with leave for childbirth when other temporary disabilities are not covered by an employer's benefit package. As we have seen above, formal equality theorists answered "no," on the grounds that such laws, if not applied to women and men alike, reinforce stereotypes about women and deter employers from hiring them. Other feminists answered "yes," arguing that inadequate leave policies constitute sex discrimination in employment and also substantially burden women's procreative rights. Maternity leave policy, however, goes beyond provision for the period of disability caused by pregnancy as a physical condition. As the excerpts below show, what is at stake is not only the place of women within the workplace during their years of childbirth and childrearing but also the priorities our society places upon the relationship between children and those who care for them in the earliest months of life.

1. THE FAMILY AND MEDICAL LEAVE ACT

FAMILY AND MEDICAL LEAVE ACT OF 1993

Pub.L. 103–03, 107 Stat. 6; 103d Cong., 1st Sess., Feb. 5, 1993.

29 USCA. ch. 28, § 2601 et seq.

[The Family and Medical Leave Act (FMLA) was first introduced into Congress in 1985. Although the bill was passed by both houses of Congress, it was vetoed by President George Bush in 1991 and in

1992, but was signed into law in the early weeks of the Clinton Administration in 1993.]

SEC. 2. FINDINGS AND PURPOSES.

(a) FINDINGS.—Congress finds that—

(1) the number of single-parent households and two-parent households in which the single parent or both parents work is increasing significantly;

(2) it is important for the development of children and the family unit that fathers and mothers be able to participate in early childrearing and the care of family members who have serious health conditions;

(3) the lack of employment policies to accommodate working parents can force individuals to choose between job security and parenting;

(4) there is inadequate job security for employees who have serious health conditions that prevent them from working for temporary periods;

(5) due to the nature of the roles of men and women in our society, the primary responsibility for family caretaking often falls on women, and such responsibility affects the working lives of women more than it affects the working lives of men; and

(6) employment standards that apply to one gender only have serious potential for encouraging employers to discriminate against employees and applicants for employment who are of that gender.

(b) PURPOSES.—It is the purpose of this Act—

(1) to balance the demands of the workplace with the needs of families, to promote the stability and economic security of families, and to promote national interests in preserving family integrity;

(2) to entitle employees to take reasonable leave for medical reasons, for the birth or adoption of a child, and for the care of a child, spouse, or parent who has a serious health condition;

(3) to accomplish the purposes described in paragraphs (1) and (2) in a manner that accommodates the legitimate interests of employers;

(4) to accomplish the purposes described in paragraphs (1) and (2) in a manner that, consistent with the Equal Protection Clause of the Fourteenth Amendment, minimizes the potential for employment discrimination on the basis of sex by ensuring generally that leave is available for eligible medical reasons (including maternity-related disability) and for compelling family reasons, on a gender-neutral basis; and

(5) to promote the goal of equal employment opportunity for women and men, pursuant to such clause.

* * *

SEC. 102. LEAVE REQUIREMENT.

(a)(1) ENTITLEMENT TO LEAVE.—* * * [A]n eligible employee shall be entitled to a total of 12 workweeks of leave during any 12–month period for one or more of the following:

(A) Because of the birth of a son or daughter of the employee and in order to care for such son or daughter.

(B) Because of the placement of a son or daughter with the employee for adoption or foster care.

(C) In order to care for the spouse, or a son, daughter, or parent, of the employee, if such spouse, son, daughter, or parent has a serious health condition.

(D) Because of a serious health condition that makes the employee unable to perform the functions of the position of such employee.

* * *

(c) UNPAID LEAVE PERMITTED.—* * * [L]eave granted under subsection (a) may consist of unpaid leave.

* * *

SEC. 104. EMPLOYMENT AND BENEFITS PROTECTION.

(a) RESTORATION TO POSITION.—

(1) * * * [A]ny eligible employee who takes leave under section 102 for the intended purpose of the leave shall be entitled, on return from such leave—

(A) to be restored by the employer to the position of employment held by the employee when the leave commenced; or

(B) to be restored to an equivalent position with equivalent employment benefits, pay, and other terms and conditions of employment.

(2) LOSS OF BENEFITS.—The taking of leave under section 102 shall not result in the loss of any employment benefit accrued prior to the date on which the leave commenced.

* * *

(c) MAINTENANCE OF HEALTH BENEFITS.—

(1) * * * [D]uring any period that an eligible employee takes leave under section 102, the employer shall maintain coverage under any "group health plan" * * * for the duration of such leave at the level and under the conditions coverage would have been provided if the employee had continued in employment continuously for the duration of such leave.

* * *

[The Act provides that an employee may bring suit for noncompliance directly under the statute, or the Secretary of Labor may sue on her behalf; it also provides for civil damages equal to lost wages and benefits, plus interests and costs, in addition to injunctive remedies such as reinstatement.]

Notes on the Family and Medical Leave Act

1. Review the "Findings" and "Purposes" sections of the Family Leave Act, above. Which feminist theorists studied in Chapter 3 are most likely to have written those sections? Do you see the influence of several strands of feminist theory? Which ones, and where? If you were to rewrite the legislative findings and purposes of the legislation based on what you know, both from this course and other sources, what, if anything, would you add or change?

2. The FMLA has a number of shortcomings from the perspective of expansive coverage, among them that the leave is unpaid and that private employers are required to comply with its provisions only if they employ 50 or more workers. 29 § U.S.C. 2611(4)(A). The Act thus covers only 11% of private sector worksites, but these employers account for almost 60% of the private workforce; together with public employees, all of whom are covered, the FMLA thus covers about 66% of U.S. employees. Holly B. Tompson and Jon M. Werner, The Family and Medical Leave Act: Assessing the Costs and Benefits of Use, 1 Employee Rts. & Employment Pol'y J. 125, 126 (1997); Commission on Leave, 104th Cong., A Workable Balance: A Report to Congress on Family and Medical Leave Policies xvi, 65 (1996). Although the Act has been very popular with the public, usage has been relatively low, with estimates running from 1% to 3.54% mean usage rates; almost 60% of the leaves are taken to address the employee's own health concerns. Tompson and Werner, above, at 138, 146. Only about 13% of leaves are taken in connection with birth or adoption of a child; some 20% are taken in connection with care for a sick spouse, child or parent, caretaking that is also heavily gendered in our society. Joseph Willis, The Family and Medical Leave Act of 1993: A Progress Report, 36 Brandeis J. Fam. L. 95, 99 (1997–98) (summarizing statistics on usage); see also Nadine Taub, From Parental Leaves to Nurturing Leaves, 13 N.Y.U.Rev.L. & Soc.Change 381, 387, n. 26 (1984–85) (wives, adult daughters, and daughters-in-law provide most of the caregiving for elderly parents and parents-in-law). Although employers predicted that the Act would be too costly in terms of replacement workers and administrative costs and strenuously opposed its passage, subsequent surveys show that most have found the Act relatively easy to comply with, and fewer than 10% report any negative business effects. Willis, above, at 100; A Workable Balance, above, at 125–30. Cost predictions have not proven to be accurate, and some early reports showed less costly turnover of employees. Tompson and Werner, above, at 149; A Workable Balance, above, at 127. In this respect, studies show that continuity of female participation in the workforce correlates with employer supportiveness, including both the length of childbearing leave provided and the ability to avoid mandatory overtime and odd shifts (late afternoon or unpredictable) upon returning to work. Jennifer L. Glass and Lisa Riley, Family Responsive Policies and Employee Retention Following Childbirth, 76 Social Forces 1401 (1998).

3. How realistic is parental leave if it is unpaid? What groups of women benefit most from such a provision? Only those whose income is secondary to another wage earner's income? (Note that single-parent families constituted about 30% of all families by 1990. Census Bureau, Household and Family Characteristics: March 1990 and 1989 7 (1990).) How does the FMLA help poor women? Does it hurt them? Should feminists support unpaid leave programs if their ultimate goal is paid leave? Why or why not?

4. Professor Maria O'Brien Hylton argues that "[t]he cost of providing some employees with parental leave will be borne by low-skill female employees who lose their jobs or fail to obtain employment because of the increased wage bill faced by the employer." Hylton, "Parental" Leaves and Poor Women: Paying the Price for Time Off, 52 U.Pitt.L.Rev. 475, 493 (1991). Thus, Hylton argues, the price of the Family Leave Act will be paid by the most vulnerable members of the workforce, especially by Black and Hispanic women. Id. at 501. Do you agree? Are employers likely to substitute male for female employees to avoid any potential costs (though the leave is unpaid)? Has this happened when employers have initiated voluntary leave programs? Consider that the wage gap between male and female workers makes men more costly employees even in relatively low-skilled positions. See Chapter 10, below. Will men take these low-paying "women's" jobs?

How many low-skilled women will actually be able to take *unpaid* leave for a longer period under such a statute than they could take in the absence of any such law? If most unskilled women can't afford to stay away longer than absolutely necessary to their health, won't employers realize this and hire them anyway? (Note, for example, that the statute allows men to take leave; yet there is no argument that its passage will deter hiring men.) Won't *some* poor women in fact be helped by the Act, since their employers won't be able to fire them for taking off whatever time is absolutely necessary? This was the situation of Lillian Garland, the plaintiff in the *Cal Fed* case. Garland, an African American woman, was a receptionist; she lost first her job, due to the lack of maternity leave, then her housing, because she had no job, and due to her lack of housing, lost custody of the daughter whose birth had incapacitated her in the first place. See Mary E. Becker, Prince Charming: Abstract Equality, 1987 S.Ct.Rev. 201, 202–03.

5. There are a variety of ways in which paid childbirth leave could be financed. Initial reports indicate that most employees taking leave under the FMLA get some kind of wage replacement, through use of accrued vacation pay, disability pay, or sick pay. A Workable Balance, above note 2, at 116. These methods place the costs of leave either upon the individual employee or the employee and the employer. Some commentators urge direct governmental financing, both because the benefits accrue to society as a whole and in order not to promote sex segregation in the workplace or overburden businesses that have a limited ability to pass on costs. Angie K. Young, Assessing the Family and Medical Leave Act in Terms of Gender Equality, Work/Family Balance, and the Needs of Children, 5 Mich. J. Gender & L. 113, 156 (1998). As we saw in the *Cal Fed* case, discussed in Chapter 3, above, some states finance childbirth leave through the temporary disability system, thus limiting paid leave to mothers. See Arielle Horman Grill, The Myth of Unpaid Family Leave: Can the United States Implement a Paid Leave Policy Based on the Swedish Model?, 17 Comp. Lab. L.J. 373, 378

(1996). Sweden finances its comprehensive system through a combination of payroll tax and general government revenue (id. at 380); the Canadian system relies upon unemployment insurance to provide payment for family leave. Donna Lenhoff and Claudia Withers, Implementation of the Family and Medical Leave Act: Toward the Family–Friendly Workplace, 3 J. Gender & L. 39, 54 (1994). Which of these systems seems to you to be the fairest? The most economically feasible? The most politically feasible in the U.S.?

6. Prior to passage of the FMLA, Nadine Taub pointed out that a leave program tied to traditional family relationships would prove inadequate in a society where the pool of formally related, and thus statutorily qualified, caregivers has been heavily reduced by divorce, step-parenting, cohabitation, extended family and other networking arrangements for child care. See Taub, above note 2, at 391–94. Professor Taub argued, in addition, that "[t]o structure a benefit program around membership in the family is to reward and attempt to channel people into an institution that has proved oppressive to many, generally women." Id. at 393. How can these problems be addressed? Administrative regulations interpreting the FMLA attempt to address these issues by defining a child as a "biological, adopted, or foster child, a stepchild, a legal ward, or a child of a person standing in loco parentis. . . . " 29 C.F.R. § 825.113(a),(c)(1993).

How would you change the definition of who is to qualify for leave under the FMLA? Does the Act reflect the diversity of family structures in our society, including both the frequency of cohabitation and family-like relationships in African American communities, as described by Dorothy Roberts in the excerpt in the previous section? The District of Columbia Family and Medical Leave Act, adopted as a result of the efforts of a broad coalition including both the lesbian and gay communities and the African American community contains a very broad definition of family, including anyone with whom a worker shares a residence and has a "committed relationship." D.C.Code § 36–1301(4)(c) (1992).

7. Despite the FMLA's gender-neutrality, do you think many men in this country will take leave at the time of childbirth? See Rosemarie Feuerbach Twomey and Gwen E. Jones, The Family and Medical Leave Act of 1993: A Longitudinal Study of Male and Female Perceptions, 3 Employee Rts & Employment Policy J. 229 (1999) (describing study showing continuing beliefs that caretaking leave is for female employees). The fact that the leave is unpaid is a substantial deterrent, along with the fact that it is limited to 12 weeks, the time typically associated with recovery from childbirth and adjusting to breastfeeding. Nancy E. Dowd, Family Values and Valuing Family: A Blueprint for Family Leave, 30 Harv. J. on Legis. 335, 347–50 (1993). Some commentators point out that this leads to a vicious circle with respect to care of children, as parenting skills are very much learned "on the job": when the mother stays home with the newborn, she both gains competence and becomes known as the one who knows how to do the tasks involved, ultimately leading both parents and the children to look to her for these functions. Young, above note 5, at 124–25. In Sweden, by contrast, childbirth leave can extend as long as 12 months, with wage replacement; but the father must take at least one month of the leave or it is lost. Grill, above note 5, at 375. Should we perhaps consider giving 12 weeks paid leave for each parent, nontransferable, so that to take advantage of 24

weeks of paid leave, the father as well as the mother would have to take 12 weeks off?

8. Care of the elderly is a task that also falls disproportionately upon women in our society. Data from the 1988 National Survey of Families and Households, which studied a large representative national sample, showed that 14.4% of women respondents who both work and fulfill traditional caregiving roles also report caring for someone with a serious illness or disability. See Carol L. Jenkins, Women, Work, and Caregiving: How Do These Roles Affect Women's Well-being?, 9 J. Women & Aging 27, 34–40 (1997). This unpaid care by women allows elderly persons to remain in the community rather than be institutionalized and often dependent upon society at large for financial support. Id. at 40. Yet caring for an elderly parent is generally not accompanied by cutting back upon employment; rather, the caregivers cut back on other duties or leisure time. Id. at 32. FMLA provides one, if rather limited, response to this problem. One author suggests that policymakers should consider the social benefits of this unpaid caregiving for the elderly and provide aid in the form of adult day care, meals-on-wheels, and respite care. Id. at 41–42. Why do you think the lion's share of caring for the elderly falls upon women in our society? What additional public or legal responses to this problem can you imagine? Why don't we hear more about the need to get men to caretake for the elderly?

2. SOME INTERNATIONAL COMPARISONS

MATERNITY LEAVE POLICIES: AN INTERNATIONAL SURVEY

11 Harv.Women's L.J. 171, 177–81, 185–88 (1988).

[The sections excerpted from this article were written by Ileana Porras, who wrote the section about maternity leave policies and practices in Chile, and Jennifer Schirmer, who wrote the section about Sweden.]

Maternity leave in Chile is mandatory. The law requires all employers to provide six weeks prenatal maternity leave and twelve weeks postnatal maternity leave. This obligation cannot be contracted away by the employer, nor can a pregnant woman waive this right. In other words, a pregnant woman may not, by law, work during her legally mandated resting times, whether she feels capable of it or not.

During the four months of imposed rest, a woman on maternity leave is generally entitled to receive a subsidy equal to her net salary. This benefit is paid through the Social Security system, as long as the woman has contributed to Social Security for at least six months, with three of those months occurring during the six months immediately preceding her leave. If, due to the employer's negligence, a woman did not start contributing to Social Security in time, the employer must bear the burden of paying the woman the equivalent of what she would have received as a benefit.

In cases where the pregnancy leads to health complications, the law continues to be generous. With an official certificate attesting to the illness, a woman may remain away from work as long as necessary. During her health-related leave, the woman will continue to receive her full salary through Social Security if she is eligible.

After the birth of the child, the law entitles women to special benefits related to their roles as mothers. Chilean maternity law provides that mothers are entitled to an hour a day, during working hours, to feed their infant children. Employers must count this hour as part of the hours worked. In contrast, the half-hour lunch break to which all workers are legally entitled is not treated as part of the working day.

In reality, the law permitting mothers to feed their infant children during working hours has little practical significance. The law only requires employers of twenty or more workers to provide and pay for child care facilities. The requirement may be satisfied by joining with other employers to run a common nursery, or by paying for external child care. The result seems to be that only a very small proportion of employers provide in-house nurseries. Most mothers, therefore, do not have the necessary access to their children during the work day to take advantage of the statutory nursing breaks.

Chilean law also provides for indefinite paid leave for the mother of a seriously sick infant under a year old. This provision is problematic in that it applies only to women. It reinforces the stereotype of women as the proper child care-takers because fathers are not equally entitled to take time off. Indeed, the very existence of the right may have a coercive effect, pressuring women to remain at home and care for the sick child, regardless of the effect it may have on their professional advancement.

Given the breadth of the rights and entitlements available to pregnant women by law, it is difficult to imagine that employers would be willing to hire women of child bearing age, or to keep them on after they become pregnant. The capacity of Chilean law to cope with this problem is difficult to gauge. The Constitution, which is gender neutral, prohibits employers from discriminating in their hiring decisions. This is taken to include a prohibition on discrimination against women. Given the rather strong disincentives for employment of women created by the maternity law, however, such protection appears weak. On the other hand, the maternity law includes an anti-firing provision which protects women already in the work force. Under that provision, a woman may not be fired during the period of time between the beginning of the pregnancy to a year after the termination of the official maternity leave. During this time she enjoys the special privilege usually reserved to union leaders, which requires judicial authorization for dismissal. Further, if a pregnant woman is fired by an employer who is unaware that she is pregnant, she must be reinstated with back pay. This entitlement not to be fired covers workers in virtually all sectors of the workplace, except women employed by households, who may be fired at will despite their pregnancy.

How is Chilean maternity law to be assessed? On its face it seems very progressive. Its net effect is to place working women in a position where childbearing will not prove an excessive economic burden. Chilean women are guaranteed their jobs, salaries, and enough time to recuperate after the birth. In a country where birth control is frowned upon and abortion is illegal except for health reasons, such provisions are extremely significant.

On the other hand, many of these laws seem to originate in a concern for the health of the fetus and infant rather than a concern for women. Since 1857, the Civil Code has provided that: "The law protects the life of he who is to be born." The constitution of 1980 repeats these words, thus reinforcing the higher protection afforded the fetus. Although this oft-stated concern for the life of the fetus is not dispositive as to whom the maternity provisions are intended to protect, it must color our understanding of the laws.

A further example of the Chilean maternity laws' heightened concern for the fetus is a provision that pregnant women employed in work considered a health risk during pregnancy must be transferred at the same level of pay to a safer job. The statute defines five categories of "dangerous" work: lifting or pushing heavy weights; work requiring standing for extended periods of time; night work; work requiring long hours; and any employment the competent authorities declare inappropriate for pregnant women. In light of this statute, many other statutes may be read as predominantly fetus-protective. The mandatory nature of maternity leave, the right to stay away from work if a child is ill, and the economic benefits for pregnant women all indicate that the statutes intend the primary beneficiary to be the child rather than the mother.

Nevertheless, easy conclusions cannot be drawn. Mandatory maternity leave may be necessary in a country such as Chile where women who are confronted with demanding and powerful employers might otherwise be forced to contract away or waive their rights. Whether the majority of women are well served by the Chilean maternity laws, or whether women would be better served by other measures are questions not easily answered.

* * *

Sweden has the longest paid parental leave of any Scandinavian country: nine months at ninety percent of income and three months at the minimum sick leave rate of 60 kr or $10.00 per day, available to both men and women. However, even in a social democratic welfare state such as Sweden, which has been committed to gender equality for decades, women experience a basic contradiction in terms of parental leave: while they are provided a relatively generous leave (in comparison to the rest of the world), they find this leave has not changed either the economic or social constraints on men and women set by the labor market or the cultural impediments to male participation in childrearing. Moreover, the leave policy divides women by class because it benefits professional women at a higher rate than it does working class women.

The statistics show that economic constraints limit Swedish men's use of parental leave. In 1983 it was reported that "about three quarters of new fathers do not take a single day of the leave" to which they are entitled. The men who do use the leave are government employees who receive full wage replacement and professionals with flexible schedules. Although it has been illegal for an employer to refuse parental leave since 1978, there remain "ways of making it clear that an extended absence may interfere with upward mobility." Thus, the single most important factor given by fathers for *not* taking the leave has been the belief that their prospects for career enhancement would suffer. Because men's ability to take advantage of the leave is largely restricted by economic class, their social responsibility as parents and partners is also limited by class.

Economic constraints are only part of the story. Men do not so easily give up traditional roles and privileges. Of the ten percent of men who took parental leave in Sweden in 1977, twenty-one percent spent only one to nine days on leave, with another thirty spending ten to twenty-nine days. Only one percent actually took from 180 to 210 days leave. Further, men were more likely to take leave if the child was male. Again, in 1983, nearly ten years after the leave legislation was passed, the average period of time taken by men remained low, ranging from ten days to one month. A key factor in determining male attitudes is the man's perception of his workmates' views. A clear majority of Swedish men approve of the opportunity for "paid days off," but many are "ambivalent" about the leave. Moreover, even if men *do* opt for the leave, it is unclear how much time they spend caring for children and doing household chores.[95]

Sweden has both a highly gender-segregated labor market and a high part-time working rate for women. Men choose from 300 occupations in Sweden while women choose from only thirty, many at the low end of the pay scale. Nearly half of all employed women work part-time, contrasted with seven percent of men. Men's working hours are on average ten hours longer per week than women's. Thus, despite generous parental leave, the typical pattern among Swedish women today is to work full-time until they have children and then to reduce their work to part-time. This practice puts them at a permanent disadvantage in the labor market and reinforces their primary responsibility to the family over the workplace.

Finally, the Swedish income-based parental leave policy may magnify differences among women. Women with a higher income receive a greater real benefit than women with lower income because a ten percent reduction in salary is a greater hardship to a woman working piece-rate in a factory than to a professional woman. Additionally, at the

95. *Cf.* a Danish study found that while upper middle-class men sometimes "helped" with child care and household tasks, it was never at the expense of their careers. Schirmer, The Limits of Reform: Women, Capital and Welfare 146–164 (1982). In Sweden, women spend an average of about 35 hours per week on housework, against 7–8 hours by men.

end of the nine months, the working-class woman is economically less able than her middle-class counterpart to stay home for another three months at a flat rate. A social policy that is meant to improve gender equality may, in reality, exacerbate class differences.[100]

The lesson to be learned from the Swedish parental leave policy is that single reforms which do not address larger economic and cultural issues can at best be palliatives; at worst, they cement traditional gender and class stratifications in both family and work life.

Notes on Maternity Leave

1. Whose responsibility is the welfare of children during infancy: the individual woman's, the father's, the employer's, or the society's? How have the Swedish answered this question? What is the Chilean position? If there were "scientific" information of a link between crime, drug use, etc. and the quality of early relationships between infants and their caretakers, would you answer the question differently?

2. Does it make a difference what policy goals (women's equality, pronatalism, fetal protection, children's welfare, protection of the disabled, keeping women in the home, etc.) underlie a maternity leave policy? What does the Chilean experience show on this point?

3. Given the experience of a government-funded parental leave policy in Sweden that is voluntary for parents and of mandatory maternal leave in Chile, it seems clear that the social context and purpose in which the policy is embedded are critical to its impact on the status of women. The history of such policies in different Western industrialized nations is instructive on this point. Nancy Dowd has described the genesis of the family policies in Sweden as having been the desire to draw women into the workforce and in France, to increase the birth rate; family leave policy in the United States, by contrast, has been advocated as a women's rights issue. Dowd, Envisioning Work and Family: A Critical Perspective on International Models, 26 Harv. J. on Legis. 311, 316–19, 328–31 (1989). Paolo Wright–Carozza suggests that the American focus on gender discrimination has had a detrimental effect upon the development of maternity policy here, by viewing it through the lens of a formal equality abstracted from parental responsibilities and family relationships. Wright–Carozza, Organic Goods: Legal Understandings of Work, Parenthood, and Gender Equality in Comparative Perspective, 81 Calif. L. Rev. 531, 574 (1993). By contrast, while the paradigm of pregnancy as an individual employment disability reigned in the U.S., Italian postwar legislation providing for childbearing and childrearing benefits and its interpretation by the courts were premised upon a more complex combination of goals, including not only equal employment but also a restructuring of family roles, so as to effectuate societal concerns about the welfare of children and

100. *Cf.* the author's research in Denmark where, until recently, a professional woman had five months paid leave and a factory worker fourteen weeks. Debates about extending maternity leave to eighteen weeks in 1983 revealed class differences among women based on distinct working conditions: white-collar and professional workers demanded the leave be extended after the birth, when they felt most tired, and working-class women demanded the leave begin earlier in order to avoid long, tiring days on their feet and to safeguard the embryo from dangerous fumes.

families. The language of U.S. law, at least prior to passage of the FMLA, instead "rested on a thin notion of equality that separates individuals from the full context of their lives and on a neglect for the interrelationship of human goods implicit in these areas of life [market work and family care] and law." Id. at 532. As a result of the broader focus in Italy, additional legislation was passed to establish nurseries on the premises of all major employers. Id. at 543. Wright–Carozza concludes that "[i]n Italy, the struggle for women's equality has been a struggle to share and socialize the responsibilities and obligations that society historically has imposed on women alone and that helped keep women out of the workforce," thus reflecting a vision of equality that sees persons—male and female—as integral wholes, participating in multiple but interconnected aspects of life. Id. at 579, 581. Given the quite different historical and social background in the United States, can you think of strategies to encourage this kind of paradigm shift here?

4. Until passage of the FMLA, the United States was the only industrialized nation without a national policy guaranteeing some type of maternity leave, causing an Equal Opportunities Unit attorney for the European Community Commission to comment that the U.S. "seems to assume that pregnancy is sort of a private hobby, which must be borne at your own expense." Sabra Craig, The Family and Medical Leave Act of 1993: A Survey of the Act's History, Purposes, Provisions, and Social Ramifications, 44 Drake L. Rev. 51, 52, 79 (1995) (quoting Orlagh O'Farrell). This comment highlights the widespread belief in the U.S. that childrearing is essentially a private affair, in which the state should not be involved, a belief that coexists with a great deal of political rhetoric about "family values." By contrast, in Sweden, the public is willing to pay very high taxes in order to finance a system of public subsidies for both parental leave and child care facilities for older children. Parents are currently entitled to a year's leave upon the birth of a child, the first 60 days paid at 90% of their salaries and the remaining 300 days at 80%, in addition to monthly allowances until the child is three and the right to reduce their work day to six hours until their children are eight years old. Arielle Horman Grill, The Myth of Unpaid Family Leave: Can the United States Implement a Paid Leave Policy Based on the Swedish Model?, 17 Comp. Lab. L.J. 373, 378–79 (1996). The result is that children in Sweden are cared for by their parents during infancy, whereas fewer than 10% of U.S. families now consist of one wage-earner parent and a homemaker. Id. at 385–88. In short, although Sweden regards childrearing as a responsibility of the society at large, the family is the social unit charged with carrying out the tasks involved. At the same time, Sweden has the world's highest labor market participation rate for females: 91% of women between 25 and 49 are employed. Id. at 381. What are the implications of this model for women? For children?

5. Fathers' participation rates in Sweden have improved in recent years, though they are still much less likely to take leave than mothers and do so for shorter periods. Participation by Swedish fathers has increased from 3% in 1974, to 23% in 1979, to 44% of fathers taking an average of 45 days parental leave by 1992. Grill, above note 4, at 377–78. A 1994 change in Swedish law, which has the effect of requiring that the father take one

month of the leave due to the couple or the full period will be lost, is expected to increase these percentages. Id. at 375–78.

6. What do you think an ideal policy for parental leave would provide? Be sure to address the following questions:

* Should it be paid or unpaid?

* What employers should be covered?

* How should it be funded and how administered?

* Should it be linked to a percentage of the employee's wages?

* Is this fair to lower paid women?

* How else might the level of pay be determined?

* Should costs be borne by the employer, by the social security system, or by unemployment insurance?

* How long a period of time should be provided and at what level of income?

* Who should be entitled to take leave?

* Should it cover both men and women?

7. Women's participation in the political process, and particularly in the legislature, seems to be central to passage of effective parental leave legislation. Women made up 21% of the Swedish parliament in the year the parental leave legislation was passed there. Angie K. Young, Assessing the Family and Medical Leave Act in Terms of Gender, Equality, Work/Family Balance, and the Needs of Children, 5 Mich. J. Gender & L. 113, 160 (1998). In 1995, the proportion was 41%. Linda Haas, Family Policy in Sweden, 17 J. Family & Econ. Issues 47, 53 (1996). In your opinion, would it be an adequate child care strategy simply to elect more women legislators in the United States?

D. CHILD CARE

Leave at the time of childbirth is only the first step in a policy to address the needs of families with small children. After the initial period of recuperation by the mother and incorporation of the child into the life of the family, human infants have many needs that must be fulfilled by adults over a long period of time. How these needs are met has profound implications both for the structure of power and well-being within the family and for women's subsequent ability to participate effectively in the workforce. The current options in the United States are relatively limited. In single-parent or dual-earner homes—currently more than 90% of all families—the option to care for the child oneself during the work day, even in infancy, is generally not available. Lacking an infrastructure of public institutions to care for preschool children, parents are forced to choose among care by relatives, a "nanny," day care provided in the home of another woman, and institutional day care facilities, all with very little public subsidy.

In this section, we address a number of issues: (1) the division of labor for child care within the family; (2) child care by third parties, including the American ambivalence about day care in general and the gender, race, and class issues implicated in the widespread employment of women of color to look after other women's children; and (3) the limited social supports that exist for child care in this country. We also discuss the implications of recent welfare "reform" legislation for mothers of small children and compare the arrangements in the United States with those available in other industrialized nations.

1. WHO TAKES CARE OF CHILDREN WITHIN THE FAMILY?

ARLIE HOCHSCHILD, THE SECOND SHIFT

33–39, 43–44 (1989).

[Together with Anne Machung, Arlie Hochschild carried out extensive interviews of 50 two-job couples, most of them several times over the period from 1980 to 1988; she also observed many of the couples in their homes, all in order to study the division of domestic labor and child care responsibilities when husbands and wives both work. Based upon her observations and interviews, Hochschild concluded that women in a two-job couple work roughly fifteen hours longer each week than men, or an extra month of 24–hour days over the course of a year.]

Nancy Holt arrives home from work, her son, Joey, in one hand and a bag of groceries in the other. As she puts down the groceries and opens the front door, she sees a spill of mail on the hall floor, Joey's half-eaten piece of cinnamon toast on the hall table, and the phone machine's winking red light: a still-life reminder of the morning's frantic rush to distribute the family to the world outside. Nancy, for seven years a social worker, is a short, lithe blond woman of thirty who talks and moves rapidly. She scoops the mail onto the hall table and heads for the kitchen, unbuttoning her coat as she goes. Joey sticks close behind her, intently explaining to her how dump trucks dump things. Joey is a fat-cheeked, lively four-year-old who chuckles easily at things that please him.

Having parked their red station wagon, Evan, her husband, comes in and hangs up his coat. He has picked her up at work and they've arrived home together. Apparently unready to face the kitchen commotion but not quite entitled to relax with the newspaper in the living room, he slowly studies the mail. Also thirty, Evan, a warehouse furniture salesman, has thinning pale blond hair, a stocky build, and a tendency to lean on one foot. In his manner there is something both affable and hesitant.

From the beginning, Nancy describes herself as an "ardent feminist," an egalitarian (she wants a similar balance of spheres and equal power). Nancy began her marriage hoping that she and Evan would base their identities in both their parenthood and their careers, but clearly tilted toward parenthood. Evan felt it was fine for Nancy to have a career, if she could handle the family too.

As I observe in their home on this evening, I notice a small ripple on the surface of family waters. From the commotion of the kitchen, Nancy calls, "Eva-an, will you *please* set the table?" The word *please* is thick with irritation. Scurrying between refrigerator, sink, and oven, with Joey at her feet, Nancy wants Evan to help; she has asked him, but reluctantly. She seems to resent having to ask. (Later she tells me, "I *hate* to ask; why should I ask? It's begging.") Evan looks up from the mail and flashes an irritated glance toward the kitchen, stung, perhaps, to be asked in a way so barren of appreciation and respect. He begins setting out knives and forks, asks if she will need spoons, then answers the doorbell. A neighbor's child. No, Joey can't play right now. The moment of irritation has passed.

Later as I interview Nancy and Evan separately, they describe their family life as unusually happy—except for Joey's "problem." Joey has great difficulty getting to sleep. They start trying to put him to bed at 8:00. Evan tries but Joey rebuffs him; Nancy has better luck. By 8:30 they have him *on* the bed but not *in* it; he crawls and bounds playfully. After 9:00 he still calls out for water or toys, and sneaks out of bed to switch on the light. This continues past 9:30, then 10:00 and 10:30. At about 11:00 Joey complains that his bed is "scary," that he can only go to sleep in his parents' bedroom. Worn down, Nancy accepts this proposition. And it is part of their current arrangement that putting Joey to bed is "Nancy's job." Nancy and Evan can't get into bed until midnight or later, when Evan is tired and Nancy exhausted. She used to enjoy their love-making, Nancy tells me, but now sex seems like "more work." The Holts consider their fatigue and impoverished sex life as results of Joey's Problem.

The official history of Joey's Problem—the interpretation Nancy and Evan give me—begins with Joey's fierce attachment to Nancy, and Nancy's strong attachment to him. On an afternoon walk through Golden Gate Park, Nancy devotes herself to Joey's every move. Now Joey sees a squirrel; Nancy tells me she must remember to bring nuts next time. Now Joey is going up the slide; she notices that his pants are too short—she must take them down tonight. The two enjoy each other. (Off the official record, neighbors and Joey's baby-sitter say that Nancy is a wonderful mother, but privately they add how much she is "also like a single mother.")

For his part, Evan sees little of Joey. He has his evening routine, working with his tools in the basement, and Joey always seems happy to be with Nancy. In fact, Joey shows little interest in Evan, and Evan hesitates to see that as a problem. "Little kids need their moms more than they need their dads," he explains philosophically; "All boys go through an oedipal phase."

Perfectly normal things happen. After a long day, mother, father, and son sit down to dinner. Evan and Nancy get the first chance all day to talk to each other, but both turn anxiously to Joey, expecting his mood to deteriorate. Nancy asks him if he wants celery with peanut butter on it. Joey says yes. "Are you sure that's how you want it?" "Yes." Then the fidgeting begins. "I don't like the strings on my celery." "Celery is made up of strings." "The celery is too big." Nancy grimly slices the celery. A certain tension mounts. Every time one parent begins a conversation with the other, Joey interrupts. "I don't have anything to drink." Nancy gets him juice. And finally, "Feed me." By the end of the meal, no one has obstructed Joey's victory. He has his mother's reluctant attention and his father is reaching for a beer. But talking about it later, they say, "This is normal when you have kids."

Sometimes when Evan knocks on the baby-sitter's door to pick up Joey, the boy looks past his father, searching for a face behind him: "Where's Mommy?" Sometimes he outright refuses to go home with his father. Eventually Joey even swats at his father, once quite hard, on the face for "no reason at all." This makes it hard to keep imagining Joey's relation to Evan as "perfectly normal." Evan and Nancy begin to talk seriously about a "swatting problem."

Evan decides to seek ways to compensate for his emotional distance from Joey. He brings Joey a surprise every week or so—a Tonka truck, a Tootsie roll. He turns weekends into father-and-son times. One Saturday, Evan proposes the zoo, and hesitantly, Joey agrees. Father and son have their coats on and are nearing the front door. Suddenly Nancy decides she wants to join them, and as she walks down the steps with Joey in her arms, she explains to Evan, "I want to help things out."

Evan gets few signs of love from Joey and feels helpless to do much about it. "I just don't feel good about me and Joey," he tells me one evening, "that's all I can say." Evan loves Joey. He feels proud of him, this bright, good-looking, happy child. But Evan also seems to feel that being a father is vaguely hurtful and hard to talk about.

The official history of Joey's problem was that Joey felt the "normal" oedipal attachment of a male child to his mother. Joey was having the emotional problems of growing up that any parent can expect. But Evan and Nancy add the point that Joey's problems are exacerbated by Evan's difficulties being an active father, which stem, they feel, from the way Evan's own father, an emotionally remote self-made businessman, had treated him. Evan tells me, "when Joey gets older, we're going to play baseball together and go fishing."

As I recorded this official version of Joey's Problem through interviews and observation, I began to feel doubts about it. For one thing, clues to another interpretation appeared in the simple pattern of footsteps on a typical evening. There was the steady pacing of Nancy, preparing dinner in the kitchen, moving in zigzags from counter to refrigerator to counter to stove. There were the lighter, faster steps of Joey, running in large figure eights through the house, dashing from his tonka truck to his motorcycle man, reclaiming his sense of belonging in this house, among his things. After dinner, Nancy and Evan mingled footsteps in the kitchen, as they cleaned up. Then Nancy's steps began again; click, click, click, down to the basement for laundry, then thuck,

thuck, thuck up the carpeted stairs to the first floor. Then to the bathroom where she runs Joey's bath, then into Joey's room, then back to the bath with Joey. Evan moved less—from the living room chair to Nancy in the kitchen, then back to the living room. He moved to the dining room to eat dinner and to the kitchen to help clean up. After dinner he went down to his hobby shop in the basement to sort out his tools; later he came up for a beer, then went back down. The footsteps suggest what is going on: Nancy was at work on her second shift.

Behind the Footsteps

Between 8:05 a.m. and 6:05 p.m., both Nancy and Evan are away from home, working a "first shift" at full-time jobs. The rest of the time they deal with the varied tasks of the second shift: shopping, cooking, paying bills; taking care of the car, the garden, and yard; keeping harmony with Evan's mother who drops over quite a bit, "concerned" about Joey, with neighbors, their voluble baby-sitter, and each other. And Nancy's talk reflects a series of second-shift thoughts: "We're out of barbecue sauce.... Joey needs a Halloween costume.... The car needs a wash...." and so on. She reflects a certain "second-shift sensibility," a continual attunement to the task of striking and restriking the right emotional balance between child, spouse, home, and outside job.

When I first met the Holts, Nancy was absorbing far more of the second shift than Evan. She said she was doing 80 percent of the housework and 90 percent of the childcare. Evan said she did 60 percent of the housework, 70 percent of the childcare. Joey said, "I vacuum the rug, and fold the dinner napkins," finally concluding, "Mom and I do it all." A neighbor agreed with Joey. Clearly, between Nancy and Evan, there was a "leisure gap": Evan had more than Nancy. I asked both of them, in separate interviews, to explain to me how they had dealt with housework and childcare since their marriage began.

One evening in the fifth year of their marriage, Nancy told me, when Joey was two months old and almost four years before I met the Holts, she first seriously raised the issue with Evan. "I told him: 'Look, Evan, it's not working. I do the housework, I take the major care of Joey, *and* I work a full-time job. I get pissed. This is *your* house too. Joey is *your* child too. It's not all *my* job to care for them.' When I cooled down I put to him, 'Look, how about this: I'll cook Mondays, Wednesdays, and Fridays. You cook Tuesdays, Thursdays, and Saturdays. And we'll share or go out Sundays.' "

According to Nancy, Evan said he didn't like "rigid schedules." He said he didn't necessarily agree with her standards of housekeeping, and didn't like that standard "imposed" on him, especially if she was "sluffing off" tasks on him, which from time to time he felt she was. But he went along with the idea in principle. Nancy said the first week of the new plan went as follows. On Monday, she cooked. For Tuesday, Evan planned a meal that required shopping for a few ingredients, but on his way home he forgot to shop for them. He came home, saw nothing he could use in the refrigerator or in the cupboard, and suggested to Nancy that they go out for Chinese food. On Wednesday, Nancy cooked. On Thursday morning, Nancy reminded Evan, "Tonight it's your turn." That night Evan fixed hamburgers and french fries and Nancy was quick to praise him. On Friday, Nancy cooked. On Saturday, Evan forgot again.

As this pattern continued, Nancy's reminders became sharper. The sharper they became, the more actively Evan forgot—perhaps anticipating even sharper reprimands if he resisted more directly. This cycle of passive refusal followed by disappointment and anger gradually tightened, and before long the struggle had spread to the task of doing the laundry. Nancy said it was only fair that Evan share the laundry. He agreed in principle, but anxious that Evan would not share, Nancy wanted a clear, explicit agreement. "You ought to wash and fold every other load," she had told him. Evan experienced this "plan" as a yoke around his neck. On many weekdays, at this point, a huge pile of laundry sat like a disheveled guest on the living-room couch.

In her frustration, Nancy began to make subtle emotional jabs at Evan. "I don't know *what's* for dinner," she would say with a sigh. Or "I can't cook now, I've got to deal with this pile of laundry." She tensed at the slightest criticism about household disorder; if Evan wouldn't do the housework, he had absolutely *no* right to criticize how she did it. She would burst out angrily at Evan. She recalled telling him: "After work *my* feet are just as tired as *your* feet. I'm just as wound up as you are. I come home. I cook dinner. I wash and I clean. Here we are, planning a second child, and I can't cope with the one we have."

* * *

UPSTAIRS–DOWNSTAIRS: A FAMILY MYTH AS "SOLUTION"

Not long after this crisis in the Holts' marriage, there was a dramatic lessening of tension over the issue of the second shift. It was as if the issue was closed. Evan had won. Nancy would do the second shift. Evan expressed vague guilt but beyond that he had nothing to say. Nancy had wearied of continually raising the topic, wearied of the lack of resolution. Now in the exhaustion of defeat, she wanted the struggle to be over too. Evan was "so good" in *other* ways, why debilitate their marriage by continual quarreling. Besides, she told me, "women always adjust more, don't they?"

One day, when I asked Nancy to tell me who did which tasks from a long list of household chores, she interrupted me with a broad wave of her hand and said, "I do the upstairs, Evan does the downstairs." What does that mean? I asked. Matter-of-factly, she explained that the upstairs included the living room, the dining room, the kitchen, two bedrooms, and two baths. The downstairs meant the garage, a place for storage and hobbies—Evan's hobbies. She explained this as a "sharing" arrangement, without humor or irony—just as Evan did later. Both said they had agreed it was the best solution to their dispute. Evan would take care of the car, the garage, and Max, the family dog. As Nancy explained, "the dog is all Evan's problem. I don't have to deal with the dog." Nancy took care of the rest.

For purposes of accommodating the second shift, then, the Holts' garage was elevated to the full moral and practical equivalent of the rest of the house. For Nancy and Evan, "upstairs and downstairs," "inside and outside," was vaguely described like "half and half," a fair division of labor based on a natural division of their house.

The Holts presented their upstairs-downstairs agreement as a perfectly equitable solution to a problem they "once had." This belief is what we might call a "family myth," even a modest delusional system. Why did they believe it? I think they believed it because they needed to believe it, because it solved a terrible problem. It allowed Nancy to continue thinking of herself as the sort of woman whose husband didn't abuse her—a self-conception that mattered a great deal to her. And it avoided the hard truth that, in his stolid, passive way, Evan had refused to share. It avoided the truth, too, that in their showdown, Nancy was more afraid of divorce than Evan was. This outer cover to their family life, this family myth, was jointly devised. It was an attempt to agree that there was no conflict over the second shift, no tension between their versions of manhood and womanhood, and that the powerful crisis that had arisen was temporary and minor.

M. RIVKA POLATNICK, WHY MEN DON'T REAR CHILDREN : A POWER ANALYSIS

In Mothering: Essays in Feminist Theory

23, 24–25, 26, 27–28, 31, 33, 37 (Joyce Trebilcot, ed. 1983).

* * * [M]en (as a group) don't rear children because they don't *want* to rear children. (This implies, of course, that they are in a position to enforce their preferences.) It is to men's advantage that women are assigned childrearing responsibility, and it is in men's interest to keep things that way.

* * *

Full-time childrearing responsibility limits one's capacity to engage in most other activities. However, the most important thing, in power terms that childrearers can't do is to be the family breadwinner. This is the job that men prefer as their primary family responsibility. It offers important power advantages over the home-based childrearing job.

* * *

First, and of signal importance, breadwinners earn money. "Money is a source of power that supports male dominance in the family.... money belongs to him who earns it, not to her who spends it, since he who earns it may withhold it."[5]

5. Reuben Hill and Howard Becker, eds., *Family, Marriage, and Parenthood* (1955), p. 790.

Second, occupational achievement is probably the major source of social status in American society.

> In a certain sense the fundamental basis of the family's status is the occupational status of the husband and father. [The wife/mother] is excluded from the struggle for power and prestige in the occupational sphere [while the man's breadwinner role] carries with it . . . the primary prestige of achievement, responsibility, and authority.[6]

Even if one's occupation ranks very low in prestige and power, other tangible and intangible benefits accrue to wage earners, such as organizational experience, social contacts, "knowledge of the world," and feelings of independence and competence. Moreover, the resources that breadwinners garner in the outside world do not remain on the front porch; breadwinning power translates significantly into power within the family. This is in direct contradiction to the notion of "separate spheres": The man reigning supreme in extrafamilial affairs, the woman running the home-front show. * * *

The correlation between earning power and family power has been substantiated concretely in a number of studies of family decision-making. These studies show that the more a man earns, the more family power he wields; and the greater the discrepancy between the status of the husband's and wife's work, the greater the husband's power. When the wife works too, there is a shift toward a more egalitarian balance of power and more sharing of household burdens.

* * *

Men have good reason, then, to try to monopolize the job of principal family breadwinner (much as they may appreciate a second income). Husbands' objections to wives working "stem from feelings that their dominance is undermined when they are not the sole or primary breadwinners."[11] There is also

> the feeling of being threatened by women in industry, who are seen as limiting opportunities for men, diminishing the prestige of jobs formerly held only by men, and casting a cold eye on masculine pretentions to vocational superiority.[12]

These feelings are quite justified; as Benson so neatly understates it, "the male fear of competition from women is not based solely on myth."[13]

Where outright forbidding of the wife to work is no longer effective, the continued allocation of childrearing responsibility to women accomplishes the same end: assuring male domination of the occupational

6. Talcott Parsons, "Age and Sex in the Social Structure" in *The Family: Its Structure and Functions,* edited by Rose Laub Coser (1964), pp. 258, 261–62.

11. Phyllis Hallenbeck, "An Analysis of Power Dynamics in Marriage," *Journal of Marriage and the Family* 28 (May 1966): 201.

12. Helen Mayer Hacker, "The New Burdens of Masculinity," *Marriage and Family Living* 19 (August 1957): 232.

13. Leonard Benson, *Fatherhood: A Sociological Perspective* 293 (1968).

world. Should all other barriers to economic power for women suddenly vanish, childrearing responsibility would still handicap them hopelessly in economic competition with men.

Of course, children are not just a handy excuse to keep women out of the job market. Most people—male and female—want to have them, and somebody has to rear them. Men naturally prefer that women do it, so that having children need not interfere with their own occupational pursuits.

* * *

By propagating the belief that women are the ones who really desire children, men can then invoke a "principle of least interest": that is, because women are "most interested" in children, they must make most of the accommodations and sacrifices required to rear them. Benson says that "fatherhood ... is less important to men than motherhood is to women, in spite of the fact that maternity causes severe limitations on women's activities." My own version would be that fatherhood is less important to men than motherhood is to women *because* childrearing causes severe limitations on the childrearer's activities.

* * *

Women too imbibe the ideology of motherhood, but men seem to be its strongest supporters. By insuring that the weight of childrearing responsibility falls on women's shoulders, they win for themselves the right of "paternal neglect." As Benson observes, "The man can throw himself into his work and still fulfill male obligations at home, mainly because the latter are minimal. [Men have] the luxury of more familial disengagement than women."

Of course, men as family breadwinners must shoulder the *financial* burden involved in raising children: they may have to work harder, longer hours, and at jobs they dislike. But even factory workers enjoy set hours, scheduled breaks, vacation days, sick leave, and other union benefits. To the extent that men *can* select work suited to their interests, abilities, and ambitions, they are in a better position than women arbitrarily assigned to childrearing. And to the extent that breadwinning gains one the resources discussed earlier (money, status, family power, etc.), financial responsibility is clearly preferable, in power terms, to "mothering" responsibility.

* * *

Performing well at the job of childrearer may be a source of feminine credentials, but it is not a source of social power or status. Of all the possible adult roles for females, "the pattern of domesticity must be ranked lowest in terms of prestige," although "it offers perhaps the highest level of a certain kind of security."[29] When a woman bears and raises children, therefore, she is fulfilling social expectations and avoid-

29. Parsons, "Age and Sex in the Social Structure," p. 261.

ing negative sanctions, but she "is not esteemed, in the culture or in the small society of her family, in proportion to her exercise of her 'glory,' childbearing."[30]

The rewards for rearing children are not as tangible as a raise or a promotion, and ready censure awaits any evidence of failure: "if the child goes wrong, mother is usually blamed."[31] Thus the male preference for the breadwinner role may reflect (among other things) an awareness that "it's easier to make money than it is to be a good father.... The family is a risky proposition in terms of rewards and self-enhancement."[32]

* * *

Childrearing, I have argued, is not a source of money, status, power in the society, or power in the family. The childrearing job is disadvantageous in terms of these major assets, but there are also drawbacks inherent in the nature of the work itself. The rearing of children "involves long years of exacting labor and self-sacrifice," but

> the drudgery, the monotonous labor, and other disagreeable features of childrearing are minimized by "the social guardians." On the other hand, the joys and compensations of motherhood are magnified and presented to consciousness on every hand. Thus the tendency is to create an illusion whereby motherhood will appear to consist of compensations only, and thus come to be desired by those for whom the illusion is intended.[40]

The responsibilities of a childrearer/homemaker are not confined to a 40–hour work-week. Margaret Benston estimates that for a married woman with small children (excluding the very rich), "the irreducible minimum of work ... is probably 70 or 80 hours a week."[41] In addition to the actual hours of work, there is the constant strain of being "on call." Thus, another consideration in why the husband's power is greatest when the children are young "may be the well-described chronic fatigue which affects young mothers with preschoolers."[42]

* * *

The allocation of childrearing responsibility to women, I have argued, is no sacred fiat of nature, but a social policy which supports male domination in the society and in the family.

Whatever the "intrinsic desirability" of rearing children, the conditions of the job as it's now constituted—no salary, low status, long hours,

30. Judith Long Laws, "A Feminist Review of Marital Adjustment Literature," *Journal of Marriage and the Family* 33 (August 1971): 493.

31. Benson, *Fatherhood,* p. 12.

32. Myron Brenton, *The American Male* (1966), p. 133.

40. Leta S. Hollingworth, "Social Devices for Impelling Women to Bear and Rear Children," *The American Journal of Sociology* 22 (July 1916): 20–21, 27.

41. Margaret Benston, "The Political Economy of Women's Liberation" in Garskof, Roles Women Play, p. 199.

42. Hallenbeck, "An Analysis of Power Dynamics in Marriage," p. 201.

domestic isolation—mark it as a job for women only. Men, as the superordinate group, don't want childrearing responsibility, so they assign it to women. Women's functioning as childrearers reinforces, in turn, their subordinate position. Thus we come back again to the causal model of my Introduction—

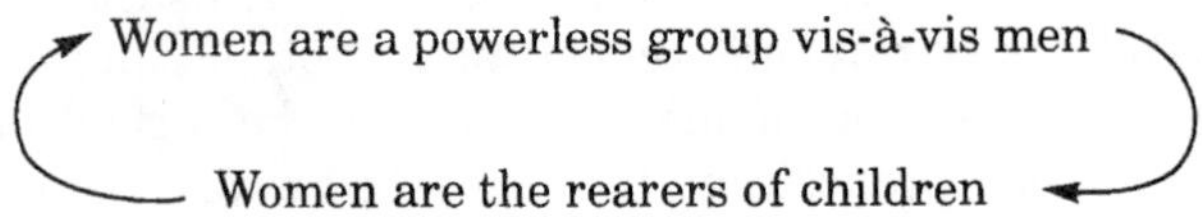
Women are a powerless group vis-à-vis men
Women are the rearers of children

—a vicious circle that keeps male power intact.

Notes on Child Care

1. In a more recent study, Arlie Hochschild describes how the hours left over for the second shift in our society have been decreasing, as the average worker, by various estimates, has added a month of work to his or her work year (citing Juliet Schor, The Overworked American: The Unexpected Decline of Leisure (1991)). Hochschild, The Time Bind: When Work Becomes Home and Home Becomes Work (1997). Official data highlight this problem, concluding that families on average have experienced a decrease of 22 hours a week (14%) in parental time available to spend with their children; this creates a "time crunch" that falls virtually entirely on women. Council of Economic Advisers, Families and the Labor Market, 1969–1999: Analyzing the "Time Crunch" 3–6, 11–13 (1999). A startling result of Hochschild's study is that many workers, especially women, report that they feel more "at home" at work—more relaxed, emotionally supported, and appreciated—than they do at home. Hochschild, The Time Bind, at 200–01. Why do you think this is so? Why do women experience this more than men? How can this reversal of home and work be addressed?

2. What options did Nancy Holt, who "chooses" to lose the battle over the second shift, have? Why didn't she exercise them? Is she doing more than her own share in part because she wants to? A national survey of 1,100 mothers reported that only about one in four thought that fathers should play a 50–50 role in raising children (although most wanted fathers to do more child care than they currently did), and two out of three mothers seemed threatened by the idea of equal participation, leading the authors to conclude that "*mothers themselves may be subtly putting a damper on men's involvement with their children* because they are so possessive of their role as primary nurturer." Louis Genevie and Eva Margolies, The Motherhood Report: How Women Feel About Being Mothers 358 (1987) (emphasis in original). What do you think explains these results? What do you think you would have done if you were in Nancy Holt's place?

3. Why do you think women rather than men are typically the primary caretakers of children? Do you find the explanation offered by Chodorow, in the excerpt included in the previous section (The Reproduction of Mothering), or that offered by Polatnick (power) more persuasive? What would a

relational feminist think causes this allocation of responsibility? A socialist feminist? A dominance/inequality theorist? How would a liberal equality theorist explain it?

4. If women "mother" because of influences upon them in early childhood, how can this system be changed? Hochschild reports that sex-role socialization has not changed much in the younger generation with respect to who is to be breadwinner and who is to be primarily responsible for caretaking and other domestic labor. Hochschild, The Second Shift, at 266 (discussing 1986 study of Berkeley seniors, to the effect that "54 percent of the women and 13 percent of the men expected to be the one who would miss an important meeting at work for a sick child"). A more recent study of "care orientation" in students in grades 6, 8, 10, and 12 found a larger percentage of the females had a value orientation characterized by, among other things, a higher priority given to children. Kimberly Badger, Rebecca Simpson Craft, and Larry Jensen, Age and Gender Differences in Value Orientation among American Adolescents, 33 Adolescence 591–96 (1998). See also Miriam Lewin and Lilli M. Tragos, Has the Feminist Movement Influenced Adolescent Sex Role Attitudes? A Reassessment After A Quarter Century, 16 Sex Roles 125 (1987) (finding no significant change in sex role stereotyping by high-school students between 1956 and 1982). What do you think explains the persistence of these attitudes?

What sort of a father is Joey (Nancy and Evan's son in the excerpt from The Second Shift) likely to be? How can he change?

5. Hochschild concluded, based on her observations of Nancy and Evan Holt's "family myth" and those constructed by other couples whose marriages she studied, that highly educated, professional, higher-income couples tend to engage more in the rhetoric of equality, without any more real equality, than couples at the other end of the socioeconomic scale. (One of the couples Hochschild observed to be *most* equitably sharing the tasks of the "second shift" also voiced very traditional and non-egalitarian rhetoric about the roles of husbands and wives in marriage. Hochschild, The Second Shift, at 59–74. Why do you think middle- and upper-middle-class couples feel the need to obscure reality? Have you observed this pattern in your friends and acquaintances? In your own life?

6. How can one break the vicious cycle Polatnick describes, in which women have less power than men and are therefore assigned the task of childrearing, which in turns keeps them from gaining more power in the workplace, and thus in the home? Can one woman do it as an individual or does the whole society have to change in order for any one to do so? What kinds of changes would be necessary?

7. Although it is a violation of Title VII not to provide disability benefits for maternity leave if other disabilities are covered by an employer, no court has ever found that the statute is violated by structuring a job so as to effectively preclude its performance by someone with child care responsibilities. Thus, for example, a law firm that requires young lawyers to bill 2500 hours per year does not violate Title VII. Can you make an argument that such practices do constitute sex discrimination? How would you go about proving your allegations? What evidence would you bring into court? Is it admissible? For a discussion of the possibility of an employment

discrimination case seeking to require an employer to provide child care assistance, see Lucinda M. Finley, Legal Aspects of Child Care: The Policy Debate Over The Appropriate Amount of Public Responsibility, in Parental Leave and Child Care: Setting a Research and Policy Agenda (Janet Shibley Hyde and Marilyn J. Essex, eds. 1991), at 149–52; Mary Joe Frug, Securing Job Equality for Women: Labor Market Hostility to Working Mothers, 59 B.U. L. Rev. 55, 61–74 (1979). See also Joan Williams, Unbending Gender: Why Family and Work Conflict and What To Do About It 104–08 (2000) (suggesting a number of antidiscrimination claims, such as Title VII disparate-impact claims and Equal Pay Act claims, to require employers to provide family-friendly policies and to protect workers who work part-time, refuse overtime or travel, and otherwise seek to accommodate work with familial responsibilities).

2. CHILD CARE BY THIRD PARTIES

RUTH SIDEL, WOMEN & CHILDREN LAST: THE PLIGHT OF POOR WOMEN IN AFFLUENT AMERICA

115–18, 128–30, 179, 184–87 (1986).

Day care is one of those murky issues on which many Americans do not really know where they stand. Are we for it or against it? Is it good for children or harmful to them? Will it facilitate their social and intellectual development or undermine their emotional well-being? Is it perhaps somewhat "un-American" for a mother to leave her child during the first few years of life? That is what the Russians, the Chinese, and the Swedes do; is that what we want to do? Why do we seem so very ambivalent about this important topic?

* * * [T]he rhetoric of the Reagan administration and its allies has undermined public perception of the need for day care by nostalgically recalling and mythologizing another era—perhaps the 1950s, more likely the 1920s—and longingly trying to recapture it.

In this image of small-town America, we are led to believe that father went to work every morning and returned home every evening to hugs and shouts of joy, that mother had hot cocoa and homemade cookies ready for well-behaved children returning from school, and that in case of an emergency grandmother was down the block, only too glad to help out when needed. Children set up lemonade stands on tree-lined streets, large families gathered for Thanksgiving dinner, and friends of long standing were available to provide mutual aid and support in times of hardship—perhaps a scene out of a Jimmy Stewart movie, with everything working out just fine in the end. There is little evidence that this Norman Rockwell image of America ever existed except, possibly, for a limited number of middle- and upper-middle-class families; it surely is not the reality of today. But this image, this rhetoric, has been used by an administration that has tried, and succeeded to a remarkable extent, in removing supports from families under the guise that they will be encouraged to return to an idyllic Never–Never Land.

Other voices, from other viewpoints, also attack day care. Recent allegations of sexual abuse of children by workers in day-care centers in California and New York have shocked parents, professionals, and the public. These incidents highlight a critical problem that has existed in American society for many years: The flagrant disregard for the well-being of children resulting in the absence of a responsible, coherent child-care policy.

* * *

Marion Blum, educational director of the Wellesley College Child Study Center, has recently written a powerful critique of day care. She points out that in our extraordinarily materialistic society, children are viewed as things, as commodities around which others can make a profit. She rightly condemns such equipment as cage-like cribs, harnesses and leashes that treat children as though they were animals rather than humans in order to minimize the number of caretakers and to maximize profits. She points out that because of the high turnover of preschool teachers, and the fact that teachers work shifts that may not coincide with the children's hours at the center, children must relate to a variety of adults during their day-care experience. She points out that eight hours or more is a long time for a three- or four-year-old to be away from home and to be required, for the most part, to behave according to preset schedules. She and others have pointed out the difficulties for over-worked caregivers trying to maintain proper sanitation, particularly in younger age groups in which the children may not be toilet trained. She points out the higher rates of colds, flu, diarrhea, and even hepatitis A in children who attend day-care centers.

Finally, Blum notes that day care has involved a "transfer of roles from one group of exploited women—mothers—to another group of exploited women—day-care staff." Day-care workers are among the lowest paid adult wage earners in our society, with little or no opportunity for advancement, little or no prestige, and very little in the way of benefits. According to the Children's Defense Fund, "Two out of three center-based caregivers earn below poverty level wages and 87 percent of family day-care workers earn below the minimum wage." The status of preschool teachers clearly indicates the lack of value we place on women and children in our society.

Why is day care so inadequate in the United States? Why is it so exploitive of children, of day-care workers, of the parents themselves who often have no other choice? Is it because day care is seen as "nonproductive" in a society so geared to materialism and productivity? Is it because it serves the needs of two groups—women and children—who are particularly powerless? Is it because in a system not committed to full employment, decision-makers really do not want women in the labor force possibly taking jobs away from men? Is it because many, particularly people in positions of power, want to maintain the patriarchal family, and day care is seen as a force undermining that power relationship? * * *

Perhaps the most significant development over the past few years has been the emergence of employer-supported child care. According to the Conference Board, a nonprofit business research organization, more than 1,800 companies are providing some form of child-care assistance to workers. Child-care support by employers takes many forms. It includes providing or participating in the provision of direct services. * * * Some companies join together to form a consortium to run a center; others sponsor family day-care arrangements.

A second form of employer participation in their employees' child-care concerns is the provision of information and referral services, either offered on the work premises or through an existing community agency. Yet another form of involvement is employer-financed subsidy. The establishment of a Dependent Care Assistance Plan was made possible by the Economic Recovery Tax Act of 1981, making child care a nontaxable benefit for employees. The fourth mechanism whereby employers help their employees with child care is through more flexible working hours—flextime, job sharing, part-time work, or home work, also called "flexi-place."

* * *

There is no doubt that employer involvement in child care is a positive development; it has, for example, undoubtedly legitimized day care in the eyes of many who may have felt doubt or even antipathy. But there are problems with relying on employers to be major providers of child care. One major difficulty is that the current wave of employer-sponsored activity is generally voluntary. Most firms or unions or institutions that move into the area of day care do it because they need to recruit and retain skilled employees, because they feel their employees will, in the long run, have more stable work histories if some of their family problems are solved, or because they feel it is good public relations. As Friedman points out, industries that cater to the family market, such as Gerber Foods and Stride Rite children's shoes, feel a greater commitment to family issues. But what of other working people in the country? Most of the companies that offer child-care options are nonunionized. Child-care benefits are, therefore, often not a right won through negotiation and guaranteed through a contract but rather a result of enlightened self-interest on the part of industry. But what happens when the industry's self-interest changes—if its profit margin shrinks and executives feel such services can be eliminated?

Which segment of the population is most likely to benefit from industry involvement in child care? Will this be yet another way of separating services for the poor from services for working people, many of whom are middle class? Corporate child-care programs are usually found in high-technology companies, insurance companies, banks and hospitals. Are we moving simultaneously toward improved child care for the fortunate few and reduced, often inferior care for the poor, the unemployed, and those workers unfortunate enough to work for companies that are either unenlightened or not making sufficient profit to consider breaking new ground in the area of child care? In addition, many of the companies now offering child-care services offer them as part of a "cafeteria" plan, whereby the worker must choose one benefit over another. Should a parent have to choose dental coverage over child care or vice versa?

Child care is still a two-class system in the United States. Those with adequate income can generally purchase first-rate care for their preschool children; those without adequate income are left at the mercy of the political and economic forces that determine social policy. While the poor, the near poor, and the working class sometimes have access to good care, more often than not they are faced with long waiting lists, inadequate teacher-child ratios, and a rapid turnover of caregivers.

* * *

Lessons From Sweden

* * *

During the 1970s the single most important family policy issue [in Sweden] was child care. Since the Swedish government, and indeed most institutions within Swedish society, had made a serious commitment both to equality between men and women and to enhancing the well-being of the family unit, the expansion of child-care facilities was considered an urgent priority.

Child-care programs are a municipal responsibility in Sweden. Facilities are generally located in residential areas, near where the children live. Unlike the pattern in countries such as China, preschool facilities at the workplace are rare in Sweden.

There are several different kinds of facilities for young children. Day nurseries, generally open from 6:30 A.M. to 6:30 P.M., take children from six months to seven years. Because of the availability of parental leave until the child is one year old and because of waiting lists for available places, relatively few children as young as six months attend.

Part-time groups generally care for older preschoolers, children ages four to six. In 1975 a law was passed requiring all municipalities to provide a preschool place for all six-year-olds. These programs usually run three hours a day, five days a week, and are comparable to kindergarten in the United States.

Yet another alternative is the family day nursery. In this instance, the municipality hires a woman to care for up to four children in her home. These facilities are supervised by the municipality.

Recreation centers, also known as "leisure time centers," are available after school and during school vacations to care for school-age children, ages seven to twelve, whose parents are working or studying full time.

* * *

Although Swedish policymakers have recognized over the past ten to fifteen years the urgent need for additional preschool facilities, particularly with increasing numbers of young women entering the labor force, their commitment to day care of extraordinarily high quality has often meant an inability to move ahead in numbers of places as rapidly as many would have liked. Swedish day nurseries are surely among the best day-care facilities in the world. From the modern, relatively spacious and somewhat avant-garde centers in Stockholm, stocked with the most up-to-date equipment, to day nurseries such as the one in the suburbs of the small city of Västerås, located in a lovely old wooden house surrounded by trees and grass, which prides itself on the close relationships among children, parents, and staff, preschool facilities in Sweden are indeed enviable. They are, almost unfailingly, warm and welcoming, and decorated colorfully, ingeniously, sometimes with Scandinavian fabrics and always with stunning posters and the children's artwork. Close attention is paid not only to the children's physical environment but to their individual development, to their health and well-being, and to their social development.

The children are sometimes grouped by age, more often today into sibling groups ages two-and-one-half to seven. The notion is that, by mixing different ages, children can have the experience of playing different roles in the group, of helping one another and of being helped, of caring for others and being cared for. The caregivers include preschool teachers, who have been trained in a two-year course following upper secondary school, and children's nurses, who are trained through a two-year program within upper secondary school or through a special one-year program. The most common ratio is one adult for every four or five children, with the infant programs having even fewer children per adult. Creative play is stressed, with children working both in small groups and singly if they prefer. The development of the individual and the child's ability to be part of the larger group are both felt to be essential learning experiences.

Special facilities are available for immigrant children ages five and six who speak a language other than Swedish in the home. These children have priority in obtaining places in preschool facilities and are offered training in their "home language." For at least four hours a week children may, on a voluntary basis, be taught by a teacher who speaks their native tongue; participate in unilingual part-time groups from the age of four; and join unilingual sibling groups at day nurseries or in a variety of other settings in which their original language is used.

In 1981 the cost of preschool care was estimated at approximately 44,000 kronor ($5,000) per child. The central government paid at that time a subsidy of just over 21,000 kronor for each child in a fully qualified day nursery. The state subsidy for family day nurseries was 3,250 kronor per place, plus 35 percent of the municipality's gross expenses for the program. Parents' fees vary from municipality to municipality and are dependent upon income, but the average fee paid by parents was approximately 4,000 kronor ($460) in 1981. Part-time preschools are free for six-year-olds and for younger children needing special care. There is no fixed fee for after-school care; the amount is often linked to the day nursery fee but is set at perhaps 40 to 50 percent of that amount.

In addition to benefits that stem from Sweden's family policy, Swedish citizens are entitled to a comprehensive variety of other benefits under their social insurance system. These include health insurance, sickness benefits, old-age pension, disability pension, work-injury insurance, unemployment insurance, and a variety of special measures to help to care for the elderly. In addition, "social assistance" is available for those individuals who are still in need after receiving other benefits.* * *

Notes on the Provision of Child Care

1. Women obtain child care during work hours from a variety of options available in this society—from relatives, from other women (in the child's or the other woman's home), in family day care homes, and in institutionalized day care facilities. See, e.g., Nat'l Research Council, Who Cares for America's Children?: Child Care Policy for the 1990s 147–64 (Cheryl D. Hayes, John L. Palmer, and Martha J. Zaslow, eds. 1990). It is estimated that over 40% of preschool children of working mothers are cared for by relatives (the parents or other relatives, such as grandmothers), but this source of day care is fast declining with the increase in female labor force participation. Jennifer L. Glass and Lisa Riley, Family Responsive Policies and Employee Retention Following Childbirth, 76 Social Forces 1401, 1406 (1998). Family day care runs the gamut from one woman offering to look after another woman's child along with her own, for some compensation, while the other woman works, to structured in-home environments that are licensed to look after a small group of preschoolers and are subject to regulation. It is difficult to estimate how many of these arrangements are used by working women because a portion of this labor takes place in the underground economy. Nat'l Research Council, above, at 151. The Census Bureau estimated that family day care accounted for 17.7 to 26.8 percent of the care of children under the age of three in the mid–1980's. See Margaret K. Nelson, The Regulation Controversy in Family Day Care: The Perspective of Providers, in Parental Leave and Child Care: Setting a Research and Policy Agenda (Janet Shibley Hyde and Marilyn J. Essex, eds. 1991), at 354. The quality of care available in family day care homes varies substantially, leading many to suggest more stringent health and quality regulation and monitoring of this in-home "industry," a move resisted by many care providers. From 50 to 90 percent of family day care is thought to be unregulated. Id. at 354–55. What are the race and class implications of increased regulation of this type of caregiving?

2. During World War II, when it was perceived to be necessary to the national economy and defense, child care was provided in some workplaces and subsidized by the government. For example, centers established under the Lanham Act included two at the Kaiser Shipbuilding plant in Portland, Oregon, which were open 24 hours a day and provided numerous services,

including care for children with minor illnesses, shopping and low cost carry-out dinners. Sidel, Women & Children Last 119–20. What are the advantages of on-site child care provided by the employer? For the employer? For the parent? For the child? What are the disadvantages for each group?

3. Most European countries devote substantial attention and public resources to provision of services to support persons who are raising children, by way of direct grants or family allowances, or by direct provision of services such as publicly funded and publicly run nurseries, or by some combination of the two. See, e.g., Sheila B. Kamerman and Alfred J. Kahn, Child Care, Family Benefits and Working Parents (1981). Despite economic downturn and the replacement of the Social Democratic government by a more conservative administration, Sweden has remained committed to providing high-quality publicly subsidized day care for all children. Linda Haas, Family Policy in Sweden, 17 J. Family & Econ. Issues 47, 80–85 (1996). Despite the commitment to sex equality at home and at work, however, gender segregation in the workplace does persist to some extent in Sweden, and women remain more likely to care for children than men. Perhaps as a result of government policies, men did increase their participation in household work from 7% of all time spent at housework in 1974 to 18% in 1991. Id. at 73–75. Would the Swedish system of child care work here? Why or why not?

France, an industrialized country without the extensive social democratic political background of Sweden, also has a comprehensive program of publicly funded child care. After 16 weeks of paid maternity leave, infant care is available in crèches collectives (infant day care centers whose directors have training equivalent to that of a registered nurse or midwife, with additional training in administration of infant care) and crèches familiares (clusters of 15 in-home care providers who look after three children each and are trained, supervised and monitored by directors comparable to those acting as supervisors in the collective centers); the centers, which are available only to working parents, are subsidized and charge according to ability to pay. Barbara R. Bergmann, Saving Our Children From Poverty: What the United States Can Learn from France 35–41, 46 (1996). There are also family allowances for parents who look after infants in the home and centers for periodic child care for them as well. Id. at 48. Free full-time nursery schools are provided for children between the ages of 3 and 6 and form an integral part of the public educational system. Id. at 28–35.

Perhaps because European industrialized countries provide these and comparable child care benefits to parents in all income classes, use of these benefits is not stigmatized and does not reinforce class differences. Nancy E. Dowd, Family Values and Valuing Family: A Blueprint for Family Leave, 30 Harv. J. on Legis. 335, 362 (1993). As a result, the percentage of 3– to 6–year-old children in publicly funded child care in Western European countries is extremely high: 72% in Sweden, 85% in Spain, 91% in Italy, 95% in Belgium, and 99% in France. Luke Harding and Emily Sheffield, Women and the Family, The Guardian, Mar. 12, 1998, at 9.

4. Why is it so hard to make arguments for government funding of child care in the United States? Apart from the American anti-tax, anti-government political culture and ideology of individualism, Barbara Berg-

man suggests that unwillingness to pay for child care in this country relates to the history of racism. For one thing, "Americans are accustomed to think that the primary beneficiaries of child care, income supplementation, and medical care programs are parents, and in particular, mothers, rather than children." Bergman, above note 3, at 19. Moreover, she states, "The anger against poor children's parents is in part connected to the problem of race relations in the United States. * * * But the widespread antagonism against black people undoubtedly contributes to the opposition to giving poor families—widely but falsely perceived to be black—any more help." Id. at 10. Do you agree with this explanation?

5. Does it make a difference *why* the government adopts a particular child care policy—that is, whether it is seen as a question of sex equality, as in Sweden; of employment necessity, as in wartime Britain and the United States; or of child welfare? How are the resulting programs likely to differ? Does it make a difference if the child care policy and programs stand alone or form part of a broader family support policy including, as in Sweden and France, comprehensive national health insurance, social insurance against unemployment, provisions for care for the elderly, etc.? Why or why not?

6. A report on the structure and attitudes of American families was released by the National Opinion Research Center (NORC) in late 1999. Tom W. Smith, The Emerging 21st Century American Family (NORC, GSS Social Change Rpt. No. 42, Nov. 24, 1999). NORC reports that American attitudes toward government assistance for child care and other types of government social welfare programs have changed with the changing structure of the American family, from the previously typical single-earner couple to a predominance of dual-earner couples and single-parent families. Single-earner couples are the most traditional in their attitudes toward gender roles, women working, and social welfare policies to assist working parents; dual-earner parents are more liberal (NORC calls them more "modern") on all these fronts; and single parents are the most supportive in their orientation to all of these issues. Id. at 16–18. NORC predicts that support for gender equality and government assistance will increase with the continuing structural changes in the family, especially as more children are raised by working mothers. Id. at 19–20. How would you assess this prediction? Do you think that structural changes will inexorably lead to a change in American views on all these subjects?

7. There has by now been a substantial amount of research concerning the effects of maternal employment upon children. Contrary to popular assumptions, the overwhelming results of longitudinal studies show that children whose mothers work suffer no detrimental effects from maternal employment per se. See, e.g., Adele Eskeles Gottfried and Allen W. Gottfried, eds., Maternal Employment and Children's Development, Longitudinal Research (1988). Controlling for other differences, including socioeconomic status, children whose mothers are employed and children whose mothers are not employed are equivalent in infant developmental status, security of attachment in infancy, toddlerhood and kindergarten years, cognitive, language and intellectual development in the preschool through school-age years, problem solving in toddlerhood, social reasoning during preschool and social maturity during the school years, emotional expressiveness during kindergarten, behavioral adjustment from ages four through seven, academic

performance in the early school years, school motivation, and sex role development in adolescence. Id. at 270. Indeed, there appear to be benefits from maternal employment beyond purely economic ones, including higher educational aspirations and attitudes, paternal involvement, and variety of children's experience. Id. at 273. This research was used by the California Supreme Court as a basis for holding that a mother's employment status could not be used to discriminate against her in deciding about child custody. Burchard v. Garay, 42 Cal.3d 531, 229 Cal.Rptr. 800, 724 P.2d 486, 493 (1986) (Rose Bird, J., concurring). Use of day care still can figure in trial court decisions about custody, however. In 1994, for example, a Michigan judge granted custody of Jennifer Ireland's three-year-old daughter to her father because Ireland relied on a day care center while she was a student at the University of Michigan. Reuters, Mother Loses Custody Over Use of Day Care, Chicago Sun–Times, July 28, 1994, at 9. Feminist groups rushed to file briefs upon appeal, and the decision was subsequently reversed.

A large-scale ongoing longitudinal study by the National Institute of Child Health and Human Development (a division of the National Institutes of Health) has shown that placing even a very young infant in child care has no significant effect upon infant-mother attachment security. NICHD Early Child Care Research Network, The Effects of Infant Child Care on Infant–Mother Attachment Security: Results of the NICHD Study of Early Child Care, 68 Child Development 860–79 (1997). Typical day care does not slow down children's development of language or other cognitive skills and may even improve it, especially for children in lower-income groups; this cognitive advantage is not shared by children in home-based day care, although family day care is apparently superior in relation to physical development and health (fewer infectious diseases). Gwen Broude, The Realities of Day Care, The Public Interest, Fall 1996, at 99, 103.

Might there be additional values to a mother's employment in that her sons may be less likely to form traditional attitudes about the proper role of women?

8. If California were to pass a law requiring employers to provide day care for women employees' children, how would the formal equality theorists who opposed the maternity leave statute in the *Cal Fed* case (see Chapter 3) respond? Would such a law be constitutional? Would it violate Title VII? What if it were written in a gender-neutral fashion, even though the state contemplated that only women employees were likely to take advantage of it? *Should* California pass such a law?

9. The costs of obtaining child care for preschool children are substantial. The U.S. Census Bureau reported that in 1993, 56% of families paid an average of $74 per week for child care; families with two or more preschoolers paid about $110 per week. This was a nation-wide average for all types of paid child care arrangements. Census Bureau, Current Population Reports, Sept. 1995, What Does It Cost To Mind Our Preschoolers?, at 3. Depending upon the family income, these expenditures amounted to 6% to 25% of their monthly income. Id. at 4. Middle-class families in large metropolitan areas often pay much more. In Chicago and suburbs, for example, the cost of in-home care had reached as much as $400–$500 per week by the fall of 2000; and one large day care center located at a hospital was charging more than

$200 per week. The race and immigration status of a caregiver may influence the cost. See Taunya Lovell Banks, Toward a Global Critical Feminist Vision: Domestic Work and the Nanny Tax Debate, 3 J. Gender, Race & Justice 1, 31 nn.139–40 (1999) (reporting that the going rate for an inexperienced woman from the Caribbean working as a live-in "nanny" in New York City was $150 per week plus room and board, that Haitians were cheaper, due to both language difficulties and Americans' fear of AIDS, but that Hispanics started at $200 per week because they were white).

10. How would you address the race and class issues raised by the types of child care available in the United States? What would be the provisions of an ideal child care policy in this country, and how would it address these problems? How would such a policy be financed? How would you describe the child care policy we have now? What sort of child care program would you want available for your own child?

MARY ROMERO, MAID IN THE U.S.A.

98–103, 32–34, 37, 39–41 (1992).

Domestic service reveals the contradiction in a feminism that pushed for women's involvement outside the home, yet failed to make men take responsibility for household labor. Employed middle- and upper-middle class women escaped the double day syndrome by hiring poor women of color to perform housework and child care, and this was characterized as progress. Some feminists defined domestic service as progressive because traditional women's work moved into the labor market and became paid work. However, this definition neglects the inescapable fact that when women hire other women at low wages to do housework, both employees and employers remain women. As employers, women continued to accept responsibility for housework even if they supervised domestics who performed the actual labor. If we accept domestic service as central to women's oppression, the contradiction, as Linda Martin and Kerry Segrave have pointed out, is that "every time the housewife or working woman buys freedom for herself with a domestic, that very same freedom is denied to the domestic, for the maid must go home and do her own housework."[4]

Although the system of gender domination places the burden of housework on women, middle class women have financial resources to escape the drudgery of housework by paying someone else to do her work. * * * In other words, hire a woman of color and pay her as little as possible to fulfill your housework duties and responsibilities. The most exploitative form of domestic service is maintained through systems of gender, class and racial domination. Thus, middle-class American women aim to "liberate" themselves by exploiting women of color—particularly immigrants—in the underground economy, for long hours at relatively low wages, with no benefits.

4. Linda Martin and Kerry Segrave, *The Servant Problem: Domestic Workers in North America*, pp. 32–33.

* * * In *Las Mujeres*, Ida Gutierrez recounted the ways in which women employers determined her working conditions:

> Some of the ladies pay Social Security, but some of them don't. It all depends. If you're lucky, you find a woman that is real nice to you. If you get to meet one of those ladies, you got it made—they pay for your gas, or they give you money. But not all people are the same. I've worked for rich ladies who thought they'd go broke if they gave me a Coca–Cola. And they make you work real hard for your money, too—clean the walls, get down on your knees and scrub the floor.[9]

The present chapter draws upon my research with Chicana domestic workers as well as studies of African American, West Indian, Japanese American, and Central American immigrant women. Interviews with domestic workers describe interactions between white middle-class women employers and working class women of color that take place outside the public eye. The accounts describe working conditions and work relations and provide insight into the function of gender in shaping interclass and interracial social relationships. Investigating daily rituals and practices involving employer and employee provides a microperspective on the process whereby systems of gender, class, and race domination are reproduced in domestic service.

WHY DO WOMEN HIRE OTHER WOMEN

Why do white middle class employers hire working-class women of color as domestics? * * *

Let us overlook, for now, the illusion common among white middle-class women that hiring a woman of color to clean their toilets is a form of social benefit, reducing the unemployment rate. It is clear that African American, West Indian, Chicana, and Japanese American domestics describe working arrangements that challenge the thesis that personal service and status are vanishing needs no longer fulfilled in the occupation. They report a broad range of tasks including personal service and emotional labor, suggesting that servitude and traditional demeanor are still expected by some employers. * * *

Physical Labor

* * *

In their efforts to escape the diffuse duties of their housewife roles, employers do not acknowledge work boundaries. Even when the worker's tasks were agreed upon in a verbal contract, employees frequently reported that employers requested additional duties. For instance, household workers commonly complained that employers did not differentiate between housework and child care. In her interviews with women hired to do child care in New York City, Kathy Dobie found that "many of the women are hired as nannies and then asked if they

9. Nan Elsasser, Kyle MacKenzie and Yvonne Tixier y Vigil, *Las Mujeres: Conversations from a Hispanic Community*, p. 70–1.

wouldn't mind straightening up a bit. They are asked if they wouldn't clean, then shop, then do the laundry, then, etc." One child care worker told Dobie:

> I give her coffee, I take care of Stephen. I do the laundry. I go out and do the shopping. I buy her birth control tablets. I couldn't believe that ... Even the light bulbs in the ceiling, I change. Even her panties, I pick them up when she drops them on the floor.[13]

Soraya Moore Coley reported similar findings in her study on African American private household workers. Mrs. Green described how her job description changed:

> When she hired me, she told me I was to only take care of the children. Then, the woman starts leaving the house and asking me if I would do this or that. Before you know it, I'm taking care of the baby and doing the work. I enjoy the children and I guess I stayed because they become so attached to me—but the woman probably knew when she hired me, she wanted me to do other work.[14]

* * *

Not all housewives structured the work to relieve themselves of the burden of housework. Workers encountered employers who disregarded their years of experience and treated them as unskilled labor that required detailed instruction and supervision. * * * In her interview with Studs Terkel, Maggie Holmes described the demeaning and unnecessary nature of supervision:

> I don't like nobody checkin' behind me. When you go to work, they want to show you how to clean. I been doin' it all my life. They come and get the rag and show you how to do it. [laughs.] I stand there, look at 'em. Lotta times I ask her, "you finished?" I say, "if there's anything you gotta go and do, I'd wish you'd go." I don't need nobody to show me how to clean.[20]

* * *

CHICANA PRIVATE HOUSEHOLD WORKERS AS WORKING MOTHERS

* * *

For Chicana private household workers, having a job meant doing paid housework during the day and returning to do unpaid housework in their own homes. At home or on the job, there was no respite from housework.

* * *

13. Kathy Dobie, "Black Women, White Kids, A Tale of Two Worlds," p. 23.

14. Soraya Moore Coley, " 'And Still I Rise': An Exploratory Study of Contemporary Black Private Household Workers," p. 213.

20. Studs Terkel, *Working: People Talk About What They Do All Day and How They Feel About What They Do*, p. 118.

These women understood all too well the plight of working women. Homemaking activities ranged from the usual housecleaning, cooking, laundry, and shopping to endless errands, nursing, and child care. Although tasks and the amount of work differed among families, mothers with younger children were faced with additional tasks related to child care, including extra laundry, cooking, and housecleaning. Child care duties were frequently socialized to other family members by women who lived near their families of orientation; babysitting nephews, nieces, and grandchildren was not unusual.

* * *

In many cases the women arranged the job so that they were always at home when their families were there. Husbands' and children's schedules were rarely inconvenienced or altered. Consequently, husbands were not faced with the need to change the division of household labor. Like so many other mothers and wives, Chicanas were expected to cook, wash, iron, vacuum, dust, and care for children. For the most part, they did not escape the sexual division of labor that dominates household work today. About half of the women described a rigid sexual division of labor in household duties. * * *

All of the women approved of their husbands helping with housework, child care, cooking and other household chores; yet this did not mean that they voiced dissatisfaction with the division of labor between wife and husband. To some degree, the issue of equity was related to the husbands' perceived position as breadwinners. The women tended to discount the importance of their economic contributions to the family, characterizing their wages as "pin money." They described their wages as providing "extras" not afforded by their husbands' incomes. Objectively, however, the items included food, clothes, tuition, and bills. Clearly, the "extras" purchased by these wage-earning mothers are necessities rather than extras. They may not indeed be necessary for survival, but these items, which husbands' paychecks cannot cover, would be considered necessary by most middle-class families.

* * *

My inquiries about husbands helping with housework were usually interpreted as having to do with child care. Descriptions of the ways in which husbands "helped out" were almost uniformly the same: when wives were not home, husbands were responsible for the children. They watched the children and sometimes fed them if the wife had prepared food before she left. However, "watching the kids" did not necessarily involve the broad range of tasks such as bathing or cleaning up after the children. Husbands were more likely to supervise older children and make sure that their chores were done. In fact, most of the married women with school age children mentioned that their husbands helped with the housework by telling the children to do their chores. Mrs. Segura's response was typical:

> No he don't [do housework]. He'll tell the kids "that doesn't go there," "pick it up and take to the hamper" or "put it in your room."

* * *

In sum, the division of household labor left all these women with the double day. Like many other working mothers, Chicanas did not have enough help with housework, child care, laundry, and cooking. Mrs. Chacon voiced a wish to be able to afford to hire someone to help her with the spring-cleaning in her own home.

> I would appreciate someone—to be able to afford someone to come in and help me instead of taking one or two weeks to do the job. Instead you'd be able to pay someone to come in and have it done the way you want it done too.

Unlike higher-paid workers, they were unable to gain relief from the double day by replacing their labor with the labor of another. As workers in a poorly-paid occupation, Chicana household workers had limited resources and certainly could not afford the same solutions as middle-class women. Rarely could they afford to take the family to restaurants, order take-out, or fill the refrigerator with expensive frozen or precooked food. Nor could they afford to pay for child care. The cost of day care can be a burden for middle class women; it is especially onerous for low-paid workers. The lack of bilingual and bicultural services was also a problem in purchasing child-care services.

* * *

For the majority of women whose extended families lived in the city, female relatives were an important resource. Relatives—particularly grandmothers and sisters—were frequently called upon to care for the children during the day. Five of the women mentioned exchanging child-care services with relatives and neighbors. Relatives were especially helpful in preparing for the holidays. However, only women residing fairly close to their relatives were able to obtain regular assistance. More frequently, relatives were a source of aid only during a crisis. Sisters and mothers provided help during sickness, childbirth and emergencies. And, of course, relatives dropping in from out of town often created additional housework rather than provided additional help.

The Chicanas that I interviewed represented their choice of employment as a conscious strategy. When I asked, "Why did you start doing housework?" their response was not, "I couldn't find any other job." Rather, they began by comparing housework with previously held unskilled jobs. Jobs as line workers, nurse's aides, waitresses, or dishwashers had fixed schedules. Taking days off from fast-food restaurants, car washes or turkey farms jeopardized their employment. Explanations about the way in which domestic service was compatible with taking care of their families followed.

They emphasized that domestic service allowed them to arrange their own hours, and they could easily add or drop employers to lengthen or shorten the workweek. As private household workers, they were able to arrange hours and the workweek to care for sick children, to attend pta meetings, or to take children to the dentist. The flexible schedule also permitted women to participate in school functions or be active in church and community activities. Having control over their own schedules permitted the women to get their children off to school in the morning and be back home when school was over. Domestic service did not demand rigid commitments of time, nor did the occupation force women to make the job their first priority. Mrs. Garcia explained:

> You can change the dates if you can't go a certain day and if you have an appointment, you can go later, and work later, just as long as you get the work done.... I try to be there at the same time, but if I don't get there for some reason or another, I don't have to think I'm going to lose my job or something.

Two-thirds of the interviewees said that they selected domestic service over other low-paying jobs because the occupation offered the flexibility to fulfill family obligations. As Mrs. Lopez related:

> That's one thing with doing daywork—the children are sick or something, you just stayed home because that was my responsibility to get them to the doctor.

Mothers with preschool children preferred domestic service over other low-paying jobs that they had held in the past. Unable to afford a sitter or day-care, domestic service offered an alternative. Mrs. Rodriquez, a thirty-three-year-old mother of two, took her preschool children to work with her:

> I could take my kids with me. There were never any restrictions to taking the children. Most of the people I've worked for like kids, so I just take the kids with me. It's silly to have to work and pay a sitter. It won't work.

Mrs. Cordova also mentioned this aspect of domestic service as grounds for selecting the occupation:

> So that's what I enjoyed about housework is that I could take the kids along and not worry about not having a reliable baby-sitter. So that's mainly the reason I did it [domestic service], because I knew the kids were going to be all right and they were with me and they were fed and taken care of.

Flexibility was not an inherent characteristic of domestic service. Neither was taking children to the job. Provisions for both had to be negotiated in informal contracts and labor arrangements with employers.

* * *

Notes on Women of Color as Child Care Workers

1. In the excerpt above, Romero implies that the employment of women of color by middle-class women to care for their children and do their housework is exploitative per se and says that this reveals a contradiction in feminism. Do you agree or disagree with her position? Why?

2. Are there ways in which the interests of women of color employed as household workers and of the women who employ them are congruent? How?

3. Taunya Lovell Banks suggests that only socialist feminism, with its emphasis upon multiple systems of oppression, the need for significant structural changes, and collective action, provides an adequate analytical framework for analyzing the intersecting issues involved in working women's employment of other women to care for their children. Banks, Toward a Global Critical Feminist Vision: Domestic Work and the Nanny Tax Debate, 3 J. Gender, Race & Justice 1, 38–40 (1999). Do you agree? How would other feminist legal theorists studied in Chapter 3 address the problems raised by the employment of women of color as child care workers?

4. As Romero points out, one way upper-income and professional women in the U.S. deal with their dual roles in the home and in the economy is to shift the burden of child care onto another group of women, many of them undocumented workers employed at or below the minimum wage and with no benefits. The nomination in late 1992 by President Clinton of corporate lawyer Zoe Baird to be Attorney General focused national attention on the fact that many of these child care arrangements take place in the underground market, without payment of taxes or Social Security for the child care worker. Indeed, Clinton's first two nominees for Attorney General both withdrew over irregularities concerning the employment of women to care for children in their homes; he ultimately appointed a woman without children, Janet Reno, as the first woman Attorney General. See Mona Harrington, Care and Equality: Inventing a New Family Politics 11–24 (1999). According to Mona Harrington, the Clinton Administration was surprised by the uproar over this issue because it had focused upon the gender issue and failed to notice the class issues involved; it was thus unprepared for the outrage of many Americans about Baird's domestic arrangements. The central problem, Harrington says, is that "we have not devised any equality-respecting system to replace the full-time caretaking labor force of women at home." Id. at 17. What do you think of this analysis? Whose equality counts the most? That of women in the workplace required to compete with men who have no caretaking duties, or that of the women looking after those women's children? How can these problems, which Harrington calls "care-equality problems," be addressed? Taunya Banks points out that feminists also missed an opportunity at the time of the so-called "Nannygate" controversy to force a more general public debate about the gendered nature of mothering and other domestic work. Banks, note 3 above, at 5.

5. In the first part of the 20th century, there was in fact a movement to improve the conditions of domestic workers by encouraging employers to

use voluntary, standardized labor contracts and by lobbying for passage of labor legislation applicable to domestic service. See Peggie R. Smith, Regulating Paid Household Work: Class, Gender, Race, and Agendas of Reform, 48 Am. U. L. Rev. 851, 882–917 (1999). A National Committee on Household Employment, chaired by Eleanor Roosevelt, drafted labor standards to govern the employment relationship. Id. at 884–85. When the New Deal labor legislation was passed, however, domestic service was excluded from the Fair Labor Standards Act, the National Labor Relations Act, and the Social Security Act. Id. at 888–89. Smith attributes these failures to a number of factors, including the economic devaluation of housework in general as non-productive work; reluctance to think of the home as a unit of production or of household employers, who were women, as requiring regulation; and unwillingness to accept interference with family privacy. Id. at 898–912. Moreover, as white women left domestic service and were increasingly replaced by women of color, political support for protection of domestic workers decreased. Id. at 915–16.

6. How can conditions be improved for the women who care for other women's children? Domestic workers are now covered by Social Security, but compliance with domestic employment laws is very low. Although Congress simplified the payment of employment taxes after the Zoe Baird fiasco by eliminating quarterly reporting requirements, increasing the threshold amount, and exempting wages paid to certain family members, the number of household employers filing employment tax returns fell from 500,000 in 1994 to 300,000 in 1995. Debra Cohen–Whelan, Protecting the Hand That Rocks the Cradle: Ensuring the Delivery of Work Related Benefits to Child Care Workers, 32 Ind. L. Rev. 1187, 1192–93 (1999). It is conservatively estimated that fewer than 25% of household employers comply with the requirements of the Social Security Act on behalf of their domestic employees. Smith, above note 5, at 921. One commentator suggests a carrot-and-stick approach to enforcing the law—selecting income tax returns of dual-income couples with high salaries and exemptions for dependents for special scrutiny, and increasing the incentive to comply by providing a deduction for child care as a business expense, thus defraying much of the cost of paying employment taxes. Cohen–Whelan, above, at 1205–07, 1213–15. In this way, domestic workers would be able to claim Social Security benefits when they retire or are disabled, as well as unemployment compensation. These measures may not address the treatment of undocumented immigrant workers, however, who typically work for lower wages and do not want their employment relationships revealed. This is not surprising, as Taunya Banks notes, given that the Congressional debates following the "Nannygate" controversy focused primarily on the problems of affluent working women and, when the interests of the women employed as child care workers were considered, upon the needs only of native-born minority workers, not of foreign-born resident child care providers. Banks, note 3 above, at 14–15.

3. THE STATE AND CHILD CARE

In contrast to other major industrialized countries, the United States has no comprehensive policy on child care. In its absence, the outlines of a policy of sorts can nonetheless be discerned indirectly, for example, in the structure of the Family and Medical Leave Act, described above; in the indirect subsidization of child care expenses through the tax code; and in the implications of recent welfare legislation for the care of children born to poor women. In this section we focus on the policy implications for child care of provisions in the Internal Revenue Code and of welfare reform requiring mothers to work.

Text Note: Child Care and the Internal Revenue Code

The cost of caring for young children is an expense incurred by mothers who are employed in the wage labor market. However, it has never been classified as a business expense under the Internal Revenue Code. In a 1939 case, a working couple claimed a deduction for the expenses of employing others to look after their young child. The Tax Court rejected classification of these costs as a business expense, explaining that:

> We are not prepared to say that the care of children, like similar aspects of family and household life, is other than a personal concern. The wife's services as custodian of the home and protector of its children are ordinarily rendered without monetary compensation. There results no taxable income from the performance of this service and the correlative expenditure is personal and not susceptible of deduction. Here the wife has chosen to employ others to discharge her domestic function * * *. But that does not deprive the same work performed by others of its personal character nor furnish a reason why its cost should be treated as an offset in the guise of a deductible item.
>
> * * *
>
> It may for practical purposes be said to constitute a distinction between those activities which, as a matter of common acceptance and universal experience, are "ordinary" or usual as the direct accompaniment of business pursuits, on the one hand; and those which, though they may in some indirect and tenuous degree relate to the circumstances of a profitable occupation, are nevertheless personal in their nature, of a character applicable to human beings generally, and which exist on that plane regardless of the occupation, though not necessarily of the station in life, of the individuals concerned.
>
> In the latter category, we think, fall payments made to servants or others occupied in looking to the personal wants of their employers. And we include in this group nursemaids retained to care for infant children.

Smith v. Commissioner of Internal Revenue, 40 B.T.A. 1038, 1039–40 (1939), aff'd, 113 F.2d 114 (2d Cir.1940).

One argument against granting a tax deduction for child care is that the greatest benefit would flow to those individuals who earn the most, whose income is therefore likely to be taxed at a higher rate, and for whom a deduction from income is thus likely to provide a greater benefit. Such a deduction would have the same regressive effect, this argument runs, as if the federal government were to provide cash payments for child care that increased as income increased. However valid this point may be, it has not prevailed with respect to those expenses which the tax law has decided to treat as business expenses, including the cost of automobiles, home offices, and business meals.

Although child care is still not deductible as a business expense, the Internal Revenue Code does now include a limited provision for a tax credit for cash spent for child care. 26 U.S.C. § 21 (1986). A credit against taxes theoretically eliminates the disparity between higher- and lower-bracket taxpayers since everyone gets the same benefit, while a deduction would provide more benefit to higher bracket taxpayers. However, the credit is of no value if the taxpayer makes so little as to not have a positive tax liability against which to offset the credit. Moreover, the credit is based on only a maximum of $2,400 spent for one child and $4,800 for two or more children, regardless of how much is actually spent; and only 30% of the amount spent may be credited, less 1% for each $2,000 in adjusted gross income above $10,000, thus making the credit worth less to middle- and upper-income taxpayers who spend large sums on child care. In addition, the credit may not be taken if the caregiver could be claimed as a dependent on the taxpayer's return, thus generally excluding payments to any relative living in the household. Hence, the credit may not be available for child care by a relative, although such care, typically by a female relative, is a very common support system for poor women.

The current Internal Revenue Code also allows an employee to pay in pretax dollars for up to $5,000 in child care, if the employer maintains a plan providing for the setting aside and reimbursement of such expenses, a provision which gives higher-bracket taxpayers a larger benefit by shielding their marginal income. The amount is taken out of the employee's income, placed in an account by the employer, and not reported as taxable income for that year; the employee then receives the amounts set aside only when she presents evidence of payments actually made for dependent care during that calendar year. By 1998, about 50% of companies with 100 or more employees offered this type of plan that helps employees pay for child care with pretax dollars. Families and Work Institute, The 1998 Business Work–Life Study: A Sourcebook v (1998) (surveying a representative sample of 1,057 companies). The tax code also allows an employer to provide child care directly in an equivalent amount, without taxing the benefit to the employee. 26 U.S.C. § 129.

In addition, the Taxpayer Relief Act of 1997 introduced a per-child credit against taxes owed for those with dependent children under the age of 17. For those with one or two children, the credit is a nonrefundable credit of $500 per child, phased out at $75,000 for single taxpayers or heads of households, and $110,000 for married taxpayers filing jointly. It is reduced by $50 for each $1,000 over these threshold amounts. Thus, the benefit is totally phased out if taxpayers with one child have more than $10,000 over the threshold and those with two children have more than $20,000 over the threshold, cutting off many middle-class households in high-cost areas of the country.

In addition to denying a business expense deduction for child care, the Internal Revenue Code supports a traditional division of labor within the family by creating other disincentives for wives to work, for example, by (1) taxing the income of the secondary earner (usually the wife, who is typically paid less, is more likely to work part time, and may enter and leave the paid workforce at various points in her life cycle) at the marginal rate of the primary earner; (2) imposing regressive Social Security tax rates (the same percentage of income is paid by all wage earners, until they reach the annual maximum amount); and (3) failing to impute income for unpaid labor by homemakers. See Nancy C. Staudt, Taxing Housework, 84 Geo. L.J. 1571, 1590–92, 1607–10 (1996); Edward J. McCaffery, Taxing Women 91–93, 120–22, 137–60 (1997).

Notes on Child Care and the Internal Revenue Code

1. According to the Tax Court in *Smith*, child care should not be deductible as a business expense in part because it is not one of "those activities which, as a matter of common acceptance and universal experience, are 'ordinary' or usual as the direct accompaniment of business pursuits," but rather is an activity which though it "may in some indirect and tenuous degree relate to the circumstances of a profitable occupation, [is] nevertheless personal . . . , applicable to human beings generally, . . . regardless of the occupation, though not necessarily of the station in life, of the individuals concerned." Deconstruct this argument. What are the interests underlying the distinction being made? With what is the court really concerned? Is this argument gender-based? Is the description by the *Smith* court dated, or does it still describe the attitude toward child care in our society?

The Canadian supreme court considered the issue of child care as a business expense more recently, in light of its constitutional prohibition of sex discrimination, but reached essentially the same decision as the *Smith* court. Symes v. Canada, 110 D.L.R. 4th 470 (1993). Ironically, although the case discussed the issue in light of the right to equality on the basis of sex as explicitly guaranteed by the Canadian Charter of Rights and Freedoms, these arguments failed on the ground that men with primary child care responsibilities were equally disadvantaged by the limitations on the deductibility of child care costs! Id. at 559.

2. Mary Louise Fellows asserts that the author of the opinion in Smith v. Commissioner "relies on accepted roles based on class, gender, and, in a less obvious way, race to create the appearance of applying tax rules objectively." Fellows, Rocking the Tax Code: A Case Study of Employment–Related Child–Care Expenditures, 10 Yale J.L. & Feminism 307, 311, 374–79 (1998). Among other things, the opinion fails to address the problem that a family in which both parents work forgoes the tax benefit of the imputed income available to them if one stayed at home and performed child care for the family unit. The mother's payment of another individual to perform these services instead is treated as a personal choice. Which is the choice involved: to have children or to enter the workforce? Does the mother go to work to earn the money to consume child care or purchase child care in order to go to work? In what sense should these be treated as personal choices?

3. Should feminists support an income tax deduction for child care, if it benefits some groups of women more than others? Why or why not?

4. Allowing pretax payments for dependent care under a benefits reimbursement account with the employer provides a subsidy for some mothers—those who are employed by large institutional employers who set up such an account—and shuts out those employed part-time or with smaller employers who do not have such accounts, with a detrimental effect on many lower-income mothers who need child care in order to find employment. It also removes pressure from Congress to acknowledge that child care should be treated as a business expense for which a deduction should be allowed. Would you eliminate it for these reasons? How would you alter this arrangement in the interests of fairness and equality?

5. In one case, the Tax Court held that welfare payments paid to a mother for the care of her disabled adult child were taxable as income to the mother, although welfare payments are generally nontaxable. Bannon v. Commissioner, 99 T.C. 59 (1992). Why must a related caregiver who uses those payments to care for the welfare recipient pay tax on them, when the welfare recipient herself is not required to do so? Why is this "income," if money given to a mother who is a homemaker by the child's father is not imputed as income to her? (Note: Child support after divorce is not taxable to the mother, although maintenance or alimony must be included in her taxable income.) What are the assumptions underlying these distinctions? See, e.g., Grace Blumberg, Sexism in the Code: A Comparative Study of Income Taxation of Working Wives and Mothers, 21 Buff. L. Rev. 49 (1971).

6. When the Internal Revenue Code creates a disincentive for wives to work, whom does this advantage? Whom does it disadvantage? Should government be creating such incentives? Why or why not? How can they be eliminated? See, e.g., Note, A Feminist Justification for the Adoption of an Individual Filing System, 62 S. Cal. L. Rev. 197 (1988). Would removing the "marriage penalty" remove the disincentive for wives to work or to marry?

Text Note: Welfare Reform

Recent changes in the U.S. welfare system have had a dramatic impact upon the relationship of women to their children. These "reforms" also mark a dramatic break from traditional views about the value of women caring for their own children in the home. The previous welfare system, Aid to Families with Dependent Children ("AFDC"), had its origins in New Deal Social Security legislation. The program was designed primarily with white women in mind—widows or women who had been abandoned—and it assumed that these women would not work. Dorothy Roberts, Killing the Black Body: Race, Reproduction and the Meaning of Liberty 205–06 (1997). Thus AFDC provided a type of income support for the children of these mothers, although it was never as generous as the level of support given to former wage-earners under the Social Security system and was in fact inadequate to support a woman and her family.

AFDC was a federal program that reimbursed states for part of the benefits provided under a state welfare scheme, so long as the state scheme complied with federal requirements. It was a so-called entitlement program, that is, there was a federally guaranteed entitlement to assistance for persons covered by its terms, and states were guaranteed a matching share of whatever amount was necessary to provide benefits to all who qualified for the program. Jane C. Murphy, Legal Images of Motherhood: Conflicting Definitions from Welfare "Reform," Family, and Criminal Law, 83 Cornell L. Rev. 688 (1998).

Initially, virtually all AFDC recipients were white; indeed, African Americans were largely excluded from the program's benefits until the 1960's. See Linda Gordon, Pitied But Not Entitled: Single Mothers and the History of Welfare 1890–1935 15, 276 (1994). As the civil rights movement and accompanying litigation forced the inclusion of women and children of color, work requirements gradually began to be added to the program. In the 1970's, women with school-age children were required to register to work, and the Family Support Act of 1988 required women whose children were three or older to work or enter training to work. Murphy, above, at 734.

A stereotype of the Black welfare mother was exploited by the New Right in the 1980's to attack the system of welfare as a whole, and presidential candidate Bill Clinton also vowed to "end welfare as we know it." Id. at 735. The Personal Responsibility and Work Opportunity Reconciliation Act (PRWORA) of 1996 was the result. 42 U.S.C. §§ 601–607. PRWORA abolished the federal entitlement system, replacing it with a block-grant program under which states were given a fixed sum, regardless of the level of need, and the states were given authority to decide eligibility requirements as well as the overall structure of the state program. However, PRWORA required two major changes in all state programs receiving funding. First, absolute time limits were imposed upon the receipt of benefits: a five-year cumulative lifetime maximum for any family, and a two-year deadline for all current recipients to find other means of support. Second, all recipients were required to work, regardless of the age of their children. Many states also added so-called "Family Caps," providing that no additional amounts would be included in a family's benefits upon the birth of a child to a mother who was already receiving benefits. Roberts, above, at 210–25.

In sum, the welfare reforms of the 1990's contradicted both the original assumptions of the AFDC program and the "family" rhetoric of the New Right—that a young child was best cared for by his or her mother. At the same time, the new program made woefully inadequate provision for child care. Although PRWORA includes funding to states for child care purposes (42 U.S.C. § 601), the Congressional Budget Office estimated that it falls $13.1 billion short of meeting the needs of mothers faced with the new work requirements during the period from 1997 to 2002. Murphy, above, at 740 n.281. A recent study reports that as a result of changes in the welfare law, "[a]bout a million additional toddlers and preschoolers are in child care because of changes in the welfare laws, but many are in low-quality care and are lagging in language and social development." Tamar Lewin, Study Finds Welfare Changes Lead a Million Into Child Care, N.Y. Times, Feb. 4, 2000, at A16 (describing a Berkeley/Yale study of 1000 single mothers moving from welfare to work).

DOROTHY E. ROBERTS, THE VALUE OF BLACK MOTHERS' WORK,

26 Conn. L. Rev. 871–78 (1994).

I. WHY MUST WELFARE MOTHERS WORK?

The common ground of contemporary welfare reform discourse is the belief that single mothers' dependence on government support is irresponsible and should be remedied by requiring these mothers to get jobs. "Workfare" is a refrain of the general theme that blames the poor, because of their dependence mentality, deviant family structure, and other cultural depravities, for their poverty. Martha Minow reveals workfare's injustice by asking the unspoken question, "why should single mothers responsible for young children be expected to work outside the home?"[2] Why does society focus on welfare mothers' dependence on public assistance rather than on their children's dependence on them for care?

Minow correctly points out that the focus on welfare mothers' dependence rather than their valuable care reflects a radical departure from the original welfare policy towards mothers. During the late nineteenth century, women successfully lobbied for public relief for widowed mothers. In her recent book, Protecting Soldiers and Mothers: The Political Origins of Social Policy in the United States, Theda Skocpol demonstrates how women's organizations and their allies exploited the ideology of motherhood to attain mothers' pensions and other "maternalist" legislation. The logic that propelled maternalist welfare policy was precisely the opposite of that backing workfare: widowed mothers needed government aid so that they would not have to relinquish their maternal duties in the home in order to join the work force. This maternalist rhetoric was powerful enough to mobilize disenfranchised women, defeat conservative opponents, and convince American legislatures to embark on social welfare programs far ahead of those of most European countries.

The current workfare proposals, then, reflect an unprecedented depreciation of welfare mothers' contribution to society. The rhetoric of motherhood has lost all of the persuasive force it wielded during the Progressive Era. The modern welfare state has increasingly degraded the work all mothers perform. It has abandoned the moral mother ideology and diminished the control of mothers over child care. As increasing numbers of women join the work force, society decreasingly rewards mothers' socially productive labor in the home. An individual's entitlement to welfare benefits now depends on his or her relationship to the market. Former workers are entitled to compensation by social insurance programs for their prior participation in the wage labor force. As unpaid caregivers with no connection to a male breadwinner, single mothers are considered undeserving clients of the welfare system.

This universal devaluation of mothers' work, however, does not explain entirely the revolution in welfare reform. When welfare reform-

2. Martha Minow, The Welfare of Single Mothers and Their Children, 26 Conn. L. Rev. 817 (1994). * * *

ers devise remedies for maternal irresponsibility, they have Black single mothers in mind. Although marital status does not determine economic well-being, there is a strong association between Black single motherhood and family poverty. The image of the lazy Black welfare queen who breeds children to fatten her allowance shapes public attitudes about welfare policy. Part of the reason that maternalist rhetoric can no longer justify public financial support is that the public views this support as benefitting primarily Black mothers. Society particularly devalues Black mothers' work in the home because it sees these mothers as inherently unfit and their children as inherently useless.

II. THE VALUE OF BLACK MOTHERING

Maternalist rhetoric has no appeal in the case of Black welfare mothers because society sees no value in supporting their domestic service. The public views these mothers as less fit, less caring, and less hurt by separation from their children. First, workfare advocates fail to see the benefit in poor Black mothers' care for their young children. To the contrary, contemporary poverty rhetoric blames Black single mothers for perpetuating poverty by transmitting a deviant lifestyle to their children. Far from helping children, payments to Black single mothers merely encourage this transgenerational pathology. Dominant images have long depicted Black mothers as unfit. * * * Modern social pundits from Daniel Patrick Moynihan to Charles Murray have held Black single mothers responsible for the disintegration of the Black family and the Black community's consequent despair.[15]

Second, workfare advocates fail to see the injury in requiring Black mothers to leave their young children. Welfare reform discourse gives little attention to the relationship between poor Black mothers and their children. The forced separation of Black mothers from their children began during slavery, when Black family members faced being auctioned off to different masters. Slave mothers knew the regular pain of seeing their loved ones "rented out, loaned out, bought up, brought back, stored up, mortgaged, won, stolen or seized."[18] The disproportionate state disruption of Black families through the child welfare system reflects a continuing depreciation of the bond between Black mothers and their children.

Finally, workfare advocates are not hindered by any disharmony in the idea of a Black working mother. The conception of motherhood confined to the home and opposed to wage labor never applied to Black women. Slave women's hard labor in the field defied the Victorian norm of female domesticity. Even after Emancipation, political and economic conditions forced many Black mothers to earn a living outside the home. Americans expected Black mothers to look like Aunt Jemima, working in somebody else's kitchen: "(o)utfitted in an unflattering dress, apron, and

15. See Charles Murray, Losing Ground: American Social Policy, 1950–1980, at 154–66 (1984) (claiming that welfare induces Black women to refrain from marriage and to have babies)* * *

18. Toni Morrison, Beloved 23 (1987).

scarf (a 'headrag'), she is always ready for work and never ready for bed."[22] American culture reveres no Black madonna; it upholds no popular image of a Black mother nurturing her child. Given this history, it is not surprising that policymakers do not think twice about requiring welfare mothers to leave their young children in order to go to work.

III. THE VALUE OF BLACK CHILDREN

The state often uses the pretext of helping children to justify regulating their mothers. What is striking about recent welfare proposals is that they do not even claim the traditional justification of promoting children's welfare. Indeed, they mandate or encourage practices traditionally regarded as harmful to children, such as mothers working outside the home and abortion. Welfare reformers cannot demonstrate that it is better for poor children to make their mothers work. Minow convincingly describes the extra dangers these children face. Their mothers' employment may actually reduce the amount of money available for their needs and jeopardize their health care; it may deprive them of their only protection against a myriad of environmental hazards. Thus, it is not mothers' wage labor itself that is harmful to children; rather, workfare's harm lies in its failure to provide meaningful support for working mothers, such as day care, jobs, housing, health care, education and a guaranteed income.

Underlying the consensus that welfare mothers should work is often the conviction that their children are socially worthless, lacking any potential to contribute to society. Welfare reform rhetoric assumes that these children will grow up to be poor and, consequently, burdens to society. The proposals dismiss any possible reason to nurture, inspire, or love these children. Minow asks at the end of her essay, "why not consider paying mothers of especially young children to care for their children?" In addition to the historic resistance to compensating mothers' work, society's response is, "because these children are not worth it."

The reason for society's bleak assessment is not only the belief that Black mothers are likely to corrupt their children, but that Black children are predisposed to corruption. * * * The powerful Western image of childhood innocence does not seem to benefit Black children. Black children are born guilty. They are potential menaces—criminals, crackheads, and welfare mothers waiting to happen. * * *

This devaluation of Black children, like the devaluation of Black mothering, is older than recent poverty discourse. It stems from a racial caste system based on white superiority and racial purity that has endured for three centuries. In this supposedly natural hierarchy, Black mothers inevitably pass down to their children a whole set of inferior traits. Racist ideology dictates that Black bodies, intellect, and character

22. Regina Austin, Black Women, Sisterhood, and the Difference/Deviance Divide, 26 New Eng. L. Rev. 877, 883 (1992).

are all inherently vulgar. This history enhances Stephanie Coontz's account of the family's political role.[34] American society's embrace of the private family as its model for social accountability is particularly devastating for Black children. According to Coontz, society's empathy extends only to people "whom we can imagine as potential lovers or family members."[35] America's legacy of racial separation makes it especially difficult—if not impossible—for most white Americans to imagine Black children as part of their family.

Notes on Welfare Reform and Child Care

1. Is the public opposition to women on welfare because they are single, because they do not work, or because they are assumed to be Black? (In fact, only 39.5% of AFDC recipients in 1990 were African American; non-Hispanic whites were 38.1%. Lucy A. Williams, The Ideology of Division: Behavior Modification Welfare Reform Proposals, 102 Yale L.J. 719, 744 (1992).) Linda C. McClain notes, as well, the gendered assumptions underlying the critique of welfare, with its emphasis upon the "irresponsibility" of mothers who procreate without either a husband or adequate economic resources, rather than upon men's failure to take responsibility for contraception, to be involved and nurturing parents, and to pay child support. McClain, "Irresponsible" Reproduction, 47 Hastings L.J. 339, 422–25 (1996).

2. The welfare reform legislation is premised upon the belief that it is possible to modify the behavior of welfare recipients by the terms of a statute. Lucy Williams challenges this reasoning by examining the false assumptions under an idea like a Family Cap, which limits the number of children for whom aid may be given. Williams, above note 1, at 736–41. The legislation assumes, among other things, that: welfare mothers have many children; they have viable family planning options; and they get pregnant in order to receive additional benefits. In reality, as of 1990, 72.5% of AFDC families had only one or two children; only about 10% had more than three. Id. at 737. Moreover, childbearing decisions appear not to correlate with economics in general; and birthrates among welfare recipients are not higher where benefits are high. Id. at 739–40. Finally, as noted in Chapter 6, poor women have little access to medical care, often have little control over the conditions under which they become pregnant, and are unable to obtain government funding for abortions. Why do you think so many false assumptions persist in the face of evidence to the contrary?

3. The welfare reform legislation also assumes that welfare recipients do not work because they do not want to; the new law is expected to modify behavior in this respect as well. In fact, poor women who are mothers do work, or try to, although there are simply not enough jobs in the economy for unskilled workers without experience. Indeed, the median stay on AFDC in 1990, prior to the reforms, was 23 months. Williams, above note 1, at 744. Jody Raphael suggests that one reason women may not be able to keep jobs, or join training programs, is domestic violence, and deliberate sabotage by

34. See Stephanie Coontz, The Way We Never Were: American Families and the Nostalgia Trap (1992).

35. Id. at 115.

the abuser of any attempt to establish economic independence of him. Raphael, Domestic Violence and Welfare Receipt: Toward A New Feminist Theory of Welfare Dependency, 19 Harv. Women's L.J. 201, 203–07 (1996). What policies are necessary to address this problem? See also Joan Meier, Domestic Violence, Character, and Social Change in the Welfare Reform Debate, 19 Law & Policy 205, 209–12 (1997) (summarizing empirical research showing that over 50% of women on welfare are presently or have recently been victims of domestic violence and describing the causal connection between the abuse and women's inability to participate in welfare-to-work programs or become economically self-sufficient).

4. Is the fact that women in general are moving into the workforce, and thus that middle-class women with children work, a good reason to require women who are on welfare to be employed as well? Why or why not? Do you believe that mothers in general should work outside the home, or only those who wish to do so? Should it depend upon whether they are able to find work that yields a benefit greater than their caretaking in the home would yield? How would you measure this?

5. Is there any way to reconcile the New Right rhetoric of family values and opposition to working mothers and day care, on the one hand, and its support for requiring welfare mothers to work, on the other? To what extent do patriarchal notions play a role in this rhetoric? Should the wife be at home because she has a husband or because she has a child? Or is racism the only explanation for this seeming anomaly?

6. Is the conservative critique of welfare consistent with opposition to abortion? What alternatives are assumed to be available to a young woman without economic resources who becomes pregnant, or is abandoned by the father of her children, or leaves him to escape domestic violence? See McClain, above note 1, at 396–408 (describing the intersection of arguments about abortion and about "irresponsible" reproduction).

7. As Roberts points out in the excerpt above, the welfare reforms "mandate or encourage practices traditionally regarded as harmful to children, such as mothers working outside the home and abortion.... Their mothers' employment may actually reduce the amount of money available for their [poor children's] needs and jeopardize their health care; it may deprive them of their only protection against a myriad of environmental hazards." Do the values embedded in the welfare reform legislation reflect a more general abandonment of the notion that it is important for mothers to care for their children and a denigration of the value of mothers' work? Or only for Black mothers and their children?

E. CUSTODY

Text Note: The Development of Custody Preferences

Well into the 19th century, fathers automatically retained custody of their children at divorce or separation because children were their father's property and under his control at all times. By the end of the 19th century, this paternal preference was replaced in most jurisdictions by a presumption that children "of tender years" (somewhere between the ages of 5 and 12 depending on the child and the judge) were best off in the custody of their mothers. When a judge regarded a child as no longer "of tender years," custody was awarded according to the best interest of the child standard, which directs the judge to place the child in that household which (in the judge's view) will be best for the child. With the advent of the second wave of the women's movement, the tender years doctrine came under attack because it treated women and men differently and was therefore inconsistent with formal equality. As a result, between 1970 and 1990, the maternal preference was replaced in almost all jurisdictions by some version of the "best interest of the child" standard.

Several other approaches have been used in recent years. Many jurisdictions have moved toward joint custody, which can mean either joint *legal* custody only (joint decisionmaking on matters such as education and health care with a primary custodial parent and visitation for the noncustodial parent) *or* joint legal custody combined with joint *physical* custody (child resides half the time with each parent). Although joint custody first developed as an arrangement set out in divorce settlement agreements by some parents and tolerated by the courts, in many places it was pressed upon divorcing parents by mediators and judges even when the parents did not agree to it, on the theory that continued close contact with both parents is always in the best interest of the child. Another approach, the "primary-caretaker" standard, was adopted in West Virginia and Minnesota, though it has now been abandoned in both jurisdictions. Minnesota returned to the best interest standard, and West Virginia has adopted the standard of the American Law Institute's Principles of Family Dissolution. The ALI standard is akin to the primary-caretaker standard but applies the underlying principle that children are likely to be best off after divorce in the care of the person who cared for them prior to the divorce in as many cases as possible, not just those in which one parent has been a *primary* caretaker. The ALI standard therefore provides that, whenever possible, the court is to apportion custody so as to approximate the proportion of time each parent spent caring for the child during marriage. Each of these approaches is discussed in the article which follows. Katharine Bartlett, the author, was the Reporter for the ALI's Principles of Family Dissolution.

KATHARINE T. BARTLETT, CHILD CUSTODY IN THE 21ST CENTURY: HOW THE AMERICAN LAW INSTITUTE PROPOSES TO ACHIEVE PREDICTABILITY AND STILL PROTECT THE INDIVIDUAL CHILD'S BEST INTERESTS

35 Willamette L. Rev. 467, 468–81 (1999).

I. The Open-Ended Best-Interests-of-the-Child Test

Let us consider the case of Jane and David. Like most couples today, both work outside the home, and both are actively involved in the caretaking of their two children, Sara, 8, and Jamelle, 10. David works longer hours and earns more money than Jane. Jane, who works thirty hours per week outside the home, assumes primary responsibility for the children. She makes the after-school arrangements, goes to the parent-teacher conferences, sees to the children's doctor's appointments, and performs a majority of the bedtime and morning routines, weekend care, and meal preparation.

Jane and David have different parenting styles. David believes in firm rules, high expectations, and regular chores. He will not negotiate bedtimes, dinner menus, homework routines, or the children's choice of movies. Jane is a freer spirit who is more spontaneous and creative with the children. She does not interrupt her quality time with the children with an artificial bedtime or rigid schedule for homework and chores. The children have more fun when they are with Jane, but they are better behaved when with David. There are other differences as well. David goes to church; Jane does not. David reads voraciously and has tried to pass on his love of literature, fine art, and classical music to the children; Jane enjoys board games, cards, television, and rock and roll.

A year ago, Jane had an affair, for which David has not forgiven her. Their relationship has deteriorated, they have decided to divorce, and now they each want custody of the children. Who should win? What rule should govern the case?

For a long time, the rule thought to best serve the child's interests at divorce was the best-interests-of-the-child test. This test simply adopts the goal as the standard itself, leaving it to the judge to determine what custodial arrangement, on a case-by-case basis considering all of the relevant facts, produces the best result for the child. The advantages of the test are obvious: (1) it relies on individualized determinations for Sara and Jamelle specifically, not generalizations about what is good for all children or the average child; (2) it focuses decisionmaking on the child, rather than on the interests of the state of Oregon or on Jane's or David's own desires; and (3) it creates the greatest amount of flexibility in decisionmaking.

As many others have pointed out, this broad, individualized standard also has a number of flaws. Most especially, the standard allows so much judicial discretion that Jane and David may find it hard to predict what the court will do. Either party may win and, thus, each has reason to secure his or her respective advantage, most likely at the expense of cooperation with the other. For example, David may ask for primary custody, even if he does not want it, to create some negotiating room. He may attempt to build his reputation as the more responsible parent by alienating Jane from the court-appointed psychiatrist, the children's teachers, or the parents of the children's friends. Jane, for her part, may begin to exclude David from decisionmaking, or suggest to the children in subtle, or not-so-subtle, ways, that their father is a real drag. None of these strategies is likely to benefit the children.

To convince the court that he or she is the better parent, David and Jane will each hire experts. These experts can be expensive. What will they do to earn their fees? Jane is likely to want experts who will give testimony in open court about how flexible, caring, and nurturing she is, and what a cold, uncaring, rigid and distant figure their father is.

David's experts, in turn, will attempt to highlight Jane's irresponsibility, her sexual immorality, and her lack of discipline of the children, while emphasizing David's rock-steady parenting skills. This dirty linen will be aired in custody reports or in open court, furthering the alienation between the parents.

After hearing from the experts, the teachers, the friends, Jane and David themselves, and perhaps even the children, how will the court decide? Under the best-interests test, any sense the court makes of the evidence will be determined by what it determines is best for children. The judge cannot separate that determination from the judge's beliefs about what matters to the child's welfare. If the judge thinks organized religion is beneficial for children, he or she will favor David on that account. If the judge thinks that what matters most is how much time a parent has spent caring for the child, Jane will have the edge, unless the judge believes that a good mother would have stayed home and spent her time caring for children rather than trying to advance her career. If the judge thinks that spontaneity and creativity are better for children than firm routines, Jane wins. On the other hand, if Jane's extramarital affair makes her a bad parent in the judge's eyes, she is more likely to lose.

No matter who gets custody, the matter is not necessarily over, for the facts may change. For example, assume Jane wins primary custody, but then her boyfriend moves in with her and the children. While the judge may have been willing to overlook Jane's marital infidelity episode before the divorce, he may feel differently about her engaging on an ongoing basis in behavior he deems immoral. David may think it is worth a try to find out. If so, the whole case will be relitigated—as it may be also if Jane decides to relocate to Idaho or takes a job that requires her to rely more heavily on day care.

II. Alternatives to the Best Interests Test

Any standard example like the one outlined demonstrates a number of difficulties with the best-interests test: uncertainty and unpredictability, stimulation of strategic behavior, encouragement of litigation, and the requirement of costly experts in a setting that emphasizes finger-pointing over cooperation. In light of these and related difficulties, policy-makers and scholars have been attempting for years to refine the best interests test, in order to achieve, with a greater degree of predictability, decisions that are best for children. It is important to see that these refinements are alternatives to the best-interests test, not alternatives to the child's best interests. They represent efforts to determine the child's interests without producing the "anti-child consequences." After examining the alternatives, this part explains why the ALI approach is the most promising one.

A. "Laundry List" Approach

The first—and by far the most common—way legislators have attempted to make the best-interests test more specific and predictable is to detail a "laundry list" of factors that courts must consider in applying the best-interests test. Oregon's statute, for example, lists the following factors: (1) the emotional ties between the child and other family members; (2) the parties' interest in and attitude toward the child; (3) the desirability of continuing an existing relationship; (4) the abuse of one parent by the other; and (5) the willingness and ability of each parent to facilitate and encourage a close and continuing relationship between the other parent and the child. Other statutes mention the child's physical, emotional, mental, religious, and social needs and the capability and desire of each parent to meet these needs, the child's preferences, and the stability of each home environment.

The laundry-list approach to determining the child's best interests appears to add specificity and concreteness. Two difficulties, however, make this approach less likely to produce a predictable result than the best-interests test itself. First, the lists focus on factors such as parenting abilities and the quality of relationships, which are as intangible and difficult to measure as the child's best interests. Second, the approach fails to prioritize the factors under consideration. A court may decide that Jane has a stronger emotional bond with her children, but that David is more mature and has better parenting abilities. Who, then, should win? When the factors do not all point in a single direction—that is, when guidelines are needed most—they leave the decisionmaker to decide which factors matters most, with no useful guidance from the rule itself.

B. Primary Caretaker Presumption

A different approach for operationalizing the best-interests test, an approach popular among scholars and commentators, is a primary caretaking presumption. A primary caretaker presumption requires a court to identify the parent who has spent the greatest amount of time caring for the child and then award custody to that parent, unless the other parent establishes that the primary caretaking parent is unfit. The approach is defended on the grounds that the parent who has been taking primary care of the child has the better parenting skills and the stronger emotional connection with the child. If the presumption is applied to the facts set forth above, Jane would win custody because she spent more time during the marriage caring for the children than did David.

The primary caretaker approach has been criticized as favoring women because women are most often the primary caretakers of children. This claim of bias is an interesting topic in itself: Should the fact that women have assumed (or been assigned) the primary responsibility for raising children in this society mean that when they get custody, the system is biased in favor of them? If so, it should also be viewed as sex discrimination to pay men more than women in paid employment, even if men have more work experience, or education, or ambition, or work longer hours, in accordance with the roles socially assigned to them.

Ironically, the experiences of the only two states that have worked with a primary caretaking presumption—West Virginia, from 1981 through 1999,[8] and Minnesota for four years between 1985 and 1989—appear to show that gender bias against mothers, especially those who do not conform to gender role stereotypes, is as least as serious a problem as bias against fathers. The problem comes from the fact that in identifying who has been the primary caretaking parent, many courts tend to reward fathers for doing more than judges expect them to do, while tending to penalize mothers who work or who are otherwise less available to their children than the traditional stay-at-home mother.[11] A number of trial courts have characterized a woman who intends to put her child in day care as an uncaring mother, while treating a father who intends to do so as simply a responsible provider.[12] Courts are also said to be harder on mothers who have had an extramarital affair than they are on fathers who have done so, or to find mothers more emotionally unstable even when that instability might be due to severe domestic abuse.[14]

If gender bias in the application of the presumption could be eliminated, the primary caretaker approach would produce more determinate results than the best-interests test. The primary caretaker approach, however, * * * presupposes that every family has a primary caretaker or, if not, that it should have one. I am talking about two

8. See Garska v. McCoy, 278 S.E.2d 357 (W.Va.1981). [The court identified a number of factors to be considered under the primary-caretaker standard:

> In establishing which natural or adoptive parent is the primary caretaker, the trial court shall determine which parent has taken primary responsibility for, *inter alia,* the performance of the following caring and nurturing duties of a parent: (1) preparing and planning of meals; (2) bathing, grooming and dressing; (3) purchasing, cleaning, and care of clothes; (4) medical care, including nursing and trips to physicians; (5) arranging for social interaction among peers after school, i.e., transporting to friends' houses or, for example, to girl or boy scout meetings; (6) arranging alternative care, i.e., babysitting, day-care, etc.; (7) putting child to bed at night, attending to child in the middle of the night, waking child in the morning; (8) disciplining, i.e., teaching general manners and toilet training; (9) educating, i.e., religious, cultural, social, etc.; and (10) teaching elementary skills, i.e., reading, writing and arithmetic.

Id. at 363.] * * *

11. See, e.g., Patricia Ann S. v. James Daniel S., 435 S.E.2d 6 (W.Va.1993) (upholding the trial court finding that neither the father, who was a full-time architect, nor the mother, who was a stay-at-home parent, was the children's primary caretaker, because father typically made the children's breakfast, cooked some weekend meals, attended some school functions, and engaged in weekend activities with the children). This same bias also affects how the trial courts apply the best-interests test. See, e.g., *In re* Marriage of Holcomb, 888 P.2d 1046 (Or.Ct.App.1995) (overturning trial court decision to place a child with the father based in part on the conclusion that the mother's plans to attend graduate school out of state, as well as her continued breastfeeding of the 19–month-old child, demonstrated that she placed her concerns for herself above those of her child); Prost v. Greene, 652 A.2d 621 (D.C.1995) (accepting trial court findings that the father assumed the greater portion of parental obligations for the children, based on evidence that focused more on what the mother did not do than on what the father did).

12. See, e.g., Tresnak v. Tresnak, 297 N.W.2d 109 (Iowa 1980) (reversing custody award to the father that had been based, in part, on an assumption that the mother's pursuit of a legal education would be detrimental to the children, while no such assumption was made about the father, who was engaged in full-time employment outside the home).

14. See, e.g., Patricia Ann S., 435 S.E.2d at 6.

different types of norms here: an empirical one—how a child has been cared for, before the divorce—and a normative one—how the child should be cared for, after the divorce. A primary caretaker rule perpetuates a particular norm—that one parent specializes (and should) in childrearing while the other parent specializes (and should) in supporting the family economically. That is a reasonable description of many families. but it is not the only reasonable reality or ideal, and it is not a reality or ideal that should be sponsored by a society that prides itself on—indeed, gives constitutional recognition to—the importance of family diversity and cultural pluralism.

* * *

C. Joint Custody Approach

Another alternative to the best-interests test, and the favored solution of many legislators, is joint custody. Joint custody, its advocates argue, serves the child's best interests by treating both parents as important to the child, with their own strengths and unique contributions to the child's well-being.

Reformers have sought to make joint custody a more likely option in custody cases by enacting measures that require judges to consider, or to prefer, joint physical custody. The strength of the presumption varies. Some states, such as Oregon, recognize a presumption in favor of joint custody only when parents agree to it. Other states have rules that affect only the burden of proof, making joint custody the default rule but allowing an order other than joint custody if one parent establishes that joint custody is not in the child's best interests. A few states impose a stronger presumption. In Florida, for example, shared parenting responsibility is required unless shown to be detrimental to the child.

Leaving aside the special practical difficulties of working out equally shared physical responsibility in many family circumstances, a joint custody rule is inadequate for the same reason a primary caretaker rule is inadequate: it presumes that one particular form of custody is best in all cases. A joint custody rule represents a judgment by the state that both parents should have equal caretaking roles with respect to their children. While this norm, again, might make sense to many of us in our individual lives, it is not the choice many families have exercised and should not be imposed as a general standard.

D. Why the Alternatives to the Best–Interests Tests Have Not Replaced It

Although both a primary caretaker presumption and a joint custody approach have their adherents, neither approach has caught on as the way to implement the goal of the child's best interests. The reason, in my view, is that neither norm is suitable as a starting point. As I mentioned above, a primary caretaker presumption presupposes that there is, and ought to be, a primary caretaking parent; there often is not, and it is inappropriate to presume that there should be. A joint custody presumption states the norm that parents should divide the caretaking responsibilities for their children more or less equally at divorce; they often have not done so up to that point, and it is inappropriate to compel them to do so in the future. Each presumption may work well for some families—or at least do little harm—but may impede achievement of the child's interests in the substantial number of cases in which it does not fit the family's circumstances.

The mismatch between the ideals of each of these presumptions and the family realities within which they must be implemented has caused substantial difficulties for courts. Few states have enacted a primary caretaker presumption. Those that have—West Virginia and Minnesota—have had a disproportionate number of appellate cases in which trial court decisions have been reviewed and often overturned. The joint custody movement has produced new laws in at least thirteen states but has not made child custody decisions substantially more predictable and certain. As noted above, those legislatures enamored of the notion of joint custody as an ideal have enacted legislation that is largely symbolic, applying only when the parties have agreed to joint custody, or as a burden of proof rule. The few states that have a stronger presumption in favor of joint custody typically follow rules that counteract its effects. * * * Because joint custody does not suit the individual needs and circumstances of many families, interest in joint custody seems to be subsiding. Montana recently repealed its joint custody preference.

E. The ALI Alternative

The ALI has proposed a set of default rules or "Principles" in the custody area that go some way toward avoiding the difficulties described above. These Principles provide that, unless parents agree otherwise, a parent should be allocated custodial responsibility in rough proportion to the share of responsibility the parent assumed before the divorce or the circumstances giving rise to the custody action.[a] Exceptions to this rule

a. Section 2.09 is the key provision of the ALI, Principles of the Law of Family Dissolution: Analysis and Recommendations (tentative Draft No. 3 (1998)):

§ 2.09 Allocation of Custodial Responsibility

(1) Unless otherwise resolved by agreement of the parents * * * or unless manifestly harmful to the child, the court should allocate custodial responsibility so that the proportion of custodial time the child spends with each parent approximates the proportion of time each parent spent performing caretaking functions for the child prior to the parents' separation or, if the parents never lived together, before the filing of the action, except to the extent required under [the provision dealing with parental neglect or abuse] or necessary to achieve any of the following objectives:

(a) to permit the child to have a relationship with each parent which, in the case of a legal parent who has performed a reasonable share of parenting functions, should be not less than a presumptive amount of custodial time determined through a uniform rule of statewide application;

(b) to accommodate the firm and reasonable preferences of a child who has reached a specific age, as set forth in a uniform rule of statewide application;

(c) to keep siblings together when the court finds that doing so is necessary to their welfare;

(d) to protect the child's welfare when, under an otherwise appropriate allocation, the child would be harmed because of a gross disparity in the quality of the emotional attachments between each par-exist, but these exceptions for the most part are either clear and easily applicable, or require that the necessary findings be established under a heightened standard of proof. * * * The Principles also require reasonable limits in access to a child to protect the child or child's parent where the other parent, regardless of the past level of caretaking, is found to have engaged in child abuse, domestic abuse, or drug or alcohol abuse. In fact, when domestic abuse is established, the abusing parent cannot be allocated custodial access without findings that the child and the other parent can be protected.

* * *

The ALI approach to allocating custodial responsibility prioritizes a factor that courts increasingly emphasize in applying the best-interests test: past parenting involvement. The approach, however, makes this reliance more explicit and predictable. In effect, it amounts to a primary caretaker presumption when one parent has been exercising a substantial majority of the past caretaking, and it amounts to a joint custody presumption when past caretaking has been shared equally in the past. It responds to all variations and combinations of past caretaking patterns between those two poles, declining to impose some average, idealized family form on all families and instead favoring solutions that roughly approximate the caretaking shares each parent assumed before the divorce or before the custody issue arose.

The benefits of the ALI alternative are substantial. First, it focuses a factfinder on historical facts rather than on subjective questions about what is good for children, comparative judgments about the quality of emotional bonds and parental abilities, or future speculation about the different outcomes that might result from different custodial arrangements. Questions about who did what in the past can be contentious, but

ent and the child or in each parent's demonstrated ability or availability to meet a child's needs;

(e) to take into account any prior agreement of the parents that, under the circumstances as a whole including the reasonable expectations of the parents and the interests of the child, would be appropriate to consider;

(f) to avoid an allocation of custodial responsibility that would be extremely impractical or that would interfere substantially with the child's need for stability in light of economic, physical, or other circumstances, including the distance between the parents' residences, the cost and difficulty of transporting the child, the parents' and child's daily schedules, and the ability of the parents to cooperate in the arrangement[.]

* * *

(3) If the court is unable to allocate custodial responsibility under Paragraph (1) because the allocation under that paragraph would be manifestly harmful to the child, or because there is no history of past performance of caretaking functions, as in the case of a newborn, or because the history does not establish a pattern of caretaking sufficiently dispositive of the issues of the case, the court should allocate custodial responsibility based on the child's best interests, taking into account the factors and considerations that are set forth in this section and in §§ 2.13 [dealing with parental neglect and abuse] and 2.20(4) [dealing with relocation of a parent] and preserving to the extent possible this section's priority on the share of past caretaking functions each parent performed.

(4) In determining how to schedule the custodial time allocated to each parent, the court should take account of the economic, physical, and other practical circumstances such as those listed in Paragraph (1)(f).

courts and court procedures are set up to resolve what happened in the past; they are not accustomed to predicting the future.

Because questions about past parenting patterns are factual and do not require normative judgments or speculative predictions, they should be answerable in most cases without resort to experts. At the same time, past caretaking patterns likely are a fairly reliable proxy of the intangible qualities such as parental abilities and emotional bonds that are so difficult for courts to ascertain. If the parent has been more involved with the child in the past, it may reasonably be supposed that parent is more experienced and emotionally connected to the child. Past caretaking patterns also are likely to mirror the strength of each parent's preference to spend time with the child, which means less distortion in the bargaining process.

Relying on past caretaking patterns also reduces the potential for bias in custody decisions, which may be based on gender, race, religion, and other prejudicial factors. Under the best interests test, it is difficult to eliminate the bias stemming from an unconscious belief that a mother's primary occupation should be raising her children, while a father should be engaged in the full-time economic support of the family. If custody must be apportioned based on each parent's past share of caretaking efforts, however, this bias has far less room to operate. A parent who obtains a greater share of custodial time because of a more extensive prior role as the caretaking parent does so not because of the court's gender bias but because of the parents' own past choices about the best way to care for the child.

Aligning post-divorce shares of custodial time with past caretaking produces better incentives for caretaking, appropriate to the circumstances and preferences of parents. A parent who expects an equal share of parenting time in the event of divorce will know that this share depends on equal caretaking participation during the marriage. In contrast, a joint custody presumption provides no incentive for a parent to increase his or her caretaking responsibility during the marriage. Even a primary caretaker presumption provides no incentive for a parent exercising little caretaking responsibility to enhance that responsibility, unless he or she is prepared to become the primary caretaker.

Notes on Child Custody

1. Does the best-interest-of-the-child standard provide sufficient guidelines for judges? What does Bartlett think? What do you think? Who are the people serving as family court judges in your jurisdiction? How do they get there? Do they want to be in the domestic relations division? Can you predict how the judges in your jurisdiction would come out in Bartlett's hypothetical involving Jane and David under a best-interest standard? Compare your answer with your classmates. Is there consensus on what "best interests" would mean in this hypothetical? Is the standard empty in terms of guidance as to what to do when there are two fit parents with different values, parenting styles, life styles, interests, religious commitments, etc.?

2. According to the readings earlier in this chapter, do mothers or fathers typically perform most of the functions outlined in the West Virginia primary caretaker standard quoted in footnote 8 in the excerpt above? As Bartlett reports, some commentators claim this standard is biased against men "because women are most often the primary caretakers of children." Barlett asks: "Should the fact that women have assumed (or been assigned) the primary responsibility for raising children in this society mean that when they get custody, the system is biased in favor of them?" What do you think? Under an unbiased standard, would men be as likely to win custody as women? What would make a standard bias-free in your view?

3. What reasons might a father have for seeking custody other than to caretake? Bartlett suggests that her hypothetical "David may ask for primary custody, even if he does not want it, to create some negotiating room." Negotiating room over what? If he doesn't want custody, what would he use the threat of seeking custody for in divorce negotiations? Is this a problem?

4. As Bartlett indicates, during the more than 18 years in which West Virginia used the primary caretaker standard, the standard as applied often favored men. In footnote 14, Bartlett cites one of these cases: Patricia Ann S. v. James Daniel S., 190 W.Va. 6, 435 S.E.2d 6 (W.Va.1993). In this case, the court awarded custody to a father who worked 12–hour days as an architect with frequent out-of-town business trips rather than to the mother who quit working as a kindergarten teacher to work as a full-time mother when she had children. Incredibly, both the trial court and the West Virginia Supreme Court found that there had been no primary caretaker because both parents had been equally involved in caretaking. The appropriate standard was therefore the best-interest standard, and the trial court, affirmed by the West Virginia Supreme Court, held that the father won under the standard. What explains cases in which judges find that the parents shared parenting equally when one gave up her career to care for the children full time at home? What does Bartlett see as the problem? Do we all tend to expect more of mothers than fathers and to be quite impressed when fathers do more than the average father does? How can we protect children and mothers from such bias in custody decisions?

5. As Bartlett points out, the bias apparent in *Patricia Ann S.*—the tendency to be over-impressed when a father does *any* caretaking—"also affects how the trial courts apply the best-interests test." As examples, she cites an Oregon appellate court's decision overruling a trial court award of custody to the father because, among other things, the mother planned to go to graduate school in another state (evidence, according to the trial judge, that she placed her own needs above those of her child) and a District of Columbia appellate court decision overturning a trial court's award of custody to the father based on its conclusion that he had done most of the parenting though the evidence focused on what the mother did *not* do rather than what the father *did*. Many other cases could be cited to illustrate this common phenomenon. Do you think that the ALI approach will eliminate this problem? Won't the determination under § 2.09 of the relative proportions of caretaking performed by each parent during the marriage be tainted by precisely the same bias? What other parts of the ALI Principles of Family Dissolution § 2.09 would give a basis for an award of most of the custodial time to a father who has not been a primary caretaker?

6. What is the ALI standard when the mother has done 70% of the caretaking during the marriage and the father has done 30% but, for practical reasons, they are unable to share custody 70%–30%?

7. Fathers, even unwed fathers, are increasingly successful in obtaining custody of newborns under the best-interest standard. See Mary Becker, The Rights of Unwed Parents: Feminist Approaches, 63 Soc. Service Rev. 496 (1989). What is the ALI standard for newborn babies? Does the ALI regard pregnancy as caretaking? Should pregnancy be regarded as caretaking? Should the ability or desire of the mother to breastfeed be relevant? See Kristen D. Hofheimer, Breastfeeding as a Factor in Child Custody and Visitation Decisions, 5 Va. J. Soc. Pol'y & L. 433 (1998) (judges are prone to give lip service to the importance of breastfeeding but award custody without regard to this factor). What do you think the proper standard is for a newborn?

8. As we have seen in Chapter 7, there are many financial hazards and long-term economic risks attached to being a traditional homemaker in an era when marriage is frequently not forever. As we have seen in this chapter and will see again in Chapter 10, being the primary caretaker of children also causes serious problems for women who work. Ann Laquer Estin points out the general silence in our society about the financial hazards of economic dependence and caregiving. Estin, Maintenance, Alimony, and the Rehabilitation of Family Care, 71 N.C.L.Rev. 721, 779 (1993). Given that fathers have also become much more likely to gain custody when they seek it, even when the mother has been a full-time homemaker like Patricia Ann S., caregivers also lack protection for their relationships to their children. How would proponents of the various feminist theories described in Chapter 3 respond to this problem? Would all of them see it as equally problematic? How would the various feminist theorists discussed in Chapter 3 address the question of selecting the appropriate custody standard? What would they look at? Which approaches would be most concerned with the desires of most women? Which with the economic position of women during and after marriage?

9. The award to the father in *Patricia Ann S.*, discussed in note 4, above, ignored not only clear evidence that the stay-at-home mother had been the primary caretaker, but also evidence that the father had physically and emotionally abused the mother, alienated the children from her, used excessive force on the children, and generally exerted a high level of control over mother and children. For example, the dissenting judge reports:

> It is clear from Mr. S.'s testimony that he ran this family with an iron hand, a significant trait in abusive relationships being the total power and control of one party. The evidence reflects that for some period of time Mrs. S. was not allowed to have a cent, not even grocery money. She was permitted to write a grocery list, and if her husband was ever-so-gracious, he would include her requests. Once she attempted to take $20 from his wallet and wound up in the emergency room after he wrestled her over it. Mr. S. testified that he actually found the whole episode rather humorous, likening his wife clinging desperately to the $20 bill by hiding it in her mouth as resembling a lizard with lettuce sticking out of its mouth.

435 S.E.2d at 19 (Workman, C.J., Dissenting). Abusive men often seek custody to maintain their control over wives as well as their children; and family court judges, who tend not to be well-trained in domestic violence, award custody to abusive fathers either (1) ignoring classic indicators of abuse or (2) as in *Patricia Ann S.*, ignoring explicit evidence of abuse. What explains this phenomenon?

10. Like the Oregon statute described by Bartlett, many best-interest statutes have friendlier-parent provisions stating that one factor that a court can consider is "the willingness and ability of each parent to facilitate and encourage a close and continuing relationship between the other parent and the child." What is the effect of such statutes on women fighting for custody against abusive partners? Does the fact that the Oregon statute also lists "the abuse of one parent by the other" as a factor judges can consider eliminate the problems the friendlier-parent provision poses for survivors of domestic violence and abuse? See Joan Zorza, Recognizing and Protecting the Privacy and Confidentiality Needs of Battered Women, 29 Fam. L. Q. 273, 285 (1995).

11. Although the Oregon best-interest statute described by Bartlett mentions "abuse of one parent by the other" as one factor a court *can* consider, it does not mandate that abuse be taken into account or given any particular weight in determining the child's best interest. There is overwhelming evidence of serious harm to children who live in households in which one adult abuses another. Such children are more likely than other children to abuse others or be abused themselves as adults, may have trouble forming healthy adult intimate relationships, or may avoid intimate relationships. See Mary Becker, Double Binds Facing Mothers in Abusive Families: Social Support Systems, Custody Outcomes, and Liability for Acts of Others, 2 U. Chi. Roundtable 13, 19–20 (1995). But under statutes simply listing abuse as one factor, judges are free to ignore the effect of spousal abuse on children. Indeed, some best-interest statutes provide that the court is not to consider conduct that does not affect a parent's relationship to the child. This sort of provision has been used by judges to explain why evidence of spousal abuse is irrelevant to the custody decision.

Other jurisdictions have statutes attempting to restrain judicial discretion in custody cases in which there is evidence of spousal abuse. Under the Louisiana statute, for example, there is a presumption that an abusive parent should not have sole or joint custody. It is rebuttable only on a showing that the abuser has completed a treatment program, is not abusing alcohol or illegal drugs, and that the child's best interest requires custody with the abuser. La. Rev. Stat. Ann. § 364 (West 1992). What do you think is the ideal approach? Should evidence of abuse be rebuttable evidence that the abusive parent should not receive custody? Irrebuttable? Under what circumstances should an abusive spouse receive custody?

12. Mothers who have been in abusive relationships are likely to look less than ideal for a number of reasons. Many abused women are angry and some are fragile after their experience; their partners may appear stable, calm, controlled, and often quite charming. The children, especially once they are over the age of five or six, may identify with and prefer to live with the abuser. The abused mother, whom they have seen demeaned and derided

all their lives, may be unable to control them. See, e.g., *Patricia Ann S.*, note 4, above (mother angry and unable to control the older two children—both boys—who now shared their father's attitude toward her, whereas he was calm and totally in control). How should we respond to these difficulties?

Text Note: The Importance of Mothers

In an article examining outcomes in appellate cases in West Virginia during the first ten years in which the primary caretaker standard was used (1981–1991), Professor Mary Becker argues for a maternal deference standard.[2] She notes that in the vast majority of families, the mother is not only the primary caretaker in terms of the factors listed in Garska v. McCoy (see footnote 8 in the Bartlett extract above), but also the primary emotional caretaker: the person who carries the baby not just in the backpack but in her mind because of her closer identification and stronger emotional bond with the child. Most mothers have much stronger connections with their child than most fathers even when they share child care. One study, in which each parent performed at least 35% of the child care, reported that:

> the women tended to be more emotionally involved with the children and to feel more strongly about them. These women worried more about their children when not with them, and found separation more distracting and harder to endure than the men. The women had more difficulty concentrating on other tasks when they themselves were not caretaking: "Fathers simply put a hold on their parenting functions when away from their children in a way women rarely do." * * * The fathers also felt generally more separate from the children they mothered than did the women who mothered. The women tended to be both the organizer and the emotional caregiver, and it is likely that these activities appear together most of the time.

Both the mothering mothers and the mothering fathers in this study report that the mothers were involved more emotionally in their children's lives and felt the connection between self and child as sharper and more unconscious. One father describes:

> Two "life and death" incidents from their daughter's early life. In one, their infant was about to fall off the changing table. Both he and his wife were present, but she lunged to catch the baby. In the second, their car slid off the road in winter. The father emerged from the car, dazed; his wife went straight for the infant. Soberly, he reflects that "the reality, the inner connection of taking our daughter as part of ourselves was different for my wife and for me. She was much more a part of my wife's life, and some of my stuff was much more romantic, much more objectifying."

> A mother in this same study:

> Says reproachfully that when it comes to their child, her partner always first thinks about what he needs, while I tend to start from "What does our son need?"[3]

2. Becker, Maternal Feelings: Myth, Taboo, and Child Custody, 1 S. Cal. Rev. L. & Women's Stud. 133 (1992).

According to Becker, the mother carries the baby, and later the child, in her mind because she has, in the vast majority of families, a much stronger emotional bond with the child, one which began during pregnancy and has been reinforced over time by her care for and relationship with her child. This is true whether or not mothers work.

Becker also notes that custodial fathers are *not* typically the child's primary caretaker. Regardless of who has custody, the primary caretaker after divorce is likely to be a woman: if not their own mother, then the father's new wife or his mother. But women are not fungible. A stepmother is not likely—given the difficulty of her role in post-divorce relationships where she may be resented by the children and treated quite differently from their mother—to carry the child in her mind the way a mother would.

Given the facts that (1) judges have a great deal of difficulty appreciating how much caretaking is done by mothers rather than fathers (and make custody decisions in light of a number of other biases having nothing to do with the child's well-being), (2) most fathers will not actually be primary caretakers after getting custody (their new partners will be primary caretakers as stepmothers), and (3) women are not fungible (stepmothers will not be as likely as women who have mothered a child even prior to birth to carry the child in their minds), Becker recommends the adoption of a maternal *deference* standard, under which judges would defer to a fit mother's judgment of what custodial arrangement is best for her children. Of all the people on earth, it is the mother who has (in the vast majority of cases) demonstrated most concern for this child and the greatest commitment to the child's well-being. The mother's recommendation as to the best custodial arrangement should therefore be adopted by the court unless she is an unfit parent.

Recent studies indicate that, in fact, children in the custody of single fathers or fathers and stepmothers are less likely to flourish according to a number of objective indicators. For example, "children living with stepmothers are significantly less likely to have routine doctor and dentist visits, or have a place for usual medical care, or for sick care. If children living with stepmothers have *regular contact* with their birth mothers (2–3 times a month), however, their health care does not suffer relative to that reported for children who reside with birth mothers." The birth children of these stepmothers did receive adequate health care. And the children living with single birth fathers, rather than birth fathers and stepmothers, did no better than those living with stepmothers.[4]

A study looking at food expenditures "by family type, holding constant household size, age, composition and income, [finds] that in those households in which a child is raised by an adoptive, step- or foster mother [rather than

3. Diane Ehrensaft, Parenting Together: Men and Women Sharing the Care of Their Children 96, 99, 114 (1987).

4. Anne Case and Christina Paxson, Mothers and Others: Who Invests in Children's Health? 21, 23 (Apr. 2000) (quote is from abstract) (available at www.wws.princeton.edu/'rpds/macarthur/workingp1.html) (visited Sept. 1, 2000).

birth mother], less is spent on food." The study found no relationship between food expenditures and the father's relationship to the children.[5]

Similar results are obtained when looking at children's educational and occupational attainment. Once socioeconomic status is taken into account, children living with their birth mothers in single-parent households are as likely to succeed as children living with both biological parents, whereas children living with single fathers or fathers and stepmothers are significantly less likely to succeed.[6]

In a study examining educational attainment in blended families, researchers find that "[c]hildren raised by adoptive fathers or foster fathers are not at risk for lower educational attainment, provided that they are raised by their birth mothers, while children raised by adoptive, step- or foster mothers are at risk—even when their birth fathers are present." These authors suggest a sociobiological explanation for the results in all these studies:

> That mothers play a more important role than fathers in the rearing of children is consistent with the fact that a woman must make a larger commitment in bearing a child. A woman is more limited in the number of children she can parent, both because she must carry each child and because women have a shorter reproductive span, which may affect the relative intensity with which she raises the children that she does bear.
>
> * * *
>
> Whether it is due to some combination of the limitations women face in the number of offspring they can successfully bear, or to differences in the physiological responses of women and men to young children's needs, it appears that investments in children are more likely to be made by women, and that birth mothers protect investments in birth children above those in non-birth children.[7]

This analysis is consistent with the insistence of sociobiologists that females have incentives to invest more in fewer children than males, who are motivated to invest less in more children. Sociobiologists see this difference as linked to the fact that women have a more limited span of time in which to reproduce and, because of the demands and burdens of pregnancy, are limited in the number of offspring they can produce, whereas men can remain fertile throughout their lives and beget many children without making significant investments in any of them. In a recent article titled Biology for Feminists, Katharine Baker suggests that feminists embrace

5. Anne Case, I-Fen Lin and Sara McLanahan, Household Resource Allocations in Stepfamilies, 89 Am. Econ. Rev. 239 (1999); Anne Case, I-Fen Lin, Sara McLanahan, How Hungry is the Selfish Gene? 3, 15 (Jan. 2000)(forthcoming in Econ. J. and available at www.wws.princeton.edu/'rpds/macarthur/workingp1.html (visited Sept. 1, 2000)). (In this last study, many—perhaps most—of the adopted children were not children adopted by strangers at a young age but children adopted by a stepmother after a father's remarriage.)

6. Timothy J. Biblarz and Adrian E. Raftery, Family Structure, Educational Attainment, and Socioeconomic Success: Rethinking the "Pathology of Matriarchy," 105 Am. J. Sociol. 321 (1999).

7. Anne Case, I-Fen Lin, and Sara McLanahan, Educational Attainment in Blended Families 17, 18 (Aug. 2000) (available at www.wws.princeton.edu/'rpds/macarthur/workingp1.html) (visited Sept. 1, 2000).

"biology, at least as a strategic device, so that we may reveal the wholly inadequate job that the law has done in controlling nature's horrors."[8] With respect to the law of child custody, Baker notes that:

> the law seems to ignore the evolutionary pressure (not to mention the abundant contemporary evidence) suggesting that men are less inclined than women to invest in children. Some men may be willing to so invest, but given the tendency men have to focus less on each child, it seems odd that the law would presume that both parents are equally fit to caretake.
>
> Finally, the law ignores differentials in the cost of losing a child. A male can, at relatively low cost, create another child. He can continue to do this, with only mildly decreased fertility rates, well into his seventies. For a female, because her eggs are so much more costly than sperm in terms of body resources, and so much more precious than sperm in terms of years of availability, the loss of a child is a very serious loss. Once she spends any time rearing a child, she has incurred huge, often prohibitive opportunity costs that can prevent her from parenting again. Thus, the cost of losing a child in a custody battle is likely to be much greater for her than for him.[9]

In another recent article, Penelope Bryan identifies women's needs at divorce, particularly with respect to child custody and post-divorce support, as an important but unfinished piece of feminist business. Given the "pain, loss, and humiliation" of many women at divorce, she urges feminists to listen to divorced women and then put aside their differences with respect to the ideal custody standard and join in supporting a primary caretaker standard. She believes that such a standard would "honor the caretaking that mothers provide" and protect women from the loss they fear most. [10]

Text Note: Outcomes in Custody Cases

There have been dramatic changes in custody doctrine in recent decades with the demise of the maternal preference standard and the rise of joint custody. Have these changes caused changes in custodial arrangements for children after divorce? Data from 1885 to 1949 indicate that mothers, as a result of settlement or litigation, received sole physical custody at very high rates, typically 80 to 95% of the time. Fathers received custody only about 10% of the time. In the remaining cases, custody would have been split between the parents in some way (e.g., one of each of two children to each parent) or awarded to a third party such as a grandparent.[11] Researchers estimate that in 1968, just prior to the abandonment of the maternal

8. Katharine K. Baker, Biology for Feminists, 75 Chi.-Kent L. Rev. 805, 805–06 (2000).

9. Id. at 822–23.

10. Penelope E. Bryan, Re-asking the Woman Question at Divorce, 75 Chi.-Kent L. Rev. 713, 742, 751–52 (2000) (Bryan prefers a maternal deference standard, but considers it unrealistic given the political climate.).

11. See William Goode, After Divorce 29 (1956); Paul Jacobson, American Marriage and Divorce 131 (1959); James A. Levine, Who will Raise the Children? New Options for Fathers (and Mothers) 184 n.23 (1976); Harold T. Christensen and Hanna H. Meissner, An Analysis of Divorce in Tippecanoe County, Indiana, 40 Soc. & Soc. Res. 247, 248 (1956).

preference standard, mothers received sole physical custody about 90% of the time at divorce.[12] We have no data on litigated cases prior to 1971.

Today, too, most children of divorce live with their mothers. As in the past, most custody arrangements are the result of the parents' agreement rather than a judge's application of a custody standard in a litigated case. Parents do, however, bargain in the shadow of the applicable standard, so parental arrangements may well be affected by what judges do.

Regional studies of custody outcomes in all divorces (not just litigated cases) suggest that changes in custody standards do not always result in changes in outcomes. For example, a study of outcomes in Alabama reveals no significant differences despite a dramatic change in the custody standard: mothers received sole physical custody 91% of the time between 1976 and 1986, though at the start of the period mothers had the advantage of the maternal preference and at the end were subject to the gender-neutral best-interest standard.[13] In many, probably most, jurisdictions, there have been dramatic increases in awards of joint *legal* custody even when mothers continue to receive sole physical custody at traditional rates.[14] On the other hand, in some jurisdictions, mothers are less likely to receive sole physical custody today than in the past. And there is clearly a great deal of variation from jurisdiction to jurisdiction in the rates at which mothers receive custody in general after divorce. For example, a study of two counties near San Francisco in the mid–1980's showed mothers receiving sole physical custody only 67% of the time, though mothers in Alabama received custody 91% of the time in the mid–1980's.[15]

Variations by region are also present in a national but non-representative survey of attorneys from the late 1980's. Respondents (members of the American Bar Association's Custody Committee) reported the results of over 1,200 cases, but the survey did not clearly distinguish between joint and physical custody. Attorneys were asked to describe results as maternal custody, paternal custody, or joint custody. Respondents indicated that in 61% of the settled cases mothers received custody; in 15% of the cases fathers received custody; and in 21% of the cases custody was joint. But

12. Lenore J. Weitzman and Ruth B. Dixon, Child Custody Awards: Legal Standards and Empirical Patterns for Child Custody, Support and Visitation After Divorce, 12 U.C. Davis L. Rev. 473, 484, 489 (1979) (1968 data shows mothers receiving custody 88.4% of the time in San Francisco and 87.7% of the time in Los Angeles); Julie A. Fulton, Parental Reports of Children's Post–Divorce Adjustment, 35 J. Soc. Issues, 126, 128 (1979) (in 1970, mothers received sole physical custody 87% of the time and fathers 8% of the time in three urban Minnesota counties).

13. See Laura E. Santilli and Michael C. Roberts, Custody Decisions in Alabama Before and After the Abolition of the Tender Years Doctrine, 14 Law & Hum. Behav. 123 (1990).

14. See Stephen J. Bahr, Jerry D. Howe, Meggin Morrill Mann, and Matthew S. Bahr, Trends in Child Custody Awards: Has the Removal of Maternal Preference Made a Difference?, 28 Fam. L. Q. 247, 256–57, 259 (1994) (finding no increase in awards of physical custody to fathers in Utah between 1970 and 1993, though there was an increase in awards of joint *legal* custody over the time of the study).

15. On the California counties, see Robert H. Mnookin, Eleanor E. Maccoby, Catherine R. Albiston, and Charlene E. Depner, Private Ordering Revisited: What Custodial Arrangements Are Parents Negotiating?, in Divorce Reform at the Crossroads 37, 54, 74 (Stephen D. Sugarman and Herma Hill Kay, eds. 1990) (fathers received sole physical custody 10% of the time, and physical custody was joint 25% of the time). For the Alabama study, see Santilli and Roberts, note 13, above.

results varied greatly by region. For example, in the South Central region, mothers received custody in settled cases 72% of the time, while in the West mothers received custody in settled cases only 58% of the time.[16]

Litigated Cases

As indicated earlier, we know of no pre–1971 data on results in litigated cases for comparative purposes. Today, the data on outcomes in litigated cases remains sparse. An early California study looks at outcomes in litigated cases from 1972 and 1976 (before and after the elimination of the maternal preference). Between these dates, there was no change in the percentage of fathers requesting custody. But there was a dramatic increase in their likelihood of obtaining custody over the period of the study: from 37% in 1972 to 63% in 1977. Yet because so few fathers sought custody, there was no significant change in the proportion of cases overall in which mothers received custody between 1972 and 1977 (88–90%).[17]

In the national survey of attorneys just described, respondents reported that in litigated cases, mothers received custody 65% of the time, and fathers received custody 29% of the time. In 6% of the adjudicated cases, judges ordered joint custody. Once again, results varied by region. The South Central region was most hospitable to mothers, awarding custody in litigated cases to mothers in about 70% percent of the cases and to fathers in less than 10% of the cases. Courts were most hostile to mothers in the Northeast, where mothers received custody only 50% of the time, fathers received custody 26% of the time, and joint custody was mandated 24% of the time in litigated cases.[18]

Outcomes in litigated cases may vary not just by region but by county, depending on who is sitting on the bench. For example, a study of the actual outcomes in litigated cases before two judges—one man and one woman—in Orange County, North Carolina, between 1983 and 1987 indicates that mothers received sole custody in only 16% of the cases, the father received sole physical custody in 62% of the cases, and 22% of the cases resulted in joint physical custody.[19] The authors of this North Carolina study compare various kinds of cases, and conclude that judges responded differently to various allegations of parental unfitness, depending upon whether the allegation was against the mother or father. For example, there were five cases in which fathers were alleged to have been unfaithful; none were denied custody (either primary or joint physical custody). Mothers were accused of being unfaithful in 16 cases; only five of these women were given joint or primary custody. In 16 cases, there were allegations of mental instability. None of the three fathers in this set of cases lost joint or primary custody, even though two were subsequently hospitalized. Of the 14 mothers accused of mental instability, however, ten lost custody. Courts were also more likely to order mental health evaluations of mothers. Nine out of 14 mothers

16. Donald H. Stone, The Moral Dilemma: Child Custody When One Parent Is Homosexual or Lesbian: An Empirical Study, 23 Suffolk U. L. Rev. 711, 715 & n.4 (1989).

17. Weitzman and Dixon, above note 12, at 475–77, 502–04.

18. Stone, above note 16, at 717.

19. The Committee for Justice for Women and the Orange County North Carolina Women's Coalition, Contested Custody Cases in Orange County, N.C. Trial Courts 1983–1987: Gender Bias, The Family and The Law 35 (2d ed., Nov. 1991).

accused of mental instability were ordered evaluated, whereas only one of the three fathers was ordered evaluated.[20]

The authors of this study report that other factors also favor paternal custody over maternal custody regardless of the allocation of responsibility for child care during marriage. These other factors include financial status and allegations of drug and alcohol abuse. Allegations of paternal abuse seldom affected custody decisions. For example, none of the three fathers proven to have sexually abused their children lost custody. Two of these fathers were given sole custody and one joint custody. Of the 19 fathers accused of spousal abuse, only three were denied sole or joint physical custody. Only one of the seven fathers accused of physical abuse lost sole or joint physical custody.[21]

Studies Trying to Understand How Judges Decide

An early study of how judges make custody decisions considered California cases between 1968 and 1977. During that period California moved both from divorce for fault to no-fault divorce *and* from the maternal preference standard to the best interest standard in all custody cases. This study looked at divorce cases from 1968, 1972, and 1977 and also interviewed 169 attorneys and 44 judges in San Francisco and Los Angeles Counties. Two years after the abolition of the maternal preference standard, 98% of the attorneys from Los Angeles said that judges still used a maternal preference in deciding who would have custody of pre-school children. And about 33% said that judges also used the preference in deciding custody for older children.[22]

These researchers found that the focus was on the mother in deciding whether to give custody to the mother or the father. The most important factors likely to result in paternal custody, in the view of attorneys, were (in this order): (1) maternal physical abuse; (2) maternal emotional abuse; (3) maternal promiscuity; (4) maternal addiction to drugs; (5) maternal mental instability; and (6) maternal alcoholism. The quality of the father's relationship with the children was the *seventh* factor and mentioned by only 10% of the attorneys.[23]

One empirical study of litigated cases in San Diego coded various facts and psychological assessments in the court's file and then used statistical analysis to try to determine what facts or psychological factors influenced judges' custodial decisions. This study identified only two strongly predictive factors: the recommendation of a counselor ordered by the court to investigate the family (75% of the time the judge ordered the custodial arrangement recommended by the counselor) and the child's preference. The counselor's recommendation could be predicted from the mother's appearance, social skills, and social adjustment (the mother was more likely to get custody when the counselor's report described her as having "good" physical appearance, social skills and social adjustment). If a father lived with a

20. Id. at 14–15, 17.

21. Id. at 14.

22. Weitzman and Dixon, above note 12, at 506–08.

23. Id. at 508.

woman, whether a girlfriend, wife, or mother, he had a 50% chance of obtaining custody.[24]

Taken together, these studies suggest that more has changed in terms of doctrine and the language of opinions than in terms of outcomes in settled cases or in the actual grounds on which judges make decisions. With respect to *legal* custody, changes have been dramatic in some jurisdictions: the number of cases in which parents share legal responsibility for decisionmaking has skyrocketed, and the number of cases in which only the mother has legal responsibility has correspondingly plummeted. With respect to *physical* custody, the change has been in the same direction—toward more paternal custody—but is more modest, though in some counties and regions women are at significant risk of losing custody of the children they have mothered when a father fights for custody.

Notes on the Importance of Mothers and on Custody Outcomes

1. Is it a mistake to mention the strength of women's emotional bonds with their children because doing so reinforces stereotypes? Is it true, in your opinion, that women have stronger emotional bonds with their children and are more likely to plan and organize to ensure children's needs are met (including, for example, health care)? Even if true, is it dangerous to mention these emotional realities? Are there dangers with both approaches—either ignoring *or* acknowledging the importance of mothering to the well-being of children? What are they? How would various feminist approaches described in Chapter 3 deal with this double bind?

2. Do you agree with Katharine Baker that feminists should use sociobiology in arguments that mothers and fathers should not be regarded as equally qualified to care for children at divorce?

3. Do the results in the single father-stepmother studies—for example, that children in the custody of single birth fathers or birth fathers and stepmothers receive inadequate health care unless a birth mother is in frequent contact—surprise you? What do you think explains these results? When you think of families you know, do you agree that women are more likely than men to invest in children and that women are likely to invest most in their own children?

4. How much weight should judges give to the fact that a father is living with another woman (his mother, a girlfriend, or a wife)? Should cohabitation with a wife or girlfriend hurt rather than help his chances of getting custody in light of the stepmother studies?

5. Is it constitutional sex discrimination for a judge to consider (1) whether a father seeking custody is living with a woman or (2) the evidence that children in general seem to be better off with their mother than with a stepmother? Is the problem the constitutional standard or that these factors should be irrelevant? If our primary concern is the best interests of children, should we ignore the results of the stepmother studies?

24. Carla C. Kunin, et al., An Archival Study of Decision-Making in Child Custody Disputes, 48 J. Clinical Psychol. 564, 567, 569, 572 (1992).

6. Were you surprised by the Alabama study indicating that the elimination of the maternal preference standard did not affect outcomes during the periods studied? What explains these results?

7. What explains the fact that attorneys often believe judges still rely on an unspoken maternal preference, especially for young children? Do the studies described above suggest that the parents' sex *is* still relevant to custody decisions? Is it realistic to think that judges actually decide custody cases as though the issue were which of two sexless parents should have custody rather than whether a mother or a father should have custody? Could you, for example, determine custody of a newborn or a toddler without reference to parental sex? Would it be better to have a more honest rule? What would a more honest rule look like? Would it be constitutional?

8. Do the stepmother studies support Becker's maternal deference standard? What are the pros and cons of such a standard? Does it raise constitutional problems? If so, what are they? How would proponents of various feminist theories examined in Chapter 3 analyze her proposal?

9. Most mothers receive custody of their children at divorce because most fathers agree to it. But if a father chooses to fight for custody against a mother who has been a primary caretaker, he is likely to have a number of advantages in litigation. Custody litigation is extremely expensive, and he is likely (because he was not the primary caretaker but the primary breadwinner even if she also worked) to have more money for lawyers and expert witnesses. If he is remarried and she is not (and men remarry at higher rates than women), his household may look better for the child because it is a traditional two-parent family. (There are many decisions changing custody from a single mother to a remarried father. See, e.g., Carla C. Kunin, et al., An Archival Study of Decision–Making in Child Custody Disputes, 48 J. Clinical Psychol. 564, 569 (1992) (reporting on study finding that if father was living with another woman, his wife, girlfriend, or mother, his chances of obtaining custody in litigated cases rose to 50%).) Biases against mothers, particularly those who do not conform to judges' images of good mothers, are also likely to hurt mothers. If the husband is abusive, he may be able to use the divorce process, as many abusive men do, to continue his abuse and ultimately obtain custody. For stay-at-home mothers as well as working mothers who have sacrificed fast-track careers to care for their children, but especially for mothers in abusive relationships, these are frightening possibilities; and loss of custody can be devastating. Given the importance of children to women and the inequities in the current custody system, why isn't the appropriate standard for child custody at divorce a priority item on the political agenda?

10. Can the feminists in your class agree on a custody standard which would better protect women and their relationships with children at divorce than the best interest standard?

F. LESBIAN AND GAY PARENTS

DAVID L. CHAMBERS AND NANCY D. POLIKOFF FAMILY LAW AND GAY AND LESBIAN FAMILY ISSUES IN THE TWENTIETH CENTURY

33 Fam. L. Q. 523, 532–42 (1999).

Many gay men and lesbians have children. They have them in the course of marriages and other relationships with a person of the opposite sex. They have them, by artificial insemination or adoption, when single or during relationships with a same-sex partner. There is very little statutory law explicitly addressing the gay parent. Lesbians and gay men who are parents or who want to become parents come into contact with the law in the same way that most heterosexuals do: when they divorce or become involved in a custody struggle with another person who claims the rights of a parent and when they apply for adoption or seek to become foster parents. Over the last thirty years, as more and more women and men have revealed themselves as lesbian or gay, these encounters with the legal system have become more frequent.

A parent's homosexuality was explicitly acknowledged in a handful of reported cases going back to 1952, but custody cases involving a homosexual parent first began appearing with some frequency in the early and mid–1970s, as the women's liberation movement and changing attitudes towards divorce made it easier for all women to leave marriages and as the gay liberation movement enabled substantial numbers of gay men and lesbians to embrace an identity they had earlier been taught to despise.

When the cases first arose in the 1970s, courts applying the prevailing "best interests of the child" standard ruled both for and against lesbian and gay parents [but usually against]. * * *

During the late 1970s, the first mental health research on the well-being of children raised by lesbian mothers was published. Using expert witnesses, advocates were in a better position to dispel recurring myths about lesbians as mothers—that lesbians were mentally ill or emotionally unstable; that a lesbian mother was likely to sexually molest her child or engage in sexual behavior in front of her child; that children raised by lesbian mothers would probably become gay or lesbian, would be confused about their gender identity, would be socially stigmatized, or would suffer other psychological harm.

By the late 1970s, numerous factors coincided to encourage a new form of lesbian and gay parenthood not tied to heterosexual marriage. The gay rights movement enabled many young adults to embrace, rather than reject, their sexual orientation. Many gay men and lesbians who, in an earlier period, would have married a person of the opposite sex out of convention, fear, or denial, no longer did so. While it may have initially appeared that parenthood would never be an option for such men and women, other cultural and medical phenomena soon resulted in a new frame of mind. Specifically, births of out-of-wedlock children no longer carried the stigma they did in earlier decades, and medical technology opened the possibilities for conception without sexual intercourse. Although there are accounts of decisions by lesbian couples to raise children together as far back as 1965, it was at some point in the late 1970s that lesbians in significant numbers, first in the San Francisco area and then around the country, began contemplating planned motherhood, primarily using alternative insemination as the means of conception, but also adopting as individual parents. Into the early 1980s, even as the conservative Christian right emerged and its influence grew, the openness, pride, and numbers of lesbian and gay families also grew.

Meanwhile, the number of reported cases of custody and visitation disputes between a heterosexual parent and a gay or lesbian parent also increased. About twenty states had reported appellate decisions in the first half of the 1980s. Decisions during this period were as mixed as those of the 1970s. In 1980, for example, the Massachusetts Supreme Court ruled that a lesbian mother could not lose her children simply because she had a lifestyle "at odds with the average."[35] The Alaska Supreme Court ruled in 1985 that a mother's lesbian relationship should be considered only if it negatively affected the child and that it was "impermissible to rely on any real or imagined social stigma attaching to mother's status as a lesbian."[36] * * *

Most courts, however, continued to rule against gay parents. Cases from appellate courts in North Dakota, South Dakota, and Virginia overturned trial court judges who had awarded custody to lesbian, gay, or bisexual parents. * * *

In May 1985, neighbors of a gay foster parent couple in Boston went to the Boston Globe to express their disapproval. The ensuing publicity sparked widespread national debate about gay men and lesbians raising children. The Massachusetts Department of Social Services removed the children from the home, and changed its policy, issuing regulations that made it almost impossible for lesbians and gay men to become foster parents. In the wake of that controversy, New Hampshire in 1986 enacted a law prohibiting adoption, foster parenting, or ownership of a child care facility by lesbians or gay men. Although the child care facility provisions were struck down as unconstitutional, the bans on adoption and foster parenting were upheld. New Hampshire became the second state with an adoption ban and the first with a legislatively mandated ban on gay foster parenting.

In the latter half of the 1980s, state courts continued to decide substantial numbers of custody disputes between a lesbian or gay parent and a heterosexual parent and continued the prior pattern of widely divergent attitudes toward parenting by lesbians and gay men. During this same period of time, advocates for gay and lesbian parents developed

35. Bezio v. Patenaude, 410 N.E.2d 1207 (Mass.1980).

36. S.N.E. v. R.L.B., 699 P.2d 875 (Alaska 1985).

new approaches to protect gay and lesbian families in which, from birth, a child had two parents of the same gender. Lawyers advocated for "second-parent adoption," a term describing the equivalent of a stepparent adoption, in which a biological parent's partner adopts her child. The term "joint adoption" was used to designate adoption of a child by both members of a couple, a practice unheard of earlier unless the couple was married. The first second-parent adoption was granted in Alaska in 1985; within months others were granted in Oregon, Washington, and California.

The mid–1980s also saw the first disputes between separating lesbian mothers who had raised a child together, between a surviving nonbiological mother and family members of a deceased biological mother, and between a lesbian mother and a semen donor, often a gay man, when disagreements arose about the donor's relationship with the child. These cases would become more prominent in the late 1980s and into the 1990s. In a particularly poignant 1989 case, a trial court judge in Broward County, Florida, awarded custody of ten year old Kristen Pearlman to Janine Ratcliffe, her nonbiological mother, reversing a decision made four years earlier, upon the death of Kristen's biological mother, Joanie, that had granted custody to Joanie's parents. In chambers, the child pleaded with the judge to permit her to live with Janine. The judge found that Kristen continued to view Janine as her primary parent figure, that it would be detrimental to Kristen to continue her separation from Janine, and that there was no evidence Janine's sexual orientation would have any detrimental effect on Kristen.

Although there have been a handful of other cases arising upon the death of a child's only legal parent, disputes about parenthood in planned lesbian and gay families have arisen primarily in two other contexts. The first is a claim by a legally unrecognized parent to continue a relationship with a child when she and the child's biological or adoptive parent separate. The second is a claim by a biological father, usually a semen donor, who demands legal parental status in disregard of an agreement with the lesbian couple that he would not assert parental rights based on biology. These cases have presented courts with two options—recognize planned lesbian and gay families and modify family law principles to protect the interests of parents and children in such families, or maintain a rigid definition of parenthood that often fails to recognize the reality of children's actual relationships with parenting figures. Courts, sometimes claiming that legislative language gave them no choice, have usually taken the latter option. Appellate courts in California and New York, the states with the largest number of planned lesbian and gay families, have both closed the door on all claims by legally unrecognized mothers and recognized the claims of semen donors.[47] Claims by legally unrecognized mothers have also been rebuffed in Ohio, Texas, Florida, and Vermont, without ever reaching the ques-

47. Alison D. v. Virginia M., 572 N.E.2d 27 (N.Y.1991); Thomas S. v. Robin Y., 618 N.Y.S.2d 356 (App.Div.1994); Z.C.W. v. Lisa W., 84 Cal. Rptr. 2d 48 (Cal.Ct.App.1999); Jhordan C. v. Mary K., 224 Cal. Rptr. 530 (Cal.Ct.App.1986).

tion of the child's best interests.[48] While appellate courts in Wisconsin, New Mexico, and Massachusetts have allowed the non-biological parent to request visitation,[49] these states are in the minority, and even they have not authorized a claim for sole or joint custody by the legally unrecognized parent, even if she was the child's primary caretaker.

The 1990s, like the preceding two decades, were filled with incongruity for lesbian and gay parents. The number of planned lesbian and gay families skyrocketed, bringing broad visibility in the media, in schools, in churches and synagogues, and in the courts. With this visibility came an increased number of heterosexual allies, people in positions of power able to influence mainstream organizations, as well as ordinary people whose children became friends with children of gay and Lesbian parents, thereby learning about gay and lesbian families in ways that break down myths, stereotypes, and fear. In 1995, the American Psychological Association issued Lesbian and Gay Parenting: A Resource for Psychologists, a review of forty-three empirical studies and numerous other articles that concluded that "[n]ot a single study has found children of gay and lesbian parents to be disadvantaged in any significant respect relative to children of heterosexual parents."[50] In 1996 and 1999, the American Bar Association passed resolutions opposing use of sexual orientation as a basis for denying custody and adoption, respectively. In some parts of the country, joint and second-parent adoptions for lesbian and gay couples became routine, and lesbians and gay men were welcomed as adoptive and foster parents for the growing number of children needing good homes.

With increased visibility came increased political volatility. Legislatures had more opportunities to debate lesbian and gay parenting. Related issues concerning children and homosexuality, such as the content of school curricula, the sexual orientation of teachers and school board members, and whether gay men can serve as Boy Scout leaders, increasingly became subjects of public controversy. The debates over same-sex marriage often included heated discussion of childrearing by lesbians and gay men. Courts today considering the fate of lesbian and gay parents issue their rulings in this volatile context.

The greatest legal accomplishment for lesbian and gay parents in the 1990s was the availability in some parts of the country of joint and second-parent adoption. After many unreported trial court decisions in the last half of the 1980s, the first reported second-parent adoption by a lesbian couple occurred in 1991 in the District of Columbia.[51] Other reported decisions came shortly thereafter, and in early 1992 the first

48. Liston v. Pyles, 1997 Ohio App. LEXIS 3627 (1977); Jones v. Fowler, 969 S.W.2d 429 (Tex.1998); Titchenal v. Dexter, 693 A.2d 682 (Vt.1997), Kazmierazak v. Query, 1999 Fla. App. LEXIS 6355 (1999).

49. *In re* H.S. H.-K., 533 N.W.2d 419 (Wis.1995); A.C. v. C.B., 829 P.2d 660 (N.M. 1992); E.N.O. v. L.M.M., 711 N.E.2d 886 (Mass.1999).

50. American Psychological Association, Lesbian and Gay Parenting: A Resource for Psychologists 8 (1995).

51. *In re* Adoption of Minor (T. and M.), 17 Fam. L. Rep. (BNA) 1523 (D.C. Super. 1991).

New York decision granting a second-parent adoption to a lesbian couple was reported in the New York Times and applauded on its editorial page.[52] Appeals courts in New York, New Jersey, Vermont, Massachusetts, Illinois, and the District of Columbia have approved such adoptions and instructed trial judges to grant them under the same best-interests-of-the-child standard used in all adoptions.[53] Appellate courts in only four states, Wisconsin, Colorado, Ohio, and Connecticut, have rejected such adoptions, in decisions narrowly construing their adoption statutes.[54] Trial courts in more than a dozen other states have granted such adoptions, and in some counties, such as those in the San Francisco Bay area, there have been hundreds, perhaps thousands, over the last fifteen years. In a 1997 settlement of a class action law suit, New Jersey became the first state in the country with a written agency policy requiring that gay, lesbian, and unmarried heterosexual couples be evaluated for joint adoption of children using the same criteria used for married couples.

From the mid–1990s on, the increasing, high profile coverage of lesbian and gay families provoked an escalation of efforts to prevent lesbians and gay men from adopting children and serving as foster parents. Legislation proposing statewide bans on adoption and/or foster parenting was introduced between 1995 and 1997 in Oklahoma, Missouri, South Carolina, Tennessee, and Washington. None passed. In 1998, however, on the heels of the nationwide publicity accorded the settlement of the New Jersey litigation, prohibitions were proposed in Arkansas, Indiana, Texas, and Utah. Restrictions passed in Utah and Arkansas in 1999.[55]

Despite these setbacks, there were also positive legislative developments. In 1999 New Hampshire repealed its ban on lesbian and gay adoption and foster parenting.[56] Upon signing the bill into law, Governor Jeanne Shaheen commented that foster and adoptive families would now be selected based on fitness, "without making prejudicial assumptions." Later in 1999, the Republican-controlled House of Representatives defeated an amendment that would have prohibited joint adoption by unmarried gay and heterosexual couples in the District of Columbia, even though the same language had passed in 1998.

52. *In re* Adoption of Evan, 583 N.Y.S.2d 997 (N.Y.Sup.Ct.1992); Ronald Sullivan, Judge Lets Gay Partner Adopt Child, N.Y. Times, Jan. 31, 1992, at B1; James D. Marks, A Victory for the New American Family, N.Y. Times, Feb. 1, 1992, at 21.

53. *In re* Dana, 660 N.E.2d 397 (N.Y. 1995); *In re* Adoption of Two Children by H.N.R., 666 A.2d 535 (N.J.Super.Ct.App. Div.1995); *In re* Adoptions of B.L.V.B. and E.L.V.B., 628 A.2d 1271 (Vt.1993); *In re* Adoption of Tammy, 619 N.E.2d 315 (Mass. 1993); *In re* Petition of K.M. and D.M., 653 N.E.2d 888 (Ill. App. Ct. 1995); *In re* M.M.D. & B.H.M., 662 A.2d 837 (D.C.1995).

54. *In re* Angel Lace M., 516 N.W.2d 678 (Wis.1994); *In re* Adoption of T.K.J., 931 P.2d 488 (Colo. 1996); *In re* Adoption of Doe, 1998 WL 904252 (Ohio Ct. App. 1998); *In re* Adoption of Baby Z., 724 A.2d 1035 (Conn.1999).

55. See A. Green, Boards Adopts Ban on Gay Foster Parents, Arkansas Democrat–Gazette, March 24, 1999, at B–3; R. Rivera, Board Defends Its Ban on Gay Adoptions, Salt Lake Tribune, October 30, 1999, at D2.

56. N.H. Rev. Stat. Ann. §§ 170–B:2 to B:4, 170–F:2 to F:6 (1994) (repealed 1999).

Although childrearing by openly gay men and women has become increasingly common, and although young gay men and lesbians have an increasing number of positive images and role models that allow them to affirm their sexual orientation, large numbers of adults still do not come out as gay or lesbian until after they have married and had children within heterosexual marriages. Their life stories look strikingly like those of their counterparts in the 1970s, and, as in earlier decades, their fate will be determined more than anything else by the state in which they live and the judge who hears their case.

The most visible custody dispute in the 1990s was the battle between Sharon Bottoms and her mother, Kay Bottoms, who challenged Sharon's right to continue raising her two year old son, Tyler, even though Sharon's former husband believed that Sharon should retain custody of the boy. Sharon lost at trial, but won in the Virginia Court of Appeals, in a decision that credited the years of research on the well being of children living with lesbian mothers.[59] The victory was short-lived, however, as the Virginia Supreme Court in 1995 reinstated the trial court's ruling, which included a prohibition on Sharon's visitation with Tyler in the presence of her partner.[60]

The continuing vulnerability of lesbian and gay parents in some parts of the country was reinforced by a series of state supreme court decisions in 1998 and 1999 from Indiana, Missouri, North Carolina, Alabama, and Mississippi.[61] Each affirmed either a change in custody or a severe restriction on visitation rights based upon the parent's homosexuality. * * *

To be sure, there were positive court decisions during the 1990s. A 1998 opinion from the highest court in Maryland overturned a trial judge's order that a gay father's partner be prohibited from being present during the father's visitation with his children,[63] in the process citing similar 1990s decisions from Illinois, Pennsylvania, and Washington.[64] Nonetheless, a review of reported disputes between gay and straight parents in the 1990s demonstrates that neither the increased visibility of lesbian and gay families, nor the mental health research on the well-being of children raised by lesbian and gay parents, nor the successes in the areas of adoption and foster-parenting have decreased the risks to a lesbian mother or gay father battling a heterosexual former spouse over custody or visitation. It is as true at the turn of the millennium as it was in the 1970s that the result of such a dispute depends largely on where the case goes to court.

59. Bottoms v. Bottoms, 444 S.E.2d 276 (Va.Ct.App.1994).

60. Bottoms v. Bottoms, 457 S.E.2d 102 (Va.1995).

61. Marlow v. Marlow, 702 N.E.2d 733 (Ind.Ct.App.1998); J.A.D. v. F.J.D., 978 S.W.2d 336 (Mo.1998)(en banc); Pulliam v. Smith, 501 S.E.2d 898 (N.C.1998); *In re* J.B.F and J.M.F., 730 So. 2d 1190 (Ala. 1998); Weigand v. Houghton, 730 So. 2d 581 (Miss.1999).

63. Boswell v. Boswell, 721 A.2d 662 (Md.1998).

64. *In re* Marriage of Pleasant, 628 N.E.2d 633 (Ill. App. Ct. 1993); Blew v. Verta, 617 A.2d 31 (Pa. Super. Ct. 1992); *In re* Marriage of Wicklund, 932 P.2d 652 (Wash.Ct.App.1996).

Notes on Family Law and Gay and Lesbian Families

1. Are you surprised by the results of the empirical studies to which Chambers and Polikoff refer, studies reporting on the well-being of children raised by lesbian mothers? The studies generally report that the children of lesbian mothers do not differ in statistically significant ways from the children of heterosexuals on measures of sexual orientation, gender identity, gender role, self-esteem, psychological health, and social adjustment. Researchers have also found no deficits in children of lesbian mothers in other areas of "personal development, including separation-individuation, locus of control, self-concept, intelligence, or moral judgment," and many studies show that "children of lesbian mothers have normal, healthy relationships with other children as well as with adults." Several studies suggest that children of lesbian mothers may experience more teasing than other children, although the problem does not appear to be particularly serious. See Mary Becker, Family Law in the Secular State and Restrictions on Same–Sex Marriage, 2001 U. Ill. L. Rev. 1, 50–52. Should children be awarded to heterosexual fathers rather than lesbian mothers to protect them from teasing?

2. One study does suggest that children raised by lesbian mothers may be somewhat more likely to become lesbian or gay for a number of reasons, including being raised in an environment more accepting of same-sex relationships. See Becker, above note 1, at 52–53. If children raised by lesbian mothers do as well as other children on measures of well-being and development, should it matter whether these children are more likely to (feel free to?) identify as lesbian or gay themselves?

3. Polikoff and Chambers describe the shift in some jurisdictions from a per se rule that lesbian mothers and gay fathers are unfit parents in custody disputes with heterosexual ex-spouses to a rule that sexual orientation is irrelevant to custody and visitation issues except to the extent that the straight parent shows a link between sexual orientation and harm to the child (the nexus test). This sounds like a decided shift in favor of lesbian mothers and gay fathers. But Susan Becker reports that hostile judges find harm based solely on sexual orientation. Before these judges, there is no difference between the per se rule and the nexus test. See Susan J. Becker, Court–Created Boundaries Between a Visible Lesbian Mother and Her Children, 12 Wis. Women's L.J. 331 (1997); Susan J. Becker, Child Sexual Abuse Allegations Against a Lesbian or Gay Parent in a Custody or Visitation Dispute: Battling the Overt and Insidious Bias of Experts and Judges, 74 Denver L. Rev. 75 (1996). What rules would best protect relationships between children and their gay and lesbian parents with respect to (1) the relevance of sexual orientation and (2) the underlying custody standard (best interest, primary caretaker, ALI proposal, etc.)?

4. When a lesbian couple gives birth as a result of artificial insemination, there are three parents: two mothers (one biologically related to the child) and a semen donor. Who do you think should have a stronger claim, a semen donor who has not given up all rights to contact with a child in writing or the non-birth mother who has mothered the child? Why have courts been more willing to recognize the claims of the semen donor than

those of the non-birth mother when she and the birth mother separate after years of co-mothering?

5. The situation is changing so rapidly that it is impossible to give an accurate snapshot of the state of the law on lesbian and gay custody and parenting issues. In their 1999 article, Chambers and Polikoff state that both California and New York have "closed the door on all claims" brought by lesbian mothers who are not biologically related to their children, referring to the New York case of Alison D. v. Virginia M., 77 N.Y.2d 651, 569 N.Y.S.2d 586, 572 N.E.2d 27 (1991). But in July of 2000, a Westchester County family court judge ruled that when a lesbian couple split up, the children had the same "right" as other children to continued contact with both parents. See Janis C. v. Christine T., V–1926–99; v–1927–99 (Westchester Co., N.Y. Fam. Ct. June 6, 2000) (described at <http://www.nylj.com/north/00/06/ns061200a2.html> (visited 9/25/2000)). What can a lesbian mother do to minimize or eliminate the risk of losing all contact with her child if she and her partner, to whom the child is biologically related, split up?

6. Gay and Lesbian Defenders (GLAD, a Boston gay rights organization) created a working group of lawyers "to develop standards to guide attorney and client conduct in queer dissolution situations." William B. Rubenstein, Divided We Propagate: An Introduction to Protecting Families: Standards for Child Custody in Same–Sex Relationships, 10 U.C.L.A. Women's L. J. 143, 147–48 (1999)(describing development of the standards). For the standards, see GLAD, Protecting Families: Standards for Child Custody in Same–Sex Relationships, 10 U.C.L.A. Women's L. J. 151 (1999). If a lesbian couple came to you to draft a waiver of all parental rights to be signed by a sperm donor, would you suggest anything to try to protect the non-biological mother's link to the child in a jurisdiction in which second-parent adoption is not possible? What might be done to minimize her risk?

G. CHILD SUPPORT

LENORE WEITZMAN, THE ECONOMICS OF DIVORCE: SOCIAL AND ECONOMIC CONSEQUENCES OF PROPERTY, ALIMONY, AND CHILD SUPPORT AWARDS

28 U.C.L.A. L. Rev. 1181, 1233, 1234–40, 1241, 1249, 1250–52 (1981).

[The statistics upon which Lenore Weitzman relied in this classic article were derived from a massive study using data from court records and interviews Weitzman conducted with judges, matrimonial lawyers and divorced individuals in California between 1968 and 1978.]

IV. Child Support

A. The Amount of Child Support

* * *

Another way of looking at the typical child support award is as a percentage of husband's income. In Ted Byrd's case, $250 out of a net monthly income of $1,000 is 25% of Ted's net income for child support. That was about the average percentage in Los Angeles in 1977, but was slightly below the average in San Francisco where child support averaged about a third of the husband's net income.

The percentage of a husband's income awarded in child support varies by the husband's income level, with lower income men typically being required to pay a greater proportion of their incomes in child support. * * * In the random sample of court dockets, men who earned less than $10,000 a year were ordered to pay 20% of their gross incomes in child support. The percentage dropped to 10% of gross income among men earning $30,000 or more. * * *

[A] man is rarely ordered to part with more than a third of his net income, no matter what his income level. Since both the judges and the attorneys we interviewed often referred to an informal limit of never ordering a man to pay more than one-half of his net income in support, we were surprised to find this lower one-third "ceiling" operating in practice.

These data were also surprising in that the amounts of support awarded were lower than the amounts suggested in the schedule that judges use to set temporary orders. While the schedule of suggested support awards is intended as a rough guideline for temporary orders, close to 60% of the Los Angeles judges said they consistently relied on them. Perhaps these schedules are being interpreted as having set an upper limit or a ceiling on award levels.

B. The Adequacy of Child Support Awards

I would suggest three standards for evaluating the adequacy of child support awards. One is to compare them with the actual costs of raising children. A second is to assess their reasonableness in terms of the husband's financial resources. Each of these standards is embodied in California law, which specifies that support be set in accordance with the parties' needs and ability to pay. A third way to evaluate them is to compare the husband's financial contribution to child support with the financial contribution of his former wife.

1. The Cost of Raising Children

Economist Thomas Espenshade has calculated that it would cost $85,163 to raise a child to age eighteen in a moderate income family in 1980. In a low income family in the United States it would cost $58,238. His calculations include only the direct maintenance costs: out-of-pocket expenditures on the child's birth, food, clothing, housing, transportation, medical care, education, and other expenses. A final component is the cost of a four-year college education at a tax-supported institution. * * *

If we use Espenshade's conservative estimates, and eliminate the cost of college (since college costs may not be included in child support), we find that it averages $4,200 a year to raise one child at a moderate income level. Because of economies of scale, a second child increases the costs roughly half as much as the first child so that the total childrearing cost for two minor children would be over $6,000 a year. Similarly, if we calculate the cost for a low income standard of living, we find the cost close to $3,000 a year for one child and over $4,500 for two children.

* * * If we assume that our hypothetical Pat Byrd would raise her children at the moderate standard, we find that her court-ordered child support award would give her $2,700 less than what she needs. Even at the poverty standard, her court-ordered child support would leave her $1,200 short.

The inadequacy of court-ordered child support is underscored by another relevant comparison. Pat Byrd's total support award of $450 per month for child and spousal support is lower than she would get from the Aid to Families with Dependent Children (AFDC) program. The AFDC level of support for a household with two children is $463 per month plus $73 in food stamps, or a total of $536 per month. The Federal Government has determined this sum to be necessary for families at the lowest economic levels; hence we see that Pat Byrd, our average divorced woman, obviously will not be able to rear her children, even at the poverty level, on the court-ordered support.

One problem with Espenshade's calculations is that they omit a major child care expense that Pat Byrd will have to bear. Since Espenshade's calculations are based on two-parent families, he assumes that one parent, typically the mother, is available full time to care for the child. But if the mother in a single-parent family has to work, she typically has to pay someone else to take care of her children. These child care costs have to be added to Espenshade's estimates in order to determine adequate child support for such single-parent families.

* * *

If we assume that Pat Byrd will work full time, then her child care costs would be about $200 a month for her daughter and $138 a month for her son. That adds up to over $333 a month—more than her entire child support award. Of course, if she is lucky enough to get the children into a public day care center with a sliding fee scale, her costs will be much less, but that typically entails a long waiting list and places her under pressure to go to work immediately.

2. *The Husband's Ability to Pay*

A second way to evaluate the adequacy of child support awards is in terms of the husband's financial resources. In a classic study of child support enforcement, Professor David Chambers established a procedure for evaluating the reasonableness of the court awards in terms of the husband's resources.[199] Chambers first looked at the father's postdivorce standard of living *without* any deductions. Following his procedures with our California data, we find, as Chambers did, that most fathers would be relatively well off. In Michigan, over 90% of the divorced fathers

199. D. Chambers, Making Fathers Pay (1979).

would be living at a level above the higher standard budget if they did not pay any support. In California, close to two-thirds of the fathers would be living at this level if no support were paid. When a father moves out, "separating himself from his family and hoarding all income to himself, the father improves his standard of living dramatically."

Next, Chambers asked what would happen to the father's standard of living if he paid the full amount of child support ordered. At the same time he asked how ex-wives and dependent children would fare on the amount of support ordered by the court. Obviously, if the family income stays constant, both units cannot maintain their former standard when living apart. In Michigan, Chambers found that "under the levels of child support that are ordered by the court . . . it is only the women and children whose standards of living decline even when the father is making payments." Chambers concluded that 80% of the fathers could maintain a comfortable standard of living (at or above the intermediate standard budget) after paying court-ordered support.

In California, we found that close to three-quarters of the fathers had the "ability to pay" the amount the court ordered without a substantial reduction in their standard of living. * * * 61% of the California fathers would be able to comply fully with the court order and still live above the high standard budget. An additional 12% would be living above the lower standard budget. Thus 73% of the men could live at a level above the lower standard budget. In contrast only 7% of the women would be living at this level. Almost all the women and children—fully 93%—would be living below the poverty level.

* * *

V. Social and Economic Consequences for the Family

A. *Postdivorce Incomes of Husbands And Wives*

The awards made in * * * two hypothetical cases illustrate how support awards structure large disparities in the postdivorce incomes of men and women. * * * [I]f Victor Thompson is ordered to pay $2,000 a month spousal support, he retains $4,000 a month or twice as much income for himself. And if Ted Byrd is ordered to pay $450 a month for spousal and child support, he retains $550 for himself or 55% of the family's income. That leaves 45%—less than half—to be shared by the three other members of his family. Judges are reluctant to consider taking more than half of a man's net income for support, but when there are children in the family, the consequences can be grossly inequitable: a wife and two children are expected to live on less than the husband has for himself.

Thus one result of the support awards discussed above is that husbands are much better off after divorce than are their former wives and children. * * *

B. *The Impoverishment of Women and Children*

* * *

These data * * * show a radical change in the two families' [those of the former husband and wife] standard of living just one year after legal divorce. Men experienced a 42% improvement in their postdivorce standard of living, while women experienced a 73% loss.[b]

* * * [D]ivorce is a financial catastrophe for most women: in just one year they experience a dramatic decline in income and a calamitous drop in their standard of living. It is difficult to imagine how they survive the severe economic deprivation: every single expenditure that one takes for granted—clothing, food, housing, heat—must be cut to one-half or one-third of what one is accustomed to. No wonder that more divorced women report that they are in a constant financial crisis after divorce and that they are perpetually worried about not being able to pay their bills. This financial crisis cannot help but affect their socio-emotional lives, and it is not surprising that divorced women report more stress and less satisfaction with their lives than any other group of Americans.

Notes on Child Support

1. Some commentators disagree with Weitzman's conclusions. Weitzman attributes the economic situation of women after divorce to the passage of reformed divorce laws and, in particular, to no-fault divorce, because it took away previous bargaining power based on the capacity to resist a divorce. Others point out that the economic situation of women and children was bad both before and after the change. See, e.g., Marygold S. Melli, Constructing A Social Problem: The Post–Divorce Plight Of Women And Children, ABF Research J., Fall 1986, at 759, 770. Professor Martha Fineman criticizes the notion that *any* legal reforms grounded in the concept of marriage as an equal partnership can provide a remedy for the post-divorce situation of women. Martha L. Fineman, Illusive Equality: On Weitzman's *Divorce Revolution*, ABF Research J., Fall 1986, at 781, 783. This is so, in Fineman's view, because such reforms are based upon a liberal feminist ideal of gender equality and independence, while the real life situation of women and children is one of need and dependence. Id. at 786. What types of child support arrangements do you think would be supported by proponents of the various "schools" of feminist theory described in Chapter 3? What do you think would be fair?

2. Professor Jane Rutherford suggests a per capita division of income upon divorce, so that a family consisting of a mother, father and three children with the mother earning $20,000 and the father earning $30,000 would result in the following division upon divorce if the mother has

b. Others disagree about the exact percentage, but all agree that women's standard of living does drop substantially in the aftermath of divorce, while men's does rise. See, e.g., Suzanne M. Bianchi, Lekha Subaiya, and Joan R. Kahn, The Gender Gap in the Economic Well–Being of Nonresident Fathers and Custodial Mothers, 36 Demography 195 (1999).

custody: mother and children receive $40,000 (a $20,000 transfer from the father), and father receives $10,000, thus allocating the total post-divorce family income of $50,000 among the individuals on a per capita basis. Rutherford, Duty in Divorce: Shared Income as a Path to Equality, 58 Fordham L.Rev. 539, 566–67 (1990). Is this a fair division? Why or why not?

3. Data compiled by the Bureau of the Census show that in 1995 only about 39% of custodial parents (85% of whom are women) who were awarded child support payments in fact received the full payment awarded; this percentage had increased from 34% in 1993. Census Bureau, Current Population Reports, Mar. 1999, Child Support for Custodial Mothers and Fathers: 1995, at 1, 4. These statistics show only the extent of nonpayment of child support where an award of child support has in fact been made, either by court order or by voluntary agreement. According to the 1995 statistics, 42% of the 13.7 million custodial parents with children from absent parents had never received any award in the first place, for a variety of reasons, most commonly that they did not feel the need for a legal agreement or that the child's other parent could not afford to pay. Id. at 2–3; Figure 2. Not surprisingly, the Census Bureau reported that about 32% of custodial parents who do not receive child support have a relatively high poverty rate. Id. at 3.

In the last two decades, Congress has enacted legislation to strengthen the enforcement of child support awards, requiring state enforcement agencies, among other things, to attempt to track down absent fathers, to require mandatory withholding of support from paychecks, and to establish guidelines to determine child support obligations. See 42 U.S.C.A. §§ 651–654 (1988). By contrast, in Sweden, if a noncustodial parent does not or cannot pay a child support award, the government steps in and pays a "maintenance advance" to the child, which the parent must repay; but if the amount of child support awarded is clearly inadequate, the government will also pay a supplementary allowance which the parent is not required to repay. Ruth Sidel, Women & Children Last: The Plight Of Poor Women In Affluent America 180–81 (1986). How does the Swedish arrangement differ from that in this country? What are the conceptual underpinnings of the two programs? Who do you think should be primarily responsible for the support of young children? On what grounds?

4. Why do you think so many fathers fail to pay child support? Harry D. Krause believes that the main reason is that defaulting fathers simply don't have the money to pay. Krause, Child Support Reassessed: Limits of Private Responsibility and the Public Interest, in Divorce Reform at the Crossroads 175 (Stephen D. Sugarman and Herma Hill Kay, eds. 1990). However, Weitzman's data from California and data gathered by David Chambers in Michigan indicate that inability to pay is certainly not the only cause. Indeed, there is little relationship between income and noncompliance with child support orders. Weitzman, above, at 1256. Chambers' study shows that strong enforcement procedures, including automatic monitoring of payment or nonpayment of child support by court personnel, a self-starting system of collection, and a high incarceration rate, correlate with high rates of compliance. David L. Chambers, Making Fathers Pay: The Enforcement of Child Support 90–93 (1979). What does this correlation show, if anything, about the reasons for nonpayment? About appropriate remedies? Why do you

think courts are reluctant to jail fathers for nonpayment of child support? Do you think they should do so?

5. Krause suggests that our society's emphasis on collecting child support from absent fathers is essentially misplaced in an era when the only familial relationship may be founded upon (1) consanguinity based on permissible recreational sex or (2) the essentially terminated post-divorce relationship between the typical father and his child. Krause, above note 4, at 181. In the past, Krause argues, children looked after their parents in old age, but this reciprocal function has now been taken over by the government, through Social Security and Medicare. The responsibility for child support should be undertaken by the public as well, Krause concludes, now that there is no real social link between many fathers and their children. What do you think of this argument? Is it likely that the government, state or federal, will undertake the responsibility for adequate child support in the United States?

6. As indirect support for Krause's theory that fathers do not pay child support because of attenuated links to their children, the Census Bureau reports that noncustodial parents who had visitation or joint custody were more likely to make child support payments: 74% with those provisions made payments and only 35% without them. Census Bureau, Current Population Reports, Mar. 1999, Child Support for Custodial Mothers and Fathers: 1995, at 3. Which do you think is the chicken and which the egg? One study of 80 noncustodial fathers showed that the fathers who were *most* likely to lose contact with their children after divorce were the very ones who had been most involved with and attached to them during the marriage, apparently because the loss of the closer connection was so painful that fathers adapted to it by becoming disengaged. Edward Kruk, Discontinuity Between Pre-and Post–Divorce Father–Child Relationships: New Evidence Regarding Paternal Disengagement, in The Consequences of Divorce: Economic and Custodial Impact on Children and Adults 195–227 (Craig A. Everett, ed. 1991). How would you address this problem?

7. Even if the full amount of child support is collected, the amounts may be meager in relation to the costs of raising a child. Different states calculate the support due in a number of different ways. See, e.g., Ira Mark Ellman, Paul M. Kurtz And Elizabeth S. Scott, Family Law 532–33 (3d Ed. 1998). One system bases the amount presumed due upon a percentage of the noncustodial parent's income, for example, 20% for one child, 25% for two, 32% for three, up to 50% for six or more children. 750 ILCS 5/505(a)(1)(2000). Thus, if a parent obliged to pay support earns $40,000 per year and takes home $32,000 as statutorily defined net income, he would owe approximately $533 per month for one child, $667 for two, $853 for three children, and so on. The custodial parent's income would not be taken into account, but she would presumably work given the meager resources otherwise available to the diminished family unit. (In other states, the income of both parents is taken into account, and the calculation would assume contributions by both toward support of the child.) Given that, even under the rather low national averages reported in the Census Bureau statistics for 1993 described above (in Section D2), the custodial parent will be required to pay between $300 and $450 per month for child care while she

works, this does not leave an adequate amount for other costs, such as housing, food, clothes, and medical care.

8. One reason frequently cited for the federal government's intense focus on collection of child support is that this will enable the movement of women and children off welfare. See, e.g., Institute for Women's Policy Research, How Much Can Child Support Provide? Welfare, Family Income and Child Support, Mar. 1999, at 1 (quoting President Clinton). Careful analysis of the factors associated with the receipt of child support challenges this hypothesis, for a number of reasons. First, women who in the past received AFDC were in fact the women least likely to be awarded child support or to collect it if awarded. Id. at 1–3. Moreover, the amount of support these women could potentially collect is quite limited; child support currently constitutes only about 11.8% of family income for this group (in contrast with 21.3% for non-AFDC but low-income families), hardly enough to move the family out of poverty. Id. at 5–6. The authors of the study conclude: "This points to the limitation of using child support as a safety net or replacement of government transfers for single-mother families on welfare, because those single-mothers who are disadvantaged in the labor market are also disadvantaged in obtaining child support." Id. at 6. What are the policy implications of this study?

9. Stephen D. Sugarman distinguishes between a conservative and a liberal view of child support. The conservative view rests upon the principles that it is morally irresponsible to have a child unless one can financially support one and that a morally responsible father will continue to support his children even if his relationship to the mother breaks down. The liberal view, by contrast, rests upon the assumption that everyone should be able to have children (and most will do so, in any event), that the resulting children should not be punished for their parents' conduct, and that the society has a collective moral obligation to support those children whose parents are too poor to do so alone. Sugarman, Financial Support of Children and the End of Welfare As We Know It, 81 Va. L. Rev. 2523, 2524–27 (1995). With which of these two perspectives do you agree, and why? What policy consequences flow from each?

10. A number of different proposals resting upon some notion of collective responsibility for the support of children have been made. Perhaps the most influential has been that of Irwin Garfinkel for a child support assurance (CSA) program. See Garfinkel, Assuring Child Support: An Extension of Social Security (1992). Under this plan, the caretaker of a child would receive either the amount paid by the noncustodial parent pursuant to a child support award or an assured benefit amount set by the government (Garfinkel proposes $2000–2500 for one child per year), whichever is higher; if child support lower than the assured benefit is paid, the government would make up the difference between the two. Id. at 47. Unlike child support allowances given to all families in a country like France, regardless of need or marital status, CSA would be available only to single parents and only to the extent the amount was not covered by the noncustodial parent. Sugarman makes a less broad-reaching proposal, suggesting that children of absent parents be covered by benefits under the Social Security system that are currently reserved for the children of parents whose absence is the result

of death. Sugarman, above note 9, at 2561. This plan, of course, would only cover children whose fathers are themselves insured under the Social Security system, leaving out, for example, many teen mothers. Id. at 2562. Which of these alternatives do you prefer? Which (if any) seems politically feasible? Can you think of other ways in which our society might undertake to protect these children?

Chapter 9

WOMEN AND EDUCATION

A. INTRODUCTION

The struggle for equality in women's education began with the demand for access and has evolved to question the very idea of education, both its content and process. Women now make up the majority of students in American colleges and universities, and by 2006 women will earn 55% of all bachelor's degrees. A statistical comparison of educational opportunities before federal legislation mandating non-discrimination in education and two decades later shows the following gains:

	1970's	1994
Female high school grads, aged 16–24, in college	43%	63%
Women completing 4 or more years of college	18%	27%
Men completing 4 or more years of college	26%	27%
Medical degrees conferred on women	9%	38%
Dental degrees conferred on women	1%	38%
Law degrees conferred on women	25%	44%
Business degrees conferred on women	8%	47%
Engineering degrees conferred on women	.5%	15%
Doctorates in science and engineering conferred on women	9%	20%
Doctoral degrees to U.S. citizens conferred on women	25%	44%
Percentage of college athletes female	15%	37%
Percentage of high school athletes female	7.5%	39%
Women postsecondary vocational education students	—	58%[1]

1. U.S. Dept. of Ed., Title IX: 25 Years of Progress 3–4, 6, 12–14 (1997). In terms of international comparisons, the U.S. fared relatively well in the number of women, aged 25–34, who had completed (a) secondary and (b) higher education degrees in 1992:

	(a)	(b)
United States	87%	23%
Japan	92%	12%
West Germany	86%	11%
United Kingdom	80%	11%
France	66%	12%

This represents extraordinary progress, particularly in light of 19th century attitudes towards the education of women, described by Florence Howe:

> * * * Scientific belief held not only that the brains of women were smaller than those of men, but also that brain size was directly related to intelligence, and that hence women were less capable than men of academic learning. More important, however, was the medical assumption that only one bodily organ functioned optimally at any one time. Thus, if women used their brains during adolescence, their uterine development would be disturbed and their child-bearing abilities impaired, perhaps so severely as to cause the production of malformed or dead infants. Indeed, higher education might in and of itself sterilize women. * * * [F]or the female scholar, intense study directly inhibited her ability to bear children, or to bear healthy normal ones, capable of surviving past infancy.[2]

The belief that education impairs women's ability to conceive and bear children was an effective tool to keep girls out of the classroom. It was not until the latter part of the 19th century that almost all public elementary schools admitted both boys and girls; in 1837 (200 years after the first American college was founded), Oberlin College admitted women, becoming the first coeducational institution of higher learning, and the first all-female baccalaureate program began at Mt. Holyoke.[3] Education for female slaves did not come until after Emancipation; it was a crime to teach slaves to read.[4]

It took another century for Congress to attempt to remedy the widespread discrimination in education, enacting the Education Amendments of 1972 ("Title IX"), mandating that women shall not "be excluded from participation in, be denied the benefits of, or be subjected to discrimination under any education program or activity receiving Federal financial assistance."[5]

Italy	43%	7%
Canada	83%	16%

2. Florence Howe, Myths of Coeducation 210 (1984).

3. Deborah L. Rhode, Association and Assimilation, 81 Nw. U.L. Rev. 106, 128–136 (1986).

4. Angela Y. Davis, Women, Race & Class 106 (1981) ("with the exception of Maryland and Kentucky, every Southern state absolutely prohibited the education of slaves").

5. 20 U.S.C.A. § 1681 et seq. (1988). The statute continues, *inter alia,* to exclude from coverage (1) religious schools; (2) U.S. military schools; (3) public undergraduate schools that have been single sex since inception; and (4) limited other special programs. See also regulations implementing Title IX, 45 C.F.R. Pt. 86 (1992). Three other federal statutes deal with sex discrimination in education: the Women's Educational Equity Act of 1974, 20 U.S.C.A. § 3041 (2000) (providing for federal financial and technical support to local efforts to remove barriers for females in all areas of education); Title IV of the Civil Rights Act of 1964, 42 U.S.C.A. § 2000c (1994) (providing for support to schools to comply with the mandate of nondiscrimination by providing funds for regional Desegregation Assistance Centers and grants to state education departments for providing more equitable education to students); and the 1976 amendments to the Vocational Education Act of 1963, 20 U.S.C.A. § 1371 (2000) (requiring states to act affirmatively to eliminate sex bias, stereotyping, and discrimination in vocational education).

Although women are now admitted to public schools, bias persists in a multitude of forms, many not readily apparent.[6] For instance, over half of girls and women at all levels of education experience sexual harassment.[7] And studies of how teachers relate to boys and girls consistently find that boys are called on more often, given more constructive criticism, and encouraged more.[8] Another, more serious issue is whether boys and girls learn differently. Some studies indicate that girls learn best through collaboration and "connected" knowing and that boys thrive on individualistic, aggressive styles. Nonetheless, the "male" style remains the norm. Gendered use of language and communication patterns further exacerbates this problem.

Textbooks, for the most part, continue to focus on the exploits of men; women are absent or are presented in passive, limited and limiting roles. Not only are women who have achieved in the public sphere often ignored, but women's accomplishments in the domestic sphere are also. This results in a distorted view of history, emphasizing military events; if women's roles in society and achievements were included in textbooks, our entire conception of historical periods, issues and circumstances would change.[9]

Girls are also discouraged, and frequently excluded, from participating in athletics, a traditional way to develop self-assurance, learn teamwork and gain recognition. It is probably in the area of athletics that Title IX has had the most profound effect. Still, athletic scholarships for women continue to lag behind those awarded to men. As of 1997, college women were awarded only about one third of all athletic scholarship dollars.[10]

Sex bias continues when women apply for financial assistance to attend college, receiving less in grants and loans, and they thus are more likely to withdraw from school due to financial problems. Additionally, in spite of the proven lack of correlation between women's performance in classwork and their scoring on standardized tests, colleges continue to use such test scores to deny admission to some women and to disqualify others from financial support.[11]

6. See generally The AAUW Report: How Schools Shortchange Girls (1992).

7. See Harassment Is Rife in Schools, Chi. Trib., Mar. 25, 1993, News § , at 3 (based upon a survey in Seventeen Magazine, over 80% of girls aged nine to 19 reported inappropriate sexual comments, gestures and looks).

8. See generally Myra and David Sadker, Failing at Fairness: How America's Schools Cheat Girls (1994).

9. Howe, above note 2, at 86, 134–35.

10. In 1971, fewer than 300,000 high school girls participated in interscholastic sports; in 1997, over 2.4 million did. Women's basketball illustrates this dramatic development: from 1972 to 1994, girls playing high school basketball increased 300 percent. Without Title IX's mandate, it is unlikely that American women would have won the 1996 Olympic gold medal in basketball. Girls and women are also participating in greater numbers in sports traditionally viewed as male only—lacrosse, wrestling, soccer, rugby, and ice hockey. Soccer has become more and more of a "girls" sport, as demonstrated by the U.S. women's team winning an Olympic gold in 1996 and the World Cup in 1999. Title IX: 25 Years of Progress, above note 1, at 15, 17.

11. See generally Isaiah Smithson, Introduction: Investigating Gender, Power, and Pedagogy, in Gender in the Classroom: Power and Pedagogy 1 (Susan L. Gabriel

The definition of "equality" in education seems more elusive the more we learn. Some educators are turning to separatism as a solution for both women and minorities. Several studies have measured the value of single-sex colleges in terms of both external achievements and internal satisfaction and have found them superior to coeducation. This forces us to ponder the following complicated question: is the concept "separate but equal," rejected for race in 1954,[12] nonetheless viable when considering gender?

This chapter will address a wide variety of issues involved in equality of education for women, beginning with single-sex education and proceeding to issues of testing and affirmative action. After discussing equality in athletic programs, the chapter concludes with an examination of two areas that are very important to acceptance of women into educational institutions on an equal footing with men: the regulation of hate speech and sexual harassment on campus.

B. SINGLE-SEX EDUCATIONAL INSTITUTIONS

MISSISSIPPI UNIVERSITY FOR WOMEN v. HOGAN

United States Supreme Court, 1982.

458 U.S. 718, 102 S.Ct. 3331, 73 L.Ed.2d 1090.

JUSTICE O'CONNOR delivered the opinion of the Court.

This case presents the narrow issue of whether a state statute that excludes males from enrolling in a state-supported professional nursing school violates the Equal Protection Clause of the Fourteenth Amendment.

The facts are not in dispute. In 1884, the Mississippi Legislature created the Mississippi Industrial Institute and College for the Education of White Girls of the State of Mississippi, now the oldest state-supported all-female college in the United States. The school, known today as Mississippi University for Women (MUW), has from its inception limited its enrollment to women.

* * *

The School of Nursing [established in 1971] has its own faculty and administrative officers and establishes its own criteria for admission.

Respondent, Joe Hogan, is a registered nurse but does not hold a baccalaureate degree in nursing. * * * In 1979, Hogan applied for admission to the MUW School of Nursing's baccalaureate program. Although he was otherwise qualified, he was denied admission to the School of Nursing solely because of his sex. School officials informed him

and Smithson, eds. 1990); Katherine Connor and Ellen J. Vargyas, The Legal Implications of Gender Bias in Standardized Testing, 7 Berkeley Women's L.J. 13 (1992).

12. Brown v. Board of Education, 347 U.S. 483, 74 S.Ct. 686, 98 L.Ed. 873 (1954).

that he could audit the courses in which he was interested, but could not enroll for credit.

Hogan filed an action * * *, claiming the single-sex admissions policy of MUW's School of Nursing violated the Equal Protection Clause of the Fourteenth Amendment. * * * Because the challenged policy expressly discriminates among applicants on the basis of gender, it is subject to scrutiny under the Equal Protection Clause of the Fourteenth Amendment. That this statutory policy discriminates against males rather than against females does not exempt it from scrutiny or reduce the standard of review. Our decisions also establish that the party seeking to uphold a statute that classifies individuals on the basis of their gender must carry the burden of showing an "exceedingly persuasive justification" for the classification. The burden is met only by showing at least that the classification serves "important governmental objectives and that the discriminatory means employed" are "substantially related to the achievement of those objectives."

* * *

The State's primary justification for maintaining the single-sex admissions policy of MUW's School of Nursing is that it compensates for discrimination against women and, therefore, constitutes educational affirmative action. As applied to the School of Nursing, we find the State's argument unpersuasive.

In limited circumstances, a gender-based classification favoring one sex can be justified if it intentionally and directly assists members of the sex that is disproportionately burdened. * * *

Mississippi has made no showing that women lacked opportunities to obtain training in the field of nursing or to attain positions of leadership in that field when the MUW School of Nursing opened its door or that women currently are deprived of such opportunities. In fact, in 1970, the year before the School of Nursing's first class enrolled, women earned 94 percent of the nursing baccalaureate degrees conferred in Mississippi and 98.6 percent of the degrees earned nationwide. * * * As one would expect, the labor force reflects the same predominance of women in nursing. When MUW's School of Nursing began operation, nearly 98 percent of all employed registered nurses were female.

Rather than compensate for discriminatory barriers faced by women, MUW's policy of excluding males from admission to the School of Nursing tends to perpetuate the stereotyped view of nursing as an exclusively woman's job.[15] By assuring that Mississippi allots more openings in its state-supported nursing schools to women than it does to men, MUW's admissions policy lends credibility to the old view that

15. Officials of the American Nurses Association have suggested that excluding men from the field has depressed nurses' wages. To the extent the exclusion of men has that effect, MUW's admissions policy actually penalizes the very class the State purports to benefit.

women, not men, should become nurses, and makes the assumption that nursing is a field for women a self-fulfilling prophecy. * * *

The policy is invalid also because it fails the second part of the equal protection test, for the State has made no showing that the gender-based classification is substantially and directly related to its proposed compensatory objective. To the contrary, MUW's policy of permitting men to attend classes as auditors fatally undermines its claim that women, at least those in the School of Nursing, are adversely affected by the presence of men.

* * *

The uncontroverted record reveals that admitting men to nursing classes does not affect teaching style, that the presence of men in the classroom would not affect the performance of the female nursing students, and that men in coeducational nursing schools do not dominate the classroom. In sum, the record in this case is flatly inconsistent with the claim that excluding men from the School of Nursing is necessary to reach any of MUW's educational goals.

* * *

Accordingly, we hold that MUW's policy of denying males the right to enroll for credit in its School of Nursing violates the Equal Protection Clause of the Fourth Amendment.

JUSTICE POWELL, with whom JUSTICE REHNQUIST joins, dissenting.

The Court's opinion bows deeply to conformity. Left without honor—indeed, held unconstitutional—is an element of diversity that has characterized much of American education and enriched much of American life. The Court in effect holds today that no State now may provide even a single institution of higher learning open only to women students.

* * *

By applying heightened equal protection analysis to this case, the Court frustrates the liberating spirit of the Equal Protection Clause. It prohibits the States from providing women with an opportunity to choose the type of university they prefer. And yet it is these women whom the Court regards as the *victims* of an illegal, stereotyped perception of the role of women in our society. The Court reasons this way in a case in which no woman has complained, and the only complainant is a man who advances no claims on behalf of anyone else. His claim, it should be recalled, is not that he is being denied a substantive educational opportunity, or even the right to attend an all-male or a coeducational college. It is *only* that the colleges open to him are located at inconvenient distances.

Notes on Hogan

1. The majority opinion in *Hogan* states that when a man alleges that he has been discriminated against because of his sex in violation of Equal

Protection, courts are to apply the "intermediate scrutiny" standard of review applicable in similar suits brought by women, rather than the rational basis standard generally applicable to claims under the Equal Protection Clause. Which is the appropriate standard when discrimination against men is alleged? Do you agree with the majority or dissent? Does it matter which standard is applied? How does this case fit with the early liberal feminist strategy of the Women's Rights Project discussed in Chapter Two?

2. In his dissent in *Hogan,* Justice Powell states that "[t]he Court in effect holds today that no State now may provide even a single institution of higher learning open only to women students." Is this a correct reading of the majority opinion?

3. Justice O'Connor warns in *Hogan* against "benign" legislation that is based on paternalistic stereotypes. Is it possible to characterize sex-specific rules, like MUW's, as benign *or* harmful? Don't such rules help some women at some times in some ways and hurt some women at some times in other ways? How did MUW's policy (a) help and (b) hurt women? How would you decide whether the costs outweigh the benefits? How should courts approach such difficult issues? Can the courts be trusted to make these determinations?

Consider Justice Powell's view that MUW's women-only policy is benign because it conforms to an honored tradition which gives women the benefit of diversity in their choice of school, i.e., it expands women's choices. David Hoffman points to three problems with this characterization:

> First, it is clearly a mistake to assume that women, or men, have unlimited freedom of choice as to the school they attend. Many students are forced, as Joe Hogan was, to attend school where their families or jobs are located. Moreover, the notion that a woman's decision to attend a sex-segregated school is truly voluntary is deeply undercut by the reality, recognized even by Justice Powell, that one of the factors that make single-sex schools attractive for women is the sexist treatment they receive at coeducational schools.
>
> Second, separate schools for women have historically been significantly inferior to comparable male facilities. This second-class status may affect not only the self-esteem of students who attend women's schools, but their careers and salaries as well.
>
> Third, the Justices' invocation of ancient tradition on behalf of single-sex schools probably does more to undermine the legitimacy of the schools than to bolster it. Women's schools were originally founded in the United States because of the exclusion of women from the established colleges and universities, and bore an unmistakable stigma on that account. Their curricula, moreover, were defined by traditional, stereotyped notions of "women's place." To the extent that women's schools have transcended these limitations, they have generally done so in spite of their heritage rather than because of it.
>
> * * *
>
> "Choice" is relatively unmeaningful for women when the range of options is largely determined by men.

Hoffman, Challenge to Single–Sex Schools Under Equal Protection: *Mississippi University for Women v. Hogan*, 6 Harv. Women's L.J. 163, 172 (1983). What criteria do you think Hoffman would utilize to determine if a single-sex school benefitted women or not? What criteria does Justice Powell use?

4. How would the feminist theorists examined in Chapter 3 approach the problems raised in *Hogan*?

5. Are women's colleges discriminatory by their very nature? Should our society approve of separatism when it is chosen by the less powerful group, rather than imposed upon it by the dominant group, and is a means toward empowerment? See Janella Miller, The Future of Private Women's Colleges, 7 Harv. Women's L.J. 153, 179–80 (1984).

6. A San Francisco coeducational academic high school adopted a policy that the student body should be divided 50/50 between boys and girls. In order to achieve this balance, it was necessary to set an admission standard of a 3.50 grade point average on a scale of 4 for girls and only 3.25 for boys. Is this constitutional? What does this policy do to a definition of equality? Is this simply "affirmative action" in reverse? See Berkelman v. San Francisco Unified Sch. Dist., 501 F.2d 1264 (9th Cir.1974).

7. Should it matter whether the government operates a sex-specific school? What arguments can you make for allowing only private single-sex institutions?

UNITED STATES v. VIRGINIA

United States Supreme Court, 1996.

518 U.S. 515, 116 S.Ct. 2264, 135 L.Ed.2d 735.

[This case, known as *VMI*, is excerpted in Chapter Two, above.]

Notes on Single–Sex Education

1. Is *VMI* consistent with *Hogan*? Does *Hogan* support sex-specific schools when such schools add diversity to a state's educational offerings? What of *Hogan*'s rejection of traditional sexual stereotypes? Does the Court in *VMI* accept such stereotypes? In *Hogan,* the Supreme Court went out of its way to emphasize that men in the classrooms did not affect teaching style or the performance of female students; does it address that concern in *VMI*? Is the difference in how the genders learn relevant to these cases?

2. How would the *VMI* issue, i.e., whether women must be admitted to a male-only state-supported college, be analyzed under the various feminist theories explored in Chapter 3? How would proponents of each of these approaches respond to the point that VMI will change, if not be destroyed, if women are admitted?

3. Does *VMI*, as Scalia indicates, sound the death knell for public, single-sex education? What about footnote 7, in which the Court stated it did "not question the Commonwealth's prerogative *evenhandedly* to support diverse educational opportunities (emphasis added)?" What criteria will such a school have to meet to pass muster after *VMI*? What about private single-sex schools? Will they be affected by *VMI*?

4. *VMI* was decided on constitutional grounds. Does Title IX impose identical requirements, i.e., are "equal protection" and non-discrimination on the basis of gender identical concepts? Are there differing standards?

5. Some states continue to experiment with single-sex education in primary and secondary public schools:

(a) New York City has a public school for girls only, the Young Women's Leadership High School. Opened in 1996, the school now has over 400 middle and high school students. As soon as the school opened, the New York Civil Liberties Union, the National Organization for Women, and the New York Civil Rights Coalition filed a Title IX complaint, but as of 1999 the Department of Education had yet to take any final action. Does the school violate Title IX? What arguments would you make in defense of the school? Is a single-sex public K–12 school unconstitutional? See Denise C. Morgan, Anti–Subordination Analysis after *United States v. Virginia*: Evaluating the Constitutionality of K–12 Single–Sex Public Schools, [1999] U. Chi. Leg. F. 381.

(b) California's former governor, Pete Wilson, set aside $5 million dollars in 1996 to fund experimental, single-sex public school academies on sites of existing middle and high schools. This program required that districts receiving funds must spend equal amounts on boys' and girls' programs, and that the money must be spent for equivalent items or purposes. See Tamar Lewin, In California, Wider Test of Same–Sex Schools, N.Y. Times, Oct. 9, 1997, at A1. Is this constitutional? Is it a violation of Title IX?

(c) In 1991, the Detroit School Board Task Force recommended establishing all-male, African American high school academies, citing the following statistics: (1) in 1989, the unemployment rate for African American males living in Detroit was 18.3%, compared with 7.1% for all males in Michigan; (2) the homicide rate for Black males between ages 15 and 24 in the county in which Detroit is located is 14 times the national rate for all males, twice the rate for African American males in Michigan, and 47 times the rate for white males in Michigan; (3) 54% of Detroit boys eventually drop out of school, and over 66% are suspended; (4) boys fall further behind the national average academically in almost every successive year of elementary and secondary school; (5) boys in the first grade perform at or above grade level on academic achievement tests, but by the twelfth grade they are over two grades behind in reading and over three grades behind in mathematics; and (6) the Detroit male dropout rate is approximately 10% higher than the female dropout rate. Note, Inner–City Single–Sex Schools: Educational Reform or Invidious Discrimination?, 105 Harv.L.Rev. 1741, 1742–43 (1992). Moreover, the Detroit public school student population is 90% Black. Id. at 1743, n. 10. However, girls, too, suffer from remarkably high dropout rates and low academic performance in the Detroit school system. Nearly 50% of female students drop out, and, on average, twelfth-grade girls score only at a ninth-grade level on standardized math tests and at a tenth-grade level on standardized reading tests. Id. at 1745, n. 32. High levels of violence, teenage pregnancy and other social problems are correlated with low academic performance. Id. at 1756.

Do you think these statistics justify the Detroit School Board's establishment of three male academies? Does the Constitution forbid dealing with one *part* of a problem before solving the whole? Especially when the alternative may be to take *no* action? What if the Detroit School Board had a plan in place to open a similar number of Female Academies on a specific date, rather than simply saying that it would do so "soon"? Would that change your opinion? See Garrett v. Board of Education, Detroit, 775 F.Supp. 1004 (E.D.Mich.1991) (granting a preliminary injunction preventing the opening of the unconstitutional educational facilities on the ground that the important purpose of the all-male academies is insufficient to override the rights of females to equal opportunities).

What does the Detroit School Board mean when it states that African American boys are "at-risk" students? Does it mean "at risk" of committing a crime? In what ways are the Detroit African American girls also "at risk"? What can you infer from the School Board's decision to address the male students' problems first?

The boys' "Rites of Passage" curriculum in the Detroit schools included topics such as "men master their emotions," "men need a vision and a plan for living," and "men acquire skills and knowledge to overcome life's obstacles." What would be included in a "Rites of Passage" curriculum for adolescent girls?

Many parents desperately wanted their children to go to the Male Academies. Within four months of the announcement that the Academies would be established, nearly 1200 children had applied for 560 slots. Accord in Detroit Would Let Girls Attend All–Boys Schools, N.Y. Times, Aug. 26, 1991, at A16. Following the ruling in *Garrett,* the Detroit School Board approved a compromise plan and admitted 38 girls to the experimental schools with the Afrocentric curriculum for the 1991–92 school year. Ron Russell, Single–Sex Schools Get New Approach in Detroit, Detroit News, Nov. 18, 1991. Does that settlement satisfy Equal Protection concerns?

6. Are there dangers in an all-male institution that are absent in an all-female institution? Are there benefits to an all-female institution that are absent from an all-male institution? What arguments can you make for permitting female-only institutions while disallowing male-only institutions? What arguments would the various feminist theorists discussed in Chapter 3 make?

7. Would separate but equal grade schools be permissible under the feminist theories explored in Chapter 3? What are the benefits and harms likely to be associated with such schools?

8. Michael Kimmel, one of the founders of the masculinities movement, addressed why boys are at risk in a speech he gave in January of 2000:

> Are boys in trouble in school? At first glance, the statistics would suggest that they are. Boys commit suicide four times more often than girls, get into fights twice as often, get lower grades on standardized tests of reading and writing, and have lower class rank and fewer honors than girls. Given these gender differences, it's not surprising that we're

having a national debate. After all, boys seem to be both doing badly and doing worse than girls.

* * *

Introducing masculinities into the discussion alleviates several of the problems with the "what about the boys?" debate. It enables us to explore the ways in which class and race complicate the picture of boys' achievement and behaviors. It also reveals that boys and girls are on the same side in this struggle, not pitted against each other. Making masculinity visible also enables us to understand what I regard as the *real* boy crisis in America. We call it "teen violence," "youth violence." Just who do we think is doing it—girls? Imagine if the killers in schools in Littleton and Jonesboro were all black girls from poor families. The entire focus would be on race, class, and gender. Yet the obvious fact that at these schools the killers were all middle-class white boys seems to have escaped everyone's notice. From an early age, boys learn that violence is not only an acceptable form of conflict resolution, but one that is admired.

If we really want to rescue boys, protect boys, promote boyhood, then our task must be to find ways to reveal and challenge this ideology of masculinity, to disrupt the facile "boys will be boys" model, and to erode boys' sense of entitlement. Because the reality is that this ideology of masculinity is the problem for *both* girls *and* boys. * * *

Kimmel, "What About the Boys?" What the Current Debates Tell Us, and Don't Tell Us, About Boys in School, Wellesley Centers for Women, 21 Research Rpt. 6 (2000). Can public education "reveal and challenge this ideology of masculinity?" How?

9. What criteria should be used to determine if public single-sex schools are "equal?" Identical curriculum? The same budget? The same number of students, size of classes and number of teachers and administrators? See, e.g., Bray v. Lee, 337 F.Supp. 934 (D.Mass.1972) (to obtain admission to Boston Latin Schools, girls had to score at least 133 out of 200 on an admissions test but the boys only had to score 120 or better because Boys Latin had twice as much capacity as Girls Latin; court held that the use of separate and different standards to evaluate the examination results to determine the admission of boys and girls constitutes a violation of the Equal Protection Clause). Revisit this question after completing this section. Does *VMI* provide guidance about what "comparability" in Equal Protection cases means? Are "comparability" and "equality" interchangeable? Is the concept "separate but equal" viable when considering gender? What about when considering race?

10. Several commentators question the assimilation of women into male society through coeducation, claiming that it fails to challenge the existing structure of society in any meaningful way. See, e.g., Deborah L. Rhode, Association and Assimilation, 81 Nw.U.L.Rev. 106 (1986); Janella Miller, The Future of Private Women's Colleges, 7 Harv. Women's L.J. 153 (1984). Adrienne Rich acknowledges that women who try to change the university will be accused of "reverse chauvinism":

> Women in the university therefore need to address themselves—against the opprobrium and obstruction they do and will encounter—to changing the center of gravity of the institution as far as possible; to work toward a woman-centered university because only if that center of gravity can be shifted will women really be free to learn, to teach, to share strength, to explore, to criticize, and to convert knowledge to power.

Rich, Toward a Woman–Centered University, in On Lies, Secrets, and Silence: Selected Prose 1966–1978 125, 128 (1979). There is no doubt that education is a powerful tool of socialization. What is the best strategy to address this issue? Does a college that admits women only offer the answer? Even if it uses a "male" curriculum? What solution would you propose?

Text Note: Classroom Experiences, Language, Learning Styles, and Self–Esteem

Many researchers have puzzled over the drop in girls' self-esteem as they go through school, even though they get better grades than boys. At least one teacher trainer, Cathy Nelson, attributes this effect to the negative messages delivered to girls by school curricula, messages that women's lives count for less than men's. The historian Linda Kerber states: "Lowered self-esteem is a perfectly reasonable conclusion if one has been subtly instructed that what people like oneself have done in the world has not been important and is not worth studying."[16]

In a year-long study designed to determine if specific day-to-day teacher practices of equity are linked to student achievement in a seventh grade classroom, researchers discovered that:

> While boys and girls reported fair treatment, both in surveys and in focus groups and interviews, they also described their experiences at school in terms of differential treatment, which *they* considered fair because boys and girls are different and "that's just the way it is." For these adolescents an understanding of differences being "natural" also led to expectations that boys did not have to pay attention during lessons but could later rely on teachers and girls in the class (since girls are "smarter") to provide extra help. Both boys and girls thought that the greater amount of time teachers spend working with boys individually or in small groups was fair because boys need more attention. Girls said that boys are "louder," "more disruptive," "more outgoing" while girls are "more shy than boys" and "normally quiet."
>
> Boys said that girls are "smarter," naturally faster at their schoolwork, better listeners, and are easily embarrassed and therefore do not like too much attention while boys "want more attention," are "more outgoing," and "don't study as much." When we asked boys if it was difficult for them to attend classes when they thought they weren't as smart as their female classmates, one boy told us, "In elementary and middle school, [girls are] like way smarter than boys, but then like when it comes to like high school and college I think boys start to get even

16. The AAUW Report: How Schools Shortchange Girls 67 (1992).

> smarter because like most of the famous scientists are like the boys * * * but you don't really see that much famous, smart girl scientists."[17]

The researchers concluded that culture constructs and reinforces these inequities under the guise of progress. Additionally, they found that:

> Consistent with national data, the girls in this study had lower self-esteem than boys, despite the fact that they got consistently higher grades in every subject area. Boys, on the other hand, felt little motivation to do well and take responsibility for their own learning, especially in subjects deemed more feminine such as language arts.[18]

As the data was reviewed further, the investigators noted "links between these girls' experience of the absence of safety in the classroom and the lack of safety in the hallways, lunchrooms, and schoolyards across the country" as a result of extensive sexual harassment and other safety issues.[19] They perceived these threats to safety to be highly gendered, with conventional notions of masculinity and femininity contributing to the threatening environment. This study thus presents a complicated picture: boys and girls perceive teachers to be fair and equitable when boys and girls are treated differently. Apparently, by the seventh grade, gender stereotypes are firmly imbedded.[20]

These classroom inequities occur in an environment in which learning styles vary greatly. For many girls and women, successful learning takes place in an atmosphere that enables students empathetically to enter into the subject they are studying, an approach called "connected knowing."[21] On the other hand, it is suggested that boys thrive in an adversarial, individualistic classroom. Even though there are no studies indicating that boys would not learn better through "connected knowing," few teachers employ it. Competition, not collaboration, is the mode of learning.

Language and communication issues further complicate the classroom experience for females. Research indicates men tend to (1) do more talking; (2) interrupt more; and (3) choose the topics of discussion in conversations with women.[22] On the other hand, in all-women conversations, the speakers regard the conversation as cooperative, not competitive; in all-men conversations, speakers view the conversation as individualistic. What is the result? According to Sally McConnell–Ginet:

> How does inequality in discourse affect what can be meant and by whom? First, men are more likely than women to have a chance to express their perspective on situations, not only because they have more frequent access to the floor but also because they are more actively

17. Michelle V. Porche and Renee Spencer, "We've Come a Long Way ... Maybe?" Wellesley Center for Women, 21 Research Rpt. 22–23 (2000).

18. Id.

19. Id.

20. See generally Myra and David Sacker, Failing at Fairness: How America's Schools Cheat Girls (1994).

21. See Mary Field Belenky, Blithe McVicker Clinchy, Nancy Rule Goldberger, and Jill Mattuck Tarule, Women's Ways of Knowing: The Development of Self, Voice and Mind 102 (1986).

22. Sally McConnell–Ginet, The Sexual (Re)Production of Meaning: A Discourse–Based Theory in Language, Gender, and Professional Writing: Theoretical Approaches and Guidelines for Nonsexist Usage 35, 43 (Francine Wattman Frank and Paul A. Treichler, eds. 1989).

> attended to. This distinction is especially important, since comprehension goes well beyond simple recognition of the linguistic structures used. In other words, where the sexes have somewhat different perspectives on a situation, the man's view is more likely to be familiar to the woman than hers is to him. This observation leads directly to the second point: men are much more likely than women to be unaware that their own view is not universally shared.[23]

Many researchers have pointed to hypercorrect grammar, superpolite forms, and questioning as distinctive characteristics of women's speech. Specifically, women were found to: (a) ask more questions; (b) make statements in a questioning tone; (c) use more tag questions ("don't you think?"); (d) lead off with questions to ensure a listener's attention; and (e) use more "hedges" or qualifiers and intensifiers ("really").[24]

Finally, coeducation appears to require women to alter the communication patterns they utilize in all-women conversations in order to participate fully in the classroom. Linguists note this dilemma:

> The collaborative patterns which are central to talk among women—drawing out other speakers, supportive listening and head nods, mutual sharing of emotions and personal knowledge, respect for one another's conversational space—are weak or "powerless" only when contrasted with their opposites. For example, open, sharing behaviors become weak only when another person in an interaction refuses to reciprocate them. Being sensitive to another's need—inviting them to take turns at talk, drawing out the topics they raise—is heard as ineffectual only when this sensitivity is not reciprocated. Revealing emotions is a disadvantage only when others are being reserved and refusing to share or to show emotion. The "powerlessness" of the speech patterns women more often use exists only relative to the power of so-called masculine patterns. When only women are told to change their behavior, and essentially to adopt "male forms," the characteristics of male speech are ignored, and the assumption of power as domination is reproduced.[25]

Thus, the classroom experience remains a difficult one for girls and women to negotiate successfully.

Notes on the Classroom Experience

1. How should teachers respond to the findings about day-to-day teacher practices and their impact on gender equity? What *does* equity mean in the classroom? "Identical" treatment? How can we make sure that gender differences don't make a difference in fair treatment in the classroom?

2. The linguists discuss women's collaborative communication patterns in positive terms; are these really survival skills of the oppressed? If so,

23. Id.

24. See generally Robin Lakoff, Language and Woman's Place 53–6 (1975).

25. Barrie Thorne, Cheris Kramarae, and Nancy Henley, Language, Gender and Society: Opening a Second Decade of Research in Language, Gender and Society 7, 19 (Thorne, Kramarae and Henley, eds. 1983).

should we be valorizing them? Do you agree that there is a hierarchy in communication patterns, with male forms considered superior? Are women taken more seriously if they use a more male speech style? However, if a woman speaks more directly and assertively, will she be dismissed as "unfeminine"? Do women, in effect, need to be bilingual—using their first language (female) when speaking on a personal level or with other women and their foreign language (male) when they need to be "taken seriously"? How do you assess the likelihood of reforming coeducational communication patterns?

3. What are the implications of the findings about communication patterns? Do women express their thoughts more tentatively? Do women have to work harder to get someone's attention? Have women internalized men's assumptions that what they have to say is not very interesting or intellectually rigorous? In your experience, do these patterns impact women's performance in law school? What is their likely impact on litigation? What is the implication of this data for coeducation?

4. The *VMI* case, excerpted in Chapter 2, above, acknowledged gendered ways of learning, holding that the "adversative" system of teaching utilized at VMI would have to be changed if women were enrolled since it negatively affected women's learning. If men and women learn differently, which system of teaching should be used? The one that favors men or women? For a more complete discussion of feminist pedagogy, see Charlotte Bunch and Sandra Pollack, eds., Learning Our Way: Essays in Feminist Education (1983); Margo Culley and Catherine Portuges, eds., Gender Subjects: The Dynamics of Feminist Education (1985); Susan L. Gabriel and Isaiah Smithson, eds., Gender in the Classroom: Power and Pedagogy (1990); Elizabeth Minnich, Jean O'Barr, and Rachel Rosenfeld, eds., Reconstructing the Academy: Women's Education and Women's Studies (1988).

5. Do you think it is possible to transform the power dynamics of the coeducational classroom from masculinist ("domination or control") to feminist ("power as energy, effective interaction or empowerment")—a solution offered by Thorne, Kramarae, and Henley, in footnote 25, above. How could this be accomplished?

Text Note: Comparisons Between Single-Sex Female and Coeducational Higher Education

In the late 1970's Elizabeth Tidball published an influential study showing that from 1910 to 1960 "graduates of women's colleges were twice as likely as women graduates of coeducational institutions to be cited for career achievements in *Who's Who of American Women*."[31] She later found similar results, i.e., greater numbers of women's colleges graduates, when she compared men and women entering medical school and obtaining natural science doctorates. These findings seemed especially true for graduates of the Seven Sisters colleges of Barnard, Bryn Mawr, Radcliffe, Mount Holyoke, Smith, Vassar, and Wellesley. This higher career achievement was explained

31. Joy K. Rice and Annette Hemmings, Women's Colleges and Women Achievers: An Update, in Reconstructing the Academy: Women's Education and Women's Studies 220 (Elizabeth Minnich, Jean O'Barr, and Rachel Rosenfeld, eds. 1988).

by Tidball to be the result of greater numbers of women faculty who could act as role models at women's colleges. These, and other similar assertions of success and achievement by graduates of women's colleges, contributed to the resurgence of women's colleges in the 1980's following the closing of many women's colleges in the mid-sixties and seventies.[32]

Two other researchers, Joy K. Rice and Annette Hemmings, have updated Tidball's studies. According to their study:

> Women's colleges flourished before the turn of the century, offering women who wanted to obtain a higher education the choice of a single-sex environment. Many of these early colleges justified their mission to educate women with the social rationale that educated women would become teachers, reformers, and culture bearers, as well as "better" mothers and wives. Although in the first half of this [the twentieth] century elite women's colleges were largely accessible only to the wealthy, they often provided a rigorous curriculum for women that was comparable to that received by men at coeducational institutions. By the late 1960s, however, federal cutbacks and economic constraints on higher education prompted many small colleges to close and universities and colleges to reduce their budgets. Educational equity and the integration of minorities and women was publicly debated, and women's colleges increasingly were seen by professionals in educational policy studies as an elitist anachronism. In 1960 there were about three hundred colleges for women; by 1970 only half of those colleges remained single-sex institutions. The majority of these were church-related schools, primarily Roman Catholic. As financial pressures grew and coeducation attracted many women to previously all-male schools, many women's colleges began admitting men. The six-month period between June and December 1968, when an astounding sixty-four women's colleges either became coeducational institutions or closed their doors, was a watermark in higher education. Today [1988], 116 women's colleges educate about 125,000 students, roughly 1 percent of all college students and 2 percent of all women college students.[33]

The researchers found data consistent with Tidball's results[34] and noted that other studies essentially replicated Tidball's major findings using *Who's Who in America* instead of *Who's Who of American Women*.[35] However, these studies also suggested that factors other than the single-sex environment may have played a role—college admissions selectivity and prior student academic achievement. Nonetheless, when Tidball reanalyzed her own data, she found that: (1) highly selective women's colleges had twice as many graduates who were achievers as did highly selective coeducational colleges; and (2) all other women's colleges were twice as likely to have high-achieving women alumnae as were all other coeducational colleges. Still, a key variable, the student's socioeconomic status, was not taken into account.

Opponents of single-sex education argue that these studies are flawed because: (1) they failed to control for such factors as pre-college backgrounds, institutional recruitment efforts, and institutional selectivity; and

32. Id. at 220–23.

33. Id. at 221–22.

34. Id. at 222–23.

35. Id.

(2) because women were not admitted to many men's colleges until the 1970's, women's colleges had the best and brightest women from which to draw their student bodies.[36] Furthermore, because studies consistently conclude that boys benefit from the presence of girls and that the "severest forms of sexism [are] found in boys' schools,"[37] opponents believe that coeducational settings are the best way to fight discrimination.

Numerous studies appear to be inconsistent in terms of improved academic performance for girls in a single-sex environment.[38] However, it is incontrovertible that single-sex education offers greater opportunities for girls to be in leadership positions. Furthermore, one effect of single-sex women's education, positive self-esteem, has remained constant in both older and more current studies: "At both secondary and postsecondary schools, female students self-report that single-sex educational environments are academically advantageous * * * . Two fairly well-accepted advantages of single-sex education are the effect of an all-girl environment on self-esteem and students' satisfaction with their academic * * * life."[39] In fact, in one poll 91% of women who attended an all-girls' school believed single-sex education helped them.[40]

DOROTHY C. HOLLAND AND MARGARET A. EISENHART, EDUCATED IN ROMANCE: WOMEN, ACHIEVEMENT, AND COLLEGE CULTURE

3–4, 8, 85–86, 88, 104 (1990).

[Holland and Eisenhart are both anthropologists. In 1979 the U.S. National Institute of Education gave a grant to the authors to learn why so few women were becoming scientists or mathematicians. They investigated this question in two southern universities: a predominantly Black university that they called "Bradford" and a predominantly white university that they called "Southern University" (SU).]

When the women in our ethnographic sample began their college careers, they had reputations as good students, and approximately half said they would major in a math-or science-related field. All stated that they expected to pursue a career after graduating from college. Yet from following these women's unfolding lives—during the study (1979–81), when the women were due to graduate from college (1983), and again when they had begun their adult lives (1987)—we know that less than a third of these bright and privileged women met their own expectations for the future. By the time they left college, they had arrived at

36. Nancy Levit, Separating Equals: Educational Research and the Long–Term Consequences of Sex Segregation, 67 G. Wash. L. Rev. 451, 475–76 (1999).

37. Id. at 499.

38. Id. at 485–92.

39. Id. at 481, 496. Research by Cornelius Riordan suggests that the positive effects of single-sex schools are the greatest for Black and Hispanic females from low socioeconomic levels. See Sandar C. Ceraulo, Separated by Sex: A Critical Look at Single–Sex Education for Girls, 76 J. Chem. Educ. 615 (1999)(book review).

40. Josette Shiner and Bonnie Erbe, Are All–Girl Schools Good for Education?, Wash. Times, Apr. 17, 1999, § A12 (citing a 1990 Yankelovich poll).

practices—to put the outcome in terms of the critical educational and feminist literature—that are key in sustaining women's subordinate positions in the society. Most had ended up with intense involvements in heterosexual romantic relationships, marginalized career identities, and inferior preparation for their likely roles as future breadwinners.

* * *

As we followed the women's experiences during the period of our study, we found that the peer system promoted and propelled the women into a world of romance in which their attractiveness to men counted most. The women were subjected to a "sexual auction block." In the shadow of the peer society, academics commanded only limited attention. The women were more or less left on their own by the university, by their peers, and to a lesser extent by their parents, to develop—or not—careers, to prepare themselves—or not—as future breadwinners.

* * *

Campus Life At Bradford and SU

Peer cultures at Bradford and SU absorbed a great deal of the students' time and energy, as they had for the students' historical counterparts. Peer-organized activities went on continually; peers were in constant attendance, day and night. For most of the women in our study * * * the academic aspects of college life paled by comparison with the peer culture. Although academic pursuits took time—sometimes large portions of the women's time—they did not capture the women's interest and attention nearly as much as the peer system did.

We also found evidence of another cultural theme * * * attributed to the college peer culture: the great emphasis on cross-gender romantic relationships. When the women came to Bradford and SU, they entered into a peer culture built around an ethos of romantic heterosexual relationships. The peer-ranking systems at both schools were intimately tied to gender relations interpreted in terms of attractiveness and romance. As a consequence, for the women in our study other kinds of relationships, as well as academic interests, became hard to establish or maintain. In particular, we found that in the ethos of the student culture, women's relationships with other women, like their interest in schoolwork, tended to be pushed aside. * * * Thus the peer culture was important ultimately in constructing women's economic marginality and their subordination to men.

Although similar in broad outline, the peer cultures at the two universities were not identical. Romance and attractiveness were prominent aspects of peer culture * * * on both campuses, but only at SU were they the major organizing principles of women's social world. At Bradford, * * * principles of female self-reliance also applied. * * *

The Pursuit Of Romance

In the world of peers encountered by the women in our study, the most exciting and popular activities included opportunities to meet men or to enact romantic relationships. The women devoted considerable time and energy to going places (bars, mixers, parties, pools) where they hoped to be noticed by men, to taking care of male friends by cleaning their apartments or cooking for them, to assisting at fraternity activities as "sweethearts" or "little sisters," and to supporting men's sports (as spectators, cheerleaders, flag girls, majorettes, and managers). In addition, their conversations frequently concerned men and romantic relationships. Women spent hours, in the dorm, in the library, on the way to class, discussing who was attractive and why, who was "going with" whom, who wanted to go out with whom, what couples were doing when they went out, how well-matched members of a couple were, what was needed to become more attractive, and so forth.

* * *

When asked about the majors or career interest of their peers, most of the women in the ethnographic study said they knew little or nothing about them. * * *

Although the women's conversations about boyfriends and about their favorite activities included references to other women, women and their relationships with each other were not a primary focus of attention. Relationships with women, although valued and enjoyed, almost always revolved around relationships with men.

Campus and community political activity also failed to interest the women very much. Vestiges of campus radicalism remained, but attracted little attention.

* * *

ATTRACTIVENESS: ANOTHER FACE OF THE DOUBLE STANDARD

On the surface, the culture of romance is based upon equality: the woman and the man are equally attractive and their exchange involves intimacy and prestige for both. The hidden inequality is revealed, however, when the different bases of attractiveness are examined. Men's prestige and correlated attractiveness come from the attention they receive from women and from success at sports, in school politics, and in other arenas. Women's prestige and correlated attractiveness come only from the attention they receive from men.

This way of seeing things was illustrated by one woman's description of how another women [sic] tried to insult her: "She told me, '[You] may be able to do calculus, but I'm dating a football player.'" Both women were well aware that dating a football player was "the big thing" at SU.

> [Note, however, that some 20% of the women in these studies did not give up their careers, and that the culture of romance gained dominance in the women's lives only as their aspirations had begun to crumble. The latter did not occur because of the culture of romance; it occurred for other reasons.]

Notes on College Studies

1. What do you think are the reasons why graduates of the Seven Sisters women's colleges are such high achievers? Have you experienced single-sex education? How do you evaluate its benefits? What, if any, are its disadvantages?

2. Are the materials presented in this section consistent or contradictory? Does the Holland and Eisenhart study suggest additional reasons why graduates of women's colleges rate higher in career achievement? After considering these materials, would you want your daughter to attend a single-sex or coeducational college?

3. Do you think that reliance on inclusion in *Who's Who,* as used by Tidball and others, is a satisfactory indicator of achievement? What other measures would you use? Rice and Hemmings note that women's colleges have increased their ethnic and socioeconomic diversity by attracting and providing support for ethnic and racial minorities and disadvantaged women. Do you agree with their conclusion that this might decrease the influence of socioeconomic status as a determinant of career achievement for women's college graduates?

4. Does it surprise you that peers are the greatest influence on women students? Does this resonate with your personal experiences?

5. Do you think that Holland and Eisenhart's conclusions are skewed because both colleges they studied were in the South? Why or why not? They paint a bleak picture for women given the fact that their prestige comes *only* from the attention they receive from men. What can be done to correct this? Does this picture end at graduation?

6. Rather than being isolated from half the population, is it important for women to learn to relate to men during the educational process? Do you think that attending women's schools inhibits females from developing necessary survival skills in a "man's" world? What arguments can you make in support of coeducation for women? Does the strength of those arguments vary with the maturity of the students? With their level of self-esteem? Do the arguments supporting single-sex women's education also support single-sex men's education? Are there reasons why males should be educated alongside females? Can you develop an optimal model for education for both sexes? What role should the law play in these issues?

C. STANDARDIZED TESTING

PHYLLIS TEITELBAUM, FEMINIST THEORY AND STANDARDIZED TESTING

In Gender/Body/Knowledge: Feminist Reconstructions of Being and Knowing 324, 325–33 (Alison M. Jaggar and Susan R. Bordo, Eds. 1989).

The issue of sex bias in standardized tests has been brought into sharp focus by a nationwide debate about the differential validity of college admissions tests—the Scholastic Aptitude Test (SAT), the Preliminary Scholastic Aptitude Test/National Merit Scholarship Qualifying Test (PSAT/NMSQT), and the American College Testing Program Assessment Exam (ACT). Phyllis Rosser (1987, 1988) has reviewed the data in this debate. * * *

According to Rosser (1987:1), on average, women consistently earn higher high school and college grades than men; yet, on average, women receive lower scores than men on all three college admissions examinations. The score difference is particularly large in math; in the SAT math section in 1986 the gap was 50 points on average on a 200–800 point scale. But even in the verbal section of the SAT, where women used to perform better than men, women in 1986 scored on average 11 points lower than men. So the total score difference on the SAT in 1986 was 61 points (50 plus 11). Because women get higher grades in college than men, Rosser (1987:3) argues that the SAT does not accurately predict women's first-year college grades. According to Rosser, "If the SAT predicted equally well for both sexes, girls would score about 20 points higher than the boys, not 61 points lower."

Score differences between women and men on the PSAT/NMSQT and on the ACT are similar to those on the SAT. Rosser (1987:5–16) points out the serious consequences of these score differences:

1. College admissions—Nearly all four-year colleges and universities use SAT or ACT scores in admissions decisions, and many use cut-off scores, particularly for admission to competitive programs (Rosser 1987:4). If women's first-year grades indicate that their test scores ought to be higher than men's, then women applicants are undoubtedly being unfairly rejected in favor of less qualified male applicants.

2. College scholarships—According to Rosser (1987:8), over 750 organizations, including the National Merit Scholarship Corporation, use SAT, PSAT/NMSQT, or ACT scores in selecting scholarship recipients. In 1985–1986, largely as a result of the PSAT/NMSQT score difference, National Merit Finalists were 64 percent male and only 36 percent female (Rosser 1987:11). The results in other scholarship programs are similar; women lose out on millions of dollars in college scholarships because of a score difference that may be invalid.

3. Entry into "gifted programs"—Rosser (1987:6–8) points out that many academic enrichment programs are offered to students who achieve high scores on the SAT, PSAT/NMSQT, or ACT. Women's lower scores result in their loss of these opportunities as well.

4. Effect on self-perceptions and college choices—There is evidence that students alter their academic self-perceptions and decide where to apply to college partly on the basis of their test scores. If the tests underpredict women's academic abilities, women may not apply to

academically demanding colleges for which they are in fact qualified, and their academic self-perceptions may be set too low.

The three tests' publishers currently argue that the tests are not biased against women. The publishers have put forward several explanations for the score differences; these explanations suggest that the scores reflect true differences in women's and men's academic preparation and/or abilities. For example, some argue that women take easier courses in high school and college than men or that women receive higher grades than men because women try harder to please their teachers.

The debate over standardized college admissions tests is important for two reasons: (1) it questions whether these tests are equally valid predictors of academic success for women and for men; (2) it points out what is at stake for women if these tests are biased against them. It is not yet clear whether the score differences are due to bias and, if so, to what kind of bias. Nevertheless, the data Rosser presents on the negative consequences for women of the score differences underscore the importance of investigating whether and how standardized tests are biased against women.

* * *

[The author describes several approaches that have been tried and currently coexist in the attempt to eliminate sex and racial/ethnic bias from standardized tests: (1) *judgmental systems* (based on a content conception of bias) eliminate sexist and racist language, assure that women and minorities are represented in content, and evaluate whether all test-takers have had an opportunity to learn the material; (2) *item bias* and *differential item performance methods* (based on a performance conception of bias) ascertain statistically whether specific subgroups of test-takers perform poorly on particular test questions and then may eliminate these questions; and (3) *differential validity methods* (based on a prediction conception of bias) focus on situations in which a test does not predict equally well for different subgroups of test-takers.]

Standardized Testing And Androcentric Knowledge

Most work currently being done on test bias accepts the basic underlying assumptions of standardized testing as given. What would happen if we questioned those assumptions from the perspective of feminist theory? What emerges is a radically different conception of sex bias as something inherent in the assumptions that underlie the content and format of standardized tests.

Feminist theorists have pointed out that what we have been taught to accept as standard scholarship is actually "androcentric" (that is, dominated by or emphasizing masculine interests or point of view). For example, the field called "history" has actually been the history of men; the history of women was simply left out. Similarly, "knowledge" and "science" are not universal; as currently taught, they are an androcentric form of knowing and of doing science.

The androcentric form of knowledge and science accepted in the twentieth-century United States is based on the theory of knowledge called positivism, which includes the following assumptions: scientific explanation should be reductionistic and atomistic, building up a complex entity from its simplest components; one can and should be objective (value-neutral) in scientific research (Jaggar 1983:356); and reason and emotion can be sharply distinguished (Jaggar 1985:2). This form of androcentric knowledge tends to be dualistic and dichotomous, viewing the world in terms of linked opposites: reason-emotion, rational-irrational, subject-object, nurture-nature, mind-body, universal-particular, public-private, and male-female (Jaggar 1985:2). It tends to be quantitative, and it takes the natural sciences as a model for all other academic disciplines. It contains an individualistic conception of humans as separate, isolated individuals who attain knowledge in a solitary, rather than a social, manner (Jaggar 1983:355). In addition, it includes a linear clock-and-calendar sense of time, rather than a circular sense of time (Wilshire 1985), and time is considered very important.

Standardized tests seem clearly to be based on this model of knowledge. In format, they are, as much as psychometricians can make them, positivistic, scientific, objective, value-free, dualistic, quantitative, linear-time-oriented, atomistic, and individualistic. In content, standardized tests reflect the androcentric model of knowledge by excluding everything that does not fit its definition of "knowledge" and everything that cannot be tested in a positivistic format.

First, consider the *format* of standardized tests:

1) The tests are "standardized" in an attempt to make them *objective and value-free*. Psychometricians hope that, if all test-takers receive the same test questions under the same standardized conditions and choose among the same multiple-choice answers, subjectivity and values can be excluded. But can they be? Test questions are written by subjective, value-laden human beings; questions and answer choices reflect the question-writer's upbringing and values, despite the question-writer's attempts to eliminate them. Test-takers bring to the test very different sets of experiences and feelings, and their interpretations of questions will vary accordingly. There is no such thing as a "culture-free" test. Every test question must assume some "common knowledge," and such knowledge is "common" only within a particular subculture of the society.

2) Multiple-choice tests are *dualistic* in that they force a choice between possible answers: one is "right"; the others are "wrong." The model is dichotomous—either/or, with no gradations. But, depending on the question, a graduated model in which several answers are "partly right" may be more appropriate. If test-takers were allowed to explain why they chose a particular "wrong" answer, we might find that it was "right" in some sense, or partly right.

3) Standardized tests are relentlessly *quantitative*. Their goal is to measure a person's knowledge or skill and to sum it up in one number. (This quantification adds to the impression that standardized tests are "objective.") The single score reflects an androcentric fascination with simple quantification and precision; though psychometricians frequently state that test scores are not precise, test scores are often taken as absolute by both the public and the institutions that use the scores in decision making.

4) Tests are usually timed; thus, measurement of speed, as well as knowledge or skill, often contributes to the final score. This *linear-time-orientation* rewards speed even in subject areas where speed is not important.

5) Standardized tests are *atomistic*. Some systems of planning test content break learning down into "educational objectives" that are as narrow and concrete as possible—for example: "Can write legibly at X words per minute" (Krathwohl 1971:21). Even when such reductionistic educational objectives are not used, tests are inherently atomistic because they try to measure particular knowledge or skills separately from all other knowledge and skills.

6) Standardized tests are *individualistic* and usually competitive. A single person's performance is measured and compared, either with others' performances or with some present standard of mastery. The ideas of "merit," of ranking, and of comparison are inherent in the testing enterprise. If there were no need to wish to compare individuals, there would be no standardized tests.

But even more important than format is *content:*

1) Standardized tests are in general designed to *test "reason" only*—the kind of knowledge that is included in the androcentric definition of knowledge. Excluded are whole areas of human achievement that contribute to success in school and work but are considered either inappropriate for testing or "untestable" from a practical point of view. Such characteristics and skills as intuition, motivation, self-understanding, conscientiousness, creativity, cooperativeness, supportiveness of others, sensitivity, nurturance, ability to create a pleasant environment, and ability to communicate verbally and nonverbally are excluded from standardized tests. By accepting and reflecting the androcentric model of knowledge, standardized tests reinforce value judgments that consider this model of knowledge more valid and important than other ways of viewing the world. Content that is not tested is judged less valuable than that included on tests.

2) Test publishers attempt to *exclude emotion* from test content. Topics that are very controversial are avoided. Emotions that test-takers feel about the test itself are labeled "test anxiety" and considered a source of "error"; test-takers' "true scores" would be based only on reason, not emotion.

Implications of This Analysis

Is an androcentric, positivistic standardized test necessarily biased against women? The answer you will give depends on whether you believe that women test-takers have completely adopted the generally taught androcentric model of knowledge and that they are as adept in manipulating its concepts as are men. If you believe that women think the way men do, that they share men's "common knowledge," that they are as comfortable with dualistic, quantitative, timed, atomistic, competitive tests as men, and that the content excluded from the tests is no more salient to women than it is to men, then you will conclude that standardized tests are not sex-biased by virtue of their androcentric origins.

If, on the other hand, you believe as I do that women and men perceive the world differently, excel in different areas, and feel comfortable with different test formats, then you conclude that an androcentric test is bound to be sex-biased. And you need not be a biological determinist to believe that such sex differences exist. It seems to me that the different life experiences that gender creates are sufficient explanation; growing up female is a different social and intellectual experience from growing up male (Farganis 1985:21).

Farganis, Sondra. 1985. "Social Theory and Feminist Theory: The Need for Dialogue." Manuscript.

Jaggar, Alison. 1983. *Feminist Politics and Human Nature. Totowa, N.J.: Rowman and Allenheld.*

Jaggar, Alison. 1985. "Feeling and Knowing: Emotion in Feminist Theory." Manuscript.

Krathwohl, David R., and David A. Payne. 1971. "Defining and Assessing Educational Objectives." In *Educational Measurement,* ed. Robert L. Thorndike. Washington, D.C.: American Council on Education.

Rosser, Phyllis. 1988. "Girls, Boys, and the SAT: Can We Even the Score?" *NEA Today* (special ed.) 6, no. 6 (January): 48–53.

Rosser, Phyllis, with the staff of the National Center for Fair and Open Testing. 1987. *Sex Bias in College Admissions Tests: Why Women Lose Out.* 2d ed. Cambridge, Mass.: National Center for Fair and Open Testing (Fair Test).

Wilshire, Donna. 1985. "Ideas presented for discussion" and "Topics for discussion." Manuscripts prepared for the "Feminist Ways of Knowing Seminar." Douglass College, Rutgers University, New Brunswick, N.J.

SHARIF v. NEW YORK STATE EDUCATION DEPARTMENT

United States District Court, Southern District of New York, 1989.

709 F.Supp. 345.

This case raises the important question of whether New York State denies female students an equal opportunity to receive prestigious state merit scholarships by its sole reliance upon the Scholastic Aptitude Test ("SAT") to determine eligibility. To the Court's knowledge, this is the first case where female students are seeking to use the federal civil rights statute prohibiting sex discrimination in federally-funded educational programs to challenge a state's reliance on standardized tests. This case also presents a legal issue of first impression: whether discrimination under Title IX can be established by proof of disparate impact without proof of intent to discriminate.

* * *

[The court reviewed the evolution of the New York State Scholarship Awards and how they are determined. After utilizing special Regents examinations for decades, in 1977, as a cost-cutting measure, the program was instructed to use a nationally established competitive examination to decide awards. The State Education Department ("SED") chose the Scholastic Aptitude Test ("SAT"), the test taken by the greatest number of students. In response to allegations that the SED's practice of relying solely on the SAT discriminated against females who consistently score below males, the legislature directed that the awards be based in part upon the student's grade point average as a measure of high school achievement. Under this procedure, using a combination of grades and SAT scores, women received substantially more scholarships than in the prior years in which the SAT had been the sole criterion. Although use of the GPA reduced the disparity between the number of men and women receiving awards, the SED recommended that the practice be discontinued, as soon as a new exam was developed, because: (1) use of GPA put an increased burden on school staff; (2) use of GPA did not provide an equitable way to compare students from different schools; and (3) use of GPA would encourage students to avoid more challenging courses in order to obtain better grades for scholarship purposes. The legislature failed to provide funds to develop a new exam or to renew its directive to use GPA's in the scholarship determination.]

The Educational Testing Service ("ETS") developed the SAT in order to predict academic performance in college. The ability of the SAT to serve this purpose has been statistically "validated." It is undisputed, however, that the SAT predicts the success of students differently for males and females. In other words, while the SAT will predict college success as well for males within the universe of males as for females within the universe of females, when predictions are within the combined universe of males and females, the SAT *underpredicts* academic performance of females in their freshman year of college, and *overpredicts* such academic performance for males. The SAT has never been validated as a measure of past high school performance.

* * *

Both the Empire and Regents Scholarships are intended to reward past academic achievement of high school students, and to encourage those students who have demonstrated such achievement to pursue their educations in New York State. It is undisputed, however, that the SAT was developed and validated to serve a different purpose—*predicting* performance *in college.* * * *

Males have outscored females on the verbal portion of the SAT since 1972, with an average score differential of at least 10 points since 1981. Males have also consistently outscored females on the mathematics portion, with an average differential of at least 40 points since 1967. In 1988, for example, girls scored 56 points lower than boys on the test. The probability that these score differentials happened by chance is approximately about one in a billion and the probability that the result could consistently be so different is essentially zero.

Statisticians have attempted to explain the score differentials between males and females by removing the effect of "neutral" variables, such as ethnicity, socioeducational status (parental education), high school classes, and proposed college major. However, under the most conservative studies presented in evidence, even after removing the effect of these factors, at least a 30 point combined differential remains unexplained.

* * *

Plaintiffs do not claim that defendants have intentionally discriminated against them based on their sex. Rather, they claim that defendants' practice of sole reliance upon SAT scores to award prestigious state scholarships disparately impacts female students. * * *

Plaintiffs * * * have established that the probability, absent discriminatory causes, that women would consistently score 60 points less on the SAT than men is nearly zero. Defendants concede that at least half of this differential cannot be explained away by "neutral" variables. Based upon the totality of evidence, then, this Court finds that plaintiffs have demonstrated that the State's practice of sole reliance upon the SAT disparately impacts young women.

* * *

The SED cannot justify its discriminatory practice because any alternative would be more difficult to administer. All states giving merit scholarship awards, with the exception of New York and Massachusetts, use GPAs, without concern for either administrative difficulties, grade inflation or the comparability of grades. Any administrative difficulties that the SED experienced in 1988, when it used a combination system, were attributable to the SED's own failure to implement and clarify specific guidelines for the collections of grades, and to provide any enforcement mechanisms to guard against cheating. * * *

Defendants' practice of relying solely upon SAT scores in awarding Regents and Empire Scholarships deprives young women of the opportunity to compete equally for these prestigious scholarships in violation of both Title IX and the Constitution's equal protection clause. Defendants are hereby ordered to discontinue such discriminatory practices and, instead, to award Regents and Empire Scholarships in a manner that more accurately measures students' high school achievement. For the present year, the best available alternative is a combination of grades and SATs. The SAT component is justified, not as a measure of achievement, but to weight the GPA component. The Court, however, does not limit the SED's discretion to develop other alternatives in the future, including a statewide achievement test.

Notes on Standardized Testing

1. Are there feasible alternatives to using standardized national tests for admission to college, awarding of scholarships, and placement in advanced courses? Peter Sacks reports that a "student's high school record alone is the best predictor of performance in the first year of college." Sacks, Standardized Minds: The High Price of America's Testing Culture and What We Can Do to Change It 7 (2000). What about personal interviews? Essays about how an applicant has overcome adversity in their life? Evaluate the added costs of each alternative.

2. If the standardized tests currently reflect androcentric knowledge, can this be corrected? Phyllis Teitelbaum suggests "gynecocentric" tests, dominated by or emphasizing feminine interests or point of view, as a possible solution. Will it harm men if we substitute a test based on "gynecocentric" knowledge? If so, which should be used—the one that favors men or the one that favors women? How would a proponent of the various feminist theories discussed in Chapter 3 respond to this question? Is there another alternative?

In fact, the SAT was revised in 1995, due in part to the criticism of the gender-related prediction differences, i.e., the overprediction of college grades of males and underprediction for females. However, the SAT gender gap continued to grow during the period 1996–99, and as of mid–1999 was at 43 points. This results in the exclusion of thousands of women from schools which rely on a minimum SAT cut-off score, even though the statistics establish that they are likely to out-perform first-year male college students. FairTest: National Center for Fair & Open Testing, http://fairtest.org/pr/8–31SATgap.htm. According to Teitelbaum, what would make the SAT more equitable, or can it be saved?

3. Teitelbaum states that women taking standardized tests operate under a dual burden: they must show mastery both of the test's subject matter and of the test's androcentric format and content. Should females receive some form of "extra credit" in their scores to mediate this extra burden? After the unexplained disparity is calculated each year, should women be awarded the point spread? Would this satisfy Teitelbaum's criticism of the tests?

4. Would a possible solution to the dilemma in *Sharif* be a quota on scholarships—50% each to men and women? How would a proponent of the various feminist theories discussed in Chapter 3 respond to this question?

Would such a quota violate any law? What is more persuasive to you, the plaintiffs' argument against relying solely on SAT scores because they discriminate against girls or the defendants' argument against using GPA's because they are not uniform, put an extra burden on school staff, and encourage students to take "easy" courses? Why?

5. Title IX regulations forbid recipients of federal funds from administering or operating any test for admission "which has a disproportionately adverse effect on persons on the basis of sex unless the use of such test or criterion is shown to predict validly success in the education program or activity in question and alternative tests or criteria which do not have such a disproportionately adverse effect are shown to be unavailable." 45 C.F.R. § 86.21(b)(2) (1992). Are schools that rely on the SAT and ACT tests in compliance with this Title IX regulation? According to the National Center for Fair & Open Testing, "an advocacy organization working to end the abuses, misuses and flaws of standardized testing and ensure that evaluation of students and workers is fair, open, and educationally sound" (FairTest), the Office for Civil Rights of the Department of Education issued a draft Resource Guide in May of 1999 (revised in December of 1999) that summarized current law and professional guidelines concerning standardized test score misuse. In order to use such tests properly, "if an exam has a significant disparate impact on minorities and women, then it is the obligation of the institution requiring it to show that the use of test scores is an 'educational necessity,' that the exam is technically sound (valid and reliable), and that there is no practical alternative mechanism of equivalent or better quality that achieves the same educational goal with less disparate impact." FairTest Examiner: Federal Standards for Standardized Tests, http://fairtest.org/examarts/summer99/FederalStandards.htm. Do you think colleges can justify continued use of the SAT under this standard?

6. To settle a gender bias complaint brought by FairTest, the Educational Testing Service (ETS) added a "writing" section to the three-hour, multiple-choice Preliminary SAT/National Merit Scholarship Qualifying Test (PSAT/NMSQT), the scores of which are the sole factor in awarding about $28 million in annual National Merit Scholarships. Even though females earn higher grades than their male counterparts in both high school and college when matched for identical courses, they won fewer than 40% of the prestigious National Merit Scholarships before this change. As of 1999, women, who represent 56% of students taking the PSAT/NMSQT, were awarded 45% of the scholarships. FairTest made this statement:

> The narrowing of the National Merit gender gap raises several important questions. Why, for example, have similar changes not been made on the SAT, the GRE and related exams which show comparable bias? Even more fundamentally, why are instruments on which results can be so quickly "adjusted" ever used as the sole or primary factor to determine college admissions or award scholarships?

FairTest: National Center for Fair & Open Testing, State-by-State Study Shows Hundreds More Females Will Win Scholarships, Apr. 21, 1999, http://www.fairtest.org/pr/psat4.21.htm. See also Kristen Poe, Note: Blinded by Results: Is Looking to GPA in Addition to Standardized Test Scores Truly a Less Discriminatory Solution to Merit Scholarship Selection?, 19 Women's

Rts. L. Rptr. 181 (1998). How would you answer the question posed above by FairTest? Although these tests do not predict school success very well, we do know that they correlate exceedingly well with income and education of one's parents. Sacks, above note 1, at 8. What does this suggest about a "meritocracy" based on standardized tests?

6. Standardized tests are now being used by the National College Athletic Association (NCAA) to deny eligibility to college athletes. As of 1995, NCAA's Proposition 16 governs initial eligibility for athletes at Division I schools. To qualify, student-athletes must have a 2.0 GPA in 13 approved academic core courses and an SAT of 1010 or a combined ACT of 86; if they do not, they are precluded from competition and may be denied athletic scholarships. A similar, moderately less restrictive rule, Proposition 48, was in effect from 1986 until 1995. According to data provided by the NCAA, had Prop. 48 been applicable in 1984 and 1985, it would have denied full eligibility to 47% of African American student-athletes who went on to graduate, but just 8% of white athletes who graduated. Research by the NCAA itself demonstrates that African American student-athletes are disqualified at a rate 9 to 10 times the rate for white students. The need for either of these two measures has been questioned, since prior to 1986 the graduation rate for African American and white student-athletes, male and female, was higher than the rate for their non-athlete counterparts—and it remains true today. Additionally, using an SAT cut-off score disproportionately harms low-income students. According to the Department of Education, Prop. 48's test score cut-off denied full eligibility to more than one-third of lower-income students, despite their classroom success. The comparable percentage was only one-tenth for higher-income students. FairTest, What's Wrong with the NCAA's Test Score Requirements?, http://www.fairtest.org/facts/prop48.htm. Sports ethicist Russ Gough noted:

> There is a strong correlation between family income and standardized test scores. The NCAA's own studies have completely ignored this well-documented and well-known correlation. The upshot here is that, under the present rule structure, the NCAA might as well throw out its standardized test score requirements and simply allow a freshman to play or not play on the basis of his family's income.

Gough, A Sporting Chance, Wash. Post, Nov. 29, 1994, at A23. In light of all of the problems, both racial and economic, why do you think the NCAA persists in relying so heavily upon standardized tests? Considering the dramatic impact on low-income students who need athletic scholarships to attend college, do you think Prop. 16 is fair? On the basis of its impact alone, should Prop. 16 be discontinued? One court found that Prop. 16 had an unjustified disparate impact on African American student-athletes and thus granted summary judgment to plaintiffs under Title VI of the Civil Rights Act of 1964 ("Title VI"), 42 U.S.C. § 2000d et seq., and certain implementing regulations promulgated thereunder. Cureton v. NCAA, 37 F. Supp. 2d 687 (E.D.Pa.1999).

7. The incredible explosion in the use of standardized tests has potential long-term effects on kindergarten through 12th grade as well as college students. Some schools are now using test scores to determine promotion and graduation. What will be the gender and race impact of such policies?

Plaintiffs lost a suit challenging Texas' use of the exit-level Texas Assessment of Academic Skills (TAAS) examination to determine high school graduation on the grounds that it discriminated against minority students. In granting judgment to the defendants, the court held that the state had articulated legitimate goals for the use of the TAAS: to hold schools, students, and teachers accountable for education and to ensure that all Texas students receive the same, adequate learning opportunities. Furthermore, even though TAAS did adversely affect minority students, the state demonstrated an educational necessity for the test and the plaintiffs failed to identify equally effective alternatives. The court found that the test itself was strongly correlated to material actually taught in the classroom, was in keeping with current educational norms, and did not perpetuate prior educational discrimination or unfairly hold minority students accountable for the failures of the state's educational system. GI Forum v. Texas Education Agency, 87 F. Supp.2d 667 (W.D.Tex.2000).

D. AFFIRMATIVE ACTION

Text Note: Affirmative Action

Racial and gender preferences and emphases in recruitment, retention, scholarships, admission, hiring, and awarding of contracts are known as different things in different contexts, e.g., affirmative action in higher education, affirmative action in employment, and so-called minority set-asides in government contracts. Many of these programs resulted in greater representation of women and minorities in jobs, schools, and businesses in which they were previously excluded, tokenized, or minimally represented. However, in the late 1980's several attacks were launched against affirmative action, arguing that these programs discriminated against whites and men ("reverse discrimination") or that the programs actually harmed those they were intended to benefit (primarily through stigmatization). The strength of the anti-affirmative action movement was realized in 1996 when the people of California, by referendum, adopted the California Civil Rights Initiative (Proposition 209) as an amendment to their constitution. Proposition 209 sweeps wide and far, providing that:

> the state shall not discriminate against, or grant preferential treatment to, any individual or group on the basis of race, sex, color, ethnicity, or national origin in the operation of public employment, public education, or public contracting.

The Ninth Circuit Court of Appeals, finding this provision to pass muster under the Fourteenth Amendment, vacated an earlier injunction against its implementation.[41] Its impact was felt immediately; a year later there was only one African American student at Boalt Hall, Berkeley's law school.[42]

41. Coalition for Economic Equity v. Wilson, 110 F.3d 1431 (9th Cir.), cert. denied, 522 U.S. 963, 118 S.Ct. 397, 139 L.Ed.2d 310 (1997).

42. In the fall of 1996, 20 African Americans matriculated at Boalt Hall; in fall of 1997, only one did (from 7.6% to .4%). In the fall of 1996, there were 19 African Americans who entered U.C.L.A. Law School; in the fall of 1999, that number was down to three (from 6.2% to .3%). Source: University of California Law School Submissions (9/10/1999 update). In Texas, the year after the *Hopwood* decision, see note

Following the anti-affirmative action success in California, several bills were introduced into Congress to "nationalize" Proposition 209, and numerous states are considering or have enacted similar legislation.

Another prong of the anti-affirmative action attack has been individual so-called reverse discrimination suits against numerous state colleges and universities, arguing that racial and/or gender preferences unfairly impacted non-minorities, resulting in denial of their admission. Some of these cases have been successful even though in 1978 the Supreme Court held in *Bakke*[43] that race was a valid consideration in the admissions process for graduate school.[44]

Underlying the large question of affirmative action is the fundamental issue of "merit." Generally, admission or employment is determined by "neutral" evaluative methods, e.g., standardized tests, and subjective assessments, e.g., interviews. There is an assumption that this system of evaluation is fair and functional, that all applicants have an equal opportunity to compete, and that the resulting meritocracy identifies the people most qualified for the position. Departures from these traditional and conventional methods to determine who is most qualified are said to be unfair to those who are ranked as most qualified under this system. The dominance of objective criteria is a relatively recent phenomenon, dating from the 1950's.[45]

Affirmative action challenges both the norms inherent in this system of meritocracy as well as the implicit understanding that all people have an equal opportunity to achieve under these norms. The following excerpt argues that the "affirmative action" debate provides an opportunity to re-examine our commitment to racial and gender fairness.

44 below, admission of Hispanic students to the University of Texas School of Law fell 64% and admissions of African American students dropped 88%. www.aauw.org/1000/affactbd.html (Jan. 2000).

43. Regents of Univ. of Cal. v. Bakke, 438 U.S. 265, 98 S.Ct. 2733, 57 L.Ed.2d 750 (1978).

44. See, e.g., Hopwood v. Texas, 78 F.3d 932 (5th Cir.), cert. denied, 518 U.S. 1033, 116 S.Ct. 2581, 135 L.Ed.2d 1095 (1996); Wooden v. Board of Regents of the Univ. of Ga., 32 F. Supp.2d 1370 (1999) (holding a dual track admittance system in which the objective academic criteria to be admitted was lower for the Black applicants unconstitutional). But see Smith v. Univ. of Washington Law School, 233 F.3d 1188 (9th Cir.2000) (upholding an admissions policy considering race as a factor).

45. James Crouse and Dale Trusheim, The Case Against the SAT 31–37 (1988). Susan Sturm and Lani Guinier note conflict that arose with the ascendancy of this understanding of merit:

> On the one hand, merit was increasingly judged on a single or dominant criterion of performance—the ability to get good grades or perform well on tests that are designed to assess general intelligence or inherent ability. On the other hand, that single criterion of performance was exactly the area in which blacks had been made most vulnerable, factually, legally, and mythologically. As a factual and legal matter, blacks' educational opportunities had been severely limited. As the subject of political and pseudo-scientific myth-makers, blacks were pervasively stereotyped as possessing less general intelligence or inherent ability. Thus, the push for greater rationality in the workplace and institutions of higher learning must be juxtaposed against efforts by blacks and other people of color to challenge both the racially discriminatory allocation of benefits and the racial stereotypes that reinforced that allocation of benefits.

Sturm and Guinier, The Future of Affirmative Action: Reclaiming the Innovative Ideal, 84 Calif. L. Rev. 953, 967 (1996).

SUSAN STURM AND LANI GUINIER, THE FUTURE OF AFFIRMATIVE ACTION: RECLAIMING THE INNOVATIVE IDEAL

84 Calif. L. Rev. 953–58, 1010 (1996).

We are witnessing a broad-based assault on affirmative action—in the courts, the legislatures, and the media. Opponents have defined affirmative action as a program of racial preferences that threatens fundamental American values of fairness, equality, and democratic opportunity. Opponents successfully depict racial preferences as extraordinary, special, and deviant—a departure from prevailing modes of selection. They also proceeded on the assumption that, except for racial or gender preferences, the process of selection for employment or educational opportunity is fair, meritocratic, and functional. Thus, they have positioned affirmative action as unnecessary, unfair, and even un-American.

Those of us pursuing the quest of racial and gender justice in a genuinely democratic society face a crucial challenge. How do we respond to this assault on affirmative action? How do we invite a deeper conversation and analysis of selection and admissions conventions in pursuit of fairness? Understandably, much of the response has been reactive. Supporters of affirmative action typically engage the debate on the terms defined by the assault: affirmative action must continue. It is fair. It is still needed to rectify continued exclusion and marginalization in the society.

Supporters of affirmative action have also put forward a critique of the fairness and functionality of existing merit standards. They marshal considerable evidence showing that these standards exclude women and people of color, and that people who were excluded in the past do not yet operate on a level playing field. They have also challenged the justification for relying on these exclusionary criteria; they argue that the selection criteria do not predict the future performance of candidates in the positions they seek to occupy. They then rely on this critique of the fairness and validity of existing merit standards to justify departing from those standards for women and people of color. Affirmative action is justified to level the playing field, to rectify the biases built into the existing selection system, and to remedy past and continuing exclusion or underrepresentation.

Despite the moral and empirical force of these arguments, there is a sense in which they are not being heard. They certainly have not reshaped the terms or tone of the public debate. The most compelling moral claims are simply dismissed as special-interest pleading. Part of the reason for this asymmetry is that proponents of racial and gender justice have responded to the debate only as it is framed by the current assault.

This narrow response has tactical, strategic, and substantive costs. As a tactical matter, proponents have accepted a paradigm that misdirects attention and energy into trench warfare, rather than into pursuing a progressive agenda. By reacting defensively to the current onslaught, they have foreclosed discussion of new, innovative strategies for racial and gender justice. Substantively, they have accepted an existing framework of selection that is fundamentally and deeply flawed for those whom it includes as well as for those left out.

In other words, affirmative action, as it is currently practiced, supplements an underlying framework of selection that is implicitly arbitrary and exclusionary. It does not challenge the overall operation of a conventional and static selection process; instead, it creates exceptions to that process. Those exceptions play into existing racial stereotypes, predictably generating backlash. By implicitly legitimizing a selection process that operates in the name of merit, affirmative action programs reinforce that backlash. Programs perceived as racial preferences also enable employers to cast issues of economic retrenchment in terms of racial conflict. Many white workers who acknowledge the lack of corporate responsibility for the economic well-being of workers still focus their wrath and blame on the workers perceived as beneficiaries of affirmative action.

It is time, we argue, for those of us committed to racial and gender equity to advance a more fundamental critique of existing selection and admission conventions. It is time to discuss how conventional assessment and predictive criteria do not function fairly, democratically, or even meritocratically for many Americans who are not members of racial or gender minorities. To reclaim the moral high ground, we must broaden and expand the terms of engagement. By revealing faulty assumptions about the concept of affirmative action and the system of selection in which it operates, we can move from an incrementalist strategy of inclusion for a few to a transformative vision of reform for the many.

To reopen the conversation on race, gender, and democratic opportunity, it is necessary to change the paradigm. Certainly, we must challenge out loud the basic assumption that affirmative action is a departure from an otherwise sound meritocracy. At the same time, we must challenge existing add-on practices of affirmative action as too conservative a remedy. The experience of women and people of color offers insights beyond showing how and why those particular people have been excluded. We need to show that the current one-size-fits-all ranking system of predicting "merit" is no longer justified or productive for anyone.

The present system of selection is unfair for people who are neither women nor people of color. It denies opportunity for advancement to many poor and working-class Americans of all colors and genders who could otherwise obtain educational competence. It is underinclusive of those who can actually do the job. It is deeply problematic as a predictor of actual job performance. Across-the-board, it does violence to fundamental principles of equity and "functional merit" in its distribution of opportunities for admission to higher education, entry-level hiring, and job promotion.

Typical among the existing criteria and selection methods are paper-and-pencil tests, such as the Scholastic Assessment Test (SAT), the Law School Admissions Test (LSAT), and civil service exams. These tests, which are used to predict future performance based on existing capacity or ability, do not correlate with future performance for most applicants, at least not as a method of ranking those "most qualified." These tests and informal criteria making up our "meritocracy" tell us more about past opportunity than about future accomplishments on the job or in the classroom.

In challenging the way these tests are used, we are not proposing a critique of merit per se. Nor are we advancing an entirely original argument. Simply stated, we seek to highlight the way that certain paper-and-pencil tests have been used as "wealth preferences" or poll taxes to determine who gets to participate as full citizens in our democracy. As Michael Lind argues in a slightly different context, these tests are used, in conjunction with subjective assessments and informal networks, to develop a class-linked opportunity structure that credentializes "a social oligarchy."[19]

The approach we develop * * * links affirmative action initiatives with the project of fundamentally rethinking how we define and practice genuine merit selection. We argue that affirmative action is an opportunity to take from the margin to rethink the whole. Affirmative action is not about exceptions to the norm; it is about the norm itself. Affirmative action, and the experience of those who have been previously excluded, provide a window on a much larger set of questions. These are the same questions that companies and educational institutions must face to meet the demands of an economy in transition: Can we define and predict ability to perform based on one-size-fits-all tests and criteria? How do we go about identifying the type of worker/student who will perform successfully under changing economic conditions? Is sameness fairness? Or must we reconsider the notion that in a complicated world there are simple and single solutions? How do we rethink the process and content of selection to better accommodate the demands of the twenty-first-century workplace?

It is time to ask a different set of questions about affirmative action, questions that address the most pressing problems facing not only people of color and women, but all of those who are unfairly excluded from participation in work and education. We need to go beyond the modest curative of affirmative action to examine more deeply our system of selecting and evaluating all workers and students. This approach to affirmative action can open up an inquiry into the adequacy and legitimacy of the one-size-fits-all approach to selection that prevails in many

19. Michael Lind, Prescriptions for a New National Democracy, 110 Pol. Sci. Q. 563, 582 (1995–96).

arenas. In this way, affirmative action provides a less reactive, more transformative critique that highlights the range of preferences implicit in conventional selection and prediction criteria.

Patterns of exclusion experienced primarily by women and people of color are, nevertheless, still important. They serve as signals. Patterns of race-and gender-based exclusion signal the possibility that bias or unfair advantage has operated in the ostensibly neutral selection process. They also signal the inadequacy of traditional methods of selection for everyone, and the need to rethink the process used to allocate opportunities to participate in work and school. In other words, patterns of exclusion provide a window on the methods for "inclusion." They are an important source of continuous critique of monolithic and monochromatic ranking and selection processes.

Rethinking our assumptions about selection is important to be able to pursue goals of racial and gender justice and fairness. Even more, it is crucial to our capacity to develop productive, fair, and efficient institutions that can meet the challenges of a rapidly changing, unstable, and increasingly complex marketplace. By using the experiences of those on the margin to rethink the whole, we may forge a new, progressive vision of cross-racial collaboration, functional diversity and genuinely democratic opportunity.

> [The authors then provide an extensive analysis of what they call the "testocracy," in which applicants are scored, ranked, and their future performance predicted based on static, closed-book, timed paper-and-pencil assessments of past ability. First, they argue that the tests are extremely limited and do not measure qualities necessary to succeed, such as motivation, creativity, perseverance and teamwork skills. Second, they note that studies have consistently shown that the tests are only weakly correlated to what they are intended to measure. Finally, they discuss the racial, gender and class discriminatory impact of these tests.]

* * *

We are proposing a shift in the model of selection from prediction to performance. This model builds on the insight that the opportunity to participate creates the capacity to perform, and that actual performance offers the best evidence of capacity to perform. There simply is no substitute for experience, both in equipping people to perform and in producing informed judgments about the functional capacity of candidates. This approach shifts the emphasis away from the design of an instrument that is separate from the performance of the job, but that can be correlated with success in that job. Instead, the emphasis is on thinking creatively about how evaluation can proceed through the observation of applicants engaged in the work of those positions. The model also emphasizes the importance of creating opportunities to succeed and of structuring fair, inclusive, and participatory mechanisms to define and assess successful performance. This approach thus embeds performance and inclusion in the design of the selection process.

Notes on Affirmative Action

1. In a highly publicized book published in 1998, William G. Bowen (former President of Princeton University) and Derek Bok (former President of Harvard University) strongly supported affirmative action after analyzing the College and Beyond Database, containing the academic, employment, and personal histories of more than 45,000 students of all races who entered certain academically selective universities in the falls of 1951, 1976, and 1989. Bowen and Bok, The Shape of the River: Long–Term Consequences of Considering Race in College and University Admissions (1998). They found that utilizing race as a criterion for admission resulted in increased educational opportunities for all students as well as increasing the number of graduates involved in volunteer activities, especially in leadership positions. Emphasizing the civic responsibilities of educational institutions, the authors argue that "[w]hat admissions officers must decide is which set of applicants, *considered individually and collectively*, will take fullest advantage of what the college has to offer, contribute most to the educational process in college, and be most successful in using what they have learned for the benefit of the larger society." Id. at 277. In agreeing that admissions must be "fair," Bowen and Bok define "fairness" as follows: "each individual is to be judged according to a consistent set of criteria that reflect the objectives of the college or university. Fairness should not be misinterpreted to mean that a particular criterion has to apply—that, for example, grades and test scores must always be considered more important than other qualities and characteristics so that no student with a B average can be accepted as long as some students with As are being turned down." Id. at 277–78. Is their position consistent with Sturm and Guinier? In what ways? Although both support affirmative action, is one argument more persuasive to you than the other? Why?

2. As noted by Sturm and Guinier, standardized tests are not very good at predicting performance; even the best employment tests only explain nine percent of the variation in predicted job performance. Sturm and Guinier, above, at 970. And, in education, "[v]alidity studies of aptitude tests used to predict performance as measured only by first-year grades show correlations similar to those in the employment context." Id. at 971. Coupled with this poor predictive ability is a strong racial disparity in test scores which, according to Bowen and Bok, shows "no signs of disappearing in the foreseeable future." Bowen and Bok, above note 1, at 51. Why do you think standardized tests are relied upon so heavily when they (1) underpredict or do not predict performance very well and (2) have such a strong adverse racial impact?

3. Some people oppose racial preferences on the principle that the Constitution demands "color-blind" equality. Instead, they propose considering class, rather than race, in order to redress economic inequities that, in fact, are experienced more by Blacks and Hispanics. However, only one in six students from families with incomes under $20,000 who finished in the top tenth of their high school class is Black or Hispanic. Bowen and Bok, above note 1, at 271. So, even if schools could afford class-based affirmative action (in terms of the additional scholarship funds that would be required),

"substitution of a class-based system would drastically reduce the quality of the eligible pool of black and Hispanic applicants, seriously impeding the goal of preparing the ablest minority leaders for society and the professions." Id. at 51. Would you support a class-based preference in lieu of racial affirmative action? See Deborah C. Malamud, Class–Based Affirmative Action: Lessons and Caveats, 74 Tex. L. Rev. 1847 (1996).

Can you think of any other alternatives to race-based affirmative action? What about being a child in a single-parent household? Are alternatives, such as class, simply intended to be "proxies" for race? If so, why is it necessary to create a subterfuge?

Bowen and Bok believe race is a legitimate criterion:

> An individual's race may reveal something about how that person arrived at where he or she is today—what barriers were overcome, and what the individual's prospects are for further growth. Not every member of a minority group will have had to surmount substantial obstacles. Moreover, other circumstances besides race can cause "disadvantage." Thus colleges and universities should and do give special consideration to the hard-working son of a family in Appalachia or the daughter of a recent immigrant from Russia who, while obviously bright, is still struggling with the English language. But race is an important factor in its own right, given this nation's history and the evidence presented in many studies of the continuing effects of discrimination and prejudice. Wishing it were otherwise does not make it otherwise. It would seem to us to be ironic indeed—and wrong—if admissions officers were permitted to consider all other factors that help them identify individuals of high potential who have had to overcome obstacles, but were proscribed from looking at an applicant's race.
>
> * * *
>
> Race almost always affects an individual's life experiences and perspectives, and thus the person's capacity to contribute to the kinds of learning through diversity that occur on campuses. This form of learning will be even more important going forward than it has been in the past. Both the growing diversity of American society and the increasing interaction with other cultures worldwide make it evident that going to school only with "the likes of oneself" will be increasingly anachronistic. The advantages of being able to understand how others think and function, to cope across racial divides, and to lead groups composed of diverse individuals are certain to increase.

Bowen and Bok, above note 1, at 278–79. Are these comments convincing? Can you articulate additional reasons why race is a legitimate criterion in hiring and admitting to school?

4. What would happen without racial affirmative action? Bowen and Bok's study illustrates the fairly severe consequences:

> First, we estimate that the adoption of a strict race-neutral standard would reduce black enrollment at these academically selective colleges and universities by between 50 and 70 percent. * * * According to these estimates, if blacks had been admitted in the same proportions as whites within each SAT interval (our definition of race-neutrality),

black matriculants in 1989 would have constituted no more than 3.6 percent of the entering classes at these schools.

Second, the most selective schools would experience the largest drops in black enrollment. The proportion of black students in these institutions would decrease from about 7 percent to roughly 2 percent of total enrollment.

* * *

Imposition of a race-neutral standard would produce very troubling results from this perspective: such a policy would reduce dramatically the proportion of black students on campus—probably shrinking their number to less than 2 percent of all matriculants at the most selective colleges and professional schools. Moreover, our examination of the application and admissions files indicates that such substantial reductions in the number of black matriculants, with attendant losses in educational opportunity for all students, would occur without leading to any appreciable improvement in the academic credentials of the remaining black students and would lead to only a modest change in the overall academic profile of the institutions.

Bowen and Bok, above note 1, at 51, 280. How would anti-affirmative action proponents respond to these results?

5. Are there "affirmative action" plans in place for whites or males? What about legacies, in which children of alumni are granted admission? For example, for several decades 20 percent of Harvard students have been admitted as legacies even though they may not be as well qualified as regular applicants under the traditional academic criteria. Laura M. Padilla, Intersectionality and Positionality: Situating Women of Color in the Affirmative Action Dialogue, 66 Fordham L. Rev. 843, 867 (1997). What about athletic scholarships and admissions? Why aren't these preferences recognized as a type of affirmative action?

6. After concluding that affirmative action preferences exacerbate intergroup tensions and perpetuate certain subtle forms of intergroup bias, Linda Hamilton Krieger nonetheless argues that they are essential in addressing societal discrimination:

> [T]endencies towards intergroup discrimination are much more subtle, stable, and pernicious than these assumptions ["that discrimination is conscious, intentional, and reasonably easy to identify" and "that absent state-sanctioned or overt discrimination by private actors* * *, intergroup relations in the United States will improve or at least remain relatively tranquil"] or their reflection in anti-affirmative action rhetoric admit. Social cognition teaches that much intergroup discrimination is both unintentional and unconscious. It occurs spontaneously as an unwanted artifact of normal cognitive functions associated with the processing of information about other people and can be corrected, if at all, only through further deliberate mental effort. Social identity theory and related research in experimental social psychology indicates that the tendencies to assist or excuse those with whom we feel closely identified and to subordinate the socially distant are far less tractable than we might wish.

> These more subtle, incremental forms of discrimination are difficult to recognize, and neither our cultural understanding nor our jurisprudential models of discrimination illuminate or provide ways to reckon with them. Without affirmative action, it remains to be seen how powerfully they will operate to exclude minorities and women from large segments of the academy, public contracting, or labor markets.

Krieger, Civil Rights Perestroika: Intergroup Relations After Affirmative Action, 86 Calif. L. Rev. 1251, 1332–33 (1998). Are you persuaded by this additional justification for affirmative action? Are there distinctions to be made between gender and racial intergroup discrimination which would justify variations in affirmative action? Recall the discussions in Chapter Two about comparing race and gender discrimination, appropriate standards, and remedies.

Text Note: Affirmative Action in the Classroom

On a substantive level, during the early 1970s women in higher education began to create and offer courses with an interdisciplinary emphasis that focused on women and were critical of the subordination of women and minorities. The Women's Studies Movement was a direct attack on the narrowness and exclusivity of the traditional male-dominated curriculum. Additionally, this new concentration was premised on effecting social change, sometimes even including an activist component. In a sense, women's studies is a type of classroom affirmative action.[52]

Florence Howe describes the basic curriculum in a mature women's studies program:

> 1. an understanding of patriarchy in historical perspective, philosophically and sociologically, its relationship to the religions of the world, and to ideas of knowledge and power—hence, an understanding of what it means to be born "permanently" into a subordinate or dominant status; a knowledge of feminist theory
>
> 2. an understanding of the complex, confusing, and still chaotic area of biological psychological sex differences; the importance of null findings
>
> 3. an understanding of socialization and sex roles, as well as of sex-role stereotyping; the relationships among gender, race, and class—all from a cross-cultural perspective
>
> 4. an understanding of women in history, not only in the United States, but throughout the world, recognizing that such study includes legal as well as medical history—the history of birth control, for example, which is essential to the study of women, even to the study of fiction about women
>
> 5. an understanding of women as represented in the arts they have produced, some of which have been buried or ignored as arts—quilt-

52. See generally Florence Howe, Myths of Coeducation: Selected Essays 1964–1983 (1984). Ms. Howe notes the novelty of this challenge to the "men's curriculum," and explains it as follows: "It is difficult to criticize adversely an institution you want access to. It is difficult also to criticize an institution you have access to but want equality in." Id. at 218.

making, for example, or the pottery of North American Indian women; and as represented in the significant literature by women of all races and nationalities that never was included in the literary curriculum; as well as an awareness that the images of women portrayed by the male-created arts have helped to control the dominant conceptions of women—hence, the importance of studying images of women on TV, in film and the theatre, and in advertising

6. an understanding of the ways in which post-Freudian psychology has attempted to control women's destiny; an awareness that other male-centered psychological constructs like those of Erikson and Kohlberg are potentially damaging to women; an understanding of new women-centered theories of female development

7. an understanding of female sexuality, including perspectives on both heterosexuality and lesbianism; special issues involved in birth control and reproduction

8. an understanding of the history and function of education as support and codifier of sex segregation and of limited opportunities for women; some perspectives on education as an agent for change in the past and present

9. an understanding of the history and function of the family in the United States and cross-culturally; of the current variety of family structures, and of the conflict between beliefs and research findings with reference especially to issues surrounding children

10. an understanding of women in the workforce through history, in the present, and cross culturally; the economy in relation to women; the relationship between money and power in personal interactions, in the family, and in society

11. an understanding of the relationship between laws affecting women and social change; the history of women and social movements.[53]

What further distinguishes this approach from the male curriculum is that class, race, and sexual orientation issues are addressed as well.

Of course, even after the need for women's studies is established, there are serious issues about implementation strategy. Should the interdisciplinary courses and materials remain segregated under "Women's Studies," or should there be a curriculum mainstreaming them in an integrationist approach? There are some very serious concerns with each approach. For instance, only the converted may take segregated courses unless they are mandatory. There are problems, as well, with the integrationist approach: "What happens to a body of feminist knowledge that is distributed by non-feminists because they have to incorporate it into their course? And what happens to the student who gets her or his feminist education from such a teacher?"[54] These concerns are equally applicable to teaching feminist theory in law schools.

53. Howe at 275–76.

54. Gloria Bowles and Renate Duelli Klein, Introduction: Theories of Women's Studies and the Autonomy/Integration Debate, in Theories of Women's Studies 1, 9 (Bowles and Klein, eds. 1983).

Similar to gender preference programs, women's studies has been criticized as devaluing or harming men. These innovations have frequently met with resistance, which are explained by Carolyn Heilbrun, referring to Christine Froula's work, in terms of power politics:

> Why are men so afraid? "I think the answer to this question," Christine Froula, a young feminist critic writes, "has to do with the fact that woman's voice threatens to discredit that masculinist culture upon which [men have] modeled their identity." Many works of the canon have constructed their "speech on the bedrock of woman's silence." "Men very commonly express the fear that feminist criticism will invert that hierarchy in which they have invested so much—will, in other words, silence *them* as patriarchal discourse has silenced women. * * * But a woman speaking does not reverse the conditions of her own silencing. She does not demand that men be silent: she only asks that men cease speaking in such a way as to silence her."
>
> All the jokes in literature about women-dominated marriages, all the horrible wives in Dickens, Trollope, and others speak to the male fear of hierarchical reversal. If men are not boss, women will be. But this is what men fear, not what women want. Women ask men only to "grant women's voices an equal position with male discourse, rescuing it from the now inevitable reactive position of either assimilation or opposition."[55]

This male fear has resulted in vitriolic attacks on attempts to reform the male curriculum, traditionally known as the "canon," in which the works of particular authors, almost exclusively white and male, establish the standards of excellence.

Another aspect of affirmative action in the classroom is what has become known as the Political Correctness (PC) Wars, a reaction to the demands of women and minorities that the canon be opened to non-white, non-male authors, issues and concerns; that racist and sexist speech which inhibits learning and poisons the learning environment not be tolerated; and that what constitutes excellence not be determined by an elite few. During the 1990's many conservative academics and politicians decried "political correctness," which, according to them, was an ideological movement stifling free discussion, destroying academic standards, and threatening the First Amendment.[56] Katherine T. Bartlett gave a spirited response to these critics:

> In any social organization, the views of the dominant tend to be taken for granted as objective and neutral. Challenges to these views—like those we are now hearing in the universities—appear to seek special favors for the "less qualified," or some compromising of academic standards.

* * *

55. Heilbrun, The Politics of Mind: Women, Tradition, and the University, in Gender in the Classroom: Power and Pedagogy 28, 30–31 (Susan L. Gabriel and Isaiah Smithson, eds. 1990).

56. See, e.g., William J. Bennett, The De-Valuing of America: The Fight for Our Culture and Our Children (1995); Jeffrey Winters, ed., PC Wars: Politics and Theory in the Academy (1994); Dinesh D'Souza, Illiberal Education: Political Correctness and the College Experience (1992).

> Some PC critics dismiss as interest-group politics requests that authors such as Toni Morrison or Mary Wollestonecraft be included in the curriculum; others malign courses in feminist theory or black studies as a "Balkanization" of the curriculum.
>
> In contrast, assignments of writings by Nathaniel Hawthorne or T.S. Eliot draw no notice and require no defense; neither does the "basic" political philosophy course that begins with Aristotle and ends with John Rawls. The difference is *not* that the standard "Western civilization" courses are apolitical. In fact, it is precisely the alignment of these courses with particular points of view—the dominant ones in our society—that makes them appear neutral. This is not to argue that such courses should be abolished, but nobody should pretend that only feminist and minority-studies courses have political content.[57]

In fact, according to Bartlett, it is the PC critics who are utilizing personal denunciation and caricature instead of honest discussion in an attempt to divert the debate. They are "using a double standard to judge those who do not respect their authority. These critics invoke important principles of academic freedom to shield themselves from criticism of classroom remarks that some students find racist or sexist."[58]

E. ATHLETIC PROGRAMS

Text Note: Gender Equity in Athletics

In no area has unequal treatment been more open, and defended, than sports. The early legal challenges to sex inequality in school athletics were based primarily on state and federal constitutional protections. These cases most frequently concerned the legality of rules that classified persons as eligible to participate in sports on the basis of their sex. In general, courts had little difficulty concluding that public school regulations prohibiting girls from participating in particular sports denied girls Equal Protection.[59] Nonetheless, many states have lawful policies prohibiting females from participating with males in contact sports.[60] In addition, when a school provides teams in particular sports for both sexes, most courts have approved the sex-segregated teams.[61] On the other hand, decisions have been inconsistent

57. Bartlett, Some Factual Correctness About Political Correctness, Wall St.J., June 6, 1991, § A, at 19.

58. Id.

59. See Hoover v. Meiklejohn, 430 F.Supp. 164 (D.Colo.1977)(soccer); Brenden v. Independent Sch. Dist., 477 F.2d 1292 (8th Cir.1973)(tennis, cross country skiing, and cross country running); Carnes v. Tennessee Secondary Sch. Athletic Ass'n, 415 F.Supp. 569 (E.D.Tenn.1976) (baseball); Reed v. Nebraska Sch. Activities Ass'n, 341 F.Supp. 258 (D.Neb.1972) (golf); Lantz v. Ambach, 620 F.Supp. 663 (S.D.N.Y.1985) (football); Clinton v. Nagy, 411 F.Supp. 1396 (N.D.Ohio 1974) (football); but see Lafler v. Athletic Bd. of Control, 536 F.Supp. 104 (W.D.Mich.1982) (finding that even though no women's division existed, female plaintiff was constitutionally denied the right to box in the flyweight division of the Golden Gloves boxing competition).

60. Title IX regulations also seem to permit this, defining contact sports broadly to include "boxing, wrestling, rugby, ice hockey, football, basketball and other sports the purpose or major activity of which involves bodily contact." 34 C.F.R. § 106.41(b) (1995).

61. See O'Connor v. Board of Educ. of Sch. Dist. No. 23, 645 F.2d 578 (7th Cir. 1981), cert. denied, 454 U.S. 1084, 102 S.Ct. 641, 70 L.Ed.2d 619 (1981); but see Yellow Springs Exempted Village Sch. Dist. Bd. of when rules prohibiting boys from participating on girls' teams are at issue. All of these reported cases involve situations in which there is no separate boys' team. Courts upholding such regulations usually rely on arguments that the exclusionary rules were substantially related to the important governmental interest in redressing overall equality of athletic opportunity and to redress past discrimination against women.[62]

More recently, plaintiffs have asserted broader claims of discrimination in athletic programs, especially in the areas of funding and scholarships. For example, in 1987 female students at Washington State University were successful in their suit, based on Washington's Equal Rights Amendment, that sought more equal funding. The trial court ordered WSU to increase incrementally the funds and scholarships allocated to the intercollegiate athletic program until it matched the percentage of women undergraduates at the university; however, the football program was to be excluded from the calculations. On appeal, the Washington Supreme Court held that the trial court had abused its discretion, stating that the state ERA "contains no exception for football."[63]

With the enactment of Title IX in 1972, it was widely predicted that equality in athletics finally was within reach.[64] In some sports, there have been amazing gains; for instance, approximately 41% of all American soccer players now are girls and women[65] and the U.S. Women's Soccer Team won the 1999 World Cup in women's soccer. The face of sports has changed over the past three decades.

Educ. v. Ohio High Sch. Athletic Ass'n, 443 F.Supp. 753 (S.D.Ohio 1978). See also Glenn M. Wong and Richard J. Ensor, Sex Discrimination in Athletics: A Review of Two Decades of Accomplishments and Defeats, 21 Gonzaga L.Rev. 345 (1985–86). Regulations under Title IX also permit separate teams for males and females "where selection for such teams is based upon competitive skill." 34 C.F.R. § 106.41(b) (1995).

62. See Clark v. Arizona Interscholastic Ass'n, 695 F.2d 1126 (9th Cir.1982), cert. denied, 464 U.S. 818, 104 S.Ct. 79, 78 L.Ed.2d 90 (1983) (excluding boys from girls' volleyball teams is a permissible means to insure equal opportunity for girls and to redress past discrimination); but see Gomes v. Rhode Island Interscholastic League, 469 F.Supp. 659 (D.R.I.), vacated as moot, 604 F.2d 733 (1st Cir.1979) (holding that Fourteenth Amendment and Title IX require school to allow plaintiff to compete on girls volleyball team); Attorney General v. Massachusetts Interscholastic Athletic Ass'n, 378 Mass. 342, 393 N.E.2d 284 (1979) (holding that exclusion of boys from girls team violates state Equal Rights Amendment).

63. Blair v. Washington State Univ., 108 Wash.2d 558, 566, 740 P.2d 1379, 1383 (1987).

64. Women have made extraordinary improvements in performance. For example, in "swimming and long-distance running, women have come to within ten percent of the best male times. Joan Benoit won the women's marathon in the 1984 Olympics in 2 hours, 24 minutes, 52 seconds, a time that would have captured the gold medal in the men's marathon in 1948, and would have won a silver medal in the men's marathon in 1952. On the other hand, gold medal-winner Don Schollander's world record-setting time in the 400–meter freestyle in the 1964 Olympics would have placed him fifth in the women's event in the 1980 Moscow Games." Karen L. Tokarz, Separate But Unequal Educational Sports Programs: The Need for a New Theory of Equality, 1 Berkeley Women's L.J. 201, 221 (1985). In 1926, the first woman to swim the English Channel, nineteen-year-old Gertrude Ederle, shattered the previous record by almost two hours. Pia Sarkar, She Was the Wave of the Future, The Record, Jan. 25, 2000, News §, at 1. The current world record of 7 hours and 40 minutes was set by female Penny Lee Dean in 1978. http://home.istar.ca.

65. Jessica E. Jay, Women's Participation in Sports: Four Feminist Perspectives, 7 Tex. J. Women & L. 1, 9 (1997).

Participation in girls' high school athletics has grown enormously. In 1971, only one in 27 girls participated in high school sports; by 1994 that figure was one in three. While this certainly constitutes progress, one out of two boys are involved in high school interscholastic athletics.[66]

College statistics are quite similar. In 1997 the NCAA released a sequel report to its 1992 "Gender Equity Study." In reviewing the progress made at Division I schools, the NCAA found that although 53% of the undergraduates were women, they constituted only 37% of student-athletes, with women's teams receiving only 23% of expenditures. Coaches of men's teams received 60% of the compensation for Division I schools; there were no female coaches in the major men's teams of football, basketball and baseball.[67]

Under Title IX, there are three main sources of gender equity: the law itself, implementing regulations, and the Title IX Athletics Investigator's Manual used by the Department of Education's Office of Civil Rights (OCR), the federal agency with responsibility for interpreting and enforcing Title IX. The OCR has identified three compliance areas: (1) athletic financial assistance; (2) equivalence in other athletic benefits and opportunities; and (3) effective accommodation of athletic interests and abilities. The second area—equivalence—has ten components: effective accommodation of interest and ability; provision and maintenance of equipment and supplies; scheduling of games and practice times; travel and per diem allowances; opportunity to receive coaching and academic tutoring; assignment and compensation of coaches and tutors; provisions of locker rooms, practice and competitive facilities; provision of medical and training facilities and services; provision of housing and dining facilities and services; and publicity. The Final Policy Interpretation adds two other factors: recruitment and provision of support services.

Under the third compliance area, effective accommodation of athletic interests and abilities, even if there is a gender disparity, the institution will not be in violation if it can satisfy one of the OCR's safe harbors:

1. Whether intercollegiate level participation opportunities for male and female students are provided in numbers substantially proportionate to the respective enrollments; or

2. Where the members of one sex are underrepresented among athletes, whether the institution can show a history and continuing practice of program expansion which is demonstrably responsive to the developing interests and abilities of that sex; or

3. Where the members of one sex are underrepresented among athletes, and the institution cannot show a continuing practice of program expansion, whether the institution can demonstrate that the interests and abilities of the members of that sex have been fully and effectively accommodated.[68]

66. Id. at 6–7.

67. Diane Heckman, ScoreBoard: A Concise Chronological Twenty–Five Year History of Title IX Involving Interscholastic and Intercollegiate Athletics, 7 Seton Hall J. of Sport L. 391, 416–18 (1997).

68. 34 C.F.R. § 106.41(c)(1)-(10) (1995); Final Policy Interpretation, Title IX and Intercollegiate Athletics, 44 Fed. Reg. 71,415, 71,418 (1979). In a rather complex scheme, the Final Policy Interpretation separates the first factor, effective accommoda-

Most schools rely in their defense on this third prong, accommodation of interests and abilities.[69] In order to satisfy this safe harbor, schools are not required to integrate their teams or even to provide the same choice of sports to both sexes;[70] they may even provide greater athletic opportunities to one gender where the other gender simply does not wish or is not able to compete.[71]

In practice, OCR has never withdrawn federal funds from any educational institution as a result of noncompliance in athletics. Thus, private parties have become much more active in filing suit under Title IX.

Text Note: Title IX Sports Litigation

There have been many cases litigated by private parties that show how pervasive unequal treatment can be in intercollegiate sports. In a 1987 class action, female students participating in (or deterred from participating in) the intercollegiate athletic program at Temple University asserted violations of both state and federal equal protection clauses as well as Title IX.[72] In considering the defendant's motion for summary judgment, the court stated that its task was "to define the 'equality' that is required, and then to

tion of interests and abilities, from the other criteria.

69. Roy Whitehead, Walter Block, and Lu Hardin, Gender Equity in Athletics: Should We Adopt a Non–Discriminatory Model?, 30 U. Tol. L. Rev. 223, 225 (1999). The authors note that "very few institutions, especially those with football programs, are able to meet the first test, proportionality. Additionally, a training session with an author of the OCR Investigator's Manual reveals that no institution, to his knowledge, has ever met the second test consisting of a history and practice of program expansion responsive to the interests and abilities of women." Id.

70. Note, Title IX in the Nineties, 15 N.Y.L. Sch. J. Hum. Rts. 561, 564–65 (1999).

71. Melody Harris, Hitting 'Em Where It Hurts: Using Title IX Litigation to Bring Gender Equity to Athletics, 72 Denver U.L. Rev. 57, 90 (1994). According to Harris:

> To evaluate this prong, courts must consider a number of factors: any surveys conducted by the institution demonstrating athletic interest or ability in the underrepresented gender; "expressed interests" of the underrepresented gender; club and intramural participation by the underrepresented gender; and participation levels in feeder schools, community programs, or physical education classes. Moreover, the manner in which the educational institution met the developing interests of men, and whether the institution actively encouraged any male sport, must also be considered. If an institution has cut an existing and viable women's team, this prong will be easily satisfied by testimony by the plaintiff athletes regarding their interests and abilities in continuing play on their former teams.

Id. According to Whitehead et al.:

> Much to the dismay of some interest groups, OCR has ruled that the third part of the test may be satisfied by the institution showing it has accommodated the interest and abilities of its female students although there may be a substantial disproportionateness of numbers between male and female athletes. According to the OCR, this may be demonstrated by showing that the opportunity to participate in intercollegiate athletics is consistent with the interests of enrolled women undergraduates who have the ability to play college sports, which can be determined by an external survey of the university's recruiting area, including high school and junior college competition, summer league competition, and sanctioned state sports. The university need only accommodate women who have the ability to play at the intercollegiate level.

Whitehead et al., above note 69, at 225–26.

72. Haffer v. Temple University, 678 F.Supp. 517 (E.D.Pa.1987).

determine whether defendants offer equivalent athletic programs to men and women student athletes."

First, the court noted that during the relevant time periods, in terms of opportunities to compete, although Temple's student body was fifty percent female, only one-third of its athletes were. Second, Temple spent $2,100 more on male athletes that it did on female athletes. Third, 84 percent of recruiting funds, or $236 more per capita, was spent on male athletes. Fourth, men's teams paid coaches more, had more coaches assigned to them, and received superior coaching (although, as the defendant noted, the proportion of women's coaches to total coaches was higher than the proportion of women athletes to total athletes). Fifth, Temple spent over twice as much on team travel for men's teams (e.g., even when teams, such as male and female basketball, were traveling to the same destination the men's team flew and the women's team took a bus). Sixth, male athletes were provided superior support in the areas of uniforms; equipment; locker rooms; supplies; facilities and scheduling for both practice and competition; housing and dining facilities, including for pre-season and holidays; preference in provision of athletic trainers and training services; academic tutoring support; and publicity. In defense of these economic disparities, Temple argued that (a) women's teams still had a higher win rate and (b) that if the "revenue" teams of football, men's basketball and women's basketball were excluded, expenditures on nonrevenue men's teams were equivalent to that spent on women's nonrevenue teams. The court rejected the proposition that comparable "win" rates meant equal treatment as well as the "revenue" team argument (or so-called "football defense") since the Temple football team lost more money than the entire expenditures on the women's sports program. Finally, the court refused to impose an intent requirement in order to find a violation of Title IX and, based upon the above facts, denied the motion for summary judgment.

After eight years of litigation, and about two months after the trial in *Haffer* began, the district court approved a settlement negotiated by the parties. In the landmark consent decree, Temple agreed to alter its athletic program over five years beginning with the 1988–89 academic year, and plaintiffs agreed to withdraw their demand for $1.8 million dollars in damages. Temple agreed specifically, among other things, to: (a) keep the percentage of athletic scholarships granted to women equal to the percentage of female participants in the school's athletic programs and (b) keep the percentage of athletic expenditures for women within 10 percentage points of the percentage of women participating (excluding coaches' salaries and benefits, home game expenses and post-season competition), e.g., if one third of the school's athletes are women, then the women's athletic program must receive at least 23% of the total athletic budget. Temple was required to file annual reports with the court and is subject to contempt if it fails to meet the terms of the decree. The University also had to pay over $700,000 in fees and costs.[73]

73. Steve Springer, After 16 Years, Title IX's Goals Remain Unfulfilled, L.A. Times, Oct. 30, 1988, Sports §, at 12.

The *Haffer* case has been followed by many other Title IX suits brought by private parties. In a class action filed after Brown University demoted the women's gymnastics and volleyball teams from university-funded varsity status to donor-funded varsity status, a downgrade which cost the teams not only university funding but also most of the other forms of support and privileges accompanying university-funded varsity sports at Brown, the First Circuit affirmed liability.[74] Two men's teams, water polo and golf, were similarly downgraded. During a trial on the merits, the district court found that:

> in 1993–94, there were 897 students participating in intercollegiate varsity athletics, of which 61.87% were men and 38.13% (342) were women. During the same period, Brown's undergraduate enrollment comprised 5,722 students, of which 48.86% (2,796) were men and 51.15% (2,926) were women. * * * [I]n 1993–94, Brown's intercollegiate athletics program consisted of 32 teams, 16 men's teams and 16 women's teams. Of the university-funded teams, 12 were men's teams and 13 were women's teams; of the donor-funded teams, three were women's teams and four were men's teams. At the time of trial, Brown offered 479 university-funded varsity positions for men, as compared to 312 for women; and 76 donor-funded varsity positions for men, as compared to 30 for women. In 1993–94, then, Brown's varsity program—including both university-and donor-funded sports—afforded over 200 more positions for men than for women. Accordingly, * * * Brown maintained a 13.01% disparity between female participation in intercollegiate athletics and female student enrollment, and "although the number of varsity sports offered to men and women are equal, the selection of sports offered to each gender generates far more individual positions for male athletes than for female athletes."[75]

The trial court then held that Brown did not meet the OCR Policy Interpretation concerning effective accommodation because it did not provide opportunities for male and female students in numbers substantially proportionate to their respective enrollments nor did it maintain an ongoing program expansion for the underrepresented sex, women. Continuing, the court held that simply eliminating or demoting several men's teams did not constitute program expansion for women. Finally, the court found that Brown had not fully and effectively accommodated women to provide equal opportunity.

On appeal, the First Circuit recognized that sex discrimination under Title IX imposes differing standards for athletics and admissions and employment. It rejected Brown's argument that the gender disparity was caused not by discrimination but by a lack of interest on the part of female students unrelated to lack of opportunities. The court explained:

> to allow a numbers-based lack-of-interest defense to become the instrument of further discrimination against the underrepresented gender would pervert the remedial purpose of Title IX. We conclude that, even if it can be empirically demonstrated that, at a particular time, women have less interest in sports than do men, such evidence, standing alone,

74. Cohen v. Brown Univ., 101 F.3d 155 (1st Cir.1996), cert. denied, 520 U.S. 1186, 117 S.Ct. 1469, 137 L.Ed.2d 682 (1997).

75. 101 F.3d at 163.

> cannot justify providing fewer athletics opportunities for women than for men. Furthermore, such evidence is completely irrelevant where, as here, viable and successful women's varsity teams have been demoted or eliminated.[76]

Furthermore, the court noted that since Title IX there has been a tremendous growth in women's participation in sports, a fact that rebuts Brown's argument that women are less interested in sports for reasons other than lack of opportunity.[77] In another case the court held that male athletes do not have a cause of action when, in response to a significant deficit in the athletic budget, the college decided to eliminate the men's, but not the women's, swimming team.[78]

When seven female University of Texas–Austin athletes filed a class action against the school claiming intentional discrimination under Title IX, the UT student body was 47% women, although their sports participation was a mere 23%. The men's annual athletic budget for nine sports was $16 to $20 million, while the women's budget for eight sports was $4.3 million. Men received $1.78 million in scholarship dollars, while women got $449,000. The attorney representing the plaintiffs, Diana Henson, said the lawsuit did not seek monetary damages but rather to force UT to add softball, soccer, rowing and gymnastics to the women's athletic competitions. In 1993 the UT settled the lawsuit, agreeing to devote 44% of its varsity athletic roster spots to women and to give women more than 42% of its athletic scholarship money. In order to accomplish this goal, UT added three women's varsity teams and slightly reduced the roster sizes of its men's varsity teams without eliminating any of them.[79]

Notes on Title IX Litigation

1. Brown also proffered an argument that a remedy with numerical requirements was a "quota" and hence unconstitutional according to Adarand Constr., Inc. v. Pena, 515 U.S. 200, 115 S.Ct. 2097, 132 L.Ed.2d 158 (1995). Do you think that the successes of the anti-affirmative action movement, discussed in the previous section, will affect remedies imposed *after* findings of liability? Are numerically-based remedies a type of quota in the context of separate sports teams for women and men? Why or why not?

2. One of the defenses asserted by Temple was that "revenue" teams, most particularly football, should be excluded from any comparisons. Many commentators believe that college football is the biggest obstacle to Title IX compliance. According to Deidre G. Duncan:

76. Id. at 179.

77. See also Favia v. Indiana Univ. of Pa., 812 F.Supp. 578 (W.D.Pa.), aff'd, 7 F.3d 332 (3d Cir.1993); Roberts v. Colorado State Univ., 814 F.Supp. 1507 (D.Colo.), aff'd in part, rev'd in part sub nom., Roberts v. Colorado State Bd. of Agric., 998 F.2d 824 (10th Cir.), cert. denied, 510 U.S. 1004, 114 S.Ct. 580, 126 L.Ed.2d 478 (1993).

78. Kelley v. Board of Trustees, 35 F.3d 265, 270 (7th Cir.1994) (holding that this was not a Title IX violation "because even after the cuts, 'men's participation in athletics would continue to be more than substantially proportionate to their presence in the university's student body.' ").

79. Carol Herwig, Female Athletes Sue Texas for Gender Bias, USA Today, July 2, 1992, Sports §, at 2; Citing Title IX, 7 Women File Suit Against Texas, Wash. Post, July 3, 1992, Sports §, at 2.

> Many coaches and athletes fear that "Title IX will be the end of major college football." College football has been referred to as the "golden goose" of college athletics. Football's attendance levels and television ratings far surpass those of any other sport. Likewise, there is no sport, men's or women's, that equals the number of players and scholarships given to football programs by university athletic departments. All of these numbers pose great problems for a university attempting to achieve Title IX compliance. * * *
>
> In Division I college football, eighty-eight scholarships are permitted per university and participation often exceeds one hundred athletes. This problem virtually precludes universities from having a ratio of male to female athletes proportionate to the general student body. With such large teams, football often costs far more money than the entire women's athletic budget. Athletic departments worry that if schools were forced to offer an equitable number of men's and women's scholarships, some schools would be able to operate only three men's sports: football, basketball, and baseball.
>
> The problem seems deceptively simple to solve—exempt college football from the proportionality requirement. However, football cannot legally be exempted. When Congress passed Title IX, the late Senator John Tower of Texas proposed an amendment that would have excluded revenue-producing sports from the Title IX equity requirement. The bill was summarily rejected. Proponents of gender equity interpret this rejection as imposing a requirement that Title IX analysis must include college football.
>
> * * *
>
> Aside from the proportionality problem, football also raises the issue of how to give credit to revenue-generating sports. Because football often contributes revenue and provides financial support for other men's and women's athletics, football supporters claim it should be exempted from Title IX analysis. They point to the fact that money raised from college football, along with the revenue earned from the NCAA Division I men's basketball tournament, assists in supporting several other nonrevenue generating sports, men's and women's. An NCAA study released in August of 1994 revealed that men's sports programs, with football at the top of the list, generated an average of sixty-nine percent of Division I–A athletic department revenue. Women's programs average only four percent of total revenues, with the remaining [revenue] coming from nongender specific sources.

Duncan, Gender Equity in Women's Athletics, 64 U. Cin. L. Rev. 1027, 1046–49 (1996). Should football be exempt from Title IX proportionality compliance requirements? Why or why not? How strong is the revenue generation argument? If there hadn't been massive exclusion of women from college sports in the past, due to discrimination, do you think that women's sports could generate as much revenue as the entrenched men's sports? What is the role of the media in deciding which sports generate the most revenue? Does the revenue generation argument come dangerously close, as a practical matter, to elevating college sports from amateur to professional status? Is this desirable? Is it reality?

3. After investigating allegations of sex discrimination, in 1992 the OCR found Brooklyn College in violation of Title IX. The findings included the fact that women made up 30% of Brooklyn College's athletes, while they were 56% of the student body. The equipment budget for men's teams was nearly seven times that for women's teams; and men's teams played more games, e.g., the men's baseball schedule included 46 games while the women's softball team played 12. Men's teams had more experienced coaches, more experienced trainers, higher food stipends, more publicity and 87% of the money spent on recruiting. Malcolm Moran, Brooklyn College at Crossroads, N.Y. Times, June 23, 1992, § B, at 15. Several months after receiving the OCR decision, the College decided to terminate its entire athletic department. Roscoe Nance, Colleges, USA Today, July 2, 1992, Sports §, at 13. Is there any remedy for this?

4. How should non-discrimination be defined in athletic scholarships and funding? Title IX regulations require only substantial proportionality in scholarships based on the percentage of females with respect to the total group of athletic participants. 34 C.F.R. § 106.37(a) (1995). Is one effect of these regulations to provide an incentive to schools not to promote participation by females? Is this regulation consistent with Title IX? Should it be amended?

MICHAEL A. MESSNER, POWER AT PLAY: SPORTS AND THE PROBLEM OF MASCULINITY

24, 33, 34, 35–37, 62, 68–69, 91, 159–60, 166–68, 170–72 (1992)

[The author conducted semi-structured interviews, ranging from one and one-half hour to six hours, with 30 male former athletes, aged 21 to 48, in order to "discover how masculine gender identities develop and change and boys and men interact with the socially constructed world of organized sport."]

Zane Grey once said, "All boys love baseball. If they don't, they're not real boys." This is, of course, an ideological statement: Some boys do not love baseball, or any other sports, for that matter. There are millions of males who at an early age are rejected by, become alienated from, or lose interest in organized sport. Yet, studies in the 1970s and the 1980s consistently showed that sport remains the single most important element of the peer-status system of U.S. adolescent males. The fact is, boys are, to a greater or lesser extent, judged according to their ability, or lack of ability, in competitive sport.

* * *

Young boys may initially find that playing competitively gives them the opportunity to experience emotionally "safe" connections with others. But once enmeshed in sport as an institution, they are confronted by two interrelated realities—hierarchy and homophobia—that undermine the possibility of boys' transcending their fears of intimacy and developing truly close relationships with others.

* * *

The extent of homophobia in the sports world is staggering. Boys learn early that to be gay, to be suspected of being gay, or even to be unable to prove one's heterosexual status is not acceptable. Though athletes are cultural symbols of masculine heterosexual virility, however, it is not true that there are no gay men and boys in sports. There is growing evidence that many (mostly closeted) gay males are competing in organized sport at all levels.

* * *

Indeed, boys learn early that if it is difficult to define masculinity in terms of what it *is*, it is at least clear what it is *not*. A boy is not considered masculine if he is feminine. In sport, to be told by coaches, fathers, or peers that one throws "like a girl" or plays like a "sissy" or a "woman" is among the most devastating insults a boy can receive, and such words can have a powerful impact upon his actions, relationships, and self-image. Sociologist Gary Alan Fine spent three years studying Little League baseball teams and noted clear and persistent patterns of homophobic banter and sexual talk about females among eleven-and twelve-year-old boys. * * *

Fine's observations demonstrate how homophobia and the sexual objectification of females together act as a glue that solidifies the male peer group as separate from females, while at the same time establishing and clarifying hierarchical relations within the male peer group. In short, homophobia polices the boundaries of narrow cultural definitions of masculinity and keeps boys—especially those in all-male environments such as organized sport—from getting too close. Through sport, a young boy learns that it is risky—psychologically as well as physically—to become too emotionally open with his peers: he might be labeled a "sissy," a "fag," or even be beaten up or ostracized from the group. He also finds that he had better not become too close to girls; he must, of course, establish his masculine status by making (and laughing at) heterosexist jokes, but he "must never let girls replace boys as the focus of [his] attention."

* * *

Indeed, my research suggests that a young man's imperative to prove himself, to perform, achieve, and win, dovetails with the hierarchic world of athletic careers in such a way that he tends to develop a certain kind of relationship to his own body. It's not simply that an athlete's body becomes "the focus of the self," but that the athlete is often encouraged to see his body as an instrument. An "instrumental male" is an alienated creature: he is usually very goal-oriented (in his work and in his personal relations), and he frequently views other people as objects to be manipulated and defeated in his quest to achieve his goals. The ultimate extension of instrumental rationality is the alienation from one's own body—the tendency to treat one's body as a tool, a machine to be utilized (and "used up") in the pursuit of particular ends. Tender feelings (toward oneself and toward others) come to be seen as an impediment, something that needs to be repressed or "worked on." Physical or emotional pain are experienced as a nuisance to be ignored or done away with (often through the use of alcohol or other drugs). A common result of this focus on the body as an instrument is violence expressed toward others, and ultimately toward oneself.

* * *

Mary Duquin and Brenda Bredemeier [sociologists], in two separate studies aimed at testing Gilligan's theory of gender difference [excerpted and discussed in Chapter 3, above], found that male and female athletes indeed engaged in different kinds of moral reasoning around issues such as rule-breaking and aggression. Female athletes tended to fear that aggression—even "within the rules"—threatened their connection with others, and thus the basis of their identities. By contrast, male athletes tended to feel affirmed by, and comfortable with, rule-bound athletic aggression.

These social-psychological analyses of athletic aggression reveal the affinity between developing masculine identities and the structure of values of the institution of sport. Within the athletic context, young males can develop a certain kind of closeness with each other while not having to deal with the kinds of (intimate) attachments that they tend to fear. Here individuals' roles and separate positions within hierarchies are determined by competition within a clearly defined system of rules that governs the interaction of participants. Although many athletes will "stretch" the rules as much as they can to gain an advantage over their opponents, most have a respect, even a reverence, for the importance of rules as a code of conduct that places safe boundaries around their aggression and their relationships with others. Without the rules, there would be chaos—both physical and psychological; there would be a frightening need to negotiate and renegotiate relationships constantly. This is what feels truly dangerous to men. * * *

For most of the men whom I interviewed, this sort of aggression "within the rules" was considered legitimate—even desirable. In fact, sociologist Peter Lyman has observed that aggression is usually not defined by men as "violent" so long as it is rule-governed, rather than anger-induced.

* * *

An interesting consensus has emerged among those who have studied gender and friendship in the United States: Women have deep, intimate, meaningful, and lasting friendships, while men have a number of shallow, superficial, and unsatisfying "acquaintances." Several commentators have concluded that men's relationships are shallow because men have been taught to be highly homophobic, emotionally inexpressive, and competitive "success objects."

* * *

Organized sport, as we know it, emerged largely as a masculinist response to a crisis in the gender order of the late nineteenth and early twentieth centuries. The world of sport gave men a retreat from what they feared was a "feminized" modern culture, and it gave white upper-class men (initially), and working-class and minority men (eventually), a means of "naturalizing" dominant forms of masculinity. Throughout most of the twentieth century, this masculine institution of sport existed alongside a vibrant but much less visible tradition of women's sport. In the early 1970s, there emerged what Stephanie Twin has called a "second wave of athletic feminism." The explosion of girls' and women's athletics in the next two decades served notice that female athletes could no longer be ignored to the extent that they once were.

How have men responded to women's recent movement into sport? There is some evidence that increasing female athleticism has caused many boys and men to adjust—and sometimes radically alter—their preconceptions of what women are capable of. Personally confronting the reality of female athleticism has caused some boys and men to question what sociologist Nancy Theberge has called "the myth of female frailty." On the other hand, there is also considerable evidence that women's sport has been institutionally contained, and thus its potential challenge to sport's construction of hegemonic masculinity has been largely defused.

* * *

Increased athletic participation for girls and for women does partially undermine sexist attitudes and assumptions among some men. Yet as long as we are simply attempting to incorporate women within an institution that is, in its dominant structure and values, a masculine construction, "equal opportunity" for females will ultimately serve to affirm and naturalize masculine superiority. The reason is this: Today's sports media—and, indeed, liberal feminists who are intent on gaining equal opportunities for female athletes—often ignore the fact that male and female bodies do tend to differ in potential physical strength, endurance, agility, and grace. Despite considerable overlap, the average adult male is about five inches taller than the average female. Can women really hope to compete with men at the highest levels of basketball or volleyball? Males average 40 percent muscle and 15 percent body fat, while females average 23 percent muscle and 25 percent body fat. Can women possibly compete at the highest levels with men in football, track and field, hockey, or baseball? On the other hand, women have some physical differences from men that can be translated into athletic superiority. For instance, * * * women's different skeletal structures and greater flexibility make for superior performances on a balance beam. In addition, women's higher body fat ratio gives them greater buoyancy in water and greater insulation against heat loss, which has translated into women's times in distance swimming, especially in cold water, being considerably faster than men's.

In other words, as long as we are intent on measuring the highest levels of physical performance, males are likely to excel in some activities, females in others. Yet given our present values and institutional arrangements, these average physiological differences between the sexes nearly always end up being translated into female physical "inferiority." The reason for this is simple: The most highly valued sports in the U.S. (especially the "money sports" like football) are at present organized according to the most extreme possibilities of the male body. "Equal opportunity" for women within these masculine-defined sports puts women at a decided disadvantage.

Significantly, though coverage of women's sport lags far behind coverage of men's sport, the sport media increasingly appear to be employing liberal conceptions of equal opportunity in their presentations of the athletic performances of women. With women competing in male-defined sports, the media can employ statistics as "objective measures of performance." Spectators can see for themselves that, for instance, though the women competitors in the Olympics are impressive athletes, the medal winners' performances would rarely be good enough to qualify them for the finals in the men's events. Equal opportunity within this system thus provides support for the ideology of meritocracy, while subtly supplying incontrovertible evidence of the "natural superiority" of males over females. Clearly, if equal opportunity for women is not to serve simply as the basis for a reconstituted ideology of male superiority, the institution of sport itself must be transformed from a masculine construction to a human construction.

* * *

What does televised sport mean to male viewers? The mythology and symbolism of today's most popular spectator sports are probably meaningful to viewers on a number of levels: patriotism, militarism, violence, and meritocracy are all dominant themes. But it is reasonable to speculate that gender is a salient organizing theme in the construction of meanings, especially with respect to the more aggressive and violent aspects of sport. For example, when I was interviewing a thirty-two-year-old white professional-class male, and I asked him how he felt about the fact that recently a woman had been promoted to a position of authority in his workplace, he replied, "A woman can do the same job as I can do—maybe even be my boss. But I'll be *damned* if she can go out on the 'football' field and take a hit from Ronnie Lott [legendary retired San Francisco 49'er safety football player who was known for being a 'hard hitter' and who had part of his little finger amputated in order to play in a scheduled game]."

At the most obvious level, we can read this man's statement as an indication that he is identifying with Ronnie Lott as a man, and the basis of the identification is the violent male body. Football, based as it is on the fullest potential of the male body (muscular bulk, explosive power) is clearly a world apart from women, who are relegated to the roles of sex objects on the sidelines, rooting their men on. In contrast to the bare and vulnerable bodies of the cheerleaders, the armored male bodies of the football players are elevated to mythical status and thus give testimony to the undeniable "fact" that here is at least one place where men are clearly superior to women. Yet it is also significant that this man was quite aware that he (and perhaps 99 percent of the rest of the male population of the United States) was probably equally incapable of taking a "hit" from the likes of Ronnie Lott and living to tell of it. I would speculate that by recognizing the simultaneous construction of identification and difference among men, we may begin to understand the major role that televised sport plays in the current gender order.

* * *

Since the institution of sport is both constructed by, and in turn helps to construct, the overall gender order, it makes no sense to speak of transforming sport in the abstract. Any fundamental changes in the values and structure of organized sport necessarily must take place within a larger movement to transform other social institutions (economy, politics, family, education, etc.). But this does not mean that attempts to change sport have no worth. I have argued here that sport is a key component of our current gender order. Further, though sport's major impact appears to support the status quo of hegemonic masculinity, there are also internal contradictions in men's experiences with athletic careers. These problems have been given potential new meaning by women's recent challenge to sport as a masculine institution.

* * *

It is possible for sport to be reorganized in such a way that its positive potentialities—which all of the men I interviewed experienced to a degree, but which, for many of them, were eclipsed by anxiety and pain—can rise to the surface. But if, as I have suggested, the current affinity between boys' and men's developing masculine identities and the institution of sport continues, then simply attempting to reorganize sport will be an exercise in futility. There are two fundamental requisites for the humanization of sport: First, boys and girls should be brought up and nurtured in an equal manner, and this work must be shared equally by men and women. Second, all of our social institutions—schools, workplaces, families, the state—must be reorganized in ways that maximize equality for all people. Girls and boys, women and men who are raised in such an egalitarian world might finally be able to enjoy sport for all that it really has to offer.

Notes on Sports, Gender, and Masculinities

1. Do you agree with Messner that the institution of sport is premised upon hierarchy and homophobia? Can you provide examples? Is the same true for "girls'" sports? Can you think of other ways in which sports perpetuate male domination? After reading the Messner excerpt, do you perceive a relationship between sports and violence against women? A 1998 study found that college football and basketball players were more abusive to

women than other college students: "[f]rom 1991–93, male student athletes comprised 3.3 percent of the male population at 10 major universities but accounted for 19 percent of the men reported to campus officials for sexual assault ... Of those, 76 percent were football or basketball players." Paul Ruffins, The Fumble of a Lifetime, 17 Black Issues in Higher Education 34 (2000). Another study documented findings "that male college students who engaged in formal athletics were more likely than other men to feel hostile towards women and engage in sexual aggression." Id.

2. Do you agree with Messner that organized sport was a "masculinist response to a crisis in the gender order of the late nineteenth and early twentieth centuries?" Does it continue to assert male superiority and dominance? In what ways? What role do the media play in perpetuating views about proper gender roles through the use of sports? Figure skating is one of the most often televised women's sports; why?

3. When she was a student at Harvard Law School, Lyn Lemaire, former member of the U.S. Women's Cycling Team, noted that the prevailing model of athletics today is "combative." According to her analysis, the fundamental reason for engaging in sports under this combative model was best expressed by Vince Lombardi, long time coach of the National Football League champion Green Bay Packers: "Winning isn't everything; it's the only thing." Lemaire points out that "this narrow view posits victory and dominance as the goals of athletic competition and thereby creates a dichotomy between the winners and the losers in sports competition." Lemaire, Women and Athletics: Toward a Physicality Perspective, 5 Harv.Women's L.J. 121, 123 (1982). She urged a new model for sports:

> In contrast to the "traditional model" of sports, which emphasizes competition for the sake of winning, the "physicality model" focuses on the value of athletic participation per se, regardless of winning or losing. The author [Lemaire] thus advocates a shift from a goal-oriented to a process-oriented view of the benefits of athletic activity. The argument does not suggest that women are incapable of competing successfully with men, that competition in itself is undesirable, or that physicality is mere recreation devoid of rigorous training. Rather, the point is advanced that competition and exertion engaged in for the joy of athletic participation could increase the number and elevate the status of women athletes.

Id. at 122. Is this a substantive equality argument? Is Lemaire's proposal similar to what is occurring in other areas of education, i.e., not just obtaining access for women to play by men's rules but serious evaluation of the game itself? How is her proposal similar or dissimilar to Messner's sports analysis?

F. SEXUAL HARASSMENT

GEBSER v. LAGO VISTA INDEPENDENT SCHOOL DISTRICT

Supreme Court of the United States, 1998.

524 U.S. 274, 118 S.Ct. 1989, 141 L.Ed.2d 277.

JUSTICE O'CONNOR delivered the opinion of the Court.

The question in this case is when a school district may be held liable in damages in an implied right of action under Title IX of the Education

Amendments of 1972 for the sexual harassment of a student by one of the district's teachers. We conclude that damages may not be recovered in those circumstances unless an official of the school district who at a minimum has authority to institute corrective measures on the district's behalf has actual notice of, and is deliberately indifferent to, the teacher's misconduct.

* * *

[The facts alleged in this case were that petitioner, eighth-grade student Alida Star Gebser, in 1991 joined a high school book discussion group led by a teacher at Lago Vista's high school, Frank Waldrop. At meetings of the book club Waldrop often made sexually suggestive comments. Later that fall, when Gebser entered high school, she was assigned to classes taught by Waldrop. His sexual comments continued; he began to direct them specifically to Gebser, including at times when they were alone in the classroom. The next spring he initiated sexual conduct with her, and the two of them had sexual intercourse several times over the next year, although never on school property. Gebser did not report the relationship to school officials because she was uncertain how to react and wanted to keep Waldrop as a teacher. When other parents complained of Waldrop's comments in class, the principal met with the teacher and advised him to be careful about his class comments. The principal did not report the complaint to the superintendent, who was the Title IX coordinator. A few months later police discovered Waldrop having sex with Gebser and arrested him. He was fired and his teaching license was revoked. During this time Lago Vista School District did not have an official sexual harassment policy or grievance procedure.]

Gebser and her mother filed suit against Lago Vista and Waldrop in state court in November 1993, raising claims against the school district under Title IX and state negligence law, and claims against Waldrop primarily under state law. They sought compensatory and punitive damages from both defendants. After the case was removed, the United States District Court for the Western District of Texas granted summary judgment in favor of Lago Vista on all claims, and remanded the allegations against Waldrop to state court. [The Fifth Circuit affirmed.] * * *

[The Court began its analysis by noting that although Title IX's express statutory means of enforcement is administrative, it recognized an implied private cause of action in 1979 and specifically established in Franklin v. Gwinnett County Public Schools, 503 U.S. 60, 112 S. Ct. 1028, 117 L.Ed.2d 208 (1992), that monetary damages are available in sexual harassment claims under Title IX. However,

Franklin did not articulate the standard for liability, which is the issue in this case. Petitioners, joined by the United States as amicus curiae, argued that Title VII employment discrimination standards used in cases involving a supervisor's sexual harassment of an employee in the workplace should be adopted; they relied on language in *Franklin* which analogized teachers sexually abusing students to supervisors sexually harassing a subordinate in the workplace. Because Meritor Sav. Bank v. Vinson [excerpted in Chapter 10] directed courts to apply common law agency principles in determining employer liability under Title VII, they argued agency principles should also apply under Title IX. Specifically, they advanced two possible standards under which Lago Vista would be liable for Waldrop's conduct: (1) vicarious or imputed liability and (2) constructive notice, i.e., where the district knew or "should have known" about the harassment but failed to uncover and eliminate it. Both of these theories are broader than that adopted by the Fifth Circuit's rule requiring actual notice.]

Congress enacted Title IX in 1972 with two principal objectives in mind: "to avoid the use of federal resources to support discriminatory practices" and "to provide individual citizens effective protection against those practices." The statute was modeled after Title VI of the Civil Rights Act of 1964, which is parallel to Title IX except that it prohibits race discrimination, not sex discrimination, and applies in all programs receiving federal funds, not only in education programs. The two statutes operate in the same manner, conditioning an offer of federal funding on a promise by the recipient not to discriminate, in what amounts essentially to a contract between the Government and the recipient of funds.

That contractual framework distinguishes Title IX from Title VII, which is framed in terms not of a condition but of an outright prohibition. Title VII applies to all employers without regard to federal funding and aims broadly to "eradicat[e] discrimination throughout the economy." Title VII, moreover, seeks to "make persons whole for injuries suffered through past discrimination." Thus, whereas Title VII aims centrally to compensate victims of discrimination, Title IX focuses more on "protecting" individuals from discriminatory practices carried out by recipients of federal funds. * * *

Title IX's contractual nature has implications for our construction of the scope of available remedies. When Congress attaches conditions to the award of federal funds under its spending power, as it has in Title IX and Title VI, we examine closely the propriety of private actions holding the recipient liable in monetary damages for noncompliance with the condition. Our central concern in that regard is with ensuring "that the receiving entity of federal funds [has] notice that it will be liable for a monetary award." * * * If a school district's liability for a teacher's sexual harassment rests on principles of constructive notice or respondeat superior, it will likewise be the case that the recipient of funds was unaware of the discrimination. It is sensible to assume that Congress did not envision a recipient's liability in damages in that situation.

Most significantly, Title IX contains important clues that Congress did not intend to allow recovery in damages where liability rests solely on principles of vicarious liability or constructive notice. Title IX's express means of enforcement—by administrative agencies—operates on an assumption of actual notice to officials of the funding recipient. * * *

Presumably, a central purpose of requiring notice of the violation "to the appropriate person" and an opportunity for voluntary compliance before administrative enforcement proceedings can commence is to avoid diverting education funding from beneficial uses where a recipient was unaware of discrimination in its programs and is willing to institute prompt corrective measures. The scope of private damages relief proposed by petitioners is at odds with that basic objective. When a teacher's sexual harassment is imputed to a school district or when a school district is deemed to have "constructively" known of the teacher's harassment, by assumption the district had no actual knowledge of the teacher's conduct. Nor, of course, did the district have an opportunity to take action to end the harassment or to limit further harassment.

It would be unsound, we think, for a statute's express system of enforcement to require notice to the recipient and an opportunity to come into voluntary compliance while a judicially implied system of enforcement permits substantial liability without regard to the recipient's knowledge or its corrective actions upon receiving notice. Moreover, an award of damages in a particular case might well exceed a recipient's level of federal funding. (Lago Vista's federal funding for 1992–1993 was roughly $120,000). Where a statute's express enforcement scheme hinges its most severe sanction on notice and unsuccessful efforts to obtain compliance, we cannot attribute to Congress the intention to have implied an enforcement scheme that allows imposition of greater liability without comparable conditions.

Because the express remedial scheme under Title IX is predicated upon notice to an "appropriate person" and an opportunity to rectify any violation, we conclude, in the absence of further direction from Congress, that the implied damages remedy should be fashioned along the same lines. An "appropriate person" under § 1682 is, at a minimum, an official of the recipient entity with authority to take corrective action to end the discrimination. Consequently, in cases like this one that do not involve official policy of the recipient entity, we hold that a damages remedy will not lie under Title IX unless an official who at a minimum has authority to address the alleged discrimination and to institute corrective measures on the recipient's behalf has actual knowledge of discrimination in the recipient's programs and fails adequately to respond.

We think, moreover, that the response must amount to deliberate indifference to discrimination. The administrative enforcement scheme presupposes that an official who is advised of a Title IX violation refuses to take action to bring the recipient into compliance. The premise, in other words, is an official decision by the recipient not to remedy the violation. That framework finds a rough parallel in the standard of deliberate indifference. Under a lower standard, there would be a risk that the recipient would be liable in damages not for its own official decision but instead for its employees' independent actions. * * *

Applying the framework to this case is fairly straightforward, as petitioners do not contend they can prevail under an actual notice standard. * * *

Petitioners focus primarily on Lago Vista's asserted failure to promulgate and publicize an effective policy and grievance procedure for sexual harassment claims. They point to Department of Education regulations requiring each funding recipient to "adopt and publish grievance procedures providing for prompt and equitable resolution" of discrimination complaints, and to notify students and others "that it does not discriminate on the basis of sex in the educational programs or activities which it operates." Lago Vista's alleged failure to comply with the regulations, however, does not establish the requisite actual notice and deliberate indifference. And in any event, the failure to promulgate a grievance procedure does not itself constitute "discrimination" under Title IX. Of course, the Department of Education could enforce the requirement administratively: Agencies generally have authority to promulgate and enforce requirements that effectuate the statute's non-discrimination mandate, even if those requirements do not purport to represent a definition of discrimination under the statute. We have never held, however, that the implied private right of action under Title IX allows recovery in damages for violation of those sorts of administrative requirements.

The number of reported cases involving sexual harassment of students in schools confirms that harassment unfortunately is an all too common aspect of the educational experience. No one questions that a student suffers extraordinary harm when subjected to sexual harassment and abuse by a teacher, and that the teacher's conduct is reprehensible and undermines the basic purposes of the educational system. The issue in this case, however, is whether the independent misconduct of a teacher is attributable to the school district that employs him under a specific federal statute designed primarily to prevent recipients of federal financial assistance from using the funds in a discriminatory manner. Our decision does not affect any right of recovery that an individual may have against a school district as a matter of state law or against the teacher in his individual capacity under state law or under 42 U.S.C. § 1983. Until Congress speaks directly on the subject, however, we will not hold a school district liable in damages under Title IX for a teacher's sexual harassment of a student absent actual notice and deliberate indifference. We therefore affirm the judgment of the Court of Appeals.

DAVIS v. MONROE COUNTY BOARD OF EDUCATION

Supreme Court of the United States, 1999.

526 U.S. 629, 119 S.Ct. 1661, 143 L.Ed.2d 839.

JUSTICE O'CONNOR delivered the opinion of the Court.

Petitioner brought suit against the Monroe County Board of Education and other defendants, alleging that her fifth-grade daughter had been the victim of sexual harassment by another student in her class. Among petitioner's claims was a claim for monetary and injunctive relief under Title IX of the Education Amendments of 1972. The District Court dismissed petitioner's Title IX claim on the ground that "student-on-student," or peer, harassment provides no ground for a private cause of action under the statute. The Court of Appeals for the Eleventh Circuit, sitting en banc, affirmed. We consider here whether a private damages action may lie against the school board in cases of student-on-student harassment. We conclude that it may, but only where the funding recipient acts with deliberate indifference to known acts of harassment in its programs or activities. Moreover, we conclude that such an action will lie only for harassment that is so severe, pervasive, and objectively offensive that it effectively bars the victim's access to an educational opportunity or benefit.

* * *

Petitioner's minor daughter, LaShonda, was allegedly the victim of a prolonged pattern of sexual harassment by one of her fifth-grade classmates at Hubbard Elementary School, a public school in Monroe County, Georgia. According to petitioner's complaint, the harassment began in December 1992, when the classmate, G.F., attempted to touch LaShonda's breasts and genital area and made vulgar statements such as " 'I want to get in bed with you' " and " 'I want to feel your boobs.' " Similar conduct allegedly occurred on or about January 4 and January 20, 1993. LaShonda reported each of these incidents to her mother and to her classroom teacher, Diane Fort. Petitioner, in turn, also contacted Fort, who allegedly assured petitioner that the school principal, Bill Querry, had been informed of the incidents. Petitioner contends that, notwithstanding these reports, no disciplinary action was taken against G.F.

G.F.'s conduct allegedly continued for many months. In early February, G.F. purportedly placed a door stop in his pants and proceeded to act in a sexually suggestive manner toward LaShonda during physical education class. LaShonda reported G.F.'s behavior to her physical education teacher, Whit Maples. Approximately one week later, G.F. again allegedly engaged in harassing behavior, this time while under the supervision of another classroom teacher, Joyce Pippin. Again, LaShonda allegedly reported the incident to the teacher, and again petitioner contacted the teacher to follow up.

Petitioner alleges that G.F. once more directed sexually harassing conduct toward LaShonda in physical education class in early March, and that LaShonda reported the incident to both Maples and Pippen. In mid-April 1993, G.F. allegedly rubbed his body against LaShonda in the school hallway in what LaShonda considered a sexually suggestive manner, and LaShonda again reported the matter to Fort.

The string of incidents finally ended in mid-May, when G.F. was charged with, and pleaded guilty to, sexual battery for his misconduct. The complaint alleges that LaShonda had suffered during the months of harassment, however; specifically, her previously high grades allegedly dropped as she became unable to concentrate on her studies, and, in April 1993, her father discovered that she had written a suicide note. The complaint further alleges that, at one point, LaShonda told petitioner that she " 'didn't know how much longer she could keep [G.F.] off her.' "

Nor was LaShonda G.F.'s only victim; it is alleged that other girls in the class fell prey to G.F.'s conduct. At one point, in fact, a group composed of LaShonda and other female students tried to speak with Principal Querry about G.F.'s behavior. According to the complaint, however, a teacher denied the students' request with the statement, " 'If [Querry] wants you, he'll call you.' "

Petitioner alleges that no disciplinary action was taken in response to G.F.'s behavior toward LaShonda. In addition to her conversations with Fort and Pippen, petitioner alleges that she spoke with Principal Querry in mid-May 1993. When petitioner inquired as to what action the school intended to take against G.F., Querry simply stated, " 'I guess I'll have to threaten him a little bit harder.' " Yet, petitioner alleges, at no point during the many months of his reported misconduct was G.F. disciplined for harassment. Indeed, Querry allegedly asked petitioner why LaShonda " 'was the only one complaining.' "

Nor, according to the complaint, was any effort made to separate G.F. and LaShonda. On the contrary, notwithstanding LaShonda's frequent complaints, only after more than three months of reported harassment was she even permitted to change her classroom seat so that she was no longer seated next to G.F. Moreover, petitioner alleges that, at the time of the events in question, the Monroe County Board of Education had not instructed its personnel on how to respond to peer sexual harassment and had not established a policy on the issue.

* * *

There is no dispute here that the Board is a recipient of federal education funding for Title IX purposes. Nor do respondents support an argument that student-on-student harassment cannot rise to the level of "discrimination" for purposes of Title IX. Rather, at issue here is the question whether a recipient of federal education funding may be liable for damages under Title IX under any circumstances for discrimination in the form of student-on-student sexual harassment.

* * *

[The Court noted that in *Gebser* it articulated a Title IX standard in which money damages will be available only where federally-funded recipients had notice of liability. The School Board argued that Title IX provides no such notice that a recipient could be liable not for its misconduct but that of a third party over whom it exercises little control. Although the Court agreed that a recipient may be liable only for its own misconduct, it disagreed that the plaintiff in this case was holding the School Board responsible for G.F.'s actions. Rather, the petitioner was seeking "to hold the Board liable for its own decision to remain idle in the face of known student-on-student harassment in its schools."]

We consider here whether the misconduct identified in *Gebser*—deliberate indifference to known acts of harassment—amounts to an intentional violation of Title IX, capable of supporting a private damages action, when the harasser is a student rather than a teacher. We conclude that, in certain limited circumstances, it does. * * * [T]he regulatory scheme surrounding Title IX has long provided funding recipients with notice that they may be liable for their failure to respond to the discriminatory acts of certain non-agents. The Department of Education requires recipients to monitor third parties for discrimination in specified circumstances and to refrain from particular forms of interaction with outside entities that are known to discriminate.

The common law, too, has put schools on notice that they may be held responsible under state law for their failure to protect students from the tortious acts of third parties. In fact, state courts routinely uphold claims alleging that schools have been negligent in failing to protect their students from the torts of their peers.

* * * If a funding recipient does not engage in harassment directly, it may not be liable for damages unless its deliberate indifference "subject[s]" its students to harassment. That is, the deliberate indifference must, at a minimum, "cause [students] to undergo" harassment or "make them liable or vulnerable" to it. Moreover, because the harassment must occur "under" "the operations of" a funding recipient, the harassment must take place in a context subject to the school district's control.

These factors combine to limit a recipient's damages liability to circumstances wherein the recipient exercises substantial control over both the harasser and the context in which the known harassment occurs. Only then can the recipient be said to "expose" its students to harassment or "cause" them to undergo it "under" the recipient's programs. * * *

Where, as here, the misconduct occurs during school hours and on school grounds—the bulk of G.F.'s misconduct, in fact, took place in the classroom—the misconduct is taking place "under" an "operation" of the funding recipient. In these circumstances, the recipient retains substantial control over the context in which the harassment occurs. More importantly, however, in this setting the Board exercises significant control over the harasser. We have observed, for example, "that the nature of [the State's] power [over public schoolchildren] is custodial and tutelary, permitting a degree of supervision and control that could not be exercised over free adults." * * *

We stress that our conclusion here—that recipients may be liable for their deliberate indifference to known acts of peer sexual harassment—does not mean that recipients can avoid liability only by purging their schools of actionable peer harassment or that administrators must engage in particular disciplinary action. We thus disagree with respondents' contention that, if Title IX provides a cause of action for student-on-student harassment, "nothing short of expulsion of every student accused of misconduct involving sexual overtones would protect school systems from liability or damages." * * *

We believe, however, that the standard set out here is sufficiently flexible to account both for the level of disciplinary authority available to the school and for the potential liability arising from certain forms of disciplinary action. A university might not, for example, be expected to exercise the same degree of control over its students that a grade school would enjoy, and it would be entirely reasonable for a school to refrain from a form of disciplinary action that would expose it to constitutional or statutory claims.

* * *

We thus conclude that funding recipients are properly held liable in damages only where they are deliberately indifferent to sexual harassment, of which they have actual knowledge, that is so severe, pervasive, and objectively offensive that it can be said to deprive the victims of access to the educational opportunities or benefits provided by the school.

* * *

Whether gender-oriented conduct rises to the level of actionable "harassment" thus "depends on a constellation of surrounding circumstances, expectations, and relationships," including, but not limited to, the ages of the harasser and the victim and the number of individuals involved. Courts, moreover, must bear in mind that schools are unlike the adult workplace and that children may regularly interact in a manner that would be unacceptable among adults. Indeed, at least early on, students are still learning how to interact appropriately with their peers. It is thus understandable that, in the school setting, students often engage in insults, banter, teasing, shoving, pushing, and gender-specific conduct that is upsetting to the students subjected to it. Damages are not available for simple acts of teasing and name-calling among school children, however, even where these comments target differences in gender. Rather, in the context of student-on-student harassment, damages are available only where the behavior is so severe, pervasive, and objectively offensive that it denies its victims the equal access to education that Title IX is designed to protect.

* * *

Moreover, the provision that the discrimination occur "under any education program or activity" suggests that the behavior be serious enough to have the systemic effect of denying the victim equal access to an educational program or activity. Although, in theory, a single instance of sufficiently severe one-on-one peer harassment could be said to have such an effect, we think it unlikely that Congress would have thought such behavior sufficient to rise to this level in light of the inevitability of student misconduct and the amount of litigation that would be invited by entertaining claims of official indifference to a single instance of one-on-one peer harassment. By limiting private damages actions to cases having a systemic effect on educational programs or activities, we reconcile the general principle that Title IX prohibits official indifference to known peer sexual harassment with the practical realities of responding to student behavior, realities that Congress could not have meant to be ignored. * * *

Applying this standard to the facts at issue here, we conclude that the Eleventh Circuit erred in dismissing petitioner's complaint. Petitioner alleges that her daughter was the victim of repeated acts of sexual harassment by G.F. over a 5–month period, and there are allegations in support of the conclusion that G.F.'s misconduct was severe, pervasive, and objectively offensive. The harassment was not only verbal; it included numerous acts of objectively offensive touching, and, indeed, G.F. ultimately pleaded guilty to criminal sexual misconduct. Moreover, the complaint alleges that there were multiple victims who were sufficiently disturbed by G.F.'s misconduct to seek an audience with the school principal. Further, petitioner contends that the harassment had a concrete, negative effect on her daughter's ability to receive an education. The complaint also suggests that petitioner may be able to show both actual knowledge and deliberate indifference on the part of the Board, which made no effort whatsoever either to investigate or to put an end to the harassment.

* * * Accordingly, the judgment of the United States Court of Appeals for the Eleventh Circuit is reversed, and the case is remanded for further proceedings consistent with this opinion.

Notes on Sexual Harassment in Schools

1. The cases discussed above show the Supreme Court developing the jurisprudence of private litigation under Title IX, a progression from establishing sexual harassment as discrimination under Title IX (*Franklin*, 1992), to adding the requirement of actual notice to an official with authority to institute corrective measures and who responds with deliberate indifference

in order to impose liability (*Gebser*, 1998), to establishing liability for peer harassment if there is actual notice to an official with authority who is deliberately indifferent and the harassment alleged is "so severe, pervasive, and objectively offensive that it can be said to deprive the victims of access to the educational opportunities or benefits provided by the school" (*Davis*, 1999). Do you think that the Court was correct to imply a private cause of action under Title IX in the first place? See Cannon v. University of Chicago, 441 U.S. 677, 99 S.Ct. 1946, 60 L.Ed.2d 560 (1979). When a court implies a cause of action not explicitly provided for by statute, what kinds of problems occur? What does a plaintiff have to allege now to survive a motion to dismiss in cases involving (a) teacher and (b) peer sexual harassment in schools?

2. In *Davis*, even though the Court affirmed a cause of action for peer sexual harassment, it appeared to impose three highly restrictive elements: (a) the defendant must have actual notice and act with deliberate indifference; (b) liability will be limited to circumstances in which the school exercises substantial control over both the harasser and the context in which the known harassment occurs; and (c) the harassment has to be so severe, pervasive, and objectively offensive that it deprives the victim of access to the educational opportunities or benefits provided by the school. What kinds of problems do you anticipate with these restrictions?

Interestingly, the Court seemed to recognize potential problems with the third aspect, noting that "schools are unlike the adult workplace and that children may regularly interact in a manner that would be unacceptable among adults," and that "[d]amages are not available for simple acts of teasing and name-calling among school children * * * even where these comments target differences in gender." Is this standard too high to protect targets, usually girls? At a time when personalities and social interaction are being developed, shouldn't there be greater rather than lesser sensitivity to harassment?

When a North Carolina school disciplined a six-year-old boy for kissing a female classmate on the cheek, there was public criticism that the innocence of childhood was being punished. See, e.g., Dan Rollins, A Kiss Is Just a Kiss . . . Or Is It?, Charleston Gazette, Dec. 4, 1996, Metro at 5. What action should the school take in such a situation? What more would you want to know before making a recommendation?

3. What does the *Davis* requirement of the educational institution's substantial control over both the harasser and context mean for colleges and universities? Is there a different standard for liability and damages? What about student interns who, as part of a college course, report for a learning experience at a placement outside of the university in order to obtain practical experience? Will a university be responsible for sexual harassment that occurs in that context? See Cynthia Grant Bowman and MaryBeth Lipp, Legal Limbo of the Student Intern: The Responsibility of Colleges and Universities to Protect Student Interns Against Sexual Harassment, 23 Harv. Women's L.J. 95 (2000).

4. In response to critics who claim that sexual harassment is not really a problem, surveys of college students in the United States have revealed that between 30 and 70% of women undergraduates think they have been

victims of some form of sexual harassment. See, e.g., Judith Berman Brandenburg, Confronting Sexual Harassment: What Schools and Colleges Can Do 15–16 (1997). For example, in relatively early studies, in 1980, 30% of the female seniors at Berkeley reported harassment by at least one male instructor, and over 43% of graduate and undergraduate female students at Iowa State University in 1983 believed they received undue attention from a professor. Elisabeth A. Keller, Consensual Amorous Relationships Between Faculty and Students: The Constitutional Right to Privacy, 15 J.C. & U.L. 21 (1988). Moreover, a survey in the Journal of College and Student Personnel in 1983 reported that 75% of students believed that most female students would be reluctant to report a professor's sexually harassing conduct; none of the students surveyed who considered themselves harassed reported such harassment to a university official. Id. Does a lack of reported complaints justify inaction in this area? Why or why not? What is the problem with a sexual harassment policy that is complaint-driven?

5. Other studies have addressed sexual harassment in primary and secondary schools as well. A 1993 survey in Seventeen Magazine, addressed to girls aged nine to 19 years old, found that 89% of the respondents suffered inappropriate sexual comments, gestures and looks; 83% responded that they had been touched, pinched or grabbed. Harassment Is Rife in Schools, Girls Say, Chi. Trib., Mar. 25, 1993, § 1, at 3. Another 1993 survey found that 85 percent of female respondents in grades eight through eleven had been sexually harassed. AAUW Ed. Fndn., Hostile Hallways: The AAUW Survey on Sexual Harassment in America's Schools 7 (1993). Do these studies suggest that sexual harassment policies are necessary for kindergarten through twelfth grade? If so, should those policies have a greater emphasis on education about what sexual harassment is? Would you make other adjustments for young children?

6. Will the holding in *Davis* apply to college date rape? A woman is more likely to be the victim of a sexual assault while at college than at any other time in her life. Nonetheless, college age women are less likely to report their rapes than victims in other age groups; only one in ten campus rape victims reports her attack to the college administration. See Terry Nicole Steinberg, Rape on College Campuses: Reform Through Title IX, 18 J.C. & U.L. 39 (1991). Can you make an argument under *Davis* that campus rape is sexual harassment violative of Title IX? What would you have to prove after *Davis*? Is campus rape sex discrimination? If a college investigates and punishes other campus crimes, but not rape, is it violating any provision of Title IX? Would it be necessary to amend Title IX to cover campus rape?

7. As early as the 1980 report by the National Advisory Council on Women's Educational Programs, researchers discovered that victims of sexual harassment in schools try to manage incidents on their own. Frank J. Till, National Advisory Council on Women's Educational Programs, Sexual Harassment: A Report on the Sexual Harassment of Students (1980). Many victims suffer in isolation; when they go "public," they express surprise to discover that they were not alone. Id. The report concluded:

> Why do victims keep silent or try to cope without invoking the authority of the school administration or the courts? Our responses and the work

> of almost all researchers indicate that there are several primary causes: fear that they—as victims—are somehow responsible for the incident, fear that they will not be believed, shame at being involved in any form of sexual incident, fear that by protesting they will call attention to their sex rather than to their work, a belief that no action will be taken, and fear of reprisals by the initiator and his colleagues.

Id. Do you think this "silencing" continues to this day? Why do you think victims of sexual harassment feel this way? Are they right in their assumptions? Are there similar responses by women to rape and sexual harassment in the workplace? See discussions in Chapters 5 and 10, respectively. Do you think the Court in *Gebser* and *Davis* was aware of this data when it imposed an actual notice standard before liability could be found?

BILLIE WRIGHT DZEICH AND LINDA WEINER, THE LECHEROUS PROFESSOR: SEXUAL HARASSMENT ON CAMPUS

118–19 (1984).

A crucial concern for both students and academicians is learning to recognize the characteristics that differentiate the lecherous professor from his colleagues. There are no infallible predictors for recognizing sexual harassment. The most pernicious behavior can occur exclusive of "giveaways," or isolated actions can be misinterpreted as sinister when they are simply examples of clumsy professional or social style. However, a tentative list of warning signs might include the following:

- *Staring, leering, ogling* These behaviors may be surreptitious or very obvious. In any case, college faculty should possess knowledge of social decorum, and must avoid such activities.
- *Frequently commenting on personal appearance of the student* In the academic setting, most professors refrain from discussing the apparel and physical traits of their students.
- *Touching out of context* Every physical gesture should be appropriate to the occasion, setting, and need and character of the individual student. Professional educators may legitimately be expected to possess the ability to make such determinations.
- *Excessive flattery and praise of the student* This behavior, exhibited with others present, is especially seductive to students with low self-esteem or high aspirations. By convincing a student that she is intellectually and/or physically exceptional, the lecherous professor gains psychological access to her.
- *Deliberately avoiding or seeking encounters with the student in front of colleagues* Depending on the type of harasser, he may either attempt to hide from or to perform for colleagues in interactions with the student. The key is that in either case his behavior with the student changes when he is being observed.
- *Injecting a "male versus female" tone into discussions with students or colleagues* A frequent behavior of verbal harassers, this

conduct signals a generally disparaging attitude toward women. Its initial effect is to make them feel outsiders in the academic environment, but it may also be an indicator of other potential forms of abuse.

• *Persistently emphasizing sexuality in all contexts* Pervasive, inordinate emphasis on sex can occur in class or outside. For the lecherous professor, sexuality becomes, in effect, the prism through which all topics are focused. Students, male and female, can usually detect this behavior readily, and such professors often acquire a reputation for "being fixated on sex" in papers, tests, and discussions.

SCHOOL SEXUAL HARASSMENT POLICIES

[The following are portions of various sexual harassment policies that have been enacted at different universities at different times.]

University of Chicago

Sexual advances, requests for sexual favors, or sexually-directed remarks constitute harassment when either:

1. submission to such conduct is used or threatened to be used as the basis for academic or employment decisions; or

2. such conduct directed against an individual persists despite its rejection.

Sexual harassment can take many forms. Without feeling constrained by specific definitions, any person who believes that his or her educational or work experience is compromised by sexual harassment should feel free to discuss the problem with a Complaint Advisor.

Northwestern University

It is the policy of Northwestern University that no male or female member of the Northwestern community—students, faculty, administrators, or staff—may sexually harass any other member of the community. Sexual advances, requests for sexual favors, and other verbal or physical conduct of a sexual nature constitute harassment when

1. Submission to such conduct is made or threatened to be made either explicitly or implicitly a term or condition of an individual's employment or education;

2. Submission to or rejection of such conduct by an individual is used or threatened to be used as the basis for academic or employment decisions affecting that individual; or

3. Such conduct has the purpose or effect of substantially interfering with an individual's academic or professional performance or creating what a reasonable person would sense as an intimidating, hostile, or offensive employment, educational, or living environment.

Antioch College Faculty-Student Consensual Sexual Relations Policy

The faculty-student relationship, however warm or caring, inherently involves disproportionate power and influence on one side and is thus liable to abuse. A sexual relationship between a faculty member and a student can not only exploit this imbalance but also distort and inhibit the learning environment. For these reasons, it is the agreement of the Antioch College faculty that sexual relationships between Antioch College faculty members and Antioch College students are unacceptable and constitute professional misconduct.

DePaul University Examples of Sexual/Gender Harassment

A. Examples of behavior that may constitute sexual harassment include, but are not limited to:

* unwelcome verbal or physical advances of a sexual nature;

* requests or subtle pressure for sexual favors, overt or implied;

* abusive or threatening behavior directed at a person;

* remarks, jokes, comments or observations of a sexual nature that demean or offend individuals on the basis of their sex, provided, however, that such expressions will not be considered sexual harassment if uttered for a valid academic purpose;

* gestures or other nonverbal behavior of a sexual nature provided, however, that such expressions will not be considered sexual harassment if uttered for a valid academic purpose;

* gestures or other nonverbal behavior of a sexual nature provided, however, that such expressions will not be considered sexual harassment if based upon a valid academic purpose; and

* display or distribution of offensive materials of a sexual nature provided, however, that such expressions will not be considered sexual harassment if used for a valid academic purpose.

B. Examples of gender harassment may include, but are not limited to, the following:

* language or physical conduct that demeans another person because of his or her gender; and

* abusive or threatening behavior directed at a person on the basis of his or her gender.

C. Sexual and gender harassment may occur regardless of sexual orientation.

D. Sexual and gender harassment under this policy may be communicated in a variety of ways including, but not limited to, oral pronouncements, notes, letters, faxes, electronic messages and displays on public workstations.

Notes on Sexual Harassment Policies

1. Which of the sexual harassment policies excerpted above is best, and why? In particular, answer the following questions:

(a) *Conduct prohibited.* What behaviors do the policies cover? Do they all cover both quid pro quo (i.e., sex in exchange for favors) and hostile or offensive environment situations? Do you think most people know what conduct "has the purpose or effect of unreasonably interfering with an individual's academic or professional performance or creating an intimidating, hostile, or offensive employment, educational, or living environment?" This language in the Northwestern policy tracks that of the Equal Employment Opportunity Commission's Guidelines on Sexual Harassment in Employment. 29 C.F.R. § 1604.11 (1992). Is it preferable to be very specific about the conduct prohibited, such as the "examples" in the DePaul University policy? Why or why not? What are "sexually-directed remarks" as referred to by the Chicago policy? Is it necessary to give some examples to educate people governed by such policies? Must the remarks be repeated in order to violate the Chicago policy?

(b) *Harassment by peers.* Do all the policies cover harassment by peers? After *Davis*, shouldn't a policy address students harassing other students? The explicit, or implicit, reason for sexual harassment policies is to protect the victim from the abuse of the harasser's power or authority over her. Is it a necessary element that the harasser be in a position of power over the victim? Do male students have power over female students? What is the nature of such power?

(c) *Consensual relationships.* The Antioch College policy prohibits sexual relationships between faculty and students, even those presumably "consensual." Should consensual sexual relationships between teachers and students be prohibited? If so, under what circumstances? Should such relationships be barred only if the student is under the direct supervision of the faculty member? What about future reliance on the faculty member for references and the like? Is there always a disparity of power between teacher and student? If so, can there be true "consent"? What if the sexual relationship preceded the teacher-student relationship? Even if the teacher is not in an immediate position of authority over the student, is there a possibility that a student's judgment may be compromised by her feelings of trust and respect? What is the impact on other students if a peer has a sexual relationship with a teacher? Do faculty members have a right of privacy to have a sexual relationship with whomever they wish, including students? See Margaret H. Mack, Regulating Sexual Relationships Between Faculty and Students, 6 Mich. J. Gender & L. 79 (1999) (arguing that sexual relationships should be prohibited as long as faculty have supervisory or evaluative control over a student); Gary E. Elliott, Consensual Relationships and the Constitution: A Case of Liberty Denied, 6 Mich. J. Gender & L. 47 (1999) (arguing that professors should be as free from regulation in their sexual relations with students as they are in their speech rights); Martha Chamallas, Consent, Equality, and the Legal Control of Sexual Conduct, 61 S.Cal.L.Rev. 777 (1988); Elisabeth A. Keller, Consensual Amorous Relationships Between Faculty and Students: The Constitutional Right to Privacy, 15 J.C. & U.L. 21 (1988).

2. What is the most appropriate legal description of the teacher-student relationship? Is it one of fiduciary and beneficiary? What legal obligation does that characterization imply? Or is the relationship more like professional and client? Are sexual relationships appropriate under either characterization? Why or why not? See Ronna Greff Schneider, Sexual Harassment and Higher Education, 65 Tex.L.Rev. 525, 552–53 (1987).

3. Does your school have a sexual harassment policy? Is it adequate in your view? If your school fails to issue a policy or grievance mechanisms to address sexual harassment complaints, can you assert a viable claim under Title IX after *Gebser*? Pursuant to its authority under Title IX, the Department of Education has issued a regulation requiring schools receiving federal funds to "adopt and publish grievance procedures providing for prompt and equitable resolution of student and employee complaints alleging any action which would be prohibited by this part [proscribing sex discrimination]." 45 C.F.R. § 86.8(b) (1992). See Alexander v. Yale Univ., 631 F.2d 178 (2d Cir.1980) (plaintiff lacked standing to bring an action against Yale for failing to provide an institutional grievance procedure that would promptly and equitably have resolved her claim of sexual harassment).

4. Draft what you think would be an ideal sexual harassment policy for your institution. Be sure to consider the role of education and the need for an enforcement mechanism in constructing the policy, as well as the problem of retaliation. Under guidelines proposed by Women Organized Against Sexual Harassment, a student group at Berkeley, an adequate sexual harassment policy must: "(1) acknowledge sexual harassment as sex discrimination, not as isolated misconduct; (2) refer to a full range of harassment from subtle innuendos to assault; (3) refer to ways in which the context of open and mutual academic exchange is polluted by sexual harassment; and (4) refer to sexual harassment as the imposition of sexual advances by a person in a position of authority." Phyllis L. Crocker, An Analysis of University Definitions of Sexual Harassment, in Reconstructing the Academy: Women's Education and Women's Studies 24, 35 (Elizabeth Minnich, Jean O'Barr, and Rachel Rosenfeld, eds. 1988). Do you agree with these guidelines? Are they too limited?

5. Do sexual harassment policies infringe on academic freedom of speech by limiting the exploration of ideas in the classroom? How? If so, how should we determine which concern should be superior? Should the answer be determined by which group is hurt more if its right is denied? Who is to decide?

G. HATE SPEECH REGULATION

Text Note: Hate Speech Codes

Some universities responded to the extraordinary increase in hostility towards students of color and women students at the end of the last century by adopting "hate speech" codes. Following a series of racial incidents at the University of Wisconsin, that school prohibited students from making remarks that demeaned others and created a hostile or intimidating educational environment. Within two years the regulation had been invoked 35 times. In October of 1991, however, a federal judge declared the rule unconstitutionally overbroad and unduly vague.[85] Two years earlier another federal district court struck down a campus hate speech code in Doe v. University of Michigan on the same grounds.[86] In 1993, Central Michigan University's speech code was declared unconstitutional, and Stanford University's rule was thrown out in 1995.[87] Because First Amendment free speech concerns are only applicable when state action is present, these decisions are limited to public institutions; private colleges and universities are free to issue and enforce hate speech regulations without running afoul of the First Amendment.

After the court challenges, many public colleges and universities drafted new hate speech policies which address the constitutional issues. These revised speech codes are carefully tailored to satisfy the fighting words doctrine, enunciated by the Supreme Court in Chaplinsky v. New Hampshire, 315 U.S. 568, 62 S.Ct. 766, 86 L.Ed. 1031 (1942), as modified by Cohen v. California, which requires the fighting words to be "directed to the person of the hearer," 403 U.S. 15, 20, 91 S.Ct. 1780, 1785, 29 L.Ed.2d 284, 291 (1971).

These attempts to regulate racist speech on school campuses are not unique; the international community has long recognized the real harms caused by racist speech propaganda and has chosen to outlaw it. The members of the United Nations have adopted an International Convention on the Elimination of All Forms of Racial Discrimination, which requires states to criminalize racial hate messages. Additionally, the United Kingdom, Canada, Australia and New Zealand all have laws restricting racist speech, leaving the United States alone among major common law jurisdictions in its complete tolerance of such speech.[88]

This section first looks at the Supreme Court's decision concerning hate crimes, and then at two authors who address what they view as the real harms that result from hate speech on college campuses.

85. UWM Post, Inc. v. Board of Regents of Univ. of Wisconsin, 774 F.Supp. 1163, 1164, 1167, 1181 (E.D.Wis.1991).

86. 721 F.Supp. 852 (E.D.Mich.1989) (holding that code was unconstitutionally overbroad both on its face and as applied and unduly vague).

87. Dambrot v. Central Mich. Univ., 839 F.Supp. 477, 481 (E.D.Mich.1993) (overturning a campus rule that prohibited any "verbal * * * behavior that subjects an individual to an intimidating, hostile or offensive educational * * * environment by demeaning or slurring individuals * * * because of their racial or ethnic affiliation"); Corry v. Stanford Univ., No. 740309 (Cal. Super. filed Feb. 27, 1995) (holding that even though policy was restricted to "fighting words," it was an impermissible content-based regulation because it proscribed only fighting words "based on sex, race, color, and the like").

88. Mari J. Matsuda, Public Response to Racist Speech: Considering the Victim's Story, 87 Mich. L. Rev. 2320, 2341 (1989). The Convention was unanimously adopted by the General Assembly on December 21, 1965, and entered into force on January 4, 1969. The U.S. was an early signatory but, although President Carter submitted the convention to the Senate for ratification in 1978, the Senate has not yet done so. Id. at 2345, 2346–48. See also Richard Delgado, Campus Antiracism Rules: Constitutional Narratives in Collision, 85 Nw. U.L. Rev. 343, 364–71 (1991).

R.A.V. v. CITY OF ST. PAUL

Supreme Court Of The United States, 1992.

505 U.S. 377, 112 S.Ct. 2538, 120 L.Ed.2d 305.

JUSTICE SCALIA delivered the opinion of the Court.

In the predawn hours of June 21, 1990, petitioner and several other teenagers allegedly assembled a crudely-made cross by taping together broken chair legs. They then allegedly burned the cross inside the fenced yard of a black family that lived across the street from the house where petitioner was staying. * * * [St. Paul charged the juvenile petitioner under the St. Paul Bias–Motivated Crime Ordinance, which provides:]

> "Whoever places on public or private property a symbol, object, appellation, characterization or graffiti, including, but not limited to, a burning cross or Nazi swastika, which one knows or has reasonable grounds to know arouses anger, alarm or resentment in others on the basis of race, color, creed, religion or gender commits disorderly conduct and shall be guilty of a misdemeanor."

* * *

> [The Supreme Court of Minnesota interpreted this statute as proscribing only "fighting words," a category of words the Supreme Court had in the past held could be proscribed because "by their very utterance [they] inflict injury or tend to incite an immediate breach of the peace." Chaplinsky v. New Hampshire, 315 U.S. 568, 572, 62 S.Ct. 766, 86 L.Ed. 1031 (1942). The Supreme Court was, of course, bound by the narrowing interpretation of the Minnesota Supreme Court.]

The First Amendment generally prevents government from proscribing speech, or even expressive conduct, because of disapproval of the ideas expressed. Content-based regulations are presumptively invalid. From 1791 to the present, however, our society, like other free but civilized societies, has permitted restrictions upon the content of speech in a few limited areas, which are "of such slight social value as a step to truth that any benefit that may be derived from them is clearly outweighed by the social interest in order and morality." We have recognized that "the freedom of speech" referred to by the First Amendment does not include a freedom to disregard these traditional limitations. Our decisions since the 1960's have narrowed the scope of the traditional categorical exceptions for defamation, and for obscenity, but a limited categorical approach has remained an important part of our First Amendment jurisprudence.

* * *

Our cases surely do not establish the proposition that the First Amendment imposes no obstacle whatsoever to regulation of particular instances of * * * proscribable expression [such as "fighting words"], so that the government "may regulate [them] freely." That would mean that a city council could enact an ordinance prohibiting only those legally obscene works that contain criticism of the city government or, indeed, that do not include endorsement of the city government. Such a simplistic, all-or-nothing-at-all approach to First Amendment protection is at odds with common sense and with our jurisprudence as well. * * *

Even the prohibition against content discrimination that we assert the First Amendment requires is not absolute. It applies differently in the context of proscribable speech [such as "fighting words"] than in the area of fully protected speech. The rationale of the general prohibition, after all, is that content discrimination "rais[es] the specter that the Government may effectively drive certain ideas or viewpoints from the marketplace." But content discrimination among various instances of a class of proscribable speech often does not pose this threat.

When the basis for the content discrimination consists entirely of the very reason the entire class of speech at issue is proscribable, no significant danger of idea or viewpoint discrimination exists. Such a reason, having been adjudged neutral enough to support exclusion of the entire class of speech from First Amendment protection, is also neutral enough to form the basis of distinction within the class. To illustrate: A State might choose to prohibit only that obscenity which is the most patently offensive *in its prurience—i.e.,* that which involves the most lascivious displays of sexual activity. But it may not prohibit, for example, only that obscenity which includes offensive *political messages.* And the Federal Government can criminalize only those threats of violence that are directed against the President, * * *—since the reasons why threats of violence are outside the First Amendment (protecting individuals from the fear of violence, from the disruption that fear engenders, and from the possibility that the threatened violence will occur) have special force when applied to the person of the President. But the Federal Government may not criminalize only those threats against the President that mention his policy on aid to inner cities. * * *

Another valid basis for according differential treatment to even a content-defined subclass of proscribable speech is that the subclass happens to be associated with particular "secondary effects" of the speech, so that the regulation is "*justified* without reference to the content of the ... speech." A State could, for example, permit all obscene live performances except those involving minors. * * *

Applying these principles to the St. Paul ordinance, we conclude that, even as narrowly construed by the Minnesota Supreme Court, the ordinance is facially unconstitutional. Although the phrase in the ordinance, "arouses anger, alarm or resentment in others," has been limited by the Minnesota Supreme Court's construction to reach only those symbols or displays that amount to "fighting words," the remaining, unmodified terms make clear that the ordinance applies only to "fighting words" that insult, or provoke violence, "on the basis of race, color, creed, religion or gender." Displays containing abusive invective, no matter how vicious or severe, are permissible unless they are addressed to one of the specified disfavored topics. Those who wish to use "fighting words" in connection with other ideas—to express hostility, for example, on the basis of political affiliation, union membership, or homosexuality—are not covered. The First Amendment does not permit St. Paul to impose special prohibitions on those speakers who express views on disfavored subjects.

In its practical operation, moreover, the ordinance goes even beyond mere content discrimination, to actual viewpoint discrimination. Displays containing some words—odious racial epithets, for example—would be prohibited to proponents of all views. But "fighting words" that do not themselves invoke race, color, creed, religion, or gender—aspersions upon a person's mother, for example—would seemingly be usable *ad libitum* in the placards of those arguing *in favor* of racial, color, etc. tolerance and equality, but could not be used by that speaker's opponents. One could hold up a sign saying, for example, that all "anti-Catholic bigots" are misbegotten; but not that all "papists" are, for that would insult and provoke violence "on the basis of religion." St. Paul has no such authority to license one side of a debate to fight freestyle, while requiring the other to follow Marquis of Queensbury Rules.

* * *

Despite the fact that the Minnesota Supreme Court and St. Paul acknowledge that the ordinance is directed at expression of group hatred, Justice Stevens suggests that this "fundamentally misreads" the ordinance. It is directed, he claims, not to speech of a particular content, but to particular "injur[ies]" that are "qualitatively different" from other injuries. This is word-play. What makes the anger, fear, sense of dishonor, etc., produced by violation of this ordinance distinct from the anger, fear, sense of dishonor, etc., produced by other fighting words is nothing other than the fact that it is caused by a distinctive idea, conveyed by a distinctive message. The First Amendment cannot be evaded that easily. It is obvious that the symbols which will arouse "anger, alarm or resentment in others on the basis of race, color, creed, religion or gender" are those symbols that communicate a message of hostility based on one of these characteristics. * * *

Finally, St. Paul and its *amici* defend the conclusion of the Minnesota Supreme Court that, even if the ordinance regulates expression based on hostility towards its protected ideological content, this discrimination is nonetheless justified because it is narrowly tailored to serve compelling state interests. Specifically, they assert that the ordinance helps to ensure the basic human rights of members of groups that have historically been subjected to discrimination, including the right of such group members to live in peace where they wish. We do not doubt that these interests are compelling, and that the ordinance can be said to promote them. But the "danger of censorship" presented by a facially content-based statute, requires that that weapon be employed only where it is "*necessary* to serve the asserted [compelling] interest." The existence of adequate content-neutral alternatives thus "undercut[s] significantly" any defense of such a statute, casting considerable doubt on the government's protestations that "the asserted justification is in fact an accurate description of the purpose and effect of the law." The dispositive question in this case, therefore, is whether content discrimination is reasonably necessary to achieve St. Paul's compelling interests; it plainly is not. An ordinance not limited to the favored topics, for example, would have precisely the same beneficial effect. In fact the only interest distinctively served by the content limitation is that of displaying the city council's special hostility towards the particular biases thus singled out. That is precisely what the First Amendment forbids. The politicians of St. Paul are entitled to express that hostility—but not through the means of imposing unique limitations upon speakers who (however benightedly) disagree.

Notes on R.A.V.

1. Can you find support for upholding the Minnesota statute in the language in *Chaplinsky* that fighting words can be proscribed because "by their very utterance [they] inflict injury or tend to incite an immediate breach of the peace"? 315 U.S. at 572, 62 S.Ct. at 769. Why didn't the Court use this language to uphold the Minnesota law?

2. Justice Scalia seems confident that the state is unlikely to be discriminating on the basis of viewpoint when "the basis for the content discrimination consists entirely of the very reason the entire class of speech at issue is proscribable." He illustrates this point by noting that a state can "prohibit only that obscenity which is most patently offensive in its prurience." Do you think that such regulation is likely to be neutral with respect to viewpoint? Think, for example, of the effect of such an approach, when applied by jurors, on gay or lesbian erotica relative to straight erotica.

3. Can you describe the distinction Justice Scalia sees between threats of violence against the President, which can be singled out from other threats of violence and punished more severely, and threats of violence against a member of a specific racial group on the basis of race, which cannot? Would it matter that a threat of violence was targeted against women rather than against a racial group? What are the implications of this reasoning for (a) the MacKinnon–Dworkin ordinance, discussed above in Chapter 5, or (b) the hostile environment prong of a sexual harassment cause of action, discussed in Chapter 10? Does Scalia consider the Title VII limits on sex discrimination in employment to be different from the statute at issue in *R.A.V.?* How is the harassing-environment prong of sexual harassment different from the St. Paul ordinance?

4. Justice Scalia seems to see the *R.A.V.* outcome as necessary to protect unpopular speakers from the tyranny of the majority: "majority preferences must be expressed in some fashion other than silencing speech on the basis of content." Is it possible that Scalia's decision is in fact counter-majoritarian in a more basic sense, i.e., it tends to support the power of white men, a minority group? How might a decision like *R.A.V.* support

the status quo, tending to perpetuate the subordinate status of women and racial minorities?

5. Under the Supreme Court's approach, are the costs and benefits of the Free Speech provision of the First Amendment borne by different groups? Are the groups harmed most by racist and sexist speech as likely to have their own speech effectively protected by the First Amendment? Are they likely to have more power in the private arena, e.g., control of media, or in the public arena? Frederick Schauer, The Political Incidence of the Free Speech Principle, 64 U.Colo.L.Rev. 935 (1993); Frederick Schauer, Uncoupling Free Speech, 92 Colum.L.Rev. 1321, 1355 (1992); J.M. Balkin, Some Realism About Pluralism, 1990 Duke L.J. 375. Consider the reasons for, and effects of, movies in which 80 to 85% of the characters are male and "[t]he few female roles are dominated by three major images: 'child temptress' (as in the film 'Crush'), 'commodity' ('Honeymoon in Vegas') and 'psycho-killer' ('Hand That Rocks The Cradle')." Merilee S. Novinson, Stop Feeding the Exploitation–Film Monster, Chi.Trib., May 9, 1993, § 6, at 11. (Novinson is chair of the advocacy committee of Women in Film/Chicago).

6. Why is the constitutional commitment to racial and sexual equality irrelevant in cases involving speech? Given that the Fourteenth Amendment (containing the equality commitment) was enacted after the First Amendment, could you argue that the latter should be read in light of the former? How might such a reading affect the analysis in a case like *R.A.V.?* See, e.g., Akhil Reed Amar, Comment: The Case of the Missing Amendments: R.A.V. v. City of St. Paul, 106 Harv.L.Rev. 124 (1992); Akhil Reed Amar, The Bill of Rights and the Fourteenth Amendment, 101 Yale L.J. 1193 (1992). Would you agree with such an approach? See also Morrison Torrey, Thoughts About Why the First Amendment Operates to Stifle the Freedom and Equality of a Subordinated Majority, 21 Women's Rts. Rptr. 25 (1999) (arguing that both the Fourteenth and Nineteenth Amendments should outweigh the First Amendment since the later amendments represent participation by a more inclusive group in the democratic process). What other arguments could be made for it?

7. Justice Scalia seems to believe that government is unlikely to suppress speech it considers undesirable by restrictions on conduct rather than speech. Is this equally true for all groups? Would it be true for lesbians and gay men? Are some government rules—such as the military ban on lesbians and gay soldiers—designed to silence them? In recent debates, much of the support for the ban is from those who wish not to exclude valuable soldiers from service, but to keep them quiet. Why does the ban look like a restriction on conduct rather than speech (or expressive conduct, which is protected as speech)?

8. MacKinnon argues that there are speech issues on both sides of the pornography debate, and that the speech of pornographers silences women (see pornography section in Chapter 5). Could a similar point be made about cross burnings? Isn't part of the message of burning a cross in the yard of an African American family that they should move away without complaint, that they most definitely should *not* continue challenging the status quo by either speech or action? Why doesn't Justice Scalia see the burning cross as an attempt to stop political action and to silence political speech of African

Americans who would change the status quo? If you do see speech issues on both sides of the case, how would you resolve them? Why does the Court analyze the case as though speech issues arise only on one side?

MARI J. MATSUDA, PUBLIC RESPONSE TO RACIST SPEECH: CONSIDERING THE VICTIM'S STORY

87 Mich.L.Rev. 2320, 2336–40, 2357–58, 2360–61 (1989).

[Also in M. Matsuda, C. Lawrence, R. Delgado, K. Crenshaw, Words That Wound: Critical Race Theory, Assaultive Speech And The First Amendment, Westview Press (1993)]

Racist hate messages are rapidly increasing and are widely distributed in this country using a variety of low and high technologies. The negative effects of hate messages are real and immediate for the victims. Victims of vicious hate propaganda have experienced physiological symptoms and emotional distress ranging from fear in the gut, rapid pulse rate and difficulty in breathing, nightmares, post-traumatic stress disorder, hypertension, psychosis, and suicide. Patricia Williams has called the blow of racist messages "spirit murder" in recognition of the psychic destruction victims experience.

Victims are restricted in their personal freedom. In order to avoid receiving hate messages, victims have had to quit jobs, forgo education, leave their homes, avoid certain public places, curtail their own exercise of speech rights, and otherwise modify their behavior and demeanor. The recipient of hate messages struggles with inner turmoil. One subconscious response is to reject one's own identity as a victim-group member. As writers portraying the African–American experience have noted, the price of disassociating from one's own race is often sanity itself.

As much as one may try to resist a piece of hate propaganda, the effect on one's self-esteem and sense of personal security is devastating. To be hated, despised, and alone is the ultimate fear of all human beings. However irrational racist speech may be, it hits right at the emotional place where we feel the most pain. The aloneness comes not only from the hate message itself, but also from the government response of tolerance. When hundreds of police officers are called out to protect racist marchers, when the courts refuse redress for racial insult, and when racist attacks are officially dismissed as pranks, the victim becomes a stateless person. Target-group members can either identify with a community that promotes racist speech, or they can admit that the community does not include them.

The effect on non-target-group members is also of constitutional dimension. Associational and other liberty interests of whites are curtailed by an atmosphere rife with racial hatred. In addition, the process of dissociation can affect their mental health. Dominant-group members who rightfully, and often angrily, object to hate propaganda share a guilty secret: their relief that they are not themselves the target of the racist attack. While they reject the Ku Klux Klan, they may feel ambivalent relief that they are not African–American, Asian, or Jewish. Thus they are drawn into unwilling complacency with the Klan, spared from being the feared and degraded thing.

Just as when we confront human tragedy—a natural disaster, a plane crash—we feel the blessing of the fortunate that distances us from the victims, the presence of racist hate propaganda distances right-thinking dominant-group members from the victims, making it harder to achieve a sense of common humanity. Similarly, racist propaganda forces victim-group members to view all dominant-group members with suspicion. It forces well-meaning dominant-group members to use kid-glove care in dealing with outsiders. This is one reason why social relations across racial lines are so rare in America.

Research in psychosocial and psycholinguistic analysis of racism suggests a related effect of racist hate propaganda: at some level, no matter how much both victims and well-meaning dominant-group members resist it, racial inferiority is planted in our minds as an idea that may hold some truth. The idea is improbable and abhorrent, but it is there before us, because it is presented repeatedly. "Those people" are lazy, dirty, sexualized, money-grubbing, dishonest, inscrutable, we are told. We reject the idea, but the next time we sit next to one of "those people" the dirt message, the sex message, is triggered. We stifle it, reject it as wrong, but it is there, interfering with our perception and interaction with the person next to us. For the victim, similarly, the angry rejection of the message of inferiority is coupled with absorption of the message. When a dominant-group member responds favorably, there is a moment of relief—the victims of hate messages do not always believe in their insides that they deserve decent treatment. This obsequious moment is degrading and dispiriting when the self-aware victim acknowledges it.

* * *

In order to respect first amendment values, a narrow definition of actionable racist speech is required. Racist speech is best treated as a *sui generis* category, presenting an idea so historically untenable, so dangerous, and so tied to perpetuation of violence and degradation of the very classes of human beings who are least equipped to respond, that it is properly treated as outside the realm of protected discourse. * * *

The alternative to recognizing racist speech as qualitatively different because of its content is to continue to stretch existing first amendment exceptions, such as the "fighting words" doctrine and the "content/conduct" distinction. This stretching ultimately weakens the first amendment fabric, creating neutral holes that remove protection for many forms of speech. Setting aside the worst forms of racist speech for special treatment is a non-neutral, value-laden approach that will better preserve free speech.

In order to distinguish the worst, paradigm example of racist hate messages from other forms of racist and nonracist speech, three identifying characteristics are suggested here:

1. The message is of racial inferiority;

2. The message is directed against a historically oppressed group; and

3. The message is persecutorial, hateful, and degrading.

Making each element a prerequisite to prosecution prevents opening of the dreaded floodgates of censorship.

The first element is the primary identifier of racist speech: racist speech proclaims racial inferiority and denies the personhood of target group members. All members of the target group are at once considered alike and inferior.

The second element attempts to further define racism by recognizing the connection of racism to power and prejudice. It is the structural subordination of a group based on an idea of racial inferiority. Racist speech is particularly harmful because it is a mechanism of subordination, reinforcing a historical vertical relationship.

The final element is related to the "fighting words" idea. The language used in the worst form of racist speech is language that is, and is intended as, persecutorial, hateful, and degrading.

* * *

A range of legal interventions, including the use of tort law and criminal law principles, is appropriate to combat racist hate propaganda. While the value of free speech can guide the choice of procedure—including evidentiary rules and burdens of persuasion—it should not completely remove recourse to the institution of law to combat racist speech. Racism as an acquired set of behaviors can be dis-acquired, and law is the means by which the state typically provides incentives for changes in behavior.

CHARLES R. LAWRENCE III, IF HE HOLLERS LET HIM GO: REGULATING RACIST SPEECH ON CAMPUS

1990 Duke L.J. 431, 452–55.

The fighting words doctrine anticipates that the verbal "slap in the face" of insulting words will provoke a violent response with a resulting breach of the peace. When racial insults are hurled at minorities, the response may be silence or flight rather than a fight, but the preemptive effect on further speech is just as complete as with fighting words. Women and minorities often report that they find themselves speechless in the face of discriminatory verbal attacks. This inability to respond is not the result of oversensitivity among these groups, as some individuals who oppose protective regulation have argued. Rather, it is the product of several factors, all of which reveal the non-speech character of the initial preemptive verbal assault. The first factor is that the visceral emotional response to personal attack precludes speech. Attack produces an instinctive, defensive psychological reaction. Fear, rage, shock, and flight all interfere with any reasoned response. Words like "nigger," "kike," and "faggot" produce physical symptoms that temporarily disable the victim, and the perpetrators often use these words with the intention of producing this effect. Many victims do not find words of response until well after the assault when the cowardly assaulter has departed.

A second factor that distinguishes racial insults from protected speech is the preemptive nature of such insults—the words by which to respond to such verbal attacks may never be forthcoming because speech is usually an inadequate response. When one is personally attacked with words that denote one's subhuman status and untouchability, there is little (if anything) that can be said to redress either the emotional or reputational injury. This is particularly true when the message and meaning of the epithet resonates with beliefs widely held in society. This preservation of widespread beliefs is what makes the face-to-face racial attack more likely to preempt speech than are other fighting words. The racist name-caller is accompanied by a cultural chorus of equally demeaning speech and symbols.

The subordinated victim of fighting words also is silenced by her relatively powerless position in society. Because of the significance of power and position, the categorization of racial epithets as "fighting words" provides an inadequate paradigm; instead one must speak of their "functional equivalent." The fighting words doctrine presupposes an encounter between two persons of relatively equal power who have been acculturated to respond to face-to-face insults with violence. The fighting words doctrine is a paradigm based on a white male point of view.[93] In most situations, minorities correctly perceive that a violent response to fighting words will result in a risk to their own life and limb. Since minorities are likely to lose the fight, they are forced to remain silent and submissive. This response is most obvious when women submit to sexually assaultive speech or when the racist name-caller is in a more powerful position—the boss on the job or the mob. Certainly, we do not expect the black women crossing the Wisconsin campus to turn on their tormentors and pummel them. Less obvious, but just as significant, is the effect of pervasive racial and sexual violence and coercion on individual members of subordinated groups who must learn the survival techniques of suppressing and disguising rage and anger at an early age.

93. The fighting words doctrine captures the "macho" quality of male discourse. It is accepted, justifiable, and even praiseworthy when "real men" respond to personal insult with violence. * * * The fighting words doctrine's responsiveness to this "male" stance in the world and its blindness to the cultural experience of women is another example of how "neutral" principles of law often reflect the values of those who are dominant. * * *

Notes on Hate Speech and Hate Speech Codes

1. Is the following hate speech code constitutional?

Speech or other expression constitutes harassment by personal vilification if it:

> (a) is intended to insult or stigmatize an individual or a small number of individuals on the basis of their sex, race, color, handicap, religion, sexual orientation, or national and ethnic origin; and
>
> (b) is addressed directly to the individual or individuals whom it insults or stigmatizes; and
>
> (c) makes use of insulting or "fighting" words or non-verbal symbols.
>
> In the context of discriminatory harassment by personal vilification, insulting or "fighting" words or non-verbal symbols are those "which by their very utterance inflict injury or tend to incite to an immediate breach of the peace," and which are commonly understood to convey direct and visceral hatred or contempt for human beings on the basis of their sex, race, color, handicap, religion, sexual orientation, or national and ethnic origin.

If you do believe this policy to be unconstitutional, can you amend it to make it constitutional? How? Does the policy cover what teachers might say in the classroom, or does it only regulate peer behavior? Should that make a difference? Is it restricted to face-to-face insults? What about academic freedom?

2. Mari Matsuda specifically addresses racist hate speech. Can her arguments be extended to sexist hate speech? Are the three characteristics of racist speech that she identifies equally applicable to women?

3. How can the harms of hate speech be established? Is the harm of hate speech more persuasive when it is put into context, i.e., when we are told the stories of specific incidents and how the victims felt? Richard Delgado writes about incidents at eight selected campuses in his article, Campus Antiracism Rules: Constitutional Narratives in Collision, 85 Nw. U.L.Rev. 343, 349–58 (1991). Would litigants be more effective if they did this type of "storytelling?" See also Cynthia Grant Bowman, Street Harassment and the Informal Ghettoization of Women, 106 Harv.L.Rev. 517 (1993).

4. What exactly are the harms of hate speech in the campus setting? It has been suggested that hate speech disrupts an equal learning environment:

> when, for example, black students hear that they "don't belong in classrooms, they belong hanging from trees," when an Asian student is told, "Die, Chink. Hostile Americans want your yellow hide," or when women students are described as "fat housewives." Such demeaning expression injures self-image, undermines self-confidence, and alienates the victimized student from her school. Hate speech hinders learning and participation in and out of class. It may also frustrate efforts to attract minority faculty and students.

First Amendment—Racist and Sexist Expression on Campus—Court Strikes Down University Limits on Hate Speech.—*Doe v. University of Michigan,* 721 F.Supp. 852 (E.D.Mich.1989), 103 Harv.L.Rev. 1397, 1399–1400 (1990).

Can you identify any other harms? Have you ever been targeted for "hate speech"? If so, how did you feel?

5. Delgado also argues that how you frame the issue determines the outcome: Is it a First Amendment problem of free speech or a Fourteenth Amendment problem of equality? Delgado, above note 3, at 345–46. He summarizes the problem as follows:

> One often hears that the problem of campus antiracism rules is that of balancing free speech and equality. But more is at stake. Each side wants not merely to have the balance struck in its favor; each wants to impose its own understanding of what is at stake. Minority protectors see the injury of one who has been subject to a racial assault as not a mere isolated event, but as part of an interrelated series of acts, by which persons of color are subordinated, and which will follow the victim wherever she goes. First amendment defenders see the wrong of silencing the racist as much more than a momentary inconvenience: protection of his right to speak is part of the never-ending vigilance necessary to preserve freedom of expression in a society that is too prone to balance it away.

Id. at 347–48. Can you find a way to solve this problem? Is there any way to reconcile the First and Fourteenth Amendments in this context? Is there the same conflict in regulating pornography? Is pornography a form of "hate speech"?

6. Do you think hate speech codes are a good idea? Haven't universities always regulated speech? Aren't the following regulations of speech equivalent to classroom speech codes, though generally less explicit: grades, syllabi, reading and writing assignments, and unspoken understandings about what is relevant to discussions? What, if any, are the differences? Why do hate speech codes look like censorship to many, resulting in successful First Amendment challenges, though there never have been First Amendment "censorship" challenges to the assignment of "the male curriculum" or the exclusion of women's perspectives or issues from academic courses? See Mary E. Becker, Conservative Free Speech and the Uneasy Case for Judicial Review, 64 U.Colo.L.Rev. 975 (1993).

Is the problem that speech codes make universities' expectations of students explicit? Intelligent discussions are possible only if there is a shared understanding of what is relevant and worthwhile. Incoherent diatribes, for example, are understood as out of place in the classroom because they are inconsistent with worthwhile intellectual discussions in an atmosphere conducive to learning. Why aren't speech codes, even in public institutions, just explicit statements of such understanding and judgments, at least when applicable to classroom discussions? A student who repeatedly engages in incoherent diatribes might receive a low grade for classroom participation or a reprimand from the teacher, but would certainly be "disciplined" in some manner, although that word probably would not be used. Is this censorship?

Do women in your law school who have been raped raise issues they consider important in criminal law classes? Do they feel "censored"? By whom? Would they consider bringing a First Amendment challenge on censorship grounds if your school is a public one? What would be the weaknesses of such a suit?

7. Would the proponents of the various feminist theories explored in Chapter 3 support hate speech regulation? On what grounds would each support or oppose it?

8. Where do civil libertarians stand on this issue? Charles R. Lawrence III, expresses his view of this dilemma:

> But I am deeply concerned about the role that many civil libertarians have played, or the roles we have failed to play, in the continuing, real-life struggle through which we define the community in which we live. I fear that by framing the debate as we have—as one in which the liberty of free speech is in conflict with the elimination of racism—we have advanced the cause of racial oppression and have placed the bigot on the moral high ground, fanning the rising flames of racism. Above all, I am troubled that we have not listened to the real victims, that we have shown so little empathy or understanding for their injury, and that we have abandoned those individuals whose race, gender, or sexual orientation provokes others to regard them as second class citizens. These individuals' civil liberties are most directly at stake in the debate.

Lawrence, above at 436. See Nadine Strossen, Regulating Racist Speech on Campus: A Modest Proposal? 1990 Duke L.J. 484 (ACLU position on regulation of hate speech). The ACLU National Board modified its position in 1993; it states "that it is constitutional for courts to impose heavier penalties when an action that is already a crime, like assault, is motivated by bigotry." Richard N. Ostling, A.C.L.U.—Not All That Civil, Time, Apr. 26, 1993, at 31.

In testimony before the Senate Judiciary Committee hearings on S.622, the Hate Crimes Prevention Act of 1999, the ACLU stated it could not support the proposed bill making violent conduct directed at a person because of race, color, national origin, religion, gender, sexual orientation, or disability a federal civil rights violation *unless* the bill was amended by adding the following evidentiary provision:

> In any prosecution under this section, (i) evidence proving the defendant's mere abstract beliefs or (ii) evidence of the defendant's mere membership in an organization, shall not be admissible to establish any element of an offense under this section.

www.aclu.org/congress/1051199a.html.

9. In an article comparing the status of university sexual harassment and hate speech codes, Jon Gould concludes that, even though the speech codes were virtually identical to Title VII's sexual harassment laws, courts strike down speech codes while enforcing sexual harassment policies. Gould, The Triumph of Hate Speech Regulation: Why Gender Wins But Race Loses in America, 6 Mich. J. Gender & L. 153 (1999). He also expresses surprise that the universities whose hate speech codes were found unconstitutional did not exert strong defenses and failed to appeal the adverse rulings:

> Perhaps, even supporters had only intended the codes as a symbolic statement—in this case, as a vehicle to highlight their concern over a receding national interest in civil rights. In either case, it is abundantly clear that the codes did not have the same level of committed support that Title VII did.

> What's more, the universities were in the difficult position of playing defense against an organized opposition. Contrary to the experience of sexual harassment litigants, the universities were not joined by any legal advocacy groups, nor did the EEOC enter the litigation on their behalf. Rather, the universities found themselves pitted against an unbending wall of attorneys affiliated with the American Civil Liberties Union and the Individual Rights Foundation.

Id. at 195–96. The court decisions were met with little protest on college campuses. Id. at 196. The author suggests that the political climate might explain the situation, citing a 1990 Gallup poll finding that almost 2/3 of Americans believe that racial equality has been achieved and that white Americans consider the civil rights crusade complete and express little willingness to address the problems faced by Black Americans; 2/3 of whites oppose new civil rights law and 77% of whites think Blacks overestimate the amount of discrimination. Id. at 216–17. However, the opposite is true for women: a significant number of Americans believe women do not have equal job opportunities as men and only 29% think there has been too much attention paid to the civil rights of women. Id. at 217. Do you think public opinion is influencing these decisions? How do you explain the lack of support for hate speech codes and the substantial support for sexual harassment policies? Do you agree that the two types of speech regulation are essentially the same?

Chapter 10

WOMEN AND WAGE LABOR

A. INTRODUCTION

From the settling of the first colonies until the industrial revolution, most Americans, women as well as men, worked in family businesses and on farms. Women and men often specialized in different chores, but women were major producers of necessities consumed by families: cloth, clothing, candles, soap, fresh vegetables and fruits from the kitchen garden, eggs and chickens, canned food, as well as meals. There were important variations in labor and conditions across race and class. Privileged, upper class women supervised slaves and servants involved in these activities. But relatively few Americans of any race, sex, or class worked for wages. As late as 1780, "64 percent of the non-native population lived in families engaged in self-employment, 20 percent were slaves, and only 16 percent were wage workers or indentured servants."[1]

In a little over 100 years, the situation changed dramatically: "[B]y 1890, there were twice as many people working for wages or salaries as there were self-employed; by 1970, there were nine times as many."[2] This astonishing transition was accompanied by the movement of much production from the home to the factory. As producer activity left the home in the 19th century, the cult of domesticity developed as the ideal for "real" women (white middle or upper class women who were not immigrants); a woman's place was in the home nurturing her children and creating a haven to which the weary breadwinner could return at night.[3] Although relatively few white women born in this country worked for wages once they were married, many women of color, immigrant, lower class, and single women worked for wages in order to survive. For example, as late as 1920, only 6.5% of married European American women worked for wages, though 32.5% of married African American women did so and 18.5% of married Asian American women. In each of

1. Teresa L. Amott and Julie A. Matthaei, Race, Gender, and Work: A Multicultural Economic History of Women in the United States 295 (1991).

2. Id.

3. See Barbara Welter, The Cult of True Womanhood: 1820–1860, 18 Am.Q. 151 (1966).

these categories, employment rates were much higher for unmarried women: 45% for European American women; 58.8% for African American women; and 38.7% for Asian American women.[4]

The single most important change in the labor force in the 20th century was the increase in female wage workers, the fastest growing segment of the wage workforce. Today, most women with children work in the wage labor market either full or part time, and African and European American women are about equally likely to work for wages. Most women continue also to be primarily responsible for the domestic sphere. Information about women's labor force participation rates are detailed in the tables that follow.

Table 1: Women's Labor Force Participation Rates Civilians Age 16 and Over[5]

1942–1996

Year	Percentage of Women in Labor Force[6]	Women as Percentage of Labor Force	Year	Percentage of Women in Labor Force	Women as Percentage of Labor Force
1948	32.7%	28.6%	1976	47.3%	40.5%
1952	34.7%	31.0%	1980	51.5%	42.5%
1956	36.9%	32.2%	1984	53.6%	43.8%
1960	37.7%	33.4%	1988	56.6%	45.0%
1964	38.7%	34.8%	1992	57.8%	45.4%
1968	41.6%	37.1%	1996	59.3%	46.2%
1972	43.9%	43.9%			

Table 2: Civilian Labor Force Participation Rates for Persons Age 16 and Over by Sex, Race, and Hispanic Origin,[7] Selected Years, Actual 1975, 1990, 1996, and Projected 2005 (in percentages).[8]

	Women					Men				
	All races	White	Black	Other	Hispanic	All races	White	Black	Other	Hispanic
1975	46.3%	45.9%	48.8%	51.3%	—[9]	77.9%	78.7%	71.0%	74.8%	—
1990	57.5%	57.5%	57.8%	56.7%	53.0%	76.1%	76.9%	70.1%	74.2%	81.2%
1996	59.3%	59.1%	60.4%	58.8%	53.4%	74.9%	75.8%	68.7%	68.7%	79.6%
2005	61.7%	62.6%	58.8%	56.7%	53.6%	72.9%	73.9%	65.8%	72.3%	76.1%

4. Amott and Matthaei, above note 1, table 9–2 at 300.

5. Information from Cynthia B. Costello, Shari Miles, and Anne J. Stone, The American Woman 1999–2000: A Century of Change—What's Next table 4–1 at 264 (1998).

6. Percentage of Civilian women aged 16 and older who were in the labor force.

7. Persons of Hispanic origin may be of any race.

8. Information from Costello et. al, above note 5, table 4–3 at 266.

9. Data unavailable.

Table 3: Labor Force Participation Rates for Mothers with Infants[10]

1976	31%	1988	51%
1980	38%	1992	54%
1984	47%	1998	59%

Among mothers with infants in 1998, 36% were employed full-time, 17% were employed part-time, and 6% were looking for work. For women with older children, labor-force participation rates are higher. For mothers without infants, 52% were working full time and 17% working part time. Women with higher levels of education and wages are more likely to return to work (and to work longer hours) after the birth of a child than other women.

Among separated, divorced, or widowed women with infants, 50% worked full time in 1998, whereas only 39% of married women worked full time with infants. Women with infants who had never married were least likely to work full time (24%).

By 1998, only 24% of families headed by a couple and with children in the household were traditional in the sense of having a breadwinning father and a full-time homemaker mother. Indeed, the "major change for the past two decades in family and economic life has not been the growth of dual-employed couples without children, but an increase in the number and proportion of couples where both child rearing and working lives are the norms for both spouses."[11]

Women's workforce participation rates no longer vary much with the number of their children. As indicated in the table above, 59% of mothers with an infant were in the wage-labor market in 1998. Mothers with one child (of any age) were in the wage-labor market at about that rate (61%) and those with two or more children were in the wage-labor market at only a slightly lower rate (57%).

The focus of this chapter is Title VII, 42 U.S.C.A. § 2000e et seq., the primary federal law prohibiting sex discrimination in employment. Two types of discrimination claims can be brought under Title VII: disparate treatment and disparate impact. Disparate treatment is proscribed by § 703(a):

> a) It shall be an unlawful employment practice for an employer—
>
> (1) to fail or to refuse to hire or to discharge any individual, or otherwise to discriminate against any individual with respect to his compensation, terms, conditions, or privileges of employment, because of such individual's race, color, religion, sex, or national origin; or

10. United States Census Bureau, Fertility of American Women, Current Population Reports June 1998 at 8 (September 2000) (mothers 15–44 years of age who have had a child within the last year and were working or looking for work).

11. Id. at 8–9, 12.

> (2) to limit, segregate, or classify his employees or applicants for employment in any way which would deprive or tend to deprive any individual of employment opportunities or otherwise adversely affect his status as an employee, because of such individual's race, color, religion, sex, or national origin.

42 U.S.C.A. § 2000e–2. Discrimination based on sex is permissible only when sex is "a bona fide occupational qualification ["BFOQ"] reasonably necessary to the normal operation of that particular business or enterprise." 42 U.S.C.A. § 2000e–2(e).

Disparate impact is proscribed by § 703(k)(1)(A):

> An unlawful employment practice based on disparate impact is established under this title only if—
>
> (i) a complaining party demonstrates that a respondent uses a particular employment practice that causes a disparate impact on the basis of race, color, religion, sex, or national origin and the respondent fails to demonstrate that the challenged practice is job related for the position in question and consistent with business necessity * * *

42 U.S.C.A. § 2000e–2(k)(a)(A).

Title VII provides both for individual suits by "aggrieved individuals" and for suits by the Equal Employment Opportunity Commission ("EEOC"), a federal administrative agency charged with enforcement of Title VII. Aggressive enforcement by the EEOC against targeted industries has had significant effects in desegregating traditionally male jobs. For example, during the 1970's significant desegregation occurred when the banking and insurance industries were targeted for enforcement actions.[12] Unfortunately, as explored in the next section, Title VII has had only limited effect in helping women combine wage work and caretaking.

B. MOTHERS IN THE WORKPLACE

Text Note: The Early Cases

The first sex-discrimination case to come before the Supreme Court, Phillips v. Martin Marietta Corp., 400 U.S. 542, 91 S.Ct. 496, 27 L.Ed.2d 613 (1971), was as important as any subsequent case. The Fifth Circuit, known at that time for its firm commitment to racial equality, had held that an employer did not violate Title VII's ban on sex discrimination by refusing to hire women with preschool children. 411 F.2d 1 (5th Cir.1969). The employer argued that this policy was not "per se discrimination on the basis of sex," presumably because some women (those without preschool children) were hired. The Fifth Circuit accepted this argument:

> A per se violation of the Act can only be discrimination based solely on one of the categories, i.e., in the case of sex, women vis-a-vis men.

12. Barbara F. Reskin and Patricia A. Roos, Job Queues, Gender Queues: Explaining Women's Inroads into Male Occupations 54–55 (1990).

> When another criterion of employment is added to one of the classifications listed in the Act, there is no longer apparent discrimination based solely on * * * sex * * *. It becomes the function of the courts to study the conditioning of employment on one of the elements outlined in the statute coupled with the additional requirement and to determine if any individual or group is being denied work due to his * * * sex * * *.
>
> As to the case *sub judice,* as [sic] assembly trainee, among other disqualifications, cannot be a woman with pre-school age children. The evidence presented in the trial court is quite convincing that no discrimination against women as a whole or the appellant individually was practiced by Martin Marietta. The discrimination was based on a two-pronged qualification, i.e., a woman with pre-school age children. Id. Phillips was not refused employment because she was a woman nor because she had pre-school age children. It is the coalescence of these two elements that denied her the position she desired. In view of the above, we are convinced that the judgment of the District Court [for the defendant] was proper * * *.

Id. at 4. The court saw congressional intent as crucial, but concluded that "[t]he common experience of Congressmen is surely not so far removed from that of mankind in general as to warrant our attributing to them such an irrational purpose" as to require that employers treat mothers and fathers of young children "exactly alike." Id.

Had the Supreme Court affirmed this decision, Title VII's ban on sex discrimination would have been nearly meaningless. But in a brief unanimous opinion the Court held that Martin Marietta had violated Title VII by adopting "one hiring policy for women and another for men." 400 U.S. at 544.

Since this initial Supreme Court decision, the courts have charted a wavering course, sometimes seeing sex discrimination and sometimes missing it. In 1976 the Supreme Court held that Title VII's prohibition on sex discrimination did not include distinctions based on pregnancy. General Electric Co. v. Gilbert, 429 U.S. 125, 97 S.Ct. 401, 50 L.Ed.2d 343 (1976). Women were shocked and outraged. Congress responded with the Pregnancy Discrimination Act or 1978 ("PDA"), which amended Title VII to provide that sex discrimination includes discrimination

> because of or on the basis of pregnancy, childbirth, or related medical conditions; and women affected by pregnancy, childbirth, or related medical conditions shall be treated the same for all employment-related purposes, including receipt of benefits under fringe benefit programs, as other persons not so affected but similar in their ability to work or inability to work * * * .

42 U.S.C.A. § 2000e(k).

As of January 2001, only one other PDA case has reached the Supreme Court. In International Union, UAW v. Johnson Controls, Inc., 499 U.S. 187, 111 S.Ct. 1196, 113 L.Ed.2d 158 (1991), the question was whether an employer could exclude women who could not prove sterility from the factory floor where workers were exposed to lead. To prove sterility, a woman had to produce a document from her doctor certifying that she could not conceive because she was post-menopausal or for some other reason. Men received no similar protection even though there was evidence of risk to the offspring of male workers. Precise levels of risk for children of women and men were unknown, but the plaintiffs included a 50–year old divorcee (most unlikely to have a child in the future) and a young married man whose wife was trying to become pregnant. Clearly the risk of harm to future life was greater as a result of the exposure of this man than of this woman.

The Court held that *Johnson Controls*' policy overtly, facially, violated Title VII:

> Johnson Controls' policy classifies on the basis of gender and childbearing capacity, rather than fertility alone. Respondent does not seek to protect the unconceived children of all its employees. Despite evidence in the record about the debilitating effect of lead exposure on the male reproductive system, Johnson Controls is concerned only with the harms that may befall the unborn offspring of its female employees. * * * This Court faced a conceptually similar situation in Phillips v. Martin Marietta Corp., and found sex discrimination because the policy established "one hiring policy for women and another for men—each having pre-school-age children." Johnson Controls' policy is facially discriminatory because it requires only a female employee to produce proof that she is not capable of reproducing.
>
> Our conclusion is bolstered by the Pregnancy Discrimination Act of 1978 (PDA), in which Congress explicitly provided that, for purposes of Title VII, discrimination "on the basis of sex" includes discrimination "because of or on the basis of pregnancy, childbirth, or related medical conditions." * * * In its use of the words "capable of bearing children" in the 1982 policy statement as the criterion for exclusion, Johnson Controls explicitly classifies on the basis of potential for pregnancy. Under the PDA, such a classification must be regarded, for Title VII purposes, in the same light as explicit sex discrimination. Respondent has chosen to treat all its female employees as potentially pregnant; that choice evinces discrimination on the basis of sex.
>
> * * * [T]he absence of a malevolent motive does not convert a facially discriminatory policy into a neutral policy with a discriminatory effect. Whether an employment practice involves disparate treatment through explicit facial discrimination does not depend on why the employer discriminates but rather on the explicit terms of the discrimination. * * * The beneficence of an employer's purpose does not undermine the conclusion that an explicit gender-based policy is sex discrimination under § 703(a) and may thus be defended only as a BFOQ.

Id. at 198–200.

Johnson Controls tried to use Title VII's BFOQ defense, which allows an employer to discriminate on the basis of sex when sex "is a bona fide occupational qualification reasonably necessary to the normal operation of that business or enterprise." The Court rejected this argument. Although there had been cases in which a BFOQ was recognized on the basis of safety concerns, the Court explained that safety concerns justify sex discrimination only when the issue is safety of those in contact with the employee during the course of her job, such as customers. Thus, a BFOQ defense is available only when "sex or pregnancy actually interferes with the employee's ability to perform the job." Id. at 204.

In claiming a BFOQ defense, Johnson Controls had argued that women employees were more costly than male employees because of the risk to offspring during pregnancy. The court rejected the relevance of cost:

> A word about tort liability and the increased cost of fertile women in the workplace is perhaps necessary. * * * It is correct to say that Title VII does not prevent the employer from having a conscience. The statute, however, does prevent sex-specific fetal-protection policies. These two aspects of Title VII do not conflict.
>
> * * *
>
> The tort-liability argument reduces to two equally unpersuasive propositions. First, Johnson Controls attempts to solve the problem of reproductive health hazards by resorting to an exclusionary policy. Title VII plainly forbids illegal sex discrimination as a method of diverting attention from an employer's obligation to police the workplace. Second, the specter of an award of damages reflects a fear that hiring fertile women will cost more. The extra cost of employing members of one sex, however, does not provide an affirmative Title VII defense for a discriminatory refusal to hire members of that gender. Indeed, in passing the PDA, Congress considered at length the considerable cost of providing equal treatment of pregnancy and related conditions, but made the "decision to forbid special treatment of pregnancy despite the social costs associated therewith." * * *
>
> We, of course, are not presented with, nor do we decide, a case in which costs would be so prohibitive as to threaten the survival of the employer's business. We merely reiterate our prior holdings that the incremental cost of hiring women cannot justify discriminating against them.

Id. at 208, 210–211.

Notes on the Early Cases

1. Why would a rational company allow young married men whose wives were trying to conceive to work in a lead exposure area but exclude 50–year-old divorced women?

2. How would you decide a case in which there is firm scientific evidence that risk associated with maternal exposure is significantly higher than the risk associated with paternal exposure? (There was no such evidence in *Johnson Controls.*) What would the outcome be under the various feminist approaches described in Chapter 3?

3. Can employers fire pregnant workers exposed to fetal hazards in the workplace? Would firing the pregnant worker from a hazardous job necessarily be in the best interest of the child? What if the fired pregnant woman would lose her insurance and no longer be able to afford adequate medical care? What if she would be unable to make mortgage payments or pay her rent?

In Hunt–Golliday v. Metropolitan Water Reclamation District of Greater Chicago, 104 F.3d 1004 (7th Cir.1997), a pregnant woman was fired after experiencing cramps (and "threatening to miscarry," according to hospital personnel who treated her) while doing heavy lifting. Hunt–Golliday had just returned from a period of disability caused by a back injury. The near miscarriage occurred on her first day back on the job; she left and went to the hospital for treatment, and then called in sick the next day. The Seventh Circuit affirmed the grant of summary judgment for the employer on her pregnancy discrimination claim, noting that she had "presented no evidence showing, for instance, that a nonpregnant employee returning from extended leave who left her job and called in sick after one day back would not have been suspended." Id. at 18. Do you think that there should have been a trial to see if her pregnancy was a factor in the decision to fire her? Under *Johnson Controls*, can an employer fire a pregnant worker with a perfect attendance record after she has cramps and almost miscarries after doing heavy lifting?

4. Suzanne Harvender learned she was pregnant in February of 1996 with a due date in late September. She was a staff technician with the Norton Company and worked with chemicals. When she informed her employer of her pregnancy, the employer asked her to obtain a letter from her doctor stating that "she should be protected from chemical exposure." She thought that Norton "requested the note so that they could place her on a light duty program as they had done before when she had gone through an earlier pregnancy." Harvender v. Norton Co., 1997 WL 793085, 4 Wage & Hour Cas.2d (BNA) 560 (N.D.N.Y.1997). Harvender gave Norton the requested letter from her doctor, and Norton responded by placing her on FMLA leave (which totals only 12 unpaid weeks of leave in a calendar year), explaining that they could not place her on light duty because of restructuring and downsizing. Norton also indicated that if she did not return to work after her 12–week unpaid FMLA leave (May 15), her employment would be terminated. Suzanne Harvender miscarried and returned to work in April. She also brought suit alleging that Norton had (1) knowingly and intentionally violated the FMLA; (2) intentionally inflicted emotional distress; and (3) breached its contract of employment. The district court granted the employer's motion for summary judgment on all three claims, and holding that employers as well as employees can invoke the FMLA because "nowhere in the act does it provide that FMLA leave must be granted only when the employee wishes it to be granted." Would Suzanne Harvender have faired better had she filed suit for pregnancy discrimination under Title VII, citing *Johnson Controls*?

In the decisions below, you will see that courts require that women present evidence that, in fact, similarly situated men were not so treated. What would be the chances that Havender could find a similarly situated male at all (regardless of how he was treated)? (As the decisions below indicate, if she cannot find a similarly situated man who was treated better she is likely to lose on a Title VII claim.)

5. Consider Armstrong v. Flowers Hospital, 812 F.Supp. 1183 (M.D.Ala.1993). Pamela Armstrong was a nurse working for a hospital that provided home services to patients. During her pregnancy, she was assigned to a patient with cryptococal meningitis, an infectious and serious illness

common among AIDS patients. AIDS patients tend to suffer from a number of opportunistic infections likely to be more dangerous to a child in utero than to a healthy adult. Armstrong told her supervisor that because she was in the first trimester of pregnancy she should not treat this patient. Her supervisor replied that it was not hospital policy to reassign nurses on the basis of unusual risks. Armstrong was given two days in which to decide whether to treat the patient or lose her job. She refused to treat the patient and was fired. As a result, she lost her health insurance prior to childbirth. She sued claiming both disparate treatment and disparate impact discrimination on the basis of pregnancy. The district court held that there had been no disparate treatment since pregnant workers were treated precisely like nonpregnant workers, a straightforward application of formal equality.

Should employers be required to offer employees particularly vulnerable to fetal hazards—typically pregnant workers and male workers whose wives are trying to conceive—safe employment during the period of vulnerability at no loss of pay? The Americans with Disability Act ("ADA") requires that employers accommodate disabilities but is no help for these workers since it does not cover temporary disabilities. Should Title VII be amended to require accommodation of the needs of workers hoping to be parents in the near future? On a theoretical level, is there any link between employers' failure to afford such accommodation and inequality between women and men? For discussions of the need to require such accommodation, see Mary Becker, Reproductive Hazards After *Johnson Controls*, 31 Hous. L. Rev. 43 (1994); Ruth Colker, Pregnancy, Parenting, and Capitalism, 58 Ohio State L. J. 61, 75–76 (1997).

TROUPE v. MAY DEPARTMENT STORES CO.

United State Court of Appeals, Seventh Circuit, 1994.

20 F.3d 734.

POSNER, CHIEF JUDGE.

In 1978, Congress amended Title VII of the Civil Rights Act of 1964 to prohibit discrimination on account of pregnancy: "women affected by pregnancy, childbirth, or related medical conditions shall be treated the same for all employment-related purposes, including receipt of benefits under fringe benefit programs, as other persons not so affected but similar in their ability or inability to work." * * *

The plaintiff, Kimberly Hern Troupe, was employed by the Lord & Taylor department store in Chicago as a saleswoman in the women's accessories department. She had begun working there in 1987, initially working part time but from July 1990 full time. Until the end of 1990 her work was entirely satisfactory. In December of that year, in the first trimester of a pregnancy, she began experiencing morning sickness of unusual severity. The following month she requested and was granted a return to part-time status, working from noon to 5:00 p.m. Partly it seems because she slept later under the new schedule, so that noon was "morning" for her, she continued to experience severe morning sickness at work, causing what her lawyer describes with understatement as "slight" or "occasional" tardiness. In the month that ended with a warning from her immediate supervisor, Jennifer Rauch, on February 18, she reported late to work, or left early, on nine out of the 21 working days. The day after the warning she was late again and this time received a written warning. After she was tardy three days in a row late in March, the company on March 29 placed her on probation for 60 days. During the probationary period Troupe was late eleven more days; and she was fired on June 7, shortly after the end of the probationary period. She testified at her deposition that on the way to the meeting with the defendant's human resources manager at which she was fired, Rauch told her that "I [Troupe] was going to be terminated because she [Rauch] didn't think I was coming back to work after I had my baby." Troupe was due to begin her maternity leave the next day. We do not know whether it was to be a paid maternity leave but at argument Lord & Taylor's counsel said that employees of Lord & Taylor are entitled to maternity leave with half pay. We must assume that after Troupe was fired she received no medical benefits from Lord & Taylor in connection with her pregnancy and the birth of her child, for she testified without contradiction that she received no monetary benefits of any kind, other than unemployment benefits, after June 7, 1991. We do not know whether Lord & Taylor was less tolerant of Troupe's tardiness than it would have been had the cause not been a medical condition related to pregnancy. There is no evidence on this question, vital as it is.

* * *

Different kinds and combinations of evidence can create a triable issue of intentional discrimination ("disparate treatment," in the jargon of discrimination law), the only kind of discrimination alleged in this case. One kind is evidence that can be interpreted as an acknowledgment of discriminatory intent by the defendant or its agents * * *. Such evidence is indeed direct evidence as distinct from circumstantial; and since intent to discriminate is a mental state and mind reading not an accepted tool of judicial inquiry, it may be the only truly direct evidence of intent that will ever be available. But circumstantial evidence is admissible too, to provide a basis for drawing an inference of intentional discrimination.

* * *

[In order to survive] summary judgment a plaintiff must produce * * * evidence from which a rational trier of fact could reasonably infer that the defendant had fired the plaintiff because the latter was a member of a protected class, in this case the class of pregnant women.

We must examine the record in the light of these principles. The great, the undeniable fact is the plaintiff's tardiness. Her lawyer argues with great vigor that she should not be blamed—that she was genuinely ill, had a doctor's excuse, etc. That would be pertinent if Troupe were arguing that the Pregnancy Discrimination Act requires an employer to treat an employee afflicted by morning sickness better than the employer would treat an employee who was equally tardy for some other health reason; this is rightly not argued. If an employee who (like Troupe) does not have an employment contract cannot work because of illness, nothing in Title VII requires the employer to keep the employee on the payroll.

Against the inference that Troupe was fired because she was chronically late to arrive at work and chronically early to leave, she has only two facts to offer. The first is the timing of her discharge: she was fired the day before her maternity leave was to begin. Her morning sickness could not interfere with her work when she was not working because she was on maternity leave, and it could not interfere with her work when she returned to work after her maternity leave because her morning sickness would end at the latest with the birth of her child. Thus her employer fired her one day before the problem that the employer says caused her to be fired was certain to end. If the discharge of an unsatisfactory worker were a purely remedial measure rather than also, or instead, a deterrent one, the inference that Troupe wasn't really fired because of her tardiness would therefore be a powerful one. But that is a big "if." We must remember that after two warnings Troupe had been placed on probation for sixty days and that she had violated the implicit terms of probation by being as tardy during the probationary period as she had been before. If the company did not fire her, its warnings and threats would seem empty. Employees would be encouraged to flout work rules knowing that the only sanction would be a toothless warning or a meaningless period of probation.

Yet this is only an interpretation; and it might appear to be an issue for trial whether it is superior to Troupe's interpretation. But what is Troupe's interpretation? Not (as we understand it) that Lord & Taylor wanted to get back at her for becoming pregnant or having morning sickness. The only significance she asks us to attach to the timing of her discharge is as reinforcement for the inference that she asks us to draw from Rauch's statement about the reason for her termination: that she was terminated because her employer did not expect her to return to work after her maternity leave was up. We must decide whether a termination so motivated is discrimination within the meaning of the pregnancy amendment to Title VII.

Standing alone, it is not. (It could be a breach of contract, but that is not alleged.) Suppose that Lord & Taylor had an employee named Jones, a black employee scheduled to take a three-month paid sick leave for a kidney transplant; and whether thinking that he would not return to work when his leave was up or not wanting to incur the expense of paying him while he was on sick leave, the company fired him. In doing so it might be breaking its employment contract with Jones, if it had one, or violating a state statute requiring the payment of earned wages. But the company could not be found guilty of racial discrimination unless (in the absence of any of the other types of evidence of discrimination that we have discussed) there was evidence that it failed to exhibit comparable rapacity toward similarly situated employees of the white race. We must imagine a hypothetical Mr. Troupe, who is as tardy as Ms. Troupe was, also because of health problems, and who is about to take a protracted sick leave growing out of those problems at an expense to Lord & Taylor equal to that of Ms. Troupe's maternity leave. If Lord & Taylor would have fired our hypothetical Mr. Troupe, this implies that it fired Ms. Troupe not because she was pregnant but because she cost the company more than she was worth to it.

The Pregnancy Discrimination Act does not, despite the urgings of feminist scholars, e.g., Herma Hill Kay, "Equality and Difference: The Case of Pregnancy," 1 Berkeley Women's L.J. 1, 30–31 (1985), require employers to offer maternity leave or take other steps to make it easier for pregnant women to work—to make it as easy, say, as it is for their spouses to continue working during pregnancy. Employers can treat pregnant women as badly as they treat similarly affected but nonpregnant employees, even to the point of "conditioning the availability of an employment benefit on an employee's decision to return to work after the end of the medical disability that pregnancy causes." Maganuco v. Leyden Community High School Dist. 212, 939 F.2d 440, 445 (7th Cir.1991). *Maganuco* and other cases hold that disparate impact is a permissible theory of liability under the Pregnancy Discrimination Act, as it is under other provisions of Title VII. But, properly understood, disparate impact as a theory of liability is a means of dealing with the residues of past discrimination, rather than a warrant for favoritism.

The plaintiff has made no effort to show that if all the pertinent facts were as they are except for the fact of her pregnancy, she would not have been fired. So in the end she has no evidence from which a rational trier of fact could infer that she was a victim of pregnancy discrimination. The Supreme Court noted recently that the age discrimination "law requires the employer to ignore an employee's age . . . ; it does not specify *further* characteristics that an employer must also ignore," such as pension expense. Hazen Paper Co. v. Biggins, 507 U.S. 604, 612, 113 S.Ct. 1701, 1707, 123 L.Ed.2d 338 (1993) (emphasis in original). The Pregnancy Discrimination Act requires the employer to ignore an employee's pregnancy, but * * * not her absence from work, unless the employer overlooks the comparable absences of nonpregnant employees * * * in which event it would not be ignoring pregnancy after all. Of course there may be no comparable absences, but we do not understand Troupe to be arguing that the reason she did not present evidence that nonpregnant employees were treated more favorably than she is that * * * there is no comparison group of Lord & Taylor employees. What to do in such a case is an issue for a case in which the issue is raised. (We do not even know how long Troupe's maternity leave was supposed to be.) We doubt that finding a comparison group would be that difficult. Troupe would be halfway home if she could find one nonpregnant employee of Lord & Taylor who had not been fired when about to begin a leave similar in length to hers. She either did not look, or did not find. Given the absence of other evidence, her failure to present any comparison evidence doomed her case.

Notes on Troupe

1. How would you characterize the tone of this opinion? Do you think it is condescending and hostile to Kimberly Troupe? What assumptions does Posner make about "morning" sickness? See Ann C. McGinley and Jeffrey W. Stempel, Condescending Contradictions: Richard Posner's Pragmatism and Pregnancy Discrimination, 46 Fla. L. Rev. 193 (1994).

2. In *Troupe*, Posner uses a hypothetical (the African American male employee in need of a kidney transplant) to dismiss any inference that Lord & Taylor discriminated against Troupe on the basis of her pregnancy although her boss had said that she was being fired because she was not expected to return to work after her baby was born. According to Posner, his hypothetical kidney patient "implies that [Lord & Taylor] fired Ms. Troupe not because she was pregnant but because she cost the company more than she was worth to it." But is Posner's hypothetical kidney patient actually on point? Do you think that Lord & Taylor would have been as likely to infer that the kidney patient would not return from short-term disability leave as it was to infer that Troupe would not return from maternity leave? Wouldn't a closer analogy be a man who had a recent record of tardiness related to medical problems, who was about to go on a medical leave which would entirely cure those problems, and who expected to become a new father during his leave? Do you think that Lord & Taylor would have been as likely to fire the about-to-be father? In the non-hypothetical real world, is there any truly analogous comparison group Troupe could use?

3. The *Troupe* case reached the Seventh Circuit on appeal from a district court decision granting summary judgment for the employer. Thus, affirmance was appropriate only if no reasonable fact finder could conclude that Troupe was dismissed because she was pregnant or a woman. Further, once a plaintiff shows that either sex or pregnancy played a *part* in an employment decision, the burden shifts to the employer to prove "by a preponderance of the evidence that it would have made the same decision even if it had not taken the plaintiff's gender into account." Price Waterhouse v. Hopkins, 490 U.S. 228, 258, 109 S.Ct. 1775, 104 L.Ed. 268 (1989). In *Price Waterhouse*, the plaintiff's evidence that gender had played a part consisted of evidence of sexual stereotyping. Hopkins was told that she did not make partner because she was too macho and aggressive and that her chances would improve if she would "walk more femininely, talk more femininely, dress more femininely, wear make-up, have her hair styled, and wear jewelry." Id. at 278. On the basis of this and similar evidence, the Court held that Hopkins demonstrated that sex was a factor, and the burden was now on her employer to demonstrate that it would have reached the same decision had it not considered her sex.

Did Troupe present evidence of sex stereotyping analogous to that presented in *Price Waterhouse*? Do you think that a reasonable fact finder might conclude that Kimberly Troupe had at least presented evidence that sex (which includes pregnancy) played *a role* in Lord and Taylor's decision? Is it credible (given her supervisor's explanation) that her pregnancy played *no role* in the decision to fire her? Isn't it likely that Lord & Taylor's assessment of the odds of Troupe returning from leave were affected by the fact that it was pregnancy leave and that she would be a new mother at the end of it? Can one seriously argue that an employer would be as likely to conclude that a male worker, about to become a father while on an extended medical leave, would not return to his job? How does Posner handle the social expectations and stereotypes about pregnant women and new mothers? For a discussion of stereotyping missed by the courts in *Troupe* and similar cases, see Judith G. Greenberg, The Pregnancy Discrimination Act: Legitimating Discrimination Against Pregnant Women in the Workforce, 50 Me. L. Rev. 225 (1998).

4. How does Posner justify the result in *Troupe*? Why does he conclude that his interpretation is the only possible one and that there is no issue for trial? Why didn't *Troupe* have enough evidence to survive summary judgment with her combination of the timing of her firing (when her morning sickness could no longer be a problem) and her supervisor's statement that she was being terminated because she was not expected to return to work after her leave? Does Posner pick her case apart by looking at one element at time and dismissing each because it, standing alone, would not be sufficient, though of course the plaintiff has not relied only on any one fact?

5. Look carefully at Posner's decision, beginning with the sentences just before his assertion that the "great, the undeniable fact is the plaintiff's tardiness." In the preceding paragraphs, Posner has explained that various combinations of evidence can create a triable issue of fact so that summary judgement is inappropriate. His first analytical sentence, applying Title VII law to the facts before him, is: "the great, the undeniable fact is the plaintiff's tardiness." How is this great fact relevant (on the employer's motion for summary judgment) given Troupe's testimony her supervisor told her she was being fired because she was not expected to return to work from her maternity leave?

6. Was Kimberly *Troupe* discriminated against because she was about to become a new mother and hadn't even been tough enough to work her scheduled hours during her pregnancy? For other cases in which women seem to have lost their jobs for being about to become mothers, see Piantanida v. Wyman Center, Inc. 116 F.3d 340 (8th Cir.1997) (affirming dismissal on summary judgment of plaintiff's claim that she had been discriminated against because she was a "new mom" on the ground that discrimination against new parents is gender-neutral); Bass v. Chemical Banking Corp., 1996 WL 374151 (S.D.N.Y.1996) (dismissing on summary judgment plaintiff's claim that she had been discriminated against because she was the mother of young children with respect to a promotion opportunity—which went to a woman without children—because the plaintiff failed to show that men with young children were treated more favorably than she). Are the cases in which about-to-be new mothers lose consistent with Phillips v. Martin Marietta, 400 U.S. 542, 91 S.Ct. 496, 27 L.Ed.2d 613 (1971) (described in the introduction to this section on mothers in the workplace)? For a discussion of recent new mother cases, see Martha Chamallas, Mothers and Disparate Treatment, 44 Will. L. Rev. 337 (1999).

7. The FMLA had yet to be enacted at the time Kimberly Troupe was fired. Would it have helped her?

8. How would a formal equality feminist analyze *Troupe*? Would she find discrimination in violation of Title VII? What about a dominance feminist? A relational feminist?

9. Would it surprise you to learn that Posner is not a supporter of the PDA?

> The requirement that the employer not differentiate among its employees on the basis of pregnancy is analytically the same as a requirement that the employer pay the same retirement benefits to male and female employees despite women's superior longevity, or a requirement that the employer grant maternity leave (in other words, agree to reinstate female employees who take time off to have or take care of their babies). In all three cases, the law compels the employer to ignore a real difference in the average cost of male and female employees. The result is inefficient, but a more interesting point is that it may not benefit women as a whole.

Richard A. Posner, An Economic Analysis of Sex Discrimination Laws, 56 U. Chi. L. Rev. 1311, 1332 (1989). Posner's point is that employers may be reluctant to hire women of child-bearing age if they must ignore real costs associated with employing them. Do you agree that the PDA has likely done more harm than good? In deciding *Troupe*, was Posner influenced by his antipathy to the statute he was interpreting? See McGinley and Stempel, above note 1, at 245–251 (noting that Posner also regards bans on sex discrimination as unlikely to help women).

Text Note: Pregnancy and Disparate Impact

In *Troupe*, Posner cites his earlier decision in Maganuco v. Leyden Community High School Dist. 212, 939 F.2d 440, 445 (7th Cir.1991) for the position that "[e]mployers can treat pregnant women as badly as they treat similarly affected but nonpregnant employees, even to the point of conditioning the availability of an employment benefit on an employee's decision to return to work after the end of the medical disability that pregnancy causes." Rebecca Maganuco claimed that her employer had discriminated on the basis of pregnancy both in terms of disparate treatment (the type of discrimination analyzed in *Troupe*) and in terms of disparate impact. As noted earlier, disparate impact occurs when an employer adopts a rule or standard that has a negative impact on a protected group; once the plaintiff shows that a policy has such an impact, the employer must drop the policy unless it demonstrates that it is sufficiently "job related" or a "business necessity." Disparate impact was first recognized and is most likely to be applied in the context of an occupational qualification or selection procedure. In that context, the question is whether a requirement or procedure disproportionately leaves out of the candidate pool qualified candidates who are (depending on the claim) African American, female, etc. In order to establish a disparate impact case, the plaintiff shows, for example, and 50% of graduates of law schools are women but that only 20% of those hired by the defendant law firm are women. Note that there are two figures for comparison here: the percentage of women in the applicant pool and the percentage of those hired who are women.

Although plaintiffs have tried to bring disparate impact claims based on pregnancy-discrimination challenges to employer rules of various kinds, these claims tend to fail. One problem is that in pregnancy cases, unlike disparate impact claims in other settings, there is no obvious way to determine impact. In Maganuco, for example, the plaintiff was a high school teacher who challenged a provision in the union contract prohibiting the use of accrued sick days for a (paid) disability leave followed by an (unpaid) maternity leave. Thus, a pregnant teacher had to choose between using her accrued sick days (accumulated at the rate of 17 days a year) and taking a maternity leave (of up to one and a half semesters without pay).If these leaves could be combined, many pregnant women would be able to take a leave for a full school year to care for a newborn. But under the policy, women had to choose between one and a half semesters of unpaid leave and paid leave for the period of their accrued sick days. In a sense, such a policy had a disparate impact on women, since only women qualified for maternity leave and only maternity leave could not follow a period of disability during which the employee used accrued sick days. Women were obviously worse off under the school district's policies than they would have been under a policy that allowed women to combine maternity leave with disability leave using accrued sick days. But there are other possible comparisons. Women were better off under the school district's policy than they would have been if the employer provided no maternity leave, just leave during the period of actual disability associated with childbirth.

There are no two obvious numbers to compare in this situation. Indeed, Rebecca Maganuco argued that the "leave policy leads women who choose to have children to accumulate a greater number of sick days than men or than women who choose to forego childbirth," id. at 444, though this result wouldn't necessarily follow. Not surprisingly, the Seventh Circuit noted that Maganuco failed to present evidence demonstrating this alleged disparate impact. The case therefore lacked the "gross statistical disparities" necessary for a disparate impact case.

Maganuco also argued that the school district's leave policies had a discriminatory impact "by forcing women to choose between using their accumulated sick days for pregnancy-related disability and taking maternity leave subsequent to childbirth." Id. But the court rejected this argument on the ground that the PDA only requires that pregnant women be given the same benefits available to others. Moreover, noted Posner, the impact Maganuco was challenging depended not just on the district's policies and the biological fact of pregnancy, but on the teacher's "choice to forego returning to work immediately in favor of spending time with her newborn child." Id. (Posner noted that the school districts policy extending a one and a half semester leave to new mothers and not to new fathers probably did violate Title VII. See 939 F.2d at 445 n.1.)

Although the *Maganuco* court held that a disparate impact pregnancy discrimination claim was possible, it did not see a valid one in the case before it. This seems to be the general fate of such claims.

Notes on Pregnancy and Disparate Impact

1. What role does the fact that a woman "chooses" to spend some time with her new baby play in Posner's analysis? Do you think this use is fair? Is

this choice the equivalent of a vacation in Tahiti or is it itself a productive and labor-intensive enterprise which can be expected to contribute to the general good? If you were writing the opinion, what would you say about the relevance of the mother's "choice" to the question of whether her needs and those of her baby should receive some accommodation from an employer?

2. Although Posner talks about the function served by disparate impact claims and states "that disparate impact is a permissible theory of liability under the Pregnancy Discrimination Act," he did not apply it in *Troupe*. Why not? What does he see as the problem with applying disparate impact in that case?

3. Would you regard as favoritism policies designed to make it as easy for women to combine pregnancy and parenting with wage work as it is for men to combine (their partner's) pregnancy and parenting with wage work? Would Posner?

4. Although there is no obvious comparison to use to determine impact in pregnancy cases, courts could interpret Title VII's ban on policies having a disparate impact on pregnant women as requiring employers to make reasonable accommodations to the needs of pregnant workers. After all, when pregnant workers need accommodation (including jobs less hazardous to the fetus), it is because a rule or policy makes it more difficult for them than for other workers to continue to work. This approach has been taken by Canadian courts interpreting very similar statutes. Why haven't American courts taken such an approach? Ruth Colker suggests that the explanation is the prevalence of "judges who are imbued in the philosophy of law and economics" in American courts. Colker, Pregnancy, Parenting, and Capitalism, 58 Ohio State L. J. 61, 82 (1997). What do you think explains this difference? Would you favor the Canadian approach?

IN RE: CARNEGIE CENTER ASSOCIATES

United States Court of Appeals, Third Circuit, 1997.

129 F.3d 290.

* * *

> [Deborah Rhett, an unmarried African American woman working as a secretary, was fired during her maternity leave. The employer needed to eliminate a secretarial position, and picked Rhett's, not on the basis of seniority or merit, but because she was out of the office. When Rhett informed her supervisors and coworkers of her pregnancy, the company controller and financial officer asked if planned on marrying, and one said that getting married was "the right thing to do." Carnegie had an informal policy under which it tried to hold jobs open for workers on maternity leave when possible, and had done so for two others in the past. The district court affirmed the order of the Bankruptcy court which had dismissed Rhett's claim of discrimination on the basis of race and sex.]

Rhett argues that Carnegie terminated her employment solely because of her absence and her absence was due solely to her pregnancy and related medical conditions. Consequently, in her view Carnegie terminated her employment because of her pregnancy. The Supreme Court has held that under the Age Discrimination in Employment Act an employer must ignore an employee's age in certain employment decisions, but not any other characteristics such as pension expense. *Hazen Paper Co. v. Biggins, 507 U.S. 604, 612, 113 S. Ct. 1701, 1707, 123 L. Ed. 2d 338 (1993).* The Court of Appeals for the Seventh Circuit has held, by analogy to Hazen, that the PDA "requires the employer to ignore an employee's pregnancy, but ... not her absence from work, unless the employer overlooks the comparable absences of non-pregnant employees...." *Troupe, 20 F.3d at 738.* This holding is entirely consistent with the plain language of the PDA * * *. This view eliminates Rhett's theory of transitivity, that if A (termination) is caused by B (absence) which is caused by C (pregnancy), then C causes A. Other courts similarly have held that "the PDA does not force employers to pretend that absent employees are present whenever their absences are caused by pregnancy."

* * *

This case is unusual in that Carnegie terminated an employee who had performed satisfactorily solely because of an economically justified reduction in force while she was away on maternity leave.

Nevertheless, the law covering this case is clear from the view of the Court of Appeals of the Seventh Circuit which it set forth in *Troupe*, that an employer legitimately can consider an employee's absence on maternity leave in making an adverse employment decision; [this view] is consistent with and, indeed, is compelled by the plain language of the PDA. Thus, *Troupe* properly requires the plaintiff employee seeking to recover under the PDA to show that the employer treated her differently than non-pregnant employees on disability leave. * * * Thus, we cannot find, as Rhett urges, that the mere consideration of an employee's absence on maternity leave is a per se violation of the PDA. In short, the PDA does not require an employer to reinstate an employee merely because she has been absent on maternity leave. Rather, the PDA is a shield against discrimination, not a sword in the hands of a pregnant employee.

Rhett has not made a showing that Carnegie treated her differently than it would have treated a non-pregnant employee absent on disability leave. Of course, it was difficult for her to make such a showing because Carnegie never has had an employee on disability leave for a protracted period for a reason other than pregnancy. Thus, we must affirm the district court's denial of her PDA claim for the reasons indicated.

* * *

In reaching our result, we have not overlooked Rhett's argument that this case is somehow different than a case based on a claim of discrimination predicated either on race or gender, because she bases her claim on both race and gender. This argument adds nothing to her case because regardless of the basis for her claim of discrimination, she cannot establish that the legitimate reason that Carnegie proffered for terminating her was pretextual. Furthermore, we have not ignored Rhett's argument that Carnegie's termination of her position had a discriminatory impact on her based on her race. Rather, we reject this contention as entirely insubstantial for an employee is not insulated from having her position lawfully terminated merely because she happens to be a minority.

* * *

CONCLUSION

We hold, in agreement with the Court of Appeals for the Seventh Circuit [and] the plain language of the PDA, * * * that an employee alleging a PDA violation must show that her employer treated her differently than it would have treated an employee on leave for a temporary disability other than pregnancy. It is not a violation of the PDA for an employer to consider an employee's absence on maternity leave in making an adverse employment decision if it also would have considered the absence of an employee on a different type of disability leave in the same way. Inasmuch as Carnegie asserted that Rhett's absence from work, rather than her pregnancy, was the reason for her termination, and Rhett has failed to show that this assertion was pretextual, her claim fails.

In view of our conclusions, we will affirm the judgment of the district court * * *.

MCKEE, CIRCUIT JUDGE, dissenting.

I agree that Deborah Rhett's claim of racial discrimination was properly dismissed. However, I respectfully dissent because I believe that the district court erred in affirming the bankruptcy court's dismissal of Rhett's claim of sex discrimination. * * *

Relying upon *Hazen Paper Company v. Biggins, 507 U.S. 604, 113 S. Ct. 1701, 123 L. Ed. 2d 338 (1993),* the majority states that "the Supreme Court has held that under the Age Discrimination in Employment Act an employer must ignore an employee's age in certain employment decisions, but not any other characteristics such as pension expense." However, I believe that *Hazen Paper* [supports the plaintiff in this case.] * * *

> [In *Hazen Paper*, the plaintiff was fired a few weeks before his pension rights would have vested based on his years of service. The Supreme Court held that firing an employee to prevent his pension rights from vesting under a plan providing for vesting based on years of service did not necessarily violate the ADEA (though it would violate ERISA). The Court explained that such a termination would violate the ADEA only if the employer fired the employee because of his age, which was analytically distinct from his years of service. The Court did remand for consideration of whether the jury had sufficient evidence to find a violation of the ADEA.]

Pregnancy and absence are not, however, analytically distinct, and an employer cannot punish for the absence occasioned by pregnancy under Title VII. As noted above, that statute states that it is an unlawful employment practice to "discharge any individual ... or otherwise discriminate ... because ... of sex," and, after the PDA, that includes discrimination "on the basis of pregnancy ... or related medical conditions." That protection is meaningless unless it is intended to extend to the "temporary" absence from employment that is unavoidable in most pregnancies. Thus, the absence endemic to pregnancy, unlike factors that may sometimes be a proxy for age, has to be protected under the facts of this case. In *Hazen Paper,* it was the employee's years of service, not his age, that occasioned the vesting of his pension. The Court was very careful to note that

> We do not consider the special case where an employee is about to vest ... as a result of his age, rather than years of service, and the employer fires the employee in order to prevent vesting. That case is not presented here. Our holding is simply that an employer does not violate the ADEA just by interfering with an older employee's pension benefits that would have vested by virtue of years of service.

507 U.S. at 613. I believe that Rhett's situation under the PDA is much closer to the situation of an employee whose pension is vesting because of age than to the plight of the plaintiff in *Hazen Paper.* Accordingly, the holding in Hazen Paper does not assist the majority nearly as much as first appears.[4]

"In using the broad phrase 'women affected by pregnancy, childbirth and related medical conditions,' the [PDA] makes clear that its protection extends to the whole range of matters concerning the childbearing process." H.R. Rep. 95–948. The holding in *Troupe*, and the majority's holding here, remove a substantial portion of the protection Congress intended. *Troupe*'s position was terminated because of conditions related to pregnancy (tardiness occasioned by her morning sickness). I do not understand, therefore, why she was not terminated "because of ... her pregnancy," in violation of Title VII.

* * *

Carnegie clearly did not put Rhett's departure on maternity leave to one side when deciding to terminate her. Rhett's absence from work was

4. I do not mean to suggest by this that the PDA requires an employer to necessarily take affirmative steps to make it easier for a pregnant employee to work. See *Troupe,* 20 F.3d at 738 ("The Pregnancy Discrimination Act does not ... require employers to ... take ... steps to make it easier for pregnant women to work."). The PDA does not provide for accommodation as does the ADA.

Nor do I suggest that an employee who is pregnant can not be fired for reasons that are not occasioned by pregnancy. For example, if Carnegie decided, in good faith, to eliminate everyone with a certain salary grade based upon its business judgment, Rhett could be terminated if she was at that salary grade whether she was on pregnancy leave or not because the termination would not be based upon a factor endemic to her pregnancy.

so inextricably intertwined with pregnancy, her protected trait, as to make the two inseparable. In its "theory of transitivity," the majority separates the events in this case into discrete entities that suggest the causal relationship between Rhett's pregnancy and her termination. The majority too easily rejects [Rhett's] position. See Maj. Op. ("This view eliminates Rhett's theory of transitivity, that if A (termination) is caused by B (absence) which is caused by C (pregnancy), then C causes A.").

TERMINATION BECAUSE OF PREGNANCY

An employer can not insulate itself from the reach of Title VII by an action that appears neutral, yet has the functional effect of disparately treating an individual based upon a protected trait. See Griggs, 401 U.S. at 430. Carnegie's action is the functional equivalent of terminating Rhett because she was pregnant.

* * *

CONCLUSION

For the reasons stated above, I would reverse the decision of the district court and remand this matter to the bankruptcy court for a determination of whether Rhett would have been terminated had her pregnancy-related absence been put aside.

* * *

Notes on Carnegie

1. The *Carnegie* majority holds that it was not discriminatory to fire Rhett if the company "would have considered the absence of an employee on a different type of disability leave in the same way." But there was no evidence of how the company would have treated a similarly situated man because Carnegie had never had "an employee on disability leave for a protracted period for a reason other than pregnancy." Do you nevertheless think that Rhett's race and pregnancy were in all likelihood factors in Carnegie's choice of whom to fire? How might her race have been relevant; what stereotypes about African American women might have been in play? Why does even the dissent agree that her race claim was properly dismissed? What would Rhett have to show to prove that race and pregnancy (particularly for a black woman outside of marriage) likely influenced Carnegie's decision to fire her rather than the least competent secretary? Why does it seem to be so difficult to frame that combined claim in a way recognizable by Title VII?

2. Take a close look at paragraphs two and three of the dissent in *Carnegie*. Is firing a worker because she is about to go on pregnancy leave (and therefore costs more to the employer than she is worth, as Posner describes the situation in *Troupe*) or because she is on leave and someone has to be cut from the payroll (as in *Carnegie*),more like firing an older worker whose pension rights are about to vest because of years in service (analytically distinct from age) or one whose rights are about to vest with

age (obviously not analytically distinct from age)? What point does Judge McKee make in these paragraphs?

3. With whom do you agree, the *Carnegie* majority or dissent, on the causation point? Was Rhett fired because of her pregnancy when she was fired because of her absence which occurred because of her pregnancy?

4. In this case the court concedes that the plaintiff could not possibly compare the employer's treatment of her with the employer's treatment of other workers; the company had never had anyone on extended disability who was not pregnant. Does the PDA protect women only at employers large enough to have a history of extended disability leaves for workers in varying circumstances? Or is finding a comparison group for pregnant workers likely to be impossible in many cases even at large employers?

5. Protection of pregnant workers is important for a number of reasons. The woman and her baby may need the medical insurance routinely given during leaves and may be uninsured without leave. Both may need the income that would come with her return to work after the baby's birth. Losing one's job at any time can be traumatic, and losing one while pregnant and facing unusual costs as well as the inability to work for some period of time is likely to be particularly traumatic. Trauma can have all sorts of negative effects on pregnancy and its outcome. A significant part of the persistent wage gap between women and men is attributable to the fact that many women take time off from wage work when and after their children are born. Being able to combine childcare (including pregnancy) and wage work is essential for women's economic equality. See Samuel Issacharoff and Elaine Rosenblum, Women and the Workplace: Accommodating the Demands of Pregnancy, 94 Colum. L. Rev. 2154 (1994). Can you think of more effective ways to protect women during pregnancy than the PDA?

BROWN v. RENTOKIL

Case C–394/96, [1998] ECR I–4185

European Union Case Law

COURT OF JUSTICE

(1998)

[In each case before it, the Court of Justice of the European Union is advised by one of nine Advocates General. The Advocate General delivers an opinion in open court recommending an outcome and rationale. As in this case, the Court routinely adopts the Advocate General's recommendations. The decision below begins with the recommendation of the Advocate General and ends with the judgment of the European Court of Justice.]

Opinion of Mr. Advocate General Ruiz–Jarabo Colomer delivered on 5 February 1998.

* * * Mrs. Brown, the appellant in the main proceedings, was employed as a driver for Rentokil Limited * * * (hereinafter "Rentokil"), the respondent in those proceedings. Her job was mainly to

transport and change Sanitact units in shops and other centres. She became pregnant and informed Rentokil in August 1990.

Her pregnancy later became complicated through a number of interrelated causes, of which details are not given in the documents before the Court. As from 16 August 1990 she submitted a succession of four-week medical certificates mentioning various diagnoses such as "symptoms of pregnancy," "bleeding in pregnancy" or "pregnant back-ache." From that time, until her dismissal, the appellant remained unable to work.

The respondent included a clause in the contract of employment under which any employee, man or women, who was incapable of work for more than 26 weeks without interruption would be dismissed. On 9 November 1990 Mrs. Brown had a meeting with two executives of the company, who informed her that half of the 26–week period had passed and reminded her that her employment contract would be terminated on 8 February 1991 if she was not back at work by that time, following an independent medical examination confirming that she was able to work. Those details were confirmed to her by letter of the same date.

The appellant did not go back to work after receiving that letter. The parties agree that there was never any question of her being able to return to work prior to the [expiration] of the 26–week period. [She gave birth on 22 March 1991.]

* * *

[The courts of Great Britain held that Rentokill did not discriminate on the basis of sex when it fired Mrs. Brown.]

The Community Legislation

The Community provisions of which an interpretation is needed for judgment to be given in this dispute are all contained in [the Equal Treatment Directive], namely Article 2(1) and (3) and Article 5(1) and (2), which provide as follows:

[The Equal Treatment Directive]

Article 2

(1) For the purposes of the following provisions, the principle of equal treatment shall mean that there shall be no discrimination whatsoever on grounds of sex either directly or indirectly by reference in particular to marital or family status.

* * *

(3) This Directive shall be without prejudice to provisions concerning the protection of women, particularly as regards pregnancy and maternity.

Article 5

(1) Application of the principle of equal treatment with regard to working conditions, including the conditions governing dismissal, means that men and women shall be guaranteed the same conditions without discrimination on grounds of sex.

(2) To this end, Member States shall take the measures necessary to ensure that:

(a) any laws, regulations and administrative provisions contrary to the principle of equal treatment shall be abolished

(b) any provisions contrary to the principle of equal treatment which are included in collective agreements, individual contracts of employment, internal rules of undertakings or in rules governing the independent occupations and professions shall be, or may be declared, null and void or may be amended.

* * *

On 19 October 1992 the Council adopted [the Maternity Leave and Pregnancy Discrimination Directive] in order to protect the health and safety of pregnant workers who have given birth or are breastfeeding * * *, which requires the Member States to adopt, before 19 October 1994, among others provisions needed to ensure that female workers enjoy a continuous period of maternity leave of at least 14 weeks, allocated before and/or after confinement, including two weeks compulsory leave. It also prohibits dismissal of a pregnant worker, in the following terms:

[The Pregnancy Directive]

Article 10

(1) Member States shall take the necessary measures to prohibit the dismissal of workers [who are pregnant, have recently given birth or are breastfeeding] during the period from the beginning of their pregnancy to the end of the maternity leave ... save in exceptional circumstances not connected with their condition which are permitted under national legislation and/or practice and, where applicable, provided that the competent authority has given its consent. ...

However, since Mrs. Brown was dismissed at the beginning of 1991, there is no need to interpret [the Pregnancy Directive in this case].

* * *

The National Legislation

* * *

[At the time of Mrs. Brown's dismissal, a woman was entitled to return to her job after pregnancy provided that she had been working for her employer for at least two years at the start of her 11th week of pregnancy, but Mrs. Brown had not been working for her employer long enough for this provision to apply to her. In addition, pregnant women, including Mrs. Brown, are entitled to up to 18 weeks paid leave at birth under British law.]

* * *

[Observations and Recommendation to the European Court of Justice]

* * * [This Court's earlier decisions in this area] illustrate well the thesis of Lucinda M. Finley, which can be summarized in the following statement:

> The fact that women bear children and men do not has been the major impediment to women becoming fully integrated into the public world of the workplace.[14]

* * *

What is involved here, ultimately, is the duty incumbent upon us all of progressively removing all traces of the discrimination which women have suffered over the centuries, a duty to which the institutions of the European Union are so deeply committed.

* * *

Starting from the premise that equality, as defined by the Constitutional Court of one of the Member States, "is not a reality or an abstract mathematical concept but rather unequal treatment of that which is unequal or equal treatment of that which is similar or alike" * * * and having regard to the settled case-law of the Court of Justice to the effect that "discrimination can arise only through the application of different rules to comparable situations or the application of the same rule to different situations," * * * I shall now consider whether the dismissal of a pregnant woman on grounds of incapacity for work arising from her condition occurs under the same conditions as dismissal of a man for incapacity for work of the same duration, arising from an illness.

* * *

I wonder whether it is still necessary, at this stage, to repeat the self-evident fact that pregnancy is a situation which affects only women, since only they can become pregnant. Pregnancy, besides being a biological situation pertaining exclusively to women, is a period limited in time, during which there may occur not only the well-known phenomenon of morning sickness but also complications such as risks of miscarriage or premature contractions associated with stress, which may compel the woman to rest absolutely for periods which may extend from two or three months to the whole of the period of pregnancy.

This Court emphatically stated, [in an earlier decision], that "the dismissal of a female worker on account of repeated periods of sick leave

14. Lucinda M. Finley, "Transcending Equality Theory: A Way out of the Maternity and the Worplace Debate," Columbia Law Review, Vol. 86:1118, p. 1119.

which are not attributed to pregnancy or confinement does not constitute direct discrimination on grounds of sex, inasmuch as such periods of sick leave would lead to the dismissal of a male worker in the same circumstances."

Can it be said, however, that the dismissal of a pregnant woman on account of repeated periods of sick leave attributable to pregnancy occurs under the same conditions as the dismissal of a man who has been on sick leave for the same period? In my opinion the answer is no.

Without wishing to meddle in matters which are the province of doctors, I should make it clear that, although * * * pregnancy is not in any way comparable with a pathological condition, no one is unaware of the existence of "high-risk pregnancies" which occur—the following being examples, not an exhaustive list—when there is a history of premature or still-births, when the placenta is lower than normal, when the woman has undergone in vitro fertilization treatment, and in cases where the woman suffers from a heart condition or diabetes. The main characteristic of such pregnancies is not that they cause the woman to be "ill" but that, normally, they require her to remain under strict medical supervision and, in some of the cases mentioned above, to rest absolutely for several months or, sometimes, throughout her pregnancy.

I cannot share the view that, in situations of that kind, where the woman is not suffering from any illness but is simply pregnant, it can be said that, in the event of dismissal for repeated absences, she is dismissed under the same conditions as a man who has been absent through illness for the same period of time. The same reasoning will apply where the incapacity for work derives from the fact that pregnancy has aggravated an existing illness or brought about conditions which may be classified as real illness.

Whilst the situation of a pregnant worker whose pregnancy prevents her from working and that of a male worker who is ill coincide in so far as neither of them can, for a period, carry out the tasks involved in her or his employment, important differences distinguish them: only women may find themselves at some time during their working life in a situation where they are prevented from working because of incapacity arising from a pregnancy and, in most cases, a woman's incapacity for work arising from pregnancy will end on a date known in advance with more or less accuracy, when she gives birth.

These factors appear to have been taken into account by the domestic law applicable in most Member States at the time of the material events in this case, which was fairly similar—only the legislation in the United Kingdom and Ireland differed radically.

Thus, [for example,] in Germany there was specific protection for women from the start of pregnancy until after confinement, whereby in that period dismissal was subject to administrative authorisation. In Denmark, the Ministry of Employment considered it discriminatory to take account, for the purposes of dismissal, of absences due to incapacity for work attributable to pregnancy, before a woman gave birth. In

France, the employer could not dismiss a woman during pregnancy, during maternity leave or during the four weeks thereafter. * * *

I consider that the dismissal of a woman whilst she is pregnant, on account of unfitness for work caused by her pregnancy, by taking into consideration a situation in which only women can find themselves, constitutes direct discrimination contrary to Article 5(1) of [the Equal Treatment Directive].

* * * If that were not the case, and the future of an employed woman, on becoming pregnant, could depend on whether or not her pregnancy involved excessive complications, I would be obliged to state, paraphrasing Papinian, that despite the passage of the centuries "there are many points in our [Community] law in which the condition of females is inferior to that of males."[42]

* * *

[Judgment of the European Court of Justice]

* * *

According to settled case-law of the Court of Justice, the dismissal of a female worker on account of pregnancy, or essentially on account of pregnancy, can affect only women and therefore constitutes direct discrimination on grounds of sex.

* * *

It was precisely in view of the harmful effects which the risk of dismissal may have on the physical and mental state of women who are pregnant, women who have recently given birth or women who are breastfeeding, including the particularly serious risk that pregnant women may be prompted voluntarily to terminate their pregnancy, that the Community legislature, pursuant to Article 10 of [the Pregnancy Directive] on the introduction of measures to encourage improvements in the safety and health at work of pregnant workers and workers who have recently given birth or are breastfeeding * * * provided for special protection to be given to women, by prohibiting dismissal during the period from the beginning of their pregnancy to the end of their maternity leave. Article 10 of [the Pregnancy Directive] provides that there is to be no exception to, or derogation from, the prohibition of dismissal of pregnant women during that period, save in exceptional cases not connected with their condition.

* * *

[D]ismissal of a woman during pregnancy cannot be based on her inability, as a result of her condition, to perform the duties which she is contractually bound to carry out. If such an interpretation were adopted, the protection afforded by Community law to a woman during pregnancy

42. "Papinianus libro trigensimo primo quaestionum. In multis iuris nostri articulis deterior est condicio feminarum quam masculorum." The Digest of Justinian, University of Pennsylvania Press, Vol. I, Book One (Human Status), p. 16.

would be available only to pregnant women who were able to comply with the conditions of their employment contracts, with the result that the provisions of [the Equal Treatment Directive] would be rendered ineffective.

* * *

It is also clear from all the foregoing considerations that * * * where a woman is absent owing to illness resulting from pregnancy or childbirth, and that illness arose during pregnancy and persisted during and after maternity leave, her absence not only during maternity leave but also during the period extending from the start of her pregnancy to the start of her maternity leave cannot be taken into account for computation of the period justifying her dismissal under national law. As to her absence after maternity leave, this may be taken into account under the same conditions as a man's absence, of the same duration, through incapacity for work.

* * *

It is well settled that discrimination involves the application of different rules to comparable situations or the application of the same rule to different situations. * * *

Where it is relied on to dismiss a pregnant worker because of absences due to incapacity for work resulting from her pregnancy, * * * a contractual term, applying both to men and to women, is applied in the same way to different situations since * * * the situation of a pregnant worker who is unfit for work as a result of disorders associated with her pregnancy cannot be considered to be the same as that of a male worker who is ill and absent through incapacity for work for the same length of time.

Consequently, application of that contractual term in circumstances such as the present constitutes direct discrimination on grounds of sex.

* * *

[Ruling]

On those grounds, THE COURT * * * hereby rules: Articles 2(1) and 5(1) of [the Equal Treatment Directive], on the implementation of the principle of equal treatment for men and women as regards access to employment, vocational training and promotion, and working conditions, preclude dismissal of a female worker at any time during her pregnancy for absences due to incapacity for work caused by illness resulting from that pregnancy.

The fact that a female worker has been dismissed during her pregnancy on the basis of a contractual term providing that the employer may dismiss employees of either sex after a stipulated number of weeks of continuous absence does not affect the answer given.

Notes on the European Law of Sex and Pregnancy Discrimination

1. Compare the tone of the decision of the European Court of Justice and that of the Seventh Circuit in *Troupe* and *Maganuco* and the Third Circuit in *Carnegie* in terms of their attitudes toward the pregnant worker. How and where does the European Court express its concern for the well-being of the woman and the child? Are similar concerns ever expressed by the American courts? What do you think explains this difference? See Ruth Colker, Pregnancy, Parenting, and Capitalism, 58 Ohio State L. J. 61, 72–73 (1997) (discussing dominance of economic analysis in PDA discussions combined with a failure to consider the needs of the newborn, and noting in particular Posner's "uncaring and callous consideration of the needs of the newborn" in Maganuco). Should the needs of the newborn be considered in creating rights for pregnant workers?

2. In reaching its decision, the European Court of Justice considers the "the harmful effects which the risk of dismissal may have on the physical and mental state of women who are pregnant, women who have recently given birth or women who are breastfeeding, including the particularly serious risk that pregnant women may be prompted voluntarily to terminate their pregnancy." Are these concerns paternalistic or troubling in any other way? Is it dangerous to provide a pregnant woman with some of the supports she needs in order to be able to afford to bear and raise a child?

3. Compare the references to American feminists in *Troupe* (Herma Hill Kay) and *Brown* (Lucinda Finley), particularly the attitude with which they are cited. Compare the United States and Europe in terms of their commitment to social safety nets and rugged individualism. Why might European culture be more open to feminist arguments on these issues?

4. Compare the American decisions throughout this text (and those you have read elsewhere) with the European Court of Justice in terms of strength of commitment to equality in the real world. In *Brown*, the Advocate General states: "What is involved here, ultimately, is the duty incumbent upon us all of progressively removing all traces of the discrimination which women have suffered over the centuries, a duty to which the institutions of the European Union are so deeply committed." The European Court of Justice has itself "expanded the equal pay principle [of the Treaty governing the European Union] into a general equality right between women and men which exists at the core of EU law." Elizabeth F. Defeis, The Treaty of Amsterdam: The Next Step Towards Gender Equality, 23 B.C. Int'l & Comp. L. Rev. 1, 6 (1999). The Treaty is the European equivalent of the United States Constitution, and the European Court of Justice is the equivalent of the United States Supreme Court. Can you imagine any justice on our Supreme Court describing sex equality as "existing at the core of our constitutional framework"?

5. Compare the benefits and protections available a pregnant worker in Great Britain before *Brown* and after *Brown* with those available to a pregnant worker in the United States today.

6. In his opinion, Advocate General Colomer states that equality "is not a reality or an abstract mathematical concept but rather unequal treatment of that which is unequal or equal treatment of that which is alike." What does he mean by stating that equality is not a reality and not a "mathematical concept"? Is it fair or accurate to state that American courts regard equality as both a reality and a mathematical concept?

7. The Brown opinion stresses that equality requires that comparable situations be treated comparably and that different situations be treated differently. (This notion of equality can be traced back to Aristotle.) Why is the second prong—that those differently situated be treated differently—never mentioned in American cases?

8. Under the European approach, the fact that only women experience pregnancy and childbirth is the basis for regarding discrimination on the basis of pregnancy, childbirth, or any factor related to them (such as being unable to work for a time because of morning sickness or childbirth) as direct sex discrimination; Sex equality demands such a rule because otherwise women workers who become parents would face handicaps not faced by male workers who become parents. In the United States, the fact that only women experience pregnancy and childbirth dooms claims of discrimination unless a woman can find a similarly situated male, an often impossible task. Does the European approach level the playing field for female and male workers or is it a form of favoritism protecting women when men are not protected? What would Posner think?

9. What do you think would happen were legislation proposed in Congress defining pregnancy discrimination as including any negative employment decision based on pregnancy, childbirth, or maternity leave or on any factor related to pregnancy and childbirth (including inability to work)? What arguments would be used to oppose such legislation? Who would support it?

10. Joan Williams proposes the use of Title VII to challenge employer norms structured for ideal workers without any significant caretaking or domestic responsibilities. For example, she suggests that a Title VII disparate impact case be used to challenge the low numbers of women in higher level jobs because of such norms. The plaintiff would argue that the standards for promotion have a disparate impact on women workers and would begin by showing "that, say, 50 percent of entry-level positions but only 20 percent of jobs in the top four corporate levels and a mere 5 percent of top management positions are held by women." Williams, Unbending Gender: Why Family and Work Conflict and What To Do About It 106 (2000). The second issue would be "whether the relative paucity of women in higher-level jobs is caused by the actions of the employer or by women's choice to quit." Id. She suggests that, even if many women regard their failure to stay on the high-powered career track as a matter of their own personal choice, judges need not:

> [The courts'] mandate is to consider whether the constraints women face constitute discrimination. If they do, the fact that many women may have internalized those constraints does not provide employers with an excuse for continuing the discrimination.

Id. Finally, the plaintiff would explain how specific policies, such as not considering part-time employees for partnership, contribute to the disappearance of women at higher level jobs. The burden would then shift to the defendant to show that the challenged practice is a business necessity. Williams concedes that the availability of the business necessity defense in her hypothetical case is arguable either way, but notes that even if the plaintiff loses on this issue, she "can win if she can prove the existence of a less discriminatory alternative, an alternative way of structuring the promotion track that has a less harsh effect on women." Id. at 107.

Given what you have seen in judicial interpretations of Title VII so far in this chapter, what do you think of Williams' proposal? Can you imagine judges concluding that even though women state that they choose not to compete on the partnership track, the employer's failure to consider part-time workers for partner constitutes sex discrimination? See Kathryn Abrams, Cross–Dressing in the Master's Clothes, 109 Yale L. J. 745, 756–57 (2000) (expressing some doubts).

Can you think of ways to promote change that might be more effective? Would you start with legislative changes giving American women paid maternity leave and the right not to be fired during pregnancy or maternity leave for any pregnancy-related reason, rights parallel to those now enjoyed by European women?

Can you think of ways to increase the numbers of women in higher positions? Consumers, clients, shareholders, and government can all exert pressure (in different ways) on employers to adopt affirmative action policies to increase the number of women in higher jobs, but again, American judges seem to be part of the problem. Return to the question of how to increase the numbers of women in higher level jobs after reading the text note comparing attitudes toward affirmative action in the United States and the European Union.

Text Note: Affirmative Action in the United States and the European Union

In a recent article, Elizabeth F. Defeis describes European law as been far more supportive of affirmative action for women than American law.[13] The only United States Supreme Court decision addressing affirmative action in employment for women, Johnson v. Transportation Agency, Santa Clara County, California, 480 U.S. 616, 107 S.Ct. 1442, 94 L.Ed.2d 615 (1987), upheld the legality of the plan before the Court, but that plan was very limited in scope. The Santa Clara plan allowed the county agency to take sex into account as one factor in selecting between qualified applicants for traditionally male jobs "in which women have been significantly underrepresented." Id. at 620–621. The case involved a challenge from a qualified man when, in mid–1980, a qualified woman became the first woman ever to hold a Skilled Craft Worker Position (prior to her promotion, all 238 of the Skilled Craft Workers were men). In upholding the plan, the Court pointed to the "manifest imbalance" of women in these positions and stressed that

13. Elizabeth F. Defeis, The Treaty of Amsterdam: The Next Step Towards Gender Equality, 23 B.C. Int'l & Comp. L. Rev. 1, 21–33 (1999).

the plan did not "unnecessarily trammel the interests" of male employees (during the period from 1978–1982, there were 111 new Skilled Craft positions and 105 went to men), that sex was only one factor taken into account in selecting among qualified applicants, and that the plan was not permanent but a temporary means to reach a balanced workforce, allowing sex to be considered as a factor when considering promotion to positions held disproportionately by men.

Since Johnson, the Supreme Court has been increasingly hostile to affirmative action in the context of race. See Adarand Constructors, Inc. v. Pena, 515 U.S. 200, 115 S.Ct. 2097, 132 L.Ed.2d 158 (1995) (holding unconstitutional Small Business Administration regulations creating a financial incentive for contractors to hire minority subcontractors); City of Richmond v. J.A. Croson Co., 488 U.S. 469, 109 S.Ct. 706, 102 L.Ed.2d 854 (1989) (holding unconstitutional a city's affirmative action plan to set aside a portion of city contracts for minority contractors). The increasing hostility to affirmative action for race—among the general population as well as the Justices of the Supreme Court—has made affirmative action for anyone increasingly unimaginable in the United States.

European law is moving in the opposite direction on affirmative action for women. Article 141 of the Treaty of Rome, the original treaty of the European Union, contained a single provision mandating sex equality: a provision mandating equal pay for equal work regardless of sex.[14] This provision is the basis for the Equal Treatment Directive quoted and interpreted in *Brown* to ban the firing of a worker during pregnancy or maternity leave for any reason connected to pregnancy or maternity leave, including inability to do the job because of temporary disability. The European Court of Justice has interpreted this directive as consistent with a German law giving a preference for civil-service promotions to women—if as qualified as male candidates "unless reasons specific to an individual male candidate tilt the balance in his favor"—for positions in which women are underrepresented. Case C–409/95, Marshall v. Land Nordrhein–Westfalen, [1997] All ER (EC) 865 (1997). The European Court of Justice noted that "such a rule may counteract the prejudicial effects on female candidates" of continuing stereotypes, including the expectation "that women will interrupt their careers more frequently, that owing to household and family duties they will be less flexible in their working hours, or that they will be absent from work more frequently because of pregnancy, childbirth, and breastfeeding." Id. at ¶¶ 28, 29, 31.

The Amsterdam Treaty of 1997 amended the original Treaty of Rome by, among other things, strengthening the commitment to achieving actual equality between women and men. In the words of Elizabeth Defeis:

> The Amsterdam Treaty goes beyond existing EU legislation regarding gender equality in employment and imposes a general obligation on the Union in all of its activities to eliminate inequalities and to promote equality. In addition to clarifying, developing and expanding the EC Treaty provisions on equality, the Amsterdam Treaty adopts the comparable worth concept first set out in [EU legislation] and requires "equal pay for work of equal value."

14. Id. at 2.

The Amsterdam Treaty also adds two new provisions to the Article 141 equality principle. The first provision requires the Council [of Europe] * * * to adopt measures to ensure equal opportunity and equal treatment of men and women in employment. The second provision allows Member States to adopt and maintain positive action provisions. It states:

> With a view to ensuring full equality in practice between men and women in working life, the principle of equal treatment shall not prevent any Member State from maintaining or adopting measures providing for specific advantages in order to make it easier for the underrepresented sex to pursue a vocational activity or to prevent or compensate for disadvantages in professional careers.

Although the term "underrepresented sex" replaces the term "women" as the focus of positive action, a declaration by Member States stipulates that such action should in the first instance aim at improving the situation of women in working life. * * *

Finally, the Amsterdam Treaty expands the scope of the equality principle and allows the Council to take action against discrimination based on sex, race or ethnic origin, religion or belief, disability, age, or sexual orientation within the limits of its powers. * * *

These amendments, declarations, requirements and provisions afford greater flexibility to the equality principle and should influence the [European Court of Justice] in future cases. They affirm the EU's commitment to promote equality between men and women in employment as well as in general. It is clear that Member States may use positive action to promote equality between men and women in employment, not only with respect to access to employment but also with respect to all other aspects of employment.[15]

Notes on Affirmative Action in the United States and the European Union

1. In Marshall v. Land Nordrhein–Westfalen, the European Court of Justice referred to continuing prejudice against and stereotyping of women in justifying a law requiring affirmative action for women against a challenge that it violated the Equal Treatment Directive. American courts, including the Supreme Court, do not speak of continuing discrimination against women. In Johnson v. Transportation Agency, the American sex-based affirmative action case discussed in the text note above, the woman who was promoted under the challenged plan and became the only woman ever to hold a Skilled Craft Worker position in the Santa Clara County Transportation Agency had herself (of course) faced discrimination and stereotyping on the job as well as in the selection process. For example, one member of an interviewing team which rated the candidates was a man who had referred to Joyce as a "rebel-rousing, skirt-wearing person." Yet the Court never once mentioned continuing discrimination as a good reason for affirmative action. And the Court's stress, in *Johnson* and other cases, on

15. Id. at 31–32.

the temporary nature of the plan suggests an assumption that discrimination is over, so that once a balanced work force is achieved, there is no continuing need for affirmative action.

As *Troupe* illustrates, American judicial decisions, again unlike European decisions, ignore that employment has been and continues to be structured to accommodate workers without significant caretaking abilities, i.e., people who are not likely to be mothers. These structural barriers to equality for women are not discrimination in the United States, as *Troupe* again illustrates. Why has the Supreme Court been unwilling to date to recognize that both discrimination and structural barriers are substantial and continuing obstacles to women's equality? Do American courts believe that equality is a reality (as well as a mathematical concept) and *cannot*, therefore, be continuing on any systemic basis? Why are European courts able to see inequality as continuing?

2. Have you been surprised by what you have learned about European law in this chapter? Is it consistent with the self-image of the United States as a leader in women's rights? What explains our conviction that we are at the forefront of sex equality around the world and our parochialism, i.e., our inattention—in the news or elsewhere in popular culture—to more progressive approaches to sex equality?

3. What are the downsides of affirmative action for women? How can individual women be hurt by such policies? What are the advantages of affirmative action for women? Do you support or oppose affirmative action for women? Would you support actual quotas or absolute preferences in any circumstances?

C. SEXUAL HARASSMENT

With the passage of the Equal Pay Act in 1963, women were entitled to equal pay for equal work. The next year, after the passage of the Civil Rights Act of 1964, employers were prohibited from making employment decisions based on sex. But many workplaces remained hostile to women. Women talking about problems in their workplaces identified a variety of practices, including demands for sex in exchange for promotions and constant sexual comments, which created a hostile work environment. Creative practitioners, working with women workers and activists, crafted a theory of "sexual harassment" as a type of sex discrimination prohibited by Title VII. Beginning in the 1970's, women brought sexual harassment test cases under Title VII's prohibition of sex discrimination.[16] These early cases were mostly rejected by trial courts for a variety of reasons, including that (1) the activity at issue was "nothing more than a personal proclivity, peculiarity or mannerism" and not company policy; (2) the company did not derive a benefit from the conduct; and 3) recognition of sexual or amorous activity at the workplace as a violation of Title VII would open the floodgates to vast litigation. Employers also argued that if sexual harassment was sex discrimination because the harasser harassed only people of the opposite sex (and not members of

16. See generally Catharine A. MacKinnon, Sexual Harassment of Working Women (1979).

the same sex), then a bisexual supervisor could harass with impunity both men and women since he would not be discriminating between one sex and another. Because this seemed odd, sexual harassment must be something other than sex discrimination.[17]

Despite a number of early dismissals, plaintiffs persisted in bringing claims of sexual harassment and a court finally recognized sexual harassment as a form of sex discrimination in 1976.[18] Two types of sexual harassment claims emerged: (1) quid pro quo, in which submission to sexual advances is a condition of an individual's hiring, firing, promotion, or receipt of an employment benefit, and (2) hostile environment, in which sexual conduct and/or speech unreasonably interferes with an individual's work performance or creates an intimidating, hostile or offensive working environment.[19]

In 1980, the agency with authority to enforce Title VII, the Equal Employment Opportunity Commission ("EEOC"), issued regulations essentially codifying the judicial holdings recognizing quid pro quo sexual harassment and anticipating the development of the hostile environment theory:

> (a) Harassment on the basis of sex is a violation of Sec. 703 of Title VII. Unwelcome sexual advances, requests for sexual favors, and other verbal or physical conduct of a sexual nature constitute sexual harassment when (1) submission to such conduct is made either explicitly or implicitly a term or condition of an individual's employment, (2) submission to or rejection of such conduct by an individual is used as the basis for employment decisions affecting such individual, or (3) such conduct has the purpose or effect of unreasonably interfering with an individual's work performance or creating an intimidating, hostile, or offensive working environment.
>
> (b) In determining whether alleged conduct constitutes sexual harassment, the Commission will look at the record as a whole and at the totality of the circumstances, such as the nature of the sexual advances and the context in which the alleged incidents occurred. The determination of the legality of a particular action will be made from the facts, on a case by case basis. * * *

29 C.F.R. § 1604.11 (revised July 1, 1992). In 1986, the Supreme Court recognized sexual harassment as a cause of action under Title VII.

MERITOR SAVINGS BANK v. VINSON

Supreme Court of the United States, 1986.

477 U.S. 57, 106 S.Ct. 2399, 91 L.Ed.2d 49.

JUSTICE REHNQUIST delivered the opinion of the Court.

* * *

In 1974, respondent Mechelle Vinson met Sidney Taylor, a vice president of what is now petitioner Meritor Savings Bank (bank) and

17. Corne v. Bausch and Lomb, Inc., 390 F.Supp. 161, 163 (D.Ariz.1975), vacated without op., 562 F.2d 55 (9th Cir.1977).

18. Williams v. Saxbe, 413 F.Supp. 654 (D.D.C.1976).

19. Miller v. Bank of America, 600 F.2d 211 (9th Cir.1979) (quid pro quo); Meritor Savings Bank v. Vinson, 477 U.S. 57, 106 S.Ct. 2399, 91 L.Ed.2d 49 (1986) (harassing environment).

manager of one of its branch offices. When respondent asked whether she might obtain employment at the bank, Taylor gave her an application, which she completed and returned the next day; later that same day Taylor called her to say that she had been hired. With Taylor as her supervisor, respondent started as a teller-trainee, and thereafter was promoted to teller, head teller, and assistant branch manager. She worked at the same branch for four years, and it is undisputed that her advancement there was based on merit alone. In September 1978, respondent notified Taylor that she was taking sick leave for an indefinite period. On November 1, 1978, the bank discharged her for excessive use of that leave.

Respondent brought this action against Taylor and the bank, claiming that during her four years at the bank she had "constantly been subjected to sexual harassment" by Taylor in violation of Title VII. She sought injunctive relief, compensatory and punitive damages against Taylor and the bank, and attorney's fees.

At the 11–day bench trial, the parties presented conflicting testimony about Taylor's behavior during respondent's employment. Respondent testified that during her probationary period as a teller-trainee, Taylor treated her in a fatherly way and made no sexual advances. Shortly thereafter, however, he invited her out to dinner and, during the course of the meal, suggested that they go to a motel to have sexual relations. At first she refused, but out of what she described as fear of losing her job she eventually agreed. According to respondent, Taylor thereafter made repeated demands upon her for sexual favors, usually at the branch, both during and after business hours; she estimated that over the next several years she had intercourse with him some 40 or 50 times. In addition, respondent testified that Taylor fondled her in front of other employees, followed her into the women's restroom when she went there alone, exposed himself to her, and even forcibly raped her on several occasions. These activities ceased after 1977, respondent stated, when she started going with a steady boyfriend.

* * *

Taylor denied respondent's allegations of sexual activity, testifying that he never fondled her, never made suggestive remarks to her, never engaged in sexual intercourse with her, and never asked her to do so. He contended instead that respondent made her accusations in response to a business-related dispute. The bank also denied respondent's allegations and asserted that any sexual harassment by Taylor was unknown to the bank and engaged in without its consent or approval.

* * *

Respondent argues, and the Court of Appeals held, that unwelcome sexual advances that create an offensive or hostile working environment violate Title VII. Without question, when a supervisor sexually harasses a subordinate because of the subordinate's sex, that supervisor "discriminate[s]" on the basis of sex. Petitioner apparently does not challenge this proposition. It contends instead that in prohibiting discrimination with respect to "compensation, terms, conditions, or privileges" of employment, Congress was concerned with what petitioner describes as "tangible loss" of "an economic character," not "purely psychological aspects of the workplace environment." * * *

We reject petitioner's view. First, the language of Title VII is not limited to "economic" or "tangible" discrimination. The phrase "terms, conditions, or privileges of employment" evinces a congressional intent " 'to strike at the entire spectrum of disparate treatment of men and women' " in employment. Petitioner has pointed to nothing in the Act to suggest that Congress contemplated the limitation urged here.

Second, in 1980 the EEOC issued Guidelines specifying that "sexual harassment," as there defined, is a form of sex discrimination prohibited by Title VII. * * *

Of course, * * * not all workplace conduct that may be described as "harassment" affects a "term, condition, or privilege" of employment within the meaning of Title VII. For sexual harassment to be actionable, it must be sufficiently severe or pervasive "to alter the conditions of [the victim's] employment and create an abusive working environment." Respondent's allegations in this case—which include not only pervasive harassment but also criminal conduct of the most serious nature—are plainly sufficient to state a claim for "hostile environment" sexual harassment.

* * *

[T]he District Court's conclusion that no actionable harassment occurred might have rested on its earlier "finding" that "[i]f [respondent] and Taylor did engage in an intimate or sexual relationship . . . , that relationship was a voluntary one." But the fact that sex-related conduct was "voluntary," in the sense that the complainant was not forced to participate against her will, is not a defense to a sexual harassment suit brought under Title VII. The gravamen of any sexual harassment claim is that the alleged sexual advances were "unwelcome." While the question whether particular conduct was indeed unwelcome presents difficult problems of proof and turns largely on credibility determinations committed to the trier of fact, the District Court in this case erroneously focused on the "voluntariness" of respondent's participation in the claimed sexual episodes. The correct inquiry is whether respondent by her conduct indicated that the alleged sexual advances were unwelcome, not whether her actual participation in sexual intercourse was voluntary.

* * * [T]he Court of Appeals stated that testimony about respondent's "dress and personal fantasies," which the District Court apparently admitted into evidence, "had no place in this litigation." The apparent ground for this conclusion was that respondent's voluntariness vel non in submitting to Taylor's advances was immaterial to her sexual harassment claim. While "voluntariness" in the sense of consent is not a defense to such a claim, it does not follow that a complainant's sexually provocative speech or dress is irrelevant as a matter of law in determining whether he or she found particular sexual advances unwelcome. To the contrary, such evidence is obviously relevant.

* * *

Finding that "the bank was without notice" of Taylor's alleged conduct, and that notice to Taylor was not the equivalent of notice to the bank, the court concluded that the bank therefore could not be held liable for Taylor's alleged actions. The Court of Appeals took the opposite view, holding that an employer is strictly liable for a hostile environment created by a supervisor's sexual advances, even though the employer neither knew nor reasonably could have known of the alleged misconduct. The court held that a supervisor, whether or not he possesses the authority to hire, fire, or promote, is necessarily an "agent" of his employer for all Title VII purposes, since "even the appearance" of such authority may enable him to impose himself on his subordinates.

* * *

This debate over the appropriate standard for employer liability has a rather abstract quality about it given the state of the record in this case. We do not know at this stage whether Taylor made any sexual advances toward respondent at all, let alone whether those advances were unwelcome, whether they were sufficiently pervasive to constitute a condition of employment, or whether they were "so pervasive and so long continuing ... that the employer must have become conscious of [them]."

We therefore decline the parties' invitation to issue a definitive rule on employer liability, but we do agree with the EEOC that Congress wanted courts to look to agency principles for guidance in this area. While such common-law principles may not be transferable in all their particulars to Title VII, Congress' decision to define "employer" to include any "agent" of an employer surely evinces an intent to place some limits on the acts of employees for which employers under Title VII are to be held responsible. For this reason, we hold that the Court of Appeals erred in concluding that employers are always automatically liable for sexual harassment by their supervisors. For the same reason, absence of notice to an employer does not necessarily insulate that employer from liability.

Finally, we reject petitioner's view that the mere existence of a grievance procedure and a policy against discrimination, coupled with respondent's failure to invoke that procedure, must insulate petitioner from liability. While those facts are plainly relevant, the situation before us demonstrates why they are not necessarily dispositive. Petitioner's general nondiscrimination policy did not address sexual harassment in particular, and thus did not alert employees to their employer's interest in correcting that form of discrimination. Moreover, the bank's grievance procedure apparently required an employee to complain first to her supervisor, in this case Taylor. Since Taylor was the alleged perpetrator, it is not altogether surprising that respondent failed to invoke the procedure and report her grievance to him. Petitioner's contention that respondent's failure should insulate it from liability might be substantially stronger if its procedures were better calculated to encourage victims of harassment to come forward.

Notes on Meritor

1. Do you think Congress intended to address sexual harassment when it passed Title VII in 1964? Why or why not? Under principles of statutory construction, should Title VII be interpreted to cover this kind of sex discrimination?

2. Did the Supreme Court perceive the *Meritor* case to be a quid pro quo or hostile environment case? Do you agree? What are the practical effects of how the issue is cast? Are there differing proof problems? Is quid pro quo harassment easier to recognize? Do you think that quid pro quo harassment is less controversial, i.e., most people agree that it is wrong? It is estimated that quid pro quo constitutes only a small portion (about 5%) of sexual harassment. See Morrison Torrey, We Get the Message—Pornography in the Workplace, 22 S.W.U. L. Rev. 53, n.17 (1992).

3. Do you think the Court adequately defined hostile environment sexual harassment? Based on the opinion, would you feel comfortable advising a client about what constitutes a hostile environment? Do you think men and women might perceive what occurs in the workplace differently? Several differences in gendered perspectives and experiences have been documented in numerous studies. See Torrey, above note 2, at 60–66. Every study that has found gender differences has concluded that women are more likely than men to perceive behaviors as harassing. See Jeremy A. Blumenthal, The Reasonable Woman Standard: A Meta-Analytic Review of Gender Differences in Perceptions of Sexual Harassment, 22 L. & Hum. Behav. 33, 46 (1998); Richard L. Wiener, Linda Hurt, Brenda Russell, Kelley Mannen and Charles Gasper, Perceptions of Sexual Harassment: The Effects of Gender, Legal Standard, and Ambivalent Sexism, 21 L. & Hum. Behav. 71 (1997) ("Although men were less sensitive to the reasonable woman standard than women, under some conditions the reasonable woman standard enabled both genders to find greater evidence of harassment."). For example, Barbara Gutek, in her 1985 book, Sex and the Workplace: The Impact of Sexual Behavior and Harassment on Women, Men and Organizations, discussed the findings of her study based on a large random sample survey of 1,257 working men and women in Los Angeles County. She discovered that even though the definition of sexual harassment differed on the basis of gender, the single largest difference was male and female reactions to and attitudes

about overtures from the opposite sex, e.g., 67% of men said they would be flattered by a woman at work making a proposition to them while only 17% of women responded they would be flattered while the remaining 63% of the women said they would be insulted. Ironically, neither sex was aware of this difference. Gutek concluded that sexual harassment is generally not a problem for men even though they report receiving social and sexual overtures from women. The majority of the male subjects indicated that young, attractive, unmarried, co-workers or subordinate women made most of the advances to them, and they neither felt coerced to submit to keep their jobs or felt that their work or opportunity for advancement was affected. Women, on the other hand, reported a completely different experience. The average male harasser was older (almost half were forty or over), married, and less attractive. In response to the harassment, over 20% of the women in the study quit a job, transferred, were fired, or quit applying for a job. Torrey at 61–62. What do you make of these differences? How can you explain them? Do they help to explain why men and women may have such different views of sexual harassment? Are men more likely to see "sex" at work as sex, while women perceive it to be an abuse of power over them? What problems do these differences cause in litigating sexual harassment cases? In what ways would you ameliorate these problems?

4. Do you agree with the Court's distinction between "voluntary" and "welcome"? What difference, if any, does it make? How can a court determine if sexual activity was "unwelcome"? Is consent the same thing as welcomeness? Note that, in general, an employee may not sign a form waiving her right to be free from unlawful discrimination on the basis of race or sex; if she could, as a practical matter, employers might require all employees to execute such a waiver on day one of the job. See generally, Charles A. Sullivan, Michael J. Zimmer and Richard F. Richards, Employment Discrimination, III 336 (2d ed. 1988). What are the risks for women of recognizing welcomeness as a defense? How can a woman demonstrate unwelcomeness? By changing the subject? Leaving the room? Or does she have to expressly tell the harasser that his behavior is unwelcome? Must she "resist"? What are the risks (for men and employers) of not recognizing such a defense? Which alternative is better and more fair? Which alternative is likely to yield the lowest number of errors?

5. Susan Estrich believes that the requirement of "unwelcomeness" imports some of the worst doctrines of rape law into Title VII cases: "Unwelcomeness has emerged as the doctrinal stepchild of the rape standards of consent and resistance, and shares virtually all of their problems." Estrich, Sex at Work, 43 Stan.L.Rev. 813, 827 (1991). Estrich argues that the consent standard shifts the focus from the behavior of the defendant to that of the plaintiff. Id. at 827. Why might this be true? Is there any way that a welcomeness standard could empower women? Or does the notion of "unwelcomeness" necessarily incorporate female stereotypes? For instance, does posing nude for magazines mean that the plaintiff "welcomes" questions from her employer about her willingness to pose nude for him in the plant? Why or why not? What assumptions underlie the positions on each side? See Burns v. McGregor Electronic Industries, 955 F.2d 559 (8th Cir.1992) (reversing the lower court's conclusion that an employee's objections to

alleged sexual harassment in the workplace were not credible in light of her having posed nude for motorcycle magazines).

6. Why does the Supreme Court in *Meritor* consider how a plaintiff dresses relevant? What assumptions must the Court be making? What effect does admission of such evidence have on women plaintiffs? Recall the Florida rape case in which the jury found that a woman who had worn a lace miniskirt with no underwear "asked for it the way she was dressed." See discussion of rape, above Chapter 5. What are the risks of allowing or disallowing such evidence? Which alternative is likely to yield the lowest error rate?

7. The *Meritor* Court says that "sexually provocative speech" is "obviously relevant." Why should the content of a plaintiff's conversations be relevant? How should a woman communicate and be an effective employee when sexual language is prevalent in the workplace? If she is non-responsive, will there be a negative impact on her employment? On the other hand, if she responds in similar language, is she indicating that the environment is "welcome"? See Ukarish v. Magnesium Elektron, 31 F.E.P. 1315 (D.N.J. 1983) (dismissing claim because plaintiff appeared to accept the sexual banter at the workplace and even to join in it).

8. How should the rules of discovery and evidence be applied in sexual harassment cases? For instance, is evidence of prior or contemporaneous sexual conduct outside the workplace admissible? See Priest v. Rotary, 98 F.R.D. 755 (N.D.Cal.1983) (defendant could not inquire as to the names of plaintiff's sexual partners during the previous ten years since any evidence obtained would be inadmissible under Federal Rule of Evidence 404, which excludes evidence of character or past acts offered to show that a person acted in conformity). Is the issue similar to the problems addressed by rape shield statutes in the criminal context? (See discussion of rape shield statutes, above Chapter 5.) In 1995, Congress revised F.R.E. 412 to extend "rape shield" protection to civil actions that claim sexual misconduct, including sexual harassment. It deems inadmissible, subject to exceptions, evidence offered to prove (1) that any alleged victim engaged in other sexual behavior or (2) any alleged victim's sexual predisposition. However, when Jane Harris Aiken analyzed how the courts were utilizing Rule 412, she found that while "[c]ourts are more willing to be suspicious of broad inquiries into a plaintiff's sexual history even at discovery," nonetheless "they are finding new relevance for such evidence when evaluating damage claims." Aiken, Sexual Character Evidence in Civil Actions: Refining the Propensity Rule, 6 Wis. L.Rev. 1221, 1224 (1997). In other words, even after Rule 412, when a plaintiff asserts a claim for mental or emotional damages, her sexual history and predisposition are likely to be discoverable and admissible.

9. Under the Civil Rights Act of 1991, Pub.L. 102–166 (Nov. 21, 1991), 105 Stat. 1071, plaintiffs under Title VII now can demand (1) punitive damages if the employer acted with malice or reckless indifference to the plaintiff's federal rights; (2) compensatory damages for future pecuniary losses, emotional pain, suffering, inconvenience, mental anguish, loss of enjoyment of life, and other nonpecuniary losses, subject to varying caps from $50,000 to $300,000 depending upon the number of workers employed

by the defendant; and (3) a trial by jury. How does this amendment to Title VII change what is at stake in sexual harassment cases? Might there be an even greater emphasis on the mental status of the plaintiff?

10. African American women have played a dominant role as plaintiffs in litigating sexual harassment claims. See Susan Brownmiller and Dolores Alexander, From Carmita Wood to Anita Hill, Ms., Jan./Feb. 1992, at 70. Why do you think this is so? Is it possible to separate sexual harassment from racism? Is this a continuing legacy of slavery, as discussed by Barbara Omolade, above Chapter 4? See also Sumi Cho, Converging Stereotypes in Racialized Sexual Harassment: Where the Model Minority Meets Suzie Wong, 1 J. Gender, Race & Just. 177, 182 (1997) (how Asian Pacific American women "are at particular risk of being racially and sexually harassed because of the combustible and recombinant reaction of race with gender that produces sexualized racial stereotypes and racialized gender stereotypes").

11. In one of the most important events to publicize sexual harassment, Professor Anita Hill testified in October of 1991 before the Senate Judiciary Committee considering the nomination of Clarence Thomas to be a Supreme Court justice. Hill, who as a young lawyer had worked under the supervision of Thomas at the Equal Employment Opportunity Commission, spoke of the numerous unwanted sexual overtures made by Thomas. Much of the hearing was televised, with Thomas claiming he was being victimized by a "media lynching." In the first six months following Hill's testimony, the EEOC logged a record number harassment complaints, 50% more than the previous six months. Jane Mayer and Jill Abramson, Strange Justice: The Selling of Clarence Thomas 352 (1994). Nonetheless, although it is estimated that between 40% and 65% of female workers claim to have experienced sexual harassment in the workplace, less than 5% file complaints. Jill Smolowe, Anita Hill's Legacy, Time, Oct. 19, 1992, at 56. How do you explain this? Should women feel a moral obligation to enforce Title VII by filing sexual harassment suits? What concerns militate against pursuing a lawsuit? What would you advise a client? What would you do yourself?

HARRIS v. FORKLIFT SYSTEMS, INC.

Supreme Court of the United States, 1993.

510 U.S. 17, 114 S.Ct. 367, 126 L.Ed.2d 295.

JUSTICE O'CONNOR delivered the opinion of the Court [which was unanimous with concurring opinions by JUSTICES SCALIA and GINSBURG].

In this case we consider the definition of a discriminatorily "abusive work environment" (also known as a "hostile work environment") under Title VII of the Civil Rights Act of 1964. * * *

Teresa Harris worked as a manager at Forklift Systems, Inc., an equipment rental company, from April 1985 until October 1987. Charles Hardy was Forklift's president.

The Magistrate found that, throughout Harris' time at Forklift, Hardy often insulted her because of her gender and often made her the target of unwanted sexual innuendos. Hardy told Harris on several occasions, in the presence of other employees, "You're a woman, what do you know" and "We need a man as the rental manager"; at least once, he told her she was "a dumb ass woman." Again in front of others, he suggested that the two of them "go to the Holiday Inn to negotiate [Harris'] raise." Hardy occasionally asked Harris and other female employees to get coins from his front pants pocket. He threw objects on the ground in front of Harris and other women, and asked them to pick the objects up. He made sexual innuendos about Harris' and other women's clothing.

In mid-August 1987, Harris complained to Hardy about his conduct. Hardy said he was surprised that Harris was offended, claimed he was only joking, and apologized. He also promised he would stop, and based on this assurance Harris stayed on the job. But in early September, Hardy began anew: While Harris was arranging a deal with one of Forklift's customers, he asked her, again in front of other employees, "What did you do, promise the guy ... some [sex] Saturday night?" On October 1, Harris collected her paycheck and quit.

Harris then sued Forklift, claiming that Hardy's conduct had created an abusive work environment for her because of her gender. The United States District Court for the Middle District of Tennessee, adopting the report and recommendation of the Magistrate, found this to be "a close case," but held that Hardy's conduct did not create an abusive environment. The court found that some of Hardy's comments "offended [Harris], and would offend the reasonable woman," but that they were not

> "so severe as to be expected to seriously affect [Harris'] psychological well-being. A reasonable woman manager under like circumstances would have been offended by Hardy, but his conduct would not have risen to the level of interfering with that person's work performance.
>
> "Neither do I believe that [Harris] was subjectively so offended that she suffered injury.... Although Hardy may at times have genuinely offended [Harris], I do not believe that he created a working environment so poisoned as to be intimidating or abusive to [Harris]."

* * *

When the workplace is permeated with "discriminatory intimidation, ridicule, and insult," that is "sufficiently severe or pervasive to alter the conditions of the victim's employment and create an abusive working environment," Title VII is violated.

This standard, which we reaffirm today, takes a middle path between making actionable any conduct that is merely offensive and requiring the conduct to cause a tangible psychological injury. As we pointed out in *Meritor*, "mere utterance of an ... epithet which engenders offensive feelings in a employee," does not sufficiently affect the conditions of employment to implicate Title VII. Conduct that is not severe or pervasive enough to create an objectively hostile or abusive work environment—an environment that a reasonable person would find hostile or abusive—is beyond Title VII's purview. Likewise, if the victim does not subjectively perceive the environment to be abusive, the conduct has not actually altered the conditions of the victim's employment, and there is no Title VII violation.

But Title VII comes into play before the harassing conduct leads to a nervous breakdown. A discriminatorily abusive work environment, even one that does not seriously affect employees' psychological well-being, can and often will detract from employees' job performance, discourage employees from remaining on the job, or keep them from advancing in their careers. Moreover, even without regard to these tangible effects, the very fact that the discriminatory conduct was so severe or pervasive that it created a work environment abusive to employees because of their race, gender, religion, or national origin offends Title VII's broad rule of workplace equality. The appalling conduct alleged in Meritor, and the reference in that case to environments " 'so heavily polluted with discrimination as to destroy completely the emotional and psychological stability of minority group workers,' " merely present some especially egregious examples of harassment. They do not mark the boundary of what is actionable.

We therefore believe the District Court erred in relying on whether the conduct "seriously affect[ed] plaintiff's psychological well-being" or led her to "suffe[r] injury." Such an inquiry may needlessly focus the factfinder's attention on concrete psychological harm, an element Title VII does not require. Certainly Title VII bars conduct that would seriously affect a reasonable person's psychological well-being, but the statute is not limited to such conduct. So long as the environment would reasonably be perceived, and is perceived, as hostile or abusive, there is no need for it also to be psychologically injurious.

This is not, and by its nature cannot be, a mathematically precise test. We need not answer today all the potential questions it raises, nor specifically address the Equal Employment Opportunity Commission's new regulations on this subject, see 58 Fed.Reg. 51266 (1993) (proposed 29 CFR §§ 1609.1, 1609.2); see also 29 CFR § 1604.11 (1993). But we can say that whether an environment is "hostile" or "abusive" can be determined only by looking at all the circumstances. These may include the frequency of the discriminatory conduct; its severity; whether it is physically threatening or humiliating, or a mere offensive utterance; and whether it unreasonably interferes with an employee's work performance. The effect on the employee's psychological well-being is, of course, relevant to determining whether the plaintiff actually found the environment abusive. But while psychological harm, like any other relevant factor, may be taken into account, no single factor is required. * * *

We therefore reverse the judgment of the Court of Appeals, and remand the case for further proceedings consistent with this opinion.

* * *

Notes on Harris

1. The Court in *Harris* does try to provide greater guidance by indicating that "hostile" or "abusive" can only be determined by looking at all the circumstances, including "frequency of the discriminatory conduct; its severity; whether it is physically threatening or humiliating, or a mere offensive utterance; and whether it unreasonably interferes with an employee's work performance." Do you agree with these factors? Can you identify others you think relevant?

2. Two of the many ironies about sexual harassment are that it both undermines a woman's self-esteem, making it less likely that she will complain about the harassment, and increases stress, which may in fact negatively affect her performance, giving her employer "legitimate" business reasons for terminating her if she does speak out. See James E. Gruber and Lars Bjorn, Women's Responses to Sexual Harassment: An Analysis of Sociocultural, Organizational, and Personal Resource Models, 67 Soc.Sci.Q. 814, 817 (1986); Joy A. Livingston, Responses to Sexual Harassment on the Job: Legal, Organizational, and Individual Actions, 38 J.Soc.Issues 5, 16 (1982). How are judges likely to respond to evidence of these reactions to harassment? As counsel for plaintiff, how might you try to handle these problems?

3. How might coping responses of victims of sexual harassment further complicate the situation? Women typically try to manage incidents on their own by ignoring the behavior, avoiding the harasser, asking the harasser to stop, or trivializing the incidents by making a joke of the harassment in the hope it will put an end to the behavior. Morrison Torrey, We Get the Message—Pornography in the Workplace, 22 Sw.U.L.Rev. 53, 69–70 (1992). How are these responses likely to affect subsequent litigation?

4. Why do most victims remain silent, or blame themselves for the incident of sexual harassment, rather than complain to management? How would you respond if your supervisor commented on your breasts? What if you were a waitress, and a customer grabbed you and kissed you; what would you do? What if you went out with a group from your office, and a supervisor from another department told you that if you slept with him he would "take care of you?" Would you report the incident to your supervisor, who is a friend of the harasser?

5. Both parties utilized expert witnesses about whether pornography in the workplace was sexual harassment in Robinson v. Jacksonville Shipyards, 760 F.Supp. 1486 (M.D.Fla.1991). The pornography that Lois Robinson and other women had to deal with on a daily basis included totally or partially nude women involved in sexually submissive behavior, including "a drawing depicting a frontal view of a nude female body with the words 'U.S.D.A. Choice' written on it . . . a dart board with a drawing of a woman's breast, with her nipple as the bull's eye . . . a picture of a woman's pubic area with a meat spatula pressed on it . . . multiple centerfold-style pictures . . . a picture of a nude woman with long blonde hair wearing high heels and holding a whip [Robinson had long blonde hair and worked with a welding tool called a whip]." Id. at 1495–98. The court found that one of plaintiff's

experts, Dr. Susan Fiske, an expert on sexual stereotyping, presented testimony supporting "a sound, credible theoretical framework from which to conclude that the presence of pictures of nude and partially nude women, sexual comments, sexual joking, and other behaviors * * * creates and contributes to a sexually hostile work environment." Id. at 1505. Should expert testimony be necessary to obtain such a conclusion? Is it likely to be necessary?

6. How free is speech at work? Are employees free to speak their minds? Who regulates speech at work? In the *Jacksonville Shipyards* case, discussed above note 5, the employer banned all political speech at work, including campaign posters, buttons, etc. Why wasn't that ban a violation of the First Amendment? Would the ban on political speech, posters, etc., have violated the First Amendment if the employer had been a government entity? Why would an employer adopt a policy banning political speech but tolerating (or even encouraging) wide-spread displays of pornography, including the type of pornography at Jacksonville Shipyards? See Mary Becker, How Free Is Speech at Work?, 29 U.C. Davis L. Rev. 815 (1996).

On appeal in *Jacksonville Shipyards*, one of the employer's arguments was that pornography alone, if not directed against any particular woman, cannot constitute sexual harassment because it is speech protected by the First Amendment. (The case settled before an appellate decision was issued following the employer's bankruptcy.) Except for early cases challenging restrictions on gender-based employment ads, e.g., Pittsburgh Press Co. v. Pittsburgh Comm. on Human Relations, 413 U.S. 376, 93 S.Ct. 2553, 37 L.Ed.2d 669 (1973) (finding gender-specific employment advertisements discriminatory), the First Amendment has been relatively dormant in the employment discrimination context. However, in the 1990's a few scholars began to argue that the First Amendment protected workplace speech from liability from Title VII. See generally Eugene Volokh, Freedom of Speech and Workplace Harassment, 39 U.C.L.A. L. Rev. 1791 (1992); Kingsley R. Browne, Title VII as Censorship: Hostile–Environment Harassment and the First Amendment, 52 Ohio St. L.J. 481 (1991). To date, however, courts have *not* applied the First Amendment so as to insulate sexual harassment employment discrimination from Title VII remedies. The Supreme Court in *Harris* failed to mention First Amendment concerns even though several amici curiae addressed the issue. See generally Richard H. Fallon, Jr., Sexual Harassment, Content Neutrality, and the First Amendment Dog That Didn't Bark, 1994 Sup. Ct. Rev. 1.

7. According to Cynthia L. Estlund, commentators on this issue range from essentially First Amendment absolutism, see, e.g., Browne, above note 6, to a position that "harassment law [is] both necessary to workplace equality and entirely consistent with free speech principles and doctrine," see, e.g., Becker, above note 6. Estlund, Freedom of Expression in the Workplace and the Problem of Discriminatory Harassment, 75 Tex. L. Rev. 687, 693 (1997). Estlund proposes an alternative: "a conception of the workplace as a 'satellite domain' of public discourse—a domain that lies outside the core of public discourse but contributes to that discourse in unique and important ways." Id. at 693–94. Specifically, she proposes:

> a compromise in the form of certain constraints on the *manner* of expression in the workplace forum. Admittedly these constraints would not be constitutional in the public forum. In particular, the proposal would leave unprotected, first, speech that is directed at a listener whom the speaker knows to be offended on the basis of race, sex, or religion, and, second, speech the manner of which is manifestly offensive on the basis of race, sex, or religion—independent of the viewpoint expressed—and that is uttered at a time and place that could not reasonably be avoided by listeners who are thus offended.

Id. at 695.

Should discriminatory speech in the workplace be insulated from Title VII liability? Or should Title VII restrictions on workplace speech be insulated from First Amendment limitations? What would be the advantages and disadvantages of recognizing speech claims in such settings? Do you think the Estlund proposal is a good compromise? How does her approach vary from regarding Title VII regulations as insulated from the First Amendment?

8. Sexual harassment often is prevalent when women attempt to work in traditionally male-dominated occupations. See Elvia R. Arriola, "What's the Big Deal?" Women in the New York City Construction Industry and Sexual Harassment Law, 1970–1985, 22 Colum. Hum. Rts. L. Rev. 21 (1990). Why might men harass women in such situations? Why might such harassment be especially frightening in industries like construction—and hence effective in forcing women out of the job?

9. Describe the harm of quid pro quo sexual harassment as a violation of (a) formal equality, (b) MacKinnon's dominance feminism, (c) relational equality, and (d) critical race feminism. What does each see as the core harm?

10. Sexual harassment is not just a problem in the United States. According to the International Labor Organization, "[o]ne in 12 women in the industrialized world is forced out of her job after being sexually harassed at work." Job Sex Harassment Hits Industrial World, ILO Washington Focus, Winter 1993, at 1. Research involving 23 industrialized countries showed pervasive sexual harassment against women. However, at that time only seven of the countries had statutes specifically mentioning the term sexual harassment (Australia, Canada, France, New Zealand, Spain, Sweden and some states in the United States); in six countries the term has been defined by judicial opinions (Australia, Canada, Ireland, Switzerland, United Kingdom, and the United States); in many other countries laws concerning unfair dismissal, tort or criminal law have implied prohibitions against sexual harassment. Id. However, in only four years there were dramatic changes: 36 countries adopted sexual harassment legislation by 1997. See ILO, World of Work, No. 19 (Mar. 1997).

Text Note: "Reasonable Woman" Standard

The *Harris* Court held that "[s]o long as the environment would reasonably be perceived, and is perceived, as hostile or abusive" the plaintiff has established a prima facie case of hostile environment sexual harassment.

How does a factfinder determine if a "reasonable" person would find an environment hostile or abusive? Who is the "reasonable person"—is there a standard that can be truly "objective"?

Although the origin of the reasonable man standard is difficult to determine, English courts adopted the standard in the 19th century and American courts soon followed.[20] The intent of the standard is to establish an objective, uniform expectation of behavior: "The actor is required to do what such an ideal individual would be supposed to do in his place. * * * He is not to be identified with any ordinary individual, who might occasionally do unreasonable things; he is a prudent and careful man, who is always up to standard."[21] The "reasonable man" has become a symbol of rational society. As Morrison Torrey notes:

> Its evolution and transformation is a comment on our cultural frustrations with attempting to assimilate women into the public life of the patriarchy. Initially stated as the "reasonable man" standard, it has been amended to become the "reasonable person" standard as a concession to the early second wave of feminism. This change was superficial only because the law continued to actually apply the formulations and perspectives of the reasonable "man." However, powerful arguments have been made to substantively modify this standard to reflect the actual perspectives of the parties involved. These arguments, based on considerable empirical data showing that men and women frequently have different perspectives and experiences of the world, have been accepted by the Equal Employment Opportunity Commission and, more recently and dramatically, by at least five federal courts of appeals and multiple district courts.[22]

Why is it necessary to apply an objective standard at all? What is the purpose of an objective standard?

In what appeared to be a groundbreaking case, the Ninth Circuit Court of Appeals adopted the "reasonable woman" standard in Ellison v. Brady, 924 F.2d 872 (1991). In that sexual harassment hostile environment case in which a co-worker wrote several letters to the plaintiff claiming to love her (even after being counseled to leave the frightened Ms. Ellison alone), the court held:

> [W]e believe that in evaluating the severity and pervasiveness of sexual harassment, we should focus on the perspective of the victim. If we only examined whether a reasonable person would engage in allegedly harassing conduct, we would run the risk of reinforcing the prevailing level of discrimination. Harassers could continue to harass merely because a particular discriminatory practice was common, and victims of harassment would have no remedy. We therefore prefer to analyze harassment from the victim's perspective. A complete understanding of the victim's view requires, among other things, an analysis of the different perspec-

20. See Laurie J. Taylor, Comments: Provoked Reason in Men and Women: Heat-of-Passion Manslaughter and Imperfect Self-Defense, 33 UCLA L.Rev. 1679, 1686 (1986).

21. William L. Prosser, Law of Torts 150–51 (4th ed. 1971).

22. Morrison Torrey, We Get the Message—Pornography in the Workplace, 22 SW.U.L.Rev. 53, 59–60 (1992).

tives of men and women. Conduct that many men consider unobjectionable may offend many women. * * *

We realize that there is a broad range of viewpoints among women as a group, but we believe that many women share common concerns which men do not necessarily share. For example, because women are disproportionately victims of rape and sexual assault, women have a stronger incentive to be concerned with sexual behavior. Women who are victims of mild forms of sexual harassment may understandably worry whether a harasser's conduct is merely a prelude to violent sexual assault. Men, who are rarely victims of sexual assault, may view sexual conduct in a vacuum without a full appreciation of the social setting or the underlying threat of violence that a woman may perceive.

In order to shield employers from having to accommodate the idiosyncratic concerns of the rare hyper-sensitive employee, we hold that a female plaintiff states a prima facie case of hostile environment sexual harassment when she alleges conduct which a reasonable woman would consider sufficiently severe or pervasive to alter the conditions of employment and create an abusive working environment.

We adopt the perspective of a reasonable woman primarily because we believe that a sex-blind reasonable person standard tends to be male-biased and tends to systematically ignore the experiences of women. The reasonable woman standard does not establish a higher level of protection for women than men. Instead, a gender-conscious examination of sexual harassment enables women to participate in the workplace on an equal footing with men. By acknowledging and not trivializing the effects of sexual harassment on reasonable women, courts can work towards ensuring that neither men nor women will have to "run a gauntlet of sexual abuse in return for the privilege of being allowed to work and make a living."

We note that the reasonable victim standard we adopt today classifies conduct as unlawful sexual harassment even when harassers do not realize that their conduct creates a hostile working environment. Well-intentioned compliments by co-workers or supervisors can form the basis of a sexual harassment cause of action if a reasonable victim of the same sex as the plaintiff would consider the comments sufficiently severe or pervasive to alter a condition of employment and create an abusive working environment.[23]

Feminist scholars have not all agreed as to the benefits of adopting a reasonable "woman" standard. Although she has reservations about the reasonable woman standard, Martha Chamallas does acknowledge an important positive aspect of this development:

What seems important about even this incremental shift in doctrine, however, is its potential to challenge the authority of the dominant group's account of events. If the victim's perspective were recognized in the law, it might not only increase plaintiffs' chances for winning but might also change the content of what is discussed, the

23. Id. at 878–80.

terms of the dialogue, and perhaps even the impact of litigation on discrimination victims.[24]

Does the reasonable woman standard imply an idealized woman? Susan Estrich imagines what such a woman would be like:

> Such a woman is tough, not "hypersensitive"; she is aggressive, not passive. Such a woman complains in a way that effectively stops the harassment. Such a woman does not suffer in silence or confide only in other women. In short, the "reasonable woman" is very much a man.[25]

These criticisms suggest that, even though the phrasing recognizes women, there still is a danger that the definition of the new standard will maintain and reinforce the norm, i.e., white, Christian, straight, middle class, male.

What alternatives are there? Professor Chamallas' proposal is to interpret "the reasonable woman to be the reasoning woman who offers a plausible account of how gender oppression operates in the workplace" so that "modifications of the reasonable person standard do not need to be fixed but could respond to plaintiff's descriptions of her community and the relationships among workers. This seems preferable to having the court decide for the plaintiff at the outset what form of discrimination she suffered."[26]

Attempting to articulate a standard that incorporates both feminist theory and practical concerns, Kathryn Abrams suggests:

> If the defendant can demonstrate that the behavior in question was not likely to create a fear of sexual coercion or a sense of devaluative sexualization among women, the court should find that the plaintiff's response was idiosyncratic.[27]

Professor Abrams allocates this burden to the defendant because it is "normatively desirable to assume that sexual behavior sufficiently offensive to drive a plaintiff to court is harassing and to put the burden on the defendant to show otherwise."[28] She even offers specific factors to assist courts in applying this standard: (1) nature of the conduct; (2) frequency of conduct; (3) extent to which the language specifically applies to, or otherwise targets, the plaintiff; and (4) precise language used.[29]

What about a totally subjective standard? Eileen M. Blackwood believes this is the only appropriate position for a variety of reasons. First, she questions whether male decisionmakers can "determine how a reasonable woman would have reacted without resorting to male defined culturally

24. Martha Chamallas, Feminist Constructions of Objectivity: Multiple Perspectives in Sexual and Racial Harassment Litigation, 1 Tex. J. Women & L. 95, 122–23 (1992).

25. Estrich, Sex at Work, 43 Stan. L.Rev. 813, 846 (1991). See also Chamallas, above note 24, at 122 (shift to a gendered standard is unacceptable because of its retention of the notion of "objectivity"); Nancy S. Ehrenreich, Pluralist Myths and Powerless Men: The Ideology of Reasonableness in Sexual Harassment Law, 99 Yale L.J. 1177, 1234 (1990) ("as long as reasonableness means abstract neutrality and pluralism means limitless tolerance, each concept will reinforce the other, and both will perpetuate an unequal status quo").

26. Chamallas, above note 24, at 136, 140.

27. Kathryn Abrams, Gender Discrimination and the Transformation of Workplace Norms, 42 Vand.L.Rev. 1183, 1211 (1989).

28. Id. at n. 116.

29. Id. at 1211–13.

biased perspectives."[30] Second, she argues that the reasonable woman standard does not create a new society consensus: "[t]he reasonable woman is just the wife of 'the man in his shirtsleeves,' who tolerates and lives with the male status quo on a daily basis. The man considers her reasonable only for as long as she tolerates the status quo, while showing appropriate feminine sensibilities."[31] Finally, she discounts as ridiculous employer fears that the idiosyncratic or hypersensitive employee will create undeserved liability. After all, liability does not attach at the first sign of sexual activity:

> It [liability] requires that the woman indicate in some way that the behavior is unwelcome. If, after receiving notice that sexual behavior is unwelcome, an employer fails to address her concerns, the woman does and should have a claim against her employer. It does not really matter whether her concerns are reasonable or not. The *subjective* effect upon her is the key consideration.[32]

Professor Blackwood further supports her position by an analogy to tort law—"[t]ortfeasors take their plaintiffs as they find them."[33]

Yet another possibility is to utilize economic analysis in approaching this problem. Gillian Hadfield argues that sexual harassment should be actionable under Title VII "whenever it would lead a hypothetical rational woman to alter her employment decisions if she could do so at little or no cost."[34]

Notes on the Reasonable Woman Standard

1. How would a factfinder determine the perspective of a reasonable woman? Would experts be required? Did the Supreme Court in *Harris*, decided two years after *Ellison*, decline to adopt the "reasonable woman" standard? See Barbara A. Gutek et al., The Utility of the Reasonable Woman Legal Standard in Hostile Environment Sexual Harassment Cases: a Multimethod, Multistudy Examination, 5 Psychol. Pub. Pol'y & L. 596 (1999).

2. What do you see as positive about a reasonable woman standard? What does Chamallas mean when she suggests that this standard may challenge "the dominant group's account of events"?

3. Would the Chamallas proposal avoid all "objectivity" and the "ideal woman" problems? What are judges worried about when they adopt a reasonable person or woman standard in sexual harassment cases? How might these concerns affect their application of the Chamallas standard?

4. Do you find Blackwood's arguments persuasive? What are the dangers of regarding as sexual harassment any activity the plaintiff claims is sexual harassment? Can you think of other approaches that might better balance women's need for equal opportunity in the workplace and the employer's interest in not being held liable *whenever* a plaintiff complains? Is an "objective" standard necessary? Do you think courts are likely to accept a subjective standard? Why or why not?

30. Ellen M. Blackwood, The Reasonable Woman in Sexual Harassment Law and the Case for Subjectivity, 16 Vt.L.Rev. 1005, 1012 (1992).

31. Id. at 1023.

32. Id. at 1025.

33. Id.

34. Gillian K. Hadfield, Rational Women: A Test for Sex-Based Harassment, 83 Cal. L. Rev. 1151 (1995).

5. What are the underlying assumptions of Hadfield's formula? Is it too objective? Does it take into consideration whether the victim enjoys her job? Whether there are comparable jobs available? Does it imply that jobs are fungible? What about a job that is close to the victim's daycare provider? Are all of these factors subsumed under the language "little or no cost"? Do women perhaps perceive the concept of "cost" differently than men might?

6. How would a formal equality feminist assess the "reasonable woman" standard? Someone applying MacKinnon's dominance approach? A relational feminist?

7. After evaluating all of the risks and dangers in a "reasonable woman" standard, do you think it is still better than the "reasonable person" standard for women? Which alternative do you think each of the feminist theorists discussed in Chapter 3 would prefer? Which of the reasonable person formulas discussed above comes closest to the Court's in *Harris*? Which one do you prefer?

ONCALE v. SUNDOWNER OFFSHORE SERVICES, INC.

Supreme Court of the United States, 1998.

523 U.S. 75, 118 S.Ct. 998, 140 L.Ed.2d 201.

JUSTICE SCALIA delivered the opinion for a unanimous Court.

This case presents the question whether workplace harassment can violate Title VII's prohibition against "discriminat[ion] ... because of ... sex," when the harasser and the harassed employee are of the same sex.

* * *

The precise details are irrelevant to the legal point we must decide, and in the interest of both brevity and dignity we shall describe them only generally. In late October 1991, Oncale was working for respondent Sundowner Offshore Services on a Chevron U.S. A., Inc., oil platform in the Gulf of Mexico. He was employed as a roustabout on an eight-man crew which included respondents John Lyons, Danny Pippen, and Brandon Johnson. Lyons, the crane operator, and Pippen, the driller, had supervisory authority. On several occasions, Oncale was forcibly subjected to sex-related, humiliating actions against him by Lyons, Pippen and Johnson in the presence of the rest of the crew. Pippen and Lyons also physically assaulted Oncale in a sexual manner, and Lyons threatened him with rape. [According to the appellate opinion, the rig was an all-male environment, and the harassment included "Pippen and Johnson restraining Oncale while Lyons placed his penis on Oncale's neck, on one occasion, and on Oncale's arm, on another occasion;" and "the use of force by Lyons to push a bar of soap into Oncale's anus while Pippen restrained Oncale as he was showering on Sundowner premises." 83 F.3d 118, 118–19 (5th Cir.1996).]

Oncale's complaints to supervisory personnel produced no remedial action; in fact, the company's Safety Compliance Clerk, Valent Hohen, told Oncale that Lyons and Pippen "picked [on] him all the time too," and called him a name suggesting homosexuality. Oncale eventually quit—asking that his pink slip reflect that he "voluntarily left due to sexual harassment and verbal abuse." When asked at his deposition why he left Sundowner, Oncale stated "I felt that if I didn't leave my job, that I would be raped or forced to have sex."

* * * [T]he district court held that "Mr. Oncale, a male, has no cause of action under Title VII for harassment by male co-workers."

* * *

Title VII's prohibition of discrimination "because of ... sex" protects men as well as women, and in the related context of racial discrimination in the workplace we have rejected any conclusive presumption that an employer will not discriminate against members of his own race. "Because of the many facets of human motivation, it would be unwise to presume as a matter of law that human beings of one definable group will not discriminate against other members of that group." * * * If our precedents leave any doubt on the question, we hold today that nothing in Title VII necessarily bars a claim of discrimination "because of ... sex" merely because the plaintiff and the defendant (or the person charged with acting on behalf of the defendant) are of the same sex.

Courts have had little trouble with that principle in cases [in which] * * * an employee claims to have been passed over for a job or promotion. But when the issue arises in the context of a "hostile environment" sexual harassment claim, the state and federal courts have taken a bewildering variety of stances. Some, like the Fifth Circuit in this case, have held that same-sex sexual harassment claims are never cognizable under Title VII. Other decisions say that such claims are actionable only if the plaintiff can prove that the harasser is homosexual (and thus presumably motivated by sexual desire). Still others suggest that workplace harassment that is sexual in content is always actionable, regardless of the harasser's sex, sexual orientation, or motivations.

We see no justification in the statutory language or our precedents for a categorical rule excluding same-sex harassment claims from the coverage of Title VII. As some courts have observed, male-on-male sexual harassment in the workplace was assuredly not the principal evil Congress was concerned with when it enacted Title VII. But statutory prohibitions often go beyond the principal evil to cover reasonably comparable evils, and it is ultimately the provisions of our laws rather than the principal concerns of our legislators by which we are governed. Title VII prohibits "discriminat[ion] ... because of ... sex" in the "terms" or "conditions" of employment. Our holding that this includes sexual harassment must extend to sexual harassment of any kind that meets the statutory requirements.

* * *

Courts and juries have found the inference of discrimination easy to draw in most male-female sexual harassment situations, because the challenged conduct typically involves explicit or implicit proposals of sexual activity; it is reasonable to assume those proposals would not have been made to someone of the same sex. The same chain of inference would be available to a plaintiff alleging same-sex harassment, if there were credible evidence that the harasser was homosexual. But harassing conduct need not be motivated by sexual desire to support an inference of discrimination on the basis of sex. A trier of fact might reasonably find such discrimination, for example, if a female victim is harassed in such sex-specific and derogatory terms by another woman as to make it clear that the harasser is motivated by general hostility to the presence of women in the workplace. A same-sex harassment plaintiff may also, of course, offer direct comparative evidence about how the alleged harasser treated members of both sexes in a mixed-sex workplace. Whatever evidentiary route the plaintiff chooses to follow, he or she must always prove that the conduct at issue was not merely tinged with offensive sexual connotations, but actually constituted "discrimina[tion] ... because of ... sex."

* * * The prohibition of harassment on the basis of sex requires neither asexuality nor androgyny in the workplace; it forbids only behavior so objectively offensive as to alter the "conditions" of the victim's employment. "Conduct that is not severe or pervasive enough to create an objectively hostile or abusive work environment—an environment that a reasonable person would find hostile or abusive—is beyond Title VII's purview." We have always regarded that requirement as crucial, and as sufficient to ensure that courts and juries do not mistake ordinary socializing in the workplace—such as male-on-male horseplay or intersexual flirtation—for discriminatory "conditions of employment."

We have emphasized, moreover, that the objective severity of harassment should be judged from the perspective of a reasonable person in the plaintiff's position, considering "all the circumstances." In same-sex (as in all) harassment cases, that inquiry requires careful consideration of the social context in which particular behavior occurs and is experienced by its target. A professional football player's working environment is not severely or pervasively abusive, for example, if the coach smacks him on the buttocks as he heads onto the field—even if the same behavior would reasonably be experienced as abusive by the coach's secretary (male or female) back at the office. The real social impact of workplace behavior often depends on a constellation of surrounding circumstances, expectations, and relationships which are not fully captured by a simple recitation of the words used or the physical acts performed. Common sense, and an appropriate sensitivity to social context, will enable courts and juries to distinguish between simple teasing or roughhousing among members of the same sex, and conduct which a reasonable person in the plaintiff's position would find severely hostile or abusive.

* * *

Notes on Oncale

1. The Court notes that some courts have held that only homosexual same-sex harassment is cognizable, because it is "motivated by sexual desire." In either *Meritor* or *Harris* did the Court describe or require a motive for harassment? What do you think does motivate a harasser? A variety of reasons have been suggested for male-female harassment: many men, as a result of socialization, can only relate to women as sex objects, not professional colleagues; others perceive women as unwanted competition and hope to force their exit; still others do not understand that their conduct is unwelcome. See generally Morrison Torrey, We Get the Message—Pornography in the Workplace, 22 Sw. U. L. Rev. 53 (1992); Maria L. Ontiveros, Three Perspectives on Workplace Harassment of Women of Color, 23 Golden Gate U.L. Rev. 817 (1993). What do you think motivated the harassers in *Oncale*?

2. According to a recent study, men often harass other men to enforce "the traditional heterosexual male gender role." Craig R. Waldo, Jennifer L. Berdahl and Louise F. Fitzgerald, Are Men Sexually Harassed? If So, by Whom?, 22 Law & Hum. Beh. 59, 61 (1998). According to the authors,

> [t]his form of behavior includes ridiculing men for acting too "feminine" and pressuring them to engage in stereotypical forms of "masculine" behavior. Such behavior can be interpreted as arising from the societal devaluation of femininity and the complementary valorization of male heterosexuality and masculinity. Thus, for men, gender harassment includes not only negative and derogatory remarks about men, and the lewd and obscene comments that also offend women, but also enforcement of the traditional male gender role.

Id. The study also discovered that such harassment between men occurs more often than previously assumed. Id. at 72. See also Hilary S. Axam and Deborah Zalesne, Simulated Sodomy and Other Forms of Heterosexual "Horseplay:" Same Sex Sexual Harassment, Workplace Gender Hierarchies, and the Myth of the Gender Monolith Before and After *Oncale*, 11 Yale J. L. & Feminism 155 (1999). Does this provide an explanation for the occurrences in *Oncale*? Joseph "Jody" Oncale, married with two children, is only 5′4″ tall. Neither he, nor the men who harassed him, are homosexual; Oncale asserts that he is "not a standard-bearer for gay rights," although he is not a "gay-basher." See Mary Judice, LA Offshore Worker Settles Sex Suit, Times–Picayune, Oct. 24, 1998, at C1; Joanna Weiss, Same–Sex Harassing Illegal Too, Court Says, Times–Picayune, Mar. 5, 1998, at A1.

3. Catharine MacKinnon filed an amicus brief on behalf of the National Organization on Male Sexual Victimization, Inc.; Men Stopping Rape, Inc.; et al. in support of Joseph Oncale. 1997 WL 471814. In that brief she argued that "sexual abuse of men by men is a serious social problem of gender inequality" since "sex-discriminatory norms long endemic to such settings [all-male work environments]—under which men may sexually victimize others—must also be addressed to make sex equality real." Id. at 12–13. More specifically, she stated:

> The denial that interactions among men can have a sexual component, and that sexual abuse of men is gendered, are twin features of the social ideology of male dominance with which amici are familiar as experts. In this ideology, men are seen as sexually invulnerable. This image protects men from much male sexual violence and naturalizes the sexual abuse of women, making it seem that women, biologically, are sexual victims. Denying that men can be sexually abused as men thus supports the gender hierarchy of men over women in society. The illusion is preserved that men are sexually inviolable, hence naturally superior, as the sexual abuse of men by men is kept invisible.

Id. at 11. In addressing sexual orientation issues, she asked:

> By definition, sexual harassment is unwanted, so victim sexual orientation is as irrelevant on same-sex facial challenges on sex-basis as it is on opposite-sex ones. The sexual orientation of the victim cannot convert aggression that is sex-based into aggression that is not, or vice-versa.
>
> Will Title VII access now turn on the sexual feelings and imagined or real sexual identities of perpetrators? Will it have one sexual harassment rule for gay sexual harassers and another for straight ones? One for those whose sexual feelings have coalesced, another for those whose sexual feelings are diverse, diffuse, denied, deniable, unknown, or simply unprovable? Oncale sued for forced sex. Why should the gender of those with whom Lyons and Pippen are sexual, when others want to be sexual with them, determine Oncale's rights against them for violating (what is conventionally considered) his manhood?

Id. at 25. Do you agree with MacKinnon that the interactions in *Oncale* had a sexual component (though all the men were heterosexual) and that their interactions were "gendered"? What does MacKinnon mean by "gendered"? What does the Supreme Court mean by "gender discrimination"? Is her approach one that you could have predicted under dominance theory?

4. Scalia gives the following as an example of how a plaintiff might show that same-sex harassment occurred because of sex (though it was not sexually motivated): "a female victim is harassed in such sex-specific and derogatory terms by another woman as to make it clear that the harasser is motivated by general hostility to the presence of women in the workplace." Is this example likely to be of any use to Joseph Oncale, working with other men in an all-male job site? What is the issue on remand in *Oncale*? What could Joseph Oncale introduce as evidence that he was harassed "because of sex" in an all-male environment where most men were not treated the way he was?

Even in an environment with women as well as men, how could Oncale prove discrimination on the basis of sex? Would similar harassment of women (by the men who harassed Oncale) support or undermine Oncale's claim? Would evidence that women were not harassed support his claim that he was harassed because of sex if *most* men as well as *all women* were *not* harassed? Or would evidence that all or some women were harassed support his claim that he was harassed because of sex if no other men were harassed? (The case was settled on the eve of the trial in October of 1998.) See Richard F. Storrow, Same–Sex Sexual Harassment Claims After *Oncale*:

Defining the Boundaries of Actionable Conduct, 47 Am. Univ. L.R. 677 (1998);

5. If Oncale shows that he was harassed because he was regarded as an effeminate man, would he prove a violation of Title VII by analogy to Price Waterhouse v. Hopkins, 490 U.S. 228, 109 S.Ct. 1775, 104 L.Ed.2d 268 (1989) (excerpt below this chapter) (Court holds that it is sex discrimination to treat an abrasive woman differently from abrasive men)? Or would recovery be denied under the cases holding that discrimination on the basis of sex under Title VII does not reach discrimination on the basis of sexual orientation? The lower courts have consistently held that Congress did not intend to reach discrimination on the basis of sexual orientation when it enacted the Title VII ban on discrimination on the basis of sex. See, e.g., DeSantis v. Pacific Tel. & Tel., 608 F.2d 327, 329–331 (9th Cir.1979); Samuel Estreicher and Michael C. Harper, Cases and Materials on Employment Discrimination and Employment Law 209 (2000).

Was Oncale harassed because he was slight and therefore perceived as somewhat feminine? Would such harassment be gender-based? Would Scalia regard such harassment as sex discrimination? Would the other Justices, who have generally regarded sex and gender as synonymous in Title VII discussions, see above Chapter 2, regard harassment of a man because of his perceived effeminacy as sex discrimination? If they did, given the widespread perception that all gay men are effeminate, wouldn't that be equivalent to holding that Title VII bans discrimination on the basis of sexual orientation?

6. Does *Oncale* support the proposition—an argument actually made by employers in early sexual harassment cases and described above this section—that Title VII cannot reach sexual harassment by the hypothetical non-discriminatory bisexual supervisor who does not discriminate on the basis of sex in selecting targets? Does this suggest that sexual harassment is not a form of sex discrimination? Or does it suggest that the Court in *Oncale* missed some key point about sexual harassment?

7. Under *Oncale* and the interpretation of Title VII as not reaching sexual orientation discrimination, see above note 5, is it likely that a gay man harassed by straight men (or a lesbian harassed by straight women) will have a cause of action under Title VII? What difficulties would such a plaintiff have in proving discrimination on the basis of sex? In practical terms, is Scalia's standard likely to be any different from the standard of those lower courts holding that same-sex sexual harassment "claims are actionable only if the plaintiff can prove the harasser is homosexual (and thus presumably motivated by sexual desire)"? How can the victim of same-sex harassment show sex discrimination other than by showing that someone of the opposite sex would not have been harassed sexually by the harasser(s)? And won't the sexual orientation of the harasser be key to that determination, under traditional ways of thinking, so that gay male harassers of straight men will be violating Title VII whereas straight harassers of gay men will not be violating Title VII? See Steven L. Willborn, Taking Discrimination Seriously: Oncale and the Fate of Exceptionalism in Sexual Harassment Law, 7 Wm. & Mary Bill Rts. J. 677 (1999) (noting that nowhere else in discrimination is such an exacting search of the "true" reason required); see also, Dabney D. Ware & Bradley R. Johnson, Oncale v.

Sundowner Offshore Services, Inc.: Perverted Behavior Leads to a Perverse Ruling, 51 Fla. L. Rev. 489 (1999) (noting that presumption of sexual desire is available to plaintiff if he can show the harasser was a homosexual). Do you agree with Mary Coombs that "gay workers may well find that *Oncale* has made them more, rather than less, vulnerable in the workplace." Coombs, Title VII and Homosexual Harassment After Oncale: Was it a Victory?, 6 Duke J. of Gender L. & Pol'y 1137, 114 (1999).

8. How would a formal equality feminist describe the harm of sexual harassment? Under what circumstances would a formal equality feminist consider sexual harassment a form of sex discrimination? For example, would heterosexual-male sexual harassment be a form of sexual harassment? What of the bisexual supervisor who harasses both men and women? The heterosexual male who sexually harasses a gay man? A gay man who sexually harasses a straight man? How would a dominance anti-subordination feminist answer these questions? A relational feminist?

9. Did Mr. Oncale have alternatives to a Title VII suit? What about criminal charges (rape or assault and battery) or a tort action (assault, battery, invasion of privacy, intentional infliction of emotional distress)? Is this true for other victims of harassment? Why not rely on a torts action? In a recent article, Mark McLaughlin Hager argues that victims of hostile environment sexual harassment by non-supervisory co-workers should seek redress through tort suits (primarily outrage and intentional infliction of emotional distress) against the perpetrators rather than a Title VII suit against the employer. Hager, Harassment as a Tort: Why Title VII Hostile Environment Liability Should Be Curtailed, 30 Conn. L. Rev. 375 (1998). He believes that the offense is one to personal dignity and autonomy and is not a type of gender discrimination. Is a tort action a better alternative? Why or why not? Could a tort suit be brought against an employer for negligence, i.e., the supervisor did nothing when informed of the conduct? Why not? See Catharine A. MacKinnon, Sexual Harassment of Working Women 88, 164–74 (1979) (arguing against the personalization of sexual harassment law through tort actions).

10. Should an employer simply prohibit *all* sexual activity or conversation in the workplace? Is that a feasible, or desirable, response? Recent studies indicate that 70 to 80 percent of people date or wed people they meet at work. See Denver Rocky Mountain News, Looking for Love? Survey Shows It's in Workplace, Bus. at 2G (Feb. 14, 1999); Florida Times–Union, First Business, at 12 (Sept. 21, 1998). A 1994 poll by the American Management Association found that about half of the workplace romances lead to marriage or a long-term relationship. U.S. Chamber of Commerce, 86 Nation's Business No. 7 (Jul. 1, 1998). In fact many employers believe that workplace romance can benefit companies since "people involved in office romance were more interested in their work, more motivated, more energized, more creative, and extra productive because they didn't want to get criticized by their peers that the romance was causing a falloff in productivity." Id. How can employers allow romance but discourage harassment? Can you draft rules reflecting this difference? Can romance gone sour become harassment?

KATHRYN ABRAMS, THE NEW JURISPRUDENCE OF SEXUAL HARASSMENT

83 Cornell L. Rev. 1169, 1205–1213 (1998).

* * *

Even before the workplace emerged as a site of struggle over gender equality, sexual harassment functioned to preserve male supremacy and reinforced masculine norms. Many "pink collar" jobs and jobs traditionally held by women were defined in order to replicate or draw on the roles women performed in the home or in sexual encounters or relationships. Furthermore, the gendered role of women workers also permitted male employees to enjoy many of the male privileges which men enjoyed outside the workplace. Some attributes of female employment roles perpetuated advantages that were not sexual in nature. A secretary, for example, made her boss's coffee, organized his worklife, and assumed responsibility for social amenities, such as the purchase of gifts. Other female employment roles perpetuated male prerogatives that were characteristically sexual. From office worker to stewardess, women were expected to dress and conduct themselves so as to be aesthetically pleasing or stimulating to male sexual desires. The men who supervised or worked with such women often considered it appropriate to comment on this physical presentation or to act on the desire it was intended to arouse, without any particular reference to the desires of the woman involved. It is in this sense that Catharine MacKinnon wrote in 1979 that sexual harassment was built into the job descriptions of many women in traditionally female jobs. Sexual harassment, along with sex segregation and the specific job requirements of women's work, was a part of the work environment that conditioned the expectations of workers and reinforced the gender hierarchy—of men over women and of masculine power and sexual subjectivity over female service and sexual objectification—that permeated the rest of society.

As more women have begun to claim equal status in society and have sought access to a wider range of jobs, male control over the workplace is no longer so hegemonic that sexualization and sexual availability are built uncontroversially into women's job descriptions. Women now realize that work roles need not replicate the roles prescribed in broader society at large. They have begun to see demands for sexual availability or titillation as extraneous, though they have not always recognized such demands as illegitimate or illegal. In the face of women's demands for equality in the workplace and their tentative exploration of new roles that secured some degree of independence from the roles of wife, mother, or sex object, harassment has begun to both follow different patterns and take on different meanings.

In some cases, sexual harassment has emerged as a means of preserving male control over the workplace, particularly where the entry of women into a particular workforce appears to call that control into question. A prime example is sexual harassment directed at women who have entered predominantly male fields. Some types of harassment within this category are particularly flagrant, including physical or sexual aggression or persistent, targeted verbal abuse so severe as to serve unequivocal notice that women are not welcome. Women targeted in this way are often compelled to leave the workplace or transfer to a job with different coworkers or another supervisor. Even when they stay, it is clear that they remain at the sufferance of their male coworkers; they have no hope of getting sufficient purchase on the workplace to make it in any sense their own.

Other forms of harassment aimed at preserving male control are slightly subtler. Supervisors or coworkers may sexualize women employees by either propositioning them directly or treating them in a manner that highlights their sexuality, as opposed to other, work related characteristics. Supervisors may demand that women workers conform to dominant feminine stereotypes that operate outside the workplace by making repeated comments or suggestions regarding the employees' physical appearance, or through instructions to behave in a feminine manner. In some cases, it may be applied categorically to signal that women are not taken seriously: that they are considered sex objects or "pets" instead of competent workers. These latter forms of harassment may not be sufficient to compel all women to leave any particular workplace. Yet they make clear—to women and the men who work with them—that mere presence is not equal to influence or control. These forms of harassment suggest that whatever professional goals women pursue, they will continue to be viewed and judged by reference to more traditional female roles and whatever careers they enter, they still will occupy subordinate roles.

A distinctive feature of these control oriented forms of sexual harassment is that they operate against women as a group. While the harassment may be directed at a particular target who suffers individual employment detriment, most harassment within this category treats individual women as representatives of their sex based group. The message communicated is not simply about a particular woman but about the suitability of all women for employment in a particular job or work environment.

Other forms of harassment are concerned not with resisting women directly but with asserting the primacy of male prerogatives or norms in the workplace. Sexism involves a hierarchy between men and women, but it is rarely concerned simply with the relations between the biological sexes. Most forms of sexism also involve a valuation of masculine norms—those practices or characteristics associated with men—and a devaluation of feminine norms—those practices or characteristics associated with women. Similarly, most forms of sexism involve a confinement of men and women to paradigmatically masculine and feminine roles. This confinement prevents women from partaking of the privilege that may flow from manifesting more socially valued characteristics. It also prevents men from compromising the hierarchy among values by embracing devalued norms. Discouraging or disciplining instances of nonconformity creates the illusion, as Franke notes, that "femininity is ... the authentic expression of female agency and masculinity is ... the authentic expression of male agency."[211] The apparently inevitable association of males with valued (or superordinate) norms and of females with devalued (or subordinate) norms also rationalizes as "natural" the subordination of women to men.

Some forms of harassment seek to enforce this gender hierarchy or gender confinement in the workplace, as they might in other spheres of life. One coworker may devalue a woman who performs a traditionally feminine task (such as secretarial work or food service) by sexualization or derogation. Another may harass a nonfeminine woman or nonmasculine man. These actions may have little to do with workplace relations between the sexes and much to do with social struggles over normative hierarchy and gender conformity.

Yet, there are other forms of sexual harassment which relate to a particular expression of gender hierarchy that occurs in the workplace. The social power of men and the social valuation of masculine norms are expressed, as they are in other social and institutional settings, through the creation of work environments that reflect these norms. Not only do masculine qualities define the effective or successful worker, but also masculine tastes and prerogatives shape the environment in which people do their jobs. Some of this male interaction, such as roughhousing, sexualized talk or pornographic images in the workplace, may not seem "masculine" so much as "the way things are done." Other examples of the entrenchment of masculine norms, such as the toleration of unilateral or even predatory sexual expression, may be recognized as such but are given little thought. All of these norms, however, may be called into question when women, to whom such norms are frequently less natural or less congenial, enter the workplace. When this occurs, male workers may assert these norms more vigorously in order to reentrench them in the workplace. Some portion of this entrenching behavior may be sexual harassment.

Workers may engage (or engage more intensely) in talk that sexualizes or derogates women. They may circulate or post sexually explicit or pornographic visual images. They may engage in practices such as bagging [unexpectedly grabbing a male's genitals] that express a vaguely sexualized form of masculine camaraderie. Such practices not only make "masculine" male workers more comfortable, but they also mark the workplace as an arena in which masculinity is appropriate or even constitutive. Workers may also express the traditionally male prerogative for initiating sex in a range of contexts and without particular reference to the desires of the target. A number of forces may motivate such practices, including actual sexual desire, the impulse to affirm a previ-

211. [Katherine M.] Franke, * * * [What's Wrong with Sexual Harassment?, 49 Stan. L. Rev. 691,] 762 [(1997)].

ously unchallenged prerogative of masculinity, or both. What is distinctive about this last category of behavior, for purposes of sexual harassment analysis, is not the particular motivation (i.e., sexual desire or nonsexual desire) but that the perpetrator feels sufficiently authorized to express himself in this way that he fails to consider the possibility of either contextual inappropriateness or injury to the target. Finally, workers may engage in vigorous disciplinary action against colleagues whose action or self-presentation threatens to undermine the primacy of masculine norms. Men or women who object to these norms or practices may be targeted, as may men who manifest nonmasculine traits.

Some of this behavior appears to be almost reflexive: it is conditioned by a structural arrangement that suggests the centrality or naturalness within the workplace of certain masculine norms, and that may suggest, at some subconscious level, the need to reassert them if workers perceive these norms to be in danger. However, some of this behavior may also be more self-aware and explicitly responsive, aimed as retaliating against women intruders or signaling that the demographic composition of the workplace may have changed but the organizing norms have not. Nevertheless, such behavior as a whole seeks to restore a balance, an orientation around masculine normative lines, that workers perceive disturbed. These norm entrenching forms of sexual harassment may be directed at women as a group—insofar as sexualization or derogation of women is an accepted mode of expressing masculinity or masculine camaraderie. They also may be directed at individual men or women whose actions or modes of self-presentation seem to pose a threat to the unquestioned (or embattled) predominance of masculine norms.

Notes on Sexual Harassment Jurisprudence

1. An alternative theory of sexual harassment is offered by Anita Bernstein:

> How, then, to understand sexual harassment? * * * Hostile environment sexual harassment, I argue, is a type of incivility or—in the locution that I prefer—disrespect. For purposes of doctrine, accordingly, hostile environment complaints should refer to respect; the plaintiff should be required to prove that the defendant—a man, or a woman, or a business entity—did not conform to the standard of a respectful person. This respectful person standard would rightly supplant references to reason and reasonableness; respect is integral to the understanding and remedying of sexual harassment, whereas reason is not.
>
> In giving content to the ideal of equality behind Tile VII as well as the ideal of individual autonomy behind dignitary–tort law, this respectful person standard would fit within the two most important legal bases for redressing sexual harassment in the workplace. Focus on respect addresses the concerns of both those who identify with the imperfect humanity of the accused harasser and those who seek foremost to purge sexual coercion from the workplace. Respect also reconciles competing perspectives on fault, simultaneously recognizing the tort–like wrong of

> sexual harassment and the Title VII emphasis on workplace discrimination. It gives shape to a problem whose outlines have been blurred and contested. Despite its apparent novelty, the respectful person standard is intelligible, easy to execute, and not especially vulnerable to abuse or confusion. In short, it is likely to help reduce the incidence of hostile environment sexual harassment and to provide a remedy for injured plaintiffs.

Bernstein, Treating Sexual Harassment with Respect, 111 Harv. L. Rev. 445, 450–51 (1997). Do you share Bernstein's optimism that the courts will easily be able to comprehend and apply her "respectful person" standard? Do you think there is a universal understanding of what "respect" is? How would you advise an employer client to convey to her employees what would be required under Bernstein's theory of sexual harassment? Would Bernstein's approach eliminate the "because of sex" element from Title VII and replace it with a requirement that all employees be treated with respect? Is there any way to reconcile her approach with the language of Title VII? How precisely is the respect standard different from the current standard? Which one is better for plaintiffs? For defendants? Why?

2. Katherine Franke offers a view of the problems with how sexual jurisprudence is currently articulated and offers yet another alternative:

> Although the Supreme Court has not provided such a theory [of sexual harassment], feminist theorists and lower courts have attempted to do so. Over time, three principal justifications have emerged for considering workplace sexual harassment a violation of Title VII's proscriptions against discrimination "on the basis of sex": (1) it is conduct that would not have been undertaken but for the plaintiff's sex; (2) it is conduct that violates Title VII precisely because it is sexual in nature; and (3) it is conduct that sexually subordinates women to men.
>
> Each of these approaches to the wrong of sexual harassment has formed the foundation for successful litigation challenging sexually hostile working environments under Title VII. Yet to varying degrees, all three of these paradigms fail to provide an adequate account of why sexual harassment is a form of sex discrimination. In this article, I will show that these theories of the wrong of sexual harassment don't do the work they purport to. When pressed, they provide indeterminate and unprincipled outcomes to both central and marginal cases of sexual harassment. What is more, these theories misdirect attention from the real problem: sexual harassment is a sexually discriminatory wrong because of the gender norms it reflects and perpetuates.
>
> According to the theory I develop * * *, the sexual harassment of a woman by a man is an instance of sexism precisely because the act embodies fundamental gender stereotypes: men as sexual conquerors and women as sexually conquered, men as masculine sexual subjects and women as feminine sexual objects. If a "technology" is a manner of accomplishing a task, or the specialized aspect of a particular field, then sexual harassment is both the manner of accomplishing sexist goals, and the specialized instantiation of a sexist ideology. Sexual harassment is a technology of sexism. It is a disciplinary practice that inscribes, enforces, and polices the identities of both harasser and victim according to a

system of gender norms that envisions women as feminine, (hetero)sexual objects, and men as masculine, (hetero)sexual subjects. This dynamic is both performative and reflexive in nature. Performative in the sense that the conduct produces a particular identity in the participants, and reflexive in that both the harasser and the victim are affected by the conduct. The account I suggest provides a better theoretical context from which to draw the inference that, in cases like *Meritor*, the sexual harassment of women by men, "without question," is discrimination "because of sex." At the same time, this framework has the advantage of furnishing a principled way to approach the increasing number of new sexual harassment cases at the margin involving same-sex sexual harassment. Neither the existing Supreme Court account of sexual harassment, nor the three dominant theories of the wrong of sexual harassment can provide an adequate or principled answer to these two questions: (1) why should we draw the inference, in cases like *Meritor*, that sexual harassment is sex discrimination?; and (2) does the sexual harassment of a man by another man constitute sex discrimination?

* * *

On my account, sexual harassment—between any two people of whatever sex—is a form of sex discrimination when it reflects or perpetuates gender stereotypes in the workplace. I suggest a reconceptualization of sexual harassment as gender harassment. Understood in this way, sexual harassment is a kind of sex discrimination not because the conduct would not have been undertaken if the victim had been a different sex, not because it is sexual, and not because men do it to women, but precisely because it is a technology of sexism. That is, it perpetuates, enforces, and polices a set of gender norms that seek to feminize women and masculinize men. Sexual harassment perpetuates these norms because it takes place within a culture and history that in large part reduces women's identity to that of a sex object, and reinforces men's identity as that of a sexual aggressor. Sexual harassment also can be understood to enforce gender norms when it is used to keep gender nonconformists in line. For example, women who work in nontraditional jobs, such as the women who worked at the Jacksonville Shipyards, frequently experience extreme sexual harassment from their male coworkers as a way of putting them in their "proper place." Similarly, sexual harassment operates as a means of policing traditional gender norms particularly in the same-sex context when men who fail to live up to a societal norm of masculinity are punished by their male coworkers through sexual means. As a tool of sexism, sexual harassment can do its dirty work in either a different-sex or a same-sex context. Thus, the sexism in sexual harassment lies not in the fact that it is sexual, but in what it does as a disciplinary, constitutive, and punitive regulatory practice.

Katherine M. Franke, What's Wrong with Sexual Harassment?, 49 Stan. L. Rev. 691, 695–96 (1997). How precisely does Franke's analysis differ from Abrams' or from MacKinnon's in her brief in *Oncale*? Which of these approaches to sexual harassment do you think is the best? Why? Which is the easiest to apply? Which best covers and explains every permutation of sexual harassment? Can you articulate an even better theory?

Text Note: Employer Liability

Once the doctrine of sexual harassment was established, the question of when employers should be held vicariously liable for the acts of their employees arose. The Court in *Meritor* did not resolve this issue, though it did refuse to impose liability on the employer for a hostile environment claim.

Both the courts and the EEOC uniformly imposed liability upon employers for quid pro quo harassment by supervisors, whether or not the employer actually knew of the conduct or the supervisor acted outside the scope of his employment.[35] But in hostile environment cases—whether the hostile environment was created by supervisors or co-workers—the lower federal courts consistently applied a negligence standard, holding employers liable only if they knew or should have known of the hostile environment.[36]

Then, in 1998, the Supreme Court issued two opinions addressing this issue on the same day, Faragher v. City of Boca Raton, 524 U.S. 775, 118 S.Ct. 2275, 141 L.Ed.2d 662 (1998), and Burlington Industries, Inc. v. Ellerth, 524 U.S. 742, 118 S.Ct. 2257, 141 L.Ed.2d 633 (1998). In *Faragher*, the plaintiff was a college student who worked during the summers as a lifeguard for Boca Raton. She asserted that her supervisors repeatedly subjected her and other female lifeguards to uninvited and offensive touching as well as lewd and demeaning remarks addressed to them personally and about women generally. Even though the City had a sexual harassment policy, it failed to disseminate it to her supervisors, and they were unaware of it. While the plaintiff talked about the offensive behavior with a supervisor, she considered these discussions as personal and not a formal complaint; the supervisor did not report the conversations to any City official. Later, however, another female lifeguard wrote to the City's Personnel Director to complain about the harassing supervisors' behavior. As a result, the City investigated and punished them.

The trial court found sexual harassment and held the City liable because: (1) the harassment was pervasive enough that the City had "constructive knowledge" of it; (2) under traditional agency principles, the supervisors were acting as agents; and (3) another supervisor had knowledge of the harassment and did not take any action. Faragher was awarded one dollar. On appeal, the court agreed with the finding of discrimination, but reversed the imposition of liability, finding that the supervisors were acting outside the scope of their employment when they were harassing; that they were not aided in their actions by the agency relationship; and that the City did not have constructive knowledge of the unlawful activity. The Supreme Court granted certiorari in order to identify "the circumstances under which

35. See, e.g., Katz v. Dole, 709 F.2d 251, 256 n. 6 (4th Cir.1983); 29 C.F.R. § 1604.11(c); EEOC Policy Guidance on Current Issues of Sexual Harassment D(1) (Mar. 19, 1990).

36. See, e.g., EEOC v. Hacienda Hotel, 881 F.2d 1504 (9th Cir.1989) (harassment by supervisors); Hall v. Gus Constr. Co., 842 F.2d 1010, 1016 (8th Cir.1988) (harassment by co-workers).

an employer may be held liable under Title VII of the Civil Rights Act of 1964, for the acts of a supervisory employee whose sexual harassment of subordinates has created a hostile work environment amounting to employment discrimination." 524 U.S. at 780.

The Court refused to impose automatic liability on employers for supervisors who harass. The Court held:

> An employer is subject to vicarious liability to a victimized employee for an actionable hostile environment created by a supervisor with immediate (or successively higher) authority over the employee. When no tangible employment action is taken, a defending employer may raise an affirmative defense to liability or damages, subject to proof by a preponderance of the evidence. The defense comprises two necessary elements: (a) that the employer exercised reasonable care to prevent and correct promptly any sexually harassing behavior, and (b) that the plaintiff employee unreasonably failed to take advantage of any preventive or corrective opportunities provided by the employer or to avoid harm otherwise. While proof that an employer had promulgated an antiharassment policy with complaint procedures is not necessary in every instance as a matter of law, the need for a stated policy suitable to the employment circumstances may appropriately be addressed in any case when litigating the first element of the defense. And while proof that an employee failed to fulfill the corresponding obligation of reasonable care to avoid harm is not limited to showing an unreasonable failure to use any complaint procedure provided by the employer, a demonstration of such failure will normally suffice to satisfy the employer's burden under the second element of the defense. No affirmative defense is available, however, when the supervisor's harassment culminates in a tangible employment action, such as discharge, demotion, or undesirable reassignment.

Id. at 807. The Court thus indicated that employers would be liable for harassment by supervisors under two circumstances: when there has been a "tangible job action" and when the employer fails to satisfy the requirements of the two-pronged affirmative defense (exercise of care by employer and failure of plaintiff to minimize the harm). *Faragher* involved no "tangible job action," and the Court imposed liability on the City because it failed to meet the requirements of the affirmative defense: a sexual harassment policy that was not distributed to the many city departments was an inadequate precaution against hostile environment discrimination.

The plaintiff in *Ellerth* alleged constant sexual harassment by one of her supervisors who threatened to make her work life harder but did not take any specific adverse actions against her. The plaintiff did not complain to anyone in authority at Burlington Industries. In its analysis, the Supreme Court noted that the former division of sexual harassment claims into those in which threats are carried out (quid pro quo) and those premised upon "bothersome attentions or sexual remarks that are sufficiently severe or pervasive" (hostile work environment) was not useful in determining employer liability. Instead, the Court reiterated the principle in *Faragher* that employers would be liable for tangible employment actions imposed by supervisors, but that employers have a possible affirmative defense to sexual harassment by supervisors when no tangible employment action is taken. The case was remanded to permit the trial court to determine whether to allow the plaintiff to amend her pleading or supplement her discovery based on the rulings in *Ellerth* and *Faragher*; the employer would then have an opportunity to assert and prove an affirmative defense. In dissent, Justices Thomas and Scalia were willing to impose liability upon the employer only if it was negligent in permitting the supervisor's conduct to occur.

In *Ellerth*, the Court offered additional guidance on what it meant by tangible employment action and explained why employers were vicariously liable for supervisor harassment *whenever the supervisor took a tangible job action against the harassed employee*. (The affirmative defense described in *Faragher* is not available when there has been an adverse and tangible job action.) The Court explained:

> Tangible employment actions are the means by which the supervisor brings the official power of the enterprise to bear on subordinates. A tangible employment decision requires an official act of the enterprise, a company act. The decision in most cases is documented in official company records, and may be subject to review by higher level supervisors. The supervisor often must obtain the imprimatur of the enterprise and use its internal processes.
>
> For these reasons, a tangible employment action taken by the supervisor becomes for Title VII purposes the act of the employer.

524 U.S. at 762. With respect to the meaning of tangible job action, the Court offered:

> In the context of this case, a tangible employment action would have taken the form of a denial of a raise or a promotion. The concept of a tangible employment action appears in numerous cases in the Courts of Appeals discussing claims involving race, age, and national origin discrimination, as well as sex discrimination. Without endorsing the specific results of those decisions, we think it prudent to import the concept of a tangible employment action for resolution of the vicarious liability issue we consider here. A tangible employment action constitutes a significant change in employment status, such as hiring, firing, failing to promote, reassignment with significantly different responsibilities, or a decision causing a significant change in benefits. Compare Crady v. Liberty Nat. Bank & Trust Co. of Ind., 993 F.2d 132, 136 (7th Cir.1993) ("a materially adverse change might be indicated by a termination of employment, a demotion evidenced by a decrease in wage or salary, a less distinguished title, a material loss of benefits, significantly diminished material responsibilities, or other indices that might be unique to a particular situation"), with Flaherty v. Gas Research Institute, 31 F.3d 451, 456 (7th Cir.1994) (a "bruised ego" is not enough); Kocsis v. Multi–Care Management, Inc., 97 F.3d 876, 887 (6th Cir.1996)(demotion without change in pay, benefits, duties, or prestige insufficient) and Harlston v. McDonnell Douglas Corp., 37 F.3d 379, 382 (8th Cir.1994) (reassignment to more inconvenient job insufficient).

Id. at 761.

Notes on Employer Liability

1. The Court in *Ellerth* holds that the employer is automatically liable for a supervisor's harassment, i.e., liable in the absence of employer negligence, only when it culminates in a tangible employment action. This is a significant change from pre-*Ellerth* law. As described above, both the lower federal courts and the EEOC had imposed automatic liability on employers for quid pro quo harassment by a supervisor. And quid pro quo harassment was understood as including implicit as well as explicit threats by supervisors. See, for example, the EEOC definition of sexual harassment at the beginning of this section. Do you see problems with this change? What is the standard of employer liability for quid pro quo harassment by a supervisor when the threat has been only implicit or has never been acted on (for instance, when the employee has complied)? Is the standard adequate to protect employees? Is it necessary to protect employers from inappropriate liability? What standard would you impose for supervisor threats (implicit or explicit) that do not result in "tangible job action"?

2. Subsequent to *Ellerth* and *Faragher*, at least one court has "concluded that extra work assignments, 'inappropriate' work assignments, and denial of the opportunity to attend a professional conference did not rise to the level of 'tangible employment action.' " Reinhold v. Virginia, 151 F.3d 172, 174–75 (4th Cir.1998). Is this consistent with *Ellerth*'s explanation of tangible job action? Is this cause for concern? Do you find the court's notion of tangible job action too narrow? Recall that automatic liability is imposed on the employer for supervisor quid pro quo harassment only when there has been an adverse employment action because it is the adverse action that makes the supervisor's act the company's act. But does this necessitate a conclusion that reassignment to a more inconvenient job is *not* a tangible job action? Can you suggest any explanation for the narrowness of the Court's standard for tangible job action?

3. When there has been supervisor harassment but no tangible employment action is taken, the employer can raise an affirmative defense (to be proven by a preponderance of the evidence): "(a) that the employer exercised reasonable care to prevent and correct promptly any sexually harassing behavior, and (b) that the plaintiff employee unreasonably failed to take advantage of any preventive or corrective opportunities provided by the employer or to avoid harm otherwise." How would you advise an employer who wishes to avoid liability? Should the employer hold special training sessions for all supervisors? Write, circulate and enforce a sexual harassment policy? What can an employer do to encourage victims to utilize the procedures of such a policy? If you experienced sexual harassment from a partner at a law firm, would you utilize the complaint procedure of a sexual harassment policy? Why or why not? Can an employer anticipate and address these concerns? How?

4. Left unaddressed by the Supreme Court is the standard for establishing employer liability for hostile environment harassment created by coworkers. What do you think the standard should be? Perhaps the Supreme Court has not been concerned about this issue because, as noted above, the lower courts have consistently held that employers are liable for hostile

environments created by co-workers, supervisors, customers, vendors, etc. only when negligent, i.e., the employer is liable only when the employer knew or should have known about the harassment and did not respond appropriately. Do you agree that this is the appropriate standard? What advice would you give a potential plaintiff to preserve the possibility of employer liability?

5. In the late 1990's another development occurred in the area of sexual harassment: high-profile class action suits. Three highly visible suits filed against Smith Barney, Merrill Lynch and Mitsubishi Motors affirmed the effectiveness of such suits. The actions against the two brokerage houses were groundbreaking in another way—the two employers agreed not to enforce the security industry's arbitration contract forfeiting employee rights to a court forum, leading the National Association of Securities Dealers (NASD) to allow job discrimination suits to bypass the mandatory arbitration requirement. The multi-million dollar settlements in the brokerage cases also utilize creative mediation, arbitration and judicial options for individual plaintiffs in the class. See Martens v. Smith Barney, Inc., 194 F.R.D. 113 (S.D.N.Y.2000); Cremin v. Merrill Lynch Pierce Fenner & Smith, Inc., 957 F.Supp. 1460 (N.D.Ill.1997); EEOC v. Mitsubishi Motor Manufacturing of America, 990 F.Supp. 1059 (C.D.Ill.1998). Publicity played a major role in all three of these lawsuits, applying enormous pressure on the defendants to settle. The National Organization for Women (NOW), a key player in public demonstrations in the cases, is now implementing a "direct action" campaign, asking the country's top 500 employers to sign a NOW pledge that "ensures a women-friendly workplace," including a workplace free of discrimination. While several major companies have signed the pledge, nearly 97% have not. See Carol Kleiman, Making an Enemy of Workplace Discrimination, Chi. Tribune, Aug. 17, 1999, at Business Section, pg. 1. Litigation, coupled with media campaigns, can be more effective than litigation alone. What kinds of strategies should we be implementing for the next century? What role could technology play in the fight against sexual harassment?

6. How would you assess the current state of sexual harassment law? Would you recommend a Congressional response to these Supreme Court opinions? What kind of legislation would you propose?

7. Perhaps the most notorious sexual harassment case to date arose when Paula Jones claimed then-Governor Bill Clinton, among other things, exposed his erect penis to her and asked her to "kiss it" after she went to his hotel room to meet him during a convention she was staffing as an Arkansas employee. Contrary to Ms. Jones' allegations of adverse employment actions taken after she refused, the judge found that the plaintiff received every cost-of-living and merit increase subsequent to the event, as well as receiving a job upgrade. After discovery was complete, and upon remand from the Supreme Court after it rejected a finding of temporary immunity for the President for a civil action arising before he assumed that office until after he leaves that office, Clinton v. Jones, 520 U.S. 681, 117 S.Ct. 1636, 137 L.Ed.2d 945 (1997), the judge granted summary judgment to the defendant on the ground that plaintiff did not establish a sexual harassment claim. Jones v. Clinton, 990 F.Supp. 657 (E.D.Ark.1998). See Susan S. Blaha, Feminism in the Wake of Jones v. Clinton: Theory, Politics, and the Law, 1

DePaul Women's L.J. 1 (1998). It was President Clinton's testimony during discovery in that case that led to Independent Counsel Kenneth Starr's accusations that the President obstructed justice and committed perjury, ultimately resulting in the House of Representatives bringing impeachment charges against the President. After the failure of impeachment proceedings in the Senate, President Clinton settled the *Jones* suit to foreclose subsequent appeals. Unfortunately, the *Jones* case, including the information contained in the deposition of White House intern Monica Lewinsky, created an atmosphere in which sexual harassment became more of a joke (or cliché) than a serious societal problem. See Christina E. Wells, Essay: Hypocrites and Barking Harlots: The Clinton–Lewinsky Affair and the Attack on Women, 5 Wm. & Mary J. Women & L. 151 (1998). Do you agree that sexual harassment has become a joke? How is it portrayed? It seems to be more and more the subject for television sit-coms and late night comedian monologues. What consequences does this have for working women?

D. SEXUALITY, STEREOTYPING, FEMININITY, AND PROFESSIONAL APPEARANCE

PRICE WATERHOUSE v. HOPKINS

Supreme Court of the United States, 1989.

490 U.S. 228, 109 S.Ct. 1775, 104 L.Ed.2d 268.

JUSTICE BRENNAN announced the judgment of the Court and delivered an opinion, in which JUSTICE MARSHALL, JUSTICE BLACKMUN, and JUSTICE STEVENS join.

* * *

Ann Hopkins had worked at Price Waterhouse's Office of Government Services in Washington, D.C., for five years when the partners in that office proposed her as a candidate for partnership. Of the 662 partners at the firm at that time, 7 were women. Of the 88 persons proposed for partnership that year, only 1—Hopkins—was a woman. Forty-seven of these candidates were admitted to the partnership, 21 were rejected, and 20—including Hopkins—were "held" for reconsideration the following year. * * *

In a jointly prepared statement supporting her candidacy, the partners in Hopkins' office showcased her successful 2–year effort to secure a $25 million contract with the Department of State, labeling it "an outstanding performance" and one that Hopkins carried out "virtually at the partner level." Despite Price Waterhouse's attempt at trial to minimize her contribution to this project, Judge Gesell specifically found that Hopkins had "played a key role in Price Waterhouse's successful effort to win a multi-million dollar contract with the Department of State." Indeed, he went on, "[n]one of the other partnership candidates at Price Waterhouse that year had a comparable record in terms of successfully securing major contracts for the partnership."

The partners in Hopkins' office praised her character as well as her accomplishments, describing her in their joint statement as "an outstanding professional" who had a "deft touch," a "strong character, independence and integrity." Clients appear to have agreed with these assessments. At trial, one official from the State Department described her as "extremely competent, intelligent," "strong and forthright, very productive, energetic and creative." Another high-ranking official praised Hopkins' decisiveness, broadmindedness, and "intellectual clarity"; she was, in his words, "a stimulating conversationalist." Evaluations such as these led Judge Gesell to conclude that Hopkins "had no difficulty dealing with clients and her clients appear to have been very pleased with her work" and that she "was generally viewed as a highly competent project leader who worked long hours, pushed vigorously to meet deadlines and demanded much from the multidisciplinary staffs with which she worked."

On too many occasions, however, Hopkins' aggressiveness apparently spilled over into abrasiveness. Staff members seem to have borne the brunt of Hopkins' brusqueness. Long before her bid for partnership, partners evaluating her work had counseled her to improve her relations with staff members. Although later evaluations indicate an improvement, Hopkins' perceived shortcomings in this important area eventually doomed her bid for partnership. Virtually all of the partners' negative remarks about Hopkins—even those of partners supporting her—had to do with her "interpersonal skills." Both "[s]upporters and opponents of her candidacy," stressed Judge Gesell, "indicated that she was sometimes overly aggressive, unduly harsh, difficult to work with and impatient with staff."

There were clear signs, though, that some of the partners reacted negatively to Hopkins' personality because she was a woman. One partner described her as "macho"; another suggested that she "overcompensated for being a woman"; a third advised her to take "a course at charm school." Several partners criticized her use of profanity; in response, one partner suggested that those partners objected to her swearing only "because it's a lady using foul language." Another supporter explained that Hopkins "ha[d] matured from a tough-talking somewhat masculine hard-nosed mgr [manager] to an authoritative, formidable, but much more appealing lady ptr [partner] candidate." But it was the man who, as Judge Gesell found, bore responsibility for explaining to Hopkins the reasons for the Policy Board's decision to place her candidacy on hold who delivered the coup de grace: in order to improve her chances for partnership, Thomas Beyer advised, Hopkins should "walk more femininely, talk more femininely, dress more femininely, wear make-up, have her hair styled, and wear jewelry."

Dr. Susan Fiske, a social psychologist and Associate Professor of Psychology at Carnegie–Mellon University, testified at trial that the partnership selection process at Price Waterhouse was likely influenced by sex stereotyping. Her testimony focused not only on the overtly sex-based comments of partners but also on gender-neutral remarks, made by partners who knew Hopkins only slightly, that were intensely critical of her. One partner, for example, baldly stated that Hopkins was "universally disliked" by staff, and another described her as "consistently annoying and irritating"; yet these were people who had had very little contact with Hopkins. According to Fiske, Hopkins' uniqueness (as the only woman in the pool of candidates) and the subjectivity of the evaluations made it likely that sharply critical remarks such as these were the product of sex stereotyping—although Fiske admitted that she could not say with certainty whether any particular comment was the result of stereotyping. * * *

In previous years, other female candidates for partnership also had been evaluated in sex-based terms. As a general matter, Judge Gesell concluded, "[c]andidates were viewed favorably if partners believed they maintained their femin[in]ity while becoming effective professional managers"; in this environment, "[t]o be identified as a 'women's lib[b]er' was regarded as [a] negative comment." * * *

The [trial] judge * * * held that Price Waterhouse had unlawfully discriminated against Hopkins on the basis of sex by consciously giving credence and effect to partners' comments that resulted from sex stereotyping. Noting that Price Waterhouse could avoid equitable relief by proving by clear and convincing evidence that it would have placed Hopkins' candidacy on hold even absent this discrimination, the judge decided that the firm had not carried this heavy burden.

The Court of Appeals affirmed the District Court's ultimate conclusion, but departed from its analysis in one particular: it held that even if a plaintiff proves that discrimination played a role in an employment decision, the defendant will not be found liable if it proves, by clear and convincing evidence, that it would have made the same decision in the absence of discrimination. * * * We decide today that the Court of Appeals had the better approach, but that both courts erred in requiring the employer to make its proof by clear and convincing evidence.

* * *

In passing Title VII, Congress made the simple but momentous announcement that sex, race, religion, and national origin are not relevant to the selection, evaluation, or compensation of employees.[3] Yet, the statute does not purport to limit the other qualities and characteristics that employers may take into account in making employment decisions. * * * Title VII eliminates certain bases for distinguishing among employees while otherwise preserving employers' freedom of choice. This balance between employee rights and employer prerogatives turns out to be decisive in the case before us.

Congress' intent to forbid employers to take gender into account in making employment decisions appears on the face of the statute. In now-

3. We disregard, for purposes of this discussion, the special context of affirmative action.

familiar language, the statute forbids an employer to "fail or refuse to hire or to discharge any individual, or otherwise to discriminate with respect to his compensation, terms, conditions, or privileges of employment," or to "limit, segregate, or classify his employees or applicants for employment in any way which would deprive or tend to deprive any individual of employment opportunities or otherwise adversely affect his status as an employee, because of such individual's ... sex." We take these words to mean that gender must be irrelevant to employment decisions. * * *

* * *

We need not leave our common sense at the doorstep when we interpret a statute. It is difficult for us to imagine that, in the simple words "because of," Congress meant to obligate a plaintiff to identify the precise causal role played by legitimate and illegitimate motivations in the employment decision she challenges. We conclude, instead, that Congress meant to obligate her to prove that the employer relied upon sex-based considerations in coming to its decision.

* * *

To say that an employer may not take gender into account is not, however, the end of the matter, for that describes only one aspect of Title VII. The other important aspect of the statute is its preservation of an employer's remaining freedom of choice. We conclude that the preservation of this freedom means that an employer shall not be liable if it can prove that, even if it had not taken gender into account, it would have come to the same decision regarding a particular person. The statute's maintenance of employer prerogatives is evident from the statute itself and from its history, both in Congress and in this Court.

* * *

[W]e hold that the plaintiff retains the burden of persuasion on the issue whether gender played a part in the employment decision * * *. [T]he employer's burden is most appropriately deemed an affirmative defense: the plaintiff must persuade the fact finder on one point, and then the employer, if it wishes to prevail, must persuade it on another.

* * *

In saying that gender played a motivating part in an employment decision, we mean that, if we asked the employer at the moment of the decision what its reasons were and if we received a truthful response, one of those reasons would be that the applicant or employee was a woman. In the specific context of sex stereotyping, an employer who acts on the basis of a belief that a woman cannot be aggressive, or that she must not be, has acted on the basis of gender.

Although the parties do not overtly dispute this last proposition, the placement by Price Waterhouse of "sex stereotyping" in quotation marks throughout its brief seems to us an insinuation either that such stereotyping was not present in this case or that it lacks legal relevance. We reject both possibilities. As to the existence of sex stereotyping in this case, we are not inclined to quarrel with the District Court's conclusion that a number of the partners' comments showed sex stereotyping at work. As for the legal relevance of sex stereotyping, we are beyond the day when an employer could evaluate employees by assuming or insisting that they matched the stereotype associated with their group, for " '[i]n forbidding employers to discriminate against individuals because of their sex, Congress intended to strike at the entire spectrum of disparate treatment of men and women resulting from sex stereotypes.' " An employer who objects to aggressiveness in women but whose positions require this trait places women in an intolerable and impermissible Catch–22: out of a job if they behave aggressively and out of a job if they do not. Title VII lifts women out of this bind.

* * *

It takes no special training to discern sex stereotyping in a description of an aggressive female employee as requiring "a course at charm school." Nor, turning to Thomas Beyer's memorable advice to Hopkins, does it require expertise in psychology to know that, if an employee's flawed "interpersonal skills" can be corrected by a soft-hued suit or a new shade of lipstick, perhaps it is the employee's sex and not her interpersonal skills that has drawn the criticism.

* * *

We hold that when a plaintiff in a Title VII case proves that her gender played a motivating part in an employment decision, the defendant may avoid a finding of liability only by proving by a preponderance of the evidence that it would have made the same decision even if it had not taken the plaintiff's gender into account. Because the courts below erred by deciding that the defendant must make this proof by clear and convincing evidence, we reverse the Court of Appeals' judgment against Price Waterhouse on liability and remand the case to that court for further proceedings.

Notes on Price Waterhouse

1. On remand, Price Waterhouse declined an opportunity, offered by the district court, to submit additional evidence. The district court then concluded that Price Waterhouse had not met its burden of showing that Hopkins would not have been admitted to partnership even absent sexist stereotyping. It therefore ordered Price Waterhouse to admit Hopkins to partnership, not to retaliate against her in the future, to pay her back compensation of $371,175 and lawyers' fees and costs of $422,460.32. In addition, Price Waterhouse was ordered to award her the appropriate number of partnership shares in return for Hopkins' contribution of the appropriate amount of capital to the partnership. Hopkins v. Price Waterhouse, 737 F.Supp. 1202 (D.D.C.1990), affirmed, 920 F.2d 967 (D.C.Cir. 1990).

2. Many of Hopkins' subordinates were women. Price Waterhouse argued on remand that this meant that the subordinates' objections to her treatment of them were nonsexist. Do you agree that women cannot be sexist? What would be the key question in determining whether the subordinates' negative reactions were discriminatory? For a discussion of the double standard for women and men with respect to emotions, see Arlie Russell Hochschild, The Managed Heart 162–84 (1983). What are the emotional consequences for women like Hopkins who are expected to manage feelings better than their peers? Might the partners at Price Waterhouse have thought that Hopkins' inappropriate treatment of subordinates could be cured by more "feminine" behavior? Why? What does this suggest about their expectations regarding interactions between men like themselves and subordinates?

3. What does it mean "to walk more femininely, talk more femininely," etc.? What is the content and meaning of "femininity" in the context in which Hopkins was given this advice? Do you think that feminine women are more likely to wear make-up, jewelry, and have their hair styled? Is there any link on psychological levels (independent of physical appearance) between being the kind of person others would consider "feminine" and being the kind of person likely to appear feminine in terms of physical appearance (by wearing make-up, etc.)? What is that link?

4. Christine Littleton points out that the Supreme Court's decision in Hopkins "strengthens the very cult of masculinity she found so hard to enter." Double and Nothing: Lesbian as Category, 7 U.C.L.A. Women's L. J. 1, 19 (1996). Do you agree? In there a sense in which the Hopkins decision strengthens the ability of employers to define high-status jobs as requiring masculine attributes?

Littleton also notes that courts have consistently refused to recognize discrimination against gay men or lesbians as sex discrimination actionable under Title VII. Had Price Waterhouse decided that Hopkins' "adoption of masculine attributes" suggested she was a lesbian and refused to promote her for that reason, there would have been no violation of Title VII. Littleton concludes, however—in light of Hopkins' victory together with the many cases upholding employer actions adverse to effeminate men (firing men with earrings, etc.)—that Title VII protects gender-bending only in one direction: "Both males and females are legally protected so long as they 'pass' as masculine; neither are legally protected if they call attention to attributes or behaviors associated with femininity or femaleness." Id. at 19. Do you agree? Do you see this as a problem?

5. Both Mary Anne Case and Katherine Franke discuss the relationship between sex and gender in articles critical of the courts' interpretations of Title VII. As discussed in Chapter 2, courts often use "gender discrimination" as a synonym for "sex discrimination." But these terms are understood as discrete phenomena in other disciplines. "Gender" refers to socially constructed norms appropriate for members of one sex: the two sexes are defined as female and male by physical characteristics, whereas the two genders are sets of social norms we call "femininity" (which we expect to see displayed by people whose physical sex is female) and "masculinity" (which we expect to see displayed by people whose physical sex is male).

Mary Anne Case on the relationship between sex and gender in law:

> [A]s things now stand, the concept of gender has been imperfectly disaggregated in the law from sex on the one hand and sexual orientation on the other. * * * When individuals diverge from the gender expectations for their sex—when a woman displays masculine characteristics or a man feminine ones—discrimination against her is now treated as sex discrimination while his behavior is generally viewed as a marker for homosexual orientation and may not receive protection from discrimination. * * *
>
> This differential treatment * * * marks the continuing devaluation, in life and in law, of qualities deemed feminine.* * *
>
> We are in danger of substituting for prohibited sex discrimination a still acceptable gender discrimination, that is to say, discrimination against the stereotypically feminine, especially when manifested by men, but also when manifested by women. Ann Hopkins, I fear, may have been protected only because of the doubleness of her bind: It was nearly impossible for her to be both as masculine as the job required and as feminine as gender stereotypes require. But the Supreme Court seems to have had no trouble with the masculine half of Hopkins's double bind; there is little indication, for example, that the Court would have found it to be sex discrimination if a prospective accounting partner had instead been told to remove her makeup and jewelry and to go to assertiveness training class instead of charm school.

Case, Disaggregating Gender from Sex and Sexual Orientation: The Effeminate Man in the Law and Feminist Jurisprudence, 105 Yale L. J. 1, 2–3 (1995).

Katherine Franke on the relationship between sex and gender in law:

> Antidiscrimination law is founded upon the idea that sex, conceived as biological difference, is prior to, less normative than, and more real than gender. Yet in every way that matters, sex bears an epiphenomenal relationship to gender; that is, under close examination, almost every claim with regard to sexual identity or sex discrimination can be shown to be grounded in normative gender rules and roles. Herein lies the mistake. In the name of avoiding "the grossest discrimination," that is, "treating things that are different as though they were exactly alike," sexual equality jurisprudence has uncritically accepted the validity of biological sexual differences. By accepting these biological differences, equality jurisprudence reifies as foundational fact that which is really an effect of normative gender ideology. This jurisprudential error not only produces obvious absurdities at the margin of gendered identity, but it also explains why sex discrimination laws have been relatively ineffective in dismantling profound sex segregation in the wage-labor market, in shattering "glass ceilings" that obstruct women's entrance into the upper echelons of corporate management, and in increasing women's wages, which remain a fraction of those paid men. The targets of antidiscrimination law, therefore, should not be limited to the "gross, stereotyped distinctions between the sexes" but should also include the social processes that construct and make coherent the categories male and female. In many cases, biology operates as the excuse or cover for

social practices that hierarchize individual members of the social category "man" over individual members of the social category "woman." In the end, biology or anatomy serve as metaphors for a kind of inferiority that characterizes society's view of women.

* * * Given the epiphenomenal relationship between identity and equality, the Fourteenth Amendment and Title VII should apply with equal force to acts of classification as well as to disparate treatment of classes. Rather than accepting sexual differences as the starting point of equality discourse, sex discrimination jurisprudence should consider the role that the ideology of sexual differences plays in perpetuating and ensuring sexual hierarchy.

A reconceptualization of the two most fundamental elements of sexual equality jurisprudence is necessary to correct this foundational error. First, sexual identity—that is, what it means to be a woman and what it means to be a man—must be understood not in deterministic, biological terms, but according to a set of behavioral, performative norms that at once enable and constrain a degree of human agency and create the background conditions for a person to assert, I am a woman. To say that someone is a woman demands a complex description of the history and experience of persons so labeled. This conception of sexual identity ultimately provides the basis for a fundamental right to determine gendered identity independent of biological sex.

Second, what it means to be discriminated against because of one's sex must be reconceived beyond biological sex as well. To the extent that the wrong of sex discrimination is limited to conduct or treatment which would not have occurred but for the plaintiff's biological sex, antidiscrimination law strives for too little. Notwithstanding an occasional gesture to the contrary, courts have not interpreted the wrong of sex discrimination to reach rules and policies that reinforce masculinity as the authentic and natural exercise of male agency and femininity as the authentic and natural exercise of female agency.

Franke, The Central Mistake of Sex Discrimination Law: The Disaggregation of Sex from Gender, 144 U. Penn. L. Rev. 1, 2–3 (1995).

Are Case and Franke making similar or opposite points? Why is Case's article about the need to disaggregate sex and gender whereas Franke's is about the need to see the interconnection?

Do you agree with Franke that biological differences are "really only an effect of normative gender ideology" (in paragraph one)? What does she mean? Is she arguing that having a child is the same physical event for women and men? What would Franke say if presented with evidence that high levels of testosterone make people more upbeat and confident (definite advantages in employment)? See Andrew Sullivan, Why Men Are Different, N,Y. Times Magazine, Apr. 2, 2000, at 46 (describing such evidence). Do you agree with Franke's definition of sexual identity (in paragraph four)? Is that what sexual identity means to you? Franke suggests that "[t]he targets of antidiscrimination law * * * should include the social processes that construct and make coherent the categories male and female." Can you give examples of how this suggestion would work: what kinds of cases could be brought? Would you advocate this approach? How would the various feminist approaches described in Chapter 3 view this proposal? How would judges react?

6. Would a man required to behave in a "masculine" manner face the same problems as those faced by Hopkins? Is there any conflict between "femininity" and successful business behavior? Between femininity and mental health? See Emily G. Tinsley, Sandra Sullivan–Guest, and John McGuire, Feminine Sex Role and Depression in Middle–Aged Women, 11 Sex Roles 25 (1984) (using a single scale [a scale measuring masculinity—androgyny—femininity] and finding positive correlation between depression and "femininity scores" for middle-aged women); Ronnie Wilson and Ed Cairins, Sex–Role Attributes, Perceived Competence and the Development of Depression in Adolescence, 29 J. Child Psych. & Psych. 635 (1988) (using separate "masculinity" and "femininity" scales [with androgyny defined as scoring high on both] and finding negative correlation between depression and "masculinity" scores in female and male adolescents, though no link between distinct "femininity" scores and depression; positive correlation found between "masculinity" [but not "femininity"] and perceptions of competence); Maggie Mulqueen, On Our Own Terms: Redefining Competence and Femininity (1992) (exploring conflict between "femininity" and competence).

Are "femininity" and "masculinity" opposite ends of the same scale, with androgyny in the middle? Or are they different things, so that androgyny would be a high rating on each scale? How would a person who scored high on both behave? What would you measure in constructing these various scales? How do you think the partners at Price Waterhouse would have answered these questions?

7. Are there analogous problems—problems analogous to the courts' failure to see masculine norms as sex discrimination—with respect to race and cultural background?

8. There is considerable evidence that elite women who seem to be rising to the top of professions or corporations hit a glass ceiling well before reaching the top. As one researcher reports:

> Surveys indicate consistently that although 30–40% of all entry level management positions are held by women, their proportions decline to 20% at middle ranks, and plummet to only 2–5% of the top positions (i.e., within three levels of management of the CEO's office). Stated differently, the higher one goes, the greater one's opportunities if one is male; the more opportunity shrinks if one is female.

Mark Maier, Gender Equity, Organizational Transformation and Challenges, 16 J. Bus. Ethics 943, 943 (June 1997). An article published in October, 2000, reports that "[a]lthough women in the United States comprise approximately 40% of all managers, in the largest corporations women hold less than 0.5% of the highest paid management jobs." Judith G. Oakley, Gender–Based Barriers to Senior Management Positions: Understanding the Scarcity of Female CEOs, 27 J. Bus. Ethics 321, 321 (Oct. 2000). According to a 1995 report, "among the top 1000 industrial firms and the 500 largest U.S. corporations of all types as ranked by Fortune magazine, 97% of senior managers are white, and an estimated 95–97% of senior managers are male." Id. at 321.

The glass ceiling is a metaphor for the many barriers women of all colors and men of color face as they attempt to rise through the management ranks. One problem discussed by both Maier and Oakley is that managers are supposed to exercise traits regarded as masculine, though there is no evidence that in fact these traits are effective in managing. Indeed, the evidence suggests that promotions to higher management levels depend primarily on skill as a politician, not as a manager. Could Title VII be used to challenge the masculine norms of corporate culture? Or the fact that workplaces are structured for workers without significant caretaking responsibilities? Why or why not?

In terms of traits valued in corporate culture, what do you make of the fact that 97% of senior managers are white?

9. Might women of all colors and other minorities tend to have skills that might make them more effective at managing than the politically-adept white men who tend to be promoted to higher levels? What is your reaction to Sally Helgesen's conclusion—after examining the leadership styles of four successful women leaders—that women as leaders have "particular aptitudes for long-term negotiating, analytic listening, and creating an ambiance in which people work with zest and spirit"? Helgesen, The Female Advantage: Women's Ways of Leadership 249 (1990).

Text Note: How Discrimination Operates

The standard for sex discrimination in disparate treatment cases under Title VII is the same as in cases under the Equal Protection Clause of the Fourteenth Amendment, described above in Chapter 2. For both kinds of cases, discriminatory "intent" or "purpose" is often said to be a requirement: the defendant must "intend" to discriminate. An explicitly sex-based classification—such as one rule for men and another for women—satisfies this standard. In the absence of such overt discrimination, however, evidence of an intent to discriminate on the basis of sex helps to establish that in fact this person was treated differently because she was a woman rather than, for example, because she was incompetent.

In *Price Waterhouse,* the Court explains what it means by the terminology it uses to describe intent, i.e., that gender was a motivating factor:

> In saying that gender played a motivating part in an employment decision, we mean that, if we asked the employer at the moment of the decision what its reasons were and if we received a truthful response, one of those reasons would be that the applicant or employee was a woman. In the specific context of sex stereotyping, an employer who acts on the basis of a belief that a woman cannot be aggressive, or that she must not be, has acted on the basis of gender.

Conflict theory, the prominent sociological explanation of discrimination, is consistent with this notion of discrimination as intentional:

> According to a conflict-theory perspective, the beneficiaries of systems of inequality protect their privileges by using the resources they control to exclude members of subordinate groups. Thus, these theories explain discrimination in terms of the strategic, self-interested actions by mem-

> bers of privileged groups who intentionally exclude and exploit subordinate-group members to protect or advance their own interests.[37]

Conflict theory, however, leaves much discrimination unexplained.

Social cognition theory, from social psychology, explores discrimination in terms of cognitive processing rather than intentional acts. Sociologist Barbara Reskin describes social cognition theory:

> In brief, social cognition theory holds that people automatically categorize others into ingroups and outgroups. The visibility and cultural importance of sex and race and their role as core bases of stratification make them almost automatic bases of categorization. Having categorized others, people tend to automatically "feel, think and behave toward [particular members of the category] the same way they ... feel, think, and behave toward members of that social category more generally." Importantly, categorization is accompanied by stereotyping, attribution bias, and evaluation bias. These, in turn, introduce sex, race, and ethnic biases into our perceptions, interpretations, recollections, and evaluations of others. These biases are cognitive rather than motivational; in other words, they occur independently of decision makers' group interests or their conscious desire to favor or harm others.[38]

Laboratory experiments reveal that when people are categorized into groups on any basis, bias results. Employment discrimination lawyer Linda Krieger describes these processes:

> [Experimental] subjects are grouped according to what they are told is some minimal similarity, and are then asked to evaluate members of their own and the other group or to allocate rewards between the two groups. In some studies, subjects were told that they had been grouped according to whether they tended to underestimate or overestimate the sizes of dots. In other studies, subjects were told that their group assignment had been based on preferences for different paintings or photographs, and in yet others, subjects were informed that group assignment was random.
>
> The experiments showed that, as soon as people are divided into groups—even on a trivial or random basis—strong biases in their perception of differences, evaluation, and reward allocation result. As soon as the concept of "groupness" is introduced, subjects perceive members of their group as more similar to them, and members of other groups as more different from them, than when those same persons are viewed as noncategorized individuals. Indeed, when offered a choice, * * * subjects prefer to view information indicating their similarity with ingroup members and their distinctiveness from outgroup members.
>
> While ingroup members perceive similarities between themselves and others in their group, they perceive outgroup members as being even more homogeneous. In other words, subjects tend to perceive

37. Barbara F. Reskin, The Proximate Causes of Employment Discrimination, 29 Contemporary Sociol. 319, 320–21 (2001).

38. Id. (quoting Susan T. Fiske, Monica Lin and Steven Neuberg, The Continuum Model: Ten Years Later in Dual Process Theories in Social Psychology (Shelly Chaiken and Yaacov Trope, eds. 1999)).

outgroup members as an undifferentiated mass, while ingroup members are more highly differentiated.[39]

Grouping people, things, events, into categories is a normal and necessary cognitive process; without it the world would be a vast wilderness of discrete phenomena. We would see no forests. But, as noted above, categorization results in stereotyping, evaluation bias, and attribution bias. Barbara Reskin explains how these occur:

> Stereotyping
>
> Stereotypes are unconscious habits of thought that link personal attributes to group membership. Stereotyping is an inevitable concomitant of categorization: As soon as an observer notices that a "target" belongs to a stereotyped group (especially an outgroup), characteristics that are stereotypically linked to the group are activated in the observer's mind, even among people who consciously reject the stereotypes. To appreciate the importance of stereotyping for discriminatory outcomes, it is helpful to distinguish descriptive and prescriptive stereotypes.
>
> Descriptive stereotypes, which characterize how group members are, influence how we perceive others and interpret their behavior. Descriptive stereotyping can precipitate discrimination because it predisposes observers toward interpretations that conform to stereotypes and blinds them to disconfirming possibilities, especially when the behavior that observers must make sense of is subject to multiple interpretations (e.g., she worked late because women are helpful, rather than she worked late because she wants a promotion). Thus, descriptive stereotypes distort observers' impressions of the behavior of members of stereotyped groups.
>
> Prescriptive stereotypes are generalizations about how members of a group are supposed to be, based usually on descriptive stereotypes of how they are. These normative stereotypes serve as standards against which observers evaluate others' behavior. Both descriptive and prescriptive stereotypes influence what we remember about others and the inferences we draw about their behavior. Thus, stereotypes serve as "implicit theories, biasing in predictable ways the perception, interpretation, encoding, retention, and recall of information about other people."
>
> Cognitive processes involved in stereotyping make stereotypes tenacious. People unconsciously pursue, prefer, and remember "information" that supports their stereotypes (including remembering events that did not occur), and ignore, discount, and forget information that challenges them. From the standpoint of social cognition theory, stereotypes are adaptive: People process information that conforms to their stereotypes more quickly than inconsistent information, and they are more likely to use stereotypes when they are under time pressure, partly because stereotyping conserves mental resources. Research on people's efforts to suppress stereotypes is relevant. In one study, subjects in-

39. Linda Hamilton Krieger, The Content of Our Categories: A Cognitive Bias Approach to Discrimination and Equal Employment Opportunity, 47 Stan. L. Rev. 1161, 1191–92 (1995).

structed to avoid sexist statements in a sentence-completion task could comply when they had enough time, but when they had to act quickly the statements they constructed were more sexist than those of subjects who had not been told to avoid making sexist statements. And according to a comparison of subjects who were and were not instructed to suppress stereotypes, the former could refrain from expressing stereotypes, but in a "rebound effect," they expressed stronger stereotypes in subsequent judgments than did subjects who had not tried to suppress their stereotypes in the first place.

Evaluation Bias and Attribution Bias

Stereotype-based expectations and ingroup favoritism act as distorting lenses through which observers assess others' performance and account for their successes and failures. Descriptive stereotypes affect observers' expectations and hence the explanations they construct. When the actions of others conform to our expectations, we tend to attribute their behavior to stable, internal propensities (e.g., ability), while we attribute actions that are inconsistent with our stereotype-based expectations to situational (i.e., external) or transient factors (e.g., task difficulty, luck, or effort). In this way, stereotype-based expectations give rise to biased attributions. For example, given the stereotype that men are good at customarily male tasks, competent performance doesn't require an explanation; men's failures do, however, and observers tend to attribute these unexpected outcomes to situational factors such as bad luck or lack of effort, none of which predict future failure. In contrast, women are stereotypically not expected to do well at customarily male endeavors, so explaining their failure is easy: They lack the requisite ability (an internal trait) and hence are likely to fail in the future. In contrast, their successes are unexpected, so they must have resulted from situational factors that do not predict future success.

Ingroup preference and outgroup derogation lead to similar attribution processes. Because observers expect ingroup members to succeed and outgroup members to fail, they attribute ingroup success and outgroup failure to internal factors [such as ability or lack of ability], and ingroup failure and outgroup success to situational factors [such as luck]. Observers also tend to characterize behavior that is consistent with their expectations in abstract terms and unexpected behavior in concrete terms. For example, give the same act—arriving late for a meeting—an observer would recall that an ingroup member was delayed, but that an outgroup member is a tardy person. Once behavior has been interpreted and encoded into memory, it is the interpretation, not the initial behavior, to which people have ready access. Thus, observers would predict that the outgroup member, but not the ingroup member, would be tardy in the future.

Power and Cognitive Biases

* * * [O]ccupying a position of power may prompt people to invest extra effort into categorizing others. In addition, power affects the degree to which people act on the propensity to stereotype. People can't afford to stereotype others on whom they depend because they need to assess them accurately, but they can afford to stereotype subordinate

groups and are more likely to do so than subordinate group members are to stereotype members of dominant groups. In addition, under conditions of perceived threat, the more stake observers have in the status quo, and hence the more to lose, the more likely they are to stereotype outgroups. The sense of entitlement that accompanies dominant-group status is likely to give dominant group members particular confidence in their stereotypes. This propensity is reinforced by the fact that powerful observers actively seek information that confirms their stereotypes and disregard disconfirming information. However, priming the powerful with egalitarian values leads them to pay closer attention to information that contradicts outgroup stereotypes. Finally, members of high-status ingroups show more bias in favor of ingroup members than do members of low-status groups. [40]

Disproportionately, white men are at the top of most workplaces, and they are likely to perceive women and minorities as members of outgroups. One should therefore expect "the devaluation of jobs that are predominantly female and predominantly minority" and the overvaluation of jobs held predominantly by white men.[41] And when members of outgroups are present in low numbers in jobs held predominantly by white men, stereotyping is likely to be particularly powerful.[42]

Courts assume not just that discrimination is motivational, but also that decisionmakers know what factors influence or determine a decision. Recall that in *Price Waterhouse*, the Supreme Court explains that by "saying that gender played a motivating part in an employment decision, we mean that, if we asked the employer at the moment of the decision what its reasons were and if we received a truthful response, one of those reasons would be that the applicant or employee was a woman." In reality, decisionmakers do not have access to such insight, explains Linda Krieger:

> [P]eople are actually quite poor at identifying the effects of various stimuli on their evaluations, judgments, choices, and predictions. In a series of experiments, [researchers] systematically manipulated some component of a complex stimulus situation such that the impact of a particular stimulus component on subjects' choices and actions could be assessed. They found that subjects were virtually never accurate in identifying the causal efficacy of the manipulated stimulus. Where the stimulus had a significant effect on their responses, subjects typically reported that it was noninfluential; in cases where a particular stimulus component had no significant causal effect, subjects reported it as having determined their response.[43]

Martha Chamallas identifies cultural domination as another important component of discrimination in the workplace. Consider a law school that admits minorities and women as students and even hires some as members of the faculty, but the law school's values and perspectives do not change to

40. Reskin, above note 37, at 322–323 (third paragraph of extract in text quotes Krieger, above note 39, at 1188).

41. Reskin, above note 37, at 322.

42. Martha Chamallas, Structuralist and Cultural Domination Theories Meet Title VII: Some Contemporary Influences, 92 Mich. L. Rev. 2370, 2379–83 (1994).

43. Krieger, above note 39, at 1214–15.

incorporate the values and perspectives of the newcomers.[44] For example, the school is reluctant to offer courses on feminism and critical race theory. When such courses are offered, they are regarded as "fluff," and those teaching them are seen as teaching odd "boutique" courses of interest to a few rather than anything either analytically rigorous or important for a quality legal education. Cultural domination is not, of course, limited to academic settings; it is a common phenomenon and present in some form in most workplaces.

Notes on How Discrimination Operates

1. Barbara Reskin and Debra McBrier suggest that certain personnel policies, such as formal evaluation and recruitment procedures with express standards (even if still subjective, such as "works well with others"), increase the numbers of women promoted to management. Reskin and McBrier, Why Not Ascription? Organizations' Employment of Male and Female Managers, 65 American Sociol. Rev. 1 (2000). Thus, good employment practices—designed to counteract cognitive biases—can decrease the amount of discrimination within an organization. Is there any way this insight could be incorporated into anti-discrimination law?

2. Describe the culture at places you have gone to school or worked. If cultural domination was present, can you describe how it operated and who benefited?

3. Do you agree with Linda Krieger that "[i]t is probably no accident that legal policymakers interpreting Title VII have constructed all disparate treatment discrimination as manifesting a conscious, discriminatory purpose." Krieger, The Content of Our Categories: A Cognitive Bias Approach to Discrimination and Equal Employment Opportunity, 47 Stan. L. Rev. 1161, 1247 (1995). She suggests that courts prefer this understanding of discrimination because it "holds the problem of intergroup bias at a safe distance, something those 'other people,' that is, 'bad people' do." Id. Do you agree? Do you think that the justices are unaware of the evidence about how discrimination operates on a cognitive level? Can you think of other explanations for the courts' holding fast to a motivational theory of discrimination despite mounting evidence over the last few decades that "discrimination is not one thing, but many"? Id. at 1248.

4. Ann McGinley discusses the implications of insights from the masculinities literature for Title VII:

> In her groundbreaking work on male behavior in the workplace, Professor Patricia Martin observes that men "mobilize masculinities" in their evaluation of women (and men) at work.[157] Professor Martin identifies a number of ways that men, perhaps unconsciously, establish

44. Chamallas, above note 42, at 2388–2389. See also David A. Thomas & Robin J. Ely, Making Differences Matter: A New Paradigm for Managing Diversity, Harv. Bus. Rev. 79 (September/October 1996) (describing three stages of workplace diversity; only in the third do the values and perspectives of the newcomers become part of the institution itself).

157. See Patricia Y. Martin, Gendering and Evaluating Dynamics: Men, Masculinities, and Managements, in Men As Managers, Managers As Men 186, 190 (David L. Collinson and Jeff Hearn eds., 1996).

> and maintain their dominance over equally qualified women in the workplace by conflating masculinity with social relations at work and with work performance. Professor Martin identifies three gender-based evaluation frames (or lenses) through which males evaluate female workers: (1) potential; (2) legitimacy; and (3) performance. For example, in evaluating potential, male managers typically see women and men workers as different. These frames, according to Professor Martin, are used generally without the manager's awareness. Male managers tend to judge men's talents and abilities as "more consonant with more valued jobs and opportunities." With respect to legitimacy, men "framed women as lacking legitimacy to hold powerful positions." This was apparent, for example, when a group of men on a search committee for a university president, missed the formal job presentation of the only woman candidate, while attending the presentations of all of the male candidates. This action was a public enactment of masculinity, according to Martin, "declaring for all to see their assumption that men are better (more important) than women." Finally, men observe women's performance through a "gender lens," frequently devaluing women's performance relative to men's. Even when men evaluate women positively, they still actively favor men by promoting them over women.[164]

McGinley, !Viva La Evolucion!, 9 Cornell J. L. & Pub. Pol'y 415, 440–441 (2000). In your experience at law school or at law firms, have you seen men judge men's "talents and abilities" as "more consonant with" being a good lawyer or law professor? Have you seen women as lawyers or law professors face legitimacy challenges not faced by their male peers? Have you seen women's performance as law students devalued by men relative to their valuation of men who are law students? Have you seen similar phenomena along racial lines? If you did observe any of these phenomena, would you describe them as conscious? Should they be seen as violating Title VII even if not conscious?

5. How would you craft a statute to try to reach unconscious discrimination? See McGinley, above note 3, at 481–84 (suggesting legislation that would define intent to include unconscious discrimination; "expand the stereotypes doctrine established in *Price Waterhouse*"; and create a strong inference of discrimination from "discriminatory racial or sexual remarks" even when not direct evidence of discrimination). Can you make other suggestions?

6. In a disparate treatment Title VII case, the plaintiff has the burden of producing enough evidence for an inference of discrimination on the basis of race or sex, such as that the employer was hiring people; the plaintiff, a woman of any color or a man of color applied, was qualified, but was not hired, and the employer continued to look for candidates to fill the position. Once the plaintiff makes this showing, the burden is on the employer to articulate a legitimate reason for its decision. (Although the burden of production shifts to the defendant, the ultimate burden of persuasion remains on the plaintiff.) After the defendant articulates a legitimate, nondiscriminatory reason, the plaintiff has the burden of showing that the articulated reason is just a "pretext" for discrimination, i.e., that in reality, the

164. See id. [at 202.]

decision was based not on the articulated factor but on the plaintiff's sex or race. See, e.g., St. Mary's Honor Center v. Hicks, 509 U.S. 502, 506–07, 113 S.Ct. 2742, 125 L.Ed.2d 407 (1993). This framework is based on the following assumption:

> [W]e know from our experience that more often than not people do not act in a totally arbitrary manner, without any underlying reasons, especially in a business setting. Thus, when all legitimate reasons for rejecting an applicant have been eliminated as possible reasons for the employer's actions, it is more likely than not the employer, whom we generally assume acts only with some reason, based his decision on an impermissible consideration such as race.

Furnco Construction Corp. v. Waters, 438 U.S. 567, 577, 98 S.Ct. 2943, 57 L.Ed.2d 957 (1978).

Krieger critiques this framework in light of what we know about human decisionmaking:

> Within the pretext paradigm, it is simply not possible for an employment decision to be both motivated by the employer's articulated reasons and tainted by intergroup bias; the trier of fact must decide between the two. * * *
>
> Pretext analysis thus rests on the assumption that, absent discriminatory animus, employment decisionmakers are rational actors. They make evenhanded decisions using optimal inferential strategies in which all relevant behavioral events are identified and weighted * * *. If an employer's proffered explanation for its decision is shown to be irrational or implausible in light of the relevant data set, the trier of fact may conclude, and to find for the plaintiff, must conclude, that the reasons given did not really motivate the decisionmaker, but were simply contrived to mask discriminatory intent. The presumption of invidiousness permits the trier of fact to infer discriminatory intent from flaws in a decisionmaker's inferential process. Without this presumption, one could only infer that an irrational decision has been made; such a decision, in the absence of a duty to discharge only for good cause, it would not be actionable.

Kreiger, above note 3, at 1179, 1181. Given these problems with the disparate treatment framework, can you make any suggestions for a better antidiscrimination law or better interpretations of existing antidiscrimination laws?

LANIGAN v. BARTLETT AND COMPANY GRAIN

United States District Court, Western District of Missouri, 1979.

466 F.Supp. 1388.

When plaintiff began working, defendant did not permit women to wear pantsuits in either the general or the executive office areas. In apparent response to employee requests, defendant announced a change in policy * * * which permitted women employees to wear pantsuits in the general offices, but not in the executive offices. * * *

Following this change of policy, plaintiff wore pantsuits to work on several occasions although she continued to work in the executive offices.

On July 25, 1974, plaintiff wore a pantsuit to work and was discharged for failure to comply with the company dress code policies. * * *

Plaintiff recognizes that application of the rule set forth in the "haircut" cases would require denial of her claim. These cases are unanimous in holding that nothing in Title VII prohibits an employer from making decisions based on factors such as grooming and dress. Plaintiff argues that these cases are distinguishable because not allowing women to wear pants perpetuates the stereotype that men are more capable than women of making business decisions. Perpetuation of this alleged stereotype, plaintiff contends, brings this case within that line of cases referred to as "sex-plus." This line of cases rests on the theory that disparate treatment of a male or female subclass violates Title VII since the employer has added a factor for one sex that is not added to the other sex as a condition of employment. The discrimination in these cases is directed against members of the protected class who possess the additional factor. In this case, the additional factor is the wearing of pantsuits. Thus, among employees in the executive offices, women wearing pants (the subclass) are subject to discharge while women wearing skirts and men wearing pants are not subject to discharge.

* * * [E]mployees in the executive offices deal with defendant's customers and members of the public. Following plaintiff's "sex-plus" analysis, the issue is whether the difference in treatment among women in the executive offices constitutes sex discrimination when compared to the treatment of men in the executive offices. Stated differently, the issue is whether a discharge based on plaintiff's sex plus her wearing pantsuits in violation of a known dress code policy constitutes sex discrimination.[2]

* * *

There is no question * * * that "sex-plus" employment policies can be challenged under Title VII. However, the "haircut cases" cannot be dismissed out of hand since they unanimously hold that disparate treatment of a subclass (men with long hair) of a protected class (males) does not violate Title VII. Reconciliation of these "sex-plus" cases with Phillips and similar cases is generally based on a perceived Congressional intent to limit application of Title VII in the "sex-plus" area to those employment policies which discriminate on the basis of (1) immutable characteristics, (2) characteristics which are changeable but which involve fundamental rights (such as having children or getting married), and (3) characteristics which are changeable but which significantly affect employment opportunities afforded to one sex.

Plaintiff does not contend that she is unable to wear clothes other than pantsuits or that she is in any way physically unable to comply with

2. It should be emphasized that plaintiff does not contend that she was discharged because she is a woman. The fact that she is a woman is important only because the particular aspect of dress code policy in question applies only to women. However, for purposes of responding to the "sex-plus" contention, it is useful to adopt that terminology in stating the issue.

the dress code. In other words, plaintiff's affection for pantsuits is not an "immutable characteristic." Plaintiff does not contend that she has a "fundamental right" to wear pantsuits to work. Plaintiff does contend that the dress code significantly affects employment opportunities because it perpetuates "a sexist, chauvinistic attitude in employment." Plaintiff asserts that the Court should find a violation of Title VII because "(T)he employer could offer no excuse whatsoever as to why his secretary could perform a job in a more efficient manner in a skirt rather than a pantsuit, and could only speculate as to whether or not a skirt could be considered more business-like."

These contentions miss the point. An employer is not required to justify any business practice in a Title VII action until and unless the plaintiff has established a prima facie case of discrimination. The fact that defendant introduced no evidence on the "business necessity" of a dress code prohibiting pantsuits on women working in its executive offices proves nothing because the Court holds that plaintiff has not established a prima facie case of discrimination. Accordingly, defendant was not obligated to justify its dress code policies.

The Court believes that there is no principled distinction between the rationale of the "haircut" cases and this case. Employment decisions, such as plaintiff's discharge, based on either dress codes or policies regarding hair length are more closely related to the company's choice of how to run its business rather than to its obligation to provide equal employment opportunities. The decision to project a certain image as one aspect of company policy is the employer's prerogative which employees may accept or reject. If they choose to reject the policy, they are subject to such sanctions as deemed appropriate by the company. An employer is simply not required to account for personal preferences with respect to dress and grooming standards. In this case, plaintiff has not demonstrated how defendant's dress code policies impermissibly restrict equal employment opportunities and her contention that the policies perpetuate a stereotype is simply a matter of opinion.

Notes on Lanigan

1. *Lanigan* is a 1979 case, but it states the current law on sex-specific dress codes. See, e.g., Tavora v. New York Mercantile Exchange, 101 F.3d 907 (2d Cir.1996) (affirming dismissal of suit brought by a man fired for failing to have short hair (required only of male employees); Hanson v. Highland Homes Holdings, Inc., 1997 WL 86456 (N.D.Tex.1997) (affirming dismissal of African American woman fired for failing to comply with her employer's grooming standards for women employees). What explains these cases? Under standard Title VII analysis in any context other than grooming codes, once the plaintiff has shown that an employer treats women and men differently (by, for example, prohibiting pants only on women), the plaintiff wins unless the defendant can show that sex is a BFOQ (bona fide occupational qualification for the job, a standard rarely met)? But in *Lanigan*, the employer wins even though " '[t]he employer could offer no excuse whatso-

ever as to why his secretary could perform a job in a more efficient manner in a skirt rather than a pantsuit, and could only speculate as to whether or not a skirt could be considered more business-like.' " What explains the different standards for dress codes and other cases involving overt sex discrimination under Title VII?

2. Why is it relevant that women can wear skirts (i.e., pants are not an "immutable characteristic")? Does Title VII only protect women from discrimination on the basis of "immutable characteristics"? Would the fact that women can attend high school mean that an employer could require women, but not men, to have a high school education for an unskilled position? Why do the courts bring up "mutability" in the context of dress codes?

3. Why are many professional women required to wear skirts either under overt dress codes, like that at issue in *Lanigan*, or under unwritten rules everyone "understands." If you are a second-or third-year law student, what was the rule, written or otherwise, at the firm you worked at last summer? Did you wear pants? Have you worked at a place where unshaven legs were acceptable when skirts were worn? Why does the ideal woman have so little hair on her body and so much on her head, and why are these proportions reversed for the ideal man? See Susan A. Basow, The Hairless Ideal: Women and Their Body Hair, 15 Psych. Women Q. 83 (1991) (women who do not primarily seek or have male partners less likely to remove body hair).

4. If you are a woman, compare how you feel in a skirt and in pants (assuming that both are part of comparable professional outfits). What are the differences? Would you feel more competent or confident or feminine in one or the other? What are some of the disadvantages of skirts of various lengths on the job? Of feeling feminine on the job?

5. In writing about the dress code cases, Katharine Bartlett makes this point:

> The real problem with the assumptions courts make about the trivial impact of dress and appearance requirements on employees and their importance to employers is not that they are never right; nor is it a problem of inconsistency. The problem is that they rely on unexamined, culture-bound stereotypes. Such judgments reflect more about the high degree of societal consensus regarding dress and appearance expectations than the value that individuals or businesses attach to dress and appearance. That a woman should wear knee-length skirts and high heels and a man should not can be understood as trivial to the employee but important to the employer only from within a culture in which women commonly wear knee-length skirts and high heels and men do not. In such a culture, a requirement that men wear knee-length skirts and high heels could not be so easily dismissed [as trivial].

Only Girls Wear Barrettes: Dress and Appearance Standards, Community Norms, and Workplace Equality, 92 Mich. L. Rev. 2541, 2558–59 (1994). Do you agree with Bartlett? Which way does Bartlett's point cut? Should discriminatory dress codes be illegal under Title VII?

6. Rules (formal or informal) that require women to wear shoes with heels cause serious physical injuries. Even a heel as low as ¾″ "increases the

peak pressure in the forefoot by 22% compared to 57% in 2″ and 76% in 3¼″ heels." Heels routinely cause severe and painful foot and back problems. Marc Linder, Smart Women, Stupid Shoes, and Cynical Employers: The Unlawfulness and Adverse Health Consequences of Sexually Discriminatory Workplace Footwear Requirements for Female Employees, 22 Iowa J. Corp. L. 295, 308 (1997). Pumps (which must pinch to stay on) and shoes with pointy toes are also harmful. Several airlines, including TWA and United, continue to require employees to wear harmful shoes some or all of the time. And many women work under informal rules requiring harmful shoes. Why has Title VII been so ineffective in eliminating requirements that women wear harmful shoes? Would you consider suing your law firm if women were required to wear heels or felt that an unspoken rule mandated heels? Would you expect to win?

7. Although courts allow sex-specific grooming codes, there are limits. Courts have not, for example, allowed employers to require only women to wear uniforms. Carroll v. Talman Federal Savings & Loan Ass'n, 604 F.2d 1028 (7th Cir.1979), cert. denied, 445 U.S. 929, 100 S.Ct. 1316, 63 L.Ed.2d 762 (1980). Nor have courts allowed employers to require women to wear revealing and sexy attire to waitress or to work in a lobby or as a stewardess. See Slayton v. Michigan Host, Inc., 144 Mich.App. 535, 376 N.W.2d 664 (1985) (waitress); EEOC v. Sage Realty Corp., 507 F.Supp. 599 (S.D.N.Y. 1981) (lobby attendant); Wilson v. Southwest Airlines Co., 517 F.Supp. 292 (N.D.Tex.1981) (stewardess). Is there some tension between these cases and cases like Lanigan? How do you think a judge would explain these different results?

8. Many of the grooming code cases have been brought by men who want to wear earrings or long hair. For a case in which a male optometrist loses his job for wearing one small earring to work, see Kleinsorge v. Eyeland Corp., 71 Fair Empl. Prac. Cas. (BNA) 1601 (E.D.Pa. 2000) (dismissing claim though female employees were allowed to wear earrings). Why would an employer care whether an employee wore one small (presumably tasteful) earring? What is the cultural meaning of a man wearing one earring? Of a woman wearing one earring? Of a man wearing two earrings? Or a woman wearing two earrings?

For cases in which men lose jobs because of long hair, see, e.g., Tavora v. New York Mercantile Exchange, 101 F.3d 907 (2d Cir.1996) (upholding dismissal though women employees allowed to wear long hair); Harper v. Blockbuster Entertainment Corp., 139 F.3d 1385 (11th Cir.1998) (same); Austin v. Wal–Mart Stores, Inc., 20 F.Supp.2d 1254 (S.D.Ind.1998) (same). Why would an employer allow women to wear long hair and forbid men from wearing long hair? What is the cultural meaning of a woman with long hair? Of a man with long hair?

9. Do you agree with the courts in the grooming cases that there is no sex discrimination when grooming codes require feminine appearance for women and masculine appearance for men? What links do you see between sex discrimination and discriminatory grooming codes? Between sex discrimination and masculine appearance as a requirement for men and feminine appearance as a requirement for women?

10. How would you analyze the *Lanigan* case under the various feminist approaches described in Chapter 3? Would any consider such a rule nondiscriminatory? Are their objections purely "formal," i.e., limited to the fact that a no-pants-on-women rule treats women and men differently? How, for example, would one analyze the core problem in this case using a formal equality or relational or dominance approach? Answer these same questions for *Kleinsorge*, above note 9 (the optometrist with one small earring). What explains the courts' tolerance of overtly-discriminatory grooming codes?

E. THE INTERSECTION OF RACE AND SEX

ROGERS v. AMERICAN AIRLINES, INC.

United States District Court, Southern District of New York, 1981.

527 F.Supp. 229.

Plaintiff is a black woman who seeks $10,000 damages, injunctive, and declaratory relief against enforcement of a grooming policy of the defendant American Airlines that prohibits employees in certain employment categories from wearing an all-braided hairstyle. Plaintiff has been an American Airlines employee for approximately eleven years, and has been an airport operations agent for over one year. Her duties involve extensive passenger contact, including greeting passengers, issuing boarding passes, and checking luggage. She alleges that the policy * * * discriminates against her as a woman, and more specifically as a black woman. * * *

[Defendant's motion to dismiss is] meritorious with respect to the statutory claims insofar as they challenge the policy on its face. The statutory bases alleged, Title VII and section 1981, are indistinguishable in the circumstances of this case, and will be considered together. The policy is addressed to both men and women, black and white. Plaintiff's assertion that the policy has practical effect only with respect to women is not supported by any factual allegations. Many men have hair longer than many women. Some men have hair long enough to wear in braids if they choose to do so. Even if the grooming policy imposed different standards for men and women, however, it would not violate Title VII. It follows, therefore, that an evenhanded policy that prohibits to both sexes a style more often adopted by members of one sex does not constitute prohibited sex discrimination. This is because this type of regulation has at most a negligible effect on employment opportunity. It does not regulate on the basis of any immutable characteristic of the employees involved. It concerns a matter of relatively low importance in terms of the constitutional interests protected by the Fourteenth Amendment and Title VII, rather than involving fundamental rights such as the right to have children or to marry. The complaint does not state a claim for sex discrimination.

The considerations with respect to plaintiff's race discrimination claim would clearly be the same, except for plaintiff's assertion that the "corn row" style has a special significance for black women. She contends that it

> has been, historically, a fashion and style adopted by Black American women, reflective of the cultural, historical essence of the Black women in American society. The style was "popularized" so to speak, within the larger society, when Cicely Tyson adopted the same for an appearance on nationally viewed Academy Awards presentation several years ago * * *. It was and is analogous to the public statement by the late Malcolm X regarding the Afro hair style * * *. At the bottom line, the completely braided hair style, sometimes referred to as corn rows, has been and continues to be part of the cultural and historical essence of Black American women.
>
> There can be little doubt that, if American adopted a policy which foreclosed Black women/all women from wearing hair styled as an "Afro/bush," that policy would have very pointedly racial dynamics and consequences reflecting a vestige of slavery unwilling to die (that is, a master mandate that one wear hair divorced from one's historical and cultural perspective and otherwise consistent with the "white master" dominated society and preference thereof).

Plaintiff is entitled to a presumption that her arguments, largely repeated in her affidavit, are true. But the grooming policy applies equally to members of all races, and plaintiff does not allege that an all-braided hair style is worn exclusively or even predominantly by black people. Moreover, it is proper to note that defendants have alleged without contravention that plaintiff first appeared at work in the all-braided hairstyle on or about September 25, 1980, soon after the style had been popularized by a white actress in the film "10." Plaintiff may be correct that an employer's policy prohibiting the "Afro/bush" style might offend Title VII and section 1981. But if so, this chiefly would be because banning a natural hairstyle would implicate the policies underlying the prohibition of discrimination on the basis of immutable characteristics. In any event, an all-braided hairstyle is a different matter. It is not the product of natural hair growth but of artifice. An all-braided hair style is an "easily changed characteristic," and, even if socioculturally associated with a particular race or nationality, is not an impermissible basis for distinctions in the application of employment practices by an employer.

* * *

Moreover, the airline did not require plaintiff to restyle her hair. It suggested that she could wear her hair as she liked while off duty, and permitted her to pull her hair into a bun and wrap a hairpiece around the bun during working hours. * * * Plaintiff has done this, but alleges that the hairpiece has caused her severe headaches. A larger hairpiece would seem in order. But even if any hairpiece would cause such discomfort, the policy does not offend a substantial interest.

Plaintiff has failed to allege sufficient facts to require defendants to demonstrate that the policy has a bona fide business purpose. In this regard, however, plaintiff does not dispute defendant's assertion that the policy was adopted in order to help American project a conservative and business-like image, a consideration recognized as a bona fide business purpose. Rather she objects to its impact with respect to the "corn row" style, an impact not protected against by Title VII or section 1981.

PAULETTE M. CALDWELL, A HAIR PIECE: PERSPECTIVES ON THE INTERSECTION OF RACE AND GENDER FROM CRITICAL RACE FEMINISM: A READER 297, 297–305 (ADRIEN KATHERINE WING, ED. 1997)

(originally published in [1991] Duke L. J. 365).

I want to know my hair again, to own it, to delight in it again, to recall my earliest mirrored reflection when there was no beginning and I first knew that the person who laughed at me and cried with me and stuck out her tongue at me was me. I want to know my hair again, the way I knew it before I knew that my hair is me, before I lost the right to me, before I knew that the burden of beauty—or lack of it—for an entire race of people could be tied up with my hair and me.

I want to know my hair again, the way I knew it before I knew Sambo and Dick, Buckwheat and Jane, Prissy and Miz Scarlett. Before I knew that my hair could be wrong—the wrong color, the wrong texture, the wrong amount of curl or straight. Before hot combs and thick grease and smelly-burning lye, all guaranteed to transform me, to silken the coarse, resistant wool that represents me. I want to know once more the time before I denatured, denuded, denigrated, and denied my hair and me, before I knew enough to worry about edges and ditches and burrows and knots, when I was still a friend of water—the rain's dancing drops of water, a swimming hole's splashing water, a hot, muggy day's misty invisible water, my own salty, sweaty, perspiring water.

When will I cherish my hair again, the way my grandmother cherished it, when fascinated by its beauty, with hands carrying centuries-old secrets of adornment and craftswomanship, she plaited it, twisted it, cornrowed it, finger-curled it, olive-oiled it, on the growing moon cut and shaped it, and wove it like fine strands of gold inlaid with semiprecious stones, coral and ivory, telling with my hair a lost-found story of the people she carried inside her?

Mostly, I want to love my hair the way I loved hers, when as granddaughter among grandsons I stood on a chair in her room—her kitchen-bed-living-dining room—and she let me know her hair, when I combed and patted it from the crown of her head to the place where her neck folded into her shoulders, caressing steel gray strands that framed her forehead before falling into the soft, white cottony temples at the border of her cheekbones.

Cotton. Cotton curled up in soft, fuzzy puffballs around her face. cotton pulled out and stretched on top of her head into Sunday pompadours. Cotton, like the cotton blooming in August in her tiny cotton field. Cotton, like the cotton that filled the other room in her house—the cotton room—the storehouse for September's harvest, a cradle to shield her pickings from wind and rain, to await baling and ginning and cashing in. Cotton, which along with a cow, a pig, and a coop of chickens, allowed her to eke out a husband-dead, children-gone independence in some desolate place, trapped in the bowels of segregation. Here, unheard, unseen, free, she and her beauty and her hair could not be a threat to anyone.

ON BEING THE SUBJECT OF A LAW SCHOOL HYPOTHETICAL

The case of *Rogers v. American Airlines* upheld the right of employers to prohibit the wearing of braided hairstyles in the workplace. The plaintiff, a black woman, argued that American Airlines' policy discriminated against her specifically as a black woman. In effect, she based her claim on the interactive effects of racial and gender discrimination. The court chose, however, to base its decision principally on distinctions between biological and cultural conceptions of race. More important, it treated the plaintiff's claims of race and gender discrimination in the alternative and independent of each other, thus denying any interactive relationship between the two.

Although *Rogers* is the only reported decision that upholds the categorical exclusion of braided hairstyles, the prohibition of such styles in the workforce is both widespread and long-standing. I discovered *Rogers* while reading a newspaper article describing the actual or threatened firing of several black women in metropolitan Washington, D.C., solely for wearing braided hairstyles. The article referred to *Rogers* but actually focused on the case of Cheryl Tatum, who was fired from her job as a restaurant cashier in a Hyatt Hotel under a company policy that prohibited "extreme and unusual hairstyles."

The newspaper description of the Hyatt's grooming policy conjured up an image of ludicrous and outlandishly coifed Cheryl Tatum, one clearly bent on exceeding the bounds of workplace taste and discipline. But the picture that accompanied the article revealed a young, attractive black woman whose hair fell neatly to her shoulders in an all-American, common, everyday pageboy style, distinguished only by the presence of tiny braids in lieu of single strands of hair.

Whether motivated by politics, ethnic pride, health, or vanity, I was outraged by the idea that an employer could regulate or force me to explain something as personal and private as the way I groom my hair.

My anger eventually subsided, and I thought little more about *Rogers* until a student in my course in Employment Discrimination Law asked me after class to explain the decision. I promised to take up the case when we arrived at that point in the semester when the issues raised by *Rogers* fit most naturally in the development of antidiscrimination law.

Several weeks passed, and the student asked about *Rogers* again and again (always privately, after class), yet I always put off answering her until some point later in the semester. After all, hair is such a little thing. Finally, in a class discussion on a completely unrelated topic, the persistent one's comments wandered into the forbidden area of braided-hair cases. As soon as the student realized she had publicly introduced the subject of braided hair, she stopped in midsentence and covered her mouth in embarrassment, as if she had spoken out of turn. I was finally forced to confront what the student had obviously sensed in her embarrassment.

I had avoided private and public discussions about braided hair not because the student had asked her question at the wrong point in the semester. Nor had I avoided the subject because cases involving employer-mandated hair and grooming standards do not illustrate as well as other cases the presence of deeply ingrained myths, negative images, and stereotypes that operate to define the social and economic position of blacks and women. I had carefully evaded the subject of a black woman's hair because I appeared at each class meeting wearing a neatly braided pageboy, and I resented being the unwitting object of one in thousands of law school hypotheticals.

WHY WOULD ANYONE WANT TO WEAR THEIR HAIR THAT WAY?

In discussing braided hairstyles, I was not prepared to adopt an abstract, dispassionate, objective stance on an issue that so obviously affected me personally; nor was I prepared to suffer publicly, through intense and passionate advocacy, the pain and outrage that I experience each time a black woman is dismissed, belittled, and ignored simply because she challenges our objectification. Should I be put to the task of choosing a logical, credible, "legitimate," legally sympathetic justification out of the many reasons that may have motivated me and other black women to braid our own hair? Perhaps we do so out of concern for the health of our hair, which many of us risk losing permanently after years of chemical straighteners; or perhaps because we fear that the entry of chemical toxins into our bloodstreams through our scalps will damage our unborn or breast-feeding children. Some of us choose the positive expression of ethnic pride not only for ourselves but also for our children, many of whom learn, despite all our teachings to the contrary, to reject association with black people and black culture in search of a keener nose or bluer eye. Many of us wear braids in the exercise of private, personal prerogatives taken for granted by women who are not black.

The persistent student's embarrassed questioning and my obfuscation spoke of a woman-centered silence: she, a white woman, had asked me, a black woman, to justify my hair. She compelled me to account for the presence of legal justifications for my simultaneously "perverse visibility and convenient invisibility." She forced me and the rest of the class to acknowledge the souls of women who live by the circumscriptions of competing beliefs about white and black womanhood and in the interstices of racism and sexism.

Our silence broken, the class moved beyond hierarchy to a place of honest collaboration. Turning to *Rogers*, we explored the question of our ability to comprehend through the medium of experience the way a black woman's hair is related to the perpetuation of social, political, and economic domination of subordinated racial and gender groups; we asked why issues of experience, culture, and identity are not the subject of explicit legal reasoning.

TO CHOOSE MYSELF: INTERLOCKING FIGURATIONS IN THE CONSTRUCTION OF RACE AND GENDER

SUNDAY. School is out, my exams are graded, and I have unbraided my hair a few days before my appointment at the beauty parlor to have it braided again. After a year in braids, my hair is healthy again: long and tick and cottony soft. I decide not to french roll it or pull it into a ponytail or bun or cover it with a scarf. Instead, I comb it out and leave it natural, in a full and big "Angela Davis" Afro style. I feel full and big and regal. I walk the three blocks from my apartment to the subway. I see a white male colleague walking in the opposite direction and I wave to him from across the street. He stops, squints his eyes against the glare of the sun, and stares, trying to figure out who has greeted him. He recognizes me and starts to cross over to my side of the street, I keep walking, fearing the possibility of his curiosity and needing to be relieved of the strain of explanation.

MONDAY. My hair is still unbraided, but I blow it out with a hair dryer and pull it back into a ponytail tied at the nape of my neck before I go to the law school. I enter the building and run into four white female colleagues on their way out to a white female lunch. Before I can say hello, one of them blurts out, "It is weird!" Another drowns out the first: "You look so young, like a teenager!" The third invites me to join them for lunch while the fourth stands silently, observing my hair. I mumble some excuse about lunch and interject, almost apologetically, that I plan to get my hair braided again the next day. When I arrive at my office suite and run into the white male I had greeted on Sunday, I realize immediately that he has told the bunch on the way to lunch about our encounter the day before. He mutters something about how different I look today, then asks me whether the day before I had been on my way to a ceremony. He and the others are generally nice colleagues, so I half-smile, but say nothing in response. I feel a lot less full and big and regal.

TUESDAY. I walk to the garage under my apartment building again wearing a big, full "Angela Davis" Afro. Another white male colleague passes me by, not recognizing me. I greet him and he smiles broadly, saying that he has never seen me look more beautiful. I smile back, continue the chitchat for a moment more, and try not to think about whether he is being disingenuous. I slowly get into my car, buckle up, relax, and turn on the radio. It will take me about forty-five minutes to drive uptown to the beauty parlor, park my car, and get something to eat before beginning the long hours of sitting and braiding. I feel good, knowing that the braider will be ecstatic when she sees the results of her healing handiwork. I keep my movements small, easy, and slow, relishing a rare, short morning of being free.

My initial outrage notwithstanding, *Rogers* is an unremarkable decision. Courts generally protect employer-mandated hair and dress codes, and they often accord the greatest deference to codes that classify individuals on the basis of socially conditioned rather than biological differences.

But *Rogers* is regrettably unremarkable in an important respect. It rests on suppositions that are deeply embedded in American culture. *Rogers* proceeds from the premise that, although racism and sexism share much in common, they are nonetheless fundamentally unrelated phenomena—a proposition proved false by history and contemporary reality. Racism and sexism are interlocking, mutually reinforcing components of a system of dominance rooted in patriarchy. No significant and lasting progress in combating either can be made until this interdependence is acknowledged, and until the perspectives gained from considering their interaction are reflected in legal theory and public policy.

Among employment discrimination cases that involve black female plaintiffs, at least three categories emerge.

In one category, courts have considered whether black women may represent themselves or other race or gender discriminatees. Some cases deny black women the right to claim discrimination as a subgroup distinct from black men and white women.[4] Others deny black women the right to represent a class that includes white women in a suit based on sex discrimination, on the ground that race distinguishes them.[5] Still other cases prohibit black women from representing a class in a race discrimination suit that includes black men, on the ground of gender differences.[6] These cases demonstrate the failure of courts to account for race-sex intersection, and are premised on the assumption that discrimination is based on either race or gender, but never both.

A second category of cases concerns the interaction of race and gender in determining the limits of an employer's ability to condition work on reproductive and marital choices associated with black women.[7]

4. *See, e.g.,* Degraffenreid v. General Motors Assembly Div., 413 F.Supp. 142, 145 (E.D.Mo.1976) (Title VII did not create a new subcategory of "black women" with standing independent of black males).

5. *See, e.g.,* Moore v. Hughes Helicopters, Inc., 708 F.2d 475, 480 (9th Cir.1983).

6. *See, e.g.,* Payne v. Travenol, 673 F.2d 798, 810–812 (5th Cir.1982) (interests of black female plaintiffs substantially conflict with interests of black males, since females sought to prove that males were promoted at females' expense notwithstanding the court's finding of extensive racial discrimination).

7. *See* Chambers v. Girls Club of Omaha, 834 F.2d 697 (8th Cir.1987).

Several courts have upheld the firing of black women for becoming pregnant while unmarried if their work involves association with children—especially black teenage girls. These decisions rest on entrenched fears of and distorted images about black female sexuality, stigmatize single black mothers (and by extension their children), and reinforce "culture of poverty" notions that blame poverty on poor people themselves. They also reinforce the notion that the problems of black families are attributable to the deviant and dominant roles of black women and the idea that racial progress depends on black female subordination.

A third category concerns black women's physical images. These cases involve a variety of mechanisms to exclude black women from jobs that involve contact with the public—a tendency particularly evident in traditionally female jobs in which employers place a premium on female attractiveness—including a subtle, and often not so subtle, emphasis on female sexuality. The latter two categories sometimes involve, in addition to the intersection of race and gender, questions that concern the interaction of race, gender, and culture.

The failure to consider the implications of race-sex interaction is only partially explained, if at all, by the historical or contemporary development of separate political movements against racism and sexism. Rather, this failure arises from the inability of political activists, policy makers, and legal theorists to grapple with the existence and political functions of the complex myths, negative images, and stereotypes regarding black womanhood. These stereotypes, and the culture of prejudice that sustains them, exist to define the social position of black women as subordinate on the basis of gender to all men, regardless of color, and on the basis of race to all other women. These negative images also are indispensable to the maintenance of an interlocking system of oppression based on race and gender that operates to the detriment of all women and all blacks. Stereotypical notions about white women and black men are developed not only when they are compared to white men, but also when they are set apart from black women.

THE *ROGERS* OPINION

The court gave three principal reasons for dismissing the plaintiff's claim. First, in considering the sex discrimination aspects of the claim, the court disagreed with the plaintiff's argument that, in effect, the application of the company's grooming policy to exclude the category of braided hairstyles from the workplace reached only women. Rather, the court stressed that American's policy was evenhanded and applied to men and women alike. Second, the court emphasized that American's grooming policy did not regulate or classify employees on the basis of an immutable gender characteristic. Finally, American's policy did not bear on the exercise of a fundamental right. The plaintiff's racial discrimination claim was analyzed separately but dismissed on the same grounds: neutral application of American's antibraid policy to all races and absence of any impact of the policy on an immutable racial characteristic or of any effect on the exercise of a fundamental right.

The court's treatment of culture and cultural associations in the racial context bears close examination. It carefully distinguished between the phenotypic and cultural aspects of race. First, it rejected the plaintiff's analogy between all-braided and Afro, or "natural" hairstyles. Stopping short of concluding that Afro hairstyles might be protected under all circumstances, the court held that "an all-braided hairstyle is a different matter. It is not the product of natural hair growth but of artifice." Second, in response to the plaintiff's argument that, like Afro hairstyles, braids reflected her choice for ethnic and cultural identification, the court again distinguished between the immutable aspects of race and characteristics that are "socioculturally associated with a particular race or nationality." However, given the variability of so-called immutable racial characteristics such as skin color and hair texture, it is difficult to understand racism as other than a complex of historical, sociocultural associations with race.

In support of its view that the plaintiff had failed to establish a factual basis for her claim that American's policy had a disparate impact on black women, thus destroying any basis for the purported neutral application of the policy, the court pointed to American's assertion that the plaintiff had adopted the prohibited hairstyle only shortly after it had been "popularized" by Bo Derek, a white actress, in the film 10. Notwithstanding the factual inaccuracy of American's claim, and notwithstanding the implication that there is no relationship between braided hair and the culture of black women, the court assumed that black and white women are equally motivated (i.e., by the movies) to adopt braided hairstyles.

Wherever they exist in the world, black women braid their hair. They have done so in the United States for more than four centuries. African in origin, the practice of braiding is as American—black American—as sweet potato pie. A braided hairstyle was first worn in a nationally televised media event in the United States—and in that sense "popularized"—by a black actress, Cicely Tyson, nearly a decade before the movie 10. More important, Cicely Tyson's choice to popularize (i.e., to "go public" with) braids, like her choice of acting roles, was a political act made on her own behalf and on behalf of all black women.

The very use of the term "popularized" to describe Bo Derek's wearing of braids—in the sense of rendering suitable to the majority—specifically subordinates and makes invisible all the black women who for centuries have worn braids in places where they and their hair were not overt threats to the American aesthetic. The great majority of such women worked exclusively in jobs where their racial subordination was clear. They were never permitted in any affirmative sense of the word any choice so closely related to personal dignity as the choice—or a range of choices—regarding the grooming of their hair. By virtue of their subordination—their clearly defined place in society—their choices were simply ignored.

The court's reference to Bo Derek presents us with two conflicting images, both of which subordinate black women and black culture. On the one hand, braids are separated from black culture and, by implication, are said to arise from whites. Not only do blacks contribute nothing to the nation's or the world's culture, they copy the fads of whites. On the other hand, whites make fads of black culture, which, by virtue of their popularization, become—like all "pop"—disposable, vulgar, and without lasting value. Braided hairstyles are thus trivialized and protests over them made ludicrous.

To narrow the concept of race further—and, therefore, racism and the scope of legal protection against it—the *Rogers* court likened the plaintiff's claim to ethnic identity in the wearing of braids to identity claims based on the use of languages other than English. The court sought refuge in *Garcia v. Gloor,* a decision that upheld the general right of employers to prohibit the speaking of any language other than English in the workplace without requiring employers to articulate a business justification for the prohibition.[15] By excising the cultural component of racial or ethnic identity, the court reinforces the view of a homogeneous, unicultural society, and pits blacks and other groups against each other in a battle over minimal deviations from cultural norms. Black women cannot wear their hair in braids because Hispanics cannot speak Spanish at work. The court cedes to private employers the power of family patriarchs to enforce a numbing sameness, based exclusively on the employers' whim, without the obligation to provide a connection to work performance or business need, and thus deprives employees of the right to be judged on ability rather than on image or sound.

HEALING THE SHAME

Eliminating the behavioral consequences of certain stereotypes is a core function of antidiscrimination law. This function can never be adequately performed as long as courts and legal theorists create narrow, inflexible definitions of harm and categories of protection that fail to reflect the actual experience of discrimination. Considering the interactive relationship between racism and sexism from the experiential standpoint and knowledge base of black women can lead to the development of legal theories grounded in reality, and to the consideration by all women of the extent to which racism limits their choices as women and by black and other men of color of the extent to which sexism defines their experiences as men of subordinated races.

Creating a society that can be judged favorably by the way it treats the women of its darkest race need not be the work of black women alone, nor will black women be the exclusive or primary beneficiaries of such a society. Such work can be engaged in by all who are willing to take seriously the everyday acts engaged in by black women and others to resist racism and sexism and to use these acts as the basis to develop legal theories designed to end race and gender subordination.

15. Garcia v. Gloor, 618 F.2d 264, 267–69 (5th Cir.1980).

Notes on A Hair Piece

1. For a recent case upholding an employer grooming code banning "braided" hair styles for women working for a "temporary legal staffing service," see McBride v. Lawstaf, Inc., No. 1:96–CV–0196–CC, 1996 U.S. Dist. LEXIS 16190, (N.D. Ga. May 28, 1996) (magistrate's recommendation), aff'd, 71 Fair Empl. Prac. Cas. (BNA) 1758, 1996 WL 755779 (N.D.Ga. 1996).Why would an employer object to corn rows? Do you think that corn rows are unprofessional or inconsistent with a "conservative and business-like image"? Would an "Afro/bush" be more consistent with such an image? What precisely is the distinction drawn by the court in *Rogers* between an "Afro/bush" and "corn rows"? Why, in the court's view, is a ban on corn rows less likely to violate Title VII than a ban on "Afro/bush" hair styles? What is the judge trying to do here? Is he successful?

2. Do employers regard "white" hair as more professional than "black" hair? What sorts of problems does any difference in our perceptions of professional hair create for African Americans in general and, in particular, for African American women?

3. How do you think Paulette Caldwell would have written *Rogers* if she had been the judge? What reasoning would she have used?

4. Does social cognition theory explain why the judge in *Rogers* thinks of a white actress when he thinks of cornrows?

5. Is *Rogers* the inevitable result of formal equality? How would various feminist approaches discussed in Chapter 3 analyze the question? Would it matter to your analysis that corn rows were worn once by a white actress in a movie? Would the result in *Rogers* have changed if Bo Derek had never worn corn rows in "10"? Why did the judge consider this factor relevant? What is the scope of what the judge sees as discrimination on the basis of race or on the basis of race and sex? What is the scope of what Caldwell sees as discrimination?

6. What does Caldwell mean when she states that the negative images of black women "are indispensable to the maintenance of an interlocking system of oppression based on race and gender that operates to the detriment of all women and all blacks"? Later, she says that black women will not "be the exclusive or primary beneficiaries" of a society that treats black women better. What is her point here? Can you give examples that illustrate these points?

7. Caldwell also states that "[C]onsidering the interactive relationship between racism and sexism from the experiential standpoint and knowledge base of black women can lead to the development of legal theories grounded in reality." Why is this needed? Can you give an examples?

JUDGE v. MARSH

United States District Court, District of Columbia, 1986.

649 F.Supp. 770.

[Plaintiff, an African American woman, seeks redress for, among other things, two promotions she did not receive as a civilian employee of the Army. The excerpt below deals with her failure to be promoted to the position of Equal Employment Opportunity Officer in 1981.]

The protected group upon which plaintiff's claims are based is that of black women. Disparate treatment of subclasses of women, based on an immutable characteristic or the exercise of a fundamental right, has been held unlawful under Title VII. Extrapolating from such "sex-plus" cases, the Fifth Circuit has determined that black women are a distinct subgroup, protected by Title VII. This outcome is logical: while accepted "sex-plus" discrimination is based on ostensibly neutral factors, both factors allegedly involved in the present case are separately accorded Title VII protection. Race discrimination directed solely at women is not less invidious because of its specificity. Thus, the Court concludes that employment actions directed against black women as a group may violate Title VII.

The difficulty with this position is that it turns employment discrimination into a many-headed Hydra, impossible to contain within Title VII's prohibition. * * * [P]rotected subgroups would exist for every possible combination of race, color, sex, national origin and religion. It is questionable whether any employer could make an employment decision under such a regime without incurring a volley of discrimination charges. For this reason, * * * [protected subgroups are] appropriately limited to employment decisions based on one protected, immutable trait or fundamental right, which are directed against individuals sharing a second protected, immutable characteristic. The benefits of Title VII thus will not be splintered beyond use and recognition; nor will they be constricted and unable to reach discrimination based on the existing unlawful criteria. Further, recognition of a new subgroup does not alter the employer's burden in a disparate treatment case. The employer still need establish merely a legitimate, non-pretextual basis for the employment decision. Plaintiff herein retains the burden, difficult though it may be, of establishing by a preponderance of the evidence that her employer's challenged decisions were based on this narrowly defined subgroup.

* * *

Failure to select Ms. Judge as EEO Officer was also not based on her status as a black woman. The testimony at trial did not reveal any unlawful discrimination at either level of the two-tiered decision-making process. General Cadoria indicated that the applicants' records were evaluated as a whole. General Rogers testified that, in ranking the top three applicants, he reviewed each applicant's record as a whole, and gave weight to the fact that both Anita Gomez Troughten and Luther Santiful were EEO Officers at the time, while Ms. Judge was an assistant EEO Officer. Further, Ms. Judge's SKAP [employee evaluation instrument] rating sheet had five Cs and no As, while neither Santiful nor Troughten had any ratings lower than B. General Kroesen accepted the Review Panel's recommendations. The respect General Kroesen accorded the selection process is further evidenced by his decision to reconvene the Review Panel once Anita Troughten declined the EEO Officer position.

Without doubt, the decisions of the evaluation panel members in ranking the applicants, and General Kroesen in twice relying upon the panel reflect subjective choices. Although the Court is sensitive to the possibility that subjective criteria in a hiring or promotion process may produce discrimination, it recognizes that such criteria "are not to be condemned as unlawful per se, for in all fairness to applicants and employers alike, decisions about hiring and promotion in supervising and managerial jobs cannot realistically be made using objective standards alone." The employer's judgment in selecting and applying subjective criteria may be poor, and it may be erroneous, but the only relevant inquiry for the Court is whether the given reasons mask unlawful discrimination. The steps in the evaluation and selection process of EEO Officer reflected only the subjectivity inherent in employment decisions. The preponderance of the evidence does not reveal that plaintiff's status as a black woman was a factor in her ranking or her non-selection. Thus, the Court finds that plaintiff has not met the ultimate burden of showing by a preponderance that her 1977 SKAP rating or her non-selection were based on her race and sex.

Text Note: Intersectionality Claims Under Title VII

As Paulette Caldwell points out in her essay on hair, women of color do not face a simple combination of sex discrimination plus race discrimination. The discrimination they face is the result of a complex interaction of racism and sexism, an interaction fueled by "myths, negative images, and stereotypes regarding black womanhood." Caldwell, above, at 302, see also, e.g., Harris, above Chapter 3.

Caldwell identifies three problems for black women bringing intersectional claims: their perceived inability to represent all African Americans or all women; bias against unwed black mothers (see, e.g., *Carnegie*, above); and bias against black women's physical appearance. We mention one other serious problem in this text note.

Courts rarely hold for plaintiffs on claims of discrimination based on both sex and race. For example, in Judge v. Marsh, the plaintiff claimed that she had been discriminated against as an African American woman. Although the court admitted that "employment actions directed against black women as a group may violate Title VII," the court regarded this position as turning "employment discrimination into a many-headed hydra." And it held that the plaintiff had failed in the end to prove discrimination on the basis of both sex and race. The court explained that once the employer articulated a legitimate non discriminatory reason for its failure to promote the plaintiff, the burden shifted to the plaintiff to show that she was discriminated against "based on this narrowly defined subgroup." And, in the end, she lost because she had "not met the ultimate burden of showing that" the decisions not to promote her "were based on her race and sex."

Carnegie is another example. There, an unwed African American mother lost her job when the employer had to eliminate one secretarial position while she was on maternity leave. Two employees in high positions had expressed discomfort with her marital status. The plaintiff alleged discrimination on the basis of sex and race, and apparently tried to show the connection between what happened to her and stereotypes of unwed black mothers, but the court said that her intersectional claim added nothing.

As these cases illustrate, although women of color routinely face complicated forms of discrimination that cannot easily be disentangled into race discrimination and sex discrimination, it is very difficult to win such a claim. Almost always, the combined claim comes to nothing once the plaintiff has presented the available proof and the court has applied the burden of proof rules of Title VII. To win, the plaintiff bringing an intersectionality claim would have to show that she was treated differently than white women and that she was also treated differently from men of color. This is not an easy task if the discrimination has been subtle rather than overt, and, of course, discrimination is seldom overt nowadays.

Notes on Intersectionality Claims Under Title VII

1. As noted by Caldwell, although many classes of racial minorities or women have been certified with only one person (someone who necessarily has only one sex and only one race) as a class representative, some courts have refused to certify African American women as class representatives for classes of either all African Americans or all women. See, e.g., Payne v. Travenol Lab., 673 F.2d 798 (5th Cir.1982) (African American women cannot represent a class including African American men); Moore v. Hughes Helicopters, Inc., 708 F.2d 475, 480 (9th Cir.1983) (African American women cannot represent a class including white women). Why might the status of African American women as representatives seem more suspect than representation of all women by white women or of all African Americans by an African American man? See Kimberle Crenshaw, Demarginalizing the Intersection of Race and Sex: A Black Feminist Critique of Antidiscrimination Doctrine, Feminist Theory and Antiracist Politics, 1989 U.Chi.Legal F. 139. Why might African American women be better able to represent a class of all women or all African Americans than a white woman or an African American man? Does the discussion earlier in this chapter of social cognition theory help explain the willingness of courts to certify white women or minority men, but not minority women, as representatives of classes including members of other races or of the other sex?

2. Often plaintiffs do not have the types of "smoking gun" evidence present in *Price Waterhouse*. What are the difficulties faced by a plaintiff like Judge? Do you think she might have been discriminated against, despite the court's ruling? Why might she have trouble winning on a discrimination claim even if the denial of the promotion was discriminatory?

3. What is the court getting at when it talks about the "many-headed Hydra"? Where does the court draw the line? Do you agree? Note that courts

routinely allow white men to sue for reverse discrimination under Title VII without any such discussion. See, e.g., Johnson v. Transportation Agency, 480 U.S. 616, 107 S.Ct. 1442, 94 L.Ed.2d 615 (1987); United Steelworkers v. Weber, 443 U.S. 193, 99 S.Ct. 2721, 61 L.Ed.2d 480 (1979). Why aren't such suits regarded as equally problematic, because brought by a distinct "sex-plus" subgroup?

4. Does the fact that one belongs to multiple "subgroups" strengthen or weaken the need for a Title VII remedy? Why, in practice, is it almost impossible to win an intersectionality claim?

5. Should discrimination against a black woman because of her race and sex be regarded as just another form of "sex-plus," equivalent to discriminating against any other subset of women, such as women with pre-school children? Is there a difference between these two "subgroups"? Is such analysis equivalent to eliminating race from the plaintiff's claim? See Peggie R. Smith, Separate Identities: Black Women, Work, and Title VII, 14 Harv.Women's L.J. 21, 40–45 (1991).

6. Should the presence of African Americans and women be interpreted as evidence that an employer does not discriminate against black women? For a discussion of cases suggesting yes, see Smith, above note 5, at 35–37.

7. As Virginia Wei has pointed out, like African American women, Asian American women have had "difficulties with their Title VII claims based on combined factors of race and sex." Asian Women and Employment Discrimination: Using Intersectionality Theory To Address Title VII Claims Based on Combined Factors of Race, Gender, and National Origin, 37 B.C.L. Rev. 771, 780 (1996). She notes that Asian women experience the convoluted interaction of at least three forms of discrimination: race, sex, and national origin. How would national origin complicate discrimination for Asian women? What other women are likely to face this triple intersection? Would you expect such claims to be easier or harder to establish under Title VII than claims of African American women that they have been discriminated on the basis of race and sex?

8. It is often assumed that minority women, as a "double minority," have an advantage in obtaining good jobs because they "count twice" for affirmative action purposes. Do you think that this is true? See Deborah J. Merritt and Barbara F. Reskin, The Double Minority: Empirical Evidence of a Double Standard in Law School Hiring of Minority Women, 65 S.Cal.L.Rev. 2299, 2301 (1992) (study reveals that "minority women who joined law school faculties during this period [between Fall 1986 and Spring 1991] began teaching at significantly lower ranks than the minority men, obtained positions at significantly less prestigious schools, and were significantly more likely to teach low-status courses like legal writing or trusts and estates."). Why are perceptions and reality so different?

9. Can an employer, say a law school, take into account the advantages of a diverse faculty—in terms of sex and race—to the effectiveness of its educational mission in hiring decisions? See David A. Thomas & Robin J. Ely, Making Differences Matter: A New Paradigm for Managing Diversity,. Harv. Bus. Rev., Sept.-Oct. 1996, at 79 (suggesting that in fact organizations can profit from a diverse workforce); Steven A. Ramirez, The New Cultural Diversity and Title VII, __ Mich. J. Race & L. ___ (2001) (forthcoming)

(arguing that diversity hiring for the bottom line should be legal under Title VII).

10. Camille Herbert has noted that sexual harassment claims and racial harassment claims can both be traced to the same Supreme Court decisions, and that racial harassment analogies have helped some "courts to understand and to demonstrate the unlawful and discriminatory nature of sexually harassing behavior." Herbert, Analogizing Race and Sex in Workplace Harassment Claims, 58 Ohio St. L. J. 819, 820 (1997). But she warns that, in recent years, courts have imported restrictive rules from sexual harassment law to racial harassment law, making it "increasingly difficult for employees to successfully establish the existence of a racially hostile or abusive work environment." Id. According to Herbert,

> one of the dangers that needs to be guarded against when analogizing race and sex is the suggestion that racism and sexism, or racial harassment and sexual harassment, are identical, rather than merely comparable in certain respects. If drawing analogies between race and sex is seen as an attempt to belittle, or even has the unintended result of belittling, the importance of race and the evil of racism, then the use of analogies between race and sex could pose more dangers than are justified by the potential benefits of such comparison.

Id. at 880. Do you agree with Herbert? What arguments can you make against extending the limitations emerging in the law of sexual harassment to the law of racial harassment?

F. SUMMARY JUDGMENT AND TITLE VII

Text Note on Summary Judgment and Title VII

Paul Mollica reports on a study of the change in summary judgment standards in federal courts over the last thirty years and on the importance of this change to Title VII cases.[45] When a judge grants a defendant's (or more rarely a plaintiff's) motion for summary judgment, the case is decided on the basis of a documents (including affidavits) filed with the court together with the parties' pleadings.[46] There is no trial.

Over the last thirty years, trials of any kind have become increasingly rare in federal courts in civil suits as increasing numbers of cases are dismissed on motions for summary judgment. This trend was already visible at the district court level by the mid 1980's, but was strengthened by three cases decided by the Supreme Court in 1985. Although none of these cases involved a civil rights or employment discrimination issue, [47]they have been interpreted by the lower federal courts as changing the standard for summary judgment in all kinds of cases, including those arising under Title VII.[48]

45. Paul Mollica, Federal Summary Judgment at High Tide, 84 Marq. L. Rev. 141 (2000).

46. Fed. R. Civ. Pro. 56.

47. See Matsushita Electric Industrial Co. Ltd. v. Zenith Radio Corp., 475 U.S. 574, 106 S.Ct. 1348, 89 L.Ed.2d 538 (1986) (antitrust suit); Anderson v. Liberty Lobby, Inc., 477 U.S. 242, 106 S.Ct. 2505, 91 L.Ed.2d 202 (1986) (libel action); Celotex Corp. v. Catrett, 477 U.S. 317, 106 S.Ct. 2548, 91 L.Ed.2d 265 (1986) (wrongful death action).

Mollica's study examines ten volumes of the Federal Reporter from 1973 and ten volumes from 1997–98 and finds a dramatic difference in the standard for summary judgment between these dates. In 1973, most appeals were from trials. In the cases in which the trial court had granted summary judgment, the reversal rate on appeal was 45.5%. In 1973, federal appellate courts showed

> extreme vigilance against treading on contested fact issues or mixed questions of law and fact—even arguable ones—reversing them for evidentiary hearings. Only a modest proffer by the non-movant was enough to demonstrate the necessity of a trial. This was especially true in cases applying indeterminate legal standards, such as reasonableness. * * *
>
> With only one exception [a defamation case], state-of-mind issues (such as intent and malice) did not terminate in summary judgment in the sample cases.[49]

In the 1997–98 sample, in contrast, most appeals were from grants of summary judgment, not trials.

> It has become common to evaluate such legal standards as intent and reasonableness on summary judgment—to evaluate, on occasion, even issues of credibility—and to default non-movants under Rule 56. [Rule 56 is the procedural rule on summary judgment.] * * *
>
> The reach of summary judgment * * * is especially pernicious in the field of employment discrimination law, where the ultimate issue in most cases is whether the employer (or, more pointedly, its agent) intended to discriminate on the basis of a protected classification * * * .
>
> In a fair number of the employment cases, the summary judgment went to the heart of the employer's alleged discriminatory intent. A few cases found that plaintiffs failed to prove even a prima facie case of discrimination. A larger number of decisions affirmed summary judgment by holding that the plaintiff could not establish discriminatory intent, either directly or indirectly.[50]

The pressure on lower federal courts to use summary judgment to eliminate Title VII cases from their dockets has increased greatly in the 1990's as the number of employment discrimination cases has gone through the roof. In the year ending December 13, 1990, 8,290 employment discrimination cases were filed. Less than a decade later, in the year ending March 31, 1997, the number filed was 23,547.[51] These numbers are high enough to overwhelm the federal courts and create great pressure on district courts to dispose of employment discrimination claims on motions for summary judgment.

48. Mollica, above note 45, at 141–170.

49. Id. at 147–150.

50. Id. at 166–169.

51. Rebecca Hanner White, De Minimis Discrimination, 47 Emory L. J. 1121, 1124 at n.14 (1998). Paul Mollica reports that in 1973, 8.5% of pending federal civil cases resulted in a trial, for a total of 8,297 civil trials. In 1999, 2.3% of pending federal civil cases resulted in a trial, for a total of 6,228 civil trials in a year. Mollica, above note 45, at 141.

As increasing numbers of Title VII cases are decided on summary judgment, it is likely to become ever harder for plaintiffs to prevail. *Troupe*, for example, held that as a matter of law, a plaintiff cannot prevail on a pregnancy-discrimination claim when an employer alleges that she was fired for absenteeism even if she can show that her supervisor said she was being fired because she was not expected to return from maternity leave. Over time, as more and more such cases are decided by summary judgment in order to control dockets and avoid trials, it will become more and more difficult for plaintiffs to prevail. In light of the numbers of employment discrimination cases filed every year in federal court, judicial determination to use summary judgment to eliminate most of these suits is understandable. But the result is the disappearance of Title VII as an effective remedy for employment discrimination.

Notes on Summary Judgment and Title VII

1. In 1989, the Supreme Court decided several Title VII cases limiting the ability of plaintiffs to seek remedies for employment discrimination in federal courts. The decisions were widely criticized and, for the most part, overturned by the Civil Rights Act of 1991. Ann McGinley has argued that the phenomenon of increasing summary judgment dispositions "is less obvious but equally destructive of Title VII, silently curtail[ing] workers' civil rights claims." There is, however, no outcry over this change nor any movement to amend the statute. McGinley, Credulous Courts and the Tortured Trilogy: The Improper Use of Summary Judgment in Title VII and ADEA Cases, 34 B.C.L. Rev. 203, 205–206 (1993).

A similar story can be told about pregnancy discrimination. Recall that in General Electric Co. v. Gilbert, 429 U.S. 125, 97 S.Ct. 401, 50 L.Ed.2d 343 (1976), the Supreme Court held that discrimination against pregnant workers is not actionable as sex discrimination under Title VII. Feminists and others in the civil rights community were outraged, and Title VII was amended by the Pregnancy Act of 1978 to include discrimination on the basis of pregnancy within the definition of sex discrimination. Yet cases like *Troupe* and *Carnegie* effectively eliminate Title VII's ban on pregnancy discrimination except in the most extreme (and unlikely) cases.

Why is there no protest over the general erosion of Title VII in summary judgment dispositions or the more particular erosion of the ban on pregnancy discrimination? How would you focus public attention on these problems?

2. The viability of sexual harassment complaints is also threatened by the federal court's increasing use of summary judgment. Isabel Medina has argued that this trend "frustrates enforcement of gender antidiscrimination norms by preventing juries, the most diverse, and most experienced in the workplace actors in the legal system, from participating in the development of [sexual harassment] norms and assisting American society to reach consensus on gender issues." Medina, A Matter of Fact: Hostile Environments and Summary Judgments, 8 S. Cal. Rev. Law & Women's Studies 311, 311 (1999). Given the cases you have read in this chapter, why might it be important that Title VII suits are decided in trials before juries rather than in summary judgment proceedings before judges?

3. Rebecca Hanner White suggests that in an increasingly determined effort to clear their dockets of the avalanche of employment discrimination cases, federal courts are increasingly holding that employers are liable for discrimination only when it is more than de minimis, i.e., only when it results in a tangible and adverse employment action. White, In De Minimis Discrimination, 47 Emory L. J. 1121 (1998). Although the Supreme Court has required tangible employment action in cases in which employers are held vicariously liable for harassment by a supervisor, White suggests that lower courts may be starting to require tangible (and negative) employment action generally for discrimination to be actionable. Can you suggest solutions to the avalanche? And to the standard for proving discrimination as well, given what we now know about human decisionmaking from cognitive theory?

G. COMPARABLE WORTH

Text Note: Comparable Worth

Although there is a great deal of variation in what jobs are considered women's and men's across various cultures and economic systems, men and women tend to do different things, and the construction of difference seems of great importance in all cultures and economic systems. Gayle Rubin suggests that "[t]he division of labor by sex can * * * be seen as a 'taboo': a taboo against the sameness of men and women, a taboo dividing the sexes into two mutually exclusive categories, a taboo which exacerbates the biological differences between the sexes and thereby *creates* gender."[52] And in all industrial or capitalist societies (where wages make values easy to compare), what men do is valued more than what women do.

Despite women's increasing participation in the wage labor market and the enactment of Title VII and the Equal Pay Act,[53] most women still work in women's jobs for women's wages.[54] In the Bible, women are valued at about 60% of the value of men.[55] This gender wage gap has been surprisingly persistent over the centuries, as suggested by the table below, which reports that in 1951, women workers (working full-time year-round) earned 63.9 cents for every dollar earned by male workers (working full-time year-round). As the table also illustrates, women workers in the United States have made significant gains since then, particularly in the 1980's.

52. Rubin, The Traffic in Women: Some Notes on the "Political Economy" of Sex, in Toward an Anthropology of Women 157, 178 (Rayna R. Reiter, ed. 1975).

53. 29 U.S.C.A. § 206(d). The Act prohibits employers from paying less to women than men for "equal work on jobs the performance of which requires equal skill, effort, and responsibility, and which are performed under similar working conditions * * *." Id. at § 206(d)(1).

54. U.S. Dept. of Labor, Women's Bureau, 20 Leading Occupations of Employed Women 1990 Annual Averages (March 1991). As Diane Balser notes, "[a]long with the massive entry of women into the wage-work force, a parallel and equally revolutionary phenomenon has been the development of a *sex-segregated wage-work force,* with men, in general, occupying the higher status and better paid positions and the majority of women holding the lower status and lower paid positions." Balser, Sisterhood & Solidarity: Feminism and Labor in Modern Times 19 (1987).

55. Leviticus 27: 3:4.

Table 3: 1998 Median Annual Earnings by Race and Sex[56]

Race/sex	Earnings	Wage ratio
White men	$36,172	100%
Black men	$27,050	74.9%
White women	$26,243	72.6%
Black women	$22,648	62.6%
Hispanic men	$22,285	61.6%
Hispanic women	$19,221	53.1%
All men	$35,345	
All women	$25,362	
Overall wage gap		73%

Table 4: 1951–1998 Wage Gap between Women and Men[57]

Year	Percent	Year	Percent	Year	Percent	Year	Percent
1951	63.9%	1963	58.9%	1975	58.8%	1987	65.2%
1952	63.9%	1964	59.1%	1976	60.2%	1988	66.0%
1953	63.9%	1965	59.9%	1977	58.9%	1989	68.7%
1954	63.9%	1966	57.6%	1978	59.4%	1990	71.6%
1955	63.9%	1967	57.8%	1979	59.7%	1991	69.6%
1956	63.3%	1968	58.2%	1980	60.2%	1992	70.8%
1957	63.8%	1969	58.9%	1981	59.2%	1993	71.5%
1958	63.0%	1970	59.4%	1982	61.7%	1994	72.0%
1959	61.3%	1971	59.5%	1983	63.6%	1995	71.4%
1960	60.7%	1972	57.9%	1984	63.7%	1996	73.8%
1961	59.2%	1973	56.6%	1985	64.6%	1997	74.2%
1962	59.3%	1974	58.8%	1986	64.3%	1998	73.0%

The wage gap has diminished by about 13% between 1970 and 1996 for two reasons: women's wages rose *and* men's fell. Between these dates, women's real wages rose by 17.1% *and* men's real wages fell by 3%. For the least educated women (those with a high school education or less) wages fell between 1980 and 1998.[58]

Job Segregation

The continuation of the wage gap is associated with persistent segregation by sex and race, with jobs held by women and minorities tending to pay

56. The Learning Network, <www.infoplease.com/ipa/A0197814.html> (visited 12/22/2000) (source: The National Committee on Pay Equity).

57. The Learning Network, <www.infoplease.com/ipa/A0193820.html> (visited 12/22/2000) (source: Dept. of Labor U.S. Women's Bureau).

58. Costello et al., above note 5, at 303; Jane Waldfogel and Susan Mayer, Differences Between Men and Women in the Low-wage Labor Market, 20 Focus 11, 16 (1998–1999) (published by University of Wisconsin–Madison Institute for Research on Poverty and available at <http://www.ssc.wisc.edu/irp/focus.htm#F20:1>, visited 12/23/2000).

less than other jobs. It is true that there have been significant declines in the level of job segregation in recent decades. But, as with the wage gap, job segregation is amazingly persistent. A few examples will illustrate this point. Between 1983 and 1996, women employed as lawyers and judges rose from 15.8% to 29.0%, women employed as physicians rose from 15.8% to 26.4%, and women employed as clergy rose from 5.6% to 12.3%. But even in 1996, women were 83.3% of grade school teachers (same percentage as in 1983), 93.3% of registered nurses (down from 95.8% in 1983), and 99.1% of dental assistants (*up* from 98.1% in 1983). And in 1996, men were 98.2% of firefighters (down from 99% in 1983), 98.8% of auto mechanics (down from 99.5% in 1983), and 98.6% of airplane pilots and navigators (*up* from 97.9% in 1983).[59]

Jobs are not evenly distributed regardless of race. In 1996, managerial and professional jobs were held by 31.5% of white women, 22.8% of black women, and 17.4% of Hispanic women, whereas 14.3% of Hispanic women were machine operators, fabricators, and laborers as compared to 11.0% of black women and 6.9% of white women.[60] Like sex segregation, race segregation has declined in recent decades. For example, in 1960, only 2% of African American women held management positions, whereas 18.6% held such jobs in 1990.[61]

Researchers measure the extent of job segregation with a segregation index. A sex segregation index of 60 means that 60% of women would have to change jobs for the sexes to be evenly distributed across occupations. A race segregation index of 30 means 30% of African American or Hispanic workers would have to change jobs for occupations to be distributed across occupations in the same way as white men. [62]The next table shows the drop in job segregation indices in recent decades.

Table 5: Segregation Indexes[63]

Year	Sex	Race
1970	67	37
1980	60	29.5
1990	53	27

Thus far, we have only described national data which combines information across workplaces. But even when national data reports that a job is *not* segregated by race or sex, at many (sometimes most) workplaces, the job will be held only by members of one group. (National data combines data from various workplaces in aggregate figures.) For example, both women and men work as textile, apparel and finishing machine operators. But they tend to work at different firms. About 64% of women in this occupation would have to work at a different job for this occupation to be integrated on a workplace-

59. Costello et al., above note 5, at 287.

60. Id. at 286.

61. Barbara Reskin, The Realities of Affirmative Action in Employment 53–54 (1998).

62. Id. at 22, 53.

63. Id. at 53.

by-workplace basis. And when women and men work at the same occupation at different firms, the workers at the firms employing men tend to pay higher wages.[64]

There are few studies reporting on level of actual segregation on a workplace basis. A 1989 survey of North Carolina workers asked about the race and sex of coworkers and reported that for 70% of all jobs, the jobs were held entirely by men or by women at the respondent's workplace. Of the 30% of jobs held by both men and women at particular work sites, most (16%) were held almost entirely by men or women. In only 15% of jobs did people actually work in workplaces in which women and men both held the position in proportion to their numbers in the workforce.[65]

Racial segregation was reported at somewhat lower levels. A majority (56%) of workers held jobs which were held only by blacks or only by whites at their workplaces. Some 30% worked at jobs that were almost entirely segregated. In only 14% of jobs were workers of both races present in numbers approximately proportional to their numbers in the work force.[66]

The Case for Comparable Worth

Segregation by race and sex would be less troubling were jobs held by men and women of various races equivalent in terms of pay, status, and opportunities for advancement. Unfortunately, that is not the reality. Many attempts have been made to explain the wage gap in terms of differences in education, training, labor force attachment, and so forth. These studies consistently report that white men earn more than women and minorities with the same education.[67] For example, in 1989, white male professionals earned more than Asian American professionals with *more* education. And the gap between the earnings of whites and African Americans is increasing, particularly for college graduates.[68]

Many studies have tried to explain the wage gap between women and men in terms of differences in education and work patterns. Men tend to have greater labor force attachment, and women are more likely to take time off to care for young children full time and temporarily, including when children are sick. Also, women are likely to work fewer hours for wages, though women who work for wages work more hours in toto (homemaking and wage employment combined) than working men. Researchers have concluded, however, that such differences explain only about one fourth to one half of the wage gap for the hours women do work for wages.[69] The remaining disparity would seem to be the result of differential opportunities afforded men and women by employers and unconscious undervaluation of *any* work done by women.[70]

64. Id. at 22.

65. Barbara A. Bergmann, In Defense of Affirmative Action 42–43(1996) (describing study by Donald Tomaskovic-Devey, Gender and Racial Inequality at Work: The Sources and Consequences of Job Segregation (1993).

66. Id. at 43–44.

67. Id.

68. Reskin, above note 51, at 42.

69. See, e.g., Greg J. Duncan, with Richard D. Coe, Mary E. Corcoran, Martha S. Hill, Saul D. Hoffman, and James N. Morgan, Years of Poverty, Years of Plenty: The Changing Economic Fortunes of American Workers and Families 161 (1984); Heidi Hartmann, Women are Paid Less—They and Their Families Deserve Pay Parity, Civil Rights Journal, Fall 1999, at 31.

70. Cross cultural studies support this explanation. In almost all cultures, women and men do different work, though what

To the extent differences between women and men do explain the pay gap, the explanation may only reflect discrimination and the disparate choices facing women and men. Observed differences would not necessarily *justify* the wage gap. For example, if many workplaces are structured (as they are) to accommodate men's life styles but not women's, though women's could readily be accommodated, then the fact that women caretake more than men or take off more time at childbirth (or are more likely to lose their jobs at childbirth, see cases section B above), will "explain" the wage gap though employers could accommodate this difference without any gap. Indeed, a comprehensive study of the relationship between sex segregation and the wage gap from the mid 1990's reports that the gap would almost disappear were women to work in the same occupations at the same establishments as men,[71] suggesting that it is occupational segregation that causes the gap rather than differences between the sexes.

One analysis of the wage gap for 26– to 33–year-old workers, which included information about sex, race, education, experience, geographic location, and scores on a test of cognitive skills, estimates that for this age group (one in which the wage gap is lower than it will be later in life), the gap due to discrimination is at least $1,522 a year for African American men relative to white men, $3,393 a year for African American women relative to white men, and $3,539 a year for white women relative to white men.[72]

"Comparable worth" is a term of art describing a remedy for the fact that workers in jobs held predominantly by women of any color and other members of minority groups tend to pay less than jobs held by whites and by men. Although a comparable worth standard could be formulated in many ways, it is typically described as requiring equal pay for "comparable" jobs, that is, jobs requiring equivalent knowledge and skills, mental demands, accountability, and working conditions. For example, a 1974 study for the state of Washington state analyzed each job and awarded a maximum of 280 points for the knowledge and skills required for the job, a maximum of 140 points for the job's mental demands, a maximum of 160 points for accountability, and a maximum of 20 for working conditions. These points were then added together to yield a composite point value representing the value of the job to the employer. Values of various jobs were then compared to wages of various jobs, making it possible to identify jobs for which the pay was low relative to the rate at which the employer paid jobs of comparable value.

women do in one culture men often do in another (and vice versa). Yet whatever it is that men do in a culture is what is most valued. See, e.g., Sherry B. Ortner, Is Female to Male as Nature Is to Culture?, in Woman, Culture, and Society 67 (Michelle Z. Rosaldo and Louise Lamphere, eds. 1974); Gayle Rubin, The Traffic in Women: Notes on the "Political Economy" of Sex, in Toward an Anthropology of Women 157, 178 (Rayna R. Reiter, ed. 1975).

71. Trond Peterson and Laurie A. Morgan, Separate and Unequal: Occupation–Establishment Sex Segregation and the Gender Wage Gap, 101 Am. J. Sociol. 329 (1995).

72. Barbara R. Bergmann, In Defense of Affirmative Action 39–41 & n.11 at 184–85 (1996). The pay gap between women and men varies significantly by state, from 85.7% in Washington, D.C., to 62.8% in Wyoming. In general, women tend to earn most in the Pacific Northwest, New England, and the Middle Atlantic states and to earn least in the Southeast and Mountain states. Institute for Women's Policy Research, Overview of the Status of Women in the States (2000) (available at <http://www.iwpr.org/states/pdf/national.pdf> visited 12/23/2000).

Large employers often set internal wages for many jobs according to assessments of the worth of various jobs, assessments obtained in a formal job evaluation study such as that performed by the state of Washington. The pay for some jobs, especially entry-level jobs, may be pegged to market wages. But the pay for most jobs is set by an internal formal analysis of the worth of various jobs.

A comparable worth standard cannot be expected to eliminate entirely that portion of the wage gap attributable to the undervaluation of women's work. All valuations are likely to be tainted by the fact that those with privilege have written the rules to value most the qualities and skills they see themselves as displaying.[73] For example, sociologist Arlie Hochschild has explored the relationship between gender and waged emotional work. In her study of stewards and stewardesses, she found that women (stewardesses) were more likely to be the recipients of hostile feelings from passengers and more likely to perform supportive emotional labor than stewards. Women's extra emotional work was not, however, compensated, though it is work *and* carries with it risks of alienation from one's own feelings.[74] Given current cultural values, however, emotional work performed by women will often be invisible or seen as something other than valuable work. Indeed, jobs involving caring work, such as child care, teaching, therapy, and nursing, "offer low pay relative to their requirements for education and skill."[75] Compare, for example, the median pay of a child care worker ($6.12 an hour) and a parking lot attendant ($6.38) in 1996.[76]

Although comparable worth cannot eliminate all gender-linked pay disparities, there is evidence that a comparable worth standard does result in a diminished gap between the wages paid to workers in men's jobs and the wages paid to those in women's jobs. Minnesota adopted a comparable worth standard for state employees some time ago, and 90% of the wage increases went to people (mostly women) in the following occupations: "secretaries, other clerical employees, teacher aides, other school aides, cooks, other food service employees, non-nursing medical employees, nurses (RN, LPN), social services employees, library employees, city clerks and clerk-treasurers, and liquor store employees."[77]

73. See Barbara F. Reskin, Bringing the Men Back In: Sex Differentiation and the Devaluation of Women's Work, 2 Gender & Soc'y 58 (1988). Reskin argues that "[d]ominant groups remain privileged because they write the rules," and the rules they write "enable them *to continue to write the rules.*" Id. at 60 (emphasis in original). Reskin maintains that "the basic cause of the income gap is not sex segregation but men's desire to preserve their advantaged position and their ability to do so by establishing rules to distribute valued resources in their favor." Id. at 61.

74. Hochschild, The Managed Heart: The Commercialization of Human Feeling (1983). For an article discussing the failure of traditional job evaluation systems to value emotional labor and suggesting how emotional labor might be valued in a job evaluation system, see Ronnie J. Steinberg, Emotional Labor in the Service Economy: Emotional Labor, its Measurement and Repercussions, 561 Annals Am. Acad. Polit. & Soc. Sci. 143, 143 (1999).

75. Paula England and Nancy Folbre, Emotional Labor in the Service Economy: The Contours of Emotional Labor: The Cost of Caring, 561 Annals Am. Acad. Polit. & Soc. Sci. 39, 39 (1999).

76. James Heintz and Nancy Folbre, The Ultimate Field Guide to the U.S. Economy 57 (2000).

77. Sara M. Evans and Barbara J. Nelson, Wage Justice: Comparable Worth and the Paradox of Technocratic Reform 159 (1989).

Comparable Worth Around the World

In the United States, the first federal legislation banning discrimination against women in employment was the Equal Pay Act of 1963, but it only prohibits wage discrimination between women and men "for equal work on jobs the performance of which requires equal skill, effort, and responsibility, and which are performed under similar working conditions."[78] It applies only when women hold the same job in the same establishment, and thus does not reach the wage gap associated with women holding undervalued women's jobs and men holding overvalued men's jobs.

Nor does Title VII reach this problem. An early and leading case is the decision of the Ninth Circuit in AFCSME v. State of Washington, 770 F.2d 1401 (1985). In 1974, Washington commissioned a study, described above, to consider whether there was a wage disparity between state employees working in women's jobs (jobs held predominantly by women) and those working in men's jobs. The study reported a disparity of about 20% in pay between jobs held mostly by women and those held mostly by men. After conducting similar studies in 1976 and 1980, Washington enacted legislation requiring that state employees doing jobs of comparable worth receive equal pay, with comparable worth being determined according to the four factors mentioned above: knowledge and skills, mental demands, accountability, and working conditions. This comparable worth scheme—i.e., plan to pay equal pay to workers holding (different) jobs of comparable worth—was to be implemented over a ten year period. AFSCME, a union of state workers, sued alleging sex discrimination in Washington's failure to pay women and men equal salaries for jobs of comparable worth during the ten-year phase-in period. The district court ruled for AFSCME finding that there was discrimination on the basis of sex in violation of Title VII on the basis of both disparate treatment and disparate impact.

The Ninth Circuit reversed, holding that there had been no discrimination on the basis of sex under Title VII. In rejecting the disparate treatment claim, the court stated:

> AFSCME contends discriminatory motive may be inferred from the Willis study, which finds the State's practice of setting salaries in reliance on market rates creates a sex-based wage disparity for jobs deemed of comparable worth. AFSCME argues from the study that the market reflects a historical pattern of lower wages to employees in positions staffed predominantly by women; and it contends the State of Washington perpetuates that disparity, in violation of Title VII, by using market rates in the compensation system. The inference of discriminatory motive which AFSCME seeks to draw from the State's participation in the market system fails, as the State did not create the market disparity and has not been shown to have been motivated by impermissible sex-based considerations in setting salaries.
>
> The requirement of intent is linked at least in part to culpability. That concept would be undermined if we were to hold that payment of

78. 29 U.S.C. § 206(d)(1)(with exceptions for differential payments "made pursuant to (i) a seniority system; (ii) a merit system; (iii) a system which measures earnings by quantity or quality of production; or (iv) a differential based on any other factor other than sex").

> wages according to prevailing rates in the public and private sectors is an act that, in itself, supports the inference of a purpose to discriminate. Neither law nor logic deems the free market system a suspect enterprise. Economic reality is that the value of a particular job to an employer is but one factor influencing the rate of compensation for that job. Other considerations may include the availability of workers willing to do the job and the effectiveness of collective bargaining in a particular industry. * * * [E]mployers may be constrained by market forces to set salaries under prevailing wage rates for different job classifications. We find nothing in the language of Title VII or its legislative history to indicate Congress intended to abrogate fundamental economic principles such as the laws of supply and demand or to prevent employers from competing in the labor market.
>
> While the Washington legislature may have the discretion to enact a comparable worth plan if it chooses to do so, Title VII does not obligate it to eliminate an economic inequality that it did not create. * * *

770 F.2d at 1406–07. In rejecting the disparate impact claim, the court stated:

> AFSCME's disparate impact argument is based on the contention that the State of Washington's practice of taking prevailing market rates into account in setting wages has an adverse impact on women, who, historically, have received lower wages than men in the labor market. * * * [T]he decision to base compensation on the competitive market, rather than on a theory of comparable worth, involves the assessment of a number of complex factors not easily ascertainable, an assessment too multifaceted to be appropriate for disparate impact analysis. In the case before us, the compensation system in question resulted from surveys, agency hearings, administrative recommendations, budget proposals, executive actions, and legislative enactments. A compensation system that is responsive to supply and demand and other market forces is not the type of specific, clearly delineated employment policy contemplated by [the Supreme Court's disparate impact cases]. * * *

Id. at 1405–06.

Although federal anti-discrimination law does not require equal pay for jobs of equal value, comparable worth has been adopted by some states as the pay standard for state employees, i.e., state employees must be paid according to a comparable worth assessment.

In addition, many other industrialized countries have some sort of comparable worth standard, including Ontario, Europe, and Australia, and apply their standards to *all* employers (not just state employees). The Ontario plan has been described by its drafter:

> [T]he *Pay Equity Act* has application in both the public and private sectors (to firms with ten employees or more), and it follows a proactive rather than a complaint-driven model which requires each employer to create plans to achieve pay equity for employees in predominantly female job classes. This means that employers must carry out job comparisons of all predominantly female job classes with predominantly male job classes on the basis of the skill, effort, responsibility and

working conditions inherent in the job. Where jobs are determined to be of equal or comparable value, the female job class must be paid at least at the same rate as the lowest paid male job class of equal value. The *Act* allows for varied approaches to job comparison by employers, as long as the system used is gender-neutral.

Separate plans must be posted for employees in each bargaining unit in the establishment, and for non-bargaining employees. Each plan must identify the group covered by the plan, define the establishment, and identify all job classes which formed the basis of the comparisons. The plan must also describe the gender-neutral comparison system used and the results of the comparisons. Finally, it must identify all the female job classes for which pay equity adjustments are required and state the date on which the first pay adjustments will be made.[79]

The European Union also has standard requiring equal pay "for work to which equal value is attributed."[80] This standard is enforced by the European Court of Justice in suits between employees and private employers.[81] The European Court of Justice has held, for example, that an employer cannot give lower hourly wages or lower (per hour worked) benefits to part-time workers than full-time workers if (as is often the case) there are significantly more women working part time than full time.[82] (Such differentials would be legal in the United States unless a woman employee could make the difficult showing that the policy was intentionally adopted to discriminate against women.)

Once a plaintiff in the EU shows that women are paid less than men for jobs of equal value, the burden shifts to the employer to show that the differential is justified.[83] The employer can prevail only on a showing that differentials "correspond to a real need on the part of the undertaking, are appropriate with a view to achieving the objectives pursued, and are necessary to that end."[84] More is needed than a subjective belief on the employer's part that the differentials are necessary, and the employer's objective justification must be proportionate to the pay differentials.[85] An economic defense is therefore possible, though the ECJ "has made little attempt to explain where it sees the balance lying as between commercial profitability of an organization and the elimination of discrimination."[86]

79. Elaine M. Todres, Women's Work in Ontario: Pay Equity and the Wage Gap, 22 Ottawa L.Rev. 555, 561–62 (1990). For additional information about the Ontario experience, see Judy Fudge, Limiting Equity: The Definition of "Employer" under the Ontario Pay Equity Act, 4 Can.J. Women & L. 556 (1990–1991); Patricia C. McDermott, Pay Equity in Ontario: A Critical Legal Analysis, 28 Osgoode Hall L.J. 381 (1990). For a recent description of comparable worth in the various Canadian provinces as well as at the federal level, see M. Neil Brown and Michael D. Meuti, Individualism and the Market Determination of Women's Wages in the United States, Canada, and Hong Kong, 21 Loy.L.A. Int'l & Comp.L.J. 355, 372–87 (1999).

80. Council Directive 75/117 (Equal Pay Directive) art. 1, 1975 O.J. (L45), 19 (interpreting article 119 of the Treaty of Rome).

81. Case 61/81, Commission v. U.K., [1982] 3 C.M.L.R. 284 (1982).

82. See Evelyn Ellis, EC Sex Equality Law 112–19 (1998) (discussing cases).

83. Id. at 119–122 (discussing cases).

84. Case 170/84, Bilka–Kaufhaous GmbH v. Weber Von Gartz, [1986] ECR 1607, 1628 (1986).

85. Case C–127/92, Enderby v. Frenchay Health Authority, [1993] ECR I–5535, 5576 (1993); see also Ellis, above note 82, at 125–126 (discussing cases and standard).

86. Ellis, above note 82, at 126.

Table 6: International Comparisons[87]

Country	Wage gap
Australia	91%
Sweden	89%
Norway	86%
Denmark	83%
France	81%
Italy	80%
Austria	78%
Greece	78%
The Netherlands	77%
Finland	77%
Germany	76%
Portugal	76%
Belgium	75%
United States	75%
Canada	72%
United Kingdom	70%
Spain	70%
Ireland	69%

In many, though not all, of the countries in the EU the wage gap between women and men is lower than in the United States, as the table above illustrates. All countries in the chart, other than the United States and parts of Canada, have a comparable-worth standard applicable to some private employers.

Notes on Comparable Worth

1. What are the arguments for and against a comparable worth standard applicable to all employers? In particular, what are the difficulties with this sort of standard? Would it be judicially manageable? Do you think it requires comparison of apples and oranges? Can you think of other (existing) legal standards presenting similar difficulties?

2. One limit on the effectiveness of a comparable worth standard in eliminating the wage gap between women and men is that it only allows

87. Joni Seager, The State of Women in the World Atlas 68–69 (1997) (1994 data). The chart in text above (based on data from the Department of Labor Women's Bureau) reports that in 1994 the wage gap in the United States was 72% whereas the international comparison reports the wage gap in the United States for that same year as 75%, a somewhat higher figure. Depending on the precise details of the calculation such as whether very young workers are included, wage gap numbers do vary slightly from each other. For a third figure for 1994, see 76.4% reported by Costello, et. al., above note 5, at 303.

challenges to wage disparities within a single employer. To the extent manufacturing jobs pay more than service jobs "of equal value," comparable worth will not provide a remedy. Can you think of a way to structure a remedy that would reach across industries?

3. Do you agree with the reasoning in AFSCME v. State of Washington (rejecting comparable-worth arguments in Title VII cases)? Do you agree with the court's assertion that "[n]either law nor logic deems the free market system a suspect enterprise"? If you regard the free market system with some suspicion, given the evidence of persistent wage gaps by race together with sex and job segregation by race and sex, how would you analyze the questions presented in *AFSCME*? Would you have found disparate treatment? Disparate impact?

4. Comparable worth accepts market driven wages with some minor adjustments. What problems and inequities does comparable worth thereby ignore? How would women of various classes and races fare under comparable worth? One commentator has observed: "it would be better, for the women's movement and for society, for feminist lawyers developing their legal theory to have as their goal a redefinition of human worth that challenges the market-based definition more directly than a pay equity [or comparable worth] theory does, and to seek a remedy that calls for some plausible modification in the organization of a workplace aimed at realizing a more nurturant and socially confirming conception of the nature of socially valuable labor." Peter Gabel, Dukakis's Defeat and the Transformative Possibilities of Legal Culture, Tikkun, Mar.-Apr. 1989, at 13, 113. In what ways is comparable worth conservative? What might a more radical claim look like? See also Johanna Brenner, Feminist Political Discourses: Radical Versus Liberal Approaches to the Feminization of Poverty and Comparable Worth, 1 Gender & Soc'y 447 (1987).

5. How would the various feminist approaches presented in Chapter 3 analyze and explain the wage gap? What remedy or remedies would each consider appropriate? Which explanation is, in your view, most accurate? Which remedies are most likely to be effective?

6. Do you think that the women's movement is more powerful in the United States than in other countries such as Australia, Canada, and the EU? If so, why is it that the United States is behind most of these countries in terms of adopting comparable worth *and* in the size of the wage gap between men and women?

Chapter 11

WOMEN AND THE LEGAL PROFESSION

A. INTRODUCTION

Women have entered the legal profession in large numbers only within the last few decades. In 1971, just 3% of all lawyers were women; by 1980 this figure had risen to 8%, and to nearly 25% in 1995,[1] an increase which owed a great deal to the passage of Title VII of the Civil Rights Act of 1964.[2] After meeting the challenge of outright exclusion, women have also been faced with other forms of bias in law schools, courts, and law firms. How women confront this challenge may determine both their success within the profession and possibly the shape of that profession in the future.

In 1869, Belle Mansfield became the first woman admitted to the bar in the United States, when she applied for and received a license to practice law in Iowa.[3] Women in other states of the union did not fare as well. Although Ada H. Kepley was the first woman to graduate from a law school in the United States when she received her degree from Union College of Law (now Northwestern) in 1870, she was denied admission to the Illinois bar until 1881.[4] Courts which considered the petitions of women seeking the right to practice law repeatedly found that woman's "nature" was unsuited for a profession that "has essentially and habitually to do with all that is selfish and malicious, knavish

1. Clara N. Carson, The Lawyer Statistical Report: The U.S. Legal Profession in 1995 3 (1999).

2. Title VII suits were necessary in the 1970's to force elite law firms to hire women. See Karen Berger Morello, The Invisible Bar: The Woman Lawyer in America: 1638 to the Present 210–15 (1986); Cynthia Fuchs Epstein, Women in Law 184–86 (1981).

3. Morello, above note 2, at 11–14.

4. Epstein, above note 2, at 50; Morello, above note 2, at 49–50 (Morello asserts that Kepley graduated from the University of Chicago Law School, but Northwestern's claim of historical and legal connectedness seems clearer than that of the University of Chicago, which was not founded until 1891 (the law school in 1902). Moreover, Northwestern has long laid claim to Kepley, while Chicago has not.)

and criminal, coarse and brutal, repulsive and obscene, in human life."[5]

Even after the passage of acts guaranteeing the right of women to practice the occupations of their choice, women who chose to become lawyers faced other barriers. Law schools were slow to admit women: Harvard, one of the last holdouts, did not admit women students until 1950, and a few other schools continued to exclude women until the 1960's and 1970's.[6] Until the 1970's, moreover, admissions quotas severely limited the numbers of women at most law schools; and, once admitted, women experienced hostility to their presence on the part of professors and male students alike.[7] Nonetheless, with the assistance of federal anti-discrimination laws, the number of women studying law has increased sharply during the last few decades—from 3.7% in 1963–64, to 8.6% in 1970, to 34% in 1980—and has hovered between 40 and 50% since 1985–86.[8]

Fierce discrimination continued to face women who sought positions with law firms. Wall Street was particularly hostile territory for women, and until the 1970's firms readily admitted that they did not hire women.[9] Sandra Day O'Connor, who in 1981 became the first woman justice on the Supreme Court, was unable to obtain any employment as a lawyer in 1952, although she had graduated from Stanford Law School with honors and served as an editor on the Stanford Law Review.[10] Those women lucky enough to be hired, moreover, did not advance within large law firms. The prestigious Wall Street firm of Sullivan & Cromwell, for example, hired its first woman associate in 1930 but did not make any woman partner until 1982.[11] Although women have been entering the profession in substantial numbers since the 1970's, their representation among partnerships is still disproportionately low.[12]

In the 1980's and early 1990's, task forces were set up in many states to study the question of gender bias in the law. The reports issued by these groups concluded that outright exclusion of women has now been replaced by subtler forms of discrimination against them by both judges and male lawyers—by sexist remarks and practices, by derogatory treatment and forms of address, and by numerous other messages which convey that women are still not completely welcome in the profession they have chosen to join.[13]

5. In re Goodell, 39 Wis. 232, 245–46 (1875). See also Bradwell v. Illinois, 83 U.S. (16 Wall.) 130, 130, 21 L.Ed. 442 (1872).

6. Epstein, above note 2, at 50. Notre Dame did not admit women until 1969 and Washington and Lee until 1972. Id.

7. Id. at 63–67; Morello, above note 2, at 103–05.

8. ABA, Official American Bar Association Guide to Approved Law Schools, 2000 Edition 450 (1999).

9. Epstein, above note 2, at 83–95; Morello, above note 2, at 194–217.

10. Epstein, above note 2, at 84 n.; Morello, above note 2, at 194.

11. Morello, above note 2, at 197; Epstein, above note 2, at 214–15.

12. Carson, above note 1, at 18–19. In 1984, the Supreme Court held that Title VII applies to law firm partnership decisions. Hishon v. King & Spalding, 467 U.S. 69, 104 S.Ct. 2229, 81 L.Ed.2d 59 (1984).

13. See Ann J. Gellis, Great Expectations: Women in the Legal Profession, A Commentary on State Studies, 66 Ind. L.J. 941 (1991); Jeannette F. Swent, Gender Bias at the Heart of Justice: An Empirical

The entry of women into the legal profession in increasing numbers has also brought demands for change. In a society in which women are the primary caretakers of both the very young and the very old, female lawyers have confronted a profession structured around the norm of a male attorney with little or no responsibility for caretaking. This confrontation has led to demands for maternity leave, part-time work and flexible tracks to partnership, which have in turn occasioned fears about a "glass ceiling," the "Mommy track," and the relegation of women to second-class status within the profession.[14] Some studies show that women lawyers suffer from higher levels of job dissatisfaction than do their male counterparts, and women's attrition rates in private law firms are disproportionately high.[15] An in-depth study of the women in the Harvard Law School class of 1974, for example, revealed that many of them left private law firms within five to ten years of graduation, primarily because they wanted to give more priority to their private lives (although most stayed within the field, in jobs that allowed more time for private life, as, for example, in-house counsel for corporations, government lawyers, or law professors).[16] Whether women will simply leave law firms or will stay and restructure the legal workplace to meet their needs remains an open question.

Some claim that women will substantially change the legal profession, not only by restructuring the workplace but also by contributing a "different voice" to lawyering—a more collaborative, cooperative, and contextual approach, with a preference for non-adversarial modes of dispute resolution, such as mediation.[17] Critics, on the other hand, point out that women, like minorities, may suffer in informal settings, if the parties are unequal in power or only one of the two is socialized to think

Study of State Task Forces, 6 S. Cal. Rev. L. & Women's Stud. 1 (1996).

14. The "glass ceiling" refers to an invisible barrier that prevents women from scaling the upper rungs on the ladder of success while allowing them to see what they are missing; the phrase "Mommy track" is used to describe the career path of women who choose to work fewer hours because of child care obligations and may therefore be shunted into less prestigious work with fewer opportunities for advancement. See, e.g., Felice Schwartz, Management Women and the New Facts of Life, 67 Harv.Bus.Rev., Jan.–Feb. 1989, at 65, 68; Women in Law, 74 A.B.A. J., June 1, 1988, at 49; Judith S. Kaye, "Mommy Track" in Practice, Nat'l L.J., May 22, 1989, at 13; Jennifer A. Kingson, Women in the Law Say Path Is Limited by "Mommy Track," N.Y. Times, Aug. 8, 1988, at A1.

15. Marilyn Tucker et al., Whatever Happened to the Class of 1983?, 78 Geo. L.J. 153, 164 (1990); A.B.A. Young Lawyers Division, The State of the Legal Profession 53–54 (1990); Janet Taber et al., Gender, Legal Education, and the Legal Profession: An Empirical Study of Stanford Law Students and Graduates, 40 Stan.L.Rev. 1209, 1222, 1224, 1251–52 (1988). But see David Chambers, Accommodation and Satisfaction: Women and Men Lawyers and the Balance of Work and Family, 14 Law & Soc. Inquiry 251, 252 (1989) (finding that women law graduates of the University of Michigan in the late 1970's were satisfied with both their careers and the balance of work and family in their lives five years after graduation); John P. Heinz, Kathleen E. Hull and Ava A. Harter, Lawyers and Their Discontents: Findings from a Survey of the Chicago Bar, 74 Ind. L.J. 735, 746 (1999) (finding no statistically significant gender difference in overall job satisfaction).

16. Jill Abramson and Barbara Franklin, Where Are They Now?: The Story of the Women of Harvard Law 1974 121–63, 301–07 (1986).

17. See, e.g., Carrie Menkel-Meadow, Portia in a Different Voice: Speculations on a Women's Lawyering Process, 1 Berkeley Women's L.J. 39 (1985).

in terms of the other party's interest rather than her own.[18] Others wonder how it is possible to fight the necessary battles over the many legal issues that affect women's lives without learning to fight "like men."[19]

Whatever their impact upon the structure and practice of law, it seems clear that unless women enter the profession and use its tools, they will be excluded from an important source of power in our society. As Cynthia Fuchs Epstein has pointed out, law provides access to important positions in business, government, and politics in the United States: "Members of the legal elite preside over power and property relationships. They play a leading role in the legislative and regulative bodies that write the law; they direct the executive agencies responsible for enforcing the law; they rule the courts that elaborate and apply the law; they guide the corporate and financial institutions that constitute the most important property interests."[20] In short, the role of women within the legal profession may prove central to their capacity to structure the rules and institutions which affect women's lives in every sphere.

B. WOMEN AND LEGAL EDUCATION

CATHERINE WEISS AND LOUISE MELLING, THE LEGAL EDUCATION OF TWENTY WOMEN

40 Stan. L. Rev. 1299, 1299–1300, 1302, 1313–16, 1320–21, 1327, 1330–39, 1341–42, 1345–48 (1988).

I.

Powerful men made American law and American law schools by and for themselves. While law faculties and the legal profession remain overwhelmingly male, law schools are admitting increasing numbers of women. Many of these women find legal education alienating. This essay documents the experiences of twenty women in the Yale Law School class of 1987 who organized and sustained a women's group in which we revealed, explored, and confronted our alienation. The sections of this essay show four faces of alienation: from ourselves, from the law school community, from the classroom, and from the content of legal education. * * *

A. Premises

Two premises underlie our study. First, men and women experience law school differently. From the moment the group organized, we identified our alienation as a women's issue. * * *

18. See, e.g., Lisa Lerman, Mediation of Wife Abuse Cases: The Adverse Impact of Informal Dispute Resolution on Women, 7 Harv. Women's L.J. 57 (1984); Richard Delgado, Chris Dunn, Pamela Brown, Helena Lee and David Hubbert, Fairness and Formality: Minimizing the Risk of Prejudice in Alternative Dispute Resolution, 1985 Wis. L.Rev. 1359.

19. See, e.g., Sarah E. Burns, Notes from the Field: A Reply to Professor Colker, 13 Harv. Women's L.J. 189 (1990).

20. Epstein, above note 2, at 13.

Our second premise is that women's alienation in law school matters. We are angry about our exclusion and want to feel engaged. Our alienation also impoverishes the intellectual and emotional life of the law school. The drowning of women's speech in a flood of men's voices squelches the diversity of ideas and styles that ought to sustain institutions of learning. Worst of all, the perspective of an outsider—one neither born to power nor raised to power by the law—is lost. Women have criticisms to make that students of the law should hear, criticisms that may unsettle the dominant and help to empower the rest. Finally, the alienation of women in law school affects the legal profession and everyone it touches. What we do in law school shapes what we will do as lawyers, which in turn affects the lives of others. Until women share equally in the learning, and thus in the practice, teaching, and making of law, we will be disabled in shaping society to fit women's needs.

* * *

II. Alienation From Self

* * *

Imagine a spectrum with two images at either extreme. At one end sits the image of Woman, embodying qualities associated with generations of women who themselves had little hand in shaping the image. She lacks public power. She serves other people. She is expected to be and often succeeds in being caring, empathetic, cooperative, and generous. At the opposite end stands the figure of Lawyer, as molded by previous generations of men. He is powerful, instrumental, and adversarial. In the middle, vacillating, both attracted to and repelled by each image, we stand. This section portrays our search for a way through law school that blended both images and discusses the alienation from self we experienced when swinging too close to either end of the spectrum.

* * *

We wanted to do what most of our mothers had not done, but without disabling ourselves to do what they had done. In the interviews, though, women expressed concern about the incompatibility of being a lawyer and a mother. * * * These women cast law and family as opposites not only for fear that there was no time for both but also for fear that the pursuit of one would make them unfit for the other. Maybe a trained adversary makes a poor mother. Maybe a builder and sustainer of family ties makes a poor lawyer.

* * *

Women feared losing one voice, drowned by another, the language of logic and argument replacing that of empathy and connection. They did not want to sit, detached like a judge, and decide for or against a relationship. Nor did they want to abuse a newfound power, of finding the flaws in every argument, by using it against loved ones.

* * *

III. Alienation From the Community

* * * The hostility and competitiveness of the law school community, which we perceived as sometimes directed against us as women, drew us together. * * * We found ourselves hurt by and hurting those who gave us strength, participating in the games of an institution that we did not trust and that produced winners and losers.

* * *

Our men-classmates seemed to embrace the rules of the game and the standards of selection. Although surrounded by picket lines [from a clerical workers' strike] and pictures on the walls [portraits of male alumni and benefactors] representing ongoing and historic exclusion, they behaved as though achievement, not arbitrariness, controlled admissions, faculty appointments, and faculty attention. They seemed eager to prove themselves and confident that their talent or strategy would lead to success. They appeared not to identify with people less confident and successful. The men seemed to work alone, possibly to protect and develop their individual knowledge, willing to risk failing alone, possibly in the hope of succeeding alone. We felt both untrained for and disarmed by the competitiveness and isolation and so sought one another out.

* * *

[O]ur competitiveness undermined how we cared about one another. It troubled us, as individuals, about our willingness to become the rivals of our friends. It spoiled our friendships as the successful and the less successful grew uncomfortable together. It fractured our group, as those more consistently successful found it difficult to criticize the institution that rewarded them and in which they had found a place. In contrast, those who had been hurt became increasingly angry, particularly when the rejections or their arbitrariness went unacknowledged.

We characterized our successes as arbitrary in part to downplay these divisions, but we had another reason as well. We didn't trust the game. In a sense, the rejection of our deserving friends only reinforced what the picket lines, the pictures, and our men-classmates' attitudes reminded us of—that we had not designed the rules. Those who had kept our mothers outsiders still ran the institution, set the standards of admission, and established the norms for success within it; they occupied the judges' chambers, sat on law firm hiring committees, and reviewed applications for teaching positions. Encounters with professors, practicing attorneys, and classmates reinforced our perceptions that the competitions did not always select for merit.

* * *

IV. Alienation From the Classroom

* * * The classroom was the crucible of our criticisms of ourselves and of the law school. There, many of us, longtime class participants, learned silence. * * *

We were hurt, angered, and silenced in different ways. Some were too "distracted by fear" or too stunned by the prevailing classroom tone to open their mouths. * * * Still others fell into cycles of participation and withdrawal, driven primarily by exhaustion with hearing the same speakers over and over again coupled with guilt about becoming like those speakers. * * *

Why did class discussion in law school silence a disproportionate number of women and trouble even those who continued to participate? The interviews suggest a number of answers. The first is obvious. Some professors and some students treat women with hostility or pretend that women don't exist in law classes. Such discrimination, although probably on the decline, still thrives. We also disengaged from classes because of more generalized aggression, not that directed against women in particular, but that directed against every person and every issue. We learned early that the classroom is a place for polarized argument, for winning points for a side. Many of us found ourselves mute or unwilling as classroom adversaries. Less common than argument, but no less silencing, is a speech pattern we (the authors) call "nonconversation" because it is characterized by the absence of exchanges. Everyone who talks sounds as if he were delivering an esoteric address to a large, silent audience. No one's words follow from anyone else's. Finally, we felt silenced by the element of showmanship called for in classes dominated by argument or nonconversation.

The hostility generally unleashed in law classes occasionally turns its force against women as women. Direct derogation of our minds and bodies still happens. * * * But more prevalent than such outspoken misogyny is a kind of willful deafness toward what women-students say, accompanied by an absence of eye contact, a physical turning away.

> There were times when women made points, and they were ignored or trivialized. Five minutes later, a man would make the same point, in three parts, and it was discussed. * * *

The message that women don't exist and aren't worth noticing if they try to exist is communicated in subtler ways as well. Many professors continue, in spite of increasingly open protest, to use male pronouns exclusively (unless the case involves a rape victim, a battered wife, or a mother fighting for custody) and to feature men in all hypothetical questions. They may also draw on knowledge in areas historically closed to women while remaining ignorant of subjects crucial to many women.

> Men presume that everyone understands a sports analogy. I would never presume to use a knitting analogy. * * *

Women also weren't "important enough" for most after-class discussions with the professor. Almost invariably, when the professor is a man, the cluster around the professor consists only of men. * * *

* * *

The dominance of the adversary model in legal training partially explains both the aggression and the competition. The courtroom is a place where lawyers use words to win fights. The classroom is the courtroom's shadow. * * * Professors who encourage polarization may be teaching adversarial skills. By setting the pace of discussion at more than normal speed, a professor may demand quick thinking. By asking a series of leading questions that nudge the student into increasingly extreme responses, a professor may provide a lesson in cross-examination. By taking an adamant, one-sided position, a professor may evoke in the student an argument worthy of an opposing advocate. But such professors also create the impression that all lawyers do is engage in ritualized combat. Even if this were true, there would remain the serious question whether it should be true. Is the profession well served by the ongoing infusion of young lawyers trained primarily to fight? * * *

Polarization banishes affect, unless it takes the form of zeal for winning the argument. In more gentle form and combined with genuine concern about the issue under discussion (rape, abortion, incest, racism), emotion reveals more vulnerability than is safe to expose in a roomful of adversaries-in-training. Polarization banishes confusion and, with it, questions, thereby imposing on us the burden of seeming sure and robbing us of opportunities for tentative exploration. On those of us who will not subsume affect in analysis nor pretend certainty, polarization imposes silence, causing everyone to miss what we have to say in the way we have to say it.

Our voices were lost in other kinds of classes as well. If we rejected interaction fueled by open aggression, we were simply dumbstruck by classes where interaction itself had fallen to what one woman called "autistic" speech patterns.

> I was annoyed when they [students] spoke in ten points, for fifteen minutes.
>
> No one listened to each other. The teachers didn't listen to the students. The students didn't listen to the teachers. The students didn't listen to one another. There was no joint project to learn something. In class, the teacher would say something. The student would respond. The teacher's response would have nothing to do with the student's comments.

* * * This is nonconversation.

* * *

The kind of communication we care about depends on the sharing of questions and thoughts to improve understanding. Talk meant to impress rather than to interest sets us off balance. Both argument and nonconversation involve an uncomfortable element of showmanship. * * *

V. Alienation From the Content of Our Education

* * *

Common criticisms of the content of legal education * * * centered around two themes: Legal education was narrow or acontextual; and legal discourse focused on a search, often by methods involving the suspension of personal conviction, for some kind of neutral, objective truth foreign to our understanding. * * *

The narrowness theme encompasses seemingly conflicting objections to legal education as "too theoretical" and "not theoretical enough." The women who found their education "too theoretical" charged it with inattention and indifference to "the real world," most often meaning the people involved, from parties in the cases to a range of others a decision affected. The women who found their education "not theoretical enough" felt that it lacked intellectual substance, that it made inadequate inquiry into the social, historical, political, or economic underpinnings of the cases. Both criticisms portray law as stripped, missing too much of what matters.

* * * Professors don't care who the parties are. Judicial opinions treat "the facts" in one paragraph and "the reasoning" in page after page. The assumption underlying this tilt toward analysis is that too close attention to the particulars of a case will frustrate its categorization and so foil the law's attempt to treat "like cases alike." But even accepting that categorization is necessary to law's goals, the women interviewed reject the notion that blindness to the facts is necessary to categorization. A judge needs her powers of description, of empathy, as well as of analysis to know, for instance, whether the constitution permits a state to threaten Michael Hardwick with imprisonment for up to twenty years for having sex with his male lover.[121] If she understood something about homosexual relationships she could not, with Justice White, categorize Michael Hardwick's claim by asserting "[n]o connection between family, marriage, or procreation on the one hand and homosexual activity on the other."

The quotations also suggest that the case method, as ordinarily employed, oversimplifies the world. * * * Whose interests were excluded to yield only two sides? * * *

LANI GUINIER, MICHELLE FINE, AND JANE BALIN, WITH ANN BARTOW, AND DEBORAH LEE STACHEL, BECOMING GENTLEMEN: WOMEN'S EXPERIENCES AT ONE IVY LEAGUE LAW SCHOOL

143 U. Pa. L. Rev. 1, 2–5, 47–55, 61–62, 65, 80, 82, 99 (1994).

In this Article we describe preliminary research[a] by and about women law students at the University of Pennsylvania Law School—a typical, if elite, law school stratified deeply along gender lines. Our

121. See Bowers v. Hardwick, 106 S.Ct. 2841 (1986) (holding that a state can constitutionally criminalize private, consensual, homosexual acts).

a. Guinier, Fine, and Balin subsequently published their research in the book, Becoming Gentlemen: Women, Law School, and Institutional Change (1997).

database draws from students enrolled at the Law School between 1987 and 1992, and includes academic performance data from 981 students, self-reported survey data from 366 students, written narratives from 104 students, and group-level interview data of approximately eighty female and male students. From these data we conclude that the law school experience of women in the aggregate differs markedly from that of their male peers.

First, we find strong academic differences between graduating men and women. Despite identical entry-level credentials, this performance differential between men and women is created in the first year of law school and maintained over the next three years. By the end of their first year in law school, men are three times more likely than women to be in the top 10% of their law school class.

Second, we find strong attitudinal differences between women and men in year one, and yet a striking homogenization by year three. The first-year women we studied are far more critical than their first-year male peers of the social status quo, of legal education, and of themselves as students. Third-year female students, however, are less critical than their third-year male colleagues, and far less critical than their first-year female counterparts. A disproportionate number of the women we studied enter law school with commitments to public interest law, ready to fight for social justice. But their third-year female counterparts leave law school with corporate ambitions and some indications of mental health distress.

Third, many women are alienated by the way the Socratic method is used in large classroom instruction, which is the dominant pedagogy for almost all first-year instruction. Women self-report much lower rates of class participation than do men for all three years of law school. Our data suggest that many women do not "engage" pedagogically with a methodology that makes them feel strange, alienated, and "delegitimated." These women describe a dynamic in which they feel that their voices were "stolen" from them during the first year. Some complain that they can no longer recognize their former selves, which have become submerged inside what one author has called an alienated "social male."

* * *

Finally, we document substantial material consequences for those women who exit the Law School after sustaining what they describe as a crisis of identity. These women graduate with less competitive academic credentials, are not represented equally within the Law School's academic and social hierarchies, and are apparently less competitive in securing prestigious and/or desirable jobs after graduation.

* * *

The hierarchy within the large first-year Socratic class also includes a hierarchy of perspectives. Those who most identify with the institution, its faculty, its texts, and its individualistic perspectives experience little dissonance in the first year. On the other hand are students who import an ambivalent identification with the institution, who resist competitive, adversarial relationships, who do not see themselves in the faculty, who vacillate on the emotionally detached, "objective" perspectives inscribed as "law," and who identify with the lives of persons who suffer from existing political arrangements. These students experience much dissonance.

A disproportionate number of women of all racial and ethnic groups also experience alienation in that they enter law school with a zeal for public interest work, but end having opted for corporate or other private sector employment. Our data suggest that there is an academic cost, and perhaps a mental health cost, to discarding passions, politics, emotions, and community-based identities that were once central to the student's identity. * * *

With remarkable consistency, students indicate that law school taught them to be "less emotional," "more objective," and to "put away ... passions." For some, this ability to suppress feelings [is] considered an enormous accomplishment; for others, it is considered a defeat. Second only to the skills of "objectivity," students report that over time they have learned to stop caring about others and have become more conservative. Some men indicate they have grown more aggressive and abrasive over their three years in law school; some women see themselves as more "humble" and "nitpicking." One woman concluded her interview by saying, "Here [at the Law School], it's okay to be intolerant."

The competitive, hierarchical format of the Law School's dominant pedagogy is also used by peers to put down some women. Many women who complained that their voices are pushed back and down, suffocated early on by hostile first-year classrooms, described how those women who spoke out felt humiliated by male, and some female, contemporaries who silenced those who publicly dared to "act like gentlemen." Ideas about women's sexuality, for example, became a basis for ridiculing individual women, especially those who spoke out in class. These put-downs may occur in informal networks that exist outside the classroom, but they are normalized by and may reproduce behavior that is performed within the classroom.

* * *

Many men attempt to "explain away" the gender and institutional aspects of the data. These men, who include students and faculty, often resort to alternative explanations, all of which identify a source unrelated to the Law School for the differences we found. For example, they proffered age, undergraduate major, and even participation in varsity sports in college as possible explanations for the differential between women's and men's performances as measured by grades in law school. We found no statistically significant difference between women and men in these categories. * * * We explored these intuitions and found that, when controlled for incoming demographics, gender alone predicted third-year law school class rank.

* * *

A. ALIENATION AND ACADEMIC PERFORMANCE WITHIN THE FORMAL STRUCTURE OF THE INSTITUTION

"Becoming gentlemen" appears to exact an academic cost for many women. Women's enfeebled participation within the formal structure of legal education occurs simultaneously with their less successful performance on the anonymously-graded examinations from which law school grades are derived. In other words, low levels of class participation in the formal, structured pedagogy correlate with weak performance on the formal, structured evaluation system.

There is also a psychological dimension to women's relatively weak academic performance. Along with a formal link between classroom participation and examination success, we suspect that there exists a psychological link between self-confidence, alienation, and academic performance. Students who are alienated by the formal classroom methodology, hierarchy, and size are arguably not psychologically prepared to succeed on the formal examinations. Those who doubt themselves or doubt whether they belong in the Law School do not perform as well.

Many students, especially many women, have simply not been socialized to thrive in the type of ritualized combat that comprises much of the legal educational method. * * *

* * *

It is important to recognize that peer relations reinforce women's silence via "hazing" imposed on women by white males. Students describe hazing as taking the form of "laughing at what I said" or "lesbian-baiting." Apparently, merely being called a "feminist" is sometimes considered sufficiently insulting to silence women who try to challenge prevailing interpretations of legal texts.

* * *

B. THE ALIENATION AND EXCLUSION OF WOMEN FROM INFORMAL LEARNING NETWORKS

[In this section the authors describe women's discomfort in various informal networks within the law school community and, in particular, their lack of interaction with and mentoring by male faculty.]

C. WOMEN WHO DO NOT BECOME GENTLEMEN ARE LESS VALUED MEMBERS OF THE LAW SCHOOL COMMUNITY

* * *

According to the difference hypothesis, women's difference makes them less equipped for law school. The way things are done in law school (the Socratic method, issue-spotting exams, large classrooms, unpatroled and informal networks) devalues and distorts those characteristics traditionally associated with women such as empathy, relational logic, and nonaggressive behavior. In this understanding, law school unintentionally uses a male-oriented baseline to measure male/female differences.

* * *

Most of this paper is about a group of women at the Law School who cannot or do not want to "become gentlemen." It is important to recognize, however, that even within this group of females, "women" is not a monolithic category. We have sought to identify the fact that some women who are alienated nevertheless do well academically; these women successfully function in the hierarchy and norms of the Law School. Accordingly, we identify two distinct "groups" of women. The first group of women fails academically as well as personally. The second group of women succeeds academically. These are women who do "become gentlemen." Within this category of successful women, there is also a subset who do well but feel alienated. This subset of women resents the sacrifices of self that law school requires them to make. These women perceive that law school is a "game." These women learn the rules in order to play the game, but they are acutely aware of the price they are paying. These women are those who have been described in some of our secondary literature as "bicultural" or "bilingual." They can act both as "women" and as "gentlemen" and they are acutely aware of the difference.

* * *

We believe that our research raises the second-generation diversity issue. If the first generation of women was challenged to demonstrate the need for access into existing, previously all-male institutions, the current (second) generation is challenged to demonstrate that mere access, especially in comparatively low status positions, is inadequate. As now designed, law school fails to equalize the experience and outcomes for all law students across gender. Whether because of difference or domination, legal education at an Ivy League institution exacts a disproportionate toll on almost half the law student population.

Formerly all-male educational institutions cannot incorporate and take advantage of difference without changing from within. Yet, the institution we studied has admitted more women students without adequately transforming itself. The major changes we observed occurred within the women who attend the school, not within or by the institution.

Second-generation diversity, however, requires some institutional transformation as a precondition for genuine inclusion. We argue that the purpose of legal education should be reconsidered critically. The problem is not simply "difference" or gendered domination—both of which play a role in the stories we have told. Nor is the problem simply that women are outsiders who opt for a powerful, stony silence. The problem lies in the system of evaluation in law schools, which functions to rank students on a hierarchy that prospective employers then use to choose who they will actually train to be a lawyer. In addition to ensuring selectivity, the law school's pedagogy socializes students to a certain adversarial practice of law. In these complementary ways, law schools perpetuate a vision of legal practice that has contributed to a crisis in the public trust of lawyers.

Notes on Women and Legal Education

1. If you are a law student, how has your experience been similar to or different from that of the 20 women students in Weiss and Melling's class at Yale? How many of these problems are related to whether you are male or female? What ideas do you have for changes in legal education that might address these problems? (The Weiss & Melling study was repeated in the class of 1997 at Yale, with similar results. Paula Gaber, "Just Trying To Be Human in This Place": The Legal Education of Twenty Women, 10 Yale J. L. & Feminism 165 (1998).)

2. Law school studies, in addition to those excerpted above, have consistently reported significant differences in class participation by gender, with women speaking far less frequently in class than men. See, e.g., Gaber, above note 1, at 183–93; Joan M. Krauskopf, Touching the Elephant: Perceptions of Gender Issues in Nine Law Schools, 44 J. Legal Educ. 311, 325–26 (1994); Suzanne Homer and Lois Schwartz, Admitted But Not Accepted: Outsiders Take an Inside Look at Law School, 5 Berkeley Women's L.J. 1 (1990); Taunya Lovell Banks, Gender Bias in the Classroom, 38 J. Legal Educ. 137, 141–43 (1988). Testing these reports, Elizabeth Mertz carried out a quantitative analysis of patterns in first-year contracts classes at eight law schools (recorded and coded by observers and verified by tapes); in six out of the eight classes studied, men had between 10% and 54% more turns to speak in class than women and took between 12% and 38% more time speaking. See Elizabeth Mertz, Wamucii Njogu, and Susan Gooding, What Difference Does Difference Make? The Challenge for Legal Education, 48 J. Legal Educ. 1, 45–46 (1998). What do you believe causes the different rates of participation of men and women in law school classrooms? Have you experienced it?

Some posit that women's silence reflects the fact that "they feel excluded and alienated from the law school classroom ... [and] subtle aspects of traditional legal education deny or even denigrate certain aspects of women's personal beliefs and values...." Janet Taber et al., Gender, Legal Education, and the Legal Profession: An Empirical Study of Stanford Law Students and Graduates, 40 Stan. L. Rev. 1209, 1256 (1988). Others suggest that "For many students the choice of silence is not a passive act; it is an expression of anger." Stephanie M. Wildman, The Question of Silence: Techniques to Ensure Full Class Participation, 38 J. Legal Educ. 147, 149 (1988). Whether passive withdrawal or act of rebellion, the problem is especially common among students of color whose life experiences and interpretations are not recognized by traditional legal discourse. See, e.g., Margaret E. Montoya, *Mascaras, Trenzas, y Grenas:* Un/masking The Self

While Un/braiding Latina Stories and Legal Discourse, 17 Harv. Women's L.J. 185 (1994).

What could be done to ensure full class participation? See, e.g., Wildman, above, at 152–55. At a summit conference on women in legal education held at Mills College in November 1997, participants debated whether establishing an all-women's law school would be a way to confront the problems of alienation, silence, and underachievement reported among women law students. See Jennifer Gerarda Brown, "To Give Them Countenance": The Case for a Women's Law School, 22 Harv. Women's L.J. 1 (1999). What do you think of this idea? Would it be constitutional?

3. Linda Wightman's extensive empirical study of almost 29,000 students entering 163 law schools in fall 1991 revealed, consistent with Guinier's findings, that women underperform in law school, both in comparison with male students and with their own undergraduate grade point averages. Linda F. Wightman, Women in Legal Education: A Comparison of the Law School Performance and Law School Experiences of Women and Men 5, 26–27 (1996). Wightman's survey results also showed that both women and men suffer drops in self-esteem, or academic self-concept, during law school; the drop is about the same, although women start law school with lower self-esteem. Id. at 54–59, 73. Why does this drop occur, in your opinion? What would be different at a law school that increased students' self-esteem rather than lowering it?

4. According to Wightman, African American women suffer a disproportionate drop in their self-esteem during the first year of law school. Wightman, above note 3, at 58. Why do you think the negative impact of law school upon academic self-confidence has a stronger effect on African American women than on any other group? How does this happen? Can you think of remedies for this problem? What are they? Law school appears to be have been an especially difficult experience for Latina professionals as well. See Montoya, above note 2; Maureen Ebben and Norma Guerra Gaier, Telling Stories, Telling Self: Using Narrative to Uncover Latinas' Voices and Agency in the Legal Profession, 19 Chicano–Latino L. Rev. 243 (1998). Gay and lesbian students also report that law school can be a chilly atmosphere for them. Janice L. Austin, Patricia A. Cain, Anton Mack, J. Kelly Strader, and James Vaseleck, Results from a Survey: Gay, Lesbian, and Bisexual Students' Attitudes About Law School, 48 J. Legal Educ. 157, 166–67 (1998) (describing defacement of posters and problematic in-class discussions of gay and lesbian issues).

5. Law school studies also discuss significant psychological distress experienced by women law students and report their diminished feelings of self-confidence over the years of their legal education. See Morrison Torrey, Jennifer Ries, and Elaine Spiliopoulos, What Every First–Year Female Law Student Should Know, 7 Colum. J. Gender & L. 267, 288–91 (1998) (summarizing the findings of various studies on stress and self-esteem in women law students). Psychological distress is apparently a phenomenon widespread among law students, as compared to other types of graduate students and the population at large. See, e.g., Marilyn Heins, Shirley Nickols Fahey, and Roger C. Henderson, Law Students and Medical Students: A Comparison of Perceived Stress, 33 J. Legal Educ. 511, 523 (1983) (finding equivalent

measures of stress but that law students were more stressed in areas of academics and fear of failing and were far less inclined to seek help from others to deal with their stress). Women law students are an especially high risk group. Stephen B. Shanfield and G. Andrew H. Benjamin, Psychiatric Distress in Law Students, 35 J. Legal Educ. 65, 68–72 (1985) (finding law students exhibit higher rates of psychiatric distress than medical students, and women law students a higher level of psychiatric symptoms than men law students, a finding not duplicated with medical students). To what would you attribute this phenomenon? What do you think can be done to address this problem? Would smaller classes and more frequent feedback help, in your opinion? Would some of these changes make law school a better place for male students as well?

6. Traditionally, law school teachers use what is loosely termed the Socratic method of teaching. The theory is that students will learn better if they have to infer generalities from questions posed to them in discussions about specific cases. Yet Guinier et al., in the study excerpted above, point to use of the Socratic method as one source of women's distress in law school, and other observers agree. See, e.g., Torrey et al., above note 5, at 281–82. Why do you think law professors rely on the Socratic method? Various answers have been offered, for example, that: it maintains the mystification of the legal process; it is an exercise of power in hierarchical relationships; it furthers the patriarchal power of the teacher while simultaneously devaluing students and undermining their confidence and self-esteem. Jennifer Jaff, Frame–Shifting: An Empowering Methodology for Teaching and Learning Legal Reasoning, 36 J. Legal Educ. 249, 260–61 (1986). Yet others argue that the Socratic method, used well, is the most effective pedagogy to teach women proficiency in the language of doctrinal legal analysis, so that they become "multilingual" in the type of discourse that models intellectual exchanges that take place in approaching legal problems and in the practice of law. Jennifer L. Rosato, The Socratic Method and Women Law Students: Humanize, Don't Feminize, 7 S. Cal. Rev. L. & Women's Stud. 37 (1997). What is your experience of the Socratic method? In what ways is it effective? Can it be used in a nonabusive fashion? If you were teaching, would you use the Socratic method? Why or why not? What pedagogical method would you use? More lecture? Discussion? Small group work? Simulation? Other methods?

7. What do you think of Lani Guinier's findings about the differential success of women and men in law school? Would a study of your school yield similar results? A number of formal and informal replication studies carried out at other law schools have contradicted Guinier's finding that women law students underachieve academically. One study, at Brooklyn Law School, where many of the pedagogical innovations recommended by Guinier (small sections in the first year, varied teaching techniques, non-exam-based feedback, and the like) had already been instituted, demonstrated that women students there both enter and graduate with academic credentials equivalent to men, yet still participate significantly less in class and experience more symptoms of distress. Marsha Garrison, Brian Tomko and Ivan Yip, Succeeding in Law School: A Comparison of Women's Experiences at Brooklyn Law School and the University of Pennsylvania, 3 Mich. J. Gender & Law 515 (1996). See also Shanie Latham, Iowa Study Defies Trend, Nat'l Jurist,

Oct./Nov. 1995, at 28; Chiu–Huey Hsia, Men, Women Perform Equally Well, Study Says, Columb. Spectator, Mar. 20, 1995, at 1, 5 (reporting that women law students at Iowa and Columbia, respectively, perform as well as men). A study of 13 years of entering classes at the University of Texas School of Law, however, confirms Guinier's findings. Allison L. Bowers, Women at the University of Texas School of Law: A Call for Action, 9 Tex. J. Women & L. 117 (2000) (finding that men outperformed women in both first-year grades and law review). What do you think could explain these differences in results among schools?

8. Professor Linda Hirshman has devised a measure called the "Femscore" to rank 158 accredited law schools according to two measures of how well women students succeed at each—the percentage of female tenured or tenure-track faculty and the percentage of women who make the school's law review. Hirshman, A Woman's Guide to Law School 125–54 (1999). Do you think that the percentage of women who make law review is an accurate reflection of women "succeeding" in law school? What about graduation rate, grade point average, or simple happiness with one's chosen field? What makes law school a "successful" endeavor for women? Hirshman found that women "underperform" in relation to their presence within the student body as a whole in 90 of the schools she examined, including such elite institutions as Yale, Harvard, and Stanford. Id. When choosing a law school, should women look to the statistical pattern of female students' success? How does the "woman-friendliness" of a school compare to its job placement or location as a persuasive reason to attend that institution? Would you have liked to know the Femscore of your law school prior to attending?

Hirshman also cautions potential women law students to investigate the political climate of law schools, researching views of prominent faculty, examining the catalogues for overrepresentation of women and minority students, and exploring how often courses of interest to women are actually offered at the school. Id. at 89–91, 106–13. Do you find an overriding political view in your school? How does it affect the education of women? How about the education of all future attorneys?

9. Sandra Janoff, a psychologist, carried out a study of modes of moral reasoning among law students at the beginning and end of their first year at Temple Law School. Janoff, The Influence of Legal Education on Moral Reasoning, 76 Minn. L. Rev. 193 (1991). She found that entering women law students reasoned predominantly from a care-oriented perspective, concerned with connection, prevention of harm, maintaining relationships, and responding to need, while male students were more likely to use rights-oriented moral reasoning. By the end of the first year, however, rights orientation was significantly more pronounced, and there was no significant difference in the care orientations of women and men. Are you surprised by Janoff's results? Does law school institutionalize a "male" method of moral reasoning? What changes would be necessary to eliminate this effect of law school education? Is it desirable to do so?

10. Might there be some advantages to approaching law school with an ethic of care? For example, many law professors complain that students spend too much time on exams regurgitating abstract black letter law rather than applying the law to the particular facts before them. This might be

addressed by encouraging the inclusion of more references to context and particular facts in class discussion. Would requiring clinical courses or other pro bono work also help? What other differences would you foresee based upon a care-based approach to legal education?

11. Some legal rights are based on notions of responsibility and care. For example, the primary caretaker standard for child custody at divorce is based on understanding the importance of caring relationships. Perhaps students using an ethic of care are better able to understand such rules. Can you think of other situations where this ethic might be helpful? Perhaps Gilligan's dichotomy between rights and care (see Chapter 3, above) is misleading, if rights may be based on an ethic of care. Should we have more such rights? Do you think this is likely as more women become legislators, judges, and lawyers?

Perhaps we should talk more about care and relationships in general and less about rights as such. For a thoughtful discussion of how Gilligan's "different voice" theories might affect feminist legal strategy, see Mary Joe Frug, Progressive Feminist Legal Scholarship: Can We Claim "A Different Voice"? 15 Harv. Women's L.J. 37 (1992); Judi Greenberg, Martha Minow, and Elizabeth Schneider, Contradiction and Revision: Progressive Feminist Legal Scholars Respond to Mary Joe Frug, 15 Harv. Women's L.J. 65 (1992).

12. In The Alchemy of Race and Rights: Diary of a Law Professor 8–9 (1991), Professor Patricia J. Williams identifies three features of legal thought: dichotomization, abstract universality, and objective norms. Are these concepts glorified in legal analysis? Are those the methods necessary to "think like a lawyer"? Does the law thereby avoid the truth of life's complexities? How? Is the law's attempt to universalize and objectify authority a device to avoid responsibility? What is the antidote?

13. How often does a law teacher ask the class how the students "feel" rather than "think" about a case's outcome? Should emotion have a greater role in the law? What about the role of empathy? Professor Lynne N. Henderson argues that the law would be more just if it were more empathetic. Do you think she is right? See Henderson, Legality and Empathy, 85 Mich. L. Rev. 1574 (1987). See also Robin West, Caring for Justice (1997). Contra Toni M. Massaro, Empathy, Legal Storytelling, and The Rule of Law: New Words, Old Wounds?, 87 Mich. L. Rev. 2099 (1989) (questioning the value of empathy in decision-making because, among other things, of judges' limited capacity for empathy and the dangers of discretionary adjudication). Can you think of an experience you have had that allowed you to empathize more with others? Has it enlarged your perspective? Made you a fairer person?

C. BIAS AGAINST WOMEN AS ATTORNEYS

CYNTHIA GRANT BOWMAN AND ELIZABETH M. SCHNEIDER, FEMINIST LEGAL THEORY, FEMINIST LAWMAKING, AND THE LEGAL PROFESSION

67 Fordham L. Rev. 249, 260–63 (1998).

* * *

C. Attempts by Women Lawyers and Academics to Attack the Problem of Gender Bias in the Profession: Task Forces and Commissions

In the 1980s and 1990s, a new form of literature began to emerge—reports from task forces and commissions established by women practitioners under the aegis of state supreme courts or bar associations.[58] The gender bias task force movement provides the most striking example of this development, which compiled and described the experiences of women in the legal system both as lawyers and litigants. The material assembled by the task forces provided data about the problems women lawyers continued to experience in the profession, and some included suggestions for change. In addition, publication of the reports was official recognition that discrimination against women in the legal profession continued to exist and thus legitimized the claims that had been emerging from the academy.

The task forces undertaking these independent investigations typically consisted of a mix of judges, practitioners, and academics; their methods of research included surveys, public hearings, and round-tables. Among other topics, each task force undertook an investigation of gender bias in the courtroom. The ABA Commission on Women in the Profession extended the investigation to discrimination against women in law firms and other settings, held public hearings, and published reports in 1988 and 1995.[59] * * *

The findings presented in these reports are astonishingly similar, lending persuasion from their sheer cumulative effect. The state court task force reports describe continuing discrimination against women lawyers in the courtroom by male attorneys and judges—for example, inappropriate and derogatory treatment, assumptions that women are less credible than men, and a variety of forms of sexual harassment. In addition, the findings demonstrate how women's and men's perceptions of discrimination differ (in effect, women see it and men don't notice).[61] Although the task force reports were largely essentialist with regard to their conclusions about the experiences of women, some included brief

58. The first reports were published in the early 1980s by task forces established by the New Jersey and New York supreme courts, at the instigation of women judges and practitioners. See The First Year Report of the New Jersey Supreme Court Task Force on Women in the Courts—June 1984, 9 Women's Rts. L. Rep. 129 (1986); Report of the New York Task Force on Women in the Courts (1986), 15 Fordham Urb. L.J. 1 (1986–1987). By now, a total of 35 states and five federal judicial circuits have issued reports as well. * * *

59. ABA 1988 Report [Commission on Women in the Profession, American Bar Ass'n, Report to the House of Delegates (1988)]; ABA 1995 Report [Commission on Women in the Profession, American Bar Ass'n, Unfinished Business: Overcoming the Sisyphus Factor (1995)]. * * *

61. For descriptions of the reports of the state task forces, see Ann J. Gellis, Great Expectations: Women in the Legal Profession, A Commentary on State Studies, 66 Ind. L.J. 941 (1991); Judith Resnik, Asking about Gender in Courts, 21 Signs: J. of Women in Culture and Soc'y 952 (1996); Jeannette F. Swent, Gender Bias at the Heart of Justice: An Empirical Study of State Task Forces, 6 S. Cal. Rev. L. & Women's Stud. 1 (1996).

references to the effect, for example, that the experiences of African American women were even worse.[62] Most of the state task forces deliberately chose to set aside questions of race or other discrimination in the legal profession for separate study, leaving the experiences of women of color (or of other marginalized groups) to fall between the cracks.[63]

Bar association studies pointed repeatedly to job segregation, pay differentials, glass ceilings, sexual harassment, and overwhelming work/family conflicts encountered by women lawyers. The 1988 ABA Report described testimony by women in law firms to the effect that they lacked mentors, were excluded from socialization with clients, were not assigned to "plum" cases or only given minor roles on them, and were required to overcome a presumption of incompetence. Moreover, the Glass Ceiling Report published by the New York City Bar Association in 1995 indicated that things might be getting worse rather than better: whereas 15.25% of female hires became partners between 1973 and 1981, only 5% of post–1981 hires did.[66]

Some have argued that the work of the various task forces and commissions constituted an exercise in feminist theory—essentially, cultural feminism—in that they listened to women's voices and focused upon women's experiences as different from men's. The theoretical grounding of the various studies carried out by the bench and the bar, however, was formal equality; this was perhaps inevitable, given the composition of the groups that authored them, which included powerful "insiders." Thus, discrimination against women was regarded primarily as an aberration perpetrated against individuals, the continuation of outdated stereotypes, and an irrationality rather than a structural problem requiring radical change in the profession. As a result of this theoretical grounding, recommendations for change tended to be incremental, partial, and aimed at a particular manifestation of the problem. As a remedy for in-court discrimination, for example, task forces recommended judicial education and better control by judges of their courtrooms. To remedy problems faced by women in law firms, recommendations included part-time work and flexible schedules.

At the same time, however, practitioners for whom these incremental changes had not worked told their stories in the legal press. Lawyers who had worked part-time or flexible hours, for instance, described how

62. See, e.g., Illinois Task Force on Gender Bias in the Courts, The 1990 Report of the Illinois Task Force on Gender Bias in the Courts 221 (1990) (reporting instances of patronizing, demeaning, and dismissive conduct by male judges toward African–American female attorneys). California, Michigan, and Florida, as well as the federal task forces for the Ninth and D.C. Circuits, made the experiences of women of color a more direct subject of study. See Resnik, supra note 61, at 974.

63. See id. at 973–77. Indeed, a number of manuals for both gender bias as well as race and ethnic bias task forces counseled separate treatment, for fear of distracting attention paid from one to the other. See id. at 975.

66. See [Cynthia Fuchs Epstein et al., Report, Glass Ceilings and Open Doors: Women's Advancement in the Legal Profession, 64 Fordham L. Rev. 291 (1995)] at 358–59.

"part-time" was interpreted as forty hours a week and resulted in guilt on their own part and resentment by others, loss of benefits and desirable work assignments, and either delay or complete derailment from the partnership track. In short, if the theory behind the task force recommendations was formal equality, the real-life experience of women lawyers was proving its limits.

Notes on Gender Bias in the Legal Profession

1. How should one evaluate the absence of women in positions of power in law firms? Some would say that this is merely a problem of transition, attributable to the recency of women's entry into the profession. However, recent studies show that women are much less likely than men to be in private practice seven to ten years after law school, which is approximately the amount of time it takes to become a partner in a large law firm. Mona Harrington reports, concerning women who graduated in the class of 1980 from Harvard Law School and were in practice in New York City in 1982 and 1989, that 54% of these women were in large firms in 1982, but only 33% remained there in 1989. Mona Harrington, Women Lawyers: Rewriting The Rules 37 (1994). She further reports that 70% of men from that class in New York City were in large firms in 1982 and 78% in 1989. Moreover, this disparity appears to be getting worse. A 1995 study of eight large New York firms—the "Glass Ceiling Report"—reported increasing gender disparity in the route to partnership. Cynthia Fuchs Epstein, Robert Saute, Bonnie Oglensky and Martha Gever, Glass Ceilings and Open Doors: Women's Advancement in the Legal Profession, 64 Fordham L. Rev. 291, 358–59 (1995). Although approximately 21% of male associates and approximately 15% of female associates made partner between 1973 and 1981, after 1981, only 17% of males made partner, and the female rate declined to 5%. If 40% of law school graduates in the last decade have been women, would one not anticipate the presence of more women partners, even assuming a six- or seven-year partnership "track"? What, in your opinion, has caused this phenomenon?

2. Another finding in numerous gender bias reports and surveys is that women attorneys are repeatedly subjected to sexual harassment by judges, opposing counsel, and partners and associates in their own firms. See, e.g., Marina Angel, Sexual Harassment by Judges, 45 U. Miami L. Rev. 817, 821–23 (1991) (describing numerous studies as well as individual cases in which judges harassed women in the courtroom); Lisa Pfenninger, Sexual Harassment in the Legal Profession: Workplace Education and Reform, Civil Remedies, and Professional Discipline, 22 Fla. St. U. L. Rev. 171, 179–81 (1994) (describing instances of men harassing women within law firms). A 1993 survey of 800 law partners and associates revealed that 51% of the women lawyers reported sexual harassment at some point during their careers; one in six reported incidents within the previous three years. See Mark S. Kende, Shattering the Glass Ceiling: A Legal Theory for Attacking Discrimination against Women Partners, 46 Hastings L.J. 17, 20 (1994) (quoting a 1993 National Law Journal Study). Given that sexually harassing behavior is both unethical and illegal in these circumstances, can you think of more effective remedies for women experiencing such conduct?

3. The American Bar Foundation Statistical Report states that:

> In 1995 the three employment settings in which female lawyers were most heavily overrepresented were government, legal aid and defender programs, and judicial departments. The total number of female lawyers employed in government was 41% greater than would be expected were they proportionally represented based on their representation in the total lawyer population. Overrepresentation was even greater in legal service programs (77%) and among judicial support personnel (82%).

Clara N. Carson, The Lawyer Statistical Report: The U.S. Legal Profession in 1995 13 (1999). How do you account for the higher percentages of women in government, legal aid, and similar settings than in private practice? Is this necessarily a bad thing? Why or why not?

Women are also disproportionately represented among the divorce bar. See Richard J. Maiman, Lynn Mather, and Craig A. McEwen, Gender and Specialization in the Practice of Divorce Law, 44 Me. L. Rev. 39 (1992). One study, based on interviews with 163 lawyers in Maine and New Hampshire, found that (1) while both male and female divorce attorneys preferred to represent women, the women lawyers were twice as likely to prefer wives because of the issues involved in their cases; and (2) the women divorce lawyers were more likely to be client-oriented, that is, to see their work in terms of helping people. Id. at 42, 48, 56. Why do you think women lawyers tend to cluster in domestic relations work? Is this the result of discrimination? Is it a good or bad thing?

4. Women were for a long time absent from positions of power within law schools. By 1986, more than 40% of law students were women, but only about 20% of full-time faculty in American law schools were women. Marina Angel, Women in Legal Education: What It's Like to Be Part of a Perpetual First Wave or the Case of the Disappearing Women, 61 Temp. L. Rev. 799, 803 (1988). Many of these women are in fact legal writing and clinical instructors, fields which are rapidly becoming "pink-collar ghettos." Id. See also Richard Chused, The Hiring and Retention of Minority and Female Faculty in American Law Schools, 137 U. Pa. L. Rev. 537 (1988). Given that entry-level candidates for law teaching positions have typically been out of law school only for a few years, this represents a clear gender imbalance in law faculties. One study shows that minority women are particularly disadvantaged in the hiring process, even in relation to minority men. Deborah J. Merritt and Barbara F. Reskin, The Double Minority: Empirical Evidence of a Double Standard in Law School Hiring of Minority Women, 65 S. Cal. L. Rev. 2299 (1992).

There are also indications that women are tenured at a substantially lower rate than men. Angel, above, at 805. Yet another study indicates that things may be improving, except at the elite law schools, where the numbers of women faculty remain very low. Robert Borthwick and Jordan Schau, Gatekeepers of the Profession: An Empirical Profile of the Nation's Law Professors, 25 Mich. J.L. Reform 191, 199–212 (1991). See also Deborah J. Merritt, Barbara F. Reskin, and Michelle Fondell, Family, Place, and Career: The Gender Paradox in Law School Hiring, 1993 Wis. L. Rev. 395 (finding that family ties and geographic constraints do not explain failure of recently hired women to attain positions at most prestigious law schools).

Professors Angel and Chused believe that women are underrepresented on law faculties at least in part because initial appointments rely heavily upon "old boy" networks and because the factors considered in the tenure decision are extremely subjective in nature. Chused discovered from his statistical study that a major factor relating to the number of women on a given faculty was the number of tenured women on that faculty: if tenured women made up more than 12% of the faculty, untenured women were denied tenure less often and they also left less often; if the percent was lower than 12%, women obtained tenure at lower rates. Chused, above, at 552. As of the late 1980's, women did not make up 12% or more of the tenured faculty at most American law schools, though. Angel, above, at 829. How does this affect what is taught? Do you think it makes any difference to the pedagogy employed in law schools? The research reflected in law review articles?

5. How should women lawyers respond when they are the object of or observe sexist comments, innuendo, or other forms of derogatory treatment in court? Should the response differ if the offending remarks are made by a judge or by opposing counsel? Does it make a difference if the woman's client is present at the time? What if the attorney has to appear before the same judge repeatedly? What factors should women lawyers take into account when responding in such situations? Are any of these factors potentially conflicting, for example, feminist convictions versus the interest of the client? How should one decide in case of conflict? Would you report such an incident to a bar disciplinary committee? Is it unethical?

6. In one case, a criminal defendant included in his issues for appeal the fact that the judge had referred to his female attorney in a belittling manner. The judge referred to her in chambers as "a nice girl" and a "pretty girl"; he also told the jury after ruling against her that:

> [C]ounsel had admitted that she did not know * * *. And she's sorry, she's apologized to the Court * * *. I hate to fuss at a pretty girl, fuss at an old man, but a pretty girl I hate to fuss. * * * But she was doing the best, she thought. But anyhow as she gains experience—if they don't give it to her all she does have to do is ask me, and I certainly will. * * * Don't hold it against her, she's a nice girl. I was young once myself, I put it to plain inexperience or whatever, but you'll get over it as you learn. So don't hold it against her. She's a nice girl.

State v. Pace, 310 S.C. 95, 425 S.E.2d 73, 75–76 (S.C.App.1992). While the appellate court expressed its concern about this treatment, stating that it was clearly gender-based, it held that the remarks did not impair counsel's ability to effectively represent her client and thus that no prejudicial error had occurred. Id. at 76. What do you think (1) of the court's ruling? (2) of litigation in the context of the underlying case to address problems of gender bias against a litigant's attorney? Is this an effective way to deal with the problem? What other routes would have been open to the female attorney in this case?

7. What are the effects of male and female speech characteristics in the courtroom? In two experiments college students listened to the testimony of

a female or male witness who used either "powerless" speech (e.g., speech patterns associated with women's speech, such as frequent use of intensifiers, hedges, and questioning intonation) or "power" speech (more assertive style associated with men) to deliver the same basic evidence. Both the experiment using tape-recorded testimony and the one using trial transcripts found that listeners evaluated the witness (regardless of actual sex) using the "powerless" style more negatively. See Bonnie E. Erickson, Alan Lind, Bruce C. Johnson, and William O'Barr, Speech Style and Impression Formation in a Court Setting: The Effects of "Power" and "Powerless" Speech, 14 J. Experimental & Soc. Psych. 2166 (1978). What are the implications of this research for the success of women as litigators? Is the answer to teach women to speak and act more like men in order to challenge the status quo? Or should we be attempting to challenge the hierarchical structure that places "male" speech at the top and "female" speech at the bottom?

8. One extensive empirical study of speech interactions in Israeli courtrooms, observing male and female prosecuting attorneys, concluded that:

> [T]he language directed to women professionals in the courtroom impeded and undermined their claims to expertise and reproduced hierarchical gender relations. The qualitative and quantitative measures both revealed that women were spoken to differently than men in ways that undermined their professional status. The quantitative analysis showed that women judges were more likely to be addressed in formal, nondeferent terms, rather than in the deferent, courtroom-specific forms; women lawyers, unlike men, were addressed using a nondeferent and possibly demeaning form by judges, and witnesses never used their professional title; women lawyers were interrupted more frequently than men, and judges interrupted even witnesses more frequently when it was a woman lawyer who conducted the examination; judges took over the examination most frequently when women prosecutors were examining; judges, especially men judges, were likely to issue directives to women lawyers....

Bryna Bogoch, Courtroom Discourse and the Gendered Construction of Professional Identity, 24 Law & Soc. Inquiry 329, 367–68 (1999). (About 2/3 of the prosecutors in Israel are women. Id. at 334.) This treatment has obvious consequences for women's ability to perform competently. How should these problems be addressed?

9. Women of color who are lawyers report especially serious problems with derogatory treatment in court—regularly being mistaken for secretaries or clerks in the presence of their clients, being addressed in a patronizing fashion, and the like. See, e.g., The 1990 Report of the Illinois Task Force on Gender Bias in the Courts 221; Maureen Ebben and Norma Guerra Gaier, Telling Stories, Telling Self: Using Narrative to Uncover Latinas' Voices and Agency in the Legal Profession, 19 Chicano–Latino L. Rev. 243, 258–62 (1998). How are the problems women of color face in this respect similar to, or different from, those faced by other women attorneys? What do you think of the gender bias task forces' strategic decisions, described in the excerpt above, to set aside questions of race for separate study, for fear that

attention paid to one form of discrimination would distract attention from the other?

10. Samantha, a fourth year associate, Steve, a second year associate, and Sam Senior Partner are in a critical meeting with Calvin Client, whose work represents a substantial portion of the billings at the law firm. It is two months prior to trial on a major case which has been in preparation for more than a year. Samantha has done most of the discovery and trial preparation and is eager for the experience of a major trial, while Steve has done only legal research on the case. Now it is time to decide who is to perform the in-court work as second chair. Sam Senior Partner begins the meeting by announcing that Judge Jones, before whom the case is to be tried, does not like women. What should Samantha do?

Assume the same facts, but Sam Senior Partner instead tells Samantha before the meeting that Calvin Client wants him to do all the in-court work himself because he feels uncomfortable being represented by a woman attorney in court. What should Samantha do?

What should the firm do (1) as a question of law, (2) as a question of justice, or (3) as a question of the best representation for the client?

LESLIE BENDER, SEX DISCRIMINATION OR GENDER INEQUALITY?

57 Fordham L. Rev. 941, 941–45, 949–52 (1989).

The prestigious male bastions of Wall Street law firms have finally done the honorable thing and opened their conclaves to significant numbers of women. Women who conform to male expectations and predictions of success may now enter and play by their rules. These institutional rules of the game, by which one "wins" success, power, prestige, security and money, were designed for persons like the named partners themselves, people without primary interpersonal caregiving responsibilities. * * * [A]s more women have been granted admission to the world of professional lawyering, the rules have changed. The required billable hours have escalated so that it has become physically impossible to participate in a big firm practice while taking personal responsibility for the care of others, be they children, parents, lovers, siblings, friends or the needy in our communities. Women (and men), unencumbered by such responsibilities, may be able to adjust their lifestyles to meet these unreasonable professional demands, at least temporarily. They are required to make their work the entire focus of their lives. Women (and men) who are primary caregivers and take those responsibilities seriously, whether because of externally-imposed or internalized gender role stereotypes, natural inclination, happenstance, or unfettered choice, often are forced to seek alternative career choices. Such alternatives include part-time employment; flextime and job-sharing; career "sequencing"; more flexible legal practices in small firms or as sole practitioners; teaching; in-house corporate counsel positions; government lawyering; perhaps public interest work; or even to drop out of law entirely.

* * *

Is there an important distinction between including more women lawyers in law firms and affirming gender equality? Between avoiding sex discrimination and eliminating gender inequality? I would argue that there is.

* * *

Women ought not be satisfied with being allowed into male-created big law firm practices and playing by their rules, or with being given less empowered, less prestigious, less remunerative options. We should not commend law firms for offering permanent part-time, temporary part-time, or dead-end tracks to accommodate those of us not willing or able to make our careers our entire lives. We ought not accept the implicit assumptions of the current construction of law practice that depend on dichotomies between devotion to family and to career, and that require unswerving fealty to work over all else. Women should demand no less than an opportunity to redefine the meanings of lawyering, law firm practice, professionalism, and professional success, all of which were created without our input, insights, needs and gender culture taken into account. The elimination of sex discrimination is not enough. We must have gender equality.

* * *

Our business/professional world has been constructed by men to reinforce and reward their gendered male characteristics. Interpersonal caregiving, which was not part of the male gender culture, was excluded and perceived as inappropriate or interruptive of the important functions of professional work. Although women have succeeded in entering the pre-constructed professional world and sharing it with men, we have not succeeded as well in shedding our primary responsibility for caregiving and in sharing the interpersonal caregiver role equally with men. Our entrance into the professional world has also not succeeded in bringing our gender culture into accepted facets of the professional culture. Interpersonal caregiving to our friends, family and community remains separate and distinct from our activities in the office. Women are now permitted to do both (participate in the professional world and continue in our caregiving), so long as we do not integrate them. The parts of our daily activities that reflect our gender culture are specifically excluded from and deemed inappropriate to our professional environment. As a consequence, in our professional communities, and, in particular, in the world of high-powered law firms, gender inequality predominates. Therefore, our goal must be to reconstruct legal institutions based on gender equality—empowering both genders and eliminating the privilege/power of one gender over another.

Feminism has approached the issues of gender inequality and sex discrimination in several ways. The women's liberation, liberal-humanist feminist approach began with the assimilationist premise that women can do anything men can do and can do it at least as well if given a fair opportunity and equal access to positions and offices. The goal of this model of feminism was getting women accepted into the big law firms based on traditional criteria of merit, competing on existing terms, and being treated equally to, that is the same as, men. A later variation on this theme developed the idea that where there are biological differences in women from men, for example, pregnancy and childbirth, women should be treated specially and not disadvantaged by these female physical differences, so that they could continue to compete equally for the brass rings.

Both models accept the implicit male norm of existing legal institutions and attempt to mold women to its expectations and demands. If success as a lawyer requires women to be aggressive, competitive, superrational, emotionally detached; to work at our careers for more than ten or twelve hours a day; to depend upon others to care for our families and our homes; to perpetuate status hierarchies within our working environment; and to create sharp divisions between family and career, then so be it. Even though we add more and more females to the quotient of persons doing the job, women who demonstrate aspects of the gendered women's culture are discouraged, badly evaluated, and seen as unfit. This is the infamous "add women and stir" model of reform. We add members of our sex to a profession, but we do not add "acceptance" of gender differences. Those women who can make themselves act and think most like the gendered male culture succeed. One of the surest ways to do this is to remain unencumbered by caregiving responsibilities. Women's participation and complicity in this structure perpetuate its inequalities for women who seek to maintain their interconnectedness with others and their women's gender culture identities, and for men who resist many of the traditional male gender traits. Despite gender assimilation, we find that these women do not "succeed" at equal paces and in equal numbers with their male counterparts. Women who have tried to deemphasize their female-gendered characteristics to prove their worth in the male world are nonetheless disadvantaged by their physical differences and the politics of gender power relations.

It is not gender equality for women to assume characteristics of the male gender or to attempt to take a male perspective and then do those jobs. Just because we are talented enough to assimilate male characteristics for the business world does not mean that that is what we want or what is best. Getting inside the law firms is a start, but if the only women who succeed and achieve the power to change the institutions are the women who are most like men and least woman-identified, then gender inequality continues unabated. Sex discrimination may be eliminated in the workforce, but gender inequality still cries out for response.

Some other feminists have advocated a modification of existing institutional requirements to accommodate women's traditional caregiving responsibilities. This approach moves beyond sex discrimination to issues of gender difference. While it recognizes women's gendered role expectations and choices, it does not solve the problem of gender inequality. This model argues that the practice of law must incorporate or accommodate the reality of women's actual life experiences—not as viewed from the outside, but as lived and experienced. It offers an option for women (and men) who want an alternative career choice to meet their family or interpersonal responsibilities, but it leaves the rest of the system intact. It does not question institutional assumptions about the gendered characteristics for or definitions of the norms of professional conduct and success.

The addition of a "mommy track," "parenting track," or "family track," which this analysis suggests as a solution, does not end gender inequality. It is an exception to the "normal" work style, a less valued (in terms of money, power, prestige), genderized woman track. This approach fails to consider the power aspects of gender-based norms and privileges, and looks only to accommodating difference. Women (and men) who are caregivers and spend time out of the wage force (or in lower paying jobs while caring for others) are subordinated and undervalued because of it. At best, with extraordinary effort and hard work, they can "rehabilitate" their careers after their aberrational and deviant behavior.

Had women been included in designing our workplaces, opportunities for caregiving and sensitivities to its requirements would have been an integral part of their structure. Since primary and cooperative caregivers now participate in legal practices and professional institutions, it has become eminently clear that the structure is deficient. We must collectively decide that caregiving is something we value as a constitutive aspect of our ideal lawyer/citizen/worker and then re-imagine a professional world that fosters that value. We must restructure the professional world of law firm practice (for that matter, the entire wage work world) from the perspective of people responsible for others in an actual caregiving sense.

Notes on Sex Discrimination and Gender Inequality in the Legal Profession

1. How do you think law firms would have been structured if women had played a major role in setting them up? If women were to restructure or redesign the lawyering profession, what modifications might they make other than accommodating or integrating caregiving? How should the ideal law firm be structured? How would it handle the demands of clients with fast-paced litigation? Would it need to confine itself to certain types of legal work? What are the economics of such a practice? The fairness? If you were the managing partner of a law firm, what is the first change you would make?

2. Are the phenomena described in this section—the initial exclusion of women from the legal profession, informal ways of keeping them out or of making them uncomfortable within the profession, the difficulty of combining a legal career with domestic caretaking duties, and the discomfort many women may feel with the law's distance and adversariness—all appropriately described as "gender bias"? Sex discrimination? Gender inequality? If so,

what precisely do we mean by these terms? What would a proponent of formal equality say? A dominance/inequality theorist? A relational feminist? A pragmatic feminist?

3. The 1988 Report of the ABA Commission on Women in the Profession concluded that discrimination in law firms includes, among other things, the absence of mentor relationships for women, assignment of women to subsidiary and less responsible roles in cases, exclusion from firm discussions and professional socialization, and a lack of responsiveness to the difficulties of combining domestic caretaking responsibilities with the necessity of billing some 2500 hours per year. ABA Commission on Women in the Profession, Report to the House of Delegates 11–16 (1988). Is there any way to address gender-biased treatment that occurs in private law firms? How?

Given the hierarchical nature of most large law firms and the disproportionate numbers of men at the top of the hierarchy, how should women attorneys respond to such treatment when it happens to them? What can women subjected to such treatment expect from a Title VII suit? See Hishon v. King & Spalding, 467 U.S. 69, 104 S.Ct. 2229, 81 L.Ed.2d 59 (1984). Alternatively, one female attorney, the first woman partner at Baker & McKenzie, sued her firm and six partners for breach of contract, alleging that because of age and sex discrimination they deprived her of clients, assignments and earnings, and subjected her to derogatory comments because she spoke out on behalf of women attorneys at the firm. Mark Hansen, Partner in Name Only: Lawyer's Suit Claims Age, Sex Discrimination Led to Loss of Choice Assignments, A.B.A. J., Jan. 1992, at 26. Do the Code of Professional Responsibility and complaints filed with local disciplinary committees offer any potential for relief? See Kandis Koustenis, Sexual Trial Tactics: The Ability of the *Model Code* and *Model Rules* to Discipline Discriminatory Conflicts Between Adversaries, 4 Geo. J. Legal Ethics 153 (1990). What are the advantages and disadvantages of each of these approaches—Title VII, contract, and disciplinary actions?

4. Annie Associate has been working diligently on a case with Male Partner Marvin. Annie is buried under paperwork in Conference Room A with the door closed. Marvin drops by frequently to check on Annie's progress. He always enters the room without knocking, puts his hands on Annie's shoulders, gives a little squeeze and says "How's it going honey?" Annie is REALLY getting annoyed. What should she do? What if Marvin comes in one day and says, "You look sexy in that suit. Is it new?"

5. Cynthia Fuchs Epstein has said that the application of a "differences approach" to the problems encountered by women lawyers, resulting in forms of special treatment for them, such as maternity leave, part-time work and a flexible partnership track, is just a new form of the protective attitude displayed by the 19th-century judges who denied women admission to the bar on the grounds that woman's nature and natural role did not fit her for work in the courtroom. Epstein, Faulty Framework: Consequences of the Difference Model for Women in the Law, 35 N.Y.L. Sch. L. Rev. 309, 317–27 (1990). What do you think of this argument? How are the forms of "special treatment" sought by women today different from the spheres to which they were consigned by Victorian paternalism? Do you think there is any danger that these accommodations may backfire and result in second-

class status for women within the legal profession? Is there any way to prevent this from happening?

6. Rand Jack and Dana Crowley Jack, an attorney and a developmental psychologist, interviewed practicing attorneys about who they were, what they did, and what they thought about practicing law; they were interested, among other things, in whether women attorneys bring a different point of view to the practice of law and how they reconcile personal values with the conflicting demands of legal practice. Jack and Jack, Moral Vision and Professional Decisions: The Changing Values of Women and Men Lawyers (1989). They describe a number of different ways in which care-oriented women lawyers adjust to practicing law: (1) by emulating the "male" rights-oriented model and denying the relational self, subjugating personal concerns to demands of the professional role; (2) by "splitting the self" into a detached lawyer at work and the caring self at home; and (3) attempting to reshape the role to conform with their personal morality. See id. at 130–51. One woman lawyer pursuing the third alternative, by designing her own domestic relations practice which reflected both her caring self and her feminist values, reported that the emotional toll was high; the authors conclude that "emotional vulnerability is one reason lawyers erect barriers of detachment and objectivity. The price of involved concern and the anxiety attached to caring may be more than they are able or willing to bear." Id. at 151. What are the advantages and disadvantages of the three paths described? Which path or approach do you think will achieve the most for women in the long run? In the short run? How would a formal equality theorist approach this question? A dominance/inequality theorist like MacKinnon? A pragmatic feminist? A hedonic or cultural feminist? Which path do you think you will choose?

7. Firms, like other businesses, may adjust to the presence of women lawyers and lawyers of color in a number of ways: (1) they may simply increase their representation and expect them to fit in to the existing model; (2) they may use them to understand and serve more diverse clientele; or (3) they may incorporate the new employees' perspectives into the work in a more fundamental way, allowing it to redefine the work that is done and how it should be done. See David A. Thomas and Robin J. Ely, Making Differences Matter: A New Paradigm for Managing Diversity, Harv. Bus. Rev., Sept.-Oct. 1996, 79–90. Under the third paradigm, a law firm would not only recognize the cultural differences of diverse lawyers and the value in those differences but also internalize their new perspectives into the work of the whole organization, so that it learns and grows because of them. Id. at 85–86. Which of these three paradigms is most characteristic of law firms today? Which is typical of your law school culture?

8. Catharine MacKinnon has said that the role of a successful lawyer in our society is fundamentally a "male" role:

> Being a lawyer is also substantially more consistent with the content of the male role, with what men are taught to be in this society: ambitious, upwardly striving, capable of hostility, aggressive not just assertive, not particularly receptive or set off from the track of an argument by what someone else might be saying or, god forbid, feeling. It also requires one to be unserious. By this I mean what I think Virginia Woolf meant when

> she spoke of "unreal loyalties." Not being present in what you say in a way that might make you vulnerable, skilled at false and manipulative passion and manufactured intensity. The lawyer role has as its implicit norms the same qualities that are the explicit norms of masculinity as it is socially defined. It is a power role.

MacKinnon, On Exceptionality: Women as Women in Law, in Feminism Unmodified 74 (1987). If this is so, is there any way that women can feel comfortable as lawyers? Or is law, in the words of the Wisconsin Supreme Court which denied Lavinia Goodell's application for admission to the bar, simply too "selfish and malicious, knavish and criminal" a profession for women? In re Goodell, 39 Wis. 232, 245–46 (1875).

9. If you interview for a position with a law firm, what questions would you ask and what information would you like to know? Based on her study of women's experiences in large corporate law firms, Marjorie Schaafsma suggests that what the firm values as measures of a productive lawyer is relevant to whether it is women-friendly. For example, if partners value lawyers who are aggressive "macho" litigators, the firm is incorporating norms of masculine behavior in its conception of competence and professionalism. If partners are more interested in the quality of legal work than the time lawyers actually spend in the firm, women may have a better chance to accommodate career advancement and family. An indication of how seriously partners are committed to advancing the careers of women can also be found in whether women partners have come up within the ranks at the law firm or have entered the firm as lateral hires. Schaafsma, Disruptive Ambitions: Women Lawyers in Large Law Firms, Ph.D. dissertation, Northwestern University Dep't of Sociology, 1998. What other questions would you think it would be wise to explore before signing on as a new associate?

D. LAWYERING IN A DIFFERENT VOICE?

CARRIE MENKEL–MEADOW, PORTIA IN A DIFFERENT VOICE: SPECULATIONS ON A WOMEN'S LAWYERING PROCESS

1 Berkeley Women's L.J. 39, 49–55, 57–59 (1985).

> [The Portia of the title is the character in Shakespeare's play The Merchant of Venice who pleads (in Act IV, Scene 1) for mercy to temper justice.]

[Carol] Gilligan's observations about male-female differences in moral reasoning may have a great deal to suggest about how the legal system is structured, how law is practiced and made, and how we reason and use law in making decisions. * * *

Two sets of questions illustrate how we might think about the impact of two voices on our legal system as presently constituted and as it might be transformed. First, how has the exclusion, or at least the devaluation, of women's voices affected the choices made in the values underlying our current legal structures? When we value "objectivity," or a "right" answer, or a single winner, are we valuing male goals of victory, exclusion, clarity, predictability? What would our legal system look like if women had not been excluded from participating in its creation? What values would women express in creating the laws and institutions of a legal system? How would they differ from what we see now? How might the different male and female voices join together to create an integrated legal system? Second, can we glimpse enclaves of another set of values within some existing legal structures? Is the judge "male," the jury "female?" Is the search for facts a feminine search for context and the search for legal principles a masculine search for certainty and abstract rules? It could be argued that no functional system could be either wholly masculine or wholly feminine, that there is a tendency for one set of characteristics in a system to mitigate the excesses of the other. Thus, the harshness of law produced the flexibility of equity, and conversely, the abuse of flexibility gave rise to rules of law to limit discretion. In this sense, the legal system could be seen to encompass both male and female voices already. Yet, even though our present legal structures may reflect elements of both sets of values, there is a tendency for the male-dominated or male-created forms and values to control. Thus, equity begins to develop its own harsh rules of law and universalistic regulations applied to discretionary decisions, undermining the flexibility that discretion is supposed to protect. Because men have, in fact, dominated by controlling the legal system, the women's voice in law may be present, but in a male form.

These two sets of questions explore a central issue, which is whether, to the extent that there are value choices to be made in the legal system, those choices will be differently made and with different results when the people who make decisions include a greater representation of women among their numbers. * * * But even if the choices of values are not themselves gendered, it may be that women will favor one set of values over another in sufficient numbers, or with sufficient intensity, to change the balance at times. Although existing structures give a glimpse of what the legal system could look like, we cannot yet know what the consequences of women's participation in the legal system will be—some fear the women's voice will simply be added on and be drowned out by the louder male voice; others fear an androgynous, univoiced world with no interesting differences.

Perhaps by examining these issues in their concrete forms we can see how Portia's different voice might expand our understanding of the lawyering process. * * *

The basic structure of our legal system is premised on the adversarial model, which involves two advocates who present their cases to a disinterested third party who listens to evidence and argument and declares one party a winner. In this simplified description of the Anglo–American model of litigation, we can identify some of the basic concepts and values which underlie this choice of arrangements: advocacy, persuasion, hierarchy, competition, and binary results (win/lose). The conduct of litigation is relatively similar (not coincidentally, I suspect) to a sporting event—there are rules, a referee, an object to the game, and a winner is declared after the play is over. * * * The adversarial model affects the way in which lawyers advise their clients ("get as much as you can"), negotiate disputes ("we can really get them on that") and plan transactions ("let's be sure to draft this to your advantage"). All of these activities in lawyering assume competition over the same limited and equally valued items (usually money) and assume that success is measured by maximizing individual gain. Would Gilligan's Amy create a different model?[b]

By returning to Heinz's dilemma we see some hints about what Amy might do. Instead of concluding that a choice must be made between life and property, in resolving the conflict between parties as Jake does, Amy sees no need to hierarchically order the claims. Instead, she tries to account for all the parties' needs, and searches for a way to find a solution that satisfies the needs of both. In her view, Heinz should be able to obtain the drug for his wife and the pharmacist should still receive payment. So Amy suggests a loan, a credit arrangement, or a discussion of other ways to structure the transaction. In short, she won't play by the adversarial rules. She searches outside the system for a way to solve the problem, trying to keep both parties in mind. Her methods substantiate Gilligan's observations that women will try to change the rules to preserve the relationships.

Furthermore, in addition to looking for more substantive solutions to the problem (i.e., not accepting the binary win/lose conception of the problem), Amy also wants to change the process. Amy sees no reason why she must act as a neutral arbiter of a dispute and make a decision based only on the information she has. She "belie[ves] in communication as the mode of conflict resolution and [is convinced] that the solution to the dilemma will follow from its compelling representation.... "[69] If the parties talk directly to each other, they will be more likely to appreciate the importance of each other's needs. Thus, she believes direct communication, rather than third party mediated debate, might solve the problem, recognizing that two apparently conflicting positions can both be simultaneously legitimate, and there need not be a single victor.

The notion that women might have more difficulty with full-commitment-to-one-side model of the adversary system is graphically illustrated by Hilary, one of the women lawyers in Gilligan's study. This lawyer finds herself in one of the classic moral dilemmas of the adversary system: she sees that her opponent has failed to make use of a document that is helpful to his case and harmful to hers. In deciding not to tell him about the document because of what she sees as her "professional vulnerability" in the male adversary system, she concludes that "the adversary system of justice impedes not only the supposed search for

b. See excerpt from Gilligan, In a Different Voice, in Chapter 3, above.

69. Id. [Carol Gilligan, In A Different Voice: Psychological Theory and Women's Development (1982)] at 30.

truth (the conventional criticism), but also *the expression of concern for the person on the other side.*"[70] * * *

So what kind of legal system would Amy and Hilary create if left to their own devices? They might look for ways to alter the harshness of win/lose results; they might alter the rules of the game (or make it less like a game); and they might alter the very structures and forms themselves. Thus, in a sense Amy and Hilary's approach can already be found in some of the current alternatives to the adversary model such as mediation. Much of the current interest in alternative dispute resolution is an attempt to modify the harshness of the adversarial process and expand the kinds of solutions available, in order to respond better to the varied needs of the parties. Amy's desire to engage the parties in direct communication with each other is reflected in mediation models where the parties talk directly to each other and forge their own solutions. The work of Gilligan and Noddings, demonstrating an ethic of care and a heightened sense of empathy in women, suggests that women lawyers may be particularly interested in mediation as an alternative to litigation as a method of resolving disputes.

Even within the present adversarial model, Amy and Hilary might, in their concern for others, want to provide for a broader conception of interested parties, permitting participation by those who might be affected by the dispute (an ethic of inclusion). In addition, like judges who increasingly are managing more of the details of their cases, Amy and Hilary might seek a more active role in settlement processes and rely less on court-ordered relief. Amy and Hilary might look for other ways to construct their lawsuits and remedies in much the same way as courts of equity mitigated the harshness of the law courts' very limited array of remedies by expanding the conception of what was possible.

The process and rules of the adversary system itself might look different if there were more female voices in the legal profession. If Amy is less likely than Jake to make assertive, rights-based statements, is she less likely to adapt to the male-created advocacy mode? * * *

Amy and Hilary might create a different form of advocacy, one resembling a "conversation" with the fact finder, relying on the creation of a relationship with the jury for its effectiveness, rather than on persuasive intimidation. * * *

In sum, the growing strength of women's voice in the legal profession may change the adversarial system into a more cooperative, less war-like system of communication between disputants in which solutions are mutually agreed upon rather than dictated by an outsider, won by the victor, and imposed upon the loser. Some seeds of change may already be found in existing alternatives to the litigation model, such as mediation. It remains to be seen what further changes Portia's voice may make.

* * *

70. Id. at 135–36.

Perhaps the most salient feature of Portia's different voice is in the lawyer-client relationship, where the values of care and responsibility for others seem most directly applicable. Amy and Hilary, with their ability to "take the part of the other and submerge the self," may be able to enter the world of the client, thereby understanding more fully what the client desires and why, without the domination of what the lawyer perceives to be "in the client's best interest." More fully developed sensitivities to empathy and altruism, as reported by Gilligan and Noddings, may enable women lawyers to understand a fuller range of client needs and objectives. * * * Where the Jakes of this world may make assumptions about the primacy of economic and efficiency considerations of their cases, the Amys and Hilarys may see a greater number of issues in the social, psychological and moral aspects. * * *

In presenting their legal cases within a differently structured system, Amy and Hilary might reason about and plan their cases with a hope of expressing feminine values in their decision-making. Amy and Hilary might create different rules of the game. If Amy "fights the hypo" to learn more facts, might she not have a different conception of relevance and admissibility in deciding a dispute? If women are more concerned with the context in which the dispute is embedded, would they not search for more facts and be less concerned about creation of a precedent of universal applicability? * * *

According to Gilligan, Amy and Hilary have trouble judging disputes in a male-created context because of their difficulty in perceiving one right answer, and also perhaps because of the price they might pay in losing the approval of one of the parties. Might more women judges affect the process of judging? Does the use of a jury provide a useful framework for a kind of judging where no single perception of the truth must prevail, but where a verdict is the product of a mediated consensus? If men and women approach the world with different substantive values, should each trial court have a team of judges, one male and one female? If the male judge emphasizes justice, might the female judge pay attention to mercy, seeking that resolution "in which no one is hurt?"

TRINA GRILLO, THE MEDIATION ALTERNATIVE: PROCESS DANGERS FOR WOMEN

100 Yale L.J. 1545, 1600, 1601, 1603–07 (1991).

[The late Trina Grillo, a law professor, had extensive experience as a mediator in California, where mediation is mandatory in all child custody cases. The italicized stories included in the article from which this is an excerpt are composites drawn from her own observation of many mediation cases.]

Emma has been in a marriage which in its early years seemed to be a good one for both Emma and her husband. She has been the primary caretaker of the children, and she is very committed to them. She has lived much of her life through her husband and her children, and has not worked outside her home. Increasingly, however, she has begun to feel that she and her husband have grown apart, and that he does not see her as a person but rather as a repository of various roles. After much agony, she has decided to end her marriage. Her departure from the marriage is a first step toward seeing her life as having separate dimensions from her husband's and children's, but her right to individuation does not seem clear to her; in fact, there are many times when it seems selfish and wrong. It is hard for her even to find the language to describe what is propelling her to turn her life, and her children's lives, upside down, but propelled she is. The marital separation was an early step toward defining her own physical and psychological boundaries. She now finds herself, however, feeling guilty, frightened, and unsure of how she will survive in the world alone.

Joan has been in a marriage in which she has been physically abused for ten years. She and her husband David have two children, whom David has never abused. She is afraid, however, that if she leaves David, he will begin to abuse the children whenever he is caring for them. Joan has been afraid to leave her marriage because David has threatened to harm her if she does so. When she separated briefly from him previously, he followed her and continually harassed her. Each time David beats Joan he shows great remorse afterwards and promises never to do it again. He is a man of considerable charm, and she has often believed him on these occasions. Nonetheless, Joan has finally decided to leave her husband. She is worried about what will happen, economically and physically, to her children and herself.

* * *

A. THE ETHIC OF CARE IN MEDIATION

* * *

Carrie Menkel–Meadow has suggested that the ethic of care can and should be brought into the practice of law—that the world of lawyering would look very different from the perspective of that ethic. Some commentators have identified mediation as a way to incorporate the ethic of care into the legal system and thereby modify the harshness of the adversary process. And, indeed, at first glance, mediation in the context of divorce might be seen as a way of bringing the woman-identified values of intimacy, nurturance, and care into a legal system that is concerned with the most fundamental aspects of women's and men's lives.

If mediation does not successfully introduce an ethic of care, however, but instead merely sells itself on that promise while delivering something coercive in its place, the consequences will be disastrous for a woman who embraces a relational sense of self. If she is easily persuaded to be cooperative, but her partner is not, she can only lose. If it is indeed her disposition to be caring and focused on relationships, and she has been rewarded for that focus and characterized as "unfeminine" when she departs from it, the language of relationship, caring, and cooperation will be appealing to her and make her vulnerable. Moreover, the intimation that she is not being cooperative and caring or that she is thinking of herself instead of thinking selflessly of the children can shatter her self-esteem and make her lose faith in herself. In short, in mediation, such a woman may be encouraged to repeat exactly those behaviors that have proven hazardous to her in the past.

In the story above, Emma is asked to undergo a forced engagement with the very person from whom she is trying to differentiate herself at a difficult stage in her life. She may find it impossible to think of herself as a separate entity during mediation, while her husband may easily be able to act on behalf of his separate self. "When a separate self must be asserted, women have trouble asserting it. Women's separation from the other in adult life, and the tension between that separation and our fundamental state of connection, is felt most acutely when a woman must make choices, and when she must speak the truth."[274]

Emma will be asked to talk about her needs and feelings, and respond to her husband's needs and feelings. Although in the past her valuing relationships above all else may have worked to the detriment of her separate self, Emma will now be urged to work on the future relationship between herself and her ex-husband. Above all, she will be asked to put the well-being of the children before her own, as if she and her children's well-being were entirely separate. Her problem in addressing her future alone, however, may be that she reflexively puts her children before herself, even when she truly needs to take care of herself in order to take care of her children. For Emma, mediation may play on what are already her vulnerable spots, and put her at a disadvantage. She may begin to think of herself as unfeminine, or simply bad, if she puts her own needs forward. Emma may feel the need to couch every proposal she makes in terms of the needs of her children. In sum, if she articulates her needs accurately, she may end up feeling guilty, selfish, confused, and embarrassed; if she does not, she will be moving backwards to the unbounded self that is at the source of her difficulties.

For Joan, the prescription of mediation might be disastrous. She has always been susceptible to her husband's charm, and has believed him when he has said that he would stop abusing her. She has also always been afraid of him. She is likely, in mediation, to be susceptible and afraid once again. She may continue to care for her husband, and to think that she was responsible for his behavior toward her. Joan, and not her husband, will be susceptible to any pressure to compromise, and to compromise in her situation might be very dangerous for both her and her children.

B. Sexual Domination and Judicial Violence

Women who have been through mandatory mediation often describe it as an experience of sexual domination, comparing mandatory media-

274. [Robin] West, Jurisprudence and Gender, 55 U.Chi.L.Rev. 1, 55 (1988).

tion to rape. Catharine MacKinnon's work provides a basis for explaining why, for some women, this characterization is appropriate. MacKinnon has analyzed gender as a system of power relations, evidenced primarily with respect to the control of women's sexuality. While MacKinnon recognizes the sense in which women are fundamentally connected to others, she does not celebrate it.[278] Rather, she sees the potential for connection as invasive and intrusive. It is precisely the potential for physical connection that permits invasion into the integrity of women's bodies. It is precisely the potential for emotional connection that permits intrusion into the integrity of women's lives.

Men do not experience this same fear of sexual domination, according to MacKinnon; they do not live in constant fear of having the very integrity of their lives intruded upon. Men may not comprehend their role in this system of sexual domination any more than women may be able to articulate the source of their feeling of disempowerment. Yet both of these dynamics are at work in the mediation setting. It may seem a large leap, from acts of physical violence and invasion to the apparently simple requirement that a woman sit in a room with her spouse working toward the resolution of an issue of mutual concern. But that which may be at stake in a court-ordered custody mediation—access to one's children—may be the main reason one has for living, as well as all one's hope for the future. And because mandatory mediation is a forced engagement, ordinarily without attorneys or even friends or supporters present, it may amount to a form of "psychic breaking and entering" or, put another way, psychic rape.

There is always the potential for violence in the legal system: "A judge articulates her understanding of a text, and as a result, somebody loses his freedom, his property, his children, even his life.... When interpreters have finished their work, they frequently leave behind victims whose lives have been torn apart by these organized, social practices of violence."[281]

The reality of this background of judicial violence cannot be discounted when measuring the potential trauma of the mandatory mediation setting. Although the mediation system is purportedly designed in part to help participants *avoid* contact with the violence that must come from judicial decisions, in significant ways the violence of the contact is more direct. Since the parties are obliged to speak for themselves in a setting to which the culture has not introduced them and in which the rules are not clear (and in fact vary from mediator to mediator), the potential violence of the legal result, combined with the invasiveness of the setting, may indeed end up feeling to the unwilling participant very much like a kind of rape. Moreover, in judging, it is understood that the critical view of the quarrel is that of the judge, the professional third

278. See C. MacKinnon, Difference and Dominance, in Feminism Unmodified, * * * at 32, 39 ("Women value care because men have valued us according to the care we give them, and we could probably use some. Women think in relational terms because our existence is defined in relation to men.").

281. [Robert] Cover, Violence and the Word, 95 Yale L.J. 1601, 1601 (1986).

party. Mediation is described as a form of intervention that reflects the *disputants'* view of the quarrel. But having the mediation take place on court premises with a mediator who might or might not inject her prejudices into the process may make it unlikely that the disputants' view will control. Thus, a further sense of violation may arise from having another person's view of the dispute characterized and treated as one's own.

That many reportedly find mediation helpful does not mean everyone does. Consensual sex may take place in a certain setting in one instance but that does not make all sex in that setting consensual; sometimes it is rape. And sometimes it may only seem to be consensual because forced sex is considered par for the course—that is, it is all we know or can imagine.

When I have suggested to mediators that even being forced to sit across the table and negotiate, unassisted, with a spouse might be traumatic, their reaction has been almost uniformly dismissive. Some mediators have denied that this could possibly be the case. Even mediators who acknowledge the possibility of trauma have said, in effect, "So what?" A few hours of discomfort seems not so much to ask in return for a system that, to their mind, serves the courts and the children much better than the alternative. But a few hours of discomfort may not be all that is at stake; the trauma inflicted upon a vulnerable party during mediation can be as great as that which occurs in other psychologically violent confrontations. As such, it should not be minimized. People frequently take months or years to recover from physical or mental abuse, rape, and other traumatic events. Given the psychological vulnerability of people at the time of a divorce, it is likely that some people may be similarly debilitated by a mandatory mediation process.

Moreover, because the mandatory mediation system is more problematic for women than for men, forcing unwilling women to take part in a process which involves much personal exposure sends a powerful social message: it is permissible to discount the real experience of women in the service of someone else's idea of what will be good for them, good for their children, or good for the system.

SARAH E. BURNS, NOTES FROM THE FIELD: A REPLY TO PROFESSOR COLKER

13 Harv.Women's L.J. 189, 193–195 (1990).

[At the time she wrote this article, Sarah E. Burns was Legal Director of the NOW Legal Defense and Education Fund and had extensive experience litigating women's rights cases at the trial, appellate, and United States Supreme Court levels. The excerpt is taken from a comment by Ms. Burns on an article by law professor Ruth Colker, entitled "Feminist Litigation: An Oxymoron?," 13 Harv.Women's L.J. 137 (1990), in which Professor Colker argued that feminist attorneys should consciously make use of feminist arguments and methods in their litigation practice.]

II. Feminist Litigation: What Is It?

In describing feminist litigation, Professor Colker mistakes feminine stereotypes—a gentleness that eschews fighting, a valuation of feeling, a concern for others and their relationships—as indicia of the truly "feminist." However, feminist litigation is not measured by its form, but rather is governed by its contribution to the larger feminist enterprise of transforming established social, economic, political, and legal power relations that work to the detriment of women.

Feminist litigation is not, and cannot be, as Professor Colker would have it, a dialogue. Litigation is a conflict between two or more adverse parties who seek to deploy the state's coercive power in favor of one party's interests over the interests of the other. The application or restraint of the force of the state is the direct result of litigation.

In some instances, litigation is necessary to avoid an application of state power in favor of a predetermined interest. In fact, virtually all of the litigation involving issues of sexual equality or reproductive rights has concerned efforts to alter a state-mandated outcome that works to the disadvantage of women. For example, Jane Roe was in court because Texas law coerced her either to undergo an unintended, financially and emotionally disastrous pregnancy or to obtain a legally and medically treacherous, expensive illegal abortion.[11]

Feminist litigation appeals to the state to apply or restrain its power in a manner consistent with the aims of feminism. The common goal of all branches of feminism is to right the wrongs of sex-based oppression and transform society so that women have full and equal share of resources and opportunities. In the abortion context, feminist litigation concerns whether and to what extent the state, or others acting through the state's mechanisms, may coerce women to function as vessels for the fetus.

Feminism is rooted in the basic premise that liberty and equality are moral rights, whatever the similarities and differences between the sexes. Feminism is not necessarily an effort to make the world conform more to "women's ways" of doing things, although the increased inclusion and involvement of women as a result of feminist action may bring about such an end. Indeed, feminism may require us to note that differences among women may be great as may be the similarities between women and men. Thus, while it may inspire us to counteract the denigration of women, and the status and actions associated with women, feminism is neither necessarily a celebration nor a rejection of women's cultures and norms. It is, however, always a rejection of women's subjugation.

Feminists litigate not because we have some fondness for courts or a belief that courts provide a special haven for us, but because circumstances require us to be there or to be silenced. We know gender bias in court is a severe and widespread problem. We know that there are

11. See Jane Roe v. Henry Wade, 410 U.S. 113 (1973).

limitations on litigation's power to transform society. Given the exclusion from and subordination of women by the legislatures, we cannot avoid advocacy in the courts on some theory that courts are elitist and that elected branches, being majoritarian, are our proper venue. Indeed, suggestions that feminists should shy away from litigation reflect naivete concerning how political outcomes are orchestrated by those with money and access to public opinion, who are generally not women.

Notes on Lawyering in a Different Voice

1. What do you think of Menkel–Meadow's speculations about the ways in which women might change the structure of the law? See also Naomi R. Cahn, Styles of Lawyering, 43 Hastings L.J. 1039 (1992); Jennifer A. Freyer, Women Litigators in Search of a Care–Oriented Judicial System, 4 J. Gender & Law 199 (1995). Can you think of areas in which women might want to maintain objective approaches and formal procedures? What are they? How are women of color likely to respond to this question? What would be the approach taken by a formal equality theorist, a dominance theorist, and a pragmatic feminist?

2. A number of writers express particular concern about requiring mediation in the context of cases involving domestic violence. Domestic violence victims, in addition to their socialization to place the interests of other parties before their own, may also have been rendered passive by repeated and arbitrary beatings. Quite apart from the sheer trauma of being forced to negotiate or participate in a mediation with her abuser, all of these factors may place an abused woman at a substantial disadvantage in the context of alternative dispute resolution ("ADR"). See, e.g., Lisa Lerman, Mediation of Wife Abuse Cases: The Adverse Impact of Informal Dispute Resolution on Women, 7 Harv.Women's L.J. 57 (1984); Robert Geffner and Mildred Pagelow, Mediation and Child Custody Issues in Abusive Relationships, 8 Behav. Sci. & Law 151, 152–53 (1990). Is there any way to ensure that mediation take account of these and other power imbalances between the parties? Does it make any difference if it is mandatory or not?

3. How is negotiation different from mediation with respect to the potential for gender bias? Empirical studies of law students in classes involving simulated negotiation exercises have not shown any statistically significant difference between the clinical negotiating results achieved by male and female law students. See, e.g., Charles Craver, The Impact of Gender on Clinical Negotiating Achievement, 6 Ohio St. J. Disp. Resol. 1 (1990). See also Lloyd Burton et al., Feminist Theory, Professional Ethics, and Gender–Related Distinctions in Attorney Negotiating Styles, 1991 J. Disp. Resol. 199 (based on surveys and interviews with practicing attorneys). What are the implications of these findings?

4. Some commentators argue that informal procedures such as mediation place persons of color at a disadvantage in general. Richard Delgado, Chris Dunn, Pamela Brown, Helena Lee and David Hubbert, Fairness and Formality: Minimizing the Risk of Prejudice in Alternative Dispute Resolution, 1985 Wis. L. Rev. 1359. Delgado et al. base this conclusion on social scientific studies which show that people who hold prejudiced attitudes are

more likely to act on those attitudes in informal than in formal settings and suggest that ADR should be reserved for disputes in which the parties are of comparable status and power. Are there any ways to address these problems short of retreating to formal adversarial settings?

5. Professor Sally McConnell–Ginet reports that "where the sexes have somewhat different perspectives on a situation, the man's view is more likely to be familiar to the woman than hers is to him" and "men are much more likely than women to be unaware that their own view is not universally shared." McConnell–Ginet, The Sexual (Re)Production of Meaning: A Discourse–Based Theory, in Language, Gender, and Professional Writing: Theoretical Approaches and Guidelines for Nonsexist Usage 35, 43 (Francine Wattman Frank and Paula A. Treichler, eds. 1989). What explains this phenomenon? What are the implications for negotiation? For litigation?

6. Women may be systematically disadvantaged by mediation in substantive ways as well. For example, there is a strong link between mediation and joint custody, apparently because mediators tend to push the concept. Jana B. Singer, The Privatization of Family Law, 1992 Wis. L. Rev. 1443, 1543–44. Mediation theory also urges focusing upon the future, rather than upon a couple's past behavior. Id. at 1544–45. How may women be disadvantaged by this fact? Finally, as Jana Singer points out, "mediation is touted most enthusiastically as a substitute for adjudication in precisely those areas—custody and visitation—where the prevailing legal standards are perceived to favor women." Id. at 1545.

7. Who has the best of the Colker–Burns debate? In other words, is lawyering according to feminist principles in our current legal system like being a pacifist in a world of warriors? Is it suicidal not to fight with the weapons other participants typically use in a legal system currently organized around adversarial, win-or-lose principles? Power and litigation involve the controlled use of violence, and the legal system is a monopoly. Hence, if "women's ways of doing" are not the ways things are done, is there any way to achieve change without sacrificing important individual and group battles along the way? On the other hand, can women ever change the way things are done if they simply adopt the methods by which the legal system has always proceeded; can they, in Audre Lorde's phrase, dismantle the master's house using the master's tools? Audre Lorde, The Master's Tools Will Never Dismantle The Master's House, in Sister Outsider: Essays and Speeches 110 (1984).

8. Can you think of ways to address the personal costs and potential burnout of being a caring lawyer without learning to adopt the stance of distance from one's client? Isn't this a problem law shares with other professions which involve "caretaking" roles, such as social workers? See, e.g., Perri Klass, Other Women's Children (1990) (female pediatrician). Can relationships among women practitioners play a role in addressing any of the problems women face in the practice of law?

9. Are there any types of cases feminist lawyers should refuse to take? What are they? Some British women barristers have refused to defend alleged rapists because the usual defense strategy involves destroying the complainant's credibility. However, in the British system, while solicitors are free to refuse rape defense cases, barristers who break the "cab-rank" rule

obliging them to accept any case within their field of work risk disciplinary action. Ironically, increasing numbers of women barristers are being actively sought as defenders in these types of cases, to communicate to a jury that the alleged rapist is getting an endorsement from the very sex he is supposed to have assaulted. See Celia Dodd, Law: An Unsuitable Job For a Woman, The Independent, Apr. 13, 1990, at 19. Is this prejudicial to the complainant? Are women attorneys who defend rapists being "used"? How can feminist attorneys who object to the traditional methods of courtroom defense register their protest and reform the process? Is it possible to do so while actively representing defendants?

Is it ethical to represent only certain types of clients in divorce cases—or only one gender? See Joan Mahoney, Using Gender as a Basis of Client Selection: A Feminist Perspective, 20 W. New Eng. L. Rev. 79 (1998) (analyzing under different schools of feminist legal theory—equal treatment, radical feminism, and cultural feminism—a Massachusetts case in which a female attorney refused to represent a male divorce client).

Chapter 12

WOMEN AND THE STATE

A. INTRODUCTION

What do women want from the state? What should women expect from the state? The state has traditionally denied women many of the rights guaranteed to men and has given men power over women. Only in 1919 did women win the right to vote in all elections. At common law, husbands had total control of the property of their wives; married women had no rights to own, control, or use property and could not contract. The state interpreted a marriage license as license to rape prior to recent reforms in some states. To this day, social safety nets and a variety of legal rules, from the consent standard in rape to economic rules at divorce, protect men better than women.

On the other hand, women tend to have fewer resources, lower status, and less power than men of their class and race in "private" realms. It is often impossible for women to exert pressure for change within private institutions at more than a snail's pace. Women have, for example, been excluded from leadership in mainstream religious organizations and even today are allowed to be clergy only in the more liberal branches and are rare in the upper echelons even there. In education, business and the professions, women are disproportionally at the bottom of hierarchies. The media, one of the most powerful institutions in the United States today, is dominated by men. Sports, an arena of great cultural importance, is dominated by male heros, coaches, and commentators. Men continue to have more power than women in families. Women have, therefore, often looked to the state for assistance in improving their well-being.

As a majority of voters today, women have the potential to use the state to force legal change and have sometimes been able to do so. Many institutions are more likely to change as a result of government intervention than as a result of women's attempts to change the balance of power by efforts entirely within the "private" sphere. For example, anti-discrimination laws applicable to private employers and educational institutions have increased considerably women's opportunities in employment, education, and sports within educational institutions. The Family Leave Act of 1993, mandating that employers with more than 50 employees give up to 12 weeks of unpaid leave during any 12 month period if a family member needs care, gives family leaves to more women than entirely "private" efforts have done to date. Although women's political power does not reflect women's majority status, it is often greater than women's power to change powerful private institutions, including market mechanisms.

This chapter explores a number of key issues related to the complex relationship of women and government. Three basic strategic questions are presented. First, is there a connection between the persistent inequality of women and the lack of supports for caregivers in the United States? Second, should women focus on increasing their share of government power and eliminating judicial limits on majoritarian processes? Third, how can women's share of political power be increased to reflect women's majority status?

We begin with the connection many feminists have come to see between persistent sex inequality and lack of public supports for caretakers. We then look at political equality, the extent to which women are present in governmental decisionmaking bodies in proportion to their presence in the population. We then turn to consider political reforms, beginning with insights from global feminism.

B. CARE AND EQUALITY

Text Note: The Missing Safety Nets

We have a number of income support systems, the most important being Unemployment Insurance, Social Security Old–Age and Disability Insurance (Social Security), Temporary Assistance to Needy Families (TANF, which replaced Aid to Families with Dependent Children (AFDC)), and Supplemental Security Income (SSI). Two of these systems were designed for (male) breadwinners: Unemployment Insurance and Social Security. These are the premier American income support systems. Both are understood to be state-run insurance plans, though the extent to which Social Security can accurately be classified as a form of insurance, rather than a transfer of income from the young to the old, is questionable.[1] Nevertheless, beneficiaries of these systems are not perceived as the recipients of charity; they are collecting insurance proceeds. Beneficiaries do not have to prove that they are poor to qualify, and benefits are not based on need. In contrast, TANF is the descendant of Mothers' Aid programs which were designed to aid the "white impoverished widows of men like those eligible for Workmen's Compensation."[2] SSI was designed as a safety net for the aged and disabled

1. For discussions of whether Social Security is an insurance or welfare system, see Nancy J. Altman, The Reconciliation of Retirement Security and Tax Policies: A Response to Professor Graetz, 136 U.Pa. L.Rev. 1419, 1424–32 (1988); William H. Simon, Rights and Redistribution in the Welfare System, 38 Stan.L.Rev. 1431, 1458–59 (1986).

2. Barbara J. Nelson, The Origins of the Two–Channel Welfare State: Workmen's Compensation and Mothers' Aid in Women,

who do not qualify for Social Security—people who were not successful breadwinners. Not surprisingly, most SSI recipients are women.

There are a number of ways in which the systems designed for successful breadwinners are better than the systems designed for mothers and others.[3] Both TANF and SSI are means-tested and perceived as forms of charity (or redistribution) rather than insurance. Income support levels are generally much lower for SSI and TANF (women's systems) than for Social Security and unemployment insurance (men's systems). For example, the maximum monthly TANF benefits for a family of three as of January, 2000, was $164 a month in Alabama, $377 a month in Illinois, and $626 in California.[4] In contrast, the average Unemployment Insurance benefit in Alabama and California was $684.67 month, and it was $1,048.67 a month in Illinois irrespective of need. [5] For workers earning high wages, the maximum Unemployment Insurance benefit in Alabama was $3,611.10 a month, in Illinois $5,332.90 to $7,060.43 a month (depending on the number of dependents), and in California it was $4,318.91 a month.[6]

Formal equality does apply to social insurance and welfare systems but only requires that similarly situated women and men be treated similarly.[7] Given the differences between most women and most men, it is easy to treat similar women and men identically, yet leave most women with inferior income protection. Formal equality does nothing about the fact that breadwinners have better safety nets than caretakers, including caretakers who also work for wages.

Although most women now work in the wage-labor force for much of their lives, Unemployment Insurance and Social Security continue to work better for men than for women. Unemployment Insurance offers

the State, and Welfare 123, 133 (Linda Gordon, ed. 1990). For additional discussion of these points, see Virginia Sapiro, The Gender Basis of American Social Policy, in Women, the State, and Welfare 36 (Linda Gordon, ed. 1990).

3. For early discussions of how safety nets for men are structured as social insurance whereas those for women are structured as welfare, see Nancy Fraser, Women, Welfare and The Politics of Need Interpretation, 2 Hypatia 103, 108–13 (1987); Barbara J. Nelson, Women's Poverty and Women's Citizenship: Some Political Consequences of Economic Marginality, 10 Signs 209, 221–23 (1984); Diana M. Pearce, Toil and Trouble: Women Workers and Unemployment Compensation, in Women and Poverty 141 (Barbara Gelpi, et al. eds. 1986). For a discussion of Unemployment Insurance problems from the perspective of women workers, see, for example, Diana M. Pearce, Toil and Trouble: Women Workers and Unemployment Compensation, in Women and Poverty 141 (Barbara C. Gelpi et al., eds., 1986).

4. Staff of the U.S. House of Representatives Ways and Means Committee, Maximum Combined AFDC/TANF Benefits for a Family of three (Parent with Two Children), July 1994–Jan. 2000, Table 7–7, in The Green Book: Background Material and Data on Programs Within the Jurisdiction of the Committee on Ways and Means 383–84 (2000) (hereinafter The Green Book.).

5. Staff of the U.S. House of Representatives Ways and Means Committee, Amount and Duration of Weekly Benefits for Total Employment Under the Regular State Programs, 1999 and 2000, Table 4.5 in The Green Book, above note 4, at 293. Recent data is not available on both UI averages and TANF maximums for precisely the same period, so we have used January 2000 amounts for TANF and 1999 averages for UI.

6. Id.

7. See, for example, Califano v. Goldfarb, 430 U.S. 199, 97 S.Ct. 1021, 51 L.Ed.2d 270 (1977).

unemployment benefits to eligible workers who lose their jobs through no fault of their own. Only 35% of unemployed men receive Unemployment Insurance, but even fewer—23%—of unemployed women do. We mention two major problems. First, women workers who lose their jobs or are forced to quit for reasons associated with caretaking—such as childbirth or inability to find reliable childcare—are not usually eligible for benefits because their job loss is seen as the result of their own actions. Unemployment Insurance does not support leave for childbirth even though FMLA (the Family and Medical Leave Act described in Chapter 8) gives slightly more than 50% of workers the right to 12 weeks of unpaid caretaking leave every year.[8]

The second major problem is that eligibility for Unemployment Insurance is based on earnings, rather than hours worked, with a relatively high minimum earnings requirement. As a result, many part-time and low-wage workers are not covered. And, disproportionally, women work for low-wages and (or) on a part-time basis.[9]

In June of 2000 the Department of Labor issued regulations allowing states to use Unemployment Insurance to cover paid leaves for workers to care for infants and newly adopted children. But as of January 2001 Unemployment Insurance does not cover such leaves in any state. To date only five states afford any form of paid leave at childbirth, and these states do so through Temporary Disability Insurance programs not available in other states. Under these programs, California, Hawaii, New Jersey, New York, and Rhode Island offer paid leave for the period of medical disability associated with childbirth.[10] Only two percent of workers have paid family leave as a result of voluntary employer policies. Most workers who take leave for family care cannot afford to take time off without pay, and 21% of low-wage workers who have to take leave to care for family members must use welfare for support.[11]

Leave policies providing pay for childbirth and infant care (it is virtually impossible to find day care for an infant younger than three months) make it much easier to combine mothering and wage work; significantly more mothers return to work when paid leave is available. And 85% of Americans support paid leave to care for "a new child or seriously ill family member."[12] With TANF severely limiting the availability of welfare to women between jobs, Unemployment Insurance

8. Vicky Lovell, Women and Unemployment: Better Check Your Insurance Coverage, Institute for Women's Policy Research, Quarterly Newsletter, Winter 2000, at 1, 3; Institute For Women's Policy Research, Fact Sheet: Women and Unemployment Insurance (Nov. 1999) (available at <http://iwpr.org> (select "PDF Reports") visited Dec. 28, 2000) (hereinafter UI FACT Sheet); Institute for Women's Policy Research, Fact Sheet: Paid Family and Medical Leave (Nov. 2000) (available at <http://iwpr.org> (select "PDF Reports") visited Dec. 28, 2000) (hereinafter Paid Family Leave Fact Sheet).

9. Lovell, above note 8, at 1, 3; Unemployment Insurance Fact Sheet, above note 8.

10. Paid Family Leave Fact Sheet, above note 8.

11. Id.

12. Id.

coverage is more important than ever. Yet no state provides for paid leaves to care for a new child or a family member with a serious illness.

Like Unemployment Insurance, Social Security is designed for workers without significant caretaking responsibilities though it is particularly important for women, who are less likely than men to qualify for employer-provided pensions. But Social Security does a much better job of ensuring financial security in old age for men than for women. Benefits are based on earnings over a 35–year career, and the average man works 39 years. The average woman works only 27 years, and her years without earnings severely depress her draw based on her own employment record when she retires. In addition, benefit levels are tied to wages, and thus are higher for men.[13] (Recall the discussion of the wage gap in Chapter 10.) The combination of lower wages and fewer years in the wage-labor market means that most married women draw benefits based not on their own earnings record, but as their husband's dependent spouse. For these couples, their Social Security benefits at retirement are calculated without any consideration of the wife's years working for wages; they draw not a penny more than they would have had she never worked outside the home.[14]

Another problem is that in most divorces, the husband walks away with significantly better Social Security protection than the wife, though it would be easy enough to divide Social Security entitlements equally as they are earned during marriage. (This problem is described in more detail in Chapter 7.)

Poverty rates are the strongest evidence that safety nets protect men better than women (and children). Overall, 15.4% of women are poor whereas 12.2% of men are poor.[15] But elderly women, particularly unmarried elderly women, and women heads of households with children—those most in need of safety nets—are poor at very high rates. Almost twice as many elderly women (13%) than men (7%) are poor. For elderly divorced women, the rate is an astounding 22%. When never-married women are included, the rate is even higher: 23.6% of elderly women living alone are poor. Black and Hispanic elderly women living alone are about as likely to be poor as not. For elderly black women living alone the poverty rate is 48.1%; for elderly Hispanic women living alone the poverty rate is 49.3%. The overall rate of poverty for elderly women is not expected to change much in the next twenty years.[16] Unfortunately, current plans to reform and (or) privatize Social Security

13. Susan B. Garland, Making Social Security More Women–Friendly, Business Week, May 22, 2000, at 103.

14. Id.; Mary Becker, Obscuring the Struggle, 89 Colum. L. Rev. 264, 276–86 (1989); Karen C. Burke and Grayson M.P. McCouch, The Impact of Social Security Reform on Women's Economic Security, 16 N.Y.L. Sch. J. Hum. Rts. 375, 375–87 (1999).

15. Cynthia V. Costello, Shari Miles, and Anne J. Stone, The American Woman 1999–2000, Table 6–3 at 332 (1998) (1995 data).

16. Id., Table 6–8 at 340; Garland, above note 13, at 104.

are likely to result in a system which is even less adequate from the perspective of women, the group that needs it most.[17]

Similarly, women living with children and without men are at particular risk, as Table 1 illustrates.

Table 1: Poverty Rates by Family Type After Cash Transfers 1999[18]

ALL FAMILIES	9.3%	HISPANIC FAMILIES WITH CHILDREN<18	25.0%
Married couple	4.8%	Married couple	16.8%
Male head only	11.7%	Male head only	26.0%
Female head only	27.8%	Female head only	46.6%
FAMILIES WITH CHILDREN<18	13.8%	ANGLO[19] FAMILIES WITH CHILDREN<18	8.0%
Married couple	6.3%	Married couple	3.9%
Male head only	16.2%	Male head only	11.9%
Female head only	35.7%	Female head only	25.4%
BLACK FAMILIES WITH CHILDREN<18	28.9%		
Married couple	8.6%		
Male head only	21.4%		
Female head only	46.1%		

Women heading households with children under 18, whether African American, Hispanic, or non-Hispanic white, are much more likely to be poor than married women and are also much more likely to be poor than single African American, Hispanic, or non-Hispanic white men heading households with children under 18.

Despite an unprecedented period of economic prosperity in the 1990's, the overall poverty rate for 1999 (11.8%) was not statistically different from the rate for 1979 (11.7%), though it was lower than for any of the years between 1979 and 1999.[20] Similarly, the poverty rate for children under 18 (16.9%) was the lowest of any year since 1979. As Table 1 indicates, children living with single mothers face a shockingly high risk of poverty, ranging from 22.1% *after cash transfers* (and before the effects of the stringent time limits for receipt of TANF benefits pinch[21]) for all such children to a rate of 28.2% for African American children and 31.0% for Hispanic children.

17. See, e.g., Karen C. Burke and Grayson M.P. McCouch, Women, Fairness, and Social Security, 82 Iowa L. Rev. 1209 (1997); Sharmila Choudhury and Michael V. Leonesio, Life–Cycle Aspects of Poverty Among Older Women, 60 Soc. Sec. Bull. 17 (1997); Nina Mojiri–Azad, Social Security Benefits to Widows: The Ongoing Favoritism of Single–Earner Families and the Impact on Elderly Women, 17 Law & Ineq. 537 (1999).

18. Joseph Dalaker and Bernadette D. Proctor, U.S. Census Bureau, Poverty in the United States, Current Population Reports: Consumer Income 1999 (P60–210), Table B–3 at B–11–19 (2000).

19. This entry is for non-Hispanic white families.

20. Dalaker and Proctor, above note 18, at vii.

21. Federal law requires that states limit benefits to a family to a total of two years at a time, with a life-time limit of 5 years of benefits. But the effects of these stringent limitations will not be known for several more years. Jason DeParle and Steven A. Holmes, A War on Poverty Subtly Linked to Race, N.Y. Times, Dec. 26, 2000, at A1, A16.

Persistent poverty in the United States is associated with an increasing gap between the rich and the poor in recent decades, as illustrated in Table 2.

Table 2: Selected Measures of Income Inequality 1967–1999 in Constant (1999) Dollars[22]

Measures Of Income Inequality	1999	1995	1990	1985	1975	1967
MEAN (AVERAGE) HOUSEHOLD INCOME BY QUINTILE[23]						
Top quintile (top 20%)	135,401	119,605	111,071	101,943	88,366	82,364
Second quintile	63,555	57,314	57,234	55,266	50,742	45,450
Third quintile	40,879	37,284	37,961	36,750	34,942	32,485
Fourth quintile	24,436	22,298	22,982	22,188	21,356	20,345
Fifth quintile	9,940	9,128	9,171	8,976	8,994	7,463
SHARES OF HOUSEHOLD INCOME BY QUINTILE[24]						
Top quintile (top 20%)	49.4%	48.7%	46.6%	45.3%	43.2%	43.8%
Second quintile	23.2%	23.3%	24.0%	24.6%	24.8%	24.2%
Third quintile	14.9%	15.2%	15.9%	16.3%	17.1%	17.3%
Fourth quintile	8.9%	9.1%	9.6%	9.7%	10.5%	10.8%
Fifth quintile	3.6%	3.7%	3.9%	4.0%	4.4%	4.0%
Gini coefficient of income inequality[25]	0.457	0.450	0.428	0.419	0.397	0.399

Table 2 shows that income disparities have increased dramatically in the United States between 1967 and 1999. Although real household income for the top fifth of households rose by 64% (an increase of $53,037), income for the lowest 20% of households increased by 33% (an increase of $2,477). And household income for the middle quintile increased by 25.8% ($8,394).

When wealth is considered, disparities are even more startling. In 1997 the richest one percent of households owned 49% of the financial wealth of the country, and the richest 10% owned 83% of the wealth. The share owned by the wealthiest one percent in 1997 was significantly higher than in 1983, when they owned only 43% of financial wealth. And almost all financial wealth is owned by whites. In 1995 the median[26] net

22. U.S. Census Bureau, Money Income in the United States, Current Population Reports: Consumer Income 1999 (P60–209), Table C at xii (2000).

23. The next five rows give average household income for selected years for each quintile (one-fifth) of the population. The top quintile is the 20% of households with the highest incomes, and the bottom quintile is the 20% of households with the lowest incomes.

24. These figures report the percentage of total household income going to each quintile. Thus, in 1999, the 20% of families with the highest household income received 49.4% of total household income for all households.

25. A frequently used measure of income inequality which varies between one (absolute inequality: one person receives all income) and zero (perfect equality: everyone receives the same income).

26. Half of households have more wealth than the median household and half have less.

financial wealth of Hispanic households was zero, and the figure for African American households was $200. For white households, the median was $18,100.[27]

Real income rose during the 1980's and 1990's (through 1997) only for households headed by married couples with working wives.[28] For families headed by women, 1997 median income ($21,023) was lower than income in 1979 ($21,429 in constant (1997) dollars).[29] Thus, the increase in income to families over the last two decades has been the result of married women working more hours in the wage-labor market.

Children in the United States are at very high risk of being poor particularly, as the data above suggests, if living with a single mother. This is true both before and after all cash and non-cash benefits under existing safety nets as Table 3 reports.

Table 3: Children in Poverty in the United States 1999[30]

	Prior to taxes but including cash benefits	After taxes and non cash benefits
ALL RACES		
All children<18	16.9%	12.0%
Children<6	18.0%	12.8%
Living with single mother	30.4%	22.1%
BLACK		
All children<18	33.1%	22.8%
Children<6	36.6%	26.0%
Living with single mother	41.0%	28.2%
HISPANIC		
All children<18	30.3%	21.9%
Children<6	30.6%	21.7%
Living with single mother	40.7%	31.0%
NON-HISPANIC WHITE		
All children<18	9.4%	6.8%

27. James Heintz and Nancy Folbre, The Ultimate Field Guide to the U.S. Economy 14, 15, 17 (2000).

28. Lawrence Mishel, Jared Bernstein, and John Schmitt, the State of Working America 1998–99, 46 (1999).

29. Id. at 47.

30. Dalaker and Proctor, above note 18, Table 5 at 28–32.

	Prior to taxes but including cash benefits	After taxes and non cash benefits
Children<6	10.0%	7.1%
Living with single mother	19.8%	15.2%

Of families with children, 14% of white families were maintained by women alone in 1997 whereas 24% of Hispanic families and 47% of African American Families were maintained by women alone.[31] About 13.6% of American children are not covered by any form of health insurance.[32]

Children in the United States are particularly likely, relative to children in other industrialized nations, to be living in households headed by single mothers. Not suprisingly, given this fact and the weakness of American safety nets for mothers and children, children are more likely to be poor in the United States than in other industrialized nations.

Table 4: Child Poverty Selected Industrial Nations Circa 1990[33]

Country	Pre-taxes and transfers	Post-taxes and transfers
Canada	23%	15%
United States	29%	25%
Australia	21%	15%
United Kingdom	29%	19%
Belgium	17%	4%
Germany	12%	9%
France	27%	7%
Netherlands	15%	8%
Sweden	18%	3%

The disparity between poverty rates for women and men is also larger in the United States than in many other nations. A recent study comparing poverty rates for women and men in eight industrialized

31. Heintz and Folbre, above note 27, at 80.

32. Costello et al., above note 15, Figure 5–8 at 321 (1995 data). Private insurance covered a smaller proportion of the population in 1995 than in 1988. And more people were without health insurance in 1995 than in 1988. In 1994, 16.7% of men and 14.0% of women were not covered by private insurance or Medicaid. Id. Figure 5–7 at 320.

33. Colin Hughes and Kerry McCuaig, When Mom Must Work: Family Day Care as a Welfare–To–Work Option Section 2, Table 1 (2000) (available at <http:www.childcarecanada.org/CPAG _CCEF/moms_welfare/two.html> visited 8/10/2000). Poverty rates vary with the definition of poverty being used.

nations reports that the United States has the highest disparity between male and female poverty rates of any nation studied. In the United States 38% more women than men are poor, yielding a poverty ratio of 1.38 (women to men). As Table 4 illustrates, women are *less* likely than men to be poor in Sweden (where only 73 women are poor for every 100 men). Of the industrialized nations in this study, with the exception of Australia, all have considerably better poverty ratios for women. The Australia ratio is lower than that of the United States, but not nearly as low as in the other countries studied. The findings of this study are summarized in Table 5.

Table 5: Poverty Ratios (Women to Men) in Selected Industrialized Countries After Cash Transfers[34]

Country	Poverty ratio (women to men)
Australia	1.30
Canada	1.13
France	1.11
Germany	1.18
Netherlands	1.14
Sweden	0.73
United Kingdom	1.20
United States	1.38

Because people sharing a household are assumed to share income, a poverty ratio other than 1 (one poor woman for every poor man) reflects the extent to which women are not living with men. Women living in households without men are likely to be poor for three reasons. First, as discussed in Chapter 10, women earn less than men in the wage-labor market. Second, women living without a male partner are more likely (than men living without a female partner) to be living with and supporting children. And third, being a parent depresses women's wages, though not men's. Indeed, motherhood depresses women's earnings even after taking into account time off for child care. Men tend to earn more when they become fathers.

Feminist Arguments for Social Support of Caretaking

Many feminists from various disciplines have argued in recent years that the state should provide better support systems for caretakers and their dependents. We briefly describe two forms of this argument.

Arguments Based on Morality and Equality

A number of feminists have made moral arguments for a social commitment to care for society's dependents and their caretakers and

34. Karen Christopher, Paula England, Katherin Ross, Tim Smeeding, and Sara McLanahan, Women's Poverty Relative to Men's in Affluent Nations: Single Motherhood and the State, Table 2 (2000) (available at <http://www.jcpr.org/wp/wpprofile.cfm?ID=126> visited 1/4/2001).

have seen such a commitment as essential to equality between the sexes. In Chapter 3, we described Robin West's argument for a politics centered on care and empathy rather than equality. Philosopher Eva Kittay emphasizes the link between acknowledging dependency and valuing caregiving, on the one hand, and equality for women on the other:

> The call for sexual equality has been with us for a long time. But until relatively recently, the demands of even the most farsighted women have assumed very traditional and gendered arrangements of dependency work. Radical visions in which dependency work is taken out of the family have left many women cold—largely, I suggest, because they have failed to respect the importance of the dependency relationship. A view of society as consisting of nested dependencies, so constituted as to provide all with the means to achieve functioning that respects the freedom and relatedness of all citizens, is a view that can only emerge now, as women taste the fruits of an equality fashioned by men—and find it wanting. This equality has not left room for love's labors and love's laborers. It is time to shape a new vision by creating new theories and by forging the requisite political will. We need to revise our social and political commitment to ourselves as dependents and as dependency workers. Only through these efforts may we come to see what it means for men and women to share the world in equality.[35]

In her recent book, Care and Equality: Inventing A New Family Politics, political scientist Mona Harrington argues that care should be "a national political value":

> The key idea for a new politics of family care * * * is to add care to the pantheon of national social values. That is, to assure good care to all members of the society should become a primary principle of our common life, along with the assurance of liberty, equality and justice.
>
> We need to elevate care to this level of importance for the basic reason that it is essential to human health and balanced development. It is also crucial to developing human moral potential, to instilling and reinforcing in an individual a sense of positive connection to others. And it is this sense of connection that makes possible the whole range of mutual responsibilities that allow the people of a society to respect and work toward common goals. As political theorist Joan Tronto puts it, thinking about care seriously, recognizing that everyone at different times is both a giver and receiver of care, underscores * * * [our] personal and social interdependence. And, she says, this insight can enhance a commitment to the responsibilities of democratic citizenship.[36]

35. Eva Kittay, Love's Labor: Essays on Women, Equality, and Dependency 188 (1999).

36. Mona Harrington, Care and Equality: Inventing a New Family Politics 48–49 (1999) (citing Joan Tronto, Moral Boundaries: A Political Argument for an Ethic of Care (1993) (arguing for recognition of care as a basic element of political morality)).

West's, Kittay's, and Harrington's arguments can all be seen as building on the work of Amartya Sen and Martha Nussbaum, who identify as the primary goal of government the creation of an environment in which each individual is given the ability to develop her or his capabilities for connections to others, autonomy, and competency.[37] A somewhat different argument, but one which also can be seen as building on the work of Sen and Nussbaum, views investment in developing children's capabilities as producing a public good which, like other public goods, requires public support.

Arguments Based on Women's Production of a Public Good

Feminist lawyers and economists have also argued that women are disproportionally poor because their productive caretaking labor is under-or uncompensated. Although the costs of raising children and developing their capabilities are disproportionally borne by women, the whole society benefits from a new generation of capable workers, citizens, and taxpayers.[38]

Economists Paula England and Nancy Folbre begin with the proposition that women invest more in children in terms of both time and money than men do. Women have significantly increased their hours working in the market to support their families in recent decades, while men have only slightly increased their caretaking and household labor. Increasing numbers of families are headed by women who receive inadequate or no child support from absent fathers. At the same time, it has become increasingly costly to develop the capabilities of children as education becomes increasingly important for economic success and the costs of college and university rise. According to England and Folbre, "[t]hat many other traditional obstacles to gender inequality have been overturned means that parental responsibilities loom large as a current cause of lower earnings and restrictions on career advancement for women."[39] They point out that, as Table 4 indicates, children in the United States are more likely to be poor than in most other industrialized countries and "[p]arents in general and mothers in particular remain highly susceptible to poverty in the United States."[40]

Traditionally, economists have viewed children as a consumption item; adults have children because the benefits they derive from doing so outweigh the costs. England and Folbre characterize this as the "children-as-pets approach." [41] But children raised in an environment allow-

37. Amartya Sen, Capability and Well Being, in The Quality of Life 30 (Martha C. Nussbaum and Amartya Sen, eds. 1993); Martha C. Nussbaum, Sex and Social Justice 39–47 (1999).

38. In addition to the work discussed in text making this argument, see Martha Albertson Fineman, Cracking the Foundational Myths: Independence, Autonomy, and Self–Sufficiency, 8 Am.U.J. Gender, Soc. Pol'y, & L. 13 (2000).

39. Paula England and Nancy Folbre, The Silent Crisis in U.S. Child Care: Who Should Pay for the Kids, 563 Annals Am. Acad. Polit. & Soc. Sci. 194, 197 (1999). See generally Nancy Folbre, Who Pays for the Kids?: Gender and the Structures of Constraint (1994).

40. Id.

41. Id.

ing them to develop their capabilities benefit society as a whole, not just their caretakers. They actually pay into Social Security the money used to support the elderly population, yet Social Security benefits are calculated without regard to whether recipients have invested in children.[42] We also benefit personally from the caretaking work of others; we have spouses, friends, neighbors, employers, employees, and coworkers who have been raised by others.[43]

Children are a "public good," that is, a benefit to the general society like a good defense system or good roads.[44] Yet society as a whole pays less than 38% of the costs of raising children. Instead, the costs are disproportionally borne by individual women who are, for that reason, more likely to be poor. Further, when children are raised by caretakers without the assets needed in today's society to develop their children's capabilities, too little is invested. Better supports would be economically efficient in the long term, though not the short term. And better supports would distribute to all taxpayers the costs of the benefits they enjoy as a result of others raising children. As this suggests, adequate supports for children and their caretakers should be seen as a long-term investment in the future, one that should be publicly supported to avoid free riders (those able to enjoy the benefits of a public good without paying the costs).[45]

Although this argument uses economic analysis to demonstrate that children are a value to a society as a whole (and their costs should not therefore be borne disproportionally by a group likely to be poor because of their caretaking of children), proponents do not mean to imply that economic factors should dominate decisions and relationships within the family. Rather, they simply mean to point out "the economic consequences of the organization of family life, which has become increasingly costly for women in the United States over time."[46]

England and Folbre point to France as one of the European countries which "impose higher taxes on the entire working-age population to defray the costs of child care."[47] Such policies, they note, can be thought of as a loan from the current generation of workers to the next, to be repaid through taxes on income earned as adults. We turn next to consider the programs supporting children and their caretakers in France.

Caring for Children and Caretakers in France

In France, families with children receive many supports from the state, with the result that although child poverty rates are about equal in France and the United States prior to governmental supports (based

42. Id. at 198–201.

43. Nancy Folbre Children as Public Goods, 84 Am. Econ. Rev. 86, 87–88 (1994).

44. See England and Folbre, above note 39, at 195 ("Economists define a public good as one that is difficult to put a price on because it is nonexcludable (someone can enjoy it without paying for it) and nonrival (one person can enjoy it without diminishing someone else's enjoyment of it.").

45. Id. at 201–04.

46. Id. at 196.

47. Id.

on parental income alone, about 24.7% of French children were poor in 1984–87 as compared to 23.3% of American children), after governmental supports, only 5.7% of French children remained poor whereas 21% of American children remained poor.[48] Similarly, although 24% of French adults and 20% of American adults were poor based on wage income alone, only 8% of French adults were poor after governmental supports whereas 16% of American adults remain poor after considering such supports. [49] And in the United States, proportionally more poor adults are women than in France. In the United States, 38% more women than men are poor, whereas in France only 11% more women than men are poor.[50]

Supports for Families

In France, many supports are available to all parents and children regardless of income. Free nursery schools are available for children (regardless of whether the mother works) from the time they are toilet trained (about 2½ years) until they enter first grade. Parents who use private centers receive cash benefits and tax breaks. When mothers of younger children work, government heavily subsidizes placements in day care centers.[51]

Day care workers in France are well trained and well paid relative to the United States. Indeed, because of the higher level of teacher training, nursery quality surpasses that of American pre schools with lower teacher-child ratios. [52] In 1991, French day care workers started at $14,153 per year and also received free housing or a tax-free housing allowance. The average yearly earnings for child care workers in the United States in 1998 was $12,000. Thus, women working for wages as caretakers are paid significantly more in France than in the United States.

The gap between men's and women's pay is smaller in France than in the United States: In the United States, full-time year-round wage-

48. Barbara R. Bergmann, Saving Our Children from Poverty: What the United States Can Learn From France, Table 1.1 at 6 (1996) (1984–87 data).

49. Hughes and McCuaig, above note 33, Section 2, Table 1 (data circa 1990).

50. Christopher et al., above note 34, Table 1 at 23.

51. Bergmann, above note 48, at 27–41. Subsidies for care of infants and toddlers vary with income level. In 1991, a family with a monthly income under $681 and one child would pay the equivalent of $4.15 per day for care of an infant or young toddler; such a family would pay the equivalent of $3.38 per day per child for two children in such care. A family with a monthly income of $1,286 would pay $7.68 and $6.45, respectively. A family with a monthly income of $2,496 would pay $15.21 and $12.60. Id., Table 3.7 at 40.

52. Id. at 31. In France, the ratio tends to be about 16 children to one adult. This would be regarded as inadequate in the United States, where:

> an adult-child ratio of 1:9 is thought to be crucial to providing high-quality care; U.S. preschools abide by this finding. However, a group of American experts on day care who observed French child-care facilities in 1989 concluded that, despite the larger number of children per adult, the quality * * * was as high or higher than the best and highest-cost American day-care centers. More systematic studies of teacher-child interactions confirm this impression. One study concluded that teacher training in France, which encourages teachers to carefully plan daily activities and constantly monitor the children, explained the good results.

Id. at 31.

earning women earn an average of $0.75 for every dollar earned by similar men, but full-time year-round wage-earning women in France earn about $0.81 for every $1.00 earned by such men.[53]

All education is free in France, from nursery school through university. And "supervised recreational programs for school-age children for the after-school hours, and during summers and school vacations, subsidized by the government, are common."[54]

Family allowances are available to all families with more than one child under sixteen (or eighteen, depending on the child's earnings from age 16 to 18) and are not income tested. The benefit varies only with the number of children, and in 1990 was $91 per month for a family with two children and $207 a month for a family with three children. In addition, every pregnant woman is entitled to a new baby allowance each month from the third month of pregnancy until the baby is three months old. In 1991, the new baby allowance was $134 per month. For low and medium income families, this allowance continues until the youngest child is three years. [55]

If parents do not live together, the government pays a minimum child support payment each month and is responsible for collecting child support from the non custodial parent. In 1991, the Child Support Assurance benefit was $66 per month per child. This benefit is not means tested.[56] Handicapped children receive an additional allowance independent of family income. In 1991, it was $304 a month for a child requiring constant help in eating, dressing, etc., and $164 a month for a child needing less help.[57] Income tax deductions for children are also available and about the same size as those in the United States on a per child basis.[58]

Mothers receive 16 weeks of paid maternity leave at the birth of a first or second child and 26 weeks on the birth of a third child. The stipend is paid by the social security agency, and in 1991 "was 84% of the mother's base salary up to a maximum of $1,742 dollars per month. "[59] In France, all families are covered by national health insurance.[60]

Finally, caretaking is made easier by the fact that the French, like other Europeans, work significantly fewer hours per year than do

53. Joni Seager, The State of Women in the World Atlas 68–69 (1997).

54. Bergmann, above note 48, at 28.

55. Id. at 58–61 and Table 4.5 at 59. All members of the European Community, even England, provide family allowances. In England, the allowance is $46 per month for one child, $92 for two children and $138 for three children. Id., Table 4.5 at 59.

56. Id. at 61–62.

57. Id. at 62.

58. Id. at 68.

59. Id. at 46. She is entitled to $192 a month if she had a job immediately before the pregnancy or during it even though she no longer has the job.

60. Id. at 70–88. Although France has national health care, it spends a smaller portion (9.9% in 1995) of its Gross Domestic Product on health care than does the United States (13.6% of Gross Domestic Product spent on health care in 1995). In the United States, 15% of whites lacked health insurance in 1997, 22% of African–Americans, 34% of Hispanic Americans, and 21% of Asian Americans. Heintz and Folbre, above note 27, at 122, 132.

Americans. Many American workers receive only 10 paid vacation days a year. In Europe, including France, the norm is at least four to six paid weeks of vacation. In the United States, full-time workers average 44 hours a week under unenforced laws setting the maximum work week at 40 hours. In France, a recent law mandates a maximum work week of 35 hours (down from 39 hours with no reduction in pay). [61] In 1997, American workers worked an average of 1,996 hours, compared to the French who worked only 1,560 hours.[62] Thus, the French worker works an average of 5.98 fewer hours per week.

Poor families with three or more children (and no new baby allowance) in France are entitled to an additional family allowance. In 1991 this benefit was $122 per month. For families of modest means ($17,669 yearly income for family with one child), an allowance of $57 is available for each child between the ages of six and ten at the start of the school year.[63] The single-parent's subsistence allowance ensures that total family income from wages, government benefits, child support, etc., reaches at least a set minimum level if there is a child under three in the family ($582 per month in 1991 for a parent with one child, with an additional $146 per month for each additional child).[64]

Substantial housing subsidies are also available to families at very low income levels, though they decline sharply as income rises.

All of these state-provided subsidies for child raising have two important effects:

1. By working, even at a minimum wage job, parents who work can pull their families out of poverty. Good supports provide no disincentive to work in France, because families remain poor unless parents work, but can rise above the poverty level if parents work.
2. Many of the supports needed by poor families are either available to all families or to all but wealthy families. Because these supports are available to all or most families, they are broadly supported.

61. Anders Hayden, France's 35–Hour Work Week, 34 Canadian Dimension, Feb. 1, 2000, at 8. The law was designed as a way to cut the unemployment rate, which has been very high (though it is now steadily falling). Prior to the new law, unemployment was 12.5%. Although there was some controversy about the legislation even among workers, some of whom worried that employers would merely require employees to do the same amount of work in a shorter amount of time, "84 per cent of workers who had their hours reduced said that there were more advantages than disadvantages, and 75 per cent said their quality of life had improved." Workers reported that they were likely to use the time to "spend more time with family and children." Employers have implemented the change in "diverse ways, such as: seven-hour days, alternating four-and five-day weeks, additional days off on an annual basis–usually 22 or 23, and 'time savings accounts' for accumulation of long periods of leaves." Many workplace agreements "have gone beyond 35 to 32 hours or given individual workers the choice of reducing their hours further." Id.

62. Elizabeth Olson, Americans Lead the World in Hours Worked, N. Y. Times, Sept. 7, 1999, at C9.

63. Bergmann, above note 48, at 64–65.

64. Id. at 65–66. When she no longer has a child under three, the single parent may qualify for additional assistance under the Minimum Income to Assist Job Entry Program. Id. at. 66–67.

BARBARA R. BERGMANN, SAVING OUR CHILDREN FROM POVERTY: WHAT THE UNITED STATES CAN LEARN FROM FRANCE

117–19 (1996).

How are we to design and pay for a system of programs in the United States that would enable more families to live above the poverty line? * * * French programs accomplish this by giving a great deal of help to parents who hold low-paying jobs. In order to do that, the French spend heavily in three areas: providing child care, providing health care, and providing income supplements, including help with rent. * * * [G]overnment help with child care and health insurance, covered by vouchers rather than by cash grants, are the necessary ingredients for protecting American children from deprivation.

Any system of programs will reflect the values of those devising the system. Many Americans put heavy weight on discouraging births outside of marriage and getting single parents to take jobs. The aim of reducing child poverty in the short and medium run goes largely unmentioned in the debate on reforming American welfare. On the other hand, many of those on the right appear willing to adopt policies that would increase child deprivation in the short run, on the ground that treating single parents harshly will teach them and others not to produce more children destined to be poor.

The French clearly put the greatest weight on keeping all children out of deprivation and do not put a great deal of emphasis on reducing improvident births. In fact, most of the components of their child welfare system were constructed with French-born married couples in mind, in the apparently vain hope that they would be induced to have more children. The unmarried are eligible for all of these pronatally motivated benefits, which—if they have an effect on births to unwed couples—might be expected to increase rather than reduce such births. On the other hand, increasing the labor force participation of single mothers, as these benefits do, may have a negative effect on the number of children they have, since women in jobs generally desire fewer children than those who do not. As we have seen, birthrates outside marriage are very similar in France and the United States, suggesting that the more generous benefits to single parents in France have not resulted in a flood of children to unmarried couples. Nonetheless, an American system more like the French one might not discourage births as effectively as would reduced benefits, promoted by U.S. politicians on the right. A system along French lines would provide a single mother who has low labor-market skills with an option she does not have under the present system—she and her children could live above the poverty line, provided she works for pay.

Even though the French system has achieved both low child-poverty rates and relatively high job-holding among single parents, would it work in the United States, with its very different history and culture? The fact is, the basic needs of families in the two countries are not at all different. Whether they live in France or the United States, preschool children must be cared for—by parents, by other family members, or by paid nonrelatives. Good child care is expensive to buy or provide in both countries. American children, like French children, have health-care needs, which are met or not met depending on their access to care. Whatever the incentives parents have to take jobs, there will be parents in both countries with low wages or no wages. Even if child care and medical care are provided, such children live in families that need financial help to purchase sufficient food, clothing, and shelter.

What is different in the two countries is not children's needs, but the sense of public responsibility for the welfare of the nation's children, the feelings of generosity toward those who are poor, the willingness to pay taxes, racial antipathies, the proportion of public funds devoted to armaments, the degree of faith in the government's ability to deliver effective and high-quality programs, and beliefs about the importance and means of limiting "dysfunctional" behavior, such as births to unmarried teenage mothers. These attitudinal differences do not preclude the design of an effective American program to fight child poverty, but they do create roadblocks to the acceptance of such a program.

While the unsatisfactory state of current American programs for health care and income supplementation is well known, the child-care issue has only recently been recognized as an important component in solving the problem of child poverty. Critical to the argument that follows is the idea that health care and good-quality child care are "big-ticket items," and that most of the jobs open to women on welfare will not provide them as fringe benefits or, alternatively, do not pay high enough wages to enable their purchase.

CAN WE AFFORD IT?

Another crucial roadblock in the way of a large-scale government program to reduce child poverty is the idea that, given the current budgetary situation, the United States cannot afford to spend more on social welfare programs, even those that would be of high value. But "cannot afford" has two quite different meanings: it can mean literally financially impossible or imprudent, or it can mean that the desire to purchase the item in question is not strong enough to warrant restructuring one's budget.

A program that would provide child care and health insurance for lower-and middle-income families could be financed by a modest rearrangement of the budget. When the politicians are saying (and the citizens are echoing) that we "cannot afford" to spend more on such programs, they are playing a word game—pretending to use the phrase in its "imprudence" sense, rather than in its "insufficient desire" sense. No politician wants to say that we have better things to do with our resources than mobilizing them to improve child welfare in this country (through higher taxes, or reducing other expenditures, or borrowing). By all measures, the United States is an extremely wealthy country, and one of the least taxed in the developed world. Saying that we "cannot afford" the programs simply rings hollow in light of our country's vast resources.

The example of France, a country very like ours, and with somewhat fewer resources than we have at our disposal, shows that the "can't afford it" rationale for continuing to tolerate widespread child poverty is one that deserves questioning. Certainly, it is possible that the French programs, and the heavy taxes that support them, detract somewhat from economic performance and raise unemployment rates. Nevertheless, the French example should prompt us to ask whether it would be worth sacrificing some aspects of high economic performance in favor of reducing the child poverty rate approaching one in four to a rate of one in eighteen, as the French have done.

A costly and activist program is the only way we will be able to make progress against child poverty. We cannot create, through government policy or moral suasion or religious revival, a society in which single mothers and their children will not need some help. We are unlikely to move anytime soon to a situation where all or almost all children are born to married couples, where almost all marriages last until death, and where all children have parents who earn enough to support them adequately. Such an alternative is closed to us, at least as the expected outcome of any series of actions by the government. If we are to make a serious attempt to design a government program to rescue millions of poor children whose predicament "cannot be countenanced by a wealthy nation, a caring people, or a prudent society," we must choose from the alternatives that are available to us. The passage of such a program must await the time when we have a president who can effectively frame and forward the required agenda, a time when generosity toward the "have-nots" is greater, and when antigovernment rhetoric has been overcome by an even more obvious need for action.

Notes on Care and Equality

1. Do you agree that caregiving is a moral act? If it is a moral act, should caretaking be its own reward? Many caretakers enjoy their work and love those for whom they care. Shouldn't the compensations associated with enjoying the work you do for those you love be sufficient? What are the strongest arguments for better public supports of caregivers? What are the strongest arguments against?

2. Do you agree with Kittay, Harrington, West, and others that women cannot attain equality without more social support for caretakers? What, if anything, do you see as the links between caretaking and inequality between the sexes?

3. Is valuing caretaking and supporting caregivers generally seen as an important aspect of social justice or connected to equality for women in philosophy, political science, or constitutional law courses, ordinary politics,

or the culture at large? Why do you think this is so? What do you see as the major obstacle to better public support for caretaking in the United States?

4. Are women full citizens today? Are caretakers full citizens? What does full citizenship mean to you?

5. What, if anything, do you see as the links between caretaking and inequalities based on race and class? Do you see inadequate support for paid and unpaid caretakers and caretaking as linked to race and class inequality as well as sexual inequality? How would poor or minority women be affected by better supports for caretakers, particularly those who work as caretakers in their own families and in other women's families?

6. What do you think of England and Folbre's economic argument for support of children and their caretakers? Is it dangerous because it encourages us to view children in economic terms? Or is it necessary because caretaking *is* productive labor, though it is seldom viewed as such?

7. What reforms of Social Security might be appropriate from the perspective of England and Folbre's analysis? Social Security, though seen as an insurance scheme, with each worker earning benefits for himself and his dependents, is actually a pyramid scheme, with younger generations paying benefits to older generations and a considerable amount of redistribution. Should women receive Social Security credits for each year they live with a child under 18? Would such a change be constitutional? Some reform proposals have suggested that unemployed workers (mostly women) with children under the age of six receive some sort of Social Security credit. Other reform ideas would give partial credits to part-time workers (mostly women) with older children. Current proposals for such credits would not help most women, however, since even with these reforms (the proposed credits are not large) they would be better off drawing as their husband's dependents rather than on their own Social Security account. See Institute for Women's Policy Research, Briefing Paper, Social Security for Women: Proposals for Change, IWPR Publication #D436 at 4–5 (1999) (can be ordered at <http://www.iwpr.org> visited 12/30/2000). Moreover, many women work full time *and* care for children. How could Social Security be adjusted to credit their disproportional contributions to the capabilities of those who will actually be supporting the elderly? Can you think of Social Security reforms that would be effective and constitutional?

8. Nancy C. Staudt has argued that women's unpaid caretaking and domestic work should be subject to income and payroll taxes, thus earning Social Security credits. Staudt, Taxing Housework, 84 Geo. L.J. 1571 (1996). Is this a solution? Could it be structured to give extra credits to mothers who are working full-time for wages *and* investing disproportionally in their children's capabilities? If it were so structured, would it be constitutional? Do you see other problems?

9. Despite the fact that French workers work far fewer hours a year than American workers and that the French pay higher taxes to provide better supports for families, the French economy has been booming of late. Indeed, "France is now the clear leader among the Big Four [European economic powers], with sustained growth rates since 1997 that are well ahead of Germany, Italy and the United Kingdom" and with unemployment "on a steady downward curve." The French stock market is now "outpacing

the Dow Jones industrial average." Christopher Dickey, France Takes Off, Newsweek, Mar. 20, 2000, at 14.

With its high hours worked per worker, the United States, not surprisingly, leads the world in per worker productivity. But the gap is small. For example, American workers produced an average of "$49,905 of goods in 1996." But the French produced "an average of $47,958 for each worker," despite fewer hours worked. Productivity gains are now rising faster in other countries, including France, than in the United States. Elizabeth Olson, Americans Lead the World in Hours Worked, N.Y. Times, Sept. 7, 1999, at C9. Thus strong public supports for *all* families, with additional supports for poor families (likely to be headed by single mothers), need not spell economic ruin for an economy. Such supports may, of course, put something of a damper on an economy. But might a world with such supports nevertheless be better for human beings though not necessarily best for the Dow Jones average?

10. In September of 2000, the Center for Policy Alternatives and Lifetime Television published the results of a national poll on women's concerns. The poll shows very high levels of support for (1) policies making it easier to combine caretaking and wage work, such as shorter working hours and flexible time; (2) job-independent health care; (3) equal pay and retirement security; and (4) greater availability of affordable quality child care. According to the published findings, 59% of mothers with children under six report that it is harder to balance the demands of family and work than it was four years earlier. Women are also concerned about the growing economic gap between the rich and the poor and would support an increase in the minimum wage. Center for Policy Alternatives and Lifetime Television, Women's Voices 2000: The Most Comprehensive Polling and Research Project on Women's Values and Policy Priorities for the Economy 14, 18, 19, 26–29, 32 (2000) (available at <http://www.stateaction.org/cpa/pressroom/archives/prcomplete.cfm?ID=131> visited 1/1/2001). Why haven't women, a majority group, been successful in demanding the kind of changes suggested by these poll results?

11. How would the various feminist theories in Chapter 3 approach the issue of the missing safety nets? Would all of them see the system of current safety nets as problematical? Which theoretical approaches would place the need for better safety nets for women and children high on their agenda? Which would not place better safety nets anywhere on their agenda?

C. POLITICAL EQUALITY IN THE UNITED STATES

Text Note: Who Runs the Show?

Although women are a majority of citizens and voters, women are not, and have never been, present in elective office in numbers that reflect these facts. Since 1975, women's numbers in elective office have been increasing. But the numbers remain low relative to the number of women in the population and relative to the one third that many women in politics regard as the critical mass necessary to make a difference in legislative bodies.

When diversity is considered in terms of both race *and* sex, the picture of who is in government is even more unlike the picture of the governed.

Executive Branches

No woman has been President or Vice President of the United States. Secretary of State Madeline Albright, appointed by President Clinton in 1996, is the highest ranking woman ever to serve in the federal Executive Branch. President Clinton also appointed Janet Reno, the first woman to serve as Attorney General.

Of the governors of the states after the 2000 election, five out of 50 (10%) are non-Hispanic white women; no woman of color has ever been elected governor of a state. Of the other 273 statewide elected officials, including lieutenant governors, state attorneys general, treasurers, and secretaries of state, 84 (30.8%) are women, down from 89 (32.6%) prior to the 2000 election.[65] Of the 323 statewide elected offices including governor, women of color held 5 (1.5%) positions[66]

Legislative Branches

It is extremely difficult to get information about the racial composition of state legislatures, but such information is available about Congress. Tables 6 and 7 demonstrate the overwhelming overrepresentation of white men relative to their numbers in the general population and the underrepresentation of women of all colors and other African, Asian, Hispanic, and Native American citizens in Congress. Non–Hispanic white men have more than twice their share of political power in both the House and the Senate. Indeed, non-Hispanic white men are only 33.9% of the general population but an astounding 84% of the Senate.

Table 6: Voices in the United States Congress 2001[67]

	% Population	% House	% Senate
Non–Hispanic white men	33.9%	77.4%	84.0%

65. Center for American Women and Politics (CAWP), Election 2000: Summary of Results for Women (2000) (available at <http://www.rci.rutgers.edu/~cawp/facts/Summary2000.html> visited 12/31/2000) (hereinafter CAWP, Election 2000). (CAWP is part of the Eagleton Institute of Politics at Rutgers, 191 Ryders Lane, New Brunswick, NJ 08901-8557.)

66. CAWP, FACT Sheet: Women of Color in Elective Office 2001 (Feb. 2001) (available at http://www.rci.rutgers.edu/~cawp/pdf/colorpdf> visited 4/6/2001) (hereinafter CAWP, Women of Color in Elective Office).

67. Julie R. Hirchfeld, Congress of Relative Newcomers Poses Challenges to Bush Leadership, CQ Weekly, Jan. 20, 2001, at 178. General population numbers and population data on race are from U.S. Census Bureau, Census 2000 Redistricting Data (P.L. 94–171) Summary File for states, Tables PL1, PL2, PL3, and PL4 as reported in Census 2000 PHC–T–1, Population by Race and Hispanic or Latino Origin for the United States: 1990 and 2000 tables 1 and 4 (internet release date Apr. 2, 2001). Non–Hispanics whites from the 2000 census data includes only people who indicated that their (only) race was white, since it seems probable that most whites in Congress would indicate that their (only) race was white. For other groups, the most inclusive categories from the 2000 Census are used. Thus, Hispanics can be of any color; African and Black Americans can also be Asian Americans or Native Americans, etc. Breakdowns on race and sex are not yet available using 2000 census data, so estimates on the numbers of women (in general, among non–Hispanic white women, Black or African American women, etc.) are based on the proportions of women in each group according to the March 2000 Current Population

	% Population	% House	% Senate
Women of all colors	51.1%	13.6%	13%
Black & African Americans (men and women)	12.9%	8.3%	0.0%
Hispanic Americans (men and women)	12.5%	4.4%	0.0%
Asian Americans[68] (men and women)	4.5%	0.9%	2.0%
Native Americans[69] (men and women)	1.5%	0.2%	1.0%[70]

Table 7: Women in the United States Congress 2001[71]

	% Population	% House	% Senate
All Women	51.1%	13.6%	13.0%
Non-Hispanic white women	35.2%	9.0%	13.0%
Black & African American women	6.9%	3.0%	0.0%
Hispanic American women	6.3%	1.4%	0.0%
Asian American women	2.3%	0.2%	0.0%
Native American women	0.8%	0.0%	0.0%

Only one woman of color has ever been a member of the Senate, Carol Moseley Braun who served from 1992–1998.

Overall, women are present in state legislatures in higher proportions than in Congress. State legislatures convening in 2001 will be 22.4% women, a slight drop from the 22.5% seats held by women prior to the 2000 election.[72] Table 8 gives the proportions of women in color in state legislative bodies alongside their percentage in the population. Table 9 gives the overall proportions of women in the five states with the highest percentage of women in the state legislature and the five states with the lowest percentage. Women are present in the five state legislatures with the fewest women in even smaller percentages than in Congress.

Table 8: Women in State Legislatures 2001[73]

	% Population	% State Legislatures
All Women	51.1%	22.4%

Survey. U.S. Census Bureau, Current Population Survey March 2000 (internet release date 3/15/2001).

68. Including Americans who have descended from Pacific Islanders.

69. Including Eskimo and Aleut peoples.

70. The numbers for African Americans, Hispanic Americans, and Asian Americans include women and men in the population column and the House column. (There are no women of color in the Senate.) Also, the other categories in the population column are not mutually exclusive, since Hispanic Americans can be any race. For sources of population data, see above note 67.

71. CAWP, Fact Sheet: Women of Color in Elective Office, above note 66; CAWP, Women in Elective Office 2000 (May 2000) (hereinafter CAWP, Women in Elective Office) (available at <http://www.rci.rutgers.edu/~cawp/Facts.html> visited 1/4/2001). For sources of population data, see above note 67.

72. CAWP, Election 2000, above note 65.

73. CAWP, Women in Elective Office, above note 71, CAWP Women of Color in Elective Office 2001, above note 72. For sources of population data, see above note 67.

	% Population	% State Legislatures
Non–Hispanic White women	35.2%	18.8%
Black and African American Women	6.9%	2.5%
Hispanic American Women	6.3%	0.7%
Asian American Women	2.3%	0.3%
Native American Women	0.8%	0.1%

Table 9: States with the Highest and Lowest Percentages of Women in Their Legislatures 2001[74]

HIGHEST STATES	% women	LOWEST STATES	% women
Washington	39.5%	Alabama	7.9%
Colorado	35.0%	South Carolina	10.0%
Nevada	34.9%	Oklahoma	10.1%
Arizona	34.4%	Kentucky	10.9%
Oregon	33.3%	Mississippi	12.6%

Judicial Branches

One hundred and thirteen people have served on the Unites States Supreme Court. Two of them have been women, both of whom, Justices Sandra Day O'Connor and Ruth Bader Ginsburg, are currently on the Court. Of the 113 people who have served on the Court as of January 2001, two have been African American men (1.77%): Justice Thurgood Marshall, whose seat on retirement was filled by Clarence Thomas, the other African American. No African American woman has ever served on the Court nor has any Asian American or Hispanic American or Native American man or woman. Thus, of the 113 individuals who have interpreted American constitutional law in a conservative system in which consistency with tradition and faithfulness to precedent is the basis of legitimacy, 109 (96.46%) have been non-Hispanic white men.

Of the nine justices on the Court as of the beginning of 2001, two are women (22.22%), one is African American (11.11%) and six are non-Hispanic white men (66.67%). Table 10 gives demographic information about judges on the thirteen federal circuit courts of appeal and on the district courts. When all three levels of the federal courts are combined, non-Hispanic white men comprise 61.09% of the federal bench. Note that federal judges, though disproportionally non-Hispanic white men, are nevertheless significantly more diverse than Congress if you compare these numbers with those in Table 6.

Women are 21% (166) of active federal judges (out of a total of 792). The federal judiciary is: "82.7% white (655), 10.7% African–American (85), 5.2% Hispanic (41), 0.9% Asian–American (7), 0.3% Native–American (2), and .1% Arab–American (1)."[75]

74. CAWP, Election 2000, above note 65.

75. Aliance for Justice, Demographic Portrait of the Federal Judiciary (July

There are proportionately more women on the United States Supreme Court than on the supreme courts of most states. Two states, Indiana (5), and South Dakota (5), have no woman on their state supreme courts. (The number in parentheses after the name of the state is the number of justices on the state's highest court.). Just over half of the states—26—have one woman on their highest court: Alabama; Alaska; Arizona, Arkansas, Delaware, Hawaii, Idaho, Illinois, Kansas, Kentucky, Maine, Maryland, Mississippi, Missouri, Montana, Nebraska, New Hampshire, North Carolina, Oklahoma, Oregon, Pennsylvania, South Carolina, Tennessee, Utah, West Virginia, and Wyoming.

Twenty-three states have two or more women on their supreme courts. One, Massachusetts has equal numbers of men and women on a six-member court. No state has a majority over women. Of the other 22 states with two or more woman, ten states have two women: Colorado, Florida, Georgia, Iowa, Minnesota, New Mexico, New York, North Dakota, Rhode Island, and Vermont. Twelve states have three women, but a majority of men, on their highest courts: California, Colorado, Connecticut, Louisiana, Michigan, Nevada, New Jersey, Ohio, Texas, Virginia, Washington, and Wisconsin.[76]

Notes on Political Equality

1. Why might it matter that women of all colors and other members of minority groups are underrepresented in positions as governmental decision-makers? Would only an "essentialist" (i.e., someone who believes that differences between women and men or between various racial groups are innate and universal) see a need for more women of all colors and members of other minority groups in government? In the context of representation in legislatures, Anne Phillips argues that "any system that claims to be democratic should be able to ensure that its representatives mirror the ethnic and sexual composition of the population," though at the same time she maintains that "these representatives should not then be viewed as 'representing' their ethnic group or their sex." She believes that it would be "profoundly *un*democratic if women representatives were considered to be speaking only or even mainly for women, particularly when there are no substantial mechanisms for establishing what their 'constituents' support." Anne Phillips, Engendering Democracy 155–56 (1991). Despite this reservation, Phillips believes it is necessary to adopt "procedures [such as quotas] that will ensure a more balanced result," i.e., procedures that will ensure that those represented mirror the sex of the population. Id. at 151–52. Do you agree with any of these points? Is Phillips necessarily inconsistent in advocating adequate representation of women by women, as judged by the numbers, and *also* insisting that women representatives should not be seen as speaking only or mainly for women? Could (and should) similar points be made about members of racial minorities?

2000) (vacancies excluded in calculating percentages) (available from Alliance for Justice, 11 Dupont Circle, 2nd Floor, Washington, D.C. 20036, (202) 822–6070).

76. Data from state supreme court official web sites visited 1/4/2001 (links to all state supreme court official web sites are available at <http://www.state.wv.us/wvsca/library/courts2.htm> visited 1/2/2001).

2. Do you think that people who have been primary caretakers of dependents are likely to be underrepresented in as judges and elected officials? Why? Why might it matter that primary caretakers are underrepresented in elective office?

3. A number of reasons have been given for women's underrepresentation in elected office. In some states, party bosses and political culture are barriers. Sex role socialization may inhibit women from seeking careers in politics, and women's family responsibilities may limit their participation. Bias against women on the part of voters may be another problem. The fact that most incumbents are men is a major problem. Incumbents have a tremendous advantage in an election, and in recent years women have been as likely to win as men once incumbency and other factors are considered. (The studies of these elections cannot, of course, eliminate the possibility that the women who run must be more qualified than the men in order to have equal chances of winning.) As will be discussed in greater detail below, the American electoral system is also part of the problem, since women tend to do less well with single-member winner-take-all electoral schemes than schemes using some form of proportional representation. For a discussion of these possible explanations, see Janet Clark, Getting There: Women in Political Office, 515 Annals 63 (May 1991). Clark ends with the problem of power and prestige:

> Finally, the power and prestige of the political office also seem to be factors in determining the level of representation of women. That is, the more desirable the office and/or the greater the competition for the office, the less likely that women will be well represented. In legislatures that are large relative to the population represented, women have more seats. Also the degree of the professionalism of the legislature determines the relative representation of women. In legislatures where the members sit full-time, receive a relatively large salary, and hold greater prestige, there will be fewer women. The hypothesis that the level of competitiveness and prestige of the legislative body affects the number of women in office seems to be confirmed by the fact that there are more women in local and state offices than in national offices. Also, even at the same level of government, women have been more likely to be elected in places where the office is considered less desirable.

Id. at 75. The higher the position, whether in government, religion, industry, education, etc., the less likely it is that a woman will hold it. What do you think explains the dwindling number of women as one ascends any hierarchy?

4. Do you think—perhaps because of socialization or perhaps because of genetic or hormonal differences—that women are less likely to run for public office because they are less competitive and have less confidence (or perhaps less arrogance)? Senator Susan Collins of Maine describes a conversation among Democratic and Republican women Senators: "At one dinner we were talking about all the men running for president—a lot of them Senators—and here we were, nine women Senators, and not a single one of us thinks of herself as president." Collins continues:

> That's got to be gender-related. I remember Lynn Martin speaking at a women's Campaign Fund event saying a man who sells Toyotas thinks

> he's an expert in international trade while a woman thinks she needs a Ph.D. in economics before she can comment. We went down the list of men who were running, and they weren't more experienced or more capable. They have a confidence, or is it an arrogance? I don't know what it is. We got up to about a dozen Senators, both sides of the aisle. We laughed about it, but the essential truth of it struck all of us.

Eleanor Clift and Tom Brazatis, Madam President: Shattering the Last Glass Ceiling 132 (2000). This is a description of the *women in the United States Senate*, nine of the most powerful women in the world. And *they* feel lacking in confidence (arrogance?) relative to their colleagues. Do you think this is part of the problem for women in politics, particularly with respect to higher positions? What are the underlying causes? Might testosterone give men an edge in competition for high positions? In a controversial essay, Andrew Sullivan argues, based on his own experiences with testosterone injections, that testosterone explains some of the persistent inequities between the sexes, especially in high-risk professions, such as "the military, contact sports, hazardous exploration, venture capitalism, politics, gambling." Sullivan, The He Hormone, N.Y. Times Magazine, Apr. 2, 2000, at 47, 69. Whatever its source, what can be done to overcome this aspect of the problem?

5. Do you think that there is continued bias against women running for office, particularly high office? Can you think of media reactions to women candidates that would not have occurred had the candidate been a man? Can you think of voter reactions to women candidates that would not have occurred had the candidate been a man? Is it, for example, as easy for a woman as a man to appear to be an authority, particularly on military and international affairs? Describe the kind of woman you think is likely to be the first woman president. What constraints would she face? See Clift and Brazatis, note 4 above (discussing many problems). Are women, for example, more likely to be seen as "too" ambitious than male candidates for high office? Soft on defense? Too liberal on spending for social welfare?

6. A woman politician is expected to have children, but is also expected to be their primary caretaker. Women who have run for office with small children or while pregnant face a double bind: trying to appear capable of devoting the necessary time to the job *and* trying to appear to be good mothers. To date, most women have avoided this dilemma by entering politics about ten years later than men, when their children are no longer young. See Clark, above note 3 and Clift and Brazatis, above note 4, at 143–61, 212–27, 255–59. How can we offset the structural disadvantages caretakers face?

7. In recent elections women who run have had as much chance of winning *open* seats (seats without an incumbent) as men. Part of the problem with women's continuing underrepresentation is that so few women run. Part of the explanation may be that fewer women are asked to run: 90% of men who run have been asked to run by party leaders and activists, whereas only 30% of women who run have been asked. See Clift and Brazatis, above note 4, at 305. Have you ever considered running for the House of Representatives of the United States Senate? What would deter

you? Are the things which would deter you in any way linked to being a woman or a man? Compare your responses with those of others in your class.

8. Can you think of advantages men who are simply voters (not candidates for office) might have over women with respect to political power? See Karen Burns, Kay Hehman Schlozman, and Sidney Verba, The Public Consequences of Private Inequality: Family Life and Citizen Participation, 91 Am. Polit. Sci. Rev. 373, 373 (1997) (considering political power of husbands and wives in light of domestic inequalities and concluding that husbands have more power than would be expected on the basis of their other characteristics because of their "control over major financial decisions and autonomy in using small amounts of time").

Text Note: Women Make a Difference

The Center for the American Woman and Politics (CAWP) at the Eagleton Institute of Politics at Rutgers has done a series of important empirical studies of women in government, asking whether women make a difference.[77] They have consistently found that, in fact, women do make a difference whether as members of the executive, judicial, or legislative branches. Two of these studies look at women in legislatures during the late 1980's and the 1990's. The first surveyed and interviewed women and men in state legislatures in 1988. This study finds that, independent of party and ideology, women are more likely to support and work on issues important to women than men. For example, 76% of liberal women (but only 67% of liberal men) were working on women's rights bills; 58% of moderate women (but only 35% of moderate men) were working on such bills; 39% of conservative women (but only 26% of conservative men) were working on such bills. Note that *conservative* women tend to be more committed to women's issues than *moderate* men. African American women were especially likely to be working on women's bills: 85% of African American women legislators (but only 57% of white women legislators) were working on such bills. Id. at 40–41. Nonfeminist women were only slightly less likely (46%) than feminist men (49%) to be working on women's rights bills. In contrast, 73% of feminist women were working on such bills, as were 34% of nonfeminist men.[78]

A second study looks at women in the 103rd Congress (1993–95). This was an unusual term. The numbers of women in Congress rose dramatically in the 1992 elections for a number of reasons. One factor was the unusually high number of open seats. Another was that the 1992 election followed the hearings over Clarence Thomas' nomination to the Supreme Court. At the hearings, Anita Hill testified—before an all-male Senate Judiciary Committee—that Thomas had repeatedly harassed her sexually when he was her boss at the EEOC. A number of Senators on the Committee brutally

77. In addition to the studies described in text, see Gender and Policymaking: Studies of Women in Office (Debra L. Dodson, ed., CAWP 1991 (an analysis of a number of studies of women in executive, judicial, and executive positions which concludes that across the board, women make a difference). See also John Gruhl, Cassia Spohn, and Susan Welch, Women as Policymakers: The Case of Trial Judges, 25 Am.J.Pol.Sci. 308 (1981); Alison Morris, Women, Crime and Criminal Justice (1987).

78. Debra L. Dodson and Susan J. Carroll, Reshaping the Agenda: Women in State Legislatures 38–47 (CAWP 1991).

attacked Hill, enraging and mobilizing many women. In the next election, women were determined to make the Senate less of a boys' club. The number of women in the Senate increased in the 1992 election from 2 (2%) to 6 (6%), a threefold increase. And the number of women in the House increased from 28 (6.4%) to 47 (10.8%). Altogether the number of women in Congress almost doubled in a single election. Not coincidentally, this is the Congress that enacted the Violence Against Women Act (VAWA) which we looked at in Chapter 5.[79]

The CAWP study on women in Congress found that, like women in state legislatures, women in Congress were more likely to support and work on causes important to women than were their male colleagues, as illustrated by the following table:

Table 10: Selected Votes of Male and Female House Members in the 103rd Congress[80]

	Republican Men	Republican Women	Democratic Men	Democratic Women
For Crime Bill (including VAWA)]	23%	67%	72%	89%
For Assault Weapons Ban	19%	58%	66%	91%
For FACE Conference Report (access to abortion clinics)	20%	75%	80%	97%
For Brady Bill (gun control)	30%	67%	70%	89%
Against Amendment to Ask Recruits if Gay, Bisexual	32%	67%	87%	100%
For Family and Medical Leave Act	21%	50%	87%	100%
Against Hyde Amendment (no federal funds for abortions for poor women)	6%	50%	58%	86%
Against Version of Don't Ask, Don't Tell	6%	17%	41%	78%

Women's presence was, however, far more important than simply the numbers of votes they were able to cast on issues important to women:

> Women members of Congress can influence the nature of the debate, the policy agenda, or the content of bills, women can also influence the face of legislation by blocking a bill in committee, extricating bills from committee, forcing a vote on a bill, participating in a "whipping" plan to muster votes, holding press conferences to influence public perception of a bill, meeting with leadership to express a collective point of view, or getting added to a bill certain provisions their male colleagues might not have considered. Women in the 103rd Congress took all these steps, thereby exerting important influences in addition to any impact to be discerned through analysis of their voting behavior of bill sponsorship.[81]

Congresswomen in the 103rd Congress felt a special responsibility to represent women. Congressman Nydia Velazquez (D–NY) describes this commitment:

79. Debra L. Dodson, Susan J. Carroll, Ruth B. Mandel, Katherine E. Kleeman, Ronnee Schreiber, and Debra Liebowitz, Voices, Views, Votes: The Impact of Women in the 103rd Congress 2–3 (CAWP 1993).

80. Id., table at 9.

81. Id. at 9–10.

> Before I came here, I worked for a Congressman. And while I worked for him, I saw that women's issues were not part of the national agenda. And that is . . . true today. It hasn't changed. So it is our responsibility to participate in every single issue that we have here, and every debate that we have here, but I understand that if we don't force others to focus on women's issues, then it will not be a part of the debate. And that is a responsibility that all of us share, especially women.[82]

And, in the words of Congresswoman Nancy Johnson (R–CT):

> We need to integrate the perspective of women into the policy-making process, just as we have now successfully integrated the perspective of environmental preservation, the perspective of worker safety .... Now, whenever something comes up, we automatically think, "Gee, how will this affect the environment? How will this affect the working people at the work site?" But we don't really think, "How is this going to affect women who work at home? Women in the workplace with home responsibilities? Women who are single parents?" And I do feel a special responsibility to participate in the public policy process in a way that assures that where something is going to affect women as well as men, that I think through how will this affect women who are at home taking care of children who need to re-enter the work force later on? How does this affect women who didn't get to go beyond high school because their family thought that only boys should go to college, and now they're stuck? I know a lot more about the shape of women's lives and the pattern of women's lives, so I need to look and see how the public policy will affect those patterns, and how it will help or hurt.[83]

Although no woman served as chair of a committee in the 103rd Congress, the report concludes:

> Women members made a difference in the 103rd Congress. The voices, views and votes of the female Representatives and Senators who served from 1993 to 1995 made themselves heard and felt in the legislative debate and in the legislation passed. Even though they were a mere one-tenth of the membership, and slightly more than half of them were freshmen, the Congresswomen found ways to have an impact within an institution in which women's perspectives have seldom been recognized and where more senior and better positioned (almost always male) members often dominate.[84]

Notes on Women in Office

1. Are you surprised that women in Congress believe that if they don't raise women's issues, no one does? Do you think that this assessment is likely to be accurate? Why or why not?

2. If you are a woman, would you feel a responsibility to represent women if you were in elected office? Why or why not? If you are a man, would you see any need to think particularly about women's needs, interests, and the effect of proposed legislation on women? Why or why not?

82. Id. at 15.

83. Id. at 15–16.

84. Id. at 24.

3. Would you give an edge to a woman candidate in deciding whom to vote for? For example, if you are pro-choice and consider that a top priority item, would you be more likely to vote for a moderate pro-choice women over a moderate pro-choice man with similar credentials? Why? Do the men and women in your class answer these questions differently?

4. Can you think of specific ways in which it might it matter that most judges are non-Hispanic white men though this group is a minority of the population? Consider not only possible conflicts of interest but also issues on which non-Hispanic white men and women of various colors and other members of minority groups might have different perceptions because of their different life experiences. Do you think women and others in minority groups might tend to view some issues differently? In what sorts of cases would you expect to see differences?

D. GLOBAL FEMINISM AND EQUALITY

Text Note: Perspectives from Global Feminism

For many American women, the Convention on the Elimination of All Forms of Discrimination Against Women (CEDAW)[85] has been their first introduction to global feminism. Many have worked for adoption of CEDAW by the United States and by various local entities, such as cities and counties within the United States.

CEDAW was adopted by the General Assembly of the United Nations on December 18, 1979, and is the only comprehensive treaty on human rights for women. It defines sex discrimination broadly as "any distinction, exclusion, or restriction, made on the basis of sex which has the effect or purpose of impairing or nullifying the recognition, enjoyment or exercise by women of human rights and fundamental freedoms in the political, economic, social, cultural, civil or any other field."[86] CEDAW requires that States Parties take positive steps to eliminate all forms of discrimination against women. Article 3 provides:

> States Parties shall take in all fields, in particular in the political, social, economic and cultural fields, all appropriate measures, including legislation, to ensure the full development and advancement of women, for the purpose of guaranteeing them the exercise and enjoyment of human rights and fundamental freedoms on a basis of equality with men.[87]

Indeed, States Parties are obligated "[t]o modify the social and cultural patterns of conduct of men and women, with a view to achieving the elimination of prejudices and customary and all other practices which are based on the idea of the inferiority or the superiority of either of the sexes or on stereotyped roles for men and women."[88]

CEDAW has important provisions for working women. It requires a comparable worth standard for pay inequities[89] and paid maternity leave or

85. Convention on the Elimination of All Forms of Discrimination Against Women, 1249 U.N.T.S. 13 (1981) (hereinafter CEDAW).

86. Id. Art. 1.

87. Id. Art. 3.

88. Id. Art. 5(a).

comparable social benefits.[90] And CEDAW requires States Parties "[t]o encourage the provision of the necessary supporting social services to enable parents to combine family obligations with work responsibilities and participation in public life, in particular through promoting the establishment and development of a network of child-care facilities."[91]

President Carter submitted CEDAW to the Senate for ratification in 1980, but the accompanying report from the State Department indicated that many reservations were necessary and the Senate "took no action."[92] In 1994, President Clinton urged Senate ratification but "with four reservations, three understandings, and two declarations."[93] After hearings, the Senate Foreign Relations Committee recommended ratification of the Convention subject to the reservation, understandings, and declarations suggested by the Clinton Administration together with an additional understanding added by Senator Helms. Again no action was taken by the Senate.[94]

Reservations, understandings, and declarations function as objections to certain treaty provisions or interpretations enabling a signatory nation to bind itself only to those parts of the treaty with which it agrees. Indeed, the United States reservations, declarations, and understandings as specified by the Senate Foreign Relations Committee were designed to ensure that if enacted, CEDAW would have absolutely no effect whatsoever within the United States. In addition, as with most other human rights treaties, the United States would have included a declaration that withheld agreement to jurisdiction of an international tribunal.[95] And the treaty would not have been self-executing, i.e., would not become part of United States law unless separately enacted. [96]

In September of 2000, Saudi Arabia became the 166th nation to bind itself to the treaty.[97] Among the nations that have not ratified CEDAW, in addition to the United States, are Afghanistan, North Korea, Iran, and Sudan. The United States does not, of course, publicly admit opposition to women's rights. Rather, it insists that American law adequately protects women's rights. But, as we have seen, the American approach denies women important rights common elsewhere and needed by American women. For example, throughout Europe, women have the right to paid maternity leave and a right not to be fired during pregnancy or maternity leave for any pregnancy-related reason (such as being unable to work).[98] Women in the United States have only the right, as indicated earlier, to a short unpaid

89. Id. Art. 11, § 1(d).

90. Id. Art. 11, § 2(b).

91. Id. Art. 11, § 2(c).

92. Malvina Halberstam, United States Ratification of the Convention on the Elimination of All Forms of Discrimination Against Women, 31 Geo. Wash. J. Int'l L. & Econ. 49, 54 (1997).

93. Id. at 55.

94. Id.

95. Id. at 60.

96. Louis Henkin, U.S. Ratification of Human Rights Conventions: The Ghost of Senator Bricker, 89 Am. J. Int'l L. 341, 347–48 (1995).

97. See <http:www.un.org/womenwatch/daw/cedaw/states.htm> (visited 12/11/2000).

98. See Case C–394/96, Brown v. Rentokil, [1998] ECR I–4185 (1998) (under European Union law, an employer cannot fire an employee during pregnancy or maternity leave for any reason connected to pregnancy, such as inability to do the job because of pregnancy-related disability) (extract in Chapter 10).

leave and can be fired while pregnant for, e.g., being late for work because of morning sickness.[99]

Gender Mainstreaming

American notions on women's rights are also quite different from emerging international standards in the political arena. CEDAW Article 7 provides:

> States Parties shall take all appropriate measures to eliminate discrimination against women in the political and public life of the country and, in particular, shall ensure to women, on equal terms with men, the right:
>
> (a) To vote in all elections and public referenda and to be eligible for election to all publicly elected bodies;
>
> (b) To participate in the formulation of government policy and the implementation thereof and to hold public office and perform all public functions at all levels of government;
>
> (c) To participate in non-governmental organizations and associations concerned with the public and political life of the country.

This may sound consistent with American notions that women cannot be formally excluded from political participation, but section (b) in particular has a much thicker meaning in the context of international women's rights. It is an expression of the political goal of the international women's movement: gender mainstreaming, which means the involvement of women at all levels of governmental policymaking and implementation in appropriate numbers (according to their presence in the population) to ensure that women's interests, needs, and concerns are taken into account consistently and throughout the process of governmental policy making and implementation.[100]

A new international norm for democratic legitimacy is emerging: a democracy is legitimate only if women participate at all levels of government in proportion to their presence in the population. Quotas to ensure women's presence in elected office at appropriate levels are seen as an appropriate means to ensure democratic legitimacy. Thus, electoral quotas for women have become an increasingly important part of the international feminist agenda. The Platform for Action of the Fourth World Conference on Women in Beijing in 1994 includes the following explanation of the importance of equality in governmental decisionmaking:

> Equality in political decision-making performs a leverage function without which it is highly unlikely that a real integration of the equality

99. See, e.g., In Re Carnegie Center Associates, 129 F.3d 290 (3d Cir.1997) (not pregnancy discrimination for employer to fire the secretary on maternity leave rather than, e.g., the one with least seniority or the lowest job evaluations, when a reduction in force was necessary) (extract in Chapter 10); Troupe v. May Department Stores Co., 20 F.3d 734 (7th Cir.1994) (not pregnancy discrimination for employer to fire pregnant worker on the day before she was to go on maternity leave even though supervisor told her she was being fired because employer thought she would not return to work; employee had been tardy or left early a number of times during pregnancy because of morning sickness) (extract in Chapter 10).

100. Fourth World Conference on Women, Platform for Action and the Beijing Declaration at 111 (1996) (Platform for Action Strategic Objective G.189).

> dimension in government policy-making is feasible. In this respect, women's equal participation in political life plays a pivotal role in the general process of the advancement of women. Women's equal participation in decision-making is not only a demand for simple justice or democracy but can also be seen as a necessary condition for women's interests to be taken into account. Without the active participation of women and the incorporation of women's perspectives at all levels of decision-making, the goals of equality, development and peace cannot be achieved. [101]

The goal, as noted earlier, is "gender-mainstreaming":

> In addressing the inequality between men and women in the sharing of power and decision-making at all levels, Governments and other actors should promote an active and visible policy of mainstreaming a gender perspective in all policies and programs so that before decisions are taken, an analysis is made of the effects on women and men, respectively.[102]

The Beijing platform for action explicitly calls for governments to use "positive measures" to correct the "low proportion of women among economic and political decision makers at the local, national, regional and international levels."[103] Governments are to "[t]ake measures, including, where appropriate, in electoral systems that encourage political parties to integrate women in elective and non-elective public positions in the same proportion and at the same levels as men."[104] When appropriate, electoral systems are to be reformed to increase women's representation,[105] and governments are to "[a]im at gender balance in the lists of national candidates nominated for election."[106]

The Council of Europe, a broader (and looser) organization than the European Union and the organization behind the European Convention on Human Rights, supports gender mainstreaming and stresses the importance of having women in 50% of all governmental decisionmaking positions for democratic legitimacy. For example, at the Fourth European Ministerial Conference of the Council of Europe on Equality between Women and Men in November of 1997, the Ministers of the Council of Europe issued a Declaration on Equality between Women and Men as a Fundamental Criterion of Democracy.[107] It recommends gender balance at all levels of governmental decisionmaking and encourages assessment and reform of electoral systems to facilitate the integration of women in proportional numbers at all levels.

101. Id. at 109 (Platform for Action Strategic Objective G.181).

102. Id. at 111 (Platform for Action Strategic Objective G.189).

103. Id. at 111 (Platform for Action Strategic Objective G.186).

104. Id. at 112 (Platform for Action Strategic Objective G.1.190(b)).

105. Id. (Platform for Action Strategic Objective G.1.190(d)).

106. Id. (Platform for Action Strategic Objective G.1.190(j)).

107. Council of Europe, Declaration on Equality between Women and Men as a Fundamental Criterion of Democracy (1997) (available at <http://www.com.coe.int/reports/cmdocs/1997/97cm203.html> visited 1/20/2001).

The European Union is also taking actions in support of gender mainstreaming. In July of 2000, the Commission of the European Communities submitted a proposal to the Council of the European Union, the European Parliament, the Economic and Social Committee, and the Committee of the Regions laying out a "Community framework strategy on gender equality." [108] This proposal identifies as the goal of equality "an inclusive democracy." Such a political structure "requires that all citizens women and men alike * * * participate and be represented equally in the economy, in decision-making, and in social, cultural and civil life." The goal is gender mainstreaming: to ensure that "[w]omen's concerns, needs, and aspirations be taken into account and assume the same importance as men's concerns in the design and implementation of policies." One of the five areas of focus is "promoting equal participation and political representation" in all areas of decisionmaking. The Commission acknowledges that the "persistent under-representation of women in all areas of decision making marks a fundamental democratic deficit which requires Community level action." Among other things, the Commission suggests an assessment of the influence of electoral systems, legislation, quotas, targets and other measures on gender balance in elected political bodies." The goal of this and other European Commission and Council actions related to political representation of women is to see women participate as 50% of the decisionmakers throughout the Union, whether the decisionmaking body is a local commission or a major institution of the Union.

The United States does not do well when compared, as Table 12 does, with other countries in terms of the presence of women in the country's highest legislative body. Indeed, with a ranking of 56, there are 55 countries around the world in which women are represented in the highest legislative body in higher numbers.

Table 11: Women in the National Legislatures of the Countries in the European Union, Canada, and the United States

As Ranked by the Inter–Parliamentary Union[109]

Rank	Country	Lower or Single House			Upper House		
		Seats	Women	% Women	Seats	Women	% Women
1	Sweden (party quotas)110	349	149	42.7%	—	—	—
2	Denmark (party quotas)	179	67	37.4%	—	—	—
3	Finland (party quotas)	200	73	36.5%	—	—	—

108. Communication from the Commission to the Council, The European Parliament, The Economic and Social Committee and the Committee of the Regions, Towards a Community Framework Strategy on Gender Equality 2001–2005 at 2–3, 7–9 (2000) (2000/0143 (CNS)).

109. Rankings of the Inter–Parliamentary Union were current as of July 15, 2000, and include every country in the world (not all of which are included in the table in text, which includes only the countries of the European Union, Canada, and the United States) and available at <www.ipu.org/wmn-e/classif.htm> visited 8/18/2000).

110. The five leading parties require that women and men alternate on party lists. Liane Hansen (anchor), Women From Around the World Look For Ways to Increase Their Numbers in Elected Positions and Leadership Roles, National Public Radio, Weekend Edition, June 11, 2000 (reporter Margot Adler speaking) (hereinafter NPR, Women Around the World).

4	Norway (party quotas)	165	60	36.4%	—	—	—
5	Netherlands (party quotas)	150	54	36.0%	75	20	26.7%
7	Germany (party quotas)[111]	669	207	30.9%	69	41	59.84%
12	Spain (party quotas)	350	99	28.3	259	59	22.58
15	Austria	183	49	26.8%	64	13	20.3%
22	Belgium (quota law)	150	35	23.3%	71	20	28.2%
23	Switzerland (party quotas)	200	46	23.0%	46	9	19.6%
30	Canada	301	60	19.9%	105	32	30.5%
33	United Kingdom (party quota in 1997)[112]	659	121	18.4%	666	105	15.8%
37	Portugal (quota law unconstitutional)[113]	230	40	17.4%	—	—	—
41	Luxembourg (party quota or other system)[114]	60	10	16.7%	—	—	—
56	United States[115]	435	56	12.9%	100	9	9%
61	Ireland (party quotas)[116]	166	20	12.0%	60	11	9%
68	Italy (quota law unconstitutional)[117]	630	70	11.1%	326	26	8%
71	France (quota law for next election)[118]	577	63	10.9%	321	19	5.9%
?	Greece	300	?	?	—	—	—

The European countries with highest proportions of women in their parliaments have both proportional representation systems *and* some sort of formal quota system either by law or party rule.

Proportional Representation

Most of the countries of the European Union—indeed, almost all the countries of the world—have some form of proportional representation. All the countries of Europe (including the United Kingdom) elect their representatives to the European Parliament by a proportional representation scheme. It has been obvious for some time that women and minority groups do better at winning elected office under proportional representation systems than under winner-take-all geographic districts, the most common electoral structure in the United States.

111. The Social Democratic Party of Germany requires that 40% of candidates on party lists be women. Id.; Voters Should Count on Women, Toronto Star, Apr. 27, 2000.

112. In 1997, Tony Blair set a quota of 50% women for Labor candidates running for open seats in Parliament, and the number of women in the House of Commons increased from 63 to 122, sweeping Blair and the Labor party into office. Alexander MacLeod, After Gains, British Women Frustrated with Politics, The Christian Science Monitor, June 27, 2000, at 7; Voters Should Count on Women, Toronto Star, Apr. 27, 2000.

113. NPR, Women Around the World, above note 110 (Jane Kramer, reporter for the New Yorker, speaking).

114. Each party has either quotas or a system favoring women candidates.

115. One hundred seventy-six countries are included in the ranking. Other countries above the United States in the ranking are: Iceland, New Zealand, Mozambique, South Africa, Bosnia and Herzegovina, Venezuela, Cuba, Grenada, Argentina, Turkmenistan, Viet Nam, Namibia, Seychelles. Australia, Monaco, China, Lao People's Democratic Republic, Croatia, Democratic People's Republic of Korea, Costa Rica, Guyana, Uganda, Estonia, Lithuania, Rwanda, Botswana, Latvia, United Republic of Tanzania, Dominican Republic, Angola, Bahamas, Czech Republic, Tajikistan, Eritrea, Ecuador, Burundi, Slovakia, Jamaica, Saint Kitts and Nevis, San Marino, and Poland.

116. In Ireland, only three of the six major parties have quotas, some as low as 20%.

117. NPR, Women Around the World, above note 110 (Jane Kramer, reporter for the New Yorker, speaking).

118. Id. (host Liane Hansen speaking); Lara Marlowe, Jospin's Wife Beats Her Own Drum, The Irish Times, Oct. 25, 2000, at 12.

In the simplest proportional representation scheme, votes are cast for parties. Before the election, the party publishes a list of the people who are running for that party in each district. Thus, for example, an electoral district might elect 10 representatives to the legislature, and each voter casts one vote for one party, say the Green, Red, or Orange Party. If the Green Party gets 60% of the vote, then the first 6 candidates on its list go to the legislature. If the Red Party gets 30% of the vote, the first 3 candidates on its list go to the legislature. And if the Orange Party receives 10% vote, the first candidate on its list goes to the legislature.

There are many variations on proportional representation, and several allow votes for individual candidates, thus maximizing accountability of those in office, who must win reelection on the basis of their personal record as well as their party's. Cumulative voting in modified at-large schemes is one such system. Under a cumulative voting at-large system, voters vote for particular candidates. But voters, not politicians determine how individuals combine into groups for purposes of representation—provided that each electoral district has at least five seats. In a district with five seats, each voter would receive five votes, which can be cast in any way desired among the candidates: a voter could cast one vote for each of five candidates or five votes for a single candidate. (Empirical studies have shown that as long as districts have at least five seats with this scheme, how the politicians draw district lines has no effect on representation in the legislature. Women do best in districts with seven to ten seats.[119])

By contrast, winner-take-all systems base representation on geographic units drawn up by politicians. Geographic districting *can* create effective democracies in countries with homogeneous populations.[120] The majoritarian systems of England and the United States may have worked fairly well at the time they were designed. In America, at the time the republic was founded, the franchise was limited to a relatively homogenous population: propertied men of European descent. But winner-take-all single-member districts make it difficult for individuals with views that are in the minority to have any voice in policy. Under a proportional representation scheme, minority views are more likely to be represented in the legislative body. And proportional representation schemes facilitate the election of women of all colors and other members of minority groups. Thus, proportional representation schemes facilitate the representation of the entire population, not just the people who form a majority in each district.

In a plurality system, like that in United States, parties can be reluctant to nominate a woman lest she lose to a male competitor. Party leaders may hate to deny the candidacy to a man who has been active in the party and who wants to run. And since there is only one candidate in a district, the party cannot balance the ticket nor appeal to a broader group of voters by backing a diverse set of candidates within the district. In a proportional representation system, a woman runs as part of a group, and this can be

119. Douglas J. Amy, Real Choices New Voices: The Case for Proportional Representation Elections in the United States 51–53, 110–11 (1993).

120. Lani Guinier, Lift Every Voice: Turning a Civil Rights Setback Into a New Vision of Social Justice 256 (1998); Arend Lijphart, Democracies: Patterns of Majoritarian and Consensus Government in Twenty-One Countries 3–4 (1984).

perceived by party leaders as a less risky strategy. In addition, the party has an incentive to include diverse candidates on its slate in order to appeal to diverse voters within the district. The list of party candidates can be balanced to represent various interests within the party, including not just women but other members of minority groups or of other identifiable party constituencies. Because it is easier for parties in a proportional representation system to field a diverse set of candidates, parties in such systems are also more susceptible to diversification pressure when other parties diversify their slates.

Not surprisingly, of the four countries with the lowest percentages of women in the lower houses of their national legislative bodies in a study of sixteen Western democracies, three have winner-take-all single-member district electoral systems inherited from feudal England (Canada, Great Britain, and the United States).[121]

Quotas for Women Candidates

Not only did the European countries with highest proportions of women in their parliaments have proportional representation systems, rather than winner-take-all single-member districts, they also had adopted a quota system ensuring that a certain proportion of those elected would be women. The five countries with the highest proportions of women in their national parliament—Sweden, Denmark, Finland, Norway, and the Netherlands, all had party quotas, as did Germany, the country ranked seventh. The party rules vary from country to country and, in some countries, from party to party. In Sweden, the five major parties have internal rules requiring that men's and women's names alternate on the party list for proportional representation. In Germany the Social Democratic party has a 40% quota for women on its lists of candidates.

The French Experience

The percentage of women in the French parliament has lagged significantly behind the level of representation of women in a number of the other countries in the European Union. French women did not obtain the vote until 1944. In 1945, France changed from a majoritarian electoral system to a proportional representation system, but returned to a majoritarian scheme in 1958.[122] By the 1990's, France was 71st in terms of representation of women, as indicated in Table 12. Women served as only 10.9% of the lower house of the French Parliament and as 5.9% of the upper house. Sweden, ranked first, had 42.7% women in its parliament; Denmark, second, 37.4%, Finland, third, 36.5%, the Netherlands, fifth, 36%, and Germany, seventh, 30.9%.

Part of the problem for French women is that France has an electoral system much like that in the United States: single-member winner-take-all districts. France adds one variation: to win in one round, a candidate must receive a majority of the votes cast; to advance to the second round (when

121. Amy, above note 119, Table 5.1 at 103.

122. University of Helsinki, Women in the European Union, Chapter 5.2; The Situation of Women in Politics; available at www.helsinki.fi/science/xantippa/wee/weetext/wee252.html; visited 8/19/2000 (France did use a proportional representation system for the 1986 parliamentary system, and that election returned an all-time high of 24.7% women to parliament).

one is necessary) a candidate must receive at least 12.5% of registered (not actual) voters. The person who gets the most votes on the second round wins.

In France, women responded to the low levels of women in parliament with a movement for "parité," which gained momentum in the late 1980's and 1990's, as the combination of proportional representation and quotas increased the level of women's participation in other European parliaments to levels much, much higher than those in France. The Parité Movement pushed for a quota to be enacted by the overwhelmingly male parliament—and succeeded. Activists published lists of men against parité, and women voted against them. Within two to three years, 80% of voters supported parité. [123]

The French Parité Movement began with a constitutional amendment in 1999. (The Italian and Portuguese Supreme Courts had struck quotas as unconstitutional.)[124] In May, 2000, the French legislature passed a statute implementing parité by requiring that every party's political slate must include as many women as men or lose its government-provided campaign financing. The effectiveness of the French Parité Movement can be seen in Table 13. At the time of the 1999 election of representatives to the European Parliament, the French law was not yet in effect. Yet on *this* list, unlike that in table 12, France ranks third in representation of women. (This success is also, of course, attributable to the fact that elections to the European Parliament, unlike those to the French Parliament, are under a proportional representation scheme.)

Table 12: Women in the European Parliament 1999 Election[125]

Country	Seats	Women	% Women
1. Sweden	22	11	50%
2. Finland	16	7	43.8%
3. France	87	35	40.2%
4. Austria	21	8	38.1%
5. Denmark	16	6	37.5%
6. Germany	99	36	36.4%
7. Spain	64	22	34.4%
8. Ireland	15	5	33.3%
9. Luxembourg	6	2	33.3%
10. Netherlands	31	10	32.3%

123. NPR, Women Around the World, above note 110 (Francoise Gaspard, leader of the French Parité Movement, speaking); Marlowe, above note 117.

124. NPR, Women Around the World, above note 110 (Jane Kramer, reporter for The New Yorker, speaking).

125. European Data Base, Women in Decision-making, <www.db-decision.de/FactSheets/EP–Results.htm> (visited 8/19/2000).

Country	Seats	Women	% Women
11. Belgium	25	7	28%
12. United Kingdom	87	21	24.1%
13. Greece	25	4	16.0%
14. Portugal	25	5	20.0%
15. Italy	87	9	10.3%
Total	626	188	30%

Notes on Global Feminism

1. Compare the definition of sex discrimination in CEDAW and the notion of sex discrimination in the constitutional cases described in Chapter 2. Would quotas for women in elections violate CEDAW? Would such quotas violate the United States Constitution?

2. What do you think of CEDAW's definition of sex discrimination? Would American women be better off with a similar definition in Title VII (applying to employment) or Title IX (applying to education) or the Constitution? What new challenges could be brought, under Title VII, Title IX, or the Constitution, were we to adopt the CEDAW definition?

3. Would any of the constitutional sex-discrimination cases you studied in Chapter 2 (see chart at the end of Chapter 2 for a quick review) come out differently under the CEDAW standard? Could a man allege sex discrimination under the CEDAW standard? Are there other possible differences? Which standard do you prefer? Why?

4. Although the United States routinely puts reservations on international treaties and conventions involving human rights, such as CEDAW, to ensure that America's law on human rights is not changed by treaty and cannot be overruled by any international tribunal, the United States has been willing to change American law and bind the United States to jurisdiction of an international tribunal in treaties dealing with free trade. See, e.g., Andrea Knox, The World Trade Organization at a Crossroads, World Trade, Oct. 1, 1999, at 34. What explains this difference?

5. The United States Constitution states that the president has the power to make treaties "with the Advice and Consent of the Senate." Do you think that there is a relationship between women's underrepresentation in the Senate (non-Hispanic white men are 84% of Senators; non-Hispanic white women 13%) and the failure of the United States to ratify CEDAW as well as the United Nations Convention on the Rights of the Child (which, among other things, bans executions of juvenile offenders and has been ratified by all countries except the United States and Somalia)? Why is the United States so unwilling to endorse treaties guaranteeing rights to women and children? Is it really, as the State Department insisted in proposing the enactment of CEDAW with reservations, declarations, and understandings ensuring that it would have no effect, that those making this assertion believe that American law adequately protects women's rights? Or is it that those in power oppose better rights for women, even when such rights are common in other similar parts of the world?

6. Compare the percentages of women in the House and Senate of the United States Congress with the percentages of women in the parliaments of the European nations and the percentages of women in the European parliament. Are you surprised by the fact that the United States ranks 56th world-wide in terms of women's representation in the national legislature as of the summer of 2000? Are you surprised by the high levels of women's representation in the European parliament, where the level is over twice that in the American Congress? What explains this difference?

7. Were you aware, before you took this course, of the use and success of electoral quotas for women in Europe and the broad support for gender mainstreaming by this means in the international feminist movement? Where did you hear about them? Has the mainstream media reported these developments?

8. Why do you think European women responded to the problem of women in elected office with pressure for quotas? Why were they successful? Why have women done so much better in Europe in terms of political equality? Why have American women failed to give the same level of attention to the need for political equality?

9. Do you agree with the Beijing Platform for Action that women's equal participation in governmental decision-making is a demand for simple justice, a demand for (real) democracy, and a necessary prerequisite for women's interests to be taken into account? Do you agree? Would most Americans agree? What do you see as the sticking points either for yourself or for Americans in general? Can you imagine a major American governmental institution conceding, as the European Commission did, that the under-representation of women in all levels of governmental decisionmaking "marks a fundamental democratic deficit" requiring immediate action on a national level? What explains these differences?

10. The Recommendation of the European Commission, described above, offers gender mainstreaming as a theoretical basis for the European and international feminist focus on political equality: In order to integrate women's needs, perspectives, interests, and concerns into all levels of governmental decisionmaking, we need to integrate women into governmental decisionmaking bodies in proportion to their numbers in the population. Do you agree or disagree with this analysis of the meaning of equality and how to achieve it? Is this vision of equality most consistent with that of formal equality, dominance feminism, pragmatic feminism, relational feminism, socialist feminism, multicultural feminism, or lesbian feminism?

11. What are the strongest arguments you can make for and against electoral quotas? Do quotas suggest that women are not qualified for public office? What are the qualifications for a good representative in a legislative body? Why might women be better representatives in some respects than men regardless of objective "qualifications"? What are the actual "qualifications" for high elective office in the United States today given how campaigns are conducted and their cost? What are the actual "qualifications" one would look for in an ideal representative, ignoring electability?

12. The Beijing Platform for Action paragraph 181, quoted above, clearly sees gender mainstreaming—equal participation by women in all levels of governmental decisionmaking—as a necessary precondition to

equality. Why? What is the reasoning behind this view? What is the platform's vision of equality in this paragraph? Do you agree? Do you think it is possible for women to achieve equality prior to obtaining parity in governmental decisionmaking?

13. Would quotas facilitate the ability of women to combine politics and mothering? Would quotas help overcome women's reluctance to go after highly competitive positions? Are these arguments for quotas? Are the women elected under a quota requirement likely to be women who will *not* push for change because, for example, they are likely to be beholden to party bosses?

14. Are quotas undemocratic? Or do they enhance democracy?

E. POLITICS OF EQUALITY

Text Note: Politics of Equality

We are so used to women's underrepresentation in elective office that we do not see it as undermining the legitimacy of our "democracy." If women were another historically disadvantaged and still subordinate majority group with similar levels of representation in a purported democracy, the legitimacy of the structure would be suspect. Christine Boyle, a Canadian scholar, poses this question in the form of a hypothetical:

> Imagine a country in which all or most of the women, but not the men, lived in one geographical area—for example, Ontario. One can then examine the laws applying to and the economic position of "Ontarians" from a neutral standpoint. It will be found that the position of Ontarians is not good in Canadian society. They have been systematically discriminated against throughout their history; for example, their property was taken from them without compensation, they had no rights to their children, enfranchisement was ridiculed and bitterly opposed, and they still rarely sit in Parliament or on the bench. They are subjected to assault and sexual abuse by non-Ontarians, and they largely work at menial tasks for which they are paid much less than non-Ontarians, or nothing. In addition, they are depicted ever more widely by various media as being less than human, as objects for the sexual gratification of non-Ontarians. One has only to attempt such an account to realize that there exist two fundamentally different groups in Canada (and, of course, elsewhere). It is submitted that an electoral system which does not reflect any confrontation of that fact is inadequate.[126]

Boyle is suggesting that we would "naturally" respond to such inequity by suggesting separate representation of Ontarians along geographic lines, i.e., that Ontarians would elect their own representatives to the legislature.

The situation of women, of course, is different from that of the hypothetical Ontarians in that women are not in certain geographic areas. The Canadian Advisory Council on the Status of Women argues that there is no

126. Christine Boyle, Home Rule for Women: Power-Sharing Between Men and Women, 7 Dalhousie L.J. 790, 796 (1983).

good reason to so privilege geographically identifiable groups over other groups with interests that are not always identical. The Canadian Advisory Council points out that women's geographic dispersion

> does not mean * * * that the problem disappears or that we should give up on the task of finding a solution. One of the fundamental underlying assumptions in our constitution is * * * that "Geography is Destiny." This has many consequences. The intense focus on federal-provincial relations, and on territorial representation, are two examples. The federalism model recognizes geographic and some kinds of cultural diversity, but makes invisible other kinds of diversity such as gender.
>
> While women in Canada may have different views about many constitutional issues (and why not?), from a feminist perspective it is important to question the territorial (originally property-based) model that works so well to keep women out of politics.[127]

One could, of course, make similar points about the United States.

Many feminists would agree, even many committed to judicially enforced formal equality,[128] that we must primarily look to women for their own creation of equality within the legal system through political participation, rather than to the Supreme Court and the lower federal courts deciding constitutional sex equality cases. Courts are institutions with little power to effect social change. Courts can only decide the cases presented according to the applicable legal rules and within their system of precedent; courts cannot order social equality. On many issues, such as economic rights at divorce or homemakers' rights to adequate Social Security, only detailed tinkering at the legislative level will yield substantive equality. Further, the grass roots mobilization necessary to elect women and create pressure for legislative reform may be key to many of the changes necessary for social equality.

The European approach—"gender mainstreaming" as it is called in the international community—is consistent with many important strands of feminist theory. An approach that focuses on using whatever means is necessary, including quotas, to ensure women's proportional share of governmental decisionmaking at all levels gives women themselves authority and allows women to determine how to integrate women's interests and needs into the public agenda, rather than relying on a Supreme Court imposing an abstract notion of formal equality.[129] This is a strategy *not* focused on men.[130] It recognizes both the conflict of interest between women and men, hence the need for women in elective office, and the fact that men are potential political allies.[131] It is consistent with feminist method, especially listening to

127. Canadian Advisory Council on the Status of Women, A Feminist Guide to the Canadian Constitution 56–57 (Lynn Smith and Eleanor Wachtel, Aug. 1992).

128. See, e.g., Ruth Bader Ginsburg and Barbara Flagg, Some Reflections on the Feminist Legal Thought of the 1970s, [1989] University of Chicago Legal Forum 9, 18 (extract in Chapter 3).

129. A number of feminists have stressed the importance of seeing women as active agents, rather than passive victims See, e.g., Angela P. Harris, Race and Essentialism in Feminist Legal Theory, 42 Stan. L. Rev. 581 (1990) (extract in Chapter 3); Martha Mahoney, Whiteness and Women, In Practice and Theory: A Reply to Catharine A. MacKinnon, 5 Yale J. L. & Feminism 211 (1993).

130. See Sarah Hoagland, Lesbian Ethics 57–58 (1988) .

131. See Harris, above note129.

women, since change will hopefully come more from the grass roots up than from the top down.[132] Indeed, in the context of sex, it is difficult to imagine effective social change coming from any other direction. Under this approach, we can stress not the universality of women's needs, which tends to be the focus in arguing to a court, but rather the need to form coalitions across race and class to address the varying needs of various women.[133]

We close with suggestions for a number of electoral reforms that would facilitate the representation of women of all colors and other minorities in numbers proportional to their presence in the population. Five types of changes are discussed here: (1) campaign reform, particularly campaign finance reform; (2) policies designed to maximize voter turnout; (3) votes for children, to be exercised by a parent or legal guardian until the child reaches 18; (4) some form of proportional representation for all elections other than the United States Senate; and (5) proportional representation for the Senate combined with a quota of 50% women (requiring a constitutional amendment).

1. Campaign reform, including reform of campaign financing. Campaigns in the United States are fantastically expensive relative to their cost in other democracies, in part because of the importance of media advertising and in part because they last so long. Compare, for example, campaigns in Great Britain, where there is a "long history of banning paid political advertising in the broadcast media" (though candidates and parties are allocated free broadcast time) and the formal period for national election campaigns is just over a month.[134] By the time a candidate wins in the United States, she is indebted to many special interests, regardless of what a majority of voters may want, and many points of view may be excluded due to the sheer incapacity to raise sufficient funds to compete.

In order to facilitate women's access to the political system, we need reform of campaigns themselves, requirements that campaigns be shorter, bans on advertisements in the broadcast media, free media time for candidates, and public financing of campaigns with stringent limits on monetary donations as well as on the ability of others, including political action committees, to spend money on behalf of candidates.

2. Maximizing voter turnout. In the 2000 presidential election, 53% of those eligible voted, a slight upturn from the 49% of voters who turned out for the 1996 presidential election.[135] In a recent mid-term Congressional election, only 37% voted. American voting rates are low relative to other countries today and low when compared to America in the past. In a pre–1996 comparison of voting rates in industrialized nations, the United States (at 53% of eligible adults voting) is nineteenth out of twenty (compare, for example, Belgium, where 94% of eligible adults vote; Austria 92%;

132. See Catharine A. MacKinnon, Consciousness Raising in Toward a Feminist Theory of the State 83 (1989) (extract in Chapter 3).

133. See Harris, above note 129, Mari Matsuda, Standing Beside ,My Sister, Facing the Enemy: Legal Theory Out of Coalition in Where Is Your Body? 63 (1996) (extract in Chapter 3).

134. Lisa E. Klein, On the Brink of Reform: Political Party Funding in Britain, 31 Case W. Res. J. Int'l L. 1, 2, 25 (1999).

135. Guinier, above note 120, at 253 (1996 election information); Associated Press, Wisconsin Ranks Third in Voter Turnout, Telegraph–Herald (Dubuque, IA), Nov. 12, 2000, at A9 (2000 election information).

Australia 90%; West Germany 87%; Italy 84%; United Kingdom 74%; Canada 72%).[136] Current participation rates are also low relative to earlier eras. Between 1840 and 1896, 78% of eligible American voters turned out to vote in presidential elections.[137] These non-participation rates surely suggest that our current political system is failing as a democracy in fundamental ways.

Although women now vote at higher rates than men, poor people (disproportionally women) and racial minorities (many of them women) are less likely than others to vote. Countries with higher voting rates usually have not just some system of proportional representation, so that all votes count and the poor are more likely to be able to vote for a candidate speaking to their interests, but also policies that foster voting. By contrast, the United States "is one of the few if not the only major democracy in the world that requires advance registration as a prerequisite to voting without the government assuming responsibility for seeing to it that all eligible people are registered."[138]

In addition to either eliminating the obligation to register in advance or making it easier to register near election day, voter participation would likely increase were elections rarer (for example, a maximum of one election day every two years, with *all* local and national elections on the same date) and on a holiday or Sunday with paid time-off for voters who work on those days. Voting might be made an obligation of citizenship. Both Belgium and Australia take this approach: citizens are *required* to vote. Belgium and Australia are two of the three top countries in terms of voter turnout of twenty industrialized democracies, though enforcement is lax and penalties light.[139]

3. Votes for children. In the United States, single-member election districts are drawn so that each district has roughly the same number of people. And it is people, not eligible voters, who are counted almost universally in districting schemes in the United States. Districts with many children or others ineligible to vote have, therefore, the same level of representation but fewer residents who can vote than districts with few such residents. Thus, in a district with many children or other people ineligible to vote, a vote counts for more. But voters who do not live in households with children often have interests that conflict with those of children and their caretakers. For example, those without children at home may be less interested in adequate funding of public education than parents with children at home.

As Jane Rutherford has argued, the basic problem with this scheme is vote dilution. The Supreme Court's one person, one vote rule (applicable in all elections except those to the Senate) is designed to guard against vote dilution which would occur were a state able to give more weight to some citizens' views than to others. Yet without proxies for parents, "that is precisely what happens to parents." [140] In the average congressional district, parents and children are 66% of the people in the district (and are all

136. Daniel Hays Lowenstein, Election Law: Cases and Materials 42 (1995).

137. Id.

138. Lowenstein, above note 136, at 48–49.

139. Id. at 33 n.2, 53.

140. Jane Rutherford, One Child, One Vote: Proxies for Parents, 82 Minn L Rev 1463, 1465, 1512 (1998).

counted for districting purposes, i.e., in allocating representatives per so many people in the population), but exercise only 54% percent of the votes.[141] People living in households without children comprise 34% of the population in the average congressional district but enjoy 46% of the votes. On a household basis, households without children have 140% "of the voting power of households with children."[142] And part of the voting power enjoyed by households without children is the result of living near households with children, though the interests of the households without children are likely to conflict with the needs of children.[143]

Rutherford points out that a household with two adults has the same amount of political weight—the same amount of representation—as a household with two adults and two children. In the first household, every member of the household has a vote. In the second household, half do not have votes. And the voters, if they are good parents, "will essentially split their votes ... so they represent their needs and the needs of their children." Giving parents proxies to vote for children redresses this problem, and evens out political weight on a per capita basis, the goal of the one person, one vote rule.[144]

Current poverty rates are the strongest indicator of the need for such an adjustment in political power. As Rutherford has pointed out, "fifty years ago it was the elderly who were poor."[145] Social Security and Medicare have eliminated most poverty among the elderly. Although these are expensive programs, they have survived because of the political power of the elderly. Today, it is disproportionally children (and their caretakers, particularly in single-mother families) who are poor. Children have no direct political power to use in pressing for effective governmental programs lowering their poverty rates. And their indirect power—through their parents—is diluted because it is folded into the parents' own vote. Yet, as discussed earlier in this chapter, children are a public good. We all benefit from having younger generations of taxpayers and workers, particularly as we age.

Votes for children (to be exercised by their custodial caretakers) are especially important to women because almost all mothers live with their children and must think about their needs and the needs of their children when they enter the voting booth. In addition, the children most likely to be poor are those living with single mothers who are also poor. Votes for children to be exercised by their custodians would give far more political clout to one of the poorest identifiable groups in our society, single mothers with children.

Although giving parents proxy votes for children is a novel idea and therefore seems strange, it may well be constitutional. There is no constitutional provision banning such an electoral structure and no constitutional

141. Id. at 1466.

142. Id. at 1512.

143. Id. at 1466, 1512, 1512 n.211.

144. Id. at 1512. Sylvia Ann Hewlett and Cornell West have also proposed proxy votes for children. Hewlett and West, The War Against Parents: What We Can Do For America's Beleaguered Moms and Dads 240–41 (1998).

145. Rutherford, above note 140, at 1465.

case definitively indicating that it would be impermissible. It is certainly consistent with one reading of the one person, one vote rule.[146]

4. Proportional representation for bodies other than the United States Senate. As noted earlier, winner-take-all systems with geographic districting *can* create effective democracies in countries with homogeneous populations.[147] Voters in this country have not been a homogeneous group for some time, and the results of using a system that works only for homogenous populations is clear from the data in Tables 6 through 9, above, showing the overwhelming overrepresentation of non-Hispanic white men in elective office, particularly at the highest levels. As Douglas Amy puts it in the opening line to his book on proportional representation, "[t]he American election system is unfair, outmoded, and undemocratic."[148] Yet few Americans "are even aware of these problems. * * * We assume that this system is the epitome of democracy and a model for the rest of the free world. But nothing could be further from the truth."[149]

Almost all younger democracies have some form of proportional representation. We inherited this archaic voting structure based on the notion that it is the land that should be represented from England.[150] And England today is reconsidering its use of single-member winner-take all districts. As noted earlier, there are many forms of proportional representation. And proportional representation schemes could be adopted without constitutional amendment for all elections other than those to the Senate. Cumulative voting in modified at-large schemes, described earlier, seems especially appropriate for the United States, since it would allow voters to continue to vote for individual candidates. Each voter would have as many votes as people to be elected but could cast all her votes for a single candidate, and each district would elect at least five representatives. As indicated earlier, under such a scheme, voters, not politicians, would determine what groups were being represented by whom.

Proportional and semiproportional representation schemes have a number of advantages:

1. Electoral systems based on proportional representation facilitate the representation of the entire population, particularly women of all colors and members of other minority groups.
2. Debates on policy issues can be substantively better when more options and interests are brought to the table.
3. Voters are more likely to vote when their vote counts and they have more options than two parties both trying to capture the middle.
4. Candidates are less likely to engage in negative campaigning and more likely to actually engage on issues, since they must maximize their own vote, not just defeat one specific opponent.
5. Because candidates can win election by expressing substantive views with which only a minority of voters agree, they are likely to talk

146. Id. at 1514–17.

147. Guinier, above note 120, at 256; Lijphart, above note 120, at 3–4.

148. Amy, above note 119, 1.

149. Id.

150. Lani Guinier, The Tyranny of the Majority: Fundamental Fairness in Representative Democracy 128 (1994).

about substantive issues rather than mouthing platitudes while projecting the right image.[151]

The standard concern with proportional and semiproportional representation systems is fear of balkanization and instability, i.e., a fear that there will many small parties, that extremist parties will therefore have a great deal of power as larger parties attempt to form coalition governments, and, as a result, that governments will collapse too often on a parliamentary vote of no confidence.[152] But proportional representation schemes can be structured to avoid this problem. Moreover, since the United States is not a parliamentary system, government will not fall because of shifting coalitions during a president's term.

Including a proportional representation component in an electoral scheme can actually stabilize a democracy. To the extent proportional representation encourages voter turnout, it is likely to contribute to stability: "democracies with lower voter turn-out levels have higher amounts of citizen turmoil and violence."[153] Hitler's rise to power has been attributed to the rapid political mobilization of a large group of new voters who had previously been disengaged.[154] Proportional representation can protect democracies from extremist takeovers by keeping more voters engaged in the political system.

In the 1990's, Cynthia McKinney, a former political science professor and a Democratic member of the U.S. House of Representatives, twice "introduced legislation to allow states to adopt proportional and semiproportional voting systems for congressional elections."[155] A proportional or semiproportional representation scheme could be designed for all legislative bodies at the state and federal level other than the United States Senate without constitutional modification.

For all legislative elections other than the Senate, we should therefore shift to a system of at-large cumulative voting in districts with at least five seats in order to realize the many benefits of proportional representation while retaining the ability to vote for specific candidates. Such a shift would not require any constitutional amendment and would greatly enhance American politics in all kinds of ways, including representation of caretakers, women, and minorities.

5. *Proportional representation for the Senate (requiring a constitutional amendment).* The Constitution requires two Senators, each with one vote, from each state. Currently, each Senator from each state is elected in a winner-take-all single-member-district election.

Without constitutional amendment, Senate elections could be reorganized to allow cumulative voting, though both Senators would be up for election at the same time. Each voter would have two votes and could cast one for each of two candidates or could cast both for a single candidate. Under such a scheme, each state would be a multi-member district of two with cumulative voting. Alternatively, the Constitution could be amended to

151. For a more thorough discussion of these and other advantages of proportional representation, see Amy, above note 119, at 1–152, Guinier, above note 120, at 251–311.

152. See id. at 157–60.

153. Guinier, above note 120, at 251.

154. Id. at 269.

155. Id. at 261.

provide for regional election of Senators with multi-member districts and cumulative voting (as opposed to the current constitutionally required form of representation: two Senators from each state).

A third, and more radical, option would require each state to send at least one woman to the Senate. Given the current constitutional standard for sex discrimination, this would violate the Equal Protection clause of the Fourteenth Amendment as interpreted by the Supreme Court and would therefore require a constitutional amendment. Mary Becker has proposed amending the Constitution with a new ERA:

> Section 1. Neither any state nor the federal government shall deprive any woman or man of life, liberty, or property, without due process of law; nor deny to any woman or man within its jurisdiction the equal protection of the laws.
>
> Section 2. Each state shall have at least one senator who is a woman. Congress shall, through appropriate legislation, establish laws to enforce this provision and may determine that it become effective only upon the retirement of male incumbents in the Senate.
>
> Section 3. Congress shall have the ultimate power to enforce this Amendment and to determine its scope and meaning.[156]

This amendment would both (1) require that one Senator from each state be a woman, and (2) give ultimate power to determine the meaning of sex equality to the United States Congress (with 50% women in its upper chamber) rather than to the United States Supreme Court.

Any of these three changes in the method of electing Senators is likely to increase the representation of currently underrepresented groups in the Senate as well as to broaden Senators' perspectives and ideas on substantive and policy issues. In addition, either of the two initial suggestions for change, both of which involve a form of proportional or semiproportional representation, could be combined with the ERA approach, requiring that at least half the Senate be comprised of women. Of the three, perhaps the best would be regional elections (cumulative voting for multi-member districts) with the ERA requirement of 50% women, since that combination seems likely to offer the greatest potential for changing the composition of the Senate in terms of race as well as sex. (In regional elections with cumulative voting, minorities would be more likely to be able to pool their votes to elect a minority Senator.) Given the current makeup of the Senate—recall that non-Hispanic white men are 87% of the Senate though only 35.11% of the population—the case for dramatic change in the way we elect Senators is particularly strong.

In addition, placing sex equality issues in the hands of a Congress with 50% women in its upper chamber will better protect women than judicial review by the United States Supreme Court, and will do so without dampening political movements for equality. Indeed, this approach will encourage political movements for equality, without binding Americans to any particular view of what equality between the sexes would look like.

156. Mary Becker, The Sixties Shift to Formal Equality and the Courts: An Argument for Pragmatism and Politics, 40 Wm. & Mary L. Rev. 209, 264 (1998).

Notes on Equality in Politics

1. The immediate problem is that even raising electoral reform for discussion in any popular forum seems impossible. Recall the furor over Lani Guinier's nomination early in the Clinton administration to head the Civil Rights Division of the Justice Department, a position requiring Senate confirmation. Guinier had advocated proportional representation as a remedy for some violations of the Voting Rights Act and had suggested that minorities might not always be treated fairly by the majority. For suggesting that American democracy might be flawed and that proportional or semiproportional representation—methods used in most of the world's democracies—might better integrate the views of those traditionally underrepresented, the Wall Street Journal castigated her as a "Quota Queen" and "out of the mainstream." Newsweek titled a story "Crowning a Quota Queen." Others used "Loony Lani," the "Czarina of Czeparatism," the "Princess of Proportionality," and "Real America's Madwoman." In the end, as a result of the media frenzy (and the administration's failure to launch any defense), Guinier's name was withdrawn by the President. Guinier, Lift Every Voice: Turning A Civil Rights Setback into A New Vision of Social Justice 36–56. (1998). Given this background, the initial problem with moving to a proportional or semiproportional representation system like those in place in most of the world is the difficulty of even raising the issue in the United States. Guinier did not in fact advocate quotas—only proportional representation. What would the reaction be to a proposal for quotas for women along the lines of parité in France?

2. In addition to the Voting Rights Act of 1965 (which has sometimes been interpreted by the Supreme Court as requiring racial balance as a remedy for violations), quotas do exist today in various forms in our governmental system and in the party structure. For example, the Federal Election Commission has six members, and no more than three are to be "affiliated with the same political party." 2 U.S.C.A. § 437c(a)(1). The Securities and Exchange Commission, 15 U.S.C.A. § 78d(a), the Federal Trade Commission, 15 U.S.C.A. § 41, and the Commodity Futures Trading Commission, 7 U.S.C.A. § 4a(a)(1), each consist of five members, no more than three to be "members of the same political party." Similar rules apply to the Board of Directors of the Federal Deposit Insurance Corporation, 12 U.S.C.A. § 1812(a)(2), and the Federal Housing Finance Board, 12 U.S.C.A. § 1422a(b)(2). Both major parties have National Committees consisting of one man and one woman from each state.

Several states have enacted gender balance legislation, providing that boards, commissions, committees, and councils of all kinds appointed by elected officials be gender balanced. Two states have enacted such legislation as binding law: North Dakota and Iowa. Iowa Code Ann. § 69.16A; N.D. Cent. Code § 54–06–19. Montana has a nonbinding gender balance resolution. Mont. Code Ann. § 2–15–108. Iowa has mandatory quotas for *elected* Judicial Nominating Commissioners, one man and one woman to be elected from each district. Iowa Code Ann. § 69.16A.

How would the case for quotas for women in elective office be similar to, and different from, the case for quotas in these settings? Are these quotas constitutional? Why or why not? See Bachur v. Democratic National Party, 836 F.2d 837 (4th Cir.1987) (holding constitutional Maryland rules implementing policies of the national party requiring voters to cast an equal number of votes for women and men as delegates to the Democratic convention). Would quotas for women be constitutional in light of Congress's power under the Nineteenth Amendment to enforce women's right to vote "by appropriate legislation"? U.S. Const. Amend. XIX (the same language as that used in the Fifteenth Amendment).

If you think that such quotas would be unconstitutional (recall that the Supreme Courts of Italy and Portugal struck gender quotas similar to France's as unconstitutional), is this another example of the conservative nature of binding judicial review? Constitutional law aside, what do you see as the major problems with quotas as a means of ensuring that women in elected office are proportional to the numbers of women in the population?

3. Should women begin by pressing for internal party quotas, such as the quota now in place in both parties with respect to membership on National Committees? European women in a number of countries, as noted above, have been quite successful in increasing levels of representation as a result of internal party quotas. Supporters of internal party quotas could publish lists of men in elected office who refused to support the internal quota, and women and other supporters of internal quotas could then vote against them at the next election. (Recall that this tactic was used in France with respect to elected officials' support of parité, the proposed law requiring that 50% of those elected be women). Would these tactics work here? Assume, as may well be true, that women will not achieve equality in any arena until they have first achieved political equality. What strategies would you adopt to achieve political equality in the United States?

4. Would you support Becker's proposed ERA? What do you like about it? What do you dislike about it?

5. How important would various feminist theorists described in Chapter 3 consider women's presence in elective office, and what means would they see as appropriate to this end? Consider these questions from the perspective of dominance feminism, formal equality feminism, hedonic feminism, socialist feminism, pragmatic feminism, postmodern feminism, critical race feminism, and lesbian feminism. How important do you consider the analysis of the political representation issue in your assessment of the overall strengths and weaknesses of these various feminist approaches? Does each feminist approach have strengths and weaknesses? What are they? Which has influenced most the way you look at the world or approach legal issues? Which do you expect to use in the future in thinking about how to resolve specific legal issues?

6. Are women focusing on political power just as real power shifts from governments to the huge multinational corporations? Are men in Europe allowing women into political power just when—as is often the case when women gain access—power shifts elsewhere? As one commentator on parité recently observed, "real power is no longer political. It's financial." Liane Hansen (anchor), Women From Around the World Look For Ways to Increase Their Numbers in Elected Positions and Leadership Roles, National Public Radio, Weekend Edition, June 11, 2000 (Jane Kramer, reporter for

The New Yorker, speaking). As of 1995, women held "only 6.2% of all ministerial positions world wide." According to Womankind Worldwide, a UK charity dedicated to women's development and women's human rights around the world, women hold 12% of seats in national legislatures worldwide, though in the least developed countries women's representation is as low as 8.5%. But women "hold only 1% of executive positions in the world's biggest international corporations." Womankind Worldwide, Gender Gap: Decisionmaking (available at <www.womankind.org.uk> visited 1/2/2001). How would you begin thinking about ensuring that women exercise their share of economic decisionmaking?

Index

References are to Pages. Italic type indicates quote or extract in text.

References are to Pages. Italic type indicates quote or extract in text.

References are to Pages. Italic type indicates quote or extract in text.

References are to Pages. Italic type indicates quote or extract in text.

References are to Pages. Italic type indicates quote or extract in text.

References are to Pages. Italic type indicates quote or extract in text.

References are to Pages. Italic type indicates quote or extract in text.

References are to Pages. Italic type indicates quote or extract in text.

References are to Pages. Italic type indicates quote or extract in text.

References are to Pages. Italic type indicates quote or extract in text.

References are to Pages. Italic type indicates quote or extract in text.

References are to Pages. Italic type indicates quote or extract in text.

References are to Pages. Italic type indicates quote or extract in text.

0-314-24110-8
90000
9 780314 241108

Civil Engineering and

Engineering Mechanics Series

N. M. Newmark and W. J. Hall, Editors

PRENTICE-HALL INTERNATIONAL, INC., *London*
PRENTICE-HALL OF AUSTRALIA, PTY. LTD., *Sydney*
PRENTICE-HALL OF CANADA, LTD., *Toronto*
PRENTICE-HALL OF INDIA PRIVATE LIMITED, *New Delhi*
PRENTICE-HALL OF JAPAN, INC., *Tokyo*

COMPUTER METHODS

PRENTICE-HALL, INC.
Englewood Cliffs, New Jersey

OF STRUCTURAL

ANALYSIS

FRED W. BEAUFAIT
Associate Professor of Civil Engineering
Vanderbilt University

WILLIAM H. ROWAN, JR.
Associate Professor of Information Engineering
Vanderbilt University

PETER G. HOADLEY
Professor of Civil Engineering
Vanderbilt University

ROBERT M. HACKETT
Assistant Professor of Civil Engineering
Vanderbilt University

COMPUTER METHODS OF STRUCTURAL ANALYSIS

Beaufait/Rowan/Hoadley/Hackett

Englewood Cliffs, N.J.

Current printing (last digit):
10 9 8 7 6 5 4 3 2 1

13–165951–0
Library of Congress Catalog Card No. 74–107394

Printed in the United States of America

To

THE SCHOOL OF ENGINEERING

Vanderbilt University
Nashville, Tennessee

PREFACE

This text is designed as a teaching tool to be used in an advanced undergraduate professional course or a first-year graduate course and as a reference book for the practicing structural engineer. The book has been developed from lecture material prepared by the authors for a short course series offered to practicing structural engineers for the past several summers and for a graduate–undergraduate elective course in the Civil Engineering Department. The use of this material proved highly successful in both applications and this fact encouraged the authors to prepare the material for textbook presentation.

The authors have tried to make the book a self-teaching text so that the lecturer need not repeat the material presented but might be free to expand upon this material. In order for the text to serve its intended purpose, the student must be aware of his responsibility *to read and study each sentence with care and to scrutinize each example problem.*

Subject. This text is concerned with the linear, elastic analysis of structural systems, i.e., the evaluation of actions and displacements produced by the application of specific distrubances. The particular structural systems to be studied are those that are composed of elements which transfer the support of loads in only one direction, i.e., beam elements. This type of system is referred to as a framed structure. Included in this category are continuous beams, planar frames, space frames, grids, planar trusses and space trusses.

With the electronic, digital computer available to perform routine computations, it is important that the engineer be familiar with the techniques which are best suited for computer operations whether he is developing his own computer programs or using commercial programs to solve his problems. Thus, this text is concerned with the development of methods of structural analysis which are suited to regimented computer procedures. The two fundamental approaches to the analysis of an indeterminate structural system, i.e., the flexibility method and the stiffness method, are developed and formulated for computer usage. However, emphasis is given to the stiffness method, the approach which is considered to be best suited for computer programming.

Prerequisites. Before undertaking the study of the material in this text, the student should have a working knowledge of basic structural mechanics and mechanics of materials. Although it is not absolutely necessary, it is desirable for the student to have had a prior introduction to the analysis of indeterminate framed structures. The student must have some knowledge of elementary calculus and differential equations before studying the advanced topics presented in Chapters 8 and 9. Also, he should be familiar with at least one computer programming language, preferably FORTRAN IV, before studying Chapters 10, 11, 12 and 13. These chapters are concerned with the development of computer programs for analyzing structural systems.

Elementary matrix algebra is used throughout the text in developing the methods of analysis for use with a digital computer; consequently, the student must be familiar with this subject before undertaking the study of structural analysis. For those students who are not familiar with elementary matrix algebra or who need some review of the subject, the various topics from matrix algebra that are prerequisites to this text are presented in Appendix A.

Outline. As the title implies, the text is concerned with methods of structural analysis that are suited for use with the digital computer. Chapters 1 through 9 are concerned with the development of the mathematical tools and theory for analyzing the framed structural systems. Chapters 10 through 13 are concerned with the development of computer programs to perform the analysis of structural systems.

Chapter 1 develops the fundamental concepts of the two basic methods of analysis, i.e., the flexibility and stiffness methods. It affords the student a brief look at the complete process of analyzing a simple indeterminate structure by the two methods before a more detailed development of these methods is undertaken. A comparison is made of the two fundamental methods in order to demonstrate the greater potential of the stiffness method for computer application.

Chapter 2 introduces the student to several techniques for solving simultaneous equations. The material presented in this chapter is not intended to be an in-depth study of mathematical theories; it is designed to equip the student with the necessary mathematical tools for analyzing structural systems. The various topics that are discussed are directly applicable to computer usage.

Chapter 3 develops the basic concepts of the flexibility method for analyzing the planar, indeterminate framed structure. The method is presented from an elementary point of view to re-acquaint the student with, or if necessary introduce him to, the coupling of the equations of equilibrium and of compatibility. Since the flexibility method does not lend itself very well to computer programming, the method is not studied in depth.

Chapter 4 establishes the basic equations for analyzing the framed structure in matrix form and discusses the process for developing the various matrices for the analysis of planar, orthogonal structures. The member stiffness matrix is defined for a typical beam element of a planar, orthogonal frame considering only flexural deformation. The flexibility method of analysis is used as a tool for evaluating the required matrices for both prismatic and nonprismatic beam elements.

Chapter 5 extends the concepts of the stiffness method of analysis developed in Chapter 4 to the analysis of planar, nonorthogonal structural systems. The member stiffness matrix is redefined for the typical beam element of a planar frame to consider axial deformations, as well as flexural deformations. In addition, the various matrices required in a stiffness analysis are developed for several different types of beam elements.

Chapter 6 expands the development of the stiffness method to the analysis of three-dimensional (space) structures. The several matrices required to describe the behavior of a beam element are developed for the typical member of a rigid space frame, a space truss and a grid system.

Chapter 7 is concerned with the analysis of large structural systems by subdividing a structure into regions or substructures. Also, the evaluation of the member stiffness matrix and the fixed end actions for a beam element using the concepts of substructures is discussed.

Chapter 8 extends the stiffness method to include consideration of the effect of axial loads upon the flexural behavior of planar frames and for determining the critical values of applied axial loads based upon the elastic stability of planar, structural systems.

Chapter 9 introduces the use of energy concepts in the development of the stiffness equations. The principle of stationary potential energy is introduced and used to develop the member stiffness matrix for a beam element and the structure stiffness matrix for complete structural systems.

Chapter 10 discusses the philosophy of developing stiffness analysis computer programs to analyze structural systems. The idea of developing a banded structure stiffness matrix and its advantages are considered. Techniques for developing efficient programs are explored.

Chapters 11, 12 and 13 describe computer programs developed in FORTRAN IV for the analysis of planar, orthogonal frames; general planar, nonorthogonal systems; and general space structures, respectively. These programs are written so that they can be used on most electronic, digital computer systems with only minor modifications. The programs are thoroughly documented so that they can be modified by the user to meet his needs. A complete listing of the programs is given in Appendices C, D and E.

The authors are of the opinion that Chapters 1 through 6 contain the essential material to be covered in an undergraduate course. Although Chapters 7, 8 and 9 have been written for an undergraduate course, the material in these chapters may be found to be more appropriate for a first-year graduate course along with Chapters 10 through 13. However, the material in any one of the Chapters 7 through 13 can be used with Chapters 1 through 6 in an undergraduate course.

Acknowledgments. The authors wish to express their sincere appreciation to

Dr. Horace E. Williams, Associate Professor of Engineering Mathematics, Vanderbilt University, for his development of the material presented in Chapter 2 and his assistance in preparing Appendix A; and to Mr. Jack R. Horner, M.S. candidate, Department of Civil Engineering, Vanderbilt University, for his help in developing the computer programs discussed in Chapters 11, 12 and 13. The authors also wish to thank Mrs. Evelyn Faw for the typing of the many drafts and final copy of this text.

CONTENTS

4
STIFFNESS METHOD OF ANALYSIS: PLANAR ORTHOGONAL STRUCTURES 78

5
STIFFNESS METHOD OF ANALYSIS: PLANAR NONORTHOGONAL STRUCTURES 143

6
STIFFNESS METHOD OF ANALYSIS: THREE-DIMENSIONAL STRUCTURES 218

7
ANALYSIS OF STRUCTURAL SYSTEMS USING SUBSTRUCTURES 296

12
PLANAR FRAME AND TRUSS PROGRAM 448

13
SPACE FRAME AND TRUSS PROGRAM 465

Appendix A
MATRIX ALGEBRA AND DETERMINANTS 478

Appendix B
STABILITY AND LOAD FUNCTIONS 491

Appendix C
PLANAR ORTHOGONAL FRAME PROGRAM 495

1 CONCEPTS OF INDETERMINATE STRUCTURAL ANALYSIS

1–1 Introduction

In undertaking the mathematical analysis of any physical system, it is first necessary to formulate an *idealized mathematical model* of the system. Many structural systems may be quite adequately represented by models which can be solved by application of the equations of static equilibrium, i.e., a ***statically determinate structural model.*** However, in order to accurately represent a vast number of structural systems having numerous constraints, it is necessary to formulate a mathematical model which is too restrained to be solved by the equations of statics alone, i.e., a ***statically indeterminate structural model.***

The numerous techniques for accomplishing an elastic analysis of a model of an indeterminate structural system can be grouped into two basic methods: (1) the ***flexibility method,*** where *actions* (shear forces, axial forces, and bending moments) are taken as the unknown quantities in the formulation of the analysis; and (2) the ***stiffness method,*** which considers *displacements* (translations and rotations) to be the unknown quantities. In analyzing the indeterminate structure, whether using the flexibility or stiffness approach, a set of independent, simultaneous equations must be established in terms of the unknown quantities (*actions* or *displacements*) and solved.

The methods of analysis are developed on the basic assumption that a linear relationship exists between applied loads and resulting displacements of the structure so that the principle of superposition is valid. Consequently, the material of the structure must obey Hooke's law, i.e., stress is proportional to strain, and must not be stressed beyond its elastic limit. This basic assumption also implies that the equations of equilibrium may be developed using the geometry of the undeflected structural model, thereby assuming that the change in geometry due to imposed deformations is negligible when compared with the original geometry of the model.

1–2
Indeterminacy

Associated with the two basic methods of analysis are two types of indeterminacy that may be used to describe a structural system: (1) ***static indeterminacy***, and (2) ***kinematic indeterminacy***. Static indeterminacy refers to the number of *actions* (shear forces, axial forces, and bending moments), external and/or internal, that must be released in order to transform a structural system into a *stable*, *statically determinate system*, i.e., one that can be analyzed by considering the available independent equations of equilibrium and equations of conditions resulting from special construction features. The degree of statical indeterminacy of a system, *defined as the number of released actions*, specifies the number of special independent equations that must be developed in terms of the released actions in order to analyze the system by the flexibility approach. These equations are developed with the idea of restoring the continuity of the structural system which was removed when the system was reduced to a statically determinate structure.

The second type of indeterminacy of a structural system, kinematic indeterminacy, refers to the number of *independent components of joint displacement* (translations and rotations), with respect to a specified set of coordinate axes, that are required to describe the response of the system when subjected to an arbitrary loading condition. The structure must be artificially restrained in order to convert the system into a *kinematically determinate structure*, i.e., a structure with all joint displacements restrained. The degree of kinematic indeterminacy, defined as *the number of unrestrained components of joint displacement*, specifies the number of special, independent equations that must be written in terms of the unrestrained components of joint displacement if the system is to be analyzed by the stiffness method. These equations are developed on the idea of establishing equilibrium of the individual joints of the structure when the artificial joint constraints are released.

Examples illustrating the degree of static and kinematic indeterminacy of various structural systems are given in Fig. 1-1. Consider, for instance, the structure of Fig. 1-1(b). Since there are five components of unknown support reaction and only three applicable equations of statics, two support reactions must be released in order to reduce the system to a statically determinate structure, hence the system is statically indeterminate to the second degree. In contrast to this, the system is kinematically indeterminate to the fourth degree due to the fact that there are four components of unrestrained joint displacement, neglecting axial deformation of the individual members.

It is important to realize that the degrees of static and kinematic indeter-

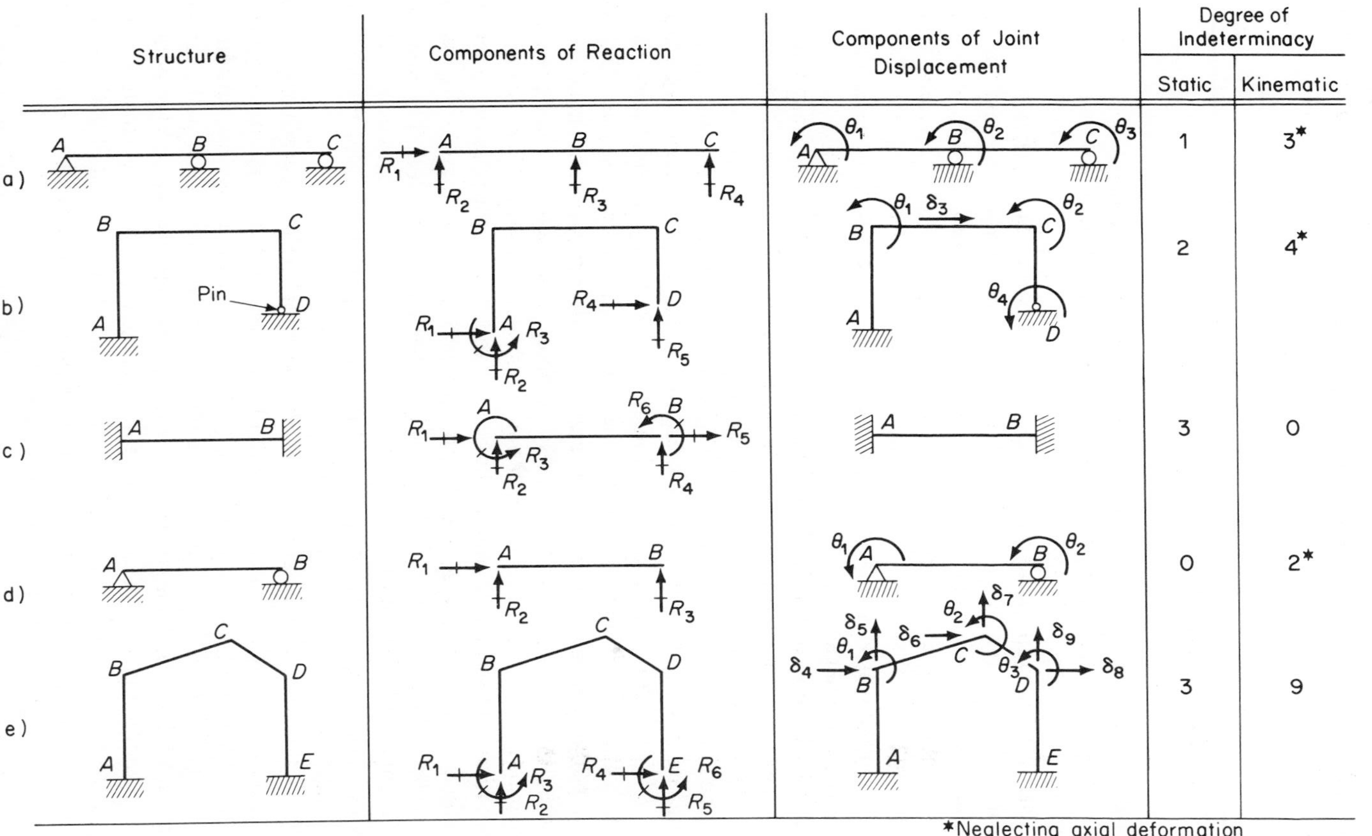

Fig. 1-1 Examples of indeterminacy.

minacy of a structural system are convenient indicators of the amount of computational effort that will be required to analyze the system by either the flexibility or stiffness method.

1–3
The Flexibility Method of Analysis

To illustrate the basic concepts of the flexibility method of analyzing an indeterminate structural system, consider the analysis of the two-span continuous beam of Fig. 1-2(a).

The initial step in the analysis of any system is to clearly define the model in terms of geometry, boundary conditions, material properties, and loading. The continuous beam of Fig. 1-2(a) has two spans of length L_1 and L_2 with roller supports at joints 1 and 2 and a fixed support at joint 3. The elements of this system may have either a variable or constant moment of inertia over their length, and the modulus of elasticity may vary within the system. A general loading of the structure is indicated.

The application of the flexibility method in analyzing an indeterminate structure requires that the structure first be reduced to a *stable, statically determinate system*. Hence, the degree of static indeterminacy of the given structure must be established and a corresponding number of actions released to create the statically determinate model, i.e., the ***released structure***. Referring to the continuous beam shown in Fig. 1-2(a), the structure is found to be statically indeterminate to the second degree, since there are five components of support reaction as identified in Fig. 1-2(b) that must be evaluated and only three independent equations of equilibrium to be utilized. Therefore, two components of action must be released in order to establish the statically determinate model. Although there are several combinations of two actions that might be removed to form the released structure, the actions A_1 and A_2 are selected as the redundant actions for this discussion. The resulting statically determinate model is shown in Fig. 1-2(c). The problem now becomes one of establishing a set of independent, simultaneous equations in terms of the redundant actions so that they may be evaluated and the analysis of the indeterminate system completed.

When the released structure is subjected to the applied loads, it will experience deformations that are not consistent with the behavior of the actual indeterminate system. However, by applying forces equal to the released actions, the deformations of the released structure are made consistent with those of the actual system. In analyzing the released structure, the displacement at the point of application and along the line of action of each redundant must be evaluated. With reference to the structure of Fig. 1-2(c), the displacement of points 1 and 2 in the released structure due to the applied loading condition are defined as δ_{10} and δ_{20}, respectively, as indicated in Fig. 1-2(d).

Although the magnitude and direction of the redundant actions are unknown

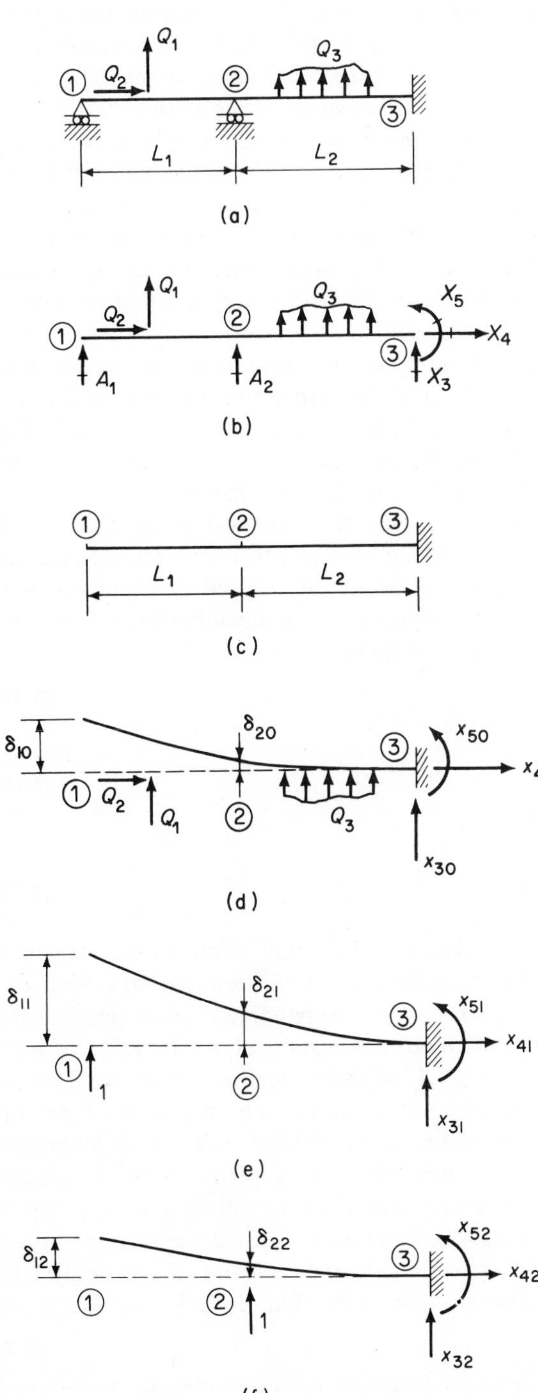

Fig. 1-2 Illustration of flexibility method of analysis: (a) the structure; (b) identification of reactions; (c) released structure; (d) displacements due to applied loads—released structure; (e) displacements due to unit of A_1—released structure; (f) displacements due to unit of A_2—released structure. *Note:* All actions and displacements are shown in an assumed positive sense.

at this stage in the analysis, the released structure can be analyzed for the application of an assumed unit value of each redundant, individually. For each case the displacement of the points of application of the redundants, along the line of action of the redundants, must be evaluated. Finally, considering the displacements of the released structure at the points of application of the redundant actions due to both the applied loading condition and the individual unit values of redundants, a set of independent, simultaneous equations can be written to describe the actual known displacement of the original indeterminate structure at each point of redundant application. Solving these equations, the magnitude and direction of each redundant required to develop the continuity of the system can be determined. For the continuous beam under discussion, the displacement of points 1 and 2 due to the application of a unit value of A_1 are identified in Fig. 1-2(e) as δ_{11} and δ_{21}, respectively, and the displacement of points 1 and 2 due to the application of a unit value of the redundant A_2 are identified in Fig. 1-2(f) as δ_{12} and δ_{22}, respectively. Now, a linear function of the two cases described in Figs. 1-2(e) and (f) can be combined with the case described in Fig. 1-2(d) so that the resulting deformation of the released structure will match that of the original indeterminate structure. Considering that points 1 and 2 are restrained against displacement along the line of action of the respective redundant—i.e., δ_{s1} and δ_{s2} are each equal to zero—the equations of compatibility which govern the superposition of the three cases are written as

$$\delta_{10} + \delta_{11}A_1 + \delta_{12}A_2 = \delta_{s1} = 0 \tag{1-1a}$$

and

$$\delta_{20} + \delta_{21}A_1 + \delta_{22}A_2 = \delta_{s2} = 0 \tag{1-1b}$$

which can be written in matrix form as

$$\begin{bmatrix} \delta_{10} \\ \delta_{20} \end{bmatrix} + \begin{bmatrix} \delta_{11} & \delta_{12} \\ \delta_{21} & \delta_{22} \end{bmatrix} \begin{bmatrix} A_1 \\ A_2 \end{bmatrix} = \begin{bmatrix} 0 \\ 0 \end{bmatrix} \tag{1-1c}$$

These equations state that the displacements of the actual indeterminate structure, δ_{si}, are equal to the corresponding displacements of the released structure, δ_{i0}, due to the imposed load condition, plus the corresponding displacements of the released structure, δ_{ij}, due to the individual application of a unit value of each redundant times the required magnitude A_j of the respective redundant. This set of equations can be solved for the unknown quantities, i.e., the *released actions*.

Once the redundants have been evaluated, any desired action or displacement of the indeterminate structure may be determined by superimposing the actions and displacements of the released structure caused by the imposed loading condition and the corresponding actions and displacements resulting from the individual application of each of the redundants to the released structure. For example, the support reaction X_5 of the indeterminate structure [Fig. 1-2(a)] is calculated as

$$X_5 = x_{50} + x_{51}A_1 + x_{52}A_2 \tag{1-2}$$

where x_{50} is the reaction of the released structure corresponding to the support reaction X_5 due to applied loads, x_{51} is the reaction of the released structure corresponding to the support reaction X_5 due to a unit of released action A_1, and x_{52} is the reaction of the released structure corresponding to the support reaction X_5 due to a unit of the released action A_2.

1–4 The Stiffness Method of Analysis

Now, consider the analysis of the continuous beam of Fig. 1-2(a) by the stiffness method. For convenience, the structure is shown again in Fig. 1-3(a). As stated before, the first step in the analysis is to clearly define the structural model with respect to geometry, boundary conditions, material properties, and loading.

The application of the stiffness method in analyzing an indeterminate structure requires that the structure first be reduced to a *kinematically determinate system*. Hence, the components of joint displacement of the structure which are unrestrained by external conditions must be identified, thus establishing the degree of kinematic indeterminacy, and a corresponding number of artificial restraints

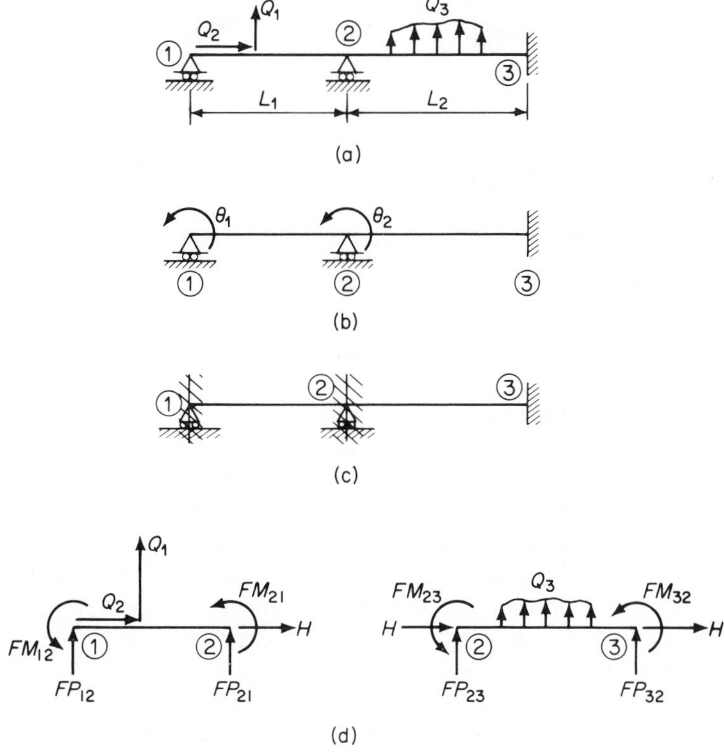

Fig. 1-3 Illustration of stiffness method of analysis: (a) the structure; (b) identification of unrestrained displacements; (c) restrained structure; (d) fixed end actions.

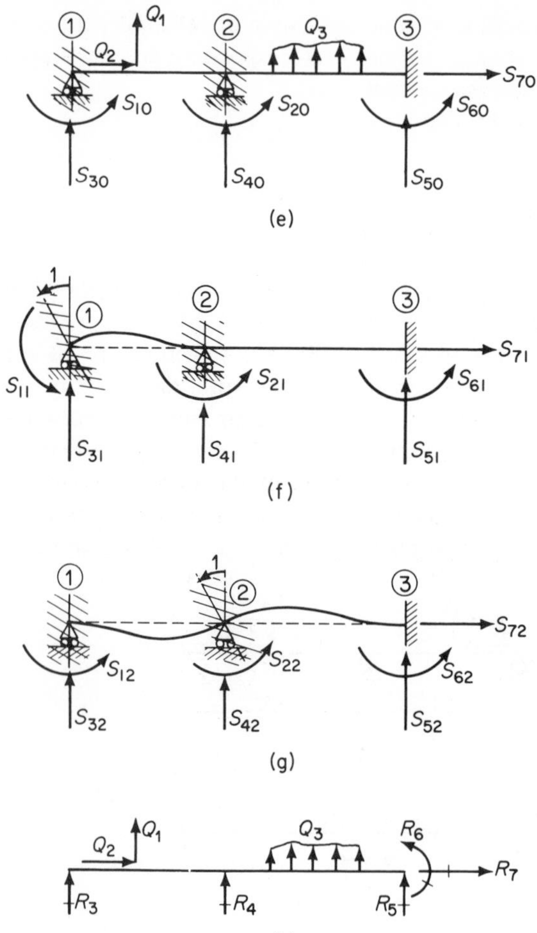

Fig. 1-3—*Cont.* (e) Reactions due to applied loads—restrained structure; (f) reactions due to unit of θ_1—restrained structure; (g) reactions due to unit of θ_2—restrained structure; (h) structure reactions. *Note:* All actions and displacements are shown in an assumed positive sense.

must be applied to the structure in order to constrain these displacements, thus creating the kinematically determinate system, i.e., the ***restrained structure***. The continuous beam of Fig. 1-3(a) is kinematically indeterminate to the second degree. There are two components of unrestrained joint displacement when neglecting axial deformations, i.e., the rotation of joints 1 and 2. These displacements are to be constrained by artificial restraints. The unrestrained components of joint displacement are identified in Fig. 1-3(b) and the restrained structure is shown in Fig. 1-3(c). In the restrained structure, joints 1 and 2 are constrained against vertical translation as well as rotation, and joint 3 is constrained against both vertical and horizontal translation and rotation.

Having defined the restrained structure, it must be analyzed for the loading condition that is imposed on the indeterminate system. The support reactions of the restrained structure for any given loading condition are simply the actions required to constrain the various joint displacements. At each joint each restraining reaction is equal the sum of (a) the corresponding *fixed end member actions* which are required to constrain the ends of the members that frame into the joint against displacements due to loads applied directly to the members, and (b) the corresponding *action equal and opposite to a similar action applied directly to the joint.* Referring to the structure under discussion, the fixed end actions resulting from the applied loads are shown in Fig. 1-3(d) in an assumed positive sense. With no applied joint loads, the support reactions of the restrained structure, identified in Fig. 1-3(e), are evaluated as follows:

At joint 1

$$S_{10} = FM_{12} \tag{1-3a}$$

and

$$S_{30} = FP_{12} \tag{1-3b}$$

At joint 2

$$S_{20} = FM_{21} + FM_{23} \tag{1-3c}$$

and

$$S_{40} = FP_{21} + FP_{23} \tag{1-3d}$$

At joint 3

$$S_{50} = FP_{32} \tag{1-3e}$$

$$S_{60} = FM_{32} \tag{1-3f}$$

and

$$S_{70} = H \tag{1-3g}$$

It should be recalled that the axial deformations of the members have been neglected and that only joint 3 has been restrained against any horizontal displacement; therefore, there is only the one component of horizontal support reaction, S_{70}, for the restrained structure and it must resist all components of horizontal force.

In addition to analyzing the restrained structure for the actual loading condition, it must also be analyzed for displacement of the artificially restrained joints. Since the required magnitude and direction of displacement of the unrestrained joints are unknown, it is convenient to analyze the restrained structure for the individual application of an assumed unit value of each of the artificially restrained joint displacements. Then, based on the fact that the artificial restraining support reactions do not exist in the actual indeterminate system, a set of independent, simultaneous equations can be written in terms of the unknown joint displacements. This set of equations expresses the summation of the support reactions of the restrained structure, corresponding to the artificially restrained joint displacements, developed by the actual loading condition and the individual displacement of the joints. By solving this set of equations, the magnitude and direction of the unrestrained joint displacements of the indeterminate system can be evaluated. With regard to the structure being discussed, the support reactions developed by the application of a unit value of the artificially restrained joint rotation of joint 1 (θ_1) to the restrained structure are identified in the assumed positive sense in Fig. 1-3(f). The support reactions developed by the application of a unit value of the artificially restrained joint rotation of joint 2 (θ_2) to the restrained structure are shown in Fig. 1-3(g) in their assumed positive sense. A linear function of the two cases described in Figs. 1-3(f) and (g) can be combined with the case described in Fig. 1-3(e) so that the artificial restraining actions vanish, i.e.,

$$S_{10} + S_{11}\theta_1 + S_{12}\theta_2 = 0 \tag{1-4a}$$

and

$$S_{20} + S_{21}\theta_1 + S_{22}\theta_2 = 0 \tag{1-4b}$$

These two equations can be written in matrix form as

$$\begin{bmatrix} S_{10} \\ S_{20} \end{bmatrix} + \begin{bmatrix} S_{11} & S_{12} \\ S_{21} & S_{22} \end{bmatrix} \begin{bmatrix} \theta_1 \\ \theta_2 \end{bmatrix} = \begin{bmatrix} 0 \\ 0 \end{bmatrix} \tag{1-4c}$$

or, from Eqs. (1-3a) and (1-3c),

$$\begin{bmatrix} S_{11} & S_{12} \\ S_{21} & S_{22} \end{bmatrix} \begin{bmatrix} \theta_1 \\ \theta_2 \end{bmatrix} = \begin{bmatrix} -FM_{12} \\ -(FM_{21} + FM_{23}) \end{bmatrix} \tag{1-4d}$$

These equations state that for each component of unrestrained joint displacement, θ_m, of the original indeterminate structure the sum of (a) the corresponding artificial constraining action S_{m0} required to maintain the restrained structure under the action of the given loading condition and (b) the corresponding constraining actions $S_{mn}\theta_n$ that are developed when subjecting the restrained structure to the individual joint displacements θ_n is equal to zero. This set of equations can be solved for the unknown joint displacements.

Once the magnitude and direction of the unrestrained joint displacements have been established, any other action or displacement of the original indeterminate system can be evaluated by superimposing the corresponding action or displacement of the restrained structure induced by the actual loading condition and by the displacement of the artificially restrained joints. For example, the final support reaction R_3, identified in Fig. 1-3(h), is equal to

$$R_3 = S_{30} + S_{31}\theta_1 + S_{32}\theta_2 \tag{1-5}$$

where S_{30} is the support reaction of the restrained structure corresponding to R_3 developed by applied loads, S_{31} is the corresponding support reaction of the restrained structure caused by the application of a unit value of θ_1, and S_{32} is the corresponding support reaction of the restrained structure resulting from the application of a unit value of θ_2.

1–5 Choice of Method of Analysis

The procedures for the analysis of an indeterminate structural system by the two basic methods reveal that there is very little difference in the fundamental philosophy of the two approaches. For this reason, the choice of one approach over the other is primarily a matter of computational convenience. With the flexibility method, there are several alternatives as to redundants, and the choice of redundants has a significant effect on the nature and amount of computational effort required. With the stiffness method, there is no question about the selection of the unknown quantities, since there is only one possible restrained structure; thus this method of analysis follows a rather set procedure. There are naturally certain advantages and disadvantages to both approaches, and when carrying out the analysis by hand computations, the method requiring the least amount of effort would certainly be selected. However, if an electronic digital computer is to be used to execute the analysis, the manner in which the required set of equations is formulated becomes the important factor in selecting the method of analysis. To have an effective computer program, the computations required to develop the equations for the analysis should not be peculiar to a particular geometry so that the analysis of each structure becomes a unique operation; the computations should also be repetitive in nature. When programming the computer, the method of analysis should require as few man-decisions as possible and should be general in application. This text, which is concerned with the application of the electronic digital computer in analyzing indeterminate structural systems, will therefore emphasize the development and application of the method of analysis best suited for use with the computer, i.e., the ***stiffness method***.

2 SOLUTION OF SYSTEMS OF LINEAR EQUATIONS

A knowledge of several efficient and accurate methods for solving the systems of linear equations that are generated in the analysis of a structural system, along with an understanding of the underlying concepts, is necessary before studying the subsequent chapters of this book. This chapter† discusses those properties of matrices which are particularly useful in analyzing systems of linear equations, and develops several efficient algorithms for solving such systems. An ***algorithm*** is defined as a systematic procedure for performing a certain mathematical operation. It is assumed that the student is familiar with the basic definitions and theorems of matrix algebra. Readers not familiar with these basics are referred to Appendix A.

2–1 Matrix Equations

A system of m linear equations in n unknowns

$$\begin{aligned} a_{11}x_1 + a_{12}x_2 + \cdots + a_{1n}x_n &= b_1 \\ a_{21}x_1 + a_{22}x_2 + \cdots + a_{2n}x_n &= b_2 \\ &\vdots \\ a_{m1}x_1 + a_{m2}x_2 + \cdots + a_{mn}x_n &= b_m \end{aligned} \tag{2-1a}$$

may be written as a matrix equation in the following manner:

$$\begin{bmatrix} a_{11} & a_{12} & \cdots & a_{1n} \\ a_{21} & a_{22} & \cdots & a_{2n} \\ \vdots & & & \\ a_{m1} & a_{m2} & \cdots & a_{mn} \end{bmatrix} \begin{bmatrix} x_1 \\ x_2 \\ \vdots \\ x_n \end{bmatrix} = \begin{bmatrix} b_1 \\ b_2 \\ \vdots \\ b_m \end{bmatrix} \tag{2-1b}$$

†This chapter was written by Dr. Horace E. Williams, Associate Professor of Engineering Mathematics, Vanderbilt University, Nashville, Tennessee.

Equation (2-1b) may in turn be expressed in shorthand notation as

$$[\mathbf{A}][\mathbf{X}] = [\mathbf{B}] \tag{2-1c}$$

where

$$[\mathbf{A}] = \begin{bmatrix} a_{11} & a_{12} & \cdots & a_{1n} \\ a_{21} & a_{22} & \cdots & a_{2n} \\ \vdots & & & \\ a_{m1} & a_{m2} & \cdots & a_{mn} \end{bmatrix} \tag{2-1d}$$

$$[\mathbf{X}] = \begin{bmatrix} x_1 \\ x_2 \\ \vdots \\ x_n \end{bmatrix} \tag{2-1e}$$

and

$$[\mathbf{B}] = \begin{bmatrix} b_1 \\ b_2 \\ \vdots \\ b_m \end{bmatrix} \tag{2-1f}$$

The notation of Eqs. (2-1c), (2-1d), (2-1e), and (2-1f) will be used throughout this chapter.

2–2 Solution of Systems of Linear Equations by Matrix Inversion

A system of linear equations may be solved using the inverse of the coefficient matrix if it exists.† Given the set of linear equations

$$[\mathbf{A}][\mathbf{X}] = [\mathbf{B}] \tag{2-2a}$$

premultiply both sides of the equation by $[\mathbf{A}]^{-1}$, yielding

$$[\mathbf{A}]^{-1}([\mathbf{A}][\mathbf{X}]) = [\mathbf{A}]^{-1}[\mathbf{B}] \tag{2-2b}$$

or

$$([\mathbf{A}]^{-1}[\mathbf{A}])[\mathbf{X}] = [\mathbf{A}]^{-1}[\mathbf{B}] \tag{2-2c}$$

then

$$[\mathbf{I}][\mathbf{X}] = [\mathbf{A}]^{-1}[\mathbf{B}] \tag{2-2d}$$

and

$$[\mathbf{X}] = [\mathbf{A}]^{-1}[\mathbf{B}] \tag{2-2e}$$

---

†See Sec. A-7 for the definition of the inverse of a matrix.

It is thus apparent that systems of linear equations may be solved by using the *inverse* of the coefficient matrix [A] if it exists. Algorithms for finding the inverse of a matrix will be developed in the two succeeding sections.

2-2.1 Adjoint Method of Computing Inverse Matrices

The matrix formed from a given square matrix [A] by replacing each element a_{ij} of [A] by its cofactor† α_{ij} is called the *matrix of cofactors* of matrix [A]. The transpose of this matrix is called the ***adjoint matrix*** of matrix [A], which will be denoted by adj[A], i.e.,

$$\text{adj}[\mathbf{A}] = \begin{bmatrix} \alpha_{11} & \alpha_{21} & \cdots & \alpha_{n1} \\ \alpha_{12} & \alpha_{22} & \cdots & \alpha_{n2} \\ \vdots & \vdots & & \vdots \\ \alpha_{1n} & \alpha_{2n} & \cdots & \alpha_{nn} \end{bmatrix} \tag{2-3}$$

If each element of the adjoint matrix is divided by $|A|$, i.e., the determinant‡ of the matrix [A], the resulting matrix is $[\mathbf{A}]^{-1}$. Obviously if $|A| = 0$, the inverse does not exist. By the adjoint method, then,

$$[\mathbf{A}]^{-1} = \begin{bmatrix} \frac{\alpha_{11}}{|A|} & \frac{\alpha_{21}}{|A|} & \cdots & \frac{\alpha_{n1}}{|A|} \\ \frac{\alpha_{12}}{|A|} & \frac{\alpha_{22}}{|A|} & \cdots & \frac{\alpha_{n2}}{|A|} \\ \vdots & \vdots & & \vdots \\ \frac{\alpha_{1n}}{|A|} & \frac{\alpha_{2n}}{|A|} & \cdots & \frac{\alpha_{nn}}{|A|} \end{bmatrix} \tag{2-4}$$

To prove that the matrix of Expression (2-4) is in fact the required inverse, develop the product $[\mathbf{A}][\mathbf{A}]^{-1}$:

$$\begin{bmatrix} a_{11} & a_{12} & \cdots & a_{1n} \\ a_{21} & a_{22} & \cdots & a_{2n} \\ \vdots & \vdots & & \vdots \\ a_{n1} & a_{n2} & \cdots & a_{nn} \end{bmatrix} \begin{bmatrix} \frac{\alpha_{11}}{|A|} & \frac{\alpha_{21}}{|A|} & \cdots & \frac{\alpha_{n1}}{|A|} \\ \frac{\alpha_{12}}{|A|} & \frac{\alpha_{22}}{|A|} & \cdots & \frac{\alpha_{n2}}{|A|} \\ \vdots & \vdots & & \vdots \\ \frac{\alpha_{1n}}{|A|} & \frac{\alpha_{2n}}{|A|} & \cdots & \frac{\alpha_{nn}}{|A|} \end{bmatrix} = \begin{bmatrix} C_{11} & C_{12} & \cdots & C_{1n} \\ C_{21} & C_{22} & \cdots & C_{2n} \\ \vdots & \vdots & & \vdots \\ C_{n1} & C_{n2} & \cdots & C_{nn} \end{bmatrix} \tag{2-5}$$

Consider the diagonal element C_{11} in the first row and first column of the product resulting from the matrix operation called for in Eq. (2-5).

$$C_{11} = a_{11}\frac{\alpha_{11}}{|A|} + a_{12}\frac{\alpha_{12}}{|A|} + \cdots a_{1n}\frac{\alpha_{1n}}{|A|} \tag{2-6a}$$

†See Sec. A-4.3 for the definition of a cofactor.

‡See Sec. A-7 for a development of determinants and their properties.

or

$$C_{11} = \frac{1}{|A|}(a_{11}\alpha_{11} + a_{12}\alpha_{12} + \cdots + a_{1n}\alpha_{1n}) \tag{2-6b}$$

The expression in parentheses on the right-hand side of Eq. (2-6b) may be recognized as a Laplace expansion† of [A] by cofactors of the first row and is equal to $|A|$. Thus, the result for this element is $C_{11} = 1$. By similar reasoning it may be seen that each diagonal element of the product matrix resulting from the matrix operations of Eq. (2-5) represents a Laplace expansion of [A], which equals $|A|$ divided by $|A|$ and is therefore equal to 1.

Now, consider the element in the first row and second column of the product matrix indicated by Eq. (2-5), i.e., C_{12}:

$$C_{12} = a_{11}\frac{\alpha_{21}}{|A|} + a_{12}\frac{\alpha_{22}}{|A|} + \cdots + a_{1n}\frac{\alpha_{2n}}{|A|} \tag{2-7a}$$

or

$$C_{12} = \frac{1}{|A|}(a_{11}\alpha_{21} + a_{12}\alpha_{22} + \cdots + a_{1n}\alpha_{2n}) \tag{2-7b}$$

The expression in parentheses on the right-hand side of Eq. (2-7b) may be recognized as a Laplace expansion of the first row of [A] by cofactors of the second row. Thus, $C_{12} = 0$. By similar reasoning it may be seen that each element not on the main diagonal of the product represents an expansion of a row of [A] by the corresponding cofactors of another row and is thus zero. The product formed is, therefore, seen to be equal to the identity matrix. Thus, the matrix $[\mathbf{A}]^{-1}$ as defined in Eq. (2-4) satisfies the definition of the ***inverse matrix***, i.e.,

$$[\mathbf{A}][\mathbf{A}]^{-1} = [\mathbf{I}] \tag{2-8}$$

Example 2-1. Find the inverse of [A] by the adjoint method and check the results.

$$[\mathbf{A}] = \begin{bmatrix} 1 & 5 & 1 \\ 0 & 4 & 2 \\ 0 & 1 & 1 \end{bmatrix} \tag{2-9}$$

STEP 1. Expand by cofactors of the first column to determine $|A|$.

$$|A| = 1 \cdot \begin{vmatrix} 4 & 2 \\ 1 & 1 \end{vmatrix} = 2 \tag{2-10}$$

The inverse exists.

STEP 2. Build matrix $[\alpha]$, the matrix of cofactors of [A].

$$\alpha_{11} = (-1)^{1+1}\begin{vmatrix} 4 & 2 \\ 1 & 1 \end{vmatrix} = 2 \tag{2-11a}$$

$$\alpha_{12} = (-1)^{1+2}\begin{vmatrix} 0 & 2 \\ 0 & 1 \end{vmatrix} = 0 \tag{2-11b}$$

---

†See Sec. A-4.3 for a discussion of Laplace expansion methods.

$$\alpha_{13} = (-1)^{1+3}\begin{vmatrix} 0 & 4 \\ 0 & 1 \end{vmatrix} = 0 \tag{2-11c}$$

$$\alpha_{21} = (-1)^{2+1}\begin{vmatrix} 5 & 1 \\ 1 & 1 \end{vmatrix} = -4 \tag{2-11d}$$

$$\alpha_{22} = (-1)^{2+2}\begin{vmatrix} 1 & 1 \\ 0 & 1 \end{vmatrix} = 1 \tag{2-11e}$$

$$\alpha_{23} = (-1)^{2+3}\begin{vmatrix} 1 & 5 \\ 0 & 1 \end{vmatrix} = -1 \tag{2-11f}$$

$$\alpha_{31} = (-1)^{3+1}\begin{vmatrix} 5 & 1 \\ 4 & 2 \end{vmatrix} = 6 \tag{2-11g}$$

$$\alpha_{32} = (-1)^{3+2}\begin{vmatrix} 1 & 1 \\ 0 & 2 \end{vmatrix} = -2 \tag{2-11h}$$

$$\alpha_{33} = (-1)^{3+3}\begin{vmatrix} 1 & 5 \\ 0 & 4 \end{vmatrix} = 4 \tag{2-11i}$$

STEP 3. Form $[\boldsymbol{\alpha}]^T = \text{adj}[\mathbf{A}]$.

$$[\boldsymbol{\alpha}]^T = \begin{bmatrix} 2 & -4 & 6 \\ 0 & 1 & -2 \\ 0 & -1 & 4 \end{bmatrix} = \text{adj}[\mathbf{A}] \tag{2-12}$$

STEP 4. Divide each element of adj[**A**] by $|A| = 2$, giving $[\mathbf{A}]^{-1}$.

$$[\mathbf{A}]^{-1} = \begin{bmatrix} 1 & -2 & 3 \\ 0 & \frac{1}{2} & -1 \\ 0 & -\frac{1}{2} & 2 \end{bmatrix} \tag{2-13}$$

Example 2-2. Solve the following system of equations by matrix inversion:

$$\begin{aligned} x_1 + 5x_2 + x_3 &= 2 \\ 4x_2 + 2x_3 &= 6 \\ x_2 + x_3 &= 4 \end{aligned} \tag{2-14a}$$

Equations (2-14a) are written in matrix form as

$$\begin{bmatrix} 1 & 5 & 1 \\ 0 & 4 & 2 \\ 0 & 1 & 1 \end{bmatrix}\begin{bmatrix} x_1 \\ x_2 \\ x_3 \end{bmatrix} = \begin{bmatrix} 2 \\ 6 \\ 4 \end{bmatrix} \tag{2-14b}$$

Since the inverse of the coefficient matrix [**A**] of this set of equations was established in the previous example, Expression (2-13), the solution of the system of equations may be expressed as

$$[\mathbf{X}] = [\mathbf{A}]^{-1}[\mathbf{B}] = \begin{bmatrix} 1 & -2 & 3 \\ 0 & \frac{1}{2} & -1 \\ 0 & -\frac{1}{2} & 2 \end{bmatrix}\begin{bmatrix} 2 \\ 6 \\ 4 \end{bmatrix} = \begin{bmatrix} 2 \\ -1 \\ 5 \end{bmatrix} \tag{2-15}$$

yielding

$$\begin{aligned} x_1 &= 2 \\ x_2 &= -1 \\ x_3 &= 5 \end{aligned} \qquad \textbf{(2-16)}$$

Unfortunately, the adjoint method of computing an inverse of a matrix is unwieldy for anything except small matrices. The method described in the next section is much more satisfactory for larger matrices.

2-2.2 Row Transformation Method of Computing Inverse Matrices

The inverse of a given ***nonsingular*** matrix [A] may be found by appropriate utilization of *elementary row transformations* performed on [A].† By proper choice of a sequence of row transformations, a nonsingular matrix [A] of order n may be transformed or reduced to the identity matrix of order n. If the same sequence of row transformations is subsequently performed on the identity matrix of order n, the resulting transformed matrix will be $[\mathbf{A}]^{-1}$. To provide a rationale for justifying this procedure note that, by the definition of $[\mathbf{A}]^{-1}$ given in Eq. (2-8) and by the fact that $[\mathbf{A}]^{-1}$ is unique, it is apparent that $[\mathbf{A}]^{-1}$ is the matrix of transformations which reduce [A] to [I]. The same transformations applied to [I] result in

$$[\mathbf{A}]^{-1}[\mathbf{I}] = [\mathbf{A}]^{-1} \qquad \textbf{(2-17)}$$

Thus, the unique set of linear transformations which reduces [A] to [I] also transforms [I] to $[\mathbf{A}]^{-1}$.

The mechanics of this method are perhaps best learned and understood through the careful examination of an illustration.

Example 2-3. Determine the inverse of matrix [A], given below, by the row transformation method.

$$[\mathbf{A}] = \begin{bmatrix} 1 & -3 & 1 \\ -2 & 4 & 2 \\ 3 & -7 & 1 \end{bmatrix} \qquad \textbf{(2-18)}$$

To simplify the computations involved, apply the appropriate row transformations to both [A] and [I] simultaneously. This can be efficiently done by applying the transformations to a new matrix formed by placing the elements of the matrices [A] and [I] side by side as

$$[\mathbf{A} \mid \mathbf{I}] = \left[\begin{array}{ccc|ccc} 1 & -3 & 1 & 1 & 0 & 0 \\ -2 & 4 & 2 & 0 & 1 & 0 \\ 3 & -7 & 1 & 0 & 0 & 1 \end{array}\right] \qquad \textbf{(2-19)}$$

†A discussion of elementary row transformations is given in Sec. A-5.

The first step is to replace all elements of column 1, except for the diagonal element, by zeros, which may be accomplished by the following transformations:

1. Add 2 times row 1 to row 2, i.e., $R_2 \rightarrow R_2 + 2R_1$
   (*read*, row 2 is replaced by row 2 plus 2 times row 1).
2. Subtract 3 times row 1 from row 3, i.e., $R_3 \rightarrow R_3 - 3R_1$
   (*read*, row 3 is replaced by row 3 minus 3 times row 1).

The result of these operations is

$$\left[\begin{array}{rrr|rrr} 1 & -3 & 1 & 1 & 0 & 0 \\ 0 & -2 & 4 & 2 & 1 & 0 \\ 0 & 2 & -2 & -3 & 0 & 1 \end{array}\right] \tag{2-20a}$$

Next, replace the diagonal element of column 2 by a 1. This is done by the following transformation:

3. Multiply row 2 by $-\frac{1}{2}$, i.e., $R_2 \rightarrow -\frac{1}{2} R_2$
   (*read*, row 2 is replaced by $-\frac{1}{2}$ times row 2).

The result is

$$\left[\begin{array}{rrr|rrr} 1 & -3 & 1 & 1 & 0 & 0 \\ 0 & 1 & -2 & -1 & -\frac{1}{2} & 0 \\ 0 & 2 & -2 & -3 & 0 & 1 \end{array}\right] \tag{2-20b}$$

Then replace the elements of column 2 not on the diagonal by zeros with the transformations:

4. $R_1 \rightarrow R_1 + 3R_2$
5. $R_3 \rightarrow R_3 - 2R_2$

The result is

$$\left[\begin{array}{rrr|rrr} 1 & 0 & -5 & -2 & -\frac{3}{2} & 0 \\ 0 & 1 & -2 & -1 & -\frac{1}{2} & 0 \\ 0 & 0 & 2 & -1 & 1 & 1 \end{array}\right] \tag{2-20c}$$

Now reduce the diagonal element of column 3 to a 1. This is accomplished by

6. $R_3 \rightarrow \frac{1}{2} R_3$

This gives

$$\left[\begin{array}{rrr|rrr} 1 & 0 & -5 & -2 & -\frac{3}{2} & 0 \\ 0 & 1 & -2 & -1 & -\frac{1}{2} & 0 \\ 0 & 0 & 1 & -\frac{1}{2} & \frac{1}{2} & \frac{1}{2} \end{array}\right] \tag{2-20d}$$

Finally, reduce all nondiagonal elements of column 3 to zeros using the transformations

7. $R_1 \rightarrow R_1 + 5R_3$
8. $R_2 \rightarrow R_2 + 2R_3$

yielding

$$\left[\begin{array}{rrr|rrr} 1 & 0 & 0 & -\frac{9}{2} & 1 & \frac{5}{2} \\ 0 & 1 & 0 & -2 & \frac{1}{2} & 1 \\ 0 & 0 & 1 & -\frac{1}{2} & \frac{1}{2} & \frac{1}{2} \end{array}\right] \tag{2-20e}$$

The resulting inverse is

$$[\mathbf{A}]^{-1} = \begin{bmatrix} -\frac{9}{2} & 1 & \frac{5}{2} \\ -2 & \frac{1}{2} & 1 \\ -\frac{1}{2} & \frac{1}{2} & \frac{1}{2} \end{bmatrix} \tag{2-21}$$

Check: $[\mathbf{A}][\mathbf{A}]^{-1} = [\mathbf{I}]$ **(2-22a)**

$$\begin{bmatrix} 1 & -3 & 1 \\ -2 & 4 & 2 \\ 3 & -7 & 1 \end{bmatrix} \begin{bmatrix} -\frac{9}{2} & 1 & \frac{5}{2} \\ -2 & \frac{1}{2} & 1 \\ -\frac{1}{2} & \frac{1}{2} & \frac{1}{2} \end{bmatrix} = \begin{bmatrix} 1 & 0 & 0 \\ 0 & 1 & 0 \\ 0 & 0 & 1 \end{bmatrix} \tag{2-22b}$$

2-2.3 Matrix Inversion Solution to Systems of Equations

It has been shown in Eqs. (2-2) that the solution to the matrix equation

$$[\mathbf{A}][\mathbf{X}] = [\mathbf{B}] \tag{2-2a}$$

is

$$[\mathbf{X}] = [\mathbf{A}]^{-1}[\mathbf{B}] \tag{2-2e}$$

provided $[\mathbf{A}]^{-1}$ exists. It should be observed at this point that should the column matrix [**B**] on the right-hand side of the equations change while [**A**] (the *matrix of coefficients*) remains unchanged, the new solution can be found by multiplying $[\mathbf{A}]^{-1}$ by the new [**B**]. This point is of particular interest in solving structural problems by matrix methods when a structure is to be analyzed for different loading arrangements. As will be seen in later chapters, changing the loading conditions will only change matrix [**B**].

It should also be observed that if $[\mathbf{B}] = [\mathbf{0}]$, the only solution when $[\mathbf{A}]^{-1}$ *exists* is $[\mathbf{X}] = [\mathbf{0}]$, called the ***trivial solution.*** Matrix equation

$$[\mathbf{A}][\mathbf{X}] = [\mathbf{0}] \tag{2-23}$$

will have a ***nontrivial solution*** when $[\mathbf{A}]^{-1}$ *does not exist,* i.e., if $|A| = 0$.

2–3 Solution of Systems of Linear Equations by Gauss Elimination

Another procedure for solving systems of linear equations which is also based on performing elementary row transformations on a matrix is the Gauss elimination method. The general procedure is (1) to reduce the coefficient matrix of a given system of equations to *upper triangular form*† using appropriate elementary transformations on the rows of the system; and (2) to find the solution to the system by solving the resultant upper triangular system found in the first step.

†Upper triangular matrices are defined in Sec. A-3.7.

The procedure will be illustrated using a system of four equations in four unknowns and its extension to higher-order systems should then be clear.

The basic principle which permits this procedure is that performing elementary row operations on a system of linear equations produces a new and equivalent set of linear equations, which means that the new set of equations may be shown to have the identical set of solutions.

Before looking at examples of this procedure, it would be well to examine the possible situations that may occur in solving systems of linear equations. Letting $[\mathbf{A}][\mathbf{X}] = [\mathbf{B}]$ represent a system of n equations in n unknowns described in matrix form, essentially three conditions may be encountered:

1. If $|A| \neq 0$, i.e., if $[\mathbf{A}]$ is ***nonsingular***, then there is a unique solution to the system which may be found by the methods of this chapter. The rank† of $[\mathbf{A}]$ is n in this case.

   If $|A| = 0$, i.e., if $[\mathbf{A}]$ is ***singular***, then there is no *unique* solution to the system. Further investigation is then required to determine whether there are any solutions to the system. To do this, construct a matrix called the ***augmented matrix***, denoted by $[\mathbf{A}_g]$, which is formed by appending $[\mathbf{B}]$ to the matrix $[\mathbf{A}]$. That is, $[\mathbf{A}_g] = [\mathbf{A} \mid \mathbf{B}]$. The following cases then may occur:

2. $[\mathbf{A}]$ has rank r while $[\mathbf{A}_g]$ has rank r_1 which is greater than r, i.e., $r_1 > r$. In this case, the system is *inconsistent* and no solutions may be found.

3. $[\mathbf{A}]$ has rank r while $[\mathbf{A}_g]$ has rank r also. In this case, there are r linearly independent equations and $n - r$ linearly dependent equations, and the system has no unique solution; but linearly dependent‡ solutions may be found. Specifically, one may solve for r of the unknowns in terms of the other $n - r$ unknowns. The Gauss elimination method described in this section is quite applicable in handling such cases as will be seen in Example 2-5.

Example 2-4. Solve the system of linear equations

$$2x_1 - 3x_2 - x_3 + 2x_4 = 15 \tag{2-24a}$$

$$-x_1 + x_2 + 2x_3 - 2x_4 = -13 \tag{2-24b}$$

$$x_1 - x_2 + x_3 + x_4 = 4 \tag{2-24c}$$

$$3x_1 + 2x_2 - x_3 - x_4 = 3 \tag{2-24d}$$

by the Gauss elimination method.

A convenient device for operating on the given system is to form the ***augmented matrix***, which is obtained by placing the matrix of coefficients of the equations and the column of constant terms side by side, i.e.,

$$\left[\begin{array}{rrrr|r} 2 & -3 & -1 & 2 & 15 \\ -1 & 1 & 2 & -2 & -13 \\ 1 & -1 & 1 & 1 & 4 \\ 3 & 2 & -1 & -1 & 3 \end{array}\right] \tag{2-25a}$$

†A discussion of matrix rank is given in Sec. A-6.

‡A discussion of linear dependence is given in Sec. A-6.

The initial step is to divide row 1 by 2 in order to reduce a_{11} to unity.

1. $R_1 \rightarrow \frac{1}{2} R_1$

$$\left[\begin{array}{rrrr|r} 1 & -\frac{3}{2} & -\frac{1}{2} & 1 & \frac{15}{2} \\ -1 & 1 & 2 & -2 & -13 \\ 1 & -1 & 1 & 1 & 4 \\ 3 & 2 & -1 & -1 & 3 \end{array}\right] \tag{2-25b}$$

Next, replace the elements below the main diagonal in column 1 by zeros. This may be done by using the row operations:

2. $R_2 \rightarrow R_2 + R_1$
3. $R_3 \rightarrow R_3 - R_1$
4. $R_4 \rightarrow R_4 - 3R_1$

$$\left[\begin{array}{rrrr|r} 1 & -\frac{3}{2} & -\frac{1}{2} & 1 & \frac{15}{2} \\ 0 & -\frac{1}{2} & \frac{3}{2} & -1 & -\frac{11}{2} \\ 0 & \frac{1}{2} & \frac{3}{2} & 0 & -\frac{7}{2} \\ 0 & \frac{13}{2} & \frac{1}{2} & -4 & -\frac{39}{2} \end{array}\right] \tag{2-25c}$$

Next, reduce element a_{22} to unity.

5. $R_2 \rightarrow -2R_2$

$$\left[\begin{array}{rrrr|r} 1 & -\frac{3}{2} & -\frac{1}{2} & 1 & \frac{15}{2} \\ 0 & 1 & -3 & 2 & 11 \\ 0 & \frac{1}{2} & \frac{3}{2} & 0 & -\frac{7}{2} \\ 0 & \frac{13}{2} & \frac{1}{2} & -4 & -\frac{39}{2} \end{array}\right] \tag{2-25d}$$

Then replace the elements below the main diagonal in column 2 by zeros. This is accomplished by the following operations:

6. $R_3 \rightarrow R_3 - \frac{1}{2} R_2$
7. $R_4 \rightarrow R_4 - \frac{13}{2} R_2$

$$\left[\begin{array}{rrrr|r} 1 & -\frac{3}{2} & -\frac{1}{2} & 1 & \frac{15}{2} \\ 0 & 1 & -3 & 2 & 11 \\ 0 & 0 & 3 & -1 & -9 \\ 0 & 0 & 20 & -17 & -91 \end{array}\right] \tag{2-25e}$$

Now reduce element a_{33} to unity.

8. $R_3 \rightarrow \frac{1}{3} R_3$

$$\left[\begin{array}{rrrr|r} 1 & -\frac{3}{2} & -\frac{1}{2} & 1 & \frac{15}{2} \\ 0 & 1 & -3 & 2 & 11 \\ 0 & 0 & 1 & -\frac{1}{3} & -3 \\ 0 & 0 & 20 & -17 & -91 \end{array}\right] \tag{2-25f}$$

Finally, replace the elements below the main diagonal in column 3 by zeros. This may be accomplished by the following transformation:

9. $R_4 \rightarrow R_4 - 20R_3$

$$\left[\begin{array}{cccc|c} 1 & -\frac{3}{2} & -\frac{1}{2} & 1 & \frac{15}{2} \\ 0 & 1 & -3 & 2 & 11 \\ 0 & 0 & 1 & -\frac{1}{3} & -3 \\ 0 & 0 & 0 & -\frac{31}{3} & -31 \end{array}\right] \tag{2-25g}$$

Since Matrix (2-25g) has been obtained by using row transformations on Matrix (2-25a), the solutions to the system of equations represented by Matrix (2-25g) are equivalent to the solutions of the original system of equations. At this point, the first part of the method has been completed and one is ready to begin the second part of the method, which is referred to as the ***backward solution.***

Matrix (2-25g) represents the following equations:

$$\begin{aligned} x_1 - \tfrac{3}{2}x_2 - \tfrac{1}{2}x_3 + x_4 &= \tfrac{15}{2} \\ x_2 - 3x_3 + 2x_4 &= 11 \\ x_3 - \tfrac{1}{3}x_4 &= -3 \\ -\tfrac{31}{3}x_4 &= -31 \end{aligned} \tag{2-25h}$$

Equations (2-25h) may now be solved by first solving the bottom equation for x_4, i.e.,

$$-\tfrac{31}{3}x_4 = -31 \tag{2-26a}$$

or

$$x_4 = 3 \tag{2-26b}$$

Next, solve the third equation for x_3, substituting in the value for x_4 found in Expression (2-26b):

$$x_3 - \tfrac{1}{3}(3) = -3 \tag{2-26c}$$

or

$$x_3 = -2 \tag{2-26d}$$

Next, solve the second equation for x_2, substituting in the values for x_3 and x_4 found in Expressions (2-26d) and (2-26b):

$$x_2 - 3(-2) + 2(3) = 11 \tag{2-26e}$$

or

$$x_2 = -1 \tag{2-26f}$$

Finally, solve the first equation for x_1, substituting in the values for x_2, x_3, and x_4 found in Expressions (2-26f), (2-26d), and (2-26b):

$$x_1 - \tfrac{3}{2}(-1) - \tfrac{1}{2}(-2) + 3 = \tfrac{15}{2} \tag{2-26g}$$

or

$$x_1 = 2 \tag{2-26h}$$

Example 2-5. Solve the system of linear equations

$$\begin{aligned} x_1 - 2x_2 + x_3 &= 1 \\ x_1 + x_2 - x_3 &= -1 \\ x_1 - 5x_2 + 3x_3 &= 3 \end{aligned} \tag{2-27}$$

by the Gauss elimination method.

If this system is investigated as per Sec. A-6 of the Appendix, the rank of [A] is found to be 2 and the rank of $[\mathbf{A}_g]$ is found to be 2. Thus, there is no unique solution to the system, but there will be solutions for two of the unknowns in terms of a third unknown. Notice that this result arises naturally when using Gauss elimination.

Form the augmented matrix of Eqs. (2-27), i.e.,

$$\left[\begin{array}{ccc|c} 1 & -2 & 1 & 1 \\ 1 & 1 & -1 & -1 \\ 1 & -5 & 3 & 3 \end{array}\right] \tag{2-28a}$$

Next, reduce Matrix (2-28a) to upper triangular form as illustrated in the previous example. This may be accomplished by the following row transformations:

1. $R_2 \to R_2 - R_1$
2. $R_3 \to R_3 - R_1$

which gives

$$\left[\begin{array}{ccc|c} 1 & -2 & 1 & 1 \\ 0 & 3 & -2 & -2 \\ 0 & -3 & 2 & 2 \end{array}\right] \tag{2-28b}$$

3. $R_2 \to \frac{1}{3} R_2$

which gives

$$\left[\begin{array}{ccc|c} 1 & -2 & 1 & 1 \\ 0 & 1 & -\frac{2}{3} & -\frac{2}{3} \\ 0 & -3 & 2 & 2 \end{array}\right] \tag{2-28c}$$

4. $R_3 \to R_3 + 3R_2$

which gives

$$\left[\begin{array}{ccc|c} 1 & -2 & 1 & 1 \\ 0 & 1 & -\frac{2}{3} & -\frac{2}{3} \\ 0 & 0 & 0 & 0 \end{array}\right] \tag{2-28d}$$

The third row is now all zeros, indicating that no further elimination may be accomplished. A back solution for x_1 and x_2 in terms of x_3 may be obtained from the final set of equations

$$x_1 - 2x_2 + x_3 = 1 \tag{2-29a}$$

$$x_2 - \tfrac{2}{3} x_3 = -\tfrac{2}{3} \tag{2-29b}$$

Thus

$$x_2 = \tfrac{2}{3} x_3 - \tfrac{2}{3} \tag{2-29c}$$

$$x_1 = 2x_2 - x_3 + 1 \tag{2-29d}$$

Substituting the solution for x_2 from Eq. (2-29c) in Eq. (2-29d) gives

$$x_1 = \tfrac{1}{3} x_3 - \tfrac{1}{3} \tag{2-29e}$$

2-4 Solution of Systems of Linear Equations by Iteration

The method of solution to be described here is a useful computer-oriented procedure for finding solutions to systems of n linear equations in n unknowns, expressed as $[\mathbf{A}][\mathbf{X}] = [\mathbf{B}]$, where $|A| \neq 0$, and is presented because of its applicability to many engineering problems. Some guidelines for convergence of the method are outlined later.

Although the procedure will be illustrated using a system of three equations with three unknowns, the ideas may be extended to systems of higher dimension with a minimum of effort.

Consider the system of equations

$$\begin{aligned} a_{11}x + a_{12}y + a_{13}z &= b_1 \\ a_{21}x + a_{22}y + a_{23}z &= b_2 \\ a_{31}x + a_{32}y + a_{33}z &= b_3 \end{aligned} \tag{2-30}$$

The general procedure involves finding by some means an *initial approximation* to the solution, then substituting this approximation into the equations, one at a time, thus generating *new approximations* to the solution. Each new approximation will be more accurate than the previous one, if the method converges, and one may iterate in this fashion to a desired degree of accuracy. To begin the process, solve the first equation for x, the second equation for y, and the third equation for z, giving

$$x = \frac{1}{a_{11}}(b_1 - a_{12}y - a_{13}z) \tag{2-31a}$$

$$y = \frac{1}{a_{22}}(b_2 - a_{21}x - a_{23}z) \tag{2-31b}$$

$$z = \frac{1}{a_{33}}(b_3 - a_{31}x - a_{32}y) \tag{2-31c}$$

An *initial approximation* to the solution may be obtained by substituting $x = 0$, $y = 0$, $z = 0$ into the right-hand terms of Eq. (2-31). The results of this substitution are†

$$x_1 = \frac{b_1}{a_{11}} \tag{2-32a}$$

$$y_1 = \frac{b_2}{a_{22}} \tag{2-32b}$$

$$z_1 = \frac{b_3}{a_{33}} \tag{2-32c}$$

†The subscripts on the variables in these and subsequent equations are used to designate the order of approximation in which they were calculated. That is, x_1, y_1, and z_1 are the values of x, y, and z found in the first approximation.

A second approximate solution is found by solving Eqs. (2-31a), (2-31b), and (2-31c) in that order, using the most current values for x, y, and z, yielding

$$x_2 = \frac{1}{a_{11}}(b_1 - a_{12}y_1 - a_{13}z_1) \tag{2-33a}$$

$$y_2 = \frac{1}{a_{22}}(b_2 - a_{21}x_2 - a_{23}z_1) \tag{2-33b}$$

$$z_2 = \frac{1}{a_{33}}(b_3 - a_{31}x_2 - a_{32}y_2) \tag{2-33c}$$

In a like manner, a third approximate solution is found:

$$x_3 = \frac{1}{a_{11}}(b_1 - a_{12}y_2 - a_{13}z_2) \tag{2-34a}$$

$$y_3 = \frac{1}{a_{22}}(b_2 - a_{21}x_3 - a_{23}z_2) \tag{2-34b}$$

$$z_3 = \frac{1}{a_{33}}(b_3 - a_{31}x_3 - a_{32}y_3) \tag{2-34c}$$

The general *recursive* relations for this procedure may be stated as follows:

$$x_i = \frac{1}{a_{11}}(b_1 - a_{12}y_{i-1} - a_{13}z_{i-1}) \tag{2-35a}$$

$$y_i = \frac{1}{a_{22}}(b_2 - a_{21}x_i - a_{23}z_{i-1}) \tag{2-35b}$$

$$z_i = \frac{1}{a_{33}}(b_3 - a_{31}x_i - a_{32}y_i) \tag{2-35c}$$

The process is continued as indicated in Eqs. (2-33), (2-34), and (2-35) until a desired degree of accuracy is acquired, as demonstrated by the inequalities

$$\begin{aligned} |x_i - x_{i-1}| &< \epsilon \\ |y_i - y_{i-1}| &< \epsilon \\ |z_i - z_{i-1}| &< \epsilon \end{aligned} \tag{2-36}$$

where ϵ represents the degree of accuracy specified for the problem; e.g., for three-decimal-place accuracy, $\epsilon = 0.0005$.

The complete conditions for convergence of this method are not entirely known; however, numerical analysis theory guarantees convergence (at a reasonably rapid rate) when the *absolute value* of the diagonal element of each row of the coefficient matrix, a_{ii}, is as large or larger than the *sum of the absolute values* of the remaining elements in the row. Stated mathematically,

$$|a_{ii}| \geq \sum_{k=1}^{n} |a_{ik}| \tag{2-37}$$

where $k \neq i$, and $i = 1, 2, \ldots n$. A matrix with this property has *diagonal dominance*. There is empirical evidence, however, that the procedure will, in general, converge well if the diagonal element has the largest absolute value of any element in that row. Nonetheless, difficulties in convergence are often found in very large problems making the method less attractive than other procedures in these situations.

Example 2-6. Solve the system of equations:

$$\begin{aligned} 8x - 3y + 2z &= 20 \\ 4x + 11y - z &= 33 \\ 6x + 3y + 12z &= 36 \end{aligned} \tag{2-38}$$

by the iterative method.

A list of approximate solutions to Eq. (2-38) obtained from four cycles of iterations is given in Table 2-1.

Table 2-1

Cycle	x	y	z
1	2.5	3.0	3.0
2	2.875	2.227	1.006
3	3.084	1.970	0.966
4	2.997	1.998	1.002

The exact solution to the system in this example may be verified to be $x = 3$, $y = 2$, $z = 1$. Notice how rapidly accuracy to two decimal places was obtained using the given iterative method.

2–5 Partitioning of Matrices

A ***submatrix*** of an $n \times n$ matrix [**A**] is defined as a matrix formed by deleting specified rows and columns of [**A**]. Partitioning a given matrix into submatrices is a very useful technique for working with large matrices, since it will be shown in the subsequent discussions that several important matrix operations may be performed by operating with submatrices.

2-5.1 Single Partitions

The matrix equation [**Y**] = [**A**][**X**] when expanded may be written as

$$\begin{aligned} y_1 &= a_{11}x_1 + a_{12}x_2 + \cdots + a_{1q}x_q + a_{1,q+1}x_{q+1} + \cdots + a_{1n}x_n \\ y_2 &= a_{21}x_1 + a_{22}x_2 + \cdots + a_{2q}x_q + a_{2,q+1}x_{q+1} + \cdots + a_{2n}x_n \\ &\vdots \\ y_n &= a_{n1}x_1 + a_{n2}x_2 + \cdots + a_{nq}x_q + a_{n,q+1}x_{q+1} + \cdots + a_{nn}x_n \end{aligned} \tag{2-39}$$

The terms of these equations may then be grouped as

$$\begin{aligned} y_1 &= (a_{11}x_1 + a_{12}x_2 + \cdots + a_{1q}x_q) + (a_{1,q+1}x_{q+1} + \cdots + a_{1n}x_n) \\ y_2 &= (a_{21}x_1 + a_{22}x_2 + \cdots + a_{2q}x_q) + (a_{2,q+1}x_{q+1} + \cdots + a_{2n}x_n) \\ &\vdots \\ y_n &= (a_{n1}x_1 + a_{n2}x_2 + \cdots + a_{nq}x_q) + (a_{n,q+1}x_{q+1} + \cdots + a_{qn}x_n) \end{aligned} \tag{2-40}$$

Equations (2-40) may subsequently be written in matrix form as

$$\begin{bmatrix} y_1 \\ y_2 \\ \vdots \\ y_n \end{bmatrix} = \begin{bmatrix} a_{11} & a_{12} & \cdots & a_{1q} \\ a_{21} & a_{22} & \cdots & a_{2q} \\ \vdots & & & \\ a_{n1} & a_{n2} & \cdots & a_{nq} \end{bmatrix} \begin{bmatrix} x_1 \\ x_2 \\ \vdots \\ x_q \end{bmatrix} + \begin{bmatrix} a_{1,q+1} & \cdots & a_{n1} \\ a_{2,q+1} & \cdots & a_{n2} \\ \vdots & & \\ a_{n,q+1} & \cdots & a_{nn} \end{bmatrix} \begin{bmatrix} x_{q+1} \\ x_{q+2} \\ \vdots \\ x_n \end{bmatrix} \tag{2-41}$$

and Eq. (2-41) may then be denoted as

$$[\mathbf{Y}] = [\mathbf{A}_1][\mathbf{X}_1] + [\mathbf{A}_2][\mathbf{X}_2] \tag{2-42a}$$

where

$$[\mathbf{A}_1] = \begin{bmatrix} a_{11} & a_{12} & \cdots & a_{1q} \\ a_{21} & a_{22} & \cdots & a_{2q} \\ \vdots & & & \\ a_{n1} & a_{n2} & \cdots & a_{nq} \end{bmatrix} \tag{2-42b}$$

$$[\mathbf{X}_1] = \begin{bmatrix} x_1 \\ x_2 \\ \vdots \\ x_q \end{bmatrix} \tag{2-42c}$$

$$[\mathbf{A}_2] = \begin{bmatrix} a_{1,q+1} & \cdots & a_{n1} \\ a_{2,q+1} & \cdots & a_{n2} \\ \vdots & & \\ a_{n,q+1} & \cdots & a_{nn} \end{bmatrix} \tag{2-42d}$$

and

$$[\mathbf{X}_2] = \begin{bmatrix} x_{q+1} \\ x_{q+2} \\ \vdots \\ x_n \end{bmatrix} \tag{2-42e}$$

It may be seen that $[\mathbf{A}_1]$ is an $n \times q$ submatrix of $[\mathbf{A}]$, $[\mathbf{A}_2]$ is an $n \times (n - q)$ submatrix of matrix $[\mathbf{A}]$, $[\mathbf{X}_1]$ is a $q \times 1$ submatrix of $[\mathbf{X}]$, and $[\mathbf{X}_2]$ is a $(n - q) \times 1$ submatrix of matrix $[\mathbf{X}]$.

A more compact notation for Eq. (2-41) may be obtained by writing the equation $[\mathbf{Y}] = [\mathbf{A}][\mathbf{X}]$ as

$$\begin{bmatrix} y_1 \\ y_2 \\ \vdots \\ y_n \end{bmatrix} = \left[\begin{array}{cccc|ccc} a_{11} & a_{12} & \cdots & a_{1q} & a_{1,q+1} & \cdots & a_{1n} \\ a_{21} & a_{22} & \cdots & a_{2q} & a_{2,q+1} & \cdots & a_{2n} \\ \vdots & & & & \vdots & & \\ a_{n1} & a_{n2} & \cdots & a_{nq} & a_{n,q+1} & \cdots & a_{nn} \end{array}\right] \left[\begin{array}{c} x_1 \\ x_2 \\ \vdots \\ x_q \\ \hline x_{q+1} \\ x_{q+2} \\ \vdots \\ x_n \end{array}\right] \tag{2-43a}$$

or

$$[\mathbf{Y}] = [[\mathbf{A}_1] \mid [\mathbf{A}_2]] \left[\begin{array}{c} [\mathbf{X}_1] \\ \hline [\mathbf{X}_2] \end{array}\right] \tag{2-43b}$$

and then adopting the convention that the submatrices in Eq. (2-43b) are to obey the same rules that apply to elements of a matrix. Performing the indicated multiplication of Eq. (2-43b) using this convention yields

$$[\mathbf{Y}] = [\mathbf{A}_1][\mathbf{X}_1] + [\mathbf{A}_2][\mathbf{X}_2] \tag{2-44}$$

which corresponds to the result derived in Eq. (2-42a).

Matrices written in the form of Eqs. (2-43) are referred to as ***partitioned matrices***, and the process represented by Eqs. (2-43) and (2-44) is referred to as *partitioning into submatrices*. It should be noted from Eq. (2-41) that $[\mathbf{A}_1]$ is compatible for multiplication with $[\mathbf{X}_1]$ and that $[\mathbf{A}_2]$ is compatible for multiplication with $[\mathbf{X}_2]$. Such a partitioning of matrices [**A**] and [**X**] so that the resulting submatrices are compatible for multiplication is called a *valid partitioning*. The partitioning of matrix [**A**] represents a *vertical partition*, while the partitioning of matrix [**X**] represents a *horizontal partition*. In order to obtain a valid partitioning of [**A**] and [**X**], the number of columns in $[\mathbf{A}_1]$ must correspond to the number of rows in $[\mathbf{X}_1]$.

The usefulness of the techniques of partitioning will be illustrated in subsequent sections.

2-5.2 Cross-Partitions

Considering again the equation [**Y**] = [**A**][**X**], let matrix [**A**] be partitioned both vertically and horizontally into four submatrices as follows:

$$[\mathbf{A}] = \left[\begin{array}{c|c} [\mathbf{A}_{11}]_{p\times q} & [\mathbf{A}_{12}]_{p\times(n-q)} \\ \hline [\mathbf{A}_{21}]_{(m-p)\times q} & [\mathbf{A}_{22}]_{(m-p)\times(n-q)} \end{array}\right]_{m\times n} \tag{2-45a}$$

and let [**X**] and [**Y**] be partitioned horizontally as follows:

$$[\mathbf{X}] = \left[\begin{array}{c} [\mathbf{X}_1]_{q\times 1} \\ \hline [\mathbf{X}_2]_{(n-q)\times 1} \end{array}\right]_{n\times 1} \tag{2-45b}$$

and

$$[\mathbf{Y}] = \begin{bmatrix} [\mathbf{Y}_1]_{p\times 1} \\ \hdashline [\mathbf{Y}_2]_{(m-p)\times 1} \end{bmatrix}_{m\times 1} \tag{2-45c}$$

Thus, the equation $[\mathbf{Y}] = [\mathbf{A}][\mathbf{X}]$ may be written as

$$\begin{bmatrix} [\mathbf{Y}_1] \\ \hdashline [\mathbf{Y}_2] \end{bmatrix} = \left[\begin{array}{c:c} [\mathbf{A}_{11}] & [\mathbf{A}_{12}] \\ \hdashline [\mathbf{A}_{21}] & [\mathbf{A}_{22}] \end{array}\right] \begin{bmatrix} [\mathbf{X}_1] \\ \hdashline [\mathbf{X}_2] \end{bmatrix} \tag{2-46}$$

A partitioning of [A] both vertically and horizontally as above is called a ***cross-partition.*** Adopting the same convention for operating with submatrices of partitioned matrices as in the previous section and performing the indicated multiplications of Eq. (2-46) yields

$$[\mathbf{Y}_1] = [\mathbf{A}_{11}][\mathbf{X}_1] + [\mathbf{A}_{12}][\mathbf{X}_2] \tag{2-47a}$$

and

$$[\mathbf{Y}_2] = [\mathbf{A}_{21}][\mathbf{X}_1] + [\mathbf{A}_{22}][\mathbf{X}_2] \tag{2-47b}$$

Notice that in order for the partitions of Eq. (2-46) to be valid for multiplication, the number of *columns* in $[\mathbf{A}_{11}]$ must correspond to the number of rows in $[\mathbf{X}_1]$, and the number of *rows* in $[\mathbf{A}_{11}]$ must correspond to the number of rows in $[\mathbf{Y}_1]$.

The partitioning process may be extended to more complex matrix products when desirable. Consider the matrix equation

$$[\mathbf{A}]_{(m\times n)}[\mathbf{B}]_{(n\times s)} = [\mathbf{C}]_{(m\times s)} \tag{2-48}$$

and partition each of the matrices of this equation into submatrices as follows:

$$\left[\begin{array}{c:c} [\mathbf{A}_{11}]_{p\times q} & [\mathbf{A}_{12}]_{p\times(n-q)} \\ \hdashline [\mathbf{A}_{21}]_{(m-p)\times q} & [\mathbf{A}_{22}]_{(m-p)\times(n-q)} \end{array}\right] \left[\begin{array}{c:c} [\mathbf{B}_{11}]_{q\times r} & [\mathbf{B}_{12}]_{q\times(s-r)} \\ \hdashline [\mathbf{B}_{21}]_{(n-q)\times r} & [\mathbf{B}_{22}]_{(n-q)\times(s-r)} \end{array}\right] =$$

$$\left[\begin{array}{c:c} [\mathbf{C}_{11}]_{p\times r} & [\mathbf{C}_{12}]_{p\times(s-r)} \\ \hdashline [\mathbf{C}_{21}]_{(m-p)\times r} & [\mathbf{C}_{22}]_{(m-p)\times(s-r)} \end{array}\right] \tag{2-49}$$

Performing the indicated multiplication on the submatrices of Eq. (2-49), using the same conventions for partitioned matrices as before, yields

$$[\mathbf{C}_{11}]_{p\times r} = [\mathbf{A}_{11}]_{p\times q}[\mathbf{B}_{11}]_{q\times r} + [\mathbf{A}_{12}]_{p\times(n-q)}[\mathbf{B}_{21}]_{(n-q)\times r} \tag{2-50a}$$

$$[\mathbf{C}_{12}]_{p\times(s-r)} = [\mathbf{A}_{11}]_{p\times q}[\mathbf{B}_{12}]_{q\times(s-r)} + [\mathbf{A}_{12}]_{p\times(n-q)}[\mathbf{B}_{22}]_{(n-q)\times(s-r)} \tag{2-50b}$$

$$[\mathbf{C}_{21}]_{(m-p)\times r} = [\mathbf{A}_{21}]_{(m-p)\times q}[\mathbf{B}_{11}]_{q\times r} + [\mathbf{A}_{22}]_{(m-p)\times(n-q)}[\mathbf{B}_{21}]_{(n-q)\times r} \tag{2-50c}$$

$$[\mathbf{C}_{22}]_{(m-p)\times(s-r)} = [\mathbf{A}_{21}]_{(m-p)\times q}[\mathbf{B}_{12}]_{q\times(s-r)} + [\mathbf{A}_{22}]_{(m-p)\times(n-q)}[\mathbf{B}_{22}]_{(n-q)\times(s-r)} \tag{2-50d}$$

The cross-partitions of the matrices in Eq. (2-49) are seen from Eqs. (2-50) to be valid for multiplication. Notice that the horizontal partitioning chosen for [C] corresponds to the horizontal partitioning of [A] and that the vertical partitioning chosen for [C] corresponds to the vertical partitioning of [**B**]. Also, the vertical partitioning of [**A**] corresponds to the horizontal partitioning of [**B**]. The process of selecting valid partitions for matrix products may be extended to any number of horizontal or vertical partitions using the principles discussed in this section. The following section will present practical applications of the partitioning principles.

2-5.3 Applications of Partitioning to Finding Inverse Matrices

Partitioning of matrices into submatrices may be used effectively to simplify the labor in inverting matrices and solving large systems of equations. Several such useful applications of partitioning techniques are developed in the following examples.

Example 2-7. Find the inverse of the matrix

$$[\mathbf{A}] = \begin{bmatrix} 1 & 1 & 0 & 0 \\ 1 & 2 & 0 & 0 \\ 0 & 0 & 3 & -1 \\ 0 & 0 & -5 & 1 \end{bmatrix} \tag{2-51}$$

Examination of matrix [**A**] reveals that a substantial number of zero elements are present. Partitioning techniques may be effectively employed to utilize this fact and reduce the amount of labor required. Matrix [**A**] may be cross-partitioned as follows:

$$[\mathbf{A}] = \left[\begin{array}{c|c} [\mathbf{A}_{11}] & [\mathbf{0}] \\ \hline [\mathbf{0}] & [\mathbf{A}_{22}] \end{array}\right] = \left[\begin{array}{cc|cc} 1 & 1 & 0 & 0 \\ 1 & 2 & 0 & 0 \\ \hline 0 & 0 & 3 & -1 \\ 0 & 0 & -5 & 2 \end{array}\right] \tag{2-52}$$

Let the desired inverse of [**A**] be denoted as

$$[\mathbf{A}]^{-1} = \left[\begin{array}{c|c} [\mathbf{B}_{11}] & [\mathbf{B}_{12}] \\ \hline [\mathbf{B}_{21}] & [\mathbf{B}_{22}] \end{array}\right] \tag{2-53}$$

Since the basic requirement placed on $[\mathbf{A}]^{-1}$ is that it satisfy the equation $[\mathbf{A}][\mathbf{A}]^{-1} = [\mathbf{I}]$, the partitions of $[\mathbf{A}]^{-1}$ in Eq. (2-53) should be chosen so as to constitute a valid partitioning conforming to the partitions chosen for [**A**] as outlined previously.

Next, form a partition of the identity matrix [**I**] to conform to the partitions chosen for [**A**] and $[\mathbf{A}]^{-1}$.

$$[\mathbf{I}] = \left[\begin{array}{c|c} [\mathbf{I}_1] & [\mathbf{0}] \\ \hline [\mathbf{0}] & [\mathbf{I}_2] \end{array}\right] = \left[\begin{array}{cc|cc} 1 & 0 & 0 & 0 \\ 0 & 1 & 0 & 0 \\ \hline 0 & 0 & 1 & 0 \\ 0 & 0 & 0 & 1 \end{array}\right] \tag{2-54}$$

Substituting Eqs. (2-52), (2-53), and (2-54) into the equation $[\mathbf{A}][\mathbf{A}]^{-1} = [\mathbf{I}]$ gives

$$\left[\begin{array}{c|c} [\mathbf{A}_{11}] & [\mathbf{0}] \\ \hline [\mathbf{0}] & [\mathbf{A}_{22}] \end{array}\right] \left[\begin{array}{c|c} [\mathbf{B}_{11}] & [\mathbf{B}_{12}] \\ \hline [\mathbf{B}_{21}] & [\mathbf{B}_{22}] \end{array}\right] = \left[\begin{array}{c|c} [\mathbf{I}_1] & [\mathbf{0}] \\ \hline [\mathbf{0}] & [\mathbf{I}_2] \end{array}\right] \tag{2-55}$$

which in turn gives, upon performing the indicated submatrix multiplications,

$$[\mathbf{A}_{11}][\mathbf{B}_{11}] = [\mathbf{I}_1] \tag{2-56a}$$

$$[\mathbf{A}_{11}][\mathbf{B}_{12}] = [\mathbf{0}] \tag{2-56b}$$

$$[\mathbf{A}_{22}][\mathbf{B}_{21}] = [\mathbf{0}] \tag{2-56c}$$

$$[\mathbf{A}_{22}][\mathbf{B}_{22}] = [\mathbf{I}_2] \tag{2-56d}$$

Solving Eqs. (2-56) for $[\mathbf{B}_{11}]$, $[\mathbf{B}_{12}]$, $[\mathbf{B}_{21}]$, and $[\mathbf{B}_{22}]$ gives

$$[\mathbf{B}_{11}] = [\mathbf{A}_{11}]^{-1} \tag{2-57a}$$

$$[\mathbf{B}_{12}] = [\mathbf{0}] \tag{2-57b}$$

$$[\mathbf{B}_{21}] = [\mathbf{0}] \tag{2-57c}$$

$$[\mathbf{B}_{22}] = [\mathbf{A}_{22}]^{-1} \tag{2-57d}$$

Thus, the inverse of [A] is seen to be

$$\left[\begin{array}{cc|cc} 2 & -1 & 0 & 0 \\ -1 & 1 & 0 & 0 \\ \hline 0 & 0 & 2 & 1 \\ 0 & 0 & 5 & 3 \end{array}\right] \tag{2-58}$$

It should be clear that the benefit obtained from using the partitioned matrices is that the solution was found by inverting 2×2 matrices rather than a 4×4 matrix and that several of the submatrices were zero matrices. In large problems, substantial savings in time and effort may be obtained when it is possible to reduce the size of the matrices with which one must actually work to obtain the solution. Matrices with a number of zero elements are frequently encountered in applications, and partitioning techniques often prove very beneficial in such cases.

Example 2-8. Solve the following system of equations

$$\begin{aligned} x_1 - x_2 &= 3 \\ x_3 - x_4 + x_5 &= 1 \\ 2x_6 + x_7 &= 1 \\ 2x_1 + x_2 &= 1 \\ 2x_3 + x_4 + x_5 &= 2 \\ -x_6 + 2x_7 &= 1 \\ x_3 + 2x_4 - x_5 &= 0 \end{aligned} \tag{2-59}$$

by Gauss elimination using submatrices.

The system of equations may be expressed in matrix form as

$$\begin{bmatrix} 1 & -1 & 0 & 0 & 0 & 0 & 0 \\ 0 & 0 & 1 & -1 & 1 & 0 & 0 \\ 0 & 0 & 0 & 0 & 0 & 2 & 1 \\ 2 & 1 & 0 & 0 & 0 & 0 & 0 \\ 0 & 0 & 2 & 1 & 1 & 0 & 0 \\ 0 & 0 & 0 & 0 & 0 & -1 & 2 \\ 0 & 0 & 1 & 2 & -1 & 0 & 0 \end{bmatrix} \begin{bmatrix} x_1 \\ x_2 \\ x_3 \\ x_4 \\ x_5 \\ x_6 \\ x_7 \end{bmatrix} = \begin{bmatrix} 3 \\ 1 \\ 1 \\ 1 \\ 2 \\ 1 \\ 0 \end{bmatrix} \tag{2-60}$$

and the augmented matrix for this system of equations becomes

$$\left[\begin{array}{ccccccc:c} 1 & -1 & 0 & 0 & 0 & 0 & 0 & 3 \\ 0 & 0 & 1 & -1 & 1 & 0 & 0 & 1 \\ 0 & 0 & 0 & 0 & 0 & 2 & 1 & 1 \\ 2 & 1 & 0 & 0 & 0 & 0 & 0 & 1 \\ 0 & 0 & 2 & 1 & 1 & 0 & 0 & 2 \\ 0 & 0 & 0 & 0 & 0 & -1 & 2 & 1 \\ 0 & 0 & 1 & 2 & -1 & 0 & 0 & 0 \end{array}\right] \tag{2-61a}$$

Considerable work may be saved in this problem by utilizing appropriate partitioning techniques to obtain zero submatrices where possible. By interchanging rows 2 and 4 and rows 3 and 7, Matrix (2-61a) may be rewritten and then partitioned as

$$\left[\begin{array}{cc:ccc:cc:c} 1 & -1 & 0 & 0 & 0 & 0 & 0 & 3 \\ 2 & 1 & 0 & 0 & 0 & 0 & 0 & 1 \\ \hdashline 0 & 0 & 1 & 2 & -1 & 0 & 0 & 0 \\ 0 & 0 & 1 & -1 & 1 & 0 & 0 & 1 \\ 0 & 0 & 2 & 1 & 1 & 0 & 0 & 2 \\ \hdashline 0 & 0 & 0 & 0 & 0 & -1 & 2 & 1 \\ 0 & 0 & 0 & 0 & 0 & 2 & 1 & 1 \end{array}\right] \tag{2-61b}$$

This partitioned matrix is now of the form

$$\left[\begin{array}{c:c:c:c} [\mathbf{A}]_{2\times 2} & [\mathbf{0}] & [\mathbf{0}] & [\mathbf{K}_1] \\ \hdashline [\mathbf{0}] & [\mathbf{B}]_{3\times 3} & [\mathbf{0}] & [\mathbf{K}_2] \\ \hdashline [\mathbf{0}] & [\mathbf{0}] & [\mathbf{C}]_{2\times 2} & [\mathbf{K}_3] \end{array}\right] \tag{2-62}$$

A matrix of this form, where all submatrices not on the main diagonal are zero matrices, is referred to as a ***band matrix***. Such matrices arise frequently in structural analysis problems.

Matrix (2-62) represents the matrix equation

$$\left[\begin{array}{c:c:c} [\mathbf{A}]_{2\times 2} & [\mathbf{0}] & [\mathbf{0}] \\ \hdashline [\mathbf{0}] & [\mathbf{B}]_{3\times 3} & [\mathbf{0}] \\ \hdashline [\mathbf{0}] & [\mathbf{0}] & [\mathbf{C}]_{2\times 2} \end{array}\right] \left[\begin{array}{c} [\mathbf{X}_1] \\ \hdashline [\mathbf{X}_2] \\ \hdashline [\mathbf{X}_3] \end{array}\right] = \left[\begin{array}{c} [\mathbf{K}_1] \\ \hdashline [\mathbf{K}_2] \\ \hdashline [\mathbf{K}_3] \end{array}\right] \tag{2-63}$$

or

$$\left[\begin{array}{cc|ccc|cc} 1 & -1 & 0 & 0 & 0 & 0 & 0 \\ 2 & 1 & 0 & 0 & 0 & 0 & 0 \\ \hline 0 & 0 & 1 & 2 & -1 & 0 & 0 \\ 0 & 0 & 1 & -1 & 1 & 0 & 0 \\ 0 & 0 & 2 & 1 & 1 & 0 & 0 \\ \hline 0 & 0 & 0 & 0 & 0 & -1 & 2 \\ 0 & 0 & 0 & 0 & 0 & 2 & 1 \end{array}\right] \left[\begin{array}{c} x_1 \\ x_4 \\ \hline x_7 \\ x_2 \\ x_5 \\ \hline x_6 \\ x_3 \end{array}\right] = \left[\begin{array}{c} 3 \\ 1 \\ \hline 0 \\ 1 \\ 2 \\ \hline 1 \\ 1 \end{array}\right] \tag{2-64}$$

Expanding Eq. (2-63) into submatrix equations gives

$$[\mathbf{A}][\mathbf{X}_1] = [\mathbf{K}_1] \tag{2-65a}$$

$$[\mathbf{B}][\mathbf{X}_2] = [\mathbf{K}_2] \tag{2-65b}$$

$$[\mathbf{C}][\mathbf{X}_3] = [\mathbf{K}_3] \tag{2-65c}$$

or

$$\begin{bmatrix} 1 & -1 \\ 2 & 1 \end{bmatrix} \begin{bmatrix} x_1 \\ x_4 \end{bmatrix} = \begin{bmatrix} 3 \\ 1 \end{bmatrix} \tag{2-66a}$$

$$\begin{bmatrix} 1 & 2 & -1 \\ 1 & -1 & 1 \\ 2 & 1 & 1 \end{bmatrix} \begin{bmatrix} x_7 \\ x_2 \\ x_5 \end{bmatrix} = \begin{bmatrix} 0 \\ 1 \\ 2 \end{bmatrix} \tag{2-66b}$$

$$\begin{bmatrix} -1 & 2 \\ 2 & 1 \end{bmatrix} \begin{bmatrix} x_6 \\ x_3 \end{bmatrix} = \begin{bmatrix} 1 \\ 1 \end{bmatrix} \tag{2-66c}$$

The equations represented by Eqs. (2-66) may now be solved rapidly using Gauss elimination methods.

The augmented matrix for Eq. (2-66a) is

$$\left[\begin{array}{cc|c} 1 & -1 & 3 \\ 2 & 1 & 1 \end{array}\right] \tag{2-67a}$$

The augmented matrix for Eq. (2-66b) is

$$\left[\begin{array}{ccc|c} 1 & 2 & -1 & 0 \\ 1 & -1 & 1 & 1 \\ 2 & 1 & 1 & 2 \end{array}\right] \tag{2-67b}$$

The augmented matrix for Eq. (2-66c) is

$$\left[\begin{array}{cc|c} -1 & 2 & 1 \\ 2 & 1 & 1 \end{array}\right] \tag{2-67c}$$

To solve for x_1 and x_4, Gauss elimination may be applied to the augmented matrix of Eq. (2-67a) as follows:

$$\left[\begin{array}{cc|c} 1 & -1 & 3 \\ 2 & 1 & 1 \end{array}\right] \tag{2-68a}$$

$R_2 \rightarrow R_2 - 2R_1$.

$$\left[\begin{array}{cc|c} 1 & -1 & 3 \\ 0 & 3 & -5 \end{array}\right] \tag{2-68b}$$

thus

$$3x_4 = -5 \tag{2-68c}$$

$$x_4 = -\tfrac{5}{3} \tag{2-68d}$$

and

$$x_1 + \tfrac{5}{3} = 3 \tag{2-68e}$$

$$x_1 = \tfrac{4}{3} \tag{2-68f}$$

To solve for x_7, x_2, and x_5 Gauss elimination may be applied to the augmented matrix of Eq. (2-67b) as follows:

$$\left[\begin{array}{ccc|c} 1 & 2 & -1 & 0 \\ 1 & -1 & 1 & 1 \\ 2 & 1 & 1 & 2 \end{array}\right] \tag{2-69a}$$

$R_2 \rightarrow R_2 - R_1$, and

$R_3 \rightarrow R_3 - 2R_1$.

$$\left[\begin{array}{ccc|c} 1 & 2 & -1 & 0 \\ 0 & -3 & 2 & 1 \\ 0 & -3 & 3 & 2 \end{array}\right] \tag{2-69b}$$

$R_2 \rightarrow -\tfrac{1}{3} R_2$.

$$\left[\begin{array}{ccc|c} 1 & 2 & -1 & 0 \\ 0 & 1 & -\tfrac{2}{3} & -\tfrac{1}{3} \\ 0 & -3 & 3 & 2 \end{array}\right] \tag{2-69c}$$

$R_3 \rightarrow R_3 + 3R_2$.

$$\left[\begin{array}{ccc|c} 1 & 2 & -1 & 0 \\ 0 & 1 & -\tfrac{2}{3} & -\tfrac{1}{3} \\ 0 & 0 & 1 & 1 \end{array}\right] \tag{2-69d}$$

thus

$$x_5 = 1 \tag{2-69e}$$

and

$$x_2 - \tfrac{2}{3}(1) = -\tfrac{1}{3} \tag{2-69f}$$

$$x_2 = \tfrac{1}{3} \tag{2-69g}$$

and

$$x_7 + 2(\tfrac{1}{3}) - 1 = 0 \tag{2-69h}$$

$$x_7 = \tfrac{1}{3} \tag{2-69i}$$

To solve for x_6 and x_3, Gauss elimination may be applied to the augmented matrix of Eq. (2-67c):

$$\begin{bmatrix} -1 & 2 & \vdots & 1 \\ 2 & 1 & \vdots & 1 \end{bmatrix} \tag{2-70a}$$

$R_1 \rightarrow -R_1$.

$$\begin{bmatrix} 1 & -2 & \vdots & -1 \\ 2 & 1 & \vdots & 1 \end{bmatrix} \tag{2-70b}$$

$R_2 \rightarrow R_2 - 2R_1$.

$$\begin{bmatrix} 1 & -2 & \vdots & -1 \\ 0 & 5 & \vdots & 3 \end{bmatrix} \tag{2-70c}$$

Thus

$$5x_3 = 3 \tag{2-70d}$$

$$x_3 = \tfrac{3}{5} \tag{2-70e}$$

and

$$x_6 - 2(\tfrac{3}{5}) = -1 \tag{2-70f}$$

$$x_6 = \tfrac{1}{5} \tag{2-70g}$$

Should one desire to invert a large matrix using computer programs that are available to him at a computer center to which he has access, but the matrix he desires to invert is too large to be used with the available computer program, partitioning techniques may be used to break the given matrix into submatrices small enough to fit the available programs. In some situations, the given matrix may not contain enough zero elements to fit the situations described in the two previous examples. A general procedure for partitioning a matrix into submatrices and inverting the matrix by submatrix techniques may be derived, and the resulting formulas do not depend upon having any zero elements in the given matrix.

Let an $n \times n$ matrix $[\mathbf{A}]$ be cross-partitioned as follows:

$$\begin{bmatrix} [\mathbf{A}_{11}]_{p \times p} & [\mathbf{A}_{12}]_{p \times q} \\ [\mathbf{A}_{21}]_{q \times p} & [\mathbf{A}_{22}]_{q \times q} \end{bmatrix} \tag{2-71}$$

where $p + q = n$.

Letting $[\mathbf{B}] = [\mathbf{A}]^{-1}$ in the equation $[\mathbf{A}][\mathbf{A}]^{-1} = [\mathbf{I}]$, partition the matrices of this equation in such a way as to form valid partitions corresponding to the partitioning of $[\mathbf{A}]$ as indicated in Eq. (2-49).

$$\begin{bmatrix} [\mathbf{A}_{11}]_{p \times p} & [\mathbf{A}_{12}]_{p \times q} \\ [\mathbf{A}_{21}]_{q \times p} & [\mathbf{A}_{22}]_{q \times q} \end{bmatrix} \begin{bmatrix} [\mathbf{B}_{11}]_{p \times p} & [\mathbf{B}_{12}]_{p \times q} \\ [\mathbf{B}_{21}]_{q \times p} & [\mathbf{B}_{22}]_{q \times q} \end{bmatrix} = \begin{bmatrix} [\mathbf{I}_1]_{p \times p} & [\mathbf{0}]_{p \times q} \\ [\mathbf{0}]_{q \times p} & [\mathbf{I}_2]_{q \times q} \end{bmatrix} \tag{2-72}$$

Performing the indicated submatrix multiplications of Eq. (2-72) gives

$$[\mathbf{A}_{11}][\mathbf{B}_{11}] + [\mathbf{A}_{12}][\mathbf{B}_{21}] = [\mathbf{I}_1] \tag{2-73a}$$

$$[\mathbf{A}_{11}][\mathbf{B}_{12}] + [\mathbf{A}_{12}][\mathbf{B}_{22}] = [\mathbf{0}] \tag{2-73b}$$

$$[\mathbf{A}_{21}][\mathbf{B}_{11}] + [\mathbf{A}_{22}][\mathbf{B}_{21}] = [\mathbf{0}] \tag{2-73c}$$

$$[\mathbf{A}_{21}][\mathbf{B}_{12}] + [\mathbf{A}_{22}][\mathbf{B}_{22}] = [\mathbf{I}_2] \tag{2-73d}$$

If the inverse of [**A**] exists and the partitions may be chosen so that the inverses of $[\mathbf{A}_{11}]$ and $[\mathbf{A}_{22}]$ exist, operating first on Eq. (2-73b) with $[\mathbf{A}_{11}]^{-1}$ gives

$$[\mathbf{A}_{11}]^{-1}[\mathbf{A}_{11}][\mathbf{B}_{12}] + [\mathbf{A}_{11}]^{-1}[\mathbf{A}_{12}][\mathbf{B}_{22}] = [\mathbf{0}] \tag{2-74a}$$

or

$$[\mathbf{B}_{12}] + [\mathbf{A}_{11}]^{-1}[\mathbf{A}_{12}][\mathbf{B}_{22}] = [\mathbf{0}] \tag{2-74b}$$

thus

$$[\mathbf{B}_{12}] = -[\mathbf{A}_{11}]^{-1}[\mathbf{A}_{12}][\mathbf{B}_{22}] \tag{2-74c}$$

Now, substituting this result into Eq. (2-73d) gives

$$[\mathbf{A}_{21}](-[\mathbf{A}_{11}]^{-1}[\mathbf{A}_{12}][\mathbf{B}_{22}]) + [\mathbf{A}_{22}][\mathbf{B}_{22}] = [\mathbf{I}] \tag{2-75a}$$

or

$$(-[\mathbf{A}_{21}][\mathbf{A}_{11}]^{-1}[\mathbf{A}_{12}] + [\mathbf{A}_{22}])[\mathbf{B}_{22}] = [\mathbf{I}] \tag{2-75b}$$

thus

$$[\mathbf{B}_{22}] = ([\mathbf{A}_{22}] - [\mathbf{A}_{21}][\mathbf{A}_{11}]^{-1}[\mathbf{A}_{12}])^{-1} \tag{2-75c}$$

Applying the same procedure to Eqs. (2-73a) and (2-73c) gives

$$[\mathbf{B}_{21}] = -[\mathbf{A}_{22}]^{-1}[\mathbf{A}_{21}][\mathbf{B}_{11}] \tag{2-76a}$$

and

$$[\mathbf{B}_{11}] = ([\mathbf{A}_{11}] - [\mathbf{A}_{12}][\mathbf{A}_{22}]^{-1}[\mathbf{A}_{21}])^{-1} \tag{2-76b}$$

Equation (2-75c) may be solved using known or obtainable submatrices from the matrix [**A**] to give $[\mathbf{B}_{22}]$. This result may then be substituted in Eq. (2-74c) to find $[\mathbf{B}_{12}]$. Matrices $[\mathbf{B}_{11}]$ and $[\mathbf{B}_{21}]$ may be found in a similar fashion.

This method, as mentioned previously, is primarily valuable for adapting an available computer program for matrix inversion to the inversion of matrices larger than those which can be inverted directly by the given computer program. In doing this, however, some thought should be given to the ever-present danger of compounding error truncation beyond the limits of tolerable accuracy.

2–6
Solution of Systems of Equations by Cholesky's Method

Certain special properties of matrices which occur in the analysis of structural systems may be utilized advantageously, particularly when solving large systems of equations. The properties to be utilized are those of *real, symmetric, positive definite, band matrices.*

Real matrices and symmetric matrices are defined in Secs. A-1 and A-3 of Appendix A. A matrix [**A**] is ***positive definite*** if and only if

$$[\mathbf{X}]^T[\mathbf{A}][\mathbf{X}] > 0 \tag{2-77}$$

for all nonzero column matrices [X]. A matrix [A] is a ***band matrix*** of width $(2m + 1)$ if all elements a_{ij} for which $|i - j| > m$ are zero. For instance,

$$\begin{bmatrix} a_{11} & a_{12} & 0 & 0 & 0 & 0 \\ a_{21} & a_{22} & a_{23} & 0 & 0 & 0 \\ 0 & a_{32} & a_{33} & a_{34} & 0 & 0 \\ 0 & 0 & a_{43} & a_{44} & a_{45} & 0 \\ 0 & 0 & 0 & a_{54} & a_{55} & a_{56} \\ 0 & 0 & 0 & 0 & a_{65} & a_{66} \end{bmatrix} \tag{2-78}$$

is a band matrix of width 3, where m, which equals 1 in this instance, is referred to as the half-band width. Stiffness matrices of structural systems, defined in later chapters, possess these properties.

If a matrix [A] is a *symmetric*, *positive definite*, *square* matrix of order n, it may be decomposed uniquely into $[A] = [G][G]^T$, where [G] is a ***lower triangular matrix*** of order n with *positive* diagonal elements.† It follows that $[G]^T$ is an ***upper triangular matrix*** of order n with *positive* diagonal elements.

Using the fact that $[A] = [G][G]^T$, the solution of the system of equations $[A][X] = [B]$ may be computationally simplified by rewriting the system of equations as

$$[G][G]^T[X] = [B] \tag{2-79a}$$

Equation (2-79a) may be solved as a pair of equations expressed as

$$[G][Y] = [B] \tag{2-79b}$$

and

$$[G]^T[X] = [Y] \tag{2-79c}$$

The simplifications in computation result from the fact that [G] and $[G]^T$ are *triangular matrices.*

An additional simplification is achieved from the fact that if [A] is a *band matrix* of band width $(2m + 1)$, then [G] may be shown to be a ***triangular band matrix*** of width $(m + 1)$. For Matrix (2-78), [G] will be of the form

$$\begin{bmatrix} g_{11} & 0 & 0 & 0 & 0 & 0 \\ g_{21} & g_{22} & 0 & 0 & 0 & 0 \\ 0 & g_{32} & g_{33} & 0 & 0 & 0 \\ 0 & 0 & g_{43} & g_{44} & 0 & 0 \\ 0 & 0 & 0 & g_{54} & g_{55} & 0 \\ 0 & 0 & 0 & 0 & g_{65} & g_{66} \end{bmatrix} \tag{2-80}$$

For a symmetric band matrix [A], utilizing computer techniques, considerable storage space may be saved, since only the nonzero elements of [A] must be stored,

†A derivation of this theorem is given in Ref. 2-3 at the end of this chapter.

and as a result of the symmetry, only an $(m+1)$ width must be stored. Thus, if [**A**] is an nth order matrix, only $(m+1)\times n$ elements of [**A**] must be stored rather than the n^2 elements required for matrices not possessing these properties. Matrix [**G**] will also require only an $(m+1)$ width to be stored. For very large problems for which m is appreciably smaller than n, the resulting efficiency gains are highly significant both in speed and in the size of problems that may be handled.

By solving iteratively the equations

$$[\mathbf{A}] = [\mathbf{G}][\mathbf{G}]^T \tag{2-81}$$

for the elements g_{ij}, an algorithm known as Cholesky's method may be derived. The algorithm steps are as follows:

1. Start with $j = 1$.
2. $g_{11} = \sqrt{a_{11}}$.
3. Let $i = j + 1$.
4. $g_{i1} = \dfrac{a_{i1}}{g_{11}}$.
5. Let $i = i + 1$ and return to step 4.
6. Repeat steps 4 and 5 until $i = n + 1$.
7. Let $j = j + 1$.
8. $g_{jj} = \sqrt{a_{jj} - \sum_{k=1}^{j-1} g_{jk}^2}$.
9. Let $i = j + 1$.
10. $g_{ij} = \dfrac{a_{ij} - \sum_{k=1}^{j-1} g_{ik}g_{jk}}{g_{jj}}$.
11. Let $i = i + 1$ and return to step 10.
12. Repeat steps 10 and 11 until $i = n + 1$.
13. Return to step 7.
14. Repeat steps 7 through 13 until $j = n$.

A flow diagram for this algorithm is given in Fig. 2-1. The numbering of blocks in the flow diagram is chosen to correspond to the numbering of the steps above.

Example 2-9. Solve the set of equations [**A**][**X**] = [**B**] where

$$[\mathbf{A}] = \begin{bmatrix} 1 & -1 & 1 & 2 \\ -1 & 5 & -3 & 0 \\ 1 & -3 & 3 & 0 \\ 2 & 0 & 0 & 7 \end{bmatrix}, \qquad [\mathbf{X}] = \begin{bmatrix} x_1 \\ x_2 \\ x_3 \\ x_4 \end{bmatrix}, \qquad [\mathbf{B}] = \begin{bmatrix} 2 \\ -4 \\ 4 \\ 1 \end{bmatrix} \tag{2-82}$$

The first step is to find [**G**] using the Cholesky algorithm.

$$g_{11} = \sqrt{a_{11}} = \sqrt{1} = 1 \tag{2-83a}$$

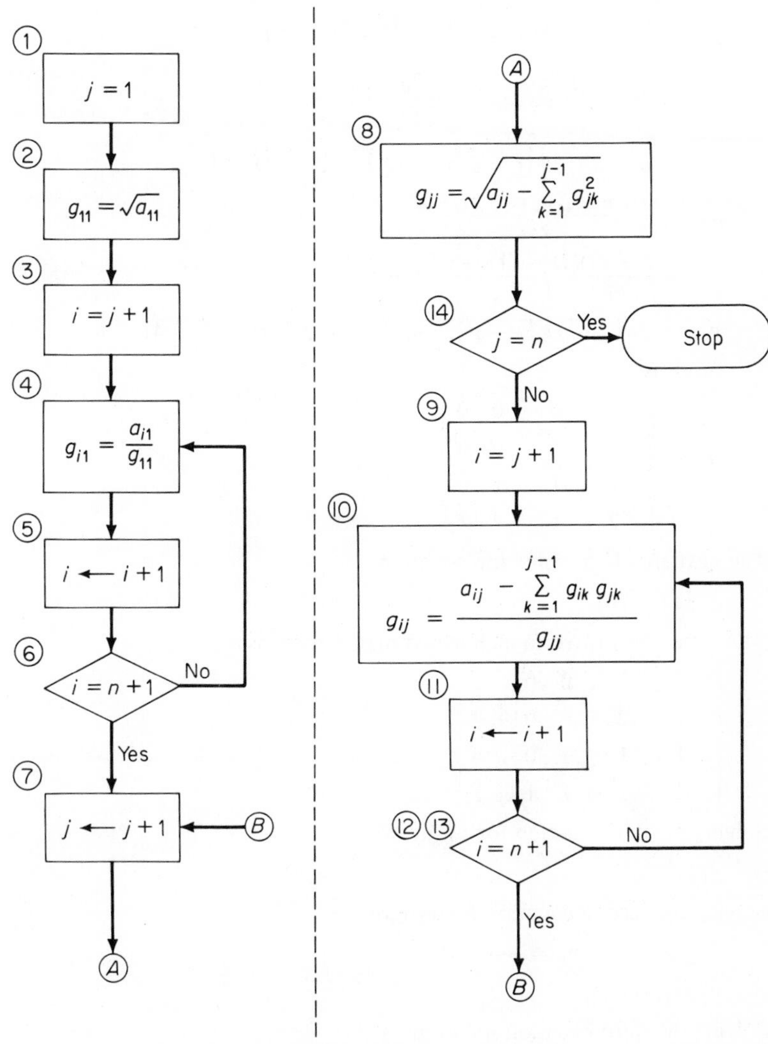

Fig. 2-1 Flow diagram for computing the elements of [G] by the Cholesky method.

$$g_{21} = \frac{a_{21}}{1} = -1 \tag{2-83b}$$

$$g_{31} = \frac{a_{31}}{1} = 1 \tag{2-83c}$$

$$g_{41} = \frac{a_{41}}{1} = 2 \tag{2-83d}$$

$$g_{22} = \sqrt{a_{22} - g_{21}^2} = \sqrt{5 - 1} = 2 \tag{2-83e}$$

$$g_{32} = \frac{a_{32} - g_{31}g_{21}}{g_{22}} = \frac{-3 - (1)(-1)}{2} = -1 \tag{2-83f}$$

$$g_{42} = \frac{a_{42} - g_{41}g_{21}}{g_{22}} = \frac{0 - (2)(-1)}{2} = 1 \tag{2-83g}$$

$$g_{33} = \sqrt{a_{33} - (g_{31}^2 + g_{32}^2)} = \sqrt{3 - (1 + 1)} = 1 \tag{2-83h}$$

$$g_{43} = \frac{a_{43} - g_{41}g_{31} - g_{42}g_{32}}{g_{33}} \tag{2-83i}$$

$$= \frac{0 - (2)(1) - (1)(-1)}{1} = -1 \tag{2-83j}$$

$$g_{44} = \sqrt{a_{44} - (g_{41}^2 + g_{42}^2 + g_{43}^2} = \sqrt{7 - (1 + 1 + 4)} = 1 \tag{2-83k}$$

The result is

$$[\mathbf{G}] = \begin{bmatrix} 1 & 0 & 0 & 0 \\ -1 & 2 & 0 & 0 \\ 1 & -1 & 1 & 0 \\ 2 & 1 & -1 & 1 \end{bmatrix} \tag{2-84}$$

The next step is to solve the equation

$$[\mathbf{G}][\mathbf{Y}] = [\mathbf{B}] \tag{2-85a}$$

which may be written in augmented matrix form as

$$\left[\begin{array}{cccc|c} 1 & 0 & 0 & 0 & 2 \\ -1 & 2 & 0 & 0 & -4 \\ 1 & -1 & 1 & 0 & 4 \\ 2 & 1 & -1 & 1 & 1 \end{array}\right] \tag{2-85b}$$

Solving the first equation for y_1 gives

$$y_1 = 2 \tag{2-85c}$$

Solving the second equation for y_2 gives

$$2y_2 = -4 + y_1 = -4 + 2 = -2 \tag{2-85d}$$

$$y_2 = -1 \tag{2-85e}$$

Solving the third equation for y_3 gives

$$y_3 = 4 + y_2 - y_1 = 4 - 1 - 2 \tag{2-85f}$$

$$y_3 = 1 \tag{2-85g}$$

Solving the fourth equation for y_4 gives

$$y_4 = 1 + y_3 - y_2 - 2y_1 = 1 + 1 + 1 - 4 \tag{2-85h}$$

$$y_4 = -1 \tag{2-85i}$$

This technique is referred to as the ***forward solution.***

The third step is to solve the equation

$$[\mathbf{G}]^T[\mathbf{X}] = [\mathbf{Y}] \tag{2-86a}$$

which may be written in augmented matrix form as

$$\left[\begin{array}{cccc|c} 1 & -1 & 1 & 2 & 2 \\ 0 & 2 & -1 & 1 & -1 \\ 0 & 0 & 1 & -1 & 1 \\ 0 & 0 & 0 & 1 & -1 \end{array}\right] \tag{2-86b}$$

Solving the fourth equation for x_4 gives

$$x_4 = -1 \tag{2-86c}$$

Solving the third equation for x_3 gives

$$x_3 = 1 + x_4 = 1 - 1 \tag{2-86d}$$

$$x_3 = 0 \tag{2-86e}$$

Solving the second equation for x_2 gives

$$2x_2 = -1 + x_3 - x_4 = -1 + 0 + 1 \tag{2-86f}$$

$$x_2 = 0 \tag{2-86g}$$

Solving the first equation for x_1 gives

$$x_1 = 2 + x_2 - x_3 - 2x_4 = 2 + 0 + 0 + 2 \tag{2-86h}$$

$$x_1 = 4 \tag{2-86i}$$

This technique is referred to as the ***backward solution.***

The final solution is then

$$x_1 = 4 \tag{2-86j}$$

$$x_2 = 0 \tag{2-86k}$$

$$x_3 = 0 \tag{2-86l}$$

$$x_4 = -1 \tag{2-86m}$$

2–7 Problems

2-1. Solve the following system of equations by iteration to two-decimal-place accuracy:

$$10x - 4y + 5z = 40$$

$$3x + 7y + 2z = 14$$

$$x - 2y + 8z = 28$$

2-2. Write a computer program to solve a system of four equations with four unknowns by the iterative technique presented. Carry the results to three-decimal-place accuracy.

2-3. Solve the following system using Gauss elimination.

$$x_1 - 2x_2 + 2x_3 + 4x_4 = -10$$

$$2x_1 - x_2 - x_3 + 2x_4 = -4$$

$$3x_1 + x_2 + 2x_3 - x_4 = 12$$
$$x_1 + 2x_2 + x_3 + x_4 = 2$$

2-4. Solve Prob. 2-3 by matrix inversion of the coefficient matrix.

2-5. Solve Prob. 2-3 if the constant matrix on the right-hand side of the equation is

$$\begin{bmatrix} 1 \\ 2 \\ 3 \\ 4 \end{bmatrix}$$

2-6. Write the following sets of equations in matrix form and solve by any desired method.

(a) $2x_1 + x_2 + 3x_3 = 5$
$x_1 - x_2 - 3x_3 = 6$
$5x_1 - 4x_2 - x_3 = 7$

(b) $x_1 + 2x_2 = 3$
$2x_1 + x_2 = 5$
$x_1 - x_2 = 3$

(c) $x_1 + x_2 + x_3 + x_4 = 4$
$x_2 + x_3 + x_4 = 3$
$x_3 + x_4 = 2$
$x_4 = 1$

2-7. Perform the indicated multiplication using the indicated partitions.

$$\left[\begin{array}{ccc:c} 3 & 2 & -1 & -1 \\ 1 & 1 & 0 & 2 \\ 2 & -1 & 1 & 2 \\ \hdashline 0 & 1 & 2 & -2 \\ 1 & -1 & -1 & 0 \end{array}\right] \left[\begin{array}{ccc:cc} 1 & 1 & 2 & -1 & -1 \\ 3 & 1 & 1 & 0 & 2 \\ 2 & 2 & -2 & 1 & 0 \\ \hdashline 0 & 0 & 1 & 1 & 1 \end{array}\right]$$

Check the result by multiplying without the benefit of partitioning.

2-8. Find the inverse of the given matrix, using the indicated partitioning, and check the result.

$$\left[\begin{array}{ccc:cc} 1 & 0 & -1 & 0 & 0 \\ 0 & 1 & -1 & 0 & 0 \\ 1 & 0 & 1 & 0 & 0 \\ \hdashline 0 & 0 & 0 & 2 & 2 \\ 0 & 0 & 0 & 1 & 3 \end{array}\right]$$

2-9. Derive the solution to the system of equations

$$a_{11}x_1 + a_{12}x_2 = b_1$$
$$a_{21}x_1 + a_{22}x_2 = b_2$$

by elimination methods and show that the result is identical to the matrix solution $[\mathbf{X}] = [\mathbf{A}]^{-1}[\mathbf{B}]$, where $[\mathbf{A}]^{-1}$ is computed by the adjoint method.

2-10. Complete the solutions of the subproblems of Example 2-8 and check the results, using matrix inversion methods.

2-11. Find the inverse of the coefficient matrix of the system of equations in Prob. 2-3 by

(a) the adjoint method;
(b) the row transformation method;
(c) the method of Example 2-9, using a 2×2 partitioning of the given matrix.

2-12. Construct a simple example for which the iterative method of this chapter does not converge.

2-13. Show that the matrix equation $[\mathbf{A}][\mathbf{X}] = [\mathbf{B}]$ is equivalent to the matrix equation $[\mathbf{X}]^T[\mathbf{A}]^T = [\mathbf{B}]^T$. Show that if $[\mathbf{A}]$ is symmetric, the solution is then $[\mathbf{X}]^T = [\mathbf{B}]^T[\mathbf{A}]^{-1}$.

2-14. Show that if $[\mathbf{A}]$ is symmetric and orthogonal, the solution to the equation $[\mathbf{A}][\mathbf{X}] = [\mathbf{B}]$ is $[\mathbf{X}] = [\mathbf{A}][\mathbf{B}]$.

2-15. Solve the given system of equations by using Cholesky's method.

$$3x + 2y - z = 2$$
$$2x + 4y + 2z = 1$$
$$-x + 2y + 4z = 2$$

2-16. By attempting to solve the system of equations in Prob. 2-3 by Cholesky's method, indicate where the method fails and explain why.

SELECTED REFERENCES

2-1 Forsythe, George, and Cleve B. Moler, *Computer Solution of Linear Algebraic Systems*. Englewood Cliffs, N.J.: Prentice-Hall, Inc., 1967.

2-2 Householder, Alston S., *The Theory of Matrices in Numerical Analysis*. Waltham, Mass.: Blaisdell Publishing Co., 1965.

2-3 James, M. L., G. M. Smith, and J. C. Wolford, *Applied Numerical Methods for Digital Computation with Fortran*. Scranton, Pa.: International Textbook Co., 1967.

2-4 Sokolnikoff, I. S., and R. M. Redheffer, *Mathematics of Physics and Modern Engineering*. New York: McGraw-Hill Book Company, 1965.

2-5 Weeg, Gerard P., and Georgia B. Reed, *Introduction to Numerical Analysis*. Waltham, Mass.: Blaisdell Publishing Co., 1966.

3 INTRODUCTION TO THE FLEXIBILITY METHOD OF ANALYSIS: PLANAR STRUCTURES

3–1 Introduction

As pointed out in Chapter 1, the potential of the ***flexibility method*** of analysis is not as great in most cases as that of the ***stiffness method***, particularly when the analysis of a structural system is coupled with the use of an electronic digital computer. There are, however, cases wherein application of the flexibility method is found to be convenient. This is particularly true where the degree of static indeterminacy is low—say, up to three—and when hand computations are to be used.

The flexibility method considers ***actions*** (*forces* and *moments*) as the ***redundants*** (*unknowns*) which when removed do not render the structure unstable. Solution of these redundants requires a set of simultaneous linear algebraic equations, describing the *continuity* of the system, with as many independent equations as redundants.

The primary purpose of this chapter is not to develop a matrix formulation of the flexibility method, but rather to discuss the basic concepts of the method and to illustrate these concepts in the analysis of a few simple structural models. A review of the use of the virtual work method in finding deformations is presented. In the solution of the virtual work integrals for obtaining deformations, the method of graphical integration is used.

3–2
Displacements by Virtual Work

Before proceeding in the discussion of the flexibility method, it is desirable to discuss the computation of displacements. Because of its general application, the method of ***virtual work*** is presented. Since this method of computing displacements is presented in detail in most undergraduate texts on structural analysis (see the references at end of this chapter), the derivation of the necessary relationships will not be given here.

3-2.1 Structures Subjected to Bending

With members subjected primarily to bending strains, the deflection of a point in a structural system is given by

$$y = \int_0^L \frac{Mm}{EI}\,dx \tag{3-1}$$

where y = deflection of the point in question;
M = moment expressed as a function of x;
m = moment due to a unit load placed at the location of the desired deflection and in the direction of the desired deflection expressed as a function of x;
E = modulus of elasticity;
I = moment of inertia (in most cases in this chapter, I will be considered constant in order to simplify the mathematics);
L = length of the structure.

Example 3-1. To illustrate the use of Eq. (3-1), consider the structure shown in Fig. 3-1. In this example, it is desired to find the deflection y at the location of the 30 k (kip) load. Substitution of the expressions for moments, M and m, and values of E and I given in Fig. 3-1 into Eq. (3-1) yields

$$y = \int_0^{120} \frac{(18x)(0.6x)}{(30{,}000)(1000)}\,dx + \int_0^{180} \frac{(12x)(0.4x)}{(30{,}000)(1000)}\,dx$$

$$y = 0.518 \text{ in.}$$

Example 3-2. For the structure shown in Fig. 3-2, the horizontal deflection at point D is desired. The moment functions and values of E and I are given in the figure. Substitution of these values into Eq. (3-1) yields

$$y = \int_0^{240} \frac{(-3840)(-192)}{(30{,}000)(2000)}\,dx + \int_{96}^{192} \frac{[-40(x-96)](-x)}{(30{,}000)(1500)}\,dx$$

$$y = 3.61 \text{ in.}$$

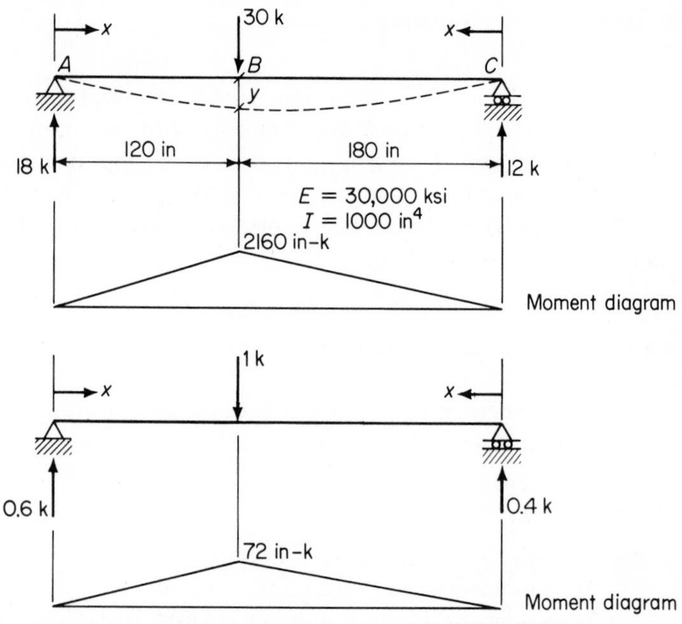

Section	x measured from	Limits on x	Moment due to real loads	Moment due to unit load
AB	A	0 → 120	$M = 18x$	$m = 0.6x$
CB	C	0 → 180	$M = 12x$	$m = 0.4x$

Fig. 3-1 Example 3-1: Deflection of simple beam.

Example 3-3. For the structure shown in Fig. 3-3, it is desired to find the slope θ at the point of application of the 30 k load. Note that the unit load is now a unit moment. Substitution of the moment functions into Eq. (3-1) yields

$$\theta = \int_0^{240} \frac{(10x)(-x/360)}{EI}\,dx + \int_0^{120} \frac{(20x)(x/360)}{EI}\,dx$$

$$\theta = -\frac{96{,}000}{EI}\text{ rad}$$

The negative sign indicates that the unit moment was applied in the direction opposite to that of the resulting rotation at the point of application of the 30 k load.

3-2.2 Numerical Integration

Although the evaluation of Eq. (3-1) is not particularly difficult, the application of the flexibility method may involve the calculation of many displacements.

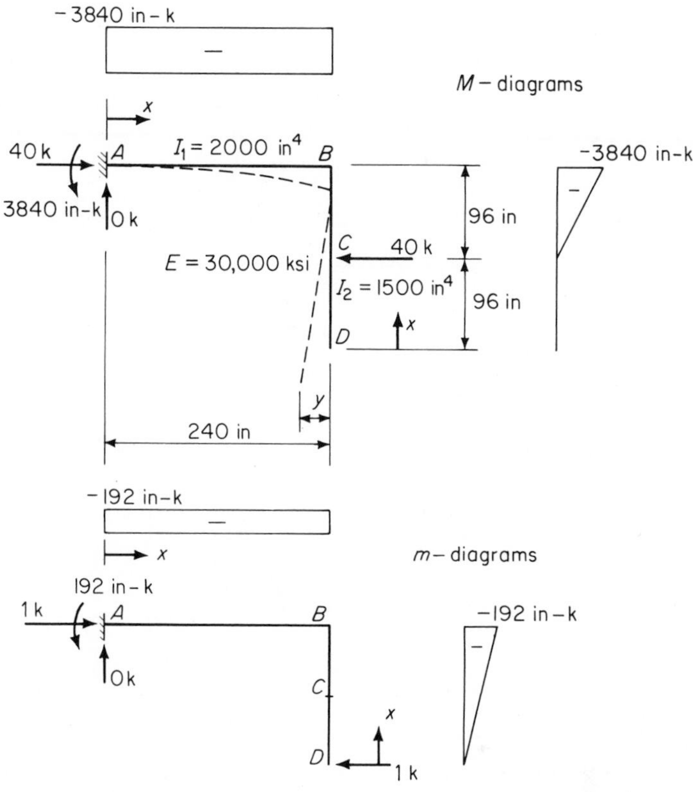

Sections	x measured from	Limits on x	Moments due to real loads	Moment due to unit load
AB	A	0 → 240	$M = -3840$	$m = -192$
DC	D	0 → 96	$M = 0$	$m = -x$
CB	D	96 → 192	$M = -40(x - 96)$	$m = -x$

Fig. 3-2 Example 3-2: Deflection of framed structure.

It would be very helpful to be able to minimize the amount of time necessary to calculate these displacements. The application of a numerical integration procedure in the evaluation of Eq. (3-1) will decrease the time involved in calculating the displacement.

First, note that the m-diagram always consists of a series of ***straight lines***, i.e., m-functions are always *linear functions* of x. This is true because the m-diagram is due to a single unit concentrated load or moment (see Figs. 3-1, 3-2, and 3-3).

Secondly, the moment functions due to the original load are nearly always

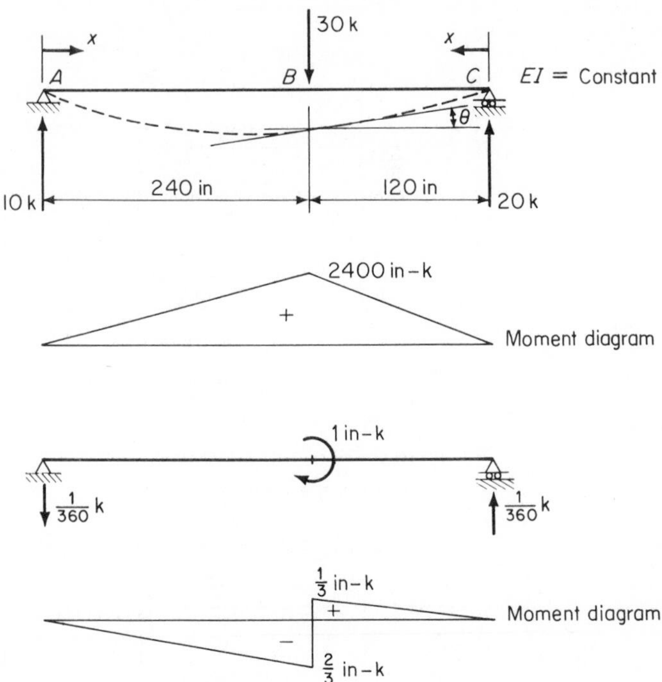

Sections	x measured from	Limits on x	Moments due to real loads	Moment due to unit loads
AB	A	0 → 240	$M=10x$	$m=-\frac{x}{360}$
CB	C	0 → 120	$M=20x$	$m=\frac{x}{360}$

Fig. 3-3 Example 3-3: Rotation of simple beam.

simple polynomials. In fact, in almost all cases these functions are either linear or second-degree polynomials (parabolas).

Equation (3-1) can be rewritten as

$$y = \int_A^B m\left(\frac{M}{EI}\right) dx \tag{3-2}$$

where M/EI is the moment function due to the original load divided by EI.

If EI is constant, then the M/EI diagram has the same shape as the M-diagram. Let

$$A_M = \int_A^B \frac{M}{EI}\, dx \tag{3-3}$$

This integral represents the area under the M/EI diagram between points A and B and is denoted by the symbol A_M [see Fig. 3-4(a)]. In addition, the m-diagram, which is always a series of straight lines, can be expressed as

$$m = c + kx \tag{3-4}$$

where c and k are constants [see Fig. 3-4(b)].

Substitution of Eq. (3-4) into Eq. (3-2) yields

$$\int_A^B m\left(\frac{M}{EI}\right) dx = c\int_A^B \left(\frac{M}{EI}\right) dx + k\int_A^B \left(\frac{M}{EI}\right) x\, dx \tag{3-5}$$

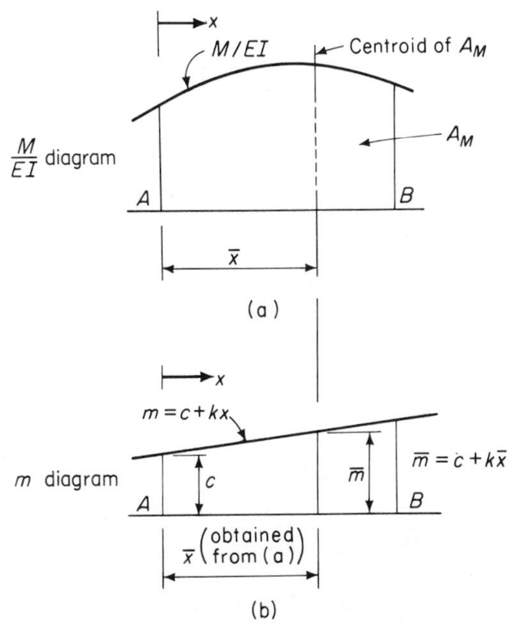

Fig. 3-4 Diagrams for numerical integration method: (a) M/EI diagram; (b) m diagram.

The integral in the second term on the right-hand side of Eq. (3-5) is the *first moment* of the area under the M/EI diagram about point A and can be written

$$\bar{x}A_M = \int_A^B \left(\frac{M}{EI}\right) x\, dx \tag{3-6}$$

where $\bar{x}$ is the x-distance from point A to the **centroid** of the area under the M/EI diagram. Substitution of Eqs. (3-3) and (3-6) into Eq. (3-5) yields

$$\int_A^B m\left(\frac{M}{EI}\right) dx = cA_M + k\bar{x}A_M = (c + k\bar{x})A_M \tag{3-7}$$

But

$$\bar{m} = c + k\bar{x} \tag{3-8}$$

where $\bar{m}$ is the value of m for $x = \bar{x}$, or the value of m ***at the same location as the centroid of the area under the M/EI diagram.*** Thus,

$$\int_A^B m\left(\frac{M}{EI}\right) dx = \bar{m}A_M \tag{3-9}$$

Note that neither A_m nor $\bar{m}$ can be evaluated across a discontinuity in either M or m, i.e., both functions for M and m between points A and B must be continuous functions of x. Should either diagram be discontinuous, the structure can be divided into segments in which both functions of M and m are continuous. The results obtained from each segment are added algebraically to obtain the total. Thus,

$$y = \sum \bar{m}A_M \tag{3-10}$$

Example 3-4. In order to illustrate the method of numerical integration, consider the beam of Example 3-1 shown in Fig. 3-1. Again, the deflection at point B is desired. Discontinuities exist in both M- and m-diagrams at the point of load application, thus the diagrams must be broken into two segments, i.e., segments AB and BC as shown in Fig. 3-5. With

$$A_M^{AB} = \frac{129{,}600}{EI}$$

$$A_M^{BC} = \frac{194{,}400}{EI}$$

$$\bar{m}_{AB} = 48$$

$$\bar{m}_{BC} = 48$$

then

$$y = \bar{m}_{AB}A_M^{AB} + \bar{m}_{BC}A_M^{BC} = \frac{48(129{,}600)}{EI} + \frac{48(194{,}400)}{EI}$$

$$y = \frac{48}{EI}(129{,}600 + 194{,}400) = \frac{48(324{,}000)}{30{,}000(1000)}$$

$y = 0.518$ in. (checks with previous solution)

Example 3-5. For a second illustration, consider the structure discussed previously in Example 3-2. Again, the horizontal deflection at point D is desired. The moment diagrams are redrawn in Fig. 3-6 thus:

$$A_M^{AB} = -\frac{921{,}600}{EI_1} = -\frac{921{,}600}{30{,}000(2000)} = -0.01535$$

$$A_M^{BC} = -\frac{184{,}320}{EI_2} = -\frac{184{,}320}{30{,}000(1500)} = -0.00409$$

$$\bar{m}_{AB} = -192$$

$$\bar{m}_{BC} = -160$$

Note that since $A_M^{CD} = 0$, segment CD does not enter into the calculations.

$$y = \bar{m}_{AB}A_M^{AB} + \bar{m}_{BC}A_M^{BC} = -192(-0.01535) - 160(-0.00409)$$

$y = 3.61$ in. (checks with previous solution)

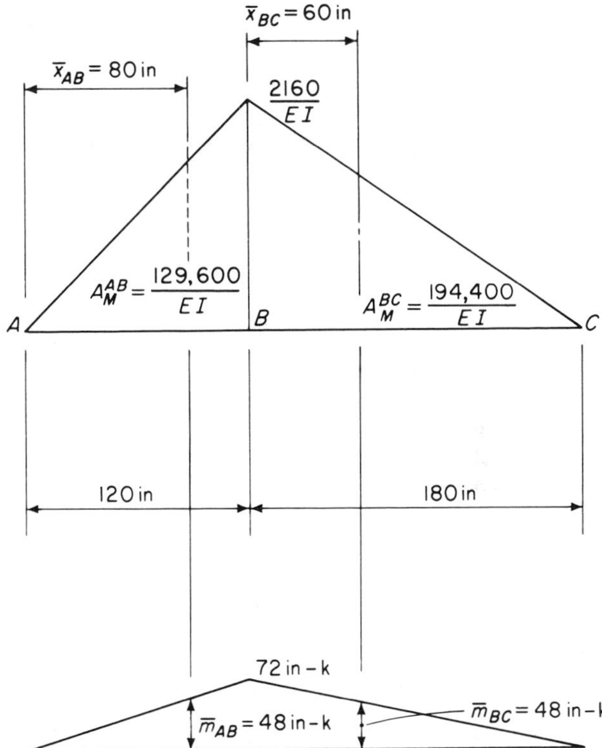

Fig. 3-5 Example 3-4: Use of numerical integration method in calculating deflections. (Moment diagrams from Fig. 3-2.)

In order to facilitate the computations of $\bar{m}A_M$, a variety of shapes for M- and m-diagrams are given in Fig. 3-7.

3-2.3 Structures Subjected to Axial Forces

In truss structures, the primary stresses are axial stresses. The virtual work equation for determining displacements in such structures is

$$y = \sum_{i=1}^{n} \frac{S_i u_i L_i}{A_i E_i} \tag{3-11}$$

where S_i = axial force in ith truss member due to the original load;
u_i = axial force in ith member due to a unit load placed at the location of the desired displacement in the direction of the desired displacement;
L_i = length of ith member;
A_i = cross-sectional area of ith member;
E_i = modulus of elasticity of ith member;
n = number of members in truss.

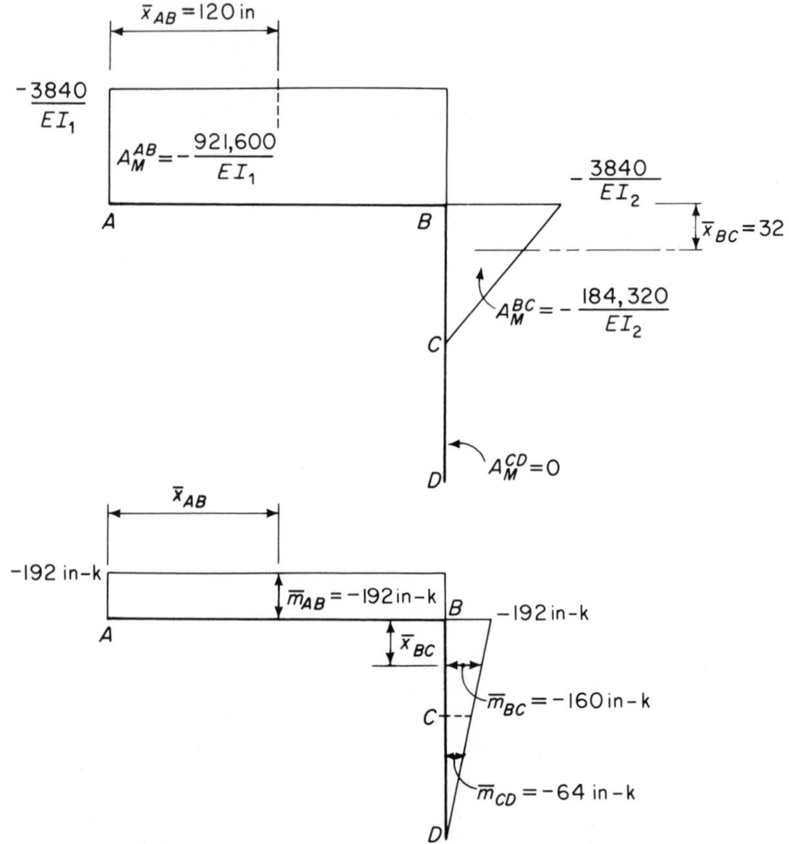

Fig. 3-6 Example 3-5: Use of numerical integration method in calculating deflection of a frame.

Example 3-6. To illustrate the use of Eq. (3-11), consider the structure shown in Fig. 3-8. In this example, the horizontal deflection of the roller support B due to the applied load is desired. In Fig. 3-8(a), the structure is shown subjected to an applied load of 12 k acting horizontally at C. Bar forces S due to the applied load and bar forces u due to the unit load placed at the point of the desired deflection and in the direction of the deflection and values of L/A are given in Fig. 3-8(c).

The sum of SuL/AE, shown in the figure, is equal to the deflection, as noted.

3–3
Basic Equations of Flexibility Analysis

An introduction to the flexibility method of analysis was given in Sec. 1-3. The basic procedure for analyzing a structural system by the flexibility method is as follows:

1. Release the original structure so that it is a ***stable determinate structure***; the ***released actions*** (*reactions* and/or *internal actions*) are called ***redundants***.

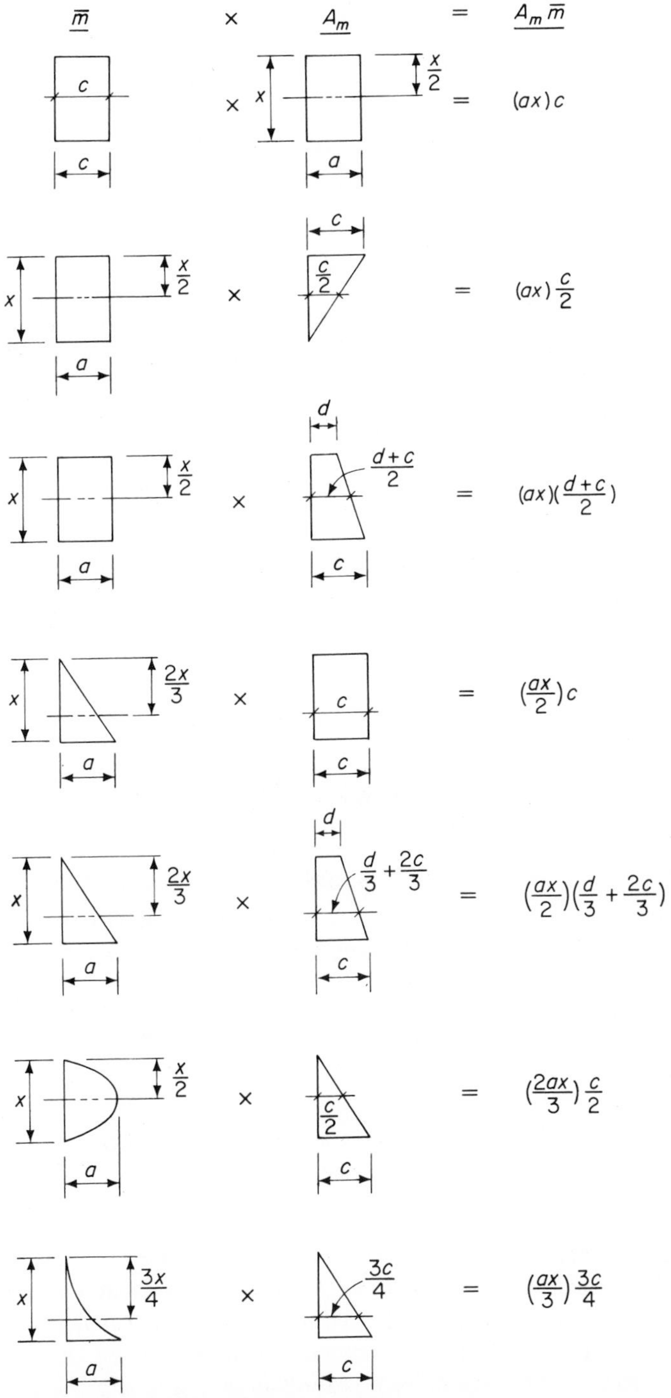

$\overline{m}$	×	A_m	=	$A_m \overline{m}$
	×		=	$(ax)c$
	×		=	$(ax)\frac{c}{2}$
	×		=	$(ax)(\frac{d+c}{2})$
	×		=	$(\frac{ax}{2})c$
	×		=	$(\frac{ax}{2})(\frac{d}{3}+\frac{2c}{3})$
	×		=	$(\frac{2ax}{3})\frac{c}{2}$
	×		=	$(\frac{ax}{3})\frac{3c}{4}$

Fig. 3-7 Evaluation of $\bar{m}A_M$ for typical moment diagrams.

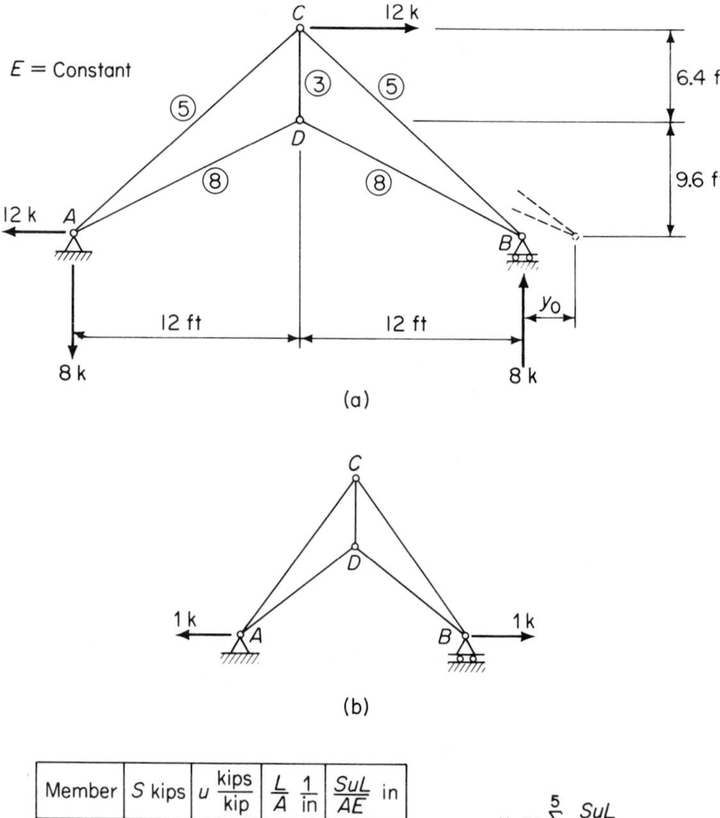

Member	S kips	u $\frac{\text{kips}}{\text{kip}}$	$\frac{L}{A}$ $\frac{1}{\text{in}}$	$\frac{SuL}{AE}$ in
AC	−5.0	−2.5	60.0	750/E
AD	+19.2	+3.2	23.1	1418/E
CD	+24.0	+4.0	25.6	2460/E
CB	−25.0	−2.5	60.0	3750/E
DB	+19.2	+3.2	23.1	1418/E
Sum	—	—	—	9796/E

$$y_0 = \sum_{i=1}^{5} \frac{SuL}{AE} = \frac{9796}{30 \times 10^3} = 0.326 \text{ in} \longrightarrow$$

(c)

Fig. 3-8 Example 3-6: Deflection of truss. (a) Original structure; (b) secondary system; (c) SuL/AE table.

2. Calculate the deformations at the locations of the released actions due to the original loads, in the direction of the released actions (redundants).
3. Apply unit values of the redundants, ***one at a time***, to the released structure.
4. Calculate the deformations at each release in the direction of the release due to the unit value of each redundant acting separately.
5. Write a continuity equation for each released action by describing the displace-

ment of the point of application of the redundants as a linear combination of the deformations calculated in steps 2 and 4.
6. Solve the set of linear algebraic equations for the unknown redundants.
7. Place the known values of the redundants back on the structure and complete the solution by using the equations of static equilibrium.

The ***sign convention*** that is used for the ***flexibility analysis*** is as follows:

1. ***Forces and translations upward or to the right are positive.***
2. ***Counterclockwise moments and rotations are positive.***

Equations (1-1) in Sec. 1-3, although written for a particular system indeterminate to two degrees, can be expanded for a system that is statically indeterminate to m degrees as follows:

$$\begin{array}{l} \delta_{10} + \delta_{11}A_1 + \delta_{12}A_2 + \cdots + \delta_{1i}A_i + \cdots + \delta_{1m}A_m = \delta_{s1} \\ \delta_{20} + \delta_{21}A_1 + \delta_{22}A_2 + \cdots + \delta_{2i}A_i + \cdots + \delta_{2m}A_m = \delta_{s2} \\ \vdots \\ \delta_{i0} + \delta_{i1}A_1 + \delta_{i2}A_2 + \cdots + \delta_{ii}A_i + \cdots + \delta_{im}A_m = \delta_{si} \\ \vdots \\ \delta_{m0} + \delta_{m1}A_1 + \delta_{m2}A_2 + \cdots + \delta_{mi}A_i + \cdots + \delta_{mm}A_m = \delta_{sm} \end{array} \tag{3-12}$$

where: A_i = ith redundant action;
δ_{i0} = displacement of released structure at ith redundant location in the direction of the redundant due to the original loads;
δ_{ij} = displacement at point i of released structure in the direction of the released redundant A_i due to a unit load at point j in the direction of the released redundant A_j;
δ_{si} = imposed displacement of ith support of real structure in the direction of the redundant.

The only new terms in the general set of equations given above, other than those discussed in Sec. 1-3, are the deformations $\delta_{s1}, \delta_{s2}, \ldots \delta_{sm}$. These are the deformations at the location of the redundants and in the direction of the redundants that may exist in the original structure. These deformations may be due to settlement, displacement of an elastic support, rotation of a semirigid fixed end support, etc. Now, Eqs. (3-12) may be expressed in matrix form as:

$$\begin{bmatrix} \delta_{10} \\ \delta_{20} \\ \vdots \\ \delta_{i0} \\ \vdots \\ \delta_{m0} \end{bmatrix} + \begin{bmatrix} \delta_{11} & \delta_{12} & \cdots & \delta_{1i} & \cdots & \delta_{1m} \\ \delta_{21} & \delta_{22} & \cdots & \delta_{2i} & \cdots & \delta_{2m} \\ \vdots & & & & & \vdots \\ \delta_{i1} & \delta_{i2} & \cdots & \delta_{ii} & \cdots & \delta_{im} \\ \vdots & & & & & \vdots \\ \delta_{m1} & \delta_{m2} & \cdots & \delta_{mi} & \cdots & \delta_{mm} \end{bmatrix} \begin{bmatrix} A_1 \\ A_2 \\ \vdots \\ A_i \\ \vdots \\ A_m \end{bmatrix} = \begin{bmatrix} \delta_{s1} \\ \delta_{s2} \\ \vdots \\ \delta_{si} \\ \vdots \\ \delta_{sm} \end{bmatrix} \tag{3-13}$$

or

$$[\mathbf{D}_0] + [\mathbf{D}][\mathbf{A}] = [\mathbf{D}_s] \tag{3-14}$$

which can be rewritten as

$$[\mathbf{A}] = [\mathbf{D}]^{-1}([\mathbf{D}_s] - [\mathbf{D}_0]) \tag{3-15}$$

where: $[\mathbf{D}_0]$ represents the deformations of the released structure at the point of application of the redundants and in the direction of the redundants due to the original loads;

$[\mathbf{D}]$ represents the deformations of the released structure at the locations of the redundants and in the direction of the redundants due to unit values of the redundants acting separately;

$[\mathbf{A}]$ represents the redundant actions;

$[\mathbf{D}_s]$ represents the deformations that exist at the location of the redundants and in the direction of the redundants in the original structure (settlements, elastic support deformations, etc.).

The $[\mathbf{D}]$ matrix is known as the ***flexibility matrix*** and the elements of the matrix are known as ***flexibility coefficients***. This matrix is a function of the geometry and material properties of the structure. Matrix $[\mathbf{D}]$ is symmetric about the main diagonal. That is, $\delta_{ij} = \delta_{ji}$ according to Maxwell's principle of reciprocal deformations, i.e., $\delta_{13} = \delta_{31}$, etc. Maxwell's principle† states:

> The deflection at one point *A* in a structure due to a load applied at another point *B* is exactly the same as the deflection at *B* if the same load is applied at *A*.

Now, suppose *n* additional actions—i.e., internal moments, shears, and reactions—were desired in addition to the *m* redundants. As stated earlier, these actions can be determined once the redundants have been evaluated by applying the equations of static equilibrium. These actions can also be defined as a linear combination of the corresponding actions of the released structure caused by the imposed loading condition and the individual application of each of the redundants, i.e.,

$$\begin{aligned}
X_1 &= X_{10} + x_{11}A_1 + x_{12}A_2 + \cdots + x_{1i}A_i + \cdots + x_{1m}A_m \\
X_2 &= X_{20} + x_{21}A_1 + x_{22}A_2 + \cdots + x_{2i}A_i + \cdots + x_{2m}A_m \\
&\vdots \\
X_i &= X_{i0} + x_{i1}A_1 + x_{i2}A_2 + \cdots + x_{ii}A_i + \cdots + x_{im}A_m \\
&\vdots \\
X_n &= X_{n0} + x_{n1}A_1 + x_{n2}A_2 + \cdots + x_{ni}A_i + \cdots + x_{nm}A_m
\end{aligned} \tag{3-16}$$

†J. N. Hoff, *The Analysis of Structures*, New York: John Wiley & Sons, Inc., 1956, page 373.

where: X_i = action desired, such as internal moment, shear, or reaction, other than a redundant;

X_{i0} = the value of the action X_i for the released structure subjected to the original applied loads;

x_{ij} = value of action X_i due to a unit value of the redundant X_j, i.e., x_{23} would be the value of the action at point 2 (assuming this action was not one of the redundants) due to a unit value of the redundant at point 3;

m = number of redundants or number of degrees of static indeterminacy;

n = number of other actions desired.

In matrix form, Eqs. (3-16) become

$$\begin{bmatrix} X_1 \\ X_2 \\ \vdots \\ X_i \\ \vdots \\ X_n \end{bmatrix} = \begin{bmatrix} X_{10} \\ X_{20} \\ \vdots \\ X_{i0} \\ \vdots \\ X_{n0} \end{bmatrix} + \begin{bmatrix} x_{11} & x_{12} & \cdots & x_{1i} & \cdots & x_{1m} \\ x_{21} & x_{22} & \cdots & x_{2i} & \cdots & x_{2m} \\ \vdots & & & & & \vdots \\ x_{i1} & x_{i2} & \cdots & x_{ii} & \cdots & x_{im} \\ \vdots & & & & & \vdots \\ x_{n1} & x_{n2} & \cdots & x_{ni} & \cdots & x_{nm} \end{bmatrix} \begin{bmatrix} A_1 \\ A_2 \\ \vdots \\ A_i \\ \vdots \\ A_m \end{bmatrix} \tag{3-17}$$

or

$$[\mathbf{X}] = [\mathbf{X}_0] + [\mathbf{x}][\mathbf{A}] \tag{3-18}$$

In order to illustrate the use of Eqs. (3-14) and (3-18), the following example is presented.

Example 3-7. The planar frame shown in Fig. 3-9(a) is indeterminate to three degrees. The reactions at points A and D are desired. The reactions at point D (A_1, A_2, and A_3) are chosen as the redundants. In Fig. 3-9(b) the redundants have been released and the corresponding deformations δ_{10}, δ_{20}, and δ_{30} computed. Note that δ_{10} and δ_{20} are translations and that δ_{30} is a rotation.

The corresponding displacements of point D due to unit values of the redundants A_1, A_2, and A_3 are given in Figs. 3-9(c), (d), and (e). Substitution of the required information from Fig. 3-9 into Eq. (3-13) and factoring out EI gives

$$\begin{bmatrix} -33{,}912 \\ -6588 \\ -2862 \end{bmatrix} + \begin{bmatrix} 2448 & 810 & 216 \\ 810 & 1308.3 & 147.5 \\ 216 & 147.5 & 31 \end{bmatrix} \begin{bmatrix} A_1 \\ A_2 \\ A_3 \end{bmatrix} = \begin{bmatrix} 0 \\ 0 \\ 0 \end{bmatrix} \tag{3-19}$$

Solving Eqs. (3-19) for A_1, A_2, and A_3 gives

$$\begin{bmatrix} A_1 \\ A_2 \\ A_3 \end{bmatrix} = \begin{bmatrix} 2448 & 810 & 216 \\ 810 & 1308.3 & 147.5 \\ 216 & 147.5 & 31 \end{bmatrix}^{-1} \begin{bmatrix} 33{,}912 \\ 6588 \\ 2862 \end{bmatrix} \tag{3-20}$$

or

$$\begin{bmatrix} A_1 \\ A_2 \\ A_3 \end{bmatrix} = \begin{bmatrix} 0.00116 & 0.00042 & -0.01003 \\ 0.00042 & 0.0018 & -0.01145 \\ -0.01003 & -0.01145 & 0.15663 \end{bmatrix} \begin{bmatrix} 33{,}912 \\ 6588 \\ 2862 \end{bmatrix} \tag{3-21}$$

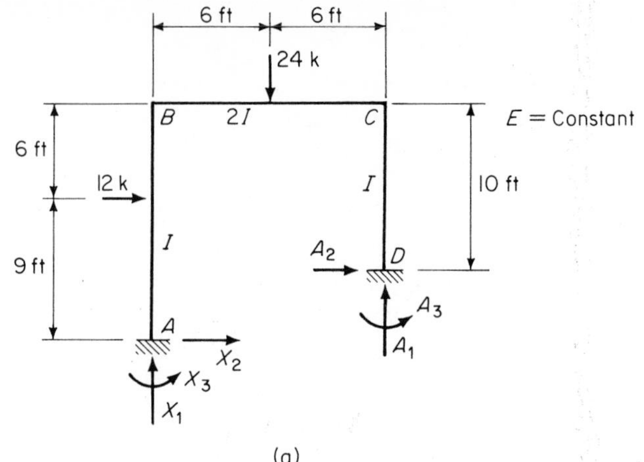

(a)

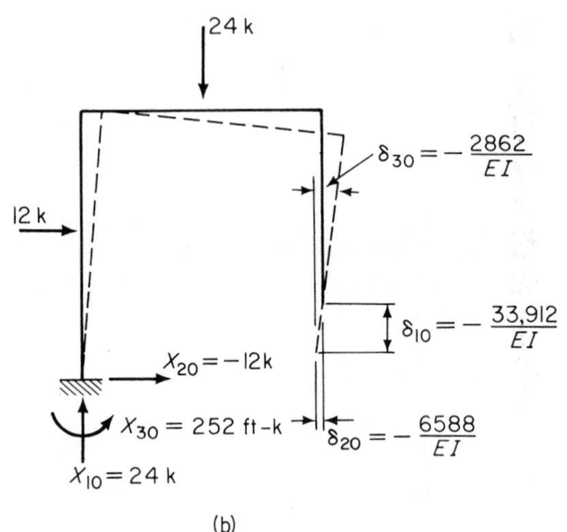

(b)

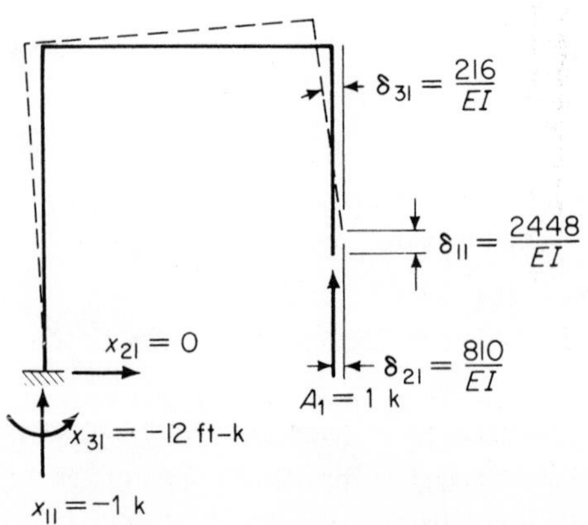

(c)

Fig. 3-9 Example 3-7: Analysis of planar frame. (a) Original structure; (b) released structure; (c) $A_1 = 1$ k.

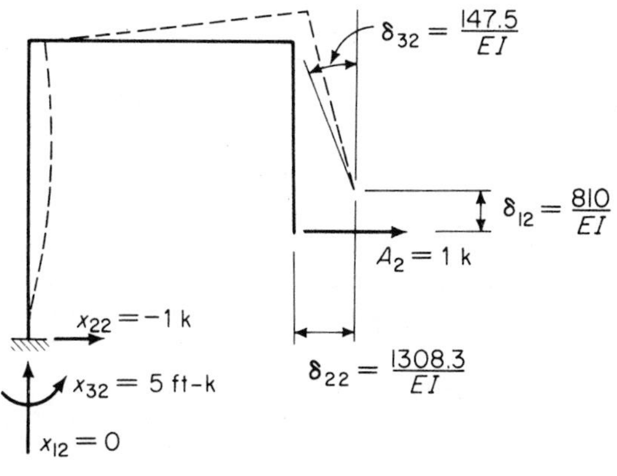

(d)

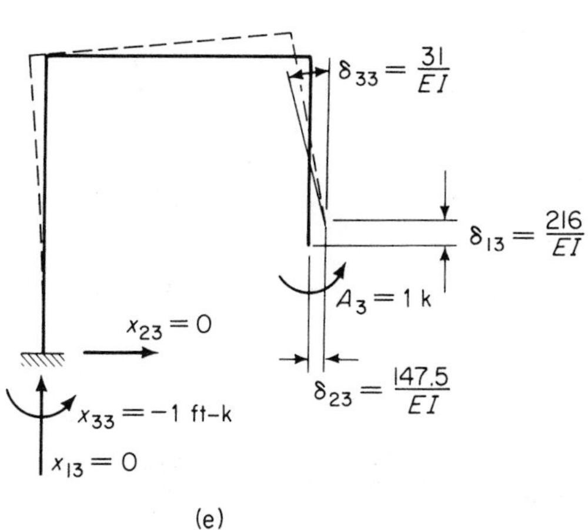

(e)

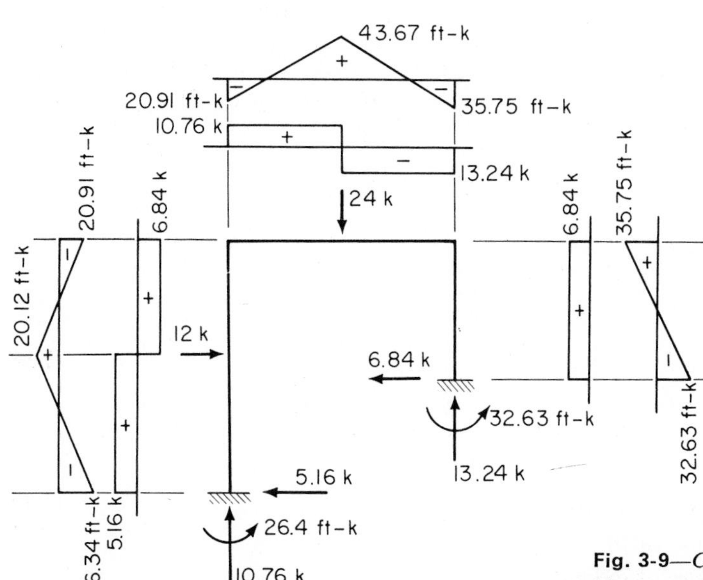

(f)

Fig. 3-9—*Cont.* (d) $A_2 = 1$ k; (e) $A_3 = 1$ k; (f) shear and moment diagrams.

which yields

$$\begin{bmatrix} A_1 \\ A_2 \\ A_3 \end{bmatrix} = \begin{bmatrix} +13.24 \\ -6.84 \\ +32.63 \end{bmatrix} \tag{3-22}$$

Thus, $A_1 = 13.24$ k $\uparrow$, $A_2 = 6.84$ k $\leftarrow$ (note that the negative sign in the above matrix indicates that A_2 is opposite in direction to that established by the sign convention), and $A_3 = 32.63$ ft-k $\curvearrowleft$.

The reactions at point A are also desired and can be obtained by Eq. (3-17). All necessary values for substitution into Eq. (3-17) are given in Figs. 3-9(a) through (e). Hence,

$$\begin{bmatrix} X_1 \\ X_2 \\ X_3 \end{bmatrix} = \begin{bmatrix} 24 & -1 & 0 & 0 \\ -12 & 0 & -1 & 0 \\ 252 & -12 & 5 & -1 \end{bmatrix} \begin{bmatrix} 13.24 \\ -6.84 \\ 32.63 \end{bmatrix} \tag{3-23}$$

which gives

$$\begin{bmatrix} X_1 \\ X_2 \\ X_3 \end{bmatrix} = \begin{bmatrix} +10.76 \\ -5.16 \\ +26.4 \end{bmatrix} \tag{3-24}$$

Thus, $X_1 = 10.76$ k $\uparrow$, $X_2 = 5.16$ k $\leftarrow$ (note that the negative sign in the matrix above indicates that X_2 is opposite in direction to that established by the sign convention), and $X_3 = 26.4$ ft-k $\curvearrowleft$.

The shear and moment diagrams for the frame are given in Fig. 3-9(f).

3–4 Flexibility Equations for Multiple-Load Cases

The matrix representation of the flexibility equations is very useful for solving multiple-load cases. Equation (3-14) can be expanded into the following form in order to handle this situation; each column matrix of Eq. (3-14) now becomes a rectangular matrix in which each column represents a given load case:

$$\begin{bmatrix} A_1^1 & A_1^2 & \cdots & A_1^p \\ A_2^1 & A_2^2 & \cdots & A_2^p \\ \vdots & \vdots & & \vdots \\ A_m^1 & A_m^2 & \cdots & A_m^p \end{bmatrix} = \begin{bmatrix} \delta_{11} & \delta_{12} & \cdots & \delta_{1m} \\ \delta_{21} & \delta_{22} & \cdots & \delta_{2m} \\ \vdots & \vdots & & \vdots \\ \delta_{m1} & \delta_{m2} & \cdots & \delta_{mm} \end{bmatrix}^{-1} \times \left(\begin{bmatrix} \delta_{s1}^1 & \delta_{s1}^2 & \cdots & \delta_{s1}^p \\ \delta_{s2}^1 & \delta_{s2}^2 & \cdots & \delta_{s2}^p \\ \vdots & \vdots & & \vdots \\ \delta_{sm}^1 & \delta_{sm}^2 & \cdots & \delta_{sm}^p \end{bmatrix} - \begin{bmatrix} \delta_{10}^1 & \delta_{10}^2 & \cdots & \delta_{10}^p \\ \delta_{20}^1 & \delta_{20}^2 & \cdots & \delta_{20}^p \\ \vdots & \vdots & & \vdots \\ \delta_{m0}^1 & \delta_{m0}^2 & \cdots & \delta_{m0}^p \end{bmatrix} \right) \tag{3-25}$$

or

$$[\mathbf{A}^p] = [\mathbf{D}]^{-1}([\mathbf{D}_s^p] - [\mathbf{D}_0^p]) \tag{3-26}$$

where: p = number of load cases;
m = number of redundants.

Note that the matrices [A], $[\mathbf{D}_s^p]$, and $[\mathbf{D}_0^p]$ contain one column of elements for each load case. If only one load case is to be investigated, Eq. (3-25) reduces to Eq. (3-13).

If other actions are desired, an expanded version of Eq. (3-17) may be used as follows:

$$\begin{bmatrix} X_1^1 & X_1^2 & \cdots & X_1^p \\ X_2^1 & X_2^2 & \cdots & X_2^p \\ \vdots & \vdots & & \vdots \\ X_n^1 & X_n^2 & \cdots & X_n^p \end{bmatrix} = \begin{bmatrix} X_{10}^1 & X_{10}^2 & \cdots & X_{10}^p \\ X_{20}^1 & X_{20}^2 & \cdots & X_{20}^p \\ \vdots & \vdots & & \vdots \\ X_{n0}^1 & X_{n0}^2 & \cdots & X_{n0}^p \end{bmatrix} + \begin{bmatrix} x_{11} & x_{12} & \cdots & x_{1m} \\ x_{21} & x_{22} & \cdots & x_{2m} \\ \vdots & \vdots & & \vdots \\ x_{n1} & x_{n2} & \cdots & x_{nm} \end{bmatrix} \begin{bmatrix} A_1^1 & A_1^2 & \cdots & A_1^p \\ A_2^1 & A_2^2 & \cdots & A_2^p \\ \vdots & \vdots & & \vdots \\ A_m^1 & A_m^2 & \cdots & A_m^p \end{bmatrix} \tag{3-27}$$

or

$$[\mathbf{X}^p] = [\mathbf{X}_0^p] + [\mathbf{x}][\mathbf{A}^p] \tag{3-28}$$

To illustrate the use of these equations, consider the following example.

Example 3-8. The truss structure shown in Fig. 3-10(a) is indeterminate to two degrees. All four reactions are required. The reactions at points 1 and 2 have been chosen as the redundants (A_1 and A_2). Two load cases are to be investigated as shown in Fig. 3-10(a). In Figs. 3-10(b) and (c), the redundants have been released and the corresponding deformations given for each load case.

The corresponding displacements of points 1 and 2 due to unit values of the redundants A_1 and A_2 are given in Figs. 3-10(d) and (e). Substitution of the required information from Fig. 3-10 into Eq. (3-25) and factoring out L/EA gives

$$\begin{bmatrix} A_1^1 & A_1^2 \\ A_2^1 & A_2^2 \end{bmatrix} = \begin{bmatrix} 10.22 & 7.33 \\ 7.33 & 10.22 \end{bmatrix}^{-1} \left(\begin{bmatrix} 0 & 0 \\ 0 & 0 \end{bmatrix} - \begin{bmatrix} -5.77 & -10 \\ -4.22 & -10 \end{bmatrix} \right) \tag{3-29}$$

or

$$\begin{bmatrix} A_1^1 & A_1^2 \\ A_2^1 & A_2^2 \end{bmatrix} = \begin{bmatrix} 0.2015 & -0.14452 \\ -0.14452 & 0.2015 \end{bmatrix} \begin{bmatrix} 5.77 & 10 \\ 4.22 & 10 \end{bmatrix} = \begin{bmatrix} 0.55 & 0.57 \\ 0.017 & 0.57 \end{bmatrix} \tag{3-30}$$

Thus,

$$A_1^1 = 0.55 \text{ k} \uparrow \quad \text{and} \quad A_2^1 = 0.017 \text{ k} \uparrow$$

$$A_1^2 = 0.57 \text{ k} \uparrow \quad \text{and} \quad A_2^2 = 0.57 \text{ k} \uparrow$$

The reactions X_1 and X_2 are found by Eq. (3-27) as follows:

$$\begin{bmatrix} X_1^1 & X_1^2 \\ X_2^1 & X_2^2 \end{bmatrix} = \begin{bmatrix} 0.833 & 0.5 \\ 0.167 & 0.5 \end{bmatrix} + \begin{bmatrix} -0.667 & -0.333 \\ -0.333 & -0.667 \end{bmatrix} \begin{bmatrix} 0.55 & 0.57 \\ 0.017 & 0.57 \end{bmatrix} \tag{3-31}$$

$$\begin{bmatrix} X_1^1 & X_1^2 \\ X_2^1 & X_2^2 \end{bmatrix} = \begin{bmatrix} 0.46 & -0.07 \\ -0.027 & -0.07 \end{bmatrix} \tag{3-32}$$

Thus,

$$X_1^1 = 0.46 \text{ k} \uparrow \quad \text{and} \quad X_2^1 = 0.027 \text{ k} \downarrow$$
$$X_1^2 = 0.07 \text{ k} \downarrow \quad \text{and} \quad X_2^2 = 0.07 \text{ k} \downarrow$$

The final reactions for the truss are shown in Figs. 3-10(f) and (g).

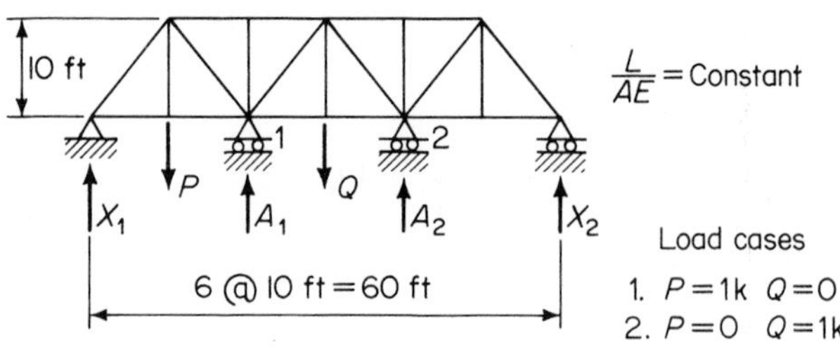

m=2 (number of redundants)
p=2 (number of load cases)
n=2 (number of other reactions)

(a)

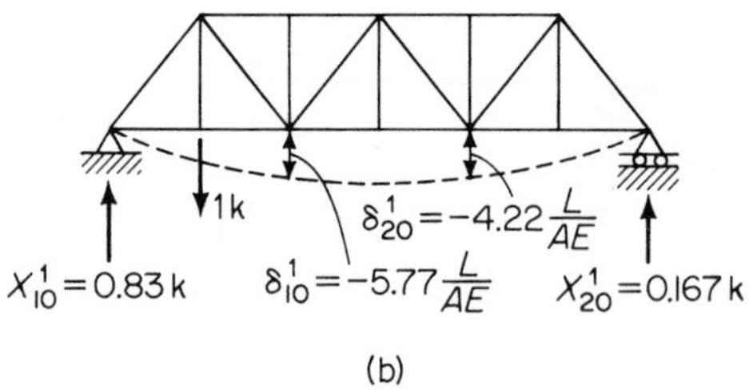

(b)

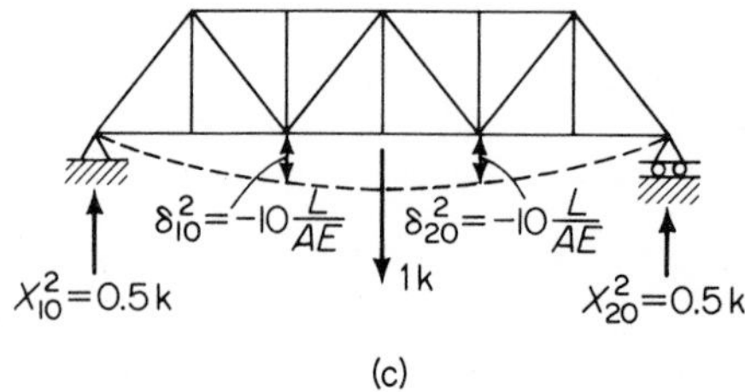

(c)

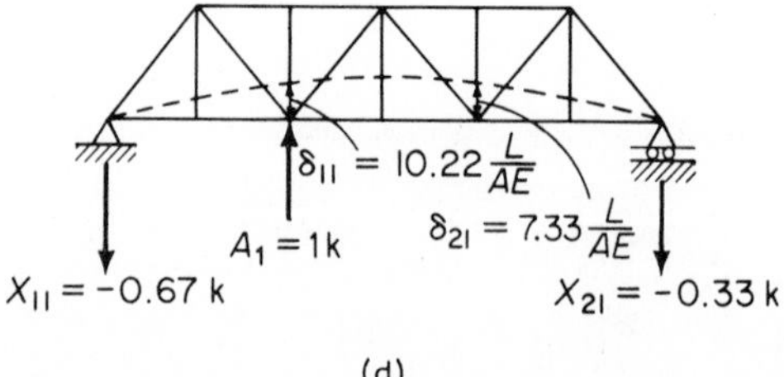

(d)

Fig. 3-10 Example 3-8: Truss analysis. (a) Original structure; (b) released structure—load case 1; (c) released structure—load case 2; (d) deflections due to $A_1 = 1$ k.

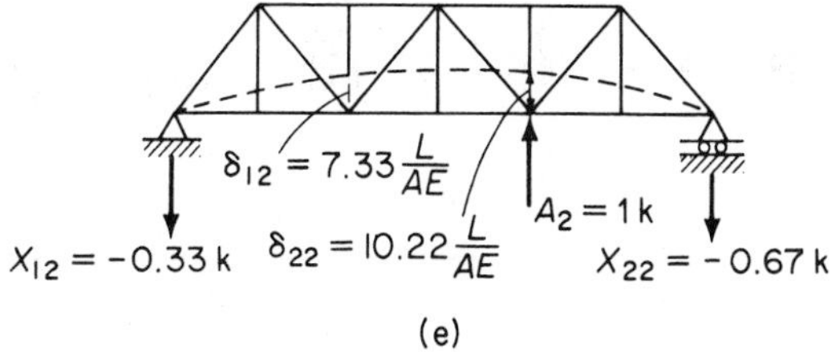

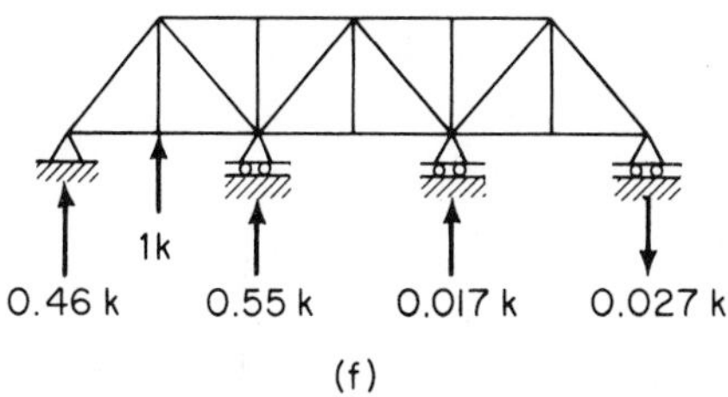

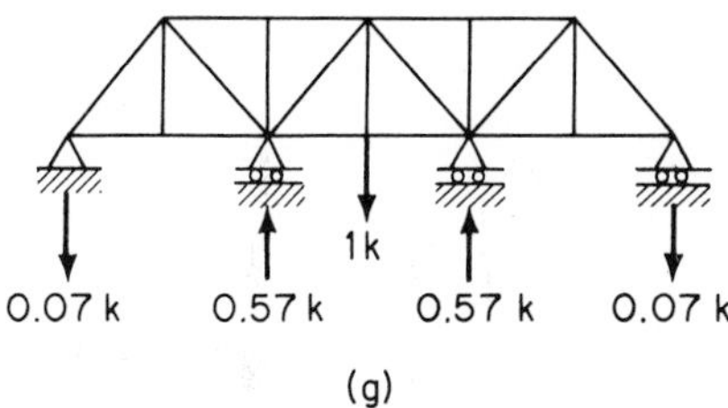

Fig. 3-10—*Cont.* (e) Deflections due to $A_2 = 1$ k; (f) solution—load case 1; (g) solution—load case 2.

3–5 Flexibility Equations for Elastic Supports

There are cases wherein the supports of a structure are considered to be ***elastic***. Equation (3-15) may be used to solve a problem of this nature; however, a few modifications are necessary before this equation can be applied. Equation (3-15) is restated:

$$[\mathbf{A}] = [\mathbf{D}]^{-1}([\mathbf{D}_s] - [\mathbf{D}_0]) \tag{3-15}$$

If any of the elastic supports are chosen as redundants, then the unknown values of $[\mathbf{A}]$ also appear in $[\mathbf{D}_s]$, since the final deformation of any elastic support chosen as a redundant is a function of the elastic support constant, i.e., $A_i = -k_i\delta_{si}$, where k_i is the ***elastic support constant*** or spring constant in units of *force per unit deformation* for the *i*th redundant. A negative sign appears in the relationship because the direction of the spring deflection is opposite to that of the reaction. Hence,

$$[\mathbf{D}_s] = -[\mathbf{k}][\mathbf{A}] \tag{3-33}$$

or

$$\begin{bmatrix} \delta_{s1} \\ \delta_{s2} \\ \vdots \\ \delta_{sm} \end{bmatrix} = -\begin{bmatrix} \frac{1}{k_1} & 0 & \cdots & 0 \\ 0 & \frac{1}{k_2} & \cdots & 0 \\ \vdots & \vdots & & \vdots \\ 0 & 0 & \cdots & \frac{1}{k_m} \end{bmatrix} \begin{bmatrix} A_1 \\ A_2 \\ \vdots \\ A_m \end{bmatrix} \tag{3-34}$$

For those redundant actions that are not elastic supports, the value of the spring constant may be taken as ***infinity***. Thus, the value of $1/k$ for that support is ***zero***.

Substitution of Eq. (3-33) into Eq. (3-15) yields

$$[\mathbf{A}] = [\mathbf{D}]^{-1}(-[\mathbf{k}][\mathbf{A}] - [\mathbf{D}_0]) \tag{3-35}$$

which can be rewritten as

$$[\mathbf{A}] = -[\mathbf{D}]^{-1}[\mathbf{k}][\mathbf{A}] - [\mathbf{D}]^{-1}[\mathbf{D}_0] \tag{3-36}$$

or

$$[\mathbf{I}][\mathbf{A}] + [\mathbf{D}]^{-1}[\mathbf{k}][\mathbf{A}] = -[\mathbf{D}]^{-1}[\mathbf{D}_0] \tag{3-37}$$

Since

$$[\mathbf{I}] = [\mathbf{D}]^{-1}[\mathbf{D}] \tag{3-38}$$

Eq. (3-37) becomes

$$[\mathbf{D}]^{-1}[\mathbf{D}][\mathbf{A}] + [\mathbf{D}]^{-1}[\mathbf{k}][\mathbf{A}] = -[\mathbf{D}]^{-1}[\mathbf{D}_0] \tag{3-39}$$

Factoring $[\mathbf{D}]^{-1}$ and simplifying, Eq. (3-39) reduces to

$$([\mathbf{D}] + [\mathbf{k}])[\mathbf{A}] = -[\mathbf{D}_0] \tag{3-40}$$

Letting

$$[\mathbf{D}_k] = [\mathbf{D}] + [\mathbf{k}] \tag{3-41}$$

which gives

$$[\mathbf{D}_k] = \begin{bmatrix} \left(\delta_{11} + \frac{1}{k_1}\right) & \delta_{12} & \delta_{13} & \cdots & \delta_{1m} \\ \delta_{21} & \left(\delta_{22} + \frac{1}{k_2}\right) & \delta_{23} & \cdots & \delta_{2m} \\ \delta_{31} & \delta_{32} & \left(\delta_{33} + \frac{1}{k_3}\right) & \cdots & \delta_{3m} \\ \vdots & \vdots & \vdots & & \vdots \\ \delta_{m1} & \delta_{m2} & \delta_{m3} & \cdots & \left(\delta_{mm} + \frac{1}{k_m}\right) \end{bmatrix} \tag{3-42}$$

Eq. (3-40) yields

$$[\mathbf{A}] = -[\mathbf{D}_k]^{-1}[\mathbf{D}_0] \tag{3-43}$$

To illustrate the use of Eq. (3-43), consider the following example.

Example 3-9. The three-span continuous beam shown in Fig. 3-11 is indeterminate to two degrees. A complete analysis of the system is desired. The reactions at points 1 and 2 have been chosen as the redundants (A_1 and A_2), thus the effect of both elastic supports will enter into Eq. (3-43). In Fig. 3-11(b), the redundants have been released and the corresponding deformations are given. In Figs. 3-11(c) and (d), the deformations due to unit values of the redundants are shown. Substitution of these deformations into Eq. (3-43) gives

$$\begin{bmatrix} A_1 \\ A_2 \end{bmatrix} = \begin{bmatrix} (0.0435 + \frac{1}{300}) & (0.0274) \\ (0.0274) & (0.0263 + \frac{1}{200}) \end{bmatrix}^{-1} \begin{bmatrix} -1.468 \\ -0.872 \end{bmatrix} \tag{3-44}$$

and

$$\begin{bmatrix} A_1 \\ A_2 \end{bmatrix} = \begin{bmatrix} 30.68 \\ 1.15 \end{bmatrix}$$

Thus, $A_1 = 30.68\ \text{k}\uparrow$ and $A_2 = 1.15\ \text{k}\uparrow$. The final reactions, shears, and moments are shown in Fig. 3-11(e) on page 66.

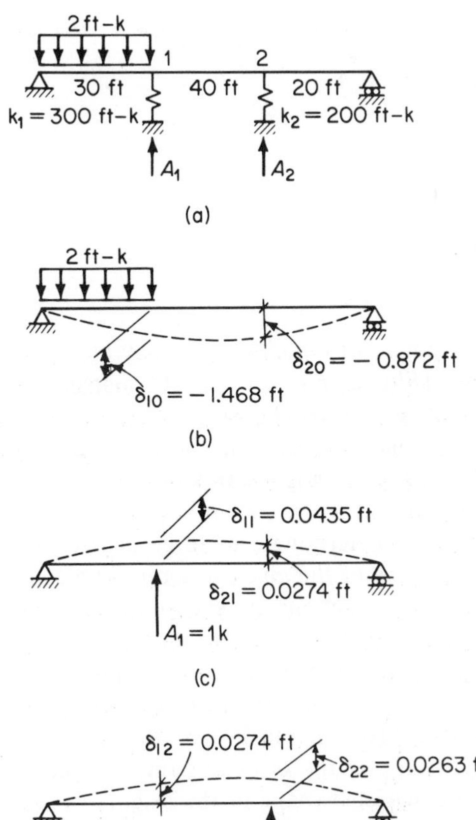

Fig. 3-11 Example 3-9: Analysis of continuous beam on elastic supports. (a) Original structure; (b) released structure; (c) $A_1 = 1\,\text{k}$; (d) $A_2 = 1\,\text{k}$.

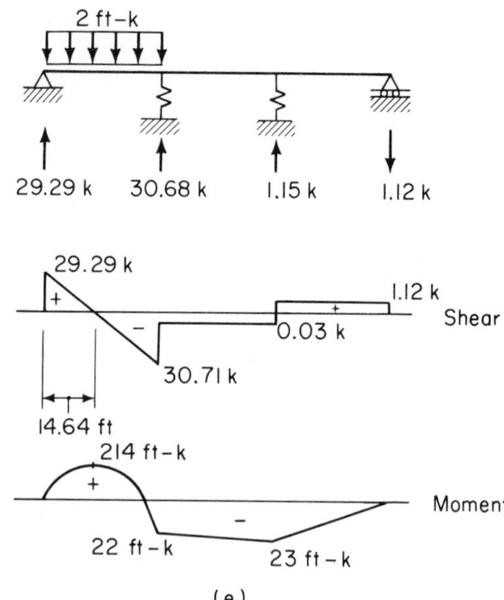

Fig. 3-11—*Cont.* (e) Shear and moment diagram.

3–6 Improving the Stability of the Flexibility Equations

In structures consisting of a large number of redundants, it may be important to make the main diagonal of the ***flexibility matrix***—i.e., the [**D**] matrix—as strong as possible. This can be done, to some extent, by choosing the redundants in such a manner that when they are removed, ***the deflected shape of the released structure approximates, as nearly as possible, that of the original structure.***

To illustrate this point, consider the structure shown in Fig. 3-12. The structure is a four-span continuous beam, indeterminate to three degrees, subjected to a load P as shown. The deflected shape of the given structure is shown in Fig. 3-12(a). In Fig. 3-12(b) the three internal reactions are chosen as the redundants, and when they are released the structure deflects as shown in Fig. 3-12(c).

In Fig. 3-12(d), the internal moments over the interior supports are chosen as the redundants. When they are released, the structure deflects as shown in Fig. 3-12(e). Although neither the deflected shape in Fig. 3-12(c) nor that in Fig. 3-12(e) is exactly like the deflected shape of the original structure, the deflected shape in Fig. 3-12(e) is closer to the deflected shape of the original structure.

To check this hypothesis, the analysis of the four-span continuous beam discussed above is given in the following example.

Example 3-10. The structure discussed in Fig. 3-12 is to be analyzed by first considering the three internal reactions as redundants and then considering the three internal moments

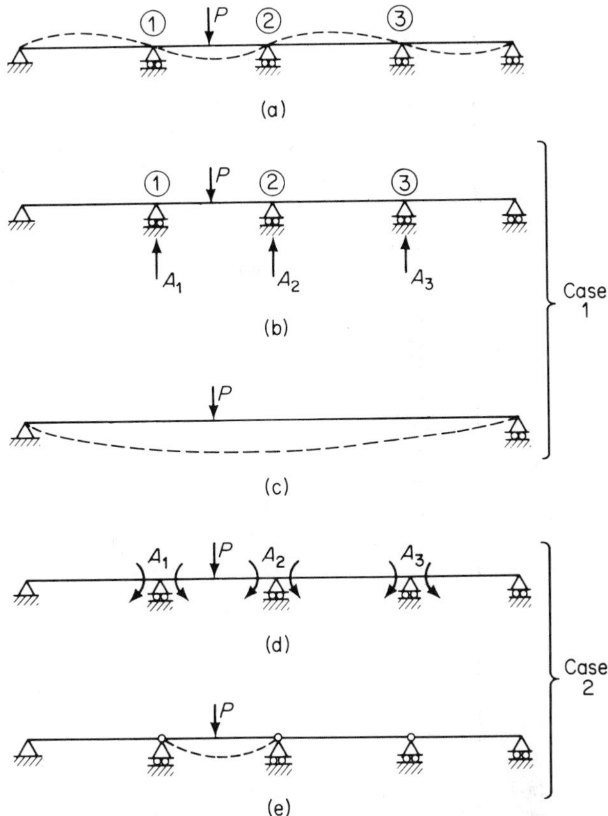

Fig. 3-12 Selection of redundants to improve mathematical stability of simultaneous equations: (a) deformation of original structure; (b) reactions as redundants; (c) deflection of released structure; (d) moments as redundants; (e) deflection of released structure.

as redundants. In the first case, the reactions at points 1, 2, and 3 (A_1, A_2, and A_3) are redundants as shown in Fig. 3-13. The redundants are released and the deflections δ_{10}, δ_{20}, and δ_{30} given. In Figs. 3-13(c), (d), and (e), the values of deformations due to unit values of A_1, A_2, and A_3 are given. Substitution of these deformations into Eq. (3-13) and factoring out EI yields

$$\begin{bmatrix} -54{,}170 \\ -70{,}000 \\ -26{,}650 \end{bmatrix} + \begin{bmatrix} 907.5 & 944.4 & 351.8 \\ 944.4 & 1500 & 612 \\ 351.8 & 612 & 296.2 \end{bmatrix} \begin{bmatrix} A_1 \\ A_2 \\ A_3 \end{bmatrix} = \begin{bmatrix} 0 \\ 0 \\ 0 \end{bmatrix} \tag{3-45}$$

Solving for A_1, A_2, and A_3,

$$\begin{bmatrix} A_1 \\ A_2 \\ A_3 \end{bmatrix} = \begin{bmatrix} 907.5 & 944.4 & 351.8 \\ 944.4 & 1500 & 612 \\ 351.8 & 612 & 296.2 \end{bmatrix}^{-1} \begin{bmatrix} 54{,}170 \\ 70{,}000 \\ 26{,}650 \end{bmatrix} \tag{3-46}$$

and

$$\begin{bmatrix} A_1 \\ A_2 \\ A_3 \end{bmatrix} = \begin{bmatrix} 0.003 & -0.002 & -0.00001 \\ -0.002 & 0.006 & -0.009 \\ -0.00001 & -0.009 & 0.021 \end{bmatrix} \begin{bmatrix} 54{,}170 \\ 70{,}000 \\ 26{,}650 \end{bmatrix} \tag{3-47}$$

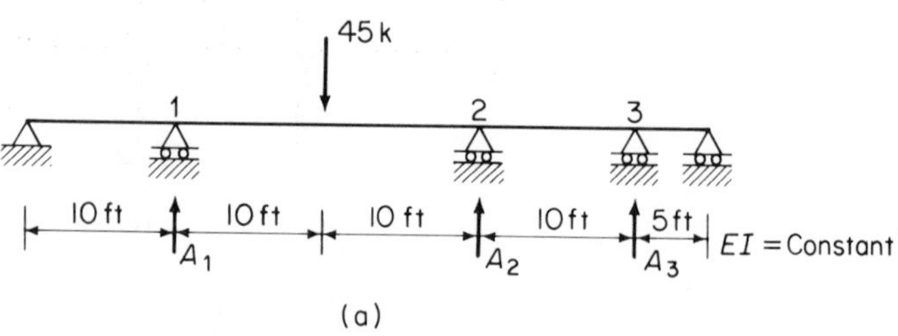

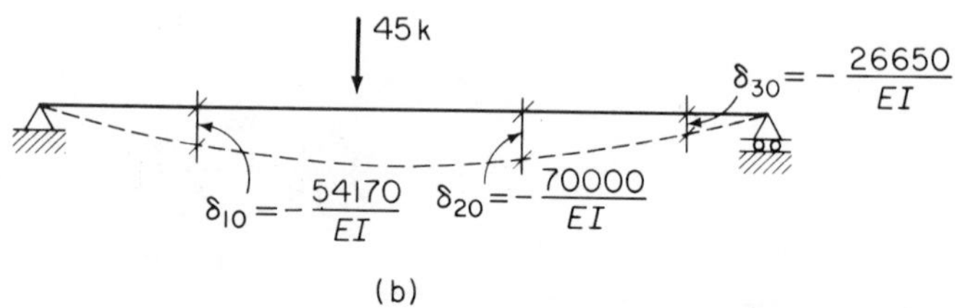

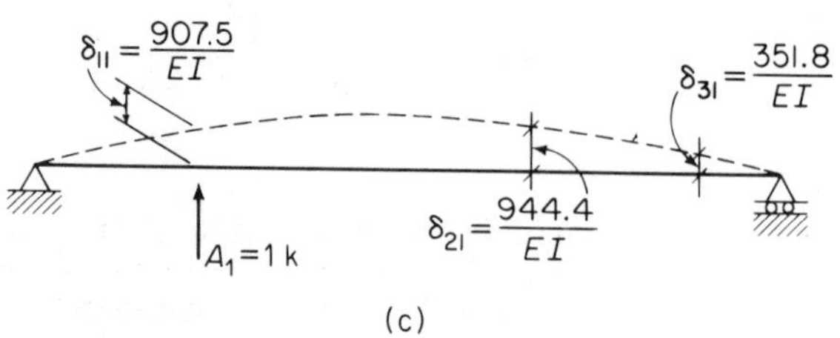

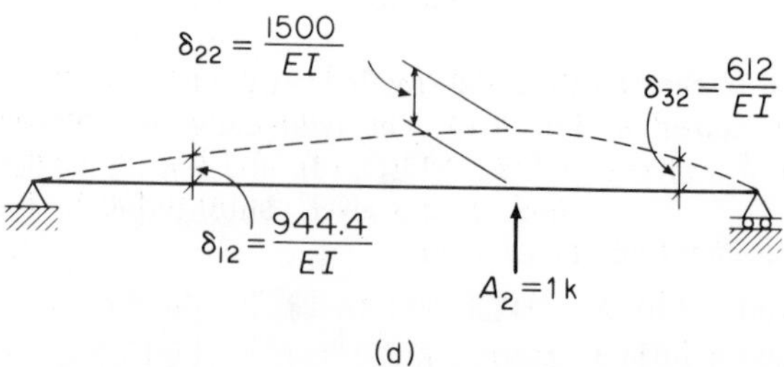

Fig. 3-13 Example 3-10: Analysis of continuous beam; reactions as redundants. (a) Original structure; (b) released structure; (c) $A_1 = 1$ k; (d) $A_2 = 1$ k.

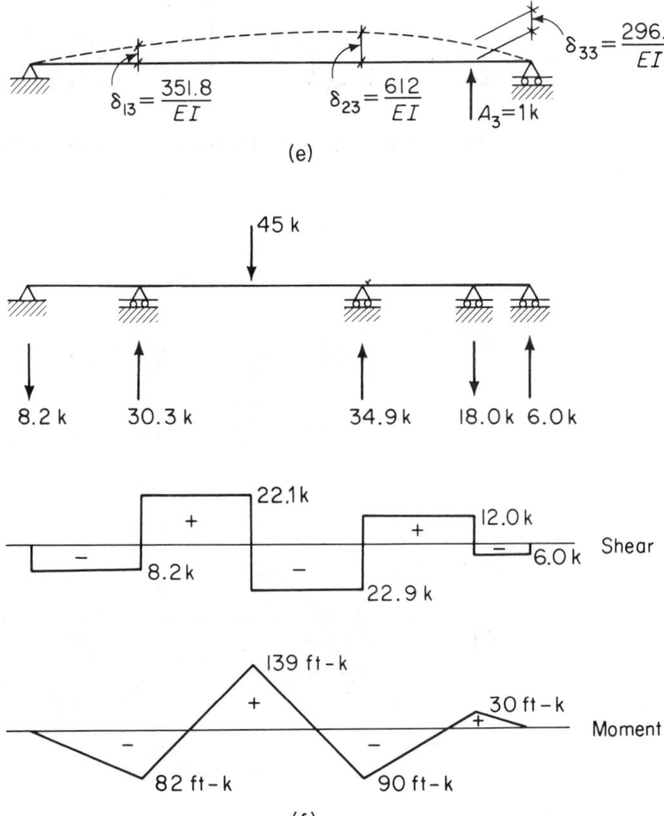

Fig. 3-13—*Cont.* (e) $A_3 = 1$ k; (f) shear and moment diagrams.

Thus,

$$\begin{bmatrix} A_1 \\ A_2 \\ A_3 \end{bmatrix} = \begin{bmatrix} 30.3 \\ 34.9 \\ -18.0 \end{bmatrix} \tag{3-48}$$

or $A_1 = 30.3$ k $\uparrow$, $A_2 = 34.9$ k $\uparrow$, and $A_3 = 18.0$ k $\downarrow$. The shear and moment diagrams are given in Figure 3-13(f).

In the second case, the same four-span continuous beam is shown with the internal moments at the three internal supports as the redundants, i.e., A_1, A_2, and A_3 (see Fig. 3-14).

In the released structure shown in Fig. 3-14(b), the redundants have been removed and the corresponding deformations computed. Note that δ_{10}, δ_{20}, and

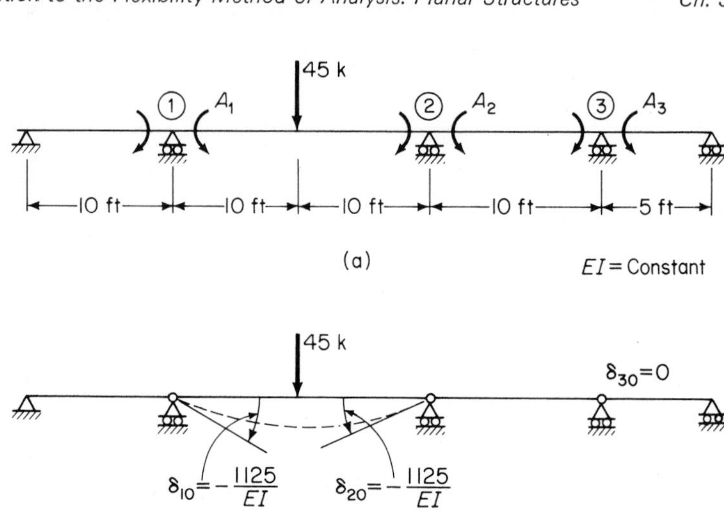

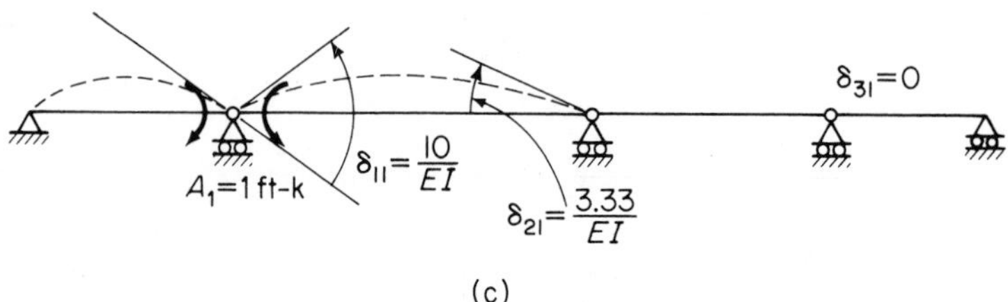

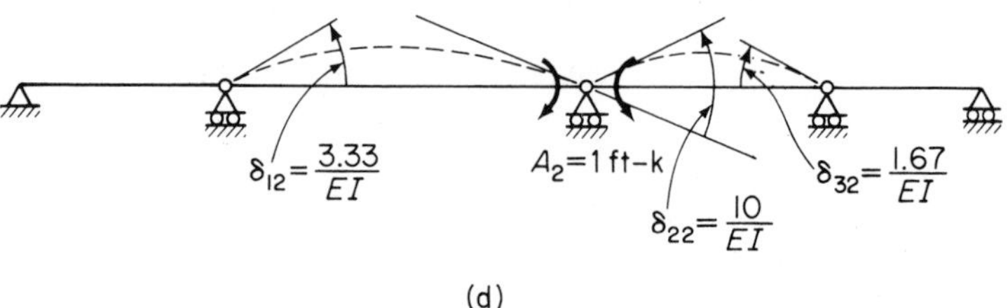

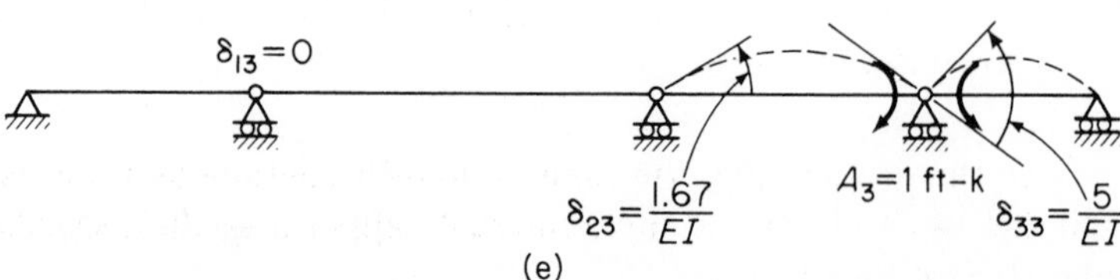

Fig. 3-14 Example 3-10: Analysis of continuous beam; internal moments over supports as redundants. (a) Original structure; (b) released structure; (c) $A_1 = 1$ ft-k; (d) $A_2 = 1$ ft-k; (e) $A_3 = 1$ ft-k.

δ_{30} are internal rotations. In Figs. 3-14(c), (d), and (e), unit values of the three redundants A_1, A_2, and A_3 are applied and the deformations computed as noted. Substitution of the computed deformations into Eq. (3-13) and factoring EI yields

$$\begin{bmatrix} A_1 \\ A_2 \\ A_3 \end{bmatrix} = \begin{bmatrix} 10 & 3.33 & 0 \\ 3.33 & 10 & 1.667 \\ 0 & 1.667 & 5 \end{bmatrix}^{-1} \begin{bmatrix} 1125 \\ 1125 \\ 0 \end{bmatrix} \tag{3-49}$$

and

$$\begin{bmatrix} A_1 \\ A_2 \\ A_3 \end{bmatrix} = \begin{bmatrix} 82.4 \\ 90.0 \\ -30.0 \end{bmatrix} \tag{3-50}$$

thus, $A_1 = 82.4$ ft-k ⤹⤸, $A_2 = 90.0$ ft-k ⤹⤸, and $A_3 = 30.0$ ft-k ⤺⤻. These moment values are in agreement with those given in the moment diagrams of Fig. 3-13.

Compare the form of the flexibility matrix in Eq. (3-46), i.e.,

$$[\mathbf{D}] = \begin{bmatrix} 907.5 & 944.4 & 351.8 \\ 944.4 & 1500 & 612 \\ 351.8 & 612 & 296.5 \end{bmatrix} \tag{3-51}$$

to the flexibility matrix in Eq. (3-49), i.e.,

$$[\mathbf{D}'] = \begin{bmatrix} 10 & 3.33 & 0 \\ 3.33 & 10 & 1.667 \\ 0 & 1.667 & 5 \end{bmatrix} \tag{3-52}$$

To facilitate a comparison, both matrices can be transformed so that the largest element, which appears on the diagonal of the two matrices, becomes unity. Thus, dividing each element of the flexibility matrix of Expression (3-51) by 1500 yields

$$[\bar{\mathbf{D}}] = \begin{bmatrix} 0.605 & 0.629 & 0.234 \\ 0.629 & 1.000 & 0.408 \\ 0.234 & 0.408 & 0.197 \end{bmatrix} \tag{3-53}$$

and dividing each element of the flexibility matrix of Expression (3-52) by 10 yields

$$[\bar{\mathbf{D}}'] = \begin{bmatrix} 1.000 & 0.333 & 0 \\ 0.333 & 1.000 & 0.167 \\ 0 & 0.167 & 0.500 \end{bmatrix} \tag{3-54}$$

Comparison of the two transformed matrices of Expressions (3-53) and (3-54) reveals that the diagonal of the matrix in Expression (3-54) is stronger than that of the matrix in Expression (3-53) relative to other elements in the matrix. Thus, the mathematical stability of the second case, where moments are chosen as the redundants, is greater.

The difference is not great in this particular example, and both solutions are quite stable mathematically; however, in large problems where the number of redundants is great, mathematical stability is very important. The proper choice of redundants is a prime consideration in such cases.

3–7
Conclusion

This chapter has been concerned with the development and application of the flexibility method of analysis in its simplest form. The purpose was not to develop a generalized matrix formulation of the flexibility method, but to introduce the basic concepts of the method and to develop some tools to be used later in conjunction with the analysis of a structural system by the stiffness method. A generalized matrix formulation of the ***flexibility method*** for analyzing a structural system, using the notion of unassembled members, is considerably more complex than the material presented here. It involves establishing the ***member flexibility matrix*** and the ***transformation matrix*** for each member of the system and the ***structure flexibility matrix*** for the whole system. These matrices are analogous to the ***member stiffness matrix***, the ***transformation matrix***, and the ***structure stiffness matrix***, respectively, that will be defined in the following chapters for the ***stiffness method*** of analysis.

As stated earlier in Chapter 1, the ***stiffness method*** for analyzing a structural system is the primary concern of this text, since it is much better suited for computer applications than is the ***flexibility method*** of analysis. For this reason, the authors do not feel it necessary to spend any more time studying the flexibility method. For a detailed discussion of the flexibility method, the reader is referred to either Ref. 3-5 or Ref. 3-6 listed at the end of the chapter.

3–8
Problems

3-1 to 3-6. Compute the deflection and rotation at points A and B of the following structural systems by the method of virtual work.

3-7 to 3-9. Compute the vertical deflection at point A of the following structural systems by the method of virtual work.

3-10 to 3-15. Compute the deflection and rotation at points A and B of the structural systems shown in Probs. 3-1 to 3-6 by the method of graphical integration.

3-16 to 3-24. Analyze completely the following structural systems using the flexibility method.

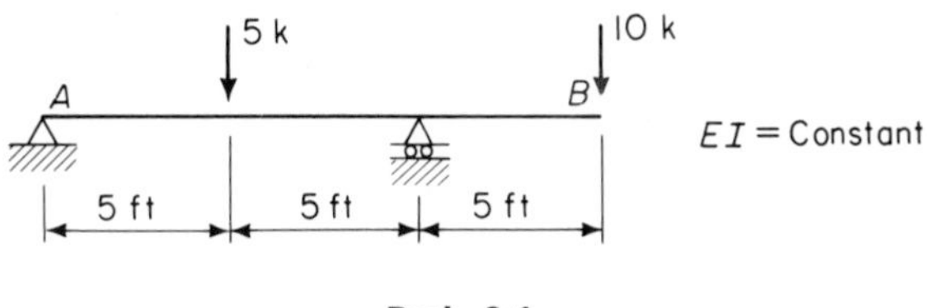

Prob. 3-1

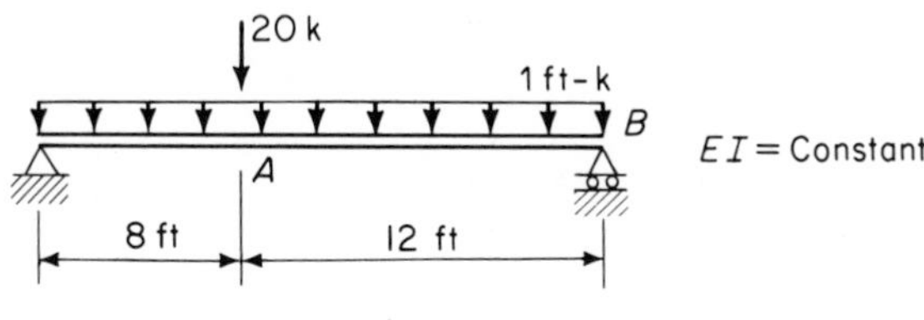

Prob. 3-2

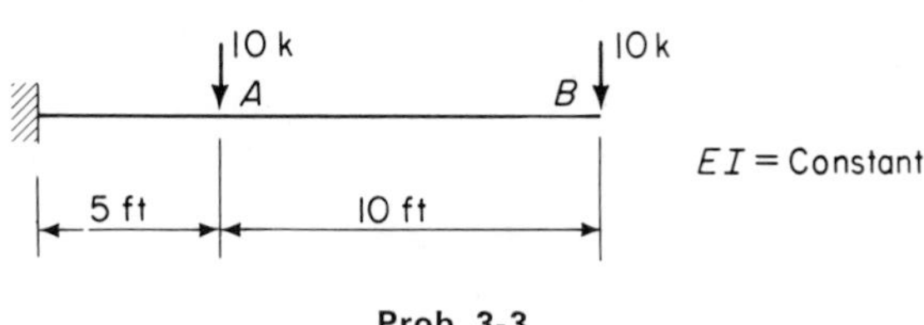

Prob. 3-3

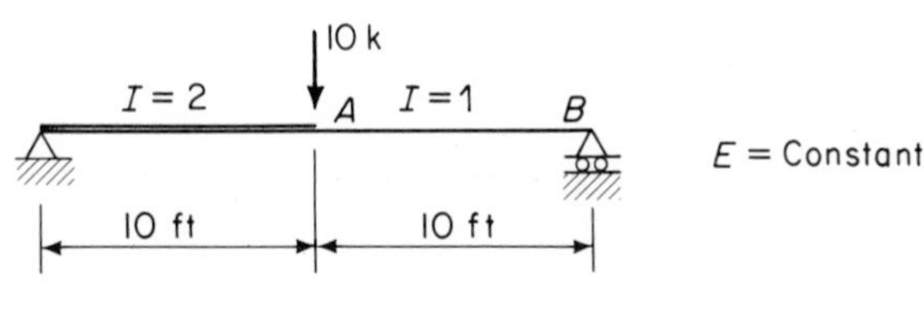

Prob. 3-4

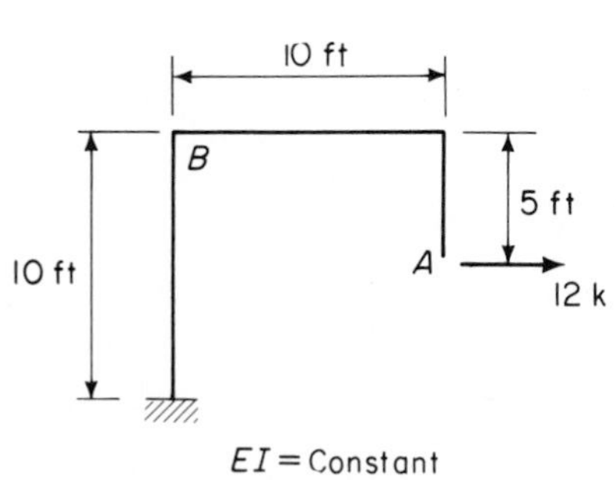

EI = Constant

Prob. 3-5

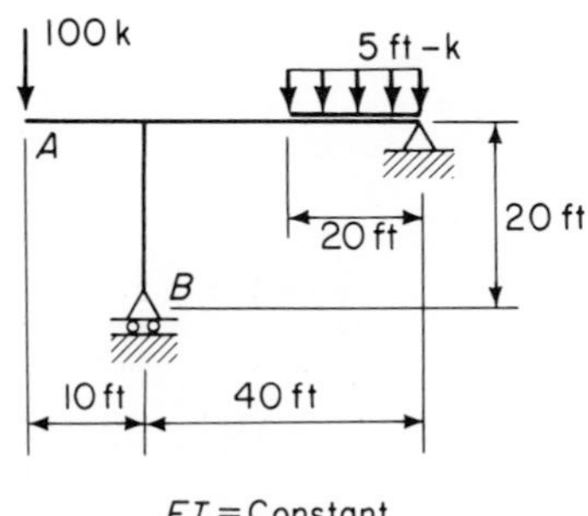

EI = Constant

Prob. 3-6

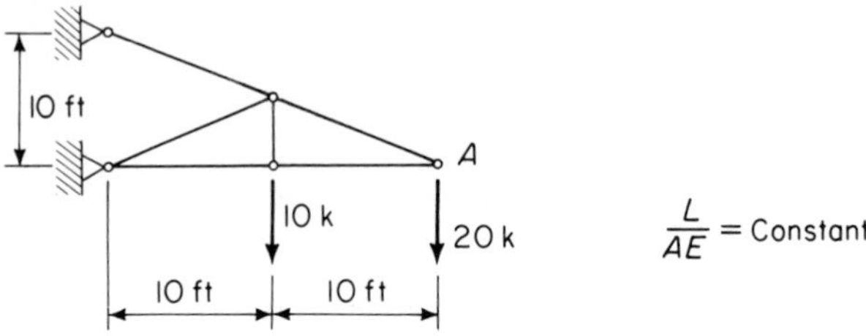

Prob. 3-7

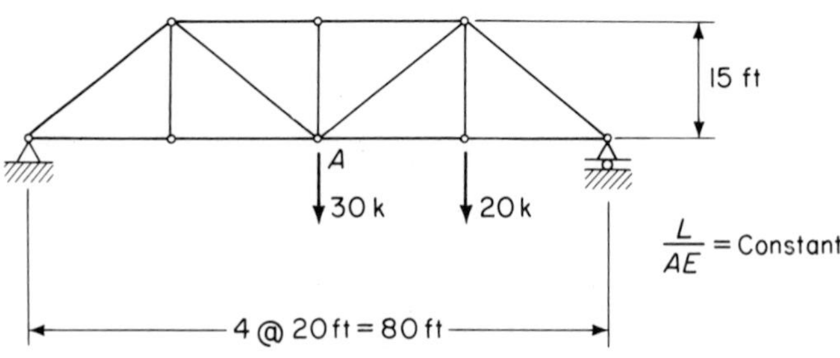

Prob. 3-8

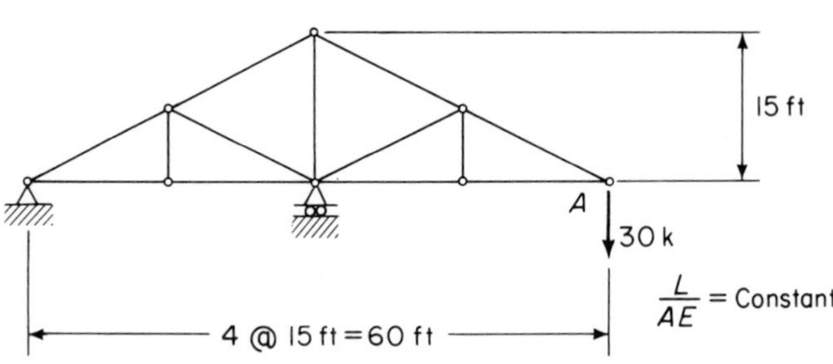

Prob. 3-9

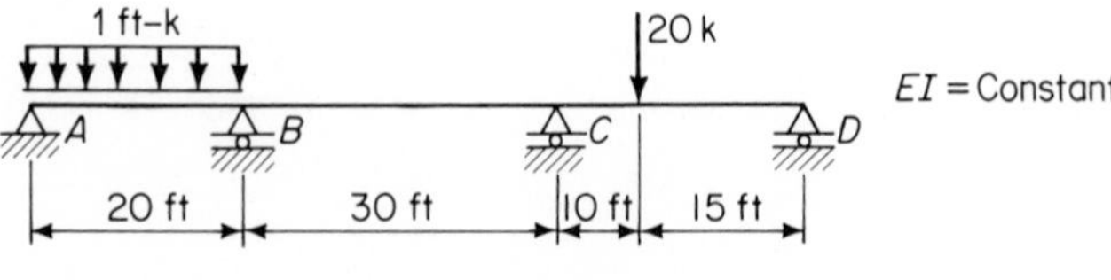

Prob. 3-16

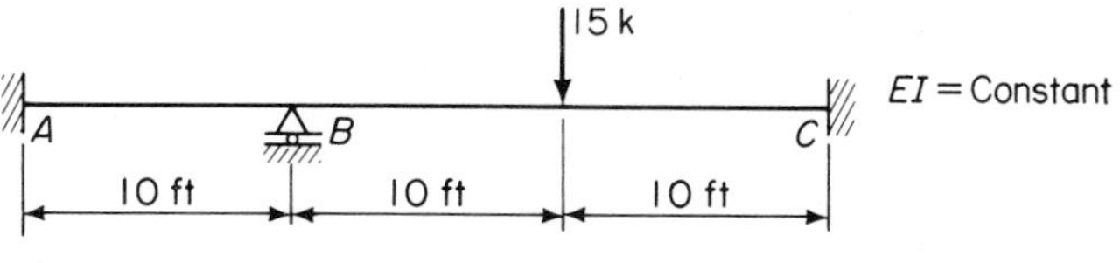

Prob. 3-17

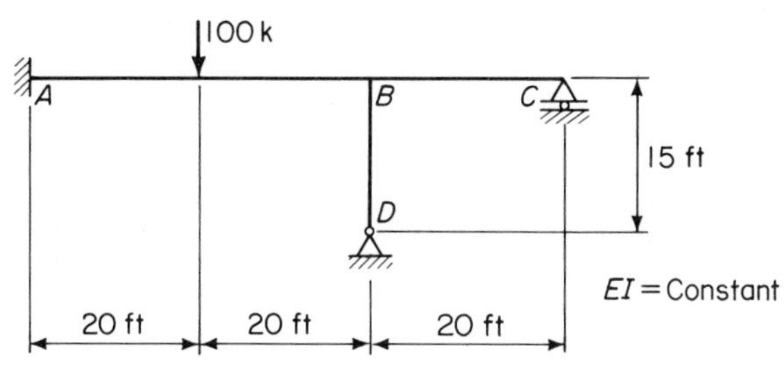

Prob. 3-18

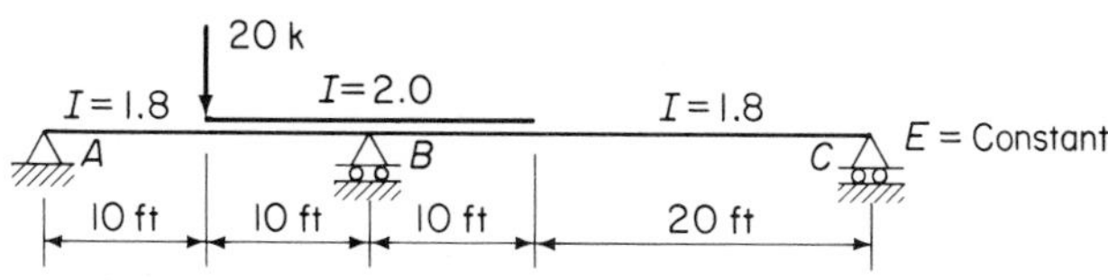

Prob. 3-19

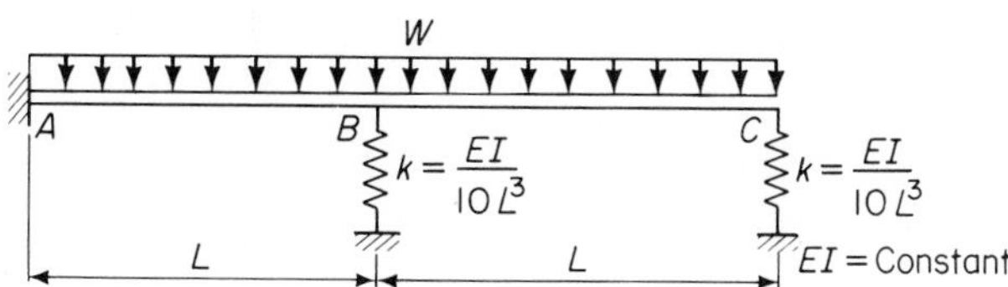

Prob. 3-20

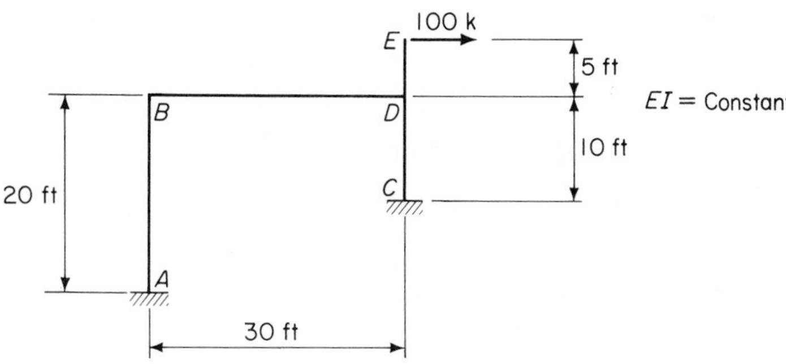

Prob. 3-21

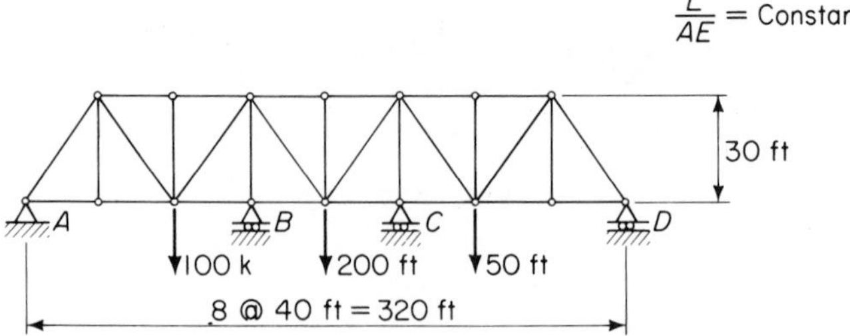

Prob. 3-22

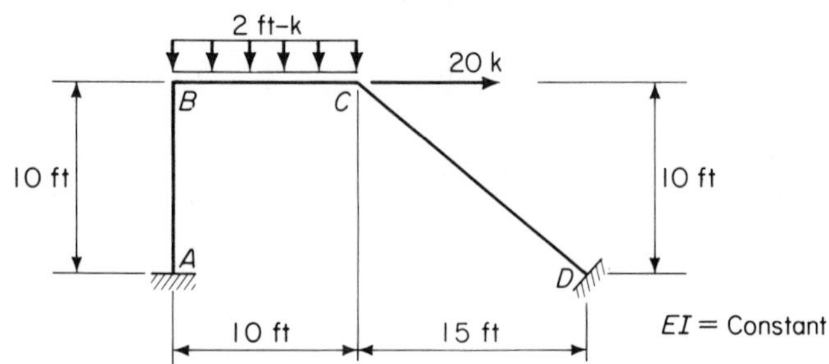

Prob. 3-23

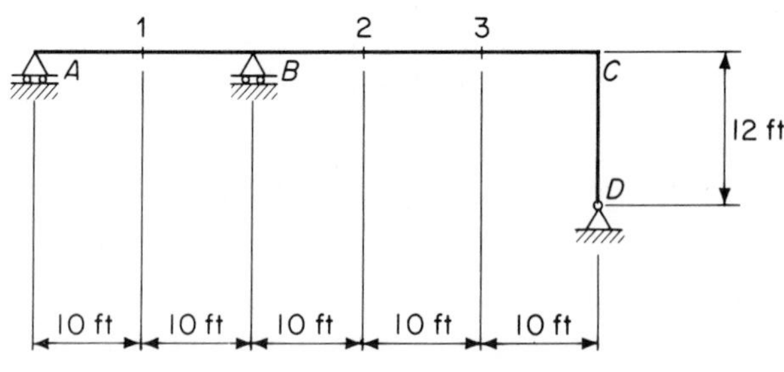

Load case 1 – a single vertical 20 k load at point 1
Load case 2 – a single vertical 20 k load at point 2
Load case 3 – a single vertical 20 k load at point 3

Prob. 3-24

SELECTED REFERENCES

3-1 Rogers, G. L. and M. L. Causey, *Mechanics of Engineering Structures*. New York: John Wiley & Sons, Inc., 1962.

3-2 Carpenter, Samuel, *Structural Mechanics*. New York: John Wiley & Sons, Inc., 1960.

3-3 Wang, C. K., *Statically Indeterminate Structures.* New York: McGraw-Hill Book Company, 1953.

3-4 Au, Tung, *Elementary Structural Mechanics.* Englewood Cliffs, N.J.: Prentice-Hall, Inc., 1963.

3-5 Hall, A. S., and R. W. Woodhead, *Frame Analysis,* 2nd ed. New York: John Wiley & Sons, Inc., 1967.

3-6 Willems, Nicholas, and William M. Lucas, Jr., *Matrix Analysis for Structural Engineers.* Englewood Cliffs, N.J.: Prentice-Hall, Inc., 1968.

4 STIFFNESS METHOD OF ANALYSIS: PLANAR ORTHOGONAL STRUCTURES

4–1
Sign Convention

The following sign convention will be used in the development of the stiffness method and its application in analyzing a planar orthogonal system:

1. ***Counterclockwise*** end moments acting on the ends of a beam element are positive;
2. ***counterclockwise*** joint rotations and joint moments are positive;
3. joint translations ***upward or to the right*** are positive, as well as joint forces; and
4. end shears acting ***upward or to the right*** on the ends of a beam element are positive.

It is implied by the assumed sign convention that the planar orthogonal structural system is positioned or viewed so that its members are vertical and/or horizontal.

4–2
The Beam Element

When using the stiffness method to study the behavior of a structural system, the restrained structure must be analyzed, as stated earlier in Chapter 1, for the application of unit values of joint displacement. However, before studying the response of the restrained structure as a whole to the application of joint deformations, it is convenient to investigate the response of an individual beam element to unit values of joint (or end) displacements. Particular attention is given to the end actions which correspond to the various components of possible joint displacement of the structure. In this discussion, only deformations of the beam element due to bending will be considered.

4-2.1 Member Stiffness Matrix: Neglecting Axial Deformations

For the purpose of discussion, consider a typical beam element i restrained at its ends with either a variable or constant moment of inertia over its length (Fig. 4-1). The ends of the member will be denoted by the letters j and k, letting j designate the *left end.* The member will be positioned in the frame of a set of orthogonal axes x_m and y_m, referred to as the ***local axes*** of the member, with the origin at the j-end and the x_m axis directed toward the k-end. The y_m axis which is oriented 90° *counterclockwise* from the x_m axis is selected such that the x_m–y_m plane defines the plane of bending of the member. The cross-sectional shape of the member is assumed to be symmetrical with respect to the x_m–y_m plane.

Neglecting axial deformations of the member, there are only two possible components of inplane displacement at each end of member i to be considered, i.e., normal translation and rotation. The rotation and translation of end j in the x_m–y_m plane will be referred to as θ_p and δ_r, respectively, and the corresponding displacements at end k will be referred to as θ_q and δ_s. By neglecting axial deformation of the beam element, any displacement of the member in a direction parallel to the longitudinal axis x_m will be that of a rigid body.

Imposing a unit rotation of end j ($\theta_p = 1$) of beam element i while preventing all other end displacements, restraining moments and shears will be required at the j- and k-ends of the member, as indicated in Fig. 4-2, in order to maintain static equilibrium. The restraining actions at end j are a moment denoted as K^i_{pp} and a shear K^i_{rp}; the restraining actions at end k are a moment K^i_{qp} and a shear K^i_{sp}. In identifying these actions, the *first subscript* indicates the nature of the action—i.e., moment or shear, by referring to the label of the corresponding

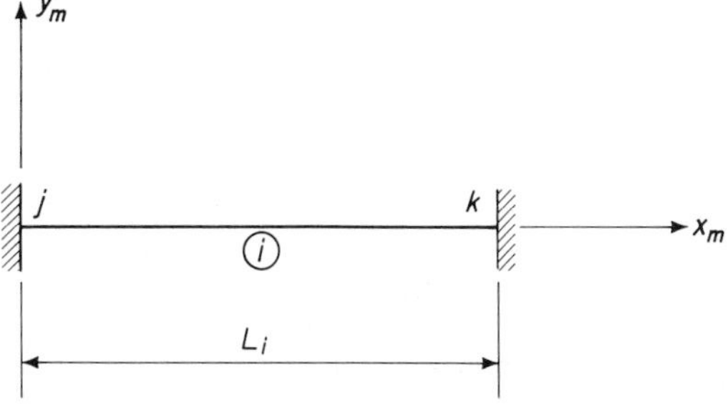

Fig. 4-1 Typical restrained beam element.

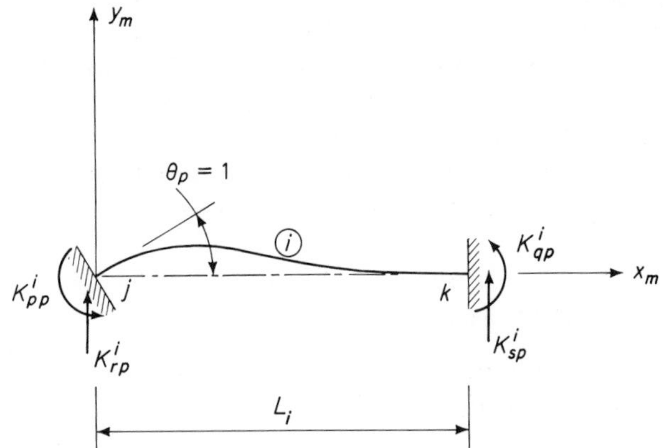

Fig. 4-2 Unit rotation of end j, beam element i.

displacement, i.e., rotation or translation—and the *second subscript* refers to the imposed displacement that causes the action. The superscript is used to refer to the member being studied. For example, K^i_{qp} is the action for member i corresponding to the end rotation θ_q, i.e., the moment at end k, caused by a unit of rotation θ_p. These actions are shown in Fig. 4-2 in their assumed positive sense. For a unit rotation of end k ($\theta_q = 1$) with all other displacements restrained, the restraining moments and shears necessary to maintain equilibrium of the deformed member are shown in Fig. 4-3. These restraining actions are designated as K^i_{pq}, K^i_{qq}, K^i_{rq}, and K^i_{sq}. Next, considering a unit translation normal to the member axis x_m of end j ($\delta_r = 1$) while restraining the other displacements, the restraining moments are K^i_{pr} and K^i_{qr} and the restraining shears are K^i_{rr} and K^i_{sr}. This case is illustrated in Fig. 4-4. Finally, when member i is subjected to a unit translation normal to the member axis x_m at end k ($\delta_s = 1$) with the other end displacements equal to

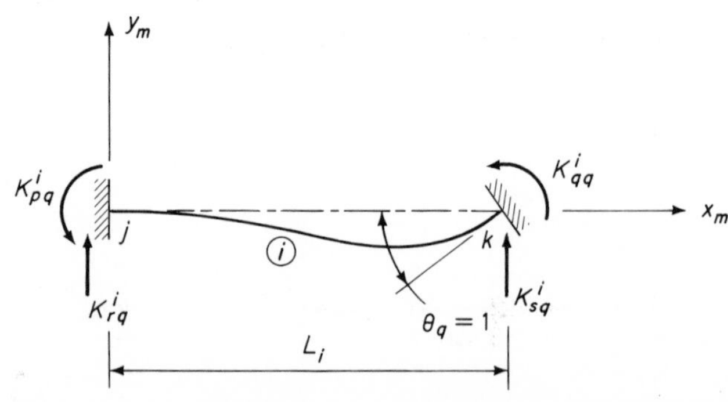

Fig. 4-3 Unit rotation of end k, beam element i.

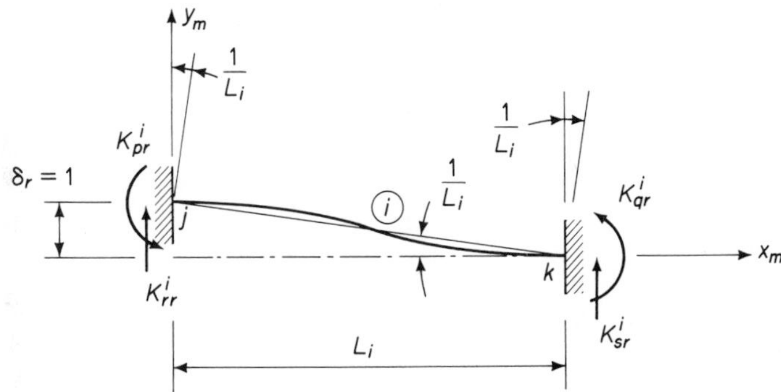

Fig. 4-4 Unit translation of end j, beam element i.

zero, the restraining actions K^i_{ps}, K^i_{qs}, K^i_{rs}, and K^i_{ss} are required (Fig. 4-5) to maintain equilibrium of the deformed member.

Should member i experience arbitrary end displacements θ_p, θ_q, δ_r, and δ_s as shown in Fig. 4-6, the corresponding end actions required to maintain equilibrium of the restrained member can be evaluated by combining a linear function of the several cases described in Figs. 4-2 through 4-5, i.e.,

$$m^i_p = K^i_{pp}\theta_p + K^i_{pq}\theta_q + K^i_{pr}\delta_r + K^i_{ps}\delta_s \tag{4-1a}$$

$$m^i_q = K^i_{qp}\theta_p + K^i_{qq}\theta_q + K^i_{qr}\delta_r + K^i_{qs}\delta_s \tag{4-1b}$$

$$p^i_r = K^i_{rp}\theta_p + K^i_{rq}\theta_q + K^i_{rr}\delta_r + K^i_{rs}\delta_s \tag{4-1c}$$

$$p^i_s = K^i_{sp}\theta_p + K^i_{sq}\theta_q + K^i_{sr}\delta_r + K^i_{ss}\delta_s \tag{4-1d}$$

Now, this set of equations can be conveniently expressed in matrix form as

$$[\mathbf{m}]_i = [\mathbf{K}]_i[\boldsymbol{\delta}]_i \tag{4-2}$$

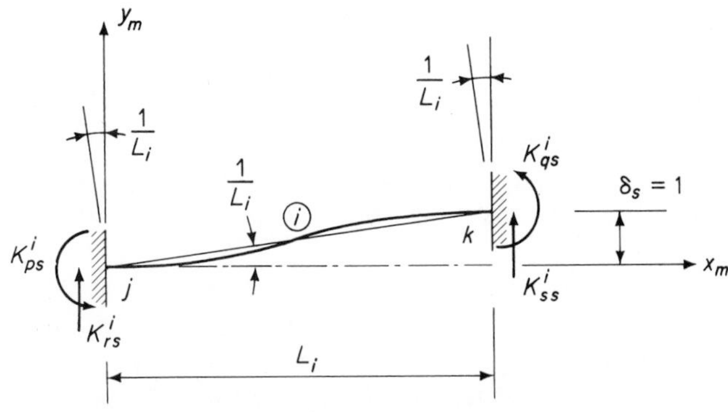

Fig. 4-5 Unit translation of end k, beam element i.

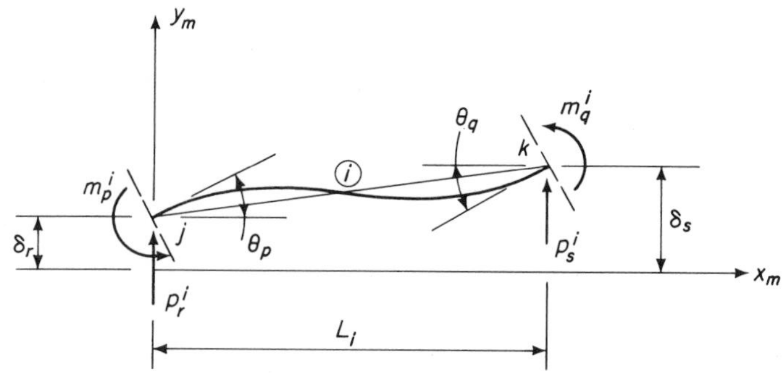

Fig. 4-6 General displacement of ends of beam element *i*.

where

$$[\mathbf{m}]_i = \begin{bmatrix} m_p \\ m_q \\ p_r \\ p_s \end{bmatrix}_i \tag{4-3a}$$

$$[\boldsymbol{\delta}]_i = \begin{bmatrix} \theta_p \\ \theta_q \\ \delta_r \\ \delta_s \end{bmatrix}_i \tag{4-3b}$$

and

$$[\mathbf{K}]_i = \begin{array}{c} \begin{matrix} p & \quad q & \quad r & \quad s \end{matrix} \\ \begin{bmatrix} K_{pp} & K_{pq} & K_{pr} & K_{ps} \\ K_{qp} & K_{qq} & K_{qr} & K_{qs} \\ K_{rp} & K_{rq} & K_{rr} & K_{rs} \\ K_{sp} & K_{sq} & K_{sr} & K_{ss} \end{bmatrix}_i \end{array} \begin{matrix} p \\ q \\ r \\ s \end{matrix} \tag{4-3c}$$

The matrix $[\boldsymbol{\delta}]_i$ represents the possible components of end displacement of member *i*, the matrix $[\mathbf{m}]_i$ represents the components of end action required to maintain equilibrium of member *i* when subjected to general end displacements, and the matrix $[\mathbf{K}]_i$ represents the various components of restraining end action of member *i* resulting from the independent application of unit values of the possible end displacements.

The matrix $[\mathbf{K}]_i$ is referred to as the ***member stiffness matrix*** and the elements of the matrix are defined as ***member stiffness coefficients.*** Examining the matrix $[\mathbf{K}]_i$, the rows are found to relate to a particular component of restraining action caused by a unit value of each possible end displacement and the columns represent the components of restraining action developed by a particular unit value of end displacement. To aid in the identification of the member stiffness coefficients, the rows and columns are labeled, as shown, with respect to their related restraining action and end displacement, respectively. It should be pointed out that the elements of this member stiffness matrix represent all of the information that must be known about the general beam element i of a planar orthogonal structural system (neglecting axial deformations) in order to formulate an analysis by the stiffness method. Should a given member have some special end condition imposed on it, such as a hinge, its member stiffness matrix will only be a modification of the member stiffness matrix given in Expression (4-3c). This point will be discussed in Chapter 5.

The stiffness coefficients of Expression (4-3c) can be defined in terms of the *four rotational stiffness coefficients* K^i_{pp}, K^i_{pq}, K^i_{qp}, and K^i_{qq}. Reviewing the response of beam element i to the unit rotation of end j while the other possible end displacements were prevented (Fig. 4-2), the required end shears can be evaluated in terms of the restraining moments by considering the static equilibrium of the member, i.e.,

$$K^i_{rp} = \frac{K^i_{pp} + K^i_{qp}}{L_i} \tag{4-4a}$$

and

$$K^i_{sp} = -\frac{K^i_{pp} + K^i_{qp}}{L_i} \tag{4-4b}$$

Similarly, for the case where the beam element is subjected to a unit rotation of end k (Fig. 4-3), the restraining shears can be defined as

$$K^i_{rq} = \frac{K^i_{pq} + K^i_{qq}}{L_i} \tag{4-5a}$$

and

$$K^i_{sq} = -\frac{K^i_{pq} + K^i_{qq}}{L_i} \tag{4-5b}$$

Referring to Fig. 4-4, the deformation imposed on the beam element when end j was translated a unit value while the other end displacements were restrained can be duplicated by first rotating both ends of the member through an angle of $1/L_i$, as shown in Fig. 4-7, while preventing any translation of the ends and then rotating the whole member as a rigid body, clockwise, through an angle of $1/L_i$. Hence, the end moments required to maintain equilibrium of the deformed member of Fig. 4-7 can be determined by combining a linear function of the two cases described in Figs. 4-2 and 4-3, i.e.,

$$K^i_{pr} = K^i_{pp}\left(\frac{1}{L_i}\right) + K^i_{pq}\left(\frac{1}{L_i}\right) = \frac{K^i_{pp} + K^i_{pq}}{L_i} \tag{4-6a}$$

and

$$K^i_{qr} = K^i_{qp}\left(\frac{1}{L_i}\right) + K^i_{qq}\left(\frac{1}{L_i}\right) = \frac{K^i_{qp} + K^i_{qq}}{L_i} \tag{4-6b}$$

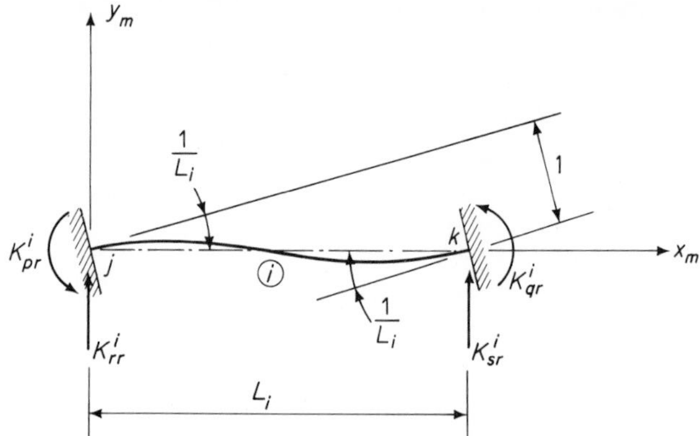

Fig. 4-7 Rotation of ends through angle of $1/L_i$ (translation of ends prevented).

Now, considering the static equilibrium of the beam element of Fig. 4-4 and the relationships expressed by Eqs. (4-6), the restraining end shears K^i_{rr} and K^i_{sr} can be obtained from the equations

$$K^i_{rr} = \frac{K^i_{pp} + K^i_{pq} + K^i_{qp} + K^i_{qq}}{L_i^2} \tag{4-7a}$$

and

$$K^i_{sr} = -\frac{K^i_{pp} + K^i_{pq} + K^i_{qp} + K^i_{qq}}{L_i^2} \tag{4-7b}$$

In a similar manner, the end actions required to maintain equilibrium of the beam element i when end k is subjected to a unit of translation with the ends restrained against any other displacement can be expressed in terms of the four rotational stiffness coefficients as

$$K^i_{ps} = -\frac{K^i_{pp} + K^i_{pq}}{L_i} \tag{4-8a}$$

$$K^i_{qs} = -\frac{K^i_{qp} + K^i_{qq}}{L_i} \tag{4-8b}$$

$$K^i_{rs} = -\frac{K^i_{pp} + K^i_{pq} + K^i_{qp} + K^i_{qq}}{L_i^2} \tag{4-8c}$$

$$K^i_{ss} = \frac{K^i_{pp} + K^i_{pq} + K^i_{qp} + K^i_{qq}}{L_i^2} \tag{4-8d}$$

Thus, performing the substitutions indicated by Eqs. (4-4), (4-5), (4-6), (4-7), and (4-8), the member stiffness matrix $[\mathbf{K}]_i$, defined by Expression (4-3c), can be written as shown in Table 4-1, Expression (4-9). The rows and columns are again labeled to indicate the ordering of the matrix and to identify the elements.

Table 4-1

MEMBER STIFFNESS MATRIX

(Local Axes System)

$$
\begin{array}{cc}
 & \begin{array}{cccc} p & q & r & s \end{array} \\
[\mathbf{K}]_i = & \left[\begin{array}{cccc}
K_{pp} & K_{pq} & \left(\dfrac{K_{pp}+K_{pq}}{L}\right) & -\left(\dfrac{K_{pp}+K_{pq}}{L}\right) \\
K_{qp} & K_{qq} & \left(\dfrac{K_{qp}+K_{qq}}{L}\right) & -\left(\dfrac{K_{qp}+K_{qq}}{L}\right) \\
\left(\dfrac{K_{pp}+K_{qp}}{L}\right) & \left(\dfrac{K_{pq}+K_{qq}}{L}\right) & \left(\dfrac{K_{pp}+K_{pq}+K_{qp}+K_{qq}}{L^2}\right) & -\left(\dfrac{K_{pp}+K_{pq}+K_{qp}+K_{qq}}{L^2}\right) \\
-\left(\dfrac{K_{pp}+K_{qp}}{L}\right) & -\left(\dfrac{K_{pq}+K_{qq}}{L}\right) & -\left(\dfrac{K_{pp}+K_{pq}+K_{qp}+K_{qq}}{L^2}\right) & \left(\dfrac{K_{pp}+K_{pq}+K_{qp}+K_{qq}}{L^2}\right)
\end{array}\right]_i \begin{array}{c} p \\ \\ q \\ \\ r \\ \\ s \end{array}
\end{array}
\tag{4-9}
$$

4-2.2 Evaluation of Rotational Stiffness Coefficients

Once the four rotational stiffness coefficients K^i_{pp}, K^i_{pq}, K^i_{qp}, and K^i_{qq} have been determined for a given beam element, the member stiffness matrix $[\mathbf{K}]_i$ can be written for the member using Expression (4-9). The flexibility approach offers a very convenient method for evaluating the four rotational stiffness coefficients for a beam element.

When analyzing a structural system by the stiffness method, the system is converted into a *kinematically determinate* structure, and when analyzing the same structural system by the flexibility method the system is reduced to a *statically determinate* structure. If the determinate systems for the two methods of analysis are *compatible*, a useful relationship between the stiffness coefficients defined in the stiffness method and the flexibility coefficients defined in the flexibility method can be developed. Now, in order for the two determinate systems to be compatible, the actions that are released to create the statically determinate structure in the flexibility analysis must correspond to the displacements that are artificially restrained to establish the kinematically determinate structure in the stiffness analysis, i.e., the same set of actions and corresponding displacements must be considered in both methods of analysis. Therefore, the determinate structure for a flexibility analysis of a beam element must be a system with end moments released—i.e., a simple beam—to be compatible with the determinate structure which has been used for the analysis of the beam element by the stiffness method considering end rotations, i.e., a fixed end beam.

The flexibility coefficients for the simple beam that are related to the rotational stiffness coefficients for the fixed end beam are identified in Figs. 4-8(a) and (b). The flexibility coefficients δ^i_{jj} and δ^i_{kj} define the rotation of ends j and k, respectively, of member i due to a unit value of moment being applied at end j [Fig. 4-8(a)]. The flexibility coefficients δ^i_{jk} and δ^i_{kk} define the rotation of ends j and k, respectively, due to a unit value of moment being applied at end k [Fig. 4-8(b)].

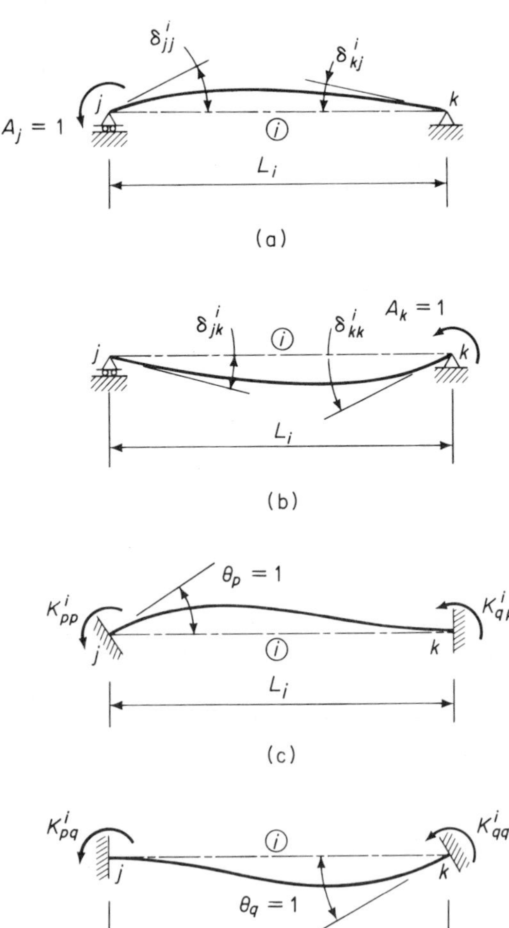

Fig. 4-8 Identification of flexibility and rotational stiffness coefficients for a beam element: (a) flexibility coefficients—unit moment applied at end j; (b) flexibility coefficients—unit moment applied at end k; (c) rotational stiffness coefficients—unit rotation of end j; (d) rotational stiffness coefficients—unit rotation of end k. *Note:* Actions are shown in assumed positive sense.

The four rotational stiffness coefficients are identified in Figs. 4-8(c) and (d). The stiffness coefficients K^i_{pp} and K^i_{qp} define the end moments required at the j- and k-ends of member i, respectively, to maintain equilibrium when the j-end is subjected to a unit value of rotation while end k is fixed [Fig. 4-8(c)]. The stiffness coefficients K^i_{pq} and K^i_{qq} define the end moments required at ends j and k, respectively, to maintain equilibrium when end k is subjected to a unit value of rotation while end j is fixed [Fig. 4-8(d)].

Now, a linear function of the two cases described in Figs. 4-8(a) and (b) can be combined to develop the deformation of the beam element described in Fig. 4-8(c) if

$$K^i_{pp}\delta^i_{jj} + K^i_{qp}\delta^i_{jk} = 1 \qquad \textbf{(4-10a)}$$

and

$$K^i_{pp}\delta^i_{kj} + K^i_{qp}\delta^i_{kk} = 0 \tag{4-10b}$$

Similarly, the two cases can be combined to develop the deformation of the beam element shown in Fig. 4-8(d), if

$$K^i_{pq}\delta^i_{jj} + K^i_{qq}\delta^i_{jk} = 0 \tag{4-10c}$$

and

$$K^i_{pq}\delta^i_{kj} + K^i_{qq}\delta^i_{kk} = 1 \tag{4-10d}$$

When writing Eqs. (4-10) for a particular beam element, the proper signs must be assigned to the values of the flexibility coefficients. ***Counterclockwise*** end rotation is assumed to be positive. Equations (4-10) can be expressed in matrix form as

$$\begin{bmatrix} \delta_{jj} & \delta_{jk} \\ \delta_{kj} & \delta_{kk} \end{bmatrix}_i \begin{bmatrix} K_{pp} & K_{pq} \\ K_{qp} & K_{qq} \end{bmatrix}_i = \begin{bmatrix} 1 & 0 \\ 0 & 1 \end{bmatrix} \tag{4-11}$$

or

$$[\mathbf{D}_r]_i[\mathbf{K}_r]_i = [\mathbf{I}] \tag{4-12}$$

where $[\mathbf{D}_r]_i$ defines the ***rotational flexibility*** of the simple beam and $[\mathbf{K}_r]_i$ defines the ***rotational stiffness*** of the fixed end beam. From Eqs. (4-12), it is seen that

$$[\mathbf{K}_r]_i = [\mathbf{D}_r]_i^{-1} \tag{4-13}$$

Hence, for *compatible* determinate structures, the stiffness matrix is equal to the inverse of the flexibility matrix. Keep in mind that in order for this relationship to be true, the actions denoted as the stiffness coefficients must correspond to the displacements defining the flexibility coefficients.

Example 4-1. Evaluate the member stiffness matrix defined by Expression (4-9) for a beam element with constant moment of inertia I and modulus of elasticity E over its length.

Using the *conjugate beam method* for determining deflections, the flexibility coefficients for the simply supported prismatic member are determined in Figs. 4-9 and 4-10. Substituting this information into Eqs. (4-11), the rotational flexibility matrix for the prismatic beam element is defined as

$$[\mathbf{D}_r]_i = \begin{bmatrix} \dfrac{L}{3EI} & \dfrac{-L}{6EI} \\ \dfrac{-L}{6EI} & \dfrac{L}{3EI} \end{bmatrix}_i \tag{4-14}$$

Hence, from Expression (4-13), i.e.,

$$[\mathbf{K}_r]_i = [\mathbf{D}_r]_i^{-1} \tag{4-13}$$

the rotational stiffness matrix for the prismatic member, $[\mathbf{K}]_i$, is written as

$$\begin{bmatrix} K_{pp} & K_{pq} \\ K_{qp} & K_{qq} \end{bmatrix}_i = \begin{bmatrix} \dfrac{4EI}{L} & \dfrac{2EI}{L} \\ \dfrac{2EI}{L} & \dfrac{4EI}{L} \end{bmatrix}_i \tag{4-15}$$

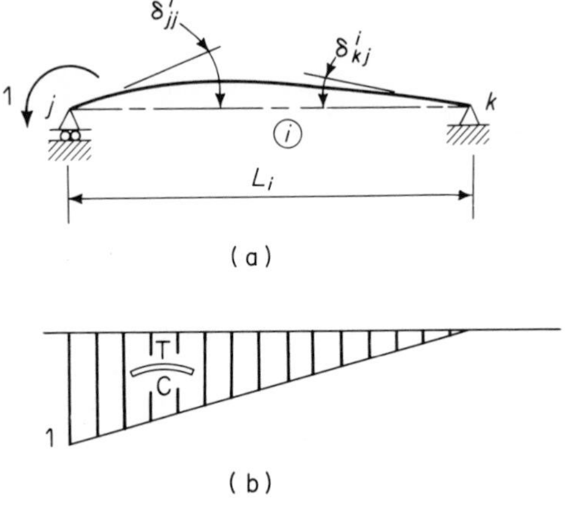

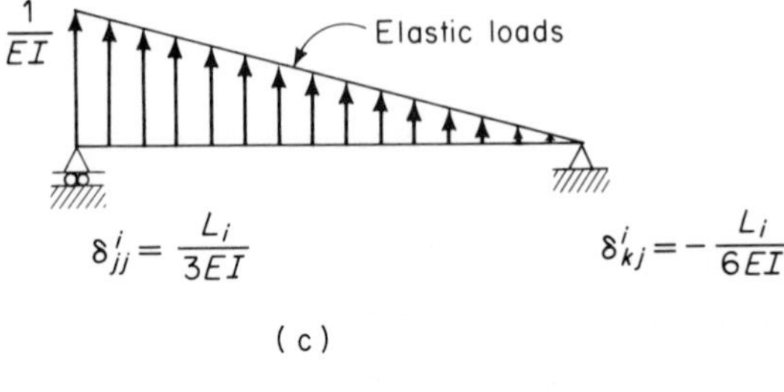

$\frac{1}{EI}$ Elastic loads

$\delta^i_{jj} = \frac{L_i}{3EI}$ $\delta^i_{kj} = -\frac{L_i}{6EI}$

(c)

Fig. 4-9 Example 4-1: Application of unit moment at j end of simple beam: (a) real beam (counterclockwise rotation assumed positive); (b) moment diagram; (c) conjugate beam.

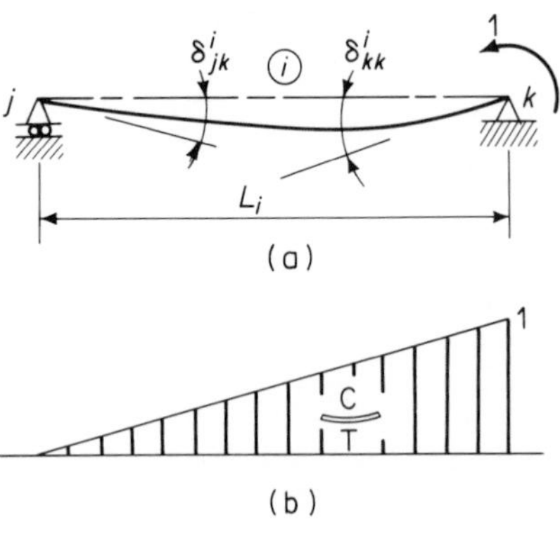

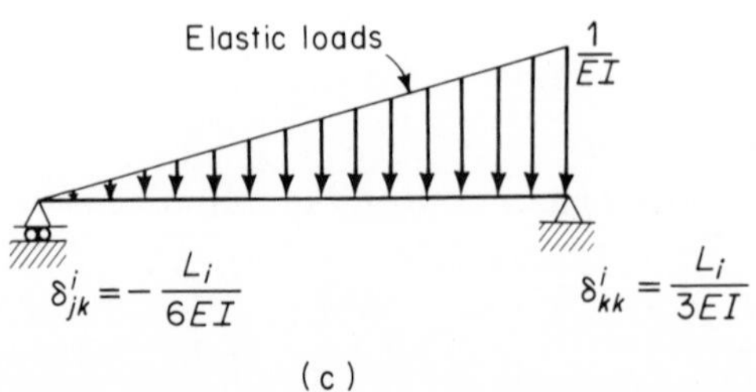

Elastic loads $\frac{1}{EI}$

$\delta^i_{jk} = -\frac{L_i}{6EI}$ $\delta^i_{kk} = \frac{L_i}{3EI}$

(c)

Fig. 4-10 Example 4-1: Application of unit moment at k end of simple beam: (a) real beam (counterclockwise rotation assumed positive); (b) moment diagram; (c) conjugate beam.

and substituting these values for the four rotational stiffness coefficients into Expression (4-9) yields

$$[\mathbf{K}]_i = \begin{bmatrix} \frac{4EI}{L} & \frac{2EI}{L} & \frac{6EI}{L^2} & \frac{-6EI}{L^2} \\ \frac{2EI}{L} & \frac{4EI}{L} & \frac{6EI}{L^2} & \frac{-6EI}{L^2} \\ \frac{6EI}{L^2} & \frac{6EI}{L^2} & \frac{12EI}{L^3} & \frac{-12EI}{L^3} \\ \frac{-6EI}{L^2} & \frac{-6EI}{L^2} & \frac{-12EI}{L^3} & \frac{-12EI}{L^3} \end{bmatrix}_i \begin{matrix} p \\ q \\ r \\ s \end{matrix} \quad (\text{columns } p, q, r, s) \tag{4-16}$$

Example 4-2. Establish the member stiffness matrix defined by Expression (4-9) for the tapered beam element described in Fig. 4-11(a). The beam has a rectangular cross-section with a width b; the beam is twice as deep at the j-end as at the k-end with a linear variation in depth over the length of the member. The cross-section at the k-end is selected as the reference section, defining its moment of inertia as I. The modulus of elasticity is constant for the member.

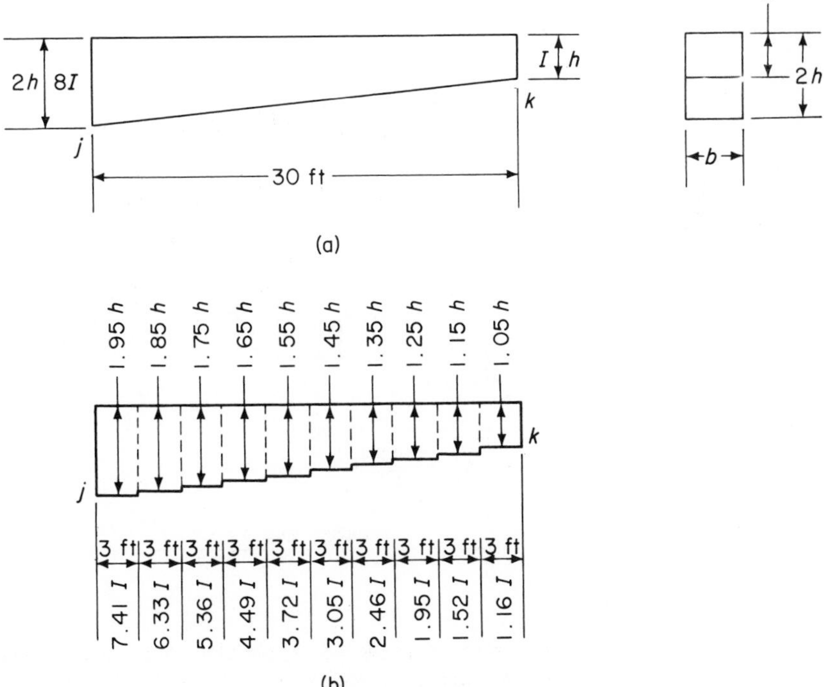

Fig. 4-11 Example 4-2: Tapered beam element: (a) beam element; (b) equivalent member.

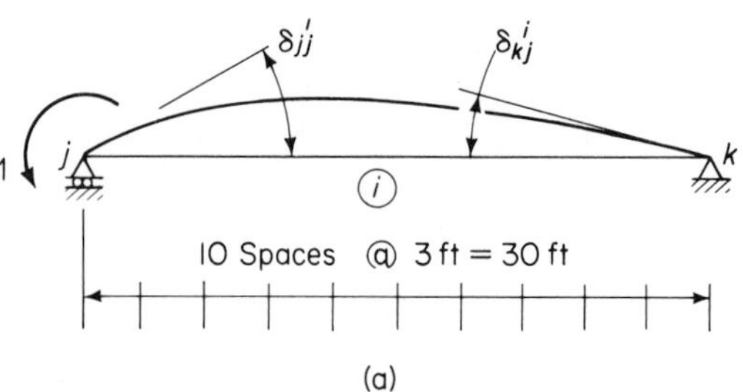

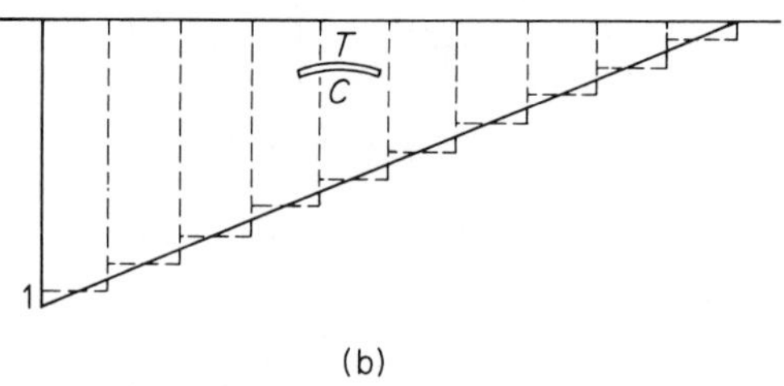

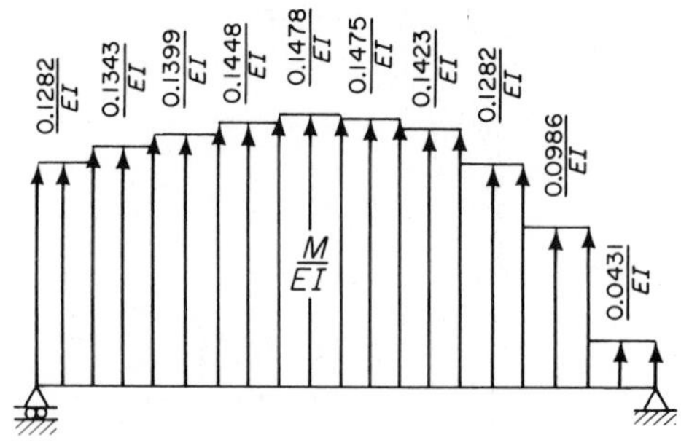

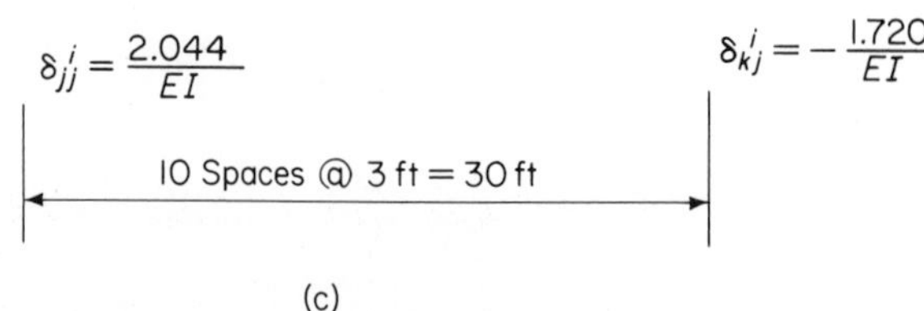

Fig. 4-12 Example 4-2: Application of unit moment at j end of simple beam: (a) equivalent beam (counterclockwise rotations assumed positive); (b) moment diagram; (c) conjugate beam.

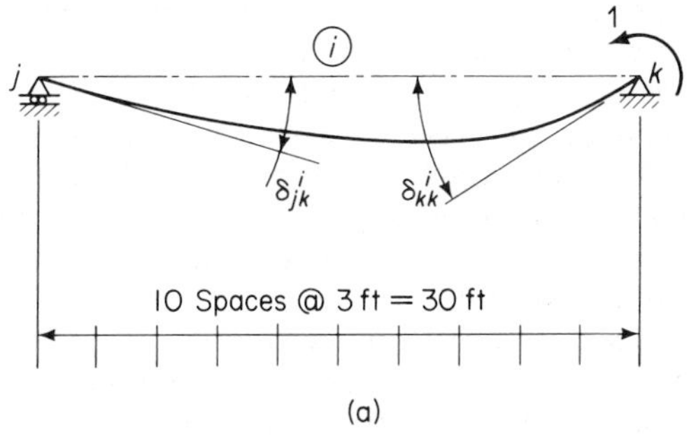

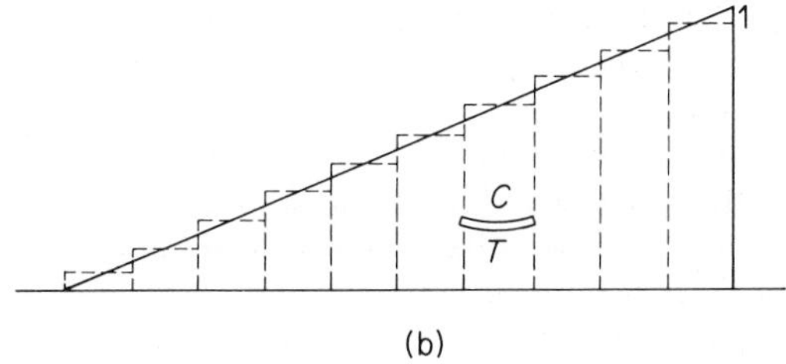

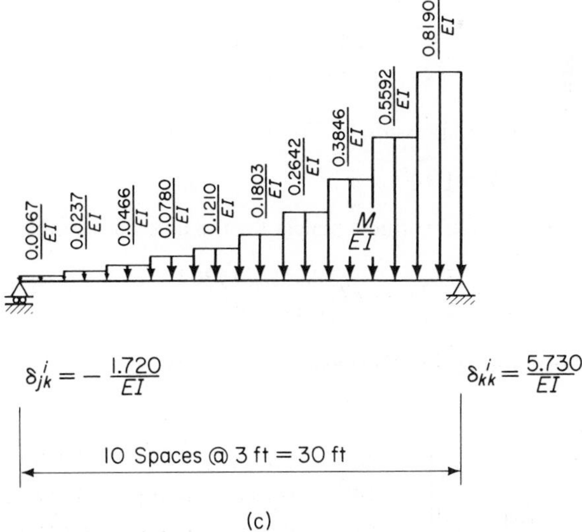

Fig. 4-13 Example 4-2: Application of unit moment at k end of simple beam: (a) equivalent beam (counterclockwise rotations assumed positive); (b) moment diagram; (c) conjugate beam.

For a ***haunched*** or ***tapered*** beam element, it is convenient to employ an *approximate solution* using a numerical procedure rather than attempting to carry out an exact solution which would involve the integration of complex terms. The approximation involves the creation of an ***equivalent beam*** by subdividing the member into convenient segments and assuming each segment to have a constant depth equal to an average depth of the real beam over the segment. The *equivalent beam* for the tapered beam element of Fig. 4-11(a) is defined, using segments 3 feet in length, as a nonprismatic beam with a constant moment of inertia over each segment of the beam; this *equivalent beam* is described in Fig. 4-11(b).

Using the conjugate beam method for calculating deflections, the rotational flexibility coefficients (δ^i_{jj}, δ^i_{jk}, δ^i_{kj}, and δ^i_{kk}) are determined in Figs. 4-12 and 4-13 for the *equivalent beam* of Fig. 4-11(b). In these computations, the elastic loads—i.e., the M/EI diagrams—applied to the conjugate beam are established using the average bending moment within each segment as if it were constant over the length of the segment. This averaging of the bending moment is a second approximation of the numerical procedure; it is in line with the approximation used in establishing the *equivalent beam.*

The prime factor that influences the accuracy of the numerical procedure that has been suggested for computing the flexibility coefficients for a haunched or tapered beam is the length of segment used in establishing the *equivalent beam.* However, it will be found that the accuracy of the numerical solution is, in most cases, rather insensitive to the size of segment used in the analysis; hence, relatively large segments, say segment length to span length ratio of $\frac{1}{10}$, can be used in the analysis and will yield acceptable results.

From the information determined in Figs. 4-12 and 4-13, the rotational flexibility matrix for the tapered beam is written as

$$[\mathbf{D}_r]_i = \frac{1}{EI}\begin{bmatrix} 2.044 & -1.720 \\ -1.720 & 5.730 \end{bmatrix} \tag{4-17}$$

and from Expression (4-13), which states that

$$[\mathbf{K}_r]_i = [\mathbf{D}_r]_i^{-1} \tag{4-13}$$

the rotational stiffness matrix for the tapered beam is written as

$$\begin{bmatrix} K_{pp} & K_{pq} \\ K_{qp} & K_{qq} \end{bmatrix}_i = EI\begin{bmatrix} 0.654 & 0.196 \\ 0.196 & 0.233 \end{bmatrix}_i \tag{4-18}$$

Substituting into Expression (4-9) yields

$$[\mathbf{K}]_i = EI \begin{array}{c} \begin{matrix} \quad p \quad & \quad q \quad & \quad r \quad & \quad s \quad \end{matrix} \\ \begin{bmatrix} 0.654 & 0.196 & 0.028 & -0.028 \\ 0.196 & 0.233 & 0.014 & -0.014 \\ 0.028 & 0.014 & 0.001 & -0.001 \\ -0.028 & -0.014 & -0.001 & 0.001 \end{bmatrix}_i \end{array} \begin{matrix} p \\ q \\ r \\ s \end{matrix} \tag{4-19}$$

If I is given in units of ft^4 and E is given in units of k/ft^2, the elements of the matrix of Expression (4-19) will be in terms of k/rad, ft-k/rad, k/ft, or ft-k/ft, whichever is appropriate.

4-2.3 Exercises

1. Calculate the stiffness coefficients of the member stiffness matrix for the beam element described in Fig. 4-14(a); E is constant.

2. Determine the member stiffness matrix for the haunched beam given in Fig. 4-14(b). The beam is 1.5-ft wide and has straight haunches at either end. Use 2-ft-long segments to approximate the haunched portion of the beam; E is constant.

3. Establish the member stiffness matrix for the beam element of Fig. 4-14(c), letting $I = 9000$ in^4 and $E = 30 \times 10^6$ psi.

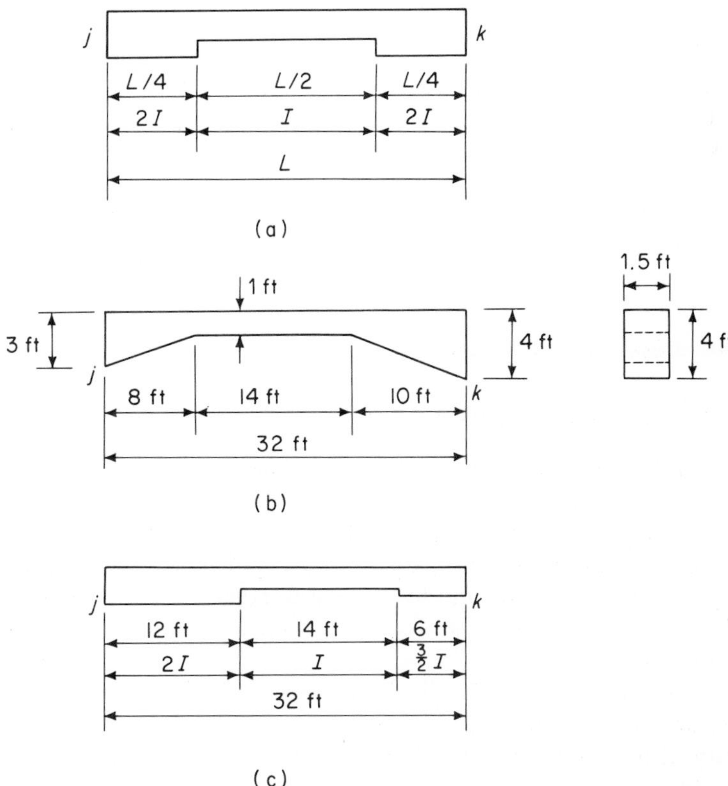

Fig. 4-14

4. Develop the member stiffness matrix for the tapered beam element described in Fig. 4-14(d). The member has a constant width of b and a variable depth; E is constant.

5. Evaluate the elements for the member stiffness matrix for the haunched beam element of Fig. 4-14(e). The beam is 1.5-ft wide and has parabolic haunches at either end described by the equation $y = kx^2$; E is equal to 3000 ksi. Use 2-ft-segment lengths in approximating the haunches in the solution.

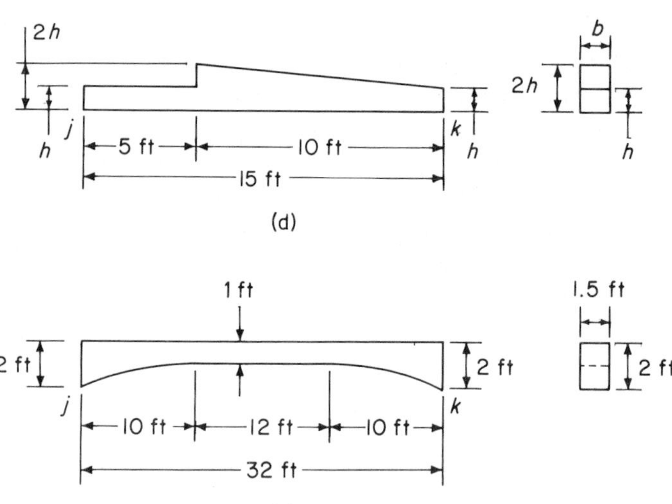

Fig. 4-14—*Cont.*

4–3
Development of Matrices

4-3.1 Equations of Analysis

The basic philosophy of the stiffness method of analysis has been stated and discussed in Chapter 1, Sec. 1-4. However, before considering the application of the stiffness method in analyzing various types of structural systems, the procedure of the analysis should be organized into a systematic program and the basic equations of the analysis should be developed in general terms. As a vehicle for doing this, consider the analysis of the orthogonal structural system described in Fig. 4-15.

The members of the rigid frame (Fig. 4-15) may have either variable or constant moments of inertia over their lengths; and the modulus of elasticity may vary within the system. The frame has a span of L and a height of H. A general loading is applied to the system as indicated in the figure. The joint labels are given in the circles adjacent to the members.

For this structure (Fig. 4-15), the possible independent components of joint displacement are identified in Fig. 4-16, with respect to the sign convention of Sec. 4-1, and *neglecting* axial deformation of the members, these displacements are labeled as indicated. The j- and k-ends of each member are also designated in Fig. 4-16. The j-end of each element was selected so that the assumed positive direction of end shears for the element corresponds to the assumed positive direction of joint forces and translation.

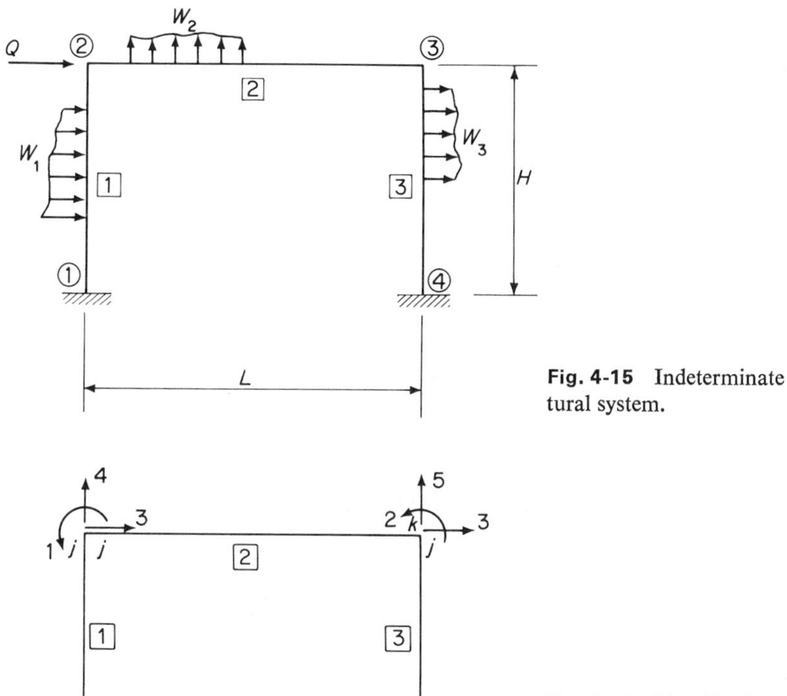

Fig. 4-15 Indeterminate structural system.

Fig. 4-16 Identification of possible joint displacements and *j* and *k* ends.

The frame (Fig. 4-15) is *kinematically indeterminate* to the third degree: joint displacements θ_1, θ_2, and δ_3 are unrestrained and joint displacements δ_4, δ_5, θ_6, δ_7, θ_8, and δ_9 are restrained by the supporting condition of the system. The given structure can be reduced to a kinematically determinate system by artificially constraining the three unrestrained components of displacement, i.e., θ_1, θ_2, and δ_3. Therefore, the ***restrained structure***, described in Fig. 4-17, is created by artificially constraining joint 2 against rotation (θ_1) and horizontal translation (δ_3) and joint 3 against rotation (θ_2); the other possible components of joint displacement (δ_4, δ_5, θ_6, δ_7, θ_8, and δ_9) are already restrained by the supporting conditions. Keep in mind that axial deformation of the members is being neglected in the analysis.

As stated in Sec. 1-4, the analysis of a structural system is achieved by superimposing (1) the solution of the restrained structure for applied disturbances, and (2) the solution of the restrained structure for joint displacements. The analysis of the restrained structure of Fig. 4-17 for the applied loads is indicated in Fig. 4-18. The support reactions of the restrained structure are identified in their assumed positive directions in Fig. 4-18(a). These reactions are denoted as S_{m0}, where the subscript m assumes the label of the corresponding displacement and

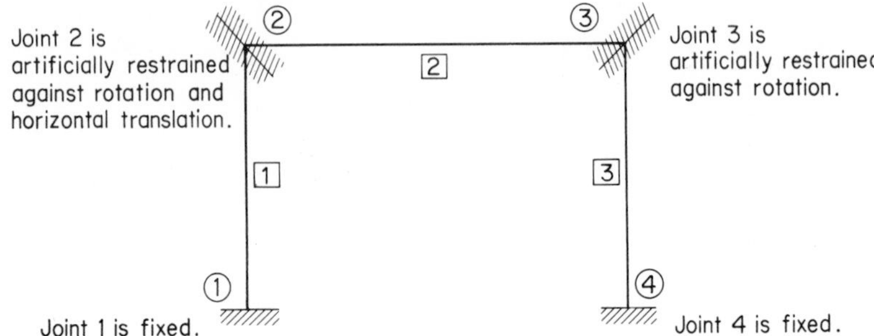

Fig. 4-17 The restrained structure.

the subscript 0 denotes that the reactions are due to applied disturbances. The support reactions are evaluated using Fig. 4-18(b). Since all joints are restrained, the actions developed at the ends of the members are simply fixed end moments and fixed end shears; the fixed end actions appearing at the end of a member are converted into actions acting on the adjacent joint by a change in direction. The fixed end moments are denoted as FM^i_m and fixed end shears are defined as FP^i_m, where the superscript i refers to the member being considered and the subscript m again takes the label of the joint displacement corresponding to the action. Considering the equilibrium of each joint yields

$$S_{10} = FM^1_1 + FM^2_1 \tag{4-20a}$$

$$S_{20} = FM^2_2 + FM^3_2 \tag{4-20b}$$

$$S_{30} = FP^1_3 + FP^3_3 - Q \tag{4-20c}$$

$$S_{40} = FP^2_4 \tag{4-20d}$$

$$S_{50} = FP^2_5 \tag{4-20e}$$

$$S_{60} = FM^1_6 \tag{4-20f}$$

$$S_{70} = FP^1_7 \tag{4-20g}$$

$$S_{80} = FM^3_8 \tag{4-20h}$$

$$S_{90} = FP^3_9 \tag{4-20i}$$

Although the magnitude and direction of displacement of the joints are unknown at this stage of the analysis, the restrained structure can be analyzed for the application of unit values of each of the possible components of joint displacement. Thus, a linear function of these solutions can be combined with the solution of the restrained structure for applied disturbances to establish a set of equations that can be used to evaluate the unknown joint displacements.

The reactions of the restrained structure resulting from the application of unit values of joint displacements are identified in Fig. 4-19. It is possible to evaluate these reactions in terms of the member stiffness coefficients that have been defined in Sec. 4-2. Consider, for example, the application of a unit value of

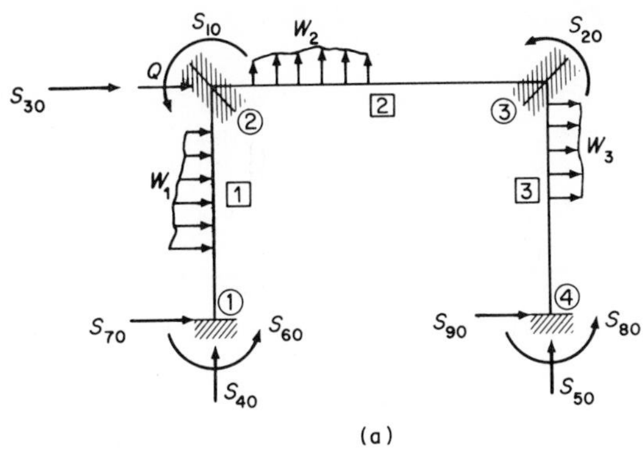

(a)

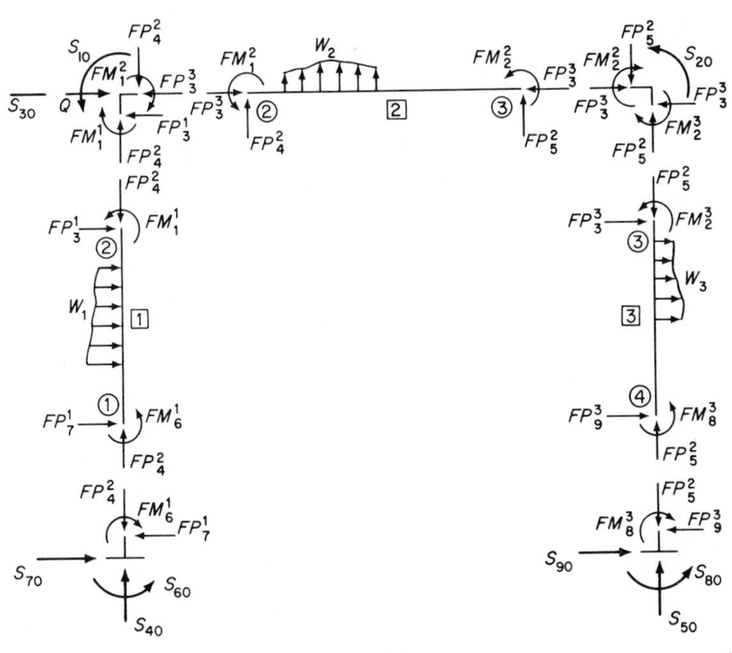

(b)

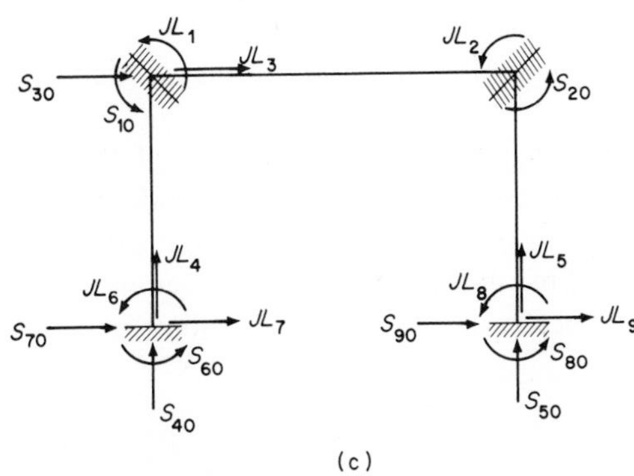

(c)

Fig. 4-18 Support reactions of the restrained structure—applied loads: (a) identification of reactions (support reactions shown in assumed positive sense); (b) evaluation of reactions (fixed-end moments and fixed-end shears shown in assumed positive sense —reactions assumed positive); (c) identification of joint loads (all actions shown in assumed positive sense).

rotation at joint 2 of the restrained structure. The resulting reactions are defined in Fig. 4-19(a). Relating member 1 of the deformed restrained structure to the typical member i of Fig. 4-2, it is seen that for a unit value of rotation at the j-end of member 1, the restraining actions required to maintain equilibrium of the deformed member are a restraining moment K_{11}^1 and a restraining shear K_{31}^1 at the j-end, and a restraining moment K_{61}^1 and a restraining shear K_{71}^1 at the k-end. Note that the subscripts assume the labels assigned to the possible joint displacements of the system in Fig. 4-16; the first subscript refers to the particular displacement that corresponds to the restraining action being defined and the second subscript refers to the displacement that has been imposed on the system. The superscript identifies the member being considered. Next, relating member 2 to the typical member i of Fig. 4-2, the restraining actions required to maintain equilibrium of the deformed member are a restraining moment K_{11}^2 and a restraining shear K_{41}^2 at the j-end, and a restraining moment K_{21}^2 and a restraining shear K_{51}^2 at the k-end. Hence, the total restraining moment required at joint 1 to maintain the deformed restrained structure [Fig. 4-19(a)] is equal to the sum of the moments required to rotate the ends of each member framing into the joint, i.e.,

$$S_{11} = K_{11}^1 + K_{11}^2 \tag{4-21a}$$

The other reactions can be evaluated in a similar manner, giving

$$S_{21} = K_{21}^2 \tag{4-21b}$$

$$S_{31} = K_{31}^1 \tag{4-21c}$$

$$S_{41} = K_{41}^2 \tag{4-21d}$$

$$S_{51} = K_{51}^2 \tag{4-21e}$$

$$S_{61} = K_{61}^1 \tag{4-21f}$$

$$S_{71} = K_{71}^1 \tag{4-21g}$$

$$S_{81} = 0 \tag{4-21h}$$

$$S_{91} = 0 \tag{4-21i}$$

In defining the reactions of the restrained structure S_{mn}, the first subscript identifies the actions by referring to the corresponding joint displacement and the second subscript denotes the particular joint displacement that has been imposed on the restrained structure.

For the application of a unit value of rotation at joint 3 of the restrained structure [Fig. 4-19(b)], the restraining actions required at the ends of each beam element can be determined by relating member 2 of the restrained structure to the typical member i of Fig. 4-3 and member 3 to the typical member of Fig. 4-2. The reactions of the restrained structure are evaluated as follows:

$$S_{12} = K_{12}^2 \tag{4-22a}$$

$$S_{22} = K_{22}^2 + K_{22}^3 \tag{4-22b}$$

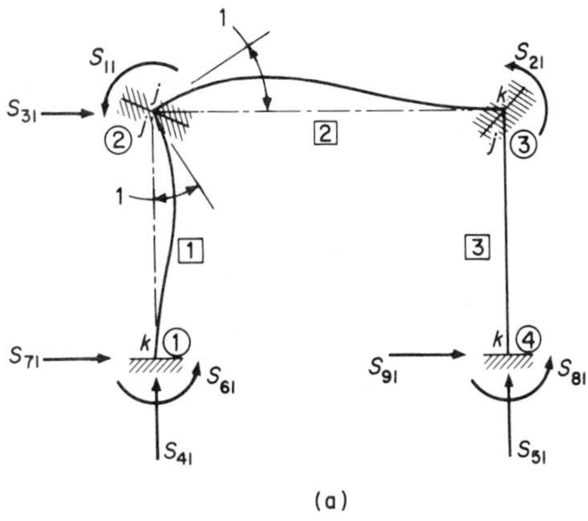

(a)

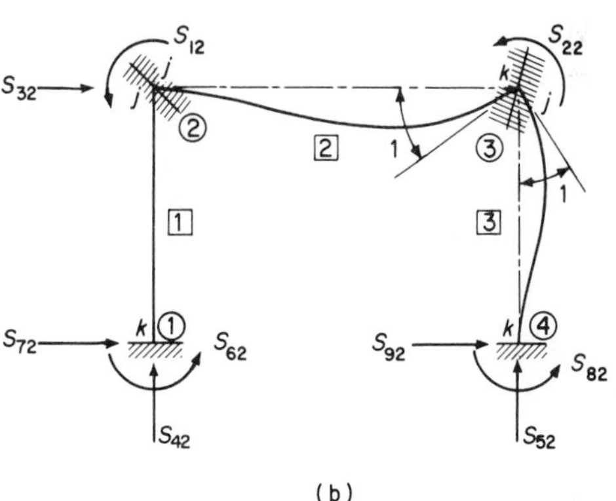

(b)

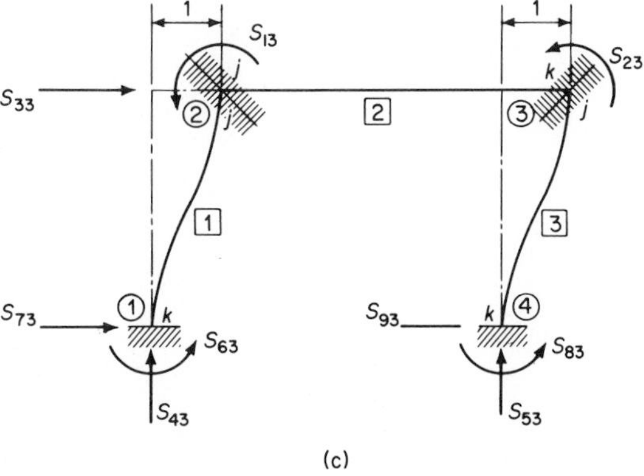

(c)

Fig. 4-19 Reactions of restrained structure due to application of unit joint displacements: (a) application of unit rotation θ_1; (b) application of unit rotation θ_2; (c) application of unit translation δ_3.

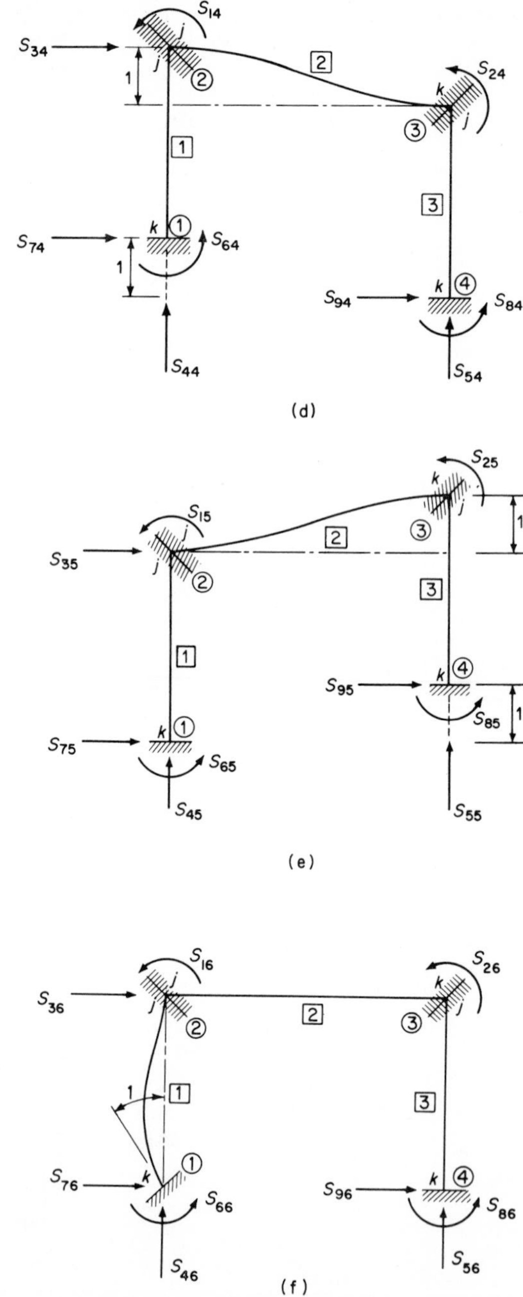

Fig. 4-19—*Cont.* (d) Application of unit translation δ_4; (e) application of unit translation δ_5; (f) application of unit rotation θ_6.

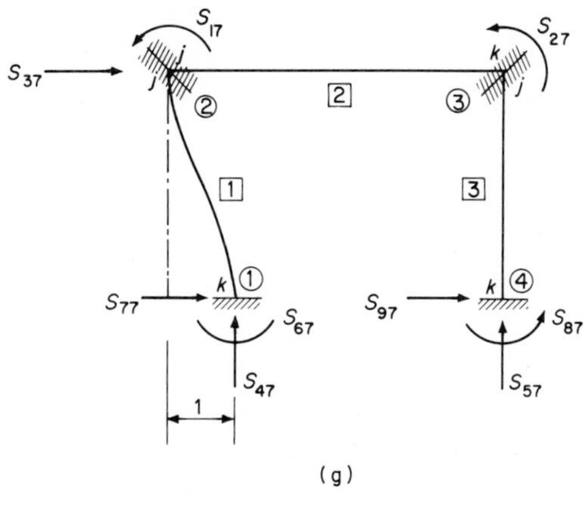

(g)

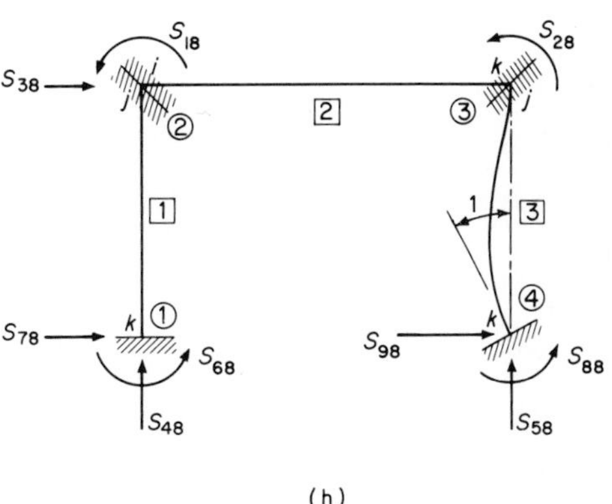

(h)

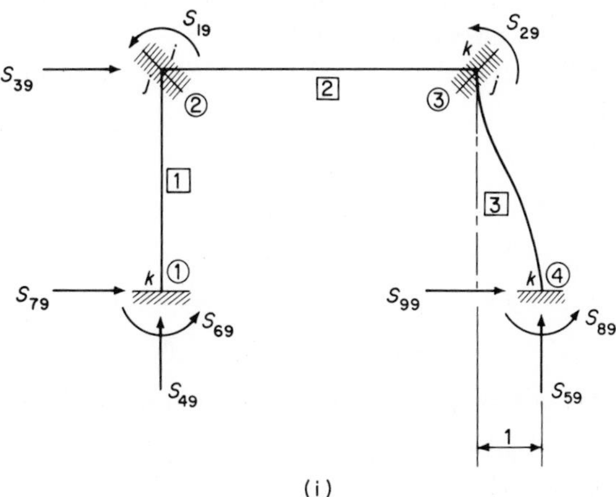

(i)

Fig. 4-19—*Cont.* (g) Application of unit translation δ_7; (h) application of unit rotation θ_8; (i) application of unit translation δ_9. *Note:* Reactions shown in assumed positive sense.

$$S_{32} = K^3_{32} \tag{4-22c}$$

$$S_{42} = K^2_{42} \tag{4-22d}$$

$$S_{52} = K^2_{52} \tag{4-22e}$$

$$S_{62} = 0 \tag{4-22f}$$

$$S_{72} = 0 \tag{4-22g}$$

$$S_{82} = K^3_{82} \tag{4-22h}$$

$$S_{92} = K^3_{92} \tag{4-22i}$$

The reactions that are developed when the restrained structure is subjected to a unit value of horizontal displacement at joint 2 [Fig. 4-19(c)] can be evaluated by first relating members 1 and 3 to the deformed typical beam element i of Fig. 4-4. For this case [Fig. 4-19(c)], the reactions of the restrained structure are defined as

$$S_{13} = K^1_{13} \tag{4-23a}$$

$$S_{23} = K^3_{23} \tag{4-23b}$$

$$S_{33} = K^1_{33} + K^3_{33} \tag{4-23c}$$

$$S_{43} = 0 \tag{4-23d}$$

$$S_{53} = 0 \tag{4-23e}$$

$$S_{63} = K^1_{63} \tag{4-23f}$$

$$S_{73} = K^1_{73} \tag{4-23g}$$

$$S_{83} = K^3_{83} \tag{4-23h}$$

$$S_{93} = K^3_{93} \tag{4-23i}$$

The reactions of the restrained structure for the remaining cases described in Fig. 4-19 are defined as follows:

For the application of a unit value of vertical translation of joint 1 [Fig. 4-19(d)],

$$S_{14} = K^2_{14} \tag{4-24a}$$

$$S_{24} = K^2_{24} \tag{4-24b}$$

$$S_{44} = K^2_{44} \tag{4-24c}$$

$$S_{54} = K^2_{54} \tag{4-24d}$$

$$S_{34} = S_{64} = S_{74} = S_{84} = S_{94} = 0 \tag{4-24e}$$

For a unit value of vertical translation of joint 4 [Fig. 4-19(d)],

$$S_{15} = K^2_{15} \tag{4-25a}$$

$$S_{25} = K^2_{25} \tag{4-25b}$$

$$S_{45} = K^2_{45} \tag{4-25c}$$

$$S_{55} = K^2_{55} \tag{4-25d}$$

$$S_{35} = S_{65} = S_{75} = S_{85} = S_{95} = 0 \tag{4-25e}$$

For a unit value of rotation of joint 1 [Fig. 4-19(f)],

$$S_{16} = K^1_{16} \tag{4-26a}$$

$$S_{36} = K^1_{36} \tag{4-26b}$$

$$S_{66} = K^1_{66} \tag{4-26c}$$

$$S_{76} = K^1_{76} \tag{4-26d}$$

$$S_{26} = S_{46} = S_{56} = S_{86} = S_{96} = 0 \tag{4-26e}$$

For a unit value of horizontal translation of joint 1 [Fig. 4-19(g)],

$$S_{17} = K^1_{17} \tag{4-27a}$$

$$S_{37} = K^1_{37} \tag{4-27b}$$

$$S_{67} = K^1_{67} \tag{4-27c}$$

$$S_{77} = K^1_{77} \tag{4-27d}$$

$$S_{27} = S_{47} = S_{57} = S_{87} = S_{97} = 0 \tag{4-27e}$$

For a unit value of rotation of joint 4 [Fig. 4-19(h)],

$$S_{28} = K^3_{28} \tag{4-28a}$$

$$S_{38} = K^3_{38} \tag{4-28b}$$

$$S_{88} = K^3_{88} \tag{4-28c}$$

$$S_{98} = K^3_{98} \tag{4-28d}$$

$$S_{18} = S_{48} = S_{58} = S_{68} = S_{78} = 0 \tag{4-28e}$$

Finally, for a unit value of horizontal translation of joint 4 [Fig. 4-19(i)],

$$S_{29} = K^3_{29} \tag{4-29a}$$

$$S_{39} = K^3_{39} \tag{4-29b}$$

$$S_{89} = K^3_{89} \tag{4-29c}$$

$$S_{99} = K^3_{99} \tag{4-29d}$$

$$S_{19} = S_{49} = S_{59} = S_{69} = S_{79} = 0 \tag{4-29e}$$

Now, the solution of the indeterminate structure of Fig. 4-15 can be obtained by summing the solution of the restrained structure for the applied loads (Fig. 4-18) and a linear function of the solutions of the restrained structure for the application of unit values of the possible joint displacements (Fig. 4-19). These solutions of the restrained structure described in Figs. 4-18 and 4-19 must be combined so that the *artificial restraining actions* which were introduced to establish the restrained structure *vanish*. In addition, the combining of these various solutions of the restrained structure must yield the true support reactions

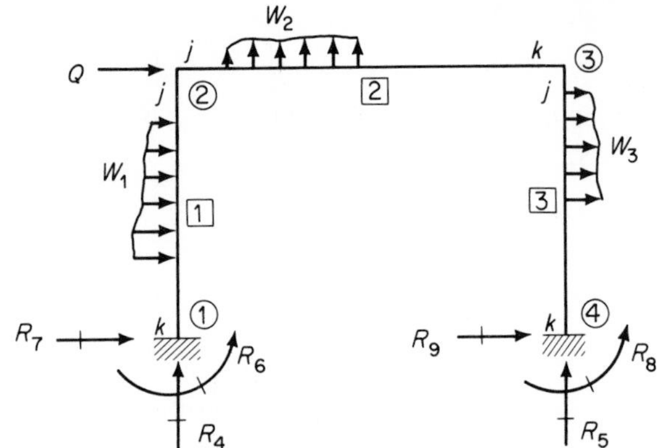

Fig. 4-20 Identification of support reactions.

acting on the indeterminate structure, as defined in Fig. 4-20. The solution of the indeterminate system can be expressed in equation form as follows:

$$S_{10} + S_{11}\theta_1 + S_{12}\theta_2 + S_{13}\delta_3 + S_{14}\delta_4 + S_{15}\delta_5 + S_{16}\theta_6 + S_{17}\delta_7 + S_{18}\theta_8 + S_{19}\delta_9 = 0 \tag{4-30a}$$

$$S_{20} + S_{21}\theta_1 + S_{22}\theta_2 + S_{23}\delta_3 + S_{24}\delta_4 + S_{25}\delta_5 + S_{26}\theta_6 + S_{27}\delta_7 + S_{28}\theta_8 + S_{29}\delta_9 = 0 \tag{4-30b}$$

$$S_{30} + S_{31}\theta_1 + S_{32}\theta_2 + S_{33}\delta_3 + S_{34}\delta_4 + S_{35}\delta_5 + S_{36}\theta_6 + S_{37}\delta_7 + S_{38}\theta_8 + S_{39}\delta_9 = 0 \tag{4-30c}$$

$$S_{40} + S_{41}\theta_1 + S_{42}\theta_2 + S_{43}\delta_3 + S_{44}\delta_4 + S_{45}\delta_5 + S_{46}\theta_6 + S_{47}\delta_7 + S_{48}\theta_8 + S_{49}\delta_9 = R_4 \tag{4-30d}$$

$$S_{50} + S_{51}\theta_1 + S_{52}\theta_2 + S_{53}\delta_3 + S_{54}\delta_4 + S_{55}\delta_5 + S_{56}\theta_6 + S_{57}\delta_7 + S_{58}\theta_8 + S_{59}\delta_9 = R_5 \tag{4-30e}$$

$$S_{60} + S_{61}\theta_1 + S_{62}\theta_2 + S_{63}\delta_3 + S_{64}\delta_4 + S_{65}\delta_5 + S_{66}\theta_6 + S_{67}\delta_7 + S_{68}\theta_8 + S_{69}\delta_9 = R_6 \tag{4-30f}$$

$$S_{70} + S_{71}\theta_1 + S_{72}\theta_2 + S_{73}\delta_3 + S_{74}\delta_4 + S_{75}\delta_5 + S_{76}\theta_6 + S_{77}\delta_7 + S_{78}\theta_8 + S_{79}\delta_9 = R_7 \tag{4-30g}$$

$$S_{80} + S_{81}\theta_1 + S_{82}\theta_2 + S_{83}\delta_3 + S_{84}\delta_4 + S_{85}\delta_5 + S_{86}\theta_6 + S_{87}\delta_7 + S_{88}\theta_8 + S_{89}\delta_9 = R_8 \tag{4-30h}$$

$$S_{90} + S_{91}\theta_1 + S_{92}\theta_2 + S_{93}\delta_3 + S_{94}\delta_4 + S_{95}\delta_5 + S_{96}\theta_6 + S_{97}\delta_7 + S_{98}\theta_8 + S_{99}\delta_9 = R_9 \tag{4-30i}$$

Making the substitutions indicated by Eqs. (4-20) through (4-29), Eqs. (4-30) can be rewritten in matrix form as shown in Table 4-2, Eq. (4-31), or in a more general matrix notation as

Table 4-2

$$
\left[\begin{array}{ccc|cccccc}
K^{1}_{11} + K^{2}_{11} & K^{2}_{12} & K^{1}_{13} & K^{2}_{14} & K^{2}_{15} & K^{1}_{16} & K^{1}_{17} & 0 & 0 \\
K^{2}_{21} & K^{2}_{22} + K^{3}_{22} & K^{3}_{23} & K^{2}_{24} & K^{2}_{25} & 0 & 0 & K^{3}_{28} & K^{3}_{29} \\
K^{1}_{31} & K^{3}_{32} & K^{1}_{33} + K^{3}_{33} & 0 & 0 & K^{1}_{36} & K^{1}_{37} & K^{3}_{38} & K^{3}_{39} \\
\hline
K^{2}_{41} & K^{2}_{42} & 0 & K^{2}_{44} & K^{2}_{45} & 0 & 0 & 0 & 0 \\
K^{2}_{51} & K^{2}_{52} & 0 & K^{2}_{54} & K^{2}_{55} & 0 & 0 & 0 & 0 \\
K^{1}_{61} & 0 & K^{1}_{63} & 0 & 0 & K^{1}_{66} & K^{1}_{67} & 0 & 0 \\
K^{1}_{71} & 0 & K^{1}_{73} & 0 & 0 & K^{1}_{76} & K^{1}_{77} & 0 & 0 \\
0 & K^{3}_{82} & K^{3}_{83} & 0 & 0 & 0 & 0 & K^{3}_{88} & K^{3}_{89} \\
0 & K^{3}_{92} & K^{3}_{93} & 0 & 0 & 0 & 0 & K^{3}_{98} & K^{3}_{99}
\end{array}\right]
\left[\begin{array}{c}
\theta_1 \\ \theta_2 \\ \delta_3 \\ \hline \delta_4 \\ \delta_5 \\ \theta_6 \\ \delta_7 \\ \theta_8 \\ \delta_9
\end{array}\right]
=
\left[\begin{array}{c}
-FM^{1}_{1} - FM^{2}_{1} \\
-FM^{2}_{2} - FM^{3}_{2} \\
-FP^{1}_{3} - FP^{3}_{3} + Q \\
\hline
-FP^{2}_{4} \\
-FP^{2}_{5} \\
-FM^{1}_{6} \\
-FP^{1}_{7} \\
-FM^{3}_{8} \\
-FP^{3}_{9}
\end{array}\right]
+
\left[\begin{array}{c}
0 \\ 0 \\ 0 \\ \hline R_4 \\ R_5 \\ R_6 \\ R_7 \\ R_8 \\ R_9
\end{array}\right]
\qquad \textbf{(4-31)}
$$

$$[\mathbf{S}_c][\boldsymbol{\Delta}_c] = [\mathbf{JL}_c] + [\mathbf{R}_c] \tag{4-32}$$

defining $[\mathbf{S}_c]$ as the ***complete structure stiffness matrix***, $[\boldsymbol{\Delta}_c]$ as the ***complete joint displacement matrix***, $[\mathbf{JL}_c]$ as the ***complete joint load matrix***, and $[\mathbf{R}_c]$ as the ***complete support reaction matrix***.

The matrices of Eqs. (4-32) can be partitioned as indicated in Table 4-2, separating the columns of the complete structure stiffness matrix $[\mathbf{S}_c]$ into two groups according to elements associated with the *unrestrained* and the *restrained* components of joint displacement, and separating the rows of all of the matrices, with respect to the unrestrained and restrained components of joint displacement. For this partitioning, Eqs. (4-32) can be expressed as

$$\begin{bmatrix} [\mathbf{S}_{uu}] & [\mathbf{S}_{ur}] \\ [\mathbf{S}_{ru}] & [\mathbf{S}_{rr}] \end{bmatrix} \begin{bmatrix} [\boldsymbol{\Delta}_u] \\ [\boldsymbol{\Delta}_r] \end{bmatrix} = \begin{bmatrix} [\mathbf{JL}_u] \\ [\mathbf{JL}_r] \end{bmatrix} + \begin{bmatrix} [\mathbf{0}] \\ [\mathbf{R}_r] \end{bmatrix} \tag{4-33}$$

where $[\mathbf{S}_{uu}]$ represents the restraining actions of the restrained structure associated with the unknown joint displacements resulting from the independent application of unit values of unknown joint displacements; $[\mathbf{S}_{ru}]$ represents the restraining actions associated with the joint displacements restrained by the real supports of the system resulting from independent application of unit values of unknown joint displacements; $[\mathbf{S}_{ur}]$ represents the restraining actions of the restrained structure associated with the unknown joint displacements developed by the independent application of unit values of the joint displacements restrained by the real supports of the system; and $[\mathbf{S}_{rr}]$ represents the restraining actions associated with the joint displacements restrained by the real supports developed by the independent application of unit values of these restrained displacements. The first subscript identifies the restraining actions of the restrained structure as to whether they are associated with unrestrained (u) or restrained (r) components of joint displacement in the actual structure and the second subscript identifies whether the imposed individual joint displacements are unrestrained (u) or restrained (r) components of joint displacement in the actual structure.

Examining Eqs. (4-31), it is seen that the elements of the complete structure stiffness matrix are established by a *summation* of the member stiffness coefficients for the members of the structure having the same subscripts.

Unfortunately, Eqs. (4-31) cannot be solved directly for the unknown components of joint displacement due to the fact that they constitute a set of *dependent* equations, i.e., $|S_c| = 0$. However, the unknown joint displacements can be evaluated by combining the solution of the restrained structure for applied loads (Fig. 4-18) and a linear function of the solutions of the restrained structure for the application of a unit value of each of the unknown joint displacements [Figs. 4-19(a), (b), and (c)] so that the artificial restraining actions vanish. This operation can be expressed as

$$S_{10} + S_{11}\theta_1 + S_{12}\theta_2 + S_{13}\delta_3 = 0 \tag{4-34a}$$

$$S_{20} + S_{21}\theta_1 + S_{22}\theta_2 + S_{23}\delta_3 = 0 \tag{4-34b}$$

$$S_{30} + S_{31}\theta_1 + S_{32}\theta_2 + S_{33}\delta_3 = 0 \tag{4-34c}$$

Looking back at Eqs. (4-30), it is realized that Eqs. (4-34) are identical to Eqs. (4-30a), (4-30b), and (4-30c) after the restrained components of joint displacement are set equal to zero. Making the substitutions indicated by Eqs. (4-20) through (4-23), Eqs. (4-34) can be rewritten as

$$\begin{bmatrix} (K_{11}^1 + K_{11}^2) & K_{12}^2 & K_{13}^1 \\ K_{21}^2 & (K_{22}^2 + K_{22}^3) & K_{23}^3 \\ K_{31}^1 & K_{32}^3 & (K_{33}^1 + K_{33}^3) \end{bmatrix} \begin{bmatrix} \theta_1 \\ \theta_2 \\ \delta_3 \end{bmatrix} = \begin{bmatrix} -FM_1^1 - FM_1^2 \\ -FM_2^2 - FM_2^3 \\ -FP_3^1 - FP_3^3 + Q \end{bmatrix} \tag{4-35}$$

Now, referring to Eqs. (4-31) and (4-33), Eqs. (4-35) can be represented by the matrix equation

$$[\mathbf{S}_{uu}][\mathbf{\Delta}_u] = [\mathbf{JL}_u] \tag{4-36}$$

The solution of this set of *independent* equations for the unknown joint displacements is indicated as

$$[\mathbf{\Delta}_u] = [\mathbf{S}_{uu}]^{-1}[\mathbf{JL}_u] \tag{4-37}$$

Keep in mind that Eq. (4-36) can be solved by any one of the several techniques discussed in Chapter 2.

Once the magnitudes and directions of the unrestrained joint displacements have been established, the support reactions for the indeterminate structure can be computed from Eqs. (4-30d) through (4-30i) after setting the restrained displacements equal to zero and substituting for the values of unrestrained displacements. Hence, using the information from Eqs. (4-20) through (4-23), Eqs. (4-30d) through (4-30i) can be written as

$$\begin{bmatrix} K_{41}^2 & K_{42}^2 & 0 \\ K_{51}^2 & K_{52}^2 & 0 \\ K_{61}^1 & 0 & K_{63}^1 \\ K_{71}^1 & 0 & K_{73}^1 \\ 0 & K_{82}^3 & K_{83}^3 \\ 0 & K_{92}^3 & K_{93}^3 \end{bmatrix} \begin{bmatrix} \theta_1 \\ \theta_2 \\ \delta_3 \end{bmatrix} + \begin{bmatrix} FP_4^2 \\ FP_5^2 \\ FM_6^1 \\ FP_7^1 \\ FM_8^3 \\ FP_9^3 \end{bmatrix} = \begin{bmatrix} R_4 \\ R_5 \\ R_6 \\ R_7 \\ R_8 \\ R_9 \end{bmatrix} \tag{4-38}$$

or, referring to Eqs. (4-31) and (4-33), as

$$[\mathbf{S}_{ru}][\mathbf{\Delta}_u] - [\mathbf{JL}_r] = [\mathbf{R}_r] \tag{4-39}$$

Finally, the end actions which are developed at the ends of the members of the indeterminate structure of Fig. 4-15 can also be determined by superimposing the solution of the restrained structure for applied loads and for joint displacements. The end actions for a member of the restrained structure resulting from the applied loading condition are simply the fixed end actions for the member; the end actions required to maintain equilibrium of a restrained beam element subjected to general displacements of its ends have been defined earlier in Fig. 4-6. Hence, the ***final end moments*** and ***end shears*** identified in Fig. 4-21 for a typical beam element of an indeterminate structure can be expressed as

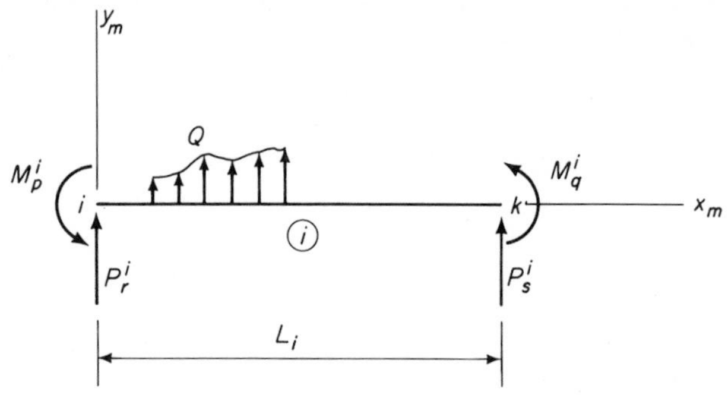

Fig. 4-21 Final end moments and shears.

$$M^i_p = m^i_p + FM^i_p \tag{4-40a}$$

$$M^i_q = m^i_q + FM^i_q \tag{4-40b}$$

$$P^i_r = p^i_r + FP^i_r \tag{4-40c}$$

$$P^i_s = p^i_s + FP^i_s \tag{4-40d}$$

where M^i_p, FM^i_p = final end moment and fixed end moment at end j of member i, respectively;

M^i_q, FM^i_q = final end moment and fixed end moment at end k of member i, respectively;

P^i_r, FP^i_r = final end shear and fixed end shear at end j of member i, respectively;

P^i_s, FP^i_s = final end shear and fixed end shear at end k of member i, respectively.

Substituting Eqs. (4-1) into Eqs. (4-40) yields

$$M^i_p = K^i_{pp}\theta_p + K^i_{pq}\theta_q + K^i_{pr}\delta_r + K^i_{ps}\delta_s + FM^i_p \tag{4-41a}$$

$$M^i_q = K^i_{qp}\theta_p + K^i_{qq}\theta_q + K^i_{qr}\delta_r + K^i_{qs}\delta_s + FM^i_q \tag{4-41b}$$

$$P^i_r = K^i_{rp}\theta_p + K^i_{rq}\theta_q + K^i_{rr}\delta_r + K^i_{rs}\delta_s + FP^i_r \tag{4-41c}$$

$$P^i_s = K^i_{sp}\theta_p + K^i_{sq}\theta_q + K^i_{sr}\delta_r + K^i_{ss}\delta_s + FP^i_s \tag{4-41d}$$

which can be expressed in matrix form as

$$[\mathbf{M}]_i = [\mathbf{K}]_i[\boldsymbol{\delta}]_i + [\mathbf{FM}]_i \tag{4-42}$$

where $[\mathbf{M}]_i$ represents the components of final end moments and final end shears of member i; $[\mathbf{K}]_i$ is the member stiffness matrix for member i; $[\boldsymbol{\delta}]_i$ represents the components of end rotations and normal translation of member i; and $[\mathbf{FM}]_i$ represents the components of fixed end moments and shears of member i. Keep in mind that the subscript p refers to the rotation of the j-end of member i, the subscript q refers to the rotation of the k-end, and the subscripts r and s refer to the normal translation of the ends j and k, respectively.

Using Eqs. (4-41) and the information obtained from Eqs. (4-35), the final end moments and end shears for the members of the indeterminate structure of Fig. 4-15 can be computed from the following equations:

Member 1

$$M_1^1 = K_{11}^1\theta_1 + K_{16}^1(0) + K_{13}^1\delta_3 + K_{17}^1(0) + FM_1^1 \qquad \textbf{(4-43a)}$$

$$M_6^1 = K_{61}^1\theta_1 + K_{66}^1(0) + K_{63}^1\delta_3 + K_{67}^1(0) + FM_6^1 \qquad \textbf{(4-43b)}$$

$$P_3^1 = K_{31}^1\theta_1 + K_{36}^1(0) + K_{33}^1\delta_3 + K_{37}^1(0) + FP_3^1 \qquad \textbf{(4-43c)}$$

$$P_7^1 = K_{71}^1\theta_1 + K_{76}^1(0) + K_{73}^1\delta_3 + K_{77}^1(0) + FP_7^1 \qquad \textbf{(4-43d)}$$

Member 2

$$M_1^2 = K_{11}^2\theta_1 + K_{12}^2\theta_2 + K_{14}^2(0) + K_{15}^2(0) + FM_1^2 \qquad \textbf{(4-44a)}$$

$$M_2^2 = K_{21}^2\theta_1 + K_{22}^2\theta_2 + K_{24}^2(0) + K_{25}^2(0) + FM_5^2 \qquad \textbf{(4-44b)}$$

$$P_4^2 = K_{41}^2\theta_1 + K_{32}^2\theta_2 + K_{44}^2(0) + K_{45}^2(0) + FP_4^2 \qquad \textbf{(4-44c)}$$

$$P_5^2 = K_{51}^2\theta_1 + K_{52}^2\theta_2 + K_{54}^2(0) + K_{55}^2(0) + FP_5^2 \qquad \textbf{(4-44d)}$$

Member 3

$$M_2^3 = K_{22}^3\theta_2 + K_{28}^3(0) + K_{23}^3\delta_3 + K_{29}^3(0) + FM_2^3 \qquad \textbf{(4-45a)}$$

$$M_8^3 = K_{82}^3\theta_2 + K_{88}^3(0) + K_{83}^3\delta_3 + K_{89}^3(0) + FM_8^3 \qquad \textbf{(4-45b)}$$

$$P_3^3 = K_{32}^3\theta_2 + K_{38}^3(0) + K_{33}^3\delta_3 + K_{39}^3(0) + FP_3^3 \qquad \textbf{(4-45c)}$$

$$P_9^3 = K_{92}^3\theta_2 + K_{98}^3(0) + K_{93}^3\delta_3 + K_{99}^3(0) + FP_9^3 \qquad \textbf{(4-45d)}$$

As demonstrated by the analysis of the indeterminate structure of Fig. 4-15, the analysis of a structural system by the stiffness method can be achieved by developing and solving the general Eqs. (4-36), (4-39), and (4-42). The unrestrained components of joint displacements are evaluated from the equation

$$[\mathbf{S}_{uu}][\mathbf{\Delta}_u] = [\mathbf{JL}_u] \qquad \textbf{(4-36)}$$

The final end actions developed at the ends of each member of the system are determined by solving the equation

$$[\mathbf{M}]_i = [\mathbf{K}]_i[\boldsymbol{\delta}]_i + [\mathbf{FM}]_i \qquad \textbf{(4-42)}$$

and the components of support reaction are obtained from the equation

$$[\mathbf{R}_r] = [\mathbf{S}_{ru}][\mathbf{\Delta}_u] - [\mathbf{JL}_r] \qquad \textbf{(4-39)}$$

Thus, the problem becomes one of formulating the various matrices of the above equations and solving these equations.

In preparation for developing the required matrices, the members and the joints of the structural system to be analyzed must be labeled, independently. The sequence of labeling is immaterial, but some logical pattern should be followed. In addition, the *j*- and *k*-ends of each member of the system must be designated so that the member can be related to the typical member of Fig. 4-6 when establishing its member stiffness matrix. For the continuous beam or orthogonal structural system, the ***left end of a beam or the top of a column must be designated as the j-end of the element;*** consequently, the right end of the beam or the bottom of the column will be the k-end. This requirement for the selection of the j-end of a member is dictated by the imposed sign convention—i.e., the assumed positive direction of normal end translation for a member must coincide with the assumed positive directions of joint translation for the structure (Sec. 4-1).

The procedure for establishing the various matrices of Eqs. (4-36), (4-39), and (4-42) will be discussed in the following sections.

4-3.2 Joint Displacement Matrix

To establish the sequence of the set of simultaneous equations represented by Eq. (4-32), identify and label all possible independent components of joint displacement (horizontal and vertical translation as well as rotation), whether restrained or unrestrained. *Label the unrestrained displacements first and then the displacements restrained by the imposed support requirements* (Fig. 4-22).

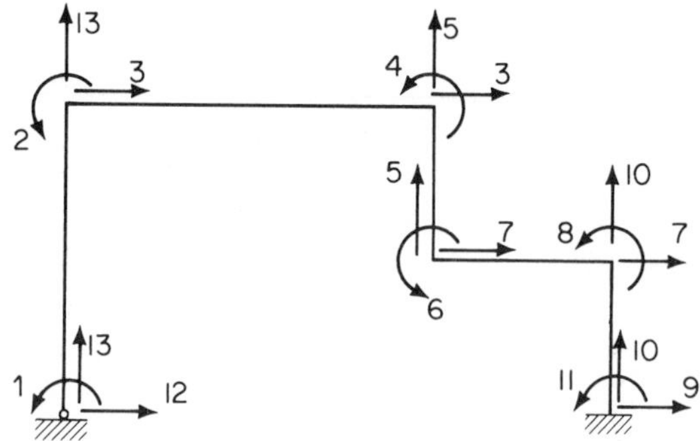

Fig. 4-22 Labeling of possible joint displacements.

It is suggested that numerical designations be used to label the possible components of displacement of the system starting with the integer 1 and numbering, sequentially, first the unrestrained displacements and then the restrained displacements. The elements of the complete joint displacement matrix $[\mathbf{\Delta}_c]$ are thus defined; they appear in the matrix in the order of their labeling. This matrix is partitioned into two parts with respect to the unrestrained and the restrained components of displacement as indicated by Eq. (4-33). The upper portion of the matrix, which contains the components of unrestrained displacement, is represented by the matrix $[\mathbf{\Delta}_u]$; the lower portion, which contains the components of restrained displacement, is represented by the matrix $[\mathbf{\Delta}_r]$.

The components of joint displacements are to be defined with respect to the sign convention given in Sec. 4-1.

4-3.3 Joint Load Matrix

The elements of the complete joint load matrix $[\mathbf{JL}_c]$, defined in Eq. (4-32), are obtained from the analysis of the restrained structure for the applied inplane loading condition. These elements, identified as JL_m, are the actions that appear at the joints of the restrained structure when the restrained structure is subjected to the applied disturbance. They are ***equal in magnitude and opposite in direction to the reactions of the restrained structure;*** thus, referring to Fig. 4-18(c),

$$JL_1 = -S_{10}$$

$$JL_2 = -S_{20}$$

etc.

and, from Fig. 4-18(b) (*following the sign convention of Sec. 4-1*),

$$JL_1 = -FM_1^1 - FM_1^2$$

$$JL_2 = -FM_2^2 - FM_2^3$$

$$JL_3 = -FP_3^1 - FP_3^3 + Q$$

etc.

Examining Eqs. (4-30) and (4-31) that were written for the analysis of the indeterminate structure of Fig. 4-15, it is seen that the reactions of the restrained structure S_{m0} due to the applied loading were transferred into joint actions by moving these terms from the left-hand side of the equations to the right-hand side. This transformation resulted in a sign change for each element. Each element of the complete joint load matrix represents a component of total joint action corresponding to one of the previously defined components of joint displacement. Each element of the matrix may be the sum of two types of joint load: (1) ***applied joint load***, and (2) ***equivalent joint load.***

APPLIED JOINT LOADS

Any load applied externally to a joint of a structure is classified as an ***applied joint load.*** These actions must be given in terms of horizontal and vertical components of force and moment. The sign convention used in describing the applied joint loads is as follows:

1. ***Counterclockwise*** moments, and
2. joint forces acting ***upward or to the right*** are assumed to be positive (Fig. 4-23).

EQUIVALENT JOINT LOADS

The joint actions which result from the loading of the members of the restrained structure along their length are referred to as ***equivalent joint loads.***

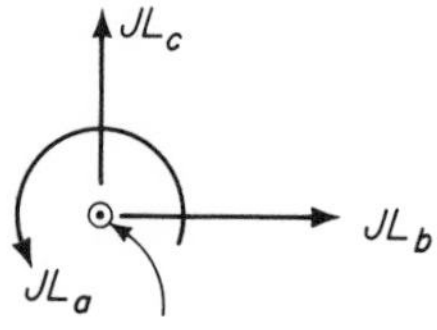

Fig. 4-23 Positive joint loads.

These joint loads are established by means of a simple transformation of the corresponding fixed end actions which are required to restrain the ends of the members against translation and rotation when a disturbance—i.e., a load, a change in temperature, a fabrication error, etc.—is applied to the member [Fig. 4-18(b)]. The fixed end actions for a beam element are identified in Fig. 4-24 and described in accordance with the following sign convention:

> 1. ***Counterclockwise*** fixed end moments, and
> 2. fixed end forces acting ***upward or to the right*** are positive (Fig. 4-24).

The equivalent joint loads are to be described in terms of the sign convention suggested for the applied joint loads. Employing these two sign conventions for fixed end actions and equivalent joint loads, *a fixed end action can be transformed into an equivalent joint load by simply reversing its sign.* The equivalent joint load must also be given in terms of horizontal and vertical components of force and moment.

The fixed end actions for the more common loading conditions of a prismatic member and a few loading conditions of particular nonprismatic beam elements can be found in available engineering handbooks. If this information is not available to the engineer, the fixed end actions can be computed by one of several techniques of structural mechanics. For example, consider the determination of the fixed end actions by the flexibility approach for a general beam element with

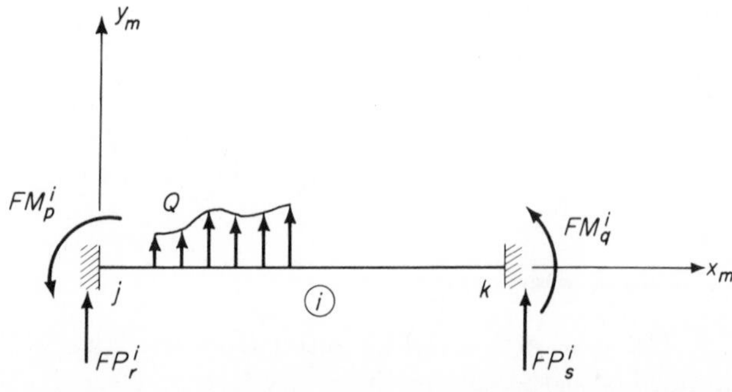

Fig. 4-24 Fixed end actions for member *i*.

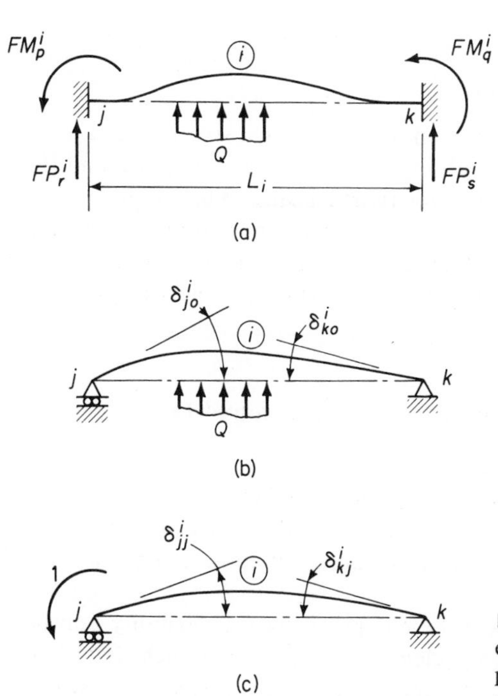

Fig. 4-25 Evaluation of fixed end actions by flexibility approach: (a) general beam element; (b) displacement of released structure due to applied loads; (c) flexibility coefficients—unit moment applied at end j; (d) flexibility coefficients—unit moment applied at end k. *Note:* All actions shown in assumed positive sense.

a general loading as described in Fig. 4-25(a). The released structure for the fixed end beam element is defined as a simple beam [Fig. 4-25(b)]. The end rotations experienced by the released structure when subjected to the applied loading condition are identified in Fig. 4-25(b) as δ^i_{j0} and δ^i_{k0} at the j- and k-ends of member i, respectively. The flexibility coefficients δ^i_{jj}, δ^i_{jk}, δ^i_{kj}, and δ^i_{kk} for the released structure are identified in Figs. 4-25(c) and (d). Now, the deformation of the simple beam due to applied loads [Fig. 4-25(b)] and a linear function of the two cases described in Figs. 4-25(c) and (d) can be superimposed to duplicate the deformation and response of the fixed end beam of Fig. 4-25(a). The combining of these three cases requires that

$$\delta^i_{j0} + FM^i_p\delta^i_{jj} + FM^i_q\delta^i_{jk} = 0 \tag{4-46a}$$

and

$$\delta^i_{k0} + FM^i_p\delta^i_{kj} + FM^i_q\delta^i_{kk} = 0 \tag{4-46b}$$

which can be expressed in matrix form as

$$\begin{bmatrix}\delta_{j0}\\ \delta_{k0}\end{bmatrix}_i + \begin{bmatrix}\delta_{jj} & \delta_{jk}\\ \delta_{kj} & \delta_{kk}\end{bmatrix}_i \begin{bmatrix}FM_p\\ FM_q\end{bmatrix}_i = \begin{bmatrix}0\\ 0\end{bmatrix} \tag{4-47a}$$

or

$$[\mathbf{D}_0]_i + [\mathbf{D}_r]_i[\mathbf{FM}_m]_i = [0] \tag{4-47b}$$

where $[\mathbf{D}_0]_i$ defines the displacement of the released structure due to applied loads, $[\mathbf{D}_r]_i$ defines the rotational flexibility of the released structure, and $[\mathbf{FM}_m]_i$ defines the fixed end moments for the restrained beam. When writing Eqs. (4-46), the end rotations were assumed to be positive in nature, i.e., *counterclockwise;* thus, when writing Eqs. (4-46) or (4-47) for a particular problem, the appropriate signs must be given to the displacement terms. Solving Eqs. (4-47) for the fixed end moments yields

$$[\mathbf{FM}_m]_i = -[\mathbf{D}_r]_i^{-1}[\mathbf{D}_0]_i \tag{4-48}$$

or making the substitution indicated by Expression (4-13),

$$[\mathbf{FM}_m]_i = -[\mathbf{K}_r]_i[\mathbf{D}_0]_i \tag{4-49}$$

where $[\mathbf{K}_r]_i$ defines the rotational stiffness coefficients for beam element i. Once the fixed end moments have been determined for a given loading of the beam element, the fixed end shears can be found by considering static equilibrium of the member.

The fixed end actions can be computed by the flexibility approach for prismatic and nonprismatic beam elements subjected to such disturbances as temperature changes, imposed deformations, support displacements, etc., as well as applied loads.

Example 4-3. Determine the fixed end moments and shears for a prismatic beam element with a localized imperfection in straightness, i.e., a bend $\mathbf{\Omega}$ present in the member at a distance of a from the j-end [Fig. 4-26(a)]. The angle of bend $\mathbf{\Omega}$ is given in radians.

The analysis of the released structure, i.e., the simple beam, is indicated in Fig. 4-26(b). The rotational flexibility coefficients for the prismatic beam element, which were determined in Example 4-2, are given by Expression (4-15). Substituting this information into Eqs. (4-49) yields

$$\begin{bmatrix} FM_p^i \\ FM_q^i \end{bmatrix} = -\begin{bmatrix} \dfrac{4EI}{L} & \dfrac{2EI}{L} \\ \dfrac{2EI}{L} & \dfrac{4EI}{L} \end{bmatrix} \begin{bmatrix} \dfrac{-(L-a)\Omega}{L} \\ \dfrac{a\Omega}{L} \end{bmatrix} \tag{4-50a}$$

which gives

$$\begin{bmatrix} FM_p^i \\ FM_q^i \end{bmatrix} = \begin{bmatrix} \dfrac{2EI\Omega}{L^2}(2L-3a) \\ \dfrac{2EI\Omega}{L^2}(L-3a) \end{bmatrix} \tag{4-50b}$$

Having evaluated the fixed end moments, the fixed end shears can be determined by considering the static equilibrium of the restrained beam element. Hence,

$$FP_r^i = \frac{6EI\Omega}{L}(L-2a) \tag{4-51a}$$

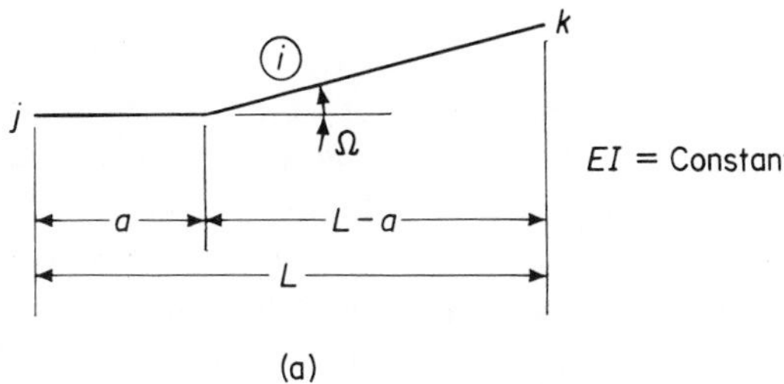

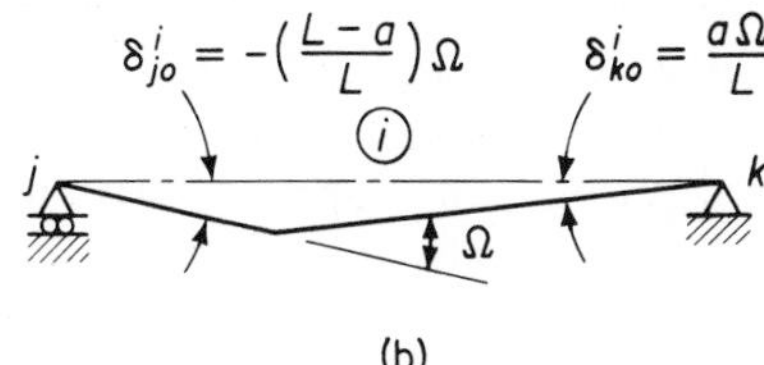

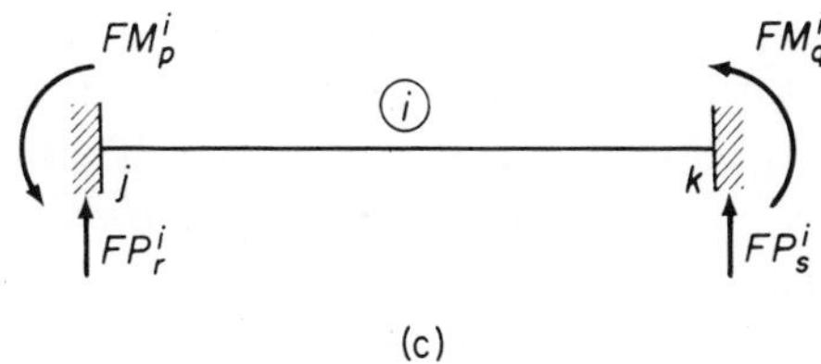

Fig. 4-26 Example 4-3: Prismatic beam element with bend: (a) beam element; (b) displacement of released structure due to kink in beam element; (c) fixed end actions. *Note:* Counterclockwise end rotations are positive.

and

$$FP^i_s = \frac{-6EI\Omega}{L}(L - 2a) \tag{4-51b}$$

These fixed end actions are identified in Fig. 4-26(c).

Each component of total joint action at a joint is obtained by combining the respective components of equivalent joint load and applied joint load. Once this component of total joint action has been established, it must be labeled to conform to the labeling of the corresponding component of joint displacement, which has been defined and labeled earlier, since the elements of the complete joint load matrix $[\mathbf{JL}_c]$ must appear in the same sequence as the corresponding elements of the complete joint displacement matrix $[\mathbf{\Delta}_c]$. As indicated in Eqs. (4-33), the complete joint load matrix should be partitioned into two submatrices: the matrix $[\mathbf{JL}_u]$, representing the components of joint load associated with the unrestrained joint displacement; and the matrix $[\mathbf{JL}_r]$, representing the components of joint load associated with the restrained joint displacements.

4-3.4 Support Reaction Matrix

As stated earlier, Eq. (4-32) respresents the superposition of the restraining actions of the restrained structure for (a) the application of applied loading condition, and (b) the independent application of joint displacements. The sum of these cases for each of the artificial restraints must be zero and for each of the existing restraints must be equal to the corresponding support reaction of the indeterminate system. These restrictions are imposed on the solution by the complete support reaction matrix $[\mathbf{R}_c]$. Thus, when partitioning the matrix with respect to the unrestrained and restrained components of joint displacement as indicated in Eq. (4-33), the upper portion becomes a null matrix and the lower portion, defined as $[\mathbf{R}_r]$, represents the components of support reaction.

In order to establish the elements of the matrix $[\mathbf{R}_r]$, the possible components of support reaction must be identified and given the same labels as the corresponding components of restrained displacement, since they must appear in the same sequence. The sign convention used in describing the support reactions is the same as that used in describing the applied joint loads.

4-3.5 Structure Stiffness Matrix

In Eq. (4-32), the complete structure stiffness matrix $[\mathbf{S}_c]$ represents the various components of joint restraining actions required to maintain the restrained structure when it is subjected to the individual application of unit values of joint displacements. For example, the element S_{uv} of the matrix is the joint restraining action of the restrained structure associated with the component of possible joint displacement u resulting from a unit value of joint displacement v. Each column of the complete structure stiffness matrix represents the analysis of the restrained structure for the application of a unit value of a particular joint displacement. Each row of the matrix represents the value of a particular restraining action resulting from the application of a unit value of each of the joint displacements to the restrained structure.

When a unit value of joint displacement is imposed upon a restrained structure, as illustrated in Fig. 4-27, the end actions required to maintain equilibrium of each member of the system that is subjected to the imposed displacement are the restraining end actions K^i_{uv}, which have been defined in Figs. 4-2 through 4-5 for various end displacements of a restrained beam element. Knowing the end actions that are developed at the ends of the members due to an imposed displacement, the reactions of the restrained structure, S_{uv}, can be evaluated by considering the static equilibrium of each joint. Thus, the joint restraining actions, which might be referred to as ***structure stiffness coefficients***, can be defined as

$$S_{uv} = \sum_i K^i_{uv} \tag{4-52}$$

In order to evaluate the structure stiffness coefficients for a given system, the member stiffness matrix $[\mathbf{K}]_i$ must first be established for each member of the system. Once the member stiffness matrix has been developed for a particular member, the elements of the matrix, i.e., the member stiffness coefficients, must be identified with respect to the labeling of the joint displacements. Each row of the member stiffness matrix is identified by the label of the component of joint

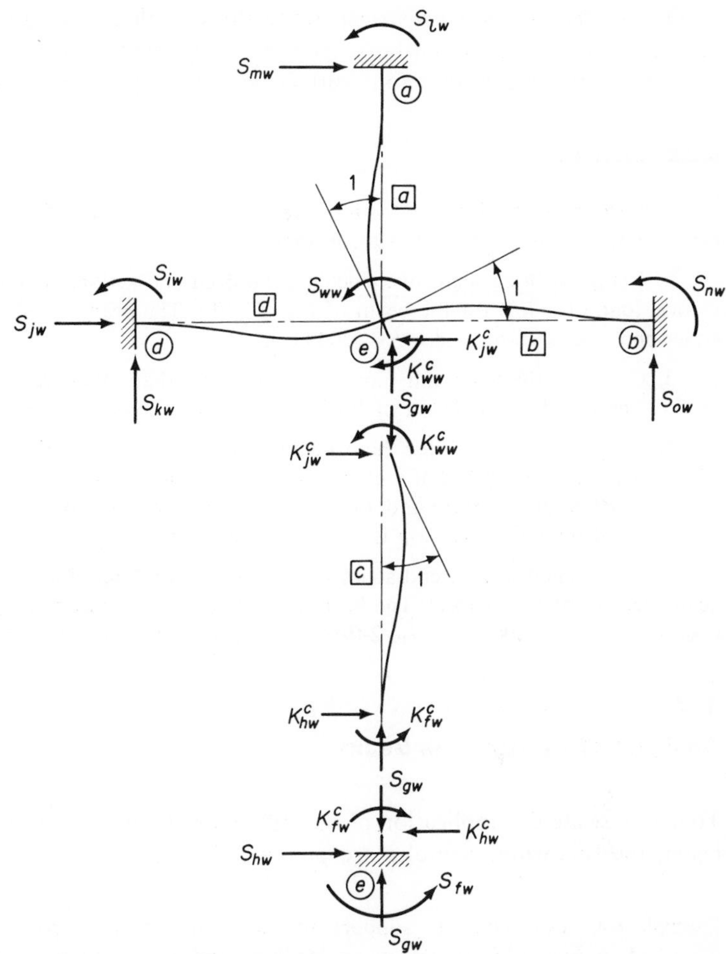

Fig. 4-27 Identification of structure stiffness coefficients. *Note:* End moments, end shears, and joint restraining actions are shown in assumed positive sense.

displacement at the end of the member that corresponds to the action referred to in the row; each column of the member stiffness matrix is identified by the label of the component of joint displacement at the end of the member that would cause the actions identified by the elements of the column. If Expression (4-9) is used to establish the member stiffness matrix for a member, the rows and columns assume the labels of the joint displacements in the following sequence: *rotation at j-end, rotation at k-end, normal translation of j-end, and normal translation of k-end.* After the member stiffness matrix has been developed for each member of the system, ***each structure stiffness coefficient is determined by summing the member stiffness coefficients that have the same labels***, *i.e.*, ***subscripts,***

as the structure stiffness coefficient. Once the complete structure stiffness matrix has been established, it can be partitioned with respect to restrained and unrestrained displacements into four submatrices: $[\mathbf{S}_{uu}]$, $[\mathbf{S}_{ur}]$, $[\mathbf{S}_{ru}]$, and $[\mathbf{S}_{rr}]$.

4-3.6 Exercises

1. Determine the fixed end actions created by a settlement of Δ of the j-end of the beam shown in Fig. 4-14(a); E is a constant.

2. Using 2-ft-long segments, calculate the fixed end actions required for a uniform vertical load of w k/ft for the beam of Fig. 4-14(b). The beam has straight haunches at either end and is 18-in. wide; $E = 3000$ ksi.

3. Calculate the fixed end moments and shears that would result from a rotation of β at the k-end of the beam of Fig. 4-14(c); E is a constant.

4. Develop expressions for the fixed end actions resulting from a linear temperature differential over the depth d of a prismatic beam of span length L. Let T_1 be the temperature at the top of the beam and T_2 be the temperature at the bottom of the beam. The coefficient of thermal expansion is α; E and I are constants.

5. Determine the fixed end actions due to a uniform load of w k/ft for the haunched beam element of Fig. 4-14(e). The beam is 1.5-ft wide with parabolic haunches at either end; E is equal to 3000 ksi. Use 2-ft-segment lengths in approximating the haunches.

4–4
Analysis of Continuous Beam

To demonstrate the application of the stiffness method for analyzing a continuous beam, the following examples are presented.

Example 4-4. Calculate the support reactions of the three-span continuous beam described in Fig. 4-28 for the given loading condition using the stiffness method of

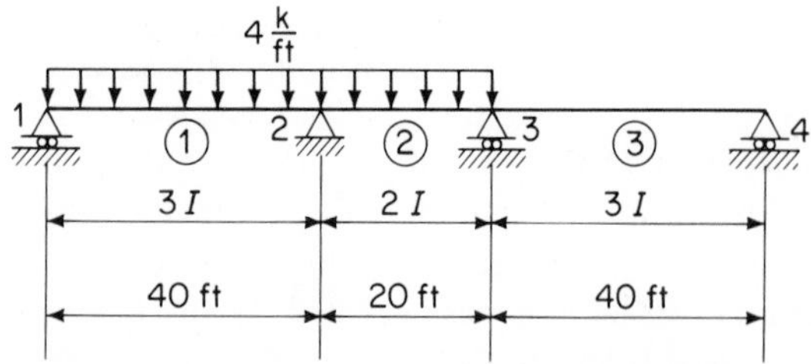

Fig. 4-28 Example 4-4: Continuous beam.

analysis (neglecting axial deformations). The relative moments of inertia for the system are given in terms of I, and the modulus of elasticity E is assumed to be a constant. The joint numbers are shown next to the supports and the member labels are the circled numbers adjacent to the members.

JOINT DISPLACEMENT MATRIX

The first step in developing the analysis of the structural system is to identify the j- and k-ends of each member and to identify and label the possible joint displacements. This has been done in Fig. 4-29. Referring to Fig. 4-29, the complete joint displacement matrix $[\mathbf{\Delta}_c]$ is written as

$$[\mathbf{\Delta}_c] = \begin{bmatrix} \theta_1 \\ \theta_2 \\ \theta_3 \\ \theta_4 \\ \hdashline \delta_5 \\ \delta_6 \\ \delta_7 \\ \delta_8 \end{bmatrix} = \begin{bmatrix} [\mathbf{\Delta}_u] \\ \hdashline [\mathbf{\Delta}_r] \end{bmatrix} \tag{4-53}$$

which is partitioned as indicated with respect to the restrained and unrestrained displacements.

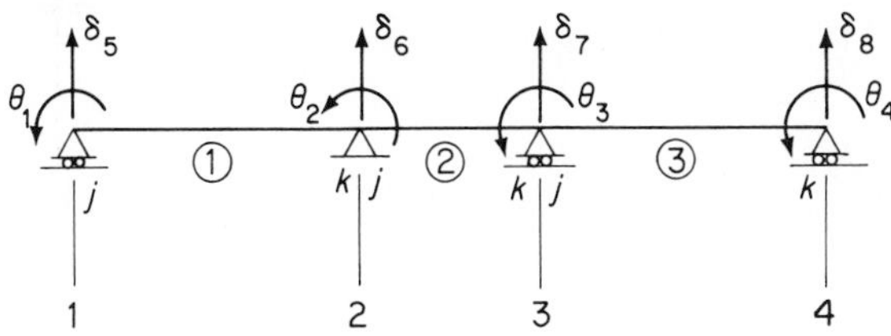

Fig. 4-29 Example 4-4: Identification of possible joint displacements and j- and k-ends.

MEMBER STIFFNESS MATRICES

Since the members of the three-span continuous beam have constant moments of inertia, the stiffness matrix for each member can be written by substituting the proper values into Expressions (4-16), relating each member to the typical member described in Fig. 4-6. To help identify the elements of each matrix, the rows and columns are labeled to correspond to the labeling of the possible displacements at the ends of the member. The sequence of the labeling is θ_p, θ_q, δ_r, and δ_s.

Member 1

$$[\mathbf{K}]_1 = \begin{array}{c} \begin{matrix} \quad 1 \quad & \quad 2 \quad & \quad 5 \quad & \quad 6 \quad \end{matrix} \\ \begin{bmatrix} \dfrac{12EI}{40} & \dfrac{6EI}{40} & \dfrac{18EI}{40^2} & \dfrac{-18EI}{40^2} \\ \dfrac{6EI}{40} & \dfrac{12EI}{40} & \dfrac{18EI}{40^2} & \dfrac{-18EI}{40^2} \\ \dfrac{18EI}{40^2} & \dfrac{18EI}{40^2} & \dfrac{36EI}{40^3} & \dfrac{-36EI}{40^3} \\ \dfrac{-18EI}{40^2} & \dfrac{-18EI}{40^2} & \dfrac{-36EI}{40^3} & \dfrac{36EI}{40^3} \end{bmatrix}_1 \end{array} \begin{matrix} 1 \\ 2 \\ 5 \\ 6 \end{matrix} \tag{4-54a}$$

which can be rewritten as

$$[\mathbf{K}]_1 = EI \times 10^{-2} \begin{bmatrix} 30.0 & 15.0 & 1.1250 & -1.1250 \\ 15.0 & 30.0 & 1.1250 & -1.1250 \\ 1.1250 & 1.1250 & 0.0562 & -0.0562 \\ -1.1250 & -1.1250 & -0.0562 & 0.0562 \end{bmatrix}_1 \begin{matrix} 1 \\ 2 \\ 5 \\ 6 \end{matrix} \quad \text{(columns 1, 2, 5, 6)} \tag{4-54b}$$

where the elements of the matrix are identified as

$$\begin{bmatrix} K_{11} & K_{12} & K_{15} & K_{16} \\ K_{21} & K_{22} & K_{25} & K_{26} \\ K_{51} & K_{52} & K_{55} & K_{56} \\ K_{61} & K_{62} & K_{65} & K_{66} \end{bmatrix} \tag{4-54c}$$

Member 2

$$[\mathbf{K}]_2 = \begin{bmatrix} \frac{8EI}{20} & \frac{4EI}{20} & \frac{12EI}{20^2} & \frac{-12EI}{20^2} \\ \frac{4EI}{20} & \frac{8EI}{20} & \frac{12EI}{20^2} & \frac{-12EI}{20^2} \\ \frac{12EI}{20^2} & \frac{12EI}{20^2} & \frac{24EI}{20^3} & \frac{-24EI}{20^3} \\ \frac{-12EI}{20^2} & \frac{-12EI}{20^2} & \frac{-24EI}{20^3} & \frac{24EI}{20^3} \end{bmatrix}_2 \begin{matrix} 2 \\ 3 \\ 6 \\ 7 \end{matrix} \quad \text{(columns 2, 3, 6, 7)} \tag{4-55a}$$

which reduces to

$$[\mathbf{K}]_2 = EI \times 10^{-2} \begin{bmatrix} 40.0 & 20.0 & 3.0 & -3.0 \\ 20.0 & 40.0 & 3.0 & -3.0 \\ 3.0 & 3.0 & 0.3000 & -0.3000 \\ -3.0 & -3.0 & -0.3000 & 0.3000 \end{bmatrix}_2 \begin{matrix} 2 \\ 3 \\ 6 \\ 7 \end{matrix} \quad \text{(columns 2, 3, 6, 7)} \tag{4-55b}$$

where the elements are identified as

$$\begin{bmatrix} K_{22} & K_{23} & K_{26} & K_{27} \\ K_{32} & K_{33} & K_{36} & K_{37} \\ K_{62} & K_{63} & K_{66} & K_{67} \\ K_{72} & K_{73} & K_{76} & K_{77} \end{bmatrix} \tag{4-55c}$$

Member 3

$$[\mathbf{K}]_3 = \begin{bmatrix} \frac{12EI}{40} & \frac{6EI}{40} & \frac{18EI}{40^2} & \frac{-18EI}{40^2} \\ \frac{6EI}{40} & \frac{12EI}{40} & \frac{18EI}{40^2} & \frac{-18EI}{40^2} \\ \frac{18EI}{40^2} & \frac{18EI}{40^2} & \frac{36EI}{40^3} & \frac{-36EI}{40^3} \\ \frac{-18EI}{40^2} & \frac{-18EI}{40^2} & \frac{-36EI}{40^3} & \frac{36EI}{40^3} \end{bmatrix}_3 \begin{matrix} 3 \\ 4 \\ 7 \\ 8 \end{matrix} \quad \text{(columns 3, 4, 7, 8)} \tag{4-56a}$$

or

$$
[\mathbf{K}]_3 = EI \times 10^{-2} \begin{bmatrix} 30.0 & 15.0 & 1.1250 & -1.1250 \\ 15.0 & 30.0 & 1.1250 & -1.1250 \\ 1.1250 & 1.1250 & 0.0562 & -0.0562 \\ -1.1250 & -1.1250 & -0.0562 & 0.0562 \end{bmatrix}_3 \quad \begin{matrix} \text{columns: } 3, 4, 7, 8 \\ \text{rows: } 3, 4, 7, 8 \end{matrix} \qquad \textbf{(4-56b)}
$$

where the elements of the matrix are identified as

$$
\begin{bmatrix} K_{33} & K_{34} & K_{37} & K_{38} \\ K_{43} & K_{44} & K_{47} & K_{48} \\ K_{73} & K_{74} & K_{77} & K_{78} \\ K_{83} & K_{84} & K_{87} & K_{88} \end{bmatrix} \qquad \textbf{(4-56c)}
$$

STRUCTURE STIFFNESS MATRIX

With eight possible joint displacements, the elements of the complete structure stiffness matrix, i.e., *the structure stiffness coefficients*, are identified as

$$
[\mathbf{S}_c] = \begin{bmatrix} S_{11} & S_{12} & S_{13} & S_{14} & S_{15} & S_{16} & S_{17} & S_{18} \\ S_{21} & S_{22} & S_{23} & S_{24} & S_{25} & S_{26} & S_{27} & S_{28} \\ S_{31} & S_{32} & S_{33} & S_{34} & S_{35} & S_{36} & S_{37} & S_{38} \\ S_{41} & S_{42} & S_{43} & S_{44} & S_{45} & S_{46} & S_{47} & S_{48} \\ S_{51} & S_{52} & S_{53} & S_{54} & S_{55} & S_{56} & S_{57} & S_{58} \\ S_{61} & S_{62} & S_{63} & S_{64} & S_{65} & S_{66} & S_{67} & S_{68} \\ S_{71} & S_{72} & S_{73} & S_{74} & S_{75} & S_{76} & S_{77} & S_{78} \\ S_{81} & S_{82} & S_{83} & S_{84} & S_{85} & S_{86} & S_{87} & S_{88} \end{bmatrix} \quad \begin{matrix} \text{columns: } 1\text{–}8 \\ \text{rows: } 1\text{–}8 \end{matrix} \qquad \textbf{(4-57a)}
$$

and are evaluated by summing the member stiffness coefficients with the same subscripts. The complete structure stiffness matrix is given in Table 4-3, Expression (4-57b), which is partitioned with respect to the restrained and unrestrained components of joint displacement into the four submatrices defined in Eqs. (4-33), i.e.,

$$
\left[\begin{array}{c|c} [\mathbf{S}_{uu}] & [\mathbf{S}_{ur}] \\ \hline [\mathbf{S}_{ru}] & [\mathbf{S}_{rr}] \end{array}\right]
$$

Now,

$$
[\mathbf{S}_{uu}]^{-1} = \frac{1}{EI} \begin{bmatrix} 3.7790 & -0.8913 & 0.2852 & -0.1426 \\ -0.8913 & 1.7825 & -0.5704 & 0.2852 \\ 0.2852 & -0.5704 & 1.7285 & -0.8913 \\ -0.1426 & 0.2852 & -0.8913 & 3.7790 \end{bmatrix} \quad \begin{matrix} \text{columns: } 1, 2, 3, 4 \\ \text{rows: } 1, 2, 3, 4 \end{matrix} \qquad \textbf{(4-58)}
$$

JOINT LOAD MATRIX

For the loading of the three-span continuous beam described in Fig. 4-28, the fixed end actions for the elements of the system are equal to

Table 4-3

$$
[\mathbf{S}_c] = EI \times 10^{-2}
\begin{array}{c}
\begin{array}{cccc|cccc}
1 & 2 & 3 & 4 & 5 & 6 & 7 & 8
\end{array} \\
\left[\begin{array}{cccc|cccc}
30.0 & 15.0 & 0 & 0 & 1.1250 & -1.1250 & 0 & 0 \\
15.0 & 70.0 & 20.0 & 0 & 1.1250 & 1.8750 & -3.0 & 0 \\
0 & 20.0 & 70.0 & 15.0 & 0 & 3.0 & -1.8750 & -1.1250 \\
0 & 0 & 15.0 & 30.0 & 0 & 0 & 1.1250 & -1.1250 \\
\hline
1.1250 & 1.1250 & 0 & 0 & 0.0562 & -0.0562 & 0 & 0 \\
-1.1250 & 1.8750 & 3.0 & 0 & -0.0562 & 0.3562 & -0.3000 & 0 \\
0 & -3.0 & -1.8750 & 1.1250 & 0 & -0.3000 & 0.3562 & -0.0562 \\
0 & 0 & -1.1250 & -1.1250 & 0 & 0 & -0.0562 & 0.0562
\end{array}\right]
\end{array}
\begin{array}{c} \\ 1 \\ 2 \\ 3 \\ 4 \\ 5 \\ 6 \\ 7 \\ 8 \end{array}
\qquad \textbf{(4-57b)}
$$

Member 1

$$FM_1^1 = +533.0 \text{ ft-k} \qquad FM_2^1 = -533.0 \text{ ft-k}$$

$$FP_5^1 = +80.0 \text{ k} \qquad FP_6^1 = +80.0 \text{ k}$$

Member 2

$$FM_2^2 = +133.0 \text{ ft-k} \qquad FM_3^2 = -133.0 \text{ ft-k}$$

$$FP_6^2 = +40.0 \text{ k} \qquad FP_7^2 = +40.0 \text{ k}$$

Member 3

$$FM_3^3 = 0 \qquad FM_4^3 = 0$$

$$FP_7^3 = 0 \qquad FP_8^3 = 0$$

Transforming these fixed end actions into equivalent joint loads, the total joint loads acting on the restrained structure are as shown in Fig. 4-30. Labeling these joint loads

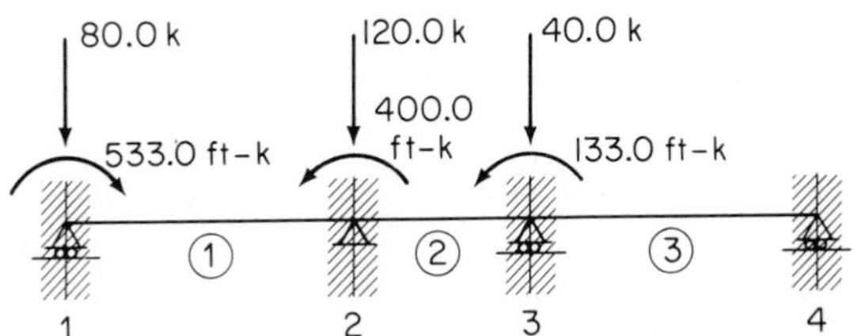

Fig. 4-30 Example 4-4: Total joint loads.

to conform to the labeling of the corresponding possible joint displacement, the complete joint load matrix is written as

$$[\mathbf{JL}_c] = \begin{bmatrix} JL_1 \\ JL_2 \\ JL_3 \\ JL_4 \\ \hdashline JL_5 \\ JL_6 \\ JL_7 \\ JL_8 \end{bmatrix} = \begin{bmatrix} -533.0 \\ 400.0 \\ 133.0 \\ 0 \\ \hdashline -80.0 \\ -120.0 \\ -40.0 \\ 0 \end{bmatrix} = \begin{bmatrix} [\mathbf{JL}_u] \\ \hdashline [\mathbf{JL}_r] \end{bmatrix} \tag{4-59}$$

SOLUTION

Using Expressions (4-53), (4-58), and (4-59), Eq. (4-37), i.e.,

$$[\boldsymbol{\Delta}_u] = [\mathbf{S}_{uu}]^{-1}[\mathbf{JL}_u] \tag{4-37}$$

which defines the unknown joint displacements can be written as

$$\begin{bmatrix} \theta_1 \\ \theta_2 \\ \theta_3 \\ \theta_4 \end{bmatrix} = \frac{1}{EI}\begin{bmatrix} 3.7790 & -0.8913 & 0.2852 & -0.1426 \\ -0.8913 & 1.7825 & -0.5704 & 0.2852 \\ 0.2852 & -0.5704 & 1.7825 & -0.8913 \\ -0.1426 & 0.2852 & -0.8913 & 3.7790 \end{bmatrix}\begin{bmatrix} -533.0 \\ 400.0 \\ 133.0 \\ 0 \end{bmatrix} = \frac{1}{EI}\begin{bmatrix} -2332.80 \\ 1112.20 \\ -143.10 \\ 71.54 \end{bmatrix} \tag{4-60a}$$

which yields

$$[\boldsymbol{\Delta}_u] = \begin{bmatrix} \theta_1 \\ \theta_2 \\ \theta_3 \\ \theta_4 \end{bmatrix} = \frac{1 \times 10^2}{EI} \begin{bmatrix} -23.3280 \\ 11.1220 \\ -1.4310 \\ 0.7154 \end{bmatrix} \tag{4-60b}$$

The rotations given by Expression (4-60b) are relative rotations of the joints. The actual rotations can be determined by substituting for E (in units of k/ft^2) and I (in units of ft^4).

FINAL END ACTIONS

Writing Eqs. (4-42) for each member, i.e.,

$$[\mathbf{M}]_i = [\mathbf{K}]_i[\boldsymbol{\delta}]_i + [\mathbf{FM}]_i \tag{4-42}$$

the final end actions for each member of the three-span continuous beam can be established. It should be realized, when writing these equations for each member of the system, that the end displacements which are restrained by the supports are equal to zero.

Member 1

$$\begin{bmatrix} M_1 \\ M_2 \\ P_5 \\ P_6 \end{bmatrix}_1 = EI \times 10^{-2} \begin{bmatrix} 30.0 & 15.0 & 1.1250 & -1.1250 \\ 15.0 & 30.0 & 1.1250 & -1.1250 \\ 1.1250 & 1.1250 & 0.0562 & -0.0562 \\ -1.1250 & -1.1250 & -0.0562 & 0.0562 \end{bmatrix}_1 \frac{1 \times 10^2}{EI} \begin{bmatrix} -23.3280 \\ 11.1220 \\ 0 \\ 0 \end{bmatrix}_1 + \begin{bmatrix} 533.0 \\ -533.0 \\ 80.0 \\ 80.0 \end{bmatrix}_1$$

$$\begin{bmatrix} M_1 \\ M_2 \\ P_5 \\ P_6 \end{bmatrix}_1 = \begin{bmatrix} 0 \\ -549.26 \text{ ft-k} \\ 66.27 \text{ k} \\ 93.73 \text{ k} \end{bmatrix}_1 \tag{4-61a}$$

Member 2

$$\begin{bmatrix} M_2 \\ M_3 \\ P_6 \\ P_7 \end{bmatrix}_2 = EI \times 10^{-2} \begin{bmatrix} 40.0 & 20.0 & 3.0 & -3.0 \\ 20.0 & 40.0 & 3.0 & -3.0 \\ 3.0 & 3.0 & 0.3000 & -0.3000 \\ -3.0 & -3.0 & -0.3000 & 0.3000 \end{bmatrix}_2 \frac{1 \times 10^2}{EI} \begin{bmatrix} 11.1220 \\ -1.4310 \\ 0 \\ 0 \end{bmatrix}_2 + \begin{bmatrix} 133.0 \\ -133.0 \\ 40.0 \\ 40.0 \end{bmatrix}_2$$

$$\begin{bmatrix} M_2 \\ M_3 \\ P_6 \\ P_7 \end{bmatrix}_2 = \begin{bmatrix} 549.26 \text{ ft-k} \\ 32.20 \text{ ft-k} \\ 69.07 \text{ k} \\ 10.93 \text{ k} \end{bmatrix}_2 \tag{4-61b}$$

Member 3

$$\begin{bmatrix} M_3 \\ M_4 \\ P_7 \\ P_8 \end{bmatrix}_3 = EI \times 10^{-2} \begin{bmatrix} 30.0 & 15.0 & 1.1250 & -1.1250 \\ 15.0 & 30.0 & 1.1250 & -1.1250 \\ 1.1250 & 1.1250 & 0.0562 & -0.0562 \\ -1.1250 & -1.1250 & -0.0562 & 0.0562 \end{bmatrix}_3 \frac{1 \times 10^2}{EI} \begin{bmatrix} -1.4310 \\ 0.7154 \\ 0 \\ 0 \end{bmatrix}_3 + \begin{bmatrix} 0 \\ 0 \\ 0 \\ 0 \end{bmatrix}_3$$

$$\begin{bmatrix} M_3 \\ M_4 \\ P_7 \\ P_8 \end{bmatrix}_3 = \begin{bmatrix} -32.20 \text{ ft-k} \\ 0 \\ -0.81 \text{ k} \\ 0.81 \text{ k} \end{bmatrix}_3 \tag{4-61c}$$

These final end actions are shown in Fig. 4-31.

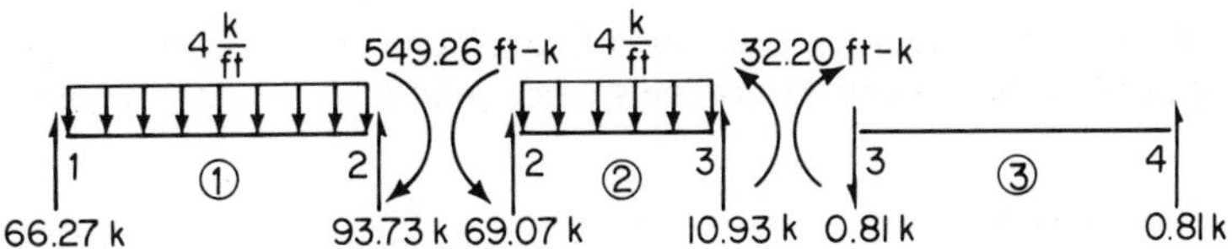

Fig. 4-31 Example 4-4: Final end actions.

SUPPORT REACTIONS

Using Expressions (4-57b), (4-59), and (4-60b), the support reactions are found by Eq. (4-39), i.e.,

$$[\mathbf{R}_r] = [\mathbf{S}_{ru}][\mathbf{\Delta}_u] - [\mathbf{JL}_r] \tag{4-39}$$

to equal

$$\begin{bmatrix} R_5 \\ R_6 \\ R_7 \\ R_8 \end{bmatrix} = EI \times 10^{-2} \begin{bmatrix} 1.1250 & 1.1250 & 0 & 0 \\ -1.1250 & 1.8750 & 3.0 & 0 \\ 0 & -3.0 & -1.8750 & 1.1250 \\ 0 & 0 & -1.1250 & -1.1250 \end{bmatrix} \frac{1 \times 10^2}{EI} \begin{bmatrix} -23.3280 \\ 11.1220 \\ -1.4310 \\ 0.7154 \end{bmatrix} - \begin{bmatrix} -80.0 \\ -120.0 \\ -40.0 \\ 0 \end{bmatrix}$$

or

$$\begin{bmatrix} R_5 \\ R_6 \\ R_7 \\ R_8 \end{bmatrix} = \begin{bmatrix} 66.27 \text{ k} \\ 162.80 \text{ k} \\ 10.12 \text{ k} \\ 0.81 \text{ k} \end{bmatrix} \tag{4-62}$$

which are shown in Fig. 4-32.

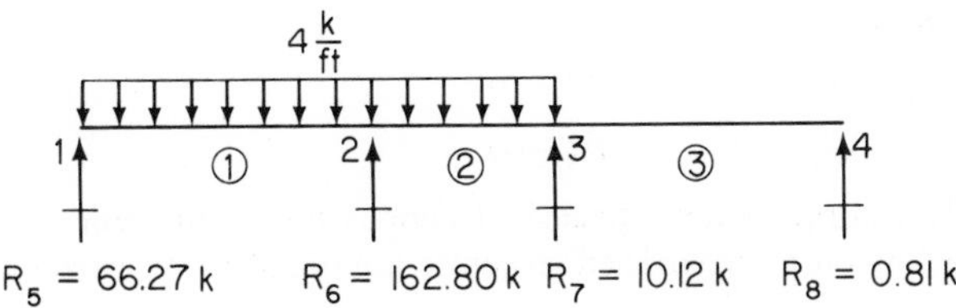

Fig. 4-32 Example 4-4: Support reactions.

Example 4-5. Analyze the three-span continuous beam of Example 4-4 for a settlement of 0.5 in. at support No. 2 (Fig. 4-33). Let $E = 30{,}000$ ksi, and $I = 1000$ in^4.

In developing the analysis of the structural system for this load condition, the complete joint displacement matrix $[\mathbf{\Delta}_c]$ and the complete structure stiffness matrix $[\mathbf{S}_c]$ as established in Example 4-4 remain unchanged, since these two matrices are dependent

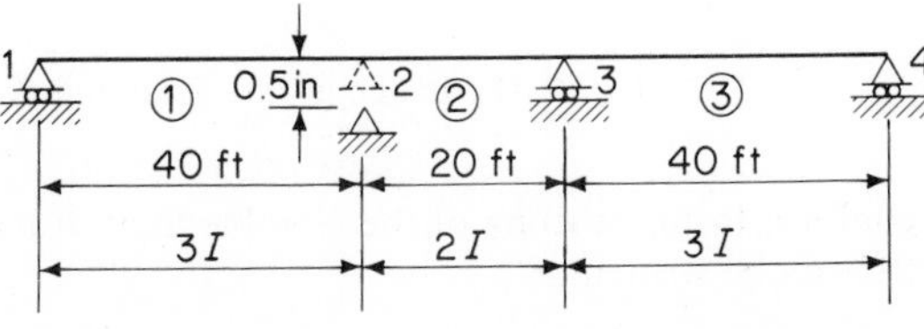

Fig. 4-33 Example 4-5: Continuous beam subjected to support settlement.

only upon the geometry and support conditions of the structural system and are independent of the loading. Hence, only a new joint load matrix is required for this analysis.

JOINT LOAD MATRIX

Initially the support settlement is assumed to act on the restrained structure and its effect is described in terms of equivalent joint loads. The fixed end actions developed by a relative displacement Δ of the ends of a prismatic beam causing a counterclockwise rotation of the member are equal to

$$FM^i_p = \frac{-6EI_i\Delta}{L_i^2} \qquad FM^i_q = \frac{-6EI_i\Delta}{L_i^2}$$

and

$$FP^i_r = \frac{-12EI_i\Delta}{L_i^3} \qquad FP^i_s = \frac{12EI_i\Delta}{L_i^3}$$

So, for a settlement of 0.5 in. of support No. 2, the fixed end actions for the members of the three-span continuous beam are given as follows:

Member 1

$$FM^1_1 = 97.66 \text{ ft-k} \qquad FM^1_2 = 97.66 \text{ ft-k}$$

$$FP^1_5 = 4.88 \text{ k} \qquad FP^1_6 = -4.88 \text{ k}$$

Member 2

$$FM^2_2 = -260.42 \text{ ft-k} \qquad FM^2_3 = -260.42 \text{ ft-k}$$

$$FP^2_6 = -26.04 \text{ k} \qquad FP^2_7 = 26.04 \text{ k}$$

Member 3

$$FM^3_3 = 0 \qquad FM^3_4 = 0$$

$$FP^3_7 = 0 \qquad FP^3_8 = 0$$

Transforming these fixed end actions into equivalent joint loads, the total joint loads acting on the restrained structure are found to be as shown in Fig. 4-34. Labeling these

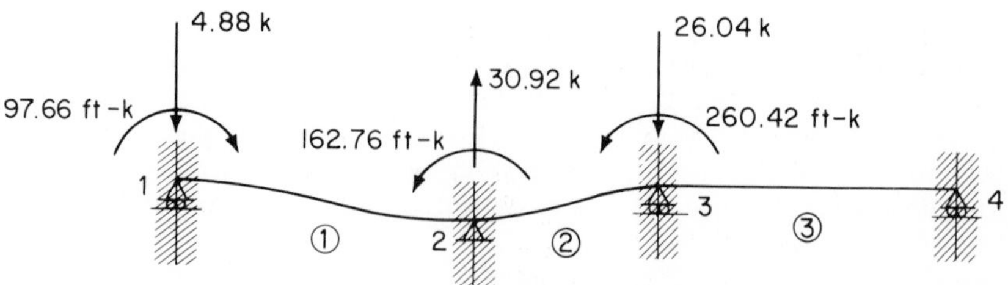

Fig. 4-34 Example 4-5: Total joint loads.

components of total joint load to conform to the labeling of the possible joint displacements, the complete joint load matrix can be written as

$$[\mathbf{JL}_c] = \begin{bmatrix} -97.66 \\ 162.76 \\ 260.42 \\ 0 \\ \text{------} \\ -4.88 \\ 30.92 \\ -26.04 \\ 0 \end{bmatrix} = \begin{bmatrix} [\mathbf{JL}_u] \\ \text{----} \\ [\mathbf{JL}_r] \end{bmatrix} \tag{4-63}$$

SOLUTION

Using Expressions (4-53), (4-58), and (4-63), the unknown joint displacements can again be determined by Eq. (4-37), i.e.,

$$[\boldsymbol{\Delta}_u] = [\mathbf{S}_{uu}]^{-1}[\mathbf{JL}_u] \tag{4-37}$$

which becomes

$$\begin{bmatrix} \theta_1 \\ \theta_2 \\ \theta_3 \\ \theta_4 \end{bmatrix} = \frac{1}{EI}\begin{bmatrix} 3.7790 & -0.8913 & 0.2852 & -0.1426 \\ -0.8913 & 1.7825 & -0.5704 & 0.2852 \\ 0.2852 & -0.5704 & 1.7825 & -0.8913 \\ -0.1426 & 0.2852 & -0.8913 & 3.7790 \end{bmatrix}\begin{bmatrix} -97.66 \\ 162.76 \\ 260.42 \\ 0 \end{bmatrix} = \frac{1}{EI}\begin{bmatrix} -439.85 \\ 228.62 \\ 343.51 \\ -171.77 \end{bmatrix} \tag{4-64a}$$

yielding

$$[\boldsymbol{\Delta}_u] = \begin{bmatrix} \theta_1 \\ \theta_2 \\ \theta_3 \\ \theta_4 \end{bmatrix} = \frac{1 \times 10^2}{EI}\begin{bmatrix} -4.3985 \\ 2.2862 \\ 3.4351 \\ -1.7177 \end{bmatrix} \tag{4-64b}$$

Again, these are relative joint rotations. The actual rotations of each joint can be found by substituting for E (k/ft^2) and I (ft^4).

FINAL END ACTIONS

Having evaluated the unrestrained displacements, the final end actions developed at the ends of each member of the structural system can be determined by writing Eq. (4-42), i.e.,

$$[\mathbf{M}]_i = [\mathbf{K}]_i[\boldsymbol{\delta}]_i + [\mathbf{FM}]_i \tag{4-42}$$

for each member. It should be realized that although a settlement was imposed on support No. 2 of the restrained structure, the supports of the three-span continuous beam will not permit any additional translation of the support joints; hence,

$$\delta_5 = \delta_6 = \delta_7 = \delta_8 = 0 \tag{4-65}$$

The effect of the support settlement is described in terms of equivalent joint loads.

Member 1

$$\begin{bmatrix} M_1 \\ M_2 \\ P_5 \\ P_6 \end{bmatrix}_1 = EI \times 10^{-2} \begin{bmatrix} 30.0 & 15.0 & 1.1250 & -1.1250 \\ 15.0 & 30.0 & 1.1250 & -1.1250 \\ 1.1250 & 1.1250 & 0.0562 & -0.0562 \\ -1.1250 & -1.1250 & -0.0562 & 0.0562 \end{bmatrix}_1 \frac{1 \times 10^2}{EI} \begin{bmatrix} -4.3985 \\ 2.2862 \\ 0 \\ 0 \end{bmatrix}_1 + \begin{bmatrix} 97.66 \\ 97.66 \\ 4.88 \\ -4.88 \end{bmatrix}_1$$

$$\begin{bmatrix} M_1 \\ M_2 \\ P_5 \\ P_6 \end{bmatrix}_1 = \begin{bmatrix} 0 \\ 100.27 \text{ ft-k} \\ 2.50 \text{ k} \\ -2.50 \text{ k} \end{bmatrix}_1 \tag{4-66a}$$

Member 2

$$\begin{bmatrix} M_2 \\ M_3 \\ P_6 \\ P_7 \end{bmatrix}_2 = EI \times 10^{-2} \begin{bmatrix} 40.0 & 20.0 & 3.0 & -3.0 \\ 20.0 & 40.0 & 3.0 & -3.0 \\ 3.0 & 3.0 & 0.3000 & -0.3000 \\ -3.0 & -3.0 & -0.3000 & 0.3000 \end{bmatrix}_2 \frac{1 \times 10^2}{EI} \begin{bmatrix} 2.2862 \\ 3.4351 \\ 0 \\ 0 \end{bmatrix}_2 + \begin{bmatrix} -260.42 \\ -260.42 \\ -26.04 \\ 26.04 \end{bmatrix}_2$$

$$\begin{bmatrix} M_2 \\ M_3 \\ P_6 \\ P_7 \end{bmatrix}_2 = \begin{bmatrix} -100.27 \text{ ft-k} \\ -77.29 \text{ ft-k} \\ -8.88 \text{ k} \\ 8.88 \text{ k} \end{bmatrix}_2 \tag{4-66b}$$

Member 3

$$\begin{bmatrix} M_3 \\ M_4 \\ P_7 \\ P_8 \end{bmatrix}_3 = EI \times 10^{-2} \begin{bmatrix} 30.0 & 15.0 & 1.1250 & -1.1250 \\ 15.0 & 30.0 & 1.1250 & -1.1250 \\ 1.1250 & 1.1250 & 0.0562 & -0.0562 \\ -1.1250 & -1.1250 & -0.0562 & 0.0562 \end{bmatrix}_3 \frac{1 \times 10^2}{EI} \begin{bmatrix} 3.4351 \\ -1.7177 \\ 0 \\ 0 \end{bmatrix}_3 + \begin{bmatrix} 0 \\ 0 \\ 0 \\ 0 \end{bmatrix}_3$$

$$\begin{bmatrix} M_3 \\ M_4 \\ P_7 \\ P_8 \end{bmatrix}_3 = \begin{bmatrix} 77.29 \text{ ft-k} \\ 0 \\ 1.93 \text{ k} \\ -1.93 \text{ k} \end{bmatrix}_3 \tag{4-66c}$$

These final end actions developed by the settlement of support No. 2 are described in Fig. 4-35.

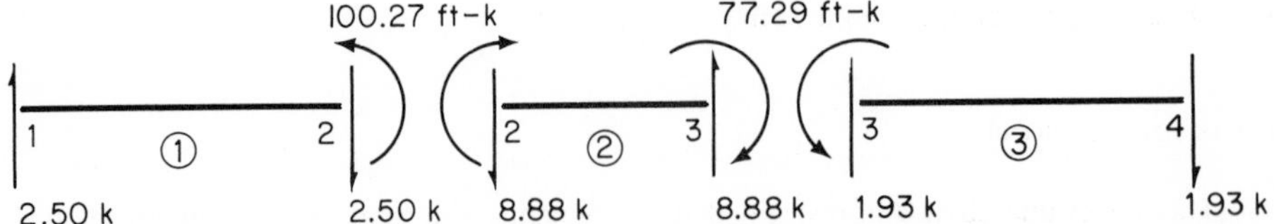

Fig. 4-35 Example 4-5: Final end actions.

SUPPORT REACTIONS

Subtituting the proper matrices of Expressions (4-57), (4-63), and (4-64b) into Eq. (4-39), i.e.,

$$[\mathbf{R}_r] = [\mathbf{S}_{ru}][\mathbf{\Delta}_u] - [\mathbf{JL}_r] \tag{4-39}$$

the support reactions (Fig. 4-36) can be evaluated:

$$\begin{bmatrix} R_6 \\ R_7 \\ R_8 \\ R_9 \end{bmatrix} = EI \times 10^{-2} \begin{bmatrix} 1.1250 & 1.1250 & 0 & 0 \\ -1.1250 & 1.8750 & 3.0 & 0 \\ 0 & -3.0 & -1.8750 & 1.1250 \\ 0 & 0 & -1.1250 & -1.1250 \end{bmatrix} \frac{1 \times 10^2}{EI} \begin{bmatrix} -4.3985 \\ 2.2862 \\ 3.4351 \\ -1.7177 \end{bmatrix} - \begin{bmatrix} -4.88 \\ 30.92 \\ -26.04 \\ 0 \end{bmatrix}$$

$$\begin{bmatrix} R_6 \\ R_7 \\ R_8 \\ R_9 \end{bmatrix} = \begin{bmatrix} 2.50 \text{ k} \\ -11.38 \text{ k} \\ 10.81 \text{ k} \\ -1.93 \text{ k} \end{bmatrix} \tag{4-67}$$

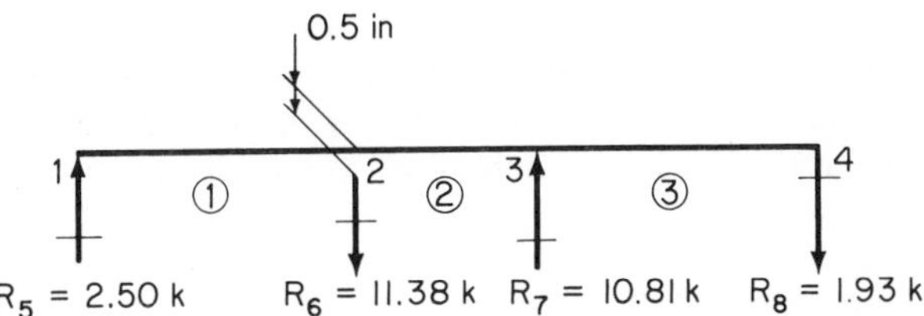

Fig. 4-36 Example 4-5: Support reactions.

4–5 Multiple-Load Cases

Reviewing the procedure followed in the analysis of the three-span continuous beam for the two load cases (Examples 4-4 and 4-5), it is seen that it was necessary to change only the matrices involving the fixed end actions, $[\mathbf{FM}]_i$, and the joint loads, $[\mathbf{JL}_c]$, in order to evaluate the unknown joint displacements $[\mathbf{\Delta}_u]$ and final end actions $[\mathbf{M}]_i$ for each load case. Thus, when a structural system is to be analyzed for several loading conditions, the various *column matrices* which have been defined previously—e.g., $[\mathbf{\Delta}_c]$, $[\mathbf{JL}_c]$, $[\mathbf{FM}]_i$, $[\boldsymbol{\delta}]_i$, $[\mathbf{M}]_i$, etc.—can be expanded into $n \times m$ matrices, where n represents the number of elements appearing in the matrix for a *single* load case and m represents the number of *load cases* to be considered. This permits the analysis of the structure for the several load cases to be carried out in one operation. *Each column* will represent the elements of the particular matrix for a given load case. For example,

$$\begin{array}{c} \\ [\mathbf{\Delta}_c] = \end{array} \begin{array}{c} \begin{array}{ccccc} 1 & 2 & 3 & \cdots & m \leftarrow \text{load case} \end{array} \\ \begin{bmatrix} \Delta_{11} & \Delta_{12} & \Delta_{13} & \cdots & \Delta_{1m} \\ \Delta_{21} & \Delta_{22} & \Delta_{23} & \cdots & \Delta_{2m} \\ \Delta_{31} & \Delta_{32} & \Delta_{33} & \cdots & \Delta_{3m} \\ \vdots & \vdots & \vdots & \vdots & \vdots \\ \Delta_{n1} & \Delta_{n2} & \Delta_{n3} & \cdots & \Delta_{nm} \end{bmatrix} \begin{array}{l} 1 \\ 2 \\ 3 \\ \vdots \\ n \leftarrow \text{displacement component} \end{array} \end{array} = [[\mathbf{\Delta}_c]_1 \quad [\mathbf{\Delta}_c]_2 \quad [\mathbf{\Delta}_c]_3 \quad \cdots \quad [\mathbf{\Delta}_c]_m] \tag{4-68a}$$

Thus, Eq. (4-36) can be expanded to consider several load cases as

$$[\mathbf{S}_{uu}][[\mathbf{\Delta}_u]_1 \quad [\mathbf{\Delta}_u]_2 \quad \ldots \quad [\mathbf{\Delta}_u]_m] = [[\mathbf{JL}_u]_1 \quad [\mathbf{JL}_u]_2 \quad \ldots \quad [\mathbf{JL}_u]_m] \tag{4-68b}$$

and Eq. (4-42) can be expressed as

$$[[\mathbf{M}]_1 \quad [\mathbf{M}]_2 \quad \ldots \quad [\mathbf{M}]_m]_i$$
$$= [\mathbf{K}]_i[[\boldsymbol{\delta}]_1 \quad [\boldsymbol{\delta}]_2 \quad \ldots \quad [\boldsymbol{\delta}]_m]_i + [[\mathbf{FM}]_1 \quad [\mathbf{FM}]_2 \quad \ldots \quad [\mathbf{FM}]_m]_i \qquad \textbf{(4-68c)}$$

4–6
Analysis of Rigid Frame

Example 4-6. Determine the member end actions and the support reactions for the rigid frame structure described in Fig. 4-37 developed by the given loading condition. Once again, the joint numbers are given adjacent to the respective joint, the member labels are given in the circles adjacent to the members and the relative moment of inertia of each member is indicated in the box adjacent to the member. The modulus of elasticity E is assumed to be constant.

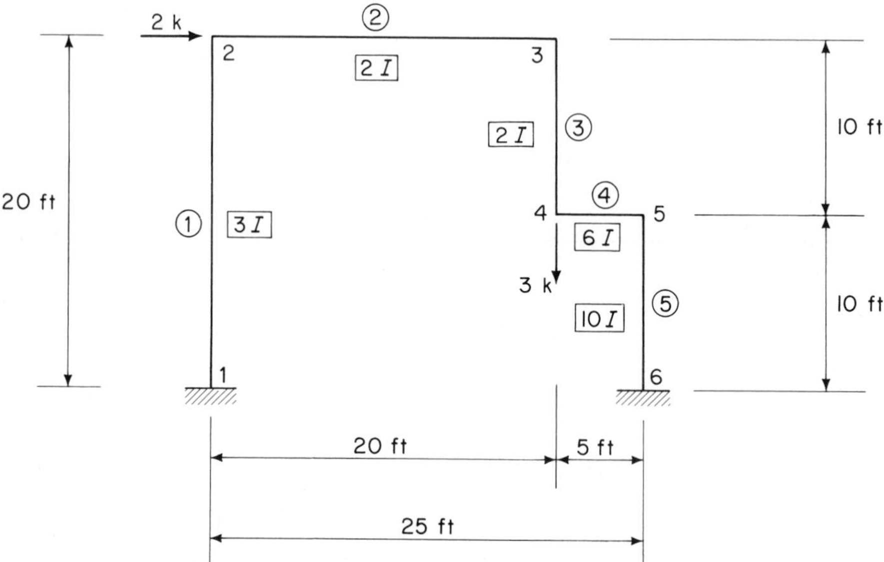

Fig. 4-37 Example 4-6: Rigid frame.

JOINT DISPLACEMENT MATRIX

The possible joint displacements are identified and labeled in Fig. 4-38, and the j- and k-ends of each member are selected as shown in the figure. The complete joint displacement matrix is written as

$$[\Delta_c] = \begin{bmatrix} \theta_1 \\ \theta_2 \\ \theta_3 \\ \theta_4 \\ \delta_5 \\ \delta_6 \\ \delta_7 \\ --- \\ \theta_8 \\ \delta_9 \\ \delta_{10} \\ \delta_{11} \\ \delta_{12} \\ \theta_{13} \end{bmatrix} = \begin{bmatrix} [\Delta_u] \\ --- \\ [\Delta_r] \end{bmatrix} \tag{4-69}$$

MEMBER STIFFNESS MATRICES

Substituting into Expression (4-16), which defines the member stiffness matrix for a member with a constant moment of inertia, the member stiffness matrix for each

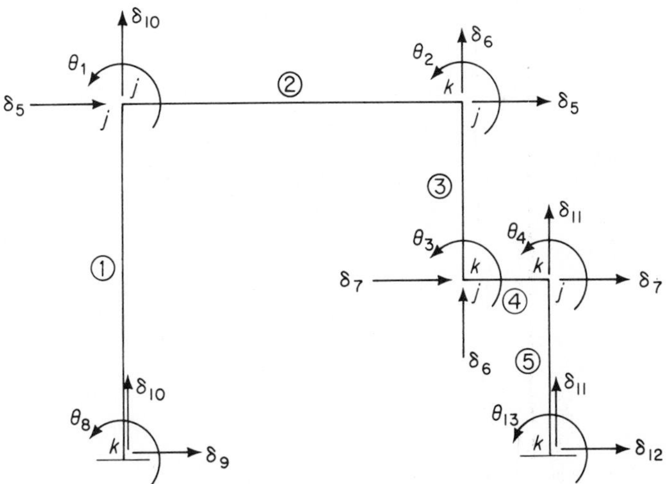

Fig. 4-38 Example 4-6: Identification of possible joint displacements and *j*- and *k*-ends.

member of the frame can be established. The rows and columns are labeled to correspond with the labeling of the related joint displacements of the system (Fig. 4-38) to aid in the identification of the elements of the matrices.

Member 1

$$[\mathbf{K}]_1 = EI\begin{array}{c} \begin{matrix} 1 & \quad 8 & \quad 5 & \quad 9 \end{matrix} \\ \left[\begin{array}{rrrr} 0.6000 & 0.3000 & 0.0450 & -0.0450 \\ 0.3000 & 0.6000 & 0.0450 & -0.0450 \\ 0.0450 & 0.0450 & 0.0045 & -0.0045 \\ -0.0450 & -0.0450 & -0.0045 & 0.0045 \end{array}\right]_1 \end{array} \begin{array}{c} \\ 1 \\ 8 \\ 5 \\ 9 \end{array} \tag{4-70a}$$

Member 2

$$[\mathbf{K}]_2 = EI\begin{array}{c} \begin{matrix} 1 & \quad 2 & \quad 10 & \quad 6 \end{matrix} \\ \left[\begin{array}{rrrr} 0.4000 & 0.2000 & 0.0300 & -0.0300 \\ 0.2000 & 0.4000 & 0.0300 & -0.0300 \\ 0.0300 & 0.0300 & 0.0030 & -0.0030 \\ -0.0300 & -0.0300 & -0.0030 & 0.0030 \end{array}\right]_2 \end{array} \begin{array}{c} \\ 1 \\ 2 \\ 10 \\ 6 \end{array} \tag{4-70b}$$

Member 3

$$[\mathbf{K}]_3 = EI\begin{array}{c} \begin{matrix} 2 & \quad 3 & \quad 5 & \quad 7 \end{matrix} \\ \left[\begin{array}{rrrr} 0.8000 & 0.4000 & 0.1200 & -0.1200 \\ 0.4000 & 0.8000 & 0.1200 & -0.1200 \\ 0.1200 & 0.1200 & 0.0240 & -0.0240 \\ -0.1200 & -0.1200 & -0.0240 & 0.0240 \end{array}\right]_3 \end{array} \begin{array}{c} \\ 2 \\ 3 \\ 5 \\ 7 \end{array} \tag{4-70c}$$

Member 4

$$[\mathbf{K}]_4 = EI\begin{array}{c} \begin{matrix} 3 & \quad 4 & \quad 6 & \quad 11 \end{matrix} \\ \left[\begin{array}{rrrr} 4.8000 & 2.4000 & 1.4400 & -1.4400 \\ 2.4000 & 4.8000 & 1.4400 & -1.4400 \\ 1.4400 & 1.4400 & 0.5760 & -0.5760 \\ -1.4400 & -1.4400 & -0.5760 & 0.5760 \end{array}\right]_4 \end{array} \begin{array}{c} \\ 3 \\ 4 \\ 6 \\ 11 \end{array} \tag{4-70d}$$

Member 5

$$[\mathbf{K}]_5 = EI\begin{array}{c} \begin{matrix} 4 & \quad 13 & \quad 7 & \quad 12 \end{matrix} \\ \left[\begin{array}{rrrr} 4.000 & 2.000 & 0.6000 & -0.6000 \\ 2.000 & 4.000 & 0.6000 & -0.6000 \\ 0.6000 & 0.6000 & 0.1200 & -0.1200 \\ -0.6000 & -0.6000 & -0.1200 & 0.1200 \end{array}\right]_5 \end{array} \begin{array}{c} \\ 4 \\ 13 \\ 7 \\ 12 \end{array} \tag{4-70e}$$

STRUCTURE STIFFNESS MATRIX

Superimposing the member stiffness matrices, the complete structure stiffness matrix $[\mathbf{S}_c]$ is obtained as shown in Table 4-4, Expression (4-71). The matrix is partitioned with respect to the restrained and unrestrained joint displacements as indicated. According to Eqs. (4-33), the four submatrices are defined as

$$\left[\begin{array}{c|c} [\mathbf{S}_{uu}] & [\mathbf{S}_{ur}] \\ \hline [\mathbf{S}_{ru}] & [\mathbf{S}_{rr}] \end{array}\right]$$

Table 4-4

$[\mathbf{S}_c] = EI$

	1	2	3	4	5	6	7	8	9	10	11	12	13
1	1.0	0.2000	0	0	0.0450	−0.0300	0	0.3000	−0.0450	0.0300	0	0	0
2	0.2000	1.2000	0.4000	0	0.1200	−0.0300	−0.1200	0	0	0.0300	0	0	0
3	0	0.4000	5.6000	2.4000	0.1200	1.4400	−0.1200	0	0	0	−1.4400	0	0
4	0	0	2.4000	8.8000	0	1.4400	0.6000	0	0	0	−1.4400	−0.6000	2.000
5	0.0450	0.1200	0.1200	0	0.0285	0	−0.0240	0.0450	−0.0045	0	0	0	0
6	−0.0300	−0.0300	1.4400	1.4400	0	0.5790	0	0	0	−0.0030	−0.5760	0	0
7	0	−0.1200	−0.1200	0.6000	−0.0240	0	0.1440	0	0	0	0	−0.1200	0.6000
8	0.3000	0	0	0	0.0450	0	0	0.6000	−0.0450	0	0	0	0
9	−0.0450	0	0	0	−0.0045	0	0	−0.0450	0.0045	0	0	0	0
10	0.0300	0.0300	0	0	0	−0.0030	0	0	0	0.0030	0	0	0
11	0	0	−1.4400	−1.4400	0	−0.5760	0	0	0	0	0.5760	0	0
12	0	0	0	−0.6000	0	0	−0.1200	0	0	0	0	0.1200	−0.6000
13	0	0	0	2.0000	0	0	0.6000	0	0	0	0	−0.6000	4.0000

(4-71)

Now,

$$[\mathbf{S}_{uu}]^{-1} = \frac{1}{EI}\begin{array}{c} \begin{matrix} 1 & 2 & 3 & 4 & 5 & 6 & 7 \end{matrix} \\ \begin{bmatrix} 1.1319 & -0.0500 & 0.1845 & 0.1440 & -3.2159 & -0.7610 & -1.0240 \\ -0.0500 & 1.4809 & -0.0748 & -0.1443 & -5.0583 & 0.6191 & 0.9300 \\ 0.1845 & -0.0748 & 1.0364 & 0.5028 & -6.3158 & -3.8223 & -2.3463 \\ 0.1440 & -0.1443 & 0.5028 & 0.6871 & -4.5322 & -2.9593 & -3.3195 \\ -3.2159 & -5.0583 & -6.3158 & -4.5322 & 111.6470 & 26.5507 & 28.0134 \\ -0.7610 & 0.6191 & -3.8223 & -2.9593 & 26.5507 & 18.5859 & 14.0864 \\ -1.0240 & 0.9300 & -2.3463 & -3.3195 & 28.0134 & 14.0864 & 24.2645 \end{bmatrix} \end{array} \begin{matrix} 1 \\ 2 \\ 3 \\ 4 \\ 5 \\ 6 \\ 7 \end{matrix} \tag{4-72}$$

JOINT LOAD MATRIX

With loads applied only at the joints of the structural system, the complete joint load matrix is written directly as

$$[\mathbf{JL}_c] = \begin{bmatrix} JL_1 \\ JL_2 \\ JL_3 \\ JL_4 \\ JL_5 \\ JL_6 \\ JL_7 \\ \hdashline JL_8 \\ JL_9 \\ JL_{10} \\ JL_{11} \\ JL_{12} \\ JL_{13} \end{bmatrix} = \begin{bmatrix} 0 \\ 0 \\ 0 \\ 0 \\ 2.0 \\ -3.0 \\ 0 \\ \hdashline 0 \\ 0 \\ 0 \\ 0 \\ 0 \\ 0 \end{bmatrix} = \begin{bmatrix} [\mathbf{JL}_u] \\ \hdashline [\mathbf{JL}_r] \end{bmatrix} \tag{4-73}$$

SOLUTION

Using Expressions (4-69), (4-72), and (4-73), the unknown joint displacements are evaluated by Eq. (4-37) as follows:

$$\begin{bmatrix} \theta_1 \\ \theta_2 \\ \theta_3 \\ \theta_4 \\ \delta_5 \\ \delta_6 \\ \delta_7 \end{bmatrix} = \frac{1}{EI}\begin{bmatrix} 1.1319 & -0.0500 & 0.1845 & 0.1440 & -3.2159 & -0.7610 & -1.0240 \\ -0.0500 & 1.4809 & -0.0748 & -0.1443 & -5.0583 & 0.6191 & 0.9300 \\ 0.1845 & -0.0748 & 1.0364 & 0.5028 & -6.3158 & -3.8223 & -2.3463 \\ 0.1440 & -0.1443 & 0.5028 & 0.6871 & -4.5322 & -2.9593 & -3.3195 \\ -3.2159 & -5.0583 & -6.3158 & -4.5322 & 111.6470 & 26.5507 & 28.0134 \\ -0.7610 & 0.6191 & -3.8223 & -2.9593 & 26.5507 & 18.5859 & 14.0864 \\ -1.0240 & 0.9300 & -2.3463 & -3.3195 & 28.0134 & 14.0864 & 24.2645 \end{bmatrix} \begin{bmatrix} 0 \\ 0 \\ 0 \\ 0 \\ 2.0 \\ -3.0 \\ 0 \end{bmatrix} \tag{4-74a}$$

hence,

$$[\Delta_u] = \begin{bmatrix} \theta_1 \\ \theta_2 \\ \theta_3 \\ \theta_4 \\ \delta_5 \\ \delta_6 \\ \delta_7 \end{bmatrix} = \frac{1}{EI} \begin{bmatrix} -4.149 \\ -11.974 \\ -1.165 \\ -0.186 \\ 143.642 \\ -2.656 \\ 13.768 \end{bmatrix} \tag{4-74b}$$

These are relative values of joint displacement. The actual value of each component of displacement can be obtained, if desired, by substituting for E (k/ft^2) and I (ft^4). Translations will be in units of feet and rotations in radians.

FINAL END ACTIONS

Writing Eq. (4-42) for each member, i.e.,

$$[\mathbf{M}]_i = [\mathbf{K}]_i[\boldsymbol{\delta}]_i + [\mathbf{FM}]_i \tag{4-42}$$

the final end actions developed at the ends of each member are

Member 1

$$\begin{bmatrix} M_1 \\ M_8 \\ P_5 \\ P_9 \end{bmatrix}_1 = EI \begin{bmatrix} 0.6000 & 0.3000 & 0.0450 & -0.0450 \\ 0.3000 & 0.6000 & 0.0450 & -0.0450 \\ 0.0450 & 0.0450 & 0.0045 & -0.0045 \\ -0.0450 & -0.0450 & -0.0045 & 0.0045 \end{bmatrix}_1 \frac{1}{EI} \begin{bmatrix} -4.149 \\ 0 \\ 143.642 \\ 0 \end{bmatrix}_1 + \begin{bmatrix} 0 \\ 0 \\ 0 \\ 0 \end{bmatrix}_1 = \begin{bmatrix} 3.97 \text{ ft-k} \\ 5.22 \text{ ft-k} \\ 0.46 \text{ k} \\ -0.46 \text{ k} \end{bmatrix}_1 \tag{4-75a}$$

Member 2

$$\begin{bmatrix} M_1 \\ M_2 \\ P_{10} \\ P_6 \end{bmatrix}_2 = EI \begin{bmatrix} 0.4000 & 0.2000 & 0.0300 & -0.0300 \\ 0.2000 & 0.4000 & 0.0300 & -0.0300 \\ 0.0300 & 0.0300 & 0.0030 & -0.0030 \\ -0.0300 & -0.0300 & -0.0030 & 0.0030 \end{bmatrix}_2 \frac{1}{EI} \begin{bmatrix} -4.149 \\ -11.974 \\ 0 \\ -2.656 \end{bmatrix}_2 + \begin{bmatrix} 0 \\ 0 \\ 0 \\ 0 \end{bmatrix}_2 = \begin{bmatrix} -3.97 \text{ ft-k} \\ -5.54 \text{ ft-k} \\ -0.48 \text{ k} \\ 0.48 \text{ k} \end{bmatrix}_2 \tag{4-75b}$$

Member 3

$$\begin{bmatrix} M_2 \\ M_3 \\ P_5 \\ P_7 \end{bmatrix}_3 = EI \begin{bmatrix} 0.8000 & 0.4000 & 0.1200 & -0.1200 \\ 0.4000 & 0.8000 & 0.1200 & -0.1200 \\ 0.1200 & 0.1200 & 0.0240 & -0.0240 \\ -0.1200 & -0.1200 & -0.0240 & 0.0240 \end{bmatrix}_3 \frac{1}{EI} \begin{bmatrix} -11.974 \\ -1.165 \\ 143.642 \\ 13.768 \end{bmatrix}_3 + \begin{bmatrix} 0 \\ 0 \\ 0 \\ 0 \end{bmatrix}_3 = \begin{bmatrix} 5.54 \text{ ft-k} \\ 9.86 \text{ ft-k} \\ 1.54 \text{ k} \\ -1.54 \text{ k} \end{bmatrix}_3 \tag{4-75c}$$

Member 4

$$\begin{bmatrix} M_3 \\ M_4 \\ P_6 \\ P_{11} \end{bmatrix}_4 = EI \begin{bmatrix} 4.8000 & 2.4000 & 1.4400 & -1.4400 \\ 2.4000 & 4.8000 & 1.4400 & -1.4400 \\ 1.4400 & 1.4400 & 0.5760 & -0.5760 \\ -1.4400 & -1.4400 & -0.5760 & 0.5760 \end{bmatrix}_4 \frac{1}{EI} \begin{bmatrix} -1.165 \\ -0.186 \\ -2.656 \\ 0 \end{bmatrix}_4 + \begin{bmatrix} 0 \\ 0 \\ 0 \\ 0 \end{bmatrix}_4 = \begin{bmatrix} -9.86 \text{ ft-k} \\ -7.51 \text{ ft-k} \\ -3.48 \text{ k} \\ 3.48 \text{ k} \end{bmatrix}_4 \tag{4-75d}$$

Member 5

$$\begin{bmatrix} M_4 \\ M_{13} \\ P_7 \\ P_{12} \end{bmatrix}_5 = EI \begin{bmatrix} 4.0000 & 2.0000 & 0.6000 & -0.6000 \\ 2.0000 & 4.0000 & 0.6000 & -0.6000 \\ 0.6000 & 0.6000 & 0.1200 & -0.1200 \\ -0.6000 & -0.6000 & -0.1200 & 0.1200 \end{bmatrix}_5 \frac{1}{EI} \begin{bmatrix} -0.186 \\ 0 \\ 13.768 \\ 0 \end{bmatrix}_5 + \begin{bmatrix} 0 \\ 0 \\ 0 \\ 0 \end{bmatrix}_5 = \begin{bmatrix} 7.51 \text{ ft-k} \\ 7.89 \text{ ft-k} \\ 1.54 \text{ k} \\ -1.54 \text{ k} \end{bmatrix}_5 \quad \textbf{(4-75e)}$$

The free body diagram for each member showing these final end actions is given in Fig. 4-39.

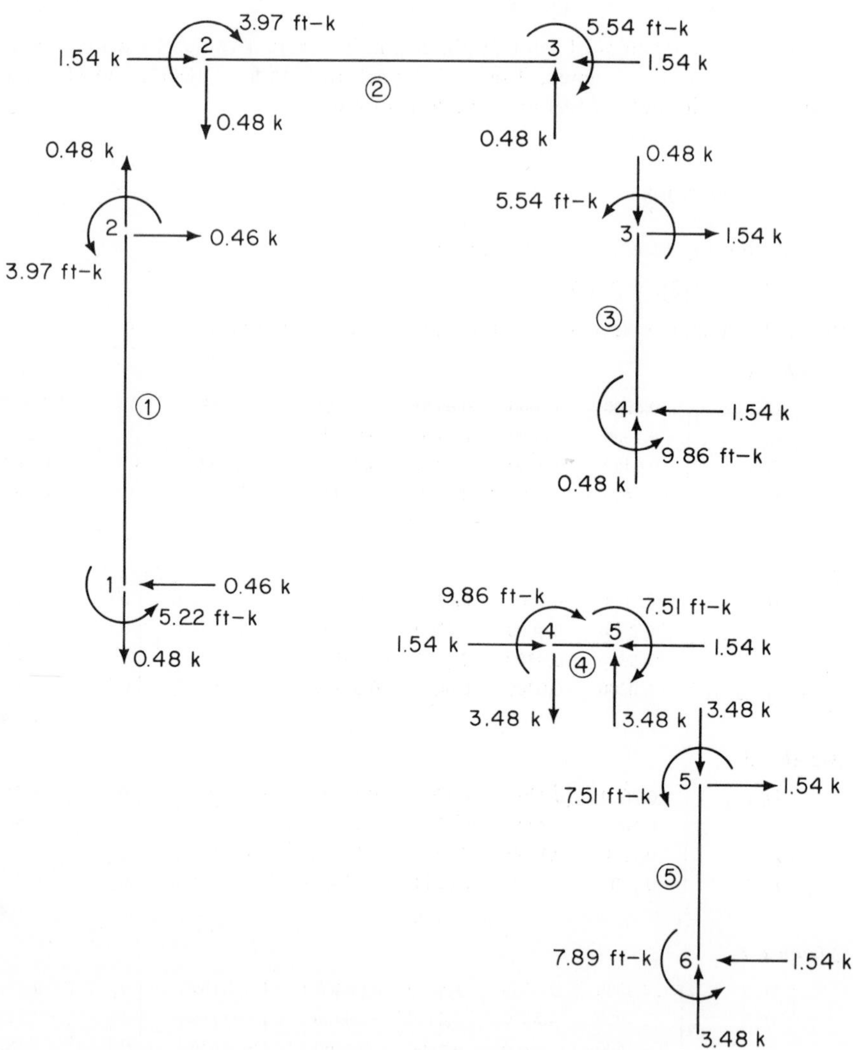

Fig. 4-39 Example 4-6: Final end actions.

SUPPORT REACTIONS

Substituting into Eqs. (4-39), i.e.,

$$[\mathbf{R}_r] = [\mathbf{S}_{ru}][\mathbf{\Delta}_u] - [\mathbf{JL}_r] \tag{4-39}$$

gives

$$\begin{bmatrix} R_8 \\ R_9 \\ R_{10} \\ R_{11} \\ R_{12} \\ R_{13} \end{bmatrix} = EI \begin{bmatrix} 0.3000 & 0 & 0 & 0 & 0.0450 & 0 & 0 \\ -0.0450 & 0 & 0 & 0 & -0.0045 & 0 & 0 \\ 0.0300 & 0.0300 & 0 & 0 & 0 & -0.0030 & 0 \\ 0 & 0 & -1.4400 & -1.4400 & 0 & -0.5760 & 0 \\ 0 & 0 & 0 & -0.6000 & 0 & 0 & -0.1200 \\ 0 & 0 & 0 & 2.0000 & 0 & 0 & 0.6000 \end{bmatrix} \frac{1}{EI} \begin{bmatrix} -4.149 \\ -11.974 \\ -1.165 \\ -0.186 \\ 143.642 \\ -2.656 \\ 13.768 \end{bmatrix} + \begin{bmatrix} 0 \\ 0 \\ 0 \\ 0 \\ 0 \\ 0 \end{bmatrix} \tag{4-76a}$$

which yields

$$\begin{bmatrix} R_8 \\ R_9 \\ R_{10} \\ R_{11} \\ R_{12} \\ R_{13} \end{bmatrix} = \begin{bmatrix} 5.22 \text{ ft-k} \\ -0.46 \text{ k} \\ -0.48 \text{ k} \\ 3.48 \text{ k} \\ -1.54 \text{ k} \\ 7.89 \text{ ft-k} \end{bmatrix} \tag{4-76b}$$

These support reactions are shown in Fig. 4-40.

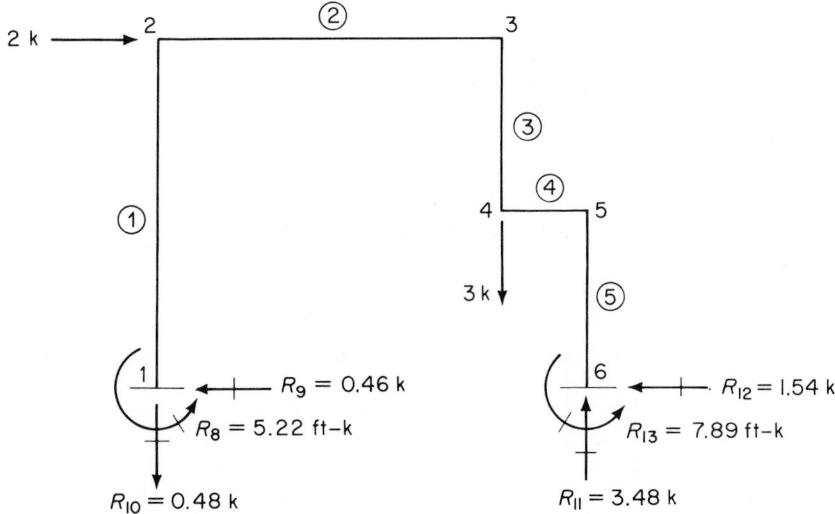

Fig. 4-40 Example 4-6: Support reactions.

4–7
Problems

4-1 to 4-6. Analyze the structural system for the indicated loading, and draw the shear and moment diagrams for each member; E = constant and the relative value of moment of inertia is indicated for each member.

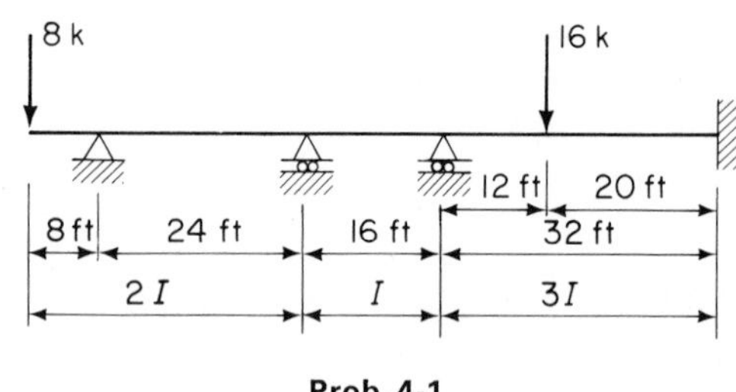

Prob. 4-1

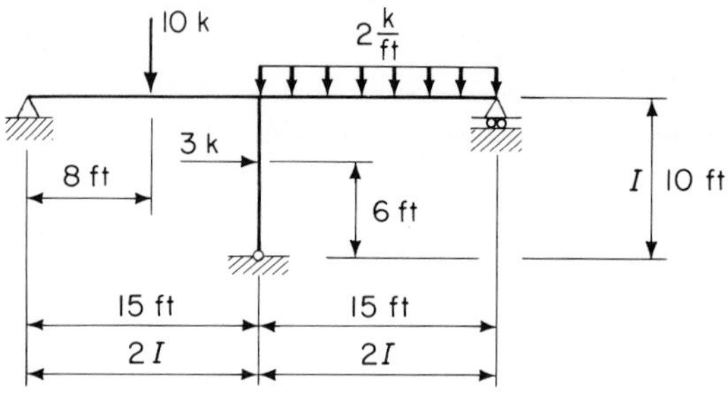

Prob. 4-2

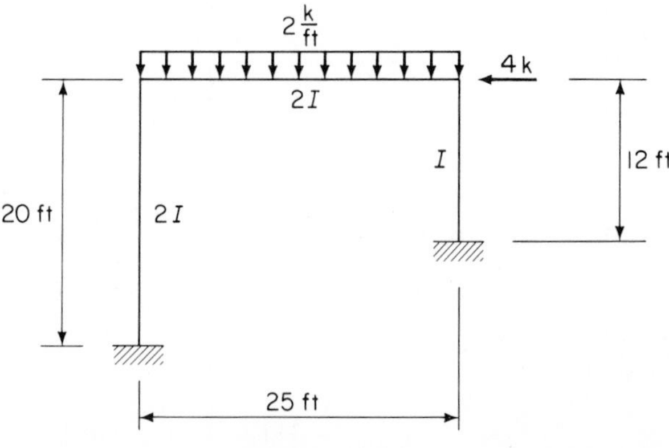

Prob. 4-3

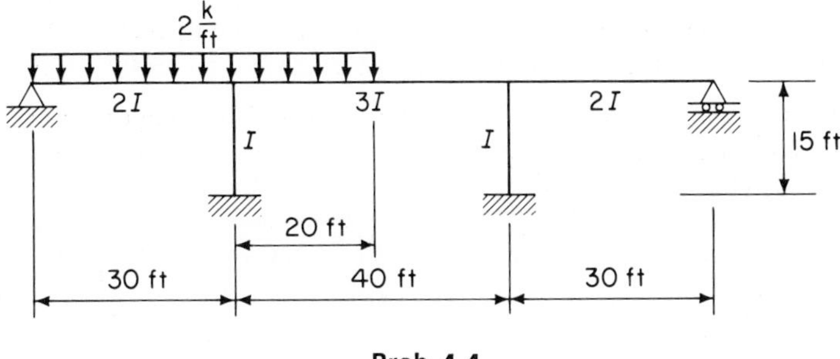

Prob. 4-4

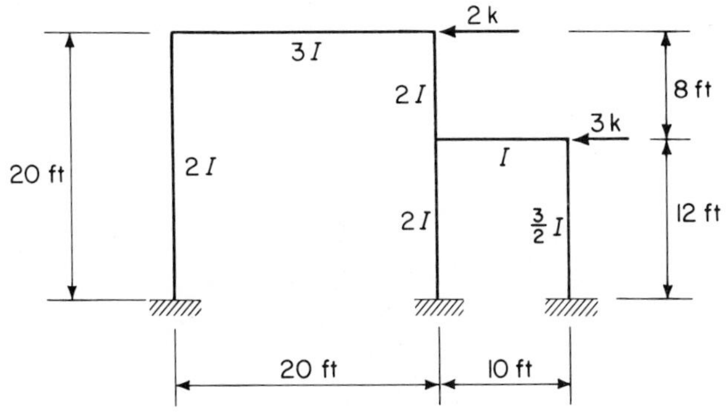

Prob. 4-5

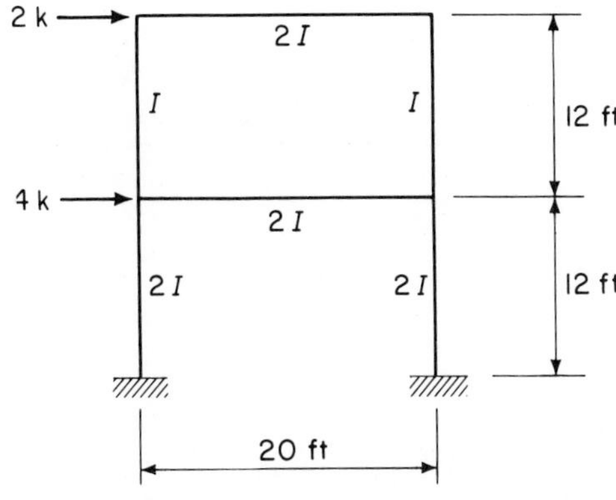

Prob. 4-6

4-7. Analyze the rigid frame of Prob. 4-2 for a settlement of the center support of 0.6 in.; $I = 500\ \text{in}^4$, $E = 30{,}000$ ksi.

4-8. Determine the final member end actions and the support reactions for the frame of Prob. 4-3 caused by a clockwise rotation of the left support of 2°; $I = 5000\ \text{in}^4$, $E = 3000$ ksi.

4-9. Analyze the planar orthogonal frame of Prob. 4-4 for a settlement of the left column support of 0.6 in. and of the right column support of 0.8 in.; $I = 6000$ in^4, $E = 3000$ ksi.

4-10 to 4-12. Calculate the final member end actions and the support reactions for the indicated loading of the structure, and draw the shear and moment diagrams for each member; $E = 30{,}000$ ksi.

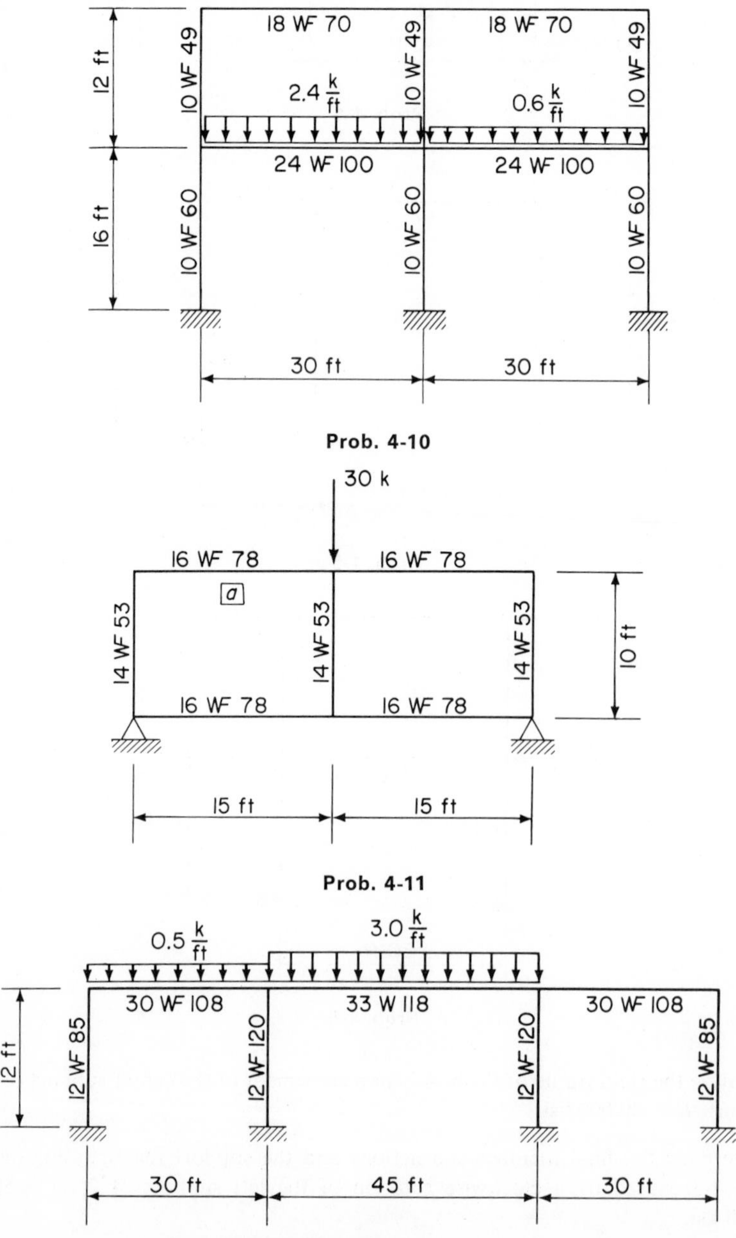

Prob. 4-10

Prob. 4-11

Prob. 4-12

4-13. Determine the final member end actions and the support reactions for the frame of Prob. 4-11 if member *a* is fabricated with a 6° bend (rotating the right end of the member counterclockwise) at a point 5 ft from the left end of the member.

4-14. Analyze the frame of Prob. 4-12 for a fabrication error of 0.75 in. which resulted in the 33 WF 118 being too short.

4-15. Analyze the continuous beam for the given loading. The beams are 1.5-ft wide and have straight haunches; $E = 3000$ ksi.

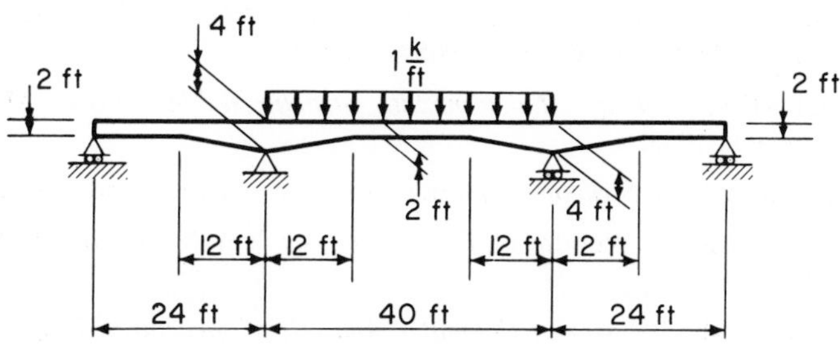

Prob. 4-15

4-16. Analyze the continuous beam for the indicated loading condition. Draw the shear and moment diagrams for each beam. The relative values of moments of inertia for each member are indicated; $E =$ constant.

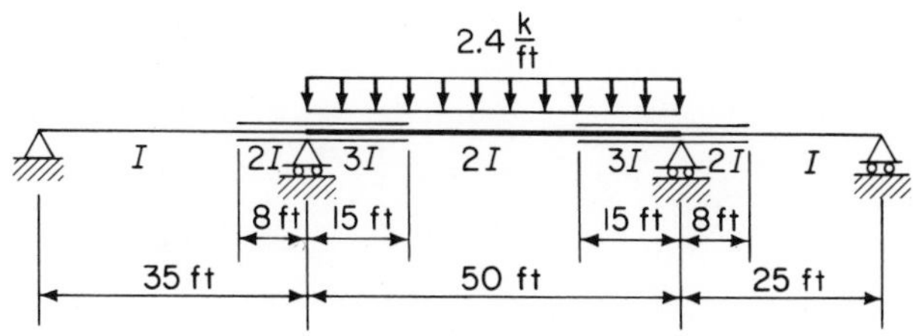

Prob. 4-16

4-17. Write a computer program using the stiffness method to analyze a continuous beam for a uniform vertical load applied to any span and acting over the entire span. Assume that the moment of inertia is constant over the span of each beam and is different for each beam; E is constant for the structure.

4-18. Develop a computer program to analyze a general planar orthogonal frame by the stiffness method for the following load cases: (1) a uniform normal load over the span of a member; (2) a normal concentrated load applied at point within the span of a member; (3) a vertical or horizontal concentrated load applied at a joint; and (4) a moment applied at a joint. Assume that the beam elements are prismatic and that E is constant for the structure.

4-19. Write a computer program to develop the member stiffness matrix and to compute the fixed end actions for a uniform normal load acting over the entire span for a nonprismatic beam element.

SELECTED REFERENCES

4-1 Pei, Ming L., "Stiffness Method of Rigid Frame Analysis," ASCE, *Second Conference on Electronic Computation.* Pittsburgh, Pa.: September 8 and 9, 1960.

4-2 Kinney, J. Sterling, *Indeterminate Structural Analysis.* Reading, Mass.: Addison-Wesley Publishing Co., Inc., 1957.

4-3 Gere, James M., and William Weaver, Jr., *Analysis of Framed Structures.* Princeton, N.J.: D. Van Norstrand Co., Inc., 1965.

4-4 Wang, Chu-Kia, *Statically Indeterminate Structures.* New York: McGraw-Hill Book Company, 1953.

4-5 Morice, P. B., *Linear Structural Analysis.* London: Thames and Hudson, 1959.

4-6 Hall, A. S., and R. W. Woodhead, *Frame Analysis.* New York: John Wiley & Sons, Inc., 1961.

4-7 Rubinstein, Moshe F., *Matrix Computer Analysis of Structures.* Englewood Cliffs, N.J.: Prentice-Hall, Inc., 1966.

4-8 Willems, Nicholas, and William M. Lucas, Jr., *Matrix Analysis for Structural Engineers.* Englewood Cliffs, N.J.: Prentice-Hall, Inc., 1968.

4-9 Livesley, R. K., *Matrix Methods of Structural Analysis.* New York: The Macmillan Company, Inc., 1964.

5 STIFFNESS METHOD OF ANALYSIS: PLANAR NONORTHOGONAL STRUCTURES

5–1 Introduction

The analysis of a structural system by the stiffness method can be achieved, as previously demonstrated, by solving the set of equations expressed in matrix form as

$$[\mathbf{S}_c][\mathbf{\Delta}_c] = [\mathbf{JL}_c] + [\mathbf{R}_c] \tag{4-32}$$

defining $[\mathbf{S}_c]$ as the ***complete structure stiffness matrix***, $[\mathbf{\Delta}_c]$ as the ***complete joint displacement matrix***, $[\mathbf{JL}_c]$ as the ***complete joint load matrix***, and $[\mathbf{R}_c]$ as the ***complete support reaction matrix***.

In the development of the several matrices of Eq. (4-32), all of the components of joint displacement, joint load, and support reaction, which form the elements of the respective matrices, must be described with respect to the same system of axes, i.e., the ***reference axes*** for the entire structure. Consequently, in order to maintain continuity of the Eq. (4-32), the complete structure stiffness matrix $[\mathbf{S}_c]$ must be written with respect to the *reference axes;* therefore, the individual member stiffness matrices $[\mathbf{K}]_i$ must also be developed within the frame of the *reference axes*.

Although the establishment of a system of reference axes was not explicitly specified in the analysis of the planar orthogonal structural system discussed in Chapter 4, a system of orthogonal axes (X–Y) was implied by the assumed sign convention for components of joint displacement and joint action in Sec. 4-1; this system of reference axes was assumed to correspond to the orientation of the structure as shown in Fig. 5-1(a). In addition, the various member stiffness matrices were established directly with respect to the implied reference axes from Expression (4-9), which was developed with respect to the member's own set of local orthogonal axes (x_m–y_m), by selecting the *j*-end of each member so that the assumed positive sense for the end shears in the frame of the local axes would coincide with the assumed positive sense in the frame of the reference axes as indicated in Fig. 5-1(a). This ability to develop the member stiffness matrices with respect to the reference axes directly is due not only to the similarity of orientation of the various systems of local axes and the reference axes, but also to the fact that the effects of axial deformations were neglected in the analysis.

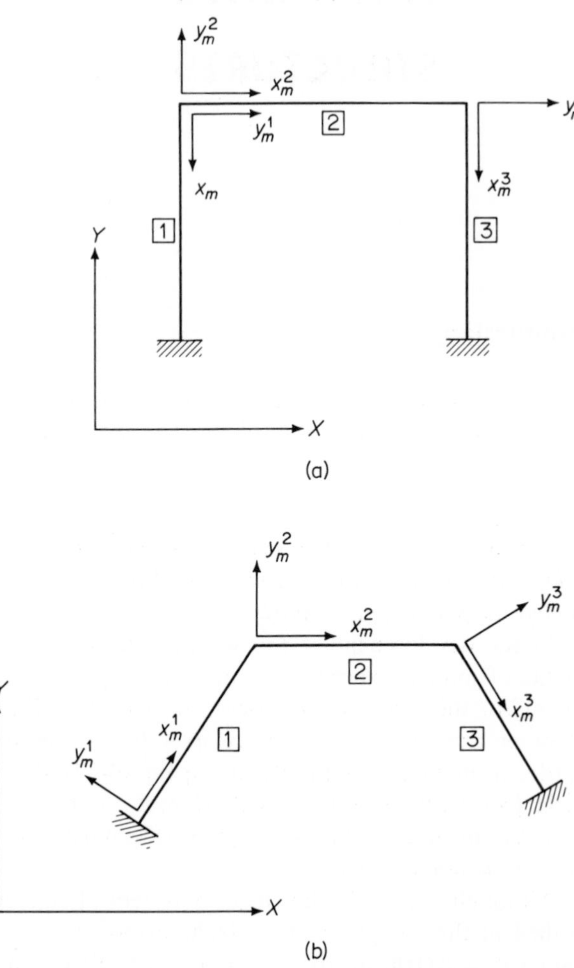

Fig. 5-1 Local and reference axes for planar structural systems: (a) orthogonal frame; (b) nonorthogonal frame.

Unfortunately, when analyzing a planar nonorthogonal structural system, the reference axes cannot be as conveniently positioned as to correspond to the orientation of the numerous systems of local axes of the structure as illustrated in Fig. 5-1(b); also, when considering axial deformations, the local axes cannot always be conveniently positioned so that the positive sense for both the end shears and end axial forces will coincide with the positive senses in the frame of the reference axes as indicated in Fig. 5-1. Hence, the member stiffness matrix, in general, cannot be written directly with respect to the reference axes while maintaining a uniform sign convention for the actions and displacements of the individual members as well as for the structure as a whole. Thus, once the member stiffness matrix has been developed in the frame of the local axes, it must be *transformed* into the frame of the reference axes. This necessary transformation will be the primary concern of this chapter.

After all of the required member stiffness matrices have been obtained with respect to the chosen system of reference axes for the structure, the complete structure stiffness matrix $[\mathbf{S}_c]$ can once again be established by *summing* of the elements of the member stiffness matrices with like subscripts. The procedure for developing the other matrices of Eq. (4-32)—i.e., the complete joint displacement matrix $[\mathbf{\Delta}_c]$, the complete joint load matrix $[\mathbf{JL}_c]$, and the complete support reaction matrix $[\mathbf{R}_c]$—is essentially the same as that outlined in Chapter 4; the only difference being that the elements of these matrices must be given in terms of components with respect to the arbitrary system of reference axes.

5–2 Sign Convention

For the analysis of a planar structural system, the sign convention established in Chapter 4 can be expressed with respect to the ***reference*** and ***local member axes*** of the system as follows:

1. ***Counterclockwise*** joint rotations and joint moments are positive;
2. components of joint translation and of joint forces ***in the direction of the positive reference axes*** X–Y are positive;
3. ***counterclockwise*** end rotations and end moments are positive; and
4. components of end translation and of end forces ***in the direction of the positive local member axes*** x_m–y_m are positive.

5–3 The Beam Element

In Sec. 4-2 the member stiffness matrix $[\mathbf{K}]_i$ was developed for a beam element considering only rotation and normal translation of the ends of the member.

This matrix can be expanded to also take into account the response of the beam element to axial displacement of its ends.

5-3.1 Member Stiffness Matrix: Considering Axial Deformation

For the purpose of discussion, consider a beam element that has either a constant or variable moment of inertia over its length and is positioned in the frame of a set of *local axes* x_m–y_m, with the origin at the j-end of the member and the x_m axis directed toward the k-end of the member. The x_m axis will define the centroidal axis of the member, and the x_m–y_m plane will define the plane of bending of the member. The cross-sectional shape of the member is assumed to be symmetrical about the x_m–y_m plane.

As shown in Figs. 4-2 through 4-5, axial end forces are not required in maintaining static equilibrium of the restrained beam element when it is subjected to a unit value of end rotation or normal translation. This is a result of the assumption that the change in length of the member due to flexural deformations is negligible. Should the j-end of the member be subjected to a unit value of axial translation along the x_m member axis ($\delta_t = 1$) while preventing any other displacement of the ends of the member [Fig. 5-2(a)], only the axial forces K^i_{tt} and K^i_{ut} at the j- and k-ends, respectively, would be required to maintain equilibrium of the member. Likewise, for a unit value of axial translation of the k-end of the beam element along the x_m member axis ($\delta_u = 1$) with other end displacements prevented [Fig. 5-2(b)], the axial forces K^i_{tu} and K^i_{uu} are the only actions

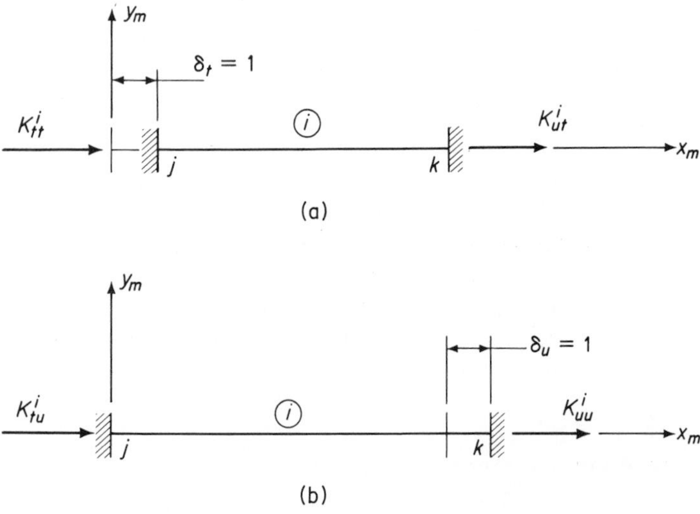

Fig. 5-2 Axial deformations of beam element i: (a) unit axial displacement of end j; (b) unit axial displacement of end k.

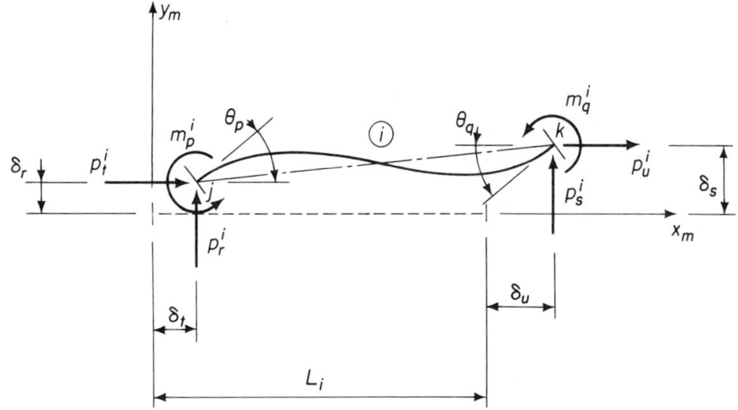

Fig. 5-3 General displacement of typical beam element with restrained ends.

necessary to establish equilibrium of the member. If the beam element is subjected to the general displacements θ_p, θ_q, δ_r, δ_s, δ_t, and δ_u of its ends as shown in Fig. 5-3, the resulting end actions required to maintain equilibrium of the deformed member can be evaluated by superimposing the corresponding end actions developed by the individual application of unit values of end displacements (Figs. 4-2 through 4-5 and Fig. 5-1) times the actual magnitude of the imposed displacement, i.e.,

$$m_p^i = K_{pp}^i\theta_p + K_{pq}^i\theta_q + K_{pr}^i\delta_r + K_{ps}^i\delta_s \qquad \textbf{(5-1a)}$$

$$m_q^i = K_{qp}^i\theta_p + K_{qq}^i\theta_q + K_{qr}^i\delta_r + K_{qs}^i\delta_s \qquad \textbf{(5-1b)}$$

$$p_r^i = K_{rp}^i\theta_p + K_{rq}^i\theta_q + K_{rr}^i\delta_r + K_{rs}^i\delta_s \qquad \textbf{(5-1c)}$$

$$p_s^i = K_{sp}^i\theta_p + K_{sq}^i\theta_q + K_{sr}^i\delta_r + K_{ss}^i\delta_s \qquad \textbf{(5-1d)}$$

$$p_t^i = \qquad + K_{tt}^i\delta_t + K_{tu}^i\delta_u \qquad \textbf{(5-1e)}$$

$$p_u^i = \qquad + K_{ut}^i\delta_t + K_{uu}^i\delta_u \qquad \textbf{(5-1f)}$$

or

$$[\mathbf{m}]_i = [\mathbf{K}]_i[\boldsymbol{\delta}]_i \qquad \textbf{(5-2a)}$$

where the matrices are defined as

$$[\mathbf{m}]_i = \begin{bmatrix} m_p \\ m_q \\ p_r \\ p_s \\ p_t \\ p_u \end{bmatrix}_i \qquad \textbf{(5-2b)}$$

$$[\boldsymbol{\delta}]_i = \begin{bmatrix} \theta_p \\ \theta_q \\ \delta_r \\ \delta_s \\ \delta_t \\ \delta_u \end{bmatrix}_i \tag{5-2c}$$

and

$$[\mathbf{K}]_i = \begin{array}{c} \begin{array}{cccccc} p & q & r & s & t & u \end{array} \\ \left[\begin{array}{cccccc} K_{pp} & K_{pq} & K_{pr} & K_{ps} & 0 & 0 \\ K_{qp} & K_{qq} & K_{qr} & K_{qs} & 0 & 0 \\ K_{rp} & K_{rq} & K_{rr} & K_{rs} & 0 & 0 \\ K_{sp} & K_{sq} & K_{sr} & K_{ss} & 0 & 0 \\ 0 & 0 & 0 & 0 & K_{tt} & K_{tu} \\ 0 & 0 & 0 & 0 & K_{ut} & K_{uu} \end{array}\right]_i \end{array} \begin{array}{c} \\ p \\ q \\ r \\ s \\ t \\ u \end{array} \tag{5-2d}$$

Comparing Eqs. (5-1) with Eqs. (4-1) of Chapter 4, it is seen that the first four equations of (5-1) are the same as the four equations of (4-1), and only the last two independent equations of (5-1) are needed to account for the effect of axial deformations. Therefore, using Expression (4-9) of Table 4-1, the member stiffness matrix of Expression (5-2d) can be written as shown in Table 5-1, Expression (5-3).

Table 5-1

MEMBER STIFFNESS MATRIX

(Local Axes System)

$$[\mathbf{K}]_i = \begin{array}{c} \begin{array}{cccccc} p & q & r & s & t & u \end{array} \\ \left[\begin{array}{cccccc} K_{pp} & K_{pq} & \left(\frac{K_{pp}+K_{pq}}{L}\right) & -\left(\frac{K_{pp}+K_{pq}}{L}\right) & 0 & 0 \\ K_{qp} & K_{qq} & \left(\frac{K_{qp}+K_{qq}}{L}\right) & -\left(\frac{K_{qp}+K_{qq}}{L}\right) & 0 & 0 \\ \left(\frac{K_{pp}+K_{qp}}{L}\right) & \left(\frac{K_{pq}+K_{qq}}{L}\right) & \left(\frac{K_{pp}+K_{pq}+K_{qp}+K_{qq}}{L^2}\right) & -\left(\frac{K_{pp}+K_{pq}+K_{qp}+K_{qq}}{L^2}\right) & 0 & 0 \\ -\left(\frac{K_{pp}+K_{qp}}{L}\right) & -\left(\frac{K_{pq}+K_{qq}}{L}\right) & -\left(\frac{K_{pp}+K_{pq}+K_{qp}+K_{qq}}{L^2}\right) & \left(\frac{K_{pp}+K_{pq}+K_{qp}+K_{qq}}{L^2}\right) & 0 & 0 \\ 0 & 0 & 0 & 0 & K_{tt} & K_{tu} \\ 0 & 0 & 0 & 0 & K_{ut} & K_{uu} \end{array}\right]_i \end{array} \begin{array}{c} \\ p \\ q \\ r \\ s \\ t \\ u \end{array} \tag{5-3}$$

5-3.2 Evaluation of Extensional Stiffness Coefficients

The four new terms that have been introduced into the member stiffness matrix, K^i_{tt}, K^i_{tu}, K^i_{ut}, and K^i_{uu}, are referred to as the ***extensional stiffness coefficients.***

These four stiffness coefficients can be evaluated for a given beam element drawing on fundamental concepts of mechanics of materials.

If an axial load P is applied to a beam element of uniform cross-section, the member will experience a change in length of

$$\delta_a = \frac{PL}{AE} \tag{5-4}$$

where L is the original length of the member, A is the cross-sectional area, and E is the modulus of elasticity. Hence, the axial load required to impose a specified axial deformation is

$$P = \frac{AE\delta_a}{L} \tag{5-5}$$

For a unit axial translation ($\delta_t = 1$) imposed at the j-end of a member with a uniform cross-section with the k-end held in position, as shown in Fig. 5-2(a), the end actions required to maintain equilibrium of the deformed member are

$$K_{tt}^i = \frac{AE}{L} \tag{5-6a}$$

and

$$K_{ut}^i = \frac{-AE}{L} \tag{5-6b}$$

Similarly, for a unit axial translation ($\delta_u = 1$) of the k-end of the member while the j-end is held in position [Fig. 5-2(b)], the end actions required to maintain equilibrium are

$$K_{tu}^i = \frac{-AE}{L} \tag{5-6c}$$

and

$$K_{uu}^i = \frac{AE}{L} \tag{5-6d}$$

Thus, using the information given in Expressions (4-16) and (5-6), the member stiffness matrix of Expression (5-3) can be written for a prismatic beam element:

$$[\mathbf{K}]_i = \begin{array}{c} \begin{array}{cccccc} p & q & r & s & t & u \end{array} \\ \left[\begin{array}{cccccc} \frac{4EI}{L} & \frac{2EI}{L} & \frac{6EI}{L^2} & \frac{-6EI}{L^2} & 0 & 0 \\ \frac{2EI}{L} & \frac{4EI}{L} & \frac{6EI}{L^2} & \frac{-6EI}{L^2} & 0 & 0 \\ \frac{6EI}{L^2} & \frac{6EI}{L^2} & \frac{12EI}{L^3} & \frac{-12EI}{L^3} & 0 & 0 \\ \frac{-6EI}{L^2} & \frac{-6EI}{L^2} & \frac{-12EI}{L^3} & \frac{12EI}{L^3} & 0 & 0 \\ 0 & 0 & 0 & 0 & \frac{AE}{L} & \frac{-AE}{L} \\ 0 & 0 & 0 & 0 & \frac{-AE}{L} & \frac{AE}{L} \end{array}\right]_i \end{array} \begin{array}{c} p \\ q \\ r \\ s \\ t \\ u \end{array} \tag{5-7}$$

If a nonprismatic beam element is described as a member with segments of constant cross-sectional area as well as constant moment of inertia, the axial deformation δ_a caused by an applied axial force P can be evaluated by the equation

$$\delta_a = P \sum_1^n \left(\frac{L_n}{A_n E} \right) \tag{5-8}$$

where L_n is the segment length, A_n is the cross-sectional area of the segment, and n is the number of segments. Thus, the axial force required to impose a specified axial deformation is defined as

$$P = \delta_a \sum_1^n \left(\frac{A_n E}{L_n} \right) \tag{5-9}$$

The four extensional stiffness coefficients identified in Fig. 5-2 can be defined using Eq. (5-9) as

$$K_{tt}^i = \sum_1^n \left(\frac{A_n E}{L_n} \right) \tag{5-10a}$$

$$K_{tu}^i = -\sum_1^n \left(\frac{A_n E}{L_n} \right) \tag{5-10b}$$

$$K_{tu}^i = -\sum_1^n \left(\frac{A_n E}{L_n} \right) \tag{5-10c}$$

$$K_{uu}^i = \sum_1^n \left(\frac{A_n E}{L_n} \right) \tag{5-10d}$$

In order to establish the member stiffness matrix of Expression (5-3) for a nonprismatic beam element, the rotational stiffness coefficients can be evaluated from a flexibility analysis of the member as discussed in Sec. 4-2.2, Chapter 4.

5-3.3 Exercises

1. Determine the four extensional stiffness coefficients for the nonprismatic beam element described in Fig. 5-4(a). The modulus of elasticity E is a constant for the member.

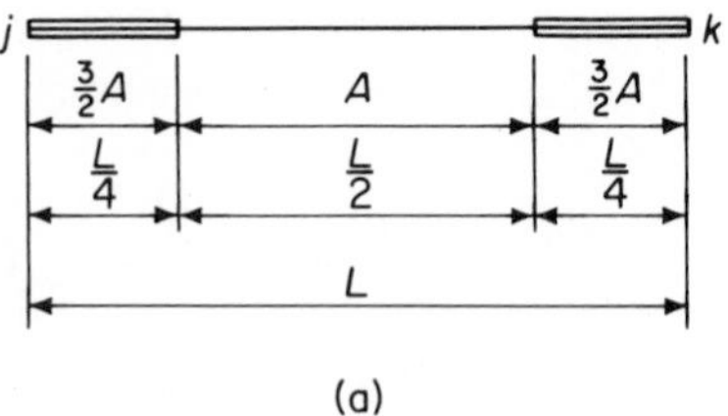

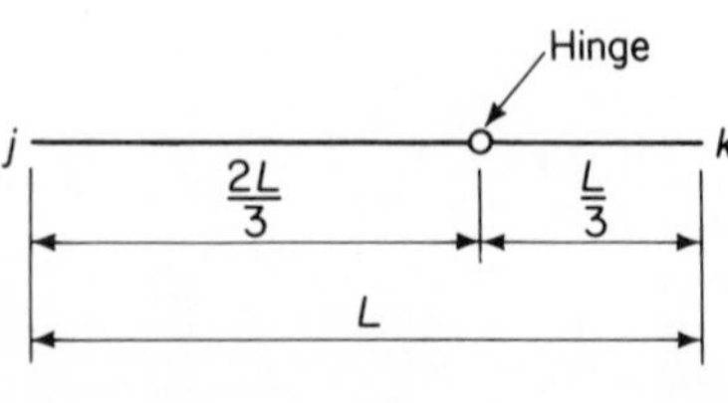

Fig. 5-4 Exercises.

2. Establish the member stiffness matrix of Expression (5-3) for the prismatic beam element with an intermediate hinge described in Fig. 5-4(b); E, I, and A are constant.

5–4
Transformation of Coordinate Systems

Consider the two sets of orthogonal axes, x_1–x_2 and y_1–y_2, with a common origin at O where the axes y_1–y_2 are rotated *counterclockwise* from the axes x_1–x_2 by an angle γ (Fig. 5-5). Defining the ***direction cosine*** as *the cosine of the angle between two axes*, the position of the y_1 axis with respect to the x_1 and the x_2 axes can be described by the direction cosines C_{11} and C_{12}, respectively, where

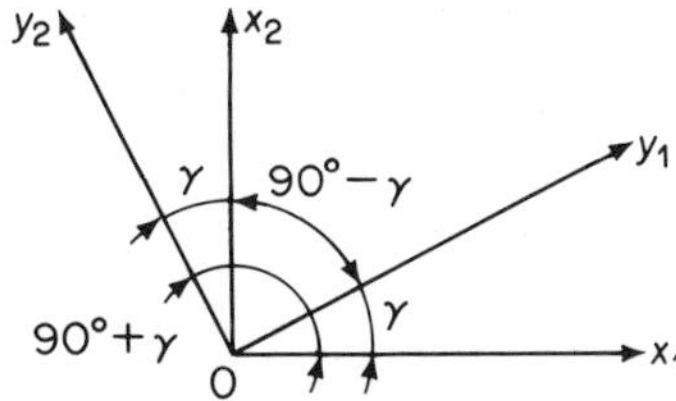

Fig. 5-5 Orientation of x_1–x_2 and y_1–y_2 axes.

$$C_{11} = \cos\gamma \tag{5-11a}$$

$$C_{12} = \cos(90° - \gamma) = \sin\gamma \tag{5-11b}$$

and the position of the y_2 axis with respect to the x_1 and x_2 axes can be described by the direction cosines C_{21} and C_{22}, respectively, where

$$C_{21} = \cos(90° + \gamma) = -\sin\gamma \tag{5-11c}$$

$$C_{22} = \cos\gamma$$

When defining the above direction cosines, the *first subscript* refers to the y_1–y_2 axes and the *second subscript* refers to the x_1–x_2 axes; the label 1 refers to the 1-axis of the particular system and the label 2 refers to the 2-axis of the system.

Now, consider a general vector V, which could represent either an end displacement or an end force of a member in a structural system, positioned in a plane acting through the origin of the two sets of orthogonal axes, x_1–x_2 and y_1–y_2, as shown in Fig. 5-6. This vector V can be described by its components in either of the two systems of orthogonal axes—i.e., by V_1 and V_2 in the y_1–y_2 system or $\bar{V}_1$ and $\bar{V}_2$ in the x_1–x_2 system—and a relationship between these two sets of orthogonal components of the vector V can be established as follows:

Inasmuch as the vector $\bar{V}_1$ in the x_1–x_2 system can be resolved into components in the y_1–y_2 system as

$$\bar{V}_1 \cos\gamma$$

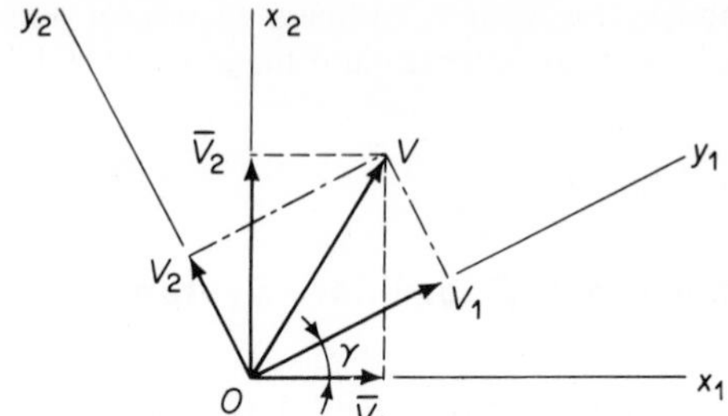

Fig. 5-6 Components of general vector with respect to x_1–x_2 and y_1–y_2 axes.

along the y_1 axis and

$$-\bar{V}_1 \sin \gamma$$

along the y_2 axis, and the vector $\bar{V}_2$, also in the x_1–x_2 system, can be resolved into components in the y_1–y_2 system as

$$\bar{V}_2 \cos \gamma$$

along the y_2 axis and

$$\bar{V}_2 \sin \gamma$$

along the y_1 axis, the total component of the two vectors $\bar{V}_1$ and $\bar{V}_2$ along the y_1 axis is found to be

$$V_1 = \bar{V}_1 \cos \gamma + \bar{V}_2 \sin \gamma \tag{5-12a}$$

and the total component along the y_2 axis is found to be

$$V_2 = -\bar{V}_1 \sin \gamma + \bar{V}_2 \cos \gamma \tag{5-12b}$$

Using the direction cosines of Expression (5-11), Eqs. (5-12) can be rewritten as

$$V_1 = C_{11}\bar{V}_1 + C_{12}\bar{V}_2 \tag{5-13a}$$

$$V_2 = C_{21}\bar{V}_1 + C_{22}V_2 \tag{5-13b}$$

and expressed in matrix form as

$$\begin{bmatrix} V_1 \\ V_2 \end{bmatrix} = \begin{bmatrix} C_{11} & C_{12} \\ C_{21} & C_{22} \end{bmatrix} \begin{bmatrix} \bar{V}_1 \\ \bar{V}_2 \end{bmatrix} \tag{5-14a}$$

or

$$[\mathbf{V}] = [\mathbf{C}][\bar{\mathbf{V}}] \tag{5-14b}$$

where the matrix $[\mathbf{V}]$ represents the components of the general vector V in the y_1–y_2 system; the matrix $[\bar{\mathbf{V}}]$ represents the components of the general vector V in the x_1–x_2 system; and the matrix $[\mathbf{C}]$ is the ***rotation matrix*** *from the x_1–x_2 system to the y_1–y_2 system.*

Similarly, resolving the vectors V_1 and V_2 of the y_1–y_2 system into components in the x_1–x_2 system, the total component along the x_1 axis is equal to

$$\bar{V}_1 = V_1 \cos \gamma - V_2 \sin \gamma \tag{5-15a}$$

and along the x_2 axis the total component is equal to

$$\bar{V}_2 = V_1 \sin \gamma + V_2 \cos \gamma \tag{5-15b}$$

Employing the proper direction cosines from Expressions (5-11), Eqs. (5-15) can be expressed as

$$\bar{V}_1 = C_{11}V_1 + C_{21}V_2 \tag{5-16a}$$

$$\bar{V}_2 = C_{12}V_1 + C_{22}V_2 \tag{5-16b}$$

which could be written in matrix form as

$$\begin{bmatrix} \bar{V}_1 \\ \bar{V}_2 \end{bmatrix} = \begin{bmatrix} C_{11} & C_{21} \\ C_{12} & C_{22} \end{bmatrix} \begin{bmatrix} V_1 \\ V_2 \end{bmatrix} \tag{5-17a}$$

or

$$[\bar{\mathbf{V}}] = [\mathbf{C}]^T[\mathbf{V}] \tag{5-17b}$$

where the matrix $[\mathbf{C}]^T$ is the ***rotation matrix*** *from the y_1–y_2 system to the x_1–x_2 system.*

Comparing Eqs. (5-14) and (5-17), it is seen that the rotation matrix of Eq. (5-17) is the *transpose* of the rotation matrix [C] of Eq. (5-14). Also, in rewriting Eq. (5-14) to solve for the components of the general vector V in the x_1–x_2 system, i.e.,

$$[\bar{\mathbf{V}}] = [\mathbf{C}]^{-1}[\mathbf{V}] \tag{5-18}$$

the *inverse* of the rotation matrix [C] is seen to be equal to the *transpose* of the matrix, i.e.,

$$[\mathbf{C}]^{-1} = [\mathbf{C}]^T \tag{5-19}$$

hence, the rotation matrix [C] is said to be *orthogonal.*

5–5 Analysis of Rigid Frame Structure

5-5.1 Transformation Matrix: Beam Element

Consider the restrained beam element i with its set of local axes (x_m–y_m) positioned in the frame of a second set of axes, i.e., the reference axes (X–Y), such that the member axis x_m is rotated from the X-axis of the reference system by an angle γ (Fig. 5-7). For general end displacements of the restrained member, the components of end actions have been defined with respect to the local axes [Figs. 5-3 and 5-7(a)]; however, from Eqs. (5-16), the components of end force with respect to the local axes (p_r, p_s, p_t, and p_u) can be resolved into components of end force with respect to the reference axes [Fig. 5-7(b)], where

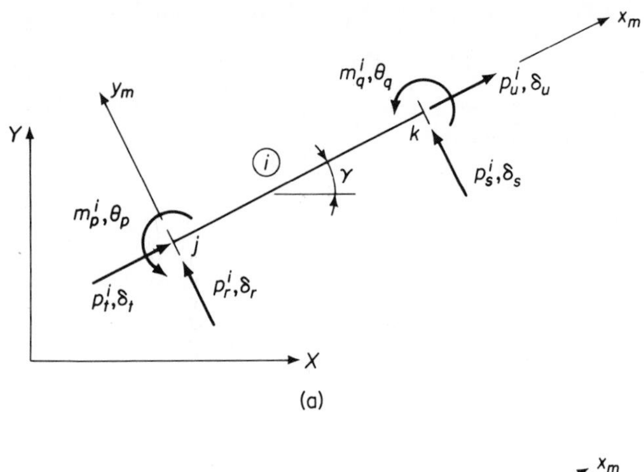

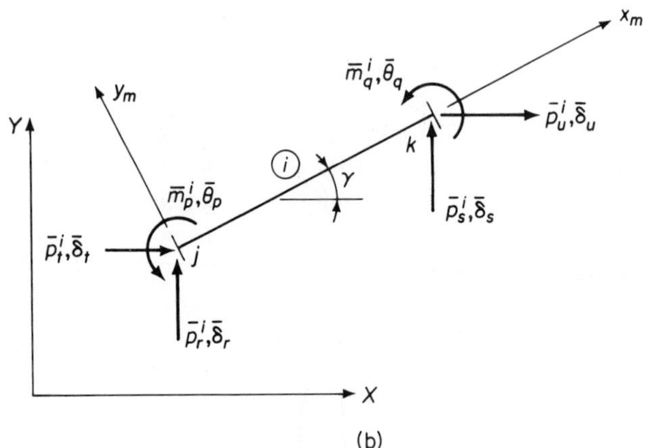

Fig. 5-7 Components of end action and displacement for beam element with restrained ends: (a) local system; (b) reference system.

$$\bar{p}_r^i = C_{22}p_r^i + C_{12}p_t^i \quad \textbf{(5-20a)}$$

$$\bar{p}_s^i = C_{22}p_s^i + C_{12}p_u^i \quad \textbf{(5-20b)}$$

$$\bar{p}_t^i = C_{21}p_r^i + C_{11}p_t^i \quad \textbf{(5-20c)}$$

$$\bar{p}_u^i = C_{21}p_s^i + C_{11}p_u^i \quad \textbf{(5-20d)}$$

and the end moments, which are independent of the orientation of the system of axes, can be defined with respect to the reference axes as

$$\bar{m}_p^i = m_p^i \quad \textbf{(5-20e)}$$

$$\bar{m}_q^i = m_q^i \quad \textbf{(5-20f)}$$

Rearranging to conform to the ordering of Eqs. (5-1), Eqs. (5-20) can be expressed in matrix form as

$$\begin{bmatrix} \bar{m}_p \\ \bar{m}_q \\ \bar{p}_r \\ \bar{p}_s \\ \bar{p}_t \\ \bar{p}_u \end{bmatrix}_i = \begin{bmatrix} 1 & 0 & 0 & 0 & 0 & 0 \\ 0 & 1 & 0 & 0 & 0 & 0 \\ 0 & 0 & C_{22} & 0 & C_{12} & 0 \\ 0 & 0 & 0 & C_{22} & 0 & C_{12} \\ 0 & 0 & C_{21} & 0 & C_{11} & 0 \\ 0 & 0 & 0 & C_{21} & 0 & C_{11} \end{bmatrix}_i \begin{bmatrix} m_p \\ m_q \\ p_r \\ p_s \\ p_t \\ p_u \end{bmatrix}_i \quad \textbf{(5-21)}$$

or, with reference to Eqs. (5-17), as

$$[\bar{\mathbf{m}}]_i = [\mathbf{T}]_i^T[\mathbf{m}]_i \quad \textbf{(5-22)}$$

where the matrix $[\mathbf{m}]_i$ represents the components of end action for member i in the frame of the system of *local axes;* the matrix $[\bar{\mathbf{m}}]_i$ represents the components of end action for member i in the frame of the system of *reference axes;* and the matrix $[\mathbf{T}]_i^T$ is the *transformation matrix rotating from the local system to the reference system* and is the transpose of the matrix $[\mathbf{T}]_i$ which is defined in Eq. (5-25).

By Eqs. (5-13), the components of end force in the frame of the local axes can be expressed in terms of the components of end force in the frame of the reference axes as

$$p_r^i = C_{22}\bar{p}_r^i + C_{21}\bar{p}_t^i \quad \textbf{(5-23a)}$$

$$p_s^i = C_{22}\bar{p}_s^i + C_{21}\bar{p}_u^i \quad \textbf{(5-23b)}$$

$$p_t^i = C_{12}\bar{p}_r^i + C_{11}\bar{p}_t^i \quad \textbf{(5-23c)}$$

$$p_u^i = C_{12}\bar{p}_s^i + C_{11}\bar{p}_u^i \quad \textbf{(5-23d)}$$

Also,

$$m_p^i = \bar{m}_p^i \quad \textbf{(5-23e)}$$

$$m_q^i = \bar{m}_q^i \quad \textbf{(5-23f)}$$

Equations 5-23 can be expressed in matrix form as

$$\begin{bmatrix} m_p \\ m_q \\ p_r \\ p_s \\ p_t \\ p_u \end{bmatrix}_i = \begin{bmatrix} 1 & 0 & 0 & 0 & 0 & 0 \\ 0 & 1 & 0 & 0 & 0 & 0 \\ 0 & 0 & C_{22} & 0 & C_{21} & 0 \\ 0 & 0 & 0 & C_{22} & 0 & C_{21} \\ 0 & 0 & C_{12} & 0 & C_{11} & 0 \\ 0 & 0 & 0 & C_{12} & 0 & C_{11} \end{bmatrix}_i \begin{bmatrix} \bar{m}_p \\ \bar{m}_q \\ \bar{p}_r \\ \bar{p}_s \\ \bar{p}_t \\ \bar{p}_u \end{bmatrix}_i \quad \textbf{(5-24)}$$

or

$$[\mathbf{m}]_i = [\mathbf{T}]_i[\bar{\mathbf{m}}]_i \quad \textbf{(5-25)}$$

where the matrix $[\mathbf{T}]_i$ is the *transformation matrix rotating from the reference axes to the local axes* and is defined as the ***transformation matrix***.

Solving Eq. (5-25) for the components of end action with respect to the reference axes and comparing the resulting equation with Eq. (5-22), it is seen that

$$[\mathbf{T}]_i^{-1} = [\mathbf{T}]_i^T \tag{5-26}$$

i.e., the matrix $[\mathbf{T}]_i$ is *orthogonal.*

Similarly, the relationship between the components of end displacement of member i with respect to the local axes x_m–y_m and the reference axes X–Y (Fig. 5-7) can be established as

$$[\bar{\boldsymbol{\delta}}]_i = [\mathbf{T}]_i^T[\boldsymbol{\delta}]_i \tag{5-27}$$

and

$$[\boldsymbol{\delta}]_i = [\mathbf{T}]_i[\bar{\boldsymbol{\delta}}]_i \tag{5-28}$$

where the matrix $[\boldsymbol{\delta}]_i$ represents the components of end displacement in the system of *local axes,* and the matrix $[\bar{\boldsymbol{\delta}}]_i$ represents the components of end displacement in the system of *reference axes,* i.e.,

$$[\delta]_i = \begin{bmatrix} \theta_p \\ \theta_q \\ \delta_r \\ \delta_s \\ \delta_t \\ \delta_u \end{bmatrix}_i \tag{5-29a}$$

and

$$[\bar{\boldsymbol{\delta}}]_i = \begin{bmatrix} \bar{\theta}_p \\ \bar{\theta}_q \\ \bar{\delta}_r \\ \bar{\delta}_s \\ \bar{\delta}_t \\ \bar{\delta}_u \end{bmatrix}_i \tag{5-29b}$$

In identifying the end actions and displacements for the typical beam element i (Fig. 5-7), the subscripts p and q refer to a moment or rotation at the j- and k-ends, respectively; the subscripts r and s refer to a force or translation in the y-direction of either the local or reference system of axes at the j- and k-ends, respectively; and the subscripts t and u refer to a force or translation in the x-direction of either system of axes at the j- and k-ends, respectively.

Now, introducing the constants

$$C_x = \cos \gamma \tag{5-30a}$$

and

$$C_y = \cos (90^\circ - \gamma) \tag{5-30b}$$

where the angle γ is measured *counterclockwise* from the X-axis of the reference system to the member axis x_m (Fig. 5-7), the direction cosines of Expressions (5-11), which describe the orientation of the local axes of member i with respect to the reference axes, can be expressed as

$$C_{11} = C_x \tag{5-31a}$$

$$C_{12} = C_y \tag{5-31b}$$

$$C_{21} = -C_y \tag{5-31c}$$

$$C_{22} = C_x \tag{5-31d}$$

and the transformation matrix $[\mathbf{T}]_i$ for member i can be written as

$$[\mathbf{T}]_i = \begin{bmatrix} 1 & 0 & 0 & 0 & 0 & 0 \\ 0 & 1 & 0 & 0 & 0 & 0 \\ 0 & 0 & C_x & 0 & -C_y & 0 \\ 0 & 0 & 0 & C_x & 0 & -C_y \\ 0 & 0 & C_y & 0 & C_x & 0 \\ 0 & 0 & 0 & C_y & 0 & C_x \end{bmatrix}_i \tag{5-32}$$

Referring to Fig. 5-8, the direction cosines C_x and C_y defined by Expressions (5-30) can be expressed in terms of the X, Y coordinates of the ends of the member i as

$$C_x = \frac{X_k - X_j}{L_i} \tag{5-33a}$$

and

$$C_y = \frac{Y_k - Y_j}{L_i} \tag{5-33b}$$

with

$$L_i = \sqrt{(X_k - X_j)^2 + (Y_k - Y_j)^2} \tag{5-34}$$

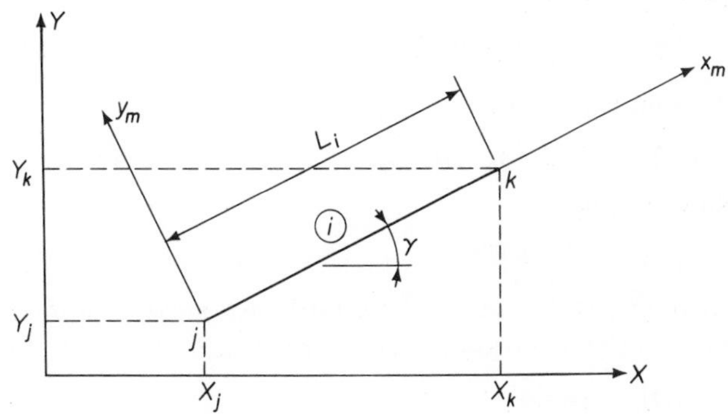

Fig. 5-8 Orientation of beam element i in frame of reference axes.

where (X_j, Y_j) are the coordinates of end j of member i in the reference system of axes; (X_k, Y_k) are the coordinates of end k in the reference system of axes; and L_i is the length of the member. The proper signs for the direction cosines C_x and C_y will result when making the required substitution into Eqs. (5-33) regardless of the orientation of the member within the frame of the X–Y system; however, before Eqs. (5-33) can be used, the j- and k-ends of the member must be designated, thus establishing the orientation of the x_m–y_m axes.

5-5.2 Member Stiffness Matrix with Respect to Reference Axes

For the restrained beam element i (Fig. 5-3), the relationship between the components of general end displacement ($\theta_p, \theta_q, \delta_r, \delta_s, \delta_t$, and δ_u) described with respect to the local axes, and the resulting components of restraining end action ($m_p, m_q, \delta_r, \delta_s, \delta_t$, and δ_u), also described with respect to the local axes of the member, has been established in Eqs. (5-1) and expressed in matrix form as

$$[\mathbf{m}]_i = [\mathbf{K}]_i[\boldsymbol{\delta}]_i \tag{5-2a}$$

When developing Eq. (5-2a) for a beam element of a structural system, the components of end displacement which correspond to the components of displacement of the joints that are connected by the member will be defined initially with respect to the arbitrary set of reference axes X–Y of the structure. For this reason, the components of end displacement which appear in Eq. (5-2a) can be defined in terms of components of end displacement in the frame of the reference axes according to Eq. (5-28). Also, by Eq. (5-25), the components of end action required to maintain static equilibrium of the restrained member when subjected to the general end displacements can be expressed in terms of components with respect to the reference axes. Thus, substituting Eqs. (5-25) and (5-28) into Eq. (5-2a) yields

$$[\mathbf{T}]_i[\bar{\mathbf{m}}]_i = [\mathbf{K}]_i[\mathbf{T}]_i[\bar{\boldsymbol{\delta}}]_i \tag{5-35}$$

which can be rewritten as

$$[\bar{\mathbf{m}}]_i = [\mathbf{T}]_i^{-1}[\mathbf{K}]_i[\mathbf{T}]_i[\bar{\boldsymbol{\delta}}]_i \tag{5-36}$$

or, from Eq. (5-26),

$$[\bar{\mathbf{m}}]_i = [\mathbf{T}]_i^{T}[\mathbf{K}]_i[\mathbf{T}]_i[\bar{\boldsymbol{\delta}}]_i \tag{5-37}$$

Now, letting

$$[\bar{\mathbf{K}}]_i = [\mathbf{T}]_i^{T}[\mathbf{K}]_i[\mathbf{T}]_i \tag{5-38}$$

where $[\bar{\mathbf{K}}]_i$ is defined as the ***transformed member stiffness matrix*** written with respect to the arbitrary system of *reference axes X–Y*, Eq. (5–37) becomes

$$[\bar{\mathbf{m}}]_i = [\bar{\mathbf{K}}]_i[\bar{\boldsymbol{\delta}}]_i \tag{5-39}$$

which describes the relationship between the components of end displacement and end action of member i in the frame of the reference axes.

Table 5-2

TRANSFORMED MEMBER STIFFNESS MATRIX

(Reference Axes System)

$$[\bar{\mathbf{K}}]_i = \begin{array}{c} \\ \\ \\ \\ \\ \\ \end{array}\overset{\begin{array}{cccccc} \bar{p} & \bar{q} & \bar{r} & \bar{s} & \bar{t} & \bar{u} \end{array}}{\begin{bmatrix} K_{pp} & K_{pq} & C_xK_{pr} & C_xK_{ps} & -C_yK_{pr} & -C_yK_{ps} \\ K_{qp} & K_{qq} & C_xK_{qr} & C_xK_{qs} & -C_yK_{qr} & -C_yK_{qs} \\ C_xK_{rp} & C_xK_{rq} & C_x^2K_{rr} + C_y^2K_{tt} & C_x^2K_{rs} + C_y^2K_{tu} & C_xC_yK_{tt} - C_xC_yK_{rr} & C_xC_yK_{tu} - C_xC_yK_{rs} \\ C_xK_{sp} & C_xK_{sq} & C_x^2K_{sr} + C_y^2K_{ut} & C_x^2K_{ss} + C_y^2K_{uu} & C_xC_yK_{ut} - C_xC_yK_{sr} & C_xC_yK_{uu} - C_xC_yK_{ss} \\ -C_yK_{rp} & -C_yK_{rq} & C_xC_yK_{tt} - C_xC_yK_{rr} & C_xC_yK_{tu} - C_xC_yK_{rs} & C_x^2K_{tt} + C_y^2K_{rr} & C_x^2K_{tu} + C_y^2K_{rs} \\ -C_yK_{sp} & -C_yK_{sq} & C_xC_yK_{ut} - C_xC_yK_{sr} & C_xC_yK_{uu} - C_xC_yK_{ss} & C_x^2K_{ut} + C_y^2K_{sr} & C_x^2K_{uu} + C_y^2K_{ss} \end{bmatrix}_i} \begin{array}{c} \bar{p} \\ \bar{q} \\ \bar{r} \\ \bar{s} \\ \bar{t} \\ \bar{u} \end{array} \tag{5-40}$$

Performing the matrix operations indicated in Eq. (5-38), the transformed member stiffness matrix $[\bar{\mathbf{K}}]_i$, defined with respect to an arbitrary system of orthogonal axes, can be written as given in Table 5-2, Expression (5-40). The columns of the matrix are labeled to correspond to the labeling of the associated components of end displacement and the rows are labeled to correspond to the labeling of the associated components of end action, both in the frame of the reference axes, to establish the ordering of the matrix.

Now that the various member stiffness matrices can be written with respect to the single set of orthogonal axes X–Y, the complete structure stiffness matrix can be developed with respect to this system of axes.

5-5.3 Equations of Analysis

The analysis of a structural system by the stiffness method entails the development of the system of equations

$$[\mathbf{S}_c][\boldsymbol{\Delta}_c] = [\mathbf{JL}_c] + [\mathbf{R}_c] \tag{4-32}$$

which must be written with respect to a single set of coordinate axes, i.e., the reference axes; from this system of equations, the independent components of unrestrained joint displacement are evaluated by solving that set of equations expressed as

$$[\mathbf{S}_{uu}][\boldsymbol{\Delta}_u] = [\mathbf{JL}_u] \tag{4-36}$$

and the components of support reaction are determined by solving that set of equations expressed as

$$[\mathbf{S}_{ru}][\boldsymbol{\Delta}_u] - [\mathbf{JL}_r] = [\mathbf{R}_r] \tag{4-39}$$

The primary problem is one of developing the various matrices. The procedure for this is essentially the same as that described in Chapter 4 for the analysis of the planar orthogonal frame; the few exceptions will be discussed in the following paragraphs.

As a first step in developing the equations for analyzing a particular structure, the elements and joints of the structure should be labeled, separately, and the j- and k-end of each element identified. The choice of end to be designated as the j-end for each member is *immaterial*; however, as with the labeling of the elements and joints, some logical pattern should be followed just as a matter of good practice. With the selection of the j-end for a member, the local member axes x_m–y_m are automatically positioned: the origin is at the j-end with the positive x_m axis directed toward the k-end and the positive y_m axis rotated *counterclockwise* 90° to the x_m axis.

Next, the X–Y reference axes for the structure must be established. Then, the direction cosines C_x and C_y defined by Eqs. (5-30) or (5-33), as well as the transformation matrix $[\mathbf{T}]_i$ of Expression (5-32), can be evaluated for each member of the structure.

To set the order of the matrices of Eq. (4-32), identify and label (number) all possible independent components of joint displacement (rotation and translation) with respect to the X–Y axes—***labeling the unrestrained components of displacement first and then the components of restrained displacement*** as demonstrated in Fig. 5-9. With this the elements of the complete joint displacement matrix $[\mathbf{\Delta}_c]$ are defined, appearing in the order of their labeling.

In developing the complete joint load matrix $[\mathbf{JL}_c]$, the joint loads acting on the restrained structure must be described in terms of components in the frame of the X–Y reference axes; these components of joint load, which are the elements of the matrix $[\mathbf{JL}_c]$, must be given the same label as their corresponding component of joint displacement so that the elements of the complete joint load

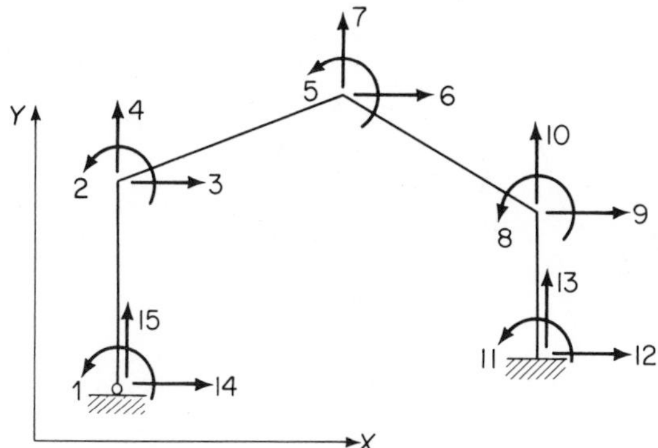

Fig. 5-9 Labeling of possible components of joint displacement.

matrix $[\mathbf{JL}_c]$ will appear in the same sequence as the corresponding elements of the complete joint displacement matrix $[\mathbf{\Delta}_c]$. When computing the equivalent joint loads for a disturbance applied along the span of a member, the components of fixed end actions calculated with respect to the local axes of the member [Fig. 5-10(a)] can be resolved into components in the frame of the reference axes [Fig. 5-10(b)] in keeping with Eq. (5-22) as

$$[\overline{\mathbf{FM}}] = [\mathbf{T}]_i^T[\mathbf{FM}] \tag{5-41}$$

where

$$[\mathbf{FM}]_i = \begin{bmatrix} FM_p \\ FM_q \\ FP_r \\ FP_s \\ FP_t \\ FP_u \end{bmatrix}_i \tag{5-42a}$$

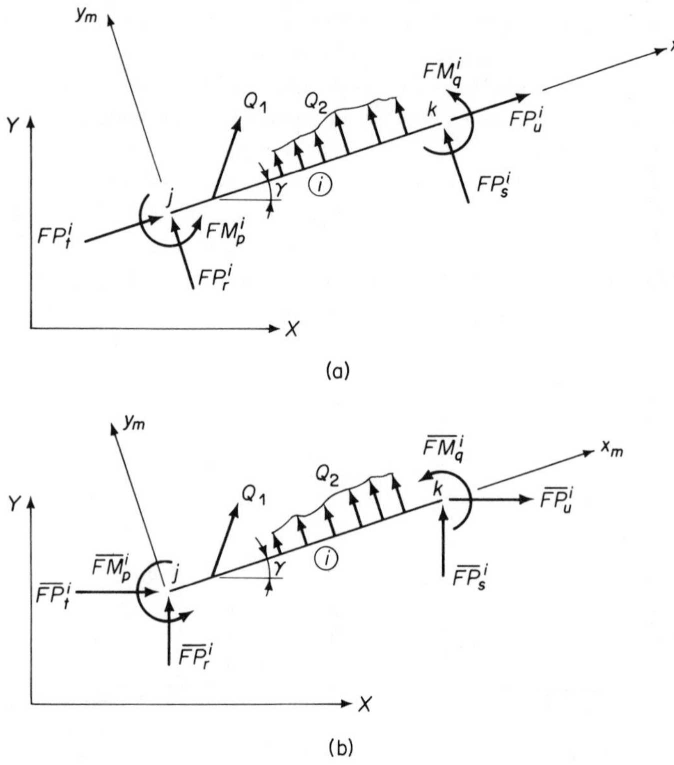

Fig. 5-10 Components of fixed end action for beam element with both ends restrained.

and

$$[\overline{\mathbf{FM}}]_i = \begin{bmatrix} \overline{FM}_p \\ \overline{FM}_q \\ \overline{FP}_r \\ \overline{FP}_s \\ \overline{FP}_t \\ \overline{FP}_u \end{bmatrix}_i \tag{5-42b}$$

Now, the ***fixed end actions*** in the frame of the reference axes ***transform into equivalent joint loads by a reversal in signs*** (Sec. 4-3.3).

The elements of the complete support reaction matrix $[\mathbf{R}_c]$ are established by identifying the independent components of support reaction for the structure with respect to the X–Y axes and giving them the same label as their corresponding component of joint displacement.

If the complete structure stiffness matrix $[\mathbf{S}_c]$ is to be developed by superposition of the numerous member stiffness matrices as suggested in Chapter 4, then these member stiffness matrices must be written with respect to the X–Y reference axes. For a particular member, the transformed member stiffness matrix $[\bar{\mathbf{K}}]_i$, written with respect to the reference coordinate system, can be determined by relating the member to the typical member i of Fig. 5-7 to evaluate the member stiffness coefficients and making the required substitutions into Expression (5-40). The elements of the transformed member stiffness matrix receive the labels of the components of displacement (in the frame of the X–Y axes) of the joints connected by the member. The order of labeling the rows and columns of Expression (5-40) must follow the indicated sequence. The member stiffness matrix $[\mathbf{K}]_i$ which is written with respect to the local axes can be obtained from Expression (5-3).

After solving for the unrestrained components of joint displacement $[\boldsymbol{\Delta}_u]$ as indicated by Eq. (4-36), the ***final end actions*** $[\mathbf{M}]_i$ developed at the ends of the individual members (Fig. 5-11) can be determined by superimposing the end actions resulting from the joint displacements of the system $[\mathbf{m}]_i$ and the fixed end actions $[\mathbf{FM}]_i$ which were used to establish the equivalent joint loads; i.e.,

$$[\mathbf{M}]_i = [\mathbf{m}]_i + [\mathbf{FM}]_i \tag{5-43}$$

or, from Eq. (5-2a),

$$[\mathbf{M}]_i = [\mathbf{K}]_i[\boldsymbol{\delta}]_i + [\mathbf{FM}]_i \tag{5-44}$$

where

$$[\mathbf{M}]_i = \begin{bmatrix} M_q \\ M_t \\ P_r \\ P_s \\ P_t \\ P_u \end{bmatrix}_i \tag{5-45}$$

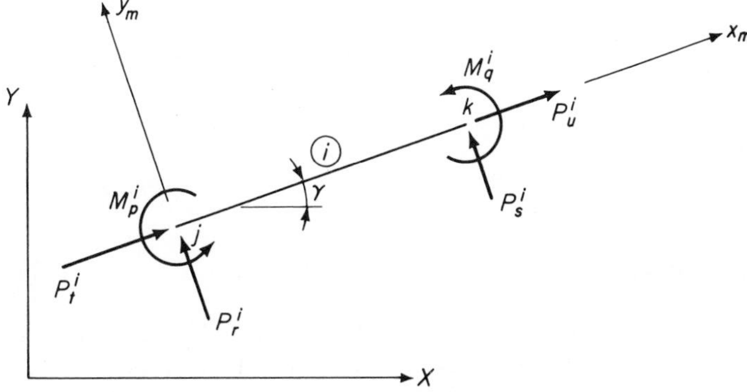

Fig. 5-11 Components of final end action for member with both ends restrained.

which are the components of final end action with respect to the local axes. Since the components of end displacement for member i will more than likely be known with respect to the X–Y reference axes, Eq. (5-44) can be rewritten as

$$[\mathbf{M}]_i = [\mathbf{K}]_i[\mathbf{T}]_i[\bar{\boldsymbol{\delta}}]_i + [\mathbf{FM}]_i \tag{5-46}$$

If desired, the final end actions can be evaluated in terms of components with respect to the X–Y system as

$$[\overline{\mathbf{M}}]_i = [\overline{\mathbf{K}}]_i[\bar{\boldsymbol{\delta}}]_i + [\overline{\mathbf{FM}}]_i \tag{5-47}$$

and the components of final end action with respect to the local axes determined by the expression

$$[\mathbf{M}]_i = [\mathbf{T}]_i[\overline{\mathbf{M}}]_i \tag{5-48}$$

In order to illustrate the application of the stiffness method for the analysis of a nonorthogonal frame, the following example is presented.

Example 5-1. Analyze the rigid frame shown in Fig. 5-12 for the imposed loading condition. For the columns of the structure, the cross-sectional area A is 30 in² and the moment of inertia I about the axis of inplane bending is 3000 in⁴; the cross-sectional area and moment of inertia for the beam are 40 in² and 6000 in⁴, respectively; E is a constant. The joint label is given in the circle next to each member.

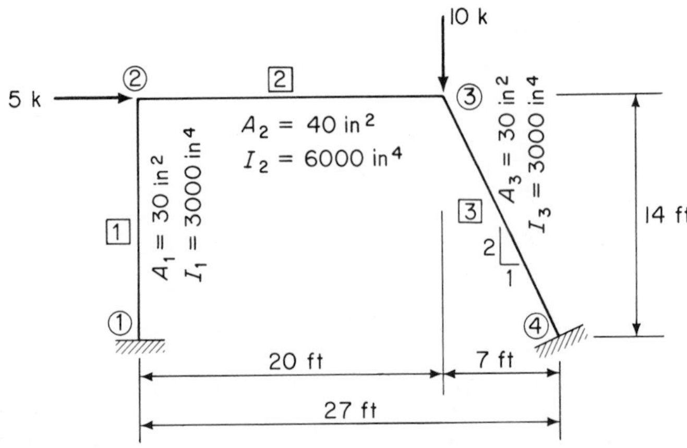

Fig. 5-12 Example 5-1: Rigid frame.

MEMBER INFORMATION

In Fig. 5-13, the j- and k-end for each member have been selected, thus establishing the local member axes for each member. In addition, the reference axes for the structure have been positioned.

The coordinates of the joints of the structure in the frame of the reference axes are given in Table 5-3. The direction cosines for each member, which were computed by

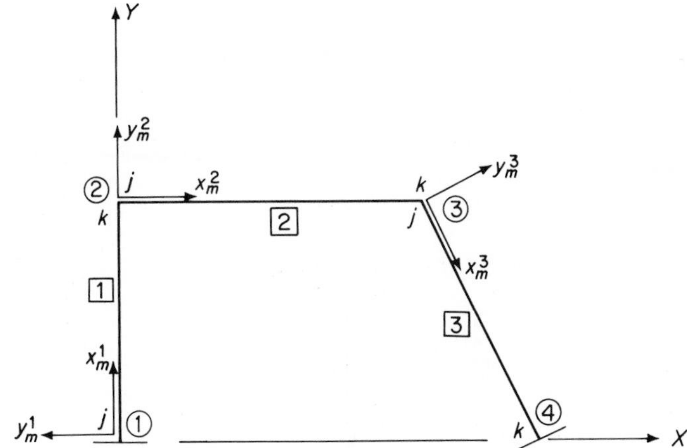

Fig. 5-13 Example 5-1: Establishment of local and reference axes.

Eqs. (5-33), are given in Table 5-4 along with the member's length, cross-sectional area, and moment of inertia.

Table 5-3

	Coordinate	
Joint	*X*, ft	*Y*, ft
1	0	0
2	0	+14.0
3	+20.0	+14.0
4	+27.0	0

Table 5-4

	Joint					Direction Cosine	
Member	*j*	*k*	*A*, ft²	*I*, ft⁴	*Length*, ft	C_x	C_y
1	1	2	0.208	0.145	14.00	0	+1.0
2	2	3	0.278	0.289	20.00	+1.0	0
3	3	4	0.208	0.145	15.65	+0.4473	−0.8946

JOINT DISPLACEMENT MATRIX

The possible independent components of joint displacement in the frame of the X–Y reference axes are identified and labeled as shown in Fig. 5-14; thus, the complete joint displacement matrix can be written as

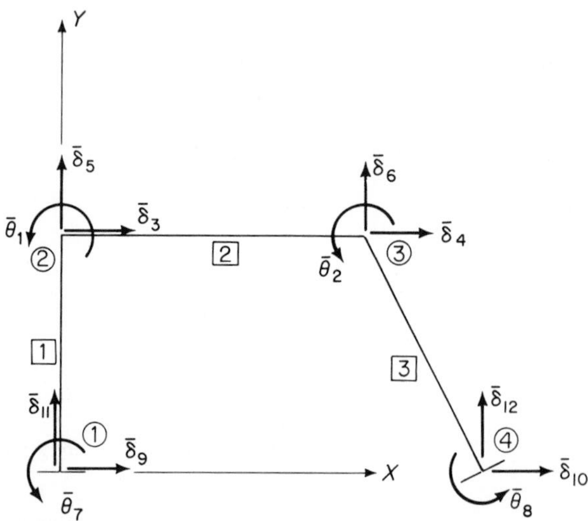

Fig. 5-14 Example 5-1: Identification of components of joint displacement.

$$[\mathbf{\Delta}_c] = \begin{bmatrix} \bar{\theta}_1 \\ \bar{\theta}_2 \\ \bar{\delta}_3 \\ \bar{\delta}_4 \\ \bar{\delta}_5 \\ \bar{\delta}_6 \\ -- \\ \bar{\theta}_7 \\ \bar{\theta}_8 \\ \bar{\delta}_9 \\ \bar{\delta}_{10} \\ \bar{\delta}_{11} \\ \bar{\delta}_{12} \end{bmatrix} = \begin{bmatrix} [\mathbf{\Delta}_u] \\ --- \\ [\mathbf{\Delta}_r] \end{bmatrix} \tag{5-49}$$

MEMBER STIFFNESS MATRICES

Substituting into Expressions (5-7) and (5-40), the member stiffness matrix with respect to the local axes, $[\mathbf{K}]_i$, and with respect to the reference axes, $[\bar{\mathbf{K}}]_i$, can be written for each member of the frame. The rows and columns of the transformed member stiffness matrix $[\bar{\mathbf{K}}]_i$ for each member must be labeled to conform to the labeling of the components of displacement, described with respect to the reference axes, of the joints connected by the member (Fig. 5-14).

Member 1

$$[\mathbf{K}]_1 = E \times 10^{-3} \begin{array}{c} \begin{matrix} p & q & r & s & t & u \end{matrix} \\ \begin{bmatrix} 41.428 & 20.714 & 4.439 & -4.439 & 0 & 0 \\ 20.714 & 41.428 & 4.439 & -4.439 & 0 & 0 \\ 4.439 & 4.439 & 0.634 & -0.634 & 0 & 0 \\ -4.439 & -4.439 & -0.634 & 0.634 & 0 & 0 \\ 0 & 0 & 0 & 0 & 14.857 & -14.857 \\ 0 & 0 & 0 & 0 & -14.857 & 14.857 \end{bmatrix}_1 \end{array} \begin{matrix} p \\ q \\ r \\ s \\ t \\ u \end{matrix} \tag{5-50a}$$

and

$$[\bar{\mathbf{K}}]_1 = E \times 10^{-3} \begin{array}{c} \begin{matrix} 7 & 1 & 11 & 5 & 9 & 3 \end{matrix} \\ \begin{bmatrix} 41.428 & 20.714 & 0 & 0 & -4.439 & 4.439 \\ 20.714 & 41.428 & 0 & 0 & -4.439 & 4.439 \\ 0 & 0 & 14.857 & -14.857 & 0 & 0 \\ 0 & 0 & -14.857 & 14.857 & 0 & 0 \\ -4.439 & -4.439 & 0 & 0 & 0.634 & -0.634 \\ 4.439 & 4.439 & 0 & 0 & -0.634 & 0.634 \end{bmatrix}_1 \\ \begin{matrix} \bar{p} & \bar{q} & \bar{r} & \bar{s} & \bar{t} & \bar{u} \end{matrix} \end{array} \begin{matrix} 7 \\ 1 \\ 11 \\ 5 \\ 9 \\ 3 \end{matrix} \tag{5-50b}$$

Member 2

$$[\mathbf{K}]_2 = E \times 10^{-3} \begin{array}{c} \begin{matrix} p & q & r & s & t & u \end{matrix} \\ \begin{bmatrix} 57.800 & 28.900 & 4.335 & -4.335 & 0 & 0 \\ 28.900 & 57.800 & 4.335 & -4.335 & 0 & 0 \\ 4.335 & 4.335 & 0.434 & -0.434 & 0 & 0 \\ -4.335 & -4.335 & -0.434 & 0.434 & 0 & 0 \\ 0 & 0 & 0 & 0 & 13.900 & -13.900 \\ 0 & 0 & 0 & 0 & -13.900 & 13.900 \end{bmatrix}_2 \end{array} \begin{matrix} p \\ q \\ r \\ s \\ t \\ u \end{matrix} \tag{5-51a}$$

and

$$[\bar{\mathbf{K}}]_2 = E \times 10^{-3} \begin{array}{c} \begin{matrix} 1 & 2 & 5 & 6 & 3 & 4 \end{matrix} \\ \begin{bmatrix} 57.800 & 28.900 & 4.335 & -4.335 & 0 & 0 \\ 28.900 & 57.800 & 4.335 & -4.335 & 0 & 0 \\ 4.335 & 4.335 & 0.434 & -0.434 & 0 & 0 \\ -4.335 & -4.335 & -0.434 & 0.434 & 0 & 0 \\ 0 & 0 & 0 & 0 & 13.900 & -13.900 \\ 0 & 0 & 0 & 0 & -13.900 & 13.900 \end{bmatrix}_2 \\ \begin{matrix} \bar{p} & \bar{q} & \bar{r} & \bar{s} & \bar{t} & \bar{u} \end{matrix} \end{array} \begin{matrix} 1 \\ 2 \\ 5 \\ 6 \\ 3 \\ 4 \end{matrix} \tag{5-51b}$$

Member 3

$$[\mathbf{K}]_3 = E \times 10^{-3} \begin{matrix} p & q & r & s & t & u & \\ \left[\begin{matrix} 37.061 & 18.530 & 3.552 & -3.552 & 0 & 0 \\ 18.530 & 37.061 & 3.552 & -3.552 & 0 & 0 \\ 3.552 & 3.552 & 0.454 & -0.454 & 0 & 0 \\ -3.552 & -3.552 & -0.454 & 0.454 & 0 & 0 \\ 0 & 0 & 0 & 0 & 13.291 & -13.291 \\ 0 & 0 & 0 & 0 & -13.291 & 13.291 \end{matrix}\right]_3 \end{matrix} \begin{matrix} p \\ q \\ r \\ s \\ t \\ u \end{matrix} \tag{5-52a}$$

and

$$[\bar{\mathbf{K}}]_3 = E \times 10^{-3} \begin{matrix} 2 & 8 & 6 & 12 & 4 & 10 \\ \left[\begin{matrix} 37.061 & 18.530 & 1.589 & -1.589 & 3.178 & -3.178 \\ 18.530 & 37.061 & 1.589 & -1.589 & 3.178 & -3.178 \\ 1.589 & 1.589 & 10.728 & -10.728 & -5.137 & 5.137 \\ -1.589 & -1.589 & -10.728 & 10.728 & 5.137 & -5.137 \\ 3.178 & 3.178 & -5.137 & 5.137 & 3.023 & -3.023 \\ -3.178 & -3.178 & 5.137 & -5.137 & -3.023 & 3.023 \end{matrix}\right]_3 \\ \bar{p} & \bar{q} & \bar{r} & \bar{s} & \bar{t} & \bar{u} \end{matrix} \begin{matrix} 2 \\ 8 \\ 6 \\ 12 \\ 4 \\ 10 \end{matrix} \tag{5-52b}$$

STRUCTURE STIFFNESS MATRIX

The complete structure stiffness matrix $[\mathbf{S}_c]$, which is developed by summing of the transformed member stiffness matrices of Expressions (5-50b), (5-51b), and (5-52b), is given in Table 5-5, Expressions (5-53). This matrix is partitioned with respect to unrestrained and restrained components of joint displacement as indicated in Table 5-5. According to Eq. (4-33) the four submatrices are defined as

$$\left[\begin{array}{c|c} [\mathbf{S}_{uu}] & [\mathbf{S}_{ur}] \\ \hline [\mathbf{S}_{ru}] & [\mathbf{S}_{rr}] \end{array}\right]$$

Now,

$$[\mathbf{S}_{uu}]^{-1} = \frac{1}{E} \times 10^3 \begin{matrix} 1 & 2 & 3 & 4 & 5 & 6 \\ \left[\begin{matrix} 0.01178 & -0.00302 & -0.01965 & -0.01678 & -0.00259 & -0.00399 \\ -0.00302 & 0.01189 & -0.01154 & -0.01304 & -0.00264 & -0.00435 \\ -0.01965 & -0.01154 & 0.85077 & 0.81136 & 0.01916 & 0.36368 \\ -0.01678 & -0.01304 & 0.81136 & 0.84300 & 0.01921 & 0.37899 \\ -0.00259 & -0.00264 & 0.01916 & 0.01921 & 0.06716 & 0.00980 \\ -0.00399 & -0.00435 & 0.36368 & 0.37899 & 0.00980 & 0.26177 \end{matrix}\right] \end{matrix} \begin{matrix} 1 \\ 2 \\ 3 \\ 4 \\ 5 \\ 6 \end{matrix} \tag{5-54}$$

Table 5-5

$$[\mathbf{S}_c] = E \times 10^{-3} \begin{array}{c} \\ \left[\begin{array}{rrrrrr:rrrrrr} 99.228 & 28.900 & 4.439 & 0 & 4.335 & -4.335 & 20.714 & 0 & -4.439 & 0 & 0 & 0 \\ 28.900 & 94.861 & 0 & 3.178 & 4.335 & -2.746 & 0 & 18.530 & 0 & -3.178 & 0 & -1.589 \\ 4.439 & 0 & 14.534 & -13.900 & 0 & 0 & 4.439 & 0 & -0.634 & 0 & 0 & 0 \\ 0 & 3.178 & -13.900 & 16.923 & 0 & -5.137 & 0 & 3.178 & 0 & -3.023 & 0 & 5.137 \\ 4.335 & 4.335 & 0 & 0 & 15.291 & -0.434 & 0 & 0 & 0 & 0 & -14.857 & 0 \\ -4.335 & -2.746 & 0 & -5.137 & -0.434 & 11.162 & 0 & 1.589 & 0 & 5.137 & 0 & -10.728 \\ \hdashline 20.714 & 0 & 4.439 & 0 & 0 & 0 & 41.428 & 0 & -4.439 & 0 & 0 & 0 \\ 0 & 18.530 & 0 & 3.178 & 0 & 1.589 & 0 & 37.061 & 0 & -3.178 & 0 & -1.589 \\ -4.439 & 0 & -0.634 & 0 & 0 & 0 & -4.439 & 0 & 0.634 & 0 & 0 & 0 \\ 0 & -3.178 & 0 & -3.023 & 0 & 5.137 & 0 & -3.178 & 0 & 3.023 & 0 & -5.137 \\ 0 & 0 & 0 & 0 & -14.857 & 0 & 0 & 0 & 0 & 0 & 14.857 & 0 \\ 0 & -1.589 & 0 & 5.137 & 0 & -10.728 & 0 & -1.589 & 0 & -5.137 & 0 & 10.728 \end{array}\right] \end{array}$$

Column numbers: 1 2 3 4 5 6 7 8 9 10 11 12; row numbers: 1–12

(5-53)

JOINT LOAD MATRIX

Since there are no loads applied along the length of any of the members in the structural system and the given joint loads are described as components of actions with respect to the reference axes (Fig. 5-12), the joint load matrix is established by referring to Figs. 5-12 and 5-14 as

$$[\mathbf{JL}_c] = \begin{bmatrix} JL_1 \\ JL_2 \\ JL_3 \\ JL_4 \\ JL_5 \\ JL_6 \\ \hdashline JL_7 \\ JL_8 \\ JL_9 \\ JL_{10} \\ JL_{11} \\ JL_{12} \end{bmatrix} = \begin{bmatrix} 0 \\ 0 \\ 5.0 \\ 0 \\ 0 \\ -10.0 \\ \hdashline 0 \\ 0 \\ 0 \\ 0 \\ 0 \\ 0 \end{bmatrix} = \begin{bmatrix} [\mathbf{JL}_u] \\ \hdashline [\mathbf{JL}_r] \end{bmatrix} \tag{5-55}$$

SOLUTION

Solving Eq. (4-36) for the unknown quantities, i.e., the unrestrained components of joint displacement, gives

$$[\boldsymbol{\Delta}_u] = [\mathbf{S}_{uu}]^{-1}[\mathbf{JL}_u] \tag{4-37}$$

Making the proper substitutions from Expressions (5-49), (5-54), and (5-55) into Eq. (4-37) yields the following set of equations:

$$\begin{bmatrix} \bar{\theta}_1 \\ \bar{\theta}_2 \\ \bar{\delta}_3 \\ \bar{\delta}_4 \\ \bar{\delta}_5 \\ \bar{\delta}_6 \end{bmatrix} = \frac{1}{E} \times 10^3 \begin{bmatrix} 0.01178 & -0.00302 & -0.01965 & -0.01678 & -0.00259 & -0.00399 \\ -0.00302 & 0.01189 & -0.01154 & -0.01304 & -0.00264 & -0.00435 \\ -0.01965 & -0.01154 & 0.85077 & 0.81136 & 0.01916 & 0.36368 \\ -0.01678 & -0.01304 & 0.81136 & 0.84300 & 0.01921 & 0.37899 \\ -0.00259 & -0.00264 & 0.01916 & 0.01921 & 0.06716 & 0.00980 \\ -0.00399 & -0.00435 & 0.36368 & 0.37899 & 0.00980 & 0.26177 \end{bmatrix} \begin{bmatrix} 0 \\ 0 \\ 5.0 \\ 0 \\ 0 \\ -10.0 \end{bmatrix} \tag{5-56}$$

which reduce to

$$[\boldsymbol{\Delta}_u] = \begin{bmatrix} \bar{\theta}_1 \\ \bar{\theta}_2 \\ \bar{\delta}_3 \\ \bar{\delta}_4 \\ \bar{\delta}_5 \\ \bar{\delta}_6 \end{bmatrix} = \frac{1}{E} \times 10^3 \begin{bmatrix} -0.0583 \\ -0.0142 \\ 0.6170 \\ 0.2669 \\ -0.0022 \\ -0.7993 \end{bmatrix} \tag{5-57}$$

upon performing the indicated matrix multiplication. These are relative joint displacements. If E is defined in terms of k/ft², the actual displacements of each joint can be obtained (translations will be in units of feet).

FINAL END ACTIONS

Substituting into Expression (5-46), i.e.,

$$[\mathbf{M}]_i = [\mathbf{K}]_i[\mathbf{T}]_i[\bar{\boldsymbol{\delta}}]_i + [\mathbf{FM}]_i \tag{5-46}$$

the final end actions resulting from the given loading of the structure can be determined for each member with respect to the local axes of the member.

Member 1

From Expression (5-32), the transformation matrix is given as

$$[\mathbf{T}]_1 = \begin{bmatrix} 1.0 & 0 & 0 & 0 & 0 & 0 \\ 0 & 1.0 & 0 & 0 & 0 & 0 \\ 0 & 0 & 0 & 0 & -1.0 & 0 \\ 0 & 0 & 0 & 0 & 0 & -1.0 \\ 0 & 0 & 1.0 & 0 & 0 & 0 \\ 0 & 0 & 0 & 1.0 & 0 & 0 \end{bmatrix}_1 \tag{5-58a}$$

and for the given loading condition (Fig. 5-12) the fixed end action matrix becomes

$$[\mathbf{FM}]_1 = [\mathbf{0}] \tag{5-58b}$$

Also, referring to Figs. 5-7 and 5-14, as well as Expression (5-57), the end displacement matrix is written as

$$[\bar{\boldsymbol{\delta}}]_1 = \begin{bmatrix} \bar{\theta}_7 \\ \bar{\theta}_1 \\ \bar{\delta}_{11} \\ \bar{\delta}_5 \\ \bar{\delta}_9 \\ \bar{\delta}_3 \end{bmatrix}_1 = \frac{1}{E} \times 10^3 \begin{bmatrix} 0 \\ -0.0583 \\ 0 \\ -0.0022 \\ 0 \\ 0.6170 \end{bmatrix}_1 \tag{5-58c}$$

Substituting Expressions (5-58) and (5-50a) into Eq. (5-46) and performing the indicated matrix operations yields

$$\begin{bmatrix} M_p \\ M_q \\ P_r \\ P_s \\ P_t \\ P_u \end{bmatrix}_1 = \begin{bmatrix} 1.53 \text{ ft-k} \\ 0.32 \text{ ft-k} \\ 0.13 \text{ k} \\ -0.13 \text{ k} \\ 0.03 \text{ k} \\ -0.03 \text{ k} \end{bmatrix}_1 \tag{5-59}$$

Member 2

For member 2,

$$[\mathbf{T}]_2 = \begin{bmatrix} 1.0 & 0 & 0 & 0 & 0 & 0 \\ 0 & 1.0 & 0 & 0 & 0 & 0 \\ 0 & 0 & 1.0 & 0 & 0 & 0 \\ 0 & 0 & 0 & 1.0 & 0 & 0 \\ 0 & 0 & 0 & 0 & 1.0 & 0 \\ 0 & 0 & 0 & 0 & 0 & 1.0 \end{bmatrix}_2 \quad \textbf{(5-60a)}$$

$$[\mathbf{FM}]_2 = [\mathbf{0}] \quad \textbf{(5-60b)}$$

and

$$[\bar{\boldsymbol{\delta}}]_2 = \begin{bmatrix} \bar{\theta}_1 \\ \bar{\theta}_2 \\ \bar{\delta}_5 \\ \bar{\delta}_6 \\ \bar{\delta}_3 \\ \bar{\delta}_4 \end{bmatrix}_2 = \frac{1}{E} \times 10^3 \begin{bmatrix} -0.0583 \\ -0.0142 \\ -0.0022 \\ -0.7993 \\ 0.6170 \\ 0.2669 \end{bmatrix}_2 \quad \textbf{(5-60c)}$$

Writing Eq. (5-46) for member 2 and solving for the final end actions yields

$$\begin{bmatrix} M_p \\ M_q \\ P_r \\ P_s \\ P_t \\ P_u \end{bmatrix}_2 = \begin{bmatrix} -0.32 \text{ ft-k} \\ 0.95 \text{ ft-k} \\ 0.03 \text{ k} \\ -0.03 \text{ k} \\ 4.87 \text{ k} \\ -4.87 \text{ k} \end{bmatrix}_2 \quad \textbf{(5-61)}$$

Member 3

For member 3,

$$[\mathbf{T}]_3 = \begin{bmatrix} 1 & 0 & 0 & 0 & 0 & 0 \\ 0 & 1 & 0 & 0 & 0 & 0 \\ 0 & 0 & 0.4473 & 0 & 0.8946 & 0 \\ 0 & 0 & 0 & 0.4473 & 0 & 0.8946 \\ 0 & 0 & -0.8946 & 0 & 0.4473 & 0 \\ 0 & 0 & 0 & -0.8946 & 0 & 0.4473 \end{bmatrix}_3 \quad \textbf{(5-62a)}$$

$$[\mathbf{FM}]_3 = [\mathbf{0}] \quad \textbf{(5-62b)}$$

and

$$[\bar{\boldsymbol{\delta}}]_3 = \begin{bmatrix} \bar{\theta}_2 \\ \bar{\theta}_8 \\ \bar{\delta}_6 \\ \bar{\delta}_{12} \\ \bar{\delta}_4 \\ \bar{\delta}_{10} \end{bmatrix}_3 = \frac{1}{E} \times 10^3 \begin{bmatrix} -0.0142 \\ 0 \\ -0.7993 \\ 0 \\ 0.2669 \\ 0 \end{bmatrix}_3 \quad \textbf{(5-62c)}$$

Using Expressions (5-62) and (5-52a) with Eq. (5-46), the final end actions are equal to

$$\begin{bmatrix} M_p \\ M_q \\ P_r \\ P_s \\ P_t \\ P_u \end{bmatrix}_3 = \begin{bmatrix} -0.95 \text{ ft-k} \\ -0.69 \text{ ft-k} \\ -0.10 \text{ k} \\ 0.10 \text{ k} \\ 11.09 \text{ k} \\ -11.09 \text{ k} \end{bmatrix}_3 \qquad \textbf{(5-63)}$$

The final end actions of the members of the structure are described in Fig. 5-15.

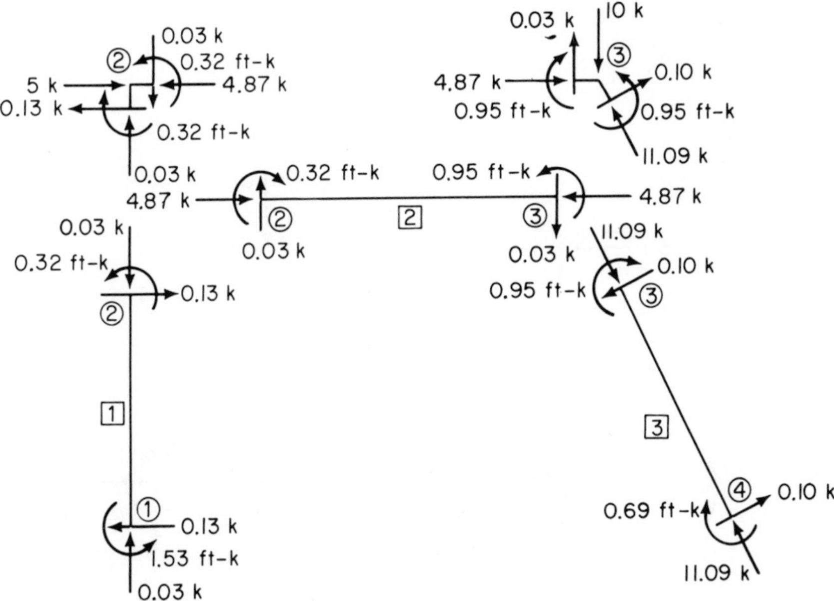

Fig. 5-15 Example 5-1: Final end actions.

SUPPORT REACTIONS

From Expressions (5-53), (5-55), and (5-57), Eq. (4-39), i.e.,

$$[\mathbf{R}_r] = [\mathbf{S}_{ru}][\mathbf{\Delta}_u] - [\mathbf{JL}_r] \qquad \textbf{(4-39)}$$

can be written as

$$\begin{bmatrix} R_7 \\ R_8 \\ R_9 \\ R_{10} \\ R_{11} \\ R_{12} \end{bmatrix} = E \times 10^{-3} \begin{bmatrix} 20.714 & 0 & 4.439 & 0 & 0 & 0 \\ 0 & 18.530 & 0 & 3.178 & 0 & 1.589 \\ -4.439 & 0 & -0.634 & 0 & 0 & 0 \\ 0 & -3.178 & 0 & -3.023 & 0 & 5.137 \\ 0 & 0 & 0 & 0 & -14.857 & 0 \\ 0 & -1.589 & 0 & 5.137 & 0 & -10.728 \end{bmatrix} \frac{1}{E} \times 10^3 \begin{bmatrix} -0.0583 \\ -0.0142 \\ 0.6170 \\ 0.2669 \\ -0.0022 \\ -0.7993 \end{bmatrix} \qquad \textbf{(5-64a)}$$

and performing the indicated operations yields

$$\begin{bmatrix} R_7 \\ R_8 \\ R_9 \\ R_{10} \\ R_{11} \\ R_{12} \end{bmatrix} = \begin{bmatrix} 1.53 \text{ ft-k} \\ -0.69 \text{ ft-k} \\ -0.13 \text{ k} \\ -4.87 \text{ k} \\ 0.03 \text{ k} \\ 9.97 \text{ k} \end{bmatrix} \tag{5-64b}$$

The free body diagram for the complete structure is shown in Fig. 5-16.

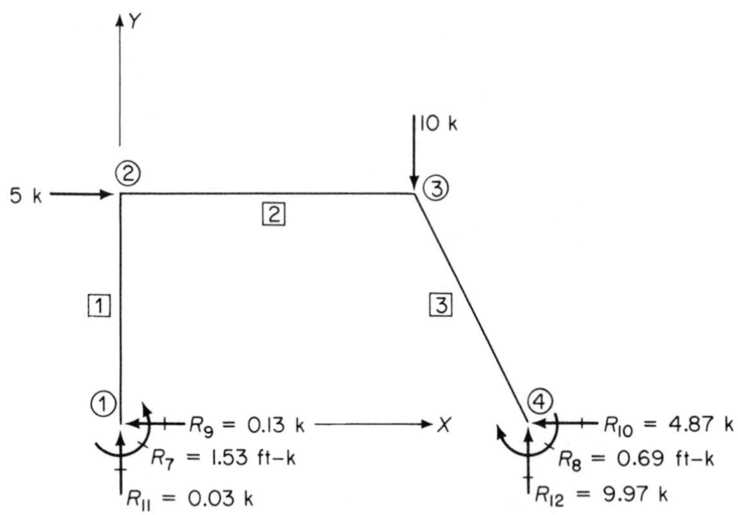

Fig. 5-16 Example 5-1: Support reactions.

5–6
Analysis of Planar Truss System

In a truss structure the joints are assumed to be *pin-connected;* consequently, the beam elements of this type of structural system can resist only axial deformations of their ends. Also, since the ends of the members which frame into a pin-connected joint are free to rotate independently of one another, there is no mechanism to relate the member end rotations at a joint; therefore, the idea of a joint rotation is meaningless in describing the independent components of displacement of a pin-connected joint. Considering these characteristics of the truss system, the various matrices required in describing the behavior of a typical truss member can be developed.

5-6.1 Transformation Matrix: Truss Member

In analyzing a truss system, there are only two possible independent components of joint translation, with respect to the reference axes, to be considered at a joint, since the joint rotations are undefined. Accordingly, with respect to the local member axes, there are two possible components of translation at each end of a truss member, and corresponding to these components of translation there are two possible components of end force with respect to the local axes at each end of the truss member [Fig. 5-17(a)]. Now, according to Eqs. (5-20a) through (5-20d), these components of end force in the frame of the local axes can be resolved into components of end forces in the frame of the arbitrary reference axes [Fig. 5-17(b)], i.e.,

$$\bar{p}_r^i = C_{22}p_r^i + C_{12}p_t^i \tag{5-65a}$$

$$\bar{p}_s^i = C_{22}p_s^i + C_{12}p_u^i \tag{5-65b}$$

$$\bar{p}_t^i = C_{21}p_r^i + C_{11}p_t^i \tag{5-65c}$$

$$\bar{p}_u^i = C_{21}p_s^i + C_{11}p_u^i \tag{5-65d}$$

expressed in matrix form as

$$\begin{bmatrix} \bar{p}_r \\ \bar{p}_s \\ \bar{p}_t \\ \bar{p}_u \end{bmatrix}_i = \begin{bmatrix} C_{22} & 0 & C_{12} & 0 \\ 0 & C_{22} & 0 & C_{12} \\ C_{21} & 0 & C_{11} & 0 \\ 0 & C_{21} & 0 & C_{11} \end{bmatrix}_i \begin{bmatrix} p_r \\ p_s \\ p_t \\ p_u \end{bmatrix}_i \tag{5-66a}$$

or

$$[\bar{\mathbf{p}}]_i = [\mathbf{T}_T]_i^T[\mathbf{p}]_i \tag{5-66b}$$

Also, as indicated by Eqs. (5-23a) through (5-23d), the components of end force in the frame of the local axes can be expressed in terms of the components of end force in the frame of the arbitrary reference axes, i.e.,

$$p_r^i = C_{22}\bar{p}_r^i + C_{21}\bar{p}_t^i \tag{5-67a}$$

$$p_s^i = C_{22}\bar{p}_s^i + C_{21}\bar{p}_u^i \tag{5-67b}$$

$$p_t^i = C_{12}\bar{p}_r^i + C_{11}\bar{p}_t^i \tag{5-67c}$$

$$p_u^i = C_{12}\bar{p}_s^i + C_{11}\bar{p}_u^i \tag{5-67d}$$

expressed in matrix form as

$$\begin{bmatrix} p_r \\ p_s \\ p_t \\ p_u \end{bmatrix}_i = \begin{bmatrix} C_{22} & 0 & C_{21} & 0 \\ 0 & C_{22} & 0 & C_{21} \\ C_{12} & 0 & C_{11} & 0 \\ 0 & C_{12} & 0 & C_{11} \end{bmatrix}_i \begin{bmatrix} \bar{p}_r \\ \bar{p}_s \\ \bar{p}_t \\ \bar{p}_u \end{bmatrix}_i \tag{5-68a}$$

or

$$[\mathbf{p}]_i = [\mathbf{T}_T]_i[\bar{\mathbf{p}}]_i \tag{5-68b}$$

The matrix $[\mathbf{T}_T]_i$ is the ***transformation matrix for a truss member*** rotating from the reference system of axes to the local system of axes. The direction cosines which make up the elements of this matrix are defined in Expressions (5-11); however, using Expressions (5-31), the transformation matrix can be written in terms of the direction cosines C_x and C_y, which define the orientation of the member axis x_m in the frame of the reference axes:

$$[\mathbf{T}_T]_i = \begin{bmatrix} C_x & 0 & -C_y & 0 \\ 0 & C_x & 0 & -C_y \\ C_y & 0 & C_x & 0 \\ 0 & C_y & 0 & C_x \end{bmatrix}_i \tag{5-69}$$

Also, comparing Eqs. (5-68b) and (5-66b), it is recognized that the transformation matrix of Eq. (5-69) is an *orthogonal* matrix, i.e.,

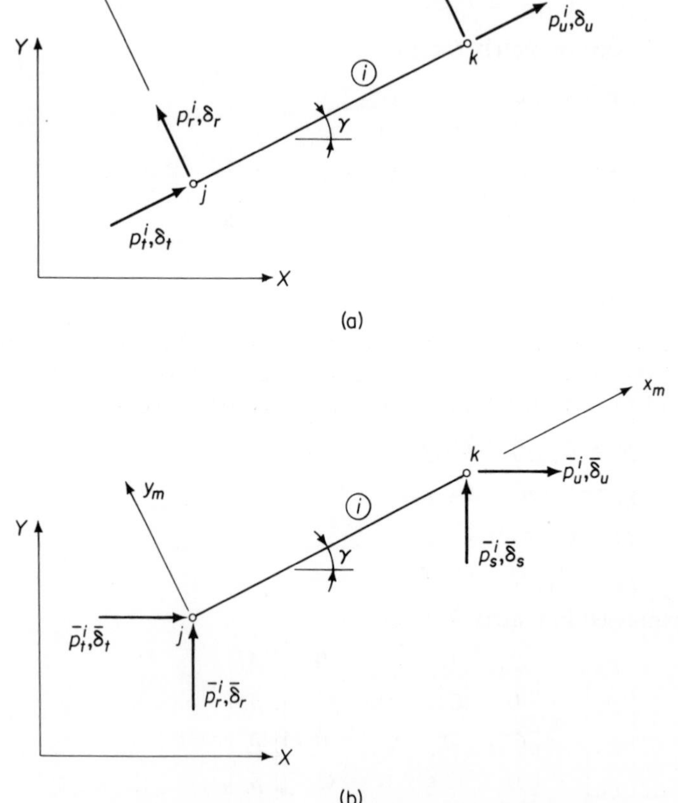

Fig. 5-17 Components of end force and end displacement for truss member: (a) local system; (b) reference system.

$$[\mathbf{T}_T]_i^{-1} = [\mathbf{T}_T]_i^T \tag{5-70}$$

The relationship between the corresponding end displacements of a truss member i in the frame of the local axes and the frame of the reference axes can be expressed as

$$[\boldsymbol{\delta}_T]_i = [\mathbf{T}_T]_i[\bar{\boldsymbol{\delta}}_T]_i \tag{5-71}$$

and

$$[\bar{\boldsymbol{\delta}}_T]_i = [\mathbf{T}_T]_i^T[\boldsymbol{\delta}_T]_i \tag{5-72}$$

where

$$[\boldsymbol{\delta}_T]_i = \begin{bmatrix} \delta_r \\ \delta_s \\ \delta_t \\ \delta_u \end{bmatrix}_i \tag{5-73a}$$

and

$$[\bar{\boldsymbol{\delta}}_T]_i = \begin{bmatrix} \bar{\delta}_r \\ \bar{\delta}_s \\ \bar{\delta}_t \\ \bar{\delta}_u \end{bmatrix}_i \tag{5-73b}$$

The components of end displacement appearing in Expressions (5-73a) and (5-73b) are defined in Fig. 5-17.

5-6.2 Member Stiffness Matrices: Truss Member

Since a member that is pin-connected at both ends in a structural system can resist only axial deformations, the components of end force in the frame of the local axes which are required to maintain equilibrium of the truss member when subject to general end displacements (δ_r, δ_s, δ_t, and δ_u) in the frame of local axes (Fig. 5-18) can be expressed as

$$p_r^i = 0 \tag{5-74a}$$

$$p_s^i = 0 \tag{5-74b}$$

$$p_t^i = K_{tt}^i\delta_t + K_{tu}^i\delta_u \tag{5-74c}$$

$$p_u^i = K_{ut}^i\delta_t + K_{uu}^i\delta_u \tag{5-74d}$$

Recalling the matrices $[\mathbf{p}]_i$ and $[\boldsymbol{\delta}_T]_i$, which have been defined in Expressions (5-68) and (5-73a), Eqs. (5-74) can be expressed in matrix form as

$$\begin{bmatrix} p_r \\ p_s \\ p_t \\ p_u \end{bmatrix}_i = \begin{bmatrix} 0 & 0 & 0 & 0 \\ 0 & 0 & 0 & 0 \\ 0 & 0 & K_{tt} & K_{tu} \\ 0 & 0 & K_{ut} & K_{uu} \end{bmatrix}_i \begin{bmatrix} \delta_r \\ \delta_s \\ \delta_t \\ \delta_u \end{bmatrix}_i \tag{5-75a}$$

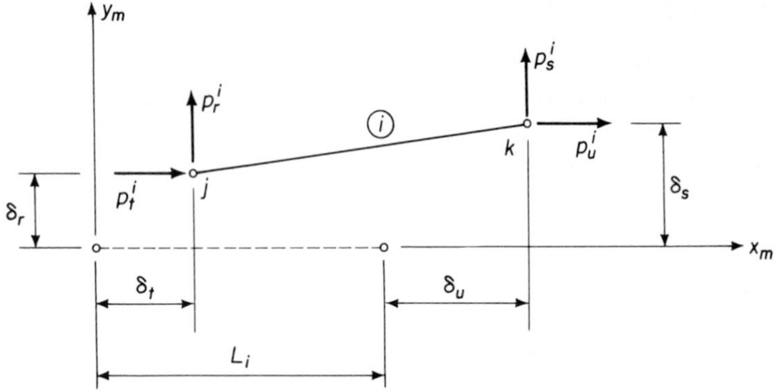

Fig. 5-18 General displacement of typical truss member.

or

$$[\mathbf{p}]_i = [\mathbf{K}_T]_i[\boldsymbol{\delta}_T]_i \tag{5-75b}$$

where the matrix $[\mathbf{K}_T]_i$ is defined as the ***member stiffness matrix*** with respect to the local axes ***for a truss member***. The matrix $[\mathbf{K}_T]_i$ can be transformed from the frame of the local axes into the frame of the reference axes by means of Eq. (5-38), which can be written as

$$[\overline{\mathbf{K}}_T]_i = [\mathbf{T}_T]_i^T[\mathbf{K}_T]_i[\mathbf{T}_T]_i \tag{5-76}$$

for the truss member. Performing the indicated matrix operations, Eq. (5-76) yields

$$[\overline{\mathbf{K}}_T]_i = \begin{array}{c} \begin{array}{cccc} \bar{r} & \bar{s} & \bar{t} & \bar{u} \end{array} \\ \begin{bmatrix} C_y^2K_{tt} & C_y^2K_{tu} & C_xC_yK_{tt} & C_xC_yK_{tu} \\ C_y^2K_{ut} & C_y^2K_{uu} & C_xC_tK_{ut} & C_xC_yK_{uu} \\ C_xC_yK_{tt} & C_xC_yK_{tu} & C_x^2K_{tt} & C_x^2K_{tu} \\ C_xC_yK_{ut} & C_xC_yK_{uu} & C_x^2K_{ut} & C_x^2K_{uu} \end{bmatrix}_i \end{array} \begin{array}{c} \bar{r} \\ \bar{s} \\ \bar{t} \\ \bar{u} \end{array} \tag{5-77}$$

If the truss member has a constant corss-sectional area over its length, the member stiffness matrix with respect to the local axes can be written as

$$[\mathbf{K}_T]_i = \begin{array}{c} \begin{array}{cccc} r & s & t & u \end{array} \\ \begin{bmatrix} 0 & 0 & 0 & 0 \\ 0 & 0 & 0 & 0 \\ 0 & 0 & \dfrac{AE}{L} & \dfrac{-AE}{L} \\ 0 & 0 & \dfrac{-AE}{L} & \dfrac{AE}{L} \end{bmatrix}_i \end{array} \begin{array}{c} r \\ s \\ t \\ u \end{array} \tag{5-78}$$

and the transformed member stiffness matrix of Expression (5-77) reduces to

$$[\bar{\mathbf{K}}_T]_i = \frac{AE}{L}\begin{bmatrix} C_y^2 & -C_y^2 & C_xC_y & -C_xC_y \\ -C_y^2 & C_y^2 & -C_xC_y & C_xC_y \\ C_xC_y & -C_xC_y & C_x^2 & -C_x^2 \\ -C_xC_y & C_xC_y & -C_x^2 & C_x^2 \end{bmatrix}_i \begin{matrix} \bar{r} \\ \bar{s} \\ \bar{t} \\ \bar{u} \end{matrix} \quad \text{(columns } \bar{r}, \bar{s}, \bar{t}, \bar{u}\text{)} \tag{5-79}$$

5-6.3 End Actions: Truss Member

Now, the *final end actions for a truss member* can be evaluated in terms of components in the frame of the reference axes (Fig. 5-19) from the set of equations

$$[\bar{\mathbf{P}}]_i = [\bar{\mathbf{K}}_T]_i[\bar{\boldsymbol{\delta}}_T]_i + [\overline{\mathbf{FP}}]_i \tag{5-80}$$

where

$$[\bar{\mathbf{P}}]_i = \begin{bmatrix} \bar{P}_r \\ \bar{P}_s \\ \bar{P}_t \\ \bar{P}_u \end{bmatrix}_i \approx \text{Components of final end actions with respect to the reference axes} \tag{5-81a}$$

and

$$[\overline{\mathbf{FP}}]_i = \begin{bmatrix} \overline{FP}_r \\ \overline{FP}_s \\ \overline{FP}_t \\ \overline{FP}_u \end{bmatrix}_i \approx \text{Components of fixed end actions with respect to the reference axes} \tag{5-81b}$$

The final end actions can also be described in terms of components in the frame of the local axes, recognizing that

$$[\mathbf{P}]_i = [\mathbf{T}_T]_i[\bar{\mathbf{P}}]_i \tag{5-82}$$

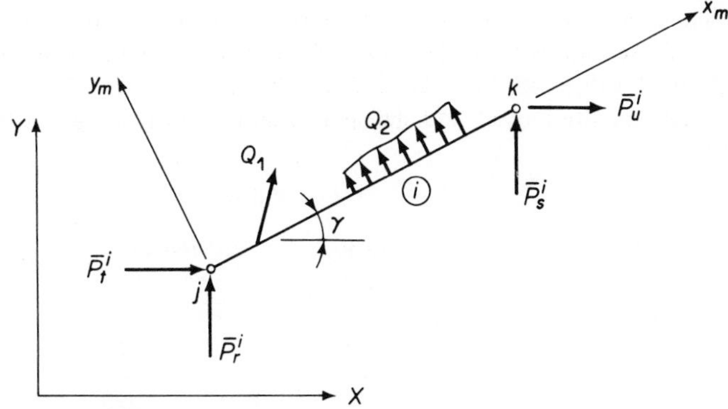

Fig. 5-19 Components of final end action in the frame of the reference axes for a truss member.

Using the various matrices associated with the truss member, the procedure for carrying out the analysis of a truss structure by the stiffness method is exactly the same as that for analyzing the rigid frame.

Example 5-2. Using the stiffness approach, calculate the displacements and actions of the truss system described in Fig. 5-20 resulting from the application of a normal, uniform load of 2 k/ft applied over the length of member 2. Each member of the truss has a constant cross-section over its length; the cross-sectional area of each member is indicated in the figure adjacent to the member. The modulus of elasticity E is constant for the structure.

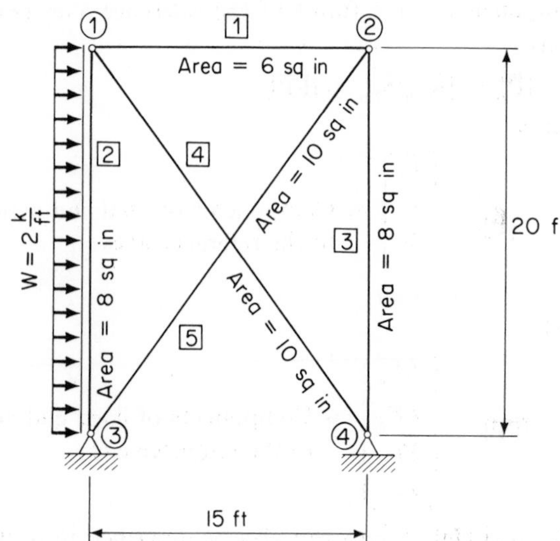

Fig. 5-20 Example 5-2: Truss system.

MEMBER INFORMATION

In Fig. 5-21, the j- and k-ends for each member are designated, thus establishing the local axes for each member, and the reference axes for the structure are positioned.

The coordinates of the joints of the structure with respect to the reference axes are given in Table 5-6. In Table 5-7 the direction cosines, Eqs. (5-33), the cross-sectional area (in square inches) and the span length (in feet) are given for each member.

Table 5-6

Joint	*Coordinate*	
	X, ft	*Y*, ft
1	0	20.0
2	15.0	20.0
3	0	0
4	15.0	0

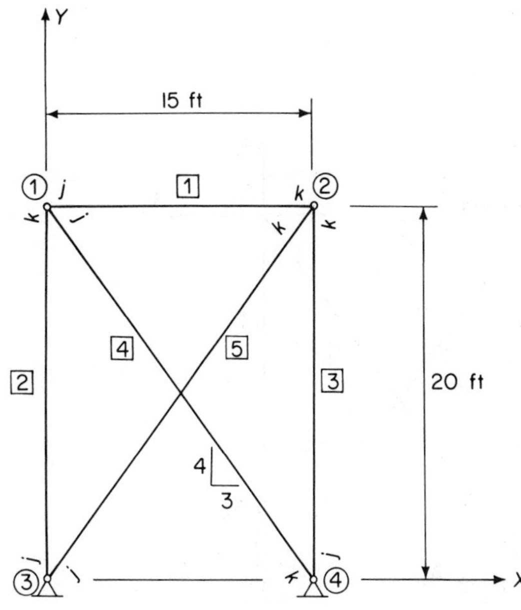

Fig. 5-21 Example 5-2: Establishment of local and reference axes.

Table 5-7

Member	*Joint* j	*Joint* k	*Area*, in²	*Length*, ft	*Direction Cosine* C_x	*Direction Cosine* C_y
1	1	2	6.0	15.0	1.0	0
2	3	1	8.0	20.0	0	1.0
3	4	2	8.0	20.0	0	1.0
4	1	4	10.0	25.0	0.60	−0.80
5	3	2	10.0	25.0	0.60	0.80

JOINT DISPLACEMENT MATRIX

Identifying and labeling the possible components of joint displacement as shown in Fig. 5-22, the complete joint displacement matrix is written as

$$[\mathbf{\Delta}_c] = \begin{bmatrix} \bar{\delta}_1 \\ \bar{\delta}_2 \\ \bar{\delta}_3 \\ \bar{\delta}_4 \\ \hdashline \bar{\delta}_5 \\ \bar{\delta}_6 \\ \bar{\delta}_7 \\ \bar{\delta}_8 \end{bmatrix} = \begin{bmatrix} [\mathbf{\Delta}_u] \\ \hdashline [\mathbf{\Delta}_r] \end{bmatrix} \qquad \textbf{(5-83)}$$

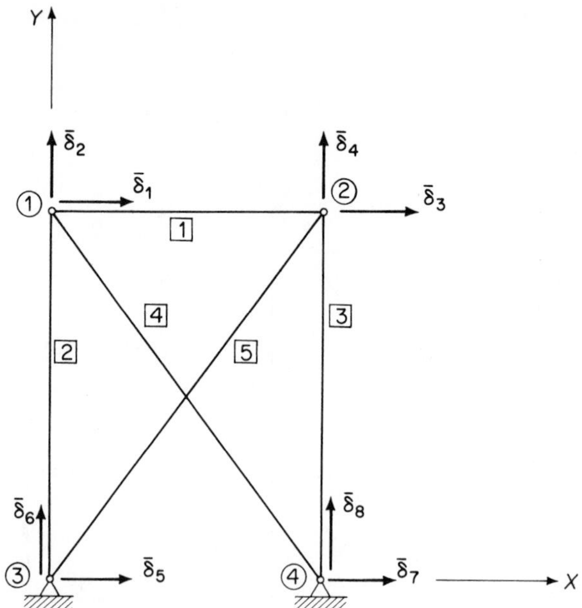

Fig. 5-22 Example 5-2: Identification of components of joint displacement.

MEMBER STIFFNESS MATRICES

Using Expressions (5-78) and (5-79), the member stiffness matrix and the transformed member stiffness matrix can be written for each member of the structure:

Member 1

$$[\mathbf{K}_T]_1 = \begin{bmatrix} 0 & 0 & 0 & 0 \\ 0 & 0 & 0 & 0 \\ 0 & 0 & \dfrac{6E}{15} & \dfrac{-6E}{15} \\ 0 & 0 & \dfrac{-6E}{15} & \dfrac{6E}{15} \end{bmatrix}_1 = 0.4E \begin{array}{c} \begin{matrix} r & s & t & u \end{matrix} \\ \begin{bmatrix} 0 & 0 & 0 & 0 \\ 0 & 0 & 0 & 0 \\ 0 & 0 & 1.0 & -1.0 \\ 0 & 0 & -1.0 & 1.0 \end{bmatrix}_1 \end{array} \begin{matrix} r \\ s \\ t \\ u \end{matrix} \tag{5-84a}$$

and

$$[\bar{\mathbf{K}}_T]_1 = 0.4E \begin{array}{c} \begin{matrix} 2 & 4 & 1 & 3 \end{matrix} \\ \begin{bmatrix} 0 & 0 & 0 & 0 \\ 0 & 0 & 0 & 0 \\ 0 & 0 & 1.0 & -1.0 \\ 0 & 0 & -1.0 & 1.0 \end{bmatrix}_1 \end{array} \begin{matrix} 2 \\ 4 \\ 1 \\ 3 \end{matrix} \tag{5-84b}$$

Member 2

$$[\mathbf{K}_T]_2 = \begin{bmatrix} 0 & 0 & 0 & 0 \\ 0 & 0 & 0 & 0 \\ 0 & 0 & \dfrac{8E}{20} & \dfrac{-8E}{20} \\ 0 & 0 & \dfrac{-8E}{20} & \dfrac{8E}{20} \end{bmatrix}_2 = 0.4E \begin{array}{c} \begin{matrix} r & s & t & u \end{matrix} \\ \begin{bmatrix} 0 & 0 & 0 & 0 \\ 0 & 0 & 0 & 0 \\ 0 & 0 & 1.0 & -1.0 \\ 0 & 0 & -1.0 & 1.0 \end{bmatrix}_2 \end{array} \begin{matrix} r \\ s \\ t \\ u \end{matrix} \tag{5-85a}$$

and

$$[\bar{\mathbf{K}}_T]_2 = 0.4E \begin{array}{c} \begin{matrix} 6 & 2 & 5 & 1 \end{matrix} \\ \begin{bmatrix} 1.0 & -1.0 & 0 & 0 \\ -1.0 & 1.0 & 0 & 0 \\ 0 & 0 & 0 & 0 \\ 0 & 0 & 0 & 0 \end{bmatrix}_2 \end{array} \begin{matrix} 6 \\ 2 \\ 5 \\ 1 \end{matrix} \tag{5-85b}$$

Member 3

$$[\mathbf{K}_T]_3 = \begin{bmatrix} 0 & 0 & 0 & 0 \\ 0 & 0 & 0 & 0 \\ 0 & 0 & \dfrac{8E}{20} & \dfrac{-8E}{20} \\ 0 & 0 & \dfrac{-8E}{20} & \dfrac{8E}{20} \end{bmatrix}_3 = 0.4E \begin{array}{c} \begin{matrix} r & s & t & u \end{matrix} \\ \begin{bmatrix} 0 & 0 & 0 & 0 \\ 0 & 0 & 0 & 0 \\ 0 & 0 & 1.0 & -1.0 \\ 0 & 0 & -1.0 & 1.0 \end{bmatrix}_3 \end{array} \begin{matrix} r \\ s \\ t \\ u \end{matrix} \tag{5-86a}$$

and

$$[\bar{\mathbf{K}}_T]_3 = 0.4E \begin{array}{c} \begin{matrix} 8 & 4 & 7 & 3 \end{matrix} \\ \begin{bmatrix} 1.0 & -1.0 & 0 & 0 \\ -1.0 & 1.0 & 0 & 0 \\ 0 & 0 & 0 & 0 \\ 0 & 0 & 0 & 0 \end{bmatrix}_3 \end{array} \begin{matrix} 8 \\ 4 \\ 7 \\ 3 \end{matrix} \tag{5-86b}$$

Member 4

$$[\mathbf{K}_T]_4 = \begin{bmatrix} 0 & 0 & 0 & 0 \\ 0 & 0 & 0 & 0 \\ 0 & 0 & \dfrac{10E}{25} & \dfrac{-10E}{25} \\ 0 & 0 & \dfrac{-10E}{25} & \dfrac{10E}{25} \end{bmatrix}_4 = 0.4E \begin{array}{c} \begin{matrix} r & s & t & u \end{matrix} \\ \begin{bmatrix} 0 & 0 & 0 & 0 \\ 0 & 0 & 0 & 0 \\ 0 & 0 & 1.0 & -1.0 \\ 0 & 0 & -1.0 & 1.0 \end{bmatrix}_4 \end{array} \begin{matrix} r \\ s \\ t \\ u \end{matrix} \tag{5-87a}$$

and

$$[\bar{\mathbf{K}}_T]_4 = 0.4E\begin{array}{c} \begin{array}{cccc} 2 & 8 & 1 & 7 \end{array} \\ \left[\begin{array}{cccc} 0.64 & -0.64 & -0.48 & 0.48 \\ -0.64 & 0.64 & 0.48 & -0.48 \\ -0.48 & 0.48 & 0.36 & -0.36 \\ 0.48 & -0.48 & -0.36 & 0.36 \end{array}\right]_4 \end{array} \begin{array}{c} 2 \\ 8 \\ 1 \\ 7 \end{array} \quad \textbf{(5-87b)}$$

Member 5

$$[\mathbf{K}_T]_5 = \begin{bmatrix} 0 & 0 & 0 & 0 \\ 0 & 0 & 0 & 0 \\ 0 & 0 & \frac{10E}{25} & \frac{-10E}{25} \\ 0 & 0 & \frac{-10E}{25} & \frac{10E}{25} \end{bmatrix}_5 = 0.4E \begin{array}{c} \begin{array}{cccc} r & s & t & u \end{array} \\ \left[\begin{array}{cccc} 0 & 0 & 0 & 0 \\ 0 & 0 & 0 & 0 \\ 0 & 0 & 1.0 & -1.0 \\ 0 & 0 & -1.0 & 1.0 \end{array}\right]_5 \end{array} \begin{array}{c} r \\ s \\ t \\ u \end{array} \quad \textbf{(5-88a)}$$

and

$$[\bar{\mathbf{K}}_T]_5 = 0.4E\begin{array}{c} \begin{array}{cccc} 6 & 4 & 5 & 3 \end{array} \\ \left[\begin{array}{cccc} 0.64 & -0.64 & 0.48 & -0.48 \\ -0.64 & 0.64 & -0.48 & 0.48 \\ 0.48 & -0.48 & 0.36 & -0.36 \\ -0.48 & 0.48 & -0.36 & 0.36 \end{array}\right]_5 \end{array} \begin{array}{c} 6 \\ 4 \\ 5 \\ 3 \end{array} \quad \textbf{(5-88b)}$$

STRUCTURE STIFFNESS MATRIX

From the transformed member stiffness matrices which have been established for the various members of the structure, the complete structure stiffness matrix can be assembled, yielding

$$[\mathbf{S}_c] = 0.4E\begin{array}{c} \begin{array}{cccccccc} 1 & 2 & 3 & 4 & 5 & 6 & 7 & 8 \end{array} \\ \left[\begin{array}{cccc:cccc} 1.36 & -0.48 & -1.00 & 0 & 0 & 0 & -0.36 & 0.48 \\ -0.48 & 1.64 & 0 & 0 & 0 & -1.00 & 0.48 & -0.64 \\ -1.00 & 0 & 1.36 & 0.48 & -0.36 & -0.48 & 0 & 0 \\ 0 & 0 & 0.48 & 1.64 & -0.48 & -0.64 & 0 & -1.00 \\ \hdashline 0 & 0 & -0.36 & -0.48 & 0.36 & 0.48 & 0 & 0 \\ 0 & -1.00 & -0.48 & -0.64 & 0.48 & 1.64 & 0 & 0 \\ -0.36 & 0.48 & 0 & 0 & 0 & 0 & 0.36 & -0.48 \\ 0.48 & -0.64 & 0 & -1.00 & 0 & 0 & -0.48 & 1.64 \end{array}\right] \end{array} \begin{array}{c} 1 \\ 2 \\ 3 \\ 4 \\ 5 \\ 6 \\ 7 \\ 8 \end{array}$$

(5-89)

where the four submatrices are defined as

$$\begin{bmatrix} [\mathbf{S}_{uu}] & [\mathbf{S}_{ur}] \\ \hline [\mathbf{S}_{ru}] & [\mathbf{S}_{rr}] \end{bmatrix}$$

Now,

$$[\mathbf{S}_{uu}]^{-1} = \frac{1}{0.4E} \begin{array}{c} \begin{array}{cccc} 1 & 2 & 3 & 4 \end{array} \\ \left[\begin{array}{rrrr} 2.503 & 0.733 & 2.052 & -0.601 \\ 0.733 & 0.824 & 0.601 & -0.176 \\ 2.052 & 0.601 & 2.503 & -0.733 \\ -0.601 & -0.176 & -0.733 & 0.824 \end{array}\right] \end{array} \begin{array}{c} 1 \\ 2 \\ 3 \\ 4 \end{array} \tag{5-90}$$

JOINT LOAD MATRIX

For this problem the only load applied to the structure is a uniformly distributed load over the length of member 2. The fixed end actions for this loading of member 2 are identified in Fig. 5-23(a) and the joint loads acting on the restrained structure are shown in Fig. 5-23(b). For this loading of the restrained structure, the complete joint load matrix is written as

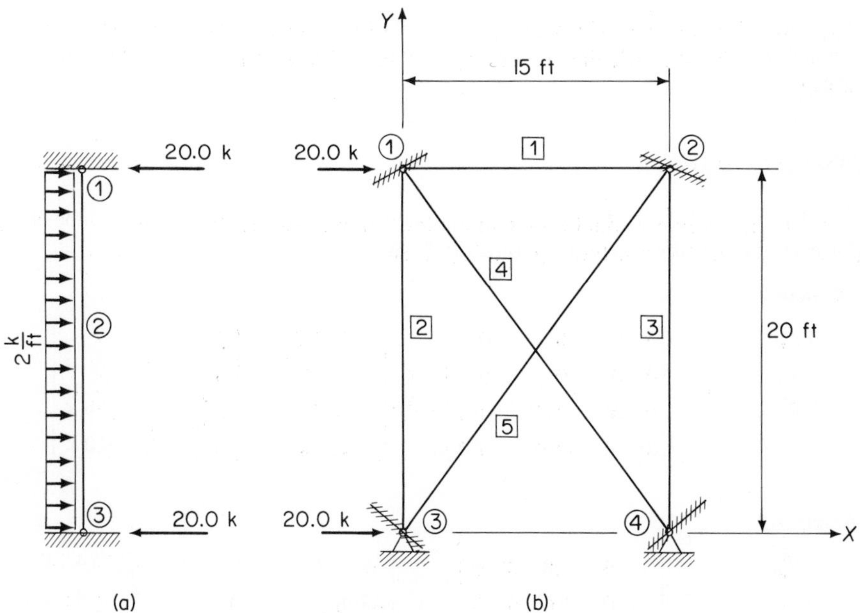

Fig. 5-23 Example 5-2: Joint loads: (a) fixed end actions; (b) joint loads.

$$[\mathbf{JL}_c] = \begin{bmatrix} JL_1 \\ JL_2 \\ JL_3 \\ JL_4 \\ \hdashline JL_5 \\ JL_6 \\ JL_7 \\ JL_8 \end{bmatrix} = \begin{bmatrix} 20.0 \\ 0 \\ 0 \\ 0 \\ \hdashline 20.0 \\ 0 \\ 0 \\ 0 \end{bmatrix} = \begin{bmatrix} [\mathbf{JL}_u] \\ \hdashline [\mathbf{JL}_r] \end{bmatrix} \tag{5-91}$$

SOLUTION

Solving Eq. (4-36) for the unrestrained joint displacements gives

$$[\mathbf{\Delta}_u] = [\mathbf{S}_{uu}]^{-1}[\mathbf{JL}_u] \tag{4-37}$$

hence,

$$\begin{bmatrix} \bar{\delta}_1 \\ \bar{\delta}_2 \\ \bar{\delta}_3 \\ \bar{\delta}_4 \end{bmatrix} = \frac{1}{0.4E}\begin{bmatrix} 2.503 & 0.733 & 2.052 & -0.601 \\ 0.733 & 0.824 & 0.601 & -0.176 \\ 2.052 & 0.601 & 2.503 & -0.733 \\ -0.601 & -0.176 & -0.733 & 0.824 \end{bmatrix}\begin{bmatrix} 20.0 \\ 0 \\ 0 \\ 0 \end{bmatrix} = \frac{1}{0.4E}\begin{bmatrix} 50.06 \\ 14.66 \\ 41.04 \\ -12.02 \end{bmatrix} \tag{5-92}$$

The joint displacements given by Expression (5-92) are relative displacements. If E is defined in units of k/in^2, the actual displacement of each joint can be obtained in units of feet.

FINAL END ACTIONS

The components of final end action in the frame of the reference axes can be obtained for each member by substituting into Eq. (5-80).

Member 1

$$\begin{bmatrix} \bar{P}_2 \\ \bar{P}_4 \\ \bar{P}_1 \\ \bar{P}_3 \end{bmatrix}_1 = 0.4E\begin{bmatrix} 0 & 0 & 0 & 0 \\ 0 & 0 & 0 & 0 \\ 0 & 0 & 1.0 & -1.0 \\ 0 & 0 & -1.0 & 1.0 \end{bmatrix}_1 \frac{1}{0.4E}\begin{bmatrix} 14.66 \\ -12.02 \\ 50.06 \\ 41.04 \end{bmatrix}_1 + \begin{bmatrix} 0 \\ 0 \\ 0 \\ 0 \end{bmatrix}_1 = \begin{bmatrix} 0 \\ 0 \\ 9.0\text{ k} \\ -9.0\text{ k} \end{bmatrix}_1 \tag{5-93a}$$

Member 2

$$\begin{bmatrix} \bar{P}_6 \\ \bar{P}_2 \\ \bar{P}_5 \\ \bar{P}_1 \end{bmatrix}_2 = 0.4E\begin{bmatrix} 1.0 & -1.0 & 0 & 0 \\ -1.0 & 1.0 & 0 & 0 \\ 0 & 0 & 0 & 0 \\ 0 & 0 & 0 & 0 \end{bmatrix}_2 \frac{1}{0.4E}\begin{bmatrix} 0 \\ 14.66 \\ 0 \\ 50.06 \end{bmatrix}_2 + \begin{bmatrix} 0 \\ 0 \\ -20.0 \\ -20.0 \end{bmatrix}_2 = \begin{bmatrix} -14.7\text{ k} \\ 14.7\text{ k} \\ -20.0\text{ k} \\ -20.0\text{ k} \end{bmatrix}_2 \tag{5-93b}$$

Member 3

$$\begin{bmatrix}\bar{P}_8\\ \bar{P}_4\\ \bar{P}_7\\ \bar{P}_3\end{bmatrix}_3 = 0.4E\begin{bmatrix}1.0 & -1.0 & 0 & 0\\ -1.0 & 1.0 & 0 & 0\\ 0 & 0 & 0 & 0\\ 0 & 0 & 0 & 0\end{bmatrix}_3 \frac{1}{0.4E}\begin{bmatrix}0\\ -12.02\\ 0\\ 41.04\end{bmatrix}_3 + \begin{bmatrix}0\\ 0\\ 0\\ 0\end{bmatrix}_3 = \begin{bmatrix}12.0\text{ k}\\ -12.0\text{ k}\\ 0\\ 0\end{bmatrix}_3 \tag{5-93c}$$

Member 4

$$\begin{bmatrix}\bar{P}_2\\ \bar{P}_8\\ \bar{P}_1\\ \bar{P}_7\end{bmatrix}_4 = 0.4E\begin{bmatrix}0.64 & -0.64 & -0.48 & 0.48\\ -0.64 & 0.64 & 0.48 & -0.48\\ -0.48 & 0.48 & 0.36 & -0.36\\ 0.48 & -0.48 & -0.36 & 0.36\end{bmatrix}_4 \frac{1}{0.4E}\begin{bmatrix}14.66\\ 0\\ 50.06\\ 0\end{bmatrix}_4 + \begin{bmatrix}0\\ 0\\ 0\\ 0\end{bmatrix}_4 = \begin{bmatrix}-14.7\text{ k}\\ 14.7\text{ k}\\ 11.0\text{ k}\\ -11.0\text{ k}\end{bmatrix}_4 \tag{5-93d}$$

Member 5

$$\begin{bmatrix}\bar{P}_6\\ \bar{P}_4\\ \bar{P}_5\\ \bar{P}_3\end{bmatrix}_5 = 0.4E\begin{bmatrix}0.64 & -0.64 & 0.48 & -0.48\\ -0.64 & 0.64 & -0.48 & 0.48\\ 0.48 & -0.48 & 0.36 & -0.36\\ -0.48 & 0.48 & -0.36 & 0.36\end{bmatrix}_5 \frac{1}{0.4E}\begin{bmatrix}0\\ -12.02\\ 0\\ 41.04\end{bmatrix}_5 + \begin{bmatrix}0\\ 0\\ 0\\ 0\end{bmatrix}_5 = \begin{bmatrix}-12.0\text{ k}\\ 12.0\text{ k}\\ -9.0\text{ k}\\ 9.0\text{ k}\end{bmatrix}_5 \tag{5-93e}$$

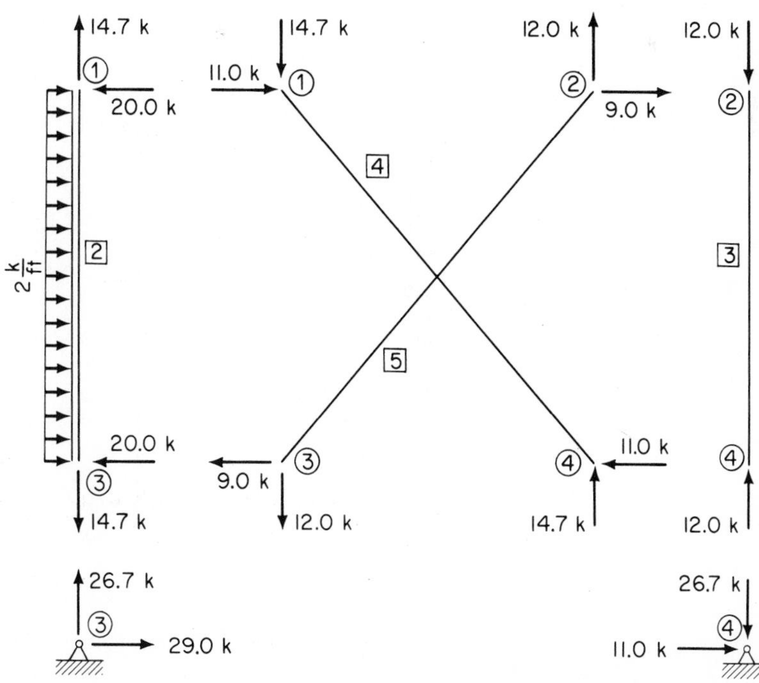

Fig. 5-24 Example 5-2: Final end actions.

The free body diagram for each member of the truss structure is shown in Fig. 5-24.

SUPPORT REACTIONS

Making the proper substitutions into Eq. (4-39), i.e.,

$$[\mathbf{R}_r] = [\mathbf{S}_{ru}][\Delta_u] - [\mathbf{JL}_r] \tag{4-39}$$

yields

$$\begin{bmatrix} R_5 \\ R_6 \\ R_7 \\ R_8 \end{bmatrix} = 0.4E \begin{bmatrix} 0 & 0 & -0.36 & -0.48 \\ 0 & -1.00 & -0.48 & -0.64 \\ -0.36 & 0.48 & 0 & 0 \\ 0.48 & -0.64 & 0 & -1.00 \end{bmatrix} \frac{1}{0.4E} \begin{bmatrix} 50.06 \\ 14.66 \\ 41.04 \\ -12.02 \end{bmatrix} - \begin{bmatrix} 20.0 \\ 0 \\ 0 \\ 0 \end{bmatrix} \tag{5-94a}$$

hence,

$$\begin{bmatrix} R_5 \\ R_6 \\ R_7 \\ R_8 \end{bmatrix} = \begin{bmatrix} -29.0\text{ k} \\ -26.7\text{ k} \\ -11.0\text{ k} \\ 26.7\text{ k} \end{bmatrix} \tag{5-94b}$$

The free body diagram of the structure is shown in Fig. 5-25.

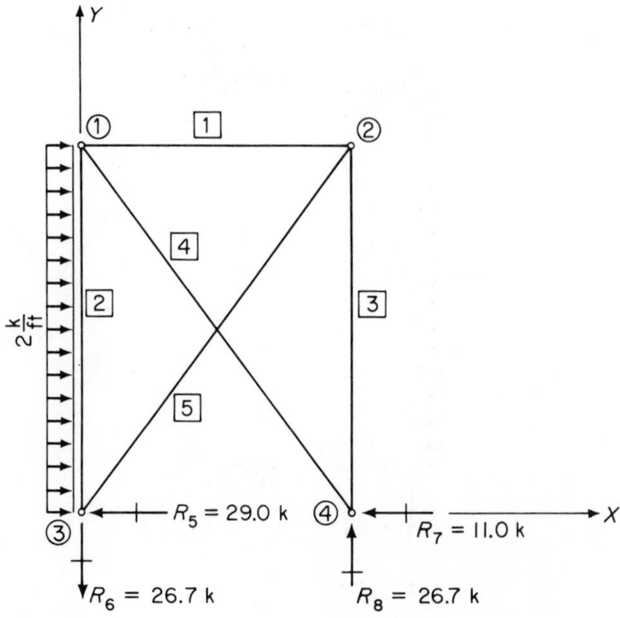

Fig. 5-25 Example 5-2: Support reactions.

5–7 Special Elements

In addition to the two basic types of beam elements which have been considered, i.e., the member with both ends restrained (Fig. 4-1) and the member with both ends pinned (Fig. 5-17), there are other types of beam elements which may be used in a structural system. For these special members, the various matrices required for the development of Eq. (4-32) and a set of equations for the final end actions similar to Eq. (5-44) can be established following the procedure used in developing matrices for the two basic beam elements.

5-7.1 Beam Element: One End Pinned, One End Restrained

Consider the beam element where the j-end is *pinned* and the k-end is *restrained* (Fig. 5-26). When subjecting the member to a unit value of each of the possible end displacements θ_q, δ_r, δ_s, δ_t, and δ_u, separately, the end actions required to maintain static equilibrium while restraining the ends of the member

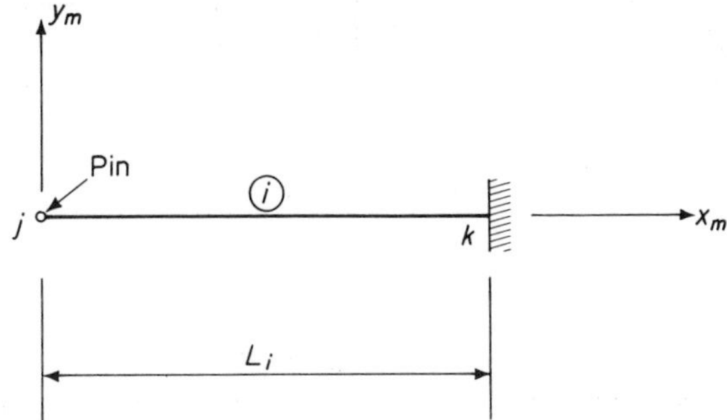

Fig. 5-26 Beam element—j-end pinned, k-end restrained.

against any other displacement are defined in Figs. 5-27. It should be recognized that the end moment at the j-end of the member must be zero since the pin permits free rotation of that end of the member; also, that the rotation of the pinned end of the member is undefined, since it cannot be related to the end rotation of other members which might frame into the same joint of the structure. This is not to say that the rotation of the joint cannot be defined should there be two or more members which are rigidly connected at the joint.

If the member of Fig. 5-26 is subjected to general displacements of its ends, the end actions which are required to maintain equilibrium of the deformed member (Fig. 5-28) can be defined as

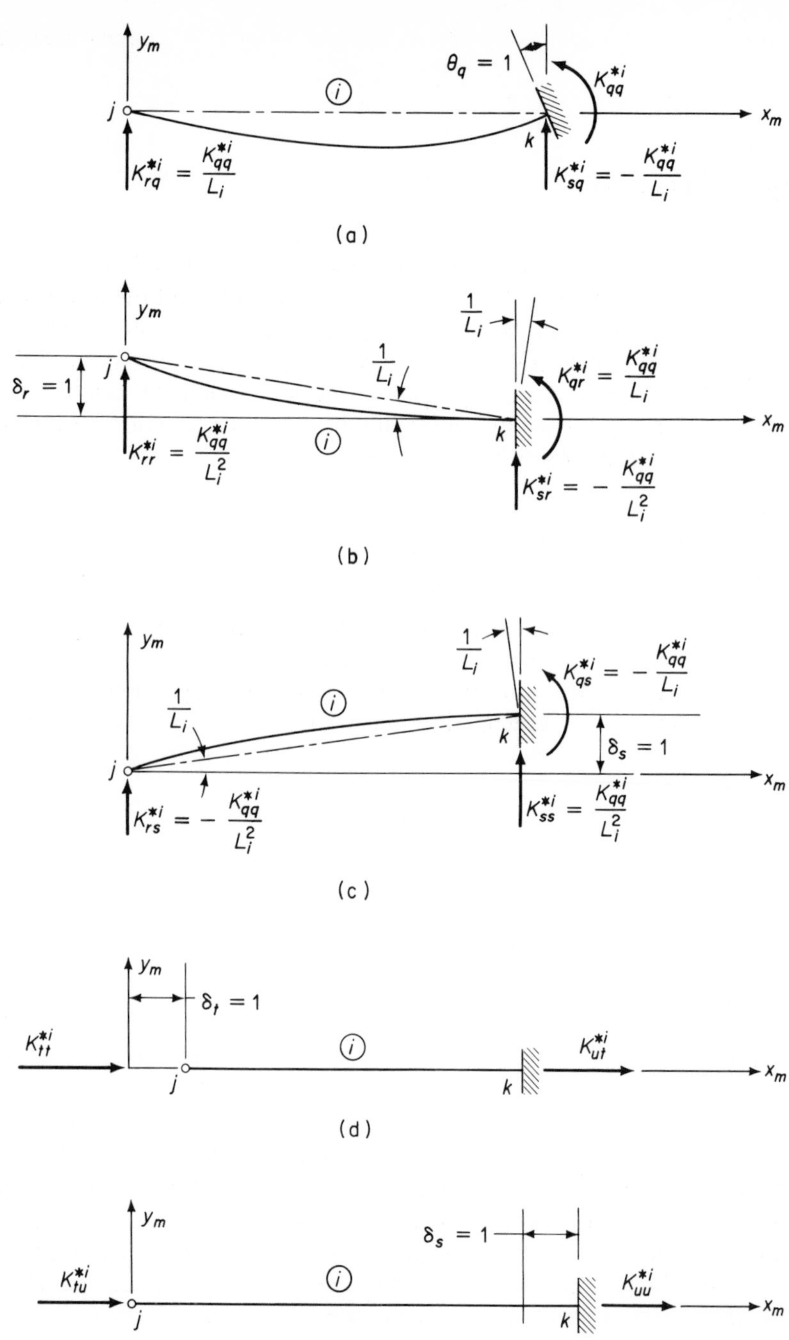

Fig. 5-27 Restraining end actions resulting from unit values of end displacement, pinned-restrained member (a) unit rotation δ_q; (b) unit translation δ_r; (c) unit translation δ_s; (d) unit translation δ_t; (e) unit translation δ_u.

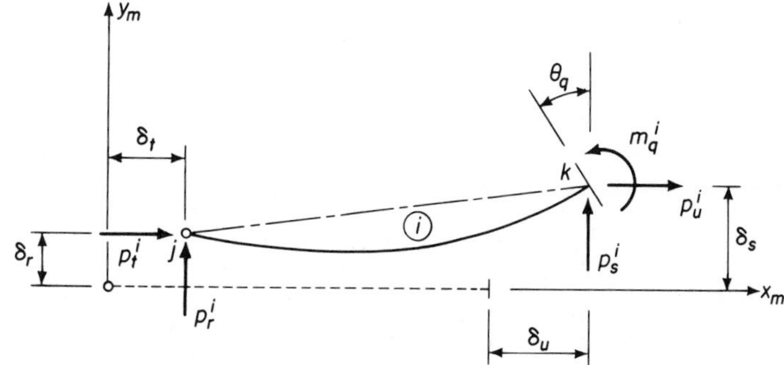

Fig. 5-28 End actions resulting from general end displacements of pinned-restrained member.

$$m_q^i = K_{qq}^{*i}\theta_q + K_{qr}^{*i}\delta_r + K_{qs}^{*i}\delta_s \tag{5-95a}$$

$$p_r^i = K_{rq}^{*i}\theta_q + K_{rr}^{*i}\delta_r + K_{rs}^{*i}\delta_s \tag{5-95b}$$

$$p_s^i = K_{sq}^{*i}\theta_q + K_{sr}^{*i}\delta_r + K_{ss}^{*i}\delta_s \tag{5-95c}$$

$$p_t^i = K_{tt}^{*i}\delta_t + K_{tu}^{*i}\delta_u \tag{5-95d}$$

$$p_u^i = K_{ut}^{*i}\delta_t + K_{uu}^{*i}\delta_u \tag{5-95e}$$

or

$$[\mathbf{m}^*]_i = [\mathbf{K}^*]_i[\boldsymbol{\delta}^*]_i \tag{5-96}$$

where

$$[\mathbf{m}^*]_i = \begin{bmatrix} m_q \\ p_r \\ p_s \\ p_t \\ p_u \end{bmatrix}_i \tag{5-97a}$$

$$[\boldsymbol{\delta}^*]_i = \begin{bmatrix} \theta_q \\ \delta_r \\ \delta_s \\ \delta_t \\ \delta_u \end{bmatrix}_i \tag{5-97b}$$

and

$$[\mathbf{K}^*]_i = \begin{matrix} & q & r & s & t & u & \\ & & & & & & \end{matrix}$$

$$[\mathbf{K}^*]_i = \begin{bmatrix} K_{qq}^* & K_{qr}^* & K_{qs}^* & 0 & 0 \\ K_{rq}^* & K_{rr}^* & K_{rs}^* & 0 & 0 \\ K_{sq}^* & K_{sr}^* & K_{ss}^* & 0 & 0 \\ 0 & 0 & 0 & K_{tt}^* & K_{tu}^* \\ 0 & 0 & 0 & K_{ut}^* & K_{uu}^* \end{bmatrix}_i \begin{matrix} q \\ r \\ s \\ t \\ u \end{matrix} \tag{5-97c}$$

(columns labelled q, r, s, t, u)

As indicated in Fig. 5-27, the member stiffness matrix of Expression (5-97c) can be expressed as

$$[\mathbf{K}^*]_i = \begin{array}{c} \begin{matrix} q & \quad r & \quad s & \quad t & \quad u \end{matrix} \\ \begin{bmatrix} K^*_{qq} & \dfrac{K^*_{qq}}{L} & \dfrac{-K^*_{qq}}{L} & 0 & 0 \\ \dfrac{K^*_{qq}}{L} & \dfrac{K^*_{qq}}{L^2} & \dfrac{-K^*_{qq}}{L^2} & 0 & 0 \\ \dfrac{-K^*_{qq}}{L} & \dfrac{-K^*_{qq}}{L^2} & \dfrac{K^*_{qq}}{L^2} & 0 & 0 \\ 0 & 0 & 0 & K^*_{tt} & K^*_{tu} \\ 0 & 0 & 0 & K^*_{ut} & K^*_{uu} \end{bmatrix}_i \end{array} \begin{matrix} q \\ r \\ s \\ t \\ u \end{matrix} \tag{5-98}$$

which, for a prismatic member, reduces to

$$[\mathbf{K}^*]_i = \begin{array}{c} \begin{matrix} q & \quad r & \quad s & \quad t & \quad u \end{matrix} \\ \begin{bmatrix} \dfrac{3EI}{L} & \dfrac{3EI}{L^2} & \dfrac{-3EI}{L^2} & 0 & 0 \\ \dfrac{3EI}{L^2} & \dfrac{3EI}{L^3} & \dfrac{-3EI}{L^3} & 0 & 0 \\ \dfrac{-3EI}{L^2} & \dfrac{-3EI}{L^3} & \dfrac{3EI}{L^3} & 0 & 0 \\ 0 & 0 & 0 & \dfrac{AE}{L} & \dfrac{-AE}{L} \\ 0 & 0 & 0 & \dfrac{-AE}{L} & \dfrac{AE}{L} \end{bmatrix}_i \end{array} \begin{matrix} p \\ r \\ s \\ t \\ u \end{matrix} \tag{5-99}$$

By defining the components of end actions with respect to the reference axes as shown in Fig. 5-29, the transformation matrix for the member with one end pinned and the other end restrained can be developed from Eqs. (5-20) or (5-23) and Expressions (5-31), i.e.,

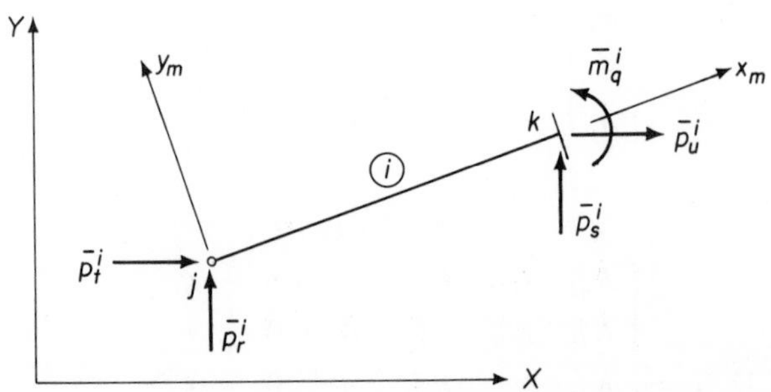

Fig. 5-29 Components of end action in the frame of the reference axes for pinned-restrained member.

$$[\mathbf{T}^*]_i = \begin{bmatrix} 1 & 0 & 0 & 0 & 0 \\ 0 & C_x & 0 & -C_y & 0 \\ 0 & 0 & C_x & 0 & -C_y \\ 0 & C_y & 0 & C_x & 0 \\ 0 & 0 & C_y & 0 & C_x \end{bmatrix}_i \begin{matrix} q \\ r \\ s \\ t \\ u \end{matrix} \quad \text{(columns } q, r, s, t, u\text{)} \tag{5-100}$$

Having established the transformation matrix, the member stiffness matrix can be transformed from the frame of the local member axes into the frame of the reference axes of the structure by the equations

$$[\bar{\mathbf{K}}^*]_i = [\mathbf{T}^*]_i^T[\mathbf{K}^*]_i[\mathbf{T}^*]_i \tag{5-101}$$

Using Expressions (5-98) and (5-100) and performing the indicated matrix operations, the transformed member stiffness matrix of Eqs. (5-101) can be written as shown in Table 5-8, Expression (5-102).

The final end actions for this member with one end pinned and the other end restrained, when part of a structural system, can be evaluated with respect to the local axes of the member from the set of equations

$$[\mathbf{M}^*]_i = [\mathbf{K}^*]_i[\mathbf{T}^*]_i[\bar{\boldsymbol{\delta}}^*]_i + [\mathbf{FM}^*]_i \tag{5-103}$$

where

$$[\mathbf{M}^*]_i = \begin{bmatrix} M_q \\ P_r \\ P_s \\ P_t \\ P_u \end{bmatrix}_i \approx \text{Components of final end actions with respect to the local axes} \tag{5-104a}$$

$$[\mathbf{FM}^*]_i = \begin{bmatrix} FM_q \\ FP_r \\ FP_s \\ FP_t \\ FP_u \end{bmatrix}_i \approx \text{Components of fixed end actions with respect to the local axes} \tag{5-104b}$$

and

$$[\bar{\boldsymbol{\delta}}^*]_i = \begin{bmatrix} \bar{\theta}_q \\ \bar{\delta}_r \\ \bar{\delta}_s \\ \bar{\delta}_t \\ \bar{\delta}_u \end{bmatrix}_i \approx \text{Components of end displacement with respect to the reference axes} \tag{5-104c}$$

If desired, the components of final end actions, as well as the components of fixed end actions, in the frame of the local axes can be resolved into components in the frame of the reference axes by the expressions

Table 5-8

TRANSFORMED MEMBER STIFFNESS MATRIX

(Reference Axes System)

$$
[\bar{\mathbf{K}}^*]_i = \begin{array}{c}
\begin{array}{ccccc} \bar{q} & \bar{r} & \bar{s} & \bar{t} & \bar{u} \end{array} \\
\left[\begin{array}{ccccc}
K^*_{qq} & \dfrac{C_x K^*_{qq}}{L} & \dfrac{-C_x K^*_{qq}}{L} & \dfrac{-C_y K^*_{qq}}{L} & \dfrac{C_y K^*_{qq}}{L} \\
\dfrac{C_x K^*_{qq}}{K} & \dfrac{C_x^2 K^*_{qq}}{L^2} + C_y^2 K^*_{tt} & \dfrac{-C_x^2 K^*_{qq}}{L^2} + C_y^2 K^*_{tu} & C_x C_y K^*_{tt} - \dfrac{C_x C_y K^*_{qq}}{L^2} & \dfrac{C_x C_y K^*_{qq}}{L^2} + C_x C_y K^*_{tu} \\
\dfrac{-C_x K^*_{qq}}{L} & \dfrac{-C_x^2 K^*_{qq}}{L^2} + C_y^2 K^*_{ut} & \dfrac{C_x^2 K^*_{qq}}{L^2} + C_y^2 K^*_{uu} & \dfrac{C_x C_y K^*_{qq}}{L^2} + C_x C_y K^*_{ut} & C_x C_y K^*_{uu} - \dfrac{C_x C_y K^*_{qq}}{L^2} \\
\dfrac{-C_y K^*_{qq}}{L} & C_x C_y K^*_{tt} - \dfrac{C_x C_y K^*_{qq}}{L^2} & \dfrac{C_x C_y K^*_{qq}}{L^2} + C_x C_y K^*_{tu} & C_x^2 K^*_{tt} + \dfrac{C_y^2 K^*_{qq}}{L^2} & C_x^2 K^*_{tu} - \dfrac{C_y^2 K^*_{qq}}{L^2} \\
\dfrac{C_y K^*_{qq}}{L} & \dfrac{C_x C_y K^*_{qq}}{L^2} + C_x C_y K^*_{ut} & C_x C_y K^*_{uu} - \dfrac{C_x C_y K^*_{qq}}{L^2} & C_x^2 K^*_{ut} - \dfrac{C_y^2 K^*_{qq}}{L^2} & C_x^2 K^*_{uu} + \dfrac{C_y^2 K^*_{qq}}{L^2}
\end{array}\right]_i
\end{array}
\begin{array}{c} \\ \bar{q} \\ \bar{r} \\ \bar{s} \\ \bar{t} \\ \bar{u} \end{array}
\qquad \textbf{(5-102)}
$$

$$[\overline{\mathbf{M}}^*]_i = [\mathbf{T}^*]_i^T[\mathbf{M}^*]_i \tag{5-105a}$$

and

$$[\overline{\mathbf{FM}}^*]_i = [\mathbf{T}^*]_i^T[\mathbf{FM}^*]_i \tag{5-105b}$$

5-7.2 Helical Spring

The helical spring (Fig. 5-30) is similar to the truss member (Fig. 5-17) which was discussed in Sec. 5-6 in that it too can resist only axial deformations. Hence, most of the matrices which were written for the truss member can be used for the helical spring; only the member stiffness matrices and the transformation matrix need be modified for this type of member.

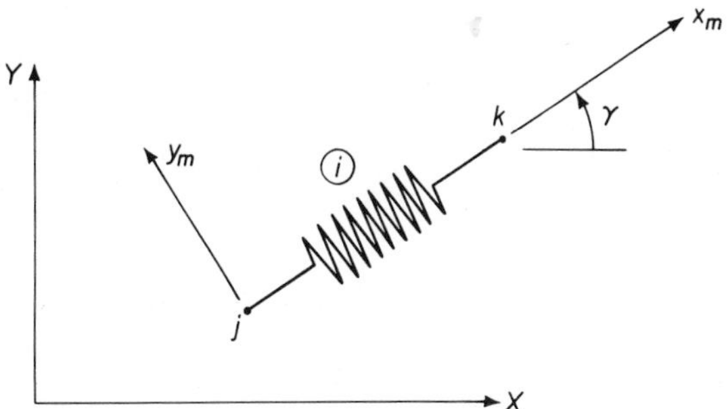

Fig. 5-30 Helical spring.

Defining the force required to impose a unit value of end displacement of the spring as the *spring constant* K_s, the member stiffness matrix with respect to the local axes can be written from Eq. (5-74) as

$$[\mathbf{K}_S]_i = \begin{array}{c} \begin{matrix} r & s & t & u \end{matrix} \\ \begin{bmatrix} 0 & 0 & 0 & 0 \\ 0 & 0 & 0 & 0 \\ 0 & 0 & K_S & -K_S \\ 0 & 0 & -K_S & K_S \end{bmatrix}_i \end{array} \begin{matrix} r \\ s \\ t \\ u \end{matrix} \tag{5-106}$$

As for the transformation matrix, since the length of the spring is usually undefined, it is advantageous to write this matrix in terms of the angle γ, i.e., the angle between the x_m axis of the member and the X-axis of the reference axes (*measuring counterclockwise*), rather than in terms of the coordinates of the j- and k-ends of the member in the frame of the reference axes. Hence, evaluating the direction cosines by Expression (5-11), the transformation matrix of Eqs. (5-68a) can be written as

$$[\mathbf{T}_S]_i = \begin{bmatrix} \cos\gamma & 0 & -\sin\gamma & 0 \\ 0 & \cos\gamma & 0 & -\sin\gamma \\ \sin\gamma & 0 & \cos\gamma & 0 \\ 0 & \sin\gamma & 0 & \cos\gamma \end{bmatrix}_i \tag{5-107}$$

Now, substituting Expressions (5-106) and (5-107) into Eq. (5-76), the transformed member stiffness matrix for the helical spring becomes

$$[\overline{\mathbf{K}}_S]_i = K_S \begin{bmatrix} \sin^2\gamma & -\sin^2\gamma & \sin\gamma\cos\gamma & -\sin\gamma\cos\gamma \\ -\sin^2\gamma & \sin^2\gamma & -\sin\gamma\cos\gamma & \sin\gamma\cos\gamma \\ \sin\gamma\cos\gamma & -\sin\gamma\cos\gamma & \cos^2\gamma & -\cos^2\gamma \\ -\sin\gamma\cos\gamma & \sin\gamma\cos\gamma & -\cos^2\gamma & \cos^2\gamma \end{bmatrix}_i \tag{5-108}$$

When developing the mathematical model for a structural system, the helical spring can be used to represent the response of the foundation of the system. Unless the structure is supported by rock or pile clusters, it is unlikely that a fixed support can be realized; however, a pin support may not be realistic either, since the supporting soil will offer resistance to the movement of a support.

5-7.3 Inclined Roller Support

As stated earlier, the displacement of a joint must be described in terms of *independent* components of displacement with respect to the reference axes, otherwise Eq. (4-36) will be singular. Now, for a roller support [Fig. 5-31(a)], the independent components of joint translation are the displacements *normal* and *tangential* to the surface guiding the roller. If this surface is oriented parallel to one of the reference axes [Fig. 5-31(a)], then no special problem will arise in defining the independent components of translation with respect to the reference axes; but if the surface is inclined with respect to the reference axes [Fig. 5-31(b)], there will be a problem in defining the displacement of the joint, since the components of joint translation with respect to the reference axes are not independent. In order to alleviate this problem the roller support can be replaced by an ***equivalent member***, as shown in Figs. 5-31(c) and 5-31(d), normal to the surface guiding the roller. This member should offer the same restraints to the joint as the roller; thus, the member should have a very large cross-sectional area ($A \rightarrow \infty$) and a length of the same order of magnitude as the other members of the system so that its axial deformation will be negligible; also, the member should offer no resistance to the displacement of the joint normal to the longitudinal axis of the equivalent member. This can be satisfied by assuming that the member has a moment of inertia equal to zero ($I = 0$) and is fixed at its base if the joint of the structure is rigid [Fig. 5-31(c)], or by assuming that the member is pinned at its base if the joint of the structure is pin-connected [Fig. 5-31(d)].

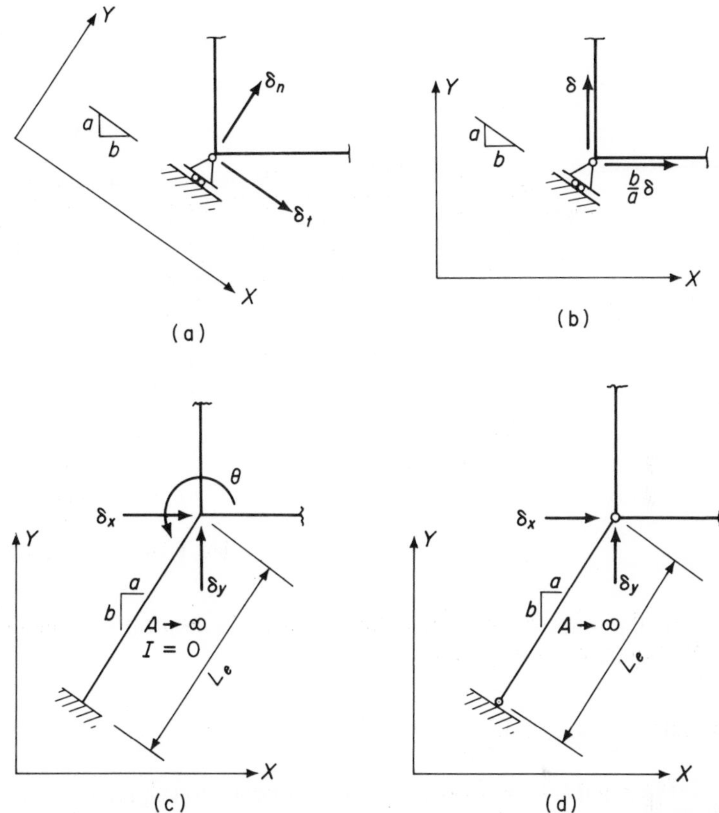

Fig. 5-31 Inclined roller: (a) surface oriented parallel to a reference axis; (b) surface oriented at an angle to reference axes; (c) equivalent support for rigid joint in system; (d) equivalent support for pinned joint in system.

5–8 Analysis of Planar Frame with Elastic Supports

Example 5-3. The final end actions of the members and the reactions of the supports resulting from the applied loading are to be determined for the structural system described in Fig. 5-32. The beams of the structure have a cross-sectional area A of 18.0 in^2 and a moment of inertia about the axis of inplane bending I of 5450 in^4; the column has a cross-sectional area A of 25.2 in^2 and a moment of inertia about the axis of in-plane bending I of 4000 in^4; and the two helical spring supports have spring constants K_S equal to 100 k/in. The modulus of elasticity E for the system is equal to 30,000 ksi. The joint numbers are given in the circles adjacent to the joints and the member numbers are indicated in the squares adjacent to the members.

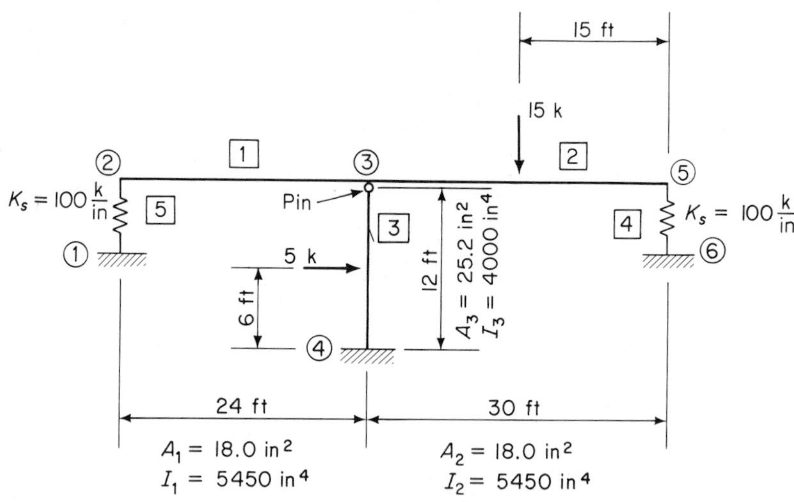

Fig. 5-32 Example 5-3: Structural frame.

At the beam–column connection, joint 3, the beam is continuous and the column is pin-connected to the beam.

MEMBER INFORMATION

The *j*- and *k*-ends of each member have been selected, establishing the orientation of the local axes for each member, and the reference axes for the structure have been positioned as shown in Fig. 5-33. In Table 5-9, the coordinates of the joints with respect to

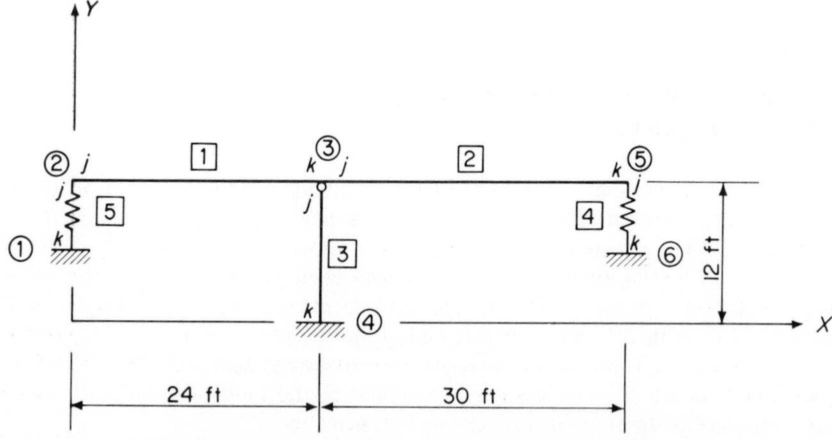

Fig. 5-33 Example 5-3: Establishment of local and reference axes.

the reference axes are listed. In Table 5-10, the direction cosines are given for each member, along with the cross-sectional area, moment of inertia, and length; the spring constant and angle γ are also given for the helical springs.

Table 5-9

	Coordinate	
Joint	X, ft	Y, ft
2	0	12.0
3	24.0	12.0
4	24.0	0
5	54.0	12.0

Table 5-10

	Joint							*Direction Cosines*	
Member	j	k	A, ft^2	I, ft^4	L, ft	K_S, k/ft	γ, degrees	C_x	C_y
1	2	3	0.125	0.263	24.0	—	—	1.0	0
2	3	5	0.125	0.263	30.0	—	—	1.0	0
3	3	4	0.175	0.193	12.0	—	—	0	−1.0
4	5	6	—	—	—	1200.0	270.0	—	—
5	2	1	—	—	—	1200.0	270.0	—	—

JOINT DISPLACEMENT MATRIX

Identifying and labeling the components of joint displacement with respect to the reference axes as shown in Fig. 5-34, the complete joint displacement matrix is written as

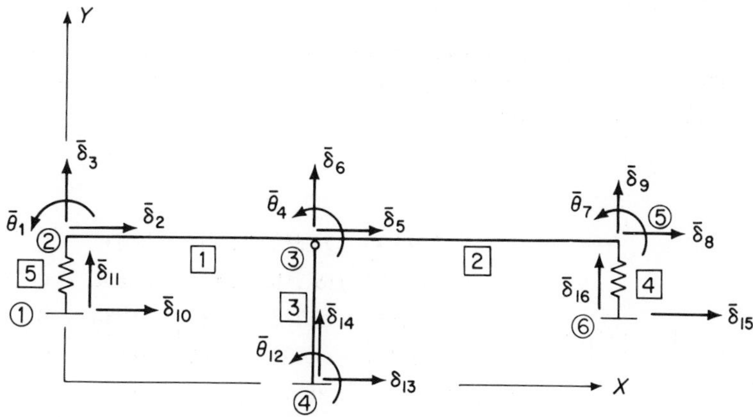

Fig. 5-34 Example 5-3: Identification of components of joint displacement.

$$[\boldsymbol{\Delta}_c] = \begin{bmatrix} \bar{\theta}_1 \\ \bar{\delta}_2 \\ \bar{\delta}_3 \\ \bar{\theta}_4 \\ \bar{\delta}_5 \\ \bar{\delta}_6 \\ \bar{\theta}_7 \\ \bar{\delta}_8 \\ \bar{\delta}_9 \\ \hdashline \bar{\delta}_{10} \\ \bar{\delta}_{11} \\ \bar{\theta}_{12} \\ \bar{\delta}_{13} \\ \bar{\delta}_{14} \\ \bar{\delta}_{15} \\ \bar{\delta}_{16} \end{bmatrix} = \begin{bmatrix} [\boldsymbol{\Delta}_u] \\ \hdashline [\boldsymbol{\Delta}_r] \end{bmatrix} \tag{5-109}$$

MEMBER STIFFNESS MATRICES

For members 1 and 2, which are restrained against rotation and translation at both ends (Fig. 5-34) in the restrained structure, the member stiffness matrices with respect to the local axes $[\mathbf{K}]_i$ can be written from Expression (5-7); and the transformed member stiffness matrices written with respect to the reference axes $[\bar{\mathbf{K}}]_i$ can be obtained from Expression (5-40). However, since the transformation matrices for these members, Expression (5-32), are identity matrices, i.e.,

$$[\mathbf{T}]_1 = [\mathbf{T}]_2 = [\mathbf{I}] \tag{5-110}$$

the transformed member stiffness matrix for each member will be the same as the member stiffness matrix for the member; this is due to the fact that the local axes have the same orientation as the reference axes.

Member 1

$$[\mathbf{K}]_1 = [\bar{\mathbf{K}}]_1 = 1 \times 10^3 \begin{array}{c} \begin{matrix} 1 & 4 & 3 & 6 & 2 & 5 \end{matrix} \\ \begin{bmatrix} 189.360 & 94.680 & 11.835 & -11.835 & 0 & 0 \\ 94.680 & 189.360 & 11.835 & -11.835 & 0 & 0 \\ 11.835 & 11.835 & 0.986 & -0.986 & 0 & 0 \\ -11.835 & -11.835 & -0.986 & 0.986 & 0 & 0 \\ 0 & 0 & 0 & 0 & 22.500 & -22.500 \\ 0 & 0 & 0 & 0 & -22.500 & 22.500 \end{bmatrix}_1 \end{array} \begin{matrix} 1 \\ 4 \\ 3 \\ 6 \\ 2 \\ 5 \end{matrix} \tag{5-111}$$

Member 2

$$[\mathbf{K}]_2 = [\bar{\mathbf{K}}]_2 = 1 \times 10^3 \begin{array}{c} \begin{matrix} 4 & 7 & 6 & 9 & 5 & 8 \end{matrix} \\ \begin{bmatrix} 151.488 & 75.744 & 7.574 & -7.574 & 0 & 0 \\ 75.744 & 151.488 & 7.574 & -7.754 & 0 & 0 \\ 7.574 & 7.574 & 0.505 & -0.505 & 0 & 0 \\ -7.574 & -7.574 & -0.505 & 0.505 & 0 & 0 \\ 0 & 0 & 0 & 0 & 18.000 & -18.000 \\ 0 & 0 & 0 & 0 & -18.000 & 18.000 \end{bmatrix}_2 \end{array} \begin{matrix} 4 \\ 7 \\ 6 \\ 9 \\ 5 \\ 8 \end{matrix} \tag{5-112}$$

For member 3, which has one end pinned and the other end restrained, the member stiffness matrix $[\mathbf{K}^*]_i$ can be written from Expression (5-99); the transformation matrix $[\mathbf{T}^*]_i$ is given by Expression (5-100); and the transformed member stiffness matrix $[\bar{\mathbf{K}}^*]_i$ can be obtained from Expression (5-102).

Member 3

$$[\mathbf{K}^*]_3 = 1 \times 10^3 \begin{array}{c} \begin{matrix} q & r & s & t & u \end{matrix} \\ \begin{bmatrix} 208.440 & 17.370 & -17.370 & 0 & 0 \\ 17.370 & 1.448 & -1.448 & 0 & 0 \\ -17.370 & -1.448 & 1.448 & 0 & 0 \\ 0 & 0 & 0 & 63.000 & -63.000 \\ 0 & 0 & 0 & -63.000 & 63.000 \end{bmatrix}_3 \end{array} \begin{matrix} q \\ r \\ s \\ t \\ u \end{matrix} \tag{5-113a}$$

$$[\mathbf{T}^*]_3 = \begin{bmatrix} 1 & 0 & 0 & 0 & 0 \\ 0 & 0 & 0 & 1.0 & 0 \\ 0 & 0 & 0 & 0 & 1.0 \\ 0 & -1.0 & 0 & 0 & 0 \\ 0 & 0 & -1.0 & 0 & 0 \end{bmatrix}_3 \tag{5-113b}$$

and

$$[\bar{\mathbf{K}}^*]_3 = 1 \times 10^3 \begin{array}{c} \begin{matrix} 12 & 6 & 14 & 5 & 13 \end{matrix} \\ \begin{bmatrix} 208.440 & 0 & 0 & 17.370 & -17.370 \\ 0 & 63.000 & -63.000 & 0 & 0 \\ 0 & -63.000 & 63.000 & 0 & 0 \\ 17.370 & 0 & 0 & 1.448 & -1.448 \\ -17.370 & 0 & 0 & -1.448 & 1.448 \end{bmatrix}_3 \end{array} \begin{matrix} 12 \\ 6 \\ 14 \\ 5 \\ 13 \end{matrix} \tag{5-113c}$$

For the two helical springs, members 4 and 5, the member stiffness matrices $[\mathbf{K}_S]_i$ can be written from Expression (5-106); the transformation matrices $[\mathbf{T}_S]_i$ can be developed according to Expression (5-107); and the transformed member stiffness matrix $[\bar{\mathbf{K}}_S]_i$ can be obtained from Expression (5-108).

Member 4

$$[\mathbf{K}_S]_4 = 1 \times 10^3 \begin{array}{c} \begin{matrix} r & s & t & u \end{matrix} \\ \begin{bmatrix} 0 & 0 & 0 & 0 \\ 0 & 0 & 0 & 0 \\ 0 & 0 & 1.200 & -1.200 \\ 0 & 0 & -1.200 & 1.200 \end{bmatrix}_4 \end{array} \begin{matrix} r \\ s \\ t \\ u \end{matrix} \quad \text{(5-114a)}$$

$$[\mathbf{T}_S]_4 = \begin{bmatrix} 0 & 0 & 1 & 0 \\ 0 & 0 & 0 & 1 \\ -1 & 0 & 0 & 0 \\ 0 & -1 & 0 & 0 \end{bmatrix}_4 \quad \text{(5-114b)}$$

and

$$[\bar{\mathbf{K}}_S]_4 = 1 \times 10^3 \begin{array}{c} \begin{matrix} 9 & 16 & 8 & 15 \end{matrix} \\ \begin{bmatrix} 1.200 & -1.200 & 0 & 0 \\ -1.200 & 1.200 & 0 & 0 \\ 0 & 0 & 0 & 0 \\ 0 & 0 & 0 & 0 \end{bmatrix}_4 \end{array} \begin{matrix} 9 \\ 16 \\ 8 \\ 15 \end{matrix} \quad \text{(5-114c)}$$

Member 5

$$[\mathbf{K}_S]_5 = 1 \times 10^3 \begin{array}{c} \begin{matrix} r & s & t & u \end{matrix} \\ \begin{bmatrix} 0 & 0 & 0 & 0 \\ 0 & 0 & 0 & 0 \\ 0 & 0 & 1.200 & -1.200 \\ 0 & 0 & -1.200 & 1.200 \end{bmatrix}_5 \end{array} \begin{matrix} r \\ s \\ t \\ u \end{matrix} \quad \text{(5-115a)}$$

$$[\mathbf{T}_S]_5 = \begin{bmatrix} 0 & 0 & 1 & 0 \\ 0 & 0 & 0 & 1 \\ -1 & 0 & 0 & 0 \\ 0 & -1 & 0 & 0 \end{bmatrix}_5 \quad \text{(5-115b)}$$

and

$$[\bar{\mathbf{K}}_S]_5 = 1 \times 10^3 \begin{array}{c} \begin{matrix} 3 & 11 & 2 & 10 \end{matrix} \\ \begin{bmatrix} 1.200 & -1.200 & 0 & 0 \\ -1.200 & 1.200 & 0 & 0 \\ 0 & 0 & 0 & 0 \\ 0 & 0 & 0 & 0 \end{bmatrix}_5 \end{array} \begin{matrix} 3 \\ 11 \\ 2 \\ 10 \end{matrix} \quad \text{(5-115c)}$$

STRUCTURE STIFFNESS MATRIX

The complete structure stiffness matrix is developed by summing the elements of the transformed member stiffness matrices with like subscripts and is given in Table 5-11, Expression (5-116). This matrix is partitioned with respect to the unrestrained and re-

Table 5-11

$[\mathbf{S}_c] = 1 \times 10^3$

	1	2	3	4	5	6	7	8	9	10	11	12	13	14	15	16	
	189.360	0	11.835	94.680	0	−11.835	0	0	0	0	0	0	0	0	0	0	1
	0	22.500	0	0	−22.500	0	0	0	0	0	0	0	0	0	0	0	2
	11.835	0	2.186	11.835	0	−0.986	0	0	0	0	−1.200	0	0	0	0	0	3
	94.680	0	11.835	340.848	0	−4.261	75.744	0	−7.574	0	0	0	0	0	0	0	4
	0	−22.500	0	0	41.948	0	0	−18.000	0	0	0	17.370	−1.448	0	0	0	5
	−11.835	0	−0.986	−4.261	0	64.491	7.574	0	−0.505	0	0	0	0	−63.000	0	0	6
	0	0	0	75.744	0	7.574	151.488	0	−7.574	0	0	0	0	0	0	0	7
	0	0	0	0	−18.000	0	0	18.000	0	0	0	0	0	0	0	0	8
	0	0	0	−7.574	0	−0.505	−7.574	0	1.705	0	0	0	0	0	0	−1.200	9
	0	0	0	0	0	0	0	0	0	0	0	0	0	0	0	0	10
	0	0	−1.200	0	0	0	0	0	0	0	1.200	0	0	0	0	0	11
	0	0	0	0	17.370	0	0	0	0	0	0	208.440	−17.370	0	0	0	12
	0	0	0	0	−1.448	0	0	0	0	0	0	−17.370	1.448	0	0	0	13
	0	0	0	0	0	−63.000	0	0	0	0	0	0	0	63.00	0	0	14
	0	0	0	0	0	0	0	0	0	0	0	0	0	0	0	0	15
	0	0	0	0	0	0	0	0	−1.200	0	0	0	0	0	0	1.200	16

(**5-116**)

strained components of joint displacement as indicated in Table 5-11. The four submatrices are defined as

$$\left[\begin{array}{c|c} [\mathbf{S}_{uu}] & [\mathbf{S}_{ur}] \\ \hline [\mathbf{S}_{ru}] & [\mathbf{S}_{rr}] \end{array}\right]$$

Now,

$$[\mathbf{S}_{uu}]^{-1} = 1 \times 10^{-6} \begin{array}{c} \begin{array}{ccccccccc} 1 & 2 & 3 & 4 & 5 & 6 & 7 & 8 & 9 \end{array} \\ \left[\begin{array}{ccccccccc} 8.292 & 0 & -38.570 & -1.102 & 0 & 0.793 & 0.358 & 0 & -3.071 \\ 0 & 735.052 & 0 & 0 & 690.608 & 0 & 0 & 690.608 & 0 \\ -38.570 & 0 & 767.615 & -18.531 & 0 & 2.255 & 6.518 & 0 & -52.695 \\ -1.102 & 0 & -18.531 & 4.534 & 0 & 0.106 & -1.624 & 0 & 12.955 \\ 0 & 690.608 & 0 & 0 & 690.608 & 0 & 0 & 690.608 & 0 \\ 0.793 & 0 & 2.255 & 0.106 & 0 & 15.796 & -0.752 & 0 & 1.808 \\ 0.358 & 0 & 6.518 & -1.624 & 0 & -0.752 & 9.100 & 0 & 32.987 \\ 0 & 690.608 & 0 & 0 & 690.608 & 0 & 0 & 746.163 & 0 \\ -3.071 & 0 & -52.695 & 12.955 & 0 & 1.808 & 32.987 & 0 & 791.127 \end{array}\right] \end{array} \begin{array}{c} \\ 1 \\ 2 \\ 3 \\ 4 \\ 5 \\ 6 \\ 7 \\ 8 \\ 9 \end{array} \tag{5-117}$$

JOINT LOAD MATRIX

For the loading of the structure as indicated in Fig. 5-32, the fixed end actions must be determined for members 2 and 3 in order to establish the joint loads for the restrained structure. For member 2, which is restrained at both ends and loaded at midspan with a 15-k normal concentrated load, the fixed end actions are equal to

$$[\mathbf{FM}]_2 = \begin{bmatrix} FM_p \\ FM_q \\ FP_r \\ FP_s \\ FP_t \\ FP_u \end{bmatrix}_2 = \begin{bmatrix} 56.250 \text{ ft-k} \\ -56.250 \text{ ft-k} \\ 7.500 \text{ k} \\ 7.500 \text{ k} \\ 0 \\ 0 \end{bmatrix}_2 \tag{5-118a}$$

as shown in Fig. 5-35(a). Member 3, which is restrained at one end and pinned at the other end, is loaded at midheight with a 5-k normal concentrated load; the fixed end actions for this member, which are shown in Fig. 5-35(b), are equal to

$$[\mathbf{FM}^*]_3 = \begin{bmatrix} FM_q^* \\ FP_r^* \\ FP_s^* \\ FP_t^* \\ FP_u^* \end{bmatrix}_3 = \begin{bmatrix} 11.250 \text{ ft-k} \\ -1.562 \text{ k} \\ -3.438 \text{ k} \\ 0 \\ 0 \end{bmatrix}_3 \tag{5-118b}$$

Transforming these fixed end actions into joint loads as shown in Fig. 5-35(c), the complete joint load matrix is written as

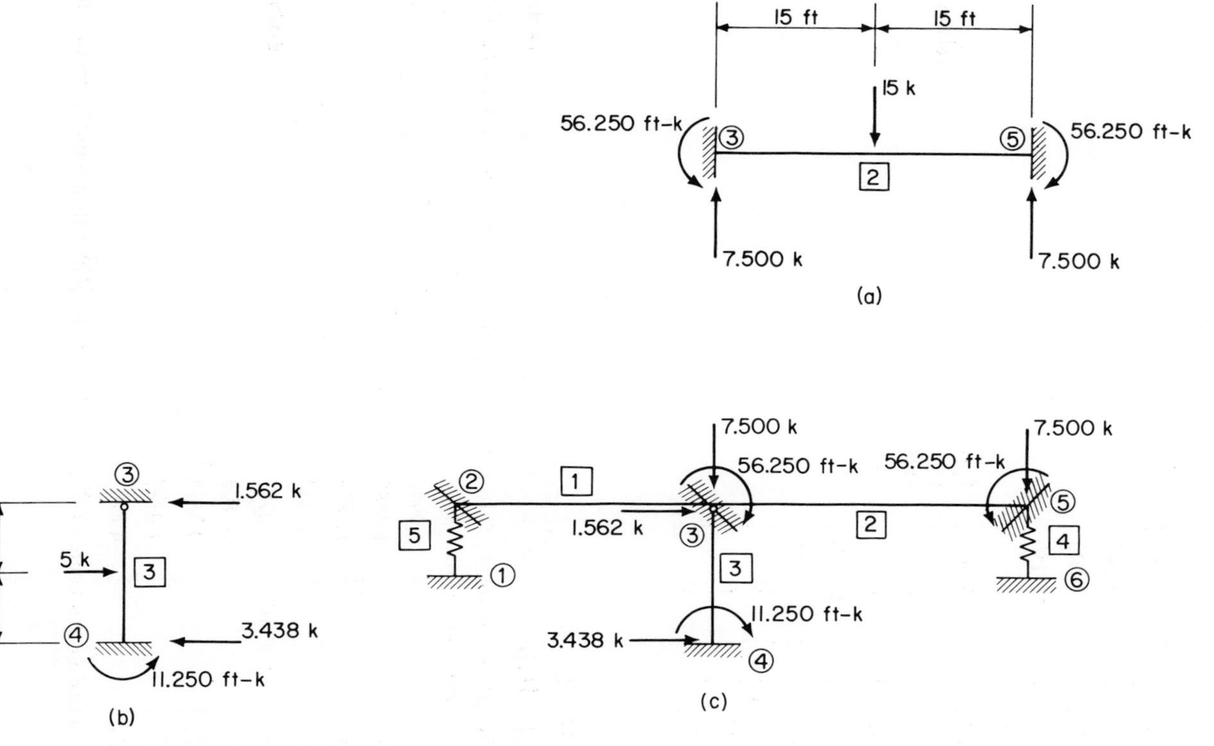

Fig. 5-35 Example 5-3: Joint loads: (a) fixed end actions—member 2; (b) fixed end actions—member 3; (c) joint loads.

$$[\mathbf{JL}_c] = \begin{bmatrix} JL_1 \\ JL_2 \\ JL_3 \\ JL_4 \\ JL_5 \\ JL_6 \\ JL_7 \\ JL_8 \\ JL_9 \\ \hdashline JL_{10} \\ JL_{11} \\ JL_{12} \\ JL_{13} \\ JL_{14} \\ JL_{15} \\ JL_{16} \end{bmatrix} = \begin{bmatrix} 0 \\ 0 \\ 0 \\ -56.250 \\ 1.562 \\ -7.500 \\ 56.250 \\ 0 \\ -7.500 \\ \hdashline 0 \\ 0 \\ -11.250 \\ 3.438 \\ 0 \\ 0 \\ 0 \end{bmatrix} = \begin{bmatrix} [\mathbf{JL}_u] \\ \hdashline [\mathbf{JL}_r] \end{bmatrix} \tag{5-119}$$

SOLUTION

From Eq. (4-36),

$$[\mathbf{\Delta}_u] = [\mathbf{S}_{uu}]^{-1}[\mathbf{JL}_u] \tag{4-37}$$

Substituting the proper matrices into this system of equations and performing the indicated matrix operation yields

$$[\mathbf{\Delta}_u] = \begin{bmatrix} \bar{\theta}_1 \\ \bar{\delta}_2 \\ \bar{\delta}_3 \\ \bar{\theta}_4 \\ \bar{\delta}_5 \\ \bar{\delta}_6 \\ \bar{\theta}_7 \\ \bar{\delta}_8 \\ \bar{\delta}_9 \end{bmatrix} = 1 \times 10^{-3} \begin{bmatrix} 0.0992 \\ 1.0787 \\ 1.7873 \\ -0.4443 \\ 1.0787 \\ -0.1803 \\ 0.3615 \\ 1.0787 \\ -4.8202 \end{bmatrix} \tag{5-120}$$

These are the actual components of displacement of the joints (translations defined in units of feet).

FINAL END ACTIONS

Member 1

Since member 1 has been considered to be restrained at both ends, the final end actions in the frame of the local axes can be obtained from Eq. (5-46), i.e.,

$$[\mathbf{M}]_1 = [\mathbf{K}]_1[\mathbf{T}]_1[\bar{\boldsymbol{\delta}}]_1 + [\mathbf{FM}]_1 \tag{5-121}$$

Recognizing that

$$[\mathbf{T}]_1 = [\mathbf{I}] \tag{5-122a}$$

$$[\mathbf{FM}]_1 = [\mathbf{0}] \tag{5-122b}$$

and

$$[\bar{\boldsymbol{\delta}}]_1 = \begin{bmatrix} \bar{\theta}_1 \\ \bar{\theta}_4 \\ \bar{\delta}_3 \\ \bar{\delta}_6 \\ \bar{\delta}_2 \\ \bar{\delta}_5 \end{bmatrix}_1 = 1 \times 10^{-3} \begin{bmatrix} 0.0992 \\ -0.4443 \\ 1.7873 \\ -0.1803 \\ 1.0787 \\ 1.0787 \end{bmatrix}_1 \tag{5-122c}$$

Eq. (5-121) can be solved, yielding

$$[\mathbf{M}]_1 = \begin{bmatrix} M_p \\ M_q \\ P_r \\ P_s \\ P_t \\ P_u \end{bmatrix}_1 = \begin{bmatrix} 0 \\ -51.4 \text{ ft-k} \\ -2.1 \text{ k} \\ 2.1 \text{ k} \\ 0 \\ 0 \end{bmatrix}_1 \tag{5-123}$$

Member 2

For member 2, which has also been treated as restrained at both ends, the final end actions with respect to the local axes can be obtained from the set of equations

$$[\mathbf{M}]_2 = [\mathbf{K}]_2[\mathbf{T}]_2[\bar{\boldsymbol{\delta}}]_2 + [\mathbf{FM}]_2 \tag{5-124}$$

considering that

$$[\mathbf{T}]_2 = [\mathbf{I}] \tag{5-125a}$$

and

$$[\bar{\boldsymbol{\delta}}]_2 = \begin{bmatrix} \bar{\theta}_4 \\ \bar{\theta}_7 \\ \bar{\delta}_6 \\ \bar{\delta}_9 \\ \bar{\delta}_5 \\ \bar{\delta}_8 \end{bmatrix}_2 = 1 \times 10^{-3} \begin{bmatrix} -0.4443 \\ 0.3615 \\ -0.1803 \\ -4.8202 \\ 1.0787 \\ 1.0787 \end{bmatrix}_2 \tag{5-125b}$$

Eq. (5-124) yields

$$[\mathbf{M}]_2 = \begin{bmatrix} M_p \\ M_q \\ P_r \\ P_s \\ P_t \\ P_u \end{bmatrix}_2 = \begin{bmatrix} 51.4 \text{ ft-k} \\ 0 \\ 9.2 \text{ k} \\ 5.8 \text{ k} \\ 0 \\ 0 \end{bmatrix}_2 \tag{5-126}$$

Member 3

For a member pinned at one end and restrained at the other end, the final end actions in the frame of the local axes can be determined from Eq. (5-103); thus, for member 3,

$$[\mathbf{M}^*]_3 = [\mathbf{K}^*]_3[\mathbf{T}^*]_3[\bar{\boldsymbol{\delta}}^*]_3 + [\mathbf{FM}^*]_3 \tag{5-127}$$

and with

$$[\bar{\boldsymbol{\delta}}^*]_3 = \begin{bmatrix} \bar{\theta}_{12} \\ \bar{\delta}_6 \\ \bar{\delta}_{14} \\ \bar{\delta}_5 \\ \bar{\delta}_{13} \end{bmatrix}_3 = 1 \times 10^{-3} \begin{bmatrix} 0 \\ -0.1803 \\ 0 \\ 1.0787 \\ 0 \end{bmatrix}_3 \tag{5-128}$$

$$[\mathbf{M}^*]_3 = \begin{bmatrix} M_q \\ P_r \\ P_s \\ P_t \\ P_u \end{bmatrix}_3 = \begin{bmatrix} 30.0 \text{ ft-k} \\ 0 \\ -5.0 \text{ k} \\ 11.3 \text{ k} \\ -11.3 \text{ k} \end{bmatrix}_3 \tag{5-129}$$

Member 4

For a helical spring, the final end actions in the frame of the local axes can be evaluated by the set of equations

$$[\mathbf{P}_S]_i = [\mathbf{K}_S]_i[\mathbf{T}_S]_i[\bar{\boldsymbol{\delta}}_S]_i + [\mathbf{FP}_S]_i \tag{5-130}$$

For member 4, this set of equations can be written as

$$[\mathbf{P}_S]_4 = [\mathbf{K}_S]_4[\mathbf{T}_S]_4[\bar{\boldsymbol{\delta}}_S]_4 + [\mathbf{FP}_S]_4 \tag{5-131}$$

and since

$$[\mathbf{FP}_S]_4 = [\mathbf{0}] \tag{5-132a}$$

and

$$[\bar{\boldsymbol{\delta}}_S]_4 = \begin{bmatrix} \bar{\delta}_9 \\ \bar{\delta}_{16} \\ \bar{\delta}_8 \\ \bar{\delta}_{15} \end{bmatrix}_4 = 1 \times 10^{-3} \begin{bmatrix} -4.8202 \\ 0 \\ 1.0787 \\ 0 \end{bmatrix}_4 \tag{5-132b}$$

Eq. (5-131) yields

$$[\mathbf{P}_S]_4 = \begin{bmatrix} P_r \\ P_s \\ P_t \\ P_u \end{bmatrix}_4 = \begin{bmatrix} 0 \\ 0 \\ 5.8 \text{ k} \\ -5.8 \text{ k} \end{bmatrix}_4 \tag{5-133}$$

Member 5

For member 5, which is a helical spring, Eq. (5-130) is written as

$$[\mathbf{P}_S]_5 = [\mathbf{K}_S]_5[\mathbf{T}_S]_5[\bar{\boldsymbol{\delta}}_S]_5 + [\mathbf{FP}_S]_5 \tag{5-134}$$

which with

$$[\mathbf{FP}_S]_5 = [0] \tag{5-135a}$$

and

$$[\bar{\boldsymbol{\delta}}_S]_5 = \begin{bmatrix} \bar{\delta}_3 \\ \bar{\delta}_{11} \\ \bar{\delta}_2 \\ \bar{\delta}_{10} \end{bmatrix}_5 = 1 \times 10^{-3} \begin{bmatrix} 1.7863 \\ 0 \\ 1.0787 \\ 0 \end{bmatrix}_5 \tag{5-135b}$$

yields

$$[\mathbf{P}_S]_5 = \begin{bmatrix} P_r \\ P_s \\ P_t \\ P_u \end{bmatrix}_5 = \begin{bmatrix} 0 \\ 0 \\ -2.1\text{ k} \\ 2.1\text{ k} \end{bmatrix}_5 \tag{5-136}$$

The free body diagram for each of the members is shown in Fig. 5-36.

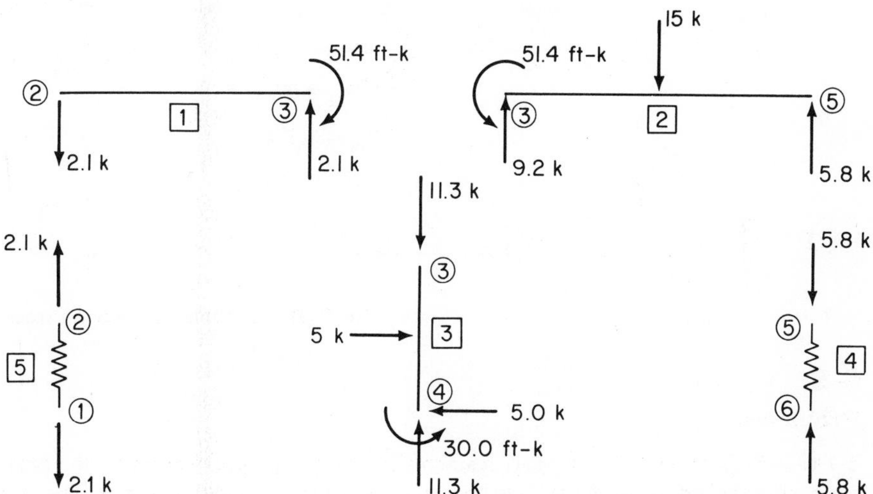

Fig. 5-36 Example 5-3: Final end actions.

SUPPORT REACTIONS

The reactions of the supports of the structural system resulting from the given loading of the structure can be determined by solving the set of equations given as

$$[\mathbf{S}_{ru}][\boldsymbol{\Delta}_u] - [\mathbf{JL}_r] = [\mathbf{R}_r] \tag{4-39}$$

Thus, substituting the proper matrices into this set of equations and performing the indicated matrix operations yields

$$[\mathbf{R}_r] = \begin{bmatrix} R_{10} \\ R_{11} \\ R_{12} \\ R_{13} \\ R_{14} \\ R_{15} \\ R_{16} \end{bmatrix} = \begin{bmatrix} 0 \\ -2.1 \text{ k} \\ 30.0 \text{ ft-k} \\ -5.0 \text{ k} \\ 11.3 \text{ k} \\ 0 \\ 5.8 \text{ k} \end{bmatrix} \tag{5-137}$$

The free body diagram for the structural system is shown in Fig. 5-37.

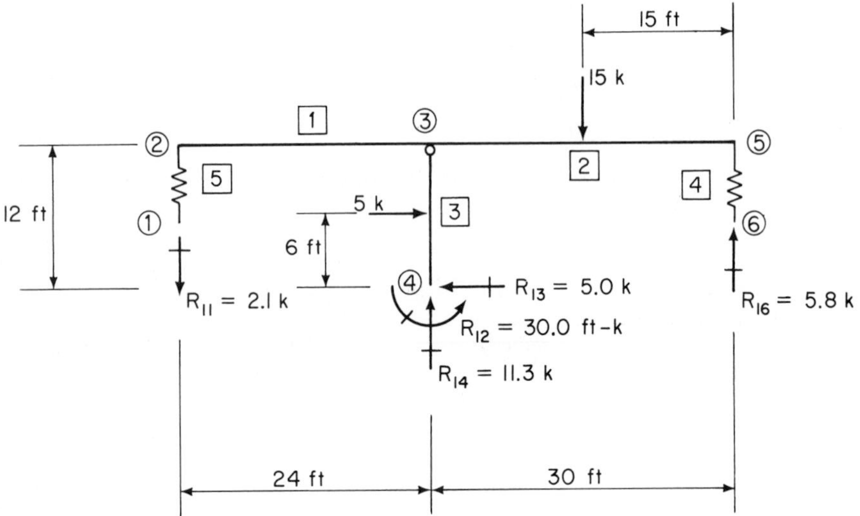

Fig. 5-37 Example 5-3: Support reactions.

5–9 Problems

5-1 to 5-7. Determine the support reactions for the structural system and the final end actions for the individual elements of the structure for the indicated loading of the system; $E = 30{,}000$ ksi.

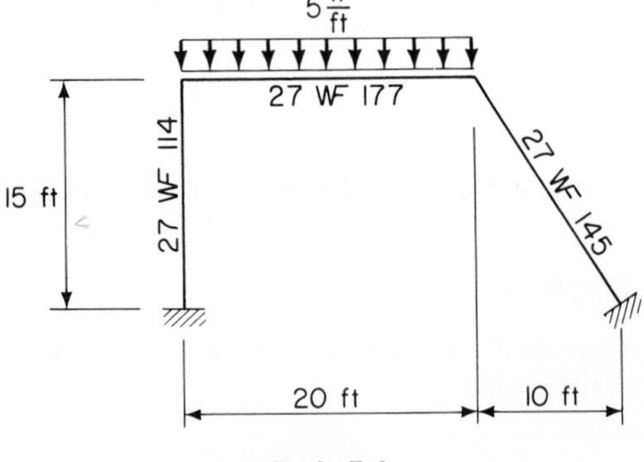

Prob. 5-1

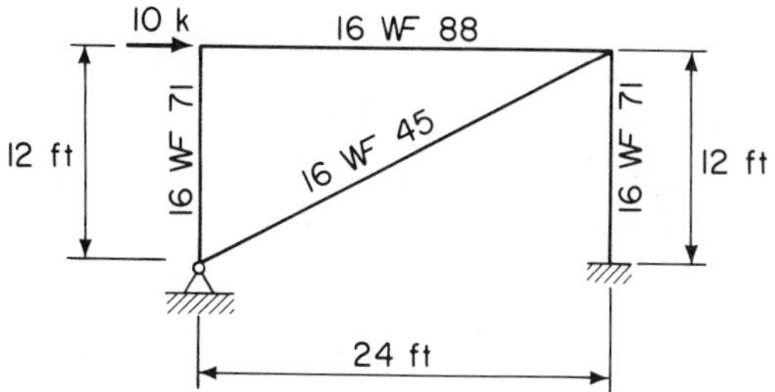

Prob. 5-2

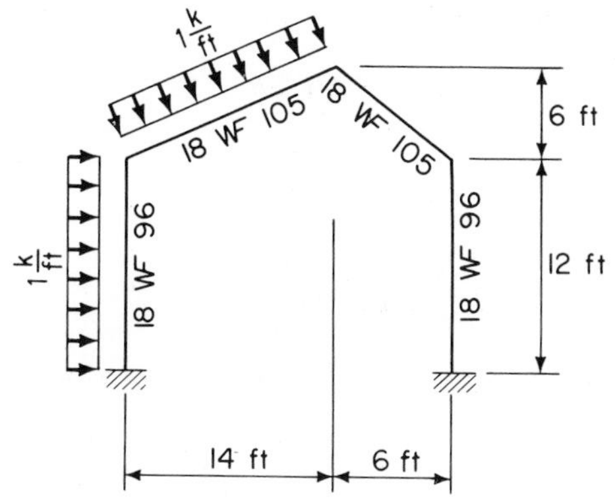

Prob. 5-3

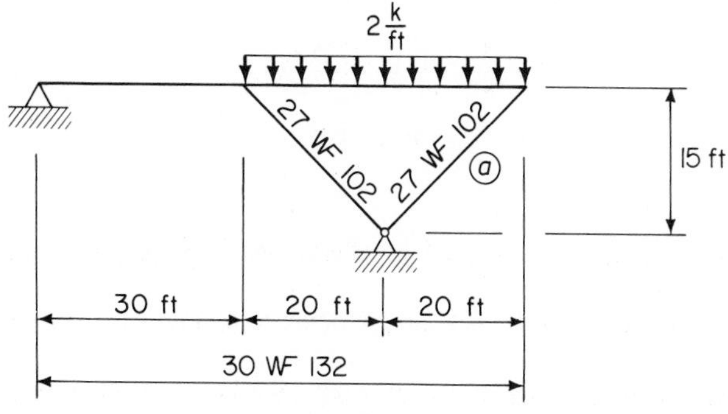

Prob. 5-4

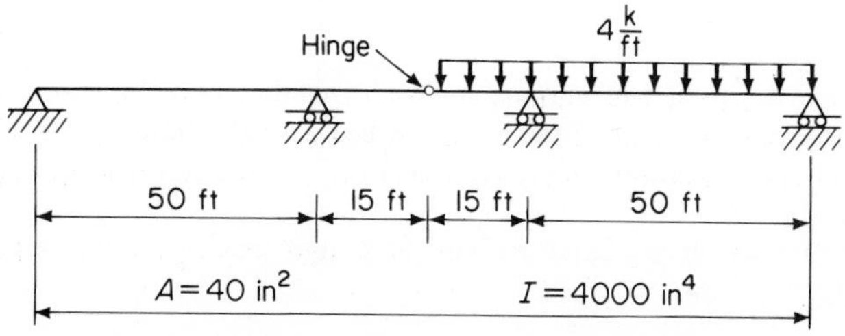

Prob. 5-5 *Note:* Axial deformation may be neglected.

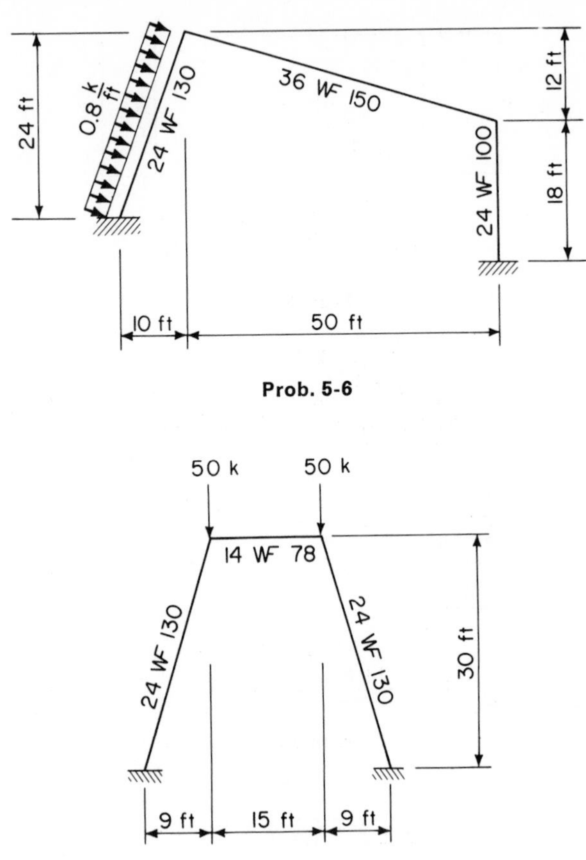

Prob. 5-6

Prob. 5-7

5-8. Analyze the structure of Prob. 5-1 for a settlement of the left support of 0.75 in.

5-9. Analyze the frame of Prob. 5-3 for a clockwise rotation of 5° of the left support.

5-10. Determine the final end actions for each member and the support reactions for the system if member *a* of the structure of Prob. 5-4 is fabricated 0.5 in. too short.

5-11. Analyze the rigid frame of Prob. 5-6 for a support settlement of 0.8 in. of the right support.

5-12. Determine the final end actions for each member and the support reactions for the structure that would result if the 14 WF 78 beam of the frame in Prob. 5-7 had a 6° bend (right end rotated counterclockwise) at a point 4 ft from the left end of the beam.

5-13 to 5-17. Determine the bar forces in the planar trusses for the indicated loading; $E = 30{,}000$ ksi.

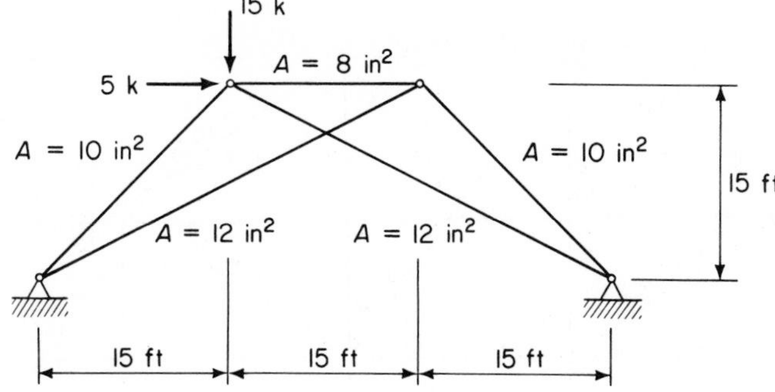

Prob. 5-13

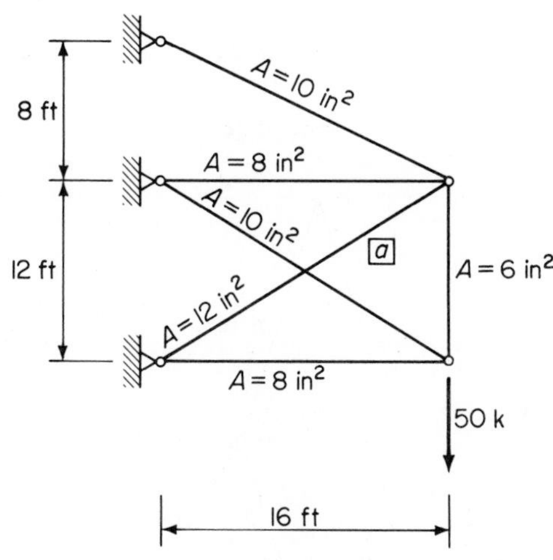

Prob. 5-14

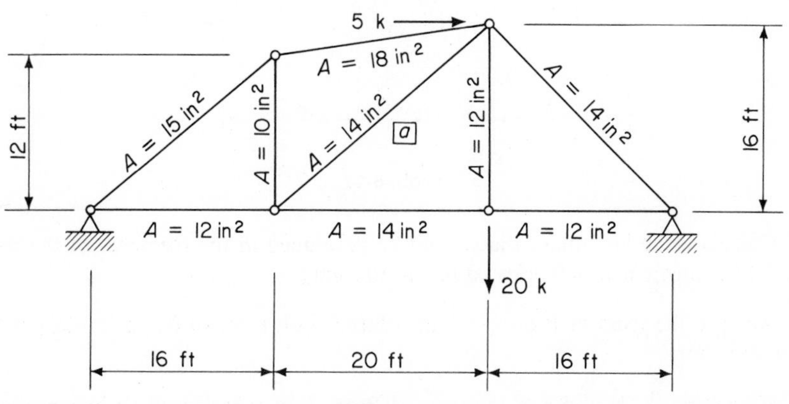

Prob. 5-15

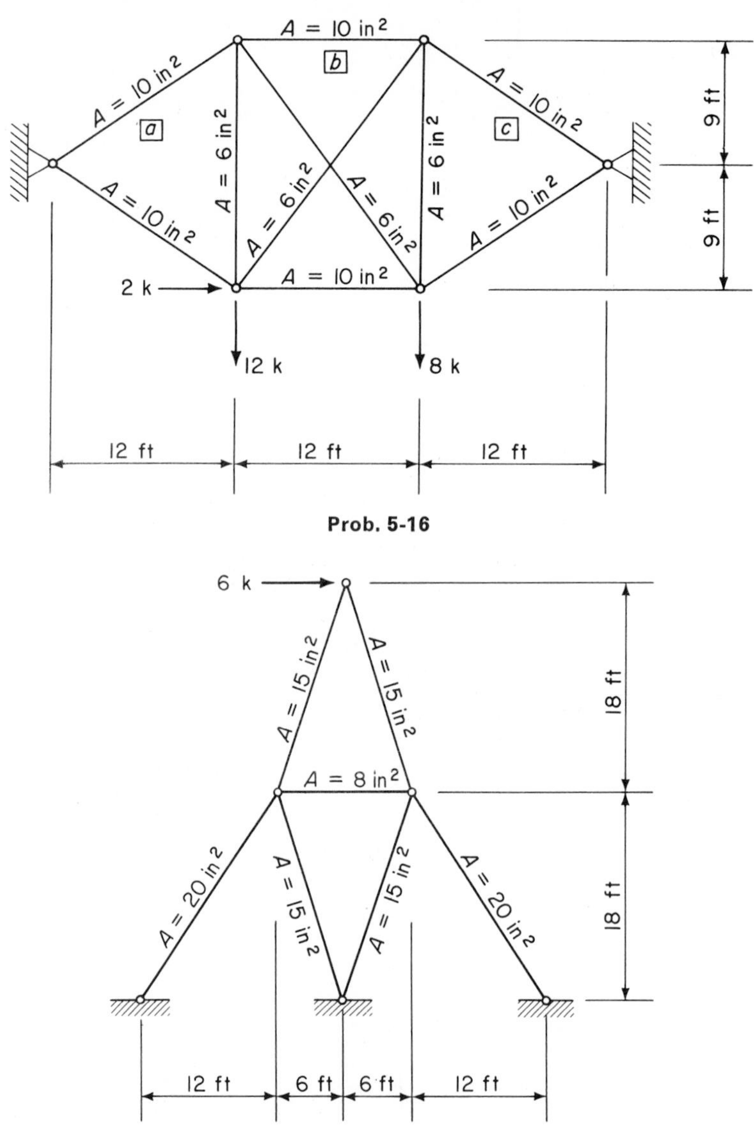

Prob. 5-16

Prob. 5-17

5-18. Calculate the bar forces that would be developed in the members of the truss of Prob. 5-14 if member *a* is fabricated 0.5 in. too long.

5-19. Analyze the truss of Prob. 5-15 for a fabrication error of 0.3 in. causing member *a* to be too short.

5-20. If members *a*, *b*, and *c* of the truss of Prob. 5-16 experienced an increase in temperature of 40° with respect to the temperature in the other members of the truss, what would be the magnitude of the axial forces developed in the members? The coefficient of thermal expansion is 0.0000065.

5-21. How much would the length of members *a*, *b*, and *c* in the truss of Prob. 5-16 have to be changed in order to chamber (displace vertically) the two lower joints 1 in.?

5-22. Analyze the two-span continuous beam for the applied load. The beam has a cross-sectional area of 20 in^2 and a moment of inertia of 6000 in^4; the spring constant for the helical spring is 10 k/in.; $E = 30{,}000$ ksi.

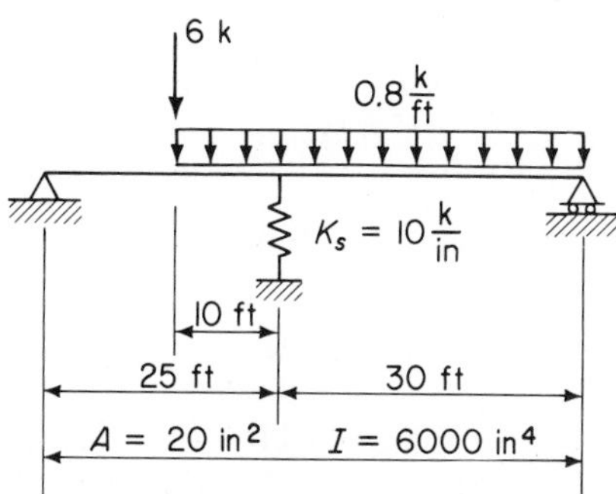

Prob. 5-22

5-23. The reinforced concrete portal frame is supported by elastic foundations represented by springs. The spiral springs, which can resist only rotational displacements, have an assumed spring constant of 5000 k-ft/rad; the helical springs, which can resist only axial displacements, have an assumed spring constant of 5 k/in. For the beam and columns, $E = 3000$ ksi. Determine the support reactions and the final member end actions for the given loading. Draw the moment and shear diagrams for the beam and columns.

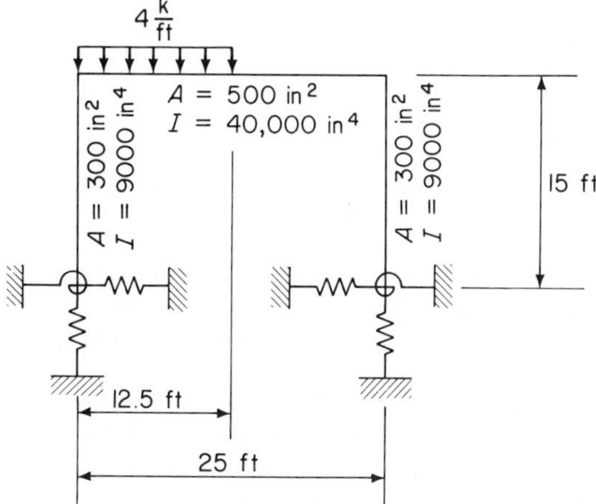

Prob. 5-23

5-24. Analyze the continuous beam for the indicated loading condition. The beam has a cross-sectional area of 30 in^2 and a moment of inertia of 800 in^4; $E = 30{,}000$ ksi. The spiral spring at the right end of the beam can resist only a rotational displacement and has a spring constant of 8000 k-ft/rad. The helical spring providing the intermediate support has a spring constant of 500 k/in.

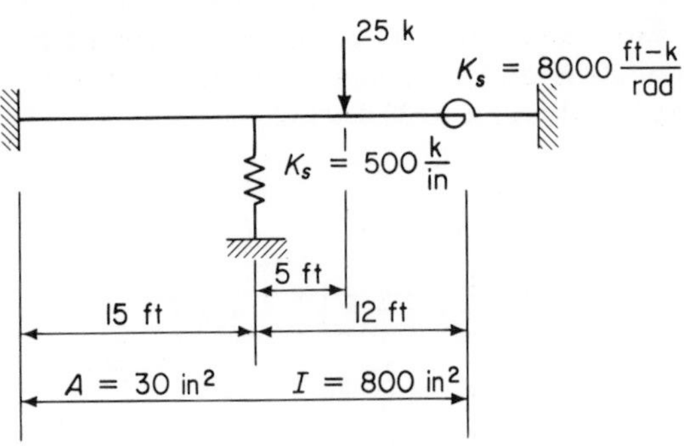

Prob. 5-24

5-25. Analyze the portal frame for the applied loading. The beam–column connections which are semirigid are represented by the pin–spring joint. The spiral springs have a spring constant of 10,000 k-ft/rad; $E = 30{,}000$ ksi.

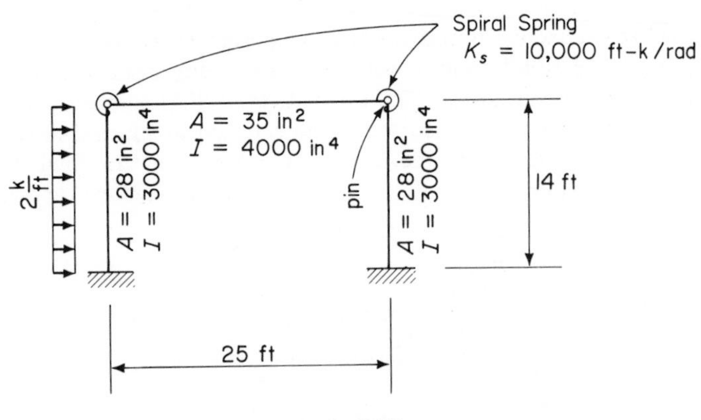

Prob. 5-25

5-26. Develop the member stiffness matrix $[\mathbf{K}]_i$ for a prismatic WF beam to account for shear deformations along with flexural and axial deformations. Let L = span length, E = modulus of elasticity, and I = moment of inertia of cross-section.

5-27. It has been stated and shown (Chapter 4) that a structure can be analyzed by the stiffness method for a support displacement by assuming that the disturbance is applied to the restrained structure, thus describing the imposed disturbance in terms of fixed end actions. Using the set of joint equilibrium equations

$$[\mathbf{S}_c][\mathbf{\Delta}_c] = [\mathbf{JL}_c] + [\mathbf{R}_c]$$

explain how a structure can be analyzed for a given support displacement without having to describe the disturbance in terms of fixed end actions.

5-28. Write a computer program to determine by the stiffness method the bar forces developed in a truss structure with loads applied at the joints.

5-29. Using the stiffness method develop a computer program to analyze a rigid planar frame. The members of the structure may be loaded with either a uniform normal load distributed over the entire length of the member or a normal concentrated load positioned at any point along the member. In addition to the member loads, the frame may be loaded at the joints.

SELECTED REFERENCES

5-1 Gere, James M., and William Weaver, Jr., *Analysis of Framed Structures.* Princeton, N.J.: D. Van Nostrand Co., Inc., 1965.

5-2 Wang, Chu-Kia, *Statically Indeterminate Structures.* New York: McGraw-Hill Book Company, Inc., 1953.

5-3 Morice, P. B., *Linear Structural Analysis.* London: Thames and Hudson, 1959.

5-4 Hall, A. S., and R. W. Woodhead, *Frame Analysis.* New York: John Wiley & Sons, Inc., 1961.

5-5 Rubinstein, Moshe F., *Matrix Computer Analysis of Structures.* Englewood Cliffs, N.J.: Prentice-Hall, Inc., 1966.

5-6 Willems, Nicholas, and William M. Lucas, Jr., *Matrix Analysis for Structural Engineers.* Englewood Cliffs, N.J.: Prentice-Hall, Inc., 1968.

5-7 Livesley, R. K., *Matrix Methods of Structural Analysis.* New York: The Macmillan Company, Inc., 1964.

6 STIFFNESS METHOD OF ANALYSIS: THREE-DIMENSIONAL STRUCTURES

6–1 Introduction

The technique which has been developed in Chapters 4 and 5 for the analysis of the planar structural system can be expanded very easily to analyze a three-dimensional (space) structure. A matrix equation similar to the matrix equation which has been written to describe the joint equilibrium of the planar structural system, i.e.,

$$[\mathbf{S}_c][\Delta_c] = [\mathbf{JL}_c] + [\mathbf{R}_c] \tag{4-32}$$

can be written to describe the joint equilibrium of the space structure; also, the matrix equation describing the equilibrium of a beam element of a planar structure, i.e.,

$$[\mathbf{M}]_i = [\mathbf{K}]_i[\mathbf{T}]_i[\bar{\boldsymbol{\delta}}]_i + [\mathbf{FM}]_i \tag{5-46}$$

can be redefined to describe the equilibrium of a beam element arbitrarily oriented in space. Thus, the analysis of a space structure by the stiffness method differs from the analysis of a planar structure only in the composition of the various matrices that are used.

As demonstrated in Chapters 4 and 5, the primary task of this method of analysis is the development of the complete structure stiffness matrix $[\mathbf{S}_c]$, which represents a *summation* of the member stiffness matrices of the individual elements of the structural system under investigation. This leads to the problem of establishing the member stiffness matrix for each beam element of the system with respect to the single set of coordinate axes established for the whole structure, i.e., ***the reference axes***.

6–2
Sign Convention

The sign convention to be used in the analysis of a three-dimensional structural system will be an extension of the sign convention introduced in Chapter 5 for the analysis of the planar system. Also, in line with the sign convention introduced in Chapter 5, a ***right-handed system of orthogonal, coordinate axes*** (Fig. 6-1) will be used for both ***the local member axes and the reference axes*** of the structure. The axes shown in Fig. 6-1 indicate the positive senses of the right-handed coordinate system.

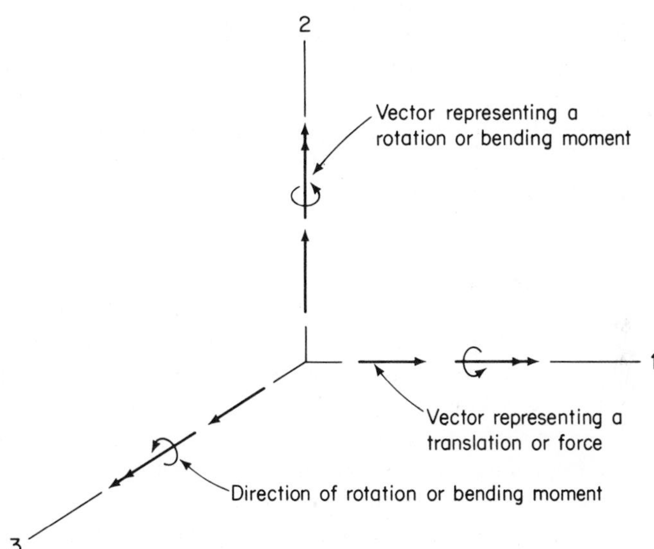

Fig. 6-1 Sign convention: three dimensional space.

When operating in a three-dimensional space, it is convenient to represent rotations and bending moments, as well as translations and forces, by vectors: a ***translation or force*** will be represented by a ***vector with a single arrowhead*** and a ***rotation or bending moment*** will be represented by a ***vector with a double arrowhead*** (Fig. 6-1). The direction of a rotation or of a bending moment will be indicated by the *curved fingers of the right hand when pointing the thumb of the right hand in the direction of the arrowheads of the vector*. The positive direction of rotation or bending moment as related to the representative vector is illustrated in Fig. 6-1.

The sign convention that will be employed can be stated as follows:

> A vector pointing in the direction of a positive coordinate ordinate axis represents a positive quantity (Fig. 6-1).

6–3
The Beam Element

When analyzing a structural system that must be described in terms of a three-dimensional space, there will be six possible components of joint displacement, i.e., a component of translation and a component of rotation with respect to each of the coordinate axes of the three space, at each joint that must be accounted for, this is to say, each joint will have *six possible degrees of freedom*. Consequently, for a given beam element of a three-dimensional structural system there will be twelve possible components of end displacement—i.e., six components at each end of the member that correspond to the displacements of the two joints connected by the member—that must be considered in establishing the end-action–displacement relationships for the member.

6-3.1 Member Stiffness Matrix

The typical beam element i of a three-dimensional structure is assumed to be arbitrarily oriented in space and positioned in the frame of a set of orthogonal axes x_m–y_m–z_m, with the j-end of the member at the origin of the system of axes and the x_m axis directed toward the k-end of the member as illustrated in Fig. 6-2. This system of axes constitutes the local axes of the member. The x_m axis defines the *centroidal axis* of the member, the y_m axis defines the *minor principal axis* of the cross-section, and the z_m axis defines the *major principal axis* of the cross-section. In addition, the *shear center* of the cross-section is assumed to coincide with the centroid of the cross-section. The beam element may have either a constant or variable moment of inertia and cross-sectional area over its length.

The twelve possible displacements of the ends of member i,—i.e., δ_t, δ_r, δ_v, θ_l, θ_n, and θ_p at the j-end, and δ_u, δ_s, δ_w, θ_m, θ_o, and θ_q at the k-end—with respect to the local axes are defined in Fig. 6-2. If the member is subjected to a unit value of each of the possible end displacements, separately, the end actions which are required to maintain static equilibrium while restraining the ends of the member against any other displacement are defined in Figs. 6-3 and 6-4. Should the element be subjected to general displacements of its ends, the resulting end actions required to maintain static equilibrium of the deformed member (Fig. 6-5) can be determined by superimposing the corresponding end actions developed by the individual application of unit values of each end displacement (Figs. 6-3 and 6-4) times the actual magnitude of the imposed displacement, i.e.,

$$p^i_t = K^i_{tt}\delta_t + K^i_{tu}\delta_u \tag{6-1a}$$
$$p^i_r = K^i_{rr}\delta_r + K^i_{rp}\theta_p + K^i_{rs}\delta_s + K_{rq}\theta_q \tag{6-1b}$$
$$p^i_v = K^i_{vv}\delta_v + K^i_{vn}\theta_n + K^i_{vw}\delta_w + K^i_{vo}\theta_o \tag{6-1c}$$
$$m^i_l = K^i_{ll}\theta_l + K^i_{lm}\theta_m \tag{6-1d}$$
$$m^i_n = K^i_{nv}\delta_v + K^i_{nn}\theta_n + K^i_{nw}\delta_w + K^i_{no}\theta_o \tag{6-1e}$$
$$m^i_p = K^i_{pr}\delta_r + K^i_{pp}\theta_p + K^i_{ps}\delta_s + K^i_{pq}\theta_q \tag{6-1f}$$
$$p^i_u = K^i_{ut}\delta_t + K^i_{uu}\delta_u \tag{6-1g}$$
$$p^i_s = K^i_{sr}\delta_r + K^i_{sp}\theta_p + K^i_{ss}\delta_s + K^i_{sq}\theta_q \tag{6-1h}$$
$$p^i_w = K^i_{wv}\delta_v + K^i_{wn}\theta_n + K^i_{ww}\delta_w + K^i_{wo}\theta_o \tag{6-1i}$$
$$m^i_m = K^i_{ml}\theta_l + K^i_{mm}\theta_m \tag{6-1j}$$
$$m^i_o = K^i_{ov}\delta_v + K^i_{on}\theta_n + K^i_{ow}\delta_w + K^i_{oo}\theta_o \tag{6-1k}$$
$$m^i_q = K^i_{qr}\delta_r + K^i_{qp}\theta_p + K^i_{qs}\delta_s + K^i_{qq}\theta_q \tag{6-1l}$$

This set of equations can be written in matrix form as

$$[\mathbf{m}^s]_i = [\mathbf{K}^s]_i[\boldsymbol{\delta}^s]_i \tag{6-2}$$

where the matrices are defined as

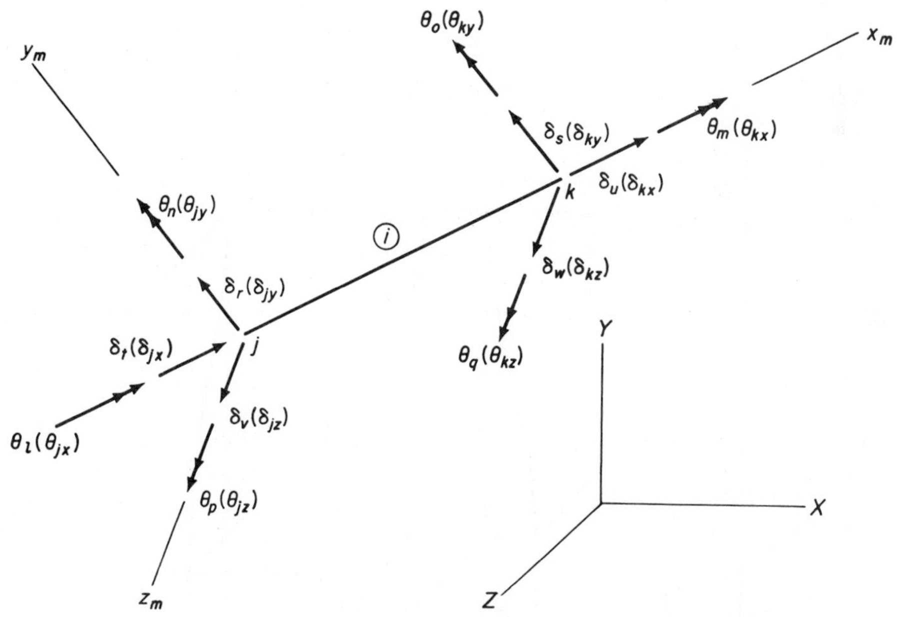

Fig. 6-2 Possible components of end displacement for beam element in three-dimensional space.

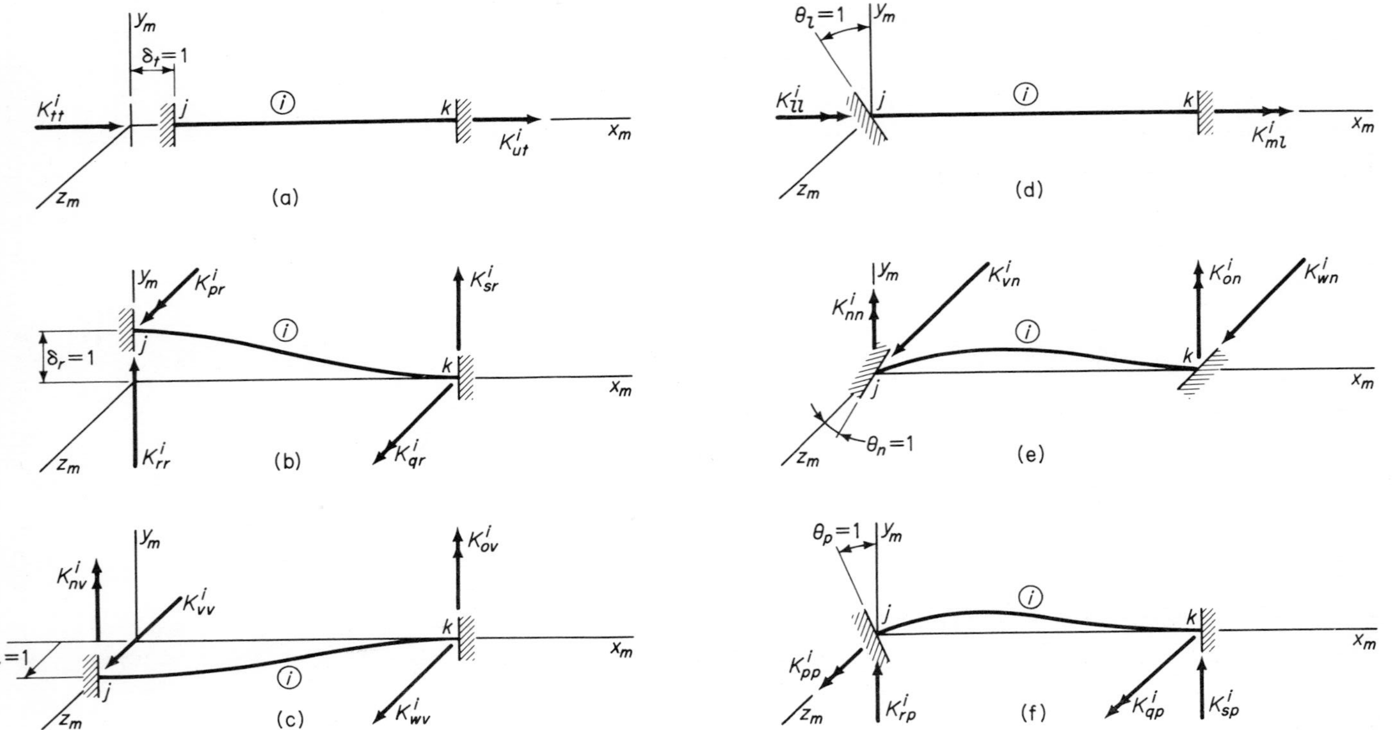

Fig. 6-3 Restraining end actions resulting from unit values of end displacements at *j*-end of member i: (a) unit translation in x_m direction; (b) unit translation in y_m direction; (c) unit translation in z_m direction; (d) unit rotation about x_m axis; (e) unit rotation about y_m axis; (f) unit rotation about z_m axis.

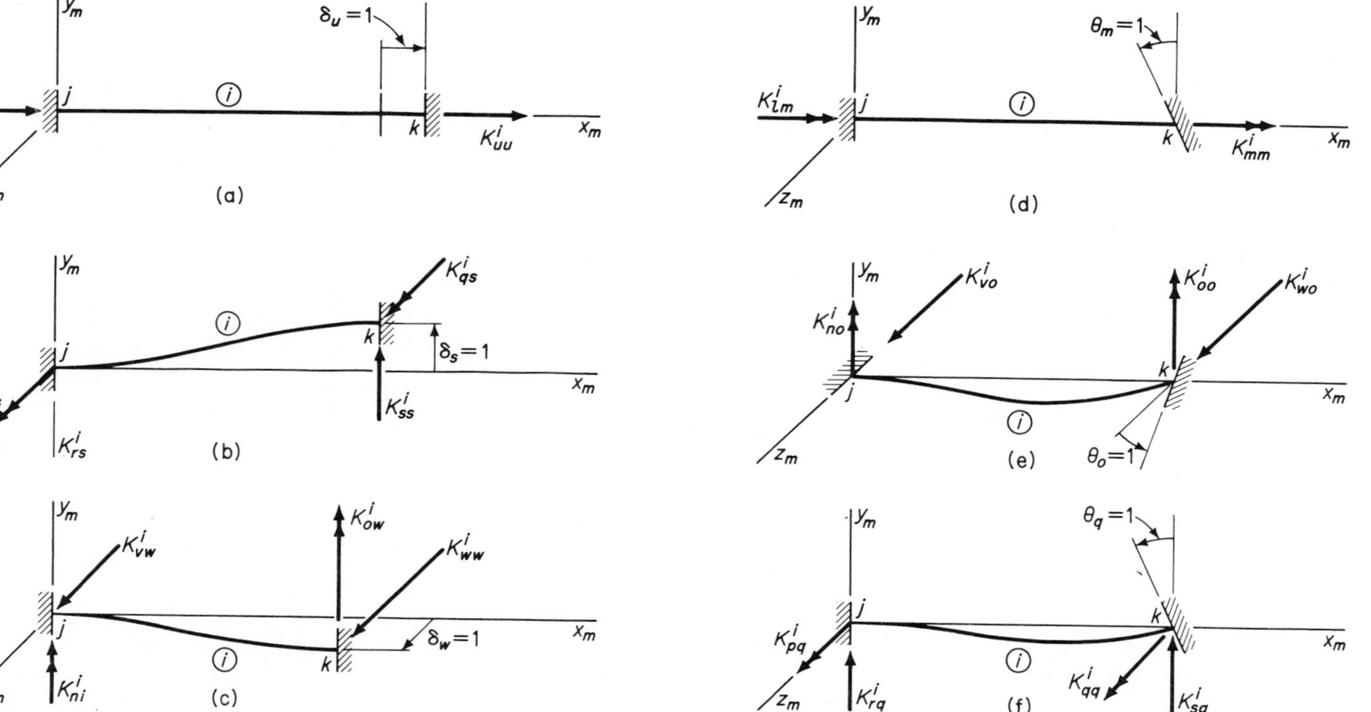

Fig. 6-4 Restraining end actions resulting from unit values of end displacements at k-end of member i: (a) unit translation in x_m direction; (b) unit translation in y_m direction; (c) unit translation in z_m direction; (d) unit rotation about x_m axis; (e) unit rotation about y_m axis; (f) unit rotation about z_m axis.

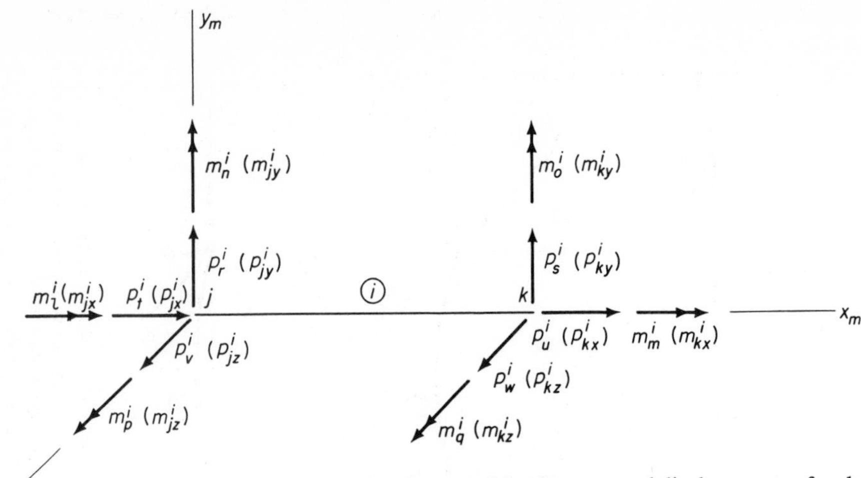

Fig. 6-5 End actions resulting from general displacements of ends of member *i*.

$$[\mathbf{m}^s]_i = \begin{bmatrix} p_t \\ p_r \\ p_v \\ m_l \\ m_n \\ m_p \\ p_u \\ p_s \\ p_w \\ m_m \\ m_o \\ m_q \end{bmatrix}_i \text{ or } \begin{bmatrix} p_{jx} \\ p_{jy} \\ p_{jz} \\ m_{jx} \\ m_{jy} \\ m_{jz} \\ p_{kx} \\ p_{ky} \\ p_{kz} \\ m_{kx} \\ m_{ky} \\ m_{kz} \end{bmatrix}_i \begin{matrix} \left.\begin{matrix} \\ \\ \\ \end{matrix}\right\} \text{components of end force at } j\text{-end} \\ \left.\begin{matrix} \\ \\ \\ \end{matrix}\right\} \text{components of end moment at } j\text{-end} \\ \left.\begin{matrix} \\ \\ \\ \end{matrix}\right\} \text{components of end force at } k\text{-end} \\ \left.\begin{matrix} \\ \\ \\ \end{matrix}\right\} \text{components of end moment at } k\text{-end} \end{matrix} \tag{6-3a}$$

$$[\boldsymbol{\delta}^s]_i = \begin{bmatrix} \delta_t \\ \delta_r \\ \delta_v \\ \theta_l \\ \theta_n \\ \theta_p \\ \delta_u \\ \delta_s \\ \delta_w \\ \theta_m \\ \theta_o \\ \theta_q \end{bmatrix}_i \text{ or } \begin{bmatrix} \delta_{jx} \\ \delta_{jy} \\ \delta_{jz} \\ \theta_{jx} \\ \theta_{jy} \\ \theta_{jz} \\ \delta_{kx} \\ \delta_{ky} \\ \delta_{kz} \\ \theta_{kx} \\ \theta_{ky} \\ \theta_{kz} \end{bmatrix}_i \begin{matrix} \left.\begin{matrix} \\ \\ \\ \end{matrix}\right\} \text{components of end translation at } j\text{-end} \\ \left.\begin{matrix} \\ \\ \\ \end{matrix}\right\} \text{components of end rotation at } j\text{-end} \\ \left.\begin{matrix} \\ \\ \\ \end{matrix}\right\} \text{components of end translation at } k\text{-end} \\ \left.\begin{matrix} \\ \\ \\ \end{matrix}\right\} \text{components of end rotation at } k\text{-end} \end{matrix} \tag{6-3b}$$

and

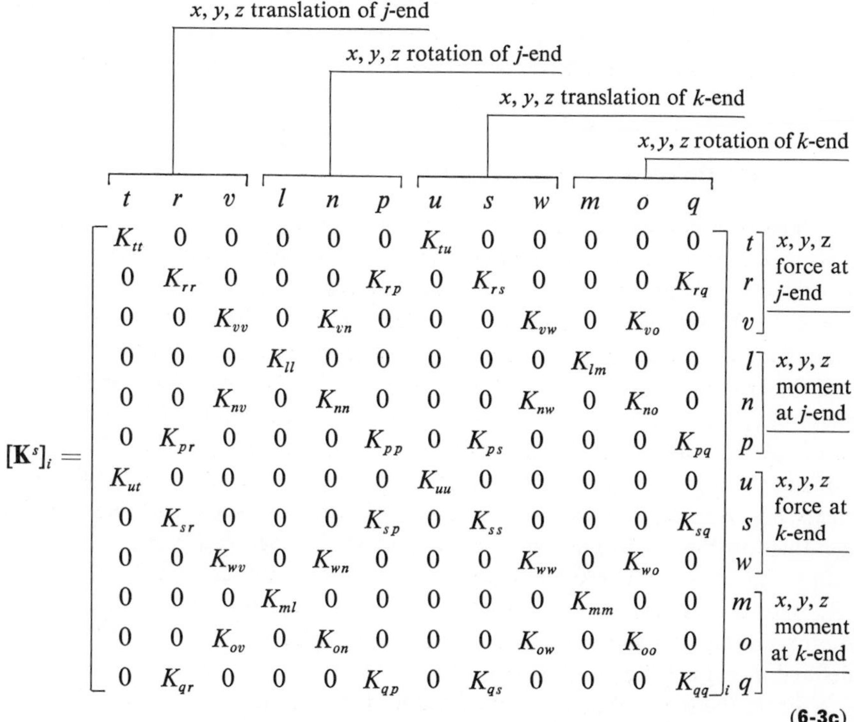

$$[\mathbf{K}^s]_i = \begin{array}{c} \\ \end{array}\begin{bmatrix} K_{tt} & 0 & 0 & 0 & 0 & 0 & K_{tu} & 0 & 0 & 0 & 0 & 0 \\ 0 & K_{rr} & 0 & 0 & 0 & K_{rp} & 0 & K_{rs} & 0 & 0 & 0 & K_{rq} \\ 0 & 0 & K_{vv} & 0 & K_{vn} & 0 & 0 & 0 & K_{vw} & 0 & K_{vo} & 0 \\ 0 & 0 & 0 & K_{ll} & 0 & 0 & 0 & 0 & 0 & K_{lm} & 0 & 0 \\ 0 & 0 & K_{nv} & 0 & K_{nn} & 0 & 0 & 0 & K_{nw} & 0 & K_{no} & 0 \\ 0 & K_{pr} & 0 & 0 & 0 & K_{pp} & 0 & K_{ps} & 0 & 0 & 0 & K_{pq} \\ K_{ut} & 0 & 0 & 0 & 0 & 0 & K_{uu} & 0 & 0 & 0 & 0 & 0 \\ 0 & K_{sr} & 0 & 0 & 0 & K_{sp} & 0 & K_{ss} & 0 & 0 & 0 & K_{sq} \\ 0 & 0 & K_{wv} & 0 & K_{wn} & 0 & 0 & 0 & K_{ww} & 0 & K_{wo} & 0 \\ 0 & 0 & 0 & K_{ml} & 0 & 0 & 0 & 0 & 0 & K_{mm} & 0 & 0 \\ 0 & 0 & K_{ov} & 0 & K_{on} & 0 & 0 & 0 & K_{ow} & 0 & K_{oo} & 0 \\ 0 & K_{qr} & 0 & 0 & 0 & K_{qp} & 0 & K_{qs} & 0 & 0 & 0 & K_{qq} \end{bmatrix}_i \tag{6-3c}$$

Columns: $t, r, v, l, n, p, u, s, w, m, o, q$; rows: $t, r, v, l, n, p, u, s, w, m, o, q$.

(6-3c)

Expression (6-3c) defines the ***member stiffness matrix with respect to the local member axes*** for a beam element of a three-dimensional structure with both ends restrained against rotation and translation. The rows are identified with respect to the end action being defined by each equation of Eqs. (6-1) and the columns are identified with respect to the end displacement causing the end actions listed in each column.

Note that the components of end displacement and end action can be defined using two subscripts as indicated in Expressions (6-3a) and (6-3b). The first subscript indicates the end of the member at which the displacement or action occurs and the second subscript indicates the direction of the displacement or action. This notation is convenient when the set of equations are arranged as are Eqs. (6-1).

From studying Figs. 6-3 and 6-4, it is seen that the response of the beam element to end displacements can be separated into two independent (uncoupled) groups: (1) the response to displacements in the x_m–y_m plane, i.e., θ_p, θ_q, δ_r, δ_s, δ_t, and δ_u; and (2) the response to displacements out of the x_m–y_m plane, i.e., θ_l, θ_m, θ_n, θ_o, δ_v, and δ_w. Consequently, when analyzing the response of a planar structure for disturbances applied in the plane of the structure (Chapter 5), it was not necessary to consider the response of the individual members, or of the structure, to possible out-of-plane displacements. Similarly, if a planar structure is to be analyzed for disturbances applied normal to the plane of the structure (to be discussed later in this chapter), it will not be necessary to consider the response of the individual members, or of the structure, to the possible inplane displacements when establishing the required action–displacement relationships. The analysis of a planar structural system is simply a special case of the analysis of the general three-dimensional structural system.

6-3.2 Evaluation of Member Stiffness Coefficients

The member stiffness coefficients for a beam element of a three-dimensional structure that are functions of bending deformations, i.e., bending in either the x_m–y_m or x_m–z_m planes, can be evaluated by the flexibility approach discussed in Sec. 4-2.2. The stiffness coefficients identified in Figs. 6-3(b), 6-3(f), 6-4(b), and 6-4(f) are a function of bending deformations of the beam element in the x_m–y_m plane, and they were expressed in Sec. 4-2 in terms of the four ***rotational stiffness coefficients*** K^i_{pp}, K^i_{pq}, K^i_{qp}, and K^i_{qq}. In a similar manner, the stiffness coefficients identified in Figs. 6-3(c), 6-3(e), 6-4(c), and 6-4(e), which are a function of bending deformations in the x_m–z_m plane, can be expressed in terms of the ***rotational stiffness coefficients*** K^i_{nn}, K^i_{no}, K^i_{on}, and K^i_{oo}. The evaluation of the ***extensional stiffness coefficients*** identified in Figs. 6-3(a) and 6-4(a) was discussed in Sec. 5-3.2. Hence, the evaluation of all of the nonzero elements of the member stiffness matrix of Expression (6-3c) for a beam element of a three-dimensional structure has been discussed with the exception of the four ***torsional stiffness coefficients*** K^i_{ll}, K^i_{lm}, K^i_{ml}, and K^i_{mm} defined in Figs. 6-3(d) and 6-4(d).

From the study of mechanics of materials,† it is known that the *angle of twist* θ_x experienced by a beam element subjected to a torsional moment M_x at its ends can be defined as

$$\theta_x = \frac{M_x L}{I_x G} \tag{6-4}$$

where L is the length of the member, G is the *shearing modulus of elasticity*, and I_x is a *torsional constant* expressed as a function of the member's cross-section. Thus, from Eq. (6-4), the torsional moment M_x required at the ends of a beam element to impose a specified relative angle of twist θ_x between the ends of the member is defined as

$$M_x = \frac{GI_x}{L}\theta_x \tag{6-5}$$

The behavior of a member with a uniform circular section when subjected to a torsional moment can be described as a pure shear deformation where a plane section before twisting remains a plane section when the member is twisted. For the member with a uniform circular section of diameter d, I_x is defined as

†S. P. Timoshenko and J. N. Goodier, *Theory of Elasticity*, 2nd ed. New York, McGraw-Hill Book Company, 1951, pp. 258–313.

$$I_x = \frac{\pi d^4}{32} \tag{6-6}$$

which is the expression for the *polar moment of inertia* for a circular section. In contrast to the rather simple behavior of the beam element with a uniform circular section, the behavior of a prismatic beam element when subjected to a torsional moment involves a *warping* of the member where a plane section before twisting experiences a distortion out of the plane when the member is twisted. However, if the member is free to warp, Eq. (6-4) or (6-5) can be used to describe the torsional-action–displacement relationship of a prismatic member if the appropriate torsional constant I_x is used.

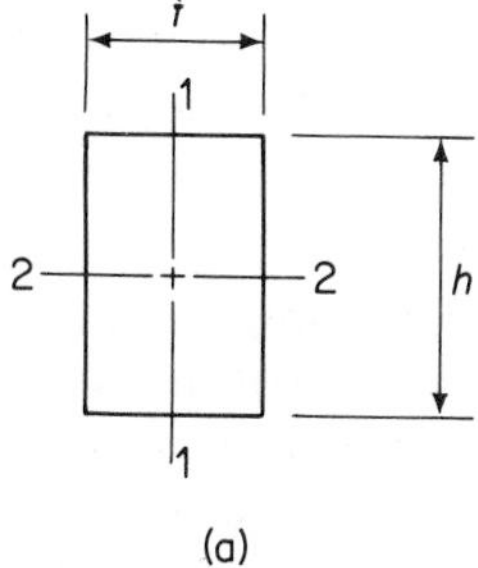

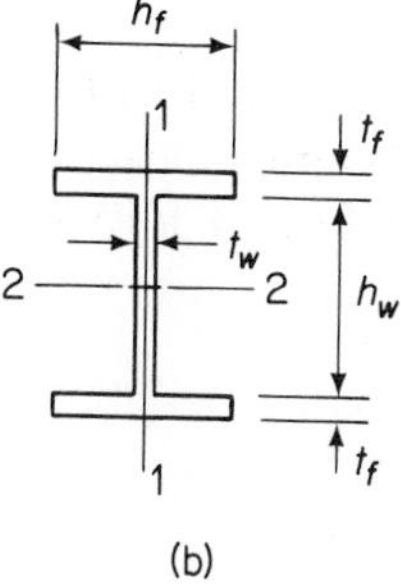

Fig. 6-6 Beam element sections: (a) rectangular section; (b) WF section.

For a beam element with a rectangular cross-section [Fig. 6-6(a)], the torsional constant I_x can be approximated by the expression

$$I_x = \frac{ht^3}{3}\left[1 - 0.630\frac{t}{h} + 0.052\left(\frac{t}{h}\right)^5\right], \qquad h \geq t \tag{6-7a}$$

or

$$I_x = \frac{ht^3}{3}\beta, \qquad h \geq t \tag{6-7b}$$

The values of β for various ratios of h/t are given in Table 6-1.

Table 6-1

VALUES OF COEFFICIENT β

h/t	β	h/t	β	h/t	β
1.0	0.422	2.5	0.748	5.0	0.874
1.25	0.539	3.0	0.790	6.0	0.895
1.5	0.587	3.5	0.820	8.0	0.921
1.75	0.643	4.0	0.842	10.0	0.937
2.0	0.687	4.5	0.860	∞	1.000

For a rectangular section which has a large ratio of h/t, Eq. (6-7) reduces to

$$I_x = \tfrac{1}{3}ht^3 \tag{6-8}$$

If the section of a prismatic member is composed of slender rectangular areas [Fig. 6-6(b)], the torsional constant I_x for the section can be approximated by the expression

$$I_x = \tfrac{1}{3}\sum ht^3 \tag{6-9}$$

where h and t are the long and short dimensions of each area, respectively.

Should one or both ends of a prismatic member be restrained against warping, the analysis† of the member becomes rather complicated; however, the torsional-action–displacement relationship for the member can be *approximated* by Eq. (6-4). The error introduced into an analysis of a system by the use of Eq. (6-4) is considered to be negligible, particularly if the beam element has a high span–depth ratio.

Using Eq. (6-5), the end actions required to maintain equilibrium of the deformed beam element i when the j-end is subjected to a unit angle of twist ($\theta_l = 1$) while the k-end is fixed in position [Fig. 6-3(d)] are defined as

$$K_{ll}^i = \frac{GI_x}{L} \tag{6-10a}$$

and

$$K_{ml}^i = \frac{-GI_x}{L} \tag{6-10b}$$

Similarly, for a unit angle of twist ($\theta_m = 1$) imposed on the k-end of the beam element i while the j-end is fixed in position, the end actions are defined as

$$K_{lm}^i = \frac{-GI_x}{L} \tag{6-10c}$$

and

$$K_{mm}^i = \frac{GI_x}{L} \tag{6-10d}$$

The member stiffness matrix of Expression (6-3c) can be written for the prismatic beam element as shown in Eq. (6-11).

†Fred B. Seely and James O. Smith, *Advanced Mechanics of Materials*, 2nd ed. New York, John Wiley & Sons, Inc., 1952, pp. 281–291.

$$
[\mathbf{K}^s]_i = \begin{array}{c} \\ \left[\begin{array}{cccccccccccc}
t & r & v & l & n & p & u & s & w & m & o & q \\
\frac{EA_x}{L} & 0 & 0 & 0 & 0 & 0 & \frac{-EA_x}{L} & 0 & 0 & 0 & 0 & 0 \\
0 & \frac{12EI_z}{L^3} & 0 & 0 & 0 & \frac{6EI_z}{L^2} & 0 & \frac{-12EI_z}{L^3} & 0 & 0 & 0 & \frac{6EI_z}{L^2} \\
0 & 0 & \frac{12EI_y}{L^3} & 0 & \frac{-6EI_y}{L^2} & 0 & 0 & 0 & \frac{-12EI_y}{L^3} & 0 & \frac{-6EI_y}{L^2} & 0 \\
0 & 0 & 0 & \frac{GI_x}{L} & 0 & 0 & 0 & 0 & 0 & \frac{-GI_x}{L} & 0 & 0 \\
0 & 0 & \frac{-6EI_y}{L^2} & 0 & \frac{4EI_y}{L} & 0 & 0 & 0 & \frac{6EI_y}{L^2} & 0 & \frac{2EI_y}{L} & 0 \\
0 & \frac{6EI_z}{L^2} & 0 & 0 & 0 & \frac{4EI_z}{L} & 0 & \frac{-6EI_z}{L^2} & 0 & 0 & 0 & \frac{2EI_z}{L} \\
\frac{-EA_x}{L} & 0 & 0 & 0 & 0 & 0 & \frac{EA_x}{L} & 0 & 0 & 0 & 0 & 0 \\
0 & \frac{-12EI_z}{L^3} & 0 & 0 & 0 & \frac{-6EI_z}{L^2} & 0 & \frac{12EI_z}{L^3} & 0 & 0 & 0 & \frac{-6EI_z}{L^2} \\
0 & 0 & \frac{-12EI_y}{L^3} & 0 & \frac{6EI_y}{L^2} & 0 & 0 & 0 & \frac{12EI_y}{L^3} & 0 & \frac{6EI_y}{L^2} & 0 \\
0 & 0 & 0 & \frac{-GI_x}{L} & 0 & 0 & 0 & 0 & 0 & \frac{GI_x}{L} & 0 & 0 \\
0 & 0 & \frac{-6EI_y}{L^2} & 0 & \frac{2EI_y}{L} & 0 & 0 & 0 & \frac{6EI_y}{L^2} & 0 & \frac{4EI_y}{L} & 0 \\
0 & \frac{6EI_z}{L^2} & 0 & 0 & 0 & \frac{2EI_z}{L} & 0 & \frac{-6EI_z}{L^2} & 0 & 0 & 0 & \frac{4EI_z}{L}
\end{array}\right]_i \end{array}
\begin{array}{c} \\ t \\ r \\ v \\ l \\ n \\ p \\ u \\ s \\ w \\ m \\ o \\ q \end{array}
\quad (6\text{-}11)
$$

For a beam element with a variable cross-section over its span length, the torsional-action–displacement relationship can be approximated by the equation

$$\theta_x = \frac{M_x}{G} \sum_{1}^{n} \frac{L_n}{I_{xn}} \tag{6-12}$$

if the member is described as an element with n segments of constant section, each segment having a length of L_n and a torsional constant I_{xn}. Using Eq. (6-12), the four torsional stiffness coefficients can be evaluated for the nonprismatic beam element.

6-3.3 Exercises

1. Develop the member stiffness matrix $[\mathbf{K}^s]_i$ for a 24 WF 110 steel beam which has 12 in. $\times$ $\frac{1}{2}$ in. $\times$ 8 ft–0 in. cover plates on both top and bottom flanges at both ends. The beam has a span length of 32 ft–0 in.

2. Compute the torsional constant I_x for a beam element made up of two 12 [35 back to back with 6 in. clear spacing and the flanges turned outward.

3. Compute the torsional constant I_x for a beam element made up of two 10 in. [24.9 with 10-in.-wide cover plates top and bottom. The member has an out-to-out dimension of 11 in. and the flanges of the two channels are directed inward. At the ends, the cover plates are $\frac{3}{8}$-in. thick for a length of 6 ft, and over the center portion of the member they are $\frac{1}{4}$-in. thick. The member has a total length of 20 ft.

6–4 Transformation of Coordinate Systems

The transformation of the components of a vector from one system of orthogonal coordinates to another system of orthogonal coordinates is basically the same for the three-dimensional space as for the two-dimensional space discussed in Chapter 5; however, the transformation in a three-dimensional space is somewhat more difficult to visualize and requires more mathematical computations in order to perform the operation.

6-4.1 General Rotation Matrix

To begin, consider a general vector V_0 which is arbitrarily oriented with respect to a given set of orthogonal, coordinate axes (y_1, y_2, y_3) as shown in Fig. 6-7. This vector can be described in terms of its components in the direction of the three coordinate axes where

$$V_1 = V_0 \cos \gamma_{01} \tag{6-13a}$$

$$V_2 = V_0 \cos \gamma_{02} \tag{6-13b}$$

$$V_3 = V_0 \cos \gamma_{03} \tag{6-13c}$$

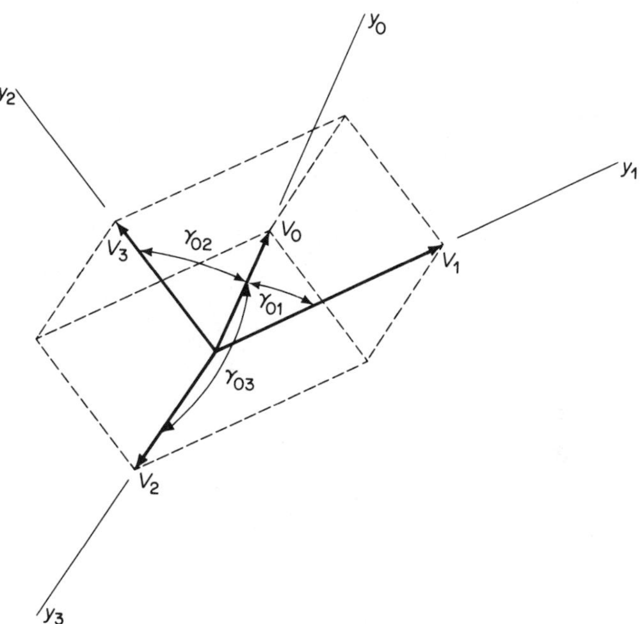

Fig. 6-7 Components of general vector in three-dimensional space.

The angles γ_{01}, γ_{02}, and γ_{03} are defined as the angles between the vector V_0 and the y_1, y_2, and y_3 axes, respectively. The terms $\cos \gamma_{01}$, $\cos \gamma_{02}$, and $\cos \gamma_{03}$ are referred to as the ***direction cosines***, describing the position of the vector V_0 with respect to the y_1, y_2 and y_3 axes. It should be remembered that a direction cosine is not an angle but is the cosine of the angle between a vector and a coordinate axis or between two coordinate axes.

The general vector V_0 can also be described in terms of its components in any other coordinate system, e.g., the vectors $\bar{V}_1$, $\bar{V}_2$, and $\bar{V}_3$, as shown in Fig. 6-8, which are the components of V_0 in the x-coordinate system. These components of the vector V_0 can be established by resolving each of the components of V_0 in the y-coordinate system—i.e., V_1, V_2, and V_3—into its own set of components in the x-coordinate system and summing. This yields

$$\bar{V}_1 = V_1 \cos \gamma_{11} + V_2 \cos \gamma_{21} + V_3 \cos \gamma_{31} \quad \textbf{(6-14a)}$$

$$\bar{V}_2 = V_1 \cos \gamma_{12} + V_2 \cos \gamma_{22} + V_3 \cos \gamma_{32} \quad \textbf{(6-14b)}$$

$$\bar{V}_3 = V_1 \cos \gamma_{13} + V_2 \cos \gamma_{23} + V_3 \cos \gamma_{33} \quad \textbf{(6-14c)}$$

where the angles γ_{ij} are defined in Fig. 6-8. Defining the direction cosines as

$$C_{ij} = \cos \gamma_{ij} \quad \textbf{(6-15)}$$

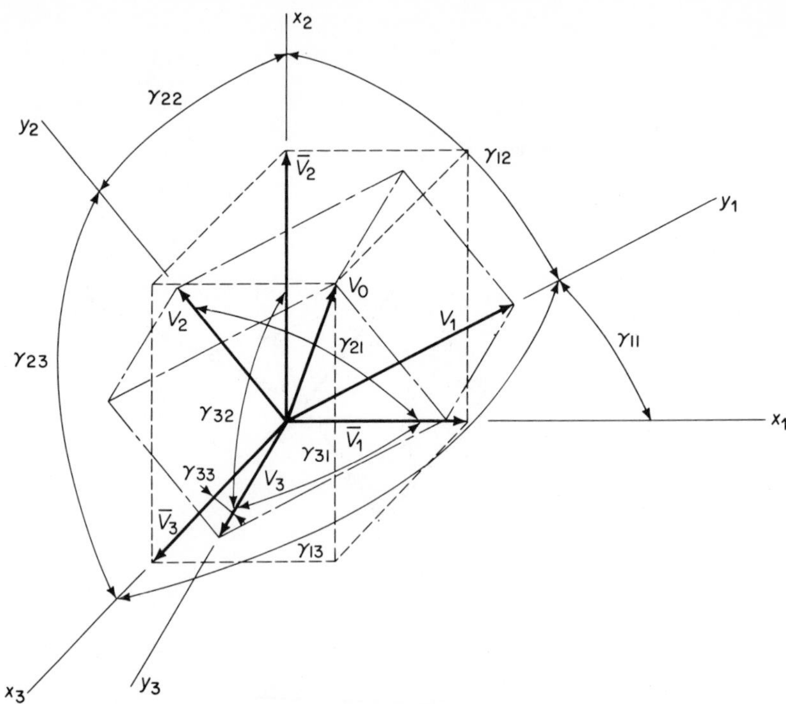

Fig. 6-8 Components of general vector in x_1, x_2, x_3 and y_1, y_2, y_3 coordinate systems.

where i refers to a particular axis of the y-coordinate system and j refers to a particular axis of the x-coordinate system, Eqs. (6-14) can be expressed in matrix form as

$$\begin{bmatrix} \bar{V}_1 \\ \bar{V}_2 \\ \bar{V}_3 \end{bmatrix} = \begin{bmatrix} C_{11} & C_{21} & C_{31} \\ C_{12} & C_{22} & C_{32} \\ C_{13} & C_{23} & C_{33} \end{bmatrix} \begin{bmatrix} V_1 \\ V_2 \\ V_3 \end{bmatrix} \tag{6-16a}$$

or

$$[\bar{\mathbf{V}}] = [\mathbf{C}^s]^T [\mathbf{V}] \tag{6-16b}$$

The matrix $[\mathbf{C}^s]^T$ is referred to as the rotation matrix from the y-coordinate system to the x-coordinate system and is the transpose of the matrix $[\mathbf{C}^s]$ defined in Eq. (6-17b).

Similarly, the component vectors ($\bar{V}_1$, $\bar{V}_2$, and $\bar{V}_3$) in the x-coordinate system can be resolved into the y-coordinate system by the equations

$$\begin{bmatrix} V_1 \\ V_2 \\ V_3 \end{bmatrix} = \begin{bmatrix} C_{11} & C_{12} & C_{13} \\ C_{21} & C_{22} & C_{23} \\ C_{31} & C_{32} & C_{33} \end{bmatrix} \begin{bmatrix} \bar{V}_1 \\ \bar{V}_2 \\ \bar{V}_3 \end{bmatrix} \tag{6-17a}$$

or

$$[\mathbf{V}] = [\mathbf{C}^s][\bar{\mathbf{V}}] \tag{6-17b}$$

where the matrix $[\mathbf{C}^s]$ is referred to as the ***rotation matrix*** from the x-system of coordinate axes to the y-system of coordinate axes.

Comparing Eqs. (6-16) and (6-17), it is seen that the rotation matrix $[\mathbf{C}^s]$ is an *orthogonal* matrix in a three-dimensional space just as its related matrix was in the two-dimensional space, i.e.,

$$[\mathbf{C}^s]^{-1} = [\mathbf{C}^s]^T \tag{6-18}$$

6-4.2 Member Rotation Matrix

Now, for a given beam element i with its set of local axes (x_m, y_m, z_m) positioned arbitrarily in the frame of a second set of coordinate axes—i.e., the reference axes (X, Y, Z), as shown in Fig. 6-9—the orientation of the longitudinal member axis x_m of the beam element can be established by the direction cosines C_x, C_y, and C_z, which are defined as

$$C_x = \cos \gamma_x \tag{6-19a}$$

$$C_y = \cos \gamma_y \tag{6-19b}$$

and

$$C_z = \cos \gamma_z \tag{6-19c}$$

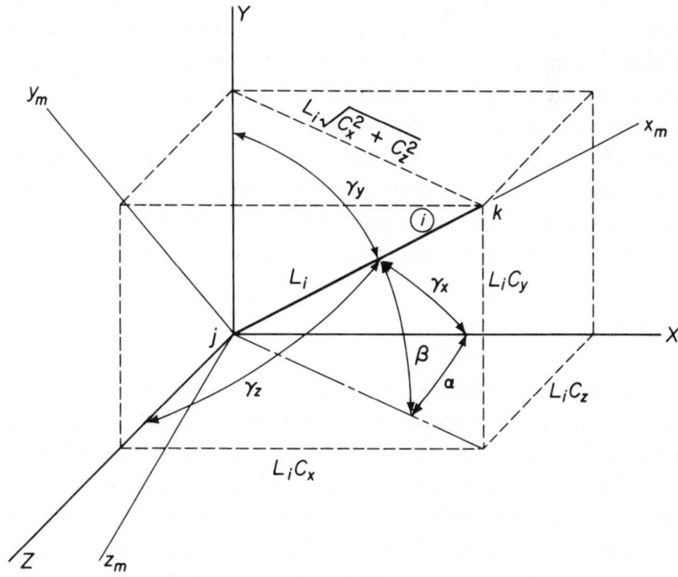

Fig. 6-9 Orientation of beam element in space with respect to reference axes.

Should the coordinates of the j- and k-ends of beam element i be known with respect to the reference axes (X, Y, Z), these direction cosines can be written as

$$C_x = \frac{X_k - X_j}{L_i} \tag{6-20a}$$

$$C_y = \frac{Y_k - Y_j}{L_i} \tag{6-20b}$$

$$C_z = \frac{Z_k - Z_j}{L_i} \tag{6-20c}$$

with

$$L_i = \sqrt{(X_k - X_j)^2 + (Y_k - Y_j)^2 + (Z_k - Z_j)^2} \tag{6-20d}$$

where (X_j, Y_j, Z_j) are the coordinates of end j and (X_k, Y_k, Z_k) are the coordinates of end k of beam element i with respect to the *reference system of axes.*

It would be convenient if the rotation matrix $[\mathbf{C}^s]$, which was defined in Eq. (6-17), could be expressed in terms of the direction cosines of Expression (6-20) as was done in Chapter 5 for the rotation of coordinate axes in a two-dimensional space. However, in a three-dimensional space these three direction cosines do not furnish all of the information needed to establish the orientation of the local coordinate axes with respect to the reference axes. One additional bit of information must be known about the positioning of the member with respect to the reference axes, and that is the value of the angle of roll or **Ψ-*angle***, which will be defined later in this discussion.

In order to define the rotation matrix of Eq. (6-17) in terms of the direction cosines C_x, C_y, and C_z and the Ψ-angle, consider again the resolution of the components of the general vector V_0 in the reference system of coordinate axes (X, Y, Z) into components in the local system of coordinate axes (x_m, y_m, z_m). This transformation from the reference axes to the local axes can conveniently be accomplished by successive planar rotations. However, in developing the general transformation in this manner, the sequence in which the planar rotations are made is very important because it influences the composition of the expressions which define the elements of the rotation matrix and the evaluation of the Ψ-angle.

Y–Z–X TRANSFORMATION

By assuming that the X-, Y-, Z-axes are initially rotated through the angle α (defined in Fig. 6-9) about the Y-axis, as indicated in Fig. 6-10, a new set of coordinate axes X_α, Y_α, Z_α can be defined. The X_α axis of the new system will coincide with the line of intersection of the X–Z and the Y–x_m planes; the X_α and Z_α axes will remain in the original X–Z plane; and the Y_α axis of the new system will coincide with the original Y-axis. The vector components $\bar{V}_x$, $\bar{V}_y$, $\bar{V}_z$ in the frame of the X-, Y-, Z-axes are resolved into vector components $V_{\alpha x}$, $V_{\alpha y}$, $V_{\alpha z}$ in the frame of the new X_α, Y_α, Z_α axes. This transformation can be accomplished by means of the equations

$$\begin{bmatrix} V_{\alpha x} \\ V_{\alpha y} \\ V_{\alpha z} \end{bmatrix} = \begin{bmatrix} \cos\alpha & 0 & \sin\alpha \\ 0 & 1 & 0 \\ -\sin\alpha & 0 & \cos\alpha \end{bmatrix} \begin{bmatrix} \bar{V}_x \\ \bar{V}_y \\ \bar{V}_z \end{bmatrix} \tag{6-21}$$

From Fig. 6-9, it is seen that

$$\sin\alpha = \frac{C_z}{\sqrt{C_x^2 + C_z^2}} \tag{6-22a}$$

and

$$\cos\alpha = \frac{C_x}{\sqrt{C_x^2 + C_z^2}} \tag{6-22b}$$

Hence, Eqs. (6-21) can be written as

$$\begin{bmatrix} V_{\alpha x} \\ V_{\alpha y} \\ V_{\alpha z} \end{bmatrix} = \begin{bmatrix} \frac{C_x}{\sqrt{C_x^2 + C_z^2}} & 0 & \frac{C_z}{\sqrt{C_x^2 + C_z^2}} \\ 0 & 1 & 0 \\ \frac{-C_z}{\sqrt{C_x^2 + C_z^2}} & 0 & \frac{C_x}{\sqrt{C_x^2 + C_z^2}} \end{bmatrix} \begin{bmatrix} \bar{V}_x \\ \bar{V}_y \\ \bar{V}_z \end{bmatrix} \tag{6-23a}$$

or

$$[\mathbf{V}_\alpha] = [\mathbf{C}_\alpha^s][\bar{\mathbf{V}}] \tag{6-23b}$$

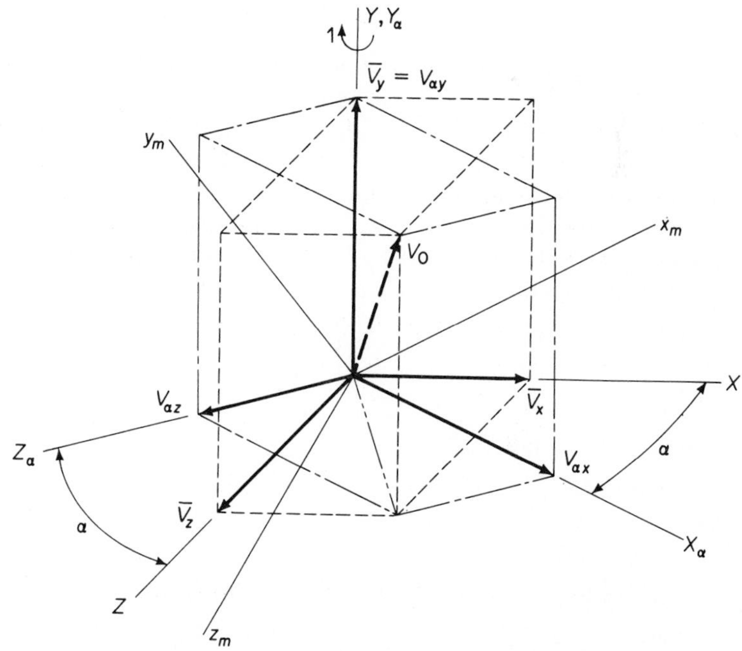

Fig. 6-10 Rotation of X, Y, Z coordinate axes about Y axis into coordinate axes X_α, Y_α, Z_α.

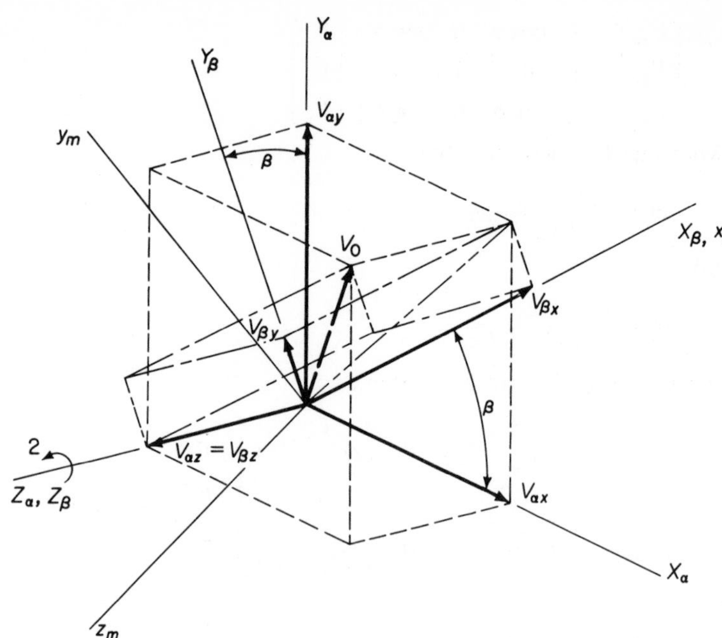

Fig. 6-11 Rotation of X_α, Y_α, Z_α coordinate axes about Z_α axis into coordinate axes X_β, Y_β, Z_β.

Next, a second system of coordinate axes X_β, Y_β, Z_β can be set up by assuming that the X_α, Y_α, Z_α axes are rotated about the Z_α axis through the angle β, which is defined in Fig. 6-9. As a result of this rotation, the X_β axis will coincide with the longitudinal member axis x_m, the Z_β axis will be the same as the Z_α axis, and the Y_β–Z_β plane will contain the y_m and z_m axes of the local system (Fig. 6-11). The set of vector components $V_{\alpha x}$, $V_{\alpha y}$, $V_{\alpha z}$ in the frame of the X_α, Y_α, Z_α axes can be resolved into a set of components $V_{\beta x}$, $V_{\beta y}$, $V_{\beta z}$ in the frame of the X_β, Y_β, Z_β axes by means of the equations

$$\begin{bmatrix} V_{\beta x} \\ V_{\beta y} \\ V_{\beta z} \end{bmatrix} = \begin{bmatrix} \cos\beta & \sin\beta & 0 \\ -\sin\beta & \cos\beta & 0 \\ 0 & 0 & 1 \end{bmatrix} \begin{bmatrix} V_{\alpha x} \\ V_{\alpha y} \\ V_{\alpha z} \end{bmatrix} \tag{6-24}$$

Referring to Fig. 6-9,

$$\sin\beta = C_y \tag{6-25a}$$

and

$$\cos\beta = \sqrt{C_x^2 + C_z^2} \tag{6-25b}$$

Substituting Expressions (6-25) into Eqs. (6-24) yields

$$\begin{bmatrix} V_{\beta x} \\ V_{\beta y} \\ V_{\beta z} \end{bmatrix} = \begin{bmatrix} \sqrt{C_x^2 + C_z^2} & C_y & 0 \\ -C_y & \sqrt{C_x^2 + C_z^2} & 0 \\ 0 & 0 & 1 \end{bmatrix} \begin{bmatrix} V_{\alpha x} \\ V_{\alpha y} \\ V_{\alpha z} \end{bmatrix} \tag{6-26a}$$

which can be written as

$$[\mathbf{V}_\beta] = [\mathbf{C}^s_\beta][\mathbf{V}_\alpha] \tag{6-26b}$$

Finally, if the X_β, Y_β, Z_β axes are assumed to be rotated about the X_β axis, which coincides with the x_m axis, the Y_β and Z_β axes can be brought in line with the y_m and z_m axes of the local system, respectively, as indicated in Fig. 6-12. Thus, defining the angle between the Y_β and y_m axes, or between the Z_β and z_m axes, as Ψ_y, the vector components $V_{\beta x}$, $V_{\beta y}$, $V_{\beta z}$ in the frame of the X_β, Y_β, Z_β axes can be resolved into vector components V_x, V_y, V_z of the general vector V_0 in the frame of the local axes by the equations

$$\begin{bmatrix} V_x \\ V_y \\ V_z \end{bmatrix} = \begin{bmatrix} 1 & 0 & 0 \\ 0 & \cos\Psi_y & \sin\Psi_y \\ 0 & -\sin\Psi_y & \cos\Psi_y \end{bmatrix} \begin{bmatrix} V_{\beta x} \\ V_{\beta y} \\ V_{\beta z} \end{bmatrix} \tag{6-27a}$$

or

$$[\mathbf{V}] = [\mathbf{C}^s_{\Psi y}][\mathbf{V}_\beta] \tag{6-27b}$$

Combining Eqs. (6-23), (6-26), and (6-27), the set of vector components in the frame of the reference axes of the general vector V_0 can be resolved directly into the set of vector components in the frame of the local axes, i.e.,

$$[\mathbf{V}] = [\mathbf{C}^s_{\Psi y}]\,[\mathbf{C}^s_\beta]\,[\mathbf{C}^s_\alpha]\,[\bar{\mathbf{V}}] \tag{6-28a}$$

However, according to Eq. (6-17b),

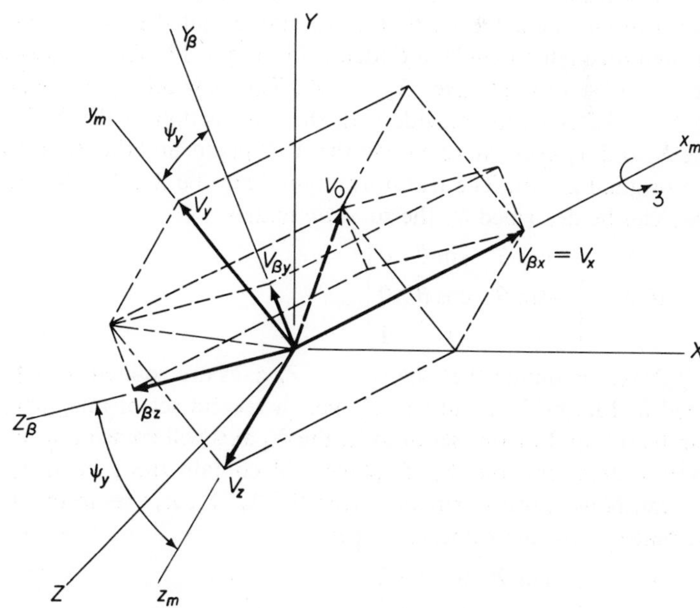

Fig. 6-12 Rotation of X_β, Y_β, Z_β coordinate axes about X_β axis into coordinate axes x_m, y_m, z_m.

$$[\mathbf{V}] = [\mathbf{C}_Y^s][\bar{\mathbf{V}}] \tag{6-28b}$$

hence,

$$[\mathbf{C}_Y^s] = [\mathbf{C}_{\Psi y}^s][\mathbf{C}_\beta^s][\mathbf{C}_\alpha^s] \tag{6-29}$$

which is defined as the ***rotation matrix for a Y–Z–X transformation***. Performing the matrix operations indicated in Eqs. (6-29), the rotation matrix relating the reference axes and a given set of local axes by way of a *Y–Z–X* transformation can be defined as

$$[\mathbf{C}_Y^s]_i = \begin{bmatrix} C_x & C_y & C_z \\ \dfrac{-C_xC_y\cos\Psi_y - C_z\sin\Psi_y}{\sqrt{C_x^2+C_z^2}} & \sqrt{C_x^2+C_z^2}\cos\Psi_y & \dfrac{-C_yC_z\cos\Psi_y + C_x\sin\Psi_y}{\sqrt{C_x^2+C_z^2}} \\ \dfrac{C_xC_y\sin\Psi_y - C_z\cos\Psi_y}{\sqrt{C_x^2+C_z^2}} & -\sqrt{C_x^2+C_z^2}\sin\Psi_y & \dfrac{C_yC_z\sin\Psi_y + C_x\cos\Psi_y}{\sqrt{C_x^2+C_z^2}} \end{bmatrix}_i \tag{6-30}$$

which gives the rotation matrix in terms of the direction cosines defining the position of the x_m longitudinal axis of the local system of axes with respect to the reference system of axes and the Ψ-angle, Ψ_y, identified in Fig. 6-12.

Z–Y–X TRANSFORMATION

The transformation from the reference system of axes to the local system of axes can also be achieved by first assuming that the *X*-, *Y*-, *Z*-reference axes are rotated through an angle of θ (defined in Fig. 6-13) about the *Z*-axis establishing a new set of coordinate axes X_θ, Y_θ, Z_θ. This new set of axes will be oriented such that the X_θ axis will coincide with the intersection of the *X–Y* and Z–x_m planes, the X_θ and Y_θ axes will remain in the *X–Y* plane, and the Z_θ axis will coincide with the original *Z*-axis. The transformation from the *X*-, *Y*-, *Z*-axes to the X_θ, Y_θ, Z_θ axes can be described by the rotation matrix

$$[\mathbf{C}_\theta^s] = \begin{bmatrix} \cos\theta & \sin\theta & 0 \\ -\sin\theta & \cos\theta & 0 \\ 0 & 0 & 1 \end{bmatrix} \tag{6-31}$$

Next, assuming that the X_θ, Y_θ, Z_θ axes are rotated through an angle λ (defined in Fig. 6-13) about the Y_θ axis, a second set of imaginary axes X_λ, Y_λ, Z_λ can be set up. For this set of axes, the X_λ axis will coincide with the x_m axis of the local system, and the Y_λ–Z_λ plane will contain the y_m and z_m axes of the local system. Now, a transformation from the X_θ, Y_θ, Z_θ axes to the X_λ, Y_λ, Z_λ axes can be made using the rotation matrix

$$[\mathbf{C}_\lambda^s] = \begin{bmatrix} \cos\lambda & 0 & \sin\lambda \\ 0 & 1 & 0 \\ -\sin\lambda & 0 & \cos\lambda \end{bmatrix} \tag{6-32}$$

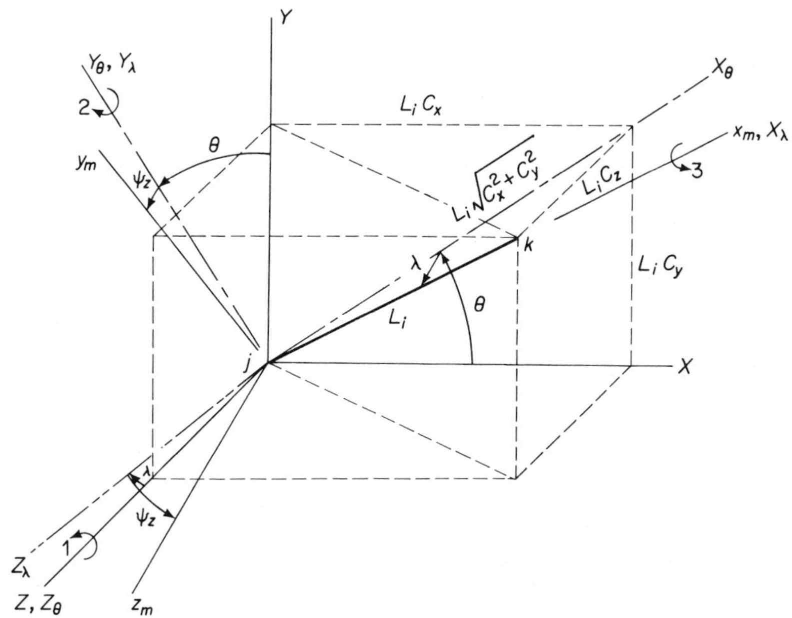

Fig. 6-13 *Z–Y–X* transformation of reference axes into the local axes for member *i*.

Finally, the X_λ, Y_λ, Z_λ system of axes can be resolved into the x_m, y_m, z_m system of local axes by assuming that the λ-axes system is rotated about the X_λ axis (which already coincides with the x_m axis) through an angle of Ψ_z, which has been defined earlier as the Ψ-angle. This transformation from the X_λ, Y_λ, Z_λ axes to the x_m, y_m, z_m local axes requires the rotation matrix

$$[\mathbf{C}^s_{\Psi z}] = \begin{bmatrix} 1 & 0 & 0 \\ 0 & \cos\Psi_z & \sin\Psi_z \\ 0 & -\sin\Psi_z & \cos\Psi_z \end{bmatrix} \tag{6-33}$$

The transformation from the reference axes to the local axes can be made directly by way of the *Z–Y–X* sequence of planar rotation using the rotation matrix

$$[\mathbf{C}^s_Z] = [\mathbf{C}^s_{\Psi z}][\mathbf{C}^s_\lambda][\mathbf{C}^s_\theta] \tag{6-34a}$$

which is defined as

$$[\mathbf{C}^s_Z]_i =$$

$$\begin{bmatrix} \cos\theta\cos\lambda & \sin\theta\cos\lambda & \sin\lambda \\ -\sin\theta\cos\Psi_z - \cos\theta\sin\lambda\sin\Psi_z & \cos\theta\cos\Psi_z - \sin\theta\sin\lambda\sin\Psi_z & \cos\lambda\sin\Psi_z \\ \sin\theta\sin\Psi_z - \cos\theta\sin\lambda\cos\Psi_z & -\cos\theta\sin\Psi_z - \sin\theta\sin\lambda\cos\Psi_z & \cos\lambda\cos\Psi_z \end{bmatrix}_i \tag{6-34b}$$

The rotation matrix $[\mathbf{C}^s_Z]_i$ is referred to as the ***rotation matrix for a Z–Y–X transformation.***

Recognizing from Fig. 6-13 that

$$\sin\theta = \frac{C_y}{\sqrt{C_x^2 + C_y^2}} \quad \textbf{(6-35a)}$$

$$\cos\theta = \frac{C_x}{\sqrt{C_x^2 + C_y^2}} \quad \textbf{(6-35b)}$$

$$\sin\lambda = C_z \quad \textbf{(6-35c)}$$

$$\cos\lambda = \sqrt{C_x^2 + C_y^2} \quad \textbf{(6-35d)}$$

the rotation matrix of Expression (6-34b) can be rewritten as

$$[\mathbf{C}^s_Z]_i = \begin{bmatrix} C_x & C_y & C_z \\ \dfrac{-C_xC_z\sin\Psi_z - C_y\cos\Psi_z}{\sqrt{C_x^2 + C_y^2}} & \dfrac{-C_yC_z\sin\Psi_z + C_x\cos\Psi_z}{\sqrt{C_x^2 + C_y^2}} & \sqrt{C_x^2 + C_y^2}\sin\Psi_z \\ \dfrac{-C_xC_z\cos\Psi_z + C_y\sin\Psi_z}{\sqrt{C_x^2 + C_y^2}} & \dfrac{-C_yC_z\cos\Psi_z - C_x\sin\Psi_z}{\sqrt{C_x^2 + C_y^2}} & \sqrt{C_x^2 + C_y^2}\cos\Psi_z \end{bmatrix}_i \quad \textbf{(6-36)}$$

For the Z–Y–X sequence of axes transformations, the angle Ψ_z (Fig. 6-13) is identified as the Ψ-angle.

In general, either the Y–Z–X transformation, Expression (6-30), or the Z–Y–X transformation, Expression (6-36), can be used to transform from reference to local coordinate systems for a member of a three-dimensional structural system. However, for a particular member, one rotation matrix may have an advantage over the other in the evaluation of the related Ψ-angle. Keep in mind that the Ψ-angles for the two rotation matrices are not necessarily the same angle; *be sure that the Ψ-angle which is evaluated is the one that is required for the rotation matrix which is to be used.*

If a member is positioned in the frame of the reference axes such that its longitudinal axis x_m corresponds to the Y-direction of the reference coordinate system, the rotation matrix for a Y–Z–X transformation becomes undefinable due to the fact that C_x and C_z become zero. Thus, the rotation matrix for a Z–Y–X transformation must be used. Similarly, for a member whose longitudinal axis x_m corresponds to the Z-direction, the rotation matrix for a Z–Y–X transformation becomes undefinable. The Y–Z–X transformation must be used for this case.

Ψ-ANGLE

The Ψ-angle is defined as the angle between the Y_β and y_m axes, or Z_β and z_m axes, for a Y–Z–X transformation [Fig. 6-14(a)]; and as the angle between the Y_λ and y_m axes, or Z_λ and z_m axes, for a Z–Y–X transformation [Fig. 6-14(b)].

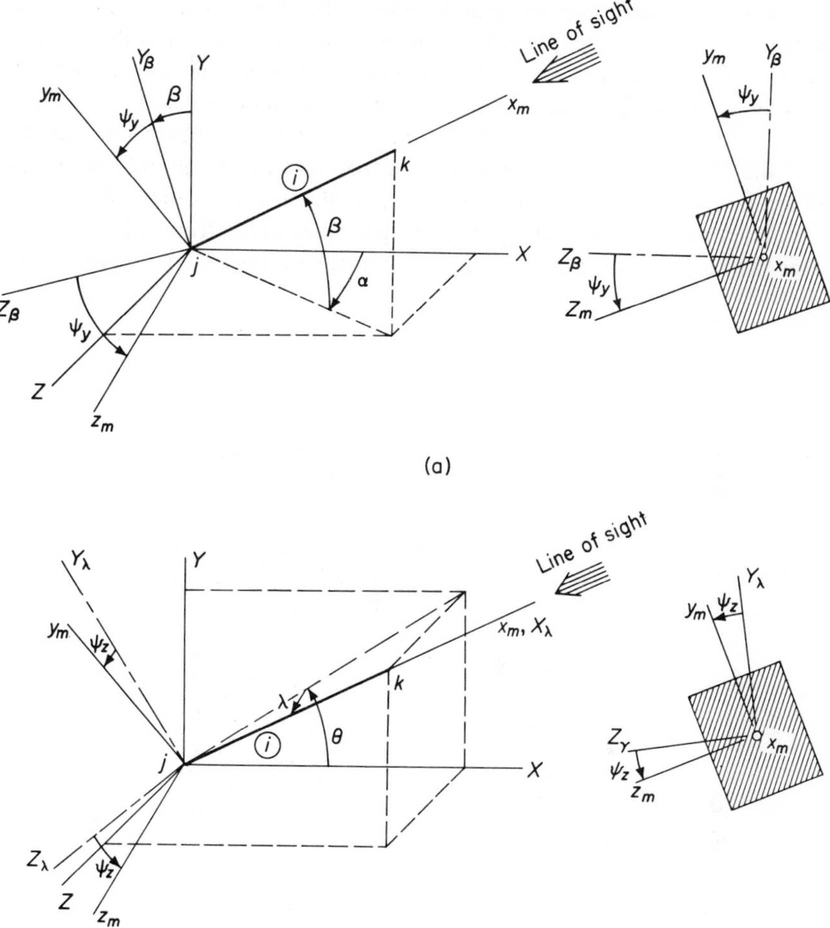

Fig. 6-14 Ψ-Angle: (a) *Y–Z–X* transformation; (b) *Z–Y–X* transformation.

In both cases the **Ψ**-angle is measured in a *counterclockwise* direction when viewing the cross-section of the member in a *negative* x_m direction, i.e., looking down the x_m axis from the *k*-end toward the *j*-end.

When describing the orientation of a particular structural member in the frame of the *X*-, *Y*-, *Z*-reference axes, the three direction cosines C_x, C_y, and C_z define the location of the longitudinal x_m axis and the **Ψ**-angle defines the location of the minor principal axis. All of these parameters are dependent upon the geometry of structure. The evaluation of the three direction cosines is a rather straightforward operation as indicated by Eqs. (6-20), but this may not be the case for the evaluation of the **Ψ**-angle.

In the more common structural systems, the members are usually oriented such that the y_m–x_m principal plane for a member will be oriented in the same direction as one of the reference axes. Consequently, when making the transformation of coordinate axes, the Ψ-angle can possibly be evaluated *by inspection* if the y_m–x_m plane contains either the Y- or Z-reference axis when studying an individual member and the transformation is initiated by a rotation about the reference axis which lies in the y_m–x_m plane. Otherwise, the Ψ-angle must be computed.

The orientation of the y_m–x_m principal plane in the frame of X–Y–Z reference axes can be established by knowing the location of a point lying in the y_m–x_m plane,

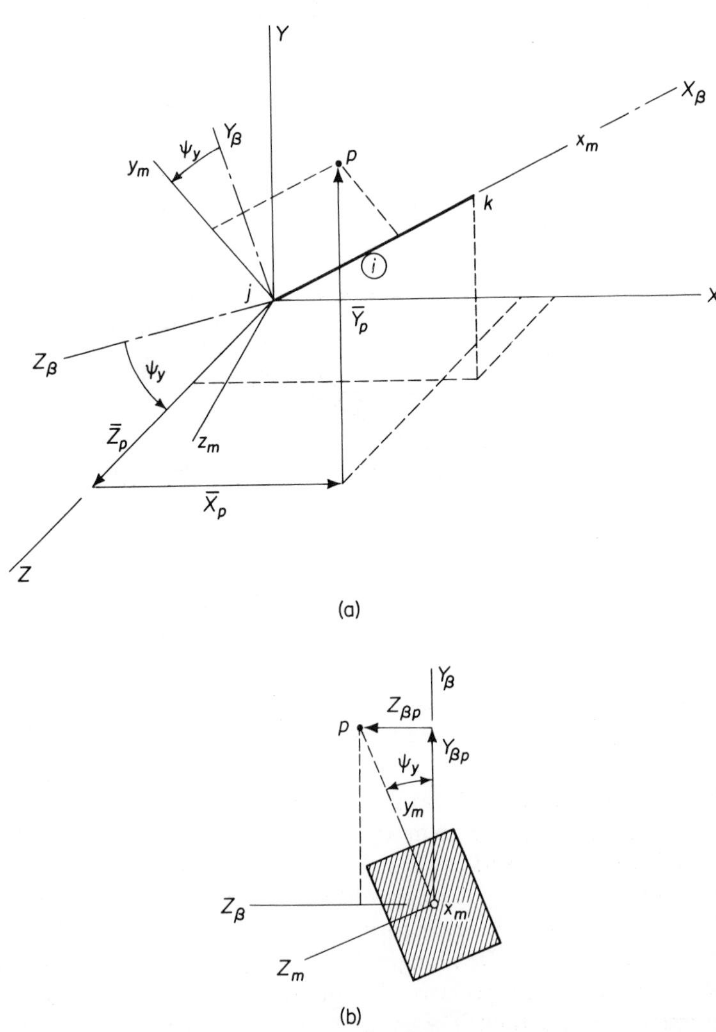

Fig. 6-15 Evaluation of Ψ-angle for Y–Z–X transformation: (a) position vectors locating point p; (b) Ψ-angle.

but not along the x_m axis, with respect to the reference axes and the location of the longitudinal x_m axis. If such a point can be conveniently identified with respect to the reference axes, the coordinates of the point will describe *position vectors* $\bar{X}_p$, $\bar{Y}_p$, $\bar{Z}_p$ with respect to the reference system of axes as shown in Fig. 6-15(a). Now these vectors can be resolved into position vectors in the X_β, Y_β, Z_β coordinate system (Fig. 6-12) by a Y–Z–X transformation of the reference axes or into position vectors in the X_λ, Y_λ, Z_λ coordinate system (Fig. 6-13) by a Z–Y–X transformation of the reference axes. For the Y–Z–X transformation, the position vectors in the β-system of axes can be evaluated by means of Eqs. (6-23) and (6-24), i.e.,

$$\begin{bmatrix} X_{\beta p} \\ Y_{\beta p} \\ Z_{\beta p} \end{bmatrix} = \begin{bmatrix} \sqrt{C_x^2 + C_z^2} & C_y & 0 \\ -C_y & \sqrt{C_x^2 + C_z^2} & 0 \\ 0 & 0 & 1 \end{bmatrix} \begin{bmatrix} \dfrac{C_x}{\sqrt{C_x^2 + C_z^2}} & 0 & \dfrac{C_z}{\sqrt{C_x^2 + C_z^2}} \\ 0 & 1 & 0 \\ \dfrac{-C_z}{\sqrt{C_x^2 + C_z^2}} & 0 & \dfrac{C_x}{\sqrt{C_x^2 + C_z^2}} \end{bmatrix} \begin{bmatrix} \bar{X}_p \\ \bar{Y}_p \\ \bar{Z}_p \end{bmatrix} \tag{6-37a}$$

which yields

$$X_{\beta p} = C_x\bar{X}_p + C_y\bar{Y}_p + C_z\bar{Z}_p \tag{6-37b}$$

$$Y_{\beta p} = -\frac{C_xC_y}{\sqrt{C_x^2 + C_z^2}}\bar{X}_p + \sqrt{C_x^2 + C_z^2}\,\bar{Y}_p - \frac{C_yC_z}{\sqrt{C_x^2 + C_z^2}}\bar{Z}_p \tag{6-37c}$$

and

$$Z_{\beta p} = -\frac{C_z}{\sqrt{C_x^2 + C_z^2}}\bar{X}_p + \frac{C_x}{\sqrt{C_x^2 + C_z^2}}\bar{Z}_p \tag{6-37d}$$

As shown in Fig. 6-15(b), the position vectors $Y_{\beta p}$ and $Z_{\beta p}$ locate the point p in the y_m–z_m plane. Thus, for a Y–Z–X transformation, the Ψ-angle is defined by the expression

$$\sin \Psi_y = \frac{Z_{\beta p}}{\sqrt{Y_{\beta p}^2 + Z_{\beta p}^2}} \tag{6-38a}$$

and

$$\cos \Psi_y = \frac{Y_{\beta p}}{\sqrt{Y_{\beta p}^2 + Z_{\beta p}^2}} \tag{6-38b}$$

Following the same procedure, an expression similar to Eq. (6-38) can be established for the evaluation of the Ψ-angle for a Z–Y–X transformation.

Example 6-1. Determine the Ψ-angle for the three members of the frame structure described in Fig. 6-16(a). The members of the frame are positioned in the system such that the y_m–x_m principal plane of each member is perpendicular to the X–Y reference plane. The j-end of each member is labeled and the positive local member axes are indicated.

Member 1

Since member 1 is oriented in the direction of the Y-reference axis, a Z–Y–X transformation must be used. The Ψ-angle, Ψ_z, is found by inspection to be 90°.

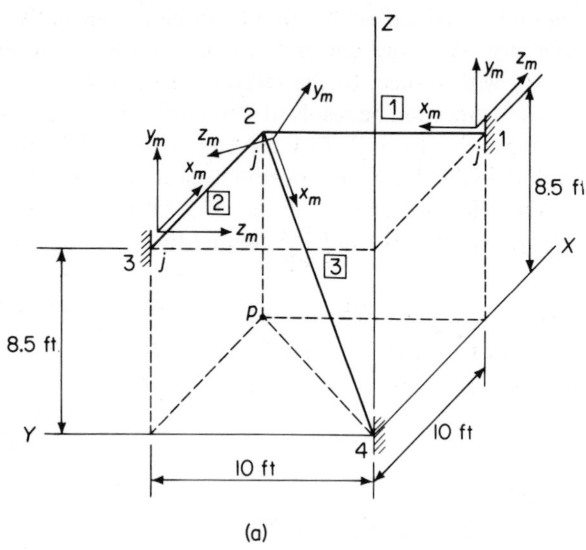

Fig. 6-16 Example 6-1: Determination of Ψ-angle: (a) structure.

Member 2

Member 2 is oriented in the direction of the X-reference axis and the y_m–z_m plane coincides with the Y–Z plane. Either a Y–Z–X or a Z–Y–X transformation could be used. In this instance, the Ψ-angle is the same for either transformation. The Ψ-angle can be obtained by inspection: $\Psi_y = \Psi_z = 90°$.

Member 3

The y_m–z_m plane of member 3 contains the Z-reference, hence a Z–Y–X transformation, shown in Fig. 6-16(b), is recommended. For this type of transformation the Ψ-angle, Ψ_z, is found by inspection to equal 90°.

For a Y–Z–X transformation, described in Fig. 6-16(c), the Ψ-angle is not readily apparent and cannot be evaluated by inspection. In order to determine the Ψ-angle for the Y–Z–X transformation from Expression (6–38), the point p is selected as the point of intersection of the y_m–x_m plane of the three members and the X–Y reference plane [Fig. 6-16(a)]. The point has the coordinates of (10, 10, 0) with respect to the reference axes for the total system, and the coordinates (0, 0, −8.5) in the reference system with respect to the j-end of member 3. Thus, the position vectors in the reference system are

$$\begin{bmatrix} \bar{X}_p \\ \bar{Y}_p \\ \bar{Z}_p \end{bmatrix} = \begin{bmatrix} 0 \\ 0 \\ -8.5 \end{bmatrix}$$

with

$$C_x = -0.606$$
$$C_y = -0.606$$
$$C_z = -0.515$$

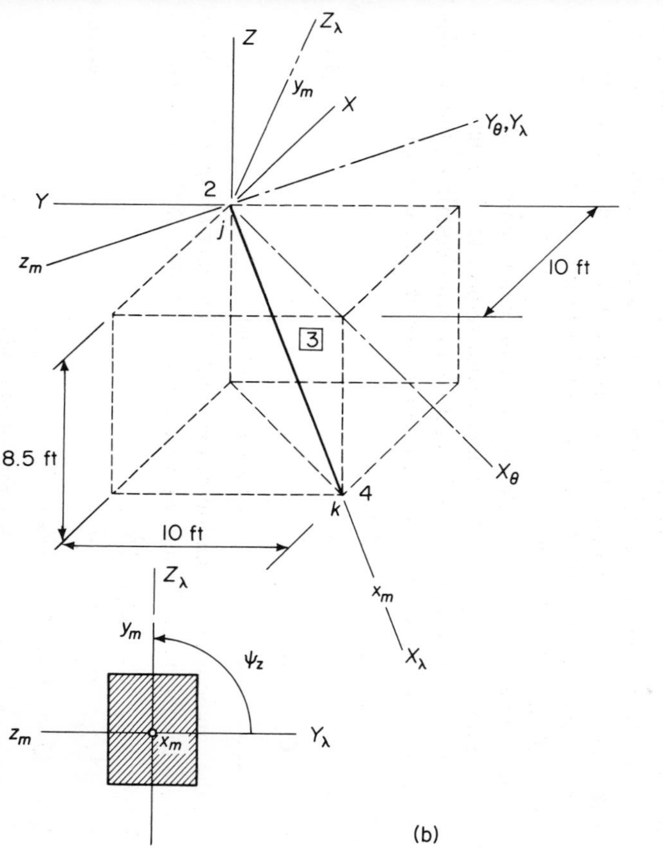

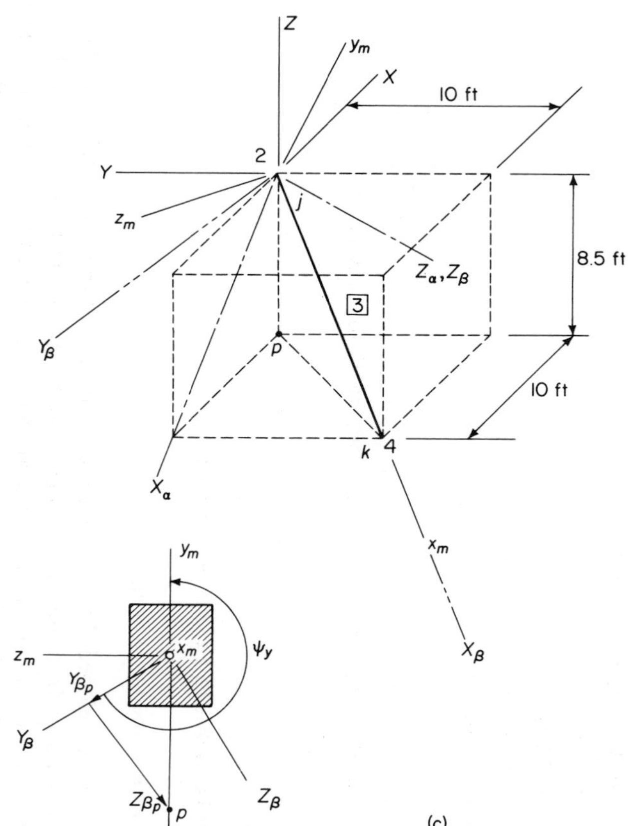

Fig. 6-16—*Cont.* (b) Ψ-angle, Z–Y–X transformation—member 3; (c) Ψ-angle, Y–Z–X transformation—member 3.

Equations (6-37c) and (6-37d) yield

$$Y_{\beta p} = +3.336$$

$$Z_{\beta p} = +6.477$$

and, from Eq. (6-38),

$$\sin \Psi_y = +0.8891$$

and

$$\cos \Psi_y = +0.4578$$

Hence, from Fig. 6-16c, the angle of roll from the Y_β to y_m axis is evaluated as

$$\Psi_y = 242.75°$$

6–5
Analysis of Rigid Frame Structure

6-5.1 Transformation Matrix

Having developed the mechanism to resolve a set of orthogonal components of a given vector from one orthogonal, coordinate system to another, the transformation of the components of end displacement or end action of a beam element from, say, the frame of the reference system of axes into the frame of the local system of axes, or from the local axes to the reference axes, can now be established.

The components of possible end displacement and corresponding components of end action with respect to both the local and reference system of axes are defined in Fig. 6-17 for beam element i which is restrained against translation as well as rotation of its ends. It is assumed that the orientation of the local axes with respect to the reference axes will be described in terms of the direction cosines C_x, C_y, and C_z of Eqs. (6-20) and the Ψ-angle.

Now, according to Eqs. (6-17), the set of vector components which describe, say, the translation of the j-end of member i with respect to the reference axes $(\bar{\delta}_t, \bar{\delta}_r, \bar{\delta}_v)$ can be resolved into a set of vector components describing the translation of the j-end with respect to the local axes of the member $(\delta_t, \delta_r, \delta_v)$ as

$$\begin{bmatrix} \delta_t \\ \delta_r \\ \delta_v \end{bmatrix}_i = \begin{bmatrix} C_{11} & C_{12} & C_{13} \\ C_{21} & C_{22} & C_{23} \\ C_{31} & C_{32} & C_{33} \end{bmatrix}_i \begin{bmatrix} \bar{\delta}_t \\ \bar{\delta}_r \\ \bar{\delta}_v \end{bmatrix}_i \tag{6-39a}$$

translation of j-end

Likewise, the components of rotation of the j-end of member i (Fig. 6-17) can be rotated from the frame of the reference axes into the frame of the local axes as

$$\begin{bmatrix} \theta_l \\ \theta_n \\ \theta_p \end{bmatrix}_i = \begin{bmatrix} C_{11} & C_{12} & C_{13} \\ C_{21} & C_{22} & C_{23} \\ C_{31} & C_{32} & C_{33} \end{bmatrix}_i \begin{bmatrix} \bar{\theta}_l \\ \bar{\theta}_n \\ \bar{\theta}_p \end{bmatrix}_i \tag{6-39b}$$

rotation of j-end

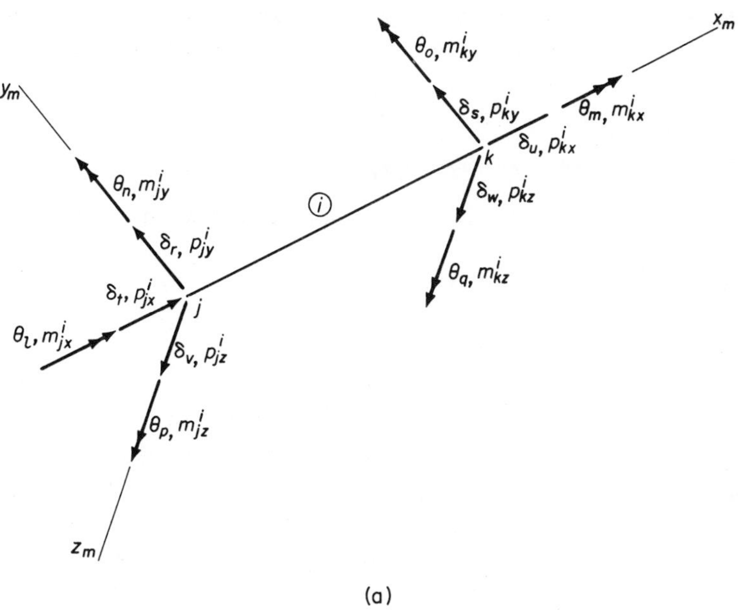

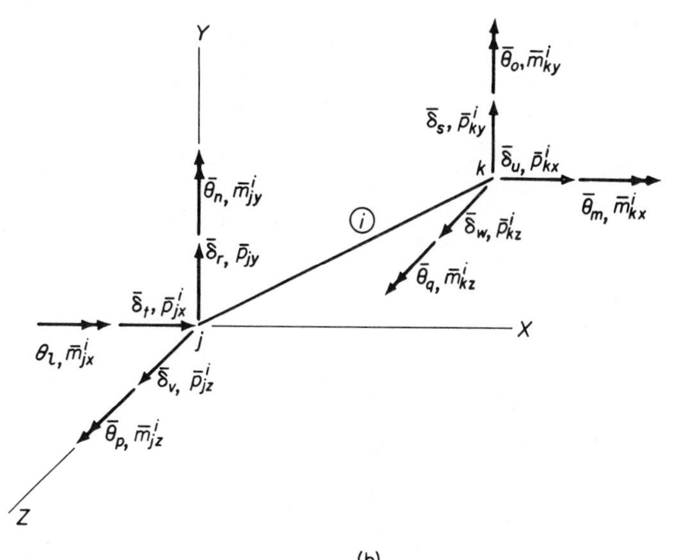

Fig. 6-17 Possible components of end displacement and end action for beam element in a three-dimensional space: (a) local coordinate system; (b) reference coordinate system.

Similarly, the components of translation and rotation of the k-end of member i (Fig. 6-17) can be rotated from the reference axes into the local axes as

$$\begin{bmatrix} \delta_u \\ \delta_s \\ \delta_w \end{bmatrix}_i = \begin{bmatrix} C_{11} & C_{12} & C_{13} \\ C_{21} & C_{22} & C_{23} \\ C_{31} & C_{32} & C_{33} \end{bmatrix}_i \begin{bmatrix} \bar{\delta}_u \\ \bar{\delta}_s \\ \bar{\delta}_w \end{bmatrix}_i \quad \text{(translation of } k\text{-end)} \tag{6-39c}$$

and

$$\begin{bmatrix} \theta_m \\ \theta_o \\ \theta_q \end{bmatrix}_i = \begin{bmatrix} C_{11} & C_{12} & C_{13} \\ C_{21} & C_{22} & C_{23} \\ C_{31} & C_{32} & C_{33} \end{bmatrix}_i \begin{bmatrix} \bar{\theta}_m \\ \bar{\theta}_o \\ \bar{\theta}_q \end{bmatrix}_i \quad \text{(rotation of } k\text{-end)} \tag{6-39d}$$

However, rather than having to consider the transformation of each set of vector components from one system of axes to another independently, Eqs. (6-39) can be combined into one operation:

$$\begin{bmatrix} \delta_t \\ \delta_r \\ \delta_v \\ \theta_l \\ \theta_n \\ \theta_p \\ \delta_u \\ \delta_s \\ \delta_w \\ \theta_m \\ \theta_o \\ \theta_q \end{bmatrix}_i = \begin{bmatrix} C_{11} & C_{12} & C_{13} & 0 & 0 & 0 & 0 & 0 & 0 & 0 & 0 & 0 \\ C_{21} & C_{22} & C_{23} & 0 & 0 & 0 & 0 & 0 & 0 & 0 & 0 & 0 \\ C_{31} & C_{32} & C_{33} & 0 & 0 & 0 & 0 & 0 & 0 & 0 & 0 & 0 \\ 0 & 0 & 0 & C_{11} & C_{12} & C_{13} & 0 & 0 & 0 & 0 & 0 & 0 \\ 0 & 0 & 0 & C_{21} & C_{22} & C_{23} & 0 & 0 & 0 & 0 & 0 & 0 \\ 0 & 0 & 0 & C_{31} & C_{32} & C_{33} & 0 & 0 & 0 & 0 & 0 & 0 \\ 0 & 0 & 0 & 0 & 0 & 0 & C_{11} & C_{12} & C_{13} & 0 & 0 & 0 \\ 0 & 0 & 0 & 0 & 0 & 0 & C_{21} & C_{22} & C_{23} & 0 & 0 & 0 \\ 0 & 0 & 0 & 0 & 0 & 0 & C_{31} & C_{32} & C_{33} & 0 & 0 & 0 \\ 0 & 0 & 0 & 0 & 0 & 0 & 0 & 0 & 0 & C_{11} & C_{12} & C_{13} \\ 0 & 0 & 0 & 0 & 0 & 0 & 0 & 0 & 0 & C_{21} & C_{22} & C_{23} \\ 0 & 0 & 0 & 0 & 0 & 0 & 0 & 0 & 0 & C_{31} & C_{32} & C_{33} \end{bmatrix}_i \begin{bmatrix} \bar{\delta}_t \\ \bar{\delta}_r \\ \bar{\delta}_v \\ \bar{\theta}_l \\ \bar{\theta}_n \\ \bar{\theta}_p \\ \bar{\delta}_u \\ \bar{\delta}_s \\ \bar{\delta}_w \\ \bar{\theta}_m \\ \bar{\theta}_o \\ \bar{\theta}_q \end{bmatrix}_i \begin{matrix} \text{translation of } j\text{-end} \\ \text{rotation of } j\text{-end} \\ \text{translation of } k\text{-end} \\ \text{rotation of } k\text{-end} \end{matrix} \tag{6-40a}$$

or

$$[\boldsymbol{\delta}^s]_i = [\mathbf{T}^s]_i[\bar{\boldsymbol{\delta}}^s]_i \tag{6-40b}$$

where

$$[\mathbf{T}^s]_i = \begin{bmatrix} [\mathbf{C}^s]_i & [\mathbf{0}] & [\mathbf{0}] & [\mathbf{0}] \\ [\mathbf{0}] & [\mathbf{C}^s]_i & [\mathbf{0}] & [\mathbf{0}] \\ [\mathbf{0}] & [\mathbf{0}] & [\mathbf{C}^s]_i & [\mathbf{0}] \\ [\mathbf{0}] & [\mathbf{0}] & [\mathbf{0}] & [\mathbf{C}^s]_i \end{bmatrix}_i \tag{6-41}$$

which is defined as the ***transformation matrix*** for beam element i arbitrarily oriented in a three-dimensional space.

This transformation matrix of Expression (6-41) serves the same purpose in the three-dimensional space as the transformation matrix of Expression (5-32) served in the two-dimensional space, and it possesses the same property as the transformation matrix for the two-dimensional space, i.e.,

$$[\mathbf{T}^s]_i^{-1} = [\mathbf{T}^s]_i^T \qquad \textbf{(6-42)}$$

This fact can be proven quite easily by rewriting Eqs. (6-39) to solve for the components of displacement in the frame of the reference axes in terms of the components of displacement with respect to the local system, recalling that

$$[\mathbf{C}^s]_i^{-1} = [\mathbf{C}^s]_i^T \qquad \textbf{(6-18)}$$

and combining the resulting equations into a single matrix operation similar to Eq. (6-40a). This results in

$$[\bar{\boldsymbol{\delta}}^s]_i = [\mathbf{T}^s]_i^T [\boldsymbol{\delta}^s]_i \qquad \textbf{(6-43)}$$

The rotation matrix $[\mathbf{C}^s]_i$, which forms the major elements of the transformation matrix of Expression (6-41), can be evaluated for a given beam element i by substituting into Expression (6-30) or (6-36), whichever is appropriate.

6-5.2 Transformed Member Stiffness Matrix: Beam Element

The components of member end action resulting from end displacement of the beam element have been defined in Fig. 6-17 with respect to both the local and reference axes. Since these vector components are similar to the vector components describing the corresponding end displacements (Fig. 6-17), the components of end action can also be transformed from the reference system of axes to the local system as

$$[\mathbf{m}^s]_i = [\mathbf{T}^s]_i[\bar{\mathbf{m}}^s]_i \qquad \textbf{(6-44a)}$$

and from the local system of axes to the reference system as

$$[\bar{\mathbf{m}}^s]_i = [\mathbf{T}^s]_i^T[\mathbf{m}^s]_i \qquad \textbf{(6-44b)}$$

where

$$[\mathbf{m}^s]_i = \begin{bmatrix} p_{jx} \\ p_{jy} \\ p_{jz} \\ m_{jx} \\ m_{jy} \\ m_{jz} \\ p_{kx} \\ p_{ky} \\ p_{kz} \\ m_{kx} \\ m_{ky} \\ m_{kz} \end{bmatrix}_i \approx \text{Components of end action with respect to local axes for member } i \qquad \textbf{(6-45a)}$$

$$[\bar{\mathbf{m}}^s]_i = \begin{bmatrix} \bar{p}_{jx} \\ \bar{p}_{jy} \\ \bar{p}_{jz} \\ \bar{m}_{jx} \\ \bar{m}_{jy} \\ \bar{m}_{jz} \\ \bar{p}_{kx} \\ \bar{p}_{ky} \\ \bar{p}_{kz} \\ \bar{m}_{kx} \\ \bar{m}_{ky} \\ \bar{m}_{kz} \end{bmatrix}_i \approx \text{Components of end action with respect to reference axes for member } i \tag{6-45b}$$

and again

$$[\mathbf{T}^s]_i = \begin{bmatrix} [\mathbf{C}^s]_i & [0] & [0] & [0] \\ [0] & [\mathbf{C}^s]_i & [0] & [0] \\ [0] & [0] & [\mathbf{C}^s]_i & [0] \\ [0] & [0] & [0] & [\mathbf{C}^s]_i \end{bmatrix}_i \tag{6-41}$$

The relationship between the components of end displacement and the components of end action with respect to the local system of axes for a beam element with both ends restrained against translation and rotation and arbitrarily positioned in the frame of the reference axes has been developed earlier and expressed as

$$[\mathbf{m}^s]_i = [\mathbf{K}^s]_i[\boldsymbol{\delta}^s]_i \tag{6-2}$$

Now, using Eqs. (6-40b), (6-42), and (6-44a), the relationship between the components of end displacement and the components of end action with respect to the reference axes can be expressed as

$$[\bar{\mathbf{m}}^s]_i = [\bar{\mathbf{K}}^s]_i\,[\bar{\boldsymbol{\delta}}^s]_i \tag{6-46}$$

with

$$[\bar{\mathbf{K}}^s]_i = [\mathbf{T}^s]_i^T[\mathbf{K}^s]_i[\mathbf{T}^s]_i \tag{6-47}$$

The matrix $[\bar{\mathbf{K}}^s]_i$ is defined as the ***transformed member stiffness matrix***, written ***with respect to the reference axes*** for the given structural system.

6-5.3 End Actions: Beam Element

The possible components of fixed end action for a beam element in a three-dimensional space resulting from a load or disturbance being applied along the span of the member are defined in Fig. 6-18 for the local and reference systems of axes. These actions may be evaluated with respect to either system of axes and transformed into the other system by means of the equations

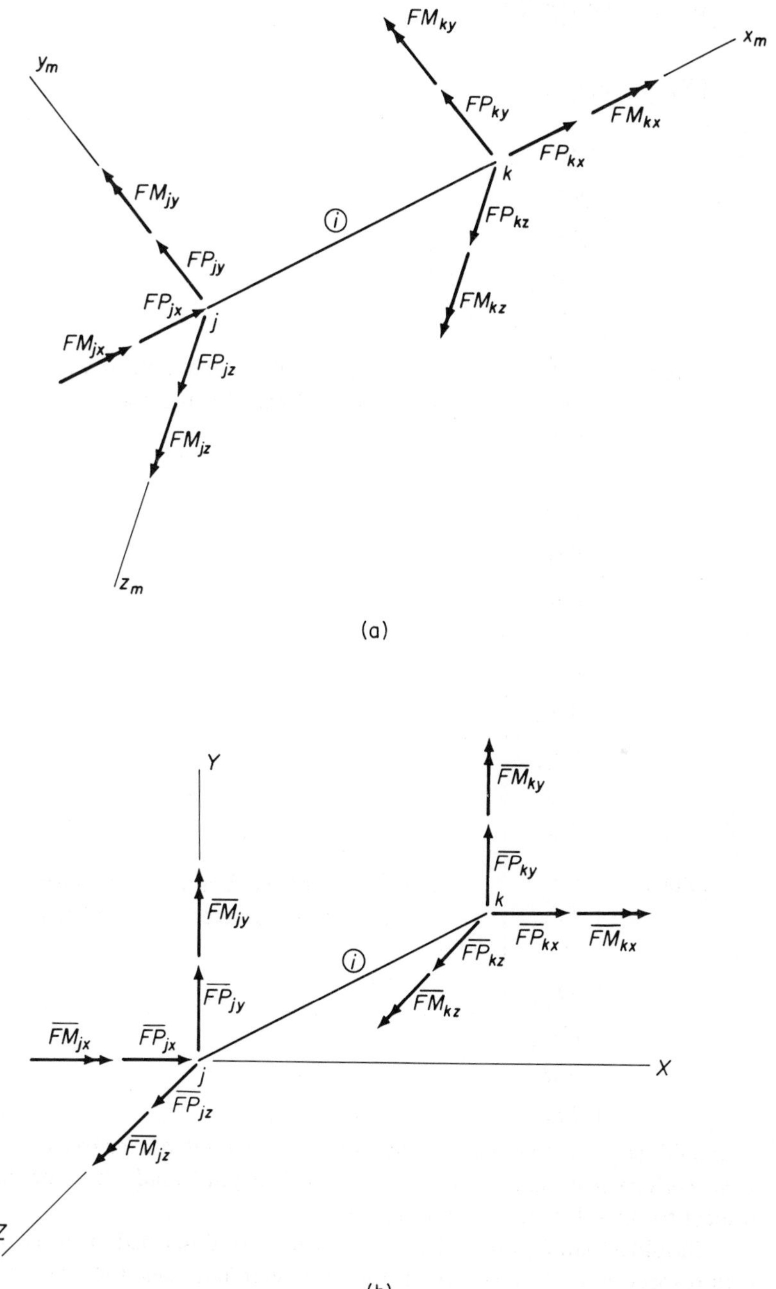

Fig. 6-18 Possible components of fixed end action for beam element in a three-dimensional space: (a) local coordinate system; (b) reference coordinate system.

$$[\mathbf{FM}^s]_i = [\mathbf{T}^s]_i[\overline{\mathbf{FM}}^s]_i \tag{6-48a}$$

or

$$[\overline{\mathbf{FM}}^s]_i = [\mathbf{T}^s]_i^T[\mathbf{FM}^s]_i \tag{6-48b}$$

where

$$[\mathbf{FM}^s]_i = \begin{bmatrix} FP_{jx} \\ FP_{jy} \\ FP_{jz} \\ FM_{jx} \\ FM_{jy} \\ FM_{jz} \\ FP_{kx} \\ FP_{ky} \\ FP_{kz} \\ FM_{kx} \\ FM_{ky} \\ FM_{kz} \end{bmatrix}_i \approx \text{Components of fixed end actions with respect to local axes for member } i \tag{6-49a}$$

and

$$[\overline{\mathbf{FM}}^s]_i = \begin{bmatrix} \overline{FP}_{jx} \\ \overline{FP}_{jy} \\ \overline{FP}_{jz} \\ \overline{FM}_{jx} \\ \overline{FM}_{jy} \\ \overline{FM}_{jz} \\ \overline{FP}_{kx} \\ \overline{FP}_{ky} \\ \overline{FP}_{kz} \\ \overline{FM}_{kx} \\ \overline{FM}_{ky} \\ \overline{FM}_{kz} \end{bmatrix}_i \approx \text{Components of fixed end actions with respect to reference axes for member } i \tag{6-49b}$$

It should be remembered that *the fixed end actions are converted into equivalent joint loads by a change in sign;* the equivalent joint loads must be described with respect to the reference system of axes.

Should a load Q_0 applied at a specific joint be described in terms of components with respect to a set of axes other than the reference axes, the given components of load Q_0 can be transformed into the reference system by Eq. (6-16), i.e.,

$$\begin{bmatrix} \bar{Q}_x \\ \bar{Q}_y \\ \bar{Q}_z \end{bmatrix} = [\mathbf{C}^s]_i^T \begin{bmatrix} Q_x \\ Q_y \\ Q_z \end{bmatrix} \tag{6-50}$$

using the proper rotation matrix for the two sets of axes. A similar transformation can be made for a load applied to a member defined in terms of components with respect to a set of axes other than the local member axes.

The possible components of final end actions in the frame of the local axes for a beam element of a three-dimensional structural system are defined in Fig. 6-19(a) and can be evaluated by means of a set of equations similar to Eqs. (5-46), i.e.,

$$[\mathbf{M}^s]_i = [\mathbf{K}^s]_i[\mathbf{T}^s]_i[\bar{\boldsymbol{\delta}}^s]_i + [\mathbf{FM}^s]_i \tag{6-51}$$

where

$$[\mathbf{M}^s]_i = \begin{bmatrix} P_{jx} \\ P_{jy} \\ P_{jz} \\ M_{jx} \\ M_{jy} \\ M_{jz} \\ P_{kx} \\ P_{ky} \\ P_{kz} \\ M_{kx} \\ M_{ky} \\ M_{kz} \end{bmatrix}_i \approx \text{Components of final end actions with respect to local axes for member } i \tag{6-52}$$

The components of final end action can also be evaluated with respect to the reference axes, shown in Fig. 6-19(b), by means of the equations

$$[\bar{\mathbf{M}}^s]_i = [\bar{\mathbf{K}}^s]_i[\bar{\boldsymbol{\delta}}^s]_i + [\overline{\mathbf{FM}}^s]_i \tag{6-53}$$

or

$$[\bar{\mathbf{M}}^s]_i = [\mathbf{T}^s]_i^T[\mathbf{M}^s]_i \tag{6-54}$$

where

$$[\bar{\mathbf{M}}^s]_i = \begin{bmatrix} \bar{P}_{jx} \\ \bar{P}_{jy} \\ \bar{P}_{jz} \\ \bar{M}_{jx} \\ \bar{M}_{jy} \\ \bar{M}_{jz} \\ \bar{P}_{kx} \\ \bar{P}_{ky} \\ \bar{P}_{kz} \\ \bar{M}_{kx} \\ \bar{M}_{ky} \\ \bar{M}_{kz} \end{bmatrix}_i \approx \text{Components of final end actions with respect to reference axes for member } i \tag{6-55}$$

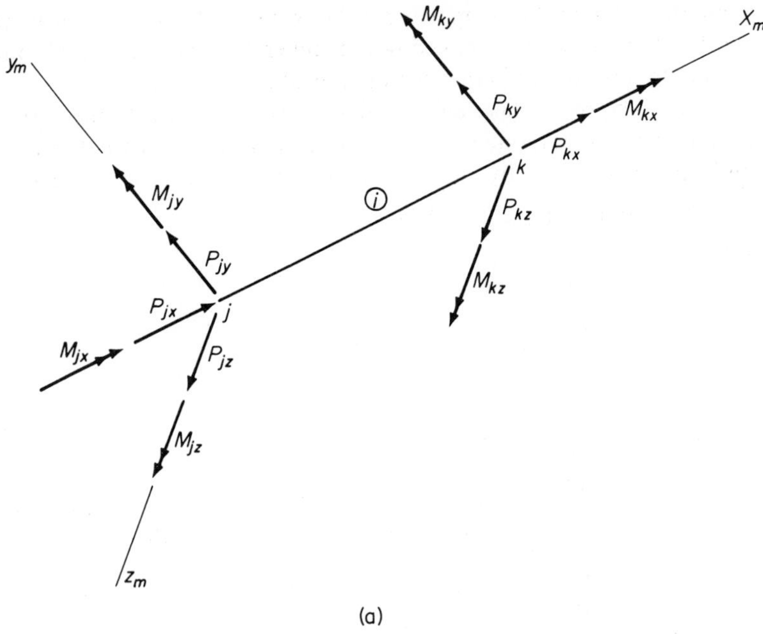

(a)

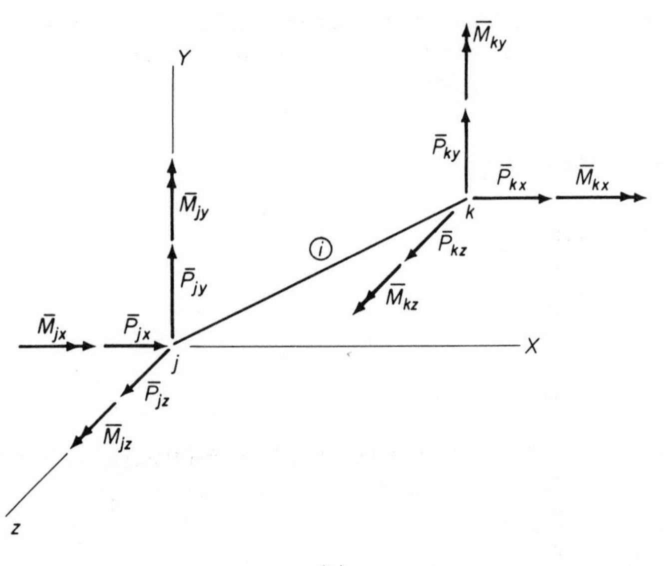

(b)

Fig. 6-19 Possible components of final end action for beam element in a three-dimensional space.

6-5.4 Equations of Analysis

The analysis of a three-dimensional structural system can be described by the same basic equations used to describe the analysis of a planar structure. Considering the total system, the static equilibrium of the joints is defined by the matrix equation

$$[\mathbf{S}_c][\boldsymbol{\Delta}_c] = [\mathbf{JL}_c] + [\mathbf{R}_c] \tag{6-56}$$

and from this set of equations, a set of independent equations, i.e.,

$$[\mathbf{S}_{uu}][\boldsymbol{\Delta}_u] = [\mathbf{JL}_u] \tag{6-57}$$

can be obtained and solved for the unknown components of joint displacement with respect to the reference axes. In addition, a second set of equations, i.e.,

$$[\mathbf{R}_r] = [\mathbf{S}_{ru}][\boldsymbol{\Delta}_u] - [\mathbf{JL}_r] \tag{6-58}$$

can be identified and used to evaluate the components of support reactions with respect to the reference axes.

Having determined the unrestrained components of joint displacement, the components of final end action in the frame of local axes can be evaluated for each member of the structure by means of Eq. (6-51), i.e.,

$$[\mathbf{M}^s]_i = [\mathbf{K}^s]_i[\mathbf{T}^s]_i[\bar{\boldsymbol{\delta}}^s]_i + [\mathbf{FM}^s]_i \tag{6-51}$$

The procedure for carrying out the analysis of a three-dimensional structure is the same as that followed for the analysis of the nonorthogonal, planar structure except for the fact that six components of joint displacement rather than three must be taken into consideration.

Example 6-2. For the structural system described in Fig. 6-20, determine the final end actions at the ends of each member and the support reactions caused by the indicated loading.

The structure is designed with members 1 and 2 in a horizontal plane meeting at right angles at joint 2 and with member 3 framing into member 2, at joint 3, perpendicular to the plane of members 1 and 2. The members are prismatic and have the same cross-sectional properties:

$$EI_y = EI_z = EI$$

$$GI_x = \frac{EI}{4}$$

and

$$EA_x = \frac{EI}{4}$$

The members are oriented in the structure so that the y_m–x_m plane of members 1 and 2 are perpendicular to the plane containing the two members and the y_m–x_m plane of member 3 coincides with that of member 2. The frame is supported at joints 1 and 4, which are assumed to be fixed.

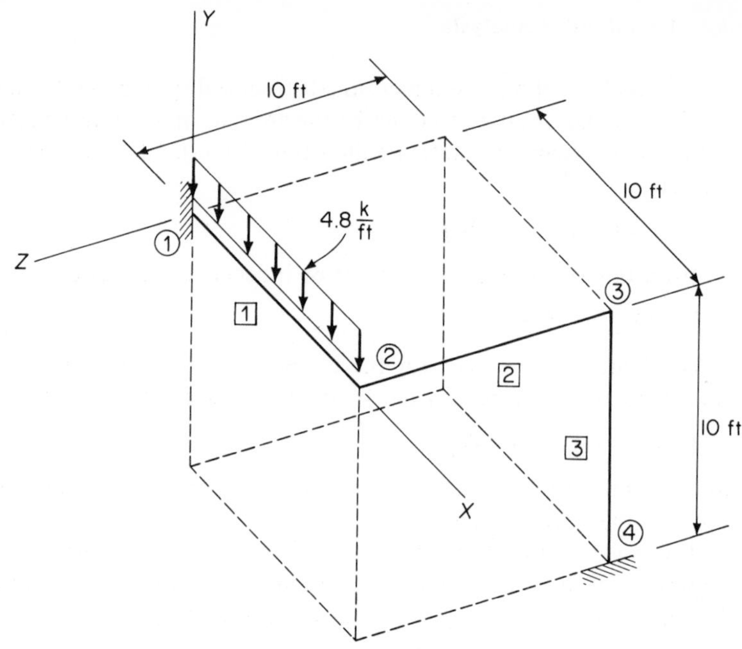

Fig. 6-20 Example 6-2: Rigid space frame.

The reference axes are located with the origin at joint 1, the X-axis along the axis of member 1, the Z-axis lying in the plane of members 1 and 2, and the Y-axis vertical.

The structure is loaded with a uniform vertical load of 4.8 k/ft along the length of member 1.

MEMBER INFORMATION

In Fig. 6-21, the j- and k-ends of each member have been selected and the orientation of the local member axes have been established. Tables 6-2 and 6-3 give the required joint and member information.

Table 6-2

	Coordinate		
Joint	X, ft	Y, ft	Z, ft
1	0	0	0
2	10.0	0	0
3	10.0	0	−10.0
4	10.0	−10.0	−10.0

Table 6-3

Member	Length, ft	Joint		Direction Cosines			Type of Transformation	Ψ-Angle
		j	*k*	C_x	C_y	C_z		
1	10.0	1	2	+1	0	0	*Y–Z–X*	0°
2	10.0	2	3	0	0	−1	*Y–Z–X*	0°
3	10.0	4	3	0	+1	0	*Z–Y–X*	90°

JOINT DISPLACEMENT MATRIX

The possible independent components of joint displacements with respect to the reference axes (X, Y, Z) are identified in Fig. 6-22. The complete joint displacement matrix is written as

$$[\mathbf{\Delta}_c] = \begin{bmatrix} \bar{\delta}_1 \\ \bar{\delta}_2 \\ \bar{\delta}_3 \\ \bar{\theta}_4 \\ \bar{\theta}_5 \\ \bar{\theta}_6 \\ \bar{\delta}_7 \\ \bar{\delta}_8 \\ \bar{\delta}_9 \\ \bar{\theta}_{10} \\ \bar{\theta}_{11} \\ \bar{\theta}_{12} \\ --- \\ \bar{\delta}_{13} \\ \bar{\delta}_{14} \\ \bar{\delta}_{15} \\ \bar{\theta}_{16} \\ \bar{\theta}_{17} \\ \bar{\theta}_{18} \\ \bar{\delta}_{19} \\ \bar{\delta}_{20} \\ \bar{\delta}_{21} \\ \bar{\theta}_{22} \\ \bar{\theta}_{23} \\ \bar{\theta}_{24} \end{bmatrix} = \begin{bmatrix} [\mathbf{\Delta}_u] \\ --- \\ [\mathbf{\Delta}_r] \end{bmatrix} \tag{6-59}$$

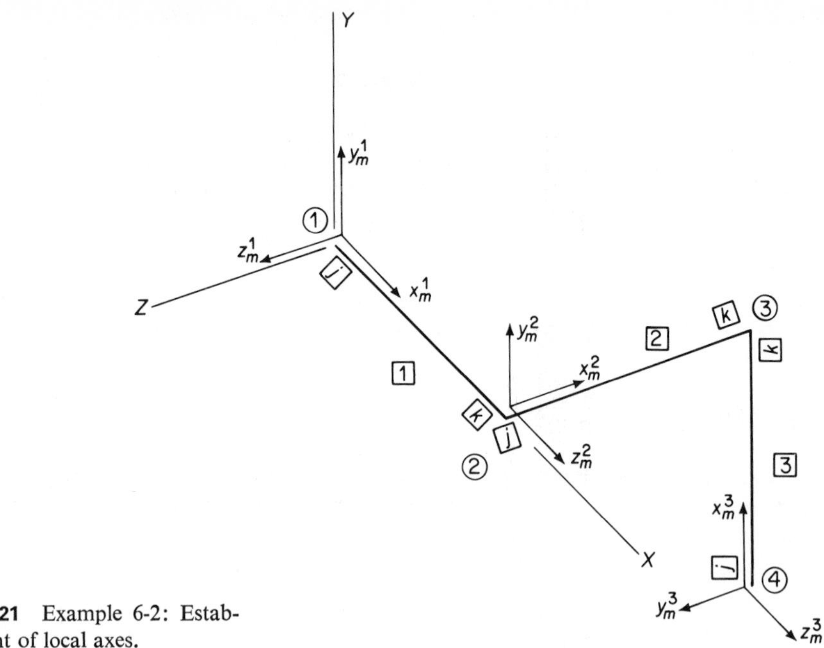

Fig. 6-21 Example 6-2: Establishment of local axes.

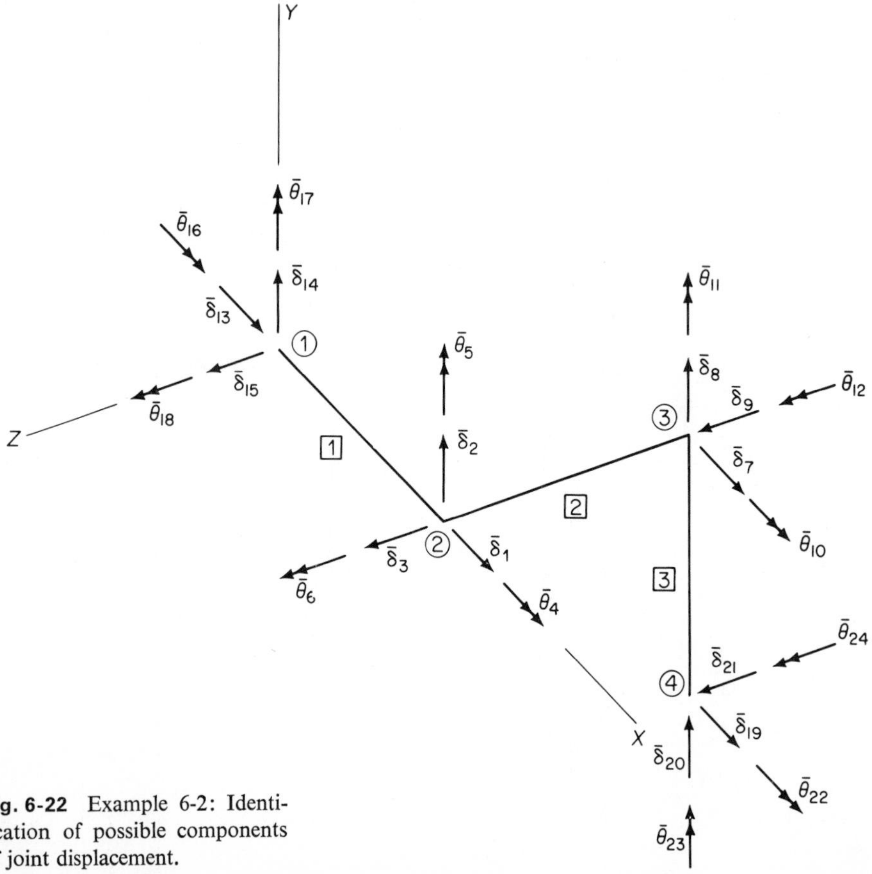

Fig. 6-22 Example 6-2: Identification of possible components of joint displacement.

MEMBER STIFFNESS MATRIX

For each beam element, the member stiffness matrix $[\mathbf{K}^s]_i$ written with respect to the local axes can be established by substituting into Expression (6-11); the transformation matrix $[\mathbf{T}^s]_i$ can be established by means of Expression (6-41), using the proper rotation matrix $[\mathbf{C}^s]_i$ of either Expression (6-30) or Expression (6-36); and the transformed member stiffness matrix $[\bar{\mathbf{K}}^s]_i$ written with respect to the reference axes can be developed by substituting into and performing the indicated operations of Eq. (6-47), i.e.,

$$[\bar{\mathbf{K}}^s]_i = [\mathbf{T}^s]_i^T[\mathbf{K}^s]_i[\mathbf{T}^s]_i \tag{6-47}$$

The rows and columns of the member stiffness matrices are labeled to correspond to the labeling of the components of displacement of the ends of the member to aid in the identification of the elements.

Member 1

With

$$[\mathbf{C}_Y^s]_1 = \begin{bmatrix} 1 & 0 & 0 \\ 0 & 1 & 0 \\ 0 & 0 & 1 \end{bmatrix}_1 \tag{6-60a}$$

$$[\mathbf{T}^s]_1 = \left[\begin{array}{ccc|ccc|ccc|ccc}
1 & 0 & 0 & 0 & 0 & 0 & 0 & 0 & 0 & 0 & 0 & 0 \\
0 & 1 & 0 & 0 & 0 & 0 & 0 & 0 & 0 & 0 & 0 & 0 \\
0 & 0 & 1 & 0 & 0 & 0 & 0 & 0 & 0 & 0 & 0 & 0 \\
\hline
0 & 0 & 0 & 1 & 0 & 0 & 0 & 0 & 0 & 0 & 0 & 0 \\
0 & 0 & 0 & 0 & 1 & 0 & 0 & 0 & 0 & 0 & 0 & 0 \\
0 & 0 & 0 & 0 & 0 & 1 & 0 & 0 & 0 & 0 & 0 & 0 \\
\hline
0 & 0 & 0 & 0 & 0 & 0 & 1 & 0 & 0 & 0 & 0 & 0 \\
0 & 0 & 0 & 0 & 0 & 0 & 0 & 1 & 0 & 0 & 0 & 0 \\
0 & 0 & 0 & 0 & 0 & 0 & 0 & 0 & 1 & 0 & 0 & 0 \\
\hline
0 & 0 & 0 & 0 & 0 & 0 & 0 & 0 & 0 & 1 & 0 & 0 \\
0 & 0 & 0 & 0 & 0 & 0 & 0 & 0 & 0 & 0 & 1 & 0 \\
0 & 0 & 0 & 0 & 0 & 0 & 0 & 0 & 0 & 0 & 0 & 1
\end{array}\right]_1 \tag{6-60b}$$

Hence,

$$[\mathbf{K}^s]_1 = [\bar{\mathbf{K}}^s]_1$$

$$= EI\begin{array}{c} \begin{array}{cccccccccccc} 13 & 14 & 15 & 16 & 17 & 18 & 1 & 2 & 3 & 4 & 5 & 6 \end{array} \\ \left[\begin{array}{cccccccccccc}
0.025 & 0 & 0 & 0 & 0 & 0 & -0.025 & 0 & 0 & 0 & 0 & 0 \\
0 & 0.012 & 0 & 0 & 0 & 0.060 & 0 & -0.012 & 0 & 0 & 0 & 0.060 \\
0 & 0 & 0.012 & 0 & -0.060 & 0 & 0 & 0 & -0.012 & 0 & -0.060 & 0 \\
0 & 0 & 0 & 0.025 & 0 & 0 & 0 & 0 & 0 & -0.025 & 0 & 0 \\
0 & 0 & -0.060 & 0 & 0.400 & 0 & 0 & 0 & 0.060 & 0 & 0.200 & 0 \\
0 & 0.060 & 0 & 0 & 0 & 0.400 & 0 & -0.060 & 0 & 0 & 0 & 0.200 \\
-0.025 & 0 & 0 & 0 & 0 & 0 & 0.025 & 0 & 0 & 0 & 0 & 0 \\
0 & -0.012 & 0 & 0 & 0 & -0.060 & 0 & 0.012 & 0 & 0 & 0 & -0.060 \\
0 & 0 & -0.012 & 0 & 0.060 & 0 & 0 & 0 & 0.012 & 0 & 0.060 & 0 \\
0 & 0 & 0 & -0.025 & 0 & 0 & 0 & 0 & 0 & 0.025 & 0 & 0 \\
0 & 0 & -0.060 & 0 & 0.200 & 0 & 0 & 0 & 0.060 & 0 & 0.400 & 0 \\
0 & 0.060 & 0 & 0 & 0 & 0.200 & 0 & -0.060 & 0 & 0 & 0 & 0.400
\end{array}\right]_1 \end{array} \begin{array}{c} \\ 13 \\ 14 \\ 15 \\ 16 \\ 17 \\ 18 \\ 1 \\ 2 \\ 3 \\ 4 \\ 5 \\ 6 \end{array} \tag{6-61}$$

Member 2

$$
[\mathbf{K}^s]_2 = EI
\begin{array}{c}
\begin{array}{cccccccccccc}
t & r & v & l & n & p & u & s & w & m & o & q
\end{array}\\
\left[\begin{array}{cccccccccccc}
0.025 & 0 & 0 & 0 & 0 & 0 & -0.025 & 0 & 0 & 0 & 0 & 0\\
0 & 0.012 & 0 & 0 & 0 & 0.060 & 0 & -0.012 & 0 & 0 & 0 & 0.060\\
0 & 0 & 0.012 & 0 & -0.060 & 0 & 0 & 0 & -0.012 & 0 & -0.060 & 0\\
0 & 0 & 0 & 0.025 & 0 & 0 & 0 & 0 & 0 & -0.025 & 0 & 0\\
0 & 0 & -0.060 & 0 & 0.400 & 0 & 0 & 0 & 0.060 & 0 & 0.200 & 0\\
0 & 0.060 & 0 & 0 & 0 & 0.400 & 0 & -0.060 & 0 & 0 & 0 & 0.200\\
-0.025 & 0 & 0 & 0 & 0 & 0 & 0.025 & 0 & 0 & 0 & 0 & 0\\
0 & -0.012 & 0 & 0 & 0 & -0.060 & 0 & 0.012 & 0 & 0 & 0 & -0.060\\
0 & 0 & -0.012 & 0 & 0.060 & 0 & 0 & 0 & 0.012 & 0 & 0.060 & 0\\
0 & 0 & 0 & -0.025 & 0 & 0 & 0 & 0 & 0 & 0.025 & 0 & 0\\
0 & 0 & -0.060 & 0 & 0.200 & 0 & 0 & 0 & 0.060 & 0 & 0.400 & 0\\
0 & 0.060 & 0 & 0 & 0 & 0.200 & 0 & -0.060 & 0 & 0 & 0 & 0.400
\end{array}\right]_2
\end{array}
\tag{6-62a}
$$

$$
[\mathbf{C}_Y^s]_2 = \begin{bmatrix} 0 & 0 & -1\\ 0 & 1 & 0\\ 1 & 0 & 0 \end{bmatrix}_2 \tag{6-63a}
$$

and

$$
[\mathbf{T}^s]_2 = \left[\begin{array}{ccc|ccc|ccc|ccc}
0 & 0 & -1 & 0 & 0 & 0 & 0 & 0 & 0 & 0 & 0 & 0\\
0 & 1 & 0 & 0 & 0 & 0 & 0 & 0 & 0 & 0 & 0 & 0\\
1 & 0 & 0 & 0 & 0 & 0 & 0 & 0 & 0 & 0 & 0 & 0\\
\hline
0 & 0 & 0 & 0 & 0 & -1 & 0 & 0 & 0 & 0 & 0 & 0\\
0 & 0 & 0 & 0 & 1 & 0 & 0 & 0 & 0 & 0 & 0 & 0\\
0 & 0 & 0 & 1 & 0 & 0 & 0 & 0 & 0 & 0 & 0 & 0\\
\hline
0 & 0 & 0 & 0 & 0 & 0 & 0 & 0 & -1 & 0 & 0 & 0\\
0 & 0 & 0 & 0 & 0 & 0 & 0 & 1 & 0 & 0 & 0 & 0\\
0 & 0 & 0 & 0 & 0 & 0 & 1 & 0 & 0 & 0 & 0 & 0\\
\hline
0 & 0 & 0 & 0 & 0 & 0 & 0 & 0 & 0 & 0 & 0 & -1\\
0 & 0 & 0 & 0 & 0 & 0 & 0 & 0 & 0 & 0 & 1 & 0\\
0 & 0 & 0 & 0 & 0 & 0 & 0 & 0 & 0 & 1 & 0 & 0
\end{array}\right]_2 \tag{6-63b}
$$

Hence,

$$
[\bar{\mathbf{K}}^s]_2 = EI
\begin{array}{c}
\begin{array}{cccccccccccc}
1 & 2 & 3 & 4 & 5 & 6 & 7 & 8 & 9 & 10 & 11 & 12
\end{array}\\
\left[\begin{array}{cccccccccccc}
0.012 & 0 & 0 & 0 & -0.060 & 0 & -0.012 & 0 & 0 & 0 & -0.060 & 0\\
0 & 0.012 & 0 & 0.060 & 0 & 0 & 0 & -0.012 & 0 & 0.060 & 0 & 0\\
0 & 0 & 0.025 & 0 & 0 & 0 & 0 & 0 & -0.025 & 0 & 0 & 0\\
0 & 0.060 & 0 & 0.400 & 0 & 0 & 0 & -0.060 & 0 & 0.200 & 0 & 0\\
-0.060 & 0 & 0 & 0 & 0.400 & 0 & 0.060 & 0 & 0 & 0 & 0.200 & 0\\
0 & 0 & 0 & 0 & 0 & 0.025 & 0 & 0 & 0 & 0 & 0 & -0.025\\
-0.012 & 0 & 0 & 0 & 0.060 & 0 & 0.012 & 0 & 0 & 0 & 0.060 & 0\\
0 & -0.012 & 0 & -0.060 & 0 & 0 & 0 & 0.012 & 0 & -0.060 & 0 & 0\\
0 & 0 & -0.025 & 0 & 0 & 0 & 0 & 0 & 0.025 & 0 & 0 & 0\\
0 & 0.060 & 0 & 0.200 & 0 & 0 & 0 & -0.060 & 0 & 0.400 & 0 & 0\\
-0.060 & 0 & 0 & 0 & 0.200 & 0 & 0.060 & 0 & 0 & 0 & 0.400 & 0\\
0 & 0 & 0 & 0 & 0 & -0.025 & 0 & 0 & 0 & 0 & 0 & 0.025
\end{array}\right]_2
\end{array}
\begin{array}{c}
\\ 1\\ 2\\ 3\\ 4\\ 5\\ 6\\ 7\\ 8\\ 9\\ 10\\ 11\\ 12
\end{array}
\tag{6-62b}
$$

Member 3

$$[\mathbf{K}^s]_3 = EI \begin{array}{c} \begin{array}{cccccccccccc} t & r & v & l & n & p & u & s & w & m & o & q \end{array} \\ \left[\begin{array}{cccccccccccc}
0.025 & 0 & 0 & 0 & 0 & 0 & -0.025 & 0 & 0 & 0 & 0 & 0 \\
0 & 0.012 & 0 & 0 & 0 & 0.060 & 0 & -0.012 & 0 & 0 & 0 & 0.060 \\
0 & 0 & 0.012 & 0 & -0.060 & 0 & 0 & 0 & -0.012 & 0 & -0.060 & 0 \\
0 & 0 & 0 & 0.025 & 0 & 0 & 0 & 0 & 0 & -0.025 & 0 & 0 \\
0 & 0 & -0.060 & 0 & 0.400 & 0 & 0 & 0 & 0.060 & 0 & 0.200 & 0 \\
0 & 0.060 & 0 & 0 & 0 & 0.400 & 0 & -0.060 & 0 & 0 & 0 & 0.200 \\
-0.025 & 0 & 0 & 0 & 0 & 0 & 0.025 & 0 & 0 & 0 & 0 & 0 \\
0 & -0.012 & 0 & 0 & 0 & -0.060 & 0 & 0.012 & 0 & 0 & 0 & -0.060 \\
0 & 0 & -0.012 & 0 & 0.060 & 0 & 0 & 0 & 0.012 & 0 & 0.060 & 0 \\
0 & 0 & 0 & -0.025 & 0 & 0 & 0 & 0 & 0 & 0.025 & 0 & 0 \\
0 & 0 & -0.060 & 0 & 0.200 & 0 & 0 & 0 & 0.060 & 0 & 0.400 & 0 \\
0 & 0.060 & 0 & 0 & 0 & 0.200 & 0 & -0.060 & 0 & 0 & 0 & 0.400
\end{array}\right]_3 \end{array} \tag{6-64a}$$

$$[\mathbf{C}^s_Z]_3 = \begin{bmatrix} 0 & 1 & 0 \\ 0 & 0 & 1 \\ 1 & 0 & 0 \end{bmatrix}_3 \tag{6-65a}$$

and

$$[\mathbf{T}^s]_3 = \left[\begin{array}{ccc|ccc|ccc|ccc}
0 & 1 & 0 & 0 & 0 & 0 & 0 & 0 & 0 & 0 & 0 & 0 \\
0 & 0 & 1 & 0 & 0 & 0 & 0 & 0 & 0 & 0 & 0 & 0 \\
1 & 0 & 0 & 0 & 0 & 0 & 0 & 0 & 0 & 0 & 0 & 0 \\ \hline
0 & 0 & 0 & 0 & 1 & 0 & 0 & 0 & 0 & 0 & 0 & 0 \\
0 & 0 & 0 & 0 & 0 & 1 & 0 & 0 & 0 & 0 & 0 & 0 \\
0 & 0 & 0 & 1 & 0 & 0 & 0 & 0 & 0 & 0 & 0 & 0 \\ \hline
0 & 0 & 0 & 0 & 0 & 0 & 0 & 1 & 0 & 0 & 0 & 0 \\
0 & 0 & 0 & 0 & 0 & 0 & 0 & 0 & 1 & 0 & 0 & 0 \\
0 & 0 & 0 & 0 & 0 & 0 & 1 & 0 & 0 & 0 & 0 & 0 \\ \hline
0 & 0 & 0 & 0 & 0 & 0 & 0 & 0 & 0 & 0 & 1 & 0 \\
0 & 0 & 0 & 0 & 0 & 0 & 0 & 0 & 0 & 0 & 0 & 1 \\
0 & 0 & 0 & 0 & 0 & 0 & 0 & 0 & 0 & 1 & 0 & 0
\end{array}\right]_3 \tag{6-65b}$$

Hence,

$$[\bar{\mathbf{K}}^s]_3 = EI \begin{array}{c} \begin{array}{cccccccccccc} 19 & 20 & 21 & 22 & 23 & 24 & 7 & 8 & 9 & 10 & 11 & 12 \end{array} \\ \left[\begin{array}{cccccccccccc}
0.012 & 0 & 0 & 0 & 0 & -0.060 & -0.012 & 0 & 0 & 0 & 0 & -0.060 \\
0 & 0.025 & 0 & 0 & 0 & 0 & 0 & -0.025 & 0 & 0 & 0 & 0 \\
0 & 0 & 0.012 & 0.060 & 0 & 0 & 0 & 0 & -0.012 & 0.060 & 0 & 0 \\
0 & 0 & 0.060 & 0.400 & 0 & 0 & 0 & 0 & -0.060 & 0.200 & 0 & 0 \\
0 & 0 & 0 & 0 & 0.025 & 0 & 0 & 0 & 0 & 0 & -0.025 & 0 \\
-0.060 & 0 & 0 & 0 & 0 & 0.400 & 0.060 & 0 & 0 & 0 & 0 & 0.200 \\
-0.012 & 0 & 0 & 0 & 0 & 0.060 & 0.012 & 0 & 0 & 0 & 0 & 0.060 \\
0 & -0.025 & 0 & 0 & 0 & 0 & 0 & 0.025 & 0 & 0 & 0 & 0 \\
0 & 0 & -0.012 & -0.060 & 0 & 0 & 0 & 0 & 0.012 & -0.060 & 0 & 0 \\
0 & 0 & 0.060 & 0.200 & 0 & 0 & 0 & 0 & -0.060 & 0.400 & 0 & 0 \\
0 & 0 & 0 & 0 & -0.025 & 0 & 0 & 0 & 0 & 0 & 0.025 & 0 \\
-0.060 & 0 & 0 & 0 & 0 & 0.200 & 0.060 & 0 & 0 & 0 & 0 & 0.400
\end{array}\right]_3 \end{array} \begin{array}{c} \\ 19 \\ 20 \\ 21 \\ 22 \\ 23 \\ 24 \\ 7 \\ 8 \\ 9 \\ 10 \\ 11 \\ 12 \end{array} \tag{6-64b}$$

STRUCTURE STIFFNESS MATRIX

The complete structure stiffness matrix $[\mathbf{S}_c]$ is established once again by summing the member stiffness coefficients given in Expressions (6-61), (6-62b), and (6-64b) with respect to the subscript identification of the elements. Rather than developing the whole matrix $[\mathbf{S}_c]$, only the two submatrices that are needed to carry out the analysis are written:

$$[\mathbf{S}_{uu}] = EI\;\begin{array}{cccccccccccc|c}
1 & 2 & 3 & 4 & 5 & 6 & 7 & 8 & 9 & 10 & 11 & 12 & \\
\hline
0.037 & 0 & 0 & 0 & -0.060 & 0 & -0.012 & 0 & 0 & 0 & -0.060 & 0 & 1\\
0 & 0.024 & 0 & 0.060 & 0 & -0.060 & 0 & -0.012 & 0 & 0.060 & 0 & 0 & 2\\
0 & 0 & 0.037 & 0 & 0.060 & 0 & 0 & 0 & -0.025 & 0 & 0 & 0 & 3\\
0 & 0.060 & 0 & 0.425 & 0 & 0 & 0 & -0.060 & 0 & 0.200 & 0 & 0 & 4\\
-0.060 & 0 & 0.060 & 0 & 0.800 & 0 & 0.060 & 0 & 0 & 0 & 0.200 & 0 & 5\\
0 & -0.060 & 0 & 0 & 0 & 0.425 & 0 & 0 & 0 & 0 & 0 & -0.025 & 6\\
-0.012 & 0 & 0 & 0 & 0.060 & 0 & 0.024 & 0 & 0 & 0 & 0.060 & 0.060 & 7\\
0 & -0.012 & 0 & -0.060 & 0 & 0 & 0 & 0.037 & 0 & -0.060 & 0 & 0 & 8\\
0 & 0 & -0.025 & 0 & 0 & 0 & 0 & 0 & 0.037 & -0.060 & 0 & 0 & 9\\
0 & 0.060 & 0 & 0.200 & 0 & 0 & 0 & -0.060 & -0.060 & 0.800 & 0 & 0 & 10\\
-0.060 & 0 & 0 & 0 & 0.200 & 0 & 0.060 & 0 & 0 & 0 & 0.425 & 0 & 11\\
0 & 0 & 0 & 0 & 0 & -0.025 & 0.060 & 0 & 0 & 0 & 0 & 0.425 & 12
\end{array} \tag{6-66}$$

and

$$[\mathbf{S}_{ru}] = EI\;\begin{array}{cccccccccccc|c}
1 & 2 & 3 & 4 & 5 & 6 & 7 & 8 & 9 & 10 & 11 & 12 & \\
\hline
-0.025 & 0 & 0 & 0 & 0 & 0 & 0 & 0 & 0 & 0 & 0 & 0 & 13\\
0 & -0.012 & 0 & 0 & 0 & 0.060 & 0 & 0 & 0 & 0 & 0 & 0 & 14\\
0 & 0 & -0.012 & 0 & -0.060 & 0 & 0 & 0 & 0 & 0 & 0 & 0 & 15\\
0 & 0 & 0 & -0.025 & 0 & 0 & 0 & 0 & 0 & 0 & 0 & 0 & 16\\
0 & 0 & 0.060 & 0 & 0.200 & 0 & 0 & 0 & 0 & 0 & 0 & 0 & 17\\
0 & -0.060 & 0 & 0 & 0 & 0.200 & 0 & 0 & 0 & 0 & 0 & 0 & 18\\
0 & 0 & 0 & 0 & 0 & 0 & -0.012 & 0 & 0 & 0 & 0 & -0.060 & 19\\
0 & 0 & 0 & 0 & 0 & 0 & 0 & -0.025 & 0 & 0 & 0 & 0 & 20\\
0 & 0 & 0 & 0 & 0 & 0 & 0 & 0 & -0.012 & 0.060 & 0 & 0 & 21\\
0 & 0 & 0 & 0 & 0 & 0 & 0 & 0 & -0.060 & 0.200 & 0 & 0 & 22\\
0 & 0 & 0 & 0 & 0 & 0 & 0 & 0 & 0 & 0 & -0.025 & 0 & 23\\
0 & 0 & 0 & 0 & 0 & 0 & 0.060 & 0 & 0 & 0 & 0 & 0.200 & 24
\end{array} \tag{6-67}$$

Now, $[\mathbf{S}_{uu}]^{-1}$ is given in Expression (6-68).

JOINT LOAD MATRIX

As shown in Fig. 6-20, the structure is loaded with a uniform vertical load of 4.8 k/ft along the length of member 1. The fixed end action matrix for member 1 can be defined as

$$
[\mathbf{S}_{uu}]^{-1} = \frac{1}{EI}
\begin{array}{c}
\begin{array}{cccccccccccc}
1 & 2 & 3 & 4 & 5 & 6 & 7 & 8 & 9 & 10 & 11 & 12
\end{array} \\
\left[\begin{array}{rrrrrrrrrrrr}
38.396 & 1.266 & -6.236 & 0.001 & 1.750 & 0.085 & 11.279 & -0.403 & -5.028 & -0.503 & 3.005 & -1.578 \\
1.266 & 210.745 & -43.160 & -21.908 & 5.487 & 30.182 & -39.151 & 11.279 & -50.707 & -13.286 & 3.124 & 7.303 \\
-6.236 & -43.160 & 102.028 & 2.421 & -11.235 & -6.537 & 50.707 & 5.028 & 84.038 & 9.312 & -2.752 & -7.543 \\
0.001 & -21.908 & 2.421 & 5.546 & -0.346 & -3.130 & 3.124 & 3.005 & 2.752 & 0.688 & -0.278 & -0.625 \\
1.750 & 5.487 & -11.235 & -0.346 & 3.048 & 0.888 & -13.286 & -0.503 & -9.312 & -1.061 & 0.688 & 1.928 \\
0.085 & 30.182 & -6.537 & -3.130 & 0.888 & 6.698 & -7.303 & 1.587 & -7.543 & -1.928 & 0.625 & 1.425 \\
11.279 & -39.151 & 50.707 & 3.124 & -13.286 & -7.303 & 210.745 & 1.266 & 43.160 & 5.487 & -21.908 & -30.182 \\
-0.403 & 11.279 & 5.028 & 3.005 & -0.503 & 1.587 & 1.266 & 38.396 & 6.236 & 1.750 & 0.001 & -0.085 \\
-5.028 & -50.707 & 84.038 & 2.752 & -9.312 & -7.543 & 43.160 & 6.236 & 102.028 & 11.235 & -2.421 & -6.537 \\
-0.503 & -13.286 & 9.312 & 0.688 & -1.061 & -1.928 & 5.487 & 1.750 & 11.235 & 3.048 & -0.346 & -0.888 \\
3.005 & 3.124 & -2.752 & -0.278 & 0.688 & 0.625 & -21.908 & 0.001 & -2.421 & -0.346 & 5.546 & 3.130 \\
-1.587 & 7.303 & -7.543 & -0.625 & 1.928 & 1.425 & -30.182 & -0.085 & -6.537 & -0.888 & 3.130 & 6.698
\end{array}\right]
\begin{array}{c}
1 \\ 2 \\ 3 \\ 4 \\ 5 \\ 6 \\ 7 \\ 8 \\ 9 \\ 10 \\ 11 \\ 12
\end{array}
\end{array}
\qquad \textbf{(6-68)}
$$

$$[\mathbf{FM}^s]_1 = \begin{bmatrix} FP_{jx} \\ FP_{jy} \\ FP_{jz} \\ FM_{jx} \\ FM_{jy} \\ FM_{jz} \\ FP_{kx} \\ FP_{ky} \\ FP_{kz} \\ FM_{kx} \\ FM_{ky} \\ FM_{kz} \end{bmatrix}_1 = \begin{bmatrix} 0 \\ 24.0 \text{ k} \\ 0 \\ 0 \\ 0 \\ 40.0 \text{ ft-k} \\ 0 \\ 24.0 \text{ k} \\ 0 \\ 0 \\ 0 \\ -40.0 \text{ ft-k} \end{bmatrix}_1 \tag{6-69a}$$

with respect to the local axes of member 1 (Fig. 6-21), and can be defined as

$$[\overline{\mathbf{FM}}^s]_1 = \begin{bmatrix} \overline{FP}_{jx} \\ \overline{FP}_{jy} \\ \overline{FP}_{jz} \\ \overline{FM}_{jx} \\ \overline{FM}_{jy} \\ \overline{FM}_{jz} \\ \overline{FP}_{kx} \\ \overline{FP}_{ky} \\ \overline{FP}_{kz} \\ \overline{FM}_{kx} \\ \overline{FM}_{ky} \\ \overline{FM}_{kz} \end{bmatrix}_1 = \begin{bmatrix} \overline{FP}_{13} \\ \overline{FP}_{14} \\ \overline{FP}_{15} \\ \overline{FM}_{16} \\ \overline{FM}_{17} \\ \overline{FM}_{18} \\ \overline{FP}_{1} \\ \overline{FP}_{2} \\ \overline{FP}_{3} \\ \overline{FM}_{4} \\ \overline{FM}_{5} \\ \overline{FM}_{6} \end{bmatrix}_1 = \begin{bmatrix} 0 \\ 24.0 \\ 0 \\ 0 \\ 0 \\ 40.0 \\ 0 \\ 24.0 \\ 0 \\ 0 \\ 0 \\ -40.0 \end{bmatrix}_1 \tag{6-69b}$$

with respect to the reference axes of the structure (Fig. 6-21). This transformation was made using Eq. (6-48b), i.e.,

$$[\overline{\mathbf{FM}}^s]_1 = [\mathbf{T}^s]_1^T[\mathbf{FM}^s]_1$$

Having defined the loading of the structure in terms of fixed end actions with respect to the reference axes, the components of fixed end action can be converted into equivalent joint loads and summed into the joint load matrix, yielding

$$[\mathbf{JL}_c] = \left[\begin{array}{c} 0 \\ -24.0 \\ 0 \\ 0 \\ 0 \\ 40.0 \\ 0 \\ 0 \\ 0 \\ 0 \\ 0 \\ 0 \\ \hline 0 \\ -24.0 \\ 0 \\ 0 \\ 0 \\ -40.0 \\ 0 \\ 0 \\ 0 \\ 0 \\ 0 \\ 0 \end{array}\right] \begin{array}{c} 1 \\ 2 \\ 3 \\ 4 \\ 5 \\ 6 \\ 7 \\ 8 \\ 9 \\ 10 \\ 11 \\ 12 \\ \\ 13 \\ 14 \\ 15 \\ 16 \\ 17 \\ 18 \\ 19 \\ 20 \\ 21 \\ 22 \\ 23 \\ 24 \end{array} = \left[\begin{array}{c} [\mathbf{JL}_u] \\ \hline [\mathbf{JL}_r] \end{array}\right] \tag{6-70}$$

↑ corresponding displacement label

SOLUTION

Making the substitutions called for by Eqs. (6-57), i.e.,

$$[\mathbf{S}_{uu}][\mathbf{\Delta}_u] = [\mathbf{JL}_u] \tag{6-57}$$

and solving for the unknown components of joint displacement yields

$$[\mathbf{\Delta}_u] = \begin{bmatrix} \bar{\delta}_1 \\ \bar{\delta}_2 \\ \bar{\delta}_3 \\ \bar{\theta}_4 \\ \bar{\theta}_5 \\ \bar{\theta}_6 \\ \bar{\delta}_7 \\ \bar{\delta}_8 \\ \bar{\delta}_9 \\ \bar{\theta}_{10} \\ \bar{\theta}_{11} \\ \bar{\theta}_{12} \end{bmatrix} = \frac{1}{EI} \begin{bmatrix} -26.984 \\ -3850.600 \\ 774.360 \\ 400.592 \\ -96.168 \\ -456.448 \\ 647.504 \\ -207.216 \\ 915.248 \\ 241.744 \\ -49.976 \\ -118.272 \end{bmatrix} \tag{6-71}$$

The values of displacement given in Expression (6-71) are relative values. If desired, the actual values of displacement can be obtained by substituting into Expression (6-71) for E (k/ft^2) and I(ft^4). The translations will be in units of feet and the rotations in radians.

FINAL END ACTIONS

Having evaluated the components of joint displacement with respect to the reference axes, the components of final end action with respect to the local axes can now be determined for each member of the structure by Eq. (6-51), i.e.,

$$[\mathbf{M}^s]_i = [\mathbf{K}^s]_i[\mathbf{T}^s]_i[\bar{\boldsymbol{\delta}}^s]_i + [\mathbf{FM}^s]_i \tag{6-51}$$

Member 1

Referring to Fig. 6-22, the end displacement matrix with respect to the reference axes is written as

$$[\bar{\boldsymbol{\delta}}^s]_1 = \begin{bmatrix} \bar{\delta}_{13} \\ \bar{\delta}_{14} \\ \bar{\delta}_{15} \\ \bar{\theta}_{16} \\ \bar{\theta}_{17} \\ \bar{\theta}_{18} \\ \bar{\delta}_1 \\ \bar{\delta}_2 \\ \bar{\delta}_3 \\ \bar{\theta}_4 \\ \bar{\theta}_5 \\ \bar{\theta}_6 \end{bmatrix} = \frac{1}{EI} \begin{bmatrix} 0 \\ 0 \\ 0 \\ 0 \\ 0 \\ 0 \\ -26.984 \\ -3850.600 \\ 774.360 \\ 400.592 \\ -96.168 \\ -456.448 \end{bmatrix}_1 \tag{6-72}$$

Now, substituting Expressions (6-60b), (6-61), (6-69a), and (6-72) into Eq. (6-51) yields

$$[\mathbf{M}^s]_1 = \begin{bmatrix} P_{jx} \\ P_{jy} \\ P_{jz} \\ M_{jx} \\ M_{jy} \\ M_{jz} \\ P_{kx} \\ P_{ky} \\ P_{kz} \\ M_{kx} \\ M_{ky} \\ M_{kz} \end{bmatrix}_1 = \begin{bmatrix} 0.7 \text{ k} \\ 42.8 \text{ k} \\ -3.5 \text{ k} \\ -10.0 \text{ ft-k} \\ 27.2 \text{ ft-k} \\ 179.7 \text{ ft-k} \\ -0.7 \text{ k} \\ 5.2 \text{ k} \\ 3.5 \text{ k} \\ 10.0 \text{ ft-k} \\ 8.0 \text{ ft-k} \\ 8.5 \text{ ft-k} \end{bmatrix}_1 \tag{6-73}$$

Member 2

Referring to Fig. 6-22, the end displacement matrix with respect to the reference axes is defined as

$$[\bar{\boldsymbol{\delta}}^s]_2 = [\boldsymbol{\Delta}_u] \tag{6-74a}$$

In addition,

$$[\mathbf{FM}^s]_2 = [0] \tag{6-74b}$$

Substituting Expressions (6-62a), (6-63b), (6-74a), and (6-74b) into Eqs. (6-51) yields

$$[\mathbf{M}^s]_2 = \begin{bmatrix} P_{jx} \\ P_{jy} \\ P_{jz} \\ M_{jx} \\ M_{jy} \\ M_{jz} \\ P_{kx} \\ P_{ky} \\ P_{kz} \\ M_{kx} \\ M_{ky} \\ M_{kz} \end{bmatrix}_2 = \begin{bmatrix} 3.5 \text{ k} \\ -5.2 \text{ k} \\ 0.7 \text{ k} \\ 8.5 \text{ ft-k} \\ -8.0 \text{ ft-k} \\ -10.0 \text{ ft-k} \\ -3.5 \text{ k} \\ 5.2 \text{ k} \\ -0.7 \text{ k} \\ -8.5 \text{ ft-k} \\ 1.2 \text{ ft-k} \\ -41.8 \text{ ft-k} \end{bmatrix}_2 \tag{6-75}$$

Member 3

Referring to Fig. 6-22, the end displacement matrix with respect to the reference axes is written as

$$[\bar{\boldsymbol{\delta}}^s]_3 = \begin{bmatrix} \bar{\delta}_{19} \\ \bar{\delta}_{20} \\ \bar{\delta}_{21} \\ \bar{\theta}_{22} \\ \bar{\theta}_{23} \\ \bar{\theta}_{24} \\ \bar{\delta}_{7} \\ \bar{\delta}_{8} \\ \bar{\delta}_{9} \\ \bar{\theta}_{10} \\ \bar{\theta}_{11} \\ \bar{\theta}_{12} \end{bmatrix}_3 = \frac{1}{EI} \begin{bmatrix} 0 \\ 0 \\ 0 \\ 0 \\ 0 \\ 0 \\ 647.504 \\ -207.216 \\ 915.248 \\ 241.744 \\ -49.976 \\ -118.272 \end{bmatrix}_3 \tag{6-76a}$$

also,

$$[\mathbf{FM}^s]_3 = [0] \tag{6-76b}$$

Substituting Expressions (6-64a), (6-65b), (6-76a), and (6-76b) into Eq. (6-51) yields

$$[\mathbf{M}^s]_3 = \begin{bmatrix} P_{jx} \\ P_{jy} \\ P_{jz} \\ M_{jx} \\ M_{jy} \\ M_{jz} \\ P_{kx} \\ P_{ky} \\ P_{kz} \\ M_{kx} \\ M_{ky} \\ M_{kz} \end{bmatrix}_3 = \begin{bmatrix} 5.2\text{ k} \\ 3.5\text{ k} \\ -0.7\text{ k} \\ 1.2\text{ ft-k} \\ 15.2\text{ ft-k} \\ -6.6\text{ ft-k} \\ -5.2\text{ k} \\ -3.5\text{ k} \\ 0.7\text{ k} \\ -1.2\text{ ft-k} \\ -8.5\text{ ft-k} \\ 41.8\text{ ft-k} \end{bmatrix}_3 \tag{6-77}$$

The free body diagram for the three members of the structure are shown in Fig. 6-23, and the free body diagrams for joints 2 and 3 are shown in Fig. 6-24.

SUPPORT REACTIONS

Substituting the proper matrices into Eq. (6-58), i.e.,

$$[\mathbf{R}_r] = [\mathbf{S}_{ru}][\boldsymbol{\Delta}_u] - [\mathbf{JL}_r] \tag{6-58}$$

and performing the indicated matrix operations, the components of support reaction with respect to the reference axes are found to be equal to

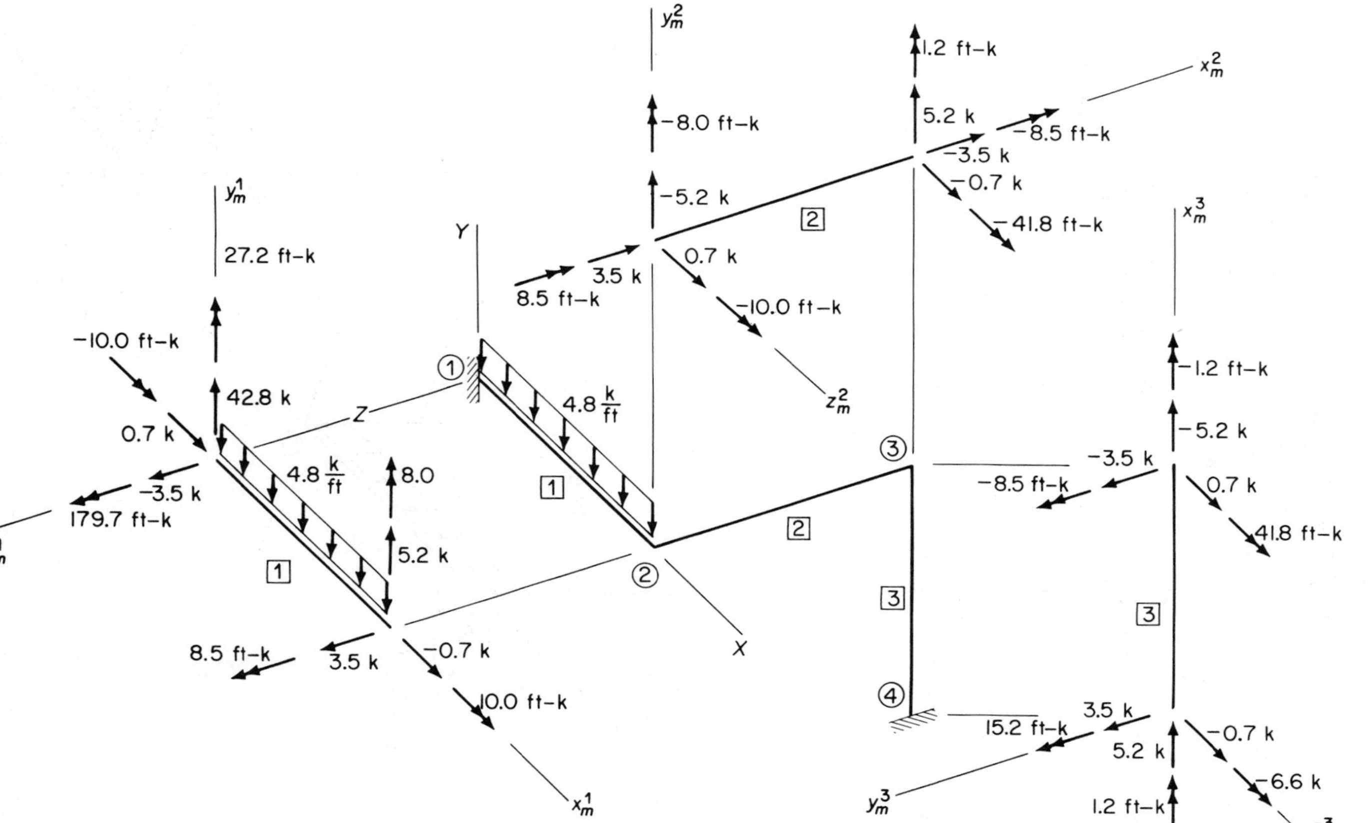

Fig. 6-23 Example 6-2: Components of final end actions.

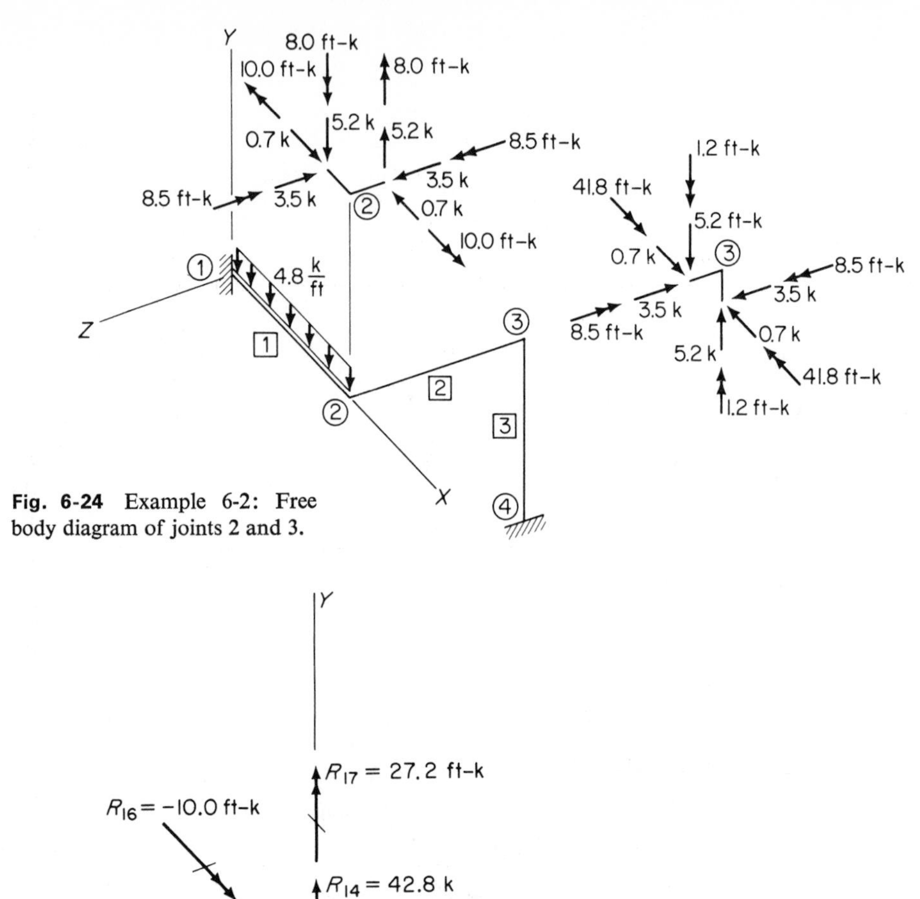

Fig. 6-24 Example 6-2: Free body diagram of joints 2 and 3.

Y
$R_{17} = 27.2$ ft–k
$R_{16} = -10.0$ ft–k
$R_{14} = 42.8$ k
$R_{13} = 0.7$ k
1
4.8 k/ft
10 ft
$R_{15} = -3.5$ k
$R_{18} = 179.7$ ft–k
3
Z
1
10 ft
2
2
3
$R_{24} = 15.2$ ft–k
X
4
$R_{21} = 3.5$ k
$R_{19} = -0.7$ k
10 ft
$R_{20} = 5.2$ k
$R_{22} = -6.6$ k
$R_{23} = 1.2$ ft–k

Fig. 6-25 Example 6-2: Components of support reactions.

$$[\mathbf{R}_r] = \begin{bmatrix} R_{13} \\ R_{14} \\ R_{15} \\ R_{16} \\ R_{17} \\ R_{18} \\ R_{19} \\ R_{20} \\ R_{21} \\ R_{22} \\ R_{23} \\ R_{24} \end{bmatrix} = \begin{bmatrix} 0.7\text{ k} \\ 42.8\text{ k} \\ -3.5\text{ k} \\ -10.0\text{ ft-k} \\ 27.2\text{ ft-k} \\ 179.7\text{ ft-k} \\ -0.7\text{ k} \\ 5.2\text{ k} \\ 3.5\text{ k} \\ -6.6\text{ ft-k} \\ 1.2\text{ ft-k} \\ 15.2\text{ ft-k} \end{bmatrix} \quad \textbf{(6-78)}$$

Figure 6-25 shows the free body diagram of the structure.

6–6 Space Truss Structure

In identifying a structural system as a truss, the joints of the structure are assumed to be pinned. Hence, the individual beam elements of the structural system are assumed to be able to resist only axial deformations. These assumptions, which were made for the analysis of the planar truss, will also be valid for the three-dimensional truss system. The various matrices required to carry out the analysis of a three-dimensional truss system by the stiffness method can be developed with very little effort from the information that has been established for the analysis of a rigid space frame.

For a beam element, arbitrarily oriented in a three-dimensional space, with *ideal spherical hinges* at either end, there are only three possible components of end displacement at each end to be considered. These are identified in Figs. 6-26 with respect to both the local axes and the reference axes; the corresponding possible components of end action with respect to both the local and reference axes are identified in Fig. 6-27. Considering the fact that a truss member can resist only axial deformation, the relationship between the possible components of end displacement and the corresponding components of end action can be expressed as

$$p_t^i = K_{tt}^i \delta_t + K_{tu}^i \delta_u \quad \textbf{(6-79a)}$$

$$p_r^i = 0 \quad \textbf{(6-79b)}$$

$$p_v^i = 0 \quad \textbf{(6-79c)}$$

$$p_u^i = K_{ut}^i \delta_t + K_{uu}^i \delta_u \quad \textbf{(6-79d)}$$

$$p_s^i = 0 \quad \textbf{(6-79e)}$$

$$p_w^i = 0 \quad \textbf{(6-79f)}$$

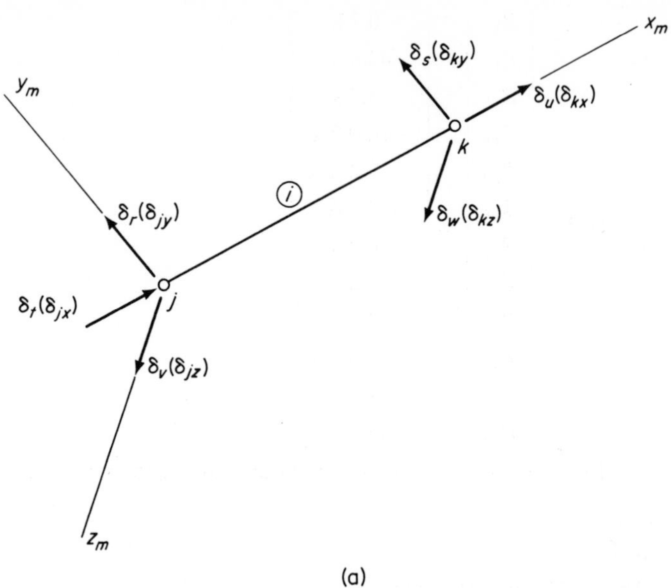

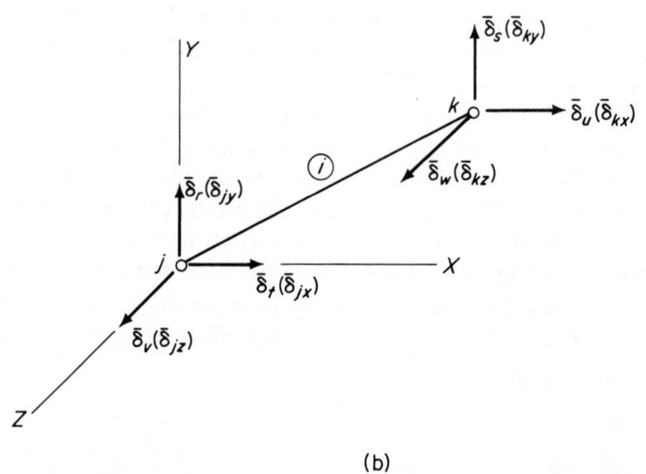

Fig. 6-26 Possible components of end displacement for truss member: (a) local coordinate system; (b) reference coordinate system.

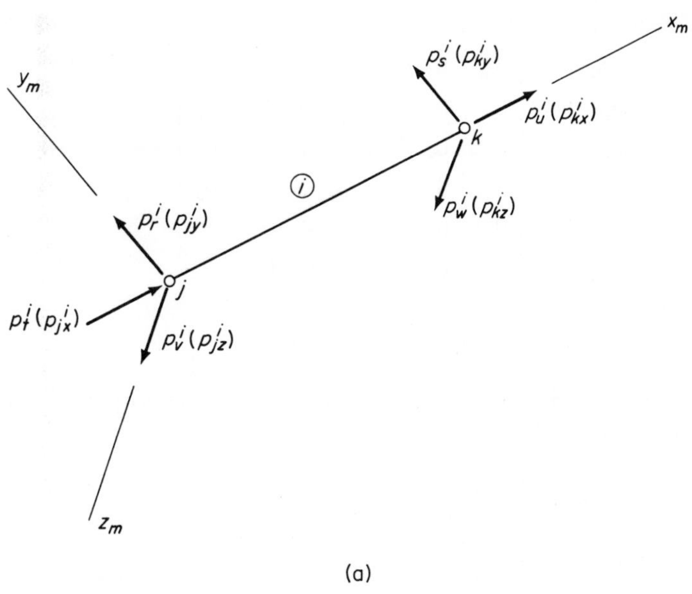

(a)

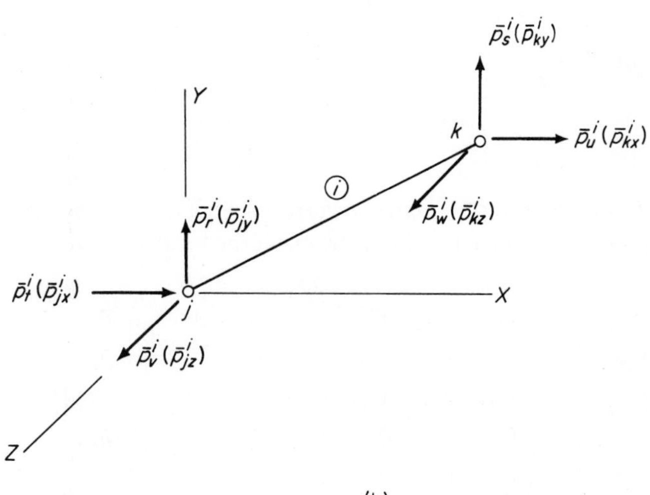

(b)

Fig. 6-27 Possible components of end action for truss member: (a) local coordinate system; (b) reference coordinate system.

which can be expressed in matrix form as

$$\begin{bmatrix} p_t \\ p_r \\ p_v \\ p_u \\ p_s \\ p_w \end{bmatrix}_i = \begin{bmatrix} K_{tt} & 0 & 0 & K_{tu} & 0 & 0 \\ 0 & 0 & 0 & 0 & 0 & 0 \\ 0 & 0 & 0 & 0 & 0 & 0 \\ K_{ut} & 0 & 0 & K_{uu} & 0 & 0 \\ 0 & 0 & 0 & 0 & 0 & 0 \\ 0 & 0 & 0 & 0 & 0 & 0 \end{bmatrix}_i \begin{bmatrix} \delta_t \\ \delta_r \\ \delta_v \\ \delta_u \\ \delta_s \\ \delta_w \end{bmatrix}_i \tag{6-80a}$$

or

$$[\mathbf{p}^s]_i = [\mathbf{K}_T^s]_i\,[\boldsymbol{\delta}_T^s]_i \tag{6-80b}$$

For convenience of notation and to insure the proper order of the matrices as defined, let

$$[\mathbf{p}^s]_i = \begin{bmatrix} p_{jx} \\ p_{jy} \\ p_{jz} \\ p_{kx} \\ p_{ky} \\ p_{kz} \end{bmatrix}_i \begin{matrix} \left.\begin{matrix} \\ \\ \\ \end{matrix}\right\} \text{end action at } j\text{-end} \\ \left.\begin{matrix} \\ \\ \\ \end{matrix}\right\} \text{end action at } k\text{-end} \end{matrix} \tag{6-81a}$$

and

$$[\boldsymbol{\delta}_T^s]_i = \begin{bmatrix} \delta_{jx} \\ \delta_{jy} \\ \delta_{jz} \\ \delta_{kx} \\ \delta_{ky} \\ \delta_{kz} \end{bmatrix}_i \begin{matrix} \left.\begin{matrix} \\ \\ \\ \end{matrix}\right\} \text{end displacements at } j\text{-end} \\ \left.\begin{matrix} \\ \\ \\ \end{matrix}\right\} \text{end displacements at } k\text{-end} \end{matrix} \tag{6-81b}$$

Using the rotation matrix defined by Eqs. (6-17), the relationship between the components of end action in the frame of the local and reference axes can be written as

$$\begin{bmatrix} p_{jx} \\ p_{jy} \\ p_{jz} \\ p_{kx} \\ p_{ky} \\ p_{kz} \end{bmatrix}_i = \begin{bmatrix} C_{11} & C_{12} & C_{13} & 0 & 0 & 0 \\ C_{21} & C_{22} & C_{23} & 0 & 0 & 0 \\ C_{31} & C_{32} & C_{33} & 0 & 0 & 0 \\ 0 & 0 & 0 & C_{11} & C_{12} & C_{13} \\ 0 & 0 & 0 & C_{21} & C_{22} & C_{23} \\ 0 & 0 & 0 & C_{31} & C_{32} & C_{33} \end{bmatrix}_i \begin{bmatrix} \bar{p}_{jx} \\ \bar{p}_{jy} \\ \bar{p}_{jz} \\ \bar{p}_{kx} \\ \bar{p}_{ky} \\ \bar{p}_{kz} \end{bmatrix}_i \tag{6-82a}$$

or

$$[\mathbf{p}^s]_i = [\mathbf{T}_T^s]_i[\bar{\mathbf{p}}^s]_i \tag{6-82b}$$

where

$$[\mathbf{T}_T^s]_i = \begin{bmatrix} [\mathbf{C}^s]_i & [\mathbf{0}] \\ [\mathbf{0}] & [\mathbf{C}^s]_i \end{bmatrix}_i \tag{6-83}$$

Similarly, the relationship between the components of end displacement in the frame of the two coordinate systems is given as

$$[\boldsymbol{\delta}_T^s]_i = [\mathbf{T}_T^s]_i[\bar{\boldsymbol{\delta}}_T^s]_i \tag{6-84}$$

Hence, the ***transformed member stiffness matrix for a truss member*** of a three-dimensional truss structure is defined as

$$[\bar{\mathbf{K}}_T^s]_i = [\mathbf{T}_T^s]_i^T[\mathbf{K}_T^s]_i[\mathbf{T}_T^s]_i \tag{6-85}$$

using Eqs. (5-38) as a guide.

The ***final end actions*** for the space truss element i can be evaluated with respect to the local axes from a set of equations expressed in matrix form as

$$[\mathbf{P}^s]_i = [\mathbf{K}_T^s]_i[\boldsymbol{\delta}_T^s]_i + [\mathbf{FP}^s]_i \tag{6-86a}$$

or

$$[\mathbf{P}^s]_i = [\mathbf{K}_T^s]_i[\mathbf{T}_T^s]_i[\bar{\boldsymbol{\delta}}_T^s]_i + [\mathbf{FP}^s]_i \tag{6-86b}$$

and can be evaluated with respect to the reference axes for the whole structure by the equations

$$[\bar{\mathbf{P}}^s]_i = [\bar{\mathbf{K}}_T^s]_i[\bar{\boldsymbol{\delta}}_T^s]_i + [\overline{\mathbf{FP}}^s]_i \tag{6-87}$$

or

$$[\bar{\mathbf{P}}^s]_i = [\mathbf{T}_T^s]_i^T[\mathbf{P}^s]_i$$

where

$$[\mathbf{P}^s]_i = \begin{bmatrix} P_{jx} \\ P_{jy} \\ P_{jz} \\ P_{kx} \\ P_{ky} \\ P_{kz} \end{bmatrix}_i \approx \text{Components of final end action with respect to local axes} \tag{6-88a}$$

and

$$[\mathbf{FP}^s]_i = \begin{bmatrix} FP_{jx} \\ FP_{jy} \\ FP_{jz} \\ FP_{kx} \\ FP_{ky} \\ FP_{kz} \end{bmatrix}_i \approx \text{Components of fixed end action with respect to local axes} \tag{6-88b}$$

The ***transformation matrix for a space truss member***, $[\mathbf{T}_T^s]_i$, can be evaluated using either Expression (6-30) or (6-36). If the truss structure is loaded only at its joints and/or if the orientation of the y_m and z_m axes is unimportant in the design or analysis of the members of the structure for internal stresses, the y_m and z_m axes of each member can be positioned so that the Ψ-angle is zero; then the rotation matrix for a Y–Z–X tranformation as defined by Expression (6-30) reduces to

$$[\mathbf{C}_Y^s]_i = \begin{bmatrix} C_x & C_y & C_z \\ \dfrac{-C_x C_y}{\sqrt{C_x^2 + C_z^2}} & \sqrt{C_x^2 + C_z^2} & \dfrac{-C_y C_z}{\sqrt{C_x^2 + C_z^2}} \\ \dfrac{-C_z}{\sqrt{C_x^2 + C_z^2}} & 0 & \dfrac{C_x}{\sqrt{C_x^2 + C_z^2}} \end{bmatrix}_i \tag{6-89}$$

and for a Z–Y–X transformation as defined by

$$[\mathbf{C}_Z^s]_i = \begin{bmatrix} C_x & C_y & C_z \\ \dfrac{-C_y}{\sqrt{C_x^2 + C_y^2}} & \dfrac{C_x}{\sqrt{C_x^2 + C_y^2}} & 0 \\ \dfrac{-C_x C_z}{\sqrt{C_x^2 + C_y^2}} & \dfrac{-C_y C_z}{\sqrt{C_x^2 + C_y^2}} & \sqrt{C_x^2 + C_y^2} \end{bmatrix}_i \tag{6-90}$$

For the case where the Ψ-angle is zero, the transformed member stiffness matrix for a space truss member, defined by Eq. (6-85), can be written as

$$[\bar{\mathbf{K}}_T^s]_i = \begin{array}{c} \begin{matrix} \bar{t} & \bar{r} & \bar{v} & \bar{u} & \bar{s} & \bar{w} \end{matrix} \\ \begin{bmatrix} C_x^2 K_{tt} & C_x C_y K_{tt} & C_x C_z K_{tt} & C_x^2 K_{tu} & C_x C_y K_{tu} & C_x C_z K_{tu} \\ C_y C_x K_{tt} & C_y^2 K_{tt} & C_y C_z K_{tt} & C_y C_x K_{tu} & C_y^2 K_{tu} & C_y C_z K_{tu} \\ C_z C_x K_{tt} & C_z C_y K_{tt} & C_z^2 K_{tt} & C_z C_x K_{tu} & C_z C_y K_{tu} & C_z^2 K_{tu} \\ C_x^2 K_{ut} & C_x C_y K_{ut} & C_x C_z K_{ut} & C_x^2 K_{uu} & C_x C_y K_{uu} & C_x C_z K_{uu} \\ C_y C_x K_{ut} & C_y^2 K_{ut} & C_y C_z K_{ut} & C_y C_x K_{uu} & C_y^2 K_{uu} & C_y C_z K_{uu} \\ C_z C_x K_{ut} & C_z C_y K_{ut} & C_z^2 K_{ut} & C_z C_x K_{uu} & C_z C_y K_{uu} & C_z^2 K_{uu} \end{bmatrix}_i \end{array} \begin{matrix} \bar{t} \\ \bar{r} \\ \bar{v} \\ \bar{u} \\ \bar{s} \\ \bar{w} \end{matrix} \tag{6-91}$$

for either a Y–Z–X or a Z–Y–X transformation. Should the truss member have a constant cross-section over its length, Expression (6-91) reduces to

$$[\bar{\mathbf{K}}_T^s]_i = \frac{AE}{L} \begin{array}{c} \begin{matrix} \bar{t} & \bar{r} & \bar{v} & \bar{u} & \bar{s} & \bar{w} \end{matrix} \\ \begin{bmatrix} C_x^2 & C_x C_y & C_x C_z & -C_x^2 & -C_x C_y & -C_x C_z \\ C_y C_x & C_y^2 & C_y C_z & -C_y C_x & -C_y^2 & -C_y C_z \\ C_z C_x & C_z C_y & C_z^2 & -C_z C_x & -C_z C_y & -C_z^2 \\ -C_x^2 & -C_x C_y & -C_x C_z & C_x^2 & C_x C_y & C_x C_z \\ -C_y C_x & -C_y^2 & -C_y C_z & C_y C_x & C_y^2 & C_y C_z \\ -C_z C_x & -C_z C_y & -C_z^2 & C_z C_x & C_z C_y & C_z^2 \end{bmatrix}_i \end{array} \begin{matrix} \bar{t} \\ \bar{r} \\ \bar{v} \\ \bar{u} \\ \bar{s} \\ \bar{w} \end{matrix} \tag{6-92}$$

Using the matrices defined in this section to describe the response of a space truss member, the analysis of a space truss system by the stiffness method can be performed following the same procedure used earlier for the analysis of a rigid space frame.

One word of caution: When developing a space truss system, be certain that the system is *geometrically stable.* All joints of the system must be sufficiently restrained in the *X*-, *Y*-, and *Z*-directions so that a joint cannot experience a large displacement in one or more directions before one or more members become active in resisting its movement. Remember that the joints of a space truss are assumed to be spherical pins, free to rotate about any axis.

6–7 Planar Grid Structure

Having now formulated the analysis of a three-dimensional structural system by the stiffness method, it should be recognized that the analysis of the planar structural system (Chapter 5) is simply a special case of the three-dimensional problem. In Chapter 5 consideration was given to the analysis of the planar structure subjected to the action of disturbances acting in the plane of the structure. What about the analysis of a planar structural system subjected to a disturbance, say a load, normal to the plane of the structure? This type of structural system is referred to as a *planar grid structure;* it too can be treated as a special case of the more general three-dimensional structure, as was pointed out earlier in Sec. 6-3. The reason for considering the planar structure, whether loaded in its plane or normal to its plane, as a special case is the immediate reduction in unknown terms generated in the analysis and the reduction in mathematical effort required to obtain a solution.

When analyzing the planar structure under the action of loads in the plane of the structure, the possible components of joint displacement that had to be taken into consideration were translations in the *X*- and *Y*-directions ($\bar{\delta}_X$ and $\bar{\delta}_Y$) and rotation about the *Z*-axis ($\bar{\theta}_Z$) as indicated in Fig. 6-28(a). However, if a planar structure is loaded normal to the plane of the structure, the components of joint displacement which are required to describe the displacement of a joint are a translation in the *Z*-direction ($\bar{\delta}_Z$) and rotations about the *X*- and *Y*-axes ($\bar{\theta}_X$ and $\bar{\theta}_Y$) as shown in Fig. 6-28(b). Thus, treating the planar grid structure as a special problem, it will be necessary to consider only three components of end displacement at each end of a typical grid member.

For the typical grid member, the local orthogonal axes will be established such that the x_m axis will again define the longitudinal, *centroidal axis* of the member and the x_m–y_m plane will coincide with the plane of the structural system, which will be defined as the *X*–*Y* plane. In this instance, the z_m axis will define the *minor principal axis* of the cross-section and the y_m axis will define the *major principal axis.* Again, it will be assumed that the *shear center* of the cross-section will coincide with the centroid of the cross-section. The grid member may have either a variable or constant cross-section along its length.

The possible components of end displacement with respect to both the local

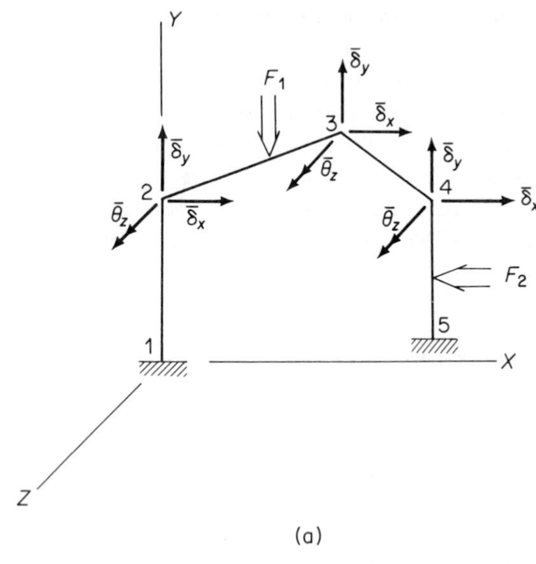

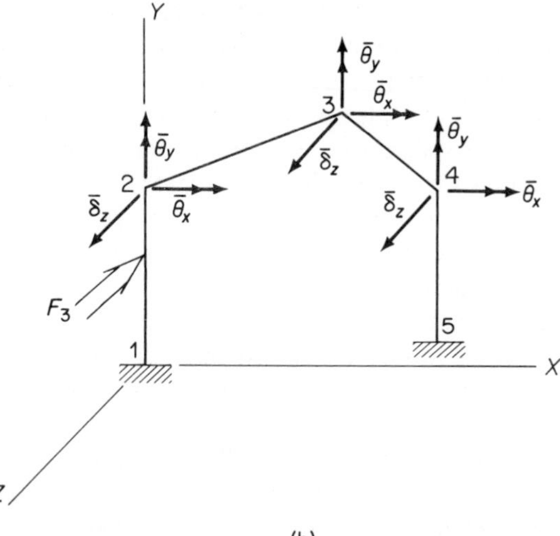

Fig. 6-28 Components of joint displacement of planar structure with loads in the plane and normal to the plane of the structure: (a) loads in the plane of the structure; (b) loads normal to the plane of the structure.

and reference coordinate systems are identified in Fig. 6-29; the corresponding components of end action for the grid member are identified in Fig. 6-30.

Referring to Fig. 6-3(c), (d), and (e) and Figs. 6-4(c), (d), and (e), the end actions required to maintain equilibrium of the grid member with both ends restrained, when it is subjected to general displacements θ_l, θ_m, θ_n, θ_o, δ_v, and δ_w of its ends (Fig. 6-31), can be determined from the equations

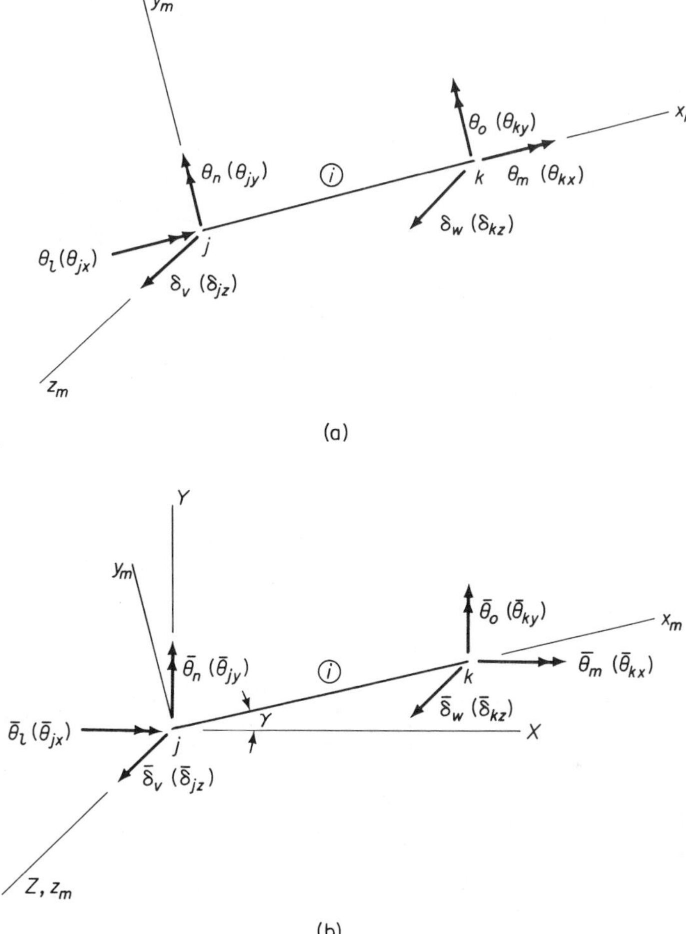

Fig. 6-29 Possible components of end displacement for grid member: (a) local coordinate system; (b) reference coordinate system.

$$m_l^i = K_{ll}^i\theta_l + K_{lm}^i\theta_m \tag{6-93a}$$

$$m_m^i = K_{ml}^i\theta_l + K_{mm}^i\theta_m \tag{6-93b}$$

$$m_n^i = \qquad + K_{nn}^i\theta_n + K_{no}^i\theta_o + K_{nv}^i\delta_v + K_{nw}^i\delta_w \tag{6-93c}$$

$$m_o^i = \qquad + K_{on}^i\theta_n + K_{oo}^i\theta_o + K_{ov}^i\delta_v + K_{ow}^i\delta_w \tag{6-93d}$$

$$p_v^i = \qquad + K_{vn}^i\theta_n + K_{vo}^i\theta_o + K_{vv}^i\delta_v + K_{vw}^i\delta_w \tag{6-93e}$$

$$p_w^i = \qquad + K_{wn}^i\theta_n + K_{wo}^i\theta_o + K_{wv}^i\delta_v + K_{ww}^i\delta_w \tag{6-93f}$$

which can be expressed in matrix form as

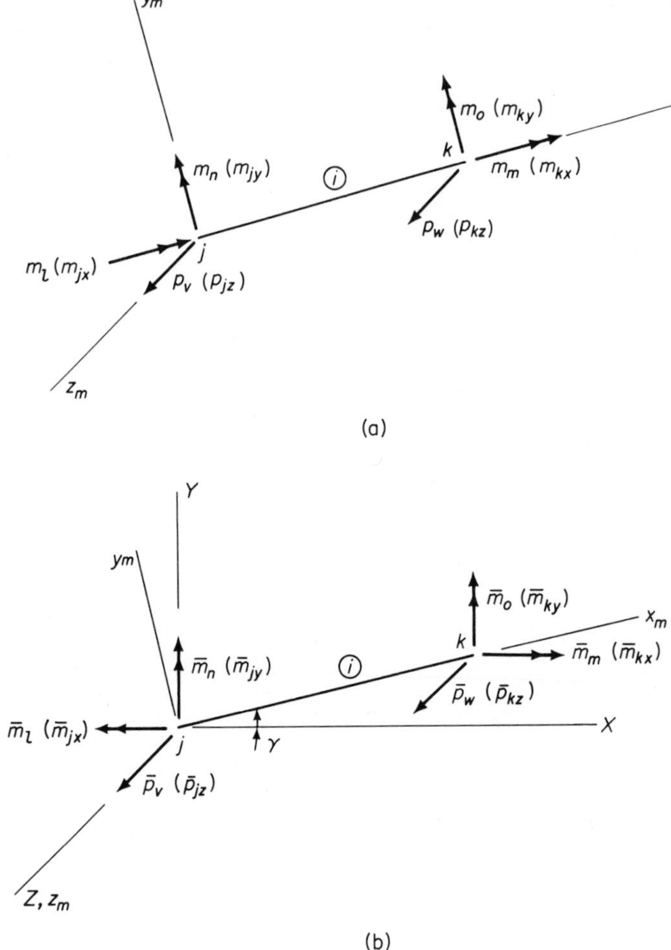

Fig. 6-30 Possible components of end displacement for grid member: (a) local coordinate system; (b) reference coordinate system.

$$\begin{bmatrix} m_l \\ m_m \\ m_n \\ m_o \\ p_v \\ p_w \end{bmatrix}_i = \begin{bmatrix} K_{ll} & K_{lm} & 0 & 0 & 0 & 0 \\ K_{ml} & K_{mm} & 0 & 0 & 0 & 0 \\ 0 & 0 & K_{nn} & K_{no} & K_{nv} & K_{nw} \\ 0 & 0 & K_{on} & K_{oo} & K_{ov} & K_{ow} \\ 0 & 0 & K_{vn} & K_{vo} & K_{vv} & K_{vw} \\ 0 & 0 & K_{wn} & K_{wo} & K_{wv} & K_{ww} \end{bmatrix}_i \begin{bmatrix} \theta_l \\ \theta_m \\ \theta_n \\ \theta_o \\ \delta_v \\ \delta_w \end{bmatrix}_i \tag{6-94}$$

or

$$[\mathbf{m}_G]_i = [\mathbf{K}_G]_i[\boldsymbol{\delta}_G]_i \tag{6-95}$$

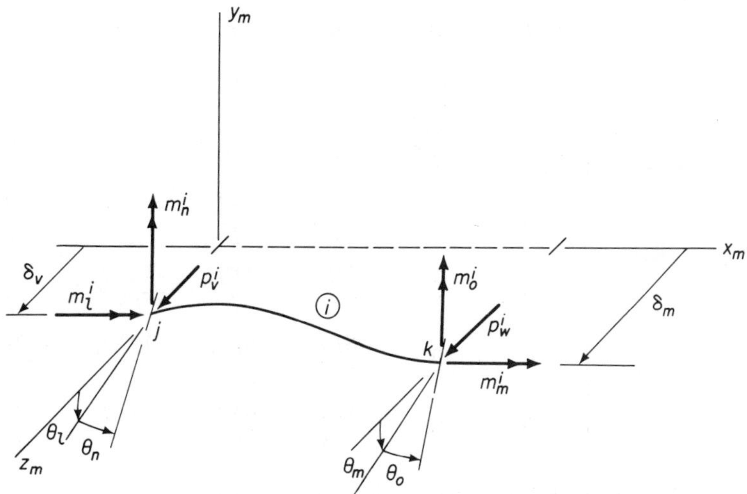

Fig. 6-31 General displacement of typical grid member with both ends restrained. *Note:* x_m–y_m plane corresponds to the plane of the structure containing member *i*.

where the matrix $[\mathbf{K}_G]_i$ is defined as the ***grid member stiffness matrix*** written ***with respect to the local axes***. Again, for convenience of notation and to clearly define the order of the matrices, the matrices representing the components of end displacement and the corresponding components of end action could be written as

$$[\boldsymbol{\delta}_G]_i = \begin{bmatrix} \theta_{jx} \\ \theta_{kx} \\ \theta_{jy} \\ \theta_{ky} \\ \delta_{jz} \\ \delta_{kz} \end{bmatrix}_i \tag{6-96a}$$

and

$$[\mathbf{m}_G]_i = \begin{bmatrix} m_{jx} \\ m_{kx} \\ m_{jy} \\ m_{ky} \\ p_{jz} \\ p_{kz} \end{bmatrix}_i \tag{6-96b}$$

For a prismatic grid member, the member stiffness matrix of Expression (6-94) will become

$$[\mathbf{K}_G]_i = \begin{array}{c} \\ \left[\begin{array}{cccccc} \frac{GI_x}{L} & \frac{-GI_x}{L} & 0 & 0 & 0 & 0 \\ \frac{-GI_x}{L} & \frac{GI_x}{L} & 0 & 0 & 0 & 0 \\ 0 & 0 & \frac{4EI_y}{L} & \frac{2EI_y}{L} & \frac{-6EI_y}{L^2} & \frac{6EI_y}{L^2} \\ 0 & 0 & \frac{2EI_y}{L} & \frac{4EI_y}{L} & \frac{-6EI_y}{L^2} & \frac{6EI_y}{L^2} \\ 0 & 0 & \frac{-6EI_y}{L^2} & \frac{-6EI_y}{L^2} & \frac{12EI_y}{L^3} & \frac{-12EI_y}{L^3} \\ 0 & 0 & \frac{6EI_y}{L^2} & \frac{6EI_y}{L^2} & \frac{-12EI_y}{L^3} & \frac{12EI_y}{L^3} \end{array}\right]_i \end{array} \begin{array}{c} l \\ m \\ n \\ o \\ v \\ w \end{array} \quad \text{columns: } l,\ m,\ n,\ o,\ v,\ w \tag{6-97}$$

When establishing the local and reference coordinate systems for a given planar grid structure, remember that a *right-handed system of orthogonal, coordinate axes* is to be used. Also, the reference axes for the whole structure are to be oriented such that the X–Y plane coincides with the plane of the grid structure; thus, the Z-axis will be normal to the plane of the structure.

Now, using the information of Sec. 5-4, the relationship between the components of end displacement with respect to the local and reference system of axes can be expressed as

$$\begin{bmatrix} \theta_{jx} \\ \theta_{kx} \\ \theta_{jy} \\ \theta_{ky} \\ \delta_{jz} \\ \delta_{kz} \end{bmatrix}_i = \begin{bmatrix} C_x & 0 & C_y & 0 & 0 & 0 \\ 0 & C_x & 0 & C_y & 0 & 0 \\ -C_y & 0 & C_x & 0 & 0 & 0 \\ 0 & -C_y & 0 & C_x & 0 & 0 \\ 0 & 0 & 0 & 0 & 1 & 0 \\ 0 & 0 & 0 & 0 & 0 & 1 \end{bmatrix}_i \begin{bmatrix} \bar{\theta}_{jx} \\ \bar{\theta}_{kx} \\ \bar{\theta}_{jy} \\ \bar{\theta}_{ky} \\ \bar{\delta}_{jz} \\ \bar{\delta}_{kz} \end{bmatrix}_i \tag{6-98}$$

or

$$[\boldsymbol{\delta}_G]_i = [\mathbf{T}_G]_i[\bar{\boldsymbol{\delta}}_G]_i \tag{6-99}$$

where

$$C_x = \frac{X_k - X_j}{L_i} \tag{5-33a}$$

and

$$C_y = \frac{Y_k - Y_j}{L_i} \tag{5-33b}$$

The matrix $[\mathbf{T}_G]_i$ is the ***transformation matrix for the planar grid member***. It should be recognized that this matrix is also an *orthogonal* matrix, i.e.,

$$[\mathbf{T}_G]_i^{-1} = [\mathbf{T}_G]_i^T \tag{6-100}$$

Similarly, the relationship between the components of end action in the frame of the local and the reference axes can be written as

$$\begin{bmatrix} m_{jx} \\ m_{kx} \\ m_{jy} \\ m_{ky} \\ p_{jz} \\ p_{kz} \end{bmatrix}_i = \begin{bmatrix} C_x & 0 & C_y & 0 & 0 & 0 \\ 0 & C_x & 0 & C_x & 0 & 0 \\ -C_y & 0 & C_x & 0 & 0 & 0 \\ 0 & -C_y & 0 & C_x & 0 & 0 \\ 0 & 0 & 0 & 0 & 1 & 0 \\ 0 & 0 & 0 & 0 & 0 & 1 \end{bmatrix}_i \begin{bmatrix} \bar{m}_{jx} \\ \bar{m}_{kx} \\ \bar{m}_{jy} \\ \bar{m}_{ky} \\ \bar{p}_{jz} \\ \bar{p}_{kz} \end{bmatrix}_i \tag{6-101}$$

or

$$[\mathbf{m}_G]_i = [\mathbf{T}_G]_i[\bar{\mathbf{m}}_G]_i \tag{6-102}$$

With reference to the discussion of Sec. 6-5.2, the grid member stiffness matrix with respect to the reference axes—i.e., the ***transformed grid member stiffness matrix***—for a planar grid member is defined as

$$[\bar{\mathbf{K}}_G]_i = [\mathbf{T}_G]_i^T[\mathbf{K}_G]_i[\mathbf{T}_G]_i \tag{6-103}$$

and can be evaluated for any given grid member by simply performing the indicated matrix operations. For the prismatic member, the transformed grid member stiffness matrix is given in Table 6-4, Expression (6-104).

Finally, the components of final end actions for the planar grid member can be determined with respect to the local axes from the set of equations

$$[\mathbf{M}_G]_i = [\mathbf{K}_G]_i[\mathbf{T}_G]_i[\bar{\boldsymbol{\delta}}_G]_i + [\mathbf{FM}_G]_i \tag{6-105}$$

or with respect to the reference axes by the set of equations

$$[\bar{\mathbf{M}}_G]_i = [\bar{\mathbf{K}}_G]_i[\bar{\boldsymbol{\delta}}_G]_i + [\overline{\mathbf{FM}}_G]_i \tag{6-106a}$$

or

$$[\bar{\mathbf{M}}_G]_i = [\mathbf{T}_G]_i^T[\mathbf{M}_G]_i \tag{6-106b}$$

where

$$[\mathbf{M}_G]_i = \begin{bmatrix} M_{jx} \\ M_{kx} \\ M_{jy} \\ M_{ky} \\ P_{jz} \\ P_{kz} \end{bmatrix}_i \approx \text{Components of final end action with respect to local axes for member } i \tag{6-107a}$$

Table 6-4

TRANSFORMED GRID MEMBER STIFFNESS MATRIX

$$[\bar{\mathbf{K}}_G]_i = \begin{array}{c} \\ \left[\begin{array}{cccccc} \bar{l} & \bar{m} & \bar{n} & \bar{o} & \bar{v} & \bar{w} \\ \frac{GI_x}{L}C_x^2 + \frac{4EI_y}{L}C_y^2 & -\frac{GI_x}{L}C_x^2 + \frac{2EI_y}{L}C_y^2 & \left(\frac{GI_x}{L} - \frac{4EI_y}{L}\right)C_xC_y & -\left(\frac{GI_x}{L} + \frac{2EI_y}{L}\right)C_xC_y & \frac{6EI_y}{L^2}C_y & -\frac{6EI_y}{L^2}C_y \\ -\frac{GI_x}{L}C_x^2 + \frac{2EI_y}{L}C_y^2 & \frac{GI_x}{L}C_x^2 + \frac{4EI_y}{L}C_y^2 & -\left(\frac{GI_x}{L} + \frac{2EI_y}{L}\right)C_xC_y & \left(\frac{GI_x}{L} - \frac{4EI_y}{L}\right)C_xC_y & \frac{6EI_y}{L^2}C_y & -\frac{6EI_y}{L^2}C_y \\ \left(\frac{GI_x}{L} - \frac{4EI_y}{L}\right)C_xC_y & -\left(\frac{GI_x}{L} + \frac{2EI_y}{L}\right)C_xC_y & \frac{4EI_y}{L}C_x^2 + \frac{GI_x}{L}C_y^2 & \frac{2EI_y}{L}C_x^2 - \frac{GI_x}{L}C_y^2 & -\frac{6EI_y}{L^2}C_x & \frac{6EI_y}{L^2}C_x \\ -\left(\frac{GI_x}{L} + \frac{2EI_y}{L}\right)C_xC_y & \left(\frac{GI_x}{L} - \frac{4EI_y}{L}\right)C_xC_y & \frac{2EI_y}{L}C_x^2 - \frac{GI_x}{L}C_y^2 & \frac{4EI_y}{L}C_x^2 + \frac{GI_x}{L}C_y^2 & -\frac{6EI_y}{L^2}C_x & \frac{6EI_y}{L^2}C_x \\ \frac{6EI_y}{L^2}C_y & \frac{6EI_y}{L^2}C_y & -\frac{6EI_y}{L^2}C_x & -\frac{6EI_y}{L^2}C_x & \frac{12EI_y}{L^3} & -\frac{12EI_y}{L^3} \\ -\frac{6EI_y}{L^2}C_y & -\frac{6EI_y}{L^2}C_y & \frac{6EI_y}{L^2}C_x & \frac{6EI_y}{L^2}C_x & -\frac{12EI_y}{L^3} & \frac{12EI_y}{L^3} \end{array}\right]_i \end{array} \begin{array}{c} \\ \bar{l} \\ \bar{m} \\ \bar{n} \\ \bar{o} \\ \bar{v} \\ \bar{w} \end{array} \quad \textbf{(6-104)}$$

and

$$[\mathbf{FM}_G]_i = \begin{bmatrix} FM_{jx} \\ FM_{kx} \\ FM_{jy} \\ FM_{ky} \\ FP_{jz} \\ FP_{kz} \end{bmatrix}_i \approx \text{Components of fixed end action with respect to local axes for member } i \qquad \textbf{(6-107b)}$$

Having defined the various matrices necessary to describe the response of a planar grid member with both ends restrained, the analysis of a planar grid structure by the stiffness method can now be carried out.

6–8 Comments

In closing this discussion on the analysis of a structural system by the stiffness method, there are a few points that need to be emphasized.

In developing the various matrices associated with a particular type of structural element, the order that was used in each case was strictly at the author's discretion and may be altered by the reader. However, it must be understood that if the order of one matrix associated with a given member is changed, all of the other matrices associated with that member must be changed in the same fashion. The organization of all of the matrices associated with a particular type of structural element must be compatible, i.e., have the same order, to insure that the proper equations are being developed and used in the analysis of the structural system.

The reader is reminded that *right-hand-oriented*, orthogonal, coordinate systems have been used in developing the stiffness method for analysis of structural systems. Hence, care must be exercised when identifying the local and reference coordinate axes to be sure that right-hand coordinate axes are used.

Although only flexural, torsional, and axial deformations have been considered in developing the member stiffness matrices for the various types of beam elements, this does not mean that these are the only deformations that can be taken into account. The effect of shear deformations can be incorporated, if desired, into the member stiffness matrix for a particular element.

Also, there is essentially no limit as to the type of element that can be considered in the analysis, e.g., the various matrices can be defined for a beam element where the shear center and the centroid of the cross-section do not coincide. The finite element method† for analyzing structural systems is simply an application of the stiffness method for the analysis of a continuous system, the major difference being the nature of the basic element that is used.

---

†O. C. Zienkiewicz, *The Finite Element Method in Structural and Continuum Mechanics*, New York, McGraw-Hill Book Company, 1967.

The stiffness method is a very powerful tool when coupled with the electronic digital computer for analyzing complex as well as simple structures. The procedure for carrying out the analysis is a very orderly, systematic procedure that is not restricted to a particular type of system. Only those matrices that are required to describe the behavior of particular structural elements are different. Thus, the problem of analyzing a given structure becomes one of developing the proper matrices to describe the response of the elements which make up the system.

6–9
Problems

6-1. Determine the final end actions developed at the end of each member and the support reactions of the rigid frame caused by the indicated loading. For each member, $I_x = 3I/2$, $I_y = 2I$, $I_z = 4I$, and $A_x = I/4$; E = constant and $G = E/2$. The relative value of I for each member is given in the box adjacent to the member. The y_m–x_m plane of each member is perpendicular to the X–Z reference.

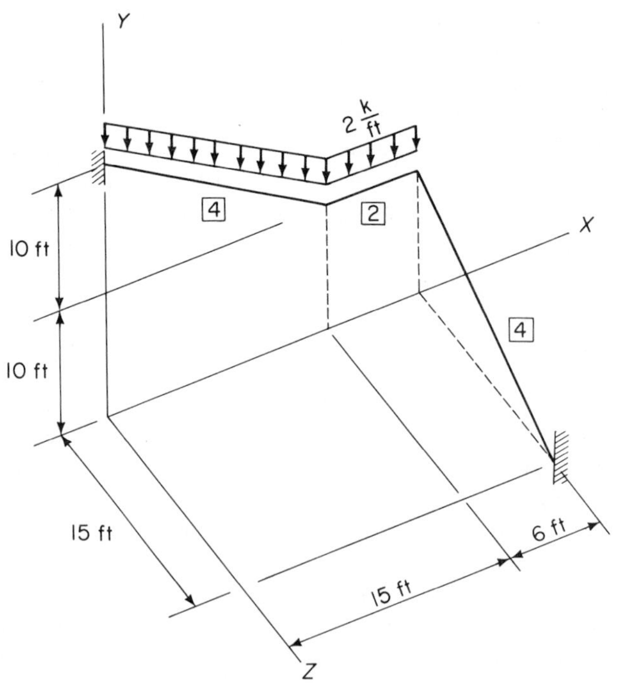

Prob. 6-1 *Note:* The y_m–x_m plane of each member is perpendicular to the X–Z plane.

6-2. Analyze the space frame for the imposed loading condition. The members are prismatic 24 WF 100 steel beams; E = 30,000 ksi and G = 12,000 ksi. The members are oriented such that the y_m–x_m plane of each beam, where the y_m axis defines the minor axis of the cross-section, is perpendicular to the X–Z reference plane.

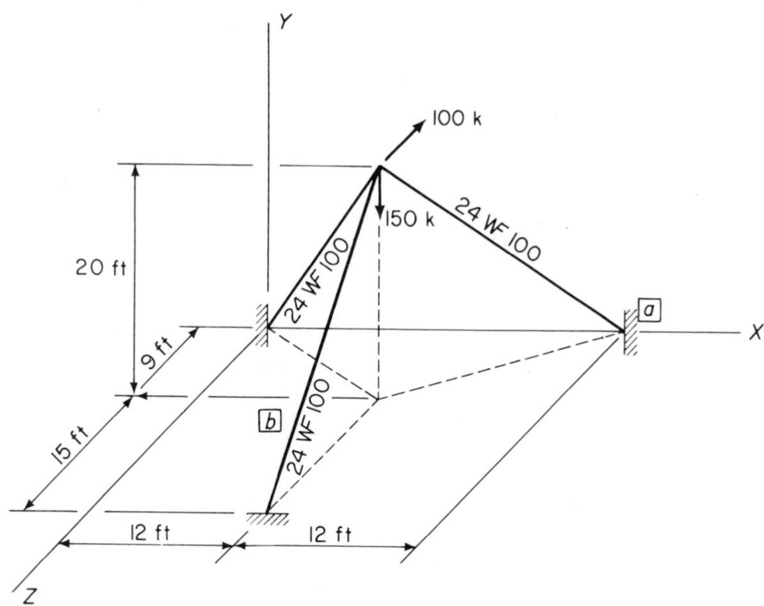

Prob. 6-2 *Note:* The y_m–x_m plane of each member is perpendicular to the X–Z plane.

6-3. Compute the support reactions and final end actions. For members 1 and 2, $I_x = 2I/3$, $I_y = I$, $I_z = 3I$, and $A_x = I/5$; for member 3, $I_x = I$, $I_y = 2I$, $I_z = 5I$, and $A_x = I/4$; $E =$ constant and $G = E/2$. The y_m–x_m plane of each beam is perpendicula. to the X–Y reference axis.

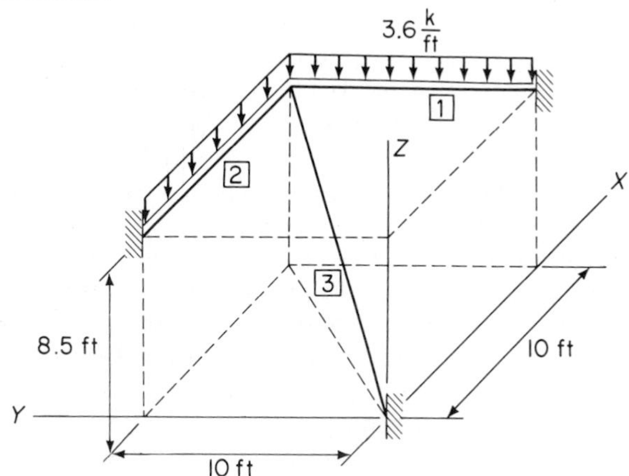

Prob. 6-3 *Note:* The y_m–x_m plane of each member is perpendicular to the X–Y plane.

6-4. The space frame is to be analyzed for the indicated loading condition. With the y_m axis defining the minor principal axis of the cross-section, the y_m–x_m plane of each beam is perpendicular to the X–Y reference plane and the y_m–x_m plane of each column is perpendicular to the X–Z reference plane; $E = 30{,}000$ ksi and $G = 12{,}000$ ksi.

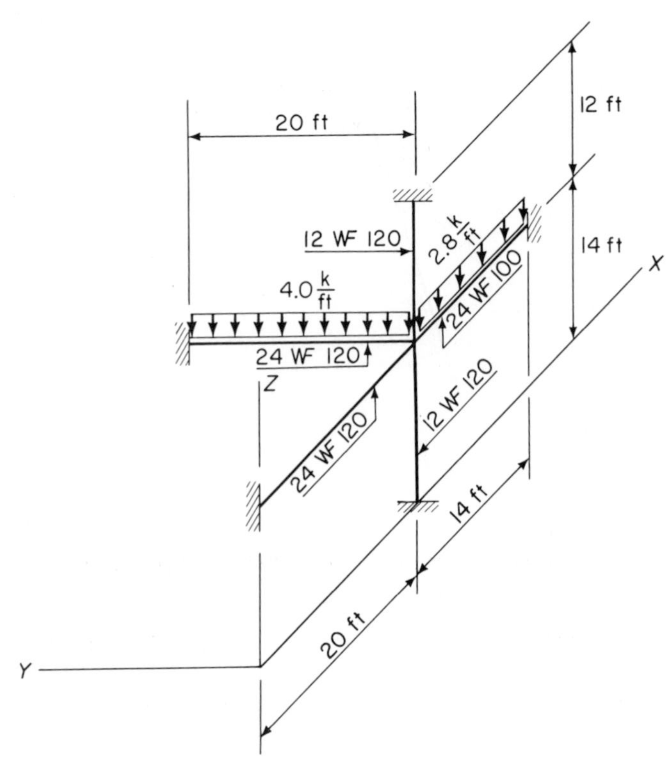

Prob. 6-4 *Note:* The y_m–x_m planes of the beams are perpendicular to the X–Y plane, and the y_m–x_m planes of the columns are perpendicular to the X–Z plane.

6-5. Determine the final end actions for each member and the support reactions for the structure caused by the applied loading. For members 1 and 2, $I_x = I/2$, $I_y = 6I$, $I_z = 8I$, and $A_x = I/5$; for member 3, $I_x = I$, $I_y = 10I$, $I_z = 10I$, and $A_x = I/4$; $E =$ constant and $G = E/2$. Letting the y_m axis define the minor principal axis of a member's cross-section, the y_m–x_m plane of members 2 and 3 are perpendicular to the X–Z reference plane and the y_m–x_m plane of member 1 coincides with the X–Y reference plane.

6-6. Develop the complete structure stiffness matrix for the rigid space frame described in the figure and set up the complete joint load matrix for the indicated loading condition. Letting the y_m axis define the minor principal axis of a cross-section, the y_m–x_m plane of each column is parallel to the Y–Z reference plane and for each beam is perpendicular to the X–Y reference plane; $E = 30{,}000$ ksi and $G = 12{,}000$ ksi.

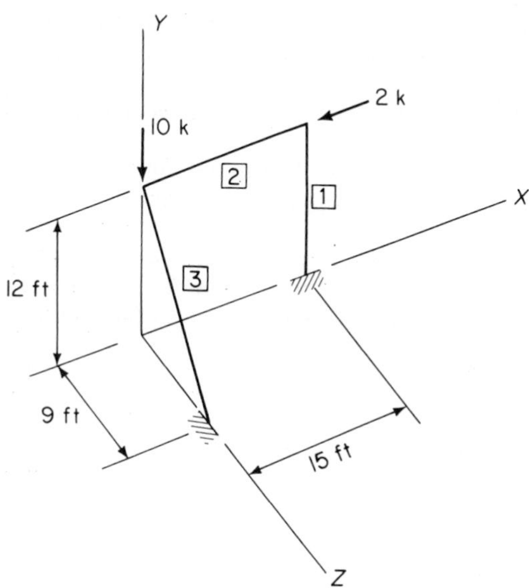

Prob. 6-5 *Note:* The y_m–x_m plane of member 1 coincides with the X–Y reference plane. The y_m–x_m plane of members 2 and 3 is perpendicular to the X–Z plane in both cases.

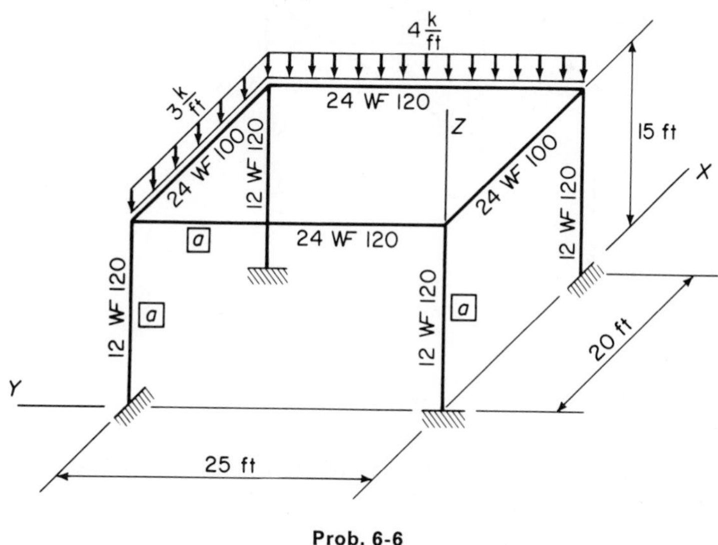

Prob. 6-6

6-7. Analyze the frame of Prob. 6-2 for a vertical settlement of 0.75 in. of the support *a*.

6-8. Determine the final end actions and support reactions developed by the rigid frame of Prob. 6-2 if member *b* is fabricated 1 in. too short.

6-9. Analyze the space frame of Prob. 6-5 for a vertical settlement of 0.5 in. of the support of member 1. Let $I = 1000$ in^4, $E = 3000$ ksi, and $G = 1000$ ksi.

6-10. Analyze the rigid space frame of Prob. 6-6 for the indicated loading.

6-11. Analyze the rigid frame structure of Prob. 6-6 for an increase in temperature of 40° of members *a* over the other members of the structure.

6-12 to 6-15. Determine the bar forces developed in the space truss. The orientation of the local axes for each member may be selected for convenience of computation; $E = 30{,}000$ ksi. The cross-sectional area of each member (in terms of sq in.) is indicated adjacent to the member.

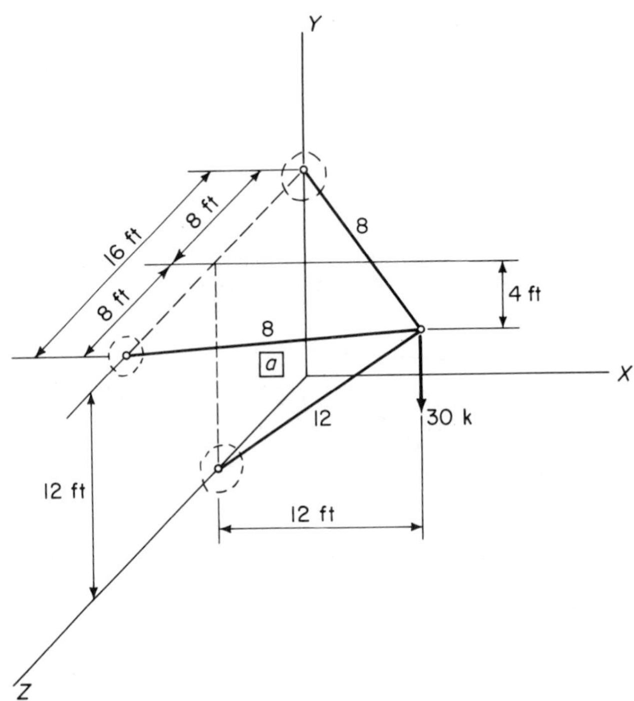

Prob. 6-12

6-16. Compute the bar forces developed in the space truss of Prob. 6-12 if member *a* is fabricated 0.5 in. too short.

6-17. Analyze the space truss of Prob. 6-13 for a settlement of support *a* of 0.75 in.

6-18. Determine the bar forces in each member and the support reactions for the structure if member *a* of the truss of Prob. 6-14 is fabricated 0.25 in. too long.

6-19. Analyze the structure of Prob. 6-15 for a fabrication error of 0.3 in. shortening the length of member *a*.

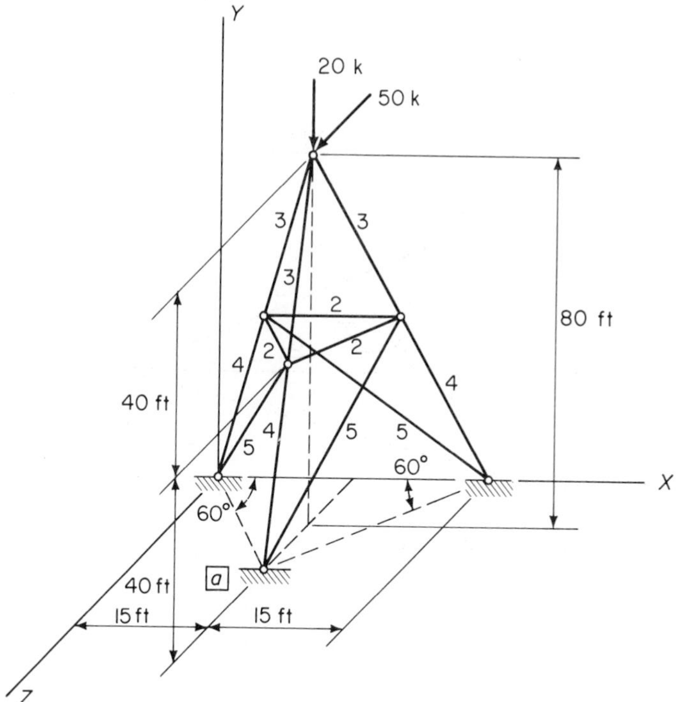

Prob. 6-13

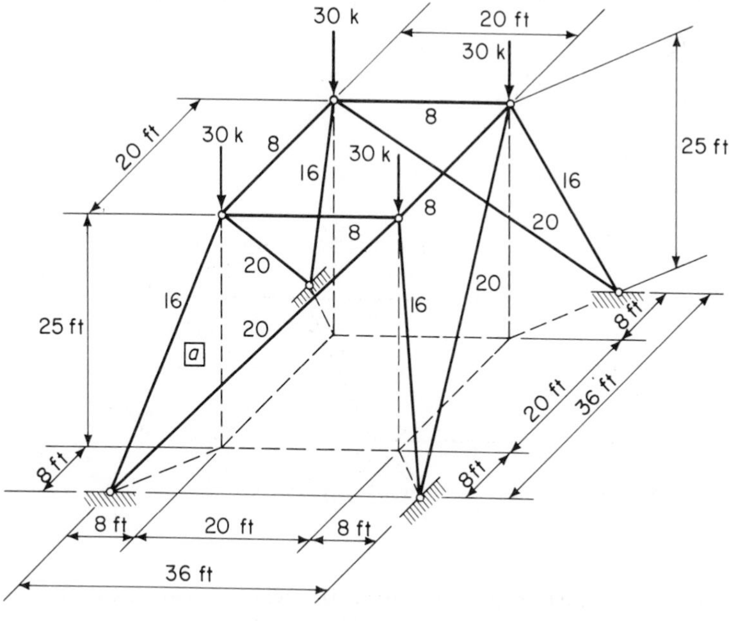

Prob. 6-14

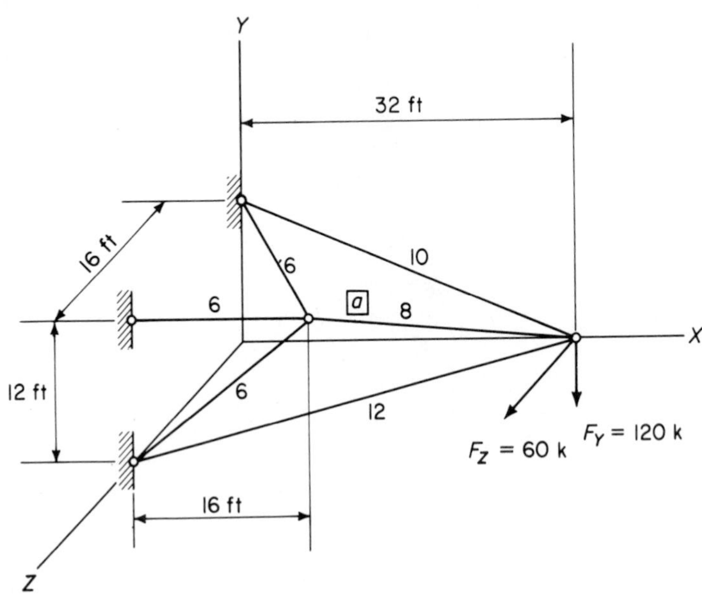

Prob. 6-15

6-20 to 6-23. Analyze the planar grid structures for the indicated loading. Each member is positioned in the X–Y reference plane so that the major principal axis (y_m) of each cross-section lies in the plane; $E = 30{,}000$ ksi and $G = 12{,}000$ ksi.

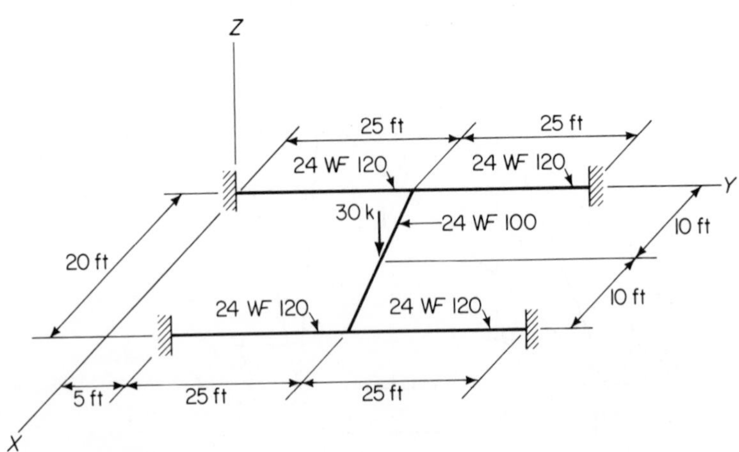

Prob. 6-20 *Note:* Major principal axis of the cross section of each member lies in the X–Y reference plane.

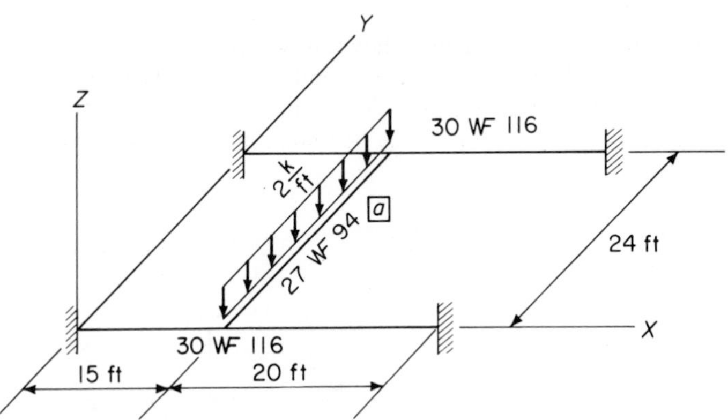

Prob. 6-21 *Note:* Major principal axis of the cross section of each member lies in the X–Y reference plane.

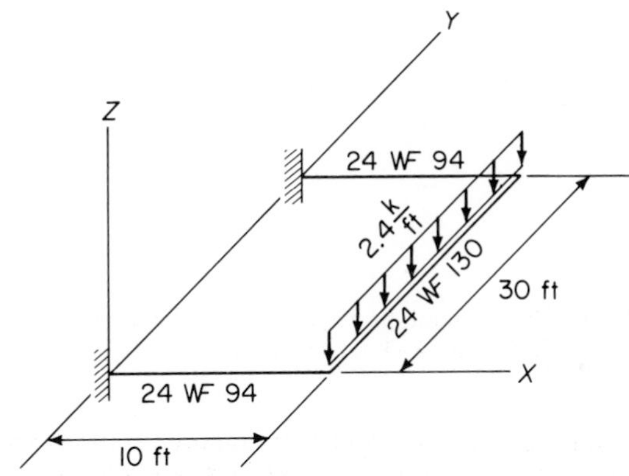

Prob. 6-22 *Note:* Major principal axis of the cross section of each member lies in the X–Y reference plane.

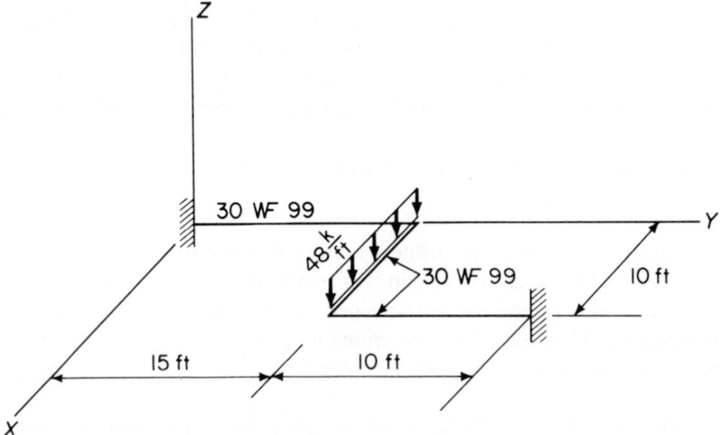

Prob. 6-23 *Note:* Major principal axis of the cross section of each member lies in the X–Y reference plane.

6-24. Analyze the planar grid structure shown in the figure for the indicated loading. For each member, $I_x = 3I/2$, $I_y = 2I$, $I_z = I$, and $A_x = I/6$. The major principal axis (y_m) of the cross-section of each member lies in the X–Y reference plane. The relative value of I for each member is given in the box adjacent to the member; $E =$ constant and $G = E/3$.

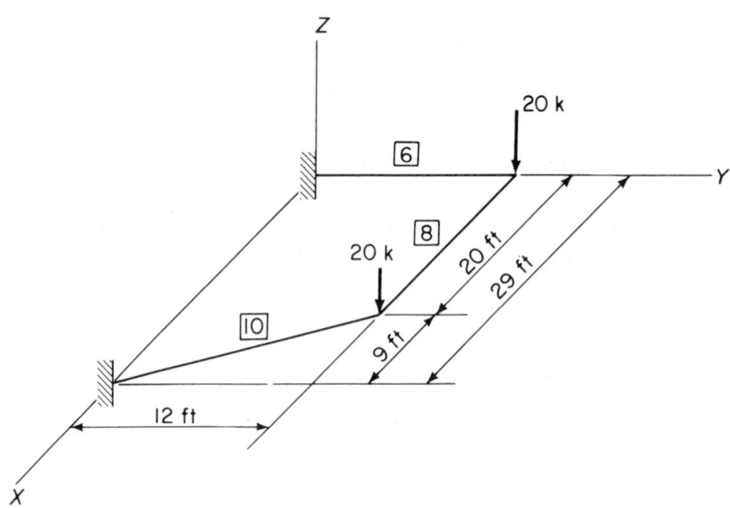

Prob. 6-24 *Note:* Major principal axis of the cross section of each member lies in the X–Y reference plane.

6-25. Determine the final end actions and the support reactions for the structure of Prob. 6-21 if member a is fabricated with a bend of 5° (rotating right end in a counter-clockwise direction) at midspan.

6-26. (a) Establish all of the matrices for a beam element with either a variable or constant cross-section over its span length, arbitrarily oriented in a three-dimensional space, with both ends of the member restrained against translation in the x_m, y_m, and z_m directions, both ends restrained against rotation about the x_m and y_m axes, and both ends free to rotate about the z_m axis so that this type of member could be handled in a stiffness analysis.

(b) Evaluate the member stiffness matrix for this beam element if it were a prismatic member.

6-27. Develop the grid member stiffness matrix $[\mathbf{K}_G]_i$ for a prismatic grid member with a pin at the j-end of the member so that it is free to rotate about the major principal axis y_m. The member is assumed to be restrained against all other possible components of end displacement. Also, establish the transformation matrix $[\mathbf{T}_G]_i$ and the transformed grid member stiffness matrix $[\bar{\mathbf{K}}_G]_i$ for this member.

6-28. Establish the member stiffness matrix $[\mathbf{K}^s]_i$ for a prismatic 12 in. [25# beam. Note that for this member the shear center and the centroid of the cross-section do not coincide. The x_m axis will define the centroidal axis of the beam and the z_m principal axis will contain both the centroid and the shear center of the channel section.

6-29. Develop a computer program to analyze by the stiffness method a planar grid frame for any possible loading condition. *Hint:* Let fixed end actions be input data.

6-30. Write a computer program to analyze by the stiffness method a space truss system for loads applied only at the joints.

6-31. Write a computer program to carry out the analysis of a rigid space frame by the stiffness method for any possible loading condition. *Hint:* Use fixed end actions as input.

SELECTED REFERENCES

6-1 Willems, Nicholas, and William M. Lucas, Jr., *Matrix Analysis for Structural Engineers*. Englewood Cliffs, N.J.: Prentice-Hall, Inc., 1968.

6-2 Gere, James M., and William Weaver, Jr., *Analysis of Framed Structures*. Princeton, N.J.: D. Van Nostrand Company, Inc., 1965.

6-3 Seely, Fred B., and James O. Smith, *Advanced Mechanics of Materials*, 2nd ed. New York: John Wiley & Sons, Inc., 1952.

6-4 Timoshenko, S. P., and J. H. Goodier, *Theory of Elasticity*, 2nd ed. New York: McGraw-Hill Book Company, 1951.

7 ANALYSIS OF STRUCTURAL SYSTEMS USING SUBSTRUCTURES

7–1 Introduction

The *direct procedure* for analysis by the stiffness method that has been discussed in Chapters 4, 5, and 6 is well suited for programming the electronic digital computer to analyze structures of moderate size. Unfortunately, for "large" structural systems—i.e., ones having a high degree of kinematic indeterminacy—this direct procedure can become quite cumbersome due to insufficient addressable core storage in the computer. A segmentation of the program with temporary storage of data on auxiliary storage devices such as magnetic tapes or discs becomes necessary. This use of auxiliary storage devices generally requires a large amount of computer time for transferring data into and out of the core memory of the computer, thus increasing the time required to solve a problem, which results in increased costs. Although there is no immediate solution to the problem of having to use peripheral storage devices when program requirements exceed the available core storage, there are techniques that can be used to make effective use of peripheral storage and to reduce the transfer of data into and out of the core memory of the computer.

The difficulty in analyzing a "large" structural system by the direct procedure arises in having to solve a large number of simultaneous equations while being restricted in the amount of core memory available to carry out the operation. There are a variety of mathematical techniques that could be used to resolve this problem, e.g., an iteration procedure or a partitioned matrix technique could be used. Unfortunately, the mathematical techniques are usually limited in their effectiveness in reducing transfer time into and out of peripheral storage. Another approach to resolving this problem is to segment the structure itself into smaller *substructures*, first analyzing each of the substructures as an independent structure and then considering these substructures as individual elements, developing the analysis of the total structure. By subdividing the total structure into substructures the number of equations that must be solved at any one time in the analysis of the total system will be reduced. This technique of using substructures has been found to be a most effective means of analyzing large structures. In order to use the stiffness approach in this method of analysis only a few modifications need to be made in the direct procedure discussed in the previous chapters.

7–2 Basic Concept

Before, when analyzing a structural system such as that shown in Fig. 7-1(a), the ***restrained structure***, which is the ***basic model*** for the stiffness method of analysis, was established by restraining all joints against displacement [Fig. 7-1(b)]; and the analysis was developed considering the response of the individual beam elements to applied disturbances and end displacements. For each component

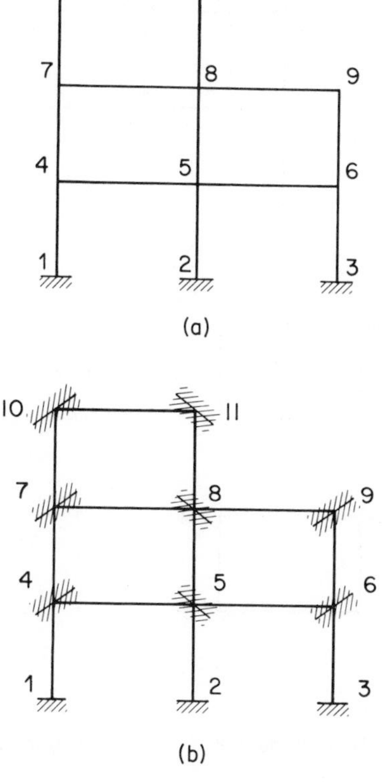

Fig. 7-1 Restrained structure using basic beam elements: (a) actual structure; (b) restrained structure.

of joint displacement that had to be *artificially* constrained in the restrained structure, an unknown was introduced into the analysis. Thus, if the structure was very large, the number of unknowns could very easily exceed ordinary computational abilities.

In contrast to the direct procedure, if the structure is conveniently *partitioned* into regions or ***substructures***, a restrained structure can be defined by assuming just those joints at the boundaries of the specified substructures to be restrained, as illustrated in Fig. 7-2(a). Defining the restrained structure in this manner, the various substructures [Fig. 7-2(b)] become the basic components to be used in the analysis of the structural system. Once the individual substructures have been analyzed for applied disturbances, as well as unit values of boundary displacements, the procedure for analyzing the total system is essentially the same as that outlined in Chapters 4, 5, and 6. The advantage realized by partitioning the structure into substructures is that the number of unknown components of joint displacement to be evaluated at any one time in the analysis of the total system is less than the number of unknowns generated by the direct procedure.

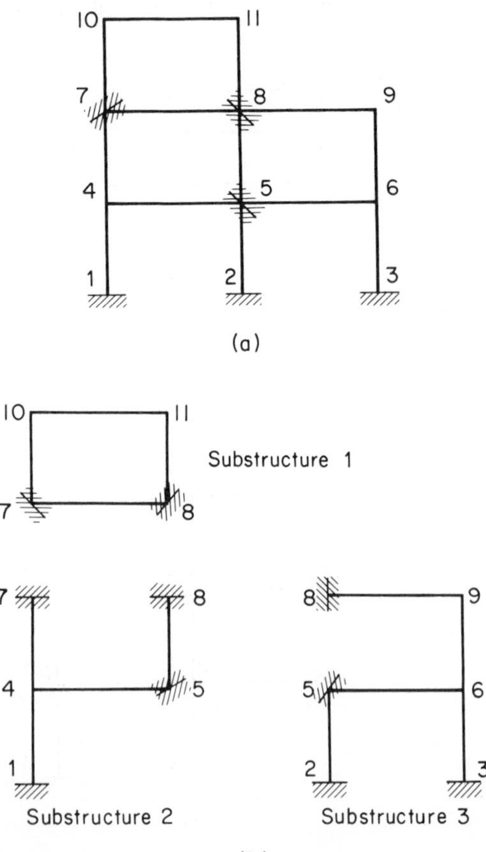

Fig. 7-2 Restrained structure using substructures: (a) restrained structure; (b) substructures.

A ***substructure*** can be defined as an element or a group of elements that form a portion of a structural system. Thus, the beam element which is used as the basic component in the direct procedure is, in fact, a substructure; however, it will become evident from later discussion that it is a unique substructure.

The analysis of the substructure with its boundaries fixed can be carried out using the direct procedure as if it were a complete system in itself. From such an analysis, the fixed boundary actions—which are analogous to the fixed end actions for a beam element—and the displacements of the unrestrained joints of the substructure can be evaluated, and the substructure stiffness matrix can also be established. Obviously, the joint displacements determined from this analysis will not be the true displacements of the unrestrained joints of the substructure, due to the fact that some of the boundaries of the substructure are artificially constrained in the basic model, i.e., the restrained structure. Therefore, these displacements must be corrected to account for the response of the substructure to the displacements of its artificially restrained boundaries, which will be determined from the analysis of the total structure. Once the actual displacements of all of the unrestrained joints of the total structure have been evaluated, the final end actions can be determined for each beam element of the structure.

The primary advantage of using substructures when analyzing a large system by the stiffness method can be illustrated with the structure of Figs. 7-1 and 7-2. If the direct procedure is followed, defining the restrained structure as shown in Fig. 7-1(b), there would be twenty-four (24) unknown components of joint displacement to be evaluated. In contrast to this, if the restrained structure were defined as shown in Fig. 7-2(a) by dividing the frame into three substructures, the maximum number of unknown components of joint displacement to be considered at any one time in the analysis would be nine (9). There are six (6) unrestrained components of joint displacement to be evaluated in the analysis of substructures 1 and 3, three (3) unrestrained components of joint displacement to be determined in the analysis of substructure 2, and nine (9) components of artificially constrained joint displacement to be solved for in the analysis of the whole structure. Thus, by using substructures, the number of unknowns to be solved for at any one time can be reduced considerably from the number of unknowns that would have to be solved for in the direct solution. This is not to say that the amount of computational effort required by the stiffness method would be reduced with the use of substructures; in fact, the computational work will usually be increased. It is the ability to reduce the amount of core storage needed to perform computations and to logically segment the analysis, thus reducing the transfer of data into and out of the core storage, that makes the use of substructures advantageous when solving large structural systems on the computer.

One should be aware of the fact that the manner in which a structure is partitioned when establishing the restrained structure will affect the composition of the substructure stiffness matrices as well as the complete structure stiffness matrix; thus, the computational operations of the analysis are affected. Therefore, some thought must be given to the actual partitioning of a structure into substructures.

7–3
Analysis of a Substructure

Once the restrained structure for a structural system has been defined, each substructure must be analyzed, independently, for (1) any disturbance applied within that region of the system, and (2) possible substructure boundary displacements. Each substructure is assumed to be isolated from adjacent regions with all of its boundaries restrained, as illustrated in Fig. 7-2(b), and is analyzed by the stiffness method using the direct procedure discussed in Chapters 4, 5, and 6 as if it were a complete structural system.

For the analysis of the nth substructure of a given structural system, the equations describing static equilibrium of the joints of the substructure can be expressed in matrix form, similar to Eq. (4-32) or (6-56), as

$$[\mathbf{S}_c^n][\mathbf{\Delta}_c^n] = [\mathbf{JL}_c^n] + [\mathbf{R}_c^n] \tag{7-1}$$

where the superscript n refers to the fact that these equations are written for the particular region denoted as substructure n. Thus, $[\mathbf{S}_c^n]$ is referred to as the ***complete structure stiffness matrix for substructure n;*** $[\mathbf{\Delta}_n^c]$ is defined as the ***complete joint displacement matrix for the nth substructure;*** and $[\mathbf{JL}_c^n]$ and $[\mathbf{R}_c^n]$ are the ***complete joint load matrix and complete boundary reaction matrix,*** *respectively,* ***for substructure n.*** Now, the equations of joint equilibrium—i.e., Eq. (7-1)—can be partitioned, as before, with respect to the unrestrained joint displacements and the restrained boundary displacements of the substructure. This partitioning is indicated as

$$\begin{bmatrix} [\mathbf{S}_{uu}^n] & [\mathbf{S}_{ur}^n] \\ [\mathbf{S}_{ru}^n] & [\mathbf{S}_{rr}^n] \end{bmatrix} \begin{bmatrix} [\mathbf{\Delta}_u^n] \\ [\mathbf{\Delta}_r^n] \end{bmatrix} = \begin{bmatrix} [\mathbf{JL}_u^n] \\ [\mathbf{JL}_r^n] \end{bmatrix} + \begin{bmatrix} [\mathbf{0}] \\ [\mathbf{R}_r^n] \end{bmatrix} \tag{7-2}$$

As mentioned earlier, the true response of a substructure, as part of a total system, can be viewed as the summation of two cases: (1) the response of the substructure, with its boundaries restrained, to applied disturbances; and (2) the response of the system to actual boundary displacements. Thus, Eq. (7-2) can be written as

$$\begin{bmatrix} [\mathbf{S}_{uu}^n] & [\mathbf{S}_{ru}^n] \\ [\mathbf{S}_{ru}^n] & [\mathbf{S}_{rr}^n] \end{bmatrix} \begin{bmatrix} [\mathbf{\Delta}_{uf}^n] \\ [\mathbf{0}] \end{bmatrix} = \begin{bmatrix} [\mathbf{JL}_{uf}^n] \\ [\mathbf{JL}_{rf}^n] \end{bmatrix} + \begin{bmatrix} [\mathbf{0}] \\ [\mathbf{R}_{rf}^n] \end{bmatrix} \tag{7-3}$$

to evaluate the response of substructure n, with its boundaries fixed, to any disturbance applied to the system, i.e., with $[\mathbf{\Delta}_{rf}^n] = [\mathbf{0}]$; and to determine the response of substructure n to the application of the true boundary displacements (to be determined from the analysis of the total structure) with all other loading removed, i.e., with $[\mathbf{JL}_{ud}^n] = [\mathbf{JL}_{rd}^n] = [\mathbf{0}]$, Eq. (7-2) can be written as

$$\begin{bmatrix} [\mathbf{S}_{uu}^n] & [\mathbf{S}_{ur}^n] \\ [\mathbf{S}_{ru}^n] & [\mathbf{S}_{rr}^n] \end{bmatrix} \begin{bmatrix} [\mathbf{\Delta}_{ud}^n] \\ [\mathbf{\Delta}_{rd}^n] \end{bmatrix} = \begin{bmatrix} [\mathbf{0}] \\ [\mathbf{R}_{rd}^n] \end{bmatrix} \tag{7-4}$$

The subscript f refers to the case where the substructure boundaries are fixed (restrained) against any movement and the subscript d refers to the case where the substructure boundaries are subjected to displacements. In Eqs. (7-3) and (7-4), $[\mathbf{\Delta}^n_{uf}]$ represents the displacements of the unrestrained joints of substructure n due to applied loads; $[\mathbf{\Delta}^n_{ud}]$ represents the displacements of the unrestrained joints of substructure n due to the application of actual boundary displacements; and $[\mathbf{\Delta}^n_{rd}]$ represents the actual displacements of the substructure boundaries that are to be evaluated from the analysis of the total structure. In addition, $[\mathbf{R}^n_{rf}]$ denotes the fixed boundary actions of substructure n resulting from the applied disturbances. These actions will be transformed into equivalent joint loads for the analysis of the total structure. Finally, $[\mathbf{R}^n_{rd}]$ represents the boundary actions that are required to maintain equilibrium of substructure n when its boundaries are subjected to the displacement $[\mathbf{\Delta}^n_{rd}]$.

Equation (7-3) can be expanded into the two equations

$$[\mathbf{S}^n_{uu}][\mathbf{\Delta}^n_{uf}] = [\mathbf{JL}^n_{uf}] \tag{7-5}$$

and

$$[\mathbf{S}^n_{ru}][\mathbf{\Delta}^n_{uf}] = [\mathbf{JL}^n_{rf}] + [\mathbf{R}^n_{rf}] \tag{7-6}$$

Now, solving Eq. (7-5) for the unrestrained components of joint displacement gives

$$[\mathbf{\Delta}^n_{uf}] = [\mathbf{S}^n_{uu}]^{-1}[\mathbf{JL}^n_{uf}] \tag{7-7}$$

and using this information—i.e., Eq. (7-7)—Eq. (7-6) can be rewritten to give an expression for determining the fixed boundary actions, i.e.,

$$[\mathbf{R}^n_{rf}] = [\mathbf{S}^n_{ru}][\mathbf{S}^n_{uu}]^{-1}[\mathbf{JL}^n_{uf}] - [\mathbf{JL}^n_{rf}] \tag{7-8}$$

Likewise, Eq. (7-4) can be expanded into the two equations

$$[\mathbf{S}^n_{uu}][\mathbf{\Delta}^n_{ud}] + [\mathbf{S}^n_{ur}][\mathbf{\Delta}^n_{rd}] = [\mathbf{0}] \tag{7-9}$$

and

$$[\mathbf{S}^n_{ru}][\mathbf{\Delta}^n_{ud}] + [\mathbf{S}^n_{rr}][\mathbf{\Delta}^n_{rd}] = [\mathbf{R}^n_{rd}] \tag{7-10}$$

Premultiplying the terms of Eq. (7-9) by $[\mathbf{S}^n_{uu}]^{-1}$ yields

$$[\mathbf{\Delta}^n_{ud}] + [\mathbf{S}^n_{uu}]^{-1}[\mathbf{S}^n_{ur}][\mathbf{\Delta}^n_{rd}] = [\mathbf{0}] \tag{7-11}$$

or

$$[\mathbf{\Delta}^n_{ud}] = -[\mathbf{S}^n_{uu}]^{-1}[\mathbf{S}^n_{ur}][\mathbf{\Delta}^n_{rd}] \tag{7-12}$$

Now, substituting Eq. (7-12) into Eq. (7-10) gives

$$-[\mathbf{S}^n_{ru}][\mathbf{S}^n_{uu}]^{-1}[\mathbf{S}^n_{ur}][\mathbf{\Delta}^n_{rd}] + [\mathbf{S}^n_{rr}][\mathbf{\Delta}^n_{rd}] = [\mathbf{R}^n_{rd}] \tag{7-13}$$

which can be rewritten as

$$([\mathbf{S}^n_{rr}] - [\mathbf{S}^n_{ru}][\mathbf{S}^n_{uu}]^{-1}[\mathbf{S}^n_{ur}])[\mathbf{\Delta}^n_{rd}] = [\mathbf{R}^n_{rd}] \tag{7-14}$$

Letting

$$[\mathbf{S}^n_s] = [\mathbf{S}^n_{rr}] - [\mathbf{S}^n_{ru}][\mathbf{S}^n_{uu}]^{-1}[\mathbf{S}^n_{ur}] \tag{7-15}$$

Eq. (7-14) can be written as

$$[\mathbf{R}^n_{rd}] = [\mathbf{S}^n_s][\mathbf{\Delta}^n_{rd}] \tag{7-16}$$

Comparing Eq. (7-16) with Eq. (5-2a) or (6-2) and recalling that the matrix $[\mathbf{R}^n_{rd}]$ refers to the boundary actions required to maintain equilibrium of the substructure when it is subjected to the boundary displacements $[\mathbf{\Delta}^n_{rd}]$, it is appropriate to define the matrix $[\mathbf{S}^n_s]$ as the ***substructure stiffness matrix***.

For the analysis of the nth substructure, the ***substructure stiffness matrix*** $[\mathbf{S}^n_s]$ and the ***fixed boundary actions*** $[\mathbf{R}^n_{rf}]$ are defined. Once this information has been established for all of the substructures that have been identified in creating the restrained structure for the total system, the complete structure stiffness matrix $[\mathbf{S}_c]$, and the complete joint load matrix $[\mathbf{JL}_c]$ can be assembled for the total structure. Hence, the familiar equations

$$[\mathbf{S}_c][\mathbf{\Delta}_c] = [\mathbf{JL}_c] + [\mathbf{R}_c] \tag{7-17}$$

which, in this instance, describe the static equilibrium of (1) the joints linking the various substructures together, and (2) the joints at the real boundaries of the total system can be written.

It should be recalled that Eq. (7-17) must be written with respect to a single set orthogonal, coordinate axes, referred to as the *reference axes*. Therefore, the information obtained from the analysis of the various substructures must be defined with respect to this set of reference axes before it can be used in the formulation of the equilibrium equations for the complete structure. For this reason, it is convenient to develop the equilibrium Eqs. (7-3) and (7-4) with respect to a set of axes that correspond to the reference axes of the total structure.

In formulating Eq. (7-17), the complete structure stiffness matrix $[\mathbf{S}_c]$, which represents the linkage of the substructures, is assembled by a *summation of the various substructure stiffness coefficients*, i.e.,

$$S_{ij} = \sum_n S^n_{ij} \tag{7-18}$$

where S^n_{ij} is the ***substructure stiffness coefficient for the nth substructure*** identified by the labels i, j. This means that a set of labels identifying the possible components of displacement of the joints linking the substructures together and the joints at the real boundaries of the actual structure must be defined independent of the displacement labels assigned to each substructure. An example of the several sets of displacement labels that are required when using substructures in the analysis of a structural system is given in Fig. 7-3, considering the frame of Fig. 7-1(a) subdivided as shown in Fig. 7-2. (Remember to *label first the unrestrained displacements and then the restrained displacements.*)

In order to establish the complete joint load matrix $[\mathbf{JL}_c]$, *the fixed boundary actions of each substructure* $[\mathbf{R}^n_{rf}]$, determined from Eq. (7-8), *must be transformed into equivalent joint loads by a change in signs* and labeled with respect to the set of displacement labels established for the total structure. Once this has been done, each element of the complete joint load matrix $[\mathbf{JL}_c]$ is determined by summing the equivalent and the applied joint loads, appearing at the joints linking the

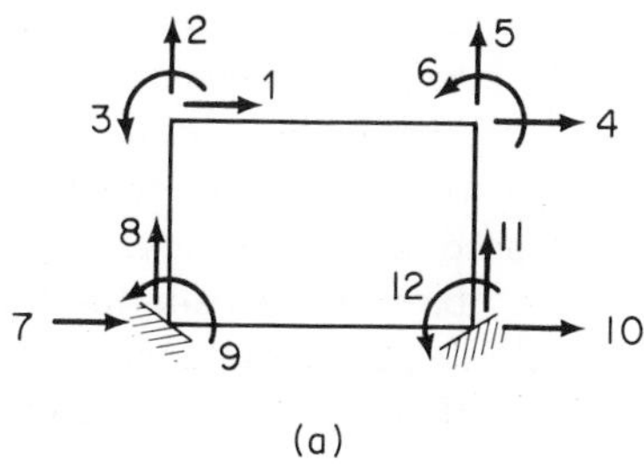

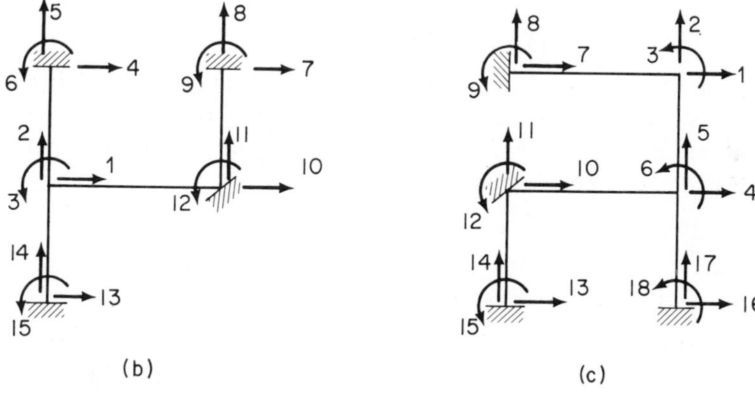

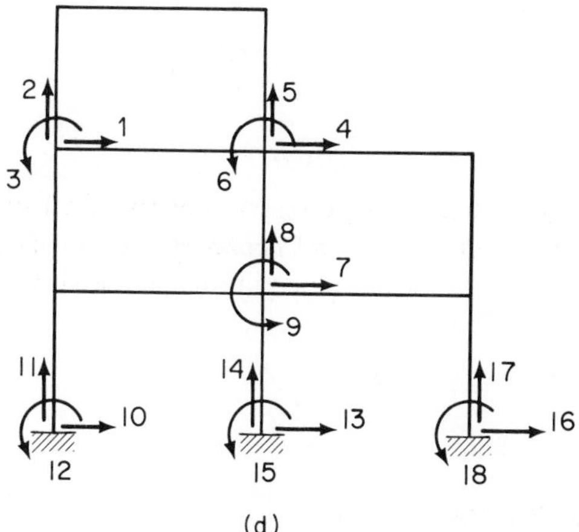

Fig. 7-3 Sets of displacement labels for analysis of substructures and total system: (a) substructure 1; (b) substructure 2; (c) substructure 3; (d) total structure.

substructures and at the real boundaries of the actual structure, that have labels which correspond to the label of the element in question. Following this procedure, any disturbance applied directly to a joint that has been designated as a substructure boundary joint will not be considered in the analysis of the substructure but will be taken into account when analyzing the total system.

Once Eq. (7-17) has been written for the total system, the matrices can be partitioned with respect to the unrestrained and restrained components of displacement of the joints linking the substructures and defining the boundaries of the actual system, i.e.,

$$\begin{bmatrix} [\mathbf{S}_{uu}] & [\mathbf{S}_{ur}] \\ [\mathbf{S}_{ru}] & [\mathbf{S}_{rr}] \end{bmatrix} \begin{bmatrix} [\mathbf{\Delta}_u] \\ [\mathbf{\Delta}_r] \end{bmatrix} = \begin{bmatrix} [\mathbf{JL}_u] \\ [\mathbf{JL}_r] \end{bmatrix} + \begin{bmatrix} [0] \\ [\mathbf{R}_r] \end{bmatrix} \tag{7-19}$$

From this set of equations, the unrestrained components of displacement of the joints common to the substructure boundaries, as well as any unrestrained component of displacement of a true boundary joint, and the components of support reactions can be determined; i.e.,

$$[\mathbf{\Delta}_u] = [\mathbf{S}_{uu}]^{-1}[\mathbf{JL}_u] \tag{7-20}$$

and

$$[\mathbf{R}_r] = [\mathbf{S}_{ru}][\mathbf{S}_{uu}]^{-1}[\mathbf{JL}_u] - [\mathbf{JL}_r] \tag{7-21}$$

Having evaluated the actual displacements $[\mathbf{\Delta}_u]$ of the joints that connect the various substructures together, the ***actual boundary displacement matrix*** $[\mathbf{\Delta}^n_{rd}]$ can be written for each substructure and the true displacements of the unrestrained joints of each substructure can be determined; i.e.,

$$[\mathbf{\Delta}^n_u] = [\mathbf{\Delta}^n_{uf}] + [\mathbf{\Delta}^n_{ud}] \tag{7-22}$$

or, using Eq. (7-12),

$$[\mathbf{\Delta}^n_u] = [\mathbf{\Delta}^n_{uf}] - [\mathbf{S}^n_{uu}]^{-1}[\mathbf{S}^n_{ur}][\mathbf{\Delta}^n_{rd}] \tag{7-23}$$

Having evaluated the true displacements of all of the unrestrained joints of the total structure, the ***final end actions*** for each of the beam elements can be computed using the appropriate equations expressing equilibrium of the member; e.g.,

$$[\mathbf{M}]_i = [\mathbf{K}]_i[\mathbf{T}]_i[\bar{\boldsymbol{\delta}}]_i + [\mathbf{FM}]_i \tag{5-46}$$

7–4
Analysis of Planar Frame

To illustrate the procedure for analyzing a structural system by the stiffness method using substructures, the following example is presented:

Example 7-1. Neglecting the effects of axial deformations analyze the planar orthogonal frame of Fig. 7-4 for the indicated applied loading. The modulus of elasticity E and the moment of inertia I are the same for each member and are constant for each member.

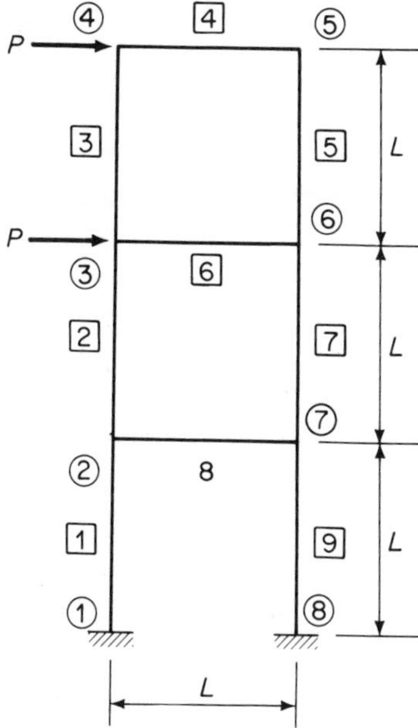

Fig. 7-4 Example 7-1: Planar, orthogonal frame.

The joint labels are given in the circles adjacent to the joints and the member labels are given in the squares adjacent to the members.

RESTRAINED STRUCTURE

The restrained structure that has been assumed for the total system is identified in Fig. 7-5(a); in defining this restrained structure, the system has been partitioned into the two substructures shown in Fig. 7-5(b).

Before the analysis of the complete system can be carried out, each substructure must be analyzed to establish the required substructure stiffness matrices and the fixed boundary matrices.

Analysis of Substructure 1

The loading and supporting conditions of substructure 1 are indicated in Fig. 7-6. Remember that the restrained boundaries at joints 3 and 6 are, in fact, artificial boundaries.

JOINT DISPLACEMENT MATRIX

The possible components of joint displacements for substructure 1, with respect to the reference axes, are identified and labeled in Fig. 7-7. The unrestrained displacements are labeled first and then the artificially restrained displacements are labeled. For this sequence of labeling, the complete joint displacement matrix for substructure 1 is given as

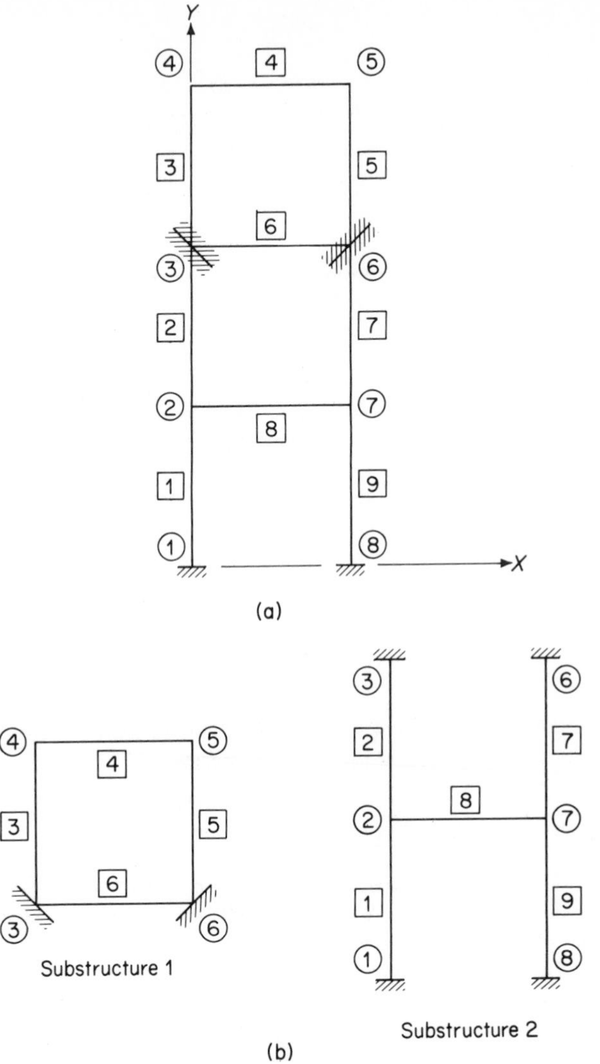

Fig. 7-5 Example 7-1: Identification of restrained structure for total system: (a) restrained structure; (b) substructures.

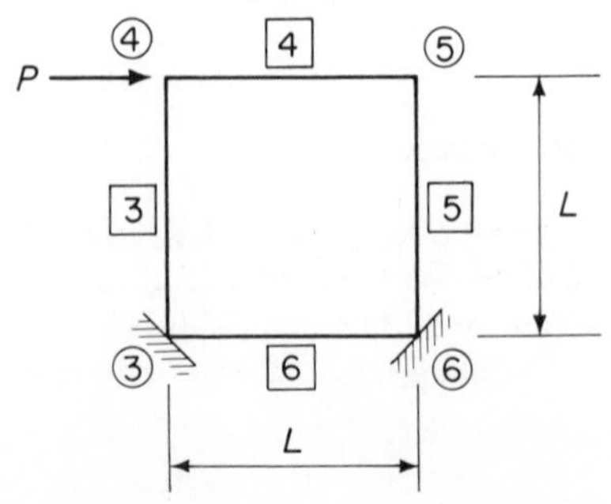

Fig. 7-6 Example 7-1: Substructure 1. (*EI* constant and equal for all members.)

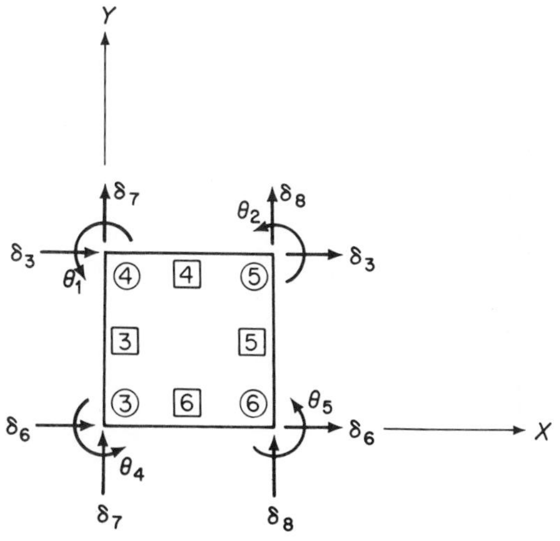

Fig. 7-7 Example 7-1: Identification of possible joint displacements (substructure 1).

$$[\mathbf{\Delta}_c^1] = \begin{bmatrix} \theta_1 \\ \theta_2 \\ \delta_3 \\ -- \\ \theta_4 \\ \theta_5 \\ \delta_6 \\ \delta_7 \\ \delta_8 \end{bmatrix} \begin{matrix} \left.\begin{matrix} \\ \\ \\ \end{matrix}\right\} \text{unrestrained displacements} \\ \\ \left.\begin{matrix} \\ \\ \\ \\ \\ \end{matrix}\right\} \text{restrained artificial boundary displacements} \end{matrix} \tag{7-24}$$

MEMBER STIFFNESS MATRICES

Following the procedure of Chapter 4 for the analysis of the planar orthogonal frames, the j- and k-ends of each member are identified as shown in Fig. 7-8.

The member stiffness matrix for each member can be written using Expression (4-16). The rows and columns of each matrix are labeled with respect to labeling of the joint displacements (Fig. 7-7) to help in identifying the elements.

Member 3

$$[\mathbf{K}]_3 = EI \begin{array}{c} \begin{matrix} 1 & \quad 4 & \quad 3 & \quad 6 \end{matrix} \\ \begin{bmatrix} \frac{4}{L} & \frac{2}{L} & \frac{6}{L^2} & -\frac{6}{L^2} \\ \frac{2}{L} & \frac{4}{L} & \frac{6}{L^2} & -\frac{6}{L^2} \\ \frac{6}{L^2} & \frac{6}{L^2} & \frac{12}{L^3} & -\frac{12}{L^3} \\ -\frac{6}{L^2} & -\frac{6}{L^2} & -\frac{12}{L^3} & \frac{12}{L^3} \end{bmatrix}_3 \end{array} \begin{matrix} 1 \\ 4 \\ 3 \\ 6 \end{matrix} \tag{7-25}$$

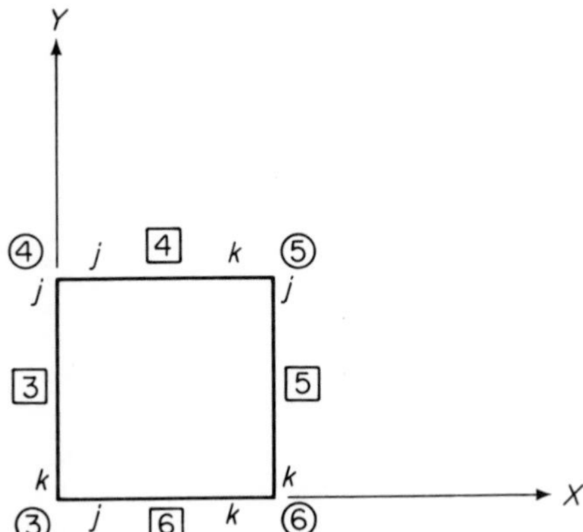

Fig. 7-8 Example 7-1: Identification of reference axes and j- and k-ends (substructure 1).

Member 4

$$[\mathbf{K}]_4 = EI\begin{bmatrix} \frac{4}{L} & \frac{2}{L} & \frac{6}{L^2} & -\frac{6}{L^2} \\ \frac{2}{L} & \frac{4}{L} & \frac{6}{L^2} & -\frac{6}{L^2} \\ \frac{6}{L^2} & \frac{6}{L^2} & \frac{12}{L^3} & -\frac{12}{L^3} \\ -\frac{6}{L^2} & -\frac{6}{L^2} & -\frac{12}{L^3} & \frac{12}{L^3} \end{bmatrix}_4 \quad \text{(columns 1, 2, 7, 8; rows 1, 2, 7, 8)} \tag{7-26}$$

Member 5

$$[\mathbf{K}]_5 = EI\begin{bmatrix} \frac{4}{L} & \frac{2}{L} & \frac{6}{L^2} & -\frac{6}{L^2} \\ \frac{2}{L} & \frac{4}{L} & \frac{6}{L^2} & -\frac{6}{L^2} \\ \frac{6}{L^2} & \frac{6}{L^2} & \frac{12}{L^3} & -\frac{12}{L^3} \\ -\frac{6}{L^2} & -\frac{6}{L^2} & -\frac{12}{L^3} & \frac{12}{L^3} \end{bmatrix}_5 \quad \text{(columns 2, 5, 3, 6; rows 2, 5, 3, 6)} \tag{7-27}$$

Member 6

$$[\mathbf{K}]_6 = EI\begin{bmatrix} \frac{4}{L} & \frac{2}{L} & \frac{6}{L^2} & -\frac{6}{L^2} \\ \frac{2}{L} & \frac{4}{L} & \frac{6}{L^2} & -\frac{6}{L^2} \\ \frac{6}{L^2} & \frac{6}{L^2} & \frac{12}{L^3} & -\frac{12}{L^3} \\ -\frac{6}{L^2} & -\frac{6}{L^2} & -\frac{12}{L^3} & \frac{12}{L^3} \end{bmatrix}_6 \quad \text{(columns 4, 5, 7, 8; rows 4, 5, 7, 8)} \tag{7-28}$$

STRUCTURE STIFFNESS MATRIX

Summing the elements of the various member stiffness matrices with like labels, the complete structure stiffness matrix for substructure 1 is written as

$$[\mathbf{S}_c^1] = EI\begin{array}{c} \begin{array}{cccccccc} 1 & 2 & 3 & 4 & 5 & 6 & 7 & 8 \end{array} \\ \left[\begin{array}{ccc:ccccc} \frac{8}{L} & \frac{2}{L} & \frac{6}{L^2} & \frac{2}{L} & 0 & -\frac{6}{L^2} & \frac{6}{L^2} & -\frac{6}{L^2} \\ \frac{2}{L} & \frac{8}{L} & \frac{6}{L^2} & 0 & \frac{2}{L} & -\frac{6}{L^2} & \frac{6}{L^2} & -\frac{6}{L^2} \\ \frac{6}{L^2} & \frac{6}{L^2} & \frac{24}{L^3} & \frac{6}{L^2} & \frac{6}{L^2} & -\frac{24}{L^3} & 0 & 0 \\ \hdashline \frac{2}{L} & 0 & \frac{6}{L^2} & \frac{8}{L} & \frac{2}{L} & -\frac{6}{L^2} & \frac{6}{L^2} & -\frac{6}{L^2} \\ 0 & \frac{2}{L} & \frac{6}{L^2} & \frac{2}{L} & \frac{8}{L} & -\frac{6}{L^2} & \frac{6}{L^2} & -\frac{6}{L^2} \\ -\frac{6}{L^2} & -\frac{6}{L^2} & -\frac{24}{L^3} & -\frac{6}{L^2} & -\frac{6}{L^2} & \frac{24}{L^3} & 0 & 0 \\ \frac{6}{L^2} & \frac{6}{L^2} & 0 & \frac{6}{L^2} & \frac{6}{L^2} & 0 & \frac{24}{L^3} & -\frac{24}{L^3} \\ -\frac{6}{L^2} & -\frac{6}{L^2} & 0 & -\frac{6}{L^2} & -\frac{6}{L^2} & 0 & -\frac{24}{L^3} & \frac{24}{L^3} \end{array}\right] \end{array} \begin{array}{c} \\ 1 \\ 2 \\ 3 \\ 4 \\ 5 \\ 6 \\ 7 \\ 8 \end{array} \tag{7-29a}$$

The matrix is partitioned with respect to the restrained and unrestrained displacements of substructure 1, defining the resulting matrices as

$$[\mathbf{S}_c^1] = \left[\begin{array}{c:c} [\mathbf{S}_{uu}^1] & [\mathbf{S}_{ur}^1] \\ \hdashline [\mathbf{S}_{ru}^1] & [\mathbf{S}_{rr}^1] \end{array}\right] \tag{7-29b}$$

JOINT LOAD MATRIX

With just the load P applied at joint 4 (Fig. 7-6), the joint load matrix of Eq. (7-3) is written as

corresponding displacement label

$$\left[\begin{array}{c} [\mathbf{JL}_{uf}^1] \\ \hdashline [\mathbf{JL}_{rf}^1] \end{array}\right] = \left[\begin{array}{c} 0 \\ 0 \\ P \\ \hdashline 0 \\ 0 \\ 0 \\ 0 \\ 0 \end{array}\right] \begin{array}{c} 1 \\ 2 \\ 3 \\ 4 \\ 5 \\ 6 \\ 7 \\ 8 \end{array} \tag{7-30}$$

INTERNAL JOINT DISPLACEMENTS

Writing Eq. (7-5) for substructure 1, i.e.,

$$[\mathbf{S}^1_{uu}][\mathbf{\Delta}^1_{uf}] = [\mathbf{JL}^1_{uf}] \tag{7-31a}$$

or

$$EI\begin{bmatrix} \frac{8}{L} & \frac{2}{L} & \frac{6}{L^2} \\ \frac{2}{L} & \frac{8}{L} & \frac{6}{L^2} \\ \frac{6}{L^2} & \frac{6}{L^2} & \frac{24}{L^3} \end{bmatrix}\begin{bmatrix} \theta_1 \\ \theta_2 \\ \delta_3 \end{bmatrix} = \begin{bmatrix} 0 \\ 0 \\ P \end{bmatrix} \tag{7-31b}$$

and solving for the unrestrained components of joint displacement yields

$$[\mathbf{\Delta}^1_{uf}] = [\mathbf{S}^1_{uu}]^{-1}[\mathbf{JL}^1_{uf}] \tag{7-32a}$$

or

$$\begin{bmatrix} \theta_1 \\ \theta_2 \\ \delta_3 \end{bmatrix} = \frac{1}{84EI}\begin{bmatrix} 13L & -L & -3L^2 \\ -L & 13L & -3L^2 \\ -3L^2 & -3L^2 & 5L^3 \end{bmatrix}\begin{bmatrix} 0 \\ 0 \\ P \end{bmatrix} \tag{7-32b}$$

where

displacement label

$$[\mathbf{\Delta}^1_{uf}] = \frac{P}{84EI}\begin{bmatrix} -3L^2 \\ -3L^2 \\ 5L^3 \end{bmatrix} \begin{matrix} 1 \\ 2 \\ 3 \end{matrix} \tag{7-33}$$

FIXED BOUNDARY ACTIONS

For substructure 1, Eq. (7-8) becomes

$$[\mathbf{R}^1_{rf}] = [\mathbf{S}^1_{ru}][\mathbf{\Delta}^1_{uf}] - [\mathbf{JL}^1_{rf}] \tag{7-34a}$$

Hence, the fixed boundary actions for substructure 1 are equal to

$$[\mathbf{R}^1_{rf}] = EI\begin{bmatrix} \frac{2}{L} & 0 & \frac{6}{L^2} \\ 0 & \frac{2}{L} & \frac{6}{L^2} \\ -\frac{6}{L^2} & -\frac{6}{L^2} & -\frac{24}{L^3} \\ \frac{6}{L^2} & \frac{6}{L^2} & 0 \\ -\frac{6}{L^2} & -\frac{6}{L^2} & 0 \end{bmatrix}\frac{P}{84EI}\begin{bmatrix} -3L^2 \\ -3L^2 \\ 5L^3 \end{bmatrix} - \begin{bmatrix} 0 \\ 0 \\ 0 \\ 0 \\ 0 \end{bmatrix} \tag{7-34b}$$

or

corresponding displacement label

$$[\mathbf{R}^1_{rf}] = \begin{bmatrix} \dfrac{24PL}{84} \\ \dfrac{24PL}{84} \\ -P \\ -\dfrac{36P}{84} \\ \dfrac{36P}{84} \end{bmatrix} \begin{matrix} 4 \\ 5 \\ 6 \\ 7 \\ 8 \end{matrix} \tag{7-35}$$

SUBSTRUCTURE STIFFNESS MATRIX

The substructure stiffness matrix for substructure 1 can be evaluated by substituting the proper matrices into the equation

$$[\mathbf{S}^1_s] = [\mathbf{S}^1_{rr}] - [\mathbf{S}^1_{ru}][\mathbf{S}^1_{uu}]^{-1}[\mathbf{S}^1_{ur}] \tag{7-36a}$$

[from Eq. (7-15)] which yields Eq. (7-36b) on page 312; performing the indicated matrix operations gives

boundary displacement label

$$[\mathbf{S}^1_s] = \frac{EI}{84} \begin{matrix} & 4 & 5 & 6 & 7 & 8 & \\ \end{matrix}$$

$$[\mathbf{S}^1_s] = \frac{EI}{84}\begin{bmatrix} \dfrac{512}{L} & \dfrac{64}{L} & 0 & \dfrac{576}{L^2} & -\dfrac{576}{L^2} \\ \dfrac{64}{L} & \dfrac{512}{L} & 0 & \dfrac{576}{L^2} & -\dfrac{576}{L^2} \\ 0 & 0 & 0 & 0 & 0 \\ \dfrac{576}{L^2} & \dfrac{576}{L^2} & 0 & \dfrac{1152}{L^3} & -\dfrac{1152}{L^3} \\ -\dfrac{576}{L^2} & -\dfrac{576}{L^2} & 0 & -\dfrac{1152}{L^3} & \dfrac{1152}{L^3} \end{bmatrix} \begin{matrix} 4 \\ 5 \\ 6 \\ 7 \\ 8 \end{matrix} \tag{7-37}$$

(Column labels 4, 5, 6, 7, 8.)

Analysis of Substructure 2

Substructure 2 is described in Fig. 7-9. It should be kept in mind that the fixed boundaries at joints 1 and 8 are real boundaries of the total structural system (Fig. 7-4) and that the restrained boundaries at joints 3 and 6 are artificial boundaries. Also, referring back to Fig. 7-4, since there are no loads applied within the region of substructure 2 there is no applied loading to be considered in the analysis of the substructure.

JOINT DISPLACEMENT MATRIX

The possible components of joint displacement for substructure 2, with respect to the reference axes, are identified and labeled in Fig. 7-10. *The unrestrained displacements*

$$[\mathbf{S}_s^1] = EI\begin{bmatrix} \frac{8}{L} & \frac{2}{L} & -\frac{6}{L^2} & \frac{6}{L^2} & -\frac{6}{L^2} \\ \frac{2}{L} & \frac{8}{L} & -\frac{6}{L^2} & \frac{6}{L^2} & -\frac{6}{L^2} \\ -\frac{6}{L^2} & -\frac{6}{L^2} & \frac{24}{L^3} & 0 & 0 \\ \frac{6}{L^2} & \frac{6}{L^2} & 0 & \frac{24}{L^3} & -\frac{24}{L^3} \\ -\frac{6}{L^2} & -\frac{6}{L^2} & 0 & -\frac{24}{L^3} & -\frac{24}{L^3} \end{bmatrix} - EI\begin{bmatrix} \frac{2}{L} & 0 & \frac{6}{L^2} \\ 0 & \frac{2}{L} & \frac{6}{L^2} \\ -\frac{6}{L^2} & -\frac{6}{L^2} & -\frac{24}{L^3} \\ \frac{6}{L^2} & \frac{6}{L^2} & 0 \\ -\frac{6}{L^2} & -\frac{6}{L^2} & 0 \end{bmatrix} \frac{1}{84EI}\begin{bmatrix} 13L & -L & -3L^2 \\ -L & 13L & -3L^2 \\ -3L^2 & -3L^2 & 5L^3 \end{bmatrix} EI\begin{bmatrix} \frac{2}{L} & 0 & -\frac{6}{L^2} & \frac{6}{L^2} & -\frac{6}{L^2} \\ 0 & \frac{2}{L} & -\frac{6}{L^2} & \frac{6}{L^2} & -\frac{6}{L^2} \\ \frac{6}{L^2} & \frac{6}{L^2} & -\frac{24}{L^3} & 0 & 0 \end{bmatrix} \tag{7-36b}$$

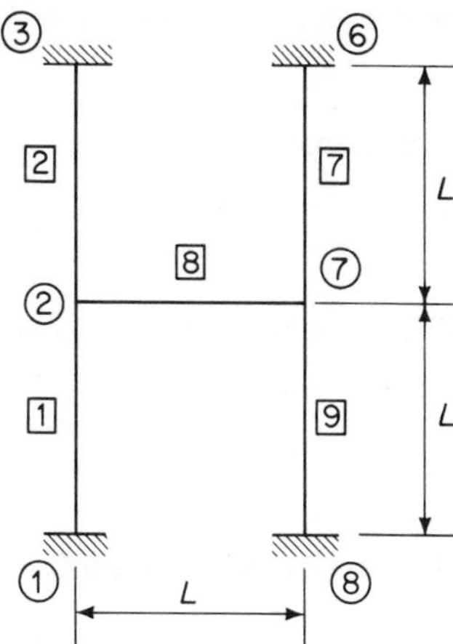

Fig. 7-9 Example 7-1: Substructure 2. (*EI* constant and equal for all members.)

are labeled first, then the artificially restrained boundary displacements are labeled, and, finally, the restrained displacements of the real boundaries are labeled. When labeling the possible displacements of the substructure, the possible horizontal translations of joints 3 and 6 must have the same label since they are connected in the assembled structure (Fig. 7-4) by a beam element—i.e., by member 6—and axial deformation is being neglected in this analysis.

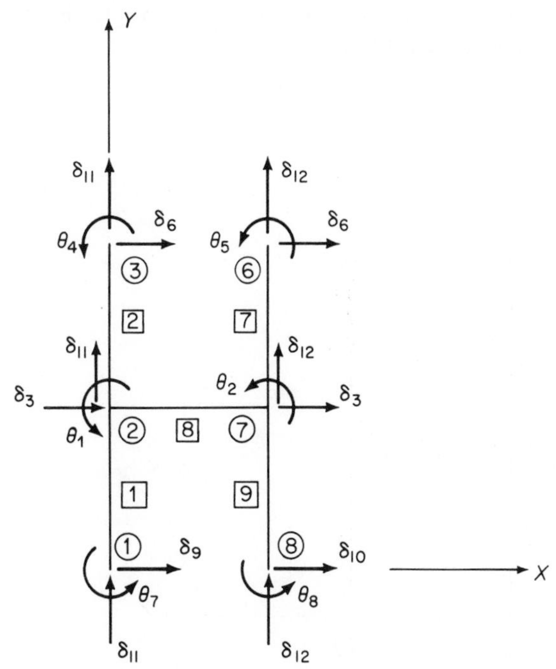

Fig. 7-10 Example 7-1: Identification of possible joint displacements (substructure 2).

The complete joint displacement matrix for substructure 2 is defined as

$$[\Delta_c^2] = \begin{bmatrix} \theta_1 \\ \theta_2 \\ \delta_3 \\ \hdashline \theta_4 \\ \theta_5 \\ \delta_6 \\ \theta_7 \\ \theta_8 \\ \delta_9 \\ \delta_{10} \\ \delta_{11} \\ \delta_{12} \end{bmatrix} \begin{matrix} \left.\begin{matrix} \\ \\ \\ \end{matrix}\right\} \text{unrestrained displacements} \\ \left.\begin{matrix} \\ \\ \\ \end{matrix}\right\} \text{restrained artificial boundary displacements} \\ \left.\begin{matrix} \\ \\ \\ \\ \\ \\ \end{matrix}\right\} \text{restrained real boundary displacements} \end{matrix} \tag{7-38}$$

MEMBER STIFFNESS MATRICES

The j- and k-ends of each member of substructure 2 are identified in Fig. 7-11 in accordance with the procedure of Chapter 4.

Using Expression (4-16), the member stiffness matrix can be written for each member. The rows and columns are labeled with respect to the labeling of the displacements in Fig. 7-10 to help identify the elements of the matrices.

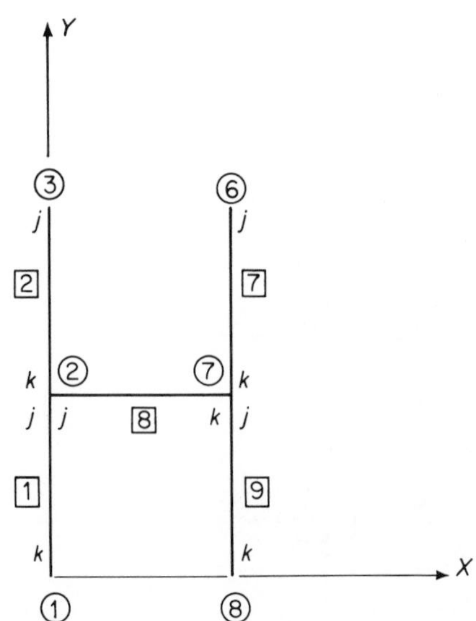

Fig. 7-11 Example 7-1: Identification of reference axes and j- and k-ends (substructure 2).

Member 1

$$[\mathbf{K}]_1 = EI \begin{array}{c} \begin{array}{cccc} 1 & 7 & 3 & 9 \end{array} \\ \left[\begin{array}{cccc} \frac{4}{L} & \frac{2}{L} & \frac{6}{L^2} & -\frac{6}{L^2} \\ \frac{2}{L} & \frac{4}{L} & \frac{6}{L^2} & -\frac{6}{L^2} \\ \frac{6}{L^2} & \frac{6}{L^2} & \frac{12}{L^3} & -\frac{12}{L^3} \\ -\frac{6}{L^2} & -\frac{6}{L^2} & -\frac{12}{L^3} & \frac{12}{L^3} \end{array}\right]_1 \end{array} \begin{array}{c} \\ 1 \\ 7 \\ 3 \\ 9 \end{array} \tag{7-39}$$

Member 2

$$[\mathbf{K}]_2 = EI \begin{array}{c} \begin{array}{cccc} 4 & 1 & 6 & 3 \end{array} \\ \left[\begin{array}{cccc} \frac{4}{L} & \frac{2}{L} & \frac{6}{L^2} & -\frac{6}{L^2} \\ \frac{2}{L} & \frac{4}{L} & \frac{6}{L^2} & -\frac{6}{L^2} \\ \frac{6}{L^2} & \frac{6}{L^2} & \frac{12}{L^3} & -\frac{12}{L^3} \\ -\frac{6}{L^2} & -\frac{6}{L^2} & -\frac{12}{L^3} & \frac{12}{L^3} \end{array}\right]_2 \end{array} \begin{array}{c} \\ 4 \\ 1 \\ 6 \\ 3 \end{array} \tag{7-40}$$

Member 7

$$[\mathbf{K}]_7 = EI \begin{array}{c} \begin{array}{cccc} 5 & 2 & 6 & 3 \end{array} \\ \left[\begin{array}{cccc} \frac{4}{L} & \frac{2}{L} & \frac{6}{L^2} & -\frac{6}{L^2} \\ \frac{2}{L} & \frac{4}{L} & \frac{6}{L^2} & -\frac{6}{L^2} \\ \frac{6}{L^2} & \frac{6}{L^2} & \frac{12}{L^3} & -\frac{12}{L^3} \\ -\frac{6}{L^2} & -\frac{6}{L^2} & -\frac{12}{L^3} & \frac{12}{L^3} \end{array}\right]_7 \end{array} \begin{array}{c} \\ 5 \\ 2 \\ 6 \\ 3 \end{array} \tag{7-41}$$

Member 8

$$[\mathbf{K}]_8 = EI \begin{array}{c} \begin{array}{cccc} 1 & 2 & 11 & 12 \end{array} \\ \left[\begin{array}{cccc} \frac{4}{L} & \frac{2}{L} & \frac{6}{L^2} & -\frac{6}{L^2} \\ \frac{2}{L} & \frac{4}{L} & \frac{6}{L^2} & -\frac{6}{L^2} \\ \frac{6}{L^2} & \frac{6}{L^2} & \frac{12}{L^3} & -\frac{12}{L^3} \\ -\frac{6}{L^2} & -\frac{6}{L^2} & -\frac{12}{L^3} & \frac{12}{L^3} \end{array}\right]_8 \end{array} \begin{array}{c} \\ 1 \\ 2 \\ 11 \\ 12 \end{array} \tag{7-42}$$

Member 9

$$
\begin{array}{c}
\quad\quad\quad\quad\; 2 \quad\quad\;\; 8 \quad\quad\;\; 3 \quad\quad\;\; 10 \\
[\mathbf{K}]_9 = EI\begin{bmatrix}
\frac{4}{L} & \frac{2}{L} & \frac{6}{L^2} & -\frac{6}{L^2} \\
\frac{2}{L} & \frac{4}{L} & \frac{6}{L^2} & -\frac{6}{L^2} \\
\frac{6}{L^2} & \frac{6}{L^2} & \frac{12}{L^3} & -\frac{12}{L^3} \\
-\frac{6}{L^2} & -\frac{6}{L^2} & -\frac{12}{L^3} & \frac{12}{L^3}
\end{bmatrix}_9
\begin{array}{c} 2 \\ 8 \\ 3 \\ 10 \end{array}
\end{array}
\tag{7-43}
$$

STRUCTURE STIFFNESS MATRIX

Superimposing the member stiffness matrices, the complete structure stiffness matrix for substructure 2 is equal to

$$
[\mathbf{S}_c^2] = EI\left[\begin{array}{ccc:ccccccccc}
1 & 2 & 3 & 4 & 5 & 6 & 7 & 8 & 9 & 10 & 11 & 12 \\
\frac{12}{L^2} & \frac{2}{L} & 0 & \frac{2}{L} & 0 & \frac{6}{L^2} & \frac{2}{L} & 0 & -\frac{6}{L^2} & 0 & \frac{6}{L^2} & -\frac{6}{L^2} \\
\frac{2}{L} & \frac{12}{L} & 0 & 0 & \frac{2}{L} & \frac{6}{L^2} & 0 & \frac{2}{L} & 0 & -\frac{6}{L^2} & \frac{6}{L^2} & -\frac{6}{L^2} \\
0 & 0 & \frac{48}{L^3} & -\frac{6}{L^2} & -\frac{6}{L^2} & -\frac{24}{L^3} & \frac{6}{L^2} & \frac{6}{L^2} & -\frac{12}{L^3} & -\frac{12}{L^3} & 0 & 0 \\
\hdashline
\frac{2}{L} & 0 & -\frac{6}{L^2} & \frac{4}{L} & 0 & \frac{6}{L^2} & 0 & 0 & 0 & 0 & 0 & 0 \\
0 & \frac{2}{L} & -\frac{6}{L^2} & 0 & \frac{4}{L} & \frac{6}{L^2} & 0 & 0 & 0 & 0 & 0 & 0 \\
\frac{6}{L^2} & \frac{6}{L^2} & -\frac{24}{L^3} & \frac{6}{L^2} & \frac{6}{L^2} & \frac{24}{L^3} & 0 & 0 & 0 & 0 & 0 & 0 \\
\frac{2}{L} & 0 & \frac{6}{L^2} & 0 & 0 & 0 & \frac{4}{L} & 0 & -\frac{6}{L^2} & 0 & 0 & 0 \\
0 & \frac{2}{L} & \frac{6}{L^2} & 0 & 0 & 0 & 0 & \frac{4}{L} & 0 & -\frac{6}{L^2} & 0 & 0 \\
-\frac{6}{L^2} & 0 & -\frac{12}{L^3} & 0 & 0 & 0 & -\frac{6}{L^2} & 0 & \frac{12}{L^3} & 0 & 0 & 0 \\
0 & -\frac{6}{L^2} & -\frac{12}{L^3} & 0 & 0 & 0 & 0 & -\frac{6}{L^2} & 0 & \frac{12}{L^3} & 0 & 0 \\
\frac{6}{L^2} & \frac{6}{L^2} & 0 & 0 & 0 & 0 & 0 & 0 & 0 & 0 & \frac{12}{L^3} & -\frac{12}{L^3} \\
-\frac{6}{L^2} & -\frac{6}{L^2} & 0 & 0 & 0 & 0 & 0 & 0 & 0 & 0 & -\frac{12}{L^3} & \frac{12}{L^3}
\end{array}\right]
\begin{array}{c} \\ 1 \\ 2 \\ 3 \\ 4 \\ 5 \\ 6 \\ 7 \\ 8 \\ 9 \\ 10 \\ 11 \\ 12 \end{array}
\tag{7-44a}
$$

Partitioning this matrix with respect to the unrestrained and restrained displacements yields

$$[\mathbf{S}_c^2] = EI\begin{bmatrix} [\mathbf{S}_{uu}^2] & [\mathbf{S}_{ur}^2] \\ [\mathbf{S}_{ur}^2] & [\mathbf{S}_{rr}^2] \end{bmatrix} \tag{7-44b}$$

JOINT LOAD MATRIX

Since there is no disturbance applied to the substructure,

$$\begin{bmatrix} [\mathbf{JL}_{uf}^2] \\ [\mathbf{JL}_{rf}^2] \end{bmatrix} = [0] \tag{7-45}$$

INTERNAL JOINT DISPLACEMENTS

For substructure 2, Eq. (7-7) is written as

$$[\mathbf{\Delta}_{uf}^2] = [\mathbf{S}_{uu}^2]^{-1}[\mathbf{JL}_{uf}^2] \tag{7-46}$$

Substituting

$$[\mathbf{S}_{uu}^2]^{-1} = \frac{1}{EI}\begin{bmatrix} \frac{6L}{70} & -\frac{L}{70} & 0 \\ -\frac{L}{70} & \frac{6L}{70} & 0 \\ 0 & 0 & \frac{L^3}{48} \end{bmatrix} \tag{7-47}$$

and

$$[\mathbf{JL}_{uf}^2] = [0] \tag{7-48}$$

yields

$$[\mathbf{\Delta}_{uf}^2] = [0] \tag{7-49}$$

FIXED BOUNDARY ACTIONS

Writing Eq. (7-8) for substructure 2

$$[\mathbf{R}_{rf}^2] = [\mathbf{S}_{ru}^2][\mathbf{\Delta}_{uf}^2] - [\mathbf{JL}_{rf}^2] \tag{7-50}$$

and making the proper substitutions gives

$$[\mathbf{R}_{rf}^2] = [0] \tag{7-51}$$

SUBSTRUCTURE STIFFNESS MATRIX

From Eq. (7-15),

$$[\mathbf{S}_s^2] = [\mathbf{S}_{rr}^2] - [\mathbf{S}_{ru}^2][\mathbf{S}_{uu}^2]^{-1}[\mathbf{S}_{ur}^2] \tag{7-52a}$$

which yields Eq. (7-52b) after the proper substitutions are made:

$$[\mathbf{S}_s^2] = EI\begin{bmatrix} \frac{4}{L} & 0 & \frac{6}{L^2} & 0 & 0 & 0 & 0 & 0 & 0 \\ 0 & \frac{4}{L} & \frac{6}{L^2} & 0 & 0 & 0 & 0 & 0 & 0 \\ \frac{6}{L^2} & \frac{6}{L^2} & \frac{24}{L^3} & 0 & 0 & 0 & 0 & 0 & 0 \\ 0 & 0 & 0 & \frac{4}{L} & 0 & -\frac{6}{L^2} & 0 & 0 & 0 \\ 0 & 0 & 0 & 0 & \frac{4}{L} & 0 & -\frac{6}{L^2} & 0 & 0 \\ 0 & 0 & 0 & -\frac{6}{L^2} & 0 & \frac{12}{L^3} & 0 & 0 & 0 \\ 0 & 0 & 0 & 0 & -\frac{6}{L^2} & 0 & \frac{12}{L^3} & 0 & 0 \\ 0 & 0 & 0 & 0 & 0 & 0 & 0 & \frac{12}{L^3} & -\frac{12}{L^3} \\ 0 & 0 & 0 & 0 & 0 & 0 & 0 & -\frac{12}{L^3} & \frac{12}{L^3} \end{bmatrix} - EI\begin{bmatrix} \frac{2}{L} & 0 & -\frac{6}{L^2} \\ 0 & \frac{2}{L} & -\frac{6}{L^2} \\ \frac{6}{L^2} & \frac{6}{L^2} & -\frac{24}{L^3} \\ \frac{2}{L} & 0 & \frac{6}{L^2} \\ 0 & \frac{2}{L} & \frac{6}{L^2} \\ -\frac{6}{L^2} & 0 & -\frac{12}{L^3} \\ 0 & -\frac{6}{L^2} & -\frac{12}{L^3} \\ \frac{6}{L^2} & \frac{6}{L^2} & 0 \\ -\frac{6}{L^2} & -\frac{6}{L^2} & 0 \end{bmatrix} \frac{1}{EI}\begin{bmatrix} \frac{6L}{70} & -\frac{L}{70} & 0 \\ -\frac{L}{70} & \frac{6L}{70} & 0 \\ 0 & 0 & \frac{L^3}{48} \end{bmatrix} EI\begin{bmatrix} \frac{2}{L} & 0 & \frac{6}{L^2} & \frac{2}{L} & 0 & -\frac{6}{L^2} & 0 & \frac{6}{L^2} & -\frac{6}{L^2} \\ 0 & \frac{2}{L} & \frac{6}{L^2} & 0 & \frac{2}{L} & 0 & -\frac{6}{L^2} & \frac{6}{L^2} & -\frac{6}{L^2} \\ -\frac{6}{L^2} & -\frac{6}{L^2} & -\frac{24}{L^3} & \frac{6}{L^2} & \frac{6}{L^2} & -\frac{12}{L^3} & -\frac{12}{L^3} & 0 & 0 \end{bmatrix} \tag{7-52b}$$

This yields

$$
\begin{array}{c}
\text{boundary displacement label} \\
\begin{array}{ccccccccc}
4 & 5 & 6 & 7 & 8 & 9 & 10 & 11 & 12
\end{array}
\end{array}
$$

$$
[\mathbf{S}_s^2] = \frac{EI}{140}\begin{bmatrix}
\frac{407}{L} & -\frac{97}{L} & \frac{300}{L^2} & \frac{57}{L} & \frac{113}{L} & -\frac{66}{L^2} & -\frac{234}{L^2} & -\frac{120}{L^2} & \frac{120}{L^2} \\
-\frac{97}{L} & \frac{407}{L} & \frac{300}{L^2} & \frac{113}{L} & \frac{57}{L} & -\frac{234}{L^2} & -\frac{66}{L^2} & -\frac{120}{L^2} & \frac{120}{L^2} \\
\frac{300}{L^2} & \frac{300}{L^2} & \frac{960}{L^3} & \frac{300}{L^2} & \frac{300}{L^2} & -\frac{480}{L^3} & -\frac{480}{L^3} & -\frac{720}{L^3} & \frac{720}{L^3} \\
\frac{57}{L} & \frac{113}{L} & \frac{300}{L^2} & \frac{407}{L} & -\frac{97}{L} & -\frac{486}{L^2} & \frac{186}{L^2} & -\frac{120}{L^2} & \frac{120}{L^2} \\
\frac{113}{L} & \frac{57}{L} & \frac{300}{L^2} & -\frac{97}{L} & \frac{407}{L} & \frac{186}{L^2} & -\frac{486}{L^2} & -\frac{120}{L^2} & \frac{120}{L^2} \\
-\frac{66}{L^2} & -\frac{234}{L^2} & -\frac{480}{L^3} & -\frac{486}{L^2} & \frac{186}{L^2} & \frac{828}{L^3} & -\frac{348}{L^3} & \frac{360}{L^3} & -\frac{360}{L^3} \\
-\frac{234}{L^2} & -\frac{66}{L^2} & -\frac{480}{L^3} & \frac{186}{L^2} & -\frac{486}{L^2} & -\frac{348}{L^3} & \frac{828}{L^3} & \frac{360}{L^3} & -\frac{360}{L^3} \\
-\frac{120}{L^2} & -\frac{120}{L^2} & -\frac{720}{L^3} & -\frac{120}{L^2} & -\frac{120}{L^2} & \frac{360}{L^3} & \frac{360}{L^3} & \frac{960}{L^3} & -\frac{960}{L^3} \\
\frac{120}{L^2} & \frac{120}{L^2} & \frac{720}{L^3} & \frac{120}{L^2} & \frac{120}{L^2} & -\frac{360}{L^3} & -\frac{360}{L^3} & -\frac{960}{L^3} & \frac{960}{L^3}
\end{bmatrix}
\begin{array}{c} 4 \\ 5 \\ 6 \\ 7 \\ 8 \\ 9 \\ 10 \\ 11 \\ 12 \end{array}
\qquad \mathbf{(7\text{-}53)}
$$

Analysis of Complete Structure

JOINT DISPLACEMENT MATRIX

For the restrained structure defined in Fig. 7-5(a), the possible components of joint displacement have been identified and labeled in Fig. 7-12. Keep in mind that only those components of displacement that are restrained in the restrained structure are considered in the analysis of the assembled system; the displacement of the unrestrained joints in the restrained structure are accounted for in the analysis of the various substructures.

Labeling first the displacements that are artificially constrained in the restrained structure and then the restrained displacements, the complete joint displacement matrix is defined as

$$
[\mathbf{\Delta}_c] = \begin{bmatrix} [\mathbf{\Delta}_u] \\ --- \\ [\mathbf{\Delta}_r] \end{bmatrix} = \begin{bmatrix} \theta_1 \\ \theta_2 \\ \delta_3 \\ -- \\ \theta_4 \\ \theta_5 \\ \delta_6 \\ \delta_7 \\ \delta_8 \\ \delta_9 \end{bmatrix} \qquad \mathbf{(7\text{-}54)}
$$

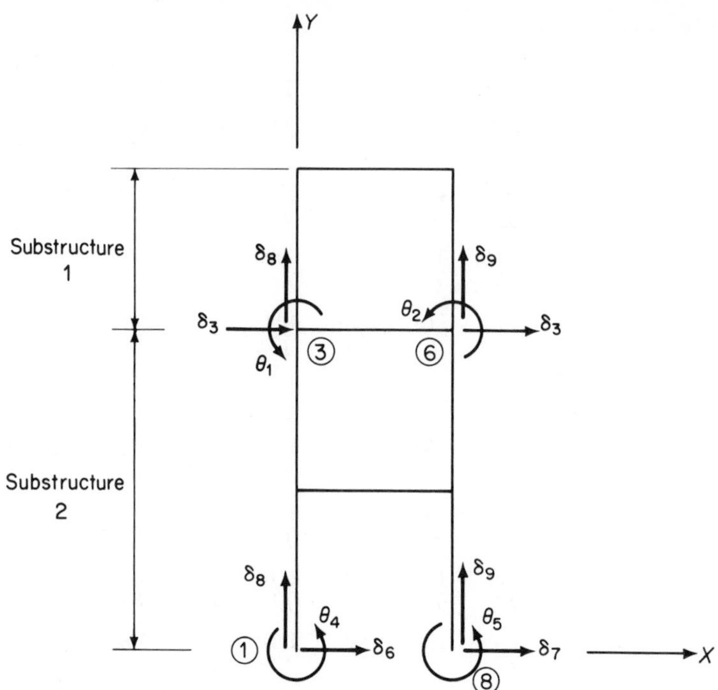

Fig. 7-12 Example 7-1: Identification of possible joint displacements (complete structure).

SUBSTRUCTURE STIFFNESS MATRICES

Although the substructure stiffness matrix for each substructure has been written, the elements of these matrices must now be labeled with respect to the labeling of the displacements in Fig. 7-12. The substructure stiffness matrices are repeated here with the rows and columns labeled to identify the elements of the matrices; the numbers across the top (column labels) and down the right side (row labels) correspond to the new displacement labels of Fig. 7-12, and the numbers given in the circles across the bottom (column labels) are the old boundary displacement labels used in the analysis of the respective substructure.

Substructure 1

Column labels across the top: 1, 2, 3, 8, 9 ← new displacement label defined in Fig. 7-12

$$[\mathbf{S}_s^1] = \frac{EI}{84}\begin{bmatrix} \frac{512}{L} & \frac{64}{L} & 0 & \frac{576}{L^2} & -\frac{576}{L^2} \\ \frac{64}{L} & \frac{512}{L} & 0 & \frac{576}{L^2} & -\frac{576}{L^2} \\ 0 & 0 & 0 & 0 & 0 \\ \frac{576}{L^2} & \frac{576}{L^2} & 0 & \frac{1152}{L^3} & -\frac{1152}{L^3} \\ -\frac{576}{L^2} & -\frac{576}{L^2} & 0 & -\frac{1152}{L^3} & \frac{1152}{L^3} \end{bmatrix} \begin{matrix} 1 \\ 2 \\ 3 \\ 8 \\ 9 \end{matrix} \tag{7-37}$$

Circled column labels across the bottom: ④ ⑤ ⑥ ⑦ ⑧ — boundary displacement label defined in Fig. 7-7

Substructure 2

new displacement label defined in Fig. 7-12

$$
\begin{array}{c}
\begin{matrix} \quad 1 & \quad 2 & \quad 3 & \quad 4 & \quad 5 & \quad 6 & \quad 7 & \quad 8 & \quad 9 \end{matrix} \\
[\mathbf{S}_s^2] = \frac{EI}{140}\left[\begin{array}{ccccccccc}
\frac{407}{L} & -\frac{97}{L} & \frac{300}{L^2} & \frac{57}{L} & \frac{113}{L} & -\frac{66}{L^2} & -\frac{234}{L^2} & -\frac{120}{L^2} & \frac{120}{L^2} \\
-\frac{97}{L} & \frac{407}{L} & \frac{300}{L^2} & \frac{113}{L} & \frac{57}{L} & -\frac{234}{L^2} & -\frac{66}{L^2} & -\frac{120}{L^2} & \frac{120}{L^2} \\
\frac{300}{L^2} & \frac{300}{L^2} & \frac{960}{L^3} & \frac{300}{L^2} & \frac{300}{L^2} & -\frac{480}{L^3} & -\frac{480}{L^3} & -\frac{720}{L^3} & \frac{720}{L^3} \\
\frac{57}{L} & \frac{113}{L} & \frac{300}{L^2} & \frac{407}{L} & -\frac{97}{L} & -\frac{486}{L^2} & \frac{186}{L^2} & -\frac{120}{L^2} & \frac{120}{L^2} \\
\frac{113}{L} & \frac{57}{L} & \frac{300}{L^2} & -\frac{97}{L} & \frac{407}{L} & \frac{186}{L^2} & -\frac{486}{L^2} & -\frac{120}{L^2} & \frac{120}{L^2} \\
-\frac{66}{L^2} & -\frac{234}{L^2} & -\frac{480}{L^3} & -\frac{486}{L^2} & \frac{186}{L^2} & \frac{828}{L^3} & -\frac{348}{L^3} & \frac{360}{L^3} & -\frac{360}{L^3} \\
-\frac{234}{L^2} & -\frac{66}{L^2} & -\frac{480}{L^3} & \frac{186}{L^2} & -\frac{486}{L^2} & -\frac{348}{L^3} & \frac{828}{L^3} & \frac{360}{L^3} & -\frac{360}{L^3} \\
-\frac{120}{L^2} & -\frac{120}{L^2} & -\frac{720}{L^3} & -\frac{120}{L^2} & -\frac{120}{L^2} & \frac{360}{L^3} & \frac{360}{L^3} & \frac{960}{L^3} & -\frac{960}{L^3} \\
\frac{120}{L^2} & \frac{120}{L^2} & \frac{720}{L^3} & \frac{120}{L^2} & \frac{120}{L^2} & -\frac{360}{L^3} & -\frac{360}{L^3} & -\frac{960}{L^3} & \frac{960}{L^3}
\end{array}\right]
\begin{array}{c} 1 \\ 2 \\ 3 \\ 4 \\ 5 \\ 6 \\ 7 \\ 8 \\ 9 \end{array} \\
\begin{matrix} ④ & ⑤ & ⑥ & ⑦ & ⑧ & ⑨ & ⑩ & ⑪ & ⑫ \end{matrix}
\end{array}
\qquad \textbf{(7-53)}
$$

boundary displacement label defined in Fig. 7-10

STRUCTURE STIFFNESS MATRIX

The complete structure stiffness matrix is developed by summing the elements of the substructure stiffness matrices with like labels. Thus,

$$
\begin{array}{c}
\begin{matrix} \quad 1 & \quad 2 & \quad 3 & \quad 4 & \quad 5 & \quad 6 & \quad 7 & \quad 8 & \quad 9 \end{matrix} \\
[\mathbf{S}_c] = \frac{EI}{420}\left[\begin{array}{ccc:cccccc}
\frac{3781}{L} & \frac{29}{L} & \frac{900}{L^2} & \frac{171}{L} & \frac{339}{L} & -\frac{198}{L^2} & -\frac{702}{L^2} & \frac{2520}{L^2} & -\frac{2520}{L^2} \\
\frac{29}{L} & \frac{3781}{L} & \frac{900}{L^2} & \frac{339}{L} & \frac{171}{L} & -\frac{702}{L^2} & -\frac{198}{L^2} & \frac{2520}{L^2} & -\frac{2520}{L^2} \\
\frac{900}{L^2} & \frac{900}{L^2} & \frac{2880}{L^3} & \frac{900}{L^2} & \frac{900}{L^2} & -\frac{1440}{L^3} & -\frac{1440}{L^3} & -\frac{2160}{L^3} & \frac{2160}{L^3} \\
\hdashline
\frac{171}{L} & \frac{339}{L} & \frac{900}{L^2} & \frac{1221}{L} & -\frac{291}{L} & -\frac{1458}{L^2} & \frac{558}{L^2} & -\frac{360}{L^2} & \frac{360}{L^2} \\
\frac{339}{L} & \frac{171}{L} & \frac{900}{L^2} & -\frac{291}{L} & \frac{1221}{L} & \frac{558}{L^2} & -\frac{1458}{L^2} & -\frac{360}{L^2} & \frac{360}{L^2} \\
-\frac{198}{L^2} & -\frac{702}{L^2} & -\frac{1440}{L^3} & -\frac{1458}{L^2} & \frac{558}{L^2} & \frac{2484}{L^3} & -\frac{1044}{L^3} & \frac{1080}{L^3} & -\frac{1080}{L^3} \\
-\frac{702}{L^2} & -\frac{198}{L^2} & -\frac{1440}{L^3} & \frac{558}{L^2} & -\frac{1458}{L^2} & -\frac{1044}{L^3} & \frac{2484}{L^3} & \frac{1080}{L^3} & -\frac{1080}{L^3} \\
\frac{2520}{L^2} & \frac{2520}{L^2} & -\frac{2160}{L^3} & -\frac{360}{L^2} & -\frac{360}{L^2} & \frac{1080}{L^3} & \frac{1080}{L^3} & \frac{8640}{L^3} & -\frac{8640}{L^3} \\
-\frac{2520}{L^2} & -\frac{2520}{L^2} & \frac{2160}{L^3} & \frac{360}{L^2} & \frac{360}{L^2} & -\frac{1080}{L^3} & -\frac{1080}{L^3} & -\frac{8640}{L^3} & \frac{8640}{L^3}
\end{array}\right]
\begin{array}{c} 1 \\ 2 \\ 3 \\ 4 \\ 5 \\ 6 \\ 7 \\ 8 \\ 9 \end{array}
\end{array}
\qquad \textbf{(7-55a)}
$$

Partitioning this matrix with respect to the unrestrained displacements (artificially constrained displacements of restrained structure) and restrained displacements (actual boundary constraints) yields

$$[\mathbf{S}_c] = \begin{bmatrix} [\mathbf{S}_{uu}] & [\mathbf{S}_{ur}] \\ \hline [\mathbf{S}_{ru}] & [\mathbf{S}_{rr}] \end{bmatrix} \tag{7-55b}$$

JOINT LOAD MATRIX

Transforming the components of fixed boundary actions obtained from the analysis of the substructures into equivalent joint loads by a change in sign, identifying the components of equivalent joint load with respect to the identification of joint displacements in Fig. 7-12, and summing the components of equivalent joint load with corresponding components of joint loads applied directly to the constrained joints of the restrained structure [see Figs. 7-4 and 7-5(a)] yields the complete joint load matrix; i.e.,

$$[\mathbf{JL}_c] = \begin{bmatrix} [\mathbf{JL}_u] \\ \hline [\mathbf{JL}_r] \end{bmatrix} = \begin{bmatrix} JL_1 \\ JL_2 \\ JL_3 \\ \hline JL_4 \\ JL_5 \\ JL_6 \\ JL_7 \\ JL_8 \\ JL_9 \end{bmatrix} = \begin{bmatrix} 0 \\ 0 \\ P \\ \hline 0 \\ 0 \\ 0 \\ 0 \\ 0 \\ 0 \end{bmatrix} + \begin{bmatrix} -\frac{24PL}{84} \\ -\frac{24PL}{84} \\ P \\ \hline 0 \\ 0 \\ 0 \\ 0 \\ \frac{36P}{84} \\ -\frac{36P}{84} \end{bmatrix} + \begin{bmatrix} 0 \\ 0 \\ 0 \\ \hline 0 \\ 0 \\ 0 \\ 0 \\ 0 \\ 0 \end{bmatrix} = \begin{bmatrix} -\frac{24PL}{84} \\ -\frac{24PL}{84} \\ 2P \\ \hline 0 \\ 0 \\ 0 \\ 0 \\ \frac{36P}{84} \\ -\frac{36P}{84} \end{bmatrix} \tag{7-56}$$

equivalent joint loads (substructure 1)
applied joint loads
equivalent joint loads (substructure 2)
total joint loads

EVALUATION OF JOINT DISPLACEMENTS

The unrestrained joint displacements—i.e., the aritficially constrained displacements of the restrained structure identified in Figs. 7-5(a) and 7-12—can be determined from the set of simultaneous equations

$$[\mathbf{S}_{uu}][\mathbf{\Delta}_u] = [\mathbf{JL}_u] \tag{4-36}$$

or

$$[\mathbf{\Delta}_u] = [\mathbf{S}_{uu}]^{-1}[\mathbf{JL}_u] \tag{7-20}$$

Hence,

$$[\mathbf{\Delta}_u] = \frac{420}{EI} \times 10^{-5} \begin{bmatrix} 28.723L & 2.070L & -9.623L^2 \\ 2.070L & 28.723L & -9.623L^2 \\ -9.623L^2 & -9.623L^2 & 40.736L^3 \end{bmatrix} \begin{bmatrix} -\dfrac{24PL}{84} \\ -\dfrac{24PL}{84} \\ 2P \end{bmatrix} \quad \textbf{(7-57)}$$

or

$$[\mathbf{\Delta}_u] = \begin{bmatrix} \theta_1 \\ \theta_2 \\ \delta_3 \end{bmatrix} = \frac{P}{EI} \begin{bmatrix} -0.1178L^2 \\ -0.1178L^2 \\ 0.3653L^3 \end{bmatrix} \quad \textbf{(7-58)}$$

Now, the joint displacements defined by Expression (7-58) are the actual displacements of the joints that are common to the various substructures. The actual displacements of the other unrestrained joints of the structural system (Fig. 7-4) can be determined by writing Eq. (7-23) for each substructure and solving.

Substructure 1

Referring to Figs. 7-7 and 7-12, the actual displacements of the boundaries of substructure 1, defined by the matrix $[\mathbf{\Delta}^n_{rd}]$, are identified as

$$[\mathbf{\Delta}^1_{rd}] = \begin{bmatrix} \theta_4 \\ \theta_5 \\ \delta_6 \\ \delta_7 \\ \delta_8 \end{bmatrix} = \frac{P}{EI} \begin{bmatrix} -0.1178L^2 \\ -0.1178L^2 \\ 0.3653L^3 \\ 0 \\ 0 \end{bmatrix} \quad \textbf{(7-59)}$$

For substructure 1, Eq. (7-23) is written as

$$[\mathbf{\Delta}^1_u] = [\mathbf{\Delta}^1_{uf}] - [\mathbf{S}^1_{uu}]^{-1}[\mathbf{S}^1_{ur}][\mathbf{\Delta}^1_{rd}] \quad \textbf{(7-60a)}$$

Making the proper substitutions yields Eq. (7-60b) on page 324, which gives

$$\begin{bmatrix} \theta_1 \\ \theta_2 \\ \delta_2 \end{bmatrix} = \frac{P}{EI} \begin{bmatrix} -0.0525L^2 \\ -0.0525L^2 \\ 0.4921L^3 \end{bmatrix} \quad \textbf{(7-61)}$$

↑ joint displacements defined in Fig. 7-7

Substructure 2

Referring to Figs. 7-10 and 7-12,

$$[\mathbf{\Delta}^2_{rd}] = \frac{P}{EI} \begin{bmatrix} \theta_4 \\ \theta_5 \\ \delta_6 \\ \theta_7 \\ \theta_8 \\ \delta_9 \\ \delta_{10} \\ \delta_{11} \\ \delta_{12} \end{bmatrix} = \frac{P}{EI} \begin{bmatrix} -0.1178L^2 \\ -0.1178L^2 \\ 0.3653L^3 \\ 0 \\ 0 \\ 0 \\ 0 \\ 0 \\ 0 \end{bmatrix} \quad \textbf{(7-62)}$$

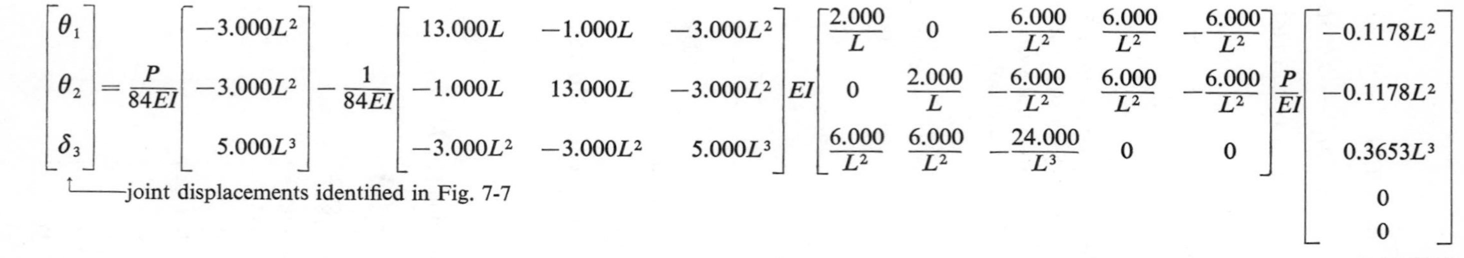

$$\begin{bmatrix} \theta_1 \\ \theta_2 \\ \delta_3 \end{bmatrix} = \frac{P}{84EI}\begin{bmatrix} -3.000L^2 \\ -3.000L^2 \\ 5.000L^3 \end{bmatrix} - \frac{1}{84EI}\begin{bmatrix} 13.000L & -1.000L & -3.000L^2 \\ -1.000L & 13.000L & -3.000L^2 \\ -3.000L^2 & -3.000L^2 & 5.000L^3 \end{bmatrix} EI \begin{bmatrix} \frac{2.000}{L} & 0 & -\frac{6.000}{L^2} & \frac{6.000}{L^2} & -\frac{6.000}{L^2} \\ 0 & \frac{2.000}{L} & -\frac{6.000}{L^2} & \frac{6.000}{L^2} & -\frac{6.000}{L^2} \\ \frac{6.000}{L^2} & \frac{6.000}{L^2} & -\frac{24.000}{L^3} & 0 & 0 \end{bmatrix} \frac{P}{EI}\begin{bmatrix} -0.1178L^2 \\ -0.1178L^2 \\ 0.3653L^3 \\ 0 \\ 0 \end{bmatrix} \quad \textbf{(7-60b)}$$

↑ joint displacements identified in Fig. 7-7

For substructure 2,

$$[\Delta_u^2] = [\Delta_{uf}^2] - [S_{uu}^2]^{-1}[S_{ur}^2][\Delta_{rd}^2] \qquad \textbf{(7-63a)}$$

which, after making the proper substitution, yields Eq. (7-63b) on page 326, from which

$$\begin{bmatrix} \theta_1 \\ \theta_2 \\ \delta_3 \end{bmatrix} = \frac{P}{EI}\begin{bmatrix} -0.1397L^2 \\ -0.1397L^2 \\ 0.1532L^3 \end{bmatrix} \qquad \textbf{(7-64)}$$

└——joint displacements defined in Fig. 7-10

For convenience, the actual displacements of each of the joints of the total system are summarized in Table 7-1.

Table 7-1

SUMMARY OF JOINT DISPLACEMENTS

Joint	*Rotation*	*Horizontal Translation*	*Vertical Translation*
1	0	0	0
2	$-0.1397\frac{PL^2}{EI}$	$0.1532\frac{PL^3}{EI}$	0
3	$-0.1178\frac{PL^2}{EI}$	$0.3653\frac{PL^3}{EI}$	0
4	$-0.0525\frac{PL^2}{EI}$	$0.4921\frac{PL^3}{EI}$	0
5	$-0.0525\frac{PL^2}{EI}$	$0.4921\frac{PL^3}{EI}$	0
6	$-0.1178\frac{PL^2}{EI}$	$0.3653\frac{PL^3}{EI}$	0
7	$-0.1397\frac{PL^2}{EI}$	$0.1532\frac{PL^3}{EI}$	0
8	0	0	0

FINAL END ACTIONS

The final end actions can be determined for each member of the structure from the now familiar set of equations:

$$[\mathbf{M}]_i = [\mathbf{K}]_i[\boldsymbol{\delta}]_i + [\mathbf{FM}]_i \qquad \textbf{(4-42)}$$

which can be written for each member. These final end actions will be identified with respect to the joint displacement labels for the substructure that the member is associated with (Figs. 7-7 and 7-10). The *j*- and *k*-ends of each member have been identified in Figs. 7-8 and 7-11.

$$\begin{bmatrix} \theta_1 \\ \theta_2 \\ \delta_3 \end{bmatrix} = \begin{bmatrix} 0 \\ 0 \\ 0 \end{bmatrix} - \frac{1}{70EI} \begin{bmatrix} 6.000L & -1.000L & 0 \\ -1.000L & 6.000L & 0 \\ 0 & 0 & 1.4583L^3 \end{bmatrix}$$

└── joint displacements identified in Fig. 7-10

$$\times EI \begin{bmatrix} \frac{2.000}{L} & 0 & \frac{6.000}{L^2} & \frac{2.000}{L} & 0 & -\frac{6.000}{L^2} & 0 & \frac{6.000}{L^2} & -\frac{6.000}{L^2} \\ 0 & \frac{2.000}{L} & \frac{6.000}{L^2} & 0 & \frac{2.000}{L} & 0 & -\frac{6.000}{L^2} & \frac{6.000}{L^2} & -\frac{6.000}{L^2} \\ -\frac{6.000}{L^2} & -\frac{6.000}{L^2} & -\frac{24.000}{L^3} & \frac{6.000}{L^2} & \frac{6.000}{L^2} & -\frac{12.000}{L^3} & -\frac{12.000}{L^3} & 0 & 0 \end{bmatrix} \frac{P}{EI} \begin{bmatrix} -0.1178L^2 \\ -0.1178L^2 \\ 0.3653L^3 \\ 0 \\ 0 \\ 0 \\ 0 \\ 0 \\ 0 \end{bmatrix} \tag{7-63b}$$

Member 1

$$\begin{bmatrix} M_1 \\ M_7 \\ P_3 \\ P_9 \end{bmatrix}_1 = EI \begin{bmatrix} \frac{4}{L} & \frac{2}{L} & \frac{6}{L^2} & -\frac{6}{L^2} \\ \frac{2}{L} & \frac{4}{L} & \frac{6}{L^2} & -\frac{6}{L^2} \\ \frac{6}{L^2} & \frac{6}{L^2} & \frac{12}{L^3} & -\frac{12}{L^3} \\ -\frac{6}{L^2} & -\frac{6}{L^2} & -\frac{12}{L^3} & \frac{12}{L^3} \end{bmatrix}_1 \frac{P}{EI} \begin{bmatrix} -0.1397L^2 \\ 0 \\ 0.1532L^3 \\ 0 \end{bmatrix}_1 + \begin{bmatrix} 0 \\ 0 \\ 0 \\ 0 \end{bmatrix}_1 = \begin{bmatrix} 0.36PL \\ 0.64PL \\ 1.00P \\ -1.00P \end{bmatrix}_1$$

↑ labels correspond to displacement labels of Fig. 7-10

(7-65a)

Member 2

$$\begin{bmatrix} M_4 \\ M_1 \\ P_6 \\ P_3 \end{bmatrix}_2 = EI \begin{bmatrix} \frac{4}{L} & \frac{2}{L} & \frac{6}{L^2} & -\frac{6}{L^2} \\ \frac{2}{L} & \frac{4}{L} & \frac{6}{L^2} & -\frac{6}{L^2} \\ \frac{6}{L^2} & \frac{6}{L^2} & \frac{12}{L^3} & -\frac{12}{L^3} \\ -\frac{6}{L^2} & -\frac{6}{L^2} & -\frac{12}{L^3} & \frac{12}{L^3} \end{bmatrix}_2 \frac{P}{EI} \begin{bmatrix} -0.1178L_2 \\ -0.1397L^2 \\ 0.3653L^3 \\ 0.1532L^3 \end{bmatrix}_2 + \begin{bmatrix} 0 \\ 0 \\ 0 \\ 0 \end{bmatrix}_2 = \begin{bmatrix} 0.52PL \\ 0.48PL \\ 1.00P \\ -1.00P \end{bmatrix}_2$$

↑ labels correspond to displacement labels of Fig. 7-10

(7-65b)

Member 3

$$\begin{bmatrix} M_1 \\ M_4 \\ P_3 \\ P_6 \end{bmatrix}_3 = EI \begin{bmatrix} \frac{4}{L} & \frac{2}{L} & \frac{6}{L^2} & -\frac{6}{L^2} \\ \frac{2}{L} & \frac{4}{L} & \frac{6}{L^2} & -\frac{6}{L^2} \\ \frac{6}{L^2} & \frac{6}{L^2} & \frac{12}{L^3} & -\frac{12}{L^3} \\ -\frac{6}{L^2} & -\frac{6}{L^2} & -\frac{12}{L^3} & \frac{12}{L^3} \end{bmatrix}_3 \frac{P}{EI} \begin{bmatrix} -0.0525L^2 \\ -0.1178L^2 \\ 0.4921L^3 \\ 0.3653L^3 \end{bmatrix}_3 + \begin{bmatrix} 0 \\ 0 \\ 0 \\ 0 \end{bmatrix}_3 = \begin{bmatrix} 0.32PL \\ 0.18PL \\ 0.50P \\ -0.50P \end{bmatrix}_3$$

↑ labels correspond to displacement labels of Fig. 7-7

(7-65c)

Member 4

$$\begin{bmatrix} M_1 \\ M_2 \\ P_7 \\ P_8 \end{bmatrix}_4 = EI \begin{bmatrix} \frac{4}{L} & \frac{2}{L} & \frac{6}{L^2} & -\frac{6}{L^2} \\ \frac{2}{L} & \frac{4}{L} & \frac{6}{L^2} & -\frac{6}{L^2} \\ \frac{6}{L^2} & \frac{6}{L^2} & \frac{12}{L^3} & -\frac{12}{L^3} \\ -\frac{6}{L^2} & -\frac{6}{L^2} & -\frac{12}{L^3} & \frac{12}{L^3} \end{bmatrix}_4 \frac{P}{EI} \begin{bmatrix} -0.0525L^2 \\ -0.0525L^2 \\ 0 \\ 0 \end{bmatrix}_4 + \begin{bmatrix} 0 \\ 0 \\ 0 \\ 0 \end{bmatrix}_4 = \begin{bmatrix} -0.32PL \\ -0.32PL \\ -0.63P \\ 0.63P \end{bmatrix}_4$$

↑ labels correspond to displacement labels of Fig. 7-7

(7-65d)

Member 5

$$\begin{bmatrix} M_2 \\ M_5 \\ P_3 \\ P_6 \end{bmatrix}_5 = EI \begin{bmatrix} \frac{4}{L} & \frac{2}{L} & \frac{6}{L^2} & -\frac{6}{L^2} \\ \frac{2}{L} & \frac{4}{L} & \frac{6}{L^2} & -\frac{6}{L^2} \\ \frac{6}{L^2} & \frac{6}{L^2} & \frac{12}{L^3} & -\frac{12}{L^3} \\ -\frac{6}{L^2} & -\frac{6}{L^2} & -\frac{12}{L^3} & \frac{12}{L^3} \end{bmatrix}_5 \frac{P}{EI} \begin{bmatrix} -0.0525L^2 \\ -0.1178L^2 \\ 0.4921L^3 \\ 0.3653L^3 \end{bmatrix}_5 + \begin{bmatrix} 0 \\ 0 \\ 0 \\ 0 \end{bmatrix}_5 = \begin{bmatrix} 0.32PL \\ 0.18PL \\ 0.50P \\ -0.50P \end{bmatrix}_5 \tag{7-65e}$$

↑ labels correspond to displacement labels of Fig. 7-7

Member 6

$$\begin{bmatrix} M_4 \\ M_5 \\ P_7 \\ P_8 \end{bmatrix}_6 = EI \begin{bmatrix} \frac{4}{L} & \frac{2}{L} & \frac{6}{L^2} & -\frac{6}{L^2} \\ \frac{2}{L} & \frac{4}{L} & \frac{6}{L^2} & -\frac{6}{L^2} \\ \frac{6}{L^2} & \frac{6}{L^2} & \frac{12}{L^3} & -\frac{12}{L^3} \\ -\frac{6}{L^2} & -\frac{6}{L^2} & -\frac{12}{L^3} & \frac{12}{L^3} \end{bmatrix}_6 \frac{P}{EI} \begin{bmatrix} -0.1178L^2 \\ -0.1178L^2 \\ 0 \\ 0 \end{bmatrix}_6 + \begin{bmatrix} 0 \\ 0 \\ 0 \\ 0 \end{bmatrix}_6 = \begin{bmatrix} -0.71PL \\ -0.71PL \\ -1.41P \\ 1.41P \end{bmatrix}_6 \tag{7-65f}$$

↑ labels correspond to displacement labels of Fig. 7-7

Member 7

$$\begin{bmatrix} M_5 \\ M_2 \\ P_6 \\ P_3 \end{bmatrix}_7 = EI \begin{bmatrix} \frac{4}{L} & \frac{2}{L} & \frac{6}{L^2} & -\frac{6}{L^2} \\ \frac{2}{L} & \frac{4}{L} & \frac{6}{L^2} & -\frac{6}{L^2} \\ \frac{6}{L^2} & \frac{6}{L^2} & \frac{12}{L^3} & -\frac{12}{L^3} \\ -\frac{6}{L^2} & -\frac{6}{L^2} & -\frac{12}{L^3} & \frac{12}{L^3} \end{bmatrix}_7 \frac{P}{EI} \begin{bmatrix} -0.1178L^2 \\ -0.1397L^2 \\ 0.3653L^3 \\ 0.1532L^3 \end{bmatrix}_7 + \begin{bmatrix} 0 \\ 0 \\ 0 \\ 0 \end{bmatrix}_7 = \begin{bmatrix} 0.52PL \\ 0.48PL \\ 1.00P \\ -1.00P \end{bmatrix}_7 \tag{7-65g}$$

↑ labels correspond to displacement labels of Fig. 7-10

Member 8

$$\begin{bmatrix} M_1 \\ M_2 \\ P_{11} \\ P_{12} \end{bmatrix}_8 = EI \begin{bmatrix} \frac{4}{L} & \frac{2}{L} & \frac{6}{L^2} & -\frac{6}{L^2} \\ \frac{2}{L} & \frac{4}{L} & \frac{6}{L^2} & -\frac{6}{L^2} \\ \frac{6}{L^2} & \frac{6}{L^2} & \frac{12}{L^3} & -\frac{12}{L^3} \\ -\frac{6}{L^2} & -\frac{6}{L^2} & -\frac{12}{L^3} & \frac{12}{L^3} \end{bmatrix}_8 \frac{P}{EI} \begin{bmatrix} -0.1397L^2 \\ -0.1397L^2 \\ 0 \\ 0 \end{bmatrix}_8 + \begin{bmatrix} 0 \\ 0 \\ 0 \\ 0 \end{bmatrix}_8 = \begin{bmatrix} -0.84PL \\ -0.84PL \\ -1.68P \\ 1.68P \end{bmatrix}_8 \tag{7-65h}$$

↑ labels correspond to displacement labels of Fig. 7-10

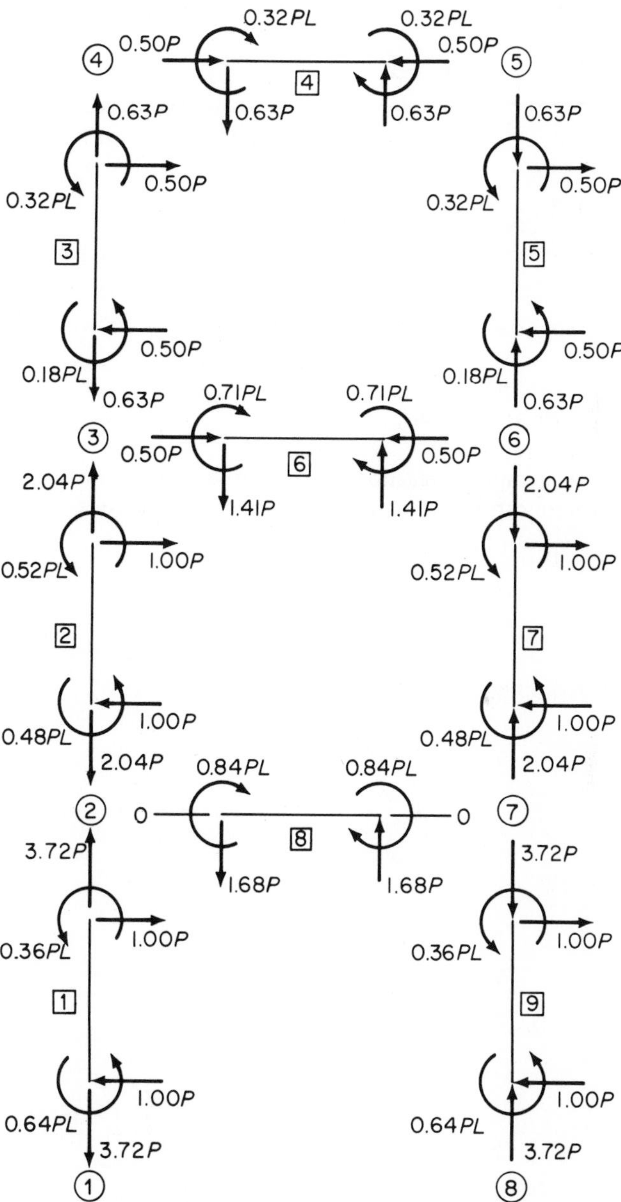

Fig. 7-13 Example 7-1: Final end actions.

Member 9

$$\begin{bmatrix} M_2 \\ M_8 \\ P_3 \\ P_{10} \end{bmatrix}_9 = EI \begin{bmatrix} \frac{4}{L} & \frac{2}{L} & \frac{6}{L^2} & -\frac{6}{L^2} \\ \frac{2}{L} & \frac{4}{L} & \frac{6}{L^2} & -\frac{6}{L^2} \\ \frac{6}{L^2} & \frac{6}{L^2} & \frac{12}{L^3} & -\frac{12}{L^3} \\ -\frac{6}{L^2} & -\frac{6}{L^2} & -\frac{12}{L^3} & \frac{12}{L^3} \end{bmatrix}_9 \frac{P}{EI} \begin{bmatrix} -0.1397L^2 \\ 0 \\ 0.1532L^3 \\ 0 \end{bmatrix}_9 + \begin{bmatrix} 0 \\ 0 \\ 0 \\ 0 \end{bmatrix}_9 = \begin{bmatrix} 0.36PL \\ 0.64PL \\ 1.00P \\ -1.00P \end{bmatrix}_9$$

↑—labels correspond to displacement labels of Fig. 7-10

(7-65i)

The free body diagram of each member is shown in Fig. 7-13.

SUPPORT REACTIONS

The support reactions of the structural system produced by the loading of the structure can be evaluated from the set of equations

$$[\mathbf{R}_r] = [\mathbf{S}_{ru}][\boldsymbol{\Delta}_u] - [\mathbf{JL}_r] \tag{7-21}$$

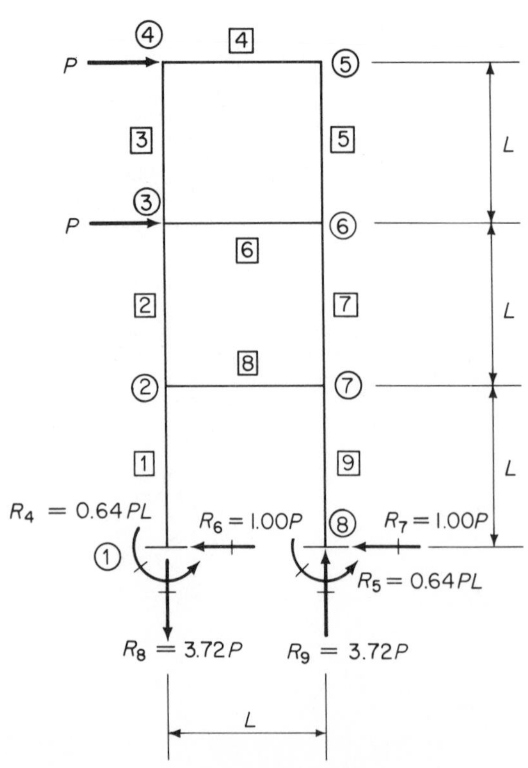

Fig. 7-14 Example 7-1: Support reactions.

or

$$\begin{bmatrix} R_4 \\ R_5 \\ R_6 \\ R_7 \\ R_8 \\ R_9 \end{bmatrix} = \frac{EI}{420}\begin{bmatrix} \frac{171}{L} & \frac{339}{L} & \frac{900}{L^2} \\ \frac{339}{L} & \frac{171}{L} & \frac{900}{L^2} \\ -\frac{198}{L^2} & -\frac{702}{L^2} & -\frac{1440}{L^3} \\ -\frac{702}{L^2} & -\frac{198}{L^2} & -\frac{1440}{L^3} \\ \frac{2520}{L^2} & \frac{2520}{L^2} & -\frac{2160}{L^3} \\ -\frac{2520}{L^2} & -\frac{2520}{L^2} & \frac{2160}{L^3} \end{bmatrix} \frac{P}{EI}\begin{bmatrix} -0.1178L^2 \\ -0.1178L^2 \\ 0.3653L^3 \end{bmatrix} - \begin{bmatrix} 0 \\ 0 \\ 0 \\ 0 \\ \frac{36P}{84} \\ -\frac{36P}{84} \end{bmatrix} = \begin{bmatrix} 0.64PL \\ 0.64PL \\ -1.00P \\ -1.00P \\ -3.72P \\ 3.72P \end{bmatrix} \tag{7-66}$$

↑ labels correspond to displacement labels of Fig. 7-12

The free body diagram of the whole system is shown in Fig. 7-14.

7–5 Determination of Member Stiffness Matrix and Fixed End Actions: Special Beam Elements

The member stiffness matrix and the fixed end action matrix can be evaluated for a special beam element by analyzing the member as if it were a substructure. Thus, the substructure stiffness matrix $[\mathbf{S}^n_s]$ defined by Eq. (7-15) is the desired member stiffness matrix $[\mathbf{K}]_i$, and the fixed boundary actions $[\mathbf{R}^n_{rf}]$ calculated by Eq. (7-8) are the required fixed end actions $[\mathbf{FM}]_i$.

In defining the beam element as a substructure, artificial internal joints may be specified at any desired location within the span of the member, e.g., at points where there is a change in the modulus of elasticity E or in the moment of inertia I.

Since the member information for a prismatic member is either familiar or can be obtained from available handbooks, it is convenient to subdivide a non-prismatic member into segments of constant EI. These segments then take on the role of beam elements which make up the assumed substructure. If the given beam element is tapered or if it has haunched ends, an approximate analysis can be made using an *equivalent beam element* with lengths of constant EI. The *equivalent beam element* can be established—as explained in Chapter 4, Sec. 4-2.2—by dividing the member into finite segments each having a constant depth equal to the average depth of the given beam element over the length of the segment.

Example 7-2. Determine the member stiffness matrix for the beam element i with one end pinned and the other end restrained (Fig. 7-15). The beam element has a constant EI and cross-sectional area A over its entire length.

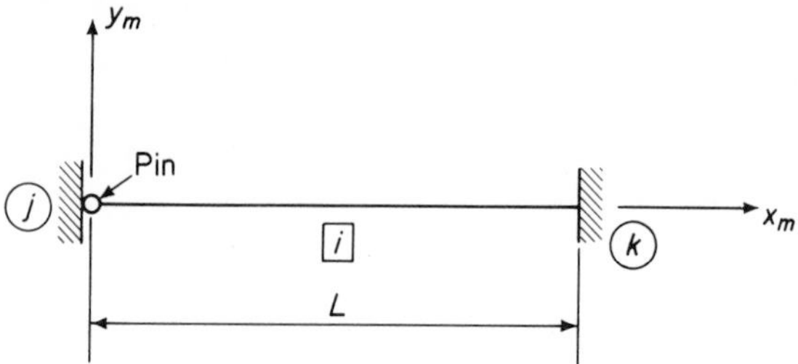

Fig. 7-15 Example 7-2: Beam element with one end pinned, one end restrained.

JOINT DISPLACEMENTS

Treating the beam element as a substructure, the possible components of joint displacement are defined with respect to the member axes as shown in Fig. 7-16. The unrestrained displacement of the substructure—i.e., the rotation at the j-end—is numbered first, followed by the numbering of the restrained displacements. Since the member has a constant EI over its length there is no need to assume internal joints. It should be recalled that the numbering of the possible displacements establishes the order of the equilibrium equations and the complete substructure stiffness matrix $[\mathbf{S}_c^n]$.

STRUCTURE STIFFNESS MATRIX

Since the restrained structure for the substructure is a beam element with both ends restrained, the complete structure stiffness matrix for the substructure is equal to the member stiffness matrix for the beam element as defined by Expression (5-7); i.e.,

$$[\mathbf{S}_c^i] = \begin{array}{c} \begin{array}{cccccc} 1 & 2 & 3 & 4 & 5 & 6 \end{array} \\ \left[\begin{array}{c|ccccc} \frac{4EI}{L} & \frac{2EI}{L} & \frac{6EI}{L^2} & -\frac{6EI}{L^2} & 0 & 0 \\ \hline \frac{2EI}{L} & \frac{4EI}{L} & \frac{6EI}{L^2} & -\frac{6EI}{L^2} & 0 & 0 \\ \frac{6EI}{L^2} & \frac{6EI}{L^2} & \frac{12EI}{L^3} & -\frac{12EI}{L^3} & 0 & 0 \\ -\frac{6EI}{L^2} & -\frac{6EI}{L^2} & -\frac{12EI}{L^3} & \frac{12EI}{L^3} & 0 & 0 \\ 0 & 0 & 0 & 0 & \frac{AE}{L} & -\frac{AE}{L} \\ 0 & 0 & 0 & 0 & -\frac{AE}{L} & \frac{AE}{L} \end{array}\right] \end{array} \begin{array}{c} \\ 1 \\ 2 \\ 3 \\ 4 \\ 5 \\ 6 \end{array} \tag{7-67}$$

The matrix is partitioned with respect to unrestrained and restrained components of displacements.

MEMBER STIFFNESS MATRIX

Now, the substructure stiffness matrix—that is to say, the member stiffness matrix for beam element i—can be determined by writing Eq. (7-15) for the substructure and solving, i.e.,

$$[\mathbf{S}_s^i] = [\mathbf{S}_{rr}^i] - [\mathbf{S}_{ru}^i][\mathbf{S}_{uu}^i]^{-1}[\mathbf{S}_{ur}^i] \tag{7-68a}$$

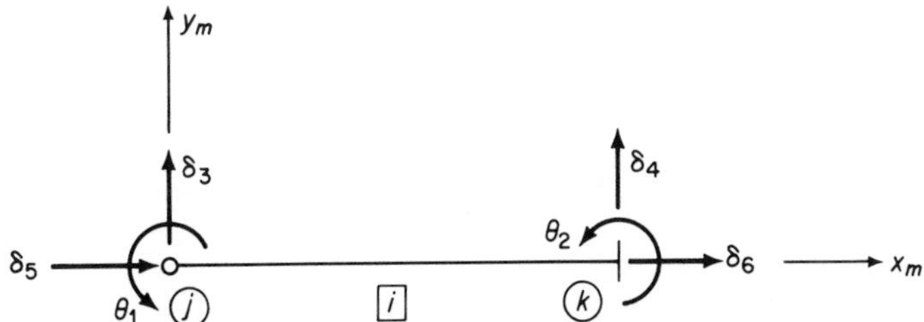

Fig. 7-16 Example 7-2: Identification of possible joint displacements.

or

$$[\mathbf{S}_s^i] = \begin{bmatrix} \frac{4EI}{L} & \frac{6EI}{L^2} & -\frac{6EI}{L^2} & 0 & 0 \\ \frac{6EI}{L^2} & \frac{12EI}{L^3} & -\frac{12EI}{L^3} & 0 & 0 \\ -\frac{6EI}{L^2} & -\frac{12EI}{L^3} & \frac{12EI}{L^3} & 0 & 0 \\ 0 & 0 & 0 & \frac{AE}{L} & -\frac{AE}{L} \\ 0 & 0 & 0 & -\frac{AE}{L} & \frac{AE}{L} \end{bmatrix} - \begin{bmatrix} \frac{2EI}{L} \\ \frac{6EI}{L^2} \\ -\frac{6EI}{L^2} \\ 0 \\ 0 \end{bmatrix} \left[\frac{L}{4EI}\right] \left[\frac{2EI}{L} \;\; \frac{6EI}{L^2} \;\; -\frac{6EI}{L^2} \;\; 0 \;\; 0\right] \tag{7-68b}$$

Performing the indicated matrix operations yields

$$[\mathbf{S}_s^i] = [\mathbf{K}^*]_i = \begin{array}{c} \\ \end{array} \overset{\begin{array}{ccccc} 2 & 3 & 4 & 5 & 6 \end{array}}{\begin{bmatrix} \frac{3EI}{L} & \frac{3EI}{L^2} & -\frac{3EI}{L^2} & 0 & 0 \\ \frac{3EI}{L^2} & \frac{3EI}{L^3} & -\frac{3EI}{L^3} & 0 & 0 \\ -\frac{3EI}{L^2} & -\frac{3EI}{L^3} & \frac{3EI}{L^3} & 0 & 0 \\ 0 & 0 & 0 & \frac{AE}{L} & -\frac{AE}{L} \\ 0 & 0 & 0 & -\frac{AE}{L} & \frac{AE}{L} \end{bmatrix}} \begin{array}{c} 2 \\ 3 \\ 4 \\ 5 \\ 6 \end{array} \tag{7-69}$$

$$\begin{array}{ccccc} q & r & s & t & u \end{array}$$

(Column labels 2–6: displacement labels defined in Fig. 7-16; column labels q, r, s, t, u: displacement labels defined in Fig. 5-28)

Referring to Chapter 5, Sec. 5-8.1, the substructure stiffness matrix defined by Expression (7-69) is the same as the member stiffness matrix $[\mathbf{K}^*]_i$ of Expression (5-99) that was defined for a prismatic member with the j-end pinned and the k-end fixed.

Example 7-3. Establish the member stiffness matrix for the nonprismatic beam element i described in Fig. 7-17 and compute the fixed end actions for the indicated loading of the member. The modulus of elasticity E is constant over the length of the member; A refers to the cross-sectional area of the member at the k-end; I is the moment of inertia of the cross-section at the k-end; and L refers to the length equal to $\frac{1}{3}$ of total span of member.

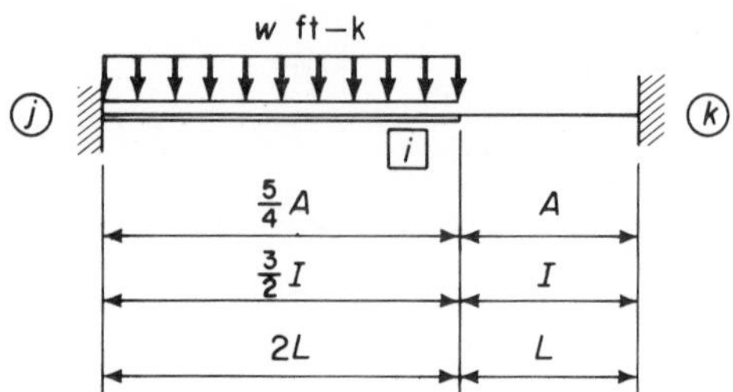

Fig. 7-17 Example 7-3: Nonprismatic beam element.

In order to develop the analysis of this nonprismatic member in terms of elements with constant EI, an internal joint is assumed at the point of change in I and A. The joints and the members of the substructure—i.e., the beam element—are labeled in Fig. 7-18.

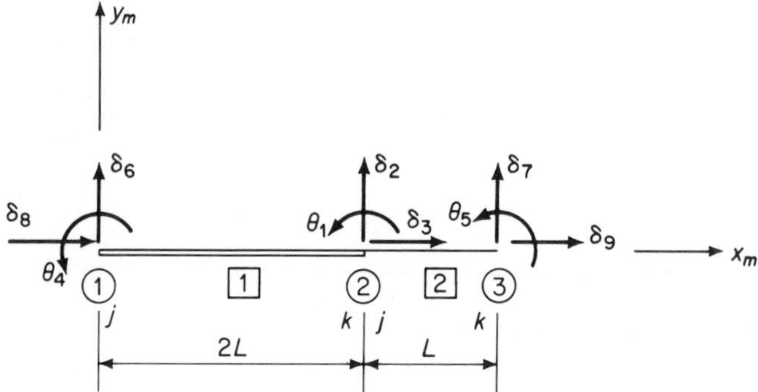

Fig. 7-18 Example 7-3: Selection of joints and identification of axes, j- and k-ends, and possible joint displacements.

JOINT DISPLACEMENT MATRIX

Taking into account axial deformations, the possible components of joint displacement are identified with respect to the member axes of the beam element and are numbered, labeling unrestrained displacements first as indicated in Fig. 7-18. The complete joint displacement matrix for the substructure is written as

$$[\Delta_c^i] = \begin{bmatrix} \theta_1 \\ \delta_2 \\ \delta_3 \\ \hdashline \theta_4 \\ \theta_5 \\ \delta_6 \\ \delta_7 \\ \delta_8 \\ \delta_9 \end{bmatrix} \begin{matrix} \left.\begin{matrix} \\ \\ \\ \end{matrix}\right\} \text{unrestrained displacements} \\ \\ \left.\begin{matrix} \\ \\ \\ \\ \\ \\ \end{matrix}\right\} \text{restrained displacements} \end{matrix} \qquad \textbf{(7-70)}$$

STRUCTURE STIFFNESS MATRIX

The j- and k-ends for each segment of the substructure are defined in Fig. 7-18. The member stiffness matrix for each segment can be written directly from Expression (5-7).

Member 1

$$
[\mathbf{K}]_1 = \frac{E}{8}
\begin{array}{c}
\begin{matrix} 4 & \quad 1 & \quad 6 & \quad 2 & \quad 8 & \quad 3 \end{matrix} \\
\begin{bmatrix}
\dfrac{24I}{L} & \dfrac{12I}{L} & \dfrac{18I}{L^2} & -\dfrac{18I}{L^2} & 0 & 0 \\
\dfrac{12I}{L} & \dfrac{24I}{L} & \dfrac{18I}{L^2} & -\dfrac{18I}{L^2} & 0 & 0 \\
\dfrac{18I}{L^2} & \dfrac{18I}{L^2} & \dfrac{18I}{L^3} & -\dfrac{18I}{L^3} & 0 & 0 \\
-\dfrac{18I}{L^2} & -\dfrac{18I}{L^2} & -\dfrac{18I}{L^3} & \dfrac{18I}{L^3} & 0 & 0 \\
0 & 0 & 0 & 0 & \dfrac{5A}{L} & -\dfrac{5A}{L} \\
0 & 0 & 0 & 0 & -\dfrac{5A}{L} & \dfrac{5A}{L}
\end{bmatrix}
\end{array}
\begin{matrix} \\ 4 \\ 1 \\ 6 \\ 2 \\ 8 \\ 3 \end{matrix}
\tag{7-71a}
$$

displacement labels defined in Fig. 7-18

Member 2

$$
[\mathbf{K}]_2 = \frac{E}{8}
\begin{array}{c}
\begin{matrix} 1 & \quad 5 & \quad 2 & \quad 7 & \quad 3 & \quad 9 \end{matrix} \\
\begin{bmatrix}
\dfrac{32I}{L} & \dfrac{16I}{L} & \dfrac{48I}{L^2} & -\dfrac{48I}{L^2} & 0 & 0 \\
\dfrac{16I}{L} & \dfrac{32I}{L} & \dfrac{48I}{L^2} & -\dfrac{48I}{L^2} & 0 & 0 \\
\dfrac{48I}{L^2} & \dfrac{48I}{L^2} & \dfrac{96I}{L^3} & -\dfrac{96I}{L^3} & 0 & 0 \\
-\dfrac{48I}{L^2} & -\dfrac{48I}{L^2} & -\dfrac{96I}{L^3} & \dfrac{96I}{L^3} & 0 & 0 \\
0 & 0 & 0 & 0 & \dfrac{8A}{L} & -\dfrac{8A}{L} \\
0 & 0 & 0 & 0 & -\dfrac{8A}{L} & \dfrac{8A}{L}
\end{bmatrix}
\end{array}
\begin{matrix} \\ 1 \\ 5 \\ 2 \\ 7 \\ 3 \\ 9 \end{matrix}
\tag{7-71b}
$$

displacement labels defined in Fig. 7-18

The complete structure stiffness matrix is formulated by summing the elements of the various member stiffness matrices with like labels; thus,

$$
[\mathbf{S}_c^i] = \frac{E}{8}
\begin{array}{c}
\begin{array}{ccc:cccccc}
1 & 2 & 3 & 4 & 5 & 6 & 7 & 8 & 9
\end{array} \\
\left[\begin{array}{ccc:cccccc}
\frac{56I}{L} & \frac{30I}{L^2} & 0 & \frac{12I}{L} & \frac{16I}{L} & \frac{18I}{L^2} & -\frac{48I}{L^2} & 0 & 0 \\
\frac{30I}{L^2} & \frac{114I}{L^3} & 0 & -\frac{18I}{L^2} & \frac{48I}{L^2} & -\frac{18I}{L^3} & -\frac{96I}{L^3} & 0 & 0 \\
0 & 0 & \frac{13A}{L} & 0 & 0 & 0 & 0 & -\frac{5A}{L} & -\frac{8A}{L} \\
\hdashline
\frac{12I}{L} & -\frac{18I}{L^2} & 0 & \frac{24I}{L} & 0 & \frac{18I}{L^2} & 0 & 0 & 0 \\
\frac{16I}{L} & \frac{48I}{L^2} & 0 & 0 & \frac{32I}{L} & 0 & -\frac{48I}{L^2} & 0 & 0 \\
\frac{18I}{L^2} & -\frac{18I}{L^3} & 0 & \frac{18I}{L^2} & 0 & \frac{18I}{L^3} & 0 & 0 & 0 \\
-\frac{48I}{L^2} & -\frac{96I}{L^3} & 0 & 0 & -\frac{48I}{L^2} & 0 & \frac{96I}{L^3} & 0 & 0 \\
0 & 0 & -\frac{5A}{L} & 0 & 0 & 0 & 0 & \frac{5A}{L} & 0 \\
0 & 0 & -\frac{8A}{L} & 0 & 0 & 0 & 0 & 0 & \frac{8A}{L}
\end{array}\right]
\end{array}
\begin{array}{c} \\ 1 \\ 2 \\ 3 \\ 4 \\ 5 \\ 6 \\ 7 \\ 8 \\ 9 \end{array}
\tag{7-72}
$$

The matrix is partitioned with respect to unrestrained and restrained joint displacements.

MEMBER STIFFNESS MATRIX

The substructure or member stiffness matrix for the nonprismatic beam element can be obtained by developing Eq. (7-15) and performing the indicated operations.

$$[\mathbf{S}_s^i] = [\mathbf{S}_{rr}^i] - [\mathbf{S}_{ru}^i][\mathbf{S}_{uu}^i]^{-1}[\mathbf{S}_{ur}^i] \tag{7-73a}$$

which yields Eq. (7-73b) on page 337 when proper substitutions are made for the matrices and gives

displacement labels defined in Fig. 7-18

$$
[\mathbf{S}_s^i] = [\mathbf{K}]_i = E
\begin{array}{c}
\begin{array}{cccccc}
4 & 5 & 6 & 7 & 8 & 9
\end{array} \\
\left[\begin{array}{cccccc}
\frac{1.917I}{L} & \frac{0.801I}{L} & \frac{0.906I}{L^2} & -\frac{0.906I}{L^2} & 0 & 0 \\
\frac{0.801I}{L} & \frac{1.444I}{L} & \frac{0.748I}{L^2} & -\frac{0.748I}{L^2} & 0 & 0 \\
\frac{0.906I}{L^2} & \frac{0.748I}{L^2} & \frac{0.551I}{L^3} & -\frac{0.551I}{L^3} & 0 & 0 \\
-\frac{0.906I}{L^2} & -\frac{0.748I}{L^2} & -\frac{0.551I}{L^3} & \frac{0.551I}{L^3} & 0 & 0 \\
0 & 0 & 0 & 0 & \frac{0.385A}{L} & -\frac{0.385A}{L} \\
0 & 0 & 0 & 0 & -\frac{0.385A}{L} & \frac{0.385A}{L}
\end{array}\right]_i \\
\begin{array}{cccccc}
p & q & r & s & t & u
\end{array}
\end{array}
\begin{array}{c} \\ 4 \\ 5 \\ 6 \\ 7 \\ 8 \\ 9 \\ \\ \end{array}
\tag{7-74}
$$

displacement labels defined in Fig. 5-3

$$[\mathbf{S}_s^i] = \frac{E}{8}\begin{bmatrix} \frac{24I}{L} & 0 & \frac{18I}{L^2} & 0 & 0 & 0 \\ 0 & \frac{32I}{L} & 0 & -\frac{48I}{L^2} & 0 & 0 \\ \frac{18I}{L^2} & 0 & \frac{18I}{L^3} & 0 & 0 & 0 \\ 0 & -\frac{48I}{L^2} & 0 & \frac{96I}{L^3} & 0 & 0 \\ 0 & 0 & 0 & 0 & \frac{5A}{L} & 0 \\ 0 & 0 & 0 & 0 & 0 & \frac{8A}{L} \end{bmatrix} - \frac{E}{8}\begin{bmatrix} \frac{12I}{L} & -\frac{18I}{L^2} & 0 \\ \frac{16I}{L} & \frac{48I}{L^2} & 0 \\ \frac{18I}{L^2} & -\frac{18I}{L^3} & 0 \\ -\frac{48I}{L^2} & -\frac{96I}{L^3} & 0 \\ 0 & 0 & -\frac{5A}{L} \\ 0 & 0 & -\frac{8A}{L} \end{bmatrix} \frac{8}{E}\begin{bmatrix} \frac{0.02079L}{I} & -\frac{0.00547L^2}{I} & 0 \\ -\frac{0.00547L^2}{I} & \frac{0.01021L^3}{I} & 0 \\ 0 & 0 & \frac{0.07692L}{A} \end{bmatrix} \frac{E}{8}\begin{bmatrix} \frac{12I}{L} & \frac{16I}{L} & \frac{18I}{L^2} & -\frac{48I}{L^2} & 0 & 0 \\ -\frac{18I}{L^2} & \frac{48I}{L^2} & -\frac{18I}{L^3} & -\frac{96I}{L^3} & 0 & 0 \\ 0 & 0 & 0 & 0 & -\frac{5A}{L} & -\frac{8A}{L} \end{bmatrix} \tag{7-73b}$$

The rows and columns of the member stiffness matrix for the beam element of Fig. 7-17 are labeled with respect to the labeling of possible end displacements of both Figs. 7-18 and 5-3 for easy reference.

JOINT LOAD MATRIX

For the loading of the system described in Fig. 7-17, the fixed end actions are

Member 1

$$FM_4^1 = \tfrac{1}{3}wL^2 \qquad FM_1^1 = -\tfrac{1}{3}wL^2$$

$$FP_6^1 = wL \qquad FP_2^1 = wL$$

$$FP_8^1 = 0 \qquad FP_3^1 = 0$$

Member 2

$$FM_1^2 = 0 \qquad FM_5^2 = 0$$

$$FP_2^2 = 0 \qquad FP_7^2 = 0$$

$$FP_8^2 = 0 \qquad FP_9^2 = 0$$

The subscripts identifying the fixed end action correspond to the label of the respective joint displacement, identified in Fig. 7-18.

Having identified the fixed end actions, the complete joint load matrix for the substructure can be developed; i.e.,

$$[\mathbf{JL}_c^i] = \begin{bmatrix} JL_1 \\ JL_2 \\ JL_3 \\ \hdashline JL_4 \\ JL_5 \\ JL_6 \\ JL_7 \\ JL_8 \\ JL_9 \end{bmatrix} = \begin{bmatrix} \tfrac{1}{3}wL^2 \\ -wL \\ 0 \\ \hdashline -\tfrac{1}{3}wL^2 \\ 0 \\ -wL \\ 0 \\ 0 \\ 0 \end{bmatrix} \tag{7-75}$$

Now, partitioning the matrix of Expression (7-75) with respect to the unrestrained displacements and restrained displacements of the system (Fig. 7-18) yields

$$[\mathbf{JL}_{uf}^i] = \begin{bmatrix} \tfrac{1}{3}wL^2 \\ -wL \\ 0 \end{bmatrix} \tag{7-76a}$$

and

$$[\mathbf{JL}_{rf}^i] = \begin{bmatrix} -\tfrac{1}{3}wL^2 \\ 0 \\ -wL \\ 0 \\ 0 \\ 0 \end{bmatrix} \tag{7-76b}$$

FIXED END ACTIONS

The fixed boundary actions for the substructure are obtained from Eq. (7-8) which is written as

$$[\mathbf{R}^i_{rf}] = [\mathbf{S}^i_{ru}][\mathbf{S}^i_{uu}]^{-1}[\mathbf{JL}^i_{uf}] - [\mathbf{JL}^i_{rf}] \tag{7-77a}$$

or

$$[\mathbf{R}^i_{rf}] = \frac{E}{8}\begin{bmatrix} \frac{12I}{L} & -\frac{18I}{L} & 0 \\ \frac{16I}{L} & \frac{48I}{L^2} & 0 \\ \frac{18I}{L^2} & -\frac{18I}{L^3} & 0 \\ -\frac{48I}{L^2} & -\frac{96I}{L^3} & 0 \\ 0 & 0 & -\frac{5A}{L} \\ 0 & 0 & -\frac{8A}{L} \end{bmatrix} \frac{8}{E}\begin{bmatrix} \frac{0.02079L}{I} & -\frac{0.00547L^2}{I} & 0 \\ -\frac{0.00547L^2}{I} & \frac{0.01021L^3}{I} & 0 \\ 0 & 0 & \frac{0.07692L}{A} \end{bmatrix}\begin{bmatrix} \frac{wL^2}{3} \\ -wL \\ 0 \end{bmatrix} - \begin{bmatrix} -\frac{wL^2}{3} \\ 0 \\ -wL \\ 0 \\ 0 \\ 0 \end{bmatrix} \tag{7-77b}$$

Performing the indicated operations yields the fixed boundary or the fixed end actions, i.e.,

$$[\mathbf{R}^i_{rf}] = [\mathbf{FM}]_i = \begin{bmatrix} 0.699wL^2 \\ -0.379wL^2 \\ 1.440wL \\ 0.569wL \\ 0 \\ 0 \end{bmatrix} \begin{matrix} 4 & p \\ 5 & q \\ 6 & r \\ 7 & s \\ 8 & t \\ 9 & u \end{matrix} \tag{7-78}$$

corresponding displacement labels of Fig. 7-18 (first column of labels)
corresponding general displacement labels of Fig. 5-3 (second column of labels)

7–6
Problems

7-1. Partitioning the system into two convenient substructures, determine the reactions for the rigid planar frame by the stiffness method of analysis, neglecting the effects of axial deformation. Also, draw the moment and shear diagrams for each member of the structure. Modulus of elasticity E and moment of inertia I are the same for each member.

7-2. Calculate the support reactions for the structure and the final end actions for each member of the structure by the stiffness method of analysis, neglecting the effects of axial deformation. Divide the system into three substructures. Modulus of elasticity E is constant for all members. The relative moment of inertia of each member is indicated adjacent to the member.

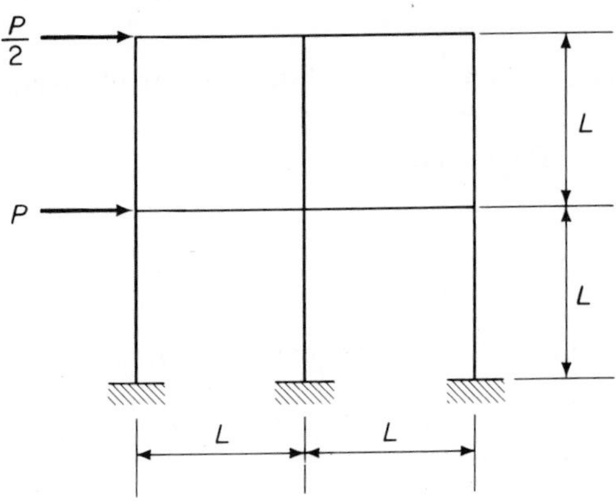

Prob. 7-1

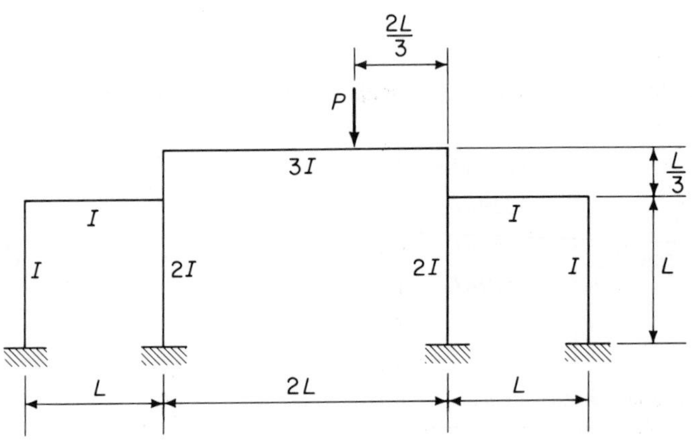

Prob. 7-2

7-3 to 7-5. Determine the member stiffness matrix and the fixed end actions for the given beam element and loading condition by the stiffness method, treating the element as a substructure; E = modulus of elasticity, I = moment of inertia, and A = cross-sectional area.

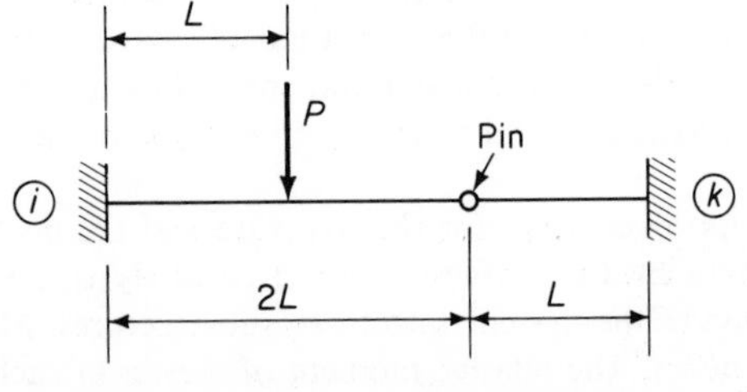

Prob. 7-3 (E, I, and A constant.)

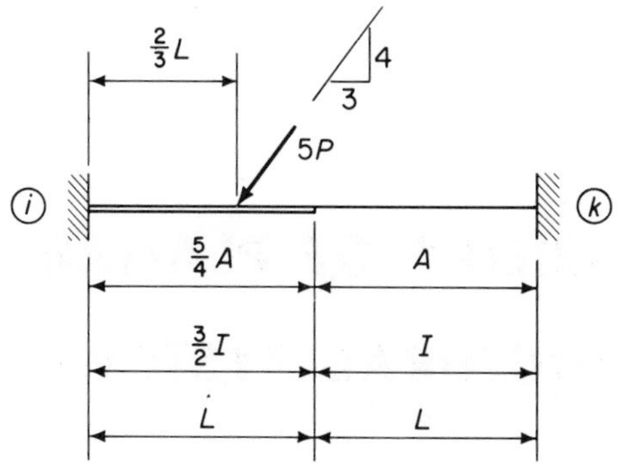

Prob. 7-4 (E constant.)

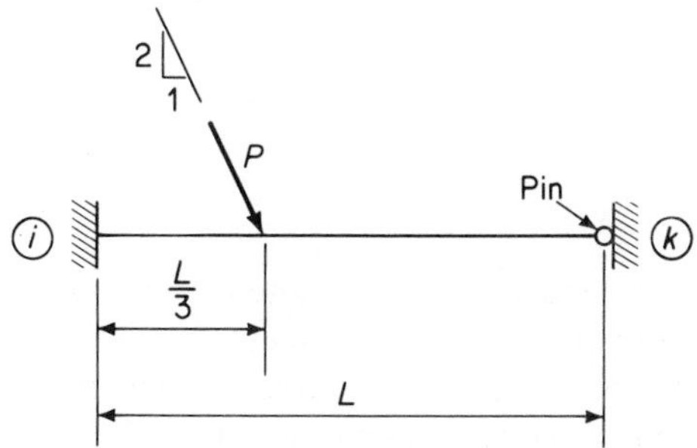

Prob. 7-5 (E, I, and A constant.)

SELECTED REFERENCES

7-1 Przemieniecki, J. S., "Matrix Structural Analysis of Substructures," *AIAA Journal*, Vol. 1, No. 1, January, 1963.

7-2 Livesley, R. K., *Matrix Methods of Structural Analysis*. New York: The Macmillan Company, Inc., 1964.

7-3 Rubinstein, Moshe F., *Matrix Computer Analysis of Structures*. Englewood Cliffs, N.J.: Prentice-Hall, Inc., 1966.

7-4 Willems, Nicholas, and William M. Lucas, Jr., *Matrix Analysis for Structural Engineers*. Englewood Cliffs, N.J.: Prentice-Hall, Inc., 1968.

8 STABILITY OF PLANAR STRUCTURAL SYSTEMS

8–1
Introduction

The analysis of elastic structural systems whose individual members are subjected to axial forces combined with bending moments necessitates an investigation of the effect of the axial forces upon the rotation and translation of the ends of the individual members. This chapter presents a method for considering the effect of axial forces upon the flexure of a planar frame and for determining the critical values of applied axial forces based upon the elastic stability of the frame. The method employs the use of certain ***stability*** and ***load functions*** which are incorporated into the equilibrium conditions as terms in the expressions relating the joint rotations, translations, and loads. The ensuing analysis may then be carried out in a conventional manner.

In light of the emphasis placed upon the ***stiffness method*** of structural analysis in this text, the derivations and applications of the stability and load functions to be presented will follow along the lines of the development of the stiffness method presented in earlier chapters. The sign convention stated in Sec. 5-2 will be adhered to in the development of the material of this chapter.

8–2
Euler Load

The value of the ***critical load*** for a compressed structural member can be obtained by considering the behavior of an ***ideal column***, which is assumed to be initially perfectly straight and compressed by a centrally applied load. Consider the case of a uniform slender, ideal column pinned and laterally restrained at both ends and subjected to an axial force P [Fig. 8-1(a)]. The member is assumed to be

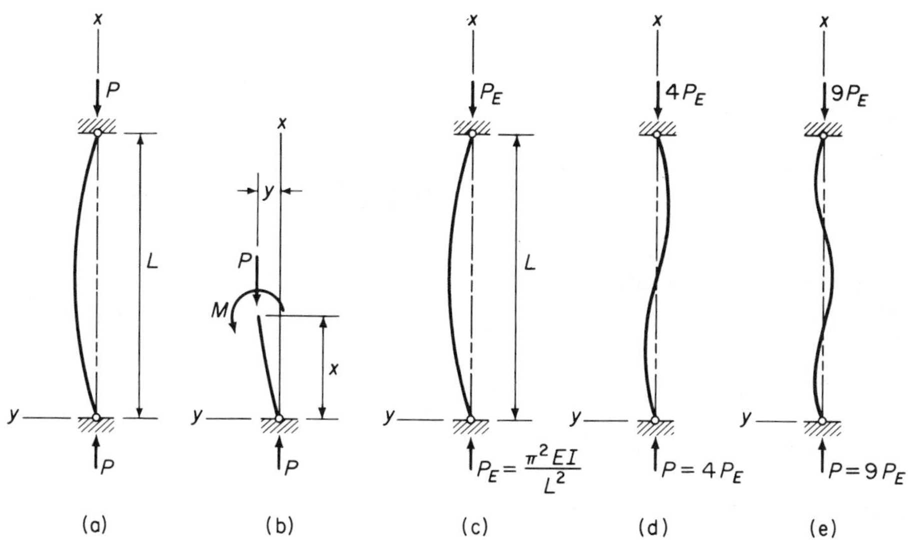

Fig. 8-1 Euler load for pinned end member: (a) axially loaded slender column; (b) free body diagram x distance from y-axis; (c) $n = 1$; (d) $n = 2$, braced laterally at midspan; (e) $n = 3$, braced laterally at third points.

weightless, perfectly elastic, and stressed within the proportional limit. If the force P is less than the critical value, the member will remain straight and undergo only axial compression. The member is therefore in a condition of stable equilibrium such that if a lateral force is applied, say, at midheight, and a small lateral deflection produced, the deflection will disappear and the member will return to its original straight form when the lateral force is removed. If P is gradually increased, a condition is attained wherein the straight form of equilibrium becomes unstable and the application of a small lateral force to the member will produce a deflection which does not disappear when the lateral force is removed. The ***critical load*** is thus defined as the axial force which is necessary to maintain the member in this slightly deflected position.

A theoretical analysis of this critical load was carried out by Leonhard Euler, the Swiss mathematician, in 1757. His analysis was based on the differential equation of an elastic curve,

$$\frac{d^2y}{dx^2} = \frac{M}{EI} \tag{8-1}$$

where M is the bending moment, E is the modulus of elasticity, and I is the moment of inertia about the axis of bending. The moment–curvature–sign relationship of Eq. (8-1) is established in Fig. 8-2. Applying Eq. (8-1) to the member shown in Fig. 8-1(a), by considering equilibrium of the free body shown in Fig. 8-1(b), yields

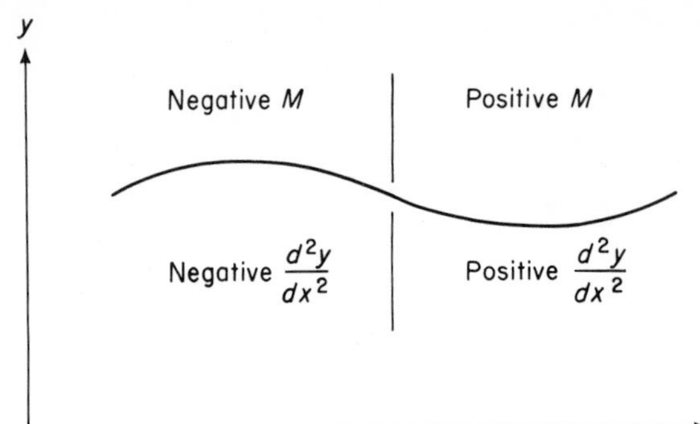

Fig. 8-2 Moment–curvature–sign relationship.

$$EI\frac{d^2y}{dx^2} = M = -Py \tag{8-2}$$

The general solution of Eq. (8-2) can be expressed in the form

$$y = A \sin\left(\frac{u}{L}x\right) + B \cos\left(\frac{u}{L}x\right) \tag{8-3}$$

where

$$u = L\sqrt{\frac{P}{EI}} \tag{8-4}$$

The parameters A and B are constants which can be evaluated from known boundary conditions. Substituting the boundary condition $y = 0$ at $x = 0$ into Eq. (8-3) yields $B = 0$. Therefore, Eq. (8-3) reduces to

$$y = A \sin\left(\frac{u}{L}x\right) \tag{8-5}$$

Substituting the additional boundary condition $y = 0$ at $x = L$ into Eq. (8-5) yields

$$A \sin u = 0 \tag{8-6}$$

Equation (8-6) is satisfied if $A = 0$, which is the trivial solution—i.e., there is no lateral deflection of the member—or if

$$u = n\pi \tag{8-7}$$

where $n = 0, 1, 2, 3 \ldots.$

Substituting Eq. (8-7) into Eq. (8-4) and rearranging yields

$$P = \frac{n^2\pi^2 EI}{L^2} \tag{8-8}$$

The value $n = 0$ is meaningless, since P would be zero. For the other values of n, the column bends into the *modes* shown in Figs. 8-1(c) through 8-1(e). Of these, the most important is the one shown in Fig. 8-1(c); the others occur with larger loads and are possible only if the member is laterally braced at the nodal points or points of zero deflection. The ***critical*** or ***Euler load*** for a pinned end uniform member is therefore given by

$$P_E = \frac{\pi^2 EI}{L^2} \tag{8-9}$$

8–3
Stability Functions

8-3.1 Rotation Functions

Consider the uniform or prismatic beam element i shown in Fig. 8-3(a), which is, when unloaded, perfectly straight and of length L_i. A unit rotation at the j-end induces restraining moments K^i_{pp} at end j and K^i_{qp} at end k. The resulting end shear forces expressed in terms of the restraining moments, considering equilibrium of the element, are

$$K^i_{rp} = -K^i_{sp} = \frac{K^i_{pp} + K^i_{qp}}{L_i} \tag{8-10}$$

Applying the differential equation of an elastic curve, Eq. (8-1), to the free body shown in Fig. 8-3(b),

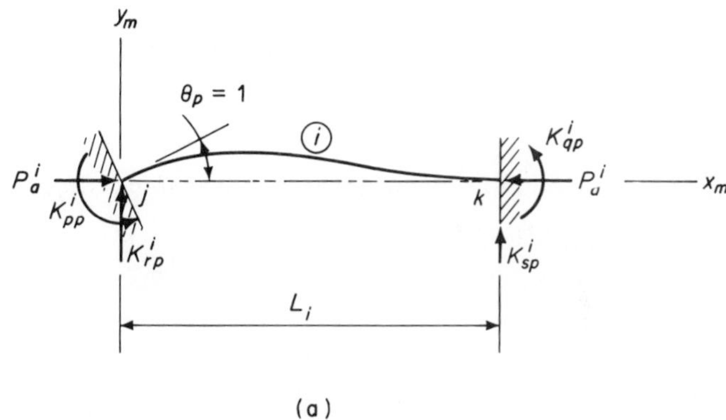

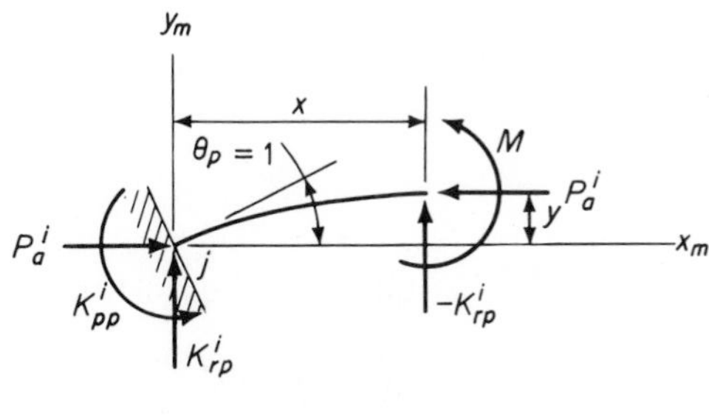

Fig. 8-3 Unit rotation of end j, beam element i: (a) free body diagram, beam element i; (b) free body diagram, x distance from j-end.

$$EI\frac{d^2y}{dx^2} = M = -(P_a^i y + K_{pp}^i - K_{rp}^i x) \tag{8-11}$$

where P_a^i is an axial force applied to the element. Substituting Eq. (8-10) into Eq. (8-11) yields

$$EI\frac{d^2y}{dx^2} = -P_a^i y - K_{pp}^i + (K_{pp}^i + K_{qp}^i)\frac{x}{L_i} \tag{8-12}$$

The axial force P_a^i can be expressed as a scalar multiple of P_E^i, the ***pinned end Euler load*** for the beam element i for buckling in the plane of the applied unit rotation; i.e.,

$$P_a^i = \Phi_i P_E^i \tag{8-13}$$

or

$$P_a^i = \Phi_i \pi^2\left(\frac{EI}{L_i^2}\right) \tag{8-14}$$

since, from Eq. (8-9),

$$P_E^i = \frac{\pi^2 EI}{L_i^2} \tag{8-15}$$

Substituting Eq. (8-14) into Eq. (8-12) and rearranging gives

$$\frac{d^2y}{dx^2} + \frac{\pi^2\Phi_i}{L_i^2}y = \frac{(K_{pp}^i + K_{qp}^i)(x/L_i) - K_{pp}^i}{EI} \tag{8-16}$$

The general solution of Eq. (8-16) can be expressed as

$$y = A\sin\left(\frac{u_i}{L_i}x\right) + B\cos\left(\frac{u_i}{L_i}x\right) + \frac{L_i^2}{u_i^2 EI}\left[(K_{pp}^i + K_{qp}^i)\frac{x}{L_i} - K_{pp}^i\right] \tag{8-17}$$

where

$$u_i = \pi\sqrt{\Phi_i} \tag{8-18}$$

Substituting the boundary conditions $y = 0$ at $x = 0$ and $y = 0$ at $x = L_i$ yields values for the constants A and B:

$$A = -\frac{L_i^2}{u_i^2 EI}(K_{pp}^i \cot u_i + K_{qp}^i \csc u_i) \tag{8-19a}$$

and

$$B = \frac{L_i^2}{u_i^2 EI}K_{pp}^i \tag{8-19b}$$

Substituting these values of A and B into Eq. (8-17) yields

$$\frac{u_i^2 EI}{L_i^2}y = -(K_{pp}^i \cot u_i + K_{qp}^i \csc u_i)\sin\left(\frac{u_i}{L_i}x\right) + K_{pp}^i\cos\left(\frac{u_i}{L_i}x\right)$$
$$+ (K_{pp}^i + K_{qp}^i)\frac{x}{L_i} - K_{pp}^i \tag{8-20}$$

Differentiating Eq. (8-20) with respect to x in order to obtain an expression for the slope of the elastic curve and rearranging,

$$\frac{u_i^2 EI}{L_i}\frac{dy}{dx} = K_{pp}^i\left[1 - u_i \sin\left(\frac{u_i}{L_i}x\right) - u_i \cot u_i \cos\left(\frac{u_i}{L_i}x\right)\right] + K_{qp}^i\left[1 - u_i \csc u_i \cos\left(\frac{u_i}{L_i}x\right)\right] \tag{8-21}$$

Substituting the boundary condition $dy/dx = 0$ at $x = L_i$ into Eq. (8-21), the relationship between the restraining moments at the j- and k-ends of the beam element can be expressed as

$$K_{qp}^i = \frac{u_i - \sin u_i}{\sin u_i - u_i \cos u_i} K_{pp}^i \tag{8-22}$$

Substituting the additional boundary condition $dy/dx = 1$ at $x = 0$ along with Eq. (8-22) into Eq. (8-21), the value of the restraining moment at the j-end is given by

$$K_{pp}^i = \frac{u_i(\sin u_i - u_i \cos u_i)}{2(1 - \cos u_i) - u_i \sin u_i}\left(\frac{EI}{L_i}\right) \tag{8-23}$$

By letting

$$r_i = \frac{u_i(\sin u_i - u_i \cos u_i)}{2(1 - \cos u_i) - u_i \sin u_i} \tag{8-24a}$$

and

$$c_i = \frac{u_i - \sin u_i}{\sin u_i - u_i \cos u_i} \tag{8-24b}$$

a set of ***rotation functions*** for the beam element i is defined.

For the special case of *zero* axial load, for which the variable u_i becomes zero, by applying l'Hospital's rule, which states that in attempting to obtain the limit of the quotient

$$\frac{f(u_i)}{g(u_i)}$$

where both $f(u_i)$ and $g(u_i)$ approach zero as u_i approaches zero, one may instead consider the quotient

$$\frac{f'(u_i)}{g'(u_i)}$$

where f' and g' are first derivations of f and g with respect to u_i, Eqs. (8-24a) and (8-24b) reduce to

$$(r_i)_{\Phi_i=0} = 4 \tag{8-25a}$$

and

$$(c_i)_{\Phi_i=0} = \tfrac{1}{2} \tag{8-25b}$$

respectively. Thus, it is seen that for the case of zero axial load, Eqs. (8-24) reduce to the conventional stiffness and carry-over factors, respectively, for a prismatic member.

The end shear forces defined by Eq. (8-10) can now be redefined in terms of the ***rotation functions*** r_i and c_i. This is accomplished by substituting the expressions for the restraining moments in terms of r_i and c_i,

$$K^i_{pp} = r_i\left(\frac{EI}{L_i}\right) \tag{8-26a}$$

and

$$K^i_{qp} = c_i K^i_{pp} = c_i r_i\left(\frac{EI}{L_i}\right) \tag{8-26b}$$

into Eq. (8-10). The resulting expressions are given by

$$K^i_{rp} = -K^i_{sp} = r_i(1 + c_i)\left(\frac{EI}{L_i^2}\right) \tag{8-26c}$$

A unit rotation at the k-end induces restraining moments K^i_{qq} at end k and K^i_{pq} at end j. The following expressions for the restraining moments and the end shear forces for this condition in terms of the rotation functions r_i and c_i,

$$K^i_{pq} = c_i r_i\left(\frac{EI}{L_i}\right) \tag{8-27a}$$

$$K^i_{qq} = r_i\left(\frac{EI}{L_i}\right) \tag{8-27b}$$

and

$$K^i_{rq} = -K^i_{sq} = r_i(1 + c_i)\left(\frac{EI}{L_i^2}\right) \tag{8-27c}$$

can be obtained through the same procedure that was applied for the case of a unit rotation at end j. It is left as an exercise for the reader to verify Eqs. (8-27).

For *negative* values of Φ_i, corresponding to *tensile* axial forces, a variable v_i can be defined as

$$v_i = \pi\sqrt{\Phi_i} = i\pi\sqrt{|\Phi_i|} = iu_i \tag{8-28}$$

where $\boldsymbol{i}$ is the imaginary unit. Since v_i is a complex variable, the following trigonometric functions are defined:

$$\sin v_i = \frac{e^{iv_i} - e^{-iv_i}}{2i} = \frac{e^{-u_i} - e^{u_i}}{2i} \tag{8-29a}$$

and

$$\cos v_i = \frac{e^{iv_i} + e^{-iv_i}}{2} = \frac{e^{-u_i} + e^{u_i}}{2} \tag{8-29b}$$

The expressions for the rotation functions r_i and c_i can then be written as

$$r_i = \frac{iu_i\left[\dfrac{e^{-u_i} - e^{u_i}}{2i} - iu_i\left(\dfrac{e^{-u_i} + e^{u_i}}{2}\right)\right]}{2\left(1 - \dfrac{e^{-u_i} + e^{u_i}}{2}\right) - iu_i\left(\dfrac{e^{-u_i} - e^{u_i}}{2i}\right)} \tag{8-30a}$$

and

$$c_i = \frac{iu_i - \dfrac{e^{-u_i} - e^{u_i}}{2i}}{\dfrac{e^{-u_i} - e^{u_i}}{2i} - iu_i\left(\dfrac{e^{-u_i} + e^{u_i}}{2}\right)} \tag{8-30b}$$

Equations (8-30) reduce to

$$r_i = \frac{u_i\left[\dfrac{e^{-u_i} - e^{u_i}}{2} + u_i\left(\dfrac{e^{-u_i} + e^{u_i}}{2}\right)\right]}{2\left(1 - \dfrac{e^{-u_i} + e^{u_i}}{2}\right) - u_i\left(\dfrac{e^{-u_i} - e^{u_i}}{2}\right)} \tag{8-31a}$$

$$c_i = \frac{u_i + \dfrac{e^{-u_i} - e^{u_i}}{2}}{-\dfrac{e^{-u_i} - e^{u_i}}{2} - u_i\left(\dfrac{e^{-u_i} + e^{u_i}}{2}\right)} \tag{8-31b}$$

Substituting the hyperbolic functions

$$\sinh u_i = \frac{e^{u_i} - e^{-u_i}}{2} \tag{8-32a}$$

and

$$\cosh u_i = \frac{e^{u_i} + e^{-u_i}}{2} \tag{8-32b}$$

into Eqs. (8-31) and rearranging, the following expressions are obtained:

$$r_i = \frac{u_i(u_i \cosh u_i - \sinh u_i)}{2(1 - \cosh u_i) + u_i \sinh u_i} \tag{8-33a}$$

$$c_i = \frac{u_i - \sinh u_i}{\sinh u_i - u_i \cosh u_i} \tag{8-33b}$$

Thus, the values of the ***rotation functions*** for the case of ***tensile axial loads*** are obtained from Eq. (8-33) by considering the *absolute* value of Φ_i.

Figure 8-6 shows the functional relationship between r_i and c_i and values of Φ_i. Tabulated values of r_i and c_i are also listed in Appendix B.

8-3.2 Translation Function

The functions r_i and c_i are associated with a *joint rotation*. Another operation to consider is a *joint translation*, Fig. 8-4(a). The ends j and k of the prismatic beam element i are restrained against rotation, but end j is translated through a unit distance relative to end k. The translation operation may be alternatively regarded as the rotation of the ends j and k through angles of $1/L_i$ [Fig. 8-4(b)] followed by a clockwise rotation of the member through an angle of $1/L_i$ during which the restraining moments K^i_{pr} and K^i_{qr} remain unchanged. The axial load in Fig. 8-4(b) differs somewhat from the axial load in Fig. 8-4(a), but for a small angle of translation the difference may be neglected.

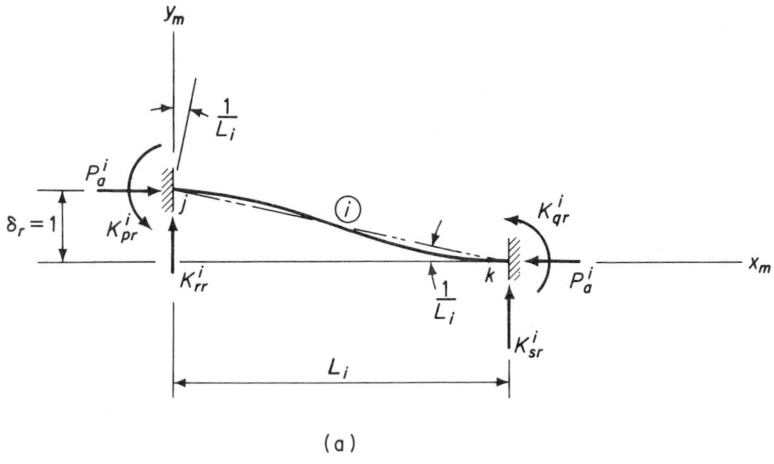

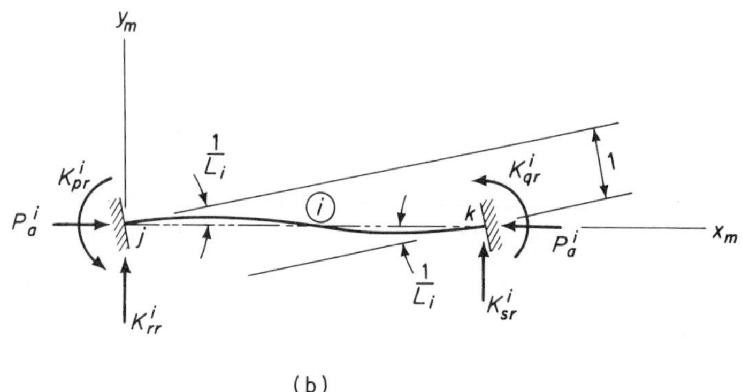

Fig. 8-4 Unit translation of end j, beam element i: (a) free body diagram, beam element i; (b) rigid body rotation of beam element i.

Taking moments about end k in Fig. 8-4(a), it is found that

$$K_{rr}^i = \frac{(K_{pr}^i + K_{qr}^i) - P_a^i(1)}{L_i} \tag{8-34a}$$

It is also obvious from equilibrium considerations of the free body in Fig. 8-4(a) that

$$K_{sr}^i = \frac{P_a^i(1) - (K_{pr}^i + K_{qr}^i)}{L_i} \tag{8-34b}$$

Due to the rotations indicated in Fig. 8-4(b),

$$K_{pr}^i = r_i\left(\frac{EI}{L_i}\right)\left(\frac{1}{L_i}\right) + r_i c_i\left(\frac{EI}{L_i}\right)\left(\frac{1}{L_i}\right) \tag{8-35a}$$

and

$$K_{qr}^i = r_i c_i\left(\frac{EI}{L_i}\right)\left(\frac{1}{L_i}\right) + r_i\left(\frac{EI}{L_i}\right)\left(\frac{1}{L_i}\right) \tag{8-35b}$$

Therefore, from Eqs. (8-35),

$$K^i_{pr} = K^i_{qr} = r_i(1 + c_i)\left(\frac{EI}{L_i^2}\right) \tag{8-36}$$

Substituting Eq. (8-36) into Eqs. (8-34) yields

$$K^i_{rr} = -K^i_{sr} = 2r_i(1 + c_i)\left(\frac{EI}{L_i^3}\right) - \frac{P^i_a}{L_i} \tag{8-37}$$

For the case of *zero* axial load, Eq. (8-37) reduces to

$$K^i_{rr} = -K^i_{sr} = 2r_i(1 + c_i)\left(\frac{EI}{L_i^3}\right) \tag{8-38}$$

The expressions for the end shear forces K^i_{rr} and K^i_{sr} for the case of *zero* axial load, Eq. (8-38), can be modified to apply to the case of applied axial load. Consider the equation

$$K^i_{rr} = -K^i_{sr} = t_i\left[2r_i(1 + c_i)\left(\frac{EI}{L_i^3}\right)\right] \tag{8-39}$$

where t_i is defined as a ***translation function***. In order to obtain an expression for t_i, the expressions for K^i_{rr} from Eqs. (8-37) and (8-39) are equated.

$$t_i\left[2r_i(1 + c_i)\left(\frac{EI}{L_i^3}\right)\right] = 2r_i(1 + c_i)\left(\frac{EI}{L_i^3}\right) - \frac{P^i_a}{L_i} \tag{8-40}$$

Substituting Eq. (8-14) into Eq. (8-40) and solving for t_i,

$$t_i = 1 - \frac{\pi^2\Phi_i}{2r_i(1 + c_i)} \tag{8-41}$$

A unit translation of the k-end induces restraining actions K^i_{qs} and K^i_{ss} at end k and K^i_{ps} and K^i_{rs} at end j. The following expressions for the restraining moments and the end shear forces for this condition in terms of the rotation and translation functions,

$$K^i_{ps} = K^i_{qs} = -r_i(1 + c_i)\left(\frac{EI}{L_i^2}\right) \tag{8-42a}$$

$$K^i_{rs} = -K^i_{ss} = -2t_ir_i(1 + c_i)\left(\frac{EI}{L_i^3}\right) \tag{8-42b}$$

can be obtained through the same procedure that was applied for the case of a unit translation of end j.

The relationship between t_i and values of Φ_i is illustrated in Fig. 8-6 and tabulated values of t_i are listed in Appendix B.

8-3.3 Member Stiffness Matrix

The member stiffness matrix as defined by Eq. (4-3c) can now be constructed for a prismatic beam element i subjected to an applied axial load P^i_a by utilizing Eqs. (8-26), (8-27), (8-36), (8-39), and (8-42):

$$\begin{array}{cc} & \begin{array}{cccc} \quad p \quad & \quad q \quad & \quad r \quad & \quad s \quad \end{array} \\ [\mathbf{K}]_i = EI & \left[\begin{array}{cccc} \dfrac{r_i}{L_i} & \dfrac{c_i r_i}{L_i} & \dfrac{r_i(1+c_i)}{L_i^2} & -\dfrac{r_i(1+c_i)}{L_i^2} \\ \dfrac{c_i r_i}{L_i} & \dfrac{r_i}{L_i} & \dfrac{r_i(1+c_i)}{L_i^2} & -\dfrac{r_i(1+c_i)}{L_i^2} \\ \dfrac{r_i(1+c_i)}{L_i^2} & \dfrac{r_i(1+c_i)}{L_i^2} & \dfrac{2t_i r_i(1+c_i)}{L_i^3} & -\dfrac{2t_i r_i(1+c_i)}{L_i^3} \\ -\dfrac{r_i(1+c_i)}{L_i^2} & -\dfrac{r_i(1+c_i)}{L_i^2} & -\dfrac{2t_i r_i(1+c_i)}{L_i^3} & \dfrac{2t_i r_i(1+c_i)}{L_i^3} \end{array}\right]_i \begin{array}{c} p \\ \\ q \\ \\ r \\ \\ s \end{array} \end{array} \tag{8-43}$$

Axial deformation of the beam element has been neglected in the derivations leading up to the development of Eq. (8-43). Expansion of Eq. (8-43) to include the effect of axial deformation follows along the lines of the development of the member stiffness matrix presented in Chapter 5. (See Prob. 8-7.)

8–4
Lateral Load Functions

The fixed end actions of a restrained member due to applied lateral loads on the member depend upon the value of the axial load on the member as well as upon the distribution and intensity of the lateral load. Two lateral loading conditions will be considered: (1) a uniform load distributed over a portion of the length of the member, and (2) a concentrated load applied anywhere along the span.

8-4.1 Uniform Load

Consider the prismatic beam element i shown in Fig. 8-5(a) loaded laterally with a partially distributed load $-w$ per unit length and axially with the compressive force P_a^i. The ends j and k are fixed against rotation and translation with moments FM_p^i and FM_q^i and shear forces FP_r^i and FP_s^i being induced.

Applying the differential equation of an elastic curve, Eq. (8-1), to the free body shown in Fig. 8-5(b),

$$EI\frac{d^2y}{dx^2} = M = -\left[FM_p^i - P_a^i(-y) - FP_r^i(x) + \frac{(-w)x^2}{2}\right] \tag{8-44}$$

The general solution of Eq. (8-44) can be expressed in the form

$$y = A\sin\left(\frac{u_i}{L_i}x\right) + B\cos\left(\frac{u_i}{L_i}x\right) - \frac{L_i^2}{u_i^2 EI}\left[FM_p^i + \frac{wL_i^2}{u_i^2} - \frac{wx}{2}\left(\frac{2FP_r^i}{w} + x\right)\right] \tag{8-45}$$

Differentiating Eq. (8-45) with respect to x yields

$$\frac{dy}{dx} = \frac{u_i}{L_i}A\cos\left(\frac{u_i}{L_i}\right) - \frac{u_i}{L_i}B\sin\left(\frac{u_i}{L_i}x\right) + \frac{L_i^2}{u_i^2 EI}(FP_r^i + wx) \tag{8-46}$$

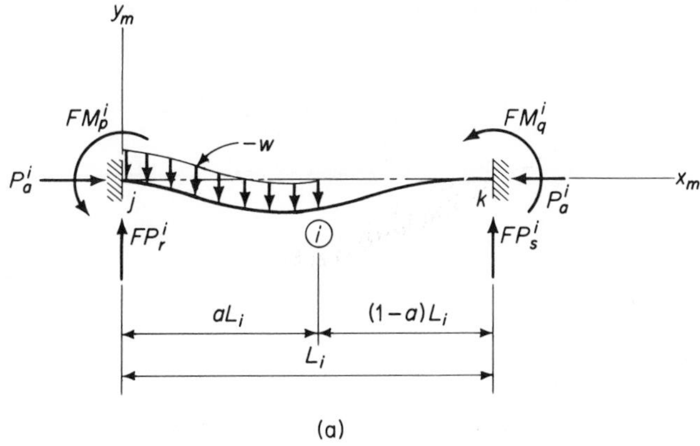

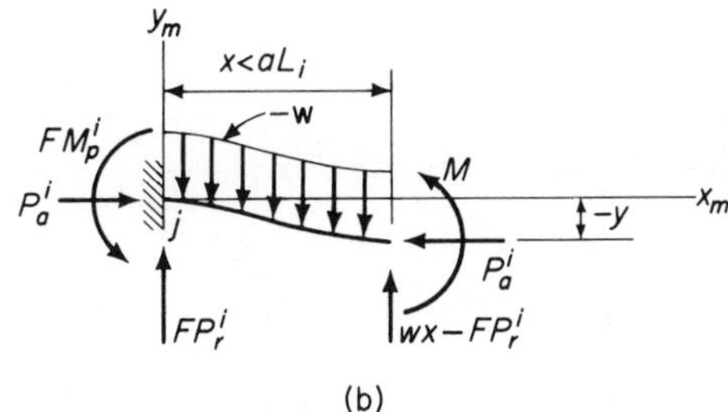

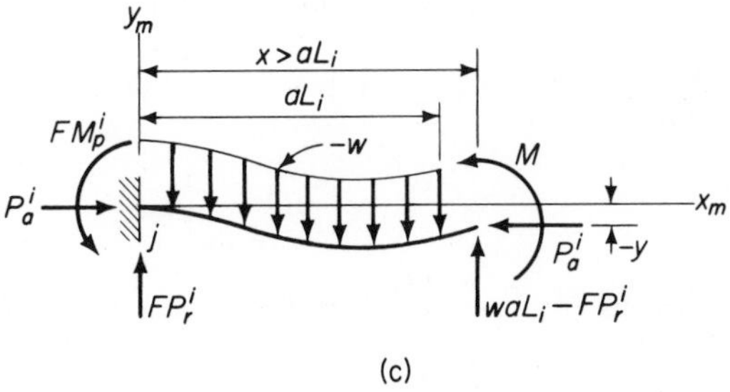

Fig. 8-5 Uniform lateral load partially distributed, beam element i: (a) free body diagram, beam element i; (b) free body diagram, x distance from j-end $< aL_i$; (c) free body diagram, x distance from j-end $> aL_i$.

Substituting the boundary conditions $y = 0$ and $dy/dx = 0$ at $x = 0$ yields

$$A = -\frac{L_i^3}{u_i^3 EI} FP_r^i \tag{8-47a}$$

and

$$B = \frac{L_i^2}{u_i^2 EI}\left(FM_p^i + \frac{wL_i^2}{u_i^2}\right) \tag{8-47b}$$

Inserting these values of A and B into Eqs. (8-45) and (8-46) and rearranging yields

$$\frac{u_i^2 EI}{L_i^2} y = \left(FM_p^i + \frac{wL_i^2}{u_i^2}\right)\cos\left(\frac{u_i}{L_i}x\right) - \frac{L_i(FP_r^i)}{u_i}\sin\left(\frac{u_i}{L_i}x\right) + \frac{wx}{2}\left(\frac{2FP_r^i}{w} + x\right) - FM_p^i - \frac{wL_i^2}{u_i^2} \qquad 0 \le x \le aL_i \tag{8-48}$$

and

$$\frac{u_i^2 EI}{L_i^2}\frac{dy}{dx} = -\frac{u_i}{L_i}\left(FM_p^i + \frac{wL_i^2}{u_i^2}\right)\sin\left(\frac{u_i}{L_i}x\right) - FP_r^i\cos\left(\frac{u_i}{L_i}x\right) + wx + FP_r^i \qquad 0 \le x \le aL_i \tag{8-49}$$

Applying Eq. (8-1) to the free body diagram shown in Fig. 8-5(c),

$$EI\frac{d^2y}{dx^2} = M = -\left[FM_p^i - P_a^i(-y) - FP_r^i(x) + (-w)aL_i\left(x - \frac{aL_i}{2}\right)\right] \tag{8-50}$$

The general solution of Eq. (8-50) can be expressed in the form

$$y = A\sin\left(\frac{u_i}{L_i}x\right) + B\cos\left(\frac{u_i}{L_i}x\right) - \frac{L_i^2}{u_i^2 EI}\left[FM_p^i + \frac{wa^2L_i^2}{2} - (FP_r^i + waL_i)x\right] \tag{8-51}$$

Differentiating Eq. (8-51) with respect to x yields

$$\frac{dy}{dx} = \frac{u_i}{L_i}A\cos\left(\frac{u_i}{L_i}x\right) - \frac{u_i}{L_i}B\sin\left(\frac{u_i}{L_i}x\right) + \frac{L_i^2}{u_i^2 EI}(FP_r^i + waL_i) \tag{8-52}$$

Substituting the boundary conditions $y = 0$ and $dy/dx = 0$ at $x = L_i$ yields

$$A = \frac{L_i^2}{u_i^2 EI}\left[\left(FM_p^i + \frac{wa^2L_i^2}{2}\right)\sin u_i - L_i(FP_r^i + waL_i)\left(\sin u_i + \frac{\cos u_i}{u_i}\right)\right] \tag{8-53a}$$

and

$$B = \frac{L_i^2}{u_i^2 EI}\left[\left(FM_p^i + \frac{wa^2L_i^2}{2}\right)\cos u_i - L_i(FP_r^i + waL_i)\left(\cos u_i - \frac{\sin u_i}{u_i}\right)\right] \tag{8-53b}$$

Inserting these values of A and B into Eqs. (8-51) and (8-52) and rearranging yields

$$\begin{aligned}\frac{u_i^2 EI}{L_i^2} y = {} & \\ & \left[\left(FM_p^i + \frac{wa^2L_i^2}{2}\right)\sin u_i - L_i(FP_r^i + waL_i)\left(\sin u_i + \frac{\cos u_i}{u_i}\right)\right]\sin\left(\frac{u_i}{L_i}x\right) \\ & + \left[\left(FM_p^i + \frac{wa^2L_i^2}{2}\right)\cos u_i - L_i(FP_r^i + waL_i)\left(\cos u_i - \frac{\sin u_i}{u_i}\right)\right]\cos\left(\frac{u_i}{L_i}x\right) \\ & + (FP_r^i + waL_i)x - FM_p^i - \frac{wa^2L_i^2}{2} \qquad aL_i \le x \le L_i\end{aligned} \tag{8-54}$$

and

$$\frac{u_i^2 EI}{L_i^2}\frac{dy}{dx} =$$

$$\frac{u_i}{L_i}\left[\left(FM_p^i + \frac{wa^2L_i^2}{2}\right)\sin u_i - L_i(FP_r^i + waL_i)\left(\sin u_i + \frac{\cos u_i}{u_i}\right)\right]\cos\left(\frac{u_i}{L_i}x\right)$$

$$-\frac{u_i}{L_i}\left[\left(FM_p^i + \frac{wa^2L_i^2}{2}\right)\cos u_i - L_i(FP_r^i + waL_i)\left(\cos u_i - \frac{\sin u_i}{u_i}\right)\right]\sin\left(\frac{u_i}{L_i}x\right)$$

$$+ FP_r^i + waL_i \qquad aL_i \le x \le L_i \tag{8-55}$$

Equating the expressions for y from Eqs. (8-48) and (8-54) and the expressions for dy/dx from Eqs. (8-49) and (8-55) for the two segment lengths aL_i and $(1 - a)L_i$ at $x = aL_i$ and introducing the relationship

$$FP_r^i = waL_i\left(\frac{a}{2} - 1\right) + \frac{FM_p^i + FM_q^i}{L_i} \tag{8-56}$$

obtained from a consideration of the equilibrium of the free body shown in Fig. 8-5(a), the following moment expressions are obtained:

$$FM_p^i = -wL_i^2\frac{\frac{a^2}{2}(1 - \cos u_i) + \left(\frac{\sin au_i}{u_i} - a\right)\left(\frac{\sin u_i}{u_i} - \cos u_i\right)}{2(1 - \cos u_i) - u_i \sin u_i}$$

$$+\frac{\left(\frac{1 - \cos au_i}{u_i}\right)\left(\frac{1 - \cos u_i}{u_i} - \sin u_i\right)}{2(1 - \cos u_i) - u_i \sin u_i} \tag{8-57}$$

and

$$FM_q^i = wL_i^2\frac{a\left(1 - \frac{a}{2}\right)(1 - \cos u_i) + \left(\frac{\sin au_i}{u_i} - a\right)\left(\frac{\sin u_i}{u_i} - \cos u_i\right)}{2(1 - \cos u_i) - u_i \sin u_i}$$

$$+\frac{\left(\frac{1 - \cos u_i}{u_i}\right)\left(\frac{1 - \cos au_i}{u_i} - \sin au_i\right)}{2(1 - \cos u_i) - u_i \sin u_i} \tag{8-58}$$

Applying l'Hospital's rule to Eqs. (8-57) and (8-58), as was done in Sec. 8-3.1 for the case of *zero* axial load, yields

$$FM_p^i = -wa^2L_i^2(\tfrac{1}{2} - \tfrac{2}{3}a + \tfrac{1}{4}a^2) \tag{8-59}$$

and

$$FM_q^i = wa^3L_i^2(\tfrac{1}{3} - \tfrac{1}{4}a) \tag{8-60}$$

which are equivalent to the moment expressions found in most structural engineering handbooks.

For the particular case wherein the uniform load is distributed over the entire length of the beam element i—i.e., $a = 1$—Eqs. (8-57) and (8-58) reduce to

$$FM_p^i = -FM_q^i = -\frac{wL_i^2}{u_i^2}\left[1 - \frac{u_i \sin u_i}{2(1 - \cos u_i)}\right] \tag{8-61}$$

or

$$FM^i_p = -FM^i_q = -m_i \frac{wL_i^2}{12} \tag{8-62}$$

where

$$m_i = \frac{12}{u_i^2}\left[1 - \frac{u_i \sin u_i}{2(1 - \cos u_i)}\right] \tag{8-63}$$

It can be shown by applying l'Hospital's rule that, when $\Phi_i = 0$, Eq. (8-61) reduces to

$$(FM^i_p)_{\Phi_i=0} = -(FM^i_q)_{\Phi_i=0} = -\frac{wL_i^2}{12} \tag{8-64}$$

The ***load function*** m_i is therefore the factor by which the standard fixed end moment due to a uniformly distributed load over the entire span, $-wL_i^2/12$ with zero axial force, is multiplied in order to obtain the fixed end moment when axial load is present.

For *negative* values of Φ_i corresponding to *tensile* axial loads, Eqs. (8-57) and (8-58) may be modified by introducing the complex variable v_i as was done in Sec. 8-3.1 to yield

$$FM^i_p = -wL_i^2\left[\frac{\frac{a^2}{2}(1 - \cosh u_i) + \left(\frac{\sinh au_i}{u_i} - a\right)\left(\frac{\sinh u_i}{u_i} - \cosh u_i\right)}{2(1 - \cosh u_i) + u_i \sinh u_i} - \frac{\left(\frac{1 - \cosh au_i}{u_i}\right)\left(\frac{1 - \cosh u_i}{u_i} + \sinh u_i\right)}{2(1 - \cosh u_i) + u_i \sinh u_i}\right] \tag{8-65}$$

and

$$FM^i_q = wL_i^2\left[\frac{a\left(1 - \frac{a}{2}\right)(1 - \cosh u_i) + \left(\frac{\sinh au_i}{u_i} - a\right)\left(\frac{\sinh u_i}{u_i} - \cosh u_i\right)}{2(1 - \cosh u_i) + u_i \sinh u_i} - \frac{\left(\frac{1 - \cosh u_i}{u_i}\right)\left(\frac{1 - \cosh au_i}{u_i} + \sinh au_i\right)}{2(1 - \cosh u_i) + u_i \sinh u_i}\right] \tag{8-66}$$

Equation (8-61) can also be modified in this same manner, thus yielding

$$FM^i_p = -FM^i_q = \frac{wL_i^2}{u_i^2}\left[1 + \frac{u_i \sinh u_i}{2(1 - \cosh u_i)}\right] \tag{8-67}$$

from which the following expression for the load function m_i results:

$$m_i = -\frac{12}{u_i^2}\left[1 + \frac{u_i \sinh u_i}{2(1 - \cosh u_i)}\right] \tag{8-68}$$

which is applicable for the case of a tensile axial load. Therefore, the fixed end moments for the condition of tensile axial load are obtained from Eqs. (8-65), (8-66), and (8-67) by considering the absolute value of Φ_i. The additional fixed end actions FP^i_r and FP^i_s can be found by considering equilibrium conditions of the beam element.

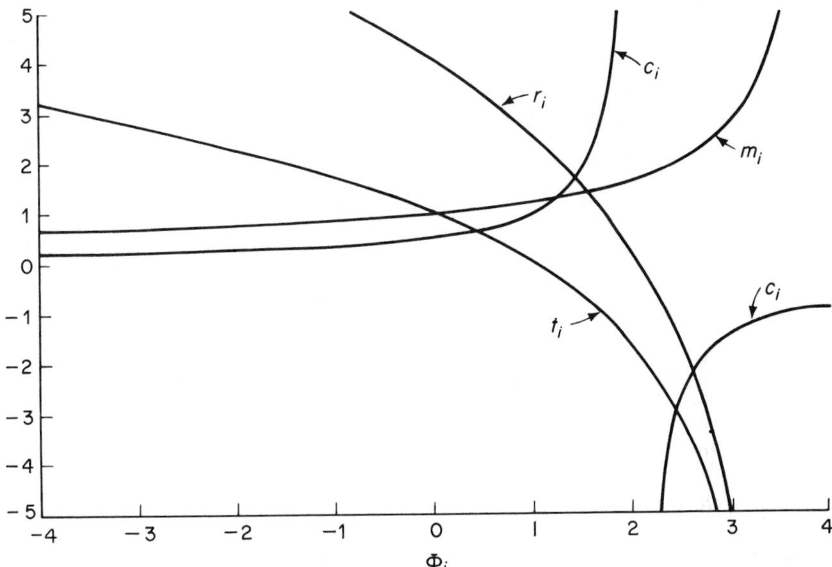

Fig. 8-6 Stability and load functions vs. Φ_i values.

The dependence of m_i upon values of Φ_i is illustrated in Fig. 8-6 and tabulated in Appendix B, and curves relating fixed end moments due to a partially distributed uniform lateral load to values of loaded-to-total span ratio a are shown in Figs. 8-7 and 8-8.

8-4.2 Concentrated Load

Consider now the prismatic beam element i shown in Fig. 8-9(a), loaded laterally with a concentrated load $-W$ and axially with the compressive force P_a^i. The ends j and k are fixed against rotation and translation with end moments FM_p^i and FM_q^i and end shear forces FP_r^i and FP_s^i thus induced.

Applying Eq. (8-1) to the free body shown in Fig. 8-9(b),

$$EI\frac{d^2y}{dx^2} = M = -[FM_p^i - P_a^i(-y) - FP_r^i(x)] \tag{8-69}$$

The general solution of Eq. (8-69) can be expressed as

$$y = A\sin\left(\frac{u_i}{L_i}x\right) + B\cos\left(\frac{u_i}{L_i}x\right) - \frac{L_i^2}{u_i^2EI}[FM_p^i - FP_r^i(x)] \tag{8-70}$$

Differentiating Eq. (8-70) with respect to x yields

$$\frac{dy}{dx} = \frac{u_i}{L_i}A\cos\left(\frac{u_i}{L_i}x\right) - \frac{u_i}{L_i}B\sin\left(\frac{u_i}{L_i}x\right) + \frac{L_i^2}{u_i^2EI}FP_r^i \tag{8-71}$$

Substituting the boundary conditions $y = 0$ and $dy/dx = 0$ at $x = 0$ yields

$$A = -\frac{L_i^3}{u_i^3EI}FP_r^i \tag{8-72a}$$

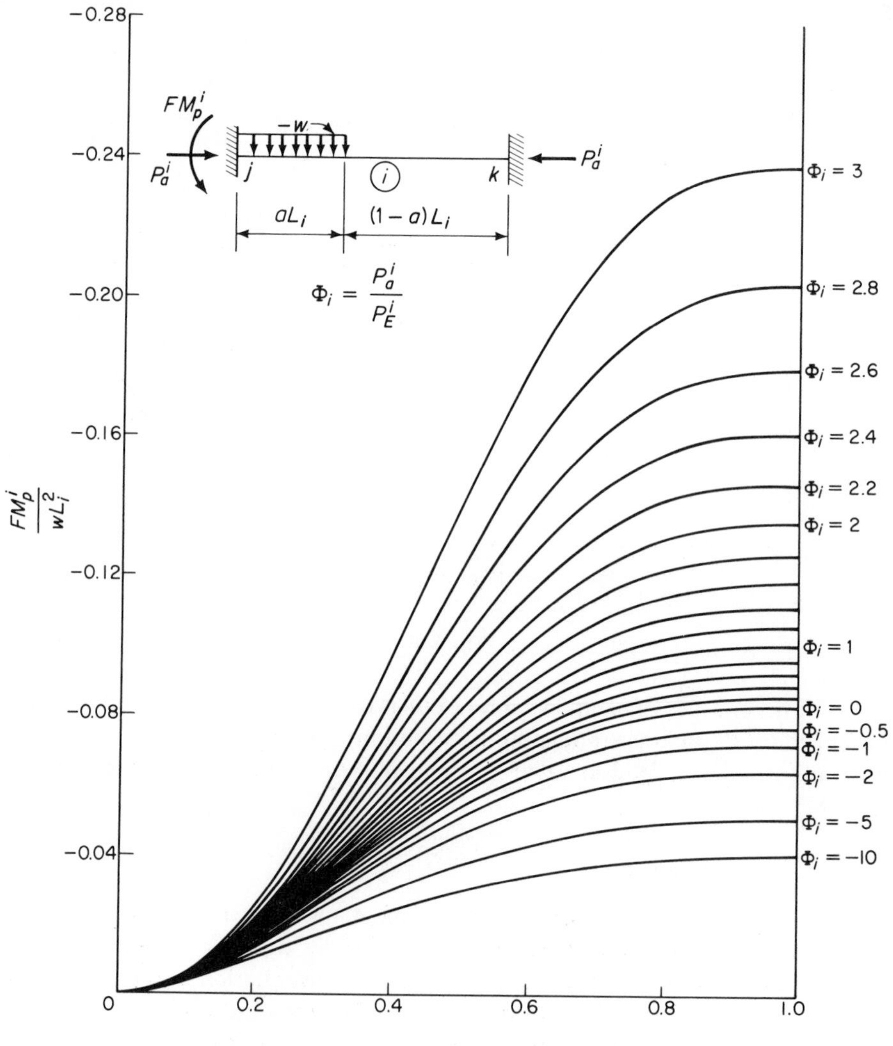

Fig. 8-7 Curves for fixed end moment at j-end due to partially distributed lateral load.

and

$$B = \frac{L_i^2}{u_i^2 EI} FM_p^i \tag{8-72b}$$

Inserting these values of A and B into Eqs. (8-70) and (8-71) and rearranging yields

$$\frac{u_i^2 EI}{L_i^2} y = FM_p^i \cos\left(\frac{u_i}{L_i} x\right) - \frac{L_i(FP_r^i)}{u_i} \sin\left(\frac{u_i}{L_i} x\right) + FP_r^i(x) - FM_p^i$$

$$0 \leq x \leq aL_i \tag{8-73}$$

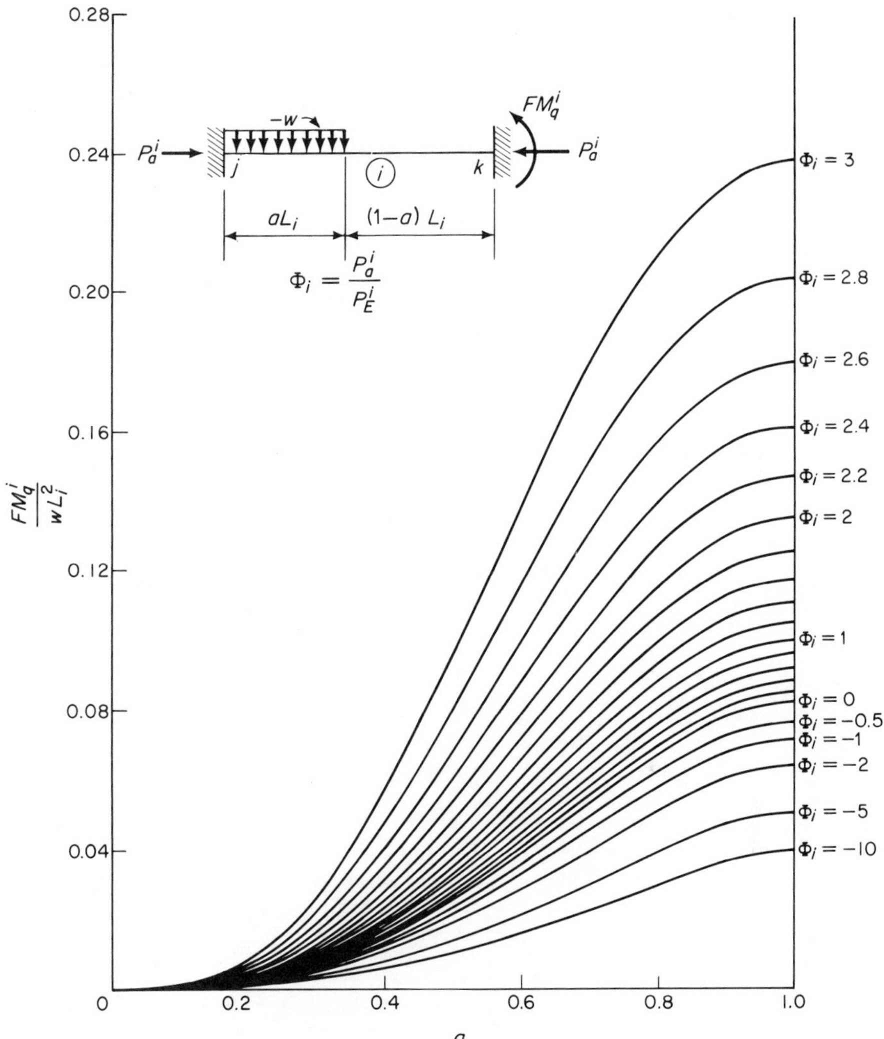

Fig. 8-8 Curves for fixed end moment at k-end due to partially distributed lateral load.

and

$$\frac{u_i^2 EI}{L_i^2}\frac{dy}{dx} = -\frac{u_i FM_p^i}{L_i}\sin\left(\frac{u_i}{L_i}x\right) - FP_r^i\cos\left(\frac{u_i}{L_i}x\right) + FP_r^i$$

$$0 \leq x \leq aL_i \qquad \textbf{(8-74)}$$

The differential equation of an elastic curve applied to the free body shown in Fig. 8-9(c) yields

$$EI\frac{d^2y}{dx^2} = M = -[FM_p^i - P_a^i(-y) - FP_r^i(x) + (-W)(x - aL_i)] \qquad \textbf{(8-75)}$$

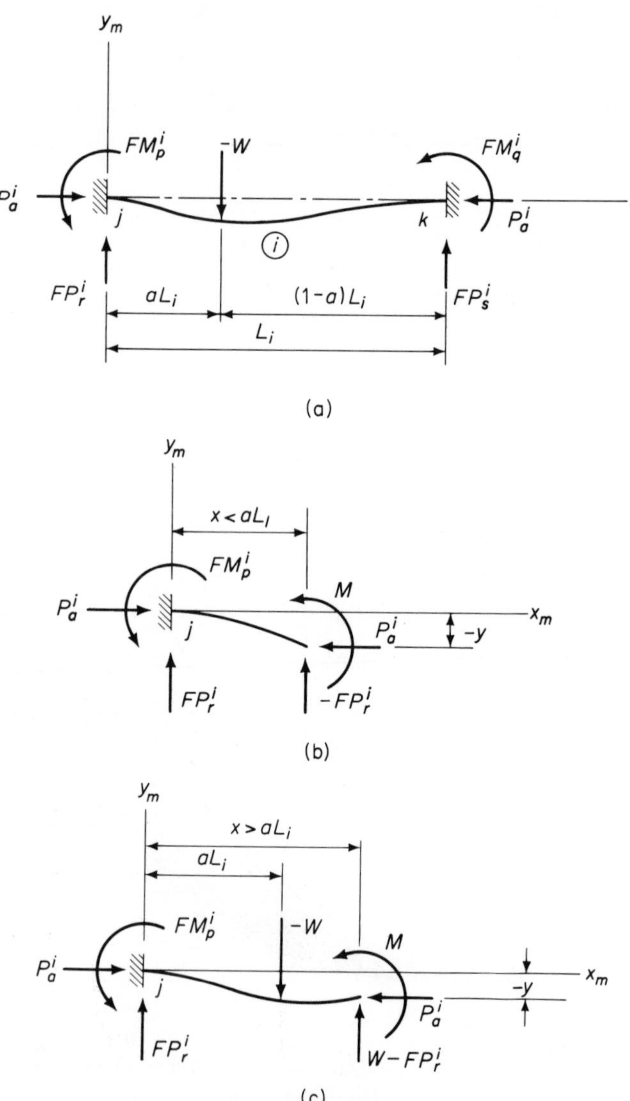

Fig. 8-9 Concentrated lateral load, beam element i: (a) free body diagram, beam element i; (b) free body diagram, x distance from j-end $< aL_i$; (c) free body diagram, x distance from j-end $> aL_i$.

The general solution of Eq. (8-75) can be expressed in the form

$$y = A \sin\left(\frac{u_i}{L_i}x\right) + B \cos\left(\frac{u_i}{L_i}x\right) - \frac{L_i^2}{u_i^2 EI}[FM_p^i + WaL_i - (FP_r^i + W)x] \tag{8-76}$$

Differentiating Eq. (8-76) with respect to x yields

$$\frac{dy}{dx} = \frac{u_i}{L_i} A \cos\left(\frac{u_i}{L_i}x\right) - \frac{u_i}{L_i} B \sin\left(\frac{u_i}{L_i}x\right) + \frac{L_i^2}{u_i^2 EI}(FP_r^i + W) \tag{8-77}$$

Equating the expressions for y from Eqs. (8-73) and (8-76) and the expressions for dy/dx from Eqs. (8-74) and (8-77) for the two segment lengths aL_i and $(1 - a)L_i$ at $x = aL_i$ yields

$$A = -\frac{L_i^3}{u_i^3 EI}(FP_r^i + W \cos au_i) \tag{8-78a}$$

and

$$B = \frac{L_i^2}{u_i^2 EI}\left(FM_p^i + \frac{L_i W}{u_i} \sin au_i\right) \tag{8-78b}$$

Inserting these values of A and B into Eqs. (8-76) and (8-77) and rearranging yields

$$\begin{aligned}\frac{u_i^2 EI}{L_i^2} y = &\left(FM_p^i + \frac{L_i W}{u_i} \sin au_i\right) \cos\left(\frac{u_i}{L_i}x\right) \\ &- \frac{L_i}{u_i}(FP_r^i + W \cos au_i) \sin\left(\frac{u_i}{L_i}x\right) \\ &+ (FP_r^i + W)x - FM_p^i - WaL_i \qquad aL_i \le x \le L_i\end{aligned} \tag{8-79}$$

and

$$\begin{aligned}\frac{u_i^2 EI}{L_i^2}\frac{dy}{dx} = &-\frac{u_i}{L_i}\left(FM_p^i + \frac{L_i W}{u_i} \sin au_i\right) \sin\left(\frac{u_i}{L_i}x\right) \\ &- (FP_r^i + W \cos au_i) \cos\left(\frac{u_i}{L_i}x\right) + FP_r^i + W \qquad aL_i \le x \le L_i\end{aligned} \tag{8-80}$$

Finally, by inserting the boundary conditions $y = 0$ and $dy/dx = 0$ at $x = L_i$ and eliminating FP_r^i between Eqs. (8-79) and (8-80), the following expression for FM_p^i is obtained:

$$\begin{aligned}FM_p^i = -WL_i\Bigg[&\frac{a(1 - \cos u_i) - (1 - \cos au_i)\left(\dfrac{\sin u_i}{u_i} - \cos u_i\right)}{2(1 - \cos u_i) - u_i \sin u_i} \\ &+ \frac{\left(\dfrac{1 - \cos u_i}{u_i} - \sin u_i\right) \sin au_i}{2(1 - \cos u_i) - u_i \sin u_i}\Bigg]\end{aligned} \tag{8-81}$$

Applying l'Hospital's rule to Eq. (8-81) for the case of *zero* axial load yields

$$FM_p^i = WaL_i(a^2 - 1) \tag{8-82}$$

which is equivalent to the expression commonly found in structural engineering handbooks.

For *negative* values of Φ_i, Eq. (8-81) may be modified by introducing the complex variable v_i to yield

$$FM_p^i = -WL_i\left[\frac{a(1-\cosh u_i) - (1-\cosh au_i)\left(\dfrac{\sinh u_i}{u_i} - \cosh u_i\right)}{2(1-\cosh u_i) + u_i \sinh u_i} + \frac{\left(\dfrac{1-\cosh u_i}{u_i} + \sinh u_i\right)\sinh au_i}{2(1-\cosh u_i) + u_i \sinh u_i}\right] \tag{8-83}$$

which is applicable for the case of a *tensile* axial load.

The fixed end moments due to a series of concentrated loads may be obtained by the method of superposition. The shear forces FP_r^i and FP_s^i can be obtained by considering equilibrium conditions of the beam element.

Curves relating fixed end moments due to a concentrated lateral load to values of span ratio a are shown in Fig. 8-10.

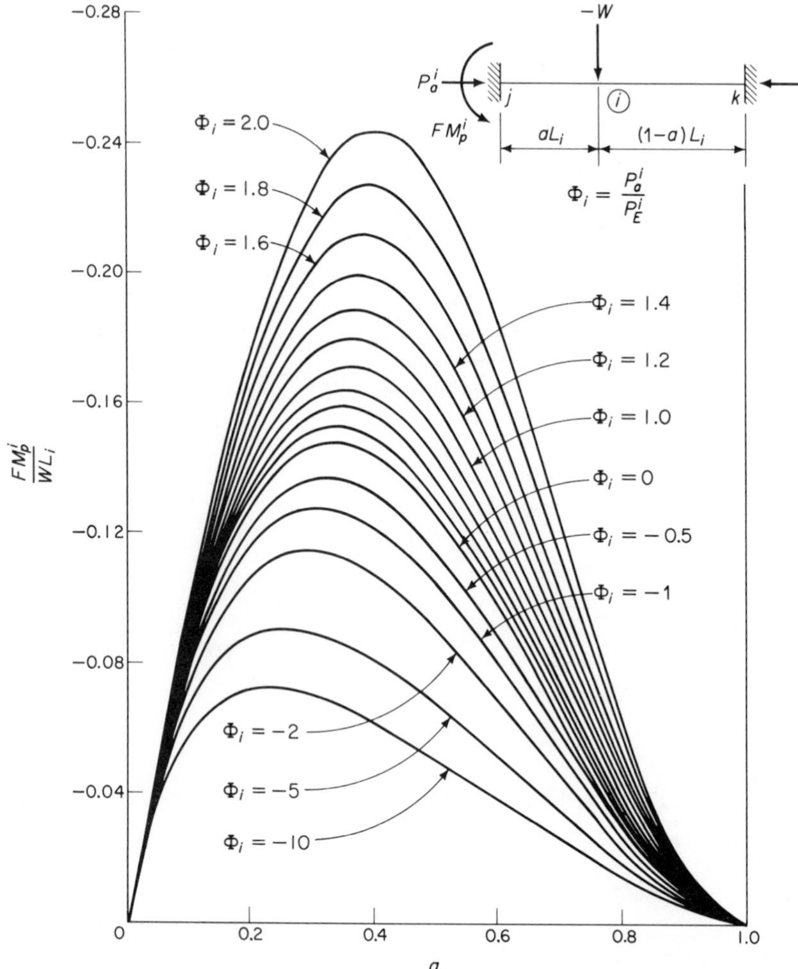

Fig. 8-10 Curves for fixed end moment due to concentrated lateral load.

8–5 Analysis of Planar Frames

The derivations of certain stability and load functions which can be utilized to determine the effect of axial forces upon the flexure of a planar frame have been presented in line with the method of analysis outlined in Chapter 4. The following example is carried out in step-by-step fashion in order to illustrate the effect of stability upon the structural behavior of a rigid frame.

Example 8-1. A planar orthogonal frame is loaded as shown in Fig. 8-11(a). The free body diagram for each member of the frame showing the final end actions obtained without considering the effect of the applied axial loads of 200 k upon the flexure of the frame is shown in Fig. 8-11(b). In the ensuing analysis, both the applied axial loads and the axial forces resulting from frame action shown in Fig. 8-11(b) are considered; however, in most cases it is not necessary to consider the latter. The ratios of these resulting axial forces to the corresponding pinned member Euler loads—i.e., the $\mathbf{\Phi}_i$ values for the resulting axial forces—are extremely small and will have little effect upon the flexure. This fact will become obvious from the calculation of the stability and load functions for member 2.

JOINT DISPLACEMENT MATRIX

The first step in developing the analysis of the structural system is to identify the j- and k-ends of each member and to identify and label the possible joint displacements. This is done in Fig. 8-12. Referring to Fig. 8-12, the complete joint displacement matrix $[\mathbf{\Delta}_c]$ is written as

$$[\mathbf{\Delta}_c] = \begin{bmatrix} \theta_1 \\ \theta_2 \\ \delta_3 \\ \hdashline \delta_4 \\ \delta_5 \\ \theta_6 \\ \delta_7 \\ \theta_8 \\ \delta_9 \end{bmatrix} = \begin{bmatrix} [\mathbf{\Delta}_u] \\ \hdashline [\mathbf{\Delta}_r] \end{bmatrix} \tag{8-84}$$

which is partitioned as indicated with respect to the restrained and unrestrained displacements.

STABILITY FUNCTIONS

The next step in the analysis is the computation of the stability functions for each member.

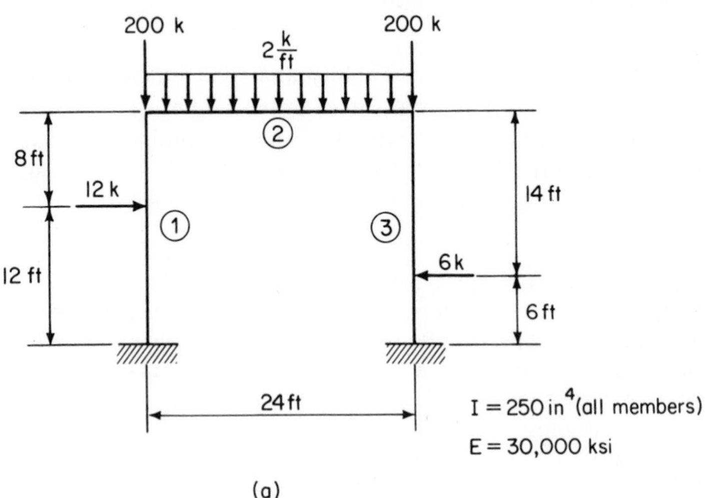

(a)

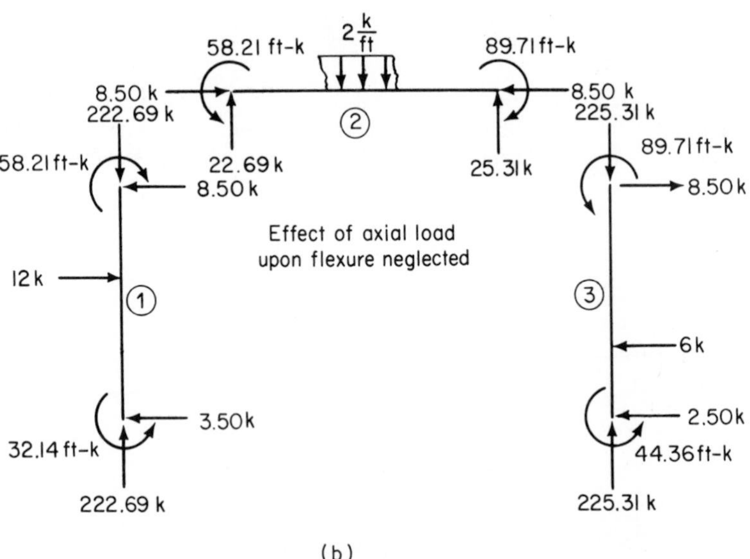

(b)

Fig. 8-11 Example 8-1: Indeterminate rigid frame: (a) frame geometry and loading condition; (b) free body diagram showing final end actions.

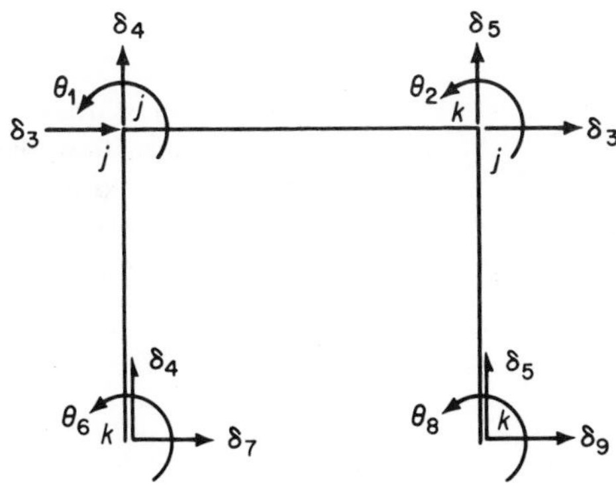

Fig. 8-12 Example 8-1: Identification of possible joint displacements and *j*- and *k*-ends.

Member 1

$$P_a^1 = 222.69 \text{ k} \qquad [\text{Fig. 8-11(b)}]$$

$$P_E^1 = \frac{\pi^2(30{,}000)(250)}{(20 \times 12)^2} = 1285 \text{ k}$$

$$\Phi_1 = \frac{222.69}{1285} = 0.173$$

$$u_1 = 1.3069 \qquad [\text{Eq. (8-18)}]$$

$$r_1 = 3.7671 \qquad [\text{Eq. (8-24a) or Appendix B}]$$

$$c_1 = 0.5469 \qquad [\text{Eq. (8-24b) or Appendix B}]$$

$$t_1 = 0.8535 \qquad [\text{Eq. (8-41) or Appendix B}]$$

Member 2

$$P_a^2 = 8.50 \text{ k} \qquad [\text{Fig. 8-11(b)}]$$

$$P_E^2 = \frac{\pi^2(30{,}000)(250)}{(24 \times 12)^2} = 892 \text{ k}$$

$$\Phi_2 = \frac{8.50}{892} = 0.0095$$

$$u_2 = 0.3062$$

$$r_2 = 3.9875$$

$$c_2 = 0.5024$$

$$t_2 = 0.9922$$

Member 3

$$P_a^3 = 225.31 \text{ k} \qquad [\text{Fig. 8-11(b)}]$$

$$P_E^3 = \frac{\pi^2(30{,}000)(250)}{(20 \times 12)^2} = 1285 \text{ k}$$

$$\Phi_3 = \frac{225.31}{1285} = 0.175$$

$$u_3 = 1.3132$$

$$r_3 = 3.7643$$

$$c_3 = 0.5475$$

$$t_3 = 0.8517$$

MEMBER STIFFNESS MATRICES

Substituting into Expression (8-43), which defines the member stiffness matrix for a member with a constant moment of inertia neglecting axial deformation, the member stiffness matrix for each member of the frame can be established. The rows and columns are labeled corresponding to the labeling of the joint displacements of the system (Fig. 8-12) to aid in the identification of the elements of the various matrices.

Member 1

$$[\mathbf{K}]_1 = EI \begin{array}{c} \begin{array}{cccc} 1 & 6 & 3 & 7 \end{array} \\ \left[\begin{array}{cccc} \dfrac{r_1}{L_1} & \dfrac{c_1 r_1}{L_1} & \dfrac{r_1(1+c_1)}{L_1^2} & -\dfrac{r_1(1+c_1)}{L_1^2} \\ \dfrac{c_1 r_1}{L^1} & \dfrac{r_1}{L_1} & \dfrac{r_1(1+c_1)}{L_1^2} & -\dfrac{r_1(1+c_1)}{L_1^2} \\ \dfrac{r_1(1+c_1)}{L_1^2} & \dfrac{r_1(1+c_1)}{L_1^2} & \dfrac{2t_1 r_1(1+c_1)}{L_1^3} & -\dfrac{2t_1 r_1(1+c_1)}{L_1^3} \\ -\dfrac{r_1(1+c_1)}{L_1^2} & -\dfrac{r_1(1+c_1)}{L_1^2} & -\dfrac{2t_1 r_1(1+c_1)}{L_1^3} & \dfrac{2t_1 r_1(1+c_1)}{L_1^3} \end{array}\right]_1 \end{array} \begin{array}{c} \\ 1 \\ 6 \\ 3 \\ 7 \end{array} \tag{8-85a}$$

or

$$[\mathbf{K}]_1 = EI \times 10^{-2} \begin{array}{c} \begin{array}{cccc} 1 & 6 & 3 & 7 \end{array} \\ \left[\begin{array}{rrrr} 18.8355 & 10.3011 & 1.4568 & -1.4568 \\ 10.3011 & 18.8355 & 1.4568 & -1.4568 \\ 1.4568 & 1.4568 & 0.1243 & -0.1243 \\ -1.4568 & -1.4568 & -0.1243 & 0.1243 \end{array}\right]_1 \end{array} \begin{array}{c} \\ 1 \\ 6 \\ 3 \\ 7 \end{array} \tag{8-85b}$$

Member 2

$$[\mathbf{K}]_2 = EI \begin{array}{c} \begin{array}{cccc} 1 & 2 & 4 & 5 \end{array} \\ \left[\begin{array}{cccc} \dfrac{r_2}{L_2} & \dfrac{c_2 r_2}{L_2} & \dfrac{r_2(1+c_2)}{L_2^2} & -\dfrac{r_2(1+c_2)}{L_2^2} \\ \dfrac{c_2 r_2}{L_2} & \dfrac{r_2}{L_2} & \dfrac{r_2(1+c_2)}{L_2^2} & -\dfrac{r_2(1+c_2)}{L_2^2} \\ \dfrac{r_2(1+c_2)}{L_2^2} & \dfrac{r_2(1+c_2)}{L_2^2} & \dfrac{2t_2 r_2(1+c_2)}{L_2^3} & -\dfrac{2t_2 r_2(1+c_2)}{L_2^3} \\ -\dfrac{r_2(1+c_2)}{L_2^2} & -\dfrac{r_2(1+c_2)}{L_2^2} & -\dfrac{2t_2 r_2(1+c_2)}{L_2^3} & \dfrac{2t_2 r_2(1+c_2)}{L_2^3} \end{array}\right]_2 \end{array} \begin{array}{c} \\ 1 \\ 2 \\ 4 \\ 5 \end{array} \tag{8-86a}$$

or

$$[\mathbf{K}]_2 = EI \times 10^{-2} \begin{array}{c} \begin{array}{cccc} 1 & 2 & 4 & 5 \end{array} \\ \left[\begin{array}{rrrr} 16.6146 & 8.3472 & 1.0401 & -1.0401 \\ 8.3472 & 16.6146 & 1.0401 & -1.0401 \\ 1.0401 & 1.0401 & 0.0860 & -0.0860 \\ -1.0401 & -1.0401 & -0.0860 & 0.0860 \end{array}\right]_2 \end{array} \begin{array}{c} \\ 1 \\ 2 \\ 4 \\ 5 \end{array} \tag{8-86b}$$

Member 3

$$[\mathbf{K}]_3 = EI \begin{bmatrix} \frac{r_3}{L_3} & \frac{c_3 r_3}{L_3} & \frac{r_3(1+c_3)}{L_3^2} & -\frac{r_3(1+c_3)}{L_3^2} \\ \frac{c_3 r_3}{L_3} & \frac{r_3}{L_3} & \frac{r_3(1+c_3)}{L_3^2} & -\frac{r_3(1+c_3)}{L_3^2} \\ \frac{r_3(1+c_3)}{L_3^2} & \frac{r_3(1+c_3)}{L_3^2} & \frac{2t_3 r_3(1+c_3)}{L_3^3} & -\frac{2t_3 r_3(1+c_3)}{L_3^3} \\ -\frac{r_3(1+c_3)}{L_3^2} & -\frac{r_3(1+c_3)}{L_3^2} & -\frac{2t_3 r_3(1+c_3)}{L_3^3} & \frac{2t_3 r_3(1+c_3)}{L_3^3} \end{bmatrix}_3 \begin{matrix} 2 \\ 8 \\ 3 \\ 9 \end{matrix} \quad \text{(columns 2, 8, 3, 9)}$$

(8-87a)

or

$$[\mathbf{K}]_3 = EI \times 10^{-2} \begin{bmatrix} 18.8215 & 10.3048 & 1.4563 & -1.4563 \\ 10.3048 & 18.8215 & 1.4563 & -1.4563 \\ 1.4563 & 1.4563 & 0.1240 & -0.1240 \\ -1.4563 & -1.4563 & -0.1240 & 0.1240 \end{bmatrix}_3 \begin{matrix} 2 \\ 8 \\ 3 \\ 9 \end{matrix} \quad \text{(columns 2, 8, 3, 9)} \tag{8-87b}$$

STRUCTURE STIFFNESS MATRIX

Superimposing the various member stiffness matrices, the complete structure stiffness matrix $[\mathbf{S}_c]$ is developed in Eq. (8-88) on page 368. Partitioning this matrix with respect to the restrained and unrestrained joint displacements yields

$$[\mathbf{S}_{uu}] = EI \times 10^{-2} \begin{bmatrix} 35.4501 & 8.3472 & 1.4568 \\ 8.3472 & 35.4361 & 1.4563 \\ 1.4568 & 1.4563 & 0.2483 \end{bmatrix} \begin{matrix} 1 \\ 2 \\ 3 \end{matrix} \quad \text{(columns 1, 2, 3)} \tag{8-89a}$$

Inverting this matrix yields

$$[\mathbf{S}_{uu}]^{-1} = \frac{1}{EI} \times 10^{2} \begin{bmatrix} 0.0372 & 0.0003 & -0.2197 \\ 0.0003 & 0.0372 & -0.2197 \\ -0.2197 & -0.2197 & 6.6048 \end{bmatrix} \begin{matrix} 1 \\ 2 \\ 3 \end{matrix} \quad \text{(columns 1, 2, 3)} \tag{8-89b}$$

JOINT LOAD MATRIX

The fixed end actions for each element of the frame due to the loading condition shown in Fig. 8-11(a) are computed:

Member 1

$$FM_1^1 = -35.76 \text{ ft-k}$$
$$FM_6^1 = +24.00 \text{ ft-k}$$

[Eq. (8-81) or Fig. 8-10]

$$
[\mathbf{S}_c] = EI \times 10^{-2}
\begin{array}{c}
\begin{array}{ccc:cccccc}
\quad 1 \quad & \quad 2 \quad & \quad 3 \quad & \quad 4 \quad & \quad 5 \quad & \quad 6 \quad & \quad 7 \quad & \quad 8 \quad & \quad 9 \quad
\end{array} \\
\left[\begin{array}{ccc:cccccc}
35.4501 & 8.3472 & 1.4568 & 1.0401 & -1.0401 & 10.3011 & -1.4568 & 0 & 0 \\
8.3472 & 35.4361 & 1.4563 & 1.0401 & -1.0401 & 0 & 0 & 10.3048 & -1.4563 \\
1.4568 & 1.4563 & 0.2483 & 0 & 0 & 1.4568 & -0.1243 & 1.4563 & -0.1240 \\
\hdashline
1.0401 & 1.0401 & 0 & 0.0860 & -0.0860 & 0 & 0 & 0 & 0 \\
-1.0401 & -1.0401 & 0 & -0.0860 & 0.0860 & 0 & 0 & 0 & 0 \\
10.3011 & 0 & 1.4568 & 0 & 0 & 18.8355 & -1.4568 & 0 & 0 \\
-1.4568 & 0 & -0.1243 & 0 & 0 & -1.4568 & 0.1243 & 0 & 0 \\
0 & 10.3048 & 1.4563 & 0 & 0 & 0 & 0 & 18.8215 & -1.4563 \\
0 & -1.4563 & -0.1240 & 0 & 0 & 0 & 0 & -1.4563 & 0.1240
\end{array}\right]
\end{array}
\begin{array}{c}
\\ 1 \\ 2 \\ 3 \\ 4 \\ 5 \\ 6 \\ 7 \\ 8 \\ 9
\end{array}
\qquad \textbf{(8-88)}
$$

$$FP_3^1 = \frac{-(12)(12) - 35.76 + 24.00}{20} = -7.79 \text{ k}$$

$$FP_7^1 = \frac{-(8)(12) - 24.00 + 35.76}{20} = -4.21 \text{ k}$$

Member 2

$$m_2 = 1.0015 \qquad \text{[Eq. (8-63) or Appendix B]}$$

$$FM_1^2 = -FM_2^2 = -\frac{(1.0015)(-2)(24)^2}{12} = 96.14 \text{ ft-k}$$

$$FP_4^2 = FP_5^2 = \frac{2(24)}{2} = 24.00 \text{ k}$$

Member 3

$$\left.\begin{aligned} FM_2^3 &= +8.04 \text{ ft-k} \\ FM_8^3 &= -18.00 \text{ ft-k} \end{aligned}\right\} \quad \text{[Eq. (8-81) or Fig. 8-10]}$$

$$FP_3^3 = \frac{(6)(6) + 8.04 - 18.00}{20} = 1.30 \text{ k}$$

$$FP_9^3 = \frac{(14)(6) + 18.00 - 8.04}{20} = 4.70 \text{ k}$$

Transforming these fixed end actions into equivalent joint loads, the total joint loads acting on the restrained structure are as shown in Fig. 8-13. Labeling these joint loads to conform to the labeling of the corresponding possible joint displacement, the complete joint load matrix is written as

$$[\mathbf{JL}_c] = \begin{bmatrix} JL_1 \\ JL_2 \\ JL_3 \\ \hline JL_4 \\ JL_5 \\ JL_6 \\ JL_7 \\ JL_8 \\ JL_9 \end{bmatrix} = \begin{bmatrix} -60.38 \\ 88.10 \\ 6.49 \\ \hline -224.00 \\ -224.00 \\ -24.00 \\ 4.21 \\ 18.00 \\ -4.70 \end{bmatrix} = \begin{bmatrix} [\mathbf{JL}_u] \\ \hline [\mathbf{JL}_r] \end{bmatrix} \tag{8-90}$$

which is partitioned as indicated with respect to the restrained and unrestrained displacements.

SOLUTION

Making the proper substitutions into Eq. (4-37), which defines the unknown joint displacements—i.e.,

$$[\boldsymbol{\Delta}_u] = [\mathbf{S}_{uu}]^{-1}[\mathbf{JL}_u] \tag{4-37}$$

yields

$$\begin{bmatrix} \theta_1 \\ \theta_2 \\ \delta_3 \end{bmatrix} = \frac{1}{EI} \times 10^2 \begin{bmatrix} 0.0372 & 0.0003 & -0.2197 \\ 0.0003 & 0.0372 & -0.2197 \\ -0.2197 & -0.2197 & 6.6048 \end{bmatrix} \begin{bmatrix} -60.38 \\ 88.10 \\ 6.49 \end{bmatrix} \tag{8-91a}$$

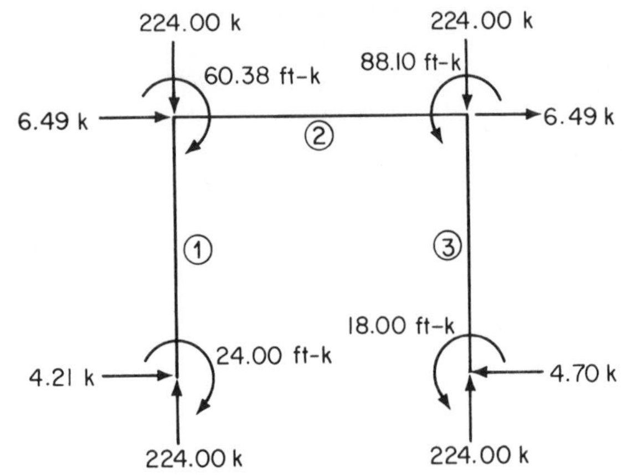

Fig. 8-13 Example 8-1: Total joint loads.

Therefore,

$$[\Delta_u] = \begin{bmatrix} \theta_1 \\ \theta_2 \\ \delta_3 \end{bmatrix} = \frac{1}{EI} \times 10^2 \begin{bmatrix} -3.6456 \\ 1.8334 \\ 36.7751 \end{bmatrix} = \begin{bmatrix} -7.0000 \times 10^{-3} \text{ rad} \\ 3.5201 \times 10^{-3} \text{ rad} \\ 0.8473 \text{ in.} \end{bmatrix} \tag{8-91b}$$

FINAL END ACTIONS

Writing Eqs. (4-42) for each member,

$$[\mathbf{M}]_i = [\mathbf{K}]_i[\delta]_i + [\mathbf{FM}]_i \tag{4-42}$$

The final end actions developed at the ends of each member are obtained as shown in Eqs. (8-92).

The free body diagram for each member showing these final end actions is given in Fig. 8-14 and the deflected frame is shown in Fig. 8-15. A comparison of final moment diagrams with and without inclusion of axial load effects is shown in Fig. 8-16.

The moment diagrams shown in Fig. 8-16 considering axial load effects can be obtained only after determining the deflection curve for the individual members. The lateral deflection of the vertical members is obtained from Eqs. (8-73) and (8-79) by substituting the proper values of end moment and end shear at the base. The ordinates of the moment curves are then computed from Eqs. (8-69) and (8-75). It is not necessary to compute the deflection of the horizontal member in order to obtain the moment diagram since there is no applied axial load.

It can be noted by comparing the resulting axial forces shown in Fig. 8-14 with those shown in Fig. 8-11(b) that there is no need to reanalyze the frame by considering the effect of the final set of resulting axial forces. It is obvious that the slight change in the resulting axial forces would not modify the final end actions. In fact, as previously stated, in most cases a frame can be analyzed considering only the effect of ***applied*** axial forces upon the flexure.

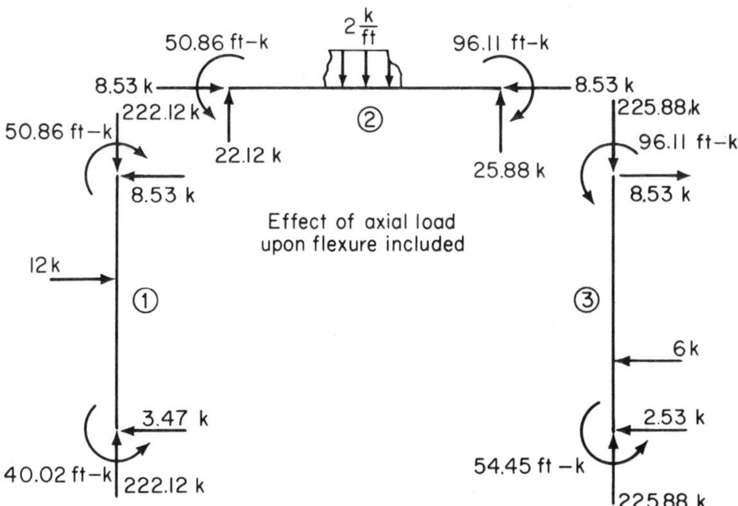

Fig. 8-14 Example 8-1: Free body diagram showing final end actions.

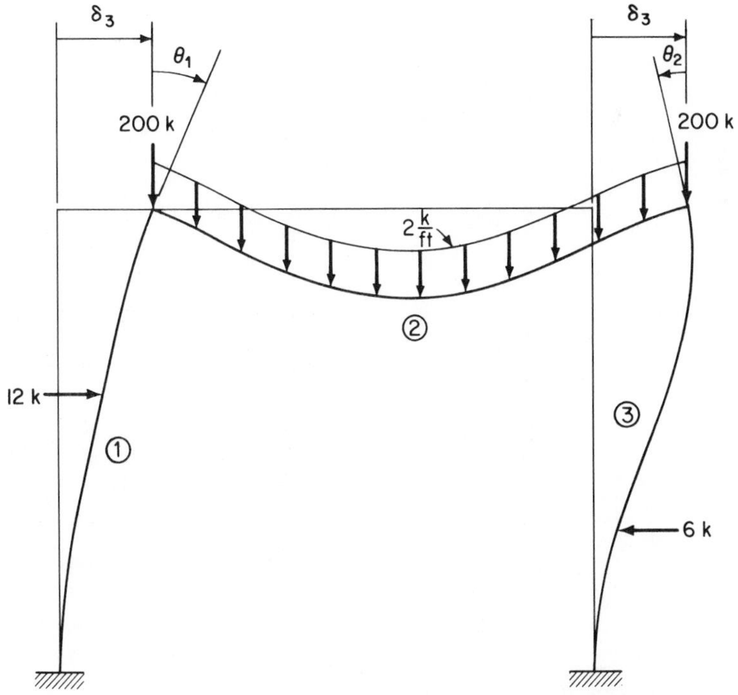

Fig. 8-15 Example 8-1: Deflected structure.

Member 1

$$\begin{bmatrix} M_1 \\ M_6 \\ P_3 \\ P_7 \end{bmatrix}_1 = EI \times 10^{-2} \begin{bmatrix} 18.8355 & 10.3011 & 1.4568 & -1.4568 \\ 10.3011 & 18.8355 & 1.4568 & -1.4568 \\ 1.4568 & 1.4568 & 0.1243 & -0.1243 \\ -1.4568 & -1.4568 & -0.1243 & 0.1243 \end{bmatrix}_1 \frac{1}{EI} \times 10^2 \begin{bmatrix} -3.6456 \\ 0 \\ 36.7751 \\ 0 \end{bmatrix}_1 + \begin{bmatrix} -35.76 \\ 24.00 \\ -7.79 \\ -4.21 \end{bmatrix}_1 = \begin{bmatrix} -50.86 \text{ ft-k} \\ 40.02 \text{ ft-k} \\ -8.53 \text{ k} \\ -3.47 \text{ k} \end{bmatrix}_1 \tag{8-92a}$$

Member 2

$$\begin{bmatrix} M_1 \\ M_2 \\ P_4 \\ P_5 \end{bmatrix}_2 = EI \times 10^{-2} \begin{bmatrix} 16.6146 & 8.3472 & 1.0401 & -1.0401 \\ 8.3472 & 16.6146 & 1.0401 & -1.0401 \\ 1.0401 & 1.0401 & 0.0860 & -0.0860 \\ -1.0401 & -1.0401 & -0.0860 & 0.0860 \end{bmatrix}_2 \frac{1}{EI} \times 10^2 \begin{bmatrix} -3.6456 \\ 1.8334 \\ 0 \\ 0 \end{bmatrix}_2 + \begin{bmatrix} 96.14 \\ -96.14 \\ 24.00 \\ 24.00 \end{bmatrix}_2 = \begin{bmatrix} 50.86 \text{ ft-k} \\ -96.11 \text{ ft-k} \\ 22.12 \text{ k} \\ 25.88 \text{ k} \end{bmatrix}_2 \tag{8-92b}$$

Member 3

$$\begin{bmatrix} M_2 \\ M_8 \\ P_3 \\ P_9 \end{bmatrix}_3 = EI \times 10^{-2} \begin{bmatrix} 18.8215 & 10.3048 & 1.4568 & -1.4563 \\ 10.3048 & 18.8215 & 1.4563 & -1.4563 \\ 1.4563 & 1.4563 & 0.1240 & -0.1240 \\ -1.4563 & -1.4563 & -0.1240 & 0.1240 \end{bmatrix}_3 \frac{1}{EI} \times 10^2 \begin{bmatrix} 1.8334 \\ 0 \\ 36.7751 \\ 0 \end{bmatrix}_3 + \begin{bmatrix} 8.04 \\ -18.00 \\ 1.30 \\ 4.70 \end{bmatrix}_3 = \begin{bmatrix} 96.11 \text{ ft-k} \\ 54.45 \text{ ft-k} \\ 8.53 \text{ k} \\ -2.53 \text{ k} \end{bmatrix}_3 \tag{8-92c}$$

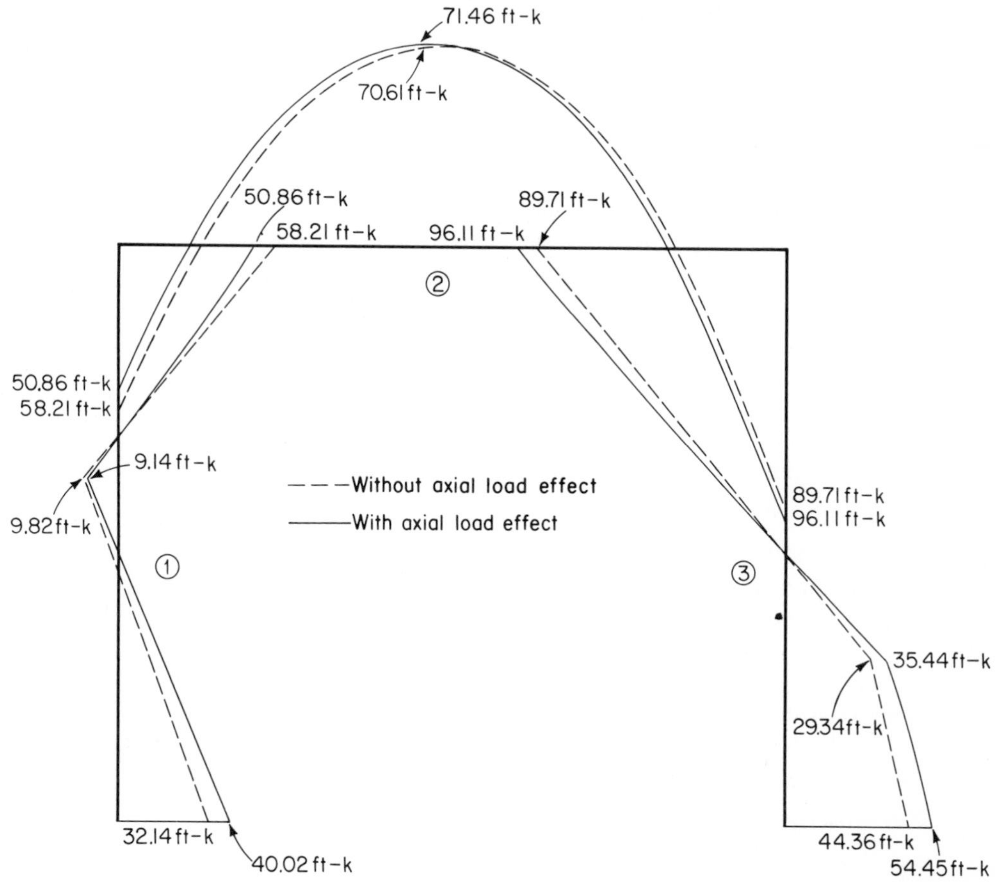

Fig. 8-16 Example 8-1: Final moment diagrams.

8–6 Critical Buckling Loads

In practice a reasonable estimate of the buckling load of a rigid-jointed structural system can usually be obtained from an elastic stability analysis of the system if it can be assumed that the *deformation* of the structure from the initial condition in which all the members are straight is *sufficiently small* for linear theory to apply.

The stability functions previously derived are applicable in determining the critical elastic buckling value of loads applied to structural systems provided *the loads act at joints of the system and can be transmitted through the structure by axial forces only*. Any structural system which (1) supports transverse loads applied within the length of a member or (2) carries joint loads that cannot be transmitted through the structure solely by axial forces must develop bending moments. The method of calculating the critical buckling load to be developed in this section *cannot* be directly applied to systems sustaining these types of loading conditions since, as the Φ_i values change, the relative stiffnesses of the members are altered, thus modifying the bending moment pattern and hence altering the axial load pattern. This interdependence between bending moments and axial load necessitates the use of an iterative method of solution of critical applied loads such as the one found in Reference 8-3.

For a structural system whose members are subjected ***only*** to the application of axial loads, neglecting axial deformations, the joint loads relative to the unrestrained joint displacements are zero at all unrestrained joints; i.e.,

$$[\mathbf{JL}_u] = [\mathbf{0}] \tag{8-93}$$

Since

$$[\mathbf{JL}_u] = [\mathbf{S}_{uu}][\mathbf{\Delta}_u] \tag{8-94}$$

the condition specified by Eq. (8-93) can be satisfied if

$$[\mathbf{\Delta}_u] = [\mathbf{0}] \tag{8-95}$$

But this is the trivial solution since it corresponds to zero displacement of the unrestrained joints.

The ***nontrivial*** solution is obtained by considering the fact that although in the buckled condition the unrestrained joints have undergone displacements, a rotation and/or a translation, the corresponding joint loads are zero—e.g., note the typical structural system shown in Fig. 8-17. In order to satisfy this condition, the determinant of the coefficients of the unknown unrestrained joint displacements—i.e., the determinant of the $[\mathbf{S}_{uu}]$ matrix—is set equal to zero,

$$|\mathbf{S}_{uu}| = 0 \tag{8-96}$$

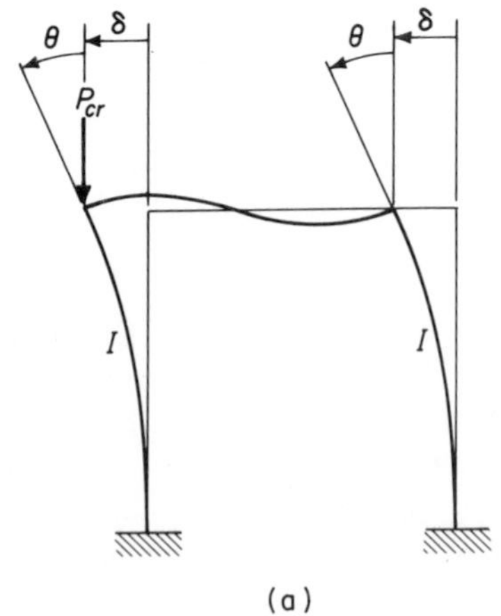

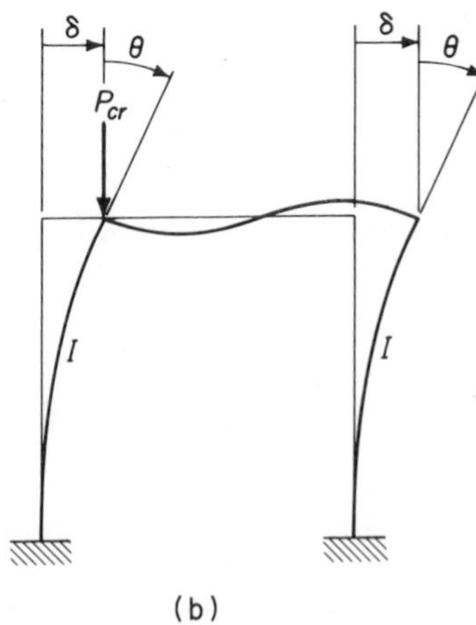

Fig. 8-17 Critical buckling modes for a typical planar structural system: (a) positive joint rotation and negative joint translation; (b) negative joint rotation and positive joint translation.

This determinant is called the ***characteristic determinant***. The expansion and simplification of Eq. (8-96) expressed in terms of the stability functions of the component members yields the ***characteristic equation*** or ***buckling condition*** for the structural system.

When the magnitude of the applied axial loads is less than the critical buckling value, neglecting axial deformations, the displacements of the unrestrained joints will be zero and the determinant of the $[\mathbf{S}_{uu}]$ matrix will be positive, which corresponds to a stable condition. When the applied axial loads exceed the critical value, the determinant of the $[\mathbf{S}_{uu}]$ matrix becomes negative, which corresponds to an unstable structure.

When more than one member of the given structural system is subjected to an applied axial load, it is necessary to establish the relationship between the Φ_i values for the loaded members based upon the relationship between the applied loads and the pinned end Euler loads for each member. When a load is applied at a joint and distributed axially to three or more members, it is necessary to carry out a preliminary analysis of the system in order to determine the value of axial load applied to each member.

Having established the critical condition and, if necessary, the relationship between two or more Φ_i values, sufficient equations have been developed to enable the value of the critical Φ_i to be obtained. From this critical value of Φ_i, the critical buckling load P_{cr} can then be determined from the relationship

$$P^i_{cr} = (\Phi_i)_{cr}\frac{\pi^2(EI)_i}{L_i^2} \tag{8-97}$$

The two following examples illustrate this method of determining the critical value of axially applied loads.

Example 8-2. It is required to determine the critical buckling load for the structural system shown in Fig. 8-18 by the method of stability functions.

JOINT DISPLACEMENT MATRIX

The j- and k-ends and the possible joint displacements are identified and labeled in Fig. 8-19. Referring to Fig. 8-19, the complete joint displacement matrix $[\mathbf{\Delta}_c]$ is written as

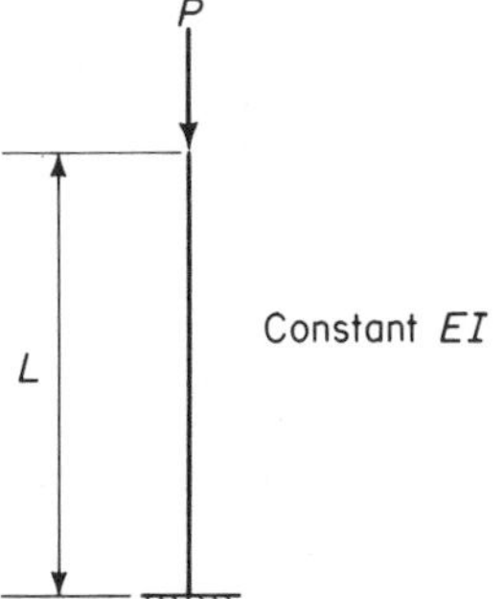

Fig. 8-18 Example 8-2: Fixed-free member.

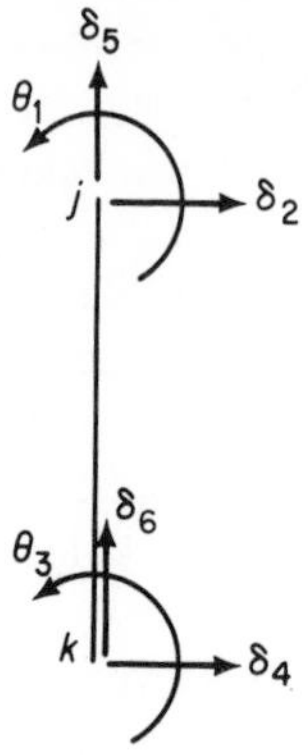

Fig. 8-19 Example 8-2: Identification of possible joint displacements and *j*- and *k*-ends.

$$[\mathbf{\Delta}_c] = \begin{bmatrix} \theta_1 \\ \delta_2 \\ -- \\ \theta_3 \\ \delta_4 \end{bmatrix} = \begin{bmatrix} [\mathbf{\Delta}_u] \\ --- \\ [\mathbf{\Delta}_r] \end{bmatrix} \tag{8-98}$$

MEMBER STIFFNESS MATRIX

Substituting into Expression (8-43), the member stiffness matrix for the single member is developed.

$$[\mathbf{K}] = EI \begin{array}{c} \begin{array}{cccc} \quad 1 \quad & \quad 3 \quad & \quad 2 \quad & \quad 4 \quad \end{array} \\ \left[\begin{array}{cccc} \dfrac{r}{L} & \dfrac{cr}{L} & \dfrac{r(1+c)}{L^2} & -\dfrac{r(1+c)}{L^2} \\ \dfrac{cr}{L} & \dfrac{r}{L} & \dfrac{r(1+c)}{L^2} & -\dfrac{r(1+c)}{L^2} \\ \dfrac{r(1+c)}{L^2} & \dfrac{r(1+c)}{L^2} & \dfrac{2tr(1+c)}{L^3} & -\dfrac{2tr(1+c)}{L^3} \\ -\dfrac{r(1+c)}{L^2} & -\dfrac{r(1+c)}{L^2} & -\dfrac{2tr(1+c)}{L^3} & \dfrac{2tr(1+c)}{L^3} \end{array}\right] \end{array} \begin{array}{c} \\ 1 \\ 3 \\ 2 \\ 4 \end{array} \tag{8-99}$$

Note that subscripts are omitted since only one member exists.

STRUCTURE STIFFNESS MATRIX

The structure stiffness matrix is obtained, in this case, by rearranging the rows and columns of the member stiffness matrix. Note that the fifth and sixth rows and columns of the matrix in Expression (8-100) contain only zero elements since axial deformation is neglected.

$$[\mathbf{S}_c] = EI \begin{bmatrix} \frac{r}{L} & \frac{r(1+c)}{L^2} & \frac{rc}{L} & -\frac{r(1+c)}{L^2} & 0 & 0 \\ \frac{r(1+c)}{L^2} & \frac{2tr(1+c)}{L^3} & \frac{r(1+c)}{L^2} & -\frac{2tr(1+c)}{L^3} & 0 & 0 \\ \hline \frac{rc}{L} & \frac{r(1+c)}{L^2} & \frac{r}{L} & -\frac{r(1+c)}{L^2} & 0 & 0 \\ -\frac{r(1+c)}{L^2} & -\frac{2tr(1+c)}{L^3} & -\frac{r(1+c)}{L^2} & \frac{2tr(1+c)}{L^3} & 0 & 0 \\ 0 & 0 & 0 & 0 & 0 & 0 \\ 0 & 0 & 0 & 0 & 0 & 0 \end{bmatrix} \begin{matrix} 1 \\ 2 \\ 3 \\ 4 \\ 5 \\ 6 \end{matrix} \quad \text{(columns 1, 2, 3, 4, 5, 6)} \tag{8-100}$$

Partitioning this matrix with respect to the restrained and unrestrained joint displacements yields

$$[\mathbf{S}_{uu}] = EI \begin{bmatrix} \frac{r}{L} & \frac{r(1+c)}{L^2} \\ \frac{r(1+c)}{L^2} & \frac{2tr(1+c)}{L^3} \end{bmatrix} \begin{matrix} 1 \\ 2 \end{matrix} \quad \text{(columns 1, 2)} \tag{8-101}$$

JOINT LOAD MATRIX

Referring to Fig. 8-18, the joint load matrix can be developed

$$[\mathbf{JL}_c] = \begin{bmatrix} JL_1 \\ JL_2 \\ \hline JL_3 \\ JL_4 \\ JL_5 \\ JL_6 \end{bmatrix} = \begin{bmatrix} 0 \\ 0 \\ \hline 0 \\ 0 \\ -P \\ 0 \end{bmatrix} = \begin{bmatrix} [\mathbf{JL}_u] \\ \hline [\mathbf{JL}_r] \end{bmatrix} \tag{8-102a}$$

where

$$[\mathbf{JL}_u] = \begin{bmatrix} JL_1 \\ JL_2 \end{bmatrix} = \begin{bmatrix} 0 \\ 0 \end{bmatrix} \tag{8-102b}$$

SOLUTION

For the nontrivial solution, the determinant of the $[\mathbf{S}_{uu}]$ matrix, Expression (8-101), is set equal to zero.

$$\begin{vmatrix} \frac{r}{L} & \frac{r(1+c)}{L^2} \\ \frac{r(1+c)}{L^2} & \frac{2tr(1+c)}{L_3} \end{vmatrix} = 0 \tag{8-103}$$

Expansion of Expression (8-103) gives

$$\frac{r}{L}\left[\frac{2tr(1+c)}{L^3}\right] - \frac{r(1+c)}{L^2}\left[\frac{r(1+c)}{L^2}\right] = 0 \tag{8-104}$$

Simplifying Eq. (8-104) yields

$$2t - c = 1 \tag{8-105}$$

which is the characteristic equation defining the critical buckling condition in terms of the appropriate stability functions. The lowest value of Φ for which this relationship is true is found from Appendix B:

$$\Phi_{cr} = 0.25$$

Then, referring to Eq. (8-97),

$$P_{cr} = 0.25\frac{\pi^2 EI}{L^2} \tag{8-106}$$

which is the classical buckling load for a fixed–free member. The critical condition is also satisfied at $\Phi = 2.25$ (Appendix B), which corresponds to the second buckling mode of the member.

Example 8-3. It is required to determine the critical value of the load applied to the structural system shown in Fig. 8-20 by applying the method of stability functions.

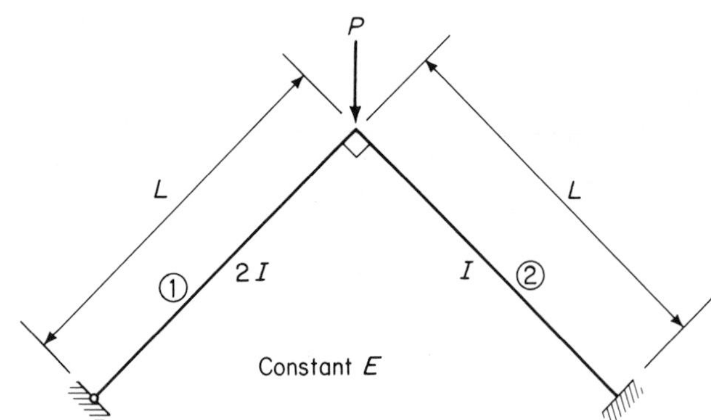

Fig. 8-20 Example 8-3: Indeterminate rigid frame.

JOINT DISPLACEMENT MATRIX

The *j*- and *k*-ends and the possible joint displacements are identified and labeled in Fig. 8-21. Referring to Fig. 8-21, the complete joint displacement matrix $[\Delta_c]$ is written as

$$[\Delta_c] = \begin{bmatrix} \theta_1 \\ \theta_2 \\ \hdashline \theta_3 \\ \delta_4 \\ \delta_5 \\ \delta_6 \\ \delta_7 \end{bmatrix} = \begin{bmatrix} [\Delta_u] \\ \hdashline \\ [\Delta_r] \\ \\ \end{bmatrix} \tag{8-107}$$

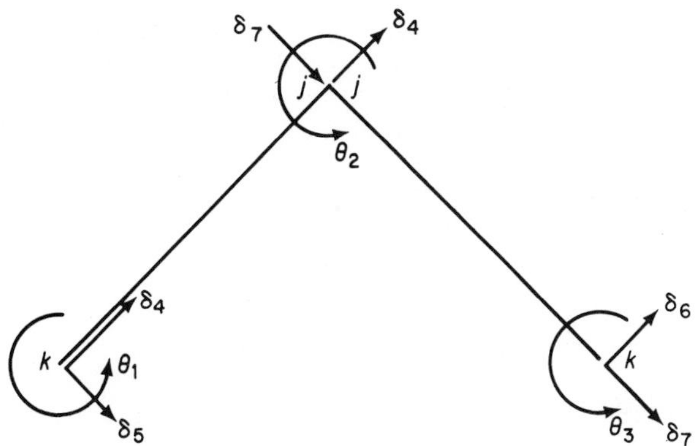

Fig. 8-21 Example 8-3: Identification of possible joint displacements and j- and k-ends.

MEMBER STIFFNESS MATRICES

Substituting into Expression (8-43), the member stiffness matrices for each member are developed.

Member 1

$$[\mathbf{K}]_1 = 2EI \begin{bmatrix} \frac{r_1}{L} & \frac{c_1 r_1}{L} & \frac{r_1(1+c_1)}{L^2} & -\frac{r_1(1+c_1)}{L^2} \\ \frac{c_1 r_1}{L} & \frac{r_1}{L} & \frac{r_1(1+c_1)}{L^2} & -\frac{r_1(1+c_1)}{L^2} \\ \frac{r_1(1+c_1)}{L^2} & \frac{r_1(1+c_1)}{L^2} & \frac{2t_1 r_1(1+c_1)}{L^3} & -\frac{2t_1 r_1(1+c_1)}{L^3} \\ -\frac{r_1(1+c_1)}{L^2} & -\frac{r_1(1+c_1)}{L^2} & -\frac{2t_1 r_1(1+c_1)}{L^3} & \frac{2t_1 r_1(1+c_1)}{L^3} \end{bmatrix}_1 \quad \text{columns/rows: } 2, 1, 7, 5 \tag{8-108a}$$

Member 2

$$[\mathbf{K}]_2 = EI \begin{bmatrix} \frac{r_2}{L} & \frac{c_2 r_2}{L} & \frac{r_2(1+c_2)}{L^2} & -\frac{r_2(1+c_2)}{L^2} \\ \frac{c_2 r_2}{L} & \frac{r_2}{L} & \frac{r_2(1+c_2)}{L^2} & -\frac{r_2(1+c_2)}{L^2} \\ \frac{r_2(1+c_2)}{L^2} & \frac{r_2(1+c_2)}{L^2} & \frac{2t_2 r_2(1+c_2)}{L^3} & -\frac{2t_2 r_2(1+c_2)}{L^3} \\ -\frac{r_2(1+c_2)}{L^2} & -\frac{r_2(1+c_2)}{L^2} & -\frac{2t_2 r_2(1+c_2)}{L^3} & \frac{2t_2 r_2(1+c_2)}{L^3} \end{bmatrix}_2 \quad \text{columns/rows: } 2, 3, 4, 6 \tag{8-108b}$$

STRUCTURE STIFFNESS MATRIX

Superimposing the two member stiffness matrices, the complete stiffness matrix $[\mathbf{S}_c]$ is developed as shown in Eq. (8-109). Partitioning this matrix with respect to the restrained and unrestrained joint displacements yields

$$[\mathbf{S}_{uu}] = EI \begin{bmatrix} \frac{2r_1}{L} & \frac{2c_1r_1}{L} \\ \frac{2c_1r_1}{L} & \frac{2r_1 + r_2}{L} \end{bmatrix} \begin{matrix} 1 \\ 2 \end{matrix} \quad \text{(columns 1, 2)} \tag{8-110}$$

JOINT LOAD MATRIX

Referring to Fig. 8-20, the joint load matrix can be developed.

$$[\mathbf{JL}_c] = \begin{bmatrix} JL_1 \\ JL_2 \\ \hline JL_3 \\ JL_4 \\ JL_5 \\ JL_6 \\ JL_7 \end{bmatrix} = \begin{bmatrix} 0 \\ 0 \\ \hline 0 \\ -P/\sqrt{2} \\ 0 \\ 0 \\ +P/\sqrt{2} \end{bmatrix} = \begin{bmatrix} [\mathbf{JL}_u] \\ \hline \\ [\mathbf{JL}_r] \\ \end{bmatrix} \tag{8-111a}$$

where

$$[\mathbf{JL}_u] = \begin{bmatrix} JL_1 \\ JL_2 \end{bmatrix} = \begin{bmatrix} 0 \\ 0 \end{bmatrix} \tag{8-111b}$$

SOLUTION

For the nontrivial solution, the determinant of the $[\mathbf{S}_{uu}]$ matrix is set equal to zero.

$$\begin{vmatrix} \frac{2r_1}{L} & \frac{2c_1r_1}{L} \\ \frac{2c_1r_1}{L} & \frac{2r_1 + r_2}{L} \end{vmatrix} = 0 \tag{8-112}$$

Expansion of Expression (8-112) gives

$$\frac{2r_1}{L}\left(\frac{2r_1 + r_2}{L}\right) - \frac{2c_1r_1}{L}\left(\frac{2c_1r_1}{L}\right) = 0 \tag{8-113}$$

Simplifying Eq. (8-113) yields

$$2r_1(1 - c_1^2) + r_2 = 0 \tag{8-114}$$

which is the characteristic equation in terms of the appropriate stability functions.

The axial force applied to each of the members of the system is, referring to the joint load matrix, Eq. (8-111a), $P/\sqrt{2}$, or

$$
[\mathbf{S}_c] = EI \begin{array}{c}
\begin{array}{ccccccc} \quad 1 \quad & \quad 2 \quad & \quad 3 \quad & \quad 4 \quad & \quad 5 \quad & \quad 6 \quad & \quad 7 \quad \end{array} \\
\left[\begin{array}{cc:ccccc}
\dfrac{2r_1}{L} & \dfrac{2c_1r_1}{L} & 0 & 0 & -\dfrac{2r_1(1+c_1)}{L^2} & 0 & \dfrac{2r_1(1+c_1)}{L^2} \\
\dfrac{2c_1r_1}{L} & \dfrac{2r_1+r_2}{L} & \dfrac{c_2r_2}{L} & \dfrac{r_2(1+c_2)}{L^2} & -\dfrac{2r_1(1+c_1)}{L^2} & -\dfrac{r_2(1+c_2)}{L^2} & \dfrac{2r_1(1+c_1)}{L^2} \\
\hdashline
0 & \dfrac{c_2r_2}{L} & \dfrac{r_2}{L} & \dfrac{r_2(1+c_2)}{L^2} & 0 & -\dfrac{r_2(1+c_2)}{L^2} & 0 \\
0 & \dfrac{r_2(1+c_2)}{L^2} & \dfrac{r_2(1+c_2)}{L^2} & \dfrac{2t_2r_2(1+c_2)}{L^3} & 0 & -\dfrac{2t_2r_2(1+c_2)}{L^3} & 0 \\
-\dfrac{2r_1(1+c_1)}{L^2} & -\dfrac{2r_1(1+c_1)}{L^2} & 0 & 0 & \dfrac{4t_1r_1(1+c_1)}{L^3} & 0 & -\dfrac{4t_1r_1(1+c_1)}{L^3} \\
0 & -\dfrac{r_2(1+c_2)}{L^2} & -\dfrac{r_2(1+c_2)}{L^2} & -\dfrac{2t_2r_2(1+c_2)}{L^3} & 0 & \dfrac{2t_2r_2(1+c_2)}{L^3} & 0 \\
\dfrac{2r_1(1+c_1)}{L^2} & \dfrac{2r_1(1+c_1)}{L^2} & 0 & 0 & -\dfrac{4t_1r_1(1+c_1)}{L^3} & 0 & \dfrac{4t_1r_1(1+c_1)}{L^3}
\end{array}\right]
\end{array}
\begin{array}{c} \\ 1 \\ 2 \\ 3 \\ 4 \\ 5 \\ 6 \\ 7 \end{array}
\tag{8-109}
$$

$$P^1_{cr} = P^2_{cr} = \frac{P_{cr}}{\sqrt{2}} \tag{8-115}$$

The Φ_i values are, referring to Eq. (8-14),

$$\Phi_1 = \frac{P/\sqrt{2}}{\pi^2(2EI)/L^2} \tag{8-116a}$$

and

$$\Phi_2 = \frac{P/\sqrt{2}}{\pi^2 EI/L^2} \tag{8-116b}$$

The relationship between the Φ_i values is therefore

$$2\Phi_1 = \Phi_2 \tag{8-117}$$

The values of Φ_1 and Φ_2 for which Eqs. (8-114) and (8-117) are satisfied are found from Appendix B by a trial-and-error procedure to be

$$(\Phi_1)_{cr} = 1.01 \tag{8-118a}$$

and

$$(\Phi_2)_{cr} = 2.02 \tag{8-118b}$$

It then follows from Eqs. (8-97) and (8-115) that

$$P_{cr} = 1.01\frac{\sqrt{2}\,\pi^2(2EI)}{L^2} = 2.02\frac{\sqrt{2}\,\pi^2 EI}{L^2} = 2.86\frac{\pi^2 EI}{L^2} \tag{8-119}$$

8–7
Summary

A means of incorporating the effect of axial loads into the stiflness method of structural analysis by the introduction of certain stability and lateral load functions has been presented in this chapter. The only limitations upon the use of these functions are those inherent in the stiffness method of analysis as presented in earlier chapters. The method of application is demonstrated and typical results are presented through an illustrative example.

The applicability of stability functions in determining the critical buckling condition in the plane of the frame for a planar structural system is also shown. The procedure outlined is straightforward in application, as illustrated, and can be utilized in obtaining computer solutions for the critical buckling loads for larger and more complex systems.

8–8
Problems

8-1 to 8-5. Analyze the structural system shown for the indicated loading using the stiffness method of analysis and stability and load functions.

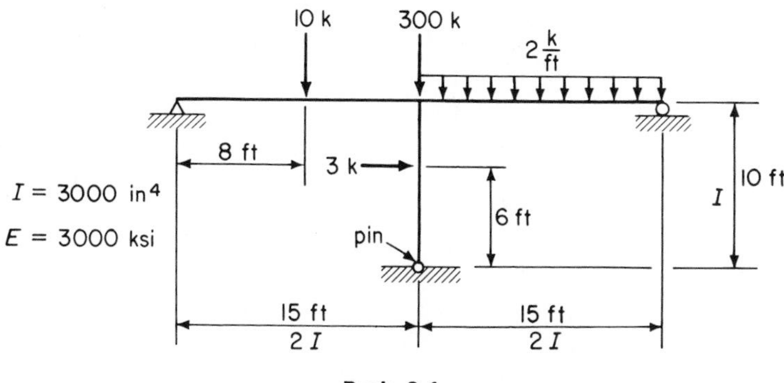

Prob. 8-1

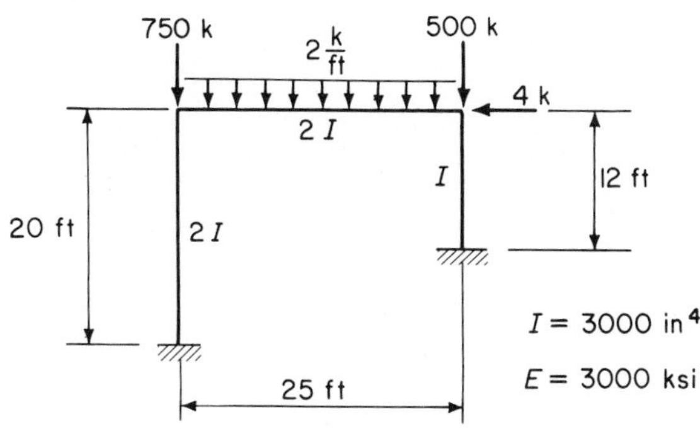

Prob. 8-2

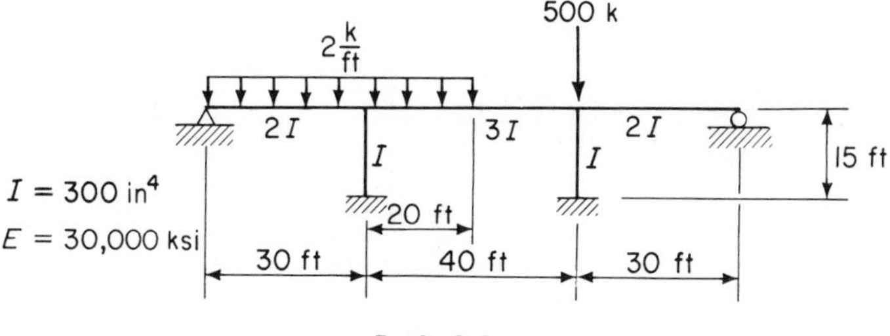

Prob. 8-3

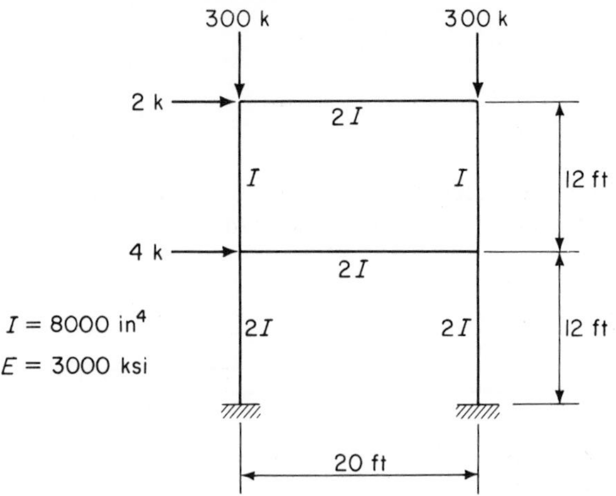

Prob. 8-4

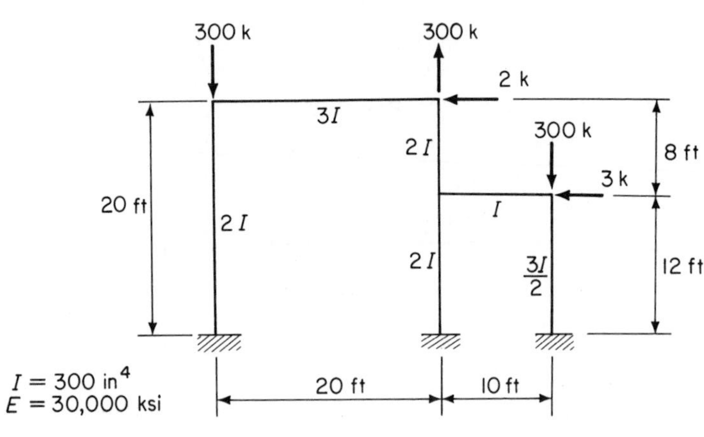

Prob. 8-5

8-6. Develop expressions for the fixed end moments for the beam element i loaded as shown.

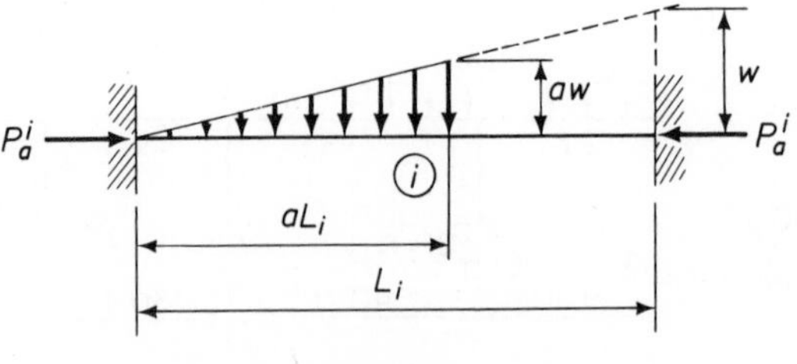

Prob. 8-6

8-7. Develop the member stiffness matrix for a typical beam element i considering axial deformation along with axial load effect.

8-8. Rework Prob. 8-1 considering axial deformations. Effective cross-sectional areas $= 143\ \text{in}^2$ (horizontal members) and $180\ \text{in}^2$ (vertical member).

8-9 to 8-13. Compute the critical buckling load for the structural system shown using the method of stability functions.

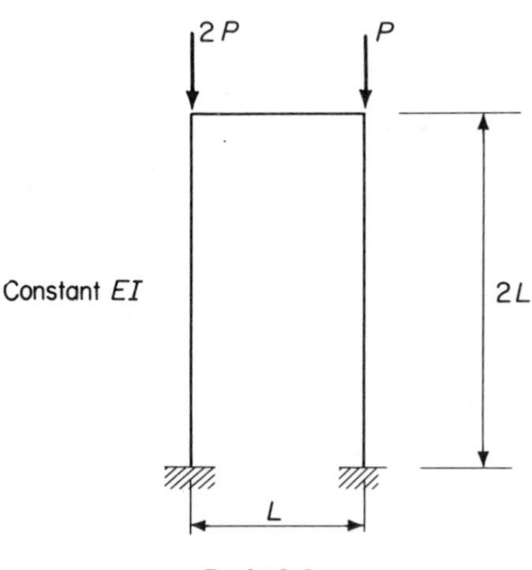

Prob. 8-9

Prob. 8-10

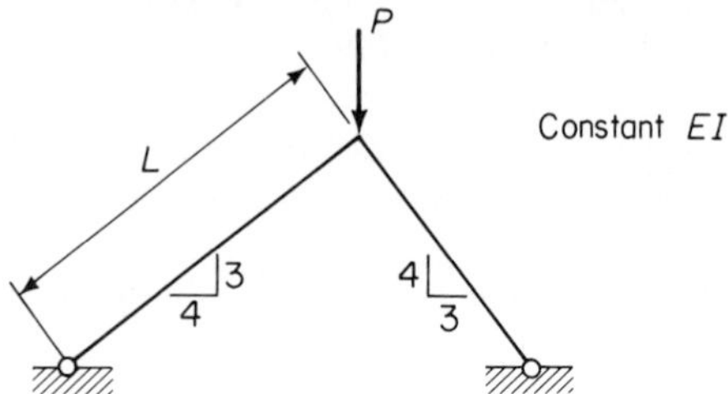

Prob. 8-11

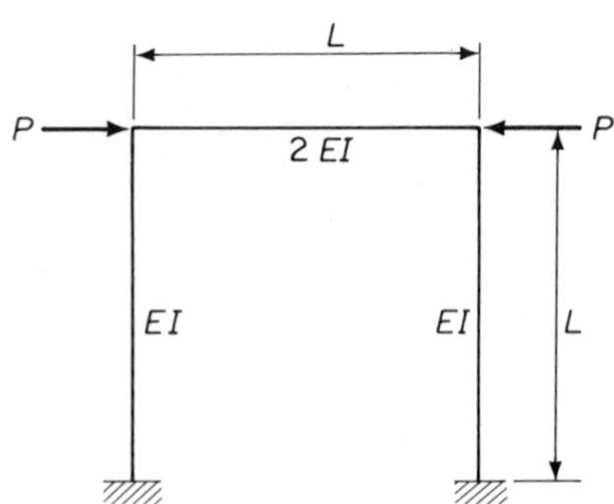

Prob. 8-12

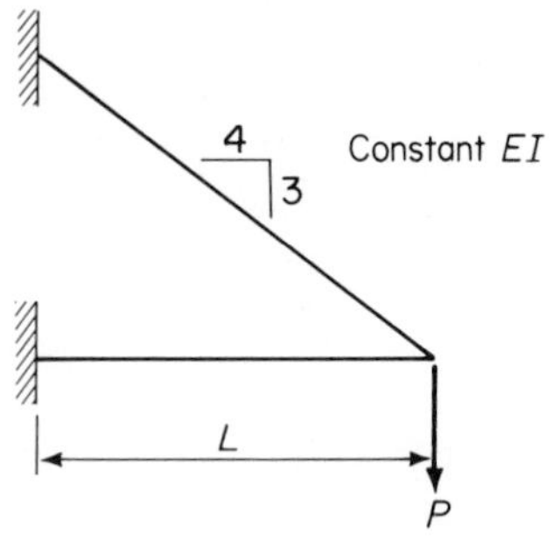

Prob. 8-13

SELECTED REFERENCES

8-1 Timoshenko, S. P., and J. M. Gere, *Theory of Elastic Stability*. New York: McGraw-Hill Book Company, 1961.

8-2 Livesley, R. K., and D. B. Chandler, *Stability Functions for Structural Frameworks*. Manchester, England: Manchester University Press, 1956.

8-3 Horne, M. R., and W. Merchant, *The Stability of Frames*. London: Pergamon Press, 1965.

8-4 Ketter, R. L., and S. P. Prawel, Jr., *An Introduction to Modern Methods of Engineering Computation*. New York: McGraw-Hill Book Company, 1968.

9 ENERGY METHODS

In previous chapters, the development and use of the stiffness method of structural analysis has been presented and illustrated. The development of the member stiffness and structure stiffness matrices was based on the basic equation relating deformations and moments; namely,

$$\frac{d^2y}{dx^2} = \frac{M}{EI} \tag{9-1}$$

where y is the displacement function, M is the moment function, and EI is the rigidity function. In this chapter, the ***principle of stationary potential energy*** is used to *derive* member stiffness and structure stiffness matrices.

9–1 The Principle of Stationary Potential Energy

The principle of stationary potential energy can be stated as follows:

> The first derivative of the total potential energy of a structural system with respect to the joint displacements is zero when the system is in a state of equilibrium.

This principle can be written in equation form as

$$\frac{\partial V}{\partial \delta_j} = 0 \qquad j = 1, 2, 3, \ldots n \tag{9-2}$$

where V is the total potential energy of the system and δ_j is the joint displacement at the jth joint.

The total potential energy consists of two parts: the *external* potential energy W_e and the *internal* potential energy W_i; or

$$V = W_e + W_i \tag{9-3}$$

The external potential energy is equal to the sum of the products of the applied loads multiplied by the corresponding displacement through which they act; or

$$W_e = \sum_{j=1}^{n} P_j \delta_j \tag{9-4}$$

where P_j is the applied load at point j and δ_j is the displacement at point j in the direction of P_j.

The internal potential energy is equal to the sum of the products of the internal stress multiplied by the internal strain; or

$$W_i = \int_v \int_0^{\epsilon} \sigma \, d\epsilon \, dv \tag{9-5}$$

where σ is the stress at an internal point and $d\epsilon$ is the incremental strain at the same internal point. The term $\int_0^{\epsilon} \sigma d\epsilon$ represents the amount of internal energy created at a point in the system. The point is represented by a unit volume of material; consequently, in order to find the total internal potential energy, one must sum over the total volume of the system. This summation (or integration) is represented in Eq. (9-5) by $\int_v$.

The internal potential energy can also be thought of as internal work. The internal work performed on the system stores energy in the system which is commonly known as strain energy U. These two forms of energy are equal and oppose one another; thus,

$$W_i + U = 0 \tag{9-6a}$$

or

$$W_i = -U \tag{9-6b}$$

Substitution of Eq. (9-6b) into Eq. (9-3) yields

$$V = W_e - U \tag{9-7}$$

Substitution of Eq. (9-7) into Eq. (9-2) yields

$$\frac{\partial(W_e - U)}{\partial \delta_j} = 0 \qquad j = 1, 2, 3, \ldots n \tag{9-8}$$

or

$$\frac{\partial(U - W_e)}{\partial \delta_j} = 0 \qquad j = 1, 2, 3, \ldots n \tag{9-9}$$

The derivation of the principle of stationary potential energy is thoroughly discussed in several texts on advanced structural analysis†; consequently, further explanation of the derivation of the principle will not be given here.

The manner in which the stationary potential energy principle, Eq. (9-9), is formulated in matrix form and is used to evaluate the member stiffness and

†Henry Langhaar, *Energy Methods in Applied Mechanics*, New York, John Wiley & Sons, Inc., 1962; Nicholas J. Hoff, *The Analysis of Structures*, New York, John Wiley & Sons, Inc., 1956; Moshe F. Rubinstein, *Matrix Computer Analysis of Structures*, Englewood Cliffs, N.J., Prentice-Hall, Inc., 1966.

structure stiffness matrices is of primary interest; but first, strain energy and external potential energy functions must be defined.

9–2 Strain Energy

There are four types of strain energy associated with the deformation of a structural system: axial, bending, shear, and torsion. Axial strain energy is the primary type of strain energy stored in truss structures, while bending strain energy is the primary type stored in beam and frame structures. Shear strain energy can be important if the structure consists of some short, relatively rigid members. Torsional strain energy is likely to be important in space frames consisting of rigid joints and, of course, would be important in the analysis of any member subjected to torsional loads. In this chapter, only axial strain energy and bending strain energy will be discussed.

9-2.1 Axial Strain Energy

For truss structures, the primary energy stored in the structure is strain energy due to axial member forces. For member i subjected to an axial force N with cross-sectional area A and modulus of elasticity E, as shown in Fig. 9-1, the strain energy is given by

$$U_a = \int_0^L \frac{N^2}{2AE} dx \tag{9-10}$$

For a uniform cross-sectional area A and a uniform modulus of elasticity E, Eq. (9-10) becomes

$$U_a = \frac{N^2 L}{2AE} \tag{9-11}$$

The axial displacements at ends j and k are defined as δ_t and δ_u, respectively. Thus, the net elongation of the member is

$$e = \delta_u - \delta_t \tag{9-12}$$

where the elongation e of a uniform member can be expressed as

$$e = \frac{NL}{AE} \tag{9-13a}$$

Rearrangement of Eq. (9-13a) to solve for N yields

$$N = \frac{AEe}{L} \tag{9-13b}$$

Substitution of Eq. (9-13b) into Eq. (9-11) yields

$$U_a = \frac{AE}{2L} e^2 \tag{9-14a}$$

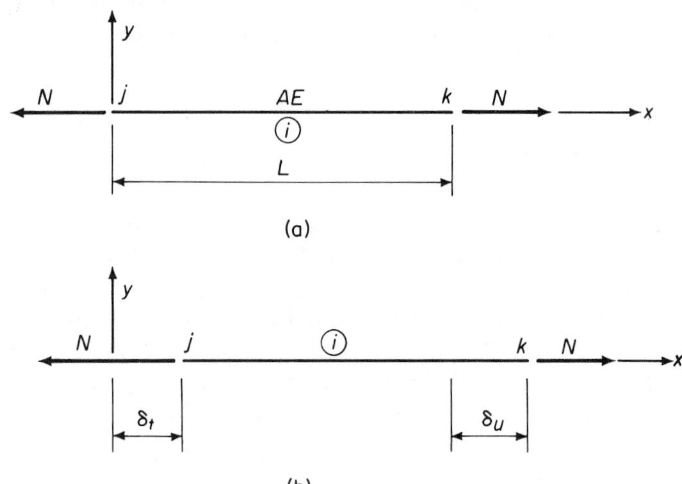

Fig. 9-1 Displacement of axially loaded member: (a) original position of member *i*; (b) displaced position of member *i*.

Substitution of Eq. (9-12) into Eq. (9-14a) yields

$$U_a = \frac{AE}{2L}(\delta_u - \delta_t)^2 \tag{9-14b}$$

The expression for the axial strain energy as given by Eq. (9-14b) is the most suitable one for use in the stationary potential energy relationship as given by Eq. (9-9), because U_a is expressed in terms of the joint displacements for the member, i.e., δ_t and δ_u.

9-2.2 Bending Strain Energy

The derivation of a useful form of the strain energy due to bending is considerably more involved than that for axial forces. Consider first the equation for strain energy of member *i* subjected to bending as expressed as a function of the moment:

$$U_b = \int_0^L \frac{M^2}{2EI}\,dx \tag{9-15}$$

where M is the bending moment in member *i* as a function of x as shown in Fig. 9-2. Note that the sign convention used in this chapter is the same as used earlier in this text, where forces and deflections up and to the right are positive, and moments and rotations counterclockwise are positive.

The elastic curve of the deflected member is related to the moment by the equation

$$EI\frac{d^2y}{dx^2} = M \tag{9-16}$$

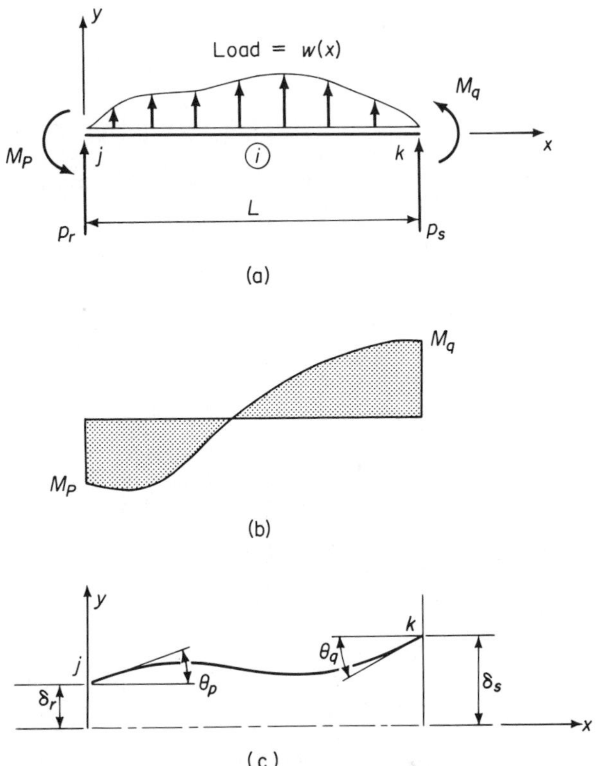

Fig. 9-2 Deformation notation for loaded beam: (a) loaded prismatic beam element; (b) moment diagram—beam sign convention ↱—↰; (c) elastic curve.

The sign convention used in Eq. (9-16) is given in Fig. 8-2.

Substitution of Eq. (9-16) into Eq. (9-15) yields

$$U_b = \int_0^L \frac{EI}{2}\left(\frac{d^2y}{dx^2}\right)^2 dx \tag{9-17a}$$

or

$$U_b = \frac{1}{2}EI\int_0^L \left(\frac{d^2y}{dx^2}\right)^2 dx \tag{9-17b}$$

if the member rigidity EI is uniform.

Before Eq. (9-17a) or (9-17b) can be used, an expression for y in terms of x and the joint displacements δ_r, θ_p, δ_s, θ_q must be found.

In order to illustrate more easily the development of the bending strain energy expression in terms of the joint displacements, consider the case shown in Fig. 9-3, where the load function w and the member rigidity EI are taken as constants. All loads, moments, shears, deflections, and rotations are shown in their positive direction.

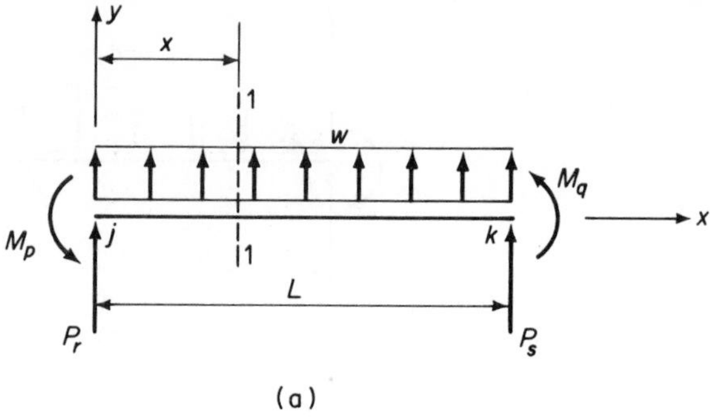

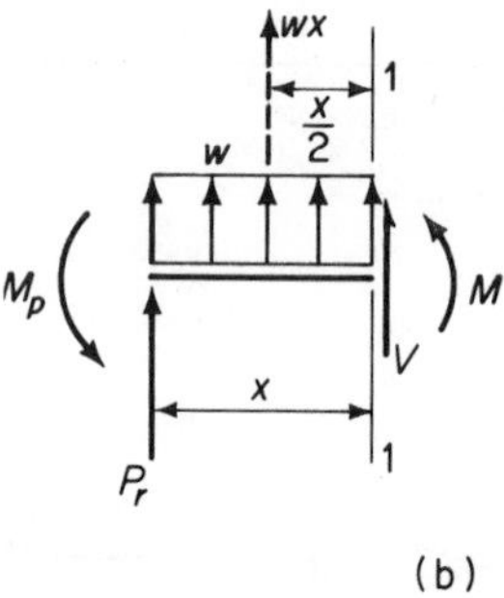

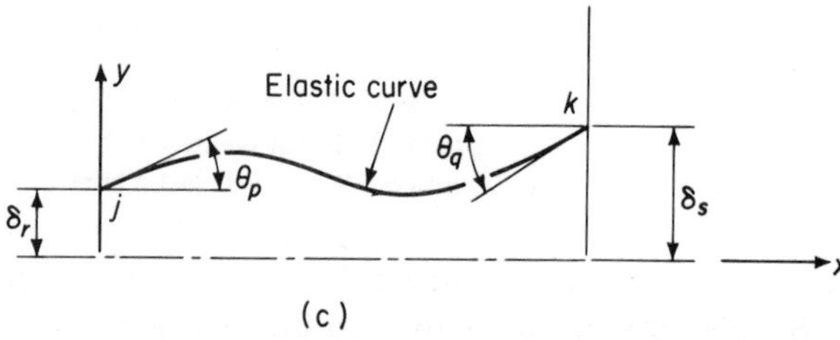

Fig. 9-3 Uniformly loaded beam element: (a) loaded prismatic beam; (b) free body diagram, Sec. 1-1; (c) elastic curve.

The moment at any point x can be written by summing moments about Sec. 1-1 to the left, yielding

$$M + M_p - P_r x - \frac{wx^2}{2} = 0 \tag{9-18a}$$

Solving for M gives

$$M = -M_p + P_r x + \frac{wx^2}{2} \tag{9-18b}$$

Substitution of Eq. (9-18b) into Eq. (9-16) yields

$$\frac{d^2y}{dx^2} = -\frac{M_p}{EI} + \frac{P_r x}{EI} + \frac{wx^2}{2EI} \tag{9-19}$$

Integrating once yields

$$\frac{dy}{dx} = -\frac{M_p x}{EI} + \frac{P_r x^2}{2EI} + \frac{wx^3}{6EI} + C_1 \tag{9-20}$$

The boundary conditions are: (1) $\frac{dy}{dx} = \theta_p, \quad y = \delta_r \text{ at } x = 0$

(2) $\frac{dy}{dx} = \theta_q, \quad y = \delta_s \text{ at } x = L$

The substitution of boundary conditions $x = 0$ and $dy/dx = \theta_p$ into Eq. (9-20) yields $C_1 = \theta_p$. Thus,

$$\frac{dy}{dx} = \theta_p - \frac{M_p x}{EI} + \frac{P_r x^2}{2EI} + \frac{wx^3}{6EI} \tag{9-21}$$

Integrating, again, yields

$$y = \theta_p x - \frac{M_p x^2}{2EI} + \frac{P_r x^3}{6EI} + \frac{wx^4}{24EI} + C_2 \tag{9-22}$$

The substitution of boundary conditions $x = 0$ and $y = \delta_r$ into Eq. (9-22) yields $C_2 = \delta_r$. Thus,

$$y = \delta_r + \theta_p x - \frac{M_p x^2}{2EI} + \frac{P_r x^3}{6EI} + \frac{wx^4}{24EI} \tag{9-23}$$

The substitution of the second set of boundary conditions—at $x = L$, $dy/dx = \theta_q$, $y = \delta_s$—into Eqs. (9-21) and (9-23) yields

$$\theta_q = \theta_p - \frac{M_p L}{EI} + \frac{P_r L^2}{2EI} + \frac{wL^3}{6EI} \tag{9-24a}$$

and

$$\delta_s = \delta_r + \theta_p L - \frac{M_p L^2}{2EI} + \frac{P_r L^3}{6EI} + \frac{wL^4}{24EI} \tag{9-24b}$$

Solving Eqs. (9-24) in terms of M_p and P_r yields

$$M_p = \frac{EI}{L}\left(4\theta_p + 2\theta_q + \frac{6\delta_r}{L} - \frac{6\delta_s}{L}\right) - \frac{wL^2}{12} \tag{9-25a}$$

and

$$P_r = \frac{6EI}{L^2}\left(\theta_p + \theta_q + \frac{2\delta_r}{L} - \frac{2\delta_s}{L}\right) - \frac{wL}{2} \tag{9-25b}$$

Since the terms $wL^2/12$ and $wL/2$ are the fixed end moment and shear at end for a uniform load, more general expressions for M_p and P_r would be

$$M_p = \frac{EI}{L}\left(4\theta_p + 2\theta_q + \frac{6\delta_r}{L} - \frac{6\delta_s}{L}\right) + FM_p \tag{9-26a}$$

$$P_r = \frac{6EI}{L^2}\left(\theta_p + \theta_q + \frac{2\delta_r}{L} - \frac{2\delta_s}{L}\right) + FP_r \tag{9-26b}$$

where FM_p and FP_r are the fixed end moment and shear, respectively. Application of the equations of equilibrium to the member shown in Fig. 9-3(a) give expressions for the end actions at k as follows:

$$M_q = \frac{EI}{L}\left(2\theta_p + 4\theta_q - \frac{6\delta_r}{L} + \frac{6\delta_s}{L}\right) + FM_q \tag{9-26c}$$

$$P_s = \frac{6EI}{L^2}\left(\theta_p + \theta_q - \frac{2\delta_r}{L} + \frac{2\delta_s}{L}\right) + FP_s \tag{9-26d}$$

where FM_q and FP_s are the fixed end moment and shear, respectively. The substitution of Eqs. (9-25a) and (9-25b) into Eq. (9-23) yields

$$y = \delta_r + \theta_p x - \frac{x^2}{L}\left(2\theta_p + \theta_q + \frac{3\delta_r}{L} - \frac{3\delta_s}{L}\right) + \frac{x^3}{L^2}\left(\theta_p + \theta_q + \frac{2\delta_r}{L} - \frac{2\delta_s}{L}\right) + G(x) \tag{9-27}$$

where

$$G(x) = \frac{wx^2}{24EI}(L - x)^2 \tag{9-28}$$

for a uniformly loaded beam. Note that all terms in Eq. (9-27) that are not functions of the joint displacements have been gathered together into the one term defined as $G(x)$. The term $G(x)$ is the deflection function for a beam with both ends fixed, i.e., joint displacements θ_p, θ_q, δ_r, δ_s equal zero. In the case above, the expression for $G(x)$ is the deflection function for a uniformly loaded fixed end beam. The advantage of this definition will become apparent shortly.

The first and second derivatives of y with respect to x, as given by Eq. (9-27), are

$$y' = \frac{dy}{dx} = \theta_p - \frac{2x}{L}\left(2\theta_p + \theta_q + \frac{3\delta_r}{L} - \frac{3\delta_s}{L}\right) + \frac{3x^2}{L^2}\left(\theta_p + \theta_q + \frac{2\delta_r}{L} - \frac{2\delta_s}{L}\right) + G'(x) \tag{9-29}$$

and

$$y'' = \frac{d^2y}{dx^2} = -\frac{2}{L}\left(2\theta_p + \theta_q + \frac{3\delta_r}{L} - \frac{3\delta_s}{L}\right) + \frac{6x}{L^2}\left(\theta_p + \theta_q + \frac{2\delta_r}{L} - \frac{2\delta_s}{L}\right) + G''(x) \tag{9-30}$$

The expression for the bending strain energy requires the square of d^2y/dx^2, which can be written as

$$\begin{aligned}(y'')^2 = {} & \frac{4}{L^2}\left(2\theta_p + \theta_q + \frac{3\delta_r}{L} - \frac{3\delta_s}{L}\right)^2 + \frac{36x^2}{L^4}\left(\theta_p + \theta_q + \frac{2\delta_r}{L} - \frac{2\delta_s}{L}\right)^2 \\ & - \frac{24x}{L^3}\left(2\theta_p + \theta_q + \frac{3\delta_r}{L} - \frac{3\delta_s}{L}\right)\left(\theta_p + \theta_q + \frac{2\delta_r}{L} - \frac{2\delta_s}{L}\right) \\ & - \frac{4G''(x)}{L}\left(2\theta_p + \theta_q + \frac{3\delta_r}{L} - \frac{3\delta_s}{L}\right) \\ & + \frac{12G''(x)}{L^2}\left(\theta_p + \theta_q + \frac{2\delta_r}{L} - \frac{2\delta_s}{L}\right) + [G''(x)]^2\end{aligned} \tag{9-31}$$

Substituting Eq. (9-31) into Eq. (9-17a) or (9-17b), integrating with respect to x, substituting in the limits, and condensing the expression would result in a fairly cumbersome equation. It turns out that those terms involving the function $G''(x)$ in Eq. (9-31) are not necessary, since they will disappear when the total potential energy is differentiated with respect to the joint displacements. The reason for this is as follows:

From Eq. (9-27), let

$$\bar{y} = \delta_r + \theta_p x - \frac{x^2}{L}\left(2\theta_p + \theta_q + \frac{3\delta_r}{L} - \frac{3\delta_s}{L}\right) + \frac{x^3}{L^2}\left(\theta_p + \theta_q + \frac{2\delta_r}{L} - \frac{2\delta_s}{L}\right) \tag{9-32}$$

and

$$y_f = G(x) \tag{9-33}$$

The expression for $\bar{y}$ is the deflection function for the member due to the occurrence of the end displacements alone and y_f is the deflection function for the member due to the applied load with both ends fixed, i.e., with all four end displacements (θ_p, δ_r, θ_q, and δ_s) equal to zero. Thus, Eq. (9-27) can be written as

$$y = \bar{y} + y_f \tag{9-34}$$

and the second derivative of y with respect to x is

$$y'' = \bar{y}'' + y_f'' \tag{9-35}$$

The substitution of Eq. (9-35) into Eq. (9-17b) gives

$$U_b = \tfrac{1}{2}EI\int_0^L (\bar{y}'' + y_f'')^2\,dx \tag{9-36}$$

or

$$U_b = \tfrac{1}{2}EI\int_0^L (\bar{y}'')^2\,dx + \tfrac{1}{2}EI\int_0^L (y_f'')^2\,dx + EI\int_0^L \bar{y}''y_f''\,dx \tag{9-37}$$

The evaluation of the first integral will result in a function of the end displacements θ_p, δ_r, θ_q, and δ_s. The evaluation of the second integral will result in a constant, since y_f'' is a function of x alone and not of the end displacements. The value of the third integral is zero. To prove that the value of the third integral is zero, integrate this integral by parts; i.e.,

$$\int_0^L u\,dv = uv\Big]_0^L - \int_0^L v\,du \tag{9-38}$$

Letting $u = \bar{y}''$ and $dv = y_f''\,dx$, then

$$du = \bar{y}'''\,dx \tag{9-39}$$

and

$$v = y_f' \tag{9-40}$$

Thus,

$$\int_0^L \bar{y}''y_f''\,dx = \underbrace{\bar{y}''y_f'\Big]_0^L}_{\text{I}} - \underbrace{\int_0^L \bar{y}'''y_f'\,dx}_{\text{II}} \tag{9-41}$$

Since y_f is the deflection function for the member when the ends are fixed, y_f' evaluated at $x = 0$ and L is zero; hence, term I in Eq. (9-41) is zero. Thus, Eq. (9-41) reduces to

$$\int_0^L \bar{y}''y_f''\,dx = -\int_0^L \bar{y}'''y_f'\,dx \tag{9-42}$$

Now, let $u = \bar{y}'''$ and $dv = y_f'\,dx$; then,

$$du = \bar{y}^{\text{IV}}\,dx \tag{9-43}$$

and

$$v = y_f \tag{9-44}$$

Thus,

$$\int_0^L \bar{y}''y_f''\,dx = \underbrace{-\bar{y}'''y_f\Big]_0^L}_{\text{I}} + \underbrace{\int_0^L \bar{y}^{\text{IV}}y_f\,dx}_{\text{II}} \tag{9-45}$$

Since y_f is zero at the boundaries of the member—i.e., at $x = 0$ and at $x = L$—term I is again zero. Term II contains the fourth derivative of $\bar{y}$ with respect to x. Differentiating $\bar{y}$, as given by Eq. (9-32), four times yields $\bar{y}^{\text{IV}} = 0$; hence, term II is also zero. Thus, Eq. (9-45) reduces to

$$\int_0^L \bar{y}''y_f''\,dx = 0 \tag{9-46}$$

Therefore, Eq. (9-37) becomes

$$U_b = \tfrac{1}{2}EI\int_0^L (\bar{y}'')^2\,dx + \text{constant} \tag{9-47}$$

The constant term in Eq. (9-47) is equal to the second integral in Eq. (9-37). The value of this constant is not important, since it will disappear after the total potential energy has been differentiated with respect to the end or joint displacements θ_p, δ_r, θ_q, and δ_s.

The second derivative of $\bar{y}$ from Eq. (9-32) is

$$\bar{y}'' = -\frac{2}{L}\left(2\theta_p + \theta_q + \frac{3\delta_r}{L} - \frac{3\delta_s}{L}\right) + \frac{6x}{L^2}\left(\theta_p + \theta_q + \frac{2\delta_r}{L} - \frac{2\delta_s}{L}\right) \tag{9-48}$$

Substituting Eq. (9-48) into Eq. (9-47), integrating, and evaluating from $x = 0$ to $x = L$ yields

$$U_b = \frac{2EI}{L}\left[\theta_p^2 + \theta_p\theta_q + \theta_q^2 + \frac{3}{L}(\delta_r - \delta_s)(\theta_p + \theta_q) + \frac{3}{L^2}(\delta_r - \delta_s)^2\right] + \text{constant} \tag{9-49}$$

Equation (9-49) is the strain energy in a member subjected to bending in terms of the end displacements. This form of the bending strain energy will prove very useful in later discussions.

9–3
External Potential Energy

The determination of an expression for the external potential energy in a structural system due to applied loads is a very simple task in most cases. It is simply the sum of the products of loads multiplied by the corresponding displacements through which they act. These displacements can be expressed in terms of the joint displacements of the structure.

For planar-truss–type structural systems, each joint has two components of displacement. Since loads are usually applied at the joints, the expression for the external potential energy is quite simple.

Consider the truss system in Fig. 9-4. Joints 1 and 2 are the only two joints in the structure which can displace. Each joint has two displacement components to describe the complete displacement picture of the structure. The displacement components of joint 1 are denoted as δ_1 and δ_2 and of joint 2 as δ_3 and δ_4. These four displacements are the joint displacements δ_j as defined in Eq. (9-2).

Since the joints are considered pinned and all loads are applied at the joints, the only type of strain energy stored in the truss is axial strain energy. The external potential energy is given by multiplying the loads by the displacements at the location of the loads and in the direction of the loads; thus,

$$W_e = (-Q)(\delta_3) + (P)(\delta_1) \tag{9-50}$$

For a beam or rigid frame structure, the same rule applies. For example,

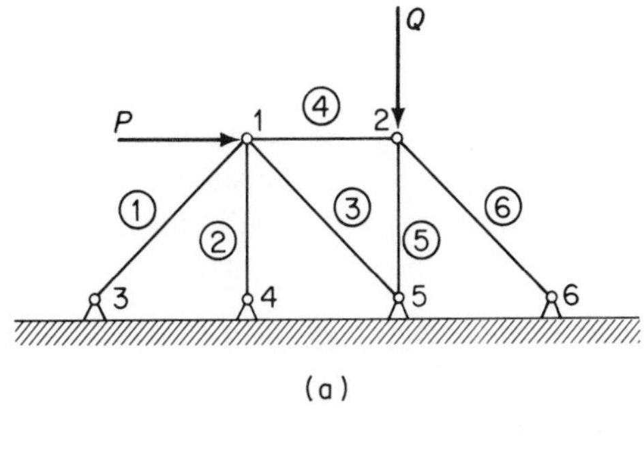

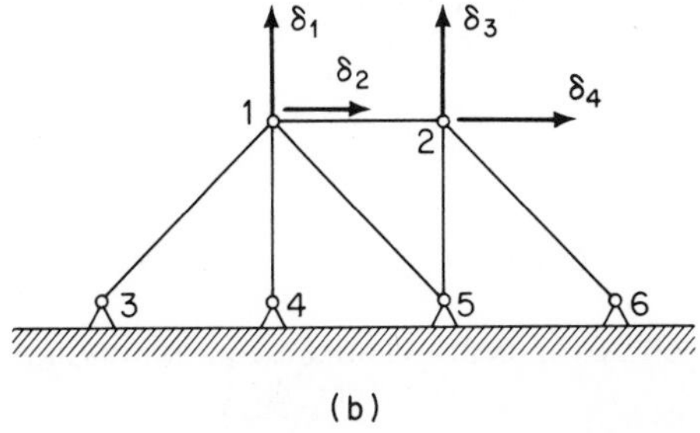

Fig. 9-4 External work for truss structure: (a) loads; (b) displacements.

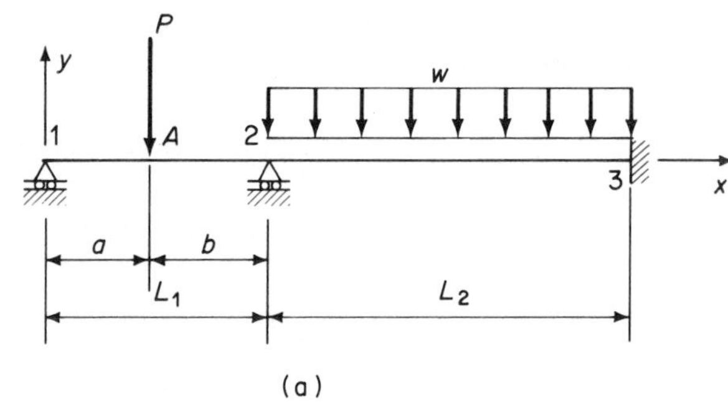

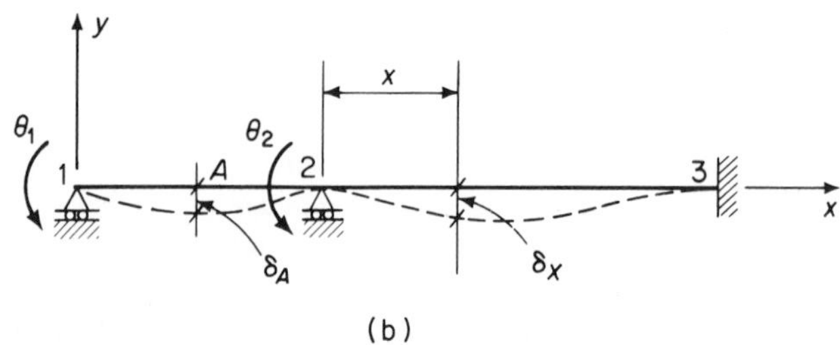

Fig. 9-5 External work for beam structure: (a) loads; (b) displacements.

consider the beam shown in Fig. 9-5. The unknown joint displacements are the rotations at joints 1 and 2 as shown in Fig. 9-5. The external potential energy is

$$W_e = (-P)(-\delta_A) + \int_0^{L_2} (-w)(-\delta_x)\, dx \tag{9-51}$$

The notation δ_x is used to indicate the value of the deflection at any distance x between joints 2 and 3. Since the given loads are not located at the joints of the structure, Eq. (9-27) must be used to express δ_A and δ_x in terms of θ_1 and θ_2.

For δ_A, the substitution of $x = a$ into Eq. (9-27) yields

$$\delta_A = \theta_1(a) - \frac{a^2}{L}[2\theta_1 + \theta_2] + \frac{a^3}{L^2}(\theta_1 + \theta_2) + G_1(a) \tag{9-52}$$

where $G_1(a)$ is the value of the deflection function for $x = a$ for beam element 1-2, assuming both ends of the element are fixed; i.e.,

$$G_1(a) = -\frac{P^3ab^3}{3EIL_1^3} \tag{9-53}$$

For δ_x, Eq. (9-27) becomes

$$\delta_x = \theta_2 x - \frac{x^2}{L}(2\theta_2) + \frac{x^3}{L^2}(\theta_2) + G_2(x) \tag{9-54}$$

where $G_2(x)$ is the deflection function for beam element 2-3, assuming both ends are fixed; i.e.,

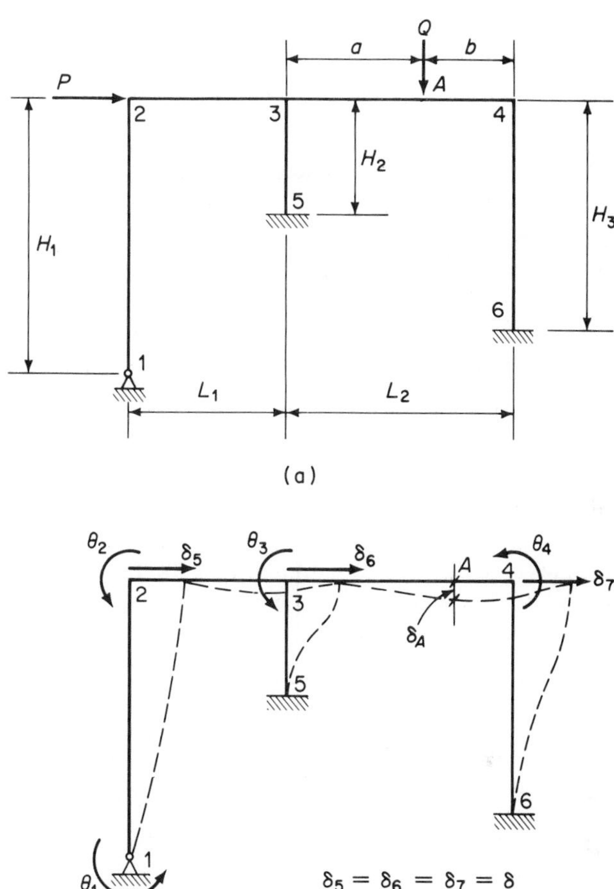

Fig. 9-6 External work for frame structure: (a) loads; (b) displacements.

$$G_2(x) = -\frac{wx^2}{24EI}(L_2 - x)^2 \tag{9-55}$$

Expressions for both $G_1(a)$ and $G_2(x)$ were obtained from the *Manual of Steel Construction*.†

As a third example, consider the frame structure shown in Fig. 9-6. If axial deformation is neglected, then $\delta_5 = \delta_6 = \delta_7 = \delta$. For this case, the joint displacements are $\theta_1, \theta_2, \theta_3, \theta_4$, and δ, and the external potential energy is expressed as

$$W_e = (P)(\delta) + (-Q)(-\delta_A) \tag{9-56}$$

†*Manual of Steel Construction*, 6th ed. New York, American Institute of Steel Construction, Inc., 1963, pp. 2–125.

The deflection at A, δ_A, can be determined from Eq. (9-27) as

$$\delta_A = \theta_3(a) - \frac{a^2}{L_2}[2\theta_3 + \theta_4] + \frac{a^3}{L_2^2}(\theta_3 + \theta_4) + G_3(a) \tag{9-57}$$

where $G_3(a)$ is the value of the deflection function at $x = a$ for beam element 3-4 for the member fixed at both ends; i.e.,

$$G_3(a) = -\frac{Q^3ab^3}{3EIL_2^3} \tag{9-58}$$

9–4
Illustrative Examples

Before deriving the member stiffness and structure stiffness matrices by the principle of stationary potential energy, first consider how this principle may be applied to the solution of several structural systems.

Example 9-1. The bar forces and joint displacements for the truss structure shown in Fig. 9-7 are desired. The joint displacements δ_j are identified as δ_1 and δ_2 and are

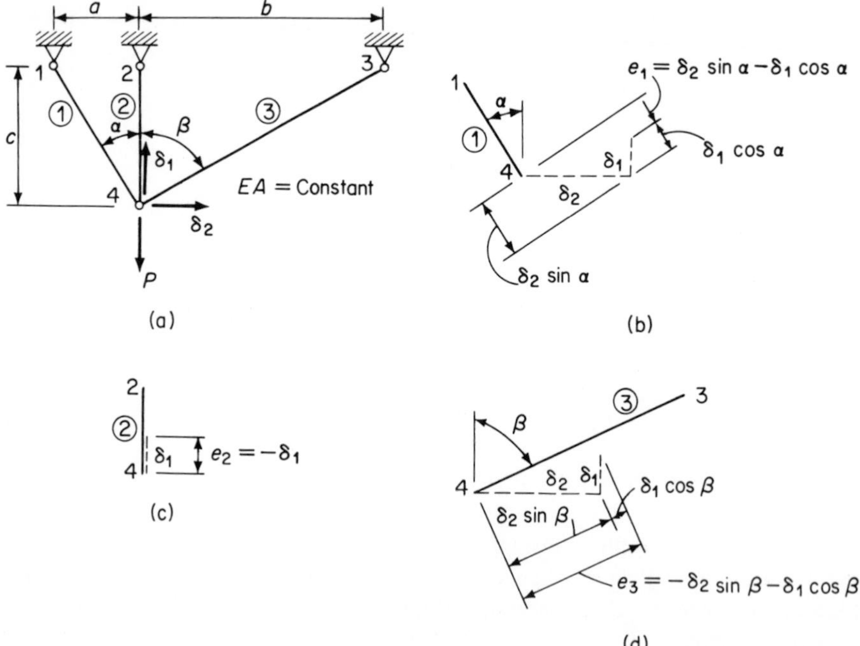

Fig. 9-7 Example 9-1: Analysis of truss structure: (a) truss structure; (b) elongation of member 1; (c) elongation of member 2; (d) elongation of member 3.

shown in the assumed positive direction. The modulus of elasticity E and the cross-sectional area A of all members are equal. Expressing the elongation of each bar, e_i, as a function of the joint displacements δ_1 and δ_2 the axial strain energy for the members of the system is given as follows [see Figs. 9-7(b), (c), and (d)]:

Member 1

$$e_1 = \delta_2 \sin\alpha - \delta_1 \cos\alpha \tag{9-59a}$$

Member 2

$$e_2 = -\delta_1 \tag{9-59b}$$

Member 3

$$e_3 = -\delta_2 \sin\beta - \delta_1 \cos\beta \tag{9-59c}$$

In the above equations, the elongation is positive when the member is subjected to tensile forces.

Modification of Eq. (9-14a) so that it represents the sum of the strain energy in each of the three members yields

$$U = \frac{EA}{2} \sum_{i=1}^{3} \frac{e_i^2}{L_i} \tag{9-60}$$

where L_i is the length of member i and e_i is the elongation or shortening of member i. The functions for e_1, e_2, and e_3 could be substituted directly into Eq. (9-60); however, the use of the chain rule in differentiation is more satisfactory when the total potential energy is differentiated with respect to δ_1 and δ_2.

The external potential energy is

$$W_e = (-P)(\delta_1) \tag{9-61}$$

The total potential energy is

$$V = U - W_e \tag{9-62}$$

or

$$V = \frac{EA}{2} \sum_{i=1}^{3} \frac{e_i^2}{L_i} + P\delta_1 \tag{9-63}$$

Now,

$$\frac{\partial V}{\partial \delta_1} = EA \sum_{i=1}^{3} \frac{e_i}{L_i} \frac{\partial e_i}{\partial \delta_1} + P = 0 \tag{9-64a}$$

and

$$\frac{\partial V}{\partial \delta_2} = EA \sum_{i=1}^{3} \frac{e_i}{L_i} \frac{\partial e_i}{\partial \delta_2} = 0 \tag{9-64b}$$

The partial derivatives of e_i with respect to δ_1 and δ_2 can be obtained by differentiating Eqs. (9-59a), (9-59b), and (9-59c). They are as follows:

$$\frac{\partial e_1}{\partial \delta_1} = -\cos\alpha \tag{9-65a}$$

$$\frac{\partial e_2}{\partial \delta_1} = -1 \tag{9-65b}$$

$$\frac{\partial e_3}{\partial \delta_1} = -\cos\beta \tag{9-65c}$$

$$\frac{\partial e_1}{\partial \delta_2} = \sin \alpha \tag{9-65d}$$

$$\frac{\partial e_2}{\partial \delta_2} = 0 \tag{9-65e}$$

$$\frac{\partial e_3}{\partial \delta_2} = -\sin \beta \tag{9-65f}$$

Equations (9-64a) and (9-64b) can be expanded to read as

$$\frac{\partial V}{\partial \delta_1} = EA\left(\frac{e_1}{L_1}\frac{\partial e_1}{\partial \delta_1} + \frac{e_2}{L_2}\frac{\partial e_2}{\partial \delta_1} + \frac{e_3}{L_3}\frac{\partial e_3}{\partial \delta_1}\right) + P = 0 \tag{9-66a}$$

and

$$\frac{\partial V}{\partial \delta_2} = EA\left(\frac{e_1}{L_2}\frac{\partial e_1}{\partial \delta_2} + \frac{e_2}{L_2}\frac{\partial e_2}{\partial \delta_2} + \frac{e_3}{L_3}\frac{\partial e_3}{\partial \delta_2}\right) = 0 \tag{9-66b}$$

Substitution of the expressions for e_i from Eqs. (9-59), and for $\partial e_i/\partial \delta_1$ and $\partial e_i/\partial \delta_2$ from Eqs. (9-65), into Eqs. (9-66) yields

$$EA\left[\frac{(\delta_2 \sin \alpha - \delta_1 \cos \alpha)(-\cos \alpha)}{L_1} + \frac{(-\delta_1)(-1)}{L_2} + \frac{(-\delta_2 \sin \beta - \delta_1 \cos \beta)(-\cos \beta)}{L_3}\right] + P = 0 \tag{9-67a}$$

and

$$EA\left[\frac{(\delta_2 \sin \alpha - \delta_1 \cos \alpha)(\sin \alpha)}{L_1} + \frac{(-\delta_2 \sin \beta - \delta_1 \cos \beta)(-\sin \beta)}{L_3}\right] = 0 \tag{9-67b}$$

Equations (9-67) can be rewritten as

$$\frac{-\delta_2 \sin \alpha \cos \alpha + \delta_1 \cos^2 \alpha}{L_1} + \frac{\delta_1}{L_2} + \frac{\delta_2 \sin \beta \cos \beta + \delta_1 \cos^2 \beta}{L_3} + \frac{P}{EA} = 0 \tag{9-68a}$$

and

$$\frac{\delta_2 \sin^2 \alpha - \delta_1 \cos \alpha \sin \alpha}{L_1} + \frac{\delta_2 \sin^2 \beta + \delta_1 \cos \beta \sin \beta}{L_3} = 0 \tag{9-68b}$$

Assuming $\alpha = 30°$, $\beta = 60°$, and $c = 1$ for the system of Fig. 9-7(a), then

$$\sin \alpha = \cos \beta = 0.5$$
$$\cos \alpha = \sin \beta = 0.866$$
$$\cos^2 \beta = \sin^2 \alpha = 0.25$$
$$\sin^2 \beta = \cos^2 \alpha = 0.75$$
$$\sin \alpha \cos \alpha = \sin \beta \cos \beta = 0.433$$
$$a = 0.578$$
$$b = 1.732$$
$$L_1 = 1.157$$
$$L_2 = 1.00$$

and

$$L_3 = 2.00$$

Substitution of the above values into Eqs. (9-68) yields

$$1.775\delta_1 - 0.159\delta_2 = -\frac{P}{EA} \tag{9-69a}$$

$$-0.159\delta_1 + 0.592\delta_2 = 0 \tag{9-69b}$$

Solving for δ_1 and δ_2 yields

$$\delta_1 = -0.58\frac{P}{EA}\downarrow \tag{9-70a}$$

$$\delta_2 = -0.154\frac{P}{EA}\longleftarrow \tag{9-70b}$$

The negative signs indicate that displacements δ_1 and δ_2 are both opposite to the arbitrarily chosen positive direction.

The bar forces N may be found by Eq. (9-13), which is rewritten below for convenience. Note that subscript i is now shown, indicating that the bar force in the ith member is to be computed:

$$N_i = \frac{A_i E_i e_i}{L_i} \tag{9-71}$$

Substitution of the values for δ_1 and δ_2 as given by Eqs. (9-70) into Eqs. (9-59) yields

$$\begin{aligned} e_1 &= \delta_2 \sin\alpha - \delta_1 \cos\alpha \\ &= -0.154\frac{P}{EA}(0.5) + 0.58\left(\frac{P}{EA}\right)(0.866) \\ &= 0.423\frac{P}{EA} \qquad \text{(tension)} \end{aligned} \tag{9-72a}$$

$$\begin{aligned} e_2 &= -\delta_1 \\ &= 0.58\frac{P}{EA} \qquad \text{(tension)} \end{aligned} \tag{9-72b}$$

$$\begin{aligned} e_3 &= -\delta_2 \sin\beta - \delta_1 \cos\beta \\ &= +0.154\frac{P}{EA}(0.866) + 0.58\frac{P}{EA}(0.5) \\ &= 0.423\frac{P}{EA} \qquad \text{(tension)} \end{aligned} \tag{9-72c}$$

Substitution of Eqs. (9-72) into Eq. (9-71) gives

$$N_1 = 0.367P \qquad \text{(tension)} \tag{9-73a}$$

$$N_2 = 0.58P \qquad \text{(tension)} \tag{9-73b}$$

$$N_3 = 0.212P \qquad \text{(tension)} \tag{9-73c}$$

To check this solution, sum vertical forces acting at joint 4. Thus,

$$N_1 \cos 30^\circ + N_2 + N_3 \cos 60^\circ = P$$

$$0.367P(0.866) + 0.58P + 0.212P(0.5) = P$$

$$1.004P \approx P$$

Example 9-2. Calculate the end moments and shears of the continuous beam shown in Fig. 9-8 and draw shear and moment diagrams. In this structure, there is only one

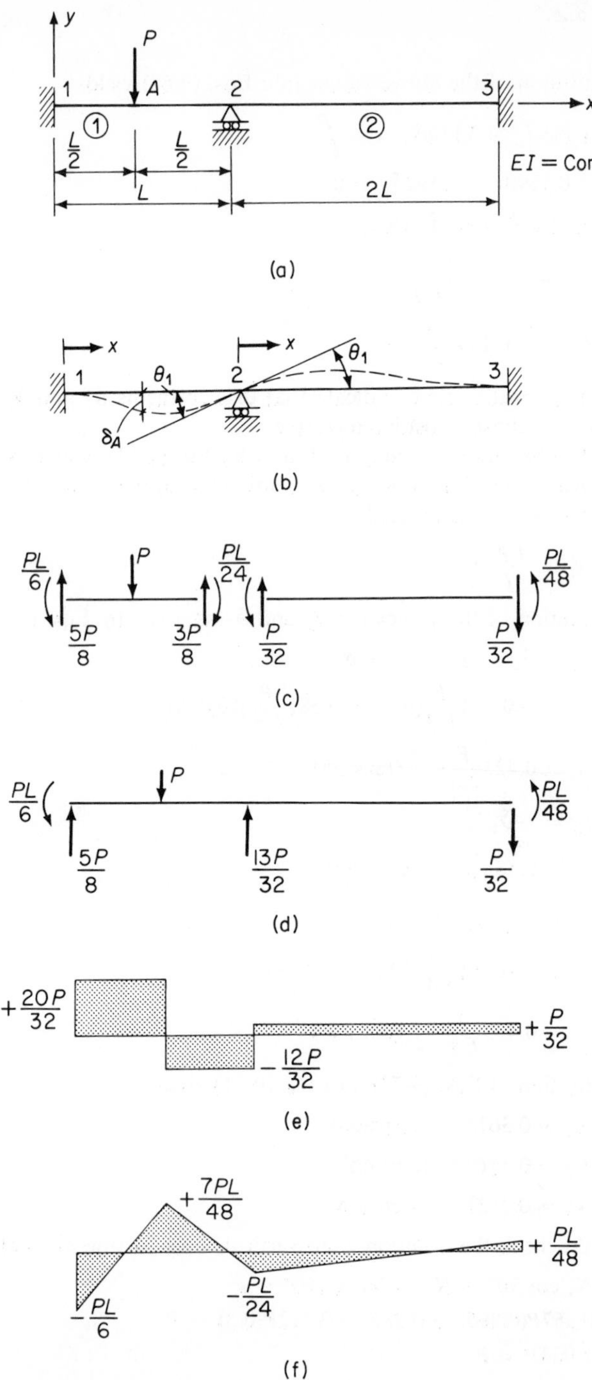

Fig. 9-8 Example 9-2: Analysis of continuous beam: (a) continuous beam; (b) displacements; (c) free body diagrams; (d) final reactions; (e) shear diagram; (f) moment diagram.

joint displacement θ_1; therefore, the total potential energy can be expressed in terms of this joint displacement.

Using Eq. (9-49), the strain energy for members 1 and 2 is

$$U_{b1} = \frac{2EI}{L}(\theta_1^2) + \text{constant} \tag{9-74a}$$

$$U_{b2} = \frac{EI}{L}(\theta_1^2) + \text{constant} \tag{9-74b}$$

The total strain energy is the sum of U_{b1} and U_{b2}, as follows:

$$U_b = \left(\frac{3EI}{L}\right)\theta_1^2 + \text{constant} \tag{9-75}$$

The external potential energy is

$$W_e = (-P)(\delta_A) = -P\delta_A \tag{9-76}$$

where δ_A is the deflection under the load P and is obtained from Eqs. (9-34); i.e.,

$$\delta_A = \bar{y} + y_f \tag{9-77}$$

Substitution into the expression for $\bar{y}$, Eq. (9-32), yields

$$\bar{y} = -\frac{(L/2)^2}{L}(\theta_1) + \frac{(L/2)^3}{L^2}(\theta_1) = -\frac{L}{8}\theta_1 \tag{9-78a}$$

The expression for y_f, the deflection under the load P if both ends were fixed, is

$$y_f = -\frac{PL^3}{192EI} \tag{9-78b}$$

Then,

$$\delta_A = -\frac{L}{8}\theta_1 - \frac{PL^3}{192EI} \tag{9-79}$$

Thus,

$$W_e = \frac{P^2L^3}{192EI} + \frac{PL}{8}\theta_1 \tag{9-80}$$

The substitution of Eqs. (9-80) and (9-75) into the expression for the total potential energy as given by Eq. (9-7) yields

$$V = \frac{P^2L^3}{192EI} + \frac{PL}{8}\theta_1 - \frac{3EI}{L}\theta_1^2 - \text{constant} \tag{9-81}$$

which by changing signs and condensing can be rewritten as

$$V = \frac{3EI}{L}\theta_1^2 - \frac{PL}{8}\theta_1 + \text{new constant} \tag{9-82}$$

Differentiation with respect to the joint displacement θ_1 and equating to zero gives

$$\frac{\partial V}{\partial \theta_1} = \frac{6EI}{L}\theta_1 - \frac{PL}{8} = 0 \tag{9-83}$$

or

$$\theta_1 = \frac{PL^2}{48EI} \tag{9-84}$$

Back substitution into Eqs. (9-26) yields

Member 1

$$M_p^1 = \frac{2EI}{L}\left(\frac{PL^2}{48EI}\right) + \frac{PL}{8} = +\frac{1}{6}PL \tag{9-85a}$$

$$M_q^1 = \frac{4EI}{L}\left(\frac{PL^2}{48EI}\right) - \frac{PL}{8} = -\frac{1}{24}PL \tag{9-85b}$$

$$P_r^1 = \frac{6EI}{L^2}\left(\frac{PL^2}{48EI}\right) + \frac{P}{2} = +\frac{5}{8}P \tag{9-85c}$$

$$P_s^1 = -\frac{6EI}{L^2}\left(\frac{PL^2}{48EI}\right) + \frac{P}{2} = +\frac{3}{8}P \tag{9-85d}$$

Member 2

$$M_p^2 = \frac{2EI}{L}\left(\frac{PL^2}{48EI}\right) = +\frac{1}{24}PL \tag{9-86a}$$

$$M_q^2 = \frac{EI}{L}\left(\frac{PL^2}{48EI}\right) = +\frac{1}{48}PL \tag{9-86b}$$

$$P_r^2 = \frac{6EI}{(2L)^2}\left(\frac{PL^2}{48EI}\right) = +\frac{1}{32}P \tag{9-86c}$$

$$P_s^2 = -\frac{6EI}{(2L)^2}\left(\frac{PL^2}{48EI}\right) = -\frac{1}{32}P \tag{9-86d}$$

The end actions given above are shown on the free bodies of each member [see Fig. 9-8(b)]. The end actions, reactions, shear and moment diagrams are given in Figs. 9-8(c), (d), (e), and (f).

9–5 Member Stiffness and Structure Stiffness Matrices

9-5.1 Member Stiffness Matrix

The principle of stationary potential energy can be used to obtain the member stiffness matrix. Although only one type of beam element will be illustrated, the method can be applied to other types of elements as well.

Consider a straight flexural member with constant stiffness throughout its length. The member is subjected to four arbitrary end displacements as shown in Fig. 9-9. Only flexural deformations are considered.

The strain energy for the member is given by Eq. (9-49) and is rewritten here for convenience:

$$U_b = \frac{2EI}{L}\left[\theta_p^2 + \theta_p\theta_q + \theta_q^2 + \frac{3}{L}(\delta_r - \delta_s)(\theta_p + \theta_q) + \frac{3}{L^2}(\delta_r - \delta_s)^2\right] + \text{constant} \tag{9-49}$$

The external potential energy is equal to the end actions required to maintain equilibrium of deformed member multiplied by the end displacements; i.e.,

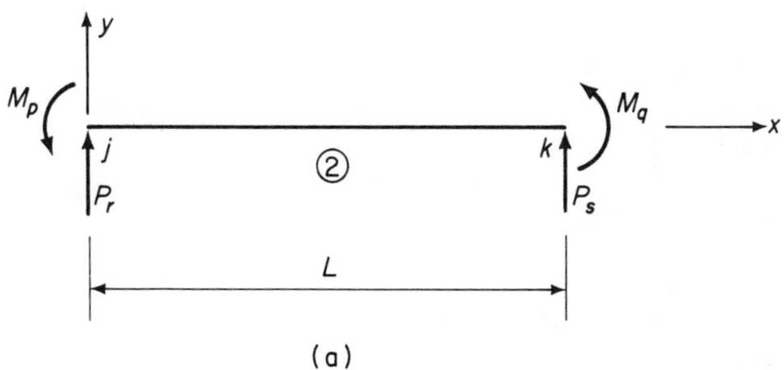

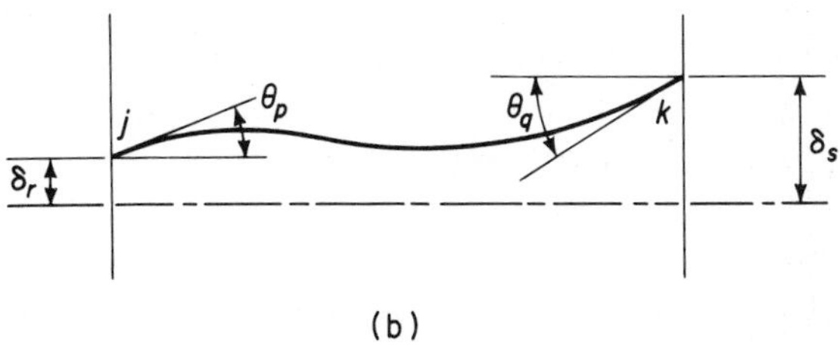

Fig. 9-9 End actions and displacements, member i: (a) end actions; (b) end displacements.

$$W_e = M_p\theta_p + M_q\theta_q + P_r\delta_r + P_s\delta_s \tag{9-87}$$

Substitution of Eqs. (9-49) and (9-87) into Eq. (9-9) yields the following set of equations:

$$\frac{\partial V}{\partial \theta_p} = \frac{2EI}{L}\left[2\theta_p + \theta_q + \frac{3}{L}(\delta_r - \delta_s)\right] - M_p = 0 \tag{9-88a}$$

$$\frac{\partial V}{\partial \theta_q} = \frac{2EI}{L}\left[\theta_p + 2\theta_q + \frac{3}{L}(\delta_r - \delta_s)\right] - M_q = 0 \tag{9-88b}$$

$$\frac{\partial V}{\partial \delta_r} = \frac{2EI}{L}\left[\frac{3}{L}(\theta_p + \theta_q) + \frac{6}{L^2}(\delta_r - \delta_s)\right] - P_r = 0 \tag{9-88c}$$

$$\frac{\partial V}{\partial \delta_s} = \frac{2EI}{L}\left[-\frac{3}{L}(\theta_p + \theta_q) + \frac{6}{L^2}(\delta_r - \delta_s)\right] - P_s = 0 \tag{9-88d}$$

The above set of equations can be placed in matrix form as follows:

$$\frac{EI}{L}\begin{bmatrix} 4 & 2 & \frac{6}{L} & -\frac{6}{L} \\ 2 & 4 & \frac{6}{L} & -\frac{6}{L} \\ \frac{6}{L} & \frac{6}{L} & \frac{12}{L^2} & -\frac{12}{L^2} \\ -\frac{6}{L} & -\frac{6}{L} & -\frac{12}{L^2} & \frac{12}{L^2} \end{bmatrix}\begin{bmatrix} \theta_p \\ \theta_q \\ \delta_r \\ \delta_s \end{bmatrix} = \begin{bmatrix} M_p \\ M_q \\ P_r \\ P_s \end{bmatrix} \tag{9-89}$$

The square matrix in Eq. (9-89) is the member stiffness matrix for a prismatic member considering flexural displacements only. Note that this matrix is the same as that given by Eq. (4-16) of Chapter 4. Axial, shear, and torsional effects can be easily included by simply adding the appropriate strain energy terms to Eq. (9-49) and by defining the additional end displacements that might be associated with these effects.

9-5.2 Structure Stiffness Matrix

The structure stiffness matrix can be obtained in much the same way as the member stiffness matrix. In order to accomplish this, the total potential energy must be written for the entire structure. To demonstrate this procedure, the same examples given earlier in the text are used. First, consider Example 4-1 given in Chapter 4, as shown again in Fig. 9-10.

Example 9-3. Determine the structure stiffness matrix for the structure in Fig. 9-10. The strain energy for each member as determined from Eq. (9-49) is as follows:

$$U_{b1} = \frac{2EI_1}{L_1}(\theta_1^2 + \theta_1\theta_2 + \theta_2^2) + \text{constant} \tag{9-90a}$$

$$U_{b2} = \frac{2EI_2}{L_2}(\theta_2^2 + \theta_2\theta_3 + \theta_3^2) + \text{constant} \tag{9-90b}$$

$$U_{b3} = \frac{2EI_3}{L_3}(\theta_3^2 + \theta_3\theta_4 + \theta_4^2) + \text{constant} \tag{9-90c}$$

where $I_1 = 3I$;
$I_2 = 2I$;
$I_3 = 3I$.

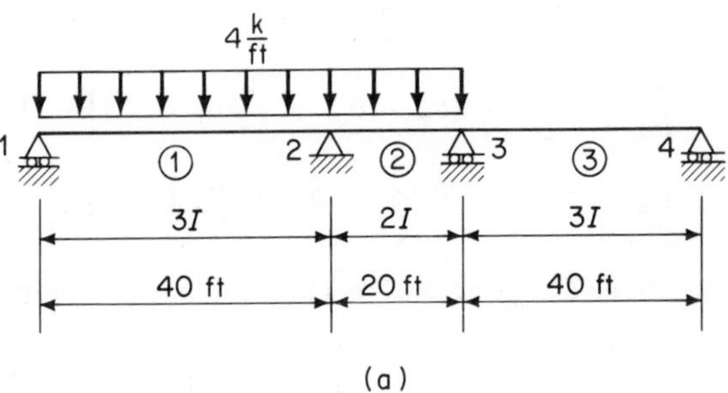

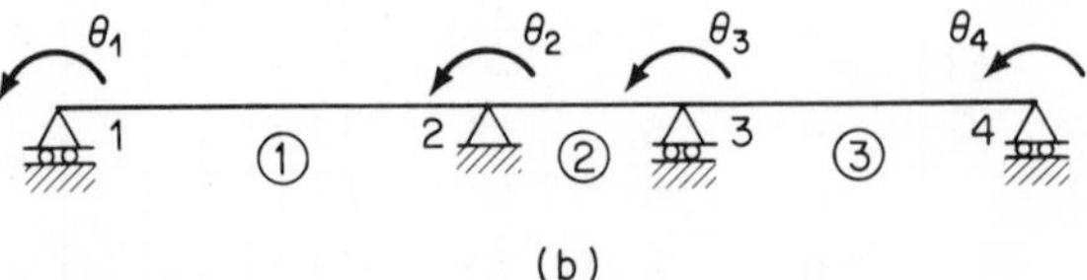

Fig. 9-10 Example 9-3: Determination of structure stiffness matrix: (a) continuous beam; (b) joint displacements.

The total strain energy is

$$U_b = U_{b1} + U_{b2} + U_{b3} \tag{9-91a}$$

or

$$U_b = \frac{6EI}{40}\theta_1^2 + \left(\frac{6EI}{40} + \frac{4EI}{20}\right)\theta_2^2 + \left(\frac{4EI}{20} + \frac{6EI}{40}\right)\theta_3^2 + \frac{6EI}{L^3}\theta_4^2$$
$$+ \frac{6EI}{40}\theta_1\theta_2 + \frac{4EI}{20}\theta_2\theta_3 + \frac{6EI}{40}\theta_3\theta_4 + \text{new constant} \tag{9-91b}$$

Again, the external potential energy W_e is a linear function in θ_1, θ_2, θ_3, and θ_4. It is not necessary to state the exact function, since only the determination of the structure stiffness matrix is of interest. Thus, W_e can be written as follows:

$$W_e = C_1\theta_1 + C_2\theta_2 + C_3\theta_3 + C_4\theta_4 \tag{9-92}$$

where C_1, C_2, C_3, and C_4 are functions of the loads and their location. Substitution of Eqs. (9-91b) and (9-92) into Eq. (9-7), and performing the differentiation with respect to $\theta_1, \theta_2, \theta_3$, and θ_4, as required by Eq. (9-9), yields the following set of equations:

$$\frac{\partial V}{\partial \theta_1} = \frac{12EI}{40}\theta_1 + \frac{6EI}{40}\theta_2 - C_1 = 0 \tag{9-93a}$$

$$\frac{\partial V}{\partial \theta_2} = \frac{6EI}{40}\theta_1 + \left(\frac{12EI}{40} + \frac{8EI}{20}\right)\theta_2 + \frac{4EI}{20}\theta_3 - C_2 = 0 \tag{9-93b}$$

$$\frac{\partial V}{\partial \theta_3} = \frac{4EI}{20}\theta_2 + \left(\frac{8EI}{20} + \frac{12EI}{40}\right)\theta_3 + \frac{6EI}{40}\theta_4 - C_3 = 0 \tag{9-93c}$$

$$\frac{\partial V}{\partial \theta_4} = \frac{6EI}{40}\theta_3 + \frac{12EI}{40}\theta_4 - C_4 = 0 \tag{9-93d}$$

Placing Eqs. (9-93) into matrix form and condensing yields

$$EI\begin{bmatrix} 0.3 & 0.15 & 0 & 0 \\ 0.15 & 0.7 & 0.2 & 0 \\ 0 & 0.2 & 0.7 & 0.3 \\ 0 & 0 & 0.3 & 0.3 \end{bmatrix}\begin{bmatrix}\theta_1 \\ \theta_2 \\ \theta_3 \\ \theta_4\end{bmatrix} = \begin{bmatrix} C_1 \\ C_2 \\ C_3 \\ C_4 \end{bmatrix} \tag{9-94}$$

unknown displacements (pointing to θ vector); structure stiffness coefficient (pointing to matrix); joint load functions (pointing to C vector)

Note that the above square matrix is identical to $[\mathbf{S}_{uu}]$ given in Eq. (4-57b) in Chapter 4.

Example 9-4. The analysis of the structure shown in Fig. 9-11 was presented as Example 5-1; however, it is desired here only to illustrate the determination of the structure stiffness matrix. Since the system is nonorthogonal, axial strain energy as well as bending strain energy must be considered in the analysis. Axial strain energy must be considered because for nonorthogonal structural systems axial elongations must be considered for joint compatibility. If axial elongation or shortening cannot be ignored, then neither can axial strain energy. The strain energy equation appropriate to the analysis of this system consists of the sum of Eqs. (9-49) and (9-14b); thus,

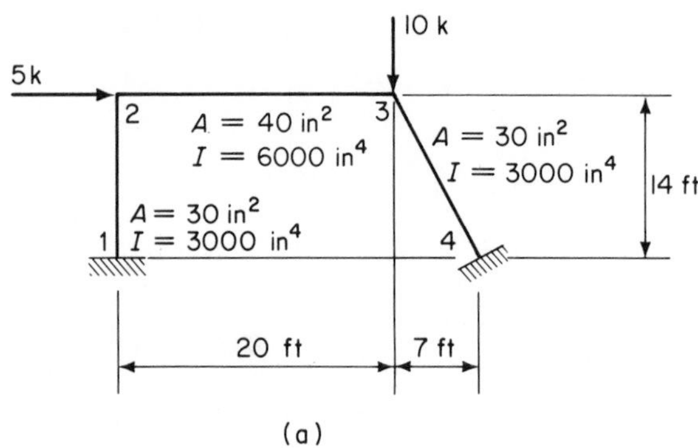

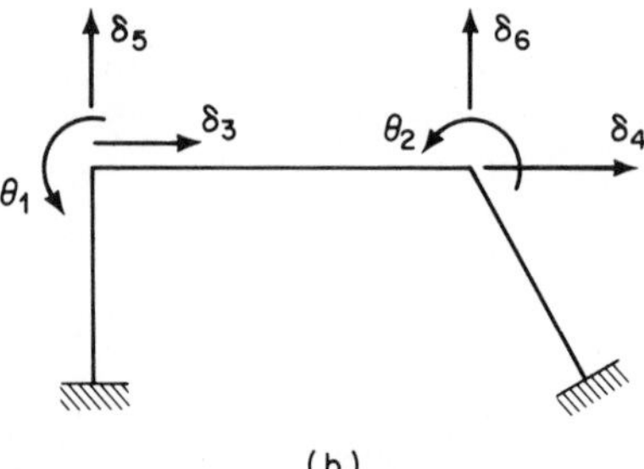

Fig. 9-11 Example 9-4: Analysis of nonorthogonal frame structure: (a) loads; (b) unknown joint displacements.

$$U = \frac{2EI}{L}\Big[\theta_p^2 + \theta_p\theta_q + \theta_q^2 + \frac{3}{L}(\delta_r - \delta_s)(\theta_p + \theta_q) + \frac{3}{L^2}(\delta_r - \delta_s)^2\Big] + \frac{AE}{2L}(\delta_u - \delta_t)^2 + \text{constant} \tag{9-95}$$

The unknown end displacements are shown in Fig. 9-11. The strain energy for each member is

$$U_1 = \frac{2EI_1}{L_1}\Big[\theta_1^2 + \frac{3}{L_1}(\delta_3)(\theta_1) + \frac{3}{L_1^2}(\delta_3)^2\Big] + \frac{EA_1}{2L_1}(\delta_5)^2 + \text{constant} \tag{9-96a}$$

$$U_2 = \frac{2EI_2}{L_2}\Big[\theta_1^2 + \theta_1\theta_2 + \theta_2^2 + \frac{3}{L_2}(\delta_5 - \delta_6)(\theta_1 + \theta_2) + \frac{3}{L_2^2}(\delta_5 - \delta_6)^2\Big] + \frac{EA_2}{2L_2}(\delta_4 - \delta_3)^2 + \text{constant} \tag{9-96b}$$

$$U_3 = \frac{2EI_3}{L_3}\Big[\theta_2^2 + \frac{3}{L_3}\Big(\frac{2}{\sqrt{5}}\delta_4 + \frac{1}{\sqrt{5}}\delta_6\Big)(\theta_2) + \frac{3}{L_3^2}\Big(\frac{2}{\sqrt{5}}\delta_4 + \frac{1}{\sqrt{5}}\delta_6\Big)^2\Big] + \frac{EA_3}{2L_3}\Big(-\frac{1}{\sqrt{5}}\delta_4 + \frac{2}{\sqrt{5}}\delta_6\Big)^2 + \text{constant} \tag{9-96c}$$

The total strain energy is

$$U = U_1 + U_2 + U_3 \tag{9-97}$$

The external potential energy W_e is a linear function of the six joint displacements; thus, it is not necessary to determine it specifically, since the structure stiffness matrix is the only matrix desired. In this form, then, W_e is as follows:

$$W_e = C_1\theta_1 + C_2\theta_2 + C_3\delta_3 + C_4\delta_4 + C_5\delta_5 + C_6\delta_6 \qquad \textbf{(9-98)}$$

where C_1, C_2, C_3, C_4, C_5, and C_6 are functions of the applied loads and their location.

Substitution of Eqs. (9-97) and (9-98) into Eq. (9-9) yields

$$\frac{\partial V}{\partial \theta_1} = \frac{4EI_1}{L_1}\theta_1 + \frac{2EI_1}{L_1}\delta_3\left(\frac{3}{L_1}\right) + \frac{4EI_2}{L_2}\theta_1 + \frac{2EI_2}{L_2}\theta_2 + \frac{2EI_2}{L_2}\left(\frac{3}{L_2}\right)(\delta_5 - \delta_6) - C_1 = 0 \qquad \textbf{(9-99a)}$$

$$\frac{\partial V}{\partial \theta_2} = \frac{2EI_2}{L_2}\theta_1 + \frac{4EI_2}{L_2}\theta_2 + \frac{2EI_2}{L_2}\left(\frac{3}{L_2}\right)(\delta_5 - \delta_6) + \frac{4EI_3}{L_3}\theta_2 + \frac{2EI_3}{L_3}\left(\frac{3}{L_3}\right)\left(\frac{2}{\sqrt{5}}\delta_4 + \frac{1}{\sqrt{5}}\delta_6\right) - C_2 = 0 \qquad \textbf{(9-99b)}$$

$$\frac{\partial V}{\partial \delta_3} = \frac{2EI_1}{L_1}\theta_1\left(\frac{3}{L_1}\right) + \frac{2EI_1}{L_1}\left(\frac{6}{L_1^2}\right)(\delta_3) - \frac{EA_2}{L_2}(\delta_4 - \delta_3) - C_3 = 0 \qquad \textbf{(9-99c)}$$

$$\frac{\partial V}{\partial \delta_4} = \frac{EA_2}{L_2}(\delta_4 - \delta_3) + \frac{2EI_3}{L_3}\left(\frac{3}{L_3}\right)(\theta_2)\left(\frac{2}{\sqrt{5}}\right) + \frac{2EI_3}{L_3}\left(\frac{6}{L_3^2}\right)\left(\frac{2}{\sqrt{5}}\delta_4 + \frac{1}{\sqrt{5}}\delta_6\right)\left(\frac{2}{\sqrt{5}}\right) + \frac{EA_3}{L_3}\left(-\frac{1}{\sqrt{5}}\delta_4 + \frac{2}{\sqrt{5}}\delta_6\right)\left(-\frac{1}{\sqrt{5}}\right) - C_4 = 0 \qquad \textbf{(9-99d)}$$

$$\frac{\partial V}{\partial \delta_5} = \frac{EA_1}{L_1}(\delta_5) + \frac{2EI_2}{L_2}\left(\frac{3}{L_2}\right)(\theta_1 + \theta_2) + \frac{2EI_2}{L_2}\left(\frac{6}{L_2^2}\right)(\delta_5 - \delta_6) - C_5 = 0 \qquad \textbf{(9-99e)}$$

$$\frac{\partial V}{\partial \delta_6} = -\frac{2EI_2}{L_2}\left(\frac{3}{L_2}\right)(\theta_1 + \theta_2) - \frac{2EI_2}{L_2}\left(\frac{6}{L_2^2}\right)(\delta_5 - \delta_6) + \frac{2EI_3}{L_3}\left(\frac{3}{L_3}\right)(\theta_2)\left(\frac{1}{\sqrt{5}}\right) + \frac{2EI_3}{L_3}\left(\frac{6}{L_3^2}\right)\left(\frac{2}{\sqrt{5}}\delta_4 + \frac{1}{\sqrt{5}}\delta_6\right)\left(\frac{1}{\sqrt{5}}\right) + \frac{EA_3}{L_3}\left(-\frac{1}{\sqrt{5}}\delta_4 + \frac{2}{\sqrt{5}}\delta_6\right)\left(\frac{2}{\sqrt{5}}\right) - C_6 = 0 \qquad \textbf{(9-99f)}$$

Using values of A, I, and L from Table 5-4 gives

$$\frac{\partial V}{\partial \theta_1} = E \times 10^{-2}[9.92\theta_1 + 2.89\theta_2 + 0.444\delta_3 + 0 + 0.433\delta_5 - 0.433\delta_6] - C_1 = 0 \qquad \textbf{(9-100a)}$$

$$\frac{\partial V}{\partial \theta_2} = E \times 10^{-2}[2.89\theta_1 + 9.48\theta_2 + 0 + 0.318\delta_4 + 0.433\delta_5 - 0.274\delta_6] - C_2 = 0 \qquad \textbf{(9-100b)}$$

$$\frac{\partial V}{\partial \delta_3} = E \times 10^{-2}[0.444\theta_1 + 0 + 1.453\delta_3 - 1.39\delta_4 + 0 + 0] - C_3 = 0 \qquad \textbf{(9-100c)}$$

$$\frac{\partial V}{\partial \delta_4} = E \times 10^{-2}[+0 + 0.318\theta_2 - 1.39\delta_3 + 1.658\delta_4 + 0 - 0.50\delta_6] - C_4 = 0 \qquad \textbf{(9-100d)}$$

$$\frac{\partial V}{\partial \delta_5} = E \times 10^{-2}[0.433\theta_1 + 0.433\theta_2 + 0 + 0 + 1.529\delta_5 - 0.0433\delta_6] - C_5 = 0 \qquad \textbf{(9-100e)}$$

$$\frac{\partial V}{\partial \delta_6} = E \times 10^{-2}[-0.433\theta_1 - 0.274\theta_2 + 0 \qquad - 0.50\delta_4 \quad - 0.433\delta_5 + 1.089\delta_6] - C_6 = 0 \tag{9-100f}$$

In matrix form, Eqs. (9-100) become

$$E \times 10^{-2}\begin{bmatrix} 9.92 & 2.89 & 0.444 & 0 & 0.433 & -0.433 \\ 2.89 & 9.48 & 0 & 0.318 & 0.433 & -0.274 \\ 0.444 & 0 & 1.453 & -1.39 & 0 & 0 \\ 0 & 0.318 & -1.39 & 1.685 & 0 & -0.5 \\ 0.433 & 0.433 & 0 & 0 & 1.529 & -0.0433 \\ -0.433 & -0.274 & 0 & -0.5 & -0.0433 & 1.0894 \end{bmatrix} \begin{bmatrix} \theta_1 \\ \theta_2 \\ \delta_3 \\ \delta_4 \\ \delta_5 \\ \delta_6 \end{bmatrix} = \begin{bmatrix} C_1 \\ C_2 \\ C_3 \\ C_4 \\ C_5 \\ C_6 \end{bmatrix} \tag{9-101}$$

The square matrix in Eq. (9-101) is the structure stiffness matrix or [$\mathbf{S}_{uu'}$.] This agrees with that obtained in Example 5-1 [see Eq. (5-49)].

9–6 Problems

9-1 to 9-7. Analyze completely the following structural systems by the method of stationary potential energy.

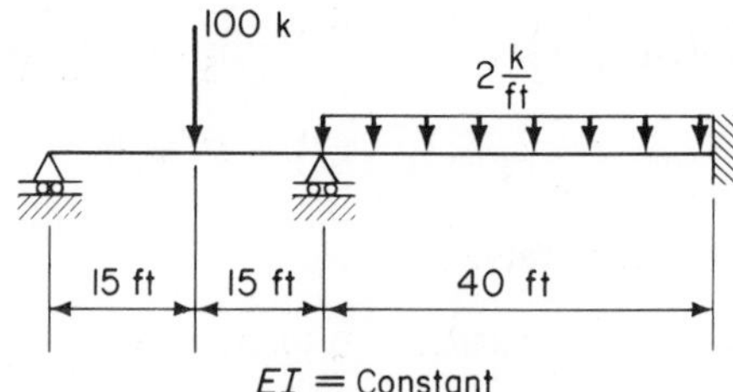

Prob. 9-1

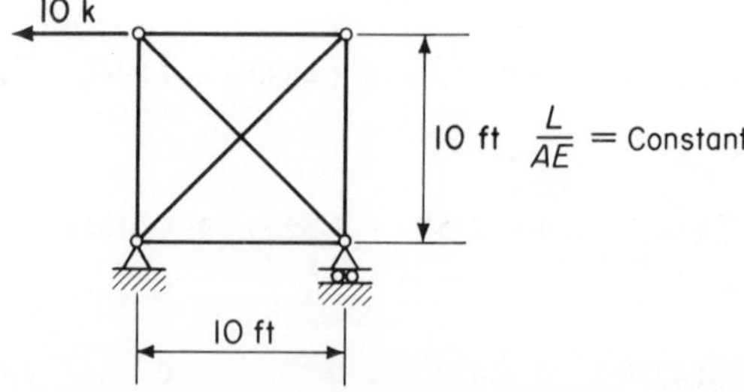

Prob. 9-2

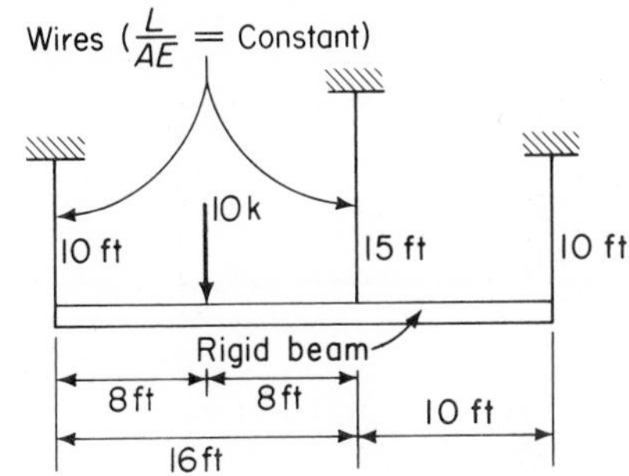

Prob. 9-3

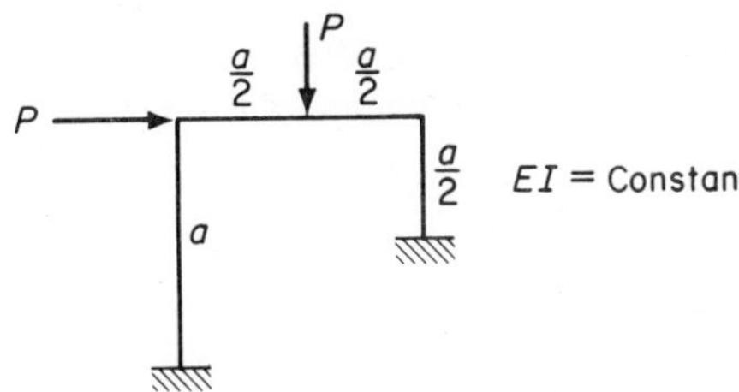

Prob. 9-4

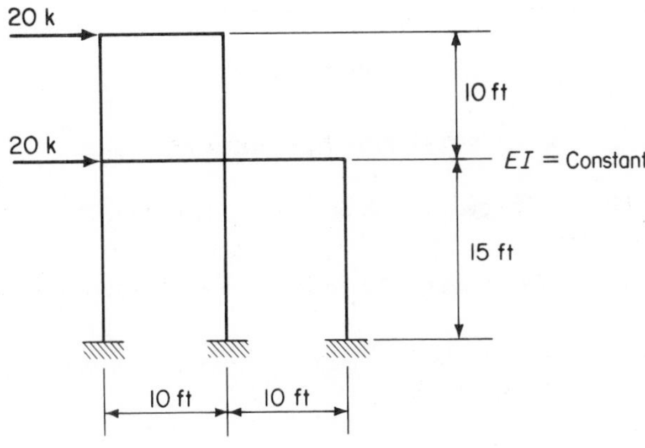

Prob. 9-5

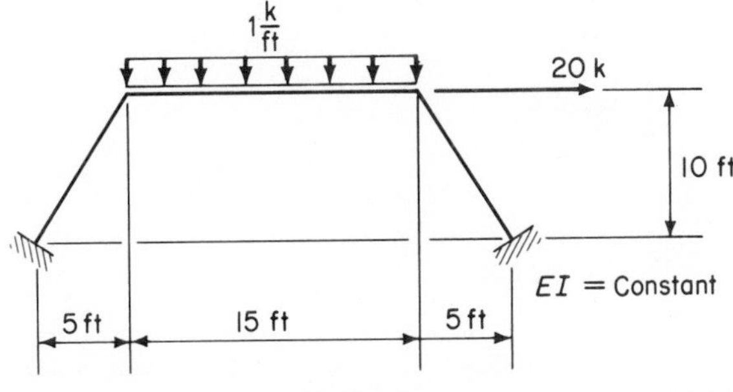

Prob. 9-6

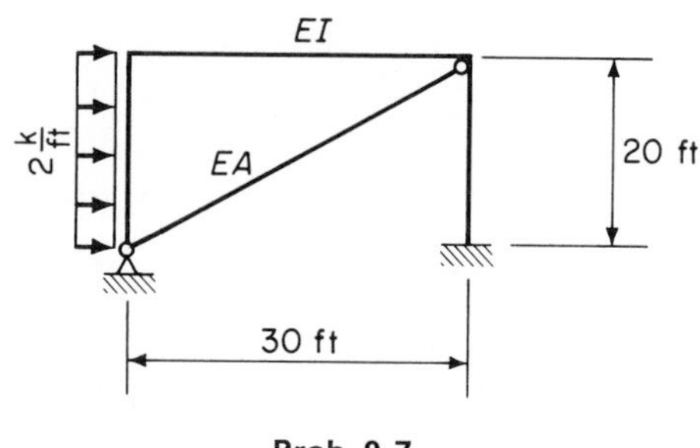

Prob. 9-7

9-8. Establish the member stiffness matrix for the tapered beam element shown below by the method of stationary potential energy (see Example 4-2).

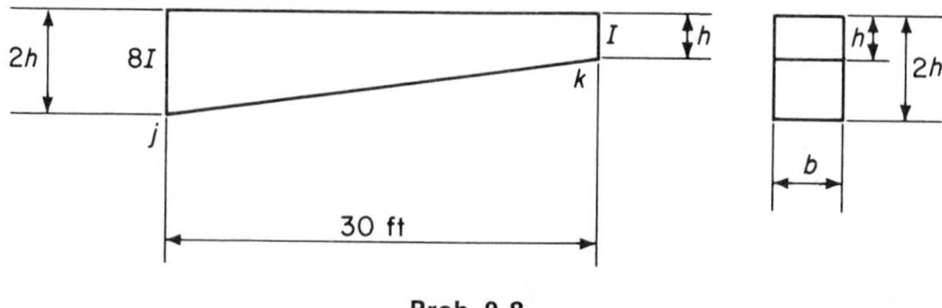

Prob. 9-8

SELECTED REFERENCES

9-1 Langhaar, Henry, *Energy Methods in Applied Mechanics.* New York: John Wiley & Sons, Inc., 1962.

9-2 Hoff, Nicholas J., *The Analysis of Structures.* New York: John Wiley & Sons, Inc., 1956.

9-3 Rubinstein, Moshe F., *Matrix Computer Analysis of Structures.* Englewood Cliffs, N.J.: Prentice-Hall, Inc., 1966.

10 INTRODUCTION TO COMPUTER PROGRAMS

10–1 Introduction

In the early days of the digital computer, application programs were developed which were usually very limited in scope. Usually, efforts were made to translate successful hand-calculation techniques directly into computer code—e.g., many of the early structural analysis programs used the moment distribution technique of Hardy Cross as a basic computer analysis tool. The direct translation of hand tools to the computer was a natural first step in the evolution of the computer age. However, it was soon realized by many analysts that the computer could, in many cases, be used much more effectively if analysis techniques were modified prior to implementation on a computer. The stiffness method of analysis, which is merely a generalization of the age-old slope deflection method, is a good illustration of this type of thinking.

The early computers were difficult to program, at best. The only means of communication with the computer was in a machine language usually requiring specific instructions and addresses to be written in a number system unfamiliar to the user. This presented the additional problem that if one wanted to solve a problem using the computer he had to communicate the problem to a computer specialist, who normally would be unfamiliar with the technical aspects of the problem. The natural evolution from this state of affairs was the concept and development of the higher-level languages, which permitted the analysts to communicate with the computer in a technical language more familiar to him. The FORTRAN language was one of the earliest higher-level languages that gained wide acceptance. FORTRAN stands for FORmula TRANslation and, as the name implies, is a language for translating algebraic expressions or formulas into machine language code automatically and generating output meaningful to the programmer. The FORTRAN language has been implemented on a wide range of digital computers.

The evolution of higher-level languages was advanced by the concept of the problem-oriented languages, which permit the user to be almost completely ignorant of the operations of the computer. The user communicates with the computer in the language of the problem he is solving. One of the earliest problem-oriented languages that gained wide acceptance among engineers was COGO,† the letters standing for COordinate GeOmetry. COGO has been used to solve surveying problems as well as a wide variety of other geometry problems. One of the earliest such languages of interest to the structural engineer was STRESS,‡ which is used primarily for analyzing framed structures, similar to those discussed in this text. STRESS employs the stiffness method as a basic analysis tool, although the STRESS user need not be familiar with the analysis techniques used in the program.

Today, through the modern technologies of data communications and computer computations, almost every engineer and scientist has access to a digital computer. The evolution of higher-level languages and problem-oriented languages has increased the direct usefulness of this tool for those not interested in becoming computer specialists.

10–2
Scope of Computer Programs

The digital computer programs discussed in this text are intended to exemplify techniques for developing flexible, efficient, and user-oriented structural analysis programs using the stiffness method of analysis and the FORTRAN IV computer language.

There are quite naturally trade-offs to be considered in developing general-purpose computer programs. Generality is usually obtained at the expense of computer efficiency—e.g., a space frame program could be used to solve a continuous beam, but this might not be a very economical approach for the individual only interested in solving continuous beams. Most likely, he would best be served by a program which concentrates on solving continuous beam problems. The programmer or program manager must weigh the advantages and disadvantages of each feature he wishes to include in a program, in light of the specifications and goals he has to meet with the finished product.

For stiffness analysis programs, the form in which the linear equations are organized and solved can be extremely important from the standpoint of computer efficiency. This is especially true for problems requiring the solution of a large number of equations. Matrix inversion techniques that require the storage of the full stiffness matrix, for example, become quite inefficient as the dimension

†See C. L. Miller, "COGO," *Department of Civil Engineering Report*, Massachusetts Institute of Technology, Cambridge, Mass., 1961.

‡See S. J. Fenves, R. D. Logcher, S. D. Mauch, and K. K. Reinschmidt, *STRESS—A User's Manual*, MIT Press, Cambridge, Mass., 1964.

of the stiffness matrix increases. Direct solution techniques such as the Gauss elimination method discussed in Sec. 2-3 have normally proved superior to matrix inversion techniques for use in general stiffness analysis programs. However, any numerical procedure for forming and solving the equations of a stiffness analysis that does not take advantage of the banded structure of the stiffness matrix may prove quite limited in terms of both the size of structure that can be handled and the efficiency of solution. The programs developed in this text take advantage of both the band structure and the symmetry of the stiffness matrix $[S_{uu}]$. The formation of the stiffness matrix into a band matrix is discussed in detail in Sec. 10-3 and the equation-solving technique used in the computer programs is discussed in Sec. 10-4.

Another important consideration in developing efficient computer programs is the use of peripheral memory devices such as magnetic tapes and discs. Peripheral devices are normally several orders of magnitude slower to access than the high-speed core memory of a computer. For example, on some computers several thousand multiplications can be performed in core memory in the same time it takes to make a single access to a magnetic tape unit or disc. It is often necessary and even desirable to use peripheral devices during the execution of a computer program; however, one should be aware of the cost in computer time for this luxury and carefully weigh the advantages and disadvantages before making the decision to use peripheral storage. The use of the compact equation-solving technique, discussed in Sec. 10-4, is an effort to minimize the use of peripheral storage devices during the equation-solving phase of the programs.

The programs of Chapters 11, 12, and 13, respectively, have been developed consistent with the theory developed in Chapters 4, 5, and 6, respectively. The programs are general in the sense that they permit the input of any structural geometry and loadings consistent with the developed theory. These programs are intended to serve a teaching function by illustrating both programming techniques and documentation methods. The documentation of each program describes and illustrates data preparation and output formats for the analysis of a framed structure. Important variable identifiers used in each program are defined along with a complete listing of the FORTRAN IV program. The logical flow of the program can be interpreted from the program listing, assuming the student is familiar with the FORTRAN IV programming language. The programs may be easily altered for different computer configurations, including different numbers and types of peripheral devices and different sizes of high-speed core memory. Such user-oriented features as flexible input–output, error detection with diagonstics, and user-controlled checking, along with efficient equation-solving techniques, are illustrated.

The planar orthogonal frame program described in Chapter 11 is developed in more detail and includes more options than the general planar frame and truss program of Chapter 12 or the space frame and truss program of Chapter 13. Chapter 11 may be used as a guide for adding additional features to the programs of Chapters 12 and 13.

10–3
Band Matrices for Stiffness Analysis

The entire structure stiffness matrix $[\mathbf{S}_{uu}]$ (defined in Sec. 4-3) need not be considered in solving for the unknown components of joint displacement, since the nature of the structural systems being studied is such that the stiffness matrix is *symmetric* and *positive definite* (defined in Sec. 2-6). Using the Cholesky decomposition method discussed in Sec. 2-6 to obtain the solution of simultaneous, linear equations, only the elements of the stiffness matrix on and below the main diagonal need be retained. The geometry of most framed structures is such that *nonzero elements* of the structure stiffness matrix may be generated compactly about the main diagonal of the stiffness matrix. Hence, only those elements below the main diagonal which fall inside the nonzero band are considered. Examine the continuous beam of Fig. 10-1. This problem is kinematically indeterminate to the 6th degree, neglecting axial deformations. The displacement designations for the unrestrained joint displacements are indicated by the letters a through f in Fig. 10-1. The six unit values of joint displacement to be applied to the restrained structure of Fig. 10-1 are shown in Figs. 10-2(a) through 10-2(f). Since each column of the stiffness matrix $[\mathbf{S}_{uu}]$ contains the restraining actions which correspond to the unrestrained joint displacements caused by a unit value of joint displacement, it is obvious that there will be no more than three nonzero actions in each column of the stiffness matrix. The task becomes one of labeling the components of unrestrained joint displacement so that the nonzero elements will be as close as possible to the main diagonal of the structure stiffness matrix. It is clear from Fig. 10-2 that displacement designation a should be as close numerically to the designation of displacement b as possible and likewise b to c, c to d, d to e, and e to f. Therefore, it is clear that, using the integers 1 through 6, there are only two ways in which one can assign displacement designations and obtain a minimum band stiffness matrix. These are: $a = 1$, $b = 2$, $c = 3, \ldots, f = 6$; or $f = 1$, $e = 2, \ldots, a = 6$. The structure stiffness matrix for either of these choices appears as

$$[\mathbf{S}_{uu}] = \begin{bmatrix} S_{11} & S_{12} & 0 & 0 & 0 & 0 \\ S_{21} & S_{22} & S_{23} & 0 & 0 & 0 \\ 0 & S_{32} & S_{33} & S_{34} & 0 & 0 \\ 0 & 0 & S_{43} & S_{44} & S_{45} & 0 \\ 0 & 0 & 0 & S_{54} & S_{55} & S_{56} \\ 0 & 0 & 0 & 0 & S_{65} & S_{66} \end{bmatrix} \tag{10-1}$$

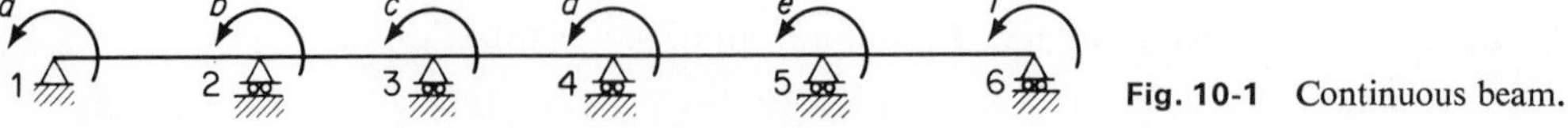

Fig. 10-1 Continuous beam.

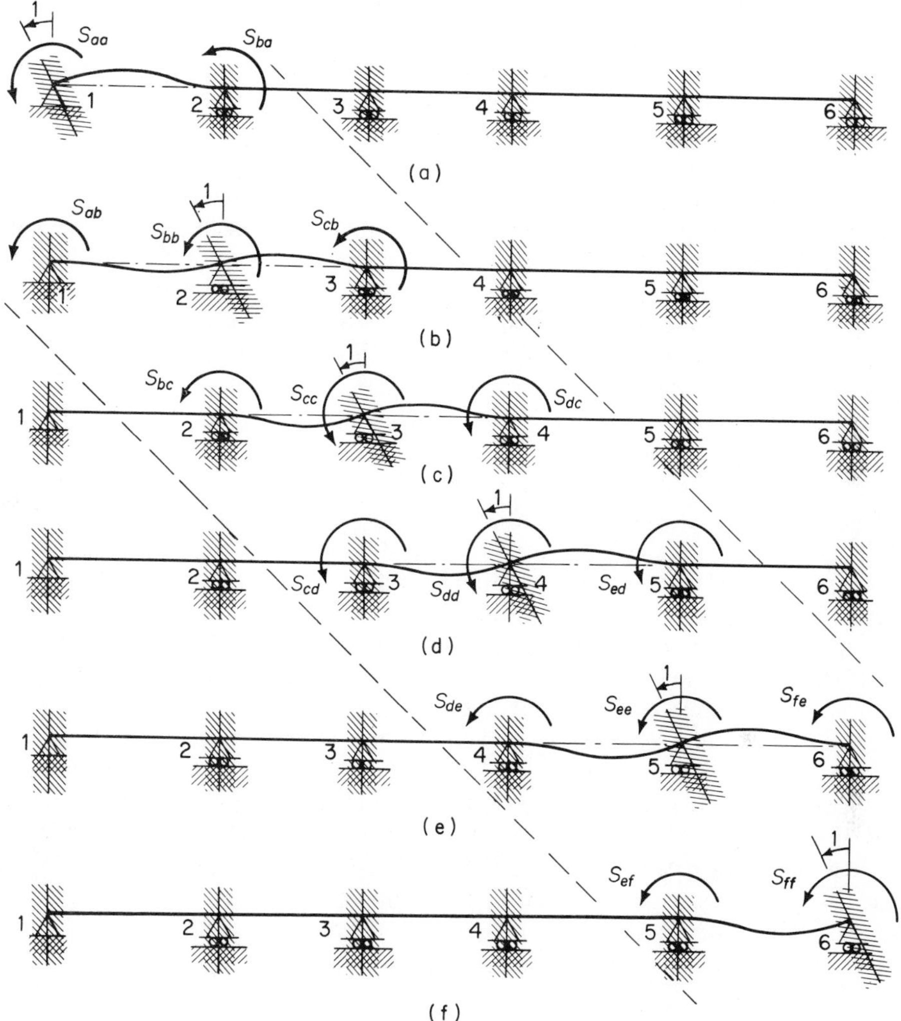

Fig. 10-2 Restraining actions resulting from unit displacements of restrained structure of continuous beam: (a) unit rotation at joint 1; (b) unit rotation at joint 2; (c) unit rotation at joint 3; (d) unit rotation at joint 4; (e) unit rotation at joint 5; (f) unit rotation at joint 6.

The nonzero elements of the structure stiffness matrix of Expression (10-1) are the nonzero restraining actions developed by the restrained structure when subjected to unit values of displacement corresponding to each unrestrained component of joint displacement. This is illustrated schematically in Fig. 10-2 by the dashed lines enclosing the area in which nonzero actions occur. It is important to observe that assignment of displacement numbers is critical in obtaining this compact form in the matrix and that only the selection of displacement numbers as indicated above will result in this form.

As pointed out previously, the structure stiffness matrix is obtained by summing the individual member stiffness coefficients of the members of the structure using the labels assigned to each component of joint displacement. If the matrix is formed using this procedure, it is important to note that the minimum half-band width for a given set of displacement designations is computed as the maximum difference in displacement designations of the unrestrained joint displacements at the ends of each member. For example, if the displacement designations for the continuous beam of Fig. 10-1 are assigned as shown in Fig. 10-3(a), then the maximum difference in displacement number of each member is 1; hence, the half-band width of the stiffness matrix is 1 as shown in Expression (10-1). However, if the displacement designations are assigned as shown in Fig. 10-3(b), the half-band width is 3 since the maximum difference in displacement numbers occurs on member 3 and is 3.

Consider the orthogonal frame of Fig. 10-4. Axial shortening of the members is to be neglected. The unrestrained components of joint displacement have been numbered in an order that yields a relatively narrow half-band stiffness matrix $[\mathbf{S}_{uu}]$. Note in Fig. 10-4 that displacements have been designated in sequence from left to right, starting at the top of the frame and moving from top to bottom, completing one floor level at a time. In Fig. 10-4, the maximum difference in displacement numbers on any member is 5; hence, the half-band width of the stiffness matrix for this displacement numbering is 5.

The numbering scheme of the unrestrained joint displacements does not change the number of nonzero elements in the stiffness matrix, but determines the positions of the nonzero elements relative to the main diagonal of the matrix. The term *codiagonal* is used to identify all of the elements of a matrix appearing a fixed number of positions from the diagonal and on the same side of the diagonal. Using this term, one may say that the numbering scheme for the structure of Fig. 10-4 results in a stiffness matrix with five nonzero codiagonals adjacent to the main diagonal. All codiagonals greater than 5 are zero.

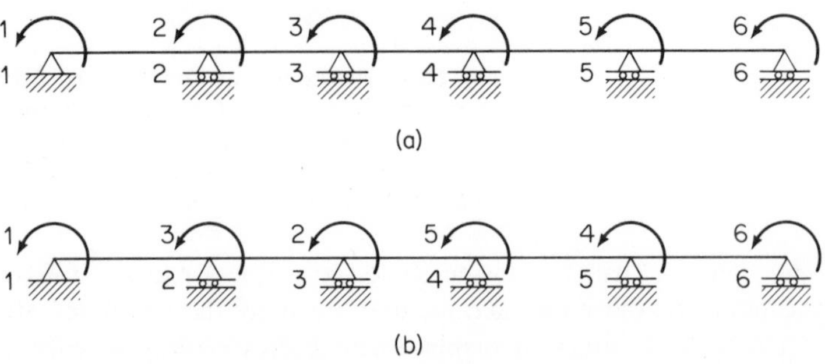

Fig. 10-3 Continuous beam with displacement labels for different half-band widths in stiffness matrix: (a) rotations numbered for half-band of 1; (b) rotations numbered for half-band of 3.

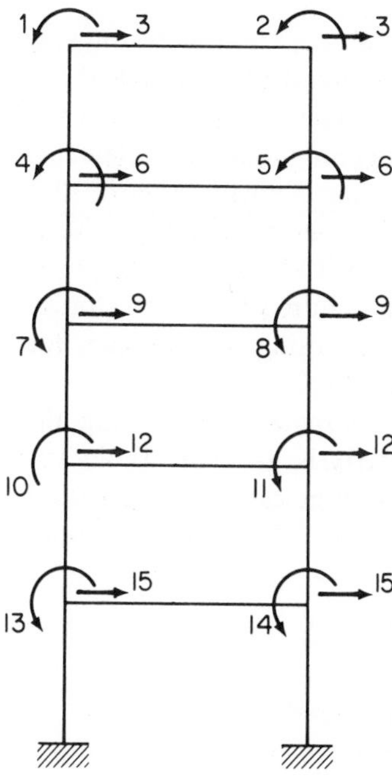

Fig. 10-4 Displacement designations for orthogonal frame to give minimum half-band stiffness matrix $[\mathbf{S}_{uu}]$.

The use of narrow band stiffness matrices can be particularly valuable from the standpoint of saving computer storage and increased efficiency in solving linear equations.

10–4
Band Matrix Equation Solving

The equation-solving technique used in each of the programs described in Chapters 11, 12, and 13 is the ***Cholesky method*** discussed in Sec. 2-6. This method can be used effectively in solving the equilibrium equations generated by the stiffness method; i.e.,

$$[\mathbf{S}_{uu}][\mathbf{\Delta}_u] = [\mathbf{JL}_u] \tag{10-2}$$

since the coefficient matrix $[\mathbf{S}_{uu}]$ is *positive definite*. It should be emphasized that this is not a procedure for solving any set of linear equations. This method should be used only for solving equations that are known to have a positive definite coefficient matrix.

The computer programs described in Chapters 11, 12, and 13 use two subroutines which are of basic importance in generating and solving the equilibrium equations. These are referred to as STORE and CHOLES.

The subroutine called STORE accepts the member stiffness matrix developed for a reference set of coordinate axes along with an ordered set of displacement labels and sums the member stiffness coefficients into a linear array. Once all members of the structure have been passed through the routine, the linear array contains the stiffness matrix $[\mathbf{S}_{uu}]$. The elements of this stiffness matrix have been stored in sequence by rows, defining only the elements within the half-band width of the matrix and the diagonal elements. Figure 10-5 illustrates the ordering of the elements of a 10×10 stiffness matrix $[\mathbf{S}_{uu}]$ with a half-band width of 3. The numbers in the squares of Fig. 10-5 indicate the position each element would occupy in the linear array. One hundred words of storage are required to store the full 10×10 matrix, but when using the compact form shown in Fig. 10-5, only 34 storage locations are required.

A comparison of storage requirements for storing all elements versus storing only the banded form of a matrix is given in Table 10-1 for several values of half-band width up to the maximum case in which the half-band becomes one less than the dimension of the matrix. The values of Table 10-1 may be computed from the equation

$$C = n(m + 1) - \frac{m(m + 1)}{2} + nd \qquad \textbf{(10-3)}$$

where C = words of storage required;
n = number of kinematic redundants;
m = half-band width;
d = number of load cases (d is assumed to be 1 in Table 10-1).

The savings in storage is significant for large matrices with relatively narrow bands. As the band width approaches the maximum value, the number of elements stored approaches the number required to store a full lower triangular matrix.

Generally, the savings in storage resulting from this arrangement of the stiffness matrix permits much larger problems to be handled directly in core storage than would be possible if a full matrix of structure stiffness coefficients

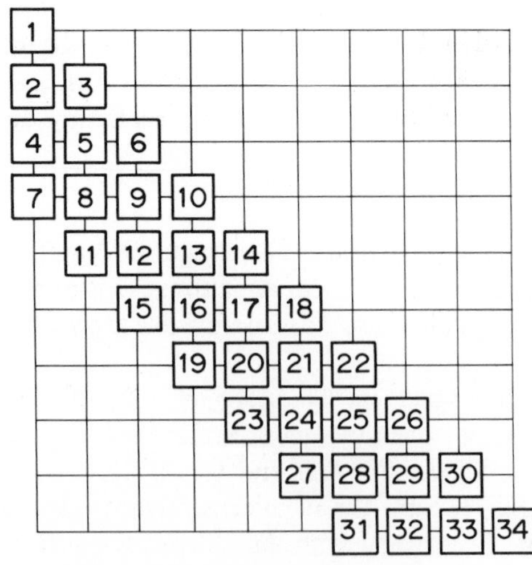

Fig. 10-5 Array numbering of stiffness elements.

Table 10-1

STORAGE REQUIRED FOR FULL MATRIX VS. HALF-BAND MATRIX

Matrix Dimension	*Number of Words for Full Matrix*	*Half-band Width*									
		4	8	12	16	19	39	59	79	99	199
20	420	110	164	202	224	230	—	—	—	—	—
40	1,640	230	364	482	584	650	860	—	—	—	—
60	3,660	350	564	762	944	1,070	1,680	1,890	—	—	—
80	6,480	470	764	1,042	1,304	1,490	2,500	3,110	3,320	—	—
100	10,100	590	964	1,322	1,664	1,910	3,320	4,330	4.940	5,150	—
200	40,200	1,190	1,964	2,722	3,464	4,010	7,420	10,430	13,040	15,250	20,300

were required. It should be pointed out, however, that the method used to solve the equilibrium equations, when stored in this compact form, must not generate any nonzero elements outside the band width and must preserve the symmetry of the matrix. The Cholesky method of factoring positive definite matrices permits such a solution to be obtained.

The subroutine CHOLES accèpts a positive definite matrix [**A**] of coefficients stored in the linear array format, plus as many right-hand-side vectors or load cases (see Sec. 4-5) as are desired and as available storage will permit. The right-hand-side vectors are stored sequentially following the coefficient matrix in the same linear array used to store the coefficient matrix. For example, the first element of the first right-hand-side vector would be stored in position 35 of the linear array for the matrix of Fig. 10-5, and the other elements of the vector would be stored sequentially in positions 36 through 44. The next vector—i.e., the first element of the second load case—would start in location 45 of the array, and so on.

The subroutine CHOLES first decomposes matrix [**A**] into the *lower triangular matrix* [**G**] using a slight modification of the decomposition algorithm of Fig. 2-1. The modification of the algorithm of Fig. 2-1 is necessary in order to consider only elements within the lower triangular half-band stiffness matrix. This is accomplished by changing the indexing parameters of Fig. 2-1 as follows:

1. Step 6 of Fig. 2-1 is modified to read $i = m + 1$, where m is the half-band width of the matrix [**A**].
2. The summation in step 8 of Fig. 2-1 is modified to read

   $$\sum_{k=q}^{j-1} g_{jk}^2$$

   where $q = 1$ if $j \leq m + 1$;
   and $q = j - m$ if $j > m + 1$.
3. The summation in step 10 of Fig. 2-1 is modified to read

   $$\sum_{k=q}^{j-1} g_{ik} g_{jk}$$

   where $q = 1$ if $j \leq m + 1$;
   and $q = j - m$ if $j > m + 1$.

The subroutine CHOLES also includes the necessary indexing computations to account for the stiffness matrix being stored by rows in a linear array. The decomposed lower triangular matrix [**G**] is superimposed on the corresponding locations of matrix [**A**]; hence, if matrix [**A**] must be preserved, then it should be stored elsewhere before entering CHOLES.

The decomposed matrix [**G**] has the same usefulness as the matrix inverse in that a *forward–backward elimination* may be performed to obtain the solution for any set of right-hand-side vectors. The CHOLES routine is divided into two major sections. The first section decomposes the coefficient matrix using the procedure outlined in the previous paragraph. The second section performs only the forward–backward elimination. This second section permits finding the solution for additional right-hand-side vectors after the coefficient matrix has been decomposed. The options and formats of the input parameters for CHOLES are given in the comment cards at the beginning of the subroutine listing in Appendix C.

After the decomposition and forward–backward elimination have been performed on the right-hand-side vectors $[\mathbf{JL}_u]$ to generate solution vectors (displacements), the solution vectors $[\mathbf{\Delta}_u]$ overlay the original right-hand-side vectors; hence, if the original vectors must be preserved, they should be stored elsewhere before entering CHOLES.

The dimensioned size of the linear array passed to CHOLES must be large enough to contain the structure stiffness matrix $[\mathbf{S}_{uu}]$ in the band format, plus as many load cases as are desired in a single pass through the subroutine. The storage available for this array depends upon the storage required for the remainder of the program and the size of the storage unit available on the particular computer used. Each of the programs developed in Chapters 11, 12, and 13 permits easy alteration of the dimension of this array. The storage required in this array for a particular problem can be computed by Eq. (10-3) with d set equal to 1.

In most structures of the type discussed in this text, the CHOLES routine can be used to give reasonably accurate results in solving the resulting linear equations. The authors have had good success solving framed structures using this routine with a 7^+ digit (32 bit) computer word. However, when solving very large structures—i.e., many unknowns—one should be aware that numerical round-off error could cause a poor solution to be obtained. Since a discussion of numerical round-off errors in machine computation is beyond the scope of this text, the reader is referred to the text by Forsythe and Moler† for a good coverage of the subject.

10–5 Problems

10-1. Suppose that the frame of Fig. 10-4 is to be analyzed considering axial deformation of the members. Show how the displacements should be numbered to obtain a minimum half-band stiffness matrix for the unrestrained displacements. What is the minimum half-band?

10-2. Determine the half-band widths for matrix $[\mathbf{S}_{uu}]$ for the given structures if the unrestrained displacements are numbered as shown in the figures on page 426.

---

†George Forsythe and Cleve E. Moler, *Computer Solution of Linear Algebraic Systems*, Englewood Cliffs, N.J., Prentice-Hall, Inc., 1967.

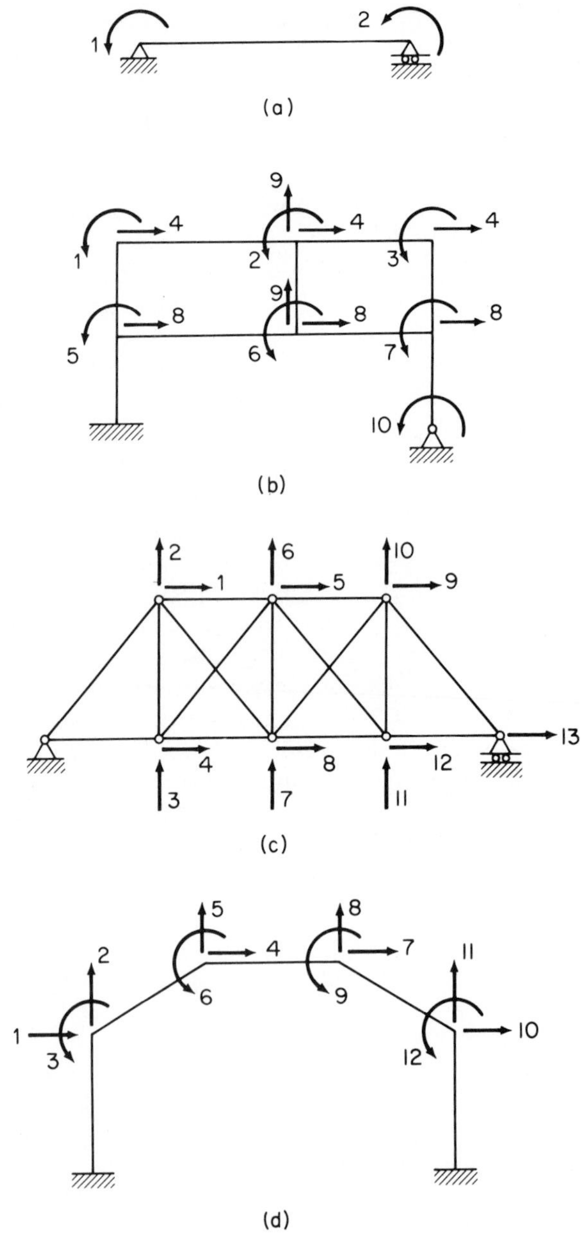

Prob. 10-2

10-3. Number the unrestrained displacements on the planar frame to give a minimum half-band matrix $[\mathbf{S}_{uu}]$, including the effects of axial shortening and bending.

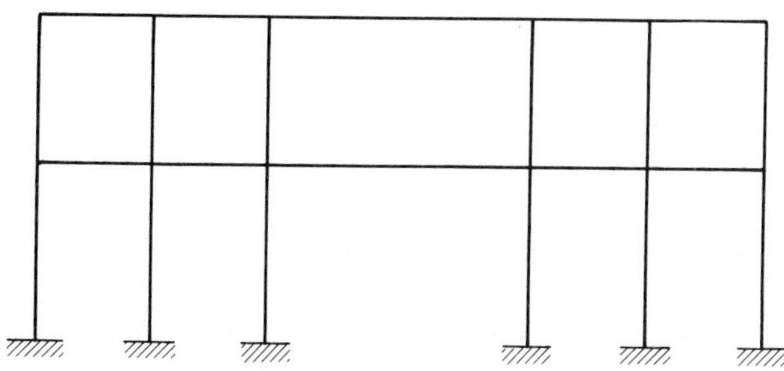

Prob. 10-3

10-4. Number the displacements for the continuous beam on an elastic foundation so that a minimum half-band matrix is obtained.

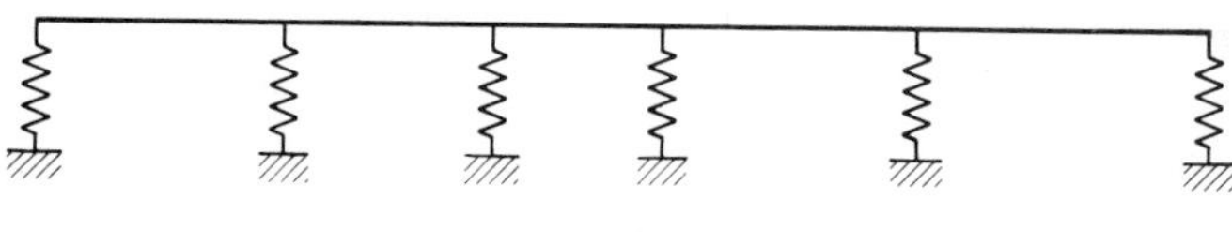

Prob. 10-4

10-5. Determine the storage requirements for storing the stiffness matrix $[\mathbf{S}_{uu}]$ and one load vector for each of the structures of Probs. 10-1, 10-2, 10-3, and 10-4 above if subroutine CHOLES is to be used to solve the equations.

11 PLANAR ORTHOGONAL FRAME PROGRAM

11–1 Introduction

The stiffness analysis of planar orthogonal frames was presented in Chapter 4. The computer program presented in this section is based on the theory, sign convention, and assumptions of Chapter 4, and the ideas of Chapter 10.

This program includes more details and options than the programs to be presented in Chapters 12 and 13. It is anticipated that this program will serve as a guide for increasing the capabilities of the programs presented in the following chapters. For example, this program contains an option that permits the evaluation of shears and moments along a particular member of the structure, whereas the programs of Chapters 12 and 13 compute only member end actions. This program also permits many output options not included in the other two.

Sections 11-2, 11-3, and 11-4 provide the basis for organizing and preparing the data for the computer program. Section 11-5 describes the organization and flow of the computer program, and the example problem of Sec. 11-6 illustrates the data preparation and output formats for a particular problem solution using the computer program.

11–2 Numbering Scheme

In preparation for computer analysis, the frame is first sketched and the components of joint displacement are identified and numbered. A distinct number is given to each component of displacement starting with the integer 1 and numbering sequentially. All unrestrained displacements of the structure are numbered before numbering the restrained displacements.

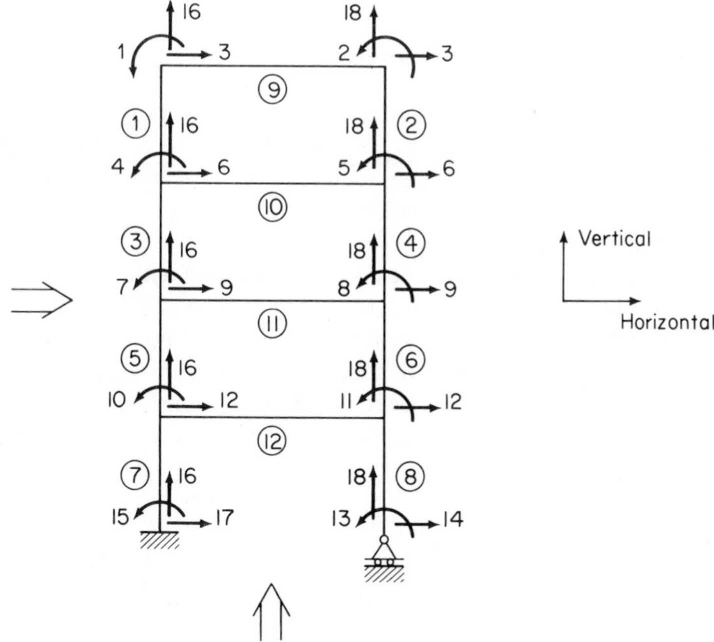

Fig. 11-1 Illustration of numbering scheme.

An example of the numbering scheme is given in Fig. 11-1. The circled numbers adjacent to the members represent the member number which must be a distinct integer for each member. They may be selected in any order desired; however, it is usually desirable to choose some systematic method that will make interpretation of the final results as simple as possible. In Fig. 11-1, for example, all of the column members were numbered in sequence prior to numbering the beam members.

Since band matrix techniques are used in the program, it is important from the standpoint of efficiency to number the displacements in an order that will result in a relatively narrow half-band matrix $[\mathbf{S}_{uu}]$. For the problem illustrated in Fig. 11-1, this is accomplished by numbering sequentially from left to right beginning at the top of the frame and working toward the bottom. It is noted that there are 14 unrestrained components of joint displacement for the frame in Fig. 11-1 and that the resulting half-band width for the indicated numbering scheme is 5. The four restrained components of joint displacement are numbered last. Since axial shortening of members is neglected in this analysis, deflection along any line of the structure is assumed to be the same at all joints along that line. This is the reason for repeating displacement numbers 3, 6, 9, 12, 16, and 18 in Fig. 11-1.

The arrows below and to the left of the frame in Fig. 11-1 indicate the direction the frame must be observed in order to determine the left end of a member—i.e., the *j*-end. As stated in Chapter 4, the *left end* of a beam and *the top* of a column must be designated as the *j*-end.

11–3
Member Load Sign Convention

The computer program permits uniform and concentrated loads to be specified normal to a member and fixed end actions to be specified at the ends of a member. The specification of fixed end actions—i.e., moments and shears—is necessary to describe any other type of disturbance applied to a member, i.e., the settlement of a structural support.

The computer program calculates fixed end actions due to concentrated and uniform loads applied normal to a member. The uniform load may cover any part of the span up to the total length of the member. Figure 11-2(a) illustrates the member load sign convention for concentrated and uniform loads applied normal to the member when the member is observed from the direction indicated in Sec. 11-2.

Figure 11-2(b) illustrates the positive directions for a member loaded with fixed end actions.

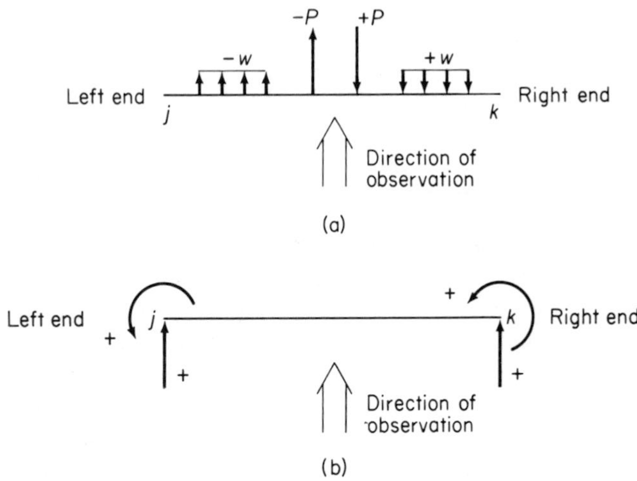

Fig. 11-2 Member load sign convention: (a) loads on span; (b) fixed end actions.

11–4
Preparation of Input Data

Preparation of input data for this program should be accomplished in the following sequence:

1. Sketch the structure and number the displacements and members as indicated in Sec. 11-2, remembering to observe the geometry of the structure in order to determine a numbering system that will keep the half-band width of the stiffness matrix as narrow as possible.

2. Define the different loading cases to be considered.
3. Compute equivalent fixed end actions (shears and moments) for any members of the structure subjected to temperature variation, misfit, or support settlement.
4. With the aid of items 1 through 3 above, prepare data cards according to the formats indicated in Tables 11-1 through 11-6.

Table 11-1

STRUCTURE DATA

Card Columns	*Identifier Name Used in Computer Program*	*Data Description*	*FORTRAN Format*
1	ICODE	The letter 'S' for structure card.	A1
2–4	N	Number of unrestrained components of joint displacement.	I3
5–7	M	Number of members.	I3
8–10	NR	Number of restrained components of joint displacement	I3
11	IPD	Leave this column blank if printout of input data is desired. Put '1' in this column to suppress printout of input data.	I1
12	IPDFL	Leave this column blank if printout of deflections and rotations is desired. Place '1' in this column to suppress printing of deflections and rotations.	I1
13	IPSM	Leave this column blank to print final end actions for each member. Place '1' in this column to print shears and moments along member at specified intervals. (See next data item.)	I1
14–15	INCR	Number of equal intervals along each member for which shear and moment is desired. Use only if '1' appears in column 13 of this card. Maximum value of INCR is 10.	I2
16	IPR	Leave blank for printout of reactions. Place '1' in this column to suppress reaction printout.	I1
17	IPRES	Leave blank for printout of residuals for equation check. Place '1' in this column to suppress printout.	I1
18–20	NL	Number of load cases to be analyzed.	I3
21–30	EG	Global modulus of elasticity for members of this structure in (k/in^2).	F10.0
31–78	IDEN	Problem identification. Any identifying information placed in this field will be reproduced at beginning of output.	12A4
78–80	——	Blank.	——

Table 11-2

MEMBER DATA

Card Columns	*Identifier Name Used in Computer Program*	*Data Description*	*FORTRAN*
1	ICODE	The letter 'M' for member card.	A1
2–4	MNUM	Member number.	I3
5–7	K1(1)	Rotational displacement designation left. (Leave blank if displacement is not defined.)	I3
8–10	K1(2)	Rotational displacement designation right. (Leave blank if displacement is not defined.)	I3
11–13	K1(3)	Translational displacement designation left. (Displacement must be designated.)	I3
14–16	K1(4)	Translational displacement designation right. (Displacement must be designated.)	I3
17	MTYPE	Member type: type 1 = 1 (see Fig. 11-3) type 2 = 2 type 3 = 3	I1
18–20	——	Blank.	3X
21–30	QL	Length of member (ft).	F10.0
31–40	QI	Moment of inertia (in^4).	F10.0
41–50	EM	Modulus of elasticity (k/in^2) for this member if different from global modulus. If same as global modulus, leave blank.	F10.0
51–80	——	Blank.	——

The input data tables (Tables 11-1 through 11-6) are organized such that the first column gives the card columns to use in positioning the data value. The second column in each of the tables—i.e., the identifier name—gives the actual identifier name used in the FORTRAN read statement that reads this card. The last column of the tables gives the FORTRAN format conversion used to interpret the input data. It should be noted that all integer values must be *right-justified* in their prescribed field. It is recommended that all real number inputs be placed in their field with the decimal point included.

The global data for a particular problem is found on the structure data card described in Table 11-1. This is the first card read by the program, and there is only one structure data card per problem.

The member data cards are read in sequence after the structure data card. One member card is required for each member of the structure, and the number of member cards must be equal to the value specified for M on the structure data card. The variable MTYPE listed in Table 11-2 identifies a member as one of three

Table 11-3

MEMBER LOAD DATA

Card Columns	*Identifier Name Used in Computer Program*	*Data Description*	*FORTRAN Format*
1	ICODE	The letter 'L' for member load.	A1
2–3	LCN	Load case number.	I2
4–6	MNUM	Member number.	I3
7	LTYPE	Leave blank for uniform load. Place '1' in this column for concentrated load. Place '2' in this column for prescribed fixed end actions.	I1
8	MTYPE	Member type: type 1 = 1 (see Fig. 11-3) type 2 = 2 type 3 = 3	I1
9–10	——	Blank.	2X
11–20	DISTB	If column 7 is blank or contains a '1', place distance from left end of member (ft) to point where load begins. If column 7 contains a '2', leave this field blank.	F10.0
21–30	DISTE	Distance (ft) from left end of member to point where load terminates. If column 7 contains a '2', leave this field blank.	F10.0
31–40	W	If column 7 is blank, enter uniform load (k/ft). If column 7 contains a '1', enter concentrated load (kips). If column 7 contains a '2', leave this field blank.	F10.0
41–50	FML	Fixed end moment action on left (ft-k) if defined. Leave blank if column 7 contains a blank or '1'.	F10.0
51–60	FMR	Fixed end moment action on right (ft-k) if defined. Leave blank if column 7 contains a blank or '1'.	F10.0
61–70	FSL	Fixed end shear action on left (kips). Leave blank if column 7 contains a blank or '1'.	F10.0
71–80	FSR	Fixed end shear action on right (kips). Leave blank if column 7 contains a blank or '1'.	F10.0

possible types described in Fig. 11-3 that can be considered by the program. In Fig. 11-3, p, q, r, and s represent the displacement designations for the member. Note that if all four displacement designations exist, the member is a type 1; if designation p is undefined, the member is a type 2; and if q is undefined, the member is a

Table 11-4

JOINT LOAD DATA

Card Columns	*Identifier Name Used in Computer Program*	*Data Description*	*FORTRAN Format*
1	ICODE	The letter 'P' for joint load.	A1
2–3	LCN	Loading case number.	I2
4–6	K11	Rotational displacement designation at joint.	I3
7–9	K22	Vertical displacement designation at joint.	I3
10–12	K33	Horizontal displacement designation at joint.	I3
13–20	——	Blank.	8X
21–30	QJM	Applied moment at joint (ft-k).	F10.0
31–40	QJV	Applied vertical force at joint (kips).	F10.0
41–50	QJH	Applied horizontal force at joint (kips).	F10.0
51–80	——	Blank.	——

Table 11-5

DUMMY LOAD DIVIDER CARD

Card Columns	*Identifier Name Used in Computer Program*	*Data Description*	*FORTRAN Format*
1	ICODE	The letter 'E' for no more loads of this type.	A1
2–80	——	Blank.	——

Table 11-6

DUMMY PROBLEM DIVIDER CARD

Card Columns	*Identifier Name Used in Computer Program*	*Data Description*	*FORTRAN Format*
1	ICODE	The letter 'C' for continue with another job. The letter 'Q' terminates the program.	A1
2–80	——	Blank.	——

type 3. The number identifying the type in Fig. 11-3 is the number to be placed in column 17 of the member data card.

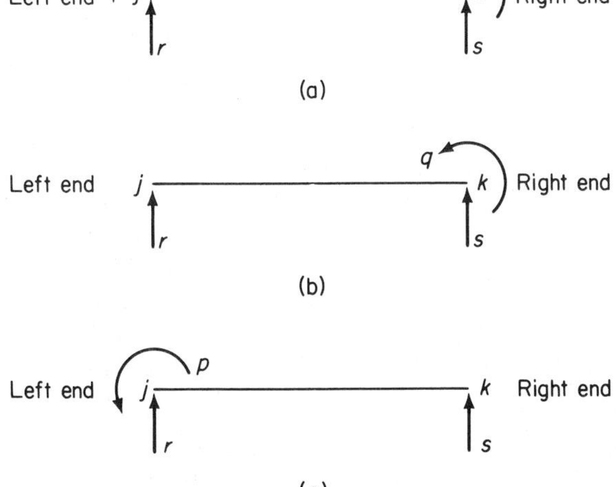

Fig. 11-3 Member type description: (a) type 1—displacements p, q, r, and s defined for member; (b) type 2—displacements q, r, and s defined for member; (c) type 3—displacements p, r, and s defined for member.

The member load data cards of Table 11-3 follow the member data cards. There must be one member load card for each load acting on a member. For example, if a single member is subjected to a concentrated load at midpoint, and there is a uniform load over the length of the span and a temperature variation that induces fixed end moments and shears in the restrained structure, then a separate member load card is required for each of these three conditions.

The member load data cards should be sequenced from the lowest-numbered member that is loaded to the highest-numbered member that is loaded. Note that member load cards are not necessary for members that are not loaded. Hence, if none of the members are loaded, no member load cards are required.

A dummy card of the type shown in Table 11-5 is used to terminate member load data cards. Note that this card is required even if there are no member load data cards.

The joint load data cards described in Table 11-4 are placed after the member load data cards. One card of this type is required for each joint of the structure that is loaded. A dummy card of the type shown in Table 11-5 is used to terminate reading of joint loads, and it must be present even if there are no joint load cards.

A single loading case is defined by the following card sequence:

1. member load data cards of Table 11-3;
2. dummy load divider card of Table 11-5;
3. joint load data cards of Table 11-4;
4. dummy load divider card of Table 11-5.

Note that two dummy cards are required for each loading case. This sequence may be repeated for up to 99 loading cases for a particular structure. The number of loading cases must correspond to the number read from the structure data card under the identifier NL.

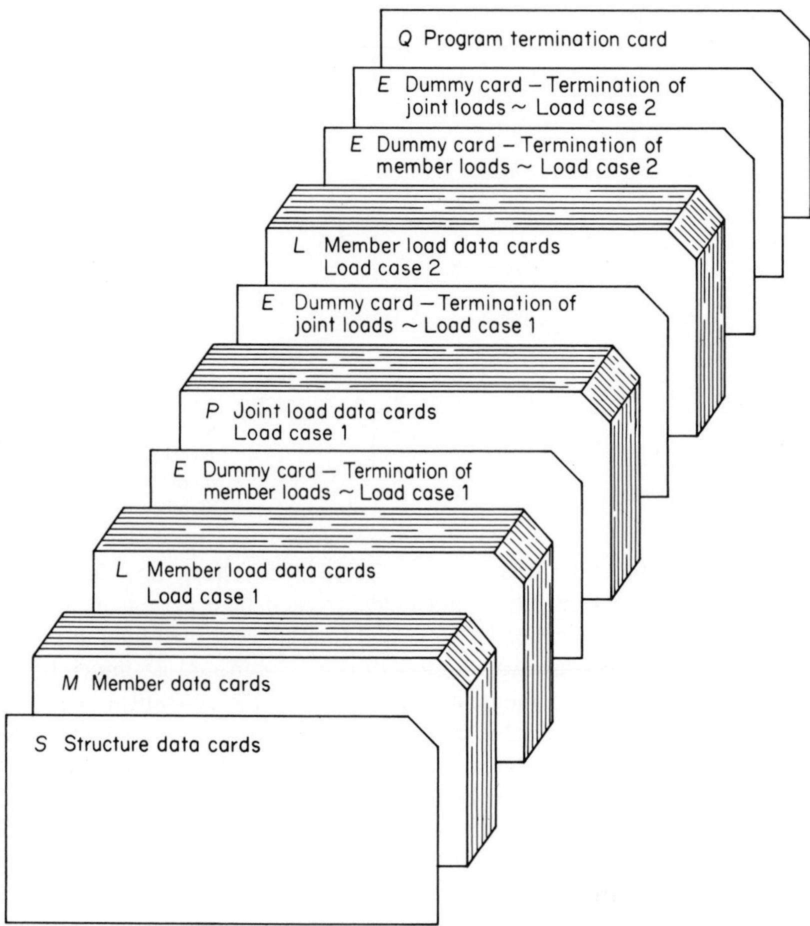

Fig. 11-4 Typical data card sequence.

After all loading cases for a structure have been processed, the dummy problem divider card of Table 11-6 is read to determine if another problem is to be run.

The letter specified in column 1 of each data card identifies the type of card being processed. A typical sequence of data cards for a structure with two load cases is illustrated in Fig. 11-4.

11–5
Program Description

The computer program is broken down into six basic segments as indicated in the abbreviated flow chart of Fig. 11-5, where the segment number is given on the left

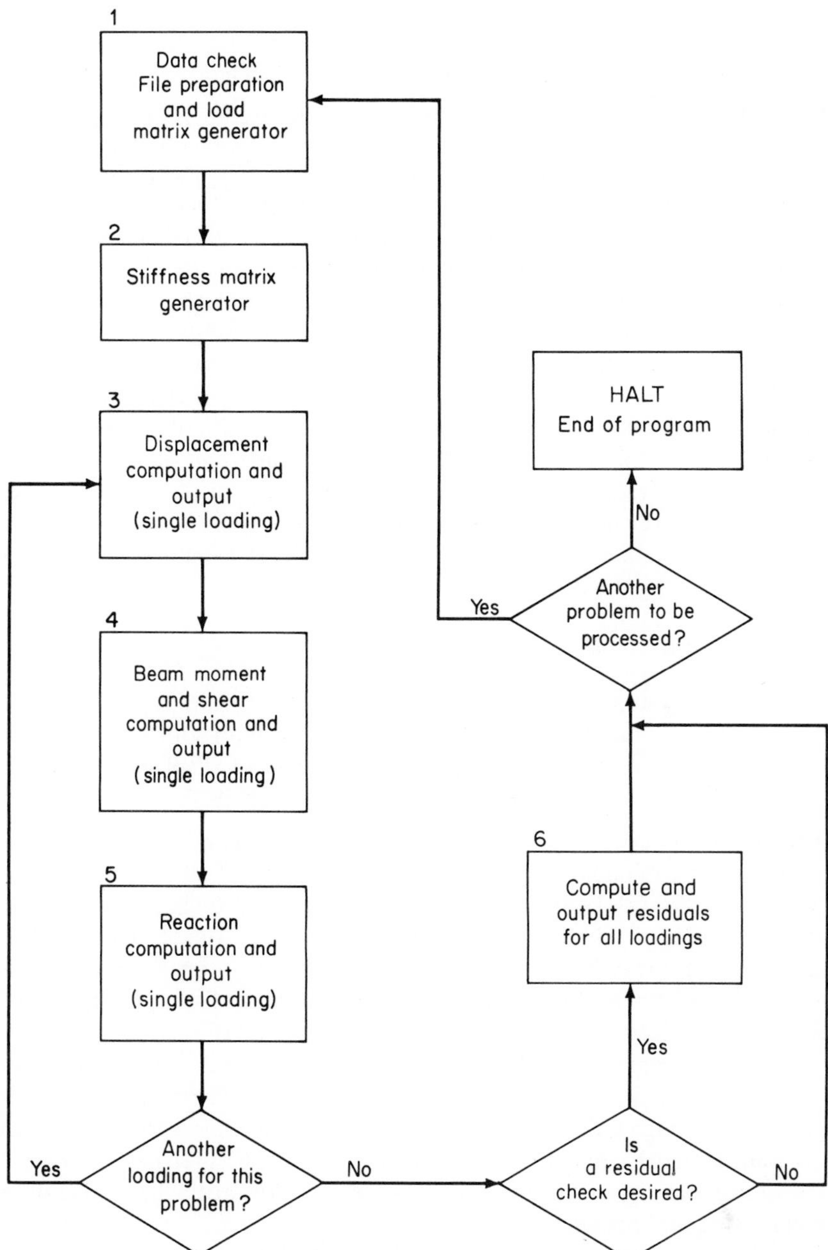

Fig. 11-5 Abbreviated flow chart of planar orthogonal frame program.

top of the rectangular blocks. The FORTRAN code assoicated with each segment is indicated on the program listing in Sec. C-3, Appendix C. Important variable and array identifiers used in the program are described in Sec. C-1, Appendix C. Segment 1 reads and interrogates the input data which has been prepared according to the format discussed in Sec. 11-4. Basic errors in data preparation may be detected during this phase of the program and indicated by a diagnostic referring to one of the error codes listed in Sec. C-2, Appendix C. Errors resulting from placing data in the improper card columns may not be detected; for this reason it is prudent to exercise the option to print out the input data for a visual check. This option is exercised by leaving column 11 of the structure data card blank as indicated in Table 11-1. In addition to data checking, this segment computes the storage required for the minimum half-band width matrix for the given displacement numbering and checks the sufficiency of available storage to handle the problem. If storage is insufficient, an error message is generated. This error message indicates the number of unknowns and computed half-band width along with the required size of the stiffness matrix array. If this error occurs, one should check the data. If the data is correct, the possibility of changing the displacement numbering to obtain a narrower half-band matrix should be investigated.

The maximum dimension required for array STIF for a particular problem can be determined by the equation

$$D_{\max} = n(m+1) - \frac{m(m+1)}{2} + n + n_r \tag{11-1}$$

where $D_{\max}$ = maximum dimension of array STIF required;
n = number of unrestrained components of joint displacement;
n_r = number of restrained components of displacement;
m = half-band width of the stiffness matrix $[\mathbf{S}_{uu}]$.

The storage allocation called for by the dimension statement in the computer program for the array STIF may be greater than the actual dimension of the array as specified by Eq. (11-1). In any case, the storage allocation in the program must be at least equal to the dimension called for by Eq. (11-1). Hence, when implementing this program, array STIF should be given as large a dimension as core storage permits. The comment cards in the computer program listing in Appendix C describe the changes needed to vary the size of array STIF.

Finally, segment 1 creates three sequential data files: one for member data, one for member load data, and one for load vectors. These files are written onto peripheral storage units, which are normally designated by control cards when the program is under control of an operating system. The user may alter the integer device assignments as indicated in the comment cards at the beginning of the program listing in Appendix C.

Segment 2 sums the member stiffness matrix into the proper locations in array STIF. The stiffness matrix is compiled in the linear array in the order described in Sec. 10-4.

Segment 3 reads the load vectors into array STIF and uses the Cholesky algorithm discussed in Sec. 10-4 to compute the displacements for each loading. The printout of displacements is optional as indicated in Table 11-1, since displacements are meaningful only if actual values of the modulus of elasticity and moment of inertia are given for each member.

Segment 4 computes the final end moments and shears for each member. It should be noted that there are two format options permitted for writing out the results:

1. If column 13 of the structure data card is blank (see Table 11-1), the final member end actions are printed out in the sign convention of Chapter 4.
2. If column 13 of the structure data card contains a '1,' moments and shears are printed out for the member end points as well as interior points equally spaced along the member. The number of equal segments along the member is specified in columns 14 and 15 of the structure data card (see Table 11-1), but must not exceed 10. Also, the moments and shears given with this option are converted to the standard beam design sign convention; that is, moments that cause *tension* in the bottom of the beam are positive and those that cause compression are negative.

Segment 5, which prints reactions, is also optional as indicated in Table 11-1. If the write option is specified, the reactions corresponding to all restrained components of joint displacement are printed for each loading.

Segment 6, which produces a residual check for each loading, is optional as indicated in Table 11-1. This segment multiplies each displacement vector by the original stiffness matrix, and subtracts the original load vector and prints the results. This gives some indication as to the numerical accuracy of the computation.

Section C-1, Appendix C, describes the important variable identifiers used in this program. This information is supplied to simplify conversions of this program to different machines and other languages when used with the program listing in Sec. C-3.

11–6 Computer Analysis of Planar Orthogonal Frame

The following example problem is given to demonstrate many of the features of data preparation for the planar orthogonal frame program, as well as to illustrate the format of the various types of output.

Example 11-1. Consider the analysis of the frame shown in Fig. 11-6 for the two load cases described in Fig. 11-7. In Fig. 11-6 the joint labels are given in the circles adjacent

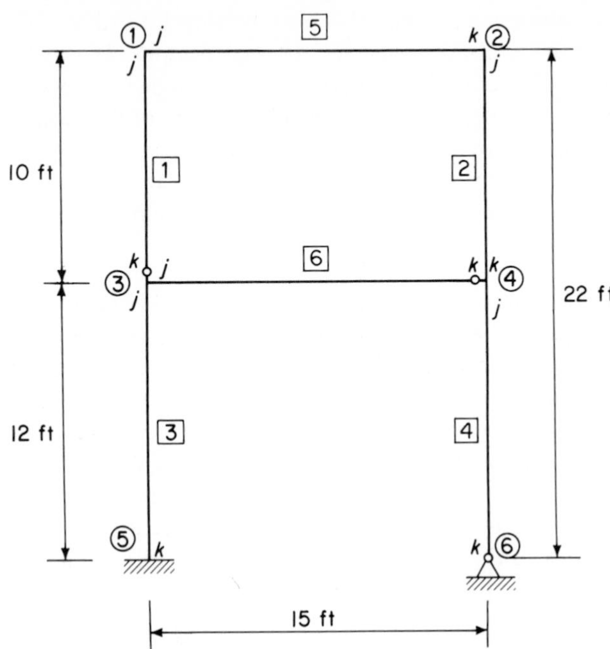

Fig. 11-6 Example 11-1: Planar orthogonal frame.

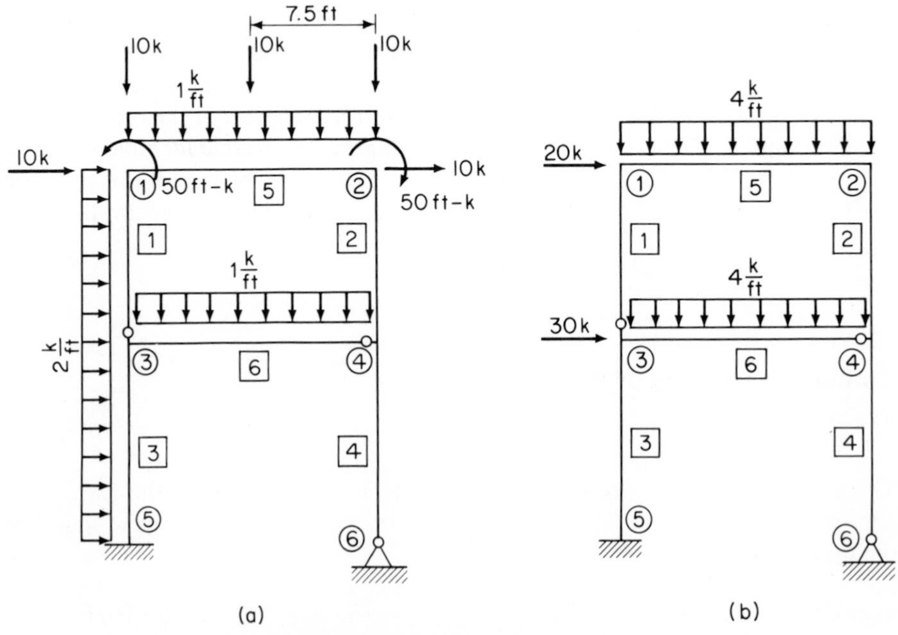

Fig. 11-7 Example 11-1: Load cases: (a) load case 1; (b) load case 2.

to the joints and the member labels are given in the squares adjacent to the members; in addition, the *j*- and *k*-ends of the members are indicated. The member properties are given in Table 11-7 and the load data is given in Table 11-8.

The following print options are desired:

1. print data for check;
2. print deflections;
3. print end moments and shears for each member;
4. print reactions;
5. print residuals.

The possible components of joint displacement are identified and labeled as shown in Fig. 11-8.

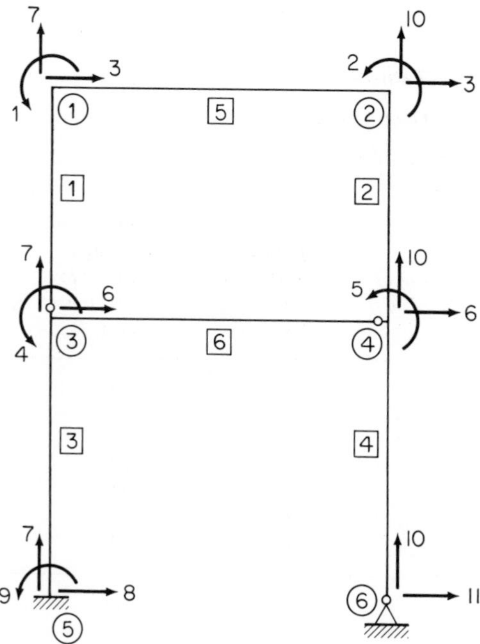

Fig. 11-8 Example 11-1: Identification and labeling of possible components of joint displacement.

The input data for this problem is given in Table 11-9 and the output is given in Table 11-10. The values of Table 11-10 are given in the following units:

1. rotations in radians;
2. translations in inches;
3. shears and axial forces in kips;
4. moments in inch-kips.

Table 11-7

MEMBER PROPERTIES

Member Number	*Type of Member* (Fig. 11-3)	*Length, ft*	*Moment of Inertia, in^4*	*Modulus of Elasticity, k/in^2*
1	Type 3	10	200	30,000
2	Type 1	10	200	30,000
3	Type 1	12	300	30,000
4	Type 3	12	300	30,000
5	Type 1	15	100	30,000
6	Type 3	15	200	30,000

Table 11-8

LOAD DATA

(a) Member Loads

Member Number	*Type of Load*	*Value of Load, k/ft or kips*	*Distance from Left End of Member to Beginning of Load, ft*	*Distance from Left End of Member to Termination of Load, ft*	*Load Case Number*
1	Uniform	−2	0	10	1
3	Uniform	−2	0	12	1
5	Concentrated	10	7.5	7.5	1
5	Uniform	1	0	15	1
6	Uniform	1	0	15	1
5	Uniform	4	0	15	2
6	Uniform	4	0	15	2

(b) Joint Loads

Joint Number	*Horizontal Force, kips*	*Vertical Force, kips*	*Moment, ft-k*	*Load Case Number*
1	10	−10	50	1
2	10	−10	−50	1
1	20	0	0	2
3	30	0	0	2

Table 11-9

INPUT DATA

Card No. \ Column No.	1 2 3 4 5 6 7 8 9 10	1 2 3 4 5 6 7 8 9 20	1 2 3 4 5 6 7 8 9 30	1 2 3 4 5 6 7 8 9 40	1 2 3 4 5 6 7 8 9 50
1	S 6 6 5	2	30000.	EXAMPLE PR	OBLEM
2	M 1 1	3 63	10.	200.	
3	M 2 2 5	3 61	10.	200.	
4	M 3 4 9	6 81	12.	300.	
5	M 4 5	6 113	12.	300.	
6	M 5 1 2	7 101	15.	100.	
7	M 6 4	7 103	15.	200.	
8	L 1 1 3	0.	10.	–2.	
9	L 1 3 1	0.	12.	–2.	
10	L 1 5 1 1	7.5	7.5	10.	
11	L 1 5 1	0.	15.	1.	
12	L 1 6 3	0.	15.	1.	
13	E				
14	P 1 1 7	3	50.	–10.	10.
15	P 1 2 10	3	–50.	–10.	10.
16	E				
17	L 2 5 1	0.	15.	4.	
18	L 2 6 3	0.	15.	4.	
19	E				
20	P 2 1 7	3	0.	0.	20.
21	P 2 4 7	6	0.	0.	30.
22	E				
23	Q				

Table 11-10

OUTPUT DATA

(a) Structure Data

N	M	NR	IPD	IPDFL	IPSM	INCR	IPR	IPRES	NL	EG
6	6	5	0	0	0	0	0	0	2	30000.00

(b) Member Data Check

ICODE	MNUM	IRL	IRR	IDL	IDR	MTYPE	QL	QI	E
M	1	1	0	3	6	3	10.00	200.00	30000.00
M	2	2	5	3	6	1	10.00	200.00	30000.00
M	3	4	9	6	8	1	12.00	300.00	30000.00
M	4	5	0	6	11	3	12.00	300.00	30000.00
M	5	1	2	7	10	1	15.00	100.00	30000.00
M	6	4	0	7	10	3	15.00	200.00	30000.00

(c) Member Load Data Check

ICODE	LCN	MNUM	LTYPE	MTYPE	DISTB	DISTE	W	FML	FMR	FSL	FSR
L	1	1	0	3	0.00	10.00	−2.00	0.00	0.00	0.00	0.00
L	1	3	0	1	0.00	12.00	−2.00	0.00	0.00	0.00	0.00
L	1	5	1	1	7.50	7.50	10.00	0.00	0.00	0.00	0.00
L	1	5	0	1	0.00	15.00	1.00	0.00	0.00	0.00	0.00
L	1	6	0	3	0.00	15.00	1.00	0.00	0.00	0.00	0.00

Table 11-10—*Cont.*

(d) Joint Load Data Check

ICODE	LCN	K11	K22	K33	QJM	QJV	QJH
P	1	1	7	3	50.00	−10.00	10.00
P	1	2	10	3	−50.00	−10.00	10.00

(e) Member Load Data Check

ICODE	LCN	MNUM	LTYPE	MTYPE	DISTB	DISTE	W	FML	FMR	FSL	FSR
L	2	5	0	1	0.00	15.00	4.00	0.00	0.00	0.00	0.00
L	2	6	0	3	0.00	15.00	4.00	0.00	0.00	0.00	0.00

(f) Joint Load Data Check

ICODE	LCN	K11	K22	K33	QJM	QJV	QJH
P	2	1	7	3	0.00	0.00	20.00
P	2	4	7	6	0.00	0.00	30.00

(g) Rotations and Deflections (Loading 1)

Displacement Number	*Displacement*
1	−0.11808474E − 01
2	−0.18479824E − 01
3	0.63164282E + 01
4	−0.24790205E − 01
5	−0.25836743E − 01
6	0.32818298E + 01

Table 11-10—*Cont.*

(h) Final End Actions (Loading 1)

Member Number	*Moment Left*	*Moment Right*	*Shear Left*	*Shear Right*
1	1721.98	0.00	4.35	−24.35
2	1306.86	571.17	15.65	−15.65
3	2141.52	5585.89	43.97	−67.97
4	−571.17	0.00	−3.97	3.97
5	−1121.98	−1906.85	−7.45	32.45
6	−2141.52	0.00	−4.40	19.40

(i) Reactions (Loading 1)

Displacement Number	*Reaction*
7	−1.85
8	−67.97
9	5585.89
10	61.85
11	3.97

(j) Rotations and Deflections (Loading 2)

Displacement Number	*Displacement*
1	−0.16517527E − 01
2	−0.68671256E − 02
3	0.59272509E + 01
4	−0.30650951E − 01
5	−0.25335774E − 01
6	0.36010895E + 01

(k) Final End Actions (Loading 2)

Member Number	*Moment Left*	*Moment Right*	*Shear Left*	*Shear Right*
1	430.07	0.00	3.58	−3.58
2	1908.40	61.54	16.42	−16.42
3	1715.10	5546.46	50.43	−50.43
4	−61.54	0.00	−0.43	0.43
5	−430.07	−1908.39	17.01	42.99
6	−1715.09	0.00	20.47	39.53

Table 11-10—*Cont.*

(l) Reactions (Loading 2)

Displacement	*Reaction*
7	37.48
8	−50.43
9	5546.46
10	82.52
11	0.43

(m) Residuals (Loading 1)

Equation Number	*Residual*
.1	0.0039
2	0.0081
3	−0.0001
4	0.0032
5	−0.0073
6	0.0005

(n) Residuals (Loading 2)

Equation Number	*Residual*
1	0.0020
2	0.0042
3	−0.0001
4	0.0073
5	−0.0039
6	0.0005

12 PLANAR FRAME AND TRUSS PROGRAM

12–1 Introduction

The stiffness analysis of planar frames and trusses was presented in Chapter 5. The computer program presented in this section is based on the theory, sign convention, and assumptions of Chapter 5, along with the discussions of Chapter 10.

This program accepts data that describes the geometry and loading of any planar frame or truss and solves for the joint displacements at each joint and the member end actions of each member.

Sections 12-2, 12-3, and 12-4 provide the basis for organizing and preparing the data for the computer program. Section 12-5 describes the organization and flow of the computer program, and the example problem of Sec. 12-6 illustrates the data preparation and output formats for a particular problem solution using the computer program.

12–2 Numbering Scheme

The structure is first sketched and the joints and members numbered. A distinct number is given to each joint and member starting with the integer 1 and numbering sequentially. The number assigned to a particular joint or member is completely arbitrary; however, one should number joints and members to make interpretation of the computer output as easy as possible.

A recommended procedure for the numbering scheme is illustrated in Fig. 12-1. In Fig. 12-1 the reference coordinate axes have been established and the origin is located in the lower left corner of the structure. Location of the coordinate axes in this manner usually facilitates the determination of joint coordinates. The joint coordinates for Fig. 12-1 are shown in parentheses after the joint number.

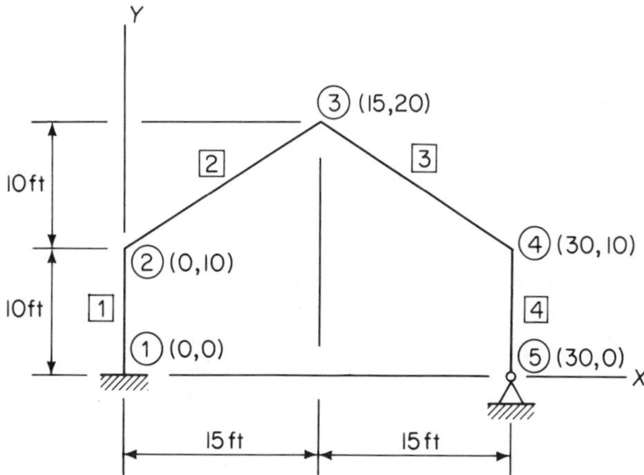

Fig. 12-1 Illustration of numbering scheme.

The computer program assigns up to three displacement numbers per joint, depending on the degree of joint restraint. These numbers are assigned sequentially based on the order in which the joint coordinate data is entered. Therefore, it is recommended that the joints be numbered and entered in a sequence that will result in as narrow a half-band stiffness matrix as possible. For example, in Fig. 12-1 the joint coordinates would be entered in the order of 1 to 5. The displacement numbering accomplished by the program for this ordering of joint coordinate data is illustrated in Fig. 12-2. Note in Fig. 12-2 that the first joint encountered (joint 1) has no free displacements and hence no displacement numbers are assigned. Joint 2, the second joint encountered, has three free displacements, and they are assigned the displacement numbers 1, 2, and 3 in the order of rotation, Y-coordinate displacement, and X-coordinate displacement. Likewise, the joint displacement numbers for the remaining joints are assigned for the free displacements in sequence as the joint coordinate data is entered. It must be realized that only the order in which the joint coordinate data is entered is of importance in the automatic assignment of displacement numbers. For example, suppose that the joint coordinates for the example of Fig. 12-1 were entered

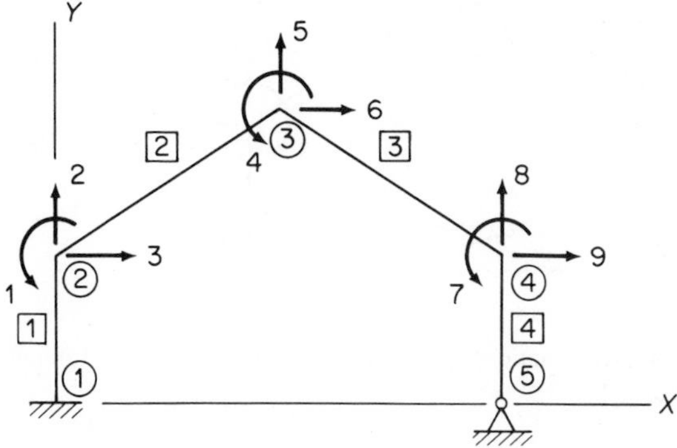

Fig. 12-2 Automatic displacement number assignment for joints entered $1 \rightarrow 5$.

in reverse order—i.e., joint 5 entered first, then joint 4, etc. The displacement numbering that would result for this ordering is shown in Fig. 12-3. It should be realized from this discussion that the half-band width of the resulting stiffness matrix is dependent upon the order in which joint coordinate data is entered; hence, the efficiency of the solution can be improved by ordering the joint coordinate data in a fashion that results in as small a half-band width stiffness matrix as possible.

If the suggestion of ordering the joint coordinate data in sequence is followed beginning with joint number 1, a good approximation of the minimum half-band stiffness matrix that results can be computed from Eq. (12-1):

$$m \leq m_a = [(|J_i - K_i| + 1)n_c - 1]_{\text{max over } i} \tag{12-1}$$

where
m = the actual half-band width;
m_a = approximate value of the half-band width;
J_i, K_i = joint numbers at ends of ith member (the term $J_i - K_i$ should be set equal to 0 if either J_i or K_i is completely restrained);
i = subscript and index indicating the member number;
n_c = maximum possible number of components of joint displacement at any joint in the structure.

The value of m_a in Eq. (12-1) is determined by finding the maximum value of the expression enclosed in brackets when considering all members of the structure. The value of n_c is 3 for planar frames and 2 for planar trusses. Equation (12-1) always gives an upper bound to the actual half-band width computed from displacement numbers directly; consequently, this relationship always gives a band width that is large enough to contain all nonzero elements.

Applying Eq. (12-1) to the structure of Fig. 12-1 gives $m = m_a = 5$. The reader is again cautioned that Eq. (12-1) is valid for this computer program only if the joint coordinates are entered in ascending order of joint number.

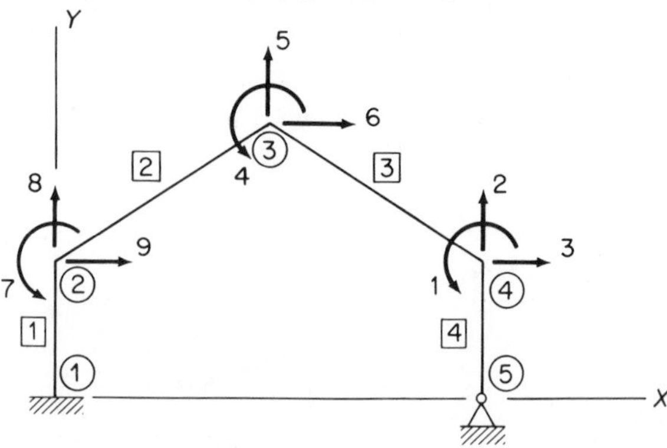

Fig. 12-3 Automatic displacement number assignment for joints entered 5 → 1.

12–3 Member Load Sign Convention

The computer program calculates fixed end actions due to concentrated and uniform loads applied to a member. These loads may be applied normal to the member or at any skew angle to the member. The sign convention for entering member loads is illustrated in Fig. 12-4. If the member is viewed such that joint j is on the left end of the member, the load is positive when applied downward in quadrants I and II and negative when applied upward in quadrants III and IV (see Fig. 12-4). The acute angle α measured between the normal line and the line of action of the load is positive in quadrants I and III and negative in quadrants II and IV (see Fig. 12-4).

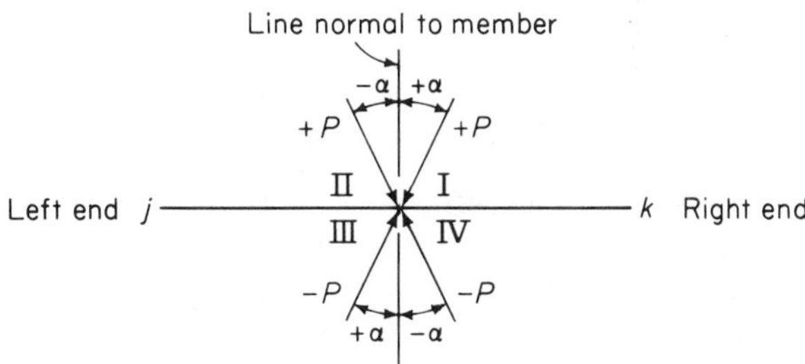

Fig. 12-4 Member load sign convention.

12–4 Preparation of Input Data

Preparation of input data for this program should be accomplished in the following sequence:

1. Sketch the structure and number the joints and members as indicated in Sec. 12-2, remembering to observe the geometry of the structure to determine the joint sequence that will keep the half-band width of the stiffness matrix as narrow as possible.
2. Establish the reference coordinate system and label the joints with the proper coordinate values.
3. Define the different load cases to be considered.
4. With the aid of items 1 through 3 above, prepare data cards according to the formats indicated in Tables 12-1 through 12-7.

The input data tables (Tables 12-1 through 12-7) are organized such that the first column gives the card columns to use in positioning the data value. The second column of the tables—i.e., the identifier name—gives the actual identifier

Table 12-1

STRUCTURE DATA

Card Columns	*Identifier Name Used in Program*	*Data Description*	*FORTRAN Format*
1	ICODE	The letter 'S' for structure card.	A1
2–4	M	Number of members in structure.	I3
5–7	NJ	Number of joints in structure.	I3
8–10	NL	Number of loading conditions for this problem.	I3
11–20	EN	Global modulus of elasticity for this problem (k/in^2).	F10.0
21–23	MUD	The half-band width of the stiffness matrix (estimated). See Eq. (12-1) for a method of estimating. If this value is unspecified or specified too small, the program will correct it at the cost of some computing time.	I3
24–75	——	Blank.	52X
76–80	JOBNO	Job identification number (any one- to five-digit number).	I5

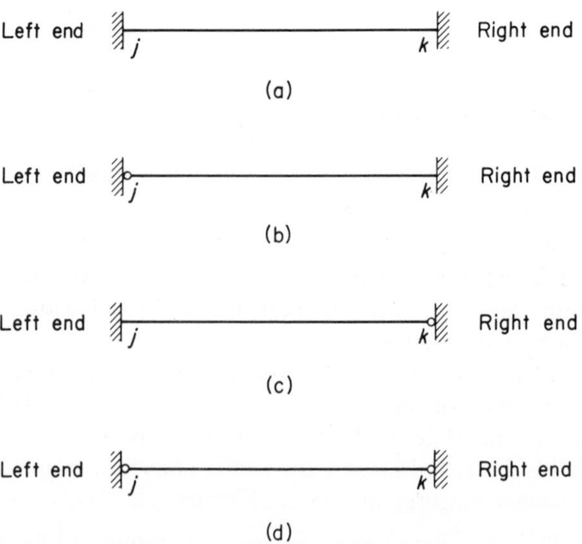

Fig. 12-5 Member type description: (a) type 0—both ends restrained; (b) type 1—*j*-end pinned, *k*-end restrained; (c) type 2—*j*-end restrained, *k*-end pinned; (d) type-3—both ends pinned.

Table 12-2

JOINT DATA

Card Columns	Identifier Name Used in Program	Data Description	FORTRAN Format
1	ICODE	The letter 'J' for joint data card.	A1
2–4	J	The joint number of this joint.	I3
5	IRR	Rotational restraint of this joint. If joint can rotate and develop moment at this joint due to rotation, leave this field blank; otherwise place '1' in column 5.	I1
6	IVR	*Y*-coordinate restraint of this joint. Leave column 6 blank if joint is unrestrained in *Y*-coordinate direction. Place '1' in column 6 if this joint is restrained against translation in the *Y*-coordinate direction.	I1
7	IHR	*X*-coordinate restraint of this joint. Leave column 7 blank if joint is unrestrained in *X*-coordinate direction. Place '1' in column 7 if this joint is restrained against translation in the *X*-coordinate direction.	I1
8–10	——	Blank.	
11–20	XCOOR	*X*-coordinate of this joint (ft).	F10.0
21–30	YCOOR	*Y*-coordinate of this joint (ft).	F10.0
31–80	——	Blank.	

Table 12-3

MEMBER DATA

Card Columns	Identifier Name Used in Program	Data Description	FORTRAN Format
1	ICODE	The letter 'M' for member data card.	A1
2–4	I	Member number.	I3
5–7	J	Joint number of end *j* of member.	I3
8–10	K	Joint number of end *k* of member.	I3
11	MT	Member type 0, 1, 2, or 3 (see Fig. 12-5).	I1
12–20	QI	Moment of inertia of member (in^4).	F9.0
21–30	QA	Cross-sectional area of member (in^2).	F10.0
31–40	E	Modulus of elasticity (k/in^2) of this member if different from global modulus. If same as global modulus, leave this field blank.	F10.0
41–80	——	Blank.	

Table 12-4

MEMBER LOAD DATA

Card Columns	*Identifier Name Used in Program*	*Data Description*	*FORTRAN Format*
1	ICODE	The letter 'L' for member load.	A1
2–4	IB1	Member number of this member.	I3
5–10	——	Blank.	6X
11–20	AB1	Value of load (k/ft if uniform load; kips if concentrated load).	F10.3
21–30	AB2	Distance from joint *j* of member along member to beginning of load (ft).	F10.3
31–40	AB3	Distance from joint *j* of member along member to termination of load (ft).	F10.3
41–50	AB4	The angle the load makes with a normal line to the member in degrees. (See Fig. 12-4.)	F10.3
51–80	——	Blank.	

name used in the FORTRAN read statement that reads this card. The last column of the tables gives the FORTRAN format conversion used to interpret the input data. It should be noted that all integer values must be right-justified in their prescribed data field. It is recommended that all real number values be placed in their field with the decimal point included.

The global data for a particular problem is placed on the structure data card described in Table 12-1. This is the first card read by the program, and there is only one structure data card per problem.

The joint data cards described in Table 12-2 are read after the structure data card. There is one joint data card for each joint in the structure.

The member data cards described in Table 12-3 follow the joint data cards. One member data card is required for each member in the structure, and the number of member cards must be equal to the value specified for M on the structure data card. The variable MT listed in Table 12-3 identifies a member as one of four possible types described in Fig. 12-5 that can be considered by the program. The number identifying the type in Fig. 12-5 is the number to be placed in column 11 of the member data card.

The member load data cards described in Table 12-4 are read after the member data cards. There must be one member load data card for each load acting on a member. These cards may be read in any order desired.

The joint load data cards described in Table 12-5 are read after the member load data cards. There must be one joint load data card for each joint of the structure that is loaded, and they also may be read in arbitrary order.

The load data is terminated by a dummy load divider card described in

Table 12-5

JOINT LOAD DATA

Card Columns	*Identifier Name Used in Program*	*Data Description*	*FORTRAN Format*
1	ICODE	The letter 'P' for joint load card.	A1
2–4	IB1	Joint number.	I3
5–10	——	Blank.	6X
11–20	AB1	Applied moment at this joint (ft-k).	F10.3
21–30	AB2	Applied force in *Y*-coordinate direction at this joint (kips).	F10.3
31–40	AB3	Applied force in *X*-coordinate direction at this joint (kips).	F10.3
41–80	——	Blank.	

Table 12-6

DUMMY LOAD DIVIDER CARD

Card Columns	*Identifier Name Used in Program*	*Data Description*	*FORTRAN Format*
1	ICODE	The letter 'N' to indicate termination of this loading condition and the beginning of a new loading condition. The letter 'E' to terminate the last loading condition for this problem.	A1
2–80	——	Blank.	

Table 12-7

PROGRAM TERMINATION CARD

Card Columns	*Identifier Name Used in Program*	*Data Description*	*FORTRAN Format*
1	ICODE	The letter 'Q' to tell the program to quit execution. This is the last card in the data deck.	A1
2–80	——	Blank.	

Table 12-6. The program permits a maximum of 999 load cases for a particular structure.

After all structures for a particular computer run have been analyzed, the program is terminated with the program termination card described in Table 12-7.

The letter specified in column 1 of each data card identifies the type card being processed. A typical sequence of data cards for a structure with two load cases is given in Fig. 12-6.

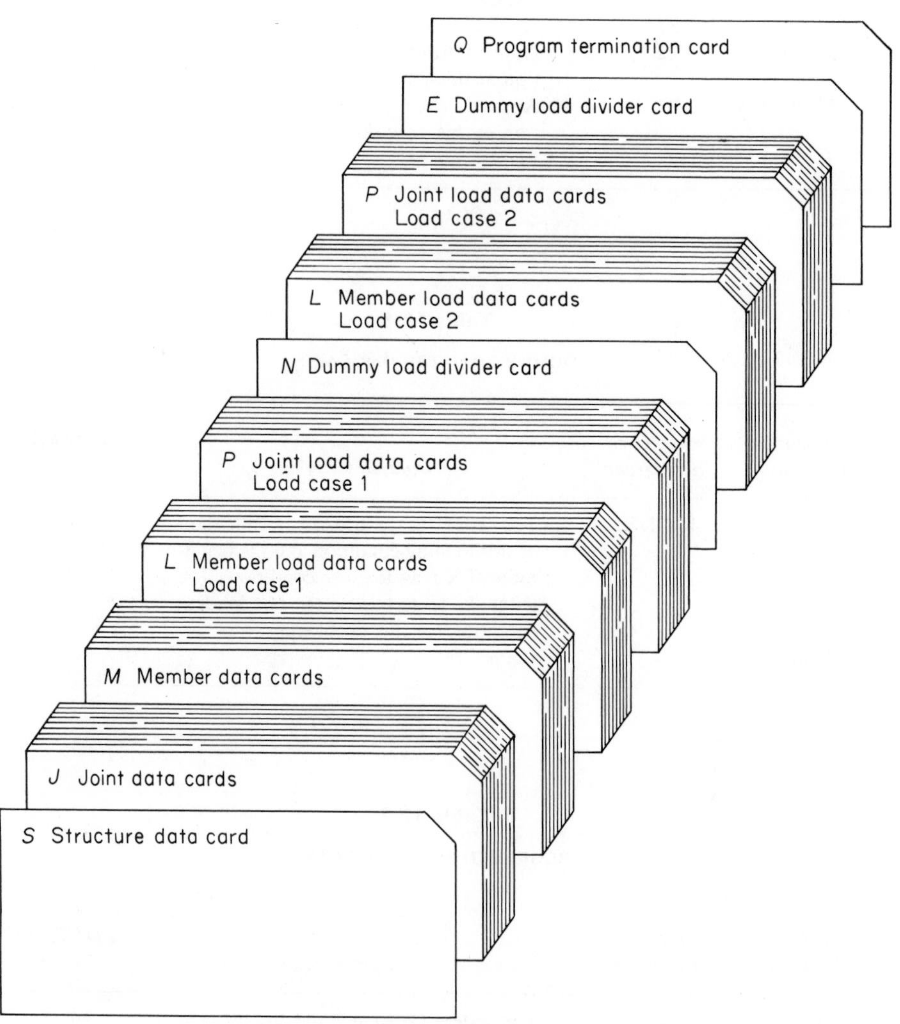

Fig. 12-6 Typical data card sequence for a structure with two load cases.

12–5
Program Description

The flow of the computer program is illustrated in the abbreviated flow chart of Fig. 12-7. Each data card read by the computer is written out for a visual check of the data as indicated in Fig. 12-6.

The joint displacement labels are assigned in sequence starting with the

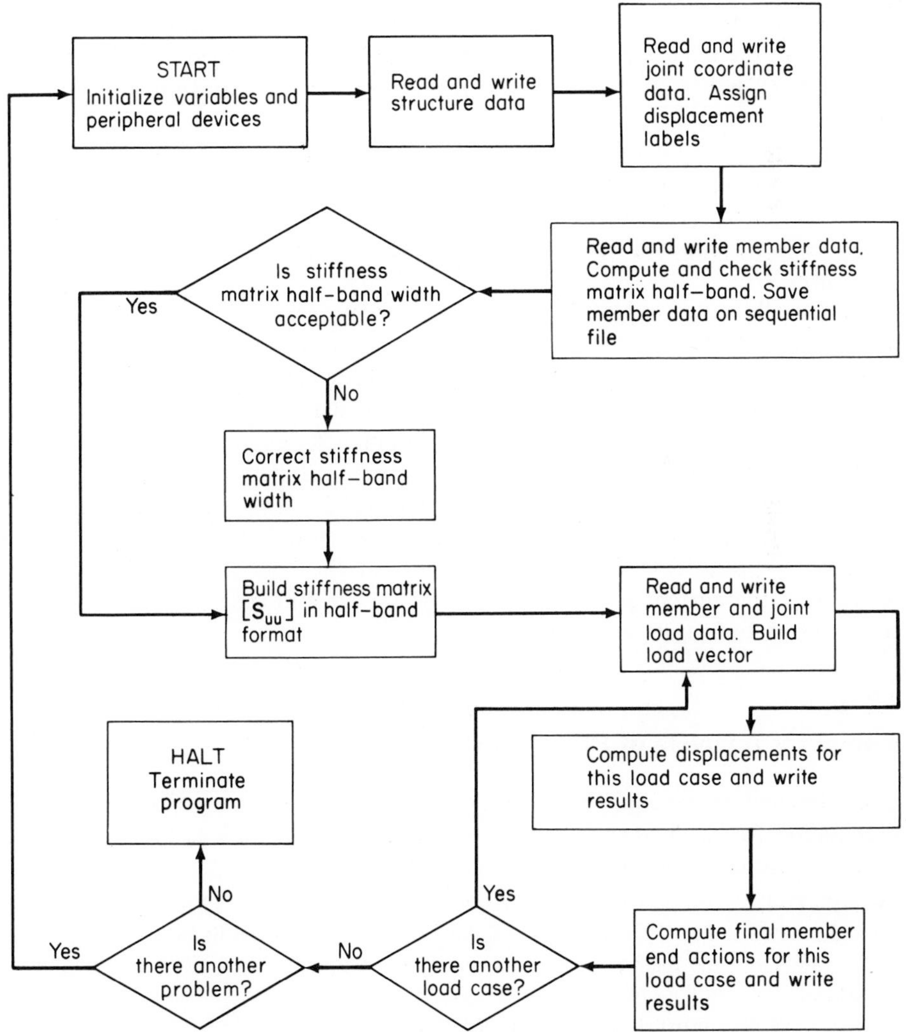

Fig. 12-7 Abbreviated flow chart for planar frame and truss program.

integer 1 as the joint data cards are read. Rotationally restrained joints and pinned joints are not labeled with a rotational displacement label (e.g., column 5 of joint data card, Table 12-2, contains a 1). Also, joints restrained in the Y-coordinate direction are not assigned a displacement label in the Y-coordinate direction, and joints restrained in the X-coordinate direction are not assigned a displacement label in the X-coordinate direction. A count of the labeled displacements determines the number of kinematic redundants for the problem and hence the dimension of the stiffness matrix $[\mathbf{S}_{uu}]$.

After all of the joint data cards have been processed, the member data cards are read and processed. The member stiffness matrix is built for each member, rotated into the reference coordinate system, and finally summed into the stiffness matrix $[\mathbf{S}_{uu}]$. The matrix $[\mathbf{S}_{uu}]$ is built in the linear array half-band format discussed in Sec. 10-4.

The member and joint load data is read and processed for each load case separately as indicated in Fig. 12-7. For each load case, the displacements at each joint in the structure and the final member end actions for each member in the structure are computed and written out before going to the next load case (see Fig. 12-7).

After all load cases have been processed, the program checks to see if another set of data is to be processed. If so, the program transfers to the beginning and begins processing the next problem; otherwise, the program stops.

During execution of the program, certain data checks are made by the program. If an error is detected, the program halts execution of the problem being processed and goes immediately to the next problem in the data stack.

Important array and variable identifiers used in the program are described in Sec. D-1, Appendix D. The FORTRAN code for this program is given in Sec. D-2, Appendix D. The comment cards at the beginning of the program listing give the current limitations of program size and indicate how to modify the program to fit different computer core sizes.

12–6
Computer Analysis of Planar Frame

The following example problem is given to demonstrate many features of data preparation for the planar frame and truss program, as well as to illustrate the format of various types of output.

Example 12-1. Consider the analysis of the frame shown in Fig. 12-8 for the two load cases described in Fig. 12-9. In Fig. 12-8 the joint labels are given in the circles adjacent to the joints and the member labels are given in the squares adjacent to the members; in addition, the j- and k-ends of the members are indicated, and the X- and Y-coordinates of each joint are shown in parentheses adjacent to each joint. The member properties are given in Table 12-8.

The input data for this problem is given in Table 12-9 and the output is given in Table 12-10. The values of Table 12-10 are given in the following units:

1. rotations in radians;
2. translations in inches;
3. shears and axial forces in kips;
4. moments in ft-k.

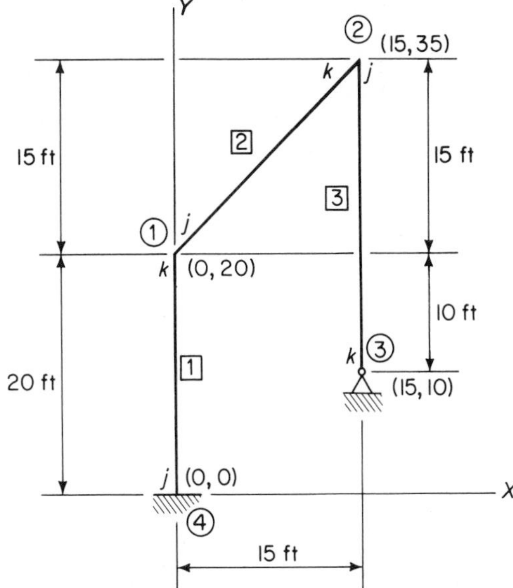

Fig. 12-8 Example 12-1: Number scheme.

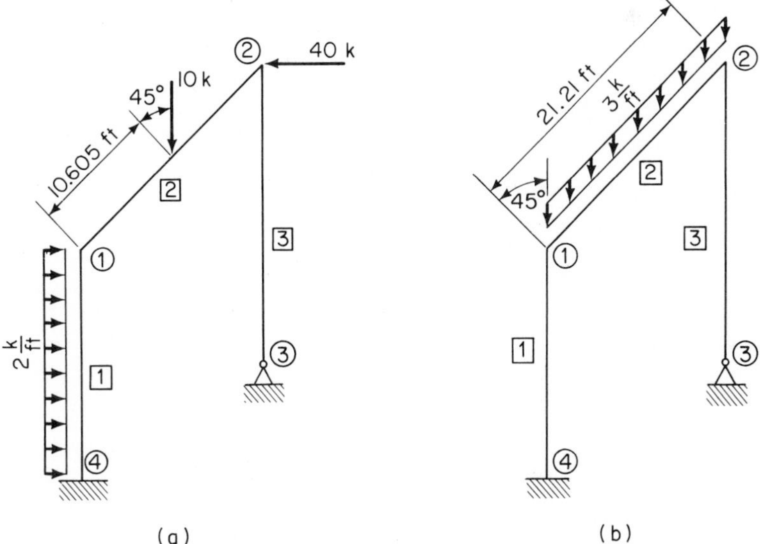

Fig. 12-9 Example 12-1: Load cases: (a) load case 1; (b) load case 2.

Table 12-8

MEMBER PROPERTIES

Member Number	*Joint J*	*Joint K*	*Moment of Inertia, in^4*	*Cross-Sectional Area, in^2*	*Modulus of Elasticity, k/in^2*
1	4	1	288	48	30,000
2	1	2	288	48	30,000
3	2	3	288	48	30,000

Table 12-9

INPUT DATA

Card No. \ Column No.	1 2 3 4 5 6 7 8 9 0 (1)	1 2 3 4 5 6 7 8 9 0 (2)	1 2 3 4 5 6 7 8 9 0 (3)	1 2 3 4 5 6 7 8 9 0 (4)	1 2 3 4 5	6 7 8 9 0 (7–8)
1	S 3 4 2	3 0 0 0 0 .	5			0 0 0 0 1
2	J 1	0 .	2 0 .			
3	J 2	1 5 .	3 5 .			
4	J 3 1 1 1	1 5 .	1 0 .			
5	J 4 1 1 1	0 .	0 .			
6	M 1 4 1	0 2 8 8 .	4 8 .			
7	M 2 1 2	0 2 8 8 .	4 8 .			
8	M 3 2 3	2 2 8 8 .	4 8 .			
9	L 1	2 .	0 .	2 0 .	0 .	
10	L 2	1 0 .	1 0 . 6 0 5	1 0 . 6 0 5	4 5 .	
11	P 2	0 .	0 .	—4 0 .		
12	N					
13	L 2	3 .	0 .	2 1 . 2 1	4 5 .	
14	E					
15	Q					

Table 12-10

OUTPUT DATA

(a) Structure Data

M	NJ	NL	E
3	4	2	30,000

(b) Joint Coordinates

Joint Number	IRR	IVR	IHR	*X-Coordinate*	*Y-Coordinate*
1	0	0	0	0.000	20.000
2	0	0	0	15.000	35.000
3	1	1	1	15.000	10.000
4	1	1	1	0.000	0.000

(c) Member Data

Member Number	J	K	*Inertia, in⁴*	*Area, in²*	*Modulus, ksi*	*Length, ft*	*Type*
1	4	1	288.000	48.000	30000.000	20.000	0
2	1	2	288.000	48.000	30000.000	21.213	0
3	2	3	288.000	48.000	30000.000	25.000	2

(d) Member Load Data (Loading 1)

Member Number	*Load*	*X-Begin, ft*	*X-End, ft*	ALPHA
1	2.000	0.000	20.000	0.000
2	10.000	10.605	10.605	45.000

Table 12-10—*Cont.*

(e) Joint Load Data (Loading 1)

Joint	*Moment, ft-k*	*Vertical Force, kips*	*Horizontal Force, kips*
2	0.00	0.00	−40.00

(f) Joint Deflections and Rotations (Loading 1)

Joint Number	*Rotation*	*Vertical Deflection, in.*	*Horizontal Deflection, in.*
1	0.0144530	−0.0099817	−3.9633951
2	0.0019268	0.0103943	−3.9999647
3		0.0000000	0.0000000
4	0.0000000	0.0000000	0.0000000

(g) Beam Moment and Shears (Loading 1)

Member Number	*J-Moment, in-k*	*K-Moment, in-k*	*J-Shear, kips*	*K-shear, kips*	*J-Axial, kips*	*K-Axial, kips*
1	−143.87	−190.49	3.28	36.72	59.89	−59.89
2	190.48	82.13	16.39	−9.32	68.32	−61.25
3	−82.13	0.00	−3.29	3.29	−49.89	49.89

Table 12-10—*Cont.*

(h) Member Load Data (Loading 2)

Member Number	*Load*	*X-Begin, ft*	*X-End, ft*	ALPHA
2	3.000	0.000	21.210	45.000

(i) Joint Deflections and Rotations (Loading 2)

Joint Number	*Rotation*	*Vertical Deflection, in.*	*Horizontal Deflection, in.*
1	−0.0063448	−0.0055146	0.4844156
2	0.0055611	−0.0063629	0.4959191
3		0.0000000	0.0000000
4	0.0000000	0.0000000	0.0000000

(j) Beam Moment and Shears (Loading 2)

Member Number	*J-Moment, in-k*	*K-Moment, in-k*	*J-Shear, kips*	*K-Shear, kips*	*J-Axial, kips*	*K-Axial, kips*
1	−1.74	−39.81	−2.08	2.08	33.09	−33.09
2	39.81	−51.94	21.93	23.07	24.87	20.13
3	51.94	0.00	2.08	−2.08	30.54	−30.54

13 SPACE FRAME AND TRUSS PROGRAM

13–1 Introduction

The stiffness analysis of space frames and space trusses was presented in Chapter 6. The computer program presented in this section is based on the theory, sign convention, and assumptions of Chapter 6, along with the discussions of Chapter 10.

This program accepts data that describes the geometry and loading of a space frame or space truss, and solves for the joint displacements at each joint and the member end actions of each member. Continuity is assumed at each internal joint of a space frame, and no special members are permitted in this program. All joints are assumed pinned in space truss problems.

Sections 13-2, 13-3, and 13-4 provide the basis for organizing and preparing the data for the computer program. Section 13-5 describes the organization and flow of the computer program, and the example problem of Sec. 13-6 illustrates the data preparation and output formats for a particular problem solution using the computer program.

13–2 Numbering Scheme

The structure is first sketched and the joints and members numbered. A distinct number is given to each joint and member starting with the integer 1 and numbering sequentially. The number assigned to a particular joint or member is arbitrary; however, one should number the joints and members to make interpretation of the computer output as easy as possible.

The numbering scheme for a simple space frame is illustrated in Fig. 13-1. The circled numbers adjacent to the joints indicate the assigned joint numbers and the numbers in boxes adjacent to the members are the assigned member num-

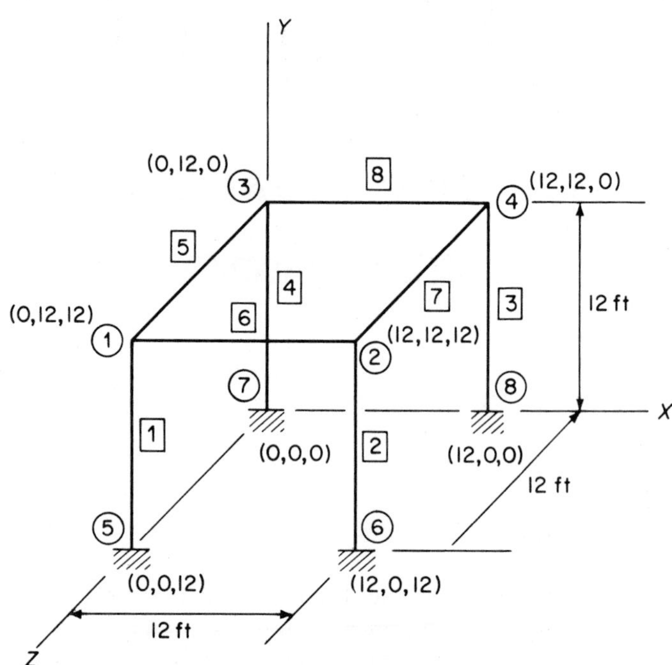

Fig. 13-1 Illustration of numbering scheme for space frame.

bers. The coordinates of each joint relative to the given reference coordinate axes are shown in parentheses adjacent to the joint numbers.

The computer program assigns six displacement designations for each unrestrained joint of the space frame. These numbers are assigned for a particular joint in the order indicated in Fig. 13-2. The single arrows in Fig. 13-2 represent translations and the double arrows represent rotations. Displacement designations are assigned only for unrestrained displacements at the joint and are assigned sequentially based on the order in which the joint coordinate data is entered. For example, in Fig. 13-1, if the joint coordinates are entered in numerical sequence by joint number, the displacement numbers 1 through 6 are assigned to joint 1, 7 through 12 to joint 2, etc. This procedure is similar to the procedure used in the numbering scheme for the planar frame and truss program discussed in Sec. 12-2, the only difference being the order and number of displacement numbers assigned at a particular joint.

If the joint coordinates are entered in numerical sequence beginning with joint 1, an approximation of the minimum half-band stiffness matrix that results can be computed from Eq. (12-1), with $n_c = 6$ for space frames and $n_c = 3$ for space trusses.

Applying Eq. (12-1) to the structure of Fig. 13-1 gives $m = m_a = 17$. Notice that when one of the restrained joints—i.e., 5, 6, 7, or 8—are encountered on the end of a member, the term $J_i - K_i$ is set equal to 0.

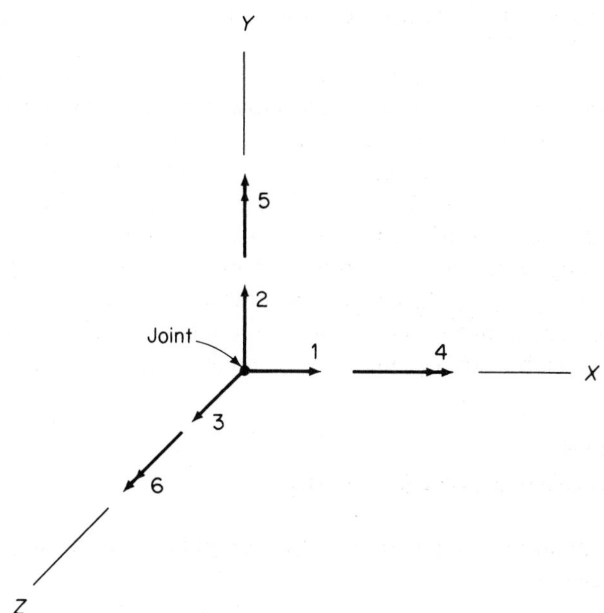

Fig. 13-2 Displacement designation sequence for space frame joint.

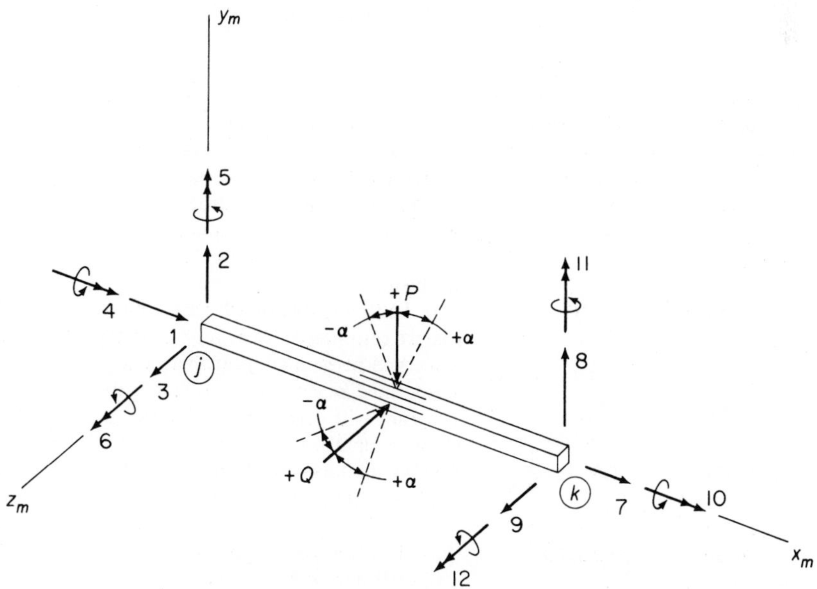

Fig. 13-3 Sign convention for member loads.

13–3 Member Load Sign Convention

The computer program calculates fixed end shears and moments due to concentrated and uniform loads applied to a member. The loads must be applied normal to one of the principal axes of inertia of the member and must pass through the shear center of the cross-section. The sign convention for entering member loads is illustrated in Fig. 13-3. Load P in Fig. 13-3 lies in the x_m–y_m plane of the member axes, and is positive as shown. Load Q in Fig. 13-3 lies in the x_m–z_m plane of the member axes, and is positive as shown. Positive and negative shew angles that the loads make with the normal are indicated in Fig. 13-3. The components of member end displacements and actions are numbered in Fig. 13-3 in the sequence in which the member stiffness matrix is compiled by the program.

13–4 Preparation of Input Data

Preparation of input data for this program should be accomplished in the following sequence:

1. Sketch the structure and number the joints and members as indicated in Sec. 13-2, remembering to observe the geometry of the structure in order to deter-

Table 13-1

STRUCTURE DATA

Card Columns	Identifier Name Used in Program	Data Description	FORTRAN Format
1	KODE	The letter 'S' for structure card.	A1
2–4	M	Number of members in structure.	I3
5–7	NJ	Number of joints in structure.	I3
8–10	NL	Number of loading conditions for this problem.	I3
11–13	MUD	The half-band width of the stiffness matrix (estimated). See Eq. (12-1) for a method of estimating. If this value is unspecified or specified too small, the program will correct it at the cost of some computing time.	I3
14–23	EN	Global modulus of elasticity for this problem (k/in^2).	F10.0
24–75	——	Blank.	52X
76–80	JOBNO	Job identification number (any one- to five-digit number).	76–80

mine the joint sequence that will keep the half-band width of the stiffness matrix as narrow as possible.

2. Establish the reference coordinate system and label the joints with the proper coordinate values.
3. Define the different load cases to be considered.
4. With the aid of items 1 through 3 above, prepare data cards according to the formats indicated in Tables 13-1 through 13-7.

Table 13-2

JOINT DATA

Card Columns	*Identifier Name Used in Program*	*Data Description*	*FORTRAN Format*
1	KODE	The letter 'J' for joint data card.	A1
2–4	J	The joint number of this joint.	I3
5	IXT	*X*-coordinate translational restraint of this joint. Leave blank if this joint is unrestrained in *X*-coordinate direction. Place '1' in this column if this joint is restrained in *X*-coordinate direction.	I1
6	IYT	Same as IXT above, except in *Y*-coordinate direction.	I1
7	IZT	Same as IXT above, except in *Z*-coordinate direction.	I1
8	IXR	Rotational restraint of this joint in *X*-coordinate direction. Leave blank if joint is unrestrained in *X*-coordinate direction. Place '1' in this column if this joint is restrained in *X*-coordinate direction. *Note:* For space truss problems, place '1' in this column.	I1
9	IYR	Same as IXR above, except in *Y*-coordinate direction.	I1
10	IZR	Same as IXR above, except in *Z*-coordinate direction.	I1
11–20	XCOOR	*X*-coordinate of this joint (ft).	F10.2
21–30	YCOOR	*Y*-coordinate of this joint (ft).	F10.2
31–40	ZCOOR	*Z*-coordinate of this joint (ft).	F10.2
41–80	——	Blank.	——

The input data tables (Tables 13-1 through 13-7) are organized such that the first column gives the card columns to use in positioning the data value. The second column of the tables—i.e., the identifier name—gives the actual identifier name used in the FORTRAN read statement that reads this card. The last column of the

Table 13-3

MEMBER DATA

Card Columns	Identifier Name Used in Program	Data Description	FORTRAN Format
1	KODE	The letter 'M' for member data card.	A1
2–4	I	Member number.	I3
5–7	J	Joint number of end j of member.	I3
8–10	K	Joint number of end k of member.	I3
11	MT	Member type. Leave column 11 blank if space frame member, place '1' in column 11 if space truss member.	I1
12–20	QIX	Moment of inertia about member X-axis (in^4).	F9.2
21–30	QIY	Moment of inertia about member Y-axis (in^4).	F10.0
31–40	QIZ	Moment of inertia about member Z-axis (in^4).	F10.0
41–50	QA	Cross-sectional area of member (in^2).	F10.0
51–60	G	Shear modulus of elasticity (k/in^2).	
61–70	SI	Angle of roll Ψ in degrees (see Fig. 6-14).	F10.0
71	ISI	If the angle of roll is specified for rotation YZX, leave this column blank. If specified for rotation ZYX, place '1' in this column.	I1
72–80	E	Modulus of elasticity of this member if different from global modulus assigned on structure data card. If same as global modulus, leave this field blank.	F9.0

tables gives the FORTRAN format conversion used to interpret the input data. It should be noted that all integer values must be right-justified in their prescribed data field. It is recommended that all real number values be placed in their field with the decimal point included.

The global data for a particular problem is placed on the structure data card described in Table 13-1. This is the first card read by the program, and there is only one structure data card per problem.

The joint data cards described in Table 13-2 are read after the structure data card. There is one joint data card for each joint in the structure.

The member data cards described in Table 13-3 follow the joint data cards. One member data card is required for each member in the structure, and the number of member cards must be equal to the value specified for M on the structure data card.

Table 13-4

MEMBER LOAD DATA

Card Columns	*Identifier Name Used in Program*	*Data Description*	*FORTRAN Format*
1	KODE	The letter 'L' for load data card.	A1
2–4	IB1	Member number of this member.	I3
5	IB2	Plane of loading. If the load lies in the member axis x_m–y_m plane, leave this column blank. (See Fig. 13-3, load *P*.) If the load lies in the member axis x_m–z_m plane, place '1' in this column. (See Fig. 13-3, load *Q*.)	I1
6–10	——	Blank.	5X
11–20	AB1	Value of load k/ft if uniform load is specified; kips if a concentrated load is specified).	F10.3
21–30	AB2	Distance from joint *j* of member to beginning of load (ft).	F10.3
31–40	AB3	Distance from joint *j* of member to termination of load (ft).	F10.3
41–50	AB4	The angle the load makes with a normal line in degrees—i.e., α in Fig. 13-3.	F10.3
51–60	AB5	Blank (used in reading joint load data).	F10.3
61–70	AB6	Blank (used in reading joint load data).	F10.3
71–80	——	Blank.	——

The member load data cards described in Table 13-4 are read after the member data cards. There must be one member load data card for each load acting on a member. These cards may be read in any order desired.

The joint load data cards described in Table 13-5 are read after the member load data cards. There must be one joint load data card for each joint of the structure that is loaded, and they also may be read in arbitrary order.

The load data is terminated by a dummy load divider card as described in Table 13-6. The program permits a maximum of 999 load cases for a particular structure.

After all structures for a particular computer run have been analyzed, the program is terminated with the program termination card described in Table 13-7.

The letter specified in column 1 of each data card identifies the type card being processed. The sequencing of data for this program is identical to that of the program described in Chapter 12. Hence, a typical sequence of data cards for a structure with two load cases is the same as that given in Fig. 12-6.

Table 13-5

JOINT LOAD DATA

Card Columns	*Identifier Name Used in Program*	*Data Description*	*FORTRAN Format*
1	KODE	The letter 'P' for joint load card.	A1
2–4	IB1	The joint number.	I3
5	IB2	Blank (used in reading member load data).	I3
6–10	——	Blank.	5X
11–20	AB1	Applied force in *X*-coordinate direction at this joint (kips).	F10.3
21–30	AB2	Same as AB1 above, except in *Y*-coordinate direction.	F10.3
31–40	AB3	Same as AB1 above, except in *Z*-coordinate direction.	F10.3
41–50	AB4	Applied moment about *N*-axis at this joint (ft-k).	F10.3
51–60	AB5	Applied moment about *Y*-axis at this joint (ft-k).	F10.3
61–70	AB6	Applied moment about *Z*-axis at this joint (ft-k).	F10.3
71–80	——	Blank.	——

Table 13-6

DUMMY LOAD DIVIDER CARD

Card Columns	*Identifier Name Used in Program*	*Data Description*	*FORTRAN Format*
1	KODE	The letter 'N' to indicate termination of this loading condition and the beginning of a new loading condition. The letter 'E' to terminate the last loading condition for this problem.	A1
2–80	——	Blank.	——

Table 13-7

PROGRAM TERMINATION CARD

Card Columns	*Identifier Name Used in Program*	*Data Description*	*FORTRAN Format*
1	KODE	The letter 'Q' to tell the program to quit execution. This is the last card in the data deck.	A1
2–80	—	Blank	—

13–5
Program Description

The description of this program is essentially the same as the description of the plane frame and truss program of Sec. 12-5, the only difference being the additional displacements that must be considered in the space structure.

Important array and variable identifiers used in the program are described in Sec. E-1, Appendix E. The FORTRAN code for this program is given in Sec. E-2, Appendix E. The comment cards at the beginning of the program listing give the current limitations of program size and indicate how to modify the program in order to fit different computer core sizes.

13–6
Computer Analysis of Space Frame

The following example problem is given in order to demonstrate some of the features of data preparation for the space frame and truss program, as well as to illustrate the format of the various types of output.

Example 13-1. Consider the analysis of the frame shown in Fig. 13-4. In Fig. 13-4 the joint labels are given in the circles adjacent to the joints and the member labels are given in the squares adjacent to the members; in addition, the *j*- and *k*-ends of the members are indicated, and the *X*-, *Y*-, and *Z*-coordinates of each joint are shown in parentheses adjacent to each joint. The problem is to be run for the single load case illustrated in Fig. 13-4. Table 13-8 gives the member properties assumed for this problem. Note that the values assumed for member properties are relative values and hence displacements obtained should be ignored.

The input data for this problem is given in Table 13-9 and the output is given in Table 13-10. The values of Table 13-10 are given in the following units:

1. rotations in radians;
2. translations in inches;
3. shears and axial forces in kips;
4. moments in ft-k.

Table 13-8

MEMBER PROPERTIES

Member Number	I_{xx}	I_{yy}	I_{zz}	*Area*	*Shear Modulus*	*Bending Modulus*
1	0.25	1.0	1.0	0.25	1.0	1.0
2	0.25	1.0	1.0	0.25	1.0	1.0
3	0.25	1.0	1.0	0.25	1.0	1.0

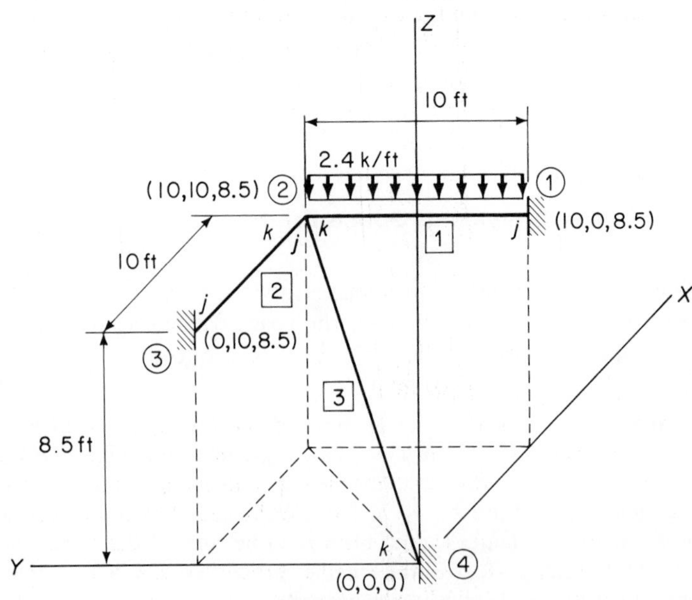

Fig. 13-4 Example 13-1: Rigid space frame.

Table 13-9

INPUT DATA

Card No. \ Column No.	1 2 3 4 5 6 7 8 9 10	1 2 3 4 5 6 7 8 9 20	1 2 3 4 5	3 1 2 3 4 5	4 1 2 3 4 5	5 1 2 3 4 5	6 1 2 3 4 5	7 0 1 2 78 9 0
1	S 3 4 1	5 1 .						0
2	J 1 1 1 1 1 1 1	1 0 .	0 .	8 . 5				
3	J 2	1 0 .	1 0 .	8 . 5				
4	J 3 1 1 1 1 1 1	0 .	1 0 .	8 . 5				
5	J 4 1 1 1 1 1 1	0 .	0 .	0 .				
6	M 1 1 2	. 2 5	1 .	1 .	. 2 5	1 .	9 0 .	1
7	M 2 2 3	. 2 5	1 .	1 .	. 2 5	1 .	9 0 .	0
8	M 3 2 4	. 2 5	1 .	1 .	. 2 5	1 .	9 0 .	1
9	L 1	2 . 4	0 .	1 0 .	0 .			
10	E							
11	Q							

Table 13-10

OUTPUT DATA

(a) Structure Data

Members	*Joints*	*Loadings*	*Global E*
3	4	1	1

(b) Joint Data

Joint Number	IXT	IYT	IZT	IXR	IYR	IZR	*X-Coordinate*	*Y-Coordinate*	*Z-Coordinate*
1	1	1	1	1	1	1	10.00	0.00	8.50
2	0	0	0	0	0	0	10.00	10.00	8.50
3	1	1	1	1	1	1	0.00	10.00	8.50
4	1	1	1	1	1	1	0.00	0.00	0.00

(c) Member Data

Member Number	J	K	IX	IY	IZ	*Area*	*Modulus*	G	*Length*	*Type*	SI	ISI
1	1	2	0.25	1.00	1.00	0.25	1.00	1.00	10.00	0	90.00	1
2	2	3	0.25	1.00	1.00	0.25	1.00	1.00	10.00	0	90.00	0
3	2	4	0.25	1.00	1.00	0.25	1.00	1.00	16.50	0	90.00	1

Table 13-10—*Cont.*

(d) Member Load Data (Loading 1)

Member Number	*Load*	*X-Begin, ft*	*X-End, ft*	ALPHA	*Type*
1	2.40	0.00	10.00	0.00	0

(e) Joint Deflections and Rotations (Loading 1)

Joint Number	*X-Deflection*	*Y-Deflection*	*Z-Deflection*	*Rotation X-Axis*	*Rotation Y-Axis*	*Rotation Z-Axis*
1	0.00000E + 00	0.00000E + 00	0.00000E + 00	0.00000E + 00	0.00000E + 00	0.00000E + 00
2	0.53166E + 04	0.53018E + 04	−0.41055E + 05	0.47115E + 04	0.11635E + 04	0.42438E + 03
3	0.00000E + 00	0.00000E + 00	0.00000E + 00	0.00000E + 00	0.00000E + 00	0.00000E + 00
4	0.00000E + 00	0.00000E + 00	0.00000E + 00	0.00000E + 00	0.00000E + 00	0.00000E + 00

(f) Final Member End Actions (Loading 1)

Member Number	J *X-Force*	J *Y-Force*	J *Z-Force*	J *X-Moment*	J *Y-Moment*	J *Z-Moment*	K *X-Force*	K *Y-Force*	K *Z-Force*	K *X-Moment*	K *Y-Moment*	K *Z-Moment*
1	−11.05	14.25	−0.21	−0.20	0.77	27.97	11.05	9.75	0.21	0.20	1.36	−5.49
2	−11.08	−0.20	0.14	−0.82	−0.99	−1.81	11.08	0.20	−0.14	0.82	−0.41	−0.19
3	18.58	−0.44	0.27	−0.40	−2.99	−4.72	−18.58	0.44	−0.27	0.40	−1.50	−2.61

APPENDIX

A MATRIX ALGEBRA AND DETERMINANTS

A–1
Basic Definitions and Notation

A ***matrix*** is defined as a rectangular array of elements. Matrices with real number elements are the ones most commonly encountered in applications and are thus given primary emphasis in this discussion. Some examples are

$$\begin{bmatrix} 2 \\ 1 \\ 3 \end{bmatrix}, \quad \begin{bmatrix} 2 & 3 & 1 \\ 4 & 6 & 7 \end{bmatrix}, \quad \begin{bmatrix} 2.0 & 3.1 \\ -6.0 & -4.2 \end{bmatrix}$$

A matrix with m rows and n columns is referred to as an $m \times n$ matrix ("m by n matrix"), where m and n denote the size or *dimensions* of the matrix. A particular element of a matrix is denoted by its *row and column position*, with these numbers affixed as subscripts to the element name. Hence, if an element of a matrix appears in the second row and third column, it is denoted by a_{23}. The first subscript denotes the row of the element and the second subscript denotes the column. A boldface letter in brackets is used to denote the entire matrix; hence, the complete notation for an $m \times n$ matrix is written as†

$$[\mathbf{A}]_{(m \times n)} = \begin{bmatrix} a_{11} & a_{12} & \cdots & a_{1n} \\ a_{21} & a_{22} & \cdots & a_{2n} \\ \cdot & \cdot & & \cdot \\ \cdot & \cdot & & \cdot \\ \cdot & \cdot & & \cdot \\ a_{m1} & a_{m2} & \cdots & a_{mn} \end{bmatrix} \tag{A-1}$$

†$m \times n$ refers to the dimensions of [**A**], and this expression is normally not shown.

A–2
Operations on Matrices

A-2.1 Addition of Matrices

Addition of matrices is possible if and only if the matrices have the *same dimensions*. The sum is formed by adding corresponding elements, i.e., elements with the same subscripts. Hence, if a_{ij} is a typical element of [**A**] and b_{ij} is a typical element of [**B**], then the sum [**C**] is formed by adding corresponding elements of [**A**] and [**B**] to form matrix [**C**]. The operation,

$$[\mathbf{C}] = [\mathbf{A}] + [\mathbf{B}] \tag{A-2a}$$

may be indicated in terms of a typical element as

$$c_{ij} = a_{ij} + b_{ij} \tag{A-2b}$$

Example A-1. Given [**A**] and [**B**] as follows:

$$[\mathbf{A}] = \begin{bmatrix} 2 & 3 & 4 \\ 1 & 0 & 1 \end{bmatrix}$$

$$[\mathbf{B}] = \begin{bmatrix} 1 & 0 & 4 \\ 0 & 8 & 2 \end{bmatrix}$$

find [**C**] = [**A**] + [**B**].

First, note that [**A**] and [**B**] are each of dimension 2 × 3 and, therefore, can be added. Hence,

$$\begin{bmatrix} 2 & 3 & 4 \\ 1 & 0 & 1 \end{bmatrix} + \begin{bmatrix} 1 & 0 & 4 \\ 0 & 8 & 2 \end{bmatrix} = \begin{bmatrix} 3 & 3 & 8 \\ 1 & 8 & 3 \end{bmatrix}$$

A-2.2 Subtraction of Matrices

Subtraction of matrices is a direct consequence of the addition law. Hence, if

$$[\mathbf{A}] + [\mathbf{B}] = [\mathbf{C}] \tag{A-3a}$$

then

$$[\mathbf{A}] = [\mathbf{C}] - [\mathbf{B}] \tag{A-3b}$$

This may be verified in the previous example by subtracting the corresponding elements of [**B**] from the corresponding elements of [**C**] to obtain matrix [**A**].

A-2.3 Multiplication of Matrices

The product of two matrices may be formed if their *contiguous dimensions are equal*, i.e., if the number of columns in the left-hand matrix being multiplied equals the number of rows in the right-hand matrix. If matrix [**A**] is of dimension $m \times n$ and matrix [**B**] is of dimension $n \times q$, the elements of the product matrix [**C**] are defined as follows:

$$[\mathbf{C}]_{(m\times q)} = [\mathbf{A}]_{(m\times n)} \times [\mathbf{B}]_{(n\times q)} \tag{A-4a}$$

$$c_{ij} = \sum_{k=1}^{n} a_{ik}b_{kj} \tag{A-4b}$$

where c_{ij} is a typical element of the product matrix [**C**]. The product matrix [**C**] will have dimension $m \times q$.

Example A-2. Given

$$[\mathbf{A}] = \begin{bmatrix} 2 & 1 & 0 \\ 1 & 0 & 1 \end{bmatrix}_{(2\times 3)}$$

$$[\mathbf{B}] = \begin{bmatrix} 3 \\ 1 \\ 2 \end{bmatrix}_{(3\times 1)}$$

find [**C**] = [**A**][**B**] (implied multiplication).

Note that [**A**] is a 2×3 matrix and [**B**] is a 3×1 matrix; thus, the left-hand matrix [**A**] has 3 columns and the right-hand matrix [**B**] has 3 rows. Hence, the contiguous dimensions are equal to 3 and the matrices are said to be conformable for multiplication in the indicated order. It should be noted also that the product [**B**][**A**] does not exist, since the contiguous dimensions for this multiplication are 1 and 2, respectively, and thus are not equal.

Forming the product [**A**][**B**] for the matrices of this example gives

$$\begin{bmatrix} 2 & 1 & 0 \\ 1 & 0 & 1 \end{bmatrix}\begin{bmatrix} 3 \\ 1 \\ 2 \end{bmatrix} = \begin{bmatrix} (2\cdot 3) + (1\cdot 1) + (0\cdot 2) \\ (1\cdot 3) + (0\cdot 1) + (1\cdot 2) \end{bmatrix} = \begin{bmatrix} 7 \\ 5 \end{bmatrix}$$

A-2.4 Scalar Multiplication of a Matrix

If k is a real number and [**A**] is a matrix containing typical elements a_{ij}, the product of the scalar k times the matrix [**A**] is defined as

$$ka_{ij} \tag{A-5}$$

In other words, to multiply a matrix [**A**] by a scalar k, every element of [**A**] is multiplied by the scalar k.

Example A-3. If

$$[\mathbf{A}] = \begin{bmatrix} 2 & 1 \\ 4 & 3 \end{bmatrix}$$

and $k = 3$, then

$$k[\mathbf{A}] = 3\begin{bmatrix} 2 & 1 \\ 4 & 3 \end{bmatrix} = \begin{bmatrix} 6 & 3 \\ 12 & 9 \end{bmatrix}$$

A-2.5 Algebraic Properties of Matrix Operations

The matrix operations which have been defined above may be shown to obey certain basic laws of algebra. If **[A]**, **[B]**, and **[C]** are arbitrary matrices of the same dimensions, then the following properties hold:

1. $[\mathbf{A}] + [\mathbf{B}] = [\mathbf{B}] + [\mathbf{A}]$ (commutative law of addition)
2. $[\mathbf{A}] + ([\mathbf{B}] + [\mathbf{C}]) = ([\mathbf{A}] + [\mathbf{B}]) + [\mathbf{C}]$ (associative law of addition)

If **[A]**, **[B]**, and **[C]** are matrices whose dimensions are such that the product of $[\mathbf{A}] \times [\mathbf{B}] \times [\mathbf{C}]$ is defined in this order, then the multiplication of matrices can be shown to be associative. That is,

3. $([\mathbf{A}][\mathbf{B}])[\mathbf{C}] = [\mathbf{A}]([\mathbf{B}][\mathbf{C}])$ (associative law of multiplication)

Again, assuming that the dimensions are such that the indicated operations may be performed,

4. $[\mathbf{A}]([\mathbf{B}] + [\mathbf{C}]) = [\mathbf{A}][\mathbf{B}] + [\mathbf{A}][\mathbf{C}]$ (distributive law of matrix multiplication with respect to matrix addition)

If a and b are real numbers, the following properties may be shown to hold:

5. $a(b[\mathbf{A}]) = (ab)[\mathbf{A}]$ (associative law of scalar multiplication)
6. $(a + b)[\mathbf{A}] = a[\mathbf{A}] + b[\mathbf{A}]$ (distributive law of scalar multiplication with respect to scalar addition)
7. $a([\mathbf{A}] + [\mathbf{B}]) = a[\mathbf{A}] + a[\mathbf{B}]$ (distributive law of scalar multiplication with respect to matrix addition)

There are three fundamental properties of multiplication in the algebra of real numbers that do not carry over to matrix algebra:

8. The commutative property, $[\mathbf{A}][\mathbf{B}] = [\mathbf{B}][\mathbf{A}]$, in general is not true.
9. The equation $[\mathbf{A}][\mathbf{B}] = [\mathbf{0}]$ does not necessarily imply that either **[A]** or **[B]** is a zero matrix.
10. The equation $[\mathbf{A}][\mathbf{B}] = [\mathbf{A}][\mathbf{C}]$ does not necessarily imply that $[\mathbf{B}] = [\mathbf{C}]$.

A–3
Special Matrices

Certain special types of matrices are frequently encountered in applications. These are defined and illustrated below.

A-3.1 The Transpose of a Matrix

The ***transpose*** of a matrix **[A]** is a new matrix denoted $[\mathbf{A}]^T$ obtained by interchanging the rows and columns of **[A]**.

Example A-4. If

$$[\mathbf{A}] = \begin{bmatrix} 1 & 2 & 3 \\ 4 & 5 & 6 \\ 7 & 8 & 9 \end{bmatrix}$$

then

$$[\mathbf{A}]^T = \begin{bmatrix} 1 & 4 & 7 \\ 2 & 5 & 8 \\ 3 & 6 & 9 \end{bmatrix}$$

Two useful algebraic consequences of matrix transposition are

1. $([\mathbf{A}] + [\mathbf{B}])^T = [\mathbf{A}]^T + [\mathbf{B}]^T$ **(A-6a)**
2. $([\mathbf{A}][\mathbf{B}])^T = [\mathbf{B}]^T[\mathbf{A}]^T$ (note the reversal of order in multiplication) **(A-6b)**

A-3.2 Square Matrices

A matrix with the same number of rows as columns—i.e., when $m = n$—is referred to as a ***square matrix*** of order n. For example, if matrix [**A**] has 6 rows and 6 columns, it is called a square matrix of order 6, or a 6th-order square matrix.

A-3.3 Symmetric and Antisymmetric Matrices

A square matrix for which $[\mathbf{A}]^T = [\mathbf{A}]$ is called a ***symmetric matrix***, and one for which $[\mathbf{A}]^T = -[\mathbf{A}]$ is called an ***antisymmetric matrix***.

Example A-5.

$$[\mathbf{S}] = \begin{bmatrix} 1 & 3 & -4 & 2 \\ 3 & 6 & -1 & -1 \\ -4 & -1 & 4 & 5 \\ 2 & -1 & 5 & 7 \end{bmatrix}$$

is a symmetric matrix of order 4 while

$$[\mathbf{T}] = \begin{bmatrix} 0 & 3 & 4 & 2 \\ -3 & 0 & -1 & 1 \\ -4 & 1 & 0 & 5 \\ -2 & -1 & -5 & 0 \end{bmatrix}$$

is an antisymmetric matrix of order 4; note that all the elements for which $i = j$ are zero in an antisymmetric matrix.

A-3.4 Diagonal Matrices

The elements of a matrix for which $i = j$ are called ***diagonal elements***, and these elements are said to constitute the ***main diagonal*** of the matrix. A square matrix in which all elements *not* on the main diagonal are zero is referred to as a ***diagonal matrix***.

Example A-6.

$$[\mathbf{D}] = \begin{bmatrix} 2 & 0 & 0 & 0 & 0 \\ 0 & 3 & 0 & 0 & 0 \\ 0 & 0 & -1 & 0 & 0 \\ 0 & 0 & 0 & 2 & 0 \\ 0 & 0 & 0 & 0 & 10 \end{bmatrix}$$

is a 5th-order diagonal matrix.

A-3.5 Identity Matrices

A diagonal matrix of order n in which all the diagonal elements are 1 is called the ***identity matrix*** of order n and is denoted by the symbol [**I**]. The identity matrix has the useful property that

$$[\mathbf{A}][\mathbf{I}] = [\mathbf{I}][\mathbf{A}] = [\mathbf{A}] \tag{A-7}$$

for all square matrices [**A**] of order n.

Example A-7.

$$[\mathbf{I}] = \begin{bmatrix} 1 & 0 & 0 \\ 0 & 1 & 0 \\ 0 & 0 & 1 \end{bmatrix}$$

is the identity matrix of order 3.

A-3.6 Zero Matrices

A square matrix of order n with all elements zero is called the ***zero matrix*** of order n. These matrices are denoted by [**0**] and have the following properties:

1. $[\mathbf{A}][\mathbf{0}] = [\mathbf{0}][\mathbf{A}] = [\mathbf{0}]$ **(A-8)**
2. $[\mathbf{A}] + [\mathbf{0}] = [\mathbf{0}] + [\mathbf{A}] = [\mathbf{A}]$ **(A-9)**

for all square matrices [**A**] of order n.

Example A-8.

$$[\mathbf{0}] = \begin{bmatrix} 0 & 0 & 0 & 0 \\ 0 & 0 & 0 & 0 \\ 0 & 0 & 0 & 0 \\ 0 & 0 & 0 & 0 \end{bmatrix}$$

is a 4th-order zero matrix.

A-3.7 Triangular Matrices

A square matrix for which all elements below the main diagonal are zero is called an ***upper triangular matrix***. A square matrix for which all elements above the main diagonal are zero is called a ***lower triangular matrix***.

Example A-9.

$$[\mathbf{A}] = \begin{bmatrix} 1 & 2 & 3 & 4 \\ 0 & 1 & 2 & 1 \\ 0 & 0 & 2 & 2 \\ 0 & 0 & 0 & 4 \end{bmatrix}$$

is an upper triangular matrix of order 4 while

$$[\mathbf{B}] = \begin{bmatrix} 1 & 0 & 0 & 0 \\ 2 & 5 & 0 & 0 \\ 4 & 1 & 2 & 0 \\ 1 & 1 & 1 & 0 \end{bmatrix}$$

is a lower triangular matrix of order 4.

A-3.8 Orthogonal Matrices

Two matrices $[\mathbf{A}]_{(m \times n)}$ and $[\mathbf{B}]_{(m \times n)}$ are said to be ***orthogonal*** to one another if

$$[\mathbf{A}]^T[\mathbf{B}] = [\mathbf{B}]^T[\mathbf{A}] = [\mathbf{I}] \tag{A-10}$$

A square matrix $[\boldsymbol{\theta}]$ of order n is said to be an ***orthogonal matrix*** if

$$[\boldsymbol{\theta}]^T[\boldsymbol{\theta}] = [\boldsymbol{\theta}][\boldsymbol{\theta}]^T = [\mathbf{I}] \tag{A-11}$$

Example A-10. The matrices

$$[\mathbf{A}] = \begin{bmatrix} 1 & 1 \\ -1 & -2 \\ 1 & 2 \end{bmatrix} \quad \text{and} \quad [\mathbf{B}] = \begin{bmatrix} 2 & -1 \\ 1 & 1 \\ 0 & 2 \end{bmatrix}$$

are orthogonal to one another, since

$$[\mathbf{A}]^T[\mathbf{B}] = \begin{bmatrix} 1 & 0 \\ 0 & 1 \end{bmatrix} \quad \text{and} \quad [\mathbf{B}]^T[\mathbf{A}] = \begin{bmatrix} 1 & 0 \\ 0 & 1 \end{bmatrix}$$

Example A-11. The matrix

$$[\boldsymbol{\theta}] = \begin{bmatrix} \frac{2}{3} & -\frac{2}{3} & \frac{1}{3} \\ \frac{1}{3} & \frac{2}{3} & \frac{2}{3} \\ \frac{2}{3} & \frac{1}{3} & -\frac{2}{3} \end{bmatrix}$$

is an orthogonal matrix, since

$$[\boldsymbol{\theta}]^T[\boldsymbol{\theta}] = [\boldsymbol{\theta}][\boldsymbol{\theta}]^T = \begin{bmatrix} 1 & 0 & 0 \\ 0 & 1 & 0 \\ 0 & 0 & 1 \end{bmatrix}$$

A–4
Determinants of Square Matrices

A-4.1 Definition and Notation

Associated with each square matrix is a scalar function or number called the ***determinant*** of the matrix. If [**A**] is a square matrix of order n, the determinant of [**A**] is denoted by either $|A|$ or det[**A**]. Before presenting the procedure for forming and defining the determinant of a given square matrix, it is helpful to first define *positive* and *negative* pairs of elements in a matrix.

Consider two distinct elements a_{ij} and a_{km} of a matrix [**A**] which are neither in the same row nor same column of [**A**], i.e., $i \neq k$ and $j \neq m$. If one of these elements lies to the left of and above the other in the array—i.e., if $i < k$ and $j < m$, or if $k < i$ and $m < j$—then the pair of elements is called a *positive* pair. If one of the elements of the pair lies to the right of and above the other—i.e., if $i < k$ and $j > m$, or if $k < i$ and $m > j$—the pair is called a *negative* pair. For example, the pair a_{31}, a_{22} is a negative pair, while a_{11}, a_{23} is a positive pair.

To form the determinant of a square matrix of order n, first form all possible products, each composed of n elements, that may be obtained by choosing one and only one element from each row and each column. It can be shown that there are $n!$ such products. For each product formed, count the number of negative pairs in the product, symbolized by σ, and multiply this product by $(-1)^{\sigma}$. Thus, if the number of negative pairs σ is even, a plus sign is attached to the product; if σ is odd, a minus sign is attached to the product. Finally, upon forming the algebraic sum of all $n!$ of these terms, the value of the determinant is obtained. This definition may be stated in formalistic terminology as

$$|A| = \sum_{\pi} (-1)^{\sigma_k} a_{1i_1} a_{2i_2} \cdots a_{ni_n} \tag{A-12}$$

where $i_1, i_2, \ldots i_n$ extend over all the $n!$ possible permutations of the numbers $1, 2, \ldots, n$; π denotes the set of all such permutations; and σ_k denotes the number of negative pairs in the kth product.

Example A-12. Find the determinant of the following matrices by applying the given definition:

1.

$$[\mathbf{A}] = \begin{bmatrix} a_{11} & a_{12} & a_{13} \\ a_{21} & a_{22} & a_{23} \\ a_{31} & a_{32} & a_{33} \end{bmatrix}$$

Applying the indicated procedure gives

$$\begin{aligned} |A| &= \begin{vmatrix} a_{11} & a_{12} & a_{13} \\ a_{21} & a_{22} & a_{23} \\ a_{31} & a_{32} & a_{33} \end{vmatrix} \\ &= (-1)^{\sigma_1}(a_{11} \cdot a_{22} \cdot a_{33}) + (-1)^{\sigma_2}(a_{12}a_{23}a_{31}) + (-1)^{\sigma_3}(a_{13}a_{21}a_{32}) \\ &\quad + (-1)^{\sigma_4}(a_{31}a_{22}a_{13}) + (-1)^{\sigma_5}(a_{32}a_{23}a_{11}) + (-1)^{\sigma_6}(a_{33}a_{21}a_{12}) \end{aligned}$$

There will be $n! = 3! = 6$ products in the solution. Negative pairs associated with each product are as follows:

$$\sigma_1 = 0, \quad \sigma_2 = 2, \quad \sigma_3 = 2, \quad \sigma_4 = 3, \quad \sigma_5 = 1, \quad \sigma_6 = 1$$

Therefore, $|A| = 1(a_{11}a_{22}a_{33}) + 1(a_{12}a_{23}a_{31}) + 1(a_{13}a_{21}a_{32}) - 1(a_{31}a_{22}a_{13})$
$- 1(a_{32}a_{23}a_{11}) - 1(a_{33}a_{21}a_{12})$

2.

$$[\mathbf{A}] = \begin{bmatrix} 1 & 2 & 3 \\ 4 & 5 & 6 \\ 7 & 8 & 9 \end{bmatrix}$$

$$|A| = 1(1 \cdot 5 \cdot 9) + 1(2 \cdot 6 \cdot 7) + 1(3 \cdot 4 \cdot 8) - 1(7 \cdot 5 \cdot 3) - 1(8 \cdot 6 \cdot 1)$$
$$- 1(9 \cdot 4 \cdot 2) = 45 + 84 + 96 - 105 - 48 - 72 = 255 - 225 = 0$$

A-4.2 Fundamental Properties of Determinants

There are some fundamental properties of determinants that greatly simplify their use in applications. These are stated below and illustrated.

1. If all the elements of a row (or of a column) of a square matrix [**A**] are zero, then $|A| = 0$.

Example A-13. Given

$$[\mathbf{A}] = \begin{bmatrix} 0 & 2 & 3 \\ 0 & 1 & 1 \\ 0 & 5 & 6 \end{bmatrix}$$

and substituting into Eq. (A-12) gives

$$|A| = 1(0 \cdot 1 \cdot 6) + 1(2 \cdot 1 \cdot 0) + 1(3 \cdot 0 \cdot 5) - 1(0 \cdot 1 \cdot 3) - 1(5 \cdot 1 \cdot 0)$$
$$- 1(6 \cdot 0 \cdot 2) = 0$$

2. If all the elements of a row (or of a column) of a square matrix are multiplied by a scalar k, the determinant of the matrix is multiplied by k.

Example A-14. Let

$$[\mathbf{B}] = \begin{bmatrix} a_{11} & a_{12} & ka_{13} \\ a_{21} & a_{22} & ka_{23} \\ a_{31} & a_{32} & ka_{33} \end{bmatrix}$$

and evaluate the determinant by means of Eq. (A-12). Each product will be found to contain the factor k; therefore,

$$|B| = k|A|$$

3. If two rows (or columns) of a matrix are interchanged, the determinant of the matrix changes sign.
4. If two rows (or columns) of a matrix [**A**] are identical, then $|A| = 0$.

Example A-15. If

$$[\mathbf{A}] = \begin{bmatrix} 1 & 1 & 1 \\ 1 & 1 & 1 \\ 9 & 6 & 5 \end{bmatrix}$$

then, from Eq. (A-12),

$$|A| = (1 \cdot 1 \cdot 5) + 1(1 \cdot 1 \cdot 9) + 1(1 \cdot 1 \cdot 6) - 1(9 \cdot 1 \cdot 1) - 1(6 \cdot 1 \cdot 1) - 1(5 \cdot 1 \cdot 1) = 0.$$

5. If two rows (or columns) of a matrix [**A**] are proportional, then $|A| = 0$.

A-4.3 Evaluation of Determinants by Laplace's Expansion

If from a square matrix [**A**] of order n the ith row and jth column are deleted, the determinant of the resulting square matrix of order $n - 1$ is called the *minor* of the element a_{ij} and is denoted by M_{ij}. The *signed minor*—i.e., $(-1)^{i+j} M_{ij}$—is called the ***cofactor*** of a_{ij} and is denoted by α_{ij}.

It may be shown that the value of $|A|$ is equal to the sum of the products of the elements of any row (or column) of [**A**], each multiplied by its own cofactor; i.e.,

$$|A| = \sum_{j=1}^{n} a_{ij}\alpha_{ij} \tag{A-13a}$$

for any fixed i, or

$$|A| = \sum_{i=1}^{n} a_{ij}\alpha_{ij} \tag{A-13b}$$

for any fixed j. This is known as Laplace's expansion.

As a corollary to the Laplace expansion, it may be shown that the sum of the products of any row (or column) of [**A**], each multiplied by the corresponding cofactors of another row (or column) of [**A**], is zero; i.e.,

$$\sum_{j=1}^{n} a_{ij}\alpha_{kj} = 0, \qquad i \neq k \tag{A-14a}$$

or

$$\sum_{i=1}^{n} a_{ij}\alpha_{ik} = 0, \qquad j \neq k \tag{A-14b}$$

Example A-16. Determine the value of $|A|$ by expanding by cofactors of the first row. If

$$[\mathbf{A}] = \begin{bmatrix} 1 & 2 & 1 \\ 4 & 0 & 2 \\ 3 & 1 & 1 \end{bmatrix}$$

then

$$|A| = \begin{vmatrix} 1 & 2 & 1 \\ 4 & 0 & 2 \\ 3 & 1 & 1 \end{vmatrix} = (-1)^{1+1}(1)\begin{vmatrix} 0 & 2 \\ 1 & 1 \end{vmatrix} + (-1)^{1+2}(2)\begin{vmatrix} 4 & 2 \\ 3 & 1 \end{vmatrix}$$

$$+ (-1)^{1+3}(1)\begin{vmatrix} 4 & 0 \\ 3 & 1 \end{vmatrix} = 1(-2) - (2)(-2) + (1)(4) = 6$$

Example A-17. Form a Laplace expansion of the matrix [**A**] of Example A-16 using the elements of the second row of [**A**] times the cofactors of the corresponding elements of first row of [**A**]. The expansion is written as

$$a_{21}M_{11} + a_{22}M_{12} + a_{23}M_{13} = (-1)^{1+1}(4)\begin{vmatrix} 0 & 2 \\ 1 & 1 \end{vmatrix} + (-1)^{1+2}(0)\begin{vmatrix} 4 & 2 \\ 3 & 1 \end{vmatrix}$$

$$+ (-1)^{1+3}(2)\begin{vmatrix} 4 & 0 \\ 3 & 1 \end{vmatrix}$$

$$= (4)(-2) - (0)(-2) + (2)(4) = -8 + 8 = 0$$

A–5
Elementary Row Transformations on Matrices

Let [**A**] be an $m \times n$ matrix. Three elementary row transformations may be defined for a matrix [**A**]:

1. the interchange of two rows;
2. multiplication of all the elements of a row by the same nonzero scalar k;
3. the addition to the elements of a given row the corresponding elements of another row or a scalar multiple of the corresponding elements of another row.

The dimensions of a matrix are obviously unchanged by a succession of elementary transformations. A valuable application of elementary transformations is that an $m \times n$ matrix [**A**] may be reduced by a succession of appropriately chosen elementary row transformations to an upper triangular matrix which has 1's or 0's for the main diagonal elements and zeros below the main diagonal. This is known as *echelon form.*

Two $m \times n$ matrices [**A**] and [**B**] are said to be *equivalent* if it is possible to pass from one to the other by a finite number of elementary row transformations. The formation of equivalent matrices using elementary row transformations is of great value in solving linear systems of equations.

A–6
The Rank of a Matrix

The ***rank*** of a matrix is defined as the dimension of the largest nonzero determinant that may be formed by deleting rows and columns (if necessary) from the matrix. Several useful properties of the rank r of a matrix may be stated as follows:

1. The minimum rank of a matrix is $r = 0$ and occurs if and only if all elements of the matrix are zero.
2. The rank of a matrix cannot exceed the smaller of the dimensions of the matrix. Thus, for a 3×4 matrix the rank cannot exceed 3.
3. The rank of a matrix is unchanged if elementary row transformations are performed on the matrix.
4. If a matrix is transformed to echelon form by elementary row operations, the rank may then be determined by counting the number of nonzero elements on the main diagonal.
5. If the rank r of a matrix is less than the number of rows, m, of the matrix, then some of the rows of the matrix are linear combinations of the other rows. Specifically, $m - r$ of the rows are linear combinations of the other r rows and are said to be *linearly dependent* upon the other r rows. If the matrix is transformed to echelon form, then $m - r$ of the rows will be reduced to all zeros. These rows are linearly dependent upon the other r rows.

Example A-18 Determine the rank of the matrix

$$[A] = \begin{bmatrix} 2 & -1 & 3 \\ 3 & 2 & 1 \\ 1 & -4 & 5 \end{bmatrix}$$

Multiply row 1 by $\frac{1}{2}$. The symbolism $R_1 \to \frac{1}{2} R_1$ is adopted (read, "Row 1 is replaced by $\frac{1}{2}$ row 1"). The transformed matrix is

$$\begin{bmatrix} 1 & -\frac{1}{2} & \frac{3}{2} \\ 3 & 2 & 1 \\ 1 & -4 & 5 \end{bmatrix}$$

Subtract 3 times row 1 from row 2; $R_2 \to R_2 - 3R_1$ (read, "Row 2 is replaced by row 2, minus 3 times row 1").

Subtract row 1 from row 3; $R_3 \to R_3 - R_1$.

The transformed matrix is

$$\begin{bmatrix} 1 & -\frac{1}{2} & \frac{3}{2} \\ 0 & \frac{7}{2} & -\frac{7}{2} \\ 0 & -\frac{7}{2} & \frac{7}{2} \end{bmatrix}$$

Multiply row 2 by $\frac{2}{7}$; $R_2 \to \frac{2}{7} R_2$:

$$\begin{bmatrix} 1 & -\frac{1}{2} & \frac{3}{2} \\ 0 & 1 & -1 \\ 0 & -\frac{7}{2} & \frac{7}{2} \end{bmatrix}$$

Add $\frac{7}{2}$ times row 2 to row 3; $R_3 \to R_3 + \frac{7}{2} R_2$:

$$\begin{bmatrix} 1 & -\frac{1}{2} & \frac{3}{2} \\ 0 & 1 & -1 \\ 0 & 0 & 0 \end{bmatrix}$$

The rank of the matrix is thus 2. The third row of the original matrix is a linear combination of, or linearly dependent upon, the first two rows.

A–7
The Inverse of a Matrix

For a given square matrix [**A**] of order n, if there exists another square matrix of order n, which will be denoted $[\mathbf{A}]^{-1}$, with the property that

$$[\mathbf{A}][\mathbf{A}]^{-1} = [\mathbf{A}]^{-1}[\mathbf{A}] = [\mathbf{I}] \tag{A-15}$$

$[\mathbf{A}]^{-1}$ is called the ***inverse*** of [**A**].

The inverse of a matrix, if it exists, is unique. The inverse of an nth-order square matrix will exist if and only if $|A| \neq 0$. Such a matrix is called a ***non-singular*** matrix. If $|A| = 0$, the matrix is called a ***singular*** matrix and no inverse exists.

Algorithms for finding the inverse of a matrix are given in Chapter 2.

Example A-19. Show that the inverse of

$$[\mathbf{A}] = \begin{bmatrix} 1 & 5 & 1 \\ 0 & 4 & 2 \\ 0 & 1 & 1 \end{bmatrix}$$

is

$$[\mathbf{A}]^{-1} = \begin{bmatrix} 1 & -2 & 3 \\ 0 & \frac{1}{2} & -1 \\ 0 & -\frac{1}{2} & 2 \end{bmatrix}$$

Now,

$$[\mathbf{A}][\mathbf{A}]^{-1} = \begin{bmatrix} 1 & 5 & 1 \\ 0 & 4 & 2 \\ 0 & 1 & 1 \end{bmatrix} \begin{bmatrix} 1 & -2 & 3 \\ 0 & \frac{1}{2} & -1 \\ 0 & -\frac{1}{2} & 2 \end{bmatrix} = \begin{bmatrix} 1 & 0 & 0 \\ 0 & 1 & 0 \\ 0 & 0 & 1 \end{bmatrix}$$

$$[\mathbf{A}]^{-1}[\mathbf{A}] = \begin{bmatrix} 1 & -2 & 3 \\ 0 & \frac{1}{2} & -1 \\ 0 & -\frac{1}{2} & 2 \end{bmatrix} \begin{bmatrix} 1 & 5 & 1 \\ 0 & 4 & 2 \\ 0 & 1 & 1 \end{bmatrix} = \begin{bmatrix} 1 & 0 & 0 \\ 0 & 1 & 0 \\ 0 & 0 & 1 \end{bmatrix}$$

APPENDIX

B STABILITY AND LOAD FUNCTIONS

Φ_i	r_i	c_i	t_i	m_i
−10.00	11.1864	0.1118	4.9678	0.4824
−9.00	10.6937	0.1185	4.7132	0.5016
−8.00	10.1754	0.1265	4.4441	0.5234
−7.00	9.6272	0.1362	4.1580	0.5485
−6.00	9.0436	0.1483	3.8512	0.5778
−5.00	8.4169	0.1639	3.5187	0.6125
−4.00	7.7367	0.1848	3.1534	0.6545
−3.00	6.9878	0.2145	2.7444	0.7070
−2.00	6.1468	0.2600	2.2743	0.7747
−1.00	5.1748	0.3381	1.7127	0.8665
−0.90	5.0681	0.3490	1.6496	0.8776
−0.80	4.9593	0.3608	1.5850	0.8891
−0.70	4.8483	0.3735	1.5187	0.9010
−0.60	4.7351	0.3872	1.4508	0.9134
−0.50	4.6194	0.4021	1.3810	0.9264
−0.40	4.5013	0.4183	1.3092	0.9398
−0.30	4.3804	0.4360	1.2354	0.9539
−0.20	4.2567	0.4553	1.1593	0.9686
−0.10	4.1299	0.4765	1.0809	0.9839
0.00	4.0000	0.5000	1.0000	1.0000
0.01	3.9869	0.5025	0.9918	1.0016
0.02	3.9736	0.5050	0.9835	1.0033
0.03	3.9604	0.5075	0.9752	1.0050
0.04	3.9471	0.5101	0.9669	1.0066
0.05	3.9338	0.5127	0.9585	1.0083
0.06	3.9204	0.5153	0.9502	1.0100
0.07	3.9070	0.5179	0.9418	1.0117
0.08	3.8936	0.5206	0.9333	1.0134
0.09	3.8802	0.5233	0.9249	1.0151
0.10	3.8667	0.5260	0.9164	1.0169
0.11	3.8531	0.5288	0.9078	1.0186
0.12	3.8396	0.5316	0.8993	1.0203

Φ_i	r_i	c_i	t_i	m_i
0.13	3.8260	0.5344	0.8907	1.0221
0.14	3.8123	0.5372	0.8821	1.0238
0.15	3.7987	0.5401	0.8735	1.0256
0.16	3.7849	0.5430	0.8648	1.0274
0.17	3.7712	0.5460	0.8561	1.0291
0.18	3.7574	0.5490	0.8474	1.0309
0.19	3.7436	0.5520	0.8386	1.0327
0.20	3.7297	0.5550	0.8298	1.0345
0.21	3.7158	0.5581	0.8210	1.0363
0.22	3.7019	0.5612	0.8122	1.0382
0.23	3.6879	0.5644	0.8033	1.0400
0.24	3.6739	0.5676	0.7943	1.0419
0.25	3.6598	0.5708	0.7854	1.0437
0.26	3.6457	0.5741	0.7764	1.0456
0.27	3.6316	0.5774	0.7674	1.0474
0.28	3.6174	0.5807	0.7584	1.0493
0.29	3.6031	0.5841	0.7493	1.0512
0.30	3.5889	0.5875	0.7402	1.0531
0.31	3.5746	0.5910	0.7310	1.0550
0.32	3.5602	0.5945	0.7218	1.0569
0.33	3.5458	0.5981	0.7126	1.0589
0.34	3.5314	0.6017	0.7034	1.0608
0.35	3.5169	0.6053	0.6941	1.0628
0.36	3.5024	0.6090	0.6848	1.0647
0.37	3.4878	0.6127	0.6754	1.0667
0.38	3.4732	0.6165	0.6660	1.0687
0.39	3.4586	0.6203	0.6566	1.0707
0.40	3.4439	0.6242	0.6471	1.0727
0.41	3.4292	0.6281	0.6376	1.0747
0.42	3.4144	0.6321	0.6281	1.0767
0.43	3.3996	0.6361	0.6185	1.0787
0.44	3.3847	0.6402	0.6089	1.0808
0.45	3.3698	0.6443	0.5992	1.0828
0.46	3.3548	0.6485	0.5895	1.0849
0.47	3.3398	0.6528	0.5798	1.0870
0.48	3.3247	0.6571	0.5701	1.0891
0.49	3.3096	0.6614	0.5603	1.0912
0.50	3.2945	0.6659	0.5504	1.0933
0.51	3.2793	0.6704	0.5405	1.0954
0.52	3.2640	0.6749	0.5306	1.0975
0.53	3.2487	0.6795	0.5206	1.0997
0.54	3.2334	0.6841	0.5106	1.1018
0.55	3.2180	0.6889	0.5006	1.1040
0.56	3.2025	0.6937	0.4905	1.1062
0.57	3.1870	0.6985	0.4804	1.1084
0.58	3.1715	0.7035	0.4702	1.1106
0.59	3.1559	0.7085	0.4600	1.1128
0.60	3.1403	0.7136	0.4498	1.1150
0.61	3.1246	0.7187	0.4395	1.1173
0.62	3.1088	0.7239	0.4291	1.1195
0.63	3.0930	0.7292	0.4187	1.1218

Φ_i	r_i	c_i	t_i	m_i
0.64	3.0772	0.7346	0.4083	1.1241
0.65	3.0612	0.7401	0.3978	1.1264
0.66	3.0453	0.7456	0.3873	1.1287
0.67	3.0293	0.7513	0.3768	1.1310
0.68	3.0132	0.7570	0.3661	1.1333
0.69	2.9971	0.7628	0.3555	1.1357
0.70	2.9809	0.7687	0.3448	1.1381
0.71	2.9647	0.7746	0.3340	1.1404
0.72	2.9484	0.7807	0.3233	1.1428
0.73	2.9320	0.7869	0.3124	1.1452
0.74	2.9156	0.7932	0.3015	1.1476
0.75	2.8991	0.7995	0.2906	1.1501
0.76	2.8826	0.8060	0.2796	1.1525
0.77	2.8660	0.8126	0.2686	1.1550
0.78	2.8494	0.8193	0.2575	1.1574
0.79	2.8327	0.8261	0.2463	1.1599
0.80	2.8159	0.8330	0.2351	1.1624
0.81	2.7991	0.8400	0.2239	1.1650
0.82	2.7823	0.8472	0.2126	1.1675
0.83	2.7653	0.8544	0.2013	1.1700
0.84	2.7483	0.8618	0.1899	1.1726
0.85	2.7312	0.8693	0.1784	1.1752
0.86	2.7141	0.8770	0.1669	1.1778
0.87	2.6969	0.8848	0.1554	1.1804
0.88	2.6797	0.8927	0.1438	1.1830
0.89	2.6623	0.9008	0.1321	1.1857
0.90	2.6450	0.9090	0.1204	1.1883
0.91	2.6275	0.9173	0.1086	1.1910
0.92	2.6100	0.9258	0.0968	1.1937
0.93	2.5924	0.9345	0.0849	1.1964
0.94	2.5748	0.9433	0.0729	1.1991
0.95	2.5570	0.9523	0.0609	1.2019
0.96	2.5393	0.9615	0.0489	1.2046
0.97	2.5214	0.9709	0.0367	1.2074
0.98	2.5035	0.9804	0.0246	1.2102
0.99	2.4855	0.9901	0.0123	1.2130
1.00	2.4674	1.0000	0	1.2159
1.10	2.283	1.111	−0.127	1.245
1.20	2.090	1.249	−0.260	1.277
1.30	1.889	1.424	−0.401	1.310
1.40	1.678	1.656	−0.550	1.346
1.50	1.457	1.973	−0.709	1.385
1.60	1.224	2.435	−0.878	1.427
1.70	0.978	3.166	−1.059	1.473
1.80	0.717	4.497	−1.254	1.522
1.90	0.439	7.661	−1.464	1.576
2.00	0.143	24.682	−1.691	1.636
2.10	−0.176	−21.074	−1.939	1.702
2.20	−0.519	−7.511	−2.210	1.774
2.30	−0.893	−4.623	−2.510	1.855
2.40	−1.301	−3.370	−2.842	1.946

Φ_i	r_i	c_i	t_i	m_i
2.50	−1.750	−2.673	−3.214	2.049
2.60	−2.249	−2.231	−3.634	2.167
2.70	−2.809	−1.928	−4.112	2.302
2.80	−3.445	−1.708	−4.664	2.460
2.90	−4.176	−1.543	−5.310	2.646
3.00	−5.032	−1.416	−6.078	2.869
3.10	−6.052	−1.316	−7.007	3.141
3.20	−7.297	−1.236	−8.159	3.480
3.30	−8.863	−1.173	−9.629	3.916
3.40	−10.908	−1.122	−11.575	4.497
3.50	−13.719	−1.082	−14.284	5.309
3.60	−17.867	−1.051	−18.326	6.527
3.70	−24.685	−1.028	−25.035	8.555
3.80	−38.173	−1.012	−38.411	12.610
3.90	−78.330	−1.003	−78.451	24.769
4.00	$-\infty$	−1.000	$-\infty$	∞

```
      GO TO 5
  140 LCNT = LCN
      MNUMT = MNUM
      IF(ITAPE.NE.1) CALL FIND(ISTIF,NDIM1,MNUMT,K1,IPRNT,QL,STIF)
      IF(ITAPE.NE.1) GO TO 122
      CALL  READA(IFILE1,MNUMT,MCOUNT,IPRNT,K1,M,QL)
      GO TO 122
  150 IF(ITAPE.NE.1) CALL FIND(ISTIF,NDIM1,MNUMT,K1,IPRNT,QL,STIF)
      DO 151 I=1,4
      IF(K1(I).EQ.0) GO TO 151
      K11 = K1(I)
      STIF(K11) = STIF(K11) -ACCFM(I)
  151 CONTINUE
      WRITE(IFILE2) MNUMT ,(BUF(I),I=27,52)
      MNUMT = MNUM
      DO 152 I=1,52
  152 BUF(I) =0.
      IF(ITAPE.NE.1) GO TO 122
      CALL  READA(IFILE1,MNUMT,MCOUNT,IPRNT,K1,M,QL)
      GO TO 122
  160 CALL ECHO3(ICODE,LCN,MNUM,LTYPE,MTYPE,DISTB,DISTE,W,FML,FMR,FSL,FS
     1R,LCOUNT,IPRNT)
      GO TO 123
  170 BUFFM(1) = FML * 12.
      BUFFM(2) = FMR * 12.
      BUFFM(3) = FSL
      BUFFM(4) = FSR
      GO TO 130
  180 CALL SIMP(BUF,W,DISTB,DISTE,LTYPE,INCR,QL,IPRNT)
      GO TO 130
  200 IF(ICODE.NE.IE) GO TO 4
      IF(LCOUNT.EQ.0) GO TO 204
      IF(ITAPE.NE.1) CALL FIND(ISTIF,NDIM1,MNUMT,K1,IPRNT,QL,STIF)
      DO 201 I= 1,26
  201 BUF(I+26) = BUF(I+26) +BUF(I)
      DO 202 I=1,4
      IF(K1(I).EQ.0) GO TO 202
      K11 = K1(I)
      STIF(K11) = STIF(K11) -ACCFM(I)
  202 CONTINUE
      WRITE(IFILE2) MNUMT,(BUF(I),I=27,52)
  204 DO 203 I = 1,52
  203 BUF(I) = 0.
      WRITE(IFILE2)MNUMT,(BUF(I),I=27,52)
  300 READ(ICARD,905)ICODE,LCN,K11,K22,K33,QJM,QJV,QJH
  905 FORMAT(A1,I2,3I3,8X,3F10.0)
      IF(ICODE.EQ.IP)GO TO 310
      IF(ICODE.EQ.IE)GO TO 320
      GO TO 6
  310 IF(ICOUNT.EQ.0.AND.LCOUNT.EQ.0) LCNT = LCN
      IF(LCNT.NE.LCN) GO TO 5
      ICOUNT = ICOUNT + 1
      IF(IPD.EQ.0) CALL ECHO4(ICOUNT,ICODE,LCN,K11,K22,K33,QJM,QJV,QJH,
     1IPRNT)
      IF (K11.GT.0) STIF(K11) = STIF(K11) + QJM*12
      IF (K22.GT.0) STIF(K22) = STIF(K22) + QJV
      IF (K33.GT.0) STIF(K33) = STIF(K33) + QJH
      GO TO 300
  320 NLT = NLT + 1
      WRITE(IFILE3)(STIF(I),I=1,LDSP)
      IF(NL.NE.NLT)GO TO 115
      REWIND IFILE1
      REWIND IFILE2
      REWIND IFILE3
      IF(ITSTR+ 9*M.GT.NDIM1) GO TO 321
      ITAPE = 0
      GO TO 322
C***                   **** END SEGMENT 1 ****
C
C***                  **** BEGIN SEGMENT 2 ****
  321 ITAPE = 1
  322 DO 400  I = 1,ITSTR
```

```
  400 STIF(I)= 0.
      DO 450 I = 1,M
      IF(ITAPE.NE.1) GO TO 401
      READ(IFILE1) ICODE,MNUM,K1,MTYPE,QL,QI,E
      GO TO 402
  401 CALL FIND1(I,MNUM,K1,MTYPE,QL,QI,E,ISTIF,STIF,NDIM1)
  402 CALL BMSTF(BM,QI,QL,E,MTYPE)
      CALL STORE(K1,BM,STIF,MLD,N)
  450 CONTINUE
C***                      **** END SEGMENT 2 ****
C
C***                    **** BEGIN SEGMENT 3 ****
      REWIND IFILE1
      ITS= ITSTR -N-NR
      IF(IPRES.EQ.0) WRITE(IFILE4)(STIF(I),I=1,ITS)
      NLT = 0
      ITS1= ITS+1
  413 READ(IFILE3)(STIF(I),I=ITS1,ITSTR)
      IF(IPRES.EQ.0) WRITE(IFILE4)(STIF(I),I=ITS1,ITSTR)
      NLT = NLT + 1
      MM=MLD+1
      IF(NLT.EQ.1)CALL CHOLES(STIF,N,MM,0,1,IPRNT,&1000)
      IF(NLT.NE.1)CALL CHOLES(STIF,N,MM,0,2,IPRNT,&1000)
      IF(IPDFL.EQ.0) CALL DISPL(STIF,ITS,N,IPRNT,NLT)
      IF(IPRES.EQ.0) WRITE(IFILE4)(STIF(J),J=ITS1,ITSTR)
C***                      **** END SEGMENT 3 ****
C
C***                    **** BEGIN SEGMENT 4 ****
      READ(IFILE2)MNUMT,(BUF(I),I=1,26)
      DO 500 I=1,M
      IF(ITAPE.NE.1) CALL FIND1(I,MNUM,K1,MTYPE,QL,QI,E,ISTIF,STIF,NDIM1
     1)
      IF(ITAPE.EQ.1)READ(IFILE1)ICODE,MNUM,K1,MTYPE,QL,QI,E
      CALL BMSTF(BM,QI,QL,E,MTYPE)
      DO 510 J= 1,4
      IF(K1(J).EQ.0.OR.K1(J).GT.N) GO TO 502
      K11 = K1(J)
      D(J)= STIF(ITS+K11)
      GO TO 510
  502 D(J)= 0.
  510 CONTINUE
      CALL ENDA(BM,PMT,D)
      DO 520 J = 1,4
      IF(K1(J).LE.N) GO TO 520
      K11=K1(J)+ITS
      STIF(K11)=  STIF(K11) - PMT(J)
  520 CONTINUE
      IF(MNUM.EQ.MNUMT) GO TO 530
      IF(IPSM.EQ.1) GO TO 504
  506 CALL ENDAO(I,PMT,NLT,IPRNT,MNUM)
      GO TO 500
  504 CALL SHRMO(PMT,QL,INCR,BUF)
      CALL DIAGO(BUF,INCR,I,IPRNT,NLT,QL,MNUM,1)
      GO TO 500
  530 DO 540 J=1,4
  540 PMT(J)= PMT(J)+ BUF(J)
      IF(IPSM.EQ.1) GO TO 550
      CALL ENDAO(I,PMT,NLT,IPRNT,MNUM)
  544 READ(IFILE2) MNUMT,(BUF(K),K=1,26)
      GO TO 500
  550 CALL SHRMO(PMT,QL,INCR,BUF)
      CALL SHRMS(BUF,INCR)
      CALL DIAGO(BUF,INCR,I,IPRNT,NLT,QL,MNUM,2)
      GO TO 544
  500 CONTINUE
C***                      **** END SEGMENT 4 ****
C
      REWIND IFILE1
C
C***                    **** BEGIN SEGMENT 5 ****
      IF(IPR.EQ.0) CALL REACT(STIF,ITSTR,NR,IPRNT,NLT,N)
C***                      **** END SEGMENT 5 ****
```

```
C
      IF(NLT.NE.NL) GO TO 413
      IF(IPRES.EQ.0) GO TO 600
  599 READ(ICARD,910)ICODE
  910 FORMAT(A1)
      IF(ICODE.NE.IQ) GO TO 10
      STOP 99999
C
C***                    **** BEGIN SEGMENT 6 ****
  600 NLT = 1
      IFIN = ITSTR + LDSP
      IF(IFIN.GT.NDIM1) GO TO 8
      IBEG = ITSTR+ 1
      REWIND IFILE4
      READ(IFILE4)(STIF(I),I=1,ITS)
  601 READ(IFILE4)(STIF(I),I= IBEG,IFIN)
      READ(IFILE4)(STIF(I),I=ITS1,ITSTR)
      CALL RES(STIF,N,MLD,ITS1,IBEG,NLT,IPRNT)
      IF(NLT.EQ.NL)GO TO 599
      NLT = NLT + 1
      GO TO 601
C***                      **** END SEGMENT 6 ****
C
    1 NEROR = 1
      GO TO 20
    2 NEROR = 2
      GO TO 20
    3 NEROR = 3
      WRITE(IPRNT,952) N,MLD,ITSTR
  952 FORMAT(9HOERROR 3 ,16HNO. OF UNKNOWNS=I3,2X,16HHALF BAND WIDTH=I3,
     12X,31HSTORAGE REQUIRED IN ARRAY STIF=I6)
      GO TO 1000
    4 NEROR = 4
      GO TO 20
    5 NEROR = 5
      GO TO 20
    6 NEROR = 6
      GO TO 20
    7 NEROR = 7
      GO TO 20
    8 NEROR = 8
   20 WRITE(IPRNT,951)NEROR
  951 FORMAT(12HO*****ERROR=I2)
 1000 READ(ICARD,963,END=1001) ICODE
  963 FORMAT(A1)
      IF(ICODE.NE.IC) GO TO 1000
      GO TO 10
 1001 STOP
      END


      SUBROUTINE  ECHO1(IPRNT,N,M,NR,NL,IPD,IPDFL,IPSM,INCR,IPR,IPRES,EG
     1)
      WRITE(IPRNT,80)
   80 FORMAT('1',25X,' STRUCTURE DATA CHECK ')
      WRITE(IPRNT,901)N,M,NR,IPD,IPDFL,IPSM,INCR,IPR,IPRES,NL,EG
  901 FORMAT(1HO,35X,2HN=I3/36X,2HM=I3/36X,3HNR=I3/36X,4HIPD=I1/36X,6HIPE
     1DFL=I1/36X,5HIPSM=I1/36X,5HINCR=I2/36X,4HIPR=I1/36X,6HIPRES=I1/36X
     2,3HNL=I3/36X,3HEG=F10.0)
      RETURN
      END


      SUBROUTINE  BAND(MLD,K1,MTYPE,N)
      DIMENSION K1(4),K11(4)
C***  UPDATED HALF-BANDWIDTH IN MLD ALSO K1 SET TO ZERO FOR PINS
      DO 5 I = 1,4
    5 K11(I) = 0
      IF (MTYPE .EQ.1) GO TO 2
      IF (MTYPE.EQ.2) K1(1) = 0
      IF (MTYPE .EQ.3) K1(2) = 0
```

```
    2 CONTINUE
      DO 1 I = 1,4
      IF(K1(I).GT.N.OR.K1(I).EQ.0) K11(I) = 10000
      IF(K11(I).EQ.10000) GOTO1
      K11(I)=K1(I)
1     CONTINUE
      MLDU = 0
      MT = 0
      DO 3 I=1,3
      K=I+1
      DO 3 J=K,4
      IF (K11(I).NE.10000.AND.K11(J).NE.10000) MT =IABS(K11(I)-K11(J))
      IF(MT.GT. MLDU) MLDU = MT
    3 CONTINUE
      IF(MLDU .GT. MLD) MLD =MLDU
      RETURN
      END


      SUBROUTINE ECHO2(IPRNT,I1,MNUM,K1,MTYPE,QL,QI,E,ICODE)
      DIMENSION K1(4)
C***  IF I1=1 THEN HEADING IS PRINTED ON A NEW PAGE
      IF(I1.EQ.1) GO TO 20
   30 WRITE(IPRNT,902) ICODE,MNUM,K1,MTYPE,QL,QI,E
  902 FORMAT(24X,A1,2X,5(I3,2X),2X,I2,3(2X,F10.2))
      RETURN
   20 WRITE(IPRNT,903)
  903 FORMAT(1H1,61X,17HMEMBER DATA CHECK)
      WRITE(IPRNT,901)
  901 FORMAT(1H0,20X,
     1          72HICODE MNUM   IRL   IRR   IDL   IDR   MTYPE       QL
     2QI              E       )
      GO TO 30
      END


      SUBROUTINE FEM(LTYPE,MTYPE,DISTB,DISTE,W,BUFFM,QL)
      DIMENSION BUFFM(1)
C***  LTYPE = 0  FOR UNIFORM LOAD ; LTYPE = 1 FOR POINT LOAD
      DISTB = DISTB * 12.
      DISTE = DISTE * 12.
      IF(LTYPE.EQ.1)WU=W
      IF(LTYPE.EQ.0)WU=W *(DISTE - DISTB)/12.
      D = QL - DISTB/2. - DISTE/2.
      TS1 = WU /(24.*QL)
      C = DISTE - DISTB
      TS2 = 24.*D*D*D/QL-6.*DISTE*C*C/QL +3.*C*C*C/QL
      TS3 = 4. * C *C - 24.*D*D
      BUFFM(1) = -TS1 *(TS2+TS3)
      TS3 = 2.*C*C -48.*D*D + 24.*D*QL
      BUFFM(2) = -TS1 *(TS2+TS3)
      TS1 = TS1 * 6./QL
      TS2 = 12.*D*D-8.*D*D*D/QL+2.* DISTE*(DISTE-DISTB)**2/QL-C*C*C/QL-C
     1*C
      BUFFM(3) = TS1 * TS2
      BUFFM(4) = WU - BUFFM(3)
      IF(MTYPE.EQ.1) RETURN
      IF(MTYPE.EQ.2) GO TO 2
      BUFFM(1)=BUFFM(1)-BUFFM(2)/2.
      BUFFM(3)=BUFFM(3)-1.5*BUFFM(2)/QL
      BUFFM(4)=BUFFM(4)+1.5*BUFFM(2)/QL
      BUFFM(2) = 0.
      RETURN
    2 BUFFM(2) = BUFFM(2) - BUFFM(1)/2.
      BUFFM(3) = BUFFM(3) - (1.5* BUFFM(1))/QL
      BUFFM(4) = BUFFM(4) + (1.5* BUFFM(1))/QL
      BUFFM(1) = 0.
      RETURN
      END

      SUBROUTINE    READA(IFILE1,MNUMT,MCOUNT,IPRNT,K1,M,QL)
```

```
      DIMENSION K1(4)
    1 READ(IFILE1)IDUM,MNUM,K1,IDUM,QL ,DUM,DUM
      MCOUNT =MCOUNT+ 1
      IF(MNUM.EQ.MNUMT) RETURN
      IF(MCOUNT.GT.M) GO TO 2
      GO TO 1
    2 WRITE(IPRNT,901)
  901 FORMAT(15HOERROR IN READA)
      END


      SUBROUTINE FIND(ISTIF,NDIM1,MNUMT,K1,IPRNT,QL,STIF)
      DIMENSION ISTIF(1),STIF(1),K1(1)
C
C***  LOOKS UP DISPL NOS. IN ISTIF ARRAY
      ISTOR = NDIM1
    1 IF(ISTIF(ISTOR).NE.MNUMT) GO TO  2
      DO 3 I=2,5
    3 K1(I-1) = ISTIF(ISTOR -I)
      QL = STIF(ISTOR -6)
      RETURN
    2 ISTOR = ISTOR - 9
      IF(ISTOR.GT.0) GO TO 1
      WRITE(IPRNT,901)
  901 FORMAT(25HOERROR IN FIND SUBROUTINE)
      STOP
      END


      SUBROUTINE ECHO3 (ICODE,LCN,MNUM,LTYPE,MTYPE,DISTB,DISTE,W,FML,FMR
     1,FSL,FSR,LCOUNT,IPRNT)
      IF(LCOUNT.EQ.1) GO TO 2
    1 WRITE(IPRNT,902)ICODE,LCN,MNUM,LTYPE,MTYPE,DISTB,DISTE,W,FML,FMR,
     1FSL,FSR
  902 FORMAT(19X,A1,4X,I2,3X,I3,4X,I1,6X,I1,2X,7(2X,F10.2))
      RETURN
    2 WRITE(IPRNT,903)
  903 FORMAT(1H1,59X,22HMEMBER LOAD DATA CHECK)
      WRITE(IPRNT,901)
  901 FORMAT(1HO,
     1          15X,114HICODE  LCN  MNUM  LTYPE  MTYPE     DISTB     D
     2ISTE        W           FML           FMR          FSL         FSR
     3)
      GO TO 1
      END


      SUBROUTINE SIMP(BUF,W,DISTB,DISTE,LTYPE,INCR,QL,IPRNT)
      DIMENSION BUF(1)
      NP = INCR+ 1
      IF(LTYPE.EQ.1) GO TO  9
      IF(LTYPE.NE.0) GO TO 100
      W=W/12.
      X = QL / INCR
      BUF(5) = 0.
      BUF(16)= 0.
      DO 1  L = 2,NP
      IF(DISTB - X) 2,4,4
    2 IF(DISTE - X) 5,3,3
    3 BUF(L+4) = -W*(X-DISTB)
      BUF(L+15)= BUF(L+4) * (X- DISTB)/2.
      GO TO 1
    4 BUF(L+4) = 0.
      BUF(L+15)= 0.
      GO TO  1
    5 BUF(L+4) = -W*(DISTE - DISTB)
      BUF(L+15)= BUF(L+4)* ((X-DISTE)+(DISTE-DISTB)/2.)
    1 X = X + QL/INCR
      RETURN
    9 X = 0.
      DO 10 L = 1,NP
      IF(X - DISTB) 20,30,30
   20 BUF(L+4)= 0.
```

```
      BUF(L+15)=0.
      GO TO 10
   30 BUF(L+4) = - W
      BUF(L+15) = -W*(X- DISTB)
   10 X = X + QL /INCR
      RETURN
  100 WRITE(IPRNT,901)
  901 FORMAT(31HERROR IN SIMP LTYPE NOT CORRECT)
      STOP
      END
```

```
      SUBROUTINE  STORE(K1,BM,STIF,MLD,N)
      DIMENSION  K1(1),BM(1),STIF(1)
      MM=MLD+1
      NS= (MLD*MM)/2
      DO 1 L=1,4
      I =K1(L)
      DO 1 K=1,4
      J = K1(K)
      IF(I.LT.J) GO TO 1
      IF(I.EQ.0.OR.J.EQ.0)GO TO 1
      IF(I.GT.N.OR.J.GT.N)GO TO 1
      LK = (L*(L-1))/2 +K
      IF(BM(LK).EQ.0.) GO TO 1
      LL = J +(I-MM)*MLD + NS
      IF(I.LE.MLD)LL= J +((I-1)*I)/2
      STIF(LL) = STIF(LL) + BM(LK)
    1 CONTINUE
      RETURN
      END
```

```
      SUBROUTINE  DISPL(STIF,ITS ,N,IPRNT,NLT)
      DIMENSION STIF(1)
      WRITE(IPRNT,901)NLT
  901 FORMAT(1H1,39X,37HROTATIONS AND DEFLECTIONS LOADING NO.I3/)
      DO 1 I=1,N
      K11= ITS+I
    1 WRITE(IPRNT,902) I, STIF(K11)
  902 FORMAT(41X,16HDISPLACEMENT NO.I3,1H=E15.8)
      RETURN
      END
```

```
      SUBROUTINE ENDA(BM,PMT,D)
      DIMENSION BM(1),PMT(1),D(1)
      PMT(1)= BM(1)*D(1)+ BM(2)*D(2)+BM(4)*D(3)+ BM(7)*D(4)
      PMT(2)= BM(2)*D(1)+ BM(3)*D(2)+BM(5)*D(3)+ BM(8)*D(4)
      PMT(3)= BM(4)*D(1)+ BM(5)*D(2)+BM(6)*D(3)+ BM(9)*D(4)
      PMT(4)= BM(7)*D(1)+ BM(8)*D(2)+BM(9)*D(3)+ BM(10)*D(4)
      RETURN
      END
```

```
      SUBROUTINE FIND1(MNUMT,MNUM,K1,MTYPE,QL,QI,E,ISTIF,STIF,NDIM1)
      DIMENSION ISTIF(1),STIF(1),K1(1)
      ISTOR = NDIM1- (MNUMT-1)* 9
      MNUM  =ISTIF(ISTOR)
      MTYPE = ISTIF(ISTOR-1)
      K1(1) =ISTIF(ISTOR-2)
      K1(2) =ISTIF(ISTOR-3)
      K1(3) =ISTIF(ISTOR-4)
      K1(4) =ISTIF(ISTOR-5)
      QL    = STIF(ISTOR-6)
      QI    = STIF(ISTOR-7)
      E     = STIF(ISTOR-8)
      RETURN
      END
```

```
      SUBROUTINE  SHRMO(PMT,QL,INCR,BUF)
      DIMENSION PMT(1),BUF(1)
      NP = INCR +1
      DO 1  J = 1,NP
    1 BUF(J+30) = PMT(3)
      BUF(42) =-PMT(1)
      X = QL/INCR
      DO 2  J = 2,NP
      BUF(J+41) = PMT(3)*X -PMT(1)
    2 X = X + QL/INCR
      RETURN
      END
```

```
      SUBROUTINE  DIAGO(BUF,INCR,I,IPRNT,NLT,QL,MNUM,IBN)
      DIMENSION BUF(1),OUT(11)
      NP = INCR + 1
      IF(I.EQ.1) GO TO 2
    1 IF(IBN.EQ.1) GO TO 10
      IF(IBN.EQ.2) GO TO 20
   10 JBIN1 = 31
      JBIN2 = 42
      JFIN1 = 30 + NP
      JFIN2 = 41 + NP
      GO TO 30
   20 JBIN1 = 5
      JBIN2 = 16
      JFIN1 = 4 + NP
      JFIN2 = 15 + NP
      GO TO 30
   30 WRITE(IPRNT,903) MNUM,(BUF(J), J=JBIN1,JFIN1)
  903 FORMAT(6HOSHEARI3,11(2X,F8.2))
      WRITE(IPRNT,904) MNUM,(BUF(J), J=JBIN2,JFIN2)
  904 FORMAT(6H    MOMI3,11(2X,F8.2))
      RETURN
    2 WRITE(IPRNT,901)NLT
  901 FORMAT(1H1,38X,44HSHEARS AND MOMENTS ALONG MEMBERS LOADING NO.I3//
     147HMEMBER NO.      DISTANCE FROM LEFT END OF MEMBER)
      OUT(1) = 0.
      DO 3 J= 1,INCR
      QJ = J
      K = J+1
    3 OUT(K) = QJ/INCR
      WRITE(IPRNT,902)(OUT(J),J=1,NP)
  902 FORMAT(1H0,7X,11(5X,F4.2,1HL))
      GO TO  1
      END
```

```
      SUBROUTINE  SHRMS(BUF,INCR)
      DIMENSION  BUF(1)
      NP =INCR + 1
      DO 1 I = 1,NP
      BUF(I+4) = BUF(I+30) + BUF(I+4)
    1 BUF(I+15)= BUF(I+15) + BUF(I+41)
      RETURN
      END
```

```
      SUBROUTINE  ENDAO(I,PMT,NLT,IPRNT,MNUM)
      DIMENSION  PMT(1)
      IF(I.EQ.1) GO TO  2
    1 WRITE(IPRNT,903)MNUM,(PMT(K),K=1,4)
  903 FORMAT(33X,I3,3X,4(2X,F12.2))
      RETURN
    2 WRITE(IPRNT,901)NLT
  901 FORMAT(1H1,42X,33HFINAL END ACTIONS FOR LOADING NO.I3)
      WRITE(IPRNT,902)
  902 FORMAT(1H0,29X,64HMEMBER NO.  MOMENT LEFT  MOMENT RIGHT  SHEAR  LE
     1FT  SHEAR RIGHT )
      GO TO 1
      END
```

```
      SUBROUTINE  REACT(STIF,ITSTR,NR,IPRNT,NLT,N)
      DIMENSION STIF(1)
      WRITE(IPRNT,901)NLT
  901 FORMAT(1H1,45X,25HREACTIONS FOR LOADING NO.I3//47X,22HDISPLACEMENT
     1  REACTION/50X,6HNUMBER//)
      NT = N
      ISTAR = ITSTR - NR + 1
      DO 1 J= ISTAR,ITSTR
      NT = NT + 1
      TEMP= -STIF(J)
    1 WRITE(IPRNT,902)NT,TEMP
  902 FORMAT(51X,I3,3X,F10.2)
      RETURN
      END


      SUBROUTINE RES(STIF,N,MUD,ITS1,IBEG,NLT,IPRNT)
      DIMENSION  STIF(1)
      WRITE(IPRNT,901)NLT
  901 FORMAT(1H1,46X,25HRESIDUALS FOR LOADING NO.I3//50X,17HEQUATION RES
     1IDUAL//)
      MM = MUD +1
      NS =(MUD* MM)/2
      NM= N*MM-NS
      DO 20  II =1,N
      IF(II.LE.MM) GO TO 5
      ID = (II - MUD)*MM + NS
      NB = MUD
      NA = MUD
      GO TO 6
    5 ID = II+((II-1)*II)/2
      NB = II - 1
      NA = MUD
    6 IF(II.GT.N-MM)NA = N-II
      K = II-1
      IN= ID -1
      SUM = 0.
      IF(NB.EQ.0) GO TO 8
      DO 7  I = 1,NB
      KK = K + NM
      SUM = SUM + STIF(IN)*STIF(KK)
      IN = IN - 1
    7 K= K -1
    8 J= II
      JJ = II
      NA = NA + 1
      DO 9 NI = 1,NA
      I = II + NI -1
      LL = J +(I-MM)*MUD + NS
      IF(I.LE.MUD)LL = J +((I-1)*I)/2
      KK = JJ + NM
      SUM = SUM + STIF(LL)*STIF(KK)
    9 JJ = JJ + 1
      KQUIT=IBEG +II -1
      ARES  = SUM - STIF(KQUIT)
   20 WRITE(IPRNT,902) II, ARES
  902 FORMAT(53X,I3,3X,F8.4)
      RETURN
      END


      SUBROUTINE BMSTF(BM,QI,QL,E,MTYPE)
      DIMENSION BM(1)
      TS1 = 2.* E * QI/QL
      TS2 = 3.* TS1 / QL
      TS3 = 2.* TS2 / QL
      TS5 = 1.5  * TS1
      TS6 =   .5 * TS2
      TS7 =   TS6/QL
      DO 1  I=1,10
    1 BM(I) = 0.
      IF(MTYPE.NE.1)GO TO 2
```

```
      BM(1) = 2.*TS1
      BM(2) = TS1
      BM(3) = BM(1)
      BM(4) = TS2
      BM(5) = TS2
      BM(6) = TS3
      BM(7) = -TS2
      BM(8) = -TS2
      BM(9) = -TS3
      BM(10)= TS3
      RETURN
    2 BM(6) = TS7
      BM(9) = -TS7
      BM(10)= TS7
      IF(MTYPE.EQ.3) GO TO 3
      BM(3) = TS5
      BM(5) = TS6
      BM(8) = -TS6
      RETURN
    3 BM(1) = TS5
      BM(4) = TS6
      BM(7) = -TS6
      RETURN
      END
```

```
      SUBROUTINE ECHO4(ICOUNT,ICODE,LCN,K11,K22,K33,QJM,QJV,QJH,IPRNT)
      IF(ICOUNT.EQ.1) GO TO 10
    1 WRITE(IPRNT,903)ICODE,LCN,K11,K22,K33,QJM,QJV,QJH
  903 FORMAT(32X,A1,3X,I3,3(2X,I3),3(2X,F10.2))
      RETURN
   10 WRITE(IPRNT,901)
  901 FORMAT(1H1,49X,21HJOINT LOAD DATA CHECK)
      WRITE(IPRNT,902)
  902 FORMAT(1H0,30X, 60HICODE LCN  K11  K22  K33      QJM          QJV
     1        QJH     )
      GO TO 1
      END
```

```
      SUBROUTINE CHOLES(A,N,MM,IB,NT,IPRNT,*)
      DIMENSION A(1)
      REAL*8  S1,T1
C
C***    A IS THE ARRAY CONTAINING THE ELEMENTS OF THE LOWER HALF BAND
C***    OF THE SYMMETRIC STRUCTURE STIFFNESS MATRIX.
C***    N = NUMBER OF EQUATIONS OR NUMBER OF UNKNOWN DISPLACEMENTS.
C***    MM= HALF BAND WIDTH + DIAGONAL ELEMENT OR MUD + 1
C***    IB + 1 = NO. OF RIGHT HAND SIDE VECTORS.
C***    NT -- IF 1 OR LESS MATRIX IS FACTORED. IF GREATER THAN 1
C***    FORWARD AND BACKWARD SUBSTITUTION PERFORMED.
C***    S1 AND T1 ARE TEMPORARY DOUBLE PRECISION VARIABLES.
C
      MUD = MM-1
      NS  = MUD*MM/2
      NM  = N*MM-NS
      IF(NT-1)30,30,31
C
C***    BEGIN CHOLESKY ALGORITHM FOR FACTORING MATRIX.
   30 DO 20 J = 1,N
      IF(J-MUD) 1,1,2
    2 IN =J-MUD
      L= IN +(J-MM)*MUD +NS
      GO TO 7
    1 IN= 1
      L= IN +(J-1)*J/2
    7 IF (J -N+MUD)103,103,105
  105 M5 =N
      GO TO 104
  103 M5 = J+MUD
  104 S1 = 0.0
      J1 = J-1
```

```
      J2 = J+1
      IF(J1)4,4,3
    3 DO 6 K = IN,J1
      T1 = A(L)
      S1 =S1 + T1**2
    6 L=L +1
    4 T1 =A(L)
      IF(T1-S1 .LT.0.) GO TO 100
      T1 =DSQRT(T1 - S1)
      A(L) = T1
      IF(J-N)19,20,20
   19 DO 18 I= J2 ,M5
      SUM = 0.0
      IF(I-MUD)68,68,71
   71 IN = I-MUD
      LL = IN + (I-MM)*MUD +NS
      GO TO 5
   68 IN = 1
      LL = IN + (I-1)*I /2
    5 IF(J1)18,18,8
    8 IF(IN -J1) 53,53,18
   53 DO 17 K = IN,J1
      LM = L+K-J
      SUM = SUM + A(LL)*A(LM)
   17 LL = LL +1
   18 A(LL) = (A(LL)-SUM) /A(L)
   20 CONTINUE
C
C***    BEGIN FORWARD SUBSTITUTION.
   31 NR = IB +1
      NB =NM +1
      DO 65 K =1,NR
      A(NB) =A(NB)/A(1)
      DO 60 I = 2,N
      IF (I -MUD) 21,21,22
   22 IN = I -MM
      KS = IN* MUD +NS
      M5 =MUD
      GO TO 27
   21 IN = 0
      M5 = I-1
      KS = M5*I /2
   27 SUM = 0.0
      DO 61 J= 1,M5
      JR = J+IN
      L   = JR +KS
      JR   = JR + NB - 1
   61 SUM = SUM +A(L)  *A(JR)
      ID = I + KS
   60 A(JR+1) =(A(JR+1) -SUM)/A(ID)
   65 NB = NB +N
C
C***    BEGIN BACKWARD SUBSTITUTION.
      NB =NM + N
      DO 75  K = 1,NR
      A(NB)= A(NB) /A(NM)
      DO 80 II = 2,N
      I = N -II +1
      IF(I-MUD)41,41,95
   95 ID =I +(I-MM)* MUD +NS
      GO TO 42
   41 ID =I +(I-1)*I /2
   42 IF(I-N+MM) 43,43,45
   45 M5 =II-1
      GO TO 76
   43 M5 = MUD
   76 SUM =0.0
      DO 81 J =1,M5
      JR = I +J
      IF(JR-MUD)98,98,99
   99 L = I +(JR-MM)*MUD+NS
      GO TO 82
```

```
   98 L = I +(JR-1)*JR/2
   82 JR =NB - N +JR
   81 SUM =SUM + A(L)*A(JR)
      JR =NB -N +I
   80 A(JR)= (A(JR)-SUM) /A(ID)
   75 NB =NB +N
      RETURN
100   WRITE(IPRNT,901)
901   FORMAT(59HSTIFFNESS MATRIX IS NOT POSITIVE DEFINITE HALT THIS PROB
     1LEM)
      RETURN 1
      END
```

APPENDIX

D PLANE FRAME AND TRUSS PROGRAM

D–1 Description of Important Identifiers

Variable Identifier†	*Type Variable*	*Dimension in Program for Array*	*Description of Identifier*
AK	Real array	6, 6	Temporary storage for member stiffness matrix relative to member axes.
AKT	Real array	6, 6	Temporary storage for member stiffness matrix relative to structure axes.
CHOLES	Subroutine	—	Cholesky decomposition routine for solving equations stored in half-band form.
CX	Real	—	Cosine of angle between member *X*-axis and structure *X*-axis.
CY	Real	—	Cosine of angle between member *X*-axis and structure *Y*-axis.
DM	Real array	6	Temporary storage for member end displacements.
FEM	Real array	6	Temporary storage for member end actions.
FEMT	Real array	6	Temporary storage for member end actions relative to structure axes.
FIX	Subroutine	—	Calculates fixed end actions for planar frame member.
FIX2	Subroutine	—	Calculates fixed end actions for planar truss member.
IHD	Integer array	200	*X*-displacement number stored by joint number.
IRD	Integer array	200	Rotational displacement number stored by joint number.
IVD	Integer array	200	*Y*-displacement number stored by joint number.
K1	Integer array	6	Temporary storage for member end displacement numbers.
MEMBER	Subroutine	—	Calculates member stiffness matrix for member axes.
MT2	Integer array	400	Member type stored by member number.

†Identifiers listed in Tables 12-1 through 12-7 are not repeated here.

Variable Identifier	*Type Variable*	*Dimension in Program for Array*	*Description of Identifier*
MUD	Integer	——	Half-band width of stiffness matrix.
NM	Integer	——	Number of words required for stiffness matrix in half-band form.
PJ	Real array	400	Fixed moment at joint *j* of member stored by member number.
QK	Real array	400	Fixed moment at joint *k* of member stored by member number.
QL1	Real array	400	Member length stored by member number.
RJ	Real array	400	Fixed shear at joint *j* of member stored by member number.
ROTA	Subroutine	——	Calculates rotation transformation matrix.
SK	Real array	400	Fixed shear at joint *k* of member stored by member number.
STIF	Real array	9000†	Stiffness matrix for unrestrained components of joint displacement.
STORE	Subroutine	——	Sums member stiffness matrix (AKT) into proper position of STIF.
T	Real array	6, 6	Temporary storage for rotation matrix.
TJ	Real array	400	Fixed axial force at joint *j* of member stored by member number.
UK	Real array	400	Fixed axial force at joint *k* of member stored by member number.
X	Real array	200	*X*-coordinate of joint stored by joint number.
Y	Real array	200	*Y*-coordinate of joint stored by joint number.

D–2
FORTRAN Code

```
C***
C***   THE DIMENSION OF ARRAY 'STIF' MUST BE EQUAL TO THE VALUE
C***       GIVEN 'NDIM1'.
C***   SET DEVICE ASSIGNMENTS AS FOLLOWS
C***       1. ICARD = CARD READER
C***       2. IPRNT = PRINTER OR OUTPUT FILE
C***       3. IFILE = TAPE UNIT OR EQUIVALENT
C***    THE DIMENSION OF ARRAYS PJ, QK, RJ, SK, TJ, UK, MT2, AND QL1
C***        MAY BE MODIFIED TO CHANGE THE MAXIMUM NUMBER OF MEMBERS
C***        THAT CAN BE PROCESSED.  THE PROGRAM AS LISTED PERMITS NO
C***        MORE THAN 400 MEMBERS IN A STRUCTURE.
C***    THE DIMENSION OF ARRAYS IRD, IVD, IHD, X, AND Y MAY BE
C***        MODIFIED TO CHANGE THE MAXIMUM NUMBER OF JOINTS THAT
C***        CAN BE PROCESSED.  THE PROGRAM AS LISTED PERMITS NO MORE
C***        THAN 200 JOINTS IN A STRUCTURE.
C***    THE ARRAY STIF IS USED TO STORE THE STIFFNESS MATRIX
C***        PLUS ONE LOAD VECTOR.  THE STIFFNESS MATRIX IS STORED
C***        IN HALF-BAND FORMAT.  AFTER OTHER DIMENSIONS ARE SET
C***        ARRAY STIF SHOULD BE GIVEN THE MAXIMUM DIMENSION THAT
C***        STORAGE WILL PERMIT.
C***
C***
C***   PLANAR FRAME AND TRUSS PROGRAM
C***
```

† To alter dimension, see comment cards near the beginning of program listing in Sec. D-2.

```
      DIMENSION DM(6),K1(6),FEM(6),FEMT(6),T(6,6),AK(6,6),AKT(6,6),
     1TS(6,6),PJ(400),QK(400),RJ(400),SK(400),TJ(400),UK(400),MT2(400),
     2QL1(400),IRD(200),IVD(200),IHD(200),X(200),Y(200),
     3STIF(9000)
      DATA IC1,IC2,IC3,IC4,IC5,IC6,IC7,IC8/'S','J','M','L','P','N',
     1'E','Q'/
      NDIM1 = 9000
      ICARD = 5
      IPRNT = 6
      IFILE = 1
  977 REWIND IFILE
      N = 0
      MX = 1
    3 READ(ICARD,921)ICODE,M,NJ,NL,EN,MUD,JOBNO
  921 FORMAT(A1,3I3,F10.0,I3,52X,I5)
      IF(ICODE.EQ.IC8) GO TO 999
C***
C***
      IF(ICODE.NE.IC1)GO TO 3
      WRITE(IPRNT,922)
  922 FORMAT(1H1,49X,30HPLANE FRAME AND TRUSS ANALYSIS)
      WRITE(IPRNT,901) JOBNO
  901 FORMAT(1H ,48X,26HSTRUCTURE DATA FOR JOB NO.I5)
      WRITE(IPRNT,902) M,NJ,NL,EN
  902 FORMAT(1H ,48X,2HM=I2,3X,3HNJ=I2,3X,3HNL=I2,3X,2HE=F10.0)
      IF(M*NJ.LE.1) GO TO 13
      WRITE(IPRNT,924)
  924 FORMAT(1H ,53X,17HJOINT COORDINATES/33X,5HJOINT,3X,3HIRR,3X,3HIVR,
     13X,3HIHR,5X,12HX-COORDINATE,8X,12HY-COORDINATE)
      DO201I=1,NJ
      READ(ICARD,923)ICODE,J,IRR,IVR,IHR,XCOOR,YCOOR
  923 FORMAT(A1,I3,3I1,3X,2F10.0)
      IF(ICODE.NE.IC2) GO TO 13
      WRITE(IPRNT,925) J,IRR,IVR,IHR,XCOOR,YCOOR
  925 FORMAT(1H ,34X,I2,6X,I1,5X,I1,5X,I1,7X,F10.3,10X,F10.3)
      X(J)=XCOOR*12.
      Y(J)=YCOOR*12.
      IF(IRR)202,203,202
  203 N=N+1
      IRD(J)=N
      GOTO204
  202 IRD(J)= NDIM1
  204 IF(IVR)205,206,205
  206 N=N+1
      IVD(J)=N
      GOTO207
  205 IVD(J)= NDIM1
  207 IF(IHR)208,209,208
  209 N=N+1
      IHD(J)=N
      GO TO 201
  208 IHD(J)= NDIM1
  201 CONTINUE
      IF(MUD.EQ.0)GO TO 307
      MM= MUD+1
      NM = N*MM - MM*MUD/2
      DO 300 L =1,NM
  300 STIF(L) = 0.
  307 WRITE(IPRNT,905)
  905 FORMAT(1H1,58X,11HMEMBER DATA/1H ,31X,6HMEM NO,3X,1HJ,3X,1HK,7X,
     17HINERTIA4X,4HAREA7X,7HMODULUS10X,6HLENGTH4X,4HTYPE)
      DO101IJK=1,M
      READ(ICARD,903) ICODE,I,J,K,MT,QI,QA,E
  903 FORMAT(A1,3I3,I1,F9.0,2F10.0)
      IF(ICODE.NE.IC3) GO TO 13
      IF(E)2001,1000,2001
 1000 E=EN
 2001 CONTINUE
      K1(1)=IRD(J)
      K1(2)=IRD(K)
      K1(3)=IVD(J)
      K1(4)=IVD(K)
```

```
      K1(5)=IHD(J)
      K1(6)=IHD(K)
      DO 90 LP =1,6
      DO 90 MP =LP,6
      IF((K1(LP).GE.NDIM1).OR.(K1(MP).GE.NDIM1)) GO TO 90
      MDI = K1(LP)-K1(MP)
      IF(MDI) 75,76,76
   75 MDI =-MDI
   76 IF(MDI-MX)90,90,85
   85 MX=MDI
   90 CONTINUE
      QL= SQRT((X(K)-X(J))**2 + (Y(K)-Y(J))**2)
      QL2=QL/12.
      WRITE(IPRNT,908) I,J,K,QI,QA,E,QL2,MT
  908 FORMAT(1H0,34X,I2,3X,I2,3X,I2,4F13.3,I5)
      MT2(I)=MT
      QL1(I)=QL
      CX=(X(K)-X(J))/QL
      CY=(Y(K)-Y(J))/QL
      IF(MUD.EQ.0) GO TO 10
      CALL ROTA(T,CX,CY)
      CALL MEMBER(T,AK,AKT,E,QI,QA,QL,MT)
      CALL STORE(K1,AKT,STIF,MUD,NDIM1)
   10 WRITE(IFILE)I,CX,CY,E,QI,QA,K1
      IF(MUD.GE.MX)GO TO 305
      MUD=MX
      REWIND IFILE
      MM=MUD+1
      NM= N*MM-MM*MUD/2
      DO 306 L=1,NM
  306 STIF(L) = 0.
      DO 310 IJK =1,M
      READ(IFILE) I,CX,CY,E,QI,QA,K1
      CALL ROTA(T,CX,CY)
      CALL MEMBER(T,AK,AKT,E,QI,QA,QL1(I),MT2(I))
310   CALL STORE(K1,AKT,STIF,MUD,NDIM1)
  305 NB =NM +1
      NEND= NM+N
      DO274IJJ=1,NL
      L38=0
      L39=0
      DO 234 I=1,M
      PJ(I)=0.
      QK(I)=0.
      RJ(I)=0.
      SK(I)=0.
      TJ(I)=0.
  234 UK(I)=0.
      DO 235 I= NB,NEND
  235 STIF(I) = 0.
 8021 READ(ICARD,904) ICODE,IB1,AB1,AB2,AB3,AB4
  904 FORMAT(A1,I3,6X4F10.3)
      IF(ICODE.EQ.IC4)GO TO 8006
      IF(ICODE.EQ.IC5)GO TO 8732
      IF(ICODE.EQ.IC6)GO TO 8008
      IF(ICODE.EQ.IC7)GO TO 8008
      GO TO 13
 8006 IF(L39.EQ.1) GO TO 393
      WRITE(IPRNT,914) IJJ
  914 FORMAT(1H1,38X,29HINPUT DATA FOR LOADING NUMBERI3//43X,6HMEMBER,
     14X,4HLOAD,7X,7HX BEGIN,5X,5HX END,5X,5HALPHA)
  393 KL = IB1
      MT=MT2(KL)
      L39 = 1
      W=AB1
      IF((AB3-AB2).GE..05) W=AB1/12.
      XX1=AB2*12.
      XX2=AB3*12.
      ALPHA = AB4
      WRITE(IPRNT,912) KL,AB1,AB2,AB3,AB4
  912 FORMAT(45X,I2,3X,F10.3,1X,F10.3,1X,F10.3,1X,F10.3)
      IF(ALPHA)8009,8010,8011
```

```
8010 COSA=1.
     SINA=0.
     GOTO8020
8009 IF(ALPHA+90.)8012,8013,8012
8013 COSA=0.
     SINA=-1.
     GOTO8020
8011 IF(ALPHA-90.)8012,8015,8012
8015 COSA=0.
     SINA=1.
     GOTO8020
8012 ALPHA=ALPHA*3.14159/180.
     COSA=COS(ALPHA)
     SINA=SIN(ALPHA)
8020 QL=QL1(KL)
     IF(MT.GT.0) GO TO 7680
     CALLFIX(W,XX1,XX2,QL,SINA,COSA,P11,P22,P33,P44,P55,P66)
     GO TO 7681
7680 CALL FIX2(W,XX1,XX2,QL,MT,SINA,COSA,P11,P22,P33,P44,P55,P66)
7681 PJ(KL)=PJ(KL)+P33
     QK(KL)=QK(KL)+P66
     RJ(KL)=RJ(KL)+P22
     SK(KL)=SK(KL)+P55
     TJ(KL)=TJ(KL)+P11
     UK(KL)=UK(KL)+P44
     GOTO8021
8732 IF(L38.EQ.1) GO TO 37
     WRITE(IPRNT,9645) IJJ
9645 FORMAT(1H1,46X,29HJOINT INPUT LOADS FOR LOADINGI2///43X,10H
    1  J5X,6HMOMENT3X,10HVERT FORCE3X,9HHOR FORCE/)
  37 J= IB1
     L38=1
     K11= IRD(J)+NM
     K22= IVD(J)+NM
     K33= IHD(J)+NM
     IF(K11.GT.NDIM1) K11 = NDIM1
     IF(K22.GT.NDIM1) K22 = NDIM1
     IF(K33.GT.NDIM1) K33 = NDIM1
     STIF(K11) = STIF(K11) + AB1*12.
     STIF(K22) = STIF(K22) + AB2
     STIF(K33) = STIF(K33) + AB3
     WRITE(IPRNT,931) J,AB1,AB2,AB3
 931 FORMAT(1H ,48X, I3, 3F12.2)
     GO TO 8021
8008 CONTINUE
     IF(L39.EQ.0) GO TO 36
     REWIND IFILE
     DO8031LLL=1,M
     READ(IFILE)I,CX,CY,E,QI,QA,K1
     CALL ROTA(T,CX,CY)
     FEM(1)=PJ(I)
     FEM(2)=QK(I)
     FEM(3)=RJ(I)
     FEM(4)=SK(I)
     FEM(5)=TJ(I)
     FEM(6)=UK(I)
     DO9997I=1,6
     FEMT(I)=0.
     DO9997J=1,6
9997 FEMT(I)=FEMT(I)+T(J,I)*FEM(J)
     DO 8291 L=1,6
     K11=K1(L)+NM
     IF(K11.GT.NDIM1) K11 = NDIM1
8291 STIF(K11) = STIF(K11) - FEMT(L)
8031 CONTINUE
  36 CONTINUE
     NP1=N-1
     IF(MUD.LE.NP1)GO TO 3000
     WRITE(6,3001)
3001 FORMAT(28X,36HMUD SPECIFIED GREATER THAN ALLOWABLE)
     GO TO 999
3000 CALL CHOLES(STIF,N,MM,0,IJJ,IPRNT,&977)
```

```
      STIF(NDIM1)= 0.
      WRITE(IPRNT,909)IJJ
  909 FORMAT(1H1,38X,43HJOINT DEFLECTIONS AND ROTATIONS FOR LOADINGI2/
     11H ,38X,4H   J7X,8HROTATION4X,22HVERT DEFL     HORZ DEFL)
      DO100I=1,NJ
      K11=IRD(I)+NM
      K22=IVD(I)+NM
      K33=IHD(I)+NM
      IF(K11.GT.NDIM1) K11 = NDIM1
      IF(K22.GT.NDIM1) K22 = NDIM1
      IF(K33.GT.NDIM1) K33 = NDIM1
  100 WRITE(IPRNT,910) I, STIF(K11), STIF(K22), STIF(K33)
  910 FORMAT(1H ,39X,I3,6X,3F12.7)
      WRITE(IPRNT,911) IJJ
  911 FORMAT(1H1,43X,31HBEAM MOMENTS AND SHEARS LOADINGI2/
     11H ,44X,69HJ MOMENT      K MOMENT      J SHEAR      K SHEAR      J AXI
     2AL      K AXIAL)
      REWIND IFILE
      DO 120 IJK= 1,M
      READ(IFILE) I,CX,CY,E,QI,QA,K1
      CALL ROTA(T,CX,CY)
      CALL MEMBER(T,AK,AKT,E,QI,QA,QL1(I),MT2(I))
      DO117II=1,6
      DM(II)=0.
      DO117JJ=1,6
      K11= K1(JJ) +NM
      IF(K11.GT.NDIM1) K11 = NDIM1
  117 DM(II) = DM(II) + T(II,JJ)*STIF(K11)
      DO130J=1,6
      FEM(J)=0.
      DO130K=1,6
  130 FEM(J)=FEM(J)+AK(J,K)*DM(K)
      FEM(1) =(FEM(1)+PJ(I))/ 12.
      FEM(2) =(FEM(2)+QK(I))/ 12.
      FEM(3) = FEM(3)+RJ(I)
      FEM(4) = FEM(4)+SK(I)
      FEM(5) = FEM(5)+TJ(I)
      FEM(6) = FEM(6)+UK(I)
      WRITE(IPRNT,9327) I,(FEM(N9),N9=1,6)
 9327 FORMAT(1H ,28X,10HMEMBER NO.I3,6F12.2)
  120 CONTINUE
      IF(ICODE.EQ.IC7)GO TO 977
  274 CONTINUE
      GO TO 977
   13 WRITE(IPRNT,1333)
 1333 FORMAT(28X,39HERROR IN INPUT DATA, GO TO NEXT PROBLEM///)
      GO TO 977
  999 CALLEXIT
      END
```

```
      SUBROUTINEFIX(W,XX1,XX2,QL,SINA,COSA,P11,P22,P33,P44,P55,P66)
      IF( ABS(XX2-XX1)-.05)1,1,2
    1 WU=W*COSA
      P11=W*SINA*(QL-XX1)/QL
      P44=W*SINA-P11
      GOTO3
    2 WU=W*(XX2-XX1)*COSA
      P44=W*SINA*(XX2-XX1)*(XX1-XX2)/(2.*QL)
      P11=W*SINA*(XX2-XX1)-P44
    3 D=QL-XX1/2.-XX2/2.
      TS1=WU/(24.*QL)
      C=XX2-XX1
      TS2=24.*D*D*D/QL-6.*XX2*C*C/QL+3.*C*C*C/QL
      TS3=4.*C*C-24.*D*D
      P33=-TS1*(TS2+TS3)
      TS3=2.*C*C-48.*D*D+24.*D*QL
      P66=-TS1*(TS2+TS3)
      TS1=TS1*6./QL
      TS2=12.*D*D-8.*D**3 /QL+2.*XX2*(XX2-XX1)*(XX2-XX1)/QL-C*C*C/QL-C*C
      P22=TS1*TS2
      P55=WU-P22
      RETURN
      END
```

```
      SUBROUTINE FIX2(W,A,B,QL,MT,SINA,COSA,P11,P22,P33,P44,P55,P66)
      IF(MT.GT.1) GO TO 8
      B1=B
      B=QL-A
      A=QL-B1
    8 IF( ABS(B-A)-.05)1,1,2
    1 WU=W*COSA
      P11=W*SINA*(QL-A)/QL
      P44=W*SINA-P11
      GO TO 3
    2 P44=W*SINA*(B-A)*(A-B)/(2.*QL)
      P11=W*SINA*(B-A)-P44
      WU =W*(B-A)*COSA
    3 IF(MT.LT.3) GO TO 14
      D= QL -.5 *(A+B)
      C= B-A
      P22=WU*D/QL
      P55=WU*(A+.5*C)/QL
      P33=0.
      P66=0.
      RETURN
   14 P55=(WU/(8.*QL**3))*(4.*QL*(A*A+A*B+B*B)-A**3-A*B*B-A*A*B-B**3)
      P22= WU-P55
      P33 = -P55*QL+.5*WU*(A+B)
      P66 = 0.
      IF(MT.EQ.2)RETURN
      P1=P11
      P4=P44
      P44= P1
      P11= P4
      P5= P55
      P2= P22
      P22= P5
      P55= P2
      P66=-P33
      P33=0.
      RETURN
      END


      SUBROUTINE ROTA(T,CX,CY)
      DIMENSION T(6,6)
      DO9991I=1,6
      DO9991J=1,6
 9991 T(I,J)=0.
      T(1,1)=1.
      T(2,2)=1.
      T(3,3)=CX
      T(4,4)=CX
      T(5,5)=CX
      T(6,6)=CX
      T(5,3)=CY
      T(6,4)=CY
      T(3,5)=-CY
      T(4,6)=-CY
      RETURN
      END


      SUBROUTINE MEMBER(T,AK,AKT,E,QI,QA,QL,MT)
      DIMENSION T(6,6),AK(6,6),AKT(6,6),TS(6,6)
      C1=2.*E*QI/QL
      C2=3.*C1/QL
      C3=2.*C2/QL
      C4=E*QA/QL
      C5= 1.5 *C1
      C6=  .5 *C2
      C7= C6/QL
      DO9992I=1,6
      DO9992J=1,6
 9992 AK(I,J)=0.
```

```
      AK(5,5)= C4
      AK(5,6)= -C4
      AK(6,5)= -C4
      AK(6,6)= C4
      IF(MT.EQ.3) GO TO 7501
      IF(MT.GT.0) GO TO 7555
      AK(1,1)= 2.*C1
      AK(1,2)=C1
      AK(1,3)= C2
      AK(1,4)= -C2
      AK(2,1)= C1
      AK(2,2)= 2.*C1
      AK(2,3)= C2
      AK(3,1)= C2
      AK(2,4)= -C2
      AK(3,2)= C2
      AK(3,3)= C3
      AK(3,4)= -C3
      AK(4,1)= -C2
      AK(4,2)= -C2
      AK(4,3)=-C3
      AK(4,4)=C3
      GO TO 7501
 7555 AK(3,3) =C7
      AK(3,4)=-C7
      AK(4,3)=-C7
      AK(4,4)= C7
      IF(MT.EQ.2) GO TO 7585
      AK(2,2)= C5
      AK(2,3)= C6
      AK(2,4)=-C6
      AK(3,2)= C6
      AK(4,2)=-C6
      GO TO 7501
 7585 AK(1,1)= C5
      AK(1,3)= C6
      AK(1,4)=-C6
      AK(3,1)= C6
      AK(4,1)=-C6
 7501 CONTINUE
      DO9994I=1,6
      DO9994L=1,6
      TS(I,L)=0.
      DO9994J=1,6
 9994 TS(I,L)=TS(I,L)+AK(I,J)*T(J,L)
      DO9995I=1,6
      DO9995L=1,6
      AKT(I,L)=0.
      DO9995J=1,6
 9995 AKT(I,L)=AKT(I,L)+T(J,I)*TS(J,L)
      RETURN
      END

C
C     *****************************************************************
C
C        SUBROUTINE STORE
C
C       THIS SUBROUTINE SUMS THE ELEMENTS OF THE 6 BY 6 ROTATED
C       MEMBER STIFFNESS MATRIX AKT INTO THE APPROPRIATE POSITIONS
C       OF THE LOWER HALF-BAND LINEAR ARRAY A.
C
      SUBROUTINE STORE(K1,AKT,A,MUD,NDF)
      DIMENSION K1(1),A(1),AKT(6,6)
C***    K1 IS THE ARRAY CONTAINING THE 6 DISPLACEMENT NUMBERS OF THE
C***    MEMBER.
C***    MUD = NUMBER OF ELEMENTS IN HALF BAND.
C***    MM = MUD + 1 (NO. OF ELEMENTS IN HALF BAND INCLUDING DIAGONAL)
C***    NDF = A NUMBER GREATER THAN THE TOTAL NUMBER OF UNKNOWN
C***    DISPLACEMENTS WHICH SOME OF THE VALUES OF THE K1 ARRAY WILL
C***    HAVE.  IT IS USED AS A CODE TO INDICATE A SUMMATION INTO A
C***    RESTRAINED OR BOUNDARY DISPLACEMENT WHICH IS NOT STORED.
```

```
C***    I AND J ARE THE ROW AND COLUMN POSITIONS IN THE STRUCTURE
C***    STIFFNESS MATRIX.  LL IS THE COMPUTED SUBSCRIPT OF THE HALF
C***    BAND ARRAY.  LL IS A FUNCTION OF I, J, AND MUD.
      IF(MUD.EQ.0) MUD=1
      MM=MUD+1
      NS=MUD*(MM)/2
      DO 621 L = 1,6
      I = K1(L)
      DO 621 K = 1,6
      J = K1(K)
      IF(I.LT.J)GO TO 621
      IF(I.GE.NDF.OR.J.GE.NDF) GO TO 621
      LL= J +(I-MM)*MUD +NS
      IF(I.LE.MUD)LL= J +(I-1)*I/2
      A(LL)=A(LL)+ AKT(L,K)
  621 CONTINUE
      RETURN
      END
```

```
      SUBROUTINE CHOLES(A,N,MM,IB,NT,IPRNT,*)
      DIMENSION A(1)
      REAL*8  S1,T1
C***    A IS THE ARRAY CONTAINING THE ELEMENTS OF THE LOWER HALF BAND
C***    OF THE SYMMETRIC STRUCTURE STIFFNESS MATRIX.
C***    N = NUMBER OF EQUATIONS OR NUMBER OF UNKNOWN DISPLACEMENTS.
C***    MM= HALF BAND WIDTH + DIAGONAL ELEMENT OR MUD + 1
C***    IB + 1 = NO. OF RIGHT HAND SIDE VECTORS.
C***    NT -- IF 1 OR LESS MATRIX IS FACTORED. IF GREATER THAN 1
C***    FORWARD AND BACKWARD SUBSTITUTION PERFORMED.
C***    S1 AND T1 ARE TEMPORARY DOUBLE PRECISION VARIABLES.
      MUD = MM-1
      NS  = MUD*MM/2
      NM  = N*MM-NS
      IF(NT-1)30,30,31
   30 DO 20 J = 1,N
      IF(J-MUD) 1,1,2
    2 IN =J-MUD
      L= IN +(J-MM)*MUD +NS
      GO TO 7
    1 IN= 1
      L= IN +(J-1)*J/2
    7 IF (J -N+MUD)103,103,105
  105 M5 =N
      GO TO 104
  103 M5 = J+MUD
  104 S1 = 0.0
      J1 = J-1
      J2 = J+1
      IF(J1)4,4,3
    3 DO 6 K = IN,J1
      T1 = A(L)
      S1 =S1 + T1**2
    6 L=L +1
    4 T1 =A(L)
      IF(T1-S1 .LT.0.) GO TO 100
      T1 =DSQRT(T1 - S1)
      A(L) = T1
      IF(J-N)19,20,20
   19 DO 18 I= J2 ,M5
      SUM = 0.0
      IF(I-MUD)68,68,71
```

```
   71 IN = I-MUD
      LL = IN + (I-MM)*MUD +NS
      GO TO 5
   68 IN = 1
      LL = IN + (I-1)*I /2
    5 IF(J1)18,18,8
    8 IF(IN -J1) 53,53,18
   53 DO 17 K = IN,J1
      LM = L+K-J
      SUM = SUM + A(LL)*A(LM)
   17 LL = LL +1
   18 A(LL) = (A(LL)-SUM) /A(L)
   20 CONTINUE
C***    BEGIN FORWARD SUBSTITUTION.
   31 NR = IB +1
      NB =NM +1
      DO 65 K =1,NR
      A(NB) =A(NB)/A(1)
      DO 60 I = 2,N
      IF (I -MUD) 21,21,22
   22 IN = I -MM
      KS = IN* MUD +NS
      M5 =MUD
      GO TO 27
   21 IN = 0
      M5 = I-1
      KS = M5*I /2
   27 SUM = 0.0
      DO 61 J= 1,M5
      JR = J+IN
      L  = JR +KS
      JR  = JR + NB - 1
   61 SUM = SUM +A(L)  *A(JR)
      ID = I + KS
   60 A(JR+1) =(A(JR+1) -SUM)/A(ID)
   65 NB = NB +N
C***    BEGIN BACKWARD SUBSTITUTION.
      NB =NM + N
      DO 75  K = 1,NR
      A(NB)= A(NB) /A(NM)
      DO 80 II = 2,N
      I = N -II +1
      IF(I-MUD)41,41,95
   95 ID =I +(I-MM)* MUD +NS
      GO TO 42
   41 ID =I +(I-1)*I /2
   42 IF(I-N+MM) 43,43,45
   45 M5 =II-1
      GO TO 76
   43 M5 = MUD
   76 SUM =0.0
      DO 81 J =1,M5
      JR = I +J
      IF(JR-MUD)98,98,99
   99 L = I +(JR-MM)*MUD+NS
      GO TO 82
   98 L = I +(JR-1)*JR/2
   82 JR =NB - N +JR
   81 SUM =SUM + A(L)*A(JR)
      JR =NB -N +I
   80 A(JR)= (A(JR)-SUM) /A(ID)
   75 NB =NB +N
      RETURN
100   WRITE(IPRNT,901)
901   FORMAT(59HSTIFFNESS MATRIX IS NOT POSITIVE DEFINITE HALT THIS PROB
     1LEM)
      RETURN 1
      END
```

APPENDIX

E SPACE FRAME AND TRUSS PROGRAM

E–1
Description of Important Identifiers

Variable Identifier†	*Type Variable*	*Dimension in Program in Words for Arrays*	*Description of Identifier*
AFM	Real array	12	Member final end actions.
AK	Real array	12, 12	Member stiffness matrix relative to member axes.
AKT	Real array	12, 12	Member stiffness matrix relative to structure axes.
CHOLES	Subroutine	——	Cholesky decomposition routine for solving equations stored in half-band form.
CJ	Real array	100	Fixed end torsion corresponding to member *X*-axis at joint *j* of member stored by member number.
CX	Real	——	Cosine of angle between member *X*-axis and structure *X*-axis.
CY	Real	——	Cosine of angle between member *X*-axis and structure *Y*-axis.
CZ	Real	——	Cosine of angle between member *X*-axis and structure *Z*-axis.
DK	Real array	100	Fixed end torsion corresponding to member *X*-axis at joint *k* of member stored by member number.
DM	Real array	12	Temporary storage for member end displacements relative to member axis.
EJ	Real array	100	Fixed end moment corresponding to member *Y*-axis at joint *j* of member stored by member number.
FEM	Real array	12	Temporary storage for member fixed end actions relative to member axes.
FEMT	Real array	12	Temporary storage for member fixed end actions relative to structure axes.

†Identifiers listed in Tables 13-1 through 13-7 are not repeated here.

Variable Identifier	*Type Variable*	*Dimension in Program in Words for Arrays*	*Description of Identifier*
FIX	Subroutine	——	Calculates fixed end actions for space frame member.
FIX3	Subroutine	——	Calculates fixed end actions for space truss member.
FK	Real array	100	Fixed end moment corresponding to member Y-axis at joint k of member stored by member number.
GJ	Real array	100	Fixed end shear force corresponding to member Z-axis at joint j of member stored by member number.
HK	Real array	100	Fixed end shear force corresponding to member Z-axis at joint k of member stored by member number.
IRX	Integer array	30	X-coordinate displacement number at joint (rotation).
IRY	Integer array	30	Y-coordinate displacement number at joint (rotation).
IRZ	Integer array	30	Z-coordinate displacement number at joint (rotation).
IXD	Integer array	30	X-coordinate displacement number at joint (translation).
IYD	Integer array	30	Y-coordinate displacement number at joint (translation).
IZD	Integer array	30	Z-coordinate displacement number at joint (translation).
K1	Integer array	12	Temporary storage for displacement numbers at ends of member.
MEMBER	Subroutine	——	Calculates member stiffness matrix for member axes.
MX	Integer	——	Computed half-band width of stiffness matrix based on assigned displacement numbering.
N	Integer	——	Contains count of components of unrestrained components of joint displacement.
NM	Integer	——	Number of storage locations required for storing stiffness matrix $[\mathbf{S}_{uu}]$ in half-band format.
NTEM	Integer	——	Number of storage locations required for storing stiffness matrix $[\mathbf{S}_{uu}]$ and one load vector.
PJ	Real array	100	Fixed end moment corresponding to member Z-axis at joint j of member stored by member number.
QK	Real array	100	Fixed end moment corresponding to member Z-axis at joint k of member stored by member number.
QL1	Real array	100	Storage of member lengths by member number.
RJ	Real array	100	Fixed end shear force corresponding to member Y-axis at joint j of member stored by member number.
ROTA	Subroutine	——	Calculates rotation transformation matrix.
SK	Real array	100	Fixed end shear force corresponding to member Y-axis at joint k of member stored by member number.
STIF	Real array	9000†	Stiffness matrix $[\mathbf{S}_{uu}]$ for unrestrained components of joint displacement.
STORE	Subroutine	——	Sums member stiffness matrix into proper position of STIF.
T	Real array	12, 12	Rotation matrix.
TJ	Real array	100	Fixed end axial force corresponding to member X-axis at joint j of member stored by member number.

†To alter dimension, see comment cards near the beginning of program listing in Sec. E-2.

UK	Real array	100	Fixed end axial force corresponding to member *X*-axis at joint *k* of member stored by member number.
X	Real array	30	*X*-coordinate of joint.
Y	Real array	30	*Y*-coordinate of joint.
Z	Real array	30	*Z*-coordinate of joint.

E–2
FORTRAN Code

```
C
C***    THE DIMENSION OF ARRAY 'STIF' MUST BE EQUAL TO THE VALUE
C***        GIVEN 'NDIM1'.
C***    SET DEVICE ASSIGNMENTS AS FOLLOWS:
C***       1. IN = CARD READER
C***       2.IPRNT = PRINTER OR OUTPUT FILE
C***       3. LTAPE = TAPE UNIT OR EQUIVALENT
C***    THE DIMENSION OF ARRAYS TJ,RJ,GJ,CJ,EJ,PJ,UK,SK,HK,DK,FK,
C***       QK,MT2,AND QL1 MAY BE MODIFIED TO CHANGE THE MAXIMUM
C***       NUMBER OF MEMBERS THAT CAN BE PROCESSED. THE PROGRAM
C***       AS LISTED PERMITS NO MORE THAN 100 MEMBERS IN A STRUCTURE.
C***    THE DIMENSION OF ARRAYS IRX,IXD,IYD,IZD,X,Y,Z,IRY,AND IRZ
C***       MAY BE MODIFIED TO CHANGE THE MAXIMUM NUMBER OF JOINTS
C***       THAT CAN BE PROCESSED. THE PROGRAM AS LISTED PERMITS
C***       NO MORE THAN 30 JOINTS IN A STRUCTURE.
C***     THE ARRAY STIF IS USED TO STORE THE STIFFNESS MATRIX
C***         PLUS ONE LOAD VECTOR.  THE STIFFNESS MATRIX IS STORED
C***         IN HALF-BAND FORMAT.  AFTER OTHER DIMENSIONS ARE SET
C***         ARRAY STIF SHOULD BE GIVEN THE MAXIMUM DIMENSION THAT
C***         STORAGE WILL PERMIT.
C
C
C***    SPACE FRAME AND TRUSS PROGRAM
C
      DIMENSION AFM(12),DM(12),K1(12),FEM(12),FEMT(12),T(12,12),
     1AK(12,12),AKT(12,12),TJ(100),RJ(100),GJ(100),CJ(100),
     2EJ(100),PJ(100),UK(100),SK(100),HK(100),DK(100),FK(100),QK(100),
     3MT2(100),QL1(100),IRX(30),IXD(30),IYD(30),IZD(30),X(30),Y(30),
     4STIF( 9000),Z(30),IRY(30),IRZ(30)
      DATA IC1,IC2,IC3,IC4,IC5,IC6,IC7,IC8/'S','J','M','L','P','N','E',
     1'Q'/
      NDIM1 = 9000
      IN=5
      IT=6
      LTAPE=3
  977 REWIND LTAPE
      MX=1
      N=0
    3 READ(IN,921)KODE,M,NJ,NL,MUD,EN,JOBNO
  921 FORMAT(A1,4I3,F10.0,52X15)
      IF(KODE.EQ.IC8)CALL EXIT
      IF(KODE.NE.IC1)GO TO 3
      WRITE(IT,922)
  922 FORMAT(1H1,30X20HSPACE FRAME ANALYSIS/)
      WRITE(IT,901)JOBNO
  901 FORMAT(1H ,28X26HSTRUCTURE DATA FOR JOB NO.I6/)
      WRITE(IT,902)M,NJ,NL,EN
  902 FORMAT(1H ,15XI3,8H MEMBERSI6,7H JOINTSI6,9H LOADINGS3X10HGLOBAL E
     1 =F11.0//)
      WRITE(IT,924)
  924 FORMAT(1H ,40X10HJOINT DATA/15X5HJOINT3X3HIXT3X3HIYT3X3HIZT3X3HIXR
     13X3HIYR3X3HIZR5X5HXCOOR8X5HYCOOR8X5HZCOOR)
      DO 201 I=1,NJ
      READ(IN,923)KODE,J,IXT,IYT,IZT,IXR,IYR,IZR,XCOOR,YCOOR,ZCOOR
  923 FORMAT(A1,I3,6I1,3F10.2)
      IF(KODE.NE.IC2) GO TO 13
      WRITE(IT,925)J,IXT,IYT,IZT,IXR,IYR,IZR,XCOOR,YCOOR,ZCOOR
  925 FORMAT(16X,I3,5XI1,5XI1,5XI1,5XI1,5XI1,5XI1,3F12.2)
```

```
      X(J)=XCOOR*12.
      Y(J)=YCOOR*12.
      Z(J)=ZCOOR*12.
      IF(IXT)202,203,202
  203 N=N+1
      IXD(J)=N
      GO TO 204
  202 IXD(J)=NDIM1
  204 IF(IYT)205,206,205
  206 N=N+1
      IYD(J)=N
      GO TO 207
  205 IYD(J)=NDIM1
  207 IF(IZT)208,209,208
  209 N=N+1
      IZD(J)=N
      GO TO 210
  208 IZD(J)=NDIM1
  210 IF(IXR)211,212,211
  212 N=N+1
      IRX(J)=N
      GO TO 213
  211 IRX(J)=NDIM1
  213 IF(IYR)214,215,214
  215 N=N+1
      IRY(J)=N
      GO TO 216
  214 IRY(J)=NDIM1
  216 IF(IZR)217,218,217
  218 N=N+1
      IRZ(J)=N
      GO TO 201
  217 IRZ(J)=NDIM1
  201 CONTINUE
      IF(MUD.EQ.0) GO TO 307
      IF (MUD.GT.N-1) GO TO 14
      MM=MUD+1
      NM=N*MM-(MUD*MM)/2
      NTEM = NM + N
      IF(NTEM.GE.NDIM1) GO TO 15
      DO 150 I=1,NM
  150 STIF(I)=0.
  307 WRITE(IT,905)
  905 FORMAT(1H0,40X11HMEMBER DATA/1H ,13X6HMEM NO3X1HJ3X1HK8X2HIX8X2HIY
     18X2HIZ7X4HAREA4X7HMODULUS8X1HG6X6HLENGTH4X4HTYPE4X2HSI3X3HISI)
      DO 10 IJK=1,M
      READ(IN,903)KODE,I,J,K,MT,QIX,QIY,QIZ,QA,G,SI,ISI,E
  903 FORMAT(A1,3I3,I1,F9.2,5F10.0,I1,F9.0)
      IF(KODE.NE.IC3) GO TO 13
      IF(E.EQ.0.0)E=EN
      K1(1) =IXD(J)
      K1(2) =IYD(J)
      K1(3) =IZD(J)
      K1(4) =IRX(J)
      K1(5) =IRY(J)
      K1(6) =IRZ(J)
      K1(7) =IXD(K)
      K1(8) =IYD(K)
      K1(9) =IZD(K)
      K1(10)=IRX(K)
      K1(11)=IRY(K)
      K1(12)=IRZ(K)
      DO 90 LP=1,12
      DO 90 MP=LP,12
      IF((K1(LP).GE.NDIM1).OR.(K1(MP).GE.NDIM1)) GO TO 90
      MDI=K1(LP)-K1(MP)
      IF(MDI)75,76,76
   75 MDI=-MDI
   76 IF(MDI-MX)90,90,85
   85 MX=MDI
   90 CONTINUE
      QL=SQRT((X(K)-X(J))**2+(Y(K)-Y(J))**2+(Z(K)-Z(J))**2)
```

```
      QL2=QL/12.
      WRITE(IT,908)I,J,K,QIX,QIY,QIZ,QA,E,G,QL2,MT,SI,ISI
  908 FORMAT(1X,15X,I3,2XI3,1XI3,1X7F10.2,6XI3,2XF7.2,I4)
      MT2(I)=MT
      QL1(I)=QL
      CX=(X(K)-X(J))/QL
      CY=(Y(K)-Y(J))/QL
      CZ=(Z(K)-Z(J))/QL
      IF(MUD.EQ.0) GO TO 10
      CALL ROTA(T,CX,CY,CZ,SI,ISI)
      CALL MEMBER(T,AK,AKT,E,QIX,QIY,QIZ,QA,G,QL,MT)
      CALL STORE(K1,AKT,STIF,MUD,NDIM1)
   10 WRITE(LTAPE)I,CX,CY,CZ,SI,ISI,E,QIX,QIY,QIZ,QA,G,K1
      IF(MUD.GE.MX) GO TO 305
      MUD=MX
      REWIND LTAPE
      MM=MUD+1
      NM=N*MM-(MM*MUD)/2
      DO 306 L=1,NM
  306 STIF(L)=0.0
      DO 310 IJK=1,M
      READ (LTAPE)I,CX,CY,CZ,SI,ISI,E,QIX,QIY,QIZ,QA,G,K1
      QL=QL1(I)
      MT=MT2(I)
      CALL ROTA(T,CX,CY,CZ,SI,ISI)
      CALL MEMBER(T,AK,AKT,E,QIX,QIY,QIZ,QA,G,QL,MT)
  310 CALL STORE(K1,AKT,STIF,MUD,NDIM1)
  305 NB=NM+1
      NEND=NM+N
      DO 274 IJJ =1,NL
      L38=0
      L39=0
      REWIND LTAPE
      DO 234 I=1,M
      TJ(I)=0.
      RJ(I)=0.
      GJ(I)=0.
      CJ(I)=0.
      EJ(I)=0.
      PJ(I)=0.
      UK(I)=0.
      SK(I)=0.
      HK(I)=0.
      DK(I)=0.
      FK(I)=0.
  234 QK(I)=0.
      DO 235 I=NB,NEND
  235 STIF(I)=0.0
 8021 READ(IN,904)KODE,IB1,IB2,AB1,AB2,AB3,AB4,AB5,AB6
  904 FORMAT(A1,I3,I1,5X,6F10.3)
      IF(KODE.EQ.IC4)GO TO 8006
      IF(KODE.EQ.IC5)GO TO 8732
      IF(KODE.EQ.IC6.OR.KODE.EQ.IC7)GO TO 8008
      GO TO 13
 8006 IF(L39.GT.0)GO TO 393
      WRITE(IT,914)IJJ
  914 FORMAT(1H1,30X35HMEMBER LOAD DATA FOR LOADING NUMBERI4//25X6HMEMBE
     1R4X4HLOAD7X7HX BEGIN5X5HX END5X5HALPHA3X4HTYPE/)
  393 KL=IB1
      L39=1
      MT=MT2(KL)
      W=AB1
      IF((AB3-AB2).GE..05) W=AB1/12.
      XX1=AB2*12.
      XX2=AB3*12.
      ALPHA=AB4
      WRITE(IT,912)KL,AB1,AB2,AB3,AB4,IB2
  912 FORMAT(26X,I3,2XF10.2,3F11.2,I4)
      IF(ALPHA)8009,8010,8011
 8010 COSA=1.
      SINA=0.
      GO TO 8020
```

```
8009 IF(ALPHA+90.)8012,8013,8012
8013 COSA=0.
     SINA=-1.
     GO TO 8020
8011 IF(ALPHA-90.)8012,8015,8012
8015 COSA=0.
     SINA=1.
     GO TO 8020
8012 ALPHA=ALPHA*3.14159/180.
     COSA=COS(ALPHA)
     SINA=SIN(ALPHA)
8020 QL=QL1(KL)
     IF(MT.EQ.0)CALL FIX(W,XX1,XX2,QL,SINA,COSA,P11,P22,P33,P44,P55,P66
    1)
     IF(MT.GT.0)CALL FIX3(W,XX1,XX2,QL,SINA,COSA,P11,P22,P33,P44,P55,P6
    16)
     TJ(KL)=TJ(KL)+P11
     UK(KL)=UK(KL)+P44
     IF(IB2.EQ.1) GO TO 7681
     RJ(KL)=RJ(KL)+P22
     PJ(KL)=PJ(KL)+P33
     SK(KL)=SK(KL)+P55
     QK(KL)=QK(KL)+P66
     GO TO 8021
7681 GJ(KL)=GJ(KL)+P22
     EJ(KL)=EJ(KL)-P33
     HK(KL)=HK(KL)+P55
     FK(KL)=FK(KL)-P66
     GO TO 8021
8732 IF(L38.GT.0) GO TO 37
     WRITE(IT,9645) IJJ
9645 FORMAT(1H1,32X27HJOINT LOAD DATA FOR LOADINGI4//10X5HJOINT5X7HX-FO
    1RCE5X7HY-FORCE5X7HZ-FORCE4X8HX-MOMENT4X8HY-MOMENT4X8HZ-MOMENT/)
  37 J=IB1
     L38=1
     K11=IXD(J) +NM
     K22=IYD(J) +NM
     K33=IZD(J) +NM
     K44=IRX(J) +NM
     K55=IRY(J) +NM
     K66=IRZ(J) +NM
     IF(K11.GT.NDIM1)K11=NDIM1
     IF(K22.GT.NDIM1)K22=NDIM1
     IF(K33.GT.NDIM1)K33=NDIM1
     IF(K44.GT.NDIM1)K44=NDIM1
     IF(K55.GT.NDIM1)K55=NDIM1
     IF(K66.GT.NDIM1)K66=NDIM1
     STIF(K11)=STIF(K11)+AB1
     STIF(K22)=STIF(K22)+AB2
     STIF(K33)=STIF(K33)+AB3
     STIF(K44)=STIF(K44)+AB4*12.
     STIF(K55)=STIF(K55)+AB5*12.
     STIF(K66)=STIF(K66)+AB6*12.
     WRITE(IT,931)J,AB1,AB2,AB3,AB4,AB5,AB6
 931 FORMAT(1H ,12XI3,6F12.2)
     GO TO 8021
8008 CONTINUE
     IF(L39.EQ.0) GO TO 36
     REWIND LTAPE
     DO 8031 LLL=1,M
     READ (LTAPE)I,CX,CY,CZ,SI,ISI,E,QIX,QIY,QIZ,QA,G,K1
     CALL ROTA(T,CX,CY,CZ,SI,ISI)
     FEM(1) =TJ(I)
     FEM(2) =RJ(I)
     FEM(3) =GJ(I)
     FEM(4) =CJ(I)
     FEM(5) =EJ(I)
     FEM(6) =PJ(I)
     FEM(7) =UK(I)
     FEM(8) =SK(I)
     FEM(9) =HK(I)
     FEM(10)=DK(I)
```

```
      FEM(11)=FK(I)
      FEM(12)=QK(I)
      DO 9997 I=1,12
      FEMT(I)=0.
      DO 9997 J=1,12
 9997 FEMT(I)=FEMT(I)+T(J,I)*FEM(J)
      DO 8291 I=1,12
      K11=K1(I) +NM
      IF(K11.GE.NDIM1) K11=NDIM1
 8291 STIF(K11)=STIF(K11)-FEMT(I)
 8031 CONTINUE
   36 CALL CHOLES(STIF,N,MM,0,IJJ,IT,&977)
      STIF(NDIM1)=0.0
      WRITE(IT,909) IJJ
  909 FORMAT(1H1,30X43HJOINT DEFLECTIONS AND ROTATIONS FOR LOADINGI4//10
     1X5HJOINT5X6HX-DEFL6X6HY-DEFL6X6HZ-DEFL4X9HROTA X-AX4X9HROTA Y-AX4X
     29HROTA Z-AX/)
      DO 100 I=1,NJ
      K11=IXD(I) +NM
      K22=IYD(I) +NM
      K33=IZD(I) +NM
      K44=IRX(I) +NM
      K55=IRY(I) +NM
      K66=IRZ(I) +NM
      IF(K11.GT.NDIM1)K11=NDIM1
      IF(K22.GT.NDIM1)K22=NDIM1
      IF(K33.GT.NDIM1)K33=NDIM1
      IF(K44.GT.NDIM1)K44=NDIM1
      IF(K55.GT.NDIM1)K55=NDIM1
      IF(K66.GT.NDIM1)K66=NDIM1
  100 WRITE(IT,910)I,STIF(K11),STIF(K22),STIF(K33),STIF(K44),STIF(K55),
     1STIF(K66)
  910 FORMAT(1H ,12XI3,6E12.5)
      WRITE(IT,911) IJJ
  911 FORMAT(1H1,45X32HFINAL MEMBER END ACTIONS LOADINGI4//2X6HMEMBER108
     1H   J X-FCE   J Y-FCE   J Z-FCE   J X-MOM   J Y-MOM   J Z-MOM   K X-FCE
     2K Y-FCE   K Z-FCE   K X-MOM   K Y-MOM   K Z-MOM/)
      REWIND LTAPE
      DO 120 IJK=1,M
      READ (LTAPE)I,CX,CY,CZ,SI,ISI,E,QIX,QIY,QIZ,QA,G,K1
      QL=QL1(I)
      CALL ROTA(T,CX,CY,CZ,SI,ISI)
      CALL MEMBER(T,AK,AKT,E,QIX,QIY,QIZ,QA,G,QL,MT)
      DO 117 II= 1,12
      DM(II)=0.
      DO 117 J= 1,12
      K11=K1(J)+NM
      IF(K11.GE.NDIM1)K11=NDIM1
  117 DM(II)=DM(II)+T(II,J)*STIF(K11)
      DO 130 J=1,12
      FEM(J)=0.
      DO 130 K=1,12
  130 FEM(J)=FEM(J)+AK(J,K)*DM(K)
      AFM(1)=FEM(1) +TJ(I)
      AFM(2)=FEM(2) +RJ(I)
      AFM(3)=FEM(3) +GJ(I)
      AFM(4)=(FEM(4)+CJ(I)) /12.
      AFM(5)=(FEM(5)+EJ(I)) /12.
      AFM(6)=(FEM(6)+PJ(I)) /12.
      AFM(7)=FEM(7) +UK(I)
      AFM(8)=FEM(8) +SK(I)
      AFM(9)=FEM(9) +HK(I)
      AFM(10)=(FEM(10)+DK(I)) /12.
      AFM(11)=(FEM(11)+FK(I)) /12.
      AFM(12)=(FEM(12)+QK(I)) /12.
      WRITE(IT,9327) I, (AFM(N3),N3=1,12)
  120 CONTINUE
 9327 FORMAT(3XI3,2X,12F9.2)
  274 CONTINUE
      GO TO 977
   13 WRITE(IT,1333)
 1333 FORMAT(15X,41HERROR IN INPUT DATA, GONE TO NEXT PROBLEM//)
```

```
      GO TO 977
14    WRITE(IT,943)MUD,N
943   FORMAT(39H BAND WIDTH TOO LARGE FOR MATRIX   MUD=I3,4H  N=I3)
      GO TO 977
15    WRITE(IT,944) NTEM,NDIM1
944   FORMAT(75H1 STORAGE AVAILABLE FOR STIFFNESS MATRIX AND ONE LOAD VE
     1CTOR IS INSUFFICENT/20X,21HSTORAGE REQUIRED=NTEM,2X,23HSTORAGE AVA
     2ILABLE=NDIM1)
      GO TO 977
      END

      SUBROUTINE FIX3(W,A,B,QL,SINA,COSA,P11,P22,P33,P44,P55,P66)
      P33=0.
      P66=0.
      C=B-A
      IF(ABS(C)-.05)1,1,2
    1 WU=W*COSA
      P11=W*SINA*(QL-A)/QL
      P44=W*SINA-P11
      GO TO 3
    2 P44=W*SINA*(A-B)*C/(2.*QL)
      P11=W*SINA*C-P44
      WU=W*C*COSA
    3 D=QL-.5*(A+B)
      P22=WU*D/QL
      P55=WU-P22
      RETURN
      END

      SUBROUTINE FIX(W,XX1,XX2,QL,SINA,COSA,P11,P22,P33,P44,P55,P66)
      C=XX2-XX1
      IF(ABS(C)-.05)1,1,2
    1 WU=W*COSA
      P11=W*SINA*(QL-XX1)/QL
      P44=W*SINA-P11
      GO TO 3
    2 WU=W*C*COSA
      P44=W*SINA*C*(XX1-XX2)/(2.*QL)
      P11=W*SINA*C-P44
    3 D=QL-XX1/2.-XX2/2.
      TS1=WU/(24.*QL)
      TS2=24.*D**3/QL-6.*XX2*C**2/QL+3.*C**3/QL
      TS3=4.*C*C-24.*D*D
      P33=-TS1*(TS2+TS3)
      TS3=2.*C*C-48.*D*D+24.*D*QL
      P66=-TS1*(TS2+TS3)
      TS1=TS1*6./QL
      TS2=12.*D*D-8.*D**3/QL+2.*XX2*C*C/QL-C**3/QL-C*C
      P22=TS1*TS2
      P55=WU-P22
      RETURN
      END

      SUBROUTINE ROTA(T,CX,CY,CZ,SI,ISI)
      DIMENSION T(12,12)
      REAL*8 S,D1,D2
      D1=3.14159265358979
      D2=180.0
      D1=D1/D2
      DO 9991 I=1,12
      DO 9991 J=1,12
 9991 T(I,J)=0.
      T3=SQRT(CX**2+CZ**2)
      IF(SI.EQ.0.) GO TO 70
      IF(SI.EQ.90.) GO TO 71
   70 CS=1.
      SN=0.
      GO TO 75
   71 CS=0.
```

```
      SN=1.
      GO TO 75
      S=SI*D1
   60 SN=DSIN(S)
      CS=DCOS(S)
   75 CONTINUE
   63 IF(ISI.EQ.0) GO TO 64
      T3=SQRT(CX**2+CY**2)
      T(1,1)=CX
      T(1,2) = CY
      T(1,3) = CZ
      T(2,1) = (-CX*CZ*SN - CY*CS)/T3
      T(2,2) =(-CY*CZ*SN + CX*CS)/T3
      T(2,3) = T3 * SN
      T(3,1) = (-CX*CZ*CS + CY*SN)/T3
      T(3,2) =(-CY*CZ*CS - CX*SN)/T3
      T(3,3) = T3 *CS
      GO TO 47
   64 T(1,1)=CX
      T(1,2)=CY
      T(1,3)=CZ
      T(2,1)=(-CX*CY*CS-CZ*SN)/T3
      T(2,2)= T3*CS
      T(2,3)=(-CY*CZ*CS+CX*SN)/T3
      T(3,1)=(CX*CY*SN-CZ*CS)/T3
      T(3,2)=-T3*SN
      T(3,3)=(CY*CZ*SN+CX*CS)/T3
   47 DO 62 K= 3,9,3
      DO 62 I= 1,3
      DO 62 J= 1,3
      IK=I+K
      JK=J+K
   62 T(IK,JK)=T(I,J)
      RETURN
      END


      SUBROUTINE MEMBER(T,AK,AKT,E,QIX,QIY,QIZ,QA,G,QL,MT)
      DIMENSION T(12,12),AK(12,12),AKT(12,12),TS(12,12)
      DO 65 J= 1,12
      DO 65 I= 1,J
   65 AK(I,J)=0.0
      C1=2.*E*QIY/QL
      C2=2.*E*QIZ/QL
      C3=3.*C1/QL
      C4=3.*C2/QL
      C5=2.*C3/QL
      C6=2.*C4/QL
      C7=G*QIX/QL
      C8=E*QA/QL
      AK(1,1)=C8
      AK(1,7)=-C8
      AK(7,7)=C8
      IF(MT.NE.0)GO TO 7499
      AK(2,2)=C6
      AK(3,3)=C5
      AK(4,4)=C7
      AK(5,5)=2.*C1
      AK(6,6)=2.*C2
      AK(8,8)=C6
      AK(9,9)=C5
      AK(10,10)=C7
      AK(11,11)=2.*C1
      AK(12,12)=2.*C2
      AK(2,6)=C4
      AK(2,8)=-C6
      AK(2,12)=C4
      AK(3,5)=-C3
      AK(3,9)=-C5
      AK(3,11)=-C3
      AK(4,10)=-C7
      AK(5,9)=C3
```

```
      AK(5,11)=C1
      AK(6,8)=-C4
      AK(6,12)=C2
      AK(8,12)=-C4
      AK(9,11)=C3
 7499 DO 66 J=2,12
      JL= J-1
      DO 66 I=1,JL
   66 AK(J,I)=AK(I,J)
      DO 9994 I=1,12
      DO 9994 L=1,12
      TS(I,L)=0.
      DO 9994 J=1,12
 9994 TS(I,L)=TS(I,L)+AK(I,J)*T(J,L)
      DO 9995 I=1,12
      DO 9995 L=1,12
      AKT(I,L)=0.
      DO 9995 J=1,12
 9995 AKT(I,L)=AKT(I,L)+T(J,I)*TS(J,L)
      RETURN
      END

      SUBROUTINE STORE(K1,AKT,STIF,MUD,NDIM1)
      DIMENSION K1(1),AKT(12,12),STIF(1)
      MM=MUD+1
      NS=(MUD*MM)/2
      DO 621 L=1,12
      I=K1(L)
      DO 621 K=1,12
      J=K1(K)
      IF(I.LT.J) GO TO 621
      IF(I.EQ.NDIM1.OR.J.EQ.NDIM1) GO TO 621
      LL=J+(I-MM)*MUD+NS
      IF(I.LE.MUD) LL=J+((I-1)*I)/2
      STIF(LL)=STIF(LL)+AKT(L,K)
  621 CONTINUE
      RETURN
      END

      SUBROUTINE CHOLES(A,N,MM,IB,NT,IPRNT,*)
      DIMENSION A(1)
      REAL*8  S1,T1
C
C***    A IS THE ARRAY CONTAINING THE ELEMENTS OF THE LOWER HALF BAND
C***    OF THE SYMMETRIC STRUCTURE STIFFNESS MATRIX.
C***    N = NUMBER OF EQUATIONS OR NUMBER OF UNKNOWN DISPLACEMENTS.
C***    MM= HALF BAND WIDTH + DIAGONAL ELEMENT OR MUD + 1
C***    IB + 1 = NO. OF RIGHT HAND SIDE VECTORS.
C***    NT -- IF 1 OR LESS MATRIX IS FACTORED. IF GREATER THAN 1
C***    FORWARD AND BACKWARD SUBSTITUTION PERFORMED.
C***    S1 AND T1 ARE TEMPORARY DOUBLE PRECISION VARIABLES.
C
      MUD = MM-1
      NS  = MUD*MM/2
      NM  = N*MM-NS
      IF(NT-1)30,30,31
C
C***    BEGIN CHOLESKY ALGORITHM FOR FACTORING MATRIX.
   30 DO 20 J = 1,N
      IF(J-MUD) 1,1,2
    2 IN =J-MUD
      L= IN +(J-MM)*MUD +NS
      GO TO 7
    1 IN= 1
      L= IN +(J-1)*J/2
    7 IF (J -N+MUD)103,103,105
  105 M5 =N
      GO TO 104
  103 M5 = J+MUD
  104 S1 = 0.0
```

```
      J1 = J-1
      J2 = J+1
      IF(J1)4,4,3
    3 DO 6 K = IN,J1
      T1 = A(L)
      S1 =S1 + T1**2
    6 L=L +1
    4 T1 =A(L)
      IF(T1-S1 .LT.0.) GO TO 100
      T1 =DSQRT(T1 - S1)
      A(L) = T1
      IF(J-N)19,20,20
   19 DO 18 I= J2 ,M5
      SUM = 0.0
      IF(I-MUD)68,68,71
   71 IN = I-MUD
      LL = IN + (I-MM)*MUD +NS
      GO TO 5
   68 IN = 1
      LL = IN + (I-1)*I /2
    5 IF(J1)18,18,8
    8 IF(IN -J1) 53,53,18
   53 DO 17 K = IN,J1
      LM = L+K-J
      SUM = SUM + A(LL)*A(LM)
   17 LL = LL +1
   18 A(LL) = (A(LL)-SUM) /A(L)
   20 CONTINUE
C
C***     BEGIN FORWARD SUBSTITUTION.
   31 NR = IB +1
      NB =NM +1
      DO 65 K =1,NR
      A(NB) =A(NB)/A(1)
      DO 60 I = 2,N
      IF (I -MUD) 21,21,22
   22 IN = I -MM
      KS = IN* MUD +NS
      M5 =MUD
      GO TO 27
   21 IN = 0
      M5 = I-1
      KS = M5*I /2
   27 SUM = 0.0
      DO 61 J= 1,M5
      JR = J+IN
      L  = JR +KS
      JR  = JR + NB - 1
   61 SUM = SUM +A(L)  *A(JR)
      ID = I + KS
   60 A(JR+1) =(A(JR+1) -SUM)/A(ID)
   65 NB = NB +N
C
C***    BEGIN BACKWARD SUBSTITUTION.
      NB =NM + N
      DO 75  K = 1,NR
      A(NB)= A(NB) /A(NM)
      DO 80 II = 2,N
      I = N -II +1
      IF(I-MUD)41,41,95
   95 ID =I +(I-MM)* MUD +NS
      GO TO 42
   41 ID =I +(I-1)*I /2
   42 IF(I-N+MM) 43,43,45
   45 M5 =II-1
      GO TO 76
   43 M5 = MUD
   76 SUM =0.0
      DO 81 J =1,M5
      JR = I +J
      IF(JR-MUD)98,98,99
```

```
   99 L = I +(JR-MM)*MUD+NS                                             CH001020
      GO TO 82                                                          CH001030
   98 L = I +(JR-1)*JR/2                                                CH001040
   82 JR =NB - N +JR                                                    CH001050
   81 SUM =SUM + A(L)*A(JR)                                             CH001060
      JR =NB -N +I                                                      CH001070
   80 A(JR)= (A(JR)-SUM) /A(ID)                                         CH001080
   75 NB =NB +N                                                         CH001090
      RETURN                                                            CH001100
100   WRITE(IPRNT,901)                                                  CH001110
901   FORMAT(59HSTIFFNESS MATRIX IS NOT POSITIVE DEFINITE HALT THIS PROBCH001120
     1LEM)                                                              CH001130
      RETURN 1                                                          CH001140
      END                                                               CH001150
```

ANSWERS TO SELECTED PROBLEMS

Section 2-7

2-1. $\begin{bmatrix} x_1 \\ x_2 \\ x_3 \end{bmatrix} = \begin{bmatrix} 2.4141 \\ 0.0482 \\ 3.2103 \end{bmatrix}$

2-3. $\begin{bmatrix} x_1 \\ x_2 \\ x_3 \\ x_4 \end{bmatrix} = \begin{bmatrix} 2.0 \\ 0.0 \\ 0.0 \\ -3.0 \end{bmatrix}$

2-6a. $\begin{bmatrix} x_1 \\ x_2 \\ x_3 \end{bmatrix} = \begin{bmatrix} 3.6667 \\ 3.3030 \\ -1.8788 \end{bmatrix}$

2-7. $\begin{bmatrix} 7 & 3 & 9 & 1 & 0 \\ 4 & 2 & 5 & 1 & 3 \\ 1 & 3 & 3 & 1 & 2 \\ 5 & 5 & -5 & 0 & 0 \\ 4 & -2 & 3 & -2 & -3 \end{bmatrix}$

2-8.

$$[A]^{-1} = \begin{bmatrix} 0.50 & 0.0 & 0.50 & 0.0 & 0.0 \\ -0.50 & 1.0 & 0.50 & 0.0 & 0.0 \\ -0.50 & 0.0 & 0.50 & 0.0 & 0.0 \\ 0.0 & 0.0 & 0.0 & 0.75 & -0.50 \\ 0.0 & 0.0 & 0.0 & -0.25 & 0.50 \end{bmatrix}$$

Section 3-8

3-1. $\theta_A = 7.50 \times 10^3 \frac{1}{EI}$

$\Delta_B = -1.89 \times 10^6 \frac{1}{EI}$ in. $\quad \theta_B = -3.75 \times 10^4 \frac{1}{EI}$

3-4. $\Delta_A = -2.16 \times 10^6 \frac{1}{EI}$ in. $\quad \theta_A = -6.00 \times 10^3 \frac{1}{EI}$

$\theta_B = 3.00 \times 10^4 \frac{1}{EI}$

3-6. $\Delta_A = 0.8724 \times 10^8 \frac{1}{EI}$ in. $\quad \theta_A = 1.80 \times 10^6 \frac{1}{EI}$

Δ_B(horizontal) $= 0.5922 \times 10^8 \frac{1}{EI}$ in. $\quad \theta_B = 1.08 \times 10^6 \frac{1}{EI}$

3-8. Δ_A(vertical) $= -4.11 \times 10^3 \frac{1}{AE}$ in.

3-16. Moment at $B = -7.52$ ft-k Reaction at $B = -11.52$ k

3-18. Moment at $A = 558.58$ ft-k
Vertical reaction at $B = 54.17$ k
Vertical reaction at $C = -8.33$ k

3-20. Moment at $A = 0.28\ wL^2$
Vertical reaction at $A = 0.81\ wL$
Vertical reaction at $C = 0.53\ wL$

Section 4-2.3

2.

$$[\mathbf{K}] = E\begin{bmatrix} 6.267 & 5.640 & 0.3721 & -0.3721 \\ 5.640 & 8.061 & 0.4282 & -0.4282 \\ 0.3721 & 0.4282 & 0.0250 & -0.0250 \\ -0.3721 & -0.4282 & -0.0250 & 0.0250 \end{bmatrix} \times 10^{-2}$$

Section 4-3.6

2.

$$[\mathbf{FM}] = w\begin{bmatrix} 105.4 \text{ ft-k} \\ -121.3 \text{ ft-k} \\ 15.55 \text{ k} \\ 16.45 \text{ k} \end{bmatrix}$$

4.

$$[\mathbf{FM}] = \frac{2EI_\alpha(T_2 - T_1)}{dL}\begin{bmatrix} -1 \\ 1 \\ 0 \\ 0 \end{bmatrix}$$

Section 4-7

4-2. Vertical reaction at left support = 2.23 k
Rotation at left support = $-0.6156 \times 10^4(1/EI)$
Vertical Reaction at center support = 17.55 k
Vertical reaction at right support = 19.15 k
Rotation at right support = $-0.9045 \times 10^4(1/EI)$

4-3. Horizontal deffection at upper left joint = $-1.769 \times 10^6(1/EI)$ in.
Rotation at upper left joint = $-2.314 \times 10^4(1/EI)$
Moment at right support = 16.19 in-k
Horizontal reaction at right support = −3.89 k
Vertical reaction at right support = −23.01 k

4-8. Horizontal deflection at upper left joint = −1.51 in.
Rotation at upper left joint = -0.6596×10^{-2}
Moment at right support = −4543.82 in-k

4-11. Vertical reaction at left support = 15.0 k
Vertical deflection at lower center joint = −0.1786 in.

4-13. Vertical reaction at left support = −192.98 k
Vertical deflection at lower center joint = −0.3705 in.

Section 5-3.3

2.

$$[\mathbf{K}] = E\begin{bmatrix} 4.0\frac{I}{L} & 2.0\frac{I}{L} & 6.0\frac{I}{L^2} & -6.0\frac{I}{L^2} & 0 & 0 \\ 2.0\frac{I}{L} & 1.0\frac{I}{L} & 3.0\frac{I}{L^2} & -3.0\frac{I}{L^2} & 0 & 0 \\ 6.0\frac{I}{L^2} & 3.0\frac{I}{L^2} & 9.0\frac{I}{L^3} & -9.0\frac{I}{L^3} & 0 & 0 \\ -6.0\frac{I}{L^2} & -3.0\frac{I}{L^2} & -9.0\frac{I}{L^3} & 9.0\frac{I}{L^3} & 0 & 0 \\ 0 & 0 & 0 & 0 & 4.5\frac{A}{L} & -4.5\frac{A}{L} \\ 0 & 0 & 0 & 0 & -4.5\frac{A}{L} & 4.5\frac{A}{L} \end{bmatrix}$$

Section 5-9

5-1. Moment at left support = −156.89 ft-k
Vertical reaction at left support = −59.37 k
Horizontal reaction at left support = 23.97 k
Horizontal Deflection at upper right joint = −0.0625 in.
Vertical deflection at upper right joint = −0.05116 in.
Rotation at upper right joint = −0.0006186

5-5. Vertical reaction at middle left support = −23.29 k
Moment at left end at right member = 718.75 in-k

5-7. Moment at left support = −1.81 in-k
Axial force in left member = 52.8 k *C*

5-12. Moment at left support = 1006.23 ft-k
Axial force in left member = 42.48 k *C*

5-13. Axial force in upper left member = 13.32 k *C*
Axial force in horizontal member = 3.25 k *C*

5-17. Horizontal deflection of top joint = 7.123×10^{-3} in.
Axial force in horizontal member = 0
Axial force in lower left member = 7.21 k *T*

5-22. Vertical deflection of beam joint at spring = −0.676 in.
Reaction at left support = 12.32 k

Section 6-3.2

1. $K_{tt} = 1.1988 \times 10^4$ k/in.
$K_{rr} = 26.76$ k/in.
$K_{vv} = 1.689$ k/in.
$K_{ll} = 198.4$ in-k

2. $I_x = 2.338$ in^4

Section 6-9

6-2. X-deflection of top joint = -1.331×10^{-8} in.
Rotation about X-axis of top joint = -1.990×10^{-4}
{Axial force in member running to origin = 109.99 k *C*
{Moment about member z-axis at origin = 0.91 ft-k
(Member x-axis runs from origin to free joint)

6-3. Y-deflection of free joint = $1.890(1/EI)$ in.
Rotation about Y-axis of free joint = $6.997 \times 10^{-2}(1/EI)$
{Axial force in diagonal member = 53.12 k *C*
{Moment about member z-axis at origin = 10.27 ft-k

6-4. Z-deflection of free joint = -3.637×10^{-3} in.
Rotation about Z-Axis of free joint = 2.884×10^{-8}
{Axial force in member parallel to Y-axis = 0.41 k *C*
{Moment about member z-axis at left end = 190.16 ft-k

6-12. Y-deflection of free joint = −0.04956 in.
Axial force in lower member = 42.43 k C

6-15. Y-deflection of joint on X-axis = −1.996 in.
Axial force in member parallel to X-axis = 200 k *T*

6-16. Y-deflection of free joint = 0.5749 in.
Axial force in member a = 752.36 k *T*

6-22. Z-deflection of free joint on X-axis = −0.2576 in.
Vertical reaction at origin = 36.0 k
Moment about member z-axis at origin = 360.0 ft-k

Section 7-6

7-1. Horizontal deflection of top joints $= 1.82 \times 10^2(L^3/EI)$ in.
Horizontal deflection of middle joints $= 1.06 \times 10^2(L^3/EI)$ in.
Moment at left support = 0.30 PL
Vertical reaction at left support $= 0.56P$
Horizontal reaction at left support $= -0.50P$

7-3.

$$[\mathbf{K}] = E\begin{bmatrix} 1.33\frac{I}{L} & 0.67\frac{I}{L} & 0.67\frac{I}{L^2} & -0.67\frac{I}{L^2} & 0 & 0 \\ 0.67\frac{I}{L} & 0.33\frac{I}{L} & 0.33\frac{I}{L^2} & -0.33\frac{I}{L^2} & 0 & 0 \\ 0.67\frac{I}{L^2} & 0.33\frac{I}{L^2} & 0.33\frac{I}{L^3} & -0.33\frac{I}{L^3} & 0 & 0 \\ -0.67\frac{I}{L^2} & -0.33\frac{I}{L^2} & -0.33\frac{I}{L^3} & 0.33\frac{I}{L^3} & 0 & 0 \\ 0 & 0 & 0 & 0 & 1.50\frac{A}{L} & -1.50\frac{A}{L} \\ 0 & 0 & 0 & 0 & -1.50\frac{A}{L} & 1.50\frac{A}{L} \end{bmatrix}$$

Moment at end $j = 0.44PL$
Vertical reaction at end $j = 0.72P$
Moment at end $k = -0.28PL$
Vertical reaction at end $k = 0.28P$

Section 8-8

8-4. Moment at left support = 23.0 ft-k
Horizontal reaction at left support = −2.94 k
Horizontal deflection at upper right joint $= 5.73 \times 10^{-2}$ in.
Rotation at upper right joint $= -7.704 \times 10^{-5}$

Section 9-6

9-1. Rotation at left joint $= -5.115 \times 10^6(1/EI)$
Moment at center support = 414.58 ft-k
Reaction at center support = 109.38 k

9-2. Horizontal deflection of top left joint $= -2.057 \times 10^2(1/E)$ in.
Axial force in left vertical member = 5.71 k *C*
Axial force in top horizontal member = 4.29 k *T*

9-6. Horizontal deflection of top left joint $= 1.49 \times 10^6(1/EI)$ in.
Moment at left support = 34.12 ft-k
Axial force in left member = 0.60 k C
Axial force in right member = 17.99 k *C*

INDEX

C

D

E

F

G

H

N

O

P